S0-BNI-717

The Encyclopedic Dictionary of Psychology

The Encyclopedic Dictionary of Psychology

Edited by

Rom Harré *and* **Roger Lamb**

The MIT Press
Cambridge, Massachusetts

First MIT Press edition, 1983

First published 1983

Library of Congress Cataloging in Publication Data

Main entry under title:

The Encyclopedic dictionary of psychology.
Includes index.
1. Psychology——Dictionaries
I. Harré, Romano II. Lamb, Roger
BF31.E555 1983 150′.3′21 83–920

ISBN 0–262–08135–0

Printed and bound in Great Britain.

CONTENTS

PREFACE

establishment of a science of psychology has been no matter. There are still those who hold that the very of a science of human thought and action is a :onception. Even if we take the restricted view of :hology as the study of the ways in which human beings ite and control their behavior, it still cannot be erstood without reference to other fields of specialist ning which psychologists neglect at their peril. It has become increasingly clear that much of what was once n to be the province of individual psychology, such as study of motives, of the emotions and of the genesis of sciousness, cannot be understood without introducing ciological dimension. In so far as psychologists are ming increasingly aware that they are not dealing just the external contingencies of action but with the ceptual systems involved in the interpretation and trol of behavior, with the structure of concepts and their rrelations, they are again bringing cognitive studies in ious forms into psychology. Finally, the developments t have taken place in neurophysiology have now made ssible to ask sensible questions about the physiological s of many cognitive processes and to expect to get non-culative answers. Human psychic functioning is poised, t were, between a social and a physiological level and olves conceptual manipulations whose understanding ns to require not only studies closely tied to the rmation processing model, but philosophical analysis vell.

lmost everything that is claimed to be part of the corpus sychological knowledge depends on presuppositions t are not, in themselves, psychological. The same tiplicity of connections has led to peculiar difficulties in eloping the field. Psychology shows little sign of uiring an accumulating body of knowledge. The work revious generations is not so much incorporated in new ions, as swept away by them.

Ve have identified three main bases for contemporary chology – cognitive psychology (concerning the uisition and processing of information), cholinguistics (the study of the most specifically human phenomenon, language), and neuropsychology, (the study of the brain and nervous system as the physical basis of thought, feeling and action). Expanding different dimensions from the core studies introduces developmental, social and personality psychology and the psychology of the emotions. The three main fields of application of psychological knowledge, educational, occupational and clinical psychology complete the basic structure. But psychology today covers the rapidly expanding study of animal behavior as well as human conduct. Finally, there are the dimensions of philosophical analysis of the basic concepts and theories of psychology and of the historical development of our understanding of human thought and behavior.

Other dictionaries of psychology have paid little attention to the ocean of "unofficial" psychology that can be found in the theories and practices of lay folk outside the academic psychological professions. We have thought it important that there should be definitive accounts of the main ideas and schools of fringe psychologies as well as of the established variety. A quite detailed exposition of these matters is a feature of this work.

Sixteen distinguished psychologists, philosophers and physiologists working in the main fields of psychological knowledge, as we saw them, have come together as initiators, advisers and critics, and this book is the consequence of their work. Each suggested fifteen major topics in their area for detailed treatment, plus up to seventy-five minor topics whose understanding was essential to a full grasp of a field.

The articles are arranged in alphabetical order, with cross references to other relevant entries. But in addition, so rich and complex is the field, we have added an index to enable the reader to look up terms which have not merited separate entries but whose sense can be grasped from their occurrence in one or more articles. In this way we hope to have made available as comprehensive a list of items as the exigencies of space allows.

Rom Harré Roger Lamb

ACKNOWLEDGMENTS

The Editors and Publisher are grateful for permission to reproduce the following illustrations:

brain and central nervous system

1 W. H. Freeman and Company. (Redrawn from R. W. Sperry, "The great cerebral commissure", *Scientific American* (January 1964).)

2 Blackwell Scientific Publications. (Redrawn from J. G. Beaumont, *Introduction to neuropsychology* (1983), p. 37.)

3 Blackwell Scientific Publications. (Redrawn from J. G. Beaumont, *Introduction to neuropsychology* (1983), p. 37.)

4 Macmillan Inc. (After Penfield and Rasmussen, *The Cerebral Cortex of Man* (1950).)

5 Blackwell Scientific Publications. (Redrawn from J. G. Beaumont, *Introduction to neuropsychology* (1983), p. 28.)

6 Blackwell Scientific Publications. (Redrawn from J. G. Beaumont, *Introduction to neuropsychology* (1983), p. 37).

7 Blackwell Scientific Publications. (Redrawn from R. Passmore and J. S. Robson, eds., *Anatomy, biochemistry, physiology and related subjects* vol. 1 (1976), p. 25.23.)

8 Blackwell Scientific Publications. (Redrawn from J. F. Stein, *Introduction to neurophysiology* (1982), p. 253.)

9 W. H. Freeman and Company. (Redrawn from J. D. French, "The reticular formation", *Scientific American* (May 1957).)

10 Hodder & Stoughton Educational. (Redrawn from David Le Vay, *Teach yourself anatomy*, p. 425.)

11 Blackwell Scientific Publications. (Redrawn from J. F. Stein, *Introduction to neurophysiology* (1982), p. 316.)

12 W. H. Freeman and Company. (Redrawn from T. H. Bullock, *Introduction to nervous systems*, p. 87.) Also, Blackwell Scientific Publications. (Redrawn from J. F. Stein, *Introduction to neurophysiology* (1982), p. 215.)

13 Holt, Rinehart & Winston, CBS College Publishing. (Redrawn from Peter Milner, *Physiological psychology* (1971), p. 84.)

14 Holt, Rinehart & Winston, CBS College Publishing. (Redrawn from Peter Milner, *Physiological psychology* (1971), p. 89.)

15 Harper & Row Inc. (Redrawn from R. F. Thompson, *Foundations of physiological psychology*, p. 96.)

16 Rockefeller University Press. (After D. M. McLean, "The triune brain, emotion and scientific bias". In *The neurosciences: second study program* (1970).)

17 John Wiley. (After J. de Groot, in *Sex and behavior*, ed. F. A. Beach (1965).)

18 Blackwell Scientific Publications. (Redrawn from J. F. Stein, *Introduction to neurophysiology* (1983), p. 189.)

19 Williams & Wilkins Co. (After R. C. Truex and M. B. Carpenter, *Strong and Elwyn's human neuroanatomy* 5th edn. (1964).)

20 McGraw Hill. (After E. L. House and B. Pansky, *Neuroanatomy* (1960).)

21 McGraw Hill. (After E. L. House and B. Pansky, *Neuroanatomy* (1960).)

22 Academic Press. (Redrawn from *Hormones and behavior*, ed. Seymour Levine (1972), p. 4.)

23 Blackwell Scientific Publications. (Redrawn from J. F. Stein, *Introduction to neurophysiology* (1982), p. 95.) Also, Academic Press. (Redrawn from P. H. Lindsay and D. A. Norman, *Human information processing* (1977), p. 73.)

24 Blackwell Scientific Publications. (Redrawn from J. F. Stein, *Introduction to neurophysiology* (1983), p. 124.)

25 Hafner (Macmillan Inc.). (After G. L. Walls, *The vertebrate eye and its adaptive radiation* (1942).)

26 Murray Hill. (After H. Davis, *Hearing and deafness: a guide for laymen* (1947).)

27 Henry Kimpton. (Redrawn from N. B. Everett, *Functional neuroanatomy*. 5th edn. (1965), p. 101.)

28 McGraw Hill. (After E. L. House and B. Pansky, *Neuroanatomy* (1960).)

29 McGraw Hill. (After E. L. House and B. Pansky, *Neuroanatomy* (1960).)

31 Liverpool University Press. (After A. L. Hodgkin, *The conduction of the nervous impulse* 4th impression (1971), p. 17.)

32 Blackwell Scientific Publications. (Redrawn from R. Passmore and J. S. Robson, eds. *Anatomy, biochemistry, physiology and related subjects*, vol. 1, 2nd. edn. (1976), p. 25.15.)

33 McGraw Hill. (After E. T. Morgan and C. Stellar, *Physiological psychology* (1950).)

34 Blackwell Scientific Publications. (Redrawn from J. F. Stein, *Introduction to neurophysiology* (1982), p. 124.)

communication: animal

Cornell University Press. (Redrawn from K. von Frisch, *Bees, their vision, chemical senses and language* (1950).)

communication: human general

Cambridge University Press. (After van Hoof, in P. A. Hinde, ed., *Non-Verbal Communication.*)

crowd psychology

Addison Wesley (Redrawn from S. Milgram and H. Toch, "Collective behavior: crowds and social movements". In *Handbook of social psychology*, ed. Lindsey and Aronson. 2nd edn. (1969), p. 532.)

display

Oxford University Press. (After S. Cramp and K. E. L. Simmons, *Birds of the western Paleartic* (1977).)

kabbalism

Hutchinson. (Redrawn from *Z'ev ben Shimon Haleui, A Kabbalistic Universe* (1978).)

locomotion

Weidenfeld & Nicolson. (Redrawn from J. Gray, *Animal locomotion* (1968), p.278.)

recognition

Oxford University Press. (Redrawn from N. Tinbergen, *The study of instinct* (1951), p.78.)

RNA

Churchill Livingstone. (After G. H. Haggis et al., *Introduction to molecular biology* (1964), p. 217.)

vocational choice

Journal of vocational behavior. (Redrawn from vol. 13 (1980), p. 289.)

CONTRIBUTORS

ffrey W. Adams JWA
unel University

ffrey R. Alberts JRAl
diana University

ving E. Alexander IEA
ke University

avid Allport DA
niversity of Oxford

win Altman IA
niversity of Utah

lia E. Annas JEA
niversity of Oxford

dgar Anstey EA
rmer Chief Psychologist, Civil Service epartment

hn Archer JA
eston Polytechnic

Michael Argyle JMA
niversity of Oxford

hris Argyris CA
arvard University

amela J. Asquith PJA
niversity of Oxford

Maxwell Atkinson JMAt
niversity of Oxford

. D. Attenborough RDA
ustralian National University

mes R. Averill JRAv
niversity of Massachusetts

harles W. Baatz CWB
ate University of New York, Binghamton

hillip J. Bairstow PJB
niversity of London

ck I. Bardon JIB
niversity of North Carolina, Greensboro

mes Barr JB
niversity of Oxford

ichael Basseches MBa
rnell University

aul Bebbington PB
niversity of London

uzanne Benack SB
nion College, Schnectady

Michael Berger MBe
University of London

Len Berkowitz LB
University of Wisconsin

Roy Bhaskar RB
University of London

Frank H. M. Blackler FHMB
University of Lancaster

Marion Blank MB
Rutgers University

Sidney Bloch SB
Warneford Hospital, Oxford

David Boadella DJB
Institute for the Development of Human Potential, London

Margaret A. Boden MAB
University of Sussex

David E. Bond DEB
Royal School for the Deaf, Margate

Chester C. Borucki CCB
University of Michigan

Malcolm Bowie MMB
University of London

David D. C. Braine DDCB
University of Aberdeen

Glynis M. Breakwell GMB
University of Oxford

Peter E. Bryant PEB
University of Oxford

J. G. Burgoyne JGB
University of Lancaster

J. Dale Burnett JDB
Queen's University, Ontario

James N. Butcher JNB
University of Minnesota

Gillian Butler GB
Warneford Hospital, Oxford

George E. Butterworth GEB
University of Southampton

Peter Byrne PBy
Birmingham Polytechnic

Hilary Callan HC
Trent University, Ontario

Anne Campbell AC
Temple University, Philadelphia

Joseph J. Campos JJCa
University of Denver

Janet Caplan JSC
Williams College, Massachusetts

Karen Stojak Caplovitz KSC
University of Denver

J. Catalan JC
Warneford Hospital, Oxford

J. K. Chadwick-Jones JKC
Saint Mary's University, Nova Scotia

Steven C. Chamberlain SCC
Syracuse University

Michael R. A. Chance MRAC
University of Birmingham

A. J. Chapman AJC
University of Leeds

Jeremy Jon Cherfas JJCh
University of Oxford

Neil M. Cheshire NMC
University College of N. Wales, Bangor

Rebecca M. Chesire RMC
University of Hawaii at Manoa

T. Matthew Ciolek TMC
Australian National University

David D. Clarke DDC
University of Oxford

Tony I. Cline TIC
Inner London Education Authority

G. Cohen GC
University of Oxford

Stanley Cohen SCoh
Hebrew University of Jerusalem

Peter Collett PC
University of Oxford

Steven Collins SCol
University of Bristol

Mark Cook MC
University of Wales, Swansea

Clyde H. Coombs CHC
University of Michigan

Cary L. Cooper CLC
University of Manchester

Joel Cooper JCo
Princeton University

John A. Corbett JAC
University of London

Thomas R. Cox TRC
University of Nottingham

Richard F. Cromer RFC
Medical Research Council, London

John H. Crook JHC
University of Bristol

Gerald C. Cupchick GCC
University of Toronto

Christopher Dare CD
University of London

Nancy Datan ND
West Virginia University

Richard J. Davidson RJD
State University of New York, Purchase

D. R. Davies DRD
University of Aston

John B. Davies JBD
University of Strathclyde

Marian Stamp Dawkins MSD
University of Oxford

Richard Dawkins RD
University of Oxford

Edward de Bono EdeB
Cambridge

Jean-Pierre De Waele J-PDeW
Vrije Universiteit Brussel

Cliff J. Denton CJD
University of Oxford

J. B. Deregowski JBDe
University of Aberdeen

Morton Deutsch MDe
Columbia University

D. W. Dickins DWD
University of Liverpool

James E. Dittes JED
Yale University

Rene Drucker-Colin RD-C
Universidad Nacional Autonoma de Mexico

Steven W. Duck SWD
University of Lancaster

Adrian J. Dunn AJD
University of Florida

J. A. Edmondson JAE
University of Texas, Arlington

Muriel Egerton ME
University of Oxford

J. Richard Eiser JRE
University of Exeter

Roger P. Elbourne RPE
Brunel University

Robert N. Emde RNE
University of Denver

Berent Enç BE
University of Wisconsin

Christopher J. G. Fairburn CJGF
University of Oxford

Fred E. Fiedler FEF
University of Washington, Seattle

Esther Flath EF
École des Hautes Études en Sciences Sociales, Paris

Ronald Fletcher RF
University of Reading (Emeritus Professor)

Gillian G. Forrest GGF
Park Hospital for Children, Oxford

John Forrester JF
Univeristy of Cambridge

John P. Fox JPF
Imperial Cancer Research Fund Laboratories, London

Fay Fransella FF
Royal Free Hospital, London

N. H. Freeman NHF
University of Bristol

Stuart D. Friedman SDF
University of Michigan

Uta Frith UF
Medical Research Council, London

K. W. M. Fulford KWMF
University of Oxford

Adrian Furnham AF
University of London

E. A. Gaffan EAG
University of Reading

David M. Galloway DMG
University of Wellington

László Garai LG
Hungarian Academy of Sciences

Patrick L. Gardiner PLG
University of Oxford

M. A. G. Garman MAGG
University of Reading

Dennis Gath DG
Warneford Hospital Oxford

Nicholas Gendle NG
University of Oxford

Marianthi Georgoudi MG
Temple University, Philadelphia

Kenneth J. Gergen KJG
Swarthmore College, Pennsylvania

Diane L. Gill DLG
University of Iowa

G. P. Ginsburg GPG
University of Nevada

Jules O. Goddard JOG
London Business School

Martin Gorin MGo
École des Hautes Études en Sciences Sociales, Paris

J. C. B. Gosling JCBG
University of Oxford

Carl F. Graumann CFG
University of Heidelberg

Richard L. Gregory RLG
University of Bristol

Sebastian P. Grossman SPG
University of Chicago

John H. Gruzelier JHG
University of London

Ronald Gulliford RG
University of Birmingham

Horst U. K. Gundlach HUKG
University of Passau

Peter Hacker PH
University of Oxford

W. Hacker WH
Institut für Ingenieurwissenschaft, Dresden

Milton D. Hakel MDH
Ohio State University

T. R. Halliday TRH
Open University

David Hargreaves DHH
University of Oxford

Rom Harré RHa
University of Oxford

Stanley G. Harris SGH
University of Michigan

Daniel P. Harrison DPH
State University of New York, Binghamton

Paul H. Harvey PHH
University of Sussex

Keith E. Hawton KEH
Warneford Hospital, Oxford

Paul Heelas PLFH
University of Lancaster

R. W. Hiorns RWH
University of Oxford

Ray J. Hodgson RJH
University of London

Robert Hogan RHo
Johns Hopkins University

J. Martin Hollis JMH
University of East Anglia

J. R. Honner JRH
Campion College, Victoria

Gary P. Horowitz GPH
State University of New York, Binghamton

Charles Hulme ChasH
University of York

Sonja M. Hunt SMH
Fairleigh Dickinson University, NJ

Carl F. Hurwitz CFH
Lesley College, Cambridge, Massachusetts

Chris M. Hutton CMH
University of Oxford

R. R. Jacobs RRJ
Pennsylvania State University

Joseph M. F. Jaspars JMFJ
University of Oxford

Robert A. Jensen RAJ
Southern Illinois University of Carbondale

E. Roy John ERJ
New York University Medical Centre

John M. Johnson JMJ
Arizona State University

Derek Johnston DWJ
University of Oxford

Alison Jolly AJ
The Rockefeller University

Gregory V. Jones GVJ
University of Bristol

Virginia Jud VJ
State University of New York

David L. Julier DLJ
University of Oxford

Shirley J. Kavanagh SJK
Thomas Coram Research Unit, London

Thomas C. Kelly TCK
London

David Kennard DK
Leicester University

Warren Kenton WKe
London

Raymond P. Kesner RPK
University of Utah

Jennifer King JK
University of Oxford

Marcel Kinsbourne MK
Eunice Kennedy Shriver Center for Mental Retardation

Walter Kintsch WKi
Center for Advanced Studies in the Behavioral Sciences, Stanford

T. M. Kitwood TMK
University of Bradford

Marga Kreckel MKr
Erlangen

Hans Kummer HK
University of Zurich

Ron Kurtz RK
Hakomi Institute, Boulder

Roger Lamb RL
University of Oxford

D. Legge DL
North Staffordshire Polytechnic

Justin Fritz Leiber JFL
University of Houston

Howard Leventhal HL
University of Wisconsin, Madison

Barbara B. Lloyd BBL
University of Sussex

J. W. Lloyd JWL
Abingdon Hospital, Oxford

Edwin A. Locke EAL
University of Maryland

Ingrid Lunt IL
Inner London Education Authority

Donna A. Lupardo DAL
State University of New York, Binghamton

D. J. McFarland DJM
University of Oxford

Robert McHenry RMcH
University of Oxford

N. J. Mackintosh NJM
University of Cambridge

Edward H. Madden EHM
State University of New York, Buffalo (Emeritus Professor)

Salvatore R. Maddi SRM
University of Chicago

Rodney Maliphant RM
University College, London

Aubrey W. G. Manning AWGM
University of Edinburgh

Peter E. Marsh PEM
Oxford Polytechnic

W. A. Marshall WAM
University of Technology, Loughborough

Maryanne Martin MM
University of Oxford

Richard A. Mayou RAM
University of Oxford

Roel W. Meertens RWM
University of Amsterdam

J. H. Mellanby JHM
University of Oxford

John E. Merritt JEM
Open University

Alexandre Métraux AM
University of Heidelberg

Janet Milewski JM
Rutgers University

Susanna Millar SMi
University of Oxford

B. Minakovic BM
University of Oxford

Martin C. Mitcheson MCM
University College Hospital, London

Don L. Mixon DLM
University of Wollongong

J. D. Mollon JDM
University of Cambridge

Jill G. Morawski JGM
Wesleyan University, Connecticut

Neville Moray NM
University of Toronto

Peter J. Mortimore PJM
Inner London Education Authority

J. Adam Morton JAM
University of Bristol

S. Moscovici SMo
École des Hautes Études en Sciences Sociales, Paris

Richard T. Mowday RTM
University of Oregon

Peter Mühlhäusler PM
University of Oxford

John R. Nesselroade JRN
Pennsylvania State University

D. K. B. Nias DKBN
University of London

Stephen Nowicki Jr SN
University of Atlanta, Georgia

Andrew P. Ockwell APO
University of Oxford

Michael W. Orr MWO
Horton General Hospital, Oxford

William Outhwaite WO
University of Sussex

Geneviève Paicheler GP
École des Hautes Études en Sciences Sociales, Paris

G. A. Parker GAP
University of Liverpool

W. L. L. Parry-Jones WLLP-J
University of Oxford

Renée B. Paton-Saltzberg RBP-S
Oxford Polytechnic

W. Barnett Pearce WBP
University of Massachusetts, Amherst

John M. Pearce JMP
University of Wales, Cardiff

David Pears DP
University of Oxford

Harry F. M. Peeters HFMP
Tilburg University, The Netherlands

Addie L. Perkins ALP
University of Michigan

Philip Pettit PP
University of Bradford

T. K. Pitcairn TKP
University of Edinburgh

Gerald M. Platt GMP
University of Masschusetts

Robert Plutchick RP
Albert Einstein College of Medicine, New York

Terry L. Powley TLP
Purdue University

Michael Pressley MP
University of Western Ontario

Dean G. Pruitt DGP
State University of New York, Buffalo

Geoffrey Pullen GPP
Littlemore Hospital, Oxford

Patrick Rabbitt PR
University of Durham

Jonathan Rée JR
Middlesex Polytechnic

Benjamin E. Reese BER
University of Oxford

Peter C. Reynolds PCR
Biped Inst., Palo Alto, Calif.

V. Reynolds VR
University of Oxford

Francis A. Richards FAR
Cornell University

Mark Ridley MR
University of Oxford

J. B. Rijsman JBR
Tilburg University

P. G. Rivière PGR
University of Oxford

Trevor W. Robbins TWR
University of Cambridge

Howard Robinson HMR
University of Liverpool

R. Rodnight RR
University of London

John C. Rowan JCR
London

Joseph F. Rychlak JFR
Purdue University

John Sabini JS
University of Pennsylvania

V. N. Sadovsky VNS
Institute for Systems Studies, Moscow

Martin A. Safer MAS
Catholic University of America, Washington

Richard C. Saunders RCS
University of Oxford

Lindsay T. Sharpe LTS
University of Freiburg

Mildred L. G. Shaw MLGS
York University, Ontario

E. W. Shepherd EWS
City of London Polytechnic

Sydney Shoemaker SS
Cornell University

J. M. Shorter JMS
University of Oxford

John D. Shotter JDS
University of Nottingham

W. Shropshire Jr WS
Smithsonian Radiation Biology Laboratory, Rockville

John J. Sidtis JJS
Cornell University

Maury Silver MS
Johns Hopkins University

Dean Keith Simonton DKS
University of California, Davis

W. T. Singleton WTS
University of Aston

Richard R. Skemp RRS
University of Warwick

Ben R. Slugoski BRS
University of Oxford

Peter K. Smith PKS
University of Sheffield

Peter D. Spear PDS
University of Wisconsin

Larry R. Squire LRS
University of California, San Diego

H. Stephen Straight HSS
State University of New York, Binghamton

Siegfried Streufert SSt
Pennsylvania State University

Donald E. Super DES
Columbia University (Emeritus Professor)

Saradha D. Supramaniam SDS
Open University

Kathy Sylva K
University of Oxford

Henri Tajfel H
University of Bristol

Charles T. Tart CT
University of California, Davis

Colin Tatton C
International Transactional Analys Association, Birmingham

David C. Taylor DC
University of Manchester

Insup Taylor I
University of Toronto

Talbot J. Taylor T
University of Oxford

Sybe J. S. Terwee SJS
University of Leiden

Irving G. Thalberg IG
University of Illinois, Chicago

Sid B. Thomas SB
State University of New York, Binghamto

John Thorp J
University of Ottawa

Noel M. Tichy NM
University of Michigan

Michael J. Tobin MJ
University of Birmingham

Richard G. Totman RG
University of Sussex

Roni Beth Tower RB
Yale University

Harry C. Triandis HC
University of Illinois, Urbana-Champaigr

Peter Trower PE
University of Leicester

J. O. Urmson JO
Stanford University (Emeritus Professor

Ladislav Valach L
University of Bern

Carol Van Hartesveldt CVan
University of Florida

Philippe Van Parijs PVan
Institut d'Economie, Louvain-la-Neuve

Philip E. Vernon PE
University of Calgary

Dirk H. G. Versteeg DHG
State University of Utrecht

Godfrey N. A. Vesey GNA
Open University

Maryse Vincent M
University of Hamburg

Mario von Cranach Mv
University of Bern

Nigel Walker NDW
University of Cambridge

Ralph C. S. Walker RCSW
University of Oxford

Patrick D. Wall PDW
University of London

Mary Warnock MW
University of Oxford

Peter B. Warr PBW
University of Sheffield

Nancy C. Waugh NCW
University of Oxford

K. Wedell KW
University of London

H. Weinrich-Haste HW-H
University of Bath

Kevin Wheldall KW
University of Birmingham

Andrew Whiten AW
University of St Andrews

Diana Whitmore DW
Psychosynthesis and Education Trust, London

Glayde Whitney GW
Florida State University

K. V. Wilkes KVW
University of Oxford

Richard S. Williams RSW
Civil Service, London

Colin Wilson CW
Gorran Haven, Cornwall

Glenn D. Wilson GDW
University of London

P. G. Winch PGW
University of London

Gordon Winocur GWi
Trent University, Ontario

Linda A. Wood LAW
University of Guelph, Ontario

Sharon Wood SW
University of Sussex

Andrew R. Woodfield ARW
University of Bristol

Steve W. Woolgar SWW
Brunel University

Anna K. Wright AKW
Surrey County Council

R. C. Ziller RCZ
University of Florida, Gainseville

Joseph L. Zinnes JLZ
University of Illinois, Urbana-Champaign

EDITORIAL NOTE

Asterisks against titles in the bibliographies indicate items suitable for further reading. The convention 1920 (*1982*) indicates a work first published in 1920 but widely accessible only in an edition of 1982, to which the publication details given refer.

Cross references to other entries are printed in small capitals in the text. Leads to further additional information can be found from the index.

Technical terms are defined in the index.

A

A priori; a posteriori An a priori proposition is one which can be known to be true a priori. Knowledge of the truth of a given proposition is a priori if no more experience is needed for that knowledge than is already required merely to understand the proposition. Some have held that substantial truths about the nature of reality can be known a priori; others that such knowledge is merely based on an understanding of linguistic conventions. An a priori concept is likewise one which has a certain independence of experience, though the best way of characterizing that independence is uncertain.

An a posteriori item is one which is not, in the above ways, a priori. JMS

able children *See* gifted children

abnormal behavior: animal Behavior resulting from stress or from a pathological condition. Experimentally induced anxiety was investigated by Pavlov who discovered that well-trained animals subjected to difficult problems often showed extreme signs of emotion. Prolonged exposure to stressful situations can lead to experimental neurosis and to physiological symptoms such as gastric ulcers. Animals subject to stress generally show loss of appetite, increased aggression and stereotyped behavior. These types of abnormal behavior sometimes occur in animals in zoos, especially if their natural behavior patterns are interrupted. DJM

absence from school and truancy "Absence from school" is failure to attend school irrespective of reason whereas "truancy" is unjustifiable absence from school without parental knowledge or consent. In England parents are required by the 1944 Education Act to ensure that their children receive education "suitable to their age, ability and aptitude" between the ages of five and sixteen. In practice, most parents do this by registering their child at a school maintained or aided by the local education authority and ensuring that he or she attends regularly unless prevented by illness or religious observance. Similar laws exist in the United States and most other developed countries although the ages of compulsory schooling vary: children in the United States, for example, are not legally required to attend school before the age of six.

There are remarkable consistencies in rates of school attendance. Cutter and Jones (1971) found a 90 per cent attendance rate in a sample of American elementary schools. Rates in Britain are similar; indeed the proportion of pupils absent has remained stable throughout the twentieth century: 89 per cent attendance at London Board Schools in 1906 (Rubinstein 1969); 89 per cent attendance in the Inner London Education Authority's schools in 1970 (Hill 1971); and a Department of Education and Science survey reported that on a given day in January 1974 90.1 per cent of all pupils aged twelve or over in England and Wales were present. This survey also showed that absence rates were highest in the final year of compulsory education, and similar trends have been found in the United States.

There has been sharp disagreement about the proportion of absent pupils who are absent illegally. Estimates range from 4 per cent (DES 1967) to 75 per cent (Reynolds and Murgatroyd 1974). A study by Galloway (1982a) showed that from a sample of British schools 4 per cent of pupils were recorded as absent illegally for at least 50 per cent of their final year. The difficulties in establishing the illegality of a pupil's absence are considerable; it is likely that many published figures have given an over-optimistic view.

Traditionally clinical practice has distinguished between SCHOOL PHOBIA, also known as school refusal, and truancy. Children referred to clinics for school phobia tend to be younger (Tyerman 1958; Hersov 1960). While Hersov and Tyerman both noted poor social adjustment, low average IQ and low educational attainments, Cooper (1966) found no evidence of educational retardation relative to IQ.

Truancy and school phobia together account for a very small proportion of absences from both primary and secondary schools. By far the most common explanations in Galloway's study (1982a) were "absence with parental knowledge, consent and approval", and "parents unable or unwilling to insist on return". It is clear that parents are aware of their children's absence in a large majority of cases, and in roughly half these cases the parents withhold their children from school. In the remainder, the child insists on remaining at home, with the parents unable or unwilling to insist on return.

Surprisingly little attention has been directed at reasons for parents condoning their children's absence from school. A high positive correlation has been demonstrated in Belfast and Sheffield between parental poverty and persistent absentee rates (Harbison and Caven 1977; Galloway 1982a). Harbison and Caven did not find this association in rural areas of Northern Ireland. It seems probable that absence from school and poverty may both arise from other variables associated with depressed inner city areas. (See also SOCIAL DISADVANTAGE.)

This suggestion received some support in a study of all persistent absentees in one area of Sheffield (Galloway 1982b). Parents of absentees were significantly more likely to be unemployed than parents of good attenders selected from the same class in school and living in the same areas. More important, a health questionnaire revealed a high prevalence of probable psychiatric illness in the mothers of absent pupils. The most common symptoms were those associated with depression. Anxiety about parental health was frequently associated with absence, but social, educational and disciplinary problems at school became increasingly important in the secondary school years.

Several studies have reported poor attenders as being less successful on tests of educational attainment and general intelligence than regular attenders. There is disagreement about whether educational retardation is the cause or the result of poor attendance. May (1975) argued that poor attenders were performing badly at school before their irregular attendance started. It has also been demonstrated that poor attenders at the age of seven were not educationally retarded at the age of sixteen, compared with their peers, if they were attending regularly at fifteen. On the other hand, continued poor attendance at fifteen was related to poor attainment. This suggests that absentees who miss a considerable amount of schooling at an early age can catch up through subsequent regular attendance, and hence that the poor attainments of the continued absentees whose teachers did not regard them as truants may be causally related to that absence. Tennent (1971) listed twenty studies of juvenile or adult offenders which reported at least 20 per cent of the sample having a history of truancy. May (1975) found that truants were more likely to have criminal records than absentees whose teachers did not regard them as truants. Galloway (1982a) found that over 20 per cent of boys whose parents condoned their absence from school had criminal records; this also applied to 19 per cent of boys whose absence was attributed mainly to illness. The general picture is one of a consistent association between truancy and DELINQUENCY, and of a slightly less consistent association between absenteeism and delinquency. Nevertheless, it should be emphasized that a majority of poor attenders are not known to offend.

There appears to be a substantial overlap between school drop-out and truancy. Many American studies on individuals who leave school without qualifications shows them to end up with low occupational status, higher likelihood of being unemployed, and decreased participation in adult education. Because truancy is associated with early school leaving, it is often difficult to tell whether it is the truancy *per se* or the lack of qualifications that leads directly to the adult outcome.

Robins and Ratcliff (1980) investigated the long-term effects of truancy on the lives of a large sample of black males, all of whom had attended ordinary state schools in St. Louis and had been above average in ability. The men were interviewed at 30–36 years of age while at the same time their records on education, housing, armed forces, police and hospital files were scrutinized. In this large group of men high truancy was found to be associated with school drop-out and later with low earnings and deviant behavior in adulthood. Naturally these poor adult outcomes were in part explained by the truants' dropping out of school and by their adolescent deviance, but the authors stress that the "truancy itself continued to have predictive power even when these intermediary events were taken into account" (p.80). On the basis of their research Robins and Ratcliff urge measures to prevent truancy which, if successful, could be expected not only to affect truancy levels, but "to forestall a variety of related deviant acts that may otherwise appear later" (p.80).

Greater attention has been paid to family and social variables in poor school attenders than to the school's own contribution in promoting regular attendance. Reynolds and Murgatroyd (1977) reported consistent differences in attendance rates between Welsh secondary modern schools with similar catchment areas (see SCHOOL DIFFERENCES), differences associated with the school's rules and policies rather than with structural variables such as size or age of buildings. More recently Rutter et al. (1 have reported significant differences in attendance between London schools, after controlling for in variables. Galloway (1982a) demonstrated signif changes in persistent absentee rates within indiv schools over a period of three years. His evidence sug that the school's influence on attendance is greate disadvantaged areas where the likelihood of absen highest in the first place.

There have been few systematic studies on eithe prognosis or the management of absence from sc Galloway, Ball and Seyd (1981a) showed that legal a is taken against only a very small proportion of persi unauthorized absentees. The prognosis following action was extremely poor, but substantial improve was associated with a change of school when this arranged for some special reason, rather than a ordinary age-related transfer (Galloway, Ball and 1981b). Many local education authorities have establ special centers for poor attenders. However, these are able to cater for a very small minority of the pup question, and systematic studies of their effec subsequent attendance are conspicuously absent.

There is no simple explanation for absence from sc Variables within the individual and within his or family, home neighborhood and school are all likely important. A comprehensive assessment is required in case, focussing on the school's provision for the pu well as on the pupil and his or her background. Succ management requires parental cooperation assistance from teachers and members of the educat and social work support services.

Bibliography

Cooper, M. G. 1966: School refusal. *Educational research* 8. 223–9.

Cutter, N. C. and Jones, E. R. 1971: Evaluation of ESEA Title VIII D Prevention Program 'Project KAPS' School Year, 1970–71. Mimeo. (in Robins and Ratcliff 1980.

Department of Education and Science, 1974: Press Notice: *Results o absence survey*, London: DES.

Galloway, D. 1982a: Persistent absence from school. *Educational rese* press.

——— 1982b: A study of persistent absentees and their families. *journal of educational psychology*. In press.

Galloway, D. M., Ball, C. and Seyd, R. 1981a: Administrative an procedures available to local education authorities in cases of poor attendance. *Durham and Newcastle research review* 9. 201–9.

——— 1981b: School attendance following legal or administrative for unauthorised absence. *Educational review* 33, 53–65.

Galloway, D. M., Ball, C., Blomfield, D. and Seyd, R. 1982: *Scho disruptive pupils*. London: Longman.

Harbison, J. and Caven, N. 1977: *Persistent school absenteeism in N Ireland*. Belfast: Statistics and Economics Unit, Dept. of Finance (No Ireland).

Hathaway, S. R., Reynolds, P. C. and Monachesi, E.D. 1969: Follow u later careers and lives of 1,000 boys who dropped out of high school. *of consulting clinical psychology* 33, 370–80.

Hersov, L. 1960: Refusal to go to school. *Journal of child psycholo psychiatry* 2. 137–45.

Hill, B. 1971: Worried about truancy, *Times educational supplement*, 2

May, D. 1975: Truancy, school absenteeism and delinquency. *educational studies* 7. 97–107.

Reynolds, D. and Murgatroyd, S. 1974: Being absent from school. *British journal of law and society* 1. 78–80.

Reynolds, D. and Murgatroyd, S. 1977: The sociology of schooling and the absent pupil: the school as a factor in the generation of truancy. In *Absenteeism in South Wales: studies of pupils, their homes and their secondary schools*, ed. H. C. M. Carroll. Swansea: University College of Swansea, Faculty of Education.

Robins, L. N. and Ratcliff, K. S. 1980: The long-term outcome of truancy. In *Out of school*, ed. L. Hersov and I. Berg. London: Wiley.

Rubinstein, D. 1969: *School attendance in London, 1870–1904: A social history*. Hull: University of Hull.

Rutter, M. et al. 1979: *Fifteen thousand hours: secondary schools and their effects on pupils*. London: Open Books; Cambridge, Mass: Harvard University Press.

Tennent, T.G. 1971: School non-attendance and delinquency. *Educational research* 13, 185–90.

Tyerman, M. J. 1958: A research into truancy. *British journal of educational psychology* 28, 217–25.

absenteeism Time lost from paid work due to frequent and repeated absence. Often used as a criterion in personnel selection research, absence rates may be measured by total days absent or number of spells of absence – one absence lasting twenty days may not have the same significance as twenty absences of one day each. Absences represent lost time to the employer, as do tardiness and unauthorized pauses for breaks. In recent years attendance and work schedules have received increased attention as organizations have experimented with flexible working schedules. Absence control policies differ greatly among organizations. There is no evidence of a unitary personal trait or disposition to be absent. MDH

Bibliography

Steers, Richard M. and Stone, Thomas H. 1982: Organizational exit. In *Personnel management*, ed. Kendrith M. Rowland and Gerald R. Ferris. Boston, Mass.: Allyn and Bacon.

accidents An accident is an unexpected event which causes injury to persons or damage to property, or both. Psychology relates to accidents through explanations of human error. Calculations of proportions of accidents due to human error are specious because there is invariably a complex pattern of preceding causal events leading up to every accident and within this pattern there are bound to be some human errors. Every psychological theory from psychoanalysis to information processing has some explanation as to why errors occur. The art of applying psychology to accident investigations is to select the appropriate mix of theories which seems relevant to the particular problem. There is a conflict between the two equally tenable concepts that errors are an inevitable concomitant of human action and that people are responsible for their actions. This is usually resolved by the compromise of "reasonable care". Accident data and evidence are always dubious and rarely comparable because of problems of definition and of reporting. However accidental injury occurs mainly in the home and in private cars. Occupational injury is relatively rare, as occupational safety has improved steadily over the past thirty years. WTS

Bibliography

Singleton, W.T. 1973: Theoretical approaches to human error. *Ergonomics* 16.6, 727–37.

acetylcholine A neurotransmitter in both the peripheral and central nervous system. Acetylcholine is synthesized from choline. Once released at the SYNAPSE, it interacts with postsynaptic receptors, and then is degraded enzymatically by acetylcholinesterase. There are two types of acetylcholine (cholinergic) receptors. Nicotinic receptors are mimicked by nicotine and blocked by α-bungarotoxin. Synapses involving nicotinic receptors are excitatory and have been postulated by McGeer, Eccles and McGeer (1978) to be ionotropic: that is, the interaction of acetylcholine and nicotinic receptors causes a direct change in the ion permeability of the postsynaptic membrane. Muscarinic receptors are mimicked by muscaine and blocked by atropine. These synapses can be excitatory or inhibitory and are thought to be metabotropic, using cyclic AMP as a second messenger (see ADENYL CYCLASE). Peripheral actions of acetylcholine include parasympathetic (muscarinic) innervation of smooth muscles and glands and nicotinic innervation of skeletal muscle (see NEURONS, ALPHA MOTOR). Centrally, acetylcholine is found predominantly in LOCAL CIRCUIT NEURONS, primarily in the EXTRAPYRAMIDAL MOTOR SYSTEM, THALAMUS and CEREBRAL CORTEX. In addition, there are cholinergic projections from portions of the LIMBIC SYSTEM to HIPPOCAMPUS. Central cholinergic synapses are predominantly muscarinic. Cholinergic systems are involved with movement and behavioral inhibition. (See also NEUROTRANSMITTER.) GPH

Bibliography

McGeer, Patrick L., Eccles, John C. and McGeer, Edith G. 1978: *Molecular neurobiology of the mammalian brain*. New York and London: Plenum.

achievement motivation This concept was developed by McClelland (see McClelland et al. 1953) and refers to the motive to achieve some standard of accomplishment or proficiency. People with a strong achievement motive (which McClelland calls need for achievement) prefer moderate to easy or hard goals or risks, want concrete feedback regarding task performance, prefer tasks where skill rather than luck determines the outcome, seek personal responsibility, have a future time perspective, and err somewhat on the side of optimism in estimating their chances for success, especially on new tasks. McClelland (1961) claims that the achievement motive is crucial in entrepreneurship and influences success in entrepreneurial occupations (e.g. selling); he has even claimed that cultural differences in achievement motivation account for differences in economic growth rates. It is argued that the need for achievement is fostered by child rearing practices which encourage independence. It is held by McClelland to be a subconscious motive, and therefore more accurately measured by projective techniques such as the Thematic Apperception Test, than by self reports. Research on achievement motivation has been criticized on numerous grounds, including: unreliability of the Thematic Apperception Test measures; inconsistency of results; excessive use of post hoc explanations when the results failed to turn out as predicted; and ethnocentrism. Heckhausen (1967) and Atkinson and Raynor (1978) have summarized much of the achievement motivation research. EAL

Bibliography

Atkinson, J.W. and Raynor, J.O. 1978: *Personality, motivation and achievement.* New York: Hemisphere.

Heckhausen, H. 1967: *The anatomy of achievement motivation.* New York: Academic Press.

McClelland, D.C. 1961: *The achieving society.* Princeton: Van Nostrand.

——— et al, 1953: *The achievement motive.* New York: Appleton-Century-Crofts.

acoustic coding Verbal symbols are said to have undergone acoustic coding when they are remembered according to what they sound like rather than what they look like or mean. Conrad (1964) and others have demonstrated that a letter incorrectly recalled in a given serial position from a recently presented list tends to be phonetically but not visually similar to the correct letter. From these results and those of related experiments (e.g. Kintsch and Bushke 1969), some psychologists have inferred that only the phonetic features of verbal information are represented in short term memory and that only its semantic (and not its phonetic) features are retained in long term memory. Later work (e.g. Craik and Kirsner 1974; Shulman 1972) has shown that that is not the case: short term memory for verbal information holds more than its phonetic characteristics; and its phonetic characteristics are often represented in long term memory as well. NCW

Bibliography

Conrad, R. 1964: Acoustic confusions in immediate memory. *British journal of psychology* 55, 75–84.

Craik, F.I.M. and Kirsner, K. 1974: The effect of speaker's voice on word recognition. *Quarterly journal of experimental psychology* 26, 274–84.

Kintsch, W. and Bushke, H. 1969: Homophones and synonyms in short term memory. *Journal of experimental psychology* 80, 403–7.

Shulman, H.G. 1972: Semantic confusion errors in short term memory. *Journal of verbal learning and verbal behavior* 11, 221–7.

acquaintance A form, or supposed form, of knowledge of things which is independent of any process of inference or any knowledge of truths. It is contrasted by RUSSELL (1910) with knowledge by description, a form of knowledge of things which does require inference and knowledge of truths. I may, for example, know the table before me as "the physical object which causes such and such sense data". According to Russell the only possible objects of acquaintance are the current data of sense (see SENSE DATUM) and of introspection, remembered data of these two kinds, UNIVERSALS, certain complex facts, and possibly the experiencing self. Acquaintance, he claims, is the necessary basis of all knowledge and of all understanding of the meanings of words. JMS

Bibliography

Russell, B.A.W. 1910: Knowledge by acquaintance and knowledge by description. *Proceedings of the Aristotelian Society* 11, 108–28.

act psychology The origins of the concept lie in Brentano's doctrine of INTENTIONALITY (though he did not use exactly this term). In his *Psychologie vom empirishen Standpunkt* (1874) he suggested the concept "intentional inexistence" to characterize the distinction between mental and physical. Unlike physical phenomena, mental phenomena are "directed upon", "point to", "mean", "refer to", or "contain" objects, which need not actually exist (for we may believe falsehoods, or try to reach for unattainable goals, etc.). In contrast to Wundt's and Titchener's introspective psychology (see INTROSPECTION) of contents, Brentano's psychology of acts asserted that mind could not be reduced to a set of elements found in consciousness: the finding of them requires mental activity of one kind or another, and, act psychologists argued, it is the way in which that activity "contains" or is "directed towards" that result which manifests the true nature of mind, not the results alone. This "directedness" of consciousness was investigated empirically by the Wurzburg school (begun by Külpe, *c.* 1900), but act psychology and its emphasis on intentionality is only now coming fully into its own, linked with an increased understanding of how people construct socially intelligible accounts of their own actions (see ETHOGENICS, ETHNOMETHODOLOGY). JDS

Bibliography

Brentano, F. 1874 *(1973): Psychology from an empirical standpoint.* London: Routledge & Kegan Paul; New York: Humanities.

Humphrey, G. 1951: *Thinking: an introduction to its experimental psychology.* London: Methuen; New York: Wiley.

ACTH Adrenocorticotropic hormone, a 39 amino acid peptide found in the anterior lobe of the PITUITARY. Its secretion from the pituitary is promoted by a chemical factor (CRF) released from the HYPOTHALAMUS (see BRAIN AND CENTRAL NERVOUS SYSTEM: ILLUSTRATIONS, fig. 22). On release from the pituitary into the blood stream, e.g. in response to stressful stimulation, ACTH reaches the adrenal gland where it stimulates the growth of the adrenal glands and the synthesis and release of steroid adrenal hormones. ACTH is also found in the brain, even following removal of the pituitary in laboratory animals. There is increasing evidence that, like the ENDORPHINS, ACTH may function as a neuromodulator in the central nervous system (CNS) (see NEUROMODULATORS). First, ACTH and the endorphins appear to be derived from the same macromolecular precursor and can be found in the same overlapping neural pathways. Second, ACTH can interact with opiate receptors and many of its effects are reversible by opiate antagonists. Finally, administration of ACTH (or its fragments) directly into the CNS have been shown to have dramatic effects on such diverse behavior as grooming and retention of avoidance learning in experimental animals. GPH

action potential (See BRAIN AND CENTRAL NERVOUS SYSTEM: ILLUSTRATIONS, figs. 30 and 31.) The electrochemical disturbance that is propagated along the length of the axon of a neuron. It is the basic unit of transmission of information from one place to another in the nervous system. Its origins lie in the fact that there is difference in potential across the neuron membrane; the inside is negative relative to the outside by approximately 70 mV. This resting potential is the result of positively charged potassium ions moving from the inside of the cell, where they are more concentrated, across the cell membrane, to the outside where there is a higher concentration of positively charged sodium ions. When a cell is stimulated it may become depolarized to a critical value called threshold. When threshold is exceeded, the resting potential collapses within 1 msec causing a transient reversal of polarity of the membrane potential at the site of stimulation due to a rapid influx of sodium ions. The resting potential is restored by an outward flow of potassium ions. This activity causes an adjacent region of the axon membrane to be stimulated and the action potential proceeds down the length of the axon toward the synaptic terminals of the cell. The amplitude of an action potential is unaffected by the intensity of the depolarizing stimulus. In myelinated axons, the action potential occurs only at breaks in the myelin sheath, called nodes of Ranvier, resulting in much more rapid conduction of the impulse. RAJ

action research Involves the creation and refinement of theory based on the application of theoretical principles of behavioural science in an effort to alter a social system. The action research model is a basic model underlying most ORGANIZATION DEVELOPMENT activities and is a data-based, problem-solving model that replicates the steps involved in the scientific method of inquiry. French and Bell (1973) postulate three processes in action research: data collection, feedback to the clients and action planning. Action research is both an approach to problem solving – a model or a paradigm – and a problem solving process – a series of activities and events.

When used as a process action research involves: systematically collecting research data about a system relative to some objective goal of that system; feeding these data back into the system; taking action by altering selected variables within the system based on both the data and hypotheses; evaluating the results of actions by collecting more data. A static picture is taken of an organization on the basis of "what exists", and hunches and hypotheses suggest actions. These actions typically entail manipulating some variable in the system that is under the control of the action researcher (this often means doing something differently from the way it has been done in the past). Later, a second static picture is taken of the system to examine the effects of the action taken. ALP/NMT

Bibliography

French, W.L. and Bell, C.H. Jr. 1973: *Organization development*. Englewood Cliffs, N.J.: Prentice-Hall.

action theory A theory concerned with the study of human goal-directed behavior and its social basis. Key terms are action, act and actor. A comprehensive definition of action includes the following characteristics: it is consciously goal-directed and planned, is motivated and deliberate behavior, is accompanied by emotions and is socially steered and controlled. An act is a unit of action which occurs in a socially defined situation and is characterized by a goal. An actor in the ideal sense is a person gifted with the capacities of self-reflection and action-related self-cognitions (e.g. identity, autonomy, competence and emotional involvement) and who is capable of experiencing and accepting responsibility.

There are many action theories. We assume, however, that these are to a great extent based on common sense social knowledge about goal oriented action as it has been described by Heider (1958; see ATTRIBUTION THEORY). Naive behavior theory has been further elaborated by Laucken (1973) who argues that assumptions about goal-directed action constitute its nucleus and that concepts such as those of goal, plan, decision, resolution and motive are part of naive action analyses and attributed by the naive psychologist to his own and others' behavior. It seems plausible that much of the basic conceptual similarity of modern action theories can be ascribed to their authors' common cultural background.

Basically, scientific problems in this field can be formulated in three questions. How is action organized, steered and controlled by the individual actor? How is it motivated (is there still room for will) and what is the role of emotion in the organization of action? How is individual action steered and controlled by society? Let us pursue the problems inherent in these questions to present a few prototypes of action theory.

"Cognitive steering" and systems approach

These theories (also referred to as "action-structure theories" or "action-regulation-theories") are based on general systems theory. Their common nucleus consists of the "sequential–hierarchical model", in which action is seen as sequentially ordered on various hierarchical levels, interconnected by feedback-circles.

As a widely known prototype, let us consider the theory of Miller, Galanter and Pribram (1960). Starting from the analogy between the program-directed computer and the plan-directed behaving organism, the authors assume that behavior is steered and controlled by cognition. Although they do not actually propose a theory of action ("action" and "behavior" are used synonymously, a goal concept is missing, etc.), they have provided some of its most essential concepts: (1) the "image" (following a notion from Boulding) as a general stock of knowledge, serving as the basis for the development of a plan. (2) The plan is a "hierarchy of instruction": instruction as far as these pieces of information direct behavior, and hierarchical since they are ordered on superposed and subordinated strategical and tactical levels. (3) The famous TOTE-unit (*T*est-*O*perate-*T*est-*E*xit) is introduced as the basic unit of the organisation of behavior, essentially a feedback-loop. TOTE-units are, in the same plan and at the same time, sequentially as well as hierarchically ordered and thus constitute sequential-hierarchical organisation.

In some of the most advanced and fertile action theories these concepts are integrated into the framework of the "Marxist theory of activity" (Rubinstein 1977). In his *Arbeits- und Ingenieur-Psychologie* Hacker (1978) presents an elaborate theory of work activity, essentially an action theory of industrial work.

Work activity is a basic concept in Marxist psychology. Work is considered the driving force of human development. All mental processes are considered as aspects of activity, since they reflect activity. Conscious reflection is considered the most important mental process (in this view, the body–mind problem does not exist). Two basic problems in the psychology of activity are the regulation of motive or drive ("Antriebsregulation") and the regulation of execution ("Ausführungsregulation"). Drive-regulation is mainly a problem of activity, execution-regulation refers to action and is the main concern of the theory. Action is a psychological unit of activity: in action, the activity's motive is dissolved into the (conscious) goal and the intent or volitional processes.

Action is a multi-level process; different levels of the hierarchy are linked with different degrees of conscious representation. Hacker distinguishes three "levels of regulation": the level of "intellectual analysis" where plans and strategies are developed (highest level); the level of "perceptive conceptual regulation" where action schemata are derived; and the "senso-motoric level" of movement orienting representations (lowest). The higher two levels have to be consciously represented, the lowest may be.

Two further concepts should be mentioned. Firstly, a differentiated concept of the "operative representation system" (OAS) is introduced, similar in function to Miller, Galanter & Pribram's "image". This refers to an internal model of all those circumstances of the production process which are relevant for the actor's own regulation of his work activity, namely the influence he thinks he can have, how much freedom he thinks he has, the characteristics of the situation, his knowledge of the work process, his means and materials and a model of the adequate procedures indicated by this information. The OAS culminates in a hierarchy of goals and plans and enables the actor to predict the actions' outcomes. Secondly, Hacker's theory contains the notion of a regulating function unit, similar to Miller, Galanter and Pribram's TOTE-unit. This is the "comparison-change-feedback unit" (VVR) which makes use of information derived from the OAS.

Motivation and emotion in action

Modern western motivation theory constitutes an equally rationalistic but more molar approach. "Motivational psychologists look at the breakpoints in the stream of behavior and try to explain to what end a new action is undertaken" (Heckhausen, in press). Motivation is seen as a product of more or less rational calculation. The basic idea of the "expectancy x value theories" is the assumption that the actor, in his choice between several action-alternatives, prefers the alternative which maximizes the product of the resulting value and the probability of success. This basic model is elaborated by the introduction of many other cognitive constructs and processes.

Consequently, the steering function of motivation is stressed and its energizing function neglected. Certainly, the nature of "mental energy" is not yet really understood. Resolve and effort, still indispensible for a realistic action theory, are however energy concepts. The question will eventually arise whether the obsolete concept of will can be dismissed in the long run, or whether it must be reintroduced (e.g. in the form of "conscious mobilization of energy").

Emotion, motivation's sibling, has been more or less neglected in rationalistic action theories. The need for a remedy is generally felt and the first models of emotional regulation, based on stress theory, have been developed.

Social steering and control

Most assumptions about social steering and control are rooted in the ideas of symbolic interactionism. This school has developed into different branches, all of which are relevant to action theory (compare e.g. Mead 1934, Goffman 1969, and the various exponents of ethnomethodology). As a common unbroken thread, there are the following ideas: human symbolic interaction leads to the establishment of a personal self concept. In the course of socialization, society transmits to its members cognitions of objects, situations, actions and the self. These constitute the basis on which to act, especially to interact and to interpret one's own and others' actions. Social steering and control therefore operate to a large degree through implanted social cognitions (indirect control as opposed to direct control, which operates through the direct enforcement of orders and norms). Here we must also mention the theory of social representations (e.g. Moscovici and Farr, in press) which stresses the systemic character and adaptive function of these socially based cognitions and considers them as the basis of social action.

However, we must consider the following questions: How strict is social control? How explicit are social prescriptions? Is there any freedom for the actor and what is the degree and importance of individual variations on these social processes? It is mainly along these lines that we find differences between theories of social control. On the pole of strictness and outside-directedness we find many psychologists who assume that the goal-structure is an attribute of the situation. In his script theory, Abelson (1976) proposes that for given situations actions are more or less completely prescribed by scripts and that the actor's activity consists mainly in the selection and execution of these prefabricated instructions. Harré & Secord (1972) start from Goffman's theater analogy; they assume that action is cognitively regulated, but follows more or less the perceived meaning of the situation and the rules and conventions which are accepted in relation to this meaning. Von Cranach and Harré (1982) grant the actor more freedom. They stress the importance of values, conventions and knowledge which the individual uses in the course of forming attitudes and making decisions about his goals and plans. These latter models can be combined

the viewpoints of systems theory mentioned above.
MvC/LV

raphy

ı, R.P. 1976: Script processing in attitude formation and decision ɛ. In *Cognition and social behavior*, ed. J.S. Carroll & J.W. Payne. New . Erlbaum.

anach, M. 1982: The psychological study of goal-directed action: sues. In von Cranach and Harré op cit.

anach, M. and Harré, R. 1982: *The analysis of action: recent theoretical pirical advances*. Cambridge and NewYork: Cambridge University

n, E. 1959: *The presentation of self in everyday life*. 2nd edn. New York: day; London: Penguin (1971).

, W. 1978: *Allgemeine Arbeits–und Ingenieurpsychologie. Psychische r und Regulation von Arbeitstätigkeiten*. Bern, Stuttgart, Wien: Hans Verlag.

R. and Secord, P.F. 1972: *The explanation of social behavior*, Oxford: lackwell. Totowa, N.J.: Rowman & Littlefield.

ausen, H. in press: Models of motivation: progressive unfolding and edied deficiencies. In *Cognitive and motivational aspects of action*, ed. W. , W. Volpert and M. von Cranach. Amsterdam: North Holland.

F. 1958: *The psychology of interpersonal relations*. New York: Wiley.

n, U. 1973: *Naive Verhaltenstheorie*. Stuttgart: Klett Verlag.

G.H. 1934: *Mind, self and society*. Chicago: Chicago University Press.

G.A., Galanter, E. and Pribram, K.H. 1960: *Plans and the structure of r*. New York: Holt.

vici, S. and Farr, R.M. in press: *Social representations*. Cambridge and ork: Cambridge University Press.

stein, S.L. 1977: *Grundlagen der Allgemeinen Psychologie*, 9. Auflage, Volk und Wissen.

ity, animal A term used to denote general muscular ity without making any distinction between particular vior patterns. Methods of measurement are usually natic and involve placing the animal in a cage with a e for monitoring differences between activity and rest. devices may include infra-red beams of light which ıvisible to the animal, each breaking of the beam by nimal being recorded by a photocell. Stabilimeter ; use a pivoted floor that tips as the animal moves s it. The movement of the floor is recorded electrically. etimes a particular activity, such as running, is ded by means of a specially designed device. Running dents can conveniently be measured by a vertically nted circular cage that rotates freely about its axis, d a running wheel: the animal runs inside the wheel, ing it to rotate, and the rotations are measured matically. Measurements of general activity are times useful in the study of CLOCK-DRIVEN BEHAVIOR, s, or other factors that influence sleep and fulness. Such measures give only a crude indication of ffects of experimental manipulations and are generally only as part of routine testing. DJM

ity psychology *See* Marxist activity psychology

ptation in evolutionary biology The process reby the biological characteristics of individuals come ones which favor survival and reproduction in their cular environment, through the long-term action of RAL SELECTION on the genetic constitution of the population in question. Alternatively it sometimes refers to a general state of adaptedness, or to a specific adaptive feature, that results from this process. In principle, the benefit conferred by an adaptive feature can be assessed in terms of its contribution to Darwinian FITNESS. In practice, however, difficulties may arise in identifying truly adaptive features, and in relating them securely to the solution of particular survival (or reproduction) problems, since these are essentially *post hoc* procedures. These difficulties are emphasized by those who argue that adaptation is an over-used concept, attractive to invoke but easily yielding empty Panglossian explanations, but these critiques generally constitute arguments for the more rigorous application of the concept rather than its abandonment (see Williams 1966, Lewontin 1978, Maynard Smith and Holliday 1979).

In other contexts adaptation is used in a variety of less restricted ways. The sense common to most of these is that of successful adjustment to some external factor, though the terms in which this adjustment is assessed vary widely.
RDA

Bibliography

Lewontin, R.C. 1978: Adaptation. *Scientific American* 239 (3), 156–169.

Maynard Smith, J. and Holliday, R. eds 1979: The evolution of adaptation by natural Selection. *Proceedings of the Royal Society*, B, 205. 435–604. London: Royal Society.

Williams, G.C. 1966: *Adaptation and natural selection: a critique of some current evolutionary thought*. Princeton: Princeton University Press.

adaptation in infants Those characteristics and processes which, in the course of development, fit the infant to the environment. Some characteristics of the newborn are preadapted to the evolutionarily predictable structures of the physical and social milieu. Behaviors essential for survival, such as sucking, are well organized and may even have been "practiced" in utero. Other behavior such as neonatal imitation, reaching for objects or looking in the direction of sound may also be preadapted, although they undoubtedly undergo further development. The process of adaptation may depend upon a considerable degree of plasticity in the nervous system. There is evidence that the nervous system adapts to repeatedly encountered characteristics of the environment during the early months of life. For example, cells in the visual cortex responsible for coding spatial orientation are subject to considerable modification in the first few weeks of life depending on the particular characteristics of the visual environment. GEB

Bibliography

Walk, Richard and Pick, Herbert L. Jr. 1978: *Perception and experience*. New York and London: Plenum.

adaptation *See above, and also* habituation; sensitization

addiction *See* dependence

adenyl cyclase cAMP and second messenger systems One of the ways in which the signal from a

NEUROTRANSMITTER, NEUROMODULATOR or HORMONE is translated into physiological changes in the target neuron or organ. In the case of synaptic transmission, neurotransmitters (e.g. NOREPINEPHRINE) are released into the synaptic cleft by the presynaptic neuron (see SYNAPSE AND SYNAPTIC TRANSMISSIONS). The neurotransmitter interacts with its receptor on the membrane of the postsynaptic neuron (see BRAIN AND CENTRAL NERVOUS SYSTEM: ILLUSTRATIONS, fig. 32). In certain types of synapses, termed metabotropic synapses, this interaction effects a series of metabolic changes in the postsynaptic neuron. It has been postulated that the neurotransmitter–receptor interaction activates an enzyme, adenyl cyclase. When activated, adenyl cyclase causes the conversion of adenosine triphosphate to cyclic adenosine monophosphate (cAMP). Cyclic AMP acts as a second messenger by catalyzing the phosphorylation of membrane proteins by another enzyme, protein kinase. By some mechanism which is yet to be elucidated, these phosphorylated proteins alter the permeability of the postsynaptic membrane to certain ions which are important in synaptic transmission. The series of events is terminated by two other enzymatic reactions by which both phosphorylated proteins and cAMP are inactivated. Other possible second messenger systems have been reviewed by Greengard (1976). GPH

Bibliography

Greengard, P. 1976: Possible role for cyclic nucleotides and phosphorylated membrane proteins in postsynaptic actions of neurotransmitters. *Nature* 260, 101–8.

Adler, Alfred *See* neo-Freudian theory; psychoanalytic personality theory

adolescence A transitional period of life between childhood and adulthood. There is more controversy than agreement among psychologists regarding the exact beginning and end of adolescence. Various physiological changes (e.g. growth spurts, maturation of reproductive organs, emergence of secondary sex characteristics–see PUBERTY) and psychological changes (e.g. emergence of logical thinking); increased interest in sexuality and the opposite sex; preoccupation with issues of IDENTITY, increased peer-conformity and increased responsibility have been identified as indicators of adolescence. However, no consensus exists on which changes define adolescence and which are frequent but non-essential characteristics of adolescents.

Adolescence is as much a social construction as an attribute of the individual. Some cultures and subcultures recognize a transitional period of a decade or more between childhood and adulthood while other cultures view the transition as occurring in the course of a brief initiation rite which may last only a few days or hours. The social construction of a lengthy adolescence has been traced to the creation of a juvenile justice system, child labor laws, and compulsory education laws during the nineteenth century emergence of an urban/industrial culture (Bakan 1971).

In practice, the study of adolescence encompasses all individuals who are psychosocially neither unambiguously children nor adults. An individual may be said to enter adolescence when he or she no longer views him/herself as a child (nor wants or expects to be treated as such), *or* when others begin to expect more mature behavior from him or her than they do from a child. Physical changes *or* psychological changes either in oneself *or* one's peers (or simply reaching a culturally specified chronological age) may precipitate this change in psychosocial status, which may then bring with it further psychological adjustments and modifications of social relations. An individual eventually achieves adult psychosocial status and leaves adolescence by successfully adopting some culturally specified adult role. This requires both the psychological capacity and willingness to perform the role on the part of the individual, and the culture's confirmation of the individual as a successful role-occupant. Historical factors often influence the difficulty of resolving the adolescent transition (e.g. high unemployment may decrease a culture's willingness to confer adult status). MBa

Bibliography

Bakan, D. 1971: Adolescence in America: From idea to social fact. *Daedalus*. Fall 1971, 979–96.

adolescence: development in The period of human development beginning with puberty and culminating in the attainment of adult maturity. It cannot be given any precise limits, but in general it covers the age-span from twelve to eighteen years.

It is a time of rapid physiological and psychological change, of intensive readjustment to family, school, work and social life and of preparation for adult roles. The processes of adolescent socialization and role-change are potentially stressful. Phase-specific maturational tasks can be identified, associated with these changes, particularly the physical, cognitive and emotional development. The sequence of physical changes at puberty involve an increased rate of growth in stature and weight (see ADOLESCENT GROWTH SPURT), development of the secondary sexual characteristics and the reproductive system (see MENARCHE) (Tanner 1962). The timing and effects of physical maturation have a number of psychological correlates and, in particular, rapid bodily change can have a powerful effect on self-concept. The variation in the age of onset and rate of the "growth spurt" and the impact of both early and late development have far-reaching effects. In boys, delayed maturation may lead to a feeling of low self-confidence and inferiority. Although the effects in girls are less marked, early menarche may be associated with negative feelings. Following puberty there is an upsurge of sexuality and an increase in heterosexual interests and behavior (Schofield 1965). There may be a passing phase of intense attachment to persons of the same sex but this does not appear to be related to adult homosexuality. The comfortable acceptance of appropriate sex-roles is an important part of identity development. Despite changing social attitudes toward sexual behavior in recent decades, in the direction of greater sexual freedom, and the pressures for early sexual experience, there is no evidence of increasing promiscuity and sexual behavior remains a major source of anxiety and uncertainty for young people. The value of sex education, and the effectiveness of different approaches is difficult to assess. The majority of adolescents, however, favor sex education in a responsible way. Changes in intellectual function have far-reaching implications for behavior and attitudes. Piaget described the transition from the stage of "concrete operations" to formal operational thinking following puberty, enabling the adolescent to think in an abstract way, to construct hypotheses and to adopt a deductive approach in solving problems (see Inhelder and Piaget 1958; Elkind 1968). These changes in adolescent reasoning are reflected in scholastic learning, in personality development, in the growth of moral judgment (see Kohlberg 1969) and political thinking. The move toward maturity requires gradual emancipation from the home, the establishment of an independent life-style, a conscious sense of individual uniqueness, commitment to a sexual orientation and a vocational direction and the development of self-control. Self-concept development in adolescence is a complex process (see Coleman 1980). Erikson's contribution to the understanding of identity formation in adolescence (1968) has had a major influence. He described the adolescent tasks of establishing a coherent identity and overcoming identity diffusion, but went further to indicate that some form of crisis was a necessary and expected phase in this process. This concept of a "normative crisis" has, nevertheless, been the most controversial part of Erikson's work and it has not been supported by research.

The course and successful completion of adolescence is influenced by a wide variety of factors. The function of parents is crucial in providing models of adult roles and in facilitating the individuation of adolescents. Despite popular views to the contrary and frequent reference to the "generation gap", conflict between adolescents and parents is rarely substantial or long-standing (see Rutter et al. 1976) and parents remain a significant influence throughout adolescence. However, the adolescent's quest for independence and challenge of parental standards, values and attainments can pose a major threat and adolescent behavior can have a disequilibrating effect on marital and family homeostasis. Further, adolescence is often a time of idealism, when society's standards and morals are examined, challenged or rejected. Outside the home, adolescence is shaped by the school, the immediate peer group and contemporary youth culture. Wider social, cultural and political factors also have direct consequences, including increasing social complexity and moral confusion (Kitwood 1980), the ambiguity in the status and role prescription for adolescents, the prolonged dependence of adolescents engaged in further and higher education, the consequences of unemployment and the effects of mixed racial society. Friendships with other young people play an important part in adolescence particularly during the period of detachment from the family. The pattern of these relationships changes during early, middle and late adolescence (Coleman 1974). The peer group has a supportive function and a powerful influence on behavior, particularly in its pressure for conformity and social popularity and, in this way, it plays an important part in adolescent socialization. The relative attractiveness of the peer group is influenced by the quality of relationships within the home, parental attitudes toward it, and the nature of the adolescent problems, since adolescents perceive parents and peers as useful guides in different areas of experience.

Some degree of anxiety and the experience of tension is likely to be related to coping with maturational changes, and the acquisition of new roles, particularly since there are no clear-cut rules about how to progress to adulthood or when the process is complete. Disturbance is most likely to occur at times of transition and the extent of the anxiety is partly a reflection of the adolescent's perception of the balance of stress and support. The idea that adolescence is characterized by "storm and stress" has been a consistent feature of major theories of adolescence. The psychoanalytic view, expressed by Anna Freud (1958) was that "adolescence is by its nature an interruption of peaceful growth" and this notion was in keeping with Erikson's concept of "identity crisis". There is substantial evidence, however, that although rapid mood swings, feelings of misery, self-doubts and self-consciousness are common in adolescence and may lead to personal suffering, only a small number show emotional distress or do experience a disturbance of identity relating to their sense of self in the present. Psychiatric disorders occurring during adolescence include those present since childhood and those arising initially in this age-period (see Rutter and Hersov 1977). The full range of disorders occurring in later age-periods may be found. The key task in diagnosis is the differentiation of psychiatric disorders from age-appropriate reactions that may settle when stress is reduced or eliminated with further development and the passage of time. WLLP-J

Bibliography

Coleman, John C. 1974: *Relationships in adolescence.* London and Boston: Routledge and Kegan Paul.

——— 1980: *The nature of adolescence.* London and New York: Methuen.

Elkind, D. 1968: Cognitive development in adolescence. In Adams, J.F., ed., *Understanding adolescent psychology.* Boston: Allyn & Bacon.

Erikson, Erik, H. 1968: *Identity, youth and crisis.* New York: Norton; London: Faber.

Freud, A. 1958: Adolescence. *Psychoanalytic study of the child* 13.255–78.

Inhelder, B. and Piaget, J. 1958: *The growth of logical thinking.* London: Routledge and Kegan Paul; New York: Basic Books.

Kitwood, T. 1980: *Disclosures to a stranger.* London and Boston: Routledge and Kegan Paul.

Kohlberg, L. 1969: Stage and sequence: the cognitive developmental approach to socialization. In *Handbook of socialization theory and research,* ed. D.A. Goslin. Chicago: Rand McNally.

Rutter, M., et al. 1976: Adolescent turmoil: fact or fiction? *Journal of child psychology and psychiatry* 17,35–56.

Rutter, M. and Hersov, L. 1977: *Child psychiatry: modern approaches.* Oxford: Blackwell Scientific; Philadelphia: Lippincott.

Schofield, Michael G. 1965: *The sexual behaviour of young people.* London: Longman; Boston: Little, Brown.

Tanner, James M. 1962: *Growth at adolescence.* 2nd edn. Oxford: Blackwell Scientific; Springfield, Ill.: C.C. Thomas.

adolescent growth spurt The period of acceleration in the rate of increase in height and weight associated with puberty. Changes in body composition take place in the adipose and lean body masses, bodily strength increases and the physique takes on an adult configuration. The growth spurt follows a phase of stable growth in late childhood and culminates in decelerating growth. It begins earlier in girls than in boys, who continue to grow at prepubertal rates for two years after the initiation of the growth spurt in girls. According to Frisch and Revelle (1971), the mean ages at the initiation of height and weight growth spurts in girls are 9.6 years, and 9.5 years, and in boys 11.7 years and 11.6 years respectively. Tanner et al. (1966) have indicated that peak height and weight velocities are reached at 12.1 and 12.9 years respectively in girls, and at 14.1 and 14.3 years in boys. Between growth spurt initiation and eighteen years approximately one-third of the growth precedes the peak height velocity and the rest occurs during the phase of growth deceleration. There is wide individual variation in the age of onset and this has psychological correlates. Early maturing boys have more favorable personalities than late maturers. WLLP-J

Bibliography

Frisch, R.E. and Revelle, R. 1971: The height and weight of girls and boys at the time of initiation of the adolescent growth spurt in height and weight and the relationship to menarche. *Human biology* 43, 140.

Tanner, J.M., Whitehouse, R.H. and Takaishi, M. 1966: Standards from birth to maturity for height, weight, height velocity, and weight velocity: British children, 1965. Parts I and II. *Archives of diseases of childhood* 41, 454 and 613.

adolescent psychiatry *See* child and adolescent psychiatry

adrenal glands (See BRAIN AND CENTRAL NERVOUS SYSTEM: ILLUSTRATIONS, fig. 22). Small, triangular organs located at the upper pole of either kidney. They consist of two distinct parts: an outer part, the adrenal cortex and a center part, the adrenal medulla which is homologous to a sympathetic ganglion. Interest in the adrenal glands was sparked by Addison's description in 1849 of patients with what we now know was an insufficiency of the adrenal cortex (Addison's disease). The adrenal cortex synthesizes and secretes a number of steroid hormones (see STEROIDS) which are essential for HOMEOSTASIS. These steroids can be divided into three groups: glucocorticoids, mineralocorticoids and sex steroids. The latter are normally secreted at a low rate. The synthesis and release of glucocorticoids is under the control of the pituitary hormone ACTH (see PITUITARY; ACTH); that of the principal mineralocorticoid aldosterone is regulated by the renin-angiotensin system. Other examples of diseases of the adrenal cortex, in addition to Addison's disease, are Cushing's syndrome due to a sustained overproduction of the principal glucocorticoid hydrocortisone, and Conn's syndrome due to primary aldosteronism. The adrenal medulla is the site of synthesis and release of EPINEPHRINE. DHGV

adrenaline *See* epinephrine

adrenocorticotrophic hormone *See* ACTH

aesthetics *See* emotion and aesthetics; experimental aesthetics

affect *See* déjà-vu and affect; emotion

affective disorders States in which mood is abnormally depressed or elated, often with associated behavioral and cognitive changes. They comprise manic-depressive psychosis, a wide variety of other less specific depressions – sometimes referred to as neurotic or reactive – and some illnesses occurring in particular settings such as puerperal psychosis and abnormal grief reactions. Although the term 'affect' has strictly a wider connotation, tradition dictates that affective disorders encompass only those disturbances where depression and elation are the moods principally involved. Mood disturbances secondary to other illnesses, for example lability accompanying an organic brain disease or the blunted emotional responsiveness sometimes seen in chronic schizophrenia, would usually not be included.

Variations of mood are of course a common and natural phenomenon, indeed an essential ingredient of our emotional lives. It is not always easy to know when such variations should be regarded as abnormal; consideration may be given to several factors: duration of the mood swing, its intensity, apparent disproportion between the circumstances and the mood, or the specific nature of the change, which in florid cases leaves the observer in no doubt about the abnormality. In practice affective disorders are seen to include brief depressive or manic reactions, more sustained states which are exaggerations of the individual's natural pattern, and distortions of emotional and cognitive functioning of all degrees of severity. Mood swings may be classed as reactive or endogenous (the latter meaning arising from within); alternatively as neurotic (understandably related to the individual's constitution) or psychotic (with depressive delusions, loss of insight and of contact with reality).

The question whether neurotic and psychotic depressions are two distinct disorders has aroused much controversy. Kendell (1968) concluded that they should be viewed as forming a single continuum; the symptoms of an individual case could be scored in such a way as to assign him or her a position on this continuum and to indicate the likely response to treatment. BIPOLAR DEPRESSION – where a manic swing has also occurred – tends to be associated with a psychotic symptom pattern. Many other types of classification have been proposed and are reviewed by Paykel and Rowan (1979). Paykel's cluster analysis subdivided depressed patients into four groups: psychotic, anxious, hostile, and younger depressives with personality ɒrders. Earlier writers had emphasized the separate :us of involutional melancholia as a form of depression cting those aged over forty-five and characterized by tation and hypochondriacal preoccupations. Recent dies have failed to confirm this. The place of anxiety tes remains controversial; by convention pure states hout significant mood change are usually classified with neuroses.

)epression is in its many forms a common disorder. In stern society prevalence rates of 3–4 per cent have been ɒted, but the figures vary greatly with the criteria for ning cases. Women seem to be affected about twice as nmonly as men, this difference being only partially ibutable to puerperal depressions. The peak age of onset ıround sixty for psychotic depression and thirty for rotic depression.

Research into the etiology of depression has identified a ge number of predisposing and precipitant causes of ich several may be operative in any one individual. tain genetic, developmental, cognitive, psychodynamic, ial and biochemical factors can be considered here. netic studies have shown a higher risk of manic-ressive psychosis (12 per cent) among the relatives of cted individuals; this is probably due to the inherited disposition, since monozygotic twins have a higher cordance rate (68 per cent) than dizygotic twins (23 per t). Unipolar and bi-polar disorders may be genetically tinct. In the course of a child's development the longed absence of a parent seems to predispose to a later dency to depression, either by undermining the ividual's sense of security or by coloring his or her erpretation of experiences of separation and loss. Such eriences are the focus of various psychoanalytic views of ression; in particular it is suggested that the deprived ividual blames himself for such losses and turns his ger inwards upon himself. Repeated experiences of being verless to avoid emotional or physical trauma can lead state described by Seligman as LEARNED HELPLESSNESS. other cognitive theory of depression was put forward by k (1967) who suggested that negative evaluations of self, the environment and the future, acquired by past erience and activated by stresses, generate a responding mood of despondency. Many social factors d understandably to depressed mood; Brown and Harris 78) identified several conditions which render women nerable to depression: preschool children at home, ence of a job or of a supportive marital relationship. ɒression is a familiar accompaniment to many physical, rmonal and biochemical abnormalities, such as ctrolyte imbalance and thyroid deficiency. In addition tain drugs such as anti-hypertensives often provoke ression. In primary depression complex patterns of ɔalance have been found in neurotransmitters emicals which enable the nerve impulse to pass from brain cell to another), particularly noradrenaline, otonin and dopamine. Antidepressant drugs have ɒortant effects on these neurotransmitters.

The diagnosis of depression is based on the symptoms l signs. These include sustained lowering of mood, netimes with diurnal variation (usually lifting in the evening): diminished interest, energy, concentration and capacity for enjoyment; headaches, heaviness in the limbs; insomnia; dry mouth, gastro-intestinal discomfort, constipation, poor appetite and weight loss. Psychotic depression may show additional features: retardation or agitation, delusions of guilt, of worthlessness, of poverty and bodily disintegration (nihilistic delusions), persecutory ideas, hallucinations of a depressive nature, pessimism and suicidal impulses. In masked depression the normal diagnostic features are unclear and other problems present: hypochondriacal preoccupations, facial pain, obsessional activity or uncharacteristic delinquent behavior (such as shop-lifting); in the elderly disturbance of intellectual function gives rise to PSEUDODEMENTIA. There are no confirmatory tests for depression, but the severity can be rated on a number of scales, for example the Beck (subjective) and the Hamilton (objective).

The choice of treatment depends on the pattern and severity of the symptoms; the more severe and the more clearly psychotic the depression the greater the likelihood of response to physical treatments. These are principally electroconvulsive therapy (ECT; see Kendell 1981), and antidepressants of the tricyclic (imipramine, amitriptyline), quaternary (mianserin), or more rarely monoamine oxidase inhibitor (MAO: tranylcypromine, phenelzine) groups. Medication continued for several months after recovery tends to prevent relapse. Lithium is a dramatically effective prophylactic in many cases of recurrent depressive or manic-depressive illness. Psychotherapy, cognitive therapy and social intervention grow in importance as the symptom pattern approaches the neurotic end of the continuum.

Mania (the term hypomania is often used for minor degrees of the condition) is a less common disorder, occurring in perhaps ten per cent of those subject to severe depressive illness, and rarely seen in the absence of depressive swings. Women predominate, but less so than with unipolar depression. According to some studies the incidence increases steadily with age. Stressful life events play a less important role in precipitating episodes of mania than of depression, and interact with effects of predisposition (largely genetic) and vulnerability.

Central symptoms of mania include: elated, disinhibited, impulsive and irritable mood; increased energy, activity, speech, social contact and enterprize; teeming thoughts and grandiose delusions. There is often an admixture of depressive mood, and where this is marked, the diagnosis of mixed affective state may be made. Hospitalization may be required to secure rest and sleep, nutrition and hydration, and to limit the consequences of the individual's distorted judgment and extravagance.

Specific treatment relies heavily on major tranquilizers (neuroleptics such as chlorpromazine and haloperidol): the manic patient may need surprisingly high doses to achieve sedation. Lithium has an important part to play, both in the acute phase and more especially in longterm prophylaxis. The course of severe unipolar and bipolar disorders tends to be one of erratic or sometimes cyclical relapses; up to 15 per cent of sufferers die by suicide, but lithium can vastly improve the prognosis.

Puerperal psychosis, occurring after about 1 in 200 births usually takes the form of a psychotic depression, the symptoms tending to be florid and varied, but the prognosis is good. The term maternity blues refers to a transient despondency often experienced soon after child-birth. The menstrual cycle is commonly associated with mood changes, often with despondency and irritability in the pre-menstrual phase; hormone adjustment and, in severe cases, lithium may be tried. Bereavement is accompanied by lowered mood lasting perhaps several months; in abnormal grief reactions the normal response may be inhibited, exaggerated or prolonged (Parkes 1972).

Future researchers will undoubtedly discover more about the biochemical mechanisms of affective disorders, leading to more effective genetic counselling, prevention and treatment. At some distant point we may have to decide whether man should have total control over his mood. DLJ

Bibliography

Beck, A.T. 1967: *Depression: clinical, experimental and theoretical aspects*. New York: Harper & Row.

Brown, G.W. and Harris, T. 1978: *Social origins of depression; a study of psychiatric disorder in women*. London: Tavistock; New York: Free Press.

Kendell, R.E. 1968: *The classification of depressive illnesses*. London: Oxford University Press.

——— 1981: The present status of electroconvulsive therapy, *British journal of psychiatry* 139, 265–83.

Parkes, C.M. 1972: *Bereavement: studies of grief in adult life*. London: Tavistock; New York: International Universities Press.

Paykel, E.S., ed. 1982: *Handbook of affective disorders*. London and New York: Churchill Livingstone.

Paykel, E.S. and Rowan P.R. 1979: Affective Disorders. In *Recent advances in clinical psychiatry*, K. Granville Grossman ed. no. 3, London and New York: Churchill Livingstone.

affix Any formative (morpheme) added to a word stem is called an affix. Those appearing word-initially (as *un-* in *unable*) are called prefixes; those appearing word-finally (such as *-er* in *runner*) are referred to as suffixes. An important distinction is that between derivational affixes whose role is to derive new lexical items from existing more basic ones (such as *freezer* from *freeze*) and inflectional affixes signalling certain grammatical categories such as tense, aspect or number. An example of the latter is the third person *-s* suffix in *sings*.

The study of inflexional affixes plays an important role in early transformational-generative grammar. Chomsky (1957) claims that affixes such as the third person *-s* with English verbs appear immediately before the verb in the grammatical deep structure and are subsequently moved to the right of the verb by a transformation called "affix hopping" as in

affix + verb ⟶ verb + affix

s + sing ⟶ sing + s ⟶ sings

If, on the other hand, there is an auxiliary in the sentence, then the -s suffix attaches to this auxiliary and not to the main verb, as in *he has come* rather than **he have comes*. The view that the affix hopping rule is psychologically real is supported, to some extent, by data from *first* and *second language acquisition*, where sentences such as **he do not drinks* and **he does not drinks* are documented. PM

Bibliography

Chomsky, Noam 1957: *Syntactic structures*. The Hague: Mouton.

ageing The general term for the study of old age. Gerontologists may be biochemists, physiologists, neurologists, psychologists or social scientists who attempt to discover how the body, brain and central nervous system change with age, how these changes affect mental abilities and behavior, and how the lives of people within society change as they grow old.

Social psychological and social studies have included, for example, how elderly people regard themselves and their changing role in society; how they feel that younger people regard them, and how they are in fact regarded; whether elderly people gradually withdraw from social contacts of all kinds ("disengagement theory") or whether they merely change the nature, and the pattern, of their social contacts.

A general question for gerontologists has always been whether old age can be indefinitely postponed, and human life indefinitely prolonged, or whether advances in medicine and social care cannot increase the maximum span of human life, though they can ensure that larger numbers of us manage to live out our full spans in good health and with our wits about us. There have been encouraging reports of spectacular longevity in isolated peasant societies such as those in Georgia in the USSR or Vilcanbanba in Ecuador, claiming that large proportions of the population are alive (and even achieve parenthood) at ages exceeding 160 or 170 years. Sadly these tales are myths. Reported ages greater than 123 years have never been satisfactorily documented. It is, of course, not impossible that science may yet find ways of prolonging life, but for the present most gerontologists believe that the overwhelming majority of us cannot expect to survive beyond our mid eighties. The most reasonable social and scientific goals are to ensure that as many of us as possible happily live out our maximum spans.

The experience of western industrialized societies bears out these hopes, and also vividly brings home the enormous social adjustments which their realization will entail. In the west, most people now aged sixteen can expect to live, in good health, until they are about seventy-two years (if they are men) and about seventy-seven years (if they are women). While techniques for treating the illnesses of old age are increasingly effective, they are also increasingly costly and unlikely to be available to all. Realistic hopes rest on much cheaper, and more effective, techniques in preventative medicine and in personal health care and maintenance of fitness. Such techniques have already been almost embarrassingly successful. In the rich west one person in every five alive today is over sixty years old. This proportion will grow, increasing the age gap, as well as the gap of prosperity between rich societies and third world countries where average life expectancies range from forty to fifty-five years. Apart from the longterm consequences of such a painful disparity of human prospects, the rich west faces urgent problems in adjusting social and economic systems to this massive, quiet, geriatric revolution.

Experiments to study changes in human mental abilities with age date from mass observations carried out by Francis Galton on visitors to the International Health Exhibition of 1883. Galton's results on changes in efficiency of memory and speed of reaction time illustrates the fundamental, unsolved question in this science. Galton could only test each of the people who visited his booth at the exhibition once. He could thus only collect *average* data for age-groups, and found that these *average* scores steadily deteriorated with age. This finding occurs with depressing regularity in all similar comparisons, though some abilities (e.g. verbal ability and verbal IQ) change much less than others (e.g. memory test scores and performance IQ scores) as older groups are sampled. However, data obtained from separate successive "cross sectional" samples of aged people do not allow us to conclude that every individual inevitably experiences a sad trajectory of progressive intellectual decline ending in senility. Recent work shows that when we look more closely at large cross-sectional samples we find that substantial numbers of people in groups aged from seventy-five to eighty-five perform as well as the average for young people aged from twenty to forty. This may mean that the clock runs faster for some of us than others, and that while some lucky people show little change in mental efficiency until they reach an advanced age, most show earlier declines. Unfortunately the only studies that can resolve this question are longitudinal surveys in which large numbers of individuals are each repeatedly tested over periods of twenty to thirty years as they pass beyond their comparatively youthful fourth and fifth decades. The evidence slowly accumulating now makes it increasingly probable that chronological age, *per se*, has little effect on human abilities. It is rather the accumulation of physiological damage over the lifespan, and the onset of diseases accompanying age, which bring a stable plateau of peak mental performance to an abrupt end in a "terminal drop" accompanying increasing pathology.

A happy and realistic goal for clinicians and psychologists is to discover what makes the fortunate "super aged" so lucky. Apart from choosing the right parents (survival runs in families), better health habits and effort to maintain intellectual as well as physical activity may allow most humans to keep their wits about them until they no longer need them.

These optimistic comments on the apparent normal course of human ageing must be contrasted with information on pathological conditions of accelerated degeneration of the central nervous system which in some respects resemble changes seen in extreme, normal, old age (dementias, Alzheimer's syndrome, etc.) (See GERONTOLOGY.) PR

aggression: conceptual issues The quest for a unitary definition of aggression, acceptable across the many specialist areas within psychology which profess an interest in the subject, has been both prolonged and largely unresolved. Recent text-books on aggression typically open with an extensive introduction to what Bandura (1973) has so aptly described as this "semantic jungle". In some cases the issue is settled by the selection of a definition which accords with a particular theoretical orientation, rather than with a more open appreciation of the variation and complexities of aggressive behavior. Thus, aggression might be viewed as a motivational state, a personality characteristic, a response to frustration, an inherent drive, or the fulfilling of a socially learned role requirement.

Alternatively, some authors viewing the whole issue as essentially irresoluble, declare that a unitary concept is not viable. Johnson (1972), for example, maintains that "it is difficult if not impossible to isolate the necessary and sufficient conditions to produce a satisfactory definition". He goes on to conclude that "there is no single kind of behavior which can be called 'aggressive' nor any single process which represents 'aggression'". Definition is further complicated by concepts and theoretical stances deriving from related disciplines such as ethology and anthropology. It is not surprising, therefore, to discover more than 250 different definitions of aggression in the psychological literature, discounting pure operationalizations for experimental purposes. An extensive volume of literature reviewing these various definitions and the conceptual stances from which they derive already exists. Rather than providing a review of the reviews it is more appropriate to isolate those components of definitions for which there is broad support and those where lack of consensus is most evident. Further elaboration is to be found in Baron (1977).

Firstly, aggression may be said to occur only between members of the same species. In other words it is distinguishable from predation, anti-predator behavior and encounters arising from competition for the same ecological niche.

Secondly, there is the notion that aggression involves the delivery of a noxious stimulus. In other words, the products of aggression must be perceived negatively by the recipient. Such a definition would allow a wide range of behavior, from nuclear bombing to sarcastic comment, to be classed as aggressive, and this stance is to be preferred to those which limit aggression to the perpetration of physical injury. It is, however, not a *sufficient* condition for aggression since noxious stimuli can clearly be delivered without any aggression present. One would rarely accuse a dentist of being aggressive when he causes pain to a person's mouth. Nor would one suggest that all injurious car accidents are attributable to aggressive drivers.

Clearly the concept of *intention* must be an essential component of any satisfactory definition. It is at this point, however, that the most severe difficulties arise since a very mentalistic concept has been introduced. And while it might be philosophically legitimate to talk of *intentionality* in a discussion of human behavior it would be absurd to use such a concept in relation to aggression in animals. To ask whether one cat *intended* to injure another is to engage in a quite untenable form of anthropomorphism.

There might also be a problem in attempting to define

aggression with reference to any limited category of behavior, even though Buss (e.g.) allows for considerable freedom in this context. This is because behavior may be exhibited only if an appropriate target is available and conditions are such that delivery of a noxious stimulus is possible. Geen (1976) attempts to overcome this limitation by adding a further necessary condition. He insists that there must be "some expectation that the stimulus will reach its target and have its intended effect".

Again, however, we are presented with rather immeasurable criteria and a distinct sense of circularity is evident. Both intention and expectation are to be gleaned only through post hoc rationalization of action. More importantly there is the continuing, restricting assumption that aggression cannot be said to exist unless there are observable, intentional acts directed at specific targets!

So, on the one hand we have an apparent desire to define aggression in terms which accord with the frames of reference of traditional, empirical psychology – i.e. overt behavior. On the other, in order to meet the constraints of simple logic and everyday human experience, mentalistic criteria are introduced (often apologetically). Lacking, however, is any indication of how intention or expectation may be determined in general or specific examples of aggression.

Because of these problems we might be forgiven for adopting Johnson's position. At the same time, however, there exists in everyday language and conceptualization the notion that aggression does indeed have a unitary nature, although the range of psychological states and patterns of behavior might be rather wider than is commonly assumed by psychologists. In everyday talk we use the term "aggression" to refer to acts of hostility, violence etc. in a pejorative manner, but at the same time we speak of an athlete running an aggressive race and of the successful, entrepreneurial businessman conducting an aggressive sales campaign. In the latter examples the sentiment is a positive one.

The two senses in which the term aggression is used have little in common in behavioral terms and in the case of the athlete it is difficult to isolate a "noxious stimulus". What unites them is the presence of competition, establishment of dominance and the subjugation of perceived rivals – a broad but meaningful constellation of psychological processes. It is suggested that this might provide the starting point for a more relevant and useful definition of aggression. Such an approach is in keeping with some ethological perspectives, and allows for comparative study. This, however, is not its primary objective. Viewing aggression in this manner allows us to evaluate more clearly the social motives of a wide range of acts which otherwise appear to be quite disparate. Rather than aggression inhering in a limited range of behaviors, it might more reasonably be seen as an internal motivational state. Resultant behavior will be a function not only of the strength of such a state but also of the target and, more importantly of extant social and cultural frameworks whose primary function is the regularising and containment of aggressive expression (see below, *ritual aggression*).

From this standpoint acts of violence, with the statu social *events*, may be distinguished clearly from aggression process itself. Aggression, under cert circumstances, may result in acts of physical injury wh can be said to constitute violence. Violence, however, is a *necessary* consequence of aggression, other means for expression of dominance and the subjugation of ri being readily available. Nor need violence necessarily preceded by a state of aggression, especially when the ta of violence is remote or when systematic dehumaniza of the target has been achieved. In such cases one mi argue that the violent acts are more akin to predation t to expressions of aggression (see Marsh 1978).

The concept of intentionality is, to a large ext redundant in this formulation because, again, aggressic not determined solely by reference to the partic behavior but may be determined by reference to relationship between individuals involved in a gi encounter and to their respective motives. This can b distinct advantage in non-laboratory research since th kinds of data are often more readily available than direct measures of particular behavior.

Major Fields of Research

Research directly concerned with the antecedent aggression has occupied the bulk of the literature over past thirty years. The nature-nurture controversy is heated in this field as in those of intelligence personality. The major theoretical approaches wit which this research has been conducted can summarized as follows:

Biological Theories: The work of Freud and his conce *Thanatos*, which recast Hobbesian notions in psychoanalytic form was later mirrored by the etholog theory of Lorenz (1966). Subsequent ethological work Eibl-Eibesfeldt (1961–1971) and Tinbergen (1953) ref some of the more mechanistic assumptions of the ea approaches, emphasized more strongly the plasticity inherited characteristics and the important role of so and cultural factors. Within this broad category perspectives we should also include work on spe genetic abnormalities – e.g. the XYY syndrome.

Drive Theories: Work by Dollard et al (1939) develo from a psychoanalytic position and gave rise to frustration-aggression model. The unworkable rigidit this model was, to some extent, tempered in subsequ models proposed by Berkowitz (1962) and the theme also been explored by Feshbach (1964), and many oth These approaches did much to encourage examinatio social factors as antecedents of aggressive behavior. approach is even more firmly evident in the third cate of approaches.

Social Learning Theories: Work by Bandura (1973) provided the basis for extensive research, most of which been laboratory based using children as subjects. Wor Geen (1976) has been particularly influential.

In addition to the numerous general textbooks aggression (e.g. Baron 1977, Johnson 1972) and th focussing on one of the major approaches (e.g.

Eibesfeldt 1979), rather extreme polarizations in the Nature-Nurture debate can be found in Ardrey (1979) and Montagu (1976).

Ritual Aggression

Work on ritual aggression has developed in two quite different fields – those of ethology and anthropology. In ethology the term ritualization was coined by Huxley and used to refer to "the adaptive formalisation or canalisation of emotionally motivated behaviour, under the telenomic pressure of natural selection". It has been employed in particular in the area of aggressive behavior by writers such as Lorenz, (1966), Eibl-Eibesfeldt (1979) and others. Evidence suggests that patterns of fighting behavior are modified to the extent that intra-species agonistic encounters result in relatively little injury to the protagonists. Potentially lethal attacks take on the nature of "tournaments" involving threat signals such as color changes, bristling of fur etc.

In anthropology ritual refers to patterned routines of behavior involving a system of signs and conventional relations between the actions in which the ritual is performed and the social act achieved by its successful completion. Many examples of tribal warfare have been described in these terms. The Dani of New Guinea, for example, were described by Gardner and Heider as engaging in highly ceremonial and ritual patterns of inter-group hostility.

More recently, writers such as Fox (1977) have brought these two major approaches together in the explanation of particular patterns of group aggressive activity. Here the assumption is that patterns of ritual aggression in man have essentially the same (largely biological) origins and perform the same adaptive functions. Work by Marsh (1978), however, which has focussed on ritual aggression among youth in Britain, suggests that the common origins argument is unnecessary in the explanation of such patterns of behavior. PEM

Bibliography

Ardrey, R. 1979: *The hunting hypothesis*. London and New York: Methuen.

Bandura, A. 1973: *Aggression: a social learning analysis*. Englewood Cliffs, NJ: Prentice Hall.

Baron, R.A. 1977: *Human aggression*. New York: Plenum Press.

Berkowitz, L. 1962: *Aggression: a social psychological analysis*. New York: McGraw-Hill.

Dollard, J., et al. 1939: *Frustration and aggression*. New Haven, Conn: Yale University Press.

Eibl-Eibesfeldt, I. 1971: *Love and hate*. Methuen; New York: Holt, Rhinehart & Winston.

——— 1979: *The biology of peace and war*. London: Thames & Hudson.

Feshbach, S. 1964: The function of aggression and the regulation of aggressive drive. *Psychology review* 71, 257–72.

Fox, R. 1977: The inherent rules of violence. In P. Collett (ed) *Social rules and social behavior*. Oxford: Basil Blackwell, Totowa, N.J.: Rowman & Littlefield.

Geen, R. G. 1976: *Personality; the skein of behaviour*. London: Henry Kimpton.

Johnson, R.N. 1972: *Aggression in man and animals*. W.B. Saunders.

Lorenz, K. 1966: *On aggression*. London: Methuen; New York: Harcourt, Brace & World.

Marsh, P. 1978: *Aggro: the illusion of violence*. London: Dent.

Montagu, A. 1976: *The nature of human aggression*. Oxford and New York: Oxford University Press.

Tinbergen, N. 1953: *Social behaviour in animals*. London: Methuen; New York: Wiley.

aggression: in developmental research A term which has several partially overlapping meanings, ranging from assertion of the self or forcefulness, to the motivation, feelings, or intent behind acts of violence, i.e., physical force used against another. These various facets have been studied developmentally by systematically observing the aggressive behavior of preschool and school children, by laboratory experiments involving aggressive play, by tests involving fantasy play, or by ratings of aggression by parents, children or peers.

Major areas of development research on aggression concern: (a) the processes whereby children acquire specific aggressive actions, e.g. by REINFORCEMENT or IMITATION; (b) socializing influences which may enhance aggression (e.g. the family, the school, television); (c) the developmental continuity of aggression; (d) the social rules and consequences of aggressive actions. JA

Bibliography

Bandura, A. 1973: *Aggression: a social learning analysis*. Englewood Cliffs, N.J. and London: Prentice-Hall.

Feshbach, S. 1970: Aggression. In *Carmichael's manual of child-psychology*, ed. Paul Mussen. 2 vols. 2nd edn. New York and Chichester: John Wiley.

aggression and emotions Aggression is one of those unfortunate terms in the behavioral sciences that have been taken over from everyday language and have a variety of meanings. Furthermore people tend to assume that the different uses of the term must have something in common since they are all covered by the same word. Most research-oriented psychologists define aggression as the intentional injury of another, and regard this form of behavior as quite different (i.e. governed by different processes) from the other actions often given the same label in ordinary speech (such as assertiveness, attempts to achieve mastery, or ritualized threat displays). What is most important about aggression is that the aggressor wants to hurt or perhaps even destroy the victim, either physically or psychologically, and is reinforced when this particular goal is achieved. Aggression in this sense has very little in common with the forcefulness shown by an "aggressive" salesman or the boastfulness demonstrated by a youthful male who is trying to impress someone by acting tough.

Distinctions have to be drawn among different types of aggression even within this somewhat limited definition. It is especially important to differentiate between instrumental aggression and what many psychologists refer to as hostile aggression. In both cases the aggressor seeks to injure someone, but when he is acting instrumentally the aggressive behavior is carried out for another, nonaggressive purpose (such as for money or social approval). The person who attacks his victim because he believes the rules of his group require him to do so is engaging in instrumental aggression, since the rule compliance brings rewards and avoids punishment. Hostile aggression, on the other hand, is primarily directed toward the injury of the victim, and is typically a response to aversive stimulation, whether in the form of an insult, some illegitimate treatment, a frustration or a foul odor. Such behavior can be affected by learning. Inhibitions prompted by social norms often govern the intensity of open hostile aggression and frequently affect its exact nature. Moreover, this behavior can also be influenced by anticipated rewards and punishments independently of the group's rules. Nevertheless, the basic instigation to the hostile action stems from the aversive stimulation. A good many of the homicides or serious violent assaults in everyday life appear to be instances of hostile aggression; they are explosive outbursts resulting from an argument or perceived insult in which the violence is often more intense than the aggressor had initially intended. The threat of capital punishment is usually ineffective as a deterrent to this form of violence because the aggressors generally do not think of any possible consequences beyond their desire to hurt (or destroy) their antagonist.

It is clear that aggression does not always arise in the same manner. Learning influences all aggression to some extent, and it is especially important in human instrumental aggression. As is the case with other instrumental actions, people use aggression to obtain their objectives if they have found that this form of behavior gets them what they want. On the other hand, many animals, including humans, may have an inborn capacity for aversively stimulated aggression, so this form of aggression can occur without prior learning, although it can be modified, strengthened or weakened by experience. Aversively stimulated aggression (the term is substituted henceforth for hostile aggression) is also more apt to be affected in an involuntary fashion by environmental stimuli. In such instances a particular stimulus in the surrounding situation facilitates the occurrence of overt aggression. One example is the "weapons effect" in which the mere presence of a weapon elicits stronger aggression than would otherwise have occurred, particularly if inhibitions against aggression are weak at the time (see Turner et al. 1977). While it is not altogether certain what causes the "weapons effect," the stimulus's associations with either previously reinforced aggression or aversive events seem to be especially important.

The theoretical perspective taken here helps to explain the now frequently observed effects of violent movies and also the repeated failures to demonstrate a "hostility CATHARSIS" as a result of engaging in either realistic or fantasy aggression. In regard to the former, scores of well-controlled studies in both laboratory and natural settings have shown that scenes of violence on the television or movie screen can increase the probability that children as well as adult viewers will behave aggressively themselves. This increased likelihood of aggression arises from several processes involving short-term influences or long-lasting learning. The temporary effects include (1) a weakening of inhibitions due to screen-induced ideas that aggression can be rewarding or is morally justified under particular circumstances, and also (2) the stimulation of aggression-facilitating ideas, feelings and motor reactions by the aggressive material on the screen (see Berkowitz 1973). As for hostility catharsis, a good many experiments have now contradicted the widely accepted notion that the display of either realistic or make-believe aggression "drains" a reservoir of supposedly pent-up aggressive "energy" somewhere within the person, thereby lessening the probability of further aggression. The aggressor may feel good when he finds that his intended victim has been appropriately injured and may even cease his attacks on this target for some time afterward. However the accomplishment of this objective is reinforcing so that in the long-run aggressive behavior is now more, not less, likely. We do not diminish the level of violence in society by encouraging people to act aggressively, even if this behavior takes place only in their imagination.

Apart from these practical questions of the consequences of aggressive behavior and the effects of observed violence, psychologists are also interested in theoretical questions regarding the anger experienced and the role of cognitions in emotional aggression. Most of the theoreticians concerned with emotions have focussed their attention on the processes leading to specific feelings. (Adopting this perspective, "anger" refers to a particular experience, whereas "aggression" is a label for a certain type of behavior.) There is considerable disagreement among psychologists as to how the different emotions such as anger arise. According to the classic James-Lange theory, people feel angry because their viscera automatically react in a certain way to external events. This conception fell into disfavor in the 1920s as it was realized that the viscera are too slow and insensitive to produce the differentiated emotional feelings. The prevailing view at that time was that the exciting occurrence activated a specific "emotion center" in the brain which created the particular feeling and resulting behavior. Many contemporary social psychologists have been attracted to a very different formulation, offered by Schachter and Singer (1962), which emphasizes the part played by cognitions. This theory holds that the arousal state generated by the exciting event is usually both ambiguous and affectively neutral. The label people apply to their feelings, which is determined to a considerable extent by the attributions they make regarding the cause of this occurrence (see ATTRIBUTION THEORY), supposedly produces the specific feelings they experience and the resulting behavior. While there is some evidence consistent with this analysis, it is now encountering increasing criticism (see Leventhal 1980). Recent research has shown that the emotional arousal engendered by the precipitating event is often not so ambiguous as the Schachter–Singer formulation maintains, so that our interpretation of our feelings is not so easily shaped by external happenings as this theory supposes. Furthermore, in many instances the sensations created by the exciting occurrence have a decided affective quality independently of how they are labeled.

All this is compatible with the analysis of aggression being summarized here. I am suggesting that an aversive stimulus, something the person ordinarily strives to escape or avoid, tends to instigate escape (the flight tendency) *and* aggression, that is, to aversively-stimulate aggression (the fight tendency). The comparative strength of these two tendencies is presumably governed by a variety of factors, including prior learning, the perceived ease of escape, the likelihood of punishment for aggression, and the stimulus characteristics of the available targets. From this perspective the experienced anger results from the individual's awareness of the reactions within him (throughout his body and not only in his viscera) blended together with his ideas and memories regarding similar occurrences. This means that the anger experience parallels the instigation to aggression and is not, in itself, the "drive" producing the aversively-stimulated aggression.

Other recent developments in the study of emotion are also in accord with this view. Research indicates that expressive-motor reactions, especially in the facial region, contribute to the feelings that are experienced, and that these reactions are linked together with classes of ideas and memories, as well as with experienced feelings, in a particular emotional set. The activation of any of the components in the network tends to elicit the other parts (see Leventhal 1980). Consistent with the arguments I mentioned earlier, this network conception suggests that situational stimuli having an aggressive meaning (such as fight scenes or weapons) tend to activate ideas, memories and feelings conducive to aggressive behavior, and that even aggression-related expressive movements might heighten the likelihood of "real" aggression if the inhibitions against this behavior are weak enough. LB

Bibliography

*Baron, R.A. 1977: *Human aggression*. New York: Plenum.

Berkowitz, L. 1973: Words and symbols as stimuli to aggressive responses. In *Control of aggression: implications from basic research*, ed. J.F. Knutson. Chicago: Aldine-Atherton.

Berkowitz, L., Cochran, S. and Embree, M. 1981: Physical pain and the goal of aversively stimulated aggression. *Journal of personality and social psychology* 40, 687–700.

Brain, P.F. and Benton, D., eds. 1981: *Multidisciplinary approaches to aggression research*. Amsterdam, New York, Oxford: Elsevier/North Holland.

*Leventhal, H. 1980: Toward a comprehensive theory of emotion. In *Advances in experimental social psychology*, vol. 13. ed. L. Berkowitz. New York: Academic Press.

Schachter, S. and Singer, J.E. 1962: Cognitive, social and physiological determinants of emotion. *Psychological review* 69, 379–99.

Turner, C.W. et al. 1977: The stimulating and inhibiting effects of weapons on aggressive behavior. *Aggressive behavior* 3, 355–78.

aggression *See above, and also* passive aggression

agonic This term together with the term HEDONIC refers to one of two extreme mechanisms of social cohesion and at the same time to the corresponding modes of mental operation.

Agonic social cohesion is typical of the general features of baboon and macaque societies, where social cohesion is maintained by predominant persistent attention to the dominant individual (usually a male) at the center of a group. This prevents continuous uninterrupted periods of attention to other matters. The low threshold of aggression of the dominant male means that all members of the group are liable to become the target of his aggression which in the form of threats can cause the individuals, after momentary withdrawal, to return to the source of the threat. This threat is responded to by spatial withdrawal and return (equilibration). (See Mason 1965 for an explanation of this phenomenon) by submission, displacement, redirection, and CUT-OFF (which prevents visual exploration) or by appropriate organized counter-threat. These responses are immediately available as a means of avoiding punishment. Hence, the monkeys of these societies must be in a high state of arousal, which, since they only manifest these types of behavior from time to time, must be simultaneously inhibited. A state of high arousal combined with inhibition is, therefore, the main feature of this hypothesized mental mode. The term agonic was chosen to label this state of latent defensive responsiveness to ally it with, but distinguish it from, "agonistic" which is the active state of social conflict taking place from time to time in agonistic social episodes. (See also ATTENTION STRUCTURE.) MRAC

Bibliography

Chance, M.R.A. 1962: An interpretation of some agonistic postures: the role of "cut-off" acts and postures. Reprinted from *Symposia of the Zoological Society of London* No. 8, pp.71–89. 1962.

——— 1967: Attention structure as the basis of primate rank orders. *Man* 2. 4.

Mason, W.A. 1965: Sociability and social organization in monkeys and apes. In Berkowitz L., ed. *Advances in experimental social psychology*, vol. 1. New York: Academic Press.

akrasia The technical term for weakness of will. Philosophers are interested in akrasia because although it is obvious enough that people often act against their better judgment, yet when one looks carefully it seems impossible that they should do so. A fat but would-be thin man is seduced by a chocolate eclair: he judges that, all things considered, he really would prefer not eating the eclair to eating it. And yet, we say, he weakens and eats it. But what is this weakening? Is it changing his better judgment? Then in eating the eclair he is not acting against his better judgment, but only against his former better judgment. Or is the weakening a matter of being overcome by passion? Then it is not a free act and we should not hold him responsible for it. In short, it seems impossible freely and deliberately to act against one's better judgment. And yet we often do. JT

Bibliography

Davidson, Donald 1969: How is weakness of the will possible? In *Moral concepts*, ed. Joel Feinberg. Oxford: Clarendon Press.

Mortimore, G.W., ed. 1971: *Weakness of will*. London: Macmillan.

alcoholism Most psychologists prefer the terms "alcohol dependence" or "problem drinking" to refer to the excessive and compulsive use of alcohol, since the label "alcoholism" is too closely associated with a simple disease model. A distinction is made between *dependence* upon alcohol and the harm caused by excessive consumption. Alcohol dependence refers to the strength of the habit, the subjective experience of compulsion and the difficulty in resisting alcohol across a wide variety of situations.

One component of dependence is usually called neurological adaptation, the state in which the brain adapts to the presence of alcohol. This state results in tolerance of alcohol and also withdrawal symptoms when blood alcohol levels decline. The term neuroadaptation is preferable to the term physical dependence, since these neurological changes do not always lead to dependence. A surgical patient, given morphine to reduce pain, for example, might experience withdrawal symptoms, but not a desire to continue using the drug. Neurological adaptation can be conditioned so that it is aroused by signals or condition stimuli in the absence of alcohol. This leads to behavioral tolerance and conditioned withdrawal.

One way of understanding psychological models of alcohol dependence is to consider the three stages of relapse. After a period of abstinence, a severely dependent problem drinker will usually start to drink again as a response to psychological and social events. Social anxieties, social pressures to drink, depression, frustration, boredom and loneliness have all been implicated in this first stage of relapse. The second stage involves the cognitive and psychophysiological effects of a few drinks. It is the processes involved in this stage which provoke the most debate. The simple disease model espoused by Alcoholics Anonymous includes the notion that "one drink leads to one drunk". Experimental work has shown that, for the severely dependent drinker, a desire to drink can be primed by a few drinks, but "loss of control" is not the inevitable result. Other processes are also involved at this stage, especially the "abstinence violation effect", a cognitive process which occurs when a resolution is broken and a feeling of helplessness sets in. In the final stage of relapse, after several days of heavy drinking, withdrawal symptoms are clearly expected when drinking stops. At this stage, one reason for continuing is to escape or avoid these unpleasant experiences.

The drinker learns to expect a variety of short-term and longterm consequences if he drinks or resists at each stage. Every antecedent event or signal is therefore linked to a pay-off matrix of expected consequences. A functional analysis is an attempt to identify important antecedent events, along with the associated pay-off matrix. Most psychologists base their treatment upon such a detailed functional analysis. Psychological treatments usually involve three related approaches. In the first, an attempt is made to *enhance sobriety* so that there is a good reason to resist drinking. For example, job-finding clubs have been used to deal with unemployment. The second approach involves facing up to temptation as a way of reality testing and altering the pay-off matrix. Deliberately accepting all invitations to events involving drink would be an example of this approach, which is sometimes called *cue exposure*. Finally, there is a great deal of emphasis upon the development of self-control or *coping strategies* to counteract craving.

Psychologists have been closely involved in the controversial view that some alcoholics can return to controlled drinking as an alternative to total abstinence for life. The research evidence indicates that severely dependent alcoholics do have great difficulty in achieving controlled drinking. On the other hand, for the early problem drinker who is less severely dependent, a goal of total abstinence is much more difficult to achieve than one of controlled drinking. As a working hypothesis, many psychologists believe that severe dependence is the result of learning and conditioning. Psychological treatments might therefore be developed which reverse this process. The simple disease model espouses the view that alcoholism is an irreversible disease and total abstinence is, therefore, the only route to recovery.

The development of dependence is not simply the result of an aberrant gene or an addictive personality. There are many routes to dependence. Research has identified links with cultural norms, as well as price and availability. In wine-producing countries, for example, continuous drinking is easy, cheap and socially acceptable. Consequently these countries have to cope with severe alcohol-related problems. Type of occupation is another associated factor: company directors, bar-tenders, theater managers, actors, entertainers, musicians, cooks and seamen tend to have a high death rate as a result of excessive consumption. Other influences are parental modelling and peer group pressures, as well as personality.

Psychological models of the development, nature and treatment of alcohol dependence are not very different from psychological models of any other area of human behavior and experience. This may appear to be a trite and commonsense observation, but in the last twenty years such an approach has been closely associated with a paradigm shift in the area of alcohol consumption. The simple disease model has now been replaced by a more complicated set of working hypotheses based, not upon irreversible physiological processes, but upon learning and conditioning, motivation and self-regulation, expectations and attributions. RJH

Bibliography

Marlatt, G.A. 1983: *Relapse prevention*. New York: Guildford Press.

alcoholism *See above, and also* drug dependence; Korsakow's psychosis

aleatoric theory A theoretical orientation employed in the understanding of cross-time change in behavioral phenomena. From the aleatory viewpoint human activity is largely embedded within historically contingent circumstances. Because the configuration of existing circumstances is not fundamentally systematic, cross-time trajectories of human activity may be viewed as dependent on chance. Aleatory theory attempts to understand developmental trajectories in terms of the contemporary context, and in doing so to speak to contemporary concerns. Such theories may be contrasted with ordered change theories that attempt to view human development as a sequence of fixed stages that occur regardless of historical context. (See also ORDERED CHANGE THEORY.) KJG

Bibliography

Gergen, K.J. 1982: *Towards transformation in social knowledge*. New York: Springer.

alienation A state or process in which something is lost by or estranged from the person who originally possessed it. Marx's concept of estranged labor refers primarily to the worker's estrangement, in capitalist relations of production, from his or her product, the art of production, the "species-being" or human nature, and from other workers. This estrangement (*Entfremdung*) is based on the alienation (*Entäusserung*) of the worker's wage-labor to the capitalist. It is therefore a matter of production relations rather than technology, though it may be particularly prominent with machine production. WO

Bibliography

Marx, Karl 1844 (*1975*): Economic and philosophical manuscripts. In *Early writings*. Harmondsworth: Penguin.

Lukes, Steven 1967: Alienation and anomie. In *Philosophy, politics and society*, ed. P. Laslett and W.G. Runciman, series III. Oxford: Basil Blackwell; New York: Barner & Noble.

alienation *See above, and also* work attitudes

altered states of consciousness Major alterations in both the content and pattern of functioning of consciousness, usually as perceived by the experiencer, but also as inferred by an observer. The major pattern connoted by "state" should not be trivialized by using the word "state" to refer to any change in condition: you are reading a different set of words from those of a moment ago, but it would be confusing to call this a change in the "state" of your consciousness in the same way that we would describe, say, the effects of psychedelic drugs on consciousness.

The common sense basis of the altered state distinction is illustrated by your answer to the question, "Do you think you are really dreaming at this moment?" You can introspectively examine specific aspects of your consciousness, or quickly scan its overall pattern of functioning, and confidently decide that the state of your mind at this moment feels like your ordinary waking state, not like dreaming. More precise versions of this definitional approach have been worked out in Tart (1975).

In its behavioristic phase, psychology neglected the study of altered states, as most of the effects are on internal experience rather than overt behavior, but work on this has much increased over the last decade. Our level of knowledge has increased greatly in such areas as HYPNOSIS or nocturnal DREAMING, but is still quite primitive for states such as mystical experiences, or those induced by MEDITATION or psychedelic drugs. Except for nocturnal dreaming, known physiological changes are undetected or minimal for altered states, and of little help in understanding them psychologically.

A further reason for the historical neglect of altered states has been western culture's implicit bias that the ordinary state is natural and best, so that all altered states represent various degrees of useless or pathological deviation from the natural norm. Realization of the arbitrary and ethnocentric nature of much of what we take to be natural about our consciousness allows a more open-minded investigation of altered states. The "psychedelic revolution" of the 1960s resulted in many people espousing a diametrically opposite bias, namely that the ordinary state was much inferior to "higher" states that could be attained by drugs and other means. Our scientific knowledge is still too primitive to comment objectively on such claims. At a minimum, it is clear that many people find experiences in altered states pleasant, interesting and often leading to important personal insights or integrations. On the other hand, experiencing altered states can also be unsettling to many people and can occasionally lead to serious maladjustment or psychosis. At some stage in the future we will probably be able to use altered states selectively to enhance insight, creativity, psychotherapy and personal growth, while minimizing possible risks. Knowledge of the nature of altered states may also shed important light on some kinds of mental illness. Meanwhile, people experimenting on their own with altered states may be running a real psychological risk, and possibly physiological and legal risks as well, when using illegal drugs to induce altered states. Given the positive gains claimed by proponents, many people apparently find the risks worth taking.

In general, altered states can result in dramatic changes in almost all aspects of psychological functioning. Perception can be altered so that real stimulus objects may not be perceived, or may be perceived in quite different ways. Objects which are not physically present may be perceived (see HALLUCINATION). The perceptual/associative meaning of perceptions may be quite changed from culturally normal interpretations, an effect which may be seen as insightful or threatening to social norms. Memories ordinarily retrievable may be forgotten or recalled in an entirely new light. Previously irretrievable or actively repressed memories may be recalled. State-specific memory may appear. Cognitive evaluation processes may become more intuitive (see INTUITION), may seem to lose coherence, or may have a special coherence (state-specific logic) which is perceptible while in the altered state, but which does not make sense out of the state. New kinds of emotions may be felt. Ordinary emotions may be triggered by unusual stimulus configurations or not triggered at all by their habitual stimuli. Processes which are only inferred (see UNCONSCIOUS DRIVES) in our ordinary state may be experienced directly. FANTASY may take on as much or more intensity and experienced reality than ordinary perception of the physical world. A person's sense of personal identity and/or personality characteristics may temporarily change. Gross motor behavior is often not altered, but the internal perception of that activity may be changed greatly. Some altered states (alcohol intoxication) do characteristically involve quite significant impairment of perceptual and motor functioning by objective test standards. The way in which space and time are perceived may change drastically: time may slow down or accelerate, or experiences may become "timeless". New sorts of apparent perceptions may be noted, such as awareness of new kinds of internal body sensations: enhanced sexual pleasure is one specific example of this for some altered states. Apparently (little scientific testing has been done) paranormal abilities are sometimes experienced (see PARAPSYCHOLOGY).

Among long term effects on individuals perhaps the most important are radical shifts in perception of self and environment that result in a semi-permanent redefinition of self, world and values. The most dramatic examples are those altered states we know least about, loosely termed "mystical experiences", which can transform a person's life in a few minutes. The enormous potential of altered states for relatively permanent value shifts, for better or worse, is one of the most pressing reasons for expanded scientific research on them. Some religious traditions deliberately attempt to induce altered states as part of facilitating desired spiritual insights and value changes.

Some examples of altered states are dreaming, LUCID DREAMING, alcohol intoxication, hypnosis, various kinds of meditative states, peak experiences, marijuana intoxication and the more profound alterations induced by such drugs as LSD, mescaline or psilocybin. Intense emotions may be usefully studied as altered states, as may certain kinds of psychoses. Exact description of altered states is not feasible at the present stage of our knowledge because of careless use of the common terms and large individual differences. Two persons may smoke marijuana, for example, and while their experiences may have enough in common to make the term "marijuana intoxication" a descriptively useful one, the particulars of their experience may differ quite significantly. It is especially misleading to assume identity of states in different individuals simply because the induction technique has been the same dosage of the same psychoactive drug: the chemical effects of psychoactive drugs are frequently greatly modified by such factors as personality variables, the social or experimental setting and the expectations and previously learned skills of the persons using the drugs. CTT

Bibliography

Davidson, D. and Davidson, R., eds 1980: *The psychobiology of consciousness*. New York: Plenum.

Tart, C., ed. 1971: *Altered states of consciousness*. New York: Doubleday.

Tart, C., 1975: *States of consciousness*. New York: Dutton.

alternative psychologies Various teachings concerning human psychology that have arisen outside and as alternatives to the types discussed in standard academic literature. These arise from (i) therapy centered applications of comprehensive analytical schemes (see JUNG, REICH), (ii) contemporary neurophysiological research, as well as other research pertaining specifically to CONSCIOUSNESS (ALTERED STATES, BI-MODALITY), (iii) religious/philosophical traditions (GESTALT THERAPY, SUFISM, TAOISM, see THEOSOPHY, TRANSPERSONAL PSYCHOLOGY, VEDANTA, YOGA PSYCHOLOGY, ZEN BUDDHISM, MYSTICISM), (iv) traditional esoteric sources (ASTROLOGY, GURDJIEFF, ḰABALISM, OCCULT), (v) popular-cultural therapeutic movements offering a variety of eclectic approaches (BODY-CENTERED THERAPY, EST, PRIMAL THERAPY, PSYCHOSYNTHESIS, RADICAL THERAPY), (vi) contemporary research into so-called "unexplained" phenomena (LUCID DREAMING, OUT-OF-THE-BODY-EXPERIENCES, PARAPSYCHOLOGY, PSYCHICAL RESEARCH).

In addition to a teaching or a doctrine, many of these psychologies provide or suggest methods of self-intervention; ways of altering various factors in personal life in order to achieve what is regarded, or defined as a more ideal or developed state (INDIVIDUATION, LIBERATION, OBJECTIVE CONSCIOUSNESS, SELF-ACTUALIZATION) entailing increased self-awareness and/or naturalness of function by virtue of specific practices (CHAKRA, MARTIAL ARTS, MEDITATION, SELF-OBSERVATION). DAL

altruism: biological An act, or some other property, of one organism (the altruist) which increases the survival of another organism while decreasing its own. Defined less formally, it is self-destruction to benefit others. Ethologists have taken the word from everyday use, where it has a rather broad meaning, and given it a narrower, technical meaning: confusion results if the common meaning is read into a technical ethological discussion. In common usage, altruism not only refers to the transfer of goods from altruist to recipient; it also implies a kindly intent in the altruist. The non-ethological usage is as much motivational as economic. Ethologists have stripped the word of all connotations of subjective intent, and recognise altruism only by its effects. An altruistic act is one that has the *effect* of benefiting another organism at the altruist's expense.

The ethological meaning, as well as some of its peculiarities, can be illustrated by some examples. The commonest form of altruism is parental care, in all its forms from the most rudimentary protection of eggs to its most extreme development in viviparity and lactation. The parental animal decreases its own survival, but increases that of its offspring. But parental care is not the only behavior which fits the definition. A development from parental care is the activity of the "helper at the nest". In many species of birds (the Florida scrub jay *Aphelocoma coerulescens* is an example) the offspring of earlier broods remain after fledging at the parents' nest and help to rear later broods. The later broods are the siblings, not the offspring, of the "helpers"; but helping at the nest conforms to the definition of altruism. Helping at the nest, and analogous forms of cooperative breeding, are being discovered in a rapidly lengthening list of species of birds and mammals. But for the most extreme developments we must look to the social insects (ants, bees, wasps, and termites). In fully social species some "worker" individuals are completely sterile, and devote all their energies to rearing the offspring of another individual (the "queen"). The poisonous sting of the honey bee worker illustrates a further point about the definition of altruism. The definition does not only refer to behavior. The sting, once inserted into the victim, cannot be removed; sting and abdomen are wrenched apart, and the individual worker dies. But her nestmates will benefit from the sacrifice: the sting is an altruistic ADAPTATION. Still stranger sounding characteristics, such as the growth rate of plants, may be discussed as examples of altruism. Plants may altruistically decrease their growth rates to benefit neighboring plants.

Let us now turn to theoretical principles. Altruism is of great interest to evolutionary theorists. On the first page of his book *Sociobiology* (1975) E. O. Wilson described it, without exaggeration, as 'the central theoretical problem of sociobiology'. But why is it so central a problem? To answer this question we must look closely into the theory of evolution: the theory of NATURAL SELECTION.

Natural selection, according to a simple and usually accurate interpretation, can only favor adaptations that cause their bearers to bear more offspring. It should favor individual selfishness. If we temporarily exclude parental care, altruism appears to be exactly what natural selection will oppose. Altruists (by definition) leave fewer offspring than non-altruists. So by natural selection the non-altruists should come to prevail in all natural populations. Darwinians believe that natural selection is the only cause of adaptation. Natural selection cannot (it seems) cause altruism. But altruism exists. That is the paradox. It has elicited four main kinds of solution, but only three of them are even in principle valid.

The one of the four which is in principle invalid is the theory of "group selection". We have so far supposed that natural selection produces only adaptations that make individual organisms live longer and leave more offspring. The group of organisms only benefits incidentally, when group benefit happens to be identical with individual benefit. The theory of group selection reverses this formula. It supposes that natural selection benefits groups, and if individual and group interests come into conflict, the group interest will, under natural selection, prevail. Group selection will favor characteristics that decrease the rate at which the group becomes extinct. Altruism is just such a characteristic, so it can be expected to evolve if natural selection favors groups rather than individuals.

But does it? When the evolutionary conflict between individual and group advantage has been mathematically modelled it has been found that the conditions for group selection to operate are so restrictive that they are probably rarely realized in nature (Maynard Smith 1976). Natural selection is much more powerful on individuals than on groups because the rate of turnover of individuals is so much higher than that of groups.

Group selection can be ruled out in principle. Nor do we need it, because we have three theories which are not incoherent in principle, and which can explain altruism. They are kin selection, reciprocal altruism, and manipulation. Kin selection is the most important. It is a theory that we mainly owe to W. D. Hamilton (1964). For exposition, it is convenient to work outwards from the case of parental care. Parental care presents no theoretical paradox. If an organism leaves more offspring by caring for them than by not, parental care will evolve, since genes which cause their bearers to care for their offspring will be found in more copies in the next generations than genes which do not cause parental care. The "parental care" genes are favored because the offspring share genes (with a known probability) with their parents.

Coefficients of relatedness (r = probability that a gene in one organism is also in the listed relative).

Relatives	*r*
offspring	1/2
parent	1/2
full sibling	1/2
half sibling	1/4
grandchild	1/4
uncle or aunt	1/4
first cousin	1/8
second cousin	1/32

But an organism's offspring are not the only ones to share its genes. All its relatives do, according to a certain probability which is called a "coefficient of relatedness" (see table). Consider again the case of helpers at the nest. An animal shares genes with a sibling with exactly the same probability as with its offspring. Natural selection will therefore favor helping at the nest if, by helping, an animal increases the number of its siblings by more than the number of offspring it would on average leave if it bred alone. These two quantities are measurable, and the tests that exist so far, although preliminary, do suggest that kin selection is a major part of the explanation of helping at the nest (Emlen 1978).

The second valid theory is called "reciprocal altruism" (Trivers 1971). It differs from kin selection in that it can explain altruistic acts among non-relatives. According to this theory, altruism is favored provided that it is repaid. It can be explained by one possible natural example. Packer (1977) found that male olive baboons often form pairs to consort with females in estrus. The pairs are better at defending the female from competing males than is a single male. But Packer observed that only one male of the pair mates with any particular female. So the other male is behaving altruistically: he is defending the female but receiving no benefit for his effort. Packer found that the altruism is favored because, when another female comes into estrus, the same pair of males tends to reform, but this time the males change roles. The olive baboons provide just one example. The process could work in many other cases. It is necessary that the animals can (in effect at least) recognize individuals so that acts of altruism can be reciprocated, and cheats (who do not reciprocate) discriminated against.

Manipulation is the third explanation. Animals carry a set of responses, which are normally appropriate. But they can be subverted. A cuckoo, for example, exploits the normal response of a parental bird to a gaping chick's bill. Examples of manipulated altruism are particularly common among the relationships of parasite and host species: but natural selection can in principle favor manipulation in intra-specific interactions as well.

There are, in sum, three theories which can in principle explain the evolution of altruism. When confronted by an actual example the ethologist may study it in detail to work out which (or which mixture) of the three is the correct explanation in that case. Few such detailed studies have been yet carried out. But ethologists have reached the stage of being reasonably confident which theories are, and which are not, valid applications of the theory of natural selection. See also BEHAVIOR GENETICS; PARASITISM; SOCIOBIOLOGY; HUMAN SOCIOBIOLOGY. MR

Bibliography

*Dawkins, Richard 1976: *The selfish gene*. Oxford and New York: Oxford University Press

——— 1979: Twelve misunderstandings of kin selection. *Zeitschrift für Tierpsychologie* 51, 184–200.

Emlen, S.T. 1978: Cooperative breeding. In J.R. Krebs & N.B. Davies (eds) *Behavioural ecology* Oxford: Blackwell Scientific; Sunderland Mass.: Sinauer Assoc.

Grafen, A. 1982: How not to measure inclusive fitness. *Nature* 298, 425–6.

Hamilton, W.D. 1964: The genetical evolution of social behaviour. *Journal of theoretical biology* 7, 1–52.

Maynard Smith, J. 1976: Group selection. *Quarterly review of biology* 51, 277–83.

Packer, C. 1977: Reciprocal altruism in *Papio anubis*. *Nature* 265, 441–3.

*Ridley, M. and Dawkins, R. 1981: The natural selection of altruism. In J. Philippe Rushton and Richard M. Sorrentino (eds) *Altruism and helping behavior*. Millsdale, New Jersey: Erlbaum.

Trivers, R.L. 1971: The evolution of reciprocal altruism. *Quarterly review of biology* 46, 35–57.

*Wilson, Edward O. 1975: *Sociobiology, the new synthesis* Cambridge, Mass.: Harvard University Press.

altruism: human A term often used synonymously with pro-social behavior or helping to indicate some form of unselfish behavior on behalf of others that may involve some self-sacrifice. Types of behavior that have been studied include the donation of blood, money etc; rendering assistance in an accident; volunteering; challenging shop-lifters; cooperating and competing during games. Many theories exist to explain why people do or do not behave altruistically. They include ideas from sociobiology, reinforcement theory, psychoanalysis, and theories about cognitive development and reciprocity norms.

However, probably the most important and influential research in this area has been the work on *bystander effect* by Latané and Darley (1970). The bystander effect refers to the consistently demonstrated fact that individuals are less likely to help when they are in the presence of others than when they are alone. Apart from the mere presence of a bystander, numerous other variables have been shown to affect altruistic responses: the age, sex and number of bystanders; characteristics of the victim or person in need of help; the help given by others; familiarity or ambiguity of the situation, cultural norms etc. Latané and Darley (1970) cite five critical steps in the process which leads to altruism: notice that something is happening; interpret the situation as one in which help is needed; assume personal responsibility; choose a form of assistance; implement the assistance.

More recently attention has been turned to wider aspects of altruism such as the development and teaching of altruism, individual differences in altruism and the help people offer one another in modern cities. (Rushton 1980). AF

Bibliography

Latané, Bibb and Darley, John M. 1970: *The unresponsive bystander: why doesn't he help?* New York: Appleton-Century-Crofts.

Rushton, J. 1980: *Altruism, socialization and society*. Englewood Cliffs, N.J.: Prentice Hall.

amnesia: retrograde, anterograde Partial or total loss of memory for events that occurred shortly before an injury or treatment that affects brain processes. For mild trauma, the amnesic period may encompass only a few seconds, but for more serious injury it may be much longer. Retrograde amnesia following trauma is evidence that serious injury has occurred.

The loss of memory for events that occur after traumatic injury to the central nervous system, disease, or administration of certain drugs is called anterograde amnesia. Anterograde amnesia can also result from psychosis, delirium, or the effects of drug induced alterations in consciousness which lead to inattention to environmental stimuli. This form of amnesia appears to reflect impairments in the process of storing new information in the brain.

Amnesia can also result from psychological factors such as anxiety, conversion and dissociative reactions, phobias, and obsessive–compulsive conditions. This type of amnesia does not involve any brain injury and the recovery of memory is sometimes spontaneous or can be achieved through professional psychological help.

See also MEMORY AND LEARNING DISORDERS. RAJ

amygdala (Greek, almond) A LIMBIC SYSTEM structure located medial to the temporal lobe near the ventral surface of the brain (see BRAIN AND CENTRAL NERVOUS SYSTEM: ILLUSTRATIONS, figs. 15, 17 and 21). The amygdala is divided into corticomedial and basolateral regions which in turn subdivide into smaller nuclear groups. Both areas project directly to the HYPOTHALAMUS but corticomedial nuclei send fibers, via the stria terminalis, primarily to diencephalic and forebrain areas while basolateral nuclei project more ventrally to midbrain and BRAIN STEM (figs. 5 and 6). Historically associated with a wide range of functions (e.g. olfaction, sexuality, information-processing), the amygdala is most consistently linked to emotional reactivity. The basolateral region appears to mediate an excitatory function in emotion since electrical stimulation of this area produces aggressive and other emotional responses while lesions have a general dampening effect. The opposite pattern is observed with respect to the corticomedial region, indicating an inhibitory function. Recent evidence suggests that the amygdala, in conjunction with the HIPPOCAMPUS, may contribute to basic learning and memory processes. GWi

analogy: linguistic The name given to a proposed mechanism of language change that involves the transfer of a pattern of regularity in existing forms to new forms. The nineteenth-century neo-grammarians used this concept to account for exceptions. They claimed that analogy corrupted the *sound-laws* (regular inheritance and change of sounds from mother to daughter language) by creating "non historical" forms. The Latin form for honor appears in the earliest writings as *honos, honoris*, the final *-s* representing an Indo-European inherited *s*. Later writers use *honor, honoris* presumably in analogy to the pattern found in forms with an IE final *-r* e.g. *cultor, cultoris*, Lyons (1969).

The structuralists took over, refined and restructured the views of their predecessors. Bloomfield (1933) suggested that analogical transfer works like a proportional equation: if one forms plurals by the addition of *s*, one will add *s* to a new singular (e.g. radio) as a matter of course.

Modern analysts, especially Kiparsky (1974), have generally argued against proportional analogy as a model of change. The principle objections have been that proportions are stated between individual lexical items, phrases, clauses or sentences. But there is good evidence that change occurs via rule, not via item-by-item alteration. Furthermore, proportional analogy fails to distinguish between absurd and legitimate cases of possible change. JAE

Bibliography

Bloomfield, Leonard 1933: *Language*. New York: Holt, Rinehart & Winston.

Kiparsky, Paul 1974: Remarks on analogical change. In *Historical linguistics II*, ed. J. Anderson and C. Jones. Amsterdam and New York: Elsevier.

Lyons, John 1969: *Introduction to theoretical linguistics*. Cambridge and New York: Cambridge University Press.

Mayerthaler, Willi 1978: Analogiebibliographie, *Working papers in linguistics of the Technical University Berlin* 1, 1–21. Berlin: Institute for Linguistics.

analogy *See above, and also* homology and analogy

anomie A state of normlessness or lack of regulation (Greek: *nomos*=law). Emile Durkheim (1858–1917) coined the term to describe a lack of the social control which he saw as essential to any human society. Human nature needed to be formed and regulated by society. Durkheim's early concept of the *conscience collective* neatly expresses the dual (cognitive and moral) aspect of this regulation. (See SOCIAL REPRESENTATIONS.)

The social division of labor may become anomic under capitalism; it needs to be regulated and given a moral character by occupational corporations similar to medieval guilds. The anomic form of suicide results from the frustration of desires which, in the absence of the necessary social regulation, have grown beyond all possibility of their satisfaction.

Durkheim's "anomie" is structurally similar to Marx's "estrangement"/"alienation", in that they describe an objective process with subjective consequences. They seem however to rest on divergent views of human nature, Durkheim stressing the need for social regulation in *any* society. WO

Bibliography

Lukes, Steven 1967: Alienation and anomie. In *Philosophy, politics and society*, series III, ed. P. Laslett and W.G. Runciman. Oxford: Basil Blackwell; New York: Barnes & Noble.

anorexia nervosa A psychiatric disorder in which there is self-induced weight loss with severe inanition; persistent amenorrhoea (or an equivalent endocrine disturbance in the male); and psychopathology characterized by a morbid fear of becoming fat. An extreme desire to be thin leads to food avoidance and in some cases self-induced vomiting or purgative abuse. Most of the physical features of the condition are a result of starvation. The disorder is largely confined to developed countries in which slimness is considered attractive. Onset is usually during adolescence. Most cases are female and the prevalence is increasing. The majority of treatment approaches are helpful in the short-term, at least as regards weight gain. Initial response to treatment does not predict enduring improvement. At follow-up most patients are found to retain the core psychopathology. See also NEUROSIS. CJGF

Bibliography

Dally, P. and Gomez, J. 1979: *Anorexia nervosa*. London: Heinemann. Chicago: Year Book of Medical Publishing.

anthropoid ape language Ape communication, whether acquired naturally or through training, can be termed linguistic if it shares essential features with human language or if it utilizes psychological or biological mechanisms that underlie language in man. Attempts have been made to teach apes both referential symbols equivalent to words (see MEANING, COGNITIVE) and rules for combining symbols into longer combinations (see GRAMMAR). However, since apes apparently have little ability to modulate voiced sounds (Lieberman 1975), experiments on ape language have used visual instead of auditory symbols to test usage. Two kinds of visual symbols have been used: manual gestures similar to those used in the sign languages of deaf humans (see, e.g., Klima and Bellugi 1979), and written symbols or objects analogous to the graphemes of a non-alphabetic WRITING SYSTEM such as Chinese, where each distinct visual shape denotes a concept not a sound in the language (Fouts 1975; Gardner and Gardner 1975; Premack 1976; Neago, personal communication; Patterson 1979; Patterson and Linden 1981; Rumbaugh 1977; Terrace 1979; Terrace et al. 1979). In addition, research using keyboard control of machine-synthesized speech is also under way (Patterson and Linden 1981).

In all of these studies, the animal is first taught a set of names for familiar objects, body parts, persons and common activities by pairing the symbol with examples of its referent. After the association is learned, the researcher notes the ape's ability to use the symbol in a spontaneous and appropriate manner and tests its ability to select the correct referent when presented only with the symbol. Whether taught with gestures, plastic tokens or computer-controlled displays, all three genera of existing anthropoid apes (gorilla, chimpanzee and orang-utan) can reliably learn a set of symbols for a set of conceptual classes and can use them on their own initiative to request services from humans or other apes. Since the criteria for judging sign acquisition can be very strict (for example, spontaneous and appropriate use on half the days of a given month), the published vocabularies of about 150 signs probably underestimate apes' abilities. The gorilla Koko's unofficial vocabulary is now over 700 signs. Also, ape sign acquisition shows parallels to human vocabulary learning, both spoken and signed, in the generalization and over-extension of words (Gardner and Gardner 1975; Patterson 1979). Home-reared apes also have some understanding of spoken English words (Fouts, Chown and Goodin 1976; Patterson 1979), but it is not known whether apes discriminate spoken words phonemically, in terms of the acoustic cues for articulatory differences among speech sound (see SPEECH UNITS), or by gross differences in the acoustic waveforms of different words, as human would discriminate a fog horn from a fire siren.

Students of ape language have tried to show that apes have syntactic as well as lexical (vocabulary) knowledge. Premack and Rumbaugh required their chimpanzees to learn rules for sequences of symbols. The apes were able to present symbols in certain prescribed orders, to fit the missing symbol in a blank space in a sequence, and to use different sequences for different meanings. However, critics have argued that the apes learned only complex conditional discrimination tasks, not syntax *per se*, because they did not understand the meaning of the manipulations they learned to perform. Another strategy has been to examine the spontaneous sign combinations of apes for evidence of syntax. Apes commonly produce combinations of two or three signs, with occasional longer, more repetitive sequences. In all cases in which the sequential order of signs was specifically recorded, there were statistically significant differences in the serial positions of different signs. Thus, in Terrace's chimpanzee, Nim, verb + *me*, verb + *Nim*, *more* + *X* (where *X* is a sign), and *give* + *X* combinations are more frequent than their opposites (Terrace et al. 1979). The gorilla Koko (Patterson 1979) used various orderings in action + object constructions such as *open bottle*; action + object for feeding verbs such as *eat* and the reverse order for social verbs such as *tickle*. In addition to order constraints, modifications of signs have been observed that are reminiscent of the puns and innovative constructions of human sign language (Fouts 1975; Patterson 1979). Several observers have also noted that a number of different semantic relations or functions appear to be implicit in the sign combinations of apes when considered in context (Gardner and Gardner 1975; Patterson 1979). These relations include nomination *(that bird)*, recurrence *(more cereal)*, non-existence *(me can't)*, affected state *(me good)*, attributive *(hot potato)*, possessive *(hat mine)*, direction toward a goal *(go bed)*, dative *(give me drink)*, and the agent, action and object relations already noted above. These semantic relations are similar to the relationships implicit in early child speech, which must also be interpreted to a large extent by the context. However, in the case of apes, where the speech does not develop into adult grammar, critics have argued that such inferred relations are conjectural (Terrace et al. 1979). However, since apes are capable of using such relationships in the observational learning of tool use and social behavior (Premack 1976), it is likely they function in communication as well. Nonetheless the range of semantic and syntactic relations that must be postulated in order to account for ape utterance types is far smaller than for children, and apes show a slower acquisition rate and a far lower level of achievement in both vocabulary and syntax. The mean number of signs in multi-sign combinations is much lower in apes, and grammatical function words, such as *Wh*-questions (*what, who*, etc.), are only rudimentary.

Critics have also recently challenged the inference of ape grammar on methodological grounds by claiming that ape sign combinations are prompted by human tutors, lack spontaneity and are highly imitative (Terrace et al. 1979). It is also claimed that apes, unlike humans, do not take turns in conversation but interrupt their tutors. However, these conclusions are based on the analysis of film and videotape materials that are unlikely to represent the animals' true abilities. Turn-taking cues are subtle; and they develop, like all language, in intimate social contexts. Such behavior is unlikely to develop under impoverished rearing conditions or to be exhibited in disruptive filming sessions. The tutorial methods commonly used may also inflate the number of prompted signs. Similarly, the criticism that ape signing can be explained by unconscious social cueing, analogous to the "counting" horse Clever Hans (Umiker-Sebeok and Sebeok 1980), is not only contradicted by successful double-blind experiments of vocabularly comprehension, but the behavior is too complex to be explained in this way. Nonetheless, these criticisms make it clear that the traditional verbal methods of recording ape sign language are too inaccurate to sustain the precise comparisons needed to assess apes' syntactic abilities, and systematic video records of the development of ape signing, such as Patterson's 250 hours of videotape, will be needed to resolve the question of ape grammar. Also, since the definitions of grammar that have been used in discussions of ape sign language were not derived from the analysis of film records of normal human conversational speech, and are not completely compatible with human signing, there is reason to question their psychological adequacy. By defining as language only those utterances that depart most from face-to-face conversational gatherings where most human language occurs, the theory underlying most studies of ape syntax forces us categorically to deny language to animals if they fail to meet the most stringent formalistic criteria and to ignore the similarities that otherwise exist.

A psychological definition of language should not focus exclusively on the features that are found only in man but should evaluate a species' linguistic competence in the light of its other cognitive and behavioral capacities. For example, the claim by (Terrace et al. 1979) that apes are little inclined to comment on conversation topics introduced by others is congruent with other aspects of simian psychology. Apes, as shown by their tool using, are also deficient compared to man in exchange of both artifacts and techniques and in the coordination of the actions of many individuals to produce a common product (Reynolds 1981). Consequently, it would not be surprising if their sign language proved to lack these features also. However, such discrepancies do not prove that apes "lack language". If human language is taken to be communication from which propositional relationships can be inferred, then linguistic ability, far from being an absolute, will vary with the capacity for intentional action on one hand and with the capacity for conceptual inference on the other. PCR

Bibliography

Fouts, Roger S. 1975: Capacities for language in great apes. In *Socioecology and psychology of primates*, ed. R. Tuttle. The Hague: Mouton.

Fouts, Roger S., Chown, B. and Goodin, L. 1976: Transfer of signed responses in American Sign Language from vocal English stimuli to physical object stimuli by a chimpanzee (Pan). *Learning and motivation* 7, 458–75.

Gardner, R.A., and Gardner, B.T. 1975: Early signs of language in child and chimpanzee. *Science* 187, 752–3.

Klima, Edward, and Bellugi, Ursula 1979: *The signs of language*. Cambridge, Mass. and London: Harvard University Press.

Lieberman, P. 1975: *On the origins of language*. New York: Macmillan.

Patterson, Francine 1978: The gestures of a gorilla: sign language acquisition in another pongid species. *Brain and language* 5, 72–97.

———, 1979: *Linguistic capabilities of a lowland gorilla*. Ann Arbor, Michigan: University Microfilms International.

——— and Linden, Eugene 1981: *The education of Koko*. New York: Holt, Rinehart & Winston.

Premack, David 1971: Language in chimpanzees? *Science* 172, 808–22.

*———, 1976: *Intelligence in ape and man*. Hillsdale, NJ: Erlbaum.

Reynolds, Peter C. 1981: *On the evolution of human behavior*. Berkeley and Los Angeles: University of California Press.

Rumbaugh, Duane M. (ed.) 1977: *Language learning by a chimpanzee: the LANA project*. New York: Academic Press.

Terrace, H.S. 1979: *Nim*. New York: Knopf.

———, et al. 1979: Can an ape create a sentence? *Science* 206, 891-902.

*Umiker-Sebeok, J. and Sebeok, T.A., eds. 1980: *Speaking of apes: a critical anthology of two-way communication with man*. New York and London: Plenum Press.

anthropomorphism The attribution to an animal of psychical capabilities like those of men and the supposition that it acts from similar motives. Among many others Darwin (1872) and one of the founders of ethology, Lorenz, assumed that animals have mental experiences and emotions similar to those of humans, and at times described their behavior in anthropomorphic terms. However, another pioneer of ethology, Tinbergen (1951), argued that there is no basis for inferring subjective experiences in other species. It is generally thought to be erroneous and unscientific to attribute human mental experiences to animals. The recent development of COGNITIVE ETHOLOGY (Griffin 1976), which attempts to study mental experiences in animals, is contrasted to anthropomorphism in that it does not assume that the experiences are the same as those of humans. PJA

Bibliography

Darwin, Charles 1872: *The expression of the emotions in man and animals*. London: John Murray.

Griffin, Donald 1976: *The question of animal awareness: evolutionary continuity of mental experience*. New York: Rockefeller University Press.

Tinbergen, Niko 1951: *The study of instinct* 2nd edn with new introduction, 1969. Oxford: Clarendon Press.

anxiety, clinical *See* clinical psychology

anxiety: social psychology The study of anxiety, as a specific subjective experience, a physiological state or a personality trait, has received attention in social psychology mainly as a determinant of affiliative behavior. Research by Schachter (1959) showed that the induction of anxiety leads to a preference for being in the company of others who are in the same emotional state. The social comparison which such company affords plays an important role in Schachter's theory of emotions, which suggests that the interpretation of emotions depends crucially upon such social comparison procedures where people are ignorant about the source of arousal which they experience.

The affiliation effect of induced anxiety appears to be stronger in first-born and only children. JMFJ

Bibliography

Schachter, S. 1959: *The psychology of affiliation*. Stanford, California: Stanford University Press.

aphasia Any disorder of speech resulting from brain damage. See SPEECH DISORDERS.

appeasement A ritualized gesture (including vocalizations and scents) of submission. It is commonly the opposite of threat gestures such as crouching which reduces apparent size and hides markings of sex and species. Many appeasement gestures mimic female or infantile behavior. (See also AGGRESSION, RITUAL AND RITUALIZATION.) AJ

appetitive behavior in animals The active exploratory behavior that precedes CONSUMMATORY BEHAVIOR. The term was introduced by Wallace Craig (1918) to describe the animal's response to the absence of a stimulus, such as food or a mate. For instance a hungry rat may actively forage for food and this appetitive behavior ceases when food is obtained.

Appetitive behavior is often exploited by scientists investigating animal learning and discrimination. Maze running and operant behavior are examples of appetitive behavior that are commonly manipulated in laboratory experiments (see OPERANT CONDITIONING). However, although favored by Lorenz and Tinbergen, the concept of appetitive behavior has not proved to be very useful in the study of natural behavior. Many animals do not show active foraging when hungry, but employ an ambush strategy. Moreover, there are many aspects of behavior to which it is not clear that the term is appropriate. Its use in connection with avoidance, and aggression, is controversial. DJM

Bibliography

Craig, W. 1918: Appetites and aversions as constituents of instincts. *Biology bulletin* 34, 91–107.

approach/avoidance conflict The conflict shown when identical or similar objects or places have been associated with both attractive and aversive consequences. In the classic demonstration a hungry rat is trained to run down a runway for food in the goal box until it reliably approaches the goal whenever placed in the start box. If the rat is then punished whenever it reaches the goal box, by being given a brief electric shock, it will show a characteristic pattern of conflict, running part of the way down the runway after being placed in the start box, but then hesitating, stopping, retracing and going forward again. Given the opportunity, it will now escape altogether from the situation by jumping out of the runway.

The rat will also engage in DISPLACEMENT ACTIVITY, and ethologists have recorded similar approach/avoidance conflicts, for example during courtship, when the male is both (for obvious enough reasons) attracted to the female, and also afraid of her – for example because she resembles a male conspecific who would attack if approached too closely. NJM

approach/avoidance conflict: social psychology One of the three possible types of conflict, distinguished by Lewin (1935), when the tendency to approach and avoid a goal are of equal strength. Approach leads to an increase of negative valence and hence to compensatory withdrawal from the goal; avoidance to a relative increase of positive valence and therefore to compensatory approach movements. The approach/avoidance conflict is relatively stable and leads to a great deal of vacillating and "übersprung" behavior, as observed by ethologists in animals. In children it may lead to minimal task performance, rejecting the goal or attempting to reach the goal in other ways.

The most influential research on approach/avoidance conflicts has been conducted by Miller (1944). However, most of his studies were concerned with learning in animals. JMFJ

Bibliography

Lewin, K. 1935: *A dynamic theory of personality*. New York: McGraw-Hill.

Miller, N.E. 1944: Experimental studies of conflict. In *Personality and behavior disorders: a handbook based on experimental and clinical research* Vol. 1, ed. J. McV. Hunt. New York: Ronald.

Aquinas and scholasticism Thomas Aquinas (*c.* 1225–75) was one among several brilliant products of that process of monastic schooling which Charlemagne had sponsored and which culminated in the great medieval universities. The men of these schools, so called scholastics, maintained a variety of theological and philosophical positions. "Scholasticism" is a generic term which refers to the traditions shaped by particular schools and particular religious orders. Aquinas, a Dominican educated in Cologne and Paris, occupied middle ground between the more speculative Bonaventure (1221–74), in whose work the influence of PLATO and AUGUSTINE remained telling, and the later Franciscans of Oxford such as Duns Scotus (*c.* 1265–1308). But Aquinas was not a manufacturer of compromises; rather, living at the height of the scholastic period, he brought its intellectual achievements to an apogee.

Aquinas's philosophical stance is partly shaped by his understanding of Sacred Scripture. In particular, his notion of "human being" is influenced by the Genesis account of creation: human kind is made in the image and likeness of God. Further, a second presupposition in his anthropology is the witness of the New Testament to immortality of the personal soul and to resurrection of the body. These assumptions do not necessarily prejudice his philosophical inquiry, however, for though all the scholastics shared the same faith, their understandings of that faith varied considerably.

Soul and body, moreover, are as much notions of Greek philosophy as they are of Judaeo-Christian belief. And if the Jewish tradition viewed the whole person as a unity, whether under the aspect of spirit or of body, the Greek focus explored a distinction between soul and body. Also, the worldview inherited by Western Christendom rested almost completely on Augustine's synthesis of neo-Platonic thought and Christian belief. Finally, the telling factor in Aquinas's contribution was the emergence of Aristotelian thought in Europe through translations of Arabic commentaries. Aquinas offers a synthesis of PLATO and ARISTOTLE in his own subtle account of human nature and knowing. If on the one hand he wished to preserve the possibility of the soul surviving the death of the body, as Plato urged, Aquinas was equally sympathetic to Aristotle's emphasis on the unity of soul and body.

Throughout the course of his writings Aquinas takes up questions about the nature of human being and knowing. His answers are based on a combination of introspection and appeal to external evidence. He consistently stresses the integrity of the human person and, at the same time, distinguishes between its spiritual and bodily aspects. It is his skill in handling these two positions which marks his contribution to the scholastic psychology.

Aquinas describes the human soul in various ways: it is the principle of intellectual activity, the first principle of life, the substantial form of the body, and it is the mind. But can such a form exist independently of a body? According to Aristotle the soul is essentially the form of a material substrate and incapable of real existence apart from the body. Aquinas argued, however, that the soul's distinct actuality is disclosed in our awareness of activities (such as volition and conscious thought) in which material conditions such as spatiality and particularity are transcended. If our minds can act at times independently of our bodies, so that the "bodily" plays no intrinsic part, then the soul must have some independence of the body. For, argues Aquinas, nothing can act independently unless it be independent. In technical terms the soul possesses a subsistent existence in as much as it performs a function in which the body has no share. Thus, though the soul cannot in any significant sense have existence prior to bodily existence it is able to exist apart from the body after death. The manner in which the human soul is a substantial form is different from the manner in which the animal and vegetative forms are described by Aristotle as being substantial forms. Taking such a stance, Aquinas can attribute this property to human likeness to God; and he can also provide for an account of resurrection. In so doing he argues that it is not natural for the soul to be separate from the body, hence the two could not be perpetually separated. The separate soul is not the person as such. The soul must be reunited with the body if the natural order is to be completed.

Aquinas also argues for the unity of soul and body, as well as for their separability. To be united to the body is not detrimental to the soul, but for its enrichment. Only in such oneness is human nature made complete; and only in this way can knowledge, which is only acquired with the help of the senses, be gained. The soul is dependent upon the body for knowledge, as well as naturally at home in the body. But in what way can soul and body be one? Not by any touching or mixing, says Aquinas, for that kind of interaction belongs to material things – and the soul transcends the material. Rather, just as emotions can powerfully move us, so also the soul is a kind of virtue or power, in modern terminology an ability or function. This is not meant to suggest that the soul acts through the body, but rather that we act through the soul. Where the body is alive, there also is the soul. The soul depends upon the body for the acquisition of its particular characteristics. One cannot identify the substance of the soul in terms of its abilities, but only in as much as the soul in its essence is an actuality, that is, a realization of what is possible to or potential in a body. The soul is the first actuality of the body (as, for example, "seeing" is an act of the eye). The union of soul and body is therefore immediate and not to be altered by accidental changes.

Bonaventure would agree with Aristotle's account of the soul as form of the body. But he would further add that the soul itself had a dignity apart from the body and was composed of its own spiritual form and matter. The soul did not exist to move the body, then, but to enjoy the vision of God. And though the soul was dependent upon the senses and upon the imagination for knowledge, as Aquinas also claimed, Bonaventure's Augustinianism went a step further: God can be known through the soul's reflection on itself and the soul has within it all that it necessary for such a process of ascent.

For Scotus, on the other hand, the death of a human being must involve the death of the whole person; but since Aquinas claimed the integrity of soul and body in the person, he should also allow for the death of the soul. Scotus therefore rejected Aquinas's position. He suggested that because the soul was essentially incomplete, it was dependent upon the senses of the body. The unity of soul and body was therefore for the perfection of both. Despite his emphasis on the priority of the senses in knowledge, Scotus also stressed that the soul could know, abstract, and will, independently of the body.

These are three representative positions of scholasticism. Aquinas's enduring contribution, if he did take the notions of soul and body for granted, is his insight into the goodness and givenness of what is bodily as well as what is spiritual: the fully human person is an indivisible unity. Further, this contribution can be shown to have a modern, analytic ring about it (as expounded in Burrell 1979). The elaborate subtleties of scholastic psychology, however, can only be fully appreciated in their own wide-ranging contexts. JRH

Bibliography

Aquinas, Thomas: *Summa Theologiae* 1a, 75–78; 1a 2ae, 22–48. London: Eyre and Spottiswoode; New York: McGraw-Hill.

Aquinas, Thomas: *Summa Contra Gentiles* 2, 47–101, Notre Dame, Ill.: University of Notre Dame Press.

*Burrell, D.B. 1979: *Aquinas: God and action*. London: Routledge & Kegan Paul; Notre Dame, Ill.: University of Notre Dame Press.

*Copleston, F.C. 1950: *A history of philosophy* vol. 2. London: Burns & Oates; Westminster, Maryland: Newman–Image.

*Kenny, A.J. 1979: *Aquinas*. Oxford and New York: Oxford University Press.

archetype *See* Jung, Carl

archival method A method of research involving the systematic analysis of previously recorded or preserved information. Archives are typically documents and public records, although research is not restricted to printed materials and may deal with artifacts such as tools, toys, architecture or clothing. The outstanding feature of archival methods is that they help with the study of psychological phenomena cross-time, and cross-culturally. The method is generally economical, permits re-analysis of materials, and involves a procedure of nonreactive or unobtrusive assessment of phenomena. On the other hand archival studies are susceptible to biases in the recording, survival and retrieval of information.

Archival materials may be subjected to quantitative analysis. The findings then often resemble social statistics as exemplified in Durkheim's classic study of suicide. Research problems requiring qualitative or higher-order analysis may use various techniques of content analysis. Archival research in psychology has conventionally been distinguished from historical research by its use of quantitative measures, but the distinction is superficial as some historians employ quantitative measures and some psychologists use qualitative ones. Owing to these mutual interests in methodology and in psychological explanations, a comprehensive account of archival methods must include studies in psychology and history.

JGM

Aristotelian view of emotion Aristotle placed the emotions in the category of passivity (changes impressed on an object); they are passions (*pathē*), not actions (*Categories*, 9^b27–34). An emotion can be distinguished from other human passions (sensations, bodily drives such as hunger and thirst) in that the efficient cause of an emotion is some judgment or appraisal. Emotions are thus cognitive in a broad sense, although they are not deliberative or logical; and being cognitive, emotions are subject to reasoned persuasion. In fact, Aristotle offered his most extended and consistent discussion of the emotions in the *Rhetoric* (Bk II), a work which deals with the art of persuasion.

In addition to specifying the efficient cause (the appraisal), a complete analysis of any specific emotion would include reference to its final cause (goal) and material cause (state of mind or bodily condition of the predisposed individual). However, not all emotions have a final cause; anger, for example, has a goal (revenge), but shame does not. Moral character or virtue is a learned disposition – to act correctly and to experience emotion, neither too strongly nor too weakly, but upon the right instigation, toward the right person, with the right motive, and in the right manner (*Nicomachean Ethics*, 1103^{a} 15–1106^{b}25).

JRAv

Bibliography

Fortenbaugh, W.W. 1975: *Aristotle on emotion*. London: Duckworth.

Aristotle Aristotle's study of the *psychē*, an enquiry not yet partitioned between psychology and philosophy of mind, is to be found in a group of short, dense and difficult works: *De Anima* ("On the Soul"), *Parva Naturalia* (a series of essays on topics such as memory, dreams, ageing) and *De Motu Animalium* ("On the movement of animals"). Inquiry into the *psychē* or "soul" of living things forms part of Aristotle's scientific study of the natural world in general, and shades off into the biological treatises. He studies the functioning of animals' capacities to perceive, think and move in a detailed, cautious and empirical way, often involving stretches of physiology which, though primitive and over-speculative by modern standards, show lively scientific curiosity. But this patient research is shaped by overall concern for a philosophically sound approach. The *De Anima* opens with criticisms of the philosophical inadequacies in previous works, from which develops Aristotle's own account of the soul as the "form" and "actuality" of the body; the specific problems of psychology are illuminated by concepts put to frequent use in his metaphysics and science.

The common sense Greek view of *psychē* is that it is what makes living things alive. Aristotle takes this as a basic fact, accepting that even plants have *psychē*. ("Soul" is, though common, very infelicitous as a translation of *psychē*.) Aristotle is also, however, aware of a religious and philosophical tradition (notably in Plato) conceiving of the (human) soul in a radically dualist way, as a distinct entity unhappily tied to the body. In clear reaction, Aristotle's formulations insist that the soul is essentially embodied. In a living thing we can distinguish the matter – the flesh, bones and organs – from the way in which these organs characteristically function – the way the living thing maintains itself by metabolism, perceives, moves. This is the soul, the form which makes the matter be the body of a living thing. "If the eye were an animal, sight would be its soul" (*DA* II 1): sight is the capacity of the eye and an eye is living tissue so organized as (normally) to see. The soul as a whole is a structured set of such capacities, and the body is living tissue so organized as to maintain itself, perceive, etc. Hence soul and body cannot be separated any more than sight can be separated from an eye: sight just is the way an eye functions. So the inquiry into the various capacities that constitute the soul must bring in both the bodily parts and the form that gives them their structure as functioning parts of a living body. The student of the soul will (*DA* I 1) investigate anger not merely as the boiling of blood round the heart (the matter) nor merely as desire for revenge (the form) but as both (the form as functioning in matter). Aristotle sees this as a point that needs making; to neglect either is to change the subject from the study of living things.

The soul is thus an enmattered, non-separable form; it cannot be adequately described in terms of the body, but it is not a metaphysically distinct entity. Because of the second point Aristotle has been claimed as a materialist or functionalist; because of the first he has been seen as a dualist who avoids only the claim that the soul is a separate substance. All such interpretations are problematic; modern positions in the philosophy of mind tend to be constructed to meet questions which Aristotle does not raise. Revealingly, he has no concepts which answer to the contrast of "mental" and "physical" so central to us, and interest in epistemological issues, often crucial to that contrast, finds no place in his discussion of the cognitive faculties. His "hylomorphist" account of the soul (from the Greek for matter and form) fits only partially into any theory structured by modern philosophical concerns, and it remains fascinatingly elusive, and very controversial, how we are to interpret him in terms of the mental/physical contrast.

Aristotle in fact finds it of limited interest to define soul in general (*DA* II 3); his concern is with the diverse and overlapping ranges of capacities in different kinds of living thing. Plants have the "nutritive" soul, the capacity to grow and reproduce themselves as self-maintaining organisms (*DA* II 4). Most of Aristotle's efforts are spent elucidating the capacity which distinguishes animals (including humans) from plants: perception (*DA* II 5–12, III 1–2, 7–8; *De Sensu*.) Perceiving is described as a physical interaction in terms taken over from the *Physics*, but Aristotle insists in various opaque formulae that it is different from other kinds of change. Some have found here a recognition of what we call the mental element in perceiving; however, Aristotle makes little of this and his main interest is not in the phenomenological side (though he does discuss "first-person" problems such as the unity of perceptual experience) but with perception as a process whereby we both gain information and interpret our environment. It ranges from sensitivity to the "special" objects of each sense, such as color, to grasp of the "common" objects available to more than one sense, to discrimination of the "incidental objects" of perception. These are problematic, but certainly include physical objects (an example is the son of Diares); Aristotle is ascribing to perception much identifying and conceptualizing more commonly ascribed to thinking. Perceiving is not merely passive reception of a sensory "given" which another faculty conceptualizes; it includes the active power to interpret what is received.

This broad approach to perceiving leads to an expansive

view of its scope. To the perceptive faculty is ascribed not only memory (*De Memoria*) but the puzzling faculty of *phantasia* or "imagination" (*DA* III 3) which is best taken as the capacity to conceive the world as it appears to one without judging whether or not it is really as it appears. As such it plays an important part in thinking, which never takes place without the "images" (phantasmata) which phantasia provides. (*DA* III 7).

The account of thinking (*DA* III 4–6) is strangely in conflict with what has gone before. Thinking alone *is* separable from the body; in fact the capacity for thought is "unmixed" with the body and has no bodily organ (which would allegedly disturb our ability to think of anything.) Aristotle is uncompromising about this unassimilable dualism in works which otherwise interpret the soul through the body. But the passage is exceptionally brief and fragmentary; and the problem is lessened when we reflect that in keeping with an expansive scope for perceiving Aristotle gives a very narrow scope to what he calls thinking. For most of the discussion he clearly has in mind only abstract thought in mathematics and philosophy. It is a real problem, how such thinking can be physically realized; Aristotle's dualism is a response to this problem (and has links with his handling of similar problems in his metaphysics and ethics). It has virtually nothing in common with modern mind/body dualisms.

Aristotle's theory of action (*DA* III 9–11, *De Motu*) analyses all animal and human movements, in a bold and compelling theory, as a product of two factors: a cognition and a desire of some kind, ranging from the simple to the sophisticated. Aristotle gives an abstract mechanical model for the structure of the movement, which supplements (rather than competing with) his account of movement in living things as teleological, aimed at some goal perceived by the animal as an achievable good. He also regiments the patterns of practical thought that lead to action, the so called "practical syllogism". This has been very variously but inconclusively studied. Clarity is made difficult by the fact that Aristotle moves between reconstructing the agent's reasoning and giving an external interpretation of the action; also by the fact that neither in the psychological works nor in related passages of the *Ethics* is there a single canonical form into which all the examples can be fitted. Some are informal, untidy pieces of means-ends reasoning directed at the attainment of a particular goal; others are pieces of valid but trivial reasoning with wide possible application. It looks as though Aristotle at some points thought that patterns of practical reasoning might be formalized, analogously to the valid patterns of theoretical inference. But if so the project did not get very far; practical reasoning is schematized only to the level of abstraction of means-ends reasoning, without developed notions of logical form or valid inference. Probably Aristotle realized, with his usual good sense, that this was the right level of generality to be useful in psychology. JEA

Bibliography

The Works of Aristotle translated into English, ed. J.A. Smith and W.D. Ross (Oxford: Oxford University Press, 1910–1952). Contains the *De Anima*, *Parva Naturalia* and *De Motu*. The *De Anima* and part of the *Parva Naturalia* are in the abridgement by R. McKeon (ed) *The Basic Works of Aristotle* (New York, Random House, 1941.). The *De Anima* and *Parva Naturalia* are translated with facing Greek text by W.S. Hett in the Loeb Library (Cambridge, Mass.: Harvard University Press, 1964.) The *De Anima* books II and III are translated with notes by D.W. Hamlyn (Oxford: Clarendon Press, 1968.) *Aristotle on Memory* is a translation with notes of the *De Memoria* by R.R.K. Sorabji (London: Duckworth, 1972.) *De Motu Animalium* is translated, with text, commentary and essays by M.C. Nussbaum (Princeton: Princeton University Press, 1978.)

Barnes, J., Schofield, M, and Sorabji, R.R.K., eds 1979: *Articles on Aristotle vol 4: psychology and aesthetics*, (London: Duckworth, 1979) reprints the following important recent articles:

Barnes, J. 1971–2: Aristotle's Concept of Mind. *Proceedings of the Aristotelian Society* 72, 101–14.

Kahn, C.H. 1966: Sensation and consciousness in Aristotle's psychology. *Archiv für Geschichte der Philosophie* 48, 43–81.

Norman, R. 1969: Aristotle's Philosopher-God. *Phronesis* 14, 63–74.

Schofield, M. 1978: Aristotle on the imagination. In *Aristotle on mind and the senses*, ed. G.E.R. Lloyd and G.E.L. Owen (Cambridge: Cambridge University Press.)

Sorabji, R.R.K. 1974: Body and Soul in Aristotle. *Philosophy* 49, 63–89.

———, 1971: Aristotle on demarcating the five senses. *Philosophical review* 80, 55–79.

Furley, D.J. 1978: Self-Movers. In Lloyd and Owen op. cit.

Hamlyn, D.W. 1978: Aristotle's Cartesianism. *Paideia*, special Aristotle issue.

Hardie, W.F.R. 1976: Concepts of consciousness in Aristotle. *Mind* 85, 388–411.

Hartman, E. 1978: *Substance, body and soul*. Princeton: Princeton University Press.

Kosman, L.A. 1975: Perceiving that we perceive: "On the Soul" III 2. *Philosophical review* 84, 499–519.

Robinson, H.M. 1978: Mind and body in Aristotle. *Classical Quarterly* 28, 107–24.

Wilkes, K.V. 1978: *Physicalism*, ch.7. London: Routledge & Kegan Paul.

arousal A psychophysiological concept that is used in all branches of psychology, particularly personality theory. The idea of arousal can be traced back to Pavlovian ideas of the excitatory strength of the nervous system, but is perhaps more widely known in the work of Eysenck (1967) and Gray (1971). Both see arousal level as an inherited biological phenomenon on which individuals may differ along a dimension. Furthermore both have the notion of an optimal level of arousal.

Russian and Polish researchers have looked at arousal in terms of the concept of reactivity of the nervous system – that is the relationship between the intensity of the stimulus and the amplitude of response. Stimuli of equal physical activity are demonstrated to evoke a lower level of arousal in low-reactive than in high-reactive subjects. The low-reactive individual augments stimulation, and the high-reactive individual reduces stimulation both aiming at maintaining or restoring a genetically fixed optimal level of activation.

Eysenck (1967) has argued that extroversion and introversion are closely related with habitual levels of arousal in the cortex (particularly the reticular activating system). Introverts have a higher level of arousal and hence are more inhibited, seek less stimulation and are better at learning, remembering and conditioning. Extroverts have a lower level of arousal and hence are more excitable, seek more stimulation and are not so good at learning, remembering and conditioning.

Numerous studies have looked at the relationship between various self-report and physiological measures of arousal (see Paisey and Mangan 1980). Much work in human experimental psychology has also concerned the effects of induced rather than inherited levels of arousal on performance. An inverted U curve has been found for the relationship between arousal level and performance at a wide variety of different tasks. At very low levels of arousal the nervous system may not function properly, whereas at very high levels it may lead to intense emotions that disrupt performance. A moderate optimal level of arousal tends to produce alertness and interest in the task at hand. AF

Bibliography

Eysenck, H.J. 1967: *The biological basis of personality*. Springfield, Ill.: C. C. Thomas.

Gray, J.A. 1971: *The psychology of fear and stress*. London: Weidenfeld & Nicolson; New York: McGraw Hill.

Paisey, T. and Mangan, G. 1980: The relationship of extroversion, neuroticism, and sensation-seeking to questionnaire derived measures of the nervous system. *Pavlovian journal of biological science* 15, 123–30.

arousal *See above, and also* sleep and arousal: physiological bases

art, psychology of A field of study and research in which psychological and aesthetic theories overlap. The terrain displays the diverse nature of both art and psychology and may be divided arbitarily into four areas of investigation: *mechanisms*: e.g. vision, perception, motor skills; cognitive *processes*: e.g. imagination, apperception, creativity; *personality*: e.g. motivation, mood, preference; and *practice*: e.g. representation, symbolization, graphicacy (see below). Broadly speaking, it makes use of the results of general psychological inquiry, including specially devised experimental techniques, some cross-cultural and comparative studies, and also clinical investigations of disturbed people's art works.

Fechner (1876, see Pickford p.4) is acknowledged as the pioneer of a genuine psychology of art, which developed in the wider context of debates about the value of memory drawings, the genius/madness controversy and the nature of perception and imagination. Many artists' concerns at that time revolved around Chevereul's and Goethe's color theories, ideas about line and proportion, Helmholtz's and Charles Henry's views on the role of science in art, and symbolism.

Fechner made a distinction between philosophical aesthetics "from above" and empirical aesthetics "from below"; the former proceeds from general principles to particular instances of art, and is the responsibility of the aesthetician, the latter starts with particulars, aspiring towards general principles via experimental verification. He investigated experimentally a dozen supposed principles of visual aesthetics, such as the principle of aesthetic threshold, of aesthetic health or increase, and so on. His interest in sensation, e.g. in "just noticeable differences" between degrees of lightness and darkness, led to his assertion that the "subjective magnitude of a sensation can be measured by the logarithm of the physical magnitude of the stimulus". This theory has been rejected, (although preferences for particular colors or shapes *can* be correlated with the intensity of a stimulus); likewise his claim regarding the special aesthetic status of the "golden section" has not been supported, it is merely one of a spread of favored rectangle ratios. Nevertheless Fechner did demonstrate that an empirical exploration of aesthetic problems could yield useful information and he inspired a number of followers including Martin, Birkhoff, Valentine, Eysenck and Pickford, who have investigated the measurement of sensation and of aesthetic discrimination experimentally. They developed sophisticated psychometric approaches to aesthetic questions; these were initially norm-referenced, i.e. the individual's score was determined by reference to a matched group average. Later, personality and individual differences were also subjected to quantification. As sense receptors present information according to individual requirements and desires, factors such as attention, bias, etc. had to be considered too in trying to understand artists' and spectators' capacities and limitations. Eysenck (1957, see Pickford p.16) posits a general factor which differentiates persons according to their aesthetic sensitivity and which approximates to some form of "absolute" criterion for determining artistic ability. The Maitland–Graves Design Judgment Test (1947) had purported to differentiate between artists and non-artists on the basis of test results derived from reponses to images. Related tests measured color perception and color preferences (e.g. the Luscher Color Test 1949), or measured related mental abilities, e.g. spatial reasoning capacities, moving the psychology of art towards the general areas of "visual thinking" and perception.

The psychology of perception which is of interest to artists and aestheticians because it investigates form, space, distance, motion, color, figure/ground, ambiguity, etc., has moved on from the idea that we are "receivers" picking up information from the world "out there" via our senses, to the idea that perception is selective, involving our testing out perceptual hypotheses, which are influenced by prior knowledge, past experience, current tastes and emotional states. In the drawing act or process we necessarily perceive the subject through symbol systems (Cassirer 1979). These symbol systems determine our perceptual performance and our capacity for visual processing. Gombrich (1960) sees "development" in art as stemming from artists' continual creation of new codes according to a mechanism of "schema and correction" which is synchronous with the mechanics of perception, linking art history to the psychology of art via information theory and optics. Using the notion of "projection" to describe how we interpret images, he analyses artists' purposes: representation, substitution, and symbolization. Gibson (1979) whose "ecological theory" presents the idea that the spatial character of the visual world is defined by information contained in the "ground" in which objects exist, claims that perception is not the processing of sensory inputs, but the extraction of invariants from the stimulus flux. He rejects the idea that sensory inputs are converted into perceptions by mental operations: they are not mediated by retinal pictures, neural pictures, or mental pictures;

perceiving is not an act, it is an achievement, an experiencing of the world rather than a having of experiences. Vision is a form of intelligence and we may speak of non-verbal thinking.

Fiedler and his followers emphasized the visual character of art production, claiming that non-discursive cognition is unique to artistic behavior. Cassirer (1979) affirms the visual basis of thinking via his "expressive function", "presentational function", and "meaning function" of symbolic forms. Art has also been considered to be a presentational symbol or form expressive of human feelings, an idea whose implications for art education have been explored recently by Witkin (1974) and others, who argue that artistic expression embodies states of feeling, initially unconscious, which when projected through expressive forms, enlarge our consciousness of our own "feeling intelligence". Art forms are the result of the reciprocal effect on each other of the impulse and the medium. They exemplify the intelligence of feeling. Arnheim (1954) says that perception and thinking are often treated separately, which encourages the belief that they are different processes. Thinking is seen to be clear and distinct. The senses are confused, and untrustworthy. He argues that people solve complex problems through visual thinking, that "imagery" is not a by-product of real thinking going on elsewhere in the mind. It is not an epiphenomenon, but the nexus of action. A new term, "graphicacy", is used to define the educated counterpart of the visual–spatial aspects of intelligence and communication, i.e. those special skills required for the understanding and communication of visual–spatial relationships.

Originally, creativity was seen as one of the numerous faculties of the mind whose products when added together made up intelligence. Spearman (Pickford p.135) later postulated a "general" intelligence, and Burt (Pickford p.121) used drawings for the first time in assessing this, but neglected creativity as such, as do various later approaches, e.g. multiple factor analysis of intelligence. However, such concepts as convergent–divergent thinking, field dependent–independent personality, crystallized–fluid ability, and lateral thinking, represent the efforts of some psychologists to come to terms with creative activity. A major problem is that certain features of art, such as "composition" seem to be resistant to quantification or experimental procedures.

The Gestalt School dealt with this to some extent; whereas the Behaviorists' atomistic view of creative activity emphasizes progressive trial and error learning, the Gestaltists' holistic approach emphasizes sudden shifts in our perception of a problem, even to the extent of seeing "style" as a Gestalt issue. However, to explain both our tendency to produce aesthetic order, and the aesthetic relevance of breaks in continuity (visual accents), Gombrich distinguishing his position from that of the Gestalt School, argues that there exists a sense of order essential for the survival of any organism. The a priori expectation of order offers the best strategy for the construction and maintainance of cognitive maps of environments through subsequent adjustments and modifications. Any increase or decrease of order impinges on our awareness.

This approach to the nature of creativity in art is exemplified by Stokes (Wollheim p.315) whose Kleinian aesthetics embodies notions of the medium being the object of attack and reparation, placing trust in "spontaneous" ordering forces, confirming form as content. Some Freudians' understanding of creativity as being something "possessing" an artist stems from the nineteenth century madness/genius controversy (Becker 1978), where we can perceive a drift from humoral to pathological models of creativity, as artists freed themselves from "conventional" forms of representation. This was often misinterpreted as evidence of disturbance. While it is true that the arts utilize existing perceptual sets, constancies and prejudices, artists habitually challenge these. Unfortunately, while Freud himself was cautious in the application of his theories to art, some of his followers, e.g. Reitman and Prinzhorn, tend to fall prey to a version of the intentional fallacy in that they sometimes erect normative and diagnostic criteria for a "proper" expression of meaning in art dependent on particular pictorial conventions. They subsequently make distinctions between expression and representation in terms of subjectivity and objectivity respectively. They then read backwards from the image to the "mind" of the artist, unaware that they are building aesthetic prejudices into their analysis. The value of psychoanalytically oriented studies of the creative arts is often underestimated as a consequence, as is the value of Jungian approaches, which have influenced some twentieth-century artists and art movements, e.g. Abstract Expressionism.

A growing interest in art's potential for therapy and for promoting personal growth has focussed attention on a wide range of group work and clinically derived approaches to creativity. Social psychologists, therapists and participants are beginning to investigate the underlying psychological processes. Byrne (1982) surveys the role and function of particular aesthetic models, e.g. art as expression, art as communication, frequently used in therapy and remedial education. Related to this is a renewed interest in children's art. Freeman (1980) holds that children *know* more than they can put down on paper. Reviewing previous theories, he re-assesses Piaget and Arnheim, and analyses childrens' representations of space, their coding of relationships in abstract tasks, and their mastery of strategies of representation on the page. His work is complemented by that of Gardiner (1980) who demonstrates that children's artistic capabilities, both their perceptions and their skills, are affected by shifts in mood. Related also is the psychology of play, as a form of individual and social learning via creative action; not only for children and adolescents who are going through phases of maximum responsiveness to social conditioning, but for adults too, who can use art and play as a way of rehearsing new attitudes and feelings. Additionally, fresh materials and ideas have been transposed into the terrain of the psychology of art through cultural and social anthropology (e.g. Billig/Barton-Bradley 1978) and through the overlapping concerns of psychology and semiology. PBY

Bibliography

Arnheim, R. 1954: *Art and visual perception*. London: Faber & Faber.

Becker, G. 1978: *The mad genius controversy*. London: Sage Publications.

*Billig/Barton-Bradley 1978: *The painted message*. Cambridge, Mass.: Scheukman Pub. Co.

Byrne, P. 1982: Inscape. *Journal of the British Association of Art Therapists* (Spring).

Cassirer, E. 1979: *Symbol myth and culture*. New Haven and London: Yale University Press.

Freeman, N. 1980: *Strategies of representation in young children*. New York and London: Academic Press.

Gardiner, H. 1980: *Artful scribbles: the significance of children's drawing*. London: Jill Norman.

Gibson, J.J. 1979: *An ecological approach to visual perception*. Boston: Houghton Mifflin.

Gombrich, E. 1960: *Art and illusion*. London: Phaidon ; New York: Pantheon.

*Pickford, R.W. 1972: *Psychology and visual aesthetics*. London: Hutchinson Educational.

Witkin, R.W. 1974: *The intelligence of feeling*. London: Heinemann Educational.

*Wollheim, R. 1973: *On art and the mind: Essays and lectures*. London: Allen Lane; Cambridge, Mass.: Harvard University Press (1974).

art *See above, and also* emotion and aesthetics

artificial intelligence (AI) the science of making machines do things that are generally done by minds. These include some examples usually assumed to require intelligence of a high degree: playing chess, solving logical and mathematical problems, planning and executing complex series of actions, writing detective stories, performing chemical analyses of unknown substances. Other mental capacities are less commonly thought of as needing intelligence partly because all normal human adults possess them, partly because their exercise does not normally require (or even admit of) conscious control or introspection. Prime examples of these are vision and speech. Another is "common sense" which is often actually contrasted with intelligence, that is with the sort of intelligence that is mere cleverness. Since a great deal of AI research attempts to provide machines with everyday visual or linguistic abilities and common sense reasoning powers (rather than with formal logic or technical knowledge) the definition sometimes given of AI as 'the science of making machines do things which would require intelligence if done by people' (Minsky 1968) may be misleading.

The machines used in AI are computers, usually digital, and the emphasis is on software (program) rather than on hardware (engineering) solutions. So a program that could attempt to decide whether a poem was written in the seventeenth or the nineteenth century by considering its vocabulary or other internal evidence would be more interesting in AI terms than a hardware module sensitive only to the chemicals in seventeenth-century ink. The focus of interest in AI is the information-handling, or symbol-manipulating, power of the system rather than its physical embodiment. What information does the system have, or look for, or infer for itself; how does it represent that information; how does it pass from one item of information to another; how does it make hypotheses; or test them; or compare alternative hypotheses; or decide to reject one because it accepts another; what knowledge does the system have and how does it use that knowledge; how does it know what knowledge it needs at a given time and how does it find it; what sorts of things can it represent (and thus have information about); and how, if at all, can it realize that it does not have the information required to complete its task? Questions like these rather than electronics are what concern workers in AI and a given program can be run on many different machines. So if an AI program is to be compared with a human equivalent, this should be the psychological functioning of the mind (and with psysiological mechanisms only in so far as they can be given psychological interpretations) rather than with the biochemistry of the brain.

Not all AI workers try to make their machines do things in the way that the human mind does them, especially if the machine is simply being asked to perform a technical task such as translating. The psychologist and the layman, however, will be interested in comparing AI programs with human psychology. Even in "technological" examples such as translation it often happens that a specific way of representing or transforming information is included in the program because the programmer has a hunch that people may rely on a similar method. And many AI programs are specifically intended as simulations, or models, of human psychology, so that at some (though not all) levels their functioning is thought to be significantly similar to human thinking. A chess or language program, for instance, may make decisions in the light of criteria comparable to those used (whether consciously or not) by people. And a vision-program may be deliberately modelled on psychophysiological knowledge about the human visual system (Marr 1976).

In principle such hypotheses can be empirically tested, and the points at which the program fails to function as people do can be used to provide pointers to further hypotheses which may be a better approximation to the human mind. Since the program has to be written in a programming language whose instructions can be followed by the machine, the information-processing has to be presented in a clear and explicit form. But much is nevertheless implicit in the program: the programmer usually does not realize all its implications and can meet with some surprises when running it on a computer. In a sense, then, running a programmed theory functions as a test of the theory itself, not of its truth (its closeness to human psychology) but of its internal coherence and inferential potential.

It is largely owing to work in AI that psychologists have come to realize the formerly unsuspected computational complexity of everyday mental abilities. The amount of knowledge and inferential power involved in the perception and understanding of speech, for example, is very great. As yet no AI program for speech-understanding can cope reliably with anything but a very limited range of vocabulary, syntax, and topic (airline reservations or chess moves). But even current programs use a variety of sorts of knowledge (phonetic, morphemic, lexical, syntactic, semantic) in computationally complex ways so as to interpret the speech-input (Woods 1976; CMU Speech Group 1977).

A recurring problem is how the program (or the psychological theory) can take account of the effects of context. Even individual sound segments such as a [p] differ in auditory characteristics according to their auditory context, and words and phrases vary in meaning depending on the conversational context. Context-sensitivity is a general feature of intelligent interpretation, and AI programs tend increasingly to be provided with large amounts of domain-specific knowledge for use in guiding information processing sensibly. For example a program unable to decide whether it has heard "move the king to KB4" or "move the queen to KB4" will ask itself such questions as whether both possibilities describe a legal move at the current state of play, and if so whether one of them is more likely than the other to benefit the opponent according to the criteria of good chess play recognized by the program. Depending on the answers it may be able to classify one alternative as more reasonable and choose accordingly. Furthermore some programs can wait for the next sentence and examine that for clues to the interpretation of the one before. But this method will not always work. If the speaker had actually advised an illegal or a self-destructive move, or had realized by way of criteria not represented in the program the advantage of an apparently suicidal move, then the program would be mistaken in rejecting that alternative. But, significantly, a human chess player might behave in the same way. In general the use of knowledge-based heuristics ("rules of thumb") that may help in generating solution-candidates or in recognizing a solution but cannot be guaranteed to do so characterizes information-processing that is intelligent but not infallible. Examples such as the king/queen to KB4 disprove the popular notion that a computer program has to rely solely on rigorous deductive reasoning without any possibility of error and so cannot be a close parallel to informal human thinking. However it is true that AI workers have so far had more success in simulating formal than informal thinking. Not only is it very difficult to recognize the domain-specific knowledge relevant in informal reasoning and to express it computationally so as to make it available to the machine, but the problem of using large knowledge-bases sensibly has not yet been solved. How can the program (how does a person?) realize when it needs a particular item of knowledge and retrieve it quickly? How should the knowledge-base be organized and indexed for easy retrieval of relevant items during informal common sense reasoning? The handling of large amounts of knowledge and the representation of learning are perhaps the two most pressing unsolved problems of current AI.

AI is relevant to the philosophy of mind. The relation between program and machine is analogous in important ways to that between mind and body (or between psychology and physiology). The feature of intentionality which characterizes thought, action and subjective experience in general also characterizes descriptions of what a program is doing. The program that hears an instruction to move the king to KB4 as one to move the queen to KB4 is mistaken, is reasonable and is relying on its knowledge of the rules and strategems of chess – all these terms are intentional concepts. So AI, far from being necessarily dehumanizing as is so widely feared, helps us to understand how it is possible for subjectivity to arise within a basically mechanistic world, and thus promises to integrate the previously opposed camps of "humanism" and "mechanism" within theoretical psychology and the philosophy of mind. MAB

Bibliography

*Boden, M.A. 1977: *Artificial intelligence and natural man*. Brighton: Harvester Press; New York: Basic Books.

*——— 1981: *Minds and mechanisms: Philosophical psychology and computational models*. Brighton: Harvester; Ithaca, N.Y.: Cornell University Press.

Chomsky, N. 1957: *Syntactic structures*. The Hague: Mouton.

CMU Speech Group 1977: *Speech understanding systems: summary of results of the five-year research effort* (second version). Technical Report, Computer Science Dept., Carnegie-Mellon University.

Marr, D. 1976: Early processing of visual information. *Philosophical Transactions of the Royal Society* 275 (942), 483–524.

Minsky, M.L. 1968: *Semantic information processing*. Cambridge, Mass.: MIT Press.

*Sloman, A. 1978: *The computer revolution in philosophy: philosophy, science and models of mind*. Brighton: Harvester Press; Englewood-Cliffs, N.J.: Humanities Press.

*Winston, P.M. 1977: *Artificial intelligence*. New York: Addison-Wesley.

Woods, W. et al. 1976: *Speech understanding systems, final technical progress report*, BBN Report No, 3438. Cambridge, Mass.: Bolt, Beranek & Newman.

aspiration level In a brilliant series of studies inspired by LEWIN, Dembo and Hoppe conducted some of the first experimental studies in human motivation. This early research indicated that the experience of success and failure depends more upon the person's aspirations than on some objective standard of performance. These studies also showed that the motivation for success does not lead to levels of aspiration which guarantee easy success. When translated into English (in Frank 1935 a, b), this research led to a flood of studies by American investigators, giving rise to important work on SOCIAL COMPARISON processes, self-evaluation, ideal self/actual self and ACHIEVEMENT MOTIVATION, and also to the use of self-anchoring scales to study patterns of human concern around the world. JMFJ

Bibliography

Frank, J.D. 1935a: Individual differences in certain aspects of the level of aspiration. *American journal of psychology* 47, 119–28.

Frank, J.D. 1935b: The influence of level of performance in one task on the level of aspiration in another. *Journal of experimental psychology* 18, 159–71.

assessment center A technique used in organizations for selecting individuals for promotion or special development and training, which involves multiple assessments and ratings by trained observers of various behavioral dimensions exhibited in situational and "work sample" tests. Assessment centers were first successfully conducted by the War Officer Selection Boards in Britain and the Office of Strategic Services in the United States during the second world war. The technique was then applied in industry and it is estimated that in 1980 more than 2,000 organizations used assessment centers, principally for selecting and promoting managers. Although assessment centers are costly and time consuming relative to other psychological measurements, many psychologists and personnel managers support them because of the high quality (reliability, validity, defensibility) of information generated through a center. A typical center might consume two days of observation time during which a staff of six assessors observes the behavior of twelve assessees in group exercises (such as leaderless group discussion and management games), individual exercises (such as in-baskets and fact finding interviews) and in other simulation measurement techniques including traditional paper and pencil psychological tests. (See also INTERVIEWING; PERSONNEL SELECTION) MDH

Bibliography

Moses, Joseph L. and Byham, William C., eds. 1977: *Applying the assessment center method*. New York: Pergamon.

association: animal An aspect of learning in which two stimuli, events or ideas become connected by virtue of their temporal contiguity. (See CONDITIONING.)

associationism Originally a philosophical theory, later a psychological theory, which sought to reduce the contents of the mind to a set of elementary sensations or ideas from which more complex ideas were built up by associations between them (Warren 1921). Associationist theory has always been reductive, in the sense that it sought to analyse complex ideas into their simpler components, and thus appealed to psychologists who saw their scientific task as one of showing that apparently complex mental activity was the product of simpler units and simple rules for combining those units. Both the original associationist philosophers and their psychological successors came under strong attack, from rationalist philosophers and Gestalt psychologists respectively, who disputed that the mind could be understood as a passive collection of simple ideas joined together by the inexorable operation of a few "laws of association". The slogan of Gestalt psychology, that the whole is greater than the sum of its parts, is to be understood as a reaction against associationism.

But even if one may doubt whether associationist theory can provide a complete account of the mind, in a weaker form there is scope for a theory that attempts to elucidate how we come to associate events together. There can be little doubt that we do associate one event or idea with another: are there laws of association that predict or explain how this happens? No two associationists, not even James Mill and his son, John Stuart Mill, would necessarily agree on the exact number of the laws of association. Some counted several such laws; others attempted to reduce them all to a single all-embracing law. But there has always been some measure of agreement: events or ideas, it has always been assumed, will be associated if they have frequently or consistently occurred together. This can be expressed as one law or can be analysed into at least three separate notions, temporal contiguity, spatial contiguity and constant conjunction. One idea will be associated with and hence give rise to another, if the events producing those ideas have occurred at the same time as one another, or in the same place as one another, or if they have consistently occurred together (see HUME). To these fairly generally accepted laws some theorists would add such subsidiary factors as similarity: one idea will give rise to another to the extent that they resemble one another.

In modern psychology, associationism has two areas of application, to the study of CONDITIONING, usually in non-human animals, and to the study of learning and memory in humans. Conditioning is often defined as a case of simple associative learning: in a typical conditioning experiment the experimenter arranges that certain events occur together, usually in close temporal contiguity, and the animal may be said to associate them. In PAVLOV's experiments, these events are a stimulus (the conditional stimulus, or CS) and a "reinforcing" event such as food; in instrumental conditioning, the delivery of the reinforcer is dependent on the animal's performance of a particular response, and response and reinforcer therefore always occur together.

Conditioning turns out to obey most of the traditional laws of association. It depends not only on the degree of temporal contiguity between CS or response and reinforcer, but also on the spatial contiguity. In a Pavlovian conditioning experiment, if both CS (a light) and reinforcer (a puff of air) come from overhead, or if both come from below the grid floor on which the animal is standing, conditioning proceeds more rapidly than if one comes from overhead and the other from below (Testa 1975). Constant conjunction is, presumably, only another name for consistency of reinforcement which is well known to affect the speed of conditioning. And there is some evidence that two similar events are more readily associated than two dissimilar events (Rescorla and Furrow 1977).

It is interesting to note, however, that the traditional laws of association are not sufficient to describe the circumstances that promote successful conditioning. Numerous experiments have established that conditioning occurs selectively, to good predictors of the occurrence of reinforcement (be they stimuli or response) at the expense of poor predictors. Suppose, for example, that a particular CS, a light, is sometimes followed by food and sometimes not. Although only imperfectly correlated with the delivery of food, the light will be associated with the food and will be conditioned. But if the experimenter now adds further stimuli, if on trials when the light is followed by food he adds a high-pitched tone and on trials when it is not followed by food he adds a low-pitched tone, he will find that conditioning to the light disappears (Wagner et al. 1968). The two tones now provide perfect information about the outcome of each trial, and the light, formerly the best available predictor of food, is now quite redundant. But notice that the addition of the tone has done nothing to alter the temporal or spatial contiguity between light and food, nor the degree of conjunction between them (the food still occurs only when the light has been turned on, although still not every time the light is turned on). These factors cannot therefore be sufficient to explain the strength of the association established between light and food: in conditioning experiments at least, it appears that some additional law of association is required (Mackintosh 1983).

Although one may quarrel with the details of associationist theory as applied to conditioning, few conditioning theorists have gone so far as to doubt that they are studying a form of associative, learning – although there are writers who prefer to talk of animals detecting contingencies between events or calculating overall correlations between them rather than associating events on a trial-by-trial basis (Rachlin 1977). Cognitive psychologists, studying learning, memory and thought in humans, have more frequently mounted a full-scale assault on associationist theory. In reaction against the traditional study of the rote learning of nonsense syllables initiated by Ebbinghaus (1885), they have stressed that learning and memory involve organization of the material to be learned and fitting it into a SCHEMA (Bartlett 1932). Although there have been impressive attempts to elaborate more complex, but still fundamentally associative, theories of human memory (Anderson and Bower 1973), many cognitive psychologists would argue that the attempt is misconceived. Perhaps their central objection is this: associationism holds that ideas are related in only one way, by being associated with one another, and that associations admit only of differences in strength or degree, not differences in kind. To the opponent of associationism this seems an impoverished view of the mind. We can surely distinguish a whole host of ways in which two ideas or concepts may be related: there may be a logical implication between them or a perceptual relationship; one may be included in the class of the other; they may be similar or opposites; they may just have occurred together in the past (been associated). To reduce this variety of relationships to variations along a single dimension, strength of association, seems perverse.

Once again, this is an argument against a strong form of associationism – that which seeks to reduce all mental activity to a few simple rules. It does not follow that one should dismiss a weak form of associationism – that which only asserts that events or ideas come to be associated and seeks to describe the laws that govern such associations. Modern theories of conditioning suggest that these laws are more interesting and complex than traditional associationist theories have assumed. There is little reason to doubt that they apply to humans as well as to other animals.

NJM

Bibliography

*Anderson, J.R. and Bower, G.H. 1973: *Human associative memory*. Washington: Winston.

Bartlett, F.C. 1932: *Remembering: a study in experimental and social psychology*. Cambridge: Cambridge University Press.

Ebbinghaus, H. 1885: *Über das Gedächtnis*. Leipzig. (English translation: *Memory*. New York: Dover (1964)).

*Mackintosh, N.J. 1983: *Conditioning and associative learning*. Oxford and New York: Oxford University Press.

Rachlin, H. 1977: *Behavior and learning*. San Francisco: Freeman.

Rescorla, R.A. and Furrow, D.R. 1977: Stimulus similarity as a determinant of Pavlovian conditioning. *Journal of experimental psychology, animal behavior processes* 3, 203–15.

Testa, T.J. 1975: Effects of similarity of location and temporal intensity pattern of conditioned and unconditioned stimuli on the acquisition of conditioned suppression in rats. *Journal of experimental psychology, animal behavior processes* 1, 114–21.

Wagner, A.R. *et al*. 1968: Stimulus selection in animal discrimination learning. *Journal of experimental psychology* 76, 171–80.

*Warren, H.C. 1921: *A history of the association psychology*. New York: Scribner.

associations and journals Most countries have their own learned psychological societies or associations. These societies establish standards in the training of psychologists, they monitor the practices of applied psychologists and facilitate communication within the psychological community through the publication of journals and the organization of conferences or other scientific meetings.

In March 1982, forty-five of these societies formed the International Union of Psychological Societies. Membership included the societies of countries in the Western and Eastern bloc, ones from South America, Asia, the Far East, China and Australasia.

The American Psychological Association (APA) was founded in 1892 and incorporated in 1925. It is the major psychological organization in the United States. With more than 52,000 members in 1982, it includes most of the qualified psychologists in the country. The chief governing body of the APA is the Council of Representatives, made up of members from each of the Association's forty Divisions and from affiliated State Psychological Associations. The Board of Directors, composed of the six officers of the Association and six members elected from the Council, is the administrative body and exercises general supervision over the affairs of the Association. There are three classes of membership of the APA: associate, member and fellow. It is also possible to become an affiliate member (e.g. foreign affiliates and student affiliates). The APA publishes twenty-four periodicals and a variety of books, brochures and pamphlets. The *APA Monitor* and the *American Psychologist* are sent free to members. The APA organizes an Annual Convention normally attended by more than 10,000 people. It also runs the *American Psychological Foundation* which was established in 1953 to receive gifts from psychologists who wish to contribute to the advance of psychology. This foundation thus sponsors work in psychology.

Most other societies are modelled to a greater or lesser degree upon the APA. The British Psychological Society was founded in 1901 and by 1982 had a membership of about 9,000. Membership is open to anyone who possesses a psychology degree recognized by the BPS or anyone who passes a qualifying exam set by the society. Students and psychologists overseas may become subscribers. Members receive the *Bulletin* free and have access to other BPS publications at reduced rates.

Like most societies the APA and BPS act to accredit degrees in psychology, particularly postgraduate vocational courses. In common with other societies across the world, the BPS is now exploring the possibility of registering all psychologists. Registrations would be restricted to those with an accredited qualification in psychology and is designed to protect the practitioner and the public from abuse.

Most societies are increasingly involved in policy-making as they are approached by governments to give the psychological viewpoint on salient social problems. To this effect, many societies have established boards to examine social questions: ethnic relations, ethics of research, women's rights, etc. The accent is upon making psychology more available to the public and simultaneously more accountable to them.

Journals
Most Associations hold a full range of journals. Journals or periodicals inaccessible elsewhere can often be acquired through the national association. The BPS, for instance, keeps most journals at the University of London Joint Psychology Library.

Every journal has its own format, editorial line and house style. Details of these can normally be obtained from the cover of any copy of the publication. Most journals will consider unsolicited articles for publication. However, they are subjected to a severe vetting procedure and most journals have a high rate of rejection. Even if accepted a journal article may wait between six and twenty-four months for publication. GMB

astrology An ancient body of knowledge concerned with the study of celestial influences and their effects upon the earth and man in particular. Its origins date back to the earliest times when it was observed that cyclic patterns and unusual events in the heavens seemed to relate to distinct rhythms and unusual episodes in the affairs of groups and individuals. Over the millenia a blend of empirical observation and enlightened speculation led to a set of cosmic principles that related the macrocosmic processes with those within a human being. From this emerged many lines of study ranging from complex systems of metaphysics through the nature of the psyche and the analysis of events, to prognostication. Because of the corruption and degeneration of knowledge astrology has acquired a dubious reputation, but now it is regaining the respect that the ancients and Renaissance accorded it, before it was eclipsed by the so-called Age of Reason.

The theoretical basis of astrology is summed up by the esoteric phrase "as above so below", in which the microcosm and the macrocosm were perceived not only to mirror each other in principle, but to resonate in sympathy or antipathy. Thus tensions in the greater world would precipitate epochs of growth or destruction in mankind. This general study was called mundane astrology. At first this was the prime area of interest for the priests of the early nations. Later, with the Greeks came the investigation into the effects of the universe on the individual. With a more precise mapping of the heavens and closer observations of the movements of the planets it was possible to draw up a chart of the moment of birth called a horoscope. The Arabs took the precision a step further by introducing a time and place, or Mundane House system, which related the birth chart and its contents to the particular way the psyche described interacted with the everyday world.

Astrological schools have different views on details, but a simple scheme will suffice to illustrate a general model of the anatomy of the psyche. The twelve-fold band of the Zodiac constitutes the twelve basic solar types of humanity. Thus a person with Sun in Capricorn at birth will have at the center of his being or self those characteristics associated with that sign. The Moon, which represents the ego or ordinary level of awareness, is likewise colored according to the sign in which it is found. The relationship between these two luminaries of consciousness is crucial, as a difficult or easy angle can make life fraught or flowing. The inner planets of Mercury and Venus represent such psychobiological processes as intelligence as well as the god-like archetypes of the trickster and beautiful youth or maid, while Mars and Jupiter, in their capacity of hero and king, influence the emotional levels of the psyche in their capacity for courage or generosity. Saturn and Uranus are seen in this system as the deep intellectual processes with the former as the ponderous symbol of reason and the latter as the genius of revelation. These would be experienced as long term thought and inspiration. Neptune and Pluto are regarded as planets of higher consciousness, and therefore are only perceived as remote or mysterious factors in the undeveloped psyche. The relationships of all these planets in their various signs and their placings in the mundane houses sets out the uniqueness of each chart at the moment of birth.

Tradition says that as the soul or psyche incarnates with its first breath, so its composition, up to that point still fluidic and moving, crystallizes according to the cosmic balance of forces present at the birth. From the picture made of that moment certain trends can be ascertained. Thus, for example, a Leo Sun in the first house squared or at ninety degrees to a Scorpio Moon could give rise to a nature that demanded attention and would not always be straightforward in obtaining it. However should the restraining planet Saturn be found in the tenth house of ambition, then practical difficulties would be imposed upon this drive for aggrandizement. The analysis and synthesis of many such combinations can give a clear picture of the strengths and weaknesses of the character, as well as the tasks to be accomplished. By skilled consideration of all these factors the kind of fate to be lived can be determined. This can be detailed up to a point by examining the planetary situation of the period being considered, or by what is called progressing the chart, that is reviewing the horoscope in relation to the Sun's position on being moved on a degree for each year of life.

From the point of view of psychology astrology offers a system of structure and dynamics that has been refined over many centuries. At the moment its techniques are being adapted to the criteria of conventional psychology. Many of Jung's discoveries were already well defined in the traditional literature of astrology. Today several astrologers are qualified psychotherapists, although more conventional scientists are still examining its statistical and predictive validity.

COSMIC CLOCK
(simplified)

As with psychotherapy, astrology pursues knowledge of oneself, but here the approach is to use the horoscope as a mirror that reflects the particular balances of the psyche's anatomy. By this means the person can relate the rhythmic and progressive effects of the planets and luminaries to the cyclic and long term changes in his life, as the application of the law "as above so below" reveals the interaction of the inner and outer worlds. When the light of the psychological sun is perceived in this way with its interior solar system, then astrology is seen to be an art and not a science. WKe

Bibliographyy

Collin, R. 1980: *Theory of celestial influence*. London: Watkins.

Carter, C. 1969: *The principles of astrology*. London: Theosophical Publishing House.

Kenton, W. 1978: *Anatomy of fate*. London: Rider.

atomism RUSSELL gave the name "logical atomism" to the theory that he worked out in the second decade of this century (1917). It is a philosophical theory modeled on scientific atomism. Starting from the ideal logical language that he devised with A.N. Whitehead (1910), Russell deduced that the ultimate constituents of the world must be unanalysable or simple, and he called them "logical atoms". They were, he thought, such things as particular SENSATIONS and their colors. WITTGENSTEIN developed a more extreme version of the theory which did not rely on the identification of logical atoms with sensory input (1921).

There is an early sketch of philosophical atomism in Plato's dialogue, *Theaetetus*: SOCRATES argues that there must be some indefinable words designating simple things. The same idea underlies Leibniz's atomism and HUME's. Hume deduced his atomism from the structure of our thoughts rather than from the structure of our language.

The word "atomism" is sometimes applied more loosely by philosophers to any theory that treats truth as something divisible into separate packages, and in this use it is opposed to HOLISM. DP

Bibliography

*Pears, D.F. 1966: *Bertrand Russell and the British tradition in philosophy*. London: Collins.

Russell, Bertrand 1917: *The Philosophy of logical atomism*. Reprinted in *Logic and knowledge*, ed. R.C. Marsh. London: Allen & Unwin, 1956.

——— 1910: *Principia mathematica*, with A.N. Whitehead. Cambridge: Cambridge University Press.

Wittgenstein, L. 1921: *Tractatus logico-philosophicus*. 2nd English edn with a translation by B.F. McGuinness and D.F. Pears. London: Routledge & Kegan Paul, 1961.

attachment An affective tie between an infant and caregiver construed either as an indicator of dependence motivation or as an organizational construct within a systems theoretic view of development. Initially concerned with the psychiatric sequellae of disturbed early development Bowlby (1969) used an evolutionary perspective in recasting explanations of early infant-caregiver interaction. He proposed that smiling, clinging and vocal signaling be viewed as functionally-related proximity maintaining devices which ensured the safety of the infant and the reproductive success of the parents. Concern with safety from predation was broadened to include a view of the primary caregiver as a secure base which allowed exploration and which provided comfort in distress. The strength of an organizational approach lies in its ability to integrate a diverse set of behavior and provide a theoretical account of individual differences and developmental changes (Sroufe and Waters 1977). Bowlby's theory provoked much empirical research, particularly into the presumed privileged status of the mother. Evidence has since shown that the mother need not be the primary attachment figure and that an infant can form bonds with a number of responsive caregivers, including other children. (See also DEPRIVATION; SEPARATION.) BBL

Bibliography

Bowlby, J. 1969: *Attachment and loss*. vol. 1. *Attachment*. London: Hogarth Press; New York: Basic Books, 1969.

Sroufe, L.A. and Waters, E. 1977: Attachment as an organizational construct. *Child development* 48, 1184–99.

attention: animal An aspect of perception in which the animal exercises choice in respect of the types of stimuli that influence its behavior. It is related to the searching image phenomenon in which animals searching for food concentrate upon a particular food type while ignoring other equally palatable foods. The animal may pay attention to one food at one time and to a different food at another time.

Selective attention in animals can be studied by means of learning experiments in which the animal is required to solve problems involving stimulus classification. A rat may be required to discriminate between a large vertical rectangle and a small horizontal rectangle. The problem can be solved in terms of the size or the orientation of the stimuli. In order to discover which cues the rat actually used, unrewarded transfer tests can be given, in which the animal is presented either with two stimuli of the same size but differing in orientation, or with two stimuli of the same orientation but differing in size. The first problem could be solved only if the animal had attended to, and learned about, orientation during the original training. The second problem could be solved only if the animal had attended to the size differences between the original stimuli. DJM

attention: in infants Attention refers to the selective, goal directed properties of perception. An attentive state is characterized by alert orienting toward a source of stimulation and a readiness to receive information. Attention in infancy is sometimes described as though the baby is "captured" by the striking or immediately salient properties of the auditory or visual environment. This results in a characteristically flighty pattern of behavior, with attention caught by one object or event after another. However, although the young infant may be more distractable than the older child, even the neonate exercises selectivity in perception. Babies from birth show visual and auditory preferences for aspects of stimulation that are informative about objects and events. GEB

Bibliography

Gibson, E. and Rader, N. 1979: Attention: the perceiver as performer. In *Attention and cognitive development*, ed. G.A. Hale and M. Lewis, New York and London: Plenum.

attention: philosophical analysis Attention, the concentration of a sense or thought upon some object, was little studied until the nineteenth century, when many theories were propounded by philosopher-psychologists. They distinguished passive (reflex) and active (volitional) attention, and theories include the affective, the conative, the reinforcement and the psychical energy theories. Some account of this is to be found in Stout's *Analytic psychology* (1896). The concept of heeding or attending figures prominently in Ryle's *Concept of Mind*, where it is explained in dispositional terms. The most thorough recent study is by Alan White (1964). JOU

Bibliography

Ryle, Gilbert 1949: *The concept of mind*. London: Hutchinson; Totowa, N.J.: Barnes & Noble (1975).

Stout, G.F. 1896: *Analytic psychology*. London: Library of Philosophy.

White, Alan R. 1964: *Attention*. Oxford: Oxford University Press.

attention: psychological investigation In the early days of modern psychology attention was seen as a central property of mental life. Attention controlled what was admitted to and maintained in consciousness. Its effect was to clarify the contents of consciousness, and to convert the raw material of sensation into perception. William James, Pillsbury, Wundt and Titchener all wrote at length on the nature of attention, and Titchener in particular carried out an impressive experimental program.

Since the main thrust of the concern with attention was in relation to the quality and content of consciousness, the rise of behaviorism led to a rejection of attention as a proper topic of study, and research languished. The need to design air traffic control and similar systems during the second world war caused a renewal of interest. The controller might receive several messages simultaneously, and it was necessary to understand how he selected one from another. In the mid-1950s Broadbent summarized much of the work, and proposed a "filter theory" to describe attention. This theory has had an enormous influence over the last thirty years, and has given rise to a vast amount of research. Although the theory has been extensively modified, its main outlines are still heuristically useful.

Broadbent noted that while an observer's sense organs might receive many messages at once, only one message at a time could be dealt with consciously, considered in detail and used to generate an accurate response. He therefore suggested that the rejected messages were held for a few seconds in a short term memory store, while a filter, acting like a uniselector switch, allowed the selected message to enter the higher processing centers of the brain. On the completion or abandonment of processing the switch could select one of the stored messages or a new current input. The switching mechanism, the "filter", was the mechanism of attention, and the message to be selected was chosen on the basis both of properties of the message, and also in the light of experience about the probability, importance, and other features of the situation as perceived by the observer. Attention thus operated by blocking inputs to the higher level information processing mechanisms.

Later research has led to a number of changes in this model. While in some situations an early filter can be shown to exist, in many situations no inputs are blocked prior to the pattern analysis mechanism of the brain. Instead, the observer sets different criteria in his interpretation of the output of the brain's pattern recognition system, and these criteria act as gates to modify the contents of consciousness. Selection is therefore much later, or deeper, into the nervous system than in Broadbent's model. Furthermore, while Broadbent originally thought of selection as occurring on the physical characteristics of messages, it is now known that much more complex qualities can be used as the basis of attention. For example, attention can be paid to one language rather than another, or to semantic content.

In place of the single limited capacity processor of Broadbent's model, it is now generally accepted that there are several "dedicated processors" which can operate in parallel. There is, for example, much less interference between simultaneously received visual and auditory messages than between two simultaneous auditory messages; or between attention to color and shape than attention to two colors. Furthermore, attention can be paid to the generation of outputs and actions at the expense of inputs, and so on.

The mechanisms of attention are currently conceived as much richer and more complex than in the original filter theory, although all subsequent models can be seen to have evolved from Broadbent's work in the 1950s. It remains true however that the content of consciousness, the information about which the observer is rationally thinking and consciously making decisions, is limited to one message at a time. To this extent modern work, while more sophisticated and often using quantitative mathematical models, is in complete agreement with the work at the turn of the century. Attention makes conscious life serial and severely limited in the rate at which information can be processed.

An important exception to this rule, and a case apparently of true parallel processing, occurs with highly practised skilled behavior. As an operator practices, he becomes able to perform even complex tasks without being conscious of so doing, without attention, and without interfering with other simultaneous tasks. "Automatization" or "habit" seems to alter the nervous system so that attentional mechanisms are bypassed. For example the early stages of learning to ride a bicycle or drive a car require complete attention, but when the skills are fully developed the operator is able to conduct conversations about a variety of topics while riding or driving.

Much applied research on attention has also occurred. By recording eye movements of pilots, drivers, radar operators, etc. it has been possible to derive equations describing the distribution of attention in dynamic environments, and such work has led to improved designs of cockpits and control systems. Operator error can be reduced by using instruments and instrument layouts which match the attentional demands of the task and the attentional resources of the human.

A different aspect of attention is the VIGILANCE problem. It was found that radar and sonar operators were often unable to maintain their attention in watchkeeping tasks for more than a few minutes. The decline in attention is now known to be mainly caused by changes in criterion (as described above) rather than to changes in observer sensitivity. Such changes in criterion are due to the observer's expectations, costs and payoffs associated with making false alarms or detecting signals, and similar subjective factors.

Perhaps the most disappointing field has been in the study of the physiological basis of attention. Although at one time it was believed that the physiological basis of the filter had been found in the centrifugal nerve fibers running from the brain outwards to the receptors, this is currently believed not to be the mechanism of selective attention. Complex changes in the pattern of neural activity have been observed at various levels in the brains of animals when their attention shifts, but no deep understanding has emerged. One or two patterns of EEG signals and evoked cortical responses have been found to relate fairly reliably to the conscious processing of information and to expectancy, and the physiology of arousal is rather well understood. However, with the increasingly complex models of attention which have emerged in the 1970s hopes for discovering their physiological bases have become fainter.

Attention, after its long period in the methodological wilderness of behaviorism, has been fully reinstated as a key to understanding behavior and mental life. It has even returned as an explanatory concept in animal learning, and in concept formation in animals and humans. The early proposals have been frequently placed on a sound empirical footing and, all in all, the field of research can be seen as an outstanding modern success, with steady progress towards our understanding of a central feature of human nature. NM

Bibliography

Broadbent, D. 1958: *Perception and communication.* Oxford; Pergamon.

Kahneman, D. 1973: *Attention and effort.* Englewood Cliffs, N.J.: Prentice-Hall.

Moray, N. 1969: *Listening and attention.* London and Baltimore: Penguin.

Parasuraman, R. 1983: *Varieties of attention.* New York: Wiley.

attention structure The principle of social organization based on information flow (mainly through visual attention) among members of a group.

The ways in which individual animals or people pay attention (visual or in other modalities) to stimuli, or select them for attention from the mass of input bombarding the senses, has long been recognized as an important variable in explaining inter-individual and inter-specific differences. For example, butyric acid is the important stimulus which a tick uses in searching for a mammalian host – for a crotaline snake (pit-viper) it is the body temperature which helps detection through the remarkable sensory pit on each side of the head, between eye and nostril. Thus these two groups of animals attend to quite different stimuli, which for each of them represents 'mammal'.

Similarly, within one species attention may be paid differentially among the stimuli presented to an individual – they exhibit selective attention. Perhaps the most extreme example of this is to be found in the ORIENTING RESPONSE investigated by Sokolov and his colleagues, which takes the form in many mammals of a cessation in breathing and an increase in heart rate to a sudden low frequency or rustling sound. That the same sort of thing occurs at the social level forms the basis for theories about attention structure:– that is, that animals/humans pay greater or lesser attention to certain particular stimuli in the social environment. These stimuli are of course other members of the group. An early example of observations in this field came in Konrad Lorenz's work (1937) on jackdaws, which indicated that alarm calls are responded to differentially by the flock, only those given by dominant birds resulting in the rising of the group.

A general theory of attention paid among group members was formulated by Michael Chance (1967), who used the idea of selective visual attention paid to other (primate) group members primarily as a framework to describe status among members of the group; but he also suggested that the way in which the attention of the animals was distributed underlay all social processes occurring within the group. The patterns of attention form what Chance called an attention structure, which served as more than simply an index of social status. This extension of attention structure forms the basis of Hinde's criticism of the theory (1974).

In all analyses done to date on attention structure (e.g. Scruton and Herbert 1970, Pitcairn 1976, Hold 1976), the focal point of the research has been on measuring visual attention. So attention has come to mean visual attention, but it is clear from Chance's 1967 paper that this was not the original meaning. Primate attention, although primarily a question of visual awareness, is more precisely awareness dependent upon visual information; the latter is simply the most convenient observational measure of such information. The emphasis is upon awareness, not visual orientation. That information flow from general awareness is the basic unit of study was also evident in Chance's (1962) theory of CUT-OFF which predates attention structure theory by some five years. The basic proposition in this earlier article was that the animal regulates its own arousal level during social interaction by manipulating its visual attention and hence information input. The basic unit of information flow was also delineated by Pitcairn (1976, p.53): 'to be able to maintain a spatial relationship with others, information must be available concerning the position, movements and behavior of conspecifics. Further, certain animals ... will be of greater importance ... than others . . These statements form the logical basis of Chance's (1967) attention structure hypothesis ....'

Information flow is therefore the important central concept of attention structure. It is related to the selective attention among individuals and gives rise to the attention structure as an emergent property of the system:

ATTENTION STRUCTURE
↑
INFORMATION FLOW
↑
SELECTIVE ATTENTION

Attention structure emerges as an organizing principle (of the social structure of the group) because of the set of biases which operate on individual assessment of the relative importance of others within the group. Two of the many possible roles for the determination of this relative importance have been outlined by Pitcairn (1976). The first involves the gradations of information given by the actions of different individuals. For example it was noted that differently ranked female monkeys in a troop reacted in differing ways to the quiet (non-threatening) approach of the dominant male. Those (high-ranking) females which sat unconcernedly in that case, but moved off rapidly when the male was displaying, provided more information for onlookers about possible future events than did those who always retreated, no matter what the male was doing. The amount of attention paid to the high-ranking females is a result of their discriminant responses.

The second rule concerns the differential behavioral responses of animals themselves, which allow them to gather more or less information and hence to be able to make more or less discriminating judgments, and to modify their own future behavior. The retreating low-ranked female, for example, is not able to modify her behavior toward the dominant male because she does not receive differential information from his types of approach due to her own cut-off behavior. She is fixed in her way of behaving which lacks flexibility.

These rules of operation illustrate the ways in which a set of biases about individuals which comprise the group are ordered into a set of priorities which relate to the importance (or relevance) each individual has to the other members. The important feature then is the members' "attention-focussing quality ... based on the adaptive strategy of securing the most relevant social information on which to base their own behaviour" (Chisholm 1976, p.245). Some individuals may then act as "referents" (Pitcairn, 1976), providing the model for others' behavior, exhibiting both an attention-focussing quality and acting as a resource in the sense of Seyfarth's model (see below).

Chance also suggests that different species exhibit different types of hierarchical action. What he calls AGONIC species have a rigid hierachy in which the important lines of communication and information flow coincide with agonistic dominance. These species show inflexibility in behavior and the dominance hierarchies remain stable over considerable periods of time. In HEDONIC species, on the other hand, information flows along different lines, such as affiliation, and the group exhibits much greater flexibility as the social spacing of the individuals is not controlled by the agonistic (fight/flight) relations of agonic species. These principles seem to relate variations in group organization to the underlying principles of information flow and attention structure.

Another theory which relates social structure to the interest an individual arouses is Seyfarth's model (1977–1980) of the attractiveness of high rank. In this case, however, the model is strictly a resource model, rather than an information one. The central idea is that high-ranking individuals (in Seyfarth's work, females in a troop of vervet monkeys) win the highest proportion of disputes they enter and have relatively free access to scarce resources such as food. Other females, therefore, compete for access to these high-ranking females, in particular through grooming as this may lead to the development of close bonds with their superiors, which will in turn lead to their being tolerated at food sites and supported during disputes. This model is really the corollary of Chance's attention structure, concentrating on the functional component of close bonds, rather than the causal component of the information available to members of the group through others' actions. (See also AGONIC; CUT OFF; HEDONIC.) TKP

Bibliography

Chance, M.R.A., 1962. An interpretation of some agonist postures *Symposium of the Zoological Society of London 8*, 71–89.

Chance, M.R.A., 1967. Attention structure as the basis of primate rank orders. *Man, 2*, 503–18. (Reprinted in Chance and Larsen, 1976).

Chance, M.R.A. and Larsen, R.R., 1976. *The social structure of attention*. London and New York: Wiley.

Chisholm, J.S., 1976. On the evolution of rules. In Chance and Larsen (1976).

Hinde, R.A., 1974. *Biological bases of human social behaviour*. New York and London: McGraw Hill.

Hold, B.C.L., 1976. Attention structure and rank specific behaviour. In Chance and Larsen (1976).

Lorenz, K., 1937. The companion in the birds' world. *Auk 54*, 245–73.

Pitcairn, T.K., 1976. Attention and social structure in *Macaca fascicularis*. In Chance and Larsen (1976).

Scruton, D. and Herbert, J., 1970. The menstrual cycle and its effect on behaviour in the talapoin monkey (*Miopithecus talapoin*). *Journal of the Zoological Society, London 162*, 419–36.

Seyfarth, R.M., 1977. A model of social grooming among adult female monkeys. *Journal of theoretical biology 65*, 671–98.

Seyfarth, R.M., 1980. The distribution of grooming and related behaviours among adult female vervet monkeys. *Animal behaviour 28*, 798–13.

attitudes Generally regarded as acquired behavioral dispositions, which are introduced in the analysis of SOCIAL BEHAVIOR as hypothetical constructs to account for variations in behavior under seemingly similar circumstances. As latent states of readiness to respond in particular ways they represent residues of past experience which guide, bias or otherwise influence behavior. By definition, attitudes cannot be measured directly but have to be inferred from overt behavior.

The concept of attitude is often treated in a global and undifferentiated way; but the etymology of the word itself and a conceptual analysis of definitions suggest that an attitude is regarded either as an implicit response, by learning theorists, or as a perceptual template, by cognitive social psychologists. These two views are combined in modern expectancy-value theories of attitudes (Ajzen and Fishbein 1980). The expectancy component of an attitude refers to the perceived instrumentality of the attitude object to the person's goals or the perception that the attitude object has certain attributes. The value component refers to the evaluation of the goals or attributes related to the attitude object. An attitude is thus defined as the sum of evaluative weighted expectancies or beliefs. As such, an attitude is not a very discriminating concept. It reflects the general and prevalent notion of behavioral decision theory that human action is guided by considerations of subjectively expected utility.

Ideally attitudes should be inferred by observing behavioral responses in a wide variety of situations. In practice it is of course not feasible to follow persons around in their natural surroundings and observe all their reactions to a variety of stimuli and hence it has become more or less standard procedure in attitude measurements to consider mainly verbal (evaluative) reactions to symbolic representations of the attitude object. Other reactions, such as cognitive and perceptual distortions and physiological measures, are sometimes used but their validity appears to be relatively low due to measurement problems. Standard procedures for measuring attitudes consist of constructing scales following traditionally either a subject, stimulus or response approach.

The most common type of attitude scale is probably the subject-centered type which was introduced by Likert (see Jaspars 1978). This approach represents a direct application of test theory as developed from the measurement of general cognitive activities. The construction of a Likert scale starts with the collection of a large number of prima facie relevant statements which are administered to a sample of subjects who are asked to indicate their agreement or disagreement with each statement. Item analysis or factor analysis is then used to remove from the initial collection those statements which do not show sufficiently high correlations with either the initial total score or other items, in order to ensure a scale with high internal consistency and reliability.

A stimulus approach, which stems from the psychophysical tradition in psychology, aims first at assigning scale values to attitude statements (Jaspars 1978) and arrives at a score for a respondent by calculating the median scale value for those statements with which a subject agrees.

The response-centred approach introduced by Guttman (see Jaspars 1978) is based on the analysis of the response patterns produced by respondents. Scale values for statements and subjects are simultaneously obtained. In recent years non-metric multidimensional scaling techniques have been developed which make use of computerized iterative procedures to obtain scale values for respondents and stimuli on as many scales as are required to account for the observed response patterns (Carroll and Arabie 1980).

The main purpose of measuring attitudes is to predict behavior. Initially the predictive validity of attitudes in this sense was tested by correlating scores obtained on general attitude scales with specific overt behavior in situ. Results were quite disappointing (Wicker 1969) but Fishbein and Ajzen have recently shown that attitudes do predict behavior quite well if the attitude measured is congruent with the behavior to be predicted and is specific rather than general. The attitude to the action itself is often more predictive than the attitude to the object. It has been realized moreover that the search for positive correlations between attitudes and behavior is a misguided effort (Jaspars 1978) because one cannot test whether a latent disposition is a determinant of overt behavior by correlating what people say and do. Path analytical models using latent variables show that attitudes do have an important effect on overt behavior. The correlation between verbal attitude measures and overt behavior is also an incorrect measure of the association between attitudes and behavior because it assumes that attitudes might be sufficient causes for behavior, but it is abundantly clear from a large number of studies that social behavior in particular situations is determined by many other factors. This leads to the typical finding of a discrepancy or asymmetric relation between what people say and do. In many situations normative influences make it more difficult or costly for a person to practice what he or she preaches and hence we find that expressing a counter-normative attitude is not very predictive of actual behavior whereas showing the behavior predicts the attitude of the person very well. Conversely the absence of counter-normative attitudes is strongly predictive of normative behavior. The verbal expression of a latent attitude appears to have a lower threshold than overt behavior, as Campbell has suggested. (see Jaspars 1978). Verbal attitudes based on direct, previous experience with the attitude object should raise the threshold of verbal attitude expressions and lead to a better prediction of behavior. This is exactly what recent research has shown to be the case.

The study of attitude change has been a major area of research in social psychology during the past 40 years. The traditional approach has been to regard attitude change as a problem of information processing based on persuasive communication. Under the influence of persuasive communication studies conducted during the second world war in the American Armed Forces and the Yale School (see McGuire 1969), numerous studies have been conducted to discover the determinants of successful persuasion. The model underlying these studies assumes that attitude change depends upon the discrepancy between the attitude originally held by the receiver and the position advocated by the source of the message. The amount of change produced in the receiver is thought to be a function of the relative weights of the source and the receiver. This proportional change model can be expressed as:

$$\triangle A_r = \frac{W_s}{W_s + W_r}(A_s - A_r)$$

where $\triangle A_r$ = change in attitude of the receiver
W_s and W_r = weights assigned to the values of the attitudes expressed or held by the source and receiver
A_s and A_r = the initial attitudes expressed by source and receiver.

A great many studies have shown that the weight of the source depends to a large extent upon the attitude of the receiver to the source of communication. In general, the greater the expertness, attraction, reward or coercive power of the source over the receiver, the greater the attitude change.

The second major category of determinants studied is related to the discrepancy between the attitudes of source and receiver as perceived by the receiver. Numerous studies have investigated the effect of the message structure on attitude change, but very few robust findings have been reported. It appears that such factors as emotional appeal, fear, arousal, style of delivery, explicit drawing of conclusions, refuting of counter-arguments, repetition and order of presentation have different effects depending upon the content of the message and the nature of the receiver.

Findings are similarly inconclusive with respect to the influence of characteristics of the receiver on attitude change. There is only weak evidence of a general factor of susceptibility. McGuire (1969) has suggested that contradictory findings about the effect of message and receiver factors can be reconciled if one assumes that many of these factors have opposite effects upon comprehension of a message and yielding once the message is understood. Experimental evidence and results from field studies largely support McGuire's explanation.

A completely different tradition of research on attitude change was instigated by Festinger's theory of COGNITIVE DISSONANCE. This theory suggests that people in general will show a tendency to reduce dissonant cognitions. One would therefore expect that when individuals are forced to comply at a behavioral level, they will tend to change their attitudes in accordance with their behavior. Experimental evidence supports this prediction although it is not clear whether dissonance reduction is the cause of the observed attitude change. Moreover it is obvious from later research that the process only appears to operate under certain conditions, one of which is that the person must perceive his or her own commitment to the action as voluntary. A third strategy of attitude change is to expose the receiver directly to the attitude object. Research has shown that

MERE EXPOSURE to a stimulus may be sufficient to induce a positive evaluation of the stimulus. Recently it has been shown that such preferences can even develop without being able to discriminate between stimuli.

It has been argued that the effectiveness of these three strategies depends upon the extent to which the content of a message is related more to the source or to the receiver of the communication. In general it is assumed that a matching of strategy and context will result in more attitude change. Thus an external source may be very persuasive when the content of the message is related to his own expertise, but less so when the communication refers to values held by the receiver. Changing the views a person holds of himself or herself should be more influenced by using the person's own behavior as a source of communication. JMFJ

Bibliography

Ajzen I. and Fishbein, H. 1980: *Understanding attitudes and predicting social behavior*. Englewood Cliffs, N.J.: Prentice-Hall.

Caroll J.D. and Arabie P. 1980: Multidimensional scaling. *Annual review of psychology* 31, 607–650.

Jaspars J. 1978: The nature and measurement of attitudes: determinants of attitudes and attitude change. In *Introducing social psychology*, ed. H. Tajfel and C. Fraser. Harmondsworth: Penguin.

McGuire W.J. 1969: The nature of attitudes and attitude change. In *Handbook of social psychology* 2nd edn. vol. 3, G. Lindzey and E. Aronson. Reading, Mass.: Addison-Wesley.

Wicker A.W. 1969: Attitudes vs actions: the relationship between verbal and overt behavioral responses to attitude objects. *Journal of social issues* 25, 41–78.

attraction In its most general usage the word refers to a positive attitude felt by one person toward another. In the most well-known of the attraction paradigms, however, (i.e. that of Byrne 1971) attraction refers specifically to the liking expressed by a subject for a *stranger*, and Byrne does not concern himself with the question of whether expressed liking reflects an inner state. For Byrne the psychologists' task is to explain why a given degree of liking is expressed and the conditions which lead to its expression. A third, and confusing, use of the word attraction is to refer to the *growth* of liking during acquaintance, and Levinger's (1974) schematic, diagrammatic approach to attraction has muddied the water by failing to distinguish terms for initial attraction and the more complex forms of liking and commitment that develop as RELATIONSHIPS grow. Fourth, the term attraction has been used (Berscheid and Walster 1978) to refer to the whole area of research into personal liking, and hence to refer to a variety of different forms of relationship (e.g. friendship, courtship, marriage) without any concern being shown for the possible differences in form, intensity and expressive nature of liking in the different forms of relationships.

The most consistent use of the term, derived from the prevailing ethos of experimentally based laboratory social psychology, takes attraction to be an individual's attitudes, with consequent structural division into affective (feelings), behavioral (action) and cognitive (intentional) components. The recent growth of research into relationships has, alternatively and more usefully, stressed the diversity of behavior and of joint social action that characterize relationships and has placed much less emphasis on the internal psychological processes occurring in only one of the individuals involved.

A wide range of work into attraction has been largely concerned with experimentally derived and laboratory tested explanations of the antecedents of liking (particularly exploring the features of individuals that make them attractive to others), although other work has explored the consequences of attraction on other social behavior, such as the likelihood of obtaining a bank loan (Golightly, Huffman and Byrne 1972), and the influence of a defendant's attractiveness on jury decision making (Mitchell and Byrne 1973). The bulk of the theoretical work has been on the nature and causes of attraction. The word allowance for this entry could be taken up just by listing some of the items studied, but readers can find examples under CO-OPERATION, EQUITY THEORY, SOCIAL EXCHANGE, COMMUNICATION NON-VERBAL, and SOCIAL SKILLS. A major limitation of all such work until recently was that it had not adequately explored the realization of such attraction in the conduct of personal relationships in human everyday social behavior.

For instance, early work on physical attractiveness drew a distinction between the static physical features of a person (hair, height, facial features) and the dynamic behavioral or interactional features that made them attractive, such as kindness or generosity (Perrin 1921). However, despite an increasing sophistication in measurement techniques and a growing subtlety of focus, most research clung to the idea that individuals possessed properties that made them *invariably* attractive to other people, while it ignored the processes by which such features exerted their influence through behavior. (Nowadays, for instance, research would recognize the importance of emphasizing the attributions about a given act of kindness, see ATTRIBUTION THEORY). Before long, researchers attempted to identify the personality features that were most generally attractive. The proposition was soon made that relationship of the personalities of the two partners was at least as important as the actual properties of either individual alone (a finding explained variously by COGNITIVE CONSISTENCY and COGNITIVE BALANCE). The main effort of research went into resolving the issue of whether similarity or complementarity of personality was more attractive. Complementarity of personality needs was proposed by Winch (1958) to explain the choice of marital partners and he argued that certain types of persons (e.g. dominant ones) would seek partners who had complementary styles (i.e. submissive, in the above example). However, some research suggested that this was simply not the case, and attacks by Tharp (1963) showed the methodological and conceptual weaknesses in the complementary needs hypothesis. An idea for resolving the similarity–complementarity debate was provided by Kerckhoff and Davis (1962) who suggested that courtship partners first assessed the attractiveness of their partners on similarity of backgrounds and interests; subsequently similarity of attitudes would become salient; and then partners would use "need fit" as the criterion – a sequence of events that they referred to as "filtering". This useful idea has not been well supported in relation to courtship, for which however it was proposed, although (importantly) it is based on a fundamental reorientation to the nature of attraction: namely, one which sees the research task as explaining the *growth* of liking rather than its initial inducement (see below).

Although the work on personality was undoubtedly important in the history of attraction research, the most famous style of research in the area, begun by Byrne (1961), was into the effects of attitude similarity on attraction to strangers. Arguing that individuals had an innate need for "effectance" (i.e. to validate themselves and demonstrate their competence at dealing with the world), Byrne and Clore (1967) suggested that attitudes, being essentially hypotheses would need to be *socially* validated (see SOCIAL COMPARISON) and that people would thus treat similarity of attitudes as confirming their own, and so find these attitudes rewarding and attractive. Byrne (1971) argued that similarity of attitudes would create attraction in direct proportion to the amount of similarity and the importance of the attitude to the person. In a cleverly designed, but much criticized, paradigm known as the Bogus Stranger Paradigm, Byrne was able to present subjects with a precisely measured amount of similarity to another person (the stranger) which he did as follows: the subject completed an attitude format; Byrne collected it and gave the subject some other task to do; Byrne then rigged another attitude format to reflect the subject's format to a precise extent (10, 20 ... 80 per cent similar) and handed it back to the subject as though it had been completed by an independent stranger. The subject's ratings of the person who was thought to have completed the attitude format were then taken as the measure of liking created by the known degree of attitudinal similarity. By use of this technique Byrne (1971) presented a mountain of evidence to show that attraction was directly related to attitudinal similarity.

Critics of Byrne (e.g. Murstein 1971) noted the artificiality of the paradigm, the fact that the subject could obviously not even meet the stranger, and the fact that attitudes expressed on an attitude format may not find adequate expression in social behavior, or may not exert the power of effect in real life that they do in Byrne's paradigm. It is now clearly recognized that, despite the strengths of the paradigm, similarity of attitudes creates attraction only through processes of communication in acquaintance (Duck 1977) and that they exert their influence most effectively only at certain points of interaction or acquainting.

The early filtering idea of Kerckhoff and Davis (1962) seems to provide the best basis for a resolution of the relative roles of attitudes, personality and communication in attraction, if one extends the idea of filtering from courtship to all friendships, and from attitudes or needs to a more complex view of the processes involved. Duck (1977) extended the idea of filtering to explain growth of attraction in friendships by suggesting a multi-stage filtering sequence and by noting the importance of communication in social acquainting. Thus, individuals are thought of as communicating by a variety of means those aspects of their cognitive make-up that will assist them and their partners to create internal models of each other through which to assess their social comparison value and their provision of validational support for each other. As the relationship grows, so the relevant filters will change, although, in this new approach, the ultimate purpose of their use is the same: seeking self validation.

The history of research into attraction has a number of embarrassing mistakes that mark its track: a too narrowly experimental base; a too narrowly focussed range of concerns; a too lengthy obsession with *initial* attraction rather than growth of relationship; artificiality in its researches; a too light dismissal of the study of real life relationships; and too little concern for the validity of its laboratory findings when extended to explain naturally occurring relationships. Its value can be seen to lie in the fact that it provided a number of small but critical building blocks for the more promising area of relationship research.

SWD

Bibliography

*Berscheid, Ellen and Walster, Elaine 1978: *Interpersonal attraction* (2nd ed.). Reading, Mass.: Addison-Wesley.

Byrne, D. 1961: Interpersonal attraction and attitude similarity. *Journal of abnormal and social psychology* 62, 713–14.

*Byrne, D. 1971: *The attraction paradigm.* New York and London: Academic Press.

Byrne, D. and Clore, G.L. 1967: Effectance arousal and attraction. *Journal of personality and social psychology* Monograph 6.

*Duck, S.W. 1977: *The study of acquaintance.* Farnborough, London: Saxon House/Teakfields/Gower Press.

Golightly, C., Huffman, D.M. and Byrne, D. 1972: Liking and loathing. *Journal of applied psychology* 56, 521–23.

Kerckhoff, A.C. and Davis, K.E. 1962: Value consensus and need complementarity in mate selection. *American sociological review* 27, 295–303.

Levinger, G. 1974: A three level approach to attraction: toward an understanding of pair relatedness. In *Foundations of interpersonal attraction*, ed. T.L. Huston. New York: Academic Press.

Mitchell, H.E. and Byrne, D. 1973: The defendant's dilemma: effects of jurors' attitudes and authoritarianism on judicial decisions. *Journal of personality and social psychology* 25, 123–29.

Murstein, B.I. 1971: Critique of models of dyadic attraction. In *Theories of attraction and love*, ed. B.I. Murstein. New York: Springer.

Perrin, F.A.C. 1921: Physical attractiveness and repulsiveness. *Journal of experimental psychology* 4, 203–17.

Tharp, R.G. 1963: Psychological patterning in marriage. *Psychological bulletin* 60, 97–117.

Winch, R.F. 1958: *Mate selection: a study in complementary needs.* New York: Harper & Row.

attribution theory A theory concerned with the study of common-sense explanations of human behavior and of its direct or indirect effects. People are said to be making attributions when they explain events by attributing them to causes. The idea that common-sense psychology is a fruitful area of study for social psychology was first suggested by Heider (1958), whose discussion of the everyday analysis of action has greatly influenced more recent work on attribution theory. The notion of common-sense psychology developed by Heider is akin to ideas put forward in ETHNOMETHODOLOGY and ETHOGENICS. However, in social psychology Heider's work has given rise mainly to experimental studies, especially in the formulations of causal attribution theory suggested by Kelley (in Kelley and Michela 1980) and Jones (1979).

Heider suggested that our everyday analysis of action is in a way analogous to experimental methods. We infer from observation whether the behavior of ourselves and of others is caused by environmental or personal forces. Among the latter Heider distinguishes power and ability (i.e. whether a person can do something) from motivation (i.e. what he is trying to do and how hard he is trying). Environmental forces are seen as divided into non-social factors (e.g. the difficulty of the task), and either interpersonal social forces such as requests or commands or objective social forces such as values. Heider argues that these factors are not seen as completely independent of each other. He points out that what a person "can" do encompasses both personal ability and situational difficulty. He also stresses the fact that in common sense, the less power or ability someone has, the more he will have to exert himself, and that in general how he performs will be determined both by what he can do and by what he is motivated to do.

Which forces are seen as causal in a particular instance depends on such factors as proximity, contiguity and the perceived strength and simplicity of connections, which determine whether actor and act or act and outcome are perceived as forming cause and effect units. Heider points out that in general a personal attribution is much more likely to occur than a situational attribution because actor and act are perceived as a much stronger unit than are situation and behavior, but he also considers that personal attribution is more common because a person is seen as a first or "local" cause beyond which we do not trace the causal chain. Our tendency in everyday thought to attribute behavior too often to personal factors has more recently been confirmed experimentally and labeled the "fundamental attribution error".

In contrast to Heider, Kelley (1967, 1973) suggested that an observer arrives at a causal understanding of perceived behavior either on the basis of observed covariation of the behavior and its possible causes or, in the case of a single observation, the configuration of the plausible causes. In the first case Kelley suggests that the process of causal attribution is a common-sense replica of the method of analysis of variance as utilized in scientific psychology where persons, entities and times/occasions are the independent variables. When an effect (action or behavior) occurs in one person only, but it occurs in him or her at various times and for various entities, the covariance suggests, according to Kelley's theory, that the effect is "caused" by some property, characteristic or predisposition of the person. However, when the behavior occurs all the time in almost everyone in respect to only one entity, the entity is seen as the cause of the behavior. Experiments conducted by McArthur and others (see Kelley and Michela 1980) confirm that consistency (same reaction occurring in different situations), consensus (same reaction occurring in different persons) and distinctiveness (reaction occurring only with respect to a particular entity) do indeed affect the attribution of causality in the way predicted by Kelley, although not all factors are of equal importance.

It appears, however, that in general people are not very good at assessing covariation. Perception of covariation in the social domain is largely a function of the pre-existing theories people have, as Nisbett and Ross (1980) have recently shown. The use of information in making causal inferences depends, as Tversky and Kahnemann (1974) have argued, on its representativeness and availability. The reason why consensus information is apparently less important for ordinary people in making causal inferences is probably because such information is less available, since it is less vivid and less direct than the entity and the actor. Only in the case of the attribution of performance to personal abilities does it appear that consensus information is used appropriately.

Kelley has also argued that the analysis of variance conception of the attribution process can be used to understand the phenomenon of attributional validity. A person can, according to Kelley, know that his perceptions, judgments and evaluation of the world are true to the extent that he can confidently make an entity attribution for a perception, judgment or evaluation. Kelley suggests, moreover, that the ratio of between-entity distinctions to within-entity variance between persons can be used as a measure of an individual's level of information.

In the case of a single observation Kelley has suggested several principles or causal schemata which observers may use to arrive at causal attributions. The first principle is known as the discounting principle, and states that the role of a given cause in producing a given effect is discounted if other plausible causes are present. The second principle is called the augmentation principle and refers to the familiar idea that when there are known to be constraints, costs, sacrifices or risks involved in taking an action, the action is attributed more to the actor than it would be otherwise. The discounting principle and the augmentation principle are examples of what Kelley calls a multiple sufficient cause schema and a compensatory cause schema. In addition to these two schemata Kelley distinguishes a multiple necessary cause schema, a person attribution schema, (one-to-one) pairing, and grouping schemata. Kelley holds that the layman has a repertoire of such schemata available in trying to interpret social reality.

The third major approach to the study of common-sense explanations of human behavior is the theory of correspondent inferences of Jones and Davis (1965), who have suggested that the fewer distinctive reasons an actor has for an action and the less these reasons are widely shared in the culture, the more informative is that action about the intentions or dispositions of the actor. More specifically, Jones and Davis argue that the disposition or the intention governing an action is indicated by those of its consequences not common to the alternative actions and the fewer such non-common effects, the less ambiguous is the attribution of the intention or the disposition (the principle of non-common effect). The second factor which affects causal attribution, according to Jones and Davis, is the belief of the observer about what other actors would do in the same situations (the principle of social desirability). If few persons would have acted as the actor does, the action is seen as revealing the person's intentions and dispositions.

In the third place Jones and Davis suggest that the observer makes a personal attribution if the action affects the person's personal welfare in a positive sense (the principle of hedonic relevance). Research based on correspondent inference theory has by and large confirmed that these factors do indeed affect causal attribution to persons.

The three approaches to attribution theory have given rise to a great deal of research during the last fifteen years. Apart from the research already mentioned, motivational aspects of attribution processes, especially the defensive nature of certain attributions, have been investigated. The most popular area of research has been, however, the study of differences in attributions made by actors and observers of the same behavior. The general finding here is that we are inclined to explain our own behavior in terms of situational factors, whereas the behavior of other people is more often explained in terms of their intentions and dispositions.

The consequences of differences in causal attributions have not been studied as often as the conditions which lead to these differences (Fincham and Jaspars 1981). Moreover, common-sense explanations have hardly been studied in social psychology as part of the natural social context in which they are called for. Interest in both problems appears to be growing, which, it is hoped, will lead to a theory of common-sense explanation which takes social factors into account. JMFJ

Bibliography

Fincham, F. and Jaspars, J. 1981: Attributions of responsibility. In *Advances in experimental social psychology* vol. 13, ed. L. Berkowitz. New York and London: Academic Press.

Heider, F. 1944: Social perception and phenomenal causality. *Psychological review* 51, 358–74.

——1958: *The psychology of interpersonal relations*. New York: John Wiley; London: Chapman and Hall.

Jones, E.E. 1979: The rocky road from acts to dispositions. *American psychologist* 34,107–17.

Jones, E.E. and Davis, K.E. 1965: From acts to dispositions: the attribution process in future perception. In *Advances in experimental social psychology* vol. 2, ed. L. Berkowitz. New York and London: Academic Press.

Kelley, H.H. 1967: Attribution theory in social psychology. In *Nebraska symposium on motivation*, ed. D. Levine. Lincoln: University of Nebraska Press.

——1973: The process of causal attribution. *American psychologist* 28, 107–28.

——and Michela, J.L. 1980: Attribution theory and research. *Annual review of psychology* 81.

Nisbett, R. and Ross, L. 1980: *Human inference: strategies and shortcomings of social judgement*. Englewood Cliffs, N.J. and London: Prentice-Hall.

Tversky, A. and Kahnemann, D. 1974: Judgement under uncertainty; heuristics and biases. *Science*, 185, 1124–31.

auditory nervous system The neural structures which participate in the conversion of physical sound waves into the sensations and perceptions of hearing. Sound waves interact with the external ear, ear canal, eardrum and three ossicles malleus, incus and stapes to produce a travelling wave along the basilar membrane in the cochlea (BRAIN AND CENTRAL NERVOUS SYSTEM: ILLUSTRATIONS, figs 26 and 27). Movement of the auditory receptors (hair cells) which rest on the basilar membrane causes sensory transduction initiating the chain of neural events that results in hearing. The auditory perception of pitch largely results from the frequency of the sound stimulus. Different frequencies in the sound stimulus cause different portions of the basilar membrane to move maximally: high frequencies stimulate the basilar membrane in the base of the cochlea; low frequencies, the basilar membrane in the apex of the cochlea. The orderly representation of stimulus frequencies as response maxima along the basilar membrane is a spatial mapping or tonotopic organization that is maintained in central auditory pathways.

The hair cells of the cochlea are innervated by NEURONS that form the spiral ganglion and give rise to the auditory branch of the eighth nerve. Fibers from the spiral ganglion terminate in the cochlear nucleus on the lateral surface of the BRAINSTEM. The interconnections of higher auditory centers are exceedingly complex. Auditory structures in the medulla include the nuclei of the superior olivary complex. At the level of the pons, ascending auditory fibers form a fiber tract (lateral lemniscus) to the nuclei of the lateral lemniscus and the inferior colliculus. The medial geniculate body is the auditory center in the THALAMUS. The primary auditory cortex lies in the superior temporal gyrus (Heschle's gyrus) (fig. 3). Other cortices involved in hearing and speech include Wernicke's area which is important for speech comprehension, the angular gyrus which receives both auditory and visual inputs, and Broca's area which controls the motor speech centers. Although there is bilateral representation of the cochlear map in primary auditory cortex, secondary auditory cortex (Wernicke's area) is often enlarged on the left side of the human brain, suggesting lateralization of language function to the left hemisphere of the CEREBRAL CORTEX.

Many parts of the auditory system are innervated by descending fibers from higher centers, including fibers from the auditory cortex to the medial geniculate, fibers from the inferior colliculus to the cochlear nucleus, and fibers in the olivocochlear bundle from the superior olivary complex to the cochlear hair cells and the afferent neurons of the spiral ganglion that innervate them. The function of these feedback connections is not well understood. Possible functions include the selective direction of attention to a particular sound. SCC

Bibliography

Brugge, J.F. and Geisler, C.D. 1978: Auditory mechanisms of the lower brainstem. *Annual review of neuroscience* 1, 363–94.

Dallos, P. 1973: *The auditory periphery. biophysics and physiology*. New York and London: Academic Press.

Evans, E.F. 1974: Neural processes for detection of acoustic patterns and for sound localization. In *The neurosciences, third study program*, ed. F.O. Schmitt and F.G. Worden. Cambridge, Mass. and London: MIT Press.

Geschwind, N. and Levitsky, W. 1968: Human brain: Left–right asymmetries in temporal speech region. *Science* 161, 186–87.

Keidel, W.D. and Neff, W.D., eds. 1974: *Handbook of sensory physiology*, Vol. V/1, *Auditory system, anatomy physiology (Ear)*. Berlin and New York: Springer-Verlag.

Keidel, W.D. and Neff, W.D., eds. 1975: *Handbook of sensory physiology*, Vol. V/2. *Auditory system physiology (CNS), behavioral studies, psychoacoustics*. Berlin and New York: Springer-Verlag.

von Békésy, G. 1960: *Experiments in hearing*. London and New York: McGraw-Hill.

Augustine, St. Augustine of Hippo, philosopher and theologian, 354 – 430 B.C., has been described as having had "a greater influence upon the history of dogma and upon religious thought and sentiment in Western Christendom than any other writer outside the canon of Scripture". (Knowles). His writings upon the nature of God and upon the city of God were of immense historical importance but cannot be considered here.

Augustine is well known to us as a man, primarily from his own autobiographical *Confessions*. This book describes his early sexual improprieties, his separation from Christianity (his mother was a Christian), and his return from a Manichaean belief to true faith partly through the influence of St. Ambrose and partly that of various Platonic or neo-Platonic writings. Throughout his writings there is an influence of Platonic epistemology which denies that the objects of sense are knowable. Nevertheless he approaches these problems in an interesting way. Arguing against scepticism *Contra academicos* he asserts that one can say, "I know that this seems white to me", (whether or not I know that it is white). Elsewhere he goes so far as to say that although we are sometimes misled by our senses, that is no reason to mistrust them completely. Nevertheless he places certainty in a formula not unlike Descartes': "Do you know that you exist? I know .... Do you know that you think? I know". (*Soliloquia*). In other words one can be certain of one's own thought processes, so one can know that one doubts, and hence know something which is certainly true. (*De Trinitate*). This knowledge of our own thoughts puts us in touch with ideas which are not evanescent like the objects of sense. The status of these ideas is not entirely clear, but it seems that we must grasp them as standards (*regulae*) if we are to make judgments. They cannot however be grasped by the unaided intellect, which requires divine illumination. The exact nature of this is again unclear, but the doctrine seems most readily understood in Platonic terms. In the *Republic* it is the Form of the Good which helps those who escape the cave of mere sense impressions to see reality. This Form is compared to the sun, which gives light to the mind.

The concept of divine illumination is related to the concept of grace. This makes us want to know truth, and it is also necessary if we are "to live justly". The choice a man makes to do good is not enough to enable him to do so. This doctrine has its disturbing side in its implication that one cannot merit salvation but must be one of those chosen, apparently in an arbitrary way. As such it was a doctrine notoriously embraced by Calvin and others in the Reformation. Just as his theory of knowledge is referred back to certainty about one's self, the doctrine of grace may also be referred back to Augustine's perceptions of his own experience. For in book VIII of *The confessions* he recounts how, for himself, "to will was not in itself to be able". Later he describes his conversion, after much indecision, by what might appear a chance event. He was sitting in the garden greatly distressed, when he heard a child's voice which repeated, "Take up and read", which he interpreted as a command from God. He opened the new testament at random, and found words of St Paul's, and "by a light . . . of serenity infused into my heart, all the darkness of doubt vanished away".

It is this reversion to his own case or to the self (although even the *Confessions* were written to glorify God rather than as autobiography) which makes Augustine peculiarly fascinating and poignant. He addressed God with the words, "*Noverim me, noverim Te*: if I know myself, I shall know You". He explained the nature of time in terms of human memory and expectation (*Confessions* XI). The preoccupation with the self and its relation to God was what made him so interesting to many people in the Reformation. His *Confessions* became a model for many, especially religious, autobiographers (St. Teresa and Petrarch as well as Calvinists like Richard Norwood). So apart from his importance in the history of medieval thought Augustine may also be significant for psychology because of his influence on writers who belong to the wave of self-exploration which was one of the first major modern developments in the (quasi) empirical study of the mind. RL

Bibliography

Augustine: *The confessions* (trans. E.B. Pusey). London: Dent.

Copleston, F. 1959: *A history of philosophy* (vol II). London: Burns, Oates & Washbourne.

Knowles, David, 1970: *The evolution of medieval thought* (4th impression). London: Longman.

aura An "atmosphere" or "energy" that supposedly exists around a person's body. Some people claim that they perceive this aura, frequently as a distinct band or bands of colored light. The halos in portraits of saints are a conventionalized artistic representation of auras. The shape and color of the aura is supposed to indicate the physical and psychological state of its possessor. There is a sharply bounded layer of warmer air around people's bodies which can be detected with special photographic techniques, but this is probably not the "psychic" aura people claim to perceive. Although auras have been described in almost all human cultures, making them an archetypal human experience, very little scientific research has been carried out to determine whether they are more than illusions or hallucinations (see Tart 1972). CTT

Bibliography

Tart, C. 1972: Concerning the scientific study of the human aura. *Journal of the society for psychical research* 46, 1–21.

aura *See above, and* epilepsy

Austin, J.L. (1911–60). The originator and the most influential of the school of "linguistic philosophers", centered on Oxford where he was White's Professor of Moral Philosophy. His best known works are:

Sense and sensibilia in which he attacks the SENSE DATUM theory of perception, particularly by endeavoring to show that it involves systematic misuse of such terms as "illusion", "delusion", "real", "looks", "seems" and "appears". All these terms are minutely examined.

How to do things with words in which he examines the use of language to perform actions which would not naturally be regarded as simple communication. He first develops the theory of performative utterances "I promise ...", "I appoint ...", "I name ...", which he then finds inadequate and replaces by a theory of speech-acts, within which are particularly distinguished locutionary, illocutionary and perlocutionary acts as abstractable elements in the total speech act.

Both these books are posthumous and based on lecture notes. Austin himself published only the text of lectures, among which "Other minds", "A plea for excuses" and "Ifs and cans" were particularly influential. He also advocated and practised a method of work which involved groups of philosophers jointly examining the usage of a group of related terms. JOU

Bibliography

Austin, J.L. 1961: *Philosophical papers.* Oxford and New York: Oxford University Press.

——— 1962: *Sense and sensibilia,* reconstructed by G.J. Warnock. Oxford and New York: Oxford University Press.

——— 1962: *How to do things with words,* ed. J.O. Urmson and Marina Sbisa. Oxford and New York: Oxford University Press.

*Fann, K.T., ed. 1969: *Symposium on J.L. Austin,* London: Routledge & Kegan Paul; New York: Humanities.

authoritarian personality A term introduced in (social) psychology as the title of a famous study of the psychological origins of anti-semitism. Heavily influenced by psychoanalytic theory, the authors of *The authoritarian personality* suggest that anti-semitism is a specific instance of a more general ethnocentric attitude which is held by individuals who have, as a result of an authoritarian upbringing, failed to internalize their superego and who exhibit a strong id and weak ego. The ambivalent attitude towards authority leads them, according to the theory, to express their hostile feelings towards members of outgroups. The authoritarian personality is supposed to be characterized by respect for convention, submission to authority, lack of introspection, superstition, stereotypical beliefs, admiration for power and toughness, destructive and cynical tendencies, projection and an exaggerated concern with sexual mores. The F (fascism) scale, which was constructed to measure the authoritarian personality and which contains questions about all of these aspects, appears to be multi-dimensional, indicating that not all aspects are related in the way the theory suggests. The F scale has in general, however, a high predictive validity which suggests that it taps some important aspects of human personality. JMFJ

Bibliography

Adorno, T.W., Frenkel-Brunswik, E., Levinson, D.J. and Sanford, R.N. 1950: *The authoritarian personality.* New York: Harper.

autism Infantile autism is a rare condition, affecting about two children per 10,000, and was first described by Kanner in 1943. The main features are: a failure to develop social relationships; specific abnormalities of language; an insistence on 'sameness'; and onset before thirty months of age. Three quarters of autistic children also have mental retardation. Stereotyped repetitive movements (e.g. finger flicking), overactivity and epilepsy are common. Although it is classified with the childhood psychoses, it bears little resemblance to adult psychoses such as schizophrenia. Autistic children come from predominantly middle-class families, and this observation was thought at one time to have causal significance. However, the true nature of the condition remains obscure, and the current view is that autism is a non-specific syndrome of biological impairment. Treatment is aimed at helping social and linguistic development, often using BEHAVIOR THERAPY. Involvement of the family in treatment is important and special schooling is usually necessary. Prognosis is closely linked to the degree of mental retardation present, and the severity of language impairment. GCF

Bibliography

Rutter, M. and Schopler, E. 1978: *Autism – a reappraisal of concepts and treatment.* New York: Plenum.

autogenic training A therapeutic system developed from the original work of Oskar Vogt by Johannes Schultz. It is similar to self-hypnosis, but is taught in graded steps: subsequent steps are not practiced until earlier steps are mastered. In a comfortable posture, in graded steps, patients learn to feel heaviness and warmth in their arms and legs, to experience the autonomy of their breathing process ("it breathes me") and feelings of peacefulness, to calm and regularize their heart beat, and to experience warmth in their solar plexus area along with coolness of their forehead. The process produces a highly relaxed state which is useful as an adjunct to many other kinds of therapy, as well as combatting stress *per se*. More advanced forms of autogenic training involve specific therapeutic suggestions. The standard reference book is by Schultz and Luthe (1959). CTT

Bibliography

Schultz, J. and Luthe, W. 1959: *Autogenic training: a psychophysiological approach in psychotherapy.* New York: Grune & Stratton.

autonomic nervous system The portion of the peripheral nervous system that inervates viseral organs, glands, and blood vessels in the control of basic vegetative functions (BRAIN AND CENTRAL NERVOUS SYSTEM: ILLUSTRATIONS, fig. 11). The autonomic nervous system, whose cell bodies are arranged in ganglia outside the SPINAL CORD, consist of sympathetic and parasympathetic divisions. The sympathetic division receives preganglionic fibers from motor cells in the thoracic and lumbar sections of the spinal cord, while the parasympathetic division originates in the cranial and sacral sections. The sympathetic division is responsible for mobilizing bodily resources and organizing physical activity appropriate to exciting or emergency conditions. Thus, sympathetic activation leads, for example, to increases in cardiac activity, blood flow to skeletal muscles, respiration rate, oxygen intake, and sweat gland activity to cool the body during exertion. On the other hand, digestive processes and activities associated with a relaxed state are inhibited. In contrast, the parasympathetic division acts to conserve bodily resources and maintain a state of relative quiescence. Thus the effects of parasympathetic activation are opposite to those of sympathetic activation. In general, the two systems may be regarded as working in a correlated but antagonistic fashion to maintain an internal equilibrium.

Autonomic activity is controlled by a part of the brain called the HYPOTHALAMUS. It is closely associated with the action of various hormones, particularly the epinephrines. Autonomic activity is important in situations involving aggression and fear and is involved in all aspects of emotion. DJM/GWi

autonomic system *See above, and* emotion and the autonomic system

autonomy Independence: ability to act according to one's own priorities or principles without being overwhelmed by external constraints or internal pressures such as unwanted but uncontrollable desires. Kant's classic definition of enlightenment also defines intellectual autonomy. Enlightenment is "man's emergence from his self-incurred immaturity. Immaturity is the inability to use one's understanding without the guidance of another person." Some modern critical theorists, however, have argued that the Enlightenment principles of freedom and reason have come to be realized in a limited form which actually *restricts* human freedom and the possibility of a rational society. In modern society reason is confined to the cataloguing of empirical facts, autonomy takes the form of individuals repressing their own reasonable aspirations for a better life, and, as Marcuse put it (1964 p.23), "Free election of masters and slaves does not abolish the masters or the slaves". WO

Bibliography

Marcuse, Herbert 1936 (*1972*): A study in authority. In *Studies in critical philosophy*. London: New Left Books.

——— 1964: *One dimensional man*. Boston; Beacon; London: Routledge & Kegan Paul.

aversion therapy A procedure based on classical conditioning that attempts to reduce the attractiveness of a particular stimulus by pairing it with an unpleasant event, for example, an alcoholic patient may receive a severe electric shock as soon as alcohol touches his lips. Aversion therapy found its main use in the treatment of alcoholism and various sexual "perversions", including homosexuality. Changed social attitudes toward homosexuality and the rise in the use of self-control procedures (see BEHAVIOR THERAPY) have made most uses of aversion therapy obsolete and it is now regarded primarily as of historical significance as an early and systematic attempt to apply a paradigm for experimental psychology to the treatment of maladaptive behavior. DWJ

avoidance If a particular action or response causes the cancellation or postponement of an event that would otherwise have occurred, the action may be said to be an avoidance response. Successful avoidance of unpleasant or harmful consequences has obvious adaptive value, but has long seemed to pose a serious problem for theories of learning. A successful avoidance response is one which is followed by the absence of an aversive event; but, it was asked, how can the absence of an event, that is to say no event, be responsible for reinforcing conditioning? One solution is to point out that there is an important difference between no event occurring and no event occurring at a time when one was expected to occur (see EXPECTANCY). Another, adopted by TWO-FACTOR THEORIES, is to assume that avoidance responses are reinforced because they reduce a state of FEAR classically conditioned to stimuli signaling the occurrence of the aversive event. A third, adopted by some radical behaviorists, is to describe the operations that appear to be required to reinforce avoidance responding and to eschew speculation about the inner processes of learning responsible. NJM

avowal Typically, use of first person, present tense, declarative sentences to indicate a psychological state of the speaker so that the avowal appears more or less infallible and ungrounded, though the equivalent third person sentence is not at all infallible or ungrounded. Examples might range from "I have toothache" to "I feel the kingdom of heaven within me". Wittgenstein stressed the importance of understanding avowals to a rebuttal of solipsism and mentalism. Recent cognitive psychology may indicate that avowals are much more fallible than has been supposed. JFL

Bibliography

Nisbett, R. and Wilson, T. 1977: Telling more than we can know: Verbal reports on mental processes. *Psychological review* 84, 231–59.

B

baby talk (Also termed motherese, or caretaker language), baby talk refers to that special, often stereotyped, reduced register of a language which is regarded as appropriate for talking to young children, lovers and sometimes the elderly. Conventionalized and conscious baby talk mainly comprises lexical items as *dindins* "food", *choochoo* "train", *geegee* "horse" or diminutive affixes, as in *girlie, housie, birdie* etc. It has to be distinguished from unconscious grammatical operation found with caretakers such as the use of a higher pitched voice, changes in the statistical distribution of questions, commands and statements, reduction of grammatical complexity and increased use of repetition.

Under the impact of Chomsky's mentalist view of FIRST LANGUAGE ACQUISITION baby talk was widely disregarded by psycholinguists during the 1960s and early 1970s. More recently the importance of input in the study of language acquisition has been demonstrated by a number of researchers (e.g. Snow and Ferguson 1977). PM

Bibliography

Snow, C.E., and Ferguson, C.A. 1977: *Talking to children: Language and acquisition.* Cambridge and New York: Cambridge University Press.

Bailey, Charles-James N. Born in 1926, Professor of General and English Linguistics at the Technical University Berlin (West), is the founder of the lectologist type of linguistic *variation theory*. His basic ideas were made available to a wider audience in *Variation and Linguistic Theory* (1973). The principles underlying Bailey's approach to linguistics include these features:

(1) variation is systematic and part of a speaker's *competence*.
(2) language mixing and creolization are common processes.
(3) a wave model accounts for the patterns of linguistic variation.
(4) understanding and production are not symmetrical.
(5) instead of positivist *behaviorist* accounts of language and mentalist transformation models (cf. *Chomsky*), Bailey proposes a conceptualist approach which combines the description of concrete surface variation with that of abstract relations among data variants.

Bailey's ideas have led to considerable progress in the description of linguistic continua, pidgins and creoles and, more recently, *interlanguage* systems. PM

Bibliography

Bailey, Charles-James N. 1973: *Variation and linguistic theory*, Center for Applied Linguistics, Arlington, Virginia.

Bailey, Charles-James N. 1981: Theory, description and differences among linguists. *Language and communication* 1, 39–66.

basal ganglia A group of forebrain subcortical nuclei located deep within the cerebral hemispheres. Although grouped in various ways the major structures include the caudate nucleus and putamen (collectively called striatum), globus pallidus, and claustrum. The amygdala, subthalamic nucleus, and substantia nigra are also sometimes included. The basal ganglia maintain vast connections with structures throughout the brain and particularly with the cortex and THALAMUS. It is a major integrative center for the EXTRAPYRAMIDAL MOTOR SYSTEM and as such plays an important role in the regulation of voluntary motor activity. Striatal influence in this regard appears to be primarily inhibitory since restrictive damage to this region induces, in animals, persistent circling movements and a hyperactive condition known as obstinate progression. In humans, a variety of motor disorders follow basal ganglia damage. Degenerative changes in the globus pallidus and substantia nigra are associated with Parkinson's Disease, a condition characterized by rigidity, tremor, and difficulty in initiating voluntary movements. Damage to the putamen results in athetosis in which the patient assumes abnormal postures, displaying slow and repetitive movements. Huntington's Chorea, a hereditary disease characterized by jerky involuntary movements as well as by speech problems and progressive dementia, involves extensive damage to the striatum. GW

basic acts Acts which an agent performs "directly"; and one is said to perform an act directly when one need not perform that act by means of intentionally performing some other act. For example, when one sharpens a pencil, the act of sharpening the pencil consists of doing certain things (holding the pencil and a sharpener and moving one's limbs in specific ways) which result in the pencil's being sharpened. But when one winks (or intentionally smiles, or intentionally moves one's finger), barring exceptional circumstances, one does not need to perform an act in order to bring about the wink: one just winks.

Consequently, it is said that winking, smiling, moving one's finger (wriggling one's ears, taking a step, kicking, etc.) are examples of basic acts; whereas sharpening a pencil (saluting, killing someone, etc.) are examples of non-basic acts.

The category of basic acts is supposed to serve two related theoretical purposes: (i) In conformity with an atomistic view of actions, it delineates the smallest unit of acts which function as the building blocks of all actions. To be an actor in an environment all one needs is a repertoire of basic acts; the rest is taken care of by the causal connections which hold in the environment. (ii) It helps to distinguish between reflex behavior and intended or unintended consequences of intentional behavior. Reflex behavior is not built out of basic acts, whereas intentional behavior has at least one basic act as a building block. BE

basic emotions *See* emotions: basic

behavior change in the classroom An approach to problems of learning and behavior in the classroom which attempts to ameliorate problems through the systematic application of theory and techniques derived from research on animal and human learning. The approach, sometimes called behavior modification, or contingency management, was originally based in the radical behaviorist philosophy of B.F. Skinner (1974), and employed the principles and techniques of applied behavior analysis (Bijou and Baer 1978). This attempts to "explain" behavior change in terms of *respondent* and *operant conditioning* and the patterns of reinforcement (the rewards, natural consequences and punishments), which have been associated with the behavior over time. Its central concern is the identification of functional relationships between observable antecedent events, the context, a circumscribed pattern of behavior

(behavior problem) and the observable consequences of that behavior. In essence, the concern is with the ways in which external or environmental events modify behavior.

In classroom applications of this approach, attention is focused on the unacceptable behavior of the pupil or class, and an attempt is made to identify how this is influenced by what the teacher and peer group do or do not do. This is known as a functional analysis and is the main tool of applied behavior analysis in classroom and other settings. It follows the model characteristic of laboratory studies of animal and human behavior and the theoretical and conceptual interpretative framework used by radical behaviorists. The problem behavior (target) is first described in behavioral terms ("pupil gets out of seat", "pupil hits other children", "only produces three or four lines of work during lesson") and an attempt is made to record its frequency, duration or other quantifiable characteristics before any intervention is made. During the pre-intervention phase, called the baseline period, the behavior of the teacher and/or peers is also monitored, the observer focussing on what they do immediately before and after the occurrence of the target behavior. When the observers have obtained a stable baseline (i.e. a reliable and representative picture of the target behavior over a period of time) the teacher is asked to follow the instructions of the behavior analyst for the intervention phase during which the behavior of both teacher and pupil continue to be recorded. In this way the observers are able to monitor the effects of their advice. If the target behavior changes in the desired direction an attempt may be made to re-instigate the problem behavior in order to ensure that it was the teacher's actions during the pre-intervention phase that were responsible for producing the unacceptable behavior. Finally, the teacher will be asked to re-introduce a program specified by the behavior analyst and will be further instructed in how to maintain, and if necessary generalize to other situations, the now acceptable behavior. If the initial prescription fails to produce the desired changes within a reasonable time, indicating that the original analysis of functional relationships was wrong, a further analysis is undertaken and the sequence repeated until the behavior changes to a more acceptable form.

The specific changes demanded of the teacher are determined by what emerged in the functional analysis. It is, for example, not unusual to find teachers giving attention, albeit by reprimands, to disruptive behavior and ignoring perhaps inadvertently, instances of acceptable behavior. The advice given by the behavior analyst under such circumstances might be to give clearcut attention, praise, smiles and the like when the pupil is behaving appropriately (i.e. reinforce the acceptable) and ignore, with due regard to the well-being of other pupils, the disruptions.

Although teacher attention (a common "social reinforcer") may work well for many pupils, there are occasions or circumstances where it has no impact. When this happens, material or other reinforcers will be introduced. A child who does not respond to teacher attention may be allowed to have an extended play time as a reinforcer for producing more work. Sometimes tokens, in the form of points or ticks on a card, are used in conjunction with the social reinforcer of teacher's praise. When a predetermined number of these is accumulated, they can be exchanged for a prize or some desired activity. Systematic token programs are called token economies and are used either with individuals or groups. In order to maximize the opportunities for reinforcement it may become necessary to introduce changes in the content or organisation of the curriculum, structural changes in the classroom or even in the school. For instance if the learning tasks are too difficult, they will need to be structured into smaller components and the teacher will be asked to reinforce success on the smaller unit rather than the whole task.

Early applications of applied behavior analysis were implemented in selective settings, usually experimental classrooms attached to colleges or universities in the USA. Since then, there have been many studies reporting applications in a wide range of settings, including special education, focused on varied problems presented by pupils of all ages (see Sherman and Bushell 1975, O'Leary and O'Leary 1977, for illustrative studies and reviews). The central ideas and especially the techniques are being increasingly incorporated in the training of teachers and there are several textbooks for teachers on the subject (e.g. Clarizio 1971). The approach has several positive and important attributes.

One is the attention it has focused on the role of external (to the pupil) influences on classroom learning and behavior. It raises questions about the interplay between the teacher's management skills and the characteristics of pupils in trying to understand classroom problems. Having identified the set of critical factors, it provides clear procedures to attempt to bring about change.

A second feature of importance is that the approach provides a systematic way of investigating aspects of classroom interactions, particularly those concerned with management. Through an emphasis on careful description and recording, it has begun to clarify the problems many teachers encounter in their day to day work. The use of direct observation by an outside observer is an important aspect here. Another noteworthy feature, perhaps not given enough emphasis, is the underlying assumption that much behavior, including many forms of classroom behavior, is learned and retains some responsiveness to external changes. The problems are not seen as faults or disorders within the pupil.

Third, and perhaps most important, is the evidence that some classroom problems at least can be positively influenced by the use of techniques which can be taught to teachers and which do not lead to segregation of pupils into special units, classes or schools, from which they might not return to mainstream schooling.

Objections to the approach have been formulated at all levels. As a philosophy of science behaviorism is seen as narrow and out of keeping with contemporary views of science; as an orientation in psychology, its mechanistic conceptions of human behavior and experience are unacceptable to many; its views of learning, the emphasis on external determinants, and the implications it carries about the nature and solution of problems faced by teachers and pupils, are often thought simplistic. The presumed power of the classroom technology of behavior change has given rise to ethical objections, particularly when applied to the control of children in schools (see Clarke 1979, O'Leary and O'Leary 1977).

While published studies on classroom applications generally show successful outcomes it would be inappropriate to be optimistic. It is not possible to know the extent of failed applications and unsuccessful studies have a limited chance of publication. Also, even when successful, changes effected by one teacher in a particular classroom do not readily continue over time, or generalize to other teachers or other settings (Wahler 1980). It should also be emphasized that techniques and their rationale could readily be encompassed by a number of other theoretical accounts which do not necessarily give rise to the objections noted above (see Bandura 1974, Agras, Kazdin and Wilson 1979).

The increasing acceptance of behavioral techniques (if not the associated theory) among educationalists can be partly understood by considering the prevalence of learning and behavior problems in ordinary and special schools, and the limitations in the training of teachers to meet these problems.

It is difficult to obtain precise estimates of the nature and frequency of problems faced by teachers because there is no generally accepted taxonomy or classification of classroom problems. This in turn leads to a high degree of subjectivity on the part of teachers as to what they identify as problems: a "definite problem" for one teacher may be no more than a minor irritant for another. (See DISRUPTIVE BEHAVIOR).

Teacher-education is concerned primarily with curriculum matters and the foundation disciplines of philosophy, psychology and sociology. Although trainees will have some supervised teaching practice there is commonly little systematic guidance on the management of the classroom difficulties. Furthermore, while much has been written (usually by experienced teachers), on the subject (e.g. Francis 1975), this literature is pejoratively referred to as "tips for teachers".

It would of course be quite wrong to see classroom problems as arising solely out of deficiencies in teacher-training. But it would be equally incorrect to ignore the possible contribution of teaching practices to the generation or maintenance of classroom problems. The approach offered by applied behavior analysis provides one way of trying to understand classroom processes and it has drawn attention to procedures which may well be integral to good teaching. MBe

Bibliography

Agras, W.S., Kazdin, A.E. and Wilson, G.T. 1979: *Behavior therapy: toward an applied clinical science.* San Francisco: W.H. Freeman.

Bandura, A. 1974: Behavior theory and models of man. *American psychologist* 29, 859–69.

Bijou, S.W. and Baer, D.M. 1978: *Behavior analysis of child development.* New Jersey: Prentice Hall.

Clarizio, H.F. 1971: *Toward positive classroom discipline.* New York: John Wiley.

Clarke, C. 1979: Education and behaviour modification. *Journal of philosophy of education* 13, 73–81.

Francis, P. 1975: *Beyond control?* London: Allen & Unwin.

*O'Leary, D.K. and O'Leary, S.G. 1977: *Classroom management* (2nd edn.). New York: Pergamon Press.

*Sherman, J.A. and Bushell, D. 1975: Behavior modification as an educational technique. In *Review of child development research, vol. 4* ed. F.D. Horowitz. Chicago: University of Chicago Press.

Skinner, B.F. 1974: *About behaviorism.* New York: Knopf.

Wahler, R.G. 1980: Behavior modification: applications to childhood problems. In *Emotional disorders in children and adolescents,* ed. P. Sholevar, R.M. Benson and B.J. Blinder. Lancaster: M.T.P. Press; New York: Spectrum Publications.

behavior genetics Is concerned with the effects of genes on the expression of behavior. Any form of genetic analysis requires the identification of differences. This may take the form of a clear distinction between the behavior of two individuals, or there may be continuous variation in the expression of some type of behavior within a population. Breeding tests or examination of relatives can then be made to establish how far such differences are genetic. Behavior genetics is not a unified field of investigation and within this broad outline are to be found a diverse set of aims and approaches which may have little contact with each other. Fuller and Thompson (1978) provide much the best survey of the whole field.

On the one hand, much research is directed toward the nature of gene action upon behavior. Single gene mutations are studied in convenient organisms such as *Drosophila* or mice, and attempts are made to relate behavioral differences between mutant and normal individuals to gene action on physiology, neural structure or neurochemisty. At the other end of the range the techniques of quantitative genetics are used to analyse the variation within a population for a complex trait like learning ability. This will certainly involve many genes and there is no possibility of identifying the action of any one, the aim may be to use genetic analysis to help partition the trait and distinguish between variation of genetic and environmental origin.

There is an inevitable diversity imposed on the field by the nature of the character being studied. Some branches of genetics are concerned with systems whose control is quite well known and where it is possible to relate the known action of genes (i.e. controlling the synthesis of proteins) to the end product. It is no coincidence that the most spectacular recent advances in genetics have come at its interface with molecular biology. Behavior presents many more problems for genetic analysis. Firstly, the phenotype itself is extremely diverse and indeed demands many completely different levels of analysis. We may be interested in the phototactic behavior of fruit flies, the control of balance and locomotion in mice, the maze-learning of rats, levels of aggression in different breeds of dog, courtship displays in chickens or spatial components of intelligence tests in human beings (all of which have been the subject of behavior-genetic analysis). Secondly, for many such phenomena the gap between gene action at the cellular level and the end-product we are studying is maximal. Nor can we expect to be able to generalize about the pathways along which genes operate to exercise their effects on such diverse behavioral phenotypes. Not all the pathways are of much interest in any case–a mutant mouse may show inferior avoidance learning, but turn out to have an elevated pain threshold to the electric shock which serves as reinforcer in the learning situation. It will always be necessary to screen out trivial effects of this type.

It has been argued that since behavior is usually manifested only intermittently as a sequence of events through time, its genetic basis exists only in so far as we can identify some underlying structure upon which it is based. Certainly some people feel that only by working with identified single genes of known effect can we hope to make any progress (see Quinn and Gould 1979 for an extreme statement of this reductionist position). However this type of approach is scarcely possible, except in one or two favored invertebrates whose genetics are well known, and much more that is of interest to psychologists has been achieved by behavior genetic analysis at other levels. We can consider some examples of each type.

Single-gene studies

There has been extensive work on *Drosophila melanogaster* where hundreds of mutant stocks are easily available, but these may have diverged genetically in other ways over generations of culturing, so it is often more useful to treat normal flies with a mutagen and screen the progeny for behavioral changes. Using this technique mutants have been isolated which affect a wide variety of behavioral phenotypes–phototaxis, locomotor activity, circadian rhythms, courtship behavior and learning ability (see Benzer 1983). Screening for behavior mutants requires some ingenuity and many trivial effects will have to be discarded along the way, e.g. flies which fail to respond because they cannot walk properly. The mutants affecting learning were mostly derived from a screening test in which flies learnt to avoid an odor which had been associated with electric shock. As their names, *dunce, amnesiac* and *turnip*, suggest their effect is to reduce learning and retention. It is obviously important to discover whether such mutants affect only olfactory conditioning, or whether they act more generally. It is not easy to get a range of learning situations for *Drosophila* but some visual, and simple operant conditioning has proved possible; *dunce* and *amnesiac* flies show some learning ability in these situations but certainly reduced from normal, (see Folkers 1982). The genes appear to have both general and specific effects and attempts are being made to link them with changes to brain biochemistry. Using special stocks of *Drosophila* it is possible to generate flies some of whose cells express the effects of a mutant gene while others are normal. Study of such mosaic individuals helps to reveal in which parts of the body the gene acts to produce its effect–its "primary focus"; (see Hotta and Benzer 1972).

Behavioral analysis involving many genes

The great majority of behavioral characters will be affected by many genes and we may not be able to identify the effects of any particular locus. Nevertheless the study of different strains of breeds or inbred lines of animals has often yielded interesting results. Nearly always they show differences on a wide variety of behavioral measures which can be shown to be of genetic origin, but the scale and sometimes direction of such genetic effects can be markedly affected by the environment. For example Henderson (1970) compared mouse strains reared in complex or standard cage environments in a feeding situation which involved exploratory behavior and agility. The genetic contribution to variance between the strains was four times greater in mice from complex cages, indicating extreme gene/environment interaction. We must expect such interactions to be the rule in behavioral development.

Artificial selection for behavioral characters has often been successful and reveals that natural populations are variable for genes affecting behavioral traits. Aggression in mice, mating speed in *Drosophila*, maze learning in rats– all have responded strongly to selection. Tryon's experiment with maze learning was one of the first of its type. He produced "maze-dull" and "maze-bright" rats with virtually no overlap in performance. However when tested in other types of learning situation the brights performed no better or even less well than the dulls. Analysis showed that Tryon's selection had isolated factors relating to the main cues the rats responded to when learning the maze. The brights were genetically predisposed to concentrate on kinaesthetic cues in which Tryon's original maze was rich; the dulls' behavior was more visually controlled. Such a result contributed to our understanding of learning and illustrates the use of genetics as a tool for the study of behavior itself over and above its intrinsic genetic interest (see Manning 1976). By separating and exaggerating the effects of components which are normally associated together behavioral analysis is facilitated.

Human behavior genetics

Human behavior genetics mainly operates in two highly contrasted areas. First there is the study of gross genetic abnormalities, both those associated with single genes such as phenylketonuria or microcephaly, and also the chromosome abnormalities responsible for Down's syndrome, Turner's syndrome and others. With the single genes the nature of the primary action is often a clear enzyme deficiency which can be related to the effects on the functioning of the nervous system and it can sometimes be counteracted using a controlled diet. Study of the genetics of brain metabolites backed up with experimental animal studies may help us to understand certain types of mental illness where neurochemistry is implicated, (see Petersen, Collins and Miles 1982; Kety 1982).

The other type of human behavior genetics uses quantitative genetic approaches to study continuously varying traits such as intellectual ability and personality. The genetic analyses can be of impressive sophistication with data from extended families, mono- and dizygotic twins reared together and apart etc. The unresolved problem concerns the realistic separation of genetic and environmental influences upon such complex and controversial traits. (See also GENETICS, EVOLUTION AND BEHAVIOR).

AWGM

Bibliography

Benzer, S. 1983: The Croonian Lecture. Genes, neurons and behavior in *Drosophila. Proceedings of the Royal Society B.*, in press.

Folkers, E. 1982: Visual learning and memory of *Drosophila melanogastor* wild type C-S and the mutants *dunce, amnesiac, turnip* and *rutabaga. Journal of insect physiology* 28.535-39.

Fuller, John L. and Thompson, William R. 1978: *Foundations of behavior genetics*. C.V. Mosby. St Louis: No UK ed. *but* Distributed in UK by: London: Y.B. Medical Publishers.

Henderson, N.D. 1970: Genetic influences on the behavior of mice can be obscured by laboratory rearing. *Journal of comparative physiological psychology*. 72. 505-11.

Hotta, Y. and Benzer, S. 1972: The mapping of behavior in *Drosophila* mosaics. *Nature* 240. 527-35.

Kety, S. 1982: Neurochemical and genetic bases of psychopathology: current status. *Behavior genetics* 12. 93-100.

Manning, A. 1976: The place of genetics in the study of behavior. pp. 327-43. In Bateson, Paul P.G. and Hinde, Robert A., eds., *Growing points in ethology*. Cambridge: Cambridge University Press and New York.

Petersen, D.R., Collins, A.C. and Miles, R.G., 1982: An overview of the genetics of psychopathology. *Behavior genetics* 12, 3-10.

Quinn, W.G. and Gould, J.L. 1979: Nerves and genes. *Nature* 278, 19-23.

behavior modification A generic term referring to the applied use of behavioral psychology to bring about changes in human behavior by workers in the helping professions (clinical and educational psychologists, social workers, teachers, etc). Based on Skinner's OPERANT CONDITIONING paradigm, its central tenet is that all behavior is primarily learned and maintained as a result of an individual's interaction with his environment, which includes other individuals, and is hence susceptible to change by control over features of that environment. The three-term analysis of behavior (or ABC model) indicates that behavior change may be achieved by manipulating either the antecedent conditions for behavior, or the consequences following behavior, in line with the law of effect. Simply stated, this means that rewarded behavior will tend to increase in frequency, while behavior followed by punishing consequences will tend to decline (see, however, REINFORCEMENT for a more precise definition).

See also BEHAVIOR CHANGE IN THE CLASSROOM. KW

behavior therapy Also called behavior modification, is the application of the methods and findings of experimental psychology to the alteration of maladaptive behavior. Rimm and Masters (1979) suggest that behavior therapy has eight main features. (1) relative to PSYCHOTHERAPY behavior therapy tends to concentrate on behavior itself rather than some presumed underlying cause. (2) It is assumed that maladaptive behavior is to a considerable degree acquired through learning. (3) It is assumed that psychological principles, especially learning principles, can be effective in modifying maladaptive behaviors. (4) It involves setting specific clearly defined treatment goals. (5) It rejects classical trait theory. (6) The therapist adapts his or her methods of treatment to the client's problem. (7) The therapy concentrates on the here and now. (8) Therapists place great value on obtaining empirical support for their techniques.

Behavior therapy has its roots in two seminal publications in the 1950s. Wolpe (1958) described his work on experimental neurosis in cats and the clinical techniques he had developed from that work, the most important and enduring of which has been systematic desensitization. Skinner's book *Science and Human Behavior* (1953) was equally influential in suggesting how the principles derived from the study of operant conditioning and in particular the effects on learning of the consequences of behavior, could be applied therapeutically. The 1960s and '70s saw a rapid increase in the use of behavior therapy and it is now the major form of therapy practiced by clinical psychologists in much of the English speaking world. Scientific publications on behavior therapy have increased explosively and there are now numerous journals on the field in general and on specific aspects of it; the three best known are *Behaviour research and therapy*, *Journal of applied behavioural analysis* and *Behaviour therapy*. The main changes in the theoretical and empirical background to behavior therapy since the 1950s have been the increasing influence of other aspects of experimental psychology as well as learning theory and in particular the role of social and cognitive factors which have been incorporated in social learning theory (Bandura 1977) which now provides the main theoretical basis for behavior therapy.

Five stages in behavioral treatment can be recognized. (1) Behavioral analysis – a detailed analysis of a client's problems and factors related to them. This is done on the basis of data gathered in various ways, including interviewing the client, direct observation of his or her behavior and self-monitoring of this behavior. There is considerable emphasis on the collection of objective numerical data, i.e. the number of journeys from home if the patient is agoraphobic, the frequency of incontinence in an encopretic child. (2) The determination of specific goals for treatment. (3) The development of a treatment plan involving the use of those techniques of behavior therapy which are applicable to the client's problem. (4) Implementation of the treatment plan. (5) Objective evaluation of the results of treatment with modification and extension of the treatment plan based on the feedback provided by such evaluation.

Applications of Behavior Therapy

Behavior therapy has now been applied with considerable success to a wide variety of the problem behavior traditionally seen as falling within the province of psychiatry, including phobias, obsessions, generalized anxiety, depression, enuresis and encopresis, drug and alcohol abuse, the effects of longterm institutionalization in psychotic patients and the mentally handicapped, marital discord, sexual inadequacy and, decreasingly, sexual deviation, aggression, delinquency and eating disorders. In addition to the application of behavioral techniques in the traditional areas of psychiatry, treatment has now been extended to deal with the problems of physical illness in a sub specialization of behavior therapy called behavioral medicine. Among the problems treated in this area are smoking, obesity, compliance with medical regimes, rehabilitation from physical illness, the direct treatment of psychophysiological disturbances such as high blood pressure, asthma and headache, and the alteration of self-damaging patterns of behavior such as the coronary-prone Type A behavior pattern.

Techniques of Behavior Therapy
Since behavior therapy is essentially applied experimental psychology, the specific techniques are numerous and in some respects less important than a general attitude toward therapy and the collection of objective data. However, five categories of therapeutic technique, not necessarily mutually exclusive, can be discerned: (1) exposure based methods; (2) contingency management procedures; (3) cognitive behavior therapy; (4) assertive and social skills training; (5) self-control procedures.

Exposure methods
Much anxiety and anxiety-related behavior, such as phobic avoidance or obsessional compulsions, arises in response to particular events. Behavior therapy tries to extinguish the anxiety and associated behavior by systematic exposure of the patient to the feared situation. The actual form of exposure varies and can be very gradual with minimal anxiety as in systematic desensitization or rapid and fear-inducing as in flooding and can be to the real situation or to imaginal representations of it. Modelling procedures are also used, in which the patient observes the desired behavior being carried out by someone else before attempting it. There is now a consensus that exposure to the real situation (in vivo exposure) is most effective. In the treatment of obsessional behavior, such exposure is often used in conjunction with response prevention to stop the patient carrying out rituals associated with exposure to the feared or contaminating object.

Contingency management
The central tenet of OPERANT CONDITIONING that behavior is maintained by its consequences forms the basis of contingency management, an all-pervasive component of behavioral practice. Behavior therapists try to determine the consequences of disturbed behavior and to ensure that such behavior is not followed by positive consequences and that desired behavior does receive positive reinforcement. Such contingency management is usually applied as part of an overall behavioral approach which uses some of the other techniques described. For example, a therapist treating an agoraphobic woman would try to ensure that her family did not attend to her solely when she was panicking and housebound and that they did positively reinforce her efforts to go out. With the very young or with institutionalized individuals with very limited behavioral repertoires contingency management may form the main form of behavior therapy as in a token economy in which practically all forms of the patient's behavior earn tokens which can later be cashed in for material rewards or privileges. Using such methods the more damaging effects of chronic institutionalization can be averted or reversed and patients can be taught to attend to their own physical wellbeing, their ward tasks and increased social interaction with other patients.

Cognitive behavior therapy
Possibly because of its roots in behaviorism and in the rejection of psychoanalytic theory, behavior therapy has until recently fought shy of dealing with non-observable private cognitive events. However, practically all therapists working with non-institutionalized adults now concern themselves to some extent with the thoughts and beliefs of their clients. Most cognitive therapies have arisen outside the field of behavior therapy but they are increasingly being incorporated into that therapy and have more affinities with it than with the more traditional psychotherapies. The three main variants of cognitive behavior therapy are Ellis's rational emotive therapy (RET) Meichenbaum's self instructional training (SET) and Beck's cognitive therapy. All these therapies are broadly similar and all attempt to enable cognitive change, now frequently called cognitive restructuring. Ellis claims that most disturbed behavior is based on irrational beliefs which he tries to change, primarily by logical argument. He claims that there are many irrational beliefs common to mankind, including for example, the belief that one must have the love and approval of all significant people in one's environment at all times. RET attempts to modify such irrational core beliefs. SET is more concerned with specific idiosyncratic irrational beliefs and attempts to modify them by making the patient first of all aware of them, and then instructing the patient in countering them by making appropriate statements while performing the desired behavior. Beck has concentrated primarily on the role of cognitions, and cognitive therapy in depression. He regards depression as having a central cognitive element and claims that the depressed display various cognitive distortions. For example, the tendency to refer all external events to oneself or to apply absolute standards in one's thinking so that everything is either all good or all bad. While Beck uses many of the behavioral techniques, particularly early in therapy with the most depressed patients, the core of his therapy is a cognitive therapy that attempts to alter distorted thinking by, for example, helping the patients to consider their problems in alternative, solvable terms, or actually to assess the extent to which their problems can be attributed to their own actions.

Assertive and social skills training
Many interpersonal difficulties and resultant maladaptive behavior arise because of patients' inabilities to assert themselves, i.e. express positive or negative emotions clearly. Assertive and social skills training have been used with a wide variety of patients in an attempt to overcome these difficulties. The most widely used techniques in this area are behavioral rehearsal, modeling and information feedback in which the patient and therapist act out troublesome situations. The therapist first of all models the correct response, then the patients produces that response while the therapist provides feedback on the patient's behavior. It the patient is markedly socially unskilled a detailed analysis of his social deficits may be followed by extensive training on specific aspects of social interaction.

Self-control
It is a common misbelief that behavior therapy is applied by potent, or even omnipotent, therapists to passive clients. Some of the early theoretical writings on behavior therapy

encourage this misconception but in reality most therapy involves the active participation of the client and increasingly therapy aims to teach the client methods of self control that will enable him or her to cope with problem situations. Practically all the techniques described above can be used by the patient as a self-control aid, and patients can therefore learn that they must, for example, expose themselves to the fearful situation if the phobia returns, that they should rehearse difficult social situations before entering them, and that they should arrange reinforcement for their positive actions and ensure that the actions they wish to discontinue are not being reinforced. In addition to the use of these standard techniques as self-control techniques, a number of procedures uniquely related to self-control have been developed, the most prominent of which is biofeedback, a technique in which the subject learns to control his own physiological responses by receiving augmented feedback, usually through some electronic device, on the activity of the physiological system in question. Such techniques have been applied to a multitude of psychophysiological disturbances, most successfully in the treatment of headache, using muscle and skin temperature feedback, and in the treatment of encopresis using feedback from the anal sphincters.

Behavior therapy offers a complex and comprehensive treatment approach to almost the complete range of maladaptive behavior. The influential review of the effects of psychological treatment by Rachman and Wilson (1980) makes it clear that behavior therapy is effective and offers an enduring solution to many patients' problems, a solution that is often more effective than that offered by the traditional psychotherapist. Behavior therapy is also largely free of negative side effects and in particular the prediction on the basis of psychoanalytic theory that maladaptive behavior successfully treated by behavioral methods would reappear in some other form ("symptom substitution") has not been confirmed. When behavior therapy has effects beyond the particular maladaptive behavior targeted these effects are likely to represent further gains for the patient. DWJ

Bibliography

Bandura, A. 1969: *Principles of behavior modification*. New York: Holt.

——— 1977: *Social learning*. Englewood Cliffs, NJ: Prentice-Hall.

Rachman, S.J. and Wilson, G.T. 1980: *The effects of psychological therapy*. Oxford and New York: Pergammon.

Rimm, D.C. and Masters, J.C. 1979: *Behaviour therapy. Techniques and empirical findings*. London and New York: Academic Press.

Skinner, B.F. 1953: *Science and human behavior*. New York: Macmillan.

Wolpe, J. 1958: *Psychotherapy by reciprocal inhibitions*. Stanford, Calif: Stanford University Press.

behaviorism The thesis that psychology is the study of behavior rather than of any inner mental life. First advanced by WATSON as a counter to introspectionist psychology, behaviorism can be given a strong or a weak definition. The weak definition says no more than that psychologists can study only observable events, that is to say what people or animals do, but allows that what a person says is an instance of behavior, and does not raise objections to the postulation of inferred, possibly observable processes in order to explain what people do or say. In its stronger form, as originally postulated by Watson, and with some important changes of emphasis by SKINNER, behaviorism rejects any appeal to mental events or processes in the explanation of behavior. Skinner's views, sometimes called radical behaviorism, are akin to those of philosophical behaviorism which asserts that the meaning of mental or psychological concepts is to be found only by reference to the behavior instantiating such concepts: there is, for example, no inner process of intelligence whose operation causes someone to be intelligent; there is only intelligent behavior, that is to say behavior appropriate to various goals, carried out in a particular way. For Skinner, the explanation of behavior is always to be found by looking at observable events – controlling stimuli or past contingencies of reinforcement. NJM

Bibliography

Watson, J.B. 1913: Psychology as the behaviorist views it. *Psychological review* 20, 158–77.

belief *See* knowledge and belief

bilingualism People are called bilinguals if "they possess sufficient skills in a second language to permit a significant part of their social and/or intellectual activities to be conducted through the medium of that language". (Segalowitz 1977, 120). A widely made distinction is that between "compound bilingualism" and "coordinate bilingualism", the former term referring to cases where two languages are used in the same functions and domains, the latter to cases where each language is used in separate non-overlapping functions and domains. In real life these types represent the idealized endpoints of a continuum of possibilities. The degree to which two language systems are kept functionally separate is reflected in the speaker's capacity to keep them structurally separate and to translate from one system to the other.

An important field of inquiry is that of bilingualism in children (Mackey and Anderson eds. 1977), in particular how this affects their general learning capacities. PM

Bibliography

Mackey, William F. and Anderson, Theodore. 1977: *Bilingualism in early childhood*, Rowley, Mass.: Newbury House.

Segalowitz, Norman 1977: Psychological perspectives on bilingual education. In *Frontiers of bilingual education* ed. B. Spolky and R. Cooper, R. Rowley, Mass.: Newbury House.

bi-modality A way of referring to the two predominant cognitive "modes" or "styles" associated with the hemispheric specialization of the human brain. (See LATERALIZATION.)

The left hemisphere specializes in verbal, rational, analytic, and logical functions. The predominant mode of operation is linear and information is processed sequentially (is temporally ordered). It is very effective for operating within and manipulating the external, three-dimensional, object world. The right hemisphere specializes in relational perception, orientation in space, and holistic (gestalt) mentation. The predominant mode of operation is relational and information is processed simultaneously. It is instrumental for grasping the patterns of relations, for receptivity and intuitiveness, body-image and movement, and all artistic endeavors.

In most activities, we alternate between the two "modes", choosing the appropriate one and inhibiting the other. But, cultural reinforcements, as well as habitual-personal "preferences", for one mode over another can readily be observed. There are, however, other instances when we operate in both modes in a complementary way; when both are fully active and integrated with each other. It has been argued that such instances are associated with creativity and that "the complementary workings of the intellect and the intuitive underlie our highest achievements". (Ornstein.)

Many view bi-modality as a way of physiologically grounding a theory of creativity and human potential that hinges on this basic duality in human awareness; a duality that when unintegrated has resulted in familiar polarizations e.g. science and religion, analysis and intuition, reason and emotion, behavior and experience, West and East, sign and symbol ... etc. The implications of a shift from opposition to integration are worked out in ALTERNATIVE PSYCHOLOGIES. DAL

Bibliography

Ornstein, Robert 1975: *The psychology of consciousness*. London: Penguin.

Lee, Philip et al. 1977: *Symposium on consciousness*. London: Penguin.

biofeedback A technique by which an individual can learn voluntarily to control internal bodily processes such as heart rate, blood pressure, skin temperature, or degree of muscle relaxation, by obtaining immediate information (feedback) about the internal events or conditions being monitored. Information about these bodily events or states is usually not available to conscious experience except through the sensors of biofeedback instrumentation. In this way many internal processes can, to some degree, be brought under conscious control.

Operant conditioning and servo-system models currently appear to be the best explanations of biofeedback. Biofeedback is a relatively new therapeutic technique and unanswered questions about its theoretical basis, generality, and utility away from the monitoring equipment remain. RAJ

bioprogram language This term was introduced and developed by Bickerton (1981). In contrast to Chomsky's LANGUAGE ACQUISITION DEVICE which defines formal principles enabling children to select a possible grammar on the basis of restricted parental input, Bickerton's bioprogram refers to a well defined set of structures and structural developments, i.e. those which arise under conditions of CREOLIZATION of an incipient pidgin. Ordinary FIRST LANGUAGE ACQUISITION is seen to involve the task of restructuring the innate bioprogram so as to approximate to adult grammar. Numerous creole constructions can therefore be expected in developing child language. A large number of the bioprogram categories (such as the punctual-non punctual distinction, that is the distinction between those processes consisting of determinate units and those made up of continuous transitions) are absent in most adult language systems. Bickerton explains this by pointing out that much of the grammar of so called "natural" languages is in fact cultural. Consequently, the search for psychologically and biologically based linguistic universals in such languages is misguided. PM

Bibliography

Bickerton, Derek 1981: *Roots of language*, Ann Arbor; Karoma Publications.

Mühlhäusler, Peter 1982: review article of Bickerton 1981, to appear in *Folia Linguistica*.

bipolar depression *See* depression, bipolar

bisexuality A term with two meanings, the first and more traditional of which is to have the physical or psychological characteristics of both sexes. Several theorists, including FREUD and JUNG, believed that masculine and feminine characteristics are present in all people. A more recent expression of this view is the concept of androgyny. A second meaning of the term is the state of being sexually attracted to and/or having relations with both sexes. RHo

blends of primary emotional expression *See* emotions, basic; facial expression and emotion

Bleuler, Eugen (1857–1959). A Swiss psychiatrist who was for many years director of the Burghölzli Clinic, near Zurich. His major works on SCHIZOPHRENIA, PARANOID STATES and ORGANIC MENTAL STATES were based on close and detailed clinical observations. In 1911 he extended Kraepelin's clinical description of dementia praecox, introducing the term schizophrenia to emphasize the splitting (or fragmentation) of the personality and to avoid the implication that deterioration is inevitable. He acknowledged the help of C.G. Jung in his main aim of applying Freud's theories of psychological processes. Bleuler distinguished 'fundamental symptoms': autism, loosening of associations, thought disorder and changes in emotional reactions. He had a more optimistic view of social outcome than Kraepelin but believed that subtle signs of an illness process could usually be detected in the premorbid personality and invariably after clinical recovery. These ideas have had very considerable influence on many later definitions of schizophrenia (especially in the United States) and on psychological theories of etiology. RAM

Bibliography

Bleuler, E. 1950: *Dementia praecox: the group of schizophrenias*. New York: International Universities Press.

blind, the: psychology and education There is no internationally-agreed definition of blindness, and in most countries the term is not restricted only to those who are totally lacking in sight. No reliable statistics are available, therefore, about global incidence, and even within any given nation the medico-legal criteria used for classification or registration purposes will encompass a very heterogeneous population. In some countries, for example the UK and the USA, the statutory regulations specify upper limits of acuity for distant vision and lower limits for width of visual field, and result in the majority of the "legally blind" having some potentially useful residual sight. A group that is so heterogeneous in visual functioning will vary also in its educational and psychological needs, as is seen by the emergence of a term such as "educationally blind" which is used for those who have to use braille for reading and writing. The age of onset of the visual impairment and the presence of additional handicaps add to the heterogeneity of those labelled as blind.

Nevertheless, some order can be obtained by partitioning along the two independent dimensions of degree of residual vision and age of onset. The growing interest in the needs of the majority of the registered blind, those at the upper end of the blindness continuum, has its origins (1) in the confirmation of ophthalmologists that most ocular disabilities cannot be made worse by normal use of sight; (2) in the findings of experimental psychologists that various aspects of perception can be improved by training; and (3) in improvements in the quality and variety of magnifiers and low vision aids. Educators (e.g. Barraga 1964) seized upon the implications of these developments and proceeded to devise assessment and teaching procedures geared to encouraging greater reliance on and interpretation of quite meagre visual information for orientation, mobility, object perception and even the reading of print (the latter now being facilitated by the use of closed circuit television magnifiers). The classification of a child or adult as blind is no longer regarded by teachers and rehabilitation staff as sufficient reason for assuming vision to be unusable, and when there are no contra-indications from the ophthalmologist, the common practice is for them to assess whether and how the learner uses, or could use, any remaining sight in recreation, classroom, and work and to devise training programs with that information in mind.

When the cut is made along the other axis – age of onset – a new set of problems arises. For those who become blind after extensive experience of operating visually, the concepts "re-adjustment" and "rehabilitation" are used but they seem less useful when applied to those who are born blind. This does not imply that congenital blindness has no impact on cognitive, perceptual and social development but rather that the growth of the total personality has its own unique shape and integrity. The handicapping consequences of blindness will be understood later, and then initially through the mediation of other people. There will be no sense of loss of body parts or functioning, nor the expectation by parents, family and advisers of overt or disguised feelings of hostility, depression and demoralization. These, however, are major problems for the newly-blinded, and are bound up with archetypal anxieties and attitudes about blindness that are themselves not just to do with the loss or absence of one of the major sensory modalities. Blindness has a symbolic content related to light and darkness, and to loss of power and control (see, for example, Monbeck 1973). It is perhaps for this reason that rehabilitation programs for the blind are a compound of skills training (to replace the lost power and control) and counseling, with the counseling sometimes extending to the members of the immediate family to enable them to accept the blindness and understand the feelings it evokes both in them and in the blind relative. But in relation to learning, great though the difficulties of the later-blinded may be in acquiring braille, independent mobility, and daily-living skills, there is ample objective and anecdotal evidence testifying to the value for the individual of having had the power of sight, even if only for a few years, as this provides a framework against which new experiences can be set and evaluated.

Extensive evidence from behavioral scales and checklists has shown that, as a group, congenitally blind infants and young children reach certain developmental milestones later than the normally sighted. Many of the items where delays are observed involve locomotor and self-care skills. In later childhood, there is evidence too of the slower growth of various perceptual and cognitive competencies, for which the expression "developmental lag" is often used. It has, however, little explanatory value. More recent research is attempting to move on from merely recording these differences to an examination of the conditions that can mitigate the deleterious effects of visual loss. The wide variations among totally, congenitally blind children are being seen as informative about the constellation of necessary conditions for activating what Russian psychologists describe as the "safe analysers" (the remaining sensory channels). Western researchers may cast the procedure in terms of selecting alternative coding strategies, and then point to the role of the parents whose own feelings about the child's lack of sight may affect the initiation and development of their own parenting skills. As an example we may cite the importance for later language development of the ability of mother and baby to monitor one another's line of gaze and so share a frame of reference and know what the other is "thinking" about, before any mutual verbal communication is possible. In the absence of this visually-based component of pre-speech communication, the mother may herself be deprived of some important stimulus and feedback, and need to be taught how vocalization and then speech may have unusual functions for the blind child – for sensing objects, for maintaining contact, for obtaining attention, and for spatially locating himself in relation to others. The fact that language seems eventually to develop normally, that object permanence and constancy are achieved, that walking may be accomplished without a preceding crawling stage, and that some blind children achieve these and other attainments at ages not very different from those of their sighted peers, may be interpreted as proof that blindness is not inevitably a brake on development. This does not deny that it can very easily restrict opportunities for learning and interfere with the emergence of facilitative behavior on the part of the care-givers.

As with sighted children, READING occupies a central place in the educational curriculum of the blind, and although modern technology is making access to information easier through cassette-recorders and devices that can convert print into a tactile format and into spelled-out or synthetic speech, braille remains the dominant system. This is because it is a reading-and-writing medium, and one that preserves the information-rich characteristics of whole-page lay-out (the ability to emphasize by indenting, paragraphing, italicizing, etc.) and the facility for rapid backward and forward checking and scanning. However, print can be read two to three times more quickly than braille, and makes smaller demands on storage capacity (short-term memory). The various explanations for the relative slowness of tactual reading can be seen to have physiological and psychological bases: the width of the finger-pad, the "tactual window", is smaller than the eye's visual field, thus reducing the amount of information that can be picked up in one fixation; the speed of movement and powers of acuity of the eye are inherently superior; the sensations in the finger leave fast-decaying traces, easily obliterated by succeeding stimuli and thus not accurately identified and transferred to longer-term storage centers; recognition of shapes by touch is akin to recognition through blurred vision; textural (dot density) features of braille are coded as well as the global and spatially-related characteristics, and especially in the early phases of learning, this can result in the adoption of inefficient strategies of coding; and the low levels of redundancy characteristic of the structure of the braille cell (as compared with printed letter shapes), combined with multiple meanings for the symbols and complex rules about the use of contracted forms, impose perceptual and cognitive loads of a higher order than those encountered in print reading. Some of these hypotheses are now being adequately operationalized (e.g. Millar 1981) and there is reason to expect significant advances in our understanding of the factors that influence braille letter and word recognition. Among the already well-attested findings are those of Nolan and Kederis (1969) to the effect that (i) growth of some of the factors basic to reading readiness occurs very slowly in blind children, (ii) the correlation between INTELLIGENCE QUOTIENT and reading is significantly higher for braille than for print reading, and (iii) the recognition times for braille words are longer than the sum of the recognition times of the individual symbols in the words, a position which is the reverse of that found for print. Whatever the causation of the slower processing of tactually-presented information, the blind are at a disadvantage vis-à-vis their sighted peers, requiring considerably more time to cover the same curriculum content and finding graphical illustration in mathematics, geography, and other science subjects difficult to interpret.

See also INTEGRATION OF HANDICAPPED CHILDREN IN NORMAL SCHOOLS. MJT

Bibliography

Barraga, N. 1964: *Increased visual behavior in low vision children.* New York: American Foundation for the Blind.

Millar, S. 1981: Tactual shapes. In Portwood and Williams, op. cit.

*Monbeck, M. E. 1973: *The meaning of blindness: attitudes toward blindness and blind people.* Bloomington and London: Indiana University Press.

Nolan, C.Y. and Kederis, C.J. 1969: *Perceptual factors in braille word recognition.* New York: American Foundation for the Blind.

*Portwood, P. F. and Williams, R. S., eds 1981: *The visually handicapped child.* Division of Educational and Child Psychology, Occasional Papers, vol 5, no. 1. Leicester: The British Psychological Society.

*Warren, D. H. 1977: *Blindness and early childhood development.* New York: American Foundation for the Blind.

blindness: in children A severe or complete loss of sight, sufficiently serious to impair the child's ability to process visual information. Only about 10 per cent of the legally blind are totally blind. Like deafness, it is not a unitary condition.

A central question in the development of blind children is whether experiential deficits, caused either by limited mobility or sensory deprivation, interfere with intellectual development. It was widely believed that the spatial concepts of the congenitally blind differ from those of the sighted, who retain the benefits of the "spatial sense". Recent research shows that blind children may have difficulty on tasks requiring "mental rotation" of spatial relations but that on other spatial tasks, such as estimation of length, their performance is equivalent to the sighted. Thus, there can be no general deficit in spatial representation, although some tasks may force the blind child to use inappropriate coding strategies that lead to error. Research with the blind is also important for understanding how children code *cross-modal* relations, since the blind may make use of information from an intact modality that is functionally equivalent to sight for the performance of complex tasks.

See also EMOTIONAL RESPONSES TO MENTAL AND PHYSICAL HANDICAP. GEB

Bibliography

Millar, S. 1981: Cross modal and intersensory perception in the blind. In *Intersensory perception and sensory integration*, ed. Richard Walk and Herbert Pick, Jr. New York and London: Plenum.

blood-brain barrier A mechanism which interferes with or selectively prevents certain types of chemicals borne in the general circulatory system from entering the brain (Kalat 1981). The barrier is actually an interface of the capillaries supplying blood to the brain with certain types of glial cells, namely astrocytes (see GLIA). The foot-like projections of the astrocytes tightly pack the capillary membranes, resulting in an insulating glial sheath around the capillaries. In order to enter the brain chemicals leaving the blood stream must pass through not only the capillary membranes, but also the glial sheath. In general, lipid soluble chemicals cross the blood-brain barrier more readily than do water soluble substances. For example the increased potency of heroin, relative to morphine, is due to its greater permeability through the blood-brain barrier, rather than any differential affinity for opiate receptors. The lack of passive diffusion across the barrier for certain compounds can be overcome by active transport mechanisms, such as for certain amino acids. The barrier presumably functions to preserve and protect the chemical environment of the brain, and is not fully developed at birth in humans. GPH

Bibliography

Kalat, James W. 1981: *Biological Psychology*. Belmont, Calif.: Wadsworth.

body centered therapy A relatively new term referring to a host of therapies whose common goal is the altering of self-image or personality through work with the physical body, either exclusively or as a major component of the therapy. Among the more influential and widely practiced therapies of this type four stand out as very distinct in their methods, while still sharing this common goal. These four are: bioenergetics, Rolfing (also called structural integration), Feldenkrais method (also called functional integration) and body centered psychotherapy (a major form of which is called Hakomi method). Other body centered therapies include: psychomotor therapy, developed by Albert Pesso, Lomi work developed by Robert Hall, Ellisa Hall, Catherine Flaxman and Richard Heckler and the Alexander technique, developed by F. Mathius Alexander. Also related, peripherally, are dance and movement therapies and the traditional approaches like Hatha Yoga and such oriental martial arts as Tai Chi, Aikido and Tai Kwan Do. Though these do not by any means exhaust the body centered therapies, they provide a wide and representative sample.

The various body centered therapies work with the body in very different ways. Primarily these are work with: (1) slow, precise movements, as in the Feldenkrais Method, Tai Chi and Alexander Technique (all three entail a careful sensing of body position and experience); (2) expressive movements and stressful postures, used to access emotionally charged material, as in bioenergetics and dance therapy; (3) the manipulation of body tissue, especially the facial sheaths to restructure the organization of the muscles of the body and the relation of the whole body to gravity, as in Rolfing and its many offshoots; (4) the body as an expression of character and the use of touch, movement and physical interactions with the therapists in an attempt to understand and process emotionally charged issues (as in bioenergetics, body centered psychotherapy and psychomotor therapy); (5) general conditioning and toning of the body to enhance health, feelings of well being, and the development of the skills of self defense and personal control, as in Yoga and the oriental martial arts. The common element among these different approaches is their use of some aspect of work with the body to influence mental health and well being.

Bioenergetics is an offshoot of Reichian therapy developed by Alexander Lowen and John Pierrakos, both of whom worked and studied with Wilhelm REICH. It is strongly influenced by psychoanalysis and uses an elaborate theory of character which is seen as being intimately related to such aspects of the body as posture, structure, "energy flow" and tensions. The therapy combines a minimum of discussion with strong expressive movements and stress postures to promote the release of "blocked" or repressed emotions. The stress postures, combined with breath work, is used to exhaust those muscles which inhibit expression, breath and the full, free experience of feelings. The therapist will use his or her fingers and fists to open blocked areas by exerting pressure or by palpating or massaging. The therapist will often encourage the client to deepen the expression of his or her feelings by pounding, kicking, sobbing or screaming till these begin to happen in a spontaneous and natural way. It is postulated that through this contact with and expression of strong emotions, especially those that have been repressed, such as hate, anger, pain, sadness and sexual feelings, an understanding and a working through of significant emotional issues can and often is accomplished. In addition, the tensions that segment the client's body can be released and a new integration formed.

In Rolfing, the practitioner, for the most part abstains from any psychotherapeutic intervention. In theory at least, Rolfing is done on the body. The intention, however, is to create changes in the client's self image and feelings about him or herself, through integration of the myofacial system (the system which binds and gives shape to the muscles of the body) and integration of the whole body in the field of gravity. Since a lot of feeling comes up and is released during the treatment, some interchange along these lines does occur. But, generally, Rolfing is totally body-orientated, a systematic attempt to realign the structure of the body. The Rolfing practitioner uses his or her fingers, knuckles and elbows to stretch muscles that need length, to separate muscle bundles that have become stuck together through improper use and to stretch and move the facial tissue that surrounds all muscle. The Rolfer works with the facial tissue to restore proper balance, coordination and freedom of movement. A minimum of ten one-hour sessions is given, with more if needed. These ten hours follow a set routine during which layer after layer of facia and muscle are stretched and realigned until the entire body has been covered. In the process breathing and energy level improve significantly and the emotional effects are often as dramatic as the changes in body structure. A very important adjunct to Rolfing is Rolf Movement Work which, by its use of movement and awareness, has a great deal in common with Feldenkrais floor work, though most Rolf Movement Work is done standing and sitting.

Feldenkrais Method combines two ways of working with the body. One consists of a one-to-one manipulation of the body, the second is a method of movement work done with a leader directing any number of people through a series of gentle movements, done mostly on the floor. What is common to both forms is the use of heightened attention to the fine details of slow, gentle movement, whether the practitioner manipulates the client's limbs, etc., or the client makes the movements, guided by a leader. This process, which Moshe Feldenkrais developed is also called Functional Integration. The general idea is to impress upon the nervous system a detailed image of the body. Feldenkrais's second book on his method is entitled, *Awareness through movement.* By moving small segments at first and then combining these into larger and more complicated patterns, always with patient, careful attention and many repetitions, the client's body image (literally the image the client's nervous system has of his or her body) is enhanced and the possibilities of movement and the movement functions, given this new body image, much improved. Since the method is directed at creating changes in the nervous system, it is not surprising that it has found application and notable success in diseases such as cerebral palsy, polio and meningitis. Its effects on self-image are seen as directly parallel to its effects on body image and it is through these that psychological changes are made.

Body centered psychotherapy, of all of these, is the most directly psychological method. Its connections with the body therapies are: (1) its extensive use of the body to evaluate the client psychologically, as in reading the body for character, and (2) the use of physical interventions such as touch, expressive movements, etc., as a vehicle for understanding mental life and (3) its view of the mind/body split as the central issue in therapy of the character processes. In both the Hakomi Method, developed by Ron Kurtz, and the Psychomotor Therapy of Pesso, the therapist combines discussion, action and awareness to access and process important emotional material. The therapist may use fantasy, psychodrama, movement, touch and, in groups, the assistance of one or more people, to create the safety and structure necessary for powerful, emotional changes. The body centered psychotherapies have borrowed widely from the fields of movement, dance, drama and all manner of psychotherapy, from analysis to Gestalt. Their unique flavor and effectiveness is in the subtle and powerful use they make of the bodily manifestations of the client's psychological makeup. RK

Bibliography

Alexander, F.M. 1974: *Resurrection of the body.* New York: Delta (Dell Publishing Company).

Feldenkrais, M. 1972: *Awareness through movement.* New York: Harper & Row.

Kurtz, R. and Prestera, H. 1976: *The body reveals.* New York: Harper & Row.

Lowen, A. 1971: *The language of the body.* New York: Macmillan.

Rolf, I. 1975: *Structural integration.* New York: Viking/Esalen.

body image The perceptions, conscious or unconscious, of one's own body. It may be distorted in personality and neurotic disorders. Examples are ANOREXIA NERVOSA and overpreoccupation with the appearance of particular body parts. Organic lesions of the parietal lobe may cause partial or complete unawareness and neglect of parts of the body. Body image concepts have been used to explain the occurrence and nature of somatic symptoms in neurotic and psychiatric disorder. RAM

Bibliography

Schilder P. 1950: *The image and appearance of the human body.* New York: International University Press.

body language *See* body-centered therapy

body *See above, and* mind-body problem

bond A relationship in which an individual maintains and restores proximity to an inanimate object (such as a nest) or to an animate object (such as a parent or mate) towards which certain behavior is exclusively or preferentially directed (Lorenz 1966; Wickler 1976). Ethology has been concerned mainly with bonding among conspecifics, which generally is mutual though not necessarily symmetric. Bonding partners recognize each other as individuals. Bond formation occurs rapidly between parent and young (see IMPRINTING). Among adults, it requires extended inter-actions (see COURTSHIP) and may then be regarded as an investment (Kummer 1978). Bonded partners tend to defend one another. Attachment theory holds that evolved behavioral and motivational systems underlie the differential preferences of individuals for forming particular bonds (e.g. Bowlby 1969; Reynolds 1976). HK

Bibliography

Bowlby, John 1969–80: *Attachment and loss*, vol. 1. *Attachment*. 1969. New York: Basic Books; London: Hogarth Press; Institute of Psychoanalysis.

Kummer, H. 1978: On the value of social relationships to nonhuman primates: A heuristic scheme. *Social science information* 17, 687–705.

Lorenz, Konrad Z. 1966: *On aggression.* New York: Harcourt, Brace and World Inc.; London: Methuen.

Reynolds, P.C. 1976: The emergence of early hominid social organization: I. The Attachment Systems. *Yearbook of physical anthropology* 20, 73–95.

Wickler, W. 1976: The ethological analysis of attachment. *Zeitschrift für Tierpsychologie* 42, 12–28.

borderline states The category borderline state (or syndrome) has been used in the United States to cover psychiatric conditions believed to be intermediate between SCHIZOPHRENIA and the neuroses and PERSONALITY DISORDER. There is no generally accepted definition and the term is not widely used outside the United States. There are three main usages: (1) an independent entity quite separate from all other diagnostic categories; (2) a mild expression of schizophrenia, called schizotypal personality in the current American classification, DSM III (American Psychiatric Association 1980); (3) a form of personality disorder with features of impulsiveness, unstable relationship, identity disturbance, unstable mood and boredom (borderline personality in DSM III). RAM

Bibliography

American Psychiatric Association 1980: *Diagnostic and statistical manual* III.

Liebowitz, M.R. 1979: Is borderline a distinct entity? *Schizophrenia bulletin* 5, 23–28.

brain and central nervous system: illustrations *See* pp. 62–73.

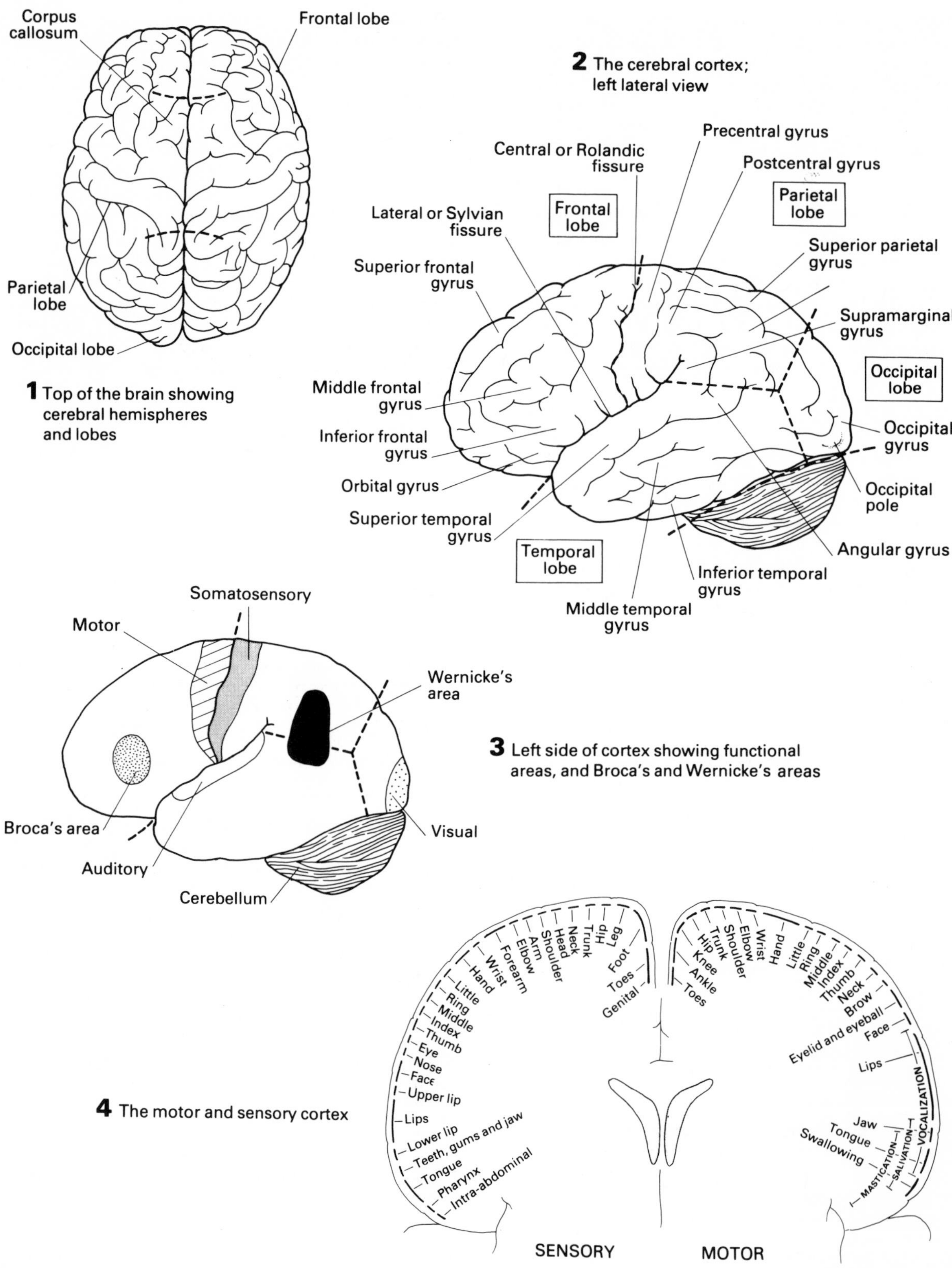

1 Top of the brain showing cerebral hemispheres and lobes

2 The cerebral cortex; left lateral view

3 Left side of cortex showing functional areas, and Broca's and Wernicke's areas

4 The motor and sensory cortex

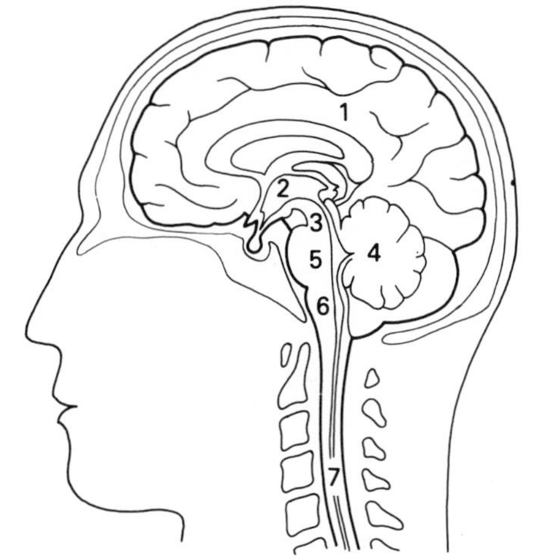

BRAIN		FOREBRAIN (prosencephalon)	TELENCEPHALON (end brain) (1)	cerebral cortex
			RHINENCEPHALON	limbic system
			DIENCEPHALON (interbrain) (2)	thalamus hypothalamus basal ganglia internal capsule
	BRAIN STEM reticular formation	MIDBRAIN	MESENCEPHALON (midbrain) (3)	midbrain
				cerebellum (4)
			METENCEPHALON (afterbrain)	pons (5)
			MYELENCEPHALON (narrow brain) (6)	medulla oblongata
SPINAL CORD (7)				

5 The regions of the brain

6 Principal structures of the brain stem and cerebellum

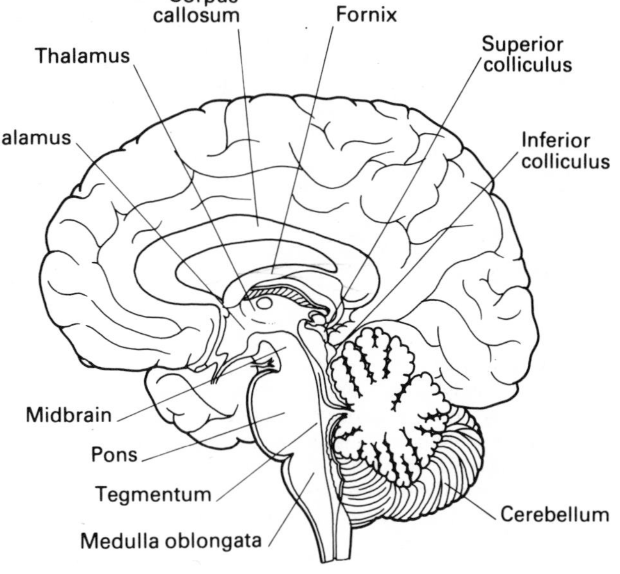

7 Dorsal view of the brain stem. The right half of the cerebellum has been removed. The left half has been drawn over to the left to expose the floor of the left ventricle

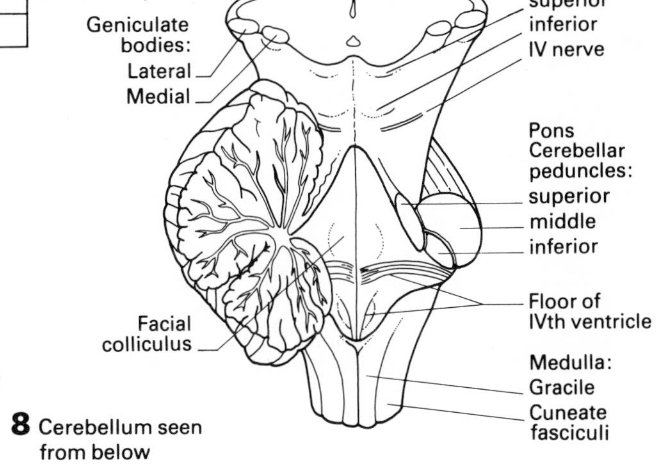

(1)
(3)
(4)
(5)
(2)

8 Cerebellum seen from below

1. Anterior lobe 2. Posterior lobe 3. Cerebellar peduncles
4. Flocculus nodule 5. Uvula

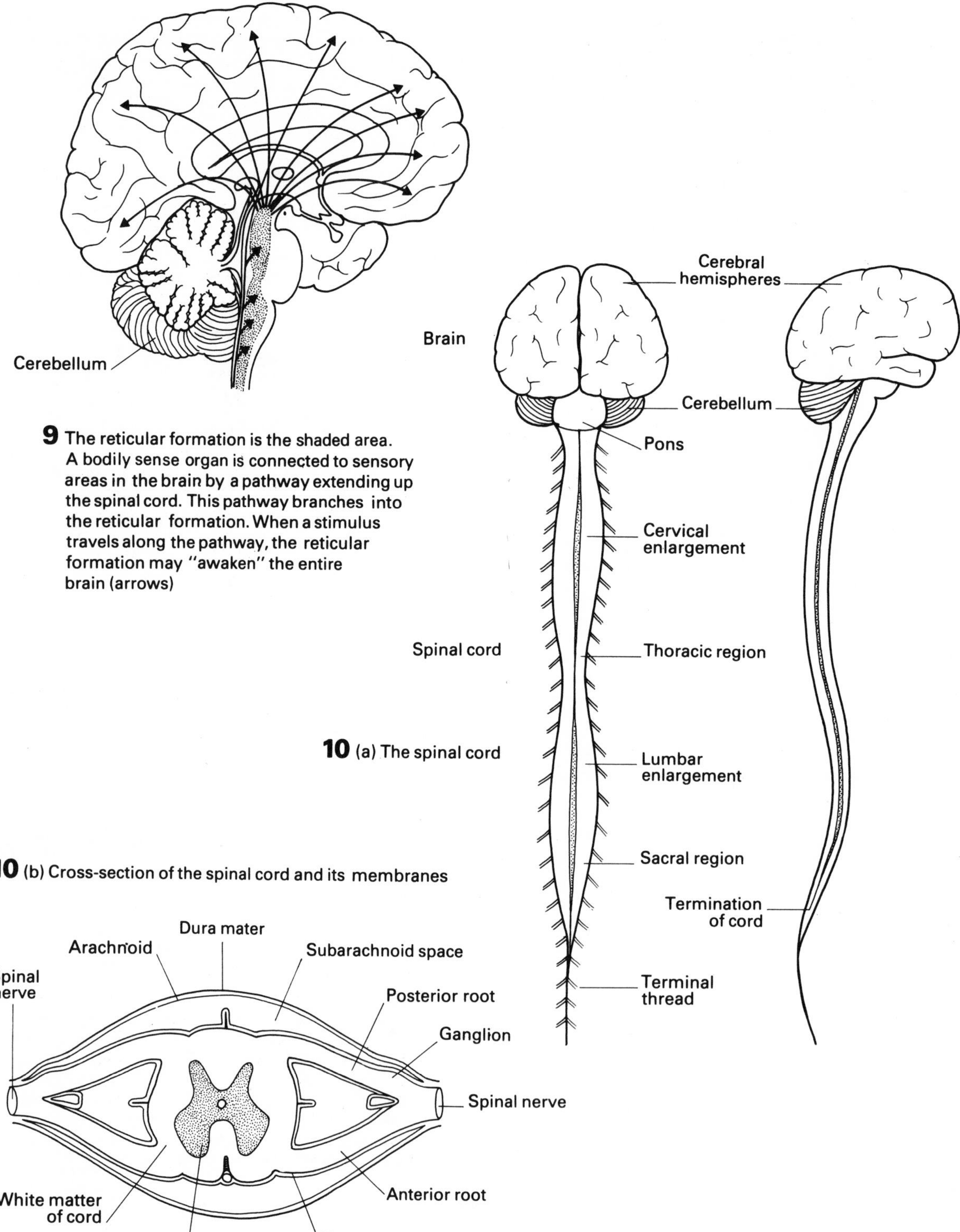

9 The reticular formation is the shaded area. A bodily sense organ is connected to sensory areas in the brain by a pathway extending up the spinal cord. This pathway branches into the reticular formation. When a stimulus travels along the pathway, the reticular formation may "awaken" the entire brain (arrows)

10 (a) The spinal cord

10 (b) Cross-section of the spinal cord and its membranes

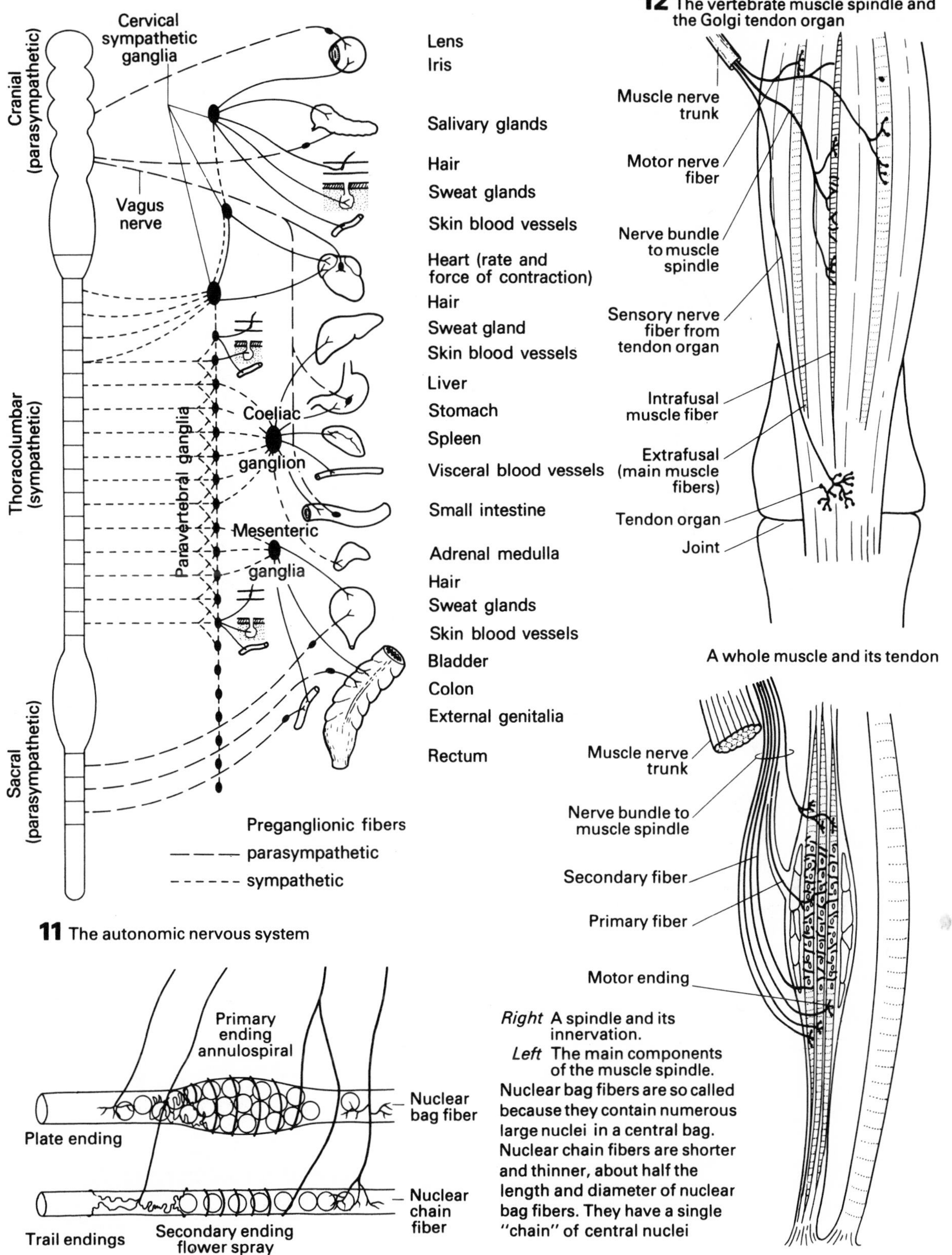

11 The autonomic nervous system

12 The vertebrate muscle spindle and the Golgi tendon organ

A whole muscle and its tendon

Right A spindle and its innervation.
Left The main components of the muscle spindle.
Nuclear bag fibers are so called because they contain numerous large nuclei in a central bag. Nuclear chain fibers are shorter and thinner, about half the length and diameter of nuclear bag fibers. They have a single "chain" of central nuclei

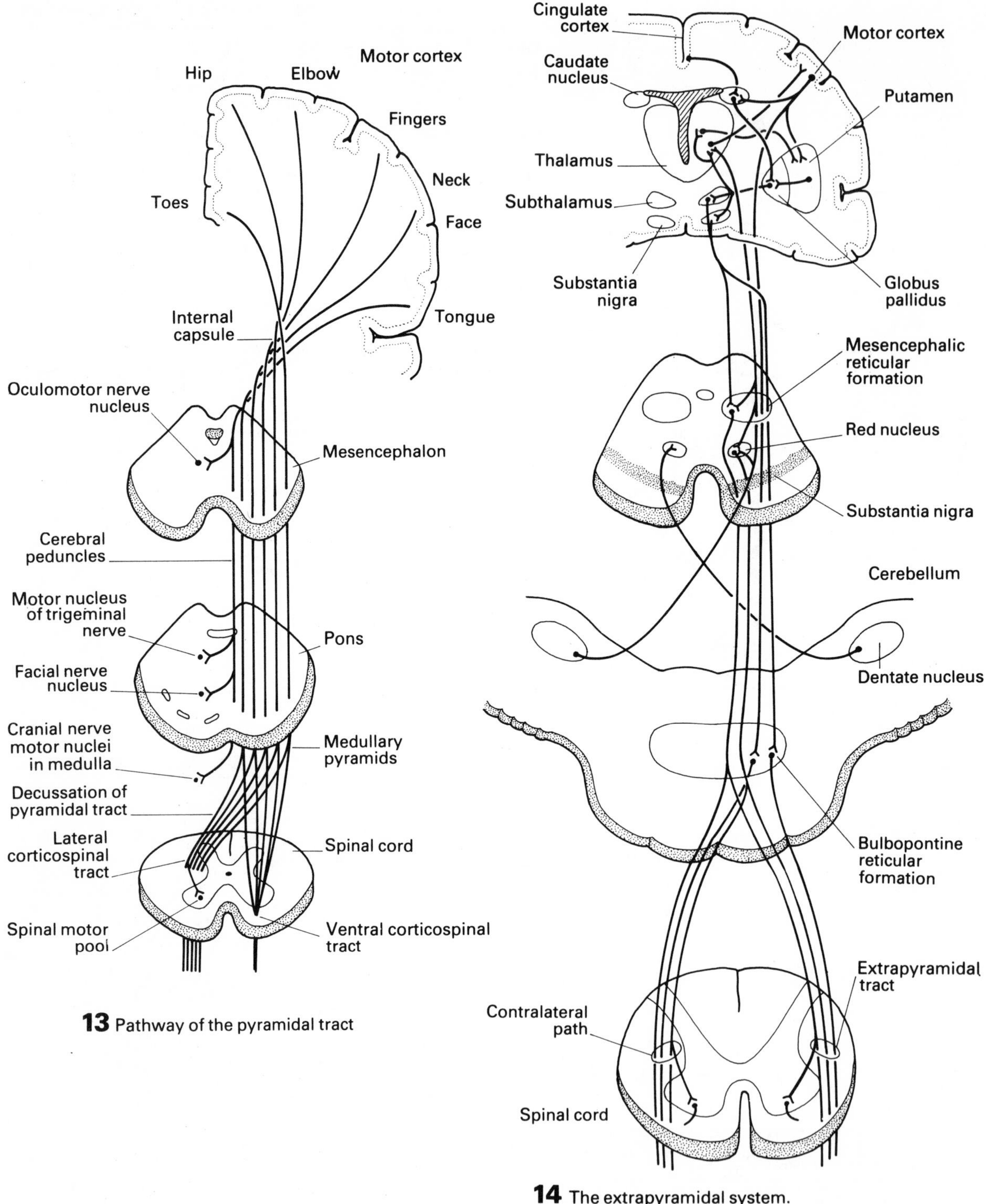

13 Pathway of the pyramidal tract

14 The extrapyramidal system.
The sections are not all to the same scale

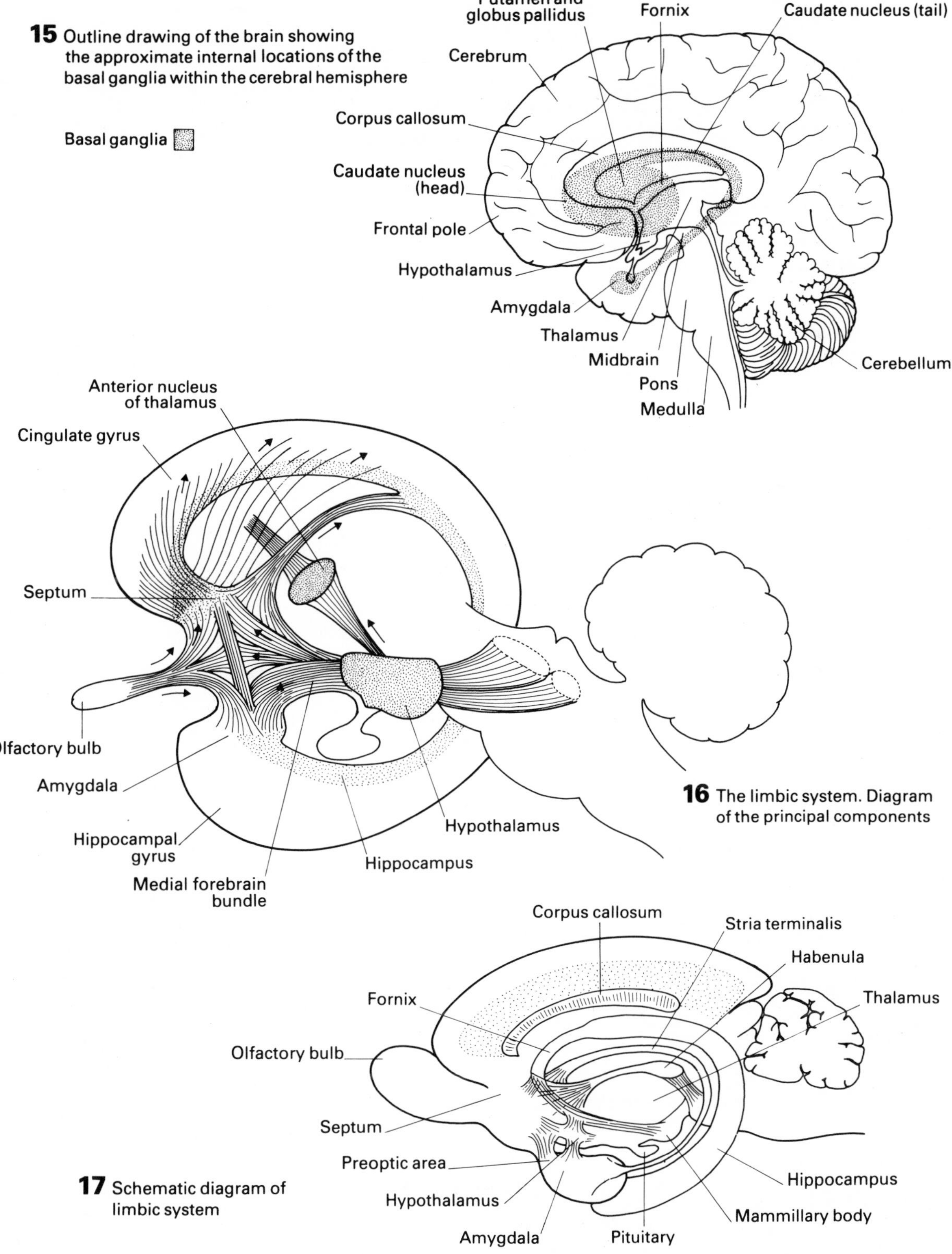

15 Outline drawing of the brain showing the approximate internal locations of the basal ganglia within the cerebral hemisphere

16 The limbic system. Diagram of the principal components

17 Schematic diagram of limbic system

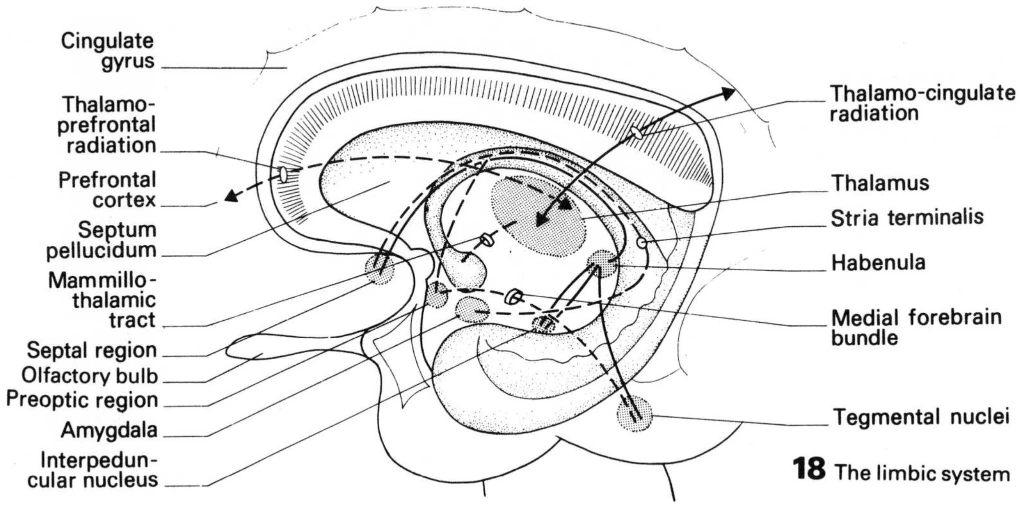

Cingulate gyrus
Thalamo-prefrontal radiation
Prefrontal cortex
Septum pellucidum
Mammillo-thalamic tract
Septal region
Olfactory bulb
Preoptic region
Amygdala
Interpedun-cular nucleus
Thalamo-cingulate radiation
Thalamus
Stria terminalis
Habenula
Medial forebrain bundle
Tegmental nuclei

18 The limbic system

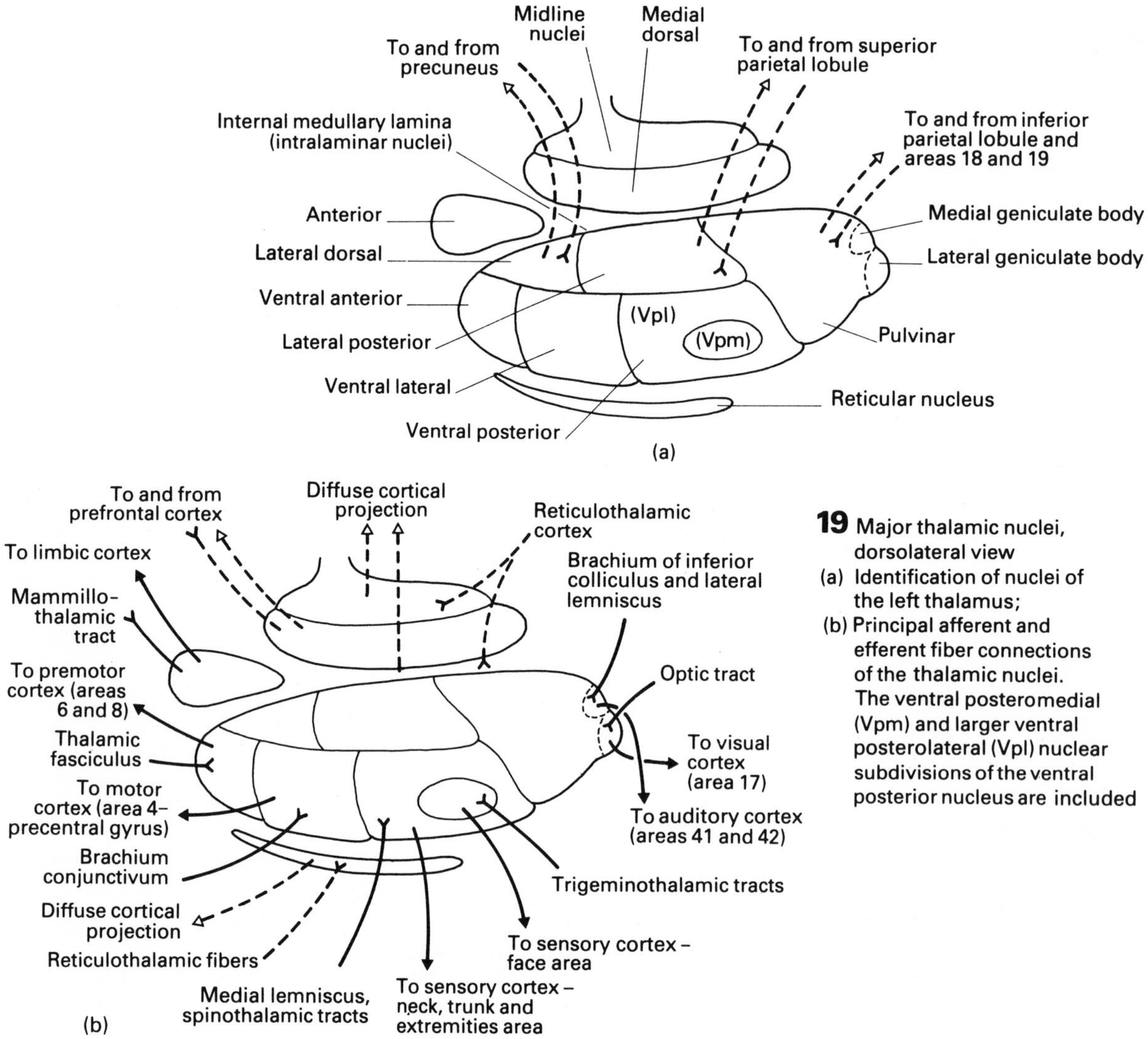

Midline nuclei
Medial dorsal
To and from precuneus
To and from superior parietal lobule
Internal medullary lamina (intralaminar nuclei)
To and from inferior parietal lobule and areas 18 and 19
Anterior
Medial geniculate body
Lateral dorsal
Lateral geniculate body
Ventral anterior
(Vpl)
(Vpm)
Lateral posterior
Pulvinar
Ventral lateral
Reticular nucleus
Ventral posterior

(a)

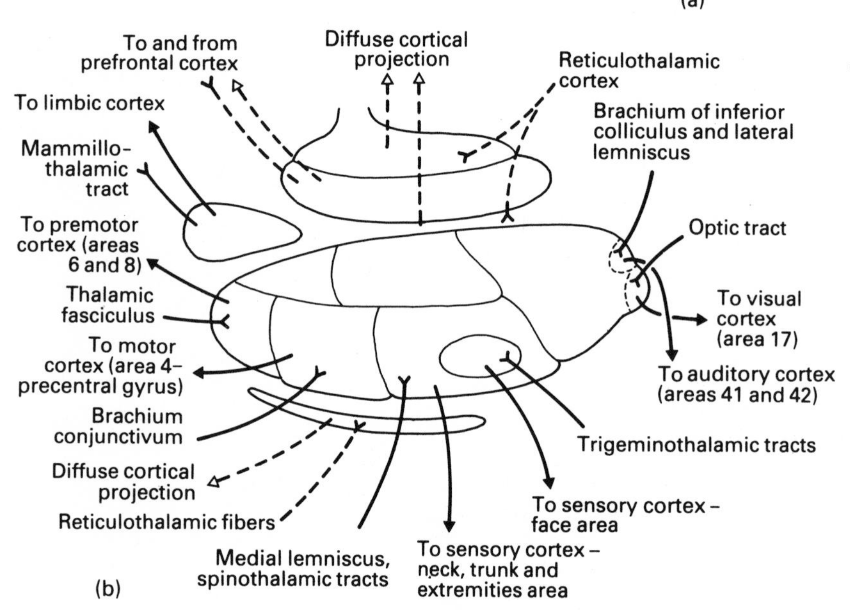

19 Major thalamic nuclei, dorsolateral view
(a) Identification of nuclei of the left thalamus;
(b) Principal afferent and efferent fiber connections of the thalamic nuclei. The ventral posteromedial (Vpm) and larger ventral posterolateral (Vpl) nuclear subdivisions of the ventral posterior nucleus are included

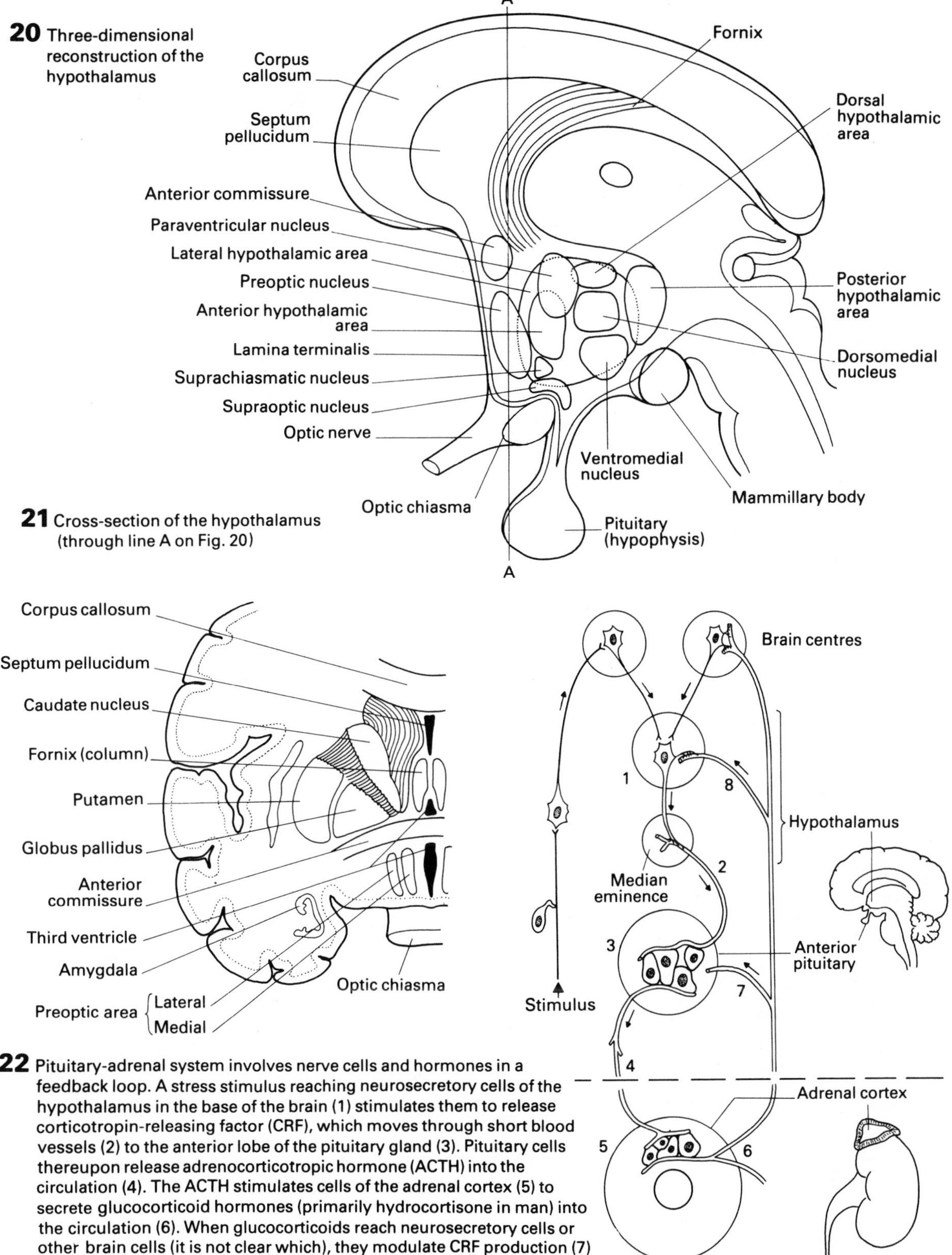

20 Three-dimensional reconstruction of the hypothalamus

21 Cross-section of the hypothalamus (through line A on Fig. 20)

22 Pituitary-adrenal system involves nerve cells and hormones in a feedback loop. A stress stimulus reaching neurosecretory cells of the hypothalamus in the base of the brain (1) stimulates them to release corticotropin-releasing factor (CRF), which moves through short blood vessels (2) to the anterior lobe of the pituitary gland (3). Pituitary cells thereupon release adrenocorticotropic hormone (ACTH) into the circulation (4). The ACTH stimulates cells of the adrenal cortex (5) to secrete glucocorticoid hormones (primarily hydrocortisone in man) into the circulation (6). When glucocorticoids reach neurosecretory cells or other brain cells (it is not clear which), they modulate CRF production (7)

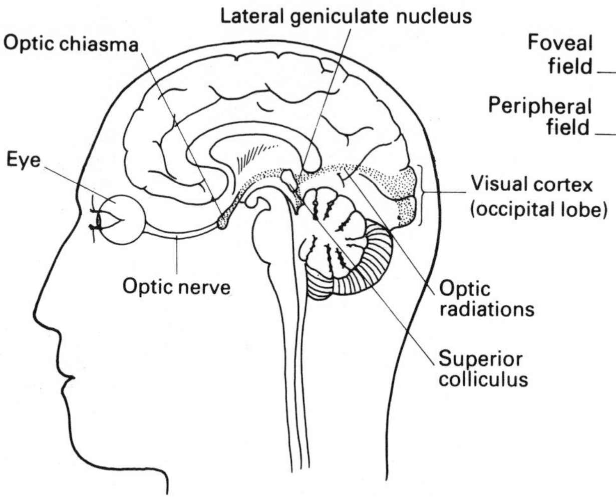

Lateral geniculate nucleus
Optic chiasma
Eye
Visual cortex
(occipital lobe)
Optic nerve
Optic
radiations
Superior
colliculus

23 Visual system. (a) Visual pathways viewed laterally

Field of vision
Foveal
field
Peripheral
field
Optic nerve
Optic chiasm
Optic tract
Lateral geniculate
nucleus
Superior colliculus
Optic radiations
(Axons from lateral
geniculate nucleus
to primary visual
cortex)
Calcarine sulcus

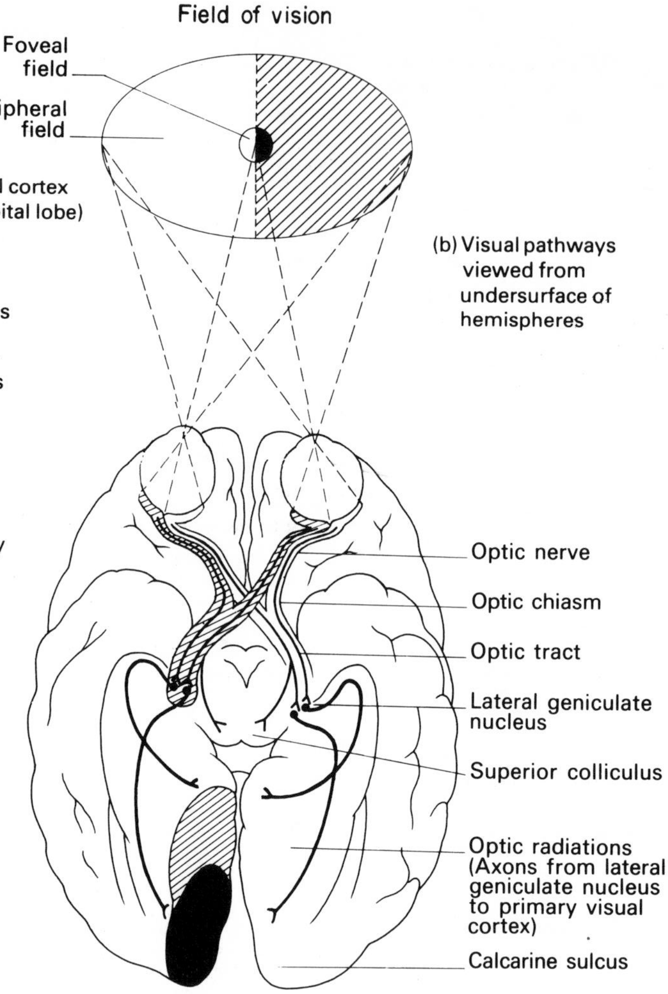

(b) Visual pathways viewed from undersurface of hemispheres

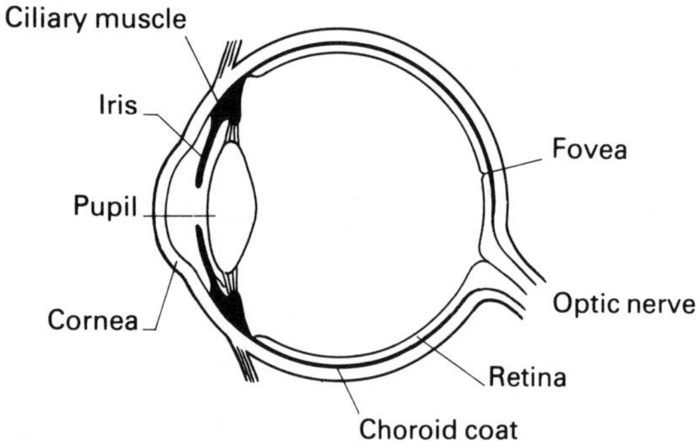

Ciliary muscle
Iris
Pupil
Cornea
Fovea
Optic nerve
Retina
Choroid coat

24 Cross-section of the eye

Pigment
epithelium
External
limiting
membrane
Rod
nucleus
Bipolar
cell
Rod
Cone
Cone
nucleus
Horizontal
cell
Centrifugal
bipolar
cell
Parasol
ganglion cell
Ganglion
cell
Internal
limiting
membrane
Receptor
layer
Outer
nuclear
layer
Outer
plexiform
layer
Inner
nuclear
layer
Inner
plexiform
layer
Ganglion
layer
Nerve
fibers
Diffuse
bipolar cell
Amacrine
cell

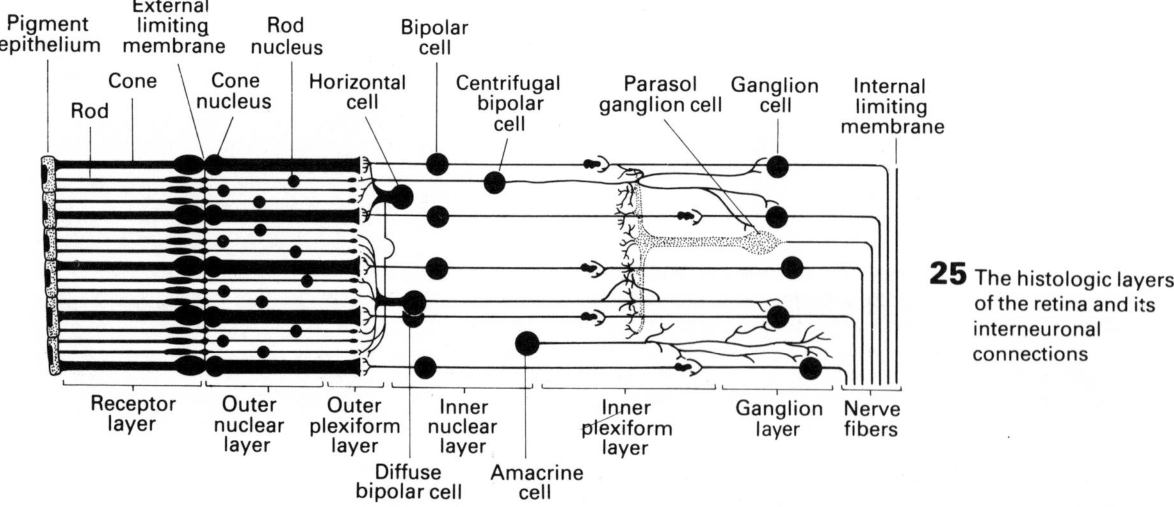

25 The histologic layers of the retina and its interneuronal connections

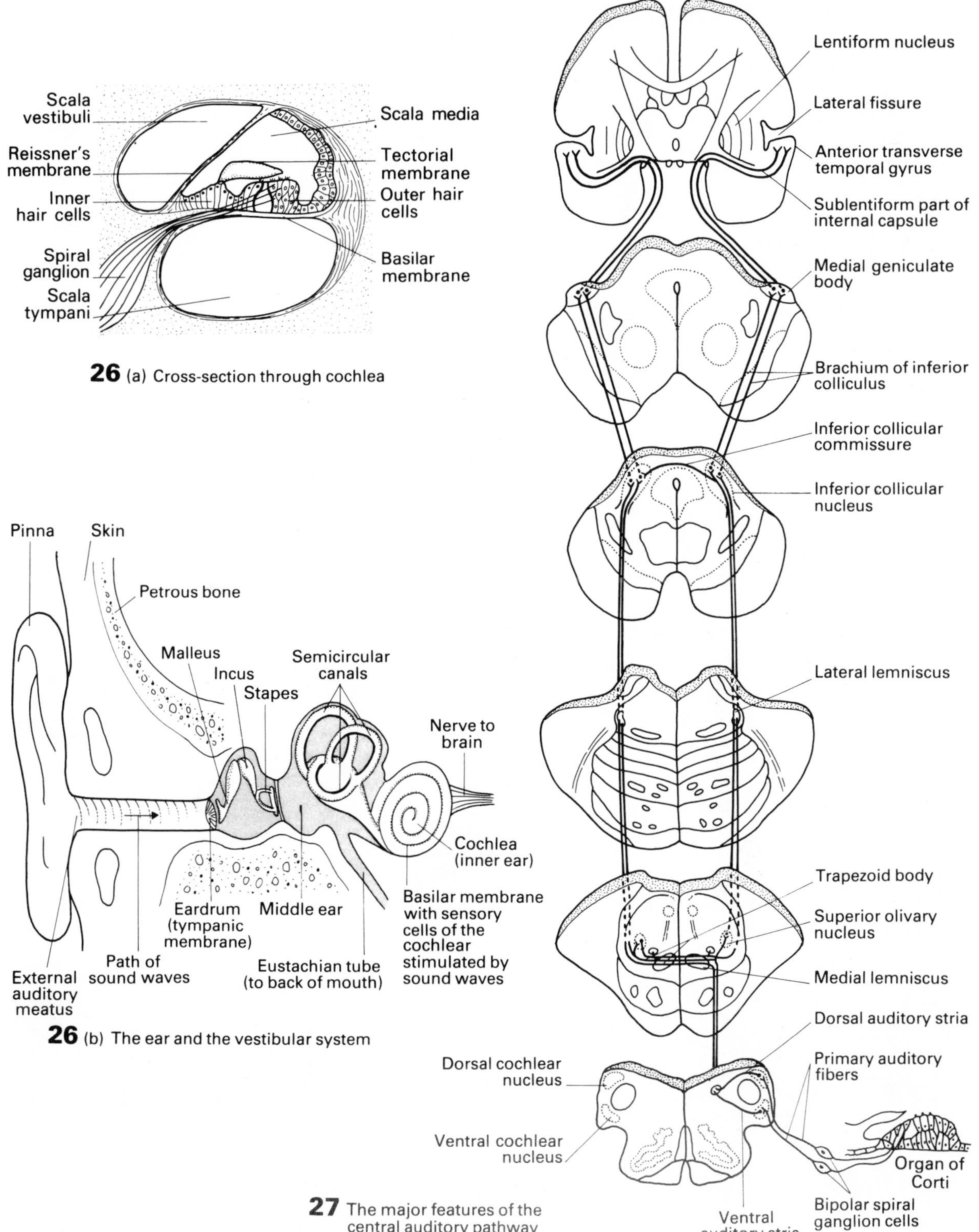

26 (a) Cross-section through cochlea

26 (b) The ear and the vestibular system

27 The major features of the central auditory pathway

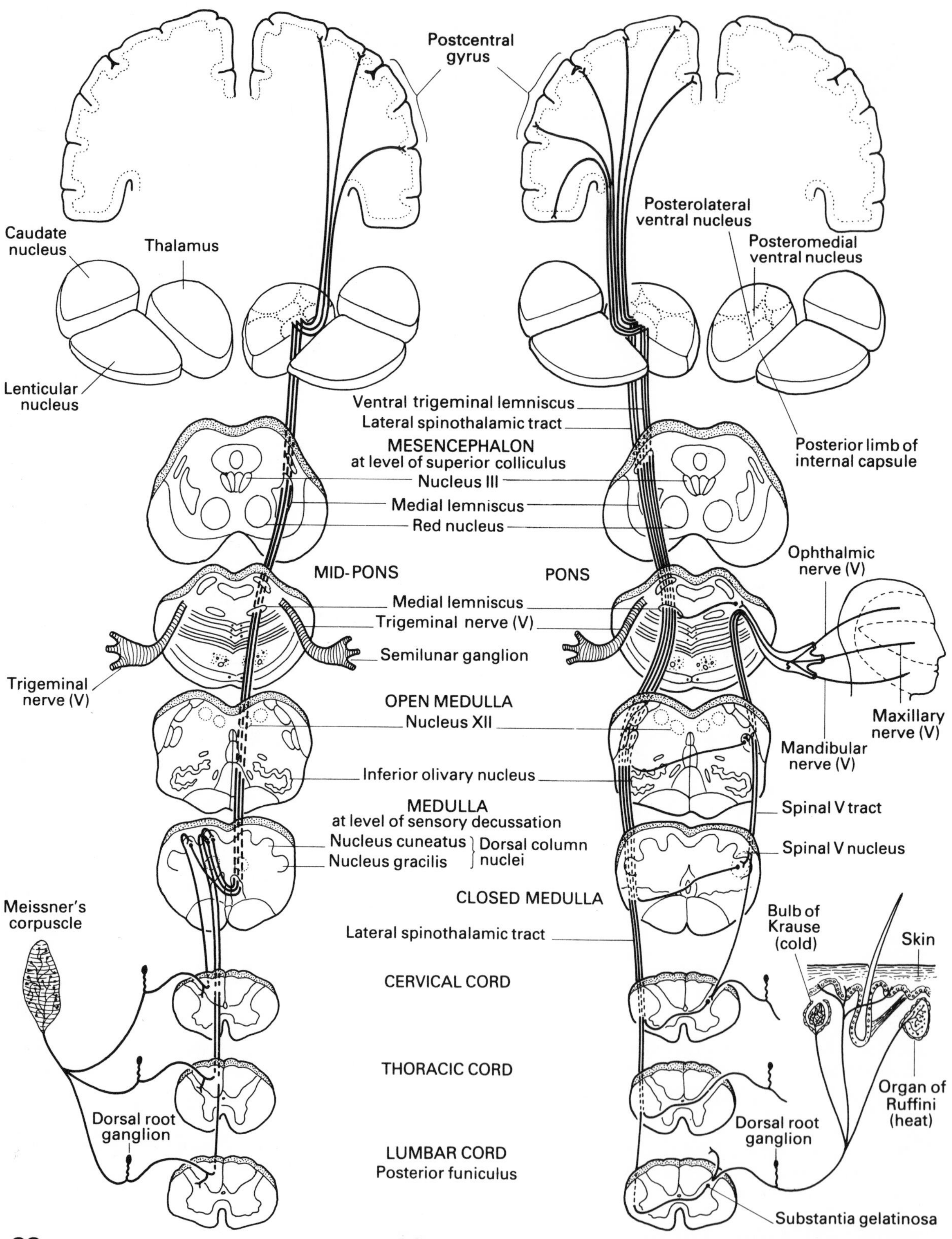

28 Pathway for tactile discrimination

29 Pathway for pain and temperature, including the types of receptors

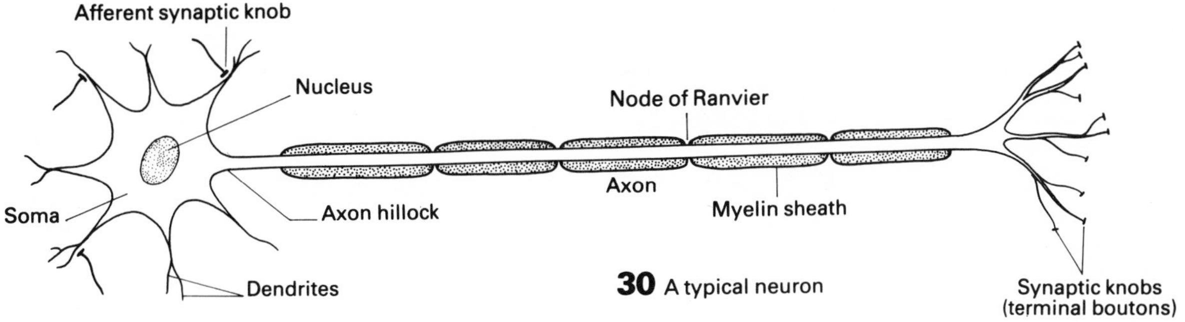

30 A typical neuron

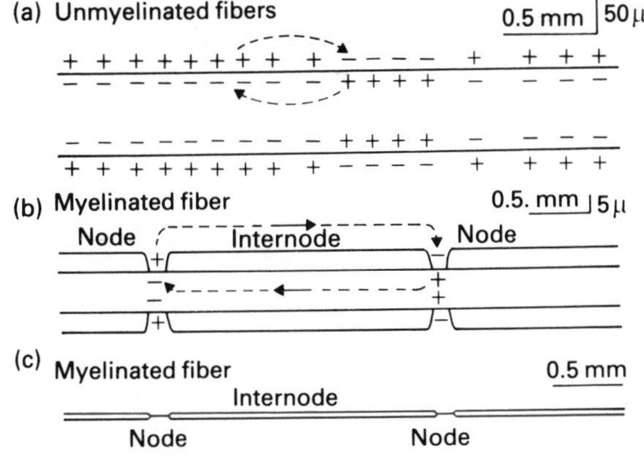

31 Propagation of impulse along a nerve fiber. In (a) there is only one line of current flow drawn in. In (b) the propagation is in a myelinated fiber, with the current flow restricted to the nodes. The dimensions in (b) are transversely exaggerated as shown by the scale, but are correctly shown in (c)

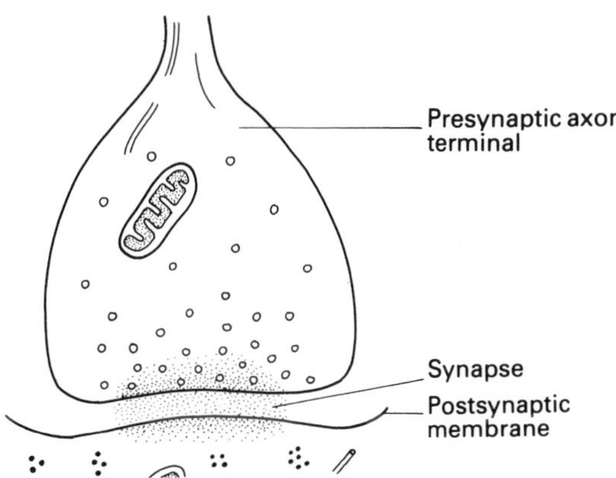

32 Diagram of a synapse. The presynaptic fiber swells to form a terminal bouton. This contains the chemical transmitter. The bouton membrane is polarized. The action potential depolarizes the membrane and the transmitter is released

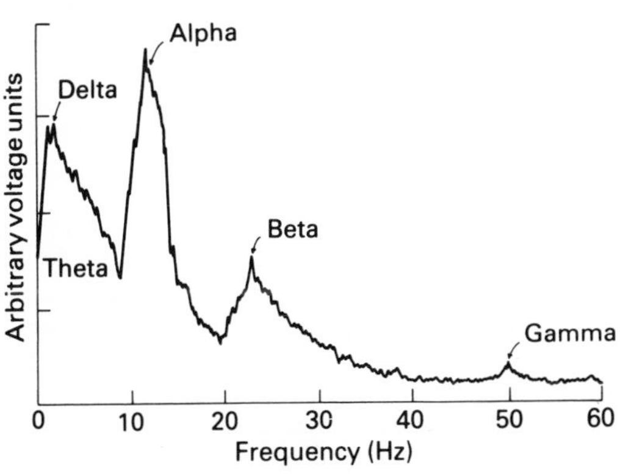

33 The frequency spectrum of brain waves. Alpha waves, 10 Hz; beta waves, 20 to 25 Hz; gamma waves, 40 to 60 Hz; and delta waves, 1 to 2 Hz. Waves of 4 to 7 Hz, between the delta and alpha waves, are called theta waves

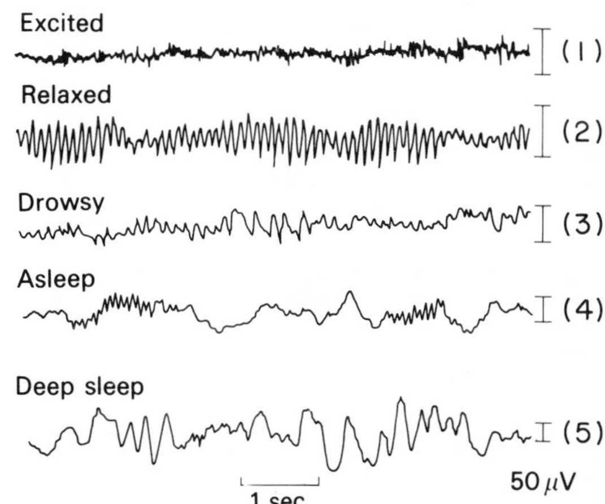

34 EEG waves: (1) β (desynchronized) wave when alert and excited; (2) α (synchronized) wave when eyes are closed and subject relaxed; (3), (4), (5) successive stages of sleep. The EEG becomes more synchronized, slower and greater in amplitude

brain and nervous system: chemistry of A major biochemical discipline, generally known as NEUROCHEMISTRY, concerned with the chemical composition of neural tissues and the functioning of the nervous system at the molecular level. Neurochemistry originated with the nineteenth-century pioneers of organic chemistry, neurophysiology and neuroanatomy, but its undoubted founder was J.L.W. Thudicum, a mid-Victorian expatriate German physician. While practicing medicine in London, Thudicum, supported by grants from government sources, conducted extensive research into brain chemistry culminating in the publication of 1884 of the classic treatise "The Chemical Constitution of the Brain" (see Drabkin 1958). Slow but steady progress over the next sixty years was followed in the post war era by an explosive growth in neurochemical knowledge. Modern neurochemistry is represented by the International Society for Neurochemistry which publishes a major journal (*Journal of Neurochemistry*) and several substantial text books (see below). It should also be emphazised that modern neurochemistry is increasingly becoming interwoven with other major disciplines in the neurosciences (e.g. neuroanatomy, neuropathology, neurophysiology, neuroendocrinology and neuro- and psychopharmacology).

Gross chemical composition. This reflects the exceptionally high ratio of surface membrane area to cell volume in the nervous system. Lipids, prominent constituents of membranes, are remarkably enriched in the brain and contribute about 50 per cent of its dry weight. Examples of lipids found only in neural tissues include galacto cerebroside (the characteristic lipid of myelin) and components of the complex class known as the gangliosides. Similarly neural tissues are greatly enriched in proteins with properties characteristic of membranes. Among the many brain-specific proteins already identified are neurafilament protein, the S-100 protein (specific to glial cells) and numerous enzymes involved in neuron-specific biosynthetic processes. Other important constituents of neural tissues are nucleic acids, nucleotides, carbohydrates, amino acids, amines and vitamins. The compounds in these categories, with certain exceptions, are found in all animal tissues but it must be emphasized that their quantitative patterns in the nervous system have many unique features.

General metabolism. The average adult human brain consumes about 49 ml of oxygen per minute or 20 per cent of the resting total body oxygen consumption. In infants this value rises to 50 per cent of the total. Under normal conditions glucose is the only substrate oxidized. Moreover the brain, unlike other organs, has only limited carbohydrate reserves and is therefore highly dependent on glucose supplied by the blood stream and exceptionally vulnerable to hypoglycaemia. In chronic starvation, however, the situation changes and the brain begins to oxidize other substrates, notably the ketone β-hydroxy-butyrate, a substance β-derived from the catabolism of fat. This explains the remarkable ability of the brain to function during prolonged starvation. The exceptionally fast rate of oxygen consumption of the brain reflects its high requirement for metabolically-derived energy in the form of the "energy-rich" compounds creatine phosphate and adenosinetriphosphate (ATP). The former functions as an energy store and the latter as the immediate source of energy for function. Both compounds are synthesized in neural tissue by enzymic pathways (glycolysis and oxidative phosphorylation) that are qualitatively similar to those in all mammalian tissues. The pattern of energy utilization in the nervous system, however, is highly distinctive. Here, major energy sources are needed for the maintenance of the ionic gradients across the nerve cell membrane that determine the membrane potential and form the basis for the conduction of the nerve impulse. (See BRAIN AND CENTRAL NERVOUS SYSTEM, figs. 30 and 31.) During conduction sodium ions enter and potassium ions leave the nerve cells through permeability changes that are independent of energy supplies. The resulting shift in membrane potential causes a relative loss in excitability and eventually the cessation of conduction. Restoration of excitability is achieved by the active transport (a process requiring energy) of sodium and potassium ions across the nerve membrane in the reverse direction. The machinery for this process (the "sodium pump") consists of a membrane-bound enzyme (known as the sodium ion-dependent adenosinetriphosphate (ATP). The energy released through this hydrolysis is coupled to ion transport by mechanisms poorly understood. In this way the incessant electrical activity of the living brain is highly dependent on a constant supply of energy, thus explaining why the brain fails so rapidly when deprived of oxygen. Other neuron-specific, though quantitively less impressive, reactions utilizing the energy of ATP include the synthesis of acetylcholine axoplasmic transport and many signal transducing processes in the sense organs.

The *in vivo* coupling of energy utilization to function in discrete areas of animal brain has been greatly advanced by the introduction by Sokoloff of the deoxyglucose technique. Carbon-labelled deoxyglucose is used as a tracer. When injected into animals the brain cells accumulate this substance at a rate proportional to their functional activity. Subsequent determination of the amount of radio-carbon in the tissue by the technique of radioautography gives an accurate quantitative measure of the activity of individual neuronal systems.

Chemical anatomy. This term covers the precise localization of molecules in tissue structures. Owing to the extraordinary cellular complexity of the nervous system progress in this area has been slow: yet such knowledge is clearly essential for the formation of hypotheses regarding the functional significance of the chemical constituents of nervous tissue. Traditional methods of regional and microdissection, cell fractionation and the preparation of subcellular structures (nuclei, mitochondria etc.) have provided limited information, but the striking advances have come from new approaches to the problem. First, extensive information on neuronal pathways has been gained by lesioning techniques in which degeneration of specific neuronal tracts is induced, either by surgical intervention or by the injection into the brain of specific cytotoxins. Subsequent analysis of the lesioned tissue alongside normal tissue from the same area provides information on the original composition of the degenerated neurons. For example the cytotoxin 6-hydroxydopamine, which causes a specific degeneration of neurons utilizing catecholamines, has been extensively used to map the projections of the dopamine and noradrenaline (see NOREPINEPHRINE) neurotransmitter systems. Secondly new developments in histochemistry have made equally major contributions. Fluorescent microscopy, a technique due to Falck and Hillarp from Sweden, has permitted the detailed mapping in the brain of neuronal systems utilizing serotonin and catecholamines as neurotransmitters. More recently immunocytochemical methods have proved invaluable, particularly since they permit the localization of antigenic molecules (e.g. enzymes and neuropeptides) to be studied at the very high magnifications available in the electron microscope. Two striking examples of the application of immunocytochemistry to the chemical anatomy of the nervous system are: the specific localization of the enzyme glutamic acid decarboxylase (responsible for the synthesis of the inhibitory neurotransmitter γ-aminobutyric acid) in the nerve terminals of the Purkinje cells in the deep cerebellar nuclei; and the demonstration of the coexistence of several neuropeptides with monoamine neurotransmitters in neurons.

Chemistry of synaptic transmission (figs. 30, 32). Communication between neurons in the mammalian nervous system occurs almost exclusively by chemical transmission. Neurotransmitters (see NEUROTRANSMITTER SYSTEMS) are chemical messengers synthesized by enzymes present exclusively in the nerve axon terminals (or presynaptic "boutons") and stored in structures known as synaptic vesicles. In general each nerve cell synthesizes and stores only one neurotransmitter, which is released into the synaptic cleft by nerve impulses traveling down the axon. After diffusing across the gap the neurotransmitter is bound to specific proteins located on the surface membrane of the postsynaptic neuron, known as receptors. The binding of neurotransmitter to its receptor initiates changes in the permeability of the postsynaptic cell membrane that either increase (excitatory neurotransmitters) or decrease (inhibitory neurotransmitters) its level of excitability, and therefore its tendency to transmit by conduction the message to further nerve cells.

The molecular events that underlie the several stages of chemical neurotransmission are only partly understood. The most complete evidence concerns the enzymic reactions involved in neurotransmitter synthesis, which are known in detail in the case of acetylcholine, γ-aminobutyric acids, dopamine, noradrenaline and serotonin. Much evidence is also available for mechanisms responsible for the inactivation of these neurotransmitters, the process that terminates transmission. Acetylcholine is hydrolyzed by the enzyme acetylcholinesterase; histochemical studies have shown this enzyme to be highly localized in the region of the synaptic cleft. The choline liberated by acetylcholinesterase action is transported back into the presynaptic terminal and utilized for further synthesis of acetylcholine. For the other neurotransmitters mentioned above inactivation occurs either through reuptake of the unchanged molecule or enzymic degradation; for example the enzyme monoamine oxidase serves to inactivate the neurotransmitters serotonin, dopamine and noradrenaline. The molecular events involved in the process of neutrotransmitter release and in neurotransmitter-receptor interaction are being intensively studied, but the current picture is far from complete. However, extensive knowledge is now available on the molecular structure of the acetylcholine receptor and work on the γ-aminobutyric acid receptor is well advanced.

Chemistry of the nervous system in man. By far the greater part of contemporary knowledge of the chemistry of the nervous system has come from studies in animals. The development of human neurochemistry has inevitably been slow because of the inaccessibility of the brain in the living subject and the unavailability of fresh human neural tissue for analysis. However, recent work has shown that for many purposes it is possible to obtain useful data by analysing tissue from cadavers taken at autopsy many hours after death. At present analysis of such material indicates that the chemistry of the human nervous system closely resembles that of other mammalian species, although it is possible that more extensive studies will reveal significant differences.

In the medical field important advances in our understanding of the pathogenesis of certain diseases of the nervous system have accrued from chemical analysis of brain tissue taken from patients after death. In Parkinson's disease (the "shaking palsy") the work of Hornykiewicz and others demonstrated a dramatic decrease in the concentration of the neurotransmitter dopamine in the basal ganglia (a brain region concerned with the control of voluntary movement – see MOVEMENT, BRAIN MECHANISMS OF) of patients dying with the disease. This discovery led to the introduction of treatment of Parkinson's disease with levodopa, a drug that increases dopamine concentrations in the basal ganglia and ameliorates many of the symptoms of the disease. In another disorder of movement, Huntington's chorea, analysis of autopsy tissue has demonstrated a significant loss of the neurotransmitter system utilising γ-aminobutyric acid, and to a lesser extent of the acetylcholine system. In dementia a more specific loss of the acetylcholine neurotransmitter system has been demonstrated. **RR**

Bibliography

Drabkin, D.L. 1958: *Thudicum: chemist of the brain*, Philadelphia: Saunders.

McIlwain, H. and Bachelard, H.S. 1971: *Biochemistry and the central nervous system*. 4th edn. Edinburgh: Churchill Livingstone.

Siegel, George J., et al., eds., 1981: *Basic neurochemistry*, 3rd edn., Boston: Little Brown.

Siesjo, B.K. 1978: *Brain energy metabolism*, Chichester and New York: John Wiley.

brain damage *See* Recovery of function after brain damage

brain mechanisms of movement Studied most often in

psychology using animal models of the symptoms of movement disorders. This approach provides an understanding of the neural bases of normal movement, and leads to discoveries of the brain areas and neurotransmitter systems responsible for abnormal movement.

Laboratory studies of brain mechanisms of movement usually take two general forms: (1) the use of experimentally-induced brain damage and/or (2) the administration of centrally acting drugs. Techniques used to produce experimental brain damage include procedures such as electrolytic or radio frequency lesions (which destroy tissue), direct infusion of neurotoxic substances into the brain (such chemicals destroy particular neuronal systems relatively selectively), aspiration of tissue and tissue transection (cutting). Centrally acting drugs are administered systemically (orally or through the muscles, skin, abdominal cavity or veins), or directly into the brain and, in general, such drugs either elicit disturbances in movement or restore more normal movement to damaged subjects. Any of these techniques may be combined in a single experiment.

The areas of greatest interest to psychologists who study movement are the motor areas of the cerebral cortex (BRAIN AND CENTRAL NERVOUS SYSTEM: ILLUSTRATIONS, figs. 3 and 4), the so-called EXTRAPYRAMIDAL system which includes a number of structures collectively referred to as the BASAL GANGLIA, the BRAINSTEM (a lower area), and the CEREBELLUM (a lower motor integration area). Areas often of special interest also include the median raphénucleus and the lateral hypothalamic area (figs. 5–8, 15 and 20). Damage or chemical manipulation of these areas can produce a variety of symptoms (varying by area) that mimic those observed in certain neurological disorders such as Parkinson's disease, epilepsy and Huntington's chorea. Some commonly studied symptoms are: Akinesia or bradykinesia (a loss or slowing of locomotion and movement), hyperkinesia (an abnormal quickening of locomotion and movement), seizure, catalepsy (the maintenance of awkward postures for long periods of time), drug-induced dyskinesias (involuntary movements of several types), tremor, muscular rigidity (which prevents normal movement), abnormalities in postural support, and impairment of righting reflexes (for detailed definitions, see Klawans 1973). Several forms of repetitive, stereotyped movements (such as those produced by amphetamines) are also studied.

A number of substances normally produced by the brain ("endogenous" substances) are known to regulate or affect movement. A few of these (putative neurotransmitters) are DOPAMINE, ACETYLCHOLINE, NOREPINEPHRINE, SEROTONIN, and gamma-aminobutyric acid (Klawans, 1973). Certain endogenous opiates, such as Beta-endorphin (Tseng et al. 1980) are also believed to affect movement. Selected symptoms, and their possible neurochemical and anatomical bases will be discussed.

Akinesia/bradykinesia often appears when dopamine systems are disrupted. In particular, manipulations that disturb the nigrostriatal dopamine system (a system that begins in the substantia nigra (fig. 14) and projects to the neostriatum) result in akinesia/bradykinesia (Hornykiewicz 1975). Thus, normal locomotion and movement depend, in part, upon intact dopamine systems. Techniques used to disrupt brain dopamine systems include focal (on a particular place in the brain) or intraventricular (through the brain's ventricles) infusion of the neurotoxin 6-hydroxydopamine (Ungerstedt 1971), a chemical that selectively destroys dopamine and norepinephrine neurons; systemic administration of drugs such as haloperidol (Hornykiewicz 1975) which block brain dopamine receptors; and electrolytic lesions of the lateral HYPOTHALAMUS (Levitt and Teitelbaum 1975), through which the nigrostriatal dopamine system courses (Ungerstedt 1971). Akinesia can also be produced by systemic injection of sufficient amounts of drugs such as reserpine (Hornykiewicz 1972), which depletes levels of dopamine, serotonin and norepinephrine; morphine and other opiate-like substances (DeRyck, Schallert and Teitelbaum 1980; Tseng et al., 1980); and general anesthetics. In Parkinson's disease (a disease in which akinesia is a prominent symptom), there is a loss of nigrostriatal dopamine neurons that can be compensated for, in part, by administration of drugs such as L-DOPA which increase brain dopamine function (Barbeau, 1962). However, the loss of excitatory dopamine systems is probably not the only mechanism that interferes with kinesia. Recent research has shown that methysergide (a serotonin receptor blocker) can reverse the profound akinesia produced by lesions of the lateral hypothalamus (Chesire and Teitelbaum 1982), and that atropine (a drug that antagonizes acetylcholine) can reverse the akinesia produced by 6-hydroxydopamine. Thus, the loss of excitatory dopamine systems in conjunction with active inhibition by intact systems may combine to produce certain forms of akinesia. *Hyperkinesia* is also a feature of certain neurological disorders, including some forms of Parkinsonism (Parkinson 1817). Hyperkinetic disorders take several forms, and vary in expression from choreatic (jerking) movements (a symptom of Huntington's chorea) to rapidly accelerating forward locomotion (seen in some forms of Parkinsonism). Lesions of the caudate nucleus (part of the neostriatum) are often used as an animal model of Huntington's chorea (figs. 14 and 15). Caudate lesions elicit a form of "cursive" hyperkinesia or "running headlong forward" during which the animal runs straight forward and is not inhibited by obstacles (Mettler 1942). In Huntington's chorea, jerky movements have been attributed, in part, to excessive effects of dopamine on neurons that have been damaged or changed by the disease process (Klawans et al., 1981). Another area that appears to be involved in hyperkinesia is the median raphénucleus, a serotonin-rich area that is part of a system involved in sleep and waking (Jouvet 1968). Although the experimental results are controversial, lesions of this nucleus can produce excessive activity and locomotion (Jacobs, Wise and Taylor 1974). Serotonin may inhibit locomotion via other areas of the brain as well. Lesions of the nucleus reticularis tegmenti pontis in the brainstem of rats produce rapidly accelerating forward locomotion that (similar to some Parkinson's patients) can coexist in the presence of severe dopamine deficiency (Cheng 1981).

When such animals recover, so that their locomotion is no longer so rapid, the serotonin receptor blockers methysergide and metergoline can fully reinstate the previous level of rapid locomotion (Chesire, Cheng and Teitelbaum 1982). Furthermore, the administration of L-5-hydroxytryptophan (which increases levels of brain serotonin) can inhibit these animals (ibid.). Interestingly, animals with damage in this nucleus are not inhibited by doses of morphine that render normal rats completely akinetic (Chesire, Cheng and Teitelbaum, in press). Thus, the nucleus reticularis tegmenti pontis may be part of a final common system that inhibits locomotion (see Cheng et al. 1981).

Among the drugs that can produce experimental *catalepsy* are haloperidol, morphine and reserpine. Reserpine is widely used in the treatment of Huntington's chorea, which has sometimes been described as the reverse of Parkinsonism (Klawans et al., 1981). Haloperidol and morphine appear to produce two very different forms of catalepsy that may reflect different adaptive states (De Ryck, Schallert and Teitelbaum 1980). Although sufficient amounts of either drug result in complete akinesia for several hours, the morphine-treated rat lacks postural support and righting reflexes (two abilities that are retained by haloperidol-treated rats). The morphine-treated rat, although rigid, lies in a posture resembling that of forward locomotion, while the haloperidol-treated rat sits crouched with a hunched spine. Thus, De Ryck, Schallert and Teitelbaum have proposed that morphine catalepsy may be organized to permit readiness for forward locomotion, while haloperidol catalepsy seems organized to permit the maintenance of stable equilibrium.

Seizure can originate at virtually any location in the brain, and may remain local or spread and become generalized (Klawans et al., 1981). There are many possible causes of seizure, including tumors, epilepsy, and brain diseases . Drugs that interfere with normal inhibitory substances in the brain can also induce seizure. These include drugs that antagonize gamma-aminobutyric acid (such as picrotoxin and bicuculline), and other convulsants (such as strychnine;). Many drugs show anticonvulsant activity, including some barbiturates such as phenobarbital.

Two forms of *tremor* are frequently distinguished: (1) intention tremor (a symptom of Wilson's and other diseases) which occurs during voluntary movement and (2) resting tremor (a feature of Parkinsonism) which usually occurs when the involved area is not engaged in voluntary movement, but may continue when such movement is initiated (Klawans 1973). Tremor may be partly dependent on serotonin systems, for it is one symptom of Parkinsonism that does not always respond as well as others to L-DOPA (Klawans 1973). In monkeys, resting tremor can be produced by lesions of the ventromedial tegmental area, and such tremor has been alleviated by administering serotonin or dopamine agonists (drugs that facilitate these systems) (Goldstein et al. 1969). However, the role of serotonin agonists in Parkinson's and other disease states has not been completely investigated, and controversy still exists (Birkmayer and Riederer 1978).

Drug-induced dyskinesias are frequently choreatic in appearance, and can occur after prolonged treatment with L-DOPA or neuroleptic drugs ("Tardive" dyskinesia) that are used to treat mental disorders (Klawans 1981). Amphetamine abuse may also produce dyskinesias (Klawans 1981). In Parkinson's disease, dyskinetic movements are frequently associated with the use of L-DOPA in high doses, or at lesser doses but in patients with a long duration of the disease (Klawans et al. 1981). In all three cases (Parkinsonism, Tardive, and Amphetamine abuse), the appearance of dyskinesia is believed to be partly a function of excessive sensitivity of dopamine receptors to the drugs (Klawans et al. 1981). RMC

Bibliography

Barbeau, A. 1962: The pathogenesis of Parkinson's disease. A new hypothesis. *Canadian Medical Association journal* 87, 802–7.

Birkmayer, W. and Riederer, P. 1978: Serotonin and extrapyramidal disorders, In *Serotonin in mental abnormalities.* ed. D.J. Boullin, New York: John Wiley.

Cheng, J.T., et al. 1981: Galloping induced by pontine tegmentum damage in rats: A form of "Parkinsonian festination" not blocked by haloperidol, *Proceedings of the National Academy of Sciences USA* 78, 3279–83.

Chesire, R.M. and Teitelbaum, P. 1982: Methysergide releases locomotion without support in lateral hypothalamic akinesia, *Physiology and behavior* 28, 335–47.

Chesire, R.M., Cheng, J.T. and Teitelbaum, P. 1982: Reinstatement of festinating forward locomotion by antiserotonergic drugs in rats partially recovered from damage in the region of the nucleus reticularis tegmenti pontis, *Experimental neurology.* 77, 286–94.

——— in press: The inhibition of movement by morphine or haloperidol depends on an intact nucleus reticularis tegmenti pontis. *Physiology and behavior.*

De Ryck, M., Schallert, T. and Teitelbaum, P. 1980: Morphine versus haloperidol catalepsy in the rat: A behavioral analysis of postural support mechanisms. *Brain research.* 201, 143–72.

Goldstein, M., et al. 1969: Drug-induced relief of the tremor in monkeys with mesencephalic lesions, *Nature* 224, 382–84.

Hornykiewicz, O. 1972: Biochemical and pharmacological aspects of akinesia. In *Parkinson's disease.* ed. J. Siegfried, Bern Stuttgart Vienna: Hans Huber.

——— 1975: Parkinsonism induced by dopaminergic antagonists. In *Advances in neurology*, ed. D.B. Calne, T.N. Chase and A. Barbeau. 9, New York: Raven Press.

Jacobs, B.L., Wise, W.D. and Taylor, K.M. 1974: Differential behavioral and neurochemical effects following lesions of the dorsal or median raphe nuclei in rats. *Brain research.* 79, 353–61.

Jouvet, M. 1968: Insomnia and decrease of cerebral 5-hydroxytryptamine after destruction of the raphe system in the cat. *Advances in pharmacology.* 6B, 265–79.

Klawans, H.L. 1973: *The pharmacology of extrapyramidal movement disorders.* Basle: S. Karger.

Klawans, H.L., et al. 1981: *Textbook of clinical neuropharmacology.* New York: Raven Press.

Levitt, D.R. and Teitelbaum, P. 1975: Somnolence, akinesia and sensory activation of motivated behavior in the lateral hypothalamic syndrome. *Proceedings of the National Academy of Sciences USA* 72, 2819–23.

Mettler, F.A. 1942: The relation between pyramidal and extrapyramidal function. *Research Publications of the Association of Nervous and Mental Diseases* 21, 150–227.

Parkinson, J. 1817 (1955): An essay on the shaking palsy. Reprinted in *James Parkinson*, ed. M. Critchley. London: Macmillan (1955).

Tseng, L.F., et al. 1980: B–Endorphin: Central sites of analgesia, catalepsy and body temperature changes in rats. *Journal of pharmacology and experimental therapeutics*. 214, 328–32.

Ungerstedt, U. 1971: Adipsia and aphagia after 6-hydroxydopamine-induced degeneration of the nigrostriatal system. *Acta Physiologica Scandinavica*. (Suppl.) 367–95–122.

brain stem The hind- and mid-brain area of the brain, located between the spinal cord and diencephalon (BRAIN AND CENTRAL NERVOUS SYSTEM: ILLUSTRATIONS figs. 5–7). The principal structures of the hind-brain are the medulla, pons, and cerebellum. The medulla is the most caudal structure in the brain stem. Several ascending and descending pathways as well as cranial nerves pass through this region which also contains nuclei concerned with basic life systems (e.g., heart action, respiration). The pons, located just anterior to the medulla, contains cell bodies for cranial nerves serving the head and face regions as well as a number of nuclei which interconnect separate brain structures. In particular there are major connections with the cerebellum, located dorsal to the medulla and pons, and primarily involved in motor co-ordination. Anterior to the hind-brain is the mid-brain which consists of the tectum and tegmentum. The tectum contains two prominences – the superior colliculus, involved in processing visual information and the inferior colliculus, which serves a similar function in audition. The tegmentum is an extension of the brain stem reticular formation which forms a central core of nuclei and pathways transmitting impulses dorsally to specific processing points at higher brain levels as well as motor impulses ventrally to the spinal cord. A separate reticular system (fig. 9) projects diffusely to cortical regions, mediating an activating function that is important for sleep, arousal, and attentional processes. GWi

brain stimulation and memory (For sites see BRAIN AND CENTRAL NERVOUS SYSTEM: ILLUSTRATIONS, figs. 2, 17, 19 and 21.) Brain stimulation via electrodes has been used as a tool for analysing the neurology of memory. Penfield and his colleagues provided some of the first reports of subjective effects of intracranial stimulation in conscious human patients during the course of surgery on the temporal lobe, as an aid to locating epileptic foci (see Penfield 1958). In roughly one third of the patients, the stimulation mimicked their characteristic epileptic auras, including not only bodily sensations, but also apparently memorial effects. For example stimulation of the medial temporal lobe induced feelings of strangeness in the present surroundings and déjà vu, whereas similar stimulation of lateral aspects of the temporal lobe repeatedly resulted in banal and stereotyped recollections, often related to emotionally significant events. Although both auditory and visual experiences occurred, together with the appropriate emotional tone, the minute detail and sense of immediacy experienced was different from that of normal recollection and resembled hallucinations. For a small number of patients the subjective sensations were not directly related to the experiential content of their spontaneous seizures.

Many aspects of Penfield's findings have been replicated. For example Bickford et al. (1958) found similar results with implanted electrodes and repeated testing involving interviews. Elicitation of that same memory could be achieved providing that stimulation parameters and neuroanatomical placement were held constant, although other studies have emphasized the variability of the responses (Stevens et al. 1969).

Although Penfield's results have been widely used in the context of the neurology of memory and in support of psychoanalytic concepts such as repression (see Kubie 1953), they can now be seen to be of more limited value. This is because the apparently memorial effects could not often be related to actual events in the subject's previous experience. The hallucinatory quality of the lateral temporal lobe effects, in particular, make it likely that many of the responses were confabulated. Mahl et al. (1964) found that momentary predispositions and thoughts at the time of stimulation were important determinants of the response. Furthermore, although the quality of the subjective phenomena have a degree of neuroanatomical specificity, similar results have been reported not only following stimulation of the hippocampus and amygdala, which are closely related to the temporal lobe, but also in medial thalamic regions (Flanigin et al. 1976). These results therefore limit the neurological significance of the effects.

Penfield also found some amnesic effects following temporal lobe stimulation, particularly in the recall of words or names. Similar effects have been found by Ojeman (1982), but also at frontal and parietal cortical sites. Ojeman has also characterized deficits in short term verbal memory resulting from stimulation to discrete frontal, parietal and occasionally temporal sites which are dissociable from sites producing naming or motor deficits in speech. Effects more similar to the amnesic syndrome have been reported in two patients following deep temporal lobe stimulation, including a retrograde amnesia for events up to a few days before the stimulation and a permanent anterograde amnesia for a short time afterwards (Bickford et al. 1958).

These results have encouraged the use of post-trial brain stimulation following training in animals to identify precise neural sites for memory processes. At currents below the threshold for seizures, motor or rewarding effects, intracranial stimulation can produce amnesia which depends on the site of stimulation and the nature of the memory task (see Kesner and Wilburn 1974).

See also PSYCHOANALYSIS; REPRESSION. TWR

Bibliography

Bickford, R.G. et al. 1958: Changes in memory function produced by electrical stimulation of the temporal lobe in man. In *The brain and human behavior*, ed. H.C. Soloman, S. Cobb and W.E. Penfield. Baltimore: Williams & Wilkins.

Flanigin, H.F. et al. 1976: Stimulation of the temporal lobe and thalamus in man and its relation to memory and behavior. In *Brain stimulation reward*, ed. A. Wauquier and E.T. Rolls. Amsterdam: North-Holland/Elsevier.

Kesner, R.P. and Wilburn, M.W. 1974: A review of electrical stimulation of the brain in the context of learning and retention. *Behavioral biology* 10 259–93.

Kubie, L.S. 1953: Some implications for psychoanalysis of modern concepts of the organization of the brain. *Psychoanalytical quarterly* 22 21–52.

Mahl, G.F. et al. 1964: Psychophysical responses in the human to intracerebral electric stimulation. *Psychosomatic medicine* 26, 337–68.

Ojeman, G.A. 1982: Interrelationships in the localization of language, memory and motor mechanisms in human cortex and thalamus. In *New perspectives in cerebral localization*, ed. R.A. Thompson and J.R. Green. New York: Raven Press.

Penfield, W. 1958: Functional localization in temporal and deep Sylvian areas. *Association for research into nervous and mental disorders* 36, 210–26.

——— and Perot, P. 1963: The brain's record of auditory and visual experience: a final summary and discussion. *Brain* 86, 595–696.

Stevens, J.R. et al. 1969: Deep temporal stimulation in man. Long latency, long lasting psychological changes. *Archives of neurology* (Chicago) 21, 157–69.

Whitty, C.W.M. and Zangwill, O.L. 1977: *Amnesia.* 2nd edn. London: Butterworth.

Buddhist psychology A form of religious thought and practice which began in the sixth century B.C. in India, with the Buddha himself, and developed in the indigenous traditions of India, Ceylon, South-East Asia, Tibet, China and Japan. In common with all other major religions of Indian origin Buddhism understands man and the universe in terms of the fundamental and interconnected ideas of transmigration or rebirth (SAMSARA), the causal role of human action (KARMA) in the process of rebirth, and the possibility of release or LIBERATION from it (in Buddhism called *nirvana*). The doctrine which distinguishes Buddhism from all other forms of Indian religion is its teaching of "not-self" (Sanskrit *anātman*, Pali *anatta*), which denies the existence of any permanent principle, any self or soul, which might be thought to undergo rebirth, or indeed to lie behind continuity in one life. In place of this hotly repudiated concept Buddhism sets the view of man as a collection of impersonal states or "moments" of mind and body.

There are two ways in which this teaching is presented, and two styles of psychological thinking which correspond to them. They may be summarized as the emphasis on doctrine as an (ultimately true) description of reality, and the use of it as an (ultimately expendable) instrument of salvation. In the first case the doctrine of not-self is presented as what Buddhism calls a "right view", which opposes other "wrong views", and is part of a process of spiritual training which sees a gradual and set pattern of "purification" in behavioral, emotional and conceptual spheres. "Purity of View" and "Purity of Behavior" are acquired together. In the second case the teaching holds that the final result and essential meaning of not-self is a kind of silent wisdom which transcends all "views", even Buddhist "right views". Here a certain attitude of moral and epistemological asceticism is imposed on all forms of conceptualization, bringing with it a particular and peculiarly Buddhist aesthetic of "emptiness". In the earlier phases of the tradition, these two sides of the doctrine were complementary; later schools, especially the Madhyamaka in India and Tibet, and ZEN BUDDHISM in Japan, strongly stressed the superiority of the second over the first, and so had a much more flexible attitude to specific details of doctrine, such as psychological analysis, and a more "spontaneous" view of liberating insight and the ways of attaining it.

In the kinds of Buddhist thought which emphasize a "right view" of psychology the aim is to specify exhaustively those impersonal elements which are brought together by karma to form the empirical human person, without the need to postulate a self or soul. These elements are grouped together in numbered lists, the most frequent of which being the "five aggregates" or "categories": form (or matter, "body"), sensations, perceptions (or ideas), mental formations (or impulses of will, volitional tendencies, inherited forces), and consciousness. Another regular list is the twelve "sense-bases", which are the six senses (the usual five plus mind, regarded as a sense in Buddhism) and their respective objects. There is a further list of eighteen "elements", which are the six senses, their objects, and the six resultant forms of "sense consciousness". The various schools of Buddhist scholasticism (the *Abhidharma* or "further doctrine") elaborated still longer lists, and in particular came to differentiate various forms of mind or consciousness, the fifth "category". For example, the Theravāda school developed a theory of a *bhavanga*-mind ("constituent of being" or "life-continuum") which continued to exist in the absence of mental processes, while the Mahasamghika school saw a somewhat similar "root-consciousness" as the unconscious vector of Karma and continuity. The Vijnanavnda school distinguished eight forms of consciousness: the six forms of sense-consciousness; a seventh called mind (but different from mind as the sixth sense, in that it had the function of unifying into a single (though illusory) ego the objects of all the six sense-consciousnesses – it thus resembles Aristotle's *sensus communis*); and finally an eighth underlying form, called the "home-" or "store-consciousness". This last was, unlike the other seven, inactive, being merely the repository in which were stored all the "seeds" of karma. (See May (1971)).

None of these theories of types of mind or consciousness contradicts the denial of a permanent soul or self, since all are seen as subject to the general fact of momentariness: that is, the Buddhist view that all elements of existence, material and mental, exist only for a moment. Estimates of the length of these "moments" varied, some assuming a sub-liminal, even infinitesimal length, others seeing a moment as roughly the length of a perception or thought (and so resembling somewhat the notion of sense-data in the West). Whatever the postulated length, these moments are seen as discrete entities, but as being held together in individual "streams". This individuation is effected in two main ways. First, there is the simple fact of the body. Mental "moments" are necessarily associated in any one lifetime with a material body, and this body is assumed necessarily to be numerically self-identical. Secondly, there are held to be certain kinds of conditioning relation in the process of karma, which explain mental continuity both in itself within one lifetime, and also over a series of rebirths, or re-embodiments. Among these conditioning relations (which resemble in many respects Humean notions of causation) the most important are contiguity between adjacent moments in a successive series, and qualitative similarity between earlier and later parts of one "stream".

The Buddhist view of conditioning is not what would be called deterministic or causal in Western thought. The doctrine is called "Dependent Co-origination" or "Conditioned Genesis", and its general formula is given in the words "when this exists, that comes into being; when this does not exist, that will not exist". The theory points to formal concomitances between things rather than a directly causal or agentive derivation of one from another. The most common way in which the short formula given above is expanded into contentful form is as a list of twelve items, each of which is taken to condition the next. Thus, "conditioned by ignorance there arise mental formations, conditioned by mental formations there arises consciousness, conditioned by consciousness there arises name-and-form (mind and body)... the six senses... sense-contact... feeling... desire... attachment... becoming... birth... old age and death". Here, characteristically, Buddhism conflates ideas which we would separate as ethics, psychology and eschatology.

In this kind of Buddhist psychology, whatever the differences in detail, all schools agree that there is a "right view" of things which opposes other "wrong views". The second form of the denial of self sees any "view" of things as ultimately inadequate to describe reality. The earlier teaching of the "selflessness of persons" is elaborated into the "selflessness of things". This latter term means two things: first, the idea that because everything is conditioned and relative nothing has an absolute existence or essence. Secondly, the word here translated as "things" is *dharma*, which is the very term used elsewhere in Buddhism to refer to the momentarily-existing impersonal elements of Buddhist psychological analysis. Thus the "selflessness of things" means that just as there is ultimately no essence of a person, no real referent of personal terms such as "self" or "soul", so ultimately there is no real referent of the terms used by Buddhist psychology to replace the idea of self. The ultimate truth of everything is "emptiness". Philosophically this thought gave rise to a vast and rich tradition of epistemology and ontology; the psychological attitude behind it can be grasped in simple form from a parable found in the earliest texts. A man who has crossed a river by means of a raft does not take it with him when he reaches dry land, but leaves it behind on the shore; so too when a man has crossed the ocean of suffering and rebirth and has reached the further shore of *nirvana*, he leaves behind the Buddhist doctrines which got him there.

Apart from the epistemological side to this idea, there is a direct connection with Buddhist ethics: we can best understand this attitude to "views", whatever their content, if we see Buddhism here as judging all conceptual products in relation to the affective dimension of desire or attachment. Instead of a dichotomy between "right" and "wrong views", we can see underlying the teaching here a kind of continuum, along which all conceptual standpoints and cognitive acts are graded according to the degree to which they are held or performed with attachment. At the lowest point on the continuum, there is the ignorant "ordinary man", and those of opposed traditions, whose "views" (such as the belief in a self) are seen simply as direct manifestations of desire; at the highest point (strictly speaking not on the continuum at all) there is the unconditioned freedom from "views" of the enlightened, desire-less and silent sage. In between these two extremes there is the "right view" of Buddhism itself, which will only lead to liberation if it is not itself made the object of desire or attachment. When Buddhism's own psychology is used in this way as an instrument of salvation, a raft to cross to the further shore, the aspirant is held to reach that enlightened state in which, as the Buddha is reported to have said, "whatever verbal designation or means of verbal designation there is, whatever expression or means thereof, whatever description or means thereof, whatever knowledge or realm of knowledge, whatever rebirth or experience of rebirth – by knowing these with super-knowledge a monk is freed".

Of the traditions of Buddhism now becoming known in the West, the Theravāda school of South Asia can best be taken to represent the first kind of Buddhist psychology; while the Japanese school of ZEN BUDDHISM best represents the second. The Tibetan tradition, still very active both in their Indian refuge and increasingly in the West, perhaps offers the clearest blend of the two. SCol

Bibliography

*Collins, S. (in press): *Selfless persons: imagery and thought in Theravāda Buddhism.* London and New York: Cambridge University Press.

*Gyatso, Tenzin (Dalai Lama XIV) 1975: *The Buddhism of Tibet and the key to the middle way.* New York: Harper Row; London: Allen & Unwin.

May, J. 1971: *La philosophie bouddhiste idéaliste.* Asiatische Studien (Etudes Asiatiques) 25.

*Robinson, R. 1977: *The Buddhist religion: a historical introduction.* 2nd. edn. Encino, Calif.: Dickenson.

Suzuki, D.T. 1959: *Zen and Japanese culture.* London: Routledge & Kegan Paul; Princeton N.J.: Princeton University Press.

bulimia In the United States this term refers both to a pattern of behavior ("binge-eating") and a specific psychiatric syndrome in which binge-eating is the principal feature; in Britain the equivalent syndrome is named bulimia nervosa. Binge-eating may be defined as a distressing episode of eating which is experienced as excessive and outside the subject's control. In bulimia nervosa, binge-eating is accompanied by compensatory self-induced vomiting or purgative abuse or both, as well as psychopathology similar to that found in anorexia nervosa. Although almost half the patients have had ANOREXIA NERVOSA in the past their body weight is usually within the normal range. Like anorexia nervosa it is confined to countries in which slimness is considered attractive. Most cases are female and the prevalence of the condition is uncertain. Vulnerability to OBESITY or DEPRESSION appears to be a predisposing factor. Treatment is difficult and the long-term prognosis is not known. See also NEUROSIS. CJGF

Bibliography

Fairburn, C.G. 1982: Eating disorders. In *Companion to psychiatric studies*, ed. R.E. Kendell and A.K. Zealley, 3rd edn. Edinburgh: Churchill Livingstone.

C

cardiac control *See* emotion and cardiac control

careers "The sequence of work-related activities and associated ATTITUDES, VALUES and aspirations over the span of one's life" (Storey 1979). An individual's career does not exist as an entity separate from the rest of his or her life; the various spheres are interdependent and a full understanding of careers must set them in the context of the individual's other activities, aims, beliefs and so on.

In everyday usage the term career seems often to be associated with upward mobility, advancement or getting on via a series of related jobs. Another view regards a career as representing occupational stability, i.e. the career soldier or career civil servant. Such career patterns as these have been given the labels "linear" and "steady state" by Driver who also writes of "transitory' and "spiral" patterns. In the former there is, in fact, no clear pattern whereas the latter is characterized by an emphasis on self-development.

Traditional views of career, as suggested by the examples given above, often associate the term with the professions where a clear series of steps can usually be identified. But a sequence of shorter steps, is apparent in other occupations: for example, craft, where apprenticeship precedes competence as a skilled worker. And as the career concept is broadened to recognize career patterns based on lateral movement so it becomes more appropriate to apply the term to blue-collar and clerical workers.

There are two aspects to the "work-related activities" element of careers: the sequence of steps or structural features of the career, and the individual's movement through that structure. As described by Milkovich et al. (1976) the sequence of steps has both length and a ceiling, and movement proceeds at a certain rate and with direction.

The sequence of work-related activities can be described as the objective or external aspect of the career. But there is also a subjective or internal (to the person) aspect, in other words the "associated attitudes, values, and aspirations". People have expectations about their careers, and it may happen that these do not coincide with what may be thought of as the "reality" of the objective career structure. This mis-match may occur for various reasons to do either with the individual, e.g. a wrong career choice, or with the employing organization.

A person's subjective experience of his or her career will change over time. The notion of change is prominent in much of the contemporary theorizing; as Van Maanen (1977, p.3) points out, "to study careers is to study change itself". The several accounts of adult development stages emphasize change (see Driver 1979 for summary) and a number of writers (e.g. Schein 1978) offer helpful reviews and syntheses of the various theories.

There appears to be a fair measure of agreement on the existence of an early exploratory or trial stage during which the adolescent or young adult is obtaining information about the self and about occupations and then making choices about suitable vocations or careers. This period in careers has been subjected to considerable theorizing (see VOCATIONAL CHOICE) and research investigation, e.g. on the transition from school to work. Much of the emphasis in vocational/careers guidance services has also been concentrated on adolescents and young adults at this early stage.

Entry into the world of work (see OCCUPATIONAL SOCIALIZATION) is likely to be a stressful period for the individual. Some exploration or trying out of jobs may well continue as the individual searches for a good match between personal values and abilities and demands of employment (see LABOR TURNOVER).

Next, comes a stage which features establishment and advancement. Various career issues face the individual during this stage. Schein, for example, suggests several, such as becoming an expert in some area, deciding whether to stay in the same organization, and deciding how to utilize experience beyond the initial area of expertise.

Some theories posit the existence of a period of mid-career crisis or transition – a period of re-thinking or soul-searching. As Schein puts it; "For many people there is a period of crisis during which a major reassessment must be made of how one is doing relative to one's ambitions and how important work and /or career is going to be in one's total life space" (page 47).

Later career may be a period of maintenance in which the individual continues along an established path. But what happens during this stage depends in large part on how the person coped with the preceding transition. Furthermore, the relative absence of empirical studies means that our understanding of this stage is patchy. The concern with passing on one's wisdom and experience may continue and preparation for retirement starts to become important. A final career stage, sometimes called "decline", sees still greater emphasis on preparation for retirement and a disengagement from paid employment.

Because they encompass the whole of an individual's career the development or stage theories represent an important advance over the earlier career theories which tended to focus rather narrowly on the period of occupational choice. Also, the stage theories typically suggest various tasks or issues which the individual may normally face during each stage. Recalling the objective/subjective distinction drawn earlier it is worth noting that Van Maanen and Schein (1977) have outlined external descriptions corresponding to each internal career stage. The propositions contained in the various stage theories will aid empirical testing of them. So far, this kind of testing has been limited: there have been relatively few studies, they have tended to concentrate on one stage or another, and they have focussed mostly on careers in isolation from the rest of life. Some studies are broadening their scope. For example, Evans and Bartolome (1980) consider work and family issues; Sofer's study of mid-career development (1970) helps somewhat to fill the gap between initial entry to work and retirement; and work on dual-career couples (e.g. Rapoport and Rapoport 1971) is helpful not only because it throws light on work and family issues but also because it helps to compensate for an over-emphasis on men's careers. RSW

Bibliography

Driver, M.J. 1979: Career concepts and career management in organizations. In *Behavioral problems in organizations*, ed. C.L. Cooper. Englewood Cliffs, NJ: Prentice-Hall.

Evans, P. and Bartolome, F. 1980: *Must success cost so much?* London: Grant McIntyre.

*Hall, D.T. 1976: *Careers in organizations.* Santa Monica, Calif.: Goodyear.

Milkovich, G.T. et al. 1976: Organizational careers. Environmental, organizational and individual determinants. In *Careers in organizations: individual planning and organizational development*, ed. L. Dyer. Ithaca, N.Y.: Cornell University Press.

Rapoport, R. and Rapoport, R. 1971: *Dual-career families.* London: Penguin.

Schein, E.H. 1978: *Career dynamics.* Reading, Mass.: Addison-Wesley.

Sofer, C. 1970: *Men in mid-career.* Cambridge and New York: Cambridge University Press.

Storey, W.D., ed. 1979: *A guide for career development inquiry.* Madison, Wisc.: American Society for Training and Development.

Super, D.E. 1957: *The psychology of careers.* New York: Harper & Row.

*——— and Hall, D.T. 1978: Career development: exploration and planning. *Annual review of psychology* 29, 333–72.

Van Maanen, J. 1977: *Organizational careers: some new perspectives.* London and New York: Wiley.

Van Maanen, J. and Schein, E.H. 1977: Career development. In *Improving life at work*, ed. J.R. Hackman and J.L. Suttle. Santa Monica, Calif.: Goodyear.

Williams, R. 1981: *Career management and career planning.* London: HM Stationery Office.

catatonia *See* schizophrenia

category The word derives from the Greek word κατηγορια which means (among other things) "predicate" or "predication". In the "Categories" Aristotle seems to base his list on mutually exclusive questions (i.e. questions with mutually exclusive kinds of answer) such as "what?" "How much/many?" "What kind?" (= substance, quantity and quality). "Category" was used by Aristotle to refer to ten broad classes, such as substance, quality, position and action. He probably had no precise idea of what distinguishes a category from any other class, but he implies that a category is a highest genus. KANT attempted to derive a list of categories from the ways in which statements are classified in logic. The resulting categories are supposed to correspond to patterns of thought which are indispensible for the making of judgment. RYLE (1938) offers the following test for category difference: if in any sentence one expression cannot be replaced by another expression without turning sense into nonsense, then the concepts expressed by each of the two expressions belong to different categories. If in "the table is nearby" we replace "the table" by "the number five", the result is nonsense; so it follows by this test that the concepts *the table* and *the number five* belong to different categories. A "category mistake" consists in treating a concept as though it belonged to a different category from its true one. Ryle claims that certain metaphysical doctrines, particularly dualistic theories of mind and body, embody such mistakes and are therefore absurd rather than simply false. (See also DISPOSITION.) JMS

Bibliography

Ryle, G. 1938: Categories. *Proceedings of the Aristotelian Society* 38, 189–206.

catharsis (Also known as abreaction.) The release of anxiety and tension by reliving and expressing an intense emotional experience. In Aristotle's *Poetics* catharsis is said to come about by watching grand tragedy on the stage. FREUD incorporated the concept into psychoanalytic therapy by emphasizing the release of repressed emotions as the first step in understanding and eliminating an underlying psychic conflict. RHo

cerebellum A large, convoluted structure in the hind-brain situated behind the medulla and pons (BRAIN AND CENTRAL NERVOUS SYSTEM: ILLUSTRATIONS figs 5–8). The cerebellum consists of two hemispheres, each covered by a cortex of gray matter which surrounds a core of white matter. A cortex contains three distinct layers in which are embedded various cerebellar nuclei. The cerebellum is attached to the brain stem by means of three pairs of peduncles containing afferent and efferent tracts which also link the structure to other parts of the central nervous system, most notably the cerebral cortex, BASAL GANGLIA, and spinal cord. A central component of the EXTRAPYRAMIDAL MOTOR SYSTEM, the cerebellum functions as part of an interconnecting system of pathways with the responsibility of coordinating motor activity in a timed and integrated fashion. The cerebellum is organized according to three functionally differentiated lobes – the flocculonodular lobe concerned with orientation and postural adjustments, the posterior lobe which exerts inhibitory control over voluntary movements, and the anterior lobe which regulates muscle tonus. A variety of motor defects follows cerebellar damage with tremor, ataxia and hypotonia among the most common symptoms. GWi

cerebral blood flow The normal brain, whether the body is sleeping or awake, requires an enormous amount of energy relative to the rest of the body. Since the metabolism of the brain is almost exclusively aerobic (i.e. oxygen requiring) and since the source of brain energy metabolism is almost exclusively glucose, under normal conditions cerebral blood flow, glucose uptake and oxygen consumption are highly correlated. This correlation can be disturbed in various pathological states, such as coma (Sokoloff 1976). The energy and oxygen requirements of the brain are reflected in the fact that, while the brain accounts for only about 2 per cent of an adult's body weight, it receives 15-20 per cent of the body's total cardiac output and accounts for about 20 per cent of the body's oxygen consumption. Recent technological advances have allowed a finer examination of blood flow to specific brain regions during various forms of mental and physical activity. One interesting suggestion from such research is that blood flow increases in the left, relative to the right, side of the brain during verbal activity (see LATERALIZATION). GPH

Bibliography

Sokoloff, L. 1976: Circulation and energy metabolism of the brain. In G. J. Siegel et al. eds, *Basic neurochemistry*. 2nd edn Boston: Little, Brown and Co.

cerebral cortex The mantle of gray matter that surrounds the cerebral hemispheres (BRAIN AND CENTRAL NERVOUS SYSTEM: ILLUSTRATIONS figs 1, 2, 5). Ninety per cent of cerebral cortex is classified as phylogenetically recent neocortex which is composed of six structurally defined layers. The convoluted surface provides numerous elevations (gyri) and depressions (sulci or fissures) which serve as useful landmarks for dividing the cortex into four principal regions – frontal, parietal, temporal and occipital lobes. The most developed part of the brain, the cortex as a whole has long been regarded as the seat of higher cognitive and intellectual function. There is also considerable localization of function, particularly involving sensory and motor processes (figs 3 and 4). Visual information is processed in an area of the occipital lobe, audition within the temporal lobe, and somatosensory input projects to the parietal lobe. A motor area in the frontal lobe is responsible for initiating movement. The capacity for speech is localized unilaterally in frontal and parietal/temporal lobe areas. Adjacent to the primary sensory and motor areas are secondary or association areas. The motor association areas are concerned with complex motor skills, while the sensory association areas integrate, store, and correlate information that is necessary for thought and perception. Damage to association areas can produce various deficits affecting the execution of skilled movements (apraxia), the ability to recognize or be aware of objects (agnosia) and the comprehension or expression of language (aphasia). GWi

channel switching If man is modelled as a single channel or limited capacity information processor the direction of ATTENTION can be thought of as switching from one channel to another. Channels are the carriers of information from different regions of the environment. As originally proposed by Broadbent they were features such as color, loudness, location, etc. Later work showed that attention can be paid to more complex characteristics such as the language of a message, and the concept of "channel" became less precise. A channel can best be regarded as any source of a message. NM

character armor *See* neo-Freudian theory

Charcot, Jean Martin (1825–1893). A most distinguished neurologist and director of the Salpêtrière Hospital in Paris, provided first descriptions of many neurological syndromes. He used the same methods of precise clinical examination and description to study HYSTERIA. Charcot believed this to be an inherited brain disease in which "stigmata" and seizures are triggered off by "hysterogenous" zones. He suggested that hysteria could be cured by hypnosis, a process which he classified into an elaborate series of stages and phenomena. Charcot's enduring importance for psychology and psychiatry results not from his beliefs, which were soon disproved, but in the interest he aroused in the study of neuroses and their treatment. He was a prominent public figures with many literary and medical friends and his regular clinical demonstrations attracted large audiences. Freud and Janet were among his pupils. RAM

chemical senses *See* senses, chemical

child and adolescent psychiatry Is concerned with persistent disturbance of emotions or behavior which affects the child's social relationships or development, and is out of keeping with the child's sociocultural background and developmental level. Psychiatric disorder may be caused by factors within the child himself; his family; or his environment. In assessing disturbed children therefore, it is necessary to examine not only the child but also the family and school and social circumstances. A multidisciplinary team approach is widely used to achieve this, with medically qualified child psychiatrists working closely with psychologists and social workers. This model forms the basis of Child Guidance Clinics.

The incidence of psychiatric disorder in school children has been estimated at between five and fifteen per cent; and ten to twenty per cent in adolescents (Rutter, Tizard and Whitmore 1981). These figures, however, do not reflect the number of children presenting for treatment, and factors such as parental anxiety may be as important as the severity of a child's disturbance when treatment is sought. Boys are twice as commonly affected as girls. Although the rate of disorder is highest in inner city areas there is no clear association with social class alone: other associated factors are parental mental illness and criminality, family discord and disruption, early separation experiences and social disadvantage. Children with central nervous system abnormalities, mental handicap, or epilepsy, and children who have been abused, form a high risk group. There has recently been considerable interest in "protective factors" (Rutter 1981), which enable some children to survive gross deprivation and psychosocial stress. Examples are: an adaptable temperament; isolated rather than all-pervasive stress; a good relationship with one parent.

The two main groups of child psychiatric disorders, which together cover more than 90 per cent of psychiatric disorder seen in children are disorders of conduct, where the child behaves in socially disapproved-of ways, e.g. lying, stealing, disobedience (see CONDUCT DISORDER) and emotional disorders, characterized mainly by anxiety symptoms, which may be accompanied by tearfulness, sadness, social withdrawal or relationship problems. They occur equally commonly in girls and boys, and are relatively short-lived compared with adult neuroses. They usually develop in response to stress in the child's environment, e.g. parental disharmony, illness in a family member. Certain children, those with especially anxious temperaments, are vulnerable to minor stresses, and it is thought that there are also critical periods in a child's life when specific stresses have a major impact, e.g. bereavement in the third or fourth years of life. Treatment usually consists of understanding the stress, and either modifying it or helping the child develop better resources to cope. The prognosis for recovery and adjustment in later life is very good.

Children diagnosed as "psychotic" are generally withdrawn and unable to form emotional relationships with adults or other children. They frequently have mannerisms such as finger flicking, twirling or spinning objects. PSYCHOSIS in childhood is very rare and is a confused area. This is partly owning to the difficulties inherent in applying adult diagnostic criteria to children who are usually unable to verbalize their inner feelings and experiences; and also partly because any process which affects relationship formation in infancy interferes with normal development. It may thus be difficult to distinguish psychosis in young children from mental retardation. Three subgroups are recognized:

(a) late-onset psychosis: these are adult-like psychoses (e.g. schizophrenia or bipolar depression) occurring in late childhood and adolescence. The treatment and prognosis is the same as for the adult condition.

(b) disintegrative psychoses: these present around the age of four with social withdrawal and loss of skills, including speech. They are due to an underlying degenerative disorder of the central nervous system, and treatment is mainly palliative and symptomatic.

(c) Infantile autism.

The outlook for recovery from psychotic conditions in childhood is not good.

In *organic mental states* there is impairment of brain functioning with "delirium" – confusion and hallucinations, which are usually visual in children. The commonest causes in childhood are high fevers accompanying infections such as measles, meningitis or pneumonia. They may also be caused by accidental self-poisoning, by overdoses of drugs such as sedatives or anticonvulsants; and by drug abuse (e.g. glue sniffing, LSD or amphetamine intoxication). Treatment is directed at the underlying cause, and the episode of delirium is usually short lived.

A number of conditions which occur on their own, not as part of a more widespread emotional or behavioral disturbance can be grouped under the heading *monosymptomatic disorders*. They include tics, enuresis (bedwetting), encopresis (soiling), night terrors, head banging, thumb sucking. Many of these can be regarded as developmental, i.e. they arise as part of a developmental stage, and resolve spontaneously with increasing age and maturity. However, treatment may be sought because of parental anxiety, or because of the child's distress if symptoms are interfering with his functioning or relationships.

Educational problems form another group of conditions. There are many reasons for a child failing to learn.

(a) General intellectual impairment, which will affect all areas of learning.

(b) A specific learning disability, affecting only one area, such as reading or arithmetic. (See DYSLEXIA; REMEDIAL MATHEMATICS; REMEDIAL READING.)

(c) Temperamental factors: Restless, fidgety children with poor concentration and high distractibility often fail to learn in ordinary classroom settings.

(d) *Conduct disordered children* have a high incidence of reading retardation. The nature of this association is not well understood. Background family factors (e.g. dismissive attitudes to learning or authority) may be relevant; or the child's failure in the classroom may lead him to act out as an alternative strategy to impress his peer group and boost his own self esteem.

(e) *Stress* – such as divorce, bereavement, illness of a family member – may lead to loss of concentration and a temporary interruption of the child's progress.

(f) *Mental illness* – depressive disorder or schizophrenia arising in adolescence interferes with learning. The teacher may be the first to notice signs of the illness as school performance declines.

Wherever a child is failing educationally, there are likely to be secondary emotional problems – poor self esteem and loss of self confidence – which may need attention in their own right. (See also ABSENCE FROM SCHOOL AND TRUANCY; SCHOOL FAILURE; SCHOOL REFUSAL.)

Treatment of disturbed children, like assessment, requires a multidisciplinary approach, and inpatient, day patient or outpatient care may be necessary. The focus of treatment may be on the individual child, e.g. through individual psychotherapy, play therapy, behavior therapy, remedial tuition, or placement in a special school. On the other hand, the focus may be on helping the family to change, and for this family therapy, or parental counseling, may be required. Liaison with schools, nurseries, and play groups may be necessary, and close working relationships with social services departments are vital for children in care, or those who are suspected of emotional or physical neglect and abuse. The combined efforts of the child psychiatric team with pediatricians, physiotherapists, speech therapists, or teachers may be needed to help children who are physically or mentally handicapped in addition to any psychiatric disturbance. Drugs are little used in child psychiatry apart from the treatment of the hyperkinetic syndrome and the adult-like psychoses.

Child abuse; non accidental injury

Each year about six children per 1,000 are abused physically, emotionally or sexually. Such children may grow up to be permanently affected by their early experiences, with impairment of their capacity to form loving relationships. Abused children may present at accident departments with multiple fractures, burns and bruising; or with failure to thrive and developmental delay. They commonly show "frozen watchfulness" in the presence of adults. Research suggests that the failure of parent-child attachment often predates the abuse, and a number of high risk factors have been identified which provide clues for possible early intervention (Lynch and Roberts 1982). These include young maternal age, a history of parental psychiatric illness; the parents themselve being abused as children; separation of mother and baby in the neonatal period, and multiple social problems. The management of child abuse may involve permanently removing the child from its parents; helping develop parenting skills in a mother and baby unit or special day center; or setting up early intervention programs for high risk mothers and their new born babies to try and promote attachment. GCF

Bibliography

*Barker, P. 1979: *Basic child psychiatry* London: Granada.

Lynch, Margaret A. and Roberts, Jacqueline 1982: *Consequences of child abuse*. London: Academic Press.

*Rutter, M. 1975: *Helping troubled children*. Harmondsworth: Penguin; New York: Plenum.

——— 1981: Stress, Coping and Development: Some issues and some questions. *Journal of child psychology and psychiatry* 22. 4, 323–56.

———, Tizard, J. and Whitmore, K., eds 1981: The Isle of Wight and its services for children. In *Education, health and behavior*. New York: Robert E. Krieber.

chimpanzee language *See* anthropoid ape language

choice Philosophical interest in choice centers on the question of its freedom (see FREE WILL), but there are subsidiary issues as well. One of these is that of the frequency of choice. On one view we make, in the course of a lifetime, relatively few significant choices, and the rest of the time we are merely playing out the choices that we have made. For example, I choose, say, to be a Catholic, and much of what I subsequently do is dictated by that choice. On another view the playing out of the choice is itself a constant activity of choosing: I constantly choose not to renege on my initial choice. The latter view was central to the moral thought of EXISTENTIALISM. Secondly, philosophers have been interested in understanding the highly complex ways in which the concept of choice overlaps with those of wanting, of decision, of action, of conation. Another philosophical problem of choice is that of its rationality. Much thought has been devoted to searching for algorithms for rational choice: the choice of right action in moral philosophy, the choice of prudential action in games theory, the choice of scientific theories in the philosophy of science. The finding of such algorithms would reduce rational choice to mere calculation; there has been much debate whether, in that case, people should be considered to be nothing more than sophisticated machines. JT

Bibliography

Daveney, T.F. 1964: Choosing. *Mind* 73, 515–26.

Glasgow, W.D. 1956: The concept of choosing. *Analysis* 20, 63–7.

Sartre, Jean-Paul 1945(1966): *Being and nothingness*. Trans. Hazel Barnes. New York: Washington Square Press.

Chomsky, Noam A. Born 1928, Professor of Linguistics at the Massachusetts Institute of Technology (MIT). Chomsky is the founder of one of the most influential schools in general linguistics and psycholinguistics, that of transformational-generative grammar (TG). TG was presented to a wider audience in *Syntactic Structures* in 1957 and subsequently developed in *Aspects of the Theory of Syntax* in 1965. Chomsky's insistence that linguistics should be a branch of cognitive psychology and his mentalist views on language learning have provoked vivid interest among psychologists (see Greene 1972).

The most influential concepts introduced by Chomsky are those of deep and surface structure, *competence* and *performance*, *acceptability* and *grammaticalness*, and the notion of generative grammar. PM

Bibliography

Chomsky, Noam 1957: *Syntactic structures*. The Hague: Mouton.

——— 1967: *Aspects of the theory of syntax*. Cambridge, Mass.: MIT

Greene, Judith 1972: *Psycholinguistics: Chomsky and psychology*, Penguin Books.

Lyons, John 1970: *Chomsky*. London: Fontana/Collins.

Christian psychology *See* Aquinas; Augustine; early Christian psychology

chromosome abnormalities Chromosomes are those parts of the body cells which carry the genetic code. In humans, the normal cell contains 46 chromosomes, 44 of which are common to both sexes (autosomal chromosomes) and 2 which differ between the sexes (sex chromosomes). In males these consist of one X and one Y (XY); in females, two matching X chromosomes (XX). A variety of abnormalities of both autosomal and sex chromosomes have now been identified, the commonest being too many or too few chromosomes. Autosomal chromosome abnormalities are generally associated with marked physical malformation and mental retardation (e.g. DOWN'S SYNDROME). Sex chromosome abnormalities are less closely associated with mental retardation; malformation of the sex organs are the most common physical abnormality and psychiatric disorder may occur. Prenatal diagosis of chromosome abnormalities is possible by sampling the amniotic fluid surrounding the foetus (amniocentesis). Subsequent termination can thus prevent the birth of an abnormal child. GENETIC COUNSELING should be offered to parents and relatives of affected children to help them decide about future pregnancies. GCF

Bibliography

Therman, E. 1980: *Human chromosomes*. Heidelberg and New York: Springer Verlag.

De Grouchy, J. and Thurleau, C. 1978: *Atlas of chromosome abnormalities*. New York: John Wiley.

circadian rhythm A cycle of internal bodily activity level with a period of about twenty-four hours. Such rhythms can be detected by measurements of body temperature, heart rate, urine secretion, plasma content or indeed any measure which indicates metabolic rate. Measurements reveal a cycle which is roughly sinusoidal with a peak at about 4.00 p.m. and a trough at about 4.00 a.m. The cycle is disturbed if there is a change in the pattern of daily activity owing for example to starting night work or to flying across the world to a different time-zone. The rate of adjustment to a new cycle varies extensively. In some individuals the phase change occurs almost at once; in others it takes weeks. On average it takes about three days for a twelve hour shift to occur.

Although these rhythms are reflected subjectively in different feelings of arousal and lassitude it is difficult to obtain a direct correlation with changes in measures of performance either in the laboratory or in the field. Such changes do occur, but they are not large and there are extensive individual differences.

Thus, although circadian rhythms are clearly relevant to policies concerning shift work or working hours of intercontinental aircrews, recommendations cannot be definitive and must also take account of psychological, social and even cultural variables. (See also CLOCK-DRIVEN BEHAVIOR.) WTS

Bibliography

Wilkinson, R. 1978: Hours of work and the 24 hour cycle of rest and activity. In *Psychology at work*, ed. P.B. Warr. Harmondsworth: Penguin.

class size Refers to the size of teaching group in schools and in further education. The most extensive research has been carried out in school settings. Most professional teachers assume that children will learn more effectively and respond more easily to group leadership in smaller classes, but research results have repeatedly challenged these common sense assumptions, yielding either inconsistent or negative results.

Studies of children's attainments at various ages and in many countries have indicated that they are not improved when class sizes are reduced. This holds good when possible intervening variables such as school size and urban/rural balance are held constant (Davie et al. 1972; Little et al. 1972). There have been methodological problems in much of the research: the criterion of attainment has often been narrow, such as a single reading test (Maxwell 1977); there has been no agreement on the range of class sizes to be studied, and some investigators have focussed on small differences in class size; for educational reasons classes with less able or difficult children are often made smaller, so that the pupil population variable confounds class size for research purposes. However, some recent studies (e.g., Shapson et al. 1980) have overcome these methodological problems, and their findings confirm the clear trend of the research evidence: the gains in basic academic achievement that are expected when school classes are reduced from 33–40 to 23–30 are not normally found – though there may be gains with groups of fewer than 16 (Glass et al. 1979).

Studies of children's behavior show similarly equivocal results (Little et al. 1972). These also suggest that teachers may not adapt their methods significantly to take advantage of decreases in class size, and Shapson et al. (1980) recently presented evidence supporting this view. However, an Australian observational study showed that in some larger first year secondary classes there was likely to be an emphasis on order and work habits with a high level of academic guidance and instruction (Keeves 1972). A fruitful line of inquiry has been the examination of how *pupils* perceive the social climate of learning in classes of various sizes. For example in one North American study they appear to experience smaller classes as consistently more cohesive and more difficult, and frequently less formal and less diverse. One important feature of the work of this research group has been that it is based on a coherent and articulate theoretical model (Anderson and Wahlberg 1972). Too much of the literature on class size has reported survey findings with post hoc explanations of limited interest. This may explain why the results have been so inconsistent and the controversy remains unresolved. TIC

Bibliography

Anderson, G.J. and Wahlberg, H.J. 1972: Class size and the social environment of learning: a replication. *Alberta journal of educational research* 18, 227–86.

Davie, R., Butler, N. and Goldstein, H. 1972: *From birth to seven: second report of the national child development study*. London: Longman.

Glass, G. and Smith, M. 1979: Meta-analysis of research on class size and achievement. *Educational evaluation and policy analysis* 1, 2–16.

Keeves, J.P. 1972: *Educational environment and student achievement.* Melbourne: Australian Council for Education Research; Stockholm: Almquist and Wiksell.

Little, A., Mabey, C. and Russell, J. 1972: Class size, pupil characteristics and reading attainment. In *Literacy at all levels. Proceedings of the 8th Annual Study Conference of the United Kingdom Reading Association*, ed. V. Southgate.

Maxwell, J. 1977: *Reading progress from eight to fifteen: a survey of attainment and teaching practices in Scotland.* Windsor, Bucks: National Foundation for Educational Research.

Shapson, S.M., et al. 1980: An experimental study of the effects of class size. *American educational research journal* 17, 141–52.

clinical psychology A branch of psychology concerned with the practical application of research findings and research methodology in the fields of mental and physical health. Clinical psychologists, whatever their theoretical backgrounds, share a strong belief in the understandability of human behavior. They are specifically skilled in the application of objective methods of observation, normative data and theories of change to human thought, feeling and action. When faced with dysfunctional behavior they will attempt to explain it in terms of normal processes, and to modify it by applying principles acquired from the study of normal learning adaptation and social interaction.

The term was first used by Witmer in 1896 to refer to assessment procedures carried out with retarded and physically handicapped children. The development of assessment procedures was further stimulated in the United States by the first world war and in the United Kingdom by the work of the War Office Selection Board during the second world war. Since then increasing numbers of nations have incorporated psychologists into their health services (Trethowan 1977), and have drawn up codes of professional practice (the American Psychological Association 1963). During the 1960s and '70s the emphasis on assessment declined after the expansion of behavioral and many other eclectic therapies, and clinical psychologists started to draw on sources other than traditional experimental psychology, e.g. social, occupational and environmental psychology and ethology.

Clinical psychology is now therefore enormously variable, as a description of the training and functions of those who make up the profession will illustrate.

Training includes the university level study of general psychology as well as specialist clinical experience, taking overall five to six years. (In some countries subsequent additional clinical experience is required before professional certification or licensing.) The graduate clinical psychologist will know something about most or all of the following:

(1) how individual experience of the world is modified by the processes involved in perception, thinking and the use of language and imagery.
(2) the processes involved in learning, memory and adaptation.
(3) what motivates human behavior, recognizing that unconscious as well as conscious motivation is possible.
(4) the course of human psychological development.
(5) norms and scales of measurement and their application to individual differences.
(6) interpersonal interaction, the formation of groups and emergence of leaders.
(7) the principles of individual and mass communication, and of the formation of attitudes, opinion and prejudice.

According to Hetherington (1964) the clinical psychologist "will, above all, have had a training in the careful observation, assessment and recording of the way people behave, and of the experiences they say they have", whether or not this behavior and experience is considered normal. This background knowledge, together with a special interest in the field of abnormal psychology (Eysenck 1973) and a variety of clinical experience, qualifies the clinical psychologist both to act as a consultant and to perform the functions outlined below.

Assessment: The purpose of assessment may be either descriptive or functional, and will vary according to which aspect of behavior, physiological, psychological (covert), or behavioral (overt) is being assessed. Descriptive assessment was primarily used (a) to compare an individual with others in a valid and reliable way, using standardized norms, e.g. an IQ test (see PSYCHOMETRICS), or (b) to describe characteristics associated with disorder as an aid to diagnosis (e.g. the M.M.P.I.). Diagnostic assessment is no longer so predominant, and newer descriptive techniques are more clearly related to the problems and progress of particular individuals. For example recent developments in behavioral assessment (Hersen and Bellack 1976) make more use of direct observation and of rating methods and take account of situational and environmental as well as individual variation. Descriptive assessment still plays an important role, e.g. in work with children with learning difficulties, with the mentally or physically handicapped and in neuropsychology. Functional assessment has increased in importance as it is a necessary first step in constructing psychological treatment programs. Its functions may be to determine the type of intervention likely to be of most value, to measure the effects of intervention or of change during therapy, or to identify factors responsible for change (Mittler 1973).

Treatment: An individual may be referred to a clinical psychologist if some aspect of the way in which he or she thinks, feels or acts is itself a problem, is causing a problem or if changing it may ameliorate a problem. The range of referrals is growing and now includes medical, developmental and rehabilitative problems as well as psychiatric ones. The precise function of clinical psychologists in treatment (rehabilitation, behavior modification, therapy, counseling, crisis intervention etc.) varies therefore according to the setting in which they work, and their theorectical orientation. Particular psychologists may specialize in BEHAVIOR THERAPY, GROUP THERAPY, family therapy, PSYCHOANALYSIS, or other PSYCHOTHERAPY and in applications to physical medicine or in rehabilitation, but they should be sufficiently well acquainted with the principles and methods of other approaches to make appropriate referrals if they do not themselves have the necessary skills. They may intervene directly with an individual or indirectly through contact with family members or direct care staff.

Because of the emphasis placed on the scientific nature of their profession, clinical psychologists have played a major part in the development of those therapies theoretically founded in academic psychology – the behavior therapies. The value of some of these procedures is now well recognized, for instance in the treatment of phobias, learning difficulties and sexual dysfunctions, and in the use of operant methods. Other areas, COGNITIVE THERAPY in particular, are not yet so well recognized, but are fast developing.

Research: Clinical psychologists have a particularly important contribution to make in the field of research since they have been trained in the use of experimental design and statistical procedures. They should for example be able to make proper use of control groups, or randomization procedures, and also remain sufficiently objective in the interpretation of observations to be willing to abandon cherished theories in the face of disconfirming evidence. They are well placed to carry out research projects as individuals or as part of multidisciplinary teams, and to advise others on appropriate use of research methodology and statistics. In performing this function the clinical psychologist is aiming to evaluate critically his own work and that of other professions so as to contribute as an applied scientist to the advancement of the health services. Examples include investigations into the value and cost effectiveness of health care interventions, into the design of health centers, or into doctor-patient communication, controlled treatment trials, testing hypotheses about the precise nature or course of dysfuntions, and detailed studies of single subjects.

Teaching: Because of their training as scientists, and their background knowledge of normal psychological development and processes, clinical psychologists are expected to contribute to the training of other health care professionals. The latter will need information about fundamental psychological principles as well as particular skills and knowledge relevant to their own specialization and interests, for instance in the cognitive changes expected with age, in the acquisition of basic skills by the mentally handicapped, in interviewing and communication skills, or in preparation for surgery. Psychologists will also be required to contribute to training for their own profession and to train others in the use of therapeutic techniques.

Administration: The deployment and organization of psychologists is of enormous importance in a small but fast growing profession. Clinical psychologists contribute to the planning and administration of health services in general, and are represented on international bodies such as the World Health Organisation (WHO 1973).

The five functions outlined above are performed in a wide variety of contexts: in psychiatric or general hospitals, in community based health centers or social work departments, in centers for the mentally or physically handicapped or for other disadvantaged groups such as geriatrics, drug addicts or epileptics, in counseling centers of all kinds and also in research establishments and government departments. The distribution of energy between functions will be determined partly by individual preferences and job demands and partly by the degree to which each country has been able to develop its psychological services within a health service or in private practice. The profession is constantly developing, as can be seen from a glance at some of the issues still under discussion. These include questions about the source of referrals to psychologists, about clinical responsibility, about the division of labor over function, and how to make best use of therapists as a scarce resource. The way in which these and other issues are resolved will determine some of the future characteristics of clinical psychology together with its national variations. GB

Bibliography

American Psychological Association 1963: Ethical Standards of Psychologists. *American psychologist* 18, 56–60.

Bellack, A.S. and Hersen, M. 1980. *Introduction to clinical psychology*, Oxford and New York: Oxford University Press.

Eysenck, H.J. 1973. *Handbook of abnormal psychology*. London and New York: Pitman.

Hersen, M. and Bellack, Alan, S. 1976: *Behavioral assessment*. Oxford and New York: Pergamon.

Hetherington, Ralph, R. 1964: The psychologist's role in society. *Bulletin of the British Psychological Society* 17, 9-12.

Korchin, Sheldon, J. 1976. *Modern clinical psychology*. New York: Basic Books.

Mackay, D. 1975. *Clinical psychology: theory and therapy*. London and New York: Methuen.

Mittler, P. 1973: *The psychological assessment of mental and physical handicaps*. London: Methuen.

Trethowan, W.H. 1977: *The role of psychologists in the health services*. London: HMSO.

World Health Organisation 1973. *The role of the psychologist in mental health services*. World Health Organisation: Copenhagen.

clock-driven behavior Rhythmic behavior driven by an endogenous clock is widespread in the animal kingdom. It is found in primitive single-celled animals and in humans. Research in the laboratory and in the field shows that many of the annual, lunar and daily rhythms of behavior found in animals are maintained by clock mechanisms that are endogenous in the sense that the rhythm persists when the animal is isolated from all possible environmental time cues. It is not sufficient, however, merely to isolate an animal in a laboratory under conditions of constant temperature, photoperiod, etc. Exogenous factors such as barometric pressure or cosmic radiation, could possibly be used by animals to keep time, and it is never possible to be sure that all such factors have been excluded. Before concluding that a rhythm is truly endogenous additional evidence is required. Experiments in which the rhythm is directly manipulated, or which control for environmental influences by transporting the experimental preparation around the globe, fall into this category.

In many cases an exogenous *zeitgeber* (time-giver) is responsible for maintaining synchrony between the endogenous rhythm and the cycle of environmental events. When an animal is isolated from the exogenous *zeitgeber* its endogenous clock drifts out of step with the environmental rhythm and is said to be free-running. Endogenous rhythms with a period of about one day are generally called circadian rhythms (*circa*, about; *dies*, a day); those of about one lunar month are called circalunar, and those of about a year are called circannual rhythms. Strictly, these terms also apply to the free-running rhythms, because the rhythm is likely to be exactly a day, etc. when under the influence of a *zeitgeber*. The action of the *zeitgeber* in synchronizing the clock to the rhythm of the environmental events is usually called entrainment.

Many animals adjust to seasonal changes in their environment by behavior that is based upon an endogenous circannual clock. Endogenous circannual rhythms have been established in some migratory birds. For example the garden warbler (*Sylvia borin*), the subalpine warbler (*Sylvia cantillans*) and the willow warbler (*Phylloscopus trochilus*) spend the summer in Europe and migrate across the Sahara desert to winter in southern Africa. If these birds are hand-raised from a few days after hatching they can be maintained under constant laboratory conditions, and the seasonal changes normally associated with migration still occur. Such captive birds show marked seasonal changes in bodyweight, food preferences, molt, testis size and migratory activity. Birds kept in cages exhibit a directional restlessness at the time when they would normally be migrating. The warblers usually migrate at night and rest during the day: in the laboratory they show nocturnal restlessness, hopping back and forth in the direction in which they would normally be migrating. The pattern of nocturnal restlessness conforms remarkably well with the pattern of activity that the migrating birds would normally show. The evidence suggests that the pattern of alternating activity and rest shown by the migratory birds is dictated by an endogenous circannual clock.

Hibernating mammals show a similar phenomenon. The golden mantled ground squirrel (*Citellus lateralis*) and the woodchuck (*Mammota monax*) show marked circannual rhythms of bodyweight and activity when maintained under constant laboratory conditions for a number of years. These animals normally build up their bodyweight before hibernation and lose weight during hibernation. This pattern persists under laboratory conditions of constant photoperiod and environmental temperature. Circannual rhythms are evidently widespread in the animal kingdom, ranging from single-celled animals to mammals. The physiological mechanisms underlying circannual clocks are not well understood, and the same is true for lunar and tidal rhythms.

A number of marine animals exhibit endogenous rhythms which correspond to lunar or tidal cycles. The sea hare (*Aplysia californica*) has nerve cells which have a rhythm of activity with a period close to the tidal cycle. The green crab (*Carcinus maenas*) has a tidal rhythm of activity, being most active at high water. This rhythm persists in constant laboratory conditions for about a week, after which it fades away. If the crab is then cooled for six hours at just above freezing point the tidal rhythm is restored.

The most investigated rhythms are the CIRCADIAN RHYTHMS which have a period of about twenty-four hours under constant laboratory conditions. As with other endogenous rhythms, the typical periodicity drifts slightly from the norm when the clock is free-running under constant laboratory conditions. Under natural conditions a twenty-four-hour periodicity is maintained by some exogenous *zeitgeber* which serves continually to reset the endogenous clock and prevent it from drifting out of phase with the cycle of environmental change. For example, lizards raised from eggs in the laboratory show a free-running rhythm of activity with a period of just under twenty-four hours. Small (amplitude 1.6°C) daily fluctuations in temperature (the *zeitgeber*) are sufficient to entrain the animals in synchrony with the exact twenty-four-hour rhythm.

Circadian rhythms in humans have been studied for many years. When a person is isolated in a subterranean bunker the rhythms of sleeping and waking, and of such physiological indices as body temperature and hormone levels, continue to follow a circadian pattern. Many people are rather poor at estimating periods of time consciously, but show a remarkable ability to wake up at a pre-set time from sleep and from hypnosis. Observations made at the South Pole and during space flight, where exogenous influences can be excluded, suggest that this unconscious type of time estimation is based upon a circadian clock.

The physiological nature of the circadian clock is not well understood. It can occur in single-celled organisms such as the protozoan *Euglena*, which shows a rhythm of swimming activity that is synchronized with the motion of the sun, but persists when the organism is maintained in continuous darkness in the laboratory. However, many of the properties of single-celled protozoans are not found in single cells of multi-celled animals, and some rhythmic phenomena may be the result of interactions between cells. This may be the case in cockroaches in which the electrical activity of cells in the optic lobe seem to be of prime importance in the maintenance of circadian rhythms of activity (Brady 1969; Roberts 1974).

Ideas about clock mechanisms are complicated by evidence that behavior can be influenced by more than one clock simultaneously. For example in one experiment green crabs (*Carcinus maenas*) were raised in the laboratory, from eggs to adulthood, under a twenty-four-hour day-night regime. The crabs showed a circadian rythm of activity, being active during the daylight hours. However, when they were given a cold shock treatment (see above) a tidal rhythm of activity also appeared, the cold shock having started an endogenous tidal clock which had lain dormant. Rats can be trained to work for food both every twenty-four hours and every 25 hours at the same time. To do this the rat has to maintain simultaneous twenty-four and twenty-five-hour rhythms of behavior, which must be based on different clocks.

The ability to keep in step with rhythmic environmental events is of considerable survival value to animals. Many animals have alternating periods of rest and activity which are synchronized with the opportunities for foraging and mating that are characteristic of the environment. The differences between diurnal and nocturnal animals is an obvious example. Animals specialized for daytime vision are at a disadvantage at night, because they are not able to forage efficiently and are in danger from predators. They usually sleep during the night in a place that is warm and safe from predators. Nocturnal animals are able to be profitably active at night. They sleep during the day in places that enable them to avoid both predators and climatic extremes, such as the heat of the desert.

Endogenous clocks play an important role in direction finding and NAVIGATION. Many birds require considerable powers of navigation on long migrations. The golden plover (*Pluvialis dominicus*), for example, breeds in Alaska and migrates to Argentina via Labrador. Much of the 11,000 km journey is over the Atlantic ocean. The green turtle (*Chelone mydas*) migrates between Brazil and Ascension Island 2,000 km out into the Atlantic ocean. Because many of the navigational aids used by animals, such as the sun, stars and moon, shift their positions in a cyclical manner, an endogenous clock is essential for precise navigation. An accurate chronometer which could be used at sea was long sought by human navigators for the same reasons. DJM

Bibliography

Brady, H. 1969: How are insect circadian rhythms controlled? *Nature* 223, 781–84.

Cloudsley-Thompson, John L. 1980: *Biological clocks, their functions in nature*. London: Weidenfeld & Nicolson.

Pengelley, Eric T. ed. 1974: *Circannual clocks: annual biological rhythms*. New York and London: Academic Press.

Roberts, S.K. de F. 1974: Circadian rhythms in cockroaches. Effects of optic lobe lesions. *Journal of comparative physiology* 88, 21–30.

cloze procedure Developed by Taylor (1953) as a tool for measuring readability. The word 'cloze' is derived from the *gestalt* notion of closure – the tendency to perceive as complete, forms which are actually incomplete.

In its application to written and oral messages approximately every fifth word of a text is omitted and native speakers are asked to complete the text. The scores obtained are used in making inferences about the difficulty of the text and the receiver's understanding of the message.

The cloze procedure is also used in determining the language impairment suffered by aphasics (see SPEECH DISORDERS). PM

Bibliography

Taylor, Wilson L. 1953: Cloze procedure: a new tool for measuring readability. *Journalism quarterly* 30, 415–33.

clumsy children These children show a difficulty in performing skilled movements which is inappropriate for their age and cannot be explained in terms of general intellectual impairment or gross sensory defects. An alternative term sometimes used for this disorder is developmental apraxia (a disorder of movement) and agnosia (a disorder of perception).

The pattern of problems experienced by individual children may vary considerably but often includes difficulties in the mastery of ordinary physical skills such as eating, dressing and tying shoe laces. Associated educational difficulties include problems with handwriting and drawing and, of course, physical education. Although recognized some time ago (see Orton 1937) until recently the problems of this group of children have received very little attention.

It is likely that in many cases clumsiness results from minor brain damage occurring early in life, possibly because of birth difficulties or neurological disease. It is not surprising therefore that there may be a variety of other difficulties associated with clumsiness such as speech problems, reading problems, hyperactivity and epilepsy.

Recognition that clumsiness may often be of consititutional origin should not be taken to mean that remediation is doomed to fail. Physiotherapy and various training exercises may improve basic physical skills and remedial teaching may help with the child's educational difficulties. Simply diagnosing and explaining the problem to parents, teachers and the child may be particularly important in helping to reduce feelings of frustration which can in turn lead to further emotional problems.

See also DYSLEXIA. ChasH

Bibliography

*Gordon, N. and McKinlay, I., eds 1980: *Helping clumsy children.*. Edinburgh: Churchill Livingstone.

*Gubby, S. 1975: *The clumsy child.* London and Philadelphia: Saunders.

Orton, S. T. 1937: *Reading, writing and speech problems in children.* New York: Norton.

code The notion that language is a code implies that particular grammars for encoding conceptualizations may differ between languages or, put differently, that linguistic surface forms may have little to do with the underlying logic of an utterance.

Among the most widely debated issues in socio-and psycholinguistics is that of the influence of linguistic categories and cultural conceptualizations on the processes underlying human thought (see WHORF). According to Bernstein (1971) a distinction can be made between elaborated codes, giving access to a wide range of knowledge and important positions in a social hierarchy, and restricted codes, which limit the speaker's access to knowledge and power. LABOV, on the other hand, argues that non-standard varieties of a language do not impose cognitive limitations.

Linguistic codes consist of subcomponents (e.g. the phonetic, phonological, lexical and syntactic components). The notion of 'subcode' refers to regional, social or stylistic variants of the same linguistic system (see DIALECT; SOCIOLECT). PM

Bibliography

Bernstein, Basil 1971: *Class, codes and control*, London: Routledge & Kegan Paul.

cognition in animals The question whether animals are capable of mental abstraction, or thinking, is a controversial one. Evidence from studies of problem solving and tool using suggests that some animals are capable of forming a cognitive map or model of their environment. When a horse scratches itself with a stick held in its mouth, it is difficult to explain the behavior without implying that the animal understands the spatial relationships between different parts of the body. When a chimpanzee makes a detour to attain a safe place from which to solicit food from a human, it is tempting to suppose that the chimpanzee has a mental map of the objects in its immediate environment (Menzel 1978). However, some scientists argue that it is not necessary, or even scientifically permissible, to endow animals with mental awareness or cognitive abilities. Some of the arguments and counter-arguments are reviewed by Griffin (1976). DJM

Bibliography

Griffin, Donald R. 1976: *The question of animal awareness*. New York: Rockefeller University Press.

Menzel, E.W. 1978: Cognitive mapping in chimpanzees. In *Cognitive processes in animal behavior*, ed. Stewart H. Hulse and Harry Fowler. Hillsdale, N.J.: Erlbaum Assoc.

cognition *See* language and cognition

cognitive abilities *See* perceptual and cognitive abilities

cognitive balance A term introduced by Heider (1958) to describe the cognitive tendency towards a balanced state in which perceived relationships between persons and/or objects co-exist without stress. Perceived relational triads are said to be balanced when all relations are positive or when one relation is positive and two are negative. Jaspars (see Eiser 1980) has shown, however, that the balanced or imbalanced state of a cognitive system depends upon the nature of the underlying cognitive representation. Cognitive balance affects the learning and completion of cognitive structures relating to social relationships. It also has an effect on the evaluation of social relationships, although other factors (agreement, positivity) have in general a stronger impact. Later research (Wyer 1974; Schank and Abelson 1977) shows that the effect is not as general as Heider originally suggested but depends on the nature of the relationships involved. JMFJ

Bibliography

Eiser, J.R. 1980: *Cognitive social psychology.* London: McGraw-Hill.

Heider, F. 1958: *The psychology of interpersonal relations.* New York: Wiley.

Schank, R.C. and Abelson, R.P. 1977: *Scripts, plans, goals and understanding.* Hillsdale, N.J.: Erlbaum.

Wyer, R.S. 1974: *Cognitive organization and chance: an information processing approach.* New York: Wiley.

cognitive complexity Reflects a style of thinking (cognition) and describes the number of dimensions and the relationship among dimensions on which a person places stimulus information in the process of translating a stimulus into a response. The use of several more or less independent dimensions of perception, judgment or behavior is called differentiation (e.g. Bieri 1961). Use of differentiated dimensions provides the person with the option of responding to the same stimulus (the same environmental situation) in a number of different ways. The outcome of differentiation could be the choice of (any) one response from those available, or it could be the use of some super-ordinate judgmental dimension(s) to select (in a strategic purposeful fashion) one of a number of behavioral options. The latter process is called integration (Streufert and Streufert 1978). The degree of cognitive complexity identified for any individual reflects the degree of differentiation and/or integration which he or she displays.

While some have argued that complexity might reflect an ability or a cognitive preference, the general opinion appears to be that the degree to which persons differentiate and integrate is a learned style. Recent evidence of physiological (cardiovascular and electroencephalographic) differences between more and less complex persons suggests the possibility of potential physiological determinants. Complexity appears unrelated to other measures of ability (including intelligence) or cognitive style.

Considerable research has shown that cognitive complexity predicts a wide range of phenomena, including attitude change, decision making and perceptual responses. Scott has provided evidence that predictions of behavior may, however, hold only for those specific cognitive domains for which a level of cognitive complexity (degree of differentiation and integration) has been established. SSt

Bibliography

Bieri, J. 1961: Complexity–simplicity as a personality variable in cognitive and preferential behavior. In *Functions of varied experience,* ed. D.W. Fiske and S.R. Maddi. Homewood, Illinois: Dorsey.

Streufert, S. and Streufert, S.C. 1978: *Behavior in the complex environment.* Washington, D.C.: Victor H. Winston & Sons.

cognitive consistency The tendency to avoid contradictory cognitions about social reality. During the 1950s Newcomb (1953), Festinger (1957), Heider (1958) and Osgood et al (1957) published, to some extent independently of each other, a number of similar theories in which the tension arising from imbalanced, dissonant or incongruent beliefs, knowledge or attitudes is seen as a motivating force in human behavior. In a general sense these theories were neither new nor remarkable. They followed in the tradition of rationalistic philosophers such as Spinoza and Herbart and can be regarded to some extent as the application of Gestalt principles in the domain of social cognition. For two decades these theories have, however, had a great influence in social psychology and stimulated an enormous amount of research. In quantitative terms Festinger's theory of cognitive dissonance has perhaps been the most productive, whereas Heider's Theory of Balanced States has been more influential in the long run because it is part of his general theory about common-sense knowledge.

The basic postulates of Festinger's theory are simple and somewhat vague. The theory states that relations between cognitive elements can be irrelevant, consonant or dissonant. Cognitive elements are only defined in a very general way as "the things a person knows". Dissonance exists between two elements when, considering these two alone, the opposite of one element follows from the other. Again it is not clear whether we are concerned here with logical or psychological inconsistency. Whatever the case may be, dissonance is, according to Festinger's theory, experienced as an unpleasant state which the individual will try to reduce by changing cognitions or by introducing new elements in his or her cognitive system. The tendency to reduce dissonance will be stronger, the higher the ratio of dissonant to consonant elements in a cognitive system is.

The strength of the theory is not its clarity but the fact that it has generated a large number of hypotheses which have been tested in a wide variety of situations. In this sense the theory has been extraordinarily fertile although not all its hypotheses have been confirmed, and for some of the phenomena alternative explanations have been offered. Originally Festinger suggested various hypotheses with respect to decision making, exposure to information, seeking of social support and acting under forced compliance. It is especially the latter application in the area of attitude change which has probably had the greatest impact. In one of the most influential experimental studies Festinger and Carlsmith (see Wicklund and Brehm 1976) showed that smaller bribes are more effective in making a person change his mind than larger payments. This counter-intuitive finding, which also seemed to contradict reinforcement theory, was derived from dissonance theory, but later research has shown that this finding only holds under particular circumstances. Two conditions are apparently very important. Although we are concerned with a situation of forced compliance, the person involved should have the impression that he or she has freely chosen to act in this particular way; and secondly it must then be impossible for the person to undo what he or she has done. Similar restrictions hold with respect to some of the other areas of research to which dissonance theory has been applied and certainly with respect to applications in the fields of marketing, politics, mass media, religion, clinical psychology, marriage counseling, gambling and treatment of smoking. A complete review can be found in Wicklund and Brehm (1976).

Heider's theory of balanced states is part of Heider's general attempt to unveil the principles of common-sense psychology. In this theory the concepts of sentiment, unit formation and balanced state play an important role. Sentiments refer to the positive or negative feelings a person can have about other persons or non-personal entities. A (cognitive) unit arises when several entities are perceived as belonging together due to proximity, similarity, common fate or other Gestalt factors. According to the theory, unit and sentiment relations tend towards a balanced state; that is, a situation in which both types of relations can co-exist without stress and do not show a tendency towards change. When balance is disturbed there will be a tendency towards restoring the balanced state. Heider distinguishes three types of balanced states. The first applies to the homogeneity of sentiment or unit relations with respect to other people, better known as the halo effect. The second group of balanced states applies to the relationship between sentiment and unit relations with respect to one other person. In this case there is a balanced state when all relations are either positive or negative. The third and most interesting group of balanced states is concerned with the relationships between a person and two other people and/or non-personal entities. Such a triadic set of relations is balanced, according to Heider's theory, when all relations are positive or when one relation is positive and the others are negative.

The theory has later been formalized and extended using graph theory, and numerous experiments have tested various predictions which follow from Heider's basic postulates. In general it appears that the strongest confirmation of the tendency towards balanced states can be found in learning and perception experiments, whereas the effect of imbalance on evaluative ratings of the social situation is much less pronounced. This is due to the fact that the pleasant or unpleasant nature of a situation is determined also by the attitude towards the other person in the situation and the extent to which persons in the situation agree with each other. In fact it is much easier to understand Heider's theory of balanced states when one realizes that the relations he is concerned with can be reformulated as linguistic relations between subject, object and verb in a sentence. This reformulation also makes clear that the balanced effects suggested are far less general than was originally thought because they depend very much upon the specific nature of the relationships.

Osgood's congruity principle and Newcomb's analysis of communicative acts do not differ essentially from the theories of Festinger and Heider and will therefore not be discussed here.

Research on cognitive consistency has decreased considerably in recent years, but the ideas of the originators are still very much alive in a disguised form in various other areas of research. Most theories about attitude change regard a discrepancy between a person's original attitude and the attitude advocated in a persuasive communication as the core of the attitude change process. One of the major strategies of attitude change derives in fact from Festinger's idea that attitude change can be brought about indirectly by first changing a person's behavior, as in a forced compliance situation, and relying on dissonance for a change of the person's attitude. JMFJ

Bibliography

Festinger, L. 1957: *A theory of cognitive dissonance*. Stanford, California: Stanford University Press.

Heider, F. 1958: *The psychology of interpersonal relations*. New York: Wiley.

Newcomb, T.M. 1953: An approach to the study of communicative acts. *Psychological review* 60, 393–404.

Osgood, C.E., Suci, G.J. and Tannenbaum, P.H. 1957: *The measurement of meaning*. Urbana: University of Illinois Press.

Wicklund, J.W. and Brehm, J.W. 1976: *Perspectives in cognitive dissonance*. New York: Wiley.

Zajonc, R.B. 1969: Cognitive theories in social psychology. In *Handbook of social psychology* 2nd edn, ed. G. Lindzey and E. Aronson. Addison-Wesley.

cognitive development, non-Piagetian studies

Although current work on cognitive development is dominated by the ideas of Piaget, there are nevertheless strands of thought about the subject whose origins owe nothing to his oeuvre, and these have an important place in the study of childhood.

One of these was the Gestalt school. Its members' main interest was in perception which they thought to be innately determined and which was in their view largely concerned with taking in patterns. This led them to argue that even very young children are aware of relative values, a belief that brought them into head-on conflict not only with Piaget and his supporters but also with the behaviorist school in America. In fact the pioneering experiments on judgments of relative size and brightness carried out in the early twentieth century by Kohler, a leading Gestalt psychologist, have been largely vindicated, and there can be little doubt that young children are as adept as Kohler claimed in dealing with relative values.

At much the same time the work of Vygotsky in Russia launched a theory and a type of experiment which have played an important role in studies of child development and have produced conclusions quite different from Piaget's. Vygotsky's central idea was that language, and particularly what he called inner speech, transforms the child's cognitive abilities. To support his hypothesis Vygotsky observed children speaking in different situations and tried to relate what they said to what they actually did when they were solving problems. He was particularly interested in any direct connection between the two, as shown by his well known story of a boy drawing a picture of a car who broke his crayon, muttered 'broken' and went on to draw a broken car.

The issue of the relationship between language and cognition was taken up by others, most notably at first by behaviorists in America and then in quite a different way by Jerome Bruner. It is a question which still awaits an answer. But the study of language acquisition per se has produced some solid data. We know a great deal not only about how children's sentences develop, thanks to the observational work of Roger Brown and others, but also about the way in which adults talk to children.

A final major strand in studies of cognitive development takes as its inspiration the notion of information processing. The notion that humans can be regarded as limited information channels is a familiar one, and it has the advantage of leading to some precise predictions. By and large when these have been made about children the idea has been that there are no great qualitative differences between them and adults, but that the major cognitive changes in childhood are quantitative – the capacity of the information channel, the size of the memory store and so on. More recently a group of psychologists interested in what they call meta-memory and meta-cognition have argued that the changes are not so much in the machine's capacity as in the correct application of the right strategies at the right time. This takes the subject into the area of education because one of the most interesting parts of this recent concentration on the extent to which children are aware of the appropriate strategies has been its application to the study of learning to read and to write. PEB

Bibliography

Gardner, H. 1982: *Developmental psychology*. 2nd edn. Boston: Little Brown and Co.

Vygotsky, Lev. S. 1962: *Thought and language*. Cambridge, Mass.: MIT; New York and London: Wiley.

cognitive development *See above, and also* Piaget

cognitive dissonance One of the consistency theories of attitude change that assumes that a person behaves in a way which will maximize the internal consistency of his or her cognitive system and that groups also strive to maximize the internal consistency of their interpersonal relations. Apart from cognitive dissonance theory (Festinger 1957) there are Heider's balance theory (1946), and Osgood and Tannenbaum's congruity theory (1955). Cognitive dissonance theory was, however, by far the most influential and dominated attitude research for over a decade.

The core of the theory is deceptively simple: two cognitive elements (thoughts, attitudes, beliefs) are said to be in a dissonant relation, if the obverse of the one would follow from the other. Because dissonance is psychologically uncomfortable, its existence will motivate a person to reduce it and achieve consonance. Further, when dissonance is present, a person will actively avoid situations and information which would be likely to increase it.

Many empirical studies have tested the theory, many of them being supportive. One of the more appealing aspects of the theory has been that it makes counter-intuitive hypotheses which are often confirmed (Festinger and Carlsmith 1959).

The theory and research is not without its critics. It has been attacked for being vague and simplistic and not clearly defining its terms "cognitive element", "follow from" etc. The very parsimoniousness of the theory is seen as a problem rather than an asset. The methodology of experiments to "prove" the theory has also been attacked because of artifacts, confounding variables and problems of external validity. Others have maintained that cognitive dissonance is a new name for an old theory, or that individual differences have been ignored. The most widely quoted as well as hotly disputed criticism of the theory is that of Chapanis and Chapanis (1964). AF

Bibliography

Chapanis, N. and A. 1964: Cognitive dissonance: Five years later. *Psychological bulletin* 61, 1–22.

Festinger, L. 1957: *A theory of cognitive dissonance*. Stanford: Stanford University Press.

——— and Carlsmith, J. 1959: Cognitive consequences of forced compliance. *Journal of abnormal and social psychology* 58, 203–10.

Heider, F. 1946: Attitudes and cognitive organization. *Journal of psychology* 21, 107–12.

Osgood, C. and Tannenbaum, P. 1955: The principle of congruity in the prediction of attitude change. *Psychological review* 62, 42–55.

cognitive ergonomics *See* ergonomics, cognitive

cognitive ethology A branch of ETHOLOGY introduced by Griffin (1976) concerned with awareness or mental experience in animals and its effects on their behavior. Griffin has suggested that animal behaviorists should reconsider the evolutionary continuity of mental characteristics between man and other animals based on evidence that animals employ some sort of internal imagery of their surroundings. Practitioners assume that man is not uniquely endowed with conscious awareness, and that it is more likely than not that mental experiences in people and animals share important properties without being completely identical. Cognitive ethology can be contrasted to ANTHROPOMORPHISM which is the attribution of human thoughts and feelings to animals. Griffin's working definitions in referring to animals are: *mental experience* – thought about objects and events that are remote in time and space from immediate sensations; *awareness* – the set of interrelated mental images of the flow of events; *intention* – a mental image of future events in which the intender places himself as participant and makes a choice as to which image he will try to bring to reality; and *consciousness* – the presence of mental images and their use by an animal to regulate its behavior. PJA

Bibliography

Griffin, Donald 1976: *The question of animal awareness: evolutionary continuity of mental experience*. New York: Rockefeller University Press.

cognitive meaning *See* meaning, cognitive

cognitive personality theory Is concerned with the development of individual differences in the processes of thinking as they affect the perceptions and behavior of individuals. While the early personality theorists (Freud, Jung, Adler) were more concerned with biological and (later) social needs, some evidence of cognitive components of personality was nonetheless present. An example is found in Freud's concept of the EGO as a (potentially) cognitive mediator between the id and the SUPEREGO. It was, however, not until the advent of neo-Freudian theory that writers such as Erikson and Sullivan utilized developmental formulations (helped in part by the work of G.H. Mead, Jean Piaget and others) to point towards emerging individual differences as cognitive in character. Sullivan, for example, distinguished between prototaxic thought (a direct series of momentary states in the sensitive organism, not unlike what James called the "stream of consciousness"), parataxic thought (identifying events that occur at the same time or in the same space as causally related), and syntaxic thought (use of consensually validated, primarily verbal thought resulting in the potential of communication among persons). Sullivan argued that cognitive development progresses from prototaxic to syntaxic cognition. Obviously, individual differences may emerge in both the degree and the rapidity of advancement toward higher syntaxic cognitive levels.

The work of PIAGET, based on experiments with children and adolescents (rather than on psychiatric observation, as was the case with most Freudian and neo-Freudian efforts) differs greatly from Freudian and even neo-Freudian viewpoints in its emphasis on the development of thought as opposed to need-states or other affective components as driving forces of the personality. Inhelder and Piaget (1958) describe the growth of formal thinking (cognition) and explore the implications of cognitive maturation as they influence personality development, resulting in specific rates of progress towards identity formation, growth of autonomy, future orientation and other cognitively more mature processes. Although it has recently been argued that the developmental sequences observed by Piaget, Kohlberg, and others are in part misplaced on the developmental time dimension (see Gelman 1978), they have been and continue to be aids for the understanding of how individual differences in cognitive characteristics of people emerge during childhood and adolescence.

It has generally been recognized that regularities and universals (i.e. the absence of differences among individuals) are greater in younger than in older children. In other words variability, including the degree of individual differences in cognitive characteristics, tends to increase with increasing age into adulthood. The lesser differences among young children are, however, often credited with being the origin of the much greater cognitive discrepancies which we see in the adult personality. As a result a number of theorists have explored the cognitive development of children to find causes for later personality characteristics. Most frequently it has been assumed that the child or adolescent can become arrested at some stage of development, producing some degree of immature adult cognition and with it inappropriate and immature behavior. Unfortunately most attempts to identify stages of development reflecting specific individual differences (for example Harvey, Hunt and Schroder's "System Theory") have suffered from the confounding of personality structure with the content of persons' attitudes or belief systems.

A somewhat different approach to cognitive personality theory grew out of the concept that individuals respond to their mental models of reality rather than to reality directly. From this point of view a person is conceived as a complex information processing system. Cognition represents the process of translating a stimulus input into a perception and, subsequently, into a potential behavioral output. Mental models would be likely to differ among people who have experienced different environments, have lived in different cultures, and have had different learning experiences. On the other hand common experiences can lead to shared mental models. People with shared models, (i.e. people who would respond to specific inputs from the environment in the same or similar fashion) are often seen as having the same personality type.

An individual's well-established mental model is likely to identify input stimuli as belonging to specific groups. Identifications of this kind are made in the attempt to organize experience into meaningful patterns. Input information may well be misinterpreted in the process. If, for example, a person's mental model would suggest that persons from country X typically behave in a certain way, then the behavior of any representative of that country would be seen in exactly that fashion, even if the actual behavior was somewhat different. In addition if the representative of that country behaved in a widely divergent way, his or her actions would probably be explained by invoking the effects of temporary environmental demands or by considering some other exception to the rule. The mental model, in other words, allows a person to view the world in a cognitively consistent (even if inaccurate) way.

Early assumptions of commonalities in behavior among certain groups resulted in theories exemplified by the identification of the Authoritarian Personality (Adorno et al. 1950). It was assumed that the authoritarian (pre-Nazi) personality had certain characteristics that would be common across cultures, but would occur with particular frequency in Germany and other one-time fascist countries. While authoritarianism was, for a time, the most popular concept in personality theory, it did not fulfill much of its promise. Authoritarians were found in all cultures. The behavior of the authoritarian was not necessarily violent as had been expected by many. Most of all, authoritarianism appeared not to be a purely cognitive concept: an authoritarian, as measured by Adorno et al. F Scale, turned out to be a person with two separate characteristics: someone with conservative attitudes or beliefs, and an acquiescent responder who is likely to agree with any strongly worded statement regardless of the content of the statement. While the first characteristic of the authoritarian represents the content (attitude, belief) of thought, the second (acquiescing in strongly worded statements) represents a cognitive characteristic. To the degree to which a person with strong liberal or politically leftwing attitudes is likely to be acquiescent, that person would, at least from the view of cognitive personality theory, be equally as authoritarian as the potential fascist.

In an attempt to develop a more pure cognitive measure of personality Rokeach (1960) focused on rigidity and on dogmatism. His dogmatism scale is designed primarily to measure fixed and strongly held (inflexible) cognitions across a number of domains. Scoring is based on agreement with dogmatic statements, even in the face of inherent inconsistencies worked into the statements. Dogmatic cognition has been shown to relate to prejudice, to attitude change characteristics, and to abnormal behavior. The work of Rokeach moved in the direction of a stylistic approach to cognition: persons are assumed to learn specific cognitive patterns i.e. styles in dealing with environmental stimulation.

Several theorists have focused on cognitive styles to explain how an individual translates a stimulus into a response. Cognitive styles are viewed as typical ways of organizing and patterning of information, i.e. the way in which an individual conceptually organizes information from the environment. The work in this area derived from the developmental stages of Piaget and others, from Lewin's concept of differentiation and hierarchical organization and, in part, from the use of factor analytic techniques in the 1950s which made it possible to relate a number of different personality measures and their underlying theoretical conceptualizations to each other. All cognitive style theories have at least one major factor in common: they tend to emphasize structure of thought rather than content of thought. Structure reflects how cognition is organized, in other words, how people think (how they relate perceptions, ideas, etc. to each other). In contrast content refers to what knowledge is available, what a person's attitudes and beliefs are, and so on.

The cognitive styles (in some cases referred to as cognitive controls) on which persons differ have been described by a number of theorists as influencing specific cognitive perceptions or behavior. Among those styles are: (1) tolerance for unrealistic experiences, the readiness to accept experiences that are at variance with conventional reality; (2) conceptual differentiation, the tendency to use many or few categories; (3) constricted-flexible control, the degree to which persons are free of influence by single powerful cues; (4) leveling-sharpening, the degree to which previous information stored in memory is integrated into present perceptions; (5) focussing-scanning, the breadth with which an individual verifies the judgments he or she makes; (6) field dependence-independence, the degree to which individuals structure their perceptual field or require externally imposed structure (see COGNITIVE STYLE); (7) category width, the range of events which individuals consider likely to occur; (8) cognitive complexity, the number and interaction of cognitive judgment dimensions brought to bear on a stimulus configuration (see COGNITIVE COMPLEXITY); and (9) reflection-impulsivity, the speed with which a person makes decisions under conditions of uncertainty. A number of attempts have been made to integrate the various cognitive styles into an overall conceptualization of cognitive personality structure. A generally satisfactory integration has yet to be found. Nonetheless a number of cognitive styles (particularly cognitive complexity and field dependence-independence) have been quite useful for the prediction of a wide range of behavior.

Recent discussions have centered around the question whether creativity as a personality characteristic is or is not cognitively determined. In part the problem of creativity is caught up with the problem of intelligence. While it has been shown that the relationship between intelligence and creativity is minimal, the attacks on intelligence as an inherent ability across a number of domains have also raised the question whether cognitive styles and creativity reflect inherent abilities, learned styles of cognition, or acquired preferences of responding. Those who argue that the creative process is a style under cognitive control nonetheless disagree on the particular style of cognition that best reflects creative thought and action. For example it has been suggested that creativity is akin to integration in cognitive complexity, that it reflects regression of thought towards simpler commonalities, or that it implies homospatial thinking – a process whereby more than one cognitive concept may occupy the same cognitive space.

The interest in cognitive approaches to personality and personality theory has certainly been on the increase in the last quarter century. In particular the interest in cognitive styles has grown considerably. Another impetus toward the emphasis on cognitive personality theory has come from ARTIFICIAL INTELLIGENCE. It has been argued that cognitive personality theory may some day become part of the wider cognitive science which is now coming into existence. By a joint effort of those who employ experimental methodology applied to cognition and cognitive personality theory and those who focus on intelligent computer software to gain greater insights into cognitive potentials, we may learn more about the characteristics and the functioning of the small scale model of the environment which guides a person's perceptions and behavior and which, to some major or minor degree, sets one person apart from all other persons. SSt

Bibliography

Adorno, T.W. et al. 1950: *The authoritarian personality*. New York: Harper.

Gelman, R. 1978: Cognitive development. *Annual review of psychology* 297–332.

Inhelder, B. and Piaget, J. 1958: *The growth of logical thinking from childhood to adolescence*. New York: Basic Books.

Rokeach, M. 1960: *The open and closed mind*. New York: Basic Books.

cognitive psychology A broad discipline, containing numerous sub-specialities, all of which include a fundamental interest in mental processes and products. A broader, but related term is cognitive science which encompasses the diverse fields of psychology, computing science–particularly that branch known as artificial intelligence, psycholinguistics, psychopharmacology–the study of the effect of drugs on consciousness, and neurobiology–the study of the nervous system. In both cases the object is to obtain an increased understanding of the human mind, although contributions may well come from a study of other minds both animate and artificial (i.e. computer). Furthermore, many of the traditional topics of psychology–the study of perception, memory, language, learning and child development are also of interest to cognitive psychologists. The major contribution of cognitive approaches is that these phenomena are now being interpreted from perspectives that make explicit mention of mental processes.

In one sense cognitive psychology is relatively new: Ulric Neisser's book, *Cognitive Psychology* 1967, is often identified as an important milestone. However during the years immediately preceeding 1967 collections of readings on cognitive psychology were already available containing articles by authors such as David Ausubel, Jerome Bruner, Carl Hovland, George Miller, Allen Newell, Jean Piaget and Herbert Simon. A more recent collection of articles has been edited by Estes (1975–78) in a six volume review of learning and cognition. For the reader whose preference lies with current statements on the state-of-the-art, Hunt's (1982) overview of cognitive science is particularly readable for the beginner, Anderson (1980) provides an excellent undergraduate level textbook on cognitive psychology and Lachman, Lachman and Butterfield (1979) focus on a research approach known as information processing, currently a dominant influence in cognitive psychology.

Essentially, the goal of information processing approaches is to model human cognitive processes, usually by means of computer programs. These models may be attempted for neural processes, for elementary information processes (e.g. retrieval from memory, recognition of simple symbols) or for higher mental processes (e.g. problem solving). Much of Simon's work has involved efforts at modelling higher mental processes (e.g. Newell and Simon 1972). Posner and McLeod (1982) emphasized elementary mental operations when they reviewed recent research which examined specific types of problems (e.g. reading, listening, viewing pictures, mental arithmetic). Lindsay and Norman (1977) provide one example of an attempt to integrate the various topics that are being interpreted from this perspective: perception, visual and auditory systems, neural networks, pattern recognition, attention, memory, language, learning, cognitive development, problem solving, stress, emotion, and even social interactions. However, many of these same topics are of interest to other cognitive interpretations besides that of information processing. Before a brief discussion of these other approaches is provided, a few comments on the way in which cognitive psychologists conduct their research deserves mention.

Much of the investigation into elementary mental operations has involved very precise measures of a subject's reaction time (the time it takes to respond in a particular fashion to a specific situation). As one example, a well-designed study by Hunt, Davidson and Lansman (1981) measured the reaction times for subjects to decide whether an item was a member of a category (e.g. is a car a vehicle?), whether two words belonged to the same category (e.g. apple–peach) or whether two words have the same name (e.g. date–date). The quick reaction times (values such as 0.653 seconds) were considered to be measures of the time required to access a well-known item from long-term memory. A careful analysis of minute differences in subjects' responses indicated statistical relationships between these measures and scores on traditional reading and vocabulary tests. Similarly, some studies rely on very precise measurements of eye movement in attempts to relate these to judgments in the similarity or difference of two items, to the process of reading or even to the playing of chess. Another methodology which is becoming more popular is called protocol analysis. Very simply, the idea is to have the subject discuss what he or she is doing while engaged in a particular task such as solving a problem. This gives the researcher two types of information: the actions taken by the subject and the subject's explanation of his actions.

In addition to considering the ways in which cognitive psychologists conduct their work, it is also important to identify the major topics that have occupied, and continue to interest, these researchers. Foremost among these topics is the study of memory. This focus has a rich tradition, including the contributions of the English psychologist Frederic Bartlett, whose book *Remembering* (1932) is recognized as one of the classics in psychology. Bartlett's approach was an important departure from the traditional study of memory through the use of nonsense syllables. Questions such as "Under what conditions can a subject remember a consonant–vowel–consonant triad such as XER?" were replaced with a concern for more realistic situations which required the remembering of faces and short stories. Bartlett's early concern for remembering images is reflected in an extensive comparison of factors influencing the memory of linguistic and pictorial images (see e.g. Paivio 1979). The study of memory is also an important topic for information processing interpretations. Terms such as short term memory (STM), long term memory (LTM), working memory, and buffers are common, representing close analogies with computer processes. The study of memory is also becoming an important consideration for those whose primary perspective is the study of knowledge, thereby helping to bring about a rapprochement between psychology and philosophy.

Work on the nature of knowledge has also benefited from the extremely strong influence of the Swiss psychologists Jean Piaget and Barbel Inhelder and their emphasis on the cognitive development of the growing child. More research has been conducted on a worldwide basis on issues relating to their work than on any other psychological topic involving children. Piaget's work began with an interest in intelligence tests and then, covering a span of almost seventy years, concentrated on the distinctive nature of children's responses to a variety of problems and showed how these differed at different age-levels. This work has, at least in one sense, come full circle to influence our current conceptions of intelligence and the nature of individual differences.

Investigations into the nature and structure of knowledge have received a strong contribution in recent years from researchers such as Roger Schank, Robert Abelson, David Rumelhart, Andrew Ortony, Allan Collins and Marvin Minsky. Schank and Abelson have developed the notion of a script closely parallel to European work on social rule systems (Collett 1978)–an organized body of knowledge related to a specific situation (eating in a restaurant) which permits us to comprehend the wide variety of phenomena associated with the situation (sitting down, reading the menu, ordering, eating, paying the bill, tipping, leaving). This is also related to work on prototypes (which is the more typical bird–an ostrich or a robin?) and questions having to do with the specific features of an object or event.

In summary, three points deserve emphasis. Cognitive psychology is a very broad field, examining a multitude of topics–perception, attention, problem solving, memory, learning, cognitive development and language. Second, there is a high degree of interaction among these various sub-disciplines. The results of one scientist's work with computers may be of intense interest to another who is working with young children. Third, and not to be underestimated, it represents a new awareness of a traditional way of approaching psychological problems, and is thought by many to have the potential to provide an integrated understanding of issues which have often been treated separately in the past. JDB

Bibliography

*Anderson, J.R. 1980: *Cognitive psychology and its implications.* San Francisco: W.H. Freeman.

Bartlett, F.C. 1932: *Remembering: a study in experimental and social psychology.* Cambridge: Cambridge University Press; New York: Macmillan.

Collett, Peter, ed. 1978: *Social rules and social behaviour.* Oxford: Basil Blackwell; Totowa, N.J.: Rowman & Littlefield.

Estes, W.K. ed.. 1975–78: *Handbook of learning and cognitive processes.* 6 vols. Hillsdale, N.J.: Lawrence Erlbaum.

*Hunt, E.B., Davidson, J. and Lansman, M. 1981: Individual differences in long-term memory access. *Memory and cognition* 9, 6, 599–608.

Hunt, M. 1982: *The universe within.* New York: Simon and Schuster.

*Lachman, R., Lachman, J.L. and Butterfield, E.C. 1979: *Cognitive psychology and information processing: an introduction.* Hillsdale, N.J.: Lawrence Erlbaum.

Lindsay, P.H. and Norman, D.A. 1977: *Human information processing.* 2nd edn. New York and London: Academic Press.

Neisser, U. 1967: *Cognitive psychology.* New York: Appleton-Century-Crofts.

Newell, A. & Simon, H.A. 1972: *Human problem solving.* Englewood Cliff: N.J.: Prentice-Hall.

Paivio, A. 1979: *Imagery and verbal processes.* Hillsdale, N.J.: Lawrence Erlbaum.

Posner, M.I. and McLeod, P. 1982: Information processing models–in search of elementary operations. *Annual review of psychology* 33, 477–514.

cognitive psychology and physiology The importance of the relationship between cognitive psychology and physiology is more commonly denied than affirmed. However there are strong reasons why they should cooperate.

The main reason for denying the significance of any relationship is that cognitive psychology (often associated with a functionalist approach to the study of intelligence, and usually relying upon work in ARTIFICIAL INTELLIGENCE) takes as *explananda* any complex systems that instantiate a certain kind of organization among their internal states, inputs and outputs. Although the most interesting such systems are human organisms, it is argued that systems constructed from different sorts of physical stuff may achieve the same kind of abstract organization among appropriately identified internal states as that found or postulated in sophisticated organisms. This view, labeled "multiple realizability", is taken to prove the near-irrelevance of the multiply-variable physical bases of cognitive capacity: these become idiosyncratic engineering details peculiar to a particular system.

There are however theoretical and methodological problems in treating cognitive psychology as a discipline quite autonomous of the physiological sciences. One difficulty is that neither side of the alleged divide has a "given" conceptual structure or taxonomy of *explananda* and *explanantia*, and in order to determine this framework each needs cooperation from the other. On the one hand, part of the appeal of cognitive psychology is that it seems to be continuous with the commonsense psychology of the layman, examining cognitive capacities familiar to all. However, the classifications of the vernacular have often proved unreliable in the physical sciences – failing to pick out natural *explananda*, or needing substantial modification before they are suitable to scientific needs – and we should not expect that commonsense psychology provides any more secure a conceptual basis for empirical research. Indeed, neuropsychological data concerning lesions such as commissurotomy and hemispherectomy, or those that produce alexia, aphasia, the various agnosias or other systematically-organized dysfunctions, have revealed much about the organization of speech, comprehension, perception and recognition that common sense or cognitive psychology, unaided, could never guess at – and these are data about cognitive abilities (see NEUROANATOMICAL FUNCTIONS AND BEHAVIOR). Cognitive psychology, therefore, should welcome a "bottom up" contribution from the neurosciences to help it develop a more detailed, reliable and fruitful taxonomy of the cognitive activities it studies.

The neurosciences, on the other hand, need "top down" contributions from cognitive psychology (and from theories in psychology generally) to assist their own theory-construction. For these sciences seek to show how the brain works *to explain behavior*; in other words, they need *explananda* from the psychological sciences, however conjectural or tentative these may be, so that they can identify appropriate *explanantia*. The great difficulty of devising adequate theoretical and conceptual frameworks has been systematically underestimated in the literature, despite the extent of disagreement about them by cognitive psychologists in particular and brain and behavioral scientists in general; no consensus is likely to emerge among cognitive psychologists unless the findings of the neurosciences are used to help decide between the competing and underdetermined theories found in the literature.

The denial of a worthwhile link between cognitive psychology and physiology looks most plausible when one considers the gulf between complex cognitive abilities and micro-level neural events. Then there seems to be an unbridgeable chasm between psychological, intentional terms and the terms used to describe synapses or electric circuits. However, the gulf is only apparent. Theories in cognitive psychology require various levels of description, since any complicated capacity (e.g. memory) may need dissection into constituent subcapacities; in the neurosciences, the functions of cerebral structure at all stages of complexity are investigated, from the hemispheres down to individual cells. Correspondingly, the terms used to describe either the subcapacities of cognitive psychology or the activities of structures such as the hippocampus or visual cortex may be neither distinctively "psychological" nor distinctively "physiological" – that old dichotomy reveals its insignificance. Indeed, whether one calls a research project "psychological" or "neuropsychological" may often prove to be an unreal question.

It can now be seen that "multiple realizability" requires relativization to particular levels of description of the system in question. It is boring that both humans and calculators can add, since the similarity holds only at a superficial level of description, suggesting nothing relevant to the more detailed study of either. It is more interesting that computers can play chess, for this complex ability presupposes a number of contributory subcapacities, some of which *may* prove to be realized in the human brain in the same sort of way as they are in the computer.

We can conclude with three points against the argument that multiple realizability secures the independence of cognitive psychology from physiology. First: theories in the neurosciences are also "multiply realizable" – one can model on computers hypotheses about, say, the activities of cerebellum or hippocampus. The feature is in no way peculiar to cognitive psychology. Second: the relevant "multiplicity" of realization is a matter of divergent explanations *at the next level down*. Thus, Ø-ing is variably realised by systems S and T if the explanation of S's Ø-ing postulates, for instance, subordinate processes *a*, *b* and *c*, while the explanation of T's Ø-ing postulates subordinate processes *b*, *d* and *e*. Now, not only may *a*, *b*, *c*, *d* and *e* be "psychological" processes themselves – proving that multiple realizability need not involve different *physical* realizations of a psychological state – but we need not suppose that the number of different realizations will be uncontrollably large. Radical multiplicity is indeed found if one makes the mistake of jumping levels and points to the indefinitely-large set of *micro*-states that (ultimately) underpin a complex cognitive activity; but this "multiple realizability", gained by jumping levels, would make *all* macro phenomena multiply realizable (the gas laws, for instance, would be "multiply realizable" by gases of different atomic constitutions). Third: multiple realizability has long been familiar to the brain and behavioral sciences, but regarded rather as an extra complexity in, than a barrier to, psycho-physical research: human brains differ slightly at all levels of organization, the brain is in some respects plastic, and many laws have to be more or less species-specific. KVW

Bibliography

Clark, Austen 1980: *Psychological models and neural mechanisms*. Oxford and New York: Oxford University Press.

cognitive style Cognitive style is defined as an individual's characteristic and consistent manner of processing and organizing what he sees and thinks about (Messick 1976; Witkin et al. 1971). Nineteen major cognitive styles have been distinguished (Messick 1976) which can be classified as one of three types.

First, there are cognitive styles which are related to abilities to perform a specific task and which are assessed in terms of the accuracy or correctness of performance (Messick 1976). An example of this cognitive style is field-independence versus field-dependence which refers to the tendency to approach situations and tasks in an analytical as opposed to a global way. It is assessed in tasks which test the ability to discriminate a figure from its background.

Second, there are cognitive styles which differ in the value which can be attributed to them. An instance of this type of cognitive style is cognitive complexity versus cognitive simplicity which refers to the extent to which people organize events, and especially social behavior, in a complex, multidimensional, and discriminating manner. In processing certain types of information a cognitively complex style is valued more highly than a cognitively simple style (Goldstein and Blackman 1977).

Third, some cognitive styles do not relate to abilities, and values are not attributed to them. An example is the cognitive style "breadth of categorization", which describes a tendency to think of specified categories as broad and inclusive or as narrow and exclusive.

A number of questions remain unresolved in cognitive style research. These include how cognitive styles are produced, e.g. consciously or unconsciously; the extent to which they are open to self-control and modification; and whether they indicate an actual capacity to process information in a certain manner or merely a preference for doing so. The conceptual adequacy of cognitive style and its related concepts has also been questioned (Kurtz 1969).

DPH

Bibliography

Goldstein, K.M. and Blackman S. 1977: Assessment of cognitive style. In *Advances in psychological measurement* (Vol. 4), ed. P. McReynolds. London and San Francisco, Calif.: Jossey-Bass.

Kurtz, R.M. 1969: A conceptual investigation of Witkin's notion of perceptual style. *Mind* 78, 522–33.

Messick, Samuel 1976: Personality differences in cognition and creativity. In *Individuality in learning*, ed. S. Messick et al. London and San Francisco: Jossey-Bass.

Witkin, H.A. et al. 1971: *A manual for the embedded figures tests*. Palo Alto, Calif.: Consulting Psychologists Press.

cognitive therapy A form of psychotherapy developed by Aaron Beck in the United States in the 1960s. Beck postulates that a person's thoughts (cognitions is the favored term here) primarily determine his or her behavior. In neurosis, and particularly in depression, where poor self-regard is a common feature, the patient's thoughts about himself are said to be incorrect because of faulty learning: erroneous premises and misconceptions are the source of such thoughts as for example, that he has achieved nothing, deserves criticism or has little to offer. Misinterpretations of reality become automatic and entrenched. In cognitive therapy the chief priority is to correct faulty conceptions and thereby eradicate negative automatic thoughts and promote realistic thinking. The therapist adopts an active role in making the patient aware of his automatic thoughts and helps him to realize that they are not true. SB

Bibliography

Beck, A.T. 1976: *Cognitive therapy and the emotional disorders.* New York: International Universities Press.

cohesiveness Refers to the forces that hold a group together. Cohesiveness is based upon the attraction that the members of the group feel for each other and/or the sharing of the common group goal. Cohesive groups are not necessarily more productive than non-cohesive groups. As Shaw (1976) noted, group members who are attracted to the group work harder to achieve its goals. If the norms of the group favor productivity, cohesiveness has a positive influence. If the norm is to avoid work, cohesive groups are less productive than non-cohesive groups.

Cohesiveness constitutes in particular a danger for decision making in groups, since it will induce pressures towards uniformity and conformity, leading to "group think". JMFJ

Bibliography

Janis, I.L. 1972: *Victims of group think.* Boston: Houghton Miflin.

Shaw, M.E. 1976: *Group dynamics: the dynamics of small group behavior.* New York: McGraw Hill.

cohort analysis The search for systematic variability that is attributable to a group of individuals having experienced the same event during the same interval of time. Forms of cohort analysis are found in sociology, demography, economics, psychology and other social and behavioral sciences (see e.g. Ryder 1965). In psychology, especially developmental psychology, cohort analysis has focussed almost exclusively on the *birth cohort,* individuals born during the same time interval, as a basis for categorizing sources of changes in, and differences among individuals. For example, differences in the average performance of twenty-year olds and seventy-year olds measured in the year 1980 on an intellectual task may be attributable to changes that are intrinsic to "ageing processes" but such differences could also be due to other influences; those associated with the fact that the seventy-year-olds were born in 1910 and have spent their first twenty years in one set of educational, political, nutritional etc. circumstances whereas the twenty-year olds were born in 1960 and have spent their first twenty years in a different set of circumstances. Individuals who differ in chronological age simultaneously differ in experienced history-specific characteristics that may be related to differences in their behavioral attributes. Important birth cohort and age differences need not be fifty-year ones; differences as small as one year were found to be significant in adolescent personality development in the 1970s (Nesselroade and Baltes 1974). Additional support for the predictive validity of cohort and age classification is found in the areas of ability and personality, verbal learning and memory, sexual attitudes and behavior, and physical attributes.

In current developmental research, papers by Schaie (1965) and Baltes (1968) have been particularly influential in establishing the value of identifying cohort and other sources of variation within and between individuals. Schaie presented a General Developmental Model in which birth cohort, chronological age, and time of measurement were identified as representing fundamental sources of variability, the magnitude of which could be estimated by means of a carefully selected set of analysis strategies. In a critique of Schaie's model, Baltes emphasized the difference between description and explanation, argued that the Schaie model was more useful as a guide to data collection than data analysis, and developed a rationale for cross-sectional and longitudinal sequences as general data collection strategies for distinguishing cohort, age and time of measurement effects. Subsequently, Schaie and Baltes (1975) agreed on the value of sequential strategies for the purpose of data collection but not on the validity of causal inferences based on data derived from them.

The determination of the magnitude of cohort, age and time effects is hindered because of dependency among the three components as they are traditionally defined. That situation has led to several developments of, and critical exchanges concerning, analytical and statistical methods for estimating cohort, age and time of measurement effects (Horn and McArdle 1980).

The concepts of cohort and cohort effects, despite their limitations for formulating explanatory accounts, constitute an important step in the evolution of ideas about development. Their discovery and study have brought about alternative ways of conceptualizing developmental phenomena and more sophisticated appraisals of the traditional longitudinal and cross-sectional research designs and methods. The substantive and methodological research efforts associated with identifying and studying cohort, age and time of measurement effects have helped to foster a significant contemporary emphasis on the study of development as a phenomenon that occurs over the life-span rather than being confined to the first eighteen or so years of life.

Cohort analysis, in explicitly recognizing the potential impact on the course of development of influences that are tied to social/environmental and biological changes has helped to focus attention on two important questions: which change phenomena are to be included in the province of developmental study and how general and permanent can one expect lawful relationships concerning development to be (Gergen, 1980). Definitive answers are yet to come but cohort analysis has underscored the importance of attending to context if developmental processes are to be more fully understood. Additional benefits of cohort analysis will be realized as cohort effects are analysed in process variable terms (Baltes, Cornelius and Nesselroade 1978). JRN

Bibliography

Baltes, P.B. 1968: Longitudinal and cross-sectional sequences in the study of age and generation effects. *Human development* 11, 145–71.

———, Cornelius, S.W. and Nesselroade, J.R. 1978: Cohort effects in developmental psychology: Theoretical and methodological perspectives. *Minnesota symposia on child psychology* vol. 11. Hillsdale, N.J.: Erlbaum Associates.

Gergen, K.J. 1980: The emerging crisis in life-span developmental theory. In *Life-span development and behavior* ed. P.B. Baltes and O.G. Brim, Jr. vol. 3. New York: Academic Press.

Horn, J.L. and McArdle, J.J. 1980: Perspectives on mathematical/statistical model building (MASMOB) in research on aging. In *Aging in the 1980s*, ed. L.W. Poon. Washington, D.C.: American Psychological Association.

Nesselroade, J.R. and Baltes, P.B. 1974: Adolescent personality development and historical change: 1970–1972. *Monographs of the Society for Research in Child Development*, 39, (serial no. 154).

Riley, M.W., Johnson, W. & Foner, A., eds. 1972: *Aging and society*. Vol. 3. *A sociology of age stratification*. New York: Russell Sage.

Ryder, N.B. 1965: The cohort as a concept in the study of social change. *American sociological review* 30, 843–61.

Schaie, K.W. 1965: A general model for the study of developmental problems. *Psychological bulletin* 64, 92–107.

——— and Baltes, P.B. 1975: On sequential strategies in developmental research and the Schaie–Baltes controversy: Description or explanation? *Human development* 18, 384–90.

collective unconscious *See* Jung, Carl

color vision The ability to distinguish different wavelengths of light (or different mixtures of wavelengths), independently of their luminance.

Our color discrimination is strictly limited: mixtures of light that are physically very different may look identical to us. The limitation derives from the most fundamental property of human color vision, that of *trichromacy*. Consider a circular matching field subtending two degrees of visual angle and divided into two halves as in the illustration. Suppose that we can illuminate the field with three fixed wavelengths, λ_1, λ_2 and λ_3, and that we also have a variable light L, which may be any wavelength or mixture of wavelengths. By arranging the lights in one of the two ways shown in the figure, it will be possible, by adjusting the intensities of λ_1, λ_2 and λ_3, to cause the two sides of the field to match. The choice of the fixed wavelengths is arbitrary (provided only that no one of them can be matched by a mixture of the other two); and they may themselves be replaced by mixtures.

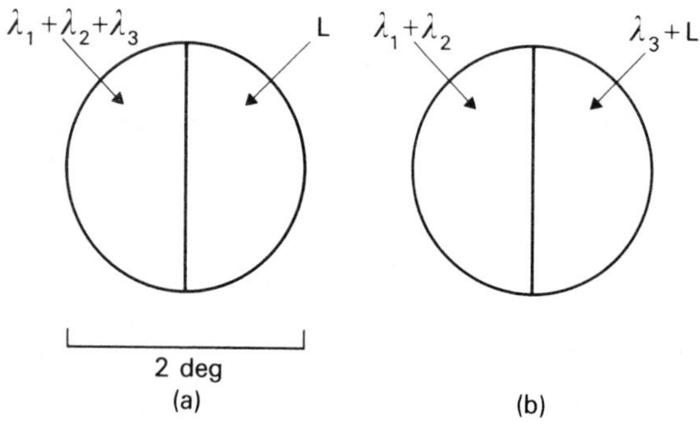

'Colourvision'

In a primitive form, the principle of trichromacy was expressed by J. C. Le Blon in his *Coloritto* (*c.* 1725), but he, and most eighteenth-century authors, took it to be a property of the world rather than of man. In 1802 Thomas Young made it clear that trichromacy was a physiological limitation and we now know that it arises because there are just three types of cone receptor in the retina, each containing a different photo-sensitive pigment (see BRAIN AND CENTRAL NERVOUS SYSTEM: ILLUSTRATIONS, fig. 25; VISUAL PERCEPTION). When measured by microspectrophotometry, the peak sensitivities of the three classes are found to lie at 420, 530 and 560 nm, but each type responds over most of the visible spectrum and there is no wavelength that stimulates only one class. Cones are thought to obey the *Principle of Univariance*: although the input can vary in intensity and wavelength, the cone's output signal can vary in only one dimension. This means that any individual cone is color blind; and thus, if the visual system is to extract information about wavelength, it must compare the rates of absorption of photons in different types of cone. This comparison is carried out by a class of post-receptoral neurons that receive excitatory signals from one or two classes of cone and inhibitory signals from other cones. Retinal ganglion cells of this "color opponent" type, and similar cells in the parvocellular layers of the lateral geniculate nucleus, are found to be excited by part of the visible spectrum and inhibited by the remainder.

Currently controversial questions are: to what extent is color analysed independently of spatial information? is there an area of prestriate cortex that is specialized for color? and, what is the relationship between the activity of "color opponent" neurons and those hues that appear to us phenomenally unmixed?

About 8 per cent of men (0.5 per cent of women) have abnormal color vision. In some forms of color deficiency the subject needs only two variables in a matching experiment; it is thought that such *dichromats* genetically lack one of the types of photopigment. Others (*anomalous trichromats*) require three variables (as in the illustration), but make matches different from those of normal observers; it is thought that one of their three types of photopigment has been replaced by a pigment with a shifted peak sensitivity.

JDM

Bibliography

*Boynton, Robert M. 1979: *Human color vision* New York and London: Holt, Rinehart & Winston.

*Mollon, J. D. 1982: Color vision. *Annual review of psychology*, 33, 41–85.

color vision in animals Color vision is widespread in the animal kingdom and is well developed in some insects (e.g. bees), reptiles, birds and primates. Some animals such as the squirrel have only two types of cone pigment and thus have imperfect color vision similar to that of a color-blind person. Some reptiles and birds have cones containing colored oil droplets in addition to the visual pigments. It is thought that these droplets act as filters, and that the wide variety of receptor types found in these animals is the result of different combinations of photopigment and oil droplet. It is difficult for us to imagine how such animals see colors, although it is possible that their perception of water differs from ours, because the proportions of the various kinds of oil droplets vary between birds which have aquatic and terrestrial habitats. DJM

commitment The question whether or not artists must be "committed" was frequently raised, particularly in France, during the 1930s, and again after the second world war. The concept of the committed writer had its fullest expression in a set of essays by J.P. Sartre which appeared in the periodical *Temps modernes* after the war, and were published in 1948 under the title *What is Literature?* Sartre argues that the writer is necessarily committed, because he cannot rise above history: he writes from where he is. But, although bound by history, he is free to choose his own values, and thus in expressing value judgments, even implicitly, he is both asserting his own freedom and helping the liberation of his readers. Sartre argues that there cannot be any other kind of literature, at least *prose* literature except *litterature engagée*. To write a work of prose is to commit yourself, deliberately. So the writer cannot escape his social responsibility. If he did not wish his readers to adopt his position, he would not write. MW

communication: animal The term 'communication' has been defined as 'the passing of information from one animal to another (and so influencing its behavior) by means of signals that have evolved for the purpose' (Deag 1980). Animals communicate with each other for a variety of reasons, in a variety of ways, and with a variety of effects. Always, however, the form their signaling takes can be assumed to be a direct or indirect outcome of natural selection: direct in the case of highly stereotyped innate signals, indirect in the case of variable signals in which a large learning component is involved.

In general, animals lower in the phylogenetic scale communicate by means of signals that are under direct genetic control and relatively free of learned inputs. Such for example is the olfactory communication of moths, by the use of pheromones. Bird communication sometimes involves learning, as for instance in chaffinch song, in which the nestling adds to an innate basis elements of the song of the parent bird. The communications of mammals are under enough genetic control to result in clear-cut, species specific signals but are often marked by individuality, and a subtle relationship to the prevailing context indicating an advanced level of cognitive control of signal emission.

Without communication animals would lack any means of collecting information about each other and passing on information to others. If we ask why animals should collect and transmit information, the answer is that such activities will tend to increase inclusive fitness. For instance a male's reproductive success is directly enhanced if he can detect that a female is in a sexually receptive condition. Likewise, a female's reproductive success will be increased if she ensures that she will be mated at the most fertile period by emitting signals to surrounding males. Hence natural selection has, in most animal groups, favored olfactory, auditory, tactile and visual signals that enable females to communicate about their sexual condition, and males to respond appropriately.

Indeed in some species, such as great-crested grebes, communication about sexual condition has been greatly extended into what can be called 'courtship' behavior prior to mating and 'pair-bond' behavior afterwards. The same is true of many other species in which natural selection has established prolonged caring for the young by a single male and a single female, or in some cases a single male and a number of females. Such monogamy occurs commonly in birds such as geese and swans, and also, though less commonly, in mammals such as badgers and some primates such as gibbons. In all these cases the maintenance of the individual relationships on which these animal 'families' are based consists of a complex set of communicative signals, in which information about personal identity is important, strangers being rejected by the bonded pair. Polygamous species include lions, deer and certain primates such as Hamadryas baboons.

Communication as described above has evolved because of its direct contribution to the reproductive success of individuals. This is not always the case. For instance worker bees, which are non-reproducing sterile females, are capable of some of the most complex kinds of communication in the animal world. Such females, or 'workers' fly out to locate flowers. Having discovered a food source they return to the hive. They then perform a 'round dance' if the distance to the flowers is less than 100 m or a 'waggle dance' if it exceeds 100 m. The speed at which the waggle dance is performed, and the number of tail waggles it contains, give the distance to the flowers, while the orientation of axis of the dance on the comb surface replicates the angle of the sun to the flight path which leads to the flowers (see illustration from von Frisch 1970).

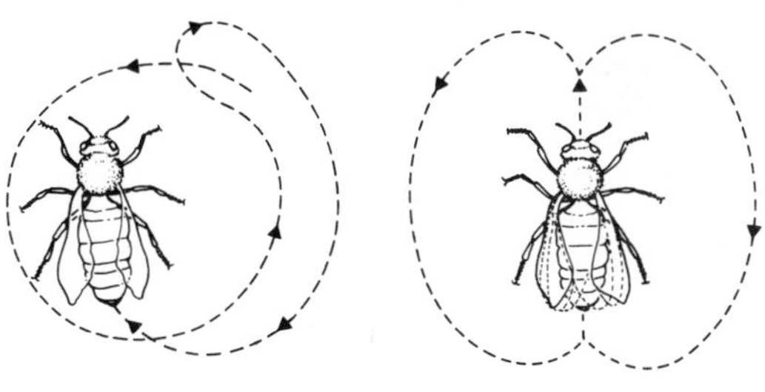

(a) round dance (b) waggle dance

Such exceedingly precise communication is at first incomprehensible in the normal terms of natural selection, when we remember that worker bees do not reproduce. Why should it have evolved? The answer does not necessitate a recourse to theories of 'mutual aid' as proposed by Kropotkin or to any other theory of group selection but can be understood as the outcome of genetic selfishness (Hamilton 1967, Dawkins 1976). Because of the nature of the reproductive process in bees, all workers are genetically very similar, and a successful genetic strategy is not for each female to reproduce individually but for one to reproduce while the rest become specialized feeders, nurses and so on. The latter has turned out, in some species, to be advantageous and in consequence the range of complex communicative processes that support it has evolved.

Besides communication within species, there are many curious features of communication that characterize prey–predator relations. These mostly relate to methods of deception or surprise. Since only prey that can avoid capture survive to reproduce, natural selection has produced extensive patterns of mimicry and camouflage. These are communicative in the sense that they relay and are received as false information by the predator. For its part, the predator's main problem is to avoid communicating its presence, owing to the existence of innate recognition reactions in the prey. Predatory activity often consists of slow, stealthy approach, or observation from a distance, followed by sudden attack before the prey can escape. This is true for both mammals such as cats and birds such as hawks, though not for some predators such as wolves or hyenas.

Finally we can consider the communication systems of our closest relatives and of ourselves. Group-living primates such as macaques and chimpanzees engage in a wide range of facial-visual signaling, as well as in a smaller range of tactile, auditory and olfactory signals. The facial expressions of these higher primates in many ways resemble those of man. Expressions such as the 'silent bared-teeth' display have been linked in an evolutionary progression to the human smile (see illustration, from Van Hooff 1972). The rather spontaneous and world-wide distribution of some human facial expressions has led Eibl-Eibesfeldt (1970) to conclude that they are innate. Probably, indeed, we should assume an innate basis to some human non-verbal communicative signals, such as the laugh, the smile, the frown, the eyebrow-flash, and the facial expressions of weeping and fear. But it is a mistake to go on from this to assume that human communication is fundamentally non-verbal, with a mere linguistic overlay. Those non-verbal elements that have an innate basis provide the background, not the foreground, to human communication. **VR**

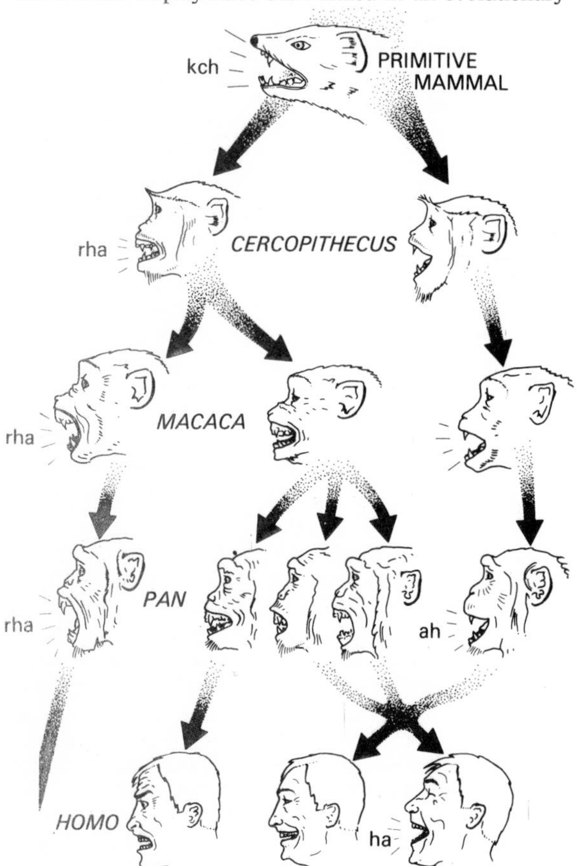

Bibliography

Dawkins, R. 1976: *The selfish gene.* Oxford University Press.

Deag, J.M. 1980: *Social behavior of animals.* London: Edward Arnold.

Eibl-Eibesfeldt, I. 1970: *Ethology, the biology of behaviour.* New York: Holt Rinehart & Winston.

Hamilton, W.D. 1967: The genetical evolution of social behaviour. *Journal of theoretical biology* 7, 1–52.

Van Hooff, J.A.R.A.M., 1972: The phylogeny of laughter and smiling. In R.A. Hinde, ed., *Non-verbal communication.* Cambridge University Press.

Von Frisch, K. 1970: *Bees, their vision, chemical senses, and language.* Ithaca N.Y.: Cornell University Press.

communication: human general Although the term "communication" is of fundamental importance in social and behavioral science there is no consensus as to its definition. There are three distinct approaches to communication: informational, interactional and relational. Despite apparent similarities of concepts, terminology and research techniques, each approach is grounded in different philosophical traditions and offers complementary yet different accounts of the phenomenon in question.

Informational approaches evolved mainly during the 1930s and 40s and have become widely accepted since then. They deal with transmission of messages, mainly factual ones, between interacting "parties" (e.g. societies, organizations, individuals, animals, telecommunication devices etc.) that are capable of sending or receiving information through some common system of signals or symbols. The theoretical roots of informational approaches are three-fold: (a) an assumption that meaning or information is encapsulated in words, gestures, appearances or objects and that these have to be untangled or decoded to have their content revealed; (b) an assumption that people's bodies, especially their faces, eyes and hands, constitute a screen on which various thoughts, emotions and attitudes are displayed; (c) an Aristotelian and Newtonian view of the world as a neutral space in which discrete entities (organisms, objects etc.) occasionally act (exert some influence) on one another. Such mutual influences are often conceptualized in terms of a linear sequence of events occurring within a dyadic framework (e.g. A acts; B reacts; A reacts to B's reaction and so forth).

There are two major groups of informational studies. The

first deals with the theory and practice of conversion of messages and meanings into various icons, signs, signals, symbols, languages or codes and their subsequent decoding. The most important model was developed by Shannon and Weaver (1949) in their work on the mathematical theory of transmission of electronic signals. Their model originally consisted of five elements: (1) an information source; (2) a transmitter (encoder); (3) a channel for transmission of signals; (4) a receiver (decoder) and (5) a destination – all arranged in a linear order. Later studies improved on this simple scheme by drawing a distinction between a "message" and its "source" and by introducing such important notions as "feedback" (destination's response which enables the source to modify its subsequent transmissions), "noise" (interference with the message traveling along a channel); "redundancy" (repetitions in coding of the message so that it is correctly decoded) and "filters" (modifiers of the message when it is arriving at the encoder or leaving the decoder). This model exhibited several virtues – simplicity, ready quantifiability and generality – making it attractive to a number of disciplines (Cherry 1957), with the result that the potential utility of other views of communication, or even their existence, tended to be overlooked.

The second group of studies in this tradition was developed mainly during the 1960s and focused on the socially organized conditions for the circulation of information between members of a given community or face-to-face gathering. The main work in this area is by Goffman, whose model of communicational exchange has four elements: (a) communicational arrangements established among a given set of individuals (e.g. direct vs. indirect; symmetrical vs. asymmetrical transmissions of messages); (b) communicational conduct (strategies) that interacting parties adopt while dealing with each other; (c) communicational constraints, that is ecological, technical, intellectual and emotional factors limiting people's choice of strategy; and finally (d) interpretational frames governing the way people perceive and account for their conduct with regard to one another. It is this model that bridges most fully the gap separating informational and interactional studies.

Interactional approaches evolved mainly in the 1960s and 70s. They define communication not as a transaction but as an occasion that individuals (mainly humans, but also animals) cooperatively establish and maintain through the skillful deployment of behavior, appearances and artifacts. This behavioral management of co-presence takes place irrespective of the wishes or intentions of the individuals engaged in it. Although they do have control over their entering into and departure from situations of co-presence, as long as the parties perceive each other's monitoring they cannot avoid continuous coordination of behavior in relation to one another. The interactional approach recognizes that every interaction involves an exchange of messages but the key research interest is in the organization of behavior rather than in "what does it mean?" The theoretical roots of this approach are three-fold: (a) the interest of behavioral sciences in fine grained analyses of human and animal behavior under a variety of circumstances, including interactions with conspecifics and the immediate environment; (b) an assumption that behavior is not so much a function of the individual's internal drives, motivations or personality as of the situation and of the social relationships established with others; (c) General Systems Theory which leads to the introduction of such fundamental notions as "systems", "dynamic equilibrium", "self-regulation", "feedback" and "program".

A number of theoretical models attempt to describe and explain the way social occasions are structured and managed by behavioral means. Five of the most important constructs are: (i) the "linguistic" model, proposed in the early 1960s by Birdwhistell (1970) which argues that despite the variety of interactions they are all constructed from the same limited repertoire of fifty to sixty elementary bodily movements and positions. It hypothetizes that behavioral sequences formed from those elementary units are organized in the way in which sequences of sound patterns are organized into words, sentences and passages of speech; (ii) the "social skill" model (Argyle and Kendon 1967) which postulates that interpersonal transactions, like other learnable skills (e.g. driving, dancing, playing card games) are hierarchically organized and formed by a series of small, goal-oriented yet often tentative and ambiguous "steps"; (iii) the "equilibrium" model (Argyle and Dean 1965) which assumes that the interacting parties always strive to maintain a certain overall "balance" in the way they deploy their behavior in relation to each other's presence and activity. Any change in the use of behavior type X is usually compensated for by appropriate changes in the use of behavior type Y and vice versa; (iv) Scheflen's "programs" model (1968) of social interaction which postulates that the overall synchronic and diachronic structure of the face-to-face encounter is generated by the operation of at least three sets of programs. The first deals with simple coordination of activities. The second controls modifications to the individuals' activities whenever some contingencies or ambiguities arise. The third program modifies the modification procedures, that is, handles the complex task of meta-communication. These programs are internalized as individuals learn to function as fully fledged members of a given group, community and culture and permit organization of diverse behavioral material into meaningful and appropriate interchanges. They are culture and context specific, that is, a given situation, a given task and a given social organization evoke performance of a given program; (v) the "systems" model (Kendon 1977) which envisages interaction as a configuration of systems of behavior each managing a separate aspect of an interpersonal transaction. So far two such systems have been identified and analysed. The first one is a system of behavior managing an "exchange of utterances" while the other one is a system of behavior managing orderly use of interactional spaces and territories.

Of these five models it is the "programs" model which displays the greatest affinity to the relational theory of communication.

The *relational* approach has been gradually developing

since the mid 1950s (Birdwhistell 1968). It postulates that people's environmental and social contexts constitute not so much the circumstances under which transfer of information and occasions of face-to-face interaction occur as the very phenomenon of communication itself. In other words, "communication" is a name for the overall system of relationships people develop between each other and with the community and habitat in which they live. Any difference (i.e. change or transformation) which makes the difference to any part of this system is called "information" (Bateson 1973). People, animals and other organisms cannot be said to engage in communication (informational approach) or participate in it (interactional approach) for they are already an indispensable part of it in the same way as they are, whether they want it or not, a part of the local as well as global ecosystem. They became immersed in it at the moment of their birth and do not leave it until the moment of their death. Three sets of theoretical developments have been instrumental in bringing the relational theory of communication about: (a) cybernetics and General Systems Theory; (b) the Theory of Logical Types which identifies discontinuities between different levels of abstraction (e.g. between a statement and meta-statement) and enables comparisons between logical structures of such diverse phenomena as play, non-play, metaphor, humor, confidence-tricks or schizophrenia; (c) the biological research on ecology and ecosystems in general and on constancy and change in the relationships between organisms and their contexts in particular.

The most important research carried out within the framework of the relational approach has been generated by the "double bind" model of psychopathology (Bateson et al. 1956). This model has, for example, challenged the traditional view of schizophrenia as a distortion in the behavior of an individual by advancing a view of schizophrenia as a permanent disturbance or distortion in the pattern of relations between an individual and other persons (Laing 1959). This distortion is thought to arise whenever people conduct themselves in such a way that (i) one or more of them is subjected to mutually exclusive demands such that to obey one is to disobey the other; (ii) this disobedience is punished; (iii) the paradoxical nature of these demands cannot be acknowledged or discussed, and (iv) people cannot escape from dealing with each other.

The relational theory of communication is in an almost embryonic stage of development. It may take several years before it will be employed as widely as is currently the case with the informational and interactional approaches. However, even at this early stage, it clearly represents one of the most seminal and revolutionary approaches to the phenomena of society, of communication, of interaction and of behavior that the social and behavioral sciences have ever known. Its strength and potential rests in the fact that it replaces the handy but restrictive framework of Aristotelian epistemology with the "Systems approach". Unlike the former, which has proved valuable for analysing simple systems, the latter has proved to be uniquely suited to dealing with moderately to highly complex phenomena. See also COMMUNICATION: NON-VERBAL. TMC

Bibliography

Argyle, M. and Dean, J. 1965: Eye-contact, distance and affiliation. *Sociometry* 28, 289–304.

Argyle, M. and Kendon, A. 1967: The experimental analysis of social performance. In *Advances in experimental social psychology*, ed. L. Berkowitz. London: Academic Press.

Bateson, Gregory 1973: *Steps to an ecology of mind: collected essays in anthropology, psychiatry, evolution and epistemology*. Frogmore: Paladin Granada Publishing Ltd.

Bateson, Gregory et al. 1956: Towards a theory of schizophrenia. *Behavioral science* 1, 251–64.

*Birdwhistell, Ray L. 1968: Communication. In *International encyclopedia of the social sciences*, ed. David J. Sills. Vol.3. New York: McMillan and Co. and The Free Press.

——— 1970: *Kinesics and context: essays on body-motion communication*. Philadelphia: University of Pennsylvania Press; London: Allen Lane (1971).

Cherry, Colin 1957. *On human communication: a review, a survey, and a criticism*. Cambridge, Mass.: MIT Press.

Goffman, Erving 1963: *Behavior in public places: notes on the social organization of gatherings*. New York: Free Press.

——— 1969: *Strategic interaction*. Pennsylvania: The Trustees of the University of Pennsylvania; Oxford: Blackwell Scientific (1970).

——— 1975: *Frame analysis: an essay on the organization of experience*. New York: Harper & Row.

*Hinde, Robert A. (Ed.) 1972. *Non-verbal communication*. Cambridge and New York: Cambridge University Press.

Kendon, Adam 1977: *Studies in the behavior of social interaction*. Bloomington: Indiana University and Lisse: Peter de Ridder.

Laing, Ronald D. 1959. *The divided self: an existential study in sanity and madness*. London: Tavistock.

Scheflen, A. 1968. Human communications: behavioral programs and their integration. *Behavioral science* 13, 44–55.

Shannon, C.E. and Weaver, W. 1949. *A mathematical theory of communication*. Urbana: University of Illinois Press.

communication: non-verbal Transmission of information by means of interactional instrumentalities (i.e. behavior, appearance and artifacts) other than language in its spoken, written, or otherwise coded form. The information exchanged by these means is diverse and can be divided into three broad categories–factual, indexical and regulatory. "Factual" messages are those dealing with requests for, and provision of, goods, services and information. They also include performance of socially significant, often ritualized behavior (e.g. decorating a person with a medal). Indexical signals convey information about the people themselves. These signals are about the sender's biological and psychological characteristics; his social and cultural affiliations; his relations with and attitudes toward those co-present; his relation to the present interaction as well as his relation to the immediate physical environment. The third category of information concerns the adequate and orderly joint management of interpersonal transactions. This consists of information about the spatial and temporal boundaries of the interaction at hand; its nature (e.g. whether a chat or an interrogation); the spatial and temporal coordination of behavior and action (e.g. the taking of turns in a conversation); definition of roles for each participant and of the required level of participants' involvement in the transaction.

For such a transmission of information to occur some communicational relationship between two or more individuals must be established. Communicating parties form such a relationship by attending to each other's deployment and usage of various interactional instrumentalities and by coordinating performances with each other. This means that people's appearance, behavior and use of objects constitute not only the source of information individuals acquire from each other but also the essential context for the acquisition of such information.

In a series of classic analyses of people's communicational conduct Goffman (1959, 1969) suggested that there are four basic types of communicational relations and that every community and every social occasion has a particular repertoire of such relations. Thus information that individuals provide (irrespective of whether it is done consciously and voluntarily) can be transmitted either directly or indirectly and, simultaneously, in either a symmetrical or an asymmetrical fashion. A direct communication (such as an exchange of smoke signals) occurs when the information is transmitted by the sender's current (usually bodily) activity, which is taking place within the operational range of the receiver's senses. Indirect communication, on the other hand, utilizes people's ability to decode messages in the form of behavioral traces or in the form of positioning and appearances of artifacts. Good examples of such disembodied messages are a burglar's footprints on a window sill, or a bouquet of red roses brought by a messenger.

Communicational arrangements differ also in the symmetry of roles adopted by the communicating parties. A symmetrical transaction is one in which people are simultaneously receiving and feeding back information. In an asymmetrical transaction (e.g. when somebody is spying or eavesdropping on someone else) the roles of senders and receivers of signals are kept separate, providing no feedback and *they* are not reversible in a given transaction.

In the course of the behavioral process appropriate conditions for transfer of information become created, defined and skilfully managed moment by moment (this process is known as "coenesis" see Ciolek, Elzinga and McHoul 1979); arrays of variously combined instrumentalities can be seen to be deployed in ever changing spatio-temporal configurations. Along acoustic channels of communication, for example, there is a widespread use of (a) speech, (b) paralanguage, (c) strepitus (non-vocal body noise), and (d) mechanically created noises and sounds. Visual communication uses (e) spacing and orientation in relation to the physical and human context, (f) body movements such as gestures, gesticulation, nods and shifts of posture, as well as facial expressions and gaze behavior; (g) physical appearance; and (h) artifacts such as dress, make-up, jewelery, etc. Transfer of information by touch and smell is usually conducted at close and very close range, and involves (j) tactile behavior such as caressing, holding, manipulation; (k) tactile and thermal appearances of the skin surface; and (l) natural bodily smells and odors, as well as their modifications by cosmetics, food, tobacco or medicaments.

Deployed behavior, appearances and artifacts are never neutral or non-significant. It has been pointed out that a given behavior can be received and reacted to at a number of levels: as a physical stimulus requiring appropriate bodily response on the part of the receiver; as a simple symptom or indicator of something else; or as a symbol or even as an element of a CODE or language of some kind. This means that in man-made environments or in the presence of other people a person cannot avoid reacting to one, at least, of these levels of behavior of other people. Similarly, no one can totally stop transmitting information of some sort, and therefore no one can stop influencing the behavior of others. Some balance, however, between the degree of sensory exposure and access can be and usually is established. This balance, often referred to as privacy of a certain degree, is, according to Altman (1975), achieved by a combined application of various control measures. These may include avoidance or modification of certain types of behavior (e.g. of the amount of mutual gaze), manipulation of spatial relationships between people, division of the environment into variously marked, controlled and defended spaces, and finally extensive reliance on furniture, barriers and concealments of various kinds. In this context it was observed that whenever the overwhelming and/or prolonged presence of others leads to a person's loss of control over the amount of information he or she receives or emits, such an individual is likely to experience a more or less acute sense of crowding.

Ways of communicating vary from community to community, from place to place and from one person to another. Cultural factors play an important role in shaping people's communicational conduct and so do numerous situational and individual variables (Argyle 1975). Another important source of variability in people's behavior is to be found in communicational transactions themselves, for these can frequently be accomplished according to more than one format or program (Scheflen 1968). There is thus a wide choice of possible strategies: sometimes people will organize their mutual conduct in terms of only one or two aspects of a single instrumentality and sometimes they will do it at the level of all the types of behavior they have at their disposal. This means that human communication can occasionally become exceedingly intricate. Further, it means that there are circumstances under which both verbal and non-verbal components of a communicational exchange form a joint system of closely interrelated instrumentalities which cannot occur separately. For this reason many researchers argue that, while the distinction between verbal and non-verbal behavior is valid, that between verbal and non-verbal communication is not always meaningful and is in fact artificial, rather like the distinction between cardiac and non-cardiac physiology (Birdwhistell 1970).

There are a number of stages in the history of communication studies, each reflecting the theoretical and methodological stance of a discipline current at the time of the research. Until the mid 1950s there was a tendency to study asymmetrical and disembodied modes of communication (Ruesch and Kees 1972). Contemporary research, however, deals primarily with those communicational arrangements which are either direct or symmetrical, or both (Kendon 1977). At the same time a significant shift in emphasis can be observed from studies of "*what* behavior means" towards research into "*how* behavior means" (Scheflen 1974). During the past twenty years these developments have led to a surge of interest in the behavioral structuring and moment-to-moment regulation of face-to-face encounters. According to the three pioneers of modern communication studies – Bateson (1973), Scheflen (1975) and Birdwhistell (1970) – all these transformations mark the steadily growing influence of the "systems approach", which has been found to constitute the most suitable tool for dealing with complex issues of human behavior. See also COMMUNICATION: HUMAN GENERAL; PROXEMICS. TMC

Bibliography

Altman, Irwin 1975: *The environment and social behavior: privacy, personal space, territory, crowding.* Monterey, Calif.: Brooks/Cole.

Argyle, Michael 1975: *Bodily communication.* London: Methuen; New York: Barnes and Noble.

Bateson, Gregory 1973: *Steps to an ecology of mind: collected essays in anthropology, psychiatry, evolution and epistemology.* Frogmore: Paladin Granada.

Birdwhistell, Ray L. 1970: *Kinesics and context: essays on body-motion communication.* Philadelphia: University of Pennsylvania Press; London: Penguin (1971).

———, Background considerations to the study of the body as a medium of "expression". In *The body as a medium of expression,* ed. J. Benthall and T. Polhemus. New York: E.P. Dutton.

Ciolek, T.M., Elzinga, R.H. and McHoul, A.W. 1979: Selected references to coenetics – the study of behavioral organization of face-to-face interactions. *Sign language studies* 22, 1–74.

Goffman, Erving 1959: *The presentation of self in everyday life.* New York: Doubleday; London: Penguin (1969).

——— 1969: *Strategic interaction.* Pennsylvania: Trustees of the University of Pennsylvania; Oxford: Blackwell Scientific (1970).

*Kendon, Adam 1977: *Studies in the behavior of social interaction.* Bloomington: Indiana University; Lisse: Peter de Ridder.

Ruesch, Jurgen and Kees, W. 1972: *Non-verbal communication: notes on the visual perception of human relations,* 2nd edn. Berkeley: University of California Press.

Scheflen, A. 1968: Human communication: behavioral programs and their integration. *Behavioral science* 13, 44–55.

——— 1974: *How behavior means.* New York: Anchor Press and Doubleday.

——— 1975: Models and epistemologies in the study of interaction. In *The organization of behavior in face-to-face interaction,* ed. A. Kendon, R.M. Harris, and M.R. Key. The Hague: Mouton.

communication network Communication between group members is often restricted by available communication channels. Communication networks are defined by the nature and number of communication channels available in a group. Communication networks can be distinguished according to their degree of centrality, peripherality and independence. A wheel structure, in which all communication is channeled through one person, has a high degree of centrality whereas a circle structure, in which members can communicate only with "adjacent" members, has a low degree of centrality. Experimental studies have shown that centralized structures are usually more efficient than more haphazard structures for simple tasks, but the reverse is true for more complex tasks. Satisfaction is generally higher in less centralized structures. Mulder (see Shaw 1976) has shown, however, that both effects do not depend wholly on the communication network available, since people can, for example, centralize a structure by deciding not to use certain channels. Cohen (see Shaw 1976) has proposed a general theory which suggests that a matching of task and communication structure leads to higher productivity. JMFJ

Bibliography

Shaw, M.E. 1976: *Group dynamics.* New York: McGraw-Hill.

communication *See above, and also* persuasive communication

compensatory education The effort to provide special education for children from poor backgrounds who have been found to be a high risk group for SCHOOL FAILURE. Although efforts in this area surged in the 1960s, the basic concept of intervening to optimize developments is not new. Education at the time of the French Revolution, for example, was marked by efforts to provide environments which would foster the development of skills in those who had until then been neglected and deemed hopeless (the mentally handicapped, the deaf, etc.; see Lane (1976) for a review of this work).

The sharp growth in compensatory efforts after the first world war can be traced to a variety of factors. First, in many industrialized western societies, there were major shifts in population with people moving from rural areas to the cities. Then after the war many middle-class families moved from the cities to the suburbs, leaving large concentrations of lower-class minorities within the inner cities. As a result increasing numbers of lower-class children were concentrated within the city schools. Since these children performed poorly in academic attainment the schools were confronted with increasingly high rates of school failure. At the same time there was increased enforcement of the laws which require all children to attend school throughout much of adolescence. As a result those children who might have dropped out of school because of failure or lack of motivation were retained.

A second major force behind the compensatory education movement derived from the changing occupational structure. As western nations became more technological there was a decline in the demand for unskilled labor and a rise in the demand for individuals who were literate and had other academic skills. The poor academic attainments of many from the lower classes therefore contributed to a high rate of unemployment among that group. The concept of compensatory education was advanced as a solution to this problem.

Third, the growing acceptance of democratic ideals led to increased demands for equality of opportunity for all. This trend was clearly shown in the Civil Rights Movement which was led by the black minority in the United States during the 1960s, and in which the demand for equal educational opportunity was central. It was felt that equality in other spheres, such as job opportunities, could not be met unless educational attainment was significantly enhanced.

These combined forces inevitably led to a focus on the school and more specifically, on the reasons for the high rate of school failure. Much use was made of a deprivation model put forward by Donald Hebb in the 1950s. The model, which stressed the concept of stimulus deprivation, was based on a series of studies documenting the environmental factors necessary for maintaining normal functioning in animals. It was found that when organisms were deprived of information to the various senses (vision, hearing and touch), their development in both the intellectual and affective realms was severely impaired. Further, studies of infants reared in the sensory-deprived environment of an institution showed comparable deficiencies in functioning (see SENSORY DEPRIVATION). Because of its power in explaining deficiencies in behavior, the deprivation model was adopted as the explanation for the problems of lower-class children. They were said to have been reared in deprived environments (see SOCIAL DISADVANTAGE) and to be in need of more stimulating environments that would compensate for the deprivation. The term 'compensatory education' logically followed from this reasoning.

Once the problem was considered within a deprivation framework, it was reasonable to focus the greatest effort on the preschool years. It was hoped that the earlier intervention was begun, the more likely it was that success would be achieved. Furthermore the dominant psychological theories, including those of Freud, Skinner and Piaget, stressed the importance of the early years in providing a foundation for all future development. Even though the failure was displayed by children of school age, it was thought that the difficulties could best be overcome by taking preventive measures during the preschool years.

A number of different efforts at early intervention were attempted. One type was based on techniques developed for the urban poor of Italy in the early 1900s by the physician Maria Montessori. The method emphasized the need for active involvement on the part of the child, in the three main areas of motor education (cutting paper, tying laces, etc.), sensory education (attention to texture, rhythms, etc.) and language, both oral and reading. Attractive and carefully structured materials were developed to foster learning while still allowing the child control over the pace and type of activity.

Other techniques used much more direct intervention. One of the most notable efforts was developed by Carl Bereiter and Siegfried Engelmann (1966). Using Skinnerian concepts of operant learning (see OPERANT CONDITIONING), they developed a language-focused method which emphasized drill, discipline and regimentation. Children worked in small groups where they were exposed to material presented in fifteen- to twenty-minute segments. The first unit might be on grammar, the second on phonics (recognizing the sounds of letters), the third on mathematics. This rigid structure stood in marked contrast to the ease and informality characteristic of most other pre-school approaches. There was an absence of free play which had long been viewed as the prime motivator of learning in young children. Instead, in line with operant principles, the rewards were externally-based motivators (e.g. food treats or praise) that had no intrinsic relationship to the tasks which the children were required to perform.

Still other methods aimed at the overall enrichment of the child. In some cases they were even called "bombardment approaches" in that they exposed the child to a vast array of stimuli in the hope of stimulating activity. (While the discussion of compensatory techniques has been limited to the educational components, it should be noted that many of them were designed for comprehensive intervention and included medical attention, nutritional enrichment and parent involvement (Zigler and Valentine 1979)).

Within a relatively short time considerable money and effort had been put into compensatory education, and efforts were also made to assess its effectiveness. Given the goal (the prevention of school failure), it would have been best to delay any assessment until the children had completed several years of formal schooling, but this was not considered feasible so it became typical for short-term evaluations to be conducted by means of tests such as intelligence tests which have been shown to correlate with academic success. There were many reports of short-term gains in IQ scores and related cognitive tests. However, the gains often seemed to disappear over time; that is, as the children moved through school, there was a lessening of the differences between those who had, and those who had not, received compensatory instruction.

Long-term follow up studies have since been made to assess the effects of preschool education on school performance and these results have been more promising (Zigler and Valentine 1979). The several hundred children who had participated in preschool programmes were found to be 40 per cent less likely to be put into special education classes, and to be 20 per cent less likely to be kept back in grade than were their peers in control groups. Further, when youths in the 16–21 year age range were studied, it was found that 37 per cent of those who had been in preschool went on to college or skilled jobs; only 8 per cent of the controls achieved this level of performance. The reason for the improvement is unclear; it could have been based upon such varied factors as changes in parents' attitudes and interactions with their children, and changes in the children's attitudes towards school and their abilities to meet the teachers' demands (see EDUCATIONAL ATTAINMENT AND EXPECTATIONS). Nevertheless the results stand in contrast to earlier reports and indicate the usefulness of continuing compensatory efforts.

While the later results are promising, their impact has not been great, for by the time they appeared considerable disillusionment had already set in and they soon became entangled in a major controversy. On one side of the controversy was Arthur Jensen who, in a famous article (1969), argued that the difficulties of lower-class minority children who fail in school derive from genetic limitations. While this paper was, and continues to be, the subject of heated debate it has nevertheless served as an important rationale for the curtailment of preschool intervention programs. Another group of researchers also questioned the basis of the preschool intervention movement (see Cazden, John and Hymes 1972 for a review of this position). They rejected the assertions that the children were either genetically or environmentally deficient and, while acknowledging that the school performance was often poor, they attributed this failure to the structure of the school system, which they saw as a reflection of the culture of the dominant social group and as a force which devalued the culture in which minority children were reared. From this vantage point compensatory education was not what was needed. Instead it was claimed that schools had to be radically altered to meet the styles of the different populations they served. While many have found this approach appealing, it has for the most part remained academic in that workable alternatives remain to be developed.

The discussion until now, like much of the actual effort itself, has been directed at the pre-school years. However, some attention has also been devoted to older age groups. For example the Follow Through program in the United States was developed to offer a continuation of special services for disadvantaged children for the first three years of formal schooling. It was hoped that by establishing continuity between the preschool years and later schooling any initial gains would be maintained. In a major evaluation of this intervention it was indeed found that those children who were given continued compensatory services achieved a higher overall performance level in later schooling than did those who only had compensatory preschool (Weisberg and Haney 1977.)

Much of the impetus for compensatory education developed in the United States, which is not surprising since the States invests more time and money in education than any other country in the world. However, compensatory education for lower-class minority groups is provided in many other countries. (See for England, Tough (1977); for Holland, Groenendaal (1978); for Israel, Frankenstein (1970) and Minkovich, Davis and Bashi (1977).) MB/JM

Bibliography

Bereiter, C. and Engelmann, S. 1966: *Teaching the disadvantaged child in the pre-school.* Englewood Cliffs, New Jersey: Prentice-Hall.

Cazden, C.B., John, V.P. and Hymes, D. 1972: *Functions of language in the classroom.* New York: Teachers College Press.

Frankenstein, C. 1970: *Impaired intelligence: pathology and rehabilitation.* London: Gordon and Breach, Science Publishers, Ltd.

Groenendaal, H.J. 1978: *Vroegtijdige hulpverlening aan zwakfunktionerende kleuters.* Amsterdam: Vrije Universiteit te Amsterdam.

Heber, R. and Garber, H. 1975: The Milwaukee project: a study of the use of family intervention to prevent cultural–familial mental retardation. In *Exceptional infant* (vol. 3), ed. B.Z. Friedlander, G.M. Sterritt and G.E. Kirk. New York: Brunner/Mazel.

Jensen, A.R. 1969: How much can we boost IQ and scholastic achievement? *Harvard educational review* 39, 1–123.

Lane, H. 1976: *The wild boy of Aveyron.* Cambridge, Mass.: Harvard University Press.

Minkovich, A., Davis, D. and Bashi, J. 1977: *An evaluation study of Israeli elementary schools.* Jerusalem: The Hebrew University of Jerusalem.

Rutter, M. et al. 1979: *Fifteen thousand hours.* London: Open Books. Cambridge, Mass.: Harvard University Press.

Tough, J. 1977: Children and programmes: how shall we educate the young child? In *Language and learning in early childhood*, ed. A. Davies. London: Heinemann.

Weisberg, H.I. and Haney, W. 1977: *Longitudinal evaluation of Head Start planned variation and Follow Through.* Cambridge, Mass.: Huron Institute.

Zigler, E. and Valentine, J. (eds.) 1979: *Project Head Start: a legacy of the war on poverty.* New York: The Free Press.

competence: linguistic According to Chomsky and other transformational-generative grammarians, competence refers to the ability of the idealized speaker-hearer to associate sounds and meanings in accordance with the rules of his or her language. A grammar of a language, in this view, is a description of this competence or knowledge. It is distinguished from the actual use of language in concrete situations, or performance (Chomsky 1965, 3–9). Transformationalist competence, like structuralist "langue" refers to invariant self-contained systems. It differs from the latter notion in that it refers to a system of generative processes rather than a systematic inventory of items.

The principal objection to the concept of linguistic competence relates to its failure to refer to an identifiable psychological reality. Linguists of the variationist type (BAILEY, LABOV) have shown that linguistic variation is highly constrained and regular and should therefore belong to competence rather than *performance*. Sociolinguists investigating the ethnography of speaking (e.g. Hymes 1974) have pointed out that, in addition to grammatical competence, actual speakers also have communicative competence, i.e. they are able to distinguish between situationally appropriate and inappropriate language use. PM

Bibliography

Chomsky, Noam 1965: *Aspects of the theory of syntax.* Cambridge Mass.: MIT Press.

Hymes, Dell 1974: *Foundations in sociolinguistics.* Philadelphia: University of Pennsylvania Press.

competition Striving to excel in order to obtain an exclusive goal; in psychology, often studied as maximizing one's own outcomes at the expense of others in game theory experiments (see GAMES). Factors which have been shown to affect cooperative and competitive behavior in these situations are: (1) the structure of the pay-off matrix; (2) the cooperative or competitive behavior shown by others; (3) attributions concerning the motives of others; (4) the possibility of communicating with adversaries. Recent evidence suggests that in humans and animals alike, competition serves to establish a social structure and to provide information about one's activities through social comparison. JMFJ

Bibliography

Passingham, R. 1981: *The human primate.* New York: Academic Press.

complex *See* Jung, Carl

componential analysis The term componential analysis is

used for a method of reducing a word's meaning to its ultimate contrastive elements. For example, from a semanticist's point of view

man is to woman
as stallion is to mare
and ram is to ewe.

All lexical items in the first column contain a semantic component "male" while the contrasting items contain a component "female", ceteris paribus. The eventual aim of componential analysis is to describe all lexical items in terms of their ultimate semantic components. Whereas some linguists (e.g. Lyons 1968, 474) have argued against assigning a philosophical or psychological status to such components, others (e.g. Katz 1964) have argued that semantic theory should designate language-independent components of a conceptual system which is part of the cognitive structure of the human mind. PM

Bibliography

Katz, Jerrold J. 1964: Analyticity and contradiction in natural language. In *The structure of language*, ed. J.A. Fodor, and J.J. Katz. New Jersey: Prentice Hall.

Lyons, John 1968: *Introduction to theoretical linguistics*. Cambridge and New York: Cambridge University Press.

computation *See* mathematics

computer-aided instruction (CAI) A method for the systematic presentation of information which relies on a computer system for program storage and retrieval. In computer-aided instruction the prospective learner interacts directly with the computer in an attempt to master the program content. Cooley and Glasser (1969) describe a CAI system in the following six steps:

(1) The goals of learning are specified in terms of observable learner behavior and conditions under which the behavior is to be manifested.
(2) The learner's initial relevant capabilities are assessed at the beginning of a course of instruction.
(3) Suitable educational alternatives are then presented to the learner, who selects or is assigned one of them.
(4) The learner's performance is monitored, recorded and continuously assessed as the session progresses.
(5) Instruction proceeds as a function of the relationships between the student's performance, available instructional activities, and pre-established criteria of competence.
(6) As instruction proceeds, data relevant to the program are generated for monitoring and improving the instructional system.

Advantages and disadvantages associated with CAI have been discussed by Goldstein (1974) and Seltzer (1971). Advantages include the tailoring of the instructional process to the unique characteristics of the learner, the immediate and accurate reinforcement, and the freeing of instructor time from the burdensome chore of bookkeeping. Among the major disadvantages associated with this form of instruction are the costs inherent in putting together a complete CAI system (including hardware and software), the degree to which learning under CAI has a carryover effect to other less structured environments requiring the same responses and the degree to which CAI is superior to other more traditional and less costly learning techniques. (See also TRAINING.) RRJ

Bibliography

Cooley, W.W. and Glaser, R. 1969: The computer and individualized instruction. *Science* 166, 574–82.

Goldstein, I.L. 1974: *Training: program development and evaluation*. Monterey, Calif.: Brooks/Cole.

Seltzer, R.H. 1971: Computer assisted instruction – what it can and cannot do. *American psychologist* 26, 373–7.

computer simulation of cognitive processes The writing of computer programs to simulate the various stages of reasoning in people engaged in intelligent activity. This may involve either abstracting general principles of reasoning as the basis of organization for solving problems; or constructing a program to perform a specific task; and in doing so mimic the various stages through which a person progresses.

In Piaget's task of seriating a number of blocks in order of size, a child makes a particular series of moves. Young (1974), in simulating these, identified a set of rules whose joint observance could account for the child's behavior at each stage of completing the task.

Categorically different behavior in children at successive stages of cognitive development was accounted for by expansion of the rule set through the acquisition of new rules. The larger problem of learning and development can then be treated as the simplified problem of understanding the acquisition of new rules which characterize these developmental differences.

Since achieving the simulation effectively depends on the strength of the underlying theory, the simulation of cognitive processes has consequences for psychological theory, perhaps highlighting areas where it is incomplete, and, for the specific problem focused upon, indicating which processes require explanation and clarification.

Some programs utilize techniques people find useful for thinking, without being psychologically valid in the above sense. NOAH (Sacerdoti 1975), a planning system, adopts the flexibility of human planning, where the ordering of actions is governed by external and necessary factors rather than being predetermined. Further, people tend to reason at initially abstract levels, confining detailed and complex problem solving to plans sufficiently refined to be considered viable. This too is reflected in Sacerdoti's program.

Capitalizing on general principles such as abstract planning encourages more effective processing through adopting "proven" (human) techniques (Newell and Simon 1972). In addition, computer programs which adopt reasoning strategies compatible with those of the user may result in more "friendly" and responsive interactive systems. SW

Bibliography

Newell, A. and Simon, H.A. 1972: *Human problem solving*. Englewood Cliffs, N.J.: Prentice-Hall.

Sacerdoti, E.D. 1975: The non-linear nature of plans. In *International joint conference of artificial intelligence* 4.

Young, R.M. 1974: Productions systems as models of cognitive Development. In *Artificial intelligence and the simulation of behavior* 1.

computer systems, on-line Computer systems are "on-line" to their users or to other devices if they communicate directly with them. "Off-line" systems, which provide no direct connection, are relatively inflexible and likely to disappear in most fields. Psychology is among the most highly computerized of the sciences; research and other professional psychologists make extensive use of large time-sharing facilities for such functions as data-processing (survey analysis, statistics) and modelling (cognitive simulation, monte carlo prediction). Smaller mini and microcomputers are widely used on-line and are to be found in most research and teaching centers. They are most commonly used in experimental psychology for stimulus preparation, equipment control, automatic data collection, etc. On-line computer systems are themselves an object of psychological study. Their complexity often creates great difficulties for users, and the processes of remembering, decision-making, communication, etc. are central to the rapidly growing field of cognitive ergonomics. (See also ERGONOMICS, COGNITIVE.) JPF

concept: animal An animal can be said to have formed a concept if it can be shown that it responds consistently to a particular aspect of a variety of stimuli presented in many different contexts. For example it has been shown that pigeons can develop the concept of 'human being' regardless of precisely what the humans look like or what they are doing. This was demonstrated by training pigeons to peck a key whenever they were shown a colored slide of a human being (which could be child, man, woman etc.) but not when they were shown animals, buildings or other pictures without human beings. The correct performance of pigeons on this and similar tasks shows an ability to form generalized concepts, not merely to respond to particular patterns. MSD

Bibliography

Herrnstein, R.J., Loveland, D.H. and Cable, C. 1976: Natural concepts in the pigeon. *Journal of experimental psychology: animal behavior processes* 2. 285–302.

concept: human To have the concept φ is either to know the meaning of the word "φ", or, while not knowing just this, to possess the sort of understanding which necessarily underlies such knowledge. For example if I understand "elasticity of demand", then I have that concept; but a shopkeeper, who wonders how altering his prices will affect the volume of his sales and his overall profits, possesses the essence of the concept even if he does not understand that expression or any synonym. Essentially to possess a concept, or set of concepts, is to be able to think about something in a certain way. To be able to think about material bodies in the way employed in Newtonian mechanics I must have such concepts as inertia, mass, force etc. To what extent the possession of concepts is inseparable from the understanding of language is a matter of controversy. Historically there has been a tendency to confuse concepts with mental images, or the capacity to form mental images. JMS

concept learning Learning to categorize different experiences. This process has been much studied using the concept identification method. A person is presented with a series of stimuli, some of which have been designated by the experimenter as instances of a new category. Success in identifying the concept is demonstrated by the ability to classify new members of the category correctly. The stimuli used have often been composed of a small number of attributes (such as color and shape), as in the classic study by Bruner, Goodnow and Austin (1956). The category to be identified consists then of stimuli that possess a particular conjunction (e.g. both *black* and *circular*), a particular disjunction (e.g. either *black* or *circular*), or some other combination of attribute-values. Considerable evidence has accumulated that learning in this type of task occurs by the formation and testing of discrete hypotheses concerning the characteristics of the concept to be acquired. It is not possible, however, to characterize many common concepts, such as *furniture*, by a simple rule. In recent years it has been shown that the acquisition of such concepts appears to center around their best instances, or *prototypes*. GVJ

Bibliography

Bruner, J.S., Goodnow, J.J. and Austin, G.A. 1956: *A study of thinking*. New York: Wiley.

*Reed, Stephen K. 1982: *Cognition: theory and applications*. Monterey, Calif.: Brooks/Cole.

concrete thinking Reasoning that is strongly tied to context or to immediate and tangible information. In Piaget's theory the concrete operational stage of cognitive development occurs between the ages of eight and eleven years. It is defined by the ability to think about problems in the "here and now" but not in the abstract and it marks a further step in the differentiation of the child from the world. The child can now reason logically in various domains such as conservation, classification and transitive inference, but only when all the information to be ordered remains immediately present. For example the child can work out the relative length of stick C by serial comparison of pairs of longer sticks A and B, to arrive at the solution by a transitive inference: $A > B, B > C \therefore A > C$. However, at the same age the child cannot solve a hypothetical version of the same problem: if John is taller than Mary and Mary is taller than Jane, who is the tallest? The ability to reason in the abstract awaits the acquisition of formal operations in early adolescence. GEB

Bibliography

Brainerd, C.J. 1978: *Piaget's theory of intelligence*. Englewood Cliffs, N.J: Prentice-Hall.

conditioning A form of associative learning which results in changes in an organism's behavior as a consequence of exposure to certain temporal relations between events. It is customary to distinguish two forms of conditioning, classical or Pavlovian conditioning on the one hand, and instrumental or operant conditioning on the other. In experimental studies of both varieties, the experimenter presents an event of biological or motivational significance usually termed a reinforcer; it may be food, water, or access to a sexual partner; or it may be a painful or distressing event such as a brief electric shock or the administration of a drug which causes nausea. Classical and instrumental conditioning differ in the other event with which this reinforcer is associated.

In classical conditioning the occurrence of a reinforcer is signaled by the presentation of a particular stimulus. In Pavlov's original experiments (1927) the reinforcer was either the delivery of food or an injection of a weak solution of acid into the dog's mouth, both of which caused the dog to salivate. Because they unconditionally elicited this response, they were called unconditional stimuli (abbreviated to US), and the salivation they elicited was an unconditional response (UR). The delivery of the reinforcer or US was preceded by the presentation of a neutral stimulus, a flashing light, a tone or buzzer or the ticking of a metronome. After a number of joint presentations of, say, the light and food, the dog would start salivating as soon as the light was turned on, before the food arrived. The light was referred to as a conditional stimulus (CS) and the response of salivating to the CS was called a conditional response (CR); the term refers to the fact that the CR is conditional upon the joint presentation of CS and US: if the light were now presented alone for a number of trials, it would lose its ability to elicit salivation. A mistranslation of 'conditional' as 'conditioned' meant that in English the CS and CR were referred to as a conditioned stimulus and conditioned response, and the verb 'to condition' was derived to refer to the process responsible for the establishment of the new CR.

Classical conditioning experiments have employed a variety of events as CS and US, and have recorded CRs ranging from discrete, reflexive responses such as salivation to food or acid as the US, blinking to a puff of air directed at the eye or flexion of the leg to a shock to the foot, to more general changes in behavior such as approaching and contacting an object associated with the delivery of food, withdrawal from an object associated with danger, or rejection of a normally palatable food whose ingestion has been artificially associated with illness and nausea. The defining criterion for saying that these are all experiments on classical conditioning is that the experimenter's rules for delivering the reinforcer or US make no reference to the behavior of his subjects. In Pavlov's experiments the dog receives food on every conditioning trial regardless of its behavior when the CS is turned on; the puff of air is directed at the eye, the shock applied to the animal's foot, or the emetic drug injected after the animal has consumed some food, and there is nothing the animal can do to prevent these things happening.

This marks the distinction between classical and instrumental conditioning. In an instrumental experiment the delivery of the reinforcer depends on the experimental subject's performance of a designated, instrumental response. The first systematic study of instrumental conditioning was by Thorndike (1911), who trained a variety of animals to escape from a puzzle box and thus gain access to food by pressing on a catch, pulling a loop of string or undoing a latch. The most commonly used procedure for studying instrumental conditioning is that developed by Skinner (1938): a rat is placed in a small chamber and presses a bar or lever protruding from one wall in order to obtain a pellet of food delivered automatically into a recess in the wall. As in Pavlov's original experiments, the reinforcer is food, but here the delivery of the reinforcer is not dependent on the occurrence of a CS, but rather on the rat's performance of a particular response, that of pressing the lever. The experimenter may be said to be rewarding this response, or if the reinforcer is an aversive or painful event, punishing it, and instrumental conditioning has occurred if the subject's behavior changes as a consequence of these 'contingencies of reinforcement' (in Skinner's phrase), that is to say if the subject comes to perform the rewarded response or refrains from performing the punished response.

The difference between classical and instrumental conditioning is thus defined in terms of the experimenter's rules for delivering a reinforcer. But this is hardly sufficient to prove that there is any fundamental distinction between the two. The fact that the experimenter can describe his experimental manipulations or operations in different ways does not imply that the subject's description matches the experimenter's or that fundamentally different processes are responsible for the changes in behavior observed in the two cases. But many psychologists have followed Skinner's lead in believing that the operational distinction may have some further significance. In the end the question is a theoretical one: whether a single theory of conditioning can encompass all the phenomena of both types of experiment.

An adequate theory of conditioning must explain why Pavlov's dog starts salivating to the CS. Pavlov's own explanation, expressed rather more clearly by his Polish successor Konorski (1948), was rather simple. Salivation is part of the set of responses unconditionally elicited by food; as a consequence of the experimenter's pairing a CS with the delivery of food the two events are associated by the subject; an association of the two events ensures that the presentation of one will activate a representation of the other (see ASSOCIATIONISM); the presentation of the CS will activate a representation of food and this activation will elicit salivation just as it would have if generated by the presentation of the food itself. Classical conditioning thus depends upon the establishment of an association between CS and US, and the CS thereby acquiring the ability to elicit responses normally elicited by the US alone.

It does not seem easy to apply this explanation to a case of instrumental conditioning: when a rat is rewarded with food for pressing a lever, this new response, not previously elicited by food, increases in probability. It is true that the last thing that will normally happen before a pellet of food is obtained is that the rat will have been in contact with the lever, sniffing it or touching it with its paw, but it remains to show how any association between these stimuli and the delivery of food could generate, via the Pavlovian mechanisms outlined above, the efficient instrumental response that rapidly emerges from the rat's initially accidental or exploratory contacts. In at least some cases, however, it turns out to be possible to apply a Pavlovian analysis. Another common instrumental procedure is to train pigeons to peck a small illuminated plastic disk on the wall of a Skinner box, rewarding them with food whenever they perform the required response. But pecking is, in fact, the pigeon's natural consummatory (or unconditional) response to food, and it turns out that the pigeon will peck the disk just as rapidly if the experimenter simply arranges to illuminate it for a few seconds before he delivers food regardless of the pigeon's behavior. The association between illumination of the disk (CS) and the delivery of food (US) is sufficient to ensure that the former comes to elicit the pecking response normally elicited by the latter alone. Here then is a purely Pavlovian explanation of what had always been regarded as a case of instrumental conditioning (Brown and Jenkins 1968).

But the fact remains that this analysis will not easily work for many cases of instrumental conditioning. It cannot easily explain why rats learn to press levers for food, still less why they can be trained to press the lever with a particular force (Notterman and Mintz 1965) or to hold it down for a particular length of time (Platt, Kuch and Bitgood 1973). It is equally unsuccessful at explaining why a dog should learn to flex a leg either to obtain food (Miller and Konorski 1928), or to avoid a puff of air directed at its ear (Fonberg 1958). Here and elsewhere instrumental conditioning occurs in accordance with Thorndike's law of effect which stated that responses are modified by the consequences, increasing in probability if followed by a satisfying consequence, decreasing if followed by an aversive consequence. Whether the law of effect is a theory or a circular description of observed data has from time to time been disputed, but it certainly captures what we intuitively see as the essential feature of voluntary actions – that they are performed because of their consequences.

If we cannot explain or describe instrumental conditioning without recourse to the law of effect, then the distinction between classical and instrumental conditioning can only be denied by dismissing Pavlov's account of classical conditioning and applying the law of effect here also. Several psychologists, notably Hull (1943), have attempted to do just this, but their attempts do not seem entirely successful. A pigeon conditioned to peck a disk whose illumination has served as a CS signalling food, will continue to do so even if the delivery of food is cancelled on those trials when the pigeon pecks at the disk. The only way for the pigeon to earn food now is to refrain from pecking when the disk is illuminated, but it is unable to do so. The association between light and food remains strong, so the pigeon cannot help approaching and pecking the light in spite of the adverse consequences of its actions (Williams and Williams 1969). There are many other examples of involuntary responses being conditioned by Pavlovian procedures in spite of their having adverse consequences. It is difficult to see how such conditioning could be analyzed in terms of the law of effect.

Unless a new, all-embracing theory is proposed, therefore, there is reason to believe that the distinction between classical and instrumental conditioning is real and important. This is not entirely surprising, for it corresponds roughly to the distinction we intuitively draw between involuntary and voluntary responses. Involuntary responses are evoked or elicited by stimuli which have been associated with, and thus make us think of, certain consequences: we cannot help salivating if we imagine someone squeezing a lemon into our mouth, or help blushing or sweating if we recall an embarrassing or frightening incident. Voluntary actions are those which we perform or refrain from carrying out because we have learned what their consequences are and because of the value we put on those consequences. We may often be mistaken in our belief that a particular response is voluntary or involuntary: the pigeon's pecking response seemed a voluntary act until experimental analysis suggested otherwise; and there is good evidence that responses we should normally regard as involuntary can sometimes be brought under voluntary control (this is the basis of BIOFEEDBACK). It is possible that the difference is one of degree rather than of kind. But that does not diminish its importance, and this suggests that we should acknowledge the reality of the two types of conditioning. NJM

Bibliography

Brown, P.L. and Jenkins, H. M. 1968: Auto-shaping of the pigeon's key peck. *Journal of the experimental analysis of behavior* 11, 1–8.

Fonberg, E. 1958: Transfer of instrumental avoidance reactions in dogs. *Bulletin de l'Academie Polonaise des sciences* 6, 353–56.

Hull, Clark L. 1943: *Principles of behavior*. New York and London: Appleton-Century.

Konorski, Jerzy 1948: *Conditioned reflexes and neuron organization*. Cambridge: Cambridge University Press. Reprinted 1968. New York: Hafner.

*Mackintosh, N.J. 1983: *Conditioning and associative learning*. Oxford and New York: Oxford University Press.

Miller, S. and Konorski, J. 1928: Sur une forme particulière des reflexes conditionnels. *Comptes Rendus des Séances de la Société de Biologie* 99, 1155–57.

Notterman, Joseph M. and Mintz, Donald E. 1965: *Dynamics of response*. New York and London: Wiley.

Pavlov, Ivan P. 1927: *Conditioned reflexes*. London: Oxford University Press. Reprinted 1960. New York and London: Dover.

Platt, J.R., Kuch, D.O. and Bitgood, S.C. 1973: Rats' lever-press durations as psychophysical judgments of time. *Journal of the experimental analysis of behavior* 19, 239–50.

*Schwartz, B. 1978: *Psychology of learning and behavior*, New York: Norton.

Skinner, Burrhus F. 1938: *The behavior of organisms*. New York and London: Appleton-Century.

Thorndike, Edward L. 1911: *Animal intelligence*. New York: Macmillan. Reprinted 1965. New York and London: Hafner.

Williams, D.R. and Williams, H. 1969: Auto-maintenance in the pigeon: sustained pecking despite contingent non-reinforcement. *Journal of the experimental analysis of behavior* 12, 511–20.

conduct disorder The commonest type of child psychiatric disorder, characterized by behavior which is antisocial, e.g. lying, stealing, aggression, firesetting, truancy. Conduct disorder occurs more commonly in boys than girls, and children from large or disrupted families living in poor social conditions are especially at risk. There is a marked association with reading retardation, and there may be associated emotional symptoms such as anxiety and low self esteem. In up to 50 per cent of children, the disorder persists into adolescence and may develop into delinquency. Psychiatric treatment may take a variety of forms. Behavioral treatments consist of setting clear limits of acceptable behavior for the child, and encouraging parents and teachers to work together in a consistent approach. Individual therapy aims at developing the child's skills and self esteem and exploring any areas of conflict; family therapy may be aimed at trying to change rejecting family attitudes. If these approaches fail it may be necessary to remove the child from the home environment, by placing him or her in a residential school, children's home, or foster family.

See also CHILD AND ADOLESCENT PSYCHIATRY; DELINQUENCY.

GCF

Bibliography

Robins, L. 1966: *Deviant children grown up*. Baltimore: Williams & Williams.

confabulation *See* memory impairment

conflict: human A psychological state of indecision which occurs when a person is influenced simultaneously by two opposing forces of approximately equal strength. According to Lewin (1935), there are three fundamental types of conflict situation:

(1) An individual may be caught at a midway point between two positive valences of nearly equal strength (i.e. the choices are equally attractive). Field theory predicts that the strength of the force toward the goal region increases as the individual approaches it; thus, chance factors alone make it likely that the individual will accidentally move toward one goal and away from the other, destroying the point of equilibrium. What results is a natural acceleration of the force toward that particular region as a consequence of an increase in proximity to the goal.

(2) An individual may be caught between two negative valences of approximately equal strength (i.e. the choices are both undesirable). Punishment is an example of this type of conflict. There are three subtypes of situations in which conflict occurs between equal negative valences: the individual is confronted by two negative valences, but it is possible to escape the situation entirely; the individual is placed between two negative valences, yet cannot leave the field; and the individual can leave an area of negative valence only by going through another region of negative valence.

(3) An individual may be exposed to opposing forces deriving from a positive and a negative valence. Conflict involving both attractive and unattractive components can also be divided into three subtypes: one situation is simply that the region, or psychological activity involved, has both negative and positive aspects. This can be recognized as the familiar Freudian concept of ambivalence. A second subtype involves an individual who is encircled by a negative region but attracted by a goal outside the negative region. In a third situation a region of positive valence is encircled by a region of negative valence. This is different from the example just cited in that the region of positive valence, rather than the region in which the person is to be found, is encircled by the negative valence.

Much research has been generated by Lewin's theoretical exploration of conflict. The most widely-known work has probably been that of Festinger's cognitive dissonance (1957) which elaborates Lewin's view that the situation prior to decision differs from that after the decision. More recent work of Deutsch's in this area was also influenced by Lewin (Deutsch 1973).

MDe

Bibliography

Deutsch, M. 1973: *The resolution of conflict*. New Haven: Yale University Press.

Festinger, L. 1957: *A theory of cognitive dissonance*. Stanford: Stanford University Press.

Lewin, K. 1935: *A dynamic theory of personality*. New York: McGraw Hill.

conflict: in animal ethology A state in which an animal is simultaneously motivated in two or more incompatible ways. A hungry rat hesitates at a short distance from the end of a runway where it has sometimes received food, sometimes electric shock. Two rival male birds face each other across the boundary between their territories. In these cases the conflict can be expressed generally as approach/avoidance, or more specifically, in the case of the rival birds, as attack/escape. When in conflict an animal may adopt a compromise posture which reveals elements of both underlying motivations. The particular compromise posture held in territorial disputes is called "threat", and elements of postures adopted during aggressive attacks and during flight can be identified. This has been taken as evidence that aggressive and escape DRIVES are independent of each other but interact to determine the final form of a behavior pattern.

AWGM

conflict: social psychology In psychology the word conflict refers mainly to a situation in which an individual is motivated to engage in two or more mutually exclusive activities, such as approaching or avoiding a goal. In social psychology the dominant interest has been in the determinants and resolution of interpersonal and intergroup conflicts. Two-person conflicts are often resolved through bargaining or negotiation. Research suggests that taking an extreme initial position, making relatively few and small concessions and convincing one's opponent that a deal with someone else is possible can facilitate an advantageous outcome. However such strategies can also lead to a deadlock. In such a case a graduated and reciprocated initiative in tension reduction, (GRIT) as suggested by Osgood (1979), may break the deadlock.

JMFJ

Bibliography

Deutsch, M. 1973: *The resolution of conflict*. New Haven: Yale University Press.

Morley, I.E., and Stephenson, G.M. 1977: *The social psychology of bargaining*. London: Allen and Unwin.

Osgood, C.E. 1979: GRIT for MBFR: a proposal for unfreezing force-level postures in Europe. *Peace research review* 8, 77–92.

conflict theory and emotion Conflict arises when the completion of a response is blocked or arrested, either by some environmental obstacle (frustration) or by incompatible response tendencies (intrapsychic conflict). Modern conflict theories of emotion are often traced to Dewey, although others (e.g. Lewin, Miller, Freud) have been more influential in developing conflict theory in diverse areas. Dewey (1894) argued that emotions arise only when a response is blocked: for example, the unimpeded avoidance of a dangerous object is not "fear". This view may be contrasted with instinct and other motivational theories, which presume that emotions accompany the free but automatic expression of certain innate or acquired drives (e.g. McDougall 1936). Both points of view contain important insights, but with respect to different subdomains of emotion. A major weakness of conflict theories is their inability to predict which emotions will result from any given conflict. Aggression is a common response to conflict, but so too are avoidance and depression; indeed, conflicting impulses may be inhibited, exaggerated, and transformed in an almost indefinite variety of ways. The specific emotion exhibited thus depends on the nature and strength of the original impulses, situational constraints and opportunities, and prior experience and socialization in similar situations. But diversity does not imply a lack of order. Biological and social evolution have provided ("selected") standardized ways of coping with widely experienced conflicts. Some common emotional reactions, such as anger, can be regarded as conflictive in this sense (Averill 1982). Hysterical (conversion) reactions are examples of more idiosyncratically shaped responses to conflict. JRA

Bibliography

Averill, J.R. 1982: *Anger and aggression: an essay on emotion*. New York, Heidelberg, and Berlin: Springer Verlag.

Dewey, J. 1894: The theory of emotion, I. Emotional attitudes. *Psychological review* 1, 553–69.

McDougall, W. 1936: *An introduction to social psychology*. 23rd edn. London: Methuen.

conflict *See above, and also* role ambiguity

congruity principle A quantitative extension of Heider's theory of balanced states suggested by Osgood and Tannenbaum (1955), in particular applicable to persuasive communication processes. According to Osgood's congruity principle, attitude change depends upon the discrepancy between the initial attitudes of the receiver towards the source and the content of the message, taking into account the positive or negative nature of the communication. Predictions of actual attitude change are only moderately sucessful and require various additional assumptions, which suggests that a weighted averaging model, in which the relative weight of the source depends on the attitude of the receiver to the source, describes attitude change better than the congruity principle. JMFJ

Bibliography

Jaspars, J. 1978: Determinants of attitudes and attitude change. In: *Introducing social psychology*, ed. H. Tajfel and C. Fraser. Harmondsworth: Penguin.

Osgood, C.E. and Tannernbaum, P.H. 1955: The principle of congruity in the prediction of attitude change. *Psychological review* 62, 42–55.

conscience A set of personal rules and values that usually parallel the norms of society and guide individual social conduct. These rules are generally thought to be learned and, are therefore, initially implanted by external influences (e.g. through the rewards and punishment of authority figures). Once the rules are internalized, however, social conduct becomes privately regulated (e.g. guilt is experienced when these internalized rules are violated). See SUPEREGO for Freud's views on the development and operation of the conscience. RHo

consciousness A term used usually very loosely to refer to one of the following:

(a) the state of an individual animal is alert and capable of action, contrasted with unconsciousness

(b) the quality that an animal species has of being capable of being aware or conscious of objects in the environment, also and probably less confusingly, referred to as sentience

(c) the state of being aware of some of one's thoughts, perceptions or emotions, also known as self-consciousness

(d) the capacity of human beings to have an organized mental life, in which each individual's experience has a particular perceived quality

(e) the system of states of mind which organize and coordinate thoughts and actions, contrasted with subconscious.

There are many connections between these five ideas. But few of them are uncontroversial. For example, (d) is often related to (c), since it is often assumed that self-awareness or the capacity to introspect is an essential characteristic of the human mind. But this assumption is by no means obvious, and one can quite intelligibly doubt whether there is such a thing as introspection. And (e) is often assimilated to (c), but this connection must be fairly loose, since there is no reason to believe that all central, organizing states consist in or are objects of awareness.

The source of this confusing overlap of meanings is the fact that the word entered European languages at a time when psychology and ordinary thought were under the influence of theories of the mind, stemming largely from Descartes and from the ideology of the Reformation, according to which the contents of a person's mind can be known and judged by that person alone. If this were true the distinctions between (c) (d) and (e) might not matter much. Unfortunately, the whole drift of modern psychology is against this assumption. Perhaps the most striking example of its influence is in the title of William James's essay "Does Consciousness Exist?" James is not doubting the existence just of *conscious* mental states, but of *all* mental states (as independent constituents of the world).

We may be able to avoid confusion by distinguishing between sentience, i.e. the capacity to perceive and also to have beliefs and desires; personhood, i.e. the capacity to have beliefs and desires *about* one's beliefs and desires (see Frankfurt 1971); and consciousness proper, i.e. the possession of a more or less continuous stream of knowledge of one's thoughts and feelings as they happen. The study of sentience could then be regarded as another name for psychology, the study of personhood, inasmuch as it is part of psychology, as the study of self-knowledge and self-deception. The remainder of this article will be restricted to consciousness proper.

Most twentieth-century theories of consciousness have tried to describe the function and operation of a psychological mechanism which directs selective attention to sensory input and to action. That is, something like (c) (d) or (e). Some, indeed, have suggested that no such mechanism exists. The reasons for this have usually been general propositions about the nature of mind and of psychology, as in Watson (1925) and perhaps Ryle (1949). Theories which do assume that there is something to be explained are mainly psychoanalytic or cognitive.

The main elements of the psychoanalytic treatment of consciousness are found in Freud's writings. In his early writings Freud argued that complex thought processes can occur unconsciously, so that the distinguishing mark of what is conscious is its rational and direct connection with behavior and its straightforward expression in social activity such as speech. Later Freud distinguished between the unconscious and the preconscious (see Freud 1915): preconsciousness consists of memories and mental processes which can become conscious when needed, while the unconscious consists of items which have been explicitly excluded from consciousness by the process of repression. On this account an individual's consciousness is created by the operation of two mechanisms: one, attention, admits of degree and is to some extent inherent in the human organism, the other, repression, is an all-or-nothing affair, and develops in the mind as a response to environmental, largely social, contingencies.

Psychoanalytic and cognitive theories both hold that consciousness is formed by the operation of processes which are also, and primarily, found in non-conscious thought. Under cognitive theories I include theories from neuroscience, cognitive psychology and artificial intelligence. In all these disciplines theories of attention, memory and coordination can be adapted and combined to give an account of some of the phenomena that one might expect theories of consciousness to explain. Thus Pribram (1980) discusses the linkage of homeostatic neural mechanisms governing attention into what he calls "feedforward" mechanisms which would have some of the characteristics of conscious attention. And Dennett (1978), building on work of Neisser (1967), suggests a complex structure of processes required for perception, memory and speech, which would capture many of the effects of consciousness. No such project will claim to be a completely adequate representation of human consciousness, but such discussion may help to clarify thinking, meaning and use of the concept of consciousness. (Sayre 1969 is explicit about this), and, for that matter, whether there is anything to be explained.

See also AVOWAL; ATTENTION: PHILOSOPHICAL ANALYSIS; DESCARTES; FREUD; INTROSPECTION; PRIVACY; SELF-DECEPTION; UNCONSCIOUS MIND. JAM

Bibliography

Davidson, Richard 1980: Consciousness and information processing. In *The psychobiology of consciousness*, ed. J.M. and R.J. Davidson. New York: Plenum.

*Dennett, D.C. 1978: *Brainstorms*. Cambridge, Mass.: Bradford Books.

Frankfurt, H. 1971: Freedom of the will and the concept of a person. *Journal of philosophy* 68.

*Freud, Sigmund 1915: The Unconscious. In *The standard edition of the complete psychological work of Sigmund Freud* vol 14. London: Hogarth Press; New York: Norton.

*James, William 1890: Chapter 9 of *The principles of psychology* New York; Holt.

Neisser, Ulric 1967: *Cognitive psychology*. New York: Appleton-Century-Crofts.

Pribram, K. 1980: Mind, brain and consciousness. In *The psychobiology of consciousness*, ed. J.M. and R.J. Davidson. New York: Plenum.

Ryle, Gilbert 1949: *The concept of mind*. London: Hutchinson.

Sayre, K. 1969: *Consciousness: a study in minds and machines*. New York: Random House.

Watson, J.B. 1925: *Behaviorism*. London: Kegan Paul.

consciousness disorders Disorders of the awareness of the self and the external environment. The main abnormalities include lowering of consciousness, dream-like disorders, and narrowing of consciousness.

(1) lowering of consciousness: *clouding of consciousness* is a reduced state of awareness, ranging from slight lowering of consciousness to stupor and coma. It is accompanied by impairment of attention, memory and perception in varying degress. Clouding of consciousness is characteristic of organic state (see ORGANIC STATES).

(2) dream-like disorders: *delirium* includes severe impairment of consciousness, with disorientation in time and place, perceptual abnormalities such as illusions and hallucinations, and motor abnormalities, such as restlessness and agitation. Delirium is also a typical picture in organic states (see ORGANIC STATES).

(3) narrowing of consciousness: twilight states where the individual remains aware of only part of the environment, as in hypnotic states, or where marked and sudden changes in consciousness are accompanied by dramatic expression of emotion such as anger or fear, and sometimes by hallucinatory experiences. Psychogenic twilight states can occur in hysteria. Organic twilight states are more often seen in epilepsy.

Psychomotor seizures are epileptic manifestations characterized by disorders of consciousness and behavior, and include epileptic automatisms, petit mal states, fugues and post-ictal disorders (see EPILEPSY). Disorders of consciousness and behavior can also occur in relation to sleep, as in the narcoleptic syndrome, somnambulism and night terrors. (Fenton 1975). JC

Bibliography

Fenton, G.W. 1975: Clinical disorders of sleep. *British journal of hospital medicine* 14, 120-45.

Lishman, W.A. 1978: *Organic psychiatry: the psychological consequences of cerebral disorder.* Oxford: Blackwell Scientific; St Louis, Missouri: C. V. Mosbye.

consciousness: alternative psychologies As ordinarily understood, consciousness may be defined as the actualized capacity for awareness, considered independently of its "content", or what the awareness is of. Taken in this sense, consciousness is at least part of what Greek philosophers must have understood by "*nous*"; part of what British and American philosophers have meant by "mind"; and also a part of what Descartes meant by "*cogitans*".

Uses of "consciousness" by philosophers tend to contrast with uses by psychologists by focussing primarily on the aspect of content as opposed to function – a factor whose state and proceedings affect behavior. Four major conceptual problems, all turning on the fact that it conjoins these two kinds of considerations, have prevented assimilation of "consciousness" to the mainstream of clarified psychological discourse.

1. The relation of consciousness to content. If "consciousness" stands for the actualized capacity for bare awareness (in a person, on an occasion), then "content of consciousness" would stand for that which the awareness (of the person, on the occasion) is *of*, when this phrase is restricted in its reference to what persons *take themselves* to be aware of (on the occasion). Otherwise, if "content" stood for something determined apart from what the person determined for himself, it would refer to something that lay outside (his) consciousness. Thus, "consciousness" refers to some state of arousal that permits one to articulate a content, or self, by producing a text (or, more precisely, a text-token, such as, e.g. the utterance of "red") in answer to the question "of what (color hue) are you presently aware?" A "content", in this use, is a momentary cross-section of a physiological process that has resulted in the arousal of some quality distinctly enough to be recognized and capable of propositional expression as a "text". The unity of a content is conferred through the unity of the meaning of the text.

2. The relation of consciousness to species of acts. Contents are determined not merely through texts in general, but through orders of qualities, articulated through corresponding orders of texts. These different orders of qualities arise, it has been found, as the result of various more or less independently aroused systems in the organism. What are termed, classically, "thinking", ("*cogitans*"), "perceiving", "remembering", "desiring", "willing", "assenting", "believing", "doubting", and so forth, are differentiations among species of content based on arousal of the relevant systems articulated by the names of these different "acts". These are acts, because one can be aware of intentionally doing them; can usually stop doing them, except sometimes in the case of desire (or in the case of seeing an array of colors in broad daylight if one's eyes are open and functioning normally). Since the doing of them affects behavior, owing to the integrative function of consciousness in bringing things together under texts, they may be termed "conscious functions", even though the systems responsible for their occurrence may be aroused and perform the same functions unconsciously (as when one drives a car without being aware of it, etc.). "Consciousness", then, would be the generic form of activity of which the other terms are species. The relative *independence* of the systems that would be aroused would explain why there are different types of content, classifiable according to the dominance of the factor operating. Their *linkage*, in patterns or chains of quality/state arousals, would both generate and explain such commonly noted phenomena as (a) various associative mechanisms, e.g. tendency to shift from a painful reality-perception state to one of hallucinated gratification of removal from that state (Freud's theory of dreams as "wish-fulfillment"); (b) state-bound content, i.e. the availability of specific recollections in specific ALTERED STATES, such as hypnosis; and (c) spontaneous interruptions in processes, such as having a tune come into one's head while speaking, etc. The representation of the different acts as species of consciousness is a recognition of the ubiquity of the attending to, and becoming aware of, the act, and all the matters distinguished from it, and from each other, on qualitative grounds. This exposition accords with John Locke's use in Bk. II, Ch. 1 of the *Essay on Human Understanding*: "Every man being conscious to himself that he thinks..."; "thinking", here, as a state in which a function is being carried out, being contrasted with perceiving, sensing, desiring, remembering, and so forth.

3. The relation of content to external facts. Whether a fact exists corresponding to the text used in articulating a particular content depends, first, on the interpretation given of the terms in it; specifically, on whether, in addition to their role in articulating a content, they are treated as having referential significance. If they are assigned no use beyond the bare articulation of the quality components of a given state, then texts are always "necessarily" true. Such a hermeneutic is proposed by so called "sense-datum" theories in philosophy, which take the stratum of experience determined by such restricted assignment of reference back to the organically conditioned qualities as evidentially and/or ontologically primordial in the analysis of perception. Widely accepted criticism of the sense datum theory in its various forms has worked strongly against the development of an empirical theory of consciousness. To treat consciousness as a real, autonomous mode of integrating factors under texts to constitute logically self-contained "contents", would suggest the revival of the framework of "given-ness", "immediacy", and so forth. By treating consciousness as empirically real, something with functions of its own, and subject to experimental investigation by checking alterations of state against alterations of content, etc., it appears that the question of the distinction between "mind" and "body" as classically posed (for example, in Descartes's *Meditations*), as a conceptual problem, is being shifted, and put on a contingent, empirical footing. Meanwhile, the use of "consciousness", as a term essentially tied to the physiological concept of "arousal", was gaining

widespread use among ALTERNATIVE PSYCHOLOGIES as well as various academic disciplines, e.g. COGNITIVE PSYCHOLOGY, the "psychology of consciousness" of Tart and Ornstein et al. This rift between the empirical notion of consciousness, emphasizing the function of its various contents, and the epistemological notion of consciousness as strictly relative to cognition, as in the classical discussions of sense perception, cannot be said to be generally resolved at present.

However, the distinction between sign and SYMBOL, can be used to account for the use of sign-tokens in a symbolic way, creating a dialectical relationship between a referring expression and its referent, in that the identification of the latter becomes more adequate as it articulates the former more precisely. This allows, conceptually, for the often *un*consciousness of what is symbolized. On the other side, the step from a "sense datum" to a "physical object" interpretation of the reference of texts in general, as a reconstruction of the old dichotomy between "idealism", and "realism", is clarified by assignment of its application to different types of content, rather than to different types of objects.

4. The relation of consciousness to "I". The first person singular pronouns are self-referential; their use calls attention back to the user. Here the distinction between articulation (of contents) and reference (to objects) is crucial, for the contents that may be *articulated* by "I", on specific occasions, cannot be construed as *referred to*, on those occasions; for, as it has been found, the contents of what-the-person-takes-himself-to-be may vary with different uses of "I", whereas a referring term, or name, is properly used only when all of its referent occurs, each time. If one says, for instance, "well, *I* don't like it..." the stressed self-reference may articulate a specific, but momentary sense of offense one has taken to a remark, or unpleasant odor, etc.; and then, later on, it may turn out that one would *not* say that, forgetting the first "I". This means that "I" cannot be construed as a name, for names refer to the same thing each time they are properly used. If "I" were construed as a name, it would refer to the self-referring gesture, itself, since that is the only feature common to all uses. The automatic or mechanical attachment of "I" by a person whenever certain types of content are entertained – representation of some sports activity, for example – would define a state or condition of "identification " with the content, a factor that might be unconscious to the person, themselves, but, as a depth-psychological configuration, exercise a general organizing control over the disposal of content, in so far as it is related to the sense of individual personhood. If there were a "psychoid" ground for an ontogenetic organization of the "identifications" made spontaneously by persons in their use of "I" it would correspond to C.G. Jung's theory of the "self" as a larger totality containing consciousness, but represented symbolically within it through use of just those tokens that spontaneously articulate identifications.

To summarize: the theory of "consciousness" is, at present, in a state of uncertainty owing to many difficulties that seem to follow from taking it one way rather than another. The two major contexts of use, in classical philosophy following Descartes, and in empirical psychology, in this century, divide the term according to its cognitive and its functional aspects respectively. In the latter context its use is tied to that which has states, and can be analyzed into contents, as event-units, related in various empirical ways to other contents and to external events. Used strictly in the context of cognition, however, "consciousness" is assimilated to the object, or that which any given case of awareness is *of*, and can be defined in terms of relations between intentional objects, rather than "contents". SBT

Bibliography

King, C. Daly 1932: *The psychology of consciousness*. New York: Harcourt, Brace.

Ornstein, R.E. 1972: *The psychology of consciousness*. San Francisco: W.H. Freeman.

consciousness, stream of Consciousness is not a stream of episodic experiences occurring in sequence; it is, as William James (1800, p.237) put it, "sensibly continuous". It consists in a flowing succession of interpenetrating phases, each containing, as he said (James, p.254), vague "feelings of tendency" of what is yet to come in terms of what has so far occurred. Although the flow may be distinguished into phases of "before" and "after", such a differentiation of the flow serves, not to separate it into a "patchwork of disjoined parts" (Dewey 1896); but on the contrary, to relate them all as aspects of the same dynamic unity. Titchener (1901–5), however, maintained that thought processes *could* be reduced to either sensations, images or feelings, where the meaning uniting them was given by their reference to the original bodily attitude in which they had their source. JDS

Bibliography

Dewey, J. 1896: The concept of the reflex arc in psychology. *Psychology review* 3, 13–32.

James, W. 1890 *(1950)*: *Principles of psychology*. New York: Dover.

Titchener, E.B. 1901–5: *Experimental psychology*. 2 vols.: New York: Macmillan.

consciousness *See above, and also* emotion and consciousness

conservation A term in Piagetian theory that refers to the knowledge that physical properties of objects remain invariant under transformations that do not involve addition or subtraction. Such knowledge is acquired between the ages of eight and eleven years, during the concrete operational period.

In the classic conservation task, the child is shown two identical beakers of liquid A and B, and will affirm that they contain an equal amount of water. The water in B is then poured into a different container C, while the child is watching, so that the height and width of the liquid is changed. The child is asked whether A and C contain the same or different amounts of water. Children from about eight years, who conserve volume, will say that the amounts are equal despite the perceptual transformation. Younger children will generally say that the container in which the water level is highest contains most, they 'center' upon or are dominated by the changing perceptual attributes of the display. Similar errors can be observed in tasks testing for conservation of length, number or weight. The question whether the child is truly dominated by appearances or simply fails adequately to understand the adult's questions, remains to be resolved. GEB

Bibliography

Donaldson, Margaret M. 1978: *Children's minds*. London: Fontana; New York: Norton (1979).

consideration Used in leadership studies to refer to the extent to which a leader shows understanding and concern for the members of his group, is considerate for their well being and is willing to explain his actions to them. Studies of how leaders' behavior might be described distinguished between consideration and INITIATING STRUCTURE. Roughly corresponding to "socio-emotional" and "task facilitative" leadership, these two dimensions of a leader's behavior are thought to be largely independent of each other and have been used to distinguish between different leadership styles.

Several studies have been concerned with the relations between group performance, members' satisfaction, and measures of a leader's consideration and initiation of structure. While some consistent findings have emerged, for example, that high consideration is required in groups where the task is unpleasant, definitive results have been few. Early hopes that consideration and initiating structure would be seen to be related to effectiveness in a straightforward manner have been disappointed. Many psychologists now prefer to explore the situational variables which moderate the outcomes of different leadership styles. See CONTINGENCY THEORIES. FHMB

Bibliography

Halpin, A.W. and Winer, B.J. 1957: A factorial study of the leader behavior description. In *Leader behaviors: its description and measurement*, ed. R.M. Stogdill and A.E. Coons. Columbus: Ohio State University, Bureau of Business Research.

*House, R.J. and Baetz, M.L. 1979: Leadership. In *Research in organizational behavior* Vol. 1, ed. B.M. Staw. Greenwich, Connecticut: JAI Press.

consolidation of memory Refers to the process whereby a recently formed labile memory trace becomes durable. The notion of "perseveration" of a neural process as necessary for the establishment of a permanent trace seems first to have been described by Mueller and Pilzecker (1900). The newly-laid trace is said to consist of the neural activity that represents an experienced event, while its stable counterpart is thought to be a structural change in the brain.

Numerous attempts (beginning with the work of Duncan) have been made to measure the time-course of consolidation in animals by administering an electroconvulsive shock (ECS) at varying intervals of time following the one-trial acquisition of a response. It was long believed that a single ECS could produce a deleterious effect on retention if it was delivered within 15 to 60 seconds after the trial. More recent work has demonstrated that the critical interval lasts less than 10 seconds.

A wide-ranging review of the literature (Chorover 1976) suggests that there may in fact exist no single time-course of consolidation, since its estimates vary widely according to such factors as the species of the animal and its experience, the nature of the task, the physical parameters of the ECS and the ECS's mode of administration. It is likely, moreover, that much ECS-induced forgetting reflects a failure in retrieval rather than the absence of a trace (Lewis 1979), since well-established memories may be disrupted by ECS or other amnestic agents.

In the human being the permanent retrograde amnesia that frequently follows head injury seldom covers a period of more than a few seconds preceding the trauma. Melton (1963) concluded on the basis of experimental data then available that in the normal human subject the consolidation process could not possibly last more than a few seconds. No subsequent evidence contradicts this conclusion. NCW

Bibliography

Chorover, S.L. 1976: An experimental critique of "consolidation studies" and an alternative "model-systems" approach to the biopsychology of memory. In *Neural mechanisms of learning and memory*, ed. M.R. Rozensweig and E.L. Bennett. Cambridge, Mass.: M.I.T. Press.

Lewis, D.J. 1979: Psychobiology of active and inactive memory. *Psychological bulletin* 86, 1054–83.

Melton, A.W. 1963: Implications of short-term memory for a general theory of memory. *Journal of verbal learning and verbal behavior* 2, 1–21.

Mueller, G.E. and Pilzecker, A. 1900: Experimentelle Beitraege zur Lehre von Gedaechtnis. *Zeitschrift für psychologie* Suppl. No. 1.

constitutional psychology Theory that specific psychological characteristics, especially personality TRAITS, are associated with aspects of physical constitution. In the 1920s Kretschmer applied this ancient idea to his psychotic patients and observed that schizophrenics tended to have a tall, linear build (asthenic or asthenic–athletic) while manic-depressives tended to be shorter and rounded (pyknic); but he did not control for the different age of onset of these illnesses. He regarded these as extreme or disordered cases of a general trend linking the temperament of schizothymia with the one build and that of cyclothymia with the other.

In the 1940s Sheldon analysed body-build into three contributory components which could each be measured objectively and used to yield standardized scores on a 7-point scale: Ectomorphy (linearity), mesomorphy (bone and muscle) and endomorphy (roundness and fat). The mixture of these components in an individual's body is its SOMATOTYPE, which can be expressed in a three-digit code. These somatic components were correlated with three parameters of temperament respectively: cerebrotonia (emotional reserve and cognitive control), somatotonia (aggressive activity) and viscerotonia (sociability, physical relaxation). Subsequent researchers have not found such high correlations, and endomorphy seems a doubtful component. Rees and Eysenck argue that two factors, one of linearity and one of size, are enough to cover the variety observed; but Parnell confirms the link between ectomorphy and schizoid intellectual temperament (see Hall and Lindzey 1978, ch. 13). Eysenck's theory of personality (1967) links two dimensions of introversion – extroversion and neuroticism – stability to the constitution of the nervous system. NMC

Bibliography

Eysenck, Hans J. 1967: *The biological basis of personality*. Springfield, Ill.: Thomas.

Hall, Calvin S. and Lindzey, Gardner, eds. 1978: *Theories of personality*. 3rd. edn. New York: Wiley.

consultation *See* process consultation

consummatory behavior in animals The behavior that terminates a period of APPETITIVE BEHAVIOR. A period of FORAGING may be terminated by the consummatory behavior of feeding. Scientists differ in opinion as to the extent to which consummatory behavior *per se* is instrumental in bringing appetitive behavior to a temporary close. Episodes of copulatory behavior, for example, are clearly terminated by ejaculation, which may be regarded as the consummatory act. In other cases, however, the situation is not so clear. Behavior such as foraging, or nest-building may be punctuated by bouts of grooming or VIGILANCE on an apparently pre-programmed basis. It is not therefore always the case that episodes of appetitive behavior are terminated by a consummatory act. DJM

contagion In contagion theories collective behavior is a process in which emotions and behavioral patterns spread rapidly and are accepted uncritically by the members of a collective. Social contagion is a form of collective excitement. It is a relatively rapid and nonrational dissemination of a mood, impulse or form of conduct. It can bring in what were initially detached observers and lead them to behave like the others involved.

Social contagion may often be seen in crowd or mass behavior. Research is mainly concerned with explaining how the absence of regulative interaction between individuals in crowds produces illusions of power and feelings of "universality" which involve a transition of responsibility to the crowd, increased similarity of the individuals' behavior and processes of emotional fusion and identification with a leader. See CROWD PSYCHOLOGY. AF

context: in psycholinguistics The term is used in two senses

(1) The context of an utterance includes the spatio-temporal situation in which it occurs, knowledge shared by speaker and hearer as well as certain culturally determined beliefs taken for granted by the interactors. Such a contextual view of meaning is associated with the Firthian School of Linguistics (see Leech 1974, pp.71–81) and the situational method of second language instruction.

(2) In a technical sense the context of a linguistic rule is defined as the conditions under which it may apply. A distinction can be drawn between context-free rules which take the general form $A \rightarrow X$ and context-sensitive rules of the form $A \rightarrow X/\ Y$ —Z (in the context preceded by Y and followed by Z). Developmentally (both ontogenetically and phylogenetically) many grammatical rules begin in a highly restricted natural context and become context free only after considerable development has taken place in a grammar. PM

Bibliography

Leech, Geoffrey 1974: *Semantics*. London: Pelican Books.

context effects Since the human cognitive system is highly interactive, the significance of a particular cue, memory trace or elementary cognitive operation cannot be determined in isolation but must be studied in context. If the overall constellation shifts, the meaning of each element changes. Context effects have been observed in perception, memory, language, thinking and problem solving. WKi

contextual theory Emphasizes the importance of contextual factors in the explanation of social, psychological and historical events. From the 1960s onwards several authors have considered contextual theory (or "contextualism") as an alternative to the traditional view that human action can be explained by reference to laws and initial conditions (the covering-law model). The search for laws–in psychology mainly correlations between dependent and independent variables–seems to detract from a careful investigation of the situation in which the action was performed. Influenced by the work of Wittgenstein, theorists working from this point of view maintain that "meaning" is not a private, subjective entity, but is created by the use of expressions in social interaction (cf. Wittgenstein's attack on private languages). So only an analysis of the context of human action can give insight into both its determinants and its meaning. See MEANING. SJST

Bibliography

*Sarbin, T.R. 1977: Contextualism: a world view for Modern psychology. In *Nebraska symposium on motivation* ed. A.W. Landfield. Lincoln: University of Nebraska Press.

Wittgenstein, Ludwig 1980: *Understanding and meaning*. ed. G.S. Baker and P.M.S. Hacker, Oxford: Basil Blackwell; Chicago: University of Chicago Press.

contingency theories An approach to understanding leadership in small groups which asserts that the effectiveness of a leader depends upon the particular circumstances in which he is operating. In exploring the relevance of contextual features contingency approaches stand in marked contrast to earlier approaches that sought to identify the personality traits that might be associated with effective leadership or to identify a universally preferred style of leadership (see CONSIDERATION; INITIATING STRUCTURE; MANAGEMENT).

One leading contingency theorist is Fiedler, who suggests that certain situations are more favorable to leaders than others. Factors which he identifies as determining "situational favorableness" are the leader's popularity with his group, the extent to which a group task is straightforward and unambiguous, and the leader's ability to administer rewards and sanctions. He predicts that task oriented leaders are more effective when easy and difficult decisions have to be made, while relation oriented leaders are more effective in situations of intermediate difficulty. An important implication of this theory is that, rather than attempting to train people to adopt new and unfamiliar leadership styles, it would be more effective to fit people into the leadership situations most suited to their characteristics. Other contingency models however have adopted a different objective, having been devised to help leaders develop more flexible approaches to their roles. Notable here is the approach of Vroom and Yetton. These writers have developed a decision-process flow chart which, according to factors such as the importance of the decision that a group has to make, its difficulty, the leader's expertise in the matter, and the degree of commitment required of the group's membership, sets out to indicate whether directive, consultative or participative styles would be the most appropriate for the leader to adopt. FHMB

Bibliography

Fiedler, F.E. 1967: *A theory of leadership effectiveness.* New York: McGraw Hill.

*Porter, L.W. et al. 1977: A symposium on leadership. In *Perspectives on behaviour in organisations*, ed. R.J. Hackman. New York: McGraw Hill.

Vroom, V.H. and Yetton, P.W. 1973: *Leadership and decision making.* Pittsburg: University of Pittsburg Press.

contingent truth A statement is said to be contingently true (or false) if it might have been false (or true). One which is not contingent (neither contingently true nor contingently false) is either necessarily true or necessarily false. In the above definition the phrase "might have been false" must be taken broadly, possibly broadly enough to cover any statement whose truth or falsity cannot be determined a priori. It is contingent that water expands on freezing however inevitable such expansion may be. It is necessary that bachelors are unmarried and that $2+2=4$, and necessarily false that 6 is an odd number. Sometimes it is said that something is not a purely contingent matter. By that it is meant that the truth of the proposition in question arises partly from the nature of the concepts employed in it. For example it may be plausibly claimed not to be purely contingent that games are played for fun. JMS

contrastive analysis of linguistic systems It is claimed by a number of applied linguists and theoreticians of SECOND LANGUAGE ACQUISITION that the best second language teaching materials are based on a contrastive analysis of the learner's first language and the target language. This view derives from the assumption that positive transfer (facilitation) and negative transfer (interference) are the most important factors in the second language learning process (see BEHAVIORISM).

Wardhaugh (1971) distinguishes between a strong and a weak version of the contrastive analysis hypothesis. The former claims that the errors and language difficulties of a learner can be predicted by a systematic comparison of the native and target languages. The weak hypothesis merely assumes that all errors can be accounted for by contrastive factors.

In spite of its superficial plausibility and wide acceptance by language teachers, neither version of the contrastive analysis hypothesis can be upheld. Empirical evidence from studies of INTERLANGUAGE suggests that contrastive errors account for only a small proportion of occurring errors. On the methodological side, contrastive linguists have failed to develop consistent criteria for the comparison of linguistic systems. PM

Bibliography

Wardhaugh, R. 1971: The contrastive analysis hypothesis. *TESOL Quarterly* 5, 223–30.

conventional and epideictic behavior These terms were given particular meanings by V.C. Wynne-Edwards (1962) in his carefully worked out theory of group selection. According to Wynne Edwards, animals control their own population densities and thereby avoid extinction. They do this by using a wide variety of homeostatic mechanisms, and these mechanisms involve competing for secondary resources such as territory instead of for food itself. It is these secondary resources that Wynne-Edwards described as "conventional", so "conventional behavior" includes territorial behavior and other behavior that leads to SPACING. The term "epideictic" refers to the effects of the DISPLAY which is involved in such activity. According to Wynne-Edwards's theory, population control comes about because when a certain number of individuals are displaying territorially, remaining potential breeders are deterred by the epideictic displays and forgo reproduction for the season.

Most ethologists now favor an alternative interpretation of such territoriality, stripping it of its group-homeostasis functions and regarding it as no more than a result of the normal inter-individual competition that forms the basis of natural selection. See also SOCIOBIOLOGY. VR

Bibliography

Wynne-Edwards, V.C. 1962. *Animal dispersion in relation to social behavior.* Edinburgh: Oliver & Boyd; New York: Hafner.

conversational implicature Term for the Gricean hypothesis that aspects of the meaning of sentences (utterances) cannot be deduced from the literal meaning of words alone, but must be inferred from the intra- and extralinguistic context. That is, what a speaker intends to communicate is partly conversationally implied or *implicated*. Conversational implicatures rest on the assumption that discourse is characterized by a cooperative effort, i.e. each participant recognizes, to some extent, a common purpose or a mutually accepted direction. The cooperative principle which participants are expected to observe is specified with the help of four maxims: make your contribution true (maxim of quality), brief (maxim of quantity), relevant (maxim of relation), and unambiguous (maxim of manner). Grice's conversational implicatures (1975) can be compared with Habermas's "ideal speech situation" (1976) which relies on four consensual presuppositions or *validity claims*, namely, that the speaker's contribution can be expected to be consensually true, comprehensible, truthful, and appropriate. Both Grice's and Habermas's approaches are aimed at providing scholars with a standard of communicative COMPETENCE against which actual communicative performance can be compared. MK

Bibliography

Grice, H.P. 1975: Logic and conversation. In *Syntax and semantics*. vol. 3. *Speech acts*, ed. P. Cole and J.L. Morgan, New York and London: Academic Press.

Habermas, J. 1976: Some distinctions in universal pragmatics. *Theoretical sociology* 3 155–67.

cooing and babbling The first two stages in child vocal communication are those of cooing and babbling. Cooing refers to the squealing–gurgling sounds made by babies between the ages of six weeks and three to six months. Cooing sounds can be elicited first by a specific stimulus, i.e. a nodding object resembling a face in the visual field of the baby. After about the twelfth week it is necessary for the face to be a familiar one to elicit smiling or cooing (Lenneberg 1967, pp.276 ff.).

Neither from the point of view of production nor from that of perception can cooing sounds be regarded as speech sounds, as the speech organs do not appear to move in a coordinated way at this stage.

Babbling, on the other hand, is clearly an example of speech sound production, though its precise relationship to later stages of LANGUAGE ACQUISITION and its communicational functions remain ill-understood. It is defined as the production of speech sounds characteristic of babies between the ages of about three months and two years. It usually peaks between nine and twelve months and with some children ceases when their first words appear. Other children continue to babble while their intelligible language develops.

During the babbling stage children produce a large variety of sounds many of which do not occur in the language of their caretakers and their peers. As babbling is also found with deaf children it is widely regarded as being related to physical maturation rather than exposure to speech.

An important psycholinguistic issue is the relationship between babbling and the child's first words (de Villiers and de Villiers 1979, pp.26 ff.). Some investigators believe that babbling is a prerequisite for normal first language acquisition, others argue in favor of a more indirect relationship between babbling and language. The study of babbling is also important in language universals research, in particular in the area of phonetic universals. PM

Bibliography

de Villiers, P.A. and J.G. 1979: *Early language*. London: Fontana; Cambridge, Mass.: Harvard University Press.

Lenneberg, Eric H. 1967: *Biological foundations of language*. New York and Chichester: John Wiley.

cooperation: animal Strong cooperation, individuals working together to achieve a common purpose, is found in humans, in social insects, and, to some extent, in a variety of other animal groups. It has been calculated that a termite mound, scaled up in relation to the size of a termite, is equivalent to a human skyscraper two miles high. As in great feats of human architecture, the termites achieve this by cooperation. Natural selection favors cooperation among social insect workers because the workers do not reproduce themselves, but are close genetic relatives of the reproductive members of their colony. A worker has nothing to gain by working for itself. All the workers gain, genetically speaking, from the survival and reproduction of the whole colony. Colony survival is served by individual cooperation. Therefore natural selection favors cooperative tendencies among workers, to the point of total self-abnegation at the individual level. The same is not true of most animals other than social insects. Rudimentary cooperation occurs in, for example, hunting bands of carnivores like lions and wolves, but this is best seen as enlightened self-interest rather than cooperation for the benefit of the whole colony. An individual hyena gets more to eat if it hunts with a group than if it hunts alone. This is because a group can bring down much bigger prey, and each individual therefore gets more to eat than it would alone. Cooperation due to 'enlightened self-interest' even occurs between members of different species. Honey guides are small African birds that have evolved the habit of leading ratels (honey badgers) or humans to wild bees' nests. The birds are good at finding nests but bad at breaking into them. The honey badgers and humans are good at breaking in but bad at finding bees' nests. Both partners benefit from the cooperation, the mammal eating the honey and the bird the grubs. Cooperation for mutual self-interest can also evolve if one partner does not benefit immediately, but only has a chance of benefiting at some time in the future, in which case it is known as 'reciprocal altruism'. There are theoretical problems with reciprocal altruism, but an adequate Darwinian rationale for it exists, and there is suggestive evidence that it occurs both within and between species. (See also ALTRUISM.) RD

Bibliography

* Dawkins, R. 1976: *The selfish gene*. Oxford: Oxford University Press.

cooperation: social psychology Working together towards the same end, purpose or effect; in psychology, especially working together for mutual benefit by maximizing joint profits or rewards and minimizing joint costs or losses. Innumerable studies have been conducted making use of matrices representing (often imaginary) pay-offs to both persons, an idea initially suggested by Von Neuman and Morgenstern (1944) and introduced in psychology by Luce and Raiffa (1957). The best known game theory paradigm of cooperation experiments is the so-called prisoner's dilemma game in which both players have to make a choice between maximizing personal or joint pay-offs, a conflict which in many conditions leads to the least preferred outcome for both parties. This and other pay-off matrices have been used extensively in studying international relations and competition in animals. JMFJ

Bibliography

Luce, R.D. and Raiffa, H. 1957: *Games and decisions: introduction and critical survey*. New York: Wiley.

Pruitt, D.G. and Kimmel, M.J. 1977: Twenty years of experimental gaming: critique, synthesis and suggestions for the future. *Annual review of psychology*. 28, 363–392.

Von Neuman, J. and Morgenstern, D. 1944: *Theory of games and economic behavior*. Princeton, N.J.: Princeton University Press.

coordination The harmonious control of muscular movements is achieved through two basic processes: central control and peripheral control. Central control involves a precise set of instructions issued by the central nervous system and followed by the muscles. The swallowing movements of humans are coordinated in this manner. Peripheral control involves FEEDBACK from sense organs in the muscles, which influences the instructions sent out from the central nervous system. For example, the coordination of limb movements in mammals is dependent upon the postural reflexes, which are based upon information from the muscles. In most cases coordination is achieved through a mixture of central and peripheral control. In the coordination of swimming movements in fish, for example, the central nervous system provides a rhythm that passes down the trunk in waves, determining the rhythmic movements of the tail and fins. In the bony fish (Teleostei), however, the fins can beat at different frequencies under certain circumstances, although they retain a degree of relative coordination.

The coordination of skilled movements in humans is interesting in that it normally starts with a high degree of peripheral control, but as the person becomes highly skilled, central control becomes predominant. The finger movements involved in expert typing and playing the piano, for example, are entirely under central control. (See DEVELOPMENT OF MOTOR SKILLS.) DJM

copula An overt verb such as English "to be" when used in normal neutral equational clauses (e.g. He is my brother). It is regarded as semantically empty and many languages do not possess a lexical item corresponding to the English copula. Its principal grammatical function is to carry temporal, modal or aspectual information (see Lyons 1968, pp.322 ff.).

The absence of an overt copula in certain varieties of English has been discussed by Ferguson (in connection with BABY TALK and FOREIGNER TALK) and for Black Vernacular English by LABOV (1969) in connection with claims made about the mental retardation of lower class black children. The development of the copula construction in FIRST LANGUAGE ACQUISITION has been studied by Brown (1970). PM

Bibliography

Brown, Roger 1970: The child's grammar from 1 to 3. In *Psycholinguistics*, ed. R. Brown. New York & London: MacMillan.

Ferguson, Charles A. 1971: Absence of copula and the notion of simplicity. In *Pidginization and creolization of languages*, ed. D. Hymes. London and New York: Cambridge University Press.

Labov, William 1969: Contraction, deletion and inherent variability of the English copula. *Language* 45, 715–62.

Lyons, John 1968: *Introduction to theoretical linguistics*. Cambridge and New York: Cambridge University Press.

coronary-prone behavior Usually refers to the Type A coronary-prone personality pattern described by Friedman and Rosenman (see TYPE-A PERSONALITY). Other psychometric work has been done, however, linking personality factors to coronary heart disease.

The conclusion from six studies using the Minnesota Multiphasic Personality Inventory (MMPI) seems to be that before their illness, patients with coronary disease differ from persons who remain healthy on several scales of the inventory, particularly those in the "neurotic" triad of hypochondriasis (Hs), depression (D), and hysteria (Hy). The occurrence of manifest coronary heart disease (CHD) increases the deviation of patients' MMPI scores further and, in addition, there is ego defense breakdown. As Jenkins (1971) summarizes: "patients with fatal disease tend to show greater neuroticism (particularly depression) in prospective MMPIs than those who incur and survive coronary disease".

Three major studies have utilized the sixteen Personality Factor inventory. All three investigations portray patients with CHD or related illness as emotionally unstable and introverted, which is consistent with the six MMPI studies. The limitation of these investigations is that they are, on balance, retrospective. That is, anxiety and neuroticism may well be reactions with CHD and other stress-related illnesses rather than precursors of it. Paffenberger, Wolf and Notkin (1966) report an interesting prospective study in which they linked university psychometric data on students with death certificates filed years later. They found a number of significant precursors to fatal CHD, one of which was a high anxiety or neuroticism score for the fatal cases. CLC

Bibliography

Jenkins, C.D. 1971: Psychological and social precursors of coronary disease. *New England journal of medicine*. 283, 244–55.

Paffenberger, R.S., Wolf, P.A. and Notkin, J. 1966: Chronic disease in former college students. *American journal of epidemiology* 83, 314–28.

correspondence inference theory *See* attribution theory

courtship: in animals Behavior patterns, often very elaborate and conspicuous, that precede, accompany and sometimes follow the act of mating. The duration of courtship varies greatly, from several days to a few seconds, depending on the extent to which males and females establish durable pair bonds. Several functions may be ascribed to courtship, such as attraction of a mate, often over a considerable distance, stimulation of the mate to sexual receptivity, and the synchronization of mating activities so that the sexual act occurs at the optimum moment. Displays used in courtship tend to show typical intensity and a high degree of species specificity, features which enable animals to recognize and mate only with members of their own species. The form of some courtship behavior suggests that the motivation of the animal performing it involves a conflict between aggression, fear and sexual behavior. (See also COMMUNICATION; REPRODUCTIVE BEHAVIOR.) TRH

creativity Many diverse definitions have been proposed, but the following is probably representative: man's capacity to produce new ideas, insights, inventions or artistic objects, which are accepted as being of social, spiritual, aesthetic, scientific or technological value. This emphasizes novelty and originality in the production of new combinations of familiar patterns, as in poetry or music, or reorganization of concepts and theories in the sciences. But unconventionality is not sufficient: a lunatic's ravings are not creative. The product must be recognized by capable people, even if initially rejected and not appreciated until later.

Traditionally, creativity was considered a rare and mysterious phenomenon, occurring mainly in a few outstanding geniuses such as Da Vinci, Mozart or Einstein, although it was realized that many other generally more mediocre artists or scientists produced occasional or minor creative works. The present trend, however, particularly in the USA is to see creativity as spread through almost the entire population, though varying in degree. The dramatic play of the young child often appears as imaginative and creative. Indeed creativity can even be observed in young animals at play or among chimpanzees who, according to Köhler (1925), display inventive thinking or "insight".

The older view often linked creativity with insanity (e.g. Lombroso and Kretschmer), though Havelock Ellis's early survey of British geniuses in 1904 found only a very small proportion who could be called psychotic. Minor emotional difficulties, ill health and neuroses were more common. Even more extensive was Terman's study (Cox 1926) of 300 emminent historical figures including many artists and scientists. Terman expected them to have possessed outstanding intelligence, but on assessing their mental capacities from their recorded achievements he found only a few with very high IQs of 170 to 200. The average was 135, and some were as low as 100–110. The geniuses were distinguished more by the character traits of perseverance and drive and the encouraging environment in which most of them were reared. Neurotic tendencies were apparent only in a minority.

Anne Roe's intensive analysis (1952) of the personalities of sixty-four highly creative living scientists, and MacKinnon's and Barron's investigations (1962 and 1969) of architects and other groups of professionals, have thrown much light on the psychology of creative individuals. Scientists, especially physical scientists, were characterized by intense absorption in their work and relative lack of interest in social or recreational activities. Though there were wide individual differences, they were the most emotionally stable group. Social scientists and Barron's writers showed more emotional disturbances, but Barron also found the writers high in ego strength, that is self-control and personal effectiveness. Many of these individuals were notably gifted as children, though not necessarily in the same special field; while others did not discover their talent and interest until early adulthood. On the other hand gifted children may be highly intelligent yet not specially talented or creative since they lack the mature technique and the strong inner drive characteristic of creative adults. Nevertheless those adolescents who do show artistic or scientific gifts, e.g. in science projects, are more likely to become involved in creative research and activities at university or in their subsequent jobs. The much lower frequency of creative accomplishments among women than among men is generally attributed to cultural expectations of sex roles, but women have also traditionally had to balance marriage and children against the ambition to follow a creative career.

A different approach is based on studying the creative process. Psychologists have reported many experiments on problem solving, a process which is certainly useful though not highly creative or original. Several writers, musicians, scientists and mathematicians have described their methods of work and the nature of their inspiration (see Ghiselin 1952). Graham Wallas (1926) recognized four main stages: first that of preparation, including the acquisition of artistic skills or scientific information relevant to the particular problem. Although creative people may rebel against accepted conventions, they must be conversant with the methods and knowledge of their field in order to have something to be creative with. Secondly there is so called unconscious cerebration, where a strong emotional drive to create interacts, largely subconsciously, with the skills or information. Next there is inspiration regarding the solution or the artistic product; this sometimes arises quite suddenly. Finally a long period of working out and elaboration occurs and, in science, of verification of the solution. This of course is an over-rigid formulation. There is often an interplay of all four stages spread over a considerable period, as in writing a symphony or novel, or developing a scientific discovery.

Much has been written on creativity by Freud and his followers. In 1908 Freud pointed out the resemblance between children's play, fantasy or daydreaming and the work of the poet. In his view all these activities are expressive of people's inner needs and their imagined solutions. But the poet's feelings and conflicts are more repressed or inhibited, and they emerge in a disguised and socially acceptable form in his finished poems. Freud further distinguished 'primary process' thinking, arising from the unconscious, from 'secondary process', which is thinking under the control of the ego. He saw both as involved in creative production.

Other writers criticized Freud's implication that artistic and scientific creation derive from the sublimation of repressed and aggressive tendencies, and that creativity is essentially a neurotic defense mechanism, for there are innumerable neurotics who are not at all creative. Kris (1952) and Koestler (1964) have modified the original theory paying more attention to the critical processes of the ego. They considered the creative artist to be a person who is more than usually in touch with his primary process fantasies and thus, like young children, more spontaneously imaginative. This underlies the original inspiration which is then taken over by the ego and fashioned through secondary process into the complete product. Moreover we gain aesthetic pleasure from a work of art because we are all prone to unconscious conflicts similar to the artist's. Kris refers to this as "regression in the service of the ego". It fits in with Barron's discussion of neuroticism and ego control among creative individuals and it helps to explain the greater part played by emotion in artistic as opposed to scientific production. Scientists do sometimes experience inspirations, but clearly most of their work is at the secondary level.

From about 1950 many industrial firms made use of schemes for stimulating creative thinking, such as Osborn's "Applied Imagination" and W. J. Gordon's "Synectics". These provide a fresh approach to such problems as designing and marketing a new product. Several staff members cooperate, and they are encouraged to put forward any suggestions that come to mind, however wild, not stopping to criticize or follow through. This is called "free wheeling", or the principle of deferred judgment. At a later session all ideas are considered critically by the group. This owes something to Freudian theory since the participants are told to relax all inhibitions and give free rein to creative imagination. Several other related techniques may be used. There is little or no scientific evidence that it works; but it has also spread from business into college courses where, it is claimed, training can be given in creative problem-solving with beneficial effects on academic work generally.

In 1950 Guilford drew attention to psychologists' neglect of creative abilities. Aptitude or achievement tests are "convergent" in the sense that the student's answers must converge to the one right solution. But some tests are available in which people are encouraged to put forward a variety of their own answers, i.e. to think "divergently". For example they may be asked to write down as many uses as they can think of for an empty tin can, and their responses are scored both for the quantity or fluency of ideas, and for quality as shown by the usefulness of the ideas. Many other similar divergent tests have been devised in the United States in the belief that American education has become too conventional and convergent, and that those children who will become the creative leaders of the next generation need to be discovered and encouraged. The tests, however, are rather trivial in content and they correlate very little with assessments or other criteria of creative behavior. As with most verbal tests girls tend to score more highly, whereas boys are more attracted to science, which chiefly involves convergent thinking. The tests are also very troublesome to score and they appear to have declined in popularity since the 1960s. PEV

Bibliography

Barron, F. 1969: *Creative person and creative process.* New York: Holt, Rinehart & Winston.

Cox, C. M. 1926: *The early mental traits of three hundred geniuses.* Stanford, Calif.: California University Press.

Freud, S. 1908: Creative writers and day-dreaming. In *Complete psychological works of Sigmund Freud,* vol. IX 1959.

*Ghiselin, B., ed. 1952: *The creative process: a symposium.* Berkeley, Calif.: University of California Press.

Gordon, W. J. J. 1961: *Syntectics: the development of creative capacity.* New York: Harper & Row.

Guilford, J. P. 1950: Creativity. *American psychologist* 5, 444–54.

Köhler, W. 1925: *The mentality of apes.* London: Kegan Paul; New York: Harcourt Brace; New York: Macmillan.

Koestler, A. 1964: *The act of creation.* London: Hutchinson.

Kris, E. 1952: *Psychoanalytic explorations in art.* New York: International Universities Press.

MacKinnon, D. W. 1962: The personality correlates of creativity: a study of American architects. *Proceedings of XIV Congress of Applied Psychology* 2, 11–39.

Osborn, A. F. 1953: *Applied imagination.* New York: Scribner.

Roe, A. 1952: *The making of a scientist.* New York: Dodd Mead.

Wallas, G. 1926: *The art of thought.* London: Jonathan Cape; New York: Harcourt Brace.

creolization The four main avenues of research into the nature of human language are (1) LINGUISTIC UNIVERSALS (see Greenberg 1963), (2) comparison with non-human communication systems (see ANTHROPOID APE LANGUAGE), (3) abnormal types of human language learning and behavior (see GENIE and LANGUAGE PATHOLOGY) and (4) creolization.

In linguistics the term "creolization" is used in two senses, that of language mixing and that of the development of a new first language when children, whose parents are of different linguistic backgrounds and therefore communicate in a makeshift pidgin language, adopt and elaborate this pidgin as a means of intercommunication. This means that children:

- are exposed to imperfect, reduced language input
- elaborate this input using new grammatical devices gleaned from internal resources, i.e. by appealing to their innate linguistic knowledge (see LANGUAGE ACQUISITION DEVICE).
- eventually speak a language which is both quantitatively and qualitatively different from that spoken by their parents and, in many cases, not intelligible to them.

Creolization in the second sense above appears to be an ideal test case for claims about the nature of the human language acquisition device and universal linguistic knowledge. The creolization hypothesis as put forward by writers such as Bickerton (1974) can be represented schematically as follows:

parents' input	mother's idiolectal pidgin (reduced language)	father's idiolectal pidgin (reduced language)
universal knowledge	Language Acquisition Device	
children's output	creole (full language)	

Whereas numerous creole languages are in existence today (e.g. French-derived creoles in the West Indies and the Indian Ocean, English-derived creoles in the West Indies, Africa and the Pacific, and Portuguese-derived creoles in Africa and Asia – altogether more than 100) there are a number of problems when it comes to testing the creolization hypothesis:

(1) observations concerning the difference between the second language pidgin and the ensuing first-language creole should preferably be made with first-generation speakers, as creoles may change through borrowing and for internal reasons, like any other language, once they have come into being. A comparison of a present-day creole with a pidgin that was spoken centuries ago is unlikely to yield satisfactory evidence.

(2) the pidgin input may vary considerably. Thus, creolization can occur a) with pidgins which are very rudimentary and unstable, i.e. so-called jargons b) with elementary stable pidgins and c) with stable expanded pidgins. These three categories reflect the fact that, even with adult second language systems, there can be considerable elaboration (see INTERLANGUAGE).

Consequently, three main types of creoles can be distinguished according to their development history:

Type 1	*Type 2*	*Type 3*
jargon	jargon	jargon
	stabilized pidgin	stabilized pidgin
		expanded pidgin
creole	creole	creole
e.g. West Indian English Creole	e.g. Torres Straits Creole	e.g. New Guinea Tok Pisin

If any second language becomes the first language of a speech community, its deficiencies need to be repaired. Depending on the development stage at which creolization occurs, different types of repair can be observed:

Type 1, with a creolized jargon: Repair is needed at all levels, i.e. there is need for a natural phonetological and semantactic system and a pragmatic system.

Type 2, with creolized stable pidgin: The repair requirements in this case include the addition of derivational depth to existing basic structures and the development of pragmatic rules.

Type 3, with creolized expanded pidgins: The main repair requirements of a nativized expanded pidgin appear to concern its stylistic and pragmatic potential. The transition between the pidgin and its corresponding creole is gradual rather than abrupt.

Of the cases of creolization which can be observed in situ today most belong to type 3 (e.g. New Guinea Tok Pisin, New Hebridean Bichelamar, West African Pidgin English) and a smaller number to type 2 (North Australian Creoles, Torres Straits Creoles). There are no known instances of type 1, the most interesting type from the point of psycholinguistic evidence, with the possible exception of Hawaiian Pidgin English, discussed by Bickerton and Odo (1976).

A careful examination of the evidence studied so far suggests the following possible universals of restructuring in creolization (see Labov 1971 and Hill ed. 1979):

(1) the development of tense and aspect systems as obligatory grammatical categories (most pidgins simply use time adverbials)

(2) the emergence of obligatory number marking

(3) the development of grammatical markers signalling EMBEDDING such as relativizers and complementizers

(4) the phonological condensation of non-content (function) words.

An example illustrating the qualitative differences between a pidgin and a creole language is the development of relativizers in Torres Straits Creole. Whereas in the mid-1960s, when it was a stabilized pidgin for most speakers, Dutton (1970) was unable to elicit overt markers of relative clauses Mühlhäusler recorded in 1978 that *we* (*etymologically* related to English *where*) was used in this function, as in *man we kam* "the man who came", among first language speakers.

The fact that the same solution for a relativizer developed – apparently independently – in West African Pidgin English, New Hebridean Bichelamar, Tok Pisin, and in various West Indian Creoles, suggests that comparative work among present-day creoles may be able to shed light on the original creolization processes (see Hellinger 1979). So far, comparative work has yielded few definite results since:

(1) the languages involved are insufficiently well documented

(2) no principled criteria for distinguishing between universally conditioned similarities, accidental similarities and historically caused similarities are known

(3) the comparative method of historical linguistics in its present form is not a reliable framework for psycholinguistic research.

Thus, in spite of its great appeal, the creolization and linguistic universals hypothesis stands in need of much further testing. It will no doubt profit from the application of VARIATION THEORIES of description and from research into FUNCTIONS OF LANGUAGE. PM

Bibliography

Bickerton, Derek 1974: "Creolization, linguistic universals, natural semantics and the brain". University of Hawaii Working Papers in Linguistics 6.3: 124–141.

Bickerton, Derek & Odo Carol 1976: *Change and variation in Hawaiian English*, Social Sciences and Linguistics Institute, University of Hawaii Honolulu.

Dutton, Thomas E. 1970: "Informal English in the Torres Straits" in Ramson, W.S. (ed.) *English transported*. Canberra: Australian National University Press.

Greenberg, Joseph H. 1963 (ed.): *Universals of language*. Cambridge, Mass. & London: MIT Press.

*Hill, Kenneth C. (ed.) 1979: *The genesis of language*, Karoma Publishers, Ann Arbor.

Hellinger, Marlies 1979: "Across base language boundaries: The Creole of Belize", in: Hancock, Ian F. *Readings in Creole studies* 315–334. Ghent: Scientific Publishers.

Labov, William 1971: "On the adequacy of natural languages I: The development of tense" mimeo. University of Pennsylvania.

*Muysken, Pieter (ed.) 1981: *Generative studies on Creole languages* Dordrecht and Cinnaminson: Foris Publications.

Valdman, Albert and Highfield, Arnold, eds 1980: *Theoretical orientations in Creole studies*. New York and London: Academic Press.

criminal psychology The study of offenders' motives, personalities and decisions. The motives for most offences – whether acquisitive, violent, sexual or connected with traffic – are normal in the sense that they are of kinds experienced by ordinary adults from time to time: greed, rage, lust, impatience, the desire for excitement. What has interested clinical psychologists, psychiatrists and psychoanalysts is the motive which is abnormal either in its strength, so that the offender finds it difficult to resist even when it is clearly dangerous to yield to it, or in its nature, sadism or pedophilia being examples.

Explanations of such motives belong to abnormal psychology: see for instance aggression, compulsive behavior etc. A few forms of mental disorder seem to be associated with certain kinds of objectionable behavior, although there is no good evidence that mental disorder in general increases the likelihood of being in trouble with the law. People who have committed serious personal violence are not infrequently found to be depressed, schizophrenic or "aggressive psychopaths". Some chronic confidence tricksters are said to have hysterical personalities. Some sexual offenders, especially against children, are found to be mentally handicapped. Arson, when committed for excitement rather than for gain or revenge, often seems to be compulsive.

The extent to which a predisposition to anti-social forms of behavior can be congenital has long been the subject of research and controversy. What cannot be disputed is the genetic transmission of a few diagnosable disorders (such as Huntington's Chorea) which sometimes involve sufferers in social trouble. There are also indisputable chromosomal abnormalities (not necessarily inherited) such as the XYY condition, which is associated with above average height, below average intelligence and a slightly increased likelihood of being involved in violence, including sexual violence.

The overwhelming majority of offenders are not suffering from such abnormalities. Their offences are often simply the result of circumstances: a speeding driver may have been late for an appointment; an assaulter may have been provoked by taunts; a sexual offender's self-control may have been reduced by alcohol or the behavior of his companion. (Indeed it is sometimes the victim's conduct that calls for explanation.) When the offence is premeditated, or repeated however, we feel the need for a fuller explanation. This may be the offender's imprudence or deliberate risk-taking; it may be lack of conscience or shame; or it may be a preference for the criminal's way of life. In other contexts what seems to call for explanation is not the frequency with which an individual offends but the frequency of offences of certain kinds among certain groups, such as vandalism among schoolboys. Current explanations may emphasize child-training methods, the values of a culture or subculture, low intelligence or impaired capacity for social learning.

Child-training methods are important because they may fail to result in the child internalizing the rules of conduct of the culture or sub-culture to which he belongs. In this case he will be readier to breach them when it seems in his interest to do so. Internalization seems most likely to take place when parents explain the reasons for a rule and withdraw affection when the child breaks it. Physical punishment, especially if harsh or erratic, seems less effective (and may teach the child violent behavior). The effect is also weaker if parents' reactions are inconsistent, or if the child's dependence on their affection is weakened (e.g. by frequent absences). There are also types of anti-social conduct which become likely only in the teens or later, when children are less influenced by their parents and more by their peers (e.g. the abuse of drugs). It may be significant that the rate of DELINQUENCY rises with every year of compulsory schooling, and begins to decline at about the age when most young people leave school and mix with older people.

In any case, the child, the teenager or the adult may belong to a *subculture* whose values do not condemn everything that the law forbids. It may for example view dishonest acquisition no more seriously than many motorists regard speeding. It may respect rather than censure a man who uses violence to settle a quarrel. In some white-collared subcultures tax evasion and the acceptance of corrupt favors are "smart". Again, an individual may belong to, or join, a subculture which condones what he or she likes doing. Even in societies which condemn pedophilia (as not all do) pedophiles can sometimes join or form like-minded groups. Such groups often adopt "neutralizing" arguments to counterbalance the condemnation of others (or in some cases their own consciences). Pedophilia is said to benefit children by introducing them to a more mature kind of affection than they get from their contemporaries. Burglars assure themselves that householders' insurance policies indemnify them. Football fans excuse their violence to rivals by claiming that the latter "began it", or "asked for it" by entering their territory. Like other groups, such as street gangs or terrorists, they may invoke loyalty to a group or a cause, which can be used to justify revenge for an injury to a group member, or an unprovoked assassination. Another technique is the denial of legitimacy: "Property is theft". The concept of "neutralization" is more often used by sociologists than psychologists, perhaps because of the latter's preoccupation with measurable characteristics.

A controversial figure is "the psychopath" (see PSYCHOPATHIC PERSONALITY). Many psychologists and psychiatrists believe that even when allowances are made for the influence of subcultures which are tolerant of dishonesty, violence, sexual promiscuity, drug abuse and other hedonistic conduct, there are some men and women whose proneness to one or more of these kinds of behavior is so impulsive or unheeding of other people's disapproval that it is in some way pathological: attributable, that is, to some sort of defect. Descriptions and explanations of the defect vary, from congenital abnormalities or perinatal brain damage to grossly affectionless upbringing. Some investigators find that samples of "psychopaths" contain individuals who do not show the normal responses to stimuli which should arouse anxiety, although the samples also seem to include others whose responses are more or less normal. Psychiatrists have succeeded in having the concept of psychopathic disorder written into legislation. For example, Section 4 of the English Mental Health Act 1959 (as amended) defines it as "a persistent disorder or disability of mind ... which results in abnormally aggressive or seriously irresponsible conduct ..." In the USA statutory definitions (e.g. of "sexual psychopaths") vary from state to state. The more precise term now approved by the American Psychiatric Association (in its *Diagnostic and Statistical Manual*) is "anti-social personality disorder" in which there is "a history of continuous and chronic anti-social behavior in which the rights of others are violated, persistence into adult life of a pattern ... that begins before the age of fifteen not due to ... severe mental retardation, schizophrenia or manic episodes". These definitions, however, are descriptive and generic, leaving room for a variety of more specific diagnoses, such as those of the International Classification of Disorders (published by the World Health Organization). It is possible that this generic group will eventually prove divisible into sub groups with more or less specific etiology; but this is unlikely to happen until research workers develop more exact diagnostic criteria and explanatory hypotheses.

An aspect of law-breaking which is only beginning to receive attention is what can be loosely called the decision-making stage, although many offences are the result of processes which can hardly be called "decisions", being impulsive, compulsive, negligent or habitual. These apart, however, even very strong motivation does not mean that every opportunity for the offence will be taken. The situation may be perceived as too risky, the penalty as too great, accomplishment as too difficult (as when a car thief is attracted by a car but desists because he would be too conspicuous, because he knows that his next prison sentence would be a long one, or because he knows that its lock is hard to force). NDW

Bibliography

Feldman, M.P. 1977: *Criminal behaviour: a psychological analysis*. New York and London: John Wiley.

Walker, N. 1977: *Behaviour and misbehaviour: explanations and non-explanations*. Oxford: Basil Blackwell; New York: Basic Books.

West, D.J. 1982: *Delinquency: its roots, careers and prospects*. London, Heinemann; Cambridge, Mass.: Harvard University Press.

crisis intervention A brief form of psychological treatment used in the case of a person whose usual methods of coping have become ineffective in the face of some personal crisis. The result is acute distress and the associated failure to function adequately in customary social roles. Crises are conveniently classified as developmental, such as adolescence and retirement, and accidental, such as a major disappointment or a breakdown in an important relationship.

The aim of therapy is relief from the effects of the crisis and possibly the development of new effective methods of coping and solving problems. The therapist provides a supportive framework within which the transiently disabled patient can have a breathing space, feel hopeful about obtaining help and receive reassurance and guidance. The patient temporarily forgoes some measure of independence, but resumes former responsibility for himself as he comes to feel and function better. SB

Bibliography

Ewing, C.P. 1978: *Crisis intervention as psychotherapy*. New York: Oxford University Press.

criterion: organizational A standard against which the accuracy of predictions may be judged, or the efficacy of a program may be evaluated. In the abstract, a criterion is an ideal measurement. It contains no bias and it is perfectly reliable (see RELIABILITY). In practice, however, operational measures used as criteria may be unreliable, contaminated and/or deficient. An actual criterion measure is contaminated when it includes elements that are not present in the ideal (or ultimate) criterion. For example, machine pacing of an assembly operation introduces a constant bias into measurements of individual productivity. An actual criterion measure is said to be deficient when it lacks elements that are part of the ultimate criterion. For example, if the ideal criterion is "student effectiveness", grades in school are deficient as an actual criterion measure. In evaluating the validity of a test or the effectiveness of a training program, it is common practice to use several criterion measures and to evaluate the predictions (or program outcomes) against each of them separately. Also, the separate measures are often combined into a composite when there is an acceptable statistical or logical rationale. MDH

Bibliography

Smith, Patricia C. 1976: Behaviors, results and organizational effectiveness: the problem of criteria. In *Handbook of industrial and organizational psychology* ed. M.D. Dunnette, Chicago: Rand McNally.

criterion: philosophical uses of The word is frequently used by philosophers, largely as a result of its employment by WITTGENSTEIN. It is not easy to see precisely what he meant by the term, and it is likely that what he intended in the earlier writings of his later period, particularly in *The blue and brown books* (1958), differs somewhat from what he meant in the later *Philosophical investigations* (1953). Two things, however, seem to be indisputable: (i) A criterion for the truth of a proposition is a state of affairs whose existence would constitute a reason for thinking the proposition to be true; and (ii) Not every such a state of affairs counts as a criterion. If it is a *purely* contingent matter (see contingent truth) that the state of affairs constitutes such a reason, then it is not a criterion but merely what Wittgenstein sometimes calls a "symptom".

All this, however, still leaves open the possibility of a variety of more precise characterizations of the notion. A criterion might be defined as something logically necessary, or logically sufficient, or logically necessary and sufficient, for what it is a criterion of. A weaker and more likely definition is one which requires only that a criterion is necessarily a reason for or evidence in favor of the truth of a proposition (Shoemaker 1962, p.4). JMS

Bibliography

Shoemaker, S. 1962: *Self-knowledge and self-identity*. Ithaca, N.Y.: Cornell University Press.

Wittgenstein, L. 1953: *Philosophical investigations*. Trans. G.E.M. Anscombe. Oxford: Basil Blackwell; New York: Macmillan.

——— 1969: *The blue and brown books*. 2nd edn. Oxford: Basil Blackwell.

critical incident analysis A procedure designed to focus attention on factors that lead to unusual success or failure on some portion of an individual's job. As early as 1954, Flanagan suggested that we could understand a great deal about an individual's performance or the characteristics of a given job by analysing the circumstances surrounding outstanding and substandard job performance. The critical incident technique relies on a supervisor or expert to observe and record unusual occurrences, both positive and negative, as they happen and to specify the event (critical incident) itself. When possible the supervisor should also note the events leading up to the critical incident and those following from it. The list of critical incidents is often segmented into categories of performance such as decision making, productivity, dependability, judgment, and initiative. Practical uses for the behavior identified via critical incident analysis include the development of job performance criteria, such as various types of rating scales and the establishment of training needs by identifying reoccurring problems of performance. RRJ

Bibliography

Flanagan, J. C. 1954: The critical incident technique, *Psychological bulletin* 51, 327–58.

critical periods: human developmental Originally an ethological concept designating a fixed time in early development when the young organism is open to forms of learning that will be essential for social adaptation and adult life. A well known example is learning of conspecifics through IMPRINTING in newly hatched goslings. In recent years the concept has been broadened to a sensitive period, to suggest simply a susceptibility for learning at a particular time rather than a crucial occasion for it.

It has been suggested by Bowlby (1969) that there may be a sensitive period for the development of attachment in humans, whereby a particular caretaker comes to acquire emotional significance for the child. It is also possible that there may be a sensitive period for the acquisition of language in early childhood. However, a more useful concept in the study of human development may lie in the general PLASTICITY of the nervous system, rather than in a very specific readiness for learning implicit in the ethological approach. GEB

Bibliography

Bowlby, J. 1969: *Attachment and loss* vol.1 *Attachment*. London: Hogarth; New York: Basic Books.

critical periods and the nervous system A period during ontogeny when specific conditions are necessary for the normal development of the nervous system (see CRITICAL PERIOD, for a description of the concept in studies of animal behavior). If the nervous system has been exposed to abnormal conditions its ability to recover from this exposure decreases quickly after the critical, or sensitive, period. Different critical periods may exist for different aspects of neural development, and although they may overlap in time, they exert their effects by different mechanisms. Nutritional deficiencies may markedly influence the overall growth and synaptogenesis of the nervous system, depending upon the time of the exposure, whereas sensory deprivation or restriction may produce selective effects upon the physiological properties of cells within sensory systems (see SENSORY DEPRIVATION AND ENRICHMENT). The nervous system's response to brain damage may also vary according to the time of occurrence of the injury, yielding different prospects for functional recovery depending upon the system involved (see RECOVERY OF FUNCTION AFTER BRAIN DAMAGE). For example, humans will show linguistic competence following damage to the language-dominant cerebral hemisphere if the injury occurs within the first decade of life. BER/RCS

critical theory A body of neo-Marxist social theory originating in the Frankfurt Institute for Social Research (hence the later term "Frankfurt School"). The Institute was founded in 1923 as a center for interdisciplinary Marxist research and began to take on a distinctive character after Max Horkheimer (1895–1973) became Director in 1930. Horkheimer and Theodor Adorno (1903–69) formed the nucleus of the Institute, but many of the leading figures of German intellectual life were associated with it at one time or another. Probably the best known are the literary theorist Walter Benjamin, the philosopher Herbert Marcuse and the psychologist Erich Fromm; others include Otto Kirchheimer and Franz Neumann (politics and law), Friedrich Pollock, Henryk Grossman and Arkady Gurland (political economy), Leo Löwenthal (literature) and Bruno Bettelheim, Nathan Ackerman and Marie Jahoda (psychology).

The Institute was forced to leave Frankfurt in 1923, settling in the USA in 1935. In 1950 it was re-established in Frankfurt, under the direction of Horkheimer and Adorno. It was the center of a distinctive conception of society and culture, represented to a greater or lesser degree in the work of individual members and associates.

Critical theory may first be viewed as part of a more general trend in western Marxism, since around 1930, towards a closer relationship with non-Marxist thought, a growing preoccupation with cultural and ideological issues at the expense of political economy, and a scholarly rather than a proletarian audience (Anderson 1976). In addition, critical theory must be seen in terms of the intellectual situation of western European Marxists, confronted in the 1930s by the unholy trio of liberal capitalism, Stalinism and fascism. The writers connected with the Institute were not content, like more orthodox Marxists, to analyse fascism as simply a mutant form of monopoly capitalism, nor, like the post-war theorists of totalitarianism, to equate Stalinism with fascism and to contrast both with an idealized image of liberal democracy. They were struck by the similarities in terms of organization, technology, culture and personality structure in all forms of society, and hence gave these phenomena a more prominent place in their analyses than had the majority of Marxist writers.

Critical theory was understood from the outset as a totalizing theory which viewed society from the standpoint of the need to change it. The theory was to be reflexive about its own status and that of its interpretive categories: "the critical acceptance of the categories which rule social life contains simultaneously their condemnation". Fascism, for example, could not really be understood in the categories of western liberalism, since this was the ideology of a social order which had produced fascism. "He who does not wish to speak of capitalism should also be silent about fascism" (cited in Jay 1973, p.156). Critical theory was also hostile to traditional disciplinary boundaries: the early *Studies in authority and the family* (1936) contained lengthy discussions of social and political thought as well as social psychological material, and *The authoritarian personality* (1950) was intended to be understood in terms of the more sociocultural analysis of *Dialectic of enlightenment* (1947), where anti-semitism is seen in the context of the rational domination inaugurated by the Enlightenment. Fascism "seeks to make the rebellion of suppressed nature against domination directly useful to domination" (1947, p.185).

The concepts of domination and authority pervade the Institute's work. Domination, although exemplified par excellence in fascism, was also the central principle of liberal societies, possibly more important than the categories of Marxian political economy. As Adorno put it in a late article, "Behind the reduction of men to agents and bearers of exchange value lies the domination of men over men". Marcuse's concept of surplus-repression, developed in his critique (1954) of Freud's *Civilisation and its discontents* (1930) is defined as "the restrictions necessitated by social domination", over and above those which, as Freud had argued, were necessary for *any* ordered society and which Marcuse calls the "rational exercise of authority" (1954, p.45).

This distinction is crucial to the critical theorists' account of the relation between reason and domination. They criticized existing social arrangements in the name of reason and of a more rational alternative society, with the conviction that "social freedom is inseparable from enlightened thought" (1947, p.xiii). At the same time, however, they increasingly saw instrumental or technological rationality as the basis of the "comfortable, smooth, reasonable, democratic unfreedom (which) prevails in advanced industrial civilisation" (Marcuse 1964, p.19). And though Marcuse's critique drew heavily on his American experience, it applied increasingly, he thought, to state socialist societies: "it is not the West but the East which, in the name of socialism, has developed modern occidental rationality in its extreme form" (1968, pp.201f.).

Marcuse's critique of industrial society in *Eros and civilisation* and *One dimensional man*, and some of his later writings, was prefigured in a more speculative form in Adorno and Horkheimer's *Dialectic of enlightenment*. Here the domination of nature by means of reason leads inevitably to the domination of man. In the lapidary formula on p.6, "enlightenment is totalitarian".

Dialectic of enlightenment also contains a critique of mass culture, or as Horkheimer and Adorno preferred to call it, the "culture industry"; they saw this as a homogeneous system of entertainment, devoid of the critical potential which high culture had once possessed and serving only to stabilize a system of domination. Here again one sees the emphasis on the interplay between sociology and psychology: "the might of industrial society is lodged in men's minds" (p.127). Cultural theory is perhaps the area for which these writers will mostly be remembered; Adorno in particular produced a substantial body of work on esthetic questions, especially on music. In philosophy, their contribution was mainly confined to expositions and critiques: Horkheimer's work on philosophies of history, Adorno's critiques of Husserl and Heidegger and Marcuse's book on Hegel, *Reason and revolution* (1941). Adorno's major work, *Negative dialectics* (1966), will surely remain as one of the classic texts of twentieth century philosophy.

Once the Institute was re-established in Frankfurt, the "Frankfurt School", as it then came to be known, had a powerful influence in an otherwise rather conservative West Germany. The major intellectual event was the School's attack on positivism and empiricism in the social sciences, the *Positivismusstreit*; the main political event was of course the challenge of the student movement and the extra-parliamentary opposition, with which the Frankfurt School had an uneasy and ultimately hostile relationship.

After the death of Adorno in 1969 critical theory developed in a more diffuse form, in the work of Jürgen Habermas, Karl-Otto Apel, Claus Offe, Alfred Schmidt, Albrecht Wellmer, and others. Habermas was a leading participant in the *Positivismusstreit* in which he linked, in a classically Frankfurt way, questions of philosophy of science with a political critique of technocracy or the "scientisation of politics". His most recent work has been concerned with "reconstructing" historical materialism as a cognitively oriented evolutionary theory of society, and to develop from this a new theory of crisis tendencies in advanced societies. In doing so he has made imaginative use of the work of Chomsky, Searle and others in linguistics, and Piaget and Kohlberg in psychology. He seems less interested than the earlier generation in psychology *per se*, though he remains fascinated by the meta-theory of psychoanalysis: the idea of a theory whose validation consists in its rationally grounded acceptance by its addressee. For Habermas, this is also the case for Marxism, understood as the critique of ideology (see EMANCIPATORY KNOWLEDGE). Habermas's latest work, *Theorie des kommunikativen Handelns* (1981) sets his earlier reflections on science and communication within a more general context of the rationalization (in Max Weber's sense) of the Lebenswelt or Lifeworld (see PHENOMENOLOGY). WO

Bibliography

Adorno, Theodor, W. et al. 1950: *The authoritarian personality*. New York: Harper.

——— 1966 (*1973*): *Negative dialectics*. New York: Seabury Press.

——— 1976: *The positivism dispute in German sociology*. London: Heinemann.

Anderson, Perry 1976: *Considerations of western Marxism*. London: New Left Books.

Freud, Sigmund 1930 (*1969*): *Civilisation and its discontents*. London: Hogarth Press; New York: Norton.

Habermas, Jürgen 1981: *Theorie des kommunikativen Handelns*, 2 vols. Frankfurt: Suhrkamp.

Horkheimer, Max and Adorno, Theodor W. 1947 (*1972*): *Dialectic of enlightenment*. New York: Herder and Herder 1972; London: Allen Lane (1973).

Institut für Sozialforschung 1936: *Studien über Autorität und Familie*. Paris: F. Alcan.

Jay, Martin 1973: *The dialectical imagination*. London: Heinemann.

Marcuse, Herbert 1941 (*1955*): *Reason and revolution*. 2nd ed. London: Routledge & Kegan Paul.

——— 1964: *Eros and civilisation*. Boston: Beacon Press.

cross-cultural psychology: general An approach which compares samples of subjects drawn from different cultures, the culture being regarded as an independent variable. There are, however, no known studies in which, as ideally should be the case, the inter-sample differences were confined to their *cultural* characteristics, i.e. in which genetic and environmental (but non-cultural) factors were controlled. This is important since these factors may interact. A seasonal grassland (environmental, non-cultural) may for example force its inhabitants to lead a nomadic life, but an ability to irrigate the land (cultural) may make it possible to ignore seasonal changes. A modification of genotypes may also take place. Mosquitoes breed in swamps (environmental) unless these are drained (cultural) and, through malaria, selectively eliminate certain genotypes from the population. Ostracism of individuals such as albinoes or twins (cultural) may also affect the genetic pool.

The term "cross-cultural" as currently used does not, therefore, imply purity of cultural effect (although it is sometimes taken to do so) and it cannot legitimately be concluded from the kind of evidence currently available that "cross-cultural" differences may easily be moderated by cultural intervention. Nevertheless cross-cultural studies do contribute important data to psychology. They do so by furnishing evidence which would be either difficult or impossible to obtain from mono-cultural samples. For example, it would be difficult to obtain a sample of totally illiterate but otherwise unhandicapped adults in Scotland or a sample of subjects with a well-ingrained left to right scanning habit from a population of Arab mono-linguals (who read from right to left).

For those who hold that psychological characteristics are evenly distributed throughout the species there is no valid justification for cross-cultural comparisons. Indeed they would argue that since one person is as likely as any other to provide a satisfactory instance of a particular variable which is being investigated, all investigations should be conducted in the most convenient place, which generally means a laboratory attached to the department of psychology of an established university.

Contrary arguments which have fostered development of cross-cultural psychology derive primarily from two sources: ethnographic studies and behaviorist studies. The former demonstrate a startlingly large variety of psychological characteristics which men may possess and the latter, by claiming that these are the result of cultural and environmental influences, offer an explanation for them.

The field was, for a long time, dominated by anthropologists and the early studies using "psychological" techniques were often carried out by them and were frequently inspired not by theoretical considerations but rather by the simplistic, but under the circumstances entirely justifiable, query, "Does this happen with them too"? Occasionally (such was the case with the studies of eidetic imagery) a rather vague theoretical underpinning was provided by an assumed analogy between the psychological processes of children and those of "primitive" people.

The great expansion of cross-cultural psychology occurred at the beginning of the second half of this century, and resulted from the increased academic activity of psychologists in developing countries, both in the newly established universities and in the applied spheres, especially those of selection and training.

Not all aspects of psychology attract cross-cultural work in equal measure. The areas in which the influence has been the strongest are briefly considered below.

Relationship between language and cognition According to the Sapir–Whorf hypothesis language (a cultural characteristic *par excellence*) affects cognitive processes. The crux of the problem lies in determining whether and to what extent apparently arbitrary, linguistic categorizations of phenomena influence the way in which these phenomena are treated by the cognitive system. If a language uses the same term for blue and green, does this mean that these colors are seen as being identical by the speakers of the language? In fact it does not. The arbitrariness of linguistic division of the color spectrum has been shown by the observation that in languages differing in color terminology in such a manner as to suggest entirely different organizations of perceptual experience, the same colors are regarded as the best examples of various segments of the spectrum. There is thus no evidence to support the view that language influences "simple" categorization.

On more complex issues, however, such as those concerning the influence of language on mnemonic and conceptual abilities, the evidence to hand is not as easily interpretable. Some interesting data on these issues has recently been obtained from studies of bilinguals; that is, of individuals in whom the linguistic influences of two different cultures co-exist. Another fecund source is the Semantic Differential technique in which bipolar scales are used to rate concepts and these ratings are analysed in search of dominant factors. This, as well as showing cultural differences of detail, has also shown a generally consistent pattern among cultures.

Studies of perception Another of the major foci of cross-cultural studies in perception incorporates the notion of clearly defined cultural influences upon perception. Cross-cultural studies of VISUAL ILLUSIONS provide the best example of this. Although illusions have engaged cross-cultural workers for over a hundred years, recent work by Segall, Campbell and Herskovits has brought the issues to general attention. Two distinct hypotheses were put forward. One of these (the carpentered world hypothesis) stated that people living in cultures such as those of the industrial west in which right angles and parallel lines are commonplace would be more prone to experience certain geometric illusions (e.g. the Müller–Lyer illusion) than the inhabitants of "less carpentered" cultures. The other hypothesis stated that people living in open country, used to wide vistas, will be more prone to such illusions as the horizontal–vertical illusion than the inhabitants of closed environments, such as dense forests, in which the visual horizon is much more restricted. These hypotheses have received a modicum of empirical support.

Another important research area is that of pictorial perception. Here, investigators are concerned with precise definition of the processes involved and with the implications of difficulties of pictorial perception, especially in illiterate cultures in which generally the difficulties appear to be particularly severe and in which, paradoxically, relatively greater reliance is placed by governments etc. on pictures as means of communication. There are definite and complex interpopulation differences both in extent of the ability to perceive that a picture represents an object (epitomic ability) and in the ability to perceive the three-dimensional nature of a depicted scene (eidolic ability). It remains a matter of controversy whether such interpopulation differences are differences of skill or of constitution.

Testing and measurement Psychological testing is of special value in populations which are unschooled. When demand for school places or for particular kinds of employment outstrips supply, testing not only attempts to increase selectors' satisfaction, but also helps to prevent the social friction which is likely to arise in divided societies.

In this sphere the work of the South African National Institute for Personnel Research led by S. Biesheuvel proved particularly influential in fostering development of new techniques and instruments. As one would anticipate, this work revealed the inapplicability of norms derived from western populations to non-western populations. It also showed up some unexpected perceptual difficulties.

Industrial psychology Aspects of cross-cultural differences in the efficiency of labor in entrepreneurial activity have also attracted attention. These range from cross-cultural differences in ergonomic characteristics (which at their very simplest may reduce to anthroprometric factors), to differences thought to result from early socialization. In this context McClelland's hypothesis of the effect of the kind of training given to the children upon the society's economic performance has been widely used, and the influence of beliefs and values upon social behavior and upon productivity has been demonstrated in some cultures. A possibility less surprising than some of the actual beliefs which were entertained!

Personality and abnormal behavior Since any theory which postulates that the early experiences of an organism are formative of its later behavior is eminently suited for cross-cultural investigation, investigations involving child-rearing practices have been undertaken in the context of a variety of personality theories, including that of Freud (see CROSS-CULTURAL STUDIES: DEVELOPMENTAL). The findings, are alas, usually nebulous.

Some theoretical considerations In an attempt to find a theoretical framework, recourse was made to Piagetian theory (which inspired many cross-cultural studies) and to the Witkinian notion of field dependence. The relevance of the latter is more apparent, postulating as it does a relationship between the extent of field dependence and the nature of the socialising process. A free non-punitive upbringing such as, it is said, prevails in traditional Eskimo societies, is particularly conducive to field independence; whilst authoritarian methods as practised in the sedentary agricultural tribes of West Africa, foster field dependence. Such social forces may be augmented by environmental conditions (see COGNITIVE STYLE).

Because these frameworks did not invariably fit the data, and because of the desire on the part of cross-cultural psychologists to dispel any suggestion that their work involved comparisons on a scale of merit, the postulate of the Emic/Etic distinction was put forward. This derives from linguistic studies (Phonemic/Phonetic). Unfortunately, it introduced difficulties of its own for its meaning is not clearly defined. It is held by some to distinguish between cultural specific (Emic) and non-specific (Etic) characteristics. Others take it to discriminate between studies done within a culture (Emic) and studies performed from the outside. Further it is sometimes said that whereas the emic approach leads to the *discovery* of a structure by an investigator the etic approach leads to the *construction* of such a structure. The utility of the distinction has yet to be established. JBDe

Bibliography

Triandis, H. et al. eds. 1980: *Handbook of cross-cultural psychology*. Boston: Allyn & Bacon.

Warren, N., ed. 1977, 1980: *Studies in cross-cultural psychology*. vols. 1 and 2. London and New York: Academic Press.

cross-cultural studies: developmental The comparative

investigation of experience and behavior across ethnic groups. Developmental studies examine the effects of the cultural milieu on patterns of physical and mental growth and are useful in distinguishing those aspects of human behavior that are universal from those which develop only in relation to specific cultural practices. An anthropological example is the work of Margaret Mead on sex role differentiation. She showed that even though behavior related to sexual role has definite biological roots, conditions of upbringing nevertheless accentuate or suppress components of sexuality in the adult. In the area of cognitive development, cross-cultural studies have also been useful in suggesting specific effects of literacy in the transition from concrete to abstract thinking. GEB

Bibliography

Lloyd, B. and Gay, J. 1981: *Universals of human thought*. Cambridge: Cambridge University Press.

cross-lagged correlation A statistical procedure to shed light on causal relationships between variables in research settings where no experimental manipulation is possible. It has been widely used in occupational psychological research within organizations (Clegg, Jackson and Wall 1977). The correlation between two variables, x and y, is calculated on two occasions (x_1 y_1 and x_2 y_2), also permitting the calculation of correlations between x on both occasions (x_1x_2), between y on both occasions (y_1y_2), and the cross-correlations which are lagged in time (x_1 y_2 and y_1 x_2). In situations where x_1 y_2 is found to be substantially larger than y_1 x_2, it is often appropriate to infer causal priority from x to y rather than in the opposite direction. PBW

Bibliography

Clegg, C.W., Jackson, P.R. and Wall, T.D. 1977: The potential of cross-lagged correlation analysis in field research. *Journal of occupational psychology* 50, 177–96.

cross-modal development Learning to use information derived from one of the senses as a standard, in order to make equivalence judgments about information from another (Jones 1981). Developmental studies throw light on assumptions about the relationships between sensory modalities and the nature of their coordination. For example, it was thought that "touch tutors vision" in development, i.e. tactual experience is necessary for perceptual development, and that verbal mediation is necessary if information obtained in one sensory modality is to be related to another.

Recent studies of chimpanzees and pre-verbal human infants show that cross-modal coding is possible from an early age without benefit of verbal mediation. This has led to a greater appreciation of sensory processes as perceptual systems whose function is to obtain information that may be equivalent between modalities. On this view the developmental problem in cross-modal coding is one of attending to and remembering the appropriate information. It is in attending to information that children may become more skilled with age, whether the equivalence judgment is to be made intra- or cross-modally, rather than in coordinating information. GEB

Bibliography

Jones, W. 1981: The developmental significance of cross-modal matching. In *Intersensory perception and sensory integration*, ed. R. Walk and H. Pick, Jr. New York: Plenum.

cross-sectional research A research design in which a range of variation in a given variable is examined by sampling several different cases at the same time: in contrast to longitudinal research in which a range of variation in a given variable is sampled by observing the same cases at different points in time. For example, a cross-sectional study of the relationship between a person's age and height would compare the heights of individuals who are at different ages, while a longitudinal study would compare the height attained by a given individual at different points in the lifespan. (See also LONGITUDINAL RESEARCH.) SB

crowd psychology The psychology of crowd and mass behavior is a psychology of history both in its subject matter and its models and in its initial aim of reforming the theory and practice of politics.

The theory of crowd psychology took shape in Europe, and more particularly in France, at the beginning of this century, after an era of traumatic events stretching from the French Revolution to the Commune of 1871, an era that saw, in Napoleon, the dazzling appearance of one of the greatest leaders of all times.

Gustave Le Bon, a true pioneer in the field addressed himself to those members of the politically conscious classes whose failure to understand the irresistible rise of crowd phenomena seemed to him a major threat to civilization (see 1903, 1910). It was Le Bon who made people recognize crowd phenomena as an essential element of social behavior in the social dynamic. His description, which still today prevails over common sense, stresses the radical difference between the psyche of the individual which is conscious, reasoned and peaceful, and that of the crowd, which is spontaneous, subconscious, passionate and even violent; in the heat generated by the crowd, the fusion of individuals into a common sentiment or spirit blurs differences of personality and social status, blunts the intellectual faculties and propels the enthusiastic and credulous mass into patterns of behavior that are sometimes heroic but, rather more often, destructive and anarchic.

An explanation for the opposition between the conscious, which is individual, and the subconscious, whose collective nature is manifested in the crowd, is to be found in the theory which fascinated Le Bon and his contemporaries, namely that of hypnosis. Hypnosis helps to explain two things: firstly, the state of suggestibility or receptivity of individuals in a crowd, and, secondly, the way in which a leader can gain control of a crowd. As Le Bon says (1903) "The leader has most often started as one of the led. He has himself been hypnotized by the idea, whose apostle he has since become" and one can add that he must be hypnotized also by the echo of his own ideas which the crowd sends back to him as it acclaims him.

Le Bon's discoveries in the psychology of natural crowds were taken up and considerably amplified by Gabriel Tarde (1901, 1910). His descriptive theory is a very general one and can be applied to all forms of social behavior. Artificial or organized crowds, henceforth called masses, become the centre of his interest. Their prototypes are the army and the church, but political parties, trades unions and all the administrative structures of the state are obviously part and parcel of the same phenomenon.

Masses, that is institutionalized crowds, become the guiding principle that explains the whole evolution of society, and implicit in all this is the resolution of a paradox. For, in the model proposed by Tarde, crowds must be capable of creativity, a quality which they lack in Le Bon's system.

The solution adopted by Tarde ascribes the advance of humanity to the progress and discoveries accomplished by the leader, who becomes the driving force behind the system.

This is possible thanks to an analogue of suggestibility, namely imitation, which ensures the cognitive and affective uniformity of the mass at the same time as its submission to the leader.

And finally one must not forget Tarde's most original contribution which makes him a precursor of the theories of mass culture. Taking as his starting point the example of the Press, he describes a type of long range, indirect, imitative suggestibility. The journalist, who is compared with the hypnotist, prefigures what today we should call a leader of opinion. Tarde foresees, therefore, from its earliest days, the era which will witness the triumph of mass communications, of crowds transformed into publics, of the masses at home.

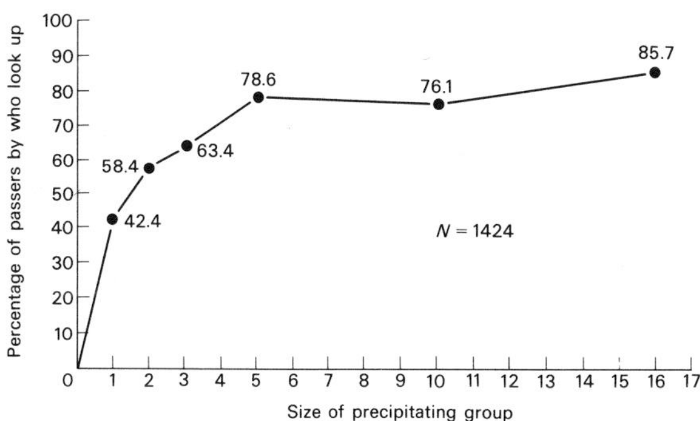

The originality and the prophetic nature of the works of Le Bon and Tarde are undeniable but it is only with Freud that their hypotheses become deductions in an all-embracing theoretical system. Freud's theory of group psychology is a generalized psychoanalytical system concerned with the history of the origins of those fundamental social institutions, the family and religion (which Freud, like his predecessors, considers as the prototype of all collective beliefs).

However, though Freud expresses admiration for Le Bon's descriptions he cannot accept his idea of a collective subconscious which might explain the changes that take place in individuals when they become part of a crowd. For Freud the subconscious springs from repression, the characteristics that an individual exhibits in a crowd are his own, and it is the individual's regression towards the mass, towards the primitive state, which provokes or permits the relaxation of this repression. "The apparently new characteristics which he then displays are in fact the manifestations of this unconscious, in which all that is evil in the human mind is contained as a predisposition. We can find no difficulty in understanding the disappearance of conscience or of a sense of responsibility in these circumstances" (1921).

Once the subconscious has been put back in its rightful place there remains the question of elucidating the nature of the mechanisms which explain the formation of the mass and the formative role played by the leader.

The intuitive suggestion by Le Bon and Tarde, that there is a kind of love that binds together the mass and the place on the one hand and the leader on the other, is taken up and clarified in Freud's concept of libido, which describes a two-fold reality: firstly, the narcissistic libido, that love of self into which the leader can and must retreat by himself if he wants to be and to remain leader, and, secondly, the erotic libido, which makes possible the social scene in general and also, in particular, what one observes in the crowd.

The second concept which is indispensable for the study of crowd psychology, identification, is a development of Tarde's theory of imitation. It expresses the differentiation of the psychic apparatus through the interiorizing of exterior authorities, of social ideals and models: "We are aware that what we have been able to contribute towards the explanation of the libidinal structure of groups leads back to the distinction between the ego and the ego ideal and to the double kind of tie which this makes possible – identification, and putting the object in the place of the ego ideal" (1921).

If one considers the two factors, Eros and Mimesis, as autonomous and irreducible, responsible both of them for the multiple conflicts that arise in their own spheres, but also for an almost permanent conflict which is due to their co-presence, one can arrive at a new and theoretically coherent explanation of the crowd/individual opposition: whereas in the individual the erotic factor dominates the mimetic factor, in the mass this relationship is reversed.

The whole system hangs together for the leader and through the leader. For the leader, thanks to the mechanisms already described; through the leader because for Freud the passage from the natural crowd to the artificial crowd is marked by that fundamental event of the psychoanalytical theory of the mass: the murder of the leader. From Moses to Mao, all the leaders in history would be, from this point of view, resurrections of one image.

The foregoing paragraphs constitute a reconstruction and an integration of the classical theories concerning the psychology of the masses. These theories were visionary in nature. The phenomenon they analyse is still unrolling today before our very eyes "on a scale hitherto unknown, hence its absolute historical novelty" (Moscovici 1981).

Moreover, these theories have had a considerable influence on recent and contemporary history. Mussolini and Hitler knew and put into practice the ideas of Le Bon. Psychoanalysis has inspired an opposing school of thought which incorporates various theoretical elements drawn from Marxism. Among the most influential tendencies we find REICH, with *The mass psychology of fascism* (1933), and above all the Frankfurt School, which saw a powerful reverberation in the social movements of the 1960s.

Another scientific tradition, based on an empirical and experimental social psychology, has, since the last world war, made an important contribution to our understanding of particular aspects of crowd phenomena.

We speak here of crowds and not of masses because by definition mass institutions and organizations, organized crowds, are excluded by epistemological distinction: "The conceptual requirements of spontaneity, planlessness, and relative lack of organization distinguish collective behavior from established groups such as the Methodist Church, Harvard University, and the Republican Party" (Milgram and Tock 1969).

The definition of the phenomenon is both simple and all-embracing. We study all human assemblies in which nearness is in itself sufficient to provoke a significant change in behavior.

Urbanization provides the sociological and ecological framework for a detailed description of the characteristics of crowds. The shape, often circular, the size, the movement, the circulation of information in the shape of a rumor and even the facilitating role of the ambient temperature, all are photographed, measured, evaluated.

Experimental studies are carried out to verify partial hypotheses. Thus, the "crowd crystals" evoked by Canetti (1962) to describe the initial formation of a crowd become, in Milgram's ingenious field experiment (1969), "precipitating groups", the efficacy of the theory being tested and measured in a busy street in New York.

This experiment is illustrative of a theoretical orientation according to which crowds are among the elementary phenomena of social life.

By way of contrast one finds theories which situate crowds in the domain of deviance or even of pathology.

To describe the homogeneity of behavior in these violent and destructive crowds, one uses terms such as "contagion" and "infection" and mathematical models derived from research into epidemics.

Closer to the psychosocial perspective of group dynamics, the Emergent Norm Theory (Turner and Killian 1957) proposes a model which dismisses the homogeneity of crowd behavior, as merely an illusion of the observer. According to this theory a small number of active participants impose on the mass of the crowd which then conforms with them, a mode of action which is perceived as a dominant norm.

In conclusion we should note that there are two distinct avenues of research in the domain of crowd psychology: the classical explicative theory whose scientific status is still rather fragile, and a corpus of research based on methods which are reputedly more rigorous but whose field of investigation is restricted by theoretical and ideological presuppositions.

One can only hope that the two currents will gather strength and come closer together. Perhaps in the street, as in Milgram's experiment. But in any case somewhere where there is a crowd to surround us. MG/SM

Bibliography

Canetti, E. 1962: *Crowds and power*. London: Gollancz.

Cantril, H. 1941: *The psychology of social movement*. New York: Wiley.

*Freud, S. 1921: *Group psychology and the analysis of the Ego*. Standard edition of the complete psychological works of Sigmund Freud. Vol. 18. London: Hogarth Press; New York: Norton.

*——— 1939: *Moses and monotheism*. Standard edition, vol. 23.

Le Bon, G. 1903: *The crowd*. London: Unwin.

——— 1910: *La psychologie politique*. Paris: Flammarion.

*Milgram, S. and Toch, H. 1969: Collective behavior: crowds and social movements. In *The handbook of social psychology*, ed. Lindsey and Aronson. 2nd edn. Reading, Mass.: Addison-Wesley.

*Moscovici, S. 1981: *L'Age des foules*. Paris: Fayard.

Reich, W. 1946: *The mass psychology of fascism*. New York: Oregon Institute Press.

Rudé, G. 1959: *The crowd in the French Revolution*. Oxford: Oxford University Press.

Sighele, S. 1901: *La foule criminelle*. Paris: Alcan.

Tarde, G. 1903: *The laws of imitation*. New York: Holt, Rinehart & Winston.

——— 1910: *L'Opinion et la foule*. Paris: Alcan.

Turner, R.H. and Killian, L.M. 1957: *Collective behavior*. Englewood Cliffs, N.J.: Prentice Hall.

crying: developmental Usually refers to a loud rhythmical vocalization associated with lowering or furrowing of the brows, which other than in neonates commonly involves tears; it is generally taken as denoting distress. Some researchers distinguish a milder behavior 'fussing' or 'fretting' on such bases as little or no rhythmicity, and the face being less contorted.

Three types of cry can be distinguished out of context, both by ear and when visually displayed as a spectrogram of the frequency distribution. These are the 'birth cry', given as the new born takes its first breaths, the 'pain cry', and the 'hunger cry' given when the baby has not been fed for several hours. But apart from these gross differences, parents tend to rely heavily on the *context* of crying, such as how long ago the last feed was, to interpret many other possible meanings of a cry, like boredom, tiredness, stomach ache or wind. AW

Bibliography

Dunn, J. 1977: *Distress and comfort*. London: Open Books; Cambridge, Mass.: Harvard University Press.

cues In cognitive psychology, the word is used more or less in its common sense in various contexts. One talks, for instance, about perceptual cues (e.g. binocular disparity is a distance cue) or syntactic cues (e.g. "that" is a cue for a subordinate clause). A cue is therefore a signal for various kinds of strategic processes (distance perception, sentence parsing, in the examples above). The term "retrieval cue" refers to a memory probe, including the specific probe itself as well as the whole context in which the retrieval is attempted. WKi

cultural deprivation *See* social disadvantage

cultural determinism The view that patterns of behavior are determined by cultural rather than biological or other factors. Some patterns of behavior persist across time within a culture although the persons who behave in a particular way are entirely different. Some customs, attitudes, values or role perceptions remain unchanged over several generations. This observation does not imply that individuals do not influence culture or that biology, situations or other determinants are unimportant in shaping human behavior. However, cultural determinism emphasizes the role of culture in the continuation of pattern across time. While humans can plan and plot they are to some extent swept along by the historic stream of their cultures. For example Kroeber and Richardson (see Kroeber 1952) examined the dimensions of women's dresses from 1605 to 1936 and found strong evidence of cultural determinism, despite attempts of dress designers to innovate and create new fashions. Learned behavior is handed down from one generation to another, creating stability which can be studied as a phenomenon. The observed continuity in such data suggests cultural determinism. This does not, of course, preclude individual innovations or variations of behavior within each culture.

HCT

Bibliography

Kroeber, A.L. 1952: *The nature of culture.* Chicago: University of Chicago Press.

cultural diffusion The spread of cultural traits through contact across societies. Some objects (customs, beliefs, attitudes, values or role perceptions) are found in one society in a particular historical period and also in neighboring societies at a later historical period. Culture change occurs through both innovation and diffusion. Among anthropologists, theoretical battles about diffusion included the question of how much cultural change is due to one or the other of these factors. A second battle was concerned with whether anthropologists should study diffusion at all, or confine themselves to examining the way institutions, operating on a single time-plane, reinforce each other. The latter, anti-diffusionist, position was championed by B. Malinowski, and is known as functionalism. Functionalism contrasts with several diffusionist schools. Three major schools can be identified: the English (Elliot Smith and W.J. Perry), German–Austrian (Father Schmidt and F. Graebner) and American (F. Boas and his students). Elliot Smith considered borrowing to be virtually the sole means by which cultures change, a view which denied the inventiveness of humans. Graebner established diffusion by noting the number of similarities and the complexity of similar cultural elements. The American school examined not only similarities but also the inner relations among the elements that were diffused, and emphasized the known historic links between the cultures where diffusion has taken place. HCT

Bibliography

Boas, Franz 1938: *General anthropology.* New York: D.C. Heath.

Graebner, Fritz 1911: *Methode der Ethnologie.* Heidelberg: Carl Winter.

Kroeber, Alfred L. 1944: *Configurations of cultural growth.* Berkeley: University of California Press.

Malinowski, Bronislaw 1961: *The dynamics of culture change.* New Haven: Yale Press.

Perry, William J. 1927: *Children of the sun.* London: Methuen.

Schaefer, J.M. 1974: *Studies of cultural diffusion.* New Haven: Human Relations Area Files Press.

Schmidt, Wilhelm 1939: *The cultural historical method of ethnology.* New York: Fortuny's.

Smith, Grafton Elliot 1927: *Culture: the diffusion controversy.* New York: Norton.

cultural lag In general, patterns of behavior frequently found in a culture are rewarding to those who behave according to those patterns. However, over time certain patterns may lose their function, but some members of the culture persist in behaving according to the no longer rewarding patterns and until they are extinguished it is possible to observe a cultural lag. For example, consider the conceptions of an ideal family size found among various populations in the world today. In many traditional societies the ideal is five or more children. Such an ideal was consistent with the survival of the group during periods when most children died in infancy, but modern public health techniques have since reduced the infant mortality rate. Yet the ideal persists, and attitudes and behavior consistent with the ideal are found in many societies. This persistence is an example of cultural lag. HCT

cultural relativism The view that patterns of understanding found in different cultures are as good as each other. This viewpoint has implications for method, philosophic position, the evaluation of values and for attitudes toward culture change. Methodologically, it implies that phenomena must be described from the perspective of adherents of a given culture. Philosophically it implies that there is no reality other than the symbolic forms which constitute culture and hence all reality is cultural (see CULTURAL DETERMINISM). Cultural relativism also guides the evaluation of values, which are seen as dependent on social organization and as varying with the modes and interests of each society. If follows that there is no way to judge the superiority of values outside the particular cultural contexts in which they were developed. Finally, this viewpoint implies that since the values of each cultural group are equally acceptable, reform should not attempt to change another group's values. Ethnocentrism is the opposite of cultural relativism. A person making ethnocentric judgments uses his or her own culture as the standard against which to measure other cultures. By contrast, in cultural relativism judgments are said to be based on experience and experience is interpreted by each individual in terms of his or her own enculturation. Judgments of right and wrong, normal and abnormal, beautiful and ugly depend on the judge's experience and are shaped by events that occur in particular ecologies and cultures. What is desirable in one ecology may be undesirable in another. Even the facts of the physical world are discerned through the acculturation screen. So the perception of time, distance, weight, size and other realities is mediated by the conventions of cultural groups. HCT

Bibliography

Herskovits, Melville J. 1972: *Cultural relativism*. New York: Random House.

culture: animal Patterns of behavior within a species whose transmission is totally dependent on non-genetic processes. This definition can be compared with that found in social anthropology, in which "culture" means the ways in which a group has come to solve the problems of life and has brought into existence normatively sanctioned modes of action. It also differs from the lay definition in which "culture" implies intellectual sophistication. In ethology, culture is taken to refer to behavior patterns arising spontaneously by individual inventiveness and transmitted to others mainly as a result of learning. A well known case is the potato- and seed-washing by Japanese macaques on Koshima Islet, S. Japan. McGrew and Tutin (1978) have suggested eight necessary criteria of culture: innovation, dissemination, standardization, durability, diffusion, tradition, non-subsistence, and natural adaptiveness. VR

Bibliography

McGrew W.C. and C.E.G. Tutin, 1978. Evidence for a social custom in wild chimpanzees? *Man* 13.234–51.

curiosity A voluntary form of exploration. The term is not used for reflex forms of exploration such as the ORIENTING RESPONSE.

Animals tend to investigate novel objects or situations by making initially tentative exploratory acts, followed by more bold investigation as the animal becomes more confident. Curiosity thus involves an element of fear combined with motivation. Animals often approach other animals of which they are undoubtedly frightened. Black-headed gulls (*Larus ridibundus*) will approach the centre of disturbance caused by a fox entering the colony. Gazelle and wildebeest will often approach and stare at predators such as hyena and cheetah (Kruuk 1972). It seems that fear of the unknown is an important aspect of curiosity.

Exploratory behavior, including play, may appear to be motivated by curiosity, but care is needed in interpreting this kind of behavior. For example monkeys will learn a puzzle task which enables them to look out of a window in their cage. Such behavior may be motivated by curiosity, but other experiments show that monkeys will learn to manipulate puzzle games without any obvious reward. Thus it may be that looking out of a window is regarded by the monkey merely as part of the puzzle game. Similarly, many animals tentatively explore and sample novel food. This may look like curiosity, but studies of FOOD SELECTION show that such sampling is an important part of learning to avoid poisonous foods, and is part of normal feeding activity.

Konrad Lorenz (1971) maintains that readiness for novel experience, defines curiosity and is characteristic of creatures which have evolved to be unspecialized. Creatures such as the raven, the rat and man can adapt to a wide range of environments and they also show the greatest curiosity. Humans often retain curiosity throughout the lifespan, in other species it may or may not be prevalent only in the earliest stages of development.

GEB/DJM

Bibliography

Kruuk, Hans 1972: *The spotted hyena: a study of predation and social behavior*. Chicago and London: University of Chicago Press.

Lorenz, Konrad 1970–1: *Studies in animal and human behavior*. 2 vols. London: Methuen; Cambridge, Mass.: Harvard University Press.

cut off An ethological term for a posture which removes a social opponent, or partner, out of sight of the actor, thereby reducing the actor's arousal in a conflict situation and increasing the potential flexibility of its own behavior.

In the course of studies on the social behavior of laboratory rats Chance and Grant discovered that when an intruder rat was introduced to the home territory or cage of another rat an approach/avoidance conflict was very evident. In close encounters the rats would adopt postures which involved raising the head so that they were unable to see each other.

The literature on the courtship of birds (e.g. several species of gulls, and especially the Booby (*Sula spp.*)), includes encounters in which either one or both of the participants could not see the other. Clearly, therefore, even if these postures were produced by conflict in the way that displacement activities are, the circumstances in which they occurred meant that they could have no effective signal value and hence an alternative explanation was sought in "cut off" which would enable the actor to more readily change its own behavior.

The concept is given added credibility from the known neurological facts about the separation of sensory (afferent) impulses in mammals along two pathways. On the one hand impulses pass via the medullary reticular and intralaminar nuclei into the cortex by a diffuse projection, bringing about arousal of the cortex and mid brain (see BRAIN AND CENTRAL NERVOUS SYSTEM: ILLUSTRATIONS). On the other, there is a point-to-point projection to the cortex via the limniscal systems providing detailed information about the stimulus source. Hence, "cutting off" the stimulus will reduce arousal even if the price is a loss of information.

Kenneth J. Wilz, studying the action of dorsal pricking in the courtship of the three-spined stickleback (*Gasterosteus aculeatus L.*), concluded that by temporarily discouraging the female from approaching the nest the male prevents her from further arousing his own aggression towards her. In this way the male effectively controls his own conflicting tendencies in favor of leading her in courtship rather than being aggressive to her. Dorsal pricking, which involves the male rising up beneath the female with the spines of his back raised enabling him to fend her off without seeing her or approaching her directly as in an aggressive encounter, is a form of "cut off".

The possibility now has to be considered that what the performance of displacement activities does for controlling arousal in the motor system, "cut off" does for the control of arousal in the sensorium. MRAC

Bibliography

Chance, M.R.A. 1962: An interpretation of some agonistic postures; The role of 'cut off' acts and postures. *Symposia of the Zoological Society of London*, 8.71–89.

Tinbergen, N. 1954: In *Evolution as a process*, ed. Julian S. Huxley, Alister C. Hardy, and Edmund B. Ford. London: George Allen and Unwin.

Wilz, K.J. 1970: Self-regulation of motivation in the three-spined stickleback (*Gasterosteus aculeatus L.*). *Nature* 226. 465 and 466.

cyclic AMP. *See* adenyl cyclase, cAMP and second messenger systems

cyclical change in history Model of the pattern of human change as a recurrent and cyclic process of growth and decay. The cyclical model of history is generally placed against two alternatives: the linear or evolutionary pattern and the discontinuous or revolutionary pattern. A cyclical model of historical change does not necessarily imply continued repetition for it may be claimed that the periods of growth are progressive ones. The works of the Italian historian, Giambattista Vico, are often cited as exemplifying a cyclical model. Sociologists interested in the processes of social change have also contemplated a cyclical model; most notable of these are Pitrim Sorokin and Vilfredo Pareto. The idea of recurrent yet developing cycles of change in phenomena has recently gained attention in psychology (Rosnow 1978). JGM

Bibliography

Rosnow, R.L. 1978: The prophetic vision of Giambattista Vico: Implications for the state of social psychological theory. *Journal of personality and social psychology* 36, 1322–331.

D

dance therapy *See* art, music and dance therapy

Darwin, Charles Born in Shrewsbury in 1809 and died in 1882. Educated at Edinburgh and Cambridge universities, his thinking was greatly stimulated by his travels as a naturalist on *HMS Beagle* from 1831 to 1836. His book *The origin of species*, published in 1859, was, together with Mendelian genetics, the foundation of the modern theory of evolution. It proposed the gradual evolution of distinct species from common ancestors via NATURAL SELECTION and the inheritance of characteristics. This evolutionary theory was extended explicitly to human beings in *The descent of man*, published in 1871. Nevertheless, the germinal ideas of both books can be traced back to the late 1830s in Darwin's unpublished notebooks (Gruber 1974). He probably delayed publication in order to build up evidence against the storm of scientific and religious controversy which he correctly estimated that the books would bring about. Darwin published the results of many other researches, including books on the effects of domestication on plants and animals, and the behavior of earthworms. Of most interest to psychologists have been *The expression of the emotions in man and animals* (1872), which foreshadows much later work on comparative ETHOLOGY and non-verbal communication; and *A biographical sketch of an infant* (1872), based on earlier diary observations of the behavior and development of his first child. PKS

Bibliography

Gruber, H.E. 1974 *Darwin on man: a psychological study of scientific creativity*. London: Wildwood House; New York: E.P. Dutton.

Darwinism, social Conventionally refers to the set of (psychological, sociological, ethnological, etc.) theories which arose from the application of Charles Darwin's views on evolution to the understanding both of social phenomena and of the processes determining the changes of sociosystems. In some instances, the term also denotes social doctrines of whatever scientific status supposedly supported by Darwinian evolutionism. This definition masks the complexity of the origins and the ramifications of this movement of thought.

The emergence of the movement of thought referred to as "Social Darwinism" took place roughly between 1850 and 1880. It reached its peak of scientific, political, social and ideological fascination and visibility in Europe and in North America between 1880 and the end of the first world war. Yet its origins can be traced back to *two* separate traditions beginning at the turn of the nineteenth century. Indeed, Malthus's *Essay on the principle of population*, first published in 1798, marks a first and decisive step in the early phase of the history of Social Darwinism, for it was instrumental in shaping both the Darwinian theory of natural selection and the theory of social evolution which eventually led to Social Darwinism proper.

Ironically, the progressive theory of natural selection drew from a work which was pessimistic in its whole outlook and politically reactionary. In his *Essay*, Malthus endeavored to rebut the theories of progress of the French *philosophes* (such as Turgot, Diderot, Condorcet) which consisted merely of "speculations on the perfectibility of man and society". According to Malthus the possibility of progress through education and political or social revolution met an insurmountable obstacle in the imbalance between the geometric increase of population and the arithmetic growth of food supply.

It was to his reading of Malthus's book that Darwin attributed his discovery of the principle of natural selection and traces of Malthus's influence on Darwin are prominent in *The origin of species* (1859) as well as in *The descent of man* (1871). But unlike Malthus, Darwin optimistically put the emphasis on the goodness of the struggle for life which results from the imbalance set forth by Malthus and pointed to the inevitability of progress through selection conceived as a law of nature (*Origin of species*, ed, cit. pp.86 and 449). Thus the frame of a sociocultural theory worked as a conceptual matrix within which Darwin discussed the main topics of natural evolution.

The second tradition of social evolutionism was prominently represented in the early nineteenth century by such authors as Hegel, Saint-Simon, and Comte. Herbert Spencer elaborated a general theory of evolution of sociosystems which directly addressed the issues raised by Malthus. His early contribution on *The proper sphere of government* (1842) and his first book on *Social statics* (1850) not only contain an attempt to find an exit from the Malthusian dilemma by means of a physiologically oriented theory of the inverse relationship between intelligence and fertility, but also include most of the ideas Spencer is said to have taken from Darwin. And though he often refers to the Lamarckian notion of individual adaptation by the constant use of the sensory, motor, secretory, etc., parts of the organism as one element of sociocultural progress, his conception resorts to the ideas of struggle for existence, survival of the fittest and other ideas of social-Darwinistic type. When the *Origin of species* was published, Spencer and his disciples welcomed its overall message as a confirmation of their own social evolutionism which would now definitely rest on a firm scientific, i.e. biological, ground (for further developments see Wiltshire 1978).

It should also be noted that Spencer had popularized the term "evolution" by 1857 and in his *Principles of biology*, the phrase "survival of the fittest". Darwin duly acknowledged this fact in the fifth edition of the *Origin* by pointing out that "I have called this principle, by which each slight variation, if useful, is preserved by the term Natural Selection, in order to mark its relation to man's power of selection. But the expression often used by Mr. Herbert Spencer of the Survival of the Fittest is more accurate, and is sometimes equally convenient" (ed. cit. p.74).

This summary makes it clear that the biological and social sciences in England developed in a parallel manner up to approximately 1860 and then converged upon a general theory of evolution in which the concepts of struggle for existence, competition, adaptation and the survival of the fittest were given great explanatory power. The summary also shows that Darwin's doctrines made possible the synthesis of the traditions mentioned above, thereby supposedly confirming in terms of biology what had already been assumed in the doctrines of sociocultural progress, so that, as Bayertz (1982, p.113) put it, one could have construed the main principles of Social Darwinism without Darwin (see also Young 1973).

When the *Origin* was published English scientists interested in the topic of evolution (whether of the cosmos, the earth, nature or society) were rapidly converted to Darwin's doctrines. Darwinism was seen as a new and valid standard within the scientific community by 1870, when the Darwinians had succeeded in taking control of the scientific institutions. And, due to the publicizing of Darwinism by such figures as Huxley, Hooker and Lyell in England, Asa Gray in the United States, and Ernst Haeckel in Germany, the new evolutionism attracted more and more intellectuals fascinated by the possibility of giving their social doctrines a scientific outlook (see Ruse 1979, pp.257–68).

Paradoxically, from 1870 on, whereas the number of severe controversies over *specific* problems of Darwinian biology grew in number, evolutionism in its trivial version of Social Darwinism – or, as Harris (1969, p.129) prefers to call it, of Biological Spencerism – became a rather fashionable ideological vehicle for the justification of social, economic and political practices.

Indeed, from the early 1870s to the mid-1890s, the economy of the industrialized nations suffered from a severe deflation. This explains why politicians and economists in Europe and in the United States sought a remedy against the economic crises in the strengthening of the policies of protective tariffs, conquest of new markets, increase of industrial production by means of reducing the impact of governmental control and stronger exploitation of colonial resources and manpower. These policies of economic *laissez-faire* and of political imperialism were argued for precisely in terms of those ideas which Social Darwinism were offering as a scientifically supported ideology (Koch, 1973, passim).

In historical accounts of Social Darwinism as ideology, however, it has often been overlooked that a rigorous adherence to the principles of struggle through *laissez-faire* economics and imperialism leads to a paradoxical situation. The paradox is that since individuals, groups, classes, states or nations are all conceived as entities or units corresponding to the organisms as units subjected to the law of natural selection, too strong a competition between individuals and groups *within* a State or nation would weaken the latter in its struggle with other States or nations. One ought therefore to distinguish analytically between the two trends of "external Social Darwinism", and "internal Social Darwinism" (Koch 1973, p.131).

The first trend postulated progress through elimination of weak, i.e. unfit, States or nations and the expansion of fit States through war, on the one hand, and, on the other, the elimination of unfit races through the deployment of eugenic techniques or, as in *National life from the standpoint of science* (1901) by the noted statistician Charles Pearson, by means of war, trade and industry.

The second trend, in contradistinction, postulated a restriction of domestic *laissez-faire* through social reform, so that the chances of survival in external struggle and competition would increase. Instead of maintaining the principle of selection modelled after that of natural selection proper, the proponents of social reform based their arguments on the possibility of man-made selection and therefore included the manipulation of social (or societal) conditions in their doctrines. A typical representative of this trend is Benjamin Kidd, whose monograph on *Social evolution* of 1894 contained a theoretical frame for social reformism, according to which the State must guarantee equal conditions of fair competition for all its members through just distribution of income and taxes, general education and change of the social and physical conditions of industrial production.

Social Darwinism as ideology had in turn some influence on the rise of the early modern social and behavioral sciences in England, the United States and in several European countries such as Germany, Austria and France. In Germany, for example, the monism of Ernst Haeckel easily amalgamated with Social Darwinism in its moderate, internally oriented version and helped to orient the hesitant steps of early German sociology and social psychology. In France, the crowd psychologists led by Le Bon and Tarde not only propagated racism, but also used social Darwinistic ideas in their theory of regression to a prior stage of evolution through suggestion by a (usually anarchistic, socialist, trade-unionist) leader. Finally, the first generation of social psychologists of the Chicago School such as Dewey and Mead had a more rigorous theory of the continuity of evolution from animal to man than their overtly ideological contemporaries blinded by Social Darwinism, and elaborated their conceptions in view of making the various techniques of social reform scientific.

Other behavioral and social scientists with a penchant for Social Darwinism or working within a frame derived from it were Lester Ward, Franklin H. Giddings, Edward B. Tylor, William G. Sumner, Edward A. Westermarck, Ludwig Gumplowicz, Alfred Fouillée (for further details see Hofstadter 1955 and Mitchell 1968). AM

Bibliography

Bayertz, K. 1982: Darwinismus als Ideologie, *Darwin und die Evolutionstheorie* (=Dialektik, vol.5), Köln: Pahl Rugenstein, 101–116.

Darwin, Charles 1859 (1958): *On the origin of species*. New York: New American Library.

Harris, M. 1969: *The rise of anthropological theory*. London: Routledge & Kegan Paul.

Hofstadter, R 1944 (1955): *Social Darwinism and American thought*. Boston: Beacon Press.

Koch, H.W. 1973: *Der Sozialdarwinismus. Seine Genese und sein Einfluss auf das imperialistische Denken*. Munich: Verlag C.H.Beck.

Mitchell, G.D. 1968: *A hundred years of sociology*. Chicago: Aldine.

Ruse, M. 1979: *The Darwinian revolution: science red in tooth and claw*. Chicago: Chicago University Press.

Wiltshire, D. 1978: *The social and political thought of Herbert Spencer*. Oxford and New York: Oxford University Press.

Young, R. 1973: The historiographic and ideological contexts of the nineteenth-century debate on man's place in nature. In: *Changing perspectives in the history of science*, M. Teich & R. Young ed. London: Heinemann.

daydream Type of waking fantasy, independent of external stimulus, possibly gratifying wishes not being satisfied in real life. Daydreams differ from night dreams in that they are generally under voluntary control, with the daydreamer fully aware of being awake. As a result, daydreams tend to be experienced as less compellingly "real" than night dreams. Daydreaming is especially common among young people, but may continue throughout a lifetime. While often dismissed as a waste of time or mere escapism, daydreaming is not inherently pathological and may have a number of adaptive properties. For example, frequent daydreamers seem better able to cope with boredom and frustration. (See also DREAMING; FANTASY). RPE

Bibliography

Singer, Jerome 1976: *Daydreaming and fantasy*. London: Allen & Unwin; New York: Harper & Row (1975).

deafness and hearing impairment in children A severe or complete loss of hearing that limits the child's ability to receive acoustic information. The incidence (in Britain) is approximately one per thousand births and it may be inherited or arise through environmental causes such as infectious diseases transmitted by the mother during pregnancy.

A primary effect is interference with communication through speech and this in turn has psychological consequences, especially for the comprehension and expression of spoken and written language. The disruptive effects on communication are most serious when deafness has its origins early in life. Remedial training may include physical aids to allow the use of residual hearing, training in lip reading, restricting the child to spoken language, training in a manual sign language or the use of "total" communication methods which comprise some combination of speech and sign. GEB

Bibliography

Meadow, K.P. 1980: *Deafness and child development*. London: Edward Arnold; Berkeley: University of California Press.

decision making The process of selecting a course of action from a behavioral repertoire. Animals usually have the motivation to perform more than one activity at a time, but are capable of only one. There must therefore be a process by which overt expression is given to one aspect of behavior while others are temporarily suppressed. This is the decision making process.

In investigating decision making in animals it is necessary to take account of the animal's motivational state, including its evaluation of external circumstances; the importance, utility, or notional cost, given by the animal to the relevant aspects of the situation; and the optimality criterion or set of decision-rules used by the animal to trade-off the various possibilities (McFarland 1977).

Research on decision making in animals is usually aimed at discovering the decision-rules employed and attempts to evaluate these in terms of the problems facing the animal in its natural environment. DJM

Bibliography

McFarland, D. J. 1977: Decision-making in animals. *Nature* 269, 15–21.

decision making and computers Decision making is the process whereby some sort of choice is made between alternatives by evaluating the information which is favorable or unfavorable to each alternative.

Computers are increasingly used to help with decision making because of their ability to analyse large amounts of information rapidly and accurately. Individual decision makers may lack experience, forget or misinterpret important material, or have insufficient time in which to formulate judgments. Computer aids have been extensively developed for medical, military and commercial applications. Some computer systems of these kinds simply analyse and summarize data, leaving the final responsibility for the decision with the human user (e.g. in company management). Other systems are given substantial responsibility for taking action (e.g. some military systems).

Historically the major techniques used by computer decision systems are logical and statistical. Large bodies of data, often quantitative, are compiled in a computer database. The database may include raw facts as in military intelligence, or carefully refined and validated facts such as accurate estimates of the probability that particular diseases will manifest particular symptoms. The computer is programmed to interpret new information or events by consulting the database and making logical or statistical calculations on the basis of the stored facts. Sometimes calculations are included which are based on theories of the system under study (as in the prediction of monetary inflation rates by simulating the interaction of economic mechanisms thought to control inflation).

There are three main ways in which psychologists have been widely involved in the development of these systems. First they have made a major contribution to the understanding of human decision making and identified a number of systematic weaknesses (conservatism in predicting the likelihood of events, overemphasis of minor or unrepresentative features of situations, conclusions formed prematurely on the basis of insufficient or unreliable information). This has helped to identify situations where computer assistance could help. Second it is not always possible to compile adequate databases of "objective" facts, and the designers of computer systems may have to rely on the use of "subjective" material obtained from people who are knowledgeable about the subject; psychologists have developed methods for obtaining such material and have identified conditions where it may be unreliable. Third "human factors" psychologists have often contributed to the evaluation of these techniques, particularly in the study of ERGONOMIC features and how computer-based decision making tools affect the organizations where they are introduced.

Notwithstanding the theoretical sophistication of many of the techniques their success is still variable. They are subject to failure from a number of causes. The data they depend upon may be unreliable or incomplete; the techniques used for making the decision may be too simple for the decision being made; and they may be rejected by the very people they are supposed to help because they are threatening, incomprehensible, or simply distrusted. Nevertheless there are many highly successful systems (see Yu 1979).

The rejection of such computer aids to decision making, even when they are successful, often has a psychological origin. The human decision-maker thinks about a decision and evaluates evidence in largely non-mathematical ways and this often means that the computer's calculations and recommendations are entirely unintelligible in human terms. (This has been a particular problem in medicine where traditionally doctors are expected to take a high degree of responsibility for their patients.)

A result of this difficulty has been the rapid growth since about 1970 of a new field known as knowledge engineering. Knowledge engineers have attempted to develop computer systems which can be easily understood by professional decision makers who are not trained in mathematics or computer science. Knowledge engineering depends upon a number of new programming techniques, but in addition it rests upon three features which are of interest to the psychologist. First, there is much less emphasis on the use of mathematical data by the computer and much more on the use of the qualitative knowledge that would be used by a human decision maker (for example the sort of material found in a medical textbook). Second, computer systems are often designed to process information in ways which emulate human thinking (they can use methods of reasoning which incorporate rules of thumb or "heuristic" rules). Finally there have been attempts to provide computer systems with the ability to explain their decisions or recommendations. Knowledge engineering is a young technology but it has a number of successes to its credit. Although the use of knowledge, the methods of reasoning, and the explanation capabilities are still relatively primitive the performance of these systems is remarkable. Their intelligibility, versatility and performance may compare very favorably with their obscure and inflexible predecessors. Modern understanding of mental processes has played an important part in their development and could be crucial in the future. JPF

Bibliography

Feigenbaum, E. 1979: Themes and case studies of knowledge engineering. In *Expert systems in the microelectronic age*, ed. D. Michie. Edinburgh: Edinburgh University Press.

Fox, J. 1982: Computers learn the bedside manner. *New scientist* 29 July, 311–13.

Tversky, A. and Kahneman, D. 1974: Judgement under uncertainty: heuristics and biases. *Science* 185, 1124–31.

Yu, V.L. 1979: Evaluating the performance of a computer-based consultant. *Computer programs in biomedicine*.

defense mechanism: in psychoanalytic theory One of a number of techniques used by the EGO to defend itself from anxiety, which may arise from three sources: when an instinctual impulse in the Id is pressing for gratification; when the SUPEREGO exerts moral pressure against a wish, intention or idea; or when there is a realistic danger of pain or injury (ego-anxiety). The aim of defense mechanisms is to divert anxiety away from the ego's consciousness. This can be done in about a dozen different ways, according to psychoanalytic literature, which vary in the extent to which they are consistent with reason and perceived reality; one that is consistent is "ego-syntonic", and one that is not is "ego-dystonic". The severity of a psychological disturbance is often assessed by the quality (in terms of ego-syntonicity) of the prevailing defenses, which PROJECTIVE

TESTS especially are designed to elicit. The ego-defenses have been extensively discussed by Anna Freud (1937) and by Laughlin (1970).

The principal defense is REPRESSION, which covers both preventing a mental element (idea, wish, anxiety, impulse, image) from becoming conscious, and rejecting from consciousness to the UNCONSCIOUS MIND one which had been. The commonest of the others are: "projection", by which one attributes to others a property of oneself and can therefore blame them instead of feeling guilt (a form of anxiety) oneself; "reaction-formation", by which one's anxiety about (say) aggressive feelings towards someone is kept at bay by overtly adopting the opposite attitude of solicitude and compliance; "identification", by which either depressive anxiety over "object-loss" is mitigated by perpetuating in one's own behavior some psychological property of (say) a parent or spouse who has been emotionally lost (cp. Freud on depression: 1917*a*, p. 239), or the threat of an aggressor is annulled by one's adopting his/her characteristics (see SUPEREGO); "denial", a relatively ego-dystonic defense because if some unpleasant feature of the perceptual world is simply denied, then this defies the "reality principle" and may lead to delusion or hallucination, whereas, if one denies some painful aspect of one's emotional make-up (say depression), one is tending towards mania; SUBLIMATION and "rationalization", both much more ego-syntonic, and the latter meaning to give an intellectual rationale for what was in fact an emotionally-determined action or response; "isolation" by which the mental image of a disturbing experience or action is disconnected in one's thinking from its temporal and associative context, drained of its feeling-tone, and left cognitively and emotionally isolated; "splitting", by which a single "object" is treated as two separate ones so that a separate set of feelings can be directed to either part-object, and the anxious dissonance between (say) wanting and rejecting the same thing be consequently resolved (see PSYCHOANALYTIC PERSONALITY THEORY for Kleinian usage); "regression", by which one reverts to the gratification techniques of an earlier psychosexual stage to compensate for a current anxiety (see PSYCHOANALYTICAL PERSONALITY THEORY for the account of "stages").

The theoretical relation between REPRESSION and the other defenses is problematic, with the exception of regression. For the latter is the only one which depends upon the chronology of personality development (Freud 1917b, ch. 22). Freud recognized (1926, ch. 11A) that he had been using the word repression to cover different forms of defense against anxiety (on the assumption that all defenses except regression would involve repression). He proposed to revert to the concept of a class of defense-mechanisms of which repression would be a particular case. Madison (1961) has argued that Freud does not maintain this program in subsequent writings. Freud also considers (1926) the possibility that the neuroses should be understood in terms of which defense mechanisms dominate their respective psychopathologies, and Fairbairn (1941) proposed a realization of this idea in the context of "object-relations theory".

Kline has reviewed a great many ingenious empirical investigations into defense-mechanisms (1981, ch. 8), and concludes that, although a number of them are poorly designed or irrelevant, there is undoubted support for repression, and a certain amount for isolation, projection, reaction-formation and denial. NMC

Bibliography

Fairbairn, W.R.D. 1941 (*1952*): A revised psychopathology. Reprinted in *Psychoanalytic studies of the personality*. London: Tavistock.

Freud, Anna 1937: *The Ego and the mechanisms of defence*. London: Hogarth; New York: International Universities Press (1946).

Freud, Sigmund 1917a; 1917b; 1926: *Mourning and melancholia* (vol. 14); *Introductory lectures* (vol. 16); *Inhibitions, symptoms and anxiety* (vol. 20). *Standard edition of the complete psychological works of Sigmund Freud*. Vols. as indicated. London: Hogarth Press; New York: Norton.

Kline, Paul 1981: *Fact and fantasy in Freudian theory*. London and New York: Methuen.

Laughlin, Henry P. 1970: *The ego and its defenses*. New York: Appleton-Century-Crafts.

Madison, Paul 1961: *Freud's concept of repression and defense*. Minneapolis: Minnesota University Press.

deindividuation A state of relative anonymity in which a person cannot be identified as a particular individual but only as a group member. Experiments by Zimbardo (1970) have shown that people show an increased tendency towards aggressive behavior in conditions of relative anonymity. The threshold for non-normative acts is lowered because sanctions cannot be easily implemented in such conditions. This in turn may lead to the weakening of such internalized controls as shame, guilt or fear. Milgram (1974) has shown that deindividuating the victim also leads to an increase in aggression. JMFJ

Bibliography

Milgram, S. 1974: *Obedience to authority: an experimental view*. New York: Harper.

Zimbardo, P.G. 1970: The human choice: individuation, reason and order versus deindividuation, impulse and chaos. In *Nebraska symposium on motivation*, ed. W.J. Arnold and D. Levine. Lincoln: University of Nebraska Press.

deixis The notion of "deixis" refers to linguistic expressions which signal the contextual existence of persons, objects and similar orientational features. Deictic words include personal pronouns, adverbials of time and place and expressions signalling an honorific dimension. They are typically speaker-oriented and serve to create textual coherence.

The presence of deictic elements in all known human languages is taken as an indication that they developed out of face-to-face interaction. PM

Bibliography

Lyons, John 1977: *Semantics*. London and New York: Cambridge University Press.

déjà vu *See* memory impairment

déjà vu and affect *Déjà vu* refers to the belief that one has already seen or experienced what one knows to be a new situation. It literally means already seen, and is often accompanied by the feeling of knowing what will happen next. The discrepancy between what one knows to be an unfamiliar situation and the subjective feeling of extreme familiarity can create considerable affect by challenging the individual's sense of reality. *Déjà vu* experiences are frequently reported by patients with epileptic activity, particularly seizures originating in the right-temporal lobe. It may last for hours or days in such patients, whereas it lasts for minutes or seconds in normal individuals.

It is possible that the feeling of familiarity in *déjà vu* results from the similarity of one's affective reactions in the old and new situations, rather than the similarity of the situations themselves (see MEMORY: STATE DEPENDENCE). One possible explanation is that the individual may have previously experienced the situation in an emotionally-charged state of consciousness, such as a dream or revelation. A related psychoanalytically-oriented explanation is that the individual actually encountered the situation previously, but no longer recalls the episode because of its association with strong unpleasant emotions. MAS

Bibliography

Reed, G. 1972: *The psychology of anomalous experience: a cognitive approach*. London: Hutchinson University Library.

delay-learning phenomenon (or delayed association) Denotes any case where associative learning depends on bridging a long interval between events. For example CONDITIONING usually proceeds with difficulty if the events to be associated (conditional and unconditional stimuli, response and reinforcer) are separated by an unfilled interval of more than a few seconds, but in certain cases, notably in associations between the quality of a food and later gastrointestinal symptoms, longer delays of minutes or hours can be tolerated. There is disagreement as to whether this phenomenon reflects a specialized adaptation of food-related learning, or unusually low levels of INTERFERENCE during the delay. Delayed-response learning, where a choice response must be made on the basis of a cue given some time previously, has been used as an assay of memory capacity and brain lesion effects in animals. (Not to be confused with Pavlov's term "delay conditioning" meaning any procedure where conditional stimulus onset precedes the unconditional stimulus without any gap between them.) EAG

delinquency Conduct disorder in young persons involving offenses against the law. In Britain, juvenile delinquents could be considered legally as persons under the age of seventeen with criminal convictions. However, no widely accepted definition exists, the term often including any antisocial, deviant or immoral behavior whether or not it forms part of a criminal offence. Delinquency is a serious cause for concern worldwide, but rates are difficult to estimate reliably. West and Farrington (1973) showed that 30.8 per cent of working-class boys in London had at least one conviction at twenty-one years. Boys have outnumbered girls in a ratio of up to ten to one. The most common offenses involve theft. A popular distinction is drawn between socialized and unsocialized delinquents (Hewitt and Jenkins 1946).

Causation is multifactorial, including genetic, psychological, social and cultural factors. Over-simplified causal explanations are misleading. Prevalence is high in depressed urban environments and one view relates delinquency particularly to disadvantaged subcultures. There is a well established connection between delinquency and disturbed home background and family conflict. Schools may have differing rates of delinquency and may play a part in fostering delinquent behavior (Reynolds 1976). Longitudinal studies suggest that future delinquents may be differentiated from others during late childhood on the basis of their attitudes and behavior (West and Farrington 1973). The "labeling" of children as failures and troublemakers, especially by teachers, contributes to the acquisition of deviant status (Hargreaves 1975). WLLP-J

Bibliography

Hargreaves, David H., Hester, F. and Mellor, S. 1975: *Deviance in classrooms*. London and Boston: Routledge & Kegan Paul.

Hewitt, Lester E. and Jenkins, Richard L. 1946: *Fundamental patterns of maladjustment: the dynamics of their origin*. Springfield, Ill.: State of Illinois.

Reynolds, D. 1976: The delinquent school. In *The process of schooling*, ed. Martyn Hammersley and Peter Woods. London and Boston: Routledge & Kegan Paul.

West, Donald J. and Farrington, D.P. 1973: *Who becomes delinquent?* London: Heinemann Educational.

*——1977: *The delinquent way of life*. London: Heinemann Educational.

delusion A delusion is a false belief, held despite evidence to the contrary, and one which is not explicable in terms of the patient's educational and cultural background. It is held with complete conviction and cannot be shaken by argument. Delusions must be distinguished from culturally acceptable beliefs and from more idiosyncratic convictions that are understandable in terms of the patient's background. The latter are called overvalued ideas. Primary delusions are those that appear to have arisen suddenly and fully formed while secondary delusions can be seen as derived from hallucinations or other psychotic beliefs. Delusions are seen most often in SCHIZOPHRENIA, severe AFFECTIVE DISORDER and ORGANIC MENTAL STATES. The content of the delusion may have diagnostic significance, for instance delusions of guilt are associated with depression. RAM

Bibliography

Jaspers, K. 1959: *General psychopathology*. Trans J. Hoenig and M.W. Hamilton. Manchester: Manchester University Press.

demand characteristics A phrase referring to the fact that certain features of the experimental setting may impose certain perceived demands upon the experimental subject. Subjects tend to act in the way that they think the experimenter would wish. Orne (1962) was one of the first to point to the demand characteristics of psychological research which he defined as "the totality of cues which convey an experimental hypothesis to the subject" (p.779). Many famous experiments such as the obedience study of Milgram (1965) have been interpreted in terms of demand characteristics (Mixon 1972). It is, of course, possible that while some subjects in an experiment will feel the need to confirm the experimental hypothesis others will not.

A related experimental artifact is evaluation apprehension, which refers to the anxiety and self-consciousness that a subject has about being observed and judged while in a laboratory or similar setting. Because subjects realize that some aspects of their behavior are being measured or observed, they may try to present themselves in a favorable light. Evaluation apprehension has been studied by Sigall, Aronson and Van Hoose (1970) who found that if subjects were faced with the choice between giving negative information about themselves while cooperating with the experimenter, and presenting positive information but negating the experimenters' demands they chose the latter. This suggests the limited effects of demand characteristics when the demand is for a display of negative aspects of the person. AF

Bibliography

Milgram, S. 1965: Some conditions of obedience and disobedience to authority. *Human relations* 18, 57–76.

Mixon, D. 1972: Instead of deception. *Journal for the theory of social behavior* 2, 145–77.

Orne, M. 1962: On the social psychology of the psychological experiment: with particular reference to demand characteristics and their implication. *American psychologist* 17, 776–83.

Sigall, H., Aronson, E. and Van Hoose, T. 1970: The cooperative subject: myth or reality. *Journal of experimental social psychology* 28, 218–24.

demystification *See* critical psychology

dendrites and dendritic spines (See BRAIN AND CENTRAL NERVOUS SYSTEMS: ILLUSTRATIONS, fig. 30). Processes of a NEURON characterized by cytoplasm like that of the cell body and often bearing numerous lateral spines. The definition is cytological. Dendritic cytoplasm is an extension of the cell body cytoplasm (perikaryon) and possesses in particular rough endoplasmic reticulum (Nissl substance) which distinguishes it from axoplasm. Dendrites are usually rapidly tapering extensions from the cell body which repeatedly branch at acute angles. They are typically packed in satellite glial cells without an individual sheath (see GLIA). Dendrites are generally the principal receptive and integrative regions of a neuron and usually do not conduct action potentials. The geometry of the "dendritic tree" determines how much various inputs will change the membrane potential at the axon hillock where nerve impulses are triggered. Although the dendritic tree is generally regarded as the input stage of a neuron (the axon is the output stage), outputs from dendrites to other dendrites are actually quite common. Such dendro–dendritic connections would appear to represent an economical way to minimize the space required for synaptic interactions. Reciprocal synapses between dendrites have been termed microcircuits and represent the most compact synaptic circuit known. Sites of reciprocal dendro–dendritic circuits include the retina, olfactory bulb, CEREBRAL CORTEX, BASAL GANGLIA, and THALAMUS.

Dendritic spines are a common feature of neural dendrites and are well displayed by the Golgi method of neuron staining. They vary from long and thin to short and fat, but a common form consists of a ball on a short thin stalk. Spines appear to be specializations for receiving synaptic inputs, although many fibers SYNAPSE onto the dendrite shaft, not onto spines. The increase in area represented by dendritic spines may be accessory to some other function since on most dendrites much of the membrane area is covered by glial processes rather than synaptic inputs. The structure of dendritic spines suggests that they help electrically to isolate groups of inputs from the electrical environment of the dendrite proper.

The above definition of dendrite is a simplification, however, and many cases arise where the term "process" may be preferable to either dendrite or axon (see Shepard 1979, for a discussion of this issue). SCC

Bibliography

Palay, S.F. and Chan-Palay, V. 1977: General morphology of neurons and neuroglia. In *Handbook of physiology*, Section 1, *The nervous system*, Vol. I. *Cellular biology of neurons*, Part 1, ed. J.M. Brookhart, V.B. Mountcastle and E.R. Kandel. Bethesda, MD: American Physiological Society.

Peters, A., Palay, S.F., and Webster, H. de F. 1970: *The fine structure of the nervous system: the cells and their processes*. New York and London: Hoeber Medical Division, Harper & Row.

Shepard, Gordon M. 1979: *The synaptic organization of the brain*. 2nd edn. New York and Oxford: Oxford University Press.

deoxyribonucleic acid *See* RNA and DNA

depressants *See* drugs, depressant

depression, bipolar Where an individual has suffered abnormal swings of mood in both directions, that is both depressive and manic illnesses, his disorder may be termed bipolar. Recurrent illnesses which are all depressive or all manic (the latter being rather rare) may be called unipolar. Perris (1976) provides evidence that unipolar and bipolar disorders are genetically distinct, but in practice it is often difficult to say with confidence that an individual belongs to the unipolar depressive category, since manic spells may go unrecognized and their emergence may be long delayed (see AFFECTIVE DISORDERS). Frank illnesses may be preceded by a tendency to the minor mood swings which characterize the cyclothymic personality. DLJ

Bibliography

*Paykel, E.S., ed. 1982: *Handbook of affective disorders*. London and New York: Churchill Livingstone.

Perris, C. 1976: Frequency and hereditary aspects of depression. In *Depression: behavioral, biochemical, diagnostic and treatment concepts*, ed. D.M. Gallant and G.M. Simpson. New York: Spectrum.

deprivation: animal A term used in ETHOLOGY to refer to a specific lack of some essential kind of stimulation during the course of normal juvenile development. Its use is therefore to be distinguished from two usages in experimental psychology. In the first, it refers to a period in which the subject has no access to an essential substance, usually food or water, so that the substance can later be used for conditioning. In the second, it refers to the exclusion of normal sensory stimulation ("sensory deprivation") in order to study the disorienting effects of this on the subject.

The idea of deprivation in ethology is closely associated with the discovery that, in most species, normal behavioral development occurs by the unfolding of genetically based tendencies in the presence of suitable environmental stimulation. If the necessary environmental stimuli are absent the result is deprivation. A closely related phenomenon, therefore, is IMPRINTING, since absence of the stimuli involved in imprinting will disturb development. Studies of deprivation in mammals have been made on dogs and monkeys. In both cases, isolation of the newborn for several months from its mother leads to the development of aberrant avoidance behavior in later development, and leads also to a lack of social and sexual competence. In the case of humans, deprivation has been described in cases where maternal care was inadequate, and it has been suggested that individuals who have suffered from maternal deprivation are likely to have mental problems in later life (see Bowlby 1953). (See also ATTACHMENT; SEPARATION). VR

Bibliography

Bowlby, John 1953: *Child care and the growth of love*. London and Baltimore: Penguin.

deprivation: human parental This term covers the many ways, emotional and physical in which parental care may be inadequate, and which may have immediate and long term consequences for the child. Bowlby (1951) suggested that separation of a young child from its mother not only causes immediate distress (protest followed by despair and detachment) but also predisposes to later PSYCHOPATHIC PERSONALITY disorder and vulnerability to AFFECTIVE DISORDER. Since then it has become apparent that the effect of separation depends on many factors including the age of the child, its previous relationship with its mother and father, and the nature of the separation. It is also apparent that the various types of parental deprivation have quite different longterm consequences. For example, lack of environmental stimulation and encouragement to learn in infancy is associated with educational under-achievement, whereas poor early emotional attachments may result in difficulties in adult social relationships.

Awareness of the consequences of maternal separation and other forms of parental deprivation has been a major influence in the development of ideas of child care whether it is undertaken by the parents, by substitute parents or by any form of educational or residential institution. RAM

Bibliography

Bowlby, J. 1951: *Maternal care and mental health*. Geneva: WHO.

Rutter, M. 1981: *Maternal deprivation reassessed*. 2nd edn. Harmondsworth and New York: Penguin.

depth psychology *See* Gurdjieff

Descartes, René (1596–1650). French scientist, mathematician and metaphysician, Descartes is remembered chiefly as a champion of modern science against medieval scholasticism, and as the advocate of a radical theoretical distinction between the mental and the physical. His writings have shaped the concepts and vocabulary of much subsequent thought about human nature.

Descartes's primary intellectual ambition was to devise a new approach to physics, through which everything in the physical world would be explained by a small set of laws of nature, i.e. equations referring to the fundamental properties of matter. His earliest systematic work, *The World* – which he abandoned in 1633 for fear of being prosecuted as Galileo had been the year before – was an attempt to apply this kind of physics not only to inanimate nature, but also to living organisms, particularly the human body. Descartes's mechanistic descriptions of digestion, blood circulation, sleep, sense-perception (especially vision), imagination, memory, emotion and purposeful movement suggested the provocative conclusion that these functions might be entirely accounted for in physical terms.

Descartes's later writings (*Discourse on method* (1637), *Meditations* (1641), *Principles of philosophy* (1644) and *Passions of the soul* (1649)) were largely concerned with defining the aspect of human nature which he considered to be inaccessible to such mechanistic explanation. His argument hung on the famous proposition *cogito ergo sum* – (I think therefore I am). Descartes claimed that, supposing one could convince oneself that the entire physical world is an illusion, one would nevertheless have an invincibly certain knowledge that one exists, if only as something "entirely distinct from body", a mere "thing that thinks" (*res cogitans*). It followed, according to Descartes, that one's own existence as a "thinking thing" was theoretically quite distinct from one's existence as a body (1911 edn, vol. 1 pp.101, 152). It was also apparent, he thought, that the nature of this "thinking thing" had been generally misunderstood, through being continually confused with physical matters such as breathing or sensation. He insisted that "there is nothing in us which we ought to refer to our soul excepting our *thoughts*" (ibid. vol. 1 p.340) and for this reason preferred to call it "mind" rather than "soul" (ibid. vol. 2 p.210). This emphatic separation of thinking from physical processes is known as *Cartesian Dualism* (see MIND AND BODY).

Descartes believed that possession of a mind in this sense explained flexibility of response and linguistic creativity (1911 edn, vol. 1 p.117), and that it distinguished humans from animals, which, however human-like in behavior, were no more than physical automata, deserving neither sympathy nor moral consideration.

Descartes held that mental states are constituted by "*ideas*" (it was he who bestowed its modern, psychological meaning on this word). He also suggested, casually but influentially, that these might be divided into three general classes – the factitious, which we form for ourselves; the adventitious, which come to us through our nerves; and the innate, which are the inborn equipment of any mind whatsoever (ibid. vol. 1 p.160). (See INNATE IDEAS.)

Descartes analysed mental acts as the outcome of the joint operation of *intellect* and *will*, the former comprising ideas of external objects (e.g. the sun, a ghost), the latter, attitudes to these ideas (e.g. belief, aversion). Ideas in the intellect might be more or less confused (as opposed to distinct) and obscure (as opposed to clear). The purpose of methodical reasoning was to clarify and distinguish one's ideas, and the ideal of human conduct in both scientific and ethical fields was to ensure that one is always governed by one's will, operating on a basis of ideas of the greatest attainable clarity and distinctness. It is debatable whether Descartes considered clear and distinct ideas to be necessarily innate.

It follows from Cartesian dualism that minds are not located, and therefore should not be conceived as being "inside" the body – "like a pilot in a ship" as Descartes sarcastically phrased it (ibid. vol. 1 pp.118, 192; vol. 2 p.102). He recognized, however, that each mind is in some way connected to an individual nervous system through which it receives its "adventitious" ideas; in this sense, it is "united to all the portions of the body conjointly". At the same time, such phenomena as illusions due to damage to the nerves made it evident that the mind "has its principal seat in the brain" – or rather, according to Descartes, at a point in an adjacent organ, the pineal gland (ibid. vol. 1 pp.345, 289, 189–199).

Although Descartes is celebrated as a "dualist", it should be noted that he insisted that purely mechanical explanations could be supplied for many of the processes commonly seen as belonging to the domain of psychology. First, all "adventitious" ideas were directly occasioned by cerebral events, and so too were the various mental perturbations which Descartes – giving a new twist to an already convoluted word – referred to as "passions". Secondly, there was behavior such as blinking which, according to Descartes, was wholly non-mental, and due entirely to the particular arrangement of "the machine of our body". This included "all the movements which we make without our will contributing thereto, as frequently happens when we ... perform those actions which are common to us and the brutes" (ibid. vol. 1 pp.339–40). In this respect, Descartes may be credited with an early conception of reflexes (see REFLEX). JR

Bibliography

Descartes, René 1897–1913: *Oeuvres de Descartes*. 12 vols., ed C. Adam and P. Tannery. Paris: Cerf.

——— 1911: *The philosophical works of Descartes*. 2 vols. Trans. Elizabeth S. Haldane and G. R. T. Ross. London and New York: Cambridge University Press.

Rée, Jonathan 1974: *Descartes*. London: Allen Lane; New York: Universe Books (1975).

desensitization, systematic A highly influential form of behavior therapy primarily used in the treatment of phobic behavior in which fear is reduced by exposing the patient to the feared object in the presence of a stimulus that inhibits such fear. It was developed by Wolpe (1958) on the basis of his work on the experimental neurosis in cats. In therapy the client imagines a series of phobic situations of ever increasing fearfulness while anxiety is inhibited by muscular relaxation. Systematic desensitization was the first behavioral technique to receive extensive experimental investigation, and numerous studies on volunteers with fears of small animals such as spiders or rats and in clinical populations with major disabling fears have shown that desensitization is an effective treatment for such behavioral disorders. In clinical practice it has now largely been superseded by exposure to the situation in reality without relaxation training. DWJ

Bibliography

Wolpe, J. 1958. *Psychotherapy by reciprical inhibitions*. Stanford, Calif: Stanford University Press.

determinism The view that some or all of our apparently free choices are really not free but have their outcomes settled from the start. The ancient idea of fate was a deterministic notion, applying not to every single detail of life but to its large events and general shape. The idea that God knows the future gave rise later on to what is now called theological determinism: if God already knows what I shall decide tomorrow, then the outcome of my decision is already settled, and alternatives are not truly open to me. Later, psychological determinism held that some or all our choices are foreordained by the deep laws of the psyche; of this view there are many versions. Neurophysiological determinism is the most recent and most compelling deterministic theory: every mental event, like a decision, is at base just a neural event; the nervous system, being part of physical nature, works by nature's causal laws. So apparently free decisions are really the inescapable outcomes of the operation of nature's causal laws. See also FREE WILL, MIND–BODY PROBLEM. JT

Bibliography

Berofsky, Bernard, ed. 1966: *Free will and determinism*. New York: Harper & Row.

Hook, Sidney, ed, 1958: *Determinism and freedom in the age of modern science*. New York: New York University Press.

determinism: psychic The theory that in a biologically intact human organism every aspect of behavior is completely determined by psychological factors. This means that without exception there are no accidents or coincidences of human behavior. This extends to hysteria, dreams and facets of psychotic behavior as well as to details of behavior such as memory lapses, random thoughts and other forms of what Freud called "the psychopathology of everyday life". A dream may be explained in terms of stresses in the life of the dreamer. Any action, moral or immoral has a cause. This suggests that the person is controlled by a chain of behavior rather than by free will and therefore is not responsible for his or her behavior. The implications of the concept for attribution of responsibility for criminal behavior is a critical concern of law. The inability of psychoanalysts to predict behavior convincingly renders psychic determinism a working hypothesis at best. Even more fundamentally, the concept assumes total knowledge or a posture of omniscience regarding the understanding of human behavior. RCZ

Bibliography

Waelder, R. 1963: Psychic determinism and the possibility of predictions. *Psychoanalytic quarterly*. 32, 15—48.

determinism *See above, and also* cultural determinism

development: psychoanalytic theories A set of related, historical–causal accounts of the development of INSTINCT and of OBJECT RELATIONS deriving from the internal psychological reality of the subject. FREUD initially sought antecedents of his patients' nervous illnesses in their life histories but a theoretical turning point was his realization that the seductions which his patients described were not real events in childhood but phantasies that had been created when they were children (Rapaport 1960). It is the incorporation of this insight which makes psychoanalytic theories of development unique.

Psychoanalytic developmental or genetic theory must be placed within the abstract, conceptual "metapsychology" which Freud created as his psychological account of that which lay beyond consciousness. The topographical, the economic and the dynamic perspectives, are, like the genetic, major parts of the metapsychology. The topographical concerns the regions of the mind, in Freud's first system, the preconscious–conscious and the unconscious. The quantities and movements of psychic energy are conceptualized within the economic perspective while the dynamic concerns the conflict of psychic forces, generally the instincts. These perspectives are interrelated and interdependent in any explanation. For example, the term "dynamic unconscious" describes the struggle of unconscious forces, usually of an infantile sexual nature, to enter consciousness. Freud created this complex apparatus to account for his patients' past and present difficulties. He was concerned with many aspects of their lives; and his genetic theory differs from the more limited developmental theories constructed in academic settings.

Genetic theory and the topographic, economic and dynamic systems were created to explain the meaning of symptoms. In *Three essays on the theory of sexuality* (1905) Freud offered explanations of adult perversions and neuroses in terms of infantile sexuality. He described the origins of adult genital sexuality in the component oral, anal and phallic sexualities of infancy and early childhood. It is important to remember that the widely known oral, anal and phallic stages of libidinal (instinctual) development were constructed primarily from the accounts and analyses of adults.

A major step in the development of object relations as well as of instinct is the Oedipus Complex, the term Freud chose to describe the child's conflicting wishes of love and hate toward its parents. Clinically the Oedipus Complex is crucial as "the nucleus of the neuroses" (Laplanche and Pontalis 1973). Individuals who do not experience the three person conflicts typical of the Oedipus Complex may develop more serious illnesses and are a therapeutic problem to psychoanalysis. But mental illness is not determined by experience alone. Freud believed that an individual's instinctual disposition contributed to the creation of neurotic symptoms (*Outline of psychoanalysis*, Standard Edition vol. 23). Both experiential and biological factors have a place in genetic theory; it is an interactionist account of development and has been compared with Piaget's model in this respect (Greenspan 1979).

In *The ego and the id* Freud introduced a second model of the mental apparatus. The older topographic system of the preconscious–conscious and the unconscious was not abandoned but maintained alongside the model of mental agencies, the familiar – id, ego and superego. The resolution of the Oedipus Complex is significant in the development of the superego. It is through identification with the parents that oedipal conflicts are successfully dealt with, that relations with the parental objects are internalized and the superego as the repository of parental ideals and prohibitions formed. A full understanding of the three agencies requires examination of them in terms of all the metapsychological perspectives but attention here is on the genetic. The ego is held to develop through the infant's adaptive encounters with reality. At birth the infant knows no reality and operates in terms of primary processes, condensation and displacement. These processes were first described by Freud in *The interpretation of dreams* and are characteristic of unconscious functioning. The ego differentiates out of the id which in the second model retained much of the identity of the unconscious. The ego functions in terms of the reality principle and its processes are described as secondary. It is this later model which is widely known in psychology, and development is often seen as an inexorable progression from id, to ego to superego as well as from oral to anal to phallic libidinal organization. Since much of metapsychological theory is ignored, these developments appear unintelligible as well as inexorable.

A further aspect of genetic theory which has wide currency is Freud's account of the development of gender identity. Freud held that human beings are bisexual and that the oral, anal and early phallic stages were essentially the same in boys and girls. Only after the child's sexual curiosity leads to the discovery that females are without a penis does further development take divergent paths (Freud 1925). Within the context of love/hate feelings for the parents in the Oedipus Complex the young boy renounces his desires for his mother in fear that his father may deprive him of his penis and the young girl is alleged to turn away from her mother in disappointment that she too is without. Ever since Freud proposed the concept of penis envy it has been controversial (Sayers 1982).

Melanie Klein extended psychoanalysis as a therapeutic technique in the treatment of very young children. She provided them with carefully chosen play material, including small models of animals and people, with which they represented their inner world (Segal 1979). Klein worked intitially within Freud's later theory of instinct, that of Eros and Thanatos or sexual and destructive instincts, but emphasized the latter more than did classical Freudian theory. From her work with young children she evolved an elaborate account of pre-oedipal development.

Moving beyond the stages of oral, anal and genital organization Klein proposed two constellations of processes, or positions as she called them. The earliest was described as the paranoid–schizoid position which characterized development in the first few months of life. The inner phantasy world of the infant was described as being unstable, made up of part objects, e.g. breasts, penises, but not the whole person of the parents. Denial, splitting into affectively good and bad, projection of the bad outward and introjection of the good were seen as dominant thought processes of the paranoid–schizoid position. These functions are metaphorically linked with the infant's bodily processes – ingestion, defecation, etc. Klein used concepts such as good and bad breasts to characterize the inner, phantasy world of the infant. That objects are not yet constituted as the symbolic wholes of the second year is an important aspect of early development and of paranoid–schizoid thought processes.

Klein suggested that by the middle of the first year the infant began to recognize that good and bad part objects emanated from a common source. The overwhelming greed for the good and the terrifying fear of the bad persecutory part object were thus moderated. The term "depressive position" marks the infant's dawning awareness of the permanence of its objects and its ambivalence about the consequences of its desires in relation to these objects.

Klein's work on pre-oedipal development led to modifications in her views of gender identity. She described the origins of the Oedipus Complex in the first year of life and held that the development of boys and girls differed. Not only were girls not phallic in the same sense as boys but she described them as more passively oral and with an early awareness of the vagina. Her views have stirred a great deal of controversy within the psychoanalytic community (Segal 1979) but through her therapeutic work with very disturbed young children and her willingness to speculate about early mental processes she has enriched genetic theory.

The treatment and study of children was also pioneered by Anna Freud, who worked within the theoretical system created by her father and developed the later topographical model, elaborating the function of the ego (1937). Careful descriptions of normal development were provided by her and her colleagues at the Hampstead Clinic (1966).

The function of infant and child observation in the construction and modification of psychoanalytic developmental theory has been a challenging one. Winnicott (1957) suggested that reconstructive work with patients provided insights about deep processes while observation offered information on early environmental events and functioned as a corrective indicating limits to infant capabilities. Nonetheless observation is not a substitute for reconstructive creation.

In recent years the extensive observation studies of Mahler and her co-workers (1975) have had an impact both on psychoanalytic and academic psychology. They describe stages of normal autism and normal symbiosis which occur prior to the psychological birth of the infant about five months after its physiological birth. The further development of self and other representations is detailed in four sub-phases of the separation–individuation process. These are – differentiation and body image development, practicing, rapprochment and consolidation of self plus initial emotional object constancy. Reopening the issue of the relationship between reconstructive interpretation, the hallmark of genetic theory, and infant observation, Peterfreund (1978) has criticized Mahler's group for overextending clinical insights in creating concepts to explain infant behavior. Indeed, he characterizes the contemporary metapsychological edifice as lacking firm roots in biology and evolutionary thinking. If Peterfreund is correct, it is a curious reflection on its creator, Sigmund Freud, whom Sulloway (1979) has described as a "crypto-biologist" and on his followers' difficulties in maintaining the complex, interactional theory he proposed. BBL

Bibliography

Freud, Anna 1937: *The ego and the mechanisms of defence.* London: Hogarth Press; New York: International Universities Press.

——— 1966: *Normality and pathology in childhood: assessments of development.* London: Hogarth Press; New York: International Universities Press.

Freud, Sigmund: *Standard edition of the complete psychological works.* Interpretation of dreams, vols. 4 & 5 (1953); Theory of sexuality, vol. 7 (1953); *The Ego and the Id*, vol. 19 (1961); Anatomical distinction between the sexes, vol. 29 (1961)' Outline of psychoanalysis, vol. 23 (1964). London: Hogarth Press; New York: Norton.

Greenspan, S.I. 1979: *Intelligence and adaptation: an integration of psychoanalytic and Piagetian developmental psychology. Psychological issues*, vol. 12, nos 3/4, Monograph 47/48. New York: International Universities Press.

Laplanche, J. and Pontalis, J-B. 1973: *The language of psychoanalysis.* London: Hogarth Press; New York: Norton, 1974.

Mahler, M.S., Pine, F. and Bergman, A. 1975: *The psychological birth of the human infant.* New York: Basic Books; London: Hutchinson.

Peterfreund, E. 1978: Some critical comments on psychoanalytic conceptualizations of infancy. *International journal of psychoanalysis* 59, 427–41.

Rapaport, A.D. 1960: Psychoanalysis as a developmental psychology. In B. Kaplan and S. Wapner eds. *Perspectives in psychological theory: essays in honor of Heinz Werner.* New York: International Universities Press.

Sayers, J. 1982: *Biological politics: feminist and anti-feminist perspectives.* London and New York: Tavistock.

Segal, H. 1979: *Klein.* Glasgow: Fontana/Collins; New York: Viking Press, 1980.

Sulloway, F.J. 1979: *Freud, biologist of the mind.* London: Burnett Books & André Deutsch; New York: Basic Books.

Winnicott, D.W. 1957: On the contribution of direct child observation to psychoanalysis. In *The maturational processes and the facilitating environment.* New York: International Universities Press; London: Hogarth Press (1965).

development of motor skills Qualitative and quantitative changes in a child's motor skill repertoire as a function of age. As they grow older, children gradually acquire a broad repertoire of motor skills. Some skills emerge more-or-less spontaneously and are later perfected with practice. For example a normal child eventually begins to walk whether or not it is actively encouraged to do so. Once on its feet, it becomes more adroit in locomotion, moving around at various speeds in a changing environment. As another example, a child will spontaneously reach for and grasp an object. This fairly rudimentary act of prehension gradually becomes perfected so that the position of the fingers and the force exerted can be delicately varied depending on the shape and the nature of the object being grasped. Such skills, emerging perhaps through mimicry (see IMITATION), but without the need for specific tuition, may be termed endogenous skills. They are acquired quite early in life and there is a marked stereotypy among normal children in their basic motor repertoire and in the order of appearance of individual skills.

Other skills tend to emerge in response to a demand by an external agent such as a parent, teacher or another child, and are perfected only if there is deliberate practice. For example, a child can learn to modify its basic pattern of locomotion for skipping and dancing. Similarly, rudimentary finger and hand movements can be modified and greatly elaborated in the acquisition of hand-writing, and the playing of a musical instrument. These skills, which come to be superimposed on the basic repertoire, may be termed exogenous. They are acquired later in life, and normal children vary greatly in the number and the degree of perfection of such skills.

It is relatively easy to measure the motoric development of children. There are two basic methods. The first involves the careful observation of a child moving freely in its natural environment, and noting how it manages the everyday tasks of locomotion, prehension, dressing and feeding. Developmental expectations can be established from observing many children. Parts of the assessment described by Gesell and Amatruda (1947) and Griffiths (1970) employ such a methodology. The advantage of an observational method is that one can be confident of examining "environmentally valid" behavior; that is, one is looking directly at the motor tasks that are of importance to the child. The disadvantage is that objective measurement of the quality of a child's performance is rarely achieved. The second method of measurement is to set up laboratory tasks that are relevant to everyday tasks demanded of a child, and ask it to perform under standard conditions (Bruininks 1978; McCarthy 1972). The advantages here are that the conditions of the task are relatively easy to control, performance can be objectively measured, and developmental norms can be established. The disadvantages are that it is difficult to choose test items that are relevant to everyday tasks, and even if they are relevant, a child's performance in the laboratory may not reflect its usual behavior (see DEVELOPMENT, METHODS OF STUDY).

While it is possible to observe and measure motoric development in children it is not at all easy to account for that development, and for the marked individual differences typically seen at each age. At the base of the problem is our incomplete understanding of what determines skilled motor behavior. For example it is relatively easy to demonstrate a developmental progression in the skill of ball catching. Two-year-old children are generally very poor at catching. If you throw a ball to a child, it does not seem to track the movement visually and does not prepare its motor response in advance of the arrival of the ball. It begins its response too late and the ball is dropped. By three to four years of age, children begin to track the movement of the ball, some anticipatory arm movements are made, and there is partial success in catching. By six to seven years of age, eye-tracking of the ball and anticipatory movements of the arms and hands are accurate. Body and hand movements are appropriately timed and placed. While young children are not good at predicting the movement of fast moving objects and making quick anticipatory movements, they can catch slow moving objects (such as a balloon).

Clearly, one has to look further than just the motor response to account for this kind of developmental progression. While a detailed task analysis of motor skills is not appropriate here, a brief account of ball catching will help to illustrate the point that motor behavior and therefore development, depends on a complex of perceptual, attentional, cognitive and motor subskills (see PERCEPTUAL AND COGNITIVE ABILITIES IN INFANCY; PERCEPTUAL DEVELOPMENT; ATTENTION IN INFANTS; COGNITIVE DEVELOPMENT). Briefly, a child must visually track the movement of a ball, attend to and comprehend its speed and trajectory, and make predicitions about its future locations. (See CROSS-MODAL DEVELOPMENT). Finally there has to be a quick grasping action of the hands and fingers at the moment of impact with the ball. Young children seem able to predict movement and formulate anticipatory responses, albeit too slowly for ball catching.

Detailed task analyses of different motor skills could highlight a number of different types of perceptual, cognitive and motor subskills contributing to performance. Each skill would have its own set of subskills, but any one subskill would be involved in a wide range of motor skills. The elucidation of the common and unique factors underlying skilled motor behavior could help in the understanding of motor-skill development, though any suggestion that performance of the whole task is simply due to the additive contribution of a number of underlying factors would be an oversimplification. It is more likely that the different factors interact in their combined contribution to skilled motor performance.

From the above considerations it becomes clear that what we observe as a progressive change in a child's motor skill repertoire might be better termed perceptual-motor development. This point can be illustrated with a study that shows a link between the development of ability to perceive and memorize kinesthetic information and the ability to write and draw. It has been shown that training a child's kinesthetic perceptual ability results in improved drawing and writing (Laszlo and Bairstow 1983).

Given the complexity of behavioral factors determining skilled motor behavior, questions relating to possible underlying neurological factors are difficult to answer, or even formulate. A computer metaphor is useful though imperfect. As a child develops there are various genetically determined "hardware" changes in the neural-network of the central nervous system (see DEVELOPMENT OF THE NERVOUS SYSTEM) in addition to other demonstrable physical changes in the structure of a child's body. These changes may critically determine the time and order of appearance of various endogenous skills. The physical structure of the body must ultimately determine the limits to skilled motor behavior at any given age, albeit in poorly understood ways. In addition it is likely that there are "software" changes in the central nervous system. A "functional structure" is superimposed on the basic physical structure of the central nervous system as a result of practicing motor skills, experiencing the sensory consequences, and receiving the concomitant rewards and punishments. These changes may underlie the appearance of exogenous skills. The metaphor breaks down when considering the longer term effects of practice and experience: the perceptual-motor experiences of a child may well (in turn) determine "hardware" changes taking place within the developing central nervous system.

Further studies of the development of motor skills need to proceed along two broad lines. The first should aim at an understanding of the behavioral factors underlying and determining skilled motor behavior, so enabling an examination of the relevant developmental changes in a child's behavior. The second would aim at elucidating the neurological bases for the development of perceptual-motor skills. If the behavioral and neurological processes behind the developmental progression were understood, developmental and other abnormalities in the skilled behavior of young children could be differentially diagnosed. PJB

Bibliography

Bruininks, R.H. 1978: *Bruininks-Oseretsky test of motor proficiency*, Circle Pines, Minnesota: American Guidance Service.

*Connolly, Kevin, ed. 1970: *Mechanisms of motor skill development*. London and New York: Academic Press.

Gesell, Arnold L. and Amatruda, Catherine S. 1947: *Developmental diagnosis*. 2nd edn. New York: Hoeber.

Griffiths, B. 1970: *The abilities of young children: a comprehensive system of mental measurement for the first eight years of life*. London: Child Development Research Centre.

Laszlo, J.I. and Bairstow, P.J. 1983: Kinaesthesis: its measurement, training and relationship with motor control. *Quarterly journal of experimental psychology*.

*Legge, David and Barber, Paul J. 1976: *Information and skill*. London and New York: Methuen.

McCarthy, D. 1972: *McCarthy scales of children's abilities*. New York: Psychological Corporation.

development of the nervous system The growing ability of the nervous system to coordinate the organism's responses to simple and complex stimuli, together with the structural and physiological changes on which this ability depends. Development is most dramatic during intra-uterine and early postnatal life. This discussion will be confined to the central nervous system and excludes physiological topics which are too complex for the space available (see also BRAIN AND CENTRAL NERVOUS SYSTEM ILLUSTRATIONS, figs. 5 and 6).

Gross Structure

Two and a half weeks after conception the disk-shaped human embryo is less than 1mm in diameter. Some cells on the dorsal surface fold to form a gutter-like "neural groove". Adjacent cells multiply and form raised walls whose top edges bend toward each other and fuse to form the neural tube, the front end of which dilates to form the brain while the remainder gives rise to the spinal cord.

Six weeks after conception five separate regions can be identified in the enlarged front end of the neural tube (Patten 1968). The hindmost will become the medulla oblongata, the next will become the pons and in front of this lies the mesencephalon or mid-brain (fig. 5).

In front of the mid-brain lies the forebrain which is itself divided into the diencephalon, in which the THALAMUS and HYPOTHALAMUS will eventually develop, and two enlargements which will become the cerebral hemispheres.

During infancy the brain grows rapidly but at a steadily decreasing rate. The brain stem, i.e. the mid-brain, pons and medulla oblongata, which contain centers essential for the maintenance of life, are quite well advanced in growth by the time of birth and show very little increase in size after the end of the first year. Nearly half the postnatal growth of the cerebral hemispheres has usually been completed by the end of the first year and they are close to their adult size by the tenth year. This growth is largely due to increase in volume of the white matter.

Cellular Structure

Multiplication of 'neuroblast' cells which will develop into neurons is most prominent from the tenth to eighteenth weeks after gestation (Dobbing 1981). The neurons grow rapidly through the remainder of pregnancy while cell multiplication declines. In late intra-uterine life, and during the first four years or so after birth, elaboration of dendritic processes (see DENDRITES) is associated with development of increasing neuronal function. Simultaneously, proliferation of the glial cells (see GLIA) continuing to the second postnatal year (Dobbing and Sands 1973), provides the main connective and supporting structure of the brain.

Myelinization begins at about the fourth fetal month, in the dorsal and ventral roots of the spinal cord. The fibers connecting higher centers in the cerebral hemispheres are generally later and some tracts are not completely myelinated for several years. After a fiber has become myelinated the thickness of the myelin sheath may continue to increase for a number of years.

The cerebral cortex develops rather slowly and it is not until the seventh fetal month that the six cell layers characteristic of the adult are apparent.

While the brain is developing its biochemical and electrical characteristics are also changing. These changes continue beyond childhood.

The Development of Function

Evidence of the degree of functional development in the central nervous system of the early embryo is provided by its movements in response to stimuli. For example, closing of the hand when the palm is touched has been demonstrated during the third fetal month. At about nine weeks, touching the mouth with a fine hair leads to bending of the whole body whereas by twelve and a half weeks, the mouth closes when it is touched and, if the touch is repeated several times, the fetus will exhibit swallowing movements. Thus a general response is replaced by a localized one appropriate to the stimulus and requiring a more highly developed nervous system.

Infants born prematurely have been studied at the gestational age of twenty-eight weeks. (Saint-Anne Dargassies 1966). They close their eyes if a light is shone on them. Nerve pathways in the midbrain and pons, which would be essential for this response, must therefore be functioning. A loud noise will awaken the infant and cause generalized movement. There is evidence of a sense of smell at this stage and there may be some taste sensation. The rooting reflex, i.e. opening the mouth and turning the head towards a part of the face which is touched, and the walking reflex are also present. The latter is demonstrated by holding the baby upright with the feet on a flat surface and moving it forward. It will walk with high stepping movements. Thus the basic functional connections in the nervous system required for the movements of walking are well developed.

By thirty weeks the neuronal connections which allow the pupil to contract when a light is shone into the eye are established. The movements of sucking and swallowing are well coordinated in relation to breathing so that the infant can suck without choking. Also, the legs stiffen when the infant is held upright, an indication that the steady output of impulses from the lower end of the spinal cord, which will later be responsible for the maintenance of muscle tone, has begun.

Premature babies of thirty-two to thirty-five weeks' gestation usually appear much more alert than younger infants. This suggests that the "arousal" mechanism within the brain may be beginning to function. Improved coordination of movement shows further development within the nervous system.

When the prematurely born infant reaches a gestational age of forty-one weeks, it will follow a light with its eyes. This implies some form of vision but does not necessarily indicate that what the infant sees has great significance for it. It does suggest that further functional links have been established between the visual input to the brain and the outflow to the eye muscles. The infant tends to respond selectively to sounds such as that of the human voice. The differences in behavior between a child born at forty-one weeks and a premature infant who has reached this age are usually slight. Whether the infant has remained in utero or has been exposed to the external environment for the preceding month or two seems to have little effect on the development of the central nervous system. The movements of the newborn full term infant are largely reflexes but they become more controlled after about five or six months, as higher centers begin to process information and relate it to movement. Responses may be observed to many different stimuli, e.g. pain, touch or pressure, changes in temperature, taste, and certain odors.

By two months of age the visual system is sufficiently well developed to allow size and shape discrimination (Fantz and Miranda 1975). The vestibular apparatus, which provides the brain with information about the position and movement of the head in space, is functioning to some extent at birth but the child is usually ten or twelve weeks old before sensory input from the eyes, the vestibular apparatus and the receptor organs in the muscles and joints become fully integrated within the central nervous system. This integration is an essential basis for well controlled voluntary movement.

Infants over the age of twelve weeks show considerable variation in the rates at which their central nervous systems develop. Ages at which developmental "landmarks" are said to be reached are generalizations and many entirely normal children will reach them either earlier or later than the norm.

After the first three months the cerebral cortex begins to influence the postural reflexes which have recently become integrated. The action of the cortex is usually to inhibit these reflexes so that the child has more voluntary control of its posture.

Effective activity in the motor areas of the cerebral cortex is shown at about the fourth or fifth month by voluntary goal-directed movements, such as grasping at an object in the field of vision. These movements become increasingly skillful as the corpus striatum, motor cortex and pyramidal tracts develop further but even after two or three years the movements may still be clumsy.

The walking reflex, which is coordinated in the spinal cord, disappears completely some months before the infant begins to crawl or walk alone because it is inhibited by higher centers of the brain as these develop. The development of independent locomotion follows a sequence which reflects the order of maturation in the regions of the motor area of the cerebral cortex in which different parts of the body are represented. The infant can creep with the help of its arms before it can use its legs to crawl, stand or walk. (See also BRAIN MECHANISMS OF MOVEMENT.) WAM

Bibliography

*Dobbing, J. 1981: The later development of the brain and its vulnerability. In *Scientific foundations of paediatrics*, ed. J. Dobbing, and J.A. Davis. London: Heinemann.

Dobbing, J. and Sands, J. 1973: The quantitative growth and development of the human brain. *Archives of disease in childhood* 46, 757–767.

Fantz, R.L. and Miranda, S.B. 1975: Newborn infant attention to form and contour. *Child development* 46, 224.

Patten, Bradley M. 1968: *Human embryology*, 3rd edn. New York and Maidenhead: McGraw-Hill.

*Saint-Anne Dargassies, S. 1966: Neurological maturation of the premature infant of 28 to 41 weeks' gestational age. In *Human development*, ed. F. Faulkner, Philadelphia and London: Saunders.

development *See above, and also* cognitive development: moral d.; personality d.; perceptual d.; prenatal d.; cross-modal d.; emotional d.; sex differences in d.

developmental psychobiology Sometimes referred to as developmental biopsychology (e.g. Tobach et al. 1977) is the study of biological processes that determine and constitute the development of behavior and its psychological components. As its name suggests, developmental psychobiology represents an amalgamation of *developmental psychology* and *psychobiology*.

Developmental psychobiology encompasses all stages of life during which the foundations for behavior are established.

The roots of developmental psychobiology can be traced to the turn of the century when many ontogenetic issues were in the limelight of scientific debate. Experimental embryology had emerged as a discipline and from within it arose some model approaches to developmental studies that were to have broad and long-lasting influences. W. Preyer (1841 – 1897), in particular, attempted to unify developmental studies in physiology, neuroanatomy and behavior. Preyer's celebrated works included comparative studies of behavioral embryology and developmental studies of the maturation of children.

Charles Darwin (1809 – 1882) can also be seen as an early advocate and practitioner of developmental psychobiology. In particular, his *The expression of emotion in man and animals* (1872) reflects some of his views of developmental study as a tool to an understanding of comparative-evolutionary aspects of behavior, as well as the nature of brain-behavior relations. Claparéde (1911) was perhaps the first developmentalist to use the term "psychobiological" in his treatment of human attention, and asked "is that which really interests us, which holds us enthralled, always that which *ought* to interest us from the point of view of our preservation, from the biological point of view?" Thereafter, as Konner (1977) points out, most of the major advances in twentieth century developmental psychology, notably those associated with Freud, Piaget, Hall, Baldwin, Gesell, Carmichael, Bower, Bowlby and Brown have been based on biological constructs.

Links with evolutionary theory and genetics

The Darwinian framework was incorporated into the thinking of many developmental psychologists (e.g. Baldwin 1895) during the later nineteenth century. Their acceptance of evolutionary views was influenced by those of contemporary embryologists who suggested that individual development (ontogeny) appears to replay (or recapitulate) the evolutionary development of the species (its phylogeny). To apply to mental development the doctrine that "ontogeny *recapitulates* phylogeny", it was assumed by many early developmental psychologists that studying the psychological development of children would provide an account of the otherwise inaccessible phylogenetic evolution of the human mind. Today, most developmentalists do not accept such views. Instead of asking what modern children can tell us about human evolution, contemporary interest tends to focus on how the nature of childhood and the developmental rules which guide it have themselves evolved (Bruner 1972; Konner 1977).

Some psychobiologically-oriented researchers conduct developmental studies because they are interested in problems derived from ETHOLOGY, COMPARATIVE PSYCHOLOGY, or ANIMAL BEHAVIOR. Indeed, ethological and comparative traditions, as articulated by Konrad Lorenz, Niko Tinbergen, T. C. Schneirla and Daniel Lehrman, placed great value on ontogenetic analyses. In particular, one goal of such behavioral approaches is to clarify *adaptive or functional* aspects of behavior, that is, to understand the means by which behavioral traits enable organisms to meet various environmental challenges and in the face of such forces of natural selection be maintained or reinforced in the species' repertoire. From this tradition comes interest in the behavior and behavioral development of young in relation to their social and physical environments. Parent-offspring relationships, affiliative behavior, the organization of motor patterns, play, imitation, recognition of parents, kin, food, prey, and basic vegetative activities have, for example, been involved in studies of the adaptive aspects of behavioral development.

The function of developmental processes is in general the achievement of adult competence. The adaptive significance of some aspects of the behavior of young, then, may lie in converting neonatal competence to adult competence: it is thought to be the case for infantile play, for example, that adaptive benefits are realized *in later life*. By contrast, some of the behaviors of young may not perform this function at all, but instead have survival value *at that point* in development. Bowlby has proposed that one such function of the human infant's attachment to its parents has been protection from predators and other threats of the environmental "niche" experienced by the infant at this vulnerable stage in its life.

The development of species-typical behavior and its evolutionary implications brings with it an appreciation of and interest in *heritable* factors that are expressed in behavior. Thus, the field of BEHAVIOR GENETICS has a relevant alignment with developmental psychobiology. Heritability, however, is a parameter of populations, not individuals, so the role of some aspects of behavior genetics exists most precisely on the level of population characteristics. The historical persistence of the so-called "nature – nuture" controversy in developmental psychobiology can be understood, in part, as a problem that has been difficult to resolve because the adversaries in the controversy are often confronting one another with analyses that are appropriate either to individuals or to populations. Behavior genetics is, however, increasingly influenced by revelations of modern molecular biology and genetics.

The complexity of modern psychobiology: parent–offspring relations

Although developmental psychobiology has a tradition of comparative study that ranges across many species, mammalian development is emphasized. This can be understood in terms of its relevance to humans, and because mammalian offspring tend to present interesting ontogenetic pictures for study – their life histories usually include dramatic transformations from infancy to adulthood. It is possible to make such a generalization because mammals are defined, as a group, on the basis of common reproductive – developmental features: live birth and the provision of milk via specialized glands on the female's body. Mammary glands are an anatomical signpost for maternal behavior. The developmental psychobiology of mammals, therefore, necessarily includes the analysis of maternal behavior or, more accurately, *parental* behavior since in many species, including man, nurturance is provided by adults other than, and in addition to the mother. Parental behavior is, in fact, a prominent feature of the reproductive efforts of many non-mammalian animals, such as some species of fish and many species of birds.

The inclusion of parental behavior in the mandate of developmental psychobiology brings with it special conceptual and methodological demands. Parental behavior is not a static or fixed form of input. The quantity and quality of parental attention tends to change over time, usually in a manner suited to the developmental status of the offspring. It is important to recognize the *developmental* nature of parental care.

The concept of developmental synchrony is very important because it stimulates awareness of the existence of the different means by which such interindividual synchrony is achieved. The effect of a parent (caregiver) on the offspring and the effect of the offspring on the parent often must be analyzed separately in order to understand the nature of their *reciprocal* controls. Developmental studies have been enhanced considerably by ability to understand the mechanisms of interactions within dyads, such as parent – offspring units.

Links with neuroscience

The problems and methods of contemporary psychobiology, physiological psychology, and the neurosciences in general, contribute to the scope and conduct of developmental psychobiology. Developmental analyses continue to be applied as *tools* to study other processes. Thus, many topics of psychobiological interest, such as learning and memory, feeding and drinking behavior, sensory processes, sleep, reproductive behavior and communication, are studied developmentally, with the aim of learning more about each problem as a result of better understanding the factors that contribute to its development.

In addition, the *methods* of contemporary neuroscience have influenced the conduct of the developmental work. In some instances a new technology has been applied to a developmental problem. This would include, for instance, basic studies of the development of neurochemical systems of the brain, behavioral pharmacology in immature animals, and neuroanatomical studies of the developing nervous system. Some of these efforts resemble or are identical to research in developmental neurobiology, a closely-aligned discipline which is best discriminated from developmental psychobiology by greater emphasis on intrinsic properties of neural tissue and systems, rather than in their relations to behavior.

The application of modern anatomical and physiological techniques of neurobiology to behaviorally-oriented investigations is usually done through "descriptive – correlative" studies, which are typical of preliminary analyses. In developmental psychobiology there are several significant examples of this approach. Neural changes during development have been described with the aid of numerous neurobiological measures, ranging from molar levels of analysis such as brain size, cortical depth and myelination patterns, to more molecular analyses such as neuronal counts, cell size and shape, or arrangement of dendritic spines. Such morphological measures are then correlated with onset of function or level of performance. Alternatively, the same kinds of neural measures can be used correlatively to assess the consequences of different early environmental conditions for rate or level of neural development.

Relevance of early experience

Ontogenetic stages during which behavior and/or morphology undergo rapid or dramatic changes are, generally speaking, especially attractive to developmental psychobiologists. It is generally believed that periods of rapid changes are more susceptible to extrinsic influences than are ontogenetic stages of stability. The assumption is that living systems in the process of reorganization or change are more easily affected by environmental events, natural or artificial, than are systems that are operating in a relatively steady state. It is for this reason, at least in part, that developmental psychobiologists are attracted to analyses of "early experience", because the "early" period is usually part of the postnatal phase when development is rapid and dramatic.

The same assumptions that highlight early life as an important period during which development is shaped, also apply to the study of the early influence of toxins or teratogens (substances that can have detrimental effects on the organism). Hence, the methods and data of developmental psychobiology are often relevant to toxicologists and teratologists interested in some organismic effects of a toxin. Toxicologists who study, for instance, potentially harmful effects of drugs on developing animals are particularly aware of the special interpretive problems, particularly in organisms that engage in extensive parent – offspring interactions. The problem is that a drug can directly affect the young organism in at least two different ways. First, the drug can act directly on the organ systems of the young animal, and perhaps have more dramatic effects than on an adult, whose tissue is less susceptible to perturbation. The second potential source of effect is less direct but can be as significant. Alterations in physical or behavioral characteristics of offspring can produce changes in the quantity or quality of parental care. Moreover, many aspects of parental care are determined, in part, by responses to proximate cues from the offspring. Drug effects, even transient ones, can affect the parent's response which, in turn, can alter the condition of the young. These effects can produce chains of interaction that can extend beyond the immediate drug effect, in time and in kind of action. JRA/AW

Bibliography

Baldwin, J.M. 1895: *Mental development in the child and in the race.* London: Macmillan.

Bateson, P.P.G. 1981: "Ontogeny." In *The Oxford companion to animal behavior*, ed. MacFarland, D.J. Oxford and New York: Oxford University Press.

Bruner, J. 1972: The nature and uses of immaturity. *American psychologist*, 27. 687 – 708.

Claparède, E. 1910 (*1911*): *Experimental pedagogy and the psychology of the child.* London.

Darwin, C. 1877: A biographical sketch of an infant. *Mind*. 2, 285–94.

Gould, S.J. 1977: *Ontogeny and phylogeny*. London: Belknap.

Hofer, M.A. 1981: *The roots of human behavior*. London: Freeman.

Konner, M. 1977: Evolution of human behavior development. In *Culture and infancy*. ed. P.H. Leiderman, S.R. Tulkin and A. Rosenfeld. London and New York: Academic Press.

Piaget, J. 1967 (*1971*): *Biology and knowledge*. Edinburgh: Edinburgh University Press; Chicago: University of Chicago Press.

Tobach, E., Aronson, L.R. and Shaw, E. 1971: *The biopsychology of development*. London and New York: Academic Press.

Trevarthen, C. 1980: Neurological development and the growth of psychological functions. In *Developmental psychology and society*, ed. J. Sarts. London and New York: Macmillan.

developmental psychology: methods of study

Developmental psychology is the study of the remarkable changes in behavior which happen as people grow older. These changes have been charted from the first moments in life, and though most of our current information about developmental changes concerns children, developmental psychology is also about the changes which take place during adulthood, since it is clear that in many ways older adults think and behave differently from younger ones.

Broadly speaking developmental psychology has two independent aims. The first is to describe what developments there are: the psychologist sets out to establish what sort of things, for example, a six-month-old child does and is capable of doing, and how these differ from a one-year-old's behavior and capacities. The second aim is to discover the causes of developmental differences. What is it, the developmental psychologist must ask, that leads a one-year-old child to behave so differently from a six-month-old?

To discover a developmental change psychologists have to compare people at different ages. There are two quite different ways of doing this, longitudinal and cross-sectional. Longitudinal studies follow the same people over time, and plot how their behavior changes as they grow older. For example a study in which a group of children is seen just before they go to school and then several times again in their ensuing school years (there are several such studies) would be a longitudinal one. The great advantage of this type of research is that one can be reasonably sure that any behavioral change that is discovered is genuinely developmental. The only room for doubt is the possibility that testing the same child several times could artificially induce a change. But the major disadvantages of the longitudinal approach are practical ones. Such studies usually take many years, are expensive, and make great administrative demands in the area of keeping in touch with all the people involved. Furthermore losing participants is itself a major hazard. Even well organized projects sometimes end up with a small fraction of their original groups, and this of course raises the danger that there is some unknown underlying difference between the two groups (those remaining and those lost) which the study would not reveal and which might make its results at best biassed and at worst wrong. A final reason why psychologists are often wary of longitudinal studies is their fear that after several years' hard work the results might not support the original hypothesis or even suggest a new one. Put together, these problems raise a considerable barrier for anyone considering doing longitudinal research, and this is probably why there are relatively few such studies. Most of the information about child development that is currently being produced relies on the other approach – cross-sectional research. This is a pity because cross-sectional studies also have their problems, and from the point of view of establishing developmental changes they are probably more serious.

Cross-sectional studies deal with different people in different age groups. An example of a cross-sectional study is one in which different age groups of five-, six-, seven- and eight-year-old children are given Piaget's well known conservation problem in two ways, and it is found that the two younger groups fail in one condition but succeed in another, while the older groups succeed in both conditions. This is a typical example of a cross-sectional study which though it spans four years of childhood can be completed within a matter of weeks. The advantages therefore are clear. Information is obtained very quickly, and if the study for one reason or another does not work very little time has been lost. But there are difficulties, and the major one is the awkward question whether the differences that emerge between different age groups are genuinely developmental ones. It is always possible that the five- and six-year-olds for example in any cross-sectional study are different from each other for quite other reasons than their age. If the project takes place in one school as such studies often do, it could be that the two age groups have had different teachers or different types of experience which have nothing to do with their ages.

It can be seen that the strengths and weaknesses of the two approaches are to a great extent complementary. Longitudinal differences are genuinely developmental apart from the problem of the effects of repeated testing, while the one advantage of cross-sectional research, apart from its practical convenience, is that it does not have this particular problem. The ideal solution, which is tried very rarely indeed, is to combine the two.

We can now turn to the actual methods used. *Observation* is the oldest, most tried method in developmental psychology. The first major insights in the subject came from the so called "baby diaries" in which parents reported on their children's progress during the first few years. The best known of these is the meticulous account written by Darwin of one of his own children. As psychology developed in the early twentieth century people began to produce observational studies of older children and of children other than their own. The method was used to study both intellectual and emotional development, and it is probably the case that most studies in child psychology up to the beginning of the second world war were observational ones. But the method was less used after 1945 partly because of the growing popularity of the experimental method, but partly too because there seemed to be a general vagueness in observational reports. The trouble mainly centered around the lack of objective criteria. If a psychologist was reporting his observations on, say, aggressive behavior, there seemed to be no check at all that his use of the term was the same as everybody else's.

The problem of objective criteria was taken up by "child ethologists" in the 1960s. Their answer, adopting methods used to study animals in their natural habitats, was to make no assumptions at all about broad categories such as aggression, but to record smaller, objectively defined pieces of behavior such as particular arm or face movements. Once these are recorded one can, using rather complex statistical procedures, see how particular acts hang together. From these consistent patterns one can infer and define the broader categories objectively. Using this method ethologists have shown that there are at least two types of apparently aggressive behavior in young children. One is genuinely aggressive, while the other, called 'rough and tumble play' is playful and not meant to hurt.

Although the first systematic reports of developmental changes were observational, the method which finally established the subject as a separate entity was undoubtedly the psychometric test. This we owe to the distinguished child psychologist Alfred Binet, who was commissioned to produce an effective intelligence test, and did so by devising a set of ingenious problems for which the main criterion was that they should be developmentally sensitive. Binet only included items which were more likely to be answered by older than by younger children. His reason for this was that whatever intelligence may be it probably increases during childhood. His method worked; at any rate it was a pragmatic success because it predicted educational progress reasonably well, and still does so. But it obviously had important theoretical connotations as well, and one of these was that it highlighted in a very systematic way the extraordinary differences in the things which young and old children can manage to do. Here for the first time was an objective demonstration of development, and more such demonstrations came thick and fast during the ensuing years.

Although these tests dramatically established a question (as well as making useful predictions about individual children) they did little, however, to provide any answer. This was the challenge taken up by experimental psychology. Experimenters also give "tests", but they can administer the same test under several different conditions, and this allows them to look at hypotheses about what underlies the often curious things that children do. The experimental method nowadays dominates child psychology, and it has made notable advances. It is to experiments that we owe, since the pioneering work of Fantz in the 1950s, the demonstration that infants can perceive and can understand a great deal more than had been generally suspected till then. Most of Piaget's best known work comes in the form of experiments, and it has been a mixture of experiments and observation which has been mainly responsible for the significant progress made in studies of the development of language over the last twenty years or so. Experiments have also helped to test theories about what causes developmental changes. If, for example, it is thought that the learning of a particular aspect of language changes the child's understanding of his environment, a very useful way of testing this would be to train children in the type of language in question and see whether this leads to any change in intellectual development. Provided the experiment is well controlled one then has a good test of the causal hypothesis. The only difficulty is that the experiment might not represent real life relationships, and so it is probably best to combine this method with others which do establish that the relationships are genuine ones.

The great advantage of experimental psychology is that it puts the psychologist in control: he can test his hypothesis by stipulating exactly what the different conditions will be in his experiments. But this is also its great disadvantage, because it means that the circumstances of the experiment often risk being artificial: to ask a child to bite on a board and then cover his head with extremely heavy equipment in order to study the movements of his eyes is splendidly scientific but it must be borne in mind that the procedure itself may influence what the child does with his eyes. Yet there seems to be little that can be done about this danger, apart from being aware of it, minimizing it where possible, and trusting in the end to the development of less intrusive techniques.

The artificiality of the experimental method has been noted by the child ethologists mentioned earlier and also by those who use more clincial methods. One that has a powerful and useful influence in child psychology is the questionnaire. Questionnaires held a very important place in child psychology during the 1950s when they were used in particular to study the ways in which children were treated by their parents. The well known study by Sears, Maccoby and Levin is a good example. These studies tended to relate the parents' behavior to the child's intellectual and emotional development. Too often, however, they assumed that any correlation must, so far as cause and effect are concerned, be one-way, and that the parents affect the child rather than the other way round. Recently, however, partly as the result of the impressive evidence from experiments that children are in many ways more aware of what is going on and more in control than had been believed earlier, it has been accepted that it could equally well be that the child is determining the parents' behavior. This makes the study of relationships between parent and child both more interesting and more difficult. Another use of questionnaires is more clinical; they have been developed, most notably by Michael Rutter, to study disturbances in childhood. There is no doubt that the answers to these questionnaires, which are usually given to parents or to teachers, do produce extremely valuable information about the problems of development. One of the most promising possibilities in child psychology is that this kind of information will be related to direct observation of the children and also to data from experiments. Indeed combining different methods is almost certainly the best way to answer most of the problems of child psychology. Longitudinal and cross-sectional studies should be done together; training studies should be combined with correlations and experiments with data from naturalistic observation and from questionnaires. None of the main methods of child psychology is perfect, but their strengths and weaknesses are often complementary. They should be used together.

PEB

Bibliography

Mussen, Paul H., ed. 1970: *Carmichael's manual of child psychology*. 2 vols. 3rd edn. New York and Chichester; John Wiley.

Vasta, Ross 1979: *Studying children: an introduction to research methods*. San Francisco: W.H. Freeman.

dialect The word is used to refer to socially or geographically determined subcodes of a language. The usefulness of the notion of dialect has increasingly come under attack because

(1) linguistic subcodes fail to correlate with pre-established social and geographical boundaries, i.e. they are not entities bounded by isoglossic bundles;

(2) it ignores the importance of a number of significant factors, in particular those of a socio-psychological nature involving linguistic differences and linguistic variation; and

(3) the criteria used in defining dialects (e.g. tests involving mutual intelligibility, shared vocabulary of social status) fail to yield unambiguous results.

Similar criticism has been levelled against the notions of SOCIOLECT and CODE. PM

Bibliography

Bailey, C.-J.N. 1977: Conceptualizing dialects as implicational constellations rather than as entities bounded by isoglossic bundles. Paper presented at *Internationales Symposium zur Theorie de Dialektes*, to appear in *Zeitschrift für Dialektologie und Linguistik* 26.

dialectic theory In its most general sense, dialectic has come to signify any more or less intricate process of conceptual or social conflict, interconnection and change, in which the generation, interpenetration and clash of oppositions, leading to their transcendence in a fuller or more adequate mode of thought or form of life, plays a key role. But dialectic is itself one of the most complex – and contested – concepts in the story of philosophical and social thought. The most important historical figures for the contemporary human sciences in this conceptual area are undoubtedly Karl Marx (1818–83) and G.W.F. Hegel (1770–1831), but Marx's dialectic cannot be understood in abstraction from its relation to Hegel's, and to understand Hegel's one must go back to the roots of western culture in ancient Greek thought.

Derived from the Greek verb meaning "to converse (or discourse)" Aristotle (384–322 BC) credited Zeno of Elea (464 BC) with the invention of the term dialectic, in his famous paradoxes (e.g. of motion) which were designed to refute his antagonists' hypotheses by drawing intuitively unacceptable conclusions from them. But the term was first generally applied to Socrates's mode of argument, or *elenchus*, which was differentiated from the Sophistic *eristic*, or art of disputation for the sake of rhetorical success, by the orientation of the Socratic dialogue towards the disinterested pursuit of truth. Plato (429–348 BC) himself regarded dialectic as the supreme philosophic method – the "coping-stone of the sciences" – using it to designate both the definition of ideas by genus and species (founding logic) and their interconnection in the light of a single principle, the Form of the Good (founding metaphysics). Aristotle's opinion of dialectic was considerably less exalted. For him dialectic was at best a propadeutic to the syllogistic reasoning expounded in his *Analytics*, in as much as, unlike the latter, it was based on premises which were merely probable, depending upon the agreement of the interlocutors. The sense of conversational interplay, involving the assertion and contradiction of theses, was retained in the practice of medieval disputation; and it was this sense that was probably most familiar to Kant (1724–1804) who also took over the Aristotelian conception of dialectic as relying upon inadequate premises and his dialectical/analytical contrast. For Kant, dialectic was that part of transcendental logic which showed the mutually contradictory or antinomic state in which the intellect fell when not harnessed to the data of experience. This spread of connotations of dialectic includes, then, argument and conflict, disputation, dialogue and exchange, but also enlightenment, demystification and the critique of illusion.

Hegel synthesized this Eleatic idea of dialectic as *reason* with another ancient strand, the Ionian idea of dialectic as *process* in his idea of dialectic as a self-generating, self-differentiating and self-particularizing *process of reason*. The second idea typically assumed a dual form, in an *ascending* dialectic, the existence of a high reality (e.g. the Forms or God) was demonstrated; and in a *descending* dialectic, its manifestation in the phenomenal world was explained.

Combination of the ascending and descending phases results in a quasi-temporal pattern of original unity, loss or division and return or reunification (graphically portrayed in Schiller's influential *Letters on the aesthetic education of mankind* (1794–5)) or a quasi-logical pattern of hypostasis and actualization. Combination of the Eleatic and Ionian strands yields the Hegelian Absolute – a logical process or *dialectic* which actualizes itself by alienating itself and which restores its self-unity by recognizing this alienation as nothing other than its own free expression or manifestation; and which is recapitulated and completed as the Hegelian System itself.

However, in addition to dialectic as a logical process, there is another inflection of the dialectic in Hegel, in which it is conceived, more narrowly, as the dynamo of this process, the second, essentially negative, moment of "actual thought". Hegel styles this moment as the "grasping of opposites in their unity or of the positive in the negative" (1969 edn., p.56). Dialectic in this narrower sense is the method which enables the dialectical commentator to observe the process by which categories, notions or forms of consciousness arise out of each other to form ever more inclusive totalities, until the system of categories, notions or forms as a whole is completed. For Hegel truth is the whole and error lies in one-sidedness, incompleteness and abstraction: its symptom is the contradictions it generates and its cure their incorporation into fuller, richer, more concrete and highly mediated conceptual forms. In the course of this process the famous principle of *sublation* is observed: as the dialectic unfolds no partial insight is ever lost. In fact the Hegelian dialectic progresses in two basic modes: by bringing out what is implicit, but not explicitly articulated, in some notion; or by repairing some want, lack or inadequacy in it.

"Dialectical", in contrast to "reflective" (or analytical), thought grasps conceptual forms in their systematic interconnections, not just their determinate differences and conceives each development as the product of a previous, less developed phase, whose necessary truth or fulfillment it is; so that there is always a tension, latent irony or incipient surprise between any form and what it is in the process of becoming.

Four main issues have dominated intellectual controversy about dialectic in the Marxist idiom: the difference between the Marxian ("materialist") and Hegelian dialectics, the role of the dialectic within Marx's work, and more broadly in any Marxian social science, the compatability of dialectics with formal logic, materialism, scientific practice and rationality generally; and the status of Engels's attempt to extend Marx's dialectic from the historical realm to encompass nature and the whole of being generally.

After his brilliant early analyses of its mystified logic and idealist concept of labor in 1843–44, Marx's critique of the Hegelian dialectic became subsumed in the works of 1844–47 under a ferocious polemical assault on speculative philosophy. But from the time of the *Grundrisse* (1857–8) on, a definite positive re-evaluation of the Hegelian dialectic occurs. The extent of this remains a matter of live controversy. But two points seem indisputable: that Marx continued to be critical of the Hegelian dialectic as such and yet believed himself to be working with a dialectic related to the Hegelian one. Thus he writes in the 1873 Afterword to *Capital* vol. I that "the mystification which the dialectic suffers in Hegel's hands by no means prevents him from being the first to present its general forms of motion in a comprehensive and conscious manner. With him it is standing on its head. It must be inverted to discover the rational kernel within the mystical shell" (Marx 1976, p.103). These two metaphors – of the inversion and the kernel – do seem to indicate that Marx thought it possible to extract part of the Hegelian dialectic without being compromised by Hegel's idealism.

For Marx, following Feuerbach here, infinite mind is nothing but the illusory projection of (alienated) finite beings and nature is transcendentally real. Thus Marx replaces Hegel's immanent spiritual ideology or *Geistodyssey* of infinite, petrified and finite mind (represented by logic, nature and spirit) with a methodological commitment to the empirically-controlled investigation of the causal relations within and between historically emergent, developing humanity and irreducibly real, but modifiable nature.

In his later work Marx often uses "dialectical" in close association with, or even just as a synonym for, "scientific". He understood his dialectic as *scientific*, because it set out to explain the contradictions in thought and the crises of socio-economic life in terms of the particular contradictory essential relations generating them; as *historical*, because it was both rooted in, and (conditionally) an agent of, the changes in the very relations and circumstances it described; as *critical*, because it demonstrated the historical conditions of validity and limits of adequacy of the categories, doctrines, practices and forms of life it explained; and as *systematic*, because it sought to trace the various historical tendencies and contradictions of capitalism back to certain structurally constitutive contradictions of its mode of production.

In the relationship between a feature of social life and its systematic misrepresentation (most generally, in IDEOLOGIES), there seems to be a species of contradiction analogous to that between a notion and its dialectical comment in Hegel. And it can be plausibly maintained that such an essence/appearance contradiction is susceptible of a purely analytical description, a possibility that is a condition of *any* human science.

The three most common positions on dialectics are that it is unintelligible nonsense, that it is universally applicable, and that it is applicable to the conceptual and/or social, but not the natural, domains. The second, universalist position must be problematic for a realist committed to the notion of the existence of nature independently of thought and for a materialist committed to the notion of its causal primacy. Yet Engels, underwriting both commitments, nevertheless took dialectic in its essentially Hegelian sense and sought to apply it to being as a whole. According to him, dialectics is "the science of the general laws of motion and development of nature, human society and thought" (1969 edn., p.169), laws which he identified as (1) the transformation of quantity into quality and vice-versa; (2) the interpenetration of opposites and (3) the negation of the negation. While Marx did not repudiate Engels's cosmology, his critique of political economy neither presupposes nor entails a dialectics of nature, and his critique of apriorism implies the a posteriori and subject-specific character of claims about the existence of dialectical, as other types of processes of reality.

The very supposition of a dialectics of nature has appeared to a line of critics from Lukács to Sartre as categorically mistaken, in as much as it involves anthropomorphically (and hence idealistically) retrojecting onto nature, categories, such as contradiction and negation, which only make sense in the human realm. Such critics do not deny that *natural science*, as part of the socio-historical world, may be dialectical; what is at stake is whether there can be a dialectics of *nature per se*. Obviously there are differences between the natural and social spheres. But are these specific differences more or less important than their generic similarities? In effect the problem of the dialectics of nature reduces to a variant of the general problem of naturalism, with the way it is resolved depending upon whether dialectics is conceived sufficiently broadly and the human world sufficiently naturalistically to make its extension to nature plausible.

Throughout its long and complex history, five basic strands of meaning in dialectic stand out:-
(1) *dialectical contradictions*, involving inclusive oppositions or forces of non-independent origins; (2) *dialectical* or discursive *argumentation*, oriented to the pursuit of groundable ideals; (3) *dialectical reason* which encompasses a spread of connotations ranging from that imaginative and conceptually flexible thinking which, under the discipline of empirical, logical and contextual constraints, plays such a crucial role in scientific development through

enlightenment and demystification to the depth rationality of emancipatory praxes; (4) *dialectical process*, involving a schema of original unity, historical diremption and eventual return, which is a recurrent and deep-rooted motif in western thought; (5) *dialectical intelligibility*, comprehending both the teleologically (in Hegel) or causally (in Marx) generated presentation of social and cultural forms (including beliefs) and their explanatory critique. In recent years there has been a tendency to return to the great classics of modern "dialectical theory", Hegel's *Phenomenology of spirit* (1807) and *Science of logic* (1812–16) and Marx's *Grundrisse* (1857–8) and *Capital* vol. I (1867). These will remain permanent resources for psychologists and other social scientists. But their critical assimilation, empirical exploitation and theoretical development have in the past been hindered by the conceptual confusions surrounding dialectics, and the political interest to which these confusions have, regrettably, become attached. RB

Bibliography

*Bhaskar, Roy 1983: *Dialectic, materialism and human emancipation.* London: New Left Books.

Engels, Frederick 1878 *(1969)*: *Anti-Duhring.* Moscow: Progress Publishers.

Hegel, G.W.F. 1812–16 *(1969)*: *Science of logic.* Trans A. Miller. London: George Allen and Unwin.

Marx, Karl 1867 *(1976)*: *Capital* Vol. I. Trans. B. Fowkes. London: New Left Review/Pelican.

———, and Engels, F. *(1975)*: *Selected correspondence.* Moscow: Progress Publishers.

diffusion *See* cultural diffusion

diglossia The term was made popular by Ferguson (1959). It refers to a situation in which two varieties of a language are used in different social functions or domains within a speech community. One of the better known instances is the use of the socially "low" popular dimotiki and the "high" katharevousa variety of Greek in present day Greece. High and low varieties are often associated with elaborated and restricted CODES respectively and the use of low varieties in education is a matter of considerable debate.

A strictly hierarchical social structure tends to perpetuate diglossic situations whereas social mobility and favorable linguistic attitudes towards other varieties lead to the development of a mesolectal continuum intermediate between the low basilect and the high acrolect (see SOCIOLECTS). PM

Bibliography

Ferguson, Charles A. 1959: Diglossia. *Word* 15, 325–40.

discourse analysis The study of regularities in the structure of linguistic units larger than a sentence. Early work of this type focussed upon how the internal parts of sentences are related to prior sentences in a particular discourse context: Pronouns, definite articles, and sentence beginnings such as "nevertheless" or "another thing" are intelligible only when the discourse establishes appropriate antecedents. The intonation of sentences, especially the differential stress among the words in it, is largely predictable on similar discourse grounds. Discourse analysis plays a pivotal role in the identification of syntactic, semantic, and pragmatic constituents within sentences (see SPEECH ACTS); examples include "given vs. new", "topic vs. comment", "subject vs. predicate", "presupposition vs. focus", and other closely intertwined distinctions.

More recent studies of longer stretches of discourse have revealed patterns that depend upon the functional properties of whole sentences and even of multi-sentence units. Conversations, for example, are analysable into "turns", with each turn categorizeable into such elements as "apologies", "insults", "excuses", and so forth. Furthermore, these units typically occur in so called "adjacency pairs": a greeting or compliment elicits an acknowledgement, an offer demands an acceptance or a rejection, a query requires a response. Other types of discourse, such as interviews, speeches, jokes, or stories, exhibit similar kinds of complex internal structure (see ETHNOGRAPHY OF SPEAKING). HSS

Bibliography

Edmonsen, C. 1981: *Spoken discourse.* London and New York: Longman.

discovery learning An approach to education which capitalizes on the child's natural curiosity and urge to explore the environment. The child learns by personal experience and experiment and this is thought to make memory more vivid and help in the transfer of knowledge to new situations. The method is especially widespread in primary school education and is associated with liberal educationalists such as Rousseau, Pestalozzi, Froebel, Dewey and Montessori. It has the support of Piaget's theory which stresses the importance of the effects of informal experience during childhood.

Limitations of the method are that there may not be sufficient time for the child to learn all it needs to know by personal discovery and that undesirable consequences, such as over-ready generalization, may ensue. Hence the teacher retains an important role in guiding the child and in supplementing teaching through more traditional methods. GEB

discrimination: animal Differential responsiveness to different stimuli. An animal can respond differently to different stimuli only when it can discriminate between them. Animals which do not initially discriminate between two stimuli can often learn to do so. For example, a pigeon given two types of grain may readily eat both. But if one type has been treated with lithium chloride and the bird vomits as a result, upon recovery it will not eat that type of grain. This form of discrimination is an important aspect of food selection.

Animals may have little difficulty in perceiving the difference between stimuli, but, nevertheless, behave towards them in the same way (see GENERALIZATION). This is the counterpart of discrimination. In learning to discriminate, the animal has both to pay attention to the relevant aspects of the stimuli, and to respond appropriately to these differences (Sutherland and Mackintosh 1971).

DJM

Bibliography

Sutherland, Norman S. and Mackintosh, Nicholas J. 1971: *Mechanisms of animal discrimination learning*. New York and London: Academic Press.

discrimination: social psychology Any behavior which implies the acceptance or rejection of another person solely on the basis of that person's membership of a particular group. In general, discrimination is seen as related to (racial, ethnic or other group) prejudice, which consists of unjustified evaluative judgments based solely on another person's group membership. Discrimination and prejudice can to some extent be explained by historically developed socio-economic conditions which may lead to competitive relations between social groups, and by psychodynamic processes which are perhaps characteristic of certain types of people (AUTHORITARIAN PERSONALITY). Recent research by Tajfel (1982) and his colleagues (see PREJUDICE) has shown that the cognitive process of categorization *per se* may already play an important role in discriminating against members of other social groups.

JMFJ

Bibliography

Tajfel, H. 1982: Social psychology of intergroup relations. *Annual review of psychology* 33, 1–39.

displaced speech The term was introduced by Bloomfield (1933) to refer to speech about events which do not relate to the immediate context of an utterance.

In their early stages of first language development children's speech is tied to the here and now. Later on the one-word stage words become detached from their original stimulus. The capacity to produce displaced speech develops in well-ordered stages. Reference to the future, for instance, always appears later than reference to the past.

The capacity for displacement is universal in human languages, but much less developed or nonexistent in animal communication systems. See also FIRST LANGUAGE ACQUISITION.

PM

Bibliography

Bloomfield, Leonard 1933: *Language*. New York: Holt, Rinehart & Winston; London: Allen & Unwin (1935).

displacement activity An activity which may appear normal, and which may be directed toward its normal external stimulus, but which occurs at an inappropriate time. For example a hungry bird shown food behind glass will often preen its wing. This might be called "displacement" preening. The name comes from the particular motivation theory which, in classical ethology, was used to account for such inappropriate actions. A DRIVE, such as hunger, denied its normal outlet (in this case feeding), "sparks over" or is "displaced" into an alternative outlet (in this case preening). In a displacement activity, unlike a redirected activity, there was no obvious functional link between the behavior pattern that was used as the alternative outlet for a drive, and the behavior pattern that was normally activated by that drive. The surplus energy theory later became unfashionable, but the name displacement activities stuck even when other motivational theories such as the "disinhibition" theory came into favor.

RD

display The term used to designate a pattern of social behavior that is species-specific and forms a part of the communicative system within or between social groups, or between individuals. An example is the "weed presentation display" of great-crested grebes which occurs between courting pairs: the partners waggle their heads, preen and then dive and rise vertically holding weeds in their beaks (see illustration, from Deag 1980). In primates many displays involve facial expressions, such as the "bared-teeth display" of macaques and chimpanzees. Ethologists make efforts to link overt displays with their underlying motivations, moods, or emotions, by context analysis. In man, non-verbal communication consists largely of gestures and expressions some of which undoubtedly have their phylogenetic roots in the displays of our primate ancestors. (See also COURTSHIP.)

VR

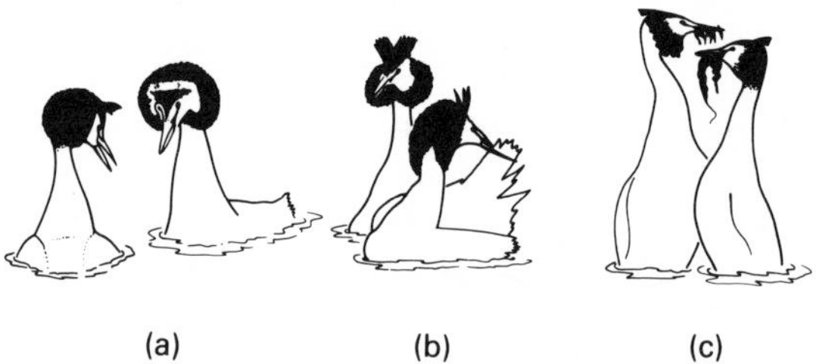

Bibliography

Deag, John M. 1980: *Social behaviour of animals*. London: Edward Arnold.

display rules *See* facial expression and emotion

disposition: philosophical usage The word "disposition" is often used in philosophical writings to cover not only such items as character traits, attitudes and inclinations but also much more broadly to include any sort of tendency, as well as such things as abilities and capacities. The principal difference between the concept of a tendency and that of an ability is that the latter is intimately connected with the idea of an aim. I may have the ability to run a marathon in that if I made the attempt I would last the course, but if nothing would induce me to try I could not be said to have any tendency or inclination to do so.

Statements ascribing dispositions have been analysed, broadly speaking, in two ways. According to RYLE (1949, ch. 5) they are purely hypothetical and say merely how something does, or would, behave in certain circumstances, or what somebody would succeed in doing if he made the right sort of attempt in the right sort of circumstances. On this view a disposition is to be contrasted with what may be called an "occurrent state" like being of a certain shape or molecular structure. Alternatively it may be claimed that a dispositional statement does ascribe an occurrent state but only in an hypothetical manner – to be brittle is to be in some (unspecified) occurrent state which makes the object in question likely to fly into fragments if struck. JMS

Bibliography

Ryle, G. 1949: *The concept of mind.* London: Hutchinson; Totowa, N. J.: Barnes & Noble (1975).

disposition: psychological usage Disposition, like temperament, character and constitution, refers to well ingrained personality characteristics or tendencies for the individual to behave in particular ways. Stable and consistent over time and across situations, the dispositional characteristics are viewed as more or less permanent or "given" personality characteristics. These characteristics, if not purely genetically endowed, are considered to be the result of genetic pre-conditions and early learning experiences which combine and interact to provide persistent reaction tendencies. For example, the individual who has an extroverted disposition may behave in a socially outgoing manner in a wide variety of situations and over a long period of time. The personality characteristics comprising extroversion (social facility, talkativeness, interest in social relationships, enthusiasm, etc.) appear to be more or less permanent aspects of the individual's personality makeup. Research has shown that extroversion has high genetic heritability. Recently, in the critical discussion of "trait" theories, it has been suggested that apparently stable dispositions are ephemeral effects of placing a person in one kind of situation, rather than another. In the latter different dispositions would be manifested (see TRAITS). JNB

disruptive pupils Pupils whose behavior disturbs their teachers. Disruptive pupils are not a new source of concern, nor is there much evidence that their numbers have increased (see McFie 1934). There is division of opinion over the relative importance of psychosocial and sociological variables. Children whose disruptive behavior culminates in expulsion from school tend to come from highly stressful family backgrounds. Some severely disruptive pupils may also be constitutionally vulnerable by reason of atypical autonomic functioning (Davies and Maliphant 1974). Many have a history of serious illnesses or accidents and reception into the care of the local authority (Galloway et al. 1982).

There are wide differences between schools in the number of pupils expelled following disruptive behavior. Demographic variables do not predict these differences, which seem to reflect policies and expectations in the schools themselves rather than the nature of their pupil intake. Social psychologists have used the concept of secondary deviance to explain the development of disruptive behavior in some schools. Teachers' initial reactions to deviant behavior may increase the probability of further deviant behavior by uniting a subgroup of pupils in opposition to the school's value system (Hargreaves et al. 1975). Psychiatric assessment is likely to regard disruptive behavior as a CONDUCT DISORDER. Psychotherapy has a poor prognosis. Special groups or centers for disruptive pupils have become popular, but systematic evaluation studies are lacking. It is widely accepted that few pupils are disruptive in all settings. Assessment should aim to identify the variables which mediate disruptive behavior. The most promising approaches to treatment aim to change the situation, the pupils' responses to the situation, or both. (See also BEHAVIOR CHANGE IN THE CLASSROOM.) DMG

Bibliography

Davies, J.G.V. and Maliphant, R. 1974: Refractory behavior in school and avoidance learning. *Journal of child psychology and psychiatry* 15, 23–31.

Galloway, D.M. et al. 1982: *Schools and disruptive pupils.* London: Longman.

Hargreaves, D., Hester, S. and Mellor, F.J. 1975: *Deviance in classrooms.* London: Routledge and Kegan Paul.

McFie, B.S. 1934: Behavior and personality difficulties in schoolchildren. *British journal of educational psychology* 4, 30–46.

dissociation An unconscious defense mechanism in which a group of mental processes are separated (or split) from the remainder of the person's activity. This may result in dissociative disorder (see HYSTERIA) in which there is a narrowing of consciousness; typical symptoms are fugues (wandering states) and multiple personality. Dissociation may also lead to conversion symptoms. RAM

distal vs. proximal variable A distinction introduced into the theory and (experimental) study of perception to separate environmental events at the periphery of, and in immediate contact with, the perceiving organism (= proximal stimuli and reactions) from those at a distance which, without being in immediate contact, affect (or are achieved by) the organism (= distal events). (In addition, there are intraorganismic or central events).

The theoretical and experimental pioneer was Egon Brunswik (1934; 1947; but see also Koffka 1935). It was mainly his research in perceptual constancy which led Brunswik to emphasize the veridicality (functional validity) of perception, which is measured by the correlation between the two distal variables, initial and terminal. To the extent that the physical values of stimulus objects are matched in perceptual responses, the distal variable is "functionally attained". While proximal variables, e.g. retinal patterns, are fluctuating and of limited "ecological validity", functional validity is higher. That it is less than perfect makes "organismic achievement" a probability function. Brunswik's theory, well known by its central "lens model", is a probabilistic functionalism.

The lens model, which explicates the various relationships between and among distal, proximal and central variables, has been modified several times, most recently by Nystedt (1972; 1981) for studying the "interaction between the objective situation and a person's construction of the situation". CFG

Bibliography

Brunswik, E. 1934: *Wahrnehmung und Gegenstandswelt.* Vienna: Deuticke.

*——— 1947: *Perception and the representative design of psychological experiments.* Berkeley, Calif.: University of California Press.

Koffka, K. 1935: *Principles of gestalt psychology.* New York: Harcourt, Brace & World.

Nystedt, L. 1972: A modified lens model: A study of the interaction between the individual and the ecology. *Perceptual and motor skills.* 34, 479–98.

——— 1981: A model for studying the interaction between the objective situation and a person's construction of the situation. In *Toward a psychology of situations.* ed. D. Magnusson Hillsdale, N.J.: Erlbaum.

distributive justice *See* equity theory

dogmatism A somewhat unfashionable term, related to the idea of closed-mindedness or the inability to form new cognitive systems of various kinds (perceptual, conceptual etc.). (See COGNITIVE PERSONALITY THEORY.)

Closed-mindedness or dogmatism is characterized by total rejection of opposing beliefs, a relatively poorly interconnected belief system and greater complexity of cognition about objects, people and groups which are positively evaluated compared to those which are negatively evaluated. The more dogmatic a person is, the more his or her cognitions are also said to depend on irrelevant desires and external authority.

Authoritarians are said to exhibit high amounts of dogmatism. They appear to have rigid and inflexible styles of thought and problem-solving abilities; to have low tolerance for ambiguity; to be highly susceptible to social influence, and to be highly conventional. To quote Eckhardt and Newcombe (1969):

> Both authoritarianism and dogmatism were negatively correlated with intellectual conviction and with education, so that the authoritarian, dogmatic, militarist is anti-intellectual. He already "knows" all that he wants to know. Knowledge is a threat to his ego-defensive orientation, and is, therefore, rejected. What he claims to be "knowledge" is actually a faith, so that the essence of dogmatism is a basic confusion between "faith and knowledge". AF

Bibliography

Eckhardt, W. and Newcombe, A. 1969: Militarism, personality and other social attitudes. *Journal of conflict resolution* 13, 210–19.

Rokeach, M. 1960: *The open and closed mind.* New York: Basic Books.

dominance *See* lateralization; zoological theories of dominance

dopamine One of the catecholamine neurotransmitters (see NEUROTRANSMITTER SYSTEMS). Dopamine is synthesized indirectly from the amino acid tyrosine. Although dopamine has been found in certain ganglia of the peripheral nervous system, most work has concentrated on its role in synaptic transmission in the central nervous system (CNS). There are two major dopaminergic pathways in the CNS. The cell bodies of the nigrostriatal pathway are located in the substantia nigra, and the neurons project to the basal ganglia (see EXTRAPYRAMIDAL MOTOR SYSTEM; BRAIN AND CENTRAL NERVOUS SYSTEM: ILLUSTRATIONS, figs. 5, 6 and 14–16). The cell bodies of mesolimbic dopaminergic neurons originate from the ventral tegmental region and project to various structures in the LIMBIC SYSTEM. Dopaminergic neurons from both sites of origin may project to certain cortical areas as well. The majority of dopaminergic synapses are suggested to be metabotropic (see ADENYL CYCLASE) and inhibitory, although excitatory dopaminergic synapses have recently been reported in the caudate nucleus. Central dopaminergic pathways are involved in the mediation of movement and emotional states, and in certain pathological states, including Parkinsonism and, perhaps, schizophrenia. GPH

double-loop learning occurs when actors alter the governing values, policies, or assumptions of a system in order to learn – that is, in order to produce a match between intention and outcome or to correct a mismatch between them. Double-loop learning is likely to involve threat to the existing system because it may make obsolete the current skills and actions and because it requires changing the underlying programs and policies.

In contrast single-loop learning occurs whenever matches are produced or mismatches are corrected without any change in the governing values. A thermostat, for example, normally acts as a single-loop learner. But a thermostat that inquired into why it was set at a particular temperature would be double-loop learning.

Single-loop learning is often adequate for getting the everyday job done, and is related to efficiency. Double-loop learning questions the rationale of a system and thereby determines its future. CA

Down's syndrome This condition, known as mongolism until the early 1960s, accounts for 25 per cent of the severely mentally retarded and is caused by a CHROMOSOME ABNORMALITY. The main clinical features are a small round head, eyes which slant upwards and outwards (giving the "mongoloid" appearance); minor abnormalities of hands and feet, and moderate to severe mental retardation. There may also be abnormalities of the heart and digestive tract. It occurs in approximately 1 in 600 live births, and the incidence increases with maternal age. The chromosome abnormality consists in over 90 per cent of cases of an extra autosomal chromosome (Trisomy 21) with a recurrence rate of 1 in 100. More rarely, there is a translocation defect of chromosomes D/G, with a high risk of recurrence; or a mixture of some cells in the body with normal chromosomes and some with abnormal chromosomes (mosaicism). The diagnosis can be made in early pregnancy by examining the amniotic fluid surrounding the fetus (amniocentesis), and it is now common practice to offer this to all older women and those who already have an affected child. GENETIC COUNSELING is important. See also MENTAL RETARDATION. GCF

Bibliography

Smith, G.F. and Berg, J.M. 1976: *Downs anomaly*. Churchill Livingstone.

dream theories Theories about why dreams occur, why they take a particular form, and what their relation is to psychological functioning as a whole. In the ancient Hebrew and Greek cultures, dreams were sent by a god as a message or warning, and for this reason they could be used for predictive purposes if their symbolism were understood: a literature of "dream-books" offering such knowledge flourished under the Roman Empire. The general idea that dreams give access to super-natural powers is still widespread.

In western Europe the idea that dreams can reflect the personal mental life, and especially the anxieties, of an individual is clearly established by the time of Shakespeare (Macbeth). The more specific thesis that dreams are composed by a kind of language translating a desire is expressed by DESCARTES alongside the view that his own famous dreams conveyed a divine command. By the latter part of the eighteenth century Lichtenberg is recommending attention to dreams in a quasi-Jungian way, as a source of expanded self-awareness (Whyte 1960, pp.86–90, 113–15). FREUD, however, felt that a sceptical reaction had set in by the end of the nineteenth century, and that he was speaking against the prevailing scientific view that they were random psychic spin-offs from physiological processes (1916, ch. 5).

For Freud, dreams provided the "royal road to a knowledge of the unconscious activities of the mind" (1900, ch. 7E) in the sense of being that part of normal and neurotic mental life which most clearly reflects the contents and processes of the UNCONSCIOUS MIND. But the "manifest content" of the dream, which is the image-sequence that the dreamer experiences and tries to report, is a systematically disguised transformation of the "latent content", which consists of those anxieties, impulses, wishes and ideas which, as an unresolved residue from the previous day's mental activity, have provoked the dream, and which the dream expresses.

The transformation of latent into manifest content is done by "dream-work" (initiated by the "dream-censor"), whose function is to codify and disguise material, already subjected to REPRESSION because unacceptable to the EGO or SUPEREGO, in such a way that it can reach consciousness. The latent material had been repressed because of its sexual, aggressive or frightening nature; and it follows that in order to understand it the course of the dream-work has to be retraced and disentangled by "interpretation".

Freud's second major publication was an account of this process and the theory underlying it (1900). The dream essentially expresses the fulfilment of a wish that is too painful or guilt-laden to acknowledge consciously, and is an example of the "primary-process" of the UNCONSCIOUS MIND achieving in hallucinatory form, according to the "pleasure-principle", the gratification of an impulse to which satisfaction is denied in reality. In this way the build-up of sleep-disrupting tension is prevented, and the dream is the "guardian of sleep" (Freud 1916, ch. 8). The primary process is a primitive, pre-rational form of ideation (contrasted with the "secondary process" of the conscious ego) which links together and transforms mental elements (images, words, ideas) according to concrete, symbolic, emotional or egocentric associations rather than to logical and empirical concepts. Since also the primary process does not acknowledge contradiction, an element may be symbolized by its opposite.

An example of perceptually "concrete" association is transforming a stimulus-element into something that happens to sound like it (without any connection of meaning). In Berger's (1963) experimental study the name "Jenny" becomes a "jemmy" and Naomi becomes "an aim to ski"; but evidence that higher-order semantic coding is also available is shown by "Gillian" becoming "a woman from Chile", evidently through a semantic transformation of the acoustically similar "Chilean". Egocentric substitution is exemplified by the boy-friend's name Richard being transformed into the dream-element "had been to a shop for a sale" by a subject who had recently been to a shop named "Richard's" for a sale. It is this personal aspect of symbolic substitution which makes it necessary to trace the significance of a manifest element through the "free-associations" and idiosyncratic complexes (to use Jung's term) of the dreamer himself. The analyst does not just translate a dream by reference to some dream-book dictionary in the manner of the ancients, but he understands the general transformational principles on which the individual creates his or her personal dream language.

Freud held, it is true, that there are some rather general symbols for some elemental and transcendent objects, events and experiences; but wrote "the range of things which are given symbolic representation in dreams is not wide: the human body as a whole, parents, children, brothers and sisters, birth, death, nakedness – and something else besides". Sexual life, however (that "something else") has "an "extraordinarily rich symbolism" (Freud 1916, ch. 10), and the appropriate occurrence of such symbolism in experimentally evoked dreams has been colorfully demonstrated by Berger and also reported by Eysenck (1957, p.171). See Kline (1981, ch. 9) for a review of empirical studies of testable aspects of the theory.

"Condensation" is an important transformation, because of its connection with "overdetermination". More than one repressed element may be condensed into a single manifest image, so that that image is the product of several determinants, each of which would have been separately sufficient to produce it (Freud 1900, ch. 6A). Elsewhere, however, Freud seems to suggest that an overdetermined image merely has two *types* or sources of determination, one from the Id (the nature of the wish) and one from the Ego (the reason for repression, or counter-will), combining to determine its form. Overdetermination also applies to symptoms. In "displacement", the apparent significance of a manifest image has been distorted by exaggerating what was trivial or contingent in the repressed idea and playing down or omitting what was central.

Freud retained these basic ideas about the nature and

purpose of the dream-work when he revised the motivational hypothesis to include the "repetition-compulsion" along with the wish-fulfilment of the "pleasure principle" (1920). The repetitive nightmare of combat-shocked soldiers, which did not abate when they were withdrawn to safety, seemed to be defying the pleasure principle, unless seen as an attempt to attach by rehearsal to the traumatic memory the ego-cushioning preparatory anxiety which had been absent (in sufficient quantities) from the event. Freud eventually rejected this hypothesis of retroactive emotional CONDITIONING, however, in favor of a revision of his basic instinct-theory to include a destructive drive (Thanatos) which was just as important and fundamental as the vital and constructive Eros.

Since JUNG's theory both of libido and of the unconscious differs from Freud's his account of dreams necessarily differs also. For him they can be forward-looking, creative, instructive, even prophetic; and they are potentially a source of personal growth, insofar as they (the "collective" dreams) draw upon the "archetypes" of the "collective unconscious". Archetypes are the common symbols, transcending time and space, which are to be found in the folk-art, religion, myths, rituals, and visions of different cultures in widely separated places and periods of time, and they are assumed to be innate in the individual. They enshrine universal, even mystical, perceptions and images; such as those of the nature of woman, in the "anima", and of balanced wholeness (whether divine or human) in the "mandala". Collective dreams, therefore, may serve to enlarge the dreamer's insight into his own resources, and even contain hints about how to solve the problems they reflect. "Personal dreams" are those that reflect more immediate concerns with the "personal unconscious", especially as personified in the id-like "shadow" (Jung 1934; 1954). Adler's view, though less specific, is closer to Jung's than to Freud's, so that Jung could say that he was "in entire agreement" with it (McGuire 1974, p.299).

Physiological accounts of dreaming provide tools for investigating such psychodynamic theories, and the discovery that dreams occur mainly during periods of "rapid eye-movement" (REM) sleep has greatly facilitated data-collection, since experimental stimuli can be introduced selectively when the subject is dream-ready, and reactions concomitant with dreaming can be measured. Use of the former technique has been discussed, and the latter makes it possible to ask, for instance, whether (as Freudian theory might suggest) these are signs of sexual arousal during dreams, other than overtly erotic ones. A study by Karacan et al. (1966), on a small sample of males, showed that the more anxious the dreams were the greater was the arousal.

More relevant, perhaps, is the disproportionate involvement in dreams of the physiological brain-activity of the non-dominant hemisphere. Bakan (1976) reports that people whose COGNITIVE STYLE favors the processes thought to be performed by the right hemisphere of the brain (i.e. "divergent") find it easier to recall dreams than do those whose style is verbal-analytic and rule-following (i.e. "convergent", the left hemisphere dominates); and that, although there is more brain-activity on the right side early in the night, the dominant hemisphere plays a larger part towards morning as reality approaches again. Creative and problem-solving dreams occur because the cognitive constraints of habitual thought-patterns ("cognitive set") are relaxed in sleep, so that ideas etc. which have been kept separate in previous waking work on a problem are able to meet and "bisociate" (Koestler 1964) into what happens to be a fruitful combination. In computer analogies of ARTIFICIAL INTELLIGENCE, dreams are seen as attempts to clear pathways and resolve informational conflicts (due to cognitive blockages and dissonances) within the system (Rose 1976, pp.303–06).

Jones (1970) has attempted to synthesize the psychodynamic and neurobiological accounts by arguing that psychic processes do not themselves *initiate* dream activity but organise and utilize the activity which has been initiated neurobiologically. NMC

Bibliography

Bakan, P. 1976: The right-brain is the dreamer. *Psychology today*. November, pp.66–8.

Eysenck, Hans J. 1957: *Sense and nonsense in psychology*. Harmondsworth: Penguin.

*Freud, Sigmund 1900, 1909, 1916, 1920: *The interpretation of dreams* (vol. 4); *The analysis of a five-year-old boy* (vol. 10); *Introductory lectures in psychoanalysis* (vol. 15); *Beyond the pleasure-principle* (vol. 18) In *Standard edition of the complete psychological worker of Sigmund Freud.* Vol. numbers as indicated. London: Hogarth Press; New York: Norton.

Jones, Richard M. 1970: *The new psychology of dreaming*. New York: Grune & Stratton.

Jung, Carl G. 1934 (*1966*): The practical use of dream-analysis. In *Collected works of C.G. Jung*. Vol. 16. London: Routledge & Kegan Paul; New York: Bollinger.

——— 1954 (*1959*): Archetypes of the collective unconscious. In *Collected works*. Vol. 9.i.

Karacan, I. et al. 1966: Erection cycle during sleep in relation to dream-anxiety. *Archives of general psychiatry*. 15, 183–9.

Kline, Paul 1981: *Fact and fiction in Freudian theory*. 2nd ed. London and New York: Methuen.

Koestler, A. 1964: *The act of creation*. London: Hutchinson.

McGuire, William, ed. 1974: *The Freud/Jung letters*. London: Hogarth; Princeton, N.J.: Princeton University Press.

Rose, Steven 1976: *The conscious brain* (revised ed.), Harmondsworth: Penguin.

*Rycroft, Charles 1979: *The innocence of dreams*. London: Hogarth.

Whyte, Lancelot L. 1960: *The unconscious before Freud*, New York: Basic Books; London: Tavistock (1962).

dreaming Hallucinatory experience during sleep, often bizarre in the telling, but usually convincing at the time. There is no clear understanding of its function. A distinction may be made between dream interpretation, based on psychoanalytic theories of personality (see FREUD, JUNG, DREAM THEORIES), and dream investigation, a branch of COGNITIVE PSYCHOLOGY.

Since dreams are not accessible to direct observation, for most of the history of dream exploration there was no other source of information about them than the subjective memory of the dreamer. The discovery in the early 1950s of a relationship between rapid eye movement (REM) sleep and the reporting of dreams in the sleep laboratory seemed to provide an objective measure of the frequency and duration of dreams. However, it is now generally accepted that there is no straightforward relationship between a particular brain state and type of mental activity, since dreamlike mentation occurs intermittently throughout sleep.

See also DAYDREAM, HALLUCINATION, LUCID DREAMING.

RPE

Bibliography

Cartwright, Rosalind 1978: *A Primer on sleep and dreaming.*Reading, Mass. and London: Addison-Wesley.

drive: ethological The output of a motivational system which energizes a specific, functionally-related set of behavior patterns. When its sexual drive is activated an animal is motivated to perform sexual behavior of all types, searching for a mate, courting, copulating, etc. when appropriate stimuli are present. Some drives are postulated to fluctuate in accordance with the internal state. Food deprivation stimulates the neural systems concerned with feeding motivation thereby ensuring that the animal's food seeking is initiated and persists until the imbalance is corrected. The drive concept is much less popular than formerly, its neural basis has remained elusive and many consider it to be impossible to define other than in terms of the observed behavior. It retains more usefulness in the consideration of conflict behavior. See also VACUUM ACTIVITY.

AWGM

drive *See above, and also* unconscious drive

drug dependence Drug dependence has been defined by the World Health Organization as: 'A state psychic and sometimes physical, resulting from the interaction between a living organism and a drug, characterized by behavioral and other responses that always include a compulsion to take the drug on a continuous or therapeutic basis in order to experience its psychic effects, and sometimes to avoid the discomfort of its absence. Tolerance may or may not be present. A person may be dependent on more than one drug.'

This replaces former definitions which attempted to sustain a distinction between drug addiction and drug habituation. The WHO Committee emphasized that the general definition should be applied separately in connection with specific drugs since the nature of the dependence varies to some extent with the type of drug (WHO 1964). This definition of dependence would exclude much consumption of psychoactive drugs. Taking drugs for medical or quasi-medical purposes to relieve specific symptoms does not constitute dependence, provided that it is for a limited period of time and that the patient experiences neither withdrawal symptoms nor a desire to continue consumption of drugs when the medication is stopped. Social consumption of drugs for hedonistic purposes, when the substance is taken on an occasional basis and where the consumer is able on each occasion to make a choice to take the drug without experiencing pressure or compulsion, may be harmful but is not drug dependence. In various societies alcohol, cannabis (both the resin and the vegetation usually referred to as marijuana) and the psychedelic drugs are usually consumed in this non-dependent fashion. Amphetamines and cocaine are also primarily taken on an intermittent basis but here the tendency to progress to a more compulsive pattern of use is greater. Sedatives such as the barbiturates and the benzodiazepine tranquillizers, and the opioid group of drugs are more likely to be consumed compulsively and continuously.

Within this range of drugs the first and most commonly consumed are likely to be those most readily available and socially accepted – in western society nicotine and alcohol. A substantial group of consumers may proceed to those drugs which are moderately disapproved of – cannabis, tranquillizers and sedatives taken for non-medical purposes, and psychedelics and amphetamines taken orally. Only a minority progress to the injection of the most disapproved drugs – cocaine and opioids including heroin (Kandel 1975).

Attempts to understand drug dependence solely on the basis of the pharmacological properties of the drug, or of a simple interaction between a drug and an animal are insufficient. Dependence is a complex interaction to which the pharmacology of the drug, the personality and situation of the subject, and the culture of the society contribute in variable degrees in varying circumstances. Social factors are inevitably involved in the interaction and include, in addition to physical access to drugs, a milieu in which drugs are socially acceptable and even, at times, within specific subcultures, encouraged. Economic and political factors are also of relevance. In particular where groups or individuals are deprived of the potential to gain success and status by legitimate means, drug-taking may provide an alternative activity.

Dependence must be understood as a continuing process. Becoming dependent may involve important factors other than those which determine the process of progression to further drug use, and again differing from the predominant factors which maintain a state of dependence once drug-taking has become a regular and established part of the individual's life.

Social factors predominate in determining the initial consumption of drugs: availability and acceptability of certain drugs; access through subcultures to the illegal drug market; the support of drug users by peers and/or a disregard of, or rebellion against the social mores of non-drug-users. Among individual factors it has been suggested that an underlying personality inclined to immediate satisfaction in disregard of possible long-term adverse consequences may pre-dispose to drug experimentation.

Continuing drug consumption will be influenced by the same factors and will be facilitated by pleasurable experiences derived from drug-taking and by an increasing identity with other drug users.

Progression to a drug-centered lifestyle or state of 'addiction' will be most likely to occur when in addition there is: social support for drug-taking behavior; a lack of gratifying alternatives, such as employment or training, and, in many individual cases, a relief from psychic or physical discomfort and pain.

The relative importance of these inter-related factors will vary between cultures and individuals and over time. Where an individual lacks personal resources and confidence to change, and where there is an obvious disparity between a society's wider expectation and the individual's capacity to achieve what are effectively unobtainable goals, the risk of progression to heavy drug use is high.

Coincidentally various factors resulting from drug-taking may amplify or reinforce this process. Developing the skills to obtain illegal drugs can earn approval within a deviant subculture and disapproval by wider society, and can modify an individual's self-image. Investment of time and energy in such activities reduces the probability of learning the skills valued in conventional society. The development of tolerance to the actions of drugs requires larger doses to maintain drug effect and hence more work is invested in obtaining supplies. The occurrence of unpleasant withdrawal symptoms which can be immediately avoided by drug administration increases the conditioned aspect of drug-taking. These factors have been elaborated in sociological and psychological theory in terms of deviancy amplification, social learning theory, and classical and operant conditioning. (See Becker 1973; Wickler 1973; Lindsmith 1968; and Young 1971.)

Conflicts between differing theories of addiction can only be reconciled by appreciating the very different circumstances pertaining in laboratory experiments with animals, pharmacological studies on human volunteers in hospital or penal settings, social studies of non-dependent cannabis consumption, and observations of the heavily dependent both on the street and in treatment.

Measures to reduce the harm of drug-taking are correspondingly complex. There is qualified support for the view that the number of individuals harmed by drug-taking will vary simply as a factor of the number of individuals who consume drugs within a society, e.g. the numbers dependent upon or suffering complications from alcohol consumption will vary according to the frequency and amount of alcohol consumption by the wider population. Hence primary prevention measures are aimed at reducing overall consumption. Most societies attempt to restrict access to drugs by increasing the cost both by taxation and by making the possession of some drugs illegal. This in turn increases the cost to the consumer both financially and in terms of time spent to acquire the drugs. Educational programs aim at persuading people to avoid or reduce their consumption of drugs. In this context simply providing information or propaganda is insufficient and increasing emphasis is being placed on helping people to improve their ability to take decisions based on such knowledge in anticipation of events (Dorn 1981). Prevention is also aimed in a general manner at providing adequate experience and skills to enable young people to cope both with intra-psychic stresses and with societal demands as adolescence and adult life are reached. However these measures can themselves have adverse consequences. Educational programs can have the unwanted effect of stimulating interest in drugs in many young people, which may make them more likely to experiment. Increasing the price of drugs will add to the burden upon the dependent user thereby reinforcing any tendency to finance drug-taking by crime. Outlawing a drug has the inevitable consequence of ensuring that only persons prepared to break the law by supplying drugs will profit from effective monopoly of supply. Decisions regarding education and social policy must therefore be based on information about the availability and demand for drugs within any particular culture.

Management of the individual's dependence upon drugs also varies. In the UK between 1920 and 1960 a few hundred opiate-dependent patients introduced to drugs in the course of medical treatment were satisfactorily managed, at least from society's point of view, by continued medical maintenance of their addiction. The same policy applied to younger gregarious drug-users in the 1960s was associated with a rapid escalation of heroin use. New users initiated with heroin from diverted medical maintenance prescriptions in North America over the past fifty years, and in Europe during the 1970s, have developed the extensive use of illegal drugs. This has been mainly in youth cultures and has been sustained primarily by illegally imported drugs. The medical management of individual users ranges from indefinite continued maintenance to immediate in-patient withdrawal. Generally it is agreed that it must include extensive social and psychological measures to enable the patient to resume a role acceptable to the wider society. The simple provision of maintenance supplies generally maintains the user within the drug subculture and on its own will rarely prevent the additional consumption of other illegal drugs. In the USA the substitution of long-term supervised maintenance with oral methadone appears to have enabled many former heroin addicts to alter their lifestyle and attain or resume conventional lives. It would be a mistake, however, to see the role of methadone in this context as purely a pharmaceutical replacement of heroin. It represents a change of status for the participant, who is no longer a person obtaining and injecting illegal drugs but one who accepts certain restraints and consumes a regular dose of medicine. That is not to dispute that even when persons have been stably maintained on methadone for a number of years they experience physical and psychological instabilities when the dose is reduced and terminated. However provided the period of maintenance has been utilized to reverse many of the social consequences of addiction and the learned patterns of behavior required to maintain an illegal drug habit, the individual is better placed to persevere through the period of discomfort and drug craving which generally follows withdrawal from opiate drugs.

A contrasting approach is practiced in drug-free therapeutic communities where the initial drug withdrawal is accompanied by considerable support from the community, and then followed by intensive use of the therapeutic community to enable the individual to learn first how to handle the difficulties without having recourse to drugs, and subsequently to generalize the skills through a progressive re-entry into society.

Morbidity and mortality rates among drug users are many times higher than among others of the same age group. The proportion of drug users able to make use of a treatment program at any one time is limited; but despite this lack of immediate cures it seems probable that in the longer term a reasonable proportion of individuals are able to avail themselves of one or another form of assistance.

MCM

Bibliography

Becker, Howard S. 1973: *The outsiders; studies in the sociology of deviance.* 2nd edn New York; Free Press.

Dorn, N. 1981: Social analysis of drugs in health education and the media. In *Drug problems in Britain, a review of ten years*, ed. G. Edwards and C. Busch. London: Academic Press.

Jaffe, J.H. 1980: Drug addiction and drug abuse. In Alfred G. Gilman, Louis S. Goodman, and Alfred Gilman, eds, *Goodman and Gilman's The pharmacological basis of therapeutics.* 6th edn New York: Macmillan.

Kandel, Denise 1975: Stages in adolescent involvement in drug use. *Science* 190, 912–14.

Lindsmith, Alfred R. 1968: *Addiction and opiates.* Chicago: Aldine.

Wickler, A. 1973: Dynamics of drug dependence, implications of a conditioning theory for research and treatment. *Archives of general psychology* 28, 611–16.

World Health Organisation 1964: *13th Report of WHO Expert Committee on Addiction Producing Drugs.* Technical Report Series no. 273.

Young, Jock 1971: *The drugtakers: the social meaning of drug use.* London: MacGibbon & Kee.

drugs, depressant A classification of psychoactive agents, the administration of which produces a general inhibition of central nervous system functions and behavior. The majority of depressant drugs are termed sedative-hypnotics, which include the barbiturates (e.g. phenobarbital), minor tranquilizers (e.g. the benzodiazepines), nonbarbituric sedatives (e.g. chloral hydrate) and alcohol (Julien 1978). In increasing doses all sedative-hypnotics can produce anxiolytic effects, excitement and euphoria (due to the inhibition of inhibitory centers in the brain), sedation, sleep and general anesthesia (the loss of consciousness, sensation and reflexes). In lethal doses these agents can result in death due to respiratory paralysis. In appropriate doses chronic administration of all sedative-hypnotics can lead to tolerance and physical dependence. In addition simultaneous administration of two or more sedative-hypnotics have at least additive effects with each other. Finally, virtually all sedative-hypnotics show cross tolerance and cross physical dependence with each other (See DRUGS, TOLERANCE AND PHYSICAL DEPENDENCE.)

GPH

Bibliography

Julien, R.M. 1978: *A primer of drug action.* 2nd edn San Francisco: Freeman.

drugs, stimulant A group of psychoactive agents which increase activity and mental alertness. Most drugs in this class have both central and peripheral nervous system effects. Stimulant drugs differ markedly in both chemical structure and mechanism of action. Amphetamines, cocaine and methylated xanthines such as caffeine all cause peripheral sympathetic nervous system activation. The central effects of amphetamines are caused primarily by their ability both to stimulate release and block re-uptake of norepinephrine and dopamine, while cocaine primarily blocks the re-uptake of norepinephrine and, to a lesser extent, dopamine. Caffeine and other methylated xanthines increase the basal metabolic rate of all cells, including neurons. While the central alerting effects of amphetamines and cocaine may be mediated primarily via stimulation of the reticular activating system, areas of the cerebral cortex may be more sensitive to caffeine than are centers in the brain stem. Nicotine is clearly a stimulant drug, as evidenced by its effects on the electroencephalogram, but both its peripheral and central mechanisms of action are complicated and dependent on time since administration. Both catecholamine and acetylcholine neurotransmitter systems appear to be involved. (See also DRUGS, TOLERANCE AND PHYSICAL DEPENDENCE.)

GPH

drugs, tolerance and physical dependence Two phenomena associated with continued use of certain drugs. Tolerance refers to a waning responsiveness following repeated administration of a given dose of a drug, or put the other way round, with repeated exposure, greater doses are needed to maintain some desired effect of the drug. Tolerance can be either dispositional (i.e. metabolic), behavioral (e.g. learning to compensate for the behavioral effects of the drug) or pharmacodynamic (i.e. decreases in the efficacy of the drug once it reaches its site of action, which may reflect compensatory alterations at the synapse). Physical dependence is a state in which the drug is needed for the body to maintain normal functioning. It is usually inferred from the consequences of terminating drug administration (i.e. withdrawal or abstinence syndrome). Interestingly, withdrawal responses are often opposite in direction from responses to initial administrations of the drug. Cross tolerance results when chronic use of one drug lessens an initial response to a different drug. Cross dependence is inferred when one drug can block the abstinence syndrome following withdrawal from chronic use of a different drug (Julien 1978).

GPH

Bibliography

Julien, R.M. 1978: *A primer of drug action.* 2nd edn San Francisco: Freeman.

drugs and animal behavior The effects of drugs on animal behavior is studied primarily as an aid to the pharmaceutical industry, especially in the evaluation and testing of possible new products. In some screening tests mice and rats are simply injected with the chemical and observed for a standard period of time. Obvious changes in behavior, and particularly abnormal behavior are noted. In other tests the animals are rated according to the extent to which they struggle when handled, for their general activity, for motor coordination, etc. Drugs are also widely used in brain research, though here it is usually their physiological effects that are monitored.

In addition to their use in investigations aimed at furthering our understanding of pharmacology and neurochemistry drugs may also be used as a tool in psychological experiments. For example one of the minor tranquilizers (sodium amytal) has been used to test the theory that the continued responding of animals that have been only partially rewarded during training is due to their greater tolerance of frustration, compared with animals that were consistently rewarded (see EXTINCTION).

The idea is that an animal that has been trained to expect a reward (see REINFORCEMENT) in particular circumstances becomes frustrated if the reward is not given. However, if the animal experiences such frustrative non-reward many times, say on 50 per cent of the trials, it will develop a tolerance of frustration. During extinction, when the animals are not rewarded at all, those which were previously partially rewarded (PR) continue to respond for much longer than those which were consistently rewarded (CR). The theory maintains that the frustration experienced by the CR animals at the beginning of extinction has a much more disruptive effect than in the PR animals, because the latter have already developed a tolerance of frustration. To test this theory Gray (1969) and his co-workers administered sodium amytal, a drug already known to have fear and frustration reducing effects in rats. In some experiments they gave the drug during training, while in others they gave it during extinction. When given during training the drug should have little effect upon CR rats because these do not experience frustration. The drug should ameliorate the effects of frustration in PR rats, thus preventing them from developing a tolerance to frustration. Therefore the administration of the drug during training should make PR animals extinguish quickly, as CR animals did during the subsequent extinction tests. This is exactly what is found.

When given during extinction the drug should have less effect upon PR animals than on CR animals, because the former (according to the theory) are already tolerant of frustration whereas the CR animals have yet to experience it. If the drug reduces the effects of frustration it should therefore have the effect of prolonging extinction in CR animals, but have little effect upon PR animals. This prediction is also confirmed by the results of experiments.

Here we have a good example of the use of a drug as a tool in experiments designed to test a psychological theory. It does not matter that the physiological action of the drug is not yet fully understood, because physiological details do not enter into the theory. The logic of the tests does not depend upon the exact action of the drug, but upon the fact that the theory predicts specified effects in different circumstances. The fact that these effects can be obtained lends support to the theory that frustration is important in the extinction of learned responses. DJM

Bibliography

Gray, J.A. 1969: Sodium amobarbital and effects of frustrative nonreward. *Journal of comparative physiological psychology* 69, 55–64.

——— 1971: *The psychology of fear and stress*. London: Weidenfeld & Nicolson; New York: McGraw-Hill.

Silverman, Paul 1978: *Animal behavior in the laboratory*. London: Chapman & Hall; New York: University Books.

drugs *See above, and also* endorphin and drug interaction

dualism *See* mind-body problem

dynamic psychology *See* psychoanalysis

dyslexic children Controversies surrounding the concept of dyslexia have given rise to much heated argument, and there is no universally accepted definition for the group of children suffering from this handicap.

The term "dyslexia" generally refers to a developmental abnormality in which there exists a difficulty in reading which is out of all proportion to the individual's intellectual competence. The definition proposed in 1968 by the World Federation of Neurology's research group on the subject, chaired by Macdonald Critchley, implies a constitutionally based reading disability free from correlates of reading failure like low intelligence, socio-cultural deprivation and gross neurological deficits. While an exclusionary definition of this type is justifiable for practical reasons, it is unsatisfactory because of its failure to aid conceptual clarity and its limitations for diagnosis. An amended definition by Critchley includes erratic spelling and lack of facility in handling written language as identifiable symptoms and suggests that the defect is capable of improvement. Nonetheless, the negative correlates continue to be central to the definition. Although Critchley insists that the diagnosis is a medical responsibility, dyslexia is not viewed basically as a medical problem by the British Medical Association (1980), which states that most doctors are not competent or willing to diagnose dyslexia without the assessment of an educational psychologist.

The first reference to such a disorder was made in a report in the British Medical Journal in 1896 describing "the paradoxical case of an intelligent boy of 14 who was incapable of learning to read". The validity of supposing that dyslexia in children is a specific inherent disorder is based on the analogy of its symptoms to the acquired loss or impairment of the ability to read, caused by cerebral damage. In order to distinguish the two conditions, it is common practice to reserve the term "alexia" for all acquired forms of reading impairment and the term "dyslexia" for the inability to learn to read. In the vast majority of cases of dyslexia, there is hardly any evidence for anatomical or physiological brain deficits. The remarkable preponderence of boys who are dyslexic makes it more difficult to explain the condition on the basis of brain damage.

The primary basis for the sustained interest in dyslexia in children is the promise that they hold as a distinct sub-group of reading disabled pupils. Although symptoms vary from child to child, case studies of dyslexic children refer to persistence in letter and word reversals, (e.g. confusions between b – d; was – saw); difficulty in repeating polysyllabic words; poor recall of sequences of letters or digits; bizarre spelling; disordered writing; frequently a history of clumsiness and late speech development. The presence of similar characteristics in many children who experience difficulty in learning to read has caused scepticism about the existence of dyslexia in children as an identifiable sub-type of reading disability. Most psychologists and educators would agree that a small proportion of problem readers may in fact have a specific learning defect which is inherent and independent of intellectual shortcomings. The symptoms of the sub-type in its current use do not help to differentiate dyslexic from non-dyslexic failing readers.

Increasing recognition that reading disability is not homogeneous has sustained the search for homogeneous sub-groups of reading-retarded children. Eleanor Boden's attempt to break these children into psychological and those with visual problems is an example (Boden, 1973). Theoretical notions about neuropsychological processes concerned with reading have been the basis for several studies using a variety of classification approaches (Vellutino, 1979). No doubt these attempts provide insights on different sub-types. However, despite their appeal for clinical and educational practice, they require evidence to show that they really are distinctive sub-types. The more recent diversity models proposed for dyslexia, as part of a continuum of language learning difficulty, hold more promise because of the shift in emphasis from treating these children as victims of pathology to providing opportunities for optimal development. SDS

Bibliography

Applebee, A.N. 1971: Research in reading retardation: two critical problems. *Journal of child psychology and psychiatry*.

Benton, A.L. and Pearl, D., eds. 1979: *Dyslexia: an appraisal of current knowledge*. Oxford and New York: Oxford University Press.

Boden, E. 1973: Developmental dyslexia: a diagnostic approach. *Developmental medicine and child neurology* 15, 663–87.

Mathis, S. 1981: Dyslexia syndromes in children: towards the development of syndrome-specific treatment programs. In *Neuropsychological and cognitive processes in reading*, ed. E.J. Pirozzolo and M.C. Mittrock. New York and London: Academic Press.

Parlidis, G.T. and Miles, T.R., eds 1981: *Dyslexia research and its applications to education*. John Liley and Sons Ltd. British Medical Association News Review.

Tansley, P. and Panckhurst, J. 1981: *Children with specific learning difficulties: a critical review of research*. London: Nelson.

Vellutino, F. 1979: *Dyslexia: theory and research*. Cambridge, Mass.: MIT Press.

E

early Christian psychology The reflections of early Christian writers, of the second to fifth centuries AD, on the spiritual and intellectual components or dimensions in man.

The sources for such teaching are: scriptural revelation, as understood by Catholic tradition, i.e. in the light of contemplative data and shared experience (introspective, liturgical, intellectual) within the Christian community; and notions borrowed from Greek philosophy, principally from those eclectic forms of middle platonism current in late antiquity. Such philosophy provides most of the speculative thought forms; but orthodox writers always attempt to correct ideas borrowed from philosophy in the perspective of biblical teaching.

The Church Fathers of the first three centuries were not for the most part directly concerned with the analysis of mind or soul, and it is not until the fourth century that major works on human nature as such begin to appear (e.g. Gregory of Nyssa, Augustine, Nemesius of Emesa). Before then, ideas about the soul or self occur in the discussion of such basic theological themes as the creation of man in the divine image, the Fall, salvation, immortality, and resurrection. The great Christological debates of the fifth century led to further precision concerning what constitutes the humanity assumed by Christ. The doctrines of creation and incarnation, in fact, provide the essential context for all patristic thought on the phenomenon of man: God created man in the beginning as a single entity, body and soul together, and this unitary nature (later flawed) was restored and given a new dignity when the Word became flesh. Even in the most platonizing writers, soul (which includes mind) is never considered entirely apart from body, since the whole nature is destined for resurrection at the end of time.

Synthesis of patristic teaching on psychology is rendered extremely difficult by the scattered and non-systematic nature of the sources. To date, no major study has been written on the subject, although there exist a number of good monographs on the doctrine of the image of God in man, as treated by individual Fathers. The problem is exacerbated by the use of inconsistent and sometimes ambiguous terminology both by patristic writers and by modern commentators.

In general, by the fourth century, one can point to a certain consensus that the principle of life and consciousness in man is a non-material, immortal spiritual substance (*psyche*, soul), created and infused into the body by God at conception. There is no agreement on such subjects as the essential nature of the soul, its parts, faculties, or relation with the body. Some, for example, adopt a basically dualist (body/soul) view of man, others – though this is often a largely terminological problem – a tripartite (body/soul/spirit); there is debate as to whether soul is properly only the rational mind, or includes the sensual and nutrient life-principles also; and while some tend to regard the passions as alien to the rational soul, others consider them as basically good, or at least capable of transformation towards the good.

By the same time (c. 400), certain speculations had effectively been discarded as inadequate expressions of the Christian vision of man: for instance, the suggestion of certain second-century apologists (Justin, Tatian) that the soul is not immortal by nature, but that survival after death is a supernatural gift of God; or notions of the pre-existence and transmigration of souls, held by Origen in the third century.

Greater precision may be gained by looking at some particular treatises which can illustrate the basic parameters of patristic psychology. The earliest Christian tract to be entitled *On the soul* is the *de anima* of Tertullian (210–213 AD), albeit this is a refutation of contemporary errors rather than a systematic exposition. Tertullian insists that divine revelation is a surer guide than philosophy; but his account is nonetheless much indebted to the Stoics, from whom he derives his curious doctrine (heterodox by later standards) that the soul, while an invisible spiritual essence, is also a "corporeal substance", composed of very refined matter. Against the Platonists, Tertullian argues that the soul is not eternal, but has an origin in time; it does not pass from body to body (transmigration), nor does it pre-exist the body. Rather, body and soul come into existence simultaneously with the act of sexual generation (this leads the author to another ultimately discredited doctrine, that of traducianism, which denies the direct creation by God of each individual soul).

Tertullian strongly maintains the unity and homogeneity of soul: soul and spirit are identical, and mind is no more than a function of soul. The soul, indeed, has numerous "powers", but not strictly speaking "parts". In the third section of his tract the author also deals with such psychological issues as the growth of the soul, sleep, dreams and consciousness after death.

More substantial reflections on soul and mind are found in the following century in two treatises of St Gregory of Nyssa, *On the making of man*, c. 380, and *On the soul and the resurrection*, 379 AD. In the former work Gregory first distinguishes various levels of soul: the "vegetative", principle of growth and nutrition, which we share with all other living things; the "sensitive" (power of sense-perception), also possessed by the animals; and the "leading" element, the *nous* or spiritual intellect, incomprehensible in nature, made in the image of God. Man is thus a microcosm, summing up in himself basic characteristics of all levels of reality. Nonetheless, the soul is unitary, not two or three spiritual entities welded together – "one in nature, intellectual and immaterial, endowed with the powers it imparts to the material body". Man is akin to God in respect to his moral attributes and reason, but different from him in that his mind must receive its information about the external world through the bodily senses. Just as there is an interdependence and interpenetration of the different levels of powers of soul, the lower serving and being animated and directed by the higher, so it is claimed that mind/soul does not reside in any particular part of the body, but acts on and is acted on by the whole.

Each person is generated at conception as a single "living and animated body", and the power of soul is gradually manifested through the material substrate. Like Tertullian, Gregory insists that neither body nor soul exists independently before birth; but he is unable to explain how the living union comes about (a miracle of divine power), nor does he offer much more than analogies to explain the relation of soul to body. Although the lower levels of soul are necessary for man's growth towards perfection in this life, it is to rational and contemplative mind that the name "soul" properly belongs, and it is this higher self which endures into the Age to Come.

In his second treatise on man, Gregory describes soul as a "created, living, intellectual substance which imparts itself to an organic body capable of sensation" – perhaps the most complete Christian definition of soul to date. However, soul is not itself an object of sense-perception: as in the case of God, we can infer its existence from its works. Being "simple and uncompounded", soul survives the dissolution of the body, but in some way retains the impressions of its physical vehicle while awaiting the resurrection of the body.

The passions, such as anger and desire, are not properly part of the essence of intellectual soul, but are modes of its existence in this life. We must aim to rid ourselves of them, or at least bring them into the service of the good. Heaven is envisaged in this tract as an ever-present contemplation of God, a *passionless* state, in which hope or regret have no place. Sense-perception (like the passions) will be no longer needed; but elsewhere, Gregory speaks of "spiritual senses", faculties of the spiritual intellect, corresponding to the physical senses, by which we apprehend transcendental realities.

Man's inner growth, even now, is a process of emancipation from the tyranny of the passions and the senses, and an "awakening" of the "eye" of the soul. The notion of spiritual senses is probably a metaphor for man's innate but often undeveloped capacity for a mystical knowledge, transcending both empirical perception and analytical reason. Gregory of Nyssa's account of mind and soul is ultimately controlled not so much by philosophical detachment, as by the vision of a mystical theologian, and by concern for salvation.

More philosophical in tendency is Nemesius of Emesa, whose work *On the nature of man* (c. 390) is a kind of *summa* of Greek patristic theological anthropology. The treatise is built on a sustained critical survey of the answers of the pagan philosophers to the question, what is mind and soul? Nemesius rejects any suggestion that mind and soul are distinct entities, or that the body is simply instrumental to the soul. The soul is a spiritual substance made for union with the body, yet subsistent in itself. Nemesius bequeaths to subsequent Greek Christian writers the doctrine of the complementarity of soul and body, each retaining a separate nature, yet mutually implied in activity, and constituting a single person, rather like the union of human and divine in Christ. It will be noted how, on the one hand, this synthesis is strong incarnational in refusing to reduce man to a purely noetic or spiritual reality; and yet, on the other hand, it sharpens the distinction within the psychosomatic unity between the composite, material body and a transcendental self, rational, incorporeal, simple and immutable. The former emphasis distinguishes the Christian thinkers of Late Antiquity from the pagan philosophers; the latter represents a significant development of doctrine from the Biblical data.

Nemesius also offers further analysis of the inner and outer senses, the passions, the will and other psychological questions. The student should certainly compare his suggestions (which are not substantially expanded by the later Byzantine Fathers) with the subtle, introspective views of his greater western contemporary, St Augustine, especially his acute reflections on mind, knowledge, memory and will.

Before leaving the Greek Fathers, it may be appropriate to bring certain points into clearer focus. First, to emphasize the teaching of the Cappadocian writers on man as microcosm, the cosmic mediator, "bridge" or "bond", who by combining in himself the material and the non-material, is able to mediate between these two orders of being, and reach beyond creation to the Uncreated. In this connection, it is important to realise that *nous* or "mind" denotes not just the discursive, analytical intellect, but also the intuitive, contemplative faculty, capable when purified of direct apprehension or "vision" of spiritual truth. It is through this "higher mind" that man knows God, and fulfils his microcosmic function in the universe.

An allied notion to *nous* is "heart", a term used (especially by Greek spiritual writers) to denote the deep, unified, psychosomatic center in man, the true inner self, in which his spiritual powers are concentrated. The "heart" is more than a metaphor for the affective or emotional; it at once subsumes and transcends sense-perception and intellection, and refers to the whole person as made in the image of God. Macarius (fourth century) calls the contemplative *nous* "the eye of the heart", of which it constitutes the innermost aspect and principle of cognition. Finally, the spiritual tradition emphasises the necessity of the "pricking of the heart", compunction and repentance, leading to a radical conversion (or perhaps extra-version) of the whole self to God. A spiritual transformation is required if the disordered, distracted and fragmented "mind" is to be "brought into the heart" and the whole man thus reintegrated. It is to this end that the entire Greek ascetical and mystical tradition is oriented, especially the practice of the contemplative "prayer of the heart" (hesychasm), which forms the kernel of Orthodox spirituality. NG

Bibliography

Augustine: *Confessions*. Trans. R.S. Pine-Coffin, 1961. Harmondsworth: Penguin. See also the treatise *de Trinitate*, especially bks. IX, X & XII.

Danielou, J. 1955: *Origen*. London.

——1980: *Gospel message and hellenistic culture*, 17. London.

Gregory of Nyssa, *Dialogue on the soul and the resurrection*. Trans. W. Moore, Library of the Post-Nicene Fathers, ser. 2 vol. V, pp. 428–68.

——*On the making of man*. Trans. H.A. Wilson, Library of Post-Nicene Fathers, ser. 2 vol. V, pp. 387–427.

Ladner, L. 1957: *The philosophical anthropology of St Gregory of Nyssa*. Dumbarton Oak Papers 12, pp.61 ff.

Nemesius of Emesa: On the nature of man. Trans W. Telfer 1955: In *Cyril of Jerusalem and Nemesius of Emesa*. Library of Christian Classics, vol. IV.

Norris, R.A. 1963: *Manhood of Christ*. Oxford: Oxford University Press.

O'Connell, R.J. 1968: *St Augustine's early theory of man*. Cambridge: Cambridge University Press.

Tertullian: *On the soul*. Trans. P. Holmes and E.A. Quain, Fathers of the Church vol. X, pp. 179–309. Washington, D.C.

Wingren, G. 1959: *Man and incarnation: a study in the biblical theology of St Irenaeus*. London.

ECT *See* electroconvulsive therapy

education: psychological assessment (US – evaluation) Refers to the investigation of educational, emotional, behavioral, developmental or other problems by applied (clinical, educational or school, and occupational) psychologists. It makes use of various procedures – interviews, observations, tests and even small-scale experiments – in order to collect and interpret information about clients and their circumstances in relation to the problem under investigation.

Assessment is a more comprehensive process than testing, and it may or may not use tests to gather the necessary information.

The assessment process is dependent to a great extent on the skills, experience and theoretical orientation of the assessor (Berger 1983). None of the differing theoretical and conceptual frameworks available has a clear position of superiority. In addition techniques such as psychological tests are prone to varying degrees and types of error, and the results they produce thus open to varied interpretations. Even the most well developed and commonly used techniques, such as tests of intelligence, are subject to these imperfections (Sattler 1982, Kaufman 1979). Finally there are no explicit rules for integrating the information obtained by these different means.

Historically, assessment was seen in narrow terms, aimed at the measurement of a limited range of attributes or characteristics by means of standardized tests. Testing and assessment were seen as synonymous. The measurement of intelligence or diagnosis of mental or physical pathology were the preponderant concerns of most applied psychologists. As some became involved in treatment and management, the range of techniques required increased, with practitioners becoming aware of the need for procedures which would have immediate implications for directing treatment. Although there were several important analyses of testing much of the early work was concerned with narrowly conceived theory and practice of measurement (psychometrics). More recently, there has been a shift towards extending the range of procedures used in assessment (Nay 1979), the emphasis being on multi-method assessment. The reasons for this change stem mainly from the inadequacies of the one or two general purpose tests which psychologists commonly used. These general tests have been found to be inadequate as guides for practice and as ways of monitoring the effects of treatment. Additionally they have been found to be insensitive to the many consequences of psychological intervention.

Nevertheless, decisions made or influenced by such tests can exert a profound effect on the lives of individuals and their families. For instance, psychological assessments developed around one or two tests are influential in decisions about schooling, particularly the transfer of pupils between ordinary (mainstream) and special schools. Such transfers can circumscribe the future choices available to the individual, can lead to the stigmatization of pupil and family and absorb scarce resources. They can also be of immense benefit in helping to provide the individual and family with forms of support which would not be made available otherwise.

Some of the negative ramifications of psychological assessment have been highlighted by the use of tests on minority group children. (See Sattler 1982 for a discussion of the impact of tests in the USA and Coard 1971 for some reactions in the UK). It is argued that the tests, commonly of intelligence and attainments are biased and prejudicial to the interests of the children, their families and others who may not share the norms of the dominant groups in the community. In some States in the USA the use of certain tests have been curbed by legislation. While there have been some recent attempts to refute the imputation of bias (Jensen 1980), the major problems arise because of the failure of test-givers to master the intricacies of test administration and interpretation (Berger 1983).

Although much of the critical debate has focussed on intelligence tests, many of the issues raised are common to most if not all psychological procedures. For instance, assessment is very much dependent on informal or systematic observation. Mitchell (1979) among others has clearly documented the many limitations of observation, including the effect of observer bias and expectation, the reactivity of the people being observed and the limitations inherent in particular systematic observation techniques.

Another recent development has been an increasing awareness of the impact on people of the contexts in which they live. In the past the concern was with measuring characteristics (pathological or non-pathological) of, or within the individual. It is now recognized that the intimate interplay between the individual and the physical and social environment has to be considered in order to obtain a realistic appraisal of problems and to formulate suitable treatment.

Assessment involves several other issues of outstanding importance. One is the conceptualization of the assessment process itself: little attention has been given to an analysis of what the process is about and why it takes the form it does. One view regards it as the application of scientific method in the investigation of the individual. This approach has been most clearly developed by Shapiro (1970). It sees investigation as being concerned with the generation and testing of hypotheses put forward to account for clinical phenomena – the presenting problems. The psychologist formulates hypotheses and uses various means to test them experimentally. That is, assessment is essentially a form of research concentrating on an individual. In the framework of this approach the distinction between assessment and treatment is no longer clear-cut and may even be irrelevant. The treatment is seen as a test of the adequacy of the hypotheses and as such is an integral part of the investigations.

A somewhat related view has been developed from a different theoretical perspective in what is known as target assessment and entails the search for functional relationships between environmental events and the problem behavior. In this approach the problem is seen in terms of a specifiable set of behavior patterns which can be clearly defined. An attempt is then made through observation and manipulation to identify the environmental antecedents and/or consequences which exert some control over the problem behavior. In so doing, both the "causes" and the means of "treatment" are identified. (See BEHAVIOR CHANGE IN THE CLASSROOM for a more detailed description of this approach.) Target assessment is one aspect of a broader approach known as behavioral assessment which concentrates on the behavior-patterns that constitute the problem, a variety of procedures being used to identify the factors which influence its expression and form. The behavioral assessment process has several stages. The first consists of problem specification, the second of selecting, implementing and eventually terminating the intervention, and the third, follow-up evaluation. Other analyses of the process have additional stages and may emphasize different aspects of the investigation and intervention, particularly ecological influences. Behavioral assessment is generally concerned with the individual and psychologists have begun to examine and develop an experimental methodology for the investigation of individual clients (e.g. Hersen and Barlow 1976).

Another important issue concerns the role of theory in assessment: some forms of assessment are presented as pragmatic and empirical, essentially exercises in testing divorced from theory while others are closely allied to a particular theoretical orientation but with little overt appreciation of the ways in which the theory influences practice.

It is not generally appreciated that theory selectively determines the form and nature of assessment. Behavioral assessment is one illustration of an approach which is closely dependent on a particular theoretical orientation. Theory provides the language, the content and the underlying models which will guide the investigations, what will be seen, and the interpretation of the outcome. It also influences the nature and evaluation of intervention. Even as common a practice as "testing intelligence" carries with it a network of assumptions and theoretical ideas about the "existence" and nature of intelligence, its measurement and its role in human functioning. A psychologist influenced by Piagetian theory and method would adopt an approach to intelligence differing substantially from that of someone whose view is based on one of several other views of intelligence (see Sattler 1982). Practitioners and the "consumers" need to be consistently aware of the implications for the individual of the adoption and adherence to a particular theoretical orientation.

Of particular relevance in the assessment of children, handicapped or not, is the need to adopt a developmental perspective and to consider the implications for assessment of the differential rates of development across the life span and the qualitative changes which occur at comparatively rapid rates in childhood. There have been some recent attempts to do so, for example in the assessment and treatment of problems in social relationships (Furman 1980).

MBe

Bibliography

*Berger, M. 1983: Psychological assessment and testing. In *Child psychiatry: modern perspectives* ed. M. Rutter and L. Hersov, 2nd edn. Oxford: Blackwell Scientific; Philadelphia: Lippincott.

Coard, B. 1971: *How the West-Indian child is made educationally subnormal in the British school system.* London: New Beacon Books.

Furman, W. 1980: Promoting social development: developmental implications for treatment. In *Advances in clinical child psychology, vol. 3.*, ed. B.B. Lahey and A.E. Kazdin. New York: Plenum Press.

Hersen, M. and Barlow, D.H. 1976: *Single case experimental design: strategies for studying behavior change.* New York and Oxford: Pergamon.

Jensen, A.R. 1980: *Bias in mental testing.* London and New York: Methuen.

Kaufman, A.S. 1979: *Intelligent testing with the W.I.S.C.-R.* New York: John Wiley.

Mitchell, S.K. 1979: Interobserver agreement, reliability and generalizability of data collected in observational studies. *Psychological bulletin* 86, 376–90.

Nay, W.R. 1979: *Multimethod clinical assessment.* New York: Gardner Press.

*Sattler, J.M. 1982: *Assessment of children's intelligence*, 2nd edn. Boston: Allyn & Bacon.

Shapiro, M.B. 1970: Intensive assessment of the single case: an inductive–deductive approach. In *The psychological assessment of mental and physical handicaps*, ed. P. Mittler. London: Tavistock; New York: Harper & Row.

education of handicapped children Education may be provided in various ways for pupils with disabilities which affect their learning and development. Ideally it should be as normal as possible in terms of the aims, curricula and methods. Many handicapped children are satisfactorily educated in ordinary classes with varying degrees of support and specialist educational, psychological and medical surveillance (see INTEGRATION OF HANDICAPPED CHILDREN INTO NORMAL SCHOOLS). Others are taught in special classes or units with possibilities for participation in ordinary classes and provision for similar support and surveillance. Special schools are needed for others, at least for part of their school life and possibly with part-time attendance at a normal school. Education through the guidance and involvement of parents should be available from birth, should continue into preschool provision and, following the normal school period, further education and vocational training should be available as required.

The aims of education and curricula should, as far as possible, be the same as for non-handicapped children although severe sensory and intellectual impairments may dictate a different emphasis in aims or require special curriculum planning. In general, the more severe the sensory or intellectual handicap the greater the need for special teaching methods. These include, first, a thorough understanding of the consequences of visual, hearing or intellectual impairments for the child's cognitive, personality and educational development as well as his or her broader personal and social needs. Second, knowledge of the methods of structuring learning, of special methods of communication (e.g. braille, language and speech, signing systems) and a variety of technical aids (vision aids, sound amplification, electronic apparatus, microprocessors, etc.)

RG

educational attainment and expectations

(1) parental expectations Research in the sociology of education has shown that parental expectations, and children's perceptions of parental expectations, have a significant independent effect on children's educational attainment. Parental expectations have been shown to have a stronger effect on attainment than teacher's expectations.

A great deal of the research on parental expectations has been in the service of discovering causal factors to explain achievement differences among ethnic groups and among groups differing in socioeconomic status. While parental expectations correlate positively with social status, parental expectations alone cannot explain achievement differences among ethnic groups, even though ethnicity correlates with socioeconomic level.

Black parents of low socioeconomic status often have expectations for their children that are equal to or higher than those of middle-class parents, although the children of these groups significantly differ in achievement levels. One possible explanation for this is that high parental expectations are not enough; parents must also provide their children with time and attention, in addition to practical strategies which can be used to achieve educational goals. In some cases, high parental expectations may actually inhibit school performance. Relatively little research has been conducted to examine the strategies parents use to implement their expectations.

Researchers have also found that high parental expectations may differentially affect different abilities. Verbal and number abilities may be more susceptible to environmental influences, such as parental expectations, than spatial abilities. Also, parental expectations tend to influence the educational attainment of girls more than boys. See also EDUCATIONAL ATTAINMENT AND PRESCHOOL EXPERIENCE; EDUCATIONAL ATTAINMENT AND SOCIAL CLASS; INTELLIGENCE AND ENVIRONMENTAL INFLUENCES.

JSC

(2) pupil expectations The expectations that pupils have about their performance in an instructional setting have profound effects on their actual performance. The concept is closely related to Merton's notion (1948) of the self-fulfilling prophecy which holds that people who have expectations about what is to occur often act in ways likely to produce that occurrence. In an educational context, those who expect to perform well, do perform better than those who do not have that expectation (Zanna et al. 1975). What has made this line of research intriguing is that the successful performance occurs even though the expectation of success is based on factors that are not relevant to performance. The expectation of success or failure may come from random selection invoked by a researcher or by factors such as race, ethnicity or socioeconomic status. While most research has focussed on the effect of successful expectations, two additional phenomena should be noted. First Aronson and Carlsmith (1962) found that pupils actively seek to confirm their expectations about themselves – even when that confirmation leads to failure. Second, the Zanna et al. study indicated that the expectations pupils have about themselves can interact with the expectations held by others. Pupils who had successful expectations, and about whom teachers also held positive expectations, actually performed worse than other students. The potentially helpful and potentially invidious effects of the expectations held by pupils has made this phenomenon an interesting one to researchers and educators.

JCo

(3) teacher expectations The study of the effect of teacher expectations on pupils' performance also derives from Merton's concept of the self-fulfilling prophecy. Rosenthal and Jacobson (1968) studied the prophecies or expectations that teachers had about children in their classes. They led teachers to believe that some of the children in their classes could be expected to do very well during the school year. Even though the children were randomly selected, those whom the teachers expected to do well actually performed much better on standardized tests at the end of the school year than did those children about whom the teachers had no expectations. This was particularly true of younger children and became less pronounced in the older grades. Teacher expectations have been shown to affect pupils' performance in a variety of areas from mathematics to swimming. Current research has continued in at least two directions. One is to place the effect of teacher expectations in a larger theoretical framework (e.g. Darley and Fazio 1980) and the other is the careful analysis of the ways in which teacher expectations are subtly communicated to students. JCo

Bibliography

Aronson, E., and Carlsmith, J.M. 1962: Performance expectancy as a determinant of actual performance. *Journal of abnormal and social psychology* 65, 178–82.

Darley, J., and Fazio, R. 1980: Expectancy confirmation processes arising in the social interaction sequence. *American psychologist* 35, 867–81.

Merton, R. 1948: The self-fulfilling prophecy. *Antioch Review* 8, 193–210.

Rosenthal, R., and Jacobson, L. 1968: *Pygmalion in the classroom: Teacher expectation and pupils' intellectual development.* New York: Holt, Rinehart & Winston.

Zanna, Mark P. et al. 1975: Pygmalion and Galatea: The interactive effect of teacher and student expectancies. *Journal of experimental social psychology* 11, 279–87.

educational attainment and institutional care Children reared in institutional care are usually the legal responsibility of a statutory or voluntary agency and live with other children in residences where they are looked after by a team of child care workers. John Bowlby has claimed that children under five who are reared in such institutions will suffer mental deficits because they lack the continuous relationship with the mother that is necessary to normal development. Some support for Bowlby's claim came from early studies showing low IQs among children reared in orphanages with poor staff ratios and few playthings.

Institutional upbringing is associated with intellectual deficit in handicapped children too. Children with Down's syndrome reared in a residential setting score lower on measures of play maturity than Down's children at home (who had more social contacts and toys).

It is difficult to pinpoint the exact cause of intellectual deficits among institutionalized children because maternal absence, poor facilities and lack of social contact are often confounded. Tizard and Hodges (1978) followed the progress of children in high quality residential nurseries, those with excellent staffing ratios, "home-like" atmosphere, and educational playthings. At the age of four nursery children did not differ on IQ measures from home-reared children with similar social backgrounds. By eight, however, the IQs of the institutionalized children had decreased markedly; in fact they were lower than scores of children living in families who had been adopted from the institution before the age of four.

It appears that institutionalization before the age of four does not impair intellectual development but that after that age institutionalization may be associated with lower intellectual functioning and school attainment. This may be due to lack of personal involvement and continuity with adults rather than inadequate facilities.

(See also INSTITUTIONALIZATION.) KS

Bibliography

*Tizard, B. 1977: *Adoption: a second chance.* London: Open Books.

——and Hodges, J. 1978: The effect of early institutional rearing on the development of eight year old children. *Journal of child psychology and psychiatry* 19, 99-118.

educational attainment and locus of control Locus of control of reinforcement refers to an individual's perception of reinforcement contingencies. The more a person sees a connection between his own behavior and what happens to him the more "internal" he is considered. Conversely, the more he does not perceive connections between his reinforcements and his actions but sees the consequences as due to luck, chance or the influence of others, the more "external" he is considered. Originating in Rotter's social learning theory (1966) locus of control orientation has been found to be related to an impressive array of significant behavior ranging from academic achievement to psychological adjustment. While there are multiple dimensional measures of locus of control available, the most popular measures for both children and adults provide a single global score.

Recent work has focussed on antecedents of, and changing of, locus of control as well as on devising procedures that take advantage of the differences in information processing associated with internal and external orientations. For example, school curricula have been designed to be consistent with children's locus of control orientation, with resultant increases in academic achievement and liking for school. SN

Bibliography

Rotter, J.B. 1966: Generalized expectancies for internal versus external control of reinforcements. *Psychological monographs* 80.

educational attainment and preschool experiences Preschool experience includes all that the child perceives or does, at home or in nursery, before compulsory schooling. A host of recent studies document the powerful influence of the home on children's preparation for school. The UK National Child Development Study found the strongest determinant of variations in reading and arithmetic attainment at seven years to be family background. Studies with even younger children show that social class influences linguistic skills and that children with more advanced language benefit the most when they go to school.

Many hypotheses have been put forward to explain the processes by which family factors affect school readiness. Observational studies indicate that high levels of maternal involvement, coupled with provision of age-appropriate and challenging playthings, foster sensory-motor competence (see PIAGET) in toddlers. Some mothers encourage intellectual development by using praise instead of criticism and allowing children to set their own pace and make decisions. Unfortunately the many factors associated with SOCIAL DISADVANTAGE such as poor jobs, housing and health make if difficult for poor families to provide a stimulating environment.

Nursery schools and playgroups have traditionally complemented middle-class homes by providing an informal curriculum of rich playthings and peer interaction. Because families living in circumstances of disadvantage rarely provide such learning opportunities, many programs of compensatory preschool education were developed to provide a "head start" for poor children before formal school (see COMPENSATORY EDUCATION). Follow-up studies (Darlington 1980) of "graduates" of American preschool programs show them to have higher rates of meeting school requirements (as measured by lower grade retention or assignment to special class) than children who had not attended preschool. Studies of children attending similar compensatory preschool programs in the UK showed significant cognitive and linguistic gains upon entry into school (Smith and James 1975).

Two factors are associated consistently with successful preschools: inclusion of sessions with structured play activities, high levels of adult–child conversation and parent involvement. Most educationalists now concentrate on the last in hopes that participating in nurseries will help parents develop confidence and skills for giving their own children a "good start". KS

Bibliography

Darlington, R.B. et al. 1980: Preschool programs and later school competence of children from low income families. *Science* 208 (April) 202–204.

*Mortimore, J. and Blackstone, T. 1982: *Disadvantage and education*. London and Exeter, N.H.: Heinemann Educational.

Smith, G.A. and James, T. 1975: The effects of pre-school education: some American and British evidence. *Oxford review of education* 1, 221–38.

educational attainment and social class Correlations have been found between parents' social class and their children's educational performance both in terms of years of schooling and level of academic achievement. The influence that a family's socioeconomic situation exerts over a child's educational attainment stems from a variety of sources, an important one being the value that a family places on education (see EDUCATIONAL ATTAINMENT AND PARENTAL EXPECTATIONS). Children of middle- to upper-class families tend to have high educational aspirations as a result of the pressure they perceive from home to continue their studies regardless of their own attitude towards school. Another factor is the effect of the values of the peer group on the children's developing standards and goals. (See also SOCIAL DISADVANTAGE; COMPENSATORY EDUCATION.) MB/JM

educational psychology That a branch of psychology should address itself to education occasions no surprise since learning and development are major concerns of both. Difficulties arise, however, in establishing the content and the limits of educational psychology, which make it hard to accord it a distinctive identity within the field of psychology.

Problems of definition and content arise from a variety of sources both within and outside psychology. Outside psychology there are the varying expectations and demands of different professional groups working with children (such as teachers, medical specialists and social workers). Meeting the psychological requirements of central and local government (particularly in relation to special educational provision) adds further complexities.

Within psychology, it would be easy to define educational psychology as the psychology of learning and teaching in school, but of course these activities are not just confined to schools. Furthermore learning and teaching extend over the entire life span. Finally what contributes to effective learning and teaching, even within schools, is much more complex and extensive than such a simplistic statement implies. However, it would be generally accepted that the subject matter and the professional practice of educational psychology are concerned with the development and education of children from birth to adulthood. Thus, a knowledge of developmental psychology, social psychology and clinical psychology is needed, to include knowledge of the basic psychological processes involved in development and learning, such as perception, cognition, memory and motivation.

Some knowledge and experience of educational practice is also required of psychologists who undertake additional professional training to work as educational psychologists (usually through teaching – see SCHOOL PSYCHOLOGICAL SERVICES). A more extensive utilization of the research skills of such people would be highly desirable if educational provision is to become more effective.

With such wide ranging subject matter, coupled with the varied professional service demands, educational psychology has inevitably been involved in many of the basic issues encountered in the general development of psychology as a science. For example controversy over the contribution of heredity and environment to educational performance still continues (see INTELLIGENCE AND ENVIRONMENTAL INFLUENCES). But since only environmental conditions are normally subject to change, they are inevitably coming under increasing attention. Precise measures of the environment, or how it is perceived, still require development. The traditional use of "social class" as an "environmental measure" can only represent a very crude first-stage level of analysis. Differences within such social groups are usually very large as is the overlap between them. Parental interest and direct parental involvement in the education of their children, particularly when young, appear important in relation to both social behavior and educational attainment. Even so, the relationship between such variables and educational performance is far from perfect, suggesting that as yet undiscovered factors may play an equal or perhaps even more important part in some children's development and educational progress (Plowden 1967).

Within schools, the expectations of teachers and their pupils as well as personality attributes have been implicated (see also EDUCATIONAL ATTAINMENT AND LOCUS OF CONTROL). The SCHOOL AS A SOCIAL ORGANIZATION that can vary in its effectiveness is also being more closely examined. More research is required in all these areas before any educational service can reliably claim to be able to identify and effectively meet the educational needs of children, however these needs are defined.

One of the distinctive contributions made by professional educational psychologists has been to identify children in need of special educational consideration and to help in making appropriate provision for them. Such children can include of course GIFTED CHILDREN as well as the HANDICAPPED and those with marked, mild or specific learning disabilities (see DYSLEXIC CHILDREN, LEARNING DIFFICULTIES, REMEDIAL MATHEMATICS, REMEDIAL READING). In establishing such needs and making such provision in the past, considerable dependence has been placed upon TESTS. These have served a useful function in the absence of better alternative techniques. It has, however, been increasingly appreciated that these instruments are not sufficiently sensitive to the wide range of individual differences in behavior that are pertinent to education. Some children too, have had experience of highly atypical environments (see e.g. SOCIAL DISADVANTAGE, DELINQUENCY, DEPRIVATION) and are consequently likely to show considerably more variability in their test performance. Caution is therefore needed in the interpretation of test performances especially those used with ETHNIC MINORITY CHILDREN.

The apparent homogeneity implicit in the labels attached to the various groups of children considered in need of special educational consideration conceals much heterogeneity in the ways in which such children actually function. Not surprisingly there is consequently a differential response to the education or 'treatment' offered. More emphasis is needed on 'process' (e.g. the learning and thinking strategies of individuals) as opposed to end-products (e.g. test results of groups). Knowledge is needed about how rather than what children accomplish. An examination of the methodology often adopted by psychologists to investigate educational problems suggests similar conclusions.

Large scale surveys supported by extensive correlational analyses have traditionally been used. These have been extremely useful in defining the broad parameters of problem areas, an inevitable and necessary first-stage level of inquiry. Such an approach has a number of limitations, however. Among these are: (1) The associations established and indexed by the correlations calculated between two variables permit no inference as to cause or the direction of effects. Furthermore they relate to group trends and not to individuals. (2) The correlated variables almost inevitably (by definition) reflect the end-product rather than the nature of the processes themselves. However some surveys, through the use of supplementary data, can point up possible causal networks more precisely (see e.g. Rutter et al. 1970). (3) Establishing the statistical significance of such correlations does not thereby establish their psychological value. Small correlations can be significant in statistical terms when large samples are used. Even large and highly significant correlations 'explain' only a proportion of the variance between variables, for example a correlation of +0.7 explains only 49 per cent ($0.7^2 \times 100$) of the variance, leaving 51 per cent as an index of ignorance or unexplained variance. (4) Various forms of factor analysis can help in the grouping and ordering of large numbers of correlations. Factor analysis is a mathematical technique, and there is no necessity for the factors, however labelled, to be equivalent to any psychological entity or variable. Furthermore it is often not easy to "fit" individuals into factor patterns so derived. There are other techniques, of course, that analyse data in relation to persons rather than by discrete variables.

Some indications of change over time can be obtained through the use of longitudinal studies which follow the same group of children over a number of years. It is thus possible to indicate at what stage in development or in a child's school career specific difficulties were identified and what happened subsequently. These procedures can provide valuable data but the method has limitations, such as: (1) The studies are time consuming and therefore expensive. (2) Samples contract in size over time for a variety of reasons such as accident, change of address, or unwillingness to continue collaboration. This reduces the value of the data. The contraction may also occur disproportionately in vulnerable sections of the sample that are central to the objectives of the research (e.g. the effects of social factors on educational performance). (3) The size of the sample needs to be sufficiently large to permit analyses and generalizations from important subgroups contained within it (e.g. those who become delinquents or who are backward in reading). (4) Important changes may take place over time that have not been adequately monitored in the research (e.g. the rapid and recent widespread increase in unemployment across all occupational groups in the United Kingdom). (5) Introducing new variables or modifying others during the course of a longitudinal study has to be avoided if maximum use is to be made of the data without confounding the results.

Cross-sectional studies using survey techniques at a given moment have an advantage in being more economical in both time and cost but cannot monitor changes over time. Some compromise arrangements merging cross-sectional and longitudinal methods in a limited way are possible.

Economic constraints, with the need to ensure more efficient and effective use of resources, will reinforce the need for more stringent evaluation of educational provision. An emphasis on more process-oriented psychological research on a smaller scale would be highly relevant to such purposes. This will require knowledge of advances within the mainstream of general psychology as well as in child development. RM

Bibliography

Baltes, P.B., Reese, H.W. and Nesselrode, J. R. 1977: *Life-span developmental psychology: introduction to research methods.* Monterey, Calif.: Brookes Cole.

Plowden 1967: *Report on children and the primary schools.* London: HMSO.

Rutter, M.L., Tizard, J. and Whitmore, K. 1970: *Education, health and behavior.* London: Longman; New York: Robert E. Krieber (1981).

EEG *See* electroencephalogram

ego: philosophical usage The word "ego" is the Latin equivalent of the English "I", but is used technically as a common noun rather than as a pronoun. The most common use is as the name of a putative substantial self distinct from the body. The most famous development of such a use is to be found in Kant's doctrine of the transcendental ego; in this theory there is no phenomenal entity, the ego or self, open to observation or introspection, but the existence of such an ego must be allowed if we are to explain mental phenomena and in particular the unity of the self. It is the transcendental ego which imposes the categories on phenomena. JOU

ego: psychological usage Although the word has a philosophical history in English as denoting the essential "self" or seat of identity (see EGO: PHILOSOPHICAL USAGE), in psychology, it has come to mean the system of rational and realistic functions of the personality. This usage is largely influenced by PSYCHOANALYTIC PERSONALITY THEORY, in which the word ego is a translation of Freud's *Ich* (1923), where it is contrasted with the instinctually impulsive "id", and with the evaluative SUPEREGO; but it is not equated with consciousness, since Freud argued that much of it would have to be unconscious or "preconscious". Its function in that theory leads to operationally definable concepts such as "ego-strength" and "ego-control", whose development in childhood and efficacy in maturity can be assessed by means independent of psychoanalysis (Cattell 1965, ch. 3). Those theorists who give greater weight to ego-processes (such as reality-perception, conscious learning and voluntary control) in their accounts of personality development and in techniques of psychotherapy are known as ego-psychologists (Hartmann 1964). See also DEFENSE MECHANISM. RMC

Bibliography

Cattell, Raymond B. 1965: *The scientific analysis of personality.* Harmondsworth: Penguin.

Freud, Sigmund 1923: The ego and the id. *Standard edition of the complete psychological works of Sigmund Freud.* Vol. 19. London: Hogarth Press; New York: Norton.

Hartmann, Heinz 1964: *Essays in ego-psychology.* London: Hogarth Press.

ego ideal Term in PSYCHOANALYTICAL PERSONALITY THEORY for the ideal standard against which the Ego evaluates its activity and qualities. Hence FREUD at one time gave it a role in dream-censorship, but for the most part he drops the term once he has attributed its function to the positive aspect of the SUPEREGO (Freud 1923, esp. pp.9–11). The young child sets up this psychic standard as part of that internalization of (or IDENTIFICATION with) parental values and controls which allows it to resolve the OEDIPUS AND ELEKTRA COMPLEXES. As such, it is "the expression of the admiration for the perfection" which the child then attributes to its parents, as opposed to representing their forbidding and punitive aspect which the superego also embodies. Elsewhere the term is used, even by Freud, synonymously with "superego". NMC

Bibliography

Freud, Sigmund 1923: The ego and the id. *Standard edition of the complete psychological works of Sigmund Freud.* Vol. 19. London: Hogarth Press; New York: Norton.

egocentrism A term first proposed in 1926 by the psychologist Jean Piaget to designate a cognitive state in which the individual comprehends the world only from his own point of view, without awareness of the existence of other possible points of view. Although typical of childish thought, egocentrism can be observed throughout the lifespan. It is a state of mind characterized by failure to differentiate between subjective and objective components of experience, with a consequent unwitting imposition of a personal point of view (see Cox 1980).

A classic example of spatial egocentrism in childhood is Piaget's "three mountains" task. The child of about five years is seated in front of a papier mâché model of three mountains and asked to imagine how the scene would appear to a doll at another position. The child consistently describes his own viewpoint as though it were characteristic of the doll's.

An example of social egocentrism from adulthood might be the case of the teacher with specialized knowledge who fails to take sufficient account of the lesser knowledge of his pupils, with the consequence that they fail to comprehend. This could be considered an example of "egocentric speech", since the teacher intends but fails to communicate. GEB

Bibliography

Cox, Maureen V. 1980: *Are young children egocentric?* London: Batsford; New York: St Martin's Press.

Piaget, Jean 1923: *The language and thought of the child.* 3rd edn. 1959. London: Routledge and Kegan Paul; New York: Humanities Press.

eidetic images *See* memory images

electroconvulsive therapy A form of therapy for the psychoses initially used to treat schizophrenics, but currently used primarily in the treatment of severe endogenous depression in individuals for whom drug therapy is either ineffective or contraindicated. With current methods patients are pretreated with a muscle relaxant to avoid undue stress on muscles and bones. An electrical current (110–170 v, low fixed amperage) is applied briefly to the head, resulting in electrical seizures.

Treatment is usually given no more than three times per week, for up to three to four weeks. In many individuals the treatment is remarkably effective in reducing severe depression. Side effects include temporary changes in the ELECTROENCEPHALOGRAM and transient retrograde and anterograde amnesia. This latter effect can be minimized by unilateral current administration. GPH

electroencephalogram (EEG) A graphic tracing of the electrical activity of the brain over time (BRAIN AND CENTRAL NERVOUS SYSTEM: ILLUSTRATIONS figs 33 and 34). An EEG is typically recorded from the surface of the scalp with an array of from six to ten electrodes placed at different locations on the head. The electrical potentials of the EEG are very small, usually around 5 to 150 microvolts, and require substantial amplification. EEG waves range in frequency from 0.5 to 50 Hz.

Several characteristic rhythms in the EEG are seen in normal individuals. Alpha rhythms have a frequency of 8 to 13 Hz and are usually seen when a person is calm and relaxed with eyes closed. Beta rhythms are low-voltage fast activity in the range of 13 to 30 Hz and are observed when an individual is aroused. Delta rhythms are large amplitude slow waves with frequencies of 0.5 to 3 Hz and appear during deep (stage 4) sleep. Theta rhythms have a frequency of 4 to 7 Hz and have been associated with memory storage processes in some studies. (See also PARADOXICAL SLEEP.) RAJ

electromagnetic senses *See* senses, electromagnetic

electrophysiology *See* neurometrics

emancipatory knowledge Knowledge of possible distortions contained in shared understandings, distortions caused by the impact of relationships of *domination* (unequal power) on the processes by which the shared understandings were formed. This definition reflects Habermas's distinctions (1971) among three human "interests" – the technical, the practical and the emancipatory – which have shaped the development of knowledge by defining its objects, methods of inquiry and criteria of validation. Technical knowledge (knowledge of lawful relations of independent and dependent variables) enables us to choose the best means of achieving agreed-upon ends. Practical knowledge (knowledge of shared meanings, norms and expectations) enables us to communicate with each other and to engage in cooperative action. Emancipatory knowledge enables us to free ourselves from shared understandings which limit our perceptions of possible goals and aspirations.

Emancipatory knowledge may be the product of any human inquiry, but it is explicitly pursued by critical social science (see CRITICAL THEORY) which includes the critique of ideology as well as some approaches to PSYCHOANALYSIS. Examples of ideas which might be proposed as emancipatory knowledge are: (1) "workers believe themselves to be incapable of democratically managing their own workplaces because they have formed their self-concepts under the influence of an educational system which is supported by and serves the interests of those who currently benefit from oligarchical management of workplaces" or (2) "sexual activity which results in feelings of guilt may do so not because sex is inherently evil, but because when we were children our powerful parents may have scolded us sharply when we touched ourselves in pleasurable ways". These ideas may increase our freedom to choose to pursue goals of workplace democratization or more fulfilling sexual experience. Validation of ideas proposed as emancipatory knowledge can only be partial or probable, and comes only when the ideas give rise to a process of continued critical self-reflection by people, culminating in the pursuit of new aspirations and in efforts to transform the conditions which presumably caused the distortion.

It is an ancient philosophical theme that true knowledge emancipates and false knowledge enslaves the knower. In the *Timaeus*, Plato suggests that true knowledge (theoria) originates in the disinterested contemplation of the cosmos, while false knowledge, or opinion (doxa), originates in the interests which guide daily life. By suppressing these interests, the knower becomes free to absorb the harmony of the cosmos and to mimic it in the conduct of daily life, thereby achieving emancipation from the enslaving force of opinion. Habermas's work reflects the evolution of the idea of emancipatory knowledge over the history of philosophy. While sharing Plato's belief that technical and practical knowledge shaped by the taken-for-granted goals of members of a society may contribute to their enslavement, Habermas argues that the Platonic dissociation of theory from daily interests, and the entire tradition of questioning our common goals and knowledge, reflects a deeper human interest in autonomy and responsibility – an emancipatory interest. MBa/FAR

Bibliography

Habermas, Jurgen 1971: *Knowledge and human interests.* Boston: Beacon Press.

embedding A term used by transformational generative grammarians to refer to sentence or clause subordination, i.e. instances where sentences or clauses appear as constituents of a superordinate matrix sentence in the deep structure (Chomsky 1965, pp.12 ff). The application of transformations on deep structures containing embeddings can lead to surface structures with no embeddings. Thus the surface sentence 'I saw the red hat' is said to be transformationally derived from 'I saw the hat which is red'.

The psychological reality of such embeddings has been subjected to numerous tests. For a discussion see Greene 1972, pp.93–188. MT

Bibliography

Chomsky, Noam 1965: *Aspects of the theory of syntax.* Cambridge Mass.: MIT Press.

Greene, Judith 1972: *Psycholinguistics: Chomsky and psychology.* Harmondsworth and Baltimore: Penguin Books.

emergence Term associated with an anti-reductionist approach to evolution popular in the 1920s. Emergentists in psychology hold that mental activity *depends* upon a sufficiently complex brain, yet it cannot be completely *reduced* to brain activity. When minds first evolved, they were a qualitatively new phenomenon in nature; a higher-than-physiological level of description is required in order to account for them.

Bolder versions of the doctrine of emergence tended to confuse the temporal process of emerging with a non-temporal relation between levels (of properties, or of discourse). For example the developmental model is clearly inappropriate to describe the relation between the mental activity in S at a given time and S's *concurrent* brain activity. This relation is better viewed as a kind of supervenience, or as contingent identity. However, emergentists were surely right in their claim that a high-level theory would not necessarily be *semantically* reducible to a lower-level theory, even if the domain of reference of the two theories were the same. There may be more than one way of describing one and the same process, and these descriptions may not be equivalent in meaning. ARW

Bibliography

Alexander, S. 1920: *Space, time and deity*. London: Macmillan; New York: Dover.

Lloyd Morgan, C. 1923: *Emergent evolution*. London: Williams and Norgate; New York: Holt.

emergent qualities Qualities found at higher levels of organization which are unpredictable from qualities found at lower levels. In the doctrine of emergence it is presupposed that things and processes have a hierarchical organization, so that it makes sense to speak of "higher" and "lower" levels. A level is a portion of the world that is marked by a set of closely related characteristics peculiar to it. The philosopher S. Alexander, in defending the older doctrine of emergent evolutionism, distinguished five levels: space – time, matter, life, mind and deity. More recently, Oppenheim and Putnam proposed six levels that are more in the spirit of modern science: elementary particles, atoms, molecules, cells, multi-cellular living things and social groups. Still, it seems that any system of levels has to make certain metaphysical assumptions. The concept of emergence is a relative concept: qualities at a higher level may be unpredictable from a single lower level theory, while they could be predicted with the help of another lower level theory.

As an example, the concept of temperature may be called emergent relative to the kinetic theory of gases: the vocabulary of this theory does not contain the concept temperature, and so nothing about temperature can be predicted on the basis of kinetic theory alone. SJST

Bibliography

Meehl, P.E. and Sellars, W. 1956: The concept of emergence. In *Minnesota studies in the philosophy of science*, vol. 1, ed. H. Feigl, M. Scriven and G. Maxwell. Minneapolis: University of Minnesota Press.

Nagel, E. 1961: *The structure of science*. London: Routledge S Kegan Paul.

Oppenheim, P. and Putnam, H. 1958: Unity of science as a working hypothesis. In *Minnesota studies in the philosophy of science*, vol. II, ed. H. Feigl, M. Scriven and G. Maxwell. Minneapolis: University of Minnesota Press.

emic vs. etic Conceptions derived from the internal logic of a culture are emic; universal conceptions, cutting across cultures, are etic. This distinction was made by Pike (1954) in discussing phon*emics* vs phon*etics*. To illustrate this emic polarity the Greek concept of *philotimia* is central to the functioning of Greek culture (Triandis 1972). It refers to a person behaving according to the norms of the ingroup – usually family and close friends. A person who is *philotimos* is highly valued; one who is *aphilotimos* is despised. People in traditional Greek culture use the word *philotimos* more often than any other to describe themselves. It is a concept that is very useful in explaining Greek culture and cannot be fully translated because of the many spontaneous associations that Greeks have with this concept.

An example of an etic concept is *social structure*. All groups have structure. That is, people communicate with others, value others, like others, respect others, avoid others, and so on in a patterned way. Sociometric studies show that some persons are over-chosen and others are under-chosen. This occurs in all cultures. Thus social structure is a concept that does not depend on a particular culture but is a universal. In cross-cultural studies researchers attempt to use emic concepts but relate them to etic constructs. By using emic concepts it is believed that one can capture some of the essence or idiosyncratic reality of a culture; by using etic constructs one attempts to communicate this information to persons outside the culture. HCT

Bibliography

Pike, K.L. 1954: *Language in relation to a unified theory of the structure of human behavior*. Glendale, Calif.: Summer Institute of Linguistics.

Triandis, H.C. 1972: *The analysis of subjective culture*. New York: Wiley.

emotion: environmental effects While some emotional reactions appear independent of former environmental stimulation, e.g. endogenous depressions, most theories postulate a high degree of interdependence between emotion and situations. Situations stimulate emotions, and emotions both color and generate situations. This interactive theme is reflected in evolutionary or ethological approaches which postulate that basic emotions reflect adaptive demands of key environmental situations; e.g. in-group and out-group identification links to acceptance–rejection; hierarchy to anger (high members) and fear (low members); territoriality to exploration and surprise; and the demands of temporal survival link to affects of mourning and myths of survival. Sociologists generate similar situation–emotion models based on analysis of group structures. In addition to these structural or correlational models, both child psychologists and anthropologists describe the processes by which emotional states and expressions integrate social behaviors in mother–infant interactions, work and family interactions and situations involving role conflicts and interpersonal regulation. These analyses range across issues such as how emotional communication generates interpersonal ties to how social (situational) rules limit the expression and potential damage of uninhibited expressions of emotions such as anger and sexuality. HL

Bibliography

Plutchik, R. 1980: A general psychoevolutionary theory of emotion. In *Emotion theory, research, and experience*, ed. R. Plutchik and H. Kellerman. New York: Academic Press.

Levy, R.I. 1973: *Tahitians: Mind and experience in the Society Islands*. Chicago: University of Chicago Press.

emotion: ethological approaches One of four major historical traditions that have attempted to describe the nature of emotions. One of these, the psychophysiological tradition, reflects the thinking of the American philosopher William James, who was concerned with a chicken-and-egg problem; which comes first, the feeling of an emotion or the physiological changes that are associated with it? This approach led to contemporary research on autonomic physiology, lie detectors and arousal. The neurological tradition, reflecting the research of Walter Cannon, a physiologist, was concerned with the effects of brain lesions on emotional expressions. Cannon's work stimulated a great deal of research concerned with mapping the HYPOTHALAMUS and the LIMBIC SYSTEM of the brain. The dynamic tradition stemmed from the work of Sigmund Freud, and was concerned mainly with the developmental changes that occur in emotions, and with their mixtures and derivatives. Freud concluded that emotions could be repressed, distorted or displaced and that their existence could only be inferred on the basis of a variety of indirect types of evidence.

The fourth major tradition, the evolutionary one, is based on the work of Charles Darwin described in *The expression of the emotions in man and animals* (1872). This work is the source of contemporary ethological approaches to emotion.

Darwin assumed that the process of evolution applied not just to anatomical structures but to the "mind" and emotions as well. He gave numerous illustrations of the basic continuity of emotional expressions from lower animals to humans. For example he pointed out that the baring of the fangs of the wolf is related to the sneer of the human adult, and that most species of animals, including humans, show an apparent increase in body size during rage (or under threat) owing to erection of body hair or feathers, changes in posture or expansion of air pouches. On the basis of many such examples, Darwin concluded that emotional expressions serve several functions in the lives of animals. They act as signals of intentions, and they are aspects of the various preparations the body makes for emergency actions. Emotional expressions convey information from one animal to another about what is likely to happen and thereby influence the chances of survival. For example a cat confronted by an attacking dog opens its mouth and shows its long incisors, pulls back its ears, erects the hair of its body, arches its back and hisses. This pattern of emotional expression, associated with mixed fear and anger, has definite value to the attacker: it signals the possibility of an attack in return. It makes the cat look larger and more ferocious and decreases the chances of a direct confrontation. This, in turn, increases survival possibilities for the cat.

Darwin also stated that many, but not all, emotional expressions are innate, or unlearned. This conclusion was based on four types of evidence: (1) some emotional expressions appear in similar form in many lower animals; (2) some emotional expressions appear in very young children in the same form as in adults, before much opportunity for learning has occurred; (3) some emotional expressions are shown in identical ways by those born blind and in those who are normally sighted; and (4) some emotional expressions appear in similar form in widely distinct races and groups of humans. Darwin also concluded that some emotional expressions are phylogenetically later than others. Expressions of fear and rage are quite primitive, while signs of grief (weeping), and frowning and blushing are relatively recent evolutionary acquisitions.

In summary, Darwin's views can be said to deal with the key issues of ethological research on emotions. He was concerned with the usefulness of a given emotional expression in the life of the animal (adaptation), with the occurrence across species of different facial and postural expressions (phylogeny), with genetic factors in expression (mechanism), and with natural selection pressures that might help to account for the appearance of particular expressions (evolution). Darwin's judgment, as well as that of ethologists today, is that emotional expressions are as reliable characters of species as are body structures, and they serve adaptive, survival functions in all organisms.

Contemporary ethologists, and to a large extent sociobiologists as well, have accepted these ideas and have tried to extend them. One form of extension has been to show more detailed parallels between lower and higher animals in emotional and social behavior. Comparing termites and monkeys, Wilson (1975) wrote: "Both societies are formed into cooperative groups that occupy territories. The group members communicate hunger, alarm, hostility, caste status, or rank and reproductive status among themselves "... Individuals are intensely aware of the distinction between groupmates and nonmembers ..."

In addition ethologists have devoted considerable research effort to studying, at many different phylogenetic levels, such emotional/social behavior as aggression, timidity, curiosity, play, courtship and sexuality. One well known list of basic adaptive, emotional patterns identifiable at most phylogenetic levels was proposed by Scott (1958). This consists of the following behavioral patterns: ingestive, agonistic, sexual, shelter-seeking, care-giving, care-soliciting, eliminative, allelomimetic (imitative), and investigative. An alternative view proposed by Plutchik (1980) is that there are eight basic behavior patterns which are the prototypes of emotions as seen in higher animals. These have been labeled with the following terms (with the subjective aspect in parentheses): protection (fear), destruction (anger), incorporation (acceptance), rejection (disgust), reproduction (joy), reintegration (sadness), orientation (surprise) and exploration (curiosity). These patterns may interact in various ways to produce the large variety of recognized emotional states.

Contemporary ethological approaches to emotion have at least four elements. As indicated above, they assume that emotions must be considered within an evolutionary context as adaptive classes of behavior. Secondly, they assume that emotions are complex chains of events that include more elements than expressive behavior alone, or subjective feelings. Emotions also include cognitive appraisals, states of physiological arousal, impulses to action, and overt behavior, all directed toward the particular events which triggered the emotional chain of response in the first place. Thirdly, it is recognized that the complexity of emotional reactions implies that their properties can be known only through a process of inference. An emotion may be conceptualized as a hypothetical construct which is known through various kinds of evidence. The types of evidence used include knowledge of: stimulus conditions preceding a reaction; an organism's behavior over an extended period of time; the species-typical behavior; how the organism's peers or conspecifics react to it; the choices an individual makes in a comparative free-choice situation; and the effect of the organism's behavior on others.

Finally, contemporary ethological thinking recognizes that emotions often mix and interact thereby producing various indirect derivatives. An example of this is the appearance of "displacement" behavior. This consists of actions that appear totally out of context. For example, two birds fighting may suddenly stop to preen their feathers. This is interpreted on the basis of the assumption that tendencies to attack and to flee occur during fighting, and that at certain times the strength of these opposing motivations are equal and opposite. Since the two responses are incompatible, neither can occur, and other activities in the animal's repertoire, such as preening, suddenly and temporarily appear. Another example of derivative expressions is seen in the variation of posture of birds and animals as a function of the relative strength of competing emotional tendencies. The zebra finch may show an "aggressive" horizontal posture associated with threat, or a "frightened" sleek, vertical, posture, or a "submissive" fluffed posture, or a specific "courtship" posture.

Intermediate postures and expressions reflect the existence of conflicts between impulses to attack and to flee. Similar mixtures of attack and withdrawal impulses have been shown for cat postures and facial expressions in the dog and the chimpanzee.

In summary it may be said that emotions are genetically programmed responses to certain common survival-related problems such as dealing with prey and predators, food and mates, care-givers and care-receivers. Emotions are attempts of the organism to achieve control over these kinds of events related to survival. Emotions are the ultra-conservative, evolutionary, behavioral adaptations that have been successful (like amino acids, DNA and genes) in increasing the chances of survival of organisms. Therefore, they have been maintained in functionally equivalent form through all phylogenetic levels. RP

Bibliography

Chance, M.R.A. 1980: An ethological assessment of emotion. In *Theories of emotion*, ed. R. Plutchik and H. Kellerman. New York: Academic Press.

Plutchik, R. 1980: *Emotion: a psychoevolutionary synthesis.* New York: Harper & Row.

Scott, J.P. 1958: *Animal behavior.* Chicago: University of Chicago Press.

Wilson, E.O. 1975: *Sociobiology: the new synthesis.* Cambridge, Mass.: Harvard University Press.

emotion: medical views of The Stoics, Kant, and many other classical writers viewed emotions as diseases of the mind. This view is no longer fashionable. Nevertheless, the emotions (variously and often vaguely defined) have found an increasingly prominent place in current medical discourse. Emotions have been linked to disease processes in six main ways.

(1) Acute emotional reactions, such as sudden fright, may have short term but sometimes fatal consequences, e.g. by inducing cardiac arrhythmias and consequent heart failure.

(2) Under conditions of chronic emotional arousal, activity of the autonomic and endocrine systems can lead directly to tissue damage in vulnerable organs (PSYCHOSOMATIC DISORDERS).

(3) The physiological changes accompanying emotional arousal may also lead to suppression of the immune system, thus increasing susceptibility to a wide range of diseases, including diseases not normally regarded as psychosomatic (e.g. neoplasms, infections).

(4) Emotional distress may also lead to changes in behavior (e.g. drug abuse, improper diet) that are pathogenic.

(5) Disease and the accompanying medical treatment can occasion intense emotional reactions (e.g. anxiety, grief, shame, anger, despair, hope); these emotional reactions may, in turn, influence symptom recognition and coping responses ("illness behavior"), and hence the course of the disease.

(6) Emotions that are not expressed for external (e.g. lack of opportunity or threat of punishment) or internal (e.g. moral) reasons may, if the stimulating conditions persist, be symbolically transformed and manifested in a manner resembling symptoms of illness (HYSTERIA). JRA

Bibliography

Stone, G.C., Cohen, F. and Adler, N.E. 1979: *Health psychology – a handbook.* San Francisco, Washington, and London: Jossey-Bass.

Weiner, H. 1977: *Psychobiology and human disease.* New York, Oxford, and Amsterdam: Elsevier.

emotion: neurobiological approach to Since the brain was first recognized as the organ of behavior scientists have been searching for the underlying brain systems which regulate and control emotional behavior. This investigative effort has primarily involved studying the effects of experimentally produced localized brain lesions on the behavior of various animal species as well as examining the emotional consequences of brain damage and the neural dysfunctions associated with psychiatric illnesses in humans.

The LIMBIC SYSTEM refers to a set of related neural structures and pathways in the brain which are importantly involved in emotion. The term is derived from *le grand lobe limbic* which was introduced by the French neurologist Paul Broca in 1878. Although Broca is best known for his discovery of the cerebral localization of certain language problems his neuroanatomical observations led him to describe the limbic lobe, which consisted of the HIPPOCAMPUS and parahippocampal gyrus, structures which formed the underlying limbus or border of the cerebral cortical hemispheres (see BRAIN AND CENTRAL NERVOUS SYSTEM: ILLS. 15–17). Anatomists working at the turn of the century conducted the first comparative anatomical studies and described a group of cerebral structures which appeared to be closely linked to the olfactory system, such as hippocampus, olfactory lobe, septal region and thus these structures were collectively named the "rhinencephalon" or olfactory brain. The AMYGDALA was also viewed as having olfactory functions since its location deep within the temporal lobe was in close proximity to the nucleus of the olfactory tract. The rhinencephalic structures identified by these anatomists were recognized to be phylogenetically older than other prominent cortical formations such as the neocortex.

A number of studies in the late 1920s linked various brain lesions to disturbances in emotional behavior (e.g. Bard 1928). However, it was not until 1937 that the rhinencephalic region came to be associated with any function other than olfaction. In that year Papez proposed that a set of anatomically related structures, which included the hypothalamus, anterior thalamic nuclei, cingulate gyrus and hippocampus mediated emotional expression and viscero-endocrine responses. Papez's suggestion was controversial at the time since it challenged existing notions of the olfactory brain. However it was becoming more apparent that the term rhinencephalic was something of a misnomer. A clear example of this was the observation that certain limbic structures are highly developed in animals which are anosmatic (e.g. the dolphin).

Papez's proposed mechanisms of emotion were elaborated upon further by MacLean (1949) who introduced the concept of the *limbic system*. MacLean noted that various rhinencephalic, thalamic and cortical structures had close anatomical connections with the hypothalamus and argued that these circuits modulated the affective response to stimuli and were responsible for autonomic effector mechanisms. He suggested that the structures of the rhinecephalon were strategically situated so as to be able to associate internal events with external stimuli. In this way, MacLean believed that the limbic system provided the emotional coloring to perceptual and cognitive processes.

The idea of an "emotional brain" was received favorably because of the popularity of Freudian thinking at the time. The concept of an ancient, deep part of the central nervous system which controls emotions and instincts unconsciously was naturally appealing to a Freudian-based psychology which ascribed great importance to the unconscious.

Around the time of Papez, Kluver and Bucy (1939) rediscovered a behavioral syndrome first observed by Brown and Schaefer (1888) Kluver and Bucy's experiments have had major impact on understanding the neurobiological substrates of emotion. They found that bilateral removal of the temporal lobe in monkeys resulted in profound changes in affective and social behavior. The lobectomized animals, formerly quite wild, became docile and tame and showed no fear reactions toward normally frightening stimuli. They displayed indiscriminate dietary behavior expressed in eating many types of previously rejected foods and attempting to eat inedible objects. Their sexual behavior changed dramatically with an increased incidence of autoerotic, homosexual and heterosexual activity. They showed a tendency to attend and react to every visual stimulus, termed "hypermetamorphosis" by Kluver and Bucy. They also showed a tendency to examine all objects by mouth, along with displaying signs of visual agnosia.

The Kluver-Bucy syndrome is not a phenomenon restricted to experimentally-lesioned animals. Many of the symptoms associated with this syndrome have also been observed in humans with a variety of neurological disorders (see e.g. Marlowe, Mancall and Thomas 1975). Additional research has indicated that the appearance of this syndrome requires both the amygdala and inferior temporal cortex to be removed bilaterally.

The functions subserved by the amygdala and hypothalamus are probably more well-studied than those for any of the other structures which comprise the limbic system. The amygdala receives input from all cortical sensory regions as well as from the internal visceral sensoria. It projects to hypothalamic, mesencephalic and lower brainstem structures. Electrical stimulaton of the amygdala induces a wide variety of autonomic changes, including effects on heart rate, respiration and blood pressure. The most commonly reported behavioral change following amygdalectomy is the loss or dimunition of the normal reaction to fear-provoking stimuli and the inability to produce appropriate defensive behavior. These findings have led investigators to associate the amygdala with species-typical defensive behavior.

It is not possible to specify a single or even major function of the hypothalamus given the complexity and anatomical diversity of this structure. It is intimately concerned with the regulation of fundamental drives and bodily needs such as feeding, drinking, sexual behavior and avoidance of injury. There appear to be both facilitory and inhibitory systems within the hypothalamus for at least some of these functions. For example lesions in the ventromedial hypothalamus induce excessive eating and eventual obesity in animals while lateral hypothalamic damage abolishes the feeding or drinking response to internal events such as changes in glucose concentration, cellular dehydration or hypervolemia.

In addition to the various subcortical structures within the limbic system, certain regions of the cerebral cortex are known to be importantly involved in emotional behavior. Jacobson (1935) was the first to report that frontal lobe removals produced dramatic affective changes. In the course of studying the behavior of chimpanzees on a variety of learning tasks following frontal lobotomy, he noticed that some of the animals became more placid after the surgery. Jacobson's observations on chimpanzees led Egas Moniz, a leading Portuguese neurologist, to propose that similar lesions in humans might relieve certain behavioral problems. In addition to establishing the questionable practice of psychosurgery, these findings highlighted the important contributions of certain cortical regions to emotional behavior. A growing body of research indicates that the frontal and temporal regions play significant roles in affective behavior in humans. For example, frontal lesions have been found to reduce the production of spontaneous facial expressions (e.g. Kolb and Milner 1981).

Recent findings on both normal and clinical populations suggest that the frontal lobes are lateralized for different affective processes (Davidson 1983). Specifically, activation of the right frontal region appears to be associated with certain negative affects while activation of the left frontal region is associated with certain positive affects. This asymmetry may represent a fundamental lateralization for approach and avoidance behavior. A number of experiments have shown that when normal individuals are exposed to negative emotional stimuli and report negative affect, EEG recorded from the left and right frontal regions shows increased right-sided activation. In response to positive affective stimuli, the EEG shows increased left-sided activation. This basic pattern has recently been observed in subjects as young as 10 months of age (Davidson and Fox 1982). Similar findings have been reported for patients with unilateral anterior cortical lesions. When the lesion is on the left side, patients are reported to display more negative emotion compared with comparable sized right-sided lesions.

The study of neurobiological substrates of emotion may provide important insights for understanding the disorders of brain function associated with various psychiatric illnesses. Already, significant advances have occurred in the treatment of schizophrenia and depression. In many important respects, these developments emerged from basic research on the neurobiology of emotion. RJD

Bibliography

Bard, P.A. 1928: A diencephalic mechanism for the expression of rage with special reference to the sympathetic nervous system. *American journal of physiology* 84, 490–513.

Brown, S. and Schaefer, E.A. 1888: An investigation into the functions of the occipital and temporal lobe of the monkey's brain. *Philosophical transactions of the royal society* 179B, 303–27.

*Davidson, R.J. 1983: Affect, cognition and hemispheric specialization. In *Emotion, cognition and behavior*, ed. C.E. Izard, J. Kagan and R. Zajonc. New York and Cambridge: Cambridge University Press.

Davidson, R.J. and Fox, N.A. 1982: Asymmetrical brain activity discriminates between positive and negative affective stimuli in human infants. *Science* 218, 1235.

Isaacson, R.L. 1974: *The limbic system*. New York: Plenum Press.

Jacobson, C.F. 1935: Functions of the frontal association areas in primates. *Archives of neurology and psychiatry* 33, 558–69.

Kluver, H. and Bucy, P.C. 1939: Preliminary analysis of function of the temporal lobe in monkeys. *Archives of neurology and psychiatry* 42, 979–1000.

Kolb, B. and Milner, B. 1981: Observations on spontaneous facial expression after focal cerebral excisions and after intracarotid injection of sodium amytal. *Neuropsychologia* 19, 505–14.

MacLean, P.D. 1949: Psychosomatic disease and the "visceral brain". *Psychosomatic medicine* 11, 338–53.

Marlowe, W.B., Mancall, E.L. and Thomas, J.J. 1975: Complete Kluver-Bucy syndrome in man. *Cortex* 11, 53–9.

Papez, J.W. 1937: A proposed mechanism of emotion. *Archives of neurology and psychiatry* 38, 725–43.

emotion: philosophical theories Otherwise called passion or feeling, emotion has been opposed by philosophers to reason, and has generally been of less interest to them than reason. David HUME, however, held that passion, not reason, was the source of morality, and emotivism, in the twentieth century, was the theory that the language of morals essentially expressed or evoked emotion, rather than stating facts. On the nature of emotion, William JAMES held that emotions were the awareness of physiological events; SARTRE thought that they were deliberately adopted ways of reacting when ordinary action was frustrated. RYLE distinguished agitations, dispositions and moods, holding that none of these was private to the individual, nor something separate and anterior to action. Recently philosophers have raised the question whether emotions are intentional (i.e. necessarily directed towards an object). MW

emotion: Piagetian view Piaget believed that cognition and affect are intricately entwined, but that neither process causes the other. Cognition is a matter of mental structures, while affect energizes behavior. Accordingly, affect can speed up or slow down intellectual development and influence what one attends to, but affect does not generate what one perceives, nor how one conceives of a problem. Similarly, cognition is linked to emotion via perception, learning and memory, but cognition cannot energize behavior.

Affect develops in six stages that roughly parallel the stages of intellectual growth. The first three stages are sensori-motor and involve (1) hereditary organizations such as alimentary instincts and curiosity; (2) the emergence of positive and negative affects linked to past experiences and circular reactions; (3) the beginnings of investment of interest in or valuation of objects. Three stages are post-representational and involve, respectively (1) the experience of the potential value that objects and persons may have; (2) the conservation of feeling states and emergence of will; and (3) the establishment of higher-order societal feelings. JJCa

Bibliography

Piaget, Jean 1981: *Intelligence and affectivity: their relationship during child development*. Paolo Alto, Calif.: Annual Reviews Inc.

emotion: satiation and starvation effects on Hunger and satiety activate emotions which complement the drive state. Drives unamplified by emotion will not activate learning or sustain behavior, but emotions are sufficient motivators in the absence of drives. For example, during periods of intense emotion, drive signals may go unnoticed, as when excitement over work inhibits or attenuates hunger pangs. The apparent urgency of hunger is a joint product of both the drive state and emotion. If a competing emotion is not present, the drive state of hunger may facilitate the activation of a relevant emotion such as interest, which will in turn amplify the drive state. In this way, emotions and drives affect one another. RJD

emotion and aesthetics The study of creative works as the embodiment of expressed emotions, and of the emotional reactions and preferences of an appreciating audience. The relationship of emotions to aesthetics has been explored by psychologists since the second half of the nineteenth century. William JAMES (1890, vol II, pp.468–74) addressed the problem when he developed his still cogent theory of emotion. James argued that emotional responses to aesthetic events have primary and secondary layers. The primary layer consists of "pure and simple" pleasures elicited by harmonious combinations of sounds, colors, and lines. These "subtle feelings" are "cognitive" or "cerebral" in nature and provide a basis for critical judgment in aesthetics. Secondary and "coarser" feelings are produced when memories and associations evoked by the aesthetic stimulus "reverberate" through the muscles and organs of the body. These coarser feelings may be "grafted" onto the subtle feelings during the unfolding of an aesthetic episode. James also applied his distinction to aesthetic preferences, associating classical preferences with subtle, cerebral feelings and romantic preferences with coarse bodily reactions.

Gustav Fechner, one of the founders of experimental psychology, introduced a systematic empirical approach to the study of aesthetics as early as 1865. He developed experimental techniques for studying the preferences and judgments of representative samples of people. The "method of choice," for example, required subjects to state their preferences from among a specified set of stimuli. By manipulating these choices researchers are able to determine the effects of theoretically important stimulus properties (e.g. the Golden Section proportion) on aesthetic preferences. The "method of production" required subjects to create an object which reflected their preferences through drawing or a similar activity. Fechner thus established an inductive analytical tradition in experimental psychology which emphasized the collection of objective facts and the examination of stimulus properties in relation to aesthetic preference. His elementary "aesthetics from below" approach is still practiced by behavioral psychologists (see Berlyne 1974). This empirical approach may be contrasted with the "aesthetics from above" engaged in by philosophers, who conceptually and deductively explore the boundaries of aesthetic beauty and truth. It also differs from the approach of art historians, who examine stylistic innovations against the background of culture and individual genius.

The major schools of psychological thought in the twentieth century, GESTALT THERAPY, INFORMATION THEORY, BEHAVIORISM, PSYCHOANALYSIS and EXISTENTIALISM have all addressed the problem of emotion and aesthetics. Gestalt psychology has contributed to our understanding of the processes underlying both subtle and coarse emotions. Gestalt psychology (Koffka 1935) maintains that perceivers are innately predisposed to organize isolated elements from visual (e.g. lines) or acoustic (e.g. tones) arrays into unified patterns (Gestalten). The "law of Prägnanz" operates through the nervous system to enhance the simplicity, regularity or symmetry in perceived patterns by filling in where necessary. Thus the appreciator may pass through stages of disorder and emotional tension during the balancing process, and his relative ability to arrive at a "good" configuration will determine aesthetic pleasure.

A second contribution, the theory of physiognomic perception, relates formal elements in the work to spontaneously and unconsciously evoked feelings and moods. The proverbial weeping willow evokes a sense of sadness by conveying "the expression of passive hanging" (Arnheim 1954). While the phenomenon of physiognomic perception has been reliably demonstrated, the foundation for this process remains something of a mystery. In general, Gestalt psychologists have drawn our attention to the complex analogical and metaphorical relationships which may exist between the formal and thematic properties in an aesthetic work.

The application of information theory principles during the 1950s (Moles 1958) provided a statistical means for evaluating not only "goodness' but also novelty of configuration. The creative work is treated as a message: an assemblage of material elements, sounds or color areas, which can simultaneously be organized into different levels of information, each with its own principles of order. One basic level of organization transmits semantic information, which denotes objects or has iconographic meaning which is related to the external world. The second basic level of information is the syntactic, which consists of relations among the formal elements in the medium. Information theorists analyse these semantic and syntactic domains in terms of gross structural or morphological properties such as uncertainty (or complexity) and redundancy (or orderliness). Goodness of configuration can be measured in terms of redundancy, while novelty of configuration can be measured in terms of uncertainty. Berlyne (1971; 1974) introduced the term "collative properties" to refer to quantifiable relations among the structural properties which could be evaluated along dimensions such as familiar–novel, expected–unexpected or simple–complex. Novel and unexpected information, either semantic or syntactic, can attract attention at least momentarily. However, long term aesthetic value and pleasure will be determined by the relationship between order and complexity or "unity-within-diversity" in the message, and the spectator's success at interpreting the emotional and intellectual meaning of the aesthetic message.

Behavioral researchers (see Berlyne 1974; Day 1981) treat aesthetic appreciation as an intrinsically motivated form of exploration or stimulus-seeking. They generally adopt the structural analysis developed by information theorists and emphasize responses to collative properties of aesthetic works. New techniques for measuring preferences and perceptions, such as multidimensional scaling and factor analysis, have been added to Fechner's "method of choice." These behavioral measures provide an objective means for verifying aesthetic theories and hypotheses. Berlyne's application of these techniques (1971; 1974) has revealed two dimensions of response, interestingness and pleasingness, which correspond to James's subtle and coarse feelings respectively. Subjects find a stimulus intellectually or cerebrally interesting in direct proportion to its structural complexity. However, subjects emotionally prefer intermediate levels of complexity, depending on their familiarity with the stimulus and state of arousal at the outset of the aesthetic experience. This emphasis on arousal reflects the natural science and reductionist bias of behavioral psychologists, who maintain that the body plays a mediating role in determining aesthetic preference. Aesthetic pleasure seems to result from moderate increases in cortical arousal or from the stimulation of pleasure centers in the brain (Berlyne 1971). The particular emotions that may be elicited by an aesthetic work and subjective emotional experience in general are considered to be of secondary importance.

The psychoanalytic approach to emotion and aesthetics emphasizes the symbolic rather than the semantic message, and has been most fruitfully applied to the study of art (Freud 1910) and literature (Jones 1955). For the Freudian, sexual or aggressive symbolism is of the greatest importance, providing the key to the unconscious desires of the creator and the appreciative spectator. The work serves the same function as a dream, enabling powerful but repressed emotions to gain expression, albeit transformed into a socially acceptable form. The appreciator can unconsciously project his own desires into the symbolic message, thereby gaining temporary satisfaction without fear of punishment or guilt (Kreitler and Kreitler 1972).

Existential psychologists maintain that the work of art or literature is an organized structure which may reveal the "world-design" of its creator or "the underlying spiritual and emotional temper of the culture" (see Binswanger and May in May, Angel and Ellenberger 1958). "Academic" styles which impose systems of meaning and reduce personal expression are abhorred; creative attempts to "pierce below surfaces" are welcomed. Modern art, as exemplified in the work of the Impressionists or Picasso, reaffirms the vitality and sincerity of aesthetic actions, and provides a fresh view of nature and the human condition. Aesthetic content (semantic information) and form (syntactic information) together reveal the emotional and intellectual world view of the artist. Fundamental emotional themes pertaining to anxiety, alienation or guilt may be directly projected into the content and character of the work. The form of the work may also express in its basic dimensions such as space (open or closed) and time (continuous or discontinuous) the phenomenology of the artist's perceptions and experience. GCC

Bibliography

*Arnheim, R. 1954: *Art and visual perception: a psychology of the creative eye.* Berkeley: University of California Press.

*Berlyne, D.E. 1971: *Aesthetics and psychobiology.* New York: Appleton-Century-Crofts.

——1974: *Studies in the new experimental aesthetics.* Washington: Hemisphere.

Day, H. 1981: *Advances in intrinsic motivation and aesthetics.* New York: Plenum.

Freud, S. 1910: *Leonardo da Vinci.* Trans. 1932 by A.A. Bull. New York: Dodds Mead.

James, W. 1890: *The principles of psychology* vol. II. Reissued 1950. New York: Dover.

Jones, E. 1955: *Hamlet and Oedipus.* Garden City, N.Y.: Doubleday.

Koffka, K. 1935: *Principles of Gestalt psychology.* New York: Harcourt, Brace.

*Kreitler, H. and Kreitler, S. 1972: *Psychology of the arts.* Durham, N.C.: Duke University Press.

May, R., Angel, E. and Ellenberger, H.F., eds 1958: *Existence.* New York: Simon and Shuster.

*Moles, A. 1958: *Théorie de l'information et perception esthétique.* Paris: Flammarion; trans. 1966. *Information theory and esthetic perception.* Urbana, Ill.: University of Illinois Press.

emotion and cardiac control Voluntary control of cardiac rate with BIOFEEDBACK and other procedures has been found to produce changes in emotion. It is known that heart rate changes during various emotions and recent evidence suggests that controlling heart rate through either biofeedback or verbal instructions changes emotional behavior. For example, when people are trained to lower their heart rates with biofeedback, they become more pain tolerant in response to noxious stimulation. When heart rate and blood pressures are lowered simultaneously, individuals report feeling particularly relaxed. Recent evidence suggests that anger, fear and sadness are associated with greater heart rate elevations compared with happiness, surprise and disgust. Therefore a lower heart rate would be expected to have a greater effect on decreasing the intensities of the first three emotions while increasing heart rate would be expected to have the greatest effect on intensifying the latter three emotions. RJD

emotion and cardiovascular disease At least two lines of investigation have linked cardiovascular disease to emotion. One is based on the hypothesis that stress causes premature illness and was advanced in 1897 by Sir William Osler, who suggested that "working the machine to its maximum capacity" may be the cause of coronary artery disease. Studies of the type-A behavior pattern, i.e. the time urgent, competitive, hard driving, individual who is overinvolved in tasks, rapid and emphatic in speech, and appears to ignore his internal states of emotional stress, shows these behaviors statistically associated with high rates of morbidity and mortality that may be mediated by stress (emotion) induced activation of the autonomic and neuroendocrine systems. The second psychosomatic approach links cardiovascular disease or high blood pressure to specific emotions, i.e. anger that is suppressed because of fear of retaliation. Evidence is accumulating implicating suppressed anger or hostility in cancer as well as cardiovascular disease. The two lines of study should converge during the coming years. HL

Bibliography

Friedman, M. and Rosenman, R.H. 1974: *Type A behavior and your heart.* New York: Knopf.

Matthews, K.A. 1982: Psychological perspectives on the Type A behavior pattern. *Psychological bulletin* 91, 293–323.

Glass, D. 1977: *Behavior patterns, stress, and coronary disease.* Hillsdale, N.J.: Erlbaum.

Graham, D.T. 1972: Psychosomatic medicine. In *Handbook of psychophysiology*, ed. N.S. Greenfield and R.A. Sternbach. New York: Holt, Rinehart & Winston.

emotion and fantasy Emotions are closely correlated with the emergence and the content of stimulus-independent thought, whether such thought is a fleeting image or an elaborate fantasy (see EMOTIONS AND CONSCIOUSNESS). The most common form of fantasy is daydreaming. Jerome L. Singer, his colleagues and students (e.g. Jerome L. Singer 1975) have repeatedly identified three separate patterns of daydreaming and have found that each pattern is characterized by both its own emotional tone and by content appropriate to that tone. Further, these patterns are relatively stable individual differences, or "trait" characteristics. The first style is that of unfocussed mind-wandering, with fleeting stereotypical fantasies and an inability to sustain any prolonged or deep emotions. The second is marked by guilty and dysphoric affect and has appropriate content. The third pattern is positive, replete with both interest and joy, and it is marked by happy memories, explorations of possibilities, or sheer playfulness with stored images. See FANTASY. RBT

Bibliography

Singer, Jerome L. 1975(*1981*): *Daydreaming and fantasy.* Oxford: Oxford University Press.

emotion and lateralization The two hemispheres of the brain appear to subserve different emotional processes. Some investigators have suggested that the right side of the brain is predominantly involved in emotion. This view has emerged from findings on brain-damaged patients which suggested that individuals with unilateral right hemisphere lesions were impaired in the perception of emotion and sometimes displayed emotional indifference. However, more recent work indicates that certain regions of the two hemispheres are differentially lateralized for certain positive and negative emotions. The left frontal region appears to be relatively more active during certain positive emotions while the right frontal region is relatively more active during certain negative emotions. The posterior association regions may be more specialized for the perception of emotion with the right side playing a greater role. RJD

Bibliography

Davidson, R.J. 1983: Affect, cognition and hemispheric specialization. In *Emotion, cognition and behavior*, ed. C.E. Izard, J. Kagan and R. Zajonc. New York and Cambridge: Cambridge University Press.

emotion and memory How emotional experiences are remembered. Experiences are stored in memory in three qualitatively different ways or codes. Motor codes represent memories for body movements, like those used in riding a bicycle. Motor memories are both difficult to describe and difficult to forget. Imagery codes represent memories which are closely related to the individual's actual perceptual experience, whether that be visual, auditory, tactile, kinesthetic, gustatory or olfactory. Symbolic codes represent memories for abstractions like words and what they signify. These abstractions are not directly related to perceptual experiences. The word "happy" is unrelated to the perceptual experience of happiness. Affective experiences are represented in memory by motor, imagery and symbolic codes.

Motor or movement codes for expressing emotions are clearly evident in infancy. The infant's expressions of pleasure and displeasure, by smiling and crying, illustrate innate motor codes for controlling facial muscle patterns. These motor codes are inherited, as the same facial movements seem to be used to express basic emotions in all cultures (Tomkins 1962). Facial movement is part of the affective memory for an emotion (see FACIAL EXPRESSION AND EMOTION).

Other skeletal and visceral muscle movement patterns associated with emotional experiences, such as increases in muscle tension, or changes in heart rate and breathing, are also stored in motor codes. One well known theory of emotions, the James-Lange theory, states that emotions are one's perception of these bodily changes. One method of training actors to express emotional feelings is to have them imagine the motor movements associated with an emotion, with the idea that the emotion itself will then follow naturally. To experience anger, the actor imagines the animal-like activities of crouching, curling his fingers, hunching his shoulders, thrusting his jaw, feeling a cold sweat on forehead and palms, breathing rapidly, and so on. The emotional state extends over the body until it is felt and expressed naturally.

The importance of motor codes for affective memories was illustrated in experiments by Lang (1979), who recorded physiological measures, such as heart rate, skin conductance, respiration and muscle tension, and verbal reports of fear when subjects were asked to imagine being locked in a sauna. The fear-arousing scene was vividly described for two groups of subjects, but one group was also asked to imagine their motor responses of rapid breathing, muscle tension, heart pounding, etc. The latter group showed stronger physiological responses and reported more intense feelings of fear.

Freud observed that patients' recall of affective experiences frequently differed sharply from the unconscious motor messages of their bodies. For example, in the case of *Dora* (p.96) he notes that "he that has eyes to see and ears to hear may convince himself that no mortal can keep a secret. If his lips are silent he chatters with his finger-tips; betrayal oozes out of him at every pore. And thus the task of making conscious the most hidden recesses of the mind is one which it is quite possible to accomplish."

Followers of Freud helped to develop the field of psychosomatic medicine, which seeks to explain the relationship of certain bodily symptoms and illnesses with psychic conflict and psychological stress. They believed that such conflicts manifested themselves in illnesses such as respiratory disorders, ulcers and hypertension. Many procedures used by psychotherapists are designed to enable their patients to recreate and control emotional feelings by activating motor memory codes for those feelings. In relaxation therapies, desensitization therapies and biofeedback, the patient learns to express, control, and counteract the muscle tension and autonomic arousal associated with affective memories. New motor behavior, such as muscle relaxation, replaces behavior which was associated with the unpleasant affective experience. Techniques used in pop therapies, such as primal screaming, dancing and massage, are also designed to counter the dysfunctional motor behavior associated with unpleasant affective memories (see PSYCHOPATHOLOGY).

Imagery codes are used to store information in memory of the emotional experience itself – what the person saw, heard, smelt, felt, and so on. Leventhal (1980) refers to the organization of imagery-coded memories of the same emotional feeling as emotional schemata. New experiences of a particular emotion are automatically stored in memory along with other experiences of that emotion. A happy experience will be linked to other episodes of happiness. In recall of the memory, the emotion is felt directly, not as the result of any cognitive reinterpretation of experience. The famous Russian acting teacher Konstantin Stanislavsky believed that actors must be able to tap into these emotional schemata to recreate spontaneous emotional feelings on the stage. The French writer Marcel Proust (1934) vividly described the involuntary flow of the memories in an emotional schema – flashback experience – which was initiated by some relatively trivial perceptual experience, such as the taste of a particular type of cake and tea.

One implication of emotional schemata is that similar emotional feelings are linked together in memory, so that an emotional feeling can act as a cue to help recover memories for similar affective experiences. Bower (1981) has shown that one's emotional state at the time of recalling an experience affects what information is recalled. Such a phenomenon is known as state-dependent memory. It was originally shown that recall of certain types of information was improved when the person was in the same drug (e.g. alcohol) state as when he or she originally learned the information. Bower showed that improved recall also occurred if the person was in the same mood state. For example in one experiment Bower hypnotically induced subjects into experiencing either a happy or a sad mood. They were then asked to recall as many childhood memories as possible. Subjects in a happy mood recalled many more happy memories than subjects in a sad mood. One may speculate that the person's mood at the time of an event becomes encoded in memory along with the event, and activation of that same mood can assist in recalling the original event (see MEMORY: STATE DEPENDENCE).

A further implication of emotional schemata is that memories of similar emotional experiences are linked automatically, with little or no conscious awareness on the part of the individual. Zajonc (1980) and his co-workers have conducted a series of experiments demonstrating the effortless, automatic build-up of feeling states in emotional schemata. They used a procedure known as the mere frequency of exposure paradigm, where subjects are presented with a series of novel stimuli. In one experiment, they saw slides of Japanese ideographs, while in another experiment, they heard unfamiliar words or tone sequences. The stimuli are presented in varying frequencies. Some are presented as many as twenty-seven times; others may be presented only once. The results of these experiments indicate that the more frequently people experience a novel stimulus, the more likely, on average, are they to say that they like it or that they think it has a good meaning. The emotional feelings for an originally novel stimulus develop without the subject's awareness of how frequently the stimulus was presented. The subject's reports of the feeling associated with a particular stimulus are elicited rapidly and reliably, even when the subject has trouble recognizing the stimulus. The emotional feeling associated with a stimulus may survive after the person can no longer recall the experience itself. One may remember liking a movie or book, but not being able to recall its contents. The independence or separation of emotional feeling from conscious awareness is frequently observed in clinical situations.

Symbolic codes for affective memories contain the appraisals of one's emotional experiences, including the verbal descriptions which are used to talk about these experiences. The information in symbolic codes is abstract and cognitive, not the movement and perceptual information of motor and imagery codes. Because movement and perceptual information is difficult to describe, there is potential for conflict between verbal appraisals or accounts of emotional experiences and what the person actually felt.

Neuropsychological evidence suggests that the left and right hemispheres of the brain may contribute differentially to cognitive and to affective information processing and memory. The left hemisphere of the brain is involved primarily in verbal skills, such as speaking and perceiving language, while the right hemisphere seems dominant for relatively nonverbal skills, such as recognizing faces, emotional facial expressions of emotion, imagery, and emotional tones of voice. It is an oversimplification to assert that only the right hemisphere is involved in emotions, since appraisal of affective memories is strongly influenced by language. Both hemispheres are involved in affective memories, but in a different and complementary fashion. This was illustrated in an experiment by Safer and Leventhal (1977), where subjects judged the effect of spoken passages which varied both in emotional content and in the tone of voice with which they were read. When listening on their right ear (left hemisphere), subjects judged the passages according to their emotional content, and when listening on the left ear (right hemisphere), they judged them according to their emotional tone of voice.

Galin (1974) speculated about the role of the two hemispheres in certain aspects of psychoanalytic theories of emotions. For example, the right hemisphere might have access to imagery-coded emotional memories which are inaccessible to the left hemisphere. The potential conflict between what is felt and what is said may be analogous to repression (see EMOTION AND LATERALIZATION). MAS

Bibliography

Bower, G.H. 1981: Mood and memory. *American psychologist* 36, 151–75.

Freud, S. 1963: *Dora – an analysis of a case of hysteria*. New York: Collier Books.

Galin, D. 1974: Implications for psychiatry of left and right cerebral specialization. *Archives of general psychiatry* 31, 572–83.

Lang, P.J. 1979: A bio-informational theory of emotional imagery. *Psychophysiology* 16, 495–512.

*Leventhal, H. 1980: Toward a comprehensive theory of emotion. In *Advances in experimental social psychology* vol. 13, ed. L. Berkowitz. New York: Academic Press.

Proust, M. 1934: *Remembrance of things past*. New York: Random House.

Safer, M.A. and Leventhal, H. 1977: Ear differences in evaluating emotional tones of voice and verbal content. *Journal of experimental psychology: Human perception and performance* 3, 75–82.

Tomkins, S.S. 1962: *Affect, imagery, consciousness (Vol. 1): The positive affects*. New York: Springer.

*Zajonc, R.B. 1980: Feeling and thinking. *American psychologist* 35, 151–75.

emotion and neurological damage Neurological damage produces changes in emotional behavior. Experiments in animals have demonstrated that damage to the frontal and temporal lobes, as well as to certain subcortical structures which comprise the limbic system, produces dramatic changes in emotional responsivity. Removal of the frontal lobes has been found to produce behavioral placidity while removal of the temporal lobes along with the AMYGDALA diminishes fear normally elicited by threatening stimuli. This latter effect is part of a syndrome produced by bilateral temporal lobectomy known as the Kluver-Bucy syndrome. In humans and certain other species damage to the left versus right side of the brain produces different emotional effects. In general anterior damage to the left side results in a more negative emotional response compared with damage to homologous right hemisphere regions. Posterior right-sided damage often results in deficits in the perception of emotional stimuli such as facial expressions. RJD

emotion and personality Concepts relating subjective feelings to the overall organization of an individual's personality, and his or her conception of it. On the whole "emotion", and "the self" have been studied as separate topics, the former dealing with the nature of emotional states as psychological conditions (Leventhal 1980), or as a common physiological condition modified by cognitive glosses (e.g. Schachter 1964); and the latter dealing with people's ideas of their own character (sometimes called the self concept) or else (in Jung's writings) referring to the most global level of psychological organization, by which all other structures and functions are subsumed – the integrated totality of the person (e.g. Storr 1973).

However, it is possible that the highest level of psychological integration and the system of emotions and motives are one and the same. The following synthesis might be proposed. Let us assume that the major psychological functions, or "parts of the mind", are related to one another by a control (or *"regulative"*) hierarchy. In other words each process typically receives information from a number of subordinate processes or channels, or commands a number of output channels or skills, while itself being one of a number of processes on the same level, which jointly contribute information to, or receive instructions from a higher level. This is not to be confused with the *constitutive* hierarchies which are more common in nature, in which each object or unit is composed of others of lower order, and is itself one of several constituents of a unit of higher order. The important distinction is that constitutive hierarchies take their properties from the bottom and are best explained by reduction, whereas control hierarchies are organized from the top, and require the opposite treatment, which is sometimes called macro-reduction. In other words, to understand objects in a constitutive structure you take them to bits to see what they are made of, but you understand units in a regulative hierarchy by piecing them together to see what they are part of.

The bottom levels of the psychological hierarchy consist of the mechanisms of perception and cognition which collect information, passing it upward through successive levels of processing in progressively fewer but more complex units; while on the output side there is the divergent hierarchy of skilled action and language in which relatively global levels of planning and activity are broken down for implementation into successively finer and more numerous units, until they are sufficiently concrete and detailed to form a motor program controlling the voluntary muscles (Powers 1973).

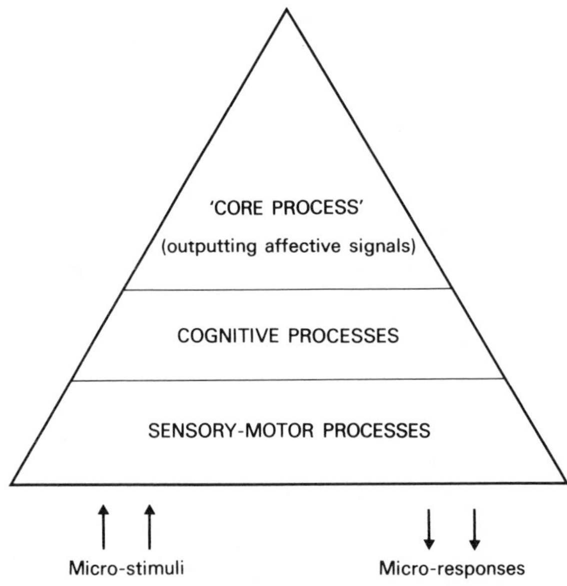

Core process theory: conscious cognitive operations under superordinate control of unattended affective/motivational centers.

The second level of the hierarchy is capable of subjective SELF-MONITORING and is the domain of subjective experience or 'conscious mental life". It is to this level of processing that the sensory hierarchy delivers highly analysed pictures, sounds and so on, and from which it takes the action units which we experience as the "will" or "intention" to move or speak, and breaks them down for fine control and implementation. Within this level of processing is a chain of sensory-motor connections, or circumstances–action contingencies, which we experience as conscious and deliberate thinking, deciding, remembering, planning and so on.

The crucial part is this. Contrary to the way we often seem to experience things, and to many theories of psychology, the uppermost level of control, and the one which is most crucial and elusive in the understanding of action has not yet been mentioned in this account. Perhaps there is a third level, which is higher than conscious or rational decision making in two senses. Firstly in the sense that it exercises a more compelling level of control, to which deliberate decision making is itself accountable; and secondly in that it produces patterns which are longer-term and broader in scope than any which are introduced into the life-course knowingly and deliberately. Deliberate voluntary control as we normally experience it is not the top part of a two-level control hierarchy, but the middle part of a three-level hierarchy of control operations or "brain programs".

Work by Zajonc (1980) has shown that affective judgments such as preferences can be made independently of cognitive evaluations such as familiarity. He suggests that emotional reactions are formulated in parallel with cognitive processing, and with greater immediacy. In the terms of the hierarchical model suggested here processing speed would be indicative *ceteris paribus* of lower order control, since the function of lower order controllers is to provide rapid and fine detailed coordination of the behavior stream. However the model is two dimensional and suggests two components of latency – the vertical movement of information (transfer time) and the lateral movement of information (process time). This makes possible paradoxical latencies, of which Zajonc's results may be an example, in which higher order processes appear to react faster because of shorter process times, and in spite of longer transfer times.

The absence of conscious maintaining from the highest level of regulation could be why interpersonal relationships and public policies are so hard to understand and so hard to put right when they go wrong. They are governed by a chain of events in the brain, the most important of which we neither monitor nor control. This is not particularly obvious in our ordinary experience of the system, because it is at a lower level of the constitutive hierarchy of behavior that we recall and label events or patterns. The misunderstanding is made worse still by trying to reduce behavior to fine elements in search of explanation, instead of regarding it as the product of a regulative hierarchy, and so looking to its gross structure for evidence of the highest levels of control that have influenced it.

Many practical problems may arise because of the same anomaly. In the medium or short-term, behavior usually seems rational and self-explanatory, freely and deliberately chosen by the individual in the light of a full and accurate understanding of the prevailing circumstances. And yet on a more global level human conduct is far more problematic and inexplicable than one would expect from an all-knowing, all-controling organism. This may be because the master control functions and the most comprehensive consolidated representations of past experience both lie outside the domain of our subjective awareness.

The life course of an individual has a hierarchical constitutive structure precisely because it is a product of the regulative hierarchy making up the "mind" of the person. In the short term the life course appears to consist of actions contingent upon circumstances. That patterns of skills or strategies, in so far as it is learned depends on past experience and learning strategies are ultimately dictated by biological endowment.

Like any system of control programs activating and modifying one another, each modification must occur under the control of a higher level. Consequently the upper levels have to be programmed first on the whole, which is why it is that in people (or for that matter in computer systems with several levels of operating system, editors, programs, sub-routines etc.) it is the earliest "experiences" which later come to exercise the most pervasive control. This is another reason for the upper level or "core process" to give rise to practical difficulties. Its response-patterns are programmed in childhood, and are therefore not only child-like, but structured according to the cognitive distinctions which were important to the child at the time. These are not readily intelligible to the child's parents at that stage, or to the adult whom the child subsequently becomes, as by then cognitive awareness will have far outgrown the terms in which it influenced the structure of the core process. This three level control hierarchy of heuristic, rational and automatic control also has parallels in artificial intelligence and the structure of industrial organizations.

There are three criteria which would suggest that the core process is functionally "above" conscious awareness and rational control:

(1) *Scope:* Its control seems to be longer-term and extends over a greater range of life activities and biological sub-systems than individual units of deliberate decision.
(2) *Many to one mapping:* For each element of the motivational system, there are many more in the cognitive system.
(3) *Control:* Motivation and emotion (perhaps tautologically, by their very definition) exert a more compelling control over thought and decision than they are subject to themselves.

The core process probably consists of a collection of representations, like very abstract maps into which a global distillation of experience is incorporated, and from which gross specifications of action are derived in the form of control signals to the cognitive plan-making level. These are experienced and labeled there as drives and feelings such as fear, excitement, sadness, and hunger.

In this way it could well be that the familiar patterns of

emotional life, which many branches of psychology have dismissed as irrelevant or disruptive to our real psychological organization, are in fact the control signals by which our highest levels of coordination are exercised. Emotion and the self may be much closer than is generally supposed. DDC

Bibliography

Schachter, S. 1964: The interaction of cognitive and physiological determinants of emotional state. *Advances in experimental social psychology* 1, 49–80, ed. L. Berkowitz. New York and London: Academic Press.

Leventhal, H. 1980: Towards a comprehensive theory of emotion. *Advances in experimental social psychology* 13, 139–207.

Powers, W.T. 1973: *Behaviour: the control of perception*. Chicago: Aldine.

Storr, A. 1973: *Jung*. Glasgow: Fontana.

Zajonc, R.B. 1980: Feeling and thinking: preferences need no inferences. *American psychologist* 35, 151–75.

emotion and physical illness Over the centuries, moralists have attributed illness to lack of balance, and overstimulation. The idea that any adaptive demand, positive or negative, evoked a common stress response, e.g. alarm, defense and exhaustion of a pituitary, adreno-cortical response pattern, was developed by Hans Selye. The hypothesis led to the studies of retrospective and prospective relationships between scores on life event scales and various illness measures. Recent studies suggest negative rather than positive life events, and the individual's perception of the event and coping skills determine the degree to which it is stressful and disease inducing. The approach of psychosomatic psychiatry is more similar to that of differential emotion theory in that particular attitudes, i.e. interpretations and modes of coping with situations, give rise to specific emotions and particular diseases, e.g. feeling deprived and wanting to get even leading to duodenal ulcer or feeling out in the cold and wanting to shut out the situation leading to asthma. Two key issues await resolution: one is the way in which short term emotional states lead to clinical disease; and the other is why stressed individuals develop different diseases. HL

Bibliography

Graham, D. 1972: Psychosomatic medicine. In *Handbook of psychophysiology*, ed. N.S. Greenfield and R..A. Sternback. New York: Holt, Rinehart & Winston.

Dohrenwend, B.S. and Dohrenwend, B.P., eds. 1974: *Stressful life events: their nature and effects*. New York: Wiley.

Levi, L. ed. 1971: *Society, stress and disease, vol. 1: The psychosocial environment and psychosomatic diseases*. London: Oxford University Press.

emotion and self These are intimately linked, although the nature of the self that influences emotionality changes dramatically with development. Young infants' selves are *biological, reactive,* and inaccessible to babies' awareness. Adults' selves are highly complex; they have been evaluated and modified by the individuals and others throughout individuals' lives.

The self influences both the *elicitation* and the *expression* of emotion. Emotions are initiated by an "appraisal" process, wherein events are related to the self. Appraisal may occur at an extremely low, reflexive level (e.g. a neonate, because of biological endowment, reacts with disgust when a foul-tasting liquid is placed in its mouth), or at a highly sophisticated level (e.g. an adult is ashamed at having made a naive remark, since this is contrary to his or her self-concept). Emotions such as shame and guilt may depend on the existence of a self concept and appear later in development than disgust or fear.

Older children or adults' selves influence their *expression* of emotion as well; expression of certain emotions may be either congruent or incongruent with persons' self-concepts (e.g. a man who is afraid may hide his fear if fearfulness is contrary to his self-image). JJCa/KSC

Bibliography

Arnold, M., ed. 1970: *Feelings and emotions: The Loyola symposium*. New York: Academic Press.

Campos, J. et al. 1983: Socioemotional development. In *Carmichael's manual of child psychology: Infancy and developmental psychobiology*, ed. M. Haith and J. Campos. New York: Wiley.

Harter, S. 1982: Developmental perspectives on the self-system. In *Carmichael's manual of child psychology: Social and personality development*, ed. M. Hetherington. New York: Wiley.

emotion and sleep Emotions are major determinants of the onset, duration and quality of sleep. Anxiety often results in insomnia and restless sleep with improved memory for dreams. Depression can be expressed in this agitated form or can result in hypersomnia, reflecting a generalized lack of energy to provoke or sustain arousal.

Emotions affect sleep most vividly by their impact on dreaming. They influence content, both in a compensatory fashion, restoring and maintaining balance in a personality, as first proposed by JUNG, and by transforming current concerns – for example, by providing wish fulfilment, as first suggested by FREUD. A third view of the relationship between dreams and emotions was originally proposed by Adler and has gathered considerable empirical support: The dreaming *process* is seen as a mechanism for resolving (not just reflecting) current emotionally-laden issues, both through the creation of possibilities and exploration of their consequences in a problem-solving fashion, and through amplifying emotion which can then generate action. (See also EMOTIONS AND CONSCIOUSNESS.) RBT

Bibliography

Cartwright, Rosalind D. 1977: *Night life: explorations in dreaming*. Englewood Cliffs, N.J.: Prentice-Hall.

emotion and social behavior Confronted by an armed robber one is understandably afraid. It is not so much the gun as the presumed intentions of the robber that provoke the emotion. It is an emotion at least partly caused by another person and to that extent social. But fear can be provoked by circumstances not at all social. A mountain climber can fear a rock slide. Other emotions, such as anger, greed, shame, guilt, envy, are social in that they involve social norms, i.e. shared expectations about appropriate conduct (Averill 1980). For instance: what makes pangs of acquisitiveness greed is not their intensity, nor the number of things the pangs stimulate one to acquire. Greed has to do with wanting more than one's due; "coveting" one's own goods is not greed. Any emotion might involve social standards – one might fear being blackballed because one hasn't lived up to them, or sorrow over their decline – but sorrow and fear can be felt over objects unconnected to standards. Some emotions are social in a strong sense: they require standards and their appraisal to be intelligible.

The idea that some emotions require an understanding of standards is new to the discipline of psychology, though Aristotle had a normative account of anger: anger is a perception of transgression wedded to an impulse toward revenge; transgression and revenge entail moral standards. Let us trace psychology's path away from standards and back again, beginning with Descartes.

In psychology's (and the British empiricists') version of Descartes's scheme, emotions are events (mental or behavioral) having causes and effects. William James, for example, analysed emotions as effects stirred up by perceptions, not as patterns of behaving and thinking intrinsically involving appraisal.

> Our natural way of thinking about these standard emotions is that the mental perception of some fact excites the mental affection called the emotion, and that this latter state of mind gives rise to the bodily expression. My thesis on the contrary is that *the bodily changes follow directly the perception of the exciting fact, and that our feeling of the same changes as they occur is the emotion*... We feel sorry because we cry, angry because we strike, afraid because we tremble... (1884 (*1968*), p.18).

James illustrates his thesis: "If we abruptly see a dark moving form in the woods, our heart stops beating, and we catch our breath instantly and before any articulate idea of danger can arise" (ibid. p.26). But why should this perception provoke trembling unless we appraise the form as dangerous? James invokes instincts: "In advance of all experience of elephants no child can but be frightened if he suddenly finds one trumpeting and charging upon him. No woman can see a handsome little naked baby without delight..." (ibid. p.20).

James realized that a nativist account makes more sense for fear of elephants than fear of a stock-market crash, so he added that once the neural pathways for fear of trumpeting elephants have been exercised, they can be pressed in to the service of stock-market dread: "A nervous tendency to discharge being once there, all sorts of unforseen things may pull the trigger and let loose the effect" (ibid. p.24). On James's account, then, the various emotions are the experience of the effects of innate patterns of neural discharge. The provocative conditions just set them off. But not all psychologists were so beguiled.

Consider Titchener's discussion of anger (1897): "It contains, e.g., the idea of the person with whom one is angry; the idea of the act of his, at which one is displeased; the idea of retaliatory action on one's own part; a mass of bodily sensations, attending the flushing of one's face, the tendency to clench the fist..." (p.13). Maranon (1924) (see Mandler 1979) tried to decide between James and Titchener. According to James if a person experiences the physical state characteristic of an emotion he or she will experience that emotion. The experimental trick is to put people in the bodily state without the context appropriate to the emotion. But to do this one has to specify the bodily state characteristic of a particular emotion. James did not consistently commit himself to any particular state for any particular emotion, but the tradition fastened on physiological arousal. Arousal of the sympathetic nervous system (producing trembling, blanching, sweating, etc.) was the plausible candidate for anger or fear. So Maranon injected subjects with epinephrine (which mimics arousal of the sympathetic nervous system), and asked them to report their experiences. The results supported Titchener. About two-thirds of the subjects reported no emotion – merely physiological symptoms. Most of the rest reported "as if" emotions, e.g. they said they felt as if they were afraid, but they weren't afraid. Sympathetic activity was not sufficient to produce emotion. Schachter and Singer (1962), in a famous, controversial experiment, sought to extend this account by showing that what sympathetic arousal lacked was the person's appraisal of the situation.

Schachter and Singer's results supported, although not strongly, the Titchnerian position. Although the replicability of the Schachter and Singer study is controversial, Zillman, in a series of studies, provided further indirect support of their position (Zillman 1979). The experimental evidence, then, is not compelling, but generally points toward a contextual account. But the view that appraisals are part of emotion has also been affected by current philosophy in the spirit of the later Wittgenstein, Ryle or Austin.

Kenny (1963), for example, argued that appraisals are part of our concept of, say, anger. While a person could be angry without perceiving a transgression, transgression is nonetheless implicated in anger. Consider this example: though we can imagine a car without an engine, the concept "car" nonetheless involves the notion of being self-propelled. In parallel, although we can understand a particular case of being angry without perceiving (or fancying) a transgression, still what defines anger is (at least in some cases) the perception of transgression. Still, all of this only shows that appraisals are central, not that social norms are essential. We must show that accounts of particular emotions divorced from social norms do not do their job. Psychology has provided a nice example of this failure.

Behaviorists analysed anger (which they called aggression, see Sabini and Silver 1982) as a response always and only produced by frustration (frustration, they allowed, was being blocked on the way to a goal). But Pastore (1952) pointed out that whether a frustration was justified or not determined whether it produced anger. For example, after you have waited for hours on a wintry street corner a friend finally arrives with his apology: contrast (A) "Sorry I'm late, I couldn't tear myself away from the television" with (B) "I'm sorry, my brother just died and I have been wandering the streets". A and B are equally "frustrating" but it would be surprising if A did not cause anger or if B did. The appraisal in anger is not "being frustrated", but, as Aristotle argued, being transgressed against. To understand what is and is not a transgression, what will or will not provoke anger one has to understand the "form of life" using accusations, justifications, excuses, mitigations, exacerbations (see Averill 1978, 1980).

Envy also involves shared standards. Silver and Sabini argued that envy involves a transgression: perceiving oneself as demeaned by another's accomplishment (or worth), and, because of that, attempting (or wanting) to undercut the other person or his or her accomplishment. Of course attacking someone or his or her "accomplishments" is not necessarily a transgression if there is truth in the attack then saying it (or wanting to say it) isn't envy but righteous indignation (see Sabini and Silver 1982). Anger and envy are social emotions in the strong sense of entailing shared social standards. Embarrassment too is a social emotion, a curious one.

The curious aspect of embarrassment is the sort of appraisal it involves. For example: you are giving a lecture; as the students begin to nod off you recognize what a miserable job you are doing. The job is so bad that you are embarrassed on seeing your students the next day. What is the appraisal here? Modigliani (1968) argues that we are embarrassed when we perceive others as perceiving us as inadequate. This also seems to explain why embarrassment is so unpleasant: it is connected to a diminution of our sense of self-worth. But suppose the lecturer knows that he or she is a good lecturer, and that the poor performance was a consequence of loss of the lecture notes and has little to do with lecturing abilities. There is no reason then to feel demeaned. But Modigliani's data (and everyday reflection) suggest that people do become embarrassed though they know that they are not at fault.

Goffman has a different approach which avoids this problem. Goffman (1967) argues that what produces embarrassment is the recognition that the self a person is sustaining in a social interaction has been upset by something he or she has done or some personal fact that has slipped out. This account avoids the difficulty but at a cost. The difficulty is avoided because what the lecturer knows about himself or herself is irrelevant to the embarrassment. The issue is whether the poor lecture upsets the consensus between lecturer and students that he or she is an adequate lecturer. This account has several virtues. For one, the appraisal involved need not be distorted. For another it can handle "positive embarrassment", e.g. the embarrassment felt on being congratulated; the pauper discovered to be a prince is embarrassed but so is the prince discovered to be a pauper. It just happens that paupers are more motivated to pretend to be princes than vice-versa. But this account cannot explain why finding one's projected self contradicted is so painful. Goffman would answer that conflicts in self presentation upset interactions. Interacting with other people is predicated on knowing how to treat them, and this requires a consensus on who they are. The power of embarrassment derives from the importance of social interactions. But, while some interactions are important, and surely the ability to have interactions is important, this does not quite explain why every social interaction should be loaded with the potential to produce embarrassment. This issue is unsettled.

This article has summarized ways in which several emotions involve social norms. Not all emotions do. Further work will, no doubt, expand the list of social emotions and the ways assessments enter them. MS/JS

Bibliography

Averill, J. 1978: Anger. *Nebraska symposium on motivation.* Lincoln: University of Nebraska Press.

——— 1980: A constructivist view of emotion. In *Emotion: theory, research, and experience*, ed. R. Plutchik and H. Kellerman. New York: Academic Press.

Goffman, E. 1967: *Interaction ritual.* New York: Anchor.

James, W. 1884 (*1968*): What is an emotion. Reprinted in *The nature of emotion*, ed. M. Arnold. London: Penguin.

Kenny, A. 1963: *Action, emotion and will.* New York: Humanities Press.

Mandler, G. 1979: Emotion. In *The first century of experimental psychology*, ed. E. Herst. Hillsdale, N.J.: LEA.

Modigliani, A. 1968: Embarrassment and embarrassability. *Sociometry* 31(3), 313–26.

Pastore, N. 1952: The role of arbitrariness in the frustration aggression hypothesis. *Journal of abnormal and social psychology*, 47, 728–31.

Sabini, J. and Silver, M. 1982: *Moralities of everyday life.* New York: Oxford University Press.

Schacter, S. and Singer, J. 1962: Cognitive, social and physiological determinants of emotional state. *Psychological review* 69, 379–99.

Titchener, E. 1897: *An outline of psychology.* New York: Macmillan.

Zillmann, D. 1979: *Hostility and aggression.* Hillsdale, N.J.: LEA.

emotion and the autonomic system Emotional behavior has historically been thought to involve arousal in the autonomic nervous system (ANS). Changes in ANS activity are believed to be a necessary, but not sufficient condition for the elicitation of emotion. A relatively large proportion of the research in autonomic psychophysiology has involved the study of emotion (e.g. Grings and Dawson 1978).

Many common-language phrases which refer to emotion include descriptions of autonomic changes. For example, "white with fear" and "red with anger" presumably refer to blood flow changes in the face while "butterflies in the stomach" refers to alterations in gastric motility. While these descriptions imply that different emotions are associated with different patterns of ANS activity this is a matter which is surrounded by considerable controversy. William James (1890) was one of the first psychologists to suggest that different emotions involve different patterns of ANS changes. James, and independently the Danish physiologist, C.G. Lange, theorized that the perception of these autonomic changes was critical for the subjective experiences of emotion. This position became known as the James-Lange theory of emotion. The theory specifically states that certain stimulus situations produce particular bodily reactions (e.g., pounding of the heart and other visceral responses) and the perception of these reactions *is* the emotion. James (1890) explains the theory in the following way:

> Common sense says, we lose our fortune, are sorry and weep; we meet a bear, are frightened and run; we are insulted by a rival, are angry and strike. The hypothesis here to be defended says that this order of sequence is

incorrect . . . that the more rational statement is that we feel sorry because we cry, angry because we strike, afraid because we tremble (pp.449–450).

The James-Lange theory was seriously challenged by Walter Cannon in the early 1900s (see Cannon 1927). Cannon presented a number of criticisms of this theory, the most significant of which include: (1) similar bodily reactions occur in widely varying emotional states, hence such changes cannot be responsible for the qualitative differences across emotion; (2) the viscera are relatively deficient in sensory nerves, and therefore we are not likely to be aware of changes occurring in these structures; and (3) autonomic reactions often have relatively long latency periods, whereas the time between the occurrence of a critical stimulus and a change in the subjective experience of emotion is often considerably shorter.

The Cannon critique of the James-Lange position was and still is very influential in psychology. The claim that patterns of autonomic arousal are similar across emotions has led to the search for the factors that are responsible for the qualitative differences in subjective feeling among emotions. The most influential theory of emotion predicated on the assumption that emotions do not differ in patterns of autonomic arousal is that proposed by Schachter and Singer (1962), who argued that emotion is comprised of (a) the activation of autonomic activity; and (b) the interpretation of this arousal as a function of environmental events. Schachter and Singer performed a series of studies designed to illustrate this theory. For example in one experiment they manipulated autonomic arousal by giving injections of epinephrine to one group of subjects and placebo injections to another. Cognitive factors were varied by providing accurate information about the drug's effect to some subjects, and misinforming and not informing other subjects. All the subjects were then left in a waiting room with an experimental accomplice who acted in either a euphoric or angry fashion. The emotional reactions of the subjects in this situation were then evaluated to determine how the combination of drug or placebo and information about the drug's effect would influence reactions to the accomplice. Schachter and Singer predicted that when subjects were not provided with accurate information about the drug's effects they would be more likely to evaluate their environment and find cues to explain their arousal. Therefore, they expected that the misinformed and uninformed groups would report themselves to experience more happiness and anger (depending upon the conditions) compared with the correctly informed group. The results from this experiment were interpreted as providing general support for the Schachter-Singer theory, although the study has been criticized on methodological and conceptual grounds (Plutchik and Ax 1967). One major problem with their conclusion about similar autonomic arousal accompanying different emotions was that no comprehensive assessment of physiological state was performed. Therefore, subjects might indeed have displayed different patterns of autonomic arousal following exposure to the happy versus angry stooge.

Although the Schachter and Singer view has been persuasive in psychology, a number of older studies have uncovered fairly convincing evidence of physiological differentiation among at least certain emotions. Both Ax (1953) and Funkenstein (1955) found that fear and anger could be distinguished on the basis of certain physiological measures. For example, Ax (1953) found that anger was associated with larger increases in diastolic blood pressure compared with fear.

Research on psychosomatic disease also supports the hypothesis of physiological differentiation among emotions. One influential theory of the etiology of psychosomatic disorders is known as the specific attitude hypothesis which asserts that (a) each psychosomatic disease is associated with its own specific attitude, and (b) each attitude has its own specific physiological characteristic (Graham 1972). Graham has found that individuals with different PSYCHOSOMATIC DISORDERS report consistently different emotional attitudes. For example patients with ulcerative colitis feel that they are injured and degraded and want to get rid of the responsible agent; those with essential hypertension feel threatened with harm and have to be alert.

One of the most striking ways in which this theory has been tested was to take healthy subjects and hypnotically induce certain emotional attitudes which had previously been found to be associated with particular psychosomatic disorders. Changes in the relevant physiological measure could then be examined to determine whether the attitudinal induction produced specific physiological patterns. In one study (Graham, Stern and Winokur 1960) subjects were hypnotized and then given instructions for the attitude associated with hives or Raynaud's disease. Hives is accompanied by increases in skin temperature while Raynaud's disease is associated with decreases in this measure. The differential effects on skin temperature of the hives versus the Reynaud's attitude could then be assessed. The predominant attitude reported by patients with hives is that they feel as though they are taking a beating and are helpless to do anything about it. The attitude associated with Raynaud's disease is that they want to take hostile gross motor action. Graham et al. (1960) found that after the attitude induction, a small but reliable difference in hand temperature developed between conditions with the induction of the hives-relevant attitude producing increases in temperature while the Raynaud's-relevant attitude produced temperature decreases. These findings support the suggestion that emotions are indeed associated with different patterns of autonomic activity and challenge the Schachter and Singer view which asserted that the same pattern of autonomic arousal occurs across emotions.

The inability of some investigators to find different patterns of ANS activity in different emotions may in part have been a function of the imprecision with which they classified emotional states. In some experiments, it was assumed that individuals would experience a particular emotional state if they were exposed to a stimulus which was selected to elicit that emotion. However, affective reactions are quite variable across people and rarely are instances of "pure" emotion elicited. In the Schachter and Singer experiment referred to above, the stooge who behaved in an angry versus joyful fashion might not have invariably elicited anger or happiness. The emotional responses of the subjects may have been a complex blend of many basic emotions. It may have been for this reason that robust ANS discrimination was not observed.

New and sophisticated methods have recently been used to measure the facial expression of emotion to select epochs of relatively "pure" emotion based upon the presence of the unique relevant facial expression. A battery of autonomic measures were recorded while subjects, self-generated emotion and the ANS measures were compared for those epochs during which pure facial expressions were present. The data from this study revealed the most robust ANS discrimination among emotions which has been found to date. RJD

Bibliography

Ax, A.F. 1953: The physiological differentiation between fear and anger in humans. *Psychosomatic medicine* 15, 433–42.

Cannon, W.B. 1927: The James-Lange theory of emotions: A critical examination and an alternative theory. *American journal of psychology* 39, 106–24.

Funkenstein, D.H. 1955: The physiology of fear and anger. *Scientific American* 192, 74–80.

Graham, D.T. 1972: Psychosomatic medicine. In *Handbook of psychophysiology*, ed. N.S. Greenfield and R.S. Sternbach. New York: Holt.

Graham, D.T., Stern, J.A. and Winokur, G. 1960: The concept of a different specific set of physiological changes in each emotion. *Psychiatric research reports* 12, 8–15.

*Grings, W.W. and Dawson, M.E. 1978: *Emotions and bodily responses*. New York: Academic Press.

James, W. 1890: *The principles of psychology*. New York: Holt.

Plutchik, R. and Ax, A.F. 1967: A critique of determinants of emotional state by Schachter and Singer (1962). *Psychophysiology* 4, 79–82.

Schachter, S. and Singer, J.E. 1962: Cognitive, social and physiological determinants of emotional state. *Psychological review* 69, 379–99.

emotion *See above, and also* Aristotelean view of e,: conflict theory and e.; play and e.

emotional aspects of physical and mental handicap Emotional disorders may occur as an adaptive response to physical and mental handicap, but may also be seen as one aspect of the underlying disorder associated with the handicap.

It is important therefore to make a distinction between those conditions which are associated with underlying brain dysfunction or damage such as epilepsy or severe mental retardation and those which are not, for example, paraplegia, orthopedic conditions, deafness and visual handicap.

Some underlying mechanisms are common to both situations, but predominate in the latter. For example the effects of labeling, discrimination, impaired functioning in day-to-day living, the individual's perception of his handicap and his temperamental or personality characteristics. In instances where the handicap is a result of brain dysfunction, factors such as the nature, site, age of onset and the effects of the dysfunction on normal brain activity may predominate. It is, however, true to say that the nature and extent of the emotional disturbance are usually a result of a complex interaction between all these factors.

In most instances the type of emotional disorder seen in association with handicap is similar to that in the non-handicapped population, although its expression may be modified as a result of the handicap or its underlying cause. Thus anxiety states and depression may occur following accident or acute illness, leading to handicap, as a direct response to a specific loss of function or inability to pursue a familiar way of life. This may then be followed by a slow process of emotional adaptation or may lead to permanent emotional disability.

The effects of handicap occurring early in life and leading to personality disorder may be offset by the increased adaptive capability of the young person.

Where handicap is associated with organic brain damage, more specific psychiatric syndromes may occur. Thus, for example, generalized epilepsy is usually associated with non-specific emotional disorders, while people with temporal lobe epilepsy have a somewhat higher frequency than normal of psychotic illness.

In the case of mental retardation, immature personality structure, language handicaps and institutionalization may be important factors. While rates of adult forms of psychotic illness are only moderately increased above those seen in the normal population, childhood psychosis or autism is more frequent in association with specific impairments in language function and impairments in social interaction. JAC

emotional behavior and the nervous system Emotion refers to an inner "state" or "feeling", but unfortunately, it is most often the overt behavior of non-verbal animals that is relied upon to determine its neural substrates. Almost every major area of the central nervous system has been implicated in emotion. However, it is generally accepted that the HYPOTHALAMUS and the LIMBIC SYSTEM, particularly the AMYGDALA (see BRAIN AND CENTRAL NERVOUS SYSTEM: ILLUSTRATIONS figs. 15–18), are most important for our emotional "state" and emotional behavior.

The hypothalamus acts as the center for emotional output. This is based on the evidence that stimulation of the hypothalamus will produce autonomic responses such as changes in heart rate. The emotional behavior altered by stimulation or lesions of the hypothalamus is, however, modified by stimulation or lesions of the limbic systems. This system, which includes the amygdala, hippocampus, septum and cingulate cortex (fig. 16) was first suspected in emotion when removal of the temporal lobes in monkeys dramatically changed their behavior. The monkeys became tame, with an apparent loss of "fear". It has since been determined that the removal of the amygdala, embedded within the temporal lobe, had caused these emotional changes (see fig. 21). The amygdala is responsible for relating external stimuli with emotional states (produced by the hypothalamus) in order to maintain proper emotional responses to the environment.

Other neural structures within the limbic system have been implicated (septum and cingulate cortex). Emotional behavior changes if these structures are stimulated or lesioned. Frontal cortex, anatomically connected with both the limbic system and hypothalamus, also plays a role in controlling emotional behavior. Frontal leucotomies are used as a medical treatment to produce docility in emotionally excited patients. RCS/BER

emotional behavior in animals The term may be used to denote a state of arousal, or certain aspects of behavior. In animal studies it is not possible to assess inner feelings, and although attempts are sometimes made to equate human and animal feelings, the scientific basis for such a comparison has been disputed (see ANTHROPOMORPHISM).

In vertebrate animals emotional behavior is usually accompanied by autonomic activity. Elevated heart beat and respiratory rate, and signs of changes in the blood supply to various parts of the body, may indicate that the animal is in an emotional state, but they do not signify particular emotions such as fear or anger.

The first important scientific work on emotion was Charles Darwin's *The expression of the emotions in man and animals* (1872). Darwin took the existence of emotion in animals for granted and addressed the question of how they might be expressed in behavior. He emphasized the communication function of emotion in animals and put forward three basic principles. His *principle of serviceable associated habits* incorporates the now accepted idea that evolutionary precursors of emotional expressions, such as defensive reflexes, could undergo ritualization and so come to serve a communicative function. Darwin's *principle of antithesis* maintains that opposite behavioral dispositions are expressed in opposite ways. The figure shows that the posture of an angry dog is in many ways opposite of its posture when fawning. Darwin's third principle is that of *the direct action of the nervous system* which recognized that many physiological adjustments are involved in a given emotional state.

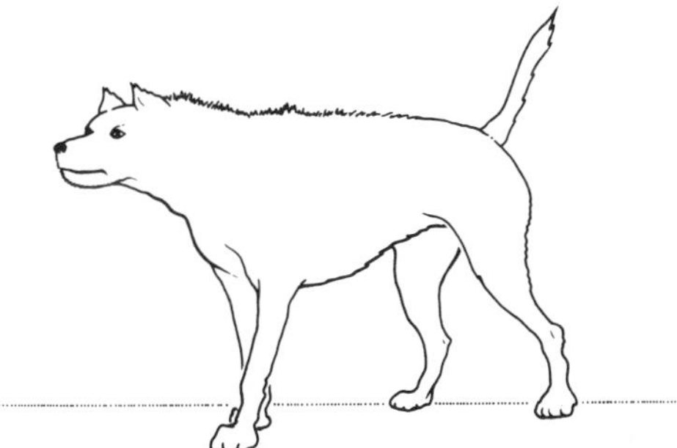

Darwin's Principle of Antithesis illustrated by the posture of a dog when submissive (above) and angry (below)

Towards the end of the nineteenth century a theory relating physiological events and emotional feelings was independently put forward by William James and Carl Lange. The James-Lange theory, as it became known, maintained that emotional feelings result directly from the perception of the physiological changes induced by the emotional circumstances. Thus to be afraid is to feel the heart pounding, the breathing quicken, etc. The theory has faltered on the failure, even with modern sophisticated methods, to detect recognizable differences in the physiological events that accompany the different emotions. A more widely accepted view, put forward by Walter Cannon (1932), is that the physiological changes associated with emotion facilitate the capacity of the body to cope with emergencies. DJM

Bibliography

Cannon, Walter B. 1932: *The wisdom of the body*. New York: Co. Co. Norton; London: Kegan Paul. Reprinted 1980. New York and London: Norton.

emotional development This refers to several dissociable but related processes which occur over the life span. It cannot be understood independently of one's definition of emotions. These are central nervous system and feeling states which are intimately associated with involuntary expressive reactions in the face, voice and gesture. Emotions motivate the individual and control numerous internal psychological processes, and are, in turn, controlled by them. Moreover, their external expressive patterns regulate interpersonal behavior in a variety of ways. They are continuous, active and adaptive processes, rather than intermittent, reactive and disruptive, as traditionally conceived. Perhaps because of their adaptive function, emotional expression patterns appear to be biologically based and pre-wired. For instance, blind infants and children with no opportunity to mimic expressions of others show remarkably similar patterns to those observable in sighted persons. At least six to eight patterns of facial expression such as anger, joy and disgust appear to be universally recognizable, and hence receptivity to these expressive patterns may also be pre-wired. In addition, emotional FACIAL EXPRESSIONS of adults, children and young infants are highly similar, permitting emotions to form a core of continuity throughout the life span (see EMOTION: ETHOLOGICAL APPROACHES).

Traditional conceptualizations have typically ignored many significant processes of emotional development, and been too simplistic about the ages of emergence of specific emotional states. Consider Bridges's widely-cited differentiation model, which posits an initial state of undifferentiated arousal in the neonate, from which first distress, then delight, differentiate at three to six weeks. At three months, anger differentiates out of distress; at four months, disgust from anger; and at six months, fear from disgust. At eight months, the positive emotion of elation differentiates from delight, and affection from elation at twelve months. Other more complex emotions such as jealousy, parental affection and envy are evident by five years.

Recent empirical work has called into question the differentiation model. There is evidence that neonates show both disgust to noxious, and delight to savory substances. They have remarkably well patterned expressions of surprise, fear, interest and possibly other fundamental emotions. Moreover, the mechanism of differentiation proposed by Bridges is not persuasive. Fear, for instance, does not seem to have expressive components similar to but more specific than disgust, nor does affection seem to share many features in common with elation.

Perhaps the most significant inadequacy of traditional conceptions of emotional development is the failure to consider different domains of development that influence which emotions are observed at different ages. Emotional behavior can change in the course of life because of changes in (1) the situations that elicit emotions; (2) the instrumental (voluntary) behavior motivated by emotions; (3) the expressive reactions indicative of emotion; (4) the emotional states themselves becoming elaborated with development; and (5) changing social conventions as to what it is proper to experience, or express, or both, as an emotion. Let us consider each of these domains in turn.

1. Emotions develop through changes in the efficacy of various eliciting circumstances, resulting from developments in perception, cognition, and learning.

These changes may sharply increase the prevalence of a given emotion in an infant's response repertoire, but it is an error to assume, on the basis of these shifts in prevalence, that the response process is changing, or that the emotional expression is not observable earlier. For instance, the smiling response blossoms at four to eight weeks of age, the frequently cited "age of emergence". However it is observable under certain conditions much earlier. Blind infants smile at the mother's voice at three weeks; drowsy infants smile to many stimuli in the first month of life; and premature infants show extensive smiling in rapid eye movement sleep states. The blossoming of the smile at four to eight weeks seems to result from new ways of seeing the face (a prepotent elicitor of smiling at that age), and from the emergence of new memory capacities (effortful assimilation to new memory stores powerfully elicits smiling at all ages).

Similarly, fear is widely believed to emerge at seven to nine months because fear of strangers, separation distress, and fear of heights and other stimuli are readily observable at those ages. However, fear is observable in response to other events much earlier: e.g. to looming stimuli by ten weeks of age, to prolonged scrutiny by a stranger at four months, and to separation from the mother in the home by five months. Accordingly, what emerges at seven months may not be a new emotion so much as a new cognitive capacity, like the ability to forecast future danger even in the absence of prior learning experiences with a specific stimulus.

Sadness is another emotional state not believed to be observable before six to eight months, when loss of a loved object is thought to be first understood by the infant. This expectation was at first supported by studies of maternal deprivation and anaclitic depression (see ATTACHMENT AND LOSS). Recent work, however, has demonstrated that sadness is observable as early as 3.5 months under conditions of severe parental abuse and neglect. Similar examples can be given for anger and other discrete emotional states. Changes in efficacy of eliciting circumstances thus constitute only one criterion of emotional development.

2. Emotional development also takes place through changes in the coping reactions of the individual.

As the infant becomes motorically and cognitively more competent, new response capabilities arise which permit new ways of reacting to old stressors. For instance, when the infant acquires the ability to crawl, it can control what happens when a stranger enters the room or the mother leaves it. Accordingly, an infant otherwise upset by a stranger can not only avoid distress, but even show friendliness. Similarly, new coping skills, such as the ability to move round objects, may prevent a child from crying or becoming frustrated with a problem. Instead of distress, the child may express joy over mastering the situation. As development continues, coping reactions become increasingly internalized, and defense mechanisms proper begin to play a role in regulating emotions. In ageing, some coping capacities may be lost, resulting in feelings of helplessness or depression.

Another major coping reaction that influences emotional development is paying attention to social cues. When infants and children are faced with ambiguous circumstances they typically look to important others for emotional information to help appraise the event (and thus to react emotionally to it). This permits emotions to be socially transmitted, by enabling individuals to mimic emotional responses without directly experiencing the positive or negative effects of the circumstances in which those responses occur.

Still another change in coping reaction to a stressor in the course of development involves the "targeting" of the object of the emotional expression. For instance, when newborns are restricted from movement, facial and vocal expressions of distress or anger are not directed at anybody, nor at the source of the distress, but by four months, infants clearly have a target – the immediate impediments – and by seven months, the target becomes both the impediment and the person who is permitting it. In adulthood, the defense mechanism of displacement illustrates a different type of coping response involving a shift in such targeting of emotions.

3. Emotional expressions can change with development. One way is by becoming less "noisy" (e.g. facial expression patterns in the neonate frequently contain components not specific to the pattern, whereas at older ages this is less so). Facial expression patterns in response to restraint of movement are similar at one and four months. However, the one-month-old typically manifests components which are not typical of anger (eye closing, tongue protrusion). The four-month-old does not.

Emotional expression patterns also communicate more complex dimensions of affect with age, especially in the first two months of life. (After two months, hedonic tone and activation dimensions are identifiable in infant facial expression much as they are with adults). In the first two months, hedonic tone (i.e., whether the experience is pleasant or unpleasant) is identifiable quite readily, but level of activation is less clearly detected, perhaps because the range of intensities of infant wakefulness is so limited in the first two months.

Expressions also become instrumental with age. That is, an expressive reaction that was once involuntarily elicited now comes under the voluntary control of the child. Both crying and smiling clearly become instrumental very early in life, perhaps as early as two months. Anger, in the form of temper tantrums, become instrumental late in the second year. Other emotional expressions can likewise become instrumental, but little is known about when they do.

4. Emotional states undergo developmental transformations. To the extent that changes in appraisal, in coping reactions, and in expressive patterning take place in the course of development, and to the extent that these processes influence the prevalence of the quality of emotional states, the feeling states of individuals must differ dramatically at different ages.

Moreover, feeling states themselves combine and synthesize in dramatic hierarchical fashion. The fundamental emotions intercoordinate into higher order, emergent emotions, and emergent emotions combine into even more complex states. Guilt is an instance of such a higher-order emotion. It is not fundamental, in so far as it shows no universally recognizable expressive pattern. It requires extensive representational abilities, may be observable by eighteen to twenty-four months of age, and seems to require the intercoordination of empathic distress with fear, sadness, and other emotions. Depression and anxiety also appear to be complex emotions which are intercoordinations of both fundamental and higher-order emotions. Anxiety seems to involve complex intercoordinations of fear, shame, anger, guilt, and interest. Depression, on the other hand, has elements of sadness, anger, disgust, contempt, guilt, and shyness. Shame, envy, and jealousy appear to be other instances of complex emotions.

5. Emotional expressions become socialized. Every culture has display rules which govern the manifestation of the expression of emotions. In some societies, for instance, the response expected at a funeral is a smile. In others, weeping and exaggerated sadness are the rule. In others, emotions are inhibited. Emotions are also socialized through the selection of appropriate channels for expression. For instance it is sometimes permissible to express anger through choice of words, but not through facial, vocal or overtly hostile behavior. JJCa/KSC/RNE

Bibliography

Bridges, K.M. 1932: Emotional development in early infancy. *Child development* 3, 324–41.

Campos, J., et al. 1983: Socioemotional development. In *Carmichael's manual of child psychology: Infancy and development psychobiology.* Vol. 2 ed. M. Haith and J. Campos. New York: John Wiley and Sons.

Sroufe, L.A. Socioemotional Development. In *Handbook of infant development*, ed. J. Osofsky. New York: John Wiley and Sons.

emotional expression and groups: The extent to which the expression and experience of emotion are influenced or shaped by the groups to which a person belongs. While there are certain universals of emotional expression, cultures vary considerably with regard to the circumstances, the manner of display and even the experience of many emotions. For example in many cultures it is more acceptable for males to express aggression than it is for females. In contrast it is more acceptable for females to express affection and to express it in particular ways (e.g. kissing) than it is for males. Similarly there are subcultural and cultural differences in the intensity and forms with which pain and grief are expressed. The display rules (Ekman 1977) which govern the expression of emotion will also reflect group appraisals of the behavior which is appropriate in various settings (e.g. church) and on different occasions (e.g. funerals). Further, the type of emotion, if any, which a person experiences on a particular occasion will, at least partially, reflect the group's interpretations of the situation. For example what counts as an "insult", and whether it is expected to move a person to anger, may be quite different in different groups.

LAW

Bibliography

Ekman, P. 1977: Biological and cultural contributions to body and facial movement. In *The anthropology of the body*, ed. J. Blacking. A.S.A. Monograph 15. New York and London: Academic Press.

emotional expression in infancy The emotional life of young infants has often been characterized as undifferentiated arousal. That view is much oversimplified. Virtually all the specific facial muscles that enter into adult emotional expressions are functional in the neonate (Oster and Ekman 1978). Infants are also capable of many variations in voice and bodily posture. Expressive reactions serve to communicate the state of the infant, and they help to establish and maintain affectional bonds with caretakers. But that is not all. Infants of two to three months of age exert, by means of expressive reactions, considerable control over their interactions with other persons, and hence over the conditions of their own development (Trevarthen 1979). Before the end of the first year expressive or emotion-like states appear, including interest, happiness, distress, surprise, anger, disgust, and fear (Izard 1979). (See EMOTIONAL DEVELOPMENT) JRA

Bibliography

Izard, C.E. 1979: Emotions as motivations: An evolutionary-developmental perspective. In *Nebraska symposium on motivation* vol. 26, ed. H.E. Howe and R.A. Dienstbier. Lincoln: University of Nebraska Press.

Oster, H. and Ekman, P. 1978: Facial behavior in child development. In: *Minnesota symposia on child psychology* vol. 11, ed. W.A. Collins. Hillsdale, N.J.: Laurence Erlbaum Associates.

Trevarthen, C. 1979: Communication and cooperation in early infancy: A description of primary intersubjectivity. In *Before speech: The beginning of interpersonal communication*, ed. M. Bullowa. Cambridge and New York: Cambridge University Press.

emotional expression *See above, and also* facial expression and emotion

emotional roles in groups: The idea that two behavioral patterns or roles will become differentiated in every group. The Instrumental or Task role is directed towards the accomplishment of specific tasks or goals; to that extent, attention will be given to emotion only in an effort to minimize emotional involvement and expression. In contrast, the expressive or socioemotional role is focused upon emotion. The concern is to ensure positive emotional experiences and to enhance the relationships between group members.

The differentiation of these roles is presumed to derive from the necessity for all groups to manage two basic problems: coping with externally imposed demands upon the group; and maintaining the internal integrity of the group by fulfilling the social-psychological requirements of its members. It was initially proposed that because the requirements of the two roles may be incompatible, the same person could not enact both roles in a particular group. Further, it was suggested that the Instrumental role is more likely to be taken by males and the expressive role by females, particularly within family groups. But these assumptions may not be warranted, depending upon such factors as the size and composition of the group, the kind of tasks involved and the group's orientation towards the task. LAW

emotions, basic Literally hundreds of emotions are recognized in ordinary language; and human beings are capable of experiencing many more emotions than are specified in any given language. One of the traditional preoccupations of theorists has been to impose some order on this array. Two general approaches have been taken: the first attempts to identify a few basic emotions, from which others can be derived as compounds or extensions; the second attempts to identify general dimensions along which all emotions presumably vary. These two approaches are not independent, and in the following discussion, both will be considered; the major emphasis, however, will be on the first (basic emotions).

The goal of some theorists is to lay out the basic emotions in a kind of periodic table. Unlike the situation in chemistry, however, there is little agreement among psychologists on which emotions are basic. An emotion can be considered basic only within the context of some broader classification scheme; and such schemes vary depending on the orientation and goal of different theorists. Five examples of classification schemes follow. These have been chosen to provide a representative list of basic emotions, and, more importantly, to illustrate the kinds of principles (logical, biological, psychological and sociological) that have been used to identify basic emotions.

(1) The first systematic attempt to classify the emotions was made by the ancient Stoics, who conceived of emotions as irrational judgments or appraisals. They divided emotions on the basis of whether the appraised object of the emotion is good or evil; and then again on whether the object is expected or already present. This yields four major categories of emotion: desire – an inclination toward an expected good; fear – a withdrawal from an expected evil; joy – an elation of the mind occasioned by some present good; and sorrow – a contraction of the mind occasioned by some present evil. Each of these categories subsumes numerous varieties of emotion, e.g. both anger (a craving for revenge) and passionate love are varieties of desire.

(2) The scheme adumbrated by the Stoics can be expanded in many ways. For example, the object of an emotion may be easy or difficult to attain (avoid). Also, an object need not be simply present or expected; a person can have an orientation toward the object that is a-temporal. By adding these criteria, Aquinas (in the thirteenth century) developed an eleven-fold classification of basic emotions: love, desire, joy, hate, aversion, sorrow, hope, despair, courage, fear, and anger. Arnold (1960) has emended and updated this scheme in her influential theory of emotion.

(3) On the basis of an analysis of facial expressions, Osgood (1966) has identified three affective dimensions: Pleasantness (P), Activation (A), and Control (C) over the situation (see also Russell and Mehrabian 1977). Presumably, emotions can lie at any point in the affective space defined by these three dimensions. Osgood found, however, that they tend to cluster around specific points. The generic names given to these basic clusters are: joy (P+, A+, C neutral), complacency (P+, A−, C neutral), loathing (P−, A+, C+), horror (P−, A+, C−), boredom (P−, A−, C+), and despair (P−, A−, C−).

(4) Kemper (1978) has proposed a classification of emotion based on the interpersonal dimensions of status and power, each of which can be excessive, adequate or insufficient. Further distinctions are made on the basis of agency (whether the self, the target or a third party is responsible for the maintenance or change in status and power relationships), and direction (whether the target of the emotion is the self or another). Finally, a temporal dimension is introduced, in that emotions can be structural (based on existing status and power relationships), anticipatory or consequent. Interactions among these dimensions and their subdivisions give rise to a large number of potential emotions. According to Kemper, there are 1,701 possible consequent emotions alone, only a small proportion of which are given distinct names in ordinary language.

(5) Clearly, as the criteria used to identify basic emotions are expanded, the number of emotions identified may become so large that it is no longer reasonable to speak of

basic emotions, but only of the criteria used to classify emotions. Since Darwin (1872) first wrote on the topic many psychologists have looked to the theory of evolution for a solution to this dilemma; that is, basic emotions are those that have served some adaptive function during the evolution of the species. After reviewing numerous proposals along these lines, Plutchik (1980) has postulated eight primary emotions, each associated with a biologically adaptive system of behavior. These emotions (and their presumed biological functions) are: fear (protection), anger (destruction), sadness (reintegration), joy (reproduction), acceptance (affiliation), disgust (rejection), expectancy (exploration), and surprise (orientation). Other emotions are presumably compounded from these primaries, e.g. love is a mixture of joy and acceptance. (See Izard 1977, for a somewhat related scheme.)

The above examples illustrate the two main approaches to simplifying the domain of emotion. The first is to identify a small number of basic emotions (e.g. fear, anger); the other is to identify a few fundamental attributes of many, if not all, emotions (e.g. pleasantness, activation). These two approaches can be combined; that is, emotions representing some combinations of fundamental attributes may be considered more "basic" than others (Osgood Example 3). Often, however, the two approaches have been conflated in an uncritical fashion, as when an attribute of many emotions is treated as a basic emotion in its own right (see the Stoic notion of desire, Example 1).

Henceforward reference is made only to basic emotions. However, many of the same considerations apply *mutatis mutandis* to approaches that emphasize fundamental attributes.

The preceding examples can be used to illustrate several features about proposals for basic emotions. Although all schemes impose some order on the vast array of emotions which humans are capable of experiencing, they differ in terms of organizing principles. Four kinds of principles can be distinguished: logical (linguistic), psychological, biological, and sociological.

(i) *Logical (linguistic) principles.* The concepts we use to refer to emotions are interrelated by a network of logical implications. For example, a person cannot hope for an event that has already occurred, nor fear an unmitigated good. Classification schemes such as those proposed by the Stoics (Example 1) and Aquinas (Example 2) rely on such logical relationships.

(ii) *Psychological principles.* An indefinite variety of classification schemes could be constructed on logical grounds; to be psychologically meaningful, such schemes must be related to the way people actually think, feel and respond when emotional. Rather than beginning with a logical scheme and relating it to behavior, many psychologists prefer to work in the reverse direction, i.e. beginning with behavior and proceeding inductively to construct a scheme that "fits" the data (e.g. Osgood, Example 3). A distinction between logical and psychological approaches cannot, however, be rigidly drawn. There is a close dialectical relationship between our concepts, on the one hand, and our experiences and nonverbal behavior, on the other.

(iii) *Biological principles.* From a reductionist view of science, biology is more "basic" than psychology. It is not surprising, therefore, that basic emotions have often been linked with biological systems of behavior (e.g. Plutchik, Example 5). Such an approach seems to have the added advantage of objectivity, since biological systems presumably exist prior to, and independent of, our conceptualization of them. Still, there are problems with this approach. For one thing it has proved no easier to obtain agreement on the number and kinds of relevant biological systems (especially in humans) than on the number and kinds of basic emotions. For another thing, empirical evidence does not support any one-to-one identification of human emotions (as ordinarily conceived) with biological systems.

(iv) *Sociological principles.* Explicitly sociological theories of emotion are few. The scheme proposed by Kemper (Example 4) is an exception, being based on the social dimensions of status and power. Other sociologists (e.g. Hochschild 1979) have emphasized the close connection between emotions and ideology. That is, experiencing the proper emotions on the proper occasions serves to validate and reinforce the beliefs of the group. From this perspective, each culture has – even creates – its own basic emotions. For example, emotions akin to reverence and awe might be basic in a theocracy; courage in a culture that is endemically at war; and envy in a culture that places great emphasis on egalitarianism.

In addition to differences with regard to principles of organization, proposals for basic emotions also differ in terms of the *level* of organization that is considered basic. That is, most schemes presume some hierarchical organization of emotional categories, but not all levels in the hierarchy are regarded as equally fundamental. Some schemes, such as that of the Stoics (Example 1), consider as basic very inclusive categories, which can then be subdivided into more specific emotions. Other schemes, such as that by Plutchik (Example 5) treat basic emotions as elementary categories, with other emotions representing compounds of these elements.

In summary, there are no basic emotions *simpliciter.* There are many ways in which emotions may be classified, on logical, psychological, biological and/or sociological grounds; and within any classification scheme, some emotions may be considered more basic than others, depending on the level of organization that is taken as the starting point for analysis. JRA

Bibliography

Arnold, M.B. 1960: *Emotion and personality.* New York: Columbia University Press.

Darwin, C. 1872: *The expression of the emotions in man and animals.* London: Murray.

Hochschild, A.R. 1979: Emotion work, feeling rules, and social structure. *American journal of sociology* 85, 551–75.

Izard, C.E. 1977: *Human emotions.* New York and London: Plenum Press.

Kemper, T.D. 1978: *A social interactional theory of emotions.* New York and Chichester: Wiley.

Osgood, C.E. 1966: Dimensionality of the semantic space for communication via facial expressions. *Scandinavian journal of psychology* 7, 1–30.

Plutchik, R. 1980: *Emotion: a psychoevolutionary synthesis*. New York and London: Harper & Row.

Russell, J.A. and Mehrabian, A. 1977: Evidence for a three-factor theory of emotions. *Journal of research in personality* 11, 273–94.

emotions, measures of Self-report, behavioral and physiological indices all provide measures of emotions. Investigators attempt to establish construct validity for emotional states by searching for concordance among various measures of emotion. Self-report measures include numerical rating scales as well as non-verbal continuous measures such as manipulating a joy stick along one or two dimensions. The most finely differentiated behavioral measure of emotion is FACIAL EXPRESSION. Detailed and reliable coding systems are now available for scoring facial expression from videotape records. Another behavioral measure which has proved useful is analysis of the voice. Certain acoustic parameters have been found to differentiate among various emotional states. Physiological measures of emotion include indices of autonomic and central nervous activity as well as of endocrine responses. The strength of concordance as well as the temporal relations among the various measures has not yet been well studied. RJD

emotions, recognition of The study of the recognition of emotions has been one of the major areas of investigation in social perception for a long time. Originally interest was mainly focussed on the problems of accuracy in recognition of emotions based on facial expressions. As this problem turned out to be largely an artifact of the stimulus material used (Brown 1965), research has shifted to the study of the process of emotional recognition and investigation of the universal nature of emotional recognition and facial expressions of emotion (Ekman and Oster 1979). Ekman has shown that there are probably only six basic emotions (happiness, sadness, surprise, fear, anger and disgust) which are expressed in the face. In addition, his cross-cultural research (Ekman and Friesen 1975) presents strong evidence for a universally similar way of expressing these emotions in different cultures, except for differences in so-called display rules. Essentially the same results have been obtained with the recognition of emotions. The six basic emotions are inferred to a large extent from similar facial expressions in different cultures. Evidence from developmental psychology supports Ekman's conclusions. JMFJ

Bibliography

Brown, R. 1965: *Social psychology*. New York: Free Press.

Ekman, P. and Friesen, W.V. 1975: *Unmasking the face*. Englewood Cliffs, N.J.: Prentice-Hall.

——— and Oster, H. 1979: Facial expressions of emotion. *Annual review of psychology* 30.

emotions and consciousness In cognitive conception consciousness is treated as awareness of a sensory state which may or may not be organized into perceptions together with the emotions evoked by the internal or external stimuli causing the sensations. From this perspective, consciousness is extended beyond general waking awareness to include states such as DAYDREAMING, SLEEP, HYPNOSIS, drug induction, MEDITATION, so involving both normal and altered conditions and capacities for reflection on one's current experience. Both intellectual and intuitive modes for consciousness can be recognized (Ornstein 1973), the former being that which is easily articulated and analysed while the latter is a non-verbal conviction of knowing. On a broad view consciousness is contrasted with a comatose state, during which the brain does not actively process information available from either inside the body or from outside of it.

Using this broad perspective Tomkins (1962, 1963), and Singer (1981) argue that emotions are always present in consciousness by definition. They hold that emotions are innate inevitable patterned responses to the density and duration of neural firing which results when stimuli (either internal or external) impinge on a person – that is, when sensation occurs. According to this view *basic emotions* are activated singly or in combination depending on the complexity, novelty and rate of presentation of the information. Each of the primary emotions itself ranges on a continuum of intensity: Interest to excitement, enjoyment to joy, surprise to startle, distress to anguish, anger to rage, disgust to revulsion, contempt to scorn, fear to terror, shame/shyness to humiliation, guilt to remorse. Four common patterns of the BASIC EMOTIONS are love, hostility, anxiety and depression. While these emotions may interact with biological drive states which result from tissue deprivation or satisfaction, they may also exist independently. When they occur alone they are time-independent, being contingent upon particular stimuli rather than biological cycles. In either case, they serve to establish a direction to consciousness by organizing perception activating learned chains of association and expectation (often labeled "*affective-cognitive structures*" or "*ideo-affective postures*"), and depending on existing beliefs of the person (see Bower 1981) directing content of consciousness. For example, a new house might be perceived as a possible new home, and so elicit joy, evoke positive attributions and so on if "home" is part of an existing conceptual structure or plan. Alternatively, construed as the locus of a new and fearful change, it could be perceived as threatening and ugly since it did not fit into beliefs and wishes about the future.

In summary, according to this view emotion is an intrinsic human state or condition and it serves two major functions in consciousness: it organizes sensations into perceptions, giving them labels and assigning attributions which aggregate into meanings, and it also directs scanning of the internal or external environment for additional information. In other words, emotion both organizes and motivates the flow of consciousness.

Piaget (see 1981 for a recent statement) has also claimed that emotion has a primary role in determining intellectual activity. He has seen affect as the motor for cognitive activity in general and for cognitive *development* (differentiation and integration) in particular. As Singer

(1973) has pointed out, Piaget demonstrated that information which is slightly discrepant from a person's expectations (schemata) evokes interest and attempts at accommodation, changing beliefs to adapt to external realities. At the same time, matching a new bit of information to schemata evokes joy, guaranteeing assimilation, the integration of understanding into what is already understood.

The study of consciousness in this broad form has also been directed toward understanding ALTERED STATES (see Ornstein 1973). It has been suggested that some "altered" states such as hypnotic trances or psychotic episodes can be understood as conditions during which a particularly intense emotion focuses and directs attention. Eastern meditative states reflect an intense focus on internal experience; sexual or tribal ecstasy are examples of alteration in a social context. Here, the affect of interest is raised to extreme levels, creating a total immersion in the activity at hand, similar to the more common "*flow*" experience described and studied by Csikzentmihalyi (1975).

A second important definition of consciousness contrasts it with a highly specific notion of *unconscious* experience. This is the psychoanalytical perspective, according to which sensations impinging on a person need not necessarily be organized into perceptions nor *must* one attend to the emotional responses they engender. A person may distort or deny experiences or repress perceptions and cognitions associated with them. The information kept from organized perception or self-awareness can be labeled "unconscious". When denial, distortion or repression occurs, energy is re-directed away from coping with the original event and its evoked emotional response. In this sense, the term "unconscious" describes a person's inability to *recognize* the stimuli affecting him or her, whether they are drawn from the external environment or from internal memories, images, thoughts, feelings, or sensations.

Recent research has provided ample evidence of such unconscious phenomena. In a particularly interesting research program Daniel Weinberger, Gary E. Schwartz and their colleagues are demonstrating selective repression of information which the perceiver considers to be counter to tolerable self-perceptions (e.g. Weinberger, Schwartz and Davidson 1979). Further brain LATERALIZATION studies have suggested a mechanism for psychoanalytic process, supporting the idea of two independent cognitive systems, housed in separate hemispheres which may interact to create a full awareness, but which can function independently. This hypothesis explains the phenomena such as the psychoanalytical type of "unconscious processing" of material which a person clearly must have grasped, or the *dissociation* of a cognition from its accompanying affect.

Perhaps another source of evidence of the impact of primary emotional states of which a person may or may not be aware abounds in literature on projective testing. Tasks which specifically request fantasy material such as the Thematic Apperception Test, or which require organization of perception with linkage to associations, such as the Rorschach inkblot test, have suggested connections between affective states and cognitive productions created during them.

Experiments in cognitive psychology are yielding abundant evidence of the power of emotions which occur naturally or are purposefully induced to direct associative, interpretive and attentional processes. Bower (1981) has confirmed the well known clinical phenomenon of "perspectivity", the organization of memories and other material into systems by reference to emotion. Bower et al. have demonstrated the influence of mood states on a range of cognitive processes which constitute consciousness. They have confirmed that information learned during one emotional state may be unavailable in other states, and that both free associations and elaborations of stories focus around the highlighted emotion. As the intensity of the emotion increases so do these effects. Interpretations are similarly affected: events and ambiguous social scenes are influenced in mood-congruent directions, imaginative stories are colored by the dominant emotion, and judgments and evaluations of others are made in a direction consistent with mood. For example, an angry person is likely to see a co-worker as hostile; when the same person later feels happy, he is likely to perceive the same co-worker as friendly. Finally, this effect extends throughout consciousness by directing attention to mood-congruent information, causing such information to be particularly salient perceptually, and facilitating mood-congruent learning, (see EMOTION AND PERSONALITY). Such effects help to explain self perception during depressed or anxious or angry states: they prime consciousness to focus on the past events with the same emotional quality, to notice similar current events, to interpret and misinterpret situations consistent with the emotion, and thus they create a self-defeating spiral. Efforts at changing such problems through directed changes in consciousness have been reported to be successful. One such effort stresses changes in the actual cognitive processes so that they are not so heavily distorted by the prevailing mood (Beck 1976); another suggests changing the contents of consciousness directly through the use of *imagery*. Both recognize the intimate relationship between emotion and consciousness. And both have achieved some success. RBT

Bibliography

Beck, A.T. 1976: *Cognitive therapy and emotional disorder.* New York: International Universities Press.

*Bower, G.H. 1981: Mood and memory. *American psychologist* 36, 129–48.

Csikzentmihalyi, 1975: *Beyond boredom and anxiety.* San Francisco: Jossey-Bass.

Ornstein, R.E., ed. 1973: *The nature of human consciousness.* New York: The Viking Press.

Piaget, J. 1981: *Intelligence and affectivity: their relationship during child development.* Palo Alto, Calif.: Annual Reviews, Inc.

Singer, J.L. 1973: *The child's world of make-believe.* New York and London: Academic Press.

——1981: *Daydreaming and fantasy.* Oxford and New York: Oxford University Press.

Tomkins, S.S. 1962, 1963: *Affect, imagery and consciousness.* Vols I and II. New York: Springer.

Weinberger, D.A., Schwartz, G.E. and Davidson, R.J. 1979: Low-anxious, high-anxious, and repressive coping styles: Psychometric patterns and behavioral and physiological responses to stress. *Journal of abnormal psychology* 88, 369–80.

emotions and facial expression *See* emotions, basic; facial expression and emotion

empathy The understanding and sharing of another person's emotional experience in a particular situation. In the early nineteenth century Lipps described empathy (an English rendering of the German *Einfuhlung*) as a process of "feeling into" the emotions expressed in the movements or dynamic postures of people, aesthetic objects or natural scenes. The spontaneous imitation of these cues produces kinesthetic sensations associated with corresponding emotions. The alternative theory of representation emphasized the need to understand the person's situation intellectually thereby evoking emotional memories previously associated with similar situations.

Empathy requires a receptive set ("taking the role of the other", Mead 1934), an appreciation of the meaning of the emotion-eliciting situation for the person and an accurate interpretation of the person's verbal and nonverbal behavior. Dymond (1949) created a measure of this kind of empathy; her test required people to make predictions about the feelings, thoughts or behavior of a person they had met briefly. Many researchers explored the correlates of this capacity for predictive empathy. This empathetic reaction can range from involuntary nonverbal and/or physiological responses to the experience of an emotion similar to that experienced by the other person. Nonverbal reactions have been associated with motor mimicry, the spontaneous and unconscious imitation of facial movements and bodily postures. Physiological responses may include for example, muscle tension and heart rate or breathing changes. These provide the material for vicarious classical conditioning according to which the observer later responds emotionally to an aversive stimulus without having been directly exposed to it. Empathetic emotional experience requires an imaginative reconstruction of the meaning of the situation for the person based on the experience of similar situations in the past and knowledge of the person, but such a reconstruction may not be sufficient to produce the emotion.

Hoffmann (1976) has studied the development of forms of empathy through childhood, and Rogers has studied the importance of empathy in the therapeutic relationship. Several psychoanalytical writers also discuss the importance of empathy in therapy; Schafer (1959) presents a model of "generative empathy" which represents the ideal, mature forms of empathy the analyst should direct toward his patient. SB/GCC

Bibliography

Dymond, Rosalind F. 1949: A scale for the measurement of empathetic ability. *Journal of consulting psychology* 13, 127–33.

Hoffmann, M.L. 1976: Empathy, role-taking, guilt and the development of altruistic motives. In *Moral development and behavior*, ed. T. Lickona. New York: Holt, Rinehart & Winston.

Lipps, T. 1965: Empathy and aesthetic pleasure. In *Aesthetic theories: studies in the philosophy of art*, ed. K. Aschenbrenner and A. Isenberg. Englewood Cliffs, N.J.: Prentice-Hall.

Katz, R.L. 1963: *Empathy*. London: Collier-Macmillan.

Mead, G.H. 1934: *Mind, self and society*. Chicago: University of Chicago Press.

Schafer, Roy 1959: Generative empathy in the treatment situation. *Psychoanalytic quarterly* 28, 342–73.

Stotland, E. 1969: Exploratory investigations of empathy. In *Advances in experimental social psychology*, Vol. 4. ed. L. Berkowitz. New York: Academic Press.

empirical methods in social inquiry Special techniques for the collection and treatment of observational data. Their importance lies in their relation to psychology in its modern phase as a behavioral science. This is because those psychologists who currently think of themselves as research scientists (and it must be remembered that not all professional psychologists would by any means place themselves in that category), claim that it is their use of such methods which makes their form of psychology scientific, and marks it off from other, supposedly nonscientific forms (psychoanalysis being the case typically cited in this respect). Although there is still no widespread agreement as to quite what it is which makes science *science*, whether there are in fact any basic methods at all (see Feyerabend 1975), empirical psychologists nonetheless see what they do as science because they proceed (a) by proposing causal theories from which (b) they derive particular hypotheses, which (c) they then test, not actually against experience, but by reference to publicly observable events–in short, because they use a version of the *hypothetico–deductive method*. It is, however, a specialized version of that method. For while empiricism as a philosophy only demands of our general theories that all their verifiable consequences are such as experience will confirm, psychologists feel that only data available to third person external observers are adequate for their purposes as behavioral scientists.

This methodological shift–a shift from a concern with experience in general (both "inner" and "outer") to its specialization solely in external observation–occurred after the débâcle of introspectionism. And under Watson's (1924) influence, psychology changed from being "the Science of Mental Life" to being the science of behavior (see BEHAVIORISM). So, while it is currently entering a cognitive phase (see COGNITIVE PSYCHOLOGY) and is now concerned with the function and structure of mental states, it still remains behaviorist in the sense of drawing all its relevant data from external observation, by use of one kind of empirical method or another.

Broadly speaking such methods may be divided into two main types: experimental and observational. In an experiment, psychologists attempt to isolate and identify the separate causal processes or mechanisms thought to underlie observed behavior. They do so by establishing the appropriate initial (controlled or closed) conditions for the alleged mechanisms to make themselves manifest. Typically, experimenters vary these initial conditions (the *independent variables*) and observe regularities in the resulting behavior (the *dependent variables*). And as the aim in such a procedure is of course to study the causes of behavior in themselves, objectively, in isolation from one another, the results ought not to be solely or predominately a function of the investigatory process itself (i.e. artifacts). As Bhaskar (1979, p.12) says, "What distinguishes the phenomena the scientist *actually* produces out of the totality of the phenomena he *could* produce is that, when his experiment is successful, it is an index of what he does *not* produce." But, as he goes on to argue, such is the case only under the *closed* conditions of the experiment. In other words, observable regularities occur because scientists have pre-arranged experimental conditions so that, as Bhaskar puts it, the constant conjunction of events obtains. Psychologists may (but only with the tacit agreement or compliance of their subjects) approximate such conditions. But normally the conditions under which psychological and social phenomena actually occur and have their being do not seem to be closed in this sense–far from it. All such circumstances must, as far as we can tell, be characterized as *open*, in which a large number of causal agents may or may not be active at the same time, and therefore in which no constant conjunctions of events certainly obtain.

Observational methods work within such open systems as given. There is no overt attempt to establish the closed conditions appropriate to experiments. Scientists merely attempt, by a combination of deductive and inductive techniques, to extract regularities from the data they collect in what they would claim to be naturalistic circumstances. Observational studies may be further subdivided into *survey* and *field* studies: in field studies, observers attempt to describe an aspect of behavior in all its different manifestations within a circumscribed sphere of life, e.g., as in a *sociometric* account of friendships among a group of people. In survey studies, a system is studied by observing its response to an input; usually but not always by studying the answers given by a sample group of people to a specially designed QUESTIONNAIRE. By arranging for such answers to be given either in one of a fixed number of categories, or on a five-point (Likert) scale, the objective data collected may be subjected to various statistical procedures, especially those of correlation and factor analysis, to reveal previously unknown relationships. In open systems, however, correlations cannot be taken as directly indicating causal relations. Hence caution is required in interpreting such results.

Questionnaire methods may also be used as *tests* of one kind or another in the exploration of both individual differences in people's abilities and in their personality characteristics, as well as the attitudes and beliefs of individuals (including their implicit theories of psychology – see ATTRIBUTION THEORY). Such tests have also been employed by cross-cultural psychologists in their field work, in an attempt to place the psychology of those they study in an intelligible relation to the psychology already familiar to them. As such they may be used as an adjunct to ETHNOGRAPHY, which cannot itself, however, be counted as an empirical method *per se*, for it also makes use of experiences gained from first- and second-person standpoints, as well as prior first-person intuitions. In fact, in this respect, even when it is claimed that "verbal reports" are being observed and studied, all data gathered from interviews and in clinical studies become suspect. It is crucial, if a method is to be truly empirical, that the third-person, external observer point of view is maintained.

Such methods, however, are not without their critics (Orne 1962; Rosenthal 1966; Harré and Secord 1972; McGuire 1973; Gergen 1973; to name but a few). Such methods, critics maintain, distort and limit the normal and open conditions of actual everyday life – the conditions necessary for our very being – and institute in its place another kind of social life. For instance, (a) surveys and questionnaires proscribe the dialogue, the continued exchanges, by which people normally avoid misunderstanding and express subtleties of opinion, attitude and belief to one another; (b) experimental situations meant to be objective contain hidden social factors; or (c) they are all structured by the overriding fact that they are exchanges between anonymous strangers observing one another – and acting under such surveillance produces a certain state of (objective) self-awareness (Duval and Wicklund 1972) inimical to normal, spontaneous behavior. Objections of this kind may be multiplied. All essentially stem, however, from the requirement that psychological data acquired by empirical methods is acquired, not from experience, but only by external observation.

Another, even more crucial objection is beginning to emerge, one of a seemingly paradoxical kind: in psychology, empirical methods do not seem to yield objective facts, i.e. facts not produced by the investigatory process itself. For, as McGuire (1973, p.449) points out, "If (an) experiment does not come out 'right', then the researcher does not say that the hypothesis is wrong, but rather that something was wrong with the experiment. . . ." And the fact seems to be, owing to the intentional nature of human action, one can always make such a claim. One can always say that what happened was not what was meant or intended to happen. What experiments test, suggests McGuire, is not whether hypotheses are true, but rather whether experimenters are "sufficiently ingenious stage managers" to demonstrate in the laboratory the effective use of a principle they already know to be true. And there is no escape from this conclusion into, for example, *field-experiments* for McGuire points out, there we merely test our abilities as "finders" of natural settings which illustrate principles we also already know to be true.

Clearly, as heirs to the modern philosophy of science (Hanson 1958; Kuhn 1962; Bhaskar 1978), we now realize that what the empirical and behavioral sciences call *data* are not simply given us in the phenomena we study, but are theory-laden, i.e., they only appear to us as the facts they are in terms of a theory constructed by us. Instead of being called data they could more correctly be called *capta* (Laing 1967, pp.52–3). For, rather than their being simply given us by Nature, we in fact *take* them out of a constantly changing flux of events. Hence, we can no longer accept that experiments provide inescapable "findings", for the results obtained depend to an extent upon our own "makings". There is a degree of arbitrary choice open to us in the determination of empirical facts. Is there anywhere else we might turn to for *data* in the sense of indubitable givens? Before embarking upon any psychological research, what we must already know, if we are to be competent members of our society, is not an arbitrary matter of our choice. The general nature of our social being is already determined (Smedslund 1980). On this view, the real *data* of experience, the givens, are what we can render explicit of what intuitively we must already know in our experience as social beings. Only these data, the facts of our mental life as persons in a society, which appear at first sight to be arbitrarily chosen, subjective, and idiosyncratic, seem in the final analysis to be inescapable, and to be the proper "givens" from which to begin. JDS

Bibliography

Bhaskar, Roy 1978: *A realist theory of science.* 2nd edn. Brighton: Harvester; Atlantic Highlands, N.J.: Humanities.

——— 1979: *The possibility of naturalism.* Brighton: Harvester.

Duval, S. and Wicklund, R.V. 1972: *A theory of objective self-awareness.* New York: Academic Press.

Feyerabend, P. 1975: *Against method: outline of an anarchist theory of knowledge.* London: New Left; Atlantic Highlands, N.J.: Humanities.

Gergen, K.J. 1973: Social psychology as history. *Journal of personality and social psychology* 26, 309–20.

Hanson, N.R. 1958: *Patterns of discovery.* Cambridge: Cambridge University Press.

Harré, R. and Secord, P.F. 1972: *The explanation of social behaviour.* Oxford: Basil Blackwell.

Kuhn, T.S. 1962: *The structure of scientific revolutions.* Chicago: University of Chicago Press.

Laing, R.D. 1967: *The politics of experience.* London: Penguin; New York: Pantheon.

McGuire, W.J. 1973: The yin and yang of progress in social psychology. *Journal of personality and social psychology* 26, 446–56.

Orne, M.T. 1962: On the social psychology of the psychological experiment: with particular reference to demand characteristics and their implications. *American psychologist* 17, 776–83.

Rosenthal, R. 1966: *Experimenter effects in behavioural research.* New York: Appleton-Century-Crofts.

Smedslund, J. 1980: Analysing the primary code: from empiricism to apriorism. In *The social foundations of language and thought: essays in honor of Jerome S. Bruner*, ed. D. R. Olsen. New York: Norton.

Watson, J.B. 1924: *Behaviorism.* Chicago: University of Chicago Press.

empirical techniques in experimental psychology Unless we invade and damage the living brain empirical techniques in experimental psychology are limited by what we can measure. Even our assessments of the performance of humans and animals with brain damage is limited by the originality and precision of our techniques of measurement. The range of things we can measure is surprisingly limited. We can time how fast a person makes a decision, or we can count how many errors he makes. We can elaborate the latter process by classifying his or her errors to attempt to discover whether some kinds of omission or confusion are more frequent than others. We can also get our subjects to use rating scales to tell us how confident they are about the decisions they make. It is salutary to reflect that the whole of the vast edifice of experimentation in human experimental psychology is based, in essence, on enormously ingenious elaborations of techniques for measuring the speed and accuracy of decisions, and rating the confidence with which people make them.

Since this edifice of experimentation in psychology *is* vast it would be out of place to do more here than to list below a few books which contain all details which the curious may desire about the basic techniques in the science of experimental psychology.

More interesting questions are what makes investigators select particular experimental paradigms and not others? How does it come to be the case that, quite abruptly, particular paradigms become "fashionable" to the point where it seems that no study which does not employ them is seriously considered by scientific journals? Why do these fashions die out as abruptly as they begin, usually leaving a fallow period until a "new paradigm" abruptly appears, again filling the journals with replications and with studies of variations?

The relationship between theories in a science and the experimental paradigms used to test them is an obscure and intriguing question not sufficiently examined by philosophers of science. This is especially true of experimental psychology, where research seems to be alternately driven from the "top down", guided by pure theoretical considerations ("theory driven research"), and driven from the "bottom up" guided by explorations of the methodological quirks of particular paradigms ("data driven" or "paradigm driven" research). If we understood better how these shifts of emphasis have occurred, and could trace better how they have been resolved, and how dissatisfactions with the *status quo* has produced new theories and new paradigms, we might learn to advance our science better. PR

Bibliography

Calfee, R.C. 1975: *Human experimental psychology.* New York: Holt, Rinehart & Winston.

Mackintosh, N.J. 1974: *The psychology of animal learning.* New York and London: Academic Press.

Stevens, S.S., ed. 1951: *Handbook of experimental psychology.* New York: John Wiley; London: Chapman & Hall.

employee participation The degree to which lower-level employees share in the management of their organization. Participation is usually viewed in terms of sharing influence, information or (less frequently) money, with differing patterns in different organizations. Employee participation in decision-making is to be distinguished from "workers' control". In the former but not the latter case final authority is retained by management.

Two principal levels are immediate and distant participation. In immediate participation employees share in decisions of direct relevance to their day-to-day work. Research has shown strong associations between positive WORK ATTITUDES and high levels of immediate participation. Distant participation is a matter of employee involvement in higher-level decision-making, for example through representatives on works councils or boards of directors. Such participation through representatives is not usually correlated with individual employees' attitudes about their work, although it is often attractive to workers and trade unions as a supplement to immediate participation (Wall and Lischeron 1977). (See also MANAGEMENT; ORGANIZATION DEVELOPMENT; WORK ATTITUDES.) PBW

Bibliography

Wall, T.D. and Lischeron, J.A. 1977: *Worker participation.* New York and London: McGraw-Hill.

employment commitment *See* work attitudes

encephalization The extraordinary development of the CEREBRAL CORTEX in humans has distinguished the human brain as being more than just a larger version of the brains in lower animals. Greater development of the neocortex was accompanied by innovations of brain function, but for the most part the changes can be described as a migration of functions from lower brain centers (brain stem, midbrain, diencephalon) to higher levels (neocortex) (see BRAIN AND CENTRAL NERVOUS SYSTEM: ILLUSTRATIONS, fig. 5). Within the cerebral cortex greatest development has occurred in the "Association" and "Motor" areas. This has allowed for the greater learning and memory capacities and for the fine motor control man possesses. Transfer of functions from lower brain centres to higher centres is readily seen by the expansion in scope of the sensory cortices. For example, in the frog all visual processing is controlled by the tectum, a midbrain structure. The equivalent in man, the superior colliculus (fig. 6), retains some visual functions, but it is the visual cortex (fig. 3) that has become most important and allows for the greater range of vision possessed by humans. The linguistic ability of humans is an example of functional innovation. In the frontal and temporal "association" cortex specialized areas have evolved for the production and comprehension of language. RCS/BER

encephalopathy *See* Wernicke's syndrome

encounter groups *See* T groups

endocrine disorders Conditions due to abnormal functioning of the endocrine glands which result in pathologically high or low levels of circulating HORMONES in the blood stream. In addition to their effect on bodily functions endocrine disorders have prominent effects on mental functions and behavior, and commonly the psychological manifestations are a characteristic feature of the clinical picture. The disorder may be due to dysfunction of the peripheral gland (e.g. thyroid, testicle), or it may be the result of abnormalities at the level of the hypophysis or the diencephalon. Endocrine disorders are caused by a variety of agents, among them: tumors, infections, trauma, immunological factors and external administration of hormonal preparations, while in a proportion of cases the cause remains unknown.

The following are examples of endocrine disorders with significant psychological and behavioral manifestations:
(1) thyroid disorders: hyperthyroidism (Graves' disease) and hypothyroidism (myxoedema).
(2) adrenal gland disorders: adrenal insufficiency (Addison's disease), endogenous overproduction of cortisol (Cushing's syndrome), phaeochromocytoma.
(3) parathyroid gland disorders: hyperparathyroidism and hypoparathyroidism.
(4) pituitary gland disorders: hypopituitarism and acromegaly.
(5) gonads: hypogonadism in man, and disorders of menstrual cycle in women.
(6) pineal gland disorders: pinealomas.
(7) pancreatic disorders: diabetes mellitus and insulinomas. JC

Bibliography

Lishman, W.A. 1978: *Organic psychiatry: the psychological consequences of cerebral disorders*, Oxford: Blackwell Scientific; St Louis, Missouri: C.V. Mosby.

endorphins *See* enkephalins/endorphins

engrams *See* representation

enkephalins/endorphins Two types of endogenous opioid peptides. After the discovery by several investigators of specific opiate binding sites in both central and peripheral mammalian systems, it was thought that these systems might also contain endogenous opioid substances which would interact with these receptors. Subsequent research has revealed two major families of endogenous opioids, both of which can interact with opiate receptors. Enkephalins are pentapeptides, with two natural forms (met and leu) differing from each other only in the terminal amino acid. Endorphins are components of β-lipotropin, a pituitary factor. The primary endorphin, β-endorphin, is a 30 amino acid peptide and is found both in the PITUITARY and in the brain. Other endorphins have also been reported, including both α- and γ- endorphin. Although the amino acid sequence for met-enkephalin is contained within the β-endorphin molecule, it is now apparent that enkephalins are not formed as degradation products from β-endorphin. Finally, although the distributions of both enkephalin-containing and endorphin-containing neurons overlap to some extent, these distributions appear to be distinct neuronal systems. Although both enkephalins and endorphins may modulate the perception of pain, endorphins may also be important in modulating mood and responses to stressful stimuli. GPH

enlightenment effects The effects of a given psychological theory on those who come to understand its premises and predictions. The most celebrated form of enlightenment effect is the self-fulfilling prophecy, initially described by Merton, in which a theory's predictions come true because of people's knowledge of the theory. Such effects may be contrasted with suicidal prophecies in which the dissemination of the theory negates its predictions. The potential for such effects has been used by both psychologists and economists to question the cumulativeness of behavioral research. If theories enter into the life of the culture, then it may be more important to ask about the potential effects of the theory than about the validity of its predictions. (See also GENERATIVE THEORY). KJG

Bibliography

Gergen, K.J. 1982: *Toward transformation in social knowledge*. New York: Springer.

Merton, R.K. 1949: *Social theory and social structure*. Glencoe, Illinois: Free Press.

enuresis A medical term applied to the involuntary passage of urine by persons more than three years old. Distinctions are made between enuresis which occurs only during the night, nocturnal and that which happens during the day, diurnal.Two thirds of the reported cases among children involve nocturnal enuresis. The reported frequency of enuresis in childhood is a function of the social characteristics of the sample studied. Rates vary for normals, children with behavior problems, institutionalized and retarded children. Rates also vary with cultural background and training. Among children whose parents have sought psychiatric advice enuresis is almost twice as common in boys as in girls and peaks between the ages of eight and eleven years. In adulthood and old age a lack of voluntary control over the discharge of urine and feces is labeled incontinence. BBL

environmental psychology The mutual relationship between people and the physical environment. Environmental psychology emerged as a field in the early 1960s, stimulated in part by environmental problems of the period and in part by changing values in traditional psychology which had previously adhered to an analytic, laboratory tradition of research and which had not studied human behavior in relationship to the large-scale physical environment (Craik 1973).

Over the years environmental psychology has since developed in the following ways: (1) *a holistic molar perspective*, in which research examines behavior in context, and attempts to study complex networks of psychological processes and environmental factors; (2) *an applied, problem solving perspective* in which research is simultaneously designed to uncover basic principles of behavior and to contribute to the solution of social problems involving the physical environment in the action research tradition; (3) *a broad and eclectic methodology* that accepts the use of laboratory experiments, field experiments, surveys and naturalistic observational studies, because the problems of the field are diverse and not amenable to study by a single procedure; (4) *a range of levels of analysis:* from micro-levels of study such as the impact of noise on task performance, to the study of social processes such as seating positions at tables in relation to social interaction and personal spacing, to moderate scale analyses of home design and use, to large-scale units of study such as community and city design, and the perception of the large scale environment of cities and countries; (5) *a range of approaches to concepts and theory:* as a young and interdisciplinary field, environmental psychology has not yet developed its own theoretical perspectives. Although the work of Barker and his associates (Barker 1968) emphasizes an approach to research that focusses on the analysis of behavior-settings that is the confluence of people, physical settings and functions or goals, the field of environmental psychology has, to date, tended to adopt substantive theoretical ideas from other areas in psychology and from other social sciences.

Environmental psychologists collaborate with researchers from other disciplines and with environmental design professionals in architecture, interior design and related fields. Collaborative work with environmental designers takes many forms, including the application of psychological principles, theories and findings to design, and evaluations and assessments of the actual and predicted impact on human functioning of environmental designs and changes. The result of cross-disciplinary projects appear in many places, most notably in the annual *Proceeding of the Environmental Design Research Association* (For descriptions of organizations, publication outlets and educational programmes see White 1979).

Research in environmental psychology encompasses a broad spectrum of topics, including perceptual and cognitive processes, orientations to places and settings, social and behavioral processes, and environmental design and environmental problems. These topics have been studied in relationship to the built or designed environments of homes, buildings, neighborhoods, cities and regions, and in relationship to "natural" environments of wilderness, parks, seashores and the like. Moreover, various psychological processes have been investigated in relation to a variety of individuals and groups, including children, families, the elderly, various cultural and ethnic groups, and special populations such as the handicapped, prisoners, institutionalized people, children, etc. (general reviews of work in the field appear in Craik 1973; Stokols 1978; Russell and Ward 1982; Altman and Wohlwill 1976–82; Baum and Singer 1978–81; Bell, Fisher and Loomis 1978).

A considerable body of research in environmental psychology has focussed on places ranging from regions and cities, to places as small as rooms or areas in rooms. Research has investigated attitudes, cognitions and perceptions of urban environments, behavior such as way-finding, helping, transportation, etc. There has also been study of the design and use of neighborhoods, institutional environments such as schools, prisons and hospitals, and housing developments for the poor, aged and other special groups. On a smaller scale, environmental psychologists have conducted research on home environments, including use of interior spaces, living and social behavior, privacy and the ways in which people define, mark and recognize territories.

An increasing body of knowledge and theory has focussed on cognitions, perceptions, meanings, attachments and attitudes to places at all levels of scale (Downs and Stea 1973). Such research includes studies of environmental meaning, the feelings people have about places, the effect of various dimensions of places on behavior, ways in which children learn about locations and the distances between places, and the preferences people have with respect to a variety of settings. This research has examined these topics in "natural" environments both because they are interesting phenomena in their own right, and to assist in the development of policies for the use and modification of such environments.

Another aspect of environmental psychology concerns social processes, such as the regulation of privacy, personal spacing and territoriality (Altman 1975). The ways in which people make themselves more or less accessible to others, through use and design of the physical environment, is a topic of emerging interest. The process of personal spacing or distancing of people from one another is one of the most well researched topics in environmental psychology. Physical distancing and separation has been studied in relation to individual factors such as personality and biography, in relation to interpersonal factors involving group composition and personal attraction, and in relation to situational factors. Territoriality, or the occupancy and control of places, has been studied in terms of different types of territories (primary, secondary and public), intrusion and reactions to territorial intrusion, and in terms of the various mechanisms for protecting and marking territories. Other research on spatial behavior involves studies of seating and physical locations in relation to social interaction, status and the like.

Another topic of concern to environmental psychology is environmental problems, such as crowding, noise, transportation, and their various associated stresses. For example, studies of crowding (Baum and Epstein 1978) have investigated the effect on behavior of the amount of space per person (spatial density), number of people in a given space (social density), and the interaction of crowding with personal and social factors. The analysis of density and crowding in relation to stress, performance, social interaction and other behavior has resulted in a large number of studies and theoretical perspectives. Studies of noise have investigated the impact of duration, predictability, controllability and other aspects of noise on physiological functioning, short- and long-term performance on intellectual and other tasks, and on social behavior. Research on other environmental problems include studies of lighting, weather, temperature, air pollution, transportation, etc.

Research in environmental psychology has been designed to develop a body of scientific knowledge regarding various aspects of human functioning in relation to various aspects of the physical environment. In addition, a considerable amount of knowledge has been accumulated about the application of environmental psychology principles and findings to the design and evaluation of different environments. This research, often involving cooperation between behavioral scientists and environmental designers, has spanned all aspects of the design process, including help in the early stages of environmental design through to the evaluation of designed or used environments when they have been occupied. In the coming decades environmental psychologists will probably work on newly emerging social problems that relate to the environment, they will continue to cooperate with other fields both inside and outside psychology in relation to methodology and theory, and they will gradually develop methods and theory unique to the study of the relationship between people and the physical environment. TA

Bibliography

Altman, I. 1975: *Environment and social behavior: privacy space, crowding and territory*. Monterey, Calif.: Brooks/Cole.

———and Wohlwill, J.F., eds. 1976–82: *Human behavior and environment: advances in theory and research*. 4 vols. New York: Plenum.

Barker, R.G. 1968: *Ecological psychology*. Stanford, Calif.: Stanford University Press.

Baum, A. and Epstein, Y.M., eds. 1978: *Human response to crowding*. Hillsdale, N.J.: Erlbaum.

Baum, A. and Singer, J., eds. 1978–81: *Advances in environmental psychology*. Series in progress. Hillsdale, N.J.: Erlbaum.

Bell, P.A., Fisher, J.D. and Loomis, R.J. 1978: *Environmental psychology*. Philadelphia and London: W.B. Saunders.

Craik, K. 1973: Environmental psychology. *Annual review of psychology*, pp. 403–22.

Downs, R.N. and Stea, D., eds. 1973: *Image and environment: cognitive mapping and spatial behavior*. Chicago: Aldine.

Russell, J.A. and Ward, L.M. 1982: Environmental psychology. *Annual review of psychology*.

Stokols, D. 1978: Environmental psychology. *Annual review of psychology*, pp.253–95.

White, W.P., ed. 1979: *Resources in environment and behavior*. Washington, D.C.: American Psychological Association.

environmentalism Proposition that behavior and personality characteristics are determined by the individual's experiences in the environment and not by innate capacities or traits. The controversy of innate versus environmental determinants of psychological characteristics was identified as the nature–nurture debate by the nineteenth-century scientist Francis Galton, who, although a hereditarian, eventually acknowledged that human development results from the interaction of native abilities and environmental experiences. The rise of the environmentalist position in the twentieth century was manifested in extensive research on the mechanics of learning, the exact ways in which the environment determines the acquisition of behavior or abilities. More recently the environmentalist proposition has been tempered by research findings concerning the nuances of the nature–nurture interaction, the significance of maturational processes, and the limits of purely deterministic models of human development.

See also BEHAVIOR GENETICS. JGM

epidemiological methods in psychiatry A series of topics linked by the epidemiological method. The topics include all aspects of the social causes, concomitants and consequences of psychiatric disorder, together with social techniques for dealing with them. The discovery of the social causes of disorder will lead to the rational development of social methods of prevention, while social influences on the course and outcome of disorder will suggest techniques of social treatment and rehabilitation.

These issues may involve the psychiatrist in the planning and evaluation of social and medical services or in the assessment of the psychiatric implications of public policy on such matters as employment, education, and housing.

The main tool of the social psychiatrist is the epidemiological method. This is essentially the study of human populations based on rates of illnesses. Two main types of rate are used, incidence and prevalence. Incidence is the number of cases of the disease in question newly appearing in a unit population at risk (often 100,000) during a given period, usually one year. Prevalence is the number of cases present in a unit population at a given time (point prevalence) or during a given period (period prevalence). Prevalence is a function of incidence and the duration of the disorder from onset to recovery or from onset to death.

The establishment of each of these rates requires the definition of a numerator (the number of cases) and a denominator (the reference population). For the rates to be comparable in different places, the definition of both numerator and denominator must be standard. Case definition implies that mental abnormalities are often most usefully regarded as diseases. The social psychiatrist is orientated toward the use of "disease" theories (see MEDICAL MODELS) in psychiatry (Wing 1978) and toward defining given diseases with more and more precision. The implication of defining SCHIZOPHRENIA say, as a characteristic psychopathological syndrome is that by doing so we hope to find out consistent and useful correlates, for example, of cause, course, outcome and response to intervention. However, not all the phenomena studied by social psychiatrists come so easily into the category of disease. SUICIDE is a clear example, ALCOHOLISM a more contentious one.

Social psychiatrists rely on no single underlying theory, but borrow at will from the disciplines of biology, psychology and sociology. The relation to sociology is particularly interesting as there is overlap of both topic and method. Because sociologists are concerned with, among other things, beliefs and values and their role in social structure and function, they are likely to be interested in the various social phenomena reflected in the relationship of society to mental illness and its sufferers. Durkheim, for instance, regarded SUICIDE as crucial to his ideas about the integration of society. Important contributions to the ideas used in social psychiatry also come from sociological studies of the family, of small groups and of social networks. Other ideas have come from studies of deviance, stratification, collective behavior and institutions. Both sociologists and social psychiatrists study populations and sociologists may also study illness rates in those populations, although they will in addition be interested in the social processes involved in formulations of illness.

In the search for associations between variables, epidemiology relies on two main strategies for studying populations. The first is the *case-control study*. Where illness is the dependent variable this has to be retrospective as illness must already be present for the case group to be identified. The *cohort study* on the other hand may be prospective or retrospective. In the prospective version, the population is divided into a group defined by the antecedent variable and a group defined by its absence. These groups are followed up and the subsequent development of illness is monitored. For both of these types of study, the selection of the control group is of paramount importance. Another type of cohort study is retrospective: whole populations are examined and the association between illness and the various antecedent variables examined. In such a study variables can be controlled for in analysis. Sophisticated statistical procedures are now used for doing this.

A major issue of interpretation in these cross-sectional epidemiological surveys is that of *causal direction*. In some cases this can be decided on logical grounds, but in others conclusions must remain tentative (see Susser 1973). One example of this problem is the association of psychiatric disorder with low social class. Does this arise because the strains involved in working-class life can precipitate psychiatric illness or because the psychiatrically ill move down the social scale? The burden of evidence favors the latter interpretation in schizophrenia, the former in minor depressions.

Epidemiological work in psychiatry has been facilitated by certain technological innovations. One of these is the use of *case registers* in which all persons using certain services in a given area are recorded. The advantages of such registers include the avoidance of selection biases and duplicate counting, reference to a defined population and the possibility of longitudinal study (Wing and Haily 1972). The problem with the study of referred populations is that it is not possible to separate factors which influence referral from those which influence the onset of a disorder. For this reason there has always been an interest in social psychiatric *surveys of the general population*. The major problem with these has been cost, which in the past led to the use of questionnaires to detect psychiatric disorders. These were really incapable of doing more than suggesting the likelihood that some kind of psychiatric disorder was present. Standardized instruments for case detection have been recently introduced. These can be linked to computer programs and incorporate procedures corresponding to those involved in psychiatric diagnosis. These include the Present State Examination in Britain and the Schedule for Affective Disorders and Schizophrenia (SADS) in the United States. Further innovations include reliable measures of other social variables, such as LIFE EVENTS and the quality of interaction between relatives.

Because of the nature and limitations of the epidemiological method, theories of social causation have tended to rely on simple linear models and to take little account of the fact that people not only are influenced by their social circumstances but have some responsibility for them.

Social causes can be regarded as *predisposing* or *precipitating*. The first group contains a variety of influences, early or late, which affect the way people respond to later circumstances. These may operate for instance by their effect on hormones and autonomic nervous system activity, on the practical options open to the person, or on the way he sees the world. Ideas about precipitating factors rely heavily on the concept of STRESS.

But there have been theories such as those of Wynne and Singer in which a cognitive factor has played a part. The advances which have been made in social explanations of psychiatric disorders have arisen because of refinements in the definition and measurement of stress. Examples include LIFE EVENTS and the way the stressful behavior of the relatives of some schizophrenics is tapped by the rating of "expressed emotion". Recently workers in social psychiatry have become interested in the concept of the *social network* and the related idea of *social support*. These have possible implications for the modifications of stress. Henderson and his colleagues have introduced two extensive interviews designed to discover a variety of aspects of a subject's social relations and the support he obtains from them.

A distinction has been made between *strategic* and *tactical* research. The former has major implications for treatment and care. Tactical research is more concerned with the action taken on the basis of such implications. Evaluation of services is an area of tactical research in social psychiatry.

Psychiatric services are made available with the object of diminishing or containing psychiatric morbidity. They are concerned, therefore, with the social consequences of psychiatric disease and they operate by affecting the treatment of the disease, by preventing chronic disabilities and by preventing the accumulation of secondary handicaps which arise because of the response of the patient and those around him to the fact of his illness. Full evaluation of a psychiatric service firstly requires an assessment of *need*, *demand* and *utilization*. The patterns of contact must be established, together with the needs of those who do contact the services being studied. An indication of the effectiveness of the current treatment and management implies explicit definitions of the treatments involved, and ways of assessing them. The requirements of those who have disorders but do not use the services must be known. Research may sometimes suggest possible new types of service, and these services should ideally be assessed when they become available. The controlled trial of social treatments involves difficulties greater than those involved in, say, a drug trial, but these difficulties should not in practice be insuperable. The principles of evaluation in social psychiatric services are laid down by Wing (1972).

PBE

Bibliography

*Bebbington, P.E. 1978: The epidemiology of depressive disorder. *Culture, medicine and psychiatry* 2, 297–341.

*Brown, George W. and Harris, Tirril 1978: *The social origins of depression*. Tavistock: London; New York: Free Press.

*Lloyd, G. and Bebbington, P. 1982: Social and transcultural psychiatry. In *Essentials of postgraduate psychiatry*, ed. P. Hill, R. Murray and A. Thorley. 2nd edn. London: Academic Press; New York: Grune and Stratton.

Susser, M. 1973: *Causal thinking in the health sciences*. London: Oxford University Press.

Wing, J.K. 1972: Principles of evaluation. In *Evaluating a community psychiatric service: The Camberwell Register 1967–71*, ed. J.K. Wing and A.M. Hailey. London: Oxford University Press.

——— 1978: *Reasoning about madness*. London: Oxford University Press.

——— 1980: Innovations in social psychiatry. *Psychological medicine* 10, 219–30.

——— and Hailey, A.M., eds. 1972: *Evaluating a community psychiatric service*. London: Oxford University Press.

Wing, J.K. et al. 1978: The concept of a 'case' in psychiatric population surveys. *Psychological medicine* 8, 203–17.

epidemiology *See above, and* life events

epigenetic sequence The biological or psychological development of the individual within his lifespan, conceived as a series of stages, each of which results from the interactions between the person and the environment and among the parts of the organism or psyche, and each of which contains new phenomena or properties not present in earlier stages. Distinguished from *phylogenetic sequence*, the development of properties in the species through biological evolution, and from *preformism*, the doctrine that all properties which arise in development are present in miniature form in the original organism. Major examples of views of psychological epigenesis are FREUD's description of personality development and PIAGET's description of cognitive development.

SB

epilepsy Acute and transitory brain dysfunction which may take the form of motor disturbances, such as convulsions, or of psychological and behavioral abnormalities. It develops suddenly, ceases spontaneously, and has a tendency to recur. It is usually accompanied by disturbances of consciousness.

Epilepsy can be classified by reference to the characteristics of the seizure, or by the nature of the cause or the underlying pathology. The study of the electrical activity of the brain by means of electroencephalography (EEG) has advanced considerably our understanding of this condition, helping to clarify its mechanisms and contributing to the process of making the diagnosis.

There are two main types of epilepsy: generalized epilepsy and focal epilepsy. *Generalized epilepsy* results from abnormalities below the cerebral cortex, and tends to spread to all parts of the cortex simultaneously, impairing consciousness from the beginning of the seizure. The attacks can take the form of "petit mal" or brief attacks usually involving disturbance of consciousness without convulsions, or "grand mal" seizures, characterized by severe and generalized convulsions with loss of consciousness. *Focal epilepsy* is due to abnormalities of specific areas of the cerebral cortex, although the electrical discharge can spread to other cortical or sub-cortical areas. The attack is usually preceded by characteristic subjective experience (aura) which can suggest the part of the brain where the discharge has its origin. For example, a discharge starting on the visual cortex tends to have an aura characterized by visual abnormalities.

The cause of epilepsy is often unknown in the case of the generalized type, although hereditary factors appear to play some part. Focal epilepsy is usually due to lesions of the particular area of the cortex involved. A variety of factors may cause such damage, among them: birth injury, congenital abnormalities, head injury, infections and tumors. Persistent febrile convulsions in childhood appear to be important in the development of temporal lobe epilepsy.

The treatment of epilepsy is mainly by means of medication, but it is important to investigate the patient carefully to rule out the presence of other conditions, such as a tumor or infection, which would require a different approach. JC

Bibliography

Lishman, W.A. 1978: *Organic psychiatry: the psychological consequences of cerebral disorder* Oxford: Blackwell Scientific; St Louis, Missouri: C.V. Mosby.

epilepsy (childhood) Recurrent, transient, brain dysfunction with altered consciousness, associated with paroxysmal electrical discharges in the brain which may be detectable by an electroencephalograph and diverse objective and subjective phenomena depending upon developmental age and the location of the discharge within the brain. It is best understood as one form of brain dysfunction which may betoken the existence of other forms of dysfunction or damage especially where the epilepsy starts early in life (particularly in the first year where there is a mortality of about 10 per cent) and is persistent. Most children survive and recover. Those who do not are more likely to show evidence of other cerebral impairments in cognition and in behavior. Otherwise behavior disorder and psychiatric disorder are increased as a function of: – the socially aversive nature of seizures leading to dread and to prejudice; the general problems of living with a chronic illness; impaired parenting of a vulnerable child; the unwanted effects of drug treatment and restrictive regimes; and poorly managed treatment programs.

Such factors in combination readily account for the 60 per cent rate of psychiatric abnormality found in children with epilepsy and brain lesions. The child's development may be biased by the brain abnormality before the onset of seizures or as a function of the disturbances in parenting engendered by the seizures. These will vary with the child's developmental age at their onset. Increased irritability and dependency, reduced learning capacity and some increased tendency towards psychosis are noted. Apart from brain dysfunction, the abnormality of parenting includes, extreme over-solicitude or severe rejection, or, what is worse, intense ambivalent wavering between these two responses to the remembered, imagined, or ever present threat of death which seizures inspire and which their mortality intermittently re-enforces. DCT

epinephrine (adrenaline) The principal compound synthetized and secreted by the adrenal medulla (see ADRENAL GLANDS; BRAIN AND CENTRAL NERVOUS SYSTEM: ILLUSTRATIONS, fig. 22). The chemical structure of epinephrine was elucidated in 1901 by Takamine (see fig.). Epinephrine was the first hormone to be synthetized (by Stolz in 1904). The N-methyalted derivative of norepinephrine (noradrenaline) is the transmitter of the post ganglionic sympathetic nerves. The adrenal glands release substantial amounts of epinephrine into the circulation in response to stressful situations. Epinephrine has profound autonomic (sympathicomimetic) and metabolic effects which together prepare the organism for the fight, flight and fright reactions. Though the presence of epinephrine in the brain was first reported in the early 1950s, it was not until 1974 that it was found in distinct neuronal systems with cell-bodies in the medulla oblongata. As central transmitter, epinephrine is thought to be involved in the regulation of neuroendocrine and autonomic processes (see TRANSMITTER SUBSTANCES). There is particularly convincing evidence for its role in the central control of cardiovascular functions. DHVG

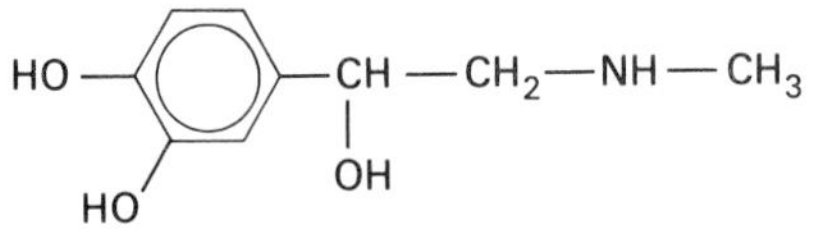

adrenaline HO—(benzene ring)—CH—CH_2—NH—CH_3
HO (on ring); OH (on CH)

epistemology *See* genetic epistemology

equity theory A theory of social behavior which suggests that individuals attempt to establish perceived equality of the outcome/input ratios in relationships. The theory has been applied to various forms of social exchange and relationships. Walster et al (1978) have studied in particular the extent to which intimate and long-term relationships are governed by the principle of equity. As yet the results of these studies are equivocal.

Judgments of fairness are, however, also based upon other rules and standards, such as equality and relative need. Each of these may be relevant in different circumstances.

If an exchange or relationship is perceived to be inequitable, equity can be and often is re-established by altering inputs, withdrawing from the relationship and/or changing one's perception of the relationship. JMFJ

Bibliography

Walster, E., Walster, G.W. and Bershid, E. 1978 *Equity: theory and research*. Boston: Allyn and Bacon.

ergonomics The application of the human sciences to the study of work, including domestic and leisure activities (see HUMAN FACTORS). The core human sciences are anatomy, physiology and psychology, but there are also contributions from other subjects such as medicine, sociology and cybernetics.

Scientific Ergonomics

The relevant aspects of anatomy are anthropometry and biomechanics. *Anthropometry* is part of morphological anatomy and *biomechanics* is functional anatomy. Both are rather different from the common clinical anatomy taught to medical students. Anthropometry (literally and actually "the measurement of man") provides data about body dimensions (height, weight, girth, etc.). This is not self-evident – (where does an arm stop or end?), there are extensive individual differences and correlations between measures are not always high. (It is possible to be tall and to have short arms.) Individual differences and some aspects of application are dealt with by the use of percentiles. Most dimensions are roughly normally distributed between people so that the 50th percentile is the same as the average, the 5th percentile is such that only 5 per cent of the population are smaller, the 95th percentile such that only 5 per cent are larger. These two limits are usually of more practical significance than the 50th percentile. For example the 5th percentile upward reach determines the maximum height of controls and the 95th percentile knuckle height determines the minimum height of controls. Biomechanics is concerned with the application of forces. Since the maximum level of forces which can be exerted is of the same order as body mass it follows that posture is of critical importance. The main body mass is in the head and trunk and the relationship of these weights to the direction of required force determines effectiveness. In short, the art of applying forces is to let the body weight do the work and to avoid shifting body mass against gravity. Consideration is also given to the muscle groups operational when a particular joint moves. Muscles are being used effectively when the largest available muscles contract for the greatest distance.

The relevant aspects of physiology are *work physiology* and *environmental physiology*. These are parts of what is sometimes called whole-body physiology as distinct from the much more widespread microphysiology. Work physiology studies the organism as a source of energy. The basic process of oxidizing food to generate energy is rather inefficient – in the human body less than a quarter of the energy appears as mechanical work, the remainder appears as heat. Hence the general body heating effect of physical work. Energy expenditure is measured by measuring oxygen consumption. All these measures require the use of a face mask, some method of determining rate or volume of respiration and the analysis of samples of expired air to determine remaining oxygen content. From these data it is possible to calculate energy expenditure and thus compare "heaviness" of work in quite different working situations and also to determine the required food intake to replace that consumed. Norms are available of what it is reasonable to expect from a worker in given circumstances of body size, sex, available food and so on in terms of a figure such as expenditure per working day. Expenditure rates for standard jobs are known. An approximate indication of energy output can be obtained more easily by measuring heart-rate which correlates with oxygen consumption but there are many complicating factors such as the level of ambient temperature. Environmental physiology studies the effects of the ambient environment on the person. The main parameters are light, heat, cold, noise and vibration. In no case is there any single physical measure which reflects the stress, demand or adequacy of a particular environmental state. For example an estimate of heat stress requires the measurement of air temperature, radiant temperature, humidity and windspeed. The environmental physiologist devises ways of combining the relevant physical parameters into stress indices and provides norms for particular kinds of people in particular circumstances. There are several important but very different limits determining respectively optimal performance levels, comfort levels and danger levels. The different environmental variables also interact in complex ways, e.g. heat and noise.

The relevant aspects of psychology are *information processing* and *organizational studies*. It is a fact that, although psychological ergonomics might be regarded as occupational psychology, the academic stimulus and support in the formative 1950s came not from traditional occupational psychology and psychometrics but from human experimental psychology. More recently there has been some rapprochement between the "fitting the job to the worker" of ergonomics and the "fitting the worker to the job" of occupational psychology through a common interest in training and in motivational aspects of the work situation.

The concept of the human operator with limited capacities as a communication channel was developed in the post-war human performance laboratories. This has obvious relevance to work in high technology industry where the operator is faced with an array of information sources; visual displays, such as dials, charts and legend plates. The ears are also used (auditory displays) and there is information feedback through the kinesthetic system as controls are manipulated. Display design deals with scales, pointers, scripts, illumination and so on, not only from the point of view of ease of discrimination but also in terms of the structuring and coding of the presented information. Control design also has psychological aspects in terms of identification, discrimination and quality of feedback. The integral concepts of the operator and the machine communicating across the operator/machine interface and the operator as an active device with identifiable properties within the control loop of the system have been developed to a high level.

People rarely work alone and the study of interpersonal interaction at work extends through teams to relations within hierarchical organizations. This can be partially treated in informational terms but it is necessary to consider also the psychology of group and organizational behavior. This scientifically rather hybrid expertise is of central importance for smoothing the impact of advancing technology from the design of the job to the structure of the supporting organization (see WORK REDESIGN). It is increasingly concentrated on the impact of computers, not only on the shopfloor but also in the office and within service organizations.

Technological Ergonomics

When dealing with practical problems the ergonomist has to develop his own expertise in addition to taking what is relevant from the supporting human sciences. Much of this expertise is concerned with issues which are critical for successful achievements: for example, experience in working as a member of an investigative team which might include not only other human scientists but also statisticians and engineers. Easy communication is always the foundation of success and this requires not only understanding the technical languages of other disciplines but also appreciating that other specialists have subtly different ways of thinking in terms of values and objectives as well as techniques. Communication with customers also is critical and again managers, accountants, economists and policy makers have their own styles and values which have to be understood and respected. There are certain conceptual and technical advances which can be attributed to ergonomics per se rather than to the separate human sciences. These include the adaptation of systems concepts and methods of field study.

Systems Ergonomics
Is about man as a system component. Early ergonomics which took the form of attempting to remedy machine and work design errors made by engineers and planners gradually gave way to a systems approach. The basic tenet is that since men and machines are bound to be involved in doing whatever the planners wish to have done there are primary design decisions on allocation of function between man and machine with procedures as a possible extra. These are colloquially described respectively as live-ware, hardware and software. Effective system design is a matter of knowing the relative advantages and limitations of the main system-components. The appropriate function allocations follow from this knowledge. In practice it is rare for the allocation of functions to be one step in the design process. More usually an attempt is made followed by preliminary validation followed by another attempt and so on so that there is iteration towards the ideal allocation. After functions have been allocated at least temporarily it is possible to continue with the design by parallel developments on the human and hardware stream thereby reducing total development time. For example it is possible to select and train operators while the machines are still being developed so that operational readiness is achieved in the shortest possible time.

Field Studies in Ergonomics
The central issue here is to arrive at a description of what a person is doing or is going to be required to do in the performance of his work. These are known as Task Analysis and Task Synthesis respectively. There are many techniques both for acquiring relevant evidence and for presenting the result in the form of a Task Description. A Task Description is an essential part of evidence relating to the allocation of functions and it later forms the basis of the design of procurement, selection, training, retraining and development schemes. If the description required must contain details of how the worker performs a task as well as what he does, it is called a Skills Analysis.

Task Analysis is currently used extensively in industries where rapid changes of technology require the implementation of sensitive job design and retraining techniques (see TASK ANALYSIS).

Finally, although Ergonomics makes an essential contribution to high technology it must not be forgotten that a continuous contribution is made to more mundane but very widespread and important problems such as chair design, work space dimensions, lifting techniques, environmental appraisal, dial design, console design and so on. WTS

Bibliography

Brown, S.C. and Martin, J.N.T., eds. 1977: *Human aspects of man-machine systems.* London: Open University Press.

De Greene, K.B., ed. 1970: *Systems psychology.* New York: McGraw Hill.

Gagne, R.M., ed. 1962: *Psychological principles in systems development.* New York: Holt, Rinehart & Winston.

Grandjean, E. 1969: *Fitting the task to the man – an ergonomics approach.* London: Taylor & Francis.

McCormick, E.C. 1976: *Human factors in engineering and design.* New York: McGraw Hill.

Murrell, K.F.H. 1965: *Ergonomics.* London: Chapman & Hall; New York: Reinhold (under the title *Human performance in industry*).

Singleton, W.T. 1972: *Introduction to ergonomics.* Geneva: World Health Organisation.

ergonomics, cognitive The study of information exchange between people and machines, with particular reference to computers. Interaction with computers involves both comprehension of features of a computer program and also the transmission of instructions from the person and information from the computer (Smith and Green 1980). Cognitive ergonomics is thus concerned with programming as a cognitive activity, the analysis of person-computer tasks, allocation of sub-tasks to person or machine, the structure of command languages, procedures for storing and presenting material in cognitively convenient forms, simulation of or alternatives to human information processing, and methods for computer systems to be easily interrogated by users. (See COMPUTER SYSTEMS, ON-LINE.) PBW

Bibliography

Smith, H.T. and Green, T.R.G., eds. 1980: *Human interaction with computers.* London: Academic Press.

error analysis As a method in applied linguistics and SECOND LANGUAGE ACQUISITION research, error analysis gained impetus in the late 1960s (see Corder 1973, pp.256–94), partly as a reaction against contrastive linguistics, partly as a means of supplementing it. It is assumed that, by systematically studying the errors of a second language learner, one can make inferences about his or her competence in that language.

Charting a second language learner's linguistic development through error analysis has psycholinguistic importance in that it submits the transfer hypothesis (see CONTRASTIVE LINGUISTICS) to critical testing. The close links of error analysis with transformational grammar is reflected in its acceptance of the competence-performance distinction. Accordingly, a distinction is made between competence "errors" and performance "mistakes".

Error analysis has been seriously hampered by the lack of adequate devices for the description of linguistic development and has therefore been replaced by studies of INTERLANGUAGE. PM

Bibliography

Corder, S. Pit 1973: *Introducing applied linguistics*. Harmondsworth and Baltimore: Penguin Books.

ESP (extrasensory perception) Introduced by J.B. Rhine in 1932 for a class of phenomena in which a person apparently "perceives" information about target events from which he is sensorily isolated. If the event is another person's thoughts, the particular form of ESP is *telepathy*. If it is a physical object or process and no person knows what that object or process is before or during the attempt to perceive it by ESP, it is *clairvoyance*. If the target will come into existence only after the act of ESP is attempted, and its particular nature is controlled by unpredictable processes, it is *precognition*. PARAPSYCHOLOGY is the branch of science which studies ESP. CTT

est An acronym for Erhard Seminar Training and Latin for "it is". *Est* is a corporation which provides "a sixty-hour educational experience which creates an opportunity for people to realize their potential to transform the quality of their lives" (*est* 1980). Attempts by outsiders to characterize more exactly this optimistic organization – as, for instance, a form of PSYCHOTHERAPY or as a mass-psychological religious movement – are not well received by insiders, although there is probably consensus that *est* belongs to the human potential movement.

One reason why *est* is not easy to characterize is that Werner Erhard, who founded the organization in 1971, drew upon a range of traditions: some religious (ZEN, YOGA, TAOISM, Subud, the PROTESTANT ETHIC and positive thinking), some psychological (GESTALT, encounter, Mind Dynamics, PSYCHODRAMA), not to speak of scientology, and what he had learnt from his work in commerce and from his reading in philosophy.

While the education received by trainees has diverse roots it is highly structured. There are two consecutive weekend sessions, 250 typically middle-class trainees spending sixty hours with a trainer. Having paid £250 each (£200 if booked in advance), and having agreed to abide by a number of ground rules (for example, to forego intoxicants, and to stay seated and silent unless called upon by the trainer), participants experience the results of the standardized techniques employed by the trainer.

The goal is "IT" and associated "recontextualization". His own "catalytic" experience of "IT" prompted Erhard to recognize that, "you can't put it together. It's already together and what you have to do is experience it being together" (see Rosen 1978, p.56). In other words, to use an *est* distinction, one cannot do much to change the "content" of life (e.g. a pressing debt), but one can change the "context" in which the content is "held" (one's experience of the debt is "transformed" if the correct context is applied) (see *est* 1980).

But what exactly is the "IT" which provides the correct context? Writes Erhard, "IT is you experiencing yourself without any symbology or any concept. Normally, I experience myself through my thoughts; I think who I am ... Well, IT is you experiencing you directly without any intervening system" (see Rosen 1978, p.63). Since this "real" self is "actually satisfied" and "perfect" (ibid, p.61), it provides the context, "power" or "source ('it cause')" to "transform your ability to experience living so that the situations you have been trying to change or have been putting up with clear up just in the process of life itself" (*est* 1980).

The strategies used by trainers are designed to "realize" the self and its powers. Two main components are "processes" (e.g. the "Danger Process" in which twenty-five trainees stand facing the audience and are reprimanded if they are not themselves) and lectures (e.g. the six-hour "Anatomy of the Mind" discourse explaining, among other things, the nature of suffering) (see Finkelstein et al. 1982). "Tapes", or patterns of thought and feeling that prevent one from experiencing one's perfection (or "completing" experiences) are destroyed; energy and satisfaction, what you create or decide, the freedom of immediate experience, take over.

Whether the strategies are best understood in terms of Erhard's rather metaphysical formulations (real and perfect self, the primacy of self/experience/consciousness/choice over the public self/objective world/belief/intellect/necessity, or whether they are best understood in terms of the more scientific language of psychotherapy raises difficult issues. (Finkelstein et al. (1982) treat *est* in terms of behavior and cathartic therapies, for example.) What is clear, however, is that the great majority of the 250,000+ *est* graduates are satisfied customers (ibid).

The challenge for psychologists is both to devise more fideistic measures of the results of *est* (how does one quantify "wholeness"?) and somehow to accommodate the possibility that "recontextualization", for example, is just as efficacious (if not more so) as more scientifically reputable processes such as FLOODING and social reinforcement. But perhaps *est* cannot be captured in terms of quantification and experimentally derived theorizing: perhaps Rosen is justified in claiming that Erhard "is, truly, providing a third dimension, opening up a 'space' for people to glimpse that cosmic perspective on their problems which is so hard to achieve in a cluttered life" (1978, p.60). PLFH

Bibliography

*Bartley, W.W. 1978: *Werner Erhard*. New York: Clarkson N. Potter.

*est 1980: *Questions people ask about the est training*.

*Finkelstein, P., Wenegrat, B. and Yalom, I. 1982: Large group awareness training. *Annual review of psychology* 515–39.

*Rhinehart, L. 1976: *The book of est*. New York: Holt, Rinehard & Winston.

Rosen, R.D. 1978: *Psychobabble*. London: Wildwood House.

ethical problems in psychology Problems arising when practices of psychologists involve harm or wrong to others, or to the practice of psychology itself. Whether described as the study of behavior or of mind, the nature of psychological research and professional practice makes ethical problems inevitable: for example, some psychologists engage in research programs that have as their goal the prediction and control of behavior; engage in therapies that aim to change thought and behavior; engage in constructing, administering, and interpreting tests that are used to determine people's life chances (cf. – American Psychological Association, 1973; Noble 1980). Only a selection of the related ethical problems can be discussed here.

Ethical issues arise in psychology, as elsewhere, when it is thought that serious good and bad are bound together in the same activity. When harm or wrong is done to animals or humans subjected to or participating in research an outsider might consider it both reasonable and humane to abandon the project. Researchers find it less simple, for they believe that harm and wrong are an incidental but inescapable part of the benefits flowing from freely chosen scientific activity. It is undeniable that world-changing benefits have come from applying scientific method to problems. The belief that benefits follow all such practice sometimes seems to be a modern article of faith.

If, as psychologists typically claim, the decision to perform a potentially harm-inducing experiment is to be based on weighing scientific benefits against costs to participants, how are the benefits and costs to be assessed? American Psychological Association guidelines (1973) contain an admirably sensitive discussion of possible costs, but declare that benefits are insured by good research design and that, in turn, good design is assured by such things as graduate training, critical reviews and research proposal evaluation. Even when alerted to possible harm, it remains all too easy to decide that an elegant design outweighs costs. To limit the assessment of benefits to design quality ignores the fact that something cast in a scientific form can be trivial. One way of providing professionals with perspective has been to set up Ethics Committees composed in part of nonprofessionals.

The means or methods used to examine a problem can, of course, be studied and alternative methods which avoid harm devised. Some research practices which lead to wrongs are not good science. For example, it can be demonstrated that the common practice of lying to participants in order to "control" their ability to pretend does not achieve the desired results (Mixon 1976).

Psychologists experiment with animals because it is believed, for example, that learning processes in animals are similar to those in humans. As property, animals have no rights, so no balancing of benefits to others and costs to them can protect them. If we need not consider their suffering there are no ethical problems. For protection animals must rely on the sensitivity of researchers (members of a profession which values detachment and objectivity), laws against wanton cruelty (where they exist), or the intervention of animal protection activists.

Psychological tests have been devised to substitute standardized, objective assessment for individual, subjective judgment. Ethical and legal problems arise when such tests can be shown to discriminate systematically against particular groups of people. Intelligence tests provide a convenient illustration. Originally devised by Alfred Binet as a placement test for French school children, the mental age score used by Binet later came to be divided by chronological age and multiplied by 100 to produce the familiar intelligence quotient (IQ). The quotient so derived reifies "intelligence", and encourages people to think of it as something innate and fixed. Further, the practice of calculating and comparing group averages introduces the possibility of characterizing one racial or ethnic group as inherently less intelligent than another (with implications for discriminatory treatment). IQ tests are challenged by imputing cultural bias – that is, instead of providing an objective and fair measure of an entity called "intelligence", the tests in part measure group-specific knowledge and so credit greater intelligence to people who possess the knowledge. Expert opinion stating that "there are *no* measures of innate capacity" (Cleary et al. 1975, p.17) does not remove the popular conviction (fed by some professionals) that the IQ test is a measure of just that.

Added to harm and wrong done to others are the effects of certain research practices on psychology itself. For example, lying to experimental participants (a practice common among a sub-group of psychologists) contributes to giving psychologists in general a reputation for lying (Weinrach and Ivey 1975). If they believe that psychologists often lie, experimental participants, facing a psychologist who gives assurances that the experiment contains no trickery, have no way of knowing whether or not the assurance is genuine or false. Psychologists who tell the truth have no way of knowing whether or not participants believe what they are told, and cannot know how many different interpretations are given to their words. Those who give psychologists a reputation for untruth justify misinforming participants by claiming that their research problems can be studied only by lying and by claiming that the importance of the information obtained outweighed any wrong done to the participant. Even if the two claims could be demonstrated (neither can) lying is not justified, for the participant is not the only one wronged: the reputation for lying puts all of experimental psychology in jeopardy (Mixon 1977).

Psychologists in some areas of research have created another ethical problem by their reluctance to do the mundane work of replicating studies. Experiments are done and the status that goes with doing experiments is claimed. Yet, lacking replication, such work lacks the certainty which is the basis for the status and repute of experimentation. In a properly functioning research community when a new discovery is made judgment is suspended until the finding can be replicated in other laboratories. Replication is necessary because the original study could be flawed, inexpertly done, the outcome due to some fluke, to fraud or to some overlooked aspect of the experimental setup, such as the subjects' attitude to the psychologist. Yet unreplicated psychological experiments become "classics" and are discussed in textbooks as though they had the status of replicated experiments. For consumers of psychological information, psychology has a problem of potential misrepresentation.

Psychology has been comparatively free of the data-fabricating scandals that regularly rock the biomedical community, just conceivably because replication is one of the means of uncovering fraud. The most talked about fraud in recent years was detected not because of replication, but because one psychologist did not like the moral and political implications of another's work and so looked at the data more carefully than is common (Kamin 1974). Openness to scrutiny and replication are two essential tools of science which must be used to insure validity and ethical integrity. DLM

Bibliography

American Psychological Association, Committee on Ethical Standards in Psychological Research 1973: *Ethical principles in the conduct of research with human participants*. Washington, D.C.: Author.

Clearly, T.A. et al. 1975: Educational uses of tests with disadvantaged students. *American psychologist* 30, 15–41.

Kamin, L.J. 1974: *The science and politics of IQ*. Potomac, Maryland: Erlbaum.

Kelman, H.C. 1967: Human use of human subjects: the problem of deception in social psychological experiments. *Psychological bulletin* 67, 1–11.

Mixon, D. 1976: Studying feignable behavior. *Representative research in social psychology* 7, 89–104.

——— 1977: Why pretend to deceive? *Personality and social psychology bulletin* 3, 647–53.

Noble, W.G. 1980: Psychologists and ethics: Report of a working party. *Australian psychologist* 15, 393–411.

Regan, T. and Singer, P., eds. 1976: *Animal rights and human obligations*. Englewood Cliffs, N.J.: Prentice-Hall.

Weinrach, S.G. and Ivey, A.E. 1975: *Bulletin of the British Psychological Society* 28, 263–7.

ethnic minority children: education Concern for the education of ethnic minority children has arisen as a result of research over the past twenty years in the United States and Great Britain indicating that these children often perform more poorly in school than the majority population. Performance differences have been documented on both intelligence tests and academic achievement measures, although differences vary depending on the ethnic group under study. The group most heavily studied has been black children.

The research prompted a number of investigators, committed to the environmentalist view of intellectual development, to devise and implement compensatory education programs. These programs, the most notable of which was Headstart in the United States, took a variety of forms but all attempted to enrich the academically-related environment of the ethnic minority child to stimulate intellectual development. As a result of contemporary trends in developmental psychology, these programs tended to concentrate on preschool-age children. Program content varied greatly; some concentrated on the child alone while others attempted to intervene and change the whole family environment.

Relatively little work has been done on educational programs for older ethnic minority children.

While a great deal of controversy surrounds the usefulness of compensatory education for ethnic minorities, evaluations to date have indicated that these programs have achieved qualified success. See also INTELLIGENCE AND ENVIRONMENTAL INFLUENCES; COMPENSATORY EDUCATION. JSC

Bibliography

Lazar, I. and Darlington, R. 1982: Lasting effects of early education: A report from the consortium for longitudinal studies. *Monographs of the Society for Research in Child Development* 47, 1–151.

ethnocentrism A term introduced in the study of the AUTHORITARIAN PERSONALITY (Adorno et al 1950) to indicate the general nature of prejudice against particular outgroups or minorities. In a series of studies, Adorno et al showed that prejudice against Jews (anti-semitism) correlated positively with prejudice against negroes and members of other minority groups, and to some extent with a politically conservative attitude. The E (ethnocentrism) scale constructed by the authors was later superseded by the ubiquitous use of the F (fascism) scale. JMFJ

Bibliography

Adorno, T.W., Frenkel-Brunswik, E., Levinson, D.J., and Sanford, R.N. 1950: *The authoritarian personality*. New York: Harper & Row.

ethnography A method of unstructured observational research developed by social anthropologists for studying the workings of human cultures "from within". It involves the researcher's participation in the everyday lives of the group under study, and its analytic potential was first demonstrated in a series of classic field studies in the Trobriand Islands by Bronislaw Malinowski who, as a German citizen, had been interned there by the British during the first world war.

Sometimes referred to as "participant observation", the method has also been widely used by sociologists for studying the behavior of particular groups and organizations in advanced industrial societies. It has been especially important in the development of approaches to sociology and social psychology which are concerned with studying human conduct in natural, rather than experimentally contrived, settings, and with obtaining observational access to the ways in which people orient to, produce and interpret their everyday activities. As such, it has featured prominently in the emergence of symbolic interactionism and ethnomethodology. JMA

Bibliography

Malinowski, Bronislaw 1922: *Argonauts of the Western Pacific*. London: Routledge & Kegan Paul.

Sudnow, David 1967: *Passing on: the social organization of dying*. Englewood Cliffs, N.J.: Prentice Hall.

Whyte, William F. 1955: *Street corner society*. Chicago: Chicago University Press.

ethnography of speaking This concept was introduced by Hymes in the early 1960s as a new approach to linguistic analysis falling between the established disciplines of anthropology, linguistics, sociology and psychology.

Its central notion is that of "speech event", the components of which include setting, participants, purposes, verbal and textual organization, manner of delivery and linguistic CODES used (see Hymes 1974).

Hymes's approach partly overlaps and is partly complementary with the views discussed under LANGUAGE: FUNCTIONS OF.

Because of the comprehensiveness of this view, which

takes the total personality as the central point of reference in all areas of behavior, progress in both theory and description has been rather slow and its use to psycholinguistics accordingly limited. PM

Bibliography

Hymes, Dell 1974: *Foundations in sociolinguistics*, Philadelphia: University of Pennsylvania Press.

Sherzer, Joel 1977: The ethnography of speaking: a critical appraisal. In *Linguistics and anthropology*, ed. M. Saville-Troike. Washington: Georgetown University Press.

ethnomethodology The study of the everyday methods of practical reasoning used in the production and interpretation of social action. Although the term now tends to be used to refer to a number of related analytic approaches it was not originally intended to denote a social scientific methodology in the sense that surveys, experiments or ethnography are methodologies. In coining the word, its originator, Harold Garfinkel, was looking for a shorthand way of describing what he had come to regard as a previously neglected, but nonetheless important, *topic* for analysis (on the origins of the word ethnomethodology, see Garfinkel 1974). In combining the words "ethno" and "methodology" to refer to the proposed new domain Garfinkel was influenced by the use of such terms as ethnobotany and ethnomedicine for referring to folk systems of botanical and medical analysis and classification. What he was recommending as a focus for study was a folk methodology, comprising a range of "seen but un-noticed" procedures or practices that make it possible for persons to analyse, make sense of and produce recognizable social activities.

Central to Garfinkel's argument and to the development of research in ethnomethodology is the idea that social scientists have paid too little attention to the implications of their own membership of, and familiarity with, the subject matter of their inquiries. Thus the claim is that any competent member of society, including the professional social scientist, is equipped with a methodology for analysing social phenomena, and that these interpretive procedures are what enable people to make sense of and to produce contextually relevant activities within the potentially infinite range of different settings they encounter in living their lives. Social scientists, however, have tended not to treat these methodic practices as matters worthy of serious investigation in their own right, but have used and relied on them as a taken-for-granted and largely unexplicated resource in carrying out their research. According to the ethnomethodologists many of the more important theoretical and methodological difficulties associated with social science result from this long-standing willingness of researchers to regard their own native competences as a resource, rather than as a topic for investigation.

In studying phenomena such as delinquency and suicide, for example, social scientists have tended to direct their efforts towards finding explanations of these forms of behavior, and a commonly used data base has been official records and statistics on the incidence of such forms of behavior. However, questions such as "why delinquency?" and "why suicide?" are also ones which are asked by laymen and in response to which there are a variety of common sense explanations. Some of the early studies in ethnomethodology focussed on the methods of reasoning used by officials to categorize behavior as "delinquent" or "suicidal", and hence to produce "the facts" that social scientists then sought to explain (e.g. Garfinkel 1967; Cicourel 1968; Atkinson 1978). A common finding from this work was that the process of arriving at official categorizations involved the deployment and testing of common sense hypotheses about causation that closely resemble those which professional researchers have proposed as "scientific" explanations. For example, evidence that a child came from a broken home would make it more likely that he would be taken to court than a child from a more stable background. Similarly, if coroners and others responsible for processing sudden deaths cannot find evidence that a deceased person had been depressed or isolated, they are unlikely to record the death as a suicide. In other words, the presence or absence of a plausible explanation of *why* a particular individual became delinquent or suicidal has been shown to be a crucially important part of deciding *that* a case is one of delinquency or suicide. Viewed in these terms, it is not very surprising that social scientists who also ask the question *why*, and who hope to find the answer by studying samples of officially categorized delinquents or suicides, tend to rediscover the common sense explanations that were used to produce the official decisions in the first place. Nor is it particularly surprising that researchers may find it difficult to convince lay persons that a causal relationship between broken homes and delinquency, or isolation and/or depression and suicide is properly to be regarded as a victory of science.

Ethnomethodological studies of official categorization procedures are sometimes regarded as being merely negative critiques of the way in which social scientists have traditionally used data from official sources for research purposes. They are also sometimes read as recommendations to the effect that previous methodological procedures should be reformed or improved, so that "more careful" or "more accurate" studies could be done in the future. These are not, however, the lessons that the ethnomethodologists themselves take from their work on official categorizations. Rather they see them as confirming the promise of treating methods of reasoning, hitherto taken for granted, as the topic for inquiry, and of the uninteresting and un-newsworthy character of research that relies on them as an unexplicated resource. Accordingly traditional approaches to the social and behavioral sciences are viewed as interesting only in so far as they, like the analyses by social workers, coroners and others, testify to the methodic ways in which people are well equipped and readily able to construct plausible descriptions and explanations of social behavior. A major challenge posed by the earlier writings of Garfinkel (1967) and other ethnomethodologists, then, was to find ways of identifying these methodic practices, and to show how they work. As such, the approach involves a marked shift away from deterministic traditions which seek to construct causal theories of behavior. Instead of trying to explain *why* some particular type of conduct occurs, ethnomethodological research sets out to describe *how* it works.

Since its emergence in the 1960s, ethnomethodology has diversified to a point where it is now somewhat misleading to refer to it as though it were a unified or homogeneous style of research. Of the various developments which have taken place, however, there can be little doubt that the approach which has had the widest interdisciplinary impact outside sociology is that which has become known as conversation analysis. As the name suggests, this work has concentrated on the study of the methodic practices used in the production of mundane conversational interaction, and its approach and findings are having a growing impact in various areas of psychology, linguistics, anthropology and sociology. Research done so far has concentrated on a range of topics, including how interactants categorize persons, actions, places, events, etc., the organization of turn-taking in conversation, how stories and jokes are constructed and responded to, the ways in which laughter can be invited and coordinated with talk, and on the production and treatment of actions such as assessments, invitations, complaints, accusations, etc.

While much of the pioneering work in this area concentrated on the analysis of everyday conversational interaction, subsequent developments have already made the term "conversation analysis" appear too narrow a descriptor for research that is conducted within this methodological framework. Thus, the approach and findings of conversation analysis are now being applied in studies of various institutional or specialized forms of interaction, including news interviews, doctor–patient consultations, courtroom interaction, plea-bargaining, classroom interaction, child language, and public speaking. A related research program being developed by Garfinkel and his colleagues involves what are becoming known as ethnomethodolical studies of work. These are concerned with identifying task-specific properties ("essential quiddities") of particular activities, such as the work of lecturing, electron microscopy, mathematics, and law.

Although research in ethnomethodology and conversation analysis has diversified over the years, there is a wide consensus among those working within the field on at least three central methodological points. The first is that the main focus of any analysis should be on how participants themselves produce and interpret their respective activities. The second is that access to the methodic practices involved depends upon the analyst adopting an orientation to interactional data which seeks to regard such materials as "anthropologically strange". In other words, analysts must be willing to treat even the most mundane and apparently ordinary events as sufficiently puzzling to be worthy of serious analytic attention. Otherwise, he too is likely to overlook, or take for granted the very taken-for-granted practices that he is trying to identify and describe. Third, there is a strong preference for working with naturally occurring interactions, rather than ones arising from experimental situations, survey interviews, or other methods involving observer intervention or manipulation.

This naturalistic approach to data collection and analysis has been greatly facilitated by the development of audio and video-recording technology, which enable real-world interactions to be preserved and subjected to repeated and detailed study. The extensive use of tape-recordings also means that the data about which analytic claims are being made are openly available for critical inspection by readers or hearers of research reports. JMA

Bibliography

Atkinson, J.M. 1978: *Discovering suicide: studies in the social organisation of sudden death*. London: Macmillan; Pittsburgh: Pittsburgh University Press.

——— and Drew, P. 1979: *Order in court: the organisation of verbal interaction in judicial settings*. London: Macmillan; Atlantic Highlands, N.J.: Humanities Press.

——— and Heritage, J.C., eds. 1983: *Structures of social action: studies in conversation analysis*. Cambridge and New York: Cambridge University Press.

Cicourel, A.V. 1968: *The social organization of juvenile justice*. New York: John Wiley.

Garfinkel, H. 1967: *Studies in ethnomethodology*. Englewood Cliffs, N.J.: Prentice Hall.

——— 1974: The origin of the term ethnomethodology. In Turner (ed.) op. cit.

Heritage, J.C. 1983: *Harold Garfinkel and ethnomethodology*. London and New York: Macmillan.

Psathas, G., ed. 1979: *Everyday language: studies in ethnomethodology*. New York: Irvington.

Sacks, H., Schegloff, E.A. and Jefferson, G. 1974: A simplest systematics for the organization of turn-taking for conversation. *Language* 50, 696–735.

Schenkein, J.N., ed. 1978: *Studies in the organization of conversational interaction*. New York: Academic Press.

Sudnow, D., ed. 1972: *Studies in social interaction*. New York: Free Press.

Turner, R., ed. 1974: *Ethnomethodology*. London: Penguin.

ethogenics A theory and associated methodology for the analysis and explanation of social interaction. Ethogenics grew out of the attempt to devise an approach to the study of social behavior that was in accordance with the most advanced understanding of the method of the physical sciences. It involved a sharp break with the positivist philosophy upon which experimental social psychology had hitherto been based. In the advanced sciences conceptual systems are used both to create "facts" and to invent hypotheses about processes by which such facts are generated. In the ethogenic approach explicit attention is given to the formulation of an analytical conceptual scheme by means of which observations and identifications of social actions, structures, etc. are made, and a coordinated explanatory scheme appropriate to the subject matter. In respect of the former feature it has much in common with aspects of ETHNOMETHODOLOGY, and in respect of the latter with the cognitive psychology of action.

Three kinds of coordinated social interaction are identified. In automatic interaction actors are not aware of either the fact or the process of coordination. Matching of postures in a conversational setting occurs without the participants being aware of it. Interaction of this sort could be set within a natural order and treated as the effect of the operation of causal mechanisms (or quasi-causal mechanisms such as habits). But in autonomous action actors are aware both of the actions they are performing and of the rules and conventions that require them (SELF-MONITORING). Ceremonial action is typically controlled by reference to explicit and known rules. Such interaction is set within a moral order, that is, people can be called to account for failures and infelicities in carrying out what was required of them. But much social interaction is not readily classified in either of these categories. The ethogenic methodology is directed to the understanding of social interaction that is neither automatic nor autonomous. It is based on the application of a conceptual system that is a generalization of that required to understand autonomous action. The actions people perform together in, say, managing a discussion, or developing a friendship, or following out the instructions of a superior, are assumed to be effective by virtue of their meanings to the actors. The genesis of meaningful action is thought to be by means similar to those by which people knowingly follow the prescriptions of a system of rules or conventions. Meanings, rules and conventions form systems of belief related to the demands of specific social situations, episodes and encounters. Included among those beliefs must be both representations of the goals appropriate for each role-player in the defined situation, and the locally accepted ways of achieving them. Like a theory in the advanced sciences the ethogenic approach exploits a system of metaphors.

A distinction needs to be drawn between the means by which a social episode is analysed so that its structure and components are revealed, and the way the production of that episode by those involved is to be explained. The ethogenic analysis of episodes depends on the three-fold distinction between behavior, actions and acts. An act is an action or several actions described or defined in a way which makes clear their social meaning, as for instance the signing of a document can be an act of surrender. Acts are realized by human actions, that is behavior carried out intentionally. The concept of "behavior" is reserved for any kind of physically realized response. The act–action–behavior distinction has also been used in ethology (Reynolds 1980). A special case of the distinction is the partition of the efficacy of SPEECH ACTS into locutionary, illocutionary and perlocutionary forces. It follows from this that the socially potent elements in an episode are defined only by the coordination of actors' intentions (the acts attempted) and interactors' interpretations (the acts as understood). It further follows that the structure of an episode is determined by semantic not by causal relations between its components. Finally it is most important to notice that acts and actions are not in 1–1 correspondence. The same act (say "farewelling") can be performed in a variety of ways (one is saying "goodbye", another is merely waving), while the same action (turning one's back) can be the expression of many different acts. This fact has profound consequences for methodology.

In studying the sequential structure of human performances in social episodes the act sequence can be related to the general typology according to which each episode is classified with respect to the social structure of the situations and encounters it includes. In courtroom encounters (such as trials) characteristic act sequences occur. But the action sequences by which act sequences are realized may be very different in different communities and cultures. To discover just what acts are being performed actors' meanings must be investigated. Since actors are not always aware of the moment by moment significance of their actions as acts, in non-ceremonial episodes, a joint method of ethnographic analysis and the collection and analysis of accounts is required to formulate hypotheses about the belief system which is being used by actors in generating typical episodes. Goffman's microsociological analyses (Goffman 1959, 1963 and 1972) have proved very helpful in suggesting ethnographic hypotheses exploiting, as they do, the dramaturgical and liturgical models of social action. But it is in the accounts that actors produce to comment on, correct and reinterpret the action that rules, conventions and other social beliefs are explicitly formulated. It is in the match between the content of accounts and the ethnographic analysis that a growing grasp of the belief system underlying the action can be achieved (Marsh, Rosser and Harré 1978).

Considered methodologically the joint method of ethnographic description and account analysis leads to competence theories, that is to theories about the knowledge and beliefs which form the resource on which competent actors draw in acting. It must be emphasized that ethogenic analysis does not lead to a set of hypotheses about what is known by individual actors. Rather it is the socially distributed knowledge located in the collectives to which they belong. Much social action is created by cognitive processes that occur in the discourse of the collective and not in the minds of individuals. For instance, one person may know what act should be performed, while another may know how that act, say "protesting", is to be performed in the existing circumstances. The cognitive processing of those components may itself be a social process, involving hierarchical relations between the actors.

The ubiquitous use of the act–action distinction (Kreckel 1981) in ethogenic analyses suggests that performance theories, about the processes by which social knowledge and belief are utilized by actors, should take a means–end form. In most cases the immediate or remote end of social action is some social effect, mediated by an act, while the proper performance of that act requires knowledge of means, that is of the right action in that milieu. Ethogenic performance theories take the form of cognitive ACTION THEORY (von Cranach and Harré 1982). Essentially this approach involves the supposition of hierarchies of means–end pairs, involving several distinctive cognitive processes, such as goal setting, goal realization, feed back and other processes, etc. Since in most cases of interest actors are not paying attention to the cognitive processes by which they are controlling their actions, account analysis has little to contribute to performance theory. However, von Cranach and others have found that when the smooth unfolding of an episode is interrupted people do become aware both of what they were trying to do (act) and how they were trying to do it (action); consciously accessing that part of the hypothetical means – end hierarchy that should have been operative at that moment in the development of the episode. By clever exploitation of this fact action psychologists have been able to make considerable progress in studying the way means – end hierarchies are developed and used (von Cranach and Harré op cit).

In this approach great emphasis has been laid on discourse (and other forms of symbolic interchange) as the main medium of social interaction. This suggests paying attention to the rhetorics of characteristic forms of discourse, including that of social psychology itself. In traditional experimental social psychology a characteristic scientistic rhetoric appears, using metaphors drawn from the superficial features of the language of the physical sciences. Typical instances are the rhetorical use of words such as "measure", "variable", "experiment" and so on, words which have a literal application in the physical sciences. In studying the use of a rhetoric one must ask for what self-presentational purposes that way of writing or speaking is chosen. This is to set it in the expressive order of action, rather than the practical order. The distinction between expressive and practical orders (or alternatively of expressive and practical motivations) is of central importance for ethogenics, since it is by reference to these orders or systems of motivation that the role of particular rhetorics is to be understood. In traditional social psychology the expressive project realized by the scientistic rhetoric is presentation of oneself as "scientist".

However, choice of one rhetoric rather than another has further consequences. The combination of positivistic philosophy with the effect of the use of superficial scientistic rhetoric had the effect of obscuring both the structural properties of social episodes and encounters and the importance of the meanings of the component acts which formed structural episodes and encounters. Adherents of the old "experimental" methodology seemed literally unable to see structures of meanings. In contrast the ethogenic approach emphasizes the importance of structure not only as a desideratum in analysis of social interaction, but also in explanation. The principal of structural explanation – "Structured products derive from structured templates", can be used to control the detailed study of performance processes. According to that principle the best hypothesis is that there is likely to be some preformed "template" in which the structure to be realized pre-exists.

A similar explanation of the orderliness of social interactions has been proposed by Abelson. People control their actions by reference to "scripts", belief-systems identical, so it seems, with the "collective social knowledge" of ethogenics. "Scripts" or "belief-systems" form the cognitive "templates" which are the basis of structural explanations. RHa

Bibliography

Collett, P., ed. 1977: *Social rules and social behavior*. Oxford: Basil Blackwell; Totowa, N.J.: Rowman & Littlefield.

Ginsburg, G.P. 1978: *Emerging strategies of social psychological research*. New York: Wiley.

Goffman, E. 1959: *The presentation of self in everyday life*. New York: Doubleday-Anchor.

——— 1963: *Stigma*. Englewood Cliffs, N.J.: Prentice-Hall.

——— 1972: *Interaction ritual*. London: Allen Lane.

Harré, R. 1979: *Social being*. Oxford: Basil Blackwell; Totowa, N.J.: Rowman Littlefield (1980).

——— and Secord, P.F. 1963: *The explanation of social behavior*. Oxford: Basil Blackwell; Totowa, N.J.: Rowman Littlefield Adams (1964).

Kreckel, M. 1981: *Communicative acts and shared knowledge in natural discourse*. London and New York: Academic Press.

Marsh, P., Rosser, E. and Harré, R. 1978: *The rules of disorder*. London: Routledge & Kegan Paul.

Reynolds, V. 1980: *The biology of human action*. Oxford: Freeman.

von Cranach, M. and Harré, R. 1982: *The analysis of action: empirical and theoretical advances*. Cambridge and New York: Cambridge University Press.

ethogram The complete behavioral vocabulary of a species, the listing of units of behavior whose occurrence in various contexts, and sequences, can be used in principle to provide a comprehensive description of behavior. The ethogram has its origins in the theories of instinct which postulated specific innate units of behavior, and ethograms are easiest to compile for the lower species. Inevitable problems in compiling an ethogram are balancing the completeness of the listing against the frequency of occurrence of rare behavior; and the issue of the lumping or splitting of particular units. In the mammals the problem is compounded by the graded nature of many types of behavior, and, in the higher primates and humans, the possibilities of intra-species variations in behavior and the possibility of deception. Nevertheless, an ethogram is an important first step in the description of a species, and human ethograms have been attempted, notably for young children. Different researchers may not agree on the ethogram of a particular species, and the construction of an ethogram may be conceived of as a psychological process involving the researcher's aims, and the perceptions of the species being studied (Reynolds 1976). (See also ETHOLOGY; OBSERVATIONAL METHODS.) PKS

Bibliography

Reynolds, V. 1976 The origins of a behavioural vocabulary: the case of the rhesus monkey. *Journal for the theory of social behaviour* 6, 105–42.

ethologism The appeal to concepts and findings derived from ethological studies of the behavior of non-human animals as a source of immediate diagnosis of the dilemmas of the human condition and of prescriptions for change. The term "ethologism" was introduced by Callan (1970) in an attempt to account for the mass appeal of works of popular ethology such as those of Ardrey (e.g. 1966), Lorenz (e.g. 1966) and Morris (e.g. 1967); and their influence on both popular and scientific conceptions of human nature. It was suggested that the roots of ethologism lay in (*a*) a loss of confidence in the solubility of human problems, such as overpopulation and warfare, by human means; (*b*) a romantic yearning for the apparent simplicity and innocence of animal life; and (*c*) the scientific success of ethology. A linguistic feature of ethologism is the adoption of terms such as "ritualization", "pair-bond" and "dominance" which have acquired a technical meaning in ethology but are nevertheless derived from human experience. These are then re-applied to social action in man under the guise of new discoveries *about* social action. Ethologism has a place in the sociology and history of ideas as a manifestation local to the scientific and popular culture of the western world of a more general – perhaps universal – human inclination to speculate about the relation of nature to that of man, and to use animal images as tools for thought about problematic or painful aspects of being human. See also ETHOLOGY; HUMAN ETHOLOGY. HC

Bibliography

Ardrey, Robert 1966: *The territorial imperative*. New York: Atheneum, 1966; London: Collins, 1967.

Callan, H. 1970: *Ethology and society: towards an anthropological view*. Oxford: Clarendon Press; New York; OUP.

Lorenz, Konrad Z. 1966: *On aggression*. London: Methuen; New York: Harcourt, Brace and World Inc.

Morris, D. 1967: *The naked ape*. London: Cape; New York: McGraw-Hill.

ethology The study of animal behavior, primarily in the natural environment of the species being observed. The domain of classical ethology was dominated by the theories of Lorenz and Tinbergen during the 1940s and 1950s. Modern ethology has broadened both the range of theoretical concepts used, and of species studied, and is now less distinct from neighboring disciplines such as comparative psychology, neurophysiology, and the experimental study of animal behavior.

The origins and rise of ethology have been described by Thorpe (1979). The immediate origins of classical ethology lay in the work of zoologists such as Heinroth in Germany, Whitman in the USA, and Huxley in Britain. These researchers combined an interest in the observation of an animal's behavior in its natural surroundings, with a concern for the adaptive value of behavior. This concern stemmed from evolutionary theory and the work of Darwin. By the late 1930s classical ethology was well under way; Huxley was instrumental in founding the Institute (now Association) for the Study of Animal Behaviour in Britain in 1936, while LORENZ and Köhler founded the German journal *Zeitschrift für Tierpsychologie* in 1937.

The work of Lorenz, Tinbergen and others led to a highly developed theory of animal behavior based on the concept of a number of DRIVES which affected responses to external stimuli; the simplest animals responded by reflexive, kinetic and taxic behavior, and more complicated animals by a chaining or hierarchy of rather stereotyped behavior forming 'fixed action patterns'. Tinbergen's book, *The study of instinct* (1951), was the culmination of this approach, which is now summarized.

A reflexive behavior is considered as an innate, relatively simple and stereotyped response involving the central nervous system and occurring very shortly after the stimulus which provokes it. Reflexive movements without orientation are referred to as kineses; the intensity of stimulation may affect rate of movement (orthokinesis) or rate of change of direction, such as turning (klinokinesis). Reflexive movements with orientation of the whole animal are referred to as taxes; for example swinging from side to side to compare stimulus intensities (klinotaxis); simultaneous comparison of two stimuli, and orientation towards one (tropotaxis); direct choice of or aversion to a source of stimulation (menotaxis); and orientation to a complex or patterned stimulus source (mnemotaxis).

Instinct theorists further postulated that such reflexive behavior units could be chained together in a sequence, or, more flexibly, considered as a hierarchical progression from higher to lower levels of APPETITIVE BEHAVIOR, ending in a consummatory act. The courtship and mating of the three-spined stickleback is a well-known example from Tinbergen's work. A fixed sequence, relatively uninfluenced by learning, is referred to as a 'fixed action pattern' (FAP).

The FAP is thought of as being set off by certain specific stimuli, called SIGN STIMULI. These 'release' the behavior by means of an INNATE RELEASING MECHANISM (IRM) which detects key features of the sign stimulus and triggers off the relevant motor neurons to activate the FAP. A SUPERNORMAL STIMULUS is one which elicits an FAP even more strongly than natural stimuli.

In Lorenz's hydraulic model of motivation (1950), which Tinbergen took over, physical energy becomes nervous energy. An instinct for a particular behavior (such as nestbuilding or finding food) builds up a reaction-specific energy or drive state. This leads to appetitive behavior (with associated kineses and taxes) and, if an appropriate sign stimulus is found, the release of FAP's which lead to a consummatory act (such as feeding, or constructing a nest). The build-up of reaction-specific energy can lower the threshold of responsiveness to external stimuli. VACUUM ACTIVITY, the expression of an FAP in the absence of sign stimuli, could occur if the reaction-specific energy built up sufficiently without finding release. DISPLACEMENT ACTIVITY occurred if the normal outlet for reaction-specific energy was prevented and the nervous energy "spilt over" from one FAP to another.

The ideas of classical ethology came under attack during the 1950s, from ethologists and comparative psychologists, especially those studying mammalian and avian species and finding that learning and flexibility in behavior was substantially greater than could be accommodated within instinct theory. It became clear that even the relatively stereotyped behavior of lower species was not as "fixed" or invariant as predicted (for example, courtship in the stickleback). Behavior patterns in birds and mammals were not simple chains or hierarchies but could only be explained by more sophisticated models. An example is the reproductive cycle of canaries, which is controlled by an interaction of internal hormonal effects, external stimuli such as day length, the behavior of conspecifics, and the physiological effects of the behavior performed.

The hydraulic model of motivation, in particular, was criticized as exemplifying a misleading confusion of physical and nervous energy. Behavioral sequences could be brought to an end by the reception of certain specific stimuli, just as readily as by the supposed discharge of energy in action. Displacement activities received alternative theoretical explanations, such as disinhibition of a response. Indeed the fundamental concept of "drive" states as in any sense usefully simplifying very complex phenomena was criticized by Hinde (1959); though the term continues in use at least as a shorthand way of describing the organization of behavior toward certain biological goals.

The 1950s and 1960s saw a rapprochement between ethologists, comparative psychologists, and neurophysiologists, such that the present disciplines are not very distinct. Although Lorenz defended a modified version of the innate/learnt dichotomy, the conceptual and practical difficulties of any simple distinction along these lines have become increasingly recognized. IMPRINTING has been an example of a type of behavior initially thought of as a largely innate process, with only the object of imprinting being learnt. The complexities of the process are now better understood. The ideas of constraints on learning, and predispositions to learn more readily in certain ways, have also been developed.

Among more recent developments in ethology has been the rapid growth of studies in primates (e.g. Chalmers 1979), with specialist journals such as *Primates* and *Folia Primatologica*. There has been increased interest in RELATIONSHIPS and SOCIAL STRUCTURE, and in more complex and flexible behavior patterns such as PLAY. Socioecology is a subdiscipline which relates social structure to the ecology of a species, notably its feeding resources and likely predators.

The growth of SOCIOBIOLOGY and behavioral ecology has led to vigorous new perspectives on animal behavior in general, and social behavior in particular. It has heightened the importance of observational studies of a sufficiently large scale to cover the behavior of a social group over several generations, so that kinship relations and medium-term reproductive success can be elucidated. It has also encouraged more detailed experimental studies of behavioral choices, for example of foraging, in terms of optimality theories. Ethological concepts and methods have also been applied to the study of human behavior, with a specialist journal, *Ethology and sociobiology* starting in 1979.

Particularly noticeable has been the advance of sophisticated quantitative models for the analysis of behavior (Colgan 1978). Two distinctive features have remained though from the earlier classical ethology. First, the emphasis on naturalistic, observational methods, at least in the initial stages of studying a new species/behavior, and the construction of an ETHOGRAM. Second, the basic framework of Tinbergen's 'four whys'; the study of the immediate causation of behavior, its development in ontogeny, the immediate adaptive value or function of the behavior, and its evolutionary history (Tinbergen 1963).

PKS

Bibliography

Bateson, Paul P.G. and Hinde, Robert A. 1976: (eds.). *Growing points in ethology*. Cambridge and New York: Cambridge University Press.

Chalmers, N. 1979. *Social behaviour in primates*. London: Edward Arnold; Baltimore; University Park Press.

Colgan, P.W. (ed.) 1978. *Quantitative ethology*. New York: Wiley.

Hinde, R.A. 1959. Unitary drives. *Animal behaviour* 7, 130–41.

——— 1982: *Ethology*. Oxford and New York: Oxford University Press.

Lehner, P. 1979: *Handbook of ethological methods*. New York: Garland.

Lehrman, D.S. 1953. A critique of Konrad Lorenz's theory of instinctive behavior. *Quarterly review of biology* 28, 337–63.

Lorenz, K.Z. 1950. The comparative method in studying innate behaviour patterns. *Symposium of the society for experimental biology* 4, 221–68.

Manning, Aubrey 1979: *An introduction to animal behaviour*. 3rd edn. London: Edward Arnold; Reading, Mass.: Addison-Wesley.

Morris, D. 1958. The reproductive behaviour of the ten-spined stickleback (*Pygosteus pungitius* L.). *Behaviour*, Suppl. No. 6, 1–154.

Thorpe, W.H. 1979. *The origins and rise of ethology*. London: Heinemann Educational.

Tinbergen, Nikolaas 1951. *The study of instinct*. Oxford: Clarendon Press.

——— 1963. On aims and methods of ethology. *Zeitschrift für Tierpsychologie* 20, 410–33.

ethology: human This refers to the application of ideas from ethology and sociobiology to the study of human behavior. The models and concepts of both classical and modern ethology began to be applied systematically in the 1960s; after a series of meetings, the International Society for Human Ethology was formally founded in 1978. Through the 1970s, human ethology has been increasingly influenced by sociobiology, and a specialist journal devoted to human applications, *Ethology and sociobiology*, commenced publication in 1979.

Despite their simplicity, some ideas of classical ethology have found human application. Theorists such as Lorenz, Tinbergen and Eibl-Eibesfeldt have looked for the presence of "sign stimuli" in humans; for example, elevated shoulders or posture-releasing submissive behavior, or babylike expressions releasing parental care. The concepts of DISPLACEMENT ACTIVITY and VACUUM ACTIVITY have been used, for example in Lorenz's controversial book *Human aggression* (1966). Eibl-Eibesfeldt has filmed and documented many "fixed action patterns" (for example facial expressions and gestures) found cross-culturally; an extensive article of his with open peer commentary (Eibl-Eibesfeldt 1979) exemplifies this fairly traditional approach to the ethological study of human behavior.

In the UK and USA, human ethologists concentrated on the observation of behavior in natural settings, without such a tight theoretical framework. Blurton Jones (1967) described the differences between rough-and-tumble play, and real aggression, in a study of nursery school children. This proved the precursor to a large number of observational studies on children, and renewed interest in sampling techniques and the problems of category definitions and the effects of the observer on behavior. These were approaches and issues which had been undeveloped since the observational studies of child development in the USA in the 1930s. Blurton Jones's edited volume, *Ethological studies of child behaviour*, proved a landmark in these respects. Because of the ease of observation, preschool children have been a goldmine for human ethological studies; other examples are aggression and dominance, attention structure, and altruism. For similar reasons, several ethological studies were carried out in medical or mental institutions. Several ethological studies have been made on autistic children.

Besides utilizing ethological concepts such as dominance hierarchy or attention structure, such studies were characterized by attempts at child or human ethograms. An ambitious example of an attempt at an ethogram for preschool children is that of McGrew (1972). Ekman and Friesen (1976) attempted to analyse human facial expression. Both these approaches, and the cross-cultural work of Eibl-Eibesfeldt, have been important influences in the study of non-verbal communication.

Following the interests of animals workers in the influence of the environment on social structure and behavior, some human ethologists have investigated areas such as the effects of crowding on behavior (McGrew 1972). Smith and Connolly (1980) combined observational methods and a child ethogram based on those of McGrew and others, together with experimental methodology, to assess the impact of different environments on the behavior of children in different preschool settings.

Some investigations were more explicitly concerned with the functional significance of certain human behaviors. The work of Bowlby (1969) on the parent–infant attachment system is a most notable example. These and other studies have considered the adaptiveness of behavior in the natural environment, often assuming that the "natural environment" of the human species – what Bowlby calls "the environment of evolutionary adaptedness" – is similar to the environment of present-day peoples living in a hunter-gatherer subsistence economy.

PKS

Bibliography

Alexander, R.D. 1980: *Darwinism and human affairs*. London: Pitman.

Blurton Jones, N.G. 1967. An ethological study of some aspects of social behaviour of children in nursery school. In D. Morris (Ed.), *Primate ethology*. London: Weidenfeld and Nicholson, pp. 347–68.

*Blurton Jones, N.G., ed. 1972: *Ethological studies of child behaviour*. Cambridge and New York: Cambridge University Press.

Bowlby, John 1969: *Attachment and loss, Vol. 1: Attachment*. London: Hogarth Press; New York: Basic Books.

Chagnon, N.A., and Irons, W. 1979: *Evolutionary biology and human social behavior: an anthropological perspective*. Massachusetts: Duxbury Press.

*Eibl-Eibesfeldt, I. 1979: Human ethology: concepts and implications for the sciences of man. *Behavioral and brain sciences* 2, 1–57.

Ekman, P., and Friesen, W.V. 1976. Measuring facial movement. *Environmental psychology and nonverbal behavior* 1, 56–75.

Lorenz, K. 1966: *On aggression*. London: Methuen; New York: Harcourt, Brace & World.

Lumsden, Charles and Wilson, Edward 1981: *Genes, minds and culture*. Cambridge, Mass.: Harvard University Press.

McGrew, W.C. 1972: *An ethological study of children's behaviour*. London and New York: Academic Press.

Ruse, M. 1979: *Sociobiology: sense or nonsense?* Dordrecht, Holland: D. Reidel Pub. Co.

Smith, P.K., and Connolly, K.K. 1980: *The ethology of preschool behaviour*. Cambridge and New York: Cambridge University Press.

Wilson, Edmund O. 1978: *On human nature*. Cambridge, Mass.: Harvard University Press.

ethology *See* cognitive ethology; emotion: ethological approaches.

etic *See* emic vs. etic

etymology The study of the origin of words. Plato's dialogue 'Cratylus' contains a discussion of the question whether there is a natural and necessary relation between things and the words which stand for them (analogist position) or whether names are merely the result of human conventions (anomalist position). The analogists argued that the origin and true meaning (etymon) of words could be traced in their shape. Similar views are held by psycholinguists working on SOUND SYMBOLISM. Because of the long-standing view in linguistics that synchronic studies are methodologically earlier than diachronic studies, etymologizing has played a somewhat subordinate role in theoretical linguistics until fairly recently (see Malkiel 1975, 101–20).

The study of folk-etymologies is of considerable interest to psycholinguists. They constitute explanations of why a certain form means what it does, based on (frequently tenuous) similarities of forms and meanings. Thus, for many speakers of English, "affricates" would be sounds characteristic of African languages. Folk etymologies reflect the speaker's desire for greater transparency. PM

Bibliography

Malkiel, Yakov 1975: Etymology and modern linguistics. *Lingua* 36, 101–20.

evaluation of training An activity designed to assess the effectiveness of a training program in relation to a set of criteria defining program success. Martin (1957) identified two classes of criteria for the evaluation of training – internal and external. Internal criteria focus attention on the effectiveness of behavior within the training environment while external criteria address issues associated with "on-the-job" performance or performance in a natural setting. Examples of internal criteria include objective exams and ratings by the trainers or trainees regarding program effectiveness. External criteria might include such things as quantity and/or quality of production following training as well as accident rates or safety records. Goldstein (1978) has taken the criteria taxonomy for training even further by suggesting that programs should be evaluated relative to the following three categories:

(1) Training Validity – Did the trainees match the criteria established for the training program? (This is similar to Martin's category of internal criteria.)

(2) Performance Validity – Did the trainees match the criteria established for success when they were back on the job? (This is similar to Martin's external criteria category.)

(3) Intraorganizational Validity – Is the program equally effective with different trainees in organizations other than the one that developed the training program?

The planning, development and execution of training programs are extremely costly so procedures for evaluating their efficacy are important, but the answer to the question of value can be multi-faceted. The many problems associated with the evaluation of training and training research have been discussed by Campbell (1971). RRJ

Bibliography

Campbell, J.P., 1971: Personnel training and development. *Annual review of psychology*.

Goldstein, I.L., 1978: The pursuit of validity in the evaluation of training programs. *Human factors* 20, 131–44.

Martin, H.O., 1957: The assessment of training. *Personnel management* 39, 88–93.

evoked potential A transient change in electrical activity that can be recorded from the brain in response to the arrival of sensory impulses. When recorded from the scalp, evoked potentials are comparable in amplitude to the current ELECTROENCEPHALOGRAM (EEG). Studies of evoked potentials have made an important contribution to our understanding of neural systems that respond selectively to different types of sensory stimulation and in the mapping of cortical and subcortical regions of the brain. Evoked potentials reflect the presence of synaptic activity but not ACTION POTENTIALS. Computer-based averaging techniques are used to make it possible to distinguish evoked potentials from a background of random brain activity. RAJ

evolution In biology, evolution refers to change from generation to generation in the genetic constitution of an animal (or plant) population. On the large scale, evolution may involve the appearance, transformation or disappearance of whole species over long spans of time, but smaller-scale changes are also forms of evolution (see Mayr 1963). The idea that species are changeable (rather than fixed, as once widely thought) has a considerable history, but was crucially strengthened by Darwin's argument for NATURAL SELECTION as a process which could bring about evolutionary change.

In the modern understanding of evolution, genetic variation may be widespread in a population and may be increased by mutation and migration: and evolutionary factors including natural selection act to change or stabilize gene frequencies in particular ways. Opinions vary as to the relative importance of different evolutionary factors – many biologists still consider natural selection in some form to be the most influential, but increasingly this has been questioned in view of the possible importance of mutation, migration, and especially genetic drift (gene frequency change at random) and founder effect (where a population's founders are unrepresentative of their population of origin). A current controversy concerns the problem of whether evolution proceeds slowly and gradually or by the alternation of long periods of stability with short episodes of rapid change (e.g. during speciation: see Stanley 1979).

In the social sciences, evolutionary theories were once widely influential (though in forms scarcely related to Darwin's theory): they were frequently uncritically used, and were eventually discredited (see Burrow 1966). Subsequently there have been attempts to revive the analogy between biological and socio cultural processes (Harré 1979; see also MEME), but much opinion still emphasizes the differences (see Harrison 1971). RDA

Bibliography

Burrow, J.W. 1966. *Evolution and society: a study in Victorian social theory.* London and New York: Cambridge University Press.

Harré, Rom 1979: *Social being* pt IV. Oxford: Basil Blackwell; Totowa, N.J.: Littlefield Adams.

Harrison, G.A. (1971): Biological evolution and social change. *Proceedings of the Royal Anthropological Institute*, 5–15.

Mayr, E. 1963: *Animal species and evolution.* Cambridge, Mass.: Harvard University Press.

Stanley, S.M. 1979: *Macroevolution: pattern and process.* San Francisco: W.H. Freeman.

evolutionarily stable strategies (ESS) In sociobiology a strategy is an ESS if, when adopted by most members of a population, it cannot be invaded by any alternative strategy. The "invasion" refers to evolutionary spread of an alternative strategy; thus an ESS is a strategy that cannot be replaced by alternatives once it becomes fixed in a population. The ESS concept was developed and formalized by Maynard Smith (1972, 1974), though several workers had independently used the same principle without emphasizing its general importance as a technique in evolutionary biology.

First, what is a strategy? A strategy is simply one of a series of possible courses of action, or allocations of effort. For an animal, "search for food" and "search for mates" could be two possible strategies. An ESS model would begin with a list of plausible strategies; precisely what is a plausible strategy must be decided by the modeller on a basis of what it seems feasible that the animal could do. The next step in the model would be an algebraic definition of how payoffs (measured in terms of FITNESS) will be allocated when individuals playing the various strategies interact. Finally, there will be a formal, mathematical analysis (based on the mathematics of game theory) to determine which strategy, if any, can be an ESS. It then remains to be established whether behavior observed in nature fits the ESS predicted by the model.

Maynard Smith pointed out that an ESS could be of two types:

(i) *pure ESS* – in a given condition always play one particular strategy.

(ii) *mixed ESS* – in a given condition play various strategies with prescribed probabilities.

There are two ways in which a mixed ESS could be achieved (Maynard Smith and Parker 1976). The population could be genetically polymorphic, so that strategy frequencies relate to genotype frequencies. (In general this poses considerable theoretical difficulty for most sexually reproducing organisms if several pure strategies must co-exist). More simply, the population could be genetically monomorphic; each individual "playing" the strategies randomly within the ESS probabilities. Some doubt exists as to whether mixed ESSs will exist in nature, rather than a set of appropriate "conditional strategies" (see below).

The formal requirements for a strategy to be an ESS have been defined by Maynard Smith (1974). For a strategy (call it strategy *I*) to be an ESS all alternative strategies must get lower pay-offs than *I* when the population consists mainly of *I*-type individuals. The mean fitness of all rare, alternative strategies must be lower than the mean fitness of the *I* strategy when *I* is common. *I* will therefore be stable, since the alternative strategies cannot spread after arising as mutations.

How does an ESS differ from a simple optimum? An ESS is in a sense a competitive optimum, or Nash equilibrium. The optimum strategy (to give highest REPRODUCTIVE SUCCESS) for an individual in an interaction against competitors often depends critically upon the strategy played by the competitors. It is under these circumstances (where payoffs to "self" depend on the strategy played by others) that the ESS approach is necessary. Two simple examples serve to illustrate this point. If an animal is constructing an overwintering nest, there may be a unique optimal solution for effort spent, reflecting the tradeoff between cost (effort = time and energy that is spent on nest-building) and benefits (improvement in survival prospects due to protection by nest against cold weather). Essentially, the animal "plays" against the environment. On the other hand, if an animal is fighting a conspecific over a territory, the optimal strategy depends on what the opponent is likely to do. If the opponent is likely to back off quickly when challenged, it pays to be persistent. Alternatively, if the opponent will persist to a costly level, it may pay to retreat. The best strategy depends on the current frequencies in the population of strategies for persisting or retreating. Selection is *frequency-dependent*; it is here we need the ESS approach.

How does the ESS approach differ from the techniques used by population geneticists who work on frequency-dependent selection? Rather little in some cases. However, population geneticists tend to be interested, say, in the equilibrium properties of two alternative alleles at a locus. The mathematics becomes very tedious as more than one locus is included, and the strategy set is therefore often very restricted. ESS theorists usually omit the problems of diploidy (dominance and recessiveness of genes) from their models, and make the assumption that strategies reproduce asexually, or that the genetic system is haploid. This sacrifice of genetic rigor allows consideration of a much bigger array of alternative strategies than would be possible using standard techniques of population genetics. In short, ESS models usually sacrifice genetic precision in the interest of having wide strategic possibilities. This has attracted some criticism (e.g. Oster and Wilson 1978) but there is reason for optimism that even with sexually-reproducing diploidy, populations can indeed evolve to an ESS (Maynard Smith 1981).

For some games there can be more than one ESS. Which ESS is achieved depends on the frequencies of strategies at the start of selection. This contrasts with simple, non-frequency dependent optimization, where there is only one solution (optimism). A further contrast is that at an ESS, the *mean fitness of the population* may well be lower than at some alternative solution though *individual fitness* is maximized in the sense that deviant mutants do worse. (In simple optimization, both mean population fitness and individual fitness are maximized at the optimum). There is no paradox in this phenomenon; characteristics do not spread because they aid the reproduction of species or populations, but because they enhance the replication rate of the genes that determine them (see e.g. Dawkins 1976, 1982).

Many ESSs are likely to be "conditional" upon circumstances. A *conditional ESS* (Dawkins 1980) prescribes what to do in alternative circumstances. For instance the conditional strategy: "retreat if smaller than opponent, escalate if larger than opponent" can be an ESS for contests between a pair of opponents over a disputed resource (Maynard Smith and Parker 1976, Hammerstein 1981). There are doubts as to whether ESSs will ever be mixed strategies, in the sense that an animal plays strategies randomly within the ESS probabilities, on the grounds that selection would favor some form of conditional ESS. The argument can be formulated as follows. If each component-pure strategy of a mixed ESS has the same expected fitness, then any mutant that behaves non-randomly can spread if it can profit by linking a given strategy with a given phenotypic state (Parker 1982). However, cases where animals have imperfect information about states, or roles, in a contest, can generate mixed ESSs that are also conditional upon an animal's estimate of its roles (Hammerstein and Parker 1981).

Difficulties with the ESS approach largely concern defining the appropriate strategy set for a particular game. It is not always easy to decide what mutant strategies may be possible, and what the payoffs would be. Further, it is not likely to be fruitful to attempt to test ESS models by trying to observe mutant strategies in nature! Despite this sort of difficulty, the fit between the predictions of many ESS models and behavior observed in nature is often encouraging, and the ESS concept must certainly be regarded as one of the major developments in SOCIOBIOLOGY.

GAP

Bibliography

Dawkins, R. 1976: *The selfish gene*. Oxford and New York: Oxford University Press.

*Dawkins, R. 1980: Good strategy or evolutionarily stable strategy? In *Sociobiology: Beyond Nature/Nurture?* ed. G.W. Barlow and J. Silverberg. Boulder, Colarado: Westview Press.

Dawkins, R. 1982: *The extended phenotype*. Oxford and San Francisco: W.H. Freeman.

Hammerstein, P. 1981: The role of asymmetries in animal contests. *Animal behavior* 29, 193–205.

Hammerstein, P. and Parker, G.A. 1981: The asymmetric war of attrition. *Journal of theoretical biology* (in press).

Maynard Smith, J. 1972: *On evolution*. Edinburgh: Edinburgh University Press.

Maynard Smith, J. 1974: The theory of games and the evolution of animal conflicts. *Journal of theoretical biology* 47, 209–221.

*Maynard Smith, J. 1979: Game theory and the evolution of behavior. *Proceedings of the Royal Society of London B* 205, 475–88.

Maynard Smith, J. 1981: Will a sexual population evolve to an ESS? *American naturalist* 117, 1015–18.

Maynard Smith, J. and Parker, G.A. 1976: The logic of asymmetric contests. *Animal behavior* 24, 159–75.

Oster, G. and Wilson, E.O. 1978: *Caste and ecology in the social insects*. Princeton: Princeton University Press.

Parker, G.A. 1982: Phenotype-limited evolutionarily stable strategies. In *Current problems in sociobiology*, ed. King's College Sociobiology Group. Cambridge: Cambridge University Press.

evolution *See above, and* genetics, evolution and behavior

existential analysis A form of psychotherapy concerned with reestablishing meaning in the lives of persons who have lost it. This psychotherapy is practiced by existential psychologists who have been influenced by philosophers such as Kierkegaard, Heidegger and Sartre. In synthesizing the work of existential psychologists and philosophers Kobasa and Maddi (1977) delineate the major assumptions about personality as follows:

(1) persons create meaning through the decision-making process;

(2) decisions invariably take the form of choosing the future (the unknown) or the past (the already familiar status quo);

(3) although choosing the future brings anxiety (fear of the unknown), choosing the past brings guilt (a sense of missed opportunity);

(4) choosing the future is desirable because it is the way of continued growth through creating meaning, whereas choosing the past leads to stagnation and eventual meaninglessness;

(5) in order to tolerate the anxiety associated with choosing the future, persons need to have developed hardiness (defined as attitudes of commitment rather than alienation, control rather than powerlessness, and challenge rather than threat) in early life;

(6) persons who tend to choose the future become individualistic, continue to grow, and feel vitality based in an expanding and deepening sense of life's meaningfulness;

(7) in contrast, persons who tend to choose the past become conformists, who change little, and increasingly experience boredom, stagnation, meaninglessness and despair about life. In addition they are vulnerable to stress-related disorders, because they experience changes as stressful, and are relatively unable to cope with them.

Although existential analysis can and is used on the entire range of psychopathological symptoms, it is especially relevant to states of meaninglessness and stress-related disorders. In providing an illustration of this approach, Maddi has synthesized the techniques employed by several existential psychotherapists, such as Binswanger, Boss, Frankl, Gendlin, Kobasa, May and himself. Existential analysis emerges as a confrontational approach, in which the therapist is active in asking difficult questions, indicating that he is not convinced, and requiring that the client accept responsibility for both actions and passivity. Needless to say, the confrontations are done in an overall context in which the client knows that he or she is cared for and supported in his or her efforts to construct a meaningful life. Therapy sessions emphasize the present and the future, dwelling less on events of the remote past. Further, the waking state is regarded as the most relevant datum, existential analysis not concerning itself with supposedly unconscious mental states. As such, there is little discussion of dreams, and when they are discussed it is in the same terms as waking experiences.

Existential analysis contrasts sharply with such humanistically-oriented therapies as person-centered counseling in being more confrontational, and such dynamic approaches as psychoanalysis in putting more emphasis on conscious experience. Typical techniques of existential analysis which underline its differences from other approaches are discussed by Maddi as follows:

(1) paradoxical intention, a technique of value when clients have symptoms which frighten them because they do not seem to be able to exercise any control over them. For example, a business executive may worry because he blushes whenever any pressure is put on him. He may feel that his whole career is jeopardized by this tell-tale sign of weakness. In employing paradoxical intention, the therapist encourages the client to exaggerate the symptom and try to blush even more under even more circumstances, so that everyone will know how threatened he feels. Clients usually resist intending paradoxically at first, then see the humor of the situation, and, once they actually adopt the suggestion, find that the symptom diminishes. From an existential viewpoint, the client has gained control over the uncontrollable symptom by attempting to increase it and thereby facing up to his or her worst fears.

(2) focussing, a technique whereby clients can identify their real feelings about a problem and then transform those feelings into something less debilitating. When the client comes up with a problem, he is asked to concentrate on the feeling it provokes. He then lets an aspect of the feeling dominate his attention. Then he is asked to find some new words or pictures to capture the feeling. The new words or pictures become the felt meaning derived from focussing. In focussing on the problem of not being able to study, clients can transcend the conventional conclusions that they are merely "lazy" or "full of self-pity", understanding instead that they are too frightened of failure to perform.

(3) Situational reconstruction, a technique whereby clients can construct a sense of options and of immutable givens in problematic circumstances. When a stressful event has occurred (e.g. a manager has been unfavorably evaluated by his superior, and failed to get promotion), he is encouraged to imagine three ways in which the situation could have been worse, and three ways in which it could have been better. Clients typically resist this instruction when they are obsessively preoccupied with the troublesome event as they remember it. But once they have succeeded in the imaginative task, they can better see the lines along which the event can be transformed mentally. Further, they will have provided themselves with ideas about how to change the circumstance itself. These ideas about change in one's person and in one's circumstances form a basis for dealing with the current problem, but also for anticipating future events beneficially.

(4) Compensatory self-improvement, a technique whereby clients confronted with a debilitating problem with which they appear incapable of coping can increase their sense of worth and control by improving their

capabilities in some other area of life. If no amount of situational reconstruction produces a sense that stressful events can be transformed, the meaning of those events is temporarily or permanently a given. In such instances attention is profitably shifted to some important deficiency that seems more changeable. By improving themselves in this fashion, clients remind themselves that they can still exercise control in other areas of life. Sometimes, they can even return to the original recalcitrant problem with greater conviction that they can cope with it.

The four techniques mentioned are useful in building hardiness. The commitment aspect of hardiness increases as the client is able to deal with problematic events of everyday life in the supportive, caring setting of psychotherapy. The control aspect of hardiness increases as the client is better able to identify feelings, discern possibilities, improve deficiencies and transform unpleasant circumstances by thought and action. The challenge aspect is increased as discussions between client and therapist clarify how the presenting problems came about because of adherence to convention and a tendency to choose the past, and how the future must be approached in a different way. This process of learning hardiness takes place simultaneously with actual attempts to choose the future in everyday life. The therapist provides understanding support in the early stages of this effort. When future-oriented decisions are reasonably common, the time to terminate therapy is near.

The techniques of existential psychotherapy are specific to it, but in the overall aim of increasing hardiness and encouraging future-oriented choices they resemble other humanistic approaches to some degree. Gestalt psychotherapy and rational–emotive therapy are fairly close in spirit to existential analysis. SRM

Bibliography

Kobasa, Suzanne C. and Maddi, Salvatore R. 1977: Existential personality theory. In *Current personality theory*, ed. R. Corsini. Itasca, Ill.: Peacock.

existentialism Existentialism is the name not of a school but of a style of philosophy, popularized especially in France after the second world war, but having its origins primarily in Germany. Its central concern was with human freedom.

The main influence on existentialist philosophers was the work of Kierkegaard (1813–55), Nietzsche (1844–1900) and Husserl (1859–1938), and the first two of these have sometimes been thought of as themselves existentialists. Sören Kierkegaard (1813–1855) aimed to release his readers from the "illusion of objectivity", and thus from the fake authority of science and of systematic philosophy, such as that of Hegel. He held that truth was essentially a personal realization, unique to each individual, and could not be ossified into dogma. He thought that the task of philosophy was to reinstate subjectivity, especially in ethics and religion.

Nietzsche equally propounded a theory within which the individual was central. The setting up of absolute standards, whether of scientific truth or of morality, was simply a species of fraud. It was a way in which the strong exercised power over the weak. A man who understood his own power, and his own free will (or will-to-power, which was the same) could establish his own criteria both of truth and morality. Freedom was freedom to overthrow the established categories within which most of us passively lead our lives.

It was the extreme individualism and the missionary demand to rethink all accepted values that passed from these philosophers into existentialism. From Edmund Husserl came the belief that the consciousness of each person is the starting point of philosophy. A conscious being (a being-for-himself) is necessarily conscious not only of things in the world which are the objects of awareness, but at the same time of himself. It is this feature which marks off the human subject; and it is from this that human freedom is derived.

The central text in existentialist philosophy is perhaps *Being and nothingness* by J.P. Sartre (1905–1980) (though some would argue that Heidegger's *Being and time* should be given this position). *Being and nothingness* was published in France in 1945. It is a vast and fruitful book. The point of its title is that existence is of two kinds, being-in-itself, the being of unconscious objects; and conscious existence. Consciousness is characterized as not only *self*-conscious (being-for-itself) but as capable of conceiving negatives, what is *not* the case, as well as what is. This is the meaning of "nothingness", (*le néant*) in the title of the book. To be able to grasp what is not, as well as what is, is to be able to conceive of possibilities, of how things might be otherwise. The human being is for ever envisaging futures which are possibilities, not actualities, and thus projecting himself forward, into action which will change the present situation. It is this that makes freedom a reality. A being which is not conscious has no freedom. It is bound by necessity to behave in accordance with its nature. But humans, in this sense, have no nature. They *are* whatever they *become* by action. Constantly aiming to leave the present for some envisaged possible future, a man makes himself whatever he chooses to be.

Both Sartre and Heidegger wanted to show that in some sense man was completely free. Though Heidegger spoke always of human beings as in the world (*Dasein*), and paid more attention to features of that world that were not under man's control, neither he nor Sartre really solved the problem of reconciling human freedom with the manifest restrictions on it imposed by the natural world. Sartre was inclined to say that social restrictions, at least, were imaginary; and he had no use for any theory of psychological necessity. If anyone claimed that, for whatever reason, he was *bound* to do something, or *could not help it*, Sartre replied that this was Bad Faith, a form of self-deception designed to lighten or evade what was otherwise an intolerable burden of responsibility. If man is genuinely free, whatever he does is done of his own choice; and even his character is simply compounded out of all the free choices he has made in the past. Thus, like Nietzsche, Sartre held that, if he is honest, a man must choose his own morality, and not fall back on the security of absolute "moral standards". Since each man is choosing for himself, and struggling to be free from the roles and categories imposed on him by others, in *Being and nothingness* Sartre argues that the existence of other people is a threat. Personal relations can never be other than a struggle for power. But some existentialists took a less gloomy view of the human predicament; some believed that man was free to be reconciled with God. Some, such as Karl Jaspers, came to existentialism through a practice of a psychiatry based on phenomenology. The common factor was a concept of freedom, which turned every act, or failure to act, into a positive choice. And in choosing, a man, having no fixed essence but only existence in time, chose what he was to be; he chose himself.

Although Sartre wrote in *What is literature?* that a writer must necessarily be "committed", as a pure existentialist it was impossible for him to be committed to any political party as having a monopoly of what is right. For that would have been Bad Faith. To take on the discipline of the party whip would be to deny freedom. But gradually pure existentialism gave way to something more constructive. It was a short-lived philosophy, which eminently suited the French under the occupation, but quite soon after the war it was swallowed up in various forms of Marxism. It had a considerable influence, however, through Sartre and other writers, on the history both of the theater and the novel, and on literary criticism; a greater influence indeed than it had on moral philosophy or metaphysics. MW

Bibliography

Olafson, F.A. 1967: *Principles and persons.* Baltimore: Johns Hopkins.

expectancy Anticipation of some future event. Tolman developed a theory of learning based on the notion of expectancy, the fundamental idea being that organisms exposed to regular sequences of events came to expect or anticipate later members of the sequence as soon as the earlier occurred. A rat that had learned to run through a maze to obtain food was said to expect that food would be delivered if it performed certain responses, or if certain stimuli (those associated with the correct path through the maze) appeared.

It can hardly be doubted that animals are sensitive to regularly repeating sequences of events. A simple demonstration is provided by an experiment on HABITUATION. If an animal is repeatedly exposed to a particular stimulus (a tap, a noise, a light) presented at regular intervals, the reaction initially elicited by that stimulus will soon habituate. But if the regular sequence is interrupted, e.g. simply by omitting the stimulus at a time when it would normally have occurred, the animal will show, by an abrupt change in its behavior, pricking its ears, turning its head towards the source of the stimulus, that it has detected this omission. To do so, it must presumably have formed some representation of the regular sequence: it must, in other words, have been expecting the stimulus to occur and been surprised when it did not.

The resistance to an expectancy theory arises from a doctrinaire adherence to a strong form of BEHAVIORISM, which requires the psychologist to study and predict only what his subject does, and does not allow him to appeal to any inner mental life to explain that behavior. But it soon became apparent that, even with inarticulate organisms (perhaps particularly with them), what an animal has learned or may be said to know is not always immediately evident in its behavior. Although it may have been true that in Tolman's theory as Guthrie said, "the rat is left buried in thought", this is paradoxically a virtue if it means that the theory stresses the gap between knowledge and action. Recent trends in the theory of learning have marked a return to Tolman's views, and few theorists today are troubled by talk of expectancies of reinforcement, differences in the effectiveness of expected and unexpected reinforcement, or animals being surprised by the occurrence of an unexpected event or the omission of an expected one.

People talk readily of expecting things to happen, or forming expectations about the outcome of some experiment. There would be something anomalous about a human psychology that refused to acknowledge expectancies. And indeed the concept is used in fields as diverse as psychophysics, studies of reaction times, utility and decision making. NJM

Bibliography

Tolman, Edward C. 1932: *Purposive behavior in animals and men.* New York: Appleton-Century Crofts.

expectancy theory In the field of WORK MOTIVATION this theory was first developed by Vroom (1964) based on earlier theories of Lewin and Tolman. Conceived primarily as a theory of choice, it asserts that the force to perform a certain act is the sum of the products of the "valences" of the outcomes of the act and the degree of expectancy that a given act will be followed by those outcomes. Valence is defined as anticipated satisfaction; thus expectancy theory is a type of calculative hedonism in that it is assumed that people will attempt to maximize satisfaction. Subsequent developments have led both to elaborations of the theory and to the questioning of some of its basic assumptions (Campbell and Pritchard 1976). The elaborations have involved positing two types of expectancies: that the subject will be able to perform the act (often a surrogate ability measure), and that if it is performed the outcome will follow (instrumentality). It has also been argued that expectancy theory predicts goal choice or goal acceptance better than it does behavior. The theory seems to predict action best when only positive valences are used, when the task situation is highly structured, and when small or moderate numbers of outcomes are considered. Theoretically, the assumption of hedonism has been criticized as has the premise that people are aware of all their values or valences (Locke 1975). EAL

Bibliography

Campbell, J.P. and Pritchard, R.D. 1976: Motivation theory in industrial and organizational psychology. In *Handbook of industrial and organizational psychology*, ed. M.D. Dunnette. Chicago: Rand McNally.

Locke, E.A. 1975: Personnel attitudes and motivation. *Annual review of psychology*, 26, 457–80.

Vroom, V.H. 1964: *Work and motivation.* New York: Wiley.

experimental aesthetics The empirical study of processes underlying aesthetic creation and appreciation. Quantified responses of a representative sample of subjects are used. In general, laboratory experiments relate specific properties (e.g. stylistic: abstract versus representational) or collative ones (e.g. complexity, novelty) to judgments and emotional (e.g. pleased or interested) responses. Correlational analyses may also be performed relating personality attributes of the subjects to the aesthetic sensibilities and preferences. Cross-cultural studies and issues of the environment and leisure have added an applied dimension to scientific aesthetics.

This scientific approach to aesthetics was preceded 100 years ago by a speculative "aesthetics from above" which treated individual experience as authoritative and derived value judgments from abstract systems (Berlyne 1971). Gustav Fechner (1801–87) was the first experimental psychologist to introduce an "aesthetics from below" which avoided value judgments and sought instead the elementary stimulus determinants of aesthetic pleasure. His "method of choice", requiring the subject to select a preferred stimulus from among an experimentally manipulated array of alternatives, is frequently used today (forced-choice paradigm). Researchers during the next half-century studied the effects of simple stimuli such as lines, colors and musical tones on aesthetic pleasure.

In the 1950s those interested in experimental aesthetics began to use concepts from INFORMATION THEORY and also new statistical procedures. Daniel E. Berlyne (1924–76) developed a research strategy which integrated information theory with a behavioral analysis of curiosity and exploration. He pioneered the use of multidimensional scaling and factor analysis for classifying aesthetic stimuli (analytic research approach) and identified basic dimensions of aesthetic response (i.e., pleasedness and interestedness). In addition, he constructed artificial stimuli (both visual and auditory) to determine the effects of his collative properties (synthetic research approach) on aesthetic responses (Berlyne 1971, 1974).

The challenge for the future is to design experiments to investigate the appreciator's search for the emotional and intellectual meaning of the stimulus during the course of an aesthetic experience. These mediating interpretive processes must be elucidated, as the reduction of aesthetic pleasure to biological reinforcement does not account for the uniqueness of aesthetic experience. The process of aesthetic creation and innovation also needs to be studied. While the information theoretic analysis of stimulus novelty in terms of uncertainty and information density may be appropriate for the synthetic research approach, it does not help us to understand the causes or the impact of aesthetic originality within the framework of a culture and its history. GCC

Bibliography

Berlyne, D.E. 1971: *Aesthetics and psychobiology.* New York: Appleton-Century-Crofts.

——1974: *Studies in the new experimental aesthetics.* Washington: Hemisphere.

Child, I.L. 1969: Esthetics. In *The Handbook of social psychology* vol. 3. Eds. G. Lindzey and E. Aronson. Reading, Mass.: Addison-Wesley.

Day, H.I. 1981: *Advances in intrinsic motivation and aesthetics.* New York: Plenum.

exploration: animal A form of APPETITIVE BEHAVIOR by which it is assumed that the animal gains knowledge of its environment. Some forms of exploratory behavior seem to be aimed at a specific goal, but other forms sometimes appear to be motivated by curiosity, and to have no obvious relevance to more material aspects of behavior, such as feeding, sexual behavior or nest maintenance. Studies of such apparently motiveless aspects of exploration, which include play, show that learning does take place, and this may be a prime function of exploration. DJM

exploration: in human development In a specific sense, exploration consists in actively seeking out and investigating novelty by means of the sensory apparatus or through motor responses or both. Its adaptive value may be that specific exploration allows the organism to test situations of potential significance and hence to reduce uncertainty concerning the properties of a complex environment. It has also been argued that exploration may, in a general sense, serve the purpose of increasing physiological arousal through active seeking of stimulation. Hence, exploration may dispel uncertainty and maintain the activation level of the nervous system at an optimum.

In developmental psychology exploration has been closely linked with PLAY and CURIOSITY. Individual differences in exploratory behavior during infancy have also been related to security of attachment. The child who is securely attached is more willing to venture on exploratory forays in strange environments, perhaps because it knows that it can always return to a safe base. GEB

Bibliography

Bruner, J.S., Jolly, A. and Sylva, K. 1976: *Play; its role in development and evolution.* Harmondsworth: Penguin; New York: Basic Books.

exposure *See* mere exposure effects

expressed emotion It was noted twenty-five years ago that schizophrenic patients discharged to family homes did less well than expected. The concept of expressed emotion (EE) has been developed to measure aspects of familial interaction which can be used to predict relapse in schizophrenics. It requires assessment of the behavior of the key relative at the time of admission, relying particularly on critical attitudes or over-involvement, and is independent of the clinical state of the patient at discharge. EE's measurement and value are now well established. Patients who return to high EE relatives with whom they are in close contact have a greater than even chance of relapse in the following nine months, even if they are on phenothiazine medication. In contrast, the relapse rate in patients returning to low EE homes is only 10 per cent. Recently Leff and his colleagues have reduced relapse rates in patients in close contact with high EE relatives to 10 per cent by reducing EE or the degree of contact with relatives. They used a composite package of education of relatives, relatives' groups and a form of FAMILY THERAPY. The clinical implications of this work are likely to be very important. PB

Bibliography

Bebbington, P.E. and Kuipers, L. 1982: The social management of schizophrenia. *British journal of hospital medicine*. In press.

Brown, G.W., Birley, J.L.T. and Wing, J.K. 1972: Influence of family life on the course of schizophrenic disorders: a replication. *British journal of psychiatry* 121, 241–58.

Kuipers, L. 1979: Expressed emotion: a review. *British journal of social and clinical psychology* 18, 237–43.

Leff, J.P., et al. 1982: A controlled trial of social intervention in schizophrenic families. *British journal of psychiatry*. 141, 121–34.

expressive behavior Serious investigation of basic forms of expressive behavior began with Darwin (1872), who proposed that FACIAL EXPRESSIONS of primary emotions in man and animals were both universal and innate.

This theme was pursued much later by ethologists in their examination of displays among birds, bees, fish and other organisms. The work of Tinbergen (1952) and Lorenz (1966) is notable in this context. Specific attention to expressive displays among higher primates is shown in the work of Van Hoof (1963) and others.

Descriptive work concerning expressions and displays in children, with no assumptions being made about underlying emotional or motivational states, has been reported by Blurton-Jones (1972) and others, who have attempted to construct a full taxonomy of expressive movements and argue that this is a prerequisite for the testing of theories concerned with the relationship between expressions and antecedent conditions.

The comparative biological approach of Eibl-Eibesfeldt has focussed on alleged innate motor patterns of expression in various human cultures. He also argues that a learning-hypothesis cannot account for the form of basic expressions since these are also found in children born blind. Emphasis is also placed on the phylogenetic continuity of expressions associated with the states of fear, anger, happiness etc.

Cross-cultural psychological studies are reported by Izard (1971) and Ekman and Friesen (1975). Their studies involved tests of recognition using standardized photographs of emotional expressions such as fear, rage, interest, joy, shame etc. Responses to more complex expressions were also analysed. Further studies were concerned with the labeling of expressions.

These studies lend considerable support to the idea that basic forms of expressive behavior are universal. This, in turn, is seen as supporting Darwin's original assumptions of innateness. It must be noted, however, that such support comes only from data relating to the expression of *primary* emotions. Where more complex blends of emotion are expressed, recognition and labeling are found to be the subject of cross-cultural variation. Culturally defined "display-rules" are also instrumental in modifying the frequency and intensity of expressive behavior. PEM

Bibliography

Blurton-Jones, N., ed. 1972: *Ethological studies of child behavior*. Cambridge and New York: Cambridge University Press.

Darwin, C. 1872: *The expression of the emotions in man and animals*. London: John Murray.

Ekman, P. and Friesen, W.V. 1975: *Unmasking the face*. Englewood Cliffs, N.J.: Prentice-Hall.

Izard, C.E. 1971: *The face of emotion*. New York: Appleton-Century-Crofts.

Lorenz, K. 1966: *On aggression*. New York: Harcourt, Brace.

Tinbergen, N. 1952: "Derived" activities: their causation, biological significance, origin and emancipation during evolution. *Quarterly review of biology* 27 (1), 1–26.

Van-Hoof, J.A.R.A.M. 1963: Facial expression in higher primates. *Symposia of the Zoological Society of London* 10, 103–4.

extension The extension of a general term is the class of all those entities to which the term may correctly be applied. The extension of "horse" is the class consisting of all horses. A language is extensional if any two terms with the same extension or reference are interchangeable in any sentence without the truth value of the sentence changing. A language containing certain psychological predicates would appear not to be extensional. Smith may be looking for a unicorn and not for a centaur, even though each of these terms has the same extension, viz the null class. JMS

extinction The process of decline in performance of learned activities which are no longer reinforced. Some aspects of learning require reinforcement for the establishment and maintenance of the response. If the reinforcement is removed the response will start to be extinguished. For example, a rat may learn to obtain food by pressing a bar. If reward is withheld, so that bar presses no longer result in food delivery, the rate of bar pressing will gradually decline to zero, and the response is said to have become extinguished.

Extinction is due to a learned inhibition of the original learned response, and not to forgetting. This can be shown by the spontaneous recovery of the original response that sometimes occurs when the animal is placed in the training situation some time after the response has been extinguished.

The rate of extinction is partly a function of the similarity between the learning situation and the conditions of extinction. The greater the difference between the two sets of circumstances the more quickly extinction occurs. This effect is known as the GENERALIZATION decrement. The rate of extinction is also affected by the reinforcement schedule that operates during learning. If the rat is rewarded for every bar press a consistent reinforcement schedule is in operation, but if only some bar presses are rewarded the animal is said to be on a partial reward schedule. Extinction proceeds at a lower rate following a partial reward schedule compared with a consistent reward schedule. This effect, known as the partial reinforcement effect, has been the subject of a large amount of research, and it remains the subject of considerable controversy (Mackintosh 1974).

DJM

Bibliography

Mackintosh, Nicholas J. 1974: *The psychology of animal learning*. London & New York: Academic Press.

extrapyramidal motor system (See BRAIN AND CENTRAL NERVOUS SYSTEM: ILLUSTRATIONS, fig. 14). Includes the BASAL GANGLIA (figs. 22 and 28) and their associated subthalamic and BRAINSTEM nuclei and connections (fig. 16). Classically the three subdivisions of the motor system are the pyramidal system (fig. 13) which connects directly from the motor cortex to the SPINAL CORD and was thought to be involved with skilled voluntary movements; the extrapyramidal system, concerned with postural adjustments; and the cerebellar system (fig. 6), involved with coordinating movement. Actually these three parts are complexly interconnected and function as a single system. The pyramidal system is phylogenetically the newest portion of the system, and its development permitted higher animals to exert separate control over individual muscles. As the pyramidal system developed, the spinal connections of the extrapyramidal system appear to have become relatively less important. In higher mammals the major action of the extrapyramidal system seems to be through the pyramidal system.

Kornhuber (1974) has suggested that both the basal ganglia and the CEREBELLUM are movement pattern generators, and that sophisticated somatosensory regulation of generated movements is accomplished by the motor cortex. In his view, the cerebellum generates patterns for fast movements and the basal ganglia patterns for slow movements (see DeLong 1974). As the somatosensory and motor portions of CEREBRAL CORTEX (fig. 3) evolved, control of those movements requiring or benefiting from elaborate analysis of tactile inputs during movement moved to the motor cortex and utilized the pyramidal system. Those movements not requiring such analysis remained in the centers of the extrapyramidal system and may still use the descending pathways of that system.

The main structures of the extrapyramidal system are the basal ganglia (caudate nucleus, putamen, and globus pallidus), the subthalamic nucleus, the substantia nigra and the red nucleus. The major inputs to the extrapyramidal system are from the cerebral cortex (including, but not solely, the motor cortex), and the thalamus (figs. 15–19). The major output is to the THALAMUS with other connections to the spinal cord via the brainstem.

Motor disorders, such as Parkinson's disease and Huntingdon's disease, involve lesions of the basal ganglia. Parkinson's disease has been an important model system for the study of neural pathology resulting from a defect in neurotransmitter metabolism. SCC

Bibliography

*Côté, L. 1981: Basal ganglia, the extrapyramidal motor system, and diseases of transmitter metabolism. In *Principles of neural science*, ed. E.R. Kandel and J.H. Schwartz. New York and Oxford: Elsevier/North-Holland.

DeLong, M.R. 1974: Motor functions of the basal ganglia: single-unit activity during movement. In *The neurosciences*, Third Study Program, ed. F.O. Schmitt and F.G. Worden. Cambridge, Mass. and London: MIT Press.

Kornhuber, H.H. 1974: Cerebral cortex, cerebellum, and basal ganglia: an introduction to their motor function. In *The neurosciences*, Third Study Program, ed. F.O. Schmitt and F.G. Worden, Cambridge, Mass. and London: MIT Press.

extra sensory perception *See* ESP

extroversion and introversion Basic attitudes which, in combination with four common functions – thinking, feeling, sensation, and intuition – form the essential descriptive concepts of JUNG's typological characterization of personality. The attitudes describe the direction of psychological interest. In introversion the focus is centered on the internal, subjective, intrapersonal aspects of psychic life; in extroversion, on the external, objective, interpersonal side. Although both attitudes are inherently present in human personality structure, one becomes dominant in consciousness during the course of early development. The other remains largely unconscious until later life. Extroverts live according to external necessity, with high concern for adaptation to environmental demands. The orientation is toward object relations in which persons and things seize interest. In the introverted attitude inner needs are decisive. The orientation is toward the preservation of ego identity which may be threatened by focus on the object. Subjective states, ideas and feelings seize interest. Adjustment is directed toward meeting inner demands. IEA

eye contact *See* gaze

F

facial expression and emotion The face is the dominant site of nonverbal signaling. The facial skin shows the state of health or the embarrassment or arousal of the individual. Intentions and emotions are conveyed by expressions such as smiles or frowns, which may be used deliberately, or may unwittingly betray states of mind. Primates have facial expressions, but expressions also appear in (e.g.) other animals' snarls. The origin of expressions may be in INTENTION MOVEMENTS such as showing the teeth ready for attack; ritualization may then have turned them into signals (threats). Such a history would lead one to expect a large innate element in the forms of human expressions, since muscular movements which display anger do not seem to have an inherently different signaling function from the white (blood–drained) or red (blood-suffused) faces brought about by action of the AUTONOMIC NERVOUS SYSTEM.

Until recently however it was the differences in expressions across cultures which seemed most striking. Klineberg (1938) looked at the descriptions of emotional expressions (not only facial) in Chinese novels, and found many unfamiliar to westerners. For example stretching out the tongue is an expression of surprise. Attempts to find cross-cultural uniformities seemed generally to founder.

This was taken to mean that the use of the face in signalling was a culture-bound affair.

Darwin (1872) however was convinced that non-verbal signals were universal, and collected testimony from missionaries in far-flung places. He asked (e.g.) whether the natives used the grief muscle as Europeans do, or expressed anger in the same way. There were also studies of blind children, for example by Thompson and by Fulcher in the 1940s, which showed that blind and sighted children used the same facial muscles in posing or making natural faces such as smiles or expressions of fear or anger. Again studies of infant smiling found how early it appears in a recognizable form and how important it is for the bond between the mother and the child. It is unlikely that an expression which has such survival value and which appears within the first month of life could be other than innate.

Ethologists in particular tended to support the innateness hypothesis. Eibl-Eibesfeldt (Hinde 1973) found the "eyebrow flash" (raising the eyebrows maximally for about 1/6 second) used in distant salutations all over the world. He also filmed deaf and blind children to see if their patterns of facial expression differed from normals. There seemed to be no such differences, even with blind/deaf thalidomide children who had no arms and could therefore not learn by touch. Support for innateness was also produced by van Hooff, who found chimpanzees using various bared teeth displays in affirmation (open-mouthed) or in appeasement (horizontal display of teeth). He suggested that these expressions may be related phylogenetically to human laughter and smiling.

There are criticisms which can be leveled at the research with blind children, although they become less plausible as the difficulties of learning increase. Clearly ordinary blind children can have learnt their facial expressions (especially to pose them) from proprioceptive information and the labels others use, but this hardly seems true of the elicited, natural expressions of those who cannot hear. Likewise differences in the structure of the face which underlies expressions may undermine direct comparisons between men and chimps. Again there is evidence of a cultural and even possibly human impact on animals' facial expressions. Van Hooff recorded a vertical bared teeth display which he thought possibly "an idiosyncratic trait of this group". Bohlwig reported that baboons in captivity had far more developed "cordial laughter" expressions than in the wild.

The best evidence for innateness therefore remains the cross-cultural comparison, which has been carried on more seriously by Ekman and his colleagues. Their approach was from the work of those interested in emotions which are "basic" i.e. different from each other in facial expression and labeling (e.g. Plutchik 1962). Having decided, on the basis of these studies, to use six basic emotions, viz happiness, sadness, anger, disgust, surprise and fear, they selected photographs "which showed the facial components they hypothesized to be specific to each". These were shown to people from USA, Brazil, Chile, Argentina and Japan and there was very good agreement about which face went with which emotion. Because these cultures may have a lot in common and the agreement therefore be based on learning, Ekman and Friesen went to New Guinea to the Fore, a preliterate people who had little contact with outsiders. They used stories, such as, "A person's mother has died", and the subject selected the correct photograph (out of three). The fear and surprise expressions were confused, but otherwise the Fore agreed with previous subjects. Other Fore people were also asked to pose expressions to fit the stories. Videotapes of these poses were shown to American students who were fairly accurate in deciphering the expressions, except again the fear and surprise.

There are objections to these studies because they use stereotypes of emotional expressions. The innateness hypothesis claims that particular expressions are produced by emotions, not that particular expressions are seen by others as appropriate to particular emotions. Obviously universality of such conventions of perception would be difficult to explain unless there were an underlying emotion/expression link. Ekman however has worked with elicited emotion. A film of sinus surgery was shown to Japanese and to American students, who were videotaped while they watched it alone and while talking to a researcher about the experience. When alone both nationalities showed very similar expressions, although they differed in company. The similarity demonstrates that the same stimuli will produce similar expressions in different cultures. Since the Japanese and Americans reported similar feelings and showed similar physiological responses, there is good evidence that their emotions were also the same.

The different expressions in company illustrate Ekman's concept of a display rule. This explains the observed differences between cultures' facial expressions. Japanese expressions are notoriously difficult to interpret, even for the Japanese. Ekman suggests that they, in common with other cultures, have their own rules about the appropriateness of emotional display. Hence there are cultural differences in control of the face. There are also different values in different cultures, so the stimuli which elicit anger, say, or disgust may vary.

The expressions in this study were coded using Ekman's Facial Affect Scoring Technique atlas, which divides the face into three areas (brows, eyes and lower face). There are in all seventy criterion photographs, and the areas of the face can be coded separately by comparison with them. Because expressions are thereby broken down into components, it is possible to see that some expressions are blends of primary emotional expressions, showing (e.g.) a mixture of happiness in one area and surprise in another. There are other possible kinds of blend, such as a rapid sequence of two primary expressions. Ekman says that "without postulating... blended expressions ... we would not be able to account for the host of complex facial expressions... and of emotion words..."

At present the innateness and universality findings seem unassailable (although the small number of cultures used hardly allows Ekman's complete confidence). Other studies which concentrate specifically on the facial muscles also support the view that the face is linked to emotion. Schwartz for instance recorded from electrodes on the surface of four facial muscles. Subjects were instructed to think of happy, sad or angry experiences. No expressions were visible but the electrical readings allowed the types of thought to be distinguished. Laird and Shimoda have separately found that changes in one's facial expression produce changes in one's feelings.

It should be remembered, however, that many uses of facial expression are conventional. The posed smile for a photograph or in greeting mother-in-law are examples. Kraut and Johnston (1979) noted that people smile at others rather than just because of pleasant circumstances. Even where emotion is connected with facial expression the process appears modifiable by learning. Buck and his colleagues have found that women's facial expressions are more recognizable than men's. Women also verbally acknowledge the emotions, while men do not. The physiological measures appear inversely related to the recognizability of one's expression. This sex difference seems learnt, as there was not one between preschool girls and boys (1977). If this shows repression by men, it seems possible that Ekman's display rules may affect the amount of emotion experienced, and hence that culture may interfere more radically in the emotional process than the superficial concept of "display" implies. RL

Bibliography

Buck, R. 1977: Nonverbal communication of affect in preschool children. *Journal of personality and social psychology* 35, 225–36.

——— Miller, R.E. and Caul, W.F. 1974: Sex, personality, and physiological variables in the communication of affect via facial expression. *Journal of personality and social psychology* 30, 589–96.

Ekman, P. and Friesen, W.V. 1975: *Unmasking the face*. Englewood Cliffs, N.J.: Prentice Hall.

*Ekman, P., Friesen, W.V. and Ellsworth, P. 1972: *Emotion in the human face*. New York: Pergamon.

Ekman, P. and Oster, H. 1979: Facial expressions of emotion. *Annual review of psychology* 30, 527–54.

Hinde, R.A., ed. 1972: *Non-verbal communication*. Cambridge and New York: Cambridge University Press.

Kraut, R.E. and Johnston, R. 1979: Social and emotional messages of smiling. *Journal of personality and social psychology*. 37, 1539–53.

Laird, J.D. 1974: Self-attribution of emotion: the effects of expressive behavior on the quality of emotional experience. *Journal of personality and social psychology* 29, 475–86.

Schwartz, G.E. 1974: Facial expression and depression: an electromyogram study. *Psychosomatic medicine* 36, 458.

Other references may be found in the bibliographies of Ekman, Friesen and Ellsworth, and of Ekman and Oster.

family, the The human group centrally concerned with biological and social reproduction and generally considered a universal unit of social organizations in its nuclear or primary form as constituted by a man, a woman and their socially recognized children. Its broader composition varies with social structural and cultural factors and its meanings reflect its use in psychological as well as in sociological and biological theories. Within psychoanalytic theory the term family romance refers to fantasies which distort the subject's relationship with its parents, e.g., that it is an adopted child, but which have their origins in the Oedipus complex. The family and particularly the mother-child relationship is held to be extremely important in early development. Psychological and social development occurring as the result of living in the family is described as primary socialization. (See also ATTACHMENT). BBL

family therapy The treatment of the family group as a unit rather than of its individual members. This form of therapy developed in the USA during the late 1940s and 1950s at a time of growing recognition of the connection between disturbance in the child and parental problems. During the last decade the family approach has become increasingly popular in the mental health field. Early family therapists worked with families containing severely disturbed individuals but, later, they were joined by those who were moving away from traditional psychoanalytic approaches with individuals. A major impetus was given by studies of communication in the families of patients suffering from schizophrenia by G. Bateson and others, which generated new concepts about family interaction, including the double-bind hypothesis, pseudo-mutuality, schism and skew in family relationships. Ackerman (1958) was one of the early pioneers.

Ideas from general SYSTEMS THEORY, cybernetics, behavior therapy (Patterson 1971), group analysis and communication theory (Watzlawick et al. 1967) have been incorporated. General systems theory has provided the most comprehensive and widely used framework, providing a model for various approaches to therapy involving intervention in the family system to change it, such as "structural family therapy" (Minuchin 1974) and "strategic therapy" (e.g. Palazzoli 1978). The theoretical base, however, remains incomplete, with no uniform agreement about the most effective use of diverse strategies. An eclectic approach in the formulation of the family's problems and treatment plan is the most appropriate. Marital or couples therapy has developed alongside family therapy. H. Dicks (1967) pioneered conjoint treatment and important contributions have been made by behavioral (Jacobson and Margolin 1979) and group analytic methods. Techniques such as family sculpting, role-playing and play-back of video recordings are often employed.

A wide range of methods of family assessment are in use (e.g. Minuchin 1974) reflecting the numerous conceptual models of how families function. Data employed range from current interactional phenomena in the family to information about the family's developmental history, the families of origin and transgenerational influences, such as family myths. The McMaster Model of Family Functioning has been influential. It is concerned with information about problem solving, communication, roles, affective responsiveness, affective involvement and behavior control. There are widely differing opinions about the precise indications and contraindications for family therapy. In general, its consideration is appropriate in disorganized, dysfunctional families, when problems are presented in relationship terms, e.g. marital problems or parent-child separation difficulties, or when an individual's symptoms appear to be the outcome of emotional conflict in the family. Outcome studies tend to have methodological weaknesses including a lack of consistency in techniques employed, poor outcome measures, and the absence of control groups. As a result, despite much partisan enthusiasm, evaluation of the efficacy of family therapy and its place in psychiatric treatments is rudimentary.

WLLP-J

Bibliography

Ackerman, N.W. 1958: *The psychodynamics of family life.* New York: Norton.

*Barker, P. 1981: *Basic family therapy.* London: Granada; Baltimore: University Park Press.

Dicks, H. 1967: *Marital tensions.* London: Routledge & Kegan Paul; New York: Basic Books.

Jacobson, N.S. and Margolin, G. 1979: *Marital therapy: strategies based on social learning and behavior exchange principles.* New York: Brunner/Mazel.

Minuchin, S. 1974: *Families and family therapy.* Cambridge, Mass: Harvard University Press.

Palazzoli, M.S. et al. 1978: *Paradox and counterparadox.* New York: Jason Aronson.

Patterson, G. R. 1971: *Families: application of social learning to family life.* Champaign, Ill: Research Press.

*Skynner, A.C.R. 1976: *One flesh: separate persons.* London: Constable.

Watzlawick, P., Beavin, J.H. and Jackson, D.D. 1967: *Pragmatics of human communication.* New York: Norton.

fantasy: Freudian theory An imaginary and organized scene or episode dramatically fulfilling a conscious or unconscious wish, in which the subject appears as one of the actors. English psychoanalysts proposed the systematic use of two spellings and employed fantasy to refer to conscious constructions and phantasy to describe the content of unconscious processes. This distinction has been ignored in American and French writings.

For FREUD fantasies can operate at either a conscious or unconscious level. Unconscious fantasies are intimately tied to repressed infantile desires; they are the structures that underpin such unconscious products as dreams and symptoms. Conscious fantasies include daydreaming and fictions which fulfill wishes that are more accessible to the conscious mind mainly because they are given coherence by the process of secondary revision. Nevertheless in analysis even conscious fantasies can be seen to be connected to unconscious ones and the wishes they articulate.

Fantasy is given a central place in OBJECT RELATIONS theories, particularly in the writings of Melanie Klein. The term comes to mean the person's inner world of unconscious feeling and impulse – the effective source of *all* human behavior. It is believed that these phantasies are the unconscious content and that the content begins in the first minutes of the infant's life when his instinctual demands have to be met by the objects in his environment. The infant's phantasies are also connected with his need to satisfy unmet needs; early phantasies articulate instinctual urges both libidinal and destructive. As the child grows phantasies are elaborated; they are found in both normal and abnormal people and are seen to be *real* to the extent that they shape the person's inter-personal relationships. It is this dynamic reality of phantasies that prompted Isaacs to distinguish conscious fantasies from primary unconscious phantasies.

A connection between conscious mental activity and unconscious wishes is exploited in projective tests which employ a variety of ambiguous stimuli, e.g., inkblots, pictures or clouds, to assess unconscious motivation. (See also DAYDREAM; DREAMING).

BBL/JWA

Bibliography

Laplanche, J. and Pontalis, J-B 1973: *The language of psychoanalysis.* London: Hogarth; New York: Norton.

Riviere, J., ed. 1952: *Developments in psychoanalysis.* London: Hogarth.

fantasy: Singer's view Fantasies are sequences of mental images occurring when attention is transferred from the external environment or some primary goal and channeled towards an unfolding series of private responses. They usually concern possible events which have varying likelihoods of actually happening.

The study of fantasy has had a checkered history in psychology. Behaviorist psychology, with its emphasis on observable behavior neglected the study of fantasy because of its private nature. Cognitive approaches, especially information processing models of man have returned psychology to the study of mental processes.

On this view emphasis is placed on the cognitive–affective functions of fantasy. Mental imagery is seen as playing a key role in learning and adaptive behavior enabling the individual to alter emotional arousal (increasing or decreasing) in anticipation of future situations, providing feedback for the self-regulation of behavior, and exploring future possibilities without commitment to action.

Normative studies reveal that while there are individual differences in the development of this skill, almost all subjects report engaging in some form of daydreaming daily. Visual imagery is the most common modality and fantasy occurs when individuals are alone and in restful motor states. The most frequently reported daydreams concern future interpersonal situations. There is some evidence suggesting that as individuals pass from adolescence through young adulthood into middle age the content of fantasy changes to become more realistic, with at least a possibility of fulfillment. Unpleasant and bizarre fantasies also decrease with age.

The use of mental imagery has been incorporated into diverse psychotherapeutic techniques with different theoretical orientations ranging from insight psychotherapy, e.g. psychoanalysis to behavior modification treatments. It has been used successfully in the relief of irrational fears (phobias) in systematic desensitization therapy as well as in the elimination of unwanted behavior by aversive conditioning. The effectiveness of these treatments suggests the power of fantasy to modify behavior.

RBP-S

Bibliography

Singer, Jerome L. 1981: *Daydreaming and fantasy.* Oxford: Oxford University Press; New York: Oxford University Press (1975).

fantasy *See above, and also* emotion and fantasy

fear: animal A motivational state aroused by specific external stimuli and promoting avoidance, defensive and escape behavior. Fear may be aroused as an innate response to certain external stimuli such as loud noise, loss of support, and pain. The influential behaviorist psychologist J. B. WATSON maintained (1924) that these were the only stimuli capable of invoking fear as an instinct, and that most fear responses were acquired through conditioning. However the work of ethologists such as LORENZ and TINBERGEN showed that there is a variety of SIGN STIMULI of which animals have an innate fear. These include hawk-like silhouettes (Tinbergen 1951), eye-like patterns (Blest 1957) and certain owl features (Hinde 1954). Fear of snakes seems to be innate in various primates including man (Hebb 1946), and detailed studies of the maturation of fear in children provide no evidence for the behaviorist view that fear is primarily acquired as a result of conditioning (Gray 1971).

On the other hand there is also plenty of evidence that fear can be acquired through learning. In addition to their innate repertoire of responses to frightening stimuli, many animals are capable of learning to fear previously neutral stimuli, and of learning new responses to avoid frightening stimuli. Fear of previously neutral stimuli may develop through the process of classical conditioning, or association. When an animal responds to a frightening stimulus it does so in the presence of other neutral stimuli, such as background sounds and the visual features of everyday life. If one of these neutral stimuli is consistently paired with the frightening stimulus it is associated with it and eventually comes to elicit fear, even in the absence of the original frightening stimulus. J. B. Watson's well-known experiment in this field involved an eleven-month-old boy called Albert, who appeared to have no fear of animals. He did, however, show signs of fear at the sound of a steel bar being struck loudly. Albert initially showed no fear of a white rat, but when the rat was repeatedly presented together with the sound of the steel bar being struck he became frightened of the rat even when it was presented without any accompanying sound. Subsequent experiments have shown that although classical conditioning is undoubtedly important in the acquisition of fear it is easier to transfer fear (by a conditioning procedure) to some stimuli than to others. Albert may well have had a latent fear of animals (such fear develops rapidly during the second year of life) and would probably not have so readily acquired fear of a more neutral stimulus.

It is thought by many psychologists that the acquisition of new avoidance patterns is accomplished in two stages. In the first stage the animal learns to fear particular environmental stimuli, as a result of a consistent association with aversive situations. In the natural environment, for example, an animal might repeatedly see a predator when feeding in a particular locality, and might consequently acquire a fear of the feeding area as a result of conditioning.

In the second stage of avoidance learning the animal learns how to prevent or remove the fear. A bird which repeatedly saw a cat in a garden might acquire a fear of the garden, but could prevent the fear from arising simply by not visiting the garden. (see AVOIDANCE).

In addition to its role in motivation, fear also has an emotional aspect which is important in communication. The fearful animal has increased autonomic activity, including elevated heart beat rate, defecation, piloerection (hair standing up), and sweating. This activity is often accompanied by facial expressions and postures that are characteristic of the species.

The manifestation of such display varies with the circumstances. For example, radio-telemetry studies show that an incubating herring gull (*Larus argentatus*) has an increasing heart beat rate when approached by a human, even though there may be few outward signs of fear. In social situations, however, herring gulls incorporate outward signs of fear into their displays. This is particularly true of threat and of the conflict that arises in dispute over territory. At the territorial boundary there is usually a balance between aggression and fear which results in a classic approach–avoidance conflict. As the animal approaches its opponent the fear becomes greater than the aggression, so the tendency to retreat predominates. As the animal moves away the fear subsides and aggression predominates once more. In these circumstances, animals often show ambivalent, threat, redirected and displacement behavior. In some species these have become ritualized in such a way that their role in communication is enhanced and the direct involvement of fear is reduced.

Fear also provides a basis for social communication in the case of alarm. In many cases an alarm signal such as the call of a bird or the bobbing white tail of a rabbit is likely to attract the attention of a predator, and the individual that issues the alarm may be endangered. Such instances of altruism in which an individual disadvantages itself to the benefit of others, are thought to evolve only when the other animals are likely to be close relatives of the animal giving the alarm. Overt signs of fear, pain, or danger are generally absent when there is no clear benefit to the kin. The cricket (*Acheta domestica*) simply stops chirping when it senses danger. The chief beneficiaries of an alarm signal would probably be rival males. Similarly, antelopes that are pulled down by predators on the African plain suffer in silence. To call for help would only endanger other members of the herd.

Many of the physiological aspects of fear are also common to aggression. From the evolutionary viewpoint this is perhaps not surprising, because both are concerned with the protection and defense of the individual, its kin and resources. In vertebrates both involve autonomic activity which prepares the animal for emergency action. During sympathetic activation the blood supply to the brain, heart, lungs and muscles is increased, making the animal ready for 'fight or flight'. Mild fear may lead to increased vigilance which may give rise to aggression or defense, depending on whether a predator or rival is detected. Many aspects of defensive behavior are highly specialized and evolved to suit the animal's ecological niche. They sometimes involve elements of both fear and aggression. The scorpion uses its sting both to poison an attacker and against its prey. Similarly, snakes use their teeth and venom both for prey capture and for defense. The horns and antlers of antelopes and deer are primarily used in aggressive encounters between rivals, but may also be used in defense against predators. Some retaliatory defensive structures have evolved primarily as anti-predator devices. Examples include the spines of hedgehogs and porcupines, and of sticklebacks. The three-spined stickleback (*Gasterosteus aculeatus*), however, also uses its spines in encounters with rival males, and to ward off over-enthusiastic females during courtship. For some species the best form of defense is attack, while for others it is escape. In many species the mixture of fear and aggression is complex. Rats and pigeons usually show signs of fear when given electric shocks in the laboratory. If, however, another member of the species is present, it may well be attacked. DJM

Bibliography

Blest, A.D. 1957: The evolution of protective displays in the Saturnioidea and Sphingidae (lepidoptera). *Behavior* 11, 257–58.

*Edmunds, Malcolm 1974: *Defence in animals*. Harlow: Longman.

*Gray, Jeffrey 1971: *The psychology of fear and stress*. London: Weidenfeld & Nicolson; New York: McGraw-Hill.

Hebb, D. O. 1946: On the nature of fear. *Psychology review* 53, 259–76.

Hinde, R. A. 1954: Factors governing the changes in strength of a partially inborn response, as shown by the mobbing behavior of the chaffinch (*Fringilla coelebs*). *Proceedings of the Royal Society* 142, 306–31 and 331–58.

Tinbergen, Nikolaas 1951: *The study of instinct*. Oxford: Clarendon Press. Reprinted with new introduction Oxford, 1969.

Watson, John B. 1924: *Behaviorism*. New York: Norton. Reprinted 1958. Chicago: Chicago University Press; London: Cambridge University Press.

feedback The effect of the consequences of behavior on future behavior. Negative feedback occurs when the consequences diminish the level of performance of, or probability of, future behavior. The consequences of feeding (i.e. intake of food) have a diminishing effect upon hunger, and the animal is less likely to eat in the near future. Positive feedback occurs when the consequences increase the level of future behavior. In some cases, for instance, it is possible for feeding to have a temporary incremental effect upon appetite and so increase the apparent level of hunger. Positive feedback tends to be unstable, leading to escalation of the behavior, and in nature it is usually kept in check by simultaneous negative feedback (as in the case of feeding) or by environmental constraints.

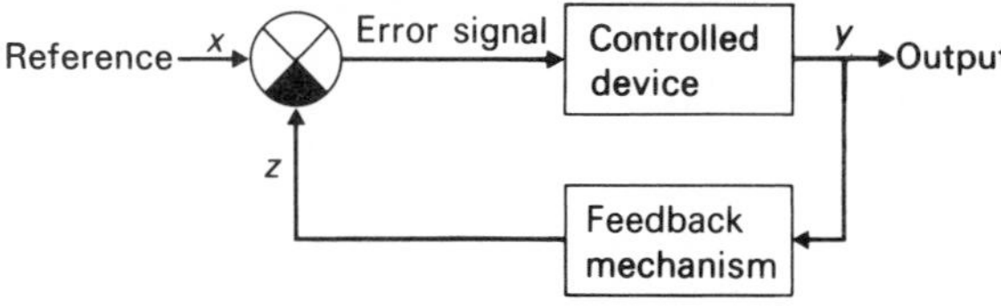

Negative feedback processes tend to have a stabilizing influence and they are particularly important in those aspects of animal behavior, such as homeostasis and orientation, in which maintenance of equilibrium is important. The essential elements of a negative feedback process are illustrated in the figure. The reference x represents the required level of output, and is usually supplied from some other part of the system. The error signal is the difference between the reference x and the feedback signal z. The error signal actuates the controlled device which produces an output y. In animal behavior studies y is usually some aspect of the behavior of the animal. The feedback mechanism monitors some aspect of the output and translates this into a signal z, which is subtracted from the reference x to give the error signal $(x\text{-}z)$. For example, the body temperature $x=39°C$ may be compared with a feedback signal (actual body temperature) of 38°C, giving an error signal of 1°C. This actuates the warning mechanisms of the body (controlled device) to increase heat output y. The consequent rise in body temperature is sensed by the feedback mechanism, and z consequently becomes larger. The feedback mechanisms that operate in real physiological and behavioral control systems are considerably more complex than that illustrated here, but the principle remains the same. DJM

feminism in psychology Over the last fifteen years political feminism has had extensive effects on social science. No social scientist predicted the rise of feminism in the 1960s, but no social science has remained subsequently untouched by it. There has been an explosion of research on women, on sex roles and on sex differences. Social science research has contributed to our understanding of sexual inequality, and has provided support for legislative action. This research has produced an extensive body of new knowledge, but, in addition, social scientists in all disciplines have been engaged in a major reconsideration of the concept of "gender", which has had a substantial effect on theory and methodology.

The early feminist-based critiques of psychological practice focussed on biasses in method – the under-representation of women in sampling, the tendency to generalize to the whole human race from all-male samples, and the fact that social scientists were inclined to ignore many areas of life which are predominantly the domain of women (Dan and Beekman 1972). As research progressed the complexity of the problems became more apparent. Research which suggested the relative unimportance of biological or innate sex differences, and undermined simple biological determinism, revealed the conflicts and paradoxes of sex roles. Attention has latterly been paid to reformulating both cultural and scientific conceptions of masculinity and femininity, in the light of inadequacies in the traditional dichotomy, since it has consistently been demonstrated that characteristics which are associated with femininity are devalued by social scientists and by society in general. It seems that Aristotle's view that "we should regard female nature as afflicted with a natural deficiency" dies hard.

The distinction between masculinity and femininity is an essential element in most cultures. Gender is the primary social category and the basis of social classification and of social relationships. We grow up aware that the basic polarity is both antithetical and symbiotic. Recent research has demonstrated that the gender dichotomy is related to many other dichotomies in symbolic classification in western culture; for example active–passive, instrumental–expressive, nature–culture, internal–external, analytic–intuitive and agency–communion (Glennon 1979). Children acquire knowledge of the cultural stereotypes of gender very early; they also learn that gender is associated with anxiety, and that there are different evaluations of masculine and feminine (Ullian 1976). Much recent research has been concerned with the nature and extent of sex stereotypes, and the way in which they affect interpersonal perception, our explanations of others' behavior, and the goals we deem to be personally desirable or unacceptable.

Stereotypical social classifications serve a number of psychological functions; they reduce complexity, they provide convenient definitions of "in" and "out" groups, and they provide simple models for emulation and for self-definition. Stereotypes can also serve to defuse threat. Clifton, McGrath and Wick (1976), for example, found that the general stereotype of women was sub-divided, particularly by men, into four categories, which they labeled "housewife", "bunny", "careerwoman" and "athlete". The first two of these categories included different aspects of the general "feminine" stereotypes; the latter two involved predominantly "masculine" characteristics. It is tempting to draw parallels with the Greek pantheon, which provided separate and distinct roles for women – Hera and Venus, the "feminine" women who related to men, and Athene and Artemis, representing wisdom and active independence, whose separateness from men was symbolized by their virginity.

The paradoxes, contradictions and evaluative connotations of stereotypical gender classification have been demonstrated in innumerable studies. Broverman, Rosenkrantz and associates found that the characteristics which were regarded as socially desirable and healthy in adults (sex unspecified), were those associated with males, but not those associated with females – a mentally healthy woman was therefore seen to be a mentally unhealthy adult (Broverman et al. 1970). Activity and general competence seem to be incompatible with feminity. If females succeed, observers and agents tend to put the success down to luck or extra effort, whereas male success is due to ability (Feldman-Summers and Kiesler 1974). When females fail, it is from lack of ability, when males do it is from bad luck or laziness.

Many forms of speech have different connotations for each sex (for example swearing, terms of endearment and expressive style), and women switch to a "neutral" form of language when they wish to be taken "seriously" (Lakoff 1973). Men make a similar adjustment when expressing intimacy and tenderness. Some subjects, for example science and technology, are seen as distinctively masculine, and to require the kind of thinking that is associated with a masculine style (Weinreich-Haste 1981).

The pervasiveness of sex stereotypes can lead to psychological conflicts for both sexes, but particularly for females. Paradoxically while a dualistic culture expects different things from males and females, coping with adult life demands a common set of capacities and skills. Women who conform to stereotypical "feminine" personality characteristics, particularly if they are engaged solely in the most stereotypically feminine activities, as wives and mothers, are more prone to depression. Women who enter non-traditional occupations, and women who hold non-traditional sex role attitudes, tend to have personality characteristics and family backgrounds (such as an active or working mother) which have either reduced the impact of social norms in childhood, or have equipped them to resist the social pressures to conform. Many women manifest role conflict; Horner, for example, found that many academically gifted women showed a "motive to avoid success" if they saw achievement to be in conflict with femininity (Horner 1970).

Psychologists have documented the conflicts and contradictions of the female role in parallel with the changes in political attitudes. The political response has been a massive effort towards redefinition of both existing and ideal social roles. The process of redefinition is difficult and painful and, for the individual, involves considerable psychological effort, which results in extensive reappraisal of the self and of social and interpersonal relations. The main outcome is that women come to define themselves in autonomous terms, not, as traditionally, in terms of their relationship to men (Goldschmidt et al. 1974). Psychologists have become aware of the extent to which they have uncritically accepted cultural assumptions concerning masculinity and femininity, and (like Thomas Aquinas) have tended to define women as "imperfect men".

Recently our understanding of the traditional symbolic male–female duality has been enlarged by the development of various concepts of androgyny. Within psychology, there are two distinct formulations of androgyny.

The first is *integrative*. It focusses on the ways in which the sexes are more alike than they are different, cf. the research of Bem (1974) and others. They devised sex role scales which broke with the traditional measures which *polarized* masculinity and femininity. Their scales measure masculinity and femininity separately, so an individual may be identified as "sex-typed" (high on one and low on the other), "androgynous" (high on both) or "undifferentiated" (low on both). It had already been suggested that a balance of masculine and feminine characteristics was desirable, and indeed it emerges from studies using Bem's scale that the androgynous person is mentally and physically healthier and more adaptable (Williams 1979). The implications are that research should be directed to identifying the social origins of gender differentiation, with a view to finding ways of reducing its effects.

The second conception of androgyny is *dualistic and dialectical*. It recognizes that there are important gender differences, in the sense that there are definable "masculine" and "feminine" styles of thought, behavior and social interaction. The main problem is seen to be the under-valuation of the feminine and the failure to acknowledge it as a valid alternative to the currently dominant masculine principle. This model seeks to identify what is specific about the feminine, and about the "feminine" pole of the various other dichotomies, Gilligan (1977), for example, has found that there is a distinctively female way of thinking about moral and personal dilemmas; whereas males (see MORAL DEVELOPMENT) focus on issues of rights and justice, females are oriented to the interpersonal and relational. Several studies have specifically addressed Bakan's distinction between *agency* (individual orientation, focus on the self and self-expansion) and *communion* (orientation to others, seeing the self as part of a social whole (Bakan 1966)). This distinction is one which matches the masculine–feminine duality. These studies demonstrate that women tend to have a greater appreciation than men of the interpersonal, and demonstrate better integration of their various biological and social roles.

There is considerable overlap between these two notions of androgyny and in practice the distinction is not always sharp. The aim of both is to provide a more balanced and accurate model of the person. The difference is in their implications for research and policy. The first conception implicitly assumes that a patriarchal society exaggerates and fosters gender differences, and that pointing out their social origins will ameliorate their potentially disastrous effects, clearly an aspect of the nature–nurture debate. The second conception recognizes the reality of gender differences, and aims for a re-evaluation of the feminine, rather than for transcendence of masculinity and femininity. An understanding of the origin of gender differences is less important for this approach. What is at issue is the dynamic relationship between masculinity and femininity within society (in both practical and symbolic forms) and within the individual.

The effects of redefinition of the social role of women are already evident. There are perceptible changes in the presentation of women in the media, and some headway has been made in removing the sexist assumptions and images from children's books and educational material. Sexual behavior has altered, apparently, with little gap now between male and female experience, and with women having greater expectations of sexual fulfilment. In both mental and physical health there is increasing recognition that the normal crises and cycles of women's lives are problematic but not pathological, and that the paradoxes and conflicts of the traditional female role cannot be ignored in any consideration of women's mental health. But perhaps the most pervasive change has been in *rhetoric*. The women's movement has created its own, and this has effectively alerted everyone to the issues of gender differentiation. The effects of the women's movement on psychology have therefore been considerable. HW-H

Bibliography

Bakan, D. 1966: *The duality of human existence.* Chicago: Rand McNally.

Bem, S.L. 1974: The measurement of psychological androgyny. *Journal of consulting and clinical psychology* 42, 155–62.

Broverman, I.K. et al. 1970: Sex role stereotypes and clinical judgements of mental health. *Journal of consulting and clinical psychology* 34, 1–7.

Clifton, A.K., McGrath, D. and Wick, B. 1976: Stereotypes of women: a single category? *Sex roles* 2, 135–48.

Dan, A.J. and Beekman, S. 1972: Male v. female representation in psychological research. *American psychologist* 27, 1078.

Feldman-Summers, S. and Kiesler, S.B. 1974: Those who are number two try harder: the effect of sex on attributions of causality. *Journal of personality and social psychology* 30, 846–55.

Gilligan, E. 1977: In a different voice: women's conception of self and morality. *Harvard educational review* 47, 481–518.

Glennon, L.M. 1979: *Women and dualism.* London: Longman.

Goldschmidt, J. et al. 1974: The women's liberation movement: attitudes and actions. *Journal of personality* 42, 601–17.

Horner, M.S. 1970: Femininity and successful achievement: a basic inconsistency. In *Feminine personality and conflict*, ed. J.M. Bardwick and E. Douvan. Belmont: Brooks/Cole.

Lakoff, R. 1973: Language and woman's place. *Language and society* 2, 45–79.

Lloyd, B.B. and Archer, J. 1976: *Exploring sex differences.* London: Academic Press.

Ullian, D.Z. 1976: The development of concepts of masculinity and femininity. In *Exploring sex differences*, ed. B.B. Lloyd and J. Archer. London: Academic Press.

Weinreich-Haste, H.E. 1981: The image of science. In *The missing half*, ed. A. Kelly. Manchester: Manchester University Press.

Williams, J. 1979: Psychological androgyny and mental health. In *Sex role stereotyping*, ed. O. Hartnett, G. Boden and M. Fuller. London: Tavistock.

field dependence/independence A dimension of individual differences in the perception of self as separate from the environment. The field dependent individual relies heavily on the visual context to establish his or her own spatial orientation, whereas the field independent person relies more on postural and gravitational cues. The dimension was first described by Witkin (1949) who used the rod and frame test (among others), to dissociate visual from gravitational cues. This test requires a rod to be adjusted to the upright position when perceived in a frame, itself at some degrees of tilt from the upright. Witkin found stable differences in adherence to the orientation of the surround (i.e. field dependence) between individuals, between the sexes (with females being more field dependent than males) and with development (with field dependence decreasing with age). There is some evidence that these differences in perception also correlate positively with other personality factors, such as authoritarianism. (See COGNITIVE STYLE.) GEB

Bibliography

Witkin, H.A. 1949: The nature and importance of individual differences in perception. *Journal of personality* 18, 145–60.

field theory A theoretical approach by which investigators have attempted to consider the phenomena under investigation as occurring in a field, that is, as part of a totality of co-existing facts which are conceived as mutually interdependent. In particular, field theory refers to the method of analysing causal relationships employed by Kurt Lewin and his students. This method assumes that the properties of any event are determined by its relations to the system of events of which it is a component and that changes of the moment are dependent upon changes in the immediate vicinity at a time just past.

Lewin stressed the need for clear understanding of the formal properties of scientific constructs, and he insisted that the determinants of behavior would have to be represented in mathematical terms if psychology were to become a rigorous discipline. As a result of this conviction Lewin formulated two different psychological geometries – topological space and hodological space – to serve as diagrammatic representations of his theoretical insights.

TOPOLOGICAL PSYCHOLOGY provides a method for diagramming relationships in field theory. Lewin was concerned with the properties of figures that remain unchanged under continuous transformation or stretching. The emphasis is on the qualitative aspects of connection and position: belongingness, membership and part–whole relationships. Concepts explained in topological terms allow one to determine which events are possible in a given life space and which are not. Some of the more important concepts defining topological space are life space, behavior, environment, person, region, differentiation, locomotion and boundary.

The most fundamental construct for Lewin was the LIFE SPACE, or the psychological field. All psychological events (thinking, acting, dreaming, hoping, etc.) are conceived to be a function of the life space, which consists of the person and the environment viewed as one constellation of interdependent factors. Life space equals the psychological field or total situation; it refers to the manifold of coexisting facts which determine the behavior of an individual at a given moment. The emphasis on the interrelatedness of the person and the environment was one of Lewin's major contributions to psychological theorizing. Psychological events, that is, changes in the life space, must be explained in terms of the properties of the field which exists at the time when the events occur. Past events can only have a position in the historical causal chains whose interweaving creates the present situation; they cannot directly influence present events.

Behavior is a function of the life space: B = f(LS). The life space is, in turn, a product of the interaction between the person (P) and his environment (E). In symbolic expression, B = f(LS) = f(P,E). The word "behavior" is employed to refer to any change in the life space which is subject to psychological laws. The characteristics of the life space (or person) are deduced from observed behavior in an observed environment. Lewin also used the word "behavior" to refer to things that are not directly observable but must be inferred, and to refer to observable interaction between the individual and the objective environment.

The word "environment" is used to refer to the objective environment or stimulus situation – the objective situation which confronts the individual at a given moment. However, Lewin also uses the term to refer to the psychological environment, which is conceived to be the environment as it exists for the individual. From this viewpoint, the psychological environment is an interactive product, determined both by the characteristics of the objective environment and by the characteristics of the person.

Lewin employed the term *person* in three ways. First, he used it to refer to those properties of the individual (his needs, his beliefs and values, his perceptual and motoric systems) which in interaction among themselves and with the objective environment produce the life space. In a second usage, Lewin regarded "person" as the equivalent to "life space" (Lewin 1936). Finally, he also used the term to refer to the "person in the life space". The person in the life space or "the behaving self" (Tolman in Parsons and Shils 1951) is the individual as related to the other entities in his life space. "The behaving self" may be thought of as the individual's perception of his relations to the environment he perceives.

Another basic concept is that of *region*, which may be defined as any distinguishable part of the life space (or person). Regions of the psychological environment refer to present or contemplated activities rather than to the objective areas in which activities are linked (Leeper 1943, pp.92–5). The degree of differentiation of a region refers to the number of subparts within it. Any region which has no distinguished subparts may be called a cell. Human development is expressed as a change of life space towards increasing differentiation. The life space of the newborn child is a field which has relatively few and only vaguely distinguishable areas. There is no time dimension or concept of past experiences in the child at this age.

Any change of position of a region within the life space is conceived to be a *locomotion*. This refers primarily to locomotion of the behaving self rather than to locomotion of parts of the psychological environment. Locomotion from one region to another involves movement of the behaving self from its present to its terminal position through a path of neighboring regions. The boundary of a region consists of those cells in the region for which there is no surrounding boundary that lies entirely within the region.

Direction in the life space is represented through the geometry of *hodological space*. The distinguished path between any two regions is the path along which the individual expects that he will move if he chooses to proceed from one region to another. It is the preferred or "psychologically best" path, determined by its attractiveness rather than its shortness. Direction is influenced by such factors as the degree of differentiation of the space into subregions, the relative prominence of whole versus parts, and the properties of the field at large. It should also be said that direction in the life space is dependent upon cognitive structure. If the individual has no clear knowledge of the sequence of steps necessary to achieve a given objective (i.e. to solve a mathematical problem) he does not know the direction of locomotion necessary to obtain his goal. Most new situations are cognitively unstructured, and behavior will be exploratory, trial-and-error, vacillating and contradictory. Lewin utilized the concept of unstable cognitive structure to give insight into the situation of adolescence. He pointed out that the change from childhood to adulthood is a shift to a more or less unknown position (Lewin 1951).

There is an interdependence between Lewin's geometrical concepts and vector psychology, which incorporates the following main dynamic concepts: tension, valence, driving force and restraining force, supplemented by the concept of potency. These dynamic concepts have the function of enabling one to determine which of a set of possible psychological events will occur.

A system in a state of *tension* is said to exist within the individual whenever a psychological need or an intention exists. Tension is a state of a region or system S which tries to change itself in such a way that it becomes equal to the state of its surrounding regions $S_1, S_2, \ldots, S_n$; it involves forces at the boundary of the region *S* in tension. A definite relation exists between the tension systems of the person and properties of the psychological environment. When a goal region which is relevant to a system in tension exists in the psychological environment, one can assert that there is a force propelling the behaving self toward the goal. From the foregoing assumptions it follows that the tendency to recall interrupted activities should be greater than the tendency to recall finished ones (Zeigarnik 1927).

A region within the life space of an individual which attracts or repels is considered to have *valence*: a region of positive valence attracts, a region of negative valence repels. *Potency* is a factor influencing the effective strengths of valences or forces.

The construct *force* characterizes the direction and strength of the tendency to change. In "The conceptual representation and measurement of psychological forces" (1938), Lewin pointed out that the strength of a force can be measured by (1) the strength of opposed driving or restraining forces, (2) the relative persistence of directed activity, (3) the velocity of locomotion or of restructuring. Driving forces correspond to a relation between at least two regions of the life space: the region of present activity and the region of a goal. Driving forces tend to lead to locomotion. Restraining forces, as such, do not lead to locomotion, but they do influence the effect of driving forces. Any region which offers resistance to locomotion, that is, any barrier to locomotion, is characterized by restraining forces at its boundary. When oppositely directed forces of about equal strength play upon the person simultaneously, conflict results (Lewin 1935).

As a specific psychological theory, field theory has little current vitality, but it has made its mark on the current general orientation of psychology. Its primary legacy has been a belief that psychological events must be explained in psychological terms; that central processes in the life space (distal perception, cognition, motivation, goal-directed behavior) are the proper focus of investigation rather than the peripheral processes of sensory input and muscular action; that psychological events must be studied in their interrelations with one another; that the individual must be studied in his inter-relations with the group to which he belongs; and that important social-psychological phenomena can be studied experimentally. A discussion of the work of those associated with Lewin may be found in Deutsch (1968). MDe

Bibliography

Deutsch, M. 1968: Field theory in social psychology. In *The handbook of social psychology*, ed. G. Lindzey and E. Aronson. Reading, Mass.: Addison-Wesley.

Festinger, L. 1957: *A theory of cognitive dissonance*. Stanford: Stanford University Press.

Heider, F. 1958: *The psychology of interpersonal relations*. New York: Wiley.

Leeper, R.W. 1943: *Lewin's topological and vector psychology: a digest and a critique*. Eugene: University of Oregon Press.

Lewin, K. 1935: *A dynamic theory of personality*. New York: McGraw-Hill.

——— 1936: *Principles of topological psychology*. New York: McGraw-Hill.

——— 1938: The conceptual representation and measurement of psychological forces. *Contributions to psychological theory* 1, No. 4.

——— 1951: *Field theory in social science*. New York: Harper.

Parsons, T. and Shils, E.A., eds. 1951: *Toward a general theory of action*. Cambridge: Harvard University Press.

Zeigarnik, B. 1927: Uber das behalten von erledigten und unerledigten handlungen. *Psychologische forschung*. 9, 1–85.

first language acquisition A term broadly used to denote the description of the acquisition by individuals of their native language. It is therefore usually confined to the study of children and their developmental progress in the acquisition of their first language as opposed to the learning of a second language or the re-learning of a language by an adult after traumatic injury.

Psychologists became especially interested in language acquisition in the late 1950s when B. F. Skinner and Noam Chomsky clashed over the theoretical assumptions necessary to explain the language acquisition process.

Skinner had attempted to formulate a theory of language acquisition in strictly behaviorist, stimulus-response terms. Chomsky, from a background in structural linguistics, argued forcibly against such a view. One of the earliest empirical studies growing out of this debate was the longitudinal study by Roger Brown who recorded in detail the language of three children throughout the early 1960s (see Brown 1973, for an overview of the early stages of language acquisition). The work of Brown and others showed that the child was actively engaged in acquiring a system of rules that allow the generation of novel word combinations. As such they lent greater support to modern linguistic views than to behaviorist accounts of the language acquisition process. Other early studies included work on the notion of PIVOT GRAMMAR to account for the regularities observed in early child utterances.

The fact that modern language acquisition studies arose from the general debate over theories of acquisition resulted in an almost total preoccupation with the structure of language.

It has become increasingly recognized by child language researchers that language acquisition encompasses a range of phenomena far beyond the bounds of syntax. While the earlier studies concentrated on the patterns of word combinations, later research began to focus on the meanings expressed by these combinations. An increasing number of studies investigated the semantic component of the grammar during language acquisition. Semantics is concerned with the meaning of words and sentences.

The renewed interest in the semantic component of language had two major consequences for the study of language acquisition. The first was the development of cognitive theories of language acquisition (see Macnamara 1972) in which it was proposed that the child's language development was dependent on prior development of particular cognitive abilities. In a Piagetian version (see PIAGET), the very ability to form word combinations was viewed as dependent on the achievement of the completion of the sensori-motor stage of cognitive development between one-and-a-half and two years of age. But though the studies engendered by such views were of interest in the continuing investigations of the relation between language and thought, they proved inadequate to explain the acquisition of the syntactic component of the grammar. It was later argued that particular developments in cognitive processes may be necessary but not sufficient to explain language acquisition. It has even been argued that the acquisition of the syntactic component of language and cognitive development are more independent than had been formerly believed, and that the development of complex linguistic forms can occur in severely retarded children with very limited conceptual knowledge.

The second consequence of the interest in semantics has been the extension of the period studied back into early infancy. Whereas some studies had concentrated on ages at which the child first begins to combine words into structured multi-word utterances, others became more interested in the processes involved in the acquisition of first words. Some work indicated that children differ in the types of the first words they begin to use, with some children tending first to acquire referential terms while others first use primarily socially expressive terms.

Much research on early word use has been directed at discovering the procedures children use when they extend their early words to refer to new instances, sometimes erroneously (overextensions). Clark (1973) found evidence that generalization of words occurs on the basis of perceptual similarities, while Nelson (1974) argued that generalizations were more often based on functional similarities. There has also been some controversy over whether children acquire criterial features that can be considered definitional of their concepts as encoded in language or whether a theory of prototypical features is more accurate.

The interest in earlier stages of language acquisition has given renewed impetus to the study of another component of language – phonology. Some studies have been concerned with processes involved in the first sounds a child makes (see COOING AND BABBLING). Others have been concerned with the acquisition and development of the phonological component of language. Of these latter studies, some have been concerned with the analysis of infant perception of auditory stimuli. Evidence has been found that speech is analysed differently from non-speech sounds even in infants as young as four weeks of age.

In studies of speech production, large individual differences have been found both in the age at which children can produce various sounds and in the order of acquisition of these sounds. Children show individual preferences for specific articulatory patterns, for particular classes of sounds, and for particular kinds of syllable structures, and use varying processing strategies. Such differences, however, do not extend beyond certain limits. While the evidence is that children actively construct their own phonologies during early development giving rise to these individual differences, there appear to be constraints and limits on their phonological output. These constraints are thought to be due both to the child's mental hypotheses and to his production and perceptual abilities at a given point in development (Leonard et al. 1980).

Various language disordered groups may differ in some aspects of the phonological component of their language perhaps due to differences in perceptual processing strategies. Phonological coding problems may be important at later stages of language acquisition. For example recent research on cognitive processes underlying SPELLING ability implicates phonological coding problems in various language disordered groups including developmental dyslexics.

A great deal of recent research on infants has been concerned with the effects of early interaction between mother and child on language acquisition. While research on mother-child interaction has failed to demonstrate convincing effects on the acquisition of syntax, such research appears to be particularly valuable for understanding the acquisition and development of pragmatics. The pragmatic component of language concerns the way in which language is used. It includes the study of the way sentences function in communication and the way the context of an utterance interacts with grammatical structure in determining meaning. Some recent research on pragmatic acquisition has been carried out by Bates (1976). (See also Rees 1978 for a review of recent experimental work on the acquisition of the pragmatic component of language.) It has been argued that some language-disordered children (for example some high level autistic children) can be characterized as having primarily pragmatic dysfunctions and may be more deficient in language use than their vocabulary and syntactic structure would suggest.

Researchers in language acquisition have become aware that language acquisition studies must be concerned with all the major domains of language – syntax, semantics, phonology and pragmatics – and the interrelations of these components with other aspects of cognitive development. At present the field is becoming increasingly complex as researchers explore problems in all these areas, as well as taking account of differences between comprehension and production in language acquisition, and the large individual differences children show in acquiring their first language. There are at present few firm conclusions regarding the processes by which language acquisition occurs. Language acquisition currently remains a mysterious process engendering a good deal of exciting research. RFC

Bibliography

Bates, E. 1976: *Language and context: The acquisition of pragmatics*. New York: Academic Press.

*Brown, R. 1973: *A first language*. Cambridge, Mass.: Harvard University Press.

Clark, E.V. 1973: What's in a word? On the child's acquisition of semantics in his first language. In *Cognitive development and the acquisition of language*. New York: Academic Press.

*deVilliers, J.G. and P.A. 1978: *Language acquisition*. Cambridge, Mass. and London: Harvard University Press.

Leonard, L.B., Newhoff, M. and Mesalam, L. 1980: Individual differences in early child phonology. *Applied psycholinguistics* 1, 7–30.

Macnamara, J. 1972: Cognitive basis of language learning in infants. *Psychological review* 79, 1–13.

*Maratsos, M. 1970: Some current issues in the study of the acquisition of grammar. In P. Mussen, ed. *Carmichael's manual of child psychology*. 2nd edn. in press. New York and Chichester: John Wiley.

Nelson, K. 1974: Concept, word and sentence: interrelations in acquisition and development. *Psychological review* 81, 267–85.

Rees, N.S. 1978: Pragmatics of language: applications to normal and disordered development. In R.L. Schiefelbusch, ed., *Bases of language intervention*. Baltimore: University Park Press.

Skinner, B.F. 1957: *Verbal behavior*. New York: Appleton-Century-Crofts; London: Methuen, 1959.

fitness In evolutionary biology "fitness" refers to Darwinian fitness – that is, the evolutionary success of an individual organism, or the average evolutionary success of organisms sharing a particular biological characteristic. In principle evolutionary success is measurable in terms of survival and reproduction, though different aspects of this are stressed in different contexts: survival, total number of offspring, or number of surviving offspring (i.e. REPRODUCTIVE SUCCESS). In practice, there may be obstacles to the measurement of these, and less satisfactory indicators may be used instead. The Spencerian phrase "survival of the fittest", though accepted by DARWIN as a summary of natural selection, is apt to mislead unless it is appreciated that it is a tautological way of expressing a principle that is nonetheless far from trivial: by definition, the fittest are those that survive (and reproduce). The more recently developed concept of inclusive fitness is a modification of Darwinian fitness to take account not only of reproductive success but also of successful aid to relatives other than offspring (see ALTRUISM; NATURAL SELECTION).

In other contexts, fitness may refer to health, physical fitness or physiological capacities. Sometimes there may be correlations between fitness in these senses and Darwinian fitness, but they are not synonymous. RDA

flooding (implosion) Techniques designed to elimate fear and avoidance by extinction. As originally described by Stampfl, the techniques require the patient to imagine the feared or avoided object in as vivid and fear-inducing form as possible while the therapist applies an additional fear-inducing commentary. Imaginal exposure to the fear object continues for some time until fear can no longer be elicited. As originally described by Stampfl, imaginal exposure to the supposed psychodynamic origins of the fear or feared situation was also attempted but his practice did not find general acceptance. While controlled trials suggested that flooding was effective in reducing phobic and obsessional behavior, it did not prove to be more powerful than other less unpleasant behavioral techniques and has now largely been superseded by real life exposure to the feared object without other fear-inducing procedures. See also DESENSITIZATION. RAM

Bibliography

Stampfl, T.G. and Levis, D.J. 1967: Essentials of implosion therapy: a learning theory-based psychodynamic behavioural therapy. *Journal of abnormal psychology* 72, 496–503.

food selection The tendency for animals to choose among available food items and so achieve a diet that is characteristic of the species. Some animals, such as the rat, are omnivorous and will eat almost anything. Others (feeding specialists) eat a single type of food, for example the koala bear (*Phascolarctos cinereus*) which eats only eucalyptus leaves. Among grazing animals food selection occurs partly as a result of the feeding technique. The buffalo (*Syncerus caffer*) selects plants on the basis of the leaf–stem ratio, preferring species with the most leaf. The plant is drawn into the mouth by the action of the tongue and lips and then pressed against the palate. A short pull of the head results in the leaves being stripped from the more fibrous stem. Feeding specialists generally have innate recognition of suitable foods and often have physiological specializations designed to cope with the restricted diet.

Omnivorous animals are more likely than feeding specialists to encounter poisonous foods and they also require more elaborate procedures for ensuring a balanced diet. Rats are notoriously good at avoiding poisoned food, and their success is achieved partly by initially avoiding novel foods. Faced with a shortage of familiar foods the rat will sample a small amount of a novel food and wait a number of hours before proceeding further. Garcia et al. (1955) discovered that if rats were fed a harmless substance and afterwards made to vomit they rapidly developed an aversion to the substance. Subsequently it was shown that a rat can learn in a single trial to avoid a novel food if consumption of the food is followed by vomiting. Such rapid and specific learning seems to be restricted to certain kinds of association, such as that between the cues that normally accompany feeding and the physiological consequences of food ingestion. A similar principle applies to specific hunger. Rodgers and Rozin (1966) found that thiamine deficient rats show an immediate, marked preference for new food, even when the new food is thiamine deficient and the old food has a thiamine supplement. The preference is short-lived. If however consumption of a novel food is followed by recovery from dietary deficiency, the rat rapidly learns to prefer the novel food. Such rapid learning on the basis of the physiological consequences of ingestion enables the rat to maintain a degree of food selection by avoiding novel foods and yet to adapt quickly and relatively safely to changing circumstances. DJM

Bibliography

Garcia, J., Kimeldorf, D.J. and Koelling, R.A. 1955: Conditioned aversion to saccharin resulting from exposure to gamma radiation. *Science* 122, 157–58.

Rodgers, W. and Rozin, P. 1966: Novel food preferences in thiamine-deficient rats. *Journal of comparative physiological psychology* 61, 1–4.

foraging Or searching for food, has several components. Before they can actually eat anything most animals must locate the area where food is to be found and then discriminate food items from inedible objects. Where food is unpredictably distributed in space, a predator may have to cover quite long distances in its search for food, expending time and energy in the process. Animals might therefore be expected to forage as efficiently as possible (gaining maximum energy in the form of food but expending as little as possible in searching for it). This is the assumption behind 'optimal foraging' models, which have attracted particular attention. On investigation, many animals including birds, fish and insects have been found to forage optimally, or nearly so. See also PREDATION. MSD

foreigner talk Foreigner talk is a conventionalized variety of reduced speech regarded by native speakers of a language as appropriate for use with foreigners. Structurally it is similar to BABY-TALK and other caretaker languages (see Clyne, ed. 1981).

As foreigner talk often constitutes the input in natural SECOND LANGUAGE ACQUISITION its study is important for the understanding of developing INTERLANGUAGE systems and pidgin languages. PM

Bibliography

Clyne, Michael, ed. 1981: Foreigner talk issue: *International journal of the sociology of language* 28.

forensic psychiatry The branch of psychiatry concerned with mentally disordered offenders. It embraces assessment, expert testimony, and treatment in various settings: ordinary psychiatric facilities, secure units, special hospitals and prisons. Many offenders show sociopathic traits, and for these the appropriateness of psychological treatment is debatable. However, one-third to one half of prison inmates suffer from other and more specific psychiatric conditions, including mental handicap, schizophrenia, epilepsy, alcoholism and drug dependency, while profound personality disorders are common among, for example, arsonists and sexual offenders. The challenge for psychiatric workers is to select those who may be helped by treatment. DLJ

Bibliography

Gunn, J. 1977: Criminal behaviour and mental disorders. *British journal of psychiatry* 130, 317–29.

forgetting *See* memory and forgetting; retention and forgetting, psychoanalytical theories

free will The idea that, contrary to the claims of DETERMINISM, the decisions and actions of agents are not foreordained, whether by fate, or by God's knowledge, or by laws of psychology, or by those of neurophysiology. The notion seems to have been first elaborated in Epicurean philosophy, in alleviation of the otherwise pervasive deterministic atomism of that system. But the idea of free will is ambiguous and this ambiguity has created much confusion in the free will/determinism debate.

One thing that people may have in mind when they speak of free will is called by philosophers freedom of spontaneity. It is the idea of unhindered expression. A free action expresses an agent's wants or his deepest longings or his truest self or something of that kind. A free decision is one uninfluenced by any form of duress or unwanted pressure. This idea of freedom is highly relative: a given act may be free from one kind of constraint but subject to another. If a person is mildly drunk and declares passionate love, then on one view he is acting freely – he is expressing his truest feelings unhindered by social conventions of reserve; on another view he is unfree – his true reasonable self is in thrall to the demon drink. However all that may be, it is clear that there is no incompatibility between freedom of spontaneity and any form of universal determinism: a being whose every action and decision is foreordained may rejoice in complete freedom: his every act may be an unhindered expression of his deepest longings, etc. Indeed it may be foreordained that it is so.

The other notion of free will is called by philosophers freedom of indifference, and it has to do with situations where an agent faces alternatives: decision and choice. Here it seems that free will is inconsistent with determinism. The determinist claims that the outcome of apparently free choices is somehow foreordained; the defender of free will claims that such apparently free choices are truly free, not foreordained.

This debate is a real one; three positions are possible and two are common. First, one might hold that determinism is true in some form and that our apparently free decisions and choices are not free but really the inevitable outcome of the workings of the laws of neurophysiology or psychology. This view has not been common. The other views are libertarianism, which defends free will and seeks to refute determinism, and compatibilism (or soft determinism), which holds that despite first appearances freedom of indifference and determinism are not really at odds after all.

Compatibilists argue that those who think that free will and determinism are inconsistent with each other suffer from a crude and inaccurate idea of free will. They point out that careful linguistic testing to exhibit the contours of the concept of freedom in contexts of decision and choice will show that it implies the absence of rather ordinary constraints – drunkenness, duress, insanity and the like – but that it does not imply the absence of universal causal determinism. That is, when in everyday life we discuss freedom, it is not freedom from universal causal determinism that we are discussing. This general thesis has been argued from various points of view with great power and subtlety. Its opponents, incompatibilists, are inclined to argue in reply that these tests of what we ordinarily mean to preclude by speaking of a decision as free do not suffice to give the true contours of the concept, which also has some unordinary but perfectly bona fide uses. The issue between compatibilists and incompatibilists (whether the latter are determinists or libertarians) is one that involves deep questions of philosophical method and metaphysics; it is unlikely to be resolvable in isolation. But the strongest argument for compatibilism is the aspect of incoherence surrounding its competitor, libertarianism.

The libertarian's view is that free will and determinism are not compatible, and that determinism is false, and so that some decisions and choices, at least, are free. The libertarian who is arguing against neurophysiological determinism, for example, will have to postulate interruptions in the physiological causal nexus – random events – to make room for free decisions. But if I decide a given way because a certain neuron randomly fires, that seems no nearer to freedom than if my decision is at the behest of a causally determined firing of a neuron. The libertarian thinks freedom is inconsistent with determinism; but give him randomness and he still does not have freedom. This is the great and deep problem for libertarianism, which gives it an aspect almost of incoherence: how can randomness in the causal nexus be identical with freedom? Freedom and randomness seem almost as incompatible as freedom and determinism.

Libertarians have to reply that while freedom is inconsistent with determinism, it is not inconsistent with randomness but merely not equivalent to it: freedom presupposes randomness. They have then to say what must be added to a random event to make it a free act. This involves difficult matters such as the ascendancy of mind over brain (see MIND–BODY PROBLEM), and what it is for an agent to do something rather than to undergo it. JT

Bibliography

Ayers, M.R. 1968: *The refutation of determinism.* London: Methuen.

*Berofsky, Bernard, ed. 1966: *Free will and determinism.* New York and London: Harper & Row.

Campbell, C.A. 1967: *In defence of free will.* London: Allen & Unwin; New York: Humanities Press.

Franklin, R.L. 1968: *Freewill and determinism.* London: Routledge & Kegan Paul.

*Hook, Sidney, ed. 1958: *Determinism and freedom in the age of modern science.* New York: New York University Press.

Kenny, A.J.P. 1975: *Will, freedom and power.* Oxford: Basil Blackwell; Totowa, N.J.: Baines & Noble.

Lucas, J.L. 1970: *The freedom of the will.* Oxford: Clarendon Press.

*Morgenbesser, Sidney and Walsh, James, ed. 1962: *Free will.* Englewood Cliffs, N.J.: Prentice Hall.

Thorp, John 1980: *Free will: a defence against neurophysiological determinism.* London and Boston: Routledge & Kegan Paul.

Freud, Sigmund (1856–1939) Founder of the branch of psychological theory and psychotherapeutic practice known as psychoanalysis. Born on the 6 May 1856 in Freiberg, Moravia, which was then within the Austro-Hungarian Empire (now Pribor in Czechoslovakia), Sigmund was the first child of the second marriage of a Jewish wool-merchant Jakob Freud, whose two sons by a previous marriage were already grown up; one of them was married and the father of a small boy, so that Freud was an uncle at birth. He had seven brothers and sisters.

The family moved to Vienna when Sigmund was only three, and the half-brothers emigrated to England (Manchester) at this time. Thereafter Freud lived in Vienna for the rest of his life, except for the last fifteen months when he too settled in England (London) after being forced to flee from Nazi persecution at home. Although family finances were very limited, the eldest son's education was fostered, and his intelligence and academic industry won him a place at the local *gymnasium*. Here, in addition to German literature and some English, he studied mainly the language and literature of the Greek and Latin classics. In his latter years at school he was consistently top of his class, putting to good use an exceptionally retentive visual and auditory memory, and his flair for writing was singled out as unusual by one of his teachers. Formal recognition of his literary achievement as an adult came with the award of the Goethe Prize at Frankfurt in 1930, three years before Hitler ordered his books to be burned in Berlin.

By the time he left school, his career plans had changed from becoming a lawyer to "desire to eavesdrop on the eternal processes" of nature, as he wrote to his boyhood friend Emil Fluss (Schrier 1969, p.424). In practice this meant registering in the medical faculty of Vienna University to study biology, physiology and anatomy. But Freud did not abandon his earlier interest in cultural and philosophical matters, for during his first few years he also sat at the feet of Franz Brentano whose theories about the object-orientation of mental processes may have influenced his own later psychological formulations (see INTENTIONALITY). As a third-year student he did laborious work on the reproductive system of the eel, but was later able to concentrate under Ernst Brucke upon neuroanatomy, the field in which he published his first scientific observations (1877). It was Brucke who eventually had to persuade Freud that he could not make a living as a research-worker and had therefore better take his medical degree. This he did in 1881.

The need for a financially gainful career became more urgent the following year when he became engaged to Martha Bernays of Hamburg. The next four years, which took him to establish such a career as a basis for marriage, produced an assiduous two-way correspondence which is a rich source for biography as well as for glimpses of Freud's view of women. The couple were married in 1886 and eventually had six children; the marriage lasted until Freud's death. During his engagement he was working in the Vienna General Hospital, mainly on neurological problems, and trying to make a mark in the medical world. He did so in 1884 with his pioneering paper on the medical and psychotropic properties of cocaine, and he consolidated this success by acquiring in the following year a teaching post at the university *(Privatdozent)* and a traveling scholarship to visit the eminent psychiatrist Jean-Martin CHARCOT in Paris. Charcot was well known for his particular interest in the pseudo-neurological symptoms (such as anesthesia, amnesia, paralysis, dysphasia) produced by some patients suffering from HYSTERIA, and in using hypnosis for their treatment. He also intuited the sexual component in many of these disturbances. It may almost be said that Freud went to Paris as a neurologist and came away as a psychotherapist. For although, when back in Vienna, he worked for another two years or so in brain-pathology (especially with children) and gathered material for an important later monograph (1891) on speech disorders arising from brain-damage (aphasia), he soon began to collaborate with Joseph Breuer in the psychological treatment of a number of hysterics. From these case-studies, published in 1895, emerged several hypotheses which have remained central in psychoanalytic theory. The question of the relation between Freud's early neurological preoccupations and his later psychological theories also remains, but at the outset he was certainly concerned to sketch an elaborate and detailed neurological model for his psychological postulates. This seminal "Project for a scientific psychology", as it is now known in English, was written only four years after the study of aphasia, but not published until 1950 (Standard Edition, vol. 1).

Crucial ideas to emerge from these first psychotherapeutic researches were (1) that the neurotic symptom, and the pattern of such psychological disturbance as a whole, are a symbolic reaction to an emotional shock; (2) that the memory of this shock, and its associated feelings, are so distressing that they have been banished from conscious recall by the mind's processes of defending itself against anxiety (see REPRESSION); (3) that these repressed elements, now located in "the unconscious", are not dormant but are part of a system of non-rational associations and transformations (the "primary process") which can indirectly influence and disrupt conscious feelings, trains of thought, recollections and perceptions, and which are most clearly evident in dreams; (4) that the business of therapy is to identify the repressed material and the reasons for its repression, and to enable the patient to accept them consciously and rationally; (5) that, in order to gain access to the unconscious, the therapist must bypass the limitations and obstructions of conscious mentation, either by hypnosis (Breuer's method, leading to the purging or "catharsis" of the repressed anxieties) or by the interpretation of free-associations, dream-material and incidental but symptomatic lapses of psychological function (Freud's substitute method based on the pervasive assumption that all such phenomena are systematically "determined": see DETERMINISM, PSYCHIC); (6) that in the course of treatment a patient forms a dependent, child-like and sometimes sexualized relationship to the therapist, in which he or she transfers to the therapist feelings, dispositions and assumptions which are derived from other relationships, especially (but not exclusively) from the childhood relationship with parents (see PROJECTION); (7) that this "transference-relationship" is a principal context for discovering and unlearning neurotic responses to anxiety and for learning healthy ones in their place (see PSYCHOANALYSIS).

The greater part of Freud's subsequent work consisted of the investigation, modification and elaboration of these central ideas, and of addressing the questions that they raise not only about the origin and treatment of emotional disturbance but also about normal personality development, motivation, thinking and the organization of mental life in general. For he was after a *general* psychology, whose principles would apply equally to the sick and the healthy, to the individual and to society. The early clinical observations had already suggested to him some more fundamental hypotheses about the structure and processes of the mind.

The idea of an emotional "trauma" in (1) and (2) above, which Freud initially identified with sexual interference by a parent-figure (the "seduction hypothesis" which he soon gave up), raised questions about the origins of anxiety, why some anxieties are intolerable, what agency initiates the defense of repression, and whether there are other defenses (see DEFENSE MECHANISM). Again, the assumptions in (3) compel one to ask how the contents of the unconscious are organized, how this evidently active system is energized, and what principle governs its indirect incursions into conscious mental life. Already by the turn of the century Freud was thinking of a motivating force *(libido)* whose aim is the satisfaction of instinctual drives towards survival, pleasure and the avoidance of pain, and whose psychological manifestation is in wish-fulfillment (see INSTINCT). This libido is in constant tension with an adaptive agency, the EGO, whose function is to regulate our actions according to reason and reality. Since the "reality principle" of the ego often requires us to delay impulse-gratification, it may conflict with the "pleasure-principle" of the libido. The frustration of libidinal gratification ultimately underlies anxiety, he argued, only to revise the idea later; and the philosophically uneasy anthropomorphic and hydraulic metaphors in which Freud depicts the psychobiological interaction between bodily instinct and mental energy are characteristic.

By the turn of the century also, the form taken by infantile sexuality in the Oedipus and Elektra Complexes had been sketched, and he was ready to illustrate in *The Interpretation of Dreams* (1900; Standard Edition, vols. 4 and 5), how "latent" unconscious feelings, images and desires are symbolically transformed and organized into the "manifest", wish-fulfilling content of normal dream-life in accordance with the "pleasure-principle" (see DREAM THEORY). The following year saw a further application to normal behavior of his hypotheses about the influence of unconscious processes, for in *The Psychopathology of Everyday Life* (1901; Standard Edition, vol. 6) Freud claims to trace a great many examples of accidents, mistakes, oversights, verbal slips, memory lapses (known collectively as PARAPRAXES) to the specific generative wishes or anxieties of which they are symptomatic expressions (see DETERMINISM, PSYCHIC).

Freud generalized his concept of libido-motivation in the theory that, in the normal course of development, the growing child gets instinctual gratification from different zones of the body at different age-levels (see PSYCHOANALYTICAL PERSONALITY THEORY). At about the time that these views were published in *Three Essays* (1905; *Standard Edition*, vol. 7), the incipient psychoanalytic movement was joined by Carl Jung of Zurich, who accompanied Freud on a lecturing invitation to Clark University, in 1909, but broke away for theoretical and personal reasons some five years later. That was three years after Alfred Adler had done the same (see McGuire 1974 and *Standard Edition*, vol. 14, pp. 48–66).

The application of his theories to cultural and sociological issues began with "Totem and taboo" (1912–13; *Standard edition*, vol. 13) and was taken up again much later in "The future of an illusion" (1927; *Standard edition*, vol. 21), "Civilisation and its discontents" (1930; *ibid.*) and "Moses and monotheism" (1934–38; *Standard edition*, vol. 23). Freud was deeply interested in the arts, with the marked exception of music, all his life; and, although originally hostile to the Surrealists' deliberate attempts to evoke unconscious associations by their painting, he changed his mind after meeting Salvador Dali in 1938 (Jones 1961, p.649). His other relevant passion was archaeology (Graeco-Roman and Egyptian), and the collection of antiquities that crowded his desk-top used to astonish his visitors. Freud made the first comprehensive statement of his theories in the *Introductory Lectures* (1916–17; Standard Edition, vols. 15 and 16), but personal tragedies and important theoretical revisions followed soon after the end of the first world war.

The post-war influenza epidemic killed his beautiful, happy and healthy daughter Sophie, mother of two young children, at the age of twenty-six. Three years later he learned of the cancer of the jaw which kept him in constant pain and frequent surgery for his last sixteen years. The first theoretical revision of his work was to some extent also a consequence of the war. The "pleasure-principle" did not allow him to explain *inter alia* why soldiers who had been traumatized in battle and removed from combat retained their recurrent nightmares. He concluded that there must be a fundamental "compulsion to repeat" which is just as basic as the pleasure-principle, and which is in the service of a more general destructive motive called the "death instinct" or *Thanatos*. A group of constructive motives contend against this. It makes up the "life instinct" or *Eros*. Many of Freud's sympathizers have misgivings about these reformulations in *Beyond the pleasure principle* (1920; Standard Edition, vol. 18), but are much happier with the "structural" revision of psychoanalytic personality theory in "The ego and the id" (1923; *Standard edition*, vol. 19), which introduce the Id as the reservoir of instinctual impulses, and the Superego or EGO IDEAL as the source of the evaluative regulation of actions and mental activity in addition to the Ego's controls. Consequently Freud can now express the goal of psychoanalysis as "where Id was Ego shall be". The theory that anxiety is transformed libido was revised in "Inhibitions, symptoms and anxiety" (1926; *Standard edition*, vol. 20) in favor of a more discriminating view in which it can be an expedient signal which calls up one or more of a range of defense mechanisms.

Freud plainly thought that both his theorizing and his therapeutic investigations were "scientific". Doubting critics, however, stress the lack of objectivity in observation, the difficulty of deriving specific testable hypotheses from the theory, the likelihood that the analyst selectively elicits certain sorts of actions or ideas from the patient, and the at least equal effectiveness of therapy based on other psychological theories (Farrell 1981: Cheshire 1975, chs. 4–7). Others argue that Freud was mistaken to think that he was giving a *causal* account of the origins of our mental life. What he provided, they say, was a way to explore and construct the idiographic meanings of that experience for each individual, as one might come to understand a linguistic text. This is the "hermeneutic" or "semiotic" approach, developed obscurely by LACAN (1973); but see also Ricoeur (1970), Blight (1981). On the other hand, there is now a considerable literature, by no means all unfavorable, about the empirical testing of Freudian theory (Kline 1981). And Einstein, having come across some events that could be explained only, as he believed, by Freud's theory of repression, concluded: "it is always delightful when a great and beautiful conception proves to be consonant with reality" (Jones 1961, p.628). Freud died in London on 23 September 1939. NMC

Bibliography

Blight, J.G. 1981: Must psychoanalysis retreat to hermeneutics? *Psychoanalysis and contemporary thought* 4, 147–205.

Cheshire, Neil M. 1975: *The nature of psychodynamic interpretation.* London and New York: Wiley.

Farrell, Brian A. 1981: *The standing of psychoanalysis.* Oxford and New York: Oxford University Press.

Freud, Ernst L., ed. 1961: *Letters of Sigmund Freud, 1873–1939.* London: Hogarth.

Freud, J. Martin 1957: *Glory reflected: Sigmund Freud – man and father.* London: Angus and Robertson.

Freud, Sigmund 1895–1938: *Gesammelte Werke.* Frankfurt am Main: S. Fischer. *Standard edition of the complete psychological works of Sigmund Freud* (24 vols.). London: Hogarth; New York: Norton.

*Jones, Ernest 1961: *The life and work of Sigmund Freud.* New York: Basic Books; London: Penguin (1964).

Kline, Paul 1981: *Fact and fantasy in Freudian theory.* 2nd edn. London and New York: Methuen.

Lacan, Jacques 1973 *(1979)*: *The four fundamental concepts of psychoanalysis.* London: Penguin.

McGuire, William, ed. 1974: *The Freud-Jung letters.* London: Hogarth; Princeton, N.J.: Princeton University Press.

Ricoeur, Paul 1970: *Freud and philosophy.* New Haven and London: Yale University Press.

Schrier, I. 1969: Some unpublished letters of Freud. *International journal of psychoanalysis* 50, 419–27.

Sulloway, Frank J. 1979: *Freud, biologist of the mind.* New York: Basic Books; London: Fontana (1980).

Fromm, Erich *See* neo-Freudian theory

frustration–aggression hypothesis *See* aggression

frustration: in animals A state of motivation that occurs when an animal's actions do not lead to the expected consequences or rewards. A hungry animal is likely to be frustrated if an expected food reward is delayed, if the food is less palatable than usual, or if the animal is physically prevented from obtaining food although it can see it.

The frustrated animal first tries harder to reach the goal, a phenomenon sometimes called the frustration effect (Amsel 1958). It may then indulge in irrelevant displacement activities such as grooming, or in aggression toward an innocent bystander.

Physiological changes during frustration are similar to those of fear, and these together with some of the behavioral manifestations of frustration are alleviated by tranquilizing drugs (Gray 1971). When animals are repeatedly frustrated in a particular situation they develop an anticipation which is aversive and leads to avoidance of the situation. This competes with the original approach motivations so that a conflict arises. When the conflicting tendencies are particularly strong and prolonged the animal may develop symptoms of acute anxiety, leading to a stress syndrome and abnormal behavior. DJM

Bibliography

Amsel, A. 1958: The role of frustrative nonreward in noncontinuous reward situations. *Psychological bulletin* 55, 102–19.

Gray, Jeffrey A. 1971: *The psychology of fear and stress*. London: Weidenfeld & Nicolson; New York: McGraw-Hill.

frustration: in humans The word frustration has been employed in three different ways in psychological literature, referring either to (1) external circumstances (2) a fairly general emotional response to circumstances, or (3) specific reactions to a particular external event. Operational definitions following the first usage have involved such things as physical barriers to a goal, the omission of a reward, threats or the actual delivery of punishment, and even insoluble problems. The internal state involved in the second usage has been discussed in terms of a measured physiological arousal or as a hypothetical variable having both energizing and directional properties. Much more specifically, the reactions involved in the third sense of the term have included regression (a return to a less mature form of behavior), fixation (an inability to modify habitual behavior), aggression, and an increased vigor of response (see Cofer and Appley 1964 for a comprehensive discussion). Most contemporary analyses seem to favor the first, external definition. One of the best examples of this usage can be found in the classic discussion of the frustration-aggression hypothesis by Dollard, et al. (1939), who formally defined frustration as "an interference with the occurrence of an instigated goal-response at its proper time in the behavior sequence", but considering the total context, it is clear that the authors were thinking more generally of a failure to obtain an anticipated goal. This is similar to Amsel's conception of frustration as the nonattainment of an expected reward (1962). Whatever the exact definition of the term, frustration must be distinguished from privation or deprivation. Where the latter concepts basically refer to the absence of a common source of gratification, frustration does not exist unless the person had been expecting to reach this particular goal and then finds it cannot be attained.

Several questions have been faced in recent years by investigators interested in the consequences of frustrations. One of these deals with why people often work harder or persist longer in a particular form of behavior after they have been thwarted. According to Amsel (1962), the increased persistence arises when nonrewarded occasions had previously been interspersed with rewarded trials so that the persons had learned to perform in the presence of frustration cues. The relationship between frustration and aggression also continues to attract considerable attention and controversy. Many critics of the 1939 formulation have argued that only illegitimate thwartings generate an aggressive inclination, but there is some evidence that supposedly legitimate frustrations can also evoke an instigation to aggression although this tendency may be suppressed because it seems "wrong" to be aggressive in that situation (see Berkowitz 1969). In line with several other writers (e.g. Ferster 1957), Berkowitz (1978, 1980) has recently held that frustrations elicit an instigation to aggression because of their aversiveness rather than their intrinsic nature as frustrations. Clearly a better understanding of the effects of frustrations on social behavior will contribute greatly to our understanding of emotions generally as well as a variety of social phenomena. LB

Bibliography

Amsel, A. 1962: Frustrative nonreward in partial reinforcement and discrimination learning: Some recent history and a theoretical extension. *Psychological review* 69, 306–28.

Berkowitz, L. 1969: The frustration–aggression hypothesis revisited. In *Roots of aggression* ed. L. Berkowitz. New York: Atherton Press.

——— 1978: Whatever happened to the frustration–aggression hypothesis? *American behavioral scientist* 21, 691–708.

——— 1980: *A survey of social psychology*. New York: Holt, Rinehart and Winston.

Cofer, C. and Appley, M. 1964: *Motivation: theory and research*. New York: Wiley.

Dollard, J., et al. 1939: *Frustration and aggression*. New Haven: Yale University Press.

Ferster, C.B. 1957: Withdrawal of positive reinforcement as punishment. *Science* 126, 509.

fugue *See* consciousness: disorders

functional autonomy Habits, skills and behavioral patterns that were originally developed in the past for instinctual satisfaction have a tendency to become, in the normal mature personality, self-motivated and independent from their historical causes.

The term originated with Gordon Allport (1937) to dispute the claim held by prominent psychologists such as McDougall (see HORMIC PSYCHOLOGY) and FREUD, that adult conduct was functionally related to and anchored in commonly held instincts, desires and needs.

Allport wanted to account for the uniqueness of each personality and the impossibility of reducing personalities to historically elementary motives. For him motivation is contemporary and independent of the original drive. The term accounts for many phenomena: (i) a human's lasting, stable interest: the mature personality depends upon an inevitable incompleteness to account for lasting interest; (ii) the persistence of habit when the incentive has been removed; (iii) the endless variety of human goals; (iv) compulsive behavior that continues after the original reason has disappeared.

The term is close in meaning to Woodworth's notion that instrumental activity may become an interest in itself – the habit may become a drive. JWA

Bibliography

Allport, G. 1937: *Personality*. London: Constable.

functional types *See* Jung, Carl

functionalism In philosophy of mind, the view that each psychological state is defined by its functional relations to inputs, outputs and other psychological states; hence that a mind is an integrated system of such states (see HOLISM). For potential causal relationships to be actualized the whole system must be realized in some physical structure. In human beings the CNS provides the "hardware". But the same functional system could be embodied in different kinds of hardware. Psychology is thus independent of the sciences which investigate particular physical or biological structures.

In a pioneering functionalist article, Putnam (1960) compared mental states to the logical states of a Turing Machine. Although this comparison is not exact (see criticisms in Block and Fodor (1972)), the analogies between minds and computers have provided a rich field for research within the functionalist framework. ARW

Bibliography

Putnam, H. 1960: Minds and machines. In *Dimensions of mind*, ed. S. Hook. New York: New York University Press.

Block, N. and Fodor, J. 1972: What psychological states are not. *Philosophical review* 81, 159–81.

functionalism (in the social sciences) An approach to society which focusses on the functions performed by customs, beliefs, institutions and other items within the social system as a whole. The term first gained wide currency in connection with the work of the social anthropologists Bronislaw Malinowski (1922) and A.R. Radcliffe-Brown (1922). Later, it spread into sociology, where it was soon used to denote what many took to be the dominant school in the field. The contours of what was denoted, however, have often been left rather fuzzy. Depending on what is supposed to be meant by the "function" of an item, functionalism admits of three main interpretations.

In one interpretation, functionalism simply consists in approaching a society *as a whole*, in studying each part of it in relation to that whole. In contrast to the historical approach from which the first functionalists had to free themselves, it does not focus on isolated customs or beliefs in order to track down their historical origins, but investigates the role each custom and each belief plays in the social system, the function it performs in it. However, as was emphatically stated by Kingsley Davis (1959) in a famous presidential address at the American Sociological Association, the functionalist point of view is nothing in itself and it is therefore unable to form the core of a distinctive approach.

This is not the case with a second interpretation, strongly suggested by some of Radcliffe-Brown's more theoretical essays, (1952) which soon became the dominant view. As outlined by the philosophers of science Ernest Nagel (1956) and Carl G. Hempel (1959) and the sociologist Robert Merton (1949), it states that the function of an item basically consists in its contribution to the survival or the good functioning of the system of which it is a part. A functionalist approach to society or to a person, consequently, consists in identifying needs (or functional requirements), i.e. the conditions whose fulfilment is required for the system to survive or to function properly, and in showing how particular customs, beliefs, etc. contribute to the satisfaction of these needs. Identifying the relevant social or psychological system and its needs may often turn out to be a tricky business, but here at least – so it was argued – functional analysis constitutes a distinctive type of inquiry.

The key question, which soon emerged is whether this type of inquiry can genuinely explain the customs, beliefs, behavior etc. with which it is concerned: a claim unambiguously present in the early functionalists' work. First of all, assuming the existence of a particular need has been established, the item considered may not be indispensable to its satisfaction. In other words, there may be *functional alternatives*. Where this is the case – which is likely to be the rule rather than the exception – showing that the item contributes to the satisfaction of a need of the system could not possibly explain why *it* is present, rather than another member of the class of functional alternatives. Secondly and more fundamentally, even when it is demonstrably indispensable for the proper functioning of the system, be it social or personal, the item considered can still not be said to have been *explained*. The most that can be said is that its presence at a given time is *predictable* from the knowledge of the (if only slightly) later fact that the system is functioning properly. It is therefore very hard to claim that, just by showing that without the item the system would not function properly, one has explained why it is there.

Faced with this fundamental difficulty authors have tended to take one of the following two stances. Many, following Nagel's and Hempel's suggestions, have attempted to give functionalism a *cybernetic* cast. Typical of the goal-directed systems studied by cybernetics is the fact that they are able to bring about, within certain limits, whatever is required to maintain themselves in a particular goal state. If a social or psychological system can be described as a goal-directed system in this sense, with its proper functioning as its goal state, then showing how a particular item contributes to the system's good functioning may be explanatory after all. This solution has been very popular in the most sophisticated theoretical statements of functionalism. But it has a serious drawback. It restricts the relevance of social scientific functionalism to the negligibly small number of situations in which the item to be explained can plausibly be said to be part of such a self-regulating device.

Other authors have attempted to preserve the wide relevance of functionalism by giving up its explanatory claim. This approach is exemplified by Parsons's later work (e.g. 1961) where the functional analysis of a social system essentially consists in classifying the problems it has to solve, within a framework provided by the four fundamental "functions" which any social system must perform: adaptation, goal-attainment, integration and latent pattern maintenance. Along the same lines, functional theory is said to consist, for the most part, in formulating a hierarchy of "reference problems" to be solved by a social system – the ultimate problem being that of "reducing environmental complexity" – and a parallel hierarchy of "equivalence domains", i.e. of sets of functionally equivalent solutions to the reference problems. Without engaging in such grand theoretical constructions most functional analyses of particular customs, institutions, etc. have tended to consist of pointing out some of the latter's "beneficial" or "problem-solving" consequences, without pretending thereby to explain *why* those customs, institutions, etc. exist, or *why* they take the form they do.

The first interpretation of functionalism suffered from a lack of distinctiveness. The second interpretation leads to the dilemma just sketched, between giving up functionalism's claim to be widely relevant and abandoning its claim to be truly explanatory. There is still a third interpretation, only recently developed in a systematic way, which avoids both shortcomings. According to this third interpretation, as foreshadowed by Larry Wright (1976) and elaborated by G.A. Cohen (1978) and Philippe Van Parijs (1981), functional statements typically made by social scientists are by no means concerned with contributions to the so called "proper functioning" of the social system. They must be understood as causally accounting for the presence of the item to which a function is ascribed, by reference to a *dispositional property* of the item which can be expressed as follows: the situation is such that, if the item (say, a rain ceremony) is or were present, its presence has or would have the consequences referred to as its function (say, the promotion of social cohesion). This move opens up the possibility of further research to justify the attribution of a dispositional property to the item. Functionalism, thus interpreted as the systematic use of a peculiar type of causal explanation, allows social–scientific functional statements to be explanatory in exactly the same way as biological functional statements advanced against the background of evolutionary theory. It not only makes explanatory sense of the functionalist approach in social anthropology; it is also able to integrate into the same framework, for example, the core of Marx's historical materialism and so-called functionalist diachronic linguistics, thus negating the criticism that functionalism is unfit for the explanation of social change.

Beyond the clarification of the logical structure of functional explanation, however, the key question for functionalism in this third interpretation concerns the nature of the underlying mechanisms: what is it that plays for the social sciences the role played by natural selection in the case of biology? Some, e.g. Cohen (1978), claim that functional explanations may be acceptable even in advance of any detailed knowledge about the mechanism. Others, e.g. Van Parijs (1981), believe that reinforcement, in a broad sense, provides the required set of mechanisms, and hence a basis for the legitimation of a wide variety of social–scientific functional explanations. Others still, e.g. Jon Elster (1982), think that no such set of mechanisms can be found. Research and argument in this area will strongly influence the future of functionalism.

See also DARWINISM, SOCIAL; HOMEOSTASIS; STRUCTURALISM.

PVP

Bibliography

Cohen, G.A. 1978: *Karl Marx's theory of history: a defence.* Oxford: Oxford University Press; Princeton, N.J.: Princeton University Press.

Davis, K. 1959: The myth of functional analysis as a special method in sociology and anthropology. *American sociological review.* 24, 757–72.

*Elster, J. 1982: Marxism, functionalism and game theory. *Theory and society* 14.

Hempel, C.G. 1959: The logic of functional analysis. In *Aspects of scientific explanation and other essays in the philosophy of science.* New York: Free Press.

Luhman, N. 1974: *Zweckbegriff und Systemrationalität.* Frankfurt: Suhrkamp.

Malinowski, B. 1922: *Argonauts of the Western Pacific.* London: Routledge & Kegan Paul.

Merton, R. K. 1949: Manifest and latent functions. In *Social theory and social structure.* New York: Free Press.

*Moore, W.E. 1978: Functionalism. In *A history of sociological analysis.* ed. T. Bottomore and R. Nisbet; London: Heinemann.

Nagel, E. 1956: A formalization of functionalism. In *Logic without metaphysics.* New York: Free Press.

Parsons, T. 1961: An outline of the social system. In *Theories of society.* vol. 1. New York: Free Press.

Radcliffe-Brown, A.R. 1922: *The Andaman Islanders.* New York: Free Press.

——— 1952: *Structure and function in primitive society.* London: Routledge & Kegan Paul.

Van Parijs, P. 1981: *Evolutionary explanation in the social sciences: an emerging paradigm.* Totowa, N.J.: Rowman & Littlefield; London: Tavistock.

Wright, L. 1976: *Teleological explanations.* Berkeley, Calif.: University of California Press.

functions of language *See* language: functions of

G

GABA (gama-amino-butyric-acid) A putative inhibitory neurotransmitter found in high concentrations in the mammalian brain and spinal cord. It is synthesized in the body from glutamic acid, a reaction which is dependent on a vitamin B6 cofactor. In humans, GABA is found in relatively high concentrations in neural elements of the EXTRAPYRAMIDAL MOTOR SYSTEM, the HYPOTHALAMUS and certain nuclei of the CEREBELLUM, while the concentration in the CEREBRAL CORTEX is relatively low. The inhibitory effects of GABA are probably due to the hyperpolarization of the postsynaptic neuron, thus making it less likely to initiate an action potential. After release, GABA may be cleared from the synaptic cleft (see SYNAPSE) via reuptake into the presynaptic neuron. It has been suggested that deficiencies of GABA may be associated with nervous system disorders such as epilepsy and Huntington's Disease (Cooper, Bloom and Roth 1978).

GPH

Bibliography

Cooper, Jack R., Bloom, Floyd E. and Roth, Robert H. 1978: *The biochemical basis of neuropharmacology*: 3rd edn. New York: Oxford University Press.

galvanic skin response (GSR) A change in the electrical resistance of the skin, related to sweating. The GSR can be produced by a minute electrical current and as such has been widely used as an unconditional response in classical conditioning paradigms. The GSR also occurs in situations which provoke emotion or anxiety. As a result it has become important in lie detection where it is used together with other measures regulated by the autonomic nervous system such as blood pressure and respiratory rate. The underlying assumption is that the individual may be capable of hiding overt expressions of emotion associated with lying, but not the autonomic responses that are beyond voluntary control. While useful in this respect these measures, including GSR, are not always reliable and are usually not admissible as evidence in a court of law. GWI

games A term referring to a variety of experimental paradigms used primarily in the study of cooperation and competition and of decision-making under conditions of uncertainty. Typically, subjects are required to choose between sets of response alternatives which can lead to a range of possible costs and benefits to themselves and/or to others with whom they interact.

The original focus of social psychological research on games was on how behavior is influenced by the structural properties of a situation defined in terms of costs and benefits contingent on alternative choices. The analysis of such costs and benefits was based on the mathematical theory of games derived from studies of economic behavior (von Neumann and Morgenstern 1944). More recent research has emphasized the importance of more cognitive variables, particularly trust and interpretation of others' intentions.

Social psychologists have been mainly concerned with games in which two or more people are (supposedly) interacting with each other, and the costs and benefits each receives are contingent both on their own choices and on the choices made by their "partners" in the interaction. By far the most frequently used game of this kind is that called the "Prisoner's Dilemma" (PD). The name refers to an imaginary situation in which two accomplices are awaiting trial, and are each individually offered lighter sentences if they plead guilty and inform on the other. If neither informs, they are likely to get away with moderate sentences. If one informs and the other does not, the informant receives a light sentence, the other a severe one, but if both inform, their sentences will be more severe than if they both kept quiet. The dilemma here is that, *if* you can trust your partner, the best *joint* outcome is for both you and your partner to keep quiet. On the other hand, whatever your partner does, you will be better off *individually* if you inform – except that if your partner thinks the same way, each of you will end up informing on the other.

In the laboratory, this dilemma is represented in terms of a two-person game where each person has a choice of two possible responses. The outcomes for each player depending on his own behavior and that of his partner are represented in terms of a pay-off matrix, as shown in Figure 1. The figures above the diagonal in each square of the matrix refer to the outcomes of player A, those below the diagonal represent the outcomes of player B. The numbers in parentheses are examples of a typical PD pay-off structure. For a game to be classed as a PD, the pay-offs must conform to the following rules:

a) $X_3 > X_1 > X_4 > X_2$; and

b) $2X_1 > (X_2 + X_3) > 2X_4$

The two response alternatives (labeled C and D) are usually referred to as "cooperative" and "competitive" moves respectively. The PD is an example of a "non-zero sum mixed-motive" game. "Non-zero sum" means that there is at least one cell of the matrix where the sum of A's and B's outcomes does not equal zero. "Mixed-motive" means that the structure could motivate subjects either to cooperate (jointly achieve X_1 rather than X_4 outcomes) or to compete (individually achieve X_3 rather than X_1 or X_4 rather than X_2).

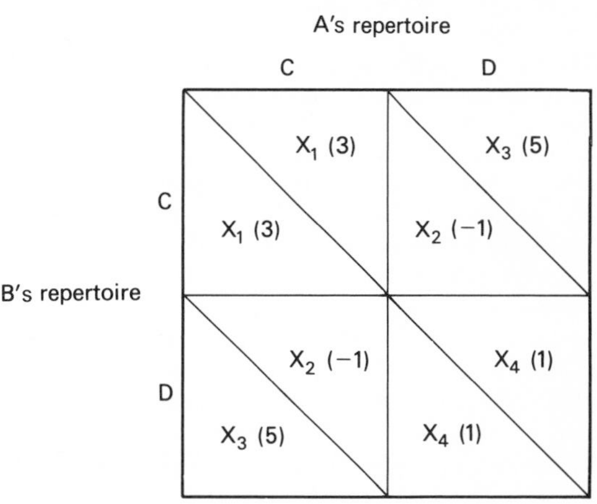

Research on the PD has shown that mutual cooperation is extremely difficult to achieve in the standard situation where subjects respond simultaneously (i.e. without knowledge of the other's choice until after they have made their own) over a series of trials. Typically, the percentage of cooperative responses is no more than about 40 per cent. The main question researchers have asked, therefore, is why cooperation is not higher.

A number of experiments have simulated the behavior of the partner, substituting a pre-programmed sequence of responses without the subjects' knowledge (Oskamp 1971). The most effective strategy in improving cooperation is when the simulated "partner" responds cooperatively only when the subject cooperates. Other studies have manipulated the real money value of the rewards and costs in the pay-off matrix, which are often notional or imaginary. Within limits, such manipulations have comparatively little effect. The *relative* sizes of the pay-offs, real or imaginary, however, can be quite effective (Terhune 1968). Other researchers have manipulated the way in which the pay-off matrix is presented to subjects (Pruitt and Kimmel 1977). Such manipulations can have quite dramatic effects on levels of cooperation, even though the pay-offs remain unaltered from a mathematical point of view. In the standard procedure players are unable to communicate with each other, and there are suggestions that this may be one of the most important factors inhibiting cooperation (Nemeth 1972). However, the effectiveness of communication depends on there being a basis of trust.

Much of the early work on the effects of trust used a "trucking game" devised by Deutsch and Krauss (1962), in which the players take the role of owners of trucking firms both needing to use a one-lane road in opposite directions. Using a PD, Kelley and Stahelski (1970) considered the factors which influence subjects to attribute cooperative or competitive intentions to their partner. They point out that, because of the structure of the PD, someone who acts competitively may also force his partner to act competitively out of self-defense. However, they argue, competitive individuals fail to discount the causative influence of their own behavior on that of their partner. Consequently, competitive individuals tend to see their partners as competitive also, whereas cooperative individuals tend to be more varied in the intentions they attribute to their partner. Miller and Holmes (1975) show that the special form of this relationship no longer applies when the structure of the game is "expanded" to include a third response option which enables players to defend themselves without their behavior being interpretable as attempts at exploitation.

Experimental games have been repeatedly criticized for their apparent artificiality and lack of generalizability (e.g. Sermat 1970). However, there may be real-life situations that can also be characterized as "mixed-motive", where short term individual gains need to be foregone if longer term mutual gains are to be achieved (cf. Pruitt and Kimmel 1977). Game-theoretical concepts and gaming analogies have been used more widely within social psychology (Thibaut and Kelley 1959), sociology (Goffman 1970) and popular writings on psychotherapy (Berne 1968) (see TRANSACTIONAL ANALYSIS). Laboratory research stresses that, in applying such concepts one must be attentive both to the structure of interactions, and to how they are interpreted by the subjects. JRE

Bibliography

Berne, E. 1968: *Games people play: the psychology of human relationships.* Harmondsworth: Penguin.

Deutsch, M and Krauss, R.M. 1962: Studies of interpersonal bargaining. *Journal of conflict resolution* 6, 52–76.

Goffman, E. 1970: *Strategic interaction.* Oxford: Basil Blackwell; Philadelphia: University of Pennsylvania Press.

Kelley, H.H. and Stahelski, A.J. 1970: Social interaction basis of cooperators' and competitors' beliefs about others. *Journal of personality and social psychology* 16, 66–91.

Miller, D.T. and Holmes, J.G. 1975: The role of situational restrictiveness on self-fulfilling prophecies: a therorετical and empirical extension of Kelley and Stahelski's Triangle Hypothesis. *Journal of personality and social psychology* 31, 661–73.

Nemeth, C. 1972: A critical analysis of research utilizing the prisoner's dilemma paradigm for the study of bargaining. In *Advances in experimental social psychology*, ed. L. Berkowitz, Vol. 6 New York: Academic Press.

Oskamp, S. 1971: Effects of programmed strategies on cooperation in the Prisoner's Dilemma and other mixed-motive games. *Journal of conflict resolution* 15, 225–59.

Pruitt, D.G. and Kimmel, M.J. 1977: Twenty years of experimental gaming: critique, synthesis, and suggestions for the future. *Annual review of psychology* 28, 363–92.

Sermat, V. 1970: Is game behavior related to behavior in other interpersonal situations? *Journal of personality and social psychology* 16, 92–109.

Terhune, K.W. 1968: Motives, situation, and interpersonal conflict within the Prisoner's Dilemma. *Journal of personality and social psychology monograph supplement* 8_S 1–24.

Thibaut, J.W. and Kelley, H.H. 1959: *The social psychology of groups.* New York: Wiley.

Von Neumann, J and Morgenstern, O. 1944: *Theory of games and economic behavior.* Princeton, N.J.: Princeton University Press.

gamma-amino-butyric acid *See* GABA

gaze Reactions to others depend on how they are perceived and how their behavior is interpreted. It follows that how much people look, and when and where they look are crucial for their social performance. Most research treats gaze only as a signal, but it operates primarily as a channel.

Gaze has a social function early in life. By the third week infants smile at a nodding head, and during the fourth week there is mutual gaze between mother and infant. Bruner found that at six weeks mother–infant interaction involves games like peek-a-boo, which consist basically of making and breaking mutual gaze. The level of gaze declines up to adolescence and then increases again.

These gaze phenomena have been found in all cultures. However, there are cultural differences. "Contact cultures", where people stand closer and touch more, also gaze more. In these cultures social relations could be more intimate (in terms of subjective feeling), or the same signals may simply have different meanings.

In every culture people notice if gaze is incorrect; this indicates the presence of cultural rules. Too much gaze is regarded as intrusive or disrespectful, too little as insincere and cold. Gaze can also vary in meaning between different cultures. Belief in the evil eye is still common in some Mediterranean countries. Certain women or priests, who have squints or deep-set eyes, are thought to cast a curse on people they look at. These ideas perhaps arise out of the discomfort of being stared at by strangers.

A person will look at someone he or she likes more than at someone disliked. Rubin found that couples who were more in love engaged in more mutual gaze than couples less deeply in love. Argyle and Dean suggested that pairs of people reach an equilibrium of intimacy, based on conflicting approach and avoidance forces. This is expressed by a combination of affiliative signals, such as gaze, proximity or smiling. If the equilibrium is disturbed, for example by an increase of distance, compensating signals would be expected, such as more gaze. Their experiments confirmed this and other findings also support it; for example, Exline found less gaze and mutual gaze when intimate topics are being discussed.

Gaze can signal other attitudes besides liking and loving. Submissive or lower status people look more, especially while listening. Hostility can be signaled by a stare, or by aversion of gaze, as when ignoring another person. Deception and embarrassment are accompanied by reduced gaze. Other emotions produce characteristic gaze patterns; for example, depression is shown by gazing downwards. In the main positive attitudes and emotions, such as liking and happiness, are shown by more gaze, and negative ones such as dislike and depression, by less. People look at those they like because the appearance and behavior of the other are rewarding. In addition, the gaze conveys further information about the attitudes and emotions of the gazer.

People being gazed at have an impression of being the object of the other's attention. In the experience of mutual gaze each person feels that he is open to the other. The general meaning of being gazed at is that the other is attending and interested. But the perceived nature of the other's interest varies.

Gaze may be interpreted as a threat. Ellsworth and others found that continuous staring caused motorists to move off more rapidly from stop-lights. Marsh found that a glance by a rival football fan may start a fight. However, gaze is only seen as a threat under certain conditions. It can lead to help if someone who has collapsed stares at the nearest person.

Gaze is used as a clue to emotions and personality. A person looking 15 per cent of the time is seen as nervous, evasive and defensive while if he looks 85 per cent of the time, he is seen as self-confident, friendly and sincere. The way the eyes are opened is also used. Emotions can be decoded with above-chance accuracy from photos of the eyes, while for certain mixed emotional states, such as pleasure and anger, this is the most informative area of the face.

In conversation, speakers use gaze at the ends of long utterances and at grammatical breaks. This is to see whether the other person has understood, agreed, and so on, or whether the listener is willing to continue listening. But there is much more gaze while listening than when speaking. It has been suggested that this is because speakers' attention is directed towards planning what to say, so they look away to avoid cognitive overload. However, this hypothesis is not supported by La France and Mayo's finding that North American Blacks look more when speaking than when listening.

During conversation people take turns in speaking and usually manage without much overlap or interruption. This is mainly through nonverbal cues, of which gaze is one. The speaker's final gaze functions as a full-stop signal. If there is no terminal gaze, it is often some time before the other person replies, at least when the conversation is hesitant.

A speaker may also use gaze as an emphasizer, sometimes by a sudden widening of the eyes. A listener indicates his attention and also his approval by looking, nodding and smiling. These glances act as reinforcers, increasing the speaker's tendency to talk about particular topics.

Gaze also plays a part in greetings. Kendon found that there is a mutual glance in the first stage, the "distant salutation", aversion during approach and another mutual gaze in the third, or close, phase, when bodily contact also occurs. These phases are reversed in partings, again with two mutual glances.

Females look more than males. The difference is greatest for mutual gaze and for looking while talking. Girls attend to faces more than boys do at six months, so there may be an innate difference. But this difference increases, and is greater for adults. Gaze is probably used more for affiliative purposes by females, and their affiliative needs are stronger. Furthermore, being looked at for a female is probably interpreted in terms of affiliation or sexual interest, rather than threat.

In conclusion, people look at each other when they are interested in each other's reactions. This leads to gaze acquiring meaning as a social signal. There may have been evolutionary development of gaze as a ritualized signal whose meaning is innate. Gaze plays a central part in communication, and is closely co-ordinated with speech. The use of gaze can go wrong in a variety of ways: aversion of gaze and staring are common in mental patients. JMA/RL

Bibliography

*Argyle, M. and Cook, M. 1976: *Gaze and mutual gaze.* Cambridge and New York: Cambridge University Press.

Argyle, M. and Dean, J. 1965: Eye-contact, distance and affiliation. *Sociometry* 28, 289–304.

Bruner, J.S. 1976: Early rule structure: the case of peek-a-boo. In *Life sentences*, ed. R. Harré. New York: Wiley.

Ellsworth, P.C., Carlsmith, J.M. and Henson, A. 1972: The stare as a stimulus to fight in human subjects: a series of field experiments. *Journal of personality and social psychology* 21, 302–11.

Exline, R. and Fehr, B.J. 1978: Application of semiosis to the study of visual interaction. In *Nonverbal Behavior and Communication*, eds. A.W. Siegman and S. Feldstein. Hillsdale, N.J.: Erlbaum.

Kendon, A. and Ferber, A. 1973: A description of some human greetings. In *Comparative ecology and behavior of primates*, eds. R.P. Michael and J.H. Crook. London: Academic Press.

La France, M. and Mayo, C. 1976: Racial differences in gaze behavior during conversation. *Journal of personality and social psychology* 33, 547–52.

Marsh, P., Rosser, E. and Harré, R. 1978: *The rules of disorder.* London: Routledge and Kegan Paul.

Geisteswissenschaftliche psychologie Originally referred to psychology as it explores the transindividual, objective mind and its products, then its relations to individual, subjective minds, whence the alleged foundation of *Geisteswissenschaften* (i.e. the humanities, historical and cultural sciences). It was put forward by E. Spranger, a disciple of Dilthey, as an elaboration of the term *Verstehende Psychologie*, with which it is now used interchangeably. HUKG

generalization: in animals Absence of DISCRIMINATION. When an animal has been trained to respond to one stimulus it may or may not respond in the same way to another stimulus. When it does so respond it is said to generalize between the two stimuli, and when it does not do so it is said to discriminate between them.

When presented with a series of stimuli of which one is familiar, animals often produce a weaker response the greater the difference between the familiar and the test stimuli, giving rise to a generalization gradient. For example, Guttman and Kalish (1958) trained pigeons to peck at colored lights to obtain food rewards. A pigeon trained to peck at a yellow light showed a progressively diminishing response when presented with lights of a different color. DJM

Bibliography

Guttman, N. and Kalish, H.I. 1958: *Scientific American* 198, 77–82.

generalization: in learning The recurrence of a learned behavior in a situation different from, but in some way resembling, that in which learning originally took place. The more similar the new situation, the more likely and complete the transfer. The decline in performance as a new situation deviates from the original is called generalization decrement; progressively greater generalization decrement as a situation becomes more dissimilar to the original defines a generalization gradient. Such gradients or stimulus control functions can show which aspects of a situation were learned about by an individual; varying a situation systematically in terms of some aspect or sensory dimension will yield a steep generalization gradient only if that aspect has been learned about originally. Steep gradients may result either where the sensory dimension is spontaneously perceived and discriminated, or where the subject has previously experienced stimuli of that kind being differentially predictive of reinforcement. Generalization may occur on the basis of abstract qualities or rules, as well as simple sensory features. WKi

generation A term originating from biology with distinct uses in social and political theory. In its strictly biological sense it refers to the coming into existence of a new organism (animal, plant, human) from the time of fertilization to its full reproductive maturity. The possibility for the spontaneous emergence of living entities, independent of any parent has led to what is known as "spontaneous generation". Controversy has centered around the issues of: (a) whether such entities develop from organic or inorganic matter, (b) whether spontaneous generation is a recurring phenomenon or one that occurred only in the past, and (c) whether such generation is attributable to chance or exhibits probabilistic regularities (Farley 1977). Today most topics relevant to biological generation form the science of genetics.

In socio-political terms a generation consists of persons in a common age group sharing the same cultural and historical experiences. The term "generational conflict" refers to the problems and conflicts observed between the younger generation trying to effect change, and the older generation trying to maintain the status quo. Many theorists have discussed the interconnection of this concept and the concept of social change. The Spanish philosopher José Ortega y Gasset, for example, considers the coexistence of various generations and the relations established between them as representing the dynamic system that makes up historic life. For Ortega, the key generational struggle takes place between those moving into middle age and those moving out of it (Sheleff 1981; Esler 1974). The German sociologist, Karl Mannheim, on the other hand, emphasized that a generation becomes an actuality when a common consciousness is aroused, i.e., when individuals participate in the social and intellectual currents of their society and period. There has been a recent resurgence of interest in the concept of generation in social and political theory. MG

Bibliography

Esler, A. ed. 1974: *The youth revolution: the conflict of generations in modern history*. Lexington, Mass.: D.C. Heath.

Farley, J. 1977: *The spontaneous generation controversy from Descartes to Oparin*. Baltimore and London: Johns Hopkins University Press.

Ortéga y Gasset, José 1974: The importance of generationhood. In Esler, op. cit.

Mannheim, Karl 1974: What is a social generation? In Esler, op. cit.

Sheleff, L.S. 1981: *Generations apart: adult hostility to youth*. New York: McGraw-Hill.

generative theory Refers to a type of theory that undermines confidence in current understandings and offers new alternatives to existing conventions of conduct. Gergen initially proposed the generative criterion as an alternative to the traditional but problematic positivist criteria for evaluating psychological theories, namely those of verification and resistance to falsification. Because symbol systems may have important shaping effects within the society, it is important to develop criteria for evaluating psychological theory that take into account the potential impact of the theory on a society that incorporates its mode of intelligibility. The generative criterion is designed to do this. (See also ENLIGHTENMENT EFFECTS.) KJG

Bibliography

Gergen, K.J. 1978: Toward generative theory. *Journal of personality and social psychology*. 36, 1344–60.

genetic counseling Advice about the risk of recurrence of congenital abnormalities. It may be offered to parents after the birth of an abnormal child, or to anyone who may be a carrier of an inheritable condition such as haemophilia. Assessment of the risk of recurrence involves an accurate diagnosis of the condition, including a search for chromosome abnormalities; a knowledge of the genetic transmission of the disorder, and a search among other family members for affected individuals or carriers. It is as important to be able to reassure parents that their child's abnormalities are not likely to recur in subsequent pregnancies as it is to warn them of a high risk of recurrence. GCF

Bibliography

Harper, P.S. 1981: *Practical genetic counselling*. Bristol: John Wright and Sons.

genetic epistemology The aim of genetic epistemology was to establish a new branch of philosophy and it had as its subject matter both the origin and the structure of knowledge. James Ward (see Ward 1883) outlined the genetic methods required by this philosophical subdiscipline, and James M. Baldwin (see e.g. Baldwin 1915) formulated its task as the reconstruction of logic from a developmental point of view, the establishment of experimental logic and the theory of the origins of cultural values.

In contemporary thought, the term genetic epistemology refers to the work of Jean PIAGET as well as to the empirical and experimental research, carried out in a Piagetian framework, on the development of concepts, logical operations and symbolic thinking in children.

Piaget's synthesis of philosophy of science and psychology draws a parallel between the evolution of the sciences and the ontogeny of thinking; in both realms there is a development from practical operations toward mathematical logic and axiomatization. Piaget thus transforms the allegedly speculative or metaphysical philosophy of science of the French constructivists into a set of testable problems in cognitive development (see Piaget 1967, 1970).

Most developmental psychologists influenced by Piaget have lost sight of this link between psychology and the philosophy of science. They limit themselves largely to elaborating on the stage-features of sensori-motor, concrete operational, pre-operational and formal operational thinking, while the processes of transition from one level to the next, remain to be determined. AM

Bibliography

Baldwin, J.M. 1915: *Genetic theory of reality*. New York and London: Putnam.

Piaget, J. 1967: Nature et méthode de l'épistémologie. In *Logique et connaissance scientifique*. Paris: Gallimard.

——— 1970: *L'Épistémologie génétique*. Paris: Presses universitaires de France.

Ward, James 1883: Psychological principles I. *Mind*.

genetics, evolution and behavior Genetic and evolutionary influences on human behavior remain controversial areas of study more than a century after Mendel's discovery of particulate inheritance and Darwin's original exposition of evolutionary theory. In the 1970s and early '80s acrimonious debate reached new depths following, for example, Jensen's publication (1969) of a review paper combining the topics of genetics, intelligence, and race, and Wilson's treatise (1975) on behavioral evolution. The current debates often involve heavy doses of polemical politics and *ad hominem* attacks. However, at the same time they often represent attempts by practitioners of academic disciplines such as anthropology, biology, genetics, psychology, and sociology to come to grips with a plethora of new information which crosses their traditional disciplinary boundaries.

Two fundamental approaches have been applied in the study of genetics. One is mechanism oriented and involves Mendelian segregation combined with physiological and cellular studies of genetic influences on the development of the phenotype of individuals. The second is a statistical approach, variously labeled biometrical or quantitative genetics, which attempts to understand the influence of genetic variation on phenotypic variation by analysing the patterns of distribution of characteristics among the members of populations. Both approaches have been applied to the investigation of psychological phenotypes.

That genetic variation can have profound influences on behavioral phenotypes of humans was unequivocally demonstrated by the discovery and subsequent investigations of phenylketonuria (PKU) beginning in the 1930s. This now-treatable form of profound mental retardation is related to a metabolic block of a particular enzymatic pathway which is itself due to homozygosity for a particular genetic allele at a single autosomal locus. The discovery of a specific genetic etiology for a particular set of retardates constituted a true breakthrough in investigations of the causes of retardation. PKU is now a classic model for a large set of genetically distinct 'aminoacidurias' and further single-gene causes of retardation. Another 'breakthrough' in understanding the genetic underpinnings of human variation was the discovery in 1959 that an extra chromosome was the cause of Down's Syndrome. It was only in 1956 that the normal diploid human chromosome number was established to be 46 (44 autosomes plus two sex chromosomes, X and Y). Having 47 chromosomes with the supernumerary being an extra copy of the chromosome labeled number 21, hence 'trisomy-21', is the cause of Down's syndrome. Females having one X chromosome rather than the normal two (45XO) were, also in 1959, discovered to display Turner's syndrome, the symptoms of which include a specific cognitive deficit and failure to mature sexually. Klinefelter's syndrome males (47XXY) have an extra X chromosome, and display sexual and personality disturbances. These and many other chromosomal anomalies associated with behavioral symptoms have been discovered in recent decades. At the present time human chromosome studies (cytogenetics) is one of the fastest expanding areas of genetic investigation with implications for psychology. Literally many hundreds of genetic alleles are now known to influence various aspects of psychological function, ranging from sensory abilities to cognition.

The biometrical approach to understanding hereditary contributions to individual differences in human behavior antedates the discovery of Mendelian genetics, having begun with investigations by Sir Francis Galton. Recent advances in methodological sophistication, especially techniques involving path coefficients and utilizing twin and adoptive family data, continue to contribute to an unraveling of the complexities of genetic and environmental influences on psychological individuality. Bouchard and McGue (1981) reviewed 111 studies, many of them recent, containing an aggregate of 526 familial correlations including 113,942 pairings dealing with genetic involvement in intellectual functioning as assessed by IQ tests. The general interpretation of the outcomes of carefully conducted studies has not changed since the inception of IQ tests early in the century; a substantial proportion of the variation in IQ appears to be mediated genetically. However, numerical estimates of the technical heritability statistic, which indexes the proportion of trait variance which is attributable to genetic variance of the population, has changed. Recent large studies point to an heritability of IQ in the vicinity of .5, rather than the .75–.8 values which were widely cited in previous decades. Large scale adoption and twin studies, some utilizing the extensive national records available in some countries (such as Denmark), are being conducted for many psychological variables. An inherited susceptibility or predisposition has been documented for many behavioral dimensions, ranging from smoking and alcoholism to homosexuality and likelihood of criminal activity, as well as diverse psychopathologies and variation in normal-range personality traits. Although specific mechanisms remain undiscovered, the evidence is unequivocal for a strong genetic dimension in the etiology of both schizophrenia and affective psychoses. Somewhat surprisingly to many, Plomin et al. (1980) point out that when genetic background is taken into account there remains no evidence for an important role of any known environmental variables in the development of schizophrenia. Although the details vary, and in most cases are poorly understood at present, it is perhaps not surprising that genetic individual differences appear to play a role in the development of individual differences on every psychological variable that has been investigated (Whitney 1976). At the present time the rapidly accumulating knowledge of genetic influences on behavior has exceeded its incorporation into general psychological theory.

Although data now outstrip general theory in the realm of psychological genetics, in the realm of human behavioral evolution theoretical speculations greatly exceed empirical data. Phenotypic variation influenced to some degree by heritable genetic variation, combined with differential reproductive success (individual Darwinian fitness or inclusive fitness) is the essence of evolution. While it is clear that heritable variation does influence most (perhaps all) dimensions of human behavior it is usually difficult to relate behavioral variation and concomitant genetical variation, at least within the normal range of variation, to differential reproductive success. Bajema (1971) has drawn together a number of papers which attempt to measure ongoing genetic evolution in contemporary societies. Unfortunately virtually every serious study is met with a wide range of criticism, much of it not scientifically grounded. Nevertheless, theoretical speculation and accounts of plausible possibilities abound in both the technical and popular literature.

Most recent accounts of human behavioral evolution remain at the level of comparisons between species and largely restrict their treatments of human behavior to species-general typological concepts. This is the case even though natural selection depends on heritable variation among individuals within the species. It has become impolite and exceedingly controversial even to discuss heritable individual differences which could involve human behavioral evolution, and academics tread lightly. Nevertheless possibilities abound, many based on quite extensive data. As an example, phenotypic intelligence as measured by the controversial IQ tests displays many of the characteristics to be expected of an evolutionarily-relevant phenotype. Phenotypic individual differences are large, measurable, and have substantial genetic influence; extreme individuals, at least at the low end of the trait continuum, are severely depressed in reproductive performance; the trait displays inbreeding depression as do many other fitness relevant traits; and a reproductive difference favoring individuals of above average intelligence is demonstrable even within some modern industralized populations. The latter finding, replicated in various independent studies (e.g. Waller 1971), is surprising to many layman who share the common observation that 'less bright' people tend to have larger families. The actual data are consistent with that observation. However, a larger proportion of the 'less bright' people also have no children at all. When account is taken of the reproductive performance of all the members of a group, including those that do not reproduce, the general outcome has been that higher intelligence is positively related to reproductive performance.

Racial variation is another taboo topic that could shed considerable light on human behavioral evolution. Of course existing biological races of humans display considerable overlap of distribution for many behavioral traits and share many of the same genes. Some geneticists and anthropologists have stated that the vast preponderance of genetic variation is among individuals within race and not among races, leading to suggestions that investigations of racial subgroups within the species would not be fruitful with regard to evolutionary interests. However Neel (1981) points out that from simultaneous consideration of only 8 genetic loci one can be correct about 87 per cent of the time in assignment of an individual to race, and greater accuracy can be obtained when dealing with small groups. Races differ in the frequency of many genes, including many of relevance to behavior. Well known examples include the genes responsible for PKU, which are predominantly found among Caucasians; Tay-Sachs disease which is almost exclusively limited to Jewish populations; and Sickle Cell Anemia which is most common in Blacks. The incidence of many behavioral phenotypes also differs substantially among races. Examples are many: the distribution of IQ scores have been found in studies from the 1920s through the 1980s to differ among races in an ordering of Americans of Asian ancestry, Americans of European Caucasian ancestry, Americans of Black African ancestry; rates of psychologically relevant phenomena such as homicide, schizophrenia, affective psychoses, and suicide differ substantially among races. Although studies of racial variation within other species have shed much light on the processes of evolution in general, the recent social climate has tended to stifle investigations of human behavioral genetics and behavioral evolution from this potentially informative perspective. GW

Bibliography

Bajema, Carl J. (comp.) 1971. *Natural selection in human populations.* New York and Chichester (W. Sussex): John Wiley & Sons, Inc.

Bouchard, T.J., and McGue, M. 1981. Familial studies of intelligence: A review. *Science 212,* 1055–9.

Jensen, A.R. 1969. How much can we boost IQ and scholastic achievement? *Harvard educational review* 39(1), 1-123.

*Lumsden, Charles J., and Wilson, Edward O. 1981. *Genes, mind, and culture.* Cambridge, Mass. and London: Harvard University Press.

Neel, J.V. 1981. The major ethnic groups: Diversity in the midst of similarity. *The American naturalist 117,* 83–7.

*Plomin, Robert, DeFries, John C., and McClearn, Gerald E. 1980. *Behavioral genetics, a primer.* San Francisco: W.H. Freeman and Company.

*Vogel, F., and Motulsky, A.G. 1979. *Human genetics.* Berlin and New York: Springer-Verlag.

Waller, J.H. 1971. Differential reproduction: Its relation to IQ test scores, education, and occupation. *Social biology 18*, 122–136.

Whitney, G. 1976. Genetic considerations in studies of the evolution of the nervous system and behavior. In R. Bruce Masterton, William Hodos and Harry Jerison (Eds.), 1976. *Evolution, brain and behavior: persistent problems.* Hillsdale, N.J.: Lawrence Erlbaum Associates, 79–106. London: distrib. by (Halsted Press Div.), Wiley, 1976.

Wilson, Edward O. 1975. *Sociobiology: the new synthesis.* Cambridge, Mass.: Belknap Press of Harvard University Press.

genetics *See above, and also* behavior genetics

Genie The name of a girl discovered by Los Angeles social workers at the age of fourteen in conditions of almost total sensory deprivation and social isolation. At the time of her discovery, in 1970, she had not acquired language. Genie's linguistic development is still being studied. It is hoped that these studies will lead to progress in the following areas:
(1) the question as to the critical age of normal first LANGUAGE ACQUISTION;
(2) the relationship between LANGUAGE AND COGNITION;
(3) the relationship between the social and the structural aspects of language.
For a recent interim report see Curtis et al. (1975). PM

Bibliography

Curtis, S., et al. 1975: To update on the linguistic development of Genie, In *Developmental psycholinguistics*, ed. D.P. Dato. Washington D.C.: Georgetown University Press.

geometrical–optical illusions *See* visual illusions

gerontolinguistics Concerns the nature of the linguistic systems used by old people and their communication problems in general. At the moment it can hardly be called a separate field within psycholinguistics, but for both social and linguistic reasons it is likely to become one in the near future. Areas of particular interest include the decrease in stylistic flexibility and reading skills in the elderly and the loss of second languages in bilinguals (Clyne 1977). PM

Bibliography

Clyne, Michael G. 1977: Bilingualism of the elderly. *Talanya* 4, 45–56.

Helfrich, Hede 1979: Age markers in speech. In *Social markers in speech*, ed. K.R. Scherer and H. Giles. Cambridge and New York: Cambridge University Press.

gerontology Involves the study of social and psychological mechanisms in ageing. It is a complex, wide-ranging and multidisciplinary subject. No sharp distinction can be drawn between the mechanisms of aging and the mechanisms of chronic degenerative illness. Research and theory in psychosomatics, behavioral medicine and psychoneuroimmunology expresses a conviction that psychological factors influence not only mental well-being in the sick and the old, but also neuroendocrine balances, immune system competence and cardiovascular function, and hence an individual's physical fitness and longevity. Evidence has accumulated which shows that the onset and course of almost every form of chronic degenerative illness are susceptible to social influences, many of which become especially acute in the lives of old people.

The main areas of research

(i) *Large-scale epidemiological surveys:* statistical surveys of rates of death and disability among populations of retired people.

(ii) *Quality of life studies:* the study of amenities, living conditions, social services and other environmental and economic factors and their relation to health and longevity in the elderly.

(iii) *Personal contact and social support:* studies of family relations, social networks, isolation and loneliness in the elderly. These involve the use of ad hoc scales as well as interview techniques.

(iv) *Studies of work and retirement:* factors affecting the adjustment of individuals who are retiring from work and descriptive studies of the transition from work to retirement.

(v) *Biographical studies:* based on the idea of life as an unfolding biographical career, this approach sets a value on forming an understanding of an individual's priorities for later life by listening to the accounts he gives of the path of his life history.

All these areas of research share the ultimate objective of prescribing measures to assist the elderly. The wider-scale survey style studies assume such measures to be general and commensurable, the smaller-scale idiographic studies reflect the assumption that caring involves sensitivity to the particular esoteric needs of an individual.

The main theories

(i) *Disengagement theory* (Cumming and Henry 1961): a functionalist theory in which ageing is represented as a process of mutual withdrawal of individual and society. The individual necessarily withdraws because of his or her diminished abilities; society withdraws because younger people are needed to fill vacant roles.

(ii) *Activity theory* (Lemon et al. 1972): opposed to disengagement theory in proposing that although role-related activity diminishes with age, level of activity nevertheless correlates with life satisfaction and perhaps health and longevity.

(iii) *Social breakdown model* (Kuypers and Bengtson 1973): ageing is characterized by the loss of an identity previously sustained through roles, norms (see NORM), and reference groups (see REFERENCE GROUP), and substitution of the identity "old person", with its connotation of incompetence and social redundancy.

(iv) *Exchange theory* (Dowd 1975): A generalization of economic exchange theory; the decline in power resources associated with age prevents the aged from becoming involved in balanced exchange relationships with other groups.

(v) *Learned helplessness model* (Abramson et al. 1978) (see LEARNED HELPLESSNESS); the diminished powers of old people give rise to attributions of uncontrollability of important outcomes. This results in a generalized helplessness set, leading to depression and perhaps illness. RGT

Bibliography

Abramson, L.Y., Seligman, M.E.P. and Teasdale, J.D. 1978: Learned helplessness in humans: critique and reformulation. *Journal of abnormal psychology*, 87, 49–74.

*Binstock, R. and Shanas, E., eds. 1976: *Handbook of aging and the social sciences*. New York: Van Nostrand.

Cumming, E. and Henry, W.E. 1961: *Growing old*. New York: Basic Books.

Dowd, J. 1975: Aging as exchange: a preface to theory. *Journal of gerontology* 30, 584–94.

Kuypers, J.A. and Bengtson, V.L. 1973: Social breakdown and competence: a model of normal aging. *Human development* 16, 181–201.

Lemon, B.W., Bengtson, V.L. and Peterson, J.A. 1972: An exploration of the activity theory of aging: activity and life satisfaction among inmovers to a retirement community. *Journal of gerontology*. 27, 511–23.

Gestalt A German word meaning "pattern" or "form", the term was introduced into philosophical psychology by the German psychologist C. von Ehrenfels, and disseminated by K. Koffka and W. Köhler. Gestalt psychologists held that in perception we, and other animals, are aware directly of a configuration or structure which is grasped as a whole and not merely as an assemblage of its parts. A favored example is that we hear a melody as a whole and not merely as a series of discreet notes, another that white paper looks lighter than grey, even when so placed as to reflect less light. The fullest account of the theory in English is that in Wolfgang Köhler's *Gestalt psychology* (1930). JOU

Bibliography

Ehrenfels, C. von 1890: Gestaltqualitäten. In *Vierteljahrsschrift für wissenschaftliche Philosophie* XIV.

Köhler, Wolfgang 1930: *Gestalt psychology*. London: Kegan Paul.

Gestalt therapy An holistic approach which is guided by the beliefs that self-support and awareness are desirable therapeutic goals; and that therapy may be most beneficial when the client is viewed as a complex process, who acts out a variety of roles which are not necessarily consistent, but which derive their meanings from their configurations in particular contexts.

Gestalt therapy has been nurtured by a number of diverse sources. On the philosophical level, it is heavily indebted to EXISTENTIALISM, with its emphasis on the here and now, wholeness of experience, freedom and responsibility and its conception of "being-as-process". PHENOMENOLOGY has also contributed significantly to the Gestalt approach via its focus on the immediacy of experience, and its dictum that the world is only as it is lived, perceived, experienced by a particular person, and that meaning is an achievement which results from the unique manner in which persons constitute their world. ZEN BUDDHISM has also provided some valuable material for the Gestalt therapist with its commentary on the self, intuition and the organization of experience.

On the psychological level the principles and procedures of perceptual organization formulated by Gestalt psychologists were transposed into motivational and social descriptions by Gestalt therapists. Personal experience is characterized as a continuum of figure–ground relationships in which specific needs receive primary attention. When a need is fulfilled, it fades into the background, and other need-configurations emerge. If a need is not fulfilled i.e. if a *gestalten* is not completed it may produce a conflict which is distracting and drains psychic energy. Full awareness of the continuous process of the formation–dissolution–reformation of gestalten, and the proper acknowledgment of one's role in that process constitute the cornerstone of healthy being. Elements of psychoanalysis and behaviorism have been incorporated into the Gestalt position, as well as some of the central insights formulated by Carl JUNG, and Wilhelm REICH.

The actual practice of Gestalt therapy varies as much as the sources which have molded its approach. Gestalt therapists have developed novel therapeutic techniques, but are not primarily concerned with the development or application of techniques, *per se*. Each therapeutic encounter provides a unique situation. The therapist attends closely to what the client is *doing* in that situation. The therapist attends to the obvious. In addition to listening to what is being said, emphasis is also put on how the client is saying it. Breathing patterns, voice inflection, emotional tone, repetition, posture, gestures, body tensions etc., are closely monitored by the therapist. These features are pointed out to the client, and the therapist may devise an "experiment" which will clarify what is being symbolized by those patterns of activity. The purpose of the experiment is to induce the client to recognize, accept and take responsibility for certain aspects and conflicts within himself, or attitudes toward others which the therapist believes may be at the root of the client's anxiety, depression, neurosis or general discomfort. A typical experiment may require the client to act out and experience bodily and emotionally the roles of significant others, or those aspects or features of the client's personality which have been suppressed and are responsible for the bevy of resistances which confront the therapist. CWB

Bibliography

Fagan, J. and Shepherd, I.L., eds. 1970: *Gestalt therapy now: theory, techniques, applications*. New York and London: Harper Colophon Books.

Loew, C., Grayson, H. and Loew, G.H., eds. 1975: *Three psychotherapies: a clinical comparison*. New York: Brunner/Mazel.

Perls, F. 1973: *The Gestalt approach an eye witness to therapy*. USA: Science and Behavior Books.

Riet, V. Van De, Korb, M. and Gorrell, J.J. 1980: *Gestalt therapy*. New York and Oxford: Pergamon Press.

gesture The word is used in several senses. Either it is used specifically to refer to communication with the hands or some other part of the body (as in the case of facial gesture) or else it is used generally to refer to communication with the whole body. This section deals only with gesture as a form of manual communication, and the reader is referred to the entry on COMMUNICATION, NON-VERBAL for a discussion of other types of gesture.

The study of manual gesture can be traced back to Cicero and Quintilian, who were concerned with rhetorical uses of the hands in oratory. However it was only during the seventeenth century, with the publication of works such as

Bonifacio's *L'Arte dei Cenni* (1616) and Bulwer's *Chirologia . . . Chironomia* (1644), that gesture acquired the status of a subject in its own right. Bonifacio and Bulwer tended to rely on literary sources rather than observation for their evidence, and their treatments were taxonomic rather than functional or pragmatic. Bulwer, however, gave a great deal of attention to gesture as a speech surrogate, and he is generally acknowledged as the first author to recognize the possibility of a codified manual language for the deaf. Since the seventeenth century there has been a growing interest in gesture and its relations to other forms of communication, and it is now possible to identify several areas in which gesture has been studied.

Gesture and the origins of language

It has been seriously proposed that the phylogenetic origins of language are to be found in gesture. The list of authors who have advanced this notion includes such notables as Wundt, Swedenborg, Romanes, Paget and Johannesson. Although there are some variations in the theories that have been offered, the basic idea is that pre-linguistic hominids started by using a gestural form of communication, and that with the development of the brain and the vocal apparatus there was a corresponding shift from a manual to a vocal protolanguage, which in turn gave way to vocal language proper. A comprehensive treatment of this topic and the relevant literature can be found in Hewes (1975).

Gesture as a language

Certain societies and groups of people possess extremely elaborate repertoires of gesture. In some cases the repertoire may simply consist of a gestural lexis which does not have the properties of a language, and where the signs are typically employed as isolated units, whereas in other cases the lexis may be associated with a grammar and therefore be a fully constituted language. There appear to be three explanations for the development of gestural systems which have the properties of language. Firstly there are those groups, such as the Cistercian monks (Barakat 1975) and the Australian Aborigines (Kendon 1980) which have committed themselves to silence and eschewed the use of speech for reasons connected with religious belief or social custom, and which have therefore developed a sign language to take the place of speech. Secondly there are peoples such as the North American Plains Indians (Mallery 1880; Taylor 1975) who have been forced to invent a *mano franca* in order to make themselves intelligible to neighboring peoples who speak another language, and finally there are the deaf who have been deprived of the ability to speak (Stokoe 1980). There are also various other groups, such as racecourse touts, Bushmen hunters, Indian merchants, as well as radio, sawmill and stock exchange personnel, who have developed sign systems because of the need to communicate across great and sometimes noisy distances, but these systems are seldom properly constituted languages. The most elaborate and thoroughly researched case of a gestural language is that of American Sign Language (Klima and Bellugi 1979). However there are other sign languages used by the deaf. These include the Paget system and finger spelling.

Colloquial gestures

Colloquial gestures are those which are not part of a sign language. They can be divided into several categories, according to whether they are iconic or symbolic, whether they accompany speech or function as a substitute for speech, whether they are produced intentionally or unintentionally, and so on (Efron 1941; Ekman and Friesen 1969). The major categories of colloquial gesture include emblems, illustrators or mimic signs and batons.

(a) *Emblems.* An emblem is defined by the fact that its shape bears no obvious relationship to its meaning; like most words in language, the link between sign and meaning is arbitrary. Examples of emblems include gestures such as the Thumbs Up, in which the thumb is extended upwards from the fist, and the Ring sign, in which the tips of the thumb and first finger are brought together to form a circle. The most thorough study of a single emblem is undoubtedly Taylor's investigation of the Shanghai or nose-thumbing gesture (1956). Numerous attempts have also been made to catalogue the emblems used by groups of people, to uncover the origins of these gestures and to explore their geographical distribution and cultural diffusion. Di Jorio (1832), for example, catalogued the emblems of Naples and traced certain Neapolitan gestures to depictions on Greek vases. Efron (1941) studied the gestural habits of first and second generation Jews and Italians in New York. Saitz and Cervenka (1972) listed and compared some of the emblems used in Columbia and the United States, and Morris et al. (1979) mapped the use and meanings of various emblems across Europe and examined the theories about the origins. Apart from these and other comparative studies, there have also been several investigations of the emblems used within a particular society. Green's (1968) analysis of Spanish gesture and Sparhawk's (1978) work on Persian gestures are examples.

(b) *Illustrators and mimic signs.* These gestures are iconic and representational and are used as a graphic means of illustrating some idea which is or is not encoded in speech. Historically there is some evidence that illustrators and mimic signs, together with onomatopoeic speech, have formed the basis of communication between people who do not share a common language (Hewes 1974). Research in this area has concentrated on the location of illustrative hand movements in relation to speech (Birdwhistell 1970; Ekman and Friesen 1972; McNeil 1979).

(c) *Batons.* As their name suggests, batons are those movements of the hands which are used to stress and orchestrate speech. Some attempt has been made to produce a taxonomy of baton postures (Morris 1977), and to examine their cultural distribution (Efron 1941), but by and large this category of gesture has gone largely unnoticed.

Although emblems, illustrators, batons and other classes of gesture can usually be distinguished, problems of classifications do arise, and the field still awaits an exhaustive taxonomic system that is applicable cross-culturally. PC

Bibliography

*Bauml, B.J. and F.H. 1975: *A dictionary of gestures*. Metuchen, N.J.: Scarecrow Press.

*Critchley, M. 1975: *Silent language*. London: Butterworth.

*Hewes, G. 1974: Gesture language in culture contact. *Sign language studies*, 4, 1–34.

*Hewes, G., ed. 1975: *Language origins: a bibliography*. The Hague: Mouton.

*Kendon, A. ed. 1981: *Nonverbal communication, interaction and gesture*. The Hague: Mouton.

*Morris, D. et al. 1979: *Gestures: their origins and distribution*. London: Cape.

All the other references referred to in this entry may be found in either Kendon (1981) or Morris et al. (1979). Useful journals to consult are *Semiotica* and *Sign language studies*.

gifted children Children who display superiority in one or more fields of human activity, in comparison with their peers, in such a way that their abilities seem to be endowed by nature. There is no doubt that children differ in their natural abilities from birth, but the degree to which these abilities are exploited and enhanced by the child's experience and teaching has been the focal point of much debate. The early research on identical twins by Galton and Pearson led the way to other such studies, from which a ratio of about 9:1 of genetic to environmental influence on INTELLIGENCE has been suggested.

The existence of a general intellective factor, called g, which is independent of other particular abilities that individuals possess was suggested independently by Binet and Simon in France and Spearman in England in the early 1900s. Tests of intelligence designed to measure this factor have since been used to classify children within their age group. Predictive validity of these tests, particularly of the Stanford developments of Binet's original scales, by Terman between 1916 and 1937 has been established in many kinds of intellectual activity. This has meant that a gifted child has been taken to mean one who scored in the top percentiles of a test of intelligence within his age group. Studies such as the longitudinal research of Terman focussed attention on this category of gifted child and provided much in the way of general insights into the characteristics that they possessed. More recently, however, attention has been focussed on a broader definition of giftedness. J.P. Guilford has suggested a model of the intellect which has 120 distinct abilities. Strengths in a particular combination of these endows an individual with his abilities in a certain field of human endeavor. The concept of CREATIVITY has evolved and is associated with giftedness in the arts and the ability to invent novel solutions to problems, both scientific and artistic.

The present meaning of giftedness is, therefore, by no means completely clear. The characteristics that a gifted child may display are those appropriate to his particular abilities. Gifted children have, in general, many characteristics and behavioral traits in common with those of lesser abilities, so that they may well, for example, wear spectacles, be thin, be pale, be impatient, but they may equally well not. The multidimensional model of the human intellect prevents the psychologist or educator from looking for general characteristics that can identify gifted children, but moves him to look at each individual and the particular combination of abilities that he has in large measure so that he can be assessed as 'gifted' or not in a particular field of endeavor. The nurturing of these gifts then has to be tailored to that individual's particular needs, his particular stage of development and his particular environment. CJD

Bibliography

Barbe, Walter B. and Renzulli, Joseph S. 1975: *Psychology and education of the gifted*. New York: Irvington.

Povey, R. 1980: *Educating the gifted child*. New York and London: Harper & Row.

George, W.C., Sanford, J.C. and Stanley, J.C. 1977: *Educating the gifted: acceleration and enrichment*. Baltimore and London: Johns Hopkins University Press..

Freeman, J. 1979: *Gifted children*. Baltimore: University Park Press.

glia Nonnervous accessory cells with special relationships to NEURONS. In mammals, glial cells occupy half the volume of the nervous system and are up to ten times more numerous than nerve cells. Although glia would seem to perform important functions, and virtually every known or suspected function of the nervous system has been assigned at some time to glia, they are probably the cellular element of the nervous system about which the least is known. Thorough description of the roles of glia in neural function remains an important research goal.

Vertebrates have five distinct types of neuroglia: astrocytes, microglia, oligodendroglia, Schwann cells and ependymal cells. Astroctyes are found in the central nervous system (CNS). They form a zone between walls of blood vessels or the coverings of the brain and spinal cord, and the nervous tissue proper. The blood–brain barrier between the circulatory system and the cerebrospinal fluid which bathes the nervous system may be due to a continuous layer of astrocytes in elasmobranch fishes (e.g. sharks), but in mammals it is the endothelial cells of the blood vessels, not the astrocytes, which form the barrier. Microglia are small cells normally uncommon in the CNS. They congregate at sites of trauma, infection, etc., where they act as phagocytes, taking up and digesting fragments of debris. There is evidence that microglia may in part derive from mesoderm, whereas other glial cell types originate from ectoderm. Oligodendroglia are the most numerous glial type, forming the sheaths of myelin around CNS neurons (BRAIN AND CENTRAL NERVOUS SYSTEM: ILLUSTRATIONS, fig. 30). Myelin sheaths permit fast information transfer along thin axons, and were essential to the evolution of the nervous systems of higher animals. Schwann cells form the myelin sheaths around neurons outside the CNS. Ependymal cells line the spinal canal and brain ventricles. They form part of the choroid plexus which participates in producing the cerebrospinal fluid. SCC

Bibliography

Orkand, Richard K. 1977: Glial cells. In *Handbook of physiology*, Section 1: *The nervous system*, Vol I. *Cellular biology of neurons*, Part 2. ed. J.M. Brookhart, V.B. Mountcastle and E.R. Kandel. Bethesda, Md.: American Physiological Society.

glossolalia Spontaneous utterances of incomprehensible sounds, often believed by the speaker to be in a real language unknown to her/him, are referred to as glossolalia or speaking in tongues.

Glossolalia is commonly distinguished from LUDLING in that it is not memorized or planned in advance. Recent research (Samarin 1972, pp.121–30) has shown, however, that speakers manipulate the linguistic variables in response to role purpose or setting of a speech event. The occurrence of speech material is restricted by the phonotactic conventions of the speaker's own language.

Glossolalia is most common in those speech communities that approve of it. The possibilities offered to psycholinguistic research include the areas of sound symbolism, phonetic universals, and cryptomnesia. PM

Bibliography

Goodman, Felicitas D. 1972: *Speaking in tongues*. Chicago and London: Chicago University Press.

Samarin, William J. 1968: Linguisticality of glossolalia. *Hartford quarterly* 8, 49–75.

———, 1972: Variation and variables in (religious) glossolalia. *Language in Society*, 121–30.

goal gradient This concept is usually applied to a particular phenomenon of maze learning in animals. When performing in a maze animals often learn not to turn into the blind alleys closest to the goal box long before they learn not to turn into blind alleys further away. This behavior is in conformity with the goal gradient hypothesis which states that blind alleys will be eliminated in reverse order beginning with the one closest to the goal. The hypothesis is based on the idea that in learning experiments prompt reward is more effective than delayed reward. The nature of the last blind alley will be learnt first because it is closest to the goal box. In fact, experiments show that blind alley entry is also affected by factors of maze design, characteristics of the animal and other variables. This may explain the conflicting results concerning the goal gradient hypothesis which have frequently been reported. RMcH

goal setting A motivational technique which involves the assigning or choosing of objectives to be reached, especially in work tasks. Similar or related concepts within organizations are: task, quota, standard, deadline and budget. Goal setting was a key element of Scientific Management (often called task management) which paved the way for Management by Objectives (Locke 1982). It is also a key component of Likert's System 4 theory and of so called organizational behavior modification.

Numerous studies of goal setting have been conducted in both laboratory and organizational settings (summarized in Locke et al. 1981). It has been consistently found that difficult goals lead to higher task performance than do easy goals and that specific goals lead to higher performance than do general goals (such as "do your best") or no goals at all. Feedback seems necessary for goal setting to work since people need to know their progress in relation to their goals. Feedback alone, however, does not necessarily lead to improved task performance; the feedback must be appraised as significant and translated into a goal for improved performance if improvement is actually to occur.

Money incentives may motivate the setting of goals where they do not already exist, but, basically, money serves to increase commitment to goals. Many studies of participation in decision making have confused goal setting with participation. Participation in setting goals does not appear to lead to better performance than simply assigning the goals; however, participation may be useful in designing plans for implementing goals. Competition is a complex form of goal setting in which the other person's performance serves as the goal; high commitment is common in competition since doing better than others is often highly valued.

Individual differences (other than ability) have not been found to affect performance in goal setting studies, probably because most studies have used assigned rather than self set goals. When goals are self set, it might be expected that people high in "need for achievement" (see ACHIEVEMENT MOTIVATION) would prefer, and work hardest, under moderate rather than very hard or easy goals.

Goal setting within organizations can best be achieved if it is introduced as a means of increasing interest in the job and if failure to attain goals is not used to threaten or punish employees. Success in achieving goals typically produces pride in performance. Informal competition among employees may serve to heighten interest and commitment.

Goal setting is an extremely reliable motivational technique with 90 per cent of studies showing significant effects on performance. In a CRITICAL INCIDENTS study, employees of a multinational high technology company cited the existence of goals and their equivalents (e.g. deadlines) as the single most frequently mentioned cause of high productivity, and their absence (e.g. no deadlines) as the single most frequent cause of low productivity. A detailed discussion of goal setting from a managerial perspective can be found in Locke and Latham (1983). EAL

Bibliography

Locke, E.A. 1982: The ideas of Frederick W. Taylor: an evaluation. *Academy of management review* 7, 14–24.

——— and Latham, G.P., 1983: *Goal setting: a motivational technique that works*. Englewood Cliffs, N.J.: Prentice Hall.

———, et al. 1981: Goal setting and task performance: 1969–1980. *Psychological bulletin* 90, 125–52.

grammar A grammar of a language is a description of the rules, regularities and laws which enable the user of a language to pair strings of sound with meaning in his or her communicative COMPETENCE. Many grammarians also refer to a speaker-hearer's knowledge of his/her language as grammar, thereby ignoring the likely discrepancy between rules and the formulation of rules.

Grammars are usually subdivided into components such as the phonetic, phonological, morphological, syntactic-lexical and semantic components. The number of components needed and the ways in which they are interrelated is a matter of debate.

There are numerous problems in connection with the definition of grammars, the most important being (1) whether grammar can be described as an autonomous entity in isolation from cultural and psychological factors, (2) the possibility that different grammars are needed for encoding and decoding and (3) the degree to which grammars reflect universals.

See also PIVOT GRAMMAR. PM

Bibliography

Givón, Talmy 1979: *On understanding grammar*. New York and London: Academic Press.

grammatical rules, psychological reality of The status of linguists' grammars as descriptions of actual mental processes employed by language users. This status has been fiercely defended by those who insist that to the extent that a grammar successfully describes a language, it necessarily stands as our best theory of the linguistic COMPETENCE of the speakers of that language. Others disagree.

The controversy surrounding psychological reality is a fairly recent one in linguistics. Before CHOMSKY, many linguists openly espoused a "reductionistic" position: Their descriptive statements were simply systematic condensations of the observed data. No theory of the psychological basis of language was to be inferred, they said, from their summary grammatical presentations. More recent work, however, has typically insisted that the analytical categories and schemata of linguistic descriptions bear a "realistic" relation to the data. Utterances are, it is said, constructed and interpreted on the basis, at least in part, of mental manipulation of items in the ways specified in the rules of the grammar. These rules, and the category symbols they contain, may not be observable in the way a word or a phrase is, but their existence is no more doubtful for all that than is the existence of well-established theoretical entities in other sciences (e.g. electrons and gravitational force in physics).

Critics of this view often adopt an "instrumentalistic" view that grammatical rules make explicit predictions about the GRAMMATICALNESS, LINGUISTIC ACCEPTABILITY, COGNITIVE MEANING, LINGUISTIC NATURALNESS, and other important properties of linguistic structures, and this explicitness makes them valuable tools for the investigation of human linguistic ability. But the way in which these rules operate – without input either in the form of overt strings to be understood or in the form of conceptual intentions to be expressed – makes them unusable in causally efficacious models of the comprehension, production, or other possible linguistic activities of even an idealized speaker-hearer. The psychological reality of grammatical rules will therefore remain in doubt until it is shown how they could be incorporated into a realistic theory of performance. HSS

Bibliography

Cooper, David E. 1975: *Knowledge of language*, London: Prism Press; New York: Humanities.

Matthews, P.H. 1979: *Generative grammar and linguistic competence*, Winchester, Mass.: Allen & Unwin.

grammaticalness A technical term used by transformational-generative grammarians such as Chomsky to describe the degree to which sentences conform to the rules of a generative grammar. A successful grammar should indicate not only that a string of words is grammatical or ungrammatical, but also that, for instance, the string *John pretended Bill to sing* is less well formed than *golf plays John*.

Grammaticalness refers to competence only and should be distinguished from acceptability which refers to performance (see Chomsky 1965, pp.3–15). Grammaticalness is only one of the factors determining the degree of acceptability of a sentence. The fact that it refers to an ideal speaker-hearer in a completely homogeneous speech community who knows his or her language perfectly makes psycholinguistic tests of grammaticality impossible. PM

Bibliography

Chomsky, Noam 1965: *Aspects of the theory of syntax*, Cambridge, Mass.: MIT Press.

greeting When two conspecifics meet, their response to one another may be hostile, but if not, and they are positively attracted to each other, they will probably engage in a more or less elaborate series of species characteristic behavior patterns toward each other. These rituals are referred to as greeting displays. Some birds such as nesting kittiwakes have elaborate greeting ceremonies the object of which is to ensure that the new arrival at the nest is indeed the mated partner of the nest-holder and will feed its own genetic offspring. Such greetings are mostly found in pair-bonded species that separate for feeding and then meet up again.

Among social mammals, greetings are extended to other members of the species as well as mates, and involve highly stereotyped behavior patterns such as the side-by-side, head-to-tail, genital sniffing of dogs. Among primates greetings are most marked in chimpanzees, and occur whenever individuals who know each other meet after a temporary spell of separation. Males frequently touch each others' testicles, while both sexes may kiss, touch hands, or hug each other.

In humans greetings are culturally specified, but the fact that they exist, and often involve hand touching, embracing and kissing indicates that their roots may lie in our primate ancestry. (See also BOND.) VR

gregariousness In ethology, the tendency of individuals to associate in groups. One way of explaining gregariousness relates to its survival value (see NATURAL SELECTION). Two main explanations in these terms have been proposed, relating to advantages accruing to gregarious individuals (or their relatives – see ALTRUISM) in predator avoidance and in food acquisition (Bertram 1978). A quite different type of explanation relates to the causal and developmental basis of gregariousness. In a well known primate study (1932) Zuckerman proposed that sexual BONDS between adult males and females were the primary factor in group cohesion, but it is now clear that this was incorrect. To say instead that groups cohere because individuals are socially attractive to each other is probably true but circular, and it may be more profitable to investigate RELATIONSHIPS AND SOCIAL STRUCTURES in a detailed way than to search for an overall explanation of gregariousness (Chalmers 1979).

RDA

Bibliography

Bertram, B.C.R. 1978: Living in groups: predators and prey. In *Behavioral ecology: an evolutionary approach*, ed. J.R. Krebs and N.B. Davies. Oxford: Blackwell Scientific; Sunderland, Mass.: Sinaues Assoc.

Chalmers, N. 1979: *Social behaviour in primates*. London: Edward Arnold; Baltimore: University Park Press.

Zuckerman, S. 1932: *The social life of monkeys and apes*. London: Kegan Paul; New York: Harcourt Brace.

group therapy A form of psychotherapy in which the same group of patients meets together regularly with one or more therapists for the purpose of obtaining symptom relief or personal change. Size varies but six to ten patients is usual, with one or two therapists. Early kinds of group therapy took the form of classroom lectures with group discussion. This method was first used in 1907 by Pratt to help tuberculous patients manage their illness. The first attempt to focus on a group's interactions was by Burrow in the 1920s. Subsequently several styles of group therapy have been developed. These may be divided into the psychoanalytic and the action-based approaches.

In the United States Slavson developed the use of PSYCHOANALYSIS in groups, focussing on individual patients in turn. In postwar England Bion and Ezriel developed a method in which the group as an entity was the focus of treatment, and Foulkes developed the method of "group analysis" in which the conductor uses the group as the instrument of treatment for the individual members.

Action-based techniques were first developed by Moreno who created psychodrama. The leader directs a spontaneous scene in which the group members may reconstruct a situation in the lives of one of them. In the 1960s action-based methods developed rapidly, influenced both by psychodrama and by psychoanalytic approaches.

These new methods included encounter groups, transactional analysis, and gestalt therapy. In many cases these and related techniques were designed for ordinary people interested in personal growth rather than for people designated as patients.

During the last decade Yalom's work (1975) on therapeutic factors in group therapy has had a major impact on the practice and training of group therapists, providing a more empirical basis for the role of the therapist.

Today group therapy is carried out in a wide variety of settings, including outpatient clinics, psychiatric hospital wards, therapeutic communities and day centers with both mixed and homogenous groups of patients. It is widely used in the treatment of neurosis, personality disorders, chronic psychosis, and the addictions (see DRUG DEPENDENCE). DHWK

Bibliography

*Whiteley J.S. and Gordon J. 1979: *Group approaches in psychiatry*. London: Routledge and Kegan Paul.

Yalom I.D. 1975: *The theory and practice of group psychotherapy*. 2nd edn. New York: Basic Books.

group training Experiential methods of training were initiated during the 1940s by Lewin and the National Training Laboratories in Bethel, Maine, USA; and by Bion and his colleagues at the Tavistock Institute in London. The experiential methods assume that 1) people can learn best from an analysis of their own immediate psychological experiences; 2) the relevant facts from which such learning can best arise are the feelings, reactions, and observations of other people with whom one interacts, but which tend to be withheld; 3) a suitably designed training workshop can overcome the forces against sharing feelings, reactions, and observations and thus make available opportunities for learning at this more immediate level; and 4) the forces to be overcome are essentially culturally acquired attitudes about the proper things to say and attitudes about the learning of new behavior.

Devices used to facilitate experiential learning range from structured role playing, followed by an analysis of each role player's performance, to unstructured sensitivity training groups (see T-GROUP). The approach has been used to increase individuals' awareness of themselves and others, to improve effectiveness of skilled performance in groups, to improve work relationships among members of a task group (see TEAM DEVELOPMENT), as well as to improve familial relationships. ALP/NMT

groups A group may be defined as two or more persons who are interacting with one another, who share a set of common goals, and norms which direct their activities, and who develop a set of roles and a network of affective relations. Many other slightly differing definitions are found in the literature, but most of these contain the key element of social interaction, or mutual influence of group members (Shaw 1981). Practically this implies a vague boundary between a group and larger social entities, such as mobs, crowds, masses and collectivities, in which direct mutual influence is not possible. Usually the line is drawn between twenty and thirty members. Most readers will be familiar with several types of groups, such as the couple, the family, playgroups, school classes, social clubs; and with groups having a wide variety of productions tasks, decision making tasks, or problem solving tasks, such as work teams, crews and committees. Rough estimates indicate that the average person in contemporary western society belongs to five or six groups at one moment, and that more than 90 per cent of all existing groups have five members or less. Groups of this size with a cognitive task, such as decision-making, or problem-solving, have been studied most intensively in a branch of social psychology usually referred to as "group dynamics" (Cartwright and Zander 1968) or "small group research" (Hare 1976). These are also the main focus of this entry.

In abstract terms, a group may be described as an open system (Bertalanffy 1962) with input, process, and resulting output. On the input side individual factors, group factors and environmental factors can be discerned (Hackmann and Morris 1975). The individual factors include properties of group members, such as biographical and personality characteristics, abilities, skills, knowledge and attitudes toward the group goals, the task, other group members, the situation and other relevant topics. They also include the physical and the social positions in the group, which may, for example, be based on the physical place in the communication network, or on age, sex, social status, formal assigned rank or function and job title. The group factors consist mainly of group size and group composition, that is, the distribution and patterning of individual characteristics in the group. An important aspect of group composition is the compatibility of individual characteristics. Generally, high compatibility leads to high group cohesiveness, and improves task performance (Hare 1976). Usually in formal groups, such as committees, the group composition is established explicitly and formally by prescribed roles, such as chairman, secretary, advisor and members. This is one form of group structure. The environmental factors include the physical and social surroundings of the group. Other environmental factors are the characteristics of the task which has to be performed, the nature of the group goal and the obstacles which block the path towards that goal.

In the interaction in groups, a distinction can be made between the pattern and the content of the interaction (McGrath and Kravitz 1982). The pattern of interaction includes the number of participating members, the length of time spent participating and the number of communications sent and received by each member. Generally, group members differ considerably in verbal participation rate, and these differences increase with group size. In addition, a strong relationship has been observed (Hare 1976; Shaw 1981) between the emitting and receiving of communication. The content of interaction includes the number of task-oriented communications in the whole group or of particular members, such as information or opinion giving, asking for suggestions and goal setting. It also includes social–emotional communications, which may be verbal or non-verbal, such as showing solidarity, agreement and tension release, or showing of antagonism, disagreement and tension.

A breakthrough in the study of the pattern and content of interaction in groups was the development by Bales (1950) of a category system which enabled observers to code (mainly verbal) behavior reliably. Since then, this category system has been modified by Bales (Bales, Cohen and Williamson 1979), or expanded by others. In addition, category systems have been developed for the coding and scoring of non-verbal behavior, such as physical distance, bodily positions, facial postures and GAZE (Argyle 1969).

In many studies which use these category systems, it has been observed that the enormous variety of interactions in groups reduces basically to four dimensions or factors (Hare 1976). The first and most important dimension is dominance versus submissiveness. Examples of dominant behavior are loquacity, many attempts to influence the others and seeking status by directing group activity. In contrast, asking for help, or showing anxiety and frustration are examples of submissiveness. The second dimension is positive social–emotional behavior (showing affection or agreement, asking graciously) versus negative behavior (unfriendly disagreement, showing antagonism). The third dimension is serious, task-oriented behavior versus expressive behavior, such as supporting others regardless of their task performance, and jocularity. The last dimension is conformity, seeking to be guided by group norms, and revealing the basic nature of the group versus non-conformity, showing tension and withdrawal, and resisting pressures to conform to group norms. Different attempts to influence the behavior, attitudes and cognitions of group members, or efforts to resist these influences usually take the form of conduct at the extreme poles of these four dimensions.

The interaction process in the group over a certain period of time results in several types of outcome. Firstly, the members become (better) acquainted with one another. Feelings of sympathy and antipathy develop, and a more or less stable ATTRACTION structure is formed. Secondly, by virtue of the group composition some members appear to behave more dominantly than others and to contribute more to goal attainment and task performance. If, at the time of group composition, an influence structure, leadership or social power structure has not been established, it will now come into being, but often only after a struggle for power takes place. Sometimes group members take over formal roles from one another, and often formal roles are supplemented by informal roles, such as the "garrulous", the "supporter", the "silent member" and the "joker" (Hare 1976). Thirdly, in task groups the most important output is, by definition, the task performance or goal attainment of the group. This may be judged on several qualitative and quantitative criteria. Fourthly, the resulting structures, and the goal attainment are usually related to the satisfaction or dissatisfaction of personal, social–emotional and task-related needs of the group members, which, in turn, are related to more or less cohesiveness in the group.

As even this rough sketch illustrates, the student of groups has to deal with a variety of input factors, process variables and outcomes, which also have complex unidirectional and bi-directional causal links over a given period of time. This multitude becomes even larger when other types of groups with different tasks and goals are considered. Not surprisingly therefore this multitude is matched by a multitude of research questions, theoretical analyses, research methods and empirical results (Cartwright and Zander 1968; Hare 1976; Shaw 1981).

The social psychological study of groups in the twentieth

century reflects two trends, namely, the development of social psychology as a science, and the study of the main problems of western society. Up to the first decades of this century, groups were mainly the object of theoretical or impressionistic analyses in which their linking function between individual and society was stressed. In the next fifteen years what are now considered to be classical studies of groups took place. These were more modest in scope, now concentrated on phenomena such as the attraction structure in groups (Moreno 1934), the development of group norms (Sherif 1936) and social influences in factory groups (Roethlisberger and Dickson 1939). However, the social psychological study of groups was shaped definitively by LEWIN and his school. (Zander 1979). Partly inspired by some of the societal problems of the 1940s and 50s, studies were conducted into theorectical and practical problems of LEADERSHIP, productivity, and group discussion. The dominant research form became the controlled experiment with small ad hoc groups in the psychological laboratory. Since then, some phenomena and processes which were originally studied as group phenomena have been studied more and more intensively in their own right (often, even without free interacting groups). Among these are: conformity, cooperation and competition (for example, in the prisoner's dilemma game, see GAMES) affiliation, and interpersonal attraction. Exceptions to this trend are studies on leadership, on processes and outcomes of decision-making groups (Brandstätter, Davis and Stocker-Kreichgauer 1982) partly inspired by the RISKY SHIFT phenomenon, and recent studies on personal relationships (Duck and Gilmour 1981–2).

See also INTER-GROUP RELATIONS, REFERENCE GROUP, SMALL GROUP INTERVENTION. RWM

Bibliography

Argyle, M. 1969: *Social interaction*. London: Methuen.

Bales, R.F. 1950: *Interaction process analysis: a method for the study of small groups*. Cambridge, Mass.: Addison-Wesley.

Bales, R.F., Cohen, S.P. and Williamson, S.A. 1979: *SYMLOG, a system for the multiple level observation of groups*. New York: Free Press.

Bertalanffy, L. von 1962: General systems theory: a critical review. *General systems* 7, 1–20.

Brandstätter, H., Davis, J.H. and Stocker-Kreichgauer, G., eds. 1982: *Group decision making*. New York and London: Academic Press.

Cartwright, D. and Zander, A., eds. 1968: *Group dynamics: research and theory*, 3rd edn. London: Tavistock; New York: Harper & Row.

Duck, S. and Gilmour, R., eds. 1981–2: *Personal relationships*. Vols. 1–4. New York and London: Academic Press.

Hackman, J.R. and Morris, C.G. 1975: Group tasks, group interaction process, and group performance effectiveness: A review and proposed integration. In *Advances in experimental social psychology*, Vol.8. ed. L. Berkowitz. New York and London: Academic Press.

Hare, A.P. 1976: *Handbook of small group research*, 2nd edn. London: Collier Macmillan; New York: Free Press.

McGrath, J.E. and Kravitz, D.A. 1982: Group research. *Annual review of psychology* 33, 195–230.

Moreno, J.L. 1934: *Who shall survive*. Washington, D.C.: Nervous and Mental Diseases Publishing Company.

Roethlisberger, F.J. and Dickson, W.J. 1939: *Management and the worker*. Cambridge, Mass.: Harvard University Press.

Shaw, M. 1981: *Group dynamics: the psychology of small group behavior*. New York, London: McGraw-Hill.

Sherif, M. 1936: *The psychology of social norms*. New York: Harper.

Zander, A. 1979: The psychology of group processes. *Annual review of psychology* 30, 417–51.

groups *See also* emotional expression in groups; emotional roles in groups; small group intervention

guilt and shame Guilt is the condition attributed to a person (including oneself) upon some moral or legal transgression. Shame is occasioned by an object which threatens to expose a discrepancy between what a person is and what he or she ideally would like to be. Thus, a person may be guilty of a crime but ashamed of the self. The degree of guilt is usually proportional to the offense committed: by contrast, the act that precipitates shame is often inconsequential in itself; its importance lies in what it reveals about the self. Both guilt and shame presume internalized standards of conduct, but guilt has a more abstract, judgmental quality than shame (e.g. one can admit to being guilty without feeling guilty, but one cannot be ashamed without feeling ashamed); and guilt is less tied to the threat of exposure. (See EMOTION AND SOCIAL BEHAVIOR). In terms of its experiential immediacy and its close relationship to self-identity, shame may be considered the more fundamental of the two emotions. In western cultures, however, guilt has been the more highly valued because of its implications for autonomous action. This prejudice is reflected in psychological theories, which tend to ignore shame as a phenomenon distinct from guilt. Psychoanalytic theories trace the origins of guilt to internalization of prohibitions imposed by early authority figures (see SUPEREGO); behaviorist theories view guilt as a conditioned emotional response to actions that in the past have led to punishment; and existentialist theories conceive of guilt as a reaction to behavior that impedes the realization of one's full potential, however that potential is defined (biologically, socially, or spiritually).

Evidence suggests that men may be more prone than women to experience guilt, and conversely with respect to shame (Lewis 1971). No single explanation can account for this and other (e.g., socioeconomic) group differences in the tendency toward guilt and/or shame. Social expectations, family dynamics, and child-rearing practices all undoubtedly play a role (see MORAL DEVELOPMENT). Entire societies have been contrasted on the extent to which they foster guilt-like or shame-like reactions as a means of social control. However, cross-cultural comparisons are made difficult by varying conceptions of guilt and shame. For example, even such cognate terms as *Scham* in German and shame in English have somewhat different meanings, the former connoting modesty as well as shame. JRA

Bibliography

Lewis, H. 1971: *Shame and guilt in neurosis*. New York: International Universities Press.

*Smith, R.W., ed. 1971: *Guilt: man and society*. Garden City, New York: Doubleday.

Thrane, G. 1979: Shame. *Journal for the theory of social behavior* 9, 139–66.

Gurdjieff, Georges Ivanovitch In dealing with Gurdjieff as a psychologist, philosopher, teacher, holy man, shaman or charlatan, all of which, among other things, he was regarded as being by various people who knew him, the factor of personal power, the effect he had on others in his presence, must be considered as an essential part of the phenomenon. "Teaching is a state of being", as it was once put, and the Sufi notion of *baraka* was taken into the schools he started, where inner connection with the sense of his presence as a living being is still sought.

This is according to his intent, which was, however not to be worshipped. One volume of his writings, the so called Third Series, titled "Life Is Real Only Then, When 'I AM' ", was to have been retained for those who had been students in such schools and achieved objective attainments; it has since been published, however. Even though Gurdjieff himself testifies to having personally renounced the use of psychic powers, such as hypnotism, at which he was reputed to be adept, the esoteric side of his activities and statements is integral to them. It is a teaching about the possibility of attaining a higher level of being, "objective consciousness", of which he is the exemplar, and the student is one who strives to attain a new, higher state of being by doing things he might not want to do, or see the point of. Everyone stands before it, and him, initially, as a student.

Apart from the factor of sheer psychic power, however, (which tends to dominate the material written about him), Gurdjieff taught a detailed and intricate doctrine about man's psychology which, though comparable at many points with ideas from other sources, stands out as a unique–though, he insists, not original–system. Only some of its major features can be given here, and possible distortion of them by being treated in abstraction from the whole should be borne in mind.

1. *The three centers.* The key to objective self-understanding is the proper understanding of the three centers, or "brains", corresponding to the moving/instinctual, feeling/emotional, and thinking/mental strata of conscious content. These are nodal points of organization of experience, separate intelligences, with their own memory record of impressions, whose physiological bases are processes controlled through the spinal column, the blood stream and the head–brain (the second, or emotional center being felt as if in the solar plexus), respectively. The analysis of what is ordinarily called "consciousness" in a person–which Gurdjieff held was not the correct use of the term–into this trichotomy of contents is unique and central to his system. Their proper relationship to one another explains how man ought to be, and function: balanced, each center playing its proper role in contributing to the whole. Their wrong relationship, explained as "one center's using the energy of another", as when one strains to stoop to pick something up, poking or snatching at it, rather than letting the fingers do their own work through the energy of the moving/instinctive center, accounts for the mechanical way man ordinarily functions. But the doctrine of the three centers is not merely intellectual, to be taken in as a concept, only; it is also a vocabulary of self-observation. The functions of the three centers are to be distinguished in oneself, contemporaneously, *as* they are making their separate contributions. The doctrine of "centers", and the deliberate initiation within oneself of a process of self-observation in terms of this doctrine and its attendant vocabulary, makes up the theoretical basis of Gurdjieff's system. The theory also holds–and this is not altogether easy to grasp at first–that it is precisely through acts of objective self-observation, that is, self-observation in terms of the vocabulary of the three centers, that an *energy* is produced, in the special sense that Gurdjieff speaks of it, which becomes the material for a new, "fourth" center of function. This is connected with a general metaphysical theory that everything existing is, in a sense, material, part of a universal process of matter–energy exchanges; and that this is also true of processes of consciousness in the individual. In its technical use "consciousness" is the name of a substance produced by those who have worked on themselves; a trace chemical compound in the brain that modifies the action of the neurotransmitters already present. Work, properly conducted, literally recreates the person. A New Man, or higher spiritual being, in the sense claimed to have been taught by Christ, might be attained in this way.

2. The situation of "man on earth". Although this is a teaching about consciousness, and purports to embody in itself the results of self-observation, objectively practiced, it by no means takes this term subjectively, but on the contrary requires a person to reverse the ordinary self-perspective, and think of himself almost as though he were outside what is ordinarily called "consciousness", namely, as a "man on earth".

In *Beelzebub's tales*, the allegory of this objective standpoint is a Martian with a gigantic telescope trained on us. From this perspective, humans are seen as beings who behave in ways that are sometimes exceedingly strange. Specifically, they are subject, among other things, to mass psychoses, outbreaks of wars and terrible destructive forces of an inner, psychic order over which they have no control. Two favorite phrases were used by Gurdjieff in describing the condition of man on earth: he "lacked his own 'I' ", and "he could not *do*. . . ". The latter meant that he lacked the capacity to carry out a course of action that would lead to the actualization of a consciously selected aim. Both these defects, which he conceals from himself by pretending to have his own "I", and to be able to "do", are traced to discontinuity of consciousness, or psychic dissociation. His ordinary waking state is that of a subjective dream. He lives, from moment to moment, disconnected from reality by the products of imagination, strung together as a sequence of experiences by conditioned reactions. There is no transcendental unity of "I" through the sequence; there is only a series of more or less separate "I's" parading on cue through consciousness, in response to what is being dreamed as taking place. This state controlled by the waking dream is that from which a person must be awakened, even if at first only fleetingly and momentarily, before any further development can proceed. In social contexts, however, people shield one another from what they really think and feel, so that people are ordinarily deprived of genuinely objective data in terms of which to observe themselves. That is to say, in social contexts, we do not ordinarily confront each other with perception of faults; yet it is just this kind of confrontation that is needed, and is provided, in schools.

3. Teachers, schools and work. The separate "I's" that occur where a single continuous consciousness and will ought to be, and is ordinarily mistaken for being, are depth psychological structures, entire personalities existing side by side with each other, each mostly ignorant of the existence of the others. This is illustrated by such phenomena as not carrying out promises honestly and sincerely made at the time. At the root of each "I" there is what Gurdjieff calls an "identification". This is a state of internalized patterning of response through mimicking others, which assimilates the sense of self, and even the use of the first person singular pronoun of self-reference, "I", to an imagined identity. These become ingrained in the work of centers. One-sidednesses of all sorts derive from identifications. "Identifications" are thus latent structures that become occurrent; and it is at the moment that they do so, that is to say, when one "I" is being replaced by another, which may be as quick as the blinking of an eye, that they may possibly be observed. It is the energy got from this, as remarked above, as well as the prodigious amount of energy that may go into producing the proper state in which such an observation of oneself may occur, that is the aim of what Gurdjieff called and taught as "The Work." At a very deep level, also, there is in each man a basic individual condition that does not want to be confronted, which is the key to the mechanical associations between "I's" as successive actors, and to the factors that appear as "personality". In order to see into himself objectively this condition that binds together the personality must be discerned, and distinguished from impulses and forms of thought that arise from what is called "essence". A person's essence is a partly inherited psychological content characterized by a particular quality of vibration, as it were, determining the sense and feel of individual existence in the formative years, before personality was acquired. Everyone in school work begins, early on, to try to observe the distinction between personality and essence in themselves. A "teacher", in general, is one who has done the work necessary to bring unity into the field of "I's"; one who has acquired his own will, and can "do". Teachers are required, and their words and deeds are required to be taken by students as laws binding on deepest conscience, and on the strongest desire "to be", in order for one-sided beings to have the opportunity of confronting themselves, and learning how to fulfill the objective requirements for personal development. SBT

Bibliography

Bennett, J.G. 1974: *Gurdjieff: making a new world*, London: Turnstone; New York: Harper & Row.

Gurdjieff, G.I. 1950–75: *All and everything*, three series of writings. London: Routledge & Kegan Paul; New York: Harcourt Brace.

Ouspensky, P.D. 1949: *In search of the miraculous*, London: Routledge & Kegan Paul; New York: Harcourt Brace.

H

habit Though the term is not currently widely used in psychology, the concept of habit as a customary manner of acting is used in various branches of psychology. In social psychology habits are examined in terms of cultural customs or norms and in clinical psychology habit usually refers to compulsive often irrational behavior while in cognitive psychology it may refer to a cognitive style or characteristic of processing information.

However the term "habit" is most often found and used in learning theory. Here the term *general habit* refers to the learned act tendency which results in a person maintaining the same relationship between corresponding stimuli and responses within a specific class of situations. In learning theory many early theorists have referred to *habit strength* which is the tendency for a particular stimulus to evoke a particular response. However there is some disagreement about the origin of habit strengths – one view stated that mere repetition of an act, regardless of the consequences, would increase the habit strength and the performance of an act, while later theorists stated that the habit strength would be increased only when the acts were followed by reinforcement. Research in skill acquisition occasionally mentions the *hierarchy* of habits (or skills) meaning that the learning of one aspect of a skill depends on the degree of mastery achieved in some lower aspect of the same skill.

From these learning principles it is possible to suggest ways in which old habits may be broken and new ones formed. One is to give the stimulus for the undesired response at a time when some incompatible response is taking place which provides a good opportunity for learning the incompatible response in place of the undesired one. Another is to repeat the cue for the habit until fatigue or action decrement prevents its occurrence. A third method is to give the stimulus for the habit with such slight intensity that the act does not occur and gradually the stimulus intensity may be increased until finally it no longer elicits the habit, even at normal tendencies. Finally of course habits may be changed by changing a person's motivation. AF

habituation A decrease in responsiveness resulting from repeated stimulation. Habituation is normally regarded as a form of learning, although it involves loss of responsiveness rather than the acquisition of new responses. A snail crawling on a table will retract into its shell if the table is tapped. It will emerge after a while and continue crawling. Another tap on the table will cause the snail to retract again, but it will emerge more quickly this time. Repeated taps will have progressively smaller effects until the snail ignores them altogether.

Habituation shows many typical features of learning including generalization and extinction. If the stimulus is withheld for a long time the habituated response reappears. (See also EMOTIONAL HABITUATION.) DJM

Halliday, Michael A.K. Born in 1925, studied Chinese language and literature at London, and general linguistics at Cambridge and Peking, Halliday is currently Professor of Linguistics at the University of Sydney. He is regarded as the leading figure in neo-Firthian linguistics and has recently made significant contributions to sociolinguistics and child language acquisition studies.

In *Categories of the theory of grammar* (1961) Halliday develops a number of notions already found in Firthian linguistics. The application of his scale-and-category grammar to language teaching is discussed in Halliday, McIntosh and Strevens (1964).

Of great importance to psycholinguistics are Halliday's studies on the development of linguistic functions in FIRST LANGUAGE ACQUISITION and his research into the relationship between function and structure. PM

Bibliography

Halliday, M.A.K. 1961: Categories of the theory of grammar. *Word* 17, 241–92.

——— 1973: *Explorations in the functions of language*. London: Edward Arnold.

———, McIntosh A. and Strevens P. 1964: *The linguistic sciences and language teaching*. London: Longman; Bloomington: Indiana University Press.

hallucinations Hallucinations are perceptions occurring in the absence of an external stimulus to the sense organs, but which are experienced as arising through the sense organs. They may occur in any sensory mordality. In normal people they are especially likely to occur while falling asleep (hypnagogic) or waking (hypnapompic) or during sensory deprivation. In the mentally ill the nature of the hallucination has some diagnostic significance. Auditory hallucinations vary in complexity from noises to conversations and are particularly associated with SCHIZOPHRENIA, severe DEPRESSION and MANIA. Visual hallucinations are characteristic of, but not confined to, ORGANIC MENTAL STATES. Olfactory and tactile hallucinations are less common but the latter are of particular value in the diagnosis and study of SCHIZOPHRENIA. In contrast pseudohallucinations are usually defined as vivid images, perceived with the mind rather than in external space, and are recognized as being unreal. A second meaning is a hallucination which the person recognizes as being unreal. Pseudohallucinations have less serious psychiatric significance than true hallucinations. RAM

Bibliography

Jaspers 1959: *General psychopathology*. Trans. J. Hoenig and M.W. Hamilton. Manchester: Manchester University Press.

hallucinogens A classification of psychoactive agents whose common property is the ability to produce pseudohallucinations and altered states of consciousness. Pseudohallucinations are based on real objects, the perception of which is distorted under the influence of the drug, and awareness that the sensory distortions are drug induced is usually retained. There are several subtypes of hallucinogens which differ, in part, in chemical structure: those which result in cholinergic blockade (e.g. atropine scopolamine), those which are derived from catechols (e.g. mescaline), the indole related hallucinogens (e.g. lysergic acid diethylamide; LSD) and the hallucinogenic anesthetics (e.g. phencyclidine; PCP). Although marijuana and hashish can, in high doses, result in sensory distortions, these agents are not usually classified as hallucinogenic. Continued use of many hallucinogens can lead to tolerance, but no physical dependence has been substantiated. GPH

handicapped children *See* education of handicapped children

hearing impaired and deaf, the: psychology and education Hearing impairment is a term used to encompass and describe all types and conditions of hearing loss, hearing problems or deafness.

Severe to total congenital (at birth) or prelingual (before language develops) hearing impairment or deafness occurs in approximately 1 to 2 per 1,000 children, excluding those who have fluctuating, intermittent or temporary conductive hearing loss caused by problems of the middle ear. The occurrence of severe to total hearing impairment in adults is approximately 3–5 per cent. As suggested by these figures, the incidence of hearing loss increases with age.

Hearing impairment or deafness usually takes one, or both, of two forms: conductive or sensory neural/perceptive hearing impairment.

Conductive hearing loss is due to a disorder in the conduction of sound from the external ear to the inner ear. It is most commonly caused by middle ear problems (Ballantyne 1977, Knight 1981).

Sensory–neural hearing loss is usually due to damage or lesions in the inner ear, i.e.: cochlea, auditory nerve, and/or auditory centres of the brain (see BRAIN AND CENTRAL NERVOUS SYSTEM: ILLS. 26 and 27). Sensory–neural hearing loss may be caused by a variety of conditions e.g postnatal causes including infection, viruses, ototoxic drugs, trauma etc. Prenatal and birth causes include: genetic factors, viral infections via the mother (e.g. maternal rubella, cytomeglovirus), ototoxic drugs taken during pregnancy; jaundice; low birth weight; anoxia, etc. (Ballantyne 1977, Knight 1981).

The degree and nature of hearing loss in childhood is usually assessed and diagnosed by an otologist and/or an audiologist. The degree of hearing loss is commonly shown on an audiogram in decibels i.e. d.b.: a logarithmic scale on vertical axis over the range of frequencies (horizontal axis) in which speech normally occurs i.e. 1.25–8.0 kilohertz (Ballantyne 1977). Other information about a subject's hearing may be obtained through freefield audiometric techniques or objective measures of hearing e.g. impedance or evoked response audiometry or electrocochleography (Knight 1981).

Categories of hearing loss based on the degree of hearing loss indicated on the audiogram tend to fall into five general categories: mild (up to 40 decibels (d.b.): moderate (41–65 d.b.) severe (66–80 d.b.): very severe (81–100 d.b.): and profound (101 d.b. or greater).

Because of the heterogeneity of the population of the hearing impaired, factors which are crucial to the understanding of the psychological, educational, auditory, linguistic, learning and behavioral needs and function of the hearing impaired, include: cause, degree and nature of hearing loss; age at onset; age at diagnosis and fitting of appropriate hearing aids; age at, and appropriateness of, audiological, educational and communicational intervention; non-verbal (practical) and verbal skills, function and abilities; motivation and aptitude; presence of additional handicapping conditions; and either enabling or handicapping nature and conditions imposed by those within the hearing impaired person's environment, or by the environment itself (Levine 1981, Moores 1978).

The psychological, educational, communicational, linguistic and social problems and needs of the prelingually hearing impaired (i.e. those whose hearing loss occurs before language is developed or established) tend to be more complex than the needs and difficulties of those who lose their hearing after language is established (Jackson 1981, Levine 1981).

Additional handicaps tend to occur more frequently in cases of congenital sensory–neural hearing impairment which may include: visual acuity, visual field, peripheral visual and visual perceptual difficulties: mental/intellectual handicap; specific learning disorders; physical and physiological difficulties (Bond 1979, Vernon 1969). Hearing impaired persons tend to have an above-average incidence of significant visual problems. (See BLIND THE: PSYCHOLOGY AND EDUCATION.)

The first few years of life are critical in communication, speech and aural language development (see Moores 1978). The normally hearing person's verbal and non-verbal or practical abilities tend to show a close positive relationship or correlation. Hearing loss occurring before language develops generally results in retardation of language and aural communicational skills, and consequently significant retardation in verbal–educational skills, in comparison with hearing peers of similar non-verbal or practical ability (Moores 1978, Levine 1981, Myklebust 1964). Even temporary, fluctuating, and intermittent hearing losses may cause retardation of verbal educational attainments and skills.

Some educators of the hearing impaired argue (with supportive evidence) that careful early diagnosis, appropriate amplification of sound through individual hearing aids, intensive enriching exposure to developmentally normative patterns of aural (auditory–oral) language and careful, consistent, parent and family guidance and training, should assist hearing impaired children to develop intelligible speech, adequate aural communicational and linguistic skills and more normative verbal–educational attainments (Nolan and Tucker 1981, Jackson 1981 section 4). Educators who are aurally (auditorily and orally) biased may suggest that there is no place for signing or natural gesture in the education of the hearing impaired.

Hearing aids (Jackson 1981) do not correct or compensate for hearing problems. The hearing aid amplifies sound to enhance whatever useful residual hearing the hearing impaired person has. Even with hearing aids, the pattern of sound may be distorted, uncomfortable and intermittent. It may not be a pleasure for the hearing impaired child to listen or to use his residual hearing.

Failure in, or inability to cope in, an aural environment usually leads to problems of attainment, adjustment and behavior (see INTELLIGENCE AND ENVIRONMENTAL INFLUENCES, and DISRUPTIVE PUPILS). Inadequancy or inappropriateness of some environments in which the hearing impaired exist, would appear to be a major factor in the higher incidence of maladaptive or disturbed behavioral and emotional patterns among the hearing impaired (Levine 1981, Mindel and Vernon 1971, Moores 1978, Myklebust 1964).

Evidence of higher, but still significantly retarded, verbal–educational attainments of hearing impaired children of hearing impaired parents (Moores 1978); severe retardation of hearing impaired children's verbal–educational attainments; above average levels of emotionally and behaviorally maladaptive, disturbed and disturbing behaviors among the hearing impaired (Levine 1981, Mindel and Vernon 1971, Moores 1978, Myklebust 1964); and concern about possible disintegration or deterioration in the "Deaf cultural group" are among factors which have motivated some educators and psychologists to advocate and support the use of sign "languages" in the education of the hearing impaired (Mindel and Vernon 1971, Moores 1978).

Sign language of the hearing impaired is a language in its own right, and consequently has different linguistic structure from other languages. Some educators of the hearing impaired have extracted the sign vocabulary for "deaf sign language" to incorporate the vocabulary into normative "hearing" aural language patterns which are acoustically amplified (individual hearing aids) and simultaneously supported with signs in normative "hearing"grammatical structure. Systems of signing which follow the above procedure include "Signed English" and "Total Communication" (Jackson 1981 section 4).

There is a diversity of educational placement and preschool services available to the hearing impaired (see INTEGRATION OF HANDICAPPED CHILDREN IN NORMAL SCHOOLS) in Britain and North America. Approximately 10 per cent or less of hearing impaired children in Britain are educated in special schools for the hearing impaired. The remainder are educated through facilities such as special classes, or small tutorial groups in ordinary schools; and many hearing impaired children, some with very severe hearing losses, cope adequately in main-stream classes. North American facilities for the hearing impaired have a similar range of preschool and school services. A few colleges in North America cater specifically for the hearing impaired.

Psychological studies of the hearing impaired appear to have moved from a pathological normative model which appeared to concentrate on features of similarity to or difference from the hearing population (Myklebust 1964) to a model based on organizing the environment and communication system to meet the needs of the hearing impaired (Levine 1981, Moores 1978).

Psychological assessment of hearing impaired children requires a clear understanding of the elements, construction, validity, reliability and purpose etc. of any test which is used, as well as understanding what the test actually measures. (See TESTS: NORMATIVE AND CRITERION REFERENCED; EDUCATIONAL ATTAINMENT; PERSONALITY). Tests which have verbal instructions, questions or content, including language which must be read, place the hearing impaired child at a disadvantage owing to linguistic retardation in comparison with non-verbal abilities. In contrast to significant retardation of verbal skills and attainments the hearing impaired tend to show a normative distribution of non-verbal or practical abilities (Bond 1979, Levine 1981, Moores 1978).

This does not mean that verbal tests should not be used with the hearing impaired as verbal tests may provide useful base-line information for comparison with peers – both hearing and hearing impaired, and for remedial programming in comparison with previous performance etc. (See TESTS: NORMATIVE AND CRITERION REFERENCED).

Careful, and appropriate early assessment, diagnosis, intervention, communication and placement, based on the hearing impaired individual's needs, abilities and aptitudes, remain crucial to enabling both the hearing impaired individual and his environment to succeed. DEB

References

Ballantyne, J. 1977: *Deafness.* 3rd edn. Edinburgh, London and New York: Churchill Livingstone.

Bond, D.E. 1979: Aspects of psycho-educational assessment of hearing impaired children with additional handicaps. *Journal of the British Association of Teachers of the Deaf* 3.3.

English, J., ed. 1978: Usher's syndrome: the personal social and emotional implications. *American Annals of the Deaf* 123, 3.

*Jackson, Anne, ed. 1981: *Ways and means 3 – hearing impairment.* Somerset Education Authority: Globe Education Publications.

Knight, N. 1981: *A medical view of hearing loss.* In Jackson, *Ways and Means 3.*

*Levine, E.S. 1981: *The ecology of early deafness: guides to fashioning environments and psychological assessments.* New York: Columbia University Press.

Mindel, E.D. and Vernon, McCay 1971: *They grow in silence: the deaf child and his family.* Maryland: National Association of the Deaf.

*Moores, D.F. 1978: *Educating the deaf: Psychology, principles and practices.* Boston: Houghton Mifflin.

Myklebust, H.R. 1964: *The psychology of deafness: sensory deprivation, learning and adjustment* 2nd edn. New York and London: Grune and Stratton.

Nolan, M. and Tucker, I.G. 1981: *The hearing-impaired child and the family.* London: Souvenir Press.

Vernon, McCay, 1969: *Multiply handicapped deaf children: medical, educational, and psychological considerations.* CEC Monograph. Washington D.C.: Council for Exceptional Children Inc.

Hebraic psychology The idea that the language and literature of the Hebrews (especially of the Old Testament period) reveal a distinctive psychological structure.

The ancient Hebrews can hardly be said to have had a psychology, in the sense of a body of formulated ideas about the operation of the mind, perception or the like. The ways in which biblical texts express the person, his actions, emotions and relations to others may however furnish some significant notions.

The main Hebrew term often traditionally rendered as "soul" is *nephesh*: a better idea of its meaning might be conveyed by an expression such as "living being". It is not a separate essence and is more like the principle of life animating the person, acting in his actions and touched by that which touches him. Thus "my *nephesh*" comes very close to "myself". In this sense "soul" has a rather "physical" tone to it. Possibly related by derivation with the breath or the throat, the *nephesh* can often have close connections with bodily areas like the heart, the liver, the kidneys and the bowels, all commonly used in expressions of emotion. These terms are indeed much more used in such expressions than to designate physical organs such as what we now call "the heart". Interestingly, the brain is seldom or never mentioned in these connections.

Again, the *nephesh* can be more or less identified with the blood as the seat of life: the eating of blood is forbidden on the grounds that "the blood is *nephesh*" (Deuteronomy 12.23), i.e. the life, and is therefore not for human consumption, perhaps because, being life, it belongs peculiarly to God. In such senses, *nephesh* is not peculiar to human beings: just as an Israelite should "know the soul of" a foreign resident, i.e. know what it is to be one, so a good man should "know the soul of" his animals (Proverbs 12.10), know what life is for them. In the creation story, plants do not count as *nephesh* but animals do: their creation is described with the words "let the earth bring forth living *nephesh*" (Genesis 1.24). In enumerations *nephesh* often refers to the persons listed: "all the *nephesh* of those who came from the thigh of Jacob were seventy *nephesh*" (Exodus 1.5); in such cases *nephesh* may be singular and collective, but may also be plural and refer to individuals. In legal texts "that *nephesh*" may mean "that (individual) person". In a rather exceptional usage, contact with a corpse is forbidden under the terms of "coming upon the *nephesh* of one dead" (Numbers 6.6, cf. 19.11). On the whole, therefore, *nephesh* does not suggest something of quite different character from the bodily and physical; it is rather the life, or the dominant life principle, animating the living.

Another group of expressions are even more clearly related to the notion of breath and depict the person in another way. Breath comes from God. In another creation narrative, God fashioned man of soil and breathed into his nostrils the breath of life, and "man became a living *nephesh*" (Genesis 2.7). Conversely, at his death man "expires": "the dust returns to the earth as it was, and the spirit returns to God who gave it" (Ecclesiastes 12.7). Further, one of the main words for "breath, wind", *ruach*, is widely used for the "spirit" of a man, which does his thinking and planning and responds to external stimuli.

Yet another conception depicts the survival of a weak, shadowy being, a "shade", after death in the underworld. In the main biblical period there was no expectation of an afterlife as a positive good, whether through resurrection or through the immortality of the soul. It was a good thing for a man that he should live to a fine old age and die among his children, being "gathered to his fathers" and if possible buried among them. This was adequate satisfaction. It would be wrong, however, to interpret this as crass materialism, as if it meant that physical life and death in our sense was the sole and ultimate criterion.

In modern times it has often been customary to contrast these Hebrew expressions with Greek views, and especially with the Platonic view of the soul as immortal, intrinsically divine, separate from the body and temporarily residing in it, while the body, being temporary and corruptible, is a burden to the soul and a corrupting force upon its purity. There is considerable validity in the comparison if we compare only the central biblical material on the Hebrew side with pure Platonism on the Greek. But if we widen the perspective to include *all* Greek ideas the comparison becomes more complex. The idea of the shadowy existence of the departed is close to ideas found in Homer; not all Greek philosophy was Platonic; also we have to consider not only what philosophers thought, but how ordinary people thought and spoke. The Hebrew image of the human spirit as breath coming from God is easily capable of extension towards the divine origin of the soul. Some of the differences may be ascribed to the fact that the Hebrews did not face the problems of formulating their psychological notions as early as Greek thinkers did; and, when they came to do it, it was partly under Greek influence, and some degree of compromise or overlap between Hebrew and Greek notions took place very easily. Internal religious developments in Judaism were of great importance. Hellenistic Judaism, stimulated by religious persecution, developed the expectation of resurrection. The torturers could destroy the body, but they could not destroy the spirit. The martyrs would rise again and receive back the life they had sacrificed. Yet their bodies were dead and must corrupt; on the other hand, they passed into the presence of God. Thus the conception of resurrection itself went hand in hand with the idea of immortality of the soul and the possibility of its continued life apart from the body. Jesus, speaking on the basis of ideas then common, distinguishes the one who can kill the body from the one who can kill the soul (Matthew 10.28). Some schools of Greek Judaism recognized the immortality and pre-existence of the soul, which is combined with the body and weighed down by the corruptibility of the latter (Wisdom 3.1, 8.19, 9.15). Such ideas are also found sporadically among the early rabbis, who had a considerable variety of notions about the soul and its relation to the body. The great medieval Jewish philosophers combine biblical passages and other Jewish traditions with concepts basically derived from the Greek philosophical traditions. Thus Maimonides, discussing *nephesh*, says that it is sometimes the rational soul, the "form" of man, while again it is sometimes that which remains of man after death (*Guide of the Perplexed* i.41; 1963 ed., p.91) – the Greek concepts are unmistakeable. One central question of dispute was whether the human "soul" that was immortal was the individual soul or a more universal intelligence.

The notion of a distinctive Hebraic psychology has been a significant cultural force, especially in the twentieth century. Matthew Arnold (1869 *(1963)*) made popular the contrast between "Hebraism" and "Hellenism" as types of literary culture. Later, theologians used the idea as an argument for the distinctiveness of biblical religion and the authority of various modern versions of it. Robinson (1925), probably influenced by L. Lévy-Bruhl, insisted on the "Hebrew conception of corporate personality" as a key to the understanding of the Bible, and this was very influential (cf. criticisms by Porter (1965) and Rogerson (1970)). The most important single presentation was Pedersen's (1926): typical of his thoughts are "the soul is an entirety with a definite stamp ... the will is the whole of the tendency of the soul" (i. 103), "the soul is more than the body, but the body is a perfectly valid manifestation of the soul" (i. 171). Pedersen was not, however, so concerned to stress the *uniqueness* of Hebraic psychology as were some others, and in fact his views were closely modeled upon Grønbech's (1909–12 *(1932)*) picture of the early Scandinavians. After about 1960, however, the tendency to take Hebrew psychology as a key to the reading of the Bible diminished under strong criticism for its misreading of linguistic evidence (Barr 1961, 1962, 1966). While works of this kind included much useful observation, they often depended on highly literal interpretations of surface phenomena of the language, taken as though they were direct indices to psychological deep structures. It is doubtful whether they demonstrated the existence of a distinctive Hebraic psychology and some of them did not even seriously try to do so. It is doubtful whether they really showed evidence of distinctiveness in depth even as against Greek thought, and they freely assimilated Hebrew psychology to supposed primitive mentality, pre-logical reasoning and the like. The network of Hebrew expressions concerning soul, spirit and the like is of deep interest for the understanding of the Bible and other Jewish literature, but it is very doubtful whether it serves as demonstration of a distinctive Hebraic psychology as such. In so far as one may speak of a "Jewish mind", it should be related not to a distinct underlying psychology tied to a particular language, but to a peculiar historical experience, literary tradition, religion and social organization. JB

Bibliography

Arnold, M. 1869 *(1963)*: *Culture and anarchy*. Cambridge: Cambridge University Press.

*Barr, J. 1961: *The semantics of biblical language*. Oxford: Oxford University Press.

——— 1962: *Biblical words for Time*. London: SCM Press.

——— 1966: *Old and New in interpretation: a study of the two Testaments*. London: SCM Press; New York: Harper and Row.

Grønbech, V. 1909-12 *(1932)*: *The culture of the teutons*. Oxford: Oxford University Press.

Lévy-Bruhl, L. 1923: *Primitive mentality*. London: Allen & Unwin.

——— 1926: *How natives think*. London: Allen & Unwin.

Maimonides: *The guide of the perplexed*, 2 vols., ed. S. Pines. Chicago and London: University of Chicago Press (1963).

*Pedersen, J. 1920 *(1926)*: *Israel: its life and culture*, 2 vols. Oxford: Oxford University Press.

Porter, J.R. 1965: The legal aspects of the concept of "Corporate Personality" in the Old Testament. *Vetus Testamentum* 15, 361–80.

Robinson, H.W. 1925: Hebrew psychology. In *The people and the book*, ed. A.S. Peake. Oxford: Clarendon Press.

Rogerson, J.W. 1970: The Hebrew conception of Corporate Personality: a re-examination. *Journal of theological studies* n.s. 21, 1–16.

hedonic Together with AGONIC this term refers to two extreme mechanisms of social cohesion and to the corresponding modes of mental activity.

Hedonic social cohesion is exhibited by chimpanzee society (and possibly also by groups of Gorilla and orang-utan). In these animals, social cohesion is periodically re-established (after periods of dispersion into groups of two, three or more), by excited sessions of mutual display in which food sharing and many forms of body contact occur: hugging, tumble play, slapping, greeting by hand touching, and pseudo sexual behavior as well as mating. In these ways social cohesion is rewarded (in contrast to the agonic form which is based on avoidance of punishment). The display sessions show a build-up of excitement to a peak, which suggests that the initial arousal is usually low and kept so by frequent body contact. Agonistic episodes are frequently followed by appeasement gestures, especially between males, who, thereby, seek reconciliation. The periodic nature of social gatherings and the low state of arousal have two consequences. (1) They allow attention to be directed continuously to environmental investigation; and (2) the arousal can fluctuate with the rise and fall of interest in aspects of the physical environment. Exploration is a self-rewarding activity and so generates a positive feedback. This keeps up the interest in any aspect of the environment for long enough for the ape to become acquainted with all its different features. Hence the power of investigation is generated. As exploration is the essential prerequisite for the operation of intelligence, (see Halstead) so also is the hedonic mode.

The discovery of the two modes was itself the result of the attempt to classify the ATTENTION STRUCTURE of primate societies. Since then it has been possible to see that they rest on an autonomic infrastructure revealed by the work of Gellhorn, who showed that in an egotropic mode, essentially the same as the agonic, the nervous system expends energy through a state of readiness for action in which heart rate increases and cortical excitation also takes place with a rise in muscular tension. In the other, the trophotropic mode, energy stores are built up, heart rate declines and cortical excitation with its accompanying muscle tension is low, as would be expected in the hedonic mode. Moreover the Laceys have shown that when the heart rate slows ability to take in information is increased and, hence, exploration made possible; thus demonstrating in another way that the hedonic mode is the essential condition for the operation of intelligence. MRAC

Bibliography

Chance, M.R.A. 1980 The social structure of attention and the operation of intelligence In Eric Sinderland and Malcolm T. Smith, eds *The exercise of intelligence.* New York and London: Garland STPM Press.

Gellhorn, E. 1966-7. The tuning of the nervous system: physiological foundations and implications for behavior. *Perspectives in biology and medicine.* 10, 559–91.

Halstead, W.C. 1951: Brain and intelligence. In L.A. Jefferies, ed. *Cerebral mechanisms in behavior.* New York: John Wiley.

Knapp, P.H. ed. 1963: *Expression of the emotions in man.* New York: International Universities Press.

Lacey, J.I. et al. 1963: The visceral level; situational determinants and behavioral correlates of autonomic response patterns. In P.H. Knapp ed. *Expression of the emotions in man.* New York: International Universities Press.

Hegel, Georg Wilhelm Friedrich (1770–1831). A German idealist philosopher whose influential psychological insights are chiefly embodied in his *Phänomenologie des Geistes* (1807) and *Geistesphilosophie* (1830). In contrast to earlier thinkers Hegel treated the individual's mental life as essentially dependent upon, and as evolving within, a communal context. Self-consciousness presupposed a developing awareness of the existence of other persons in which the subject could find his own identity confirmed; the genesis of this process, as schematically described in the *Phänomenologie*, was portrayed as involving a struggle for mastery between opposed individuals that was only finally resolved through mutual recognition. Elsewhere Hegel insisted upon the need to connect the growth of the mind with changing historical conditions, stressing both the conflicts which affect the individual personality when it is estranged from its social environment and the deceptive modes of thought and consciousness to which such conflicts give rise. PLG

Bibliography

Hegel, G.W.F. 1807 (*1977*): *Phenomenology of spirit.* Trans. A.V. Miller. Oxford: Clarendon Press.

——— 1830 (*1971*): *Philosophy of mind.* Trans. W. Wallace and A.V. Miller. Oxford: Clarendon Press.

Sklar, Judith 1976: *Freedom and independence: A study of Hegel's 'Phenomenology of mind'.* Cambridge: Cambridge University Press; Binghamton, N.Y.: Vail-Ballou Press.

*Taylor, Charles 1975: *Hegel.* Cambridge: Cambridge University Press.

hermeneutic interpretative theory The theory of human understanding in its interpretative aspect. In particular, a hermeneutic is a set of practices or recommendations for revealing an intelligible meaning in an otherwise unclear text or text-analogue. Essentially the character of the hermeneutical process consists in introducing into something already partially specified a further degree of specificity, such that what is strange, alien, foreign or unfamiliar is made familiar, or comprehensible, or simply expressible. Whether beyond this it is possible to speak of a single such process, and of a *correct* interpretation, is a matter for debate – hence the proliferation of theories in this area.

Debate revolves mainly around the following three issues. Firstly, the question of whether interpretation takes place in an already fixed and existing world, or in an evolving one, a world which is already specified to a degree but which remains open to further specification, with each interpretation actively contributing to its further development – a world which, as Hegel and Marx argued, is possibly still progressing towards its own true self-comprehension, but which does not yet possess the appropriate practical social conditions for other than "illusory" understandings of a "false" reality. Secondly there is the not unrelated question as to whether interpretation is a process taking place within a formal system of already existing categories, or whether it is a much more fundamental process, one which works to provide, prior to any explicit understandings, a specific structure of "pre-understanding" (to use Heidegger's term), a structure upon which all our more explicit, categorical understandings must rest. Thirdly, "dualistic" and "monistic" positions may be distinguished, in the sense that the hermeneutical task can either be considered as directed towards grasping a spiritual or objective "inner reality" in people's "outer" expressions, or towards a more practical aim, i.e. attempting to realize concretely the possibilities for further human being implicit in our current structures of pre-understanding – where our current categories of understanding are to be seen as a parochial commitment to a particular, historically determined mode of pre-understanding.

The oppositions set out above emerge in setting the early modern hermeneutics of Schleiermacher and Dilthey over against the later views of Heidegger and Gadamer. The earliest recorded usage (1654) and probably still the most widespread meaning of the term "hermeneutics" refers to canons of biblical exegesis. But the search for a secure method or system by which to divine the true but hidden meaning of a text was clearly active even in Old Testament times. The distinction of first formulating a systematic "historical hermeneutics" with a "psychological" approach to interpretation, *and* of reconceptualizing hermeneutics as concerned with the general problem of human understanding, must go to Schleiermacher (1768–1834). Others (e.g. Wolff 1759–1824; Ast 1778–1841) had previously agreed that the hermeneutical task involved the discovery or reconstruction of a larger unity, lost or hidden within the aggregate of fragments provided by a text or texts. They were clear that in order to render comprehensible what was, owing to its isolation and singularity, impervious to understanding, the hermeneutical process must move perpetually back and forth from the particular to the whole it indicates and back again to the particular, each polarity providing a corrective for the other. Interpretation must work, in other words, within what Ast called "the hermeneutical circle". But to say this was only to describe a part of what people do in their attempts to clarify their understanding. What was still missing was any reference to what Schleiermacher took to be the foundational act of all hermeneutics: the ordinary, everyday acts of understanding in which people come to a direct and immediate grasp of each other's meanings in their discourse with one another. To the existing grammatical and philological canons, Schleiermacher added psychological ones: hermeneutics must accomplish by conscious effort and technique what ordinary conversationalists achieve effortlessly, namely a grasp of the contents of one another's "minds". To do this, hermeneutics must restore what is lost when the immediacy of a direct, living contact between people is lost, i.e. the background, historical context in which people act. The task is to reconstruct the subjective "inner reality" within which historical actors saw their expressions as originally making sense.

Such a view requires, for the purposes of interpretation, that we split reality into two: into an "outer" reality which can be *explained* casually, and an "inner" reality which must be *understood*. Continuing in the same tradition as Schleiermacher (of romantic individualism), Dilthey (1833–1911) attempted to establish this interpretative dualism as the basis for a special methodology for the human sciences (or the *Geisteswissenschaften* as he called them, in his translation of J.S. Mill's term, "the moral sciences") – a methodology radically different from that of the natural sciences. Rather than *erklaren* (to explain) their task must be *verstehen* (to understand); where understanding was to be achieved by a psychological re-enactment or imaginative reconstruction of the experience of those to be understood, Dilthey's hermeneutics was, therefore, a hermeneutics of authors not of texts. And the special method of "the sciences of the spirit" worked to reveal (what was inaccessible to the method of the natural sciences), the hidden subjectivity, the intentions and purposes, of the historical actors and authors which informed the texts they left behind them.

This "subjective" approach is now, however, under attack, both in Anglo-Saxon philosophy under the influence of the later Wittgenstein and on the Continent. One strand of this criticism issued from Heidegger (1889–1976). He, like Dilthey, saw in hermeneutics intimations of a more general process, one in which human conduct reveals itself to itself, so to speak. But unlike Dilthey, he emphasized the practical, non-cognitive aspects of understanding, the embodied structures of "pre-understanding" people acquire in the course of their immediate, unplanned encounters with one another (Heidegger 1962). In such activities, people do not simply come to a subjective understanding of something before unknown to them, their very *being* is re-structured. And it is this pre-structuredness of their being which then makes it possible for them to exercise particular modes of understanding upon a subjective or cognitive level – and denies other modes to them. While in previous, more "dualistic" views, people could simply express themselves as they pleased, in Heidegger's view they must *participate* in a communal linguistic process with its own dynamic. Rather than people expressing their *selves* by their language, it is their language which expresses *them*, so to speak, for it determines the nature of their being and hence what they find intelligible. In other words, their "reality" is constituted for them by the very language they use in their attempts to describe it. In this "ontological" interpretation of hermeneutics, the task ceases to be that of merely clarifying or evaluating already known data with the aim of conceptual mastery; it becomes that of recognizing and expressing the new possibilities for human being implicitly present but dispersed within the texts and "text" of everyday forms of life. Heidegger's radical deepening of Schleiermacher's concern with the general problem of understanding results ironically in hermeneutics returning to its traditional concern with authorless texts – but with now an ontological rather than an epistemological concern.

Such new "truths of being" – "truth" here being truth as

disclosure rather than as correspondence to a pre-existing reality – cannot, however, be revealed methodically, by the use of pre-structured modes of understanding. For strictly, methods can only render explicit the kind of truths already implicit within them. This is the theme of Gadamer's *Truth and method* (1975). Rather than the manipulation and rearrangement of things within categories already thought of, a quite different kind of thought or mental activity is required. Indeed, Gadamer, like Heidegger, is critical of what he sees as our surrender to technological modes of functioning in everything that we do. What is required is a dialectical or dialogical approach, an active participation in the subject matter of the text. In other words, a text is understood, not by attempting to reconstruct the world within which it had its original being, nor by re-living the subjective experience of its author, but by letting the text itself "have its own say", so to speak, by letting it address one in one's own world. The kind of understanding which results here is that described by Wittgenstein (1953) when he says: "Try not to think of understanding as a 'mental process' at all ... But ask yourself: in what sort of case ... do we say, 'Now I know how to go on' ". In other words, one's aim is the practical one of enlarging (and transforming) one's current reality to incorporate a text's message, its subjective strangeness being rendered familiar in the process. *Leben* (or forms of life) replace *Geist* (or mind) as the central focus in this hermeneutics.

But does this mean that, if our interpretations gain a consensus agreement, they are true? That depends, suggests Habermas (1972, 1976) following Marx on whether in fact our current form of life allows the kind of "undistorted communication" required for a properly critical appreciation of the interpretations offered. For unless "a structure of human life" exists which "constitutes itself in a self-formative process" (Habermas 1972, p.194) – i.e. unless all a society's newborns are socialized as autonomous *persons*, all able to participate equally in negotiating meanings – the consensus reached is likely to be a false consensus, representing hidden sectional interests.

The current quickening of interest in hermeneutics in Anglo-Saxon philosophy and social theory reflects an interesting convergence between its problems and those raised by the philosophy of the later Wittgenstein. Both reject logical empiricism as an adequate approach to mental phenomena – a rejection currently echoed in psychology by the determination to study the *actions* of *agents* rather than merely *behavior* in general (see ETHOGENICS). In such a context it is not surprising that there is a return to Dilthey's claim that the natural and the human sciences require radically distinct methodologies. Yet remarkably, it is not a claim which has been unreservedly welcomed, and the unity of all the sciences is once again being asserted: but, all are now being claimed to be equally hermeneutical (see e.g. Bhaskar 1979, p.195)! Duhem (1906) had already noted long ago (around the turn of the century) that natural scientific assertions were not tested one by one against experience, but required interpretation within a theory as a whole. Kuhn (1962), however, has been most influential in this respect, arguing that the proper interpretation of theoretical statements requires reference to the context of scientific traditions and practices within which they have their currency.

But as Taylor (1980) points out, to claim that there is no essential difference between the human and the natural sciences on the grounds that both possess an interpretative component, is to forget that the aim of the natural sciences is to give an account of the world independently of the meanings it might have for individual subjects. This is achieved in the natural sciences by the use of idealizations and formal systems of interpretation which determine, prior to any further investigations the kinds of things being sought. The human sciences, however, cannot so limit themselves. For they must discover not only what kind of activity it is which makes the natural sciences possible, but they must also account for those human activities which make possible their own disciplines. To select a methodology for this task would be to pre-judge the issue; this need not, however, preclude the use of methodologies for other purposes. Controversy about this issue can be expected to continue.

JDS

Bibliography

Bhaskar, R. 1979: *The possibility of naturalism*. Brighton: Harvester Press.

Bauman, Z. 1978: *Hermeneutics and social science*. London: Hutchinson.

Duhem, P. 1906 (1962): *The aim and the structure of physical theory*. New York: Atheneum.

Gadamer, H.-G. 1975: *Truth and method*. Revised edn. London: Sheed and Ward.

Habermas, J. 1972: *Knowledge and human interests*. Trans. J. Shapiro. Boston, Mass: Beacon Press; London: Heinemann (1976).

——— 1976: *Legitimation crisis*. Trans. T. McCarthy. London: Heinemann.

Heidegger, M. 1962: *Being and time*. Oxford: Basil Blackwell; New York: Harper & Row.

Kuhn, T.S. 1962: *The structure of scientific revolutions*. Chicago: University of Chicago Press.

Palmer, R.E. 1969: *Hermeneutics: interpretation theory in Schleiermacher, Dilthey, Heidegger, and Gadamer*. Evanston, Ill: Northwestern University Press.

Rorty, R. 1980: *Philosophy and the mirror of nature*. Princeton, N.J.: Princeton University Press; Oxford: Basil Blackwell.

Taylor, C. 1980: Understanding in human science. *Review of Metaphysics*. 34, 3–23.

Wittgenstein, Ludwig 1953: *Philosophical investigations*. Trans. G.E.M. Anscombe. Oxford: Basil Blackwell; New York: Macmillan.

hierarchy The word has been used in two quite different contexts in ethology. In the field of motivation various ethologists during the 1940s developed branching (or nested) hierarchical models of the underlying control of behavior. The best known is that of Tinbergen, often illustrated by the example of the three spined stickleback, *Gasterosteus aculeatus*. Each major behavior system was called an instinct: for instance there was a reproductive instinct and a feeding instinct. Corresponding to each instinct was a 'center', a locus in the brain, which was 'charged up' over time with drive, or action potential, specific to that instinct. This drive would be released by appropriate external stimuli and discharged, ultimately in overt behavior. But instead of being discharged directly it would activate *sub*-centers. For example the reproductive instinct of the stickleback was thought to have a nest-building sub-center, a courtship sub-center etc. The hierarchy had many levels. The courtship sub-center in turn discharged into a series of sub-sub-centers, corresponding to various courtship behavior patterns. The hypothetical hierarchy went on sub-dividing until individual muscle units were reached.

The total behavior of the animal could therefore be thought of as being controlled by something like the hierarchical chain of command of an army. This is an obviously efficient system of organization, and there is likely to be some truth underlying the early hierarchical models. The models have been criticized, but usually for reasons only distantly connected with their hierarchical nature. They have been accused of neglecting the important role of feedback in bringing behavior to an end: in the simplest version of the classical models behavior came to an end when it ran out of action specific energy rather than when feedback signaled that it had achieved its goal. The models have been accused of physiological naiveté, of postulating unitary centers in the brain where the reality may be distributed and diffuse. Some modern ethologists feel that the basic idea of hierarchical organization is too important to throw out just because the classical models can be criticized.

The other context in which the word hierarchy has been used is in social relationships. Animals in groups are often described as forming dominance hierarchies. The classic example is the 'pecking order' of farmyard hens. Each hen learns the identity of the others in her group, learns to defer to individuals that usually beat her in fights, and learns to expect immediate surrender from those that she usually beats. In the simplest cases a linear hierarchy is discerned such that A pecks B, B pecks C, C pecks D etc. Dominance hierarchies are not always simply linear in this way; sometimes nontransitive relationships develop in which A pecks B, B pecks C, but C pecks A. Dominance hierarchies are not always recognized by overt aggression. The ethologist is free to look for a hierarchy expressed by any behavior pattern. For instance primatologists sometimes count whether particular monkeys get out of the way of other particular monkeys: A is described as dominant to B if B gets out of A's way, but A walks straight on when B is in his path. Other hierarchies have been constructed according to who looks at whom, who is the center of attention (see ATTENTION STRUCTURE).

True dominance hierarchies depend upon individual recognition. Various kinds of apparent dominance hierarchy can arise when there is no individual recognition. An observer may note that A usually beats B who usually beats C etc. He may conclude that he has seen a dominance hierarchy, but in fact there may be no individual recognition at all. The hierarchy may be based directly on size: A is the largest, B the next largest, etc. Or A may simply be the individual with the most aggressive disposition. True dominance hierarchies with individual recognition have often been interpreted as beneficial for the whole group, because they cut down the amount of overt aggression in the group. Groups of hens that have formed a stable dominance hierarchy produce more eggs than groups that are continually fighting to establish a dominance hierarchy. Nowadays, however, accounts in terms of benefit to the group are not generally thought to have any explanatory power, and the existence of dominance hierarchies has to be explained in terms of benefits and costs to individuals surrendering or not surrendering in particular circumstances. RD

Bibliography

*Tinbergen, N. 1951: *The study of instinct*. Oxford: Clarendon Press.

*Dawkins, R. 1976: Hierarchal organization: a candidate principle for ethology. In *Growing points in ethology*, ed. P.P.G. Bateson and R.A. Hinde. Cambridge and New York: Cambridge University Press.

higher-order need strength Based on the work of Hackman and Oldham (1980), this concept is derived from Maslow's theory which asserts that needs exist in a hierarchy of prepotency from lower (physiological: e.g. safety) to higher (social: e.g. self-esteem, and self actualization) and from Alderfer's modification which posits three levels of needs: existence, relatedness and growth. Hackman and Oldham argue that employees who have high higher-order need strength will respond more positively to job enrichment (with respect to performance and/or job satisfaction; see WORK DESIGN) than will employees who have low higher-order need strength. The results of this prediction have been mixed. White (1978) takes a pessimistic view of the findings, as do Griffin, Welsh and Moorhead (1981). One problem with the research may be that inadequate measures of need strength have been used. Also, from a career growth perspective, job enrichment changes tend to be very modest; they may only involve changing the job so that 60 per cent of the workers' mental capacity is used instead of 30 per cent, so that need strength differences are irrelevant. EAL

Bibliography

Griffin, R.W., Welsh, A., and Moorhead, G. 1981: Perceived task characteristics and employee performance: a literature review. *Academy of management review* 6, 655–64.

Hackman, J.R. and Oldham, G.R. 1980: *Work redesign*. Reading, Mass.: Addison-Wesley.

White, J.K. 1978: Individual differences and the job quality-worker response relationship: review, integration, and comments. *Academy of management review* 3, 267–80.

hippocampus (Greek, seahorse) A large, multi-layered paleocortical structure in the limbic system of the brain (BRAIN AND CENTRAL NERVOUS SYSTEM: ILLUSTRATIONS, figs. 15–17). Composed of two interlocking components, Ammon's Horn and the dentate gyrus, the hippocampus extends from its most dorsal position below the cingulate gyrus, in a lateral and ventral direction, until just near the AMYGDALA in the medial temporal lobe region. Through its connections with the entorhinal cortex, which is linked to a complex system of afferent pathways, the hippocampus receives input from all sensory modalities. The major ouflow from the hippocampus is the fornix which projects antero-ventrally, giving off some fibers to the septum and terminating in the mammillary bodies of the

HYPOTHALAMUS, (figs. 20 and 21). Historically identified with olfaction and emotion, recent research involving animals and humans implicates the hippocampus in learning and memory operations. There is considerable controversy concerning the precise role of the hippocampus, but, in broad terms, a cognitively-oriented function involving information processing is indicated. GWI

historical psychology Is concerned with cross-time alterations or transformations in patterns of human conduct and their psychological bases. In principle the historical psychologist is concerned with all patterns of change, ranging from the momentary to the millenial. For example, an historical psychologist might apply a theory of dialectic change with equal facility to momentary shifts within conversations, the development of the individual over a life span, generational change, and to cultural change spanning centuries. Yet, while broadly applicable, the vast share of interest within historical psychology has been devoted to patterns of change exceeding the life span of individuals. In this sense historical psychology has much in common with diachronic linguistics and the kind of historical sociology exemplified by Norbert Elias's *The civilizing process.* Although the concerns of the historical psychologist overlap with those of the historian, the two disciplines tend to differ in (1) the focus of study and (2) the place of theory within the research process. In the first instance traditional historians have typically focussed their concerns on incidents within the governmental, economic and military spheres, while the historical psychologist is typically more concerned with common psychological processes (perception, cognition, valuation, etc.) and their manifestations in general social patterns. With respect to theory, traditional historians have tended to leave theoretical predilections unarticulated, while attempting to vindicate a particular descriptive narrative. In contrast, for the historical psychologist theoretical concerns are generally paramount, and often dictate the historical eras to be studied and the particulars of concern within these eras.

The founding of historical psychology is most reasonably attributed to Wilhelm WUNDT. Although Wundt devoted the majority of his career to the laboratory study of mental structure and its physiological coordinates, the last twenty years of his life were devoted to his ten volume work, *Volkerpsychologie.* Wundt argued that the laboratory study of isolated, reflex-like events was insufficient for the understanding of more general patterns of human conduct including cultural values and institutions. For such understanding Wundt proposed an historical orientation. From this perspective, understanding of contemporary patterns is achieved by tracing their origins and vicissitudes through history. For example an understanding of contemporary race relations in England would, from this perspective, require that one trace the conditions under which various racial minorities immigrated into the country, their economic and educational experiences within the country since this time, the effects of various civil policies in various periods and so on. Wundt's orientation continued to have an impact on psychology for some years. For example, the Murchison *Handbook of social psychology* (1935) contained four chapters devoted to an understanding of cultural patterns through historical analysis. However, with the hegemony of the positivist orientation in psychology, and its handmaiden behaviorism, historical psychology was largely obscured from view, though scattered works continued to appear. McClelland's analysis (1961) of the dependency of achievement motivation on historical circumstances, van den Berg's study (1961) of the changing character of human nature, Vygotsky's discussion (1934) of the dependency of cognitive process on cultural conditions, and Fromm's inquiry (1941) into the historical basis for fascism, are notable in this respect. However, only within the past decade has historical psychology once again, begun to play a significant role in psychological study.

The reasons for this renaissance of interest are many and complex. Among them must be included the general deterioration of confidence in the basic tenets of positivist–empiricist philosophy. This philosophic view favored the stimulus–response form of psychological theorizing, along with the method of experimentation. Psychologists typically believed that through laboratory study they could elucidate the functioning of basic mechanisms or processes. These mechanisms, or processes, it was assumed, stood outside history. It was believed for example that the laws of conditioning operate identically regardless of historical era. Yet, as confidence in the positivist–empiricist meta-theory began to erode, so did corresponding beliefs in the mechanistic character of human conduct, the dependency of human behavior on environmental antecedents, and the capacity of experimentally manipulated conditions to furnish reliable information regarding patterns of human conduct. Theorists could begin to give serious consideration to the possibility that human behavior is largely governed by historically contingent rules as opposed to determinative mechanisms of the mind, that behavior is self-directed as opposed to environmentally determined, and that reactions to laboratory manipulations might have little to do with normal patterns of conduct within society more generally. These latter views have each favored a concern with the historical embeddedness of human activity. One is invited to see contemporary patterns of behavior as embedded within an historical sequence, the contours and implications of which may be altered through scholarly enlightenment.

A second important influence on the re-emergence of historical psychology may be traced to Marxist criticism of capitalist economic principles. As Marx argued, such principles are typically treated as both temporally unbounded in their generality and as value neutral. Yet, as Marx also demonstrated, capitalist economics appeared to be an historical contingent system and capitalist economic doctrine typically served to legitimate and mystify an economic structure which favored the proponents of the doctrine. Such argumentation later became expanded within various treatments of the sociology of science and within critical sociology more generally (Habermas 1971).

As a result of such expansion, wide ranging critical analysis has been directed toward various forms of seemingly general and value neutral theory. Although largely severed from its Marxist origins, critical analyses have focussed on the valuational investments or implications of conflict theory, cognitive psychology, stimulus–response models, moral development theory and traditional historical treatments of psychology. Such work has served to enhance consciousness of the historical conditions giving rise to various psychological theories (cf. Buss 1979), and of the ways in which theories themselves may alter social patterns.

Contemporary inquiry in historical psychology can be divided into three major forms. First, many investigators have focussed on psychosocial patterns occurring in differing historical eras. Such work usually attempts to throw into relief the historical contingency of contemporary, taken-for-granted assumptions about human nature, by documenting periods in which differing patterns existed. Exemplars of this approach include Erikson's treatment of perception in the medieval period and Verhave and van Hoorn's discussion (in press) of the self-concept over history. Certain historical treatments, particularly those of the *Les Annales* school are also of interest to such concerns. Badinter's analysis (1981) of the historical vicissitudes of the "maternal instinct" has been of special interest to psychologists.

The second major form of research in historical psychology is employed by theorists arguing for universal principles of human functioning, but simultaneously holding that historical conditions establish the values of variables within the theory. One theory will make differential predictions in differing historical periods. Historical research is used in this case to justify such conclusions. For example Simonton (1979) has used wide ranging research to argue that certain historical configurations will favor a high creative output. Specifically, if there are numerous role models in the two preceding generations and a period of nationalistic revolt, the period is likely to be a creative one across wide ranging domains, from science to the arts. Similarly, Secord's research employs gender ratio theory to make predictions about the character of heterosexual relations in various historical climes. This approach is perhaps the most conservative in the historical psychology movement, as researchers remain committed to the view of universal, deterministic theories.

The third major form of research in historical psychology has focussed on patterns of change across time. Historical research in this case is typically used to vindicate a particular theory of change. An example of this orientation is Martindale's work (1975) on alterations in aesthetic taste. As he argues, regardless of aesthetic domain, the evolution of aesthetic fashion over time undergoes a similar pattern, which can be largely attributed to basic psychological make-up.

Research in a number of other domains also contributes to the historical psychology movement. Much life span developmental inquiry is concerned with the socio-historical conditions giving rise to various life span trajectories. Research employing cohort analysis has been particularly important in documenting the dependency of such trajectories on the particular age cohort (Baltes and Schaie 1973). Inquiry into biography and psychohistory furnishes insight into the vicissitudes of historical trajectory, sensitivity to temporal background of contemporary pattern, and understanding of the processes of historical construction itself. Finally, historical inquiry in psychology, particularly that which focusses on various ideological inputs into theory and the process of historical accounting bear importantly on the development of historical psychology. KJG/HFMP

Bibliography

Badinter, E. 1981: *Mother love*. New York: Macmillan.

Baltes, P.B. and Schaie, K.W. 1973: On life span developmental research paradigms, retrospects and prospects. In *Life span developmental psychology: Personality and socialization*. New York: Academic Press.

Buss, A.R., ed. 1979: *Psychology in social context*. New York: Irvington.

Elias, N. 1939 (*1978*): *The civilizing process*. New York: Urizen.

Fromm, E. 1941: *Escape from freedom*. New York: Rinehart.

Habermas, J. 1971 (*1976*): *Knowledge and human interest*. Boston, Mass.: Beacon Press; London: Heinemann.

Martindale, C. 1975: *Romantic progression: the psychology of literary history*. Washington, D.C.: Hemisphere.

McClelland, D.C. 1961: *The achieving society*. New York: Van Nostrand.

Simonton, D.K. 1979: Multiple discovery and invention: Zeitgeist, genius, or chance? *Journal of personality and social psychology*. 37, 1603–16.

Secord, P.F. 1983: Love, misogyny and feminism. In Gergen and Gergen, op. cit.

van den Berg, J.H. 1961: *The changing nature of man*. New York: Norton.

Verhave, T. and van Hoorn, W. 1983: The temporalization of the self. In K.J. and M.M. Gergen, eds. *Historical social psychology*. Hillsdale, N.J.: Erlbaum.

Vygotsky, L.S. 1934 (*1961*): *Thought and language*. Cambridge, Mass.: MIT.

Wundt, W. 1900–16: *Volkerspychologie*. 10 vols.: Leipzig: Engelmann.

historical relativism A consequence of many varieties of HISTORICISM: the abandonment of an absolute standpoint in historical thinking implies the relativity of all norms and values. This relativism poses problems both for philosophy and the *Geisteswissenschaften* which were discussed, first in nineteenth-century Germany, by thinkers such as Dilthey and Troeltsch. Against historical relativism it is argued that the relativism of all philosophies and *Weltanschauungen* can only be recognized from an ideal of valid truth. Relativism seems to be a paradoxical position. As a philosophical doctrine, historical relativism was in a sense rehabilitated after the second world war because of developments in the philosophy of science (e.g. Kuhn's thesis of the incommensurability of paradigms) and the philosophy of mind (Wittgenstein's later work). The criticism of opponents (e.g. Popper) remained essentially the same: they maintain that relativism cannot be defended coherently and fear that it leads to scepticism and ultimately to irrationalism. SJST

Bibliography

Kuhn, T.S. 1970: Logic of discovery or psychology of research? In *Criticism and the growth of knowledge*. ed. I. Lakatos; and A. Musgrave, Cambridge: Cambridge University Press.

Popper, K.R. 1962: Facts, standards and truth: a further criticism of relativism. In *The open society and its enemies*. Vol. 2. London: Routledge & Kegan Paul.

historicism A term indicating the tendency to regard all cultural phenomena, including philosophies and worldviews, as the result of a historical development. The word historicism (German: *Historismus*) has been used with various meanings since the beginning of the nineteenth century (Schlegel, Von Ranke, Dilthey, Croce, Troeltsch, Collingwood); historicism as an intellectual movement is still older (Vico, Herder). With the growing awareness that the past is fundamentally different from the present, historicism considered itself as a *Weltanschauung* which recognized the historical character of all human existence. Each age must be viewed through its own values, and attempts by historians of the Enlightenment to measure the past by the norms of their own time were rejected. At the beginning of this century historicism came to mean "historical positivism", an investigation of historical facts for their own sake, without inquiring into their meaning and relation to the present.

K.R. Popper introduced the word in *The open society and its enemies* in a new, critical sense: here, historicism is a general term for all social philosophies (especially that of Marxism) which believe that they have discovered laws of history which enable them to prophesy the course of future events. Popper distinguishes this historicism from "historism": a theory which maintains the determination of common sense and scientific knowledge by history. Popper's distinction is not generally accepted. Historicism is also used to indicate HISTORICAL RELATIVISM. SJST

Bibliography

Popper, K.R. 1962: *The open society and its enemies*. London: Routledge. 2 vols.

Troeltsch, Ernst 1923: *Christian thought: its history and application*. London.

historicity Refers to the historical contingency of human action. The term is frequently employed by opponents of those traditional forms of psychology that assume the trans-historical stability of behavior patterns. As maintained by the critics, virtually all patterns of behavior are embedded within a particular confluence of historically contingent circumstances and thus subject to alteration or decay over time. It is said that virtually all patterns of human action are subject to historicity. The term has its roots in the longstanding historicist debate within the social sciences more generally. (See also HISTORICISM.) KJG

historiography Refers most specifically to the writing of history or the rhetoric of historical scholarship. More generally historiography is the study of the theories or models used to narrate, interpret or explain the past. It examines how knowledge about the past is organized and communicated through coherent and intelligible statements. In this broader sense historiography resembles the philosophy of history and encompasses the study of analytic methods, modes of explanation and narration, as well as the possibilities for objectivity and causal judgments in history (see HISTORICAL RELATIVISM). The problem of generating intelligible accounts of human actions is central to historiographical thinking, making historiography an appropriate, though largely neglected subject for psychologists studying human change (see HISTORICAL PSYCHOLOGY). JGM

Bibliography

Stern, F., ed. 1972: *The varieties of history*. New York: Vintage.

historiography of psychology The history of psychology cannot be confined to a chronicle of events in academic psychology. It must include a study of people who possess, prospect for, profess to possess, or are considered to possess accurate, inaccurate or delusive knowledge in psychology as well as those who make use of, seek to make use of, or who profess or are considered to use such knowledge. The history of psychology must also include an account of the animals, plants, things and artifacts which have been used in prospecting for knowledge in psychology or upon whom/which such knowledge has been used, or has been professed to have been used.

History of psychology should investigate the relations that obtain among those humans, animals, plants, things artifacts, i.e. the systems they constitute and the economic, sociological, political and cultural environments of these systems. As history it focusses on past states and changes of these systems and their environments, and it looks for regularity, order and law in these changes.

This delineation of the field of the history of psychology encompasses various general aspects: knowledge (theory) as well as practice; action for the generation of knowledge (experience) as well as action in applying knowledge adequately, inadequately or erroneously: accurate, inaccurate and delusive knowledge; expert as well as lay knowledge. This allows us to incorporate a naive or folk psychology (in the sense of popular ideas about psychological matters) and an ethnopsychology (in the sense of culture specific ideas about psychological matters) and therefore to investigate relations and interactions between academic psychology and nonacademic psychologies.

This broader schema takes in the eight main perspectives that have been used in the history of psychology so far.

(1) The *Big (Hu)man* approach highlights eminent individuals and their knowledge and action to the neglect of their embeddedness in systems and environments.

(b) The *Nations or Volksgeist* approach focusses on the psychology/ies dominant in one nation (or State) and tends to adopt national mentalities as explanatory principles.

(c) The *Zeitgeist* approach attempts to place ideas and practices into broadly conceived epochal cultural environments, discounting other determinants.

(d) The *History of Ideas* approach traces ideas, terms, concepts and theories in psychology and shows little regard for the conditions of their origin, usage and mutation.

(e) The *History of Problems* approach depicts psychology's occupation with selected problems and restricts itself as a rule to academically treated problems and corresponding research realms and interests.

(f) The *History of the Discipline* approach narrows itself to psychology as an academic discipline and a few (sometimes anachronistically conceived) antecedents.

(g) The *History of the Science* approach restricts itself further to that part of psychology it considers scientific; problems of demarcation and a restricted perception for wider issues ensue.

(h) The *Social History* approach emphasizes the social and economic frameworks in which psychology/ies develop and also the humans affected by the practice of psychology. The extent to which psychologies are shaped by their fields of inquiry is sometimes only dimly perceived.

No delineation of the field of history of psychology can be more precise than its central component; psychology. It is not helpful to answer the question "what is psychology?" in a nominalist or a pragmatist way since this would make psychology and history of psychology dependent on labels such as "psychology" or "psychologist" and their specific history (which nevertheless may be of some interest for the history of psychology). Obviously a realist answer is needed, an answer to the question "what is psychology about?" which would allow one to identify a transtemporal domain as the realm of the history of psychology. This question, to be sure, has to be answered by psychology, not by history of psychology. As long as there is no general agreement on the realm of reference of psychological terminology and theory no clear guideline offers itself, at least for modern times.

The most pervasive motif in the history of modern psychology is the influence of "adjacent sciences". The impression that there are a growing number of regularities and laws discovered or constructed for biosystems by the sciences of biology, physiology, etc and for sociosystems by the sciences of sociology, statistics, economics, etc has led to an increasing effort being put into the discovery or construction of comparable *amounts* of regularities and laws for a fuzzily defined intermediate realm (i.e. psychology). Regularities and laws from these macro- and microsystems (and also from chemistry and the physical sciences) are taken as paramorphs for the modelling of psychological regularities and laws.

At the same time a continuing tendency towards idiography and culturally specific studies can be recorded (Heelas and Lock, 1981). HUKG

Bibliography

Watson, Robert I. 1978: *The history of psychology and the behavioral sciences. a bibliographical guide.* New York: Springer

Heelas, P and Lock, A. eds. 1981: *Indigenous psychologies.* London and New York: Academic Press.

history of psychology The birth of psychology is frequently dated as 1879 when Wundt founded his psychological laboratory. Anything before that date is philosophy, and therefore not empirical, or what Thouless called "pre-scientific psychology", which reports empirical findings, but in anecdotes about individual cases or perhaps in other methodologically inadequate ways. Thouless says psychology is a science because of "its concern" with "the systematization of facts gathered by the methods of observation and experiment". "Control" is also an important element in these methods. Wundt's laboratory represents the institutional recognition of psychology. More arbitrarily it represents a starting point for the surge of effort to apply quantification, statistics and experimental method to phenomena of human behavior and experience. There have been disputes about the methods and even about the phenomena. A conventional text book may attribute to Wundt the establishment of scientific psychology, and then sneer at him for adherence to the fuzzy and outmoded procedure of introspection.

More serious writers ask why this institutional recognition came when it did. Miller (1964) suggests that Wundt looked "at the psychological problems posed by the British philosophers with the eyes of a man trained in . . . German physiology". This establishes plausible parenthood. During the nineteenth century Weber, Fechner, Müller, Helmholtz and others had enormously increased the knowledge of sensory physiology and their work (e.g. Weber's on just noticeable differences) resembles psychology experiments, where interest in responses to observably and measurably different stimuli is common.

British philosophers had discussed emotion, motivation, what and how people come to know, etc. There were also thought experiments like Locke's concern with whether a man born blind and later gaining his sight could immediately distinguish shapes without using touch (*Essay concerning human understanding* II.9). But many investigations on topics now taught as psychology were carried out by neither philosophers nor physiologists. Darwin is an academically accepted example, both for his baby book (1877) and for *The expression of the emotions . . .* But Bulwer in the seventeenth century and Di Jorio were earlier investigators of non-verbal communication, while Mrs Thrale in the eighteenth century kept an account of the development of her thirteen children. There was plenty of interest in facts about people, in knowledge "capable of being verified through sensory observation by anyone who is prepared to make the effort to do so" (Nagel). The question arises whether such knowledge is psychology.

Travel books, for instance, which dealt with "manners and customs" were common. Generally they were anecdotal. Sometimes, however, the information was collected more systematically. Sixteenth century navigators opened new lands and anthropological fieldwork was carried out on some of these trips. Hariot, for example, went to Virginia in 1585 and wrote an account of the natives. Earlier still Marco Polo had "endeavored, wherever he went, to obtain correct information" on customs and manners. This was not only to feed an appetite for the exotic. In the nineteenth century Mayhew investigated the way of life and the attitudes and beliefs of the London poor. This interest in contemporary social history was hardly new. In Britain alone it goes back to such as Giraldus Cambrensis and William FitzStephen in the twelfth century.

Even when carefully empirical, this work seems addressed to the discovery of particular facts rather than lawlike generalizations. But Mayhew does present the attitudes of, say, costermongers. His presentation, like that of clinical psychologists, often pivots on extended individual accounts, but the purpose is to report beliefs which are common to a class. Even here, however, there is no serious attempt to explain these facts by reference to underlying mechanisms, let alone to make or test predictions. It is the formulation of general statements which will lead to precise predictions that characterizes a science. So these data collections were not part of a scientific project despite their empiricism. Yet this model of science is more demanding than Thouless's "systematization of facts".

It would be crass to suppose that students of human behavior before the 1870s did not have a grasp of method and theory. Hartley, in 1749, stated that the way to do psychology was "to establish the general laws . . . from well attested phenomena, and then to explain and predict the other phenomena by these laws. This is the method recommended and followed by . . . Newton". This is certainly the scientific model, complete with an appeal to physics.

Hartley was a physician, not a philosopher. While his *Observations on man* does not concern itself with experiments, it is not without possibly empirical observations. For example, he describes how "ideas are associated with words, beginning from childhood" and asserts "the name of the visible object, the nurse, for instance, is pronounced and repeated by the attendants to the child, more frequently when his eye is fixed upon the nurse, than when upon other objects . . .". This passage may be criticized as anecdotal, influenced by observer's preconceptions or doubtfully empirical, but it is not obviously worse than some 1960s accounts of children's intentions in using utterances such as "Mommy dress".

Over a century earlier Bacon (1561 – 1626) recommended observation of behavior. Much of *The advancement of learning* is devoted to a "human philosophy". The discussion is abstract, but in his essays Bacon returns to psychology. There is no detailed evidence or suggestion how the theories might be tested. But there are (loose) theories. In essay LVII "Of Anger" Bacon gives three chief causes of anger: (1) "to be too sensible of hurt", (2) "the construction of the injury . . . to be . . . full of contempt", (3) "opinion of the touch of a man's reputation". He also suggests how to avoid "mischief" from one's own anger and how to "raise" and "appease" anger in others.

Such practical matters concerned Chesterfield (1694–1773) and Machiavelli (1467–1527). Their books testify to an interest in predicting and manipulating others' behavior on the basis of generalizations about human conduct. When Chesterfield says "The audience will form their opinion of you upon your first appearance ... and so far it will be final, that it will never totally change", this appears to state the "primacy effect" studied more recently by (e.g.) Luchins. This might be a commonplace, but it seems to be falsifiable. Men such as Chesterfield or Queen Elizabeth I's Burghley, who wrote advice for their sons, presumably believed their theories true. Burghley stressed "experience" in learning about others, so he believed there was something to be learnt, and learnt empirically. Such knowledge could be formulated for others to predict behavior without having experience of their own. Such advice was not "literary" or for amusement like Overbury's *Characters* or even Montaigne's *Essays*, but even these are concerned with psychological insight.

So by the early seventeenth century there was, even in backward England, an empirical attitude coupled with a belief that there could be a "systematization of facts" about human behavior. Nor need we stop there. Even if it were improper to infer from Chaucer (or Beowulf) that generalizations about human nature are always welcome, there is no doubt that Machiavelli took himself to be systematizing facts, nor that medieval thinkers had a grasp of scientific technique. Ockham (1284–1349) advised assessing the medical use of herbs by experiment, and propounded ideas about induction which are similar to Mill's canons. Yet, if Ockham appears in a history of psychology it is likely to be because his theory of knowledge is taken as a (pre-scientific) theory about the mind. Acceptance of psychology's descent from philosophy might lead the naive to think that no one before 1879 was observing people's behavior except in the most anecdotal way. All else was theory, with no empirical support. Such advisers as Burghley or Machiavelli were not just theorizing but may have been using isolated incidents from their own experience; or did they consider they had evidence outside their own experience?

One source, which Machiavelli used, was history. Classical and early modern historians claimed they were providing useful data about human nature. Thucydides (fifth century BC) and Polybius (second century BC) are examples, the latter saying it is better to learn by others' mistakes than one's own. Machiavelli used Livy's history, but Polybius and Thucydides say they used first-hand research, through interviews and "field trips". It was also common for classical historians to generalize. Polybius describes how paranoia spreads and men come to regard others' kindness "as a cover for trickery". Thucydides describes cities affected by civil wars: "Words had to change their usual meanings. What had been thoughtless violence was now courage . . . etc." This is a systematization of facts about what people say (noncommittal about what they think) under particular stresses. It is also based on evidence even if not questionnaires.

This could count as psychology. But Aristotle is more likely to be cited in histories of psychology. He had a medical background and was interested in research, but the *de Anima* is conceptual and concerned with definition. Furthermore some of his empirical statements, such as that small people have bad memories, or that after-images are the same color as eliciting stimuli seem doubtful.

Medicine, however, is a major aspect of Greek rationalism. In 500 BC Alcmaeon discovered the nerves by dissection and by Galen's time (AD200) most of the naked eye anatomy of the nervous system was complete. Accompanying this growth of knowledge was replacement of traditional explanations of (e.g.) mental illness or epilepsy, by explanation in terms of physical dysfunction. The idea of spirit possession was not unknown to Greeks, but Hippocrates (fifth century) sneers at faith healers and charlatans who see epilepsy as "sacred" and not natural. The desire to explain naturalistically was part of the rationalist enterprise, whether scientific or not. In Herodotus for instance alcoholism and congenital epilepsy are cited as explanations of madness. Debate about nature and nurture (or culture) appears in his pages and was widespread in his lifetime. Even "pre-scientific" psychology is engaged in an investigation, if not an empirical investigation, and is not an "indigenous" psychology or "inherited conglomerate" (see Heelas and Lock). Greek optics were certainly scientific. Greek personality typology was espoused by (e.g.) Wundt and Eysenck, who regarded the distinctions among the types and the attempt at physiological explanation as well-judged even if the physiology itself (the four humors) was shaky.

McDougall claimed that "biology" and "comparative psychology" are "preconditions of a general scientific psychology" and added that Darwin was necessary to "convince men of the continuity of human with animal evolution as regards all bodily characters". But the Greeks practiced comparative anatomy, and Aristotle's usual conception of the psyche assumes continuity from vegetable through animal to thinking forms of life. Physiology had this sense of continuity in modern times. Harvey (1578 – 1657), who discovered blood circulation and was also the first accredited user of the word "psychologie" in English, firmly believed in comparative anatomy. Willis's suggestion (1664) that the cerebellum governed involuntary movement was based on animal experiments.

Willis brings us back to the British empiricists, since he was Locke's teacher at Oxford. G.S. Rousseau suggested that the physiological discoveries of Willis and the associationism of Locke gave rise to a "science of man" immediately. This implies that Locke did not have to wait two hundred years to become a father. Certainly there was not a hundred years of desolation between Locke and the beginnings of German psychophysiology. Apart from the empiricists, who were important for their appeal to experience to support arguments as well as for their interest in mind, there were Hartley, Condillac, Bonnet and, by the end of the century Bichat and Cabanis. In physiology there were Hales's and Galvani's interests in the twitches of frogs' legs. Cabanis formulated the theory of the hierarchical organization of spinal and brain activities, a theory not yet exhausted. Bichat founded histology and suggested that mental diseases should have a physiological explanation. By the early nineteenth century Pinel was classifying mental disorders, while Pestalozzi, Herbart, Froebel and Itard were studying cognitive growth in children and the design of stimulating environments and easily assimilable curricula to help such growth. At the same time Young and Purkinje were investigating color vision.

This seems a long and venerable history. One could therefore ask whether psychology in the last hundred years is different in quality rather than in quantity from what went before. Certainly a great development has taken place in statistics as in physiology. Certainly, too, the laboratory became the home of the academic psychologist and scientific self-consciousness grew. The six men around whom Miller wrote his history are Pavlov, Wundt, James, Binet, Galton and Freud. Most would add Piaget and many would add Thorndike, Ebbinghaus, Watson, Wertheimer and Skinner. Among these it is the students of animal behavior, and specifically of conditioning who were working in a way peculiar to academic psychology, and Pavlov, a physiologist, despised psychology. The heirs of Freud and Galton may hardly count as psychologists, the former being therapists who might deny the usefulness of the experiment, the latter having perhaps grown up as statisticians. Furthermore many who have had most influence on modern psychology are not counted as psychologists. Chomsky, Lorenz and Goffman, not to mention Darwin, are in this class, while Fisher's statistical techniques have probably been as important for many practicing psychologists as any work of their professional predecessors.

Psychologists sometimes seem to be left a model of scientific method which presumably does not fit the modus operandi of most psychologists (who are less hypothetico-deductive than the model requires) and is philosophically dubious. They also have a place (the laboratory) which is respectable but has serious disadvantages since the artificial environment casts doubts on the generality of findings about the behavior of organisms which find it artificial (Orne). Some critics say that such findings are obviously not generalizable, but that must be decided empirically, not a priori. Modern psychologists have anyway imported methods (ARTIFICIAL INTELLIGENCE, ETHOLOGY, INTERVIEWS, QUESTIONNAIRES and studies of developmental, social or clinical phenomena "in the field") which do not employ controlled laboratory experiments. This does not mean that ideals of evidence, observer reliability, precise quantification or even controls have been abandoned. But of course such ideals, though sometimes less precisely, have informed much of the work mentioned in this article. RL

Bibliography

Bacon, F. 1605 (1974): *The advancement of learning*. Oxford: Clarendon Press.

Bacon, F. 1625, N.D.: *Essays*. London: Dent.

*Esper, E.A. 1964: *A history of psychology*. Philadelphia: Saunders.

Farrington, B. 1949: *Greek science* (2 vols). Harmondsworth: Penguin.

Heelas, P. and Lock, A. 1981: *Indigenous psychologies*. London: Academic Press.

Mayhew, H. 1851 (1969): *Mayhew's London*. P. Quennell, ed. London: Hamlyn.

McDougall, W. 1919: *Social psychology* (14th edition). London: Methuen.

*Miller, G.A. 1964: *Psychology, the science of mental life*. London: Hutchinson.

*Murphy, G. 1949: *Historical introduction to modern psychology*. London: Routledge & Kegan Paul (5th edition).

Orne, M.T. 1962: On the social psychology of the psychological experiment. *American psychologist* 17. 776 – 83.

Polybius, 1889: *The histories* (trans. E.S. Shuckburgh). London: Macmillan.

Rousseau, G.S. 1975: Nerves, spirits, and fibres. In *Studies in the eighteenth century III*. R.F. Brissenden and J.C. Eade.

Thouless, R.H. 1937: *General and social psychology* (2nd edn). London: University Tutorial Press.

Thucydides 1954: *The peloponnesian war* (trans. R. Warner). London: Penguin.

holism To claim that the mind is holistic implies that each element is related to, or integrated with, every other element. Various theses asserting global inter-relatedness have been explored in recent philosophy of mind: (1) The effects of a given belief or desire on S's behavior depend upon S's total set of background beliefs and desires. (2) To ascribe a given belief to a person one must make assumptions about his or her other beliefs, and other mental states. (3) The ascription of content to any of S's beliefs is regulated by a "Principle of Charity" to the effect that S is rational on the whole. Rationality is variously construed as e.g. not believing contradictions, following the rules of logic, or having beliefs that are by and large justified by the evidence.

While it is an empirical truth that human beings generally aim to maintain overall consistency in their beliefs, strong versions of holism insist that this must be so, as a condition of the possibility of their beliefs having content, and hence, that intentional explanations of action are subject to an *a priori* constraint not found in other kinds of causal explanations. ARW

Bibliography

Davidson, D. 1970: Mental events. In *Experience and theory*, ed. L. Foster and J.W. Swanson. Amherst, Mass.: University of Massachusetts Press.

Dennett, D. 1971: Intentional systems. *Journal of philosophy* 68, 87–106.

Quine, W.V.O. 1960: *Word and object*, Cambridge, Mass.: MIT Press.

Peacocke, C. 1979: *Holistic explanation*. Oxford: Clarendon Press.

holophrases Single-word utterances having one primary stress and one terminal intonation contour. In early child language such one-word utterances contain the meaning of what adults would normally express in a longer string of words, not necessarily a sentence as is widely claimed. Thus, the word apple uttered by a fourteen-month-old baby may mean "I want an apple" or "give me your apple".

Related to the emergence of holophrases in FIRST LANGUAGE ACQUISITION is the emergence of prefabricated pattern in SECOND LANGUAGE ACQUISITION and pidginization, where utterances such as "that is all" and "I don't know" are memorized as unanalysed wholes. PM

Bibliography

Hakuta, K. 1974: Prefabricated patterns and the emergence of structure in second-language acquisition. *Language learning* 24, 287–97.

Rodgon, M.M. 1976: *Single word usage: cognitive development and the beginnings of combinatorial speech*, Cambridge and New York: Cambridge University Press.

homeostasis Literally "staying the same". Living organisms and some self-regulating machines (such as thermostatically controlled heating systems, or automatic pilots) have the ability to resist change, and to keep certain properties or variables constant, even when factors are present which would tend to change them. This is most commonly done by means of negative FEEDBACK, an arrangement whereby any small fluctuations of the property in question are detected and messages fed back to an earlier point in the causal chain, where compensatory changes are made to cancel out the original fluctuations; hence the name negative feedback.

Homeostatic mechanisms are responsible for many important aspects of automatic self-regulation in animals, from the stabilization of blood chemistry, to the fine control of motor behavior. DDC

homology and analogy In evolutionary biology, both terms refer to similarities between organisms, but they are of contrasting types. Homology refers to similarities between two or more species which are due to shared characteristics inherited from a common evolutionary ancestor; whereas analogy refers to similarities which are due to factors other than common ancestry, such as convergent evolution, where species not closely related develop similar characteristics through subjection to similar natural selection pressures (see Immelmann 1980). Similarities based on homology tend to be close, detailed and structural: similarities based on analogy, however, tend to be general, superficial and functional. Comparative evolutionary arguments have repeatedly revolved around the distinction between homology and analogy, and they have been particularly acute in ethology, as behavioral comparisons across species have often been made, but homology is difficult to demonstrate. LORENZ (1973) has defended the use of an ethological approach that is frankly based on analogy, but while this is undoubtedly preferable to a confusion of the two, there remains a widespread caution about placing undue reliance on either homologies or analogies, especially in relation to behavior (see Barnett 1981). RDA

Bibliography

Barnett. S.A. 1981 *Modern ethology: the science of animal behavior*. New York, Oxford: Oxford University Press.

Immelmann, K. 1980 *Introduction to ethology*. New York, London: Plenum Press.

Lorenz, K. 1973 Analogy as a source of knowledge. *Science* 185, 229–34.

homosexuality and lesbianism Sexual interest directed at members of one's own sex. Estimates of prevalence in western countries vary considerably; high estimates, such as Kinsey's oft-cited one in three, include any homosexual experience whatever, whereas low estimates limit themselves to life-long exclusive homosexuality. Homosexual behavior is no longer illegal in Britain and North America, nor is it regarded as a form of mental illness. Homosexual behavior is permitted in many non-Western societies, but subject to social control. Recent research (e.g. Bell and Weinberg 1978) argues that homosexuals are not an identifiable class apart, but are as varied as heterosexuals, having only their sexual orientation in common. A few vulgar misconceptions about homosexuals still exist: few male homosexuals are effeminate; few females are correspondingly masculine; few homosexuals cross-dress; few molest children.

Theories of the origin of homosexuality fall into two broad classes: the biological and the social. Biological theories look for physical or physiological differences between homosexuals and heterosexuals, and tend to assume an inherited element. Social theories are more varied, ranging from the psychoanalytic theory of the unresolved Oedipus complex, to McGuire et al.'s theory of social learning mediated by self-reinforced fantasy (1965). Some theories argue that homosexuality is fear of the opposite sex more than a preference for one's own. Homosexual behavior sometimes results from force of circumstance, such as unavailability of the opposite sex rather than from inner dispositions. In some cultures homosexual behavior is required, at certain ages or on certain occasions, so explanations based on individual differences would not apply. JHC

Bibliography

Bell, A.P. and Weinberg, M.P. 1978: *Homosexualities: a study of diversity among men and women.* London: Mitchell Beazley.

McGuire, R.J., Carlisle, J.M. and Young, B.G. 1965: Sexual deviations and conditioned behaviour: a hypothesis. *Behaviour research and therapy* 2, 185–90.

hormic psychology Denotes the school of purposive psychology in general, and more specifically William McDougall's theory of instincts on which he based the subdisciplines of differential, clinical and social psychology. The name itself was suggested by T.P. Nunn in derivation from the Greek noun όρμη (impulse, drive). According to McDougall, who argued his theory against the mechanistic approaches of the time (Watson and McDougall 1929), all behavior is rooted in the instinctive endowments of organisms, (McDougall 1934). In addition, human behavior is guided by intentionality (McDougall 1912, pp.233–4). Nonetheless, all patterns of behavior, whether animal or human, belong to an unbroken "continuity" (McDougall 1928, pp.407–8).

Although intended to be purely scientific, McDougall's theory goes beyond the realm of science and merges with that of metaphysics. It conflates methodological purposivism as a device for the identification of the units of behavior and metaphysical purposivism which stresses the reality of spirit. AM

Bibliography

McDougall, William 1912: *Psychology: the study of behavior.* London: Williams & Norgat.

——— 1928: *An introduction to social psychology.* 21st edn. London: Methuen.

——— 1934: *The frontiers of psychology.* London: Nisbet.

Watson, J.B. and McDougall, W. 1929: *The battle of behaviorism: an exposition and an exposure.* New York: Horton.

hormones Chemical substances secreted by the endocrine glands and transported in the blood stream to sites of action in various parts of the body. Hormones have profound influences on physiology and behavior and play an important role in the development of certain aspects of behavior.

Hormones are present in the blood in very small quantities and the life of individual molecules is short. To have a sustained effect, therefore, hormones have to be secreted continuously in precisely controlled quantities. In some glands secretion is actuated by the nervous system, in others it is stimulated by other hormones. Control is achieved by FEEDBACK. A high level of circulatory hormone tends to inhibit further secretion, and this inhibition is reduced when the level falls. Hormones are very specific in their actions, affecting only certain parts of the body, called target organs. These may include the adrenal glands and the sex glands, which themselves secrete hormones.

The main endocrine glands of man, showing their products and function

Gland	*Hormone*	*Function or Target*
anterior pituitary	growth hormone	growth
	trophic hormones:	
	ACTH	adrenal cortex
	TSH	thyroid
	FSH	gonads
	LH	gonads
	prolactin	mammary glands
posterior pituitary	vasopressin	kidney, blood pressure
	oxytocin	mammary glands, uterus
thyroid	thyroxine	development, metabolic rate
parathyroid	parathormone	calcium, phosphorus metabolism
adrenal cortex	sex hormones	(see below)
	glucocorticoids	metabolism of carbohydrates, protein, and fat
	mineralocorticoids	electrolyte, water balance
adrenal medulla	norepinephrine	circulatory systems,
	epinephrine	glucose release
pancreas:		
cells	glucagon	glucose release
cells	insulin	glucose transfer, utilization
ovaries:		
Follicles	estrogen	development and maintenance of sexual anatomy, physiology, and behavior
Corpus luteum	progesterone	
testes	testosterone	

ACTH adrenocorticotrophic hormone
TSH thyroid stimulating hormone
FSH follicle stimulating hormone
LH luteinizing hormone

The brain has a considerable influence upon hormonal activity, and this is exercized primarily through the pituitary gland, which is situated at the base of the brain just below the HYPOTHALAMUS to which it is neurally connected (see BRAIN AND CENTRAL NERVOUS SYSTEM: ILLUSTRATIONS, figs. 15 and 20). The pituitary gland has an anterior and a posterior part which have different embryonic origins. The anterior pituitary secretes a hormone responsible for growth and a number of trophic hormones, as indicated in the table. The trophic hormones have other endocrine glands as their target organs. The role of the brain in controlling the activity of the anterior pituitary is essentially regulatory. For example, some trophic hormones are first secreted at puberty and influence the growth and development of the sex glands. Thereafter the level of circulating sex hormones is regulated by feedback via the anterior pituitary.

The brain has a more direct influence upon the posterior pituitary and the adrenal medulla. The posterior pituitary produces two hormones in mammals, vasopressin and oxytocin, which can be released very quickly in response to circumstances. For example when a young animal attempts to suckle, messages from the mammary glands are received by the brain which instructs the posterior pituitary gland to release oxytocin. This hormone is responsible for milk let-down, and the young animal must stimulate this chain of events in order to obtain milk from its mother.

The hormone vasopressin has a similar quick acting role in inducing changes in blood pressure. The adrenal medulla secretes adrenalin hormones which play a role similar to that of the AUTONOMIC NERVOUS SYSTEM and are released during fear and in other situations involving emotion.

Hormones affect behavior in a variety of ways. The most important is that they alter the animal's predisposition to indulge in certain types of behavior such as sexual behavior and migration. For example, females of many species have periods of heat during which they are capable of ovulation and are receptive to advances from males, or may actively seek out males. During this period there is a peak in the blood concentrations of estrogen and progesterone, two hormones produced by the ovary under the influence of the pituitary gland. This cycle of hormonal activity, called the estrus cycle, corresponds with the development of eggs in the ovary. The females become receptive when the eggs are ready for fertilization.

In some primates, including humans, all apes and some monkeys, the estrus cycle is replaced by a different type of cycle, called the menstrual cycle. This is characterized by periodic bleeding, called menstruation, from the uterus and vagina of sexually mature females. Menstruation occurs as a result of complex interactions among the circulating hormones. The ovarian follicles (incipient eggs) develop under the influence of follicle stimulating hormone (FSH) released by the anterior pituitary gland. Under the influence of FSH the uterus develops a rich blood supply in readiness for the implantation of the fertilized egg. The ovary also produces estrogen (or estradiol) which has a feedback effect on the pituitary gland, causing it to release more FSH. After about fourteen days the follicle ruptures under the influence of a surge of luteinizing hormone (LH) produced by the anterior pituitary gland. The rupture of the follicle releases the egg and the remaining follicular cells develop into the corpus luteum, which secretes the hormone progesterone. This has a negative feedback effect on the pituitary gland and leads to a reduction in FSH secretion. Fertilization may occur at this stage of the menstrual cycle, in which case the egg becomes implanted in the wall of the uterus and the hormonal changes characteristic of pregnancy are initiated. If fertilization does not occur, the rich blood supply of the uterine wall disintegrates and is shed into the vagina, resulting in the characteristic menstrual flow.

The hormonal balance of female Barbary doves is strongly influenced by participation in courtship and this form of communication is important in establishing cooperation between the mated pair. In the early stages of courtship the male shows aggression towards the female and this has the effect of inhibiting her reproductive cycle until the male's hormonal condition has time to change. Another aspect of behavior in which social relationships are important is dominance. Males with high levels of testosterone tend to be socially dominant and their aggressiveness towards inferiors may result in hormonal changes due to stress. In this way the reproductive potential of subordinate animals may be suppressed as a result of the action of hormones from the adrenal cortex, secretion of which is characteristic of stress. DJM

Bibliography

Leshner, A. I. 1978: *An introduction to behavioral endocrinology*. New York: Oxford University Press.

Horney, Karen *See* neo-Freudian theory

human factors Is concerned with the interaction of human operators and new technology. The term and associated concepts originate in the USA; the overlapping European term is ERGONOMICS but the two are not synonymous. Human Factors is predominantly a psychology/engineering partnership aimed at increasing system efficiency, whereas ergonomics incorporates a stronger anatomical/physiological/medical component and pays considerable attention to health and well-being as well as to efficiency.

The stimulus for the progress of human factors lies in the needs of military and similar high-technology systems such as civil aviation and space research. The basic concepts have a strong engineering and mechanical bias (information theory, control theory and decision theory) with the overall aim of incorporating expertise about the human component into engineered systems. In recent years the field has extended to all forms of transport, power generation and distribution, chemical processing and inspection tasks. WTS

Bibliography

Sheridan, T.B. and Farrell, W.R. 1974: *Man-machine systems*. Cambridge, Mass.: MIT Press.

human relations school This school of thought held that the most important influences on employee performance and satisfaction were relationships among people, specifically intra-group relations, inter-group relations, and supervisory-subordinate relations. Implicit in this view was the premise that job satisfaction leads to high productivity. The school grew out of the well known Hawthorne studies done at the Western Electric Co. during the 1920s and 1930s (see, for example, Roethlisberger and Dickson 1956). Ironically, these studies were quite poorly designed and were probably widely misinterpreted (Franke and Kaul 1978). Nevertheless the human relations school has had enormous influence. One consequence was the study of leadership or supervisory style, which has not proved very fruitful at least with respect to the prediction of work group performance. However, it is widely accepted that leadership as such plays a crucial role in organizational effectiveness (Yukl 1981).

Another outcome was the study of WORK ATTITUDES. Job satisfaction has not been found to lead to greater productivity, but has come to be studied in its own right as a desirable outcome of work experience. Group dynamics have been widely studied by both psychologists and sociologists. Group norms have been verified as important influences on employee morale and motivation and can serve to enhance or subvert organizational goals. It is now conceded that while social factors are important (Likert 1961), they are only one of many aspects of the job that affect employee productivity and attitudes so that the views of the human relations school are not now accepted in their entirety. EAL

Bibliography

Franke, R.H. and Kaul, J.D.: The Hawthorne experiments: first statistical interpretation. *American sociological review*, 1978, 43, 623–43.

Likert, R. 1961: *New patterns of management*. New York: McGraw Hill.

Roethlisberger, F.J. and Dickson, W.J. 1956: *Management and the worker*. Cambridge, Mass.: Harvard University Press.

Yukl, G. 1981: *Leadership in organization*. Englewood Cliffs, N.J.: Prentice Hall.

humanistic psychology An approach to psychology which includes love, involvement and spontaneity, instead of systematically excluding them. The object of humanistic psychology is not the prediction and control of people's behavior, but the liberation of people from the bonds of neurotic control, whether these derive from the structure of society or from the psychological condition of individuals.

Humanistic psychology emerged from the confluence of ten different streams: (1) Group dynamics, particularly in the area of T-groups; (2) The doctrine of self-actualization (Maslow 1968); (3) The person-centered approach to counseling, therapy and education (Rogers 1961); (4) The theories of Wilhelm REICH and his emphasis on the body; (5) Existentialism – particularly as interpreted analytically by Laing (1967) and practically/experientially by Perls (Fagan and Shepherd 1972); (6) The results of the use of mind-expanding drugs – particularly LSD (Stafford and Golightly 1967); (7) ZEN BUDDHISM particularly in its idea of "letting go"; (8) TAOISM, particularly in its ideas of "centering" and the yin–yang polar unity; (9) TANTRA, particularly in its emphasis on the importance of the body as an energy system; and (10) Peak experiences as revelatory and enlightening (Rowan 1976a).

Humanistic psychology is not a tidy and coherent body of knowledge, but a way of dealing with human problems by reference to a set of paradigmatic experiences:

1. A deep and intense group experience resulting in a general realignment of attitudes to self and others.

2. Ecstatic or peak experiences, in which a sense of unity and pattern of both the human and natural world is achieved.

3. The existential experience of being completely independent and totally responsible for one's thoughts and actions.

The main practitioners of humanistic psychology have all been through experiences of these kinds. This has led to the idea of body of knowledge which can be acquired and/or appreciated only by following the same experiential path.

Humanistic psychology is directed strongly to practical ends. The central concepts are *personal growth* and *human potential*. They imply that people can change by "working" on themselves. Humanistic psychology has developed a large number of different methods for self-intervention which can be ranged under four headings:

Body methods: Reichian therapy, bioenergetics, rebirthing, Rolfing, Feldenkrais method, Alexander technique, sensory awareness, holistic health, etc.

Feeling methods: Encounter, psychodrama, Gestalt awareness, primal integration, Rogerian counseling, co-counseling, etc.

Thinking methods: Transactional analysis, personal construct approach, family therapy, neuro-linguistic programming, rational–emotive therapy, etc.

Spiritual methods: Transpersonal counseling, psychosynthesis, enlightenment intensive workshops, dynamic meditation, sand play, dream work, etc.

Most of these methods can be adapted to work in any field. Humanistic practitioners operate in personal growth, counseling, psychotherapy, holistic health, education, social work, organizational theory and consultancy, management training, community development and self-help groups, creativity training and social research (Rowan 1976b).

It has been understood recently that humanistic psychology entails a new paradigm of how research should be carried out with human beings, if it is to yield practical knowledge. The people being studied are recruited as co-researchers, who participate fully in the planning of the research, in its execution, and in making sense of the results. This process yields a more many-layered kind of knowledge than the old paradigm of research could offer, and it is knowledge which can be used immediately (see Reason and Rowan 1981).

Several concepts have been elaborated on the basis of this research:

The real self: Though dropped from some radical psychologies, this is a key concept for humanistic psychology. It is common to Rogers (1961), Maslow (1968), Laing (1967) and many others. It presumes that we can dive beneath the surface appearance of roles and masks to a permanent, underlying self (Shaw 1974). Some large-scale research studies which bear on this have been put together by Hampden-Turner (1971). Simpson (1971) shows that there is a political aspect to the idea of the "real self". From this point of view sex roles could be seen as concealing "real selves" and hence as oppressive, as the Women's Movement has argued. These connections have been suggested by Carney and McMahon (1977).

Subpersonalities: This is a concept put forward in various forms by Assagioli and others (Ferrucci 1982). It implies we have a number of subpersonalities, which I have suggested come from several sources: the collective unconscious (see JUNG); the cultural unconscious; the personal unconscious; long standing conflicts and problems; long term roles and social frames; and fantasy images of how we would like to be. The original suggestion, by Ornstein (1972) of two modes of consciousness, has been greatly elaborated in recent studies (see Fadiman and Frager 1976).

Abundance motivation: Most orthodox psychology is based on a homeostatic model, which is deficiency oriented. Action is thought of as initiated by a need or want. Human beings (and animals) however, seek for tension creating and maintaining situations, as well as for tension reduction. Achievement motivation (McClelland 1953); need for varied experience (Fiske and Maddi 1961) etc. can be comprehended under the concept of abundance motivation. Any kind of action may be done out of abundance motivation. Motivation cannot be inferred from the performance. It is known only to the actor.

Finally, humanistic psychologists believe that attention to one's own states and motives makes possible the avoidance of self-deception and facilitates the discovery of a "real self". JCR

Bibliography

Carney, C.G. and McMahon, S.L. 1977: *Exploring contemporary male/female roles: a facilitator's guide*. La Jolla: University Associates.

Fadiman, J. and Frager, R. 1976: *Personality and personal growth*. New York: Harper & Row.

Fagan, J. and Shepherd, I.L., eds. 1972: *Gestalt therapy now*. London: Penguin.

Ferrucci, P. 1982: *What we may be*. Wellingborough: Turnstone Press.

Fiske, D.W. and Maddi, S.R. 1961: *Functions of varied experience*. Dorsey Press.

Hampden-Turner, C. 1971: *Radical man: the process of psycho-social development*. London: Duckworth; Cambridge, Mass.: Schenkman.

Laing, R.D. 1967: *The politics of experience*. London: Penguin.

McClelland, D. et al. 1953: *The achievement motive*. New York: Appleton-Century-Croft.

Marrow, A.J. 1969: *The practical theorist*. New York: Basic Books.

Maslow, A.H. 1968: *Motivation and personality*. New York: Harper & Row.

Ornstein, R. 1972: *The psychology of consciousness*. London: Penguin.

Reason, P. and Rowan, J., eds. 1981: *Human inquiry: a sourcebook of new paradigm research*. New York and Chichester: John Wiley & Sons.

Rogers, C.R. 1961: *On becoming a person*. London: Constable; Boston: Houghton Mifflin.

Rowan, J. 1976a: *Ordinary ecstasy: humanistic psychology in action*. London: Routledge & Kegan Paul.

——— 1976b: You're never alone with yourself. *Psychology today* (British edition) January issue.

Shaw, J. 1974: *The self in social work*. London: Routledge & Kegan Paul.

Simpson, E.L. 1971: *Democracy's stepchildren. A study of need and belief*. San Francisco: Jossey-Bass.

Stafford, P.G. and Golightly, B.H. 1967: *LSD: the problem-solving psychedelic*. Award Books.

Humboldt, Wilhelm von (1767–1835). Humboldt is regarded as one of the founders of scientific linguistics. As minister of public instruction in Prussia he was instrumental in promoting Sanskrit and Indogermanic studies. He was a profuse writer and many of his ideas have been adopted by twentieth-century linguists.

The Sapir-Whorf hypothesis (see WHORF) develops Humboldt's suggestion that there is a world-view implicit in each language. Chomsky (1965) adopted the following ideas proposed by Humboldt:

(1) the distinction between deep and surface structure corresponds to Humboldt's distinction between inner and outer form;

(2) language is seen as a creative ability (energeia) not as a mere product (ergon);

(3) speakers of a language can make infinite use of finite linguistic resources.

Another important contribution to linguistic theory is Humboldt's distinction between isolating, agglutinative and flexional languages according to their morphological properties (see AFFIX). PM

Hume, David (1711–1776). Scotland's greatest philosopher, and a distinguished historian, Hume produced his first book at the early age of 28 (1739). The centerpiece is his account of the idea of causal necessity, which he treats neither as a product of reason nor as a construction with an adequate basis in experience, but, rather, as a projection onto the world of the natural human tendency to make causal inferences. He also gives a similar account of morality: value-judgments are based on nothing more solid than natural human sentiments. It is not surprising that he was often taken to be a sceptic. Certainly, his attitude to religion was sceptical (1779). However, there is another way of interpreting his analysis of the belief in causal necessity, on which he thought that all scientific knowledge of the external world is based. It can be argued that it is the unsuccessful attempt to found this belief on reason that leads to scepticism and that Hume's less ambitious foundation, human nature, does give it a limited kind of objectivity.

Hume's second philosophical book (1748) reaffirms the main doctrines of the first in a less complicated way. The main difference is that he makes a simpler use of the theory of the association of ideas. His method was to search for the laws governing their association. He needed a theory to explain the natural tendencies of the human mind, which, in their turn, would explain its more audacious constructions. Even if he did not achieve his philosophical goal by this method, he set an example for a century of work in what was later called "psychology", and in philosophy itself his accounts of causal necessity and personal identity are still influential. DP

Bibliography

Hume, D. 1754–1762: *History of England*.

——— 1739 (*1911*): *A treatise of human nature*, London: J.M. Dent.

——— 1748 (*1902*): (Everyman Library). *An enquiry concering human understanding*: Ed. L.A. Selby Bigge, Oxford: Oxford University Press.

——1779 (1935): *Dialogues concerning natural religion.* Published posthumously. London: Nelson (2nd edn. 1947).

Stroud, Barry 1977: *Hume*. London: Routledge & Kegan Paul.

humor Among various entries for "humor" in *The Shorter Oxford English Dictionary* there is reference to the excitement of amusement, the expression of amusement, and temporary and habitual conditions of the mind. In everyday language, therefore, "humor" can apply to a stimulus, a response or a disposition. On the disposition side virtually all respondents in surveys and interviews are reported as rating themselves as "above average" for sense of humor; and Frank Moore Colby, through implication, scarcely exaggerated the importance attached to humor when he said; "men will confess to treason, murder, arson, false teeth or a wig. How many of them will own up to a lack of humor?"

There is no doubt that in modern times a good sense of humor has come to be regarded as thoroughly healthy and desirable. Historically humor was more typically characterized as base and degenerate, fit solely for the ignorant and foolish. Classic Greek and Roman scholars evidently believed that laughter is rooted in deformity and shabbiness; it was said to be degrading to art, morals and religion. In the Bible humor and laughter are very rarely mentioned, and, less in keeping with the quick than the dead, the present-day Penguin *Dictionary of psychology* defines "Laughter" anachronistically as "an emotional response, expressive normally of joy, in the child and the *unsophisticated* adult" (emphasis added).

Until recently psychologists and other social scientists regarded humor and laughter as either taboo or trivial topics for systematic inquiry, while at the same time textbook authors occasionally pointed to their ubiquitous nature. It is only in the last ten years or so that psychologists have begun to contribute significantly to knowledge: there has been a genesis and development of several substantial strands of investigation, although laughter remains largely dormant as an area of research. By and large humor researchers tend to disregard laughter. This is partly because it is seen as an essentially social response and hence a poor index of humor appreciation. It can accompany any number of emotional states, most of them having nothing to do with humor or amusement. Even when contiguous with humor its quality and quantity may be governed principally by the constitution and behavior of the surrounding company. Perhaps more to the point, it is rarely engendered in its explosive or effusive form under contrived and sterile laboratory arrangements. It is likely that humor loses its potency and maybe some of its character under laboratory scrutiny, and laboratories remain the speciously-safe haunt of most empirically-minded psychologists; as a consequence, much of the research has been truncated and even asocial, and there has been rather a dearth of trenchant empirical work.

Theories abound in the psychological literature but, with few exceptions, they are in effect statements of function or statements of properties: they are descriptive and taxonomic accounts rather than explanations as to *why* humor occurs and *why* laughter is emitted, and remarkably few draw on general principles within psychology. Generally speaking the quest for a grand theory has been abandoned, the consensus being that no single theory could usefully embrace all facets of creation, initiation and reaction. Instead there has been a proliferation of mini-theories in recent years, dwelling separately on aspects of stimulus variables–content, structure and complexity; of individual differences–personality, motivation, physiology, cognitions and psychodynamic reactions; internal amusement and of expressive responsiveness – subjective ratings and nonverbal reactions; and companionship variables, as well as other social psychological matters.

Previously philosophers and littérateurs had promoted theories on a much grander scale, and the ancestry of many present-day views is readily detected in pre-twentieth century writings. For example, Plato and Aristotle drew attention to the malevolent and invective nature of some humor, and their thoughts were precursors to derision and superiority theories which remain in vogue today. Plato (in *Philebus*) saw the weak as a justifiable target for humor, and he regarded malice as essential to laughter. Aristotle (in *Poetics*) maintained that infirmity and ugliness are prime sources of the ludicrous. By the seventeenth century Thomas Hobbes's writings on humor (in *Leviathan* and *Human Nature*) incorporated most of the essential rudiments of contemporary superiority theory. Writers in the eighteenth and nineteenth centuries – notably Beattie and Schopenhauer – were the forerunners of contemporary incongruity theorists.

It was Herbert Spencer more than a century ago who first advanced the conception of laughter as a "safety valve" against surplus energy, and at the turn of the century Freud, synthesizing relief, conflict and incongruity theories, similarly saw laughter as an outlet for discharging psychic energy. Then and later Freud described the relief action as operating when the superego has effectively censored other uses of built-up energy. Freud discriminated between "the comic", "wit" and "humor" in a manner which only his most ardent followers have done since. The discharge of energy through laughter was said by Freud to be pleasurable because of gratification derived from economic expenditures of thought (in the case of the comic), inhibition (for wit) or feeling (for humor). In humor, potentially damaging events were said to be relegated to lesser significance by the ego assuming an infantile state after energy has been displaced onto the superego.

Before the 1970s most empirical research was centered on Freudian notions but this emphasis has been superseded by widespread attention to cognitive dimensions, and particularly by work in an information-processing vein. A disparity between expectations and perceptions is generally taken to be a necessary but not a sufficient condition for humor. It is this disparity which is termed "incongruity". For humor an incongruity has to be made meaningful or appropriate; or some would say that a cognitive rule has to be found which renders the incongruity explicable within the context of the humor. A partial or complete "resolution" of the incongruity is considered to be an essential component of the humor process.

The salience of the social context is apparent in analyses

of infants' humor and laughter where the necessity for a playful mood is emphasized. Developmental psychologists in general see humor as a form of play involving symbols, images and ideas. It is first manifested at about eighteen months of age as the child acquires the ability to manipulate symbols. However, operating according to a different definition of humor, some researchers argue that humor is experienced by children as young as four months: theirs is a broader definition and one which does not embody any reference to symbolism (or capacities for playing games of pretend or make-believe); it merely requires that incongruities can be resolved by the infant, and that particular incongrous events are perceived as safe and playful. It is agreed that incongruity is never sufficient: the perception of something unexpected might lead to laughter but, if there is no playful mood, it may lead instead to fear, curiosity, problem-solving or concept learning.

Humor, through laughter and smiling, can serve a wide variety of social functions. For example, there is already research indicating that it can assist the flow of an interaction, reveal attitudes with relative impunity, communicate allegiances, induce changes in group esteem, form an integral part of a coping strategy, assist in the maintenance of a status hierarchy, and help to test the standing of relationships. It is multi-dimensional and, depending primarily upon content and social context, single instances may cause multiple and diverse effects amongst initiators, recipients and bystanders. The effects on the recipients are mediated in part by the perceived values and motives of the initiator, who in turn is influenced by responses to the humor.

The neglect of expressive responses, particularly laughter and smiling, and the neglect of the social climate will become yet less tenable as humor researchers begin to extend their breadth of inquiries. For no obvious reason, other than convenience, they have so far placed heavy emphasis on *responsiveness* to humor: we still await rigorous and heuristic work on aspects of the creation and instigation of humor. Typically in studies to date the experimenters have selected jokes, cartoons or comedy films and presented them to subjects from whom they then elicit funniness ratings. In this way research has endeavored to focus on the structure, content and psychological functions of humor, and it has ignored behavioral consequences. Also studies of groups have tended to overlook the fact that groups have their own histories and cultures: they are not *ad hoc* assemblies of individuals, and the richness of humor will not become manifest so long as they are regarded as such for laboratory purposes. Fundamental questions about how, why, when and where humor is initiated are not likely to be addressed squarely until humor is recorded as it naturally occurs; and that is usually in social situations, just before laughter. AJC

Bibliography

Chapman, A.J. and Foot, H.C. 1977: *It's a funny thing, humor.* Oxford and New York: Pergamon Press.

McGhee, P.E. and Chapman, A.J. 1980: *Children's humour.* Chichester and New York: Wiley.

McGhee, P.E. and Goldstein, J.H. (in press). *Handbook of humor research.* New York: Springer-Verlag.

hunger and the nervous system Hunger is a psychological state that serves a regulatory function, matching energy intake with expenditure. Homeostatic mechanisms within the nervous system regulating food intake are also influenced by signals from glucostatic, lipostatic and thermostatic receptors along with peripheral signals from the stomach and mouth. The interaction of these factors in the nervous system determines the initiation and termination of feeding.

Damage to the base of the brain, in or near the HYPOTHALAMUS can lead to obesity in man. It was proposed from experiments with animals in the 1950s and 1960s that the hypothalamus regulates feeding by the interaction of its ventromedial nucleus or "satiety center" with its lateral nucleus or "hunger center" (BRAIN AND CENTRAL NERVOUS SYSTEM: ILLUSTRATIONS, figs. 15 and 20). Activity of the "hunger center" initiates eating while activity in the "satiety center" inhibits eating. Recent advances, however, have called into question the simplicity of the dual-center hypothesis. Attention has been attracted towards the learning and cognitive factors influencing hunger and feeding. Responses of single cells in the primate hypothalamus and AMYGDALA have emphasized the importance of learning in food selection. RCS/BER

hunger and thirst: animal A psychological state that arises primarily as a result of a physiological requirement for nutrients, but may also be due to psychological factors.

Primary hunger is the result of food deprivation and a consequent physiological deficit. The exact nature of the deficit may vary from species to species, depending upon the constitution of the normal diet and upon the animal's physiological tolerance. Small animals which have a high metabolic rate, such as song birds (Passeriformes), quickly suffer an energy shortage when they are unable to obtain food. To maintain its bodyweight and normal activity the great tit (*Parus major*) must feed every few minutes. At night, when feeding is impossible, some birds become torpid, lower their body temperature and conserve energy. Other animals are able to draw upon energy reserves and may live for long periods without food. For example, during the rut a red deer stag may eat little or nothing for six weeks. Incubating jungle fowl do not eat for weeks and eat little even if food is placed next to the nest.

Animals may suffer from a deficiency in one of a number of specific elements of the diet that are essential for good health. These include salt, vitamins and various minerals. Such deficiences are said to lead to *specific hungers*. Failure to satisfy them may result in death. In some cases, and especially with salt and water, the specific hunger results in an increased sensitivity to the missing dietary ingredient, and the animal can readily detect its presence in food. Most minerals and vitamins, on the other hand, cannot be detected in food by taste or smell. Many animals, however, quickly learn to recognize and select those foods which promote recovery from dietary deficiency.

Thirst may have a number of causes. Primary thirst

arises from a negative water balance which results in dehydration of the body tissues. Secondary thirst may arise from the intake of dehydrating agents such as food or alcohol, or from changes in environmental temperature.

All animals require water to maintain their metabolic processes, but water is continually lost from the body as a result of excretion, thermoregulation and evaporation from the body surface. Lost water has to be replenished and this is done by drinking in the majority of animals. A few land animals can survive without drinking. Thus the flour moth (*Anagaster kuehuiella*) relies entirely upon the water content of its food. Aquatic animals do not need to drink, and most amphibians absorb water through their skin.

When drinking is not possible the body suffers a negative water balance as a result of a continuing water loss. Some automatic corrective adjustments take place (see HOMEOSTASIS) but these can only serve to cut down on the rate of water loss. Water loss through excretion can be reduced by reabsorption of water in the kidney and small intestine, but some loss remains necessary because the waste products of digestion and metabolism have to be excreted. Many animals eat less when thirsty and this helps to reduce water losses in excretion. Water loss through thermoregulation can sometimes be reduced. By taking less exercise and eating less food animals produce less heat, and by seeking a cool place an animal can conserve some of the water normally lost in keeping cool (see THERMOREGULATION).

Primary thirst results in dehydration of tissue cells. The osmotic pressure of the blood rises and this is monitored by osmoreceptors in the brain, first discovered by Verney (1947). Stimulation of osmoreceptors in the HYPOTHALAMUS and preoptic areas of the brain leads to the secretion of antidiuretic hormone from the posterior part of the PITUITARY gland. The presence of antidiuretic hormone in the bloodstream leads to a decrease in the amount and an increase in the concentration of urine excreted by the kidneys. Damage to the pituitary gland or associated area of the hypothalamus results in diabetes insipidus. The symptoms include excessive drinking and urination. Antidiuretic hormone is thus an important factor in water conservation.

Another important hormone is angiotensin, produced from a precursor in the kidney. Angiotensin in the bloodstream leads to an increase in blood pressure. It is also monitored by the brain, where it acts as a primary thirst stimulus. There are thus two bodily states that elicit primary drinking. (1) Water loss from cells due to a high concentration of salts in the body fluids resulting from food intake or water loss. This is monitored by the osmoreceptors. (2) Low fluid volume in the bloodstream as a result of haemorrhage, etc. This is monitored by the kidney, which stimulates angiotensin production, which in turn raises blood pressure as a short-term means of compensating for the fluid loss, and induces thirst. Angiotensin also suppresses feeding, which also helps to conserve water.

Secondary thirst is purely psychological and arises in situations in which the behavior of the animal is likely to induce a future primary thirst. For example, many animals drink in response to an increase in environmental temperature. Andersson (1964) showed that goats could be induced to drink by warming the anterior part of the hypothalamus. By drinking in direct response to a temperature increase the animal is making water available for thermoregulation. If the animal did not drink at this stage, its thermoregulatory water losses would induce a primary thirst. Similarly, many animals drink in association with meals. This type of secondary drinking anticipates the primary thirst-inducing consequences of food intake.

Species vary greatly in their requirements for water. Some such as the budgerigar (*Melospittacus*) and the kangaroo rat (*Dipodomys*) have such efficient water conservation mechanisms that they can survive without drinking. They obtain a little water from their food, which usually consists of seeds, and they will drink if water becomes available. Camels can manage for long periods without water, but when given a chance to drink they take in a large amount: a male camel weighing 325 kg. can drink over 100 litres of water. A very thirsty man can drink about two litres.

Some animals can make use of sources of water that are denied to others. The pack rat (*Neotoma*) can metabolize oxalic acid which is toxic for most other animals. This enables it to use water from cacti which would otherwise be poisonous. A number of reptiles and birds have special salt glands which excrete salt in a highly concentrated solution. They can therefore drink water with a salt concentration that would be lethal for other animals. Salt glands are found not only in marine animals such as the marine iguana (*Amblyrhynchus*) and many sea birds, but also in desert reptiles and in birds such as sand partridges (*Ammoperdix*) and roadrunners (*Geococcyx*). Some fresh water birds, such as ducks and flamingos, also have salt glands which enable them to exploit salt marshes and other marginal habitats.

Similarly they can learn to avoid foods which make them sick (see FOOD SELECTION).

In addition to the physiological aspects of hunger, there are a number of psychological influences. Many animals have distinctive meal patterns which are repeated day after day under constant conditions. Just as humans experience hunger at habitual meal times, so the feeding tendency of animals can be governed by time of day. In conditions in which the environment changes little from day to day animals quickly establish a daily routine of activities and eat at particular times even when food is continuously available.

Physiological processes may become attuned to the routine. In humans, for example, the liver may cease to mobilize glycogen just before a meal is due. This leads to a fall in blood sugar level in anticipation of the increase that will occur when the meal is digested. Experiments have shown that such physiological adjustments can readily undergo conditioning in relation to the time-of-day.

Another important psychological factor in hunger is the increase in appetite that occurs at the beginning of the meal. Once an animal has started to eat there is an apparent increase in hunger, the size of which depends upon the palatability of the food. This positive feedback effect is short-lived and seems to be part of a mechanism designed to enable animals to exploit feeding opportunities.

Despite a large amount of scientific work the question of which physiological factors initiate eating remains something of a mystery. The influential psychologist Walter Cannon thought (1932) that stomach contractions and other peripheral factors were responsible. However in humans, when the nerves from the stomach are cut, or the stomach is removed for medical reasons, eating is largely unaffected. Several theories have suggested that receptors within the brain are sensitive to the presence of nutrients in the blood. Substances such as glucose, amino acids, or fats, might be used as indices of dietary requirements. The level of glucose in the blood increases during digestion, but it also changes in other circumstances, such as in autonomic arousal and in anticipation of meals. Mayer and Thomas suggested (1967) that the brain responds to the utilization of glucose rather than to its availability. This suggestion is supported by the results of recent research, but the evidence remains inconclusive. Some scientists doubt whether direct monitoring of the nutrient state of the body is of prime importance in hunger. Although the fact that animals are able to respond to dietary excesses or deficits is suggestive of direct monitoring and regulation, there are alternative possibilities. Animals suffering from a particular deficiency tend to sample a wider range of foods and quickly learn to choose appropriate foods. The evidence suggests that such learning is based upon general sensations of sickness and health, rather than upon detection of specific deficiencies.

The factors that lead animals to cease eating vary considerably. Those which have internal storage organs or which eat bulky food usually finish eating before there have been any significant changes in blood composition as a result of digestion and absorption. For example, a pigeon which eats a meal of about a hundred grains of wheat will still be storing all the food in its crop an hour after the meal has ended. A snake which eats its prey whole, or a lion which eats a large meal every few days is likely to rely on stomach distension as a signal for satisfaction. On the other hand in an animal which nibbles its food like a rat, or an animal with a high throughput of food like a small bird, internal physiological changes occur while the animal is eating and stomach distension is relatively unimportant.

Animals may learn to recalibrate their short-term satiation mechanisms as a result of learning about the physiological consequences of digesting food. Le Magnen (1969) fed two differently flavoured but nutritionally identical diets to rats, and injected them with glucose immediately after they had eaten one diet. The rats associated the flavour of this food with greater absorption of calories, and subsequently ate less food of that particular flavour. There is also evidence that feeding habits may change in association with changes in body weight and fat reserves. DJM

Bibliography

Andersson, B. 1964: Aspects of the interrelations between central regulation of body temperature and food and water intake. In *Brain and behavior* II, ed. M. Brazier. Washington, D.C.: American Institute of Biological Sciences.

Cannon, W. B. 1932: *The wisdom of the body*. London: Kegan Paul.

*Hokanson, J. E. 1969: *The physiological bases of motivation*. New York and London: John Wiley & Sons.

Mayer, J. and Thomas, D. W. 1967: Regulations of food intake and obesity. *Science* 156, 328–37.

*Milner, P. M. 1970: *Physiological psychology*. New York and London: Holt, Rinehart and Winston.

Le Magnen, J. 1969: Peripheral and systemic actions of food in the caloric regulation of intake. *Annals of the New York Academy of Science* 157, 1126–57.

Verney, E. B. 1947: The antidiuretic hormone and the factors which determine its release. *Proceedings of the Royal Society* 135, 25–106.

hunger and thirst: physiological determinants *Hunger* and *thirst* are terms representing the intervening variables that have been posited to account for the discontinuous, episodic occurrence of feeding and drinking. Many workers have postulated complementary sets of stimuli of *satiety* that must work to inhibit or curtail the processes of hunger and thirst before the relevant imbalances are fully redressed. At another level of analysis the three terms are also used to refer to the reportable experiences or sensations of an individual inclined to eat or drink in the case of hunger or thirst and inclined not to eat or drink in the case of the respective satieties. Failure to distinguish clearly these levels of discourse has produced considerable confusion on occasion. Little physiological information is available on the determinants of the experiential dimension, and therefore the present analysis is restricted to identification of the physiological determinants responsible for the postulated intervening variables.

In the case of hunger the physiological determinants include the visceral and metabolic events associated with insufficient energy within the body. The organism clearly needs a variety of nutrients and, consistent with these requirements, the specific dimensions of the types of utilization that are monitored by the body are multiple. Several of these visceral and metabolic consequences of energy have been shown to operate as determinants of hunger under at least some conditions. Their relative contributions to the control of feeding in an intact animal are the subject of controversy still. Rather than list them in the order of their importance, most accounts follow the strategy used herein of listing them arbitrarily by hierarchies of class of action or site of receptors.

Both practically and conceptually, the determinants of feeding behavior fall into two categories depending on whether they serve to accomplish *short term control* of feeding or to affect the *long term control* of intake. The former mechanisms include those that operate to influence the hour-by-hour pattern of feeding or the meal-to-meal episodes of hunger, whereas the latter controls correct day-to-day or even week-to-week deviations in energy balance. In the case of the short term controls of hunger, one of the first stimuli recognized was blood sugar. Jean Mayer (1955) suggested that meal-to-meal feeding was determined by a *glucostatic mechanism*. According to this widely cited view, falling glucose utilization (as measured by the difference in glucose levels between arterial and venous blood) of an area of the HYPOTHALAMUS in the brain is a signal that stimulates feeding. Numerous variations of this theory, many of them emphasizing other alternative or additional sites (such as the liver) for the detectors, have been developed. The theory has the attractive features that (1) blood glucose is the major source of energy utilized by the brain and (2) specific cells within the brain and the body have been shown to respond to glucose.

Another mechanism thought to influence short term control of hunger is a *thermostatic mechanism* proposed by Brobeck (1960). Recognizing that different types of food seem to have different satiating capacities roughly correlated with the heat produced in their metabolism, Brobeck suggested that the thermic effects of nutrient metabolism, or specifically the "specific dynamic actions" of foods were sensed and modified feeding in order to regulate the energy supply. Since the glucostatic theory and the thermostatic hypothesis do not readily account for all feeding behavior in all short term situations, some scientists have recently proposed different variants of an energy sensing model in which some universal factor in energy metabolism (e.g. pyruvate production) is the adequate stimulus for a hypothetical receptor that controls hunger.

Feeding is also promoted by gustatory and olfactory stimuli. Although it has been traditionally recognized that taste and smell are important in identifying and selecting foods, recent research has served to identify another role–one of motivation–of taste and smell in feeding. Sensory contact with appropriate and palatable food serves to elicit and energize feeding behavior, and in that manner gustatory and olfactory stimuli may be considered signals of hunger. At the end of a meal, taste and smell may also participate in an "oral metering" process which may promote the termination of feeding.

Another analysis of the short term determinants of hunger has been the attempt to identify those controls of *satiety* which serve to limit or eliminate hunger. It has been shown that distension of the stomach as well as nutrient stimulation of gastric chemoreceptors can inhibit food intake or limit hunger. It has also been demonstrated that cholecystokinin, a hormone secreted by the small intestine when it is stimulated by food, reduces the size of a meal. Other hormones of the gastrointestinal tract may also have satiating consequences. Although the loci for the effects are controversial, food also has other satiating effects after it is absorbed from the gastrointestinal tract and enters the circulation.

In terms of long term determinants of hunger, the most widely discussed mechanism is the *lipostatic control* first hypothesized by Kennedy (1953). This view argues that some form of lipids or a related metabolite is monitored and that hunger and feeding are responses mobilized by a lipostatic control in order to correct a deficit in the level of fat stores (over 90 per cent of the total energy stored in the body is in the form of fat). Long term control exercised by this mechanism is taken to be responsible for the striking day-to-day constancy in body weight and fat stores maintained by most adult animals, including those individuals with extremely high (obese) or low (thin) but stable values.

Recent analyses, stimulated by some of the inadequacies of the traditionally recognized determinants of hunger to account for the bulk of feeding, have suggested that there are important *nonhomeostatic* determinants of hunger as well. This view suggests that hunger, except in emergency cases, is in considerable part the result of learned strategies and of endogenous "programs" that have been selected for in the process of evolution to a given ecological niche and that produce feeding behavior in cycles or patterns that anticipate and avoid the onset of homeostatic imbalances. According to some investigators, the factors of taste and smell mentioned above are not under tight homeostatic control, and this situation accounts for why exposure to a surfeit of palatable foods can lead to overeating or hyperphagia and obesity.

Several brain systems are responsible for the control of feeding. The medulla oblongata (see BRAIN AND CENTRAL NERVOUS SYSTEM: ILLUSTRATIONS, fig. 6) contains the circuitry necessary to make ingestion and rejection responses to taste stimuli and to make simple adjustments in these responses on the basis of the presence of food in the gastrointestinal tract. The hypothalamus contains neural circuitry important to the normal operation of hunger. This circuitry includes one system or set of systems in the *ventromedial hypothalamus* (fig. 20). Destruction of this region by brain lesions leads to the classical ventromedial hypothalamic syndrome characterized by excessive eating, obesity and finickiness with respect to the taste qualities of nutrients. The hypothalamus also includes a second system in and traversing the *lateral hypothalamus*. Damage to this system leads to a constellation of deficits in feeding including aphagia, anorexia, finickiness, permanent reductions in the maintained level of body weight and deficits in arousal or the sensorimotor integration necessary for feeding. Electrical recording from neurons in these hypothalamic regions indicates that neural activity there is influenced by several metabolites and visceral events already mentioned. Other mechanisms including the LIMBIC SYSTEM and particularly the AMYGDALA (figs. 15 and 21) play key roles in the analysis and integration of sensory inputs and experience in the control of hunger.

Thirst, meaning the condition that accounts for drinking or the consumption of water, has a reasonably well defined set of controls analogous to those outlined for hunger. Water debt has impact on two dimensions of the body fluid compartments that are sensed by strategically located receptors and that are ultimately translated into thirst. This dual compartment/dual stimulus or "double depletion" hypothesis has been recently articulated by Fitzsimons (1979), Epstein (1982) and a number of others. In its basic form, this double depletion hypothesis postulates that osmotic and volemic changes in water balance within the body generate thirst.

Osmotic stimulation to drink occurs when the water intake lags behind the rate of loss that occurs because of respiration, sweating and excretion. As this happens, a relative increase in electrolyte concentration or osmolarity occurs in the cells of the body, the extracellular space, and the blood as well. Hypovolemic stimulation results when body water and electrolytes are lost simultaneously or at corresponding rates (such as when body fluids move into the digestive tract or the individual loses fluids by diarrhea or hemorrhage). Hypovolemia means a lowering of blood volume.

The osmotic stimuli for thirst operate on *osmoreceptors* found in both the brain and the periphery. One of the first identified concentrations of these osmoreceptors is located in the lateral preoptic area of the hypothalamus (fig. 20), an area adjacent to the supraoptic nucleus and the nucleus circularis, both of which have been implicated in the osmotic controls of antidiuretic hormone release for conserving water. Other areas of the body including sites in the liver may also contain osmoreceptors. The lateral preoptic area of the hypothalamus is particularly central to osmotic drinking insofar as lesions of this region produce a profound adipsia or lack of drinking to osmotic stimulation.

The receptors monitoring hypovolemia are located in the circulatory system, particularly on the venous side where they serve as *baroreceptors* by continuously monitoring the stretch produced on tissues by the blood volume. Activation of these stretch receptors leads to a cascade of neuroendocrine events that liberates the active form of the hormone angiotensin in the blood stream. Angiotensin, sometimes called the hormone of thirst, serves not only to mobilize physiological adjustments which tend to offset the decrease of blood volume but also to activate directly brain mechanisms of volemic thirst. In the brain, angiotensin acts at specialized receptor tissues found adjacent to the ventricles. The subfornical organ and the organum vasculosum of the lamina terminalis are the two best studied of these receptor sites. These circumventricular sites are interconnected, and they apparently project to the lateral hypothalamus. Lesions of the receptor tissues or the lateral hypothalamus can produce profound volemic adipsia. Current evidence suggests that osmotic thirst and volemic thirst mechanisms work in an additive fashion to determine the amount of water consumed.

Satiety signals separate from simple repletion of the water deficit seem to play less of a role for thirst than the analogous signals do in the case of feeding. This situation presumably stems from the fact that, unlike complex macronutrients, ingested water is rapidly absorbed from the gastrointestinal tract and rapidly equilibrates in the body water compartments. Still, research has suggested that some water satiety may involve factors other than elimination of the stimulus of thirst. Oral metering and gastric metering, the latter by distension and osmoreceoptors in the stomach, seem to inhibit drinking in some situations before water is absorbed from the gastrointestinal tract.

Some determinants of thirst are considered nonhomeostatic. Some drinking appears to occur from habit or rhythmic patterns of behavior and may operate so as to stave off the development of water deficits that might activate osmotic and volemic controls. Similarly, meal-associated or *prandial drinking* may result from the local stimulus of a dry mouth or the need to moisten food for swallowing, rather than from a deficit signal. Some researchers in the field argue that these nonhomeostatic determinants may serve to operate as anticipatory mechanisms and may account for a large percentage of ad libitum drinking behavior. TLP

Bibliography

Brobeck, J.R. 1960: Food and temperature. *Recent progress in hormone research* 16, 439–66.

Code, C.F., ed. 1967: Control of food and water intake. Vol. 1, sect. 6 of the *Handbook of physiology*. Washington, D.C.: American Physiological Society.

Epstein, A.N. 1982: The physiology of thirst, In *The physiological mechanisms of motivation*, ed. D.W. Pfaff. Heidelberg, Berlin and New York: Springer-Verlag.

———, Kissileff, H.R. and Stellar, E., eds. 1973: *The neuropsychology of thirst: new findings and advances in concepts*. Washington, D.C.: V.H. Winston & Sons.

Fitzsimons, J.T. 1979: *The physiology of thirst and sodium appetite*. Cambridge and New York: Cambridge University Press.

Kennedy, G.C. 1953: The role of depot fat in the hypothalamic control of food intake in the rat. *Proceedings of the Royal Society, London, Series B* 140, 578–92.

Mayer, J. 1955: Regulation of energy intake and the body weight: The glucostatic theory and the lipostatic hypothesis. *Annals of the New York Academy of Science* 63, 15–42.

Morgane, P.J. and Panksepp, J., eds. 1980: *Handbook of the hypothalamus, Volume 3–Part A*. New York and Basel: Marcel Dekker, Inc.

Silverstone, T., ed. 1976: *Appetite and food intake*. Berlin: Abakon Verlagsgesellschaft.

Husserl, Edmund (1859–1938). German philosopher, best known as the founder of phenomenology. He sought a descriptive basis for philosophy in the study of mental phenomena but expected this study to reveal necessary truths about the essences of such phenomena. The method was to be phenomenological. One set out to describe the phenomena under the constraint of two "reductions". The transcendental reduction meant not assuming that there was an extra-mental reality: this, in order to subvert the tendency to apply non-mental categories to mind. The eidetic reduction meant concerning oneself only with essential features of the phenomena studied: features which could not be varied in imagination. Epistemologically, Husserl shared the Cartesian concern with establishing foundations, though he came to think that these would only be found in the everyday "life-world". Metaphysically he flirted with idealism, without ever clearly espousing it.

Husserl had an important influence on Martin Heidegger and Jean-Paul Sartre, though in his thought about the life-world he may himself have been influenced by the former. Both Heidegger and Sartre were moved by the idea that phenomenology could attain a radical level of description, unprecedented in philosophy and unparalleled in other disciplines. They used what they regarded as phenomenological description, not in the service of a foundational epistemology or idealist metaphysics, but with a view to building an ontology that left a distinctive place for the human being *vis-à-vis* reality. Heidegger emphasized that the human subject was the locus at which reality revealed itself, being brought to articulation in language. Sartre tended towards a more constructivist view, emphasising the radical freedom of the individual to see things now this way, now that. For their common insistence on such human distinctiveness, and on the fact that people usually conceal the distinctiveness from themselves, they came to be described under a common label, as existentialists. PP

Bibliography

Pivcevic, Edo 1970: *Husserl and phenomenology*. London: Hutchinson.

Solomon, Robert C., ed. 1972: *Phenomenology and existentialism*. New York: Harper & Row.

Huxley, Sir Julian Born 1887, died 1975. Educated and later a lecturer in zoology at Oxford University, he spent three years in the USA, returned to Oxford and was later professor of zoology at King's College, London. He was Secretary of the Zoological Society of London from 1935 to 1942, and Director-General of UNESCO from 1946 to 1948. Lorenz has referred to Huxley as one of the founding fathers of ethology. His 1914 publication on the courtship habits of the great crested grebe was a landmark of objective naturalistic study of "instinctive" behavior patterns. Fifty years later he organized a Royal Society symposium entitled *A discussion on ritualization of behaviour in animals and man* (1965). His interest in evolutionary theory was profound; and his 1942 book is a classic. He was also instrumental in furthering the ideas of scientific humanism, and eugenics. PKS

Bibliography

Huxley, J.S. 1942 (1974): *Evolution: the modern synthesis*. 3rd edn. London: Allen and Unwin; New York: Hafner.

hypercorrection A socio- and psycholinguistic term referring to an incorrect analogy with a linguistic form in a prestige variety which the speaker has imperfectly mastered (see SOCIOLECT; DIGLOSSIA). Hypercorrection reflects social insecurity in a context of social mobility. In its most common form, lower-middle-class speakers go beyond the highest status group in their tendency to use the forms considered correct and appropriate for formal styles (see Labov 1972, p.244).

Examples of hypercorrection are particularly frequent in the mesolectal (see SOCIOLECT) varieties of a Creole-English continuum. In Jamaican Creole English [θ] is realized as [t], so that "three" and "tree" fall together as [tri]. Many schoolteachers insist that their pupils restore the [θ]. As a result a [θ] restoration rule is generalized to apply to words which do not have it in English so that a "filter" is frequently called a "filther". This form is also supported by folk-etymology i.e. "something which removes filth". PM

Bibliography

Labov, William 1972: *Sociolinguistic patterns*, Philadelphia: University of Pennsylvania Press.

hyperkinetic states These childhood states are characterized by motor restlessness, fidgetiness, poor attention, distractability, impulsiveness and excitability. They occur more often in boys than in girls, and may be accompanied by clumsiness, learning difficulties, emotional disturbance and anti-social behavior. They are diagnosed much more frequently in North America than in Britain, possibly owing to some overlap in the diagnostic criteria used for hyperkinetic states and conduct disorder. Research into etiology has indicated a number of relevant factors, including genetic, structural or physiological brain abnormalities, toxic or allergic reactions, and family factors (maternal depression, early deprivation and poor family organization). Treatment with stimulant drugs and BEHAVIOR THERAPY produces improvements in many children. Diets low in allergens or food additives (e.g. the Feingold diet) are also used, but are still at an experimental stage. The outlook for hyperkinetic children with associated behavior problems and learning difficulties is not good; although overactivity itself decreases in adolescence. GCF

Bibliography

Black, D. 1982: The hyperkinetic child: two views. *British medical journal* 284, 533–34.

hypnosis and hypnotism The word hypnosis is a shortened form of neurohypnosis or "nervous sleep" first used by James Braid (1795–1860) to refer to a trance-like state which could be observed in patients who had undergone certain verbal or non-verbal procedures aimed at inducing such a state. The act of carrying out these procedures is known as HYPNOTISM.

The notion that an individual can be placed in a state somewhat different from normal awareness in which he or she becomes vulnerable to suggestion probably dates back as far as the cult of Aesculapius in the fourth century BC. However, the popularity of hypnosis in Europe stemmed from the practices of Franz Anton Mesmer (1734–1815) who claimed to be able to cure a variety of ailments by redistributing body fluids by the use of "animal magnetism". Mesmer's action of "passing" a magnet over the patient's body and the atmosphere in which he held his healing sessions influenced some individuals to have "fits", to behave in a somnambulistic way, to experience hallucinations and apparently to become impervious to pain.

Although, upon careful investigation, these phenomena were found to be attributable to the imagination and gullibility of the patients, Mesmer's results impressed later, more respectable, practitioners such as Braid and Esdaile (1808–59) who used hypnosis for surgical operations, and Charcot (1825–93), Freud (1856–1939) and others who used it in the treatment of emotional disorders.

Before the beginning of experimental research on the topic in the 1920s it was generally believed that hypnosis could bring about certain conditions in the patient not otherwise attainable, for example, analgesia, age regression, post-hypnotic amnesia, sensory changes like blindness, an increase in physical strength, and willingness to commit anti-social acts.

The results of sixty years of carefully controlled experiments suggest that these effects and others result not from some alteration in the hypnotized persons' capacities, but from a number of interacting factors influencing them, for example, prior knowledge of how hypnotized persons behave, expectations, willingness to volunteer and eagerness to experience something unusual, the "demand characteristics" of the situation (Orne 1962) such as the behavior of the hypnotist and the instructions given, and individual motives and beliefs. Physiological tests have so far failed to produce any consistent criteria of hypnosis, and brain patterns are those of relaxation rather than sleep.

Current theories of hypnosis tend to fall into two groups; those emanating from the psychodynamic and clinically orientated therapists who still maintain that hypnosis represents an altered state of consciousness with special and unique effects, and those put forward by experimentally oriented social psychologists who see hypnosis as a consequence of "role playing" and/or the influence of a number of social variables. One member of this group, T. X. Barber writes 'hypnosis' in parentheses to indicate his conviction that the word is unnecessary, since the associated phenomena can be more easily explained in other terms (Barber 1969).

Some of the discrepancies in research findings from these two groups may stem from the very different subjects they use and the settings in which they work.

Hypnosis is still widely and successfully used by practitioners, especially in dentistry, obstetrics and psychotherapy. The patient's belief in the efficacy of hypnosis and trust in the hypnotist seems to exert a powerful influence, probably as a variant of the placebo effect. SMH

Bibliography

Barber, T.X. 1969: *Hypnosis: a scientific approach.* New York: Van Nostrand.

Gordon, Jesse, E., ed. 1967: *Handbook of clinical and experimental hypnosis.* London: Collier-Macmillan.

Orne, M.T. 1962: On the social psychology of the psychological experiment with particular reference to demand characteristics and their implications. *American psychologist* 17, 776–83.

hypochondriasis An excessive preoccupation with bodily symptoms (especially pain) often accompanied by fears of a serious physical illness, such as cancer and heart disease. It may be a feature of a wide variety of psychiatric disorders including depression, hypochondriacal PERSONALITY DISORDER, anxiety, HYSTERIA and SCHIZOPHRENIA. It has been argued that there is a primary hypochondriacal neurosis but investigation suggests that most of such patients are suffering depressive illness and the remainder from some other primary disorder (Kenyon 1964). In treatment, once a physical illness has been excluded, the main aims are to control the demands for excessive medical investigation and at the same time treat the underlying psychological disorder appropriately. Minor problems can be satisfactorily managed by reassurance and simple counselling. RAM

Bibliography

Kenyon, F.E. 1964: Hypochondriasis: a clinical study. *British journal of psychiatry* 110, 478–88.

hypomania This commonly designates a mild state of mania, the latter term being avoided in some contexts because of its alternative meanings (that is, mania as an undifferentiated madness with disturbed behavior, or a morbid compulsion). The hypomanic state comprises restlessness and overactivity, disinhibited and extravagant behavior, racing thoughts and elated mood, often with irritability. It is usually seen within the context of an AFFECTIVE DISORDER, in most cases alternating with depression (see DEPRESSION, BIPOLAR). More rarely a brief episode may be understandable as a reaction to an emotional upset; psychoanalysts use the term manic or hypomanic defense where they speculate that the ego breaks free temporarily from the inhibiting effect of the superego.

A hypomanic illness usually remits spontaneously after a few weeks, but recurrence is likely. DLJ

Bibliography

Paykel, E.S., ed. 1982: *Handbook of affective disorders.* London and New York: Churchill Livingstone.

hypothalamus (See BRAIN AND CENTRAL NERVOUS SYSTEM: ILLUSTRATIONS, figs. 5 and 6.) A small but vital brain structure located at the base of the diencephalon. It maintains widespread connections with other brain areas through such principal afferent pathways as the fornix which originates in the hippocampus, the medial forebrain bundle from the anterior forebrain and the stria terminalis from the AMYGDALA (figs. 15–18, 20 and 21). Major efferent projections are to the THALAMUS (mammillothalamic tract) and the brain stem (mammillotegmental tract). The hypothalamus, consisting of a densely packed collection of nuclei, acts as the control center for the AUTONOMIC NERVOUS SYSTEM (fig. 11). Posterior and lateral hypothalamic nuclei regulate sympathetic functions while anterior and medial nuclei are concerned with parasympathetic discharge. The hypothalamus has important links with the endocrine system and influences the secretion of hormones which affect metabolism, growth, electrolyte balance and secondary sex characteristics (e.g. fig. 22). Areas of the hypothalamus also control a wide range of vegetative or life sustaining functions which include feeding and drinking, temperature control and sexual behavior. Damage to these areas produces growth abnormalities. The hypothalamus is also involved in emotionality. Animals with hypothalamic lesions often show only fragmentary emotional responses and appear incapable of integrated reactions of fear or anger. GWi

hypothetical constructs and intervening variables Terms in scientific propositions which respectively refer to unobserved entities and processes; or else serve only as calculational conveniences, to link observed events and quantities but without any reference or surplus meaning beyond their mode of use, and their definition in terms of observables.

For a realist, hypothetical constructs are legitimate conjectures about the world beyond the set of observation statements, which are necessary but not sufficient for the support of a theory (hence the claim by Popper that scientific generalizations are empirically falsifiable, but not verifiable). For an instrumentalist, only intervening variables are legitimate, and their value or meaning is confined to the instrumental one of organizing and interrelating observables, and the stating of empirical laws whose truth is necessary and sufficient for the more limited claims made by the concept of intervening variable.

In marginal cases it can be open to debate as to whether a concept is to be read as an intervening variable or a hypothetical construct. For the latter interpretation the general principle of scientific realism must be acceptable, and the construct must be compatible with other related forms of knowledge. DDC

Bibliography

MacCorquodale, K. and Meehl, P. 1948: On a distinction between hypothetical constructs and intervening variables. *Psychological review* 55, 95–107.

hysteria Neurotic disorder in which psychological and/or physical functioning is disturbed (e.g. in respect of emotional control, movement – coordination, sensory reactions or state of consciousness) without any evidence of physical pathology, and with some indication of psychological motivation. The term derives from the Greek word for womb (*hysteron*) because in antiquity the complaint was thought to be an exclusively female one related to the functioning of that organ. Towards the end of the last century interest developed in the susceptibility of hysterics to hypnosis as a means of removing their symptoms and even of discovering their cause. See Veith (1965) for an account of changing medical concepts of the disorder. Freud's first psychotherapeutic investigations were into cases of hysteria, whose symptoms he regarded as the symbolic expression of wishes that had been subjected to repression because of their connection with sexual guilt. For Eysenck (1957), as for Jung, the "dimensions" of hysteria are associated with unstable extroversion. NMC

Bibliography

Breuer, Joseph and Freud, Sigmund 1895: *Studies on hysteria, Standard edition of the complete psychological works of Sigmund Freud*. Vol. 2. London: Hogarth Press; New York: Norton.

Eysenck, Hans J. 1957: *Dimensions of anxiety and hysteria*. London:Routledge & Kegan Paul.

Veith: Ilza 1965: *Hysteria: the history of a disease*. London and Chicago: Chicago University Press.

I

IC analysis *See* Immediate Constituent analysis

id *See* psychoanalytic personality theory

idea In the philosophy of the seventeenth and eighteenth centuries, starting with DESCARTES, an idea is usually defined as "whatever is the object of the mind when it thinks". This use, so different from the use of the term in ancient and medieval philosophy to stand for some objective entities independent of the mind, arose from the standard colloquial use of *idée* in French and idea in English to mean picture or image. It entered philosophy in connection with a theory that perception was of ideas or mental pictures caused by physical objects and that thought was the reproduction of these pictures in memory or imagination. A wide variety of types of ideas were distinguished, principally by LOCKE, such as simple and complex, concrete and abstract, particular and general, experiential and innate. (See also IMPRESSION.) JOU

ideal self An image or representation of oneself as one would like to be. Derived from societal values and significant others, the ideal self is composed of wished for (but possibly unattainable) modes of behavior, values, traits, aspects of personal appearance etc. A disparity between the ideal self and SELF-CONCEPT (i.e. image of oneself as one really is) is taken to be a sign of poor mental health, and its reduction a primary goal of psychotherapy (see Rogerian therapy in RADICAL THERAPY). The self-ideal disparity has consequences for the regulation of behavior since it is intrinsically ANXIETY producing. Recent work in experimental social psychology has sought to explicate these regulative processes by studying the conditions under which a self-ideal comparison is likely to be induced and then subsequently dealt with by the individual (see OBJECTIVE SELF AWARENESS, SUPEREGO). BRS

idealization In the widest sense, this is the process of regarding a person as perfect. It involves overlooking or denying attributes of the person that do not fit the idealized picture and, in this respect, it differs from admiration.

In Freudian psychoanalytic terminology it refers to the mental process whereby objects may be construed as ideally good. The love-object "is aggrandised and exalted in the subject's mind" (Freud). This over-evaluation involves the transfer or displacement of an excessive quantity of libido from the ego to the object. Identification with idealized objects, especially parents, plays a part in the construction of ideal models that contribute to the formation of character. Some authors emphasize the defensive functions of idealization e.g. Klein's conception of splitting of objects into 'good' and 'bad' as a defence against anxiety. WLLP-J

Bibliography

Freud, S. 1953–74: *On narcissism: an introduction. Standard Edition of the Complete Works of Sigmund Freud*, vol. XIV, 94. London: Hogarth Press; New York: Norton.

Klein, M., 1952: In *Developments in psycho-analysis*, ed. Joan Rivière. London: Hogarth Press.

identification A core concept in psychoanalytic theory denoting the process through which the subject assimilates aspects of others (objects) and constitutes its personality from the resulting products. A legacy of Freud's use of the term in successive theoretical formulations is a set of related meanings. Noting that the assimilative process may involve extension of the subject's identity into another, a fusing with another or the borrowing of identity from another, Rycroft (1968), lists four types of identification. *Primary identification* in infancy is problematic in that the subject is scarcely differentiated from the other. The sense of the term most widely employed in psychology is *secondary identification*. It functions as a defense best known in the Oedipus Complex where assimilation of the parents replaces the ambivalent feelings of love and hostility towards them and leads to the formation of the superego. *Projective* and *introjective identification* are also defenses and involve fantasies in which the subject either is inside and in control of another or has taken the object, or part object inside the self. Identification is distinguished from incorporation which is linked with the oral stage of development and fantasies of ingesting the object, and from internalization which denotes the assimilation of relations such as that of the subject to the authority of the father. BBL

Bibliography

Rycroft, C. 1968: *A critical dictionary of psychoanalysis*. London: Nelson; New York: Basic Books.

ideology Any false, and more especially categorically mistaken, ensemble of ideas, whose falsity is explicable, wholly or in part, in terms of the social role or function they, normally unwittingly, serve. Among the more discussed ideological phenomenon are the representation of sectional or particular interests as universal; the screening of social conflict and contradiction; the naturalization of the social status quo making it seem eternal; and the creation of the impression that the social order is the product of mere conventions (e.g. in social contract theory).

The term "ideology" was initially coined by Destutt de Tracy (1754–1836) to designate the scientific study of ideas, but was used pejoratively by Napoleon Bonaparte (1769–1821) to refer to the fanciful and impractical schemes of the Enlightenment. This connotation was extended and then transformed by Marx (1818–83) and Engels (1820–95) in *The German ideology* (1845–6) to characterize the mystified and mystifying abstraction of the thought of their contemporaries from the real processes of history. In the schematic topography of historical materialism such ideas were designated as part of the superstructure, ultimately explicable in terms of the economic base; while in Marx's critical work this characteristic pattern of critical explanation was employed to take in not just German philosophy, but utopian socialism, so-called classical political and vulgar economy and mystificatory thought generally, linking up with aspects of the Baconian, Kantian and Hegelian critiques of illusion.

Subsequently the radical historical tradition, in both its Marxian (e.g. Gramsci (1891–1937)) and non-Marxian (e.g. Mannheim (1893–1947)) avatars, played down the "negative" connotation of false consciousness and emphasized the "positive" notion of ideology as expressing the values or world-view of a particular social group or milieu. More recently there has been a tendency, e.g. within modern structuralism, for ideology to become effectively identified with the entire cultural sphere. Marx's original concept of ideology has clear affinities with Freud's (1856–1939) concept of rationalization, and some writers (e.g. Habermas (b.1929)) have modelled ideology-critique on depth-analysis. Among the topics of contemporary investigation are the criteria for differentiating ideology from science; the relation between ideologies and systems of domination; and the socio-psychological mechanisms at work in the reproduction and transformation of ideological forms. RB

Bibliography

Bhaskar, Roy 1983: *Philosophical ideologies*. Brighton: Harvester Press.

Larrain, Sorge 1979: *The concept of ideology*. London: Hutchinson.

idiographic method *See* individual psychology; methodology

idiolect The term idiolect or personal dialect was introduced by Bloch (1948) in an attempt to overcome the descriptive problems stemming from linguistic variation and borrowing. It is said to be "the totality of the possible utterances of one speaker at one time in using a language to interact with one other speaker" (Bloch 1948, pp.7–8). In a more loose sense idiolects are the speech habits of a single person.

Recent research has undermined the assumption that idiolects are a useful concept in linguistic analysis. In particular, LABOV has shown that idiolects do not form single coherent systems. Numerous styleshifts occur in situations such as the ones postulated by Bloch. Like the notion of an "ideal speaker-hearer" the notion of an idiolect is likely to have little import for psycholinguistic research. PM

Bibliography

Bloch, Bernard 1948: A set of postulates for phonemic analysis. *Language* 24, 3–46.

imagery *See* mental imagery

imagination The word "imagine" and its cognates are commonly used to express a variety of differing but closely interrelated concepts. Philosophers have often found it convenient to discuss the general topic of imagination under three principal headings, the imaginative, the imaginary, and MENTAL IMAGERY. The term "imagination" has also been given by some philosophers, notably HUME (1738) and KANT (1781, 1787), to a faculty claimed to be necessarily involved in sense-perception.

The notion of imaginativeness is closely akin to those of inventiveness and creativeness. A person is said to be imaginative in so far as he or she is able to think of things which other people cannot think of. This capacity may be exercised in any sphere where thought of a more than purely routine nature is required, whether in composing a piece of music, performing it, thinking of a scientific hypothesis or devising a way of testing it, writing a poem or novel, acting in a play, and so on. It is, however, a wider notion than inventiveness or creativeness. It is also required for the understanding and appreciation of the imaginative creations of others, the feelings of other people, and so forth. In this aspect imagination shows itself as perceptiveness and sensitivity rather than as inventiveness or creativity. Not that these two aspects can be very clearly separated one from another. Sensitivity to another is akin to a readiness to make hypotheses about him, and it has been plausibly claimed (Croce 1902) that to appreciate a work of art one must be able to recreate something of the experience of the original artist. However, such freedom must operate within some appropriate discipline if imaginativeness is not to degenerate into mere fancifulness. The nature of these disciplines will vary with the activity involved and what exactly they are is at its clearest where that activity has a clear and definite purpose. I may think of a highly novel way of routing the traffic through a town center, but it hardly counts, except ironically, as "imaginative" if it is clear that it would not work. On the contrary, my inability to see that it will not work is a good indicator of my lack of imagination. The fullest discussions of imaginativeness have occurred in connection with literature and the arts (Engell 1981).

We can say "N imagines that p" meaning no more than that N mistakenly thinks that p. A person deceived by a mirage may be said to imagine that he sees an oasis. This is not quite an application of the concept of the imaginary. The oasis is not a figment of the imagination since the deceived person has reason to believe that he sees it. The notion of the imaginary is that of unfounded rather than of merely false belief. My fears, for example, are imaginary in so far as my belief that I am in danger is not based on evidence. There is a link with the idea of imaginativeness. The dangers I believe to exist are, so to speak, my own invention. They are not produced in me by my acquaintance with any palpable evidence.

The expression mental imagery covers at least seeing things in the mind's eye, hearing a tune running in one's head, and so on. Sometimes it is used more widely to include other sorts of images such as eidetic or hypnagogic ones. After-images are better seen as belonging to the category of sensation and referred to as 'after-sensations'. Discussion of mental imagery has centered largely on the nature of the likeness between imaging and perceiving, and the relation between imaging and thinking. There has been a tendency to write as though an image were a sort of picture which could be seen, heard, examined etc. by, and only by, its owner (see Galton 1883). This model, in which an image is analogous to something perceived, has been attacked by Sartre (1940) and Ryle (1949). The latter also criticizes a second model according to which an image is analogous not so much to the object before our eyes as to the sensation we have when we see that object. Whereas Ryle's total rejection of the first model has obtained wide acceptance (but see Hannay 1971), his rejection of the second is more controversial. In this rejection he does not deny all likeness between imaging and perceiving, only that the former involves anything like sentience. Perception proper, Ryle maintains, involves both sentience and something else which may be called "in a strained sense" thinking. Imaging is a special form of thought, the form of thought involved in perception; it is perception minus sentience. Some philosophers accept some such view as this (e.g. Ishiguro 1967). Others (e.g. Shorter 1952) argue that this does not do full justice to the likeness between imaging and perceiving.

Ryle's account of perception and its connection with imaging is reminiscent of Kant's view of the role of imagination in perception. Kant held that more was required for the perceptual experience of a self-conscious being than the passive reception of sensations, and he ascribed some of this extra – just how much of it is rather obscure – to the work of imagination. Our perceptions are fragmentary and fleeting. But such a fleeting and fragmentary perception has typically the character of being a perception of a more enduring object of some sort. This is true even if I can characterize my experience only as, for example, seeing a dark patch against the foliage. Where this is not so my experience will be one of complete bewilderment. "Imagination" is the name given by Kant to the power, or perhaps to part of the power, so to connect one perception with other possible perceptions, or with other perceptions not currently occurring, that it can have this typical character of being the perception of an enduring object, and of an enduring object of a certain type. For how can I see a tree, and see it as a tree, unless I am capable of regarding different perceptions occurring at different times as being perceptions of trees, and of the same tree as the one I am now seeing? We must somehow apply concepts if we are to have perceptual experience at all.

Some such claim as the above seems indubitably true. It is less clear why this function should be ascribed to the imagination. On a Rylean account of perception the justification would be via the notion of mental imagery. There are suggestions of a similar sort of justification to be found in Wittgenstein's discussion (1953) of seeing aspects of ambiguous figures. Strawson (1970) while not endorsing a Rylean account also argues plausibly for a connection with power to produce images, as well as for links with imaginativeness and the imaginary. JMS

Bibliography

*Abrams, M.H. 1953: *The mirror and the lamp: romantic theory and the critical tradition.* New York and Oxford: Oxford University Press.

Croce, B. 1902 (*1922*): *Aesthetics.* Trans D. Ainslie. London: Macmillan.

Engell, J. 1981: *The creative imagination: enlightenment to romanticism.* Cambridge, Mass. and London: Harvard University Press.

Galton, F. 1883: *Inquiries into human faculty and its development.* London: Macmillan.

Hannay, A. 1971: *Mental images – a defence.* London: Allen and Unwin; New York: Humanities Press.

Hume, D. 1738: *A treatise of human nature.* Bk I, pt IV, sect. II.

Ishiguro, H. 1967: *Imagination. Proceedings of the Aristotelian society.* Suppl. vol. 41, 37–56.

Kant, I. 1781 (1950): *Critique of pure reason.* Trans Norman Kemp Smith. London: Macmillan.

Ryle, G. 1949: *The concept of mind.* London: Hutchinson; Totowa, N.J.: Barnes and Noble (1975).

Sartre, J-P. 1940: *L'imaginaire.* Paris: Gallimard.

Shorter, J.M. 1952: Imagination. *Mind* 61. 244, 528–42.

Strawson, P.F. 1970: Imagination and perception. In *Experience and theory*, ed. L. Foster and J.W. Swanson. University of Massachusetts Press; London: Duckworth.

*Warnock, Mary 1976: *Imagination*. London: Faber & Faber; Berkeley: University of California Press.

Wittgenstein, L. 1953: *Philosophical Investigations*. Oxford: Basil Blackwell; New York: Macmillan.

imitation: animal The process by which one animal copies the behavior of another. The most simple form of imitation is social facilitation in which behavior by one individual encourages others to do the same, usually without involving any new behavior on the part of the imitator.

Imitation that involves new behavior is usually called observational learning. There are many anecdotal reports of this type of behavior. It has been reported that puppies reared with a cat foster-mother develop cat-like behavior. A more reliable example is the report from many bird-watchers that blue tits and great tits learn to open milk bottles by copying each other. In England milk is delivered in bottles and left on doorsteps. The habit of opening the metal-foil top and taking some of the cream has spread throughout the country and is a simple form of culture.

Experimental studies indicate that there are some aspects of behavior, such as bird song (see COMMUNICATION) where imitation is highly developed, but that there are few examples outside the primates of a general ability to imitate. DJM

imitation: in human development Can be defined as placing one's own actions into correspondence with the behavior of others, implying an active process of matching or rendering equivalent behavior. Such a definition stresses the social functions of imitation in maintaining interpersonal relations and group identity.

Imitation may also serve the useful purpose of disseminating knowledge acquired by individuals to other groups or across generations. In the latter case, what is inherited is not the particular, adaptive behavior itself, but a generalized capacity to imitate and thus rapidly benefit from the accumulated learning of others. Recent evidence from developmental studies suggests that the ability to imitate may be innate. It has been shown that babies in the first month of life can imitate movements of the mouth and tongue (Meltzoff 1982). Such an ability may be very useful in helping the infant rapidly to produce the particular sounds of the language into which it is born. GEB

Bibliography

Meltzoff, A.N. 1981: Imitation, intermodal co-ordination and representation in early infancy. In *Infancy and epistemology*, ed. G.E. Butterworth. Brighton: Harvester; New York: St. Martin's.

imitation and observational learning Learning achieved not by practice or by direct experience on the learner's part of the consequences of performing a particular action, but solely by observation of another agent.

Thorndike (1911) was one of the first psychologists to study imitation as a species of observational learning in animals – with uniformly negative results. Having taught a cat to escape from a puzzle box by pressing a catch, he wanted to see if a second cat could be taught the solution simply by observing the trained cat performing the correct response. Finding no evidence of any such learning he concluded that in animals other than man, at least, all learning was by direct trial and error.

It remains unclear why Thorndike's experiments were so unsuccessful. Later experimenters, at any rate, have had little difficulty in demonstrating that animals can learn the solution to a problem by observing the performance of another, trained animal. It is important, however, to distinguish several ways in which observation of another animal may affect behavior.

1. The simplest possibility is sometimes called "social facilitation". A domestic chick given the opportunity to feed from a pile of food will eventually stop, apparently satiated. But if it now sees other chicks feeding, it will start again (Turner 1965). There is a sense in which the chick is imitating the others, but it is not clear that it has learned anything very important from observation of them – for it already knows how to eat and that food is available. It would be more parsimonious to conclude that among the stimuli that can elicit feeding is the sight (or sound) of conspecifics feeding.

2. A demonstration of true observational learning requires, at the least, that the observer would have been unlikely to respond the way he does, had he not learned something relatively specific from observing the model. But even where this condition is satisfied, it is not always easy to show just what it is that the observer has learned. An untrained rat may observe a trained rat pressing a lever and obtaining food, and may then show an increased tendency to press the lever itself when given the opportunity. But it is possible that all the observer has learned is that some parts of the apparatus are more interesting than others.

There are, fortunately, studies which have established more precise conclusions than this. In one (Darby and Riopelle 1959), two monkeys took it in turns to act as observer and demonstrator in solving a series of two-choice discrimination problems. The observer would watch the other monkey receive a single trial on which he was given the opportunity to choose between two novel objects, one of which was "correct" (i.e. choice of it was rewarded with food) and the other incorrect. On the next trial the observer was allowed to choose between the same pair of objects, and was rewarded for choice of the correct object. The role of demonstrator and observer changed for the next problem, when two new objects were presented. The demonstrator, being confronted with two entirely novel objects, had no way of knowing which was correct and chose at random. But the observer, when it came to his turn, showed that he had benefited from watching the demonstrator's trial, and scored well above chance.

This experiment provides clear evidence of observational learning. But it is important to notice that the observer was not simply imitating the demonstrator's actions. If he had been, he would have copied the demonstrator's choice even when it was wrong. In fact, the observer was rather *more* likely to choose correctly when the demonstrator had been wrong than when he had, by chance, been right. So here is a case where the observer is learning something about the consequences of another animal's actions, but does not necessarily choose to imitate those actions.

3. True imitation requires the observer to copy the demonstrator's or model's actions – perhaps even regardless of the consequences of those actions. This last condition is not easily satisfied in animal studies, but there are experiments establishing imitation of a model's actions. Dawson and Foss (1965) trained several demonstrator budgerigars to obtain food from a covered receptacle; one learned, for example, by tearing the cover off with its beak, another by clawing it off with one foot. Observers were permitted to watch one of these demonstrators in action, and, when presented with the covered box themselves, obtained food in the same way (either with beak or with claw) as the particular demonstrator they had watched. They were clearly imitating a particular action, rather than learning that food was to be found in the box.

There is thus good analytic evidence from experimental studies of imitation and observational learning in a variety of animals. More naturalistic studies suggest that this is indeed an important form of learning. Young birds of many species learn to sing their species typical song by being exposed to it at an early age: in the absence of exposure at a critical period, a normal repertoire of song may fail to develop (Hinde 1969), but under normal circumstances the year-old bird will start singing the song it was exposed to during the critical period. A celebrated example of imitation is provided by the behavior of a troop of Japanese monkeys who, although living in the wild, obtained much of their food from scientists who lured them out into the open, the better to study their behavior, by leaving piles of sweet potatoes and wheat on the sea shore (Tsumori 1967). Although the monkeys were happy to eat these provisions they had to put up with sand in their food until one enterprising juvenile female discovered that sand could be washed off sweet potatoes by rubbing them in the hands under water, and that if a handful of wheat plus sand were thrown into a pool of water, the sand would sink leaving the wheat floating on the surface. In due course these novel solutions spread through the entire troop, and since it was the family and immediate companions of the original inventor who first started copying her and the conservative adult males who were the last to acquire the new practice, one may be reasonably confident that this was a case of imitation or observational learning rather than an independent series of chance discoveries.

That other primates should show good evidence of such learning is hardly surprising, for even the most casual observation suggests that young children learn a great deal by observing their parents or other children or by watching television. A baby's first sounds may be produced spontaneously, without regard to what it hears (for totally deaf infants start babbling normally), but very soon the developing child starts copying the sounds it hears. Bandura (1977) has undertaken an extensive experimental analysis of observational learning and imitation in young children. Here again, it is important to distinguish between the two concepts: the tendency of a child to copy or imitate the actions of a model depend on a variety of factors – including for example the perceived consequences of those actions for the model – and for the child if it does copy them. Failure of imitation certainly does not imply failure to have learned, by observation, what the model was doing. If children watch a model acting aggressively, for example, their tendency to copy such actions will depend on whether the model was rewarded or punished for his actions. But if the observing children are then offered incentives to repeat the model's actions, those who saw the model being punished are as capable of copying his actions as those who saw him being rewarded. Unwillingness to imitate an action is not necessarily due to having failed to observe what the action was. NJM

Bibliography

Bandura, A. 1977: *Social learning theory*. Englewood Cliffs, N.J.: Prentice-Hall.

Darby, C.L. and Riopelle, A.J. 1959: Observational learning in the rhesus monkey. *Journal of comparative and physiological psychology* 52, 94–8.

Dawson, B.V. and Foss, B.M. 1965: Observational learning in budgerigars. *Animal behaviour* 13, 470–4.

Hinde, R.A. 1969: *Bird vocalizations*. Cambridge: Cambridge University Press.

Thorndike, E.L. 1911: *Animal intelligence*. New York: Macmillan.

Tsumori, A. 1967: Newly acquired behavior and social interactions of Japanese monkeys. In *Social communication among primates*, ed. S.A. Altmann. Chicago: University of Chicago Press.

Turner, E.R.A. 1965: Social feeding in birds. *Behaviour* 24, 1–46.

immediate constituent analysis (I-C analysis) A method of utterance segmentation developed in structuralist linguistics. Its point of departure is the fact that native speakers of a language hear an utterance not as a linear string of words or morphemes but in terms of successive components consisting of groups of words, contiguous or discontiguous, and of single words.

In I-C analysis the constituents of a construction are determined, beginning with the largest unit (typically a sentence) and ending with the smallest unit (words or morphemes). The best known notational device of I-C analysis is the tree diagram. Using this device, the sentence *The dog bites the postman* is analysed as follows:

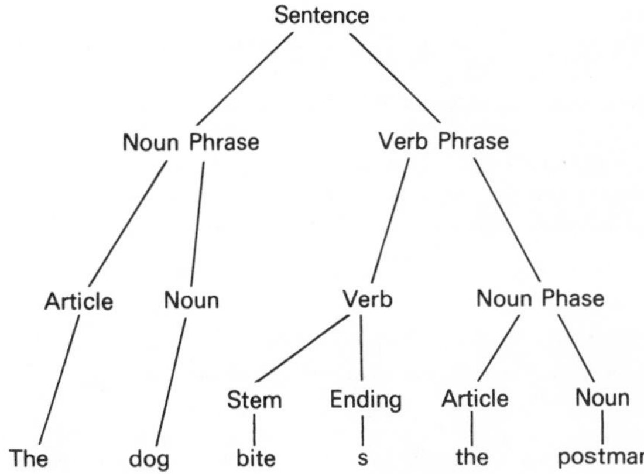

In the above example, article and noun are immediate constituents of the noun phrase, verb and noun phrase are immediate constituents of the verb phrase, and so on. It remains unclear to what extent I-C analysis reflects what a naive native speaker knows about his or her language. PM

implicit personality theory A term used to describe naive observers' assumptions about the co-occurrence of personality traits. Studies in impression formation, stimulated by the pioneering work of Asch (1946), have shown that people often assume personality traits to be present or absent in a person on the basis of limited information about only a few traits. Multivariate analysis of these assumptions (factor analysis, cluster analysis) shows that people use only a few judgmental dimensions in forming impressions of others. Rosenberg and Sedlak (1972) showed how such analyses can reveal a writer's implicit notions about human personality.

In Kelly's PERSONAL CONSTRUCT THEORY this idea has been developed and elaborated into a cognitive personality theory and an instrument for clinical diagnosis and research.

Recent reseatch in person perception has been influenced by Rosch's work on natural categories. Mervis and Rosch (1981) have suggested that prototypes and basic categories in Rosch's sense play an important role in the development and use of a person's implicit personality theory. JMFJ

Bibliography

Asch, S.E. 1946: Forming impressions of personality. *Journal of abnormal and social psychology* 41, 259–90.

Mervis, C.B. and Rosch, E. 1981: Categorization of natural objects. *Annual review of psychology* 32, 89–117.

Rosenberg, S. and Sedlak, A. 1972: Structural representations of implicit personality theory. In *Advances in experimental social psychology* Vol 6, ed. L. Berkowitz. New York: Academic Press.

impression This term is used by Hume to denote what Locke called an idea of sense (Hume 1738). He rejected the commonly used term "idea" because in colloquial use in the seventeenth and eighteenth centuries an idea was always a picture or representation, and Hume did not wish to be committed to a representative theory of perception. But the term "impression" does suggest some causal theory and Hume refers cautiously to "the unknown causes" of impressions, though he disclaims such implications for the term. Like "idea", "impression" could be used to refer to mental states such as pleasant feelings as well as to the objects of outer sense. The term "sense-impression" is still sometimes used in twentieth century philosophy. See also IDEA. JOU

Bibliography

Hume, D. 1738: *A treatise of human nature.* Bk I, pt I, sect. I.

imprinting Originally the name given to the process by which a young animal forms a lasting attachment to and preference for some object, usually its parent. The concept has now been extended to encompass many kinds of preference. It was first studied in detail by Lorenz (1935) who discovered that young presocial birds, which are active and leave the nest shortly after hatching, would treat almost any conspicuous moving object as they normally treat their mother. Imprinting objects have ranged from a matchbox to a large canvas hide and many inappropriate living objects, including people. Indeed, the sight of a gaggle of goslings following the youthful Lorenz is one of the seminal images of ethology.

Two types of imprinting were distinguished in the early days, filial imprinting, for the attachment of young bird to parent, and sexual imprinting, for the more broadly based attachment to the species of the imprinting object, later used as the basis for selection of a mating partner. Lorenz used the word *prägung* to denote the rapidity and irreversibility of the process, likening it to die-stamping. He noted properties of imprinting that seemed to set it apart from other forms of behavior: it took place only during a brief critical period early in the life of the organism; its effects were irreversible, and might be manifested only after a long delay. Each of these has been investigated in some detail, but the modern consensus is that imprinting is not a unique process but is a form of perceptual learning.

The critical period can be demonstrated by exposing chicks of various ages to an imprinting object for a brief period and measuring their preference for that object some time later. Ramsay and Hess (1954), using mallard ducklings (*Anas platyrhynchos*), found a very sharp peak of imprintability about fifteen hours after hatching. Boyd and Fabricius (1965) exposed ducklings to a moving object at different ages and found a gradual decline in the readiness of the bird to follow the model over the first ten days of life. The criticality of Lorenz's critical period thus depends on exactly how it is measured. Nevertheless it is clear that imprinting takes place very much more readily at certain times than at others and indeed may be impossible outside the limits of a sensitive, rather than a critical, period.

The factors that control the timing of the sensitive period are poorly understood (see Bateson 1979). It seems to begin as soon as the neuro-muscular coordination of the bird is sufficiently advanced to permit it to follow a moving object, although following per se is not necessary for the bird to imprint. Developmental age and time since hatching both play a part in the onset of the sensitive period. The end of the period is more of a problem. Young birds do not avoid novel objects, but as they mature they begin to respond to novelty with fear and flight, and this prevents approach and imprinting. The very process of imprinting, forming an attachment to some object in the environment, may bring sensitivity to an end. Birds reared without an imprinting stimulus in an impoverished environment remain sensitive longer than birds raised in social groups. And if a bird is imprinted very early in the sensitive period it becomes difficult to imprint it on another object even within the normal sensitive period.

The irreversibility of imprinting has also come under scrutiny. Lorenz took this to mean that an attachment, once formed, could not be transferred to a different object, probably because the critical period had passed, but imprinting is normally self-limiting in that the attachment formed serves to prevent the bird from coming into close and prolonged contact with another object to which its attachment could be transferred. The experimental evidence is confusing. Filial imprinting can be reversed if the young bird is confined with a novel stimulus and prevented from fleeing. Sexual imprinting seems more permanent, but is less absolute. Turkeys (*Meleagris gallopavo*) imprinted on humans will court turkeys, but given a choice between a turkey and a person they prefer the person. The same is true for zebra finch (*Taenopygia guttata*) males cross-fostered by Bengalese finches (*Lonchura striata*); they will court female zebra finches if forced to, but given a choice prefer the unreceptive and uncooperative Bengalese finch female to the encouraging zebra finch. It appears that there is a bias to imprint upon members of the same species, but that experience of a different species will lead to a permanent preference for that species as a mating partner.

The long delay between learning and performance apparently sets sexual imprinting apart from other forms of discrimination, although song learning in birds can also include a delay of similar length. A year or more may elapse between exposure to an imprinting stimulus and subsequent selection of that stimulus as a partner for reproduction.

Imprinting occupies a curious place in the pantheon of learning. No reward is needed to obtain the response, although in the natural world the mother is a source of heat, food, and protection. The response itself is not necessary for the discriminative ability to be learned. Once an animal has formed an attachment to an object, that object can be used as a reinforcer to modify behavior. Chicks and ducklings will perform an operant behavior to present themselves with the object they are imprinted on. The process of imprinting itself also acts as a reinforcer. Bateson placed naive chicks in a modified Skinner box, where the weight of the chick on a pedal switched on an imprinting stimulus. Even before the chick had formed an attachment to the stimulus or learned its characteristics it would stand on the pedal and make the stimulus appear. Chicks will also work to present themselves with novel views of the imprinting object, and as they learn more about the stimulus so the amount of discrepancy they will work for decreases. The young animal thus plays an active role in becoming imprinted; it seeks out objects on which to imprint, and its preference for slight novelty during imprinting has been interpreted as a mechanism to ensure that it sees, and learns about, all visual aspects of the parent. Different views – front, back, side and so on – are then integrated to form a perceptual model of the parent.

The ease with which birds can be imprinted and the strength of their learning measured (as a preference for one object over another) have made imprinting a key part in studies of the biochemistry of learning. Horn and his colleagues have shown that there are specific biochemical changes in localized areas of the brain, notably the hyperstriatum ventrale, and that these changes are consequent upon the specific experience of imprinting. Destruction of these areas after exposure to an imprinting stimulus prevents the bird from showing any preference.

The biological functions of imprinting must be considered separately for filial and sexual imprinting. Filial imprinting serves to identify the parent and keep the young close to it. In this way the young learn about food and shelter and gain protection against predators. Sexual imprinting is more problematical. It seems to provide the animal with a model for the sexual partner; in monomorphic animals, where both sexes have similar coloration, both imprint, but in dimorphic species it is often only the male that shows sexual imprinting. Once thought to identify the species for the animal, sexual imprinting is now thought to proscribe certain members of the species. Bateson has shown that quail avoid as sexual partners the animals they were raised with, while nevertheless preferring that type over others. Brown quail raised with albinos avoid the albinos they were raised with but prefer novel albinos over novel brown quail. Bateson interprets this in terms of 'optimal outbreeding', and argues that sexual imprinting provides a mechanism whereby animals can avoid incest, as the imprinting objects will generally be close kin. A similar phenomenon has been observed among children of the kibbutz: those raised together never marry.

Imprinting has also been applied to other phenomena in which a lasting preference is formed relatively quickly. Thus a mother (human and goat) is said to imprint upon her young shortly after birth, young animals to imprint upon the odor of their nest and the flavor of the mother's milk, and so on. JJC

Bibliography

Bateson, P.P.G. 1966: The characteristics and context of imprinting. *Biological reviews* 41, 177–220.

Boyd, H. and Fabricius. 1965: Observations on the incidence of following of visual and auditory stimuli in naive mallard ducklings (*Anas platyrhynchos*). *Behavior* 25, 1–15.

——— 1979: How do sensitive periods arise and what are they for? *Animal Behaviour* 27, 470–86.

——— 1981: Optimal outbreeding and the development of sexual preferences in Japanese quail, *Zeitschrift für Tierpsychologie* 53, 231–44.

——— 1982: Preferences for cousins in Japanese quail. *Nature* 295, 236–37.

Hinde, Robert A. 1982: *Ethology*. London: Fontana; New York and Oxford: Oxford University Press (hard cover).

Horn, G. 1981: Neural mechanisms of learning: an analysis of imprinting in the domestic chick. *Proceedings of the Royal Society of London (Series B)* 213, 101–37.

Lorenz, Konrad 1935: Der Kumpan in der Umwelt des Vogels. Reprinted as: Companions as factors in the bird's environment, in K.Z. Lorenz *Studies on animal and human behaviour*. London: Methuen; Cambridge, Mass: Harvard University Press.

Ramsay, A.O. and Hess, E.H. 1954: A laboratory approach to the study of imprinting. *Wilson bulletin* 66, 196–206.

incentive An aspect of motivation that results from expectation of reward or punishment. The concept was first introduced into behavior theory by Hull (1931) and it has since developed into a variety of formulations (Bolles 1975). Basically, incentive is a learned form of motivation in which certain external stimuli acquire motivating properties because the animal associates them with reinforcement. If a rat is rewarded with food for pressing a bar (see operant behavior) presentation of the bar on a future occasion may increase the animal's motivation to obtain food. On the other hand if the rat receives an electric shock for pressing the bar subsequent presentation of the bar will probably have a negative incentive effect. Similar effects are observed in humans. DJM

Bibliography

Bolles, Robert C. 1975: *Theory of motivation*. 2nd edn New York and London: Harper & Row.

Hull, C.L. 1931: Goal attraction and directing ideas conceived as habit phenomena. *Psychology review* 38, 487–506.

incentives/rewards Incentives are something of potential value (see VALUES), an offered or available reward whose function is to motivate an individual to take a specific course of action. Rewards are something of actual value, given in payment for some action or achievement. The fundamental incentive and reward offered in employment settings is money, since money is instrumental in fulfilling many values and needs (not just so called lower order needs as is commonly believed; see WORK MOTIVATION). Other commonly used occupational incentives and rewards are: achievement (resulting from achieving goals or success in some endeavor); credit and recognition (praise); increased responsibility; time off; and promotion (which combines increased pay and responsibility with a new job title). Rewards are mostly likely to be tied to actual work performance in private, profit-making organizations where there is a strong incentive for objective performance appraisal and where the ultimate success of the organization can be clearly measured. EAL

indeterminacy of translation *See* translation, indeterminacy of

indeterminism Has had two different senses. What we might call psychological indeterminism is the view that some acts of the mind are not the inevitable outcome of causal laws, but are spontaneous. Indeterminism in this sense is substantially identical with free will. Descartes was famous for his indeterminism, holding for example that the will is never constrained to assent or dissent by evidence: no matter how overwhelming the evidence may be in favor of a proposition, still the will is free to dissent from it. Indeterminism in another sense refers only to the physical world: it is the view that not all physical happenings are the inevitable outcome of physical causal laws. Indeterminism in this sense has been taken not as identical with free will, but as its precondition, by those who think the mind to be governed by the workings of the brain. The first to hold this view was Epicurus, who taught that the mind was material, but allowed for its freedom by postulating the occasional uncaused "swerve" of mind atoms. The view has had a renaissance in recent times in the work of Popper and Eccles, among others. See also MIND–BODY PROBLEM, DETERMINISM, FREE WILL. JT

Bibliography

Descartes, René (*1897–1910*): Les principes de la philosphie, Part I, sect. 32–9. In *Oeuvres de Descartes*, ed. Ch. Adam and P. Tannery, vol. viii.

Prior, A.N. 1962: Limited indeterminism. *Review of metaphysics* 16, 55–61.

Popper, Sir Karl and Eccles, Sir John 1977: *The self and its brain*. Berlin and New York: Springer International.

indexical expressions A term used by philosophers and social scientists in referring to expressions, statements or utterances which can only be understood with reference to the context in which they occur. The most obvious examples are words such as "here", "there", "now", "then", "me", "my", "you", etc. But there is a wider sense in which almost any expression whatever can be regarded as indexical. This latter view has been important in the development of ethnomethodology, and a useful discussion of its implications for social scientific research is to be found in Garfinkel (1967, pp.4–7).

One of Garfinkel's main points is that a conceptual distinction between "objective" and "indexical" expressions has been central to most debates about scientific method. Sciences can be viewed as involving determined attempts to transcend or avoid the problems of ambiguity, vagueness, imprecision, subjectivity, etc. that are associated with the use of indexical expressions. Scientific method can thus be conceived as a set of procedures or methods which facilitate the substitution of "objective" expressions for "indexical" ones. But there is no perfect or absolute way of accomplishing this in practice, which means that scientists have to rely on a range of *ad hoc* procedures which enable the substitution to be effected "for all practical purposes". Such methods or practices, however, tend to be largely taken for granted, and have seldom been fully explicated. One of the aims of ethnomethodological inquiries, then, is to identify what these practices are and to describe how they work.

Substituting objective for indexical expressions is not a process which is exclusively confined to the work of scientists. Indexical expressions are encountered by everyone in the course of everyday life. And, while any and every expression they come across may "in principle" be open to a multiplicity of possible interpretations, making sense of any particular expression depends in practice on people making decisions as to which interpretation is to be treated as the "objectively" correct one for the practical purposes at hand, and in the light of what they know about the context in which it occurs, the course of the interaction thus far, the identity, biography and intentions of their co-interactant, etc. In other words, the process of achieving mutual understanding in the course of everyday interaction can itself be viewed as involving participants in repeatedly substituting objective for indexical expressions. And, in so far as the methods of interpretation used to accomplish this are, like those used in the production of scientific interpretation, largely taken for granted, they too are regarded as part of the subject matter for ethnomethodological investigations. See also ETHNOMETHODOLOGY; TACIT KNOWLEDGE. JMA

Bibliography

Garfinkel, Harold 1967: *Studies in ethnomethodology*. Englewood Cliffs, N.J.: Prentice Hall.

indigenous psychology The study of man as he conceives himself in terms of his collective representations. The term "indigenous" emphasizes cultural views, theories, conjectures, assumptions and metaphors; draws attention to what is generally available (see SOCIAL REPRESENTATION) to man in his attempts to make sense of and organize his psychological life. On occasion, however, psychologies developed by means of experimental, philosophical and religious inquiry percolate through to the indigenous level.

Among other things, the term "psychology" refers to the manner in which the individual or person is conceptualized, the divisions made within the individual, the powers attributed to the self, the location of controlling agencies (internalized or externalized), the way in which action is conceived, the way in which emotions are classified and evaluated, the properties attributed to dreams, episodes of mental abnormality or unusual states of consciousness, and to the nature of personality judgments.

The United States has recently been described as "the Psychological Society" (Gross 1978). Psychobabble is rife (a nice example is the psychoanalytically oriented dentist who told the *New York Times* that the mouth, "acts as a barometer of the personality set of the individual"). Americans use psychology in the course of many daily activities: the salesman who has been taught the value of positive thinking (see EST); those who practice the advice contained in books such as *Baby and child care* and *Understanding your dog*. And Americans turn to psychology when they seek explanations of, and responses to, suffering. It is estimated that over seven million receive psychological intervention annually. Tending to assume that suffering is unnatural, the "healthy" but distressed person seeks a cure. Tending also to abnegate self-control and responsibility (on the grounds that the unconscious largely controls what people do and feel), Americans turn to specialists for what used to be called salvation (see PRIMAL THERAPY).

The tendency in American culture is away from Riesman's "other directed" man (receiving life cues from outside sources) towards psychologically inspired man. But not only do indigenous psychologies change with time – they also show marked cross-cultural variation. Although there are no societies in which the psychological is not acknowledged at all a number use allegorical or surrogate ways of talking about the individual, thereby muting comprehension of the autonomous self. The issue here is one of differences in the locus of the psychological (including LOCUS OF CONTROL). We think in terms of our being informed from within, of being able to act on the world, of exercising our will-power and self-control. And our apprehension of ourselves as autonomous beings is encapsulated in the notion "mind": "*I* make up *my* mind"; "*I* put *my* mind to it". The Dinka of the southern Sudan, however,

> have no conception which at all closely corresponds to our popular modern conception of the "mind" as mediating and, as it were, storing up the experiences of the self. There is for them no such interior entity to appear, on reflection, to stand between the experiencing self at any given moment and what is or has been an exterior influence upon the self (Lienhardt 1961–149).

In contrast to the western view, the Dinka individual is the object, and the external world (specifically religious "powers") provide the locus of controlling "mentalistic" agencies. Dinka speak of "memories" being activated by powers, not by the self, as when we say, "I recall to mind the time that . . ."

Despite the pioneering work of Tylor, Lévy-Bruhl and others, the anthropological study of indigenous psychologies is not far advanced. But together with the contributions of cultural historians (going back to Burckhardt and Nietzsche), scholars of English literature, Sinologists, classicists (e.g. Snell 1953), social psychologists (e.g. Wegner and Vallacher 1977), and so on, there is material enough to show that there is remarkably little consistency in the manner in which man's psychological attributes have been envisaged across cultures and through time (see Heelas and Lock 1981 for ethnographic illustrations; see also HEBRAIC PSYCHOLOGY, EARLY CHRISTIAN PSYCHOLOGY). But why should psychologists be interested in indigenous psychologies?

At first sight it appears that psychologists have as little reason to attend to the indigenous as astronomers have to take astrology seriously. Indigenous notions generally appear to be culturally contingent, present contradictory claims in any given culture (let alone cross-culturally), and often take a curious if not "erroneous" form (emotions located in the liver, as the Chewong of Malaysia maintain? (see Howell 1981)). Why should psychologists use such suspect evidence to map the psychological when they can use experimental and quantifiable techniques to explore the psychological as it "really" is?

On looking again however, one sees that psychologists are not in the position of astronomers, studying objects which exist and function independently of how they are conceived. In Hampshire's words, "The nature of the human mind has to be investigated in the history of the successive forms of its social expression" (1959, p.234). The psychological culture in which people are raised has a profoundly *constitutive* impact on their psychological performance. At the present time it is not possible exactly to demarcate the extent of constitutive processes, or the extent to which psychological phenomena operate and exist independently of how they might be conceptualized. There does however appear to be a spectrum – between the exogenous (culture dependent) and the endogenous (culture independent) – in terms of which the psychological significance of indigenous psychologies can be assessed.

At one extreme lies, for example, motivation. Rosaldo's aim in *Knowledge and passion* (1980) is to interpret Ilongot (northern Luzon) activities "from the point of view of self-conceptions – accounts of how and why to act – that must inform the social lives of actors" (p.61). Ilongot headhunting, she argues, is explicable in terms of Ilongot psychological notions, not their religious beliefs: "Not gods, but 'heavy' feelings were what made men want to kill; in taking heads they could aspire to 'cast off' an 'anger' that 'weighed down on' and oppressed their saddened 'hearts'."(p.19). Social psychological and anthropological concerns meet when what is under examination is the role of what Hallowell calls the "behavioural environment" (1971, p.87) in sustaining the individual as a social being.

At the other extreme lie psychological processes (such as memory and perception) which largely operate independently of folk "theories". In between the exogenous and endogenous lies more debatable territory. Different theorists of emotions, for example, attach varying degrees of importance to cultural factors. But although there has been something of a shift back to endogenous theories, those who advocate such a shift of emphasis have not generally gone so far as to deny a role to the exogenous component of the cultural appraisal of "emotional" arousal. Given this role, a psychological account of the emotions as they are organized and managed in any particular culture must include consideration of how the emotions are regarded: whether, for example, as with the Chewong, display of most "emotions", including anger and joy, are associated with fear inducing images – this plausibly indicating that "anger" is colored by "fear" to the extent that participants do not live with the same emotional repertoire as we in the west (see Howell 1981).

It is apparent that the more social the psychologist, and the more "anthropomorphic" the psychologist's model, the greater the attention that should be paid to what is most explicitly anthropomorphic: that is, how man envisages himself. However, indigenous psychologies do not provide comprehensive and automatically reliable paths to psychological nature. Indigenous formulations might be adventitious (see Needham's (1972) argument that "belief" does not describe a universal psychological phenomenon or might well not acknowledge what is actually occurring).

Indigenous psychological notions are of greatest interest to the psychologist when they bear on phenomena which appear to be under the influence of sociocultural constitutive processes. Even apparently "erroneous" beliefs here have psychological validity: Dinka psychological thought presumably would have to be taken into account if an attribution theorist were to research in that culture (see O'Hare and Duck 1981), and Chewong thought by emotion theorists who were studying the Chewong. Freudian theory might be no more scientific than astrology, but like astrology, only to a greater extent, it is psychologically significant. PLFH

Bibliography

Gross, M. 1978: *The psychological society*. New York: Simon and Schuster.

*Hallowell, A. 1971: *Culture and experience*. New York: Schocken Books.

Hampshire, S. 1959: *Thought and action*. London: Chatto & Windus.

*Heelas, P. and Lock, A., eds. 1981: *Indigenous psychologies*. London and New York: Academic Press.

Howell, S. 1981: Rules not words. In *Indigenous psychologies*, ed. P. Heelas and A. Lock. London and New York: Academic Press.

Lienhardt, G. 1961: *Divinity and experience*. Oxford: Clarendon Press.

*Needham, R. 1972: *Belief, language and experience*. Oxford: Basil Blackwell; Chicago: University of Chicago Press.

O'Hare, D. and Duck, S. 1981: Implicit psychology and ordinary explanation. In Heelas and Lock op cit.

Rosaldo, M. 1980: *Knowledge and passion*. Cambridge and New York: Cambridge University Press.

Snell, B. 1953: *The discovery of the mind*. Oxford: Oxford University Press.

Wegner, D. and Vallacher, R. 1977: *Implicit psychology*. New York: Oxford University Press.

individual psychology: history of The obsolete name differential psychology, was used by several founders of the field (Münsterberg 1891; Oehrn 1895; Binet and Henri 1896; Kraepelin 1896). In his systematic presentation of the methodological foundations of the new discipline, Stern (1911) rejected the term, arguing that, as "individual psychology" referred to all aspects of the psychological life of the individual, including also the general psychology of human beings, according to its already established meaning, it should be contrasted with social psychology and ethnopsychology. Besides, differential psychology also having as its object the investigation of differences between groups, he considered its older designation to be completely inadequate. On the other hand the reduction of individual persons to mere carriers of interindividual differences was incompatible with W. Stern's personalistic philosophy (1911). Therefore, individuals conceived as relatively self-contained entities were incorporated in his differential psychology as the converse of the distribution of one or more characteristics over a group of individuals. In other words, according to W. Stern, one of the basic data of differential psychology was constituted by a matrix of m characteristics exhibited by n individuals, so that one could concentrate either on the distributions and the correlations of the characteristics or on one or more individuals in whom they jointly occurred. In the latter case, the investigation of a large number of traits manifested by one individual and the analysis of their internal relationships would lead to a psychography, a term first used by Baade (1908) (cf. also Ostwald 1909), whereas it would be the task of a *Komparationslehre* to examine in how far and under what aspects two or more individuals resemble each other. Still, W. Stern must have felt that he hadn't done full justice to the individual person for he added that, in order to bridge the gap between the nomothetic and the idiographic approach, the individualizing function of psychographies had to be supplemented by biographies. In his view the basic presupposition of biography is the unity of personality whereas psychography takes as its starting point a multiplicity of traits so that both are complementary to each other.

About half a century earlier than W. Stern's decisive contribution, J.S. Mill (1851) had put forward the idea that character which had been left out of the picture by association psychology should become the object of a new science: Ethology. For similar reasons, Samuel Bailey (1858) insisted on the necessity of developing a new discipline of individual and personal character which he conceived as separate and distinct from psychology. On the continent, J. Bahnsen's plea for a characterology (1867) lead to the development of typologies or theories of characterology such as the one championed by L. Klages as the basis of his system of graphology. Most of them remained separated from psychology, or as was the case with L. Klages, were openly hostile to it. Wundt on the other hand suggested the creation of "a practical psychology namely a characterology, which should investigate the basic and typical forms of individual character with the aid of principles derived from a general theoretical psychology". Other authors who were also acutely conscious of the inability of the psychology of their times to deal with the problem of human individuality pleaded for a science of personality but unfortunately limited their efforts to the coining of new names. Mercier (1911) thought that the new discipline should be called "praxiology" whereas J.C. Smuts (1926) suggested the term "personology" which was later adopted by H.A. Murray (1938).

However all these new scientific programs remained sterile for their proponents had not clearly spelled out the far reaching consequences these programs implied. Indeed, in order to realize their objectives nothing less was required than a redefinition of the object of psychology, and the development of new methods of investigation – tasks which they were neither prepared nor willing to undertake. Because he attempted all of them, W. Stern achieved a major break-through for individual psychology.

At about the time W. Stern published his second book on differential psychology (1911) A. Adler who had just broken with Freud developed his own theory which he called individual psychology in order to emphasize his conception of the individual as a unified totality. Years later, in 1930, Adler summarized his basic theory thus: "The fundamental fact in human development is the dynamic and purposive striving of the psyche . . . The unity of personality is implicit in each human being's existence. Every individual represents both a unity of personality and the individual fashioning of that unity."

When through G.W. Allport's and H.A. Murray's contributions personality psychology had achieved academic status, Adler's theory was already so well known that it had monopolized the appellation of "individual psychology." Consequently various research orientations, clinical and assessment activities which in fact belonged to the field of individual psychology, received other names (case-study; personology; life-history approach; etc.) and the terminological diaspora which ensued prevented the clear delimitation of a specific domain.

The virtual disappearance of personality psychology during the period extending from the end of the 1950s up to the late '70s eliminated individual psychology almost completely from the field of current concerns. As R. Carlson noted in an important review of 226 articles published in the 1968 volumes of two major journals publishing research on personality: "Although the literature as a whole has elicited a wide range of potentially important informations about persons, no single investigation either noted or utilized much information about any individual subject. Thus the task performances of subjects in current research remain uninterpretable as personality data in the absence of anchoring information."

And further: "Not a single published study attempted even minimal inquiry into the organization of personality variables within the individual."

One of Carlson's major conclusions, was that the goal of studying whole persons had apparently been abandoned. This diagnosis is fully confirmed by the number of individual case-studies referred to in *Psychological abstracts* from 1960 to 1978. During this period only about 1 per cent of published articles were devoted to the investigation of single persons and no trend whatsoever that could be considered symptomatic of the existence of individual psychology as a specific field was noted. The variety of the studies was so great that Shontz's classification of case-studies (1965) could not be applied. Instead, a new two-dimensional classification emerged based on: (i) the kind of individuals it examined; and (ii) the goals pursued by the investigators proved to cover the field more adequately. Among the individuals studied, the following groups could be distinguished:

(a) Problematic persons who are the source of assessment or taxonomic problems (e.g. individuals whose personality is difficult to conceptualize within current frame-works, historical personalities, or the author of the article himself).
(b) Well known individuals posing no diagnostic problems.
(c) Groups of individuals (families, siblings) considered as a unit.

As to the goals of individual case-studies, six groups emerged:

(a) Assessment of an individual's personality and formulation of explanatory hypotheses susceptible to generalization.
(b) Detailed investigation of specific psychological processes.
(c) Illustration of a theory, a technique, a particular kind of therapy or of an interesting or rare case.
(d) Explorative studies.
(e) Theory testing either by confirmatory cases or by falsifying instances.
(f) Biographies and life-histories.

A few clear-cut conclusions can be drawn from the distribution of observed frequencies. First of all the major category of studies is constituted by the illustration of various techniques of behavior-therapy applied to known cases. On the other hand biographies and studies in which the investigation of a single person is regarded as a goal in itself are extremely scarce. Correspondingly, case-studies are concentrated in the field of clinical psychology whereas they are conspicuously absent in personality psychology. As to the methods used, they consist predominantly of tests and QUESTIONNAIRES. It is also interesting to note that, with the exception of the increase of publications devoted to behavior-therapy, no differences can be observed between the decade preceeding and the seven years following R. Carlson's important paper. In the absence of any explicit and scientifically founded justification of this state of affairs, the evolution of individual psychology is obviously in great need of scrutiny by historians and sociologists of science.

J-PDeW

Bibliography

Baade, W. 1908: Psychographische Darstellungen über normal begabter Individuen. *Zeitschrift für angewangte Psychologie*. 1, 274–7.

Bahnsen, J.F.A. 1867: *Beiträge zur Charakterologie*. Leipzig: F.A. Brockhaus.

Bailey, Samuel 1858: *Letters on the philosophy of the human mind*. 2nd series. London: Longmans, Green.

Binet, A. and Henri, V. 1896: La Psychologie individuelle. *Année psychologique*. 2, 411–65.

Kraepelin, E. 1896: Der Psychologische Versuch in der Psychiatrie. *Psychologische arbeiten*. 1, 1–91.

Mercier, C. 1911: *Conduct and its disorders*. London: Macmillan.

Mill, J.S. 1851: *System of logic*. Vol. II. London: J.W. Parker.

Münsterberg, H. 1891: Zur Individual Psychologie. *Zentual blatt für Nervenheilkunde und Psychiatrie*. 14, 196–8.

Murray, H.A. et al. 1938: *Explorations in personality*. New York: Oxford University Press.

Oehrn, A. 1895: Experimentelle Studiën zur Individual Psychologie. Diss. Dorpat, *Psychologische Arbeiten*. 1, 95–152.

Ostwald, W. 1909: *Grosse Männer*. Leipzig: Akademische Verlagsgesellschaft.

Shontz, F.C. 1965: *Research methods in personality*. Century Psychology Series; New York: Appleton-Century-Crofts.

Smuts, J.C. 1926: *Holism and evolution*. New York: Macmillan.

Stern, W. 1911: *Die Differentielle Psychologie*. Leipzig: J.A. Barth.

individual psychology: methodology Personality means a person considered in its uniqueness, as a singular entity. Since PERSONOLOGY investigates the general aspects of individual persons, its mode of approach is nomothetic. However, individual psychology is also interested in personalities and should therefore also proceed idiographically The question which must now be elucidated is how the exact relationship between nomothesis and idiography can be defined and more precisely whether a specific idiographic domain exists and, if so, how it is to be characterized. Du Mas (1955) whose important contribution has not received all the attention it merits, proposes that we should regard nomothesis as that method of science which studies data obtained from more than one individual, whereas idiography makes use of data yielded by one individual. A second assumption is that the basic data of nomothetic as well as of idiographic sciences are observations. Let O denote an observation. According to a third assumption an observation is always made of an entity at a particular occasion. Using here interchangeably entity and individual, let individuals be denoted by 1, 2, 3, . . . i . . . N and let successive occasions be denoted by 1, 2, 3, . . . k . . . L. A fourth assumption which must be introduced is that an individual always has more than one property which will be denoted 1, 2, 3, . . . j . . . M. The illustration, which corresponds to Cattell's co-variation chart (*see* Cattell 1950) gives a graphic representation of these assumptions. It also represents all observations collected from every individual in a sample or a population. Thus an observation O (ijk) corresponds to a point at coordinates i, j and k. Group or population studies are made of observations obtained from vertical sections of the cube while single case studies are made of observations collected from horizontal sections of the same volume.

Let K denote that data are collected. Then the collection K(ojk) means that observations are made and recorded of the jth characteristic, at the kth time, on the individuals 1, 2 . . . N. An observation O(ijk) may be regarded as a point and a specifically defined group as a set or domain. Domain A is identical to domain a if A and a are the same set of points. Domain B contains domain A if the set of points in B includes the set of points of A and one or more additional points. Domain A is contained in domain B, if the set of points of A is included in the set of points of B and B has one or more additional points.

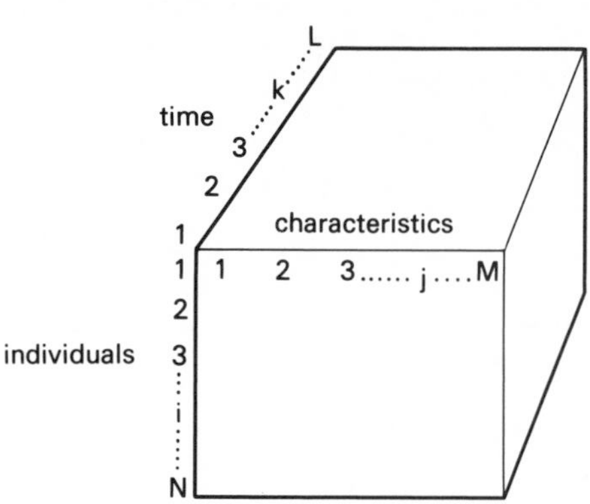

All possible domains of nomothesis ($n > 1$) and idiography ($n = 1$) can now be represented within the three-dimensional system that has been outlined. These domains are represented in the table together with some methods of data collection proper to each domain. In this way five nomothetic and five idiographic domains can be defined among which two are identical: A and a are identical as basic data and E is identical to e because both contain all the available information. Therefore the interesting comparisons to be made concern the domains B,b,C,c,D, and d. An examination of their relations of inclusion brings forth a few important conclusions:

(1) The three nomothetic domains B,C,D, are richer in information than the three corresponding idiographic domains. Indeed C can account for b and D for c, since b is included in C and c in D. It also looks as if there existed an asymmetry of inclusion between nomothesis and idiography favouring the nomothetic domains C and D. As the data collected in these domains contains information concerning single cases, it would apparently be true that from a nomothetic knowledge of a sample, information could be derived about single cases, whereas from an idiographic knowledge of single cases almost nothing can be inferred about the sample. But, the first part of this conclusion is wrong because in drawing it one overlooks the fact that the idiographic data are irreversibly included in the nomothetic domains. The treatments to which they are submitted by the methods corresponding to these domains only yield aggregate propositions (Bakan 1967) about collective properties characterizing the

	Nomothetic N > 1	Domains	*Idiographic* N = 1
	O_{ijk} Basic datum E.g. Rating of a characteristic	A a A identical to a both contained in all Nomothetic and Idiographic domains.	O_{ijk} Basic datum E.g. Rating of a characteristic
Individuals	$\overset{N}{\underset{i=1}{K}}(O_{ijk})$ E.g. Population distribution and parameters Scoring system { Contains domains A, a Contained in C, D, E, a }	B b	$\overset{L}{\underset{k=1}{K}}(O_{ijk})$ Occasions E.g.–Trends and change as a function of time –Reliability and individual variability { Contains domains A, a Contained in C, E, d, e }
Individuals and Time	$\overset{L}{\underset{k=1}{K}}\ \overset{N}{\underset{i=1}{K}}(O_{ijk})$ E.g.–Changes in population distribution and parameters due to time factors. Longitudinal Studies S factor-analysis (one test administered to N persons at different times. Correlations between persons) and T factor-analysis (one test administered to N persons at different occasions–correlations between occasions). { Contains A, B, a, b Contained in E, e }	C c	$\overset{M}{\underset{j=1}{K}}(O_{ijk})$ Characteristics E.g.–Configuration of ratings for a single individual. –Cross-sectional study of an individual. { Contains domains A, a Contained in domains D, E, d, e }
Characteristics and Individuals	$\overset{M}{\underset{j=1}{K}}\ \overset{N}{\underset{i=1}{K}}(O_{ijk})$ E.g.–Trait intercorrelations –Profiles, clusters, configurations –Cross-sectional studies of population –Q and R factor analyses. { Contains domains A, B, a, c Contained in E, e }	D d	$\overset{L}{\underset{k=1}{K}}\ \overset{M}{\underset{j=1}{K}}(O_{ijk})$ Characteristics and occasions E.g.–Changes in configurations as a function of time. –Intercorrelation of characteristics in a single individual, –O and P factor analyses. { Contains domains A, a, c Contained in E, e }
Characteristics and Individuals and Occasions	$\overset{L}{\underset{k=1}{K}}\ \overset{M}{\underset{j=1}{K}}\ \overset{N}{\underset{i=1}{K}}(O_{ijk})$ E.g.–Changes in profiles or configurations due to time factors –longitudinal studies of configurational changes in the population { Contains all nomothetic and idiographic domains except o identical to domain c. }	E e	$\overset{L}{\underset{k=1}{K}}\ \overset{M}{\underset{j=1}{K}}\ \overset{N}{\underset{i=1}{K}}(O_{ijk})$ Identical to domain E

group data but which are not applicable to the individuals composing the group. Therefore, once included, the individual data are lost, the methods used for analysing group data making it impossible to retrieve them.

(2) The question whether there exists a specific idiographic domain must be answered positively. Indeed while d contains A and a (the basic data) and is contained in E and e (the totality of the information available) it is not contained in any other domain. This specific idiographic domain is one in which several characteristics exhibited by one individual at identifiably different occasions are studied.

This conclusion bears out Windelband's intuition that idiography is the approach appropriate for the study of processes and the representation of concrete evolving entities. It also confirms and retrospectively justifies W. Stern's insistence on supplementing psychography by biography, since his two-dimensional scheme lacked a third dimension along which occasions could be ordered. Still, there is an aspect of the idiographic domain which escaped the attention of both these authors. Indeed, whereas the succession in time of the moments at which observations are gathered refers to the situations in which the observed phenomena take place, it is quite possible to compare a set of situations without taking into account the temporal order in which they occurred. Consequently, the definition of the idiographic domain must be rephrased in order to accommodate the two possibilities covered by the term "occasion". Accordingly the idiographic domain is one in which several characteristics manifested by one individual in identifiably different temporally ordered *or* unordered situations are studied. Biography is an example of idiographic investigation where consideration of the temporal order of situations is essential. On the other hand, a cross-sectional study of the ways an individual deals with the various situations confronting him, is an illustration of the second kind of idiographic approach. In both cases the objective is to discern patterns of consistency characterizing the individual person. J-PDeW

Bibliography

Allport, G.W. 1967: *Pattern and growth in personality*. New York: Holt, Rinehart & Winston.

——— 1972: The general and the unique in psychological science. *Journal of Personality*. 40, 1–16.

Bakan, D. 1969 *On method: toward a reconstruction of psychological investigation*. San Francisco: Jossey Bass.

Blanshard, B. 1965: *The nature of thought*, 2 vols.

Cattell, R.B. 1950: *Personality: a systematic theoretical and factual study*. New York: McGraw-Hill.

De Waele, J.P., and Harré, R. 1976: The personality of individuals. *In Personality*, ed. Rom Harré. Oxford: Basil Blackwell.

——— 1979: Autobiography as a psychological method. In *Emerging strategies in social psychological research*, ed. G.P. Ginsburg New York: Wiley.

Du Mas, F.M. 1955: Science and the single case. *Psychological reports* 1, 65–75.

Lamiell, J.T. 1981: Toward an idiothetic psychology of personality. *American psychologist*. 36, 276–89.

Levy, L. 1970: *Conceptions of personality: theories and research*. New York: Random House.

Shontz, F.C. 1965: *Research methods in personality*. Century Psychology Series. Appleton-Century-Crofts.

Smuts, J.C. 1926: *Holism and evolution*. New York: Macmillan.

Stern, W. 1906: *Person und Sache*. Leipzig: Barth.

——— 1919: *Die menschliche Persönlichkeit*. Leipzig: Barth.

——— 1911: *Die Differentielle Psychologie*. Leipzig: Barth.

Tyler, L.E. 1959: Toward a workable psychology of personality. *American psychologist*. 14, 75–81.

Tyler, L.E. 1978: Human possibilities and personal choice. In *The psychological development of men and women*. San Francisco: Jossey Bass.

Windelband, W. 1894: *Geschichte und Naturwissenschaft*. Strassburg: Heitz.

Wundt, W. 1895: *Logik*, II. Stuttgart: Enke.

individuality: conceptual issues Although Kluckhohn, Murray and Schneider (1953) were undeniably right in asserting that "every man is in certain respects (1) like all other men, (2) like some other men, (3) like no other men", this often quoted statement reveals the need for an elucidation of the concept of individuality but doesn't provide one. To begin with its adequate explication requires the distinction of two pairs of contrasted concepts in which the term "individual" appears with two different meanings and which are both indispensable to the definition of individual psychology as the study of whole single persons across time and situations.

The first contrast is that between an individual conceived as a unitary undivided entity and a totality, population or structure of which it constitutes an identifiable part or element. The origin of this meaning is to be found in the fact that *individuum* is the Latin translation of the Greek *atomos* i.e. that which is indivisible. In spite of its etymological origin, "individual" in the sense of indivisible, unitary entity does not preclude either a multiplicity of attributes or a complexity of structure.

The second contrast involved opposes individual and general (or universal) taken as the extremes of a series of terms hierarchically ordered in kinds and species. Among these the individual occupies the lowest level because it cannot be further divided logically. This lowest term is also called singular. The big question to which very diverging answers have been provided is whether and how the unique entity referred to by a singular term can be an object of scientific knowledge. According to Aristotle, science is the knowledge of the essence of things which finds its formulation in a definition "per genus proximum et differentiam specificam". Genus and species belong to the *praedicabilia*, i.e. that which can be predicated of a subject. And as they can be predicated of more than one subject they are said to be universal. Whereas the genus is that part of the essence of anything which is predicable also of other things differing from it in kind, the differentia is that part of the essence which distinguishes it from other species within the genus. Equally included in the praedicabilia is the *proprium* (Greek: *idion*) which is an attribute common to some or all members of a species or to several species but not constitutive of their essence and therefore not bearing upon their definition. Accidents are also non-essential praedicabilia whose presence or absence leaves unchanged the essential nature of the subject to which they are attributed. A series of terms ordered according to a hierarchy of genera and species exhibits as the lowest step of the differentiation of essence the "infima species" (Greek: *to atomon eidos*, i.e. the indivisible species) below which there are no essential differences left which might define new species. Since the individual or singular term doesn't correspond to a general concept it excludes any further logical division. However as "infima species" it subsumes an undetermined number of individuals which differ only "numero" i.e. by their mere existence in certain numbers, but not "specie" i.e. by the essence proper to their kind. Thus, for Aristotle as well as for his later followers such as A. Arnauld and P. Nicole, the authors of the influential Logic of Port-Royal (1683) there exists only numerical but not qualitative individuality. This theory should not be confused with the indefensible position taken by K. Pawlik (1972) who states that: "representatives of idiographic personality research (such as G.W. Allport) understand individuality as the unique *qualitative* characteristic of the individual, whereas representatives of the nomothetic variety (such as J.P. Guilford) consider it as the unique *quantitative* characteristic (in the sense of a uniqueness of the individual configuration of factor values in the relevant ability and personality factors)".

Consequently, it is only as a member of the species man that we can know this unique Tom Brown, but not as an individual. For as the schoolmen's saying summarizes the whole matter: "Scientia non est individuorum". This rather formidable limitation resulting from Aristotle's theory inevitably raises the problem of individuation and the search for a principle of individuation which in addition to belonging to a species might confer concrete singular existence on a being. For Aristotle and Aquinas, this principle is "matter" so that Tom Brown and John Smith can only be distinguished, as individuals, by the "matter" they are made of. To quote the Stagirite "the skin and bones are different, humanity is the same".

It is the difficulties inherent in this view as well as the problems of the reality of the *praedicabilia* defining the essence of a thing which during the Middle Ages set in motion the memorable debate between realists and nominalists, a discussion which, although generating less heat, is still going on. In fact it is only for the adherents to a realist conception of universals that there exists a problem of individuation because this view confers priority on the general. For nominalists, on the contrary, individuals are the primary reality and universals have to be abstracted from them and hence exist only "in mente". The nominalists however are confronted by a new problem: how does it come about that individual entities manifest characteristics which, because of their repetition in single instances, are general?

That this problem is still with us is demonstrated by the fact that Burt's four factor theorem concerning the measurement of any individual for any one of a given set of traits (see Burt 1941), reproduces in factor-analytic terminology the four aristotelian praedicabilia.

Leibniz (see Broad 1975), who attempted to look at the question from a new angle, considered that the differences by which individuals are distinguished from each other are not of a different nature from those which differentiate the species of a same kind, but the analysis of these characteristics would require an infinite process. Still according to this view the existence of complete notions of individuals has to be admitted, i.e. notions which exhibit no indeterminate or variable aspect capable of further determination.

Another leading conception of individuality is to be found in the Hegelian "concrete universal" which is said to be universal because it can be applied to an unlimited number of instances while remaining concrete since it also constitutes a unique and indivisible totality. English idealist philosophers have particularly emphasized this last aspect and Bosanquet (1912) has summarized this conception by defining the individuality achieved by a concrete universal as "macrocosm constituted by microcosms".

From this brief overview of the philosophical issues involved in the concept of individuality several conclusions of interest to psychology can be drawn.

(1) Whatever philosophical position one chooses to endorse, the two associated meanings of the concept of individuality must be distinguished because they originate in different operations. The first one (the individual as an indivisible unitary entity) results, at least in principle, from a real division, whereas the second (the individual as the ultimately concrete reality) is generated by a conceptual and logical division.

(2) Provided certain presuppositions are given up, a solution to the problem of individuality can be formulated which is fully consonant with current scientific thinking and practice.
Renouncing idealism which fuses both operations of division is necessary to prevent the conflation of the two meanings of individuality in the notion of concrete universal.
If one rejects the presuppositions that the subject-predicate relation reflects the structure of reality, it is no longer necessary to invoke subjects that cannot be exhaustively defined by predicates, i.e. substances.
If the separation of essence from existence is replaced by a complementary relationship, the gap between numerical (i.e. existential) and qualitative (i.e. essential) individuality disappears.
The relationship between the general and the individual can then be summarized as follows:
Every real thing or process is individual, but only as a whole and not in its particular determinations.
Each aspect or characteristic of an individual real thing is general because it is common to others. For if it didn't repeat itself it would be unknowable. But in each and every real thing its various features and relationships combine to form a unique configuration.
As the general features, by their combination, do not lose their generality, it may be said that the general inheres in the individual. This constitutes the reality of the general and the reason for the inseparability of the individual from the general.
Scientific knowledge is a perpetually oscillating movement of individualization and generalization

which progresses in ever widening spirals.

(3) It should be borne in mind that the concepts of idiography and nomothesis introduced by Windelband (1894) to designate the polarity constituted in most science by generalizing and individualizing approaches is in fact theoretically neutral. Although the term "idiography" originates in the aristotelian terminology concerning the *praedicabilia*, the term "nomothesis" is a neologism. Besides, it is difficult to ascertain what Windelband's position was on the question of individuality. Neither W. Stern nor G.W. Allport have explicitly stated their views on this point. Allport, however, having introduced Windelband's and Stern's terminology into Anglo-Saxon personality psychology (Allport 1937), has unfortunately added to the existing confusion by giving particular prominence to the notion of *proprium* which he has defined in one of his later works as the individual quality of organismic complexity (Allport 1955) – tracing back the origin of this additional meaning to E. Swedenborg (ed. Bigelow 1907), who used it in the special sense of selfishness and pride. J-PDeW

Bibliography

Allport, G.W. 1937: *Personality: a psychological interpretation.* New York: Henry Holt.

——— 1955: *Becomings.* Yale University Press. New Haven and London.

Arnauld, A. and Nicole, P. 1970: *La Logique ou l'art de penser.* Paris: Flammarion.

Bosanquet, B. 1912: *The principle of individuality and value.* London: Macmillan.

Broad, C.D. 1975: *Leibniz: an introduction.* Cambridge and New York: Cambridge University Press.

Burt, C. 1941: *The factors of the mind.* New York: Macmillan.

Kluckhohn, C. and Murray, H.A. 1953: Personality formation: the determinants. In *Personality in nature, society and culture*, ed. C. Kluckhohn and H.A. Murray. New York: Knopf.

Murray, H.A. et al. 1938: *Explorations in personality.* New York: Oxford University Press.

Pawlik, K. 1972: Individuality. In *Encyclopedia of psychology*, ed. H.J. Eysenck, W. Arnold and R. Meili. New York: Heider & Heider.

Swedenborg, E. 1907: *Proprium*, ed. J. Bigelow. New York: New Church Board of Publication.

Windelband, W. 1894: *Geschichte und Naturwissenschaft.* Strassburg: J.H.E. Heitz.

individuation *See also* Jung, Carl

inferiority complex *See* neo-Freudian theory

information processing *See* artificial intelligence; serial and parallel processing

information processing: social psychology A term used to describe the encoding, integration, representation and decoding of information in making (social) judgments. Attribution theory suggests that behavioral information is encoded by making causal inferences about latent, more or less invariant characteristics of the person and/or the situation. such attributes are then thought to be integrated mainly by a weighted averaging process, which takes into account inconsistency in the information and results in a representation (e.g. IMPLICIT PERSONALITY THEORY) and final (evaluative) judgment or category assignment. Recent research by Nisbett and Ross (1980) and Kahneman, Slovic and Tversky (1982) has revealed many biases in human judgment and has suggested that information processes rely heavily upon simplifying cognitive heuristics in which prototypes play an important role. JMFJ

Bibliography

Kahneman, D., Slovic, P. and Tversky, A. 1982: *Judgment under uncertainty: heuristics and biases.* Cambridge and New York: Cambridge University Press.

Merris, C.B. and Rosch, E. 1981: Categorization of natural objects. *Annual review of psychology* 32, 109–115.

Nisbett, R.E. and Ross, L. 1980: *Human inference: strategies and shortcomings of social judgment.* Englewood Cliffs, N.J.: Prentice-Hall.

information theory In its technical sense, linguistic "information" can be defined as patterns: a written word is a pattern of letters; a newspaper picture a pattern of dots.

The information content of a pattern (message) is measured by the number of permutations in which the elements forming the pattern can be arranged. A two letter pattern, using A and B only, can be written in four possible ways, i.e. AA AB BA BB. The information content, usually expressed as the logarithm to the base 2, is in this case $\log_2 4 = 2$ bits (binary digits).

A single letter pattern with a choice of twenty-six letters would produce twenty-six different arrangements, thus the information content of a single letter in the English alphabet is $\log_2 26 = 4.7$ bits. An indecipherable single letter message represents in fact a loss of twenty-six possible messages.

The main application of information theory is in electrical communications. Other more recent applications are in linguistics, neurophysiology, cryptography, psychology, genetics and biology.

As developed by Shannon and Weaver (1949) information theory is frequently used in psycholinguistics as a model of the events that take place when one speaker communicates a single message to a single hearer (see IDIOLECT) as in:

source → channel → receiver
↑
noise

Such a model is oversimplistic when applied to real speech events and alternative models of the nature and functions of language and speech events are preferred by sociolinguists and psycholinguists (see FUNCTIONS OF LANGUAGE; ETHNOGRAPHY OF SPEAKING). BM/PM

Bibliography

Bell, D.A. 1968: *Information theory*, London: Pitman.

Cherry, C. 1966: *On human communication*, Cambridge, Mass.: MIT Press.

Raisbeck, G. 1964: *Information theory*, Cambridge, Mass.: MIT Press.

Rosie, A.M. 1965: *Information and communication theory*, London: Blackie.

Shannon, E.C. and Weaver, W. 1949: *The mathematical theory of communication.* Urbana, Ill.: University of Illinois Press.

ingroup and outgroup Summer (1906) was the first to use the terms "ingroup", "outgroup" and "ethnocentrism", but the concepts are used mainly in research and theorizing which concern intergroup relations. Quite literally a person's ingroup is the group to which he sees himself as belonging, and the outgroup the group to which he does not see himself as belonging. Numerous experiments have shown that the mere act of categorizing people into groups can lead them to discriminate in favor of their ingroup and against their outgroup. However, ingroup and outgroup allegiances may change if the ingroup ceases to contribute to the individual's sense of positive social identity. See also PREJUDICE. AF

Bibliography

Summer, W. 1906: *Folk ways*. New York: Ginn.

inhibition: general A demonstrable nervous activity or a hypothetical process which holds in abeyance some neural and/or behavioral activity which might otherwise occur. At the interneuronal level in the central nervous system inhibition as an accompaniment to excitation clearly expands the logical possibilities of neural functioning in 'computer circuit' terms, and some of its roles, e.g. in sharpening sensory input (Hartline and Ratliff 1957) and in feedback control of muscles, have been elegantly analysed (Eccles 1969).

It has long been clear (Sherrington 1906) that the contractions of particular sets of muscles must entail the suppression of activity in other muscles for coordinated individual movements to emerge, and the same notion has been applied to the motivational problem of how a specific sequence of action is selected by an animal at any one time from its total behavioral repertoire. The ethological concept of CONFLICT entails inhibitory relations between behavior tendencies, and Andrew (1956) and van Iersel and Bol (1958) postulated that it was the balanced mutual inhibition between powerful drives such as flight, fight or sexual attraction (e.g. in courtship or agonistic situations) which cleared the stage for the occurrence of the more mundane displacement activities (the 'disinhibition hypothesis'). Incomplete inhibition might result in alternation between one behavior and another ambivalent behavior, or the truncated intention movements.

With qualifiers such as 'internal', 'external' or 'conditioned' inhibition, and inhibition 'of delay' (Pavlov) 'reactive' inhibition and 'latent' inhibition (Lubow and Moore 1959), learning theorists and comparative psychologists have used the term inhibition in a plethora of ways (see e.g. Boakes and Halliday 1972). Indeed, several kinds of "neuropsychological" (Hebb 1949) inhibition had been postulated on largely behavioral grounds before the demonstration by physiologists of inhibitory synapses and presynaptic inhibition in the brain. Although clear links may sometimes be demonstrable, it is important not to assume that there is necessarily any direct correspondence between inhibitory processes at synaptic or ganglionic levels and those postulated at behavioral levels of explanation. DWD

Bibliography

Andrew, R.J. 1956: Some remarks on behavior in conflict situations, with special reference to Emberiza spp. *British journal of animal behaviour* 4.41–5.

*Boakes, Robert A. and Halliday, Michael S., eds., 1972: *Inhibition and learning*. New York: Academic Press.

Eccles, John C. 1969: *The inhibitory pathways of the central nervous system*. Sherrington Lectures. Liverpool: Liverpool University Press; Springfield, Ill.: Thomas.

Hartline, H.K. and Ratliff, S. 1957: Inhibitory interaction of receptor units in the eye of *limulus*. *Journal of general physiology* 40. 357–76.

Hebb, D.O. 1949: *The organization of behavior*. New York: Wiley.

Iersel, J.J. van and Bol, A.C.A. 1958: Preening of two tern species. A study on displacement activities. *Behaviour* 13.1–88.

Lubow, R.E. and Moore, A.U. 1959: Latent inhibitions: the effect of non-reinforced preexposure to the conditioned stimulus. *Journal of comparative and physiological psychology* 52.415–19.

Roeder, K.D. 1967: *Nerve cells and insect behavior* 2nd edn. Cambridge, Mass.: Harvard University Press.

Sherrington, C.S. 1906: *Integrative action of the nervous system*. Cambridge: Cambridge University Press.

initiating structure A term used to refer to the task oriented behavior of a leader of a small group. It refers to the extent to which a leader defines his own role, specifies the duties of group members, indicates procedures and standards to be used, and evaluates group achievements. In combination with measures of the extent to which leaders show concern for the feelings and welfare of their group, measures of initiating structure have been used to identify different leadership styles and to explore their effects on productivity and satisfaction. See CONSIDERATION; GOAL SETTING; MANAGEMENT. FHMB

innate behavior Behavior that is present at birth; an inborn control system for action. The term innate is sometimes used interchangeably with the concept of instinct to designate pre-programmed behavioral systems, the implication being that such activities are not learned. In recent years however, the distinction between innate and acquired behavior has been superseded by an interactionist approach. Even innate behavior may have some learned components (e.g. thumb sucking may have been learned in the womb). Other inborn behavior that does not appear until later in the life cycle, such as nest building in birds, has also been shown to depend upon an interaction between endogenous and environmental factors.

In the case of the human infant the repertoire of innate behavior was until recently thought to be limited to a few reflexive responses, but it is now clear that infants are capable of fairly complex behavior soon after birth. For example newborn babies can imitate facial movements such as tongue protrusion; they show complex coordinations between seeing and hearing and will search with their eyes for a sound. GEB

Bibliography

Castillo, M. and Butterworth, G. 1981; Neonatal localisation of a sound in visual space. *Perception* 10, 331–8.

Meltzoff, A. and Moore, M.K. 1977: Imitation of facial and manual gestures by human neonates. *Science* 198, 75–8.

innate ideas The opinion that certain ideas are innate or inborn, rather than acquired through experience, has two forms. The weak form asserts that an idea must be regarded as innate if it is universally believed but not derived from any source in common experience; in the strong form, innate ideas are specific mental structures without which thought would be impossible. With rare exceptions (e.g. Bacon 1605) it has been assumed that if an idea is innate then it must also be correct, just or true.

Although the doctrine of innate ideas can be traced back as far as Plato, there is no full statement of it before the seventeenth century, when Herbert of Cherbury (1624) argued that certain "common notions" based on "natural instinct" were the basis for true religion and morality. The strong form of the doctrine was initiated by DESCARTES (1641), who was also the first to use the phrase "innate ideas". Descartes argued in particular that there could not be a mind which lacked the idea of God. It was the attack on "Innate Principles" at the beginning of Locke's *Essay* (1690) that gave notoriety to the doctrine. Locke's arguments appear to have been directed only at its weak form, and mostly depended on the debatable assumption that it would be impossible to have innate ideas without being constantly aware of them. Locke's position was ingeniously opposed by Leibniz (published posthumously 1765); but despite this, derision for "innate ideas" became a commonplace among philosophers of the "enlightenment". However, Kant (1781) regarded his own theory that space, time and the twelve "categories" constitute the indispensable synthetic principles of all experience as a reformulation of the doctrine of innate ideas. In this sense some version of the strong form of the doctrine would be accepted by many philosophers today.

More recently, Noam CHOMSKY (1966) has argued that observed similarities between natural languages, together with the remarkable rapidity of children's language acquisition, are evidence of inborn knowledge of grammatical schemata, and that this in turn vindicates the seventeenth-century advocates of innate ideas. It is doubtful, however, whether they would have welcomed his patronage. JR

Bibliography

Bacon, Francis 1605: *The advancement of learning.*

Chomsky, Noam 1966: *Cartesian linguistics.* New York and London: Harper & Row.

Descartes, René 1641 (*1911*): *Meditationes de prima philosophia.* In *The philosophical works of Descartes.* Trans. Elizabeth S. Haldane and G.R.T. Ross. London and New York: Cambridge University Press.

Herbert, Edward 1624 (*1937*): *De Veritate.* Trans. M.H. Carré. Bristol: University of Bristol.

Kant, Immanuel 1781 (*1929*): *Kritik der reinen Vernunft.* Trans. Norman Kemp Smith. London and New York: Macmillan.

Leibniz, Gottfried Wilhelm 1765 (*1916*): *Nouveaux essais sur l'entendement humain.* Trans. A.G. Langley. Chicago: Open Court.

*Stich, Stephen P. ed. 1975: *Innate ideas.* Berkeley: University of California Press.

innate releasing mechanism and releaser In classical ethological motivation theory there were two distinct roles for external stimuli. They could contribute, as 'priming' stimuli, to the build-up of action specific energy or drive. But, with or without priming stimuli, action specific energy to perform a particular behavior pattern was thought to build up spontaneously with time since that behavior pattern was last performed, in the same way as water pressure builds up behind a dam. The major role of external stimuli was to open the sluice gates. The innate releasing mechanism was a block, a gate holding back the specific drive. Each gate was unlocked by a specific key from the outside world, an appropriate stimulus or releaser perceived by the senses. The word releaser has been used in different senses. Some authors use it for any stimulus that releases behavior, including, for example a stone that elicits pecking in a bird. Others insist on reserving it for a stimulus specifically designed by natural selection to release behavior in another individual. According to this definition a stone would not qualify but the red spot on the bill of a herring gull, which releases food begging in chicks, would qualify. The releasing function has sometimes been sharply distinguished from 'directing': one stimulus, the releaser, was thought to unlock the sluice gates and allow the behavior to occur. Once the behavior pattern had been released it would usually not be directed randomly with respect to the environment, but would be orientated. Stimuli perceived via the sense organs would be used to orientate the behavior, but these stimuli would not necessarily be releasers. The behavior had, by now, already been released. Sometimes, as in the case of the red spot on the herring gull's bill, the same stimulus might serve both a releasing and a directing function. RD

Bibliography

Manning, A. 1979: *An introduction to animal behaviour.* 3rd edn. London: Edward Arnold; Reading, Mass.: Addison Wesley.

inner speech The study of inner speech is concerned with:
(1) the measurement of latent articulatory movements accompanying silent reading, listening or thinking
(2) the determination of its grammatical and semantic properties
(3) its relationship with overt speech in first *language acquisition*
(4) its role in speech production.

Experimental evidence such as electromyographic measurements, carried out mainly within Soviet psycho- and neurolinguistics, suggests that different forms of thinking are accompanied by differential physiological activity of the articulatory organs. Less reliable evidence is available, mainly from speech disorder research, on the grammatical and semantic properties of inner speech. It is widely held that it is a condensed and reduced form of language.

As to its role in child language acquisition, it is seen as a development out of interpersonal communication rather than out of the egocentric monologues of young children. Its principal function is that of programming a special class of non-speech acts, such as problem solving. Consequently, it cannot be regarded as a stage in external speech production which is controlled by different grammatical processes.

One of the most fruitful areas of inner speech research is its comparison with other reduced forms of language such as sign language (see *non-verbal communication*) and pidgins. PM

Bibliography

Průcha, Jan 1972: *Soviet psycholinguistics*. The Hague: Mouton.

Vygotsky, L.S. 1962: *Thought and language*, trans. E. Haufmann and G. Vakar, Cambridge, Mass.: MIT.

insanity A condition, usually of persons or of minds, in which the capacity for rational thought and/or behavior is seriously impaired. By long tradition, certain kinds of insanity are important both in medicine and in law, though the term insanity (like its close synonyms madness and lunacy) signifies so wide a range of conditions that its use as a technical term has been largely discontinued. In this article insanity will be considered first in medicine, then in law, and then in the common ground between these two disciplines.

Since classical times, and in most cultures, at least some forms of insanity have been regarded as, or as a product of, disease. Just which forms of insanity are properly so regarded has, however, been variously interpreted. Historically, the "disease theory" has had to compete with religious or spiritual theories, usually of demonic influence as in medieval Europe, sometimes of divine. Nowadays, although such theories persist in some parts of the world, opposition to the "disease theory" has come mainly from such disciplines as sociology, psychoanalysis, psychology and political science (Caplan, Engelhardt and McCartney 1981). These disciplines, indeed, have produced a spate of alternatives to the "disease theory" which, notwithstanding the many successes of modern medicine, shows no signs of abating.

It is of course the "disease theory" that has been most influential in medicine, doctors on the whole having confined their interest to those insane conditions that are most generally, and least contentiously, regarded as disease. In recent years the study of these conditions has been pursued largely along empirical lines: by clarifying their description and classification; by developing reliable methods for their identification; and by exploring their causes and effects (Wing 1978). It is in the context of work of this kind that the term "insanity" has now been abandoned as too emotive and too imprecise for technical use in medicine. In the Iinternational Classification of Disease (WHO1978), for example, the nearest approximation to "insanity" is PSYCHOSIS. But this term here designates a carefully defined group of conditions characterized by the presence of DELUSIONS and/or HALLUCINATIONS, and distinguished one from another by differences in the form and content of these phenomena, and by the presence or absence of various associated symptoms and signs.

The importance of insanity in law rests on the idea that the insane, being irrational, are not always fully responsible for what they do. It follows from this idea, as a principle of natural justice, that while it may sometimes be necessary to restrict the rights of the insane (for their own protection or for the protection of others), they should not normally be held liable under the law to the same extent, or in the same way, as those who are sane. This principle, however, although acknowledged by as early a writer as Aristotle (*Nicomachean Ethics*, Bk. III), has been subject to considerable difficulties of interpretation, and, in consequence, the details of its application, and the legal terminology employed, have varied widely (Walker 1968).

These difficulties of interpretation are well illustrated by the treatment of the insane in law in England and Wales at the present time. This is governed by a complex body of legislation and precept, the more important statutory provisions being contained in no fewer than four Acts of Parliament: the Criminal Justice Bill, 1948, the Homicide Act, 1957, the Mental Health Act, 1959, and the Criminal Procedure (Insanity) Act, 1964. In this legislation, the insane are variously identified and, for different legal purposes, differently defined. Several distinct legal species of insanity have therefore to be carefully distinguished, though the legislation, taken as a whole, is extremely comprehensive. Thus, it provides, inter alia, for remand, on bail or in custody, for psychiatric reports; for (possibly indefinite) admission to hospital without trial if an accused person is found to be "unfit to plead" by reason of mental disorder; for complete acquittal by the "special verdict" of "not guilty by reason of insanity", where the accused is found to be not responsible for his actions according to law (the test of which remains the McNaghten rules); for a reduction in the charge from murder to manslaughter in cases of unlawful homicide, if the responsibility of the accused is found to be "substantially reduced" by "abnormality of mind" (so called "diminished responsibility"); and for wide discretionary powers in sentencing, including orders for admission to hospital and for guardianship under the care of a local authority. Similarly, in civil law, insanity remains a sufficient ground for divorce, and is generally accepted as good evidence for testamentary and for contractual incapacity.

The difficulties presented by insanity are nowhere more evident than in the area of overlap between medicine and law, and it is in this area in particular that, notwithstanding the success of empirical methods in medicine, problems arise in medical practice in relation to insanity that are not, or not primarily, empirical in nature. Some of these may be circumvented: in regard to the establishment of criminal responsibility, for example, and the closely related question of civil capacity, doctors may seek to restrict their witness as experts to matters of fact – a policy which is endorsed by the recent Report of the Committee on Mentally Abnormal Offenders (Butler 1975). But others, as in the case of involuntary or compulsory treatment, may not be: the justification for such treatment is similar to the justification for the special treatment of the insane in law (that, being irrational, they are not always fully responsible); and it is indeed commonly given statutory legal authority (as in the Mental Health Act, 1959); but its proper use is a matter of ethics not of science, and of specifically medical ethics at that. In relation to such issues, therefore, the "disease theory" of insanity, at least in its modern highly empirical form, is insufficient even for the particular and special purposes of medical practice. The growing recognition of this, together with the increasing importance of non-empirical problems in medicine generally, provides perhaps one important reason for the appearance in recent years of so many proposed alternatives to the "disease theory", however adequate or inadequate these may yet prove to be. (See MEDICAL MODELS.) KWMF

Bibliography

Butler, Rt. Hon., the Lord, (Chairman) 1975: *Report of The Committee on Mentally Abnormal Offenders*. London, Cmnd., 6244, HMSO.

*Caplan, A.L., Engelhardt, H.T. and McCartney, J.J. 1981: *Concepts of health and disease*. Reading, Mass., London and Amsterdam: Addison-Wesley.

*Walker, N.1968: *Crime and insanity in England*. Edinburgh: Edinburgh University Press.

*Wing, J.K. 1978: *Reasoning about madness*. Oxford and New York: Oxford University Press.

World Health Organisation 1978: *Ninth revision of the international classification of diseases*. Geneva: WHO.

insight A term used by the Gestalt psychologist Wolfgang Kohler (1925) to denote a form of intelligent problem solving. Kohler set adult chimpanzees tasks that required solution by indirect means, for example, retrieval of bananas out of reach by means of a stick or by stacking boxes to form a step ladder. The chimpanzees succeeded only when all the constituent elements of the problem had first been seen within the same field of view. They behaved as though their perception of the problem had undergone a sudden radical restructuring and they would then rapidly arrive at an appropriate solution. When the elements were widely separated in space, 'insightful' learning did not occur and the chimpanzees continued to attempt ineffective 'trial and error' strategies.

Insightful problem solving similar to that observed by Kohler can be seen in human infants at about eighteen months. Thereafter, with the acquisition of language, this capacity may be greatly extended since language as a medium of representation may allow the child to "bring together" elements of a task which would otherwise remain spatially distinct in immediate perception. GEB

Bibliography

Kohler, Wolfgang 1925: *The mentality of apes*. New York: Kegan Paul.

instinct: in animal ethology A set of behavior patterns which contribute to a common function (reproduction, feeding), which are shared by all members of a species, and which develop in the absence of conventional learning or practice. TINBERGEN saw instincts as based upon hierarchically arranged neural systems sharing a common source of motivation (see HIERARCHY). Instinct was commonly understood to imply that the whole behavioral system was inherited, and there was a tendency to ignore the role of the developing animal's environment. For this reason the term is now less used. It is more common to refer to the various elements of a functionally related set, e.g. reproductive behavior as examples of 'instinctive behavior'. The different elements may develop at different rates and be affected by distinct factors during development. Thus certain elements of male sexual behavior can develop in the absence of testosterone, while other elements require this hormone, and still others may require social experience for their full development. AWGM

instinct: in general and human psychology Those patterns of experience and behavior which – as universally distinctive among the members of a species as their anatomical features – emerge within the process of maturation, are adapted to normal environmental conditions, and are inherited (*not* learned, though learning is significantly related to them). They comprise: (a) specific neuro-physiological conditions, and elements of (b) perception (sign stimuli), (c) conation (drive), motivation, exploratory and appetitive behavior, (d) consummatory acts (fixed pattern reactions and associated reflexes) and (e) emotion attendant upon fulfilment or thwarting. Their maturational order marks critical periods of development and learning (e.g. IMPRINTING), the effects of which seem enduring and irreversible. The presence of instinct does not signify the absence of intelligence or learning (a common misunderstanding); its degree of flexibility being related to the degree of complexity of the species-organism. Before, in, and after the work of Darwin, instinctual experience and behavior has been held to exist in man, though here the element of drive in particular, and flexibility in relation to learning, are emphasized. Also, man's biological inheritance being always overlaid by a cultural heritage, the accommodation of the one to the other leads to the establishment of *sentiments*, entailing non-rational as well as rational elements. The significance of instinct for sentiment-formation, learning, personality and character development, and the operation of cultural influences has entered psychological and sociological theories in many ways. Examples are: McDougall (Social Psychology); Shand (Foundations of Character); Freud (see INSTINCT; PSYCHODYNAMICS); Cooley and Mead (the importance of primary group communications during the early years of family and play-group experience in the growth of the 'self' in society); Pareto (regarding the instinctual dispositions of the human mind as "residues" exerting continual and powerful influences of a "non-logical" kind in the many theories ("derivations") which men construct about the world and society, and in the struggles between elites); and Westermarck (Origin and Development of the Moral Ideas). Always criticized in its application to man, the concept of instinct remains important in the human sciences. RF

Bibliography

Cooley, Charles Horton 1902 (*1964*): *Human nature and the social order*. New York: Schocken.

——— 1909 (*1962*): *Social organization*. New York: Schocken.

Fletcher, Ronald 1968: *Instinct in man*. London: Allen & Unwin.

McDougall, William 1908: *An introduction to social psychology*. London: Methuen.

Shand, Alexander, F. 1914: *The foundations of character*. London: Macmillan.

Westermarck, Edward 1903: *The origin and development of the moral ideas*. 2 vols. London: Macmillan.

instinct: psychodynamics A term which refers both to innate and fixed behavior patterns common to most members of a species and to a motivational force usually distinguished by its goal. In his writing Freud used the German word *instinkt* for the former and *trieb*, sometimes translated as drive, for the latter. He developed his theory of instinct (*trieb*) in the context of his psychoanalytic investigations of sexuality. Freud described an instinct as having a source within the body and a pressure or quantity of energy which was seeking release, related both to its somatic source and to its object. A subject's choice of object and method of gaining satisfaction or aim are constructed in the course of development and represented psychologically. Freud viewed instinct as 'a borderline concept between the mental and the physical' (Freud 1915). In a wider sense Freud was a dualist, initially placing EGO or self-preserving, and sexual or species perpetuating, instincts in competition, but in his final formulations opposing eros (love, both self and sexual instincts) and thanatos (instinct of death and disorder). BBL

Bibliography

Freud, S. 1915 (1957): *Instincts and their vicissitudes. Standard Edition of the Complete Works of Sigmund Freud*. vol. XIV, London: Hogarth Press; New York: Norton.

institution An established practice or custom recognized within a particular society. An institution may be social, economic, legal, political, religious, etc., and it may combine some or all of these aspects simultaneously. This is particularly true of simple societies in which many aspects are embedded in the same relationship. Examples include marriage, infanticide, law courts and forms of land inheritance. Institutions change, and divorce, for example, now constitutes an institution in most western societies. Some writers use the term to refer to a group of people who share a vested interest, but this usage is uncommon.

The study of society in practice involves the study of specific social institutions, although some social sciences assume that the institutions of a given society are functionally interrelated. Social scientists of different theoretical persuasions privilege different institutions in their accounts. PGR

institutional care *See* educational attainment and institutional care

institutionalization A syndrome of apathy, social withdrawal and lack of initiative which is associated with long periods in any unstimulating institution, including prisons, childrens' homes, mental retardation hospitals and psychiatric hospitals (Goffman 1961). In chronic schizophrenia (which is characterized by negative symptoms of withdrawal and lack of volition) there is a particular vulnerability to institutionalization. Patients may become mute, and suffer considerable social deterioration. This used to be common in the large asylums and still occurs to a less severe extent in hospital and residential care and in schizophrenics at home. Prevention and treatment require individually planned rehabilitation aiming at slow improvement to the optimal level of function. RAM

Bibliography

Goffman, E. 1961: *Asylums*. New York: Doubleday.

Wing, J.K. and Brown, G.W. 1970: *Institutionalization and schizophrenia*. Cambridge and New York: Cambridge University Press.

institutions and institutionalization In the broader sociological sense, the term "institution" or "social institution" refers to the major organized systems of social relationships in a society (see INSTITUTION). Institutionalization refers to the process whereby norms, values and ways of behaving are transformed into enduring, standard and predictable patterns.

In psychology, however, and in everyday language, the term "institution" has a much narrower and more specific meaning. It refers to certain specialized organizations and establishments for processing or changing people. The goals of such institutions include reform, treatment, re-education, re-socialization, punishment and rehabilitation. The people who find themselves in such institutions are usually called inmates, patients or clients and usually belong to one or other deviant or dependent group. Examples of such institutions are prisons, mental hospitals, old people's homes and children's homes. Being sent to these places is often referred to as "being institutionalized".

An important subgroup of such institutions has become known as "closed" or (following Goffman) "total" institutions. These are places where "a large number of like-situated individuals, cut off from the wider society for an appreciable period of time, together lead an enclosed, formally administered round of life" (Goffman 1961). Time spent in a total institution might be an enforced form of punishment or treatment (prisons, mental hospitals), a voluntary retreat from the world (convents, monasteries) or a process of education or service (army barracks, boarding schools).

The immediate and long term psychological effects of prolonged experience of these regimes and communities is usually described as "institutionalization". In psychiatric terms, the effect is seen as pathological – "institutional neurosis" (Barton 1966) – and is characterized by withdrawal, lethargy, childlike dependency and (at the extreme) an inability to survive outside the institution. Sociologists tend to see institutionalization (and specific forms such as "prisonization") not solely as pathological, but as a form of secondary socialization. The inmate learns gradually how to adjust to the regime and its deprivations, particularly by taking on the norms of the informal inmate *subculture*. This process often subverts or undermines the formal aims of the organization. These learnt strategies of "making out" or survival may or may not facilitate later adjustment outside and (as certain studies have shown e.g.

Cohen and Taylor, 1981) will depend in form and intensity on the inmates pre-institutional identity. SCoh

Bibliography

Barton, R. 1966: *Institutional neurosis.* Bristol: John Wright.

Cohen, S. and Taylor, L. 1981: *Psychological survival: the experience of long term imprisonment.* Harmondsworth: Penguin.

Goffman, E. 1961: *Asylums: essays on the social situation of mental patients and other inmates.* New York: Doubleday: Harmondsworth: Penguin (1968).

institutions, rationality of Standards or criteria against which reasoning practices within particular cultural and organizational settings are deemed adequate. Social life can be thought of as a complex of activities in which people are continually interpreting, explaining, understanding and categorizing features of their environment, which include the actions of others, their own actions and the objects and events around them. In short, people are continually making sense of their world. Traditionally, the notion of RATIONALITY implies the existence of criteria by which the adequacy of these sense-making activities can be assessed: such criteria are assumed to exist independently of the context or setting of the reasoning practice; and the reasonableness of action is thought to be indicated by the extent to which individuals match up to these criteria. By contrast, the notion of rationality of institutions.

(1) holds that criteria of adequacy in reasoning are institutionally circumscribed; and
(2) suggests that these criteria are best regarded, not as a pre-existing independent set of procedural rules, but as an argumentative resource drawn upon by participants.

The implication of (1) is that what counts as adequate will depend on the particular INSTITUTION in which reasoning is being adjudged. Thus the empirical findings of research influenced by ETHNOMETHODOLOGY demonstrate that the adequacy of sense-making is contingent upon the immediate practical purposes of actors in the organizational environment. For example, the accuracy of medical records is not a matter for analysis of correspondence between documents and the "actual facts of the matter", but a question of whether the records are "good enough" for the immediate use to which they will be put (Garfinkel 1967).

Although "rationality" clearly varies between different environments, it is not clear to what extent particular forms of rationality can be ascribed to particular institutions. On the one hand there is the general argument that certain forms of rationality characterize whole social institutions; for example, that what counts as the correct use of evidence is characteristic of the law. On the other hand the implication of (2) above is that forms of rationality should not be attributed in this way. Such is the interpretive flexibility of any procedural criterion that what counts as rational practice can vary with each occasion of use. From this "radical situationist" point of view, the emphasis switches from an attempt to discern which forms of rationality are peculiar to an institution, to an attempt to document the ways in which different notions of rationality are used by participants as a means of characterizing both their own and others' practices.

In certain institutions, questions about adequacy of procedure are especially lively for participants themselves. For example, practitioners in science, the law and psychiatry often reveal explicit concern with the adequacy of reasoning practices. Science, in particular, is sometimes thought to embody the most stringent and well-defined criteria of procedural adequacy. However, recent ethnographic investigation of scientific practice suggests that even in science what counts as adequate depends crucially on the practical exigencies of the laboratory situation (Latour and Woolgar 1979). The construction of scientific facts thus arises out of a series of localized, contextual and highly variable criteria as to procedural adequacy. In the course of such work various abstract canons of scientific procedure are invoked by scientists, but these feature as an evaluative resource in the post hoc characterization of practice rather than as a principle which guides that practice. SWW

Bibliography

Garfinkel, H. 1967: *Studies in ethnomethodology.* Englewood Cliffs, N.J.: Prentice-Hall.

Latour, B. and Woolgar, S. 1979: *Laboratory life: the social construction of scientific facts.* Beverley Hills, Calif.: Sage.

instruction *See* computer-aided instruction

instructional technology Mechanical, optical, electronic and computer aids to information presentation in education. Instructional technology ranges from simple aids such as the blackboard, through film projectors to complex computer systems. Most of this technology has originated for business and entertainment purposes and been applied to education as part of the continuous search for stimulating learning environments.

The most widely used examples of electronic instructional technology are *audio-visual aids* such as the slide projector, overhead projector, movie projector, tape recorder, television, video tape and video disk. The uses of such audio-visual media are generally to give pupils classroom experience of situations which cannot be experienced at first hand on account of cost, time or distance.

Variants of the tape recorder in the form of *language laboratories* have made a major impact on language training. Digital computers, and in particular low-cost microcomputers, are the latest additions to the range of instructional technology and are already in widespread use at all levels of the educational system (see PROGRAMED INSTRUCTION). MLGS

Bibliography

Dale, E. 1969: *Audiovisual methods in teaching.* New York: Holt, Rinehart & Winston.

integration of handicapped children in normal schools A method of providing education for handicapped children while maintaining direct and regular contact with non-handicapped peers, referred to in the USA as "mainstreaming". While both physically and mentally handicapped children have special educational needs, their social needs can probably best be met by mixing with normal peers. Successful integration consists of achieving the optimal balance between the provision of specialized teaching and equipment, and work and leisure contact with peers. Schemes have varied from special units on a school campus to complete membership by handicapped children in normal classes. The arguments in favor of segregating handicapped children have been: first, that their educational and physical needs can be met more efficiently; and second, that they can be protected from possible social rejection. The arguments in favor of integration are based essentially on the moral argument that an integrated society must not have segregated schools, whatever the basis for segregation. There is no evidence that segregation produces better educational results than integration, either for physically handicapped children (Cope and Anderson 1977), or for mentally handicapped children (Gunzburg 1974). Some integration schemes enable children suffering particular handicaps to be educated in groups within normal schools. The necessary special equipment is used for some teaching, and some takes place in normal classes. Evidence on the attitudes of normal children towards handicapped peers with whom they have had contact indicates that acceptance or rejection depends on many factors, including the level of integration achieved, and the attitudes of teachers (Gottlieb 1975). With a carefully designed scheme of integration, special educational needs can be met while achieving levels of social contact which can be beneficial to both handicapped and non-handicapped participants. SJK

Bibliography

Cope, C. and Anderson, E. 1977: *Special units in ordinary schools: an exploratory study of special provision for disabled children.* University of London Institute of Education.

Gottlieb, J. 1975: Public, peer and professional attitudes toward mentally retarded persons. In *The mentally retarded and society: a social science perspective*, ed. M.J. Begab and S.A. Richardson. Baltimore: University Park Press.

Gunzburg, H.C. 1974: Educational planning for the mentally handicapped. In *Mental deficiency: the changing outlook*, ed. A.D.B. and A.M. Clarke. London: Methuen.

intelligence The all-round mental ability (or thinking skills), either of human or of lower animal species. The term derives initially from the Greek philosopher's distinction between cognitive or intellectual, and affective or emotional, faculties of mind. In more recent times intelligence was often regarded as the quality which distinguishes man's adaptability, his capacity to learn and to reason, from the instinctive and reflex processes of animals. Though intelligence is already present in the ability of lower species to sense and react to objects and to learn at a primitive level, it evolved with the enormous growth in size and complexity of the higher brain centers and the cortex. Mammals can generally adapt more readily and cope with more complex tasks than fish and insects; while monkeys and apes are more intelligent than other mammals, apart from man.

To try to define intelligence in terms of mental powers or faculties such as memory, imagination, reasoning, etc. is of little help since these too are vaguely defined and non-observable. Modern psychology is concerned more with the analysis of behavior and mental processing than with some hypothetical causal entity in the brain. It is not a "thing" like red hair; but a quality of diverse forms of human activity. By measuring the success or failure of children of different ages, or adults, in a wide range of cognitive tasks, it is found that some persons are consistently more successful than others. The common element in all such performances was designated by C. Spearman as the General or *G* factor; and he showed how to determine what mental functions are most characteristic of intelligence, e.g. grasping relationships, abstracting, problem solving; or which are relatively independent, e.g. rote memory, sensory processes, etc. Thus it is possible to measure intelligence by appropriate tests, although one cannot see it or define it precisely. American psychologists tend to lay less stress on this general intelligence than on more specific types or factors of ability, verbal, memorizing, spatial, etc., which may be called group factors or primary factors.

Many writers consider that the term intelligence has outlived its usefulness since it gives rise to much misunderstanding and controversy (see Resnick 1976). An alternative approach is the experimental study of mental processes involved in taking in information, coding and storing it, and using this knowledge in coping with problems and in thinking. It is also hoped that the construction of computers which display "artificial intelligence" will throw further light on human intelligence (see ARTIFICIAL INTELLIGENCE).

Intelligence was regarded as an innate capacity, dependent on the genes inherited from the parents. But, in the light of such work as Piaget's on child development, and D.O. Hebb's neurological theories, it was realized that inborn brain power does not develop into effective intelligence without stimulation from the environment; also that an unstimulating or deprived environment can inhibit its growth (see INTELLIGENCE AND ENVIRONMENTAL INFLUENCES). Like all other genetic attributes it is the product of interaction between the organism and its environment. PEV

Bibliography

Hebb, D.O. 1949: *The organization of behavior.* New York: Wiley.

Piaget, J. 1950: *The psychology of intelligence.* London: Routledge & Kegan Paul.

Resnick, L.B., ed. 1976: *The nature of intelligence.* New York: Wiley.

Spearman, C. 1927: *The abilities of man.* London and New York: Macmillan.

intelligence: animal An index of ability in tasks requiring cognition. There is no generally agreed measure of animal intelligence. There are numerous examples and demonstrations of intelligent behavior, but the validity of tests of intelligence is open to criticism on the grounds that it is not possible to devise a PROBLEM SOLVING test that is not biased in respect of one species or another. Some birds can provide good imitation of sounds but not of actions; tool using is found in some species and not in others, but there are no obvious differences in intelligence between animals that use tools and those that do not. DJM

intelligence: human *See* cognitive development

intelligence and environmental influences The growth of an individual's intelligence from the fetal stage to adult maturity is affected by many aspects of the environment in which he or she is reared. Even before birth the infant's development is hindered if the mother's health or nutrition are inadequate; and environmentally produced injury to the brain may occur at birth. However, it is difficult to assess the effects of such perinatal conditions since they tend to be more frequent among lower class or minority group families than in white middle class families. Hence they may be confounded with genetic or social class differences. Malnutrition, leading to poor growth of body and brain, is particularly characteristic of children in underdeveloped countries.

Recent investigations of infancy show the importance of mother–child interactions in the first year for perceptual, linguistic and conceptual development. The mother's (or other main caretaker's) conversations and play with the child stimulate his vocalization and other responses; while poorly educated or harassed mothers are much less effective. The value of a rich and varied environment in early life was demonstrated by Hebb's work with dogs and rats. Those reared in a restricted environment showed poorer learning capacities later on than those with a more stimulating environment. Severe deprivation occasionally occurs if a child's environment provides no social contacts or access to the world of people and things. The resulting mental and even physical retardation may be almost irremediable. However there are recorded cases of severely deprived children who were transferred to a more normal environment at six or seven years old, and did catch up with other children in speech and intelligence within a few years. A striking study in this area is that by Skeels (1966), who tested twenty-four orphaned children at an average age of eighteen months, when they were living in a very unstimulating institution. Later thirteen of them were transferred to another home where there was better care and attention, and then adopted into foster homes. When traced twenty-five years later, the transferred group were normal, self-supporting adults, some in highly skilled jobs; whereas the non-transferred were still institutionalized, or in very low grade jobs.

Another study which has received considerable publicity was carried out in Milwaukee by Garber and Heber (1977). Here twenty black infants living in very poor homes were brought daily to a center for an intensive program designed to stimulate sensori-motor, perceptual, language and thinking skills. They were compared on numerous tests with another twenty matched infants who had no such treatment, and who were expected to reach an IQ of 80 or below in later childhood. Initially the two groups scored the same on developmental scales, but from two to four years their IQs averaged 122 and 96 respectively. The program ceased when the children entered school at six; and when tested at eight to nine years the experimental group averaged IQ 104, the controls 80. This is a very large improvement; but we cannot tell how permanent it is going to be until the results of further follow-up and fuller details are reported. We are not entitled to claim that an IQ deficit of over 20 points can be completely eliminated by psychologically planned child-rearing. In any case the program was far too elaborate and costly to be applied to large numbers.

Other, more haphazard types of "intervention" have proved generally ineffective, notably the American Head Start programs which were provided for thousands of preschool children from poor environments in the 1960s, in the hope that this COMPENSATORY EDUCATION would improve their learning capacities and adjustment to schooling. The schemes varied quite widely, but though some have been claimed to be beneficial, careful follow-up investigations showed that any gain in mean IQ or achievement in the first year at school usually faded out in another year, till there was no difference between Head Start children and others with comparable background who had received no special treatment. (See COMPENSATORY EDUCATION on longer term effects).

Several less ambitious experiments have been reported where children aged one to three years gained on average some 10–15 IQ points (Bronfenbrenner 1974). These programs were likewise planned to stimulate mental growth, but they generally involved training the mothers, either at home or in a clinic, to interact more effectively with their children. These projects have mostly lacked adequate control groups, and there is little evidence as to the permanence of the gains. Kagan and others (1976) showed that children reared largely in daycare centers obtain the same IQ levels as others reared entirely at home. Much has been written about the dangers of maternal DEPRIVATION, e.g. separation of child from mother because of prolonged hospitalization of either. Later investigations have not confirmed them; children may show considerable anxiety and even become apathetic; but they seem to overcome these effects quite rapidly. Much depends on the age at separation, its length and particularly on the provision of a substitute mother figure.

Parental socioeconomic class always shows some relationship to children's mental growth. Those from wealthy homes where there is more care, more materials such as educative toys and books, and more stimulating activities, obtain higher IQs and school attainments on average. But the effect is probably due in part to parental genes, not wholly to superior environment. The parents' education, in fact, is more influential than their material wealth and home comfort. A major factor is the kind of language used in the home. Bernstein (1971) has claimed that middle class, as contrasted with lower class, speech tends to develop more logical thinking and abstract concepts, rather than just expression of feelings; also to convey such values as planning for the future, self-responsibility and motivation for education. In the USA some work has been done in recent years on the effects of different kinds of home upbringing on children's development, though there are immense difficulties in this follow-up research. Probably the most influential factors are the warmth, acceptance and emotional security provided by the parents; varied experiences and contacts with other children, avoidance of overprotectiveness and encouragement of independence; and a "democratic" discipline (which expects high standards of conduct), rather than permissiveness or authoritarianism.

While it has been proved that lack of any schooling hinders the development of intelligent thinking, there seems to be little difference attributable to different kinds of schooling. Many measures believed to foster educational development, such as small classes, open plan classrooms, individualized instruction, use of visual and other aids, streaming or not streaming by ability, addditional incentives, provision of nursery schools and kindergartens, drilling in arithmetic or spelling, etc., have not been shown to have any consistent effects. Intensive remedial work with retarded children may produce some gains in reading and arithmetic – usually rather temporary; but it does not affect the overall ability level that we call intelligence. This is not because some children are genetically superior to others so that schooling makes no difference, but because, by the age of five or six, the genes interacting with the home environment have laid down a certain level of mental functioning, which the school cannot do much to alter. This level, however, as measured by intelligence tests, is by no means constant. It can fluctuate quite widely between, say, six and eighteen years; and though tests given at six can forecast eighteen-year IQ fairly accurately in the majority of cases, earlier tests from one to five have very little predictive value. Some of the variations occur because tests for different ages vary in content, or because of chance irregularities in administration and other conditions of testing. The main factor is likely to be the changes in development following on changes in environment; but we know little about which features of environment bring about speedier, or slower, growth.

There are indeed difficulties in isolating the major components of good or bad environments and measuring their effects. Far too often if one factor is shown to be ineffective, psychologists think up some other explanation without adequate proof (see Jensen 1973). Also there is so much overlapping between factors of health, family climate, education, etc. that it is hardly possible to prove which are the major causes. Admittedly, changes of thirty points or over in IQ can result from much improved environment, but this does not mean that genetic factors are not also important. Indeed the modification of intelligence level by environment does seem to be limited. We have no recipe for improving, or lowering, children's intelligence at will. Many investigations based on resemblances and differences among twins, siblings, foster children etc. have tried to specify the relative influence of heredity and environment, but without reaching a consensus. There are too many complications, such as environmental differences *between* different families, and differences between siblings *within* the same family. Often heredity and environment cooperate, or "co-vary"; that is, children born of parents with superior intelligence are more likely to be supplied with a stimulating environment than those of duller parents. Moreover, to quite an extent, children make their own environments, as well as being made by the environment. The intelligent child provokes more interaction from his mother, seeks out stimulating experiences as in reading advanced books, is more curious and more inventive; whereas the duller child is relatively apathetic and does little to develop his own thinking.

No mention has been made of differences attributable to the cultural environments of different racial or ethnic groups. The topic is highly controversial (see JENSEN CONTROVERSY) and is hardly soluble in so far as intelligence always develops through the interaction between genes and environment. The concepts and the thinking styles of, say, children in China reflect a different environment from that of American whites. They would require different tests to measure adequately their own levels of intelligence. On the other hand, Chinese-Americans and Caucasians can be compared on the same test, because their environments are largely identical. PEV

Bibliography

Bernstein, B.B. 1971: *Class, codes, and control.* London and Boston: Routledge & Kegan Paul.

*Bronfenbrenner, U. 1974: Is early intervention effective? *Teachers College Record* 76, 279–303.

Garber, H. and Heber, R. 1977: The Milwaukee project. In *Research to practice in mental retardation*, ed. P. Mittler. Baltimore: University Park Press, 119–27.

Hebb, D.O. 1949: *The organization of behavior.* New York: Wiley.

*Jensen, A.R. 1973: *Educability and group differences.* New York: Harper & Row.

Kagan, J., Kearsley, B. and Zelazo, P.R. 1976: Day care is as good as home care. *Psychology today* May, 36–7.

Labov, 1973: The logic of non-standard English. In *Language and social context*, ed. Pier Paolo Giglioli. London: Penguin.

Skeels, H.M. 1966: Adult status of children with contrasting early life experiences: A follow-up study. *Monographs of the Society for research in child development* 31, No. 105.

*Vernon, P.E. 1979: *Intelligence: heredity and environment.* San Francisco: W.H. Freeman.

intelligence quotient A number or "score" derived from performance on an intelligence test which expresses an individual's success on that test relative to the performance, on the same test, of a comparable group. There are several methods for computing an IQ, each of which can give a slightly different number. Most current tests adopt a standard procedure. This expresses an individual's score in terms of its deviation or distance (i.e. above or below) the average of the scores of the reference or normative group. By convention, the group average is commonly set to 100.

(See also TESTS, INTELLIGENCE; TESTS, NORMATIVE AND CRITERION-REFERENCED). MBe

intelligence *See above, and also* artificial intelligence

intention movement A somewhat unfortunate technical term, because it seems to have subjective connotations.

When the term was fashionable in ethology this was no difficulty because objectivism was so dominant in the thinking of ethologists. An intention movement is simply an incomplete movement. An animal is said to perform an intention movement when it starts to perform an action pattern recognizable from the species repertoire, but then breaks off before the action is completed. For example the sequence of movements leading to take-off and flight in a bird typically begins with a stretching of the neck. Birds on the ground, particularly when a little frightened, sometimes stretch the neck as though about to take off, but then do not do so. This might be called an 'intention flight movement'.

Intention movements play an important role in ethological theories of the evolution of animal signals. Neck stretching in a bird is, statistically speaking, likely to be followed by flight. Tooth-baring in a dog is statistically likely to be followed by biting. Natural selection therefore is supposed to favor the evolution of what looks like anticipatory behavior in animals after they have perceived an intention movement in another individual. A dog whose rival bares its teeth may flee as if in anticipation of being bitten. Selection thereupon, according to the theory, favored the ritualization of tooth-baring as a threat display. In the same way, many other ritualized signals have been supposed to evolve from intention movements. RD

Bibliography

Manning, A. 1979: *An introduction to animal behaviour*. 3rd edn. London: Edward Arnold; Reading, Mass.: Addison Wesley.

intentional action The analysis of intentional action has been a preoccupation of western philosophy and jurisprudence through most of their history, from Aristotle onwards. The issue is highly complex; we can perhaps resolve it into three interconnected questions.

1. Conceptual terrain. Many older discussions of intentional action assumed that the conceptual terrain was rather straightforward: that all actions were either intentional or unintentional, that the notion of "intentional" was identical to that of "voluntary" or "willed", and that an agent is responsible for all and only his intentional actions. This assumption led to a focussing of the inquiry on the pursuit of a single necessary ingredient in virtue of which an action was intentional. The grip of this simple scheme was very strong, but it has been eroded by the work of Austin (1956), Anscombe (1957) and others. (Interestingly, Aristotle's discussion of the subject is in this modern anti-simplistic vein.) It is now generally recognized that the linguistic tests for the true contours of concepts show (a) that the voluntary and the involuntary apply only to fairly narrowly muscular actions and that they are not exhaustive of such actions: if I distractedly brake the car at a green light, the action seems not correctly describable as either voluntary or involuntary; (b) that "willed" and "unwilled" are terms not so much of art as of artifice, having little place in ordinary language; (c) that the question of responsibility is no sure guide to that of intentionality: we are often held responsible for unintentional actions or omissions (strict liability), and we may not be held responsible for intentional actions, e.g. if we are insane.

2. Rules governing the outward spread of intentionality. It is a commonplace that a given single action may be redescribed as another single action which includes some consequences of the first: the action of pulling the trigger may also be described as the action of firing the gun, or as the action of shooting the policeman, or even as that of killing him. These larger descriptions spread forward in time. They may also spread laterally, when the consequences are simultaneous with the initial given action: the action of entering the room is also the action of altering the room's acoustic properties. In general, of course, an action may be intentional under one description but not under others; but sometimes intentionality *is* carried to other descriptions of an action. What rules govern this spread? If I do not and could not know of some consequences of an act, the act will not be intentional under a description which includes those consequences. Gavrilo Princip intentionally killed the Archduke Ferdinand, but he did not intentionally trigger the first world war. If I do not know but should have known of those consequences, the act under the wider description will still be unintentional, though I may be liable for it. A doctor who mistakenly prescribes a lethal drug kills his patient unintentionally, but he is liable. If I do know the consequences but do not wish them the question of intentionality is moot. In dropping the bomb on Hiroshima Truman's intention was to bring a speedy end to the war; in doing so he killed and maimed a hundred thousand innocent civilians. Was the latter an intentional act? There are similarly hard cases generated by circumstances of drunkenness, insanity, imbecility, self-deception, neurosis, hypnotism, brain-washing, torture and the like. But in all such cases the question of intentionality perhaps becomes academic once it is realized that moral liability is directly bound up with intentionality.

3. What makes an act intentional in the first place? Leaving aside hard cases of the spread of intentionality among descriptions of an act, what is it, even in an easy case, for an act to be intentional? A traditional answer stipulated that those acts are intentional which are caused by VOLITIONS; another similar answer saw them as the actions caused by the WILL. There are many difficulties with these answers. Volitions are not detectably present before all intentional actions, and to postulate them when they are undetectable is not philosophically attractive. The will too is an unsatisfactory postulate because its operations are undetectable and unimaginable: it strongly invites, though it resists, analysis into other things. Another line of answer has held that what makes an act intentional is that it fulfils or subserves a purpose of the agent, that is, that it is caused after the manner of TELEOLOGY. But in order to be intentional the action must not merely happen to subserve such a purpose, it must be *intended* by the agent to subserve the purpose: so this definition seems inescapably circular. There are similar problems with holding that what makes an act intentional is that it subserves an agent's desires or

wants. Another general answer has held that the central cases of intentional action are those caused, not by other events, but by agents. (See BASIC ACTS.) However it proves very hard to maintain agent causation as a pure unanalysable form of causation in the face of physiological analysis into event causation: for an agent to cause his arm to go up is just, for certain neurophysiological events, to cause the arm to go up. Perhaps the most common modern view of intentional action is the "coherentist" view, according to which actions are intentional if they fit in appropriate ways with prior and subsequent behavior, including verbal behavior, of the agent: roughly, an action is intentional if the agent can say why he did it. This first approximation of the coherentist view needs much refinement, of course, but even with that refinement many would say that at best the coherentist view can tell us how to detect an intentional action, but not what such an action really is. Others would claim, though, that there is no difference between these two. JT

Bibliography

Anscombe, G.E.M. 1957: *Intention*. Oxford: Basil Blackwell; Ithaca: Cornell University Press.

*Austin, J.L. 1956: A plea for excuses. *Proceedings of the Aristotelean Society* 57, 1–30.

*Danto, A.C. 1973: *Analytical philosophy of action*. Cambridge: Cambridge University Press.

Fitzgerald, P.J. 1961: Voluntary and involuntary acts. In *Oxford essays in jurisprudence*, ed. A.G. Guest. Oxford: Clarendon Press.

Goldman, Alvin I. 1970: *A theory of human action*. Englewood Cliffs, N.J.: Prentice Hall.

Imlay, R.A. 1967: Do I ever directly raise my arm? *Philosophy* 42, 119–27.

Kenny, A.J.P. 1966: Intention and purpose. *Journal of philosophy* 63, 642–51.

intentionality Intentionality is a property of at least certain mental acts and states. An intentional act or state is a functional phenomenon, in the sense that it can be properly identified only through being related to a larger context. It is not easy to say what distinguishes intentional acts within the general class of functional phenomena.

A negative approach to the question emphasizes that the context required to identify an intentional act cannot be gleaned from a knowledge, however complete, of a person's physical surroundings. This point is usually illustrated by reference to the unquestionably intentional phenomenon of judgment. We can know what judgment someone makes if and only if we have knowledge of the proposition expressing the content of his judgment. Indefinitely many propositions may fill that role compatibly with a person's physical surroundings. So knowledge of that person's surroundings will not guarantee that we can identify the judgment he makes, even concerning those surroundings.

The negative approach emphasizes the following points about intentional acts such as the judgment that a glass is full of water, all of which support the view that knowing about a person's physical environment may not help us to discern the propositional object of his judgment. The proposition may be false, the glass being only half full. It may fail in at least certain sorts of existential presuppositions, there being no water, only a reflection. More technically, if the proposition in question is expressed by the sentence "p", then it is not guaranteed that the person believes that q just because "q" is equivalent, even logically equivalent to "p" and has the same referent: just because it represents the same state of affairs, as we would say. If "q" represents that state of affairs differently from how "p" represents it, then the person may believe that p but not that q. Thus he may believe that the glass is full of water and not that the glass if full of H_2O; he may not know that water is H_2O.

The positive approach to the question of what distinguishes intentional from other functional phenomena emphasizes the concept of meaning. The idea is that if someone judges that p, we can know the propositional object of his judgment if and only if we know what "p" means to him. Whether this is known by knowing (and understanding) a public synonym of "p", for example an utterance of an appropriate English sentence, is a debated question.

Within the philosophical literature on intentionality a number of distinct issues have been broached. These concern the criterion, the range, the analysis and the status of intentionality.

The question about the criterion of intentionality is that discussed above. Phenomenologists have tended towards the positive approach, seeking exact descriptions of how mind relates to meaning in a phenomenon like judgment (see Husserl 1900–01). Analytic philosophers have preferred the negative approach trying to construct necessary and/or sufficient conditions for intentionality out of the features mentioned above. (See Chisholm 1967). In virtue of such features a sentence like "John judges that p" is what is (unhappily) known as an "intensional context". Analysis in terms of intensionality has probably done as much to obscure as to illuminate intentionality (see Kneale 1968).

The question about the range of intentionality has to do with whether, as Brentano (1874) claimed, all mental phenomena are intentional. Nowadays it is generally assumed that they are not, in view of such apparently non-intentional phenomena as pains. The concept of intentionality is so extended however that besides judgment it applies to other propositional attitudes such as believing, fearing or desiring, and to acts and states of mind which bear, not on propositions, but on particular real or would-be objects, events and situations: e.g. seeing, hearing, recognizing or imagining (see Anscombe 1965).

The question about the analysis of intentionality is whether in an intentional act or state we must always be able to distinguish an object (propositional or particular) whose existence does not entail the existence of anything other than the person who performs the act or enjoys the state. Those who believe such objects can be distinguished will probably take intentionality to involve a view of the mind as related directly to its own representations, and only indirectly, via them, to the real world. Brentano and Husserl were troubled by this issue (see Carr 1975) and it remains a live question in contemporary philosophy. It is related to the subsidiary question whether intentionality involves abstract, Platonic entities.

The question about the status of intentionality has to do with whether intentional phenomena must or even can be countenanced in a final account of what there is. Many have wanted to deny them a place. Intentionality attracts hostility for a variety of reasons: because it seems to require Platonic entities like propositions; because it gives rise to problematic intensional idioms; or because it is thought to create difficulties for materialism. The best known attack is probably Quine's (1960). The majority view at present is that intentionality is at least compatible with a final account of what there is and that we could cease to countenance intentional entities only at the cost of giving up our treatment of one another as persons.

It was said at the beginning that the intentional act or state is a functional phenomenon. A judgment is intentional–functional insofar as its proper understanding presupposes an awareness of a wider context: specifically, a wider meaning-context. However, such a judgment, according to functionalism, is also causal–functional: it plays a crucial role in the causal context in which perceptual input connects with behavioral output. This dual functionality raises the problem of whether judgments and such phenomena should be individuated by intentional or causal function. The problem has only recently come to be appreciated (see Woodfield 1982). PP

Bibliography

Anscombe, G.E.M. 1965: The intentionality of sensation. In *Analytical philosophy*, ed. R.J. Butler. 2nd series. Oxford: Basil Blackwell; Totowa, N.J.: Barnes & Noble.

*Aquila, R.E. 1977: *Intentionality: a study of mental acts.* University Park: Pennsylvania State University Press.

Brentano, Franz 1874: *Psychologie vom empirischen Standpunkte.* Leipzig: Von Duncker und Humblot.

Carr, David 1975: Intentionality. In *Phenomenology and philosophical understanding*, ed. Edo Pivcevic. Cambridge: Cambridge University Press.

Chisholm, R.M. 1967: *Perceiving: a philosophical study.* Ithaca, New York: Cornell University Press.

Husserl, Edmund 1900–01: *Logische Untersuchungen.* Halle:

Kneale, W. 1968: Intentionality and Intensionality. *Aristotelian society supplementary volume* 42, 73–90.

Marras, A., ed. 1972: *Intentionality: a study of mental acts.* Chicago: University of Illinois Press, Mass.

Quine, W.V.O. 1960: *Word and object.* Cambridge, Mass.: MIT Press.

*Woodfield, Andrew, ed. 1982: *Thought and object: Essays on Intentionality.* Oxford and New York: Oxford University Press.

interactionism: social psychology An approach to the study of social behavior which argued that behavior is a function of the person and the situation. In a general sense this position has never been disputed but in the 1960s this position received more attention when it was shown that the statistical interaction of person and situation usually explained a great deal more of the variance in questionnaire responses than consistent differences between persons. Although the debate which followed initial publications was riddled with artifacts, there can be no doubt that general personality factors explain much less variance in social behavior in situ than was originally expected. JMFJ

Bibliography

Argyle, M. 1978: *The psychology of interpersonal behavior*. Harmondsworth and Baltimore: Penguin.

interference Forgetting occurs because of the *interference* or competition from other memory traces (though some forgetting due purely to decay may also be observed). Early demonstrations showed that subjects remembered much more when they were asleep during most of the retention interval than when they were awake. These observations were later elaborated and extended, giving rise to the interference theory of forgetting, which dominated verbal learning research until the mid-1960s. Retroactive interference occurs when new learning interferes with what has been learned before. Both unlearning and response competition have been suggested as interference mechanisms. Classically, interference was regarded as an interaction between specific associative bonds, while emphasis was placed later on such factors as list differentiation (how well the learner can tell the old from the new) and rules of response selection (LEARNING STRATEGIES). Proactive interference occurs when previous learning increases the difficulty of acquiring similar new materials. WKi

inter-group relations A term which has to some extent replaced the more traditional terms prejudice and discrimination. The change in terminology reflects a shift in emphasis away from the purely negative connotations of prejudice and discrimination and their motivational implications. Evaluative differentiation between groups occurs already under minimal conditions and appears to be a function of the general tendency to establish a positive social and personal identity (see PREJUDICE). JMFJ

Bibliography

Tajfel, H. 1982: Social psychology of inter-group relations. *Annual review of psychology* 33, 1–39.

interlanguage The term was introduced by Selinker (1972). It refers to a separate dynamic linguistic system and can be regarded as a reflection of the psycholinguistic process of interaction between the learner's mother tongue and the target language in SECOND LANGUAGE ACQUISITION. Interlanguage systems are described in terms of time-incorporating grammatical rules i.e. rules which describe developments and rule-changing creativity, such as those developed by BAILEY.

Interlanguage research concentrates on natural sequences of second language acquisition. One of the most startling results so far is that this acquisition appears to follow a natural language-independent "syllabus" where contrastive factors (see CONTRASTIVE ANALYSIS OF LINGUISTIC SYSTEMS) play only a minor role. This syllabus parallels the development of pidgin languages from less complex to more complex systems and nativized creoles (see CREOLIZATION).

PM

Bibliography

Selinker, L. 1972: Interlanguage. *International review of applied linguistics* 10, 219–31.

Corder, S. Pit & Roulet, E., eds 1977: *The notions of simplification, interlanguage and pidgins and their relation to second language pedagogy.* Geneva, Librairie Droz.

internalization In social psychological terms the adoption of attitudes or behavior patterns by an individual. Indeed much of socialization and education is involved with encouraging the individual to internalize the behavioral norms, morals and values of his or her group. A child's behavior is shaped or guided by example, encouragement, rewards and punishments, and hence directed into particular channels by external instruction and intervention. However, as the child develops he or she becomes able to give him or herself these instructions. Full internalization is reached when the behavior takes place not just because it is rewarded or punished, but because it is seen to be correct or appropriate. In psychoanalytic theorizing the term is often used synonymously with introjection or identification and describes the process by which objects or norms in the external world are molded into permanent mental representations. The ego defense mechanism of identification is the way in which an individual attempts to take on the characteristics of someone who is more important than himself. Identifications may be made on the basis of guilt feelings, the need for punishment, or strong emotional attachments.

AF

interpretative theory *See* hermeneutic interpretative theory

intervening variables *See* hypothetical constructs and i.v.

interviewing A personal interview is a face-to-face discussion between two people, directed towards some specific purpose. This may, for example, be assessment of suitability for a job, or giving advice about a problem.

In a selection interview the aims are, first to match the candidate's qualifications with job requirements, and second to predict to what extent he or she is likely to work hard and be successful. The interview usually follows a biographical approach: starting from the written information on the application form, the interviewer asks the candidate to highlight the main events in his or her upbringing, education, employment, and leisure activities to date, and also to explain why he or she has applied for the job. The interviewer should follow up in depth any points which seem important. Non-verbal interaction between the two parties, smiling, nodding etc, may also have a considerable influence on what they think of each other (see Argyle, 1972).

One of the greatest pitfalls of the interview is "halo effect", the tendency when meeting another person to form a general impression, favorable or otherwise or the reverse, and to allow this general impression to affect all other judgments. One way of guarding against this is to use an interview rating form. Specimen forms are presented in Anstey (1977). Using a form of this kind compels the interviewer to make separate assessments of each aspect of personality before arriving at a final overall assessment, and to weigh the factual evidence obtained from the interview itself and from other sources, before making a decision.

Interviewing needs to be studied as a science, to be practiced as an art. There are three stages in developing the skills of interviewing:

1. The casual, unplanned approach typical of many untrained interviewers.
2. The careful, systematic approach of the interviewer who has received some training, but is still preoccupied with asking the right questions of the candidate rather than with interpreting the answers.
3. The development of sensitivity to a candidate's attitudes and feelings as well as the content of his or her replies, in a word, establishing rapport. Once rapport has been achieved the actual questions matter less, and the interview is likely to yield reasonably reliable information. An experienced interviewer may hope to achieve rapport in about 75 per cent of personal interviews.

Though one-to-one interviews are the most common, board or panel interviews are often used by large organizations when filling senior appointments. A panel of three is usually most cost-effective, preferably with members varied in age, sex, and experience. Subjectivity is reduced through pooling different impressions, but because of the shorter time available to each member for questioning it is harder to achieve rapport than in a personal interview.

Widely used though the interview is, it is still a subject of considerable controversy. Views on interviewing are affected by two contrasting views of human personality. The first holds that a person's intelligence and other basic characteristics are largely innate and enduring, and also capable of measurement. In the 1950s and 1960s such writers as Eysenck (1953) and Mayfield (1964) published evidence that these basic characteristics are measured more accurately by written tests of intelligence or temperament than by interview. It should be noted, however, that nearly all the interviewers involved had been given little or no training in how to interview, and this fact may well have had a bearing on the results obtained. According to this school of thought, interviewing is so subjective and unreliable that it should be used only as a last resort.

The opposite view is that even intellectual abilities are greatly affected by early upbringing and changes in environment. Written tests measure abilities at a point of time. On the other hand, interviewers can, by studying how an individual has progressed relative to the opportunities available to him or her, make reasonable predictions of likely future development. Interviewing, for all its obvious limitations, has the merit of two-way contact and of considering the individual in the round.

Each point of view deserves some respect. Even the strongest advocates of interviews should reinforce them by other means. Due note must be taken of academic, professional or technical qualifications where these are relevant. When selecting for any job in which a particular skill is required it is obviously sensible first to administer the relevant test, and to interview only those who reach the qualifying standard.

Promotion interviews differ from selection interviews in that solid information is available about a candidate's record within the organization, usually in the form of a series of written reports on performance. These written reports can be used in conjunction with interview information to predict how far the candidate could develop to meet the responsibilities of higher grade work.

Appraisal interviews were first generally recognized as a desirable ingredient in improved personnel management policy in the late 1950s (see Maier 1958). The purpose of an appraisal interview is for a manager to discuss a subordinate's performance with him or her, and consider how this performance can be improved and the subordinate's potential developed. Most of the early appraisal schemes failed to fulfil the hopes expected of them, mainly because they were introduced without adequate explanation or training, and because interviewers tended to adopt too authoritarian an approach. A second wave of appraisal schemes introduced in the late 1960s achieved much better results. More emphasis was placed on preparation and training for the interviews, on a problem-solving approach, on directing the interview towards specific limited objectives which were capable of achievement, and on regular feedback of information on how the scheme was working. For the outcome of research into the factors making for success or failure in appraisal schemes, see Anstey, Fletcher and Walker (1976). If, and only if these conditions are fulfilled, the general consensus now is that appraisal interviews can make a worthwhile contribution towards making the best use of staff and maintaining their morale.

Since the interview is directed towards a specific purpose its usefulness will depend critically upon both parties knowing this purpose and preparing accordingly. In selection it is up to the employer to disseminate accurate information about requirements for the job and how selection will be made. It is up to an applicant to study this information carefully, to learn about the organization, and to prepare replies to questions likely to be asked at interview. In appraisal, it is up to the manager to review the subordinate's performance over the past year and previous discussions between them. It is up to the subordinate to consider any difficulties which may have prevented him or her from achieving more.

Training for interviews is critical. Talks on how to interview are almost useless unless followed immediately by practice interviews in which students can try out the suggestions made. The best training courses include at least two practice interviews, giving each student opportunity to improve performance during the course, reinforcing good points and learning from mistakes, sometimes by watching video-tape feedback. Advice on selection training is given in Goodworth (1979), and on appraisal training in Anstey et al. (1976). Advice to interviewees is equally important. Fletcher (1981) provides guidance in self-preparation and presentation.

Another kind of interview is the counseling interview, in which the interviewer gives guidance about choice of career, about problems with people, or about personal or financial problems. While a counselor can sometimes make positive suggestions, the most important function is often to listen sympathetically and, by offering factual information or impartial comments, help the client to make up his or her own mind on which course to follow.

There are also survey or market research interviews in which the sole function of the interviewer is to elicit opinions on political or other topics, or on the relative merits of various products.

Finally, in all occupational interviews, the possibility of unfair racial or sexual discrimination is assuming increasing importance. In both the USA and the UK this is theoretically prohibited by law, but "Discriminating Fairly" (1980) lists some common sources of bias which can lead to unfair discrimination. One example (p.16) is "the tendency of the employer to recruit in his own image", and hence unwittingly to prefer someone of the same race and color, and possibly also from the same social background. Where members of ethnic minority groups are involved it is even more important that sound interviewing principles should be resolutely enforced, and that interviewers should supplement their interview impressions wherever possible by reference to objective data. (See also ASSESSMENT CENTER; PERSONNEL SELECTION.) EA

Bibliography

Anstey, E. 1977: *An introduction to selection interviewing* London: H.M. Stationery Office.

Anstey, E., Fletcher, C. and Walker, J. 1976: *Staff appraisal and development* London: Allen and Unwin.

Argyle, M. 1972: *The psychology of interpersonal behaviour* London and Baltimore: Penguin.

Discriminating fairly: a guide to fair selection. 1980: Runnymede Trust, London and British Psychological Society, Leicester.

*Downs, C.W. et al. 1980: *Professional interviewing.* New York: Harper & Row.

Eysenck, H.J. 1953: *Uses and abuses of psychology.* London and Baltimore: Penguin Books.

Fletcher, C. 1981: *Facing the interview.* London: Allen & Unwin.

Goodworth, C.T. 1979: *Effective interviewing for employment selection.* London: Business Books.

*Higham, M. 1979: *The ABC of interviewing.* London: Institute of Personnel Management.

Maier, N.R.F. 1958: Three types of appraisal interview. *Personnel* March, 27–40.

Mayfield, E.C. 1964: The selection interview: a reevaluation of published research. *Personnel psychology* 17, 239–60.

*Moffat, T.L. 1978: *Selection interviewing for managers.* New York: Harper & Row.

intracellular chemistry *See* memory and learning, intracellular chemical theories

introspection A form of self-observation in which individuals direct their attention supposedly towards the contents of their own consciousness. The belief in the possibility of such a process results from the espousal of a dualistic philosophy and the idea that all knowledge is acquired by observation. Introspection was the principle technique used in Titchener's psychology of contents. As such, it was not a casual process of "looking in", for observers had to be highly trained, being especially warned not to commit "the stimulus error", i.e., the error of not describing thoughts themselves but of reporting after the event what the thought was about. This "error", however, was unavoidable; and for this and other reasons Titchener's brand of introspective psychology fell to the onslaughts of BEHAVIORISM. It cannot be denied, though, that some kind of inward apprehension of mental phenomena is possible; and it would be foolish to dismiss out of hand all the findings reported from this era (see e.g. Humphrey 1951). JDS

Bibliography

Humphrey, G. 1951: *Thinking: an introduction to its experimental psychology*. London: Methuen; New York: Wiley.

introversion *See* extroversion and introversion

intuition The word has been used by different philosophers to describe a variety of objects of knowledge, belief or understanding, as well as the ways in which such objects are known. In each case such knowledge is supposed to be in some way or other independent of inference, justification or theory. DESCARTES, for example, contrasted the intuition by which we know self-evident mathematical axioms with the demonstration needed in the case of an unobvious theorem. Kant used the word to refer to an awareness of things which is immediate in that it does not depend on the mediation of CONCEPTS. Nowadays our pre-theoretical beliefs, about what is right or wrong for example, are called (moral) intuitions, and a man is said to have an intuitive understanding of a concept if he can employ it but is unable to give a theoretical account of it. JMS

IQ *See* intelligence quotient

IRM *See* innate releasing mechanism and releaser

J

James, William (1842–1910) Influential American psychologist and philosopher, author of *The Principles of Psychology*, one of the few classics in the history of psychology. In this book James effectively demolished the experimental introspective psychology of Wundt and helped prepare the way for different approaches to human behavior such as FUNCTIONALISM, BEHAVIORISM, humanistic psychology and the psychology of personality.

Wundt insisted that relational experiences such as "to the right of", "louder than", "brighter than" can be reduced to, or analysed into, a set of sensory and affective elements, an "element" being an independent and irreducible *Vorstellung* out of which all complex experience is compounded. James, however, argued that experienced relations are just as introspectively irreducible as the experience of sensory elements such as "blue", "sweet", and "hard". Later he argued that the whole concept of building blocks is a misguided one. No state of consciousness, he wrote, once gone can recur in an identical state. For an identical sensation to recur, the brain state at t_2 would have to be identical with the state at t_1. However, since a brain unmodified between t_1 and t_2 is physiologically impossible, an unmodified sensation is equally impossible. In his usual colorful way James concluded that "a permanently existing 'idea' or 'Vorstellung' which makes its appearance before the footlights of consciousness at periodical intervals, is as mythological an entity as the Jack of Spades" (*Principles*, p. 246).

Furthermore, James argued, we do not experience discrete sensory units but *interpreted events which have experienced affinities*. Unfortunately, these experienced affinities have been ignored by psychologists because introspective attention to affinities is difficult to achieve and when achieved tends to destroy them. Calling attention to affinities is like grasping a snowflake in the hand – it is no longer a crystal but a drop. Instead of an affinity, "we find we have caught some substantive thing, usually the last word we were pronouncing, statically taken, and with its function, tendency, and particular meaning in the sentence quite evaporated" (*Principles*, p. 244). However, phenomenologically the flights as well as the perches are to be found in the stream of consciousness, and this fact renders preposterous the assumption of discreteness clung to by the elementarists.

In general James was phenomenologically inclined in contrast to the analytical set of the Wundtians, and this inclination is nowhere more clearly revealed than in his nativistic views on spatial extension and depth perception in contrast to the elementarists' genetic accounts of how these experiences are learned.

James utilized his psychological insights in his philosophical view of "radical empiricism". He can best be understood as steering a middle course between the completely loose universe of the Humean and the block universe of the absolute idealist. There must be sufficient introspectively and ontologically irreducible relations in the world to account for the stable and enduring objects of everyday life but enough independence to avoid the doctrine of internal relations. To achieve this intermediate position, James supplemented the traditional epistemic base with spatial, temporal and causal relations. Here there is an important temporal as well as logical development in his thought. As early as the 1870s James argued that we immediately apprehend spatial and temporal relations. While these relations are not dynamic or substantial bonds of union, they still in some sense unite the heterogeneous into a universe. Later, in "The Feeling of Effort", "The Experience of Activity" and *Some Problems of Philosophy*, he showed that causal relations are also sometimes irreducibly given and that such causal connections add the final or substantial bond of union. With the doctrine of the complete independence of events thereby subverted, there is no need to "construct" physical objects out of independent sense data. Hence, James was just as much an opponent of the phenomenalism of J.S. Mill and Ernst Mach as he was of the block universe of the absolute idealists.

EHM

Bibliography

James, W. 1890 (1956): *The principles of psychology*. New York: Dover.

Ayer, A.J. 1968: *The origins of pragmatism*. London: Macmillan; San Francisco: Freeman Coopes

Janet, Pierre (1859–1947). Neurologist, philosopher and professor of experimental psychology at the College de France, Janet was a pioneer of psychodynamic psychiatry. He is best known for his descriptions of the clinical features of hysteria and his use of cathartic treatment (1965). Influenced by the teaching of CHARCOT, the fundamental concept of his psychopathology was "psychasthenia" a weakness of the highest integrative function of the brain which predisposes to NEUROSIS. He believed that treatment should provide stimulation and among the methods he investigated were hypnosis, suggestion and discussion and guidance aimed at "re-education". RAM

Bibliography

Janet, Pierre 1965: *The major symptoms of hysteria*. New York: Hafner.

Jaspers, Karl (1883–1969). Philosopher and psychiatrist, Karl Jaspers was a member – together with Gruhle, Schneider and Mayer-Gross – of the Heidelberg School, renowned for its studies of mental phenomena. His work on morbid jealousy in 1910 revealed his astonishing powers of observation and description. In 1913 he published the first edition of his *General psychopathology* which remains unsurpassed in its objective analysis and categorization of psychic events, their evolution and their consequences. He also defined the scope and limitations of various methods of exploring the psyche; in particular he distinguished those disorders whose development can be understood through empathic understanding from those where causal connexions must be inferred.

He has come to be seen as one of the founders of existential psychology. DLJ

Bibliography

Jaspers, Karl 1962: *General psychopathology*. Trans J. Hoenig and M.W. Hamilton. Manchester: Manchester University Press; Chicago: University of Chicago Press.

Jensen controversy The contributions of hereditary and environmental factors to general intelligence, as measured by standard tests, has been disputed since the 1920s. By the 1960s the majority of American psychologists and sociologists believed that differences in intelligence were mainly due to children's home upbringing and learning. They particularly rejected any genetic differences between racial or ethnic groups. Hence the uproar in 1969 when Arthur Jensen published an article in the *Harvard educational review*, which marshaled the extensive evidence of innate individual differences, and hypothesized that the large IQ difference between American blacks and whites was partly due to genetic factors. Leftwing student groups and black activists threatened him with physical violence, and many reputable social scientists condemned him more on ideological than scientific grounds. His subsequent writings have shown that much of the evidence they cited was unsound. However, some researches have supported and others rejected his hypothesis, and Jensen now admits that we lack an adequate methodology for proving it. PEV

Bibliography

Jensen, A.R. 1972: *Genetics and education*. London: Methuen; New York: Harper & Row.

job characteristics, intrinsic and extrinsic Intrinsic job characteristics are those associated with the content of a job itself, whereas extrinsic characteristics are those deriving from the context or work environment. This distinction has been important in research into WORK ATTITUDES, WORK MOTIVATION and WORK REDESIGN. Intrinsic characteristics are generally thought to include opportunities for challenge, achievement, recognition, growth and responsibility, and extrinsic characteristics to include such factors as pay, fringe benefits, job security, company policies and administration, supervision and working conditions. Whereas earlier approaches to motivation and satisfaction at work had emphasized extrinsic features, more recent applied research has concentrated upon increasing and measuring the impact of intrinsic characteristics. RTM

job involvement *See* work attitudes

job satisfaction *See* work attitudes

journals *See* associations and journals

Jung, Carl (1875–1961) The contributions to personality theory of the Swiss psychiatrist C.G. Jung were developed over a period of more than fifty productive years and now reside in the twenty volumes of his collected works (ed. Read, 1953–79). None of these, however, is devoted to a systematic discussion of what has come to be known as Jungian theory, nor do any of these volumes present an entire theory in brief outline. The task of systematizing the work was left to others. The better-known attempts have been offered by Jacobi (1962), F. Fordham (1966) and Hall and Nordby (1973).

Jung's earliest interest in the study of personality stemmed from his attempt to understand the dynamic relationship between conscious and unconscious processes (*CW* vols. 1, 2; 1961). This work led to an alliance with Sigmund Freud in the early development of psychoanalysis as a theory of personality and as a method of therapy. His defection from the psychoanalytic school founded by Freud, after five years of intense participation, was occasioned by his dissatisfaction with Freud's pansexual explanation of the origins of personality development and Freud's reluctance to approach the deeper layers of the unconscious which he feared would be associated with mysticism.

The publication in 1912 of Jung's book, *Symbols of transformation*, heralded his departure from the psychoanalytic ranks and he began a lonely, tortuous path, largely unaided by others until later life, to understand the nature of personality. In this book, in which the spontaneous fantasy productions of a single individual are analysed, much of the material that constituted the basis for a lifetime of original work are to be found in nascent form.

In general outlines Jung thought of the personality as a series of interacting bipolar energic subsystems whose undifferentiated potentialities existed at birth in a vast realm he labeled the "collective unconscious". The encounter with life forced a differentiation of the inherently dominant poles into consciousness to shape and form conscious experience. The path through life was guided by the ultimate pull to make the potential actual, to reconcile or balance the opposites, to make available to consciousness the implicit potential latent in the original structure. This life-long process he designated as "individuation". Energy was inferred from change created by the tension of opposites.

From a structural point of view Jung described personality as consisting of two dynamic, interacting realms, consciousness and the unconscious. Within consciousness he delineated two structures, the ego and the persona. The ego he designated as the center of the conscious field, the experiencing "I" or "me", the source of the individual feeling of identity and continuity. Surrounding the ego is the persona, the individual's "face to the world", the constellation of roles, attitudes and behavior by which a person presents who he or she is to the world in response to societal demands. The ego, of necessity allied with the persona, must guard against an overidentification with this public mask to the exclusion of the expression of inner promptings from unconscious sources. Such an imbalance leads to tension resulting in psychological distress.

Jung divided the unconscious into its personal and collective aspects. The personal unconscious consists largely of experiences that were once either dimly conscious or too painfully salient to maintain a consistent persona image. Through repressive kinds of mechanisms they are kept from easy access to consciousness. Some semblance of order is postulated to exist in the personal unconscious through the formation of complexes, an adherence of relevant experiences around an attracting nucleus. Thus all repressed thoughts, feelings, memories and wishes relating to experience with one's mother are described as part of a "mother complex".

The deeper layers containing the primal, universal material without which the ultimate aspects of personality cannot be forged are thought to reside in the collective unconscious, a concept unique to Jungian psychology. He conceived of mind as being capable of generating images prior to and independent of conscious experience, similar in form in all people, prototypical or archetypal in nature. In and of themselves they are the raw materials which often appear in dreams, fantasies and other creative human products, usually called forth by the imbalances caused by the demands of conscious existence. When intuitively factored they reflect the central themes with which human beings have struggled throughout history. These include good and evil, gender, power and mortality among many others. Jung personified these clustered images by giving them various names. The gender archetypes Anima and Animus referred to the hidden opposite side of the male and female, respectively. The Wise Old Man and the Great Mother were names assigned to the authoritative power figures appearing in unconsciously derived imagery. Archetypal figures or structures are all collective but not necessarily unconscious. The ego and the persona are archetypal in structure yet largely conscious in content while the shadow, a collective term which includes all that is primitive and all that is hidden about personality, contains a large segment of material that was once conscious. The flow of psychological life is conceived as a continuous engagement between consciousness and the unconscious within the confines of a relatively closed system. The development of personality, although influenced by the outside world, is pictured basically as an internal struggle.

In the search for an operating framework in which to describe the manifestations of personality, Jung settled on a typological schema which because of its empirical possibilities has had more impact in academic psychological circles than any other aspect of his theoretical work. In his classic volume *Psychological types* (1933), Jung attempted to bring order into the diversity presented by individual differences in personality through the delineation of a conceptual model which included two basic attitudes and four essential psychological functions common to humankind. The attitudes were termed "introversion" and "extroversion," probably biologically determined, which influenced the direction of energy, or interest, in the psyche. In introversion the focus of interest was centered on the internal, subjective, intrapersonal aspects of psychic life, in extroversion, on the external objective, interpersonal side. As in all major Jungian concepts, a bipolarity is intended. The functions were described as thinking and feeling, a rational pair, and sensation and intuition, a perceptual pair. Thinking and feeling are evaluative or judgmental functions, the former emphasizing the use of cognitive and intellectual information, the latter relying upon affective cues. The data they utilize are in the service of settling value issues, such as whether something is good or bad, liked or disliked. The perceptual functions are concerned with the processes related to the identity of things rather than their value. Sensation operates as the function concerned with facts or the apparent, concrete nature of the world. Intuition is directed toward the elaboration of the possibilities or relational aspects of perceptual data.

In describing personality Jung assumes that both attitudes and all four functions are part of the inherent endowment of all human beings. During the course of development, as a result of the mix of individual propensities, familial and more general cultural pressures, one of the attitudes and one of the functions are most clearly differentiated and become the conscious, operating framework of the personality. Thus, as a first approximation, personality may be described by the combination of the dominant attitude and the first function. For any person this would result in one of eight possibilities, either introversion or extroversion in tandem with one of thinking, feeling, sensation and intuition. Further complexity is added by the differentiation into consciousness of an auxiliary function, one of the pair of functions orthogonal to the first function. An individual would then have as descriptors of personality three identifying features, a dominant attitude, a first function and an auxiliary function. The general schema that emerges is a sixteen category typology. The behavioral and imaginal characteristics of each type are elaborated in the work of Isabel Briggs-Meyers (1962) whose Type-Indicator represents the most sophisticated attempt to measure individual type structure.

The concept of development, although central to Jung's teleological view of personality, focussed little on the problems of early childhood and socialization. Initially he was content to adopt the Freudian view. In later years the contributions of Frances Wickes (1966) and Michael Fordham (1947) related Jung's ideas to the experiences of childhood. Jung's picture of development remained at a much more global level. He conceived of the progression of life as basically divided into two parts. The first half, roughly marked by the end of the fourth decade, was directed toward the adaptational problem of establishing one's position or place in the world. This he saw proceeding through the development of the dominant attitude and the first function and all that such development intended in the essential choices of occupation, object attraction, mate selection, values and more general interests. As a result of this necessarily one-sided emphasis, there grows over time a pressure for expression of the neglected, more unconscious aspects of the personality contained in the opposite attitude and the fourth function, the polar opposite of the first. The occurrence of this psychological unrest may be related phenomenologically to what is commonly termed the mid-life crisis, a mark of entry into the period Jung called the second half of life. During this stage the adaptational problem shifts from finding one's way into the world to that of finding one's way out, the ultimate confrontation with mortality. In a poetic vein Jung described the entire process as an exploratory trek of traversing a mountain in which the initial energy is devoted to reaching the summit with limited concern for what lies beyond. When the peak is reached, a set of new problems is revealed in how to descend and negotiate all that is involved in concluding the task.

Thus the path of personality development is directed toward an ultimate outcome which Jung called "individuation". In its most general sense the process of individuation mirrors the sequential progression of physical existence. The templates of the physical structures are given at conception, differentiate at different rates, are strengthened or impeded by different experiences and form different integrations with each other at various times in the life history. The ultimate outcome under positive circumstances is a well-articulated, smooth-functioning physical system equipped to do in the species sense what it is capable of doing. This model Jung basically used for psychological individuation. He delineated the essential system parts (consciousness and the unconscious), the structural units within those parts (the archetypes), the stylistic framework in which these structural units operated (the attitudes and functions), and provided a dynamic rule of order by which the system and its parts were governed (the law of opposites). The energic aspects of the interaction of the system parts were guided by the principles of equivalence and entropy borrowed from the laws of thermodynamics.

In yet another vein Jung described the individuation process as directed toward the achieving of selfhood. Since the self in Jungian thought represents the totality of psychic life, we must interpret that statement as meaning the achievement of the most differentiated and integrated state of psychological development. In a metaphoric sense, as in alchemy, when the primal ingredients are put together in an appropriate mix, there will emerge an ultimate substance which will be greater than the sum of its parts. For Jung the press toward individuation is accelerated in the second half of life largely as a result of the imbalances created by the necessary adaptations during the first half of life. He identified the essential steps in the achieving of selfhood. These included relinquishing an absolute identification with the ego, accepting the power of the collective unconscious aspects of the psyche, making all the functions and the non-dominant attitude conscious and thus available for use, and similarly integrating the archetypes of the collective unconscious into conscious experience. The successful result of such a continuing set of efforts is largely ideal and hardly permanent. It creates a state of internal harmony through which both the immediate problems of living and the larger problems of life may be filtered.

While Jung thought of individuation as a universal human process, he also pointed out that the path did not necessarily resolve into an individual human struggle. Institutionalized, symbolic, non-conscious forms have emerged in the development of culture to deal with these very problems. Religious systems and their ritual practices may speak directly to these issues. Jung saw the individual need to "know oneself"as both an affliction and a blessing in that the progress of humankind is reflected in the expansion of consciousness which involves pain as part of the price of achievement.

See also SYMBOL/SYMBOLISM IEA

Bibliography

Fordham, F. 1966: *An introduction to Jung's psychology*. Harmondsworth: Penguin.

Fordham, M. 1947: *The life of childhood*. London: Kegan Paul.

Hall C.S. and Nordby, V.J. 1973: *A primer of Jungian psychology*. New York: New American Library.

Jacobi, J. 1962: *The psychology of C.G. Jung*. New Haven: Yale University Press.

Jung, C.G. 1933: *Psychological types*. New York: Harcourt.

——— 1961: *Memories, dreams, reflections*. (Recorded and edited by Aniela Jaffé) New York: Pantheon.

Meyers, I.B. 1962: *The Meyers-Briggs type indicator*. Princeton: Educational Testing Service.

Read, H. et al eds. 1953–79: *The collected works of C.G. Jung*. Princeton: Princeton University.

Wickes, F. 1966: *The inner world of childhood*. Rev. edn. New York: Appleton-Century.

K

Kabbalism The esoteric teaching of Judaism and the mystical base of western occultism. It deals with the nature and relationships of man, the universe and God.

Kabbalistic psychology, though ancient in origin, has undergone many reformations so that we find the principles of inner transformation expressed in the story of Exodus through the symbolism of a disorganized body of slaves being forged into an integrated nation in the Sinai desert before entering the Promised Land; set out in the contemporary mode of each epoch. Kabbalah has always adapted itself to the language of its time and place and so modern terms are used in this article.

The central model of Kabbalah is the Tree of Life. This is based on a metaphysical diagram of the Divine Attributes as manifested in ten sefirot or qualities, plus one non-sefirah, and their arrangement in columns, triads and paths. This format is also seen to be the basis of the human psyche which is made in the image of the Divine. All the laws of existence are expressed in the Tree of Life and their application to the psyche is perceived as relating to the moral or soul level of a four world scheme of reality as set out in Kabbalah.

In this multi-leveled model the psychological tree occupies a place between the physical world of elements and action and the two higher worlds of spirit and divinity. In this way the psyche has access to and is influenced by what goes on in those worlds. Thus the lower part of the psychological tree has contact with the body and the ego, while the central sefirah of Tiferet or the self is the link to the upper and inner worlds of the individual unconscious and the collective unconscious. The emotional soul triad of Judgment, Mercy and Beauty acts as the place of synthesis between the pillars of force and form, or dynamic and structure, while the central column holds the axis of development up the middle from matter to spirit and the divine.

The detailed anatomy of the psyche when set out on the tree is as follows: at the base is the sefirah of Kingdom or the elemental body which can be seen as the central nervous system. Above is the ego or Foundation, as it is traditionally called, which forms the focus of several triads. This is the ordinary mind that is concerned with thinking, feeling and

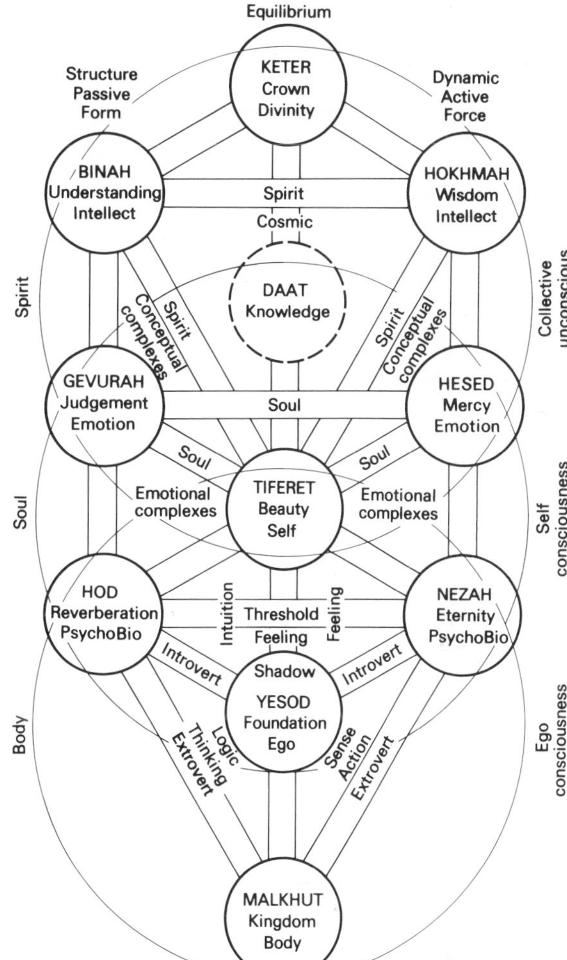

Kabbalistic tree or psyche

acting, whose triads lie below the twin sefirot of Reverberation and Eternity. These two sefirot represent the functional parts of the psyche and hold the path of the threshold between the normal consciousness of ego and what lies beyond. Above the threshold is the triad of awakening which completes what is called the lower face of the tree. This contains the four psychological sub-triads of sense, logic, feeling and intuition as well as their introvert and extrovert aspects. On either side of the self are the triads of psychological complexes. These relate to the sefirot of active and passive emotion and intellect traditionally called Mercy and Judgement, and Wisdom and Understanding. The left side contains all those emotional and intellectual complexes that hold and support the psyche such as discrimination and reason; while the right hand sefirot operate the active emotional and intellectual triads through motivations such as love and inspiration. The soul triad is seen as conscience, in that it is self-conscious. Self-consciousness is not a function but the place where the person reviews and acts upon his inner life. Traditionally it is the battle ground of good and evil. Here one's personal devil and angel try to influence the soul as it exercises the gift and responsibility of free will.

The soul level is a major stage in the progression up the central column of the tree. Beyond it lies the great triad of the spirit which allows access to the next realm of Creation. Here is found the sefirot of Knowledge or the dark glass in which the Kabbalist glimpses the great world of the macro cosmos. Seen psychologically this is the collective unconscious with its universal principles and archytypes. Here reside all the things in the psyche that have been passed down over many generations or from the higher worlds. The scale of this triad is cosmic and yet even this is reduced to a dot in relation to the triad of the divine at the Crown of the Tree. This level of consciousness brings everything into psychological integration in preparation for the higher stages of spiritual experience and union with God.

The journey of ascent from the physical level through the psyche and spirit to the divine world is described by kabbalists in ritual, allegory and metaphysics. However, despite these differences of presentation the objective is the same. This is to help an individual to become an intermediary between the various worlds and aid their unification. Thus as a person brings about development within himself so he becomes a channel for the higher influences that can flow directly down through his being and into the lower worlds. This helps the evolution of Existence. The purpose of Kabbalah is to assist in this process so that God might behold God in the perfection of its image. WKe

Bibliography

Scholem, G. 1974: *Kabbalah*. Jerusalem: Keter.

Fortune, D. 1970: *Mystical Qabalah*. London: Benn.

Halevi, Z. 1979: *Adam and kabbalistic tree*. London: Rider.

Kant, Immanuel (1724–1804). In his philosophy of mind as in much of the rest of his work, Kant reacted against the empiricism of HUME. When Hume turned in upon himself he could find no such thing as a SELF but only particular thoughts or perceptions; he therefore concluded that the self was a fiction. Kant thought this conclusion only showed the inadequacy of a philosophy which sought to ground all knowledge upon experience.

Kant claims that we do have knowledge which is not derived from experience, but recognizes the need to show how this is possible. He believes he can establish that certain conditions must hold if experience is to be possible at all, or at least experience of the same general kind as ours. We can therefore find out that these conditions hold without acquiring the information from experience, but just by reasoning from the fact that we do have experience, regardless of what the content of our experience may be. Reasoning of this kind he calls transcendental. One of the conditions for experience according to the *Critique of pure reason* (1781) is that whatever happens must have a cause; another is that the self must be considered to be a unity, and to be something more than the perceptions Hume was able to observe.

Kant thought it could not be an accident that such conditions hold. What guarantees they do is that the world as we experience it, the familiar world of things in space and time, is actually a *construction* which our minds make in accordance with principles they themselves supply – and supply in such a way as to ensure that the conditions needed for experience do obtain. Thus the principle that every event has a cause is provided by the mind in its construction: the series of events in time is arranged by us in accordance with it. This amounts to a kind of idealism about the world as we know it. Kant calls it transcendental idealism; it differs from other forms of idealism in its concern with the conditions necessary for experience, and also in that he admits that behind the everyday world we construct there lies a reality truly independent of us, the world of things as they are in themselves. The world as we know it he calls the phenomenal world, or world of appearances; the world of things in themselves, or noumenal world, is forever unknown to us just because of its radical independence.

This raises a question about the self. A unitary subject had to be presupposed as a condition for experience; but whereas the claim that every event has a cause could be guaranteed in the world as we know it because of the way our minds construct that world, our minds could hardly guarantee their own existence, as unitary subjects, in a similar fashion. They could not be simply a feature of their own construction, but must belong to the noumenal world. On the other hand, the noumenal world was supposed to be quite unknowable. Kant compromises here, and many have found his compromise unsatisfactory: he says I am *conscious that I am*, but can have no further knowledge than this about my noumenal nature. He criticizes DESCARTES for inferring from the premise "I think" that I am a simple, unitary thinking substance; I must indeed *think* of myself in this way, but nothing about the noumenal nature of anything follows from how we think about it. Thus, although I cannot avoid ascribing to myself a whole lot of present and remembered mental states, I have absolutely no guarantee that all these states actually do belong to the same noumenal subject. I take it for granted that they do, but the matter is not one about which knowledge is possible.

Whatever I can find out by experience or by introspection belongs to the world of appearances only, and tells me nothing about the underlying nature of myself as I am in myself. The distinction between the noumenal self and the empirically observable person is crucial for Kant's moral philosophy. Since within the world of appearances every event has a cause, every action we can observe ourselves or others to perform, and every mental state we can introspect or discover about empirically, is determined by causal law. Like many other moral philosophers Kant holds that if our wills were wholly subject to causal determination we could never be held responsible for what we did; but unlike most of them he thinks he can find a place for responsibility without denying the truth of a determinism which is complete and thoroughgoing within the world of appearances. For however determined the phenomenal event of my choosing may be, as something that belongs to the world of appearances, the underlying noumenal self may still act freely and make its decisions quite independently of any causes. The causal determinism that governs the world of appearances does not carry over to the noumenal world, or at least there could be no possible reason to think it does. Indeed, since we could not be moral agents unless we were noumenally free Kant considers that for practical purposes we are entitled to assume that we are. His views on this are developed in the *Critique of practical reason* (1788) and the *Groundwork of the metaphysic of morals* (1785).

This attempt to combine free will and determinism is ingenious, but unsatisfactory. If a decision is determined in the phenomenal world it is hard to see how the free noumenal self could do anything to alter it. The phenomenal events must occur in the way they do, and nothing can prevent them without disrupting the pattern of causal laws which governs the world of appearances. The noumenal self's free choices could influence what happens only by affecting the entire series of causes and effects that makes up the phenomenal world. This however would not give us what we want: we want to praise and blame one another for particular acts and particular decisions, not for the entire causal order. Kant has not found a way in which we can legitimately do this. RCSW

Bibliography

Broad, C.D. 1978: *Kant: an introduction*. Cambridge and New York: Cambridge University Press.

Kant, I. 1781, 1787 (1929): *Critique of pure reason*. Trans. N. Kemp Smith, London: Macmillan.

—— 1785 (1964) *Groundwork of the metaphysic of morals*. Trans. H.J. Paton. New York: Harper & Row. (Also under the title *The moral law*. London: Hutchinson (1948).)

—— 1788 (1956) *Critique of practical reason*. Trans. L.W. Beck. New York: Liberal Arts.

*Kemp, J. 1968: *The philosophy of Kant*. London, New York and Toronto: Oxford University Press.

*Körner, S. 1955: *Kant*. London: Penguin.

*Walker, R.C.S. 1978: *Kant*. London: Routledge and Kegan Paul.

karma An idea found in all major Indian and Indian-derived religious traditions, which sees an individual's own actions (in previous lives as well as in the present) as the most important explanation of his good or bad fortune, and of continued existence in the round of rebirth (SAMSARA). In early Indian religion, and still in some specialized forms of Hinduism, *karma* refers only to the limited sphere of activity in ritual sacrifice. Elsewhere, particularly in Buddhism, it is generalized to all actions, and points not merely to external behavior, but more importantly to the intention behind it. In popular religious culture, the idea co-exists with other explanations of fortune (such as ASTROLOGY, witchcraft, the "grace" of a god, etc.) and often comes to mean little more than "chance" or "fate". SCol

kinesis A form of orientation in which the animal's speed of locomotion depends upon the intensity of stimulation. For example, flatworms (*Platyhelminthes*) tend to aggregate in dark places because they move or turn more quickly under high illumination and consequently slow down, or even stop when they happen to reach a dark place. Kinesis is regarded as a fundamental type of orientation (Fraenkel and Gunn 1940), although it is not a very common one. DJM

Bibliography

Fraenkel, Gottfried S. and Gunn, Donald L. 1940: *The orientation of animals*. Oxford: Clarendon Press. New edn 1961. New York: Dover.

kinship In ethological terms a relationship determined by genealogical descent. This is a narrower definition than is found in social anthropology etc. in which affinal kin (through marriage), and fictional kin are also included. Kinship is of interest to ethologists primarily because of the existence of kin selection, a form of natural selection in which genetically transmitted behavior that increases the chance of close relatives surviving or reproducing is selected. Thus Bertram (1976) has argued that kin selection in lions could be responsible for communal suckling, males' tolerance toward cubs, and the lack of competition for estrous females. The existence of close kinship links was demonstrated in the 1950s in Japanese macaques, with the discovery by Japanese anthropologists of ranked matrilineages. In the society of these monkeys, all the offspring of a particular grandmother, through the female line, share a higher rank than all the offspring of a second grandmother who is of lower rank than the first. This phenomenon results from "dependent rank", by which monkeys achieve their social status during childhood through the intervention of their parents in competitive situations. VR

Bibliography

Bertram, B.C.R. 1976: Kin selection in lions and in evolution. In Paul P.G. Bateson and Robert A. Hinde, eds *Growing points in ethology*. Cambridge and New York: Cambridge University Press.

knowledge and belief Knowledge is the state of being in or having attained the intellectual goal in respect of propositions or facts, subjects or whole fields of study, languages, skills and other objects described as "known" in common speech: the goal involved, as a capacity, is "intellectual" in so far as it involves intelligent adjustment to "truth" or to the "facts". (Ryle 1949, made plain the variety of the objects of knowledge.) In the case of propositions or facts, the goal is to be in a state of firm and true assent, not just accidentally but as the result of a rationally proper or appropriate approach. "Degrees" of knowledge are described in terms of the adjective "certain": things are described as "certain" in so far as they are firmly based in such a way as to provide a reliable basis of inference to other conclusions.

The most common use in the philosophy of mind of the word "believe" is to cover every example of assent to a proposition, which is the primary subject of the attributes truth and falsity. Belief, thus conceived, may be defined as the pro-attitude towards a proposition in respect of its truth or falsity (see A. Phillips Griffiths, in Phillips Griffiths 1967). Because the pro-attitude expressed is in respect of truth, it is absurd to say "I believe that P, but P is not true", just as it is absurd to say "I approve of X, but X is wrong". Degrees of belief are expressed in terms of the adjective "sure", rather than of the adjective "certain": a claim to certainty is a claim to have obtained the objective goal, whereas an ascription of sureness is rather the indication of a psychological state.

There is a tendency, first found in the writings of Plato and Aristotle to use the term "belief" to denote an inferior state less than, and exclusive of, knowledge, and often with supposedly inferior objects. Also, the use of the word "believe" to suggest the absence of knowledge reinforced the idea that knowledge and belief are exclusive.This idea has also derived support from the scepticism of modern man who regards all assent as tentative or merely probable, and considers it as typically based on reasons, whereas knowledge is intuitive and certain. But these contrasts between belief and knowledge are all questionable.

Both in the theory of knowledge in philosophy, and in cognitive psychology, two very different approaches may be found, one of which I label aggregative or atomistic, and the other of which I label holistic or normative. In the first, the "aggregative" approach, the "act" of belief is supposed to be fundamental and knowledge is conceived of as a complex in which belief, qualified by the property of being sure, is supplemented by truth in the proposition believed and by good grounds for believing this proposition, possibly combined with some other features. In this approach belief is taken as the fundamental notion and explanations of the basis of objectivity, of the relation of knowledge and belief, and of the exact nature of good grounds for believing are matters for philosophers. The analysis of knowledge as true belief with a reason, appeared first in Plato's *Theaetetus*, and recurs constantly in the history of modern philosophy, prominently in the writings of A.J. Ayer, Chisholm (e.g. 1957, p.16 1966) and implicitly in most followers in the empiricist tradition. This approach was first attacked by Plato himself in the *Theaetetus*, was subject to acute criticism by Gettier (Phillips Griffiths 1967), implicit attack by Ryle (1949) and Austin (1961) and systematic criticism by Braine (1971). Gettier's implicit requirement that the attainment of firm and true assent be non-accidental implies the need of supplementary conditions liable to make the explanation of knowledge in terms of belief circular. Braine argues that the notions of ground or reason, and of good ground or reason, for belief need to be explained in terms of what is appropriate to bring one non-accidentally to knowledge, i.e. in terms of the notion of knowledge, rather than vice versa.

The tendency to consider the notion of belief fundamental encourages the idea that every object of assent is given to the intellect not as true but only as either probable or seeming true. Normally associated with these tendencies, whether or not necessarily, is the conception of a mass of *prima facie* true or provisional statements of belief, each isolable from the rest, so that the aggregative approach to the explanation of the concept of knowledge tends to generate an aggregative or constructional approach to the theory of the determination of what is known. This kind of empiricistic atomism, attacked by the idealists, has recently been subject to potent criticism by Quine and his followers.

In the second approach which I label holistic, the normative, standard or typical cognitive or intellectual act of the human mind is taken to be that of knowledge rather than belief, even though knowledge is intrinsically relational and cannot, like belief be imagined to be a non-relational isolable state of consciousness. This view allows justice to be done to Ryle's perception of the broad use of the word "know", and to the objections of Gettier, Braine and others to the aggregative approach. Not only is the explanation of the notions of ground and good ground to be in terms of what is appropriate to bring one non-accidentally to firm and true assent, but, in general, cases other than those of knowledge are to be considered according to their similarities to the case of knowledge or according to the ways in which they fall short of it. The standard, though not the sole, case of faith, i.e. belief upon testimony (believing people), may be taken to be the case in which a knower communicates knowledge with the authority of the witness or expert. Taking perception as an example of an area or mode of knowledge, on the holistic approach one's basic account will concern the proper and normal functioning of man in his use of his sensory powers to attain the goal of knowledge; and one will expect numerous and quite separate, merely ancillary accounts of the varied different sorts of way defects may enter in, illusion, delusion, etc. (Austin 1961, Hamlyn 1957); one will not expect one's account of the *anatomy* of perception to be shaped by one's conception of what must be regarded as abnormal or *pathological* cases.

Many of the accounts whose basic form stems from aggregative and constructional approaches turn out upon examination to incorporate holistic elements: Hume's incorporation of ideas about the cause of belief into the very notion of belief, and Popper's conception of "objective" knowledge are two random examples of this. In regard to the latter, if knowledge is conceived of as a goal, this goal may be conceived of as including some community in the holding of knowledge. So one meets the conception of knowledge as a public possession built up through the ages (Popper's "objective" knowledge), and an emphasis in many philosophers on some supposedly institutional aspects of knowledge, viz. as something peculiarly apt to provide the basis for a claim to authority of some kind, such as may make knowledge by belief upon testimony reasonable, and thus make knowledge intrinsically communicable. Then individual memory may be considered as a particular case of community memory and what is enshrined in books as an example of community memory.

Further, whereas it is natural to think of knowledge as a structured whole, which includes elements with varying degrees of certainty, it is difficult to avoid thinking of beliefs as isolable opinions or states of individual minds. Accordingly, in the case of a whole theory or belief-system, whether in the history of science or as studied in anthropology, it is often more instructive to think of the ways in which as a whole body it falls short of the goal of knowledge, than to consider it atomistically in terms of the evidence for or against its member beliefs taken individually.

The holistic approach predominates in Plato's Republic, in Aristotle's approach to the basis of knowledge, recurs in Hegel and some of his successors, but has not been systematically developed in modern times.

The dominance of the aggregative or atomistic approach in modern times has arisen in two main ways. The first may be located in Descartes who perhaps misguidedly conceded to the sceptic that the fundamental sensory element within perception is something common both to normal cases free from delusion or illusion and to abnormal cases subject to such defects. It is only against this background that the doubt may be raised as to the cause of these fundamental sensory elements, e.g. as perhaps a malevolent demon. In (modern) central state materialism in place of Descartes's malevolent demon one finds substituted the clever surgeon, but the role in argument is the same (Armstrong, 1968, pp.109, 229–30).

The second main root of the aggregative approach in modern times has been the dominance of atomistic, non-teleological, approaches to the consideration of the genesis of knowledge. Perceptual states may be conceived of as states of belief, possibly accompanied by images, both these conceived of as mental entities of some kind. It has come to seem natural to describe the particular effect of external stimuli on the sense organs in physiological terms, rather than in teleological ones related to the states of knowledge and belief which are their appropriate end product. The multiplicity of individual stimuli described is conceived of as having effects via connections in the nervous system and via ways of structuring these shared effects, ways which are partly innate, belonging to the structure of the brain, and partly the result of training. In this way a causal approach is built up to perception and to perceptual belief and in parallel with it a causal approach to one's account of the genesis of belief, probable, certain or otherwise, in all other cases. Indeed, Armstrong (1968) and others treat perception as merely a particular case of the causal genesis of belief. DDC

Bibliography

Armstrong, D.M. 1968: *A materialist theory of the mind.* London: Routledge & Kegan Paul.

Austin, J.L. 1961: Other Minds. *Philosophical papers.* London: Oxford University Press.

*Braine, David 1971: The nature of knowledge. *Proceedings of the Aristotelian Society.*

Chisholm, Roderick, M. 1957: *Perceiving: a philosophical study.* Ithaca, N.Y.: Cornell University Press.

*Chisholm, Roderick, M. 1966: *Theory of knowledge.* Englewood Cliffs, N.J.: Prentice-Hall.

Hamlyn, D.W. 1957: *The psychology of perception.* London: Routledge & Kegan Paul.

*Phillips Griffiths, A. ed. 1967: *Knowledge and belief.* London: Oxford University Press.

Ryle, Gilbert 1949: *The concept of mind,* chs 2 and 9 (sect. 7). London: Hutchinson; Totowa, N.J.: Barnes & Noble (1975).

Korsakov's syndrome (or Korsakov's psychosis) In 1889 the Russian neuropsychiatrist Korsakov described a chronic syndrome in which memory deficit was accompanied by confabulation and irritability. Nowadays the term is used in various ways. Some psychiatrists and psychologists apply it to any amnesic syndrome; that is, profound and lasting impairments of recent memory and of time-sense, with relative preservation of remote memory and good preservation of other cognitive functions. Others apply it only to a combination of the amnesic syndrome and confabulation (giving an elaborate account of events that never occurred in order to fill gaps in the memory). Others do not find the term useful.

Disorders of this type are often due to thiamine deficiency, which usually results from many years' abuse of alcohol but also from other causes such as persistent vomiting. The syndrome often follows WERNICKE'S SYNDROME. At post mortem examination of the brain, hemorrhagic lesions are found in the gray matter around the third and fourth ventricles and the aqueduct. DG

Kraepelin, Emil (1856–1926), an influential psychiatrist, teacher and writer (his textbook first appeared in 1883). Kraepelin is generally regarded as one of the founders of modern psychiatry, largely by virtue of his work on the classification of disorders (see NOSOLOGY). He described manic-depressive insanity, and in 1896 gave the name "dementia praecox" to the group of illnesses which Bleuler in 1911 was to call the schizophrenias. He considered that this illness resulted from some irreversible happening in the brain, the natural outcome being dementia; he nevertheless documented some spontaneous remissions. He also pointed the way to several techniques of investigation, notably by studying whole-life case histories and family histories, so that he was able to explore the interplay of genetic and environmental factors. DLJ

Bibliography

Kraepelin, E. 1906 *Lectures on clinical psychiatry.* Trans T. Johnstone. London: Baillere, Tindall and Cox.

L

labor turnover Workers leaving the employment of an organization for any cause. Turnover may be initiated by the organization as in discharging employees for poor work performance or laying off an employee due to lack of work. Promotions and transfers from one set of job duties to another may or may not be counted as turnover. Turnover might also be initiated by the employee as in voluntarily quitting a job. Turnover and its converse, tenure, have frequently been used as criterion measures in personnel research on both employee selection and job satisfaction. It is useful to distinguish between voluntary and involuntary turnover and also desired and undesired turnover. Replacement of productive employees is quite costly. MDH

Bibliography

Mobley, W.H. 1977: Intermediate linkages in the relationship between job satisfaction and employee turnover. *Journal of applied psychology* 62, 237–40.

Steers, R.M., and Stone, T.H. 1982: Organizational exit. In *Personnel management*, ed. K.M. Rowland, and G.R. Ferris. Boston: Allyn and Bacon.

Labov, William Born in 1927, Labov is Professor of Linguistics at the University of Pennsylvania. He is best known for his work on linguistic variation theory. In *The social stratification of English in New York City* (1966) he develops a descriptive apparatus capable of handling variable data. Linguistic variation is no longer relegated to performance but seen as a normal aspect of linguistic competence.

In demonstrating the logic and regularity of allegedly confused language of Black American children, Labov proposes a "difference hypothesis" to replace Bernstein's "deficit hypothesis" (see CODE).

Labov's studies on semantic boundaries and fuzzy semantics are now being used in aphasia research (Zurif and Blumstein 1978). The application of variation theory to FIRST LANGUAGE ACQUISITION is discussed by Labov and Labov (1976). PM

Bibliography

Labov, William 1966: *The social stratification of English in New York City*. Washington D.C.: Center for Applied Linguistics.

——— 1972: *Language in the inner city*. Philadelphia: University of Pennsylvania Press; Oxford: Basil Blackwell.

——— and Teresa 1976: Learning the syntax of questions. Paper presented at the Conference of Psychology and Language, Stirling, Scotland.

Zurfif, Edgar B. and Blumstein, Sheila E. 1978: Language and the brain. In ed. M. Halle, (et al.) *Linguistic theory and psychological reality*, Cambridge Mass. and London: MIT Press.

Lacan, Jacques (1901–81). Flamboyantly and stylistically baroque French psychoanalyst and psychiatrist, whose own history is that of the schisms and divisions of French psychoanalytical societies in 1953, 1964 and 1980. Lacan trained as a psychiatrist in the French clinical tradition in the 1920s in Paris and as a psychoanalyst in the 1930s, and was a member of surrealist and philosophically avant-garde circles of the period. He was an early champion of Heidegger and much influenced by Kojève's lectures on Hegel, infusing psychoanalysis with philosophy and poetry. In 1936 he outlined his notion of the MIRROR-PHASE. His approach was always marked by an extraordinary fidelity to Freud, an immense erudition, an emphasis on psychic structure rather than development, and a recognition of the privileged place of language in accounting for the Freudian discoveries and the nature of the psychoanalytic dialogue.

The main lines of his theory were laid out on the occasion of the first institutional schism in 1953, in his famous Discours de Rome (see Wilden (1968)): the focus was always to be on the functions and theory of language and speech in psychoanalysis. One aphorism, "the unconscious is structured like a language", offers a clear sense of Lacan's project. Firstly, he wished to indicate that the working material of psychoanalysis, speech, is what allows a conceptualization of the processes discovered by Freud in the dream, in slips of the tongue and in jokes – Freud's condensation and displacement are alternative names for the processes of metaphor and metonymy at work in language. Second, Freud's discovery that symptoms are symbolic, representing repressed thoughts, indicates that symptoms (and by inference, the unconscious) are structured linguistically. The key to the unraveling of their meaning is found, as all analysts agree, in the process of transference, during which the patient's discourse slowly translates the symptoms, phobias, patterns of behavior and character traits into speech offered to the analyst. The analyst is thus cast as the witness to the patient's revelation, or as the other conjured into existence through the mediation of speech.

Employing a theory of language derived in part from Hegel and Heidegger, but equally from the structuralism of SAUSSURE, Jakobson and Lévi-Strauss, Lacan emphasized the structure of linguistic elements which determine the material offered by patients in analysis, so that interpretation and analysis are to be viewed as working synchronically on the linguistic elements unique to each patient – in other words, the linguistic elements which are lost, distorted and transformed in constructing both symptoms on the one side, and the patient's distinctive subjectivity, on the other. Lacan questioned the parallelism of the two systems of signifier and signified which, according to Saussure, make up language. He stressed instead the priority of the signifier in determining meaning. But he emphasized less the formal systemic features of language than the dynamic relation between the subject and his speech. Starting from his theory of the mirror-phase, with its accompanying concept of the Imaginary, he distinguished between the ego, an imaginary constructed unity, and the subject, diversified as it is in complex relations with the ego, the other (the ego's imaginary counterpart) and the Other. This last, or "big Other", is the locus of the linguistic code, the guarantor of meaning, the third party in any dual relationship such as that of analysis or of love. The subject's speech is vouched for by this Other, yet is distorted and transformed in having to pass via the fantasy structure in which figure the ego and its relations to its objects. The relation of the subject to the Other is thus the mainline of the unconscious, for which analysis aims to clear the way.

Lacan's remarkable close readings of Freud's texts supported and illuminated each turn in his theory's development. The theory of the mirror-phase is linked closely to Freud's concept of narcissism and to the notion that both the ego and love are fundamentally narcissistic in character. He highlighted the concept *nachträglich* (deferred action), the retrospective mode of causality proper to the unconscious, a formal consequence of the battery of signifiers that make it up. Similarly Freud's account of the origin of society and law in *Totem and taboo* is read as a myth that highlights the essential function of the father in the constitution of the human subject. In contrast to other recent psychoanalytic theories, which stress the preeminence of the mother–child relation (pre-Oedipal, pre-genital), Lacan affirms the centrality for the subject's history of the triadic Oedipus complex, in which the function of the father is both essential and mythical. Essential, since the father is the representative of the law, in the last instance the law of language, and supplies the third term or mediating function that allows the child to find a place in the symbolic order (language) and escape from the murderous fascination of the image (other) of the mirror-phase, experienced in fantasy as fascination with the mother. Mythical, because the father's function is strictly metaphorical – the functions neither as real father (flesh and blood), nor as imaginary father (though the latter figures in fantasy as an ideal and punitive agency), but as the Name of the Father, with his name assigning the child a place in the social world and allowing the child to become a sexed being through the phallic function to which the Name of the Father refers. Lacan's account of the entry of the child into the Symbolic, by courtesy of the father's mythical function, is thus a revised version of Freud's Oedipus complex. The Oedipus complex represents the way in which infants become sexed (through their various responses to being deprived of the phallus), and become human (in escaping from the mother of the mirror-phase, whose own incompleteness renders the child's sense of wanting insupportable, into the Symbolic, in which lack is symbolizable through the generation of desire). With the triad of concepts appropriate to each sector (need/Real, demand/Imaginary, desire/Symbolic), Lacan continues his criticism of those versions of psychoanalytic theory which equate Freud's instincts *(Triebe)* with biologically determined need, arguing instead that the true realm of psychoanalytic action is the world of desire, which is created by language transforming need into desire in answer to the unsatisfiable demands of the other (mother) for love. Desire, like the Freudian instinct, is never fulfilled, always there, continually displaced and transformed.

Lacan's later theories (from the mid 1960s on) concentrated on the relation between the signifier, the Other and the object *a* (a concept linked, on the one hand, with the other of the mirror-phase and, on the other hand, with the privileged objects of Freudian instincts – the breast, feces, urine, penis, to which Lacan adds the voice and the gaze). His concern was to specify the formal characteristics of psychoanalytic discourse – an extension of his emphasis on speech as the uniquely efficacious medium of psychoanalysis. The linguistic aspect of the teaching was replaced by a more formal mathematical approach, including an attempt to define the properties of the various "spaces" postulated by psychoanalytic theory (e.g. inside/outside) – not only the space of the unconscious, distinct and yet continuous with consciousness (and thus well represented by a Möbius strip), but also the Borromean knots in which the signifying chains of demands and desires are linked together by the subject. The close alliance with mathematics (topology and number theory) and philosophy (epistemology and logic) further his attack on "psychologism". For him, psychoanalysis, rather than being a psychology of the individual or a quasi-biological account of adaptation to the environment, is more akin to the Socratic dialogue, whose aim is truth. The Freudian discovery consists in showing how desire is necessarily implicated in the truth sought by the subject along the paths opened up by the signifier. JF

Bibliography

Bowiek, M. 1979: Jacques Lacan. In *Structuralism and since*, ed. J. Sturrock. Oxford: Oxford University Press.

Lacan, J. 1966: *Ecrits*. Paris: Seuil.

——1977: *Ecrits: a selection*. London: Tavistock; New York: Norton.

——1977: *The four fundamental concepts of psychoanalysis*. London: Hogarth Press; New York: Norton.

Lemaire, A. 1978: *Jacques Lacan*. London & Boston: Routledge & Kegan Paul.

Wilden, A. 1968: *The language of the self*. Baltimore: Johns Hopkins University Press.

Laing, R.D. Scottish psychiatrist, born 1927. He has been instrumental in demonstrating the degree to which we are alienated from our own experience; how we have come to rely upon external criteria and appearances for our understanding of ourselves. "No one can begin to think, feel or act now except from the starting point of his or her own alienation". In his emphasis on therapy viewed as a social and political activity Laing calls into question the foundations of our popular cultural awareness, especially our notion of sanity, or what constitutes the accepted continuum between the poles of "normal" and "abnormal", "sane" and "insane", "appropriate" and "deviant". According to Laing, in *The politics of experience*, "the 'normally' alienated person, by reason of the fact that he acts more or less like everyone else, is taken to be sane". And, "our collusive madness is what we call sanity". Laing has also set the tone for this "radical" therapy by stating: "Psychotherapy must remain an obstinate attempt of two (or more) people to recover the wholeness of being human through the relationship between them". The popular shift towards the various ALTERNATIVE PSYCHOLOGIES represents the search for such wholeness. (See RADICAL THERAPY.) DAL

Bibliography

Laing, R.D. 1967: *The politics of experience*. New York: Pantheon Books.

language: functions of Refers to uses to which language is put in actual communication. Functional models of language attempt to relate linguistic choices to social skills (see COMMUNICATIVE COMPETENCE).

Whereas it is widely held that the cognitive function of language is the primary one (a view which may reflect only what is true of adult, male, middle-class, middle-aged academics of the "first" world) the study of other linguistic functions has become a legitimate pursuit within socio and psycholinguistics.

Research is still in a pre-theoretical phase. There are a great number of functional classifications, the best known ones being the three-function model (developed originally by Buehler 1934) and Jakobson's six-function model where a distinction is made between the cognitive, expressive, poetic, phatic, conative and metalinguistic functions of language (Jakobson 1960).

The development of functions in FIRST LANGUAGE ACQUISITION has been studied by Halliday; preliminary remarks about the role of functions in second language learning have been made by Mühlhäusler (1980). PM

Bibliography

Buehler, K. 1934: Sprachtheorie: *Die Darstellungsfunktionen des Sprache*, Jena: Gustaf Fischer.

Halliday, M.A.K. 1973: *Explorations in the functions of language*. London: Edward Arnold.

Jakobson, Roman 1960: Closing statement: linguistics and poetics: In *Style in language*, ed. T.A. Sebeok. Cambridge, Mass.: MIT Press.

Mühlhäusler, P. 1980: Structural expansion and the notion of creolization. In *Theoretical orientations in Creole Studies*, ed. Albert Valdman and Arnold Highfield. New York and London: Academic Press.

language: variation theories Although it is clear that all languages (with the exception of incipient pidgins) vary along the dimensions of time, style, and geographic and social space the study of linguistic variation is a very recent branch of linguistics. Scholars working within the structuralist and transformationalist frameworks had hitherto argued that the only proper subject of linguistic description was an abstract IDIOLECT.

Two main approaches to the study of linguistic variation can be distinguished. One is the quantitavist approach which measures the variable linguistic behavior of members of pre-established social groups. In as much as it claims to be psychologically real it assumes that the human mind can handle variability on a very large scale and is capable of learning and maintaining linguistic probabilities. The quantitavist approach is closely associated with LABOV. The second approach is the lectological or dynamic approach (associated with Bailey) which proposes that variability results from the spread of language rules through time and space. As a result the implicational ordering of the rules of language is the same for all members of a language community. Individual speakers, however, will command only a subset of the rules of the language depending on their age, social group membership or geographic origin. The greatest appeal of the lectological view to psycholinguistics is that it enables investigators to distinguish between productive and perceptive competence. As a method of description it is particularly useful when applied to developing linguistic systems such as child language or INTERLANGUAGE. PM

Bibliography

Bailey, C.J.N. 1976: The state of non-state linguistics. *Annual review of anthropology* 5, 93–106.

language acquisition *See* first language acquisition

Language Acquisition Device The notion of LAD (Language Acquisition Device) was introduced by CHOMSKY (1964). This device is said to enable the native speaker to acquire his/her internalized grammar for a language on the basis of primary linguistic input data. The function of the LAD can be represented as follows:

Input	Device	Output
Primary Data ⟶	LAD ⟶	Internalized Grammar

The LAD is independent of individual languages as children can acquire any natural language.

An important aspect of Chomsky's views on FIRST LANGUAGE ACQUISITION is that the primary data to which a child is exposed are full of performance errors.

The question to what extent children are equipped with a biologically-based innate capacity for language acquisition is not settled (see also BIOPROGRAM LANGUAGE.) The limitations of Chomsky's views on this question include: the neglect of the important role of structured input (BABY TALK); the unsuitability of a static transformational-generative model of description to capture dynamic development; and the inability to account for the discrepancy between production and perception in language acquisition. PM

Bibliography

Chomsky, Noàm 1964: *Current issues in linguistic theory*. The Hague: Mouton.

language and cognition Traditionally conceived of as a field of research which attempts to answer such questions as "How far is language necessary for thought?" and "What intellectual capacities are required for an individual to develop and sustain language?". In practice, further questions have been raised concerning both "language" and "cognition". "Is language confined to humans?". "At what point can young children be said to have acquired language?", and "Are sign languages (or other communicative systems based on non-verbal symbols) really types of language?" are all questions which test our understanding of the concept of language. They force us to decide whether, and where, to draw lines across the terminological continuum from "linguistic" through "paralinguistic" to "nonlinguistic" communication. (See also COMMUNICATION, NON-VERBAL.) It may prove impossible to point to formal properties which serve as critical attributes of language (Lyons 1972).

Questions have also been raised about "cognition". The modern field is wider in scope than the study of thinking: a reasonable definition would refer more generally to "the mental processing of information", and contributing disciplines include psychology, linguistics, ARTIFICIAL INTELLIGENCE and neurology (see also NEUROLINGUISTICS). There are many different, and some widely divergent, subfields within it, including speech perception, visual perception, word recognition and reading, memory, learning and attention, and so on. Consequently one person's view of cognition may be very different, both in content and methodology, from another's; controversial issues from one point of view are pseudo-controversies from another (Ades 1981): and precious few attempts are made these days to present an overall picture (though Campbell 1979, for language acquisition, attempts a stimulating dualistic statement, with "inner", truly cognitive, processes interacting with "outer", sensory-motor processes, and with a flexible boundary between these two domains).

Much work has centered on the theory of language

developed by CHOMSKY and his associates during the last quarter-century, and Chomsky (1981) represents, for many, the flowering of a truly cognitivist linguistics at last. But many linguists have dissented from this approach, warning that grammar-writing, like map-making, crucially involves selection, abstraction and distortion (Matthews 1979). For many psycholinguists, the Chomskyan notion of a "mental organ" of language is misguided, inasmuch as presently-known language abilities can be accounted for by appeal to nonlinguistic properties of human cognition; thus, just as there are no "organs of speech" as such (rather, organs for eating, breathing, drinking, etc.) so we have no specifically linguistic cognitive capacities (rather, other capacities are recruited to linguistic ends – Bever 1970).

Developmentally, the Behaviorist view of language acquisition as a triumph of human learning has been effectively challenged by Chomsky. His position stresses the difficulties faced by the child in constructing an appropriate grammar, given (a) the complexity of the linguistic system and (b) the apparently inadequate nature of the primary linguistic data (the forms of language the child is exposed to). Accordingly, the Chomskyan view looks to some innate potential for language acquisition, which is part of the cognitive endowment of the "prelinguistic" child, (see also LANGUAGE ACQUISITION DEVICE). Further, this capacity is specifically linguistic, hence differs radically from Piaget's concept of language (1959) as an outgrowth of general cognitive development.

Extreme difficulties lie in the way of resolving such issues. The existence of child language forms such as *sitted* (for *sat*), *foots* (for *feet*), etc., which cannot have been modelled by adult speech, suggests that very simple learning processes are not adequate; but it is still an open question how far aspects of learning are involved in, and interact with, other, possibly innate, cognitive skills in the language acquisition process. While certain language/cognition parallels (such as the coincidence of early vocabulary growth with the ability to search for displaced objects) are compatible with the Piagetian view, it is not easy (a) to establish a sufficient number of such correlations, nor (b) to determine the direction of the causality, cognition → language. Research by Donaldson (1978) into such areas as conservation and class inclusion has uncovered the importance of the interaction between linguistic forms and the perceived context for these forms; not only can children be shown to "have" these concepts much earlier than conventional Piagetian estimates allow, but (more importantly) the possession of these concepts cannot be realistically disentangled from their linguistic means of expression.

This might seem to favor the Chomskyan view of language as part of a richly structured cognitive system at the outset; but there are procedural difficulties (at the very least) here also, inasmuch as the nature of the child's specific linguistic resources is gauged on the assumption of the inadequate properties of the linguistic input to the child. Recent studies on the language addressed to young children ("motherese" and related phenomena such as BABY TALK – Ferguson and Snow 1977) have considerable potential in this connection, in uncovering aspects of clarification and simplification in speech to children which are not present in speech to adults. However, it is not yet clear whether the role of input language is crucial in language acquisition; it *might* represent such an effective (albeit unconscious) teaching strategy that learning theory once more becomes viable, or it might turn out to be a massive epiphenomenon, bound by culture and geography. The answer probably lies somewhere between these extremes, in which case we may have to consider a selective role for input – perhaps in providing enhanced contexts for the acquisition of certain types of linguistic features over others (e.g. abstract formal features which play only an indirect role in message structure, such as subject-verb inversion in English question forms).

Thus far we have considered the ontogenesis of language; we now turn to what we may call its microgenesis (the moment-by-moment, or "on-line", processing of language, both in comprehension and production), where language/cognition interactions also take place. If language abilities in adults are sustained through the operation of some stable and discrete mental organ, we should expect them to be immune from variation in relation to modality and task differences (just as they are predicted to be independent of other aspects of cognition in development). Against this view, there is the "cognitive resources" position already referred to, according to which context (along with other pragmatic factors) continues to play a role in language processing beyond the point of maturity, and modality differences (e.g. reading vs. writing, speech vs. auditory processing) may at least partially determine the nature of the processing that takes place. For instance, it may seem reasonable to assume a "search for message" strategy in comprehension, but a "search for expression units" strategy in production, and such strategies seem to involve radically different types of ability (and can indeed be differentially impaired in language pathology). Conversely, parallels in strategies may be found between language processing and other aspects of cognition (e.g. the perception of ambiguity in utterances and in visual stimuli). Again, these issues are not easy to resolve, since it appears to be impossible to develop techniques of investigation that are at once rich and non-intrusive, and to devise models of linguistic behavior that are simultaneously adequate to account for observational facts and precise enough to bear on specific hypotheses.

For example, consider the fundamental opposition between "top down" (analysis-by-synthesis) vs. "bottom up" (analysis-by-analysis) models of language perception (Fodor, Bever and Garrett 1974). Evidence exists, in both reading and auditory processing studies, to support and deny each type of model, and a good guess would therefore be that we actually employ a mixture of processing strategies; that largely automatic feature detectors call out stimulus properties for the operation of higher level synthesizing abilities, within a hierarchy towards the head of which stand "attention" and even "consciousness". Such a "model" currently beckons, but no formulation of it has rigor, and hence it has none of the properties we require of a model; most importantly, it cannot be falsified.

Finally, we should emphasize the richly differentiated

nature of language. Even restricting our discussion to conventional verbal communication, we find a hierarchy of skills, rooted in more than one sensory modality and extending across a wide range of motor control functions, yet reaching up to the highest levels of intellectual operations. In view of this, the importance of language as an object of study in the field of cognition is not surprising; but by the same token we should not expect it to yield up its secrets easily. MAG

Bibliography

Ades, T. 1981: Time for a purge. *Cognition* 10, 7–15.

Bever, T.G. 1970: The cognitive basis for linguistic structures. In J.R. Hayes, ed. *Cognition and the development of language*. New York: Wiley.

Campbell, R.N. 1979: Cognitive development and child language. In *Language acquisition: studies in first language development*, ed. P. Fletcher and M. Garman. London & New York: Cambridge University Press.

Chomsky, N. 1981. *Lectures on government and binding*. Dordrecht: Foris.

Clark, H.H. and E.V. 1977. *Psychology and language an introduction to psycholinguistics*. New York: Harcourt Brace Jovanovich.

*Donaldson, M. 1978. *Children's minds*. London: Croom Helm; New York Norton.

Fergusen, C. and Snow, C. 1977: *Talking to children: language input and acquisition*. London and New York: Cambridge University Press.

Fodor, J.A., Bever, T.G. and Garrett, M.F. 1974. *The psychology of language: an introduction to psycholinguistics and generative grammar*. New York: McGraw-Hill.

Lyons, J. 1972: Human language. In R.A. Hinde, ed. *Non-verbal communication*. London and New York: Cambridge University Press.

Matthews, P.H. 1979. *Generative grammar and linguistic competence*. London: George Allen and Unwin.

Mehler, J., ed. 1981. *Cognition* 10. (Tenth anniversary volume) Lausanne: Elsevier Sequoia S.A.

Piaget, J. 1926 (1959). *The language and thought of the child*. London: Routledge & Kegan Paul; New York: Humanities.

Language Assessment, Remediation and Screening Procedure (LARSP) is a linguistically based method for the analysis and remediation of the grammatical disorders of adults and children. Conceived by D. Crystal, P. Fletcher, and M. Garman at the University of Reading, LARSP was developed with the pragmatic aim of providing the speech therapist with a systematic procedure by which an individual's grammatical disability could be assessed in terms which facilitate subsequent remedy.

The procedure, as described by Crystal et al. (1976), consists of three stages. First, a sample of the patient's speech is recorded, transcribed, and grammatically analyzed. This analysis is then entered onto the LARSP profile chart where it is interpreted according to a developmental metric. Finally the interpretation is used to determine strategies for attaining remedial goals. The transition from assessment to remediation is helped by the developmental framework of the major part of the profile. The order in which grammatical structures are presented in the chart reflects the order in which children normally acquire them. Because grammatical disorders are pictured in terms of acquisitional delay, the LARSP therapist, working either with adults or children, is able to plot the progress of the patient according to a consistent metric, and to answer, at each stage in the treatment, the essential remedial question: "Which structure to teach next?" In addition to its widespread use in speech clinics, LARSP has been adapted for use by school teachers in an assessment and remediation model entitled "Structural Analysis of the Language of School-Age Children" (SALSAC). (See also SPEECH DISORDERS.) TJT

Bibliography

Crystal, D., Fletcher, P., and Garman, M. 1976: *The grammatical analysis of language disability*. London: Edward Arnold.

language death The term refers to a number of phenomena, the two most important being

(1) Cases where a socially inferior language is gradually replaced by a dominant language through a process of continued borrowing and mixing. This is favored in diglossic situations (see DIGLOSSIA).

(2) Cases where the speakers of a socially weaker language are made to shift to a dominant language.

The first case is of particular interest to psycholinguists as there are numerous parallels between the loss of grammar occurring with dying languages and that associated with aphasia. Differences may reflect the extent to which pragmatic factors affect the principle of "first acquired-last lost". PM

Bibliography

Dressler, W. and Leodolter, P., eds 1977: Language death issue. *International journal of the sociology of language* 12.

latent learning Learning which is not manifest in overt behavior at the time learning takes place, but may become evident in a later transfer test. For example animals may learn that one neutral event follows another (sensory preconditioning) or learn the layout of a maze through exploration without any incentive to follow a particular route. Generally, they may learn what stimuli occur in a given context even though those stimuli are not currently reinforcing; latent learning may be revealed by subsequently rendering some of these stimuli reinforcing, whereupon appropriate behavior is evinced (or acquired more rapidly than by inexperienced control subjects). Latent learning provides crucial support for cognitive learning theories such as Tolman's which characterize learning as the acquisition of knowledge or expectancy, to which changes in behavior are merely secondary. EAG

lateralization The organization of brain function such that the two hemispheres are specialized to control different psychological operations. In contrast to sensory, perceptual, and motor functions which are represented in both cerebral hemispheres, mechanisms for certain sophisticated verbal and nonverbal skills are usually found in only one hemisphere. For example, speech and language functions, at least in right-handed people, are exclusively lateralized in the left hemisphere. This has been determined by observing the effect of electrical stimulation of the brain, studying individuals with cerebral damage, and by using sodium amytal, a drug that selectively anesthetizes speech areas in the fully conscious patient. The right hemisphere, on the other hand, is dominant for nonverbal activities related, for example, to imagery, artistic expression, and performance on tasks requiring spatial skills. There is some evidence that lateralized functions affected by unilateral brain damage are taken over by the opposite hemisphere. This, along with the fact that children show less hemispheric specialization than adults, suggests that cerebral dominance may be a part of a development pattern involving differential suppression of function in each hemisphere. It has been suggested that since the two hemispheres process information in quite different ways, relative differences in cerebral dominance could affect the nature of human consciousness both between individuals and across cultures. GWi

Bibliography

Levy, J. 1981: Lateralization and its implications for variations in development. In E. Gollin (ed.) *Developmental plasticity*. New York: Academic Press.

leadership By "leadership" we mean the direction, supervision, or management of a group or an organization. Leaders are ubiquitous. They may be "emergent" (informally acknowledged); elected by the group; or appointed by the organization of which the group is a part. A leader may thus be a gas station manager, the chief executive officer of a multinational company, or the person who happens to be most influential in a group. Although the topic of leadership has been a focus of interest since the dawn of recorded history, its scientific examination began only in 1904, and did not get into its stride until the second world war.

Emergent Leadership

Early investigations were preoccupied with the question of how one attains a leadership position, and in particular, whether there are certain personality attributes or traits which enable a person to become a leader, or to be effective as a leader. We usually identify emergent leaders by means of sociometric scales, that is, by asking such questions as, "Whose opinion do you value most in this group?" "Whom would you most like to have as your leader?"

Various studies have shown that emergent leaders do not differ markedly from their followers in personality attributes or traits. They tend to be just slightly more intelligent, slightly larger, more visible and socially adept than members. Their leadership status seems to derive more from the group members' perception that a person is able to provide the needed skills, economic, or political resources to help the group to achieve its goals than from personality.

Moreover, almost everyone is a leader of at least some groups and a follower in innumerable others. It is difficult to see, therefore, how a particular trait could identify a leader.

Leadership Effectiveness

The many attempts to find leadership traits and attributes which would distinguish effective from ineffective leaders have had similarly limited success. It is of interest to note, therefore, that there is a wide divergence between practitioners and theorists in their treatment of personality attributes and characteristics.

In practice, the most commonly used predictors of leadership performance, e.g. in hiring or assigning managers, are intellectual abilities, technical competence and leadership experience. On the other hand, the major contemporary theories of leadership practically ignore these cognitive abilities and knowledge: McGregor's Theory X/Y (1960); Likert's System 1–4 (1967); House's Path Goal Theory (1971); Fiedler's Contingency Model (1967); or Vroom and Yetton's Normative Decision Model (1974), etc., either do not discuss the role of intellectual abilities or experience as important elements in their formulations, or mention them only in passing. Instead, their main focus is on such socioemotional variables as managerial attitudes or philosophies, participative management and leadership style.

The concern with socioemotional behavior was also embodied by a ground-breaking study by Lewin, Lippitt and White (1939). It investigated the effect of democratic, laissez-faire, and autocratic leaders on group climate, participation and member involvement. Boys' clubs were organized under leaders who were instructed to behave in a predetermined manner. The study was interpreted as showing that a democratic, participative style produced better results than either of the others. Above all, this study demonstrated that leadership phenomena could be examined in laboratory experiments and became the model for most empirical leadership research for the next two decades.

The Lewin studies were part of a humanistic, employee-centered movement in management thinking which championed personal growth, employee self-actualization, and participative management practices. These theories, proposed by such leading figures as McGregor, Likert, Maslow, and Mayo, had considerable impact on management thinking but neither the theories nor training programs based on them have been consistently supported by empirical research.

Leaders' Behavior

A major theme, beginning in the 1940s, was a concentrated effort to identify behavior associated with effective performance. The research, most prominently associated with a group at Ohio State University, found two important factors: "Consideration" (socioemotional, expressive behavior indicating concern for the opinions, feelings, and welfare of subordinates) and "Structuring" (assigning roles and tasks to group members, setting standards and evaluating performance). These behavior factors have played a major part in understanding the leader's role in shaping the group interaction. They did not identify practically useful differences between effective and less effective leaders. Considerate leaders had more satisfied group members and in some studies, leaders who were both structuring and considerate tended to be somewhat more effective than leaders who were not considerate or structuring. Other studies did not find these results (Korman 1967).

Contingency approaches
The Contingency Model of Leadership Effectiveness (Fiedler 1967) led to the abandonment of the notion that there was one best leadership style or behavior for obtaining effective performance. The theory classifies leaders as motivated primarily by the need to accomplish assigned tasks or to develop close and supportive relations with members of their group. The situation is classified as giving a high, moderate or low degree of power, influence and control to the leader. Situational control indicates, in essence, the probability of being able to accomplish the task. The theory and supporting research showed that task-motivated leaders perform best in high-control and in low-control situations; relationship-motivated leaders perform best in moderate-control situations.

The Contingency Model has generated considerable controversy but has been extensively validated (Strube and Garcia 1981). The theory implies that leader effectiveness can be improved by changing either personality or situational factors, and that it is considerably easier to change the latter. A training program was therefore developed to teach leaders how to modify critical components of the leadership situation (e.g. leader–member relations, task structure, position power). The effectiveness of this "Leader Match" method has been demonstrated in a variety of evaluation studies in military and civilian settings (Fiedler, Chemers and Mahar 1976; Fiedler and Mahar 1979).

Path–Goal Theory
Involves the interaction of behavior and situation and was developed by House (1971). It states that the leader must motivate the subordinates by (a) emphasizing the relationship between subordinates' own needs and the organizational goals, and (b) clarifying and facilitating the path which will enable them to fulfill their own needs as well as the organization's goals.

The theory predicts that structuring behavior (i.e. coaching, direction, specifying goals) will have positive effects when the job is unclear; considerate behavior (support, warmth, concern) will have beneficial effects when the job is boring or aversive. Research supports the theory's prediction of employees' job satisfaction and subordinates' motivation; predictions on performance have not been well supported.

Normative Decision Model
Vroom and Yetton's (1974) model prescribes the conditions under which leaders should make decisions autocratically, in consultation with group members, or with group members fully participating in the decisions. The theory assumes that (a) individual decisions are more time-effective than group decisions, (b) subordinates are more committed to a decision if they participate in its formulation and (c) complex and ambiguous tasks require more information and consultation for reaching high quality decisions. The model prescribes the way in which decisions are to be made under various conditions. Up to now, tests of this theory have been based on retrospective reports, and further research is required to evaluate the predictive validity of the theory.

Transactional Approaches
These theories deal with the way in which leaders interact with subordinates. Hollander (1978) showed, for example, that the leaders' status increases in proportion to their contribution to the group goal. Leaders must prove their worth by competence and commitment to group values, for which they then receive "idiosyncracy credits". These credits allow the leader to diverge from accepted group norms and standards, to strike out in new directions, or to be forgiven for minor transgressions.

Cognitive Approaches
Leadership theorists have returned increasingly to the study of cognitive processes. In studies of leader judgments, Green and Mitchell (1979) found that leaders attribute more blame when a subordinate's behavior had adverse consequences than if the same behavior had no negative consequences. These and similar studies show why leaders reward certain types of behavior and punish others.

A series of studies (Fiedler et al. 1979) showed that military leaders effectively utilized their intellectual abilities but not their experience when they had relatively stress-free relations with their boss. They effectively utilized their job-relevant experience, but not their intellectual abilities when stress with their boss was high. These studies suggest that intelligence and job-knowledge were prematurely abandoned by leadership theorists.

Task characteristics and formal rules and customs, as well as technologies, may guide worker activities, and therefore, substitute for leadership. These phenomena have been studied by Osborn and Hunt (1975). Leadership research is likely to focus to an increasing extent on the role of task characteristics and on the cognitive components of the leadership process. FEF

Bibliography

Fiedler F.E. 1967: *A theory of leadership effectiveness.* New York: McGraw-Hill.

——— Chemers, M.M. and Mahar, L. 1976: *Improving leadership effectiveness: the Leader Match concept.* New York: Wiley.

——— and Mahar, L. 1979: The effectiveness of contingency model training: validation of Leader Match. *Personnel psychology* 20, 1–14.

——— et al. 1979: Organizational stress and the use and misuse of managerial intelligence and experience. *Journal of applied psychology.* 64, 635–47.

Green, S.G. and Mitchell, T.R. 1979: Attributional processes of leaders in leader–member interactions. *Organizational behavior and human performance.* 23, 429–58.

Hollander, E.P. 1978: *Leadership dynamics: a practical guide to effective relationships.* New York: Free Press.

House, R.J. 1971: A path–goal theory of leader effectiveness. *Administrative science quarterly.* 16, 321–38.

Korman, A. 1967: "Consideration", "Initiating Structure", and organizational criteria. *Personnel psychology.* 18, 349–60.

Lewin, K., Lippitt, R. and White, R.K. 1939: Patterns of aggressive behavior in experimentally created social climates. *Journal of social psychology.* 10, 271–301.

Likert, R. 1967: *The human organization.* New York: McGraw-Hill.

McGregor, D. 1960: *The human side of enterprise.* New York: McGraw-Hill.

Osborn, R.N. and Hunt, J.G. 1975: An adaptive–reactive theory of leadership: the role of macro variables in leadership research. In *Leadership frontiers.* J.C.Hunt and L.L. Larson, ed. Carbondale: Southern Illinois University Press.

Strube, M.J. and Garcia, J.E. 1981: A meta-analytic investigation of Fiedler's

Contingency Model of leadership effectiveness. *Psychological bulletin.* 90, 307–21.

Vroom, V.H. and Yetton, P.W. 1974: *Leadership and decision-making.* New York: Wiley.

learned helplessness This term was introduced by Martin Seligman(1975) to denote a state of apathy which may be induced experimentally in animals and which is similar to some states of depression occurring naturally in humans. He described experiments in which dogs were subjected to electric shocks without the possibility of escaping from them. After a time the animals became inactive and submissive, lost appetite and failed to escape from shocks which they had previously known how to avoid.

Seligman suggested that depression in humans could be caused by the repeated experience of being unable to act in such a way as to achieve a desired outcome or to avoid emotional trauma. Such experiences in childhood may predispose an individual to depression, whereas the development of a sense of control over the environment may render him immune. The theory thus has etiological (see AFFECTIVE DISORDERS), preventive and also therapeutic implications, forming the basis of one type of cognitive therapy. Seligman also suggests that "unmerited" reward may have similar effects. DLJ

Bibliography

Seligman, Martin E.P. 1975: *Helplessness.* San Francisco: Freeman.

learning: animal A change of an animal's behavior in a particular situation attributable to its previous experience of the situation, and excluding changes due to sensory adaptation, muscular fatigue, injury or maturation.

Many behavioral phenomena are usually included under the general heading of learning, without it being necessarily assumed that they are caused either by common or by entirely distinctive underlying mechanisms: the most studied instances include habituation and sensitization (Groves and Thompson 1970); classical conditioning (Pavlov); operant conditioning (Skinner) or instrumental learning (Thorndike); other kinds of associative learning intermediate between classical and operant conditioning like sign-tracking (Hearst and Jenkins 1974) and observational learning; learning seemingly restricted to critical or sensitive periods in ontogeny like IMPRINTING (Lorenz) and song learning (Catchpole 1979); and performance on more complex tasks such as learning sets (Harlow 1959), delayed matching to sample (Roberts and Grant 1976), serial pattern learning (Hulse 1978), and the manipulation of symbols (Premack 1978) which many feel justify the descriptive if not the explanatory use of "cognitive" terminology (Hulse, Fowler and Honig 1978) without infringing the law of parsimony (Lloyd Morgan's canon). The extent to which maturational factors (envisaged as the execution of a genetic program) can be disentangled from experiential (learned) factors in the ontogeny of behavior probably depends mainly upon how research has been done into the behavior concerned: in intensively researched areas, such as song learning in passerine birds, interactions between genetic and experiential factors of fascinating diversity and varying from species to species are being found.

For most of the twentieth-century experimental psychologists, especially the so called 'learning theorists' (Hilgard and Bower 1975), have endeavored to establish general laws of learning perhaps common to all animal species. So far as they exist, these could reflect (i) homologous or evolutionarily convergent mechanisms perhaps delimited by fundamental neuronal mechanisms; (ii) commonalities in what is required of information systems for the selection of predictive correlations caused by the logical constancies of the universe: (iii) limitations in the conceptual and technical ingenuity of contemporary experimenters.

Recently, under the influence of ethology the degree of generality of such laws has been questioned (Seligman 1970) and the notion of constraints on learning (Shettleworth 1972) – i.e. that a particular species may have a considerable facility to learn certain things but little or none to learn others, or that specific kinds of association may be governed by specific kinds of laws – has stimulated much empirical research (such as the great volume of work on conditioned food aversion, reviewed, e.g. by Goudie 1980).

Also ethology's historic emphasis on functional explanations of behavior has recently begun to interact with both psychological and zoological studies of animal learning in a potentially fruitful way: efforts are being made both in laboratory and field to assess the way in which the learning abilities of higher vertebrates may actually be put to use and contribute to Darwinian fitness in an ecological setting such as in FORAGING (e.g. review by Lea 1981). Yet another field of interdisciplinary endeavor covering the whole breadth of the neurosciences is the long quest to understand the neural bases of learning and memory (the search for the 'engram') and here the study of relatively short-term changes in behavior and of animals with very simple nervous systems such as the mollusc *Aplysia* (Kandel 1976) is every bit as exciting as the much more voluminous literature on brain mechanisms underlying associative and instrumental learning in birds and mammals whose brains in both their anatomy and their functioning would seem to be amongst the most complex systems in the known universe. DWD

Bibliography

Catchpole, C.K. 1979: *Vocal communication in birds.* London: Institute of Biology. Studies in Biology. 115, Edward Arnold.

*Fantino, E. and Logan, C.A. 1979: *The experimental analysis of behavior: a biological perspective.* San Francisco: W.H. Freeman.

Goudie, A.J. 1980. Conditioned food aversion: an adaptive specialisation of learning? *International research communication system journal of medical science* 8. 591–4.

Groves, P. and Thompson, R. 1970: Habituation: a dual-process theory. *Psychological review.* 77.419–50.

Harlow, H.F. 1959: In Koch. S., ed., *Psychology: a study of a science.* Study I, vol. 2. New York. McGraw-Hill.

Hearst, Eliot and Jenkins, H.M. 1974: *Sign tracking: the stimulus-reinforcer relation and directed action.* Monograph of the Psychonomic Society. Austin, Texas: Psychonomic Society.

Hilgard, Ernest R. and Bower, Gordon H. 1975: *Theories of learning*. 4th edn. Englewood Cliffs, N.J. and London: Prentice Hall.

Hulse, S.H. 1978: Cognitive structures and serial pattern learning by animals. In Hulse, Fowler and Honig.

Hulse, Stewart H., Fowler, Harry, and Honig, Werner K. 1978: *Cognitive processes in animal behavior*. Hillsdale, N.J.: Lawrence Erlbaum Associates.

Kandel, Eric R. 1976: *Cellular basis of behavior: an introduction to behavioral neurobiology*. San Francisco: W.H. Freeman.

Lea, S.E.G. 1981: In Peter Harzem, and Michael D. Zeiler, eds. *Advances in analysis of behavior: vol. 2. Predictability, correlation and contiguity*. Chichester and New York: Wiley.

Premack, D. 1978: In Hulse, Fowler and Honig.

Roberts, W.A. and Grant, D.S. 1976: Studies of short-term memory in the pigeon using the delayed matching-to-sample procedure. In Douglas L. Medin, William A. Roberts, and Roger T. Davis, eds., *Processes of animal memory*. Hillsdale, N.J.: Lawrence Erlbaum Associates.

Shettleworth, S.J. 1972: Constraints on learning. In Daniel S. Lehrman, Robert A. Hinde and Evelyn Shaw, eds., *Advances in the study of behavior*. New York and London: Academic Press.

Seligman, M.E.P. 1970: On the generality of the laws of learning. *Psychological review* 77. 406–18.

learning: state-dependent Learning in which the degree of recall depends on the degree of similarity of the physiological state of the animal at the time of training to the animal's physiological state at the time of retention testing. In studies of state-dependent learning an animal is trained under the influence of a drug or some other agent and then tested at a later time either under drug or no-drug conditions. Animals demonstrating state-dependent learning show better retention when tested under the drug condition than the no-drug condition. In other words, habits learned while an animal is in one physiological state do not transfer well when the animal is tested in a different physiological state. This phenomenon is sometimes referred to as drug-induced dissociation. RAJ

learning: theories of Theories usually derived from conditioning experiments with animals designed to describe the most general features of learning and how behavior changes with learning. The heyday of learning theory was in the thirty years between 1930 and 1960, when a number of rival, global theories or systems were proposed, associated with the names of Thorndike (1911), Hull (1943), Tolman (1932) Guthrie (1935) and Skinner (1938). Although these theories were based almost exclusively on work with animals in restricted and no doubt artificial experimental situations, the theories were freely extrapolated to man. As Tolman wrote:

> I believe that everything important in psychology (except such matters as the building up of a super-ego, that is everything save such matters as involve society and words) can be investigated in essence through the continued experimental and theoretical analysis of the determiners of rat behavior at a choice point in a maze. Herein I believe I agree with Professor Hull and also with Professor Thorndike (1938, p.34).

Theories of learning were developed to answer at least three separate, but not altogether unrelated questions. First, *what* does an organism learn; secondly, what are the sufficient and necessary conditions producing learning; and thirdly, how does learning affect behavior? To these questions, they tended to give different answers and, because the questions are linked, differences in answers to one question implied differences in answers to another. There was a fourth question, often not explicitly asked, but often implicitly answered: how far can the results of conditioning experiments in rats and dogs be applied to other animals, including man, solving other kinds of problem? On this point, as the quotation from Tolman suggests, there was rather general agreement.

There was also a measure of agreement in their answers to the second question: what are the conditions under which learning occurs? Here an associationist bias suggested to all theorists that learning is a matter of association, and that temporal contiguity between the events to be associated is the single most important determinant of successful learning (see ASSOCIATIONISM). An important point at issue was whether temporal contiguity was sufficient to produce learning or whether some additional process was necessary. This amounts to asking whether Pavlov's or Thorndike's account of reinforcement is correct, and one plausible answer is that both are correct for different varieties of conditioning, Pavlov for classical and Thorndike for instrumental (see CONDITIONING).

The main points at issue revolved round the answers to the first question, what is learned, and the associated answers the theorists gave to the third question, how is learning translated into performance. The answers proposed by Thorndike, Hull and Guthrie were that learning consists of the establishment or strengthening of stimulus–response connections, and that such learning is seen as a change in behavior rather directly, for a stimulus which did not elicit a particular response before will now do so as a consequence of learning. Stimulus–response analyses of behavior have been popular with psychologists since WATSON (1913) announced the dawn of BEHAVIORISM. But their origin antedates that event by many years. Classical REFLEX theory attempted to analyse behavior into stimulus–response units: the reflex arc provided the direct connection between stimulus input and response output. Reflexes are, of course, relatively fixed, inborn patterns of behavior: the same stimulus always elicits the same response. It is obvious that learning causes behavior to change, but it might be possible to explain learning as the formation of new stimulus–response connections.

Thorndike developed such an account of the behavior of animals in his puzzle boxes. Where at first the animal struggled ineffectually and eventually hit upon the correct response which gained its release purely by chance, with continued training it would efficiently perform the required response as soon as it was placed in the apparatus. The set of stimuli produced by being placed in the apparatus now immediately elicited a response which they had only slowly and haphazardly elicited at the outset of training: a new stimulus–response connection had been formed.

Learning is undoubtedly quite often evidenced by an increase in the probability of the learner performing some particular response. But it does not follow even here that such learning can be understood as the establishment or strengthening of a stimulus–response connection. At the very least, this conclusion requires that successful solution of the sort of problem set by Thorndike should depend on the animal having had the opportunity to perform the required response in this situation and that an association between situation and response should then have been strengthened (presumably because the response was followed by some consequence). Thorndike himself thought he had provided such evidence: he spent much fruitless time and energy seeing whether animals could learn the way to escape from one of his puzzle boxes simply by observing the correct solution being performed by someone else. Finding no sign of successful IMITATION or OBSERVATIONAL LEARNING, he concluded that learning did indeed depend on the strengthening of a stimulus–response connection. But in fact there is now ample evidence that animals can learn by observation, without the opportunity to practice.

There are other reasons for questioning whether learning can always be understood as the establishment of stimulus–response connections. Learning frequently leads to no immediate or obvious change in behavior at all. The young white-crowned sparrow will not fully develop its typical species' song unless exposed to that song in the first two months of its life. During this period it must be supposed that the young sparrow learns to identify the critical features of white-crowned sparrow song. But so far as anyone can tell, there is no evidence in the bird's behavior that it has learned anything at all until the following spring when it starts practicing what it learned six months earlier (Marler 1970). Tolman and his colleagues reported numerous experiments on what they called LATENT LEARNING which implied much the same conclusion: a satiated rat given the opportunity to run through a maze which contained food at the end of one path but not others might show no tendency to choose the path that led to food until it was made hungry, at which point it would show that it had profited from its past experience by choosing that path immediately and consistently.

Learning is probably not, therefore, always a matter of strengthening responses: it is more usefully regarded as the acquisition of knowledge which may or may not produce an immediate change in behavior, just as Tolman had argued (Dickinson 1980). The connection between learning and performance is much less close than stimulus–response theories imply. But there are also reasons for questioning not only the gross oversimplification of learning implicit in a stimulus–response analysis, but also the assumption common to most of the classic learning theorists that experiments on conditioning in rats were sufficient to reveal all the important laws of learning. This assumption has been attacked by some psychologists ever since Köhler's celebrated study of problem solving by chimpanzees (1925). Köhler tested the ability of his chimpanzees to obtain food that lay out of their reach by improvising rakes to draw the food through the bars of their cage or by piling boxes on top of one another so that they could climb up and reach the banana hanging from the ceiling, He found no evidence of trial and error attempts at solutions in the behavior of his chimpanzees and concluded that they must have relied on insight into the nature of the problem. As a matter of fact, Köhler was probably wrong, for subsequent investigation has suggested that chimpanzees need experience with related problems, gained if need be during the course of play, in order to solve the sort of problem he set them (Schiller 1952).

But the issue raised by Köhler's critique remains. Theories of learning have typically been based on extrapolation from some very simple experimental procedures. Is it really plausible to suppose that all forms of learning can be understood by appeal to the same simple processes that are sufficient to explain conditioning? Although advanced explicitly or implicitly by most classic learning theorists, and still advanced by Skinner, it is doubtful whether many psychologists today would accept such a claim. Indeed, so far has the tide of opinion flowed in the opposite direction that conditioning experiments are now often derided as trivial and irrelevant to any understanding of human behavior. This is probably an over-reaction. Skinner and his followers have done some service by pointing to numerous examples from everyday life of behavior that can easily be analysed in terms of a simple theory of learning. The fond parents who hasten to pick up their crying baby may well be rewarding the baby for crying and thus increasing the chances that it will do so again whenever it is bored or alone. And when they subsequently refuse to respond immediately the baby starts crying, but still give in eventually if it goes on long enough, they are probably instituting a schedule of partial and delayed reinforcement which, as many animal experiments have established, is nicely calculated to prolong rather than put a stop to the baby's new-found habit.

But it is equally important to recognize that some aspects of human behavior are probably not illuminated by analogies with animal conditioning experiments. Theories of learning based on such experiments are surely insufficient to explain the way in which young children learn to speak their native language or to solve differential equations. Indeed, it is unlikely that such theories will explain the learning capacities of the chimpanzee. Just how far chimpanzees have progressed in learning anything approximating to language is a matter of some dispute. Yet although some aspects of language learning may be relatively simple (the meanings of concrete nouns, for example, can probably be learned by a rather simple associative process), some chimpanzees have clearly progressed beyond this stage. Premack (1976) has shown that the chimpanzee Sarah is capable of understanding and using symbols meaning "is the color of" (as in "red is the color of apple") or "is the shape of" or "is the name of" as in "apple is the name of apple"). She is also, as Gillan, Woodruff and Premack (1981) have shown, capable of solving quite complex analogical reasoning problems of the kind popular in IQ tests ("shoe is to foot as glove is to . . . "). A theory of learning based on conditioning experiments with rats or pigeons (there is good reason to believe that pigeons would be unable to solve these problems) does not take us very far in understanding the cognitive processes involved in this sort of behavior.

NJM

Bibliography

*Bower, G.H. and Hilgard, E.R. 1981: *Theories of learning*, 5th edn. Englewood Cliffs: Prentice Hall.

*Dickinson, A. 1980: *Contemporary animal learning theory*. Cambridge: Cambridge University Press.

Gillan, D.J. Woodruff, G. and Premack, D. 1981: Reasoning in the chimpanzee: I. Analogical reasoning. *Journal of experimental psychology, animal behavior processes* 7, 1–17.

Guthrie, E.R. 1935: *The psychology of learning*. New York: Harper.

Hull, Clark L. 1943: *Principles of behavior*. New York and London: Appleton-Century.

Köhler, Wolfgang 1925 (*1973*): *The mentality of apes*. London and Boston: Routledge & Kegan Paul.

Marler, P. 1970: A comparative approach to vocal learning: song-development in white-crowned sparrow. *Journal of comparative and physiological psychology monograph* 71, No. 2, Part 2.

*Premack, D. 1976: *Intelligence in ape and man*. Hillsdale: Erlbaum.

Schiller, P.H. 1952: Innate constituents of complex responses in primates. *Psychological review* 59, 177–91.

Skinner, B.F. 1938: *The behavior of organisms*. New York and London: Appleton-Century.

Thorndike, Edward L. 1911: *Animal intelligence*. New York: Macmillan.

Tolman, E.C. 1932: *Purposive behavior in animals and men*. New York: Century.

——— 1938: The determiners of behavior at a choice point. *Psychological review* 45, 1–41.

Watson, J.B. 1913: Psychology as the behaviorist views it. *Psychological review* 20, 158–77.

learning: Thorndike's laws The law of effect and the law of exercise. The law of effect states that a response followed by a satisfying or pleasant consequence (i.e. a response that is rewarded) tends to be repeated, while one followed by an annoying or unpleasant consequence (i.e. one that is punished) tends not to be repeated. To explain these empirical generalizations (sometimes referred to as the empirical law of effect) Thorndike assumed that satisfying consequences strengthen stimulus–response connections, while annoying consequences weaken them. The law of exercise states that, other things being equal, the more often a response is performed in a given situation, the more likely it is to be repeated.

Thorndike had no doubt that the law of effect was the more important of the two: only if two responses had similar effects would the law of exercise come into play to increase the probability of the more frequently performed response. And in both theoretical and empirical forms the law of effect has had much the greater impact on later psychologists. Hull attempted to explain all learning in terms of Thorndike's theoretical law of effect; while Skinner defined instrumental or operant conditioning as the establishment of responses by their consequences in accordance with the empirical law of effect. NJM

Bibliography

Thorndike, Edward L. 1911: *Animal intelligence*. New York: Macmillan.

learning: two factor/single factor theories Single factor theories of conditioning assume that classical and instrumental conditioning differ only in the experimental operations used to study them, not in any underlying process, while two factor theories assume that the two forms of conditioning are fundamentally distinct.

Two factor theorists insist that different theories are needed to account for classical conditioning, where a response initially elicited by one stimulus comes to be elicited by another solely as a consequence of the association between the two stimuli, and for instrumental conditioning where a response is modified because of its consequences. Single factor theorists attempt to reduce one type of conditioning to the other: historically the most important version of such a theory was that of Hull, who argued that all responses were modified by their consequences.

Two factor theorists assume that any such reduction of one type of conditioning to the other is impossible, but they have assumed that both processes usually occur together in any experiment. In particular they have assumed that classical conditioning to stimuli occurring at the same time as the reinforcer in an instrumental experiment endow those stimuli with classically conditioned motivational states which influence the performance of the instrumental response. NJM

learning, human: methods of studying Any attempt to list all the empirical methods which have ever been used to study human learning would produce an endless catalogue of little help or interest to anyone. A more plausible goal is a sketchy history of assumptions which have been made about the nature of human memory and forgetting, and the kinds of experiments which have been carried out to test and extend these assumptions.

Applied research into human memory dates at least from the third century BC when associational mnemonic techniques were taught in schools of philosophy and rhetoric to help speakers remember catalogues of details or complex events, or to deliver long speeches without notes. These techniques depended heavily on the use of imagery. For example students learnt to image at will arbitrary structures (e.g. "The Palace of Memory"; the "Theater of Memory", etc. etc.) with detailed imaged "locations" into which they mentally placed images of concrete objects as cues for particular topics which they wished to recall (e.g. an anchor for Naval matters; a bag of grain for farm prices etc. etc.). Such techniques have proved remarkably successful and many hundreds of years later have been investigated by Bower (1970), and others in modern laboratories.

In the intervening centuries many vivid adventurers such as "Colonel" Benkowski, of Prague, and academics such as Dr Richard Pick of Magdalen College, Oxford, incremented their incomes by developing and teaching mnemonic systems. Perhaps the most famous was Gregor von Feinagle, immortalized in Byron's *Don Juan*. This rich background of general information about very successful, practical memory aids may have contributed, indirectly, to the Lockeian idea that the efficiency of retention in human memory is determined by the number and diversity of "associations" which can be made between stored "facts". Alas, as in other areas of science the existence of this highly developed and successful *technology* of memory had remarkably little impact on hypotheses formulated about the nature of memory or on experiments made to test these hypotheses. It is no exaggeration to say that Feinagle's (1812) (pirated) published lectures could have launched an extremely effective experimental program anticipating work carried out by Bartlett by a hundred and twenty years. Bartlett's work, in turn, has taken a further fifty years to find proper appreciation.

As so often in psychology a rich harvest of "unofficial' knowledge about human abilities was lost because of the influential pertinacity of a brilliantly misguided scientist. Herman Ebbinghaus (1850 to 1909) conceived the idea that memories are stamped in by "mental work". He was aware that words or concepts frequently associated with each other might be very rapidly learned under experimental conditions. Thus he tried to use items with no existing associations, inventing "nonsense syllables" (usually a consonant, a vowel and a consonant selected at random from the alphabet) for this purpose. Ebbinghaus was his own subject, laboriously discovering how many repetitions it took him to learn lists of nonsense syllables of different lengths, how the learning of one list interfered with the learning of a subsequent list (proactive interference), or how subsequent learning interfered with retention of previous material (retroactive interference). He also showed that attempting to learn many lists immediately after each other ("massed practice") is much less efficient than learning lists at spaced intervals ("distributed practice"). It would be wrong to assume that Ebbinghaus neglected the possible effects of the associative structure of material to be learned upon the efficiency of its learning and retention. He was careful to check his results with nonsense syllables by teaching himself very long passages from *Don Juan*. He confirmed that much the same general principles applied.

The experimental techniques developed by Ebbinghaus set the pattern of laboratory work until 1930, because they were so easily assimilated to the investigation of hypotheses of mutual inhibition and facilitation between learned responses developed from work by animal learning theorists such as Pavlov, Watson, Hull and later Skinner. Indeed this tradition persisted, especially in Mid-Western Universities in the United States, until the late 1950s and mid 1960s in spite of more naturalistic experiments carried out by Sir Frederick Bartlett in Cambridge England, and published in his book *Remembering* (1932). Bartlett gave his subjects prose passages and naturalistic pictures to inspect and recall. His interest in social psychology made him sensitive to the fact that people from different cultures recall entirely different details of the same passage or picture and, as time passes, details become "conventionalised" to fit increasingly closely into their idiosyncratic expectations. Bartlett was the first to suggest that our knowledge of the world becomes incorporated into dynamic structures which he termed "schemata". These are not passive, knowledge storage devices, but rather active encoding structures which selectively assimilate and transform new information from the perceptual world.

In 1932 the ideas of computing systems and of information processing technology, let alone the concepts of "Artificial Intelligence Theory" were far in the future. Bartlett's vivid originality inspired his students at Cambridge but was not immediately appreciated elsewhere. During the 1950s it had been noted that syllables were not completely "nonsensical". Some were more "word-like", and so had more associations than others, and were correspondingly easier to learn. There followed Bousfield's discovery that lists of nouns made up of instances of easily recognized superordinate categories such as animal names, precious stones, etc. etc., were more easily recalled than random lists. From this modest beginning came a revolution in the 1960s and early 1970s with an increasing interest in subjects' use and description of relationships and of organizational structures within verbal material. If the structures which people detected, and which made their recall easier, could be discovered, it was supposed that the rules used by the brain to order and store experience might become accessible. Chomsky had pointed out that sentences in any language can be described in terms of higher order structures. Much effort was expended following up Chomsky's idea that the rules of thought could best be deduced form the rules of syntactic structure. This approach is now seen to be too limited. Allowance must also be made for semantic and propositional content, and for the use of "knowledge of the world".

The 1970s also saw an interest in memory for other types of material then words. Verbal learning had become the stock in trade of psychologists studying memory because materials were so easily collected, standardized and presented. The discovery by Haber and Standing that quite ordinary people can recognize up to 90 per cent of 5,000 or more pictures each of which they have inspected, briefly, only once before, forced psychologists to appreciate that human brains are not primarily adapted to recognize and recall words. Rather we are visual creatures who have an extraordinary facility in recognizing and imaging complex scenes. It became implicitly clear that to study the organization of memory we must be able to describe organization schemata for complex pictures as well as for lists of words and connected sentences.

At present the main difficulty facing psychologists is to find descriptions for knowledge structures which are applicable not only to techniques of data storage and retrieval in computers, but to the ways in which the human brain assimilates and retrieves information. At this juncture experimentation is, perhaps, less useful than originality in the development of abstract models for the ways in which knowledge about the world, and propositions about relationships between things in the world, can be represented in data-storage systems. Until such models become more sophisticated experiments on memory will be very trite and limited essays, hardly increasing the fragmentary understanding of complex processes which we have so far gained. PR

Bibliography

Bartlett, Frederick 1932: *Remembering: a study in experimental and social psychology*. Cambridge: Cambridge University Press; New York: Macmillan.

Bower, G.H. (1970):Analysis of a mnemonic device. *American scientist* 58, 496–510.

learning and motivation: animal studies There are two related questions here: (i) to what extent are motivational factors necessary for learning to take place and (ii) how are motivational factors involved in the initiation and regulation of conditioned behavior?

Experiments investigating the first question have involved LATENT LEARNING and sensory preconditioning procedures. In the latter, subjects initially receive paired presentations of two motivationally neutral stimuli, such as a light and tone, which will not produce any overt evidence of learning. One of these stimuli is then paired with a motivationally significant event, such as shock, and as a consequence the other will be capable of eliciting a conditioned response. Such a result could only be possible if subjects had learned about the light–tone relationship during the first stage of the experiment. This has led to the view that motivation may not be necessary for learning to occur but it is essential if the effects of that learning are to be demonstrated.

In answer to the second question theorists have subdivided motivational factors into those determined by biological needs, e.g. hunger, and those determined by the reinforcer for the conditioned response. According to Hull's formal account of the relationship between learning and motivation (1952), biological needs are related to a central state, Drive (D), and the properties of reward influence incentive motivation (K). Hull maintained that the repeated pairing of a response with reward resulted in the gradual strengthening of the response as a HABIT. Whether or not a habit would be executed and its resultant intensity (E) is given by Equation 1, where H represents the conditioned strength of the habit.

$$E = H \times D \times K \qquad (1)$$

Once a response has acquired some habit strength, the likelihood of its being performed depends upon there being a measure of drive and incentive motivation present.

As far as manipulations of drive are concerned Equation 1 is reasonably accurate when only one motivational state is involved. The hungrier an animal is the more vigorously it will perform an instrumental response to obtain food. Alternatively, the stronger an electric shock the more rapidly will an animal run to escape it. A more controversial feature of Hull's theory is the claim that drive is general, that is, that different biological needs combine to determine the resultant level of activity of this central state and that this state can energize all types of behavior. The consequent prediction that the energizing influence of drive should be independent of the need(s) responsible for its arousal has met with conflicting evidence. In support it has been found that giving a rat a mild shock before it runs in an alley for food increases the speed of this response. In contrast attempts to enhance drive by increasing food deprivation have failed to show a corresponding increase in the speed at which animals will run to escape shock. This type of result has led some theorists to accept the unparsimonious view that each need state is associated with its own drive condition (e.g. Estes 1969).

In view of its assumed general properties Hull's drive was theoretically incapable of exerting a guiding influence on behavior. The selection of responses that led to a goal appropriate to a subject's needs was left to drive stimuli. A drive stimulus was hypothesized to be a pattern of stimulation that was unique to a particular deprivation state and could serve as an eliciting stimulus for any habit strengthened in its presence. Somewhat surprisingly it has proved rather difficult to demonstrate the existence of these stimuli (see Bolles 1975, pp.270 ff, for a review). Recent research has shown that animals can associate a drive stimulus with reward (Capaldi and Davidson 1979), but it remains to be shown unequivocally that such stimuli can elicit habits.

Hull's initial proposal that drive was the only motivational influence on instrumental responding was rejected on the basis of an experiment by Crespi (1942). This study demonstrated for rats that rapid changes in the speed of running down an alley for food could be produced by manipulating the size of reward. Hull regarded these changes as being too rapid to be explained by variations in habit strength. Accordingly, he proposed that stimuli which precede the consumption of reward, such as those encountered in the alley, elicit anticipatory goal responses (r_g) that in turn arouse incentive motivation. Since a change in goal magnitude should produce a corresponding change in r_g and hence incentive motivation, Equation 1 can explain Crespi's results.

This incentive feature of Hull's theorizing has been developed in a variety of ways. Some theorists (e.g. Mowrer 1960; Bindra 1972) extended his views to such an extent that habit learning was not considered to play any role in guiding behavior. Very broadly, they proposed that stimuli preceding reward aroused positive incentive motivation while stimuli associated with aversive events excited negative incentive motivation (Bindra's terminology). By approaching stimuli that increase positive incentive and avoiding those that arouse negative incentive, animals should behave adaptively by being guided towards reward and away from aversive events. The postulation of two incentive systems has been accompanied by the proposal that they are interconnected by inhibitory links, so that increases in negative incentive will suppress appetitive responding and vice versa (see Dickinson and Pearce 1977 for a review). This feature enables incentive theories to explain many of the interactions obtained when appetitive and aversive conditioning procedures are intermixed.

If, as Hull maintained, incentive motivation is aroused by r_g then changes in the frequency of these responses should be correlated with changes in the intensity of instrumental responding. Unfortunately a considerable number of experiments have failed to reveal any support for this prediction. In reviewing these data Rescorla and Solomon (1967) concluded that stimuli that reliably precede reward will excite a central nervous state (incentive motivation) as well as eliciting overt r_gs. The consequent implication that the occurrence of r_gs will not provide a behavioral index of incentive motivation has led to two reactions. Trapold and

Overmier (1972), for example, warn against invoking central states that are unobservable as mediators of performance. They, propose, therefore, that r_gs should be regarded, in a manner similar to that initially intended by Hull, as events with response cueing but not incentive properties. Whereas theorists such as Bolles (1975) have used this opportunity to regard the central state as being cognitive rather than motivational, replacing the term "incentive" with "expectancy". Whether the properties of the goal for responding influence performance by response cueing, incentive motivational or cognitive processes remains a matter of continuing debate. At present this issue is decided more by theoretical predilection than by experimental evidence. JMP

Bibliography

Bindra, D. 1972: A unified account of classical conditioning and operant training. In *Classical conditioning*, ed. A.H. Black and W.F. Prokasy. New York: Appleton.

*Bolles, R.C. 1975: *Theory of motivation*. New York: Harper & Row.

Capaldi, E.D. and Davidson, T.L. 1979: Control of instrumental behavior by deprivation stimuli. *Journal of experimental psychology: animal behavior processes* 4, 355–67.

Crespi, L.P. 1942: Quantitative variation of incentive and performance in the white rat. *American journal of psychology* 55, 467–517.

Dickinson, A. and Pearce, J.M. 1977: Inhibitory interactions between appetitive and aversive stimuli. *Psychological bulletin* 84, 690–711.

Estes, W.K. 1969: New perspectives on some old issues in association theory. In *Fundamental issues in associative learning*. ed. N.J. Mackintosh and W.K. Honig. Halifax: Dalhousie University Press.

Hull, C.L. 1952: *A behavior system*. New Haven: Yale University Press.

Mowrer, O.H. 1960: *Learning theory and behavior*. New York: Wiley.

Rescorla, R.A. and Solomon, R.L. 1967: Two process learning theory: relationships between Pavlovian conditioning and instrumental learning. *Psychological review*. 74, 151–82.

Trapold, M.A. and Overmier, J.B. 1972: The second learning process in instrumental learning. In *Classical conditioning*. ed. A.H. Black and W.F. Prokasy. New York: Appleton.

learning and motivation: in children Motivation in the sense in which one person may be highly motivated and another lack motivation, is a concept used to explain different amounts of effort or persistence shown by different people on the same task. At one time psychologists conceptualized motivation in terms of drives or needs, i.e. something upsetting the HOMEOSTASIS of the organism. Later there was more concentration on the ways in which the environment could arouse, or motivate a person or an animal. Some things would operate as incentives which would produce effort. Much of the experimentation on animal learning has involved the interaction between rewards such as food and the animal's needs such as hunger. The animal is induced to learn something by being rewarded for its trouble. The response it makes is the instrument by which it obtains what it wants. On the other hand animals explore their environment out of curiosity. Although such exploration may be phylogenetically related to survival through the discovery of dangers or potential rewards, the individual animal's efforts may be continued with no reward (Harlow, Harlow and Meyer). Children are also explorers. But formal education may present disincentives in the form of hard work and self-denial. One major problem in education is to encourage curiosity beyond the point at which its returns are intrinsically rewarding. The attempt to do this by offering extrinsic reward in the form of approval or prizes may diminish a child's interest in what it is doing (Lepper, Greene and Nisbett 1973).

Difficulties are also created by the fact that school success may be instrumental in producing undesired as well as desired ends. Lacey, for instance, quotes a grammar school boy: "When ... I had passed (the 11+) ... I was treated as a 'puff' and was a 'brainy soft-arsed mardy'." This difficulty does not only involve peer group pressure, although, as Beloff and Temperley report, "the relatively adult-oriented and socialized children are ... the unpopular ones". There are also assumed to be pressures or encouragements from the home. In 1948 Davis suggested that different goals are regarded as desirable in different social classes. Middle class children generally do better than working class children in school. The middle class children also score better on IQ tests, but Douglas reported that 26 per cent of upper middle-class children worked "very hard" as against 7 per cent of working class children. Since hard work does affect exam success (hard workers doing better and poor workers worse than IQ scores would predict) the motivation which affects the effort is an important variable in improving such success. If it is assumed that exam performance measures learning, this motivation is clearly influencing learning.

It has been suggested that middle-class children have more stimulating home environments and are encouraged to do well at school. From the time of Froebel attempts have been made to make schools stimulating, to feed the child's natural curiosity. The success of such attempts to increase intrinsic motivation has been dubious. Programs of discovery-learning in British schools have been reported in government publications to produce minimal improvements and to be detrimental in some subjects. Hence, if the school cannot offer successful extrinsic rewards in itself the child with high ACHIEVEMENT MOTIVATION has an advantage in coping with learning. Some would regard this as an unfair advantage.

McClelland is the most famous student of achievement motivation, despite some doubts about his use of projective tests. His well known cross-cultural studies were influenced by Winterbottom (1958) who found that boys with high need for achievement had mothers who claimed that they had demanded independence from their sons. For twenty-two countries McClelland discovered a high correlation ($r = 0.53$) between the average number of achievement themes in children's readers published in 1925 and the increase in electric power consumption per head (used as an index of economic growth) between then and 1950. The themes in the children's readers were taken to show the emphasis the society placed on achievement. Further studies within societies, using different measures tended to support this assumption. This naturally implies that one's culture (or sub-culture) may instil or repress the need for achievement. This was the implication of Winterbottom's work, and Rosen and D'Andrade provided support in a study in which parents could help their sons in experimental tasks. Parents of boys with high achievement needs had higher expectations and involvement, as well as rewarding and punishing more than parents of those with low needs. But later research has had very mixed results, and has certainly not confirmed these theories about the learning of achievement motivation. Moreover the idea that parents' behavior may be a response to children's behavior as much as a cause of it has been a commonplace in recent years (Bell 1968). Meanwhile doubt has been cast on the usefulness of need for achievement scores by their failure to predict school success (Entwisle 1972).

Yet it remains a natural assumption that parental attitudes, values and involvement will influence children's motivation. If the parents simply assume that their child must be interested in and do well at school, the child is unlikely to be unaffected by this. Many researchers have said that parental interest influences school progress. Fishbein has built into his model of the connexion between attitude and behavior the assumption that the attitudes of "significant others" should be included in the predictive equation. Interestingly Kolb found that only boys of high socioeconomic status showed long term benefits from a program designed to increase underachievers' motivation. The implication was that the low status boys lost their initial improvements because of their background values.

On the other hand, according to Swift, there is no class bias (in Britain) in the assumption that school is "a good thing". Although assumptions about the role of the school might differ according to class, other factors will presumably influence the individual's effort to succeed academically. Anxiety for instance has been implicated in achievement. Holt has detailed anecdotes about children's fears in the classroom, while experimental evidence has shown that highly anxious people have more difficulty in learning, except at the top and bottom of the ability scale (Spielberger). The problem of anxiety was however taken into account by Atkinson who hypothesized that "achievement-oriented activity" would be affected by approach and avoidance forces, viz the motive to succeed and the fear of failure. This fear is said to be learnt through previous failure and its attendant shame.

More recent work has concentrated on the perceptions of success and failure, and the expectations of future performance. Clearly if one expects to fail one's anxiety and fear of failure may well be greater than if one expects to succeed. Rosenthal and Jacobson showed that teachers' erroneous beliefs about pupils' different abilities correlated highly with the pupils' achievements in class. Presumably the pupils' own beliefs may also affect their performance, whether or not the effect is mediated by anxiety. Rosenbaum found that attributions of failure to stable causes (inability, or difficult task) led to lower expectation of future success than did attributions to unstable causes (lack of effort, or bad luck), while attributions of success to stable causes led to higher expectations. It has also been suggested that those who have a high opinion of themselves will tend to attribute their success to a stable characteristic of their own, and their failure to unstable aspects (perhaps of the environment). Ames and others found that children with high social status in class were more likely to attribute a social success to themselves and a failure to external causes than were children with low status. Dweck and Reppucci showed that subjects who produced good performance after repeated failures tended to ascribe failure to low effort. Perception of the efficacy of effort may be related to perception of one's own ability. Weiner and others found that effort was believed to affect outcome most on tasks of intermediate difficulty. "Difficulty" was a matter of how many people succeed on the tasks, but difficulty may obviously be assessed in terms of one's beliefs about one's own ability. If the task is too difficult, there is less point in making an effort.

Katz in Australia and Bernstein in England both suggested that working class children are not encouraged to have a sense of control over their environment, and that they perceive success as "limited in possibility of attainment by factors over which the individual has no control". Perception of the efficacy of effort may be effected by at least two factors which could reduce a child's efforts to learn (1) a poor self-image and (2) a belief in luck as a cause of success. The latter and perhaps the former may be present in lower class children more than in middle class children, quite apart from any scepticism about the worth of education or tendency to perceive school as a repressive institution rather than an instrument for success. RL

Bibliography

Bell, R.Q. 1968: A reinterpretation of the direction of effects of socialization. *Psychological review*, 75, 81–95.

Beloff, H. and Temperley, K. 1972: The power of the peers. *Scottish educational studies* 4, 3–10.

Bernstein, B. 1962: Social class, linguistic codes and grammatical elements. *Language and speech* 5, 221–40.

Davis, A. 1948: *Social class influences upon learning*. Cambridge, Mass.: Harvard University Press.

Douglas, J.W.B. 1964: *The home and the school*. London: MacGibbon and Kee.

Fishbein, M. and Ajzen, I. 1975: *Belief, attitude, intention and behavior*. Reading, Mass.: Addison-Wesley.

Harlow, H.F., Harlow, M.K. and Meyer, P.R. 1950: Learning motivated by a manipulation drive. *Journal of experimental psychology* 40, 228–34.

*Holt, J. 1964: *How children fail*. London: Pitman.

Katz, F.M. 1964: The meaning of success. *Journal of social psychology* 52, 141–48.

Lacey, C. 1970: *Hightown grammar school*. Manchester: Manchester University Press.

McClelland, D.C. 1961: *The achieving society*. Princeton, N.J.: Van Nostrand.

Rosenthal, R. and Jacobson, L. 1968: *Pygmalion in the classroom*. New York: Holt, Rinehart & Winston.

Spielberger, C.D., ed. 1972: *Anxiety: behavior*. New York: Academic Press.

*Weiner, B. 1980: *Human motivation*. New York: Holt, Rinehart & Winston.

Swift, D.F. 1966: Social class and achievement motivation. *Educational research* 8 2, 83–95.

Winterbottom, M.R. 1958: In *Motives in fantasy, action and society*, ed. J.W. Atkinson. Princeton, N.J.: Van Nostrand.

All other references may be found in the bibliography of Weiner.

learning difficulties (Note: For the sake of brevity the word "child" includes "young person")

The term "learning difficulties" may be used either to

refer to particular aspects of learning, in which a child may have difficulty, or in a more general way, to the fact that a child has difficulty in learning. This latter use of the term was introduced in the British Report of the Committee of Enquiry into the Education of Handicapped Children and Young People (Warnock Report, DES 1978). In this Report it was recommended that the previously used categories of handicap should be discarded and that children should be considered in terms of their special educational needs. Consequently it was suggested that the term "educationally subnormal" should be replaced by "children with learning difficulties", and qualified by the terms "severe", "moderate" and "specific". "Severe" and "moderate" learning difficulties were intended to refer respectively to severe and moderate levels of subnormality. The term "learning difficulty" was subsequently incorporated into the wording of the British 1981 Act on Special Education, where a child with special educational needs was described as one who had a "learning difficulty which calls for special educational provision to be made for him". Furthermore, a child with learning difficulty was defined as one who "has a significantly greater difficulty in learning than the majority of children of his age" or who "has a disability which either prevents or hinders him from making use of educational facilities of a kind generally provided in schools".

The concept of learning difficulty adopted in the Act's definitions is not elaborated further, but would appear to include the level and nature of curricular content which would be regarded as appropriate for the children concerned, in line with the administrative connotation of the definition of "special educational need".

In the USA the term "learning disability" has been incorporated into the Education for all Handicapped Children Act of 1975 (PL 94–142). The Act includes a definition of the term indicating that it refers to deficiencies in processes underlying educational performance but excluding other forms of primary causation (e.g. environmental deprivation). This "definition by exclusion" has been criticised by Hallahan and Bryan (1981) among others.

"Learning difficulties" in the sense of a term referring to difficulties in particular aspects of learning has been used in a number of ways. One of the most common themes in its definition has been concerned with discrepancies in the levels of a child's performance. It has been noted that a child's level of performance in certain aspects of educational attainment, of communication, or of behavioral adequacy, may be lower than in other aspects of his performance or functioning, and that in certain instances these are assumed to be the result of *specific* difficulties in learning which are primary, and not the consequence of emotional disturbances, of deprivation of experience, or of sensory or motor impairment. In so far as the difficulties represent *discrepancies* in levels of performance, it is also assumed that they are not a concomitant of a generally low level of intelligence (Wedell 1975). These considerations involve two sets of assumptions – those concerned with the nature of the difficulties, and those concerned with their causes.

The account of the nature of learning difficulties outlined above has to be seen in the context of a growing doubt about INTELLIGENCE as a unitary concept. Historically, learning difficulties had been defined in terms of "backwardness" and of "retardation" (Tansley and Pankhurst 1981). These terms tended to be defined in terms of the discrepancy between a child's educational attainment and either his chronological age (backwardness) or his level of "intelligence" (specific retardation: retardation in this sense should be clearly distinguished from "mental retardation"). Specific retardation, therefore, contrasted a child's attainment with his "potential" (intelligence) and these children were therefore called "under achievers". Experts in psychometrics have questioned the validity of the concept of under achievement and of the discrepancy model in general (Thorndike 1963) Learning difficulty as defined in terms of a discrepancy between actual and expected performance is an uncertain concept.

Children's difficulties in learning have been manifested and described in a variety of ways. A common description has been in terms of syndromes of difficulties, such as DYSLEXIA. These syndrome names are derived from clinical neurological studies of adults, who have lost the capacity to perform in particular ways as the result of various forms of neurological impairment. The extension of the use of these terms to children is questionable since in these cases they refer not to a loss of a capacity, but to a failure to develop or acquire it (Wedell 1975). Furthermore, in clinical neurology, syndromes are established on the basis of the demonstrated co-occurrence of symptoms, and the evidence for this, for example, in children described as dyslexic, is contradictory (eg. DES 1972). Doubt also applies to syndrome terms such as "hyperactivity", used to describe restlessness and short attention-span in children. Schacher Rutter and Smith (1981) have pointed out that hyperactivity in many children is situation or task specific and cannot be used to describe a child in a general way.

The above accounts of learning difficulties also have associations with assumptions about their cause, and much of the literature refers to learning "disabilities". This is already often implicit in the discrepancy model of learning difficulty. Accounts of the syndrome models almost invariably also refer to disabilities underlying the symptomology. These disabilities are described in terms of the dysfunction of psychological processes which is thought to cause the impaired performance, such as defects in perceptuo-motor functions, in language and in memory. Difficulties in reading and spelling are ascribed, for example, to defects in intermodal association, and attention difficulties to defects in perception. Much research has been devoted to investigating these associations, but the evidence, while supporting many of these hypotheses, has not proved conclusive. Wedell (1973) pointed out that the causal relationship between the hypothesized underlying processes and performance on the target tasks was likely to be more complex than had been acknowledged. For example, any particular performance might be subserved by different combinations of processes and the ways in which a child had been taught the task was also likely to exert an important influence.

Much research has been devoted to attempts to discover the organic bases of learning difficulties, and some of the early studies were particularly concerned with this. In the face of insufficient evidence for associations with demonstrable neurological impairment, some have put forward the notion of "minimal cerebral dysfunction"; a hypothesis that some forms of learning difficulty might be caused by subclinical forms of neurological impairment.

Approaches to the assessment and treatment of learning difficulties have been derived from the various conceptualisations mentioned above. Delacato (1966), for example, devised means of assessing delayed and impaired neurological function, and also training procedures aimed at rectifying these. However, doubt has been expressed about these approaches by the American Academy of Cerebral Palsy. Many batteries of tests to assess the psychological processes thought to underlie learning difficulties have been produced, for example the Illinois Test of Psycholinguistic Abilities and the Frostig Developmental Test of Visual Perception. These batteries have been linked with remedial programs for the particular functions assessed. However, studies designed to investigate the effectiveness of these programs have only partly substantiated their effectiveness in improving children's performances on the test batteries, and only rarely shown the children to improve significantly more in the target educational performances (eg Hammill and Larsen 1974). Similarly, attempts by means of early identification procedures to assess these functions in children at the early stages of schooling, in order to predict which children would later have difficulties in learning, have had little success (Lindsay and Wedell 1982).

The above findings have contributed to the conclusion already mentioned above, that the causation of learning difficulties is very complex and this, in turn, has led to attempts to help children with learning difficulties through "direct instruction". These approaches involve the specification of the target task which the child is required to learn in terms of "behavioral" objectives. The sequence of instruction is based on task-analysis aimed at identifying the successive steps necessary for the child to master the target task. The methods employed in teaching are derived from operant learning theory, but many of the approaches to task analysis are based on notions similar to those underlying the "process" approach to learning difficulties (Wedell 1973). An important feature of this teaching approach is the detailed recording of the child's progress towards each objective, by means of "precision teaching" (Haring et al 1978). This teaching approach is still at the early stages of development, but has the advantages that the evaluation of its effectiveness is integral to it.

This brief account of learning difficulties has indicated that the phenomenon to which the term refers is well demonstrated, but that the understanding about how the difficulties are caused and how they should best be remedied is still a matter of controversy. The issues involved represent an interesting aspect of the meeting of psychology and education.

DMG

Bibliography

Delacato, C. H. et al. 1966: *Neurological organisation and reading*. Springfield, Ill.: C. C. Thomas.

Department of Education and Science 1972: *Children with specific reading difficulties* London HM Stationery Office.

——— 1978: *Special educational needs (The Warnock Report)* London: HM Stationery Office.

Hallahan, D. P. and Bryan, I. H. 1981: Learning difficulties. In *Handbook of special education*, ed. J. M. Kaufman and D. P. Hall. Englewood Cliffs, N.J.: Prentice Hall.

Hammill, D. D. and Larsen, S. C. 1974: The effectiveness of psycho-linguistic training. *Exceptional children* 41, 5–14.

Haring N. G. et al. 1978: *The fourth R: research in the classroom*. C. E. Merrill.

Lindsay, G. A. and Wedell, K. 1982: The early identification of educationally "At Risk" children revisited. *Journal of learning disabilities* 15, 212–17.

Schacher, R., Rutter, M. and Smith, A. 1981: The characteristics of situationally and pervasively hyperactive children: implications for syndrome definition. *Journal of child psychology and psychiatry* 22, 375–920.

Tansley, P. and Panckhurst, J. 1981: *Children with specific learning difficulties*. National Foundation for Educational Research.

Thorndike, R. L. 1963: *The concepts of over and under achievement*. New York: Columbia University Teachers' College.

Wedell, K. 1973: *Learning and perceptuo-motor disabilities in children*. New York and London: Wiley.

——— 1975: Specific learning difficulties. In *Orientations in special education*. New York and London: Wiley.

learning sets Or "sets to learn" (Harlow 1949) refer to the acquisition by an individual of the ability to learn a particular kind of task, or solve a particular kind of problem, progressively more efficiently as a result of experiencing a variety of examples of such tasks or problems. For example rhesus monkeys required to discriminate between pairs of objects for food reward learn the first few pairs slowly, but after learning several hundred different pairs are able to learn any new pair very rapidly – an object-discrimination learning set. A simpler task where a learning set may also develop in many species is serial reversal; a single pair of discriminanda is used (e.g. left and right sides of a maze, a black and a white object) and first one and then the other must be chosen to obtain food reward, the rewarded member being switched (reversed) whenever the subject is consistently choosing the currently correct one. Early reversals are learned slowly, later ones more rapidly. In general, any class of problem where there is a common rule or CONCEPT to guide solution – e.g. choose pictures showing people, choose left and right in double-alternating sequence – it may give rise to a learning set. It is recognized that learning set formation reflects the abandonment of inappropriate strategies or "error factors", including the forgetting of irrelevant preferences derived from previous problems. In addition it may reflect acquisition of the underlying rule or concept; or it may be that the concept was already present but masked by error factors.

In many cases subjects may show some degree of learning set formation, i.e. some improvement in problem-solving rate, without attaining the maximum speed or generality indicative of having learnt the precise rule. The rate and completeness with which various learning sets are acquired has often been proposed as a test of comparative intelligence across animal species, but recent work suggests little consistency within orders or even within single species; learning set capacity seems to depend more on procedural or ecological variables than on any "general intelligence" factor supposedly characteristic of a phyletic grouping. Nonetheless, insofar as they demonstrate an ability for abstraction and wide transfer of learning, learning sets illustrate an important aspect of cognitive capacity in animals. EAG

Bibliography

Bessemer, D.W. and Stollnitz, F. 1971: Retention of discriminations and an analysis of learning set. In Schrier and Stellnitz, op. cit.

Harlow, H.F. 1949: The formation of learning sets. *Psychological review* 56, 51–65.

*Warren, J.M. 1973: Learning in vertebrates. In *Comparative psychology*. ed. D.A. Dewsbury and D.A. Rethlingshafer. New York: McGraw-Hill.

A.M. Schrier and F. Stollnitz, ed. 1971: *Behaviour of nonhuman primates*. Vol 4. New York: Academic Press.

learning strategies Activities that are engaged in with the goal of increasing learning. Since they are goal directed they are executed intentionally. Such strategies may be those of a learner in which case they are either internal cognitive strategies (e.g. imagery) or external strategies (e.g. note-taking). Alternatively, they may be the strategies of authors who modify materials to make them easier to learn (e.g. by providing pictures, by adding italics to important points in a text or by organizing the material in a helpful way).

There is a long history of research on the types of strategies that people spontaneously use when they are attempting to learn. During the last two decades researchers have traced out the development of this spontaneous use of strategies. An excellent example is the work on the development of rehearsal in recall (e.g. when learners are presented with a list of words and must recall them in a test). A second example of the development of the spontaneous use of a strategy involves semantic-elaborative strategies in associative learning. These strategies include elaborative imagery (e.g. imagining a turkey sitting on a rock for the paired associate turkey–rock) and verbal elaboration (e.g. thinking "the turkey sat on the rock" for the pair turkey-rock). When late adolescents are asked to learn such paired associates, they are much more likely than younger children to employ these elaborations. Recently, the spontaneous use of strategies in everyday tasks (such as learning from text) have been examined. For a review, see Pressley et al. (1982).

Some theorists have argued that sophisticated strategy deployment on occasions when it is appropriate is at the very heart of intelligence (e.g. Borkowski, in press). A great deal of effort has also been expended in order to determine when children who do not spontaneously produce an efficient strategy can be taught to use learning strategies (see Pressley et al. 1982). For instance young schoolchildren often do not spontaneously produce rehearsal strategies when they are given a list of words to learn so that it can be reproduced later, but it is usually possible to increase these children's recall by instructing them to use rehearsal strategies. This can be the case even with late adolescents. It is also possible to instruct young schoolchildren and even preschool children to use elaborative strategies in associative learning. On the other hand children's imagery-elaborative skills lag behind (e.g. Pressley 1982), a point which emphasize that not all failures at spontaneous strategy usage can be remedied by instruction. Sometimes the learner is unable to generate a strategy because of cognitive-developmental constraints (probably the case with imagery), and sometimes for other reasons.

Just as those interested in spontaneous strategy usage have turned their attention in recent years to more practical everyday tasks, so have those interested in strategy instruction. Researchers have been instructing learners to paraphrase text, to make internal mental images of concrete stories, and to use a variety of rehearsal and imagery strategies to prepare for multiple-choice tests. In addition learning strategies are being developed for a variety of tasks such as vocabulary learning, spelling, learning social studies and the learning of face–name associations. (See Pressley et al. 1982 for examples of research in all these areas).

One particularly heartening aspect of research on strategy usage is the usefulness of strategy instruction in improving the learning of deficit populations. Disabled children do not develop some strategies until later than normal children. Retarded children are even more profoundly deficient with respect to spontaneous strategy usage. However, simple instructions to use strategies produce increased learning for these populations at least with respect to some strategies some of the time (Pressley et al. 1982 reviews work on these topics; also Pressley and Levin 1983 and Levin and Pressley 1983). However it must be emphasized that simple strategy instruction does not always work. See Bender and Levin (1978) for an example of ineffective strategy instructions with retarded children.

A variety of material aids have been designed to increase learning. In virtually every case the benefits associated with a particular type of aid have been found to be situationally specific. To illustrate this point, consider the learning gains associated with two types of adjunct aids for prose learning – questions and pictures.

When an author adds questions to a text they can be put either before the relevant material or after it, and their positioning will have a great effect on which aspects of the text are especially well learned. The presence of questions, either before or after the text, enhances the retention of material specifically covered in the questions. However, the effects of pre- versus post-questions are very different for material not specifically covered in the questions. In the case of post-questions, recall of material other than the question-relevant material is enhanced. However, pre-questions tend to reduce recall of material not specifically included in the question, presumably because the pre-questions focus the learners' attention on the question-relevant material at the expense of the material incidental to the questions. Anderson and Biddle (1975) provide a comprehensive discussion of questioning effects.

Do pictures aid prose learning? Levin and Lesgold (1978)

carefully reviewed this issue and concluded that improvement in learning happens only when young children are the learners and when the pictures accurately represent the text. Also, the prose should consist of concrete stories, orally presented, and the test should consist of short-answer questions. Thus, as in the case of questions, there are specific limitations on the extent to which learning gains are associated with pictures.

In addition to questions and pictures, a number of other aids can be added to text, and in every case positive effects are observed only some of the time. For instance, Ausubel (1963) proposed that texts be accompanied by advanced organizers which are designed to relate to-be-learned materials to already available knowledge, but research has only occasionally confirmed the effectiveness of organizers. There is great debate about whether the strategy is ineffective or whether researchers have failed to construct organizers consistent with Ausubel's theory. Recent evidence indicates that advanced organizers affect memory of higher-level conceptual knowledge, but have no impact on lower-level knowledge (see Mayer and Bromage 1980 for an overview of advanced organizer effects). Similarly, the available research indicates that overviews and behavioral objectives are effective only some of the time (Melton 1979).

There are many issues left to be resolved. The testing of learning strategies is increasingly being conducted in the classroom rather than the laboratory with many new methodological difficulties (e.g. Pressley et al. 1982; Pressley and Levin 1983; Levin and Pressley 1983). Nonetheless, there is enough positive evidence in support of the learning strategies approach to warrant the effort necessary to do real-world studies of learning strategies' effects. MP

Bibliography

Anderson, R.C. and Biddle, W.B. 1975: On asking people questions about what they are reading. In *The psychology of learning and motivation*, ed. G. Bower. Vol. 9. New York, San Francisco and London: Academic Press.

Ausubel, D.P. 1963: *The psychology of meaningful verbal learning*. New York and London: Grune and Stratton.

Barclay, C.R. 1979: The executive control of mnemonic activity. *Journal of experimental child psychology* 27, 262–76.

Bender, B.G. and Levin, J.R. 1978: Pictures, imagery, and retarded children's prose learning. *Journal of educational psychology* 70, 583–8.

Borkowski, J.G. in press: Signs of intelligence: Strategy generalization and metacognition. In *The development of reflection*, ed. S.R. Yussen. New York: Academic Press.

Levin, J.R. and Lesgold, A.M. 1978: On pictures in prose. *Educational communication and technology journal* 26, 233–43.

Levin, J.R. and Pressley, M., eds. 1983: *Cognitive strategy research: educational applications*. New York: Springer-Verlag.

Mayer, R.E. and Bromage, B.K. 1980: Different recall protocols for technical text due to advance organizers. *Journal of educational psychology* 72, 209–25.

Melton, R.F. 1979: Resolution of conflicting claims concerning the effect of behavioral objectives on student learning. *Review of educational research* 48, 291–302.

Pressley, M. 1982: Elaboration and memory development. *Child development* 53, 296–309.

——— et al. 1982: Memory strategy instruction. In *Progress in cognitive development research*, ed. C.J. Brainerd and M. Pressley, Vol. 2. New York: Springer-Verlag.

——— and Levin, J.R., eds 1983: *Cognitive strategy research: psychological foundations*. New York: Springer-Verlag.

learning theory A general term to describe the systematic body of theory and data generated by the study of learning, i.e. classical and instrumental conditioning, and usually applied to the theories and controversies current in the American psychology of learning before and immediately after the second world war and in particular the work of Hull, Guthrie, Tolman and Skinner. Learning theory formed the initial theoretical basis for much of behavior therapy but has largely been superseded by social learning theory which in addition to emphasizing, as previous theories did, the role of conditioning and reinforcement also stresses the importance of cognitive processes, self-reinforcement and imitation in the development of normal and abnormal behavior. DWJ

Lenneberg, Eric H. (1921–1975). Professor of Psychology at the University of Michigan, Lenneberg trained in the psychology of language and in general neurological and medical sciences. He made a number of important contributions to the understanding of the relationship between language and the brain. The findings presented in his *Biological foundations of language* (1967) became a major source of information for both transformational-generative grammar (see CHOMSKY) and psycholinguistics.

While Lenneberg's most important function was to serve as a synthesizer of knowledge found in the disciplines of psychology, linguistics, anthropology, neurology, physiology and genetics, he also made important contributions in the areas of localization of speech in the brain, child language development and speech disorder research. PM

Bibliography

Lenneberg, Eric H. 1967: *Biological foundations of language*. London & Sydney: J. Wiley & Sons.

Miller, George A. and Lenneberg, Elisabeth, eds 1978: *Psychology and biology of language and thought: essays in honour of Eric Lenneberg*. New York and London: Academic Press.

lesbianism *See* homosexuality and lesbianism

Lewin, Kurt German psychologist. Born 9.9.1890 in Mogilno (Posen) and died 12.2.1947 in Newton (Massachusetts, USA). Lewin studied psychology in Berlin from 1909–14. In 1922 he became *Dozent* and in 1927 professor of psychology at the same university, as one of the younger representatives of GESTALT psychology. He emigrated to the US in 1933 and was at first at Cornell, then moved to the University of Iowa in 1935. After the second world war he became the director of the Research Center for Group Dynamics at the Massachusetts Institute of Technology.

Lewin has had a great influence in many areas of psychology. His work formed in various ways a bridge between Gestalt psychology, the study of personality and motivation and social psychology. He was the founder of

FIELD THEORY in psychology, which regarded behavior primarily as a function of the person and the present situation. Lewin attempted to formalize this theory by making use of topology, but this work has been less influential than his research in group dynamics. JMFJ

His main works are: *A dynamic theory of personality* (1935); *Principles of topological psychology* (1936); *Resolving social conflicts* (1948); *Field theory in social science* (1951).

lexical analysis Both the function of the lexicon vis-a-vis other components of grammar and the nature of the lexicon itself remain among the least well understood areas of linguistics.

The notion of "lexical analysis" is usually restricted to the linguistic analysis of word-level lexical items. The most important areas of research are (see Mühlhäusler 1979, 2):

(1) lexical information. Form and cognitive meaning are only a subset of lexical information. Other components include various types of non-cognitive meaning, information about the syntactic behavior and the susceptibility of a given item to word-formation processes (e.g. differential behavior of color adjectives in causatirization: to redden, to blacken but not* to greenen,* to pinken).

(2) lexical decomposition (see COMPONENTIAL ANALYSIS)

(3) lexical field properties and lexical hierarchies, in particular universal implicational hierarchies of semantic areas such as color names (see Brown 1977).

A number of applications of lexical analysis to psycholinguistic problems are discussed in Miller (1978): 75–118). PM

Bibliography

Brown, Cecil H. 1977: Lexical universals and the human language facility. In *Linguistics and anthropology*, ed. Muriel Saville-Troike. Washington DC: Georgetown University Press.

Miller, George A. 1978: *Linguistic theory and psychological reality*. Cambridge, Mass., and London: MIT Press.

Mühlhäusler, P. 1979: *Growth and structure of the lexicon of New Guinea Pidgin*. Canberra: Pacific Linguistics.

liberation A term in Indian philosophies referring to the individual's release from SAMSARA. Some kind of liberation is the goal of almost all Indian religious practice, yet descriptions of it differ in the different schools.

In Hinduism some schools hold that liberation is possible while the individual is still alive (*Jivan-mukti*), whereas others say it can occur only at death.

Some schools see it as the permanent detachment of the individual spirit from the universe of matter, others see it as the merging of the individual self into the Cosmic Self. The buddhist equivalent is NIRVANA. (See also BUDDHIST PSYCHOLOGY, TANTRIC PSYCHOLOGY, YOGA PSYCHOLOGY, VEDANTA.) DA

life events The jargon term "life events" covers all significant social changes and adversities which people may experience. Rigorous standards of assessment are necessary to test the hypothesis that change, particularly if stressful, can lead to various physical and mental conditions. Two methods have been developed, the inventory (Holmes and Rahe 1967) and the interview schedule (Brown 1974). Each method has its particular problems (Tennant et al. 1981).

In general, an excess of life events is reported before the onset of many physical diseases (Birley and Connolly 1976) and mental conditions such as SCHIZOPHRENIA and DEPRESSION and especially before SUICIDE attempts.

However, the association is fairly weak. Modifying factors and particularly the mediating mechanisms are unclear. Insidious illness can itself generate such events. The subject and the researcher may share the bias that stress has important effects. Finally psychiatric disorders, particularly depression, have a significant bearing on the way in which we view and report our experiences. PBe

Bibliography

Brown, G.W. 1974: Meaning, measurement and stress of life events. In *Stressful life events: their nature and effects*, ed. B.S. and B.P. Dohrenwend. New York: John Wiley.

Holmes, T.H. and Rahe, R.H. 1967: The social readjustment rating scale. *Journal of psychosomatic research* 11, 213–18.

Tennant, C., Bebbington, P.E. and Hurry, J. 1981: The role of life events in depressive illness: is there a substantial causal relation? *Psychological medicine* 11, 379–89.

life space Refers to the psychological field, and was employed by LEWIN (1936) to indicate the manifold of co-existing facts which determine the behavior of an individual at a given moment. This is the most fundamental concept in Lewin's theoretical system; and the emphasis on the interrelatedness of the person and the environment has been one of his most important contributions to psychology.

The life space is a product of the interaction between the person (P) and his environment (E). Person in Lewin's terminology may be used in three ways: as equivalent to the "life space" itself; in reference to the individual in the life space, the "behaving self"; and, finally, as a direct reference to the psychological properties of the individual. In the last sense, "person" is extended to incorporate the needs, beliefs, values and perceptual and motoric systems which in interaction among themselves and with the objective environment produce the life space (see FIELD THEORY).

Lewin used the word environment to refer both to the objective and the psychological environment. The psychological environment, or the environment as it exists for the individual, is a part of the life space. Its properties are determined by the characteristics of the person as well as by the characteristics of the objective environment. A Region (i.e. area of psychological activity) of the psychological environment may often be considered attractive or repulsive by the individual when this particular quality is absent in the objective environment.

During development the life space changes towards increasing differentiation. One of these changes involves a time dimension. Plans extend further into the future along with an increased tolerance of delay, and activities of increasingly long duration are organized as one unit. There is also an increasing differentiation of a reality–irreality dimension. Irreality, which corresponds to fantasy, is a more fluid medium and more closely related to the central layers of the person. For instance a daydream has less reality than an action; a faraway "ideal" goal is less real than a goal which determines immediate action.

Since Lewin's introduction of life space and other field theory concepts, the idea that it is pointless to speak of behavior without reference to both the person and the environment has become commonly accepted. To understand behavior requires not only a knowledge of the person's past experience, but also a knowledge of present attitudes, capabilities and the immediate situation. MDe

Bibliography

Lewin, K. 1936: *Principles of topological psychology*. New York: McGraw-Hill.

lifespan psychology The lifespan perspective in developmental psychology is relatively recent. The study of development began in the nineteenth century as the study of growth-related change in infancy, childhood and adolescence. Maturational changes were thought to occur in a universal ONTOGENETIC SEQUENCE, paralleled by universal stages in psychological development. For example it is reasoned that while there is some variation in the age at which walking or talking begins, or the age of first menstruation, both sequence and timing are relatively predictable within broad bounds. Furthermore, in a given culture, it can be expected that children or adolescents will, at any given age, be working on the same set of developmental tasks, tasks representing the intersection of biological readiness and social institutions. For example, six-year-olds in one culture may be starting school, in another learning to hunt.

The lifespan perspective recognizes the need to search for a general sequence of change over the entire life course, notwithstanding the absence of maturational markers (the menopause in women is considered the only universal maturational change in adulthood), and the diversity of social roles in a pluralistic age-graded system. One cannot become a parent, for example, before puberty, nor contract a marriage independent of parental consent before reaching the age of political majority. Child labor laws restrict the participation of the young in the labor force, and mandatory retirement in certain occupations excludes the elderly.

Within these very broad bounds, however, there is much possible variation and no single sequence of roles. First marriage and parenthood may occur at twenty or earlier, at thirty, at forty, or later; the peak of a career will occur early for those in certain fields (for example professional athletes, musicians and mathematicians) and later in others (art, literature, the social sciences). The sequence of roles is not invariant: a first marriage may be followed by a second; career peaks may be followed by career changes. Consideration of the entire life cycle is complicated by the fact that the maturational timetable of the first portion of the life span is absent in adulthood, and the range of variation so great.

The scientific study of the life span began in the 1940s, building on such bases as G. Stanley Hall's book *Senescence: the last half of life*, published in 1922; Charlotte Buhler's distinction between the biological and the biographical life curves, published in 1933; and Else Frenkel-Brunswik's studies of the life span, begun in Berkeley during the 1930s. The concept of developmental tasks was developed by Robert Havighurst at the University of Chicago during the 1940s, combining the drive toward growth, or maturational timetable, of the individual with the constraints and opportunities in the social environment. In 1950 Erik Erikson published *Childhood and society*, widely considered to be the most influential book of the period and an introduction for many readers to the concept of development over the life cycle.

Although Erikson's work built on that of others, his model of eight stages of the life cycle was the first widely received model of development extending the notion of developmental stages into adulthood. Paralleling Freud's ONTOGENETIC SEQUENCE for the first part of the life cycle, Erikson poses the following "nuclear crises" or stages in psychosocial development:

Stage	*Approximate age*	*Freudian equivalent*
basic trust vs. mistrust	infancy	oral
autonomy vs. shame and doubt	toddler	anal
initiative vs. guilt	preschool	phallic/oedipal
industry vs. inferiority	school age	latency
identity vs. role confusion	adolescence/young adulthood	none
intimacy vs. isolation	young adulthood	genital
generativity vs. stagnation	middle adulthood	none
ego integrity vs. despair	later adulthood	none

Erikson's theory is an extension of Freud's in the following ways: first, he expands the concept of stages of development to embrace the entire life cycle; second, he recognizes more explicitly the interaction of the individual with the social context; third, the content of those stages for which there is no Freudian equivalent adds new substance to our understanding of development over the life span. The stage of identity vs. role confusion is the stage at which the young adult finds a place in society; generativity vs. stagnation marks the stage of responsibility for the next generation, not only through parenthood but through any form of care and concern for the young; the stage of ego integrity vs. despair marks the point when one's one and only life cycle is accepted, when one can look back over the life course without despair.

Recognition of personality development in adulthood was greatly enhanced by the work of Bernice Neugarten and her colleagues at the University of Chicago in the Kansas City Study of Adult Life, carried out over the decade 1954–64. Although she found a regular progression toward increased interiority of personality, there was no comparable regularity of change in social behavior. On the basis of these findings, she challenged the disengagement theory of Cumming and Henry, suggesting that life satisfaction was associated with sustained activity throughout the life cycle. A major contribution of Neugarten's work is expanded understanding of the developmental changes in middle age, hitherto thought to be a period of stability. Her work marks the beginning of a life-span perspective, uniting child developmental studies at one end of the life cycle with GERONTOLOGY at the other.

Since its beginnings in the study of personality development over the life course, life-span psychology has seen major advances in the study of family and intergenerational relations; cognitive development; age grading and the social system; and social policy. Not only does life span psychology encompass the life course of the developing individual, but the broader social and political context in which the individual's development occurs. See also VOCATIONAL CHOICE. ND

Bibliography

*Baltes, Paul B. and Schaie, K. Warner, eds. 1973: *Life-span developmental psychology: personality and socialization*. New York and London: Academic Press.

Datan, Nancy and Ginsberg, Leon H., eds. 1975: *Life-span developmental psychology: normative life crises*. New York and London: Academic Press.

*Datan, Nancy and Lohmann, Nancy, eds. 1980: *Transitions of aging*. New York and London: Academic Press.

*Erikson, Erik H. 1963: *Childhood and society* 2nd edn. New York: W.W. Norton; Harmondsworth: Penguin.

Goulet, L.R. and Baltes, Paul B., eds. 1970: *Life-span developmental psychology: research and theory*. New York and London: Academic Press.

*Neugarten, Bernice L., ed. 1968: *Middle age and aging*. Chicago and London: University of Chicago Press.

limbic system A group of interconnected structures located primarily in the telencephalon of the brain (BRAIN AND CENTRAL NERVOUS SYSTEM: ILLUSTRATIONS figs. 15–18). Areas most often included in the limbic system are the cingulate gyrus, hippocampus, entorhinal cortex, septum, and amygdala. The anterior thalamus and mammillary bodies of the diencephalon fig. 5, because of their anatomical and functional connections with limbic structures, are often considered part of this system. Historically designated rhinencephalon or "smell brain", the term limbic system was adopted when it became apparent that this part of the brain played a smaller role in olfaction than had originally been thought. The limbic system is frequently referred to as the visceral brain, implying a collective role in emotionality. In practice attempts to characterize the limbic system as a single functional entity seem inappropriate. Through its various structures the limbic system is involved in a range of specific operations bearing on emotional and motivational behavior as well as learning and memory processes. GWi

linguistic acceptability In transformational generative linguistics acceptability relates to *performance* in the same way that *grammaticalness* relates to *competence*. An acceptable utterance is one which has been or might have been produced by a native speaker in an appropriate context. The acceptability of a sentence depends on both its structural properties and its social appropriateness. With regard to the former one can distinguish between phonological (presence or absence of an accent), syntactic (grammatically correct or deviant) and semantic (meaningful or meaningless) acceptability. Social appropriateness, on the other hand, involves conventions for the use or non-use of structurally acceptable utterances. It is widely held that acceptable utterances or sentences are a subset of grammatical utterances and that the study of *grammaticalness* has to precede any examination of acceptability.

Whereas acceptability tests are frequently used in psycholinguistic research, the results of such tests have to be interpreted with great care as the precise relationship between pragmatic and structural factors is not well understood (Lyons 1968, pp.137–142). In post-transformational models of linguistic description, in particular those concerned with COMMUNICATIVE COMPETENCE, the distinction between acceptability and grammaticalness is no longer regarded as significant. PM

Bibliography

Lyons, John 1968: *Introduction to theoretical linguistics*, Cambridge and New York: Cambridge University Press 1968.

linguistic backsliding According to Selinker (1972, 216) backsliding is "the regular reappearance of fossilized errors that were thought to be eradicated" in SECOND LANGUAGE ACQUISITION. It usually results from the learner's difficulty in expressing particular semantic notions and from stress-provoking social settings. Otherwise a learner will produce more advanced and correct forms of the second language.

Hyltenstam (1977, 408) has shown that backsliders strictly adhere to the overall implicational pattern ("inbuilt syllabus") underlying the sequential appearance of grammatical constructions in second language acquisition.

Research into backsliding behavior can shed light on both the relationship between pragmatic and structural considerations in language development and the concept of structural difficulty in linguistics.

While the term backsliding is usually reserved for second language acquisition, the use of simplified registers such as BABY TALK can be associated with a reversal to earlier learning stages of a speaker's first language. PM

Bibliography

Hyltenstam, Kenneth 1977: Implicational patterns in interlanguage Syntax Variation'. *Language learning* 27, 2: 283–411.

Selinker, L. 1972: Interlanguage. *International review of applied linguistics* 10: 209–231.

linguistic naturalness A property often claimed for linguistic rules, categories or analyses proposed since the mid-1960s. Those interested in naturalness have been concerned to define and apply the notion "natural" in the treatment of some linguistic level or subdiscipline, e.g. one speaks of "natural" phonology, "natural" morphology, "natural" syntax, "natural" rules, etc.

In order to justify employing an attribute such as natural as a measure of evaluation, one must first establish how to recognize it. Generally, the evidence proffered by linguists can be divided into two subtypes: *system-internal* and *system-external* evidence. Language system-internal properties that count as natural include: (a) *change* – a natural category or rule is more resistant to change than unnatural category or rule; (b) CREOLIZATION – in the loss of function-words during pidginization natural rules or categories survive longest and reappear first during CREOLIZATION; (c) *typology* – natural rules or categories are more frequent in the world's languages; (d) *frequency* – tokens of natural categories or applications of natural rules are more frequent within one language; (e) *neutralization* – natural categories are the surviving members of a merger between two categories; (f) *analogy* – natural categories are the template of change; unnatural categories undergo the change; (g) *phonology* – natural categories or rules are ones easier to produce or perceive; (h) *morphology* – natural categories are not zero encoded, i.e. they have some exponent: (i) *syntax* – natural rules or categories are ones with a perceptual or production function: and (j) *mappings* – natural rules do not produce intermediate forms that are not also acceptable surface forms. Language system-external properties include: (a) *language acquisition* – natural rules and categories are acquired earlier or less subject to suppression; (b) *speech errors* – natural rules or categories are less subject to error; (c) *language disturbance* (see NEUROLINGUISTICS) – natural rules or categories resist breakdown longer; (d) *language death* – natural rules or categories are longer survivors in the dissolution of a language.

The area of linguistic naturalness with the largest literature is undoubtedly phonological naturalness. Much of this interest arose from reactions to the influential *The sound pattern of English* (SPE) by Chomsky and Halle (1968). According to Darden (1974) these reactions can be divided into controversies about five issues.

One specific and voluminous area of controversy in generative phonology in the post SPE-era bears on the degree of *abstractness* of phonological representation. The SPE-model assumes that an underlying or abstract form is mapped by rules onto a concrete, surface phonetic form. If no restrictions are placed on potential rules or representation then nothing prevents one from assuming underlying forms quite "distant" from the surface. Some of the major research supporting a more abstract phonology includes especially Gussmann (1980). Those works favoring a more restricted and concrete "natural generative phonology" include Hooper (1976) and Vennemann (1974).

The central ideas in neutral generative phonology (NGP), according to Hooper and Vennemann, are threefold: (a) The *True Generalization Condition* requires that speakers formulate generalizations about the sound structure of their language to relate surface forms one to another, not rules relating underlying to surface forms; (b) the *No Ordering Condition* bars any (extrinsic) rule ordering; and (c) *Lexical Representation* contains the words of a language, not just the stems plus rules on how to change them, e.g. *sing*, *sang* and *sung* would all be listed separately. These three conditions severely (the first named group of linguists above would say too severely) limit the type of grammars available to describe natural language phonology. In particular there could be no cases in NGP of *absolute neutralization*, sound segments that never survive to the surface of a language, but which influence derivations, e.g. there would be no "silent *e*" in English phonology in *mute* that could be appealed to in accounting for the lack of [yu] in *mut* and *moot*.

A second area of controversy about naturalness in phonology concerns the manner of *evaluating competing analyses*. In SPE counting phonological features was considered the primary criterion. Therefore, the rounding of front vowels e→ö and the rounding of back vowels $\gamma \rightarrow$o would require the same number of feature changes, i.e. the features [- round] would change to [+ round] or vice versa. However, in terms of natural properties – frequency, change, acquisition, etc. – back vowels round far more easily than front vowels. What is needed, say those favoring a more natural approach, is some universal theory of phonological markedness, a set of principles assigning segments "markedness values" and characterizing the "markedness status" of rules.

The third area addressed by those advocating naturalness in phonology concerns *distinctions in types of rules*, and Vennemann (1974) argues that one must treat differently phonetically conditioned and morphologically or lexically conditioned changes. For instance, the first can be illustrated with the backing of a nasal when followed by a back consonant, e.g. *ban* vs. *bang*; the second by the insertion of vowels before an *s*-plural whenever the noun stem ends in an *s*-like-sound, e.g. ra*tes*, mo*des*, wa*ves* vs. fa*ces*, ca*ges*, chur*ches*. In the first example reference need be made only to the phonological composition of the string; in the second reference has to be made to a morphological category *plural*. Vennemann (1974) advocates a lexicon of "words" (instead of morphemes, affixes, etc) listing all forms of a paradigm separately with rules within the lexicon relating the various forms. For regular paradigms the rules are highly redundant; for suppletive paradigms, such as *go*:*went*:*gone*, the rule would be correspondingly idiosyncratic. These two rule types would be in different components of the grammar and would fulfil different functions.

The fourth area of interest of natural phonology is *sound change*. BAILEY (1982) divides change into two subtypes: *connatural* and *abnatural* change. The first corresponds to system-internal unmarking, the reduction of markedness ("unnaturalness") because of internal pressure. Some sounds are less frequent, more subject to change, acquired by children later, etc. These tend to alter to forms with less cognitive cost (because less marked) by means of well-known phonological processes. For example, in old English a qualitative suffix -*th*[þ] was added to adjectives and some verbs, e.g. *long*:*length broad*:*breadth*, *wide*:*width*. If, however, the stem ended in a spirant such as [-f] or [-x], which was spelled -*gh* and later disappeared from English, then this -*th* qualitative suffix changed via a phonological process called *dissimilation* into a -*t*, e.g. *high:height, drive:drift, dry:drought*. The system-internal motivation for this change rests in the phonetically implausible and difficult sequence of two spirants. Abnatural change, on the other hand, is change brought about by borrowing, for example. English has taken initial [v-, z-, j-], as in *very, zest*, and *just*, from French, enlarging the inventory of distinctive sounds in the language, cf. Bloomfield (1933:447). Bailey pleads that both natural changes, connatural and abnatural, are needed to maintain the natural balance of synthesis and analysis.

Finally, natural phonology has emphasized the role of *language acquisition* in theory construction. Especially prominent in this area have been the works in natural phonology, e.g. Stampe (1979). Stampe's major claim is that a child acquires the phonological rules and representations of his language by restricting and suppressing an innate, "language-innocent" inventory of unrestricted sounds and rules to just those of his environment. Three strategies children employ are: (a) *suppression* of one of two contradictory processes; (b) *limiting* the set of segments to which a rule applies; and (c) *ordering* a previously unordered pair of rules. Consonants become voiceless because oral constriction impedes the airflow required to cause phonation. Therefore, children must learn to suppress this pole of a pair in order to be able to produce a voice-voiceless contrast. As an example of limiting, children tend to devoice all final consonants as soon as they learn to produce postvocalic segments. Children acquiring English must then limit this rule's application just to those cases of voiceless consonants. German children do not need to learn to limit this rule, as German always devoices such final consonants. Examples of ordering in children's speech are too involved to present here, see Stampe (1979, pp. xiv-xv) for illustrations.

Naturalness in morphology is a more recent development than phonological naturalness. It has primarily been the product of European linguists. As Dressler (1982) characterizes it, morphological naturalness incorporates notions from: (a) language universals; (b) perception; (c) acquisition; (d) functionalism; (e) aphasia; and (f) language change. The most important investigator in this area is Mayerthaler (1980, 1981). In assessing morphological naturalness, he first assigns a cognitive value to a linguistic category, e.g. cognitively plurality is more marked (less natural) than singularity. He, then, assigns a markedness value to the encoding of this cognitive category. The assessment of "natural" encoding of words is based upon laws. The Law of Iconicity demands, for instance, that something cognitively more marked be encoded iconically, by an additive exponent marking that asymmetry. Thus *boy:boys* is an unmarked encoding of plurality, whereas *foot:feet* is a marked encoding, since the contrast relies only on a modulatory and not an additive strategy. The plural formation *fish:fish* is least desirable, i.e. is overmarked and quite subject to change, late acquisitions and errors.

A corollary to the Law of Iconicity is often called Humboldt's Universal and can be stated as: one form, one meaning. Encodings in the unmarked case should preserve perceptual constancy. A single exponent should not be used for more than one morphological function and each morphological category should, in the ideal case, have at most a single exponent. The English inflectional -*s* provides a striking counterexample to this universal, since it encodes three morphological categories: plurality, possession and 3rd person singular present tense. A more typical instance of the pressure of Humboldt's Universal can be seen in the dislike native speakers have for those adverbs in -*ly* from adjectives that already end in -*ly*, cf. *Drive friendly*! (an actual US road sign) not *?Drive friendlily*.

Encoding is also subject to the effects of *Markedness Reversal*. A marked encoding may become unmarked in a marked environment, just as a person wearing clothing is marked in a nudist camp. Some objects naturally come in groups and rarely as individuals. These are examples, of marked environments and markedness reversal may occur. In English *police* is a natural plural and has an additively encoded singulative form *policeman*.

Naturalness in syntax has certainly played a less prominent role than naturalness in the previously discussed subdisciplines. Bartsch and Vennemann in unpublished work have proposed that the True Generalization Condition should be valid for syntax as well as for the phonology of natural language, claiming, for example, that *passive* is a rule relating two surface structures, not one connecting underlying forms. While use has been made of the properties of a natural rule-change, acquisition, breakdown, etc. – no comprehensive proposal has been made. JAE

Bibliography

Bailey, Charles-James 1982: *On the yin and yang nature of linguistics*. Ann Arbor: Karoma Press.

Bloomfield, Leonard 1933. *Language*. New York: Holt, Rinehart and Winston.

*Bruck, Anthony, Robert Fox and Michael LaGaly, eds. 1974: *Papers from the parasession on natural phonology*. Chicago Linguistics Society.

Chomsky, Noam and Morris Halle 1968: *The sound pattern of English*. New York, Evanston, and London: Harper & Row.

Darden, Bill J. 1974: Introduction. In *Papers from the parasession on natural phonology*, ed. A. Bruck, R. Fox and M. LaGaly. Chicago Linguistics Society.

Dressler, Wolfgang 1982: Plenary session papers. The XIIIth International Congress of Linguists. Tokyo, Japan.

Gussmann, Edmund 1980: *Studies in abstract phonology*. Cambridge, Mass. and London: MIT Press.

*Hooper, Joan 1976: *Introduction to natural generative phonology*. New York and London: Academic Press.

*Mayerthaler, Willi 1980: Morphologischer Ikonismus, *Zeitschrift für Semiotik* 2, 19–37.

——— 1981: *Morphologische Natürlichkeit*. Wiesbaden: Athenaion.

Stampe, David 1979: *A dissertation on natural phonology*. New York and London: Garland.

Vennemann, Theo 1974: Words and syllables in generative grammar. In *Papers from the parasession on natural phonology*, ed. A. Bruck, R. Fox and M. LaGaly. Chicago Linguistic Society.

linguistic universals Properties shared by all languages, especially properties inherent in language as a pan-human mental and behavioral trait. Although interest in "universal grammar" dates back at least to the Enlightenment (e.g. Condillac), recent discussions of linguistic universals have drawn upon increasingly detailed descriptions of the world's languages and growing research into the evolutionary, psychological and social-interactional bases of language.

The most elementary linguistic universals are simple, overt linguistic units such as consonants and vowels, conjunctions and pronouns, direction terms and body part names, or commands and questions, which all languages are believed to possess. Universals of this type have been posited in every realm of linguistic description, including phonetics, syntax, semantics, and pragmatics. In some cases, these universals are "implicational": if unit or property x is present, then unit or property y will also be. For example, languages in which the verb usually appears at the beginning of sentences tend to have function-specifying particles (e.g. prepositions) coming before nouns, while verb-final languages more often have post-posed particles. Note also that in this example the universal is stated in terms of tendencies rather than absolutes. This sort of "quantitative" or "statistical" quality is widespread among the universals so far proposed.

Perhaps the most complex kind of implicational universals are "hierarchical": particular units are recognized as being more complex or more prone to exhibit certain distributional properties than others in a relatively fixed set of similar units. The presence or distribution of a unit thus implies things about all units beneath it in the identified hierarchy. Two examples: (1) the presence of nasalization as an invariant feature of a vowel implies the presence of a vowel identical to it in every respect but nasality (see LINGUISTIC NATURALNESS). (2) If an indirect object can appear as the head noun for a relative clause (e.g. *The man who was given the prize*), then so can direct objects (e.g. *The prize which was given*) and subjects (e.g. *The jury who gave him the prize*), but not necessarily other sentence constituents. (English, unfortunately, delves so deep into this relativization hierarchy that examples of disallowed relativization are hard to come by, (see Keenan and Comrie 1977).)

More abstract universals, many of which are implicit in the phrasing of attributes that all languages exhibit, though in a large number of substantively different ways. Examples include relativization (see above) and other kinds of inclusion of one clausal unit in another (see EMBEDDING), temporal order as an indicator of the syntactic or pragmatic function of words, and ellipsis.

Studies in generative grammar (see CHOMSKY) typically employ a rather different use of the term "linguistic universal" than the one discussed so far. Rather than being properties shared by all languages, linguistic universals provide a universal descriptive framework for languages. "Substantive universals" constitute the basic features and categories with which to describe the properties of individual linguistic units. "Formal universals" prescribe the types of rule that govern the combination of the substantive primitives into actual linguistic units. This very abstract and highly ambitious theory has produced various distinct and hotly debated alternative expositions of such a "universal grammar".

Equally abstract but less controversial linguistic universals are those that Hockett (1960) has called "design features of language". Hockett cites such elements as "arbitrariness" (linguistic forms typically bear no physical correspondence to the things they represent), "discreteness" (utterances are divisible into a fixed set of recurring physical units that combine to represent a larger but still determinate set of conceptual units), and "duality of patterning" (the principles that govern the combinations of physical units into minimal meaningful units are separate and distinct from the principles that govern the combinations of those minimal units in larger conceptual structures; that is, phonology and syntax are independent). Other such universals are vocal sufficiency (all languages can be transmitted intelligibly over a solely vocal-auditory communication channel; gestural and other information – however helpful – is not essential for the emission or recognition of words), pretense (there is no necessary connection between utterance meaning and belief), and anatomical adaptedness (the organs of speech production and comprehension are biologically adapted to the task). Disputes over these and other proposed design features (over twenty so far) have arisen when Hockett and others have claimed that given features are or are not present in other communication systems (see ANTHROPOID APE LANGUAGE).

All the universals mentioned so far are synchronic. There are also, however, diachronic linguistic universals, pertaining to how languages change over time, whether historically or ontogenetically. To some extent, such diachronic universals are merely derivative from the synchronic: Language change will not result in violations of established universals. But there are also universals concerning such essentially dynamic phenomena as how imbalances or gaps in phonetic or lexical inventories will be resolved, or how contact between speakers of different languages will affect their languages. One of the best known examples of a diachronic universal is the pattern of basic color term evolution described by Berlin and Kay (1969). Their review of cross-linguistic and historical evidence supports very strong inferences as to the order of emergence of labels for both spectral and non-spectral colors.

Announcements of newly found linguistic universals invariably provoke two interrelated challenges, one methodological and the other theoretical. First, is the universal proposed merely because a large number of languages exhibit a particular property? If so, how can it be certain that all languages – unknown, extinct, or potential – will exhibit that property? The only defenses against this challenge are caution (Say only that all languages so far examined exhibit the property.) and industry (Look at all the languages you can, with as large a variety of other properties separating them as possible, before suggesting a universal.).

The second, more theoretical, challenge is, how is this universal to be explained? Is it merely a product of shared history or circumstance (All languages have a word meaning *moon*, for example.), or is it truly "inherent in language as a pan-human mental and behavioral trait"? This challenge is, of course, avoidable by the disclaimer that it is a property shared by all known languages, and whether it is shared because it is "inherent" is somebody else's question. Most linguists, however, rise to this challenge. Many alleged universals, most notably generative grammar's "formal universals", have in fact been "explained" by appeals to "innateness", on the grounds that no one has shown how to explain them on the basis either of historical or circumstantial accident or of universal extra-linguistic facts about human beings. This (often rather vague) argument from ignorance has provoked much similar (and sterile) counter-argument. But there has also been considerable (and increasingly fertile) research directed at showing how one or another linguistic universal may derive from universals of human anatomy, perception, sociality, ontogeny, communication, and so forth. HSS

Bibliography

Berlin, Brent and Kay, Paul 1979: *Basic color terms: their universality and emergence*. Berkeley, Calif.: University of California Press.

*Brown, Cecil H. and Witkowski, Stanley R. 1980: Language universals. In *Toward explaining human culture: a critical review of the findings of worldwide cross-cultural research*, ed. David Levinson and Martin J. Malone. New Haven, CN: HRAF Press.

Chomsky, Noam 1965: *Aspects of the theory of syntax*. Cambridge, Mass.: MIT Press.

Comrie, Bernard 1981: *Language universals and linguistic topology*. Oxford: Basil Blackwell; Chicago: University of Chicago Press.

Hockett, Charles F. 1960: Logical considerations in the study of animal communication. In *Animal sounds and communcation*, ed. W.E. Lanyon and W.N. Tavolga. Washington, DC: American Institute of Biological Sciences. 30

Keenan, Edward and Comrie, Bernard 1977: Noun phrase accessibility and universal grammar. *Linguistic inquiry* 8, 63–99.

Greenberg, Joseph F., ed. 1963: *Universals of language*. Cambridge, Mass.: MIT Press.

——— 1966: *Language universals*. The Hague: Mouton.

linguistics: diachronic The distinction between synchronic and diachronic linguistics was introduced by SAUSSURE, who held that the diachronic or historical study of language involved methods and principles different from the study of synchronic systems. Up to the development of variation theories diachronic considerations were regarded as irrelevant to the description of existing linguistic systems ("langue" or COMPETENCE).

The exclusion of diachronic considerations from linguistic descriptions has resulted in a compartmentalization of the discipline of linguistics. Furthermore, diachronic descriptions were considered merely to involve the comparison of synchronic systems at different points in time. Consequently synchronic linguistics was regarded as methodologically prior. The restriction of diachronic studies to the comparison of states has forced linguists to exclude variation and gradient changes from their field of interest. The suitability of such restricted methods of diachronic language study to the investigation of child language development or speech disorders is highly questionable. PM

Bibliography

Bailey, C.-J.N. 1980: Old and new views on language history and language relationships. In *Kommunikationstheoretische Grundlagen des Sprachwandels*, ed. H. Luedke. Berlin and New York: De Gruyter.

linguistics: synchronic Synchronic (descriptive, minilectal or static) linguistics is a term introduced by SAUSSURE. Its object is the description of a linguistic system as used by a set of speakers at a given point in time, during which it is assumed that no change takes place. It is regarded as methodologically prior to *diachronic linguistics*, which involves the comparison of a number of synchronic stages. Synchronic analysis is concerned primarily with the COMPETENCE, as reflected in his linguistic IDIOLECT, of an ideal speaker-hearer.

The principal problem with any synchronic linguistic analysis is that it is removed from the actual reality of speaking since it ignores the manner in which language users communicate despite time-related speech differences. Older and newer forms are related to style, social class, geographic provenance, sex or age of a speaker. Any linguist who ignores the fact that speakers are polylectal deprives him/herself of the most valuable psycho-linguistic data (see VARIATION THEORIES).

Contrary to the claims of Saussure and CHOMSKY, it can be argued that diachronic linguistics should be considered methodologically prior since development can explain its endpoint or state but not vice versa. There are also strong arguments for abandoning a strict separation of diachronic and synchronic linguistics in favor of time-incorporating developmental linguistics (see BAILEY). PM

literature and psychology Both terms, in their commonest current senses, are of recent date and it is only in the last hundred years that "literature" and "psychology" have become the objects of separate, institutionalized academic study. The organization of our present-day academic disciplines has often produced a bizarrely restricted view of what each subject comprises and of what its major texts are. Works which might be thought to be of equal interest to both fields – Plato's *Timaeus*, say, or Augustine's *Confessions*, Hobbes's *Leviathan*, Vico's *Scienza Nuova*, Kierkegaard's *The Concept of Dread* – have in practice received scant attention from either. Literature and psychology as university subjects have interacted correspondingly little. Certain literary scholars would readily acknowledge artistic merit in, say, William James's *Principles of psychology*, just as certain psychologists would allow Henry James's *Portrait of a lady* to be a work of extraordinary psychological understanding. But such moments of contact have seldom altered the ways in which each discipline defines its characteristic tasks. The psychological sciences have drawn from the world of myth and literature a few technical or semi-technical terms (narcissism, the Oedipus complex, sadism, masochism, etc), have made occasional use of literary figures (Hamlet, Don Quixote, Don Juan, Emma Bovary, Raskolnikov) as a shorthand method of denoting various personality types, and, in so far as introspective reports on the operations of the mind are thought to possess scientific value, have cited certain writers as precursors or allies: Bacon, Montaigne, Rousseau, Goethe, Coleridge, Proust. Literary studies in their turn have made use – albeit in approximate and diluted forms – of the technical vocabulary of psychology, especially in analyzing the behavior and motivation of characters in drama or prose fiction and the role of images in poetry. By far the richest interaction between literature and psychology is to be found in the works of FREUD. Although he wrote, in his essay on "Dostoyevsky and Parricide", that "before the problem of the creative artist analysis must, alas, lay down its arms", psychoanalysis suggests numerous ways in which the workings of the literary text can be better understood. Freud made extensive use of literary examples and analogies and wrote illuminatingly on Homer, Sophocles, Rabelais, Shakespeare, Goethe, Hoffmann and Ibsen. His own contribution to letters was large, as stylist, essayist, autobiographer and as the fashioner from psychoanalytic case-material of "characters" – Dora, the Rat-Man, the Wolf-Man, Little Hans – who have proved captivating to the literary imagination. Although Freud performed certain extended analyses of literary works (see, in particular, his *Delusions and dreams in Jensen's "Gradiva"*), literary studies have been more memorably energized by his general theories of mental functioning. Freud's discussion of such mechanisms as repression, condensation, displacement and over-determination, and of jokes and slips or "parapraxes", has provided students of literature with a range of new perspectives on to the literary text considered as an indirect and multi-layered mode of utterance. Freud's detailed scrutiny of "facts of language" in the handling of his case-material has been continued by Jacques LACAN and the so called "French Freudians". This fertile tradition has in recent years done much to heal the breach between literary studies and psychology and to outline fully collaborative ways in which they might study the determining roles of language both in the individual human subject and in culture at large. MMB

Other approaches, to literature which were influenced by Freud turned sometimes in a sociological direction (see CRITICAL THEORY) and sometimes towards myths and folk tales. JUNG's ideas are behind a range of studies of myth and the mythical element in literary texts. More conventional post-Freudians, for example Bettelheim (1976), have written on popular folk tales such as Cinderella. There are some however who feel that the glamor of psychoanalytic theorizing has had an unfortunate impact on the relationship between literature and psychology. Psychoanalysts and analytically oriented critics have not been slow to lay themselves open to ridicule by offering heavily excremental and libidinal accounts of whimsical children's stories. The use of artists' work as if it were clinical material has not disappeared. There are plenty of analyses of artists' traumatic infancies based largely on their novels, poems (or paintings). On the other hand more conventional psychology has offered little to help those who might be interested in applying psychological concepts to the elucidation of literary texts. I.A. Richards (1924) was one of the few important critics who attempted to make use of contemporary psychological approaches in writing about literature. His famous 1929 experiment designed to clarify some of the processes and problems of literary appreciation has hardly been followed up seriously by critics who, if slightly interested in psychology, have prefered dilute Freud or the folk-psychology implied in the work of Richards's contemporary, F.R. Leavis.

More recently there has been a different psychological interest in texts as evidence. Lévi-Strauss has attempted to expose the underlying structure of myths with an apparent aim of getting at the structures of human cognition. Less ambitious investigators have used children's books (McClelland 1961) or folk tales (Roberts et al. 1963) to compare enculturation differences in different societies. There is now also a growing interest in the use of literature and artifactual evidence for the study of HISTORICAL PSYCHOLOGY. With caution one may obtain from literature information about how people behaved, spoke and even thought or felt at different periods (see Collett 1984).

As for the influence of psychology on literature itself, it has again been the psychoanalytic and Jungian traditions which have had something to offer to writers. This may be only in their theory of their craft, in their practice (e.g. Surrealism), or it may appear explicitly in their texts, as, for instance in Svevo's *La coscienza di Zeno*, or in Thomas's *The white hotel*. MMB/RL

Bibliography

Bettelheim, B. 1976: *The uses of enchantment*. London: Thames and Hudson.

Collett, P.C. 1983: History and the study of expressive action. In *Historical social psychology*, ed. K. Gergen and M. Gergen. New York: Erlbaum.

McClelland, D.C. 1961: *The achieving society*. Princeton: Van Nostrand.

Richards, I.A. 1924: *Principles of literary criticism*. London: Routledge and Kegan Paul.

——— 1929: *Practical criticism*. London: Routledge and Kegan Paul.

Roberts, J.M., Sutton-Smith, B. and Kendon, A. 1963: Strategy in games and folk tales. *Journal of social psychology* 61, 185–99.

Trilling, Lionel 1950: Freud and literature. In *The liberal imagination*. London and New York: Oxford University Press.

local circuit neurons *See* neurons, local circuit

Locke, John (1632–1704) The founder of British empiricism. Impressed by the growth of science, but unsure of its foundations, Locke undertook a critical review of human knowledge (1689). His method, like that of DESCARTES, was to start from the evident contents of the mind and to infer by careful steps the nature of the external world. He put less trust in pure reason than did Descartes and was more critical of the legacy of medieval philosophy, especially of the idea of substance and its use to explain personal identity. Nevertheless, there is a strong element of rationalism in some of Locke's conclusions, e.g. in his account of scientific explanation. It was left to Berkeley and HUME to push empiricism to the limit. Locke's fundamental principle was that our knowledge of the contents of our own minds is independent of any knowledge of their external causes and effects. Total acceptance of this principle makes it difficult to avoid scepticism in philosophy and it leaves psychology with a single resource, introspection. Locke's political philosophy was a measured defense of the Revolution of 1688 based on the requirement that government should be by consent (1690). DP

Bibliography

Locke, John 1689 (*1975*): *An essay concerning human understanding*, ed. P.H. Nidditch. Oxford and New York: Oxford University Press.

——— 1690 (*1924*): *Two treatises on civil government*. London: J.M. Dent.

*Yolton, John W. 1968: *John Locke and the way of ideas*. Oxford and New York: Oxford University Press.

locomotion The coordinated muscular movements which displace the whole body of an animal. Many very small animals float freely in air or in water, but these movements are entirely passive and do not count as locomotion. A great variety of means of locomotion is found among animals.

The techniques used for locomotion in water include undulating swimming such as that of eels, water snakes and some marine worms (polychaetes); rowing as in ducks, water beetles and ciliated protozoa; hydrofoil swimming which is found in tunnies and other fast-swimming fish, marine turtles, penguins and auks; and the jet propulsion of squid, octopus and dragon-fly larvae. The physical principles involved in aquatic locomotion have received considerable study and are well understood.

Flight has evolved in few groups of animals, probably because it requires extreme anatomical specialization which can be achieved only by animals which are already adapted for an agile life on land. Insects were the first animals to develop flight and there were numerous types of flying insects 300 million years ago. Flying reptiles appeared about 170 million years ago and were abundant up to about 70 million years ago. Birds evolved during the same period, the early forms being similar to flying reptiles. Flying mammals (bats) appeared about 40 million years ago. Even today there are some incipient flying animals, including flying marsupials, such as the gliding possums (*Petaurus*) and flying squirrels (*Glaucomys*). There are also flying lizards, snakes and fish. All these animals have a short-range primitive type of gliding flight. Nevertheless, the potential for evolution to more sophisiticated forms is present.

Modern birds and insects are able to exploit many principles of aerodynamics and exhibit many forms of flight, including gliding, flapping flight and hovering flight. Aerodynamic principles dictate that larger animals fly faster and require less frequent wing beats. Only very small birds, such as humming birds, and insects can perform hovering flight in which there is no forward locomotion. Very large birds have to run to attain sufficient speed to become airborne. This requirement is reduced if they take off into the wind. Large birds have proportionally larger wings and their flapping flight requires considerable energy expenditure compared to that of small birds. For this reason most large birds prefer gliding flight and tend to exploit conditions where this is possible. Natural up-currents occur where the wind strikes a hill or sea cliff. Seagulls can often glide along a cliff when there is a sea breeze. Over land, up-currents called thermals may occur where there are features, such as rocky areas, which induce differential heating. Large birds, such as vultures, may save more than 90 per cent of the energy required for flapping flight, by exploiting thermals as they search for prey.

Locomotion on land occurs in a number of forms in animals without legs. Amoeboid movement is found in some single-celled animals and various types of crawling occur in worms, leeches, etc. Waves of muscular contraction pass down the body of an earthworm producing a form of concertina crawling. The serpentine crawling used by snakes exploits irregularities on the ground, such as stones and tufts of grass. Lateral pressure against these enables the snake to glide forward.

Locomotion on legs occurs mainly in the arthropods and vertebrates. Among two-legged animals there are three basic types of gait, the walk, the run and the hop. During walking there is always one foot on the ground, whereas both feet may be momentarily off the ground during running. Hopping on two legs, as in kangaroos and many birds, involves simultaneous propulsion from the two legs.

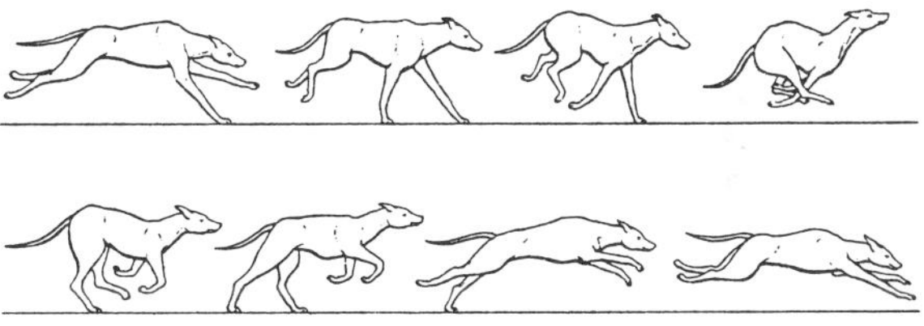

Whippet running (from Gray 1968)

Animals have numerous possible gaits, depending upon the order in which the feet touch the ground, as illustrated. In four-legged animals the main propulsion comes from the hind feet, but in many mammals the stride is lengthened by bending the back so that the hind feet may touch the ground in front of the fore feet during galloping.

Jumping from a running or standing start occurs in many mammals but few can jump much more than their own height. Some insects have a special catapult mechanism which enables them to jump many times their own height from a standing start.

Moving in trees occurs in a variety of animals and many different methods are employed. On vertical tree trunks, birds grip the bark with their claws and use their tail to brace the body. Squirrels brace their fore and hind limbs against each other. When descending vertically they rotate their hind feet so that the toes point backwards and the bark can be gripped by the claws. Cats cannot rotate their feet in this way and so cannot walk down vertical surfaces. Horizontal movement in trees may be similar to locomotion on the ground, as in small birds and mammals which run along branches. Primates swing from branch to branch with their arms and tail, a form of locomotion called brachiation.

The mechanics of locomotion have received considerable study and it has been discovered that animals use a wide variety of devices including the lever, spring, aerofoil, etc. Animals are remarkably well engineered and adapted to achieve maximum economy of movement. DJM

Bibliography

Gray, J. 1968: *Animal locomotion.* London: Weidenfeld & Nicolson; New York: Norton.

Carlsöo, Sven 1972: *How man moves: kinesiological studies and methods.* London: Heinemann.

Wickstrom, Ralph L. 1970: *Fundamental motor patterns.* Philadelphia: Lea & Febiger.

locus of control A concept first developed by Phares (1957) relating to beliefs about internal versus external control of reinforcement. It is assumed that individuals develop a general expectancy regarding their ability to control their lives. People who believe that the events that occur in their lives are a result of their own behavior and/or personality characteristics are said to have an "expectancy of internal control", while people who believe events in their lives to be a function of luck, chance, fate, powerful others or powers beyond their control or comprehension are said to have an "expectancy of external control". Various questionnaires have been devised to measure this belief system, of whch the best known are the Rotter (1966) I-E scale, the Levenson (1974) IPC scale, and the Collins (1974) scale. Each of these has been criticized on psychometric grounds. The concept has been widely used and applied in cross cultural studies, studies on health beliefs and behavior, investigations of mental illness and many other areas of research. AF

Bibliography

Collins, B. 1974: Four components of the Rotter internal–external scale: belief in a difficult world, a just world, a predictable world and a politically responsive world. *Journal of personality and social psychology* 29, 381–91.

Levenson, H. 1974: Activism and powerful others: distinctions within the concept of internal–external control. *Journal of personality assessment* 38, 377–83.

Phares, E. 1957: Expectancy changes in skill and chance situations. *Journal of abnormal and social psychology* 54, 339–42.

Rotter, J. 1966: Generalized expectancies for internal versus external control of reinforcement. *Psychological monograph* 80, No. 1.

logical construction A term introduced by RUSSELL (1905) to describe anything which could be alluded to only by means of an incomplete symbol, a symbol which has no meaning in isolation but only in the context of a sentence. Such symbols, it is claimed, are theoretically dispensible by analysis of the sentences containing them, and the logical constructions to which they allude are not, metaphysically speaking, ultimate constituents of the universe. It is doubtful whether there are any symbols which are not incomplete, but according to Russell such a "complete" symbol is one whose meaning is its REFERENCE (it has no sense) and whose reference is an object of ACQUAINTANCE. An item of one sort is said to be a logical construction out of items of another sort if and only if any sentence about items of the first sort can be translated into a set of sentences about items of the second sort, but not vice-versa. JMS

Bibliography

Russell, B.A.W. 1905: On denoting. *Mind* 14, 479–93.

logical positivism *See* positivism

logical thinking: developmental Reasoning according to the FORMAL rules of INFERENCE, so that conclusions follow validly from premises. The most influential account of the development of logical thought is Piaget's. He argued that children between the ages of eight and eleven years, in the concrete operational period, are in possession of reversible mental operations which allow logical reasoning with respect to things and events in the immediate present. The concrete operational child is aware for example, that a superordinate class must include a subordinate class or that properties of substances are conserved despite changes in their appearance. However, the systems of mental operations remain relatively isolated from each other until adolescence and the advent of formal operations. Now the child can consider the possible as well as the actual and makes systematic deductions concerning the truth or falsity of relations between propositions. The developmental transition is from an intra to an interpositional logic with an accompanying shift from concrete to abstract content. GEB

Bibliography

Flavell J.H. 1963: *The developmental psychology of Jean Piaget.* Princeton, N.J. and London: Van Nostrand.

loneliness The unpleasant experience of a discrepancy between the social relationships a person wishes or expects to have, and the kind of relationships he or she actually has. Relationships may be deficient in quantity, quality or both, but it is the person's own subjective view which is involved. Loneliness is not the same as objective physical or social isolation, although it may sometimes be associated with isolation.

Loneliness is most frequently thought of as a mood, emotion or feeling, but it may also refer to an attitude towards social relationships, to a life style, or to a condition of life (e.g. that of an elderly widower living alone). Experiences of loneliness are probably more frequent among younger than among older people, but equally frequent among men and women. However, there are likely to be group differences in the type of loneliness experienced and in the willingness to admit to loneliness.

There are many possible sources of loneliness, both situational or circumstantial (e.g. death of a loved one, unemployment, moving) and personal or psychological (e.g. shyness, poor health, poor social skills). Experiences of loneliness and their intensity will usually reflect some combination of these factors. LAW

Bibliography

Peplau, L.A. and Perlman, D. eds. 1982: *Loneliness: A sourcebook of current theory, research and therapy.* New York: Wiley.

long term memory (LTM) A memory system that keeps memories for periods of weeks, months or years. Long term memory has a very large capacity and the information appears to be stored in a more organized and processed manner than in SHORT TERM MEMORY (STM). This is shown by the finding that recall from STM is likely to lead to acoustic confusions while recall from LTM leads to semantic confusions. There is evidence indicating that memories are stored first in short term memory and then transferred to long term storage through a process known as CONSOLIDATION OF MEMORY. The biological basis of long term memory is not at present known.

See also MEMORY, SHORT TERM AND LONG TERM. RAJ

longitudinal research A method of study which involves repeated measures on the same individuals over a period of time. This is one of several methods by which developmental change is studied. Longitudinal research measures change over time in a particular sample. CROSS-SECTIONAL RESEARCH compares different age groups at the same point in time. The cross-sequential method, a method by which different age groups are studied longitudinally, allows the researcher to distinguish cohort effects from age effects. "Cohort effect" refers to the effect of being born at a particular time and into a particular historical context. "Age effect" refers to the effect of chronological age. Both contribute to developmental change. See also COHORT ANALYSIS. ND

Bibliography

Baltes, Paul B., Reese, Hayne W., and Nesselroade, John R. 1977: *Life-Span developmental psychology: introduction to research methods*. Belmont, Calif.: Brooks Cole.

Lorenz, Konrad Born in Vienna in 1903; was a medical student and then lecturer at the University of Vienna before becoming head of the psychology department at the University of Königsberg during the war years. From 1961 he was director of the Max Planck Institute for the Physiology of Behavior. During the 1930s and 1940s, Lorenz published a series of influential papers, mainly based on observation of bird behavior, which amounted to a comprehensive theory of instinctive behavior. Instincts were seen as inherited, stereotyped behavior patterns which were released by specific stimuli, or even without them if the reaction-specific energy had accumulated sufficiently in the organism. Later subject to heavy criticism (e.g. Lehrman 1953), the theory was instrumental in providing a framework for the systematic growth of ETHOLOGY. Lorenz's writings have continued to be controversial, as for instance in his approach to human behavior in books such as *On aggression* (1966) and *Behind the mirror* (1977). He shared the Nobel Prize for Physiology or Medicine in 1973 with von FRISCH and TINBERGEN. PKS

Bibliography

Lehrman, D.S. 1953: A critique of Konrad Lorenz's theory of instinctive behavior. *Quarterly review of biology* 28, 337–63.

Lorenz, Konrad Zacharias 1966: *On aggression*. New York: Harcourt, Brace & World, Inc. London: Methuen.

——— 1977: *Behind the mirror*. New York: Harcourt Brace; London: Methuen.

——— 1970 *Studies in animal and human behaviour*, Vols I and II. Cambridge: Harvard University Press; London: Methuen.

love An act of full attention and giving that accepts and attaches to someone as he or she is, thereby enhancing the potential of what that person can become. Research into love has not been extensive and according to Reik, Freud said at the conclusion of his career "we really know very little about love". (1976). However, in the past twenty years some useful research on certain aspects of the subject has taken place.

Attachment and bonding in early development have been studied by Harlow (1959), Bowlby (1969) and Klaus and Kennell (1976). Harlow's research with monkeys revealed that attachment to a maternal figure is vital to healthy development and socialization. Bowlby's studies of institutionalized infants showed common patterns of pathological reaction to separation from the mother, such as apathy and unresponsiveness. Klaus and Kennell have looked at bonding (the close physical and emotional interaction after birth) as a sensitive period which evokes strong attachment behavior between mother, father and child.

Kaplan (1979) describes the feelings of oneness in early attachment, and the moulding of mother's and child's bodies into one. What follows is the opposite pole of separateness, and the baby's need to sense the body as a mode of self-definition and as an expression of the fear of losing himself by merging with the mother. According to Fromm (1956) the attachment phase carries with it the sense of love as being loved, and with the struggle for separateness the universal paradox manifests "that two beings become one and yet remain two".

Psychoanalytic theory describes the attachment phase as the setting for narcissism. Narcissism in this sense does not refer to love of self, in contrast to love of others, Geller and Howenstine in Pope (1980) describe it as our first erotic disposition, in the sense that before we know that other bodies exist or what it is to like other bodies, we direct our libido towards our own bodies. This understanding of narcissism parallels Piaget's definition (1936) of egocentrism as a failure to discriminate external objects in the child's environment. Psychologists maintain that throughout life the struggle between narcissism and object love characterizes all erotic relationships. Object love refers to the later ability to differentiate between another's needs and one's own.

The family is the setting for the early stages in the development of love. The young child experiences a prolonged and intense emotional attachment to a parent, who is associated with the gratification of needs. The limited perspective of the child leads to the belief that this relationship is the most important, and perhaps the only one, in which the parent is involved. The growing child soon learns that not all his needs can be fulfilled in that relationship, and that he or she has to compete with another adult for the desired parent's affection. In most families, the marital relationship, the incest taboo, and the process of maturation prevent the child from becoming too dependent, thus leading him or her to look for fulfilment elsewhere.

According to Friedlander and Morrison's Freudian conception (Pope 1980), one of the major characteristics of romantic love that distinguishes it from early attachment and mature love is idealization. The child develops an idealized fantasy relationship with the parent of the opposite sex, who is of course not completely possessable. Idealization is seen as a result of the unfulfilled need to possess the parent. This tension is partly resolved by identifying with the same sex parent. The child achieves partial gratification through identifying with the person who is most highly regarded by and who is seen to possess the desired parent. Hero worship is another variant of romantic idealization which also combines with identification. A child may idealize a popular sports figure, but then, consistent with the motive for identification, subsequently tries to become like this idealized person. From a developmental viewpoint, idealization and fantasy can be seen as precursors of a more mature love for another person, because they lead to greater discrimination of someone beyond oneself. However, development may be retarded if idealization and fantasy become substitutes for genuine gratification in real relationships.

Farber (Pope 1980) indicates that in adolescence feelings of tenderness largely experienced in the family can become blended with the newly emerging sexual feelings when focussed on an individual outside the family. Falling in love is experienced when there is a combination of sexual attraction and intimacy. Having crushes from a distance may substitute for actual involvement if the person is tentative about approaching another individual. Crushes can be likened to practise emotions which prepare a person for later interpersonal contact. Similarly "chum" relationships, which play an important part in emotional development, are intimate same-sex friendships. Both types of relationships involve loving someone like oneself and they represent a mid-point between the stages of loving oneself and loving another person.

Erickson (1968) emphasized that adolescence is a time for defining one's identity. He maintained that a stable sense of identity is a prerequisite to establishing loving intimacy. Yet the attainment of a stable identity is closely connected with the ability to communicate with others in an intimate manner. People who avoid falling in love may have fears of loss of self or being engulfed by others. Nevertheless, the experience of loving contributes to knowing oneself, as the sense of knowing oneself contributes to being able to know another. Love of self, an affirmation of one's innate value and potential, is fundamental to the attainment of a wholesome identity. Unfortunately, self love is not sufficiently encouraged because it is often confused with selfishness.

Love in adulthood and the decision to marry are among the most important choices a person makes. Adult love appreciates the limits of romantic love. There is little likelihood that a love relationship can survive without a supporting framework of interpersonal skills, mutual interests, and occupational skills. It is not uncommon for couples to say that it took about ten years before true love developed. True love implies the acceptance of even the undesirable aspects of another person. Also, with the passing of years, unrealistic expectations of the other person (some of which have their origin in parental relationships) are shed.

Mature love, according to Fromm (1956) is active rather than passive. For the child, love means being loved, and many adults continue to expect this from their spouses. For the mature person, love means giving love, as well as receiving it. It is a positive act rather than a passive affect. Many people identify love with intense feelings and when the intensity subsides they wonder whether the love has gone. By doing this they miss the more essential dimension of love as an action, of which feelings are a byproduct. Also many partnerships get stuck in a need-bartering phase of "I'll do this for you if you'll do that for me" which can lead to a destructive struggle to get something from the partner. It is also asserted that people who come to psychotherapy with complaints about not being loved frequently discover that they themselves are not giving love.

Much of the research on love has focussed on definitions of the concept and the psychosocial dimensions of the experience. Current research methodology has in general proved inadequate in investigating the phenomenology, or inner experience of loving. Phenomenological contributions, which in the past have been largely ignored by academic psychology, also need to be considered.

Csikszentmihalyi (Pope 1980) investigated people's experience of enjoyment in sport, chess, mountain climbing and loving. A common pattern emerged which he called the "flow experience". The flow experience is satisfying in itself and involves a sense of oneness between the individual and his activity. The attention is focussed and feedback from the situation is clear. There is a balance between the challenges of the activity and the skills developed to meet them. Loving is seen by Csikszentmihalyi as an investment of attention in another person, with the intention of realizing that person's goals or those that are shared by both partners. The growth and enjoyment of the love relationship depend upon the development of interpersonal and other skills to meet the challenges that arise in the pursuit of shared goals.

Sadler (1969) describes loving as a dual mode of experience in which the sense of "we" is greater than the sense of "me". The perception of time is different from the everyday awareness of linear, continually moving clock time. Love's time is more timeless in that one is simply present, with another, without anticipating a later moment for fulfilment. The perception of space changes into something very personal and familiar. One feels at home when loved and loving. Similarly, individuals feel "in place", instead of trying to find their place in career or social settings. In phenomenological terms, "place" refers to the site of experience of the world, which is acknowledged in the act of loving.

Scheler (1954) emphasizes that a person in a loving relationship sees the other as he or she is, and has no desire to change the person. Love is awareness directed to people as they are, which allows for the value and potential in them to emerge and become realized in the course of time.

Finally, Buber's I–Thou relationship (1970) describes the sense of complete involvement that is central to the act of loving. Buber says that we normally experience people in two ways: "I–It" or "I–Thou". "I–It" relationships refer to the normal way of experiencing others according to their characteristics such as social background, sex, appearance and what is needed from them. In the "I–Thou" relationship the whole person is encountered as "Thou" (or "You") rather than "You are this and that for me".

The study of love and relationships which are generally assumed to be founded on love is now beginning to increase, and is greatly needed. The development of an effective understanding of how people learn to love and to preserve relationships would have practical benefits as well as removing our surprising ignorance of an aspect of people which we are supposed to think both fascinating and valuable. TCK

Bibliography

Bowlby, J. 1969: *Attachment and loss.* London: Hogarth Press; New York: Basic Books.

Buber, M. 1970: *I and thou.* New York: Charles Scribner.

Erickson, E.H. 1968: *Identity: youth and crisis.* New York: Norton; London: Faber & Faber.

*Fromm, E. 1956: *The art of loving.* New York: Harper and Brothers.

Harlow, H.F. 1959: Love in infant monkeys. *Scientific American.*

Kaplan, L.J. 1979: *Oneness and separateness.* London: Jonathan Cape.

Klaus, M.H. and Kennell, J.H. 1976: *Maternal–infant bonding.* Saint Louis: C.V. Mosby Company.

Piaget, J. 1936 *(1966)*: *The origins of intelligence in children.* New York: International Universities Press.

*Pope, K.S. and Associates 1980: *On love and loving.* San Francisco, Washington, and London: Jossey-Bass.

Reik, T. 1976: *Of Love and lust.* New York: Pyramid Books.

*Sadler, W.A. 1969: *Existence and love.* New York: Charles Scribner.

Scheler, M. 1954: *The nature of sympathy.* London: Routledge & Kegan Paul.

LTM *See* long term memory

lucid dreaming A rare but important variant of ordinary dreaming in which the dreamer feels he has awakened and is conscious, but experientially he still remains located in a sensorily real dream world. Ordinary DREAMING, strongly associated with stage 1 ELECTROENCEPHALOGRAPH pattern and conjugate rapid eye movements (REMs) is characterized by apparent sensory vividness and reality, but an unquestioning, passive quality of consciousness, as retrospectively judged by ordinary waking state standards. In lucid dreaming the dreamer both knows that the apparently real world he finds himself in is actually a dream, and, importantly, by checking the quality of his mental functioning, he experiences it as very like full wakefulness. Lucid dreamers may exercise conscious control over subsequent dream events (van Eeden, in Tart 1969), a skill which may have important therapeutic applications (Tart 1979). Recent research indicates that lucid dreams also occur in conjunction with a stage 1 electroencephalographic pattern and REMs, and that a lucid dreamer may deliberately signal to an experimenter during the lucid dream through previously agreed upon patterns of eye movements and muscle tensings. CTT

Bibliography

Tart, C. 1969: *Altered states of consciousness.* New York: John Wiley & Sons.

Tart, C. 1979: From spontaneous event to lucidity: a review of attempts to consciously control nocturnal dreaming. In *Handbook of dreams: research, theories and applications*, ed. B. Wolman, M. Ullman and W. Webb. New York: Van Nostrand Reinhold.

ludling The term was introduced by Laycock (1972) to refer to "the result of one or more transformations ... acting regularly on an ordinary language text, with the intent of altering the form but not the content (backslang *woman – namow*)" or other language games. The ability of speakers to cope with puns, SPOONERISMS, knock-knock jokes etc. form part of a speaker's communicative COMPETENCE. The study of the acquisition of this kind of competence has become an important area of child language development research (Bauman 1977). PM

Bibliography

Bauman, R. 1977: Linguistics, anthropology, and verbal art: toward a unified perspective, with a special discussion of children's folklore. In Saville-Troike, Muriel *Linguistics and anthropology.* Washington DC: Georgetown University Press 13–36.

Laycock, Donald C. 1972: Towards a typology of ludlings or play languages. *Linguistic communications* 6, 61–113.

M

Machiavellianism A personality factor which is characterized by the ability to manipulate others through flattery, threat and deceit. Is named after Machiavelli, on whose political advice in *Il Principe* research is based. The Machiavellian scale devised by Christi and Geis (1970), correlates it with sex (males score higher), urban background, age (young people score higher) and professional status (people-oriented professions score higher). Machiavellianism is also related to success in bargaining, and Machiavellians are more successful at resisting the influence of others. They violate conventional moral standards more often, by stealing and coolly denying this when accused. Even at the age of ten, differences in Machiavellianism appear to have an effect, in the successful manipulation of other children. Machiavellian children appear to have Machiavellian parents. In later life occupational success is related to Machiavellianism, particularly among women and those who have had a college education. JMFJ

Bibliography

Christi, R. and Geis, F.L., eds 1970: *Studies in Machiavellianism.* New York: Academic Press.

machine learning The emulation of human knowledge acquisition processes through algorithms programmed for a digital computer system. The possibility of machines learning about the world and how to control it has been significant in engineering studies for many years with recent developments in control, communication and computer systems stemming from Norbert Wiener's concept of a science of *cybernetics* encompassing both man and machine.

In the past decade computers have been used increasingly for such studies and the scope has been broadened to cover all aspects of ARTIFICIAL INTELLIGENCE including pattern recognition, perceptual-motor skills and linguistic activity (Winston 1977). The switch in emphasis has made it apparent that learning is only one aspect of human intelligence and that we have little hope of emulating the learning of a task if we are not able to emulate the final performance of that task.

The significance for education of work on machine learning and artificial intelligence is the insight into the processes of human learning and instruction. This has led to the use of the term cognitive science to cover all aspects of the study of intellectual processes whether in people or machines. For example much of the material published by Andreae (1977) on his *Purr Puss* learning system is concerned with the training techniques necessary to help the system to acquire knowledge. Work on expert SYSTEMS (Michie 1979) which encode and emulate human skilled activity for practical purposes has led to new understanding of these skills which in turn makes it easier to teach them to people. More advanced COMPUTER AIDED LEARNING systems also incorporate artificial intelligence techniques in their operation (Sleeman and Brown 1981) but given the limited information available from the student-computer interaction there is still the problem of measuring even part of the student's knowledge structure. (See PROGRAMMED INSTRUCTION). MLGS

Bibliography

Andreae, J.H. 1977: *Thinking with the teachable machine.* New York and London: Academic Press.

*Michie, D., ed. 1979: *Expert systems in the micro electronic age.* Edinburgh: Edinburgh University Press.

Sleeman, D.H. and Brown, J.S., eds. 1981: *Intelligent tutoring systems.* New York and London: Academic Press.

*Winston, P.H. 1977: *Artificial intelligence.* Reading; Mass. Addison-Wesley.

machine translation The conversion of sentences or connected texts (input as typescript, not continuous speech) from one natural language into another by means of a computer program. Dictionary-based methods are less sensitive to context than are thesaurus-based or script-based methods. A script is a partially ordered set of coherent themes which forms the semantic skeleton of a discourse and can guide understanding and question-answering as well as the translation of individually ambiguous words. Faithful translation of random texts (even confined to a given field with specialist vocabulary provided) is not yet a realistic goal. The aim is rather to achieve a translation good enough to indicate the advisability of hand translation. Machine translation may be combined with précis: a précis-program takes input and produces output in one language, and its output is translated by another program. (See also ARTIFICIAL INTELLIGENCE.) MAB

Bibliography

W.J. Hutchins 1978: Machine translation and machine-aided translation. *Journal of documentation* 34, 119–59.

management Attempts at definitions of management are problematical. They range from the common sense (getting things done through people, arranging for needs to be met), to the complex. The problem is that any definition reflects an explicit or implicit underlying view of the nature of organizations. An economic view of the firm would cast the manager in the role of rational economic decision maker. Structural/functional views of organizations cast the manager as the receiver of objectives and delegator of sub-objectives, with associated activities of monitoring, controling, reporting, etc. Certain "systems" views of organizations interpret managers as nodes in a network of information flows and decision points. More "political" interpretations of organizations as arrangements for working together cast managers as middlemen in a trade of power and influence, continuously involved in finding a way forward through compromise and negotiation. Interactionist views of organizations interpret managers as involved in the creation and maintenance of the organization's meanings, and through this, of its structures and processes.

All these partially inter-penetrating views of organizations and management may capture some aspects of reality. From a conceptual point of view the interactionist position is arguably the most satisfactory, since the other perspectives can be fitted into it. There is an empirical tradition of research in this area (e.g. Mintzberg, 1973; Stewart 1967). Such research often produces valuable insights but it is caught in the paradox of needing a prior definition of management to decide whom to study, and some observational categories with which to work. These categories inevitably carry certain assumptions about the nature of management.

Fascinating questions arise from the various definitions of management. For example, is it an entity, a function, a social class or a process? Is it a social definition that can be applied in certain situations or is it a process present by definition in all organizations? What is to be made of the many kinds of organization that do not have explicit "management" activities, roles or functions (professional partnerships, universities, churches, the military, etc.)? The idea of management, both in theory and as a social label for a practical activity is time-bound and has a history (Child 1969) in which the meaning has changed in a changing historical and social context. In different cultures too, there is an enormous variation in conceptions of management.

The concept of "management" is clearly going to remain problematical for everyone, from those concerned to serve it with psychological technology through to those who suspect it of having an insidious and possibly malign influence on how psychological questions are framed and addressed. Addressing the issue of management is likely to be an activity in which psychologists will find themselves alongside members of other social sciences and the intellectual consequences of this are potentially very exciting.

See also SCIENTIFIC MANAGEMENT. JGB

Bibliography

Burrell, G. and Morgan, G. 1979: *Sociological paradigms and organisational analysis*, London and Exeter, New Hampshire: Heinemann.

Child, J. 1969: *British management thoughts; a critical analysis*. London: Allen.

Heather, N. 1976: *Radical perspectives in psychology*. London and New York: Methuen.

Mintzberg, H. 1973: *The nature of managerial work*. New York and London: Harper & Row.

Stewart, R. 1967: *Managers and their jobs*. London: Macmillan.

marketing psychology The psychology of economic choice, and in particular the analysis of consumer behavior.

A marketplace is simply a forum in which economic exchange takes place. As such, it lends itself to behavioral analysis: economic choices are made daily by everyone; the choices are observable; experimentation is easy; and data describing, for example, the brand choice sequences of households, are plentiful. Indeed, markets are one of the richest natural laboratories in which to develop and test theories of human behavior.

It is, of course, the laboratory in which economists work; and its most influential product is the concept of rational economic man. This is a model of man, particularly as he appears in the neo-classical mainstream of economic theory, that is unashamedly behavioristic and deterministic.

His rationality resides in his omniscience and infallibility. Psychologically, for example, he is transparent both to himself and to others (who are, themselves, equally transparent): he knows his own values, needs and tastes; and the world he inhabits, including the full range of options open to him, is an open book. Nothing holds any surprises for him. So completely is his behavior guided by informed reason that, in effect, his choices are made for him by the logic of the particular situation in which he finds himself. In short, economic man has no personality and no choice. He has been stripped of any psychological identity, complexity or realism.

To predict his behavior, all that need be known are the combinations of economic options between which he is indifferent. To quote Pareto (1906), "the individual can disappear, providing he leaves us his photograph of his tastes". And Shackle (1977) asks the rhetorical question, "If 'choice' is a *mere* response to tastes and circumstances, both kinds being given and known, does 'choice' originate anything?"

Psychological interest in the market as an object of study represents, for the most part, a reaction against what is increasingly seen as an excessively narrow and sterile view of rational choice. The development of a more substantively psychological model of economic behavior has been an attempt to give back to economic man his individuality and his freedom. For example the Austrian school of economists, borrowing heavily from psychological theory, has stressed the necessity of including inter-personal *differences* in knowledge, beliefs and expectations in any explanation of economic behavior. For this school of thought, economic man is characterized by: *imperfect* knowledge of his own tastes and the options available to him; *fallible* interpretations of his own situation, including the actions of others; *speculative* forecasts of events and actions in the future; and *inquisitive* alertness to novel opportunities, and inventiveness in seeking them out.

Here, economic behavior is quintessentially a process over time of discovery and coordination, not of instantaneous adjustment to prevailing conditions. Man is now the *subject* – the originator of states of affairs – and not simply an object. Indeed, Hayek (1952), the leading modern Austrian economist, has argued that "it is probably no exaggeration to say that every important advance in economic theory during the last hundred years was a further step in the consistent application of subjectivism."

In marketing literature, a whole range of psychological theories has been imported and synthesized to give conceptual support to this subjectivist stance and thereby lend greater realism to the models of consumer behavior originally inherited from economics. For example, one class of models (Engel, Blackwell and Kollatt 1978; Nicosia 1966; Howard and Sheth 1969) has aimed at presenting an integrated view of how the consumer processes inputs (information) into outputs (choices). Looking into the "black box" between input and output researchers have drawn upon concepts and findings in the psychological literature of perception, evaluation, motivation and learning to map the stages through which consumers pass to reach a purchasing decision. For example, theories of selective attention, perceptual distortion, concept formation, symbolic encoding, hierarchical memory, attitude structure and stability and habituation are all shown to have direct application to understanding the behavior of consumers. JOG

Bibliography

Engel, J.F., Blackwell, R.D. and Kollatt, D.T. 1978: *Consumer behavior* 3rd edn. New York: Holt, Rinehart & Winston.

Hayek, F.A. 1952: *The counter-revolution of science*. New York: The Free Press of Glencoe.

Howard, J.A. and Sheth, J.N. 1969: *The theory of buyer behavior*, New York: Wiley.

Nicosia, F.M. 1966: *Consumer decision processes*, Englewood Cliffs, N.J.: Prentice-Hall.

Pareto, V. 1906 (*1971*): *Manual of political economy*, New York: A.M. Kelly.

Shackle, G.L.S. 1977: New tracks for economic theory, 1926–39. In *Modern economic thought*, ed. S. Weintraub. Philadelphia: University of Pennsylvania Press; Oxford: Basil Blackwell.

*Tuck, M. 1976: *How do we choose? A study in consumer behavior*, London & New York: Methuen.

marketing research Inquiry that seeks answers to questions asked by sellers about buyers. The questions are many and varied. Some ask for facts (how big is the market? who buys the product?); others, for diagnoses (why are sales down this year? how do buyers choose between the competing brands?).

Marketing research is almost exclusively conducted or commissioned by business firms. The object is to provide the firm with cost-effective information for the planning and control of its marketing strategy. This involves the design of its products, their pricing, advertising, distribution and sales support.

Marketing itself is a form of managerial thinking that treats competition between firms as essentially a battle between alternative theories of market behavior. Rival firms often differ dramatically in their predictions of how the market will respond to a particular stimulus, such as a change in price, or the introduction of a new product. Pursuing the allegory, the firm is the embodiment of its theory of competitive market response, acting rationally in the light of its own assumptions; the marketplace is the testing ground for the quality of each firm's theories, as expressed in their product offerings; and profit is the prize for consistently outperforming one's rivals in the prediction of the market's responses. In these terms, marketing research may be defined as embracing all those forms of inquiry that enhance the realism of the firm's model of its market.

Green and Tull (1975) distinguish three broad classes of research in marketing:

Exploratory studies are those that seek to raise more questions than they answer, if only better to define the significant problems and opportunities facing the firm. The aim may be to formulate provisional diagnoses of the firm's health – hypotheses that can be tested later by more formal methods – or it may be to come up with new product ideas or changes in strategic direction.

Descriptive studies are those which set out to measure and map the product perceptions, buying motivations and shopping behavior of the market in which the firm is competing. Usually built around a survey or an experiment, but sometimes relying entirely on published information, they often amount to little more than exercises in data-gathering. The aim is to answer some such questions as "who buys which brands how often and for what reason?" The answers go a long way to furnishing the firm with a working knowledge of the nature and size of the market, and the demographic and psychographic profiles of their respective buyers. Mostyn (1978) has reviewed the wide variety of techniques used by marketing researchers.

Causal studies are those which try to reveal the structural relations between the characteristics of the brands on the market and the psychological and behavioral characteristics of their buyers. In this sense, causal studies begin at the point where descriptive studies leave off, attempting to explain, say, a buyer's brand preferences in terms of his attitudes. Typically, the analytical techniques used in causal studies are data reduction methods and related multivariate statistical tools. Of these, multidimensional scaling and conjoint measurement are particularly popular. JOG

Bibliography

*Churchill, G.A. 1979: *Marketing research: methodological foundations* 2nd edn. Hinsdale, Ill.: Dryden.

Green, P.E. and Tull, D.S. 1975: *Research for marketing decisions*. 3rd edn. Englewood Cliffs, N.J.: Prentice-Hall.

Mostyn, B. 1978: *A handbook of motivational and attitude research techniques*, Bradford: MCB.

*Worcester, R.M. and Downham, J. 1978: *Consumer market research handbook*. 2nd edn. Wokingham, Berks.: Van Nostrand Reinhold.

martial arts The traditional Chinese and Japanese systems of physical and psychic training for combat. Kung Fu and Tai Chi Chu'an belong to the former tradition, whereas Judo, Kendo, Aikido and Karate belong to the latter. The Japanese martial arts were cultivated by the Samurai warriors, who developed self-mastery and fearlessness in the face of death by negating the individual ego.

Combat in the martial arts is seen as the interaction of natural, impersonal forces, and victory is gained by being in harmony with one's own natural psycho-physical force, known as Ki or Chi, and using the opponent's force to his disadvantage.

One gains mastery over the Ki by breathing exercises, and concentrating on a point called the Hara, just below the navel.

The Japanese tradition distinguishes between martial arts and martial skills by the suffixes –do and jutsu. Thus Kenjutsu and Jujutsu are techniques for destroying the enemy using the sword or one's own limbs, whereas in Kendo and Judo the emphasis is not on aggression towards the enemy but on self-development through combat. DA

Marxian personality psychology A psychological meta-theory deriving its assumptions from Marx's materialist philosophy of history and applied to the historical development and social relations of personality. Its philosophical basis, historical materialism, unlike other materialist philosophies, takes neither nature nor the spirit as its principle. Its starting point is "production", which is just as much defined by spatio-temporal dimensions as is nature, and just as creative as is mind.

S. Rubinstein (1959) derived four principles from this philosophy. These principles were to be applied both to a Marxian activity psychology and to personality psychology. They are: (1) the principle of objectivity – mental phenomena refer to objects in the space–time of the material world; (2) the principle of activity – mental dispositions develop in the activity they regulate; (3) the principle of historicity – mental states bear the marks of their history; and (4) the principle of sociality – mental characteristics are socially determined.

None of these principles, considered separately, is characteristic of a Marxian psychology. It is their combination which is specific to the psychological meta-theory derived from historical materialism. This combination is brought about by a specific interpretation of each principle:

1. A manufactured object is conceived as produced by an activity of man and as reciprocally that activity together with man. Marx *Economic and philosophical manuscripts*

claims the world of manufactured objects to be the "inorganic body" of man.

2. Activity is pictured as a necessary everyday cycle of production and reproduction. The cycle is interrupted occasionally by moments of free creation in which new values are introduced to be reproduced by subsequent necessary everyday cycles of activity.

3. History is conceived as composed of autonomous human acts restricted by social laws. These social laws are actualized by the autonomous acts of others.

4. Society is pictured as based upon relations of object appropriation and as establishing property relations (Marx, *Grundrisse*).

Rubinstein did not apply his four principles in their entirety. He considered the personality as an internal mediator of external determinants and as originating from other external determinants internalized in the past. According to his metaphor the personality of a man is his "socially determined nature".

This pattern is highly typical of allegedly Marxist personality psychologies. The personality psychology outlined by Rubinstein turned out to be an amalgam of a social cognitivism and a social behaviorism. It describes the emergence of a personality by the notion of socialization and the social functioning of a personality is described in terms of attitude (or the proximate but not identical central notion of set in Uznadse's theory), of social interaction, of communication, etc. None of these points is particularly characteristic of a Marxist approach.

In other cases the application of some of the above principles in isolation from others results in a kind of psychoanalytic personality theory. The central problem of a marxizing personality theory of psychoanalysis is the interdependence of the personality structure and the structure of society.

For W. Reich (1970) the structure of a repressive society determines an authoritarian personality structure through sexual repression in family education. E. Fromm (1963) claims that it is the structure of a competitive society based on private property that, by frustrating a need for secure relationships with others, fixes the personality on a dependent level as "escaping from freedom". A. József (1972) states that the distortion of the personalities of both the capitalist and the worker is determined by the fundamental distortion of the capitalist society. While the society is both the subject and the object of production (that is, in the process of production, reproduces itself) and of socialization which he identifies with it, the person as a worker is only the subject of production and the object of the socialization. The only subject of socialization is the person as capitalist, being at the same time the only social object of the production. This produces neurotic personalities of either a mere social object with only technical intercourse and no orgasm or a mere social subject with only impotent libido.

In contrast to the above considerations, for H. Marcuse (1962) it is not the structure of an actually given social relation (e.g. between capitalists and workers in a capitalist society) that more or less distorts the structure of a personality and still less does it depend on how repressive or liberal is that social relation. It is "civilization" which is opposed as such to "Eros" and transforms it by repression into aggression. A group of followers of LACAN and Althusser (Bruno et al. 1973) hold that besides nature the only reality is discourse and its structure. There exists a strict distinction between the discourse of the subject and that of Other, while there are no principles regulating that distinction on the level of a meta-language. The meta-level regulation of proper discourse and the personality distorted by it both are but an ideology. The ideology is the discourse produced by a dominating place in the discourse structure, but this ideology presents itself either as corresponding to an objective reality or as a mere subjective belief system of individual selves that may be opposed by that of others.

It was in controversy with such theories as well as the humanistic philosophy (Garaudy) going back to the early Marx that Lucien Sève (1969) advanced his psychological meta-theory of personality. He rejected the basic thesis of the theories of Reich, Marcuse and so on, sketched above, that there is an alienation of the personality distorted by empirically given social relations from its intrinsic, specifically human generic essence *(Gattungswesen)* given in advance of any social relations. Nevertheless he argued that there is an essence of human personality. It is neither intrinsic nor given in advance but is borne by the historically developed totality of relations of production. Furthermore, it is neither generic, nor intimately characteristic of a given individual, but the totality of relations of production is in a special way addressed to each of the particularities (i.e. classes) of that totality. For example, the human essence that characterizes a worker in a capitalist society as a personality is defined by the relations in which his personal power is reproduced as a concrete use value producing abstract exchange value for the capitalist and, at the same time, as an abstract exchange value producing concrete use value for the worker himself.

L. Garai and his team (1979) tried to extend the validity of such a production-centered approach to those aspects of the historical development and social relationship of personality which are not directly connected with production as such. For that purpose they adopted L. Vygotsky's idea (1978) of analysing a mental context according to a paradigm derived from an economic context. Vygotsky's basic argument was that man utilizes as psychic tools signs that are psychic products of his previous activity and, as such, constitute a special (i.e. mental) category of means of production brought into being as products of production. A. Léontjew (1969) set out from a psychology describing man's activity as oriented to such an object taken both as a means and a product, and attempted to derive from it a personality psychology that describes the agent of that activity with his characteristic hierarchy of motives.

Garai took personality psychology as independent of activity psychology, which has a special *mental context* to be analysed according to a paradigm obtained from another economic context, i.e. that of class relations (Garai 1977). The main paradigmatic point of class relations is claimed to be the representation of the common law of different classes by only one of them. Neither the detection of personality differences nor finding out general laws of the functioning of personalities is supposed to interest Marxist personality psychology. It investigates how, during its development, a personality establishes its differences and similarities according to or in contrast with a common pattern represented by someone with reference to whom the personality also has to distinguish or identify itself. At the beginning the elaboration of nuances of identities and differences of individuals with regard to a social situation into categorical identities and differences (see SOCIAL CATEGORIZATION) is not presented by a series of conscious acts but takes place by means of an elaboration of physical entities such as sex, height or color (as well as all kinds of body activity) into signs. These entities unconsciously symbolize, by the identities and differences of their structures, the parallel elaborated identities and differences of social structures (Köcski and Garai 1978). The emergence of the conscious self is then mediated by the confrontation between the personality's self-definition and general laws represented by others.

A further point to be stressed by a Marxist personality psychology is related to the economic fact that the part of the physical world produced by men as means of production may be expropriated by a class that becomes, by virtue of its property, the class representing the common pattern for all the classes. This has implications for personality development: (1) the above mental elaboration of physical entities into signs that mediate the unconscious mental elaboration of the personality's social world is preformed by the property relations of that social world; (2) so is the emergence of the conscious self since it is mediated by the confrontation of the personality's (unconscious) self-definition with that property-related common pattern. Thus, it is stated that personality development in a socialization process depends upon the individual's privileged or under-privileged position with regard to the property relations interpreted either in a strict economic sense or paradigmatically. The main paradigmatic point of property relations is that the property condition of occupying the position privileged to frame a law or pattern of socially approved personality is established by that law itself (Garai 1977). Those in an under-privileged position can ensure their personality development only by introducing radical changes into their self-establishing social world.

Personality development is not conceived by Marxist personality psychology as a joint effect of biological maturation and a social shaping process which a passive individual would be submitted to. Instead, it is represented as the result of an individual's activity, organized according to the paradigm of the work activity: the need-motivated reproduction cycles are interrupted by life crises which may provoke creative inventions and these become patterns to be reproduced in renewed cycles by the force of a specifically human need for a need-free activity.

The production-centered meta-theory of Marxist personality psychology is the same as that applied in Marxist activity psychology. Hence there is a real possibility of basing an integrated psychology on this meta-theory instead of reproducing the traditional distinction between a "scientific" *(Naturwissenschaftliche)* and a "humanistic" *(geisteswissenschaftliche)* psychology. LG

Bibliography

Althusser, Louis 1969: Freud and Lacan. *New left review* 55, 48–65.

Bruno, Pierre et al. 1973: La psychologie sociale: une utopie en crise. *La Nouvelle Critique* 62, 72–78; 64, 21–28.

Fromm, Erich 1963: *Marx's concept of man*. New York: F. Ungar.

Garai, László 1977: Conflict and the economical paradigm. *Dialectics and humanism* 2, 47–58.

——— et al. 1979: Towards a social psychology of personality: Development and current perspectives of a school of social psychology in Hungary. *Social science information* 18, 1, 137–66.

József, Attila 1972: Hegel, Marx, Freud. *Action poétique* 49, 68–75.

Köcski, Margit, and Garai, László 1978: Les débuts de la catégorisation sociale et les manifestations verbales. Une étude longitudinale. *Langage et société* 4, 3–30.

Léontjew, Alexei 1969: *Problems of mental development*. Washington: Joint Publications Research Service.

Marcuse, Herbert 1962: *Eros and civilisation*. New York: Random House.

Reich, Wilhelm 1970: *The mass psychology of fascism*. New York: Simon and Schuster.

Rubinstein, Sergei 1959: *Principles and ways of mental development*. (In Russian). Moscow: Publishing House of Soviet Academy of Sciences.

*Sève, Lucien 1969: *Marxisme et la théorie de la personnalité*. Paris: Editions Sociales.

Vygotsky, Lev 1962: *Thought and language*. Cambridge: MIT Press.

——— 1978: *Mind in society. The development of higher psychological processes*. Cambridge, Mass.: Harvard University Press.

Marxist activity psychology The concept of object related activity *(Gegenständliche Tätigkeit)* is the main concept of Marxist psychology. It is the part of human behavior which relates man to his social and natural environment, to other persons and to himself. (In German and Russian the words *Tätigkeit* and *dejatelnost* have different meanings from the words *Aktivität* and *aktivnost*. The English word activity does not mean what *Tätigkeit* or *dejatelnost* mean in Marxist psychology).

Man is the subject of his activity. The activity of the individual is characterized by its sociohistorical determination, its relation to an object *(Gegenständlichkeit)*, its goal directedness, the goal oriented organization of its components, and consciousness (Marx, *Capital* vol. II).

The attribute "object related" designates the pivotal feature; "in fact the very notion of activity implicitly contains the notion of an object of activity ... objectless activity bears no sense" (Leontjew 1972, p.152). On the one hand, the object is "an independently existing entirety subordinating activity of the subject" (p.152). On the other hand, the mental representation of the object is a result of activity, which in turn regulates activity.

Different categories of activity may be distinguished by means of the dominating type of motivation, especially affective or impulsive activity, instinctive activity and voluntary activity (Lewin 1926). Marxist activity psychology mainly deals with voluntary activity. The development of voluntary activity, from a phylogenetic and historical point of view, is connected with the development of work.

Marxist activity psychology tries to overcome the barrenness of the controversy between mentalist and behaviorist approaches. A main methodological principle is the unity of mental phenomena (processes, states and traits) and activity. All these mental phenomena develop and realize themselves in the kind of activity in which they are necessary for orientation and regulation. The key function of mental phenomena within activity is regulative. The development of mental phenomena within and by means of activities reveals a dialectical nature: on the one hand, mental phenomena are the results of activities; on the other hand, individuals will develop mental phenomena which are then realized in man-made objects and settings (e.g. toys, tools, towns). Mental phenomena may only be analysed in activity. The principle of the unity of mental phenomena and activity has broad consequences for the methodology of research and for psychodiagnostics. The decisive role of activity in the development of mental processes, states and traits was elaborated in two empirically based theoretical approaches:

(a) The Galperin approach of the stepwise interiorization from complete overt object related actions up to mental processes (1972). According to this view, mental processes develop in a child from his or her movements being verbally interpreted by adult speakers; they then pass through many increasingly abbreviated sensori-motor steps up to the "pure idea" of an object or process, i.e. mental representation. Such steps of abbreviation and interiorization are, for instance, talking loudly with oneself and internal talking while manipulating an object (Vygotsky 1962).

(b) The "assimilation hypothesis" of Leontjew (1969), in which the decisive link in the development of mental representations (especially perceptions) is a "motor copy" of the object or process perceived, formed by kinesthetic feedback of the muscles in the sense organs or used by them. The modality-specific information of the specific sense organs is integrated into these motor copies. Leontjew analysed these relations, referring *inter alia* to the role of the activity of the voice muscles for precise hearing.

The psychologically relevant chunk of activity is *action*. Actions include *operations*. In the Leontjew approach (1969), activities are separated from one another by motives, and actions by their different goals. Operations are subordinate means of achieving the goals of action; often they are sensori-motor skills, which do not need conscious mental regulation. "Action" is therefore a main concept in the Marxist psychology of activity. Actions are the smallest psychologically relevant units of voluntary activities. Actions are defined by their goals, i.e. in anticipation of the future results. This anticipation is combined with the intention of bringing about the anticipated result (Luria 1973). Mental representations of goals are the most important mental regulators of action. Further categories of such representations are those of the initial states (e.g. of raw materials) or of the possible transformations between such initial states and the anticipated results (Hacker 1980). Each action includes cognitive processes (perceptions, decisions, mental reproduction), motivation (goal-setting), and sensori-motor processes. So action is a psychomotor process.

Goal directed actions simultaneously present a cyclic feedback structure and a hierarchical organization (Bernstein 1967). Units consisting of goals, action programs, and feedback or control processes are nested into one another. Although this hierarchical feedback structure seems to be common to all actions, their individual structures depend on the task, defined by the individual's goal, on the subjective significance of this goal, and on its conditions of realization.

The psychological analysis of actions is not limited to the obvious "surface" sequence of motions, but includes the regulating mental "deep structure". Main aspects of this psychological analysis of action are (Tomaszewski 1978):

(a) goal setting;

(b) working out how to achieve the goal;

(c) designing or producing the necessary means;

(d) deciding to employ one means rather than another, if there is any choice;

(e) controlling the implementation by comparing the procedures and results with the program and the goal. The last four processes may not all be equally conscious. Intellectual processes are conscious in so far as they are verbalized or represented symbolically. Sensori-motor processes are predominantly unconscious. Perceptive processes regulating actions have an intermediate or limited consciousness. WH

Bibliography

Bernstein, N.A. 1967: *The co-ordination and regulation of movements.* Oxford and New York: Pergamon.

Galperin, P.J. ed., 1972: *Probleme der Lerntheorie.* Berlin: Volk und Wissen.

Hacker, W. 1980: Objective and subjective organization of working activities. In *The analysis of action*, ed. M. von Cranach and R. Harré. Cambridge: Cambridge University Press.

Leontjew, A.N. 1969: The significance of the concept of reflection for scientific psychology. In *The XVIII International Congress of Psychology.* Moscow: International Union of Scientific Psychology Organizing Committee.

——— 1972: On the importance of the notion of object-activity for psychology. In *Short communications prepared for the XX International Congress of Psychology*, ed. B.F. Lomow. 146–64. Moscow: USSR Society of Psychologists.

Lewin, K. 1926: Untersuchungen zur Handlungs- und Affektpsychologie: Vorbemerkungen über die psychischen Kräfte und Energien and über die Struktur der menschlichen Seele. In *Psychologische Forschung* 7.

Luria, A.R. 1973: *The working brain: an introduction to neuropsychology.* London: Penguin; New York: Basic Books.

Tomaszewski, T. 1978: *Tätigkeit and Bewusstsein. Beiträge zur Einführung in die polnische Tätigkeitspsychologie.* Weinheim: Beltz.

Vygotsky, L.S. 1962: *Thought and language.* Cambridge, Mass.: MIT Press.

materialism *See* mind–body problem

mathematical modelling: applications The concepts and procedures of psychological measurement have always been closely related to the development of mathematical psychology. This was especially true in the 1940s, when an important change in the conceptualization of measurement took place. Until then it had been held by many distinguished writers on science that true measurement could only be obtained if it were possible to find an empirical operation that had properties similiar to those of the arithmetical operation of addition. This was a serious problem, because such an operation appeared to be nonexistent in psychology.

A way out of this impasse was provided by Stevens (1946). Stevens defined different levels or scales of measurement, the distinguishing feature of each level having to do with the uniqueness property of the numbers obtained. At the highest level, the measurement numbers were unique up to a multiplicative constant, the level typically found in the physical sciences. At lower levels the measurement numbers might be unique only up to a monotonic or order preserving transformation.

The immediate effects of Stevens's classification scheme were twofold. First, it meant that mathematical psychologists who wished to work at the highest level of measurement, need not waste their time searching for the non-existent physical-addition operation, but could instead concentrate their efforts on constructing mathematical models which were sufficiently strong to impose a high degree of uniqueness on the unspecified parameters of the model. And second, the classification scheme implied that it was perfectly acceptable, and useful, to work with weaker models, those containing parameters having a lesser degree of uniqueness. The value of such models could be in their greater generality or applicability. This later approach was used in the scalogram model of Guttman (1944), the unfolding model of Coombs (1950), and the latent class model of Lazarsfeld (1950).

Quite a different approach to obtaining high levels of measurement began to be pursued in the 1950s. The previous approach, starting with Thurstone, could be called a top-down approach, because it starts with abstract, unobservable concepts or processes and then attempts to reason downward to observable predictions. The other approach, a bottom-up or axiomatic approach, starts with simple statements or assumptions about observable properties, and then tries to reason upward to some abstract conceptualization or model implied by these properties. If the properties are shown to be experimentally valid, it is possible to conclude that the model is appropriate. It is also possible to conclude something about the uniqueness properties of the parameters of the model. The aim of this bottom-up approach is to find simple, plausible assumptions – certainly those not requiring physical addition – which nevertheless lead to parameters having a high uniqueness.

Three highly influential examples of this bottom-up approach may be noted: the von Neumann and Morgenstern (1953) axioms for measuring utility, which required only that people be able to make judgments between pairs of gambles; the choice axiom of Luce (1959), which assumed only that choices from sets of stimuli varying in size should be related in a certain, simple way; later developed as conjoint measurement axioms which specified some simple properties concerning the joint effect of two or more factors. In all three cases, the assumptions are stated directly in terms of observables, are relatively simple to test, and if verified result in parameters having a high degree of uniqueness. Work along these lines continues at the present time, especially by those who feel that theories should be built up from directly verified assumptions.

Test theory. Measuring people, as well as stimuli or items, has been a major issue in psychology ever since the earliest attempts, around the turn of the century, to measure intelligence. However, not until relatively recently were the underlying models falsifiable. One of the most interesting of these newer models, the Rasch model (1960), has a special property, called "specific objectivity", which makes it possible to estimate the two parameters of the model, the item parameter and the person parameter, independently of each other. Important generalizations of the Rasch model have been given by Lord (1980). A recent emphasis in the testing field is the development of adaptive or tailored tests, those which are administered by computers. The object of the modelling here is to make it possible to take into consideration all the responses that a person has made to previously presented items, and therefore to be able to make more optimal decisions on each trial as to which item to present (Lord 1980).

Learning. The mathematical modelling in the field of learning developed intensely following the publication of the stochastic learning models of Estes. The earlier attempts of Thurstone (1919) were not particularly influential in the learning field, while the monumental efforts of Hull (1943) did not lead to a rich mathematical system, one having a large number of predictions relative to the number of assumptions made. This is exactly what characterized the stochastic modelling that took place in the 1950s. The assumptions made about the learning process were extremely simple, and involved very few unspecified parameters. At the same time, by using the mathematical machinery of stochastic processes, it was possible to derive detailed predictions for a large number of different types of learning tasks and different types of statistics. Particularly simple and effective Markov models were developed by Bower (1961) to explain paired associate learning, and by Restle (1962) to explain concept identification learning.

Starting in the late 1960s, the learning models became quite a bit more complicated as theorists attempted to account for a broader range of phenomena, involving, for example, the dynamics of memory, how knowledge is structured, modified and retrieved (Estes 1982). Some of the mathematical modelling became sufficiently complex that some theorists resorted to computer simulation models. However, these computer simulation models are difficult to evaluate, because it is difficult to determine how they can be tested, or even whether they can be falsified. Estes has suggested that the computer simulation models and the more traditional mathematical models may not be completely competitive, but rather may be complementary. While the entire computer simulation model may be too complicated to be expressed mathematically, it may be possible to express subsystems of the model in mathematical form, and this might permit deeper analyses of various aspects of the learning process.

Multi-Attribute Models. Most of the previously described models have focussed on simple stimuli in simple experimental situations. However, the question of how complex stimuli are organized or perceived is actually a very old question and was considered almost from the beginning of mathematical psychology. In the very earliest issues of *Psychometrika*, the mathematical groundwork was laid by Eckart and Young (1936). The basic idea was to represent the stimuli or people as points in some multidimensional, euclidean space, the dimensionality of the space being determined by the number of relevant attributes of the stimuli, and the interpoint distances by the degree of similarity of the stimuli. With the mathematical machinery developed, it was possible to determine the location of the points in the space, as well as the dimensionality of the space, merely from a knowledge of the interpoint distances, that is, from some measure of the similarity between pairs of stimuli.

However, not until high speed computers became available did these multidimensional methods become practical. In the 1950s Torgerson's approach was based on a multidimensional generalization of the Thurstone comparative judgment model. The multidimensional generalization was achieved by associating a normal distribution with the interpoint distances, rather than with the stimuli themselves. More recent multidimensional approaches have made different distributional assumptions or have made use of non-euclidean spaces (Borg 1981). The non-euclidean spaces appear to be necessary for certain types of stimuli.

Quite a different multidimensional approach was developed by Shepard (Shepard 1980). His approach required no distributional assumption whatever, and in fact made use only of the rank order of the interpoint distances. What Shepard showed, quite unexpectedly, is that from such information about the interpoint distances it is possible to locate the points rather precisely in the space and to determine the dimensionality of the space as well. This nonmetric approach has generated considerable interest and has been followed up by many improvements and variations on the same theme (Schiffman et al. 1981).

Other non-geometric approaches for dealing with complex, multi-attribute stimuli are also being developed extensively. One of the most comprehensive is the information integration theory of Anderson (1982). Anderson uses very simple algebraic models, generally involving only the adding and subtracting of the relevant attributes, but has achieved an impressive range of predictions in widely different experimental contexts.

Perhaps one of the most striking aspects of the current modelling is the way in which the models from the different fields are beginning to make contact with each other. Learning theorists are increasingly adding structural details to their models, while measurement and choice theorists are increasingly making use of the more cognitive and dynamic aspects of the learning models. Perhaps, one can even hope that the distinction between learning models and measurement models will disappear altogether. JLZ

Bibliography

Anderson, N.H. 1982: *Methods of information integration theory.* New York and London: Academic Press.

Borg, I., ed. 1981: *Multidimensional data representations: when and why.* Ann Arbor, Mich.: Mathesis Press.

Bower, G.H. 1961: Application of a model to paired-associate learning. *Psychometrika* 26, 255–80.

Coombs, C.H. 1950: Psychological scaling without a unit of measurement. *Psychological review* 57, 145–58.

Eckart, C. and Young, G. 1936: The approximation of one matrix by another of lower rank. *Pschometrika* 1, 211–18.

Estes, W.K., ed. 1975 vol. 1: 1976 vol. 2–4: 1978 vol. 5–6: *Handbook of learning and cognitive processes.* Hillsdale, N.J.: L. Erlbaum Associates.

——— 1982: *Model of learning, memory and choice.* New York: Praeger.

Guttman, L. 1944: A basis for scaling qualitative data. *American sociological review* 9, 139–50.

Hull, C.L. 1943: *Principles of behavior.* New York: Appleton-Century-Crofts.

Lazarsfeld, P.F. 1950: The logical and mathematical foundations of latent structure analysis. In *Measurement and prediction.* Vol. IV. ed. S.A. Stoufer et al. Princeton, N.J.: Princeton University Press.

Lord, F.M. 1980: *Application of item response theory to practical testing problems.* Hillsdale, N.J.: Lawrence Erlbaum.

Luce, R.D. 1959: *Individual choice behavior: a theoretical analysis.* New York: Wiley, 1959.

Rasch, G. 1960: *Studies in mathematical psychology, I. Probabilistic models for some intelligence and attainment tests.* Copenhagen: Danish Institute of Educational Research.

Restle, F. 1962: The selection of strategies in cue learning. *Psychological review* 69, 329–43.

Schiffman, S.S. et al. 1981: *Introduction to multidimensional scaling: theory, methods and applications.* New York and London: Academic Press.

Shepard, R.N. 1980: Multidimensional scaling, tree fitting and clustering. *Science* 210, 390–8.

Stevens, S.S. 1946: On the theory of scales of measurement. *Science* 103, 677–80.

Thurstone, L.L. 1919: The learning curve equation. *Psychological monograph* 26, No. 3.

von Neumann, J. and Morgenstern, O. 1953: *Theory of games and economic behavior.* Princeton, N.J.: Princeton University Press.

mathematical modelling: principles The use of mathematical models and techniques to explain psychological phenomena. The term "mathematical psychology" has been in use at least since 1936 when the Psychometric Society and its journal, *Psychometrika*, were founded to encourage, according to the subtitle of the journal, "the development of Psychology as a quantitative rational science".

Louis Thurstone, the first president of the Society, emphasized at their first meeting that what "may be called mathematical psychology" (Thurstone 1959, p.3) had to involve both quantification and rationalization. Quantification was to be used during the initial phases of a scientific study to describe experimentally observed results, but quantification by itself was not sufficient. It was not sufficient merely to fit a hyperbola to a learning curve. It was necessary for the mathematical psychologist, during the later phases of an investigation, to attempt the more demanding task of rationalizing the quantitative description by deducing it and other consequences from a small number of postulates about the nature of the underlying psychological process involved. To rationalize a learning curve meant to deduce it and other properties of learning from a few basic assumptions about how learning takes place on each learning trial.

Thurstone's conceptualization of mathematical psychology is completely modern in all essential respects, although the term "rationalization" is no longer used. Instead it is customary to speak of constructing a mathematical model to explain certain data or phenomena. Thurstone's distinction between statistics and mathematical psychology is also completely valid today. Statistical methods are used to evaluate how well the theory and experimental results agree. A knowledge of statistical theory, therefore, needs to be part of the stock in trade of the mathematical psychologist, but the development of statistical techniques is not his primary focus.

Although a good deal of mathematical psychology was carried out by Thurstone and others, this work remained largely restricted to a few areas of psychology, principally to psychological measurement and test theory. After about 1950 this changed drastically. Interest in mathematical psychology intensified considerably and gradually penetrated into all areas of experimental psychology. This was stimulated largely by the stochastic learning models of Estes (1950), Estes and Burke (1952), and Bush and Mosteller (1951), and by the many workshops in mathematical psychology held at that time. All this flurry of mathematical activity required additional outlets and led to the founding in 1964 of the *Journal of mathematical psychology* and to the publication of the three volume *Handbook of mathematical psychology* (Luce, Bush, and Galanter 1963, 1965). At the same time, the *British journal of statistical psychology* became the *British journal of mathematical and statistical psychology*. At present mathematical models and related issues appear in most of the major journals of psychology and in specialized, technical books.

Early Quantitative Psychology

Mathematical ideas and techniques have been used in psychology for some time, certainly since Gustav Fechner's *Elements of psychophysics* in 1860. However, true mathematical modelling appears to have begun with Thurstone's own efforts, first in the field of learning (Thurstone 1919) and later in psychophysics (Thurstone 1927). The earlier mathematical ideas lacked at least one of the two essentials of such modelling: falsifiability and what Thurstone called "rationalization". Falsifiability means that it should be possible to derive non-tautological predictions from the model that can be tested experimentally. It need not, however, be necessary to justify or identify experimentally every concept or process employed in the model.

The early attempts at quantification frequently lacked falsifiablity because they contained too many unspecified variables or parameters. William James's statement, in his *Principles of psychology* (1890), that Self-Esteem equals Success divided by Pretensions sounds tantalizing, but without some explanation as to how the three terms in this statement are to be measured the statement cannot be tested. Even Fechner's psychophysical law, that sensation is a logarithmic function of physical intensity, cannot be tested without a procedure for measuring sensation, and about this there continues to be no consensus.

Rationalization, the other essential ingredient of true mathematical modelling, tended also to be missing from these early attempts at quantification. Hermann Ebbinghaus and Edward Thorndike, near the end of the nineteenth century, fitted learning curves to learning data, but they did not derive these curves from fundamental considerations about the nature of learning. This is equally true of Fechner's psychophysical law. No underlying model was provided which would explain, among other things, why people should confuse some stimuli in the first place.

Thurstone's Comparative Judgment Model. Thurstone's own model for pairwise judgments (Thurstone 1927) can be used to illustrate some of the key aspects of the modelling process. There are just two assumptions of the model. The first is that the effect of each stimulus on the experimental subject can be summarized by a single number, one that varies from trial to trial but whose distribution over trials is that of a normal distribution. The second assumption concerns the decision rule that the subject follows when presented with two stimuli and is asked to choose between them with respect to some specified attribute. It is assumed that the subject selects the stimulus associated with the larger number of each trial.

Is the model falsifiable? Yes, the model is falsifiable even though it has a large number of unspecified parameters. For every pair of stimuli, there are five unknown parameters: two means, two variances and one unknown correlation. Still it can be shown that when there are at least three stimuli and three pairwise choice probabilities, the model has definite predictions which can be falsified.

Working out all the observable properties of a model, especially those that are both necessary and sufficient for the model to be valid, is one of the most basic aspects of the modelling process. Except for certain special cases, this has yet to be worked out for the Thurstone model. The special cases which have been studied have the effect of reducing the number of unknown parameters. This, at the same time, has the desirable consequence of increasing the specificity of the predictions of the model and making it easier to test.

Can the model be generalized to other types of experimental tasks or is it just purely descriptive of a certain domain of data? Yes, by simple extensions of the decision rule, the model can be made applicable to many different types of tasks, such as those requiring choices from sets containing more than two stimuli, rank order choices, detection, recognition, and identification tasks. Also by adding parameters to account for response biases, the model can explain the asymmetric effects caused by assigning different outcomes to correct and incorrect responses. This is not to suggest that this type of model is completely successful at explaining all these different types of judgments. Indeed, a continuing concern of mathematical psychologists is to explain, from a single conceptual model, all the effects that have been observed with these different tasks (Luce 1977).

How can the values of the unknown parameters of the

model, the means, the variances and the correlations, be determined from a knowledge of a person's pairwise choices? This problem, called the estimation problem, consists of working out practical procedures which can be shown to give good estimates of the unknown parameters of the model. It should also consist of some indication as to how accurate those estimates are likely to be. Determining optimal estimation procedures can be difficult, because simple analytical expressions frequently do not exist and instead it is necessary to develop efficient iterative methods. Excellent procedures have been worked out for the Thurstone model when it can be assumed that all the intercorrelations are zero or constant. However, good estimation procedures have yet to be worked out for the general model.

How uniquely can the parameters of the Thurstone model be determined? This uniqueness problem involves determining the admissible set of parameter values, those which, for a given set of data, are indistinguishable. Any set of parameter values from the admissible set can explain the data as well as any other values from the set. It is essential to determine the degree of uniqueness of the parameter estimates, because without such knowledge it is not possible to avoid making statements about the phenomenon being studied which are scientifically meaningless. Statements are scientifically meaningless when their falsehood depends on which parameter values are selected from the admissible set, not on any intrinsic property of the phenomenon.

Solving the estimation problem can also be difficult, when there are many different types of parameters and when these parameters are constrained to satisfy certain relations. For the Thurstone model it has only been solved for the simplest case, when all the intercorrelations are zero or constant and all the variances are equal. It can then be shown that the means are uniquely determined up to a linear transformation.

How does the Thurstone model compare with other competing models? Ideally this question should be answered by determining the observable properties of the model which clearly discriminate it from competing models. However, this ideal all too often does not seem to exist. There are a number of important models, which conceptually are quite distinct from the Thurstone model, but which nevertheless are extremely difficult to discriminate experimentally from the Thurstone model (Luce 1977). Still this remains a constant concern for the mathematical psychologist: how to design experiments so that different classes of models can be distinguished. JLZ

Bibliography

Bush, R.R. and Mosteller, F. 1951: A mathematical model for simple learning. *Psychological review* 58, 313–23.

Egan, J.P. 1975: *Signal detection theory and ROC analysis*. New York and London: Academic Press.

Estes, W.K. 1950: Toward a statistical theory of learning. *Psychological review* 57, 94–107.

——— and Burke, C.J. 1952: A theory of stimulus variability in learning. *Psychological review* 60, 276–86.

Luce, R.D. 1977: Thurstone's discriminal processes fifty years later. *Psychometrika* 42, 461–90.

——— Bush, R.R., and Galanter, E. eds. 1963: vol. 1–2: 1965 vol. 3: *Handbook of mathematical psychology*. New York: Wiley.

Thurstone, L.L. 1919: The learning curve equation. *Psychological monograph* 26, No. 3.

——— 1927: Psychophysical analysis. *American journal of psychology* 38, 368–89.

——— 1959: *The measurement of values*. Chicago: University of Chicago Press.

mathematics Originally the collective name for arithmetic (computation), geometry and algebra, however mathematics today includes so many areas of study (such as number theory, calculus, topology, analytical geometry, set theory and its derivatives) that counter-examples could be found for almost any attempt at an inclusive definition. There are, moreover, considerable differences in viewpoint. A pure mathematician might describe mathematics as the study of internally consistent formal structures, derived by specified rules from logically compatible sets of axioms. "We then take any hypothesis that seems amusing, and deduce its consequences. *If* our hypothesis is about *anything*, and not about some one or more particular things, then our deductions constitute mathematics", writes Russell (1929), going on to say that one of the chief triumphs of modern mathematics consists in having discovered what mathematics really is: it is identical with formal logic.

Although this approach has contributed to the development of mathematics as a rigorous intellectual discipline, the view of mathematics which it presents is incomplete. Gödel (1931 *(1962)*) has shown that the consistency of a formal system cannot be proved within the system itself. Nor does it offer any way of knowing which formal systems might be more usefully studied than others, since utility does not enter into this approach to mathematics. Referring to his mathematical activities, Hardy (1940) wrote "I have never done anything *useful*". Utility is however an essential feature of mathematics for those such as scientists, engineers, navigators, accountants and others who find it an essential tool for understanding, predicting and sometimes controlling events in their physical environment and to a lesser degree in their social environment. This accords with the viewpoint of Bruner (1966), who sees mathematics as a tool for amplifying human ratiocinative capacity.

The view which will here be developed is that mathematics is a particularly concentrated and powerful example of the functioning of human intelligence. The product of many minds, it is a cultural inheritance which, as emphasized by PIAGET (1952) and others, has to be constructed anew by each individual in his own mind. But when it has been acquired, it can greatly increase his ability to understand and control his environment.

This environment is bound to be variable. No two experiences are exactly the same: even the same object is seen on different occasions at varying distances, angles of view, differently lit. Learning is possible only because we are able to discover common properties of experiences, and store them mentally in such a way that we can recognize them on future occasions. This mental representation of a common property is what we call a concept; and the process of "pulling out" similarities and ignoring differences is called abstracting. Classifying is thus a basic activity in intelligent learning; and the concept of a set, which is a well-defined class, is a basic concept of contemporary mathematics.

Whenever we see or hear something in our physical environment which we recognize, a concept has been evoked. By attaching symbols to them, however, these concepts can be evoked independently of the environment. They become mental objects which can be manipulated, contemplated, organized. We can string them together to form a plan for action; and from several alternative plans, we can choose that which we think most likely to achieve our purpose. More: we can use our classifying ability at a higher level, by grouping concepts themselves together, abstracting another common property, and thereby forming a higher order concept. Having through our senses discovered regularities of the physical world, by mental activity we go on to discover regularities among these regularities, and so on to find higher and higher order regularities. This process of repeated abstraction is particularly characteristic of mathematics, resulting in concepts which in spite of their highly abstract quality have again and again proved their power in helping us to understand, and achieve our goals in, the physical world. How can this be?

Any plan of action depends for its success on having some kind of mental representation of the physical environment: or rather, of those features of the environment which matter for the success of the plan. A stereotyped plan, appropriate only to a particular category of situations, is a habit. Habits are closely tied to action, and lack adaptability. Moreover, given the variety of situations in which we find ourselves, the learning and remembering of a sufficient set of habits to deal with all these situations imposes ever-increasing cognitive strain. A much more effective way to store the necessary information is in the form of a conceptual structure, in which are embodied and interrelated regularities abstracted from a wide variety of experiences. These conceptual structures correspond to the schemata of Bartlett (1932), and the conceptual maps of Tolman (1948). (The term "schema" is used differently by Piaget, and is more closely tied to action.)

Within an appropriate conceptual structure, a mental model can be formed of a particular situation or class of situations, at whatever level of generality is most useful for a particular purpose. From such a model can be derived predictions of particular events, and plans to achieve particular goals. The wider the variety of actual situations which can be modelled within a particular schema, and the greater the number of possible plans which can be derived from this model, the more powerful for action is this organization of knowledge.

The abstract, general, and thereby powerful, schemata of mathematics contain possibilities for constructing models of such a wide variety as to be remarkable when we begin to consider it. Space allows no more than two examples. First, the natural numbers. Each particular number is a property abstracted from a set of sets, ignoring both the nature of the objects and their spatial configuration, and collecting together those sets whose members can be put in one-to-one correspondence. In such a way we might get the concept 4. Other collections of sets might give rise to the concepts 7, 3. We now have the beginning of a set of new concepts, alike in one way (they are the property of *any* set of sets chosen in the way described) and different in other ways. On the basis of their similarity we call all of these concepts numbers, and on the basis of their differences we can begin to organize our new set of numbers; e.g. by putting them in order, 3, 4, 7. We also see gaps to be filled; and the sequence invites extrapolation, upward and downward. Even at this level, the process of mental creativity is evoked. Still at the level of natural numbers, there is much else which space does not allow to be even touched on here. Further abstraction takes us into algebra, in which statements such as $a(p+q) = ap+aq$ represent what is common to an infinite number of particular cases such as $7(5+8) = 7\times5+7\times8$, just as each of these represents an infinite number of possible statements about actual objects.

In combination with the concept of a unit, we now have an extensive and multi-purpose schema from which particular models can be constructed to represent almost any physical object or event. Thus, with appropriate units, $a/b = c$ can represent the relationship between distance, time and speed (so we can use it to plan a car journey or run an airline). It can represent the relationship between electrical power, electromotive force ("voltage"), and current (so we can decide whether to use a 3A or 13A fuse). It can represent the relationship between mass, volume and density (so we can decide how much buoyancy material we need for our lifejacket). The fact that we use different letters as mnemonics for what they represent should not cause us to overlook that mathematically,

$$\frac{\mathrm{d}}{\mathrm{t}} = \mathrm{s}, \frac{\mathrm{W}}{\mathrm{E}} = \mathrm{I}, \frac{\mathrm{m}}{\mathrm{v}} = \mathrm{d}$$

are the same. By simply changing the units, we have adapted them for very different jobs; and this adaptability is a key feature both of intelligence in general, and of mathematics as a special case.

As a second example, consider $\sin\theta$. (We shall assume knowledge of this concept, and use it to illustrate the present argument further.) Some of the lower order regularities on which it is based are: sets of similar triangles; ratio and proportion; angles in general, and right angles in particular; measures of length (involving an expansion of the concept of counting number to measuring number); and a relation between the first and second of these, that for any set of similar triangles, the ratios of the lengths of pairs of corresponding sides are in the same proportion. This illustrates the concentration of conceptual information, nested within nests, which are handled by this concept. Now consider just three of the many situations for which $\sin\theta$ can act as a model. One is navigation. Here, one triangle is small enough to go on a map or chart, the other (though not actually drawn) is on the earth's surface.

Another is in optics. By combining this with the preceding model we get

$$\frac{\sin i}{\sin r} = \mu$$

which some will recognize as Snell's law describing a regularity in the change of direction of a ray of light as it passes from air to glass, from air to water, or between any other two transparent media. A third use of this concept gives the instantaneous value of an alternating current, in the formula $I = I_{max} \cos \omega t$.

The reader is invited to seek for himself other examples of the multipurpose nature of mathematical concepts; and also of their high level of abstraction, since this is one of the major stumbling blocks in the learning and teaching of mathematics.

As we have seen, one of the strengths of mathematics is the way in which it enables its users to handle a great concentration of information within a small number of highly abstract concepts. A consequence of this is that a few lines of mathematics contains as much information as perhaps a page or more of less abstract material. In teaching mathematics, it is easy to overlook this, and give out information faster than it can be taken in by the learner.

We have also seen how at every stage, the learning of new mathematical concepts is dependent on the learner having already available an appropriate conceptual structure. Learning with understanding takes place if and only if the new concepts are assimilated to this schema. If teaching is not carefully sequenced in such a way that the progressive building up of the successive levels of abstraction can take place, genuine mathematical understanding is impossible and the learner can only, at best, resort to the rote memorizing of rules without reasons.

Yet another way in which learners can go astray is in their conception of the nature of the learning task. The situation in which pupils are placed conduces to the belief that what they are supposed to be learning is a collection of methods for getting right answers to mathematical questions. The true nature of the task, however, is threefold. First, they need to construct in their own minds mathematical schemata, i.e. conceptual structures of the abstract and hierarchical kind already described. Second, they need to learn how to derive from these schemata particular methods for particular tasks. For novel tasks, this constitutes problem-solving ability. Many mathematical tasks are however of kinds frequently encountered, so it is also desirable to build up a set of ready-to-hand methods by which routine tasks can be done with a minimum of effort. This also has the advantage, when these routine tasks occur within a context of problem-solving, of freeing attention to concentrate on the novel, which is to say the problematic, aspects of the tasks. Thirdly, it is necessary to acquire fluency and accuracy in the execution of these tasks. These three components of mathematical ability we may call knowing-that, knowing-how, and being able. In combination, they form one of the most powerful and adaptable mental tools which mankind has yet devised. RRS

Bibliography

Bartlett, F. 1932: *Remembering*. Cambridge: Cambridge University Press.

Bruner, J.S. 1966: *Towards a theory of instruction*. Cambridge, Mass.: Harvard University Press.

*Chapman, L.R., ed. 1972: *The process of learning mathematics*. Oxford and New York: Pergamon.

Gödel, K. 1931 (*1962*): *On formally undecidable propositions*. New York: Basic Books.

Hardy, G.H. 1940: *A mathematician's apology*. Cambridge: Cambridge University Press.

*Newman, J.R. 1956: *The world of mathematics*. New York: Simon and Schuster.

Piaget, J. and Szeminska, A. 1952: *The child's conception of space*. London: Routledge & Kegan Paul.

Russell, B. 1929: *Mysticism and logic*. New York: Norton.

*Skemp, R.R. 1971: *The psychology of learning mathematics*. Harmondsworth: Penguin.

*——— 1979: *Intelligence, learning, and action*. New York and Chichester: Wiley.

Tolman, E.C. 1948: Cognitive maps in rats and men. *Psychological review* 55, 189–208.

meaning Naively we distinguish natural and conventional meaning: word meaning, sentence meaning, discourse meaning; cross-cutting these speaker's meaning, listener's meaning, language meaning; cross-cutting once more, extensional meaning (actual referent), intensional meaning and psychological meaning. More globally we distinguish syntactic meaning, semantic meaning and pragmatic meaning. Similarly, and again globally, J.L. Austin (1962) suggested that we distinguish what we say (locutional meaning) from what we do in so saying (illocutionary force). Most theoretical disagreement occurs in attempts to explain (or explain away) one or another of these in terms of the others.

Distinguishing natural and conventional meaning, F. de Saussure held that the linguistic sign has an arbitrary and conventional connection with its referent, thus distinguishing natural-meaning (1) from conventional-meaning (2).

(1) Those sores mean herpes.

(2) "Nonce" means for a single occasion.

However, it might be argued that the difference is merely that in (1) we grasp the simple causal connection, while in (2) the story is just more round about, taking in the complex development of a language and a species, not the simpler interaction of a virus and a mammalian organism. In (1) we trace the character of some superficial lesions back to their source in the life cycle of a virus. In (2) we would have to trace a phonological structure into the syntactic structures of English, semantics and cultural history, human cognition and so on. If we replace words with sentences, as in (3), where we have two sentences flanking the equational "meant", we find the syntactical resources determining equivalence in a systematic manner.

(3) When she said "It is not the case that he was absent" she meant that he was here.

(4) When he said "Like father like son" he meant that a son often resembles his father.

(5) When he said "I think you are looking tired", he meant to tell you to leave.

With (4) there is undoubtedly a semantic equivalence , as there might be between sentences in different languages, but not one available in the syntactical properties of English. In (5) we perhaps need, in addition to syntactic and semantic, a pragmatic, social–contextual analysis. And surely, these last sentences suggest that one will want to distinguish what speaker, hearer and disinterested observer might take as said. finally, and more fine-grainedly, one distinguishes both for word and sentence, the literal reference (thing, fact) from the sense (intension, proposition) that determines that reference psychologically or abstractly. G. Frege is noted for insisting on this final distinction, insisting as in (6), that both the Evening Star and the Morning Star have Venus as their extensional meaning, but this reference is attained through quite distinguishable intensional meanings; similarly, he maintained that the proposition (6) is not of the form "A = A".

(6) The Morning Star is the Evening Star.

J.S. Mill agreed with Frege in making this distinction but Mill took intensions to be psychological items while Frege held them to be abstract entities. Frege revived medieval realism in that he held that the subject matter of arithmetic and logic was real, quite apart from human conceptual psychology or conventional symbolic systems. Mill, on the other hand, propounded a version of medieval conceptualism.

Ogden and Richards, and W.V.O. Quine are recent champions of medieval nominalism, of the reduction of meaning to extension: to know the meaning of a word is to know what non-linguistic object(s) it stands for. Quine did feel that mathematics and science generally required one sort of abstract entities, namely, sets. But since a set could be given simply by specifying its membership (i.e. extensionally), Quine felt that "mysterious" intensions could be avoided. This had the troublesome consequence that (6) and (7) are true in the same way as "A = A".

(7) Heat = the mean motion of molecular particles.

Recent Oxford philosophers such as J.L. Austin, P.F. Strawson and M.A.E. Dummett, and quite recently the Harvard philosopher H. Putnam, have argued a Kantian or conceptualist line that often stresses the communal and operational aspects of meaning. Dummett has arged that to know what a mathematical proposition means is rather like knowing what a proof of it would have to look like; similarly, to understand "empirical" propositions may be to have some idea of how one goes about determining their truth. Both Austin and Putnam have argued that the meaning of one's words often, and rightfully, depends on what one takes other people to be able to do. And Austin and Strawson have stressed that the ascertainable existence of other language users is a presupposition of meaningful language use.

On the other hand Kripke (1972) and others have tried to capture intentionality by the quasi-extensional notion of possible worlds. (6) and (7) are necessary truths in that what is picked out on this and other possible worlds by the first term of the equation is the same in all cases as that which is picked out by the second term.

Some have argued that meaning is not a unitary notion or perhaps not a distinguishable notion at all. Chomsky (1980) has argued that most semantic and pragmatic features belong outside linguisitics and its formal specification of meaning. Skinner (1957) would find little distinction even between (1) and (2), reducing meaning to stimulus–response regularities. JFL

Bibliography

Austin, J.L. 1962: *How to do things with words*. London: Oxford University Press.

Chomsky, N. 1980: *Rules and representations*. Oxford: Basil Blackwell; New York: University of Columbia Press.

Dummett, M.A.E. 1978: *Truth and other enigmas*. Cambridge, Mass: Harvard University Press.

Frege, G. 1892 (1952): On sense and reference. In *Translations from the Philosophical Writings of Gottlob Frege*, ed. P. Geach and M. Black. Oxford: Oxford University Press.

Kripke, S. 1972: Naming and necessity. In *Semantics of natural language*, ed. D. Davidson and G. Harman. Dordrecht: D. Reidel.

Ogden, C.K. and Richards, I.A. 1922: *The meaning of meaning*. London: Routledge & Kegan Paul.

Putnam, H. 1978: *Meaning and the moral sciences*. London: Routledge & Kegan Paul.

Quine, W.V.O. 1960: *Word and object*. New York: Wiley.

Skinner, B.F. 1957: *Verbal behavior*. New York: Appleton-Century-Crofts.

meaning: cognitive The study of cognitive meaning (also referred to as conceptual, denotative, referential or logical meaning) is concerned with the questions of truth value and reference. It is regarded as the central aspect of semantics in human communication by the majority of linguists. Such a view implies that there is a constant, speech-independent referential potential underlying actual instances of speech. It also assumes that a clear-cut distinction can be drawn between cognitive meaning and other types of meaning (cf Leech 1974: 10–27).

The notion of the primacy of cognitive meaning has come under attack from anthropological linguists such as Silverstein (1977: 39–52), who point out that it merely reflects a subculture-specific folk-view of language, and from researchers into child language developments, since in FIRST LANGUAGE ACQUISITION, the emergence of cognitive meaning, i.e. the use of language in its referential FUNCTION, is developmentally late (see Halliday 1974). PM

Bibliography

Halliday, M.A.K. 1974: *Explorations in the functions of language*. London: Edward Arnold.

Leech, Geoffrey 1974: *Semantics*. Harmondsworth and Baltimore: Pelican Books.

Silverstein, Michael 1977: Cultural prerequisites to grammatical analysis. In *Linguistics and anthropology*, ed. M. Saville-Troike. Washington DC: Georgetown University Press.

mechanical senses *See* senses, mechanical

mechanistic theory The description of behavior exclusively through causal concepts employed in traditional natural (Newtonian) science, where a complete account of things is attempted through the use of material causes (the substance comprising things) and efficient causes (the impetus moving things). No use is made of purpose or intention. To use these would require that the "formal" cause (a pre-existing pattern of meanings) or final cause (selection of meanings that are to be achieved in action) be used as basic principles of explanation. Since mechanistic theory holds that the same natural laws which move inanimate events move the behavior of living organisms, a uniformity and predictability is achieved suggestive of a machine-like process taking place throughout nature. Thus, people are said to behave due to such underlying systematic (mechanistic) processes without meaningful understanding or choice. (See also PURPOSIVISM, VOLUNTARISM.) JFR

medial forebrain bundle A large ascending and descending fiber tract that connects the septal regions in the anterior forebrain and the ventral tegmentum in the midbrain (BRAIN AND CENTRAL NERVOUS SYSTEM: ILLUSTRATIONS, figs 5, 6, 16 and 18). The medial forebrain bundle passes through the HYPOTHALAMUS and gives off important collaterals to the lateral hypothalamic areas fig. 20. Mild electrical stimulation at all points throughout the medial forebrain bundle produces pleasurable or rewarding effects as evidenced by animals' readiness to respond for such stimulation. Other brain areas also support self-stimulation but the effect is most reliable and dramatic for the medial forebrain bundle which can yield response rates in a Skinner box of up to 10,000 per hour. Stimulation-produced reward has been compared to the effects of natural reinforcers (e.g. food, water) but differences in animals' behavior in relation to the two types of reinforcers, suggest that different mechanisms may be activated. For example, responding for brain stimulation extinguishes more rapidly, is optimal at short inter-response intervals, and requires considerably more prodding to re-establish after the delay. This pattern suggests that electrical stimulation of the medial forebrain bundle and related structures may activate, in addition to a reward system, a drive system to sustain motivation for continued behavior. By contrast natural reinforcers produce only the rewards since motivation is provided by the animal's deprived state. GWi

medical models The classical medical model of diagnosis consists of a sequence of history taking, physical examination and laboratory investigations. This model represents an orientation towards "disease" which is defined as a named medical entity, generally without definition of the cause. The medical model has been strongly criticized for being incomplete and omitting such areas as the exploration of patients' ideas, concerns and expectations, non-verbal communication and other aspects of the doctor–patient relationship. These areas are compatible with an alternative "holistic" approach to medical care in which any problem is defined simultaneously in terms of its physical, psychological and social components (Pendleton et al. in press). This is related, in turn, to the suggestion that medical care should pay greater attention to "illness" than to "disease". Illness is seen as social phenomenon rather than a medical entity and takes account of the meaning attached to a problem by the patient. This subjective interpretation can strongly affect the patient's decision to seek medical help and to comply with medical advice.

Psychological models of medical care focus upon this "patient-centered" perspective. Research suggests that the behavior of people who consider themselves ill is influenced by the way in which they perceive their symptoms as well as by many social and cultural factors which affect attitudes to pain, health, illness and health services. The most popular approach is the Health Belief Model (Becker 1974) which states that the likelihood that an individual will take action with regard to an illness will depend upon certain health beliefs: general concern about health, perceived susceptibility to and severity of the illness, and the benefits weighed against the disadvantages of the recommended action or treatment. Other research suggests, in addition, that patients' *causal explanations* of their illness significantly affect their ability to cope and to seek medical help. "Folk models" of infection often affect the management of minor illness (Helman 1978).

The traditional medical model is therefore limited in scope and has been extended towards a broader view of diagnosis which takes account of both the scientific discipline of the disease perspective and the psychological and social characteristics of the patient. In psychiatry the medical model of mental disorder has frequently been criticized both from a BEHAVIORIST and from a more HUMANISTIC perspective (e.g. Laing and Esterson 1964). Both schools think that learning and adaptation are the mechanisms which produce the behavior regarded by psychiatrists as symptoms. The current criticisms being leveled at medical models in general medical practice clearly cast greater doubt upon the always questionable derivative usage in psychiatry. JK

Bibliography

Becker, M.H. 1974: *The health belief model and personal health behavior*. Health education monographs. 2.

Helman, C. 1978: Folk models of infection in an English suburban community and their relation to medical treatment. *Culture, medicine and psychiatry*. 2, 107–438.

Laing, R.D. and Esterton, A. 1964: *Sanity, madness and the family*. London: Tavistock.

Pendleton, D.A. et al. (in press) *The consultation: an approach to learning and teaching*. Oxford and New York: Oxford University Press..

meditation The practice of mind, thought, attitude or psychophysiological transformation generally in the context of some spiritual tradition; technique for inducing ALTERED STATES OF CONSCIOUSNESS often called "mystical". Knowledge that consciousness may be experienced in different ways is extremely ancient. Natural mysticism among primitive peoples, arising from both solitary and group practices often involving repetitive dance and chant rhythms, seems to be the original basis for the institutionalization of consciousness changing practices in the major world religions. Hindus, Buddhists, Sufis, Jews and Christians all have literatures containing manuals of meditative techniques. The prime characteristic of all of them is the loss of self-identifying awareness and a sense of absorption in a wider consciousness however that may be defined (Coleman 1977). There may well be a universal need for such experience which twentieth-century western culture with its emphasis on rationality has denied (Crook 1980). Contemporary movements promoting meditation spring from the urge to meet that need outside conventional religion and its consequent commercialization in a consumer economy.

The prime feature of the mind in its normal consciousness is that sensory experience is edited or filtered by a system of mental categorization so that the world is experienced primarily as represented by the categories by which it is mapped. All such conceptual systems are the result of social conditioning from babyhood and are closely related to the human capacity for language. In particular, an association between bodily experiences and contingent effects of behavior in an environment leads to the inference that the self exists as an agent or "me" (ego). This waking state of "objective self-awareness" (Duval and Wicklund 1972) is characterized by classification of self versus others and comparative evaluations of experience in the continuum of time past, present and future. Problems of self-esteem and its maintenance in a world of comparative social evaluations lie at the root of social anxiety or disquiet. Meditational techniques that induce (a) calming, (b) catharsis of tension, (c) insight into the nature of the personal process, are often of considerable therapeutic value. Further, a training in meditation can lead to selfless experiences of being, bliss and love held to be of the highest value in world religions and which lead to a more altruistic attitude towards fellow sentient beings (Naranjo and Ornstein 1971).

Most traditional meditation techniques utilize a combination of exercises concerned with one or more of the following: control or regulation of breathing, focussed attention, relative perceptual deprivation, "yogic" body postures, and the mental visualization of scenes or symbols representing desired goal states or stages. All practices induce shifts in the electrophysiological condition of the psychosomatic system in ways that are still little understood or researched. Among the known effects of one recently researched tradition (Transcendental Meditation or TM) the following have been established: the induction of alpha brain waves and, in deeper meditation, theta waves together with a synchronization of waves at the front and back of the brain during a session and synchrony in the two hemispheres, changes in galvanic skin responses, lowered respiration rate and oxygen consumption and other biochemical changes (see BIOFEEDBACK; ELECTROENCEPHALOGRAM).

TM consists of quiet relaxed breathing and the mental repetition of a mantra especially chosen for the subject. It is an easily acquired technique nowadays carefully taught by a multitude of trained instructors all over the world. It is based upon an ancient Hindu technique popularized by the Maharishi Mahesh. Much of its scientific evaluation has been suspect especially where it has been conducted by advocates of the system by which it is promoted commercially (Bloomfield et al. 1976). Where independent evaluation has been attempted some of the positive effects have however been confirmed (West 1979). TM does reduce arousal especially in easily stressed individuals and this is valuable for those suffering from anxiety, tension and their concomitant effects. Some long term effects have been reported and are likely to be dependent upon persistence in practice.

TM and other calming meditations have close resemblances to the autogenic training of J.H. Schultz, a German doctor concerned with stress relief and self-control of bodily conditions early in this century. In this procedure the subject is told to hold his attention firmly on some bodily condition – the weight of an arm, coolness of the forehead, warmth in the hands or an assertion "I am at peace". There is a similarity here with the firm body posture and mental repetition of mantras found in TM and Buddhist meditations and especially with the "mindfulness" of the body found in Vipassana and described in one of the earliest sutras of the Buddha. Holding the attention firmly upon an inner condition seems to reduce the tendency of the mind to wander in a reverie of anxiety producing themes.

In Zen meditation the main intention is the establishment of an alert awareness both of environment and of one's own body and mental processes rather than the induction of quiescent trance. This awareness can break open the narrow categories by which self's action as an agent and respondent are cognitively confined, and experiences of oneness with the world may arise.

Close observation of the functioning of the mind (as in the Samatha meditation of the Theravada or in the similar Zazen of the Soto Zen school) is clearly the experiential basis for the models of mind found in Buddhist psycho-philosophical texts. The experience of "sitting" shows that after some hours of repetitive practice the calming effect reaches a more or less stabilized condition in which subtle shifts in the mental condition are easily observed. As the environmental stimuli change so the conscious concomitants of the auditory, visual or other senses vary in prominence as attention increases or decreases its focus on particular sources of stimulation. As memories arise and concomitant emotional conditions are produced, the way in which the "inherent ego" appears and disappears with its hopes, fears, rationalizations and vanity becomes very clear and the whole "script" of one's life may be observed with an insight which can have markedly therapeutic effects.

In Rinzai Zen a deliberate effort is made to press the rationalizing mind and its ego-defensive operations beyond the realm of words and ideas. To this end the meditator is given a Koan or paradoxical question to solve and is forced at intervals in a retreat to bring his answers to an alertly critical master (Sekida 1975; Kapleau 1965). When the meditator reaches a point of desperation, struggling with the meaning of "What is the sound of one hand clapping" for example, he may break out into an intuitive realization that beyond words is the world itself, directly apprehensible and *there* in its own nature, with which the meditator senses his own belonging. The "emptiness" of thought which is the essence of these "enlightenment experiences" is the key to the understanding of the vast Mahayana literature upon which the concept rejecting practices of Zen are based (Kapleau 1965). Such training leads to the development of the "renouncing mind" of the Bodhisattva in which selfish egoism gives way to the use of the ego in the service of others. Such "opening" experiences seem particularly to involve a process of disidentification from habitual concepts of "me" and "mine".

Meditation training in the Gelugpa order of Tibetan monks is based on the discursive intellectual presentation of Buddhist psychology rather than on intuition. Extensive study of texts is linked to "checking meditation" in which the ideas are matched against experience in the subjects' own life in a test of their personal validity. All teachings are treated in this way and if the course is a long one it is at least extremely thorough. Mistakes that can arise in following the short-cuts of Zen are thus avoided.

Tibetans have also developed the tantric meditations of Hindus within a Buddhist framework. Tantra involves extensive visualization and the deliberate identification of the subject with the internalized icons. (See TANTRIC PSYCHOLOGY). These pictures of Buddhas and the like, in both their benign and horrific forms, represent psychological forces which the adept can learn to manipulate. The practice is often associated with visualizations of bodily processes using the categories of ancient Hindu physiology. Breathing exercises and advanced yogic practices combine to produce powerful effects. No novice should attempt such practice without an appropriate teacher who will ask for preliminary preparation and initiation before advanced practice can begin. Textual research suggests strongly that the sexual imagery in much of tantric practice refers to the origin of these exercises in group rites in which sexual interaction was normal. With a suitable partner this may sometimes be the case today. The mutual endeavor is, however, on a plane of sublimation that requires subtle control of sexual physiology if it is not to degenerate into mere indulgence. It is not surprising therefore that these powerful exercises are rarely taught outside the circle of carefully prepared initiates.

Powerful psychophysiological changes referred to as "raising the Kundalini" (Gopi-Krishna 1976) etc. are unlikely to be fictitious but as with Tantra none of them have yet been researched by accredited scientists. There are similarities to the bioenergetic therapies based upon the work of Wilhelm REICH (Lowen 1975; Boadella 1975). Research on the relations between advanced yoga of this type and bioenergetics may have great value for the future.

The value of meditating for an individual depends on attitude and context. In the spiritual market place many contemporary cults of meditation, with their emphasis on gurus and membership of self-defining elitist institutions, may perhaps be seen as an expression of the disintegration of the family system in the modern West and attendant uncertainty regarding parental and sexual roles and mores. Young people, often desperate for guidance, find parental substitutes in strange places and are liable to become brain-washed practitioners of powerful psychosomatic exercises, access to which is made dependent on cult membership and financial contribution. Only where meditation is used as a means to personal development, insight and above all autonomy can its true potential be realized. JHC

Bibliography

Bloomfield, H.H. et al. 1976: *TM: how meditation can reduce stress*. London: Unwin.

Boadella, D. 1975: Between coma and convulsion. *Energy and character*. 6.1, 4–24; 6.2, 18–27; 6.3, 27–38.

Coleman, D. 1977: *The varieties of meditative experience*. London: Ryder.

*Crook, J.H. 1980: *The evolution of human consciousness*. Oxford and New York: Oxford University Press.

Duval, S. and Wicklund, R.A. 1972: *A theory of objective self-awareness*. New York: Academic Press.

Gopi-Krishna, P. 1976: *Kundalini: path to higher consciousness*. New Delhi: Orient.

*Kapleau, P. 1965: *The three pillars of Zen*. Boston: Beacon Press.

Lowen, A. 1975: *Bioenergetics*. New York.

*Naranjo, C. and Ornstein, R. 1971: *On the psychology of meditation*. New York: Viking.

Sekida, K. 1975: *Zen training; methods and philosophy*. New York: Weatherhill.

West, M. 1979: Meditation. *British journal of psychiatry* 135, 457–67.

meditation *See above, and also* transcendental meditation

meme A term introduced by Dawkins (1976) in his proposed analogy between biological and cultural evolution, to refer to the hypothetical cultural counterpart of the gene – a 'unit' of cultural inheritance. Suggestions that socio-cultural change has some of the properties of biological evolution have been made repeatedly, and early ones have long been discredited (see EVOLUTION). Recently, however, a number of subtler models have been proposed and debated (see Plotkin and Odling-Smee 1981). Some schemes suggest that cultural traits change in frequency according to their effects on the biological fitness of their bearer, but Dawkins's idea differs in suggesting that memes change frequency simply according to their capacity for cultural transmission from one individual to another. Dawkins (1982) also distinguishes between memes (units of information residing in the brain) and meme products (their outward and perceptible manifestations). This speculative scheme has stimulated a continuing debate (see Dawkins 1982, Staddon 1981, Harré 1979.) RDA

Bibliography

Dawkins, R. 1976: *The selfish gene*. Oxford: Oxford University Press.

——— 1982: *The extended phenotype: the gene as the unit of selection*. Oxford, San Francisco: W.H. Freeman.

Harré, Rom 1979: *Social being* part IV. Oxford: Basil Blackwell; Totowa, N.J.: Littlefield Adams.

Plotkin, H.C. and Odling-Smee, F.J. (1981): A multiple-level model of evolution and its implications for sociobiology. *Behavior and brain science* 4, 225—68.

Staddon, J.E.R. 1981: On a possible relation between cultural transmission and genetical evolution. In *Perspectives in ethology, 4: advantages of diversity*, ed. P.P.G. Bateson ad P.H. Klopfer. New York and London: Plenum Press.

memory: echoic The term *echoic memory* was introduced by Neisser (1967) to denote the transient store in which auditory information is contained in some unsegmented or linguistically uncategorized form. Estimates of the lower bound of the echoic trace's duration vary from two seconds (Crowder 1971) to six or eight seconds (Routh and Mayes 1974 to 20 seconds (Watkins and Todres 1980).

Echoic memory was once believed to hold only the "extrinsic" properties of aural linguistic stimuli (location, timbre, pitch) as opposed to their "intrinsic" properties (meaning, emotionality, frequency of usage in the language). This conclusion was based on studies of the stimulus suffix effect (SSE) in which any speech-like sound that immediately follows a list to be serially recalled depresses the retention of the last item. A widely accepted hypothesis regarding the SSE states that the last item in a supraspan series is normally retrieved from echoic memory, and that the suffix exerts its deleterious effect on retention by displacing that item from echoic memory (or precategorical acoustic storage: Crowder and Morton 1969). The SSE is attenuated when the suffix's acoustic properties (such as its fundamental frequency) differ from those of the items to be recalled; and it is generally not observed when the suffix is a non-linguistic sound, such as a burst of white noise.

Recent evidence, however, raises questions about the strictly precategorical nature of the suffix (and therefore of echoic memory): suffixes that are semantically related to the terminal list item have been shown to facilitate its retention (e.g. Salter and Colley 1977); and a given sound may act as a suffix or fail to do so according to whether the subject expects it to have been produced by a human voice or by a musical instrument (Ayres et al. 1979). NCW

Bibliography

Ayres, T.J. et al. 1979: Differing suffix effects for the same physical stimulus. *Journal of experimental psychology: human learning and memory* 5, 315–21.

Crowder, R.G. 1971: Waiting for the stimulus suffix: decay, delay, rhythm, and readout in immediate memory. *Quarterly journal of experimental psychology* 23, 324–40.

Crowder, R.G. and Morton, J. 1969: Precategorical acoustic storage (PAS). *Perception and psychophysics* 5, 365–73.

Routh, D.A. and Mayes, J.T. 1974: On consolidation and the potency of delayed stimulus suffices. *Quarterly journal of experimental psychology* 26, 472–79.

Salter, D. and Colley, J.G. 1977: The stimulus suffix: a paradoxical effect. *Memory and cognition* 5, 257–62.

memory: episodic The term is used to describe personal memories, as distinguished from general knowledge or semantic memory. The memory trace contains not only a certain content but also the context in which it was established. Originally all memory traces have a personal, episodic character, though some traces become decontextualized as a function of repeated exposure. The episodic memory system is not distinct from semantic memory, but the two form a continuum. Episodic memory and general knowledge are often intermixed (e.g. one's memory of a city is partly decontextualized, general knowledge, the origin of which has been forgotten and no longer matters, partly personal experiences, still embedded in their original context of acquisition). WKi

memory: iconic Refers to the transient visual trace described by Sperling (1960), who addressed the question of why more information than a subject can report should be available for a short time after the offset of a brief visual stimulus consisting of verbal items. To circumvent limitations imposed by the span of immediate apprehension (approximately four items), the subject in Sperling's study was asked to give a partial report of a stimulus (e.g. 12 digits arranged in three rows of four): an auditory cue, either coterminous with the stimulus array or occurring at an interval of up to 1,000 msec after its offset, indicated which row the subject was to report. His accuracy in recalling this set of items allowed the total number of symbols available to him immediately after the offset of the stimulus to be inferred. For a cue coterminous with the stimulus, that number is nine. The number does not increase with exposure – duration of the stimulus over a range of 15 to 500 msec.

Iconic memory was long believed to be totally prelinguistic: the subject can select items to report on the basis of physical variables such as their location, brightness, color or direction of motion; but he cannot do so on the basis of the items' membership in a linguistic category. Recent experimental results now suggest, however, that iconic memory may not be entirely prelinguistic.

The icon has sometimes been said to be nothing more than an after-image. However the icon can be formed at light-intensities much weaker than those required for the formation of after-images. It can, moreover, survive a post-exposure field strong enough to saturate the rods. The icon is accordingly a central rather than a peripheral sensory trace. This conclusion is consistent with the fact that the icon and the phenomenon of direct "visible persistence" are governed in different ways by the same experimental variables. NCW

Bibliography

*Coltheart, M. 1980: Iconic memory and visible persistence. *Perception and psychophysics* 27, 183–228.

Sperling, G. 1960: The information available in brief visual presentations. *Psychological monographs* 74, 11.

memory: in philosophical theory The word "remember" is used in a wide variety of constructions. Someone can be said to remember doing something, to do something, how to do something, that something is the case (to mention only a few of them). What they all have in common is the implication that, as a result of some past experience or experiences, the rememberer does something or is able to do something which has an appropriate sort of correspondence with that initiating experience. The nature of that initiating experience and of the correspondence between it and the later acts and abilities of the rememberer will vary with the type of remembering involved. Thus in the case of "skill" memory, remembering how to do something I will be able to do something I previously learned to do. If I remember to do something I do that thing as a result of a previously formulated intention to do it. In the case of the other constructions listed above the initiating experiences will consist in the acquisition of information which I am later able to call to mind. The exact nature of the connection between the initiating event and the later performance or ability, which must hold if it is to be a genuine case of remembering, is difficult to formulate. But it is clear that not *any* sort of causal link between the two is adequate to justify a memory claim (Martin and Deutscher 1966).

In general what I remember, the object of memory, will be quite distinct from the initiating experience. For example I may recollect that King Harold was struck in the eye by an arrow at the battle of Hastings, but I do not have to have been present in order to remember that fact. I may well have forgotten the initiating experiences which probably took place in early childhood. Personal memory, as it is sometimes called, remembering playing a round of golf for example, is an exception. Here the experiences remembered are themselves the occurrences which "initiate" the later recollections.

Many philosophers have written as though memory is, from an epistemological point of view, radically different from other sorts of knowledge; as though it were a way of acquiring knowledge about the past, rather as perception is a way of acquiring knowledge about the present (e.g. Hume 1739, Bergson 1896, Russell 1921). Such a viewpoint leads to, or at least exacerbates, problems about the grounds we use in judging that we are remembering, rather than imagining, and to theories about memory which are somewhat analogous to traditional answers to the problem of perception. It appears, however, that such a viewpoint is mistaken, since in the main personal memory is distinguished merely by the first hand nature of the initial acquisition of the remembered information. JMS

Bibliography

Bergson, H. 1896: *Matière et memoire.* Paris.

Holland, R.F. 1954: The empiricist theory of memory, *Mind* 63. 252, 464–86.

Hume, D. 1739: *A treatise of human nature.* Bk I, pt III, sect. IV.

Martin, C. and Deutscher, M. 1966: Remembering. *Philosophical review* 75, 161–96.

Russell, B. 1921: *The analysis of mind.* London: Allen and Unwin; New York: Macmillan.

memory: short term and long term The distinction between short term and long term memory (STM and LTM) was made by Melton in 1962: STM was defined as retention over intervals of up to five minutes, while LTM referred to retention over longer intervals. Other investigators have drawn the line at intervals as brief as ten seconds; most, however, have assumed that short term memory spans a maximum interval of thirty seconds to three minutes. The accuracy with which a verbal item can be recognized or recalled has been said to decline monotonically in time from its moment of initial encoding.

The distinction between STM and LTM is one of convenience and is difficult to defend for two reasons. First, STM and LTM are governed in similar ways by the same variables. Second, if the subject's attention is suitably controlled, memory for a given item does not decline as the retention interval increases from one to thirty-two seconds. What does cause it to do so is not the passage of time as such but rather the amount of *non-specific interference*, or the number of shifts of attention, which follow the initial registration of an event (Waugh and Norman 1968).

It is now accepted that STM is subserved by two independent systems, primary and secondary memory (PM and SM). PM is a limited-capacity store in which verbal information is retained in the exact order in which it occurred. Such a store is essential if we are to understand spoken language. The trace of a given event registered in PM does not decay autonomously in time but is overwritten by the traces of later attended-to events, irrespective of their similarity to the trace in question. Secondary memory, on the other hand, seems to be a store of effectively unlimited capacity. It is, however, full of gaps and distortions. The accessibility of information in SM – which may perhaps be loosely identified with episodic memory – is subject to *specific interference* from the traces of similar events.

Retrieval from PM is significantly faster than retrieval from SM; and time to retrieve information from either store increases throughout the adult years, retrieval time from SM increasing at a relatively rapid rate (Waugh et al. 1978).

Information recalled after even a brief retention interval may already have been displaced from PM. It may however, be available in SM. Hence it is not surprising that STM and LTM share common properties.

It has sometimes been claimed that the best evidence for the existence of two independent post-sensory stores underlying STM comes from studies of patients suffering from a global anterograde amnesia. Such individuals have a nearly-normal digit-span (i.e. they can reproduce a list of approximately seven digits in their original order immediately after they have seen or heard the list), and yet after a brief period of distraction they may have no memory of performing that task. They accordingly would seem to have an intact PM but a grossly impaired SM. And yet they still remember the meanings of words and the rules of grammar, so that they can understand and enunciate ordinary sentences.

In these individuals, then, such well-established skills as the ability to remember syntactic and semantic features of language, to use the rules of arithmetic, or to read and to write are seemingly intact. This fact suggests the existence of a third system, *tertiary memory*, which (along with secondary memory in the normal subject) underlies memory tested after relatively long retention intervals. Information can often be recovered from tertiary memory more rapidly than from primary memory; and time to retrieve information from tertiary memory does not seem to increase throughout the adult years. NCW

Bibliography

Melton, A.M. 1962: Comments on Professor Peterson's paper. In *Verbal behavior and learning: problems and processes*, C.N. Cofet and B.S. Musgrave. New York: McGraw-Hill.

——— 1963: Implications of short-term memory for a general theory of memory. *Journal of verbal learning and verbal behavior* 1, 1–21.

Waugh, N.C. and Norman, D.A. 1968: The measure of interference in primary memory. *Journal of verbal learning and verbal behavior* 7, 617-26.

Waugh, N.C. Thomas, J.C. and Fozard, J.L. 1978: Retrieval time from different memory stores. *Journal of gerontology* 33, 718-24.

memory: state dependence Events learned in one mental state are remembered better when one is put back into the same state. The state may be one that occurs naturally or one that is induced by hypnosis or by drugs such as alcohol and marijuana. The individual's state at the time of learning becomes associated with what is being learned. Reactivation of that state facilitates retrieval of relatively inaccessible information which is stored in memory. For example, persons who are hypnotically induced into experiencing a happy mood will recall more pleasant childhood memories than persons who are induced into experiencing a sad mood (Bower).

Drug state-dependent memory was originally demonstrated by psychopharmacologists in learning experiments with animals. The effect of both pharmacologically-induced state-dependent memory and hypnotically-induced mood state-dependent memory have been demonstrated in humans. Returning to the same state as at the time of learning leads to improved recall of events, particularly when one must remember the exact temporal order among the events. MAS

Bibliography

Bower, G.H. 1981: Mood and memory. *American psychologist* 36, 151–75.

Weingartner, H. 1978: Human state-dependent learning. In *Drug discrimination and state-dependent learning* ed. B.T. Ho, B.W. Richards, and D.L. Chute (eds): New York: Academic Press.

memory: theories of Three research issues are discussed first, and some representative current theories of memory are then outlined. All the work discussed here is within the domain of cognitive psychology. Neural and biochemical approaches are not considered.

short term/long term memory distinction
(See also MEMORY: SHORT TERM AND LONG TERM) Short term memory has a capacity of about five items if there are no competing resource demands, somewhat less if attention must be divided between short term maintenance of information and other processes (about two items are recalled from short term memory in free-recall tasks). If maintenance rehearsal is not permitted information is lost from short term memory at a rate approximated by an exponential function which starts at 100 per cent and decays to its asymptote in 20 – 30 seconds. The asymptote of the curve represents long-term memory. James (1890) referred to short-term memory as primary memory and distinguished it from secondary memory. Primary memory contains information that has never left consciousness; once an item leaves primary memory/consciousness, it recedes into a passive unconscious state from which it can be returned to consciousness only by a process of retrieval, which may or may not be successful.

Techniques to separate behaviorally the short and long term memory components of retention involve interference with the short term components of recall. If subjects are given a list of, say, fifteen words to study, their recall will show a recency effect, in that the last four to five items will be recalled better than the items in the middle of the list. This recency effect is only obtained, however, if recall follows immediately upon the presentation of the list, when subjects typically produce the last items of the list first, presumably from their still active short term buffer. If a thirty second period filled with some rehearsal-preventing task such as backward counting intervenes before subjects are allowed to start recalling, the recency effect is wiped out, presumably because the contents of the short term buffer have been lost. Studies such as this have traditionally been considered to indicate separate, distinct short term and long term memory stores. However recent research has shown that not all of the recency effect normally observed can be ascribed to short term memory effects, some of it being due to special learning strategies adopted by the subjects in such memory experiments.

Statistical techniques are also used to separate short and long term retention components. They are based on the assumption that total recall at any serial position in a list of words is composed of two independent components, the short and long term memory contributions: $R = (S + L) - (S \cdot L)$, where R, S and L are the probabilities of recall, short term and long term memory, respectively. It is assumed that the value of L is the same for all items of a list (except for those showing a primacy effect) and is equal to the observed recall (R) for the items in the middle of a list (where there is no recall from short-term memory). Hence both R and L can be estimated empirically and values for S can be computed.

This traditional model of short and long term memory is a good first approximation, though care must be taken not to treat the "separate boxes" metaphor too seriously. In many ways there is a continuity between the two stores, and a more accurate metaphor would be to describe the short term store as the momentarily active portion of long term memory: consciousness is only able to illuminate a small section of memory at a time, as a tiny flashlight might produce a circle of light in a huge dark room. So long as an item is caught in this light it is active and accessible to conscious experience, but as soon as the light is needed elsewhere, it is lost and special retrieval procedures are needed to find it again.

Short term memory processes, because of their limited capacity, appear to constitute a bottleneck for many complex cognitive processes (problem solving, discourse comprehension); hence, short term memory buffers figure as crucial components in many cognitive theories.

Levels of Encoding
How well information can be retrieved from long term memory depends on how it is encoded at the time of study and on the retrieval cues used. In considering encoding processes the relevant dimensions appear to be ones of depth of encoding and elaborateness. The metaphor of encoding depth refers to the nature of the encoding processes, which may vary from superficial, shallow levels (such as reading a word, pronouncing it, attending to its

graphic features, etc.) to deep, meaningful levels (attending to the meaning of a word, forming an image, noting its emotional value, relating it to oneself in one way or another, and finding a place for it in some overall organizational schema). Deep levels of encoding produce better learning and retention than do shallow levels. Indeed, if persons whose memory is poor are induced to encode learning materials deeply, they are often able to overcome their memory deficits.

Elaborateness plays a similar role: it helps to encode the remembered material in many different ways, in different situations and contexts, and at different times. Encoding variability ensures retrieval efficiency: makes it possible for a wide variety of retrieval cues to reproduce it.

The memory trace can be considered to be a by-product of whatever perceptual or cognitive processing has occurred. There is no separate process "storage in memory". Instead, we remember what we do. But some of the things we do are more memorable than others: the more meaningful the processing, the more the processing involves relating one item to others or to pre-existing memory traces, the more memorable the processing.

Retrieval

The success of retrieval depends on how well the retrieval cue reinstates the original conditions of encoding. The retrieval cue must (partially) match a memory structure before it can produce it. Hence the memory trace and the retrieval cue must share some significant component for a partial match to occur (the "encoding specificity" principle).

Organization plays a role in memory because it facilitates retrieval: the memory trace which is to be retrieved can be specified (partially) by its content but also by its location in a memory structure. Whenever some learning material is structured in accordance with some knowledge already available (e.g. words from different conceptual categories, or sets of thematically related words), the pre-existing knowledge structure is used to organize the new learning material (e.g. in text comprehension, pre-existing knowledge forms a schematic structure to which the new text that is being read can be tied). When recall is attempted later on, the same knowledge schemata are used to guide the retrieval process. If a learner is confronted with unorganized material, organization of that material will still be attempted, except that the outcome of this process varies from individual to individual and is unpredictable ("subjective organizations"), while in more structured situations everyone will employ more or less the same schema for organizing the material.

Formal Models of Memory

Several formal models of memory exist today that account adequately for a large number of the memory phenomena that have been studied in the laboratory. The following approaches do so by invoking rather different principles. Raaijmakers and Shiffrin (1981) have developed a search model of memory retrieval. A given retrieval cue matches and implicitly retrieves a memory trace, with a likelihood depending on the relative amount of overlap between the two. Once a trace is implicitly retrieved it is not necessarily produced: the absolute amount of overlap between the retrieval cue and the trace determines whether or not an implicitly retrieved item is actually recalled. The composition of the retrieval cue is strategically controlled in this model, while the actual retrieval mechanism is automatic. Metcalf and Murdock present a distributed memory model in which retrieval is treated quite differently. The memory trace as well as the retrieval cue are considered to be vectors of features, and the retrieval cue selects the memory trace that resonates most strongly by a process of intercorrelation. While the basic assumptions these models make about memory differ drastically, they account for approximately the same range of data. In addition there is at least one other general theory of memory of equal scope. At present we have no way of ranking these theories: memory theorists essentially agree on the important laboratory phenomena to which their theories are addressed, and they agree at the level of principles and processes, but not about the underlying mechanisms. Different theories predict the same phenomena at the behavioral level, but behavioral data alone may not provide sufficient constraints for modelling the underlying mechanisms. WKi

Bibliography

James, W. 1890: *Principles of psychology*. New York: Holt.

*Kintsch, W. 1977: *Memory and cognition*. New York and London: Wiley/Krieger.

Metcalf, J. and Murdock, B.B. 1981: An encoding and retrieval model of single-trial free recall. *Journal of verbal learning and verbal behavior*. 20, 161–89.

Raaijmakers, J.G.W. & Shiffrin, R.M. 1981: Search of associative memory. *Psychological review*. 88, 93–134.

memory *See* brain stimulation and memory; brain lesions and memory; computer simulation of cognitive processes; emotion and memory

memory and forgetting: psychoanalytic theories As with all theoretical and clinical systems, evolution over time has allowed some features of psychoanalysis to be changed and others to remain unaltered and the nature of memory and the process of forgetting as understood within psychoanalysis can be portrayed by describing the historical developments.

Psychoanalysis began with Breuer and Freud's clinical observations (see Freud 1893–95) that the symptoms of hysteria could be interpreted as symbolic representations of traumatic memories that could not be recalled because of the meaning, for the subject, of the content of the memories. Therapeutic help consisted, in the early days of Freud's psychotherapeutic work, of pressurizing the patient to rediscover the covered up memories. Freud noted that, in fortunate circumstances, recovering lost memories produced apparent cure; the symptom as a disguised form of remembrance was replaced by a direct memory, accompanied by some of the feelings appropriate to the originating traumatic experience. The events of the traumatic experience were, according to Freud's observations, sexual in nature and not available for conscious recall because social conventions forbade the sexual arousal in the (usually) young person. The event was commonly thought to have been a seduction by a household member or the witnessing of sexuality between family members. Hysterical patients were said to be suffering from "reminiscence" and psychotherapy consisted of the development of actual recall so that what had before been unconscious would now become conscious. Memory and forgetting became, thereby, central preoccupations of psychoanalysis, and have remained so to this day despite the fact that there have been vast changes in the formulation of psychoanalytic theories, and the techniques and subject matter of psychoanalytic therapies.

In his earliest psychoanalytic writings Freud considered that recall of the traumatic circumstances underlying the development of neurotic symptoms was prevented by the quantity of emotion tied up in the original experience, or evoked by the events of the trauma somehow being on the threshold of recall. The prevention of access of uncomfortable or disturbing memories to consciousness was described as *defense* and this notion, so relevant to the psychoanalytic theory of memory and forgetting, remains central to this day.

The next step in the development of the subject came in a series of unpublished letters from Freud to Wilhelm Fliess which are known as a "Project for a Scientific Psychology" (Freud 1950) written in 1895. In this document perception and memory were ascribed to separate systems of the nervous system, an idea that has been retained within contemporary psychoanalytic thinking. Moreover Freud emphasized, in these writings, the importance of motivation affecting memory and recall and he differentiated between conscious logical rational thinking (known as "secondary process thinking") which utilized memories in ways acceptable to the waking, public aspects of thinking and those forms of thought observable in dreams and in neurotic symptom formation. In this form of thinking ("primary process thinking") memories are laid down according to the pressure of strong instinctual forces e.g. the sex drives ("libido") whose "energies" (hypothesized as having potentially measurable qualitative and quantitative aspects) distort the form of the memories and, above all, determined the pressure with which such memories seek access to consciousness and are substantially opposed by the forces mobilized by the waking, conscious mind: primary process thinking shows an absence of control by the rational waking mind. Memories are linked by emotional association, by chance associations, by processes of symbolization, a part can stand for a whole and vice versa and several memories may be contained within one thought ("condensation").

These conceptualizations became greatly elaborated and firmly enshrined in psychoanalytic theory in Freud's *Interpretation of dreams* (1900) in which an extensive account of a model of the mind was given. In this, consciousness was ascribed to but a small area of the mind and of mental activity. It was assumed to be the quality of thinking in the "system Conscious" within which thoughts and memories became conscious by receiving sufficient "attention cathexis". A subjacent layer of the mind, the "system Preconscious" contained thoughts and memories which could be recalled relatively easily by receiving attention cathexis. Within this system thoughts proceeded according to the secondary processes, that is to say they were largely rational and could be expressed publicly without being regarded as strange or disordered. The system Preconscious was considered to be separated from yet a deeper layer of the mind, the "system Unconscious". Here thoughts were marked by the imprint of intense emotionally charged sexual energies. Connections between trains of thought in this system were marked by the primary process that characterizes the thinking of dreams, the formation of myths, poetic and artistic images, and which underlie the meaningfulness that psychoanalytic clinicians see in slips of the tongue, symptomatic acts and neurotic and psychotic forms of disturbed thinking. Memories within the system Unconscious are forcibly kept out of consciousness and are said to be, thereby, dynamically unconscious.

Because of the intensity of the instinctual drive derived from energies attached to the memories and wishes within the system Unconscious they are considered to be seeking expression ("discharge") in the form of actions or conscious representation and recall. Such expression is prevented by a hypothetical "censor" located between the two deepest layers of the mind that serves as an agency of defense. At the censor, unconscious memories are processed by disguise and distortion until they can be expressed in the more conscious layers of the mind without threatening the survival of the person or giving offense to social constraints.

This model of the mind ("the topographical model") remains in clinical use by psychoanalysts although many contemporary theorists have abandoned the notions of mental energies or have retained them only as metaphorically useful. The notion that forgetting can be seen as a forceful expulsion of unwelcome, disruptive or socially unacceptable thoughts, is completely retained and is ascribed, to this day, to a variety of defensive activities ("the mechanisms of defense"). The distortion and control of memories by primary process thinking whereby recall is inhibited or modified by reason of the meaning attached to the thoughts, is a fundamental aspect of contemporary psychoanalytic thinking. Moreover, it was postulated by Freud, in the early years of this century (Freud 1905) that early childhood memories were all subject to massive repression constituting the "amnesia of childhood". Freud himself thought that the large scale suppression of childhood memories was due to their being linked to the intense and forbidden sexual wishes of the child. Later Freud and other psychoanalysts added the intensity of sadistic, aggressive childhood wishes to the reasons for this repression. Yet other analysts have suggested that the strong anxieties and envy proposed as dominating childhood mental life may also account for the infantile amnesia.

Other psychoanalysts have put forward the notion that the amnesia is mainly the consequence of the shedding of redundant wishes and patterns of activity and expression. Whatever the reasons thought to account for the paucity and distortion of early childhood memories, the fact of childhood amnesia is important in psychoanalytic theory and clinical practice: the reconstruction of an outline knowledge of a patient's childhood experiences is a regular part of psychoanalytic psychotherapy.

In the third decade of this century Freud revised his model of the mind (Freud 1923 and 1926) by proposing a tripartite division into the ego, the superego and the id (the "structural model") (see FREUD). Memory was given as a function of the ego which was also conceived as having control of recall, conscious logical thinking, of carrying out defensive functions and of synthesizing and integrating the overall activity of the mental apparatus. This reorganization of the psychoanalytic model of the mind was thought necessary in order to express the fact that defensive operations causing memory lapses, for example, were directed against unconscious impulses affecting the content of the memories but the operations were themselves also unconscious and inaccessible to recall (except during and by means of the process of psychoanalysis).

The major innovation of the model was the idea of the superego. This was put forward as an agency of the mind in which the rules for behavior, parents' prohibitions and aspirations for their children, become incorporated within the mind of the growing child and become, in the end, rules, ideals and requirements which consciously and unconsciously govern not only behavior but also attitudes towards the self.

In the structural model personal expression, symptom formation and identity are considered to be the outcome of the pressures of the instinctual drives coming from the id, which are controlled and shaped in their expression by the balance of ego and superego activities.

The memories of the relationship with the parents and other significant adults, are enshrined within the mind as having major effects on personality. Increasingly, contemporary psychoanalytic theory is concerned with the way in which internalizations of personal experiences in relation to significant others are the dominating memory systems, built up into a representational world structuring large aspects of experience including processes of memory and forgetting. CD

Bibliography

Freud, S. 1893–1895: Studies on hysteria. *Standard edition of the psychological work of Sigmund Freud*. Vol II. London: Hogarth Press. New York: Norton.

——1895: Project for a scientific psychology. *Standard edition* vol I.

——1905: Three essays on sexuality. *Standard edition* vol VII.

——1900: Interpretation of dreams. *Standard edition* vols IV & V.

——1923: The ego and the id. *Standard edition* vol XIX.

——1926: Inhibitions, symptoms and anxiety. *Standard edition* vol. XX.

memory and learning: physiological bases This is concerned with (a) the neurophysiological, neurochemical and neuroanatomical foundations of the structural organization of memory and (b) the neurobiological mechanisms associated with alterations of memory (plasticity) as a function of experience (learning).

On a conceptual level the structure of longterm memory (LTM) is assumed to be the repository of most of our knowledge and skills. Information within LTM has been divided into episodic and semantic memory components. Episodic memory records information about spatio-temporal dated events which have autobiographical reference (context). The context consists of the external environment and the internal states of the organism, including affect. Semantic or reference memory concerns our permanent knowledge of the world and primarily concerns concepts and rules. It can be subdivided into (a) sensory – perceptual knowledge, which concerns the processing of sensory information, the generation of images and the storage of cognitive maps, (b) procedural – motoric knowledge, which concerns the processing of motor skills (e.g., skiing or speech production), and (c) declarative or propositional knowledge which includes our knowledge of general facts.

Contemporary views assume that these function systems are organized as a network of interconnected nodes. The connections, links or associations between and within nodes are assumed to be organized in a multi-level heterarchical fashion, that is components at one level subsume a structured set of components at a lower level, and are themselves subsumed within yet higher level units. Each node is subdivided into levels and each level is composed of attributes.

The LTM system can be in either an inactive or active state. To be in an active state the LTM system has to be triggered by sensory or data-driven input and/or by conceptually or memory-driven input. Once a subset of nodes is activated in LTM, activation will spread to other interconnected nodes (spreading activation) and will last for a short time (short-term memory) or a somewhat longer time (working memory), depending upon the degree of attention, rehearsal or consolidation (controlled processing). The greater the amount of controlled processing the longer the duration of activation, and the greater the probability of change within the LTM network of nodes.

On a neurobiological level it is thought that the anatomical structure subserving LTM is either distributed, that is the whole central nervous system codes every memory (mass action) or is relatively localized, that is specific neural "units" participate in mediation of specific memories. Even though there is a problem in defining the critical neural unit of analysis (e.g., SYNAPSE, synaptic conglomerate, synaptic assembly, NEURON, neural assembly, junctional thicket, simple circuit, neural region, system or complex system) the contemporary view is that specific neural regions, though overlapping and interacting to a great extent, contribute to a subset of nodes which comprise the structure of LTM. Many neural regions contribute to LTM structure, but at the highest level of organization there are a few regions that appear to be of critical importance. These include the CEREBRAL CORTEX, hippocampal formation, amygdaloid complex and caudate nucleus. The cerebral cortex subserves all the functional systems involved with semantic memory; the HIPPOCAMPUS is involved in processing the environmental contextual component of episodic memory; the amygdaloid complex contributes to the coding of internal states including affect; and the caudate nucleus processes additional information involved in procedural knowledge.

The cerebral cortex can be divided into major interconnected regions such as frontal, temporal, parietal, and occipital lobes which include primary sensory and motor areas as well as association areas. It has been suggested that the functional unit that corresponds to lower-level nodes might be the small cortical columns within the sensory and motor cortical areas. The functional unit that mediates higher-order level nodes might be the larger cortical columns within the association cortical areas (Eccles 1980).

Based on lesion, electrical stimulation, and electrical recording techniques as well as brain pathology in both animals and humans, it has been possible to uncover dissociations which imply specificity of function of the cortical columnar organization subserving the semantic node network.

For example, language (verbal) information is mainly, but not exclusively, stored on one side of the cerebral cortex (usually the left in humans), while visuo-spatial (nonverbal) information is stored mainly on the right side of the cortex (see LATERALIZATION). Support for this verbal – nonverbal dissociation is derived from the observation that (a) brain damage to the left cerebral cortex produces primarily language problems, while brain damage to the right cerebral cortex produces primarily visuo-spatial problems, and (b) a cut of the corpus callosum which disconnects the two sides of the cerebral cortex results in patients who can process and store primarily language information with the left side and primarily visuo-spatial information with the right (Gazzaniga and LeDoux 1978; Geschwind 1970).

Within the language semantic memory network a neural region within the left frontal lobe known as Broca's area mediates motoric aspects of language knowledge, while a neural region within the left temporal lobe known as Wernicke's area mediates propositional aspects of language knowledge.

Within the visuo-spatial semantic memory network the frontal lobe mediates egocentric or personal space (space based on perspective), while the parietal lobe mediates allocentric or absolute space (space based on invariance, i.e., cognitive map) (Semmes et al. 1963).

In contrast to the cerebral cortex involvement with semantic memory the hippocampal formation is a critical neural region involved in the mediation of the environmental contextual component of episodic memory. This conclusion is based on the observation that bilateral medial temporal lobe damage including the hippocampal formation in animals and humans produces an extensive and durable memory loss for new episodic information (Kesner 1983; Milner 1974). Patients with hippocampal damage appear to forget rather quickly events that occur in their daily life: they are usually unable to tell you where they are, what they had for breakfast or when they met you previously. In contrast they are able to converse normally at least about events that occurred before their brain damage, their verbal skills are intact and they can carry out mental arithmetic. Furthermore they can reasonably well learn and retain a variety of rules of specific procedural–motoric knowledge skills (tracking, mirror tracing, eye-lid conditioning) and declarative knowledge skills (mirror reading, rule-based verbal paired-associate learning, rules of card games) while not remembering having previously performed the task, the specific contingencies of the task, or when and where they learned the task (see MEMORY AND LEARNING DISORDERS).

Changes from an inactive to an active state in critical neural regions that comprise LTM can be indexed by dynamic changes in electrical firing patterns and biochemical functions. The duration of this active state is influenced by a large number of parameters. One neural mechanism that could mediate and maintain an active state for a long time is known as longterm potentiation. It can be measured readily in the hippocampal formation. Longterm activation (consolidation) increases the probability that relatively permanent changes (learning) might occur within the structure of LTM. Support for the idea that longterm activation might be necessary for new learning comes from the observation that pharmacological and electrical brain stimulation treatments can modify the storage and subsequent retrieval of new information within LTM (McGaugh and Herz 1972); on a time-dependent basis (that is, treatments are effective in altering information for only a limited duration after exposure to a new learning experience).

On neurophysiological, neurochemical and neuroanatomical levels of analysis, changes in neuronal firing patterns, in phosphorylation of membrances, in synaptic efficacy, and formation of new peptides, proteins, and synapses as well as dendritic differentiation have been proposed as critical mechanisms capable of mediating the restructuring of LTM.

The goal is to understand the mechanisms of plasticity within specific neuronal "units" in order to characterize and describe further the dynamic and structural aspects of long term memory. RPK

Bibliography

Eccles, John C. 1980: *The human psyche.* Heidelberg: Springer Verlag.

Gazzaniga, M.S., and LeDoux, J.E. 1978: *The integrated mind.* New York: Plenum Press.

Geschwind, N. 1970: The organization of language and the brain. *Science* 170, 940–44.

Kesner, R.P. 1983: Mnemonic functions of the hippocampus: correspondence between animals and humans. *Conditioning: representation of neural function,* ed. C.D. Woody. New York: Plenum Press.

Lachman, R., Lachman, J.L., and Sutterfield, E.C., eds. 1979: *Cognitive psychology and information processing: introduction.* Hillsdale, N.J.: Lawrence Erlbaum Associates.

McGaugh, J.L., and Herz, M.M. 1972: *Memory consolidation.* San Franciso: Freeman.

Milner, B. 1974: Hemispheric specialization: scope and limits. In *The neurosciences: third research program,* ed. F.O. Schmitt and F.G. Warden. Cambridge, Mass.: MIT Press.

Rosenzweig, M.R., and Bennett, E.L., eds. 1976: *Neural mechanisms of learning and memory.* Cambridge, Mass.: MIT Press.

Semmes, J. et al 1963: Correlates of impaired orientation in personal and extrapersonal space. *Brain* 86, 747–72.

Teyler, T., ed. 1978: *Brain and learning*. Stamford, Connecticut: Greylock Inc.

Whitty, C.W.M., and Zangwill, O.L., eds. 1977: *Amnesia: clinical, psychological and medicolegal aspects*. London and Boston: Butterworth.

memory and learning: synaptic structure theories and intracellular chemical theories These theories postulate that the changes in nervous tissue underlying learning and the formation of memory involve either the growth of new synapses or the alteration of the properties of existing synapses. A SYNAPSE is the area of communication between one nerve cell and another. The communication usually occurs when a signal (ACTION POTENTIAL) in one NEURON leads to the release of a chemical transmitter from its terminals. The transmitter diffuses across the synaptic gap and combines with a receptor molecule in the membrane of the postsynaptic cell. This combination then leads either to activation (excitation) or depression (inhibition) of activity in the postsynaptic cell. Synapses may occur on the cell body (soma and dendrites) or on the initial segment of the axon of a neuron, in which case they can either excite or inhibit the generation of the action potential. Synapses may also be present on the axon terminals, in which case their action is to modulate the release of transmitter from the terminals when a nerve action potential arrives down the axon.

Before much was known about the nature of synaptic transmission Hebb (1949) suggested that the formation of long term memories could occur via the development of new synaptic knobs which would thus increase the area of contact between the axon of one neuron and the cell body of another. As more information became available, he also included the possibility that an existing synapse might become more effective perhaps through an increase in the amount of transmitter in the presynaptic terminal. There is some evidence that large changes in environmental conditions (such as a change from dark to light in previously dark-reared young animals (Rose 1980)) lead to changes in the number of synapses detectable by anatomical methods. However, the majority of present theories of the physical basis of learning and memory propose modification of existing synapses. The types of changes which have been proposed include: altering the width of the synaptic gap (Hyden 1974); altering the effectiveness of the presynaptic action potential in activating transmitter release (Kandel 1978; Mark 1979); altering the affinity or number of postsynaptic receptors for the neurotransmitter (Rose 1980). Such modification could lead to either an increase or a decrease in the efficacy of transmission at a synapse. Any particular memory would presumably involve modification of a large number of synapses. The memory would then be coded in terms of which synapses were modified and in each case whether the modification involved depression or activation. This point of view concerning how a memory is coded need, in principle, require only one species of synaptic molecule, which would be either increased or decreased in number or activity. There might be a number of ways in which the modification of this molecule could be brought about, but the hypothesis does not require a vast range of different molecules to code for different memories.

In the late 1950s and 1960s the climate of scientific opinion was different and there was a surprisingly wide acceptance of the idea that memories should be coded molecularly – one memory, one molecule. This led to the search for such memory molecules. The major strategy in this search was to train animals on a task and then kill them and administer homogenates or extracts of their brain (or even of their whole bodies in the case of planaria) to naive animals and see whether the memory was transferred. A number of positive results were reported. However they were difficult or impossible to replicate, and in the case of the transfer of information between planaria by cannibalism it was found that the animals had not learnt the task but had merely been pseudoconditioned (Jensen 1965). Another problem with the early transfer experiments was that they purported to show transfer of an RNA code from one animal to another via oral ingestion or by injection, and yet the RNA would have been most unlikely to have remained intact or if it had to have been able to gain access to brain cells. For these reasons, the idea of memories being coded individually by RNA has fallen into disrepute.

However, one sort of transfer experiment has been replicated in some laboratories. This is the ability of a peptide (named scotaphobin) apparently formed in the brain of rats during training in a one-trial dark avoidance situation to cause dark avoidance in mice injected with it (Ungar, Desiderio and Parr 1972). While the significance of this finding is not understood it is probably related to the finding that a number of other peptides which are found in the brain and elsewhere, which are whole or are parts of neurohormones (viz. vasopressin, oxytocin, the 4–10 part of ACTH, encephalins, etc.) can have profound and fairly specific effects on behavior including learning and memory (de Wied and Jolles 1982). It is perfectly possible that the synthesis, release and action of these and other peptides is involved in the modulation of synaptic activity underlying learning and memory.

Research into the biochemical basis of learning and memory has involved experiments both on complex animals learning complex tasks and also on simpler "models of learning". In both cases two main approaches have been used; the interventional and the correlational. In the first the strategy is to look for drugs which have a well-defined action at the molecular level and see whether they interfere with learning and memory storage and/or retrieval. In the second approach, animals are taught a task and then a search is made for biochemical/physiological changes in the nervous system correlated with the acquisition of the memory. A major problem in this latter sort of experiment is what controls should be used since even "rested" controls may be learning something and "yoked" controls (which for example receive matched non-contingent shocks every time an experimental animal receives a contingent shock) undoubtedly learn something (e.g. "whatever I do I can't get away from the shock").

Simple models of learning include single synapses such as the neuromuscular junction of vertebrates. Here it is well known that synaptic efficacy can be increased for periods as long as an hour if the nerve is stimulated tetanically, that is by a rapid repetition of the stimulus, (say 30 shocks/second for 60 seconds) – post-tetanic potentiation. The molecular basis of this process is not fully understood, but it is likely to involve increased effectiveness of an action potential in the presynaptic terminal in opening the calcium channels of the presynaptic membrane. (These channels allow calcium to enter and activate, by an as yet unknown mechanism, the release of transmitters from presynaptic vesicles probably by exocytosis).

Changes in the presynaptic release mechanism have been postulated to occur in another model of learning, that is long-term facilitation of synaptically-generated field potentials in the mammalian HIPPOCAMPUS (Bliss 1979). The hippocampus is an area of the brain which is widely believed to have a role in learning and memory in man and other mammals. It has been shown that infrequent repetition of tetanic stimulation of inputs such as the perforant path (which runs from the entorhinal cortex to the granule cells of the dentate gyrus) leads to potentiation of the granule cells' responses to single stimuli to the perforant path. This potentiation can last for many weeks and may well be a component of memory systems.

Another example of presynaptic changes underlying long-term alteration of synaptic efficacy has been elegantly demonstrated by Kandel (1978) in the marine snail, *Aplysia.* The gill withdrawal reflex of this animal in response to stimulation of the siphon or the mantle has been shown to habituate or under different circumstances to become sensitized. Such habituation and sensitization while not falling within a classical definition of learning has been used as a simple model of learning (and more recently, associative learning has also been demonstrated in this animal). Long term habituation, lasting days or even weeks, is produced if four training sessions, of ten stimuli each, are given on consecutive days. The habituation of responses has been postulated to involve a decrease in the number of calcium channels in the axon terminals of the sensory nerve cell in consequence of its own prolonged activity. Such a change could be brought about via presynaptic autoreceptors for the transmitter being released, or via changes in intraterminal ion content or might be more directly related to the presynaptic action potential. Similarly, the contrasting sensitization to noxious stimuli can also last for periods of weeks if the pattern of training is suitably chosen. In this case the mechanism is heterosynaptic, involving facilitation of the synaptic release of transmitter from the sensory nerve terminal by the terminal of an axon originating in the head of the animal, which synapses upon the sensory presynaptic terminal. It appears that the transmitter released from this presynaptically facilitating neuron may be 5-hydroxytryptamine (5HT) and there is some evidence that its effect may be exerted via an increase in the intracellular level of cyclic AMP which somehow increases the effectiveness of the voltage-dependent calcium channels in the sensory neuron terminal. Such an effect means that each nerve impulse in the sensitized sensory neuron would release more transmitter than before sensitization. This work of Kandel and his associates is the nearest that research has got to a molecular and physiological understanding of any learning process. Such work has become increasingly relevant to learning in "higher" animals as it has been extended into the study of associative learning (Kandel and Schwarz 1982).

It is of importance to emphasize that in all those cases where changes in synaptic efficacy have been demonstrated as an integral part of a model learning system, the changes have occurred presynaptically. It is also of considerable interest that the changes observed were qualitatively similar in *Aplysia* for both short-lived (up to a day) and long-lasting (weeks) habituation and sensitization.

These hypotheses which propose that modulation of presynaptic efficacy underlies learning and memory do not in themselves explain the long-lasting nature of the changes. Any theory of the biochemical basis of memory must take into account the remarkable durability of some memories – for example, childhood memories can persist into extreme old age in humans. The synaptic growth theory of course would appear to account for this durability of memory. If, however, memory involves near-permanent activation or inactivation of specific existing synapses, then we need to assume that there are new molecules synthesized as a correlate of learning which are involved in this modification. For example, if we consider the long-term sensitization of the *Aplysia* reflex, activation of a 5 HT-mediated synapse leads to activation of the enzyme adenylate cyclase which leads to an increase in cyclic AMP which acts via activation of another enzyme (probably a protein kinase) to depress activity in a membrane potassium channel. (Potassium current in this channel is required in the repolarization of the presynaptic membrane and hence in closing the calcium channels.) Long term changes in the effectiveness of transmitter release could involve long term changes in the properties of the protein kinase or the potassium channel itself. Such long term effects would probably require a change in the nature of the protein synthesized (perhaps production of different subunits). For this to occur, a signal must pass from the nerve terminals back to the cell body of the sensory neuron. This signal would then (say) switch on, either at the level of transcription of DNA in the nucleus, or at the level of translation in the cytoplasm, the synthesis of the new protein. The new protein would then be transported down the axon to be incorporated into the nerve terminal membrane. (Kandel and Schwarz, 1982, have hypothesized that the signal is cyclic AMP and that the new protein is a high affinity regulatory subunit of a protein kinase which is activated by cyclic AMP and interacts with the potassium channel. This theory would explain the permanence of long-term sensitization in *Aplysia* and proposes that cyclic AMP has the role both of the short-term sensitizing agent and the long term signal.)

It has often been suggested that memory involves the synthesis of new proteins. As mentioned earlier, these proteins do not need to be specific to any particular memory. There is ample evidence from correlational experiments that both learning of tasks such as a Y-maze discrimination task in rats, and models for learning including imprinting in chicks, are associated with increased incorporation of radioactive precursor into RNA, simple proteins and glycoproteins (Matthies 1979; Rose 1980; Routtenberg 1979). Furthermore, interventional studies, using drugs which inhibit protein synthesis have shown that it is possible to block either long term storage or long term retrieval processes by massively blocking protein synthesis (e.g. Squire and Barondes 1973). Such inhibition does not necessarily interfere with learning, although it can do where the learning procedure involves many trials.

Time-dependent changes in the susceptibility of memories to disruption are well known and have been built into a number of theories of memory formation. Mark (1979) studying one-trial aversion learning in the chick (they learnt not to peck an attractive object painted with nasty-tasting methyl-anthranilate) used ouabain to block the sodium pump (which normally pumps potassium ions into and sodium ions out of cells, and is responsible for keeping intracellular concentration of these ions constant). If the ouabain was given at the time of exposure to the aversive situation it blocked subsequent memory, but ouabain had no effect if administered after learning. In contrast, inhibition of protein synthesis with cycloheximide at the time of learning left memory unaffected for about half an hour, but later caused amnesia. Mark interpreted these findings by suggesting that activity at the "learning" synapses led to a small increase in intracellular sodium which activates the sodium-pump. He suggested that the increased flow of sodium out of the cell is an essential component of the memory formation and is coupled to an increase in the rate of entry of amino acids which would then stimulate protein synthesis (presumably at the cell body). This protein synthesis is necessary for the formation of the long-term memory. While there is no evidence either for or against such a suggestion, the protein concerned could of course be involved in the calcium channel as was proposed for the *Aplysia* synapse.

Another hypothesis which incorporates time-dependent changes in memory is the cholinergic theory of Deutsch (1973, ch. 3, pp. 59–76). There is a wealth of information, including clinical data, that cholinergic systems are involved in memory. Deutsch apparently showed that the susceptibility of memory (for a light-discrimination task) in rats to drugs which interact with cholinergic synapses, varied in a time-dependent way. He suggested that the formation of memory (and/or its retrieval system) involved a gradual increase in the efficacy of the nerve action potential in causing acetylcholine release in the hippocampus. He further proposed that forgetting involved a decrease in this efficacy. While not all Deutsch's findings are readily reproducible (see George and Mellanby 1974) the theory has been of value in providing readily testable predictions and in the discussion of clinical findings, including the memory deterioration found in old age and more dramatically in Alzheimer's disease.

In conclusion, it appears likely that the long-term changes underlying learning and memory involve presynaptic transmitter release mechanisms modulated via changes in the amounts or activity of membrane proteins.

JHM

Bibliography

Bliss, T.V.P. 1979: Synaptic plasticity in the hippocampus. *Trends in neuroscience* 2, 42–5.

Deutsch, J.A. 1973: *The physiological basis of memory*. New York and London: Academic Press.

de Wied, D. and Jolles, J. 1982: Neuropeptides derived from pro-opiocortin: behavioral, physiological, and neurochemical effects. *Physiological review*, 62, 976–1043.

George, G. and Mellanby, J. 1974: A further study of the effect of physostigmine on memory in rats. *Brain research* 81, 133–44.

Hebb, D.O. 1949: *The organization of behavior*. New York: John Wiley & Son; London: Chapman & Hall.

Hyden, H. 1974: A calcium-dependent mechanism for synapse and nerve cell membrane modulation. *Proceedings of the national academy of sciences*, New York. 71, 2965–8.

Jensen, D.D. 1965: Paramecium, planaria and pseudolearning. *Animal behaviour*. Supplement 1, 9–20.

Kandel, E.R. 1978: *A cell-biological approach to learning*. Grass Lecture Monograph 1. Bethesda, Maryland: Society for Neuroscience.

——— and Schwarz, J.H. 1982: Molecular biology of learning: Modulation of transmitter release. *Science*. 218, 433–43.

Mark R. 1979: Sequential biochemical steps in memory formation: evidence from the use of metabolic inhibitors. In *Brain mechanisms in memory and learning*, ed. M.A.B. Brazier. New York: Raven Press.

Matthies, H. 1979: Biochemical, electrophysiological and morphological correlates of brightness discrimination in rats. In *Brain mechanisms in memory and learning*, ed. M.A.B. Brazier. New York: Raven Press.

Rose, S.P.R. 1980: Neurochemical correlates of early learning in the chick. In *Neurobiological basis of learning and memory*, ed. Y. Tsukada and B.W. Agranoff. New York: John Wiley & Sons.

Routtenberg, A. 1979: Anatomical localization of phosphoprotein and glycoprotein substrates of memory. *Progress in neurobiology* 12, 85–113.

Squire, L.R. and Barondes, B.H. 1973: Memory impairment during prolonged training in mice given inhibitors of cerebral protein synthesis. *Brain research* 56, 215.

Ungar, G., Desiderio, D. and Parr, W. 1972: Scotophobia. *Nature* (London), 238, 198.

memory and learning disorders Difficulties in acquiring new information and/or in remembering past events. These disorders have many causes and can take a variety of forms. An initial classification can be made by distinguishing disorders of functional, or psychogenic, origin from disorders that result from neurological injury or disease. The former are relevant to psychiatry in that the nature of the disorder in any individual is believed to be related to conflict, repression and personality structure, the latter are relevant to neurology and neuroscience in that the nature of the disorder is related to the organization of memory in the normal brain (see MEMORY IMPAIRMENT).

Functional disorders of memory typically involve the loss of personal, autobiographic memory from part of a person's past, sometimes including his or her own identity. While the disorder persists, the ability to establish a record in memory of daily events can be normal, as can be the ability to remember external events (such as news items) that occurred during the affected time period.

This type of amnesia may be the best known, having been the subject of considerable dramatic treatment in films and literature. It is not, however, so common as the disorders of learning and memory that result from brain injury, disease or certain other agents having known effects on the central nervous system. These disorders mostly occur in the context of other neurological problems such as dementia, loss of vigilance, aphasia, or inattention. To some extent of course memory cannot be considered in isolation from other functions. If attention is poor acquisition of memory will be impaired. If language dysfunction occurs it may be difficult to remember or to recall words with the usual facility. One reason why memory complaints are so common in neurological and psychiatric clinics is that many kinds of neurological disorders affecting higher cortical functions have some impact on memory, even if the disorder does not primarily affect it.

These facts notwithstanding, neurological disorders of memory can also occur as a strikingly circumscribed deficit in which learning and memory are affected out of proportion to any other deficit of higher function. Amnesia can occur for a variety of reasons, e.g. after temporal lobe surgery, chronic alcohol abuse, head injury, anoxia, encephalitis, tumor or vascular accident. It has been known for almost 100 years that this disorder depends on disruption of normal function in one of two areas of the brain, the medial surface of the temporal lobes and the diencephalic midline of the brain in the region of the THALAMUS and HYPOTHALAMUS.

The amnesic patient who has sustained damage to one of these brain regions can appear normal to casual observation. Such a patient may have normal intellectual capacity, normal ability to hold information in immediate memory (digit span is normal), intact social skills and may retain knowledge acquired earlier in life. The defect lies in acquiring new memories and in recalling some recently acquired ones. Memory for the pre-morbid period is affected in a lawful way, so that recent memories are most, and old memories least, affected. Amnesia often occurs in the absence of confabulation or confusion and with awareness by the patient of his condition. The memory deficit is non-selective, that is it affects all sorts of information regardless of its importance and regardless of the sensory modality (visual, auditory, olfactory) through which information is presented.

This generalization holds when the involvement of the critical areas of the nervous system is bilateral. When involvement is unilateral, however, the amnesic disorder is material-specific, rather than global, i.e. the deficit in learning and memory involves either verbal material, in the case of left-sided injury or disease, or non-verbal material, in the case of right-sided injury or disease (see LATERALIZATION).

In the case of transient memory disorders, which can occur after head trauma, transient ischemic episodes, or electroconvulsive therapy, there are lawful features to the course of recovery. Anterograde amnesia, or loss of new learning capacity, gradually diminishes while retrograde amnesia, or loss of pre-morbid memory, gradually shrinks in a spontaneous fashion. During shrinkage of retrograde amnesia oldest memories tend to recover first and most recent memories last. This order is not absolute, however, and recovery often occurs by the emergence of islands of memory which join up to form a continuous record of past experience. Retrograde amnesia can continue to shrink after anterograde amnesia has subsided, but all patients are left with some lacuna in memory, consisting of the time during which anterograde amnesia was present together with some retrograde amnesia. The persisting retrograde amnesia is usually brief, perhaps just a few seconds, but it can sometimes cover several weeks or months prior to the onset of amnesia.

Neurological disorders of learning and memory can be usefully classified according to which region of the brain has been damaged. In amnesia caused by damage to the midline of the diencephalon (e.g. alcoholic Korsakoff syndrome) the memory deficit appears to involve a failure of registration or initial encoding of information in long term memory. Patients with this form of amnesia benefit from repetition, and exhibit normal forgetting rates for material they are able to learn. By contrast, in amnesia caused by medial temporal lobe dysfunction, the memory deficit seems to involve a failure of memory consolidation that ordinarily occurs after initial registration or encoding. These patients exhibit abnormally rapid forgetting of information they are able to learn.

Although amnesia can be severely disabling the deficit is narrower than was once thought. Amnesia does not affect all domains of learning and memory. Amnesic patients can exhibit learning of motor skills, as well as perceptual skills such as mirror-reading, and cognitive skills such as puzzle solving. Day-to-day learning of these skills can proceed normally in amnesia, despite the fact that patients may deny having performed such tasks before. The preservation of skills in amnesia has suggested a distinction between what has been termed procedural and declarative knowledge. Procedural learning, which is spared, is thought to result in the modification of tuning of existing schemata, and in knowledge that is implicit, i.e. accessible only by engaging in or applying the procedures in which the knowledge is contained. Declarative learning, which is not spared, refers to all the specific-item information that is the subject of conventional memory experiments such as faces, words and places. Memory for these facts is dependent on the brain regions damaged in amnesia. Thus amnesia involves a specific disorder in establishing and using declarative representations about past events.

The existence of severe disorders of learning and memory inevitably raises questions of treatment and rehabilitation. The memory disorder itself cannot be reversed because the disorder derives from damage to brain cells, which cannot be replaced. In general conditions that help normal memory also help impaired memory. Thus improved concentration, the use of imagery and repetition may all be useful to patients with disorders of learning and memory except in the most severe cases. Patients with left unilateral brain damage can benefit particularly from the use of imagery, because this strategy seems to engage right hemispheric brain systems to some degree and compensates in part for the effects of brain damage. There has also been considerable recent interest in the theory that memory disorders might be responsive to drug treatment. This hope springs from the discovery of the special role of dopaminergic neurons in Parkinson's disease and from the development of L-dopa for its treatment. Might some memory disorders reflect the disproportionate loss of one brain neurotransmitter system (see NEUROTRANSMITTER

SYSTEMS) that could respond to treatment with appropriate agonists? Despite a large body of experimental work, especially with drugs that influence the activity of cholinergic neurons (e.g. physostigmine, choline, lecithin) and with hormones (e.g. vasopressin), pharmacological treatments with clinical promise are not yet available..

Meanwhile the study of learning and memory disorders continues. It is of considerable scientific interest, both because of the frequency of memory problems in clinical patients and because analysis of these disorders can reveal so much about the neurological foundations of normal memory. (See also MEMORY AND LEARNING: PHYSIOLOGICAL BASES). LRS

Bibliography

Squire, L.R. 1982: The neuropsychology of human memory. *Annual review of neuroscience* 5, 241–73.

Squire, L.R., and Davis, H.P. 1981: The pharmacology of memory: a neurobiological perspective. *Annual review of pharmacology and toxicology* 21, 323–56.

Whitty, C.W.M., and Zangwill, O.L., eds. 1977: *Amnesia: clinical, psychological and medicolegal aspects.* London: Butterworth.

memory and mood Recent research has demonstrated that mood influences the type of material retrieved from memory. Past, positive personal experiences and certain positive words are more likely to be recalled when a person is in a happy mood than when he or she is in a depressed mood. Conversely, past, negative personal experiences and certain negative words are more likely to be recalled in a depressed mood than in a happy mood. State-dependent learning provides a plausible explanation of these findings (see LEARNING, STATE DEPENDENT). Clinically the effects of mood on memory are important because they may give us insight into the processes that control mood states. Cognitive theories of depression propose that certain negative thoughts produce depressed mood and many of the other symptoms of depression. Studies of the effects of mood on memory suggest that once an individual becomes depressed there is an increase in the frequency of just those cognitions that might maintain depression and a decrease in the frequency of those cognitions which might alleviate it. This reciprocal relationship between depressed mood and cognition could form the basis of a vicious circle that would serve to perpetuate depression. MM

Bibliography

Bower, G.H. 1981: Mood and memory. *American psychologist* 36, 129–48.

Teasdale, J.D. in press: Negative thinking in depression: cause, effect or reciprocal relationship? *Advances in behaviour research and therapy.*

memory images (eidetic images) Information stored in memory may either be language-derived or propositional, or it may be derived from sensory experiences, i.e. imagery processing. Imagery appears to be located in the right or nondominant hemisphere of the brain. The verbal and nonverbal abilities of people are known to be largely independent. It is possible to interfere specifically with verbal or imagery information in memory. Imagery is often taken as evidence of support for analogue processing (as opposed to discrete, propositional processes). However, arguments have been made that analogue and digital processes are formally equivalent. Forming mental images greatly enhances memory for verbal materials.

Eidetic images are of an almost photographic clarity. The eidetic image is, in fact, a visual experience rather than a true memory image. Persons with eidetic capability can read details off such images much as normal people can from an actual visual image. The ability declines after adolescence. Well-documented research cases with adults are rare. WKi

memory impairment Memory has several stages or processes which can show impairment in a global or generalized way, or in an isolated fashion. These stages are: *registration*, or ability to add new information; *retention*, or ability to store and consolidate information; *recall*, or ability to bring back consolidated material; and *recognition*, or ability to identify previously encountered data.

Memory functions can be impaired by organic factors, such as tumors, head injury, nutritional, metabolic and other conditions affecting the brain, or by psychological factors. In each case, the features of the memory dysfunction can help to identify the cause and the site of the lesion.

Amnesic states of organic origin can be due to damage to specific areas of the brain, or to generalized and diffuse cerebral disorder. The areas of the brain which are implicated in amnesic states are the hypothalamic–diencephalic region in the base of the brain, and the hippocampal area in the temporal lobe (see BRAIN AND CENTRAL NERVOUS SYSTEM: ILLUSTRATIONS fig. 11). Damage to these areas produces a characteristic picture of memory disturbance with ability to register information for very short periods but with very defective retention and recall. The ordering of events and time sense are seriously impaired. Remote memories may be preserved. Confabulation, or production of a false but coherent account of recent events, is typical of lesions to the hypothalamic–diencephalic area, as in Korsakoff's psychosis. Diffuse and generalized cerebral disorder, as in acute organic reactions or in dementia, tends to produce global impairment of memory, together with other cognitive disorders (see ORGANIC MENTAL STATES).

Psychogenic factors can cause memory impairment. Anxiety or depression can lead to inattention or poor concentration which, in turn, can prevent registration of new information. In dissociative hysteria the individual may suffer global amnesia with loss of personal identity or of memory for important aspects of the person's life, while the ability to register and retain information is usually maintained (see MEMORY AND LEARNING DISORDERS). JC

Bibliography

Lishman, W.A. 1978: *Organic psychiatry: the psychological consequences of cerebral disorders.* Oxford: Blackwell Scientific; St Louis, Missouri: C.V. Mosby.

memory in animals The retention of novel behavior or perception. In animal behavior we know about perception only through the behavior of the animal. By analogy with our own experience, however, we can distinguish between the recognition memory of sensory stimuli and the memory of how to perform certain activities.

An animal's repertoire of behavior is made up of innate patterns and of activities acquired through experience. We can distinguish between behavior due to instinct and that due to learning. The term memory is normally reserved for the retention of behavior acquired by the animal during its lifetime. It is not normally used for the retention of innate behavior.

Memory involves learning, storage and retention of information. In experiments with animals, however, tests that these processes have occurred must involve some form of recall, recognition, or relearning. An animal may be required to recall a particular type of operant behavior to obtain food. It may be required to choose between an array of stimuli, a task requiring recognition of stimuli previously encountered. Or it may be given a previously encountered learning task, the aim being to see whether the animal learns more quickly the second time. Memory is measured by the savings that the animal shows in relearning the task.

Animal learning is not perfect and animals do not retain all that they learn. Two basic theories try to account for this phenomenon: the decay theory, which maintains that memories simply fade with time if the behavior is not rehearsed, and the interference theory, which maintains that the maintenance or recall of an existing memory is interfered with by the establishment of new memories and may be obliterated.

Psychologists also recognize three basic types of memory: immediate, short-term and long-term. Immediate memories last fractions of a second and have been recognized in research on humans as an aspect of the initial encoding part of the memory process. It is very difficult to study this aspect of memory in animals not capable of verbal responses.

Short-term memory lasts a number of minutes and research on humans has shown that the amount of information that can be held in short-term memory is limited. Experiments on short-term memory in animals often employ CONDITIONING procedures. In the delayed response test an animal is required to make a response a certain time after a signal indicating which response is to be made. For example a pigeon may be trained to peck one of three disks to obtain a reward. On a given trial one of the disks is briefly illuminated and then there is a delay before the pigeon is allowed to peck. A refinement of this technique is the delayed match-to-sample test. The animal is presented with a particular stimulus (the sample) and after a delay it is shown an array of stimuli including the sample stimulus. The correct response is to choose the sample stimulus. With considerable practice pigeons can perform correctly with delays of up to 60 seconds. Monkeys can manage delays of up to 120 seconds as can the bottle-nosed dolphin when trained in an auditory version of the problem.

Animals may appear to have poor short-term memory when tested in one way, but a good memory when tested in another. For example rats and dogs perform poorly in delayed response tasks unless they are able to rely on the orientation of parts of the body during the delay period. Rats are particularly good at spatial memory problems and dogs are adept at finding bones hidden in a field, but perform poorly when tested in an analogous way in the laboratory. A dog can be restrained for a considerable time after seeing a bone placed in one of several places, and can then retrieve it.

Once an animal has mastered a laboratory problem it may remember it for many months. Such long-term memory and its counterpart, forgetting, have been the subject of considerable scientific research. It has been discovered that fear-based behavior is particularly resistant to forgetting, though interestingly, this type of memory is less marked in young animals.

Study of the age-retention effect shows that memory for aversive stimuli is very poor during the early stages of development. Rats conditioned to an aversive flavor at ten days old quickly lost their avoidance behavior but rats conditioned at eighteen days old retained their response to the aversive flavor for at least fifty-six days. It seems likely that it is adaptive for young animals to forget aversive experiences which seldom recur. Repeated occurrence of aversive stimuli, however, leads to reinstatement of the memory. Some psychologists believe that the young forget more easily because they are more exposed to novel stimuli by virtue of their relative inexperience. The succession of novel stimuli interferes with the memory process in young animals, but this effect is not so marked in adults. An alternative view is that the age-retention effect is a specially adaptive type of memory decay. DJM

Bibliography

Hulse, Stewart H., Fowler, Harry and Honig, Werner K., eds 1978: *Cognitive processes in animal behavior*. Hillsdale, N.J.: Erlbaum.

Tarpy, Roger M. and Mayer, Richard E. 1978: *Foundations of learning and memory*. Glenview, Ill. and London: Scott, Foresman.

memory organization Memory may be metaphorically compared to a huge warehouse containing millions of stored pieces of information. However, the contents of this warehouse are not arranged randomly but organized. Items that belong together (because they were acquired at the same time, because they are similar, or because they are often used in the same context, to mention just a few principles of organization) are stored together. Consequently, retrieving one item makes available other items that are close to it in the memory structure, e.g. by a process of spreading activation. However, it must be noted that the spatial image used here is no more than a useful metaphor and does not imply a spatial organization at the neural level. WKi

menarche The onset of menstruation in adolescence. It takes place relatively late in the developmental sequence of puberty, always after the peak growth velocities have been reached. On average, it occurs at 12.9 years, 3.3 years after the onset of the adolescent growth spurt and 1.1 years after peak height velocity is attained (see Frisch and Revelle

1970). Timing is influenced by genetic factors, nutrition, illness and geographical location. There is evidence that the age of menarche has been decreasing during the last century by a few months each decade although the trend may have slowed down (see Tanner 1978). The causation of this secular trend remains controversial but it has been linked with improved nutrition, general health and standards of living. The age of onset has different psychological consequences. Early menarche associated with precocious puberty may generate a negative self-image stemming from feelings of isolation and difference from peers but generally delayed menstruation is not a source of distress. WLLP-J

Bibliography

Frisch, R.E. and Revelle, R. 1970: Height and weight at menarche and a hypothesis of critical body weights and adolescent events. *Science* 169, 397.

Tanner, J.M. 1978: *Foetus into man*. London: Open Books; Cambridge, Mass.: Harvard University Press.

menopause The permanent cessation of menstruation occurring during the middle period of life. It is associated with the end of ovulation and with atrophy of the female reproductive organs. It is not known to occur in other mammals, and its evolutionary origin is probably associated with the prolonged period of infant care in humans.

Symptoms specific to the menopausal period include vasomotor, genital and psychological changes. Some normal aspects of ageing (e.g. dryness of the skin, loss of proteins from the bones, leading to brittleness, or osteoporosis) – are exaggerated by aspects of the postmenopausal bodily state, such as lack of estrogen.

The most common and well known vasomotor symptom is the hot flush, produced by impairment of the neural mechanism controlling the blood vessels, and this may be further exaggerated by emotional factors. The principal symptoms affecting urinary and sexual functioning are dryness of the vagina and the urethra. Psychological symptoms such as irritability, depression, insomnia and feelings of nervousness, as well as general somatic symptoms such as headaches and giddiness, are also reported.

While the main physical changes (hot flushes, genital symptoms), probably result from declining estrogen levels, the cause of the psychological changes is controversial. One view is that they derive directly from a change in hormone balance, specifically from the decline in estrogen levels. Another is that they result from the physical consequences of hormonal changes, e.g. sweating or incontinence may lead to insomnia, and hence to tiredness and irritability, which produces further interpersonal conflicts and stresses, and eventually depression. A third view is that any symptoms of a decline in general health, or signs of depression or emotional problems occurring around the time of menopause will be attributed (generally incorrectly) to it. Major stresses, mostly involving the death of close friends and relatives, or children leaving home, often coincide with the time of the menopause. These stresses could be responsible for many of the general health and psychological symptoms. JA

Bibliography

Weideger, Paula 1975: *Menstruation and menopause*. New York: Knopf; London: Women's Press 1978 (*Female cycles*).

Bart, P.B. 1971: Depression in middle-aged women. In *Women in sexist society*, ed. V. Cornick and B.K. Moran. New York: Basic Books.

mental disorders *See* psychotherapeutic drug treatment of mental disorders

mental handicap Can be defined as "that condition where intellectual deficit is associated with social, physical or psychiatric handicap, and requires special services or treatment" (Corbett 1977). (Mental handicap is also sometimes used to describe conditions where intellectual deficit appears to be present because of social inadequacy resulting from chronic psychiatric disorder. This has led to much confusion, and the term is not used in this sense here.)

Intellectual deficit is assessed by standardized tests of intelligence, such as the Wechsler Adult Intelligence Scale (WAIS). An intelligence quotient of less than two standard deviations below the mean (i.e. an IQ of less than 70) is usually taken as the cut off point for legal and administrative purposes. There are two main categories of mental handicap, mild (IQ 50–70) and severe (IQ below 50). Most severe mental handicap is associated with organic brain disease.

A number of epidemiological surveys in various countries have reported the incidence of mild mental handicap to be 20–30 per 1,000 population, and the incidence of severe mental handicap between 3 and 4 per 1,000 population aged 15–19. Variations in findings are related to differences in the concepts of mental handicap used – some studies base their findings on measures of IQ alone; others use a combination of IQ and social criteria. There is a strong association between mild mental handicap and low socioeconomic status: poor housing, overcrowding, poverty, poor nutrition, inadequate stimulation and education.

The commonest genetic cause of mental retardation is DOWN'S SYNDROME (mongolism) – a chromosome abnormality accounting for 25 per cent of severely retarded hospitalized patients. Other genetic conditions include the inherited metabolic disorders (e.g. phenylketonuria); tuberose sclerosis; neural tube defects. Clinically, these disorders are recognized by the presence of various physical abnormalities with intellectual deficit. Some conditions (e.g. the chromosome abnormalities) can be diagnosed antenatally if amniocentesis is undertaken. Although genetic defects cannot be corrected, there are some genetic conditions where treatment is possible to prevent further intellectual impairment (e.g. a special diet for phenylketonuria; surgical treatment of hydrocephalus associated with spina bifida). In mild mental handicap, it is believed that polygenic inheritance plays an important part, in association with the adverse social circumstances already described. Incidentally, there is some evidence that children of mentally handicapped parents tend to have higher IQs than their parents ("regression to the mean").

The distribution of intelligence in the population means that a certain proportion of mentally handicapped people are to be expected as a result of normal variation. During pregnancy, the growth and development of the fetus's brain and nervous system can be harmed in a variety of ways: e.g. by maternal infections such as rubella (german measles); high blood pressure or toxemia which affects placental function; antenatal hemorrhage; rhesus incompatibility; drugs such as thalidomide; poisons such as coal gas; alcohol and smoking. During birth, damage may occur from birth trauma, lack of oxygen or low blood pressure. In the immediate postnatal period, the damaging factors include neonatal seizures, infection, hypoglycemia (low blood sugar), hypothermia, severe jaundice, intraventricular hemorrhage, and the other complications of prematurity, such as the respiratory distress syndrome. Trauma to the skull and underlying brain may be caused accidentally during this period, or as a result of non accidental injury (child abuse). Brain infections (meningitis, encephalitis); prolonged hypoxia due to respiratory or cardiac arrest, poisoning by carbon monoxide or lead may all cause mental handicap in a previously normal child. Infantile spasms, a form of epilepsy which develops during the first year of life, may also be accompanied by mental handicap.

Children with severe mental handicap present early in childhood with delay in attaining their developmental milestones, together with the signs of any accompanying physical disorder (e.g. cerebral palsy). Most of these children will be recognized during their first year of life. Some, such as those with Down's Syndrome, will be recognised at birth, and their parents given a prediction of the degree of mental handicap to be expected.

Mild mental handicap may go unnoticed until the child starts school, or even later if little attention is paid to educational achievement. Learning problems or behavior disturbance in the school setting will then alert the teacher to the need for psychometric assessment by a psychologist. The finding of low scores on all subtests of intelligence will confirm intellectual deficit and the child will then be placed in an appropriate educational environment, such as a special unit or school. Occasionally, previously unrecognized mentally handicapped adults present with behavior disturbance when faced with a life stress such as the death of their parents, or a change in management of the firm where they have been happily carrying out a simple job for years.

In addition to general intellectual deficit a full assessment of individual difficulties may then reveal handicap in any (or all) of the following areas:

Physical: defects of motor coordination and movement, hearing, vision or speech; epilepsy occurs in 30 per cent of severely retarded children.

Social: problems may range from social incompetence (inability to ask for and follow directions, handle money, use a telephone, etc.) to antisocial behavior (masturbating or urinating in public, taking other people's possessions, making overt sexual advances in public).

Psychiatric: children and adults with intellectual deficit have an increased risk of psychiatric disorder. This is accounted for by many factors, including brain malfunction, temperament, immaturity, the effects of social rejection, and institutional care. The types of psychiatric disorder seen are the same as those occurring in people of normal intelligence; i.e. conduct and emotional disorders in children; schizophrenia, affective psychoses, neuroses and personality disorders in adults. The following are more commonly associated with mental handicap: infantile AUTISM, HYPERKINETIC STATES, stereotyped repetitive movements and pica.

Prevention and Treatment. It is now possible to prevent mental handicap in a number of ways such as:

GENETIC COUNSELLING for prospective parents in cases where there is a high risk of the occurrence of an abnormal fetus.

Amniocentesis in pregnancy, detecting fetuses with genetic abnormalities such as Downs Syndrome at a stage when termination of pregnancy can be considered.

Ultrasonic scanning in pregnancy to detect abnormalities such as spina bifida.

Careful antenatal and obstetric care.

Good neonatal care of the newborn baby, reducing brain damage caused by treatable conditions such as hypoglycemia, phenylketonuria and congenital hypothyroidism.

Rubella immunization of all schoolgirls, to prevent congenital rubella.

Enriching the child's environment in deprived areas, as was done in the Milwaukee early intervention program.

Additional social and psychiatric handicaps may be preventable by early recognition of mental handicap through developmental screening. The family can then be supported from an early stage, and helped to develop the child's skills and counter any behavior problems before they become established. Later, appropriate school and occupational placement; training in social skills; improving the quality of institutional care; and changing society's attitude toward the mentally handicapped from rejection to acceptance may all contribute to the prevention of other difficulties.

A number of research studies have now shown that mentally handicapped adults and children in longstay hospitals have fewer skills, more disturbed behavior and a lower level of functioning than those living at home or in small "family" units. This has led to a reappraisal of the role of hospitals in the care of the mentally handicapped. There is growing acceptance of the view that this should be limited to the short-term treatment of problems such as disturbed behavior, seizure control or psychiatric illness, except for the most severely mentally and physically handicapped who need continuous nursing care. Most others can be cared for much more appropriately in the community, in small group homes, foster homes, hostels, etc. Special secure facilities may be necessary for adolescents and adults whose aggressive or antisocial behavior cannot be contained in any other setting.

The mentally handicapped living in the community need education, occupation, recreation and opportunities to take part in as many everyday activities as possible. Their families need support – financial, practical and emotional – and opportunities for relief from the stresses of coping with a handicapped child or adult for shorter or longer periods. Children and their families can often attend a pediatric department or assessment center, which provides a range of assessment and treatment facilities. In some areas preschool counsellors or specially trained health visitors visit at home to provide stimulation for the child and guidance for the parents. Attendance at the nursery class of a special school can start when the child is two and continue to sixteen, or even longer in some cases. Short-term care is usually provided through foster parents or children's homes. Resources for adults are often scarce. They should include different types of living accommodation, to meet their varying levels of dependency; and provide short and long term care; and a range of occupational activities, e.g. Adult Training Centers, sheltered workshops or sheltered employment. Community based multidisciplinary teams of professionals (psychologists, nurses, social workers, etc.) are available in many areas to offer expert help with specific problems and support families. Voluntary organizations also form an important part of the network of community support and often provide valuable resources through fund raising activities.

The life expectancy for the mentally handicapped is now greater than ever before, and many are reaching their sixties and seventies. Where there is an underlying physical condition the severity of this, and its treatability, will affect life expectancy. The prognosis for associated behavioral and psychiatric difficulties depends on a number of factors including the family background, placement in an institutional environment, and the availability of occupation and training facilities. GCF

Bibliography

Caldwell, B.M., Bradley, R.H. and Elardo, R. 1975. Early intervention. In *Mental retardation and developmental disabilities* vol. VII, ed. E.J. Wortis. New York: Brunner Mazel.

Corbett, J. 1977. Mental handicap – psychiatric aspects. In *Child psychiatry, modern approaches*, ed. M. Rutter. Oxford: Blackwell Scientific; Philadelphia: Lippincott.

Tizard, J. 1960: Residential care of mentally handicapped children. *British medical journal*, 1041–46.

mental imagery The supposed "inner representations" to which people refer in imagining, remembering and INTROSPECTION. Imagery, once regarded as too mentalistic for empirical study is now an important area of research in COGNITIVE PSYCHOLOGY, as well as in medicine. Research revolves around people's abilities to "scan" and manipulate their mental images, as well as the nature of the mental image (Neisser 1976). The role of "guided imagery" is also being studied in psychotherapy and in the diagnosis and cure of illness (Jaffe and Bresler 1980). Once in existence, images can be "observed" and manipulated as if themselves objects – a process Coleridge called *fancy* to distinguish it from *imagination* which "dissolves, diffuses, dissipates, in order to recreate; or . . . at all events it struggles . . . to unify". (*Biographia literaria* ch. XIII). Images only appear as "sensorial imaginations . . . which can be held before the mind for an indefinite time", in what James (1890, p. 243) called the "substantive parts" of the stream of thought, at its "resting places"; in its "transitive parts" their character must be more vague, i.e., less objective, and not separable from the activity in which they are involved (see Warnock 1976, pt IV). JDS

Bibliography

Jaffe, D.T. and Bresler, D.E. 1980: Guided imagery: healing through the mind's eye. In *Imagery: its many dimensions and applications*, ed. J.B. Shorr et al. New York: Plenum Press.

James, W. 1890: *Principles of psychology*. New York: Holt.

Neisser, U. 1976: *Cognition and reality*. San Francisco: Freeman.

Warnock, M. 1976: *Imagination*. London: Faber and Faber; Berkeley: University of California Press.

mental processes *See* neural control of higher mental processes

mere exposure effect The fact that repeated exposure to a neutral stimulus is sufficient to induce positive reactions to that stimulus. Zajonc (1968), who was the first to discover this effect, has presented a good deal of evidence in support of it.The effect is not restricted to interpersonal attraction. Repeated exposure also affects our evaluation of verbal, visual and auditory stimuli of various kinds (words, symbols, etc.) and can provide, at least in part, an explanation for early attachment in animals. Recently Zajonc has shown that such preferences can develop without conscious recognition or discriminations (Zajonc 1980).

In many circumstances other factors may, of course, have a much stronger effect on liking, attitudes or attractions and overshadow the effect of mere exposure. JMFJ

Bibliography

Zajonc, R. 1968: Attitudinal effects of mere exposure. *Journal of personality and social psychology monograph supplement* 9, 1–27.

——— 1980: Feeling and thinking: prefererences need no inferences. *American psychologist* 35, 151–175.

meta-communication Communication about communication. For instance, a signal may be given by an animal to a conspecific, and this signal has a particular "meaning" or effect in the communicative system of the species. However, a second signal, or set of signals, may accompany the first, changing its basic significance. This second signal is the meta-communicative one. Meta-communication has not been described outside mammals. Among mammals it is found, for instance as a characteristic of PLAY in macaques, baboons and chimpanzees. Such play is not necessarily juvenile. The playful animal may bite, chase or perform some other aggressive action, which is then modified by particular facial expressions, vocalizations or body postures to indicate that the hostility is not "real". Similar activity is prevalent among humans who laugh or smile to indicate that harsh words or aggressive actions are not to be taken at face value. VR

meta-memory Knowledge of the processes involved in information storage and retrieval that can be used voluntarily to regulate remembering. Many developmental psychologists have noted improvements with age in meta-memory.

The child or adult who has some awareness of the workings of his or her own mind will make use of this knowledge in memorizing new materials. For example, new information will be systematically categorized before being committed to memory. This knowledge is complemented by an awareness of the nature of forgetting, so that external memory aids such as a diary or a knot in a handkerchief come to be used as reminders. In both examples, the ability to "reflect" upon the memory process enables the voluntary introduction of superordinate monitoring and control processes. Other meta-mnemonic processes include checking, planning, testing, revising and evaluation.

Meta-memory is an aspect of reflective self-awareness, the capacity to think about one's own cognitive processes. Like other forms of knowledge, children's meta-cognition undergoes systematic changes with development. GEB

Bibliography

Flavell, J.H. and Wellman, H.M. 1977: *Metamemory*. In *Perspectives on the development of memory and cognition*, ed. R.V. Kail and J.W. Hagen. Hillsdale, N.J.: Erlbaum.

methods *See* empirical methods in social inquiry; empirical techniques in experimental psychology

mid-life crisis A term denoting any of several types of behavior in the middle years, from the private awareness of the finitude of the life span to the life style rearrangements of career change or divorce and remarriage. The term was introduced to describe phenomena which, arise as a consequence of demographic changes – increased longevity and the quickening of the life cycle of the family, producing a normative expectation of an extended post-parental period. Increased scientific attention to the middle years has shown that this middle phase of life is not a plateau but a time of changes, and has given rise to the popular term "mid-life crisis". The awareness of biological decline, the irrevocability of decisions made earlier in the life cycle, possible stagnation in marriage and career, declining opportunities with advancing age: in brief, intrinsic and extrinsic causes, maturational, social and existential, contribute to change as well as to the sense of crisis in middle life. ND

Bibliography

Norman, William H. and Scaramella, Thomas J., eds. 1980: *Mid-life: developmental and clinical issues*. New York: Brunner/Mazel.

migration Has been defined by Baker (1978) as the "act of moving from one spatial unit to another". If, within this definition, we set aside first of all *species migration*, which covers changes in the geographical range of a species over a number of years, secondly the *accidental migration* of individuals, and thirdly the common but not universal tendencies of individual animals towards *exploration and dispersal* from their birthplace, we have passed through a number of acceptable definition of migration leaving only the most familiar (and emphasizing the possibility of evolutionary continua between it and the others): that of significant journeys between two spatial units, eventually involving return to units previously visited. Long-term migrations of the latter type include *ontogenetic returns*, as in those of some fish returning after several years and over thousands of miles to breed near their birthplace and *annual returns* as shown by some birds between breeding and wintering grounds. Much research has concentrated upon the guidance mechanisms involved in the latter (see NAVIGATION). AW

Bibliography

Baker, Reginald R. 1978: *The evolutionary ecology of animal migration*. London: Hodder and Stoughton; New York: Holmes & Meier.

*Davies, C. 1981: Migration. pp380–387 In D. McFarland, ed. *The Oxford companion to animal behaviour*. Oxford and New York; Oxford University Press.

mimicry In evolutionary biology, a close resemblance between two organisms, or parts of organisms, evolved by natural selection as a result of the advantage accruing to one or both from the resemblance. Classically, mimicry is an adaptation of prey species: a harmless species (the mimic) may resemble a dangerous or unpalatable one (the model), or a number of dangerous or unpalatable species may resemble each other, presumably because these result in decreased predation. Predators themselves, however, exhibit mimicry on occasion too, presumably because resemblance to a harmless species aids predatory success. It has also been suggested that mimicry occurs within species, and may constitute an evolutionary origin of social communication. Many examples of mimicry are based on form and colour, visually detected, but mimicry may relate to other senses too, and may also be behavioral. (See Wickler 1968). RDA

Bibliography

Wickler, W. 1968: *Mimicry in plants and animals*. London: Weidenfeld and Nicolson; New York: McGraw Hill.

mind The most general term for intellectual competence. Broadly speaking, "the mind" is taken to include everything one is inclined to call "mental" – thoughts, feelings, emotions, perception, sensation, moods, dispositions – but intellectual activity has always been its most central element.

Historically, the term succeeded and supplanted the Aristotelian notion of *psyche*, which denotes all the functions that distinguish the animate from the inanimate. Hence *psyche* includes metabolism, nutrition, growth and locomotion as well as the mental phenomena listed above. The transition from *psyche* to (the core of) "mind" is economically seen in Descartes (1641 (*1967*), pp. 149–57) and was largely justified by the attempt to combat scepticism: statements about conscious mental events seemed to enjoy immunity from sceptical doubt, since such events are private to their possessor, who is immediately and non-inferentially aware of them and who therefore cannot be mistaken about them. The Cartesian and neo-Cartesian stress upon epistemological reliability led to a characterization of the mental, and hence the mind, which emphasized consciousness above all else. The crucial feature of privacy fostered the metaphors of the mind as either an "inner theater", in or on which mental events appeared, or as the "ghost in the machine", the genuine subject or observer of conscious phenomena. These metaphors proved impossible to interpret literally, and the stress on privacy led to the problem of our knowledge of other minds; moreover the oscillation between the "inner theater" and "inner observer" metaphors created difficulties in understanding personal identity which became apparent with Locke and Hume.

The importance of consciousness and epistemological security were much weakened by Brentano's revival of the medieval notion of the "intentional inexistence" of the objects of mental acts. Brentano characterized the mental, and hence the mind, in terms of intentionality rather than consciousness. Freud (who studied under Brentano) developed the postulate of an unconscious mind, thus further weakening the assumption that consciousness is all-important. (See INTENTIONALITY.)

Whether one emphasizes consciousness or intentionality, it would probably be generally agreed that the mental phenomena comprising "a mind" must have some substantial degree of integration, unity and coherence. Those who put particular weight on conscious mental events require a "unity of consciousness" for the ascription of a single mind, and take the split consciousness seen in commissurotomy patients under experimental conditions to justify talk of two minds, and even two persons (see Puccetti 1973). Arguably, however, a less artificial and more pervasive lack of integration is required before we withhold ascription of a single mind.

The use of the term in science is primarily to act as an umbrella-term for the subject matter of non-behaviorist psychologies. KVW

Bibliography

Descartes, René 1641 (*1967*): *Philosophical works*, ed. E.S. Haldane and G.R.T. Ross, vol. I, Cambridge: Cambridge University Press.

Puccetti, R. 1973: Brain bisection and personal identity. *British journal for the philosophy of science* 24, 339–55.

mind–body problem The problem can be expressed in the question: "Is the mind a different sort of entity from the body and, if so, how are they connected?" A thought-experiment will bring out why the mind might be held to be radically different from the body. Imagine that Smith knows everything about the neurophysiology of hearing, but is deaf. It would seem that he will not know the nature of the *experience* of hearing; that is, he will not know what it is like to hear. As, *ex hypothesi*, he knows all about the physical processes involved, the experience must be something over and above such processes. Put like this, the problem of mind is a problem about states of consciousness. It seems that the nature of such states is fully knowable only to those who have them, whereas physical states can, in principle, be observed by anyone (see PRIVACY).

An alternative formulation of the problem was given by Brentano (1973), who based his argument on the nature of thought, rather than the nature of sensory consciousness. Thought, he argued, essentially possesses the property of INTENTIONALITY; that is, it is directed onto something other than itself. Thus I might have a thought *about* the Tower of London or *about* Zeus, who does not even exist. This feature of "about-ness" – that is, of being directed onto some (possibly non-existent) thing beyond itself – does not rank among the sorts of property described in physical science and is the mark of the mental and proof of its non-physicality.

These lines of thought lead to a dualism of mind and body. Many problems then arise concerning the relation of mental states to each other and to the body. Are the mental states bound together in one mind by belonging to one mental substance, as DESCARTES thought (*Meditations on first philosophy*), or does the mind consist simply of a concatenation or bundle of these states, as HUME (*Treatise of human nature*) believed? Does the mind interact with the body, as common sense dictates? If so, by what means do two totally different types of entity interact, and would not such interaction infringe the principle of the conservation of physical energy, as physical energy is expended to produce a non-physical state? The trouble with dualism is not that it fails to fit the facts nor that it is open to knock-down objections, but that it seems to import mystery rather than shed light. For example, while it is not incoherent to explain the interaction of mind and body by saying that it is just a brute fact that they interact, we feel that we need an explanation of how and by what mechanism, and this sort of question seems to be answerable only for physical processes. In addition to these specific problems, the very idea of dualism is offensive to some philosophers and scientists. The success of physical science has led increasingly since the seventeenth century to the belief that a complete materialist account of the world ought to be possible (though there were, of course, materialists in the ancient world and before the advent of modern science).

There are three possible strategies one might employ to deal with the problem of consciousness and resolve the mind–body problem in the materialists' favor. First, one might deny that consciousness exists. Second, one might try to analyse statements about consciousness in a way which shows that they are really statements about bodily states or events. Third, one might accept that there are irreducible mental states but deny that these present any threat to materialism, because, though not themselves material, they are states of a material thing, namely the body.

The first strategy was employed by certain early behaviorists (e.g. Watson (1925)) and by proponents of the "elimination" or "disappearance" theory of mind (e.g. Rorty (1965–6)). According to these theories, pains, sensations and consciousness in general do not exist: such entities supposedly formed part of a primitive attempt to explain behavior, but now we explain behavior by physical causes.

The difficulty for such a radical theory is to explain what, if there is no such thing as a pain sensation, constitutes the *unpleasantness* of breaking a leg, for example. Simply behaving in a certain way – even being caused to do so by a brain process – is not *ipso facto* unpleasant: we pain-behave in *response* to *experienced* pain. Indeed, the very notions of pleasantness and unpleasantness seem to attach to *experiences*, which these theories want to eliminate. Are they, therefore, denying that breaking a leg is really unpleasant?

The second and more common strategy has been to provide a translation, analysis or paraphrase of psychological language which exhibits it as referring only to physical states. The most influential original form of this approach was analytical BEHAVIORISM. According to this theory, any sentence of the form "S is in mental state M" translates or analyses into one of the form "S is behaving in manner B". It was immediately obvious that not every mental state shows itself in observable behavior. Ryle (1949) therefore altered the analysans into "S is *disposed* to behave in manner B", to allow for the case in which an experience is not associated with any overt behavior. This approach faced two difficulties. First, such states as pains seem to consist of more than dispositions to behave. (Ryle himself recognized this and always allowed bare sensations to fall outside his analysis, reserving it for moods, capacities and traits of character.) Second, it is difficult to provide an adequate understanding of the concept of DISPOSITION. In response to the first problem Smart (1963) proposed the identity theory of mind. He said that sensations etc. are not mere dispositions but are identical with brain states. Statements about sensations cannot be translated into statements which are explicitly about brain states, any more than they can be translated into statements about behavior, but they can be translated into what Smart called "topic neutral" statements. A topic neutral statement is one which identifies something by means of an accidental feature of the thing reported, without revealing anything of its essential or intrinsic nature. "Whatever causes cancer" is a topic neutral expression, for it reveals nothing about the actual nature of the thing referred to (for example, whether it is a virus, or a germ, or what its chemical structure is) but refers to it only *via* its causal property of bringing about cancer. Examples of topic neutral paraphrases of psychological reports would be the analysis of "I am in pain" as "something-I-know-not-what is going on in me of the sort which goes on when my body is damaged", or "something-I-know-not-what is going on in me which tends to cause me to pain-behave". The "something-I-know-not-what" is assumed to be a brain process, though it requires empirical science to confirm that.

In response to the second problem, Armstrong (1968) proposed that dispositions in general were identical with structural causes (for example, the disposition to brittleness of glass is identical with its molecular structure) and that a disposition to human behavior in particular was identical with an internal cause of behavior – assumed again to be a brain process. He combined this idea with Smart's, and argued in his important book *A materialist theory of the mind* that mental states are nothing but internal causes of behavior, about which we have only topic neutral knowledge and which are in fact only states of the brain.

It is not possible to discuss such sophisticated theories briefly. However, one central difficulty for the theories of Smart and Armstrong concerns the idea that we have only topic neutral knowledge of our experiences. It has been said that such theories require us to pretend that we are anesthetized. If we know nothing about what it is actually like to feel pain or to see a horse, how is this different from not really being conscious of these things? And if I do not know what it is like to experience the world, how can I know what the world which features in my experience is like?

Putnam (1975), Dennett (1979) and others have tried to modify behaviorism in a different way from Smart and Armstrong. They argue that a mental state is a functional state of an organism, and this means that it stands in a relation to the body somewhat analogous to that in which a computer program stands to the hardware of the computer. Mental states are, thus, not identical with states of the body; they are *realized* in the body in the way programs are *realized* in the hardware. A problem for this theory is to see how it differs from a sophisticated behaviorism, expressed using language and analogies from computer science. A functional state is one which primes a body to serve a certain function – that is, to emit a certain output – under the appropriate circumstances. This seems to be essentially similar to a disposition to behavioral response, given the appropriate stimulus (see FUNCTIONALISM).

The third general strategy is to allow that a physical body may possess some irreducibly special mental properties. This is called the dual aspect theory because it allows that some objects possess two aspects, one mental, the other physical, and neither reducible to the other. Unfortunately this theory has serious drawbacks as an alternative to dualism, for many of the same mysteries that arise concerning the relation of mental and physical within a dualist theory also darken the dual aspect theory. Does the mental aspect influence what happens to the physical states and if so how does this influence occur? If there is no influence then mental states will be mere epiphenomena, having no influence on the physical world, which is surely implausible; the feeling of pain (for example) clearly influences our physical behavior. Furthermore, the concept of substance is sufficiently obscure to lead us to ask what precisely is meant by the claim that though there is a dualism of properties they all belong to the same substance. And, if this substance possesses both mental and physical properties, is it not a mental substance just as much as it is a physical one?

It remains, therefore, very doubtful whether a materialist theory has been devised which can provide a convincing account of consciousness.

Brentano's problem with intentionality is more difficult to assess. Computers behave in ways which appear to exhibit intentionality. They appear to be able to handle propositions about things and therefore to think about them. They also take things as their objects and are concerned about them in practical ways. For example, a rocket which is programmed to home in on a target even when that target takes evasive action has that target as the object of its activity in a way similar to that in which human intelligent behavior is concerned with or about things. The fact that there is a strong analogy between the formal feature of human intentionality and the behavior of some machines suggests that whether one believes that human intentionality possesses a feature not present in the behavior of computers or robots will depend on whether one thinks that machines omit something in human intelligent behavior over and above the formal features of intentionality: for example, whether one is inclined to deny that machines can think *strictu sensu*, on the grounds that machines are not conscious, so that what they do only counts as "thinking". In this case the problem moves back from intentionality as such to consciousness.

Although materialism is relatively popular among modern philosophers, there is still widespread discontent with the available materialist treatments of consciousness: at the same time not many philosophers are happy with the obscurities and elusiveness of dualism. The mind–body problem has by no means reached a resolution. HMR

Bibliography

Armstrong, D.M. 1968: *A materialist theory of the mind*. London: Routledge & Kegan Paul; Atlantic Highlands, N.J.: Humanities Press.

*Borst, C.V., ed. 1970: *The mind–brain identity theory*. London: Macmillan; New York: St. Martins Press.

Brentano, F. 1874 (*1973*): *Psychology from an empirical standpoint*. London: Routledge & Kegan Paul; Atlantic Highlands, N.J.: Humanities Press.

Dennett, D.C. 1979: *Brainstorms*. Brighton: Harvester; Cambridge, Mass.: MIT Press.

Putnam, H. 1975: Minds and machines. In *Philosophical papers*, vol. II, pp.362–85. Cambridge and New York: Cambridge University Press.

*Robinson, H. 1982: *Matter and sense*. Cambridge and New York: Cambridge University Press.

Rorty, R. 1965–6: Mind–body identity, privacy and categories. *Review of metaphysics* 17, 24–54.

Ryle, G. 1949: *The concept of mind*. London: Hutchinson; Totowa, N.J.: Barnes and Noble (1975).

Smart, J.J.C. 1963: *Philosophy and scientific realism*. London: Routledge & Kegan Paul; Atlantic Highlands, N.J.: Humanities Press.

Watson, J.B. 1925: *Behaviorism*. New York: Norton (revised edn 1930, reprinted 1980).

*Wilkes, K. 1978: *Physicalism*. London: Routledge & Kegan Paul; Atlantic Highlands, N.J.: Humanities Press.

mirror-phase Moment in infant development postulated by Jacques LACAN (1936), based on infant observation, animal ethology and psychoanalysis of adults. Between six and eighteen months, infants exhibit a characteristic fascination with their image in a mirror – or similar surface such as the mother's eyes – a moment of watchful jubilation, often punctuated by an inquiring look to an accompanying adult. Lacan sees in this moment the foundation of the ego; the mirror-image is taken as the ideal ego, representing a self-sufficient unity in contrast with the child's sense of its own powerlessness and incoordination; it finds itself in this first "other", its own image. In seizing on its image as its self, this initial alienating identification is typical of the ego's primary function: misunderstanding, misrecognition and, more broadly, fantasy. Language (the Symbolic) allows the child to find a way out of the aggressive dyadic mirror-relation to the other (Imaginary), leaving as a residue the Real (that which cannot be symbolized). JF

Bibliography

Lacan, J. 1936 (*1977*): The mirror stage as formative of the function of the I as revealed in psychoanalytic experience. In *Ecrits: a selection*, trans. A. Sheridan, London: Tavistock; New York: Norton.

MMPI, the The Minnesota Multiphasic Personality Inventory is an objective personality inventory developed as an aid in assessing clinical problems. It is the most widely researched personality measure with substantial validity studies supporting its use. The information available on its scales has encouraged the broad use of automated (computer based) interpretation. The MMPI clinical scales were devised according to a strategy of empirical scale construction. Items which validly discriminated the clinical group from normals were included in the scale. Scales were devised to assess hypochondria, depression, hysteria, psychopathic deviation, psychasthenia (obsessive–compulsive behavior), schizophrenia, and mania. In addition, there are several validity scales to alert the clinician to deviant response attitudes such as lying (L Scale), faking (F Scale) and general defensiveness (K Scale). JNB

mnemonic systems Mnemonics are rules of learning that improve recall. Many are known, some of which go back to classical antiquity. However, to achieve really dramatic results through their use, a great deal of effort and concentration is required. Mnemonic techniques generally rely on facilitating two processes basic to memory: chunking (that is, forming higher-order subjective units of the material to be learned) and retrieval. Efficient retrieval systems employ prelearned, automatized structures to which the learning material is tied and which serve as a guide for retrieval. The best known mnemonic technique is the method of places: the to-be-remembered items are deposited via mental imagery along a well-studied route, which is traversed in a fixed order when retrieval is attempted, picking up the stored memory traces. Another method is the key word procedure, which helps to form a bridge between two items that are to be remembered together. Peg word systems are also used frequently, in which learning material is associated with a fixed system of peg words to guide retrieval. WKi

models: role in theories Analogical (and idealized) representations of things, processes, etc. and more recently of formal systems. A specialized use for the term has appeared in psychology, as a synonym for 'theory'. In most scientific contexts a model is distinguished from a theory, in that a theory is taken to be a discourse about a model.

In engineering and the physical sciences models play a very large part both in the design of experiments and in the construction of theories. The uses of models can best be understood through the distinctions between a model, its subjects and its source. A doll is both a model *of* a human infant (subject) and modelled *on* a human infant (source). Source and subject are identical. Such models are homoeomorphs. Natural selection is modelled *on* domestic selection but it is a model *of* the unobservable real process of speciation. Source and subject are different. These are paramorphs.

Homoeomorphic models are used to bring out features of systems we already know about. For example, a hydraulic network can be used as a model of an electric circuit, suggesting certain otherwise unnoticed features of the circuit. Models are also used creatively when the behavior of a class of physical objects or substances is known but the process that produces that behavior is unobservable. Paramorphic models are used to represent the unknown productive mechanisms. Such models must be functionally equivalent to the unobservable productive process, that is the imagined model must behave like the real process. For example, a machine computational process which produces results like those produced by people who are thinking about a particular type of problem may be used as a paramorphic model of the unknown cognitive process by which the real thinker solves a problem. The success of a paramorphic model in modelling the behavior of the real system it represents is not enough to guarantee that it is a true representation of that system, but it will be seen as a probable representation if it continues successfully to simulate the thinker's cognitive processes and has no equally plausible rival.

If explanations were merely formal discourses, deductively related to that which they purported to explain, there would be indefinitely many explanations for any given set of phenomena. The use of a paramorphic model not only allows for a plausible interpretation of the theoretical terms in a favored formal theory, but serves to eliminate all those others which are incompatible with it. There is no known formal criterion which will serve the same purpose. Models, then, are indispensible for developing theoretical explanations to the point at which their plausibility as representations of the real processes productive of the phenomena of interest can be tested.

Models are analogues of whatever they represent. The principles by which models are used in scientific reasoning are part of the 'logic of analogy'. An analogue has three comparative relations with its subject, a positive analogy (likenesses), a negative analogy (differences), and a neutral analogy (those properties of the model and its subject which have not been tested for likeness or difference one with another). The assessment of the plausibility of a model can be made fairly rigorous in terms of the balance between positive, negative and neutral analogies. For instance, if there are many likenesses, few differences and not much unexplored, a model is likely to be found acceptable by its users as a true representation of the process it simulates.

Discussion of the use of models in the sciences has centered on two issues: (1) Under what conditions are models to be taken as good guides to hypotheses about unobserved processes and structures? Commentators who have concentrated only on examples of homoeomorphic or heuristic models have tended to argue that models are dispensable and should be treated as part of the psychology of scientific thinking. Those who have studied the creative uses of paramorphic models have tended to argue that novel representations of previously unknown processes could not have been achieved without the use of a model. (2) A corresponding argument has developed around the issue of the role of metaphor and simile in scientific discourse. The two issues are closely related since a system of metaphors (say the role–rule theory in social psychology) may be introduced into a scientific discourse on the basis of a model-source (say 'man as actor'). On the basis of the actor analogy the unobservable determinants of regularities in behavior are likened to rules and conventions, and the process of the regulation of behavior to rule-following. RHa

Bibliography

Black, M. *Models and metaphors.* Ithaca, N.Y.: Cornell University Press.

Bunge, M. *Model, matter and method.* Dordrecht: Reidel.

Collins, L. ed.: *The use of models in the social sciences.* London: Tavistock.

Harré, R., 1972: *The principles of scientific thinking.* London: Macmillan; Chicago: Chicago University Press (1973).

Hesse, M.B. 1963: *Models and analogies in science.* London and New York: Sheed and Ward.

mongolism *See* Down's syndrome

moral development Psychologists' definition of the "moral" broadly encompasses the avoidance of anti-social action and the performance of pro-social (altruistic) action. There are several different approaches to the explanation of moral development which reflect differing assumptions about basic human nature, and about the desirable outcomes of moral development; for example, conformity to social norms versus autonomy.

We can outline three approaches to moral development by asking three questions. Firstly, how does the individual come to be a properly socialized member of the society into which he or she is born? This is about the acquisition of good habits and constraining motives, and learning how and when to conform. It implies the development of "character"; a set of virtues, enduring traits and consistency of action. Secondly, how does the individual come to be able to make moral decisions? Behind this question is the assumption that a moral act has to be *intended* in order to be deemed "moral". However, within this approach action itself is less important than how the individual comes to *understand the moral,* how he or she develops the ability to make a *reasoned moral judgment* about the behavior of self and others. Thirdly, why do otherwise apparently normal and virtuous people act cruelly or heartlessly, or allow others to perform such acts? "Bystander apathy" (failure to intervene in an emergency), obedience to "immoral" commands, and conformity to pressures which induce anti-social behavior or inhibit pro-social behavior all happen in ordinary life, and they can also be induced under laboratory conditions (Latané and Darley 1970; Milgram 1974; Zimbardo 1974). Such findings tend to undermine the conventional assumption that adequate socialization of individuals makes for predictably "moral" action. Clearly, *situational* factors and social processes are powerful agents in creating *immoral* behavior; perhaps they are also responsible for much *moral* behavior.

There are several different and conflicting assumptions behind these questions. One assumption is that most people will behave morally so long as the socialization process inculcating the right habits and motives has been adequate and successful. Another is that some people will behave more morally than others, especially under social pressure; in other words most people's morality is adequate for ordinary interpersonal encounters and for the maintenance of a reasonable level of honesty and virtue, but does not extend to the unusual or demanding situation. A third assumption is that social situations provide the main stimulus to action (or inaction), and that individual variability in socialization or level of moral development at best mediates or moderates these social processes.

Developmental explanations of morality can be broadly divided into models of acquisition and models of growth. The first imply that morality is *learnt*: through conditioning and learning individuals acquire the motives of guilt, shame and concern for others and these constrain and regulate their behavior. Habits, skills and values become internalized in the individual and provide a repertoire of behavior and appropriate responses. The child comes to *monitor* its own behavior. According to this model, effective moral development depends upon effective reinforcement, and the kind of relationship with adults which provides good role models and good conditions for imitation and identification. Development is a slow process of acquiring habits and motives and strengthening conscience (Aronfreed 1976).

In contrast, according to *growth* models, moral development progresses through *transformation* and *restructuring*. Development is *change*, not accumulation. This model has been applied to the study of moral reasoning. Moral reasoning reflects the way the individual makes sense of the world, how he or she conceptualizes the rules and norms which govern behavior. The individual does not acquire *more* rules or learn of more rights and duties but develops greater *understanding* of the *function* of rules and norms, and comes to take into account more factors in the situation, and more points of view on the issues. Progress and development results in more *differentiation* and greater integration of these factors and perspectives. Kohlberg (in Lickona 1976) has proposed six stages of moral reasoning. Each stage is a consistent system of moral reasons. Kohlberg's stages are shown in the table.

KOHLBERG'S SIX STAGES IN THE DEVELOPMENT OF MORAL JUDGMENT

Level 1—Preconventional level

STAGE I Punishment and obedience orientation–the physical consequences of an action determine its goodness or badness. Unilateral respect for authority, law defined by the voice of authority, avoidance of punishment reason for doing right.

STAGE II Instrumental relativist orientation–right action consists of that which instrumentally satisfies one's own needs and occasionally the needs of others. Concern with 'fairness' and reciprocity, in a pragmatic, quid pro quo, sense.

Level 2–Conventional level

STAGE III Interpersonal concordance or "good-boy–nice-girl" orientation–good behavior is that which pleases or helps others and is approved by them. Conformity to stereotyped images of what is "natural " behavior. Emphasis on good intentions and being "nice", mutuality of relationships, concern for others.

STAGE IV "Law and order" orientation–importance of maintaining social order, obligations, social duties, to avoid breakdown of system. Law and constituted authority ultimate arbiters. Emphasis on doing one's duty, public and societal function of which is perceived.

Level 3–Post conventional level

STAGE V Social contract legalistic orientation–ultilitarian overtones, concern with individual rights and the greatest good for the greatest number. Awareness of the relativism of values and the fact that laws are agreed tools of social organization, and that they can be changed by discussion if they fail to fulfil social utility.

STAGE VI Universal ethical principle–right is defined by appeal to ethical principles. These principles are abstractions. Moral and legal rules are clearly separate, and the idiosyncrasy of each situation is recognized, and each dealt with on its own merits by an appeal to the abstract principle.

The emphasis in this approach is on cognitive processes and the organization of appraisal. The researcher elicits the individual's stage of moral reasoning by presenting him or her with hypothetical moral dilemmas. These dilemmas focus upon rights and justice and the conflict between legal and moral rules and obligations. Some critics, however, have argued that this is too narrow a definition of what constitutes the "moral"; the focus on justice and rights is peculiarly restricted to certain aspects of western industrial society. Gilligan has also argued that there is an important sex difference; women are more likely to think about moral questions in terms of relationships between people, and the interdependence of people which generates mutual responsibilities (Gilligan 1982). Kohlberg's longitudinal study was with males only, and the preoccupation with rights and justice may be more of a masculine style.

Kohlberg's original subjects were ten to sixteen years old, and his longitudinal data cover twenty years of their thinking. There have been other, shorter, longitudinal studies and several cross-sectional studies of adolescents and adults. From this data it is clear that under good conditions a person will progress "through" a stage in about two and a half years. Most adults, however, do not reach post-conventional reasoning; the majority studied operate with stage 3 or stage 4. What are the implications of this? Is there a connection between moral reasoning and moral action? Does moral reasoning relate to reasoning about social or political issues? The evidence is that moral stage correlates *to a degree* with behavior, but it is not a straightforward relationship (Blasi 1980). Moral stage does not, on the whole, predict the avoidance of anti-social behavior, for example, cheating. On the other hand, moral stage does predict certain forms of pro-social behavior – particularly behavior stemming from action performed in support of a principle, or in defiance of pressures to conform. The most extensive data on this has come from several studies of student activism. These studies demonstrate a close relationship between political action and moral stage (e.g. Haan, Smith and Block 1968). In a study of "bystander intervention" McNamee found that higher stage individuals were considerably more likely to intervene to help someone in distress and to disobey the instructions of an experimenter in order to do so (McNamee 1977). Milgram found that only post-conventional individuals resisted pressures to inflict electric shocks on a "subject" in a learning experiment (Milgram 1974).

This is evidence of some relationship between judgment and action. So it would appear that the higher the level of moral reasoning, the more "moral" the behavior to be expected. However, studies which examine the relationships between cognitive processes and morality consistently indicate the importance of *appraisal* in moral reasoning *and* in moral action. If we consider first the stages of moral reasoning, what is clear is that people at different stages perceive the situation differently. Consequently, they perceive their own responsiblity and involvement in the situation in different ways. Haan, Smith and Block's study demonstrated that students of different moral stages perceived what was going on in the confrontation at Berkeley differently. McNamee's study indicates that people at different stages had different perceptions as to whether they should help the distressed drug-user and whether they were personally responsible for giving such help. So, in fact, the relationship between moral reasoning and moral action is very complex. The actor, depending on his or her moral stage, interprets differently what is going on and what action is appropriate.

There are other cognitive perspectives on moral behavior besides those concerned with stages of moral reasoning. Hoffman (1976), for example, argues that *empathic motivation* is a source of moral, particularly pro-social, behavior. The basis of his argument is that empathy depends upon the child's developing understanding of role-taking, and ability to take the perspective of the other. According to Hoffman, the state of sympathetic distress promotes action, but if action does not occur, the individual feels guilty. Guilt is a state which may promote further action, but guilt may also cause the individual to *redefine* the situation in such a way that the situation no longer induces sympathetic distress.

Another approach which focuses upon cognitive processes is *equity theory*. This approach explains altruistic behavior or pro-social intervention in terms of the observer's perception of *imbalance*; the injured or distressed person is in a state of *inequity* vis-à-vis the observer. To restore equity the observer must (a) act to remove or alter the injury or distress; (b) distort the situation by diminishing its importance; (c) degrade the victim; or (d) deny responsibility. This is not a model of empathic *affect*, but essentially a social *cognitive* model.

Models of character consistency have always been undermined by the early failure of Hartshorne and May to find satisfactory intercorrelations between different areas of morality. Since then, there has been a constant tension between approaches which treated each area of morality (resistance to temptation, guilt, altruism, moral judgment, etc) as separate entities, requiring different explanations, and approaches which sought some unifying overall theme. The unifying theme has usually been some concept of "moral competence", identified with strength of motive or consistency of character – allied to "will". The cognitivist perspective, in contrast, focuses upon the individual's appraisal of the situation and perception of responsibility for action within that situation. In a comprehensive review of the field, Rest has proposed that it is *cognitive* competence which relates (a) the complexity of moral judgment, (b) the individual's potential for action, and (c) the individual's own personally perceived responsibility for taking action. However, though this model presents an integration of judgment and action (including habits) it only partly integrates the affective element in morality. HW-H

Bibliography

Aronfreed, J. 1976: Moral development from the standpoint of a general psychological theory. In *Moral development and behaviour*, ed. T. Lickona. New York: Holt, Rinehart & Winston.

Blasi, A. 1980: Bridging moral cognition and moral action: a critical review of the literature. *Psychological bulletin* 88, 1–45.

Gilligan, C. 1982: *In a different voice*. Cambridge, Mass: Harvard University Press.

Haan, N., Smith, M.B. and Block, J. 1968: Moral reasoning of young adults. *Journal of personality and social psychology* 10, 183–201.

Hoffman, M.L. 1976: Empathy, role taking, guilt and the development of altruistic motives. In *Moral development and behaviour*, ed. T. Lickona, New York: Holt, Rinehart & Winston.

Latané, B. and Darley, J.M. 1970: *The unresponsive bystander: why doesn't he help?* New York: Appleton-Century-Croft.

Lickona, T., ed. 1976 *Moral development and behavior*. New York: Holt, Rinehart & Winston.

McNamee, S. Moral behavior, moral development and motivation, *Journal of Moral Education* 7, 27–32.

Milgram, S. 1974: *Obedience to Authority*. New York: Harper & Row.

Morality. In *Handbook of Child Psychology*, J. Flavell and E. Markmam, volume on Cognitive Development. New York: Wiley.

Zimbardo, P.G. 1974: On the ethics of intervention in human psychological research: with special reference to the Stanford prison experiment. *Cognition* 2, 243–56.

morale A complex attitude to one's colleagues and work tasks. High morale is reflected in positive feelings about the work-group and confidence that difficult goals can be attained. Because of its multidimensional nature, morale has in recent years been less studied than other WORK ATTITUDES such as job motivation and attitude to colleagues. PBW

morbid jealousy The essential feature of morbid jealousy (pathological jealousy, Othello syndrome) is a delusion that the marital partner is unfaithful. The belief is held on inadequate grounds and is unaffected by argument. Characteristic behavior includes intense seeking for evidence of infidelity, with repeated cross questioning of the partner and allegations which may lead to violent quarrels. The frequency of the condition is unknown but it is not uncommon in psychiatric practice and is a major cause of murder and other violence. Morbid jealously is associated with many types of psychiatric disorder, most commonly SCHIZOPHRENIA, DEPRESSION, ALCOHOLISM and PERSONALITY DISORDER. There is a considerable risk of violence and once this has occurred there is a high risk of repetition. RAM

Bibliography

Sheperd, M. 1961: Morbid jealousy: some clinical and social aspects of a psychiatric symptom. *Journal of mental science* 107, 687–704.

motion, apparent *See* visual illusions

motivation: animal The state of an animal that is immediately responsible for the control of its behavior. Motivational changes are usually temporary and reversible in contrast to the more permanent changes in behavior that are brought about by learning, maturation, or injury.

In everyday language the term motivation is used to describe the urges, desires or reasons that are thought to account for people's behavior. In the early days of behavioral science motivation was envisaged in terms of the drive that was necessary for the manifestation of behavior: sexual behavior was due to the sex drive, eating to the hunger drive, etc. This is no longer a prevalent view and it is generally recognized that it is not necessary to account for behavior in terms of motive forces, rather that a particular activity is the result of an animal being in a particular motivational state.

It is important to distinguish between an animal's motivational potential for behavior and the motivational state that characterizes its behavior at a particular time. These are sometimes called the primary and secondary aspects of motivation. Primary thirst results from the brain's measurements of the physiological state of the body. This provides a motivational potential for drinking, which may or may not be realized according to the circumstances. A thirsty animal may not drink because there is no water available, or because some other activity is more important. Secondary thirst is an aspect of motivation that is closely related to the situation at the time of drinking. An animal might drink more than the amount required by its primary thirst because it had just eaten, or because the environmental temperature was high. Similarly, primary hunger depends upon the animal's nutritional state, whereas secondary hunger is determined by such factors as the palatability of the food or the time of day.

Within the repertoire of any given species certain activities will be incompatible with other activities in the sense that the animal cannot do them simultaneously. In other words animals can do only one thing at a time. For example an animal engaged in territorial defense may have the motivational potential for foraging, sleep, etc. The primary motivation for many activities may be simultaneously strong, but the secondary motivation associated with the performance of the relevant behavior will exist for only one of the potential activities.

The behavior observed at a particular time is usually that which has the strongest primary motivation, but this is not always the case. Sometimes there is conflict between equally strong tendencies to perform different activities. This may result in a compromise in which the animal takes up a posture intermediate between the two activities. The most common type of compromise occurs in approach-avoidance situations in which the animal is simultaneously motivated to approach an object, such as a food source or a rival, and to avoid it on account of fear of an unfamiliar situation, or of attack. Such behavior has frequently been the subject of ritualization during evolution, resulting in a characteristic display. For example the male three-spined stickleback (*Gasterosteus aculeatus*) is aggressive towards intruders into its territory. Near the boundary of the territory the aggression is mixed with fear and the stickleback typically adopts a head-down threat display. This display is thought to be a ritualized form of the sand-digging that occurs at the beginning of nest-building (Tinbergen 1952).

It is a common observation that animals perform seemingly irrelevant activities in moments of conflict. For example fighting cockerels may suddenly peck at the ground as if feeding. Such activities are called displacement activities and they are thought to be an example of behavior which does not correspond to the animal's strongest primary motivation or behavioral tendency. Displacement activities are thought to occur when the tendency for a motivationally dominant activity is suddenly reduced, thus removing its inhibition on other aspects of motivation with the potential for overt activity.

This type of disinhibition process can occur as a result of conflict, frustration, or as a part of time-sharing strategy (see DECISION-MAKING). An activity is said to be disinhibited when the inhibition from a stronger motivational tendency is removed. An example is provided by the courtship of the male smooth newt (*Triturus vulgaris*). This animal breathes air but carries out its courtship under water. During courtship there is a build-up of motivation to visit the surface of the water to breathe, but this is usually suppressed by the stronger courtship tendency. If however the courtship founders owing to the uncooperative behavior of the female, there is disinhibition and the male makes a rapid ascent to breathe (Halliday and Sweatman 1976).

Observation of behavior often indicates that certain activities tend to occur in temporal association. We might see a bird flying to some bushes, scratching at the ground, and apparently searching for something. We might then see it fly off to its nest with a twig in its bill. If we saw the bird inserting the twig into its nest we would probably conclude that it was involved in nest-building. On the basis of its temporal organization, the behavior can be divided into a searching, appetitive phase and a more stereotyped consummatory phase. (See APPETITIVE BEHAVIOR; CONSUMMATORY BEHAVIOR.) Some consummatory patterns are so inflexible as to be called fixed-action patterns. These are usually of a reflex nature, though they may involve fairly complex routines.

Close temporal association among activities suggests that they share common causal factors, such as a common influence from hormones, a common GOAL, etc. Such suggestions can often be investigated by means of laboratory experiments.

The fully controlled laboratory experiment involves careful procedures to ensure that all sources of variation are kept constant, or their effects monitored, apart from those that the experimenter intends to manipulate. In investigating primary motivational states the animals must be maintained on a regime involving controlled laboratory climatic conditions and a strict daily routine. Changes in known aspects of the maintenance conditions can then be introduced and their effects noted. For example the animals may be subjected to changes in environmental temperature, changes in diet, or injected with a substance with a known physiological effect, such as a hormone. Standardized tests are then given to assess the effects of different treatments, and the experimental animals are compared with control animals which had no change in their maintenance conditions.

In investigating secondary motivational changes similar standardized procedures are used, but all animals are usually given the same treatment up to the time of testing, and they are then tested in different ways. For example, in investigating the effects of frustration the animals will be deprived of food for a particular period and then provided with food in an experimental test. Some may have food freely available, others may have to work for it, while others may only be allowed to see the food through a glass partition. All these animals will have the same primary hunger, but their secondary motivational states will differ.

The maintenance of a stable internal physiological environment is an important aspect of motivation (see HOMEOSTASIS), and many animals are able to compensate for physiological malfunction by means of appropriate behavior. Some animals can learn to compensate for dietary deficiences, or poisoning, by altering their feeding habits (see FOOD SELECTION). They can learn to avoid unfavourable environments (see THERMOREGULATION) and to exploit new resources.

In addition to the maintenance of the internal *status quo*, changes in primary motivation are often programmed on a seasonal basis. This is often controlled by an internal biological clock which exerts its effects through the medium of hormones (see CLOCK-DRIVEN BEHAVIOR). For example the seasonal reproductive activity of some birds is directly dependent upon their hormonal state, which changes throughout the year under the combined influences of hours of daylight and the circannual clock (Pengelley 1974). Migration and hibernation are annual activities that are controlled in a similar manner.

The more psychological secondary aspects of motivation are less well understood than the principles underlying primary motivation. The minute-to-minute behavior of animals is influenced by many factors including the behavior that has just been performed, the current external stimulus, and the consequences of current behavior. If the consequences are favorable, there is often a positive feedback effect such that the motivation to continue with the current activity is increased. This is particularly noticeable when an animal eats a favorite highly palatable food. When the consequences are unfavorable and the animal does not obtain the expected feedback, a number of things may happen. Initially an animal will often try harder to obtain the desired consequences of its behavior. If unsuccessful it will usually switch attention to other aspects of the environment and this may result in a temporary change in behavior. If lack of success is prolonged the behavior will be subject to extinction as the animal learns that the behavior is not profitable. In psychological terms success is associated with incentive motivation and failure with frustration and eventual EXTINCTION of the response. The situation is complicated, however, by motivational competition from other potential activities. While an animal is foraging successfully its secondary motivation may be raised sufficiently to postpone a change to some other activity, such as territorial defense. If the foraging is unsuccessful the animal may switch earlier to an alternative activity, but if it remains hungry it will soon return to foraging. At any time the foraging may be interrupted by the powerful stimulus of a territorial intruder which has to be chased away. At other times the motivational priorities will change because the animal has become satiated.

Thus changes in behavior that appear to be the same to the outside observer may have very different motivational causes. DJM

Bibliography

*Bolles, R. C. 1975: *Theory of motivation*. New York: Harper & Row.

Halliday, T. R. and Sweatman, H. P. A. 1976: To breathe or not to breathe: the newt's problem. *Animal behaviour* 24, 551–61.

Pengelley, E. T., ed. 1974: *Circannual clocks*. New York: Academic Press.

Tinbergen, N. 1952: Derived activities: their causation, biological significance, origin and emancipation during evolution. *Quarterly review of biology* 27, 1–32.

motivation: philosophical theories of Orthodox philosophical analyses of motivation are meant to cover most cases where people are said to "have" so called *conative* and *affective* attitudes which influence their conscious voluntary behavior. Reasons for acting, desires and aversions, goals or intentions, sudden impulses and abiding proclivities as well as more or less transitory moods and emotions may all count as motivational, inasmuch as they allegedly move or could move people to act in one way instead of another.

Purely cognitive states and processes seem to be impotent by comparison. For example, one might be thoroughly informed regarding a set of circumstances, the available courses of action and the likely results thereof. But if one does not care about (detest, cherish, feel attracted – or repelled by) any of the options, it is not clear what could move one to action. Presumably threats would not be effective if one did not care what happened. HUME appears to be right (*Treatise of human nature* Bk II, pt III, sect. III): mere intellectual awareness or "reason" alone cannot move us to do anything. Of course normally when we act on our desires, fears, and so forth, it seems due in part to our *cognitive* state, to a belief, for instance, that things are not as they ought to be. Yet there appear to be cases of action caused only by a desire or mood. For instance, someone might be so euphoric, or so overwhelmed by an urge to shout, that he does so. His shout really is an action. It is not an involuntary response, like blushing from embarrassment or salivating.

This example highlights two widely accepted distinctions. First, some mental states seem capable of triggering action, while others – such as cognitive states – apparently have a more subordinate role. Second, some behavior qualifies as motivated action, but some does not.

There is less agreement on another contrast originally drawn by PLATO and recently defended at length in Peters's important monograph. Plato's Socrates, seated calmly in his prison cell, imagines someone "saying that the reason why I am sitting here is that my body is composed of bones and sinews, and ... the sinews, by lessening or increasing [their] tension, make it possible for me ... to bend my limbs". Socrates complains that this leaves out something crucial, namely that "inasmuch as the Athenians have thought it better to condemn me, I ... think it better to sit here ... and submit to ... punishment ... If I did not possess ... bones and sinews and so on ... I shouldn't be able to do what I had resolved upon; but to say that I do what I do because of them ... and not because of my choice ... would be ... extremely careless ..." (Phaedo, 98C–99B).

In latter-day terminology, are motives or reasons different from the kind of causes of behavior mentioned by Socrates? Articulating a view held by many recent philosophers, Peters characterizes motives as "reasons for action ... of the [goal-] directed sort" (1958, pp.31f.). It follows that not all action is motivated – done for reasons or directed toward some goal. The spontaneous yell is an example of unmotivated action, and according to Peters (p.152) so is a rote or habitual performance. But the unorthodox and much-debated claim of Peters and his allies is that motives and reasons should not be ranked as causes of motivated action. Peters talks of explaining a "genuine action ... as opposed to [an instance of] suffering something": "*causal explanations* are *ipso facto* inappropriate as sufficient explanations ... To ascribe a point [or goal to someone's] action is *ipso facto* to deny that it can be *sufficiently explained* in terms of causes, though ... there will be many causes in the sense of *necessary* conditions. A story can ... be told about underlying mechanisms; but this does not add up to a sufficient explanation, if ... action ... has to be explained" (p.12).

Peters thinks we can adequately account for action only within a non-causal "means-to-ends ... framework", which allows us to fit human behavior into a "rule-following purposive pattern" (pp.7ff.) Socrates's muscular and skeletal goings-on would belong, according to Peters, to the set of causally necessary conditions for action. The workings of cerebral gears, pulleys and springs imagined by such early materialists as Hobbes; the more refined "underlying mechanisms" substituted by today's mind–brain "identity theorists"; even the conscious or unconscious "drives", tensions, and states of need, anxiety or "affective arousal" postulated by psychologists would also be such conditions. On Peters's view, the occurrence of these conditions is not to be equated with having motives, and action is not an effect of the latter. Opponents naturally grumble that the relationship of motives to deeds is then too mysterious, and some undertake to show that means–ends and rule–compliance accounts are nothing but a species of causal explanation (see Davidson 1980, essays 1, 4, 5, 14).

This debate is hardly over. In any case proponents of motive–deed causation must acknowledge obscurities on their own side. For instance: what exactly is a motivational state? Can we describe, identify and study it apart from the motivated actions it supposedly engenders? How does a person's desire, together with relevant associated beliefs and other desires produce appropriate behavior? When someone is pulled in opposite directions, because he has diverse goals and the chance to pursue only one, what does it mean to say a particular motive is the "strongest"? Is strength the same as intensity? Is the intensity of a motive like that of a headache? Finally, supposing we understand what it is for someone to have preponderant reasons in favor of doing *X* rather than any of the alternatives. Will such a person always do *X* if the opportunity arises, he or she is aware of it, uncoerced, sane, and endowed with the ability, means and right to do *X*? Plato thought so, while ARISTOTLE argued that people clearly sometimes fail to do what they have overriding reasons to do. There is still no consensus, either about why the agent must do *X*, or how he fails (see AKRASIA; Mortimore 1971; Davidson 1980, essay 2).

Two other comparatively popular debates over motivated behavior – what it is to aim selfishly only for one's personal advantage, and what it is to do something for pleasure – are regarded as settled. Butler (1726) made it clear that people cannot be motivated exclusively by "self-love"; for pursuing self-interest is going after things one wants, and personal advantage *simpliciter* cannot be one of them. Similarly with regard to doing *X* for pleasure: RYLE and Peters (1958, pp.22f., 138–42) argue convincingly that this does not consist in doing *X*, then awaiting a quiver of delight; instead it is doing *X* eagerly, joyously, attentively, energetically – not under duress or just to make a living. ITh

Bibliography

Davidson, D. 1980: *Essays on actions and events*. Oxford: Clarendon Press.

Hume, D. 1739 (*1888*): *A treatise of human nature*, ed. L.A. Selby-Bigge. Oxford: Oxford University Press.

*Mortimore, G.W., ed. 1971: *Weakness of will*. London: Macmillan; New York: St. Martin's Press.

*Peters, R.S. 1958: *The concept of motivation*. London: Routledge & Kegan Paul.

Plato: *Phaedo*. Trans. R. Hackforth. Indianapolis: Bobbs-Merrill, 1955.

motivation *See above, and also* achievement motivation; learning and motivation; social motivation.

motor neurons *See* neurons, alpha and gamma motor

motor skills *See* development of motor skills

motor system *See* extrapyramidal motor system

music, psychology of In its broadest sense, this refers to the study of people's responses and behavior towards music or quasi-musical material (e.g. generated statistically or by computer), using established psychological theories and/or methods. There are advantages in attempting to restrict the term "psychology of music" to studies which aim to say something about actual responses to music *per se*, and to exclude those studies whose purpose is to illuminate a particular psychological theory unconnected with music, but which incidentally happen to use musical material. However, this distinction is not always easy to make, and in some instances both purposes may be served to some extent.

Psychological studies of music fall into a number of broad areas, and a major one of these is perception. It is important to distinguish between studies which concentrate upon the physical stimulus properties of music and their perception, and studies which take account of the effects of context and configuration. Studies of the first type might typically involve the perception of individual tones, measurement of temporal resolution capacities, timbre effects, frequency sensitivities, pitch-loudness and pitch-frequency interactions, subjective scaling (e.g. the MEL scale) and so on. Studies of the second type are often less amenable to precise control, and include recognition of familiar or distorted melodies, interference effects of tonal (diatonic) or atonal (non-diatonic) contexts upon diatonically or non-diatonically related tonal groups, transposition experiments, and the study of configuration or other Gestalt-type effects. The implications of studies of the first type are often mainly sensory rather than overtly musical; whereas the intention in studies of the second type is to illuminate some aspect of musical cognition. There are however frequent disagreements about procedures and interpretations and it is sometimes argued that certain studies of the second type in fact have features more in common with sensory experiments of the first type due to the failure of a researcher to understand the operation of context or configuration effects.

Music is temporal rather than spatial and in so far as any experiment seeks to investigate responses to music in context, so a memory component is necessarily involved. Since memory for music appears to differ from memory for other types of material (e.g. see evidence on laterality; Bever and Chiarello (1974)) a particular musical memory is postulated. The argument as to whether a particular piece of work is cognitive or "merely" sensory frequently resolves into an argument about the presence or absence of a "musical memory" component in the study, or about the presence or absence of material having "valid musical content". This is a version of the atomistic versus holistic debate which goes back many years (e.g. Seashore (1938)). However, there are large areas of overlap between studies, and the fact that different pieces of work are construed differently by different people suggests that the argument is often a matter of opinion. Accordingly, the psychology of music is perhaps best taken to include both approaches.

In recent years, the problem of internal representations has led to some fascinating debates. Some ingenious experiments have suggested the importance of a learned internal "template" of a culture-specific type. Such a template, which appears fundamental to the musical experience, has no fixed position in terms of frequency, and enables a heard tune to be perceived musically rather than sensorially, regardless of key. Within such a representation, different tones have differing degrees of stability, and the notes of the scale have specific identities rather than being mere points of reference on a prothetic frequency continuum. The best account of this to date is given in Krumhansl (1979).

Musical ability has been studied as a mental faculty, and a number of tests of musical ability, abilities, and aptitudes have been devised, those of Wing (1948) and Bentley (1966) being among the better known. Many tests exist, however, and these differ from each other in their underlying philosophy. Some emphasize sensory or psychophysical judgments, perhaps splitting music up into a series of separate abilities in accordance with an atomistic doctrine. Others emphasize judgments made in musical contexts, use extracts of real music, and are based on a holistic notion. While evidence suggests that there are merits in both approaches (which perhaps serve different purposes) tests of the second type seem to meet with wider acceptance especially among musicians and music teachers as their greater face validity recommends them. It has also been shown that musical responses can be made by people with substantial degrees of hearing deficit, indicating that musical ability is more than just a high degree of sensory acuity. On the other side of the coin, however, in tests using more overtly musical material, test constructors have not always been able adequately to take into account differences in test scores that might arise from differences in musical learning and experience, as opposed to different "levels" of "innate aptitude". It is clear that in some tests of the holistic type, children with musical experience, particularly if this is of a classical nature, will have a distinct advantage over those from musically more impoverished backgrounds, or whose experience is of some form of music other than the Western Classical tradition. A topic arising from the issues involved in testing is the extent to which musical talent is genetically transmitted, rather than acquired through learning. The issues here run parallel to those involved in the nature/nurture debate over intelligence. A comprehensive account of musical ability is given in Shuter (1968).

Psychological studies of musical performance have been on the increase in recent years. Some studies use musical performance in a fairly precisely-defined psychological context, as when for example speed of playing, sight-reading skill, or error rate are related to an information theory description of the stimulus material, an information processing model of the performance itself, or a particular description of motor programming. Other studies however have less clearly defined roots in a particular body of theory, and seek simply to illuminate a particular task in whatever way seems immediately helpful. Such studies might include investigations of pitch variation in the playing of stringed instruments, embouchure pressure exerted by expert and non-expert brass players, or the relationship between "reading ahead" and skill in sight-reading. While some studies of the latter type might be criticized for being too *ad hoc*, or for lacking clear theoretical implications within psychology, they nonetheless frequently have more immediate relevance for music teachers than do some studies of the first type.

The area of aesthetics is a broad one covering a wide range of investigative approaches. In the area of EXPERIMENTAL AESTHETICS pioneered by Berlyne (1971), most attention has been concentrated on the visual arts but a certain amount of work exists in which the postulation of an inverted-U function relating preference to complexity is examined with musical material. Some attempts have failed to find such a relationship (e.g. Vitz (1966)), but retrospectively this failure seems attributable to uncontroled context effects, and other studies find positive support for the theory (e.g. Heyduk (1972)). The search for meaning in music has gone in quite a different direction, and appears to suffer from problems with basic concepts. Subjects may be asked to make subjective statements about musical extracts, and an attempt made to identify a common theme or affect; but in most cases there is little consensus. In addition, composers' own comments have sometimes been used as a guide to what the music "really" means, which rather begs the question. At the moment, empirical evidence suggests that this approach may be misconceived. Only the most general "mood" connotations emerge with any regularity at all, and seem to depend on non-melodic aspects like tempo and rhythm. All in all, the idea that music "really" has a specifiable pattern of meaning, perhaps some sort of quasi-verbal significance as suggested by Cooke (1959) in which particular groups of notes "mean" particular things, has received little empirical support. Evidence from factor analyses, whilst perhaps more defensible from a methodological standpoint, has also proved a little disappointing and tends to identify factors which are very general, and rather stereotyped (e.g. gloom/gaiety; solemn/trivial; "rhythm"; "melody"). It may be that the search for meaning in music has become bogged down in the search for an analogy to linguistic meaning which may well not exist. Finally in the area of aesthetics, a limited number of workers have examined the role of social factors in preference, and noted age and class differences in preference, and the effects of such things as "composer credibility" upon musician's evaluations and accuracy of performance.

A number of other areas falling under the heading of "the psychology of music" exist, though these have perhaps been less well explored by psychologists. Worth mentioning are studies of the possible role of music in industry, and various claims that productivity or work satisfaction are improved when particular kinds of music are played; though in many cases, it looks as though the claims that are made by some commercially-interested organisations go rather further than is warranted by the data. The use of music in therapeutic settings is a developing area of great potential, and whilst much of the data here are "soft" rather than experimentally rigorous, there seems no reason to doubt that musical experiences can prove helpful and rewarding for many individuals who perhaps show limited signs of expression or interaction in other modalities. Lastly, cross-cultural studies have occasionally compared the music and musical abilities of different cultural groups, the most common comparisons being made between Western classical music and what is sometimes ethnocentrically referred to as "primitive" music. Sometimes, levels of perceptual and motor skills are revealed which tax the ability of Western listeners to comprehend, especially in the areas of rhythmic and modal complexity. By and large, however, the literature of ethnomusicology is a richer source of material on these things than the limited number of psychological studies.

While the bulk of work by psychologists with musical materials concerns perception, cognition, musical abilities, and performance, and to a lesser extent, aesthetics, the area is potentially very wide and almost any psychological theory or approach could be applied to some aspect of music and musical behavior, and thereby fall under the heading of "the psychology of music". The area is rich in unanswered, and unasked, questions.

JBD

Bibliography

Bentley, A. 1966: *Musical ability in children, and its measurement*. London: Harrap; New York: October House.

Berlyne, D.E. 1971: *Aesthetics and psychobiology*. New York: Appleton Century Crofts.

Bever, T.G. and Chiarello, R.J. 1974: Cerebral dominance in musicians and non-musicians. *Science* 185, 4150, 537–9.

Cooke, D. 1959: *The language of music*. Oxford: Oxford University Press.

*Davies, J.B. 1978: *The psychology of music*. London: Hutchinson; Stanford, Calif.: Stanford University Press.

——— 1981: Memory for melodies and tonal sequences: a theoretical note. *British journal of psychology* 70, 205–10.

Heyduk, R. 1972: Static and dynamic aspects of rated and exploratory preference for musical compositions. In *Pleasure, reward, preference*, ed. D.E. Berlyne and K.B. Madsen. New York: Academic Press.

Krumhansl, C.L. 1979: The psychological representation of musical pitch in a tonal context. *Cognitive psychology* 11, 346–74.

*Radocy, R.E. and Boyle, J.D. 1979: *Psychological foundations of musical behavior*. Illinois: Charles C. Thomas.

Seashore, C.E., ed. 1938: *Psychology of music*. New York: McGraw-Hill.

*Shuter, R. 1968: *The psychology of musical ability*. London: Methuen; New York: Barnes & Noble.

Vitz, P.C. 1966: Affect as a function of stimulus variation. *Journal of experimental psychology* 711, 74–9.

Wing, H.D. 1948: Tests of musical ability and appreciation. *British journal of psychology*. Monograph supplement 27.

mysticism A type of visionary religious experience in which the mystic "sees God", or believes himself or herself to have had direct experience of God. Traditional religion is based upon the belief in the reality of God, but accepts that humans are trapped in a material world whose nature prevents them from 'knowing' God in any direct sense. Mystics of all ages have been convinced that, under certain conditions, the soul can have some kind of apprehension of God or ultimate reality.

Most mystics have agreed that this vision is "ineffable", inexpressible in words. Many of them, from Plotinus to St John of the Cross and Jacob Boehme, have nevertheless written extensively about their experience, the underlying assumption of all such writings seeming to be the notion that what our senses tell us of the material world is somehow false, or at least based upon false assumptions. Most mystics also seem to be agreed upon some version of the proposition that the soul itself is of the same nature as God. In Hindu theology, the *atman*, the individual human soul, is *Brahman*, the divine ground of reality. The Christian assertion "the kingdom of God is within you" seems to mean the same thing.

Mysticism may be divided into two types, which could be labelled inclusive and exclusive. The inclusive mystic sees all reality as a manifestation of God; it may be regarded as a form of pantheism, based upon some form of direct perception rather than belief or argument. William Blake expressed the essence of "inclusive" mysticism in the line "to see a world in a grain of sand . . .". Exclusive mysticism takes as its starting point a turning away from the world and from sensory reality; it seems to accept the notion of God as entirely other-worldly – a darkness or void. Yet typically, the two are closely connected, and most mystics would insist that they are in no way contradictory. As Baudelaire says, "our pale reason hides us from the infinite". Mysticism insists that our senses somehow distort the world, reduce it to a lesser reality, in a way that a black-and-white television reduces the reality seen by the cameras to something altogether cruder and simpler. Its position therefore has much in common with the tradition of western philosophy typified by KANT, Bradley and HUSSERL, which argues that our senses "filter" reality, and present us, so to speak, with an edited — perhaps even bowdlerised — version. CW

Bibliography

Ferguson, John, 1976: *An illustrated encyclopedia of mysticism*. London: Thames & Hudson.

Underhill, Evelyn 1911: *Mysticism*. London: Methuen.

O'Brien, Elmer 1965: *Varieties of mystical experience*. New York: Mentor Books.

Staal, Frits 1975: *Exploring mysticism*. Harmondsworth: Penguin books.

N

narcissism After the Greek myth of Narcissus, either (i) a sexual perversion in which a person treats his or her own body as the preferred sex-object, or (ii) in Freudian theory any investment of libido in, and hence cathexis of, aspects of the self as opposed to external objects (see PSYCHOANALYTICAL PERSONALITY THEORY). In the latter sense narcissism is not necessarily pathological, since some positive self-regard may be both intrinsically healthy and also necessary to forming stable relationships with other people (Freud 1917, ch. 26).

Hence (a) narcissistic "object-choice", where an object is chosen because of its similarities to oneself; (b) "narcissistic hurt", which is a blow to self-esteem or morale; (c) "narcissistic supplies", which are the reassuring feedback as to their own worth which infants and young children seek from their mothers as a basis for forming their own identity (individuation); and later any affection or attention from any source which enhances self-esteem (Kohut 1971). NMC

Bibliography

Freud, S. 1917: *Introductory lectures*, part 3. *Standard edition of the complete psychological works of Sigmund Freud*. Vol. 16. London: Hogarth Press; New York: Norton.

Kohut, H. 1971: *The analysis of the self*, New York: International Univerisity Press.

narcotics A name given to the natural or synthetic derivatives of opium which have the ability to produce both sleep and analgesia (Julien 1978). Narcotic opiates can be classified as those which occur naturally in the exudate of the opium poppy (e.g. morphine), semisynthetic derivatives (e.g. heroin) and synthetic opiates (e.g. methadone). The primary medical uses of opiates in general are in the treatment of persistent coughing, in diarrhea and for relief of moderate to severe pain. The more potent opiates such as heroin or morphine can also produce euphoria, or a sense of well-being, which contributes significantly to their recreational abuse. Continued use of virtually all the opiates can lead to tolerance and physical dependence. Their mechanisms of action are complex and not fully understood, but appear to be mediated via interactions with endogenous opiate receptors (see ENKEPHALINS/ENDORPHINS). GPH

Bibliography

Julien, R.M. 1978: *A primer of drug action*. 2nd edn. San Francisco: Freeman.

natural kind The expression was introduced by J.S. Mill (1843) to cover any class "which is distinguished from all other classes by an indeterminate multitude of properties not derivable from one another". Thus *man* and *dog* are natural kinds, but *snub-nosed* and *white* are not. All kinds, says Mill, are strictly speaking natural, and all classifications man-made. But we may call a kind "natural" in a more restricted sense if recognition of it in our scheme of classification is forced on us by the nature of things, namely the concatenation in a large number of beings of a whole inexhaustible cluster of common properties. JMS

Bibliography

Mill, J.S. 1843 (*1973*): *A system of logic*. Toronto: Toronto University Press; London: Routledge & Kegan Paul.

natural selection Natural selection is the biological process whereby some members of an animal (or plant) population survive and reproduce more successfully than others, and transmit to their offspring the inherited basis of the characteristics which enabled them to do so. In any environment, individual animals live for differing lengths of time, and produce differing numbers of offspring. They also differ in their physical and behavioral characteristics, and such differences sometimes have a genetic basis. Where these patterns of variation are related, so that possessors of one genetically inherited characteristic regularly survive and reproduce more successfully than possessors of an alternative one, natural processes are in effect selecting one characteristic in the animal population at the expense of another. Acting over many generations, selection of this kind will generally result in the retention and spread through the population of those characteristics which confer the greatest advantages on their possessors, given the survival problems posed by their particular environment. Sometimes selection may act directionally, so bringing about biological changes in a population; at other times it may simply act against departures from the common form of a characteristic, thus having a stabilizing effect. Through natural selection, members of an animal population come to have characteristics which render them well adapted for living and breeding in the environment where the selection has taken place. This concept of ADAPTATION by natural selection, combined with modern understanding of the origins and inheritance of genetic variation, forms a powerful theory of the working of biological evolution – the neo-Darwinian theory.

The idea of natural selection was proposed by Darwin and Wallace (1859). In their account of how the differential survival and reproduction of individuals with different biological characteristics lead to changes in the overall frequencies of those characteristics in a natural population, the process was summed up as 'natural selection', by analogy with the artificial selection practiced by breeders of domestic animals and plants, and the term has been used ever since. The force of their proposal lay in the suggestion that the effects of natural selection, even if imperceptibly small in any particular generation, have no definite limits and so may cumulatively be very large over long periods of time. This theory, entailing biological evolution and the emergence of new species, appeared against the background of a belief in the fixity of species, and although it was by no means the first theory to challenge that doctrine, it was more cogent than earlier evolutionary theories, and it soon became embroiled in a now famous controversy. As the nineteenth century proceeded, the idea of natural selection became very influential in biology, and in the twentieth century, with the rise of classical and population genetics, Darwin and Wallace's proposal has been developed in a number of ways but not fundamentally revised. Today virtually all biologists probably consider natural selection to be a well established phenomenon, and many would also consider it the main process underlying biological evolution (though other processes are also considered – see EVOLUTION).

Darwin also proposed a theory of sexual selection, whereby characteristics were favored which enhanced reproductive success via advantages in sexual competition rather than in survival: and he suggested that this occurred in two main ways, competition between males and mate choice by females. This theory has been less consistently upheld by subsequent evolutionary biologists than the main natural selection theory, and for some time it was in partial eclipse. More recently, however, it has been widely reinstated in a developed form (see O'Donald 1980, Short 1977). Scope for the action of sexual selection is probably greatest in polygynous species, but it may nonetheless be responsible for some biological differences between the sexes in other species also. Nowadays many biologists probably consider sexual selection an aspect of natural selection rather than a distinct process.

Darwin himself envisaged that behavior (habits, instincts) would in principle be subject to natural selection in the same way as any other characteristic of an animal species; and, although it took some time to be widely accepted, this recognition became an important feature of the behavioral disciplines of ETHOLOGY and SOCIOBIOLOGY. Evidently, however, natural selection is expected to operate on behavioral characteristics only where those characteristics are genetically influenced, and where they have an impact on an animal's survival and reproduction. The genetic inheritance of behavior patterns has been precisely analysed only in a few cases: but there are undoubtedly numerous other cases where genes play an important role, including many where both genetic and environmental factors have a substantial effect on behavior (see BEHAVIOR GENETICS). The most striking indications of the influence of genes on behavior, and also of the presumed impact of natural selection on behavioral characteristics, are to be seen in the numerous behavioral differences between animal species, and these provided an important line of evidence for the founders of ethology.

In the most widely accepted form of the theory, frequently invoked in ethology, natural selection operates, as described above, on the biological and behavioral characteristics of individuals, and predominantly within species. Evolutionary ideas are in a state of considerable ferment, however, and there are less orthodox versions of natural selection theory in currency, some of which are relevant to behavioral questions. One suggestion repeatedly made in recent years is that natural selection may operate on groups (i.e. via differential extinction and fission of groups) and result in increased adaptation of groups themselves rather than the constituent individuals. Wynne-Edwards was interested in how animal populations avoid over-exploitation of resources, and he proposed that the ecologically successful groups were those whose members abstained from reproducing in response to certain social signals (see CONVENTIONAL AND EPIDEICTIC BEHAVIOR) – a system which, he proposed, was maintained by group selection, to the benefit of the group. Various other authors have proposed versions and mathematical models of group selection theory (e.g. Wilson 1980). Despite considerable debate in recent years, however, the theory has not gained general acceptance: it appears that, even though group selection may be a viable mechanism in principle, the conditions under which it is expected to outweigh individual selection are limited, and may occur rarely if at all in nature. Another large scale unit of selection is proposed in species selection theory, where it is argued that evolutionary pressures are acting between species, rather than being concentrated within them (Stanley 1979) – a proposition still under considerable debate.

A contrasting elaboration of Darwinian natural selection theory is that involved in kin selection. Hamilton was interested in the special case of the social insects, where many individuals are non-reproductive, and he argued, by an extension of the ordinary explanation of parental care, that altruism directed toward any related individual would be favored in natural selection (subject to certain specified constraints). This evolutionary explanation of altruism between kin (referred to by the terms kin selection and inclusive fitness) has gained more general acceptance among biologists than the group selection theory of altruism, at least as an explanation of the extreme altruism found among social insects and possibly for other cases too (see KINSHIP). To some authors (especially Dawkins 1982), the logical conclusion from kin selection theory is to propose the gene rather than the individual as the unit of natural selection: others, while accepting the principle of kin selection, argue for the continuing importance of the individual as an entity on which natural selection acts, or suggest that it may not be fruitful to insist on a single unit or level of selection.

Natural selection may, according to one hypothesis, operate in different ways under different ecological conditions: in particular there may be a continuum of modes whose opposite poles are termed r-selection and K-selection (Pianka 1970). K-selection, it is proposed, is the mode characteristic of relatively constant or predictable ecological conditions, and r-selection of relatively variable or unpredictable ones. The evolutionary consequences of these contrasting selective regimes are considered to be contrasting sets of characteristics in the organisms affected – in the case of K-selection, slow development, large size, late reproduction, intensive parental care, and high learning capacity; and in the case of r-selection, the opposites of those characteristics. Distinctions along the r-K continuum are sometimes drawn on a large scale (e.g. between terrestrial vertebrates and terrestrial invertebrates) and sometimes in the smaller scale comparison of closely related species (Richardson 1975). A number of authors have found this r-K distinction a useful one, but like many in this area, it has its limitations also.

See also SOCIOBIOLOGY. RDA

Bibliography

Darwin, C. 1859: *The origin of species by means of natural selection*. London: John Murray (Penguin edition 1968).

Darwin, C. and Wallace, A. 1859: On the tendency of species to form varieties; and on the perpetuation of varieties and species by natural means of selection. *Journal of the proceedings of the Linnean Society (Zoology)* 3, 45–62.

Dawkins, R. 1982: *The extended phenotype: the gene as the unit of selection*. Oxford and San Francisco: W.H. Freeman.

Hinde, R.A. 1982: *Ethology: its nature and relations with other sciences*. Oxford and New York: Oxford University Press.

Maynard Smith, J. 1975: *The theory of evolution*. 3rd edn. Harmondsworth and New York: Penguin.

O'Donald, P. 1980: *Genetic models of sexual selection*. Cambridge, New York and Melbourne: Cambridge University Press.

Pianka, E.R. 1970: On r- and K-selection. *American naturalist*. 104, 592–7.

Richardson, B.J. 1975: r and K selection in kangaroos. *Nature* 255, 323–4.

Short, R.V. 1977: Sexual selection and the descent of man. In *Reproduction and evolution* (4th International Symposium on Comparative Biology of Reproduction), ed. J.H. Calaby and C.H. Tyndale-Biscoe. Canberra: Australian Academy of Science.

Stanley, S.M. (1979): *Macroevolution: pattern and process*. San Francisco: W.H. Freeman.

Williams, G.C. 1966: *Adaptation and natural selection: a critique of some current evolutionary thought*. Princeton: Princeton University Press.

Wilson, D.S. 1980: *The natural selection of populations and communities*. Menlo Park (California), London and Sydney: Benjamin/Cummings.

naturalness *See* linguistic naturalness

navigation In the broad sense includes all non-random movement, but is usually distinguished from mere orientation in the following way. Orientation refers to movement which has direction relative to some physical entity, but which is not guided by information about the location of a goal: this latter ability is what distinguishes navigation.

Some birds migrating for the first time use the sun or stars as a compass to maintain orientation, coping with the relative movements of the sun by means of an internal biological clock or of the stars through the patterning of constellations. Following a fixed compass orientation for a specific distance normally delivers them to the species wintering grounds but experimental displacements of these birds at right angles to their migratory route produces a corresponding displacement in final destination. That experienced adult birds may return to habitual areas despite such displacement is evidence for navigation.

Navigation in this sense is often divided into pilotage, which involves homing to a destination by known landmarks, and true navigation involving homing by other means. Release experiments in novel areas have shown that pigeons are capable of true navigation, and, in addition to using a sun compass, appear to use a magnetic compass in overcast conditions. However a compass, although sufficient for orientation, is insufficient for navigation: information which is equivalent to a map must supplement it. The nature of the bird's map remains unknown, despite vigorous current research into such possibilities as the use of smells and atmospheric cues, and unsuspected abilities to sense polarized light, ultrasound and barometric pressure. (See also MIGRATION; CLOCK-DRIVEN BEHAVIOR). AW

Bibliography

Keeton, W.T. 1981: Navigation pp.400–05. In D. McFarland, ed. *The Oxford companion to animal behavior*. Oxford and New York: Oxford University Press.

needs That which is necessary for an organism's health and well being. Human needs are of two types. Physical needs are requirements for a healthy body (e.g. food, water, air). Psychological needs are requirements for mental health (e.g. self esteem, pleasure, growth). Need deprivation initially produces feelings of pain or discomfort, while need satisfaction leads to feelings of pleasure and well being. Need deprivation does not necessarily lead to an attempt at satisfaction. That depends upon whether or not the organism expects that some appropriate action will satisfy the need. Nor is there any compelling evidence to support claims that needs exist in a hierarchy of prepotency starting with bodily needs and ending with self actualization (a concept which is not clearly defined). The fact that a need is not met may or may not lead to appropriate behavior, since people can make errors in choosing courses of action. Specific choices and actions are guided by values (see VALUES). EAL

negotiation A verbal interchange aimed at reaching a joint decision among parties who perceive that their interests diverge on the issue(s) under consideration. Other procedures for making decisions under such circumstances include unilateral pre-emptive action, coercion, norm following, tacit bargaining, and decision by higher authority. Multiple parties may be involved, though most theory and research concerns the two-party case. Negotiation is found in all realms of society including the family, workplace, marketplace, and the arenas of labor/management and international relations. It can be viewed as a mild form of conflict which often results in genuine conflict resolution and which, so long as it continues, has the potential for averting more serious struggles.

Theoretical and empirical contributions to the study of negotiation are found in most branches of social science. The earliest work was done by economists, who developed several formal models (see Young 1975). More recently, significant contributions have been made by sociologists (e.g. Bacharach and Lawler 1981), political scientists (e.g., Zartman 1978), anthropologists (e.g. Gulliver 1979), industrial relations specialists (e.g. Walton and McKersie 1965), international relations scholars (e.g. Ikle 1964), and social psychologists (e.g., Druckman, 1977; Pruitt, 1981; Rubin & Brown, 1975).

Sometimes only one issue (e.g. the price of an antique) is under consideration in negotiation. But more often there are multiple issues creating a problem of cognitive overload. This problem can be handled by (a) developing an agenda; (b) placing more fundamental issues early in the agenda so that a simple formula or "framework agreement" can emerge as a guide for later, more detailed discussions; and (c) parceling out issues among several representative committees. These procedures help organize decision making but add to the complexity of the task by producing still more issues requiring joint agreement.

Positional Bargaining

Research has shown that negotiators who make higher demands and slower concessions usually achieve more favorable outcomes for themselves if agreement is reached, but their agreements are reached more slowly and they are less certain to reach agreement. High demands and slow concessions are made to the extent that (a) negotiators have high levels of aspiration, (b) they have attractive alternatives to reaching agreement, (c) they expect the other party to make large concessions in the long run, (d) they have the capacity to mount effective threats, (e) time spent in negotiation is not costly to them, and (f) a deadline for reaching agreement is not imminent. Also, representatives tend to make higher demands and slower concessions than do individuals negotiating on their own behalf, especially when they are highly accountable to, distrusted by or under the surveillance of their constituents.

Negotiators defend their proposals by means of competitive (or, as they are sometimes called, "distributive") tactics, such as (a) presenting arguments that favor their demands, (b) committing themselves not to moderate their demands so that the other party must accept them if agreement is to be reached, (c) imposing a deadline, and (d) threatening to punish the other party for not agreeing to their terms. Though often successful in eliciting concessions, competitive tactics tend to be resented and are frequently answered in kind, starting a conflict spiral.

Prominent Solutions

Sometimes a single alternative stands out in a negotiator's thinking as the most proper or most likely solution to an issue, for example, a 50-50 division of a prize, a mediator's suggestion about an appropriate hourly increase, a river or historical boundary in a border dispute. If the same alternative stands out in the other party's thinking, and each party knows that this is true of the other, a "prominent solution" is said to exist (Schelling 1960). Research suggests that the existence of a prominent solution increases the likelihood that agreement will be reached, speeds concession making, thus reducing the time spent in negotiation, and dampens the impact of other determinants of demand level and concession rate. However, if different alternatives stand out in the two parties' thinking, concessions are probably slower than they otherwise would be and agreement is likely to be jeopardized.

Problem Solving

While capable of establishing some of the boundary conditions that will delimit the final agreement, positional bargaining is often incapable of producing agreement (Fisher and Ury 1981). Prominent solutions sometimes emerge to fill this gap, but they are by no means a certain development. Hence, there is often a need for problem solving or mediation.

"Problem solving" refers to any effort to locate or move towards a mutually acceptable solution. It can be an individual or joint enterprise. An example of individual problem solving would be the activity of a negotiator who seeks information about the other party's interests, devises an alternative that seems to reconcile these interests with his or her own, and proposes this alternative to the other party. An example of joint problem solving would be a frank discussion between the two parties in which they reveal the interests underlying their proposals and their priorities among these interests and then brainstorm in search of a way to reconcile those interests that seem to be opposed.

Activities of the kind just described are quite risky in the sense of producing high potential cost if the other party is not genuinely interested in problem solving but is intent on extracting as many concessions as possible (Pruitt 1981). Problem solving activity may make one appear weak (i.e. willing to make extensive future concessions) and may reveal information that can be used by the other party to devise effective threats and locate alternatives that are just barely acceptable. In addition there is a danger that the other party will treat one's tentative proposals as concessions that provide a starting point for further negotiation. Hence, parties who wish to engage in problem solving but do not trust the other's intentions often employ less risky tactics. These include sending conciliatory signals, transmitting messages through disavowable intermediaries, and attending unofficial "backchannel" meetings with the other party. All these procedures can be employed on an exploratory basis while maintaining a rigid competitive stance in the formal negotiation.

The outcome of problem solving can be a compromise on a single issue, an exchange of concessions on two or more issues, or the recasting of an issue or issues in such a way that new, more mutually satisfying alternatives are found.

There are many advantages to employing problem solving in addition to or instead of positional bargaining. As mentioned earlier, agreement is more likely to be reached. The agreement reached is often better for both parties (i.e. more "integrative") because it reconciles their separate interests. Hence, it is likely to be more lasting, more supportive of the relationship between the parties, and more beneficial to any overarching social entity that includes both parties (e.g. a firm in which the parties are departments, or society at large). However positional bargaining cannot usually be avoided altogether, because it is encouraged by self interest. Rather, a two-step process is frequently found, in which positional bargaining is pursued until a deadlock is reached, followed by problem solving to agreement. The final agreement reflects both the forces that affect demand level (e.g. the relative cost to the two parties of time elapsed or their relative threat capacity) and the inventiveness and flexibility of the problem solving effort.

There is a danger that when engaged in problem solving negotiators will become so interested in the other party's interests that they lose sight of their own. If this happens unilaterally, the other party may gain an unnecessary advantage. If it happens bilaterally, a simple compromise may be quickly negotiated and opportunities for discovering more mutually beneficial agreements overlooked. It follows that problem solvers should take special care to be firm about their interests while remaining flexible about how these interests are to be achieved.

A desire to engage in problem solving is encouraged by, (a) a recognition that the negotiation is in a deadlock, (b) a fear that the controversy will escalate, (c) warm feelings towards or a sense of common identity with the other party, (d) a positive mood, (e) future dependence on the other party together with farsightedness about the future, and (f) freedom from constituent surveillance during negotiation. Constituent surveillance must be distinguished from accountability for the ultimate agreement to constituents. The latter encourages firmness about one's interests and, hence, in the context of problem solving activity, can lead to the development of agreements that provide high benefit to both parties.

Mediation

Problem solving is not always possible or successful, and mediation by third parties is often essential for reaching agreement in negotiation. Mediators can take either a process approach, a content approach, or both (Rubin 1981). Process mediation involves encouraging problem solving, reconciling the parties to one another, improving communication, educating the parties about the dynamics of conflict, etc. Content mediation involves suggesting possible agreements, providing decommitting formulas, providing incentives for particular concessions, etc. The most effective mediators are those who have rapport with both parties, a condition that often but not always requires impartiality between the parties. Timing is important in mediation, in that third party assistance is most welcome when the negotiators become aware that they cannot solve the problem on their own or that uncontrollable forces (e.g. escalation of the conflict) threaten the future of negotiation. Mediation must be distinguished from arbitration, in which the third party imposes a settlement. Arbitration encourages rapid, cost-effective conflict resolution. But since it takes decision making out of the hands of the conflicting parties it runs the danger of overlooking opportunities for the development of mutually beneficial agreements.

DGP

Bibliography

Bacharach, S.B. and Lawler, E.J. 1981: *Bargaining: power, tactics, and outcomes*. San Francisco: Jossey-Bass.

Druckman, D., ed. 1977: *Negotiations: social-psychological perspectives*. Beverly Hills, Calif.: Sage.

Fisher, R. and Ury, W. 1981: *Getting to YES: negotiating agreement without giving in*. Boston: Houghton Mifflin.

Gulliver, P.H. 1979: *Disputes and negotiations: a cross-cultural perspective*. New York: Academic Press.

Ikle, F.C. 1964: *How nations negotiate*. New York: Harper.

*Pruitt, D.G. 1981: *Negotiation behavior*. New York: Academic Press.

*Rubin, J.Z., ed. 1981: *Dynamics of third party intervention: Kissinger in the Middle East*. New York: Praeger.

Rubin, J.Z. and Brown, B.R. 1975: *The social psychology of bargaining and negotiation.* New York: Academic Press.

Schelling, T.C. 1960: *The strategy of conflict.* Cambridge, Mass.: Harvard University Press.

*Walton, R.E. and McKersie, R.B. 1965: *A behavioral theory of labor negotiations: an analysis of a social interaction system.* New York: McGraw-Hill.

Young, O.R. 1975: *Bargaining: formal theories of negotiation.* Urbana, Ill.: University of Illinois Press.

Zartman, I.W., ed. 1978: *The negotiation process.* Beverly Hills, Calif.: Sage.

neo-Freudian theory A term used of the approach of psychoanalytic theorists who have rejected, added to, or modified significant portions of Freud's original theory. The term is used by different writers with varying levels of specificity. In its most general sense it can apply to a wide range of psychoanalytically-orientated psychologists whose theories diverge from Freud's in greater or lesser degrees: in this sense for example, Carl Jung, Erik Erikson, Otto Rank and object relations theorists could all be considered neo-Freudians, even though Erikson accepts the basic premises of Freudian analysis while Jung rejects many of them. Usually, however, the term neo-Freudian is reserved for a smaller group of psychoanalysts whose theories share two core features: (1) they reject Freud's "libido theory", his view that the primary motivators in personality are innate biological instincts of sexuality and aggression which are specific to childhood; and (2) they correspondingly emphasize the importance of social needs, the influence of cultural and interpersonal factors and the role of the self in personality development.

The four theorists most frequently described as neo-Freudians in this more restrictive sense are Alfred Adler, Karen Horney, Erich Fromm and Harry Stack Sullivan. The following brief discussion first describes the major contributions of these thinkers and then summarizes what their theories have in common.

Alfred Adler was born in Vienna in 1870. He was a member of the original small group of psychoanalysts which met at Freud's house to discuss analytic theory, and was the first president of the Vienna branch of the Psychoanalytic Society. He came to reject some basic tenets of Freud's theory, however, including the notion that sexual trauma is the basis for neurosis, and resigned from the society in 1911 to form his own school which he named INDIVIDUAL PSYCHOLOGY. Adler sees the person as a united whole, indivisible, responsible for his actions, free and striving towards conscious goals. The major tenets of his theory are contained in six key concepts: (1) *fictional finalism*, the notion that people are motivated not primarily by past events, but by their images and expectations for future possibilities; (2) *striving for superiority*, the individual's innate tendency to develop his capacities to the full and to strive for perfection; (3) *inferiority feelings*, which Adler sees as the normal response to the realization of being less than perfect and which motivate all efforts towards self-actualization; (4) *social interest*, the innate tendency to be interested in other people and in the social group, manifested in cooperation, empathy, altruism and, ultimately, the desire for a perfect society; (5) *style of life*, the different unique forms in which individuals strive for perfection; and (6) the *creative self*, the active, constructive center of personality which interprets experience and chooses a response to it.

Karen Horney was born in Germany in 1885. She was associated with the Berlin Psychoanalytic Institute from 1918 to 1932, then emigrated to the USA where she founded an association and a training institute. Horney saw herself as remaining within the Freudian tradition, though she tried to correct what she saw as the limitations of Freud's approach: his biological and mechanistic orientation. She accepted Freud's notions of psychic determinism, unconscious motivation and the importance of irrational emotional experience. The root of neurosis for Horney is the childhood experience of basic anxiety and the strategies adopted in response to it. The helpless, totally dependent child encountering rejection, inconsistency or harsh treatment from its parents, feels that its safety and fundamental security are threatened. The child can adopt various strategies to cope with this, and these can become permanent features of personality and eventually take on the status of needs in their own right. Horney catalogues ten of these neurotic needs; they all mirror needs of normal people, but in an unrealistic, exaggerated and insatiable form: for example, the need for perfection, for total love, for complete control. Horney does not believe that the experience of basic anxiety is an inevitable part of development; it can be avoided if the child is treated with love, respect and consistency.

Like Horney, Erich Fromm was born in Germany and emigrated to the United States in the early 1930s. Fromm's work was influenced by the writings of Karl Marx and by existentialism as well as by psychoanalytic theory. He calls himself a "dialectical humanist". The central notion in Fromm's theory is his description of the human condition. Humans, he says, are animals and thus part of nature; however, because of their distinctively human nature they are also more than an animal and experience a separation between themselves and the natural world and between themselves and other people. This separateness from the natural order gives human beings the freedom to choose their lives; this freedom gives human life its meaning and potential, but it also gives rise to anxiety. As a result, people often try to relinquish their freedom through conformity or submission to authorities. Like Freud and Adler, Fromm believes that there is a species-specific, innate human nature which is independent of culture. However he has also emphasized the role that social context plays in determining the way in which the individual deals with basic human needs. Different societies and different groups within society create particular types of "character". Moreover Fromm judges societies on the basis of how well they meet the basic human needs of their members; he argues that no present society makes an adequate job of this task, and calls the form of society that he believes would do so "Humanistic Communitarian Socialism".

More than any of the other neo-Freudians, Harry Stack Sullivan moved away from Freudian theory and articulated a model of personality that is thoroughly social and interpersonal. In fact Sullivan claims that the notion of personality, conceived in terms of the single individual, is hypothetical, an illusion. Personality, he argues, consists in the relatively enduring patterns of interpersonal relations which are manifested in our lives – our relations both with real others and with the imagined others which make up the content of our thoughts, feelings and fantasies. He was strongly influenced by social psychology and anthropology, particularly by George Herbert Mead and other theorists at the Chicago School of Sociology. He was born in 1892 in New York and trained as an analyst. Sullivan described six stages in personality development, each of which represents a new interpersonal constellation. In *infancy* the child relates to the mother via its oral activity towards the nipple and develops notions of the good and bad other, and the correct and the wrong other. In *childhood* with the beginning of language, the child begins to relate to playmates and to form more cognitive representations of others. In the *juvenile* period (first school) the child learns to relate to the peer group and to authorities outside the home. In *pre-adolescence* "chum" relations with same sex peers are central for learning cooperation, mutuality, reciprocity and intimacy. The development of patterns of heterosexual relationships become the focus in *early adolescence*, as puberty brings the beginning of the lust dynamism and this becomes differentiated from companionship and intimacy. Finally, in *late adolescence*, a long period of education in varying social roles and relations brings about the transition to the complexity of adult social living and citizenship.

All four theorists share several core orientations which characterize the neo-Freudian approach. First, they all take a more positive and optimistic view of human nature than does classical psychoanalysis; they stress the striving for self-actualization, for active adaptation to the environment and for social relatedness and harmony, in contrast to Freud's emphasis on antisocial impulses of sexuality and aggression. Where Freud sees the individual as in inevitable conflict with the society which demands restriction of his impulsive acts, the neo-Freudians propose a more harmonious relationship between the individual and society. They see social life as a fulfilment of basic human nature, not a repression of it. In addition, these writers pay as much attention to the role of conscious conflicts and experiences in adolescence and adulthood as to unconscious conflicts in early childhood. Finally, they stress the effects of the social milieu in determining personality. (See also COGNITIVE PERSONALITY THEORY.) SB

Bibliography

Adler, A. 1927: *The practice and theory of individual psychology*. New York: Harcourt, Brace & World.

Ansbacher, H. L. and R. R., eds. 1956: *The individual-psychology of Alfred Adler*, New York: Basic Books.

Fromm, Erich 1941: *Escape from freedom*, New York: Rinehart.

——— 1947: *Man for himself*, New York: Rinehart.

——— 1955: *The sane society*, New York: Rinehart.

Hall, Calvin S. and Gardner Lindzey 1978: *Theories of personality*, 3rd edition, New York and Chichester: John Wiley.

Horney, Karen 1942: *Self-analysis*, New York: Norton.

——— 1950: *Neurosis and human growth*, New York: Norton.

Munroe, Ruth L. 1955: *Schools of psychoanalytic thought*. New York: Dryden Press.

Sullivan, H. S. 1953: *The interpersonal theory of psychiatry*, New York: Norton.

nervous system *See* auditory n.s.; brain and n.s., chemistry of; brain and nervous system: illustrations

neural bases *See* sensory systems, neural bases of

neural control of higher mental processes Certain neural systems in the brain are specialized to regulate higher mental functions. The study of these systems in relation to the behavior they control is called neuropsychology. Although any organism with a central nervous system may be the object of neuropsychological inquiry, most of what we know derives from the study of brain damaged and normal humans. Four methods are applicable: (1) the identification of the particular behavioral changes that occur when the brain is damaged; (2) the relation of each behavioral change to a particular site of damage using neurological evidence of the location and extent of the lesion; (3) the description of behavior in normal people that reflects the way in which their brains are organized; and (4) the monitoring of patterns of activity in the brain while people are engaged in particular tasks.

When a restricted area of brain is damaged by naturally occurring disease (stroke, brain tumors, trauma etc.), is surgically removed or is temporarily anesthetized, certain skills become unavailable. The patient may lose the ability to understand speech or speak intelligibly (receptive and expressive aphasia respectively), to recognize objects or patterns in sight, hearing or touch (agnosia), to perform skilled actions (apraxia), to recognize and use spatial relationships (visuo-spatial disorientation), or to remember events (amnesia). But the way in which the patient behaves does not simply reflect the loss of an ability because other systems readjust in order to minimize the impact of the deficit on adaptive living. Nor are the effects of brain damage always negative. Foci of irritable nerve cell discharge may be established, resulting in paroxysms involving behavioral fragments out of context, such as paroxysmal speech or arrest of speech, laughing or crying. Or the lesion may disinhibit a lower level system, causing behavioral exaggerations such as hallucinations and perceptual distortions. Still other systems work in terms of shifting balance between opponent processes. Damage may skew such a balance so that one process is permanently in the ascendant, such as turning right versus turning left, concluding a task prematurely versus unduly persevering in it, attending over a wide or within a narrow focus (Pribram and McGuinness 1975). In this way, the behavioral repertoire falls apart, revealing its components (Lashley 1931).

Relating these components to different sections of brain (localization of function) is not straightforward either, as the damaged area may be central to the lost activity, or may merely incorporate an input or output communication channel. It is therefore necessary to let multiple sources of evidence converge in support of a particular localization before accepting it as definitive. One source of corroboration is obtained through monitoring the brain by objective methods capable of determining which of its parts are active when people think or act in certain ways. The active areas generate identifiable electrical phenomena detectable on the ELECTROENCEPHALOGRAM, measurable increases in regional cerebral blood supply, and metabolic rate increase which is demonstrable by positron emission tomography. These methods can be applied both to brain damaged and to normal people.

Normal people have been found to behave in ways that reveal the effects of brain organization. Because in most people language is represented on the left side of the brain and because each half brain is responsive to the opposite side of space, they exhibit perceptual asymmetry in that they are quicker and more accurate in identifying verbal messages, by ear and by eye from the right rather than from the left. Converse asymmetry is found for certain tasks involving relationships in space, which tap the specialization of the right half brain. Also, when one half brain is active, while performing its specialized function, bodily movements towards the opposite side of space may occur. While thinking in words or speaking, people may look to the right (Kinsbourne 1972) or gesture with the right hand (Kimura 1973). Finally, it is possibly to determine the interconnection in the brain of the areas subserving two activites by seeing how well people can do both at the same time (Kinsbourne and Hicks 1978). For example people whose speech is left sided in the brain are better able to perform unrelated finger movements of the left hand than of the right hand while speaking: the control areas for speech and right finger movement share the same (left hemispheric) space and interfere with each other. This "cross talk" interference occurs because, although different parts of the brain are differently specialized, they are all, to a varying degree, interconnected within the neural network. It therefore becomes possible to construct two separate but parallel maps of the brain, one derived from specific lesion effects, and another charting a brain behavioral space based on task interactions in normal people.

Findings from these sources support certain general conclusions. Input analysis is represented in a posterior location in the cerebral cortex relative to the first cortical relays of information flow in the various sensory modalities. Output functions are represented in an anterior location relative to the cortical final common pathways for movement control. In almost all right-handers, language is left-lateralized with speech reception posterior to speech expression. Other left-lateralized functions include the recognition and production of items in proper sequence, the identification of objects, letters and colors, and the programming of individual acts in proper sequence. Overall, the specialized contribution of the left hemisphere is reasonably well summarized as the extracting of item information from incoming messages, and the programming of the specifics of response. The right hemisphere establishes the context within which those specifics are extracted and encoded. It provides a spatial framework into which sequentially processed items can be entered, to establish and conserve their relationship to each other in space. Its role in temporal organization is less well established, but it does appear to be involved in perception of melody. Syndromes of deficit that result from right hemisphere damage include inability to orient in space (visuo-spatial agnosia), to read maps (topographical aphasia) and to recognize faces (topographical apraxia).

A skill that is embarrassed by lesions on either side is the ability to copy designs, but the type of "constructional apraxia" differs depending on the side of lesion. Left damage results in roughly adequate but simplified renderings, whereas right damage results in a copy in which the individual components are identifiable, but their relationships in space are grotesquely distorted. This is a particularly clear demonstration of the way in which the specialized functions of each hemisphere make simultaneous complementary contributions to the overall mental effort.

Also, each hemisphere controls the ability to shift attention toward the opposite side; hemisphere damage may result in unilateral "neglect" of the opposite side of the person and of space. When the hemispheres are disconnected (by surgical section of the interconnecting corpus callosum) each hemisphere remains uninformed of specific information made available only to the other side (Sperry 1966). However, the person remains able to orient himself within ambient space (Trevarthen 1974). It appears that the "disconnection syndrome" applies only to those functions which are unilaterally represented in the brain. The attempts that have been made to attribute to each hemisphere a separate consciousness, or even merely a distinct cognitive style, (Bogen 1969) are misconceived. In "splitbrain" man higher mental function is controlled by one hemisphere at a time, control shifting from hemisphere to hemisphere depending on the nature of the task.

When one hemisphere is surgically removed (by "hemispherectomy") the other over time exhibits compensatory ability (particularly, but not only, when the operation is performed early in life, when the neural network remains relatively "plastic"). Virtually all the specialized functions of each hemisphere are also potentially represented in the other, and this compensatory potential is present to some degree at any age. Paradoxically, many unilateral hemisphere syndromes appear only in minor form when much or all of the other hemisphere is lost. This suggests that in normal functioning, each hemisphere inhibits tendencies on the other side of the brain with similar cognitive potential. Extensive damage releases such territories from inhibition, whereupon they assume a compensatory role.

The variation of brain organizations between individuals and between different gender groups is controversial, but it is clear that in non-right-handers (about 11 per cent of the general population) lateralization may deviate from that outlined above (Milner 1974). Specifically, there may be a high degree of bilateral representation of customarily lateralized processes, or there may be a mirror reversal, with language right-lateralized and spatial relationships represented on the left. It appears, however, that these deviations from the dextral carry no penalty in efficiency of function. Non-right-handers in the general population are no less intelligent in any respect than right-handers (Hardyck, Petrinovich, and Goldman 1976).

Neuropsychological study has shown that different brain mechanisms communicate with each other to excite or inhibit. Our present model of brain control of behavior, therefore, includes communication channels and positive and negative feedback mechanisms. The efforts of behavioral scientists to generate models of the brain and to design simulations of aspects of human behavior, are relevant to how the brain actually works only if they too incorporate communication channels and feedback loops in their design. Neuropsychological findings are useful in testing the validity of psychological inferences. Behavior that is dissociable by focal brain damage cannot be modeled as unitary, and behavior that is regularly comparably implicated by focal damage should be incorporated within the same hypothetical system. This use of neuropsychological information is a recent, but constructive, development in behavioral science. MK

Bibliography

Bogen, J.E. 1969: The other side of the brain II. An appositional mind. *Bulletin Los Angeles Neurological Society* 34, 135–62.

Hardyck, C., Petrinovich, L.F. and Goldman, Roy D. 1976: Left-handedness and cognitive deficit. *Cortex* 12, 266–79.

Kimura, D. 1973: Manual activity during speaking I. Right Handers. *Neuropsychologia* 11, 45–50.

Kinsbourne, M. 1972: Eye and head turning indicate cerebral lateralization. *Science* 176, 539–41.

Kinsbourne, M. and Hicks, R.E. 1978: Functional cerebral space: a model for overflow, transfer and interference effects in human performance. In J. Requin, Ed., *Attention and performance VII*. Hillsdale, N. J.: Lawrence Erlbaum.

Lashley, K.S. 1931: Mass action in cerebral function. *Science* 73, 245–54.

Milner, B. 1974: Hemispheric specialization: scope and limits. In F.O. Schmitt and F.G. Worden, eds., *The neurosciences*. Third study program. Cambridge, Mass.: MIT Press.

Pribram, K.H. and McGuinness, D. 1975: Arousal, activation and effort in the control of attention. *Psychological review* 82, 116–49.

Sperry, R.W. 1966: Brain bisection and consciousness. In J.C. Eccles, ed. *Brain and conscious experience*. New York: Springer.

Trevarthen, C. 1974: Functional relations of disconnected hemispheres in the brain stem and with each other: Monkey and man. In M. Kinsbourne and W.L. Smith, eds., *Hemispheric disconnection and cerebral function*. Springfield, Ill.: Thomas.

neuroanatomical functions and behavior The principal issue is the localization of behavioral or psychological function in the brain. Contemporary psychologists generally agree that psychological processes or states that underlie behavior are the end product of activity in nerve cells in the brain. There is far less agreement when it is asked whether a better understanding of psychological functions and/or behavior can be gained from an examination of their physical substrates. Quite apart from the philosophical issues concerning the relation between brain and "mind", which will not be discussed here, it is not entirely clear that a unique relationship can always be unambiguously demonstrated between specific psychological states and related behavior, on the one hand, and, on the other, activation or inhibition of activity in identifiable subdivisions of the brain.

Human brains (as well as those of other mammals) consist of billions of nerve cells, called NEURONS (see BRAIN AND CENTRAL NERVOUS SYSTEM: ILLUSTRATIONS, fig. 30), that are extensively interconnected. (One neuron may be able to exchange information with thousands of others.) Neurons tend to form aggregates or groups called NUCLEI; and the often long fibers that interconnect them may form bundles called "pathways". Anatomists have mapped the location of all nuclei and pathways. The resulting atlases of the topography of the brain reveal not only enormous complexity but also the fact that the brains of all members of a species are essentially alike while even the brains of quite different species share a common general organization.

Herbert Spencer (1820–1903) suggested in the mid-nineteenth century that in the course of evolution new levels of organization are added to primitive brains as a result of the need for ever more complex behavioral as well as physiological adjustments to the environment. Hughlings-Jackson incorporated this idea into his well known writings on the organization of brain function published around the turn of the century. Luria (1973) has made this idea the cornerstone of his more recent analysis of the organization of the brain. Not all neuroscientists agree that the functions of complex mammalian brains can best be understood in this fashion. It will nonetheless provide a useful basis for the present discussion.

All mammalian brains consist of two nearly identical right and left halves (fig. 1). They communicate with the body's sensory organs and muscles via nerves that emanate either directly from the brain or from the SPINAL CORD (fig. 10). The latter is an extension of the brain and contains many sensory and motor pathways. It also contains extensive interconnections between peripheral sensory receptors and muscles or glands. These connections permit a good deal of integration of physiological functions and simple, "reflexive" behavioral responses to specific sensory stimuli. Among these are not only the classic spinal stretch reflexes first described by Sherrington in 1906 but also more complex reactions such as withdrawal, support, scratching, penile erection, and pelvic thrusting.

The BRAINSTEM (figs. 5–7) is essentially a continuation of the spinal cord inside the head. Its lower third, the hindbrain, contains discrete nuclei that coordinate many basic physiological functions. The area also receives sensory information from most areas of the face and from the vestibular system which provides essential information about our position in space. When all brain above the lower brainstem is removed or the connections with higher structures are severed, complex postural reflexes that permit righting and orienting remain intact. Apparently normal sleep/waking cycles occur, and sensory stimuli elicit simple behavior such as hissing, growling, chewing, licking, and swallowing. Spontaneous arousal and goal-directed behavior are missing.

The middle portion of the brainstem, the midbrain (fig. 5) contains relay stations for sensory pathways from the eyes, ears, and mouth, as well as nuclei that relay information to and from a large, nearly round structure, the CEREBELLUM, which arises from the surface of the midbrain. The cerebellum contains integrative mechanisms which are responsible for the complex postural adjustments that permit walking, sitting, etc. When all the brain above the midbrain and cerebellum is destroyed, animals respond to stimuli from all sensory modalities except for olfaction (smell), and walk, swim, jump, and climb when stimulated. Also present is so called automatic behavior such as grooming and the rejection of food when sated. In the absence of intense stimuli, the animals tend to be inactive.

The upper third of the brainstem, the diencephalon, contains two discrete structures: the THALAMUS which is the last major relay station for many sensory pathways, and the HYPOTHALAMUS which contains mechanisms that are responsible for basic motivational influences such as hunger, thirst and sexual arousal as well as affective reactions (fig. 6). Animals deprived of all brain above the diencephalon will spontaneously emit complex voluntary behavior that is however, typically poorly directed and often appears at random. Such animals tend to be excessively active and reactive to stimulation and it has been suggested that the hypothalamus may provide energizing effects on behavior.

The BASAL GANGLIA (fig. 15) are large oval structures that are located on both sides of the upper brainstem. They exercise complex integrative functions that permit an interaction of automatic and voluntary movements so that the organism can perform biologically adaptive sequences of behavior including the search for and subsequent ingestion of food and water. When the brain remaining above this level is removed, the principal impairments are a lack of behavior which manifests apparent foresight (i.e. hoarding, construction of nests etc.), impaired or absent reactions to patterns of sensory input, an inability to coordinate complex movement sequences and a lack of control over fine movements.

The components of the brain discussed so far are essentially surrounded by the cortex ("rind") of the cerebral hemispheres (figs. 1–4) which consists of several layers of nerve cells and their interconnections. In primitive animals there are only two or three layers of cells and the total amount of cortex, relative to the brainstem and basal ganglia, is small. In complex mammals such as cats and monkeys, much of the cortical tissue is organized in six layers and the amount of cortex, relative to other brain tissue increases dramatically. This development of a so called neocortex is most pronounced in man and that has given rise to the expectation that the neocortex should be the substrate for complex psychological functions such as thought, language, memory etc. that seem to be peculiarly developed in humans. Extensive investigation of cortical function has shown that all sensory pathways (except those carrying olfactory information) terminate in cortical "receiving" areas that are surrounded by "association" areas which appear to process sensory information to give rise to complex perceptions of the environment. Neocortex is also the origin of a system of motor pathways that are responsible for the organization of complex voluntary movements. Adjacent to the primary motor area from which these pathways emanate (fig. 3) is a premotor region which is responsible for the organization of patterns of movements that eventually lead to a distant goal.

In man and other complex mammals, the simple two- and three-layer cortex typical of simpler organisms is found only in the HIPPOCAMPUS and associated structures that are mostly buried inside the cerebral hemispheres. It is commonly believed that this LIMBIC SYSTEM (figs. 15–18) may mediate affective reactions in concert with influences from the hypothalamus (fig. 20).

This brief review of functional neuroanatomy suggests that there is a very close relationship between brain structure and function. This is certainly true when one considers the most basic regulatory functions of the brainstem that control the activity of other organs and glands of the body. It also applies to the principal input and output channels of the brain.

Major interpretational problems arise, however, when one inquires into the localization of complex psychological processes that intervene between the perception of environmental change and the elaboration of reactions to it. Although some complex information processing, such as man's ability to speak and understand language, has been localized in specific portions of the cortex, others, such as memory, abstract thought, affects, etc. have remained elusive in spite of concerted efforts by scientists from numerous disciplines. Infrahuman mammals do not lose their ability to learn and remember even when all cortex is removed (rudimentary memories have even been demonstrated in the spinal cord of animals). Similarly, there appears to be no portion of cortex in man that is essential for learning or recall (damage to the phylogenetically old cortex of the hippocampus interferes with memory formation or recall in some way, but this impairment is not as general as was once thought.) Affective reactions do seem to depend upon information processing in the primitive cortex of the limbic system and associated subcortical regions. Nevertheless, the specific contribution of the many components of this diffuse and complex system, or the influence of neocortical mechanisms (particularly from the frontal lobe) are still to be elucidated.

Even simple brain functions are not so rigidly localized as a cursory reading of neuroanatomical texts might lead one to believe. Damage to a particular brain region does typically impair or abolish specific physiological or psychological functions. However, considerable recovery generally occurs. This suggests that other areas of the brain may be capable of assuming responsibility for a function after its "primary" representation has been destroyed.

These and related observations have led to the postulation of "mass action" or "equipotentiality" (Lashley 1931), that is, to suggestions that most, if not all, brain functions may potentially be exercised by all portions of the brain. A modern version of this idea is Pribram's suggestion (1971) that memories might be distributed throughout the brain much as a holographic representation of an object exists in every portion of the photographic film used to store it. Electrophysiologists (e.g. John 1967) have similarly proposed that information processing may not be the result of electrical activity in any single portion of the brain but, reflect the pattern of activity throughout most or all of it.

SPG

Bibliography

Hughlings-Jackson, John (1932): Remarks on dissolution of the nervous system as exemplified by certain post-epileptic conditions. In J. Taylor, ed., *Selected writings of John Hughlings-Jackson*, vol.2. London: Hodder and Stoughton.

John, E.R. 1967: *Mechanisms of memory*. New York and London: Academic Press.

Lashley, K.S. 1931: Mass action in cerebral function. *Science* 73. 245-254.

*Luria, A.R. 1973: *The working brain*. Harmondsworth: Penguin.

*Pribram, K.H. 1971: *Languages of the brain*. Englewood Cliffs, N.J.: Prentice-Hall.

Sherrington, C.S. 1906: *The integrative action of the nervous system*. New Haven: Yale University Press.

neurobiology *See* emotion, neurobiological approach to

neurochemistry and behavior The study of neurochemistry in relation to behavior is an attempt to understand the chemical processes occurring in the brain that underlie the expression of behavior. Research in this area has focussed on two rather distinct problems: the chemical mechanisms of learning and the molecular nature of memory; and a "chemical coding" of behavior which occurs because specific aspects of behavior are frequently associated with the use of specific brain pathways which use specific chemical NEUROTRANSMITTERS.

Much of the chemistry of the brain cells is not distinct from that of other cells in the body. However, the human brain uses 20-25 per cent of the oxygen consumed by the body in the resting state, and more than half the energy produced is used to maintain the electrical activity of the brain. For this reason the use of specific brain pathways is associated with local changes in energy consumption. Measurement of changes in CEREBRAL BLOOD FLOW and glucose uptake (see Sokoloff 1977) can be used to indicate changes in electrical activity, and hence the involvement of particular brain structures or pathways with particular behavior.

The chemicals most often implicated in memory are RNA and proteins. Inhibitors of protein synthesis impair the formation of long-term memory and, on the basis of substantial evidence of this type, most investigators now believe that protein synthesis is necessary for the formation of permanent memory (see Dunn 1980). Nevertheless the specific proteins involved have not been identified. The earlier idea that the proteins might be specific to the memories has now largely been discarded, and current thinking is that changes may occur in proteins normally found in the brain. Similar but more equivocal evidence has implicated RNA in memory. Studies initiated by Hydén in the 1940s indicated that the metabolism of RNA in nerve cells (neurons) was unusually sensitive to changes in nervous system activity. With the discovery by Watson and Crick that the sequence of bases in DNA was the genetic code, the possibility that memories might be coded in the base sequences of RNA molecules was entertained. Work from a number of groups in the 1960s indicated that increases in the synthesis of RNA occurred during learning in animals. However, no specific RNA molecules were found, nor any evidence for any functions of RNA in the brain that do not occur in other tissues. Both the biochemical and behavioral analyses used in the studies of RNA in relation to learning have been severely criticized (see Dunn 1980). The relationship of RNA to brain function is still an enigma, but few scientists believe that RNA is specifically related to memory. More recent evidence indicates that changes in certain protein derivatives, such as glycoproteins and phosphoproteins occur during learning and may be related to memory (see Routtenberg 1979, Matthies 1979).

Each NEURON in the brain is characterized by its neurotransmitter. The distribution of neurotransmitters among neurons is not random, but such that particular neurotransmitters may be associated with specific functions. Most psychoactive drugs have highly specific effects on a particular neurotransmitter, so that the effect of a drug is a chemical coding of behavior on particular nerve cells.

Particularly good examples of this are the effects of drugs active on DOPAMINE. Parkinson's disease is relatively common in elderly humans and affects the control of movement so that sufferers exhibit tremor and slowness of movement. Pathological studies have established that the disease is associated with the death of dopamine-containing cells in the brain. Drugs that antagonize dopamine functions in the brain can produce parkinsonian symptoms. On the other hand, drugs that promote dopamine's actions can ameliorate the symptoms of parkinsonian patients; L-DOPA, the drug most frequently used, is highly effective in the treatment of Parkinson's disease.

Another example is the anti-psychotic drugs used to treat schizophrenic patients. These drugs all appear to antagonize dopamine's actions in the brain. It is therefore believed that the expression of the psychotic behavior is produced via dopaminergic neurons. It should not be assumed that the psychosis is *caused* by a disorder of these neurons; extensive investigations have failed to produce good evidence that this is the case. Psychotic behavior probably involves a different set of dopamine neurons from those involved in the symptoms of Parkinson's disease.

Drugs specific for particular neurotransmitters have proved extremely useful for elucidating brain mechanisms, and particularly for identifying the brain circuits underlying particular behavior. Current evidence suggests that important controls can be exerted by the receptors for the neurotransmitters on the receiving cells. These receptors are proteins that recognize the neurotransmitters and are located on the external surface of the membranes that enclose receptive cells. Many drugs can bind to these receptors either to mimic or to antagonize the actions of the neurotransmitter. There is often more than one receptor type for each neurotransmitter, permitting even more specificity in the use of drugs with selective actions on the different receptor types. It now appears that regulation of these receptors may be an important mechanism for behavioral regulation. Increased numbers of receptors can produce an increased sensitivity to the neurotransmitter, and decreased numbers of receptors, decreased sensitivity. Such changes have been documented following chronic treatment with drugs active on neurotransmitter receptors. There is now speculation that changes in the sensitivity of receptors may underlie behavioral adaptation and even certain disease states. Certainly, chronic treatment with anti-psychotic or antidepressant drugs result in changes of receptor sensitivity in the brain, and these changes may parallel the therapeutic effects of the drugs (Burt et al. 1977).

The neuropeptides form a new class of neurotransmitters in the brain. The ENDORPHINS are the most well known of these neuropeptides, but more than twenty have been discovered. The neuropeptides can violate Dale's principle (see NEUROTRANSMITTER) and may appear in the same cells as other neurotransmitters, but not in any consistent pattern. The neuropeptides appear to be even more specific than the other neurotransmitters for particular types of behavior: the ENDORPHINS may be involved in the suppression of pain, while *substance P* may accentuate it. *Angiotensin II* can specifically induce drinking, and *cholecystokinin* causes cessation of eating. The neuropeptides are different from the other neurotransmitters in a number of respects. Minute quantities are necessary to elicit specific types of behavior and they may act as long-distance messengers within the brain, communicating between cells located in different parts of the brain via the extracellular or cerebrospinal fluid. AJD

Bibliography

Burt, D.R., Creese, I. and Snyder S.H. 1977: Antischizophrenic drugs: chronic treatment elevates dopamine receptor binding in brain, *Science* 196, 326–28.

Dunn, A.J. 1980. Neurochemistry of learning and memory: an evaluation of recent data. *Annual reviews of psychology* 31, 343–90.

Matthies, H. 1979. Biochemical, electrophysiological, and morphological correlates of brightness discrimination in rats. In Mary A.B. Brazier, ed., *Brain mechanisms in memory and learning: from the single neuron to man.* New York: Raven Press.

Routtenberg, A. 1979: Anatomical localization of phosphoprotein and glycoprotein substrates of memory, *Progress in neurobiology* 12, 85–113.

Sokoloff, L. 1977: Relations between physiological function and energy metabolism in the central nervous system, *Journal of neurochemistry* 29,13–26.

neurolinguistics the application of the methods and models of linguistics, particularly psycholinguistics, to the study at the neurological level of language production, reception, processing and acquisition as well as the disturbance of each of these (Lebrun 1976). Neurolinguistics encompasses aspects of linguistics, psychology and the brain sciences and consequently research in this area is often carried out by interdisciplinary teams working in conjunction with medical facilities.

The problems most typically studied, under this discipline have been primarily in two areas: language pathology and the underlying neural mechanisms of normal speech, but not every facet of disturbed verbal behavior has received equal attention. In practice neurolinguistics usually limits itself to examining organically caused impairments of language competence or language acquisition, and especially to the linguistic implications of aphasic speech and language. Stuttering, schizophrenia, mutism, DOWN'S SYNDROME, the special needs of the deaf and of laryngectomy victims have not occupied a place in the center of research. Even studies of normals have frequently grown out of their use as control groups or background studies in conjunction with disturbed speech.

With respect to research methods, neurolinguistics relies on traditional case studies, particularly in older accounts of language impairment and linguistics. But more recent investigations have increasingly emphasized experiments rather than compilations of symptomatology, lesion site, cause, prognosis, and so on. Indeed some feel that it is in experimental findings that neurolinguistics has the best chance to make its mark on linguistics as a whole and to contribute to overlapping disciplines. The need to elicit data from test subjects here, as in linguistics and psychology generally, is often crucial, since the phenomena under study may not occur sufficiently frequently in spontaneous speech for the testing of hypotheses.

With respect to the kinds of language functions investigated, neurolinguistics follows linguistics in preferentially focusing on the production and reception of spoken language. As a consequence, neurolinguistic studies of deficits in reading (dyslexia) or writing (agraphia) tend to be in a minority. The study of aphasic language usually begins by selecting groups of subjects who have been classified into impairment types by means of clinical diagnoses and psychological testing, e.g. the Boston diagnostic Aphasia Examination. Though there are many different classificatory systems for aphasics the nineteenth-century dichotomy identified by the Frenchman Paul Broca and the German Carl Wernicke is still the most commonly employed. Broca's (or motor) aphasia is linked to damage to the anterior language area (the third frontal convolution of the dominant hemisphere), while Wernicke's (or semantic) aphasia is associated with lesions in the posterior language area (angular, supramarginal and superior temporal gyri of the dominant hemisphere). Once selected the groups are asked to demonstrate their performance on some subpart of the language system. These subparts are: semantics (meaning) and lexicon (vocabulary), syntax and grammar, phonology (sound systems) and prosody (intonation, loudness, word accent). Results can then be compared as a function of aphasia type. There has also been considerable research attempting to uncover the relationship between language acquisition in children and language dissolution due to stroke, tumor, epilepsy, wounds, traffic accidents or other causes of aphasia. Still other investigators have examined the sequence of recovery from aphasia in bi-or multilinguals.

Work on word-semantics and lexicon looks at the psychological reality of organizational patterns and strategies of word retrieval. The simplest experiment of lexical organization is word association (see WORD

ASSOCIATION TESTS). The behavior of normals indicates the existence of a system of direct and indirect associations that can be quite dense with common words such as *man* but becomes more diffuse with less frequently employed words (Lesser 1978:79). According to Schuell (1950) and Rinnert and Whitaker (1973) aphasics have word finding or naming difficulties (*anomia*) that resemble the kind of retrieval problem that normals have, but their degree of difficulty is much more acute. At least, the parallel holds for Broca's patients. It does not extend to Wernicke's aphasics, however, who were found by Howes (1964) to produce inappropriate or even no associations.

Simple word association tests fail to consider the effect of one word clues on subsequent associations. This factor turns out to be quite significant. Luria and his associates in the Soviet Union emphasized the influence of a concept known as semantic fields which seems to represent a combination of sound and meaning units. Weigl (1970) makes crucial use of semantic fields, for example, in his work on deblocking. Deblocking of anomia can be effected by means of word clues in the same semantic field. Interestingly, a polysemous word given as a clue will deblock all semantic fields in which it partakes, e.g. *spring* would presumably deblock names of seasons as well as names of machine parts.

Another concept from linguistic analysis that has been tested among aphasics is the semantic feature. In order to account for the apparent cross-classificatory nature of verbs and accompanying nouns Chomsky (1965) proposed a scheme of restrictions based on binary features such as [+human]. This feature can, for example, become active in determining the choice in English between the relative pronouns *who* and *which*. Zurif et al. (1974) tested Broca's patients and normals to discover whether they could abstract out a feature [+human] from a list of words. The patients were asked to identify associated groups of words such as *mother, wife, husband* from a list containing the names of animals, fish and reptiles. Generally, Broca's aphasics were capable of abstracting this feature. Wernicke's patients, however, could not, but produced bizarre and inappropriate combinations and groupings.

One final study of the disruption of the lexicon (and also phonology) is especially interesting and relevant for neurolinguistics. Kehoe and Whitaker (in Goodglass and Blumstein 1973) reported on a twenty-three-year-old female who suffered a subdural hemotoma in the left hemisphere that produced lesions in the posterior language area (a small area in the supramarginal gyrus as determined at autopsy). No other damage was found. This patient had been tested by a speech pathologist who indicated "no systematic aphasic symptoms". Yet upon close detailed examination the patient showed very specific unsuspected deficits. Reading and oral manipulation (spelling and defining) of words of Latin origin with two or more syllables resulted in consistent breakdown of some English compounding rules. Words such as *constitutionality* were repeated with an 80 per cent error rate. The authors hypothesized that the patient had lost the ability to derive morpho-phonologically and semantically a form from the stored base. Latinate vocabulary items such as: *degradation, feminity, secessionist, citizenry, practicality*, were totally blocked. The following items, many of which are post-medieval neo-Latin coinings: *vehicular, pathological, siberian, revolutionary* could be repeated only after several false starts. And finally the following non-Latinate words of equal length and complexity caused no problems: *Mesopotamia, Mississippi, glamorousness.* Made-up words were also reproduced perfectly. This kind of very specific deficit affecting only derivationally complex words would seem to support the view that real words are listed individually and subsequently subject to derivational rules.

In addition to the abnormality shown at the semantic level, aphasics also show syntactic anomalies in their speech. The grammatical disturbance associated with anterior damage, Broca's aphasia, is known as agrammatism; that associated with Wernicke's area, paragrammatism. The first, according to Goodglass (in Goodglass and Blumstein 1973:183), is typified by: loss of articles, prepositions and personal pronouns; incorrect substitutions of these categories; substitution of the infinitive for inflected forms of the verb (in German and French); loss of coordinating and subordinating conjunctions so that sentences resemble the telegraphic style. There is also disturbance of sentence intonation as it reflects the breaking of a sentence into its syntactic constituents, i.e. phrasing. Fluent Wernicke's aphasics, on the other hand, may have considerable subordinate structure remaining. At first encounter this latter group might even seem not to be impaired, but their sentences have a characteristic meaninglessness, resulting from transpositional errors and word finding difficulties. Jakobson (1956) was one of the first to apply linguistic descriptions to these error patterns. Broca's aphasics suffered, in his view, from paradigmatic disturbances (e.g. different realizations of a form in an inflectional paradigm) while Wernicke's aphasics had *syntagmatic* disturbances (problems in sequencing) (see PARADIGMATIC AND SYNTAGMATIC RELATIONS IN GRAMMAR). Jakobson also predicted that *government* (the *s* in *father's hat*) should be more fragile than *agreement* (the *s* in *he grows tomatoes*), and that an *s* marking a semantic category such as plurality (*house/houses*) would be most stable. The predicted hierarchy of difficulty was, however, not confirmed in Goodglass's experiments. On reception tests both types of aphasics found it more difficult to discover missing agreement inflection, than government inflection. A missing plural *s* was the easiest to ascertain. Wh-questions (with *who, which, when, where*, etc) and imperatives caused less difficulty than simple declaratives, which in turn were easier than yes-no questions (those beginning with *do, can*, etc.), conditionals (beginning with *if*) and subordinate clauses. Some specific errors found in Broca's patients were over-use, correct and incorrect, of the present progressive, and considerable difficulty with the passive. Broca's sufferers omitted unstressed utterance-initial words (i.e. words which are both phonologically and psychologically less prominent than stressed ones) more often than Wernicke's patients.

Work by Zurif and Caramazza (1976, 1978) has indicated that some aphasics exploit plausibility and knowledge of the world to compensate for their syntactic deficits. They can thereby mask debilities that are ascertainable only in specifically designed tests. Zurif and Caramazza report that Broca's patients, when confronted with center-embedded sentences, i.e. noun phrase-relative clause-verb phrase, depended on semantic as well as syntactic information in their processing. Four subtypes of this structure were tested: (1) syntactically well-formed and semantically meaningful and plausible sentences, e.g. *the apple that the boy is eating is red*; (2) relative clauses containing reversible verbs, which means that purely syntactic information is crucial to understanding, e.g. *the boy that the girl is chasing is fat*; (3) syntactically well-formed but semantically implausible sentences, e.g. *the boy that the dog is petting is fat*; and (4) declaratives without relative clauses. Type (4) sentences were generally comprehended best and type (3) sentences least well. It was significantly easier for aphasics to recognize semantic deviance than to understand clues that depend on syntactic encoding. Zurif and Caramazza conclude that if a patient cannot rely on word order, semantic information or lexical constraints, his comprehension is markedly reduced. This kind of study has found, quite surprisingly, that even Broca's aphasics show well-profiled syntactic deficits, even though most previous investigations suggested that Broca's aphasia results only in output disturbance leaving the representation of language itself intact.

Phonological studies of aphasic speech are also being used to test linguistic hypotheses (see LINGUISTIC NATURALNESS). Blumstein (in Goodglass and Blumstein 1973), for example, took as a starting point two concepts from phonological theory: markedness and distinctive features. She tried to find support for these ideas in the performance of a variety of aphasic patients. By markedness she understood the relative frequency or infrequency with which a particular sound occurs in the languages of the world or its ability to enter into phonological processes such as assimilations, metathesis, etc. The English sounds [þ] and [ð], corresponding to the *th* in *breath* and *breathe*, are not often encountered. Further they are acquired late by children and disappear in some varieties of English. They are therefore held to be more marked than say [t]. Blumstein defined distinctive features as linguistic elements needed to state phonological rules, which break sounds down into units of analysis finer than the structuralist phonemes. Distinctive features offer the advantage of enabling an error to be regarded as incorrect feature selection instead of its having to be assumed that one entire phoneme has been substituted for another. On the basis of the theory of markedness and distinctive features one would predict that paraphasias would tend to result from a phonological segment's becoming less marked, and from substituting one single feature. Missing a targeted segment by two distinctive features or more should be rarer. Blumstein's results did indeed show that substitutions of one feature were most common and that there is a tendency towards unmarking regardless of lesion site. Particularly prone to disintegration was the *s* sound and the other fricatives [f], [v]. A careful study of the error types indicates that the following disruptions can occur: devoicing of final consonants, lack of control of aspiration, mistargeting (i.e. unsystematic changes in the place of articulation) of vowels and inappropriate nasalization.

Finally, neurolinguistics and language pathology has investigated the so called regression hypothesis (Jakobson 1968). It was speculated that language acquisition and language breakdown in aphasia represent inverse processes of one another. Those elements of grammar last acquired are most susceptible to disturbance, those first acquired are most stable. Zurif and Caramazza (1978) entertain this hypothesis and conclude on the basis of tests such as those discussed above that the regression hypothesis as it stands is untenable. While there are some similarities between children's speech and that of Broca's patients there are also some points of irreconcilable difference. Furthermore Wernicke's patients do not correspond to any stage in the language acquisition process. In a sense this result is not too surprising, despite outward and misleading similarities: a brain exposed to language for years or decades could hardly perform after injury in the same way as an uninjured brain only first encountering language.

A series of other techniques has also been used to obtain information about language manipulation in normals or in aphasics. These include: brain wave studies with the ELECTROENCEPHALOGRAPH or electrocortiograph; direct electrical stimulation of the language area during neurosurgery, which may result in an aphasia during the stimulation; studies of evoked potential, which results when cortical neurons are stimulated; language behavior during the Wada Test, (the injection of sodium amytal into the blood supply of one hemisphere); *brain scans* for tumors or other irregularities; radiological studies of *blood flow* to various parts of the brain during speech; *dichotic hearing* or *tachistoscopic vision* studies (which are based on the neurological property that the right ear or eye, which directly connects to the dominant (usually left) hemisphere, can process speech and language slightly better than the other ear or eye) and work with split brain patients. JAE

Bibliography

Chomsky, N. 1965: *Aspects of the theory of syntax*. Cambridge, Mass.: MIT Press.

*Goodglass, H. and Blumstein, S. (eds) 1973: *Psycholinguistics and aphasia*. Baltimore and London: Johns Hopkins University Press.

Howes, D. 1964: Application of the word frequency concept to aphasia. In *Disorders of language*, eds A. V. S. DeReuck and M. O'Conner. London: Churchill.

Jakobson, R. 1956: Two aspects of language and two types of aphasic disturbances. In *Fundamentals of language*, eds R. Jakobson and M. Halle. The Hague: Mouton.

——— 1968: *Child language, aphasia and phonological universals*. Janua Linguarum Series Minor 72. The Hague: Mouton.

Lebrun, Y. 1976: Neurolinguistic models of language and speech. In *Studies in neurolinguistics*, eds H. and H. Whitaker, vol. 1. New York, San Francisco, London: Academic Press.

Lesser, R. 1978: *Linguistic investigations of aphasia*. London: Edward Arnold.

Rinnert, C. and Whitaker, H. 1973: Semantic confusions by aphasic patients. *Cortex* 9, 56–81.

Schuell, H. 1950: Paraphasia and paralexia. *Journal of speech and hearing disorder* 15, 291–306.

Weigl, E. 1970: Neuropsychological studies of the structure and dynamics of semantic fields with the deblocking method. In *Sign, language, culture* ed. A. Greimas. Janua Linguarum Series Major 1. The Hague: Mouton.

Whitaker, H. and H., eds. 1976–1980: *Studies in neurolinguistics*, vols 1–4. New York, San Francisco, London: Academic Press.

Zurif, E. and Caramazza, A. 1976: Psycholinguistic structures in aphasia. In H. and H. Whitaker, eds ibid.

Zurif, E. and Caramazza, A. (eds) 1978: *Language acquisition and language breakdown: parallels and divergencies*. Baltimore and London: Johns Hopkins University Press.

Zurif, E., Caramazza, A., Myerson, R. and J. Galvin 1974: Semantic feature representations for normal and aphasic language. *Brain and language* 1, 167–187.

neurological damage *See* emotion and neurological damage

neurometrics It has long been known that small, variable electrical voltages, on the order of tens of microvolts, can be recorded from large (5 mn) electrodes attached with conductive paste to the surface of the human scalp. At first, these slowly fluctuating voltages were thought to reflect the summated electrical fields produced by the discharge of large numbers of nerve cells, or neurons. With the advent of microelectrode techniques, which permitted observation of the discharge of single neurons in the brains of experimental animals and their correlation with slow potentials, this view changed. It is now believed that these fluctuating voltages largely reflect the integrated, post-synaptic potentials of large populations of neurons. Since post-synaptic potentials alter the excitability of the cell, slow waves recorded from the scalp can be considered to be proportional to the probability of synchronous or coherent discharge in large ensembles of neurons.

Two classes of slow waves can be recorded from the human scalp: (1) spontaneous fluctuations of voltage, referred to as the ELECTROENCEPHALOGRAM, or EEG; and (2) transient sequences of voltage, oscillations which are time-locked to environmental stimuli, referred to as evoked potentials (EPs) or event-related potentials (ERPs). ERPs can be extracted from the EEG by computer averaging methods. A special class of EPs is the so-called "far-field" or brainstem evoked potential (BSEP), which is recorded from the vertex of the scalp and reflects volume conduction of potentials from the brainstem in response to auditory or somatosensory stimuli.

Reflection of brain functions in EEG or ERP features
Voluminous evidence demonstrated that a wide variety of important aspects of brain functions are reflected in the EEG and ERPs. Many neurological diseases cause changes in the amplitude, frequency spectrum, bilateral synchrony or symmetry of the EEG, or produce waveshapes with a morphology characteristic of certain disorders.

ERPs elicited by sensory stimuli of different modalities display waveshapes more or less typical for each modality. These waveshapes tend to be of maximal amplitude over the corresponding sensory cortical projection areas (BRAIN AND CENTRAL NERVOUS SYSTEM: ILLUSTRATIONS, fig. 3), but are also detected over other cortical regions, usually with different waveshapes. An important feature of ERPs is that their morphology changes as a function of a number of different parameters: the focus of attention of the subject, the information content of the stimulus, whether or not a priori expectancies about the stimulus have been engendered in the subject by the context in which the stimuli occur, and the semantic or symbolic significance of the stimuli.

It is useful to consider the morphology of the ERP as consisting of a succession of waves, each primarily reflecting a step in sequential processing of the information contained in the stimulus as it is evaluated by the subject in terms of prior experience and the immediate context in which the stimulus is received. Since these steps are necessarily sequential, wave components of increasing latency (time elapsed after stimulus delivery) correspond to later stages of information processing.

Unfortunately substantial differences exist across individuals with respect to the morphology of the ERP, the latency of particular components elicited by a particular stimulus, and the clarity with which particular components can be identified. It is not known whether this variability primarily reflects inherent differences in anatomical organization of functional systems mediating various processes, differences in the functional state of different subjects, or differences in the time required by different subjects to perform the sequence of functions involved in processing sensory input. For these reasons it is difficult to specify the precise latencies and amplitudes of ERP components expected in an individual subject under specified stimulus conditions. The simplest solution to this problem is achieved by using each subject as his own control. A more complex statistical approach is discussed below.

Correspondence between steps in information processing and latency of ERP components
Nonetheless, bearing these reservations in mind, a temporal schema can be constructed giving the approximate latencies of the sequences of steps involved in processing information about a sensory stimulus. Such a schema, for visual stimuli, is as follows:

Receptor activation
↓
Afferent input
↓
Cortical registration (50–100 ms)
↓
Analysis of contrast (100–150 ms)
↓
Attentional processes (100–200 ms) (reflects both internal state and prior experience)
↓
Perception (200–240 ms) (Classification of input requiring memory access)
↓
Expectancy (300–360 ms) (Evaluation of stimulus probability in prior context)
↓
Match from memory of prior event(s) (420–450 ms)

Semantic significance (450–500 ms)

(For more detailed information about the experimental evidence supporting this proposed sequence of processes, encompassing aspects of sensation, perception and cognition as reflected in the ERP, see Thatcher and John 1977.)

Exogenous versus endogenous processes
Consideration of this schema reveals that, on purely logical grounds, it is possible to distinguish between aspects of the ERP determined by the physical stimulus and the state of the afferent pathways ("exogenous" processes) and those influenced by the prior experience, expectation or semantic processes of the subject ("endogenous" processes). In this framework, what psychologists call "sensation" represents an exogenous process, "attention" is partly exogenous and partly endogenous, in that centrifugal outputs due to fatigue, habituation or arousal can inhibit afferent input and "perception" and "cognition" are primarily endogenous. Microelectrode studies, using microelectrodes chronically implanted in unrestrained animals, have revealed that two types of neurons can be indentified in many brain regions. So called "stable cells", which respond to physical features of the stimuli independent of their meaning, are believed to participate in exogenous processes. "Plastic cells", which show firing patterns correlated with subsequent behavioral responses independent of the physical features of the stimulus, are believed to participate in endogenous processes (Ramos, Schwartz and John 1976.)

"Readout" or "emitted" potentials
In studies of differential generalization in differentially conditioned animals, it has been reported that the presentation of ambiguous stimuli with parameters midway between those of differential conditioned stimuli elicits ERPs with different morphologies, reliably predictive of subsequent differential behavioral responses. Since the different ERP morphologies cannot plausibly be attributed to the neutral physical stimulus, which is identical and ambiguous whenever presented, and since the different ERP morphologies elicited closely correspond to the morphologies of the ERPs elicited by the differential stimuli used in establishing the different conditioned responses, these findings have been interpreted to reflect readout from memory of temporal patterns of coherent firing in neuronal ensembles (Ramos, Schwartz and John 1976).

Analogous reports have been published on human subjects, either in differential generalization (Begleiter and Platz 1969) or in production of so called "emitted potentials" when expected stimuli fail to occur (Sutton et al 1967).

A number of other obviously endogenous processes have been repeatedly reported in the ERP literature. The best known of these is the so called $P_{\overline{300}}$, which is a late positive component in the ERP with an amplitude which increases the *less* predictable or *more* significant the eliciting stimulus (Sutton et al. 1965). In information theoretical terms, the more unlikely a stimulus, the larger will be $P_{\overline{300}}$.

Another important endogenous process is revealed in match–mismatch procedures, in which the second member of a pair of events is compared to the first member for adherence to any of a variety of logical rules, i.e. same–different, true-false or semantic equivalence. Conformity of the second stimulus to the first with respect to the particular logical rule imposed on the subject is reflected by a late positive component at about 450 ms (Thatcher and John 1977).

A particularly interesting endogenous process was recently described (Kutas and Hillyard 1980). When a word is presented in a context which is semantically improbable, such as "I drink my coffee with sugar and *cement*", the unexpected word elicits a large, negative component in the ERP at about 480 ms.

These various types of evidence demonstrate unequivocally that analysis of the ERPs elicited in carefully controlled experimental situations can provide access to reflections of brain mechanisms related to *mental activity*. For this reason, ERP research is of unique importance in psychology and has philosophical implications perhaps transcending any other phenomena for an understanding of the physical and physiological basis of mind.

Brainstem or "far-field" potentials
A special class of ERPs, perhaps totally exogenous in origin (although the contributions of fatigue, habituation and attention have not yet been totally ruled out), is the so-called brainstem evoked potential. This waveshape, sometimes referred to as the "far-field" evoked potential, arises in the brainstem and can be detected at the vertex because of volume conduction. Since it is extremely small, on the order of 0.25 microvolts, very low noise amplifiers and averages of as much as 2,000 responses are required to extract the BSEP from the ongoing EEG, which is 2–4 orders of magnitude larger in amplitude. The auditory BSEP characteristically displays 7 peaks in an epoch of about 12 ms post-stimulus. The latency of each peak corresponds to the depolarization of ensembles of neurons at successive relay nuclei in the lateral lemniscal pathways of the auditory system between the auditory nerve entry to the BRAINSTEM and the inferior collicubes. Since the variability of latency in normal subjects for each peak is on the order of 1 200 microseconds, and relative amplitudes fall within predictable ranges, the auditory BSEP provides an exquisitely sensitive technique for evaluation of the functional status of lateral lemniscal pathways. Although less widely used, the somatosensory BSEP provides comparable information about the medial lemniscus.

It should be obvious from the cursory summary above that the EEG and ERP not only afford a unique insight into a variety of brain functions of considerable importance for the resolution of basic research issues in neurophysiology and physiological psychology, with substantial philosophical implications, but can be of great value in diagnosis and treatment of a wide variety of disorders and dysfunctions of the brain. A major obstacle in the practical application of these electrophysiological methods has been the qualitative nature of subjective evaluations of EEG and ERP phenomena, as well as the wide variability of such phenomena across samples of healthy, normally functioning individuals.

With the advent of powerful minicomputers and

economical microprocessors, a radically different approach to evaluation of EEG and ERP data has become possible. This approach is called "Neurometrics" (John et al. 1977; John 1977) Neurometric technology has several distinctive and essential aspects: (1) Precise specification of the environment of the subject and the physical characteristics of all stimuli; (2) Automatic computer controlled rejection of artefacts and presentation of stimuli, to ensure standardization of data; (3) Objective computer extraction of quantitative EEG and ERP features of clinical utility, based upon automatic algorithms of demonstrated concordance with clinical judgements; (4) Transformation of all extracted diagnostic features to relative probability, by use of the Z transform based upon the mean and standard deviation of identical features extracted from a large sample of healthy, normally functioning individuals the same age as the subject; (5) Construction of *abnormality vectors* representing each subject as a vector in an n-dimensional space of electrophysiological features, each dimension scaled according to the common metric of relative probability. The direction of the abnormality vector in the measure space defines the *quality* or nature of the abnormality, and the length of the abnormality vector defines the *quantity* or severity of the abnormality.

Clinical applications

Perhaps the most important single finding from the application of neurometric techniques has been the discovery that the relative (percent) power in the delta (1.5–3.5 Hz), theta (3.5–7.5 Hz), alpha (7.5–12.5 Hz) and beta (12.5–25 Hz) band of the resting, eyes closed EEG shows a systematic alteration with age (see EEG and fig. 33). This alteration is characteristically different for fronto-temporal, temporal, central and parieto-occipital electrode derivations. Regression equations have been derived which describe this systematic change in the relative power frequency spectrum as a function of age. These regression equations accurately describe the distribution of EEG relative power in these different frequency bands in large samples of healthy, normally functioning children from a wide variety of cultural and ethnic backgrounds. The incidence of z-values beyond the 0.05 probability level was equal or less than expected by chance in healthy children from the US, Sweden and Barbados. Healthy children from different socioeconomic strata, of different ethnic backgrounds, or of different sexes were not discriminable from each other. Thus, these descriptors of the resting EEG seem to provide a culture-fair estimate of brain maturation independent of cultural, ethnic, socioeconomic or sexual factors. In contrast, children at risk for a wide variety of neurological diseases or with learning disabilities of unknown origin displayed 40–64 per cent of abnormal values for these EEG parameters (John et al 1980;). Multivariate, independently replicated discriminant functions indicate that the discriminability of normal from learning-dysfunctional children based on neurometric EEG features is of the order of 75 per cent.

Space precludes a detailed review of further clinical findings. Neurometric features of a wide variety of neurological diseases have been reviewed by Harmony (1981). Significant and consistent features of neurometric abnormality have been found in children of normal intelligence disabled in verbal vs. arithmetical learning, in normally functioning vs dysfunctional elderly patients (John et al. 1977), in patients after traumatic head injury, in chronic alcoholics, in manic-depressive psychosis and in a variety of other diseases.

Conclusion

Electrophysiological evaluations of brain functions, in general, and neurometric evaluations, in particular, provide a powerful, unique and relatively new window into psychological processes of basic and practical interest. With the increasing focus of attention on computer evaluation of electrophysiological processes, and with the rapidly decreasing cost of microprocessors whose computational capability is escalating at an exponentially increasing rate, the information available from quantitative evaluation of electrical correlates of brain functions can be expected to become increasingly important in our understanding of the relationship between brain and behavior. ERJ

Bibliography

Begleiter, H. and Platz, P. 1969: Cortical evoked potentials to semantic stimuli. *Psychophysiology* 6, 91–100.

Harmony, T. 1981: *Functional neuroscience, vol. III: Neurometric diagnosis of neuropathology*. Hillsdale, N.J.: Lawrence Erlbaum.

John, E.R. 1977: *Functional neuroscience, Vol. II: Neurometrics: clinical applications of quantitative electrophysiology*. Hillsdale, N.J.: Lawrence Erlbaum.

——— and Alter, I. 1981: Evaluation of coma patients with the brain state analyzer. In *Seminars in neurological surgery* ed. R.G. Grossman and P.L. Gildenberg. New York: Raven Press.

——— et al. 1977: Neurometrics: numerical taxonomy identifies different profiles of brain functions within groups of behaviorally similar people. *Science* 196, 1393–410.

——— et al. 1980: Developmental equations for the electroencephalogram. *Science* 210, 1255–8.

Kutas, M. and Hillyard, S.A. 1980 Reading senseless sentences–brain potentials reflect semantic incongruity. *Science* 207, 203–5.

Ramos, A., Schwartz, E. and John, E.R. 1976: Stable and plastic unit discharge patterns during behavioral generalization. *Science* 192, 392–6.

Sutton, S. et al. 1965: Evoked potential correlates of stimulus uncertainty. *Science* 153, 1187–8.

——— 1967: Information delivery and the sensory evoked potential. *Science* 155, 1436–9.

Thatcher, R.W. and John, E.R. 1977: *Functional neuroscience, Vol. I, Foundations of cognitive processes*. Hillsdale, N.J.: Lawrence Erlbaum.

neuromodulators Substances that convey information to nerve cells through mechanisms other than neurotransmission. The concept of neuromodulation is relatively new and not yet fully established. It was introduced and further developed as the result of increasingly numerous demonstrations of the existence of endogenous substances which do not change neuronal membrane potential directly as do neurotransmitters (see SYNAPSE AND SYNAPTIC TRANSMISSION), but still affect the efficiency of the neurotransmission process. The term "synaptic modulator" was originally introduced by Krivoy et al. (1963) to describe the action of Substance P and other so called neurotropic peptides on synaptic excitability in the spinal cord. Krivoy and co-workers defined a synaptic modulator as "a substance that alters (increases or decreases) the efficiency of the neurotransmission process without per se producing a propagated response associated with a reversal of the membrane potential". This, like the definition which opens the paragraph, is a *definitio per exclusionem*, and it does not include a statement of either site or mechanism of action. It is now clear that neuromodulating substances form a very heterogenous class from the viewpoint of both chemical structure, and sites and mechanism of action. Substances traditionally classified as hormones or neurotransmitters may be neuromodulators or have neuromodulator functions as well. Neuromodulators are thought to be of importance in the regulation of a wide variety of behavioral, neuroendocrine and autonomic processes.

Peptides predominate among the newly discovered endogenous compounds which have been added to the list of substances involved in communication between nerve cells in the central and the peripheral nervous system. This emphasis on peptides is partly the result of new techniques being available. Sophisticated immunohistochemical methods developed in recent years have enabled these neuropeptides to be visualized in neuronal systems and the various neuronal networks to be traced. Double-staining techniques allow more than one substance to be visualized in a single tissue section. This allows the localization of possible interaction between networks. Double-staining has also led to the surprising and intriguing discovery of the coexistence, in single neurons, of neuropeptides and representatives of classical neurotransmitters in apparent violation of Dale's Principle ("one neuron, one neurotransmitter"). Among the neuropeptides are many substances previously known as pituitary or intestinal hormones so that the list of neuropeptides now includes: thyrotopin releasing hormone (TRH), luteinizing hormone releasing hormone (LHRH), somatostatin (growth hormone release-inhibiting hormone), vasopressin, oxytocin, ACTH (see also ACTH), enkephalins, endorphins (see also ENKEPHALINS/ENDORPHINS), growth hormone, prolactin, insulin, glucagon, angiotensin, secretin, gastrin, Substance P, neurotensin, cholecystokinin, vasoactive intestinal peptide (VIP), carnosine and bombesin (see Hökfelt et al. 1980). Specific binding sites for the neuropeptides have been found in the central and peripheral nervous systems. This was achieved by measuring the specific *in vitro* binding of radiolabelled ligands and their displacement by non-labelled compounds and by using autoradiography for microscopic visualisation of many of the neuropeptides. Although a neurotransmitter role has been suggested in various cases, many of the neuropeptides are presently thought to function as neuromodulators. This role is postulated not only from the results of behavioral, electrophysiological and neurochemical studies, but also from the notion that the dynamics of synthesis, storage and bio-inactivation of neuropeptides differ markedly from those of the classical neurotransmitters. This aspect of neuropeptides suggests the existence of slow-reacting regulatory mechanisms in peptide-containing neurons (see Hökfelt et al. 1980; Barker and Smith 1980). In contrast, the synapse in neurotransmitter-containing neurons must be capable of immediate recovery and return to the pre-activation condition; rapidly operating mechanisms for the adaptation of synthesis and release processes are essential.

As it is still difficult to make a rigid classification of substances with neuromodulatory effects, there are conflicts between the classifications so far proposed. Functional criteria suggest three subclasses (see Elliott and Barchas 1980; Barker and Smith 1980):

(1) Synaptic neuromodulators act between nerve cells in synaptic contact. The effect of a synaptic neuromodulator is local and restricted to one cell postsynaptic to the one from which the neuromodulator is released.

(2) Hormonal neuromodulators affect the neuronal activity of neurons at a relatively great distance from their site of release. In principle hormonal neuromodulators can act on a large population of nerve cells, viz. on those cells that possess neuromodulator-specific recognition sites whether membrane-bound or cytoplasmic. Substances considered as classical hormones and which are released from peripheral sources (e.g. adrenal steroids) can also have modulating effects on specific populations of neurons in the central nervous system (see also STEROIDS). There are neurons, both in the peripheral autonomic nervous system and in the hypothalamic neurosecretory systems, with axons which do not make synaptic contacts with target cells or other neurons. There is recent morphological evidence that there occur noradrenaline-containing terminals in the cortex and dopamine-containing terminals in the caudate nucleus which also appear to be devoid of synaptic contacts. Such evidence suggests that noradrenaline and dopamine released from these terminals function as hormonal neuromodulators rather than as neurotransmitters (for references see Vizi 1980).

(3) The third subclass of neuromodulators is formed by substances that act postsynaptically to their site of release as neurotransmitters by evoking a propagated response, and that simultaneously modulate their own release or synthesis via presynaptic mechanisms. Since this modulation leads in all cases to decreased neuronal activity, it is called auto-inhibition. Auto-inhibition mediated by presynaptic autoreceptors is a feature of many neurotransmitter systems in both the central nervous system and the periphery (see Vizi 1980).

The exact mechanism of action of most of the putative neuromodulators has not yet been found. The definitions given above, however, allow the prediction that any of the processes involved in neurotransmission and neurotransmitter metabolism in the "target-synapse" of a neuromodulator are potential sites for its amplifying or damping effect on neuronal activity. Neuromodulators can elicit their effects through specific membrane receptors, via membrane-bound enzymes or other proteins or via cytoplasmic or soluble recognition sites. Neuromodulators can act on processes preceding or following the membrane depolarization or hyperpolarization induced by transmitters. For example, through their effects on ion transport systems neuromodulators can elevate or depress thresholds for de- or hyperpolarization, thereby attenuating or facilitating neurotransmission. Intracellular processes can be influenced directly or via the activation of membrane receptors and the consequent activation of receptor-linked adenylate or guanylate cyclase systems. The latter possibility holds for both pre- and postsynaptic neuromodulator-specific receptors. The effects can be exerted on synthesis, uptake, storage or metabolism of the substance which acts as a neurotransmitter in the "target-synapse" of the neuromodulator. Neuromodulators can also act by influencing the affinity of neurotransmitter receptors for their endogenous agonists by exerting allosteric effects on these receptors, thereby increasing or decreasing receptor efficiency.

Substances with neuromodulating actions do not necessarily originate from nerve terminals or even from neuronal cells. Evidence has been presented for a modulating role of prostaglandins in synaptic transmission. Prostaglandins of the E-type, which are released from the postsynaptic cell as a consequence of its activation by the transmitter, reduce neurotransmitter release through presynaptic effects on Ca^{2+} ion fluxes. A similar action has been suggested for adenosine (transsynaptic modulation).

DHGV

Bibliography

* Barker, J.L. and Smith, T.G. 1980: Three modes of intercellular neuronal communication. In P.S. McConnell et al., eds, *Adaptive capabilities of the nervous system*, Progress in brain research, vol. 53. Amsterdam and New York: Elsevier/North-Holland Biomedical Press.

Elliott, G.R. and Barchas, J.D. 1980: Changing concepts about neuroregulation: neurotransmitters and neuromodulators. In D. De Wied and P.A. Van Keep, eds, *Hormones and the brain* Lancaster: MTP Press.

* Hökfelt, T. et al. 1980: Peptidergic neurons. *Nature* 284, 515-21.

Krivoy, W.A. et al. 1963: Synaptic modulation by substance P. *Federation proceedings* 38, 2344-47.

Vizi, E.S. 1980: Non-synaptic interaction of neurotransmitters: presynaptic inhibition and disinhibition. In E.S. Vizi (ed.) *Modulation of neurochemical transmission, advances in pharmacological research and practice* vol. 2 Proceeding of the 3rd Congress of the Hungarian Pharmacological Society, 1979. Budapest: Pergamon Press/Akadémiai Kiadó.

neuron (See BRAIN AND CENTRAL NERVOUS SYSTEM: ILLUSTRATIONS, figs. 30–32.) A nerve cell with all its processes. Neurons are specialized to receive signals, process them and pass them on to other neurons or effector organs such as muscles or glands. The neuron doctrine, as originally proposed, holds that neurons form the basic developmental, structural and functional units of the nervous system. Classically, each neuron possesses DENDRITES which receive inputs and integrate them, an axon which conducts a nerve impulse to the synaptic terminals where the signal is passed to another cell and a cell body which carries on the metabolic activities of the cell. Recently it has become clear that the neuron is not always the functional unit of the nervous system. Rather, localized portions of several neurons may be connected to performs a task relatively independently of other parts of the neurons involved (see Shepard 1979).

Generally the dendrites of a neuron receive connections, often from many other neurons. These connections, or SYNAPSES, (fig. 32) may provide either excitatory or inhibitory input which is mediated electrically or chemically. In an electrical synapse, an electrical signal in one neuron is relayed to a second neuron via a low resistance pathway. In a chemical synapse a substance is released from one neuron which causes currents to flow through the cell membrane of another neuron. In either case, all the inputs onto the dendrites are integrated in space and time to produce a single voltage at the spike initiation zone (axon hillock). Here analog signals are converted to digital signals as nerve impulses (action potentials) are triggered when the membrane voltage exceeds threshold. Nerve impulses are unitary events which propagate from the axon hillock toward the synaptic terminals. At the terminals electrical or chemical transmission proceeds to other cells. Chemical transmitters released by neurons at synapses include ACETYLCHOLINE, DOPAMINE, SEROTONIN, and GAMMA-AMINOBUTYRIC ACID. Special proteins, called neuropeptides, such as substance P and ENKEPHALINS may also be released by neurons. The cell body may not participate directly in the electrical activities of the neuron, but performs the metabolic activities characteristic of all cells. Since the axons of neurons may be as long as several meters, mechanisms exist for the rapid transport of materials from the cell body to the synaptic terminals and back (axonal transport).

Neurons show great diversity in structure and function. Not all cells generally regarded as neurons have all the normal properties associated with neurons. For example, cells which are connected to neurons, but which have only some of the characteristic features of neurons include those specialized for nonspecific secretion (neurosecretory cells) and sensory receptors (hair cells, rods and cones, etc.). Similarly, although propagated action potentials are characteristic of neurons, not all nerve cells conduct them.

SCC

Bibliography

Bullock, T.H., Orkand, R. and Grinnell, A. 1977: *Introduction to nervous systems*. San Francisco: W.H. Freeman.

Kandel, E.R. 1976: *Cellular basis of behavior: an introduction to behavioral neurobiology*. San Francisco: W.H. Freeman.

——— and Schwartz, J.H. 1981: *Principles of neural science*. Oxford and New York: Elsevier/North-Holland.

Shepard, G.M. 1979: *The synaptic organization of the brain*, 2nd edn. Oxford and New York: Oxford University Press.

neurons: alpha and gamma motor alpha and gamma motor neurons are nerve cells in the ventral horn of the SPINAL CORD whose activity controls the state of contraction of extrafusal and intrafusal muscle fibers respectively. *Skeletal muscle* fibers are of two types. Extrafusal muscle fibers are innervated by alpha motor neurons and are responsible for the work performed by muscles. The whole set of muscle fibers innervated by a single alpha motor neuron is called a *motor unit*. Motor units range in size from only a few to a thousand or more muscle fibers. Small motor units provide fine control of movements. The force that muscles generate can be graded in two ways. First, the rate of firing of a given alpha motor neuron can be changed. Second, the number of motor units activated can be varied. Smooth movements that result from the progressive activation of motor units start with the smallest units and recruit progressively larger motor units as the force generated increases.

Intrafusal muscle fibers (nuclear bag fibers and nuclear chain fibers) form *muscle spindles* which signal the length of muscles to the central nervous system. Primary spindle afferents (Ia) innervate all intrafusal fibers, whereas secondary spindle (II) afferents innervate only nuclear chain fibers. The length of muscle spindle fibers is controlled by gamma motor neurons. Nuclear bag fibers are innervated by dynamic gamma motor neurons and nuclear chain fibers, by static gamma motor neurons. Gamma motor neurons are necessary to maintain the loading of the muscle spindle as the length of the muscle as a whole changes. Otherwise sudden contraction of the muscle, for example, would unload the muscle spindles and inactivate them. Another simpler innervation pattern in which one motor neuron innervates both intra – and extrafusal muscle fibers is used in simpler vertebrates and persists, in part, through carnivores and possibly to man. Exactly why two separate motor innervations have evolved is problematic, since it appears that alpha and gamma motor neurons are usually coactivated.

Motor neurons are activated or inhibited directly by muscle spindle and *Golgi tendon organ* afferents (Ib) (e.g. myotactic and inverse myotactic reflexes) and by descending inputs from the CEREBRAL CORTEX, reticular formation, and vestibular system. Motor activities such as locomotion, for example, appear to involve the expression of a motor program embodied in the spinal circuitry including the reflexive effects of afferents, modulated by descending inputs from supraspinal centers. SCC

Bibliography

Harris, D.A. and Henneman, E. 1980: Feedback signals from muscle and their efferent control. In *Medical physiology*, Vol. I., ed. V.B. Mountcastle. St. Louis and London: C.V. Mosby. Pp. 703–717.

Henneman, E. 1980: Organization of the spinal cord and its reflexes. In *Medical physiology*, 1, ed. V.B. Mountcastle. St. Louis and London: C.V. Mosby. Pp. 762–786.

Kandel, E.R. and Schwartz, J.H. 1981: *Principles of neural science*. New York and Oxford: Elsevier/North-Holland.

neurons: local circuit Nerve cells concerned with processing only within a local region of the nervous system. The nervous system may be structurally and functionally divided into regions or centers such as the HIPPOCAMPUS, the THALAMUS, the CEREBRAL CORTEX, etc. Neurons whose cell bodies lie within a given center are usually of two types. Some cells, termed principal, projection, relay or Golgi Type I neurons, have DENDRITES within the center, but project their axons to other centers. Such neurons relay information between neural centers. Other cells, called local circuit neurons, interneurons, intrinsic neurons, or Golgi Type II neurons, have all of their processes within the neural center and are involved only in the activity of that local region. Often local circuit neurons make complex synaptic connections with each other and processes of principal cells that include reciprocal dendro–dendritic synapses (see DENDRITES AND DENDRITIC SPINES). SCC

Bibliography

Kandel, E.R. and Schwartz, J.H. 1981: *Principles of neural science*. New York and Oxford: Elsevier/North-Holland.

Rakic, P. 1976: *Local circuit neurons*. Cambridge, Mass. and London: MIT Press.

Roberts, A. and Bush, B.M.H. 1981: *Neurones without impulses*. Cambridge and New York: Cambridge University Press.

Shepard, G.M. 1979: *The synaptic organization of the brain*. 2nd ed. Oxford and New York: Oxford University Press.

neuropsychiatry Usually refers to the branch of psychiatry concerned with the cognitive, emotional and behavioral effects of manifest brain disorder (that is, excluding those disturbances where coarse brain disease is absent or is not currently demonstrable). The neuropsychiatrist concerns himself with such illnesses as epilepsy, dementia, endocrine and cerebral-vascular abnormalities, and infections and tumors of the brain.

The term may also be used to designate the combined disciplines of neurology and psychiatry which in some countries constitute a single specialization. DLJ

Bibliography

Lishman, W.A. 1978: *Organic psychiatry, the psychological consequence of social disorders*. Oxford: Blackwell Scientific; St Louis, Missouri: C.V. Mosby.

neurosis Neuroses are exaggerated forms of normal reactions to stressful events. There is no evidence of any kind of organic brain disorder, patients do not lose touch with external reality, and, although often associated with a degree of PERSONALITY DISORDER, the personality is not grossly abnormal. They may occur acutely at times of stress or may be chronic and associated with longstanding social difficulties. The term "neurosis" originated in the eighteenth century and was used with a variety of meanings during the nineteenth century. The present meaning is largely attributable to FREUD who defined a group of psychoneuroses of psychological etiology.

There is a distinction between the various neurotic syndromes described below and individual neurotic symptoms (for example anxiety and depression) which are extremely common in the general population and may be associated with many psychiatric disorders. Estimates of prevalence of neurotic disorder vary according to the strictness of the criteria used (see Goldberg and Huxley 1980). They make up the majority of the psychiatric cases seen in general practice, where they usually present with an undifferentiated clinical picture. The more severe neuroses can be divided into the specific syndromes, even though in clinical practice there is considerable overlap between them. Other categories listed in the current ninth edition of the International Classification of Disease (WHO 1978) and the American classification, DSM III (American Psychiatric Association 1980) are *acute reactions to stress* and *adjustment reactions*. These are used for the acute and the more prolonged emotional reactions occurring following severe stress in those with no evidence of previous psychiatric abnormality. It is difficult to distinguish between these normal (i.e. appropriate reactions) and neurosis. The traditional diagnoses of HYPOCHONDRIASIS and neurasthenia are now not normally regarded as primary psychiatric syndromes.

The neuroses have a very variable prognosis (see Goldberg and Huxley 1980). The majority of recent onset cases seen by doctors improve within a few months but a minority have a much more prolonged course. This is more likely if the initial problems are severe, if there are severe social difficulties and if the patient lacks social support and friendships. Prolonged psychological symptoms are usually associated with severe social handicaps.

Etiology Etiological factors can be considered in two groups, predisposing and precipitating. Predisposing factors include general social conditions, family difficulties or support, and to a limited extent genetic factors. Abnormalities and vulnerability of personality have frequently been described but there is no close relationship between the type of personality and the type of neurosis. Epidemiological research has described the role of protective (e.g. intimate marriage) and vulnerability factors (e.g. young children, poor marriage, lack of a job) in the patient's social circumstances (Brown and Harris 1978). Precipitating factors are stressful events such as childbirth, marriage, retirement and moving home. The principal theoretical approaches to explaining the interaction between stress and personality have been psychoanalytic (see Kaplan et al., 1980). Very different are learning theories which attempt to explain neuroses in terms of early experience and make use of learning mechanisms identified in the study of animal behavior (see Kaplan et al, 1980).

Treatment There are three main approaches to treatment: the relief of symptoms, help to solve the patient's problems, and treatment to alter vulnerability to neurosis. When the symptoms are mild and seem to be a temporary response to a stress that is likely to resolve quickly, support is all that is required. There is only a limited role for symptomatic relief by using anxiolytic drugs for a short period. Longer term drug treatment is ineffective and may lead to drug dependence. Frequently, however, it is necessary to help the patient with active steps to deal with problems in his life. As far as possible the patient is encouraged to make his own plans to solve his difficulties but practical help from a doctor or social worker may also be needed. More fundamental treatment by psychotherapy should be considered when it seems that neurosis has resulted from persistent maladaptive behavior and difficulties in personal relationships. In practice this varies between brief counseling and prolonged psychoanalytic treatment.

Clinical Features

Anxiety neurosis (or anxiety state) is a syndrome in which there are various combinations of physical and mental symptoms of anxiety, which are not attributable to real danger, and which occur either in attacks or as a persistent state. Apart from anxiety itself, psychological symptoms include irritability, difficulty in concentration and restlessness. Physical symptoms include signs of arousal of the autonomic nervous system including palpitations, sweating, nausea and diarrhea. In addition there may be tremor, difficulty in breathing or overbreathing, dizziness and headache. In some patients the physical symptoms predominate and physical disorder must be carefully considered in differential diagnosis. In treatment, short term anxiolytic drugs can be useful and specific medication can also have a limited use in the treatment of palpitations and other autonomic symptoms. Relaxation training is often as effective as medication in less severe cases. A more elaborate and varied form of BEHAVIOR THERAPY, anxiety management training, is even more effective.

In *phobic anxiety neuroses* there is an abnormal fear of certain objects or specific situations together with a strong wish to avoid them. There are three main groups: simple phobias, agoraphobia and social phobias (Marks 1969). Simple phobias are specific fears of objects or situations such as heights, thunder storms, spiders and mice. They are common in children and most adults have minor unreasonable fears. More severe phobias can cause considerable suffering and social limitations. Agoraphobia is anxiety when traveling from home, mixing with crowds or in any situation which a sufferer cannot easily leave. The fear, panic attacks and avoidance cause those with the most severe symptoms to be very restricted and perhaps housebound (Mathews et al., 1981). Sudden onset or worsening of agoraphobia or other phobic symptoms can be secondary to an AFFECTIVE DISORDER. The first step in treatment is, therefore, to look for, and if necessary treat, underlying depressive illness. Anxiolytic drugs may provide temporary relief but lasting improvement requires behavioral treatment to overcome the avoidance. Desensitization and other forms of behavior therapy are appropriate.

Depressive neurosis is a less severe form of affective disorder in which disproportionate depression has followed on upsetting events, meeting the definition of neurosis. It is, however, difficult to differentiate from affective disorder and there is considerable controversy about the classification of depression. Even so it is evident that depression and related symptoms, such as poor concentration, fatigue, poor sleep and irritability, are common neurotic symptoms both as a depressive syndrome or as part of the other syndromes.

The main feature of *hysteria* is evidence of physical symptoms in the absence of organic pathology, which have been produced unconsciously and are not caused by overactivity of the autonomic nervous system. The very long history of varying usage and the great variability in the clinical picture has led to severe problems in clear definition. It is usual to separate two groups of symptoms: (1) *conversion symptoms*, which derive from Freud's original formulation (Freud and Breuer (*1955*)) and include the physical symptoms such as paralysis, disorder of coordination, sensory disturbances, and a variety of pain syndromes; (2) *dissociative symptoms*, in which there is an apparent dissociation between different types of mental activity. These include amnesia, hysterical fits, somnambulism and multiple personality. In addition there are more general clinical features which include symbolic meaning, secondary gain and belle indifference. Although usually stressed in the literature they are not always present. Apart from these two groups clinical variants include epidemic hysteria (particularly among young girls in schools or other groups) and Briquet's syndrome, a name that has been used to describe a group of patients with chronic multiple symptoms including both hysterical and other neurotic symptoms. Careful physical assessment is always necessary before making the diagnosis of hysteria. Apart from treatment of the underlying neurotic problem, management is concerned to relieve the presenting symptoms. This is best achieved by a firm and optimistic yet sympathetic approach which avoids reinforcing the symptoms and also provides the patient with a face-saving opportunity for recovery. The prognosis is good in recent onset cases but when there is a long history symptomatic improvement is less likely.

The principal symptom in *obsessive compulsive neurosis* is a feeling of subjective compulsion to carry out an action or to dwell on an idea to an extent that is regarded as inappropriate or not sensible. The compulsion is accompanied by a subjective resistance with ideas that are regarded as inappropriate and absurd. Obsessional neuroses are uncommon. Their main symptoms are obsessional thoughts, images, ruminations, impulses and rituals. Although most episodes improve over a period of months the more severe disorders can be extremely persistent. It is necessary to exclude other primary disorders such as depression as the cause of obsessional symptoms.

In *depersonalizaton* perception is disturbed and external objects or parts of the body are experienced as having changed in quality, being unreal, remote or automotized. The symptom is common as a feature of other syndromes but primary depersonalization neurosis is rare. See also ANOREXIA NERVOSA; BULIMIA NERVOSA. RAM

Bibliography

American Psychiatric Association 1980: *Diagnostic and statistical manual* III.

Brown, G.W. and Harris, T. 1978: *Social origins of depression*. London: Tavistock.

Freud, S. and Breuer, J. (1955): *Studies on Hysteria*. Standard Edition of the Works of Sigmnd Freud vol. II. London: Hogarth; New York: Norton.

Goldberg, D. and Huxley, P. 1980: *Mental illness in the community*. London: Tavistock.

Kaplan, H.I., Freedman and Sadock, B.J. 1980: *Comprehensive textbook of psychiatry*. 3rd edn. Baltimore: Williams and Wilkins.

Marks, I.M. 1969: *Fears and phobias*. London: Heinemann; New York: Academic Press.

Mathews, A.M., Gelder, M.G. and Johnston, D.W. 1981: *Agoraphobia, nature and treatment*. New York: Guildford Press.

World Health Organisation 1978: *Mental disorders: glossary and guide to their classification in accordance with the ninth revision of the International Classification of Diseases*. Geneva: WHO.

neurotransmitter system A group of neurons which synthesize and release the same neurotransmitter is called a neurotransmitter system. Since each neurotransmitter system now known is distributed throughout more than one part of the nervous system, much of the current research in this area is focussed on determining whether a neurotransmitter system functions as a single unit in regulating physiology and behavior, or whether there are subsystems with different functions. The answer to this question is important not only for understanding normal human brain processes, but also for treating the consequences of abnormal brain function. Considerable effort has been made to determine the neuroanatomy of each known neurotransmitter system, and its possible role or roles in physiology and behavior.

The neuroanatomical analysis of neurotransmitter systems includes locating the cell bodies of neurons which produce a particular transmitter, determining where the input to them originates, and finding where their output goes. This is an extremely active research area due to the frequent exciting discoveries of new chemical substances in the brain, and the technological advances in methods for locating and identifying them. The results of these studies have shown that there is a wide range in the extent to which the different neurotransmitter substances are distributed throughout the brain and spinal cord. Some neurotransmitters such as ACETYLCHOLINE are found in neurons in many brain regions, each with its own unique set of inputs and outputs. Other neurotransmitters such as DOPAMINE are located in neurons whose cell bodies are found in relatively restricted parts of the brain, yet their outputs may still go to several different brain regions. For example, some dopamine-containing neurons communicate with the BASAL GANGLIA, while others send information to the LIMBIC SYSTEM (e.g., Cooper, Bloom and Roth 1978). These neuroanatomical findings suggest that each neurotransmitter system may have more than one behavioral or physiological function.

Long before neurons producing specific neurotransmitters could be precisely localized there was widespread interest in the possible behavioral functions of these substances. Most drugs which act to change mood or behavior affect some aspect of SYNAPTIC TRANSMISSION, and thus involve neurotransmitters. As the mechanisms of action of the drugs have been discovered, their behavioral effects have been associated with the neurotransmitter system upon which they act. However, even drugs thought to be specific to one neurotransmitter system often affect several different aspects of behavior, which may represent the effects of the drug at different neuroanatomical sites. In order to discover which subsets of a single neurotransmitter system are responsible for the different behavioral effects of a drug, special experimental techniques have been employed. Injection of drugs with known mechanisms of action into various brain regions in animals has revealed several important facts. First, different drugs injected into the same region of the brain may elicit different types of behavior; this is known as the chemical coding of behavior (Miller 1965). Second, more than one neurotransmitter is involved in any complex behavior. Finally, the same drug injected into different brain regions may elicit either the same or widely differing types of behavior. For example, acetylcholine injected into many parts of the limbic system will elicit drinking, but when injected into other limbic system sites it elicits aggression, and when injected into the basal ganglia it induces tremor. These principles suggest that when referring to a neurotransmitter system in a functional or behavioral sense, a subset of the entire system must be defined.

The current interest in the roles of neurotransmitter systems in behavior stems both from recent discoveries regarding certain degenerative disorders of the nervous system, and from the tremendous success of drug therapy in treating some psychiatric disorders. More than twenty years ago it was discovered that persons with Parkinson's disease, who have symptoms such as tremor, rigidity of the limbs, and a decrease in spontaneous motor movements, also have degeneration of the dopamine-containing neurons which communicate with the basal ganglia. The behavioral symptoms can be improved remarkably by replacing the missing dopamine either by giving drugs which act like dopamine, or drugs which the brain can convert into dopamine (Hornykiewicz 1975). Parkinson's disease has become a model for studying the roles of neurotransmitters in a variety of neurological disorders in order to discover rational drug therapies. Another neurological disorder, Huntingdon's chorea, involves abnormal involuntary movements and a gradual deterioration of cognitive function. In this hereditary disease there is degeneration of neurons which produce acetylcholine and GABA in the basal ganglia and neocortex (Wu et al. 1979). New therapies currently being tested include drugs and diets which enhance the actions of these diminished neurotransmitters. Finally, at least one form of senile dementia (Alzheimer's disease) is marked by the degeneration of some of the neurons which produce acetylcholine and communicate with the neocortex (Whitehouse et al. 1981). Since blockage of acetylcholine interferes with memory formation in normal people, it is possible that the loss of acetylcholine-containing neurons underlies the memory deficit in Alzheimer's disease. Again, new experimental therapies include drugs which act in place of the missing neurotransmitter.

The second source of interest in the behavioral roles of neurotransmitter systems in people stems from the remarkable success of drug treatment for certain psychiatric disorders. When behavioral symptoms can be relieved by a drug which acts to block or enhance a particular neurotransmitter it is possible that some disorder involving this substance may have been the cause of the symptoms. For example, drugs effective in treating schizophrenia block dopamine. It has therefore been suggested that some schizophrenics may have hyperactivity of one of the dopamine subsystems (Carlsson 1978). Similarly, depression can be treated with drugs which enhance the effectiveness of neurons which utilize NOREPINEPHRINE, dopamine, and possibly SEROTONIN. Depression has therefore been viewed as a disorder in which there may be a deficiency of one or all of these chemicals in the brain (Maas 1975).

While these hypotheses are attractive in that they provide a possible biological mechanism for emotional disorders which is consistent with the effects of the drugs used to treat them, it has been difficult to obtain direct evidence of the hypothesized differences in the brains of persons with these disorders. Unlike the known pathological changes in Parkinson's disease, Huntington's chorea, or senile dementia, there is no documented loss of neurons associated with a specific neurotransmitter substance in either schizophrenia or depression. Investigators must search for changes in the level of activity in the suspect neurons, rather than for degeneration. It is difficult, if not unethical, to assay the brains of living patients for increases or decreases in the activities of specific neurons; the researcher must settle for measures of neurotransmitter function in the cerebrospinal fluid, blood, or urine, none of which give accurate or uncontaminated measures of neurotransmitter activity in the brain. Differences in enzymes and hormone levels have been discovered in the blood of both schizophrenics and depressive persons, but none of these changes points unequivocally to a disorder of a single neurotransmitter system (e.g. Orsulak et al. 1978).

Postmortem examinations of the brains of schizophrenics and depressives provide a more direct way of testing neurotransmitter theories of emotional disorders. Workers studying schizophrenia are searching for changes in dopamine activity in the limbic system and basal ganglia, and some recent results support these expectations (Mackay et al. 1980). However, the interpretation of these findings is complicated by the fact that many of the patients had been prescribed drugs which affect dopamine. In addition, many other factors such as diet, general state of health before death, and agonal state may affect brain chemistry.

Because the blockage of dopamine in the basal ganglia may lead to motor symptoms resembling those of Parkinson's disease, it would be preferable to design a drug for schizophrenia which would act more selectively at limbic system sites. This now seems possible due to biochemical differences in the various dopamine subsystems. Knowledge of the neuroanatomy, biochemistry, and behavioral aspects of a neurotransmitter system can help in the design of drugs which are not only effective, but are also selective in their effects. As additional neurotransmitter systems are identified, further progresss can be made in understanding normal brain function, and in designing treatments for behavioral disorders. CVaH

Bibliography

Carlsson, A. 1978: Antipsychotic drugs, neurotransmitters, and schizophrenia. *American journal of psychiatry* 135,164-73.

* Cooper, Jack R., Bloom, F. E., and Roth, Robert H. 1978: *The biochemical basis of neuropharmacology*, 3rd edn. New York: Oxford University Press.

Hornykiewicz, O. 1975: Parkinson's disease and its chemotherapy. *Biochemical pharmacology* 24, 1061-65.

Maas, J. 1975: Biogenic amines and depression. *Archives of general psychiatry* 32, 1357-61.

Mackay, A.V.P. et al. 1980: Dopaminergic abnormalities in postmortem schizophrenic brain. *Advances in biochemical pharmacology* 24, 325-33.

Miller, N.E. 1965: Chemical coding of behavior in the brain. *Science* 148,328-38.

Orsulak, P.J. et al. 1978: Differences in platelet monoamine oxidase activity in subgroups of schizophrenic and depressive disorders. *Biological psychiatry* 13,637-47.

Pincus, Jonathan H., and Tucker, Gary J. 1978: *Behavioral neurology*, 2nd edn. New York: Oxford University Press.

Snyder, Solomon H. 1980: *Biological aspects of mental disorder*. New York and Oxford: Oxford University Press.

Whitehouse et al. 1981: Alzheimer disease: evidence for selective loss of cholinergic neurons in the nucleus basalis. *Annals of neurology* 10,122-26.

Wu, J.-Y. et al. 1979: Abnormalities of neurotransmitter enzymes in Huntington's chorea. *Neurochemical research*, 4,575-85.

neurotropism The tendency displayed by developing or regenerating axons for growth in a particular direction in the nervous system. The determinants of this attractive influence are unknown, but the presence of chemical signals as neurotropic "lures" has been postulated. An alternative, though not necessarily mutually exclusive hypothesis proposes that the formation of appropriate connectivity in the nervous system is simply a function of temporally constrained mechanical factors that guide and direct growth. BER/RCS

noise, exposure to Generally defined as unwanted sound, exposure to noise can impair hearing, affect task performance, alter psychophysiological activity and produce feelings of annoyance and irritation. The intensity of the noise, measured in decibels using a sound level meter, its frequency composition (the frequency of sound being measured in hertz) and the duration of exposure to the noise all determine the nature of the effect that is observed. Three kinds of hearing loss can result from exposure to intense noise: (1) a temporary and reversible hearing loss; (2) a permanent hearing loss, affecting speech comprehension, resulting from repeated exposure over several years; (3) acoustic trauma resulting from brief exposure to extremely intense noise. The performance of tasks involving the continuous processing of complex information is particularly likely to be impaired by loud noise, although very large individual differences exist in the response to environments which are apparently identical with respect to their noise characteristics. DRD

Bibliography

Broadbent, D.E. 1979: Human performance in noise. In *Handbook of noise control*, ed. C.M. Harris, 2nd edn. New York: McGraw Hill.

Davies, D.R. and Jones, D.M. 1982: Hearing and noise. In *The body at work: biological ergonomics*, ed. W.T. Singleton. Cambridge and New York: Cambridge University Press.

Jones, D.M. and Davies, D.R. 1983: Individual and group differences in the response to noise. In *Noise and society*, ed. D.M. Jones and A.J. Chapman. Chichester and New York: Wiley.

nomological A nomological regularity, generalization, or implication is one which is lawlike rather than accidental. Such a generalization supports the corresponding counterfactual. Thus "sugar is soluble in water" supports "if this sugar had been immersed in water it would have dissolved". By contrast "all men using ball points were alive after 1900" does not support "if Disraeli had used a ball point he would have lived into the present century". JMS

non-verbal communication *See* communication, non-verbal

norepinephrine (noradrenaline) One of the catecholamine neurotransmitters found in the peripheral and central nervous system. Norepinephrine is synthesized from DOPAMINE by dopamine β-hydroxylase, an enzyme that serves as a marker for norepinephrine (noradrenergic) neurons. Peripherally, norepinephrine is an important neurotransmitter in the sympathetic nervous system. Centrally, a major site for the cell bodies of noradrenergic neurons is the locus coeruleus of the BRAIN STEM. Noradrenergic projections descending from this region synapse at lower brain stem nuclei and in the spinal cord. Ascending noradrenergic pathways, including the MEDIAL FOREBRAIN BUNDLE and the dorsal bundle, project to various brain regions, including the cerebral cortex, and nuclei in the THALAMUS, HYPOTHALAMUS, HIPPOCAMPUS and RETICULAR ACTIVATING SYSTEM. Other noradrenergic neurons project from locus coeruleus to the CEREBELLUM. Norepinephrine synapses can be either excitatory or inhibitory. Behavior associated with increased noradrenergic functioning includes behavioral arousal, alertness, mood elevation, and responses to stimulants. Decreases in norepinephrine levels have been associated with the initiation of paradoxical sleep. GPH

norms: social psychology A norm is a rule or standard for action. Social norms are shared definitions of desirable behavior. They can be enforced in various ways. To the extent that a norm is effective, it leads to uniformity of behavior, but as a standard for evaluating behavior a norm does not necessarily describe the most common actual behavior. As such the term should be distinguished from concepts like statistical measures of central tendency, customs, folkways or mores.

Norms play an important role in social influence processes which are manifested in the general tendency towards CONFORMITY. Although compliance with norms depends to some extent upon the enforcement of positive and negative sanctions, the sheer unanimity with which a norm is endorsed by members of a group is in itself a factor which can induce compliance with a norm. As Moscovici (1976) has shown, the effect of active minorities in this respect is different from the effects of a dominant majority.

Deviation from norms and the origin and maintenance of norms have mainly been studied by sociologists. In social psychology the related concept of RULES has become more important in recent research. JMFJ

Bibliography

Moscovici, S. 1976: *Social influence and social change*. London and New York: Academic Press.

nosology The science of the definition of disease-entities. It is concerned with the principles by which illnesses can be differentiated from one another and with the classification of illnesses as a basis for the making of diagnoses. A satisfactory nosological system would describe for each discrete disease a specific cause, presenting picture, time course and outcome, and in addition would ideally provide confirmatory objective tests and specific treatments. In psychiatry we are far from the ideal. Until a century ago mental illness was conceptualized as a unitary psychosis, with stages from melancholia to furor, delusional madness and finally dementia. With Kraepelin, Jaspers and Bleuler, studies of genetics, phenomenology and life histories led to the current classification into the broad categories of organic and functional psychoses, neuroses, character disorders and mental handicap. DLJ

Bibliography

Clare, A. 1979: The disease concept in psychiatry. In *Essentials of postgraduate psychiatry*, ed P. Hill, R. Murray and A. Thorely. London: Academic Press; New York: Grune and Stratton.

nutrition and the nervous system Since the human body cannot manufacture everything it needs for its development and maintenance it is not surprising that abnormal states of nutrition can have dramatic effects on the developing nervous system. General malnourishment or specific vitamin deficiencies due to poor diet during the early stages of life can have pronounced effects on intellectual functioning. In adults much of the nervous system pathology that results from chronic alcoholism may be secondary to poor nutrition. Wurtman and Fernstrom (1976) have shown that variations in normal dietary intake are reflected in the synthesis, and perhaps release, of various neurotransmitters. In rats fed a meal comprised primarily of carbohydrates, concentrations of SEROTONIN in the brain are subsequently increased. Meals high in protein content result in increased brain levels of DOPAMINE and NOREPINEPHRINE. Brain levels of ACETYLCHOLINE can similarly be modified by the ingestion of foods rich in its precursor, choline. Changes in levels of neurotransmitters may be reflected in behaviors mediated by them, and the alteration of NEUROTRANSMITTER SYSTEMS by the manipulation of diet may have important therapeutic applications. GPH

Bibliography

Wurtman, R.J. and Fernstrom, J.D. 1976: Control of brain neurotransmitter synthesis by precursor availability and nutritional state. *Biochemical pharmacology* 25, 1691-96.

O

obedience As a technical term the word became popular in psychology through the work of Milgram (1974), who wrote: "Obedience is the psychological mechanism that links individual action to political purpose. It is the dispositional cement that binds men to systems of authority. Facts of recent history and observation in daily life suggest that for many people obedience may be a deeply ingrained behavior tendency, indeed, a prepotent impulse overriding training in ethics, sympathy and moral conduct" (p.1).

Obedience, in this special psychological sense, may be defined as a particular form of compliance where behavior is performed in response to a direct order. Social psychologists have done extensive research into compliance, conformity, persuasibility and obedience, particularly obedience and conformity. Yet as Milgram noted obedience and conformity may be distinguished in the following ways: (i) Hierarchy: whereas conformity regulates the behavior of equal status subjects, obedience links one status to another; (ii) Imitation: whereas conformity is imitation, obedience is not; (iii) Explicitness: in obedience the prescription for action (an order) is explicit whereas in conformity the requirement for going along with the group is implicit; (iv) Voluntarism: because conformity is a response to implicit pressure, the subject interprets his or her own behavior as voluntary, but as obedience is publicly defined as a situation devoid of voluntarism, the subject can use the public definition of the situation as a full explanation of his or her action.

Milgram's studies on obedience have been criticized in terms of ethical problems, experimental artifacts, lack of generality, and conceptual confusion. AF

Bibliography

Milgram, S. 1974: *Obedience to authority*. London: Tavistock.

obesity Refers to the presence of an abnormally high proportion of body fat whereas "overweight" refers to a body weight which is above an arbitrary standard. These words are often used interchangeably. Obesity is associated with many disorders which increase morbidity and mortality. Its prevalence is increasing in developed countries. Since the majority of obese people eat no more than their normal weight peers, obese people as a group are deficient in their utilization of energy. Psychological and social factors are also of etiological importance. Treatment aims to establish an energy deficit with energy expenditure exceeding energy intake. In general, emphasis is placed on the reduction of energy using dietary advice, behavioral intervention, anorectic drugs, or surgery. The long-term results are disappointing. CJGF

Bibliography

Schachter, S. 1971: *Emotion, obesity and crime*. New York: Academic Press.
Stunkard, A.J. 1980: *Obesity*, Philadelphia: W.B. Saunders.

object permanence Knowledge of the continued material existence of an object, even when the object itself is not accessible to direct sensory awareness. In Piaget's theory, it is argued that the concept of object permanence is a belief that is only slowly acquired in development. Piaget's evidence was that babies below approximately eight months will not search manually for a hidden object but behave as though it has ceased to exist. This led him to suppose that "out of sight was out of mind" so far as the baby was concerned.

An alternative is that the perception of object permanence is one of the constancies (Bower 1972). Just as the size and shape of an object are perceived as invariant under transformation, so is the existence of an object perceived as continuing despite temporary occlusion. The primary developmental problem may not lie in acquiring the concept of object permanence, but in making use of perceptually specified information to control manual search. GEB

Bibliography

Bower, T.G.R. 1972: *Development in infancy*. 2nd edn. San Francisco: Freeman.

Piajet, J. 1937 (*1954*): *The construction of reality in the child*. New York: Basic Books.

object relations A term used frequently by contemporary psychoanalytic writers, its shades of meaning reflecting a theoretical movement away from a model of the subject as isolated and biologically (instinctually) motivated toward a view which encompasses the subject's interactions with its surroundings – its interpersonal relations. Use of the word *object* to refer to persons derives from the commitment of psychoanalysts to an instinct theory. The object through which instinctual gratification is held to be achieved is usually a person, an aspect of a person or a symbolic representation of a person toward which the subject directs its actions or desires. Technically "object relations" refers to the mental representations of the self and other (the object) which are an aspect of ego organization and not to external interpersonal relationships. (See also INSTINCT.) BBL

objective consciousness *See* Gurdjieff

objective self-awareness *See* self awareness, objective

observational learning *See* imitation and observational learning

observational methods A distinctive feature of ETHOLOGY from its origins, and one which has proved more durable to the present day than some of its specific theories, has been its insistence on the importance of observation (see Tinbergen 1963, Thorpe 1979). This does not imply avoidance of experimentation or of laboratories: rather it reflects a stress on meticulously detailed observational descriptions of animal behavior, whatever the context. Ethologists also try to ensure that the categories used for describing observed behavior are objective – that is, that they refer to its observable form and consequences, and are capable of consistent use over time and between observers. Ethologists do recognize, however, that objectivity in this sense is not perfectible, and also that the actual designation of behavior categories studied is invariably selective (see Reynolds 1976). Errors which ethologists hope to avoid in their descriptions include choosing behavior categories that are too crude to be useful, describing behavior in ways that do not distinguish clearly between observation and interpretation, and ANTHROPOMORPHISM.

For much of ethology's development, observational methods have largely been based on prolonged immersion in observation and becoming a 'good observer', compiling a behavior catalogue or ETHOGRAM, extended recording of observations, and analysis in predominantly verbal terms. In recent decades, however, the emphasis has shifted towards quantification and the use of computer and other technology in both the recording and analysis of observed behavior (see e.g. Bramblett 1976). RDA

Bibliography

Bramblett, C.A. 1976: *Patterns of primate behavior*. Palo Alto (California): Mayfield.

Reynolds, V. 1976 The origins of a behavioural vocabulary: the case of the rhesus monkey. *Journal of the theory of social behaviour* 6, 105–42.

Thorpe, W.H. 1979 *The origins and rise of ethology: the science of the natural behaviour of animals*. London, Melbourne: Heinemann; New York: Praeger.

Tinbergen, N. 1963 On aims and methods of ethology. *Zeitschrift für Tierpsychologie 20*, 410–433.

observer's paradox The observer's paradox in linguistic research as postulated by Labov (1972, p.209) refers to the fact that the aim of linguistic research is to find out how people talk when they are not being systematically observed, and yet one can only obtain this data by systematic observation. Labov suggests a number of procedures to overcome this obstacle. PM

Bibliography

Labov, William 1972: *Sociolinguistic patterns*. Philadelphia: University of Pennsylvania Press.

occult Derived from the Latin *occultus*, hidden, occultism has traditionally meant hidden knowledge, and is used in that sense in the title of Cornelius Agrippa's *Occult philosophy*, published in 1531. As a medical term it means "subconscious" – as in "occult anxiety". The legendary founder of occult philosophy was Hermes Trismegistos – "Thrice Great Hermes" – to whom is attributed the most famous of all magical dicta: "As above, so below." This meant that the laws of the heavens – the macrocosm – were reflected in man himself – the microcosm. The only version of this belief which survives in our own time is ASTROLOGY, which is based on the notion that the positions of the planets can exert some influence upon the character and destiny of human beings. (A modern statistician, Michel Gauquelin, has produced some impressive if controversial scientific evidence that the position of the planets at birth may influence a baby's character.) But in ancient times "as above, so below" also implied a complicated system of "correspondences" between the heavens and the earth. Each planet was associated with a "cosmic principle" – Venus with love, Saturn with wisdom, Mars with war, and so on – also with a number, a color, a metal, a precious stone, a flower, and innumerable other things. Ritual magic was an attempt to make use of this "knowledge" – so that, for example, in Rome in 1628, the writer Campanella performed elaborate magical ceremonies involving lights – symbolizing the planets – and various colors, jewels, flowers, etc, to ward off an eclipse which the Pope was convinced would cause his death. (He lived another sixteen years.)

It is important to recognize that many "magicians" of earlier centuries were eminent scholars or scientists –

Paracelsus, Agrippa, Giordano Bruno, John Dee – even Isaac Newton was an enthusiastic student of alchemy, while Kepler was a believer in astrology. In Lynn Thorndike's classic *History of magic and experimental science* (8 volumes) the two traditions are in fact treated as one, but the history stops at the time of Newton, when science became the more powerful identity. It could probably be said with fairness that the history of magic since that time has been a matter of either charlatanism or romanticism – often so closely intermingled as to be almost indistinguishable. Cagliostro, Eliphaz Levi, Madame Blavatsky, Aleister Crowley, all had elements of the charlatan and showman; yet no one who studies their careers with an open mind can deny that all seem to have had certain "paranormal" powers – for example, the ability to induce "spirit knockings". It is easy to understand how a writer like Bulwer Lytton came to accept the reality of magic – a novel such as *A strange story* shows a strong disposition to seek out the startling and extraordinary for purely "artistic" reasons. Again, in the early poetry of W.B. Yeats, it is easy to see the close connection between his dislike of modern life and his interest in fairies and magic.

Yet although it is important not to lose sight of this element of pseudo-science and wishful thinking in "occultism", it must be recognized that there is also a strong element of "escapism" in the wholly sceptical outlook of many modern investigators. The evidence for various types of "spirit manifestation" is too strong and too plentiful to be dismissed wholly as fraud or imagination. Such phenomena aroused widespread public interest in the late 1840s, when a series of loud bangs and rappings occurred in the home of the Fox sisters in Hydesville, N.Y. Within ten years, "mediums" all over America were producing not only "spirit messages" but so called "materializations", in which a mysterious substance called ectoplasm seemed to issue from the medium's body and to form itself into human shapes. In Paris in the 1850s fashionable society discovered that if a group of people sat around a table, their finger-tips spread out and touching, the table would often bounce and rock around, and even float into the air – this is still a relatively easy phenomenon to duplicate. In 1882, the Society for Psychical Research was founded, mostly by sceptics, to try to reach some positive conclusions about these phenomena. A century later "positive conclusions" seem as far away as ever, yet there is an enormous and impressive body of evidence for the reality of many "paranormal" effects.

One of the most interesting observations made by these early psychic investigators was that so called "poltergiest manifestations" – which usually involve unexplainable noises and objects flying through the air – are often associated with the presence of a "disturbed adolescent". This led some of them to conclude that the phenomena could be produced *unconsciously* by the adolescent. And this notion – that "paranormal effects" may be produced by some unknown power of the human mind – is now held by the majority of those researchers who are not wholly sceptical. An experiment conducted in the early 1970s by the Toronto Society for Psychical Research, under the direction of Dr George Owen, seemed to provide conclusive evidence for this theory. The group invented the story of a man called Philip, who was supposed to have committed suicide in the time of Oliver Cromwell; they then attempted to "conjure up" Philip during seances. Eventually, they succeeded, and the table obligingly repeated Philip's history – using a code of knocks – and even waltzed around the room in front of TV cameras.

Another school of thought believes that this evidence is not conclusive – that although the unconscious mind may possess the power to produce certain paranormal phenomena, this is not conclusive evidence that "spirits" are non-existent. And in fact, anyone who studies the history of the poltergeist (the earliest recorded case dates back to 858 AD) will probably end by admitting that the theory of "recurrent spontaneous psychokinesis" (RSPK) simply fails to explain more than 50 per cent of the cases. There are dozens of cases in which the RSPK explanation needs to be supplemented by the older belief that "disembodied spirits" actually exist and can, under certain conditions, manifest themselves.

Certainly, one of the oddest things about the history of magic and witchcraft is that their basic beliefs have been unchanged over the course of at least three thousand years, and that they can be found in all parts of the world. All primitive peoples believe in the existence of spirits – both "nature spirits", and the spirits of the dead – and that these spirits can be contacted by human beings such as witch doctors and mediums. There is also a widespread belief, extending from ancient Mesopotamia to modern Brazil, that such spirits can be persuaded to "serve" human beings under certain strict conditions, and that these conditions include the precise performance of magical rituals. Understandably most psychical investigators (with a few rare exceptions, such as Guy Lyon Playfair) totally reject all such notions, and continue to look for semi-psychological explanations. Yet it is worth bearing in mind that the older explanations have the virtue of consistency, as well as of unanimity throughout various historical periods.

The most comprehensive history of modern "occultism", beginning with the early nineteenth century, can be found in James Webbs two scholarly volumes *The occult underground* (published in England as *The flight from reason*) and *The occult establishment*. Written from a sceptical point of view these nevertheless show the remarkable range and the persistent vitality of "occultism" in the post-scientific era. Interest in this whole field is now more widespread than ever, and would seem to indicate that we are far from having heard the last word on the subject. CW

Bibliography

Cavendish, R. 1967. *The black arts*. London: Routledge & Kegan Paul; New York: Putnam.

Encyclopedia of occultism and parapsychology, 1978: Ed. Leslie A. Shepard (2 vols), Detroit; Gale Research Co.

Playfair, Guy Lyon 1976: *The indefinite boundary*. London: Souvenir Press.

Wilson, Colin 1971: *The occult*. London: Hodder & Stoughton; New York: Random House.

Yates, Frances 1964: *Giordano Bruno and the hermetic tradition*. London: Routledge & Kegan Paul; Chicago: University of Chicago Press.

occupational socialization *See* socialization, occupational

Oedipus and Elektra complexes After the Greek legends in which, respectively, King Oedipus inadvertently killed his father, and Elektra avenged the murder of her father by assisting in the murder of her mother, these terms refer in PSYCHOANALYTIC PERSONALITY THEORY to two clusters of mainly unconscious feelings and ideas which set in at the "phallic" stage of psychosexual development. The child's attachment to the opposite-sex parent becomes sexualized, so that the child wishes to possess him or her and get rid of the other parent. The boy's rivalry with the father produces "castration anxiety", the female parallel of which is "penis envy". The child deals with the associated anxieties by eventually "identifying" with the same-sex parent (see DEFENSE MECHANISM) and "introjecting" his or her prohibitions as a basis for the primitive SUPEREGO, and his or her positive values as EGO IDEAL (Freud 1917, ch. 21). Some non-clinical studies of dreams and PROJECTIVE TESTS do seem to support some of the constituent hypotheses of these complexes (see Kline 1981, ch. 6). NMC

Bibliography

Freud, Sigmund 1917: *Introductory lectures*, part 3. *Standard edition of the complete psychological works of Sigmund Freud*. Vol. 16. London: Hogarth Press; New York: Norton.

Kline, Paul 1981: *Fact and fiction in Freudian theory*. 2nd edn., London and New York: Methuen.

ontogenetic sequence The Freudian model of psychosexual development, derived by analogy from the epigenetic development of embryology, in which each organ or organ system undergoes a CRITICAL PERIOD of rapid growth and differentiation at a specific time and in a particular, fixed sequence. Failure to develop during the critical period dooms the organ or organ system, and thus the organism, to developmental defects. Freud considered the psychosexual development of the individual to undergo a similar series of critical periods, or stages: the oral stage, the anal stage, the oedipal stage, the latency period, and the genital stage. Failure or fixation at any stage endangered the subsequent stages and the individual's development. ND

operant conditioning Also known as instrumental learning or Skinnerian learning, is the study of the learning of operants, the term introduced by Skinner (1938) to describe responses that are emitted without an obvious eliciting stimulus, in contrast to responses for which there are clear eliciting stimuli. Skinner and his followers have described in detail the effects of reinforcement, i.e. stimuli contingent upon operants, and have shown how the particular frequency of reinforcement systematically affects the rate and frequency of operant behavior. They have also emphasized the role of shaping in the development of new behavior whereby successive approximations to the desired behavior are reinforced. The application of operant principles in behavior modification, termed contingency management has been highly successful (see BEHAVIOR THERAPY) while Skinner's theoretical writings on the role of cognition in a scientific explanation of behavior have contributed sharply to the controversies on cognitive behavior therapy and have fuelled the belief held by a minority of behavior therapists that an adequate theory of human behavior and of behavior therapies is possible without concern for cognition and, indeed, that such concerns are harmful to the development of satisfactory theories and therapies. DWJ

Bibliography

Skinner, B.F. 1938: *The behaviour of organisms*. New York and London: Appleton Century.

operationalism A doctrine in the philosophy of science which holds that the meaning of a scientific concept is given by the set of operations by which it is measured. It was first formulated by the chemist B.C. Brodie (1869) and revived by the physicist P.W. Bridgeman (1927).

The doctrine is important to BEHAVIORISM because it provides a philosophical rationale for the reduction of mental terms to physical terms. For example, the concept of perception is translated into sensory discrimination.

Within the radical behaviorism of Skinner it has a distinct, specialized meaning, referring to the operation of functionally analysing the control of a word as a unit of verbal behavior (Skinner 1945). This is referred to by Skinner as "operational definition". AO

Bibliography

Bridgeman, P.W. 1927: *The logic of modern physics*. New York:

*Schlesinger, G. 1967: Operationalism. *The encyclopaedia of philosophy*. New York: Macmillan.

Skinner, B.F. 1945: The operational analysis of psychological terms. *Psychological review* 52, 270–7.

optical illusions *See* visual illusions

ordered change theory Refers to a class of developmental theories describing human action over time in terms of an orderly and reliable sequence. Such theories are most frequent within the domain of child development, but in principle could apply within any branch of psychology concerned with cross-time pattern. A prime exemplar of an ordered change theory is Piaget's ontogenetic theory of cognitive development. As Piaget argues, during normal development the quality of the child's thought undergoes a series of orderly transitions from the primitive and concrete to the abstract and adaptive. Ordered change theories may be contrasted with other theoretical forms emphasizing either cross time stability in pattern or non-replicable, historically contingent trajectories. (See also ALEATORIC THEORY; HISTORICITY.) KJG

organic mental states Abnormalities of psychological functions (consciousness, memory, perception, thinking or mood) and behavior, which result from disorders of the brain. Organic mental states are usually accompanied by physical symptoms which are characteristic of the underlying condition. Many alternative terms have been used, among them: organic psychoses, exogenous reactions, symptomatic psychoses, psycho-organic syndromes, brain syndromes and organic reactions. Such terms suggest, with variable degree of success, the presence of psychological and physical manifestations in these conditions. Physical diseases of the brain tend to produce similar patterns of psychological disturbance, irrespective of the actual cause (Bonhoeffer 1909, Bleuler 1951). However, psychological symptoms taken together with physical signs, especially the neurological manifestations, can be of considerable help in locating the site of the lesion.

Organic mental states can be classified by reference to their clinical picture into two principal types: acute and chronic organic mental states.

Acute organic mental states

These are usually self-limited and reversible conditions, of sudden onset, and presenting a characteristic picture and course. The main symptom at the outset is clouding of consciousness (see CONSCIOUSNESS DISORDERS). The individual's attention is impaired and concentration is poor, with a tendency to lose track during conversation. The person may appear drowsy, and time sense (e.g. time of day, estimation of time) may be lost. Clouding of consciousness tends to fluctuate, and it is usually worse in the evening. Motor activity can be considerably reduced, especially with severe clouding of consciousness. In other cases, the individual may be restless, showing intermittent agitation and repetitive behavior involving stereotyped movements, as in delirium. Here the individual may suffer perceptual abnormalities involving the visual and auditory fields, as well as bodily sensations. There are frequent and short-lived *misinterpretations* and *illusions*, and *hallucinations*, usually visual, are a prominent feature of the clinical picture. *Thinking* is commonly slow, with failure to grasp, and is often disconnected and incoherent. *Delusional ideas*, especially involving persecution or threat, are very common, and their content tends to be colored by the individual's personality and background (Wolff and Curran 1935). *Memory functions* are severely affected, and the individual has difficulty registering new information, storing data or recalling material. Memory for recent events is poor, and disorientation in time and place is common (see MEMORY DISORDERS). The patient's *mood* is also affected, anxiety and fear being frequent features. Anger and suspiciousness can be present, especially in association with delusional ideas or hallucinations. As the acute organic state improves, sleep becomes restful and prolonged, and recovery follows although memories surrounding the event remain hazy. A deteriorating course would usually progress toward coma, and in some cases, the individual may lapse into a chronic organic state.

Chronic organic mental states

These present a characteristic picture, usually with a progressive course. They may develop after an acute organic state, or they may have a gradual onset, with evidence of general intellectual decay, especially in memory and thinking, and showing personality changes with suspiciousness, uninhibited behavior or affective changes such as depression. As the condition progresses, the individual may show lack of interest and activity, social withdrawal and neglect in personal appearance and standards. The person's *memory* suffers global deterioration with forgetfulness at first, and then with more definite lapses of memory, and disorientation in time is usually present. Registration of new information is reduced and retention and recall are also affected. Confabulation may be present. Poverty of *thinking* is characteristic, and the patient's thoughts are slow and muddled, with difficulty thinking in abstract terms. Delusional ideas, usually involving persecution or threat, can develop and contribute to suspicion and abnormalities of *mood*. The latter may include anxiety and hostility. Inappropriate or superficial emotional responses may be present.

When the organic mental state is the result of localized rather than generalized brain damage the clinical picture may have characteristic psychological and neurological symptoms, in addition to those associated with an acute or chronic course. The main psychological features of focal brain damage are as follows (see also BRAIN AND CENTRAL NERVOUS SYSTEM: ILLUSTRATIONS, figs. 1, 2 and 3).

frontal lobe: cognitive impairment in chronic disorder is similar to that seen in generalized disorders, but there may be prominent personality changes with disinhibition, impulsivity and euphoria, or with lack of drive and psychomotor retardation.

parietal lobe: damage to the dominant parietal lobe is associated with specific language difficulties involving the production or understanding of words. Non-dominant hemisphere lesions may lead to problems recognizing the body image, so that parts of the body may be perceived as missing. The outside space may also be misperceived. Visuospatial difficulties may be present with lesions of either parietal lobe, so that the person has difficulties placing objects in space or finding the way about.

temporal lobe: memory disturbances are characteristic of bilateral damage to the temporal lobes (see MEMORY DISORDERS). Language difficulties may follow lesions to the dominant temporal lobe, while non-dominant lesions may be associated with visuospatial symptoms. Personality changes, with aggressive outbursts may be present.

occipital lobe: visual symptoms are prominent here, with difficulties in recognizing written material, color or objects. Visual hallucinations may also occur.

Organic mental states can be caused by a great variety of agents, some producing damage to the brain itself and some resulting from disorders in other parts of the body which have indirect effects on the central nervous system (Lishman 1978). Acute organic reactions can result from the following disorders, among others

(a) Brain lesions caused by:

trauma: head injury can lead to concussion, with a period of unconsciousness or clouding, and this can be followed by an *acute* post-traumatic delirium or other disorders.

tumors: in addition to the general feature of the acute reaction, the individual may have symptoms which suggest the location of the tumor.

infection of the central nervous system or the meninges, as in viral conditions or syphilis.
vascular disorders, such as cerebral hemorrhage or thrombosis.
degenerative conditions such as dementia, complicated by other disorders such as infections or vascular accidents.
epileptic disorders, especially psychomotor seizures (see EPILEPSY).
(b) Conditions affecting other systems which have effects on brain function:
metabolic disorders: e.g. acute disease of the liver or kidney.
endocrine disorder: e.g. of the thyroid, parathyroid, adrenal glands (see ENDOCRINE DISORDERS).
nutritional disorders: such as vitamin deficiencies.
lack of cerebral oxygen: as in cardiovascular and respiratory disorders.
infection: e.g. pneumonia and septicemia.
toxic conditions: e.g. effect of drugs (alcohol, barbiturates) or their withdrawal, or of poisons such as lead or mercury.

Chronic organic states can be caused by similar agents to those producing acute reactions, but here the structural damage is more persistent and the condition is less likely to be reversible. They often follow on from acute organic states. Chronic organic states can be the result of brain lesions or generalized disorders:
(a) Brain lesions:
trauma: post-concussional syndrome, post-traumatic dementia and psychotic states may follow severe head injury.
infections: e.g. syphilis (general paralysis of the insane) (Hare 1959), viral encephalitis.
degenerative conditions: the dementias: senile, arteriosclerotic, Alzheimer's, Huntington's, and the rare dementia due to abnormal pressure hydrocephalus which is important because of its potential reversibility (Lishman 1978).
tumors: the symptoms have localized significance.
(b) Conditions affecting other systems, among them:
metabolic diseases: e.g. chronic and severe liver and kidney conditions.
endrocrine disorders as in acute reactions.
nutritional as in thiamine deficiency (Wernicke's encephalopathy).
toxic conditions: e.g. damage from alcohol (Korsakoff's psychosis), barbiturates or poisons.
lack of cerebral oxygen: e.g. cardiovascular and respiratory diseases.

JC

Bibliography

Bleuler, M. 1951: Psychiatry of cerebral diseases, *British medical journal 2*, 1233–8.

Bonhoeffer, K. 1909: Exogenous psychoses. In *Themes and variations in European psychiatry*, ed. S. R. Hirsch and M. Shepherd. Bristol: John Wright.

Hare, E.H. 1959: The origin and spread of dementia paralytica. *Journal of mental science 105*, 594–626.

*Lishman, W.A. 1978: *Organic psychiatry: the psychological consequences of cerebral disorder*. Oxford: Blackwell Scientific; St Louis, Missouri: C. V. Mosby.

Slater, E. and Roth, M. 1969: *Clinical psychiatry*. London: Bailliere, Tindall and Cassell.

Wolff, H. and Curran, D. 1935: Nature of delirium and allied states. *Archives of neurology and psychiatry 35*, 1175–215.

organization *See above, and also* memory organization

organization development The generic name for efforts designed to change organizations that: are long-range; are organization-wide; are aimed at increasing organizational effectiveness; are intended to have beneficial effects for individuals within the organization; focus on the organization's culture; are assisted by a change agent; apply principles developed by psychologists and other behavioral scientists (French and Bell 1973; Beckhard 1969).

An essential component of organization development is an ACTION RESEARCH orientation. A change agent (usually from outside the organization) in collaboration with organization representatives, diagnoses an organization's culture by way of systematic data collection. The findings are then fed back to organization members, and discussion about their meaning and implications leads to plans for action. Action is taken, evaluated, and new plans are drawn; the cycle then recurs.

Streams of influence of organization development
This is a relatively young subject. Its beginnings can be traced to three confluent streams of influence. First there is GROUP TRAINING, a method for increasing the awareness of members of small unstructured groups about themselves and their interpersonal relations. This type of training evolved from workshops on group dynamics held during the late 1940s, in both the USA and the UK. The focus was initially on free-standing groups created solely for training individuals. These were called T-GROUPS (T standing for training). Principles were later applied to organizational settings, and group training within organizations became one basis of organization development.

The second stream is survey research with feedback. This involves surveys of organization members' attitudes about their work environment and the subsequent presentation and discussion of findings from these surveys. These steps are the first two in survey-guided action research. Of course it is possible to collect data by other means (e.g. document searches, interviews with a few important people), but assessment of a wider range of attitudes is an important part of organization development (see SURVEY FEEDBACK).

The third stream is the HUMAN RELATIONS movement, which sprang from the work of Mayo and his colleagues during the 1920s and '30s. These Hawthorne studies emphasized the influence of the informal work group upon productivity and worker satisfaction, leading to a greater interest in the application of social psychology to organizations. The value of considering the worker's "humanness" was recognized and encouraged.

Characteristics of organization development efforts
Features of organization development include diagnosing the organization's current state, planning improvement strategies, selecting intervention techniques, planning and taking action, and evaluating the effects of the intervention (Tichy and Beckhard 1978).

Data collection for the diagnosis can include any one or any combination of five procedures: questionnaire survey, observation, interviews, workshop diagnostic meetings, and examination of documents and records. Once collected, the data are interpreted for the purpose of guiding plans for organizational improvement. The main question addressed here is: "What are the problems in this organization that we–the team composed of a change agent and organization members–can deal with?" The next step is to plan how to address these problems. The members of the change team seek agreement on a strategy for change. Once this is established, the particular intervention techniques that can best be used to carry out the strategy are chosen, then implemented and amended as necessary in the light of experience. Finally, the effects of the interventions are evaluated, using some combination of the data collection procedures employed in the diagnosis. In evaluation, however, the purposes of data collection are to assess whether and why interventions had their intended effects, as well as to serve as a basis for further action planning.

Beckhard (1969) and French and Bell (1973) list the characteristics that describe organization development work as follows:

There is a planned program involving the whole system.

Plans are measured against goals set by organization members at different levels and from different sections. (Beckhard; French and Bell).

The leaders of the organization assume responsibility for management of the project (Beckhard).

Organization development efforts affect the organization's goals in that the change ought to make the goals more easily attainable (Beckhard).

The effort takes a long time. Pressure to show results in the short term should be avoided (Beckhard).

Organization development differs from TRAINING in that changes are directly related to interrelationships at work; training, on the other hand, is often intended to increase individual capabilities that in turn can affect work performance (Beckhard).

Organization development focusses on the feelings, behavior, and attitudes of people. It involves a normative education strategy for change; that is, the VALUES held by organization members are the target of change efforts (Beckhard; French and Bell).

Organization development is an "ongoing interactive process"; interventions and responses occur in a continuous though modifiable series. It is not a "one-shot" activity (French and Bell).

Programs use principles derived from any of the behavioral sciences, including psychology, sociology, anthropology, political science, economics, and psychiatry (French and Bell).

Organizations are viewed as systems, a salient quality of which in the interrelatedness of components. Thus, what happens in one part of the system is expected to have effects on other parts, and these should be examined (French and Bell).

The action research orientation calls for the collection of data about the system. This is an essential aspect of the diagnostic and evaluative phases of organization development. Underlying such projects, then, is a belief in the utility of data-based action planning (French and Bell).

Since changes in values and behavior are to occur, it is necessary for learning to be based in experience. "People learn by doing" is an important aspect of organization development philosophy (Beckhard; French and Bell).

Basic to organization development is the belief that intact work groups or teams should be the focal point for interventions in the system. Individual behavior is deeply affected by group norms; members of intact work groups face each other continuously; and individuals learn most about organizational life from their peers (Beckhard; French and Bell).

Values and assumptions

Those who engage in organization development tend to hold a common set of values and assumptions. About *individuals* in organizations the assumptions are that: (a) people will fulfil themselves if given the proper working conditions to do so; and (b) most people want to contribute to the greater good. About *group* behavior the assumptions are that: (a) people want to be accepted by others; (b) there must be a division of labor for effective functioning; (c) feelings not expressed often give rise to dysfunctional behavior; (d) the typical work group does not work cooperatively enough; and (e) change in groups involves changing relationships, so that all parties should be involved. About *organizations* it is assumed that: (a) the organizational context for groups strongly affects them; and (b) groups are interrelated through people who act in more than one. About the *client organization*, it is assumed that all organization members are to be valued, and that the best solutions are those that include gain for all. Finally, many change agents believe that: (a) feelings are important and must be an acceptable part of organizational reality; (b) participation in decision-making increases feelings of self-worth among organization members, and ought to be fostered where it is appropriate; and (c) as role models change agents must be open about their needs and expectations.

Kinds of organization development interventions

Bennis (1969) describes interventions in terms of their underlying themes, including:

discrepancy: contradictions are pointed out and discussed

theory: behavioral science theory is used to shed light on issues

procedural: critiques of method or operating procedure

relationship: investigations of interpersonal relationships

experimentation: tests are made to determine optimal alternatives for action

dilemma: a point of conflict is highlighted to illustrate some underlying problem in the system

perspective: past and future influences are considered as well as the present

organization structure: groupings of people are rearranged

cultural: values, beliefs, and attitudes of the organization are explored.

French and Bell (1973) present three separate schemes for classifying organization development interventions according to: (a) whether the intervention is process vs. task focussed, and individual vs. group focussed: (b) the people at whom the intervention is aimed, from the individual up to and including the total organization; and (c) the mechanism that is thought to underlie the change process and the techniques associated with it (e.g. increased communication is an underlying mechanism, survey feedback is the associated technique). Further details of activities are included elsewhere in this Dictionary (see GROUP TRAINING, PROCESS CONSULTATION, SOCIO-TECHNICAL SYSTEM, T-GROUPS, TEAM DEVELOPMENT, WORK REDESIGN).

Critique of the organization development field

Despite its clear successes, there is a danger that organization development tends to serve the interests of management rather than those of all organization members. There is a difficult balance for practitioners, who often espouse humanistic values while working primarily in the interests of task effectiveness (Tichy 1974). Second, the conceptual basis of organization development is not well defined, nor is there a theory that is clear and testable. This is due in part to the overemphasis on action as opposed to research. Third, much of the work in organization development focusses on interpersonal processes as the target of change. Kahn (1974) and others argue that long-lasting improvements in organizations are more likely to result from changes in structure. Practitioners must therefore develop (a) a broader knowledge base in areas of management action, including organization design and strategic planning; (b) a closer link with more traditional areas of human resource management (e.g. PERSONNEL SELECTION, appraisals, reward systems, and TRAINING); and (c) greater skill in coping with the political dynamics of organizational life (Tichy 1977) (see also WORK ATTITUDES; EMPLOYEE PARTICIPATION; MORALE; NEEDS; VALUES). SDF/NMT

Bibliography

Beckhard, R. 1969: *Organization development: strategies and models.* Reading, Mass.: Addison-Wesley.

Bennis, W. 1969: *Organization development: its nature, origins, and prospects.* Reading, Mass.: Addison-Wesley.

*French, W.L. and Bell, Jr., C.H. 1973: *Organization development.* Englewood Cliffs, N.J.: Prentice-Hall.

*Friedlander, F. and Brown, L.D. 1974: Organization development. *Annual review of psychology* 75.

Kahn, R.L. 1974: Organization development: some problems and proposals. *Journal of applied behavioral science* 10, 485–502.

Tichy, N.M. 1974: Agents of planned change: congruence of values, cognitions and action. *Administrative science quarterly* pp.164–82.

——— 1977: Demise, absorption, or renewal for the future of organization development. In *The cutting edge: current theory and practice in organization development*, ed. W.W. Burke. La Jolla, Calif.: University Associates.

——— and Beckhard, R. 1978: Managing behavioral factors in human service organizations. In *Management handbook for public administrators*, ed. J.W. Sutherland. New York: Van Nostrand Reinhold.

organizational climate A relatively enduring quality of the internal environment of an organization that (a) is experienced by its members, (b) influences their behavior, and (c) can be described in terms of the values of a particular set of characteristics (or attributes) of the organization (Tagiuri and Litwin 1968, p.27). The basic premise is that organizations have a set of generalizable conditions that affect the experience and behavior of people within those organizations. Organizational conditions often viewed as dimensions of climate include degree of routine, pressure for output, power hierarchy, risk taking, social support for employees under strain, progressiveness, individual autonomy, and reward orientation. SGH/NMT

Bibliography

Tagiuri, R. and Litwin, G.H., eds. 1968: *Organizational climate: explorations of a concept.* Cambridge, Mass.: Harvard University Press.

organizational commitment *See* work attitudes

orgastic potency *See* Reich, Wilhelm

orientation the maintenance of position and posture in relation to the external environment. Two aspects of orientation are usually distinguished: primary or positional orientation and secondary or GOAL orientation. Positional orientations guide the animal to its normal stance and maintain it in physical equilibrium. Included in this category are position with respect to gravity, postures associated with balance, etc. Goal orientations have to do with position and locomotion in relation to external goals, such as a source of food, or a social companion.

Positional orientation is closely tied to the preference positions that are characteristic of each species. Thus schooling fish not only maintain a particular position with respect to gravity, but also with respect to the surface of the water, the substratum, and to each other. Positional orientation is an important aspect of camouflage and the positional preferences of many species are related to their body coloration. Thus the bark-like underwing moth *Catocala* is normally active at night and spends the day resting on tree trunks. Experiments with blue jays (*Cyanocitta cristata*) show that the moths are much less subject to predation when resting in the vertical preferred position compared with other orientations. In the preferred position the moth's bark-like markings most closely conform with the background.

Positional orientation is attained by FEEDBACK from sense organs, usually mechanical or visual. For example the orientation of fish with respect to gravity is attained by feedback from the statocysts, but many fish also show a dorsal light reaction. This involves positioning the body in such a way that light always falls on the dorsal surface. Experiments using a centrifuge combined with controlled light directionality show that the contributions of the various sense organs involved in maintaining a vertical body position are summed algebraically in the central nervous system. However the weighting given to the different components may vary with the state of arousal of the fish. Thus sleeping fish rely entirely upon the statocysts, whereas active fish respond more to visual cues.

Goal orientation involves a spatially distant target or end-point, which may be proximate or distal. Proximate orientation implies direct sensory contact with the goal, whereas distal orientation may include NAVIGATION and MIGRATION, where there is no such contact. Goal orientation may involve a very simple form of response to environmental stimuli, as in kinesis. This is a form of orientation in which the animal's response is proportional to the intensity of the stimulation. Woodlice (*Porcellio scaber*) for instance, are active at low humidity levels and less active at high humidities. Their rapid locomotion in dry places increases the chances of discovering damper conditions. Consequently woodlice tend to aggregate in damp places beneath fallen logs, etc. Taxes involve movement directly toward or away from a source of stimulation. The negative photo-taxis of the maggot larva of the house fly (*Musca domestica*) provides an example. The maggot has a simple eye on its head, capable of registering light intensity but not of forming images. As the maggot crawls along it moves its head from side to side, measuring the light intensity on each side of its body. If a turn results in an increase in perceived brightness it tends not to be repeated and the maggot changes its course and moves away from the light source. Such successive comparison of stimulus intensity, called klino-taxis, is found in a number of species, but simultaneous comparison is more common. This is called tropo-taxis and is characterized by a straight course toward or away from the source of stimulation. To achieve this type of orientation it is necessary to have more than one sense organ. The pill woodlouse (*Armadillidium*), for example, has a pair of compound eyes on its head and can move directly toward a light source. When one eye is blacked out the animal describes a circle, showing that simultaneous comparison is a necessary component of the orientation. Those animals which have eyes which can provide information about the direction of light by virtue of their structure are capable of telo-taxis, which does not require simultaneous comparison from two sense organs. The image-forming eye, for example, provides the necessary directional information.

Distal orientation generally involves navigation, for which it is necessary to have some form of compass. Ants and bees use the sun as a compass and are able to compensate for the movement of the sun throughout the day. Compass orientation is essentially a form of telo-taxis in which the animal maintains a particular angle between its body axis and the direction of the sun. By means of an internal clock ants and bees can progressively alter this angle to match the changing direction of the sun. Clock-compensation is also found in bird navigation and in various species of fishes.

Flying animals face additional problems of orientation and navigation, because of the influence of the wind. The course of a flying animal is its locomotory direction with respect to the surrounding air, and its track is its path with respect to the ground. An animal heading in a particular compass direction may have to compensate for differences between its intended course and its actual track over the ground. The angle between the track and the animal's course direction, called the drift angle, depends upon the strength and direction of the wind. The navigating animal has to compensate for changes in wind speed and direction by changing its flight speed and drift angle. This is done with respect to visual landmarks or with reference to a compass. The compensation thus involves a comparison between the intended track and the feedback that the animal obtains about the consequences of its locomotory behavior.

The sun compass is not the only form of compass used in distal orientation. Bees and pigeons can detect the plane of polarization of sunlight and thus obtain compass bearings in overcast conditions. A number of species, including bacteria, bees, snails, and birds are sensitive to the earth's magnetic field and can use this information for orientation purposes. The electromagnetic sense is not completely understood but seems to be based upon the presence of iron-rich molecules within certain cells. The direction of migration of European robins (*Erittacus rubecula*) can be experimentally altered by superimposing an artificial magnetic field. Homing pigeons fitted with magnets become disoriented when the sky is overcast and they are not able to use the sun as a compass.

Orientation reactions are not entirely REFLEX responses, but may also involve changes in the goal of the orientation. Although an animal may normally respond to movement in its visual field, this may not occur when the movement is a consequence of the animal's own behavior. The most widely accepted explanation of this phenomenon is the REAFFERENCE theory of von Holst and Mittelstaedt. In essence the reafference principle suggests that when an animal intends to change direction the brain produces a representation of the expected consequences of the change. If the actual consequences match the expected consequences the two cancel and no movement is perceived. So if an animal moved its direction of vision 10° to the right, the visual field as first registered by the brain would move 10° to the left. This, however, would be cancelled by the representation of the intended movement (10° to the right) and no movement would actually be perceived.

Reafference theory applies not only to vision but to many aspects of orientation and locomotion. Any movement made by an animal produces consequences which must be distinguished from independent changes in the external environment, whether perceived visually, proprioceptively, or electrically. Reafference is thus an integral aspect of perception. DJM

Bibliography

Fraenkel, G. S. and Gunn, D. L. 1961: *The orientation of animals*. New York: Dover Publications.

Howard, I. P. and Templeton, W. B. 1966: *Human spatial orientation*. London and New York: John Wiley and Sons.

Schmidt-Koenig, K. 1979: *Avian orientation and navigation*. London and New York: Academic Press.

von Holst, E. 1954: Relations between the CNS and the peripheral organs. *British journal of animal behaviour* 2, 89–94.

orienting response A reflex response in which the animal focusses attention upon a suddenly presented stimulus. For example, a strange noise may cause a cat to turn its head, prick its ears and look towards the source of the sound.

When the disturbance is very marked the orienting response is usually preceded by a startle response in which the animal jumps and experiences a marked increase in heart beat rate. Repeated presentation of a stimulus leads to HABITUATION of the orienting response, but there is usually very little GENERALIZATION of the habituation. When repeated presentation of a particular stimulus leads to a decline in the orienting response, presentation of a slightly different stimulus will cause the orienting response to reappear. DJM

other minds How can I know there are any? "Man, though he have great variety of thoughts, and such from which others as well as himself might receive profit and delight, yet they are all within his own breast, invisible and hidden from others, nor can of themselves be made to appear" (Locke, *Essay concerning human understanding*, 1961, II, II). The problem has traditionally been viewed as an epistemological one, to be solved by an argument from analogy (Mill 1889, pp. 243–4; Russell 1948, pp. 501–5; Ayer 1954, pp. 191–214). The classic formulation of this solution is that by Mill: "I conclude that other human beings have feelings like me, because, first, they have bodies like me, which I know, in my own case, to be the antecedent condition of feelings; and because, secondly they exhibit the acts, and other outward signs, which in my own case, I know by experience to be caused by feelings."

The standard objection to this solution is that the reasoning is based on the observation of a single instance ("my own case"). Malcolm propounds what he regards as a more interesting objection: "Suppose this reasoning could yield a conclusion of the sort 'It is probable that that human figure' (pointing at some person other than oneself) 'has thoughts and feelings.' Then there is a question as to whether this conclusion can *mean* anything to the philosopher who draws it, because there is a question as to whether the sentence 'That human figure has thoughts and feelings' can mean anything to him" (1958, pp. 969).

How Malcolm's question arises can be explained as follows. (a) If someone asks me whether *someone else*, Jones, has thoughts and feelings, such as a feeling of pain or sadness, then I observe Jones's behavior, ask him how he feels, and so on, and answer accordingly. If someone asks me whether *I* am in pain I do not have to observe my behavior, etc. I can say straight away whether or not I am in pain. This could be expressed by saying that there are first-person and other-person uses of words such as "pain" and "sad", and that whereas other-person uses are based on observation of behavior, first-person uses are not. (b) first-person uses of words like "pain" and "sad" are based on awareness of the feelings in question. In this they are unlike other person uses. I *infer* the existence of feelings in others, on the basis of my observation of their behavior. My knowledge of the feelings of others may thus be said to be "indirect". My awareness of my own feelings, on the other hand, is direct. Nobody else can be directly aware of my feelings. They are "private". (c) Words have meaning by being names of things (physical objects, qualities, feelings, etc.) to which they refer. Learning the meaning of a word is a matter of being aware of the thing for which the word stands, and realizing that the word stands for it. (d) Since such words as "pain" and "sadness" are names of feelings, and the only feelings I can be aware of are my own, the only meaning they can have for me is as names of my own feelings. But with this meaning, if I am not in pain then there is no pain. In other words, learning the meaning of "pain" and "sadness" in this way does not equip me to understand talk of there being pain which I do not feel. Hence it does not equip me to understand talk of pain in other people. In general it leaves me with the question how "That human figure has thoughts and feelings" can have any meaning for me.

Wittgenstein (1953, I, §350) imagines someone responding

> "But if I suppose that someone has a pain, then I am simply supposing that he has just the same as I have so often had." To this response he objects as follows. "That gets us no further. It is as if I were to say: 'You surely know what "It is 5 o'clock here" means'; so you also know what 'It's 5 o'clock on the sun' means. It means simply that it is just the same time there as it is here when it is 5 o'clock." . . . In exactly the same way it is no explanation to say: the supposition that he has a pain is simply the supposition that he has the same as I. For *that* part of the grammar is quite clear to me: that is, that one will say that the stove has the same experience as I, *if* one says: it is in pain and I am in pain.

A slightly more perspicuous example would be "it is afternoon here" (said, for instance, by someone on the telephone in England to someone in New York), for our use of this expression is such that it is true if it is used at a time and place such that the sun is past the zenith but not yet over the horizon, and it is patently obvious that there cannot, at any time, be a place on the sun where the sun is past the zenith. There is no passage from the meaningfulness of "it is afternoon here" to earth-dwellers to the meaningfulness of "it is afternoon here" to sun-dwellers. Similarly, *if* learning the meaning of "pain" is a matter of being aware of pain, and realizing that the word stands for it, then there is no passage from the meaningfulness of "I am in pain" to the meaningfulness of "someone else is in pain".

The "it is afternoon here" example is instructive. There is little temptation to explain the meaning of "afternoon" in terms of a thing for which the word stands. Instead one thinks of the meaningfulness being dependent on facts of nature such as that the earth revolves on its axis relative to the sun. The spell of the name–object model for meaningfulness is broken. Once the spell is broken we are freed to consider the possibility that the public meaningfulness of "pain", also, is dependent on facts of nature, facts such as that there is a natural expression of pain, and a natural response to this expression in others. "Here is one possibility: words are connected with the primitive, the natural, expressions of the sensation and used in their place. A child has hurt himself and he cries; and then adults talk to him and teach him exclamations and, later, sentences. They teach the child new pain-behaviour" (Wittgenstein 1953, I, §244).

Wittgenstein's dissolution of the other minds problem, as a problem of meaning, has not won general approval. Strawson, for example, rejects it in favor of saying that what a person feels when he is in pain is, in some sense, *the same thing* as what others can observe about him (1964, 109).

See also PRIVACY. GNAV

Bibliography

Ayer, A.J. 1954: *Philosophical essays*. London: Macmillan; New York: St Martin's Press.

Locke, J. 1690 (*1961*): *An essay concerning human understanding*. Ed. John W. Yolton, London: Dent; New York: Dutton.

Malcolm, N. 1958: Knowledge of other minds. *Journal of philosophy* 55, 969–78.

Mill, J.S. 1889: *Examination of Sir William Hamilton's Philosophy*. 6th ed. London and New York: Longmans Green & Co.

Russell, B. 1948: *Human knowledge: its scope and limits*. London: Allen & Unwin; New York: Humanities Press.

Strawson, P.F. 1964: *Individuals*. London: Methuen.

*Vesey, G. 1974: Other Minds. In *Understanding Wittgenstein*, ed. G. Vesey, London: Macmillan; New York: Cornell University Press (1976).

*Wisdom, J. 1952: *Other minds*. Oxford: Basil Blackwell; New York: Philosophical Library.

Wittgenstein, L. 1953: *Philosophical investigations*. Trans G.E.M. Anscombe. Oxford: Basil Blackwell; New York; Macmillan.

outgroup and ingroup *See* ingroup and outgroup

out-of-the-body experiences When a person experiences his consciousness as functioning in a pattern very much like his ordinary state of consciousness (see ALTERED STATES), with his experiences of the world around him seeming quite real, but knowing at the time that his consciousness is not located where his physical body is located, he is having an out-of-the-body experience. These can arise from ordinary dreaming, but also frequently occur when a person nearly dies. Experients often see their physical body from an outside perspective. Experimentally out-of-the-body experiences are similar to LUCID DREAMING, and may sometimes be the same phenomena, except that on occasion the person having the out-of-the-body experience experiences travelling to some distant place, perceives events about which he could not have normally known, and later, after waking, verifies what he perceived, thus convincing himself that in some sense he really was at the distant place. The handful of laboratory studies that have been done on out-of-the-body experiences suggest that out-of-the-body experiences sometimes have this kind of parapsychological element (see PARAPSYCHOLOGY), and deserve further study. The out-of-the-body experience is probably the experiential basis of the concept of soul. See Green (1968), Monroe (1971), and Tart (1977) for scientific and experiential data. CTT

Bibliography

Green, C. 1968. *Out-of-the-body experiences*. Oxford: Institute for Psychophysical Research.

Monroe, R. 1971. *Journeys out of the body*. New York: Doubleday.

Tart, C. 1977. *Psi: scientific studies of the psychic realm*. New York: Dutton.

overlearning Results from OVERTRAINING in a learning task. The basis of performance often changes with extensive practice. For example, skilled motor performance may initially be organized in small units of movement with constant feedback monitoring, but with practice "open-loop" motor programs take over which coordinate longer sequences of movements without the need for high-level monitoring. This is an example of the transition from "controlled" to "automatic" processing which occurs in highly predictable environments. Other changes resulting from overlearning of simple tasks may be attributable to reduced frequency of errors, increased susceptibility to frustration after nonreinforcement, and changes in ATTENTION or orienting to cues controlling discrimination; these may affect ease of extinction or reversal. EAG

Bibliography

Holding, D.H., Ed., 1981: *Human skills*. Chichester: John Wiley

overload. *See* role ambiguity, conflict and overload

overtraining Means training or practice on some task over and above what is required initially to learn it to some criterion. Most skills receive extensive overtraining during an individual's life. Overtraining usually results in gradual improvements in efficiency and may also lead to changes in the way in which performance is controlled. See OVERLEARNING. EAG

P

pain: gate control system Pain is a sensory experience associated with injury or spoken of in terms of injury. To separate physiological mechanisms from a sensory experience smacks of dualism (Melzack and Wall 1982). Nociceptive nerve fibers in peripheral nerves detect injury. Impulses in these fibers enter the spinal cord from the body. At the first central synapses these impulses enter a gate control system (Melzack and Wall 1965). Their further progress to trigger pain reactions depends on the convergence of other impulses from the periphery which may be of innocuous origin. This convergence can inhibit or exaggerate the transmitted message and forms the basis of many folk and modern therapies. The gate control is also strongly affected by control systems descending from the brain and this may form the basis for the marked effect of attitude, experience etc. on pain. The entry control region includes the substantia gelatinosa which is the site of action of opiates as analgesics and contains an elaborate selection mechanism which is rapidly controlled by the gate control and slowly by connectivity control mechanisms. In their further course, impulses signaling the presence of injury are subject to detailed control at each stage. The relationship of injury to pain is contingent and variable. (Wall 1979). PDW

Bibliography

Melzack, R. and Wall, P.D. 1965: Pain mechanisms: a new theory. *Science* 150, 971–9.

——— 1982: *The challenge of pain*. Harmondsworth: Penguin.

Wall, P.D. 1979: *Pain* 6, 253–4.

pain: philosophical concern with Through Ludwig Wittgenstein's *Philosophical investigations* the concept of pain became a focal point for philosophical reflections in theories of language, mind and knowledge. A natural inclination and a long philosophical tradition alike suggest that psychological predicates such as "pain" ("looks red", "want") have a meaning in virtue of correlation with a subjective experience. Hence understanding such a predicate must consist in correlating it with an item in one's experience. Moreover, each of us knows with certainty whether we are in pain. Self-knowledge, on this venerable picture, consists in introspecting what goes on in the self. Knowledge of the pains of others is conceived to be inferential and hence less certain. A common corollary of this conception is that language has foundations in an array of simple unanalysable predicates in terms of which all complex concepts are defined. This array consists of items given in subjective experience to which a speaker attaches a name by private ostensive definition.

Wittgenstein argued that this picture is incoherent. It misconceives the notions of the meaning of words, self-consciousness, knowledge of others' states of mind. It results from misunderstanding the relations of language to behavior and to experience. There can be no such thing as a private ostensive definition, since a private mental sample can provide no criterion of correctness for the use of an expression. One no more acquires the *concept* of pain by hurting oneself than one acquires the concept of a negative number by running up debts. Psychological predicates are explained by specifying the *criteria* for their application, i.e. the circumstances in which certain behavior justifies their ascription to others. "Pain" does not mean pain-behavior, but pain-behavior in painful circumstances justifies asserting "he is in pain". What of self-knowledge? It is true that "I doubt (am not sure) whether I am in pain" is nonsense, but it does not follow that I am certain that I am in pain. Knowledge and certainty are possible only if doubt and ignorance make sense. In the case of pain they do not. Hence "I know I am in pain" means no more than "I (really) am in pain". Pain avowals are a learnt extension of natural pain-behavior (crying), not a form of indubitable knowledge. I do not avow my pain on the ground of inner observation any more than a baby cries on the grounds of introspection. Knowledge of others' pain rests on observed behavior which, though it is defeasible, suffices to confer certainty if it is not defeated.

Wittgenstein used the example of the concept of pain to find a *via media* between behaviorism and mentalism. He used it to try to demonstrate the logical priority of the public over the private, the physical over the mental. The framework for his reflections was exactly his attempt to repudiate the conception of language as a vehicle for the expression of language-independent thoughts. In its place he put his picture of language as a form of activity. PH

pain: psychiatric and psychological aspects Pain is probably the least understood and most ineptly treated subject in medicine today. Perhaps for these reasons alone it has little difficulty in retaining its position as the most complex and certainly the most fascinating of medical problems.

It must be significant that opium, first used in the third century BC, is still the most commonly used systemic analgesic.

The existence of an adequate theory of the mechanism of pain would do much to reduce our ignorance and an attempt to achieve this end was made by Melzack and Wall (1965) who introduced the gate theory. This postulated the existence of a filter or gate in the substantia gelatinosa of the spinal cord where susceptive stimuli were modified in the light of previous experience and emotional state at the time. If, as a result of these modifying factors, the critical threshold for firing-off was not reached, then pain would not be felt. This fact has been used to explain the fact that soldiers who were shot in battle felt no pain at all. As with other theories the gate theory is no longer acceptable in its present form and has been extensively modified to provide a role for the endogenous opioid peptides and enkephalins which have been recently isolated and provide an exciting prospect for the future.

There are many gaps in our knowledge regarding mechanism but some of these have been filled in by experience gained largely from pain clinics. These are excellent but have limited scope as they have no beds and many workers believe that it is not possible even to skim the surface of the problem in a twenty-minute out-patient interview. It should be remembered that these patients have all been treated before, unsuccessfully, and look upon the pain clinic as their last hope. It is small wonder that success in this field, if achieved, is always hard earned.

The patients have intractable pain i.e. pain that has been present for over a month and is unremitting, despite treatment. It is usually associated with malignancy, but that need not be the cause. Despite the undeniable fact that cancer pain can be intractable, it is surely no more so than the pain in a patient who has had three laminectomies, two spinal fusions and is still in pain.

Hospices have made an immense contribution to the management of the terminally ill cancer patient (see Saunders 1967). The very word "cancer" tends to be emotive but this should not be allowed to obscure the abject misery to which many patients with non-malignant pain are condemned for many years. It can be extremely damaging both physically and mentally, not only to the patient, but also to his family.

Today the existence of pain centers, or units, which are virtually autonomous, having their own beds, nursing staff and treatment rooms, has allowed the practice of a multi-disciplinary approach to the problem (Bonica 1974). Patients can be admitted directly from general practitioners or from other hospitals and a thorough assessment can be made at leisure. Problem cases can be seen by attending consultants from other specialities if necessary.

Many patients will take two or three days to relax and appreciate the aims of the unit, which is to understand their problem and help their pain. Because of their previous shuttling from doctor to doctor with no improvement there are some who think nobody believes that they are in pain. This leads to an inevitable depression and lack of confidence in themselves and their medical attendants. Management of these patients is time-consuming and often unrewarding. The placebo effect is very much in evidence in pain centres but the "negative placebo" effect also lurks just beneath the surface if a patient's equilibrium is upset.

The standard methods of treatment available are interruption of pain transmission by nerve blocks or by drug therapy. Both of these need to be bolstered by supportive counseling.

All patients attending pain clinics will have been on drugs at some stage, but their use tends to be disappointing in chronic pain. Perhaps their most effective role is in the management of terminal cancer. The final breakthrough will almost certainly be achieved in the pharmacological field, but until that time nerve blocks, by various means, serve a very important function. JWL

Bibliography

Bonica, J.J. 1974: Organisation and function of a pain clinic. In *Advances in neurology*, ed. J.J. Bonica vol. 4, 433–43.

Melzack, R. and Wall, P.D. 1965: Pain mechanisms: a new theory. *Science* 150, 971.

Saunders, C.M. 1967: *The management of terminal illness*. London Hospital Medicine Publications.

pain and the nervous system (see BRAIN AND CENTRAL NERVOUS SYSTEM, fig. 29) Sensation of pain is a submodality of the SOMATOSENSORY system and usually results from noxious stimuli. Pain is mediated by nociceptors (receptors responding to noxious stimuli). Mechanical nociceptors are activated by strong mechanical stimulation such as that inflicted by sharp objects. Heat nociceptors respond to temperatures above about 45°C. Mixed nociceptors respond to a variety of noxious stimuli. Nociceptive axons form two groups: small, myelinated Aδ fibers which mediate fast pain, a sudden, sharp sensation; and small, unmyelinated C fibers which mediate slow pain, a sickening, burning sensation. Pain afferents from the body have synapses in the dorsal horn of the spinal cord. Second-order NEURONS send fibers carrying information about painful stimuli in the anterolateral tracts (spinoreticular and spinothalamic fibers) to large regions of the BRAINSTREAM and to the THALAMUS (see BRAIN AND CENTRAL NERVOUS SYSTEM: ILLUSTRATIONS, figs. 6, 7 and 19). Fibers from the head and neck innervate these regions via the trigeminal system. In the thalamus two different regions receive pain fibers from the anterolateral tracts and project to CEREBRAL CORTEX. Blunt stimulation of neurons in the thalamus, however, does not mimic the sensory quality of pain, suggesting that spatio-temporal patterning of pain and touch inputs may be as important a determinant of pain sensation at this level as the specific pathway over which excitation arrives. Thalamic-cortical connections may be more useful for localizing painful stimuli to body sites than in the perception of pain itself. Cortical ablation rarely relieves the sensation of pain but commonly increases tolerance of the sensation.

Neural connections exist which modify the information in ascending pain pathways and reduce the sensation of pain (analgesia). Electrical stimulation of portions of the brainstem (e.g. region of the dorsal raphe nucleus) produces analgesia. A lessening of pain can also be produced by opiates (ENKEPHALINS/ENDORPHINS) and neural opiate receptors have been identified in the brain. Converging lines of evidence suggest that enkephalin/endorphin-containing interneurons may serve to inhibit the transmission of pain information in the dorsal horn of the spinal cord itself. These interneurons may be driven by descending fibers from those very regions of the brainstem where electrical stimulation produces analgesia. Other kinds of analgesia, such as that introduced by novel STRESS, do not appear to involve opiates in their mode of action, suggesting multiple mechanisms for modifying incoming sensory information about pain-producing stimuli. SCC

Bibliography

Bonica, J.J., ed 1980: *Pain. Research publications: association for research in nervous and mental disease*. New York: Raven Press.

Burgess, P.R. and Perl, E.R. 1973: Cutaneous mechanoreceptors and nocioceptors. In *Handbook of sensory physiology*, vol. II, *Somatosensory system*, ed. A. Iggo. Berlin and New York: Springer-Verlag.

Kandel, E.R. and Schwartz, J.H. 1981: *Principles of neural science*. Oxford and New York: Elsevier/North-Holland.

pain in animals An aspect of emotion which is entirely subjective. Although human pain is often associated with cries for help, this is not always the case with other animals. It is impossible to know to what extent animals feel pain, but in the interests of animal welfare it is usually considered right to assume that, during stress, they suffer in the same way as we do. (Dawkins 1980).

Pain gives warning of tissue damage, both internal and external to the body. Pain due to noxious stimuli on the body surface is usually easy to locate compared with internal pain. Internal disorders sometimes induce peripheral pain, known as *referred* pain. For example the heart disorder called angina causes a burning pain on the underside of the upper arm. Pain may also be *projected* to another part of the body: it is common for people who have lost part of a limb to experience pain that seems to come from the missing part.

Pain receptors exist in all tissues except the brain and the non-living parts of bone, nail, teeth and hair. The receptors cannot be identified anatomically and may simply be undifferentiated nerve endings. All pain nerves enter the spinal cord and their messages are thence relayed to the brain. DJM

Bibliography

Dawkins, Marion 1980: *Animal suffering: the science of animal welfare*. London: Chapman and Hall.

pain *See above, and also* mind–body problem

paired-associate learning In paired-associate learning the subject learns a list of stimulus response pairs, a process similar to learning the vocabulary of a foreign language. This procedure dominated verbal learning research until the 1960s, in part because of its close similarity to the conditioning paradigm of behavioristic psychology. Two procedural versions are used: in anticipation learning each stimulus is presented, the subject makes a response, and then the correct response is shown, until the whole list is cycled through; in the study-test method all stimulus response pairs are shown first, followed by a test of all stimulus pairs. In both cases repeated trials are usually given. Lists usually contain about 10 to 15 pairs, depending on such factors as the meaningfulness, frequency and imagery value similarity of the learning material, which influence the difficulty of the learning task. The phenomenon most extensively investigated with this procedure is forgetting caused by INTERFERENCE among the items to be learned. WKi

Papez's circuit A neural circuit identified in 1937 by the neuroanatomist J.W. Papez. It consists of the mammillary bodies in the HYPOTHALAMUS, anterior THALAMUS, cingulate gyrus, entorhinal cortex, HIPPOCAMPUS, and their interconnecting fibers (see BRAIN AND CENTRAL NERVOUS SYSTEM: ILLUSTRATIONS). Papez suggested that these structures comprise a closed reverberatory system mediating emotional experience and behavior. Emotional reactions are seen as developing on the basis of central and peripheral input. The central signals originate in the cerebral cortex and are conveyed to the hippocampus. From the hippocampus, they are transmitted to the mammillary bodies where they combine with visceral and sensory impressions from the hypothalamus. The information is then projected to the anterior thalamus, up to the cingulate gyrus where emotions are experienced, and finally, via the entorhinal cortex and hippocampus, back to the hypothalamus where expression is regulated. Although influential for some time, it is now apparent that Papez's formulations were based on questionable anatomical and clinical data. While parts of the circuit (e.g. the hypothalamus), can be linked to emotion, in recent years various structures have also become associated with other functions, particularly those related to learning and memory processes. GWi

paradigmatic and syntagmatic relations in grammar According to SAUSSURE the linguistic sign has two principal characteristics: it is arbitrary and linear. It is the latter property which calls for a distinction between paradigmatic (originally called "associative") and syntagmatic relations.

Paradigmatic relations are those holding between comparable elements in particular positions within linguistic structures, e.g. the relationship between the initial consonants of "take", "make" and "bake". Paradigmatic relations are relations in absentia, since the terms consist of an item present and others not actually present in an utterance.

Syntagmatic relations hold between successive members of a given utterance and are therefore relations in praesentia. Thus, in the word "take" [teik], the segments [t] [ei] and [k] or, at a more abstract level, Consonant Diphthong Consonant, appear in a certain grammatical arrangement.

Many word-association tests are based on the distinction between paradigmatic and syntagmatic responses (see Herriot 1970, pp.34–66). PM

Bibliography

Herriot, P. 1970: *An introduction to the psychology of language*. London: Methuen.

paralinguistic features A term used in suprasegmental phonology for characterizing certain features of utterance which are the direct result of *physiological* mechanisms such as pharyngeal, oral, and nasal cavities. Different authors give differing lists of features (e.g. nasal friction, tension of muscles, vocal cord amplitude) and arrive at different types of paralinguistic features (e.g. voice qualifiers such as whisper, husky, breathy and voice qualifications such as laugh, giggle, sob; see, *inter alia*, Crystal 1969). However, most scholars differentiate between linguistic features of tone and voice (e.g. stress, intonation), extralinguistic features (permanent vocal effects such as voice quality) and paralinguistic features (short or medium term changes in the tone of voice such as a harsh phonatory setting to express anger). Thus paralinguistic vocal effects contribute to the quality of the speaker's voice when transmitting specific emotions. Since they are phonetically discontinuous, paralinguistic "additions" to the normal flow of speech are usually easy to detect. MK

Bibliography

Crystal, D. 1969: Prosodic systems and intonation in English. Cambridge and New York: Cambridge University Press.

parallel processing *See* serial vs parallel processing

paranoid states A group of psychotic disorders in which paranoid DELUSIONS are prominent but HALLUCINATIONS and deterioration of personality are uncommon. They are distinguished from paranoid syndromes secondary to other psychiatric disorders such as ORGANIC STATES, AFFECTIVE DISORDERS and paranoid SCHIZOPHRENIA. The category of paranoid states is to some extent a temporary diagnostic grouping for cases whose classification in relation to other psychiatric disorders is uncertain. The diagnosis of a paranoid state is therefore used for acute and chronic paranoid states which are closely similar to schizophrenia but lack the generally accepted diagnostic features. Kraepelin distinguished two principal forms, paraphrenia and paranoia. The former was a paranoid psychosis with conspicuous hallucinations in middle life, which is now normally regarded as being indistinguishable from paranoid schizophrenia. Paranoia was described as a chronic psychosis with systematized delusions but without developed evidence of hallucination or thought disorder. This syndrome is extremely rare and it is doubtful whether it can be distinguished as a separate category. In current psychiatric practice the terms paraphrenia and paranoia are probably best avoided, although the diagnosis "late paraphrenia" is widely used for the schizophrenia-like paranoid illnesses of old age. Paranoid states are among the causes of a number of uncommon paranoid psychiatric syndromes, such as MORBID JEALOUSY. RAM

Bibliography

Kendler, K.S. and Tsuang, H.T. 1981: Nosology of paranoid schizophrenia and other paranoid psychoses. *Schizophrenia bulletin* 7, 594–610.

Lewis, A. 1970: Paranoia and paranoid: a historical perspective. *Psychological medicine* 1, 2–12.

parapraxis In psychoanalytic theory, the disruption of a specific action or mental process by a determinant, such as a wish of anxiety, which has become unconscious as the result of REPRESSION. Disruption takes the form of omission, as in forgetting, or substitution, as in speech-error (known popularly as the "Freudian slip"). Freud discussed such errors extensively in *Psychopathology of everyday life* (Freud 1901) in order to demonstrate that healthy people also have the unconscious processes which produce neurotic symptoms. The particular action which is disrupted may be only rather indirectly or symbolically associated with the repressed material, but Freud distinguishes degrees of awareness of the source of the error. One may be aware of the "disturbing intention" but not have seen its connection with the "disturbed intention", or one may be quite unaware of the former intentions and vigorously resist acknowledging it (Freud 1916, ch.4). Various attempts have been made to explain away Freud's and others' examples by means of "simpler" hypotheses (e.g. Timpanaro 1976). NMC

Bibliography

Freud, Sigmund 1901; 1916: *Psychopathology of everyday life* (vol.16); *Introductory lectures* (vol.15), *Standard edition of the complete psychological works of Sigmund Freud*. London: Hogarth Press; New York: Norton.

Timpanaro, Sebastiano 1976: *The Freudian slip*, trans. Kate Soper, London: New Left

parapsychology Literally the study of that which is beyond (para) ordinary psychology, refers to the study of psi phenomena, various forms of experience and behavior which imply that human beings can gather veridical information about the world or each other (various kinds of extrasensory perception, ESP) and/or alter physical events (psychokinesis, PK) in the absence of known physical mechanisms for these phenomena. The basic kind of real-life observation leading to the idea of psi is an experience (like a dream or a hunch) that provides veridical information about distant events (a typical example would be peril or injury of a loved one) when known physical energies could not convey the information, and when the event was not predictable from information already known to the percipient. Thousands of well-documented cases of this sort exist, and a majority of the American population believe that they have personally experienced such events. It is difficult absolutely to rule out ordinary explanations of such apparent psi events, such as distortions of memory, poor observation, fraud etc., as well as difficult to assess just what "coincidence" is in such cases. Laboratory research where all relevant conditions could be reliably assessed, was begun around the turn of the century. It reached sophisticated form in the work of J. B. Rhine (1895–1980) and his colleagues at Duke University, which started in the 1930s.

The basic Duke procedure for testing various kinds of postulated ESP consisted of thorough shuffling of a deck of special target cards, the Zener cards, to ensure randomization of order. The deck consisted of five cards each of five different geometric symbols. In comparing a subject's calls of the shielded cards, basic statistical analysis showed that an average of five hits per deck were expected by chance, and various deviations above or below mean chance expectation could be straightforwardly evaluated for statistical significance. If an agent or sender, usually in a distant room, looked at the target cards while the subject tried to call them, the procedure was ostensibly a telepathic one. If no one looked at the target cards while they were called, it was a clairvoyant procedure, as results would imply a direct perception of the state of material affairs. When the cards were not to be shuffled until some time *after* the subject's calls had been recorded, the procedure was precognitive.

The publication of Rhine's very successful results (Rhine and others 1934) created a sensation in the scientific and psychological community, as the existence of ESP implied a quality of the mind that was unexplainable by contemporary physical understanding of the world, or any reasonable extrapolation of that understanding. Some sixty critical articles by forty different authors were published in response, clearly establishing what a satisfactory experiment in ESP would require. From 1934 to 1939, the Duke group published seventeen satisfactory studies, of which eighty-eight per cent showed statistically significant evidence for ESP at the .01 or better level of significance. Thirty-three studies by scientists not connected with the Duke group were published, sixty-one per cent of which were significant, giving an overall seventy per cent success rate of some fifty experiments. A number of other successful replications were *not* published by their authors, who feared ridicule from sceptical colleagues! Rhine and his colleagues also began publishing significant experiments on PK at this time, in which subjects were asked to influence, by wishing alone, the machine throw of dice.

In the ordinary course of science, a period of intensive research by many investigators should have resulted eventually in discovering what the nature of psi phenomena was and integrating them into the growing body of psychological knowledge. For a variety of non-scientific reasons, such as some investigators' fears that psi phenomena somehow brought religion back as a real belief instead of simply superstition, this did not happen. It has been suggested that historical events constituted a kind of repression after the 1930s' debates: while there was no good evidence of widespread flaws which would invalidate the successful psi experiments, most scientists apparently felt that there had to be something wrong somewhere because psi was *a priori* impossible. Funding was not forthcoming, publication in mainstream journals was suppressed and parapsychology largely disappeared from the view of mainstream science. The few scientists working in the area established their own journals (*Journal of Parapsychology, Journal of the American Society for Psychical Research, Journal of the Society for Psychical Research* and *European Journal of Parapsychology*) and continued small-scale research. A 1978 survey (see Tart 1979) indicated that fewer than two dozen full time scientists were working in parapsychology, with all the major American laboratories having a miniscule combined yearly budget of about half a million dollars.

Over the years more than 700 published experiments on the four major methods of testing for psi (telepathy, clairvoyance, precognition and PK), constituting an enormous amount of evidence for the existence of the phenomena, has accumulated. Starting in the 1950s, most scientists working in the area were convinced of psi's existence, and of the fact that convincing the general scientific community of this was no longer a rational enterprise, so they began to shift research emphasis to questions about the nature of psi. Research was conducted on personality correlates of degrees of success in psi tests; the main finding was that disbelievers in ESP, who were statistically naïve, frequently scored *below* chance expectation, suggesting that they unconsciously used ESP to get 'poor' test scores which appeared to support their belief that there was no ESP. Mechanically shuffled decks of cards are now being replaced with electronic random number generators. Dice in PK tests have also been replaced by electronic generators: of fifty-four experiments published as of 1978, thirty-five showed statistically signifi cant shifts in output when subjects "willed" them to shift.

ESP tests are no longer limited to multiple choice such as card guessing, as objective methods of evaluating "free response tests" where the target may be anything, have been developed. "Remote viewing" experiments were initiated at the Stanford Research Institute. For example, an outbound experimenter hides at a randomly selected one of dozens of possible sites within a twenty-minute drive of the laboratory, while a subject tries to describe what the site looks like through words and drawings. A series of such trials at different sites are collected. Randomized sets of descriptions and site lists are given to an outside judge who is asked to rank the degree of similarity of each description to each site. Statistical analysis shows that subjects frequently give much better descriptions of unknown target sites than would be expected if they produced only generalities and chance matches. Similar significant results have been obtained from a number of ganzfeld studies, in which a subject isolated in a ganzfeld (white noise – noise consisting of a multitude of frequencies sounding together – and uniform visual field) describes his imagery while a distant sender tries to influence it to match target pictures.

Some other contemporary lines of research, sampled from the 1980 meeting program of the Parapsychological Association, the international professional association of researchers, include effects of formal education on psi ability, use of biological systems as targets in PK experiments, effects of psychological response habits and biases on psi performance, comparisons of subliminal perception and ESP, refinement of statistical analysis techniques, time-displaced PK, effects of MEDITATION and other procedures for inducing ALTERED STATES on psi performance, whether feedback on performance alters ESP performance, tests of possible causal theories derived from quantum physics considerations, physiological correlates of psi cognition, and qualities of experiments that affect psi elicitation in subjects.

Contemporary parapsychological research is becoming of interest to some physicists, who feel that some puzzling features of mind must be integrated into our physical view of the world. Parapsychologists are concerned with the lack of discrimination in the scientific community between their well-controlled research and popular fads and superstitions, a confusion that is increased by pseudo-critics who deliberately lump these things together as part of an effort to discredit the little research activity that does go on. Parapsychologists see their primary problems as gaining mainstream acceptance so that adequate research effort will be expended to clarify the field; discovering how to make psi work more reliably so that it can be demonstrated (and, more importantly, studied) on demand, and finding a theoretical structure to make sense of psi phenomena. CTT

Bibliography

*Bowles, N. and Hynds, F. 1978: *Psi search*. New York: Harper and Row.

Rhine, J., McDougall, W. and Prince, W. 1934 (1964): *Extrasensory perception*. Boston Society for Psychic Research. Boston, Mass.: Bruce Humphries.

*Tart, C. 1977: *Psi: scientific studies of the psychic realm*. New York: Dutton.

Tart, C. 1979: A survey of expert opinion on potentially negative uses of psi, United States government interest in psi, and the level of research funding of the field. In *Research in parapsychology 1978*, ed. W. Roll Metuchen, N.J.: Scarecrow Press.

*White, R. (ed.) 1976: *Surveys in parapsychology*. Metuchen, N.J.: Scarecrow Press.

*Wolman, B., et al. 1977: *Handbook of parapsychology*. New York: Van Nostrand Reinhold.

parasitism In its normal meaning parasitism is a way of making a living by feeding on the tissues of another organism without first killing it. A mosquito sucks blood from a living human. An aphid sucks sap from a living oak tree. Parasites are distinguished from predators who first kill their prey then eat it, but the distinction is not always clear cut: parasites often eventually kill their hosts; predators such as hyenas start eating their prey before it is dead; digger wasps paralyse prey by stinging them, so that their larvae can eat them alive; grazing animals take leaves and stems from grass plants without necessarily killing the plants themselves.

The concept of parasitism is often generalized to include cases other than direct feeding on the living tissues of the host. A tapeworm resides in the gut of a pig and diverts to its own use food that the pig has worked to procure and digest. In the domain of overt behavior, the name "kleptoparasitism" is sometimes given to the habit, shown by some seabirds for instance, of systematically robbing other individuals of prey. One of the most interesting special cases of parasitism is brood-parasitism or cuckooism, which has arisen not just in cuckoos but in several families of birds, bees, wasps, ants, fish and probably many other animal groups. Brood parasites typically lay their eggs in the nest of another species, and the host parents are duped into feeding the young brood parasite. In the case of ants it is not the host parents that are duped but host workers. The parasite queen invades a host nest, typically kills the host queen and is then adopted as queen by the host workers who tend her eggs and unwittingly rear a new generation of parasite queens and males. Most ant nests are parasitized by beetles, crustaceans and a mixed crew of other animals, who feed on the food gathered by the ants, or on the ant brood. They are tolerated by the ants often because they secrete chemical substances that mimic the natural communication chemicals of the ants, or even that appear to work as addictive drugs on the ants. There is scarcely any way of life that cannot in some senses, be regarded as parasitic on other organisms. RD

Bibliography

Rothschild, M. and Clay, T. 1952: *Fleas, flukes and cuckoos*. London: Collins; New York: Philosophical Library.

parent-offspring conflict Conflict between a parent and its offspring over the extent of PARENTAL INVESTMENT (PI). Formerly it was generally expected that selection would always favor the strategy (see EVOLUTIONARILY STABLE STRATEGY) that results in the maximum number of surviving offspring, and that PI would be apportioned to each offspring in accordance with this principle. However, Trivers (1974) argued that this will be true only with asexually reproducing species. He suggested that in sexually reproducing diploids, selection will be opposed on the parent and on the offspring. It will be to the advantage of genes acting in the parent to allocate PI so as to produce the maximum number of surviving offspring. However, it will be to the advantage of genes acting in the offspring to take more than this parental optimum PI. The extent of parent-offspring conflict will depend on the mating system, and on how an offspring can affect the behavior of its parent. In a series of evolutionarily stable strategy models, Parker and Macnair (1979) deduced that parent-offspring conflict would generally resolve as a compromise between the interests of the parent and those of the offspring; parents would give more PI than their optimum, but not so much as is optimal for the offspring, who would nevertheless continue to solicit further attention. GAP

Bibliography

Parker, G.A. and Macnair, M.R. 1979: Models of parent-offspring conflict. IV. Suppression: evolutionary retaliation by the parent. *Animal behavior* 27, 1210–1235.

Trivers, R.L. 1974: Parent-offspring conflict. *American zoologist* 14, 249–264.

parental investment (PI) Any investment or expenditure on a given offspring that reduces a parent's capacity to produce future offspring. This concept probably dates back to the "parental expenditure" of Fisher (1930), but was developed extensively in an important paper by Trivers (1972). The notion conveyed by PI is that if a parent invests care and provisioning in a particular offspring this improves the viability and REPRODUCTIVE SUCCESS of the offspring, but reduces the number of future offspring that can be generated because the parent has a limited total REPRODUCTIVE EFFORT.

The relative PI of each sex in a given species is important in determining the intensity of intrasexual competition (a component of sexual selection). Males of most species show less PI than females; often male PI is virtually zero (the sperm itself). Thus the theoretical maximum reproductive potential of a male is far higher than that of a female, and intense competition is likely to occur between males over females. Another aspect of PI is that parents may be in conflict with their offspring (PARENT-OFFSPRING CONFLICT) over the amount of PI given to each offspring (Trivers 1974). GAP

Bibliography

Fisher, R.A. 1930: *The genetical theory of natural selection*. Oxford: Clarendon Press.

Trivers, R.L. 1972. Parental investment and sexual selection. In: B. Campbell (ed.): *Sexual selection and the descent of man, 1871–1971*. Chicago: Aldine Atherton.

——— 1974: Parent-offspring conflict. *American zoologist* 14, 249–64.

partial reinforcement effect The increase in persistence, or resistance to EXTINCTION, produced by scheduling reinforcement on only some conditioning trials. If two groups of rats are trained to run down a runway for food in the goal box, with one group finding food on every trial and the other on only a random 50 per cent of trials, the former, consistently reinforced group will stop running very much sooner than the latter, partially reinforced group, when the food is omitted on all trials in extinction.

The partial reinforcement effect poses a problem if it is supposed that consistent reinforcement should produce stronger conditioning and that persistence in extinction directly reflects the strength of conditioning. The most generally accepted explanation is that partially reinforced animals, unlike consistently reinforced ones, have been reinforced for responding in the presence of stimuli associated with the absence of reinforcement and will therefore continue to respond in the presence of such stimuli in extinction. NJM

participation *See* employee participation

passive-aggression Behavior characterized by indirect resistance to demands for adequate performance in either social or work settings. This is accomplished by such tactics as forgetting appointments, procrastination and misplacing important materials. The term is derived from the assumption that the individual is expressing resentment and aggression in a non-assertive fashion. Passive-aggression is often used to resist the demands of authority; children often use this tactic on their parents. Passive-aggressive behavior in several aspects of an individual's life, particularly when more adaptive behavior is possible, results in general ineffectiveness. This condition, along with other factors, may lead to a diagnosis of passive-aggressive personality disorder according to criteria set out in the DSM-III. RHo

Pavlov, Ivan Petrovich (1849–1936) Physiologist and pioneer of the study of CONDITIONING. Pavlov was born in Ryazan, Russia and entered the University of St Petersburg in 1870. He graduated in natural science in 1875 and entered the Military Medical Academy. He obtained his doctorate in 1883 and then spent a few years in Germany, studying with Carl Ludwig in Leipzig. He became professor of pharmacology at the Military Medical Academy in 1890 and professor of physiology in 1895. He received the Nobel Prize for Medicine in 1904 for his work on the physiology of digestion.

Pavlov noticed that dogs sometimes salivated in anticipation of receiving food. This led him to the discovery of the conditioned reflex, now regarded as a fundamental aspect of learning. From 1902 until his death Pavlov concentrated his researches on the phenomena of CONDITIONING, and he is responsible for many of the basic concepts current in this field of study today. DJM

peer group The concept is used in two different senses: first, as a term for a small group of friends or associates who share common values, interests and activities; second, as a term for virtually all persons of the same age, a definition which reflects the fact that schools tend to be age-graded. Peer group influence can therefore be the influence that friends exercise on one another or the influence exerted by a much wider category of age-mates. The term "peer-group influence" is generally restricted to discussions of young people or adolescents, despite the fact that there is little evidence that peer group influence among adolescents is either highly distinctive or greater than among other age groupings. Using the first sense of the term, educational researchers have drawn heavily on the theory of group dynamics in social psychology. The sources and effects of influence are related to concepts such as leadership, conformity and self-concept. Using the second sense of the term, researchers have been more interested in youth subcultures within any one of which many smaller friendship groups can be contained. The differences between subcultures are usually explained with reference to the broader social class subcultures in society.

In some studies, such as Coleman's classic account (1961), the different senses of peer groups and their influence are brought together. In most studies there is a tension, as yet not adequately clarified, between two ideas: on the one hand pupils come to school already sharing subcultural values which influence attitudes to school and educational achievements; on the other hand the school itself plays an active role in the formation of subcultures and friendship groups, perhaps especially in the formation of oppositional (or counter-cultural) groups who are alienated by their school experience, and these peer groups then influence educational attitudes and aspirations. A further unresolved problem is that of determining the relative power of family and peer group to influence adolescents.

The subculture varies with age-level. In childhood, when dependence on parents is high, the peer group serves as an extension of the socialization mediated by the family and peer associates are likely to be governed by parents. In adolescence its quality and functions change as orientation shifts away from the family. The adolescent peer group may be part of a subculture that is at variance with the parental culture although generally its influence is congruent with parental values. The extent to which the peer group is relied upon by the adolescent, as a reference group depends on the degree of estrangement from parents, parental attitudes to the peer group and the nature of the dilemma, since adolescents perceive parents and peers as useful guides in different areas (Brittain 1968). During adolescence the peer group plays an important part in providing social support and identity, although some of its pressures e.g. for conformity and social acceptability, may generate difficulties. Its effects may be important in the development of antisocial behavior and delinquency although they are difficult to estimate.

It is now widely recognized that research has hitherto focussed excessively on peer groups which are male, working-class and deviant at the expense of groups which are female or middle class or non-deviant. This bias is being corrected in current research. DHH/WLLP-J

Bibliography

Coleman, J.S. 1961: *The adolescent society.* Glencoe Ill.: Free Press.

Bany, M.A. and Johnson, L.V. 1964: *Classroom group behaviour.* London and New York: Collier-Macmillan.

Brake, M. 1980: *The sociology of youth culture and youth subcultures.* London and Boston: Routledge & Kegan Paul.

Brittain, C.V. 1968: An exploration of the basis of peer-compliance and parent-compliance in adolescence. *Adolescence* 2, 445–58.

Conger, J.J. 1977: *Adolescence and youth: psychological development in a changing world.* New York: Harper & Row.

perception: animal The appreciation of the world through the senses depends upon the information received by the brain. All perception is initiated by stimulation of specialized nerve cells called receptors, which are sensitive to specific chemical or physical events. The receptors, together with ancillary structures, make up the sense organs.

Sense organs are adapted for the reception of events or stimuli from outside the nervous system. The stimuli may be internal such as temperature within blood vessels (see THERMOREGULATION) or external such as auditory or visual stimuli. Each receptor is associated with some kind of transducer mechanism which converts energy into an electrical potential by which the receptor cell can influence other nerve cells. The receptors within a sense organ connect to other cells of the nervous system.

Sensory quality depends on which nerve is stimulated, not on how it is stimulated. This doctrine of specific nerve energies was first suggested by Johannes Muller in 1834. It is not the stimuli that determine sensory quality but the nerves activated by the stimuli. For example auditory sensations in man can be generated by sound waves reaching the ear, or by mechanical or electrical stimulation of the auditory sense organs. Any kind of activation of the auditory nerves will produce auditory sensations, because the nerve goes to the auditory system of the brain. Similarly activation of the optic nerve produces visual sensations because the optic nerve transmits information to the visual system of the brain. As a rule different receptors provide information about different aspects of sensory quality and variations in the message transmitted along a nerve provide information about the intensity of the stimulation.

Animals are responsive only to certain sets of stimuli and these differ considerably from species to species. Humans respond to a restricted range of visual stimuli. People cannot detect ultraviolet radiation, whereas some bees can do this. Humans are insensitive to infra-red radiation, whereas some rattlesnakes (*Crotalus*) are directionally sensitive to infra-red radiation and use this information in attacking warm-blooded prey. The human eye cannot detect the polarization of light, but pigeons and bees can do this and use it as a navigational aid.

This diversity arises from the fact that different species occupy different ecological niches and consequently have different sensory requirements. Because of this diversity it is not possible to provide a useful answer to the often asked question – how many senses are there? However, those usually regarded as being the most important are the chemical senses, including taste and smell; the electromagnetic senses including the ability of some animals to detect magnetic fields; the mechanical senses including hearing and the sense of balance; and vision. In addition there are sensations arising from specialized receptors within the brain itself which provide information concerning hunger, thirst and thermoregulation.

A certain amount of perceptual selectivity is imposed by the sense organs themselves. In the mammalian ear each receptor responds in a proportional manner to the bending of an associated hair-like projection within the cochlea situated within the inner ear. Each hair cell is stimulated only by tones of a certain pitch, and it transduces the sound energy associated with that pitch. The auditory range of a mammal is therefore associated with the structure of the sense organs themselves. Similarly, the ability to discriminate colors is associated with pigments in the retina of the eye which are differentially sensitive to the wavelength of the light entering the eye (see COLOR VISION). In some animals considerable visual processing occurs at the retinal level. Frogs have nerve cells in the retina which are specialized for the detection of small objects moving across the visual field. These 'bug detectors' enable the animal to respond quickly to flying insects – the frog's normal prey.

Specializations of sense organs are usually highly correlated with the animal's way of life. Most vertebrates have a hemispherical receptive surface (retina) behind the lens, ensuring that all parts of the visual field at the same distance from the animal are focussed on the retina. In horses, however, the upper part of the retina is further from the lens than the lower half. This means that nearby objects lying below the level of the eye will be in focus at the same time as more distant objects above eye level. The effect of this arrangement is that the grazing horse can focus upon its food at the same time as keeping a look-out for predators.

The structure of the eye, and of the other sense organs, determines the limits of the animal's perceptual capabilities. We can imagine that the animal lives in three concentric worlds. The outermost is the physical world which includes all that it is possible for an animal to detect. Inside this is the world which the animal is capable of perceiving and this world is different for different species. For any one species the world of capability can move about within the physical world through evolutionary change. For instance, certain nocturnal moths (*Noctuidae*) which are preyed upon by bats have evolved the ability to hear the very high frequency pulses emitted by flying bats. Inside the world of capability is another world consisting of information which is either responded to or stored for future reference. Here we are distinguishing between what an animal can perceive and what it does perceive in particular circumstances. For example, Tinbergen (1951) and his co-workers discovered that male grayling butterflies (*Eumensis semele*) have marked color preferences when visiting artificial (scentless) flowers in search of food. During courtship, however, they behave as though they are completely color blind. Males prefer darker females, but take no notice of the color. For many years behavioral scientists maintained that cats were color blind. Neurophysiological investigations of the visual system, however, subsequently showed that cats ought to be capable of discriminating colors. Using improved behavioral testing techniques psychologists then demonstrated that cats are capable of color discrimination.

Stimulation of sense organs is of benefit to animals only in so far as they can interpret the information in terms of objects and events in the physical world. Most animals see coal as black and paper as white, even though brightly illuminated coal sends much more light to the eye than does a sheet of white paper in dim light. Animals must be able to interpret incoming signals in accordance with the context in which they occur and this must occur at higher levels in the nervous system. Experiments with animals show that many species are capable of accurate depth perception and judgment of distance. Squirrels leap unerringly from bough to bough, while frogs and chameleons (*Chamaeleontidae*) shoot out the tongue to the correct distance to catch an insect. Depth perception must result from processing of information in the central nervous system because each eye receives only a two-dimensional image. There are a number of cues that can be used by animals to form a three-dimensional representation of external objects: (1) motion parallax occurs when the animal moves its head from side to side. Nearby objects are swept across the retina more quickly than distant ones, and many animals use this as a cue to distance. For examples, locusts (*Acridoidea*) characteristically move their heads in this way when preparing to jump across a gap. (2) The retinal image of an object is larger when the object is nearer to the eye. In laboratory experiments stationary objects can be made to increase in apparent size. Many animals, including crabs, frogs, chickens, kittens, monkeys and human infants, run away, duck or flinch when presented with such a stimulus. This indicates that they interpret the increase in size as meaning that the object is moving toward them. Thus it appears that increasing size of the retinal image, sometimes called the looming cue, is a widespread aspect of distance judgment among animals. (3) Each eye has a slightly different view of the world and there is therefore a disparity between the retinal positions of the image of an object in the outside world. This retinal disparity is greater when the object is nearer to the animal. It is known that some insects such as the praying mantis (*Mantis religiosa*) and some birds and primates use retinal disparity as a cue to depth. (4) The extent to which the eyes converge when fixating an object depends upon the distance of the object, and this information is used by chameleons as well as by man. Many of the cues which are used by animals in depth perception or in the judgment of distance require the use of both eyes and do not depend upon fixed properties of the sense organs themselves. Depth perception depends upon sophisticated processes in the central nervous system, based upon relatively simple information from the sense organs. Many aspects of perception, including the judgment of size, the localization of sounds, and the navigational abilities of animals, depend upon intelligent interpretation of sensory information which enables the animal to build up an inner representation of the outside world.

While many aspects of perception seem sophisticated others seem overly simple. Male European robins (*Erithacus rubecula*) attack other red-breasted robins that trespass on their territory. They will also attack a stuffed robin placed in the territory, but only if it has a red breast. It appears that the red breast is a powerful stimulus for labeling another robin as an intruder. Indeed the territory owner will vigorously attack a bunch of red feathers while ignoring a stuffed robin which has no red breast. No one doubts that a robin is capable of distinguishing between a real bird and a bunch of feathers, but in territorial defense robins appear blind to all attributes except the red breast. Such phenomena are common in animal behavior, and the relatively simple stimuli that elicit the animal's response are generally called sign stimuli. The prime characteristic of sign stimuli is that the animal responds only to a small fraction of the stimulus complex that it is capable of appreciating.

It would, or course, be impossible for an animal to take note of every change in the environment that is monitored by the sense organs. Some selectivity is essential. An important aspect of this selectivity is attention. Three types of attention may be distinguished: (1) An animal may direct its sense organs toward a particular source of stimulation. A dog spying a rabbit directs his eyes, ears and nose to it, often turning head and body in the direction of the rabbit. This type of orienting response tends to result in the exclusion of other stimuli in the environment, partly as a result of the posture taken up by the dog. (2) An animal may attend selectively to some aspects of an object and ignore others. In the natural environment it is the sign stimulus that is generally the subject of this selective attention, but the phenomenon can be readily demonstrated in the laboratory where the significance of the stimuli is entirely learned (see ATTENTION). (3) The third type of attention is concerned with stimuli connected with a particular GOAL. An animal searching for food may have a SEARCH IMAGE of a particular type of food. The animal may pay particular attention to certain types of food, while ignoring other equally desirable foods. This phenomenon can be demonstrated both in the laboratory and in the field.

In addition to perceptual organization with respect to the external world, animals have to deal with the information from the sense organs that detect changes in their own body. To a large extent the coordination of muscular movements is automatic and does not involve higher nervous centers. Information from the skin and from sense organs in the muscles and tendons leads to reflex adjustments in posture and locomotion. To some extent also, messages from the internal sense organs that monitor the state of the blood (e.g. its pressure, temperature, osmosity, etc.) give rise to automatic physiological responses which form part of the general processes of HOMEOSTASIS. Nevertheless, humans can perceive some of the changes that occur in their own bodies, and pay attention to them from time to time. There is no reason to think that other animals are any different in this respect.

DJM

Bibliography

Ewert, J. P. 1980: *Neuroethology*. Berlin and New York: Springer-Verlag.

*Marler, P. R. and Hamilton, W. J. 1966: *Mechanisms of animal behavior*. New York: John Wiley & Sons.

Tinbergen, N. 1951: *The study of instinct*. Oxford: Clarendon Press.

perception: philosophical issues Perception, understood as awareness of the world about us by means of the senses, is a philosophical problem because certain facts about the nature of perception and certain theories about how it takes place appear to show that what we are aware of is not an objective world of physical objects but certain ideas, impressions, images or sense-data which are distinct from such a world. The question then arises how we can have knowledge of such a world or even have reason to believe in its existence. Because of such familiar facts as perspective, refraction and dependence of color on lighting, an accurate description of what appears to us could not be a description of the world as we ordinarily take it to be; still less could it be a description of the world as presented by any scientific theory. Moreover, sense-perception appears to be the end result of a long causal chain of which the object we claim to see is at best a distant and theoretically dispensable link.

Faced with this problem, philosophers have disagreed about its solution. Some have adopted some form of causal theory, according to which our ideas or sense-data are caused by an inferred physical reality. The simplest version of such a theory is probably representationalism in which what we perceive is taken to resemble the physical objects which cause it. No great philosopher has been a pure representationalist; but the overwhelming majority of philosophers and scientists at least from the time of Democritus have held a semi-representationalist theory; thus atomists, including Locke and Newton, held that mechanically relevant, measurable primary qualities such as shape, size and motion are the same in both atoms and the ideas they cause, whereas smell, taste, color, heat, and the like are taken to be caused by atoms which are odorless, tasteless, colorless and neither warm nor cold.

But this notion of the physical world as essentially inaccessible to perception has not satisfied empirically-minded philosophers, who have agreed with Kant that we can know nothing of a transcendent world of things in themselves or even, like those who accept the verification principle, declare that talk of such a world must be meaningless. Many of these philosophers have accepted either subjective idealism, according to which the world is composed of essentially mental ideas, or a phenomenalism which substitutes neutral sense-data for these mental entities. Anticipating Russell's principle of replacing inferred entities by logical constructions, Berkeley declared that physical objects were mere "bundles of ideas" whilst Mill said that they were "permanent possibilities of sensation". In a similar vein modern phenomenalists said that they were "logical constructions out of sense-data". To talk of the physical world is therefore merely a compendious way of describing and predicting the course of our sense-experience, while science should not be regarded as telling us of a world beyond our senses but as constructing models and theories the whole function of which is to explain and predict the course of our sense-experience. Berkeley clearly adumbrated this view, of which Mach is a classical exponent.

Both the traditional causal theorist and the phenomenalist accept the arguments which claim to show that we cannot be aware of physical objects directly but must either infer to them or regard talk about them as merely a commodious and compressed way of talking about ideas or sense-data. The view that we are sensibly aware of physical bodies was disparagingly known as "naive realism". But a minority of philosophers has always been dissatisfied with the arguments outlined at the beginning of this article. The description of how things appear, our everyday description of the physical world and the account of that world given by scientists should not be regarded as descriptions of a veil of appearance and of two worlds lurking behind it but as three equally legitimate descriptions of one and the same world. Similarly the physiologist does not tell us what happens instead of our seeing objects but how we see an object. No doubt physical objects cause a long chain of events in the central nervous system, but what we perceive is not, for example, an elliptical sense-datum caused by a round coin, but a round coin that looks elliptical. Or again, this minority holds, when we say that a tomato is red we are expressing no view whatsoever about the nature of the ultimate particles of matter; it is a gross error to suppose that because science assigns no color to the particles it is a mistake to speak of ordinary bodies as colored. Perhaps the most powerful argument that can be put for this view is the following: if the empirical facts about perceptual illusion and the empirical findings of the sciences are held to constitute an empirical refutation of the view that we perceive physical objects directly it must be possible to conceive of a world in which the empirical facts were compatible with "naive realism". How would objects look in such a world? Would coins look round from all angles, for example? The difficulty of answering such questions might suggest that the theory which generates them is confused. The best known exponent of this minority position is J. L. Austin. JOU

Bibliography

Austin, J.L. 1962: *Sense and sensibilia*. Oxford: Clarendon Press; Cambridge, Mass.: Harvard University Press.

Berkeley, George 1710: *A treatise concerning the principles of human knowledge*. (many editions).

Locke, John 1690: *An essay concerning human understanding* Bk II, ch viii. (many editions).

perception: psychological issues As a term in psychology perception refers to the apparently direct and immediate knowledge of the world, and also of our own bodies, by neural signals from the eyes, the ears, the nose, the tongue, and the many other sense organs which include the skin senses of touch and hot and cold and pain; and also organs of balance in the inner ear, and the unconscious monitoring of forces on the muscles and joints to signal the positions of the limbs. We usually think of our own perceptions as our consciousness of the world around us, and of ourselves; but much of the perception by which behavior is initiated and controled is totally unconscious, and awareness of the perception of things and states of affairs, by which we act is never more than fragmentary. We are never fully aware of what features of sensory signals are being used for the perceptions by which we survive in a hostile world, and are intelligent. This has several important implications: that we cannot be altogether responsible for what we do if "responsibility" requires awareness; and it shows that experiments are essential for discovering not only processes of perception but even what it is we perceive to recognize things, walk around without bumping into things, drive a car, or read a book. It also throws severe doubts on the notion that consciousness is causally significant for behavior. However this may be, we do talk about perception in animals, even though we may doubt whether they have consciousness at all like ours. The simple animals are however not generally thought to have perception at all as we do, but only more or less rigid and predictable tropisms and reflexes, by which behavior is more or less stimulus-determined. This distinction between behavior controlled rather directly by stimuli and far less directly by perception is important, for although there is no general agreement on how best to think about, or explain perception yet it at least seems clear to most psychologists and physiologists working on these problems that perception is essentially the reading of meanings from sensory signals; so that behavior is, generally, appropriate to all manner of hidden characteristics of objects, and situations, and is not merely triggered and guided by the stimuli that happens to be available. Perception is more than a matter of reflexes and tropisms, for it uses subtle "cues" of many kinds to make inferences to what the objects around us are like; and it is predictive. To be predictive in unusual situations, it has to draw intelligent analogies from a rich store of generalized knowledge of the world. This cognitive, knowledge-based, aspect of perception allows appropriate intelligent behavior even when there is very little available information from the senses; and even our eyes, which probably command more of the brain than all the other senses, cannot transmit anything like so much information in "real time" as they seem to do. When we open our eyes and immediately, without any apparent effort, see a room or a view all at once like a superb photograph; the perception is not at all like a photograph, but is created essentially from guesses as suggested by cues from sensed shapes of contours and textures which are essentially inferred as objects, and shadows and so on.

This view of perception as brain-descriptions based on inferences from sensory data is quite a new idea. It is associated especially with the modern founder of Physiological Optics, as it is sometimes called, the German physiologist and physicist, Hermann von Helmholtz (1821–94) who described perception as being given by Unconscious Inference. A much earlier and very different view (which was held by the Greeks including the great geometer Euclid who wrote a book on optics) and which is still in various forms accepted by some psychologists today, especially the distinguished writer on perception the late James J. Gibson, is that visual perception is not derived by inferences from sensed data: but is given directly from the world, or at least from surrounding patterns of light. In Gibson's well known phrase, this is direct "Pick up of Information from the Ambient Array". This approach has revealed a great deal about which features, textures, and so on are accepted and used for perception. So, even if one feels this philosophy to be inadequate or even ultimately misleading there is no doubt that the experiments inspired by it are extremely useful. Here though we will take a more Helmholtzian approach, based not so much on Gibson's ambient array, but rather on the reading of neural signals from the image forming eye. Retinal images and selection of visual features by eye movements are, rather curiously, hardly mentioned and even rejected altogether by the stricter Gibsonians; so, the reader will appreciate that we are in a somewhat stormy sea of controversy from the very outset.

There are, as can be seen by looking into an eye with a suitable ophthalmoscope photograph-like optical images in the eyes. These are the upside down and laterally reversed, as cast onto the retinas at the back of the eyes by the curved corneas and the internal crystalline lens. The retinas are more however than mere screens for the ever changing optical images from the world: for they are mini computers, performing the first stages of processing of the electrical signals of the incoming ("afferent") nervous system for vision. All the information that we receive from any of the senses is coded by electrical impulses running in nerve fibres at about the speed of sound, and increasing in frequency from about 5–800 impulses per second as the intensity of the light (or the pressure on the skin) or whatever increases. It is a remarkable fact that all we know and experience of the world is provided by patterns of these electrical impulses – ACTION POTENTIALS – running in bundles of fibers into the dark silent brain. The action potentials from all the senses are, physically essentially the same from all the senses; and the action potentials sending (efferent) signals to the muscles are also essentially the same. So, why do some provide sensations of color, and others of sound or touch or pain? What matters is which parts of the brain receive the action potentials. If nerves from one sense were transposed to the region of brain normally fed from another sense – then the sensations would be reversed. We might then hear light and see sounds!

The organs of sense, such as the eyes and the ears, are in engineering terms transducers; as they detect patterns of energy from the external world (and in some cases from the body) and convert the received physical energy patterns into the coded messages, transmitted by action potentials. They are incredibly sensitive, so that the light receptors of the retina (the rods, for black-white vision, and the "cones" for color) respond to a single photon, which is the physically smallest possible packet of energy. If the ears were any more sensitive, we would hear the random movement of the molecules of the air banging against the ear drum.

How are the signals from the senses read by the brain? This is the big question (at least for a Helmholtzian approach) for understanding perception, and it can at present only be partially answered. As by far the most is known about VISUAL PERCEPTION – though of course the other senses are extremely important and in their own ways perhaps as interesting – we shall consider only visual perception here but many of the same principles apply to other senses. It is now known that the signals arriving from the million or so fibers of the optic nerves are processed in many successive stages, and that an important early stage (taking place in the striate cortex, at the back of the brain where, somewhat curiously the signals go, to work forwards as they are analysed and read for their meanings) is selection of a few simple features – such as orientations of contours or edges, and movements. Thus single cells in the striate cortex fire to particular features. This was discovered by two American physiologists, David Hubel and Torsten Wiesel, and was a key discovery to how the brain reads sensory signals. The point is that the initial picture at the eye is soon lost, as features are selected and represented by combinations of firing brain cells. These patterns of electrical activity are essentially *descriptions* of the scene; and this description depends very much upon stored knowledge of objects which is given by later stages of processing which are not understood in detail. This is obvious, when one comes to realize that we act upon all manner of features of things which cannot be sensed, at least when we perceive them. Thus we perceive an ice cream as cold before we touch it; and far more subtly, we see that a person is angry or pleased from his expression or a gesture. Actually we may not be able to say just how we can see the mood of a person – or the distances or sizes or shapes of objects, or what they are made of or what they are doing or likely to do next. As we have said, but little of this complex richness or perception is available to consciousness.

Partly because consciousness is really rather unimportant for perception as a whole – even if it does dominate how we think of the visual and musical arts it is a useful step to consider and investigate perception in animals, and perhaps more surprisingly also in machines designed to accept and make sense of signals. The new science of ARTIFICIAL INTELLIGENCE is extremely important for making explicit, and for testing, theoretical ideas of how the brain may function to confer perception and intelligence, and these are closely linked. It is now known that computers can be fed with visual signals from TV camera "eyes", and programmed to read the video signals, so that they can describe and respond appropriately to external objects. It is important to allow the computer to accept as little as possible, to prevent it being overloaded with unimportant detail: what is accepted must convey a lot of information. It turns out that corners and edges of objects are extremely important features and textures of surfaces considerably less so. It is very likely that we, also, derive most of our useful visual information from edges and from shapes such as converging lines indicating depth and orientation in depth of objects; as converging lines in the retinal image is often due to shrinking of the image (exactly as for a camera) with increasing distance – to generate perspective shapes, which may be accepted as usually reliable evidence of distances, for things such as tables, rooms and roads which are usually rectangular. It follows though that when objects are queer shapes – such as actually converging to one end – then powerful illusory distortions can be generated; as the signals from the eye are misread by assumptions of rectangularity, or other common shapes. Illusions of many kinds can also be caused by adaptation of neural mechanisms, as occurs with after-images to bright lights, or to continuous motion which produces illusory, apparent, motion in the opposite direction.

Adaptations of the channels of the senses can be used to reveal what the channels are, and their characteristics, so adaptations of this kind are important as research tools for relating physiological processes and mechanisms with perception. Other kinds of illusions, such as those of perspective misapplied, reveal how and what kinds of knowledge or assumptions are accepted for reading sensory signals; for they can be read with inappropriate assumptions, to generate cognitive illusions which are a give away to how we use, and in some situations misuse, stored knowledge for seeing the world and ourselves – in terms of the past, for predicting and so surviving into the immediate future where all threats and promises wait upon our intelligent perception. RLG

Bibliography

Barlow, H.B. and Mollon, J.D.: 1982: *The senses*. Cambridge and New York: Cambridge University Press.

Frisby, John P. 1979: *Seeing: illusion, brain and mind*. Oxford and New York: Oxford University Press.

Gibson, J.J. 1950: *Perception of the visual world*. London: Allen & Unwin.

Gombrich, E.H. 1960. *Art and illusion*. Phaidon.

Gregory, R.L. 1966. *Eye and brain*, London: Weidenfeld.

———1970: *The intelligent eye*. London: Weidenfeld.

Helmholtz, H. von. 1867 (1963): *Handbook of physiological optics*, ed. J.P.C.S. Southall. New York: Dover.

perception *See above, and also* social perception

perceptual and cognitive abilities in infancy Those processes and capacities that give rise to sensory experience, the acquisition of knowledge and the formation of beliefs during the first eighteen months of life. Research in this branch of developmental psychology has flourished in recent years and has challenged the popular conception of the young baby as an "incompetent" organism.

A particularly interesting aspect of this research is the light it throws on our philosophical assumptions concerning the original nature of mind. The traditional empiricist hypothesis, that much of perception is learned during the earliest months of life, has gradually given way as research has progressed to a nativist position which emphasizes the presocial, preadaptive organization of human sensory systems. Thus, although the motor abilities of the newborn are limited, the baby's sensory capacities are relatively well developed. The force of much recent research has been to show that even very young infants are well equipped to obtain information about their environment. All sensory systems are functional at or soon after birth; neonates are capable of discriminating odors, they show taste preferences, and are sensitive to visual, tactile and auditory stimulation (Werner and Lipsitt 1981).

Perhaps the most interesting questions about infant perception concern the structure of early experience. It is here that traditional theories have been most influenced by philosophical preconceptions concerning the nature and origins of space perception. The empiricist philosophers explained perception of an extended, three dimensional space and perception of substantiality by the correlation of visual with tactual-motor experience during early infancy. Developmental theories based on these assumptions, such as Piaget's (1954), were naturally led to characterize the pre-locomotor infant as deficient in space perception and as lacking intersensory coordination. Investigators did not expect, and perhaps not surprisingly, did not find evidence for space perception or for sensory coordination in the first few months of life.

In recent years, however, an information based approach to perception has won increasing favor. The informative value of sensory stimulation was particularly stressed by Gibson (1966) in his theory of direct perception. He argued that the senses have evolved as perceptual systems whose function is to "pick up" information which specifies properties of objects and events. Perception is by means of invariant information that may be common to the various modalities, as well as modality specific. The developmental implication is that prolonged learning may not be necessary to extract significant information from sensory experience or to relate information obtained in one modality to another.

Among the first people to test this theory with young infants was Bower. He showed, in many studies with pre-locomotor babies, (0–6 months) that they perceive visual constancy of size and shape and that their vision can specify some of the tangible properties of things before they have learned the invariant properties of objects by correlating vision with touch. Further evidence that perception is coherently organized came from Bower's studies of perception of the continued existence of objects that disappear temporarily from view (Bower 1979). Others have shown space perception in the pre-locomotor infant and auditory-visual coordination in neonates (see Butterworth 1981a). This has led to the gradual realization that even very young babies may be capable of sophisticated feats of perception, which in turn has prompted a re-examination of the origins of cognitive development in infancy.

While there is still an important function for active tactual and motor exploration in infancy, one implication of recent research on visual and auditory perception is that the distance senses (vision and audition) may also contribute in important ways to early experience through the mechanisms of selective attention and storage of information. For example, techniques for measuring auditory discrimination have shown that newborn babies are particularly sensitive to the intonation patterns and syllabic structure of speech (Bertoncini and Mehler 1981). Further insights into language relevant perceptual mechanisms have been obtained with the discovery that neonates can imitate movements of mouth and tongue (Meltzoff and Moore 1977). Attending to the visual configuration of the adult's mouth may help the infant in articulating his or her own speech sounds.

That there is an inborn ability for imitation may also have important implications for the development of social relations and the transmission of culture. Indeed, some theorists, notably Trevarthen (1982) have stressed that the primary function of infant sensory preadaptations is to allow babies to relate to other people.

There is evidence that a new phase of development begins at about forty weeks and may depend upon acquisition of the ability spontaneously to retrieve information from memory. The child can now coordinate its activities with people and things, bringing both social and physical worlds together in play; it will search for hidden objects and shows fear of strangers. These phenomena suggest that the baby now has access to stored information. (There is evidence that the infant stores information and recognizes things from the neonatal period onwards; this new ability is to do with recall not simply recognition.) This capacity for representation develops rapidly so that by the end of infancy the child is well able to plan activities mentally before putting them into effect.

Another ability, easily observed in the second year of life, is the capacity to make elementary inferences. The baby will infer that if an object it has seen disappear cannot be found at one point along its path of movement, it must be elsewhere. Babies will search persistently for desirable objects even if their movements are not directly visible. Piaget (1937) says that this indicates that the baby has acquired the object concept, a belief in the permanence of objects. Coupled with an ability for delayed imitation (Piaget 1946) this may mark the beginnings of symbolism, the onset of language and the end of infancy. Although research on the perceptual abilities of young infants has led to a fundamental revision of the popular stereotype of the helpless, passive infant, we still know little of how fundamental sensory processes give rise in development to higher order capacities. The solution of this problem stands on a firmer base, now that the sophisticated perceptual capacities of babies have been recognized. (See also IMITATION; ADAPTATION IN INFANTS; PIAGET; SENSORI-MOTOR STAGE.)

GEB

Bibliography

Bertoncini, J. and Mehler, J. 1981: Syllables as units in infant speech perception. *Infant behavior and development* 4, 247–80.

Bower, T.G.R. 1979: *Human development*. San Francisco: Freeman.

Butterworth, G.E. 1981a: The origins of auditory visual perception and visual proprioception in human development. In *Intersensory perception and sensory integration*, ed. R.D. Walk, and H. Jr Pick. New York: Plenum Press, 37–70.

*Butterworth, George, ed. 1981b *Infancy and epistemology: an evaluation of Piaget's theory*. Brighton: Harvester; New York; St Martins Press (1982).

Gibson, James J. 1966: *The senses considered as perceptual systems*. Boston: Houghton Mifflin; London: Allen & Unwin (1968).

*Hofer, M.A. 1981: *The roots of human behavior*. San Francisco: Freeman.

Meltzoff, A. and Moore, M.K. 1977: Imitation of facial and manual gestures by human infants. *Science* 198, 75–8.

Piaget, J. 1937 (*1954*): *The construction of reality in the child*. New York; Basic Books.

——— 1946 (*1951*): *Play, dreams and imitation in childhood*. London: Routledge and Kegan Paul.

Trevarthen, C. 1982: The primary motives for cooperative understanding. In *Social cognition: essays on the development of understanding*, ed. G. Butterworth and P. Light. Brighton: Harvester; Chicago: Chicago University Press.

*Walk, R.D. 1981: *Perceptual development*. California: Brooks Cole.

Werner, J.S. and Lipsitt, L.P. 1981: The infancy of human sensory systems. In *Developmental plasticity behavioral and biological aspects of variations in development*, ed. Eugene S. Gollin. New York and London: Academic Press.

perceptual defense Term in experimental psychology for delays or blockages in identifying anxiety-provoking stimuli which are presented only briefly. Typically, the exposure-time necessary to read emotionally neutral words is established, and then words of the same length which have been experimentally linked with anxiety (e.g. pain, failure), or which are socially "taboo" are introduced. When the subject needs a significantly longer exposure to identify such words, perceptual defense is said to be operating. A similar effect may be produced by introducing "cognitive dissonance" (see COGNITIVE PSYCHOLOGY) into non-verbal stimuli, such as playing-cards with suits of the wrong color (e.g. red spades); and the perceptual task may, of course, be auditory. The phenomenon is reviewed by

Brown (1962), and is often taken as evidence for repression (see Kline 1981, pp.210–28). NMC

Bibliography

Brown, W. P. 1962: Conceptions of perceptual defence. *British journal of psychology*. Monograph supplement no.35.

Kline, Paul 1981: *Fact and fantasy in Freudian theory* (second edn.), London: Methuen.

perceptual development There are a few texts on the development of perceptual skills: Gibson (1969), Piaget (1969), Vurpillot (1976). The field is vast, ranging from tactile sensitivity to comprehension of the basis of visual metaphor. How can one disentangle what is specifically perceptual from more general mental changes?

With children, from preschool to early adolescence, the aim is to describe (a) sensory information to which they seem sensitized, (b) their perceptual knowledge (Flavell 1978) and (c) symbolic skills to which they have gained access. One can often check a psychological theory against physical laws. For example, since light does not travel round corners, this must be a feature of children's visual environment. But only when children have built a database about its predictable effects can these effects become incontrovertible facts of visual experience for them. Without such perceptual knowledge, covert or overt, they can neither hide properly (head-in-the-sand syndrome) nor seek efficiently. This is not a trivial point for anyone who has had to ask a child to try again to find something on a shelf. An intimate relationship exists between possession of perceptual knowledge and preparation of appropriate action.

Yet perceptual skills are difficult to bring to the level of awareness. Take size-perception: we all have extensive visual experience of body-parts, yet few people notice that a relaxed hand will typically cover from brow to chin. That is evident in untutored drawings at all ages. The problem is often posed as arising from the existence of two types of knowledge, procedural and declarative. Much perceptual skill seems to pertain to the former, to knowing how to organize information within particular contexts, rather than to the build up of solid facts across contexts.

The straight-line law of light-projection specifies that perceptual habits must be organized to deal with parallelism, angular inclination and the like. Some clear demonstrations of perceptual skill have been based on children's sensitivity to geometrical frames of reference, But, by the same token, they have high-lighted children's problems with visual-symbolics. The ability precisely to interpret pictorial linear perspective develops late, in middle childhood, yet the basic laws of perspective are the straight-line rule and size-distance relations. Even when such simple perceptual rules are grasped, they still have to be welded into a *symbolic system*. In that sense, perceptual development is something which can continue throughout life.

Mandler (1982) questions "whether it is possible to have a perceptually sophisticated organism without a related conceptual system integrated". She adds, "much of our knowledge of the world, even as adults, is organized around expectations of what we will see next or what will happen next". The more knowledge one can deploy, the less continuous attention has to be paid, and the more advance planning can be allocated to checking expectations by categorizing perceptual input. Perceptual processing can actually be physically tiring. The development of mental labor-saving devices enables effort to be concentrated upon analysing input efficiently. If one knows that landmarks have not only to be physically salient but distributed in a manner informative about one's route, it will be easier to avoid one's attention being distracted by attractive, non-informative things. Children can be acute at noticing things that could be landmarks, far less so in restricting attention to those which actually are.

In sum, though the senses can repeatedly be *recalibrated* with age and tuition, there is no reason to seek a unique motor of development in new sensory capacities "coming on stream". Behind the monitoring of sensations, which may be stable over development lies the assessment of the consequences of the sensations. These may be grave for short-range senses such as touch or taste. "All novel sensations of taste and smell are actually viewed with suspicion until their consequences have been assessed" (Engen 1979). What happens if children become "hooked" on a high salt dosage, say? "As in the case of too much sugar . . . learning must have overcome whatever innate preferences and body wisdom there might have been" (Engen 1979). the influence of cultural norms and social setting, with a new chemical sensation, can be profound (Galef 1982). For these "evolutionarily ancient" senses there is no childhood development after infancy, only the acquisition of good and bad habits, and the engagement with, or avoidance of, intelligent assessment of consequences. How we get children of different developmental status to make the assessment is quite a different matter.

Piaget, who had an acute eye for developmental discontinuities, denied the existence of perceptual stages. Even where age-related differences are sharp, one looks to the underlying interpretative skills for a reasoned account of changes in strategic skills in the use of senses. There are two important provisos. First, counter-instances can be found. Thus, Mayer (1977) reported development in anisotropy (differential sensitivity to lines differing in orientation). Yet the theoretical basis, that such development should demonstrably be of adaptive significance in relation to the geometry of the environment, is questionable (Switkes et al. 1978). The second proviso is that, as new techniques enable researchers finely to decompose the elements of an array, future models will have to contain some very subtle developmental parameters (Dowd et al. 1980).

A case example of perceptual development is with orientation. Bodily stability requires collation of external visual cues and internal balance cues. Butterworth and Cicchetti (1978) showed that when infants manage to sit unaided, visual motion cues cause them to sway in over-compensation. This again happens when learning to stand. But motor-retarded Downs' syndrome infants compensate comparatively less at the sitting stage and stagger more at standing, arguably as a result of doing less work at collation at the earlier stage. Rosinski et al. (1978) estimate that compensation is normally fully developed by age six, to about 50 per cent of what an ideal system would do. This is an impressive achievement.

If contextual sensitivity can be sharpened so early, what is left to develop are strategies for controlling it. One research tool is to manipulate the number of diagonals in the visual field, for even adults find them difficult to encode. Children find it easier to align two square targets than two diamonds, but this square-advantage vanishes if alignment has to be done under conflict: squares within diamond frames and diamonds within square frames. A simple explanation is that children distribute finite available encoding-resources over both target and context. The corollary is that a diagonal anywhere in the field uses up a constant amount of perceptual effort. The effects hold up to the age of seven or eight (Freeman 1980). Only after that can children reasonably be expected to focus perceptual effort on demand. That may possibly be part of a more general tendency for young children not to utilize their analysis of stimulus dimensions where an adult almost compulsively may do so (Ward 1980).

Yet this leads to a puzzle, With complex pictures, children sometimes concentrate on parts, sometimes on wholes (Vurpillot 1976). Pre-schoolers may be sensitive to both height and width yet fall back on just height for judging the "bigness" of a rectangle–so much so that five-year-olds may be worse than three-year-olds, (Maratsos 1973). Strategies for gathering information depend upon development of the conceptual categories which the perceptual information is supposed to serve. Andersen (1975) reports a beautiful study of perceptual widening and narrowing between the ages of three and twelve, when searching for a cup. Children also have to learn to control the odd biases, built up during normal wide-ranging perceptual exploration, in the interests of working hard at a specific perceptual puzzle. Every case of age-related perceptual bias will have to be theorized in terms of possible normal adaptive significance. One can see how spread of resources could be triggered by cues associated with overlearned skills, such as stability, and over-selectivity in cases of puzzling out the unique referent which the adult apparently intends. Finally, children develop ideas about when it is appropriate to shut off entirely: use of gaze-aversion can only be understood by going beyond perceptual mechanisms to the child as a person in social contexts. NHF

Bibliography

Andersen, E.S. 1975: Cups and glasses: learning that boundaries are vague. *Journal of child language* 2, 79–103.

Butterworth, G.E. and Cicchetti, D. 1978: Visual calibration of posture in normal and motor retarded Downs' syndrome infants. *Perception* 7, 513–25.

Dowd, J.M., et al. 1980: Children perceive large-disparity random-dot stereograms more readily than adults. *Journal of experimental child psychology* 29, 1–11.

Engen, T. 1979: The origin of preferences in taste and smell. In *Preference behaviour and chemoreception*, ed. J. Kroeze London: IRL.

Flavell, J.H. 1978: The development of knowledge about visual perception. In *Nebraska Symposium on Motivation*, vol.25., ed. C.B. Keasey. Lincoln: University of Nebraska Press.

Freeman, N.H. 1980: *Strategies of representation in young children: analysis of spatial skills and drawing processes*, London and New York: Academic Press.

Galef, B.G. 1982: Development of flavour preference in man and animals: the role of social and nonsocial factors. In *The development of perception: psychobiological perspectives*, vol.I. ed. R.N. Aslin, J.R. Alberts and M.R. Petersen. New York and London: Academic Press.

Gibson, J.J. 1969: *Principles of perceptual learning and development*, New York: Appleton-Century-Croft.

Mandler, J.M. 1982: Representation. In *Cognitive development*, ed. J.H. Flavell and E.M. Markman, New York: Wiley.

Maratsos, M.P. 1973: Decrease in understanding of the word "big" in preschool children. *Child development* 44, 747–52.

Mayer, M.J. 1977: Development of anisotropy in late childhood. *Vision research* 17, 703–10.

Piaget, J. 1969: *The mechanisms of perception*. London: Routledge & Kegan Paul; New York: Basic Brooks.

Rosinski, R.R., Degelman, D. and Mulholland, T. 1978: Intermodal relationships in children's perception. *Child development* 49, 1084-95.

Switkes, E., Mayer, M.J. and Sloan, J.A. 1978: Spatial frequency analysis of the visual environment: anisotropy and the carpentered environment hypothesis. *Vision research* 18, 1393–99.

Vurpillot, E. 1976: *The visual world of the child*. London: Allen & Unwin; New York: International Universities Press.

Ward, T.B. 1980: Separable and integral responding by children and adults to the dimensions of length and density. *Child development* 51, 676–84.

performance: linguistic Chomsky (1965, p.3) distinguishes between competence and performance, the latter being what a speaker actually does in speech. Performance is a direct reflection of competence only under idealized conditions, i.e. with abstract ideal speaker-hearers in a completely homogeneous speech community. According to Chomsky (1965, p.10) "the investigation of performance will proceed only so far as understanding of underlying competence permits".

It is widely held that COMPETENCE (i.e. abstract grammatical structures) should be the concern of linguists, and performance (mainly research into factors determining acceptability) that of psychologists or sociologists. However, it is difficult to see how such a compartmentalization of the field of language study can be maintained, in particular since:

(1) it is impossible to draw a clearcut line between competence and performance

(2) it is difficult to establish the boundary between linguistic performance and non-linguistic behavior

(3) it is not clear why competence studies should be methodologically prior to studies of performance, though it is difficult to see how performance data (the only empirically justifiable data) can even provide psycholinguistic evidence for competence within a transformational-generative framework of linguistics (see Greene 1972, pp.94–100). PM

Bibliography

Chomsky, Noam 1965: *Aspects of the theory of syntax*. Cambridge, Mass.: MIT Press.

Greene, Judith 1972: *Psycholinguistics: Chomsky and psychology*. Harmondsworth and Baltimore: Penguin.

person: concept of Though SELF CONCEPT, a system of

beliefs an individual comes to form about him or herself, and SOCIAL IDENTITY, the social category to which people assign themselves and to which they are assigned by others are well established in psychology, the concept of "person" has mainly attracted the attention of philosophers. This is unfortunate since such a concept is heavily involved in theorizing about others (see ATTRIBUTION THEORY) and in the making of moral judgments.

Philosophical interest in the concept of person centers on whether the concept refers to a primary, indecomposable entity or to a secondary conglomerate of more basic units. In the Cartesian tradition persons are composite beings requiring the union, though not the fusion, of a mind and a body. This conception of a person has been bedevilled by two main problems; how do these disparate components interact? (the MIND–BODY PROBLEM); and since we are aware only of the bodily envelope of others, how do we know that they too "have" minds (the problem of other minds). (See also SELF: PHILOSOPHICAL.)

A more satisfactory concept of person has recently been identified by Strawson (1959). On his view persons are basic beings, publicly identified by the possession of a cluster of different kinds of attributes, some bodily, some behavioral and some mentalistic. The key step in the argument for adopting this concept of person is the suggestion that though our grounds for attributing states and conditions to ourselves and to others may be different, the meaning of first person and other person attributions is the same. Though there has been considerable critical discussion of this proposal (Ayer 1964) it has much to recommend it. Latterly it has appeared in the theory of human cognitive development as a public-collective model for the acquisition of an individual's sense of personal identity (Harré 1983).

The concept of "person" has been problematic in psychology partly because human beings are not to be distinguished as persons in virtue of their physical characteristics. Being a person, suggests Abelson (1977), is to have a special *status* bestowed upon one by one's fellow agents. Persons assign to one another the *right*, not only to make first-person avowals, such as "I like you", "I am hungry", "I have changed my mind", but also to have them taken seriously, i.e. acted upon. However, such a privilege may be lost if one cannot at the same time fulfill a *duty*: that of monitoring what one says and does to ensure that it is acceptable in socially shared terms. While the concept of person includes that of SELF, it is not identical to it. Personhood is a cultural universal (Geertz 1973), while selves may exhibit different forms: the western "individualistic" self; the "impersonal" self of the Eskimo; the "bifurcated" self of the Javanese, with an "inside" and an "outside" self; the "player" self of the Balinese; and so on (Geertz 1975). Although the ability to make reference to self-knowledge is essential to being a person, that ability develops only slowly. However, this cannot mean that human beings in society have first to qualify as persons before being treated as such. Indeed, the facts of psychological development are that human beings only develop the appropriate self-referential abilities by being treated as if already possessing them. This interdependency – of people relying upon one another for their personhood – has been termed "psychological symbiosis" by Spitz (1965). Such an interdependency also allows for the possibility of *depersonalization*: if people's actions are treated by others as lacking significance, they can experience themselves as not present in the world of ordinary, everyday life, and may lose their sense of agency (see e.g. Goffman 1961). RHa/JMS

Bibliography

Abelson, R. 1977: *Persons: a study in philosophical psychology*. London: Macmillan.

Ayer, A.J. 1964: *The concept of a person*. London: Macmillan.

Geertz, C. 1973: *The interpretation of cultures*. New York: Basic Books.

——— 1975: On the nature of anthropological understanding. *American scientist* 63, 47–53.

Goffman, E. 1961: *Asylums: essays on the social situation of mental paitnets and other inmates*. New York: Doubleday.

Harré, R. 1983: *Personal being*. Oxford: Basil Blackwell.

Spitz, R.A. 1965: *The first year of life: a psychoanalytic study of normal and deviant development of object relations*. New York: International Universities Press.

Strawson, P.F. 1959: *Individuals*. London: Methuen; Atlantic Highlands, N.J.: Humanities (1960).

personal construct theory In 1955 George A. Kelly proposed a total psychology of the person. He employed the model of the individual as a "scientist", trying to predict and gain control over a personal world. This model has since aroused interest internationally.

Kelly's psychology focusses on how individuals construe events. He suggests that our understanding of and interactions with others is based on "getting inside" their psychological world. He sees people's feelings, thoughts and actions as intimately bound up with their system of constructs. Kelly's theory is therefore not strictly a cognitive one (see COGNITIVE PSYCHOLOGY).

All this stems from Kelly's model of the person as a scientist. He argues that it need not only be professionals conducting experiments who are scientists. He suggests it might be useful to look at people "as if" they were all developing theories about events, and deriving hypotheses from those theories which were then put to the test. The more their predictions or anticipations are proved correct, the better control they have over their personal world.

An unusual feature of Kelly's psychology is that behavior becomes the experiment. It is by behaving that people test their conceptions or constructs. If they do not like the answers they get from their behavioral experiments they may change constructs–and then their subsequent behavior.

The philosophical theme of constructive alternativism runs through personal construct theory and its practical applications. Kelly proposes that *one should assume that all present interpretations of the universe are subject to revision or replacement*. There are alternative ways of looking at any event. There is no fact that is "true". There is an objective reality "out there", but no one has direct access to it. All that is possible is to interpret it. This leads to a science that does not concern itself with the accumulation of facts, but with the testing of hypotheses which account best for events as currently understood. At some later date an alternative construction will emerge giving rise to new questions and the search for new answers.

Personal construct theory is formally stated in a fundamental postulate that a person's activities are determined psychologically and controlled by the ways in which he anticipates events. This is then elaborated by eleven corollaries.

This psychology is essentially about individuals in action. There is no need to explain why people act since, as living creatures, they are "forms of motion". What needs explaining is why people do what they do. Motivation is partly built in to the idea that to construe is to anticipate. A construct is a discrimination in which some events are seen as sharing qualities which, in turn, make them different from other events. Construing a person as "friendly" means one predicts certain responses and not others from him, and acts accordingly.

A child's interminable questions about the nature of its environment are attempts to form constructs. By questioning, it eventually determines where similarities in, say, various "floors", lie and what makes them different from pavements or walls. The child now anticipates that, whenever something is construed as a "floor" it will be relatively flat and safe to walk on and, conversely, will *not* suddenly shift to a position above its head.

The construct "floor–not floor" is, of course, a very simple one. But invalidation of those descriptions of the physical world that are taken for granted creates great confusion. This may happen in some forms of interrogation. For instance, invalidation of "time" by alteration of clocks and the day/night ratio, results in great confusion and anxiety.

It is here that Kelly brought emotion into his theoretical system. People experience emotion whenever they are aware that their system of constructs is in a state of change or that their ways of construing the world are inadequate. The person who finds he is unable to anticipate that day regularly follows night and that hours are precisely the same length, will experience anxiety because he will be aware that the events with which he is confronted lie outside the range of convenience of his construct system.

Kelly, who started life as a physicist and mathematician, outlined two techniques to help gain insight into another's personal world. The repertory grid assesses the relationship between constructs. It has been developed in a variety of ways and is particularly widely used in research and the clinic (see Fransella and Bannister 1977). The self-characterization invites people to describe themselves in the third person, as if sketching a character in a play. Both techniques are widely used for personal exploration and in psychotherapy.

It is important to emphasize that the words people use are not necessarily the same as the construct to which they are attached. Indeed, some constructs have no verbal labels at all. Kelly did not feel that the distinction implied in the use of the term "unconscious" (see FREUD) was sufficiently comprehensive to encompass the complexities of construing. He preferred to use the term "levels of awareness". There is preverbal construing. This refers to those ways in which the young child has come to discriminate between events in its environment but which have no words attached to them. Those not verbalized before adulthood can result in behavior which is inexplicable to the agent himself. If, on meeting strangers, you take an instant dislike to them and "feel in your guts they are no good", you are probably using a preverbal construct.

Everyone does not experience events in the same way; people differ from each other in the construction of events (Individuality Corollary). However, to the extent that one person employs a construction of experience which is similar to that employed by another, his psychological processes are similar to those of the other person (Commonality Corollary). Here is an example of Kelly's use of the bi-polarity of constructs. Personal construct psychologists typically focus on individual constructions in, say, psychotherapy and on shared constructs when studying cross-cultural differences. Repertory grids can be used in either context.

Merely sharing constructions with another does not guarantee a successful relationship. For that one needs at least to make some effort to see things through the other's eyes. Communication is dependent on the extent to which one person construes the construction processes of another (Sociality Corollary). This is the central point at which social psychology comes into Kelly's theory.

Personal construct theory has been found useful in many areas of psychology, but particularly the clinical field. Kelly felt that the psychotherapeutic setting was where his theory was centrally applicable. Here one individual struggles to step into another's shoes so as to look at the world through the other's eyes. Only in this way is it possible to understand why a person is experiencing problems. Fixed role therapy is an example he gave of how his theory might be applied in a practical context. Here a character sketch is written based on a person's self-characterization. The new character is not the opposite of the existing one, but different in a number of ways. The person is then encouraged to live the life of this person for a specified time. Implicit in fixed role therapy is the idea that people can re-create themselves and have already created the person they currently are.

Personal construct psychology is truly reflexive. It accounts for the psychotherapist's conceptions as much as for the client's. Equally it accounts for Kelly's formulation of his theory as it does for the unique human being that is you or I. The full range of application of personal construct theory is far from being determined. But wherever there are individuals to be understood, whether by psychologists, priests, sociologists, historians or friends, the personal construct model can be, and is being, found useful. FF

Bibliography

Bannister, D. and Fransella, F. 1980: *Inquiring man*. 2nd edition. London: Penguin Books; New York: Krieger.

Fransella, F. and Bannister, D. 1977: *A manual for repertory grid technique*. London and New York: Academic Press.

Kelly, G.A. 1955: *The psychology of personal constructs.* New York: Norton.

Landfield, A.W. and Leitner, L.M. 1980: *Personal construct psychology: psychotherapy and personality.* New York: Wiley.

personal identity The philosophical problem of personal identity is the intersection of a number of central philosophical problems: the problem of what it is for one and the same thing to exist at different times, the mind–body problem, the problem of the nature of the "self" and of self-awareness, and problems relating to the special concern persons have for their own survival and future well-being. While views on this topic are implicit in philosophical writings from Plato onwards, its career as a distinct philosophical topic is usually taken to begin with John Locke's discussion in his *Essay concerning human understanding*.

The problem is commonly formulated by asking what the continued identity over time of persons "consists in", or what the "criteria" of personal identity are. A seemingly commonsensical answer to such questions is that the identity of a person is nothing more nor less than the identity of a living human body. It is significant that throughout the history of the discussion of this topic this has been very much a minority view among philosophers (for a defense of the weaker view that bodily identity is necessary for personal identity, see Williams 1956). This may be in part a legacy of dualist views, like those of Descartes, which view the mind as an immaterial substance which is only contingently linked to any body. But even philosophers unsympathetic to dualism have felt that there is something special, and especially problematic, about the identity of persons, and have been resistant to the idea that personal identity is just a special case of the identity of "bodies" or material things. Two factors have contributed to this. One is the special access each person has, in memory, to facts about his own identity: while my knowledge that the man before me is (is identical to) the man I saw yesterday might plausibly be said to be grounded on evidence that the human body I see now is the one I saw then, my memory knowledge that I am the person who did such and such yesterday does not seem to be grounded on evidence of bodily identity. The other factor is the special importance we attach to personal identity. With most sorts of things, exact similarity is as good as identity: as long as I now have a watch just like the one I bought yesterday, it is a matter of indifference to me whether it is numerically the same one or an exact duplicate of it. But one is inclined to say that only a monster could feel this way about his children, and that only a madman could feel this way about himself. It would seem *prima facie* absurd to suggest that my interest in existing in the future would be equally well served if I were destroyed and replaced by an exact duplicate (but see Perry 1976 for an interesting defense of this suggestion). A satisfactory account of personal identity ought to account for this special access and this special importance. It is natural to feel that the view that personal identity consists in bodily identity can account for neither.

John Locke wrote: "Should the soul of a prince, carrying with it the consciousness of the prince's past life, enter and inform the body of a cobbler, as soon deserted by his own soul, everyone sees he would be the same person with the prince accountable only for the prince's actions. . . ." (*Essay*, II, xxvii, 15; reprinted in Perry 1975). A similar story, which avoids the dualistic overtones of Locke's, would involve the brain of a prince being transplanted into the body of a cobbler (see Shoemaker 1963). If, as seems plausible, the resulting person (supposing there is one) would remember the past life of the prince rather than that of the cobbler, and would have personality traits, etc. like those of the prince, then it also seems plausible to draw Locke's conclusion and say that this person would be the prince, despite having the cobbler's body. Locke held that personal identity consists, not in the identity of any substance (whether material or immaterial) but in sameness of "consciousness". This has commonly been interpreted as meaning that personal identity is somehow definable in terms of memory: roughly, that someone now is identical to someone who existed yesterday if and only if he remembers in a certain way (from the inside, as it were), or is capable of so remembering, that person's actions and experiences. Many subsequent philosophers have developed accounts along these lines. An attraction of such accounts is that they promise to explain the privileged access we have to our own identities; for it is precisely in remembering that we have this access.

Locke's view (interpreted as a memory theory) was sharply criticized by Joseph Butler (see Perry 1975) and Thomas Reid and descendents of their criticisms continue to be influential. The best known objection is Reid's "brave officer" case: schematically, B (the brave young officer) remembers an earlier action of A (a small boy), and later on C (an old general) remembers actions of B (as a young officer) but none of A (as a small boy). Reid argues that on Locke's view C is both identical to A (for he is identical to B, who is in turn identical to A) and not identical to A (because he remembers nothing of A's actions), and thus that the view is self-contradictory. More recent versions of the memory theory avoid Reid's objection by defining personal identity in terms of "memory continuity"; roughly, the small boy stage and the old general stage in Reid's example count as stages of one and the same person, despite the lack of a direct memory link between them, because they are indirectly linked via direct memory links to intervening stages (e.g. Grice 1941, reprinted in Perry 1975). A descendant of one of Butler's objections is that the memory theory is circular, because memory must be defined in terms of personal identity: according to this, to distinguish genuine remembering from mere seeming to remember we must impose the condition that in order to remember a past event one must be identical to someone who witnessed the event at the time of its occurrence. Memory theorists have attempted to meet this objection, and similar ones, by invoking the concept of causality. There are independent reasons for holding that the remembering of a past event involves there being a causal connection between that past event and the subsequent memory impression of it (see Martin and Deutscher 1966), and it has been held that by using this requirement to distinguish between genuine remembering and mere seeming to remember, we can avoid having to invoke the notion of personal identity in making this distinction, and thus avoid the threatened circularity in the definition of personal identity in terms of memory (see Shoemaker 1970). But once we have thus invoked the notion of causality, there seems no reason to hold that the only causal connections relevant to personal identity are ones involving memory. Reflection on the "brain transfer" version of Locke's prince–cobbler case suggests that the identity of the brain recipient with the prince consists as much in the fact that his personality, interest and skills are causally due to the prince's past history (via a distinctive sort of causal chain) as in the fact that his memories are causally linked to events in the prince's past life which they represent. This would suggest that personal identity consists in a sort of "psychological continuity and connectedness" (see Parfit 1971, reprinted in Perry 1975), that is in there being such causal links between successive phases of a person's mental life, and that memory continuity is just a special (but important) case of this.

In rejecting Locke's view that personal identity is definable in terms of memory, Butler and Reid did not offer an alternative definition; on the contrary, they maintained that personal identity is indefinable. A similar view has been held by some recent writers (Chisholm 1976; Swinburne 1974). In Butler and Reid this went with the view that whereas personal identity is identity in a "strict and philosophical sense", the identity of artifacts and organisms is identity in only a "loose and popular sense". The fact that we count artifacts and organisms as the same even though they have undergone replacement of parts was taken as showing that their identity is a fiction. Locke had held that the identity of organisms and the identity of persons are analogous; in the former different parts are related by the "same life", while in the latter different parts, or different substances, are united by the "same consciousness". David Hume combined this view of Locke's, that personal identity is on a par with the identity of organisms, with the view of Butler, that the identity of organisms is not identity in the strict sense: as Hume puts it, "The identity, which we ascribe to the mind of man, is only a fictitious one, and of a like kind with that which we ascribe to vegetables and animal bodies" (*Treatise*, I, iv, 6; reprinted in Perry 1975). Hume's account of how we come to believe in the existence of personal identity stressed the causal connections that hold between the different "perceptions" we take as belonging to a single person, and to that extent he can be seen as anticipating contemporary psychological continuity accounts; but unlike proponents of such accounts, Hume thought that strictly speaking there is no genuine identity of persons over time. His reason for holding this was his belief, which modern writers on the subject are unanimous in rejecting, that genuine identity over time is incompatible with any sort of change. Hume's attack on the notion of personal identity was also an attack (and an influential one) on the notion of the self, or mind, as something over and above our fleeting "perceptions" (feelings, sensations etc.).

Recent discussion of personal identity has focussed on the special importance it seems to have for us: its links with moral notions such as those of responsibility and obligation (e.g. the fact that someone can be rightly held responsible for an action only if he is identical to the person who did it), and, what is closely connected with these, the special concern each person has for his own survival and future well being. All of this is left unexplained by the view that personal identity is indefinable, and also by the view that it consists in the identity of the body.

Some proponents of the view that personal identity consists in psychological continuity and connectedness (e.g. Parfit 1971) have tried to explain it by contending that what matters, what is really important to us, is not the identity *per se* but rather the psychological relationships that are (normally) constitutive of it. A useful case to consider in thinking about this is the (purely hypothetical) case of "fission". Let us, for example suppose that someone is about to be split into two people, each of whom will remember his past and be in other respects psychologically continuous with him. There seems to be strong reasons for denying that either of the offshoots will be him (they cannot both be him, apparently (but see Perry 1973), yet each would have as good a claim to be him as the other). Yet it seems plausible to suppose that such a person would have a "self-interested" concern for the well-being of both his offshoots, and that his offshoots, in turn, should feel responsible for his actions and feel bound to fulfill his obligations. On the other hand it is also tempting to say that the reason why it is reasonable for me to be especially concerned about the future well-being of the future person who stands in certain psychological relations to me (e.g. who will remember my life as I have experienced it) is just that that person will be me – and this would suggest that what matters is personal identity *per se*, and not the psychological relationships which supposedly constitute it. It is because of such warring intuitions that personal identity has not lost its ability to cause philosophical perplexity. SS

Bibliography

Chisholm, R. 1976: *Person and object*. La Salle, Illinois: Open Court Publishing.

Martin, C.B. and Deutscher, M. 1966: Remembering. *Philosophical review* 75.

Perry, J. 1973: Can the Self Divide? *Journal of philosophy* 69.

*———, ed. 1975: *Personal identity*. Berkeley, Los Angeles and London: University of California Press. (Contains texts by Butler, Locke and Hume and articles by Grice and Parfit cited in the text).

——— 1976: The importance of being identical. In Rorty op cit.

*———1981: Personal identity and the concept of a person: 1963–1975. In *Chronicles* vol. IV, ed. G. Fløistad. *Philosophy of mind*. Institut International De Philosophie.

Reid, T. 1969: *Essays on the intellectual powers of man*. Cambridge Mass., and London: MIT Press.

*Rorty, A., ed. 1976: *The identities of persons*. Berkeley, Los Angeles and London: University of California Press.

Shoemaker, S. 1963: *Self-knowledge and self-identity*. Ithaca, NY: Cornell University Press.

——— 1970: Persons and their pasts. *American philosophical quarterly* 7.

Swinburne, R. 1974: Personal identity. *Proceedings of the Aristotelian Society* 74.

Williams, B. 1956: Personal identity and individuation. *Proceedings of the Aristotelian Society*.

personality An individual's enduring persistent response patterns across a variety of situations. It is comprised of relatively stable patterns of action often referred to as TRAITS, dispositional tendencies, motivations, attitudes and beliefs which are combined into a more or less integrated self-structure. Personality includes the characteristics and attributes that distinguish the individual from others. Although different theoretical perspectives on personality assign different degrees of importance to genetic, social learning or broader socio-cultural elements most views consider each of these as important causal factors in the development of personality attributes. In general, most contemporary theories of personality consider both genes and environment as important formative influences in personality. Theories of personality vary according to the prominence placed on the central organizing process (e.g. self or ego) and on certain structural elements (e.g. traits, motives, drives) of personality characteristics. JMB

personality development Personality is defined as those characteristics of an individual which determine the unique adjustment he makes to his environment. Development begins at birth and continues throughout the lifespan.

Published work on the development of personality deals mainly with children. It is useful to distinguish two main approaches to this area. One emphasizes measurement at the expense of theory. A typical study uses data from assessments of the individual's personality throughout infancy or childhood in an attempt to discover regularities and continuities in development. The other approach deals mainly with the theory of personality development and systematic observation of behavior is less important. Freud's well known theory (Freud 1910) of psychosexual development is an excellent example of this type of theory.

Freud believed that instinctual forces, primarily sexual in nature, were the basis of all human behavior (see DEVELOPMENT: PSYCHOANALYTIC THEORIES). He termed these forces "libido". Libido is sexual in a very broad sense, and during infancy and early childhood libidinal energy is associated with the various orifices of the body. The first stage is associated with the mouth and is known as the *oral* stage. Freud assumed that the extent to which libidinal drives are gratified or frustrated by the environment may lead to *fixation* at that stage. This means that a disproportionate amount of libidinal energy will be invested in a particular bodily zone. Those fixated at the oral stage are expected to develop personalities which make them compulsive eaters, smokers, talkers, etc.

Following the *oral* stage is the *anal*. Freud assumed that the baby derives pleasure from the process and products of his own excretions and that this pleasure is opposed by those who socialize him. If fixation occurs at this period, Freud expected that the child would develop later problems with relationships to authority and the need for self control. The third stage is called *phallic*. Here, the child is said to engage in specifically sexual play and to show sexual curiosity. It shades into the final or *genital* stage of early psychosexual development. During this stage, the boy's feelings and fantasies toward his mother (the primary libidinal object from the beginning) assume a specifically sexual character. (See OEDIPUS COMPLEX.) According to Freud, this is a very important period for children from both sexes because many anxieties and conflicts have to be dealt with. Freud claimed that most of the individual's later patterns of traits and defenses are determined by the particular ways in which the genital conflicts are resolved.

Freud, therefore, saw personality as fully developed or at least determined by about the age of four years. His critics often reject this view and, in addition, point out that he overinterpreted as universal and instinctual certain aspects of human nature which were specific to the time and place in which he worked. Even modern theorists generally sympathetic to his views have almost rejected the emphasis on sexual drives and paid more attention to the social and interpersonal aspects of personality development. Erikson (1963) and Sullivan (1953) are both influential theorists of the psychoanalytic school who constantly stress interpersonal relationships across the individual's lifespan as determining the capacity for other personal adjustment and development. Nevertheless, four characteristics of Freud's theory have persisted and influenced modern work on personality development. Firstly, interaction with a social environment is necessary for each successive stage to unfold. Secondly, adult personality is largely a function of interactions likely to occur within a nuclear family. Thirdly, early personality development often occurs as a resolution of internal conflicts and is likely to be unobservable (and therefore difficult for the behaviorist to "understand"). Fourthly, events in early childhood determine personality to a greater extent than do later events.

Observational studies, as mentioned earlier, lay little stress on theory and seek instead to sample the activities of individuals (usually from birth) with the object of discovering regularities and continuities in personality. There is a limited range of activities engaged in by the newborn but observations have been made of the frequencies of sucking and crying and on the lengths of periods of sleep and wakefulness. (Korner et al. 1981.) Such observations are made of the same children at regular intervals. Results suggest that most individuals show an unstable pattern of behavior in early life (0–6 months) and only moderately stable patterns thereafter (Thomas et al. 1963). The extent to which these inconsistencies are due simply to problems of measurement is not clear. There are obviously problems both in sampling individual behavior properly and in relating behavior in infancy to later behavior (Nunally 1973). Despite these problems certain consistencies have been found. Some of the main discoveries are that (a) locomotor activity level is moderately consistent in infancy and childhood and there is a link between high activity and lack of self control in adulthood (Escalona and Heider 1959); (b) passivity and submissiveness tend to be consistent characteristics (Honzik 1964); (c) dominance is a consistent characteristic during childhood and adolescence (Bronson 1967). Other longitudinal studies (e.g. Kagan 1960) for age periods from infancy to twenty years indicate that individuals tend to have a consistent approach to social situations. At the same time, there are instances in these and other longitudinal studies which show that personality development involves large and abrupt adjustments to the environment. Many personality traits seem not to be fixed in the individual but changeable throughout the life-span.

Although it is interesting simply to describe and to assess personality, it is also important to try and specify its origins and the causes of permanence and change. Efforts have been made to determine the extent to which personality characteristics are inherited. Such studies of inheritance have not met with conspicuous success either in identifying the traits most likely to be inherited or the degree to which any such traits are inherited. Research into the personalities of monozygotic and dizygotic twins (e.g. Goldsmith and Gottesman 1981) yield moderate estimates of the heritability of "extraversion", "anxiety", "persistence" and "fearfulness". However, because twin data are used, even these moderate heritabilities are likely to be overestimates. This evidence that personality traits owe little to inheritance probably goes against popular belief. Prenatal experience is another variable which is widely expected to influence personality development. Yet, here again the data are poor and no clear trends can be reported.

The best researched and most fruitful investigations into the causes of individual personality development are concerned with the impact of specific early experiences. Most work here has been done in an attempt to refine the statements of Bowlby (1951) on maternal deprivation in early infancy. In his widely quoted and influential book, Bowlby declared that "mother love in infancy and childhood is as important for mental health as are vitamins and proteins for physical health". Bowlby and others offer evidence that a child deprived of proper mothering in the first two years of life will be poorly adjusted psychologically and be unable to develop close affectional ties with others.

Bowlby's body of evidence has been carefully dissected during the past twenty years (Rutter 1981). Bowlby (heavily influenced by Freud) appears to have exaggerated the irreversibility of deprivations in infancy and early childhood. Although infantile experiences are still held to be important, the efforts of early deprivations of attachment can be reversed if opportunities for long term attachments are offered in childhood and adolescence. Furthermore, experiences at all ages can probably have a profound influence on personality development. However, there is a shortage of evidence available on adult personality development and thus it is not yet possible to evaluate this idea fully. That work which has been done certainly does not suggest that personality is ever fixed from one period to another (see, for example, Neiner and Owens 1982).

Our grasp of this area is still tentative. Nevertheless, certain basic facts are emerging. These are:

(1) The organization of personality into traits probably takes place after birth: evidence for the heritability of global and organized characteristics is poor.

(2) Individual differences in personality and its development are strongly influenced by the processes of caretaking and socialization.

(3) Many personality characteristics develop as a result of internal psychological conflicts which are unobservable.

(4) Later socialization experiences, even those in adulthood, can greatly modify earlier trends. Early experience is not as fundamental to the later course of personality development as was once thought.

RMCH

Bibliography

Bowlby, J. 1951: *Maternal care and mental health.* World Health Organization, Geneva.

Bronson, G.W. 1967: Adult derivatives of emotional expressiveness and reactivity control: developmental continuities from childhood to adulthood. *Child Development* 38, 801–18.

*Clarke, A.M. and Clarke, A.D.B. 1976: *Early experience: myth and evidence.* London: Open Books.

*Erikson, E.H. 1963: *Childhood and society* 2nd edn. New York: Norton.

Escalona, S.K. and Heider, G.M. 1959: *Prediction and outcome.* New York: Basic Books.

Freud, S. 1910: Infantile sexuality. Three contributions to the sexual theory. *Nervous and mental disease monographs*, no. 7.

Goldsmith, H.H. and Gottesman, I.I. 1981: Origins of variation in behavioral style: longitudinal study of temperament in young twins. *Child development* 52, 91–103.

Honzik, M.D. 1964: Personality consistency and change: some comments on papers by Bayley, Macfarlane, Moss, Kagan and Murphy. *Vita humana* 7, 139–42.

Kagan, J. 1960: The long term stability of selected Rorschach responses. *Journal of consultational psychology* 24, 67–73.

Korner, A.F., Hutchinson, C.A., Koperski, J.A., Kraemer, H.C. and Schneider, P.A. 1981: Stability of individual differences of neonatal motor and crying patterns. *Child development* 52, 83–90.

Neiner, A.G. and Owens, W.A. 1982: Relationships between two sets of biodata with 7 years separation. *Journal of applied psychology* 67, 146–50.

Nunally, J.M. 1973: Research strategies and measurement methods for investigating human development. In *Life-span developmental psychology: methodological issues*, ed. J.R. Nesselroade and H.W. Reese. New York: Academic Press.

*Rutter, M. 1981: *Maternal deprivation reassessed.* 2nd edn. Harmondsworth and New York: Penguin.

Sullivan, W.S. 1953: *The interpersonal theory of psychiatry.* New York: Norton.

Thomas, A. et al. 1963: *Behavioral individuality in early childhood.* New York: New York University Press.

personality disorders The term implies a variation from the average in the enduring characteristics of personality to an extent that causes the patient or other people distress or difficulty. It is usually recognizable by adolescence but may become less obvious in middle or old age. The disorder may affect all aspects of personality in one or more of its components. It is essential to distinguish this psychiatric category from mere abnormality of personality in the sense of any variation, favorable or unfavorable, from the average (see Schneider 1950). Just as it is difficult to make a distinction between normal and abnormal it is difficult to classify types of personality disorder in terms of a restricted number of categories. Two main approaches have been used. The first is a purely descriptive typology using terms such as aggressive or inadequate. The second also implies etiology for it defines the abnormal personality by reference to a syndrome of illness which it partially resembles. For example, schizoid personalities (who are eccentric, socially withdrawn and lack emotional rapport) are so called because of a supposed relationship to schizophrenia. In clinical practice it is often preferable to describe personality traits in a sentence or two rather than to attempt to fit patients in to a limited series of personality types.

The most useful descriptions of the most generally recognized types of personality disorder are those in the ninth edition of the International Classification of Disease (WHO 1978). Unfortunately, however, these incoporate both the descriptive and the etiological approach in its nomenclature and descriptions. There are eight main categories.

Paranoid: in which there is excessive sensitiveness to setbacks or to what are taken to be humiliations and rebuffs, a tendency to distort experience by misconstruing the neutral or friendly actions of others as hostile or contemptuous, and a combative and tenacious sense of personal rights. There may be a proneness to jealousy or excessive self-importance. Such persons may feel helplessly humiliated and put upon; others, likewise excessively sensitive, are aggressive and insistent. In all cases there is excessive self-reference.

Affective: characterized by lifelong predominance of a pronounced mood which may be persistently depressive, persistently elated, or alternately one then the other. During periods of elation there is unshakeable optimism and an enhanced zest for life and activity, whereas periods of depression are marked by worry, pessimism, low output of energy and a sense of futility.

Schizoid: in which there is withdrawal from affectional, social and other contacts with autistic preference for fantasy and introspective reserve. Behavior may be slightly eccentric or indicate avoidance of competitive situations. Apparent coolness and detachment may mask an incapacity to express feeling.

Anankastic (obsessional): characterized by feelings of personal insecurity, doubt and incompleteness leading to excessive conscientiousness, checking, stubborness and caution. There may be insistent and unwelcome thoughts or impulses which do not attain the severity of an obsessional neurosis. There is perfectionism and meticulous accuracy and a need to check repeatedly in an attempt to ensure this. Rigidity and excessive doubt may be conspicuous.

Hysterical (histrionic): characterized by shallow, labile affect, dependence on others, craving for appreciation and attention, suggestibility and theatricality. There is often sexual immaturity, e.g. frigidity and over-responsiveness to stimuli. Under stress hysterical symptoms (neurosis) may develop.

Asthenic (dependent, inadequate): characterized by passive compliance with the wishes of elders and others and a weak inadequate response to the demands of daily life. Lack of vigor may show itself in the intellectual or emotional spheres; there is little capacity for enjoyment.

Personality disorder with predominantly sociopathic or asocial manifestation: characterized by disregard for social obligations, lack of feeling for others, and impetuous violence or callous unconcern. There is a gross disparity between behavior and the prevailing social norms. Behavior is not readily modifiable by experience, including punishment. People with this personality are often affectively cold and may be abnormally aggressive or irresponsible. Their tolerance of frustration is low. They blame others or offer plausible rationalizations for the behavior which brings them into conflict with society (see PSYCHOPATHIC PERSONALITY; SOCIOPATHIC PERSONALITY).

Explosive: characterized by lability of mood with liability to outbursts of anger, hate, violence or affection. Aggression may be expressed in words or in physical violence. The outbursts cannot be readily controlled by the affected person, who is not otherwise prone to antisocial behavior.

The current American classification, Diagnostic and Statistic Manual III (American Psychiatric Association, 1980) includes further categories, such as the schizotypical, borderline, narcissistic, avoidant and passive aggressive. The first two of these are derived from the various descriptions of the so called borderline syndrome (see BORDERLINE STATE).

Since rather little is known about factors accounting for normal variations in personality it is unsurprising that the causes of personality disorder are poorly understood. Psychopathic personality has been studied in greater detail than any other sub-type. Adequate prospective research is made difficult by the need for a very prolonged follow-up after the events in early life that are potentially relevant. There is some evidence both that genetic influences are determinants of childhood temperament and adult traits and also that the quality of adult social relationships depends upon early experience (Rutter 1981). Psychoanalytic and other psychodynamic theories have proposed detailed explanations of the development of personality (see Neal 1971).

The definition of personality disorder implies that they are life long. However, clinical impression suggests that abnormalities may become rather less severe with age. Aggressive behavior, for instance, is much less common after the age of forty years but other difficulties in relationships are more persistent. Although potential for personality change is small, after early adult life many people are able to modify their social circumstances so as to find a way of life to which they suited and in which there is less likelihood of distress for themselves and other people.

There are two main approaches to treatment. First an attempt to change personality, secondly a more modest attempt to help people to adjust their lives in ways which would provide greater satisfaction and fewer conflicts and problems. The former aim usually requires PSYCHOTHERAPY and is easier in those who are younger and whose personalities are less clearly fixed. Success depends upon motivation and an adequate degree of insight and may require prolonged treatment. It is usually much easier and also more appropriate to concentrate on helping the patient to decide how to improve his or her social circumstances. The most severely handicapped may require support and encouragement over a very prolonged period. RAM

Bibliography

American Psychiatric Association 1980: *Diagnostic and statistical manual* III.

*Kaplan, H.I., Freedman and Sadock, B.J. 1980: *Comprehensive textbook of psychiatry*. 3rd edn. Baltimore: Williams & Wilkins.

Neal, A. 1971: *Theories of psychology: a handbook*. London: University of London Press.

Rutter, M. 1981: *Maternal deprivation reassessed*. 2nd edn. Harmondsworth and New York: Penguin.

Schneider 1930: *Psychopathic personality*. 9th edn. Vienna: F. Derlicke.

World Health Organisation 1978: *Mental Disorders: Glossary and guide to their classification in accordance with the Ninth Revision of the International Classification of Diseases*. Geneva: WHO.

personality labeling *See* sociopathic personality

personality psychology *See* Marxist personality psychology

personality research: methodology Personality research is the study of the structure of a person's thoughts, feelings and behavior. The methods of inquiry must meet the criteria of objectivity, reliability and validity.

The information gathering methods in personality research include naturalistic observation; content analysis; interview, questionnaires and photography; personality tests, including the assessment of the biopsychological system; and the experimental method. Since human subjects are involved in the research ethical and moral considerations involving the rights, safety and comfort of the potential subjects must be scrutinized (see American Psychological Association, Committee on Ethical Standards in Psychological Research 1973).

Naturalistic observation
Systematic observation in everyday settings is particularly useful in the exploratory phase of inquiry. Darwin (1936) devoted five years to the careful, detailed field observations of thousands of plants and animals during the preparation of *The Origin of Species*. Similarly, Sigmund Freud, who was greatly influenced by Darwin, spent years observing a wide range of behavior, dreams, fantasies, physical illnesses and emotional difficulties which led to insights into individual behavior and provided clues to the structure and function of personality in general.

Observations in natural settings do not distort life as laboratory observation may and do not require the subject to have descriptive skills or even assume that he or she is willing to respond. However, the approach cannot control irrelevant variables or use precise measures. Precision can be improved, however, through the use of trained reliable observers, unbiassed recording techniques (see Bales 1950), the development of coding techniques which focus on critical behavior, and sampling behavior across time.

Variations of the approach include the phenomenological technique where the subjects themselves record observations from their own point of view, and indirect studies of non-verbal behavior (including smiles, nods, and posture, but also choice of bumper stickers or room decorations).

Content analysis Content analysis also involves categorizing behavior, specifically oral and written communications, including conversations, speeches, diaries, photograph albums, recorded fantasies and even archival materials such as census reports and crime statistics. As in naturalistic observations, the subjects need not be aware of the analysis. For example, Winter (1976) analysed the announcements and speeches of several 1976 presidential candidates for various components of motivation such as achievement, affiliation and need for power. The procedure involves the selection of the material to be analysed, the type of communication whose content is to be analysed, selecting the unit of analysis such as word, sentence, or paragraph, categorizing the units of analysis such as the use of "I" or "we" as indicating self as opposed to other orientations and finally summarizing the information through quantification such as the relative length of speeches of political candidates.

Interviews, Questionnaries and Photography
These approaches involve systematically asking people about themselves. Interviews are probably most useful when we are interested in learning about someone's thoughts, feelings and goals. The process consists of the following steps: (1) formulating objectives; (2) deciding on a format, developing questions; (3) conducting pilot tests with preliminary instruments, and (4) revising and refining the instruments.

The process may also involve the use of non-verbal responses such as asking the subject to take a set of photographs which reveal something about him or her (Ziller 1981) followed by open-ended questions about the meaning of the photographs and a content analysis of them. Two of the major concerns of the interview approach are motivating persons to participate and avoiding bias through the nature of the questions.

Questionnaires, when administered anonymously, can evoke a greater degree of honesty than the face-to-face interview, though responses may be colored by the respondents' attempt to present themselves favorably and are subject to error of response sets such as stylistic tendencies to agree or disagree regardless of the nature of the question (see QUESTIONNAIRES).

Questionnaires may be open-ended or closed. For example, an open-ended question may ask "What does the 'good life' mean to you?" A closed questionnaire presents a series of alternative responses from which the respondent selects.

The investigator often sets out to demonstrate a relationship between variables. For example, a relationship between a child's self-esteem as measured by a personality test may be related to reading achievement in the first grade. Instruments designed to measure facets of personality are involved in most personality research. These may include the assessment of life history, biopsychological assessment, behavioral approaches to assessment, objective and projective techniques and the assessment of cognitive abilities and competence.

The assessment of life history is essentially the case study approach. Biopsychological assessment concerns the relation of bodily characteristics to personality. How do our daily cycles of bodily functioning effect our behavior; what are the effects of drugs on behavior; how is behavior related to the dominance of the left or right brain hemisphere? In investigating these areas the researcher has recourse to a vast array of equipment and techniques such as the electroencephalograph (EEG) which records "brain wave" rhythms or the polygraph, popularly known as the "lie detector" which along with measures of changes in the galvanic skin response, respiration, blood pressure and heart rate may be used to study reactions to stress.

In the behavioral approaches to assessment, observers record a person's behavior. For example, interactions within the family of a delinquent child are recorded with a specific emphasis on aversive statements or negative remarks directed at the child. Observations are made over a one-month period to establish the "baseline" of behavior which is to be changed in order to facilitate an atmosphere conducive to personal growth and development.

In objective techniques of personality "the subject does not know on what aspect of his behavior he is really being evaluated" (Cattell 1965). In addition to the polygraph these have included reduction of exploratory behavior in response to electric shock, measures of fatigue on motor tasks (Eysenck's pursuit rotor), and various perceptual tests, such as picture completion tasks or the rod-and-frame test (see Witkin 1967). Scores on such tests, or batteries of them, are claimed to correlate with personality traits or factors as measured by other means.

Projective techniques are more disguised and ambiguous procedures using a wide variety of stimuli and evoking a variety of responses. The technique derives from psychoanalytic theory and requires the interpreter to view the results as a sign of underlying personality dynamics. The Rorschach has been the most widely used projective technique. It requires the subject to describe various ink blots in terms of what he or she sees. Its validity has been questioned.

Finally, intellectual activities are involved in the assessment of cognitive abilities and competence, as they are in intelligence tests. The fundamental difference between the experimental method and the case study is that the experimental method permits researchers to manipulate and influence a given (independent) variable while observing changes in a second (dependent) variable. It is thought that there may be a causal connection between the independent and dependent variables, but causes are difficult to identify clearly. They must be demonstrated beyond reasonable doubt, and this cannot be achieved by other approaches to the same extent as it can in the experimental approach. It is necessary to include controls, which ensure that the changes in the dependent variable are actually associated with the independent variable and not produced by some other variable which was not even considered, let alone controlled for. For example, in examining the association between the personality of judges and their sentencing, it is necessary to control for such variables as the length of time the judge has been on the bench and the size of the community.

In laboratory experiments subjects are assigned to the two experimental conditions on the basis of chance to eliminate the possible effect of extraneous factors. Other approaches to the control of extraneous variables include holding the conditions constant across experimental groups, for instance, by using the same instructions and even tape recording them. More than one independent variable can be studied in the same experiment. For example, in examining the association between physical attractiveness and the way subjects present themselves to others it improves the design to include a measure of self-complexity because complex-attractive women may be expected to present themselves in a way very different from simplex-attractive women. Similarly attractive and less attractive women may present themselves differently in different settings such as social or task settings. Here two contrasting settings may be included in the design along with the independent variable of attractiveness (high, low) and interactions between these independent variables may be shown by statistical techniques such as analysis of variance. In this case the inclusion of setting takes into account the person-environment interaction. RCZ

Bibliography

Bales, R.F. 1950: *Interaction process analysis.* Cambridge, Mass.: Addison-Wesley.

Cattell, R.B. 1965: *The scientific analysis of personality.* Harmondsworth: Penguin.

Darwin, C. 1858 *(1936)*: *The origin of species.* New York: Random House.

Sundberg, N.D. 1977: *The assessment of persons.* Englewood Cliffs, N.J.: Prentice-Hall.

Winter, D.G. 1976: What makes the candidates run? *Psychology today* 10.

Witkin, H.A. 1967: Cognitive studies across cultures. *International journal of psychology* 2(4).

Ziller, R.C. 1981: Self, social, environmental orientation through auto-photography. *Personality and social psychology bulletin* 7, 338–43.

personality tests *See* tests, personality

personality theory, psychoanalytical There are two main strands to personality theory in the Freudian tradition, and the relation between them still poses problems. One is a "dynamic" theory of an instinctual drive whose satisfaction or frustration at different stages of a child's development gives rise to particular TRAITS or dispositions; the other is a "structural" description of how various mental functions are organized and interact.

(i) Personality is shaped by the way in which a person deals with instinctual drives, and with the anxieties associated with them. This part of the theory is about the form taken by those drives (known as "libido") and by the anxiety produced when libido is blocked, and about the DEFENSE MECHANISMS used by the EGO to reduce psychic tension and preserve a balance of forces consistent with adaptive action. Libido is satisfied or discharged mainly through bodily pleasure associated with the meeting of biological needs; it is therefore "sexual" in Freud's revised technical sense of "obtaining pleasure from zones of the body" (1938; *SE*, p.152). But since successful ego-functioning is necessary for some pleasures to be possible, such as self-preservation and self-esteem, the ego must have its own instinctual energy which is known as "narcissistic libido" (see NARCISSISM). The process by which an instinct latches onto an appropriate object, whether material or psychological, as a medium for its discharge, is "cathexis"; so that a person, place, activity etc. which has become a source of pleasure is said to have been "cathected" or invested with libido. Obstruction of cathexis, and hence of libidinal discharge, produces tension which is experienced as anxiety, unless the libido can be "displaced" onto a substitute object serving the same purpose. Displacement onto abstract, intellectual or cultural–aesthetic objects is called SUBLIMATION.

In the course of normal psychological development, libido is concentrated successively on different zones of the body, and its satisfaction or frustration at each stage is accompanied by particular emotional reactions. Those that are particularly intense or preponderant become consolidated as habitual dispositions. Too much of either satisfaction or frustration at a particular stage may lead to libido becoming "fixated" there, so that personality is dominated by the traits associated with that level and psychosexual maturity is not achieved. The young baby's emotional gratification centers on oral activities such as sucking, swallowing, spitting and biting. The first two of these responses mediate pleasure, acceptance, security and affection, and are conducive to an attitude of "basic trust" (Erikson 1963, ch.7): the latter two express rejection, hurtfulness and destructiveness, characteristic of "basic mistrust". The question whether traits allegedly arising from oral satisfaction (e.g. optimism, generosity, tolerance) do cluster together, and separately from those attributed to oral frustration (e.g. jealousy, impatience, hostility), has been statistically analysed by Kline and Storey who demonstrated two separate factors, "oral optimism" and "oral pessimism", closely resembling Erikson's trust and mistrust above (Kline 1981, pp.41-6).

At the time of toilet-training, libido is focussed on the anal zone and its processes, and this is when the infant "is first obliged to exchange pleasure for social respectability" (Freud 1917; *SE* 16, p.315). Tension-reduction must be confined to approved times and places; and this learning of impulse-control is a seed of ego-development. The issues are retention–release, giving–withholding, mess–cleanliness, obstinacy–flexibility, approval–shame. The significant grouping of associated traits known as the anal triad (orderliness, meanness and obstinacy – Freud 1905; *SE* 7) has also been confirmed statistically (Kline 1981, ch.3).

From about the fourth year, the phallic part of the genitalia, i.e. penis or clitoris, becomes the focal zone, representing for the child physical prowess, competence and worth (or their apparent absence). Necessarily the theory diverges for the sexes, and it also asserts that the child's feelings about parents are now intensified in the OEDIPUS AND ELEKTRA COMPLEXES whose dominant anxieties are castration-fear and penis-envy. Associated phallic personality features are recklessness, self-confidence and courage, but these have not been validated in the way oral and anal traits have. But the existence of a latency period, between the oedipal stage and pre-puberty, in which sexual and aggressive fantasies are relatively dormant, has been given some support by Friedman (Kline 1981, p.134).

The final genital phase is characterized by a move away from mere self-satisfaction toward a pleasure-giving relationship with an opposite-sex partner, with the aim of reproduction. Psychological correlates are group activities, social awareness and constructive and protective schemes. The relative security and dominance of this stage in the mature personality depends upon how much libido has been shed at the pregenital stages, like troops left behind to fortify precarious positions (in Freud's own simile, 1917; SE 16, p.341). The stage at which the strongest force was left is that to which a person most readily "regresses" under stress (see DEFENSE MECHANISMS).

(ii) From the structural point of view (Freud 1923; *SE* vol. 19), the mental apparatus is seen as made up of three main systems: ID, EGO and SUPEREGO. The concept of an "id" *(das Es)* was borrowed immediately from Groddeck (1923), but has a longer history as a murky, mysterious and sinister realm of the mind. For Freud it is specifically the reservoir of biological instincts and primitive emotions which press non-rationally for gratification according to the pleasure-principle. It forms a major part of the UNCONSCIOUS MIND. The ego, by contrast is rational and realistic, and has developed out of the id as the young child learns to delay and adapt his demands in the light of physical and social realities (chewing before swallowing, waiting for the potty before defecating). It is the ego that checks whether and how satisfaction of a particular wish, fantasy or impulse would be consistent with reality-constraints ("reality-testing"), and to do this it is equipped with "perceptual-consciousness". Freud had realized, some thirty years before PAVLOV, that early reality-learning is achieved especially through auditory verbal CONDITIONING, and therefore gave the ego a "hearing-cap" (i.e. an auditory lobe) in his notorious diagram (1923; SE 19, p.24). The extent to which a person can "keep his head" and regulate his actions adaptively on the basis of perception, learning and memory, even when under emotional pressure, is consequently called "ego strength" and has been independently confirmed as a valid personality trait by Cattell (1965, pp.71–5).

Behavior is checked and steered not only by reality factors but also by evaluative considerations as to what actions, thoughts, feelings etc. are good, bad, right and wrong. This is the work of the superego. A process fundamental to the formation of both ego and superego is "identification". In "primary identification", which predates the ego developmentally, the neonate does not distinguish perceptions of himself from perceptions of the mother, and in that sense is identified with her. But "secondary identification", which presupposes individuation and a sense of separate objects, refers to building into one's own personality, for some emotional reason, the perceived characteristics of another. In "goal-oriented" identification, it is done in order to gain for oneself the pleasure that the other has from that characteristic; it has something in common with "projective identification" in Kleinian theory (Segal 1979). Thus a person might dress or talk in the same way as another who is perceived as happier, cleverer, more attractive, stronger etc. (For "object-loss identification" and "identification with aggressor", see EGO IDEAL and SUPEREGO.)

(iii) Personality is also described in psychoanalysis by

reference to clinical conditions whose features or dynamics a personality shows on a small scale without being clinically disturbed (because those dynamics are under "ego-control"). An obsessional personality takes pleasure in (i.e. has "cathected") precision, orderliness, rules, regularity, cleanliness, safety, punctuality etc., and is irritated by their absence. But that person's general psychological functioning is not disrupted by washing-rituals or by catastrophic anxiety about untidiness, as in an obsessional illness. The same goes for "depressive", "hysterical', "paranoid" and "schizoid" personality (see also CONSTITUTIONAL PSYCHOLOGY).

Non-orthodox followers in the broad Freudian tradition have gone in two contrasted directions: whereas the Kleinians have placed even greater emphasis on very early sexual-aggressive phantasies in infants, the NEO-FREUDIANS have held that Freud exaggerated the part played by early instinctual factors in personality development, and have given more weight to the ego's role both in shaping personality through later social learning and in overcoming emotional problems in therapy.

As a result of applying psychoanalytic principles to the therapeutic interpretation of young children's play, Melanie Klein produced an account of personality development in which emotional "object-relations", and especially unconscious phantasies about them, are crucially formative from the earliest months (Segal 1979). The infant conceives of the source of pleasurable experiences as separate from that of unpleasant ones, and therefore constructs in phantasy a good and a bad object. He loves and takes in (incorporates) emotionally the "good" object, but rejects and attacks the "bad" one; but he also fears that the one he hates and attacks will attack him back. Here we have the basis of "schizoid" (splitting) and "paranoid" dynamics, and the infant is in the "paranoid-schizoid position". But half-way through the first year, the baby realizes that the objects of his love and hate are not two but one and the same, so that he is after all attacking and destroying the one he loves. Guilt and the "depressive position" set in. From this he emerges only by recognizing that he can make up for the hurt he is causing the loved object by acts of "reparation" such as cooperating with toileting. On this view, personality is determined by the quality of these object-relations, and by the anxieties and fantasies they arouse, and personality structure is understood as an "inner world" of internalized objects whose qualities and relationships a person tends to "project" more or less appropriately onto the outside world in which he lives.

(iv) Two contemporaries of Freud whose personality theories also diverged from his were Carl Jung and Alfred Adler. Both rejected Freud's picture of childhood sexuality, but Jung retained the notion of libido as a general psychological life-force while Adler substituted a kind of will-to-power as the basic motivating drive.

Jung elaborated the theory that there are two constitutionally determined "psychological types": introvert and extrovert. In the former, the libido is mainly turned inward upon the person's thoughts, feelings, plans, imagination; in the latter, it is turned outward via perception to the material world and other people (Jung 1921). There are, therefore, in the manifest personality (known as the personal) two sets of traits which characterize the two types in descriptive behavioral terms. The introvert tends to be reflective, cautious, solitary, emotionally reserved and controlled, while the extrovert is more active, emotionally spontaneous, confident and impulsive. The validity of the behavioral distinction is experimentally endorsed by Eysenck (1967). For Jung, as for Freud, the libido passes through maturational stages in childhood; however such stages are concerned with feelings about growth and are given much less importance. There is also a "dark" side of the personality, known as the "shadow", which inhabits the "personal unconscious" and consists of uncivilized wishes, feelings and images rejected from the persona. At a still deeper level there is an unconscious counterpart to a person's dominant sexual identity: for a man the "anima", for a woman the "animus" (see DREAM THEORIES). Apart from the difference of "types", personality differences depend upon which of the four "functions" – thought, feeling, intuition and sensation – a person uses predominantly to relate adaptively to the world.

Since for Adler the basic motivating drive is a wish to be powerful, dominant and superior to others, it follows that the fundamental source of anxiety is feelings of inferiority; and that personality-characteristics are formed by situations and perceptions which induce such feelings, and by the defense mechanisms used to combat them. Reality-factors which induce anxiety will therefore include actual physical limitations, such as poor eyesight, speech-defect, conspicuous nose, short stature, and these are said to give rise to "organ-inferiority". Intellectual, social and emotional inadequacies (as well, of course, as imagined limitations) can similarly become the focus of inferiority-feelings. A person may give in to these feelings by becoming over-dependent and a "chronic complainer", or he may compensate by striving to demonstrate power in other areas.

Everybody experiences as a child the reality of being inferior, both physically and psychologically, so the structure of the "family-constellation" is a fundamental determinant of personality. The eldest child, for example, although for a while physically and mentally superior to his or her siblings, is inferior to the parents and will have had the unsettling experience of being "dethroned" from exclusive possession of the parents by the next-born. This tends to encourage early identification with adults, and (in theory) a mature, conservative, independent personality. The last-born is inferior on all sides, and is therefore the most likely candidate for a "chronic complainer" or for intense, potency-demonstrating compensation. A typical youngest-male fantasy is that one day he will have the rest of the family at his mercy, so that they are dependent upon him. For Adler the biblical story of Joseph and the many-colored coat is an example of just such a fantasy having passed into legend (Adler 1928, ch. 5 and 8). Much subsequent empirical research has confirmed the influence of birth-rank and family-size, but the latter is perhaps more important than the former; and, although Adler seems to have been right about the conservatism and caution of first-borns in relevant cultures, he was wrong about their emotional independence (Schachter 1957; Grinder, 1978, pp.259–63). NMC

Bibliography

Adler, Alfred 1928: *Understanding human nature.* Trans. W.B. Wolfe. London: Allen & Unwin.

*Brown, James A.C. 1961: *Freud and the post-Freudians.* Harmondsworth: Penguin.

Cattell, Raymond B. 1965: *The scientific analysis of personality.* Harmondsworth: Penguin.

Erikson, Erik H. 1963: *Childhood and society.* 2nd edn. Harmondsworth: Penguin.

Eysenck, Hans J. 1967: *The biological basis of personality.* Springfield, Ill.: Thomas.

Freud, Sigmund 1895–1938: *Standard edition of the complete psychological works of Sigmund Freud.* (24 vols.). London: Hogarth Press; New York: Norton. Referred to as *SE*.

Grinder, Robert E. 1978: *Adolescence.* 2nd. ed. New York: Wiley.

Groddeck, George W. 1923 *(1949)*: *The book of the Id.* (Trans. V.M.E. Collins). London: Vision Press.

Jung, Carl G. 1921 *(1971)*: *Psychological types.* Trans. H.G. Baynes. London: Routledge & Kegan Paul.

Kline, Paul 1981: *Fact and fantasy in Freudian theory.* 2nd edn. London and New York: Methuen.

Schachter, Stanley 1957: *The psychology of affiliation.* London: Tavistock.

Segal, Hannah 1979: *Klein.* London: Fontana.

*Storr, Anthony 1960: *Integrity of the personality.* London: Heinemann.

personality theory and astrology Astrology provides some of the earliest personality theories, with origins dating back to pre-historic times. Today we have an abundance of overlapping and even contradictory theories which link the positions of the sun, moon and planets at the moment of our birth with character development and destiny. With regard to the signs of the zodiac, the first positive demonstration that there might be some truth in the claimed link between the cosmos and life on earth came using a conventional personality questionnaire. With a sample of over 2,000 people, it was found that outgoing extraverted types tended to be born during the odd-numbered signs (such as Aries) while reserved introverted types tended to be born during the even-numbered signs (such as Taurus). This finding was consistent with the astrological personality descriptions laid down by ancient Greek astrologers. Subsequent research, however, has indicated that the results were due to a self-fulfilling prophecy. People answering a questionnaire tend to be influenced by their knowledge of astrology; a person born during Aries is more likely to endorse such questions as, "are you bold and energetic?" if he happens to know that these attributes are traditionally associated with Aries. The hypothesized link between signs of the zodiac and personality is not apparent when research subjects are carefully screened for knowledge of astrology. Other claims of astrology have been investigated by numerous researchers, the most noteworthy being Geoffrey Dean, and almost without exception the claims are found to be false or at best, not proven.

The strongest support for astrology has emerged from the work of the French psychologist, Michel Gauquelin, who discovered that many eminent people had been born when one of the major planets was just above the horizon or just past the point of upper culmination. For famous actors it was Jupiter, for celebrated scientists Saturn, and for international sportsmen Mars. The sports finding has been the subject of independent research. For each group studied, and there are now five sets of samples ranging from 100 to 1,500 sportsmen, the results are similar. The combined probability that such a pattern is due to chance is many millions to one against. Research has also revealed that it is eminent people with personalities typical of their profession who are most likely to have been born "under" the astrologically appropriate planet. Independent ratings of personality descriptions taken from their biographies show that those with predominantly extraverted traits tend to be born "under" Mars or Jupiter while introverted types tend to be born "under" Saturn. In general, these findings are consistent with ancient Greek astrology: Mars as the god of war is associated with bold and assertive traits, Jupiter with joviality and Saturn with a saturnine temperament.

The evidence for this obtained link between planetary positions at the moment of birth and personality has been rigorously checked and evaluated, so far without any flaws being detected. The findings cannot be explained in terms of knowledge of astrology and self-fulfilling prophecies since very few people know the positions of the planets at the moment they were born. We are left with evidence of planetary effects, for which chance is a highly unlikely explanation, and for which there is no known physical or causal mechanism. As in the case of extra-sensory perception, psychokinesis and other apparently demonstrable para-normal phenomena, the effects are at present outside the realm of scientific possibility. DKBN

Bibliography

Dean, G.A. et al. 1977: *Recent advances in natal astrology.* UK: Recent Advances, 36 Tweedy Road, Bromley, Kent; USA: Para Research, Rockport, Mass.

Eysenck, H.J. and Nias, D.K.B. 1982: *Astrology: science or superstition?* London: Temple Smith; New York: St. Martin's.

personality theory *See above, and also* phenomenology in psychology

personality types *See* authoritarian p.; extroversion

personnel selection A field of application and research in human resource management and industrial psychology. From an organization's perspective, identifying and hiring the best qualified and most productive individuals is the central goal of personnel selection. From the individual's perspective, finding the most satisfactory position is the central question. Laws differ greatly from country to country with regard to the prerogatives of employers and employees. Yet in every case selection, hiring and placement decisions are extremely important. This is especially clear where law or custom provides for lifelong employment.

In many organizations selection decisions are made subjectively by one or a few managers. Larger organizations will have more sophisticated procedures which might include standardized aptitude, ability or achievement tests, work sample tests, simulations, standardized interviews (see INTERVIEWING), ASSESSMENT CENTERS, reference checks, medical examinations and other procedures.

Development of a formal selection and placement program begins with an analysis of the tasks and duties to be performed on a job (see TASK ANALYSIS). The content of the job serves as the basis for all elements of a personnel management system, ranging from compensation procedures to orientation, training and development programs. In the case of selection and placement, job content serves as the basis for a job description used in advertising and recruiting for the position; inferences about the skills, abilities, knowledge or other characteristics that are required to perform the work effectively; the identification of predictors such as tests, simulations and other measures; the development of validation criteria and of information for providing realistic job previews. In addition, job content serves as the basis for comparing jobs with each other – an activity needed both for classifying jobs into an occupational structure and also for aiding the placement of individuals in jobs that maximize the match between job requirements and personal qualifications across the organization.

Job content clearly plays a dominant role in the creation of a reliable and equitable selection and placement program. There are many other important factors as well. Three factors which combine to determine the utility or economic impact of a selection program are the proportion of applicants who could succeed on a job if hired, the proportion of applicants that must be hired to fill the available vacancies, and the accuracy with which such people can be identified and selected.

All pre-employment information may be gathered from every applicant and then combined into a decision – either by subjective or by actuarial means. In some selection programs, an applicant's strength in one qualification area is permitted to offset weakness in another area. This is known as a compensatory selection procedure. In other programs applicants must meet certain minimum qualifications. Applicants not meeting those qualifications are automatically excluded. This strategy is sometimes called a multiple hurdle approach. Regardless of the procedure used for combining information, selection decisions and measurements leading up to them should be scrutinized in validation research (see TESTS: VALIDITY OF).

MDH

Bibliography

Cascio, Wayne, M. 1982: *Applied psychology and personnel management*. 2nd edn. Reston, Virginia: Reston Publishing Company.

Tenopyr, Mary L., and Oeltjen, Paul D. 1982: Personnel selection and classification. *Annual review of psychology* 33, 581–618.

personology Since INDIVIDUALITY, in its two senses, can be attributed to any thing or process, its application to psychology must be considered. In order to do so, the two meanings must be temporarily separated from each other. Put into operation in the psychological field, the individual sense "unitary entity" yields the concept of person and its associated domain of inquiry, personology. For this reason, individual psychology is the psychology of persons. Authors such as Korchin (1976) use the word "personology" to refer to the study of the inside structuring and the psychodynamic patterns of the individual. In this way personology can be roughly delimited from the vast and ill-defined field of differential studies focused on variables of personality in populations of subjects. However, it would be completely inappropriate to restrict the field of personology to the internal organization of the person at a given time. The person in which personology is interested is situated in a life-world of its own in which it acts and relates to other persons which recognize each other as such. Besides, it possesses a history which is always in the making so that at any moment of its life it appears as the joint product of its history and of its biographically situated projects. Besides personology does not address an immutable entity rooted in an unchangeable human nature. Indeed, the study of historically determined forms of personal individuality as they can be found in various past and present-day socioeconomic conditions with their particular cultures and ideologies also belongs to the field of personology.

At the present day, personology is not only a little practiced discipline, but whatever personological researches are being performed, it is difficult to summarize because the kind of data used and the theoretical and methodological orientations are so divergent as to suggest a state of complete disarray. Therefore, the most useful overview of personology that can be given can only consist of an enumeration of its most pressing tasks.

Among these the first concerns the conceptual analysis of personhood and the logical as well as genetical reconstruction of the kind of structured and functional whole a person is conceived to be. It is indeed too often forgotten that definitions of personality, abundant as they are, far from replacing, in fact presuppose a definition of the notion of person, i.e. of personhood. Even if the formulation of the necessary and sufficient attributes of personhood may seem too ambitious a task, mention of some necessary conditions can help to dispel current confusion on this subject.

CONSCIOUSNESS with its basic characteristic of intentionality and consequently also the basic modes of fulfillment of intentional acts (Searle 1983) is a first candidate without which the whole realm of the self is inconceivable. Next comes "personification" as the process which, proceeding through the successive stages of initially non-reciprocal and ultimately reciprocal attributions of intentionality issues in the social construction of the person. Rule-governed and value-oriented activities with their alternatively corresponding and antagonistic technical-instrumental and social-interactional processes are another basic aspect of personhood which find their expression in dramaturgically staged roles and self-presentations and in relationships regulated by exchange principles. Personhood also implies the production and communication of meanings not only through linguistic means but also on the level of action. One of the most potent meaning-structures associated with personhood is represented by an individual's more or less coherent ideology on which his basic accounting schemes are founded.

Consideration of structural aspects is also relevant to the definition of personhood. The various degrees of unity which a person is capable of manifesting is a first question that must be dealt with. Identity, directly experienced as well as socially defined is another basic category of personhood. Much less conspicuous but nonetheless important is the notion of the delimitation of the person, i.e. of its boundaries which do not necessarily coincide with those of the body. Unity, identity and delimitation of the person are not fixed once and for all. They are achieved through successive constructions and reconstructions imposed by the fact that in any situation at any time, it is never the whole person which is involved, although a person's unity and identity, as well as the outline of its boundaries constitute basic characteristics pertaining to it as a whole. Consequently, changes instigated by internal organic causes or originating in situational requirements will inevitably lead to successive readjustments in the structure of the person.

The analysis of personhood however is not the only task of personology. Besides knowing what persons are and how they can be distinguished from non-persons, a question which has scarcely been asked must be answered: why do persons exist? In other words, what are the relationships between the development of persons and the functions they fulfill? The answer to this question can be found in authors as widely divergent in their ideological commitments as Gehlen (1940) and Galperin (1980). The atrophy of instinctive mechanisms, the extraordinarily high degree of cephalization, the slowness of development through maturation and learning and the length of life following the reproductive phase are closely related aspects of the biological consitution of human beings which makes it both possible and necessary for them to become part of a process of self-domestication through early, intensive and extensive forms of socialization. Thereby new action-structures emerge, the most crucial of which is work which enables man to produce his means of subsistence. Within this context of new competences – including language – which for their performance require an ensemble of social relationships, action patterns no longer depend on configurations of stimuli triggering off innate behavior-mechanisms sensitized by varying internal states. Needs and situations are now mediated by cognitive processes, activities and their affective regulations whose coordination and organization within the network of existing social relations constitute the functional foundation of personhood. In other words, according to this view, the person is the socially structured organization which, in the course of anthropogenesis, substitutes itself for the innate organization of instinctive mechanisms.

The person is so closely articulated with social relationships that it cannot possibly be reduced to either a superstructural or infrastructural component of social structure. In fact, to use L. Sève's happy expression (1975), it can best be described as manifesting a "juxtastructural" articulation with the basic components of social structure. Within the framework of historical materialism this means that the basic attributes of personhood entering into the construction of the person are technical-instrumental activities (belonging to productive forces), social-interactional and interpersonal relationships (corresponding to social relations of production) and the interpretation and justification of the latter under a form of a "*Weltanschauung*" (derived from the ideological superstructure).

The emergence of a developed person through a series of reorganizations imposed on the structure of its social relations and its world-view by the latter's growing technical-instrumental competencies, is made possible by the pecularities of human ontogeny and the resulting duration of the human life-span as it unfolds in a historically determined socioeconomic formation. This means that at any moment a person can only be understood as the product of its biography and that, considering the totality of its temporal extension, it is identical with it.

As Conrad (1963) has shown, linking the development of personality to the highly specific characteristics of human ontogeny also offers the possibility of explaining the origin of individual differences in certain mental and physical traits as resulting from differential growth patterns. Thus, he was able to derive a corrected version of Kretschmer's typology from the duality of a conservative and a progressive growth tendency each of which favors the body proportions proper to different developmental stages. In this way new perspectives are opened on the unitary process through which the person is constituted while individualizing itself along a set of parameter values. J-PDeW

Bibliography

Conrad, K. 1963: *Der Konstitution typus*. Berlin: Springer.

Galperin, P.J. 1980: *Zu Grundfragen der Psychologie*. Pahl-Rugenstein.

Gehlen, A. 1940 (*1950*): *Der Mensch*. Bonn: Athenäum Verlag.

Korchin, S. 1976: *Modern clinical psychology*. New York: Basic Books.

Searle 1983: *Intentionality*. Cambridge and New York: Cambridge University Press.

Sève, L. 1975: *Marxisme et théorie de la personalité*. 4th edn. Paris: Éditions Sociales.

persuasive communication *See* attitudes

phenomenology: in philosophy The word phenomenology came into use in philosophy with the publication in 1807 of Hegel's *Phenomenology of the spirit*. This was an introduction to his vast metaphysical system, designed to trace the evolution of consciousness as the recipient of phenomena or appearances, from the simplest to the most complex form.

Phenomenology did not become a kind of philosophy in its own right, however until the works of Edmund Husserl (1859–1938). Husserl acknowledged great debts to Franz Brentano (1838–1917) whose course of lectures on Descriptive Psychology, delivered in Vienna in 1888, had

"Phenomenology" as its alternative title. Brentano distinguished between introspection, deliberate self-examination, which was subject to error, and inner perception, the direct awareness of our own psychic phenomena, an awareness which he claimed accompanied all experience and was infallible. The fundamental function of consciousness was to represent. Judging and feeling emotions were both dependent on representation. Consciousness must be consciousness of something. This function he called Intentionality. Phenomenological philosophy was dependent on the description of consciousness as they appeared, that is, as representations.

According to Husserl, then, philosophy was concerned with the description of pure phenomena, with the experiences, regardless of whether they referred to concretely existing objects, to fictions, or to themselves. Purity was ensured by the deliberate refusal of the philosopher to make any assertion of existence about any of the phenomena in question. To pursue this course the philosopher had to undertake a "reduction" (epoche). He had to put aside (in brackets) all that is known, or normally assumed, about the objects of perception or thought, in order to analyse them as appearing in experience.

In addition to being the bearer of experience, in Husserl's theory consciousness also had a creative role. Our consciousness constructs the objects of our experience out of what, without it, would be a mass of chaotic, indescribable, non-recurring data. (At this point the influence of Kant is clear. Consciousness has the role of the imagination in Kant.) It would be completely impossible to produce an accurate psychological description of these raw data in the mind. Even the purest of pure phenomena is already imbued by us with sense, or meaning, in terms of which we understand what we experience as part of the universe we inhabit. Intentionality, in Brentano the essential feature of consciousness, now comes to mean that aspect of consciousness which creates or discovers meanings.

The discovery of meaning in experience is connected with the discovery of universality, or essences. Husserl thought that there was a special kind of immediate experience in which universal or general essences were grasped. In seeing a particular white object, for example, and concentrating on the experience of it, one is experiencing whiteness itself. Every particular item in experience points beyond itself. If you listen to a sustained note you cannot hear each separate moment of it, without hearing it as pointing to the same note in the past and in the future. This is what the particular momentary experience means. What I hear at any given moment is not wholly "in" the mind. Because it points to more than can be heard at that moment, it is not "immanent" but "transcendent".

So in concentrating on immediate experience, shorn of assumptions or presuppositions phenomenological philosophy discovered more in it than mere experience. The consciousness grasps essences in perception. This grasping was called *Wesensschau*, and was meant to be scientific, the source of true systematic knowledge. The method invited us to put the world in brackets and as it were dismember things ordinarily taken as objects in the world, in order to show how they were constructed as objects for us. And so their meaning for us will be revealed.

Phenomenology was the dominant philosophy in Germany from its beginnings until the 1930s. Husserl's most famous successor was Martin Heidegger (1889–1976), but in his hands, the philosophical method changed, and Heidegger is not to be thought of as a true phenomenologist. The search for meanings, "hermeneutics" nevertheless continued to be his primary concern, but without the limitation to the immediate objects of consciousness which marks phenomenology itself.

Phenomenology was introduced into France by J.-P. Sartre, and both he and Maurice Merleau-Ponty owe a great debt to Husserl, though their philosophy had no pretensions to being scientific, indeed was if anything, hostile to the methods of science. But even in Sartre's later philosophy, for example in *The question of method* (1957) the influence of Husserl and phenomenology can be seen in the proposal that Existentialism should "interiorize" Marxism. It should concentrate on the question of how the worker experiences his world, and what meanings he gives it.

In England, in a different way, both Ryle in *The concept of mind* (1949) and Wittgenstein in *The philosophical investigations* (1964) show the influence of phenomenology. MW

Bibliography

Pivcevic, Edo 1970: *Husserl and phenomenology*. London: Hutchinson.

Ryle, Gilbert 1949: *The concept of mind*. London: Hutchinson; Totowa, N.J.: Barnes & Noble (1975).

Spiegelberg, H. 1965: *The phenomenological movement*. The Hague: Mouton.

Wittgenstein, Ludwig 1953: *Philosophical investigations*. Oxford: Basil Blackwell; New York: Macmillan.

phenomenology: in psychiatry This term may be used to refer to the ensemble of mental symptoms and signs in an individual case or group of cases or in a disorder. In its stricter usage it is the study, description and classification of the evidence of mental activity. Jaspers (1962, pp.55–60) considers four groups of phenomena.

1. The individual's subjective experiences, perceptions, thoughts, impulses and self-awareness.
2. Objective mental performances, such as measurable evidence of memory and intelligence.
3. Somatic accompaniments of mental events, such as autonomic nervous system activity.
4. Meaningful objective phenomena which can be seen as evidence of the individual's intentions.

Subjective phenomenology forms the cornerstone of existential psychology and of existential analysis in which mental disorders are seen as the individual's attempt to reconcile various aspects of his experience. DLJ

Bibliography

Jaspers, Karl 1962: *General Psychopathology*. Trans J. Hoenig and M.W. Hamilton. Manchester: Manchester University Press; Chicago: University of Chicago Press.

phenomenology: in psychology The analysis of the

person–world relationship in terms of its intentionality. Phenomenologically, intentionality means that any human experience, or action has an object, which is conceptually distinct from that experience or action, and may or may not exist independently. The house which I see over there, the pain which I feel in here, or the pythagorean theorem which I hold to be true – are all objects of my present mental acts of seeing, feeling, believing, and as such they are said to be "intended" by these mental acts. The relationship between phenomenology and the human sciences has always been a case of selective exposure. It has been well documented by Merleau-Ponty (1973), Natanson (1973), Schütz (1962), Spiegelberg (1972) and Strasser (1963). What we gather from these sources is: (a) what phenomenological philosophers learnt from the human sciences, mainly psychology; and (b) what human scientists could have learnt from phenomenology. What we hardly find at all is: (c) what human scientists did take from phenomenology; and (d) what phenomenologists could have learnt from the human sciences.

The assessment, accordingly, is ambiguous. Spiegelberg (1972, xli), e.g. says: "in this century phenomenology has influenced psychology and psychiatry more than any other movement in philosophy", but (p.364), "phenomenology is the concern of only a small and unrepresentative minority". Similarly, in the 1950s, Merleau-Ponty (1973, p.50) assumed that what psychologists think about phenomenologists would be humiliating for the latter. He, nevertheless, believed that "it is in the problems and difficulties [that psychology] has encountered that we shall find both an influence of phenomenology and a harmony of two parallel investigations into common problems of the time" (ibid).

The fact is that from phenomenology the human sciences took different things at different times in a very selective manner, a state of affairs facilitated by changing emphases in phenomenological research. Four such emphases may be considered important, at least for their impact on psychology.

(1) From the beginning, phenomenology has been interpreted as the *method of faithful description of phenomena* in order to get "to the things themselves" *(zu den Sachen selbst)*. Psychologists familiar with Brentano and Husserl considered the unbiassed description of psychological phenomena the most elementary lesson to be learnt. Phenomenological descriptions have been given of the world of things (of colors, of touch), of inner experience, later, albeit rarely, of behavior. The methodological claim has been to place description first in the process of scientific investigation, before experimental or other forms of data reduction take place. Historically, however, it has been ethnomethodologists and related sociologists and anthropologists, even human ethologists, rather than psychologists who followed suit.

(2) *Phenomenology as a critical science* is another aspect which was taken up by psychologists. The criticism meant here is closely connected with the descriptive aspiration: to be critical with respect to one's own assumptions as a prerequisite of unbiassed description. Husserl warned the investigator "not to hunt deductively *(von oben her)* after constructions unrelated to the matter in question *(sachfremd)*, but to derive all knowledge from its ultimate sources ... not to be diverted by any prejudices, by any verbal contradictions or indeed by anything in the whole world, even under the name of 'exact science', but to grant its right to whatever is clearly seen ..." (quoted from Spiegelberg 1960, I, 128). Robert Macleod (1974, p.194) later expected social psychologists to adopt "an attitude of disciplined naiveté. It requires the deliberate suspension of all implicit and explicit assumptions ...".

(3) *Phenomenology as the science of meaning.* This is less a procedural than a substantive aspect resulting from the central role of the conception of intentionality. Every experience of reality is an experience of unities of meaning. For Husserl and, mainly, Schütz the "life-world" is a universe of significations, a framework of meaning which we incessantly interpret. This challenge was taken up by interpretive sociology, but largely ignored by mainstream psychology after *Verstehende Psychologie* was discontinued. Although the problem of meaning was recognized by behaviorists as well as by Gestaltists, it was not solvable in terms of conditioning or organization; nor will it be under the spell of the computational metaphor, i.e., in terms of information-processing, while the alternative ethogenic approach (Harré 1979) explicitly deals with the social constitution of meaning.

(4) *Phenomenology as the science of the life-world.* In the history of phenomenology the analysis of the life-world came late. After Husserl's *Crisis* it was mainly Schütz's work which focussed on the life-world as the correlate of our natural attitude, the unquestioned basis of all human (including scientific) activities. While a (positivistic) preference for laboratory experimentation shielded psychology from everyday life, recently at least everyday (or "naive") conceptions and "implicit theories" have become topics of research (Wegner and Vallacher 1977). However, the structure of everyday situations is hardly analysed. Exceptions, i.e. examples of a phenomenologically oriented psychology, are rare.

In conclusion, the major phenomenological emphases for psychological research are as follows:

(a) "Psychology is the scientific study of the situated person" (Linschoten 1953, p.246). While psychology traditionally focusses on the individual, phenomenological psychology is *situation-centered.* The first emphasis, therefore, is on the intentional person–world relationship in the context of individual or social *Umwelten.* That is, things and events, as intentional correlates, have meanings and values, and as such bear reference to actual or potential behavior. We encounter them less as "data", than as "agenda", i.e. something to be dealt with. To analyse the person–world relationship in terms of its intentionality makes explicit what Merleau-Ponty (1973, p.176) calls the "human dialectic".

(b) If we focus on a person's world phenomenologically it is revealed as *Umwelt,* as inhabited place. No analysis of behavior is complete without an adequate description of the place in which and with respect to which behavior "takes place". This *spatiality* of human existence is the infrastructure which facilitates or inhibits behavior.

(c) Its correlate is the *bodily* nature of the behaving subject. Whether a person perceives or acts, the world is encountered within the potentialities and limits of the body, articulated in perspectives, within or beyond our reach, etc. (Schütz 1962).

(d) Equally, the intentional relationship is to be understood as *temporal* reference. Intentional correlates may be present as perceived, past as remembered, future as anticipated. Phenomenologically more important is the fact that what we experience as being there now, as a rule, impresses us as having been there before we looked, and still being there when we turn away. Things and persons appear to have a history of their own, yet related to ours.

(e) We are born into a world of other people and of things which we have learnt to name and to handle by the mediation of others. Even the world of things carries social meaning as a world of man-made or, at least, man-ordered objects. Again, many of these things serve as media for interpersonal communication. This *sociality* of our experience and behavior is another phenomenologically essential feature of human existence. To remind psychologists of the essentially social, historical, spatial and bodily condition of the situated person has for a long time been the critical function of phenomenology in psychology. Judging from the present state of psychology this phenomenological critique has had little impact so far. CFG

Bibliography

Harré, E. 1979: *Social being.* Oxford: Basil Blackwell; Totowa, N.J.: Littlefield Adams.

*Husserl, E. 1936: *The crisis of European sciences and transcendental phenomenology.* Evanston, Ill.: Northwestern University Press (1970).

Linschoten, J. 1953: Naaword. In *Persoon en wereld.* Utrecht: Bijleveld.

MacLeod, R.B. 1974: The phenomenological approach to social psychology. *Psychological review* 54, 193–210.

Merleau-Ponty, M. 1973: *Phenomenology and the sciences of man.* In Natanson, op. cit. I, 47–108.

Natanson, M., ed. 1973: *Phenomenology and the social sciences,* 2 vols. Evanston, Ill.: Northwestern University Press.

*Schütz, A. 1962–6: *Collected papers,* 3 vols. The Hague: Nijhoff.

Spiegelberg, H. 1960: *The phenomenological movement,* 2 vols. The Hague: Nijhoff.

——— 1972: *Phenomenology in psychology and psychiatry: A historical introduction.* Evanston, Ill.: Northwestern University Press.

Strasser, S. 1963: *Phenomenology and the human sciences.* Pittsburgh: Duquesne University Press.

Wegner, D.M. and Vallacher, R.R. 1977: *Implicit psychology – an introduction to social cognition.* New York: Oxford University Press.

pheromone A chemical smell substance released by one member of a species that has a highly specific effect on a conspecific. Pheromones are most highly developed in insects. For instance it has been shown experimentally that the antennae of the male silk moth are exceptionally receptive to just one chemical substance, bombykol, and are able to respond to a single molecule of it. Female silk moths release minute amounts of bombykol, and are located by males who fly upwind along the scent trail. Pheromones are used extensively by social insects such as bees, and ants. In bees there is a "queen substance" pheromone that actually controls the sexual development of colony females, rendering them infertile workers. Ants find their way to food along trail pheromones, and give up the food they bring back to the nest only to others emitting the correct pheromone.

Among mammals scent-signals are often implicated in sexual arousal, being most often given when a female is in estrus, i.e. sexually receptive. They have the effect of stimulating male sexual activity. This is true of primates such as the rhesus monkey. In humans, research has shown the ability of men to detect and be aroused by what may be pheromones emitted by women; in general, however, human sexual approach is characteristic of both women and men, and is made up of a vast complex of non-olfactory signals.

See also COMMUNICATION; REPRODUCTIVE BEHAVIOR. VR

phobia An unrealistic and disproportionate fear of an object or situation. Characteristically a phobia cannot be reasoned away and is beyond voluntary control; intense anxiety or panic is evoked by the prospect or actuality of exposure to the feared situation which tends to be avoided. Phobias constitute a form of NEUROSIS, and may be subdivided into agoraphobia, social phobias, animal phobias, various other specific phobias (for example of thunder or heights) and illness phobia.

There are two main approaches to the understanding and treatment of phobias. Psychodynamic theories regard the fear as the displacement onto an external object of anxiety aroused by unacceptable impulses from the unconscious; resolution is through PSYCHOANALYSIS or PSYCHOTHERAPY. By contrast behaviorists emphasize the learning of associations between the object and anxiety responses in the formation of a phobia; treatment is directed at learning to confront the object without anxiety (BEHAVIOR THERAPY). DLJ

Bibliography

Marks, I.M. 1969: *Fears and phobias.* London: Heinemann; New York: Academic Press.

phonetic symbolism *See* sound symbolism

phonetics and phonology The study of human speech sounds is often divided into phonetics and phonology. Phonetics is the description of the sounds of individual languages or the universal constraints on speech sounds in terms of their articulatory, acoustic and auditory properties. Phonology, on the other hand, is concerned with the syntagmatic and paradigmatic patterning of sound in a particular human language or human language in general.

With the recent shift in emphasis from more abstract to more concrete (cf. LINGUISTIC NATURALNESS) models of phonology, the distinction between these two aspects of language study has become less important, and linguists are beginning to talk about "phonetology". At the same time, the traditional strict division between phonology and other components of *grammar* is less rigorously maintained, as phonological rules (such as contraction in he is = he's) are sensitive to syntactic information. This can be seen from the contrasting grammaticality of she's not stupid but he is with (ungrammatical)* she's not stupid but he's. PM

Bibliography

Ladefoged, Peter 1976: *A course in phonetics*. New York: Harper & Row.

Sommerstein, Alan A. 1977: *Modern phonology*. London: Edward Arnold.

physical treatment *See* psychiatry, physical treatment in

Piaget, Jean A Swiss biologist who began his work on the nature of children's intellectual development during the 1920s and continued it until his death in 1980 at the age of eighty-three. During that long time he produced a massive body of research and developed a theory about childhood which is the single biggest influence on child psychology today. The central idea in this theory is that children at first lack the capacity either to understand their environment or to reason about it coherently, and that they gradually acquire these abilities through the informal experiences with the world around them. Piaget was concerned not only with the extent of children's intellectual capacities at different ages but also with the kind of experiences which lead to intellectual growth; it was mainly because of this latter interest that Piaget's ideas have played so large a part in recent debates about education.

From the beginning his main interest in child development centered around logic. It was Piaget more than anyone else who promoted the idea that logical reasoning cannot be taken for granted in humans and is to a large extent out of the range of young children's capacities. This idea seems to have come to him during his first systematic experience of research with children while on a visit to Simon's laboratory in Paris. Simon, an erstwhile colleague of Alfred Binet, suggested that Piaget should try out some intelligence tests which involved syllogisms. Piaget did so and was so struck with the difficulty which children as old as eight and nine years had with these apparently simple logical tasks that he decided to explore the possibility that children originally lack certain logical capacities and that much that is important in child development is the result of the gradual but inexorable growth of logic during childhood.

Piaget's first studies, reported in *Language and thought of the child* (1923) and in *Judgement and reasoning in the child* (1924), concentrated on the young child's knowledge of his physical and social environment. This early work suggested that young children are egocentric, in the sense that they do not realize when they talk to others that these other people have different viewpoints from theirs and know different things. It also suggested that young children's thoughts are "animistic" – a term which Piaget used to describe a failure to distinguish animate from inanimate things–and are also characterized by "artificialism", which meant that children often do not seem to be able to distinguish between man-made and naturally formed objects in their environment.

Nearly all this early work was based on conversations between Piaget and young children or on conversations between children which were overheard by him. Soon however Piaget's work acquired a more experimental and a less conversational bent. The change came about in two ways. The first was that Piaget turned much of his attention to very young children in their first two years of life who could not converse. The second was that he decided to tackle the problem of logical abilities more directly by giving older children a series of problems which involved more experimental manipulations and less interrogation on the part of Piaget and his colleagues.

The work on the first two years of life which Piaget calls "the sensori-motor period" was based on observations of his own three children and various experiments with them. It is described in two books *The child's construction of reality* (1937) and *The origin of intelligence in the child* (1936) which still exert a powerful influence on current research on infancy. Piaget tried to show that children are born with a few built in behavior patterns such as sucking, grasping with the hand and looking at moving objects, which he called reflexes. Apart from these basic activities infants are incapable of understanding their environment or of coping with it in any way. But these reflexes provide the experiences which lead the child by the end of the two years to have a reasonable idea of the world around him, and to understand in a simple way space, time and causality. Much of this development is due to the eventual coordination of the different reflexes. For example Piaget claimed that for the first four months of life the baby does not have a proper idea of its own physical existence because its reflexes are not coordinated. The child moves his arm and feels it moving. He also sees it moving, but these two perceptions are quite unconnected. To him his own arm has exactly the same status as any other passing object. He does not know that it is his own, and only makes the connection when at four to five months of age he begins to be able to reach for things which he sees. This coordination and others allow him by the age of six months or so to have a reasonable idea of himself as a separate physical entity. But according to Piaget there is still a lot for the baby to learn, and his next major development must be to discover more about the properties of the objects around him. The major discovery which the child has to make is that these are not evanescent: they are durable and have an independent existence quite regardless of whether the baby is perceiving them at the time or not. Piaget claimed that babies at first do not understand that objects still exist when they are no longer visible, on the basis of some observations which he made that up to the age of about eight months they lose interest in a toy which they see placed under covers even though they could in principle perfectly easily retrieve it. Even when they begin to recover these hidden objects their performance remains very shaky. One of Piaget's best known and most provocative observations was of the so called A not B error. Babies between about eight and twelve months manage to retrieve a toy hidden in place (A) but then when they see it hidden somewhere else (B) they often wrongly look for it in its original hiding place. Piaget's explanation for this phenomenon was that it showed that the child could not separate the object's existence from his own actions: he actually thinks that his original action of reaching to place A somehow recreated the object. If Piaget is right it is not until the child gets over this sort of curious mistake that he really understands that the existence of the objects around him is by and large independent of his own actions. By the age of two years however the child has achieved what Piaget called a "practical" understanding of this and of other basic concepts, such as causality and space and time. However there is still a long way for the child to go. He still has, according to Piaget, to find out how to solve logical problems and to use logic to solve every day problems, and this takes to the end of what Piaget called "the concrete operations period".

The concrete operations period lasts, in Piaget's theory, until roughly thirteen years of age, During this time the child's major underlying intellectual achievement is to free himself from the domination of his immediate perception, a liberation which allows him to be logical and which indeed explains logical development. Suppose for example that an experimenter has three sticks of varying size, so that $A > B > C$. Suppose too that the child is shown them in two pairs: $A > B$ and $B > C$. In Piaget's theory these two presentations, because they represent two separate perceptions would so far as the child of five, or six, or even seven or eight is concerned remain separate. While he is perceptually dominated he cannot combine the two and this means that he cannot make the logical deduction that $A > C$. Perceptual domination thus prevents logic, and this is the theme which unites the many, varied experiments which Piaget carried out on children between the ages of three and thirteen years. There is for example the well known conservation experiment, described in such books as *The child's conception of number* (1941) and *The child's construction of quantities* (1941). The child is shown two identical quantities – say two identical glasses containing the same amounts of liquid. He compares them and judges them to be equal. The liquid from one is then poured into a thinner container which means that its level is now higher than that of the liquid which was left as it was. The child is then asked to say whether or not the two containers contain the same amount of liquid, and his usual answer is that they do not. The one with the higher level is usually said to have more than the other by children up to the age of eight years or so. Piaget's explanation for this striking error was that the perceptually dominated child has to treat a perceptual change as a real one, and as a consequence does not understand the principle of invariance. Both the explanation and the conclusion about the young child's incapacity have always been controversial, but the experiment itself is without doubt one of the most important and one of the best known in psychology. But Piaget's list of the things which a child of below about eight years cannot do did not stop there. He cannot, Piaget added, understand the logical inclusion of classes; he cannot understand Euclidean spatial relationships; he cannot even understand that someone sitting opposite him has a different viewpoint to his own. All these difficulties he documented in ingenious, but some would say flawed, experiments. Certainly his pessimism about the child's rank inability is under strong dispute at the moment, even though there is universal admiration both for the elegance of the actual theory and the ingenuity of the simple tests which Piaget and his colleagues devised.

The last developmental period in Piaget's theory was the formal operations period. It lasts roughly the length of adolescence. Of the three major periods which made up Piaget's theory this one is the Cinderella. Piaget himself did not write very much about it, and very few people have tried to repeat his experiments on children of this age range. Broadly speaking Piaget argued that this was the time when scientific thought, or at any rate the possibility of it developed. In his view this demanded not just logic, but also the ability to isolate first the variables which are relevant to the logical argument. His major evidence for this idea came from experiments in which adolescent children were basically asked to design experiments to isolate causes – such as the cause of the extent of the swing of a pendulum. The question was whether they could manage to look at one variable at a time, holding all others constant, This was something which seemed quite out of the range of the young adolescent, though many managed later on. They managed it, Piaget claimed, because they began to reflect on their own thought processes, a quality which Piaget thought of as the quintessence of development at this time and indeed the crowning glory of intellectual development. It was a summit which later on he was ruefully to agree always eluded many children and adults too.

With this one exception Piaget concentrated on development which he regarded as inevitable and indeed universal. Although the child depended on his informal experiences with the environment to lead him from one intellectual stage to the next, this experience led him along the same path as everyone else. The mechanisms which Piaget thought caused intellectual change are to be found in his theory of equilibrium. Piaget thought that children, and adults too, are content with their own intellectual experiences provided that these give a satisfactory and above all a consistent explanation of what happens around them. If they do the child is said to be in a state of equilibrium. But inevitably, according to Piaget, the child will find that he has two quite contradictory explanations of the same event, and his failure to reconcile them throws him into conflict. The conflict causes disequilibrium, and the child is forced to reorganize his intellectual processes to rid himself of the conflict which is causing all the trouble; hence the consequent intellectual change. These ideas are most forcefully described in two of Piaget's last books, *Experiments in contradiction* (1974) and *The development of thought* (1975). It must be said that there is little direct evidence for the causal side of Piaget's theory, and yet, with its stress on the importance of informal experiences and of the child making his own discoveries, it is the part of Piaget's work which has had the strongest effect on educators.

His interest in universal developmental changes was obviously guided by his enduring involvement with biology and his consistent wish to link that subject and philosophy. He became a psychologist almost by default. He simply wanted a scientific, biological explanation of the growth of knowledge. No one has done more to achieve that than he did himself.

See also EMOTION, PIAGETIAN VIEW. PEB

Bibliography

Boden, M.A. 1979: *Piaget*. Brighton: Harvester; New York: Viking Press 1980.

Gruber, H.E. and Voneche, J.J. 1977: *The essential Piaget*. London: Routledge and Kegan Paul I; New York: Basic Books.

Piaget, Jean 1923 (*1959*): *Language and thought of the child*. 3rd edn. London: Routledge & Kegan Paul; New York: Humanities.

——— 1924 (*1962*): *Judgment and reasoning in the child*. London: Routledge & Kegan Paul; New York: Humanities.

——— 1936 (*1953*): *The origin of intelligence in the child*. London: Routledge & Kegan Paul; New York: International Universities Press (1966), *The origins of intelligence in children*.

——— 1937 (*1955*): *The child's construction of reality*. London: Routledge & Kegan Paul; New York: Basic Books (1954), *The construction of reality in the child*.

———1941 (*1952*): *The child's conception of number*. London: Routledge & Kegan Paul: New York: Norton (1965).

——— 1967 (*1971*): *Biology and knowledge*. Edinburgh: Edinburgh University Press; Chicago: University of Chicago Press.

——— 1974: *Experiments in contradiction*. London: Routledge & Kegan Paul; New York: Norton.

——— *The development of thought*. London: Routledge & Kegan Paul. New York: Norton.

——— and Inhelder, Barbel 1941 (*1974*): *The child's construction of quantities*. London: Routledge & Kegan Paul; New York: Basic Books.

pineal gland A small brain structure (weight approximately 150 mg) lying along the quadrigeminate groove between the superior colliculi (see BRAIN AND CENTRAL NERVOUS SYSTEM: ILLUSTRATIONS fig. 6). The gland was first described in the third century BC by Alexandrian anatomists who believed it was a sphincter which regulated the flow of thought. According to Descartes (1596-1650) the gland was the site of the "rational mind". In fish and amphibia the pineal cells have an eye-like, light-sensitive function. The function of the pineal gland in higher vertebrates, including man, has not been established unequivocally, though it clearly has an endocrine role, probably related to gonadal function. The nerve supply to the pineal gland consists of postganglionic sympathetic fibers. Part of the input to the pineal gland via these fibers originates from the hypothalamic suprachiasmatic nucleus (figs. 15 and 20) which is believed to be a biological "clock". The pineal gland contains, and probably secretes, a number of biologically active compounds. These are mainly small peptides and biogenic amines, among which the serotonin derivative melatonin has been most extensively studied. The activity of pineal enzymes, e.g. those involved in melatonin synthesis, is dependent on the light-dark cycle. DHGV

pituitary A gland at the base of the brain which is connected to the ventral surface of the HYPOTHALAMUS (see BRAIN AND CENTRAL NERVOUS SYSTEM: ILLS 15 and 20). The pituitary has two lobes which are critical in neuroendocrine-behaviour relationships (see BRAIN AND CENTRAL NERVOUS SYSTEM: CHEMISTRY OF). The posterior lobe (or neurohypophysis) is derived embryologically from neural tissue, while the anterior lobe (or adenohypophysis) is derived from the same tissue as the roof of the mouth. The neuropeptide hormones, vasopressin and oxytocin, are synthesized in the HYPOTHALAMUS but are stored and released upon hypothalamic stimulation from the posterior pituitary into the blood stream. The anterior pituitary releases several hormones into the blood stream, including ACTH, thyrotropin, somatotropin, gonadotropins and prolactin. The release of anterior pituitary hormones is controlled by releasing factors secreted by the hypothalamus and carried in the hypophysial portal system to the anterior pituitary.

GPH

pivot class The term "pivot class" along with "open class" was introduced by Braine (1963) to distinguish the types of words found in two-word utterances in early FIRST LANGUAGE ACQUISITION.

Pivot words are statistically much more frequently used than open class words. In the utterance *this good, this come, this doggie, this red,* "this" is the pivot word, whereas all the other lexical items belong to the open class.

Pivot words can only be described with reference to the child's own grammar and not in terms of adult categories, such as functional words.

The following objections have been raised against the notion of "pivot class":

1. statistical considerations should not enter the description of linguistic COMPETENCE
2. the distinction between the two classes is gradual particularly when seen from a developmental point of view
3. there are significant inter-individual differences as regards membership of lexical items in pivot and open class.

PM

Bibliography

Braine, M.D.S. 1963: The ontogeny of English phrase structure: the first phase. *Language* 39, 1–13.

pivot-open grammar The terms "pivot" and "open" were introduced by Braine (1963) following a distributional analysis of child speech during the two-word phase. Children were found to distinguish between two syntactic word-classes: a relatively closed pivot class and a constantly growing open class. Pivot words express the grammatical relations of modification (allgone, big) and predication (there, come, want).

The grammatical reality of the pivot-open distinction is derived from the observation that only combinations of the type P + O, O + P and O + O (not P + P) are encountered.

The principal limitation of this distinction is its being restricted to surface sequences rather than to deeper semantic relations. PM

Bibliography

Bowerman, Melissa 1973: *Early syntactic development*. Cambridge and New York: Cambridge University Press.

Braine, M.D.S. 1963: The ontogeny of English phrase structure', *Language* 39. 1–13

McNeill, D. 1970: *The acquisition of language*. New York and London: Harper & Row.

plant psychology An aberrant explanation of plant behavior operating on the assumption that plants have human-like characteristics of thinking and feeling. Despite popular belief to the contrary there is no scientific evidence that plants have feelings, emotions, consciousness or any recognition of self, in the way that some animals do; i.e., they have no psychology. Nevertheless plants do possess an extensive sensory physiology in which they respond by changes in behavior to a wide variety of stimuli. They respond to many chemical and physical stimuli, such as light, pressure, stretch, chemicals and gravity. Plant physiologists, biochemists and biophysicists have studied and described these elaborate sensory systems for over a hundred years and a good deal of data exists in the scientific literature.

Internally the responses in one part of the plant are integrated with the plant as a whole by complex mechanisms. This integration is known to occur by the movement of specific biochemical substances known as plant hormones or growth regulators. In addition the movement of ions and small molecular weight substances can generate bioelectric potentials within individual cells or over extended tissues and organs. Even though much is known about these processes and they have been studied extensively they remain largely unknown in the molecular details of how they function at the cellular level in controlling plant growth, development and behavior.

Because the sensitivity of these sensory systems changes as a function of the immediate past history of stimuli which the plant has received (known in physiological terms as adaptation or range-adjustment), naive observers have occasionally been led to conclude that plants respond in a way indicative of human thought processes. Bizarre claims have been made including one that plants have the ability to sense injury or the death of other organisms at a distance. Measurements in uncontrolled experiments of bioelectric potentials were used as evidence that plants could count, respond to music, predict storms or display various kinds of conditioned reflexes.

Whenever such claims have been made they have often received popular acclaim in the general press and acceptance by persons unfamiliar with the requirements of scientific research. There appears to be an underlying desire by many to counter the methods of science and to attribute ill-defined and romantic explanations to observed behavior. Attempts to reproduce these claims under controlled conditions and by independent investigators have uniformly failed. Since these observations have not led to a body of testable and provable hypotheses, scientists (especially plant physiologists) remain skeptical about the existence of any plant psychology. The incredible diversity and complexity of plant sensory systems which are reproducible can be explained so far in terms of known scientific principles. Meanwhile the details of the behavioral responses of plants to stimuli are gradually being described.

WS

Bibliography

Galston, A.W. and Slayman, C.L. 1979: The not-so-secret life of plants. *American scientist* 67, 337–44.

Shropshire, W., Jr. 1979: Stimulus perception. *Encyclopedia of plant physiology*, vol. 7; *Physiology of movements*, ed. W. Haupt and M.E. Feinleib. Berlin and Heidelberg: Springer-Verlag.

plasticity Has two distinct meanings in general psychology which, although overlapping, possess very different implications. First, theorists such as Hollis use the term in referring to the view of the human as environmentally determined. To invoke this plasticity argument is to hold that individual action is principally a product of external rather than innate forces. Much weaker versions of this concept of plasticity are also found among those who believe that behavior and capabilities are principally determined by genes, but that development is influenced by the environment, at least during certain critical periods. In contrast, the concept of plasticity is used by others in arguing that human life trajectories are not frozen or fixed by early life experiences. Plasticity in this case refers to the capacity of the organism to undergo transformation at any time during the life course. (See also ENVIRONMENTALISM, VOLUNTARISM).

KJG

Bibliography

Hollis, M. 1977: *Models of man*. Cambridge and New York: Cambridge University Press.

plasticity: physiological concept Plasticity refers to the capacity of neurons in the central nervous system to grow beyond their normal developmental period, or to regenerate or reorganize after injury or environmental change. Although the term is sometimes used to refer to any reorganization of neural connections observed after an experimental manipulation, its use is most appropriate when referring to changes that have functional significance for the organism. At the level of the neuron, or nerve cell, the structural changes that subserve plasticity involve the growth of axons and dendrites, which are fibers that extend from the cell body of the NEURON, and are involved in the transmission of neural impulses, as well as the formation of new synapses, which are the interconnections between neurons. Such structural changes are most prominent during early development, but may be possible throughout adulthood in fish and amphibians. In mammals, a significant capacity for plasticity appears to be limited to a period early in post-natal development, which has been called the "sensitive" or "critical" period (See SENSITIVE PERIOD). In addition to referring to the structural changes that can be observed in axons, dendrites and synapses the term plasticity is used to refer to functional changes that are not accompanied by observable alterations in structure. The functional changes to which the term is applied may occur at the neuronal level, where the function of pre-existing synapses may change, or at the behavioral level, where the recovery of some behaviour after neurological damage occurs without evidence of neural growth.

Plasticity has been studied with several procedures, each of which emphasizes a different aspect of change in the central nervous system. Where the emphasis is on observing structural changes in neurons, tissue samples can be obtained, and a staining agent applied so that neurons can be identified microscopically. With this technique the axons, dendrites and synapses of normal tissue samples can be compared with those identified in tissue obtained from organisms that were subjected to some type of experimental manipulation, such as a radical environmental change or a surgical lesion. At this level of analysis, plasticity may be observed in any or all of several ways. Particular neurons form synapses at identifiable points, called target areas, with other specific neurons. Plasticity can occur through the formation of new synapses at an old target area (sprouting), or through the formation of new synapses in a different target area of the same neuron (spreading). A third type of plastic change can be observed when synapses are formed between neurons that do not typically share target areas. This third type of change is called extension.

Although the microscopic observation of stained tissue samples provides direct evidence of structural neuronal changes, it does not yield evidence of functional neuronal changes. The demonstration of functional change requires that the activity of neurons be measured in a behaving organism. One way in which this can be achieved is by recording the electrical activity of neurons. This approach, known as electrophysiology, encompasses a variety of techniques ranging from recording the activity of a single neuron using a microelectrode implanted in the cell itself, to recording the gross activity of whole regions of the brain using electrodes placed on the scalp. Electrophysiological recordings of single neurons have been used extensively to study plasticity, especially in the visual system.

In the visual cortex of many mammals there are neurons that only respond to stimulation of one eye, as well as those that respond to stimulation of either eye. The former are called monocular cells, the latter are called binocular cells. Although most neurons in the visual cortex are binocular, binocular cells tend to have a bias in their responding. That is, in normally raised animals, binocular cells on one side of the brain are more effectively activated by stimulation of the eye on the opposite side. So, for example, stimulation of the right eye will produce a greater response in the binocular cells of the left visual cortex than will stimulation of the left eye. This bias is known as ocular dominance, and it reflects an organizational principle in the central nervous system that is subject to both plasticity and a SENSITIVE PERIOD.

The phenomenon of ocular dominance can be observed by making electrophysiological recordings of the activity of neurons in the visual cortex of normally raised experimental animals, such as cats. Plasticity can be induced, however, by radically altering the animal's environment during early development. Kittens normally open their eyes after the first eight to ten days of life. If the lid of one eye is stitched closed at some point during the first few months of life, a physiological reorganization can be observed in the visual cortex. After a period of monocular deprivation during early development, almost all of the binocular cells are lost and the remaining monocular cells respond only to stimulation of the experienced eye. If the animal is allowed to use only the eye that had previously been sutured, it is functionally blind. There is a specific period of time during which the developing kitten is susceptible to the effects of monocular deprivation. This sensitive period begins at about the third week of life and extends to about the fourth month. The visual cortex appears to be extremely plastic during this time, when as few as three days of monocular deprivation during the fourth week of life is sufficient to produce changes in the normal pattern of ocular dominance.

In humans there is some indication that the brain remains plastic for language during a critical period in development. In most adults language functions are lateralized to the left cerebral hemisphere. For the right-handed population, the incidence of left hemisphere language is well above 90 per cent. Most left-handed individuals also have left hemisphere language, but as a group, there is a higher incidence of language being represented in either the right hemisphere, or both hemispheres. One of the consequences of language lateralization is that for right-handed people, damage to the left hemisphere due to stroke, tumor or trauma will frequently produce a language dysfunction. However, comparable damage to the right hemisphere in right handed adults rarely produces problems with language. The prognosis for recovery of language function after left hemisphere damage depends on the extent of the damage and the type of language dysfunction present. Although the physiological basis for recovery of function in adults is not well understood, it is generally acknowledged that the observed improvement is not due to the plastic changes seen during the early development of the central nervous system.

In very young children, on the other hand, there tends to be a much greater recovery of function following lateralized brain injury than is observed in adults. Young children who have suffered extensive damage to, or even surgical removal of the left hemisphere lose the language function they have developed just as adults do after left hemisphere injury. If the left hemisphere of a young child is damaged prior to the acquisition of language, however, language may develop in the intact right hemisphere. In the developing human, then, there appears to be some plasticity for language function in so far as the hemisphere not normally involved in language may acquire this function in response to severe damage to the language hemisphere. Such plasticity in language development is found only in childhood, and although there is no general agreement as to the length of the critical period, it appears that plasticity in language function sharply declines after the initial acquisition of language.

The term plasticity, then, generally refers to functional changes in the developing organism that are induced by external influences, and are referable to the organization of the central nervous system. Plasticity is observable at synaptic connections between axons and dendrites, in the electrical activity of single neurons, and in the behavioral recovery of function after damage to the central nervous system. JJS

Bibliography

Blakemore, C. and Cooper, G. 1970: Development of the brain depends on the visual environment. *Nature* 228, 477–8.

Gazzaniga, M.S., Steen, D. and Volpe, B.T. 1979: *Functional neuroscience.* New York and London: Harper & Row.

Jacobson, M. 1978: *Developmental neurobiology.* New York and London: Plenum Press.

Marx, J.L. 1980: Regeneration in the central nervous system. *Science* 209, 378–80.

Woods, B.T. and Carey, S. 1979: Language deficits after apparent clinical recovery from childhood aphasia. *Annals of neurology* 6, 405–9.

Woods, B.T. and Teuber, H.-L. 1978: Changing patterns of childhood aphasia. *Annals of neurology* 3, 273–80.

Plato (c. 429–347 BC) Plato's early work was largely ethical. It contains, however, assumptions about human motivation and rationality, in particular that everyone wants and only wants to take the best course. Assuming rationality, deliberation will yield what is considered the best action, given a view of the best outcome. Further, Plato holds that goodness is an objective property; in wanting what is best we all want the same thing, though some may mistake its nature. His assumption of rationality was strong: it seemed unintelligible that people should knowingly not do what they thought best. There is (a) no opposition of desires and (b) no vacillation in belief. (a) Apparent weakness of will is really ignorance. (b) Once information on what is best is acknowledged, belief follows automatically: emotional acceptance cannot lag behind rational proof. Plato vacillates between saying that we want what is best, that we want the best life, and we want our own good. In the *Protagoras* he explores a hedonistic version of the last. He probably hoped to collapse the three into one. (See *Euthydemus* 278–82, *Protagoras* 253–358, *Gorgias* 466–70, *Meno* 77–9; and modern discussions in Crombie 1962, Irwin 1977 and Santas 1979).

The result is a streamlined version of the human person: behavior is a function of what is thought best at any given time. The implausibility did not long escape Plato. We find a growing recognition, first, of desires which do not involve a view as to what is best, and second, of the possibility of a person's believing something to be bad but doing it. First, conflict is acknowledged between "bodily" desires and desire for order, etc. This starts a dualism between the changing body, whose satisfaction is unattainable, and the rational soul, whose satisfaction is found in the understanding and attainment of order. In the *Republic* he distinguishes between the desires of reason, those of the body and what might briefly be characterized as a desire for respect (the "spirited" element). This last involves beliefs about what is good and noble and will be manifested, for instance, in anger and indignation: it is allowed that bodily desires might overcome "spirit", and thereby belief as to what is best. Those with full understanding of what is best, however, will always act accordingly. Acceptance of the picture of opposing desires is less than whole-hearted. He simultaneously inclines towards a picture of a single desire-force attracted by different objects, one attraction distracting it from others. (See *Gorgias* 493–505, *Phaedo* 64–84, *Republic* 435–45 and 485; and modern discussions in Annas 1981, Crombie 1962 and Irwin 1977).

Previously Plato saw differences of character as differences in belief about what is best. He now saw people as able to be dominated by different desires; only those whose reason rules will show uniformity of life style. All except the last show distortion or defective growth. Every *psyche* has the same structure. Sexual differences are physiological only. (See *Republic* 451–57 and 543–92; and modern discussions in Annas 1981 and Crombie 1962).

Acknowledgement of conflict went hand in hand with a dualism of mind and body partly because the obvious non-rational desires were "bodily" ones. This led to vacillation on what constitutes a person. In the *Phaedo* it is reason; in the *Republic* bodily desires and "spirit" are included; in the *Timaeus* these form the mortal part of the soul; in the *Phaedrus* myth they survive death. (See *Phaedo* and *Republic* as above and also *Phaedrus* 246–56, *Timaeus* 69–71; and modern discussion in Crombie 1962).

The dualism is also motivated by epistemological concerns: the senses cannot supply knowledge *(episteme)*; something capable of discerning general natures reflected in transient phenomena is required, which must be similar in nature to what it comprehends. Since these natures are immaterial and eternal, so must the soul be. Plato adduces other considerations: the soul is not destroyed by its bad states; the soul is a self-mover. He never takes the more modern starting point of privileged access to one's own experiences as against a dubious grasp of external substance. *Episteme* consists in grasping the eternal plan of how it is best for things to be. Sense perception, in constant change and supplying only description, is incapable of yielding this. We start with an inchoate grasp of the plan and an inclination to reason about it. At best the senses stimulate this innate understanding into activity. The interaction of mind and body is taken as unproblematic metaphysically, though interesting physiologically. (See *Meno* 80–6, *Phaedo* 64–85 and 95–106, *Republic* 507–11, 522–34 and 608–11, *Phaedrus* 245–6, *Timaeus* 28–37 and 48–53, *Cratylus* 438–40, *Theaetetus* 156–72 and 179–86; and modern discussions in Crombie 1962 and Runciman 1962).

The interdependence of mind and body is taken for granted in education. Proper exercise is needed alongside appropriate music to produce harmonious personalities. They soothe "spirit" without emasculating it. This gives some defense against bodily desires. This is important since bodily desires are considered intemperate in tendency. Reason develops too late to save us. (See *Republic* 376–411, *Laws* 652–75; and modern discussions in Shorey 1935 and Crombie 1962).

In his earlier remarks on punishment Plato considers that it should primarily be aimed at the reform of the criminal. It is best to do no wrong, next best to be punished for one's wrongdoing. By the time of the *Laws* he had come to feel that punishment appealed to fear and so was inappropriate for those whose control of their fears had been developed along with their understanding. For them the proper tool is reason. If that fails they must be incurable and the only appropriate course is execution. The aim of the legislator is the development of a reasonable society, and so while the law must have sanctions it must also be shown to be reasonable. Every law is to be preceded by a preamble setting out the reasons for it. (See *Gorgias* 25, *Laws* 716–24, 862 and 899–909; and modern discussions in Crombie 1962 and Morrow 1960). JCBG

Bibliography

(The page numbers given for Plato's works in the text refer to the standard pagination used in translations of Plato's texts.)

Annas, J. 1981: *An introduction to Plato's Republic*. Oxford and New York: Oxford University Press.

Crombie, I.M. 1962: *An examination of Plato's doctrines*. London: Routledge & Kegan Paul; New York; Humanities Press.

Irwin, T. 1977: *Plato's moral theory*. Oxford and New York: Oxford University Press.

Morrow, G. 1960: *Plato's Cretan city*. Princeton: Princeton University Press.

Runciman, W.G. 1962: *Plato's later epistemology*. Cambridge: Cambridge University Press.

Santas, G.X. 1979: *Socrates' philosophy in Plato's early dialogues*. London and Boston: Routledge & Kegan Paul.

Shorey, P. 1935 and 1937: *Plato's "Republic"*. London: Heinemann; New York: Putnam.

*Taylor, A.E. 1948: *Plato: the man and his work*, fifth edn. London: Methuen; New York: Humanities Press. (Contains a sketch of the contents of every dialogue).

*Vlastos, G., ed. 1971: *Plato*. London: Macmillan; Garden City, N.Y.: Anchor Books.

play: animal A type of activity which can be defined structurally by the re-ordering, exaggeration, repetition and fragmentation of behavior. Such characteristics would be uneconomic for goal-directed activity; therefore, functionally, play is usually described as having no clear immediate benefit.

Play has only been reliably documented in warm-blooded animals, and much more frequently and extensively for mammals than birds. Typically, play activities increase rapidly in frequency during the infancy period of mammalian development, peak, and decrease to low levels by sexual maturity. Play in adult mammals is usually with offspring. Adult monkeys may use play to distract youngsters from suckling, or from other companions.

The simplest kind of mammalian play takes the form of generalized physical activity; for example, rapid hopping back and forth in young wallabies (Kaufmann 1974). In addition, among the social mammals play fighting and/or chasing are commonly observed, the form depending on the particular species: for example, stalking, chasing, pawing and wrestling in lion cubs; rearing, pawing and biting in ponies; wrestling, biting and chasing in young rhesus monkeys. Sexual play has also been described in many species, and play mothering in monkeys. Manipulative play with objects has been documented, most noticeably with the higher primates. Manipulative play often follows exploration, but is distinguished from exploration by being less stimulus directed and more characterized by positive affect.

Lazar and Beckhorn (1974) have argued that play should not be seen as a separate kind of behavior, rather, activities of immature animals may be seen to be exaggerated, reordered or incomplete because this is an inevitable aspect of ontogenetic development, leading to adult behavior. This is a minority view although it may hold force for descriptions of play mothering, and perhaps sexual play. In the case of animal play fighting and chasing however, such activities may coexist developmentally with real fighting and chasing. The play activities may differ from the real activities according to structural criteria similar to those which Loizos proposed. Furthermore, sequences of play fighting and chasing are typically preceded by play invitation or marker signals (such as open-mouth face, exaggerated walk or bow) which only appear in such contexts and are not seen in adult non-play behavior.

The characteristics of playful behavior are compatible with a learning approach which emphasizes the reinforcing nature of sensory stimulation, especially varied and novel stimulation, for the young organism. This is usually coupled with an arousal-level model which postulates that sensory stimulation is only reinforcing if it keeps the organism within an optimal arousal zone (Baldwin and Baldwin 1977). This can explain age changes, but it would require supplementing by postulates as to why particular kinds of stimulation, such as those in play fighting, are so motivating.

Since play does not have clear immediate benefits to the animal, there has been considerable speculation as to its biological function. One approach has been to argue that play functions to maintain optimal arousal (Ellis 1973), but this merely defers the problem to explaining the benefits of arousal level, which can anyway be mediated by the other behavior. More plausibly, arousal level may be part of the proximal mechanism by which playful behavior develops, rather than the ultimate function for which playful behavior was selected. Associated theories are that play functions as a neural primer, and/or as a means of reducing information load (Hutt 1979).

Spencer's theory of "surplus energy" is now of only historical interest. "Surplus" energy can be stored, and there is no biological advantage in just getting rid of it. However a slight change in the logic produces the physical training hypothesis (Fagen 1981). This argues that active physical play serves to train muscle strength and general bodily capacity and stamina; it is further argued that there is a critical period for such training, during the infant/juvenile period. The hypothesis is considered to explain certain design features of play, notably its varied but repetitive nature, and the combination of short high-intensity with long low-intensity bouts. Increases in active play are predicted after physical confinement or exercise deprivation; there is some evidence for this.

The physical training hypothesis would not explain specifically social play, nor manipulative play with objects. Until recently, social play was thought by most ethologists to help in socializing the young into the group (see RELATIONSHIPS AND SOCIAL STRUCTURE). It was hypothesized to have social bonding functions, and/or to facilitate the learning of social DOMINANCE and of species-specific communication (Poirier and Smith 1974). Studies by Harlow and others found that monkeys deprived of social play in infancy, showed poor social adjustment later.

However the inference that social play is essential for adjustment is suspect, as the monkeys were typically deprived of any kind of social interaction during isolation (Bekoff 1976).

The socialization hypotheses have been recently called into question. Firstly, naturalistic studies have found examples of some animal groups (e.g. some troops of squirrel monkeys) showing no social play, because of ecological circumstances such as food dispersal; yet these groups functioned normally in terms of cohesion, hierarchy and reproduction. Therefore, social play is not essential for socialization (Baldwin and Baldwin 1977). Secondly, socialization hypotheses do not explain the design features of social play, much of which is quasi-agonistic. Thirdly, socialization hypotheses assume that individual behavior is for the benefit of the social group. Recent thinking in SOCIOBIOLOGY directs more attention to competitive individual benefit in considering the adaptive function of behavior.

Developing these last two criticisms, Symons has carried out detailed studies of play fighting and chasing in rhesus monkeys, and elaborated an alternative functional hypothesis. The design features of play fighting are argued to be attempts to seek advantage, such as to play bite the partner without being bitten, resulting in unstereotyped competitive behavior which would serve as safe practice in juveniles for unstereotyped competitive aggression in adults. Such aggressive competition is important in reproductive success, especially for adult males. It is therefore correctly predicted that play fighting is more frequent in juvenile males than females. Symons develops a corresponding argument that play chasing is practice for predator (avoidance) skills.

Manipulative play has been hypothesized to be functional in providing practice for adult tool use, and also as a source of behavioral innovation (Fagen 1981). It is only commonly observed in the higher primates. In baboons and macaques, manipulative play is relatively infrequent in the wild and shows no regular pattern. It may not have been directly selected for, though Parker and Gibson (1977) suggest its importance for feeding activities.

This argument is stronger in the case of the cebus monkeys and great apes; notably for the chimpanzee, where manipulative play is quite frequent in the young, and may well be functional as practice for tool-using skills such as termite-fishing and leaf-sponging, which are important for subsistence (McGrew 1977). Here, manipulative play serves as practice for species-specific skills. The argument that play was selected for as a source of behavioral innovation suffers the drawback that significant beneficial innovations are rare in non-human species.

PKS

Bibliography

Aldis, Owen 1975: *Play fighting*. New York and London: Academic Press.

Baldwin, J.D. and Baldwin, J.I. 1977: The role of learning phenomena in the ontogeny of exploration and play. In Suzanne Chevalier-Skolnikoff and Frank E. Poirier, eds., *Primate bio-social development*. New York and London: Garland.

Bekoff, M. 1976: The social deprivation paradigm: who's being deprived of what? *Developmental psychobiology* 9, 497–98.

Ellis, Michael J. 1973: *Why people play*. Englewood Cliffs, NJ and Hemel Hempstead: Prentice-Hall.

Fagen, Robert M. 1981: *Animal play behavior*. New York and Oxford: Oxford University Press.

Hutt, C. 1979: Play in the under-fives: form, development and function. In *Modern perspectives in the psychiatry of infancy*. Modern perspectives in psychiatry, *8*, ed. John G. Howells. New York: Brunner/Mazel.

Kaufmann, J.H. 1974: Social ethology of the chiptail wallaby. *Animal behavior* 22, 281–369.

Lazar, J. and Beckhorn, G.D. 1974: Social play or the development of social behavior in ferrets (*Mustela putorius*)? *American zoologist* 14, 405–14.

McGrew, W.C. 1977: Socialization and object manipulation of wild chimpanzees. In Suzanne Chevalier-Skolnikoff and Frank E. Poirier, eds., *Primate bio-social development*. New York and London: Garland.

Parker, S.T. and Gibson, K.R. 1977: Object manipulation, tool use, and sensorimotor intelligence as feeding adaptations in cebus monkeys and great apes. *Journal of human evolution* 6, 623–41.

Poirier, F.E. and Smith, E.O. 1974: Socialising function of primate play. *American zoologist* 14, 275–87.

play: concepts and criteria There is no agreed definition of play. Innumerable attempts have been made, but they have failed to be accepted universally. The difficulty of defining play is not, in fact, accidental. It stems directly from our main method of categorizing behavior by its outcome or function. It is precisely the hallmark of play that the relation between the activities and their outcome or apparent goal looks paradoxical (Millar 1968). Friendly aggression, exploring the apparently familiar, pretense that is not intended to deceive are typical examples.

The criteria we use to classify behavior are, to a large extent, arbitrary. But attempts to classify play by mood or emotion have not proved successful. It is difficult to score emotion objectively. More importantly, the level of excitement varies considerably for different types of play. Similarly, there is no single or prototypical activity by which play could be defined. Almost any voluntary activity could be performed playfully, or in a play context. Here again typical aggressive, sexual or feeding activities take their significance from obvious endstates or outcomes. Uncertainties over classifying sometimes occur also with marginal instances of aggression or sex. But the uncertainty is whether the instance belongs to one or other agreed category. There is no doubt over the goal or function once the behavior is classified. With play, by contrast, the observer may be fairly certain that a child dressing a doll, or foxcubs tumbling over one another are instances of play. But he can only guess at the goal of the individual or the function for the species in either case. Such guesses are more in the nature of hypotheses that require testing rather than criteria by which the activities can be defined.

Play is more easily recognized than defined. Recognition is not infallible but a number of characteristics are typical. The most important of these are firstly that the behavior is *voluntary*:– reflex actions and acts to which the animal is constrained by others or by necessity do not count as "play". The second is the *paradoxical or peculiar nature of the relation between activities and their outcomes*. The paradox is in the eye of the beholder because the function is not obvious. An object which is being endlessly manipulated may still hold novel features for the child. Friendly fights may be necessary because they yield practice in safe conditions. But activities that lead to obvious goals are not called "play". Two further characteristics that are observed very frequently are *repetition and repetition with variations.* Specific activities or sequences of activities are repeated over and over again in games such as "mothers and fathers" by human children, or "king of the castle" games that seem to be equally popular with monkeys. Repetition with variations, called, "diversive exploration" by Berlyne (1960), is apparently directed more to what can be done with an object or a skill than to novel features. It occurs more in species with complex brains and behavior. Word repetition with variations of intonation and stress patterns is common when infants first learn to speak. Another characteristic that has been observed in play of animals below primates is that play bouts tend to consist of *parts of* behavior that belong to quite *different behavioral categories*, following each other in rapid succession. *Incomplete behavior* which is arrested before the endstate or goal is achieved (e.g. "toying" with prey by satiated animals) has also sometimes been listed. *Exaggerated movements* are common.

Many species have special signals which signify that the animal is about to play. Among the most common is the relaxed open mouthed "play-face" that occurs both in monkeys and human children. Particular chirping sounds (Altmann 1962) exaggerated "galumphing" gaits (Loisos 1966), special tones of voice in children (Garvey 1977) are used as signals for play. Looking at your partner through your legs, used by the rhesus monkeys, and young baboons of both sexes "presenting" to the play partner, are invitations to play. Play signals typically occur prior to, and also during *social* play. But the same sort of signs are also sometimes found in solitary play. It is not quite clear as yet under what conditions they occur in solitary play.

Theories of play center on the "useful/useless" dichotomy of behavior which derives from our preference for defining behavior by its functions. This is not only arbitrary, but the fact that we do not know what functions given types of behaviors have does not entitle us to assume that they have no function. However, most theories of play consist either of attempts to explain the apparent uselessness of play, or to supply and argue for a particular function (see PLAY: ANIMAL).

Spencer in the mid-nineteenth century embodied a surplus energy theory of play in his theory of evolution. Animals with more complex brains and behavior play because not all their time has been taken up with food getting. A link with creative art was implied. Overspill from instincts, or a pre-run of parts of these before they are properly sequenced was a later version by ethologists. The analogy with hydraulic systems served as the main model of behavior also for behaviorists until the mid-twentieth century. Berlyne (1960) proposed a use for play as diversive exploration which restores the organism's arousal to an optimal level when external stimulation was too low to maintain this.

Specifically developmental theories started with Hall's recapitulation hypothesis, at the turn of the century. Development of the individual was supposed to be a re-run of development of the species. Freudian psychoanalysis assigned a cathartic function to play at various stages of emotional development. For Piaget (1951) play and imitation were pure forms of assimilation and accommodation respectively, which he assumed to be the two main biological forces responsible for *cognitive* development. The child assimilates new information by applying to it the action schemas he has developed so far. Manipulative play, symbolic play and play with rules follow a sequential course with innately set ceilings. Vygotsky (1933) also assumed that play had a function in cognitive development.

A separate, unitary instinct "to practice other instincts" was proposed by Groos at the turn of the century. It was intended to account for human creative art also. Very similar assumptions are made by a number of current theories; some stressing the *practice*, and some the *innovative* element in play (Bruner, Jolly and Sylva 1976). Current models use analogies with computer systems, and some embody ideas from sociobiology (Fagen 1981).

Evolutionary theory makes it likely that behavior that occurs in many different species is not fortuitous, but has definite biological advantages. But it is not necessary to assume that all the activities we label "play" because their functions are not obvious have the *same* function. Millar (1968, 1981) argued that different types of play relate to different behavioral systems, and belong to *establishing control mechanisms* which regulate these, particularly although not solely, during development and acquisition. "Superfluous" gross motor activity such as frisking gambolling may be homoestatic controls, ensuring stimulation that is necessary for growth, and for toning up after short periods of confinement. Practice or repetitive sensory-motor play could belong to the establishment of motor programs by incorporating feedback information and automatic subroutines. Object manipulation and diversive exploration which were distinguished by Hutt (1966) from specific exploration, would provide information not merely about the object, but about new uses for it or for the activity in question. Sylva (see Bruner, Jolly and Sylva 1976) has provided some evidence that responses are more divergent after play than after more structured activity. Pretend, fantasy or imagination play (e.g. Singer 1973) is likely to relate to the organization of symbolic activities rather than to "feints" that are sometimes useful in aggressive bouts. Rehearsal and reorganization of information is needed for its later flexible use. Pretend play could be an overt form of this. Social play is probably concerned with the regulation of social relations within species. But the functions even of "play-fighting" could vary from establishing dominance hierarchies before the eruption of canine teeth makes biting lethal in species such as the polecat, to group cohesion in species such as monkeys and man where the older, heavier animals handicap themselves when play-fighting with younger ones. But we need to know a great deal more about the conditions which elicit specific types of play before any guesses at functions can be formulated sufficiently precisely for adequate testing.

The assumption that play activities belong to the control systems of a number of different behavioral functions explains the difficulty of finding a prototypical activity by which play could be defined. It also suggests that answers to questions "why" should wait on answers to questions "how" in studies of play. SMi

Bibliography

Altmann, S.A. 1962: Social Behavior of anthropoid primates: Analysis of recent concepts. In *Roots of Behavior*, ed. E.L. Bliss. New York: Harper.

Berlyne, D.E. 1960: *Conflict arousal and curiosity*. New York: McGraw Hill.

Bruner, J.S., Jolly A. and Sylva, K. 1976: *Play: its role in development and evolution*. New York: Basic Books; London: Penguin.

Fagen, R. 1981: *Animal play behavior*. Oxford and New York: Oxford University Press.

Garvey, C. 1977: *Play*. London: Fontana.

Hutt, C. 1966: Exploration and play in children. *Symposium of the Zoological Society, London* 18, 23–44.

Loisos, C. 1966: *Play in mammals*. Symposium of the Zoological Society, London.

Millar, S. 1968: *The psychology of play*. London: Penguin.

——— 1981: Play. In *The Oxford companion to animal behaviour*, ed. D. McFarland. Oxford and New York: Oxford University Press.

Piaget, J. 1951: *Play, dreams and imitation in childhood*. Boston: Routledge & Kegan Paul.

Singer, J.L. 1973: *The child's world of make-believe*. New York: Academic Press.

Vygotsky, L.S. 1933: Play and its role in the mental development of the child. *Soviet psychology* 3, No. 5.

play and emotion Play is behavior that (i) occurs outside its primary context: (ii) is under the control of the organism; and (iii) is intrinsically rewarding. In addition to these criteria, playful responses can be recognized because they tend to be exaggerated, repetitive, fragmented, and unpredictable, i.e., combined in unusual sequences. Also, many species have distinct play signals, including, perhaps, laughter in humans. Most, if not all, mammalian species, many birds, and a few reptiles (crocodilians) play. The concept of play overlaps with emotional concepts such as mirth and amusement. However play is not simply another positive emotion. It is essential to the development of a wide range of responses, including emotional responses, that would be dangerous or unpleasant to acquire in a more direct fashion. (See EMOTION AND FANTASY; PLAY: CONCEPTS AND CRITERIA.) JRAv

Bibliography

Fagan, R. 1981: *Animal play behavior*. New York and Oxford: Oxford University Press.

Smith, P.K. 1982: Does play matter? Functional and evolutionary aspects of animal and human play (with open peer commentary). *Behavioral and brain sciences* 5, 139–84.

pleasure From the very beginnings of philosophy the notion of pleasure – often in conjunction with its supposed opposite, pain – has figured prominently in philosophical arguments, usually in arguments about conduct. That is not surprising, since the question of pleasure – and of the avoidance of its "opposite" – clearly does often arise in our considerations of what to do, of why people do things, of what is worth doing and so on. But many philosophers have used the notion in a more systematic way, to achieve a radical *simplification* in the philosophy both of human motivation and of value, and much philosophical argument has been concerned with the merits of this project.

On the first point, it has been maintained (most explicitly by Bentham in *Principles of morals and legislation*) that the prospect of pleasure, or of the avoidance of pain, is the unique and invariable motive of all voluntary human action; on the second, that the realization of pleasure (more strictly, of a favorable balance of pleasure over pain) is the unique intrinsically good thing, and of its "opposite" the unique intrinsically bad thing. It is thus rather uncomfortably maintained (by Bentham and also, for instance, J.S. Mill in *Utilitarianism*) both that people always and unavoidably do pursue pleasure, and also that they ought to. It is clearly not easy to maintain both, particularly if one wishes to hold that what people ought to pursue is the *general* good ("the greatest happiness (i.e. pleasure) of the greatest number"); for it seems certain that this is not what people always and unavoidably do pursue.

The thesis that pleasure – at any rate the pleasure of the agent himself – is the unique motive can be given a certain plausibility, because of the undoubted link between pleasure and *wanting*. It seems true in some sense that, when we act voluntarily, we do what we want to do. But is not "what we want to do" that which we know, or believe, we will take pleasure in doing, or which will give us pleasure? If so, the prospect of pleasure *is* wanting; and since wanting is a necessary constituent of voluntary action, pleasure is the fundamental and ever-present motivating factor.

It will be clear that this short argument is debatable at every step. That we always do what we want to do may be true in some sense, but in what sense? If I want (decide, choose) to risk my life in battle, is it true – must it be true – that I anticipate pleasure in doing so? Even if I do expect to take pleasure in something that I want, is it pleasure that I really want – that really "moves" me – or the thing itself? Is every goal that is voluntarily pursued, whether by saints or sinners or ordinary citizens, really to be reduced to the same goal, namely pleasure? The notions of voluntariness, choice, wanting, desire, enjoyment, and satisfaction are themselves complex, and it is only by violent distortion that all of them can be "reduced" to the pursuit of pleasure.

The thesis that (a favorable balance of) pleasure is the unique good can also be given a certain plausibility. It has seemed reasonable to many to accord a unique, fundamental value to *happiness*; and it is not wholly implausible to contend, or even, like the utilitarians, to put forward as a matter of definition, that happiness consists in a satisfactory accumulation of pleasures. It is not absolutely impossible to believe that pleasure is the only good thing, and that whatever yields equal pleasure is equally good, but it seems doubtful whether anyone does really believe that. Suppose that I take pleasure in causing pain to other people. How many would really be prepared to argue that I ought to indulge this propensity, on the sole condition that I enjoy it very much – sufficiently, that is, for my pleasure to outweigh the pain that I cause? If I am doing something bad – as, for instance, deliberately causing pain – does it really make things better that I take pleasure, perhaps intense pleasure, in doing it?

Underlying these theses and countertheses about pleasure – and all too often, through remaining unraised and unanswered, confusing them – is the difficult question, what pleasure *is*. It seems natural, but is not very illuminating, to say that it is "a feeling" – we feel pleased, we feel pleasure. But what sort of feeling? It is surely not a sensation, that we feel in some part of, or even diffusedly throughout, our body – that is why it is not really the "opposite" of pain, which literally is felt as a (more or less disagreeable, even disabling) sensation. But if it is a feeling more as emotions are feelings, is it one emotion? Is the pleasure of, say, listening to music the same as that of, say, playing football? We enjoy many different things, and the enjoyment of one is not in general the same as (identically substitutable for) that of another; it seems, similarly, that a wide variety of "states of feeling" may be brought under the heading of "pleasure", and that, while there is reason in each case for that term to occur in this characterization, these are not the *same*, and may perhaps even have no introspectible common character. But if pleasure is not one thing – one sensation, one feeling – it must clearly be doubtful whether "it" could, even in principle, be deployed in the reductive, simplifying role which some philosophers have cut out for it, either in the theory of action or the theory of value. MW

Bibliography

Ryle, G. 1949: *The concept of mind*. London: Hutchinson; Totowa, N.J.: Barnes & Noble (1975).

political psychology The application of methods and concepts in social, developmental and personality psychology to the explanation of political attitudes and behavior. Broadly, research in this field covers the political consciousness and political action of the citizen, the characteristics and practice of leadership, processes of decision-making and policy-making, and the management and resolution of conflict. The aims of researchers working in this field are rapprochement between psychologists, political scientists and historians, and collaboration with practicing politicians and policy-makers in the application of psychological understanding to national and international politics. The focus of the field is applied, and the approaches within it eclectic.

Political psychology grew particularly in the 1960s in response to the nuclear threat: social psychological approaches contributed to studies of conflict resolution, negotiation and bargaining behavior, and the use of gaming and simulation in these contexts. Small group research offers much material on decision-making and leadership; one example is the application of Janis's concept of "groupthink" – the tendency of groups to generate consensus which reduces their effective use of information – to recent political and military catastrophes. The study of political leadership has drawn both from small group dynamics research, and from psycho-biographical accounts and analyses of specific leaders.

Political socialization, and by extension, political education, is an important aspect of political psychology. One approach to explaining the origin and socialization of political attitudes focusses on the relationship between ideology and personality, and the function of ideology in sustaining the self (e.g. AUTHORITARIAN PERSONALITY studies). Other, more cognitive, approaches ask what makes for an internally consistent set of political beliefs, or how does the individual develop a world view which enables him or her to make sense of political and social issues.

National and group identity and stereotypes have long been recognized as important in the development of children's attitudes and world views; the rise of political consciousness among minority groups and women further highlighted the importance of intergroup relations and social identity in political socialization and the mobilization of political action. Examples of different ways in which political psychologists approach issues can be seen in studies of the upsurge of youth protest movements during the last two decades; for some psychologists the question is, "who are the activists?"; for others the question was "what is the interrelationship between historical context, political climate and the psychological factors in individual response." HW-H

polygamy In anthropology, polygamy refers to forms of marriage where individuals of either sex have two or more spouses, usually simultaneously. The main forms of polygamy are polygyny, where a man has two or more wives, and polyandry, where a woman has two or more husbands. Both are contrasted to monogamy, where one man and one woman are married.

In ETHOLOGY, by an intended analogy, polygamy and its related terms are applied to relationships between individuals as observed in animal behavior: however, the criteria are necessarily different, being based on sexual behavior rather than marriage, and sometimes applied to mating relationships that are successive within a breeding season rather than simultaneous. Sometimes cooperation of both sexes in rearing the young is considered a further criterion. Polygamous and monogamous mating relationships are both contrasted to promiscuous mating behavior, where restricted mating relationships of substantial duration are not evident. These mating systems occur with varying frequencies in different animal groups, and there have been attempts to describe and explain the ecological and social correlates of mating systems on the basis that they result from NATURAL SELECTION (see Krebs and Davies 1981).

Biological and anthropological views of mating systems usually diverge. Nonetheless, behavioral definitions of polygamy and monogamy, based on the restriction of regular sexual activity, are sometimes applied to both humans and animals, reflecting a new approach which may offer new insights (see Hiatt 1980, Dickemann 1979). At present such approaches are at an exploratory stage. RDA

Bibliography

Dickemann, M. 1979: The ecology of mating systems in hypergynous dowry societies. *Social science information, 18*(2), 163–195.

Hiatt, L.R. 1980: Polyandry in Sri Lanka: a test case for parental investment theory. *Man* n.s. 15, 583–602.

*Keesing, R.M. 1981: *Cultural anthropology: a contemporary perspective*, 2nd ed. New York and London, Sydney: Holt, Rinehart & Winston.

Krebs, J.R. and Davies, N.B. eds 1981: *An introduction to behavioural ecology*. Oxford: Blackwell Scientific; Sunderland, Mass.: Sinauer.

positivism Auguste Comte, 1798–1857, was the founder of the original school of positive philosophy (1844). He divided the history of mankind into three stages, the theological, the metaphysical and the positive or scientific. Science alone yielded knowledge and anything that could not be put on a scientific basis should be discarded.

The Logical Positivists, who flourished in Vienna between the two wars, took over Comte's promotion of science and rejection of metaphysics and developed it as a theory of meaning. They maintained that our sensory contact with the material world gives us not only all our knowledge of truth, but also all our understanding of meaning. This empirical theory of meaning was not new: the novelty was its systematic development, begun by Ernst Mach (1900) and continued by the philosophers of the Vienna Circle, who first called themselves "Logical Positivists". The motto of this school was the Verification Principle: the meaning of a proposition is the method of its verification. The idea was developed in different ways by Rudolph Carnap (1935), Friedrich Waismann (1965), Karl Popper (1959) and A.J. Ayer, who adapted it and imported it into English philosophy (1959). The two main variables were the choice of a particular empirical basis for the theory of meaning – should the basic propositions be about sensations or about things in the physical world? – and the method of building the superstructure of language on the chosen basis. What was common to all versions of the theory of meaning was a ruthless pruning of all the more tender and adventurous shoots of language and thought.

DP

Bibliography

Ayer, A.J. 1936: *Language, truth and logic*. London: Gollancz 2nd edn. with a new introduction by the author, 1946.

——— ed., 1959: *Logical positivism*. Glencoe, Ill.: London: Allen & Unwin.

Carnap, Rudolph 1935 *(1937)*: *The logical syntax of language*. London: Kegan Paul.

Comte, Auguste 1844: *Discours sur l'esprit positif*. Paris.

Mach, Ernst 1900: *Die Analyse der Empfindung*. Jena.

Popper, Karl 1934 *(1959)*: *The logic of scientic discovery*. London: Hutchinson.

Waismann, Friedrich 1965: *The principles of linguistic philosophy*. Ed. Rom Harré. London: Macmillan.

power semantics The study of power semantics is concerned with the use of language in maintaining and consolidating differential power in a society and the manipulation of people by means of language.

The principal areas of study include address pronouns (Lambert and Tucker, eds. 1976), sex-related speech differences, political indoctrination (O'Barr and O'Barr 1976) and advertising.

An example of how differential power is expressed in language is the use in a number of European languages of a T (from French *TU*) pronoun by masters to address their servants, whilst the servants address their master with the V (from French VOUS) pronoun.

The study of power semantics is closely related to that of linguistic relativity as proposed by WHORF.

PM

Bibliography

Lambert, W.E. and Tucker, G.R., eds 1976: *Tu, vous, usted: A socio-psychological study of address patterns*. Newbury House, Rewley, Mass.

O'Barr, W.M. and J.F., eds 1976: *Language and politics*. The Hague, Mouton.

practical syllogism That form of reasoning running from premises which state an intention or consensual belief to a conclusion involving an action. In his *Nicomachean ethics*, Aristotle described it as having a universal premise (e.g. "Everything sweet ought to be tasted"), a particular premise (e.g. "This thing before me is sweet"), and a conclusion pertaining to an action. Aristotle's treatment leaves two questions unanswered: is the practical syllogism formally valid? and, does the conclusion assert a truth-claim about an action, reflect a decision whether to act, or constitute the performance of an action? Aristotle was aware of the problematic relation between the premises and the action prescribed: he specified that "the man who *is able* and *is not prevented is bound* to act accordingly at once" (1147a, Martin Ostwald, trans. emphasis added). The qualifiers "able" and "not prevented" are external to the syllogism. Further, the term "is bound to act" seems qualitatively different from the logical necessity of a valid syllogism. The action entailed by the premises of the practical syllogism is somehow different from the proposition that one *should* act. In Lewis Carroll's words, practical necessity does not "take you by the throat and *force* you to do it".

Modern commentators have responded in four ways. Perelman and Olbrechts-Tyteca (1969) assume that the "power of deliberation" may be usefully applied to domains in which exact calculation, experiment and logically valid deduction are impossible. The result is "rhetoric" or "argumentation": the methods of proof used to secure adherence about logically uncertain or contingent matters. Kenny (1966) developed criteria for demonstrating the validity of practical reasoning leading to propositions prescribing that one *should* act. Aune (1977) argued that the conclusion of the practical syllogism is neither the performance of an action nor a proposition about an action but a decision about an action. As such, practical reasoning may be evaluated from the perspective of Bayesian decision theory in addition to logical standards. For social scientists, the work by Anscombe (1963) and von Wright (1971) is the most useful of these modern treatments of practical reasoning. Their key move is the treatment of action as intentional, interpreted events within the context of language-games and forms-of-life which provide explanatory frames. Within these contexts, the practical syllogism provides a structure for organizing the reasoning actors *use* in deciding what to do and the reasons actors and/or observers *give* when explaining actions. Anscombe (1963, p.84) argued that "intentional" acts are distinguished by the "form of description" which are applied to them. Those which are described using the practical syllogism are judged by the speech community as "intentional". Von Wright (1971) championed the practical syllogism as the structure of explanation for those branches of social science which envision humans as purposive. Von Wright (1978) cautioned that the practical syllogism in which the first premise is written in the first person (e.g. "I want X) should not be taken as an accurate representation of the reasoning which "causes" a person to act. However, he argued that the syllogism in which the first premise is written in the third person can be used "retrospectively" to identify premises which justify or explain actions, and "prospectively" to predict subsequent actions. In both instances, the result is "understanding", or the locating of an action as appropriate within the language games of the community. In von Wright's formulation, the practical syllogism has this form:

A intends to bring about Y;
A knows that Y will not occur unless he does X;
Therefore, A sets himself to do X.

At least five lines of social science research employ or are consistent with the practical syllogism as the structure of explanation. Harré's "ethogeny" (1977) is the most philosophically sophisticated of a number of "dramaturgical" or "interpretive" schools of thought which analyse "both the social force and explanatory content of the speech produced by social actors as a guide to the structure of the cognitive resources required for the genesis of intelligible and warrantable social action by those actors" (Harré 1977, p.284). Harré argues that social interaction is a social product of intentional acts based on cognitive templates. The product of ethogenic research is a description of those templates and the manner in which persons achieve intelligibility in their performance. "Competent people 'contain' templates" (ibid. p.289), although they probably cannot articulate them fully. Ethogenists can identify a number of different types of templates, including "plans", formal causes of nonstandard action pattern, and "rules", formal causes of the structure of standard action sequences. These templates are that which is designated as "Y" in the first premise of the practical syllogism. Actions are justified or interpreted by showing their connection to the template. The statement of that connection is the warrant for the minor premise.

A less transparent use of the structure of the practical syllogism can be found in Jackson's "Return Potential Mode" (1966, 1975). Jackson assumes that a person's intentions are clear and powerful, but there are various means by which they could be realized. He locates the necessity or imperative force of the practical syllogism in "the distribution of potential approval and disapproval by Others for various alternatives of Actors' behavior . . ." in a given defined situation (Jackson, 1966, p.36). "Intensity" represents the deviation of the mean response from "indifference", while "crystallization" expresses the degree of consensus of the group. The quantitative measures of intensity and crystallization provide measures of the force of the necessity from the practical syllogism which impinges upon the relevant action. If intensity or crystallization are either or both low, then practical force will be low, expressed in a premise such as "a person A knows that if he does X, Y may or may not occur".

Pearce and Cronen's (1980) theory of "the coordinated management of meaning" postulates "logical force" as the "necessity" explaining patterns of social action. Persons seldom if ever act capriciously; they perceive their actions necessarily entailed because of the actions of others, their own concept of self, the demands of a situation, their intentions, etc. Pearce and Cronen treat these "perceived entailments" as scalar variables, the combination of which comprises a "logic of meaning and action" which has variable force. The entailments from preceding acts or previously established meanings is described as "prefigurative force"; the entailments from an act to subsequent acts by self or other and to meanings to be established subsequently is described as "practical force." The implications of this move are to make the practical necessity of performing an entailed action a measurable force as perceived by actors rather than an attribute of the arrangement of propositions in a syllogism; and to subsume practical necessity within an explanatory framework which includes prefigurative force.

Pearce and Cronen treat communication as a process of creating/maintaining interpretations during attempts to coordinate activity with others. This process is inherently problematic since individuals can never be certain that they have accurately perceived the other's interpretations. Researchers can develop a "portrait" of social episodes by graphing the way the logical forces of the actors intermesh. Such portraits have usefully described the occurrence of recurring patterns known to and unwanted by the actors, violence in families, and difficulties in intercultural communication. WBP

Bibliography

Anscombe, G.E.M. 1963: *Intention*. 2nd edn. Ithaca: Cornell University Press.

Aune, Bruce 1977: *Reason and action*. Dordrecht, Holland and Boston: D. Reidel.

Harré, Rom 1977: The ethogenic approach: theory and practice. In *Advances in experimental psychology*, ed. Leonard Berkowitz. New York: Academic Press.

Jackson, J. 1966: A conceptual and measurement model for norms and roles. *Pacific sociological Review* 9, 35–47.

——— 1975: Normative power and conflict potential. *Sociological methods and research* 4, 237–63.

Kenny, A. 1966: Practical inference. *Analysis* 26, 65–73.

Pearce, W. Barnett and Cronen, Vernon 1980: *Communication, action and meaning*. New York: Praeger.

Perelman, Chaim and Olbrechts-Tyteca, L. 1958 *(1969)*: *The new rhetoric: a treatise on argument*. Notre Dame, Indiana: Notre Dame Press.

Schwartz, S.H. 1973: Normative explanations of helping behavior: A critique, proposal, and empirical test. *Journal of experimental social psychology* 9, 349–64.

——— 1974: Awareness of interpersonal consequences, responsibility denial, and volunteering. *Journal of personality and social psychology* 30, 57–63.

von Wright, Georg, 1971: *Explanation and understanding*. Ithaca New York: Cornell University Press.

——— 1978: On so-called practical inference. In *Practical reasoning*, ed. Joseph Raz. Oxford University Press.

pragmatism Less a philosophical doctrine than a loosely agreed upon way of dealing with traditional philosophical issues. There are pragmatic theories of knowledge, meaning and truth, and numerous other concepts. Their common core is some reference to the manipulation of what is given, until knowledge, meaning and truth emerge from incoherent data. The pragmatists can best be understood as revolting against the classical British empiricists' "spectator" theory of knowledge and as putting a "participant" theory in its place. You cannot know the world by staring at it; you come to know it by doing things to it and discovering what happens as a result.

A strong emphasis on praxis pervaded C.S. Peirce's analysis of the concept of meaning. There is no meaning prior to use; meaning is constructed. The meaning of a proposition is the whole set of practical consequences which will occur if the proposition is true. Hence, "this diamond is hard" means "if I push it across a piece of glass it will scratch the glass", and so on. By "practical" Peirce meant experimental or manipulative interventions to see what the results would be. The meaning of a proposition consists in the whole set of such results. But how can one say of the diamond at the bottom of the sea that it is hard when it cannot be put to the test? Peirce modified his pragmatic theory so that the meaning of a proposition consists in the whole set of results which *would* occur provided the necessary manipulations *could* be made.

William James's pragmatic claim that a true proposition is one that works, is useful, or – as he put in his usual picturesque way – carries us prosperously from one part of our experience to another, has often been caricatured. If one successfully lies then one has told the truth! James, of course, meant something technical by his everyday words, namely that a proposition is true if it *predicts* what is to come, helps us prepare for the future and systematically *coheres* with other propositions which play the same role. James again was emphasizing that there is a relation between the action to which a true proposition leads and the concept of truth. It is not clear, however, whether James meant the active feature – propositions as successful leading principles – to be a sign or criterion of "truth" or whether he thought it to be part of the meaning of "truth".

According to traditional empiricism we receive knowledge of the external world passively through our sense organs. But John Dewey argued that seeing an object as yellow and of a certain shape does not constitute knowledge of it. We strike the object and find it malleable, we spin it into wire and conduct electricity through it, we ascribe to it an atomic number, and so on; only then can it be said that we have a knowledge of copper, an awareness of the structure of copper that allows us to control and utilize it.

James's *Principles of psychology*, particularly the chapters on attention and reasoning, which James characterized as *functional* ways of dealing with the environment, was the crucial influence on Dewey's form of pragmatism, which he called instrumentalism. EHM

Bibliography

Ayer, A.J. 1968: *The origins of pragmatism*. Oxford: Oxford University Press.

James, William 1907: *Pragmatism*. London: Longmans Green.

praxis The Marxist conception of human activity or production, embedded within and, simultaneously creating socio-historical conditions.

Marx specifically emphasized praxis as uniquely characterizing the human mode of production in the sense that, although itself a part of nature, the human being is able to transcend nature through his or her productive activity. In attempting to meet his or her physical needs, the individual engages in labor, and through labor recreates these needs into cultural and social activities. For example, the needs for food, shelter and procreation are recreated or transformed into agriculture, property, and family which in turn initiate more complex activities. These activities constitute both society as a progressive process of social relations and the way through which human capacities and potentialities are actualized. In this sense praxis aims both at the transformation of the world (e.g. economic, material, historical conditions) and at the individual's own self development (Janoušek 1972). It exemplifies the Marxist belief in the unity of individual and society, thought and action, and recognizes their fusion in human experience or in the human mode of production itself (see DIALECTIC THEORY, MARXIST PERSONALITY THEORY). MG

Bibliography

Janoušek, J. 1972: On the Marxian concept of praxis. In *The context of social psychology: a critical assessment*, ed. J. Israel and H. Tajfel. London: Academic Press.

Marx, Karl: German ideology; Economic and philosophical manuscripts. In *Karl Marx: Selected writings*, ed. D. McLellan. Oxford: Oxford University Press (1977).

PRE *See* partial reinforcement effect

predation A concern with the nature and implications of predatory behavior has arisen in the heated debate over the extent to which aggression is biologically determined. Writers such as Ardrey (1979), following Dart (1953) have argued that Man's instinctive hostility to his fellows derives from his emergence as a predatory hominid. His use of primitive weapons for the killing of prey were also used in conflicts with other hominid rivals and, coupled with territoriality, led to the evolution of a "killer" species. Montagu (1976), on the other hand argues that predation in Man has been overemphasized and is largely irrelevant in the discussion of the origins of aggression. Marsh (1978) has argued that aggression and predation should be seen as quite separate processes – hunting behavior being quite different in form from patterns of conspecific fighting and display in both animals and humans. He suggests, however, that the unique ability of Man is to manipulate symbols and thereby *dehumanize* his rivals. Where others can successfully be demoted to the role of prey, typical predatory acts are then, and only then, manifested. PEM

Bibliography

Ardrey, R. 1979: *The hunting hypothesis*. London and New York: Methuen.

Dart, R. A. 1953: On the predatory transition from ape to man. *International anthropology and linguistic review*.

Marsh, P. 1978: *Aggro: the illusion of violence*. London: Dent.

Montagu, A. 1976: *The nature of human aggression* Oxford: Oxford University Press.

prejudice The term "prejudice", as used in psychology, is in some ways broader and in some ways narrower than its dictionary definition in the *The Concise Oxford Dictionary* as a "preconceived opinion, bias (against, in favor of, person or thing)". Prejudice in psychological usage is broader because it includes not only biases of beliefs or opinions but also their evaluative and emotional connotations. It is narrower for two reasons. The first is that it is generally applied to people's views about social groups and their members rather than more generally to "persons" or "things". The second is that, in practice, the term has been mainly restricted in psychological theory and research to hostile or unfavorable views about human groups other than one's own ("outgroups"). It has been used by psychologists in the context of intergroup hostility, conflicts, persecution or discrimination.

Prejudice is therefore, in psychology, an ATTITUDE which has two aspects: the *cognitive*, which consists of the nature and contents of the opinions, beliefs and views about certain social groups; and the *affective* which consists of the associated emotions and values. These attitudes must be distinguished from the actual behavior towards certain groups or their members which is often referred to as "discrimination". Prejudice against a group may sometimes be present without the existence of clear and objective marks of discrimination. This may be so for a variety of reasons, such as legal or moral prohibitions, political and economic motives, etc. Conversely, there may be forms of discrimination against a group which are not necessarily associated with prejudice. For example, some people may propose restrictions on immigration without necessarily harboring hostile attitudes towards the groups upon which they wish to impose limitations of this kind. But these theoretical distinctions often do not work in practice. Attitudes of prejudice which remain for long without being capable of some form of expression in behavior tend to weaken. Discrimination against certain groups which may start from an absence of hostility often ends up as discrimination accompanied by prejudice.

Several trends of thought and research can be distinguished in the history and the present directions of the study of prejudice in psychology. An excellent review of the earlier work can be found in Allport (1954). Looking back a quarter of a century later, it appears that a twofold general distinction can be made: between research and theory concerned with prejudice as an outcome of certain individual psychological processes; and research and theory starting from the individuals' group membership and looking at its effects upon behavior and attitudes towards other groups (see Tajfel and Fraser 1978, chs 16 and 17).

Some of the "individual" conceptions of prejudice focussed upon its motivational or affective aspects; others were more concerned with the nature and contents of the beliefs about outgroups, i.e. the cognitive aspects of prejudiced attitudes.

Most of the conceptions about individual motives determining prejudice have been powerfully influenced, directly or indirectly, by ideas deriving from the Freudian theory. There is not room here for details of the theoretical links which Freud established between his general theories of human personality and his "group psychology" (see e.g. Freud 1922), particularly as his conceptions about these links changed from the earlier to the later period of his work. His two basic ideas relevant to prejudice were: the inevitability of outgroup hostility, and its function in holding the group together. As he once wrote: "It is always possible to bind together a considerable number of people in love, as long as there are other people left over to receive the manifestations of their aggressiveness" (1930, p.14).

These views were very much a part of the *Zeitgeist*. The ingroup-preserving functions of aggression against other groups fitted in with the general conceptions of SOCIAL DARWINISM and were not very different from the ideas expressed earlier by social scientists, such as Sumner (1906), who first popularized the terms "ethnocentrism", "ingroup" and "outgroup" and who also felt that the cohesion and survival of the "we-group" depended upon the availability of external enemies. Freud derived his views from certain transpositions to group attitudes and behavior of the emotional entanglements through which, according to him, each individual human being had to go in his or her (mainly his) early childhood. Sumner's ethnocentrism was an "umbrella concept" principally derived from what appeared to him to be the universal and undeniable features of social reality.

These ideas found strange bedfellows in some versions of BEHAVIORISM popular in the 1930s. A book on *Frustration and aggression* published in 1939 by Dollard and his colleagues, a group of Yale behaviorists, started from a theoretical sequence very different from that postulated by Freud and finished with very similar conclusions. Although these views underwent later a number of revisions, in which some concessions about their general validity had to be made, the basic sequence was a stark and simple one: all aggression is preceded by frustration; all frustration is followed by aggression. When aggression against the agent of the frustration cannot be "discharged" directly, because it is inhibited by external or internal impediments, it becomes displaced, i.e. directed towards a substitute target which happens to be available. In the case of relations between social groups, the outgroups and their members provide often the most convenient target for this displaced aggression. The frustration–aggression hypothesis was later revised and modified by e.g. Berkowitz (1962) who extended the concept of "frustration" in a cognitive direction through including in it the "failure of expectancies", denied the inevitability of the frustration–aggression sequence, and tried to describe, more clearly than was possible from the earlier versions of the theory, the nature of the processes guiding the choice of a particular target of aggression. But the basic idea behind all this work, from before Freud until the 1960s and later, remains that prejudice against outgroups can be accounted for by the inevitability of individual hostile motivations which somehow are joined together to create the socially shared phenomenon of prejudice. The major difficulty with such a view is its assumption that very large numbers of people happen to find themselves in a similar motivational state which sometimes lasts for very long periods of time, since in many cases prejudice against certain groups goes on for generations or even centuries (see Billig 1976).

The horrors and systematic massacres of the second world war and the persistence in its aftermath of hostile attitudes towards certain minorities in the United States led a group of refugees from Nazi Germany to attempt to answer the question: what kind of people were they who either did or potentially could commit acts of that nature? The result was the large and influential study *The authoritarian personality* published in 1950 by a team which included refugees from the Frankfurt Institute for Social Research and their American colleagues (Adorno et al. 1950). As in the ideas about prejudice described earlier, here again the influence of psychoanalytic theory (in a much modified form) was clearly visible. The sociopolitical background of the Frankfurt exiles led them to focus their attention upon the links between family structure and its wider framework in the surrounding society. Their conviction that psychological processes had to be taken into account in the understanding of intense hostility against outgroups made them look at the psychological effects of early emotional experiences in certain kinds of family relationships of which a rigid authoritarianism was the hallmark. The result of all this was the concept of "authoritarian personality". Such personalities were, according to the authors, characterized by the need to work out their inner problems and difficulties by transposing them into hostility towards the weaker, the alien, the unusual and the "different". The F ("fascist") and E ("ethnocentric") scales were among the empirical outcomes of this work; the scales were claimed to measure predispositions to hostile attitudes and actions towards certain outgroups. The validity of these scales, their reliability and their capacity to encompass the wider aspects of prejudice, by no means always associated with certain personality "types", led to many controversies, some of which are still with us today.

It could be said that the research on authoritarian personality was mainly concerned to find out why some people hate or dislike "alien" groups under most conditions, rather than why most or many people are capable of developing long-lasting prejudiced attitudes towards outgroups in some conditions. In addition to the "motivational" theories discussed earlier, three other recent trends of research focussed upon the latter of these two questions. One of them was mainly concerned with the cognitive aspects of prejudice, i.e. with the systems of beliefs about outgroups which hostile attitudes towards them usually include. The other two took as their point of departure the psychological effects of various forms of conflict or competition between social groups.

The systems of beliefs about outgroups in which unwarranted (and often unfavorable) generalizations are made about groups as a whole or their individual members are known in psychology as social stereotypes. Allport (1954) was one of the earliest authors to insist that the functions served by these stereotypes had to be understood in the more general context of the human activity of categorizing the environment, physical and social. These categorizations consist of systematizing the world around us in terms of classes of objects and events. Items within each of the classes are considered as approximately equivalent for purposes of action or of understanding the complexities of what happens around us. Thus, social categories segment our social environment into groups of people who (we assume) can be considered similar in terms of their common characteristics and of the attributions of causality concerning their actions, intentions, personal traits, individual and collective behavior. Because of the usefulness that these preconceived ideas have both in simplifying the social world around us and in preserving intact our value systems, we tend to select, interpret and accentuate the information we receive about other people in accordance with what we know or think we know about the categories to which they belong. The stronger our emotional involvement in separating between sheep and goats on certain social criteria, the stronger will be the tendency to "filter" accordingly the relevant information. This leads to a number of clear-cut effects on judgments of other people which are determined by the social category to which they are assigned (see Tajfel 1981).

These social categorizations become particularly salient and effective in conditions of conflict or competition between a group to which we belong and other groups. The classic studies on the psychological effects of such conflicts were conducted over the years by Sherif and his collaborators and summarized by him in a book published in 1966. It was found that a conflict (manipulated by the psychologists) between two groups of boys in a holiday camp, which was based on several competitions in which one of the groups only could win, led to all the usual manifestations of intergroup prejudice and hostility, including the development of ingroup rituals and of unfavorable stereotypes about the outgroup, and also, in some cases, the breakdown of previously existing individual friendships between boys who found themselves in opposing camps.

A number of more recent studies have shown, however, that biases in favor of one's group (and correspondingly, unfavorable treatment of, or ideas about, an outgroup) can develop even in the complete absence of an explicit conflict of interests or competition between groups (see Tajfel 1981; Turner and Giles 1981). Membership of some groups is important; it includes commitment and an emotional involvement in the group. Salient aspects of our self-concepts or self-images are then tied in to the image of the group as a whole. In turn, the favorable or unfavorable connotations of these collective images acquire most of their significance when comparisons of the ingroup are made with certain selected outgroups. In other words, the quality and significance of the social or group identity of individuals are largely derived from the ways in which their groups can be compared in certain important respects with other groups which, because of the nature of their relations with the ingroup, invite comparability. Many of the present-day industrial conflicts about "differentials", as well as the multiplicity of social and political movements concerned with ethnicity, are based on an interaction between the pursuit of the "objective" interests of the groups involved and these psychological processes of social identity and social comparisons. Prejudice against selected outgroups is one aspect of this interaction. The development and functioning of hostile intergroup attitudes cannot be understood in isolation from their historical, social, political and economic background; but their proper understanding requires in addition an analysis of the complex social psychological processes which also form an indissoluble part of our social reality. HT

Bibliography

Adorno, T.W. et al. 1950: *The authoritarian personality*. New York: Harper.

*Allport, G.W. 1954: *The nature of prejudice*. Cambridge, Mass.: Addison-Wesley.

Berkowitz, L. 1962: *Aggression: a social psychological analysis*. New York: McGraw-Hill.

*Billig, M. 1976: *Social psychology and intergroup relations*. European Monographs in Social Psychology, No. 9. London: Academic Press.

Dollard, J. et al. 1939: *Frustration and aggression*. New Haven: Yale University Press.

Freud, S. 1922 (*1976*): Group psychology and the analysis of the ego. *Standard edition of the complete psychological works of Sigmund Freud*. London: Hogarth; New York: Norton.

——— 1930 (*1976*): Civilization and its discontents, *Standard edition*. London: Hogarth; New York: Norton.

Sherif, M. 1966: *In common predicament: social psychology of intergroup conflict and cooperation*. Boston: Houghton Mifflin.

Sumner, W.G. 1906: *Folkways*. New York: Ginn.

*Tajfel, H. 1981: *Human groups and social categories: studies in social psychology*. Cambridge and New York: Cambridge University Press.

*Tajfel, H. and Fraser, C., eds. 1978: *Introducing social psychology*. London: Penguin Books.

*Turner, J.C. and Giles, H. eds. 1981: *Intergroup behavior*. Oxford: Basil Blackwell; Chicago: University of Chicago Press.

prenatal development Is of interest to development psychologists mainly from two aspects: first in relation to the maturation of sensory and motor capacities that occur during prenatal life, and second on account of the influence of factors affecting prenatal development on the later behavior of the infant. In relation to the latter, research interest has been focussed on: the maternal diet (which can affect brain maturation); drugs, alcohol and smoking during pregnancy; irradiation; fetal anoxia; maternal emotional state. These influences have been investigated in both human clinical studies and animal experiments. With the exception of irradiation, the various agents affect the fetus indirectly, via changes in the maternal blood supply, since a wide variety of pharmacological, hormonal and nutritional agents can pass through the placenta. JA

Bibliography

Joffee, J.M. 1969: *Prenatal determinants of behaviour*, Oxford and New York: Pergamon.

preparedness Certain combinations of stimuli, responses and reinforcers produce more rapid and effective conditioning than others; this may be described, if not explained, by saying that organisms are prepared to associate certain combinations of events and not others. The best documented example is the conditioning of aversions to food. If rats are made ill after eating or drinking some novel substance, they will show a marked aversion to the flavor of that substance, but not to other stimuli (auditory or visual) which accompanied its ingestion. But if they are punished by a brief shock to the feet for eating or drinking this substance, they will show little or no aversion to its flavor, but be most reluctant to eat or drink anything in the presence of the auditory or visual stimuli present when they were punished. Flavors are readily associated with illness; auditory or visual stimuli with an external source of pain. NJM

Bibliography

Seligman, M.E.P. 1970: On the generality of the laws of learning, *Psychological review* 77, 406–18.

primacy and recency effects In serial recall tasks, the two or three items at the beginning of a sequence are recalled better than items in the middle of the sequence. This is called the primacy effect. It can be attributed to better attention and greater resource availability at the beginning of a task. The last four or five items of a sequence are also recalled better, which is the recency effect. In part, the recency effect is due to the continued availability of the final items in short term memory, but in part it has other, strategic origins. WKi

primal therapy A clinical system, formulated by A. Janov (*The primal scream*, 1973), which forces patients to relive painful emotional experiences in order to free them from neurosis. The term "clinical" is appropriate in that Janov is reductionistic, biologically rather than psychologically orientated: "We don't recall with emotion – the Freudian abreaction. We relive. Recall and "remember" are mind phenomena; relive is a total neurophysiologic one ..." (quoted in Rosen, 1978, p.156; c.f. Janov, 1978). His system leaves no room for the therapeutic efficacy of understanding and reformulating the circumstances and current self commitments which engender suffering (see PSYCHOTHERAPY and PSYCHOANALYSIS). It is a subterranean therapy, emotions working according to processes which lie below meaning-infused mental operations; it is anti-cognitive: "The beginning of feeling is the end of philosophy". Working with a psychodynamic or hydraulic model, Janov attributes neurosis to early childhood experiences. The child's basic needs, in particular to be loved, are not gratified. The primal trauma (anger, pain) results (c.f. the frustration-aggression hypothesis), and the child responds defensively. The defense system, providing "a set of behaviors which automatically function to block Primal feelings" (Janov, 1973, p.60), is manifested in neurotic activities: bed wetting and the like, or, having been stored, in smoking, over-eating and so on during adult life.

Blocking the pain produces neurosis; feeling the pain undoes it. Therapy is required to shatter defenses, allowing the patient to get in touch with his pain and then purge what he could not cope with as a child. Therapy begins with a twenty-four hour period of isolation during which the patient is not permitted to nurture his defenses (no tension-diverting activities). There follows a three-week period during which the patient receives one open-ended therapy session a day from a qualified therapist who aims to "bust" (not have "head trips" with) his subject. Spread-eagled on a couch, the patient is encouraged to call out for his parents, and, if all goes well, he erupts with primal screams: "I hate you; Daddy, for Christ's sake, *be* nice". Group sessions follow over a six-month-period (or, as with Janovian-inspired communities such as Atlantis in Ireland, become the basis of a life-style (James, 1980)). Having gone through the hell of reliving his pains, the post-primal person has satisfied or completed his childhood needs (he no longer has to ask for the love that he needed but did not receive). He has vented his pain and anger. He no longer has any need for energy consuming defenses because the energy is now used to improve physiological functioning, etc. (see Janov, 1978). Without neurotic defenses, he is more "real", "feels" everything, and can build on the basically good nature which existed before adverse childhood experiences.

Would that life (and therapy) were so simple and true (Janov does not accept that any other approach is valid). Criticisms are legion, the most important being that there is no evidence that endogenous processes *alone* govern the paths of emotions and neurosis. However, it should be born in mind that patients do undergo primal therapy, the results being "remarkable" (Kovel 1978, p.195), and that Freud himself never entirely relinquished the idea that emotional display can be consummative in the therapeutic setting. We know so little about how the emotions work. By emphasizing endogenous processes, by treating traumas in psychodynamic fashion, Janov at the very least has set up an interesting naturalistic experiment. PLFH

Bibliography

*James, Jenny 1980: *They call us the screamers!* Firle: Caliban Books.

*Janov, Arthur 1973: *The primal scream.* London: Sphere Books.

——— 1978: *The anatomy of mental illness.* London: Sphere Books.

Kovel, Joel 1978: *A complete guide to therapy.* Harmondsworth: Penguin.

Rosen, R. 1978: *Psychobabble.* London: Wildwood House.

privacy Being perceptible by only one person. Medieval Aristotelians taught that intellect is a capacity best known through its exercise in intelligent behavior. For them there was no problem of privacy. But DESCARTES defined "thought" as "a word that covers everything that exists in us in such a way that we are immediately conscious of it" (1911 edn, II, 52). A corollary was that belief in the existence of anything other than one's own thoughts involves a questionable process of inference. The ground was laid for the notion that other people's thoughts are inaccessible, whereas one has some sort of "privileged access" to one's own.

What is the nature of one's access to one's own thoughts? LOCKE distinguished between "reflection", the mind's turning inward upon itself, and "sensation", the source of one's ideas of external things. Apart from the first being internal, and the second external, he regarded them as being very similar modes of observation. He evidently regarded sensation as being the more familiar, for he explained reflection in terms of it. "Though it be not sense, as having nothing to do with external objects, yet it is very like it, and might properly enough be called internal sense" *Essay concerning human understanding*, (I, 78).

Brentano, more consistently Cartesian than Locke, drew attention to a respect in which internal perception is unlike external: it is infallible. Strictly speaking, he said, so-called external perception is not really perception at all. One does not *perceive* external objects; one *infers* their existence from one's ideas or sensations of them. So, far from it being appropriate to assimilate internal perception to external perception, we should describe mental phenomena as "the only phenomena of which perception in the strict sense of the word is possible" (1973, p.91). Brentano did not intend this as a definition of the mental. (His definition was in terms of "intentionality".) But when Schlick referred to the difference Brentano had noted between internal and external perception it was in the context of an attempt to define the physical. Schlick concluded that "the physical is that reality which *on principle* is *only* accessible through indirect experience" (1925 §32).

Moore, in his seminal paper on "The subject-matter of psychology" (1909–10), introduced some of Brentano's ideas on the mental into British philosophy of mind. He asked "What kinds of entities are mental, and how are those which are mental distinguished from those which are not?" He said that acts of consciousness undoubtedly seem mental, but that being an act of consciousness is not the only characteristic of mentality. There is, Moore said, a characteristic which cannot be said to be a *meaning* of the term "mental", but which may be proposed as a *criterion* of what is mental: the characteristic of being directly known by one mind only. Moore was doubtful whether privacy is a characteristic of all mental acts. Perhaps the abnormal phenomena of co-consciousness in a case of split personality constitute an exception. Brentano had expressed no doubt. Since mental phenomena are the objects of inner perception "it is obvious that no mental phenomenon is perceived by more than one individual" (1973 edn, p.92).

Experimental psychologists have tended to by-pass the methodological problems attendant on mental phenomena being private by defining "psychology" as the science, not of the psyche, but of "behavior". Their use of the word behavior might be thought to be unusual (the word "behave" is colloquially opposed to "misbehave"); nor do such psychologists mean what one might reasonably suppose them to mean (viz, that "behavior" refers to a person's actions, such as kicking a football, as opposed to mere responses, such as the knee-jerk reflex). The opposition implied in psychologists' use of the term "behavior" seems to depend on views about the proper manner of psychological investigation (not by introspection) and the proper level of psychological explanation (not the level of physiological explanation). Behavior is publicly observable, and is "molar".

Philosophers have had second thoughts about the characterization of the mental in terms of "privacy" of "privileged access". Most influential in this reconsideration has been Wittgenstein, in his later work. Wittgenstein explicitly rejects what Locke and Brentano unquestioningly accept, namely that there is a perfectly proper epistemological question "How is it that a person can say what he himself believes, expects, hopes, etc?", to which the answer is that he must have observed, inwardly, a mental operation, process, state, or whatever, of believing, expecting, hoping, etc. Of such verbs as "believe", "expect" and "hope" Wittgenstein says that there is an asymmetry between the *third* person singular, present tense, use of the verb, and the *first* person singular, present tense, use (1967 §472). That *someone else* believes something, expects something, etc., *is* something *I* find out about by observation; that *I* believe something, expect something, etc., is typically *not* something *I* have to find out about. I do not need to have something to go on, to be entitled to say "I hope you'll come to my party". It is an "avowal", not a report of something inwardly observed.

The implications of Wittgenstein's view for Cartesian introspectionism and anti-Cartesian behaviorism have been spelt out by Malcolm:

> First-person psychological utterances are *not based on observations*. The error of introspectionism is to suppose that they are based on observations of inner mental events. The error of behaviorism is to suppose that they are based on observations of outward events or of physical events inside the speaker's skin. These two philosophies of psychology share a false assumption, namely, that a first-person psychological statement is a report of something the speaker has, or thinks he has, observed. (Wann 1964, p.151).

The alternative to introspectionism and behaviorism is to recognize what Malcolm calls "the autonomous status of self-testimony". From this point of view recognizing the autonomous status of self-testimony is a way of avoiding what is objectionable about behaviorism (namely, that people are treated as objects), without embracing what is objectionable about introspectionism (namely, the thesis that there is a realm of what is in principle publicly inaccessible).

See also BEHAVIORISM; OTHER MINDS. GNAV

Bibliography

Brentano, F. 1874 (*1973*): *Psychology from an empirical standpoint*. London: Routledge & Kegan Paul.

*Cook, J.W. 1965: Wittgenstein on privacy. *Philosophical review* 74, 281–314.

Descartes, R. (*1911*): *The philosophical works of Descartes*. Trans. Elizabeth S. Haldane and G.R.T. Ross, Cambridge: Cambridge University Press; New York: Dover.

*Kenny, A. 1966: Cartesian privacy. In *Wittgenstein: The philosophical investigations*, ed. G. Pitcher. New York: Doubleday; London: Macmillan (1968).

Locke, J. 1690 (*1961*): *An essay concerning human understanding*, ed. John W. Yolton. London: Dent; New York: Dutton.

Moore, G.E. 1909–10: The subject-matter of psychology. *Proceedings of the Aristotelian Society*, n.s. 10, 36–62.

Schlick, M. 1925: *Allgemeine Erkenntnislehre*. Berlin: Springer.

*Wann, T.W., ed. 1964: *Behaviorism and phenomenology*. Chicago: University of Chicago Press.

Wittgenstein, L. 1967: *Zettel*. Oxford: Basil Blackwell; Berkeley and Los Angeles: University of California Press.

problem solving: animal A test of animal intelligence. The problem solving abilities of animals have been the subject of considerable research particularly by early psychologists such as Thorndike (1911) and Kohler (1925). Much of this work was aimed at understanding cognition in animals, but its early promise has not been fulfilled.

Animals are so varied and have so many specialized abilities that it is difficult to come to any general conclusion about their intelligence. For example a commonly investigated problem is that in which the direct and obvious route to a goal is blocked and the animal has to make a detour to arrive at it. Some animals have great difficulty with this. For example, a chicken presented with food on the far side of a short wire fence will persist in attempting to penetrate the fence and will only by accident discover the detour round the end of it whereas a dog would have little difficulty with this type of problem. Chameleons are particularly good at spatial detour problems, but they would not normally be considered to be especially intelligent. Many birds perform feats of navigation that would tax an able schoolchild given the same information.

DJM

Bibliography

Kohler, W. 1925 (*1957*): *The mentality of apes*, London: Pelican Books.

Thorndike, E. L. 1911: *Animal intelligence*. New York: Macmillan.

process consultation A technique for assisting a work group in diagnosing and resolving its own difficulties in carrying out its work (Schein 1969). An expert, or consultant, assists in problem identification and solution discovery, with special reference to interpersonal problems and ineffectual decision-making. Joint diagnoses of problems is a critical feature of this method. In the ideal outcome of a process consultation the group learns to act independently in dealing with its problems and the consultant's services are regarded as no longer necessary.

Process consultation has not, so far, been proved to enhance task performance. The approach may be effective only for work groups that clearly suffer from process problems; applicability to normally functioning groups with only minor problems may be limited (Kaplan, 1979) (see also ORGANIZATION DEVELOPMENT, T-GROUPS, GROUP TRAINING, AND TEAM DEVELOPMENT). SDF/NMT

Bibliography

Kaplan, R.E. 1979: The conspicuous absence of evidence that process consultation enhances task performance. *Journal of applied behavioral science* 15, 346–60.

*Schein, E.H. 1969: *Process consultation: its role in organization development.* Reading, Mass.: Addison-Wesley.

process theory Denotes a class of theories concerned with cross-time change in patterns of action and interaction. Such theories are typically contrasted with mechanistic and structural theories, both of which are primarily concerned with stable and reliable features of behavior. Process theories are most frequently employed in developmental psychology, where theorists are typically concerned with the changing character of behavior over time. However, dialectic theorists, among others, have shown how process theories can be employed throughout psychology. From this perspective traditional research, guided as it is largely by theories of the mechanistic or structural variety, has been overly restrictive. KJG

programmed instruction Structured teaching material designed for individual student use with little, or no, teacher interaction. Early material was in programmed texts with linear presentation in a form easy to assimilate, or in a branching presentation dependent on student responses. Later developments mechanically or electronically automated the presentation and the branching. In recent years computers have been used to allow increasingly detailed analysis of student responses and patterns of response.

One of the major attractions of programmed instruction has been the provision of individualized education (Suppes 1967). The shift in emphasis from simple automation to improved education can be seen in Lumsdaine and Glasers's collection (1960) of a sequence of key historic papers on teaching machines and programmed learning covering the period 1924 to 1959, and in Galanter's symposium (1959) on automatic teaching at the end of that period. Lumsdaine and Glaser begin with Pressey's original teaching machines of 1924 and quote (p.47) his discussion of "the coming 'industrial revolution' in education" which will result in "freeing the teacher from the drudgeries of her work". Thirty-five years later Galanter (1959, p.4) is looking for a machine that will "be able to make plans for itself, and also able to diagnose the plans and ideas that the student has formed".

As programmed instruction became computer aided instruction or learning (CAI, CAL) individualization became more attainable, though it proved difficult to develop systems that would model the learner, his plans and ideas (Mitchell 1981). These considerations led to Bunderson's development (1974) of learner managed instruction in which the user rather than the computer controlled the individualization. Recent research on knowledge representation in studies of personal construct systems (Pope and Shaw 1981; Pope and Keen 1981) and artificial intelligence (see MACHINE LEARNING) has led to a far greater understanding of the processes necessary to represent knowledge structures.

During the past five years reductions in the cost of micro electronics have made it feasible to introduce microcomputers into schools and use them throughout the curriculum (Tagg 1980). Some applications involve forms of programmed instruction but this is only one component of the wider uses of the computer for simulation, information retrieval and the provision of a variety of learning environments (Papert 1980).

In conclusion it should be noted that the effectiveness of programmed instruction is crucially dependent on the quality of the teaching material used, both in terms of the content and the method of presentation, regardless of the sophistication of the technology. MLGS

Bibliography

Bunderson, C.V. 1974: The design and production of learner-controlled courseware for the TICCIT system: a progress report. *International journal man-machine studies* 6(4), 479–91.

Galanter, E. 1959: The ideal teacher. In *Automatic teaching: the state of the art*, ed. E. Galanter. New York: John Wiley, 1–11.

*Lumsdaine, A.A. and Glaser, R., eds. 1960: *Teaching machines and programmed learning.* Washington: National Education Association of the United States.

Mitchell, P.D. 1981: Representation of knowledge in CAL courseware. In *Computer assisted learning*, ed. P.R. Smith. New York and Oxford: Pergamon Press.

Papert, S. 1980: *Mindstorms: children, computers and powerful ideas.* Brighton: Harvester Press; New York: Basic Books.

Pope, M.L. and Keen, T.R. 1981: *Personal construct psychology and education.* New York and London: Academic Press.

Pope, M.L. and Shaw, M.L.G. 1981: Personal construct psychology in education and learning. In *Recent advances in personal construct technology*, ed. M.L.G. Shaw. New York and London: Academic Press.

Suppes, P. 1967: On using computers to individualize instruction. In *The computer in American education*, ed. D.D. Bushnell and D.W. Allen. New York: John Wiley.

*Tagg, E.D., ed. 1980: *Microcomputers in secondary education.* Amsterdam: North Holland: Elsevier.

projection A defense mechanism in which persons have no awareness of some anti-social impulse in themselves, instead attributing it erroneously to others. Like other defense mechanisms, projection serves to protect persons from the anxiety and guilt they would feel if they were to become conscious of their underlying anti-social impulses. As described by Freud and his followers, projection is regarded as relatively immature (being characteristic of the developmental stages of the first two years of life). When projection forms a major part of an adult's character structure, it is a sign of a fixation (or arrest of development) having taken place early in life. Fixations are likely when parents are either over-indulgent or overpunitive with their children. The form of projection in which the persons around one are typically perceived as having aggressive designs is often regarded as an aspect of latent homosexuality. SRM

projective tests Psychological tests devised to measure global aspects of personality and personality dynamics. They include a range of instruments such as the Rorschach, Thematic Apperception Test (TAT), Sentence Completion, and Draw-A-Person Test, which provide generally vague, ambiguous stimuli and require the subject to respond with his or her own constructions. The individual's response, since it cannot be attributed to the stimulus itself, is believed to reflect the individual's basic personality makeup. Projective tests have been popular instruments in clinical settings as a means of gaining understanding about the patient's psychodynamics. Recently, however, projective tests have waned in popularity partly as a result of their generally low reliability, questionable validity and the increased emphasis upon behavior treatment in clinical settings. See also TESTS, RELIABILITY; TESTS, VALIDITY. JNB

proxemics Study of the ways in which people use space and physical environment in the course of their social interactions. Originally: "the study of how man unconsciously structures microspace – the distance between men in the conduct of daily transactions, the organization of space in his houses and buildings, and ultimately the layout of his towns" (Hall 1963). Proxemic research is concerned with: (a) the phenomenon of personal space and the body buffer zones which people establish when dealing with each other and with objects; (b) the cultural patterning of sensory (visual, acoustic, tactile, olfactory) interlock during social encounters; (c) the spatial architecture (postures, spaces, distances, orientations) of face-to-face interactions; (d) the spatial distribution, placement, and orientations of people in the indoor and outdoor settings; and (e) interactional properties of semi-fixed (e.g. furniture) and fixed (e.g. walls, partitions) environmental features. Proxemics has made major contributions to studies in human communication, territoriality, crowding and privacy and constitutes an important source of data to architects and environmental designers. (See COMMUNICATION, NON-VERBAL.) TMC

Bibliography

Hall, Edward T. 1963: A system for notation of proxemic behavior. *American anthropologist* 65, 1003–26.

pseudo dementia This term is used to designate a mental condition in which there are symptoms and signs which erroneously suggest dementia, that is, progressive and irreversible loss of intellectual function (see ORGANIC MENTAL STATES). The sufferer presents with loss of memory, of attention span and general knowledge. His apparent dementia may be caused by drug intoxication or other sources of transient confusion; or by depression, which in the elderly may be initially difficult to distinguish from dementia; or by a state of hysterical dissociation; or more rarely by malingering. DLJ

Bibliography

Lishman, W.A. 1978: *Organic psychiatry: the psychological consequences of cerebral disorder*. Oxford: Blackwell Scientific; St Louis, Missouri: C. V. Mosby.

psyche A Greek word meaning breath, soul or spirit (or later mind) which was distinguished from the body. Psyche is usually contrasted with "soma", as mind is contrasted with body. To the Greeks the psyche was the personification of life, the vital principle and represented the totality of mental acts or determinants of behavior. Early modern writers used the terms synonymously with mind or mental acts, along with the two adjectives derived from this term – psychical and psychic. AF

psychiatry The branch of medical science concerned with the study, diagnosis, treatment and prevention of mental disorders. Psychiatry deals with disorders which present mainly with disturbances of emotion, thought, perception and behavior, whereas the subject of neurology is disease of identifiable parts of the nervous system. There is much overlap between these two disciplines since both are concerned with aspects of brain function, and in some countries they are practiced as one (see NEUROPSYCHIATRY).

Psychiatry has been slow to develop within the framework of medicine, detaching itself with difficulty from mythology and religion, and more recently from philosophy and politics. Until the nineteenth century there were two popular theories as to the nature of mental disorder. One was that the sufferer was possessed by demons, and could be cured by prayer, confession, exorcism or execution. The second view, propounded by Hippocrates (*c*.470–*c*.400 BC) held that madness resulted from an imbalance of the elements (earth, water, air and fire) and of the humors (blood, phlegm and bile). The humors were thought to determine the four temperaments: sanguine, choleric, phlegmatic and melancholic. Treatment was directed at redressing the imbalance through baths, diets and emetics, as recommended by Galen (AD 129–199).

The nineteenth century witnessed the introduction of scientific principles. Kraepelin studied the evolution of his patients' illnesses and their family histories, and established the basis of our present system of classification. Jaspers described and categorized mental phenomena as a basis for the discipline of psychopathology. Since then the various disciplines have developed to illuminate mental mechanisms and disorders. Neuroanatomy and physiology have identified brain pathways subserving alertness (reticular activating system), emotion (limbic system), drive and motivation, as well as centers for the control of many endocrine functions and of the autonomic nervous system. Biochemistry and pharmacology are discovering various transmitter substances in the brain responsible for passing a nerve impulse from one cell to another; some disorders (particularly manic-depression and schizophrenia) are thought to be associated with abnormalities of these transmitters, and treatment can be directed at correcting these.

Psychology has contributed many concepts and techniques important to the understanding of mental disorder. One area of knowledge concerns child development, the growth of affectional bonds, and intelligence. Another area, that of learning theory and conditioning, is relevant to neurotic problems and to BEHAVIOR THERAPY. A further field of study has made it possible to measure certain aspects of intellectual and emotional functioning. Anthropology (the study of man, especially in relation to cultural influences), sociology (the study of humans in groups) and ethology (the study of animals in their natural environment) all continue to contribute to the foundations of psychiatry.

Psychiatric NOSOLOGY (the science of the definition of disease entities) encompasses many different approaches (Clare 1979). Some conditions, for example brain infections, may readily be viewed as disorders with a specifiable etiology and pathology. Others may be defined in terms of clusters of symptoms and signs, as with depression or schizophrenia. But with many disorders there is a need to specify several other aspects of the case, and multi-axial classification may be advocated; one such system in child psychiatry involves three axes: (1) the clinical psychiatric syndrome; (2) intellectual level; and (3) associated or etiological physical conditions. A radically different approach is to abandon the concept of diagnostic categories, and to describe the individual in terms of his position on a number of dimensions, for example Eysenck's psychoticism, neuroticism and introversion/extroversion dimensions for which reliable methods of measurement are available. The terms psychosis and neurosis feature in most classification systems. PSYCHOSIS denotes severe disruption of psychological function, often with DELUSION, HALLUCINATION and loss of insight, whereas a NEUROSIS can be understood as an exaggeration of a natural reaction, often comprising anxiety. No single classification of mental disorders commands the allegiance of all psychiatrists, so the following should be viewed as a sample.

Organic psychoses (see ORGANIC MENTAL STATES): there is manifest brain pathology of a toxic, metabolic, infective, traumatic or neoplastic nature, and the symptoms usually include disorientation and disturbed consciousness. The alternative term "symptomatic psychoses" indicates that the psychological disturbance must be recognized as evidence of physical disease which should be the target of treatment. A typical example would be brain tumor.

Functional psychoses: No certain pathology and no associated disorientation are to be found, but a typical cluster of symptoms for each of two psychoses comprising this group. SCHIZOPHRENIA (initially called by Kraepelin "dementia praecox") is characterized by specific disturbances of perception and thinking together with variable impairment of emotional responsiveness and drive. A good response is to be expected in many cases with medication and rehabilitative measures, but relapse is common and schizophrenics still constitute a high proportion of those needing longterm psychiatric hospitalization. AFFECTIVE DISORDERS comprise extreme mood swings into depression or mania, and recurrent episodes may be solely of one extreme – unipolar – or of both extremes – bipolar. Treatment usually relies heavily on medication or electroconvulsive therapy (ECT), and recurrences may often be prevented by long-continued medication; sometimes it is possible to identify and eradicate precipitant stresses.

Neuroses can usually be understood as exaggerations of natural reactions, anxiety being one major component. Examples of the neuroses are pure anxiety states, phobias where the symptoms are evoked by particular situations or objects, obsessive-compulsive disorders and hysterical states. PSYCHOSOMATIC DISORDERS may be included here. Treatment can be usefully directed at resolving associated stresses, at unlearning neurotic patterns of responding and learning appropriate behavior (see BEHAVIOR THERAPY). Medication has some part to play.

PERSONALITY DISORDERS *and behavior disorders* comprise a mixture of conditions in which there is an ingrained maladaptive pattern of behavior. Subcategories are based on the identification of a particularly prominent and troublesome character trait or type of activity, for example, schizoid (withdrawn), obsessive or psychopathic personality disorders, or alcohol and drug dependence. Treatment, where appropriate, may include some form of PSYCHOTHERAPY.

MENTAL HANDICAP (retardation, subnormality) is a condition of arrested or incomplete development of mind, characterized especially by subnormality of intelligence. It may occur without other pathology as part of the natural distribution of intelligence, or in association with genetically determined anomalies or brain damage. Special schooling, occupational and residential arrangements may be needed.

From this basic classification it is evident that psychiatry is concerned with a wide range of disorders: at the one extreme those identifiable in terms of physical pathology and amenable to conventional medical treatments, at the other those where variants of natural attributes and behavior patterns are viewed in relation to social norms and where management relies on counseling and social or penal measures. The middle ground is occupied by disorders – schizophrenia and manic-depressive psychosis – where the functional disturbances may be so gross that the failure so far to find an organic cause (other than tentatively in terms of biochemistry) is surprising. The diversity and ambiguity inherent in psychiatry have promoted many changes in the discipline. Firstly, there has been a proliferation of subspecialities, facilitating both more specialized research and more specific provision of service: CHILD AND ADOLESCENT PSYCHIATRY, FORENSIC PSYCHIATRY, PSYCHOGERIATRICS, MENTAL HANDICAP. Social psychiatry is among the latest offspring, concerning itself with the many environmental factors that influence the course of an illness, and in the treatment sphere with rehabilitative processes. Secondly, psychiatry has allied itself with several other disciplines not only in the broadening of its scientific basis – which we have already seen – but in the enrichment of its therapeutic skills: PSYCHOANALYSIS, various schools of counseling, social work, CLINICAL PSYCHOLOGY, these have made such major contributions that Eysenck (1975) has put forward the controversial proposal that psychological (as distinct from physical) treatments should become the province of a discipline distinct from medicine.

Finally it is evident that psychiatry is an area for debate and controversy. SZASZ, who challenged the concept of mental illness, is seen as one of the leaders of the "anti-psychiatry" movement. Several of the controversial issues have been reviewed by Clare (1976). Such vigorous controversy indicates that psychiatry has now reached a healthy adolescence. DLJ

Bibliography

*Alexander, F.G., and Selesnick, S.T. 1967: *The history of psychiatry*. London: Allen & Unwin; New York: Harper & Row.

Clare, A.W. 1976: *Psychiatry in dissent*. London: Tavistock.

——— 1979: The disease concept. In *Essentials of postgraduate psychiatry*, ed. P. Hill, R. Murray and A. Thorley. London: Academic Press; New York: Grune & Stratton.

Eysenck, H.J. 1975: *The future of psychiatry*. London and New York: Methuen.

psychiatry: physical treatments There is a long tradition in psychiatry of the use of physical methods in the management of psychological symptoms. Treatments have often varied from the naive to the bizarre, and many widely applied treatments of the past, such as insulin coma therapy, have no present day relevance. Three main forms of physical treatment are in current use and clinical practice. These are psychosurgery, electroconvulsive therapy and chemotherapy.

PSYCHOSURGERY aims at the removal or modification of certain symptoms or disordered behavior by the selective destruction of discrete areas of the brain which are presumed to be involved in their pathogenesis or their expression. The term does not refer to the surgical treatment of patients with psychiatric symptoms who are also suffering from recognizable lesions in the brain such as tumors, cysts, scars, epileptic foci and vascular anomalies. The first operations, which were pioneered by Egar Moniz, were frontal lobotomies in patients with severe phobias, severe anxiety and severe obsessionality. The standard leucotomy was devised by Freeman and Watts in the 1950s and was widely applied, but these early operation involved relatively large lesions and led to damaging effects on the patients' subsequent adjustment. Indeed, despite improved techniques and a restriction of the size of lesions to the minimum necessary, fewer patients are now offered psychosurgery as less invasive alternative treatments have become available. The indications are therefore limited and are restricted to a relatively small group of patients suffering from intractable anxiety or obsessional symptoms who have not responded to any other treatments. In addition, a strict code of practice ensures that valid consent to psychosurgery is given and, in the absence of consent, that the reasons for surgery are agreed by independent specialists.

Electroconvulsive therapy (ECT) involves the induction of a generalized convulsion by the controlled passage of an electrical current through the brain. The use of electrical stimulation in the treatment of cerebral conditions dates back to Galen who treated patients with headaches by applying the electrically charged torpedo fish to the body. John Wesley spoke in 1756 of the "unspeakable good" done to patients by the delivery of electrical shocks, but the current use of ECT stemmed from the relatively recent work of Cerletti and Bini in the 1930s. The passage of an electrical current through the brain has marked and widespread effects in the body. These include a massive seizure discharge all over the brain, an activation of the peripheral autonomic nervous system, an increase in the output of hormones from endocrine glands and marked muscle contractions. Thus, although there is no shortage of biochemical or physiological concomitants to ECT, there have been difficulties in identifying those changes induced by ECT that are crucial to its therapeutic effects. The mode of action of ECT has, therefore, yet to be clarified, but most recent research suggests that its therapeutic action could be mediated by an increase in the sensitivity of receptors in the central nervous system induced by the convulsions.

Although ECT was initially used in a wide range of psychiatric disorders, recent research has shown that its efficacy is most readily confirmed in patients suffering from severe forms of retarded depression. It is however also used in mania and in the treatment of depressive symptoms in schizophrenia. Most patients receive between six and twelve treatments and side effects are minimal. While ECT is acknowledged to be an effective acute treatment of severe despressive illness, there is however no evidence to suggest that it exerts any significant influence on the subsequent natural course of a depressive episode. It is therefore frequently used in conjunction with chemotherapy.

Chemotherapy, the rationale for treatment of psychological symptoms with drugs is that, if biological processes are involved in the pathogenesis of mental disorders, drugs acting on or influencing such processes should have an effect on the course or nature of mental illness. PSYCHOPHARMACOLOGY is the branch of clinical pharmacology that is concerned with the classification and the investigation of the pharmacokinetics, pharmacodynamic effects and the mode of therapeutic action of drugs used in the treatment of psychiatric disorders. The clinical use of these drugs is monitored by the Committee on Safety of Medicines and there is a wide range of preparations available. The groups of drugs in most common use are the anxiolytic drugs, antidepressant drugs and the neuroleptic (antipsychotic) drugs.

Anxiolytic drugs are represented chiefly by the benzodiazepines which are widely prescribed for the relief of symptoms of anxiety, whether these are primary or secondary. They are reported to exert a calming and sedative effect and can also induce sleep. They induce changes in physiological measures of AROUSAL which accompany their clinical effects and, while their efficacy in relieving anxiety symptoms is recognized, their relevance to chronic anxiety states has been questioned, particularly as it is now known that both psychological and physical dependence can occur with this group of drugs.

Antidepressant drugs are the treatment of choice for depressive illnesses in which there is evidence of an underlying biological disturbance. Such evidence is usually based on the presence of certain clinical signs as there are no clear biochemical markers of depressive illness. A distinction is therefore made in clinical practice between changes in mood occurring in association with a presumed dysfunction in cerebral mechanisms mediating mood and changes in mood that have no clear association with any underlying disturbance and which usually reflect life crises.

Antidepressant drugs are presumed to act by increasing the amount of brain monoamines at postsynaptic receptor sites. The rationale for their use is based on the monoamine theory of depression which holds that depressed mood is associated with a deficiency of functionally active monoamines at critical receptor sites in the brain, and that antidepressant drugs compensate for such a deficiency. The most widely used have been the tricyclic antidepressants and the monoamine oxidase inhibitors (MAOI), though clinical trials have tended to favor tricyclic antidepressants over MAOIs. A new generation of non-tricyclic antidepressants is now available and these are reputed to be as effective as tricyclic antidepressants.

Neuroleptic drugs are the mainstay of the treatment of schizophrenia and of psychotic symptoms occurring in other forms of psychiatric illness. The parent drug in this group, chlorpromazine, was synthesized in 1950 and was first given to patients in 1952. Initial results were significant and convincing and this gave rise to a wave of therapeutic enthusiasm that has had few parallels in the history of medicine. The more overtly non-specific physical treatments of the past could be safely abandoned and clinical psychiatry could claim a place among other specialities in clinical medicine. Hitherto unrevealed potential for rehabilitation in previously inaccessible patients was dramatically unveiled, and for many of these a return to the community was finally possible. The efficacy of these drugs in acute schizophrenia has been confirmed in a large number of studies, but their role in chronic schizophrenia has been questioned. Despite difficulties raised by such studies and some continuing controversy, neuroleptic drugs are still firmly established in the clinical management of both acute and chronic schizophrenia. All neuroleptic drugs block dopamine receptors in the central nervous system and dopamine blockade is believed to be crucial to their therapeutic action. This has led to the dopamine hypothesis of schizophrenia, which suggests that schizophrenia may be due to a hyperdopaminergic state in the mesolimbic cortex.

Physical treatments in psychiatry have tended to follow, albeit erratically at times, developments in research on the pathophysiology of mental disorders. The non-specific treatments used in the early part of this century reflected a paucity of knowledge about the etiology of mental illness which is still apparent today, despite significant advances in neuroanatomy, neurophysiology and neurochemistry. The physical treatments described above could therefore prove to be equally non-specific in the future. MWO

Bibliography

Sargant, W. and Slater, Elliot 1972 *Introduction to physical methods of treatment in psychiatry*. 5th edn. London: Churchill Livingstone.

psychical research A general term for the scholarly, naturalistic, and scientific study of events ordinarily deemed "supernatural". By treating these matters as researchable it contrasts with a priori dismissal of such events as nonsensical or incapable of study, or of simply accepting prevailing religious interpretations of them. A major stimulus to develop psychical research was the emergence of spiritualism as an important religion in the nineteenth century.

In 1847 apparently inexplicable rapping sounds, which responded to questions, appeared around two young sisters, Margaret and Kate Fox, in Hydesville, New York. Factions immediately developed, either declaring that the raps were fraudulently produced or that the apparent intelligence behind them proved that deceased spirits could communicate with the living through psychically producing physical sounds. A new idea swept through the world which seemed to relieve the intense conflict between science and religion: you didn't have to *believe* in survival, a central tenet of Christianity and other religions, you could empirically test and demonstrate its reality. All you needed to do was go to a special person who acted as intermediary, a medium, communicate with deceased spirits and have them prove their identity!

Spiritualism quickly became a comforting religion for many, but a few scattered investigators tried scientifically testing the claim that survival could be demonstrated, as well as related claims of ostensible psychic abilities among the living. The founding of the Society for Psychical Research in London in 1882, and its members' subsequent work, gave a central focus to psychical research. As the complexity of spiritualistic phenomena and other apparently psychical events was recognized, many topics were investigated which later became part of mainstream psychology, such as hypnosis, motor automatisms, subconscious processes, abnormal psychology, and psychosomatic effects. There was so much a priori dismissal of the concept of survival and psychic abilities, however, that psychical researchers were unsuccessful in promoting large scale scientific investigation of these topics.

Although some spiritualist mediums did produce verifiable knowledge about deceased persons that they could not normally have known, the apparent experimental demonstration of ESP abilities in living people led to a counter-hypothesis that the alleged spirits were simply unconscious aspects of the medium's mind, unconsciously using ESP to pick up occasional facts which added verisimilitude, a difficult hypothesis to refute. PARAPSYCHOLOGY evolved from psychical research by limiting itself to simpler psychic phenomena that were amenable to rigorous laboratory study (see ESP) and largely abandoning work on survival. Parapsychology is generally viewed as a narrow and specialized scientific profession, while psychical research includes scholarly and humanistic studies, as well as scientific ones. CTT

Bibliography

Inglis, B. 1977: *Natural and supernatural: a history of the paranormal*. London: Hodder & Stoughton.

Mauskopf, W. and McVaugh, M. 1980: *The elusive science: origins of experimental psychical research*. Baltimore: Johns Hopkins University Press, Baltimore.

psychoanalysis A subject linked inextricably with the name of its originator, Sigmund FREUD. Freud (1916) pointed out that the word as he used it referred to three subjects: a general psychology, a treatment (a form of PSYCHOTHERAPY), and a research methodology. It is difficult to consider any one of these aspects without at the same time considering the other two, and the problem of definition is still more complex because over the passage of time psychoanalysis has also come to refer to a highly organized movement which, apart from being involved in training, treatment and research into psychoanalysis, is a quasi-political organization in the sense that it attempts to influence the training of psychiatrists, clinical psychologists and social workers. In addition, and despite a specific denial of this from Freud, psychoanalysis has become part of general culture. ("As a specialist science, a branch of psychology ... it is quite unfit to construct a *Weltanschauung* of its own." Freud 1933: 158). It has become an influence within sociology (Parsons 1965); anthropology; literary criticism (Faber 1970) and philosophy (Wollheim 1974) and, especially in certain circles, it has become an intrinsic part of intellectual attitudes and verbal currency. Because psychoanalysis has been in existence for nearly 100 years, because of the many highly speculative and imaginative aspects of its writings and, above all, because of its widespread and imprecise applications, definitions of the essence of the subject, are extremely difficult. The following five features have been organized as "the basic assumptions" (Sandler, Dare and Holder 1972) and summarize many disparate attempts to encapsulate its nature.

The first assumption is that despite its origins in the consulting rooms of a psychotherapist in private practice in Vienna at the turn of the nineteenth century, psychoanalysis is a general psychology and not solely a psychopathology: a continuity between the mental functioning of "normality" and "abnormality" is assumed, just as there is central belief in a causal continuity between mental states in infancy, childhood and adulthood. Within these continuities the function of motivational instinctual drives and conflict of motivation affecting all aspects of mental life are extremely important and are mentioned later.

Secondly, and this embodies a particular view of the philosophical issue of the body/mind relationship, psychoanalysis supposes the existence of a "mental apparatus", a construct implying a mental system in interaction, that is, making an in-put to and having an in-put from the physiological systems such as the cardio-vascular and the nervous systems. The mental apparatus is discussed in terms of structures (that is to say with processes whose rate of change is slow) and with non-structural elements which are experiential. This latter is a very crucial notion, for the basic topic of psychoanalysis is that of subjective experience rather than the observable actions, behavior, or verbal communications themselves which are the source of information about subjective experience.

Thirdly, the concept of psychological adaptation is embodied in all versions of psychoanalytic psychology. Adaptation is always assumed to be an attempt to reach a "steady" state (by analogy with the physiological notion of homeostatic equilibrium) in the face of pressures from external, environmental sources; from internal, physiological sources and from equally important and powerful sources within the mental apparatus itself. Here again it can be seen that conflict is regarded as inevitable as an organizer of psychoanalytic psychology. DEFENSE MECHANISMS, postulated as omnipresent in the control and modification of conflicting motivational tendencies, are constant elements in the psychoanalytic understanding of short-term and long-term adaptational processes. The adaptational change of mental functioning over the course of psychological development, leading to the persisting imprint of many such adaptations at different stages of life, is an important part of the psychoanalytic view of the mental world.

Fourthly, psychoanalysis is based upon an assumption of what is somewhat confusingly called determinism. Because of philosophical controversies current at the time of his education it was necessary for Freud to take a strong stand as to the possibility of finding causes for all mental activity without resort to elements either of divine inspiration or governance or of chance. Psychoanalysts still hold to this view, although it seems much less necessary to argue the case at length, and the concept of psychic determinism has become combined with the principle of overdetermination, whereby most mental events are believed to become outwardly expressed because of their origins in multiple, converging psychological processes.

Fifthly, and of extreme importance, psychoanalysis is built on the assumption that mental life can be thought of as progressing both in ways that can be brought into consciousness and at levels of functioning quite inaccessible, as a rule, to introspective awareness. The unconscious aspects of thought which are for the largest part inaccessible to the conscious mind, are described as being dynamically unconscious. They are thought to become consciously registered only under specific circumstances such as dreams, in some psychotic states, or are implied by the symbolic meanings of symptoms, parapraxes and slips of the tongue and, above all, can be constructed by the process of the clinical method of psychoanalysis.

The five assumptions underlie the different models of mental functioning which were developed by Freud and have been extended and modified by the generations of psychoanalysts since. There has been an increasing move away from an emphasis upon sexual drives as the major motivational system. First there has been the inclusion and integration of an aggressive drive paralleling the sexual drive ("the libido"). Until the 1950s there was little challenge from within psychoanalysis of Freud's suggestions of sexual and aggressive drives as specific sources of particular mental energies. Over recent years, however, this has no longer been thought to be the case. Experiences in the early stages of life are consolidated to interact with innate tendencies for the infant to be orientated toward the mother and attendant caretakers. The mental apparatus is now thought to be structured by the pressure to remain close to and to enact specific relationship needs. The psychoanalysts who have developed these ideas are referred to as the "object relations" school (e.g. Klein 1965, Winnicott 1965, Balint 1952, Bowlby 1969, 1973, 1980).

The change away from a model emphasizing the impingement of specific drives toward an accentuation of the object-attaching quality of the thrust of mental life, can be seen as the outcome of 100 years of psychotherapeutic practice, which remains the major field of activity of psychoanalysts.

Initially Freud saw himself as reconstructing features of the patient's unconscious mental life by the constructions he was able to put upon the patient's encouraged flow of thoughts ("free associations"). Symptoms, casual thoughts and dreams were the principle stimuli for freely expressed thoughts, and interpretation of the psychoanalyst's understanding of the unconscious meaning of the stream of thought was held to be therapeutic by a process of enlightenment. The balance of conflicting forces within the mind was thought to be changed. Over time, however, Freud came to realize that the main interest of the psychoanalytic provision of confidentiality and reliability in frequent (usually daily) sessions, lay in revelations about the nature of the patient's thoughts and beliefs, attitudes and longings, hatred and loves concerning the analyst. These complex feelings ("transferences") demonstrated the many experiences structured by the infantile and juvenile mind in relation to crucial people in the patient's earlier life. The provision of a new, ambiguous but reliable relationship with the analyst, combined with a careful discussion with the patient of the meaning of the unconscious mental orientations toward the psychoanalyst, has become the major activity of psychoanalytic psychotherapy; it is believed to be the source of the therapeutic improvement in the patient's abilities to make satisfactory relationships outside the therapy and to develop realistic life goals.

The analysis of the therapeutic relationship can be seen to be likely to direct the theoretical thinking of the psychoanalyst toward relationship models ("object relations theory") of the mind. It can also be seen to be related to the application of psychoanalytic ideas to therapy in stranger groups ("group analysis" or family therapies).

The peculiar nature of the psychoanalytic treatment setting consists in the unusual feature of the communications. The patient is encouraged to speak simply and as completely as possible the thoughts that come into his mind. The psychoanalyst gives no commitment to speak or respond in any way, other than to facilitate the flow and understanding of the supposedly underlying meaning of the thoughts. Questions from the patient are unlikely to be regularly answered and requests for reassurance about the patient's present condition or its future course will not, usually, elicit a response. Yet the psychoanalyst expresses a concerned and detailed interest in all aspects of the patient's life and devotes up to 200 hours a year to helping the patient. This devotion, combined with the unpredictability and peculiarities of the timing of the psychoanalyst's responses and the rule of free association, give a very special quality to the nature of the material expressed by the patient. The uniqueness of the communications, within the setting, contribute the research interest of psychoanalysis. Using the psychoanalytic method gives particular and special insights into the nature of mental life in differing psychological states. CD

Bibliography

Balint, M. 1952: *Primary love and psycho-analytic technique*. London: Tavistock.

Bowlby, J. 1969, 1973 and 1980: *Attachment and loss*. 3 vols. London: Hogarth Press; New York: Basic Books.

Faber, M.D. (ed.) 1970: *The design within: psychoanalytic approaches to Shakespeare*. New York: Science House.

Freud, S. 1913: New introductory lectures on psycho-analysis. Reprinted in *Standard edition of the complete psychological works of Sigmund Freud*, vol. XXII. London: Hogarth; New York: Norton.

——— 1915–16: Introductory lectures on psycho-analysis. Reprinted in *Standard edition*, vols XV & XVI.

Klein, M. 1965: *Envy and gratitude and other works 1946–1963*. London: Hogarth Press; Boston, Mass.: Seymour Lawrence.

Parsons 1965: *Social structure and personality*. Glencoe, Ill.: Free Press.

Sandler, J., Dare, C., and Holder, A. 1972: Frames of reference in psychoanalytic psychology. III A note on the basic assumptions. *British journal of medical psychology* 45, 143–7.

Winnicott, D.W. 1972: *The maturational processes and the facilitating environment*. London: Hogarth Press; New York: International Universities Press.

Wollheim, R. (ed.) 1974: *Philosophers on Freud*. New York: Jason Aronson.

psychobiology *See* developmental psychobiology

psychodrama A range of therapeutic techniques in which the individual acts out various roles designed to engender catharsis-like experiences and insights into self and/or others. The term is generally attributed to J.L. Moreno, a Rumanian born psychiatrist, and founder of the Psychodramatic Institute in Beacon, New York. In psychodrama the individual typically performs before a therapist-trainer and a support group, the latter usually enjoined to furnish insightful reactions to the performance. A variety of techniques are employed within psychodrama, including the soliloquy (in which the individual verbalizes his or her psychological reactions to various imagined or remembered events), the self-presentation technique (in which the individual plays the part of various significant others), the self-realization technique (in which the individual enacts his or her life plan), role reversal (in which the individual take the part of another person with whom he or she is interacting) and the mirror technique (in which a member of the audience attempts to copy the behavior of the individual so that he or she may see self from another's standpoint). KJG

Bibliography

Moreno, J.L. and Ennis, J.M. 1950: *Hypnodrama and psychodrama*. Boston: Beacon House.

Greenberg, I.A., ed., 1974: *Psychodrama: theory and therapy*. New York: Behavioral Publications.

psychogeriatrics The term is probably best used to refer to the branch of psychiatry concerned with all types of mental disorder in elderly people, that is, aged sixty-five and over. In some contexts it may refer only to confused elderly people, and in other contexts to those in whom physical and mental disease occur concurrently. Its claims to be considered as a discipline distinct from general adult psychiatry rests firstly on its greater concern with organic disorders, particularly dementias, and secondly on the need to liaise closely with a specialized range of community facilities.

The demand for psychogeriatric services is increasing rapidly. In western Europe some 13 to 16 per cent of the population are aged sixty-five or over; approximately 10 per cent of these show some degree of dementia and a further 13 per cent have other psychiatric disorders. DLJ

Bibliography

Post, F. 1965: *The clinical psychiatry of later life*, Oxford and New York: Pergamon.

psychohistory In a strict etymological sense a form of history in which the empirical and theoretical discoveries of psychology are explicitly used to explain past events. By current practice, however, psychohistory entails the more specialized application of psychoanalytic theory to the interpretation of historical events and, especially, historical personalities. Psychohistory includes both psychobiographies of specific historical figures and the highly reductionistic "group-fantasy" analysis that treats whole cultures or collections of individuals – though some practitioners, most notably deMause (1982), tend to reserve the term for the psychoanalysis of groups. Since psychohistorians themselves may be either trained psychoanalysts or professional historians, psychohistory may be classed as an interdisciplinary enterprise.

The practice of psychoanalysing historical people began with the father of psychoanalysis, Sigmund Freud, whose psychobiography of Leonardo da Vinci (1910) has become a classic of its kind. Freud also produced analyses of Dostoyevski and Woodrow Wilson (the latter in collaboration with William C. Bullett). However, Freud's work was often criticized for being excessively ahistorical; a Renaissance personality such as Leonardo's is placed on a modern, and rather procrustean, psychiatrist's couch without due reference to the peculiarities of the time and place in which that artist lived. In contrast, Erikson's more truly psychohistorical inquiries into the lives of Martin Luther and Mahatma Gandhi took more care to embed the analysis in the proper historical setting (see e.g. Erikson 1958). Furthermore by not confining himself to the tenets of orthodox Freudianism Erikson broadened the theoretical basis of the discipline. The interest of historians in this form of historical explanations was accelerated when Langer delivered his presidential address "The Next Assignment" to the American Historical Association (1958). Journal articles and books purporting to be psychohistories of major personalities, such as American presidents, have now become commonplace. Moreover, the advent and development of group-fantasy analysis, particularly in the hands of deMause, the founding president of the International Psychohistorical Association, has immensely expanded the aims of some psychohistorians. The long-standing desire to explain the psychological motivations of past historical actors is often complemented if not replaced by an oracular fascination with the interpretation of contemporary events and the prophecy of their future course. As a result it is fair to say that psychohistorians vary greatly in professional respectability, some being true academics who impose some self-restraint while others veer closer to the excesses of "pop psychology".

Psychohistory must be distinguished from those methodologies in psychology which also make successful use of historical or archival data (see Simonton 1981). In particular it should be separated from what is sometimes called "historiometry", a methodology represented by such classics as Cox's study of 301 geniuses (1926). For one thing, unlike historiometry, which is merely interested in using historical data to test scientific hypotheses about human behavior (e.g. the relationship between intelligence and achieved eminence), psychohistory is committed to applying already discovered psychological principles to historical events and persons (e.g. the role of the Oedipal Conflict in Leonardo's extraordinary investigative curiosity). Where historiometry advances inductively from the particular to the general, psychohistory proceeds deductively from the general to the particular. In this sense psychohistory is more an applied than a pure or basic science. Or, more precisely, its stress on explicating the particular rather than enlarging the store of psychological laws renders it more akin to history than to science; specific and somewhat standardized psychoanalytic concepts merely supplant the common sense psychology formerly used by historians to understand the motives of their subjects. Of course in so far as psychoanalytic therapy can be considered a science, or at least a technology, psychohistory may be viewed in similar terms, a historic patient merely taking the place of a contemporary nonentity. In any event, since psychohistorians must begin their deductive procedure with some theoretical basis, they have no choice but to commit themselves to some theory a priori, that theory invariably being psychoanalytic, the only broad-scope theory of human behaviour available when psychohistory first emerged as an intellectual discipline. In contrast, historiometry is not obliged to make any such theoretical commitments; it is solely engaged in testing theoretical propositions. The historiometric method can even be used to test predictions derived from psychoanalytic theory. Moreover, these two rival psychological methodologies go about using historical data in contrary ways. On the one hand psychohistory, like its parent psychoanalysis, is clearly devoted to qualitative analysis, to logical and often imaginative disquisition. Historiometry, on the other hand, is explicitly involved in the quantitative analysis of historical data using established measurement and statistical techniques. This makes historiometry more the cousin of psychometrics and cliometrics. Accordingly, where the psychohistorian would be intrigued with identifying the course of Leonardo's Oedipal conflict, a historiometrician would want to assess Leonardo's IQ (at least 150) and his eminence (52nd out of Cox's 301), repeat the process for the remaining 300 geniuses sampled, and then determine the statistical relationship between the two variables. As this example suggests, psychohistory is prone to take the individual case as the basis for analysis, whereas historiometry groups numerous historical personages together as part of a search for the nomothetic principles (or natural laws) of human behavior. Consequently, though superficially similar and sometimes confused with one another, psychohistory and historiometry pertain to two distinct, even rival disciplines.

Practically ever since its conception, psychohistory has come under severe attack both as history and as science (see Barzun 1974; Stannard 1980). The most frequently heard criticisms may be summarized as follows: (i) the historical record is not sufficiently complete, especially with regard to key childhood experiences, to provide a firm basis for psychoanalytic explanation; (ii) the psychohistorian all too often compensates for this dearth of fact by loosely surmising the existence of undocumented childhood events from adulthood personality and then, in a subtle form of circular reasoning, uses these inferences as actual facts for interpreting adulthood motivations; (iii) like psychoanalysis generally, psychohistory tends to be a highly subjective intellectual exercise whose interpretations are vulnerable to many equally plausible alternative accounts; (iv) despite all corrective efforts, psychohistory remains ahistorical, especially in its disregard for the possibility that psychoanalytic theory may be both era- and culture-bound and therefore inapplicable to other times and places; (v) psychoanalytic theory itself is not a validated scientific theory, nor even a successful foundation for therapy, and consequently its use to explicate history is premature; (vi) even if psychoanalytic theory were sound in the restricted sphere of its origins, there is no assurance that principles derived from clinical practice and introspective self-analysis will have applicability to non-psychiatric populations; and (vii) even if this extrapolation were justified, psychoanalytic theory, as a model primarily of unconscious motivation, may be simply irrelevant to our understanding of a good many historical events, such as those that concern attribution, decision-making, or group-dynamic processes. To such arguments most psychohistorians respond that psychoanalytic theory, particularly if suitably revised, does indeed offer a scientifically valid and universally applicable framework for historical explanation whenever it is feasible to obtain adequate materials on early childhood conditions. Nonetheless, some psychohistorians have suggested that it may be time to forfeit any strict allegiance to psychoanalytic theory. As an alternative, psychohistorians could be more eclectic, freely exploiting any psychological discovery that has explanatory value. Psychohistory might even find it advantageous to utilize more fully the growing number of generalizations that have emerged from the historiometric analysis of past creators and leaders. If the theoretical basis of the discipline were enlarged, the word psychohistory could be used in a way which was etymologically more correct to refer to studies that have only a historical, not a logical link with psychoanalytic theory. Whether psychohistory will move in this direction remains to be seen. DKS

Bibliography

Barzun, Jacques 1974: *Clio and the doctors: psycho-history, quanto-history, and history*. Chicago: University of Chicago Press.

Cox, Catherine 1926: *The early mental traits of three hundred geniuses*. Stanford, Calif.: Stanford University Press.

deMause, Lloyd 1982: *Foundations of psychohistory*. Planetarium Station, New York: Creative Roots.

Erikson, Erik H. 1958: *Young man Luther: a study in psychoanalysis and history*. New York: Norton.

Freud, Sigmund 1910 (*1957*): *Leonardo da Vinci and a memory of his childhood*. Translated Alan Tyson. *Standard edition of the psychological works of Sigmund Freud*. London: Hogarth; New York: Norton (1964).

Langer, W.L. 1958: The next assignment. *American historical review* 63, 283–304.

Simonton, D.K. 1981: The library laboratory: archival data in personality and social psychology. In *Review of personality and social psychology* vol. 2, ed. L. Wheeler. Beverley Hills and London: Sage Publications.

*Stannard, David E. 1980: *Shrinking history: on Freud and the failure of psychohistory*. New York and Oxford: Oxford University Press.

psycholexicology The psychological study of words and their meanings. Although many different approaches to this study have been pursued, the term psycholexicology has not achieved great currency. Presumably coined by George A. Miller in the early 1970s (Miller and Johnson-Laird 1976, p. vi), the term remains closely associated with Miller and Johnson-Laird's "*procedural semantics*", which emphasizes the importance of perceptual and other essentially computational operations that language users supposedly employ in determining the applicability of words. HSS

Bibliography

Lyons, John 1977: *Semantics*, Vols. I and II. Cambridge: Cambridge University Press.

Miller, George A. and Johnson-Laird, Philip N. 1976: *Language and perception*. Cambridge, MA: Harvard University Press.

psycholinguistics A sub-discipline of linguistics dealing with the psychological mechanisms underlying language acquisition, language processing, and language use. Psycholinguistics may be viewed either as the continuation of earlier traditions of research into language learning and the cognitive basis of language (see LANGUAGE AND COGNITION) or as a relatively new area of research focussing on the issue of the psychological reality of the rules and units postulated by modern linguistic theory (see GRAMMATICAL RULES and SPEECH UNITS). The relation between linguistics and psycholinguistics has often been clouded by the imprecise status assigned to the linguist's notion of the grammar of a language (see GRAMMAR). Consequently, the question whether linguistic analyses can be proved or disproved by psychological tests remains open. Similar imprecisions effect the relations between psycholinguistics and NEUROLINGUISTICS.

Early research that may be classified as psycholinguistic concerned the documentation of the stages of first language acquisition. This tradition continued into the twentieth century and still remains strong, owing to the stimulus given to language acquisition research by the nativist theories of generative grammar. Another important tradition is the Gestaltist approach to language. Wundt, for example, objected to the physicalism of neo-grammarian accounts of language change (see LINGUISTICS, DIACHRONIC) and stressed general perceptual and creative principles. He distinguished two levels of linguistic performance: the holistic or sensory-motor as opposed to that of the higher, more abstract cognitive structures. Gestaltist views on language have been recuperated by those generative psycholinguists who view the sentence, not as a sequence of linear transitions from one stimulus to the next but as a formal whole, structured hierarchically.

One of the most important schools of psycholinguistics has been behaviorism, with its intellectual roots in American Pragmatism and in the work of J.B. Watson and Pavlov. Behavioral psycholinguists see language learning as a particular application of general learning abilities. New sentences are held to be produced and understood as the result of the development of associative links (stimulus-response) between surface forms. Concepts such as introspection and consciousness are mistrusted in behaviorist psycholinguistics, and the study of behavior is limited to the observation of "objective" regularities or habits. Watson's word association theory claimed that speakers learn to associate sounds and their referents, and in learning sentences they learn the relations between the component words. Hull (1943) was not committed to the idea that all learning takes place by reinforcement and introduced the notion of a mediated response. Mediated responses include classes of segments such as phoneme, morpheme, verb. The most noted Behaviorist psycholinguist, Skinner, postulated that speakers learn structural frames or patterns as a basis for sentence composition. He took operant rather than classical conditioning to be the psychological process behind language learning. The operant is pictured as the basic unit of verbal response and conditioning takes place by a post hoc reinforcement. The result is that the organism learns to predict and control response probabilities. Other neo-behaviorist linguists are Mowrer (1960) and Osgood (1957). Mowrer concentrated on the way in which word-referent associations are established and modified the S-R learning model to include mediated responses. As with other behaviorists, reward and punishment are held to be the impulses for learning. Osgood is noted for his study of how words acquire connotative meaning and of how this can be scientifically measured. He denied the simplistic equation between (a) behavior in response to a sign and (b) behavior in response to the corresponding object. The former was held to be only a small part of the latter.

Behaviorist learning theory and structural linguistics came under attack in the late 1950s in the influential writings of CHOMSKY, who criticized Skinner's behaviorist account of language learning. Chomsky argued that language is free of stimulus control and that absence of stimulus does not limit the frequency of use of a word. He also claimed that the behaviorist notion of reinforcement and many other notions from learning theory were inapplicable to linguistic analysis. Most importantly, behaviorist psycholinguistics was held to be incapable of explaining how native language users could produce and understand sentences they had never before encountered. Chomsky denied the behaviorist claim that linguistic ability could arise as the result of generalizations from experience and pointed instead to the child's frequent exposure to deviant and ungrammatical utterances. Nevertheless, Chomsky argued, in spite of such misleading input, the child still succeeds in constructing the correct grammar of the language. An innate mechanism (the LANGUAGE ACQUISITION DEVICE) was postulated to account for this achievement, and the psycholinguist was urged to focus his attention on the discovery of the principles regulating that mechanism.

Equally significant for the development of psycholinguistics was Chomsky's distinction (1965) between LINGUISTIC COMPETENCE and PERFORMANCE as well as his claim that linguistics is a branch of cognitive psychology. The motivation behind much of contemporary psycholinguistic research stems in a large part from these early principles of Chomsky's work. Owing to Chomsky's influence, language universals became an important topic of discussion in linguistics and psycholinguistics. It was assumed that, by studying what was universal to all languages, the linguist could discover the details of the child's innate language-learning mechanism. In recent years, however, there has been a renewed interest in studies of the mother's input to the child's acquisition of language as well as a greater awareness of the interactional context of language learning (see BABY TALK).

The question of the psychological reality of grammatical structures has been explored in a number of ways. Steinberg (1982) holds that the study of the speech encoding process cannot be based on Chomsky's syntax-based grammar but must accept a meaning-based grammar such as that proposed by generative semantics. Other researchers have focussed on speech errors as evidence of encoding mechanisms (Fromkin 1968). The issues in this domain are clouded by Chomsky's shifting attitude toward the question whether language performance should be taken as a reflection, direct or indirect, of underlying competence (Fodor, Bever, Garrat 1974).

The study of speech perception and decoding processes has been equally contentious. Fodor and Bever (1965) sought to demonstrate the psychological reality of constituent and clause boundaries by examining the way subjects "mishear" clicks superimposed on input utterances. Other studies have related transformational and derivational complexity to decoding ease (i.e. processing time) and have attempted to decide between alternative grammatical models on the basis of processing plausibility.

The diversity of psycholinguistic studies increased during the 1970s. Many psycholinguists have begun to question some of the linguistic principles on which Chomsky based his early attacks on behaviorism. Nevertheless, generative grammar remains the dominant linguistic model. Some psycholinguists claim that the topic of native speaker intuitions belongs to the study of linguistic performance and that these do not directly reflect competence as Chomsky had argued. Others argue that if the notion of linguistic competence cannot be linked to psychological mechanisms it should be abandoned. Indeed, some child language theorists are now returning to the study of imitation and association, topics neglected during the anti-behaviorist revolution. In recent years the domain of psycholinguistics has become even more broad and now overlaps with neighboring investigations of ANTHROPOID APE LANGUAGE, ARTIFICIAL INTELLIGENCE, SECOND LANGUAGE ACQUISITION, SPEECH DISORDERS and BILINGUALISM. CMH/TJT

Bibliography

*Cambell, R. and Wales R. 1970: The study of language acquisition. In Lyons, *New horizons in linguistics*. Harmondsworth: Penguin.

Chomsky, N. 1965: *Aspects of the theory of syntax*. Cambridge, Mass.: MIT Press.

*Fodor J. and Bever T. 1965: The psychological reality of linguistic segments. *Journal of verbal learning and verbal behavior* 4, 420.

——— and Garrat M. 1974: *The psychology of language: an introduction to psycholinguistics*. New York; McGraw-Hill.

Fromkin V. 1968: Speculations on performance models. *Journal of linguistics* 4, pp.1–152.

*Greene J. 1972: *Psycholinguists*, Harmondsworth and Baltimore: Penguin.

Hull C. 1943: *Principles of behaviour*. New York: Appleton-Century-Crofts.

Mowrer O. 1960: *Learning theory and symbolic processes*. New York: Wiley.

Osgood C., Suci G. and Tannenbaum P. 1957: *The measurement of meaning*. Urbana, Ill.: University of Illinois Press.

*Steinberg D. 1982: *Psycholinguistics, language, mind and world*. London and New York: Longman.

Watson J. 1924: *Behaviorism*. New York: Norton.

Wundt W. 1900: *Die Sprache*. Leipzig: Englemann.

psychology: history of the term As much contention surrounds the history of the term as the history of the subject. According to the *Shorter Oxford English Dictionary* the word *psychology* can be traced back to 1693, *psychological* to 1776, *psychologist* to 1727, and *psychologic* to 1787. However, the term psychology, like many of those related to it with a shared prefix such as psychodynamic, psychometric and psychopath, has changed in meaning and usage over time. Compare the modern meaning of the use of the term *psychometrics* to mean the application of mathematical and statistical concepts and empirical measurement to psychological data, particularly mental testing and experimental results with the 1854 definition: "The alleged faculty of divining, from physical contact or proximity only, the qualities or properties of an object, or of persons or things that one has been in contact with". Certainly the term psychology and many others using a similar prefix had become part of everyday conversation by the middle of the last century. AF

psychopathic personality A PERSONALITY DISORDER characterized by antisocial, irresponsible, aggressive and impulsive behavior. However the term has an alternative meaning and Schneider (1950) and some other German writers have used it to cover the whole range of PERSONALITY DISORDERS and NEUROSES. Because of the pejorative associations of the word "psychopathic" and of the very considerable confusion as to its precise definition, the alternatives of antisocial or sociopathic personality are often preferred. Psychopathic personality is associated with parental deprivation and a history of childhood disturbance. Aggressive traits are most obvious in early adult life, but although these improve, other features do not. Lack of motivation to change and lack of insight both make treatment difficult, but limited success can be obtained by longterm support and by residential group therapy in a therapeutic community. Psychopathic personality is a common finding among recidivist offenders. The diagnosis has an important legal status in many jurisdictions as a reason for compulsory psychiatric hospital admission for both offenders and non-offenders. DLJ

Bibliography

*Kaplan, H.I., Freedman and Sadock, B. J. 1980: *Comprehensive textbook of psychiatry*. 3rd edn. Baltimore: Williams and Wilkins.

Schneider, K. 1950: *Psychopathic personality*. 9th edn. Vienna: F. Deuticke.

psychopathology The area of scientific study concerned with the manifestations of psychological disturbance and the mechanisms underlying these. The term can also be used to designate a body of knowledge and theories related to the specified topic, for example, the psychopathology of aggression. There are two main branches of study: descriptive psychopathology deals with the definition and classification of morbid symptoms and signs (also called phenomenology), JASPERS (1962) being one of its leading exponents; etiological psychopathology explores the ways in which morbid manifestations are generated by various influences, such as genetic, physiological and psychological. Among the latter, dynamic psychopathology is of interest to PSYCHOANALYSIS in postulating links between early childhood experiences and later illness patterns. Taylor (1966) provides a critical account.

The terms psychopath and psychopathy are misleading since they no longer refer to disorders within the whole field of psychopathology but are restricted to those involving persistently aggressive and anti-social behavior. In current usage the term SOCIOPATHIC PERSONALITY may be preferred so as to avoid this confusion.

Psychopathology has developed as a science since the end of the nineteenth century (Kraft-Ebbing first used the word in 1875). Hippocrates (c.470–c.400 BC) had of course recognized the brain as the seat of the emotions and of mental illness, but later centuries had lost sight of this in the pursuit of fanciful notions of possession by demons, an imbalance in the elements and humors, and, in women, the supposed migration of the womb within the body as the basis of hysteria. The growth of neurology in the last century revived interest in the central nervous system and with it the hope that neuropathologists would discover macroscopic and histological changes in the brain of those with mental illness, thereby explaining the symptoms. As this hope was fulfilled in only a minority of illnessess, there arose a need for the separate study of mental pathology.

Descriptive psychopathology, in defining and classifying the manifestations of mental disturbance, provides the raw material for on the one hand the making of diagnoses based on clusters of symptoms and signs, and on the other hand the understanding of causation. It is concerned with patterns of behavior and communication, both verbal and non-verbal, in relation to form and content, and with all types of subjective experience. The latter can be grouped into cognitive (percepts, images, thoughts, memories), affective (emotions, moods), and conative (impulses, desires, motives); a further dimension is added by introspection and self-observation.

For a description and discussion of individual symptoms the reader is referred to a more detailed text such as Jaspers (1962) and Taylor (1966). Among the most important symptoms of cognitive disorder are: illusions, HALLUCINATIONS, DELUSIONS, THOUGHT DISORDERS, obsessions, MEMORY DISORDERS and dementia. In the field of affective disturbance we have: emotional lability, anxiety, PHOBIAS, manic and depressive mood, and emotional blunting. In the conative field: states of overactivity and stupor, compulsive disorders, sexual perversions and amotivational states. All types of function may be affected by CONSCIOUSNESS DISORDERS. It is interesting to note that all these symptoms may be experienced by normal subjects, but mildly (as with phobias), transiently (as with amnesia), in a drowsy state (as with hallucinations), or in a hypnotic trance (as with psychogenic anesthesia).

Recent research into descriptive psychopathology has aimed at achieving greater reliability in the recognition of symptoms, and at identifying and rating morbid states by means of questionnaires (Mann and Murray 1979).

The second main area of work in psychopathology is concerned with the etiology of mental disorders. It is helpful to think in terms of two groups of causes: precipitant causes are those events, experiences and physiological mechanisms which lead immediately to the emergence of morbid symptoms; predisposing causes are those which enhance an individual's vulnerability without producing symptoms. Of course, these two groups of causes are not necessarily different in nature; the same cause, for example lack of oxygen supply to the brain, may have either a predisposing or a precipitant role. Furthermore, different causes are commonly seen to act in combination, having an additive effect. Such is the complexity of predisposing factors in any individual that it is often difficult to predict the effect of a specific precipitant. A severe blow on the head may predictably cause unconsciousness, but the death of a pet dog may lead to anything from a mild transient distress to the most severe and protracted psychotic depression. Nevertheless, some success has been achieved in allotting relative weights to various stressful experiences in such a way as to compile for an individual at a particular time a life events score which gives a rough guide to the likelihood of mental symptoms developing (Paykel et al. 1976). Experimental work tends to be restricted by practical and ethical considerations, and the limitations of using animals instead of human subjects.

Precipitant causes need to be understood in terms of both physiological and psychological mechanisms. The central nervous system may be seen from one viewpoint as a network of neurons, many with specialist functions, supported by a complex apparatus to maintain nutrition and homeostasis; if the integrity and physical harmony of that system are disturbed, symptoms may result. This can occur, for example, through changes in cerebral circulation, oxygenation, chemical balance, hormone regulation, temperature and electrical potential; or through alterations in the pharmacology of the brain, particularly its diverse NEUROTRANSMITTERS which transfer messages from one cell to another. Alcohol and drugs, or their withdrawal, readily unbalance the system. Two subsystems of crucial importance are the RETICULAR ACTIVATING SYSTEM, which regulates the level of consciousness, and the AUTONOMIC NERVOUS SYSTEM, which controls involuntary function such as heart rate and sweating and which can generate widespread and varied symptoms.

From another viewpoint the central nervous system emerges as a means of receiving and filtering information from the body and the environment, assessing it in relation to past experiences and current aims, and responding to it affectively and conatively. Difficulties may arise if there is too little incoming information (sensory deprivation) or too much; or when the information is incomprehensible or excessively alarming; when it reawakens disturbing or distorted memories; when it faces the individual with challenges he sees himself as unable to meet (see LEARNED HELPLESSNESS).

The nature of the precipitant cause will not usually by itself determine the nature of the morbid manifestation. However, it may be true that the more immediate and dramatic causes, especially physiological ones, tend to lead to a specific form of disturbance. For example, a high fever provokes a confusional state; nevertheless the content of an individual's talk when confused is determined by his pre-existing thoughts and memories. Most psychological precipitants result in disorders whose form and content are both largely dependent on the individual's predisposition and mental apparatus.

Freud and his associates emphasized the importance of internal psychological precipitants. These are seen as arising from primitive impulses (usually erotic and aggressive) from the unconscious threatening to break into consciousness; they are resisted by the ego with the aid of various defense mechanisms such as denial or sublimation (see Taylor 1966 p.290). But the defense itself may be so extreme as to lead to symptom formation; for example, denial may bring hysterical dissociation. Psychoanalysts have also described related predisposing causes in the shape of traumatic childhood experiences and conflicts; incompletely assimilated and resolved, these may be re-awakened later, and, along with them, pathogenic ways of coping with the associated anxiety. This theme has been extensively developed (see Brown 1964; also Erikson 1965).

There are many other formulations of psychological predisposing causes. Genetic factors as well as early experiences undoubtedly play a major role in personality development, and Eysenck (1967) has claimed to measure two stable attributes, neuroticism and introversion-extroversion, which show correlations with subsequent symptom patterns. Learning theory accounts for the evolution of maladaptive patterns of behavior in terms of classical or respondent conditioning; this has important implications for the understanding of phobias, obsessions and some forms of depression. Social theories ascribe a major role to the social environment in conditions such as sociopathy and reactive depression.

Physiological predisposing causes may sometimes be more easily recognized, as in the case of brain damage, neurological disease or ageing processes. However, many more subtle mechanisms undoubtedly await discovery in a way that will revolutionize our view of the etiology of the functional psychoses (manic-depressive illness and schizophrenia). DLJ

Bibliography

Brown, J.A.C. 1964: *Freud and the post-Freudians*. Harmondsworth: Penguin.

Erikson, Erik H. 1965: *Childhood and society*. Harmondsworth: Penguin Books.

Eysenck, H.J. 1967: *Biological basis of personality*. Springfield: C. Thomas.

*Jaspers, Karl 1962: *General psychopathology*. Trans. J. Hoenig and M.W. Hamilton. Manchester: Manchester University Press; Chicago: University of Chicago Press.

Mann, A., and Murray, R. 1979: Measurement in psychiatry. In *Essentials of postgraduate psychiatry*, ed. P. Hill, R. Murray and A. Thorley. London: Academic Press; New York: Grune & Stratton.

Paykel, E.S., McGuiness, B. and Gomez, J. 1976: An Anglo-American comparison of the scaling of life events. *British journal of medical psychology* 49, 237–47.

*Taylor, F. Kräupl 1966: *Psychopathology. Its causes and symptoms*. London: Butterworth.

psychopharmacology A discipline concerned with chemical substances (psychotropic drugs) that influence behavior, emotions, perceptions and thought processes by direct action on the central nervous system. Drugs with these actions may be divided (with some overlap) into three main categories:
(*a*) those mainly used for social, non-medical or culture-specific purposes; (*b*) drugs employed for the treatment of mental illness; and (*c*) the psychotomimetics, now used mainly in research.

(*a*) Centrally acting drugs have been used for social and non-medical purposes at least since the dawn of history. In many cultures alcohol has been and remains an outstanding example, although worldwide it is probable that more caffeine (from tea and coffee) is consumed. The psychological effects of smoking or chewing tobacco are mainly due to the central action of the nicotine present in tobacco. Other examples abound: cannabis in Muslim cultures; cocaine (from chewing the leaves of the coca plant) among Andean Indians; and hallucinogens, also of plant origin, in many tropical forest cultures. Abuse of drugs in this category leads to psychological and eventual physical dependence (or addiction) and severe, and sometimes fatal, reactions on withdrawal. Addiction to narcotics (e.g. opium, heroin) is one extreme example, but the abuse of many other drugs, taken for non-medical reasons, such as barbiturates and amphetamines, leads to similar results.

(*b*) The past thirty years has seen a phenomenal increase in the number and variety of drugs used for the treatment of mental illness. Until around 1950 only non-specific sedatives and hypnotics, such as chloral hydrate, and the barbiturates were available. The revolution began with the introduction of chlorpromazine for the treatment of schizophrenia and continued a few years later with the discovery of the antidepressants. The outstanding feature of these new drugs which distinguished them from their predecessors was their ability to alleviate the symptoms of mental illness without inducing disabling sedation, stupor or sleep. The main classes are summarized in the table.

The neuroleptics, of which more than twenty are available, are used for the treatment of schizophrenia and also in the short term to quieten acutely disturbed patients whatever the underlying psychopathology. They are mainly represented by three chemical groupings: the phenothiazines (e.g. chlorpromazine), the thioxanthenes (e.g. thioridazine) and the butyrophenones (e.g. haloperidol). In acute schizophrenia the neuroleptics alleviate the delusions, hallucinations and thought disorder characteristic of the condition to the extent that many patients are able to lead normal lives in the community. Some schizophrenics only require treatment with these drugs during the acute phase, but for others longterm treatment is needed to prevent relapse. The neuroleptics are, however, less effective against the apathy and withdrawal characteristics of some cases of chronic schizophrenia. Their main drawback is a tendency to induce extrapyramidal symptoms or disturbances of voluntary movements which may become particularly distressing during longterm treatment.

For the relief of anxiety and mild insomnia a new class of drugs – the benzodiazepenes – has almost entirely replaced the barbiturates. A major advantage of these drugs is that they are less toxic and therefore safer in overdose than the barbiturates. The best known example is diazepam (or valium) which is probably at present the most widely prescribed psychotropic drug. Chronic use of benzodiazepenes may lead to dependence and on withdrawal to symptoms of agitation, tension and insomnia; convulsions may occur after chronic use of high doses.

There are two main groups of antidepressants: the tricyclics (structurally related to the phenothiazines) and the monoamineoxidase inhibitors (MAOIs). There are now nearly twenty tricyclics available, of which imipramine was the first. In appropriate patients (not all respond) they alleviate severe depression and decrease fatigue, but often at the expense of unwanted side-effects (see table). It is of interest to note that the tricyclics have no effect on mood in normal subjects. The MAOIs have similar clinical actions but their administration requires strict control of diet and the intake of other drugs. This is because many foods and drugs contain amines with potent pharmacological actions on the cardiovascular system. In normal circumstances these amines are inactivated by the enzyme monoamine oxidase (MAO, mainly in the liver) before reaching the systemic circulation.

Lithium salts were introduced in the late 1950s for the treatment of acute attacks of mania. Lithium carbonate was found to be remarkably effective in quietening overactive euphoric patients. Later work demonstrated conclusively that given prophylactically lithium salts also stabilize mood in patients suffering cyclic swings of mania and depression and they are now widely used for this purpose. The main problem with their administration is their narrow therapeutic/toxic ratio which makes it essential to monitor plasma lithium concentrations during treatment. Toxic effects from too high a dose are potentially hazardous and may be fatal.

Stimulant drugs, represented by the amphetamines, are rarely used in clinical practice. They have no useful antidepressant action. Their proven ability to delay the onset of fatigue in normal subjects is well known, but after this effect has worn off most subjects experience lassitude, depressed mood and tension. The longterm effects of taking amphetamines habitually are serious and may result in psychopathic behavior and even paranoid psychosis resembling acute schizophrenia.

(*c*) Although certain of the psychotomimetics are used in primitive cultures for ritual purposes and are sometimes abused by addicts in western society, they are mainly of interest as research tools. Administered to normal subjects at relatively low dosage they induce profound disturbances in perception, thought and mood; these drugs are often said to elicit a "model psychosis", but the resemblance to clinical psychosis is only partial.

The main chemical groups of the psychotomimetics are: lysergic acid derivatives (e.g. lysergide or LSD); certain phenylethylamines (e.g. mescaline); methylated indolalkylamines (e.g. dimethyltryptamine); and miscellaneous compounds such as the anticholinergic drug N-methyl-3-piperidyl benzilate and phencyclidine (known as "angel dust").

The syndromes elicited by the first three groups are similar, but differ in time course. The effects of the first two last for seven to twelve hours, while those of the third group have a short duration (one to three hours). All three stimulate sympathetic centers and induce marked somatic reactions – nausea, sweating, tremor are common. As these subside the central effects increase. These may include intense visual hallucinations, anxiety succeeded by euphoria, paranoia and cognitive disturbances. True loss of insight is rare, but withdrawal and inability to communicate or recall sensations are common. However, individuals differ markedly in their reactions and the variety and intensity of symptoms seem to be partly determined by the personality of the subject.

Piperidyl benzilate and certain other anti-cholinergics induce a syndrome characterized by disorientation in time and space, incoherence and hallucinations, usually with loss of insight. The effects of phencyclidine are complex, but include disturbances in position and touch senses and in cognitive functions. However, hallucinations are rare and somatic effects less marked than with the other drugs.

Psychotropic drugs have proved extremely powerful tools in investigating the chemistry and physiology of normal behavior and in providing clues as to etiology of mental illnesses. For example, the most effective neuroleptics used in the treatment of schizophrenia block neurotransmission at dopaminergic synapses, suggesting that this TRANSMITTER SYSTEM may be overactive in the disorder. The tricyclics, among other actions, inhibit the re-uptake of noradrenaline and serotonin in the synaptic cleft, leading to the suggestion of a deficiency of these transmitters in depression. The receptor for the

Some drugs used in clinical psychopharmacology

Class	*Typical drugs*	*Main clinical effects*	*Unwanted side-effects*
Major tranquilizers or neuroleptics	Chlorpromazine Thioridazine Haloperidol	Sedation without impairment of consciousness; ameliorate psychotic symptoms including thought disorder.	Most serious are disturbances in the control of voluntary movements (dystonia, akathisia and tardive dyskinesia); also hypotension.
Anxiolytics and hypnotics	Diazepam Chlordiazepoxide Nitrazepam	Alleviate severe anxiety and induce mild sedation (anxiolytics) and sleep (hypnotics).	Include drowsiness, dependence and occasionally severe withdrawal reactions after longterm administration.
Anti-depressants	(1) *Tricyclics* Imipramine Amitriptyline Mianserin	Alleviate severe depression; decrease fatigue.	Many, and may include constipation, blurred vision and sweating, and with some drugs sedation.
	(2) *Monoamine-Oxidase Inhibitors* Phenelzine Tranylcypromine	In appropriate patients similar to the tricyclics but with less sedation.	As with tricyclics. Also administration requires strict dietary control to avoid interactions resulting in severe cardiovascular problems.
Mood-stablizing agents	Lithium salts	Specific use to quieten overactive, euphoric patients suffering attacks of mania; also prevents depression in manic-depressive psychosis.	Many, depending on dose and including gastrointestinal symptoms, weight gain and tremor. Severe toxic reactions result from too high a dose.
Stimulants	Dexamphetamine Methylphenidate	Main clinical use to increase wakeful periods in narcolepsy. No useful anti-depressant action. In normal subjects may improve psycho-motor performance and counteract fatigue.	Many, and include insomnia, anxiety and anorexia. Chronic use frequently leads to dependence and severe paranoid psychosis.

benzodiazepine drugs in the brain is closely associated with the function of the γ-aminobutyric acid neurotransmitter system. In rats high doses of amphetamine give rise to a syndrome of stereotypy which some consider an animal model for schizophrenia. These and many other observations using psychotropic drugs are providing powerful insights into the molecular basis of brain function.

RR

Bibliography

Cooper, J.R., Bloom, F.E. and Roth, R.H. 1982: *The biochemical basis of neuropharmacology*. 4th edn. Oxford and New York: Oxford University Press.

Lader, M.H. 1980: *Introduction to psychopharmacology*, Kalamazoo: Upjohn.

Lipton, M.A., DiMascio, A. and Killam, K.F. 1978: *Psychopharmacology: a generation of progress*. New York: Raven Press.

Shepherd, M., Lader, M.H., and Rodnight, R. 1968. *Clinical psychopharmacology*. London: English Universities Press.

psychosexual disorders Seriously impaired sexual performance of various kinds.

Disorders

The more common sexual disorders of women are: impaired libido – interest in sex is reduced or absent; orgasmic dysfunction – inability to obtain orgasm, or great difficulty in doing so; vaginismus – sexual intercourse is difficult or impossible because of spasm of the muscles surrounding the entrance to the vagina; dyspareunia – discomfort or pain is experienced during sexual intercourse. The sexual disorders of men are: impaired libido; erectile impotence – difficulty in obtaining or sustaining an erection; premature ejaculation – ejaculation occurs very soon after vaginal penetration, or even beforehand; ejaculatory failure – ejaculation is either impossible, or never occurs with a partner, or is very delayed.

Sexual disorders can also be classified as primary (the problem has always been present) or secondary (normal sexual functioning preceded the onset of the problem). They can be caused by a wide range of psychological and physical factors. Until the advent of sex therapy the causes of sexual disorders were usually understood in terms of Freudian theory of early sexual development and how this might be disturbed (see FREUD). The causes are now usually postulated in terms of simple psychological mechanisms (Jehu 1979). The most common cause of sexual disorders is anxiety, which may result from many factors including fear of failure, sexual inhibition and lack of confidence about personal appearance. Another contributing factor is ignorance, including lack of sexual information, and belief in incorrect facts or sexual myths. Sexual disorders are often accompanied by other marital or relationship disorders; sometimes they are the cause of these problems, but more commonly they are the result of such difficulties. Poor communication between partners is also likely to contribute to sexual disorders. Depression usually causes impaired libido and may cause other sexual problems.

Many physical illnesses can cause sexual disorders. These include, for example, ENDOCRINE DISORDERS, especially affecting the production of sex hormones, and also diabetes, neurological diseases such as multiple sclerosis, and heart and kidney disease. Sexual disorders may also occur in some patients following surgery, including mastectomy, prostactectomy and amputation. Sometimes the disorder is the result of a direct effect of the illness or operation on anatomical mechanisms responsible for sexual response; in other cases it is the result of the psychological responses to the illness or procedure.

A number of medicines can cause sexual disorders, including some used to treat hypertension, major tranquilizers and antidepressants. Sexual disorders are common in individuals who suffer from ALCOHOLISM or DRUG DEPENDENCE.

The treatment of couples with sexual disorders was revolutionized in 1970 when Masters and Johnson introduced their approach to sex therapy. Treatment consists of a careful assessment of each partner, after which the couple are given instructions in a step-by-step program through which they gradually rebuild their sexual relationship beginning with non-genital caressing exercises. Advice is given on how to improve verbal and non-verbal communication. Treatment is provided by either two co-therapists, one male and one female, or by one therapist. The couple are seen daily and at each session report back on progress. Any difficulties which they may have encountered are discussed and means of overcoming them found. Education is provided about sexual anatomy and response. The Masters and Johnson approach has been successfully modified for use in the National Health Service in the United Kingdom (Hawton 1982).

Patients without partners can also be helped. Barbach (1975) has introduced a masturbation training program for women who have not been able to have an orgasm; sometimes such treatment is provided in groups of five to eight women by two female therapists. Zilbergeld (1979) has suggested ways of helping with the sexual disorders of men who do not have partners. This treatment may also be provided in a group.

The principles of sex therapy can be used in the treatment of some disabled patients and those with chronic physical illness. Where medicine is the cause of sexual disorder, management consists of finding a suitable alternative treatment whenever possible. Sexual disorders resulting from abnormalities of sex hormones can be treated by hormone replacement. For sexual disorders which are the result of marital disharmony, some form of marital therapy rather than sex therapy is usually indicated.

The results of sex therapy reported by Masters and Johnson (1970) were outstanding. Other workers report more modest results, with two-thirds of couples usually having a good outcome (Hawton 1982). The best results are obtained in the treatment of orgasmic dysfunction, vaginismus and premature ejaculation. Severe marital disharmony and psychiatric disorder in one or other partner often indicate a poor prognosis. Although Masters and Johnson (1970) found that hardly any of the couples they had treated successfully had relapsed five years later, little other information is available concerning the longterm prognosis following sex therapy, or of the prognosis of people with sexual disorders who do not receive treatment.

Deviations

The term sexual deviation is used to describe any sexual activity that is preferred to, or displaces, heterosexual intercourse, or one that involves very unusual methods of sexual arousal, especially when the activity violates the norms of society. Whether a form of sexual behavior is regarded as deviant depends to a great degree on social values. These can change with time.

Homosexuality describes both sexual behavior with, and sexual interest in, members of a person's own sex. The sexual interest of some people exclusively involves their own sex; others may show a range of sexual interest in both their own sex and the other sex, and may be referred to as bisexual. The precise incidence of homosexuality in the general population is not known. Kinsey and colleagues (1948) estimated that among men aged thirty, 7 per cent were largely or entirely homosexual in their orientation. It has also been estimated that between 2 and 4 per cent of females are homosexual. In the United Kingdom, under the Sexual Offences Act of 1967, the legal age of consent for male homosexuality is twenty-one. Except in the armed forces there are no laws specifically concerning female homosexuality.

A transsexual is a person who has a disturbance of GENDER INDENTITY and has a powerful urge to change sex. Transsexuals may be of either sex although male transsexuals are more common. They usually seek surgery and hormone treatments to bring about sex change.

Fetishism describes sexual behavior in which an object, usually a particular form of clothing, is the main source of sexual arousal. It is probably confined to men. Similarly transvestism refers to cross-dressing in which a man gets pleasure and usually sexual satisfaction from wearing female clothing.

Exhibitionism describes behavior in which gratification is sought through displaying the genitals to members of the opposite sex, usually strangers in public places. Indecent exposure is the legal offense associated with this behavior. This is the most common sexual offense in the United Kingdom and is frequently committed by young males.

There is no definite information, but a large number of theories, about the causes of sexual deviations. It has been suggested that disturbed relationships with parents may contribute to the development of homosexuality but evidence is lacking. Similarly, the disturbance of gender identity found in transsexualism has been related to disturbed upbringing in which behavior more appropriate to the opposite sex is encouraged. Genetic causes have also been postulated. It has been suggested that genetic factors may make an individual susceptible to becoming homosexual if he or she is later exposed to appropriate environmental influences. Abnormalities in levels of sex hormones before or shortly after birth have also been suggested; this has some support from experiments in animals. However, no reliable differences are found between homosexual and heterosexual adults in terms of either their hormonal or physical characteristics. It has been postulated that transvestism and fetishism are the result of CONDITIONING in which sexual arousal at an early age occurs by change in relation to a particular object or female clothing.

Exhibitionists often suffer from sexual dysfunction and inferiority, and the deviant behavior may be a means of compensating for these difficulties.

Patients often seek treatment to rid themselves of their deviant interest when this is either not appropriate (e.g. well-established homosexual interest in middle-aged men with no heterosexual interest) or they are not well-motivated (e.g. after having been convicted of a sexual offense). Very careful assessment of the patient is therefore imperative. Sometimes deviant sexual interest appears to be related to sexual inadequacy – when treatment as for a sexual disorder may be indicated.

Aversion therapy, in which electric shocks or drug-induced nausea are paired with deviant sexual thoughts or activities, used to be popular. It is now rarely used, because of ethical problems and lack of efficacy. Other self-control techniques may be used (see BEHAVIOR THERAPY). These have been well described by Bancroft (1974). Sometimes patients need help to improve their skills in forming a relationship with a member of the opposite sex (see SOCIAL SKILLS AND TRAINING). Drugs which suppress libido are occasionally used, but can have dangerous side-effects and can pose ethical problems. Some patients do not wish to give up their deviant sexual interest but require help in adjusting to it. There are now wide ranges of self-help organizations suitable for such patients. Transsexual patients usually seek sex re-assignment, including hormonal treatment, social skills training and surgery.

Treatment aimed at modification of homosexual interest is not very successful, especially if the interest has been long established and there is no current or previous heterosexual interest. Treatment aimed at helping patients develop control over exhibitionism, fetishistic or transvestite behavior is more successful, especially with well-motivated patients. However, patients who commit more than one sexual offense (e.g. exhibitionists) usually have a poor prognosis. KEH

Bibliography

*Bancroft, J. 1974: *Deviant sexual behaviour: modification and assessment.* Oxford: Oxford University Press.

Barbach, L. 1975: *For yourself: the fulfilment of female sexuality*. New York: Doubleday.

Hawton, K. 1982: The behavioural treatment of sexual dysfunction. *British journal of psychiatry* 140, 94–101.

Jehu, D. 1979: *Sexual dysfunction; a behavioural approach to causation, assessment, and treatment*. New York and Chichester: John Wiley.

*Kaplan, H. 1974: *The new sex therapy*. London: Bailliere Tindall.

Kinsey, A.C., Pomeroy, W.B. and Martin, C.E. 1948: *Sexual behavior in the human male*. Philadephia: Saunders.

*Masters, W.H. and Johnson, V.E. 1970: *Human sexual inadequacy*. London: Churchill; Boston: Little, Brown.

Zilbergeld, B. 1979: *Men and sex*. London: Souvenir Press.

psychosis This term is commonly used to denote a serious disorder of mental functioning, as in organic, affective or schizophrenic psychosis. Beyond this there is no general agreement on its usage. In some contexts it denotes a disturbance that has the features of a clear-cut illness (for example, a psychosis resulting from thyroid under-activity) as opposed to a condition that could be seen to evolve from natural reactions and personality characteristics, which would be termed a NEUROSIS. In other contexts it specifies a mental state encompassing DELUSIONS and HALLUCINATIONS, or the loss of insight. Psychoanalysts view the mental content of psychoses as deriving from the unconscious Id which erupts unchecked into consciousness. JASPERS draws a distinction between mental phenomena which can be understood empathically, and others (encountered in the psychoses) which are accessible only to causal explanations. DLJ

psychosomatic disorders Illnesses whose development is thought to be importantly determined by psychological factors. Among the diseases speculatively grouped under this heading are: various skin conditions, essential hypertension, coronary artery disease, asthma, peptic ulcers and ulcerative colitis. Studies attempting to define the mechanism of the psychological contribution have explored the possibility of a common personality type, a specific emotional conflict, a particular set of childhood experiences, or a certain life stress. Alternative terms are psychophysiological disorders and organ neuroses, the latter being used especially by psychoanalysts to refer to situations where a persistent emotional disturbance leads to change in the physiology of an organ. DLJ

Bibliography

Alexander, F. 1952: *Psychosomatic medicine, its principles and applications.* London: Allen and Unwin.

psychosomatic disorders and the nervous system Those afflictions which display organic, or physiological, symptoms yet are regarded as lacking an underlying organic origin. The psychosomatic disorders, now more commonly known as psychophysiological disorders, are said to be psychogenic in origin. However, they are to be contrasted with other psychopathological conditions involving somatic complaints (e.g. conversion hysteria) where there are no organic manifestations of the illness. Emotional stress, through its concomitant physiological expression in the AUTONOMIC NERVOUS SYSTEM, may give rise to various somatic disease conditions, such as peptic ulcers, asthma, and essential hypertension (see also EMOTION AND THE NERVOUS SYSTEM). BER/RCS

psychosurgery A method of treating severe psychological disorders with brain surgery. Psychosurgery became an accepted treatment in the 1930s after experimental studies showed that selective brain lesions have a calming effect on animals displaying abnormal emotional behavior in stressful or conflict situations. The most common psychosurgical procedure is the frontal lobotomy which involves severing connections between the frontal cortex and the thalamus. The temporal lobe and its related structures have been another important target area, particularly in the control of aggressive behavior. Despite early reports of success it soon became apparent that many patients were not benefiting from psychosurgery and that some may indeed have deteriorated as a result of the operation. Psychosurgery patients often displayed decreased initiative, apathy, impaired concentration, general indifference, and personality changes that precluded the resumption of normal life. There have been attempts to reduce these side-effects by developing more sophisticated surgical techniques whereby localized damage is produced stereotaxically in specific brain regions (e.g. the hypothalamus, amygdala), thought to be directly involved in emotional behavior. Results, however, are mixed and psychosurgery, for clinical and ethical reasons, remains a highly controversial treatment. GWi

psychosynthesis Created by the Italian psychiatrist Roberto Assagioli. Soon after having completed psychoanalytic training and having been considered by Freud and Jung as a representative of psychoanalysis in Italy in 1910, Assagioli broke away from Freudian orthodoxy and gradually created his own approach. In 1926 he founded the Istituto di Psicosintesi in Rome. A few years later, the hostility of the fascist regime forced this institute to close, Persecution, fascist at first then nazi, prevented Assagioli from continuing his work. When the war was over, he started a new cycle of writing and teaching. He also began to encourage the creation of new psychosynthesis centers throughout the world. His two main books *Psychosynthesis* and *The act of will* were published respectively in 1965 and 1973.

Assagioli noticed that a great deal of psychological pain, imbalance and meaninglessness are felt when the diverse inner elements in the psyche exist unconnected side by side, or clash with one another. But he also observed that when they merge in successively greater wholes, the individual experiences a release of energy, a sense of well being, and a deeper meaning in his life. Seeing that this process tends to occur naturally in all human beings, but that it often gets blocked, Assagioli devised various ways of evoking and facilitating it, and gave to this system, the name of psychosynthesis.

Assagioli's typology has been expressed in his well known "egg diagram" which represents our total psyche. The three horizontal divisions of the oval stand for our past, present and future. All three are active in us, although in different ways. The "lower unconscious" (1) mainly represents our personal psychological past in the form of repressed complexes and long-forgotten memories.

If we wish to encourage our growth we need to investigate our lower unconscious. Otherwise it may be the source of trouble, storing repressed energy, controlling our actions, and robbing us of our freedom.

The "middle unconscious" (2) is where all skills and states of mind reside which can be brought at will into our "field of consciousness" (4).

Our evolutionary future comprises the states of being, of knowing, and of feeling which we call the "superconscious" (3). In the words of Assagioli, the superconscious is the region from which "we receive our higher intuitions and inspirations – artistic, philosophical or scientific, ethical 'imperatives' and urges to humanitarian and heroic action. It is the source of higher feelings, such as altruistic love; of genius and of the states of contemplation, illumination and ecstasy". The exploration of the superconscious is one of our great tasks.

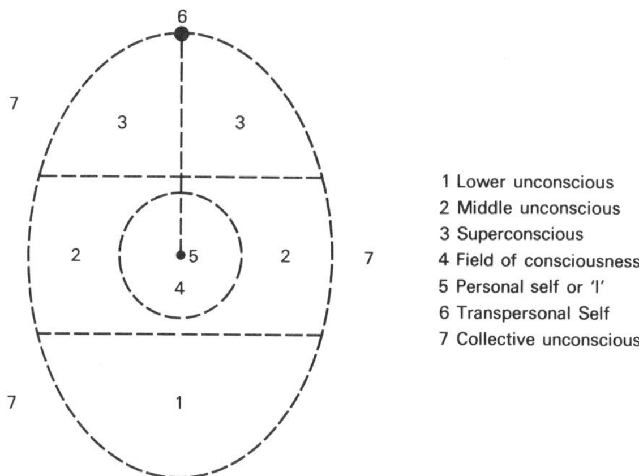

The distinction between the "lower" and the "higher" unconscious, or superconscious, is developmental, not moralistic. The lower unconscious merely represents the most primitive part of ourselves. It is not bad, it is just earlier. Conversely, the superconscious constitutes all that we can still reach in the course of our evolution. It is not, however, a mere abstract possibility, but a living reality, with an existence and powers of its own.

Our psyche is not isolated. It is bathed in the sea of what Carl Jung called the "collective unconscious" (7). In Jung's words, the collective unconscious is "the precondition of each individual psyche, just as the sea is the carrier of the individual wave". Notice that in the diagram all the lines are dotted to signify that no rigid compartments impede interplay among all levels.

The Self experiences all these levels. In the earlier stages of human development, awareness of the Self is nonexistent. For most of us, it exists later in a more or less veiled and confused way. But it can be experienced in its pure state as the personal self, or "I". (5).

The personal self is a reflection or outpost of the Transpersonal Self (6) – enough to give us a sense of centeredness and identity. It lives at the level of individuality, where it can learn to regulate and direct the various elements of the personality. Awareness of the personal self is a precondition for psychological health.

Identification with the Transpersonal Self is a rare occurrence – for some individuals, the culmination of years of discipline; for others, a spontaneous extraordinary experience. It was described in ancient times with the Sanskrit words *sat-chit-ananda*: being – consciousness – bliss. The Transpersonal Self, while retaining a sense of individuality, lives at the level of universality, in a realm where personal plans and concerns are overshadowed by the wider vision of the whole. The realization of the Transpersonal Self is the mark of spiritual fulfilment.

Personal and Transpersonal Self are in fact the same reality experienced at different levels: our true essence beyond all masks and conditionings.

The psychosynthetic approach is primarily pragmatic. It uses a number of techniques which could be grouped into the following categories:

Analytical techniques. These help to assess the blocks and the potentials of the personality, enable the exploration of the underworld of the unconscious, and reach the roots of psychological complexes. Imagery, free drawing, critical analysis, writing and subpersonality work are used for these purposes

Mastery techniques. Full awareness and understanding of harmful images and complexes may help to disintegrate them, but does not necessarily produce permanent positive change. The cognitive work needs to be complemented by the active and gradual training of all psychological functions, (sensation, desire, impulse, feeling, imagination, thinking, intuition, will). In this way we can coach and develop the archaic immature elements of our being. Special emphasis here is given to the discovery of the "I" and to the cultivation of the will as a skilful agent, capable of harmoniously regulating and coordinating the various aspects of the personality.

Transformation techniques. The step beyond understanding and mastery consists in enabling the seeds of change to come to full bloom. This phase, often the most spectacular, may bring about reversals in values, and other profound developments. Of particular relevance in this phase is visualization, with its power to trigger significant psychological and behavioral changes. The end goal is the reconstruction of the personality around a new center.

Meditative techniques. Specific tools are designed for exploring the superconscious. Various forms of MEDITATION help the individual to awaken the intuition, stimulate imagination, creativity, release higher feelings, and facilitate a wider integration.

Grounding techniques. Although superconscious experiences may be beautiful and satisfying it is better for the individual if he can express the meaning of these and if they play a role in shaping his attitudes and behavior. Moreover higher states of consciousness are not by themselves a guarantee of effective psychological functioning, and, when improperly handled, they can cause a wide variety of problems, a true pathology of the sublime. Therefore psychosynthesis attempts to harmonize the personal with the superconscious realm in the human being and to enable his free and effective expression at all levels.

Relational techniques. Healthy interpersonal relationships are the natural counterpart of individual growth. The individual can learn to deal with the common obstacles to relationships, to cultivate interpersonal qualities such as openess, love, and empathy, to acquire new communication skills, and to evoke the awareness of belonging to a greater whole.

From a historical perspective, because of its emphasis on the creative potentialities inherent in every human being, psychosynthesis can be regarded as a Humanistic and TRANSPERSONAL PSYCHOLOGY, along with the work of pioneers such as A.H. Maslow, R. May, V. Frankl, and C. Rogers. Other factors however – the attempt to relate eastern insight to western research, the variety of practical methods, the richness of possible applications, the inclusiveness of its vision – make of Assagioli's work a unique contribution to contemporary psychology. DW

Bibliography

Assagioli, Roberto, 1965: *Psychosynthesis: A manual of principles and techniques*. Harmondsworth: Penguin Books.

———, 1973: *The act of will*. London: Turnstone Press, New York: Viking Press.

psychotherapeutic drug treatment of mental disorders In the absence of knowledge of underlying pathology, treatment with psychotherapeutic medication is only a provisional remedy for mental disorders (see NEUROCHEMISTRY AND BEHAVIOR). Of late neuropharmacology has provided important insights into the nature of brain dysfunction in psychopathological states. Yet despite the initial optimism that followed the benefits from a single compound, L-dopa, in Parkinson's disease, no corresponding success has been found with other illnesses.

Schizophrenia was a term coined by Bleuler in 1911 and applied to psychotic conditions having in common certain disturbances of association. Bleuler used the term in the plural recognizing that several pathological conditions were probably represented. Present day consideration of the constellations of symptoms, natural history, response to medication and prognosis of the schizophrenias suggests that it is likely that at least two distinct pathological conditions exist, only one of which achieves significant response to psychotropic medication. Illnesses arising insidiously, often in adolescence, and characterized by blunted emotions, interpersonal difficulties, cognitive rigidity and shallowness have a poor prognosis and reveal only a partial response to treatment. In contrast acute illnesses which have florid symptoms and an obvious precipitant typically respond to drug treatment without any residual symptoms. Even so drugs are not curative. They facilitate recovery or reduce symptoms. This is not to decry their important social benefits through the making of patients more accessible to social management.

Despite evidence for differing syndromes schizophrenic patients are all medicated with similar drugs. The majority belong to the phenothiazine, butyrophenone or thioxanthine classes. The effects of these drugs, also termed neuroleptics, are threefold. They have a tranquilizing action in reducing psychotic features such as hallucinations, delusions and thought disorder, an action which may be delayed for several weeks. This antipsychotic action relates to the blockade of dopamine post-synaptic receptor sites in the mesolimbic system. They have an immediate sedative effect, to which tolerance develops, in reducing agitation, restlessness and excitement. Sedative as well as hypotensive effects correlate with blockade of α-noradrenergic receptors. They cause extrapyramidal side effects and sometimes tardive dyskinesia (that is, patterns of abnormal movement affecting certain parts of the body more than others). Extrapyramidal symptoms occur from dopamine blockade in the nigrostriatal system and compensating anticholinergic activity that ensues. Tardive dyskinesia also appears to involve this system, possibly owing to over compensation of dopaminergic activity.

Whereas nonpsychotic individuals are particularly susceptible to sedative effects at low doses, psychotic patients respond best at moderate to high doses ranging between 300 and 600 mg/day of chlorpromazine or the equivalent, with higher doses useful mainly for refractory cases. There is ample evidence that maintenance on long acting depot injections of neuroleptics after symptoms have remitted or been reduced minimizes the likelihood of a return of symptoms. Anticholinergic drugs are administered to control the Parkinsonian side effects but the long term value of their administration has been questioned.

Despite these generalizations it is not possible to predict differential effects of the various neuroleptic drugs on individual symptoms or demographic or other clinical features and so predict the response of an individual patient reliably. Beliefs about differences between drugs may stem from differences in their side effects when administered in doses with comparable antipsychotic potency (Hirsch 1982). Nevertheless the fact that individual patients will differ in their response to various drugs is in keeping with differences in chemical structure and variations in metabolism. Recent developments have focused on the role of endorphins and of β-adrenoceptor blocking drugs prescribed in large doses either as sole medication or in combination with neuroleptics.

The other type of major psychosis is the affective disorders which may take the form of depression or hypomania (Paykel and Coppen 1979). These may occur alone or together episodically. A unipolar affective illness is where only depression occurs and a bipolar illness where both depression and hypomania occur. Hypomania and depression are treated differently and may arise with or without obvious precipitants.

Endogenous depression, thought to be secondary to changes in monoamine neurotransmitters such as norepinephrine, dopamine and serotonin, responds to antidepressants all of which increase the concentration of monoamine transmitters and facilitate transmission. Presumably an underlying biochemical abnormality is corrected as long as the drugs are administered. The main classes of antidepressants are tricyclics, tetracyclics and monoamine oxidase inhibitors (MAOIs). Tricyclics raise concentrations of serotonin and norepinephrine and, depending on the direction of their selectivity, have sedative effects if the balance is in favor of serotonin or alerting actions if in favor of norepinephrine. Tetracyclics, developed from tricyclics, have fewer adverse side effects and are therefore preferable. MAOIs act by inhibiting the enzyme MAO responsible for the destruction of neurotransmitters. One of their complications is their preservation of monoamines with hypertensive sympatheticomimetic actions.

Hypomania responds to the same major tranquilizers recommended for the florid symptoms of schizophrenia. Typically they are administered in high doses which are tapered off as the condition improves. In conditions where hypomania recurs, and is therefore not simply an isolated response to an obvious stressor, lithium, which is ineffective in controlling florid symptoms, is of prophylactic value in preventing the reoccurrence of most hypomanic and some depressive episodes. Lithium is not without side effects which include hypothyroidism.

Just as the major tranquilizers are effective for both hypomania and schizophrenia so too is lithium implicated in both disorders, but as yet definitive studies in schizophrenia are lacking. This also raises the vexed problem of mixed diagnoses where symptoms of schizophrenia are coupled with symptoms of depression or hypomania. Recent evidence suggests that the role of affective symptoms has been undervalued in schizophrenia and may be integral to the disease entity.

Anxiety is conceptualized as an exaggeration of the fight or flight reflex to a threat real or imagined. It takes the form of maladaptive coping procedures as seen in obsessive–compulsive states, hysterical conversion or dissociation states, and phobias, or alternatively, as generalized anxiety unrelated to particular situations. Drug treatment for anxiety distinguishes between somatic manifestations and subjective feelings of anxiety.

The involvement of the limbic system, known to be implicated in emotional behavior, has been of central interest in understanding the neuropharmacology of anxiety. This is thought to involve the inhibitory neurotransmitter gamma-amino butyric acid (GABA). GABA is enhanced by the commonly prescribed benzodiazepines which include diazepam or valium. This and other benzodiazepines have a similar efficacy in reducing anxiety levels; nevertheless there are individual differences in the preferred drug for a particular patient. The required dose level for the individual is thought to reflect the subjective level of anxiety and should be lowered as anxiety abates. The tranquilizing properties are coupled with sedation and hence their use as hypnotics. They are available in both short and long acting forms and act quickly because they are rapidly absorbed. Benzodiazepines are being prescribed with increasing caution in view of their habit forming properties and unpleasant withdrawal effects. The sedative effects also impair psychomotor skills and perceptual judgment such as those required when driving a motor vehicle. They also reduce capacity for alcohol.

Somatic signs of anxiety such as palpitations, sweating, tachycardia, abdominal tensions and nausea which are mediated via the autonomic nervous system and controlled by limbic-hypothalamic centres are commonly treated with β-adrenoceptor blockers such as propranolol. As these drugs cause hypotension and tachycardia a test dose is usually given. In view of the cardiovascular effects they are contraindicated where there is a history of asthma, bronchospasm, heart block, cardiac failure and diabetes. In view of their antipsychotic properties, behavioral and psychophysiological effects their actions may not be restricted to physiological concomitants of anxiety. As in the treatment of psychosis combined therapy with tranquilizers is usually more effective.

Propranolol is also effective in treating explosive aggressive outbursts. Another approach is anticonvulsant medication with the rationale that temper tantrums accompany epilepsy for which anticonvulsants are indicated. The major tranquilizers have nonspecific actions which may depend on their sedative actions.

Drugs are also used to control the restlessness and agitation that is a component of dementia and other confusional states that result from toxic drug-reactions, metabolic disorders, nutritional deficiences, physical stress, endocrine disorders and cerebral anoxia. In the elderly the excessive prescribing of sedatives or psychotropic drugs can lead to agitation, in which case a withdrawal or reappraisal of medication is indicated. Drugs that control restlessness include chlormethiazole which is chemically related to vitamin B_1, phenothiazines and butyrophenones. Where confusability is regarded as secondary to impairments in cerebral circulation drugs that claim to promote cerebral circulation and metabolism may be applied (Laurence, 1980). Vitamin concentrates such as parentrovite are sometimes effective. JHG

Bibliography

Hirsch, S.R. 1982: Medication and physical treatment of schizophrenia. In *Handbook of psychiatry*, ed. J. Wing. III. Cambridge and New York: Cambridge University Press.

Laurence, D.R. 1980: *Clinical pharmacology*, 5th edn. Edinburgh: Churchill Livingstone.

Paykel, E.S. and Coppen, A. eds. 1979: *Psychopharmacology of affective disorders*. Oxford and New York: Oxford University Press.

psychotherapy The treatment of emotional and personality difficulties by psychological means. Most definitions of psychotherapy highlight the role of the therapist-patient relationship. For example Hans Strupp, a distinguished American psychotherapy researcher, has described psychotherapy as "an interpersonal process designed to bring about modifications of feelings, cognitions, attitudes and behavior which have proved troublesome to the person seeking help from a trained professional" (Strupp 1978). The therapist-patient relationship is different from other forms of relationship in important and basic ways: the person who makes himself (or herself) available as a therapist is in effect a socially sanctioned healer, a professional who commits himself to help others in need of his expertise.

The person who seeks out the therapist does so usually because of an overwhelming need. It may be to reduce distress, or to learn how to cope more effectively with life's demands or to discover how to live more creatively and fulfillingly. In many patients the need is somewhat blurred and may amount to a general sense of dissatisfaction and malaise. But however covert the problems, the essential point is that the patient decides that he (or she) is in need of help and chooses someone who has been socially sanctioned as able to provide that help.

Psychotherapy is a generic term under whose rubric are

to be found literally dozens of different forms of treatment. In an attempt to classify treatments that are customarily regarded as examples of psychotherapy the plural form of the term is more appropriate. One classification revolves around theory. We have classical Freudian psychoanalytic psychotherapy and its many variants, devised by such theorists as C.G. Jung, Alfred Adler and Melanie Klein; the client-centered therapy of Carl Rogers; existential psychotherapy; Gestalt psychotherapy; transactional analysis; behavior therapy; cognitive psychotherapy; and many more beside (Patterson 1980).

An alternative approach to classification is according to the target of treatment (Bloch 1979). The examples here include family and marital therapy, in which attention is given to the relationship between members of a family on the premises that it is in the sphere of relationships that the problem lies, and sex therapy, where the focus is obviously some difficulty in a sexual relationship.

A third way to classify the therapies is in terms of the aims of treatment (Bloch 1979). Categorizing the psychotherapies thus shows up their diverse nature, as no standard classification is available. The following represents a commonly cited approach. First, *crisis intervention* – as the name indicates the therapist intervenes in the midst of a crisis which has overwhelmed the patient, and the therapist's aim is that of helping the patient to overcome the crisis. Second, *Supportive psychotherapy* – the term depicts the goal of therapy, which is the provision of support to a patient who cannot manage without it, either in the short or long-term. There is an obvious overlap between crisis intervention and supportive psychotherapy in as much as support is fundamental to both, but supportive therapy is the term commonly applied to treatment of those patients with a need for prolonged support, often life-long: for example, patients with chronic schizophrenia or severe disorders of personality. Third, *Symptom-oriented psychotherapy* – no substantial change in personality is attempted and there is no need for the patient to achieve understanding about the nature and origins of his problems. The therapist sets out specifically to help the patient gain relief from distressing or disabling symptoms. Example, of this form of psychotherapy are the various psychological procedures to reduce anxiety; a wide range of techniques is practiced, from Eastern approaches like transcendental meditation and yoga to muscular relaxation.

A fourth approach is *insight-oriented psychotherapy* – the category of psychological treatment usually referred to when the generic term of psychotherapy is mentioned. Insight-oriented therapy is the opposite of the previous category because its chief goal is that the patient will acquire insight into what has been formerly unintelligible and bewildering. The Freudian notion (Freud 1917) that therapy should seek to make conscious what was previously unconscious is at the core of this category of therapy: three chief elements are involved. The first is the recognition and understanding of the unconsciously determined form of relationship that evolves between patient and therapist during the course of treatment, the so-called transference. According to the concept of transference, the patient transfers on to the therapist feelings and attitudes which have their roots in an earlier crucial relationship, usually with a parent or sibling. Teasing out the transference patterns enables the patient to achieve important insights about the nature and origins of his problems. The second element is the patient's identification of the unconsciously determined strategies he has used customarily to ward off unpleasant or threatening feelings, thoughts and fantasies. These mechanisms of defense include repression – a process of active forgetting of material, which is kept under control in the unconscious, denial – a self deception, whereby the harsh truth of a situation is avoided, and projection – placing intolerable feelings outside of oneself and attributing them to others. The third strand of insight involves the exploration and understanding of the relationship between current personal qualities and patterns of behavior, and key events of the past, usually from childhood.

The issue of insight raises the question of whether it is automatically followed by behavioral or personality change. One body of opinion holds that once a patient acquires self-knowledge behavioral change is inevitable on the grounds that normal psychological growth is no longer blocked by his neurosis and can develop freely.

The function of insight is best examined in the context of the basic factors which appear to underlie all forms of psychotherapy. It is highly likely that these explain the common finding that practitioners of different theoretical schools of therapy by and large achieve similar results (Luborsky et al 1975; Smith and Glass 1977). J.D. Frank (1971) the doyen of psychotherapy research, has highlighted the relevance of specific features of psychotherapy which are shared by most clinical approaches. He regards the following six factors as common to all forms of treatment, and necessary, although not sufficient in themselves, for treatment to operate:

1. An intense, emotionally charged confiding relationship with a helping person. The description of the type of relationship is revealing. Unlike an ordinary social interaction it has an intense quality with patient and therapist meeting on serious business. The relationship could not be otherwise but emotionally charged since the patient is invariably distressed or disabled and often desperate for help. The confiding nature of the relationship is intrinsic to psychotherapy. For therapy to work the patient must disclose his problems, feelings and fantasies – disclosures which are typically painful, threatening or embarrassing – and he must feel secure that everything he does reveal is completely confidential.

2. A rationale which contains an explanation of the patient's problems and of the methods of treatment for their solution. A person who seeks help through psychotherapy is usually baffled by his experience. The therapist's provision of a rationale – even giving a symptom a name is helpful – contributes to a reduction in the patient's bewildered state. Paradoxically, the content of the rationale does not seem crucial. More important is the confidence held by the therapist that his theoretical propositions and the related practical methods he applies in treatment are beneficial. Equally important is the patient's

acceptance of the rationale as making sense and offering some order to his state of disarray.

3. The provision of new information about the nature and origin of the patient's problems and of ways of dealing with them. This factor is closely allied to that of insight, mentioned earlier. It is not so much the learning by the patient of a precisely accurate explanation of his problems, but an account which is coherent, logical and illuminating. In some schools of psychotherapy the learning process is one of self-discovery, with the therapist acting as a facilitator. In other approaches the therapist assumes a more strictly pedagogic role, teaches the patient about the nature and causes of his difficulties and/or instructing him on how to set about solving them.

4. Hope in the patient that he can expect help from the therapist. A person consults a therapist in the belief that he will benefit (Wilkins 1973). His choice of a professional helper is not accidental: he usually has some idea about the professional status of the therapist and surmises that he has undertaken a program of training and must, therefore, know something about the job of helping people like himself. The other side of the effect of hope is the therapist's personal qualities. The therapist who displays a sense of optimism will usually transmit that optimism to his patient. The mere fact that the therapist takes on the patient for treatment indicates that he has some confidence that improvement is possible.

5. An opportunity for experiences of success during the course of therapy and a consequent enhancement of the sense of mastery. Often a patient enters therapy with the idea that his achievements are negligible and his chances of enjoying success slender. Therapy allows him to reverse this image: as he overcomes his difficulties, begins to appreciate the nature of his problems, and enjoys new favorable experiences during therapy, he develops a growing feeling of self-confidence and a sense that he is capable (Bandura 1977).

6. The facilitation of emotional arousal. Psychotherapy devoid of emotion is most unlikely to prove profitable. A patient's detached, rational view of himself is rarely followed by a substantial change. In ways which are difficult to define, the patient must repeatedly enter into a state of emotional arousal. Through such a process he begins to discover the feelings that are central to his experience and to appreciate what relevance they have to his problems. SB

Bibliography

Bandura, A. 1977: Self-efficacy: Towards a unifying theory of behavioral change. *Psychological review* 84, 191–215.

Bloch, S. (ed) 1979: *An introduction to the psychotherapies*. Oxford: Oxford University Press.

*——— 1982: *What is psychotherapy?* Oxford: Oxford University Press.

Frank, J.D. 1971: Therapeutic factors in psychotherapy. *American journal of psychotherapy* 25, 350–61.

Freud, S. 1917 (*1963*): *Introductory lectures on psychoanalysis. Standard Edition* volumes 15 and 16, London: Hogarth Press; New York: Norton.

Luborsky, L., Singer, B. and Luborsky, L. 1975: Comparative studies of psychotherapies. *Archives of general psychiatry* 32, 995–1008.

Patterson, C.H. 1980: *Theories of counseling and psychotherapy*. New York: Harper and Row.

Smith, M.L. and Glass, C.V. 1977: Meta-analysis of psychotherapy outcome studies. *American psychologist* 32, 752–60.

Strupp, H.H. 1978: Psychotherapy research and practice: An overview. In: *Handbook of psychotherapy and behavior change*, ed. S. Garfield and A. Bergin. New York: Wiley.

Wilkins, W. 1973: Expectancy of therapeutic gain: An empirical and conceptual critique. *Journal of consulting and clinical psychology* 40, 69–77.

psychotomimetic drugs *See* drugs

psychotropic drugs *See* drugs

puberty The process of sexual maturation and other physical changes marking the transition from childhood to adult maturity. It is accompanied by the development of secondary sexual characteristics and culminates in the capacity for reproduction. Various psychological changes, e.g. cognitive development, also take place (see ADOLESCENCE).

Puberty is initiated and controlled by changes in hypothalamic and anterior pituitary function. Changes in the reproductive system occur over two to three years and are related to the ADOLESCENT GROWTH SPURT. Puberty occurs approximately eighteen to twenty-four months later in boys than in girls and the growth spurt takes place at an earlier point in the pubertal sequence in girls than in boys. The sequence of outward signs in boys is, accelerated growth of the testes and scrotum with the appearance of pubic hair; penile growth, coinciding with the onset of the growth spurt; the first seminal discharge; deepening of the voice. In girls the process begins with the appearance of breast buds and of pubic hair. Menstruation begins near the completion of the sequence, after the peak velocity of the growth spurt (see MENARCHE). Tanner (1962) has described stages in breast growth in girls and genital development in boys.

There is wide individual variation in the age of onset and rate of progress, with different psychological correlates. Late maturation in boys, for example, may be followed by difficulties in personal adjustment. WLLP-J

Bibliography

Tanner, James M. 1962: *Growth at adolescence*. Oxford: Blackwell Scientific; Springfield, Ill.: C.C. Thomas.

punishment If the performance of a particular response results in an aversive consequence the response is being punished. Punishment was little studied by earlier learning theorists, and when it was they questioned its effectiveness. There can, however, be no question but that immediate, consistent and severe punishment of a particular action will effectively stop that action being performed. But there do remain legitimate doubts. Punishment may cause people to refrain from performing the punished action only when they believe that they will be punished again: the child smacked by his parent for performing some undesirable action may simply go and do it elsewhere far from the parent's view. Punishment may have undesirable side effects: painful or harmful consequences may generate a state of fear or stress, and the punished child may become very anxious. Finally, it is always important to ask whether the infliction of pain on another person or on an animal is morally justified. NJM

purposivism A theory of behavior in which it is assumed that the course of action is carried out according to a reason, strategy or series of steps designed to attain a projected end. In psychology, purposivism takes two forms. There is teleological purposivism in which it is held that the organism can act as a self-determining agent, freely choosing the ends and course of behavior to be enacted intentionally. There is also purposive behaviorism, in which it is assumed that purpose is a mediating pattern or "cognitive map" coming between stimulus-input and response-output, but a pattern which itself has been input via external influence rather than uniquely created internally by the organism. Whether or not organisms (including people) are self-determined agents is one of the most hotly debated questions in psychology. (See also MECHANISTIC THEORY; VOLUNTARISM.) JFR

Q

questionnaires Also known as surveys and self-report inventories, questionnaires include a number of "instruments" such as check-lists (simple lists of items which the respondent understands and "checks-off" his or her response to), rating scales (usually attitude statements or people that are rated on a number of carefully chosen and independent 3, 5 or 7 point rating scales) and inventories (usually longer questionnaires which have a number of rating scales on which the respondent is asked to respond in a particular way and which give a single score or a number of subscores). Respondents are usually required to read various questions themselves and provide some sort of written answer (a tick, a sentence etc), although the questions are occasionally given orally as in public opinion poll surveys. They are used to assess everything from attitudes to personality traits, and values to behavioral patterns. Although some questionnaires are open-ended in the sense that the respondent is relatively free in the quality and quantity of his or her responses, most questionnaires in psychology have predetermined response categories which, though restricting variety, facilitate coding and analysis.

In order for a valid, reliable and unambiguous questionnaire to be devised a number of decisions have to be made and considerable pilot work done. Oppenheim (1966) has noted three major decisions that have to be made in the initial phase: Firstly there is the decision about the methods of data collection such as interview, mailed questionnaires and self- or group administered questionnaire, each of which has particular problems associated with it. Secondly there are problems of question sequence and question type such as the use of filter questions (which start with broad issues and progressively narrow the scope of the questions onto specific points), the proportion of open and closed questions, how to ask tricky or sensitive questions and how to code the answers. Finally there are decisions to be made as to how to cope with missing data or lost information.

One of the most problematic aspects of questionnaire design relates to the wording of questions. Factual, rather than attitudinal or opinion questions are usually easier to phrase but are not without their problems. Oppenheim (1966) for instance points to the problem involved in the simple question "When do you usually have tea?" which in England can mean a beverage, a light meal in the afternoon or an evening meal. Loaded, leading, double-barrelled or double-negative questions should always be avoided and instructions should be clear and concise.

It has long been established that all self-report questionnaires are open to a range of specific response biases (Furnham and Henderson 1982). These biases include: *Faking good* or a social desirability/prestige bias where respondents reply in the manner that they believe is expected of normal well-adjusted people and hence present themselves in a socially acceptable way; *faking bad* in which respondents intentionally give an answer which will give a bad (deviant, amoral, sick) impression of themselves and hence present themselves in a socially unacceptable way; *acquiesence* or yea-saying in which respondents have a tendency to agree or say yes to questions irrespective of their content; *opposition* or nay-saying where respondents have a tendency to disagree or respond negatively to all questions irrespective of their content; *"mid-point" response set* where respondents tend to choose mid-point or neutral responses to all questions; and *carelessness, inconsistency* and *incomplete answers*. Because these response biases threaten the validity and reliability of results, numerous strategies are used to overcome them. Some questionnaires include a measure of response bias (a lie scale) which may be used to detect unreliable subjects; some questionnaires are administered along with a social desirability questionnaire of which there are quite a number; some attitude or personality questionnaires include factual or intelligence questions to check that the respondent is reading the questions; some questionnaires have "trick" or "repeated" questions so that some reliability may be tested; and still others have been deliberately subjected to experiments where respondents have been asked either to fake good or to fake bad and the results compared with those of a control group.

Most questionnaires are concerned with measuring attitudes. There are four principal scaling methods for the measurement of attitudes, each of which has certain advantages and disadvantages. (1) The method of *equal-appearing intervals* (Thurstone) in which judges compare all items, two at a time, judging which of the pair was more positive or negative in order that all the items may be scaled in relationship to one another. This enables the tester to assign a value to each item and place each respondent on a continuum according to the median scale value of the item endorsed. (2) The method of *summated ratings* (Likert) in which subjects place their answers on a continuum from strongly agree to strongly disagree. These are given simple linear weights (e.g. from 1 to 7) and then totaled. (3) *Social*

Distance Scaling (Bogardus) in which subjects are required to indicate to what extent they are willing to accept a close degree of relationship with another nationality or group (e.g. "Would you let your daughter marry a young socialist?"). (4) *Cumulative Scaling* (Guttman) which is a procedure that allows the investigator to determine from a respondents' score exactly which items he or she has endorsed. With careful preparation items in the scale are ordered and cumulative so that one can determine to what extent respondents' attitudes deviate from an ideal scale pattern. AF

Bibliography

Oppenheim, A. 1966: *Questionnaire design and attitude measurement*. London: Heinemann.

Furnham, A. and Henderson, M. 1982: The good, the bad and the mad: response bias in self-report measures. *Personality and individual differences* 3, 311–20.

R

radical therapy In 1967 an extraordinary book appeared – *The politics of experience*, by R. D. LAING. During the next ten years, all the issues raised in that book were acted on in various ways by different groups. In England, *People not psychiatry* was formed as a network of people willing to help each other, the Philadelphia Association was formed by Laing and others, and the Arbours Association followed, with Joe Berke and Morton Schatzman among others. The theoretical issues in psychology were taken up by magazines such as *Red rat* and *Humpty dumpty*, which were angry, campaigning and radical. As a result of these efforts, the medical model has now been widely abandoned even by the orthodox: the very conservative British Psychological Society, for example, came out in the late 1970s as saying that neurosis was not a medical but a psychological problem: and in America the highly respectable five-volume *Handbook of social psychology* said the same thing. Also as a result of these efforts, there is much more general awareness of problems such as racism, sexism, classism and ageism: for example, the US Department of Health, Education and Welfare issued an official kit entitled *Shattering sex-role stereotypes*, which went to all agencies concerned with alcohol, drug abuse and mental health. The same tendency was also reflected in legal changes and changes in quota regulations, etc. In the US, for example, the use of intelligence and personality tests was severely curtailed by legislation and court decisions following the contention that they were used to discriminate against blacks and others. Leon Kamin's book *The science and politics of IQ* was important in this area.

Perhaps the biggest positive change was the enormous increase in various kinds of peer counseling, starting with Re-evaluation Counseling and resulting in 1982 in four different networks of co-counseling in Britain alone. Harvey Jackins's *The human side of human beings* is where the idea began but there are more recent books by Rose Evison and Richard Horobin, and by John Southgate and Rosemary Randall, which make the technique much more accessible and understandable through the copious use of cartoons and diagrams. Self-help groups also increased, and there is now an Association of Self Help and Community Groups in Britain. One of the most influential groups was *Red therapy* in the late 1970s, and out of this came the Ernst and Goodison book *In our own hands*, basically addressed to the women's liberation movement but also useful to mixed groups or men's groups. The main point it makes is that consciousness-raising is not enough, because "unconscious feelings formed by our childhood conditioning would continue to sabotage our conscious choices for liberation". So what is needed is "unconsciousness raising", and in their book they describe how this is to be done.

Radical therapy sees the individual as part of a wider social scene, and believes that social problems need social solutions. The difficult task of relating the personal to the social so as to do justice to both was tackled by Nick Heather *(Radical perspectives in psychology)* and by John Rowan *(Ordinary ecstasy)* on the theoretical level, and by the organizations mentioned above in a practical way – to which we may now add the Institute of Psychotherapy and Social Studies in London, which is running courses based on this view of therapy. There are also some classic anthologies in this field which are still worth reading, such as *Radical psychology* (Phil Brown), *The radical therapist* (R.T. Collective), *Going crazy* (Ruitenbeek) and *Readings in radical psychiatry* (Claude Steiner). JCR

Bibliography

Brown, Phil 1973: *Radical psychology*. London: Tavistock Publications.

*Ernst, S. and Goodison, L. 1981: *In our own hands: A book of self-help therapy*. London: Women's Press.

Evison, R. and Horobin, R. 1979: *How to change yourself and your world*. Sheffield: Co-counselling Phoenix.

*Heather, N. 1976: *Radical perspectives in psychology*. London: Methuen.

Jackins, H. 1965: *The human side of human beings: The theory of re-evaluation counselling*. Seattle: Rational Island Press.

Kamin, L. 1974: *The science and politics of IQ*. New York: John Wiley.

*Laing, R.D. 1967: *The politics of experience* and *The bird of paradise*. Harmondsworth: Penguin.

R.T. Collective 1974: *The radical therapist*. Harmondsworth: Penguin.

Rowan, J. 1976: *Ordinary ecstasy: humanistic psychology in action*. London: Routledge & Kegan Paul.

Ruitenbeek, H.M. 1972: *Going crazy*. New York: Bantam Books.

Southgate, J. and Randall, R. 1978: *The barefoot psychoanalyst*. London: AKHPC.

Steiner, C. et al. 1975: *Readings in radical psychiatry*. New York: Grove Press.

radical translation *See* translation, radical

rapid eye movement *See* sleep, paradoxical

rating scale, behaviorally anchored A rating scale format used in personnel research and performance appraisal in which the rating points or levels are defined (or anchored) by examples of behavior which denote the various levels of effectiveness. This format was originated by Smith and Kendall (1963) and was expected to lead to more reliable and more relevant performance measures for use in personnel research and human resource management. From a psychometric viewpoint these hopes have not been realized. Nevertheless, the behaviorally anchored rating scale and its variants are clearly superior to other formats in providing raters with clear definitions of what is to be rated (Jacobs, Kafry and Zedeck 1980). MDH

Bibliography

Jacobs, Rich, Kafry, Ditsa, and Zedeck, Sheldon 1980: Expectations of behaviorally anchored rating scales. *Personnel psychology* 33, 595–640.

Smith, Patricia C. and Kendall, Lorne, M. 1963: Retranslation of expectations: An approach to the construction of unambiguous anchors for rating scales. *Journal of applied psychology* 47, 149–55.

rationality Has a variety of meanings in the social sciences. (1) Of agents: capacity for sound judgment in thought and action; (2) of groups or institutions: ability to express the interests of members in an effective, transparent way; (3) of systems (e.g. the physical universe or the social world); possession of an intelligible order.

Rationality of thought and action has often been held to distinguish humans from all other creatures. It has featured in many definitions of a person, as, for instance, a rational animal (Aristotle), an individual substance rational by nature (Boethius) or "a thinking, intelligent being that has reason and reflection and can consider itself as itself" (Locke). What exactly is to be meant by "rationality" is disputed, however, and it is best to discuss rational thought and rational action separately.

Rational thought is usually construed as thought which conforms to a canon of deliberation. It must at least be coherent, responsive and self-critical. Correspondingly, a person holds beliefs irrationally, if one conflicts with another, if he does not adapt them in the face of superior argument and contrary evidence or if he refuses to question their assumptions. Only part of this canon is clear, namely the requirements of deductive and inductive reasoning (and even they can be disputed). For the rest, an informal, quasi-forensic notion of what counts as defensible belief leaves a good deal of latitude. A rational person need not hold each and every belief through constant or conscious deliberation – there may be scope for intuition, authority or habit – but he must be able to muster a good defense when occasion demands.

Failure to formalize the canon, at least in detail, may suggest that thought is rational only relative to rules which vary with place and time. Philosophically this raises old issues of scepticism. Are there universal rules of rational judgment? On the one hand, clear and incisive accounts of *the* rules of logic, probability and statistics are on offer; on the other, it is plain that these fields have a long, changing and unfinished history, and not necessarily one of advance towards a definitive account. This tension shows up in the social sciences too, notably in debates about whether logic itself belongs to the subject matter of the sociology of knowledge, about whether there exist peoples whose thought displays a pre-logical mentality and about whether mentally ill people are intellectually defective or merely deviant. Such questions are of general importance for hermeneutics.

Rational action has also been a difficult topic in philosophy, ever since Plato and Aristotle tried to establish the role of belief in moving a rational man to action and to explain the relation between rational action and moral action. But, for purposes of social science, a clear start is provided by the crisp analysis proposed in Decision Theory and exploited in microeconomics. Here rationality is a relation between preferences, actions and outcomes. An ideally rational agent has a number of actions which he could perform, knows the consequences of each and has a complete and consistent order of preferences among them. He acts rationally provided that there is no other feasible action whose consequences he would prefer. This gestures to the idea of the rational agent as a maximizer of his own utility. It is silent about the source of utility and has nothing to say about the rationality of ends. Rationality lies in the informed and well calculated choice of means to whatever goals the agent may have. See especially Max Weber (1968).

In the simplest case the agent knows the various consequences with certainty. Decision Theory also provides for risk and uncertainty, however, and other technical refinements. The commonest approach is to discount the utility of an outcome by the likelihood of achieving it, thus making the rational agent a maximizer of his *expected utility*. Other discounts also need to be reckoned in, especially for costs, for the passage of time before the outcome is reached and for various matters to do with acquiring information. This all creates deep theoretical problems but the broad idea is enough to make sense of the basis of microeconomics and to yield premises for much of economic theory.

Further useful technicalities are supplied by the Theory of Games, which studies choices where the benefit to each actor depends on what others choose. It is important that choices can be individually rational for each, while summing to a result inferior for all. For instance each gardener in a drought may be rational in using water, even though it would be better for all, if none did. Such "Unseen Hand" effects (sometimes, as here, mischievous, sometimes for the public good) are central to any rational-man theory of processes and institutions.

This neat account of rational action can be challenged. The charge of assuming a crude egoism in human nature is easily rebutted, since the account requires only that a rational agent seeks to satisfy his desires (be they selfish or altruistic). More serious doubts concern the associationist or, often, behaviorist psychology underlying rational-man models. Here it is harder to establish what assumptions are essential, as opposed to merely common. Even in its blander versions, however, the account is deeply Humean in maintaining that desire is the only motive force to action. This is fiercely disputed by Kantians and others, who would have a rational agent moved by belief, judgment or moral reflection. Relatedly, its strictly instrumental, means – ends notion of rationality is rejected by those who hold that fully rational action must be morally wise or in the agent's real interest or expressive of his true identity.

The division of the topic made here into rational thought and rational action is merely expository and should not be allowed to beg questions in moral psychology, the philosophy of mind, ethics, politics and the Theory of Action. JMH

Bibliography

Hume, D. 1738: *A treatise of human nature.* Bk II, pt iii. esp. sect. 3.

Luce, D.R. and Raiffa, H. 1957: *Games and decisions: introduction and critical survey.* New York: Wiley and Son.

Kekes, J. 1976: *A justification of rationality.* Albany: New York State University Press.

Nagel, T. 1970: *The possibility of altruism.* Oxford: Oxford University Press.

Olson, M. 1965: *The logic of collective action.* Cambridge, Mass.: Harvard University Press.

Weber, M. 1968: Basic sociological terms. In. *Economy and society,* ed. G. Roth and C. Wittich. New York: Bedminster Press.

Weintraub, E.R. 1975: *Conflict and cooperation in economics.* London: Macmillan.

Williams, B.A.O. 1981: Internal and external reasons. In: *Moral luck.* Cambridge and New York: Cambridge University Press.

Wilson, B., ed. 1971: *Rationality.* Oxford: Basil Blackwell; New York: Schocken Books.

rationalization A DEFENSE MECHANISM in which persons have no awareness of the real reason why they do or think something, while giving themselves a reason that is more socially acceptable. A forty-year-old man who still lives with his widowed mother may actually be gaining considerable satisfaction of the incestuous impulses of pregenital sexuality, although he remains unconsious of this by the rationalization that, in her dependent state, it is his responsibility as a son to remain near, take care of, and love her. As described by Freud and his followers, rationalization is regarded as a reasonably effective defense (being characteristic of developmental stages of mid-childhood). But when rationalization forms a major part of an adult's character structure the result is an over controlled appearance of rational understanding, with self-interest going unrecognized. SRM

reaching The development of skilled reaching undergoes a transition from visually elicited, swiping movements of the arm, (which can be observed in the neonate) to visually guided movements of the hand at around five to six weeks. Visually elicited can be distinguished from visually guided reaching because the former is pre-programmed, or ballistic and cannot be corrected in the course of the action, whereas the latter is under continuous voluntary control. It can be corrected should an error occur in the trajectory of the hand to the object. It was thought that the acquisition of voluntary control may depend on feedback from the sight of the hand but evidence of normal development of reaching in blind babies now suggests that this may not be necessary. GEB

Bibliography

Bower, T.G.R. 1982: *Development in infancy.* 2nd edn. San Francisco: Freeman.

reading: cognitive skills Reading may be defined as the extraction of information from text; the process by which we get meaning from a printed message. In recent years cognitive psychologists have devoted a considerable amount of effort to trying to understand the processes involved in this complex skill.

Research on reading is generally conducted within a human information processing framework. The processes by which people read are explicitly fragmented into separate stages and the processes operating at these stages are systematically investigated in experiments. There are several sub processes which are often distinguished in discussions of reading.

To begin with the reader must perceive the visual patterns of the words on a page. An average rate of reading for normal adults is somewhere in the region of 250–300 words per minute. A widely held belief, which accords with our subjective experience, is that as we read our eyes sweep smoothly along the printed line. This impression is, in fact, quite false, as first shown by Javal (1879) (see Huey 1908, p.16). Our eyes move along a line of print in a series of small rapid jerks, which are called saccades. These saccades are punctuated by short periods when the eyes are still, called fixations. On average fixations last around 1/5th to 1/3rd of a second, and the saccades happen much more quickly, taking around 1/50th of a second. The perception of the printed material occurs only during fixations; during the saccades no clear vision is possible. In most situations about 94 per cent of reading time is devoted to fixations.

During the reading of a line of print the eyes sometimes move backwards towards the beginning of the line to re-read some of the material. These backward movements are known as regressions, Regressions are related to the difficulty of the material being read. When the material is difficult more regressions occur. When one line of print has been read the eyes make a long return saccade to fixate the beginning of the next line.

The mechanisms responsible for the pattern of eye movements observed during reading are the subject of a good deal of research. So called structural factors, such as the fact that visual acuity is highest at the fovea of the eye and falls off rapidly towards the periphery, and limitations on the rate at which people can understand material presented to them, will certainly place constraints on the pattern of eye movements observed. Recently, some ingenious experiments in which changes are made to a text which subjects are reading while their eyes are moving, have revealed a great deal about how eye movements are controlled (Rayner 1975).

On the basis of the visual information picked up by the eye, the reader must decode the meanings of the individual words present. This process involves going from a visual representation of a word to some stored representation of that word's meaning. According to current theories of this process the meanings of words which the reader knows are stored in a kind of internal dictionary or "lexicon". The problem is to specify the processes by which the stored information in the lexicon is accessed.

A major issue here is the type of visual perceptual information which is used in order to recognize a word. A straightforward approach to this question is to assume that a word is recognized by recognizing each of its component letters. Given that the letters within each word are recognized at the same time as each other (in parallel) and that readers utilize knowledge about the predictability of letter sequences within words to reduce the perceptual word load, it is possible to produce models which can explain much of what we know about how people recognize words (e.g. McClelland and Rumelhart 1981).

It has also often been suggested, however, that the recognition of a word may not simply be the result of recognizing its component letters. Rather, in addition to information about letters in the word, the reader may extract information about what have been called supra-letter features. The most common idea is that the reader uses information about the overall shape of the word. Processing the shape of the whole word would be an even quicker process than identifying each letter separately.

It seems likely that both these sorts of processes complement each other in skilled word recognition. Logically it is obvious that information about the component letters in a word will be important for its identification, but the putative role of supra-letter features such as word-shape is a far less obvious matter. Some recent evidence, however, does indicate a possible role for word shape information as a cue for recognition. For example, if subjects are asked to read a passage and detect misspelt words, misspellings which alter the overall shape of a word are found to be easier to detect than those which preserve word shape.

It has often been remarked that reading, historically and developmentally, is secondary to speech. It seems quite plausible to suppose, therefore, that at some stage reading will engage processes previously developed for the understanding of speech. When recognizing individual words it is possible that we translate the letters in the printed word into a representation of the word's pronunciation. Understanding the word might then depend on the operation of the same mechanisms responsible for recognizing spoken words. The evidence for this view remains inconclusive at present. It appears that some impairments of reading observed in people with brain damage (dyslexias) can be explained in terms of such a process and its disorders (Coltheart, Patterson and Marshall 1980) but considerable controversy surrounds the possible importance of this process in normal skilled readers (e.g. Parkin 1982).

This discussion of how we recognize words has given no consideration, so far, to the context provided by other words. This is undoubtedly artificial since it is well established that such context can facilitate recognition. Having previously seen "bread" leads us to respond more quickly to a related word such as "butter" (Meyer and Schvaneveldt 1971). Although processes like these, and others such as constraints imposed by grammatical structure, are probably important, it seems reasonable to suppose, in the absence of evidence to the contrary, that their effect is one of general facilitation, not a radical departure from the processes outlined so far.

Having identified the meanings of the individual words in a sentence, the reader must undertake a syntactic analysis. That is, he must relate the meanings of the individual words in a sentence according to the rules of the grammar of his language. The meaning of a sentence will depend not only upon the individual words present, but also upon the way in which they are combined. It appears that in order to perform the syntactic analysis of written messages readers hold the string of words in the form of internal speech. Using speech may be a very good way of remembering the order of words, which is clearly crucial in understanding sentences, and when our ability to do this is impaired comprehension suffers (Kleiman 1975; Baddeley, Eldridge and Lewis 1981).

Finally, the meaning of individual sentences within a passage must be related to each other to reach an understanding of the passage as a whole. A good deal of the work of psychologists grappling with these complex questions has recently been reviewed by Sanford and Garrod (1981). It seems clear that in these later stages of the reading process, models of written sentence and text comprehension will merge with theories of language comprehension in general. The reader is in a sense, performing a kind of problem solving exercise. The ease of understanding a text will not only depend upon the characteristics of the passage such as its grammatical form but also upon the reader's past experience, his familiarity with the concepts involved and the previous knowledge he brings to bear.

This undeniable complexity of the reading process is nicely captured in the following quotation from Huey (1908, p.6) one of the fathers of modern research into reading. "And so to completely analyze what we do when we read would almost be the acme of a psychologist's achievements, for it would be to describe very many of the most intricate workings of the human mind, as well as to unravel the tangled story of the most remarkable specific performance that civilization has learned in all its history." It is clear that we are a long way from achieving a complete analysis of the reading process, but it seems certain that the challenge this poses will continue to engage the efforts of psychologists and those in related disciplines for many years to come.

See also: DYSLEXIC CHILDREN; READING; REMEDIAL READING; SPELLING. ChasH

Bibliography

Baddeley, A., Eldridge, M., and Lewis, V. 1981: The role of subvocalization in reading. *Quarterly journal of experimental psychology* 33A, 439–54.

Coltheart, M., Patterson, K., and Marshall, J. C., eds. 1980: *Deep dyslexia*. London and Boston: Routledge & Kegan Paul.

*Gibson, E.J., & Levin, H. 1975: *The psychology of reading*. Massachusetts: MIT Press.

Huey, E. B. 1908 (*1968*): *The psychology and pedagogy of reading*. Cambridge, Mass.: MIT Press.

Kleiman, G.M. 1975: Speech recoding in reading. *Journal of verbal learning and verbal behavior* 14, 323–339.

McClelland, J.L. & Rumelhart, D. 1981: An interactive activation model of context effects in letter perception: Part 1. An account of basic findings. *Psychological review* 88, 357–407.

Meyer, D.E., and Schvaneveldt 1971: Facilitation in recognizing pairs of words: Evidence for a dependence between retrieval operations. *Journal of experimental psychology* 90, 227–34.

Parkin, A.J. 1982: Phonological recoding in lexical decision: Effects of spelling-to-sound regularity depend on how regularity is defined. *Memory and cognition* 10, 45–53.

Rayner, K. 1975: The perceptual span and peripheral cues in reading. *Cognitive psychology* 7, 65–81.

Sanford, A.J., and Garrod, S.C. 1981: *Understanding written language: explorations in comprehension beyond the sentence.* New York and Chichester: John Wiley & Sons.

*Smith, F. 1982: *Understanding reading.* New York: CBS College Publishing.

reading: origins and learning The processes involved in responding to language in its written form: these processes include the perception and recognition of individual letters, the recognition of significant letter combinations, their association with relevant sounds and meanings and the interpretation of meaning relationships in written language. The term "reading" can be used to refer to any or all of the processes mentioned in the above definition.

In its origins, reading can be thought of as a natural development of earlier modes of communication. For example, in the gesture language of early man it was necessary to "read" meanings conveyed by hand signals. Symbolic meanings were also encapsulated in pictures drawn on sand, bark or stone.

The use of sequences of pictures, each representing a single idea, brought reading as we know it a stage nearer. These pictures became more and more conventional in form in the course of time. Writing systems based on such "ideographs" are still used in some countries today, notably in China, where successive attempts to introduce the western alphabet have had little success.

Learning to read in such a system is a laborious process as it is necessary to learn some thousands of symbols or characters. Hence, over a period of time, symbols came to be used in some writing systems to represent the sounds in words, rather than their meanings, so that eventually a fairly small number of symbols could be used in different sequences and combinations to represent all the words in the language.

Symbols were used to represent syllables in the Mycenaen script (the earliest written records of Greek) although this script also included some pictorial characters. The ancient Semitic writing systems used by the Phoenicians and the Hebrews were syllabaries, and these persist in modified form in modern Hebrew writing and the Arabic script used in the Middle East. The Japanese continue to use a mixture of pictorial characters (the kanji), derived from Chinese, and syllabic script (the kana).

In ancient Greece the Mycenaen syllabary gave way to a system in which each consonant and vowel, that is, each segmental phoneme, had its own symbol, and this writing system was the forerunner of our present European alphabets.

As the Greek alphabet was taken up first by the Romans, and subsequently in other countries, the relationship between each sound and its unique letter tended in some cases to become rather tenuous. In Italian, Spanish, and Finnish, there is still a fairly close relationship between spelling and pronunciation. In English, however, there are only twenty-six letters available to represent a spoken language which uses some forty-five different phonemes and the spelling conventions represent a diverse mixture of imports and adaptations. Added to this, pronunciations have changed over the centuries but spellings have tended to be conservative, becoming more so with the invention of print.

The difficulties this presents both for learning to read and learning to spell have led to various attempts to simplify English spelling conventions since the introduction of print. These are well documented by Pitman and St. John (1969). Such attempts have been rather more successful in other countries, notably Norway and Holland, where official spelling reforms have been made. As an alternative to spelling reform, some educators have introduced diacritics – marks added to letters to signal pronunciation, e.g., mat; *m*ate – as a means of simplifying the learning task. Other schemes use colored letters or colored backgrounds for letters to provide cues to pronunciation. Another approach is the selection of words with very simple spellings in designing materials for the early stages of learning to read, e.g., "A man is in a tan van", with more complex spellings being introduced in the later stages at a controlled rate. Another widespread alternative is the initial use of a very small vocabulary, irrespective of spelling, so that children do not have to learn to recognize too many words at once.

In the late 1950s there was an experiment in the use of an initial teaching alphabet of forty-four characters (i.t.a.) for use in the early stages of learning to read, with transfer to the traditional spelling system once the child could read with a reasonable degree of fluency. Many educators, however, have insisted that children can learn to cope quite adequately with our spelling system if we make full use of their own language patterns in early reading materials. This concept has informed the design of a number of modern reading schemes. The principle is more closely followed, however, when children read what they, and other children, have written with the help and guidance of the teacher – the "language-experience" approach, (Stauffer 1970).

With the coming of universal education, the complexities of written English brought the problems of teaching reading to the fore in all English-speaking countries. This led to a vast amount of reading research and, in the United States particularly, to the growth of many very powerful publishing firms producing material for all stages of reading development. The teacher is now faced with a bewildering choice of materials and suggested methods for teaching reading.

The "Great Debate" in this field (Challe 1967) centred for many years on the question of whether children learn best if they start with the parts of words and learn to build them up to make meaningful "wholes" or start with the "wholes" and analyse them as and when the need arises. One school of thought emphasizes the teaching of letters and sounds, and how they go together to make up words, e.g., "ku-a-tu" says "cat" – the "phonic" approach. The other school emphasizes the importance of words of greater interest to children, e.g., words such as "elephant" or "aeroplane", and insist that these can be recognized by their overall shape – much as we learn to recognize most other things in everyday life. This is referred to as the "whole word" approach (see READING: COGNITIVE SKILLS).

It was evident even at the beginning of this century (Huey 1908), that such arguments took too narrow a view of the nature of the reading process and the demands on the adult reader. Nevertheless, it is only since the early 1960s that research has led to the development of more sophisticated models of the reading process (reviewed in Singer and Ruddell 1976), a more realistic appraisal of the reading demands of the adult world (Murphy 1973) and research into the teaching implications (Guthrie 1981).

Information science has shown how much of the information in spoken and written communication is technically redundant (Smith 1978) and linguistic research has indicated many of the factors contributing to this redundancy (Shuy 1977). This evidence has provided substantial support for Huey's early insistence on the importance of context cues. Thus, presented with the following:

The glenks strove drortibly to lift it, encouraged
by the elders of the tribe

the reader pronounces the unfamiliar "words" without hesitation, because of his familiarity with a wide range of letter sound associations and sequences, and attributes a great deal of meaning to them as a result of responding to the various meaning relationships within the sentence. Had one of the "words" not been encountered previously in print, but was nevertheless in the reader's spoken vocabulary, then even if the spelling was also largely unfamiliar the fluent reader would have little difficulty in pronouncing it. By analogy, the reader has little difficulty with, e.g., "He climbed into the laught" (loft).

The vast majority of letter-sound associations to which a child learns to respond, and the "whole words" he learns to recognize, are not in fact taught, but are learned inductively in this way. Current emphases in the teaching of reading take advantage of the insights provided by this type of observation, insisting on a primary attack on context and meaning rather than attending first to letters and sounds.

Studies of reading comprehension have tended to focus on a logical analysis of what is involved in analyzing a text, the underlying intellectual abilities, and, more recently, the relationships between text content and the existing knowledge of the reader. The first type of study has led to the production of lists of skills, often hierarchically organized, and tests purporting to measure them. These might include tests of the ability to identify facts and main ideas, to make inferences, to note similarities and differences, to reorganize information, and so on. Studies of underlying intellectual abilities have drawn heavily on the factor analytic techniques used in studies of human intelligence – with broadly similar results. Studies which focus on conceptual structures and knowledge structures lie in the main stream of current research in cognitive psychology and artificial intelligence.

Text analysis now provides a substantial contribution to studies of reading at all levels. It covers such aspects as legibility and lay-out, grammatical structure, conceptual structure, and attitudinal features. Another important area, not yet as extensively researched, is what might be termed, "the ethnography of reading" – who reads what, when, why, and to what effect (Murphy 1973). This area is likely to become more important as society becomes more dependent on access to relevant information from an ever increasing data base. All of this has many implications for education.

The teaching of reading includes the provision of any practical experiences that the teacher may think necessary for the child's understanding and appreciation of what is read and opportunities for developing oral language relating to these experiences. Within this context the teacher seeks to develop a growing awareness of what print is, and does, as a prelude to teaching specific reading skills, that is to say, all that is involved in the effective achievement of the reading task – or in simply enjoying reading. This can include clarifying reading purposes, locating and selecting reading materials likely to be suitable for achieving these purposes, strategies for dealing with different kinds of text for different kinds of purpose and ways of evaluating both the particular reading outcome and the processes involved in achieving the outcome, with such evaluation leading to decisions about how best to bring about further self-improvement. Thus, the teaching of reading can now be viewed within the more general context of information science and the growing technology relating to information storage and retrieval, as well as being part of the teaching of English generally. Although the actual definition of reading may continue to be restricted as indicated above, the practicalities of teaching reading inevitably relate to this much broader setting. JEM

Bibliography

Challe, Jeanne 1967: *Learning to read: the great debate.* New York: McGraw Hill.

Guthrie, J.T., ed. 1981: *Comprehension and teaching: research reviews.* Newark, Delaware: International Reading Association.

Huey, E.B. 1908 *(1968): The psychology and pedagogy of reading.* Cambridge, Mass.: MIT Press.

Murphy, R.T. 1973: *Adult functional reading study: final report.* Princeton, N.J.: Educational Testing Service.

Pitman, Sir J. and St John, J. 1969: *Alphabets and reading; the initial teaching alphabet.* London: Pitman.

Shuy, R.W., ed. 1977: *Linguistic theory: what can it say about reading?* Newark, Delaware: International Reading Association.

Singer, H. and Ruddell, B., eds. 1976: *Theoretical models and processes of reading.* 2nd edn. Newark, Delaware: International Reading Association.

Smith, F. 1978: *Understanding reading: a psycholinguistic analysis of reading and learning to read.* 2nd edn. London and New York: Holt, Rinehart & Winston.

Stauffer, R.G. 1970: *The language-experience approach to the teaching of reading.* New York: Harper & Row.

reafference A theory that sets out to explain how animals distinguish between stimuli that result from their own behavior and those emanating from the environment. For example when we move our eyes in a voluntary manner the image moves on the retina, but we have no perception of movement, but when the image on the retina moves as a result of movement of an object in the environment, we do see movement. Reafference theory explains this difference by assuming that during voluntary movement the brain forms an image (known as the efference copy) of the expected consequences of the movement. If the actual (reafferent) consequences correspond to the expected consequences, no movement is perceived. Stimuli emanating from the environment (exafferent stimuli) do not correspond to any efference copy and so their perception is not cancelled.

The reafference principle was developed by von Holst and Mittelstaedt (1950) and has been applied to many aspects of animal behavior, including perception, orientation and motivation. DJM

Bibliography

von Holst, Erich and Mittelstaedt, Horst 1950: Das Reafferenzprinzip: Wechselwirkungen zwischen Zentralnervensystem und Peripherie. *Naturgewissenschaft* 37, 464–76.

reasoning Drawing conclusions from premises expressed in argument or represented in thought. In psychology Piaget's theory has been most influential in describing qualitative changes in reasoning that occur with development although it is not universally accepted. He describes the reasoning of the pre-operational child aged between approximately two and eight years as transductive. That is, it is neither inductive nor deductive but proceeds by haphazard connections between elements that may not actually be related. Only with the acquisition of concrete operations between eight and eleven years does the child become capable of systematic deductions with respect to objects in the real world. With adolescence and the acquisition of formal operations the child becomes able to engage in hypothetico-deductive reasoning with respect to abstract propositions. (See also LOGICAL THINKING.) GEB

Bibliography

Siegel, L.S. and Brainerd, C.J. 1978: *Alternatives to Piaget*. New York: Academic Press.

recency *See* primacy and recency effects

recognition In ethology this term is used most frequently to describe the perception of species specific characteristics. These are recognized both between and within species. Between species the commonest forms of recognition occur between predators and their prey. Tinbergen (1951) illustrates a model of a bird used in experiments with young ducks and geese (see fig.).

When moved overhead to the left, this model produced no reaction, but when moved to the right it elicited escape responses. From this and many other similar experiments, it was concluded that most, if not all prey species have innate mechanisms for the recognition of predators, linked neurally to appropriate escape mechanisms.

In the case of recognition within species, the commonest forms concern species specific smells, sounds, and coloration. For instance rats recognize fellow group members by smell, sheep mothers recognize their offspring by smell, and wood ants recognize colony members by smell. Birds recognize conspecifics by their calls, as do certain insects such as crickets, and many mammals. Color patterns are important in recognition among birds, where the young often have particular coloration, and among mammals where the same is often the case; they are quite unimportant among insects such as ants. Owing to the existence of innate recognition mechanisms, many species have developed mimicry to protect themselves or further their own ends: eyespot mimicry among moths and butterflies has evolved by increasing the rate of survival of those individuals who were mistaken by predators for big-eyed creatures unsuitable for food.

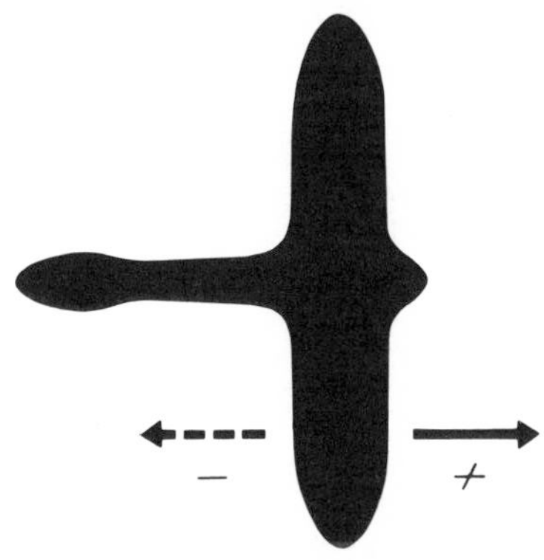

In man recognition relates largely to inter-individual recognition, a phenomenon that definitely occurs in primates and among other mammal species. Studies of infant behavior by ethologists have, however, shown that human babies have an innate smile reaction to the shape of the face, together with a number of other reactions in which innate recognition mechanisms appear to be involved. At first these are non-specific, but individual recognition (of the parent) occurs as development proceeds. VR

Bibliography

Tinbergen, Nikolaas 1951: *The study of instinct*. Oxford, Clarendon Press.

recovery of function after brain damage The return to normal levels of performance by the brain-damaged subject following any initially disruptive effects. There are several hypotheses which emphasize events and mechanisms occurring over time which may be relevant to the recovery from brain damage. Functional substitution refers to the condition whereby one neural subsystem can take over the role of another in the event of damage to the latter. This is particularly relevant to recovery from brain damage sustained in infancy where assignments of function to structure are considered to exhibit a degree of plasticity. This view has grown from observations on the restoration of speech in patients suffering early damage to the left hemisphere speech areas (see CRITICAL PERIODS AND THE NERVOUS SYSTEM). Diaschisis, functional shock suggests that some aspects of recovery can be attributed to the re-emergence of function of depressed neural areas outside the primary site of damage. Re-organizational compensation, whereby neural subsystems interact in a new way to solve an old problem, may also account for the recovery. Similarly with behavioral compensation the use of novel behavioral strategies compensates for lost skills and abilities. RCS/BER

redirected activity A technical term of classical ethology which is sometimes confused with DISPLACEMENT ACTIVITY and with VACUUM ACTIVITY. A redirected activity is an activity, recognizable from its form as being usually directed toward a particular stimulus, but on this occasion directed toward another stimulus. The classic human illustration is the aggressive man slamming his fist into the table instead of into an opponent. Aggressive gulls may sometimes violently peck the ground instead of the rival. In motivational theories of classical ethology the aggressive drive was said to be prevented by fear from achieving its normal outlet – pecking the rival – and instead found outlet in the redirected activity – pecking the ground. RD

reference The reference of a singular term (i.e. proper name, demonstrative, abstract noun etc.) is the entity singled out by the use of that term, usually in order that something may be said about it. Frege (1892) distinguished between the sense and reference of a singular term. Thus in the sentence "the highest mountain is Everest" the expressions "Everest" and "the highest mountain" have the same reference but different senses. JMS

Bibliography

Frege, G. 1892 (*1952*): On sense and reference. In *Translations from the philosophical writings of Gottlob Frege, ed.* Peter Geach and Max Black. Oxford: Oxford University Press.

reference group Reference group theory, according to Merton and Kitt (1950; 50–51), who gave the term prominence in sociology and social psychology, "aims to systematize the determinants and consequences of those processes of evaluation and self-appraisal in which the individual takes the values or standards of other individuals and groups as a frame of reference." The concept of reference group was first employed by Hyman (see Merton 1957) in studying the psychology of status and by Newcomb (see Merton 1957) in the well known Bennington College study. Stouffer (see Merton 1957) used the related notion of relative deprivation to explain the relatively high degree of dissatisfaction of soldiers in the US army, which appeared to depend on the perceived level of the groups to which they compared themselves rather than any absolute level. JMFJ

Bibliography

Merton, R.K. 1957: *Social theory and social structure*. New York: Free Press.

Merton, R.K. and Kitt, A.S. 1950: Contributions to the theory of reference group behavior. In *Continuities in social research: studies in the scope and method of the American soldier*, ed. Merton R. and Lazarsfeld, P.F. Glencoe, Illinois: Free Press, 40–105.

reflex An automatic reaction to external stimulation. In a simple reflex the central nervous system receives a message from a sense organ and converts this directly into instructions for muscular contraction or glandular secretion. For example, an increase in illumination on the retina results in a reflex contraction of the iris so that the pupil of the eye becomes smaller, cutting down the amount of light falling on the retina.

Reflexes are particularly important in the COORDINATION of limb muscles. Changes in the length of muscles, measured by muscle spindles, or in muscular tension, measured by tendon organs, are automatically signaled to the spinal cord where there are connexions with the nerves responsible for controlling muscular tension. The postural reflexes enable muscles to adjust to the mechanical forces that result from shifts in the centre of gravity during LOCOMOTION. Such reflexes often work in reciprocation, so that incompatible sets of muscles can operate in succession, thus achieving smooth coordination of limb movements.

Pavlov discovered that, although many reflexes are inborn, some can be modified or established by conditioning. The automatic depression of the brake pedal by a car driver in an emergency is an example of such a conditioned reflex. DJM

refractory period, psychological The period during which there can be no response following a previous response. The psychological refractory period is about 0.5 sec. and the most reasonable explanation is not that nothing is happening during the period but rather that the central mechanisms are occupied by feedback from the previous response.

The phenomenon was of considerable theoretical importance in post-war human experimental psychology because the effect is readily reproducible and measurable in well controlled laboratory tasks and because it formed the basis of speculation about the fundamental "single channel" nature of human performance. Since the output mechanism can be so narrowly and consistently blocked, it must follow that the human operator can only do one thing at one time. There are however complications due to grouping; the individual can perform a complex response to a complex stimulus as one integral "thing". This reduces the practical importance of the phenomenon because, with training and experience, operators in real systems can carry out very complex activities as integral units within which immediate feedback is not required. Nevertheless the effect exists and compared with the speed of engineered mechanisms 0.5 sec. is a long time. Care is needed to ensure that the refractory phase does not create a hiatus in the control of a system. (See SKILLS.) WTS

Bibliography

Welford, A.T. 1968: *Fundamentals of skill*. London: Methuen; New York: Barnes and Noble.

regression In common use, the appearance of behavior appropriate to an earlier life stage, triggered by stress. Examples include the adolescent who "regresses" to whining or tantrums when parental demands are imposed; the young child who "regresses" to bedwetting or thumbsucking with the birth of a younger sibling. The term derives from Freud's ontogenetic model of development, in which the individual passes through a series of developmental stages. Ideally, progress requires a balance of gratification and frustration; either excessive frustration or excessive gratification leads to fixation. In reality, normal development inevitably entails a less than perfect balance, and earlier stages leave residues in the form of minor fixations. Regression represents a return to an earlier stage, commonly a stage at which gratification was experienced. ND

rehabilitation In psychiatric practice is concerned with the prevention of social disablement following mental illness, especially SCHIZOPHRENIA. Social disablement results from:
(i) Continuing psychological dysfunctions (e.g. THOUGHT DISORDER, DELUSIONS and HALLUCINATIONS).
(ii) Social disadvantages (e.g. unemployment).
(iii) Personal reactions to the two previous factors (Wing and Morris 1981).

The impoverished environment and custodial attitudes of psychiatric hospitals in the past increased the patients' disabilities, leading to the apathetic and dependent state of institutionalism (Barton 1959; Wing and Brown 1970). The provision of useful occupation (e.g. in sheltered workshops) has often been the first step in reform, and it remains important.

The process of rehabilitation starts with the formulation of realistic individual goals. BEHAVIOR THERAPY can sometimes be useful, especially a form of OPERANT CONDITIONING – the "token economy". Staff reward desired behavior by the giving of tokens exchangeable for cigarettes, meals, etc. The social therapeutic approach places more emphasis on the patients' perception of his problems. GPP

Bibliography

Barton, R. 1959: *Institutional neurosis*. Bristol: John Wright & Sons.

*Clark, D.H. 1981: *Social therapy in psychiatry*. 2nd edn. Edinburgh: Churchill Livingstone.

Wing, J.K. and Brown, G.W. 1970: *Institutionalism and schizophrenia*. Cambridge: Cambridge University Press.

Wing, J.K. and Morris, B. 1981: *Handbook of psychiatric rehabilitation practice*. Oxford: Oxford University Press.

rehearsal In its most general form rehearsal can be considered a process that results in focusing the learner's attention on the information presented. Research such as that conducted by Peterson and Peterson (1959) shows that new information presented to an individual is lost rather rapidly unless the individual can review or rehearse that information. Rehearsal can take the form of silent review, vocalization of the material or even active review of such things as body movements. Rehearsal can also be considered a form of attention in that the learner is spending additional time "attending" to the information. Rehearsal and attention are also linked in experimental procedures in which distracting tasks, such as counting backwards by threes from a randomly selected number, are used to prevent the learner from rerehearsing. In training programs an important interval between information presentation and performance allows the trainee to rehearse the information. From a sequential standpoint we ask trainees to attend to information, to learn the information, to retain the learned information, and to use the information in performing the tasks. Since rehearsal promotes attention and increases learning, it plays a pivotal role in TRAINING. RRJ

Bibliography

Peterson, L.R. and Peterson, J.M. 1959: Short term retention of individual verbal items. *Journal of experimental psychology* 58, 193–8.

Reich, Wilhelm (1897–1957) Began his career as a psychiatrist after six years of graduate and post-graduate training at the University of Vienna. His professional life can be divided into four phases: his psychoanalytic work in Vienna; his sociological work in Berlin; his biological work in Scandinavia; and his work with orgone energy in America.

The Viennese period (1920–1930)
Reich trained in psychoanalysis under Freud, and became a prominent and controversial member of the group of young analysts who surrounded Freud at that time. Reich became involved very early on with the energy-source that sustained the emotional stasis of neurosis. By careful investigations into the qualities of the emotional and sexual lives of the patients who came to him for analysis, Reich concluded that every neurotic imbalance was sustained by a blockage to sexual satisfaction. Reich took up the libido theory of Freud, at a time when Freud himself was moving more into ego-psychology, and began to look on libido as a pleasurable excitation that could be either free-flowing or dammed-up in the body. By 1924 he had formulated the orgasm theory, which saw orgasm as the principle libidinal regulator, or energy valve, in the body. Reich was making fine discriminations in the qualities of satisfaction that people experienced in orgasm, dependent on the degree of commitment and surrender that they were able to bring to their love lives. In his book *The function of the orgasm* (1927) Reich described the basic dimensions of orgastic potency – the ability to surrender to the full depth of involuntary excitement without compensatory tensions or holding back; and of orgastic impotence, where sexual health was prevented by various forms of obstruction to the processes of charge and discharge of sexual energy in the body.

From 1924 to 1930 Reich was director of the Vienna Technical Seminar that was set up at his instigation as a forum where analysts could study the effects of their analytic techniques. Reich began to study how patients' resistance to getting well was organized and stratified into well-integrated defense systems by means of neurotic character formation. Reich focused the attention of the seminar on the analysis of these character defenses, rather than of the repressed contents, for he claimed that successful character-analysis would lead systematically to the resolution of the neurotic conflict, and to the freeing of the dammed-up excitation in a way that would lead to a more joyful existence and to a better regulated sexual life – a sound sexual economy.

Marxist period (1927–1937)
Reich's concern with character defenses led him into radical political involvement from 1927 onwards, as he came into conflict with the cultural forces which he felt instigated and perpetuated neurotic anxiety. Reich embraced the Marxist critique of capitalist society. In 1928 he became Vice-Director of the Psychoanalytic Polyclinic in Vienna where free psychoanalysis was made available to working-class people. In January 1929 Reich formed the Socialist Society for Sex Consultation and Sexological Research, which was a pioneering counseling center with six clinics under its control, aiming at the prevention of neurosis by the provision of good advice on birth, birth-control, advice to mothers on upbringing, and counseling on sexual problems. Reich was associated with the Communist Youth Movement for six years, and sought to gain mass acceptance for his sexological reforms in political circles. He moved to Berlin in 1930 where the political climate was more radical, and in Dusseldorf in 1931, under Reich's direction, the German Association for Proletarian Sexual Politics held its first congress. Some 40,000 members were affiliated, drawn by a revolutionary program of progressive sexual reforms. The "sex-pol" movement foundered owing to the opposition it received from the official Communist parties that looked on sexuality as a "bourgeois deviation", and owing to the deterioriating political situation in Germany that led Hitler to put a price on Reich's head for his outspoken critique of Nazism in *The mass psychology of fascism* (1933). Reich was forced to flee Germany after the Reichstag fire in February 1933.

Reich's attempt to combine Freud and Marx in a deeper synthesis of sex economy and political psychology was pursued for a few more years, but he came to feel betrayed by the left-wing movement, and began to focus his attention on the struggle between authoritarian and democratic forces in the everyday interactions of work and on a wide-ranging critique of social irrationalism as a form of psychosocial epidemic (of which fascism was a prime example), which he called "the emotional plague".

Scandinavian period (1933–1939)
In Copenhagen (1933), Malmo (1934) and Oslo (1935–9) Reich continued his work as a character analyst and political psychologist, but became increasingly involved in new research into the physiology of emotion and the biology of pulsation.

The study of character armor, and the analytic work to dissolve this, had led him to the theory that neurotic disequilibrium was physiologically anchored in the form of muscular tensions and disturbances in the rhythm of respiration. Reich's idea was that the muscular "armor" was organized in rings of tension distributed down the length of the body, and that the entire balance of functioning in the organism could be thrown out of phase by these blockages to the pleasurable flow of libidinal energy through the body. The involuntary (or vegetative) nervous system was implicated in all psychosomatic imbalance. So Reich came to see libidinal energy as equivalent to vegetative energy that could be in a state of over-charge or under-charge in any part of the body. He developed his therapeutic method in ways that worked directly with muscle tension and breathing patterns, and which facilitated much more expressive emotional release than ever occurred in conventional analytic work. Reich called this work at this time "vegetotherapy", and saw its aim as the loosening of the tension rings in the body so as to permit a free pulsation of energy and sensation throughout the tissues, leading into a rhythmic sequence that Reich at first called the "orgasm reflex" and later the "life reflex".

At the Psychological Institute at Oslo University Reich conducted a series of experiments designed to investigate the bioelectrical aspects of pleasure and anxiety. He was exploring some of the elementary processes of pulsation in both cellular and molecular structures. His work on "bions" (primitive vesicles produced in the process of disintegration), which is still little understood, led to scientific controversy in Oslo; Reich came under increasing pressure from conservative biologists, and at the outset of the second world war he moved to the USA to begin the final period of his career.

The American period (1939–1957)
In the USA Reich's work developed in unexpected directions. A biological radiation had been detected in the bion cultures, and was termed by Reich the "orgone" radiation. Attempts to isolate this radiation in a form of Faraday cage led to the construction of a cabinet which appeared to accumulate a form of atmospheric energy. Reich spent the next several years studying the relationships between organismic and atmospheric energy, and concluded that space was full of the energy he termed "orgone" and that it could be concentrated in his orgone accumulator (built out of alternating layers of organic and inorganic material), and used beneficially as a medical treatment for a variety of illnesses.

For over ten years a team of physicians working at Reich's Orgone Institute, first in New York, and later in Rangeley, Maine, explored the efficacy of this treatment (orgone therapy), particularly its effects on cancer, which he saw as a psychosomatic shrinking disease generated by emotional suppression and fueled by cellular oxygen suffocation. Treatment in the orgone accumulator, it was claimed, tended to reverse this shrinking sickness and to slow or stop the development of tumors, though Reich never claimed to have found a cure for cancer, as he saw its causes as deeply embedded in the patterns of character and culture.

Reich's orgone research ("orgonomy") was rejected by the scientific establishment of his day for its unorthodoxy. It functioned at the borderline of knowledge where biological and terrestial or cosmic energy fields interact. In the last twenty years some research has appeared to support Reich's findings, using a different terminology, and to support the basis of his work in atmospheric medicine, but this must remain the subject of considerable controversy.

The judgment of the scientific establishment remains "not proven".

In his last years Reich studied weather formation, and its effects on health, experimented with the interaction between nuclear energy and the atmosphere, and became involved in research into planetary pollution and desert formation. This led to him being prosecuted by the Food and Drug Administration for promoting an unrecognized form of medical treatment, and he was sentenced to two years' imprisonment for contempt of court in refusing to give up his medical and research work. He died, in Lewisburg Penitentiary, Pa., of a heart attack in March 1957. DJB

Bibliography

Reich, Wilhelm: *The Discovery of the orgone:* Vol. I: *The function of the orgasm;* Vol. II: *The cancer biopathy.* New York: Orgone Institute Press, 1942 and 1948; London: Panther Books (1966).

Boadella, David 1973: *Wilhelm Reich: the evolution of his work.* London: Vision Press; Chicago: Henry Regnery.

Mann, Edward 1973: *Orgone, Reich and eros.* New York: Simon and Schuster.

reinforcement The rewards and punishments obtained by animals during learning have the effect of strengthening and weakening the learning process. In the study of animal psychology the term reinforcement is used to describe these effects. A pigeon rewarded with food for pecking at a disk is likely to learn to repeat the response. The learning can be said to be positively reinforced. Conversely, a pigeon punished with a mild electric shock is likely to learn not to peck the disk in future and the pecking response is said to be negatively reinforced. For some psychologists the term reinforcement is synonymous with reward and punishment. Others reserve the term reinforcement for the processes of strengthening and weakening that occur as a result of the receipt of rewards and punishments. The situation is complicated by controversy over the question of whether reinforcement is necessary for learning. Some psychologists argue that all learning requires reinforcement since this is the process of strengthening and weakening stimulus-response connections. Others maintain that learning can occur in the absence of overt reward or punishment. IMPRINTING and song-learning in birds are cited as examples of this.

A major step in the development of ideas about reinforcement was Thorndike's Law of Effect.

> The Law of Effect is that: Of several responses made to the same situation, those which are accompanied or closely followed by satisfaction to the animal will, other things being equal, be more firmly connected with the situation, so that, when it recurs, they will be more likely to recur; those which are accompanied or closely followed by discomfort to the animal will, other things being equal, have their connections with that situation weakened, so that, when it recurs, they will be less likely to occur. The greater the satisfaction or discomfort, the greater the strengthening or weakening of the bond ... By a satisfying state of affairs is meant one which the animal does nothing to avoid, often doing such things as attain and preserve it. By a discomforting or annoying state of affairs is meant one which the animal commonly avoids and abandons (Thorndike 1911, pp.244–5).

An important feature of Thorndike's theory is that it emphasizes connections between situations and responses (S–R connections). For Thorndike, reinforcement strengthened (or weakened) a connection between a preceding response and the stimulus situation in which it had occurred. For Pavlov, on the other hand, reinforcement elicited a pattern of behavior which was associated with the prevailing environmental stimuli, and would subsequently be elicited by stimuli preceding the reinforcer (S–S connections). These two principles of reinforcement, Thorndike's law of effect and Pavlov's principle of stimulus substitution remain the most important analyses of reinforcement to this day. (Mackintosh 1974.)

Thorndike's law of effect was extended by Skinner, who saw reinforcement as any contingency which causes the behavior to increase (or decrease) in frequency. Thus if delivery of food is made contingent upon a particular response and the response is observed to increase in frequency, delivery of food counts as reinforcement. Skinner also assumed that the nature of the reinforcement, of the response, and of the prevailing stimulus are essentially arbitrary. For Skinner, the connection between any stimulus and any response can be strengthened by any means of reinforcement provided the response is within the animal's repertoire and the stimulus within its sensory range. There have been two major developments which throw serious doubt on Skinner's position. The first is the discovery that the relationship between response and reinforcement is not arbitrary, and the second is that even in classical Skinnerian situations the reinforcement does not necessarily have to be contingent upon the response.

Pigeon inspects the square illuminated key on which a stimulus is projected, pecks it and obtains a food reward delivered into a hopper located below the keys.

Modern evidence indicates that a given type of reinforcement is more effective in strengthening (or weakening) a response if the response is already motivationally related to the reinforcement. Rats readily learn to avoid food with a particular flavour if consumption of the food is followed by vomiting, but if it is followed by electric shock they usually fail to associate the flavour with the subsequent punishment. Similarly, if different response patterns of the golden hamster are systematically followed by the presentation of food, certain responses are reinforced but others are not. Moreover those responses which are susceptible to reinforcement by food are those, such as digging and rearing, which the animal would normally show when deprived of food. Responses which are resistant to food reinforcement, such as face-washing and scent-marking, are not normally associated with food or hunger (Shettleworth 1973).

The techniques of OPERANT CONDITIONING can be used to train animals to perform particular behavior patterns or tasks. Suppose we wish to train a pigeon to peck an illuminated key to obtain food reward. After one or two days of food deprivation in its home cage, the pigeon is placed in a small cage equipped with a mechanism for delivering grain. The key is situated on the wall of the cage at about head height as illustrated. Delivery of food is signalled by a small light which illuminates the grain. The pigeon soon learns to associate the switching on of the light with the delivery of food and approaches the food mechanism whenever the light comes on. The next stage is to make food delivery contingent upon some aspect of the animal's behavior. Pecking is frequently used and is encouraged by limiting rewards to movements which become progressively more similar to a peck at the illuminated disk. This procedure is called shaping. When the pigeon has learned to approach the key for reward it is rewarded only if it stands upright with its head near the key. At this stage the pigeon usually pecks the key spontaneously: slow learners can be encouraged to do this with a grain of wheat temporarily glued to the key. When the pigeon pecks the key it closes a sensitive switch in an electronic circuit which causes the food to be delivered automatically. From this point on the pigeon is rewarded only when it pecks the key and manual control for reward is no longer required.

This method is similar to that used in training circus animals and it is also used by psychologists in training animals to perform for television commercials, etc. One such team of psychologists reported on behavioral peculiarities which often occur during such training sessions. A pig was trained to pick up large wooden coins and place them in a money box. The pig was required to deposit a number of coins to obtain a reward. It learned the task easily, but with increasing practice it developed the habit of dropping the coins and rooting at them before placing them in a box. It seemed that the pig was treating the coins as though they were food items and responding to them in an instinctive manner. This type of instinctive drift has been described in a number of species (Breland and Breland 1961).

Laboratory investigations show that animals often respond to reinforcement in a motivationally biassed manner. In the case of the key-pecking pigeon mentioned above, film analysis shows that the pigeon pecks the key with a typical food-getting peck. Under a water reinforcement regime pigeons peck the key with a different style of peck reminiscent of that used when they take droplets of water. Once the pigeon has associated the key with food it behaves toward it as though it were food. Key pecking behavior can be obtained from a naive bird without any shaping at all. All that is necessary is that food should be presented soon after the pigeon's attention is drawn to the key. This can be done by switching on the key light and then presenting food. if this is repeated many times the pigeon comes to peck the key. This procedure, generally called autoshaping, can be explained in terms of Pavlovian conditioning in which the key becomes directly associated with food (S–S learning), without any recourse to the notion that the pecking response is necessary for learning to occur (S–R learning). If a pigeon is allowed to see its mate for a short period after illumination of a light, and this procedure is repeated many times, it starts to direct its courtship behavior toward the light, as though the light were a pigeon of the opposite sex. Demonstrations such as these have led some psychologists to doubt the role of reinforcement in establishing S–R connections. As every operant conditioning situation provides an opportunity for Pavlovian conditioning it may be that S–S connections are all that is necessary in an account of reinforcement (Moore 1973). Whatever the theoretical interpretation of autoshaping experiments it is clear that Skinner was incorrect in asserting that reinforcement is arbitrary in the sense of establishing connections between any type of stimulus and any element of the animal's behavior repertoire. DJM

Bibliography

Breland, K. and Breland, M. 1961: The misbehavior of organisms. *American psychologist* 16, 661–64.

Hinde, Robert A. and Stevenson-Hinde, Joan eds 1973: *Contraints on learning.* London and New York: Academic Press.

*Mackintosh, Nicholas J. 1974: *The psychology of animal learning.* London and New York: Academic Press.

Moore, B. R. 1973: The role of directed Pavlovian reactions in simple instrumental learning in the pigeon. In Hinde and Stevenson-Hinde.

Shettleworth, S.J. 1973: Food reinforcement and the organization of behavior in golden hamsters. In Hinde and Stevenson-Hinde, op. cit.

*Tapp, Jack T. ed 1969: *Reinforcement and behavior.* New York and London: Academic Press.

Thorndike, Edward Lee 1911: *Animal intelligence.* New York: Macmillan. Reprinted 1965. New York and London: Hafner.

relationships A new feature of research in social psychology in the 1980s, is concerned with the joint social action that makes a relationship work: thus research explores the taxonomizing, description and explanation of the different forms of naturally occurring personal relationships (e.g. friendship, mother–child relations, courtship, adolescent relations). Although the social psychological origin of the research on real life human interactions was a natural extension of work on ATTRACTION, the area came together as a result of seminal work by Hinde (1979) who brought together the common themes of work carried out in ethology, developmental psychology, clinical psychology and social psychology. Pointing to the inadequacy of the descriptive base upon which social psychologists had founded theories of attraction, while ethologists had descriptive categories but few theories, Hinde presented a system for understanding relationships. He noted that social psychologists had concentrated almost exclusively on liking and on attraction to strangers, without developing systematic approaches to the ways in which liking was expressed in relationships, nor the different styles of behavior that differentiated one recognizable form of relationship from another. Hinde (1981) proposed eight categorical dimensions by means of which relationships could be investigated and differentiated:

(a) the content of interactions (i.e. what the participants do together);

(b) the diversity of interactions (whether solely one type or several types of interaction are involved);

(c) the qualities of interactions (the ways in which participants do what they do);

(d) the relative frequency and patterning of interactions;

(e) the extent to which the relationship is based on reciprocity (where partners, for example, do the same thing alternately), or complementarity (where partners do different things which nonetheless complement one another to serve a common goal);

(f) the degree of intimacy;

(g) the interpersonal perceptions held by the partners about each other and their relationship;

(h) the degree of commitment of the partners to the relationship.

Although basing his work on a call for greater description of relationships in some of the dimensions outlined above, Hinde stresses that the ultimate goal is not the description of relationships but the understanding of their dynamics which springs from such a descriptive base.

Hinde's observations and productive suggestions take their starting point from several different schemes of thought. Indeed many researchers have addressed the topic of relationships from such disciplines as ethology, developmental psychology, sociology, social psychology, network analysis and studies of organizational management. A valuable part of Hinde's contribution has been the demonstration of some of the ways in which such an interdisciplinary science of human social relationships can be built, despite different interests and viewpoints on the total problem.

From the social psychological point of view, however, the greatest importance attaches to the development of a view of *growth* of liking and intimacy rather than merely of initial attraction, and in part the ripeness of the time for Hinde's suggestion is found in methodological advances in ETHOGENICS and in research on ACQUAINTANCE (Duck 1977). An excellent survey of methodological points in this area has been provided by McCarthy (1981) who identifies the strengths and weaknesses of much past and present research on relationship growth. Specific examples of innovative work are provided by Huston and others (1981) who have adopted a new approach to courtship development based on couples' retrospective accounts of the trajectory of their courtship from first meeting to marriage.

In part also the growth of the area has become possible because of theorists' growing recognition of the importance of COMMUNICATION in developing acquaintance, (Duck 1977) not only in terms of the ways in which partners self-disclose and indicate the geography of their selves to one another (Duck 1976) but also because changes in the form of communication actually serve to define and develop the relationship (Morton and Douglas 1981). These last authors have thus studied and been able to tie together several different lines of research on information processing, exchange and communication.

An extremely wide range of issues is studied under the egis of the term relationships, as might be expected, given the interdisciplinary origins of its study. While some workers (Andreyeva and Gozman 1981; La Gaipa 1981) are concerned to study and explain the effects of the social context in which relationships occur, others are concerned with their conduct and the consequences of the relative patterns of equity in partners' behavior (Hatfield and Traupmann 1981), and other workers have studied different types of relationships, for instance, sexual relationships (Przybyla and Byrne 1981), relationships in marriage and the family (Burgess 1981) and relationships at work (Mangham 1981).

Several other major areas of the work concern the development of relationships with age, disordered personal relationships and the dissolving of relationships. In the first category, work focuses mostly on mother–infant relationships and their role in the subsequent development of social relationships. SOCIAL SKILLS and SOCIAL EXCHANGE notions (Pawlby 1981). The folly of ignoring the role of parent–child interactions in the middle years of childhood and the friendships of children with their peers has been noted by Shields (1981) and La Gaipa (1981). Despite its social importance, work on the relationships of adults, especially elderly adults, has been very little studied and the role of relationships in preventing illness or premature death in the old is only just being researched (Chown 1981).

A further field that is full of social importance concerns the disorders that occur to relationships and the relationships of disordered people. Most research has so far been devoted to the study of marital disruption and divorce (Burgess 1981), but the larger problems of LONELINESS and social isolation have recently been addressed by Perlman and Peplau (1981) who suggest a new theory of loneliness. Their suggestion is that loneliness cannot sensibly be seen as mere absence of friends but as a discrepancy between desired and achieved levels of social interaction. By relating these ideas to ATTRIBUTION, Perlman and Peplau (1981) are able to make a number of testable hypotheses about the effects and antecedents of loneliness, social skill and social exchange.

Dissolution of relationships is a topic which awaits major attention from researchers beyond those working in marital dissolution (Burgess and Wiggins 1981). The major theoretical issue is whether breakdown of relationships can be seen as the mere reverse of the growth of liking and the development of relationships (Duck 1981) and, given social psychologists' poor conceptualization of the growth of commitment, it seems unlikely that an answer will be found soon. One method that could clearly be used with advantage to understand breakdown or dissolution of relationships would be the account methodology used in ethogenics, and this would provide a natural counterweight to the use of such methods in tracing the growth of courtship (Huston and others 1981).

For researchers to begin to make useful inroads into the complexities of relationships, the beginnings and development of relationships need greater study; whereas for those wishing to make inroads into social problems, it is the disorder and dissolution of relationships that represent the more urgent problems. SWD

Bibliography

Duck, S.W. 1976: Interpersonal communication in developing acquaintance. In *Explorations in interpersonal communication*, ed. G.R. Miller. Beverly Hills, California: Sage Annual Reviews.

——— 1977: *The study of acquaintance*. Farnborough and London: Saxon House, Teakfields and Gower Press.

——— and Gilmour, R. 1981: *Personal relationships: 1 Studying personal relationships, and 2 Developing personal relationships*. London and New York: Academic Press.

Gilmour, R. and Duck, S.W. eds 1981: *Personal relationships: 3 Personal relationships in disorder*. London and New York: Academic Press.

Hinde, R.A. 1981: *Towards understanding relationships*. London and New York: Academic Press.

All the other references cited in this article may be found either in Duck and Gilmour 1981, or in Gilmour and Duck 1981.

relationships and social structure, in ethology Two abstract hierarchical levels invoked in the description of societies and derived from behavioral interactions between individuals (Hinde 1979). According to Hinde a relationship results from sequences of interactions between two individuals. The nature of any interaction will be influenced by other interactions in that relationship and reflect properties inherent in both participants. The kind of patterning of all relationships realized by individuals interacting over a period of time will produce the structure of the group.

On describing relationships and structures

Traditionally, the descriptive units of social behavior exhibited by a species are enumerated and empirically classified into different categories, for example, agonistic or sociopositive behavior, on the basis of their temporal and/or functional associations. This allows us to describe relationships and social structures in terms of absolute and relative frequencies of behavioral units or categories which occur among individuals. In addition, proximity data portray relationships and subgroups by representing the spatial arrangement of individuals. Demographic parameters such as group size and sex/age composition are also used in characterizing social organizations. The more comprehensive list of social qualities compiled by Wilson (1975) draws attention to more abstract properties of social structures, such as the network of communication, the permeability or openness of a group, the degree of behavioral specialization among the group members and the kinds of subgroups. McBride's questionnaire (1976) lists an even larger number of parameters useful in the characterization of animal social groups. While illustrating the diversity of social phenomena in animals, such descriptions do not reflect the fact that similar surface structures may result from entirely different processes involved in their formation.

Most of the traditionally-used measures convey a static picture of what in reality constitutes a continuously changing system where even apparently stable properties will rely on processes conserving them. Individuals enter and leave relationships and groups while kinds of relationships and structures are preserved over generations. The framework developed by Hinde (1975) for studying relationships and structures includes the notion of historically developed entities, the current state of which cannot be understood without reference to the past.

Hinde's framework involves three levels: interaction, relationships and structure. Interactions consist of behavioral exchanges between individuals: one participant directs a particular behavior toward another that may or may not show an immediate response. What an individual does to a partner will partly depend on the identity of this partner. Interactions, therefore, have properties not present in the behavior of either participant alone. Relationships are operationally defined in terms of the content, quality and temporal patterning of their constituent interactions. Labels like "mother–child", "dominant–subordinate" or "male–female" refer to the types or content of the interactions realized in the respective relationship. Relationships not only vary in what the participants do together but also in how they are doing it, for example, in the intensity of an interaction or in its coordination between the partners. Relationships develop over time. The attributes of the partners that primarily govern the interaction pattern are likely to change. At early stages, external qualities such as sex and size will draw individuals together, while more hidden qualities, such as skills and idiosyncrasies may shape the interactions of mature relationships. A social structure is seen by Hinde as the content, quality and patterning of relationships. Mason, in contrast to Hinde, considers the operation of factors external to the social group (Mason 1978). He distinguishes three levels: an individual's behavioral repertoire and social propensities define its potential contribution to the structure of the group. The expression of this potential will be modified by the social setting of the group and the expression of their social attributes. Finally, the environment of the whole social system includes non-social factors that affect individual behavior and group structure.

An animal relationship often begins with aggressive interactions; in time it may proceed to ever more intimate interactions such as mutual grooming. It may eventually develop into a BOND. The stage reached is in part predictable by the sex, age and DOMINANCE status of the two individuals. Experimental addition of a third individual may cause the original relationship to regress permanently to an earlier stage, illustrating the mutual influence among relationships within a social structure (Kummer 1975). Some animal social structures are stratified. In the four-level society of hamadryas baboons (Abegglen in press) members of the same lower-level unit (e.g. families) interact more frequently and at more intimate stages than individuals sharing only the highest unit (the troop).

Causal aspects of relationships: learning paradigms

Hinde (1979) reviews how three classical learning

paradigms relate to inter-individual relationships: exposure learning, classical conditioning and operant conditioning. For both humans and animals, it has been shown that the mere repeated perception of another individual may induce a change in behavior towards that individual. Mutual attraction is the likely outcome of increased familiarity even in the absence of positive reinforcement and may thereby create possibilities for interactions (see KINSHIP). The view that relationships are the outcome of mutual response conditioning is held in particular by Gewirtz (1972) for human social bonds. In Bowlby's (1972) view, the attachment between mother and infant results, in part, from the operation of unconditioned stimuli (releasers) rather than the result of a learning process. A review of critique of social learning theories applied to BONDS is given by Rajecki et al. (1978).

Individualized relationships are not a prerequisite of complex social structures, as the example of the social insects shows. Individual behavior may be directly affected by the composition of the group. For example, the sex reversal in some fish species is contingent upon the sex composition of the social group. The tasks performed by an individual social insect are influenced by other colony members and the caste composition of the colony. In primates, interindividual preferences may co-vary with the sex composition of the group and the effect of relationships on one another may range from mediation to suppression: a female's ability to interact with an infant may depend on the nature of her relationship with its mother whereas a male hamadryas baboon having observed that two conspecifics form a pair is inhibited from interacting with either of them (Kummer et al. 1974).

Functional aspects of relationships

Kummer (1978), in his heuristic scheme, discusses the value of primate social relationships for the reproductive survival of the individual member. A relationship is seen as a potential for useful interactions in the future, built by interactions in the past. An individual monitors the general qualities, the behavioral tendencies and the availability of a companion, and presumably improves them by the longterm effects of his own contributions to the interactions. It also defends the availability of the companion, since one of the problems faced by a personal relationship is that it must resist the impersonal sign stimuli displayed by other group members. Ethological research on social monitoring and longterm effects of particular interactions is still in its initial phase.

Since social animals are both cooperators and competitors, conflicts of interest are frequent, and the asymmetry of attachment and interests in the dyad may change over time. Yet completely asymmetric exploitative relationships are rare and transient, presumably because either member disposes of evolved strategies that aim at an optimal cost–benefit ratio in terms of its individual fitness (see SOCIOBIOLOGY). Relationships of long standing may be more efficient than newly-formed ones in problem-solving and in terms of the number of young reared by a pair.

Group structure is ultimately determined by individual behavior and component relationships and will not, in animals, take on an existence and value of its own (Hinde 1974). The social structure is the statistical summation of individual behavioral strategies. Social behavior that benefits the whole group can mostly be explained as behavior evolved for the benefit of the actor. HK

Bibliography

Bowlby, J. 1972: *Attachment and loss*, vol. 1, *Attachment*. New York: Basic Books; London: Hogarth Press; Institute of Psycho-Analysis.

Gewirtz, J.L. 1972: Attachment and dependence: Some strategies and tactics in the selection and use of indices for those concepts. In *Communication and affect*, ed. L.K. Allowey and P. Pliner. London and New York: Academic Press.

Hinde, R.A. 1974: *Biological bases of human social behavior*. New York and London: McGraw-Hill.

——— 1975: Interactions, relationships and social structure in nonhuman primates. In Shiro Kondo et al. eds. 1975. *Proceedings from the symposia of the fifth congress of the International Primatological Society*. Tokyo: Japan Science Press.

*——— 1979: Towards understanding relationships. *European monographs in social psychology* 18. London and New York: Academic Press.

Kummer, H. 1975: Rules of dyad and group formation among captive gelada baboons (Theropithecus gelada). In Shiro Kondo et al., eds. *Proceedings from the symposia of the fifth congress of the International Primatological Society*. Tokyo: Japan Science Press.

——— 1978: On the value of social relationships to nonhuman primates: a heuristic scheme. *Social science information* 17, 687–705.

———, Götz, W. and Angst, W. 1974: Triadic differentiation: an inhibitory process protecting pairbonds in baboons. *Behavior* 49, 62–87.

Mason, W. 1978: Ontogeny of social systems. In D.J. Chivers and J. Herbert, eds., *Recent advances in primatology*, vol. 1. New York: Academic Press.

*McBride, G. 1976: The study of social organization. *Behaviour* 59, 96–115.

Rajecki, D.W., Lamb, M.E. and Obmascher, P. 1978: Toward a general theory of infantile attachment: a comparative review of aspects of the social bond. *Behavioral and brain sciences* 1 (3), 417–964.

relativism *See* cultural relativism

relearning Occurs when a training or acquisition experience is repeated some time after original learning. If the training is carried out in the same way on both occasions, the degree to which relearning is accomplished more rapidly than the original (savings) can be used as a measure of retention of the original. Conversely, in so far as relearning is necessary, forgetting of original learning can be inferred. Sometimes, even when there is no sign that the ability to perform a task has been retained, the more sensitive relearning test may reveal some memory. Relearning rates are also used to assess the effects of an intervening treatment, e.g. a brain lesion, upon retention of a task. Caution is required, as relearning measures may be contaminated by maturational, motivational or other effects of time lapse unrelated to memory. See also RETENTION AND FORGETTING. EAG

releasers *See* innate releasing mechanism and releasers

releasers: human development Are social stimuli which are especially effective in producing a response by another individual. The term also implies that both the stimulus features and the responsiveness have become mutually adapted during the course of their evolution. The term was originally used in early ethological writings. (See INNATE RELEASING MECHANISM AND RELEASERS.) In developmental psychology the concept is most readily applied to the infant's attachment responses to its caregiver, such as smiling and crying, which are regarded as resulting from selective pressures favoring proximity-seeking signals. JA

Bibliography

R.A. Hinde 1982: *Ethology*. New York and Oxford: Oxford University Press.

reliability *See* tests, reliability

religion: psychology of The psychological study of religion can: (1) provide descriptive accounts of devotional, mystical, conversion or other experiences reported as "religious"; (2) discover the degree of correlation, if any, between various elements of religiosity, such as religious practices, beliefs, moral preferences and intense experiences; (3) identify background or personality factors that may shape these religious elements; (4) trace out the consequences and functions, for an individual or a group, of any of the religious elements; (5) contribute to or borrow from philosophical or theological reflections on human nature. Psychologists pursue these studies with quantified empirical data, case studies, field studies, culling of historical and biographical materials and with armchair reflections.

In principle psychologists aspire to generalizations that would apply universally to human experience of religion. In practice, studies are usually limited to available groups (e.g. clinic patients, university students, church members) in mainstream western religions.

It is convenient to distinguish broadly between three approaches. The first tends to define religion in terms of *behavior* that is *distinct*, sometimes dramatically so, from other behavior. Church affiliation is sharply distinguished from other institutional participation, with assumed distinct psychological meaning and function – a belief in God which is distinguishable from other beliefs and attitudes, and prayers and mysticism which are unlike other intense introspective experiences, etc. The second approach regards such *behavior* as *illustrative* of whatever psychological principles apply to any membership, belief, etc. Religion might be cited as an example in any chapter in a psychology textbook, but would not warrant a chapter of its own. This approach tends not to produce any distinctive "psychology of religion", and will therefore drop out of further discussion in this article. In the third approach, religion is defined not in terms of behavior, but as a more subjective and fundamental dimension or orientation of personality and human existence, as the way a person or group deals with such issues as trust and mistrust, commitment, evil, ideals and their frustration, with personal wholeness, fragmentation, and shortcomings, and with death.

The first and third of these approaches, to be termed here simply "objective" and "subjective", will provide the framework for the rest of this article. The distinction corresponds to a fundamental distinction made by religious persons, roughly between "conservatives" and "liberals": whether religious importance is attached primarily to objective creeds, forms and institutions (which liberals term "literalism") or to existential pilgrimage wherever, as they see it, God is at work (which conservatives term "secularism"). The distinction is recognized by what is undoubtedly the most cited terminology in the field, Allport's categories of "extrinsic" and "intrinsic" religion, and accounts for the persistent popularity of these terms, despite their patent conceptual and empirical shortcomings (see Batson and Ventis 1982, Dittes 1969).

The "objective" approach favors substantive definitions of religion as "belief in God", participation in public worship or private devotions, etc. It often assumes the uni-dimensional nature of religion, i.e., intercorrelation and interchangeability among these various indices, and often assumes one such index sufficient to assess the degree of a person's religiousness. Among researchers (e.g. Argyle and Beit-Hallahmi 1975) using quantifiable empirical data with relatively large samples, the typical study correlates religion with social or personality variables, similarly defined "objectively". Typical and repeated findings are that religion is "greater" among women, young adolescents and those past middle age, among the less educated and less intelligent (when class differences are held constant), among the middle class, and among those who have more conservative attitudes on social questions, more racial prejudice and more authoritarianism. The findings suggest to some that religion encourages socially dysfunctional behavior and attitudes, to others that religion attracts those who feel most marginal, i.e. those who "need" it. Some studies attempt to connect religion with identifiable effects, such as desirable behavior or improved mental health.

The question of uni-dimensionality, i.e. the intercorrelation among the serveral indices, has been answered empirically, largely through factor analyses. Religion appears as a single factor when respondents and questionnaire items are religiously unsophisticated; "religion" then appears as an undifferentiated cluster, with the church building the most visible marker. But when respondents are limited to more religiously experienced persons and when questionnaire items permit differentiation, multiple factors appear and different elements of religion are seen to play different roles.

The "subjective" approach favors functional definitions. Religion is whatever yields trust, reduces guilt, integrates personality, increases social responsibility or helps people to cope with death, etc. As is apparent, some such functions are more conventionally identifiable to psychologists than others. This approach does not assume uni-dimensionality of religion but examines behavior, whether conventionally regarded as "religious" or other kinds. This approach is not limited to clinical or field studies (e.g. Erikson 1958) but is also used by empiricists with quantifiable data (e.g. Batson and Ventis 1982, Yinger 1970). It is also more closely connected to the thought of theologians (e.g. Tillich 1953).

Risks or accusations of "reductionism" are especially rife in the psychology of religion, because it is thought that the reality of the religious belief or practice, as understood by the practitioner, is challenged or denied by the demonstration of psychological motives or functions, especially motives not consciously recognized by the practitioner. Logically, there should be no problem. The truth or correctness of religious belief and practice is determined by philosophical or theological inquiry and by criteria entirely independent of psychological analysis. True or false belief can be equally motivated; or, to put it theologically, God may or may not use psychological processes. The "genetic fallacy" has been soundly disclaimed by every major writer in the psychology of religion, including Freud (1927) who carefully defined "illusion" as he applied it to both religion and to science, to refer to certain wish-fulfilling functions, not to objective validity. But logic aside, believers are often threatened by analysis, feeling, in effect, "I believe *either* because it is true, *or* because I need to", and analysis is sometimes used as a hostile attack on religion. Such behavior probably deserves its own psychological study.

Historically, the psychology of religion has been prominent from the beginning of modern psychology. Empirical techniques (especially sophisticated scaling and factor analytic methods) and personality theories have not only been applied readily and promptly to religion but have been developed in part in order to deal with the elusive and dramatic phenomena of religion. The earliest book to bear the title "Psychology of Religion" appeared in 1899 (Starbuck). During the early decades of this century church institutions and theological schools encouraged psychology of religion as an aid to the task of religious formation and religious education, but in the middle of the century this gave way to a preoccupation with the adaptation of therapeutic and counseling skills for clergy. More recently, especially in the US, the rapid growth of non-doctrinal, objective and analytic "religious studies" particularly in secular universities, has again encouraged the discipline. The principal organization for psychologists and sociologists of religion is the Society for the Scientific Study of Religion which has published a quarterly journal since 1960. JED

Bibliography

Argyle, Michael and Beit-Hallahmi, Benjamin 1975: *The social psychology of religion.* Boston: Routledge & Kegan Paul.

*Batson, C. Daniel and Ventis, W. Larry 1982: *The religious experience: a social-psychological perspective.* New York and Oxford: Oxford University Press.

*Dittes, James E. 1969: Psychology of religion. In *Handbook of social psychology* 2nd edn. Ed. G. Lindzey and E. Aronson. Boston: Addison-Wesley.

Erikson, Erik H. 1958: *Young man Luther.* New York: Norton.

Freud, Sigmund 1912 *(1953)*: *Totem and taboo. Standard Edition of the complete psychological works of Sigmund Freud,* vol. 13. London: Hogarth Press; New York: Norton.

——— 1927 *(1961)*: *The future of an illusion. Standard Edition* vol. 21.

James, William 1902: *The varieties of religious experience.* New York and London: Longman.

Starbuck, Edwin Diller 1899: *The psychology of religion: An empirical study of the growth of religious consciousness.* New York: Scribner.

Tillich, Paul 1953: *The courage to be.* New Haven, Connecticut: Yale University Press.

Yinger, J. Milton 1970: *The scientific study of religion.* New York and London: Macmillan.

REM sleep *See* sleep: human paradoxical

remedial mathematics Although arithmetic disability is seldom encountered apart from reading disability, the literature in remedial education is predominantly concerned with reading. Reference to remedial mathematics is minimal.

There is widespread uncertainty among teachers about both content and methods of teaching mathematics to slow learners, and there has been a lack of consensus about the proper emphasis in mathematics instruction: computational and conceptual approaches, maintain an uneasy balance.

Although efforts to reform the mathematics curriculum aim at introducing basic concepts of the discipline as early as possible, computational skills form a major part of children's experience in primary school mathematics. Speed and accuracy for computation appear to improve with practice, hence drill has been used as a justifiable means of building arithmetic skills. But various arguments, particularly the objection that drill cannot develop mathematical thinking, have been put forward against using it as the main method of instruction. Proponents of instruction in the concepts which underlie computations have claimed that understanding these concepts enhances children's ability to apply their knowledge in novel situations.

Computer assisted instruction programs use the computer as a basis for providing individual practice on computational skills and giving continuing feedback. The importance of feedback is not as reinforcement, but as a way of providing information to enable the pupil to correct errors. Scope for adjustments in problem presentation and difficulty level mean that children do not have to work on problems that are too easy or too difficult, and represents a deliberate attempt to enhance motivation.

Those who make much of the distinction between simple computational skills and an awareness of mathematical concepts often believe that efforts should be made to teach the fundamental structures of mathematics in ways that take into account children's intellectual capabilities. The use of structure oriented materials such as Diene's blocks and Cuisenaire rods is intended to help children to discover and refine concepts as they engage in manipulations of the materials which embody the mathematical properties. The structure oriented methods and materials raise questions about the nature of mathematical understanding and about the sorts of structures they actually teach.

Little is known about children's mathematical learning, and teaching methods have not been adequately evaluated. Most children routinely carry out computations and demonstrate a basic understanding of number concepts and quantity. Being mathematically competent involves more than knowing a range of concepts and mastering computation. The importance of problem solving with the use of particular heuristic strategies is widely recognized in mathematics teaching. Suggestions for remedial work in this area stem more from a commonsense approach to mathematics instruction than from any clear understanding of mathematics problem solving processes. Setting up problems of the real world in which actual mathematical problems are encountered, simplifying the text in which the problem is formulated and establishing a strategy for what is known and what must be found out are the guidelines given to teachers in their efforts at remedial work. SDS

Bibliography

Bell, A.W. et al. 1980: *A review of research in mathematical education. Section A: research on learning and teaching.* University of Nottingham: Technical Report Shell Centre for Mathematical Education.

Ginsburg, H. 1977: *Children's arithmetic.* New York: Van Nostrand.

Resnick, L.B. and Ford, W.W. 1981: *The psychology of mathematics instruction.* Hillsdale, N.J.: Lawrence Erlbaum.

remedial reading Teaching methods for reading acquisition may broadly be classified under one of two groups, one with its emphasis on decoding written language, the other on extracting meaning from text. The different methods are generally not dramatically opposed to one another, except that each tends to focus on a particular aspect of the total reading process. Individual schools in the UK have considerable freedom in the choice of method, and materials used for the teaching of reading. Although the popularity of particular methods varies from time to time, different methods and ideas concerning the teaching of reading may co-exist depending on their appropriateness for use with children who vary in reading ability.

Over the past decade there has been a sudden increase in the publication of materials which represent attempts to fulfill the needs expressed by teachers who are helping pupils who have difficulty learning to read in the regular classroom. Apart from the accent on drill and continual revision the bulk of this material is not distinguishable from materials available for use with beginning readers. With a few exceptions the majority of remedial methods do not provide a theoretical rationale for their effectiveness in meeting specific needs. Some have grown out of experience and have been developed on a pragmatic basis. This is hardly surprising in view of the fact that the preponderance of research on reading difficulty is devoted to diagnosis. The long term effect of specific remedial methods receives hardly any attention.

Several remedial methods are designed for use with children having moderate to severe reading problems. Remedial techniques focusing on decoding skills include the diacritical marking system, i.e. color coding of either letters or words, and other techniques which aim to establish sound-symbol associations leading on to the development of word recognition. Multi-sensory methods are based on the premise that some children learn best when content is presented in several modalities. Kinesthetic and tactile stimulation are frequently used along with the visual and auditory modalities. Some research supports the use of the multi-sensory method with retarded readers. Instructions for the use of these methods despite their emphasis on decoding skills reflect the important principle that the learning activities should always be meaningful and interesting.

The Method of Repeated or Simultaneous reading also called the Impress Method in the United States literature is a technique with theoretical and empirical support currently in use in remedial work. The focus is on deriving meaning from what is heard and what is read. Claims for its effectiveness are not only for remedial purposes but for developing fluent reading in beginners. The method relies crucially on the pupil reading while simultaneously hearing the text read aloud by a competent reader. Both accuracy and speed are said to improve. This suggests that although not complete in itself the method improves reading fluency and has a positive effect on pupils' confidence in their ability to read. The rationale for the success of this method is based on its potential to facilitate comprehension by the chunking of information or reducing the attentional burden of slow decoding. The technique possibly assists the child in the process of exploiting its ability to cope with spoken language and so derive meaning from written language.

On a higher level several techniques are encouraged for use in remedial work to develop reading comprehension and effective study skills. These include an introduction to the passage to serve as an advance organizer, pictures appropriate to the text, activities which involve sequencing and organizing scrambled text, setting a purpose for reading a passage, prediction of events when reading fictional material, and producing such things as graphs, tables and diagrams from text. Most of these methods are inspired by the recent theoretical analysis produced by Frank Smith (1971) and Kenneth Goodman (1982) which stresses the importance of childrens' desire to extract meaning from passages which they read and of the rather complex and sophisticated hypotheses which they use to do this. SDS

Bibliography

Goodman, K.S. 1982: *Language and literacy.* Vols. I & II. London: Routledge and Kegan Paul.

Naidoo, S. 1981: Teaching methods and their rationale. In *Dyslexia research and its applications to education,* eds G. Th. Pavlidis and T.R. Miles. John Wiley & Sons Ltd.

Samuels, S.J. 1978: What research has to say about reading inclination. Newark, Delaware: International Reading Association.

Smith, F. 1971: *Understanding reading: a psycholinguistic analysis.* New York: Holt Rinehart and Winston.

Strang, R. 1975: *Reading diagnosis and remediation.* Newark, Delaware: International Reading Association.

Renaissance psychology "The Renaissance" is considered here as bounded roughly by the dates 1300 and 1600. From about 1400 onwards western Europe underwent a long period of expansion in population, productivity and trade, accompanied by intense political conflict and religious controversy. Under these conditions many psychological issues came to the fore, related to government, diplomacy, civic life, commerce, marriage and education. More generally, there was a heightened concern to understand the resources of human nature, and the forces controlling each person's destiny. With the growth of merchant capitalism a new idea began to be accepted: that the pursuit of self-interest can be a valid principle in explaining human actions. Renaissance thought is extremely diverse; but its pyschology, whether pious (Dante, More, Luther) or wordly (Machiavelli, Montaigne), whether Aristotelian (Pomponazzi) or Platonist (Ficino), may be characterized broadly as an attempt to explore the possibilities envisaged for human beings under the economic and social conditions following the breakdown of medieval feudalism. And here the primary cultural resources were those of the Middle Ages, together with ideas from ancient texts that had recently become available via Byzantium and the Arab world. Most Renaissance writers treat the latter with great reverence, although there are signs of a more critical and historicizing approach towards the close of the period. It was during the sixteenth century that the term *psychology* came into use, meaning the discipline of knowledge about the soul. However, whereas the Renaissance produced certain avowedly "value-free" sciences such as anatomy and mechanics, it did not do so in the field of human behavior and mental function.

Possibly the most potent new insights into human nature arise from the teaching of Marsilio Ficino (1433–99) and Pico della Mirandola (1463–94) in Florence. Both thinkers employed a syncretistic method which neither allowed for fundamental discrepancies between authorities nor envisaged the historical development of ideas. Their aim was to recover the true system of knowledge, the strands of which were already present in different sources. They were strongly influenced by Plato and the neo-Platonist texts of the early Christian era, and depended heavily on the Hermetic writings, which they believed to have come from ancient Egypt. Pico drew also on the Jewish occult tradition, and made free use of more recent sources such as Islamic philosophy. In his work now commonly known as the *Oration on the dignity of man* the neo-Platonist psychology of the Renaissance finds its most clear and succinct expression.

In one passage of the *Oration* God is envisaged as speaking thus to Adam. "In conformity with thy free judgment, in whose hands I have placed thee, thou art confined by no bounds ... Thou, like a judge appointed for being honourable, art the moulder and maker of thyself; thou mayest sculpt thyself into whatever shape thou dost prefer. Thou canst grow downwards into the lower natures which are brutes. Thou canst again grow upwards from thy soul's reason into the higher natures which are divine." (Trans. Wallis 1965, p.7). Here Pico assumes the prevailing cosmology, with its three main regions, supercelestial, celestial and sublunary; and the parallel division of human nature into intelligence, soul and body, so that each person is a kind of microcosm of the whole. But these concepts are radically transformed. Human nature is not only seen as flexible, but positively welcomed as such. There lies within each person the possibility of choosing, at one extreme, the way of the senses, the life of the brutes; and at the other, contemplation and partaking in the life of God. Human being are not hopelessly corrupted by sin, nor need they be the passive victims of astral influences. A person who chooses the highest way can draw on the powers of both the celestial and supercelestial regions, and can bring wonderful works into effect. To be "in God's image" means far more than bearing the Creator's imprint; at its highest it means to be a magus, to have creative power that is indeed divine, to participate in the restoration of heaven upon earth. This vision provided an inspiration both to many artists of the Italian Renaissance, such as Botticelli, and to utopian thinkers such as Campanella.

Renaissance neo-Platonism provided, primarily, a doctrine of male human nature. There was, however, no necessary reason why it could not have applied to the female sex, especially since some branches of occult thought such as the Cabala favor androgynous conceptions. In fact these possibilities were not fully worked out; and the notion of woman as an incomplete version of the male, as taught by Aristotle and endorsed by the late medieval Church, prevailed throughout the period (see AQUINAS).

The ideas of Ficino and Pico led to a distinct theory of the deepest human relationships ("Platonic love"). The lover takes into himself an image of the beloved, and his mind becomes like a mirror in which the form of the beloved is reflected. The beloved recognizes himself in the lover, even perhaps needs the lover in order to know himself. This psychology had special implications also for the theory of memory. There was a classical mnemonic art, well-known in the Middle Ages, whereby images are associated with the different rooms of a building, and so readily re-called in order. The Renaissance neo-Platonists, notably Giordano Bruno (1548–1600), re-worked this conception, using it not for the technical purpose of memorization but in order to imprint powerful, magical images, associated with the different parts of the universe. A person who had memorized the complete set of images reflected the whole cosmos in his mind, was in harmony with its forces, and had magical and creative powers.

Ficino himself was a physician as well as philosopher and priest, and his teaching had an influence on medical practice. Here the most significant figure is Theophrastus Bombastus ab Hohenheim, self-styled Paracelsus (1493–1541). In the course of his travels he made detailed studies of mental disorders such as melancholia, compulsions, delusions, hysteria and epilepsy. He rejected interpretations of these conditions based either on theology (e.g. devil-possession, divine punishment) or sorcery (e.g. spells, curses), insisting that they should be explained through the operation of natural causes, and that the sufferers should be seen as patients needing treatment. The good physician is a kind of magus, who works with Nature in the healing process. In Paracelsus there is a marked separation of psychology from theology, and evidence of a clear empirical method in describing abnormal conditions.

Neo-Platonism was largely displaced from orthodox natural philosophy by the late seventeenth century, as mechanistic forms of explanation rose to dominance (see DESCARTES; LOCKE). In literature, however, and in radical and occult movements, it remained influential for a long time; eventually to re-surface, greatly transformed, in the depth psychology and anti-positivistic movements of the twentieth century (see JUNG, HUMANISTIC PSYCHOLOGY). TMK

Bibliography

Burckhardt, J. 1860 (1958): *The civilisation of the renaissance in Italy.* New York: Harper & Row.

Cassirer, E. 1968: Giovanni Pico della Mirandola. In *Renaissance essays: From the Journal of the history of ideas,* ed. P.O. Kristeller and P.P. Wiener. New York: Harper & Row.

Debus, A.G. 1977: *The chemical philosophy.* New York: Neale Watson.

Kristeller, P.O. 1972: *Renaissance concepts of man, and other essays.* New York: Harper & Row.

Maclean, I. 1980: *The Renaissance notion of woman.* Cambridge: Cambridge University Press.

Pico della Mirandola (1965): *On the dignity of man.* Trans C.G. Wallis. Indianapolis: Bobs Merrill.

Yates, F. 1964: *Giordano Bruno and the hermetic tradition.* London: Routledge & Kegan Paul.

repertoire The linguistic repertoire of a speaker is the entirety of communication skills that he or she can draw upon in speech exhange. A repertoire not only includes subsystems, such as DIALECTS and SOCIOLECTS, but may also subsume two or more separate linguistic systems (see BILINGUALISM). The terms repertoire and IDIOLECT are sometimes used as synonyms.

A repertoire relates to communicative COMPETENCE in a fashion similar to the relationship between performance and competence. PM

repression The principal DEFENSE MECHANISM in psychoanalytic theory. The process by which a wish, idea etc. is kept out of consciousness because it is unacceptable either to the EGO (because maladaptive) or the SUPEREGO (because offensive to moral precepts). "Primary" repression is what prevents the idea of an instinctual impulse from ever emerging into consciousness, so that much of the UNCONSCIOUS MIND consists of Id-impulses; while "secondary" repression rejects from consciousness also ideas associated with, or symbolic of, such an impulse (Freud 1915). Repression differs from inhibition in that in the former the energy of the impulse is opposed by a counter-force, whereas in the latter the energy of the impulse itself is withdrawn. If repression is excessive, impulses find indirect expression in neurotic symptoms rather than in constructive sublimitations, and normally repressed material is expressed in disguised form in dreams (see DREAMING) or in the mild disruption of everyday psychological functioning (see PARAPRAXIS). NMC

Bibliography

Freud, S. 1915 (1957): Repression. In *The standard edition of the psychological works of Sigmund Freud,* vol.14, pp. 143–58. London: Hogarth Press; New York: Norton.

reproductive behavior Encompasses the many and varied activities shown by animals which promote the production and rearing of offspring. It includes not only behavior directly associated with mating, but also aggressive behavior directed toward obtaining mates and the resources essential for successful reproduction, and parental behavior by which the young are fed and protected. So diverse are the behavior patterns subsumed under the heading of reproductive behavior, that it is difficult to draw a clear distinction between reproductive behavior and other major behavioral categories. For example, when AGGRESSION is directed toward the defense of a territory that contains the food resources required to feed the young, it becomes essentially a matter of opinion whether such aggression should be labelled as reproductive behavior or, together with behavior shown in other contexts, included under the general category of aggression (see also TERRITORIALITY).

Since the crucial variable upon which natural selection acts is the number of progeny that an individual organism leaves in succeeding generations, it could be argued that virtually all behavior patterns can be described as reproductive behavior, since anything an animal does may affect its chances of surviving and reproducing. However, a distinction is usually made between those activities which directly promote reproduction and those which maintain the survival and growth of the individual. Other categories of behavior, such as aggression or feeding, cut across this dichotomy. On some occasions an animal may be fighting or feeding to maintain its own survival, on others to promote its reproductive output.

In the great majority of animals, but with the exception of hermaphrodites (animals capable of producing male and female gametes), individuals show very different forms of reproductive behavior depending on whether they are male or female. The biological basis of all other gender differences is the difference between female and male gametes, eggs and sperm. Since sperm are relatively very small and thus metabolically cheap to produce, they are typically produced in much larger number than eggs. As a result, males have a greater reproductive potential than females. In many animals this difference in potential is expressed in very disparate forms of reproductive behavior. Whereas females commonly devote much of their time to the care, nourishment and protection of their offspring, males tend to direct much of their effort toward competing with one another for matings. This pattern is not, however, seen in all species. In some, males and females share the parental components of reproductive behavior, and in a minority of animals, it is the males which devote greater effort to the care of the young and the females which compete with one another for access to males.

How the various aspects of reproductive behavior are apportioned between the sexes varies greatly from one species to another and depends on a complex interaction between several factors. For each species, reproductive behavior takes place within a distinctive set of social interactions called the mating system of that species. In a monogamous mating system, males and females form pair bonds of varying durability. In polygynous animals certain males mate with several females, and in a polyandrous species individual females may mate with several males. Promiscuity is a term sometimes used to describe systems in which both males and females mate with several partners.

The nature of the mating system largely determines the

forms of reproductive behavior shown by each sex. In monogamous species, males and females typically share such activities as nest-building and parental care. In many polygynous animals, males carry out little or no parental care but devote nearly all their effort to fighting with other males for the possession of females. Polyandry is associated with sex role "reversal", females tending to be the more dominant sex, competing for males which carry out most of the parental care.

Monogamy is more common among birds than other groups of animals. This is probably because, for birds more than for other groups, males can enhance their own REPRODUCTIVE SUCCESS significantly by staying with one female and sharing the parental duties with her, rather than by seeking to mate with other females. In birds, males can incubate eggs and feed chicks just as effectively as females. In mammals monogamy is rare and polygyny more common. Only female mammals can produce the milk on which the young are reared and males can offer only protection to the developing offspring.

Another factor that can determine the form of the mating system is the nature of the mating act. For example, among fishes there is a tendency for the parental role to be the prerogative of the male rather than the female in those species in which the eggs are fertilized outside the female's body. Conversely, female care is commoner in species in which fertilization is internal to the female. Essentially, parental care falls on the partner that is closest to the eggs when they are fertilized.

Virtually all animals show marked periodicity in their reproductive behavior. In many species there is an annual breeding season which, in extreme cases, is limited to one or two days each year. The timing of the breeding season is typically linked to seasonal changes in the environment so that reproduction occurs at the most propitious time for the successful production and rearing of offspring. In most birds that breed in temperate climates, egg laying is timed to precede the dramatic increase in the availability of plant and insect food that occurs in the spring and summer. In some mammals, including humans, there is little or no seasonal periodicity, but a continually cycling system, in which females regularly become reproductively active (come into estrus). Whatever the periodicity of reproductive behavior, cycles are physiologically controlled by reproductive hormones secreted within the body by various endocrine glands. Hormone production, particularly in species which breed annually, is triggered by a variety of external influences such as temperature, day-length and the behavior of members of the opposite sex. Hormones commonly have a range of physiological effects, influencing many aspects of reproductive behavior. For example, testosterone has a major influence on both mating activity and aggression in males, as well as playing a role in sperm production. Female sex hormones, such as estrogen and progesterone, can be involved in the control of nest-building, mating and parental care. In general, the role of sex hormones in reproductive behavior is to bring the whole physiology of males and females into a state of reproductive preparedness and receptivity. The exact timing of the various components of reproductive behavior, and of mating in particular, is typically a function of behavioral interactions occurring between males and females.

The critical point in the reproductive process is the act of mating which is usually associated with a category of reproductive behavior referred to as COURTSHIP. Courtship involves the coordination of male and female behavior necessary for successful mating and, in some species, provides an opportunity for animals to choose their mating partners from among a wide range of potential mates. In monogamous animals which form durable mating partnerships, courtship may continue after mating has occurred and can be important in maintaining the pair bond during the parental phase of the reproductive process.

In a few animals the reproductive behavior of parents is augmented by the efforts of other individuals which act as helpers. In a number of birds, helpers provide food for the young and assist in defense of the brood against predators and other enemies. In most cases, but not all, helpers are genetically related to the individuals they are assisting. They may, for example, be previous offspring of one or both parents and thus be full or half-siblings of the young for whom they are caring. Such cooperative breeding groups are essentially extended families (see ALTRUISM) TRH

Bibliography

Halliday, T.R. 1980: *Sexual strategy*. Oxford: Oxford University Press; Chicago: Chicago University Press (1982).

Daly, M. and Wilson, M. 1978: *Sex, evolution and behavior*. North Scituate Massachusetts: Duxbury.

Hutchison, J.B., ed. 1978: *Biological determinants of sexual behaviour*. New York and Chichester: Wiley.

reproductive effort Time and energy allocated directly to producing progeny. It can be measured by the fraction of time and energy at a given age that is devoted to reproduction. In a Darwinian sense all animal activity must be related ultimately to REPRODUCTIVE SUCCESS, but it is often helpful to differentiate between effort that results directly in the production and care of progeny (reproductive effort) and effort that, although ultimately contributing to this end, is not itself directly concerned with progeny. Maximum reproductive success will result from a trade off between the two forms of effort. Those interested in the study of life history strategies are much concerned with the timing and extent of reproductive effort. GAP

reproductive success A measure of the number of offspring produced by a given individual which manage to survive to a given age. Lifetime reproductive success is the sum of all the annual reproductive successes of a given individual. Relative lifetime reproductive success is a measure of individual FITNESS. If individuals show heritable differences in relative reproductive success, selection will be acting to favor genes that confer higher than average reproductive success. Absolute reproductive success is less important than relative reproductive success in determining the outcome of selection. GAP

resource-holding potential (RHP) A measure of the ability of one of a pair of animal contestants to win or to score against its opponent in a fight, assuming both were to employ the same strategy (see EVOLUTIONARILY STABLE STRATEGIES). Thus RHP defines how contest costs will accrue to each opponent if they fight in similar fashion. This parameter, introduced by Parker (1974), is important in the modelling of animal contests, since disparities in RHP will affect the payoffs achieved by opponents in a dispute. It is clear that RHP is often equivalent simply to fighting ability, which is itself a reflection of size, strength and experience. However, in many instances environmental features may also affect an individual's ability to win a score against its opponent. For example, in fights between male insects for the possession of a female, the male originally in possession may have much better prospects (owing to its prior grasp on the female) than the attacker, even though the attacker may be larger (Sigurjonsdottir and Parker 1981). Riechert (1978) has suggested that RHP may best be defined as "relative holding power", since it is the relative difference between the two opponents that is important in determining payoffs.
GAP

Bibliography

Parker, G.A. 1974: Assessment strategy and the evolution of fighting behavior. *Journal of theoretical biology* 47, 223–43.

Riechert, S. 1978: Games spiders play: behavioral variability in territorial disputes. *Behavioral ecology and sociobiology* 3, 135–62.

Sigurjonsdottir, H. and Parker, G.A. 1981: Dung fly struggles: evidence for assessment strategy. Behavioral variability in territorial disputes. *Behavioral ecology and sociobiology* 8, 219–30.

retention and forgetting A (long term) forgetting curve plots the amount retained against time on the abcissa, measured in hours and days. The data fit exponential functions, with different types of decay rates depending on the material to be retained (nonsense syllables are forgotten faster than meaningful text) and type of test (recall, recognition, savings on relearning). What happens during the retention interval also affects the rate of forgetting: rest and sleep produce the least forgetting, study of similar materials interferes most. Most, perhaps all, forgetting is due to interference rather than to spontaneous decay of the trace, If two items are learned equally well, the older one will be retained longer.

Short term forgetting is measured in seconds. The functions are, once again, exponential, starting at 100 per cent retention for immediate tests, and reaching asymptote in about 20–30 seconds. The asymptote of the short term forgetting curve forms the starting point of the long term curve, though in practice the two kinds of curves are not always comparable, because short term curves plot the retention of individual items while long term curves typically plot the retention of whole lists of items or other, larger units. A short term memory unit is called a "chunk," with chunk size dependent on how well integrated the information is. Short term forgetting rates also depend on the nature of the activity during the retention interval: no forgetting is observed as long as the subject is permitted to actively rehearse the material; the greater the attention and resource demands of competing tasks, the more rapid short term forgetting. See MEMORY: SHORT TERM AND LONG TERM.
WKi

reticular activating system The arousal of the brain is the function of the reticular activating system (RAS) (see BRAIN AND CENTRAL NERVOUS SYSTEM: ILLS 6 and 9). The reticular formation consists of a diffuse collection of neurons located in medial regions of the brain stem. This formation extends from the medulla through the pons and mid-brain to the thalamus. Lesions of this brain region produce persistent sleep, while electrical stimulation of the reticular formation will arouse a sleeping animal. Not only does RAS activation lead to awakening, but it also produces increased levels of arousal once awake. All sensory pathways to the cortex send branches to the RAS. Although this sensory information is very nonspecific, it serves to stimulate the RAS which, in turn, activates the cortex so that the incoming message can be interpreted. Additionally, there are descending neural pathways from the cortex that may excite the RAS which will, in turn, more fully activate the cortex.
RAJ

retrieval Memory requires both encoding (or storage) and retrieval (or production). Retrieval failure appears to be the main cause of forgetting: it is believed that all memory traces that are successfully encoded (attended to) are permanently stored in long term memory, but only a fraction of them are retrievable. Retrieval depends on how successfully the context of encoding is reinstated at the time of retrieval. The retrieval cue must match at least in part the encoding context. This implies that there are no encoding procedures or retrieval cues that are uniformly good (or poor): what matters is, rather, the encoding-retrieval interaction. In an efficient retrieval system each retrieval cue produces not only the memory trace that it was designed to contact, but also another retrieval cue, which leads to the retrieval of further information. Retrieval time from long term memory varies depending on the effectiveness of the retrieval cue; retrieval time from short term memory is about 40 msec. per item.
WKi

reversal learning Learning the opposite of a discrimination that has previously been acquired; having learned to choose A not B from a pair AB the reversal would be learning to choose B. Like EXTINCTION, reversal does not result in mere "unlearning" of the original response; for example, RELEARNING of the initial task following reversal is often more rapid than original learning. Ease of reversal learning is affected by the extent of practice on the original discrimination; paradoxically, OVERTRAINING on the original task sometimes (not always) speeds up reversal. This may occur because reversal, while superficially seeming to represent pure negative transfer, contains elements of positive transfer in that the reversal involves similar attention or orienting behavior to the original task. If the same discrimination is repeatedly reversed and reinstated (serial reversal) the rate of learning improves progressively (reversal learning set) in most species, rats and monkeys for example being capable eventually of reversing a simple discrimination reliably after a single error. EAG

reversibility In Piaget's theory of intellectual development, that property of a system of mental operations that enables return to a particular point of departure. Two kinds of reversible operation are acquired during the concrete operational period and allow a new flexibility of thought. These are (1) Inversion (negation). Any mental operation that can be carried out in one direction can be carried out mentally in the opposite direction. The child who understands that $2 + 4 = 6$ should also understand that $6 - 2 = 4$. (2) Compensation (or reciprocity). For any mental operation there exists another that will compensate or nullify its effects within a total system of transformations. For example in the conservation of liquid-volume task, (see PIAGET) the child who has entered the concrete operational period can, according to Piaget, mentally compensate for an observed change in the height of liquid by noting the change in width. This helps the child to comprehend that the volume stayed constant despite a change in its appearance. GEB

Bibliography

Brainerd, C.J. 1978: *Piaget's theory of intelligence*. Englewood Cliffs, N.J.: Prentice Hall.

revolution: explanations Modern revolution, especially, refers to significant cultural and social changes in society. It is often also characterized as political, rapid and violent (Huntington 1968). Several of the great revolutions have been, more or less, violent, rapid and directed toward political change, but revolutionary cultural and social changes have occurred without violence, over long periods of time, and have had significant consequences for peoples' lives in realms other than the political. The Russian Revolution of October 1917, for example, was political and violent to be sure, but it was also directed at the economic development of then backward Russia. Furthermore it had its origins as far back at least as the Russian Revolution of 1905. Similarly the so called Industrial Revolution took 300 years to evolve, and though it did so with considerable struggle and pain to the persons and societies involved, in the conventional meaning of the term it was not violent. The effects of the Industrial Revolution on the economic and occupational lives of individuals are inestimable and persistent. Finally, the revolutionary democratization of the western family during the late nineteenth and early twentieth century had considerable consequences for peoples' daily lives but occurred without armed struggle.

Revolutions are also distinguishable from other forms of collective action sometimes referred to as revolts. For example, palace coups d'état (which involve rotating military elites but little policy change), insurrections, rebellions and riots; Though directed to political ends, violent and rapidly evolving, these frequently accomplish no fundamental social change or affect only local political conditions and are not revolutions.

It is therefore change in society's fundamental organizing principles and their implementation in practical social arrangements, either through violent action or through evolution, that is constitutive of revolution. The English Civil War of 1642 reduced the power of the monarchy and elevated the political and social position of the common man (the word revolution came into the English language in about 1600, however Cromwell meant by it not change but restoration of the old order). The French Revolution of 1789 changed principles for the attribution of personal worth from inherited privilege to citizenship, performance and contribution to society; from qualities associated with aristocracy to those associated with the third estate. And in both British and French societies the revolution not only changed principles but also brought with it, more or less, stably institutionalized forms of republican government.

It has been assumed that revolution is set in motion by social circumstances among which class has been generally thought the most important, though religion, age and shared psychological disposition have also been cited.

Marx and his followers in particular have focused upon social class as the source of revolutionary activity. The general Marxist thesis being that social class interests, particularly those related to a rising class's contribution to society and those in connection with exclusion from political and economic power motivates the class to revolt against the existing order and to replace it with one consistent with the interests of the rising class. Marxists have used this form of analysis to explain the English Civil War and the French Revolution. It has been suggested that a rising English gentry and a rising French bourgeoisie, both desirous of political and economic power overthrew an exclusionary aristocracy in order to establish a government compatible with their interests (Wallerstein 1974).

However class analysis of revolution is not exclusive to Marxists; liberal social scientists have employed it to explain mass movements directed at fundamental societal changes. Lipset (1963) suggested that the Nazi movement was the result of working-class commitment which developed because of their psychological obedience to authority. And a recent extensive quantitative study of voting patterns in Germany between 1924 and 1932 suggests that it was the middle classes, and not the working classes, which supported Hitler (Hamilton 1982). Despite the unresolved controversy between these studies they both use social class as the variable which explains the revolution's support.

Religious fervor, often with millenarian overtones, has also been viewed as the base for revolutionary participation. Puritan believers, and beliefs, have been described as the initiators of the English Civil War (Walzer 1969) and of the American Revolution of 1776 (Bailyn 1967). The young, both on account of their vitality and impatience and as the carriers of new and different values are also often thought of as instigators of revolution. The Nazi movement (Loewenberg 1971) and the French and

American radical and counterculture movements of 1968–9 (Keniston 1971) have been depicted as youth movements.

The use of social circumstances to explain revolutionary origins has produced some excellent and detailed studies of such movements (see, e.g., Calhoun 1982), many of which have been noted above. This form of analysis is dominant and persistent in the social sciences. It is a form of analysis consistent with the common-sensical and scientific logic of antecedent categories causing consequent effects. It is also consistent with a dominant social scientific belief that action is motivated by shared interests embedded in people's social positions (Tilly 1978). And it is persistent because social scientists want to have measurable categories in their efforts to conduct objective, and sometimes statistical, analyses. However, some social scientists disagree that social positions are a superior mode for analysing revolutions.

Recent studies have indicated that revolutionary participants and their opponents (i.e. counter-revolutionaries, so called entrenched elites, etc.) are drawn from similar backgrounds, from similar social classes, ages and religious affiliations (Hamilton 1982), and that what appears analytically salient for the study of revolution is the heterogeneous composition of classes, ages and religions, etc. A number of studies have therefore turned to cultural and ideological commitments and subjective orientations in their effort to explain the heterogeneity of revolutionary participants while simultaneously attempting to explain the phenomenon of revolution (Platt 1980).

Culture and ideology are central to the study of revolution because they define the nature and direction of change. Revolutions have brought about changes consistent with Max Weber's ideal-typical conceptions of rational–legal or traditional societies. The great revolutions (that is, the so called "progressive" or "left" revolutions) such as the English Civil War, the French, Russian and Chinese revolutions have effected changes in the direction of rational–legal societies. The cultural and ideological values underlying these revolutions are those of justice, freedom, rationality, individualism, performance and universal inclusion. The twentieth-century revolutions made in the name of Marxist thought exhibit these same values because Marx's thinking stands in a line with the enlightened and liberal doctrine of Locke and Rousseau.

By contrast, the German, Italian and Japanese fascist movements of the 1930s and '40s were directed at establishing or re-establishing traditional societies. This meant institutionalizing cultural and ideological values stressing nationalism, folk relations, political, economic and social activities based upon ascriptive ties such as those of birth, blood, race and giving special emphasis to collective solidarity and hierarchy.

A correlative of these "left" and "right" cultural and ideological orientations are differences in the movements themselves. First for example the revolutionaries of the left have been future-oriented, filled with hope for more just, almost utopian, societies. In contrast the right revolutionaries want to restore a lost, glorious and often idealized past. Second, the left revolutionaries view their struggle, and even their violence, as reactive; a necessary evil caused by the need to overthrow the yoke of oppression in establishing a new order – the conflict and the violence will stop with the flowering of the "new society" and the "new man". But for the right revolutionaries conflict and violence are exulted; violence is a sign of the full nature of manhood. Third, the left revolutionaries stress rationality, education, disciplined and objective analysis of reality (Walzer 1969). By contrast, the right emphasizes personal ties, brotherhood, clan, kinship, personal impulse and human will in shaping reality. Finally, the left stresses non-hierarchical, more egalitarian relations between leader and led; this came to its height among the left radicals of the 1960s with their insistence upon "participatory democracy" in all decisions. However, the right insists upon hierarchical relations between leaders and followers (see Weinstein 1980, pp.120–36 for an elaboration of these points).

These are ideal-typical conceptions of "left" and "right" revolutionaries. They are not exact reflections of the subtle differences between the many groups on both sides of the spectrum. However, there is enough historical truth in these formulations to justify, and to substantiate, the importance of cultural and ideological analyses of revolutions.

Beyond cultural and personal influences social conditions obviously foster the revolutionary impulse. There are two traditional views regarding social conditions for fomenting revolutions. In the Marxist tradition it is worsening circumstances, the increasing degradation of the working classes, or, more generally stated, it is declining expectations regarding want satisfaction which produce the motive to revolt. However, de Tocqueville suggests that better conditions, the loosening of oppression, a sudden affluence, or conditions of rising expectations spark the desire for revolution. According to de Tocqueville, continuous degradation men can endure, but the glow of success ignites "fire in the minds of men" (Billington 1980).

Marx and de Tocqueville are both correct: revolutions have been incubated in rising and in declining conditions of want satisfaction. So it can be generalized that it is unsettling conditions of social strain which incite the revolutionary impulse (Platt 1980). GMP

Bibliography

Bailyn, Bernard 1967: *The ideological origins of the American Revolution*. Cambridge, Mass.: Harvard University Press.

Billington, James H. 1980: *Fire in the minds of men: origins of the revolutionary faith*. New York: Basic Books.

Calhoun, Craig 1982: *The question of class struggle: social foundations of popular radicalism during the industrial revolution*. Chicago: University of Chicago Press.

Hamilton, Richard 1982: *Who voted for Hitler?*. Princeton, N.J.: Princeton University Press.

Huntington, Samuel P. 1968: *Political order in changing societies*. New Haven: Yale University Press.

Keniston, Kenneth 1971: *Youth and dissent*. New York: Harcourt Brace Jovanovich.

Lipset, Seymour Martin 1963: *Political man: the social bases of politics*. Garden City, N.Y.: Anchor Books/Doubleday.

Loewenberg, Peter 1971: The psychohistorical origins of the Nazi youth cohort *American historical review* 75, 1457–502.

Platt, Gerald M. 1980: Thoughts on a theory of collective action; language, affect, and ideology in revolution, In: *New directions in psychohistory: the Adelphi Papers in honor of Erik H. Erikson* ed. Mel Albin. Lexington, Mass.: Lexington Books.

Tilly, Charles 1978; *From mobilization to revolution*. Reading, Mass.: Addison-Wesley.

Wallerstein, Immanuel, M. 1974: *The modern world system: capitalist agriculture and the origins of the European world-economy in the sixteenth century* New York: Academic Press.

Walzer, Michael 1969: *The revolution of the saints: a study in the origins of radical politics*. New York: Atheneum.

Weinstein, Fred 1980: *The dynamics of Nazism: leadership, ideology and the holocaust*. New York: Academic Press.

rewards *See* incentives/rewards

rhythm *See* circadian rhythms

rhythms Periodically repeated features of behavior which may recur over time scales of any duration. Rhythms can arise as a result of clock-driven behavior, as a result of responses to rhythmically occurring external stimuli, or as relaxation oscillations which arise as a result of the physiological or mechanical organization of the animal.

Clock-driven rhythms result from the endogenous time-keeping ability of animals, and may give rise to circannual, circalunar or circadian periodicity in behavior. The timing of annual migration and hibernation is organized in this way, as are the daily routines of many animals.

Responses to exogenous rhythmicity occur in adjustment to the seasons, the weather and daily fluctuations in the availablity of food. Relaxation oscillations occur whenever there is a build-up and release of behavioral potential, as in hunger and in many aspects of locomotion. See CLOCK-DRIVEN BEHAVIOR. DJM

ribonucleic acid *See* RNA, DNA

risk taking There are two conceptual specifications of this sort of action, one emerging from SOCIAL PSYCHOLOGY and the other from the psychology of DECISION THEORY: (1) Risk taking behavior occurs if the risk-taker places something at stake, where a stake exists only if both positive and negative outcomes are possible, *and* if the risk-taker recognizes that something is or will be at stake, *and* if the risk-taker takes action which by its nature and context makes the stake irreversible and in the normal course of events will lead to some outcome (Blascovich and Ginsburg 1978). (2) Risk taking entails choosing among options which are associated with outcomes that will be of benefit or harm, but for any option the occurrence of one or the other of its set of outcomes is uncertain. A gamble is an archetypal case of each definition; so are most forms of investment, provided the returns are not guaranteed.

The social psychological study of risk-taking subsequently became extremely active in the wake of a counterintuitive finding that individuals in a group setting take greater risks than they do when acting on their own. The phenomenon came to be known as the RISKY SHIFT, and during the next several years hundreds of studies were conducted under that rubric (see Dion, Baron and Miller 1970 for a review of the early material). Considerable effort was devoted to experimental assessment of competing theories of the underlying mechanisms, which included proposals of a risk-taking norm, the role of persuasive arguments, various social comparison processes, and the spread of responsibility. Eventually it became apparent that most (but not all) of the research had little if anything to do with risk-taking, and the findings became re-interpreted as instances of group polarization, in which there is a "group-produced enhancement of a prevailing individual tendency" (Lamm and Myers 1978, 146) and has no necessary connection to risk-taking. The immense popularity of the risky shift as a research topic was due in part to its counter-intuitive nature; in part to its potential relevance to a wide range of important decision contexts, such as medicine and surgery, emergencies, and judicial sentencing; and in part to the existence of a simple questionnaire – the CDQ, or choice dilemmas questionnaire – as the criterion measure of risk-taking. Unfortunately the CDQ was a personality measure and not a measure of risk-taking behavior, which made irrelevant the 80 per cent of the studies that had used it. The absence of an adequate conceptual analysis of risk-taking made possible the adoption of such a measure (see Blascovich and Ginsburg 1978; also see Cartwright 1973 for an historical review and commentary).

Risk taking has not been consensually defined in the decision making arena either, but the criterion task by which the "risk" being taken is measured is the choice by the risk-taker of one from among two or more options. Risk taking from the standpoint of decision making has been conceptualized within a framework of rational choice, which in turn had emphasized a criterion of the maximization of expected utility (or of subjective expected utility, in the absence of objective values and probabilities). However, it now is clear that the choices which people make do not necessarily conform to the technical requirements of the EU model (see Coombs and Huang 1976) and more realistic models have been proposed. One of these is prospect theory (Tversky and Kahneman 1981) which takes into account individual differences among risk takers in the environmental information which they take into account and in the ways in which they integrate and weight that information. The EU maximization model holds that a rational individual will choose among risky options so as to maximize the expected utility of the choice, which in turn is construed as a product of the probability (p) of occurrence of the outcome associated with that choice and the value (v) of that outcome. The Prospect model assumes that each person has a changeable, neutral reference point, and that outcomes are evaluated as positive or negative deviations from that reference point. Moreover, people differ in the importance attributed to various probabilities; usually, small probabilities have greater impact on decisions than high or moderate probabilities. This is reflected in a weighting factor, Π, and in the use of the "decision weight" Πp instead of simple probability p as in

EU. Thus, in the Prospect model of risky choice, outcomes are evaluated as deviations from a reference point, which itself may be a desired state, a current state, a feared state, an earlier state, the state of some comparison group, and so on; and some probabilities can be given more importance than others through the weighting factor; and sequential decisions can be made in which different criteria and different weights can be applied at each stage of the process.

It is unfortunate that the social psychological study of risk taking has ceased to be of investigative interest, because the decision theory models of risky choice have advanced to a stage where social processes and conditions can be taken into account. A blend of the two approaches would be synergistic. GPG

Bibliography

Blascovich, J. and Ginsburg, G.P. 1978: Conceptual analysis of risk-taking in "risky shift" research. *Journal for the theory of social behavior* 8, 217–30.

Cartwright, D.A. 1973: Determinants of scientific progress: the case of research on the risky shift. *American psychologist* 28, 222–31.

*Coombs, C.H. 1975: Portfolio theory and the measurement of risk. In *Human judgment and decision processes*, ed. M.F. Kaplan and S. Schwartz. New York and London: Academic Press.

——— and Huang, L.C. 1976: Tests of the betweenness property of expected utility. *Journal of mathematical psychology* 13, 323–37.

Dion, K.L., Baron, R.S. and Miller, N. 1970: Why do groups makes riskier decisions than individuals? In *Advances in experimental social psychology* vol. 5, ed. L. Berkowitz. New York and London: Academic Press.

Lamm, H. and Myers, D.G. 1978: Group-induced polarization of attitudes and behaviors. In *Advances in experimental social psychology* vol 11, ed. L. Berkowitz. New York and London: Academic Press.

Tversky, A. and Kahneman, D. 1981: The framing of decisions and the psychology of choice. *Science* 211, 453–8.

risky shift A term which describes the fact that groups often take riskier decisions that the individual members of the group would take. This phenomenon, which counters the popular belief that groups are more conservative than individuals, was first put forward in an unpublished dissertation by Stoner in 1961. Many studies have used a choice dilemma questionnaire, developed by Kogan and Wallach (1967), in which a person or a group is asked to estimate what the odds for success would have to be in order to recommend the more risky and more valuable course of action in a two-choice situation. More recent research has shown that groups can also be more conservative than the average individual and hence the term group polarization has replaced the term risky shift. The direction of the polarization depends first of all upon the initial positions of the individual members. The group decision shifts in the direction of the majority. Although various explanations have been offered for group polarization, it appears that informational influence, based on the availability of more arguments in one direction rather than the other, explains the phenomena (Lamm and Myers 1978). JMFJ

Bibliography

Kogan, N. and Wallach, M.A. 1967: Risk taking as a function of the situation, the person and the group. In *New directions in psychology*, Vol. 2, ed. G. Mandler et al. New York: Holt, Rinehart and Winston.

Lamm, H. and Myers, D.G. 1978: Group induced polarization of attitudes and behavior. In *Advances in experimental social psychology*, Vol. II, ed. L. Berkowitz. New York and London: Academic Press.

ritual A variously conceived term which can be taken to refer to activities, of any kind but usually formalized, involving non-technological instrumentality. A rite (Greek *dromenon*, "a thing done") is a supra-scientific way of obtaining results.

One characteristic of ritual is the elaboration of means to obtain empirical ends. Following the conventions of casting spells to ensure a successful harvest is different from technological action, controlled by trial-and-error and based on what is scientifically necessary. A number of theories, generally psychological, have been devised to explain erroneous instrumentality (Beattie 1970, Jahoda 1970, Shweder 1977).

Another characteristic type is the elaboration of means to obtain meaning-dependent ends. Rather than being orientated to changing physical states of affairs, ritual of this sort is orientated to expressing or saying something. Such rituals work through non-technological instrumentalities as for example, by wearing this uniform I communicate ...; by swearing this oath I ...; by shaking hands I ...; by being the groom I ...; etc. Understanding this kind of ritual does not require a theory of erroneous instrumentality (Tambiah 1979). There is a problem in accounting for non-rational instrumentality, for example in accounting for why we shake hands rather than rub noses. Explanations have been offered by human ethologists (Eibl-Eibesfeldt 1979); and by anthropologists (Turner 1967).

The main contribution from ethology and psychology (especially psychodynamic theory) has been to examine the grounds of ritual; the main contribution from anthropology and social psychology (e.g. Goffman 1967) has been to examine meanings and functions. PLFH

Bibliography

Beattie, John 1970: On understanding ritual. In *Rationality*, ed. B. Wilson. Oxford: Basil Blackwell.

Eibl-Eibesfeldt, Irenaus 1979: Ritual and ritualization from a biological perspective. In *Human ethology*, ed. M. von Cranach, K. Foppa, W. Lepenies, and D. Ploog. Cambridge: Cambridge University Press.

Goffman, Erving 1967: *Interaction ritual*. New York: Anchor Books.

Jahoda, Gustav 1970: *The psychology of superstition*. Harmondsworth: Penguin.

Parsons, Talcott 1937: *The structure of social action*. New York: McGraw-Hill.

Shweder, Richard 1977: Likeness and likelihood in everyday thought: magical thinking in judgements about personality. *Current anthropology* 18, 637–98.

Tambiah, S.J. 1979: *A performative approach to ritual*. London: British Academy.

Turner, Victor 1967: *The forest of symbols*. Ithaca, N.Y.: Cornell University Press.

ritual and ritualization In anthropology, ritual refers to a prescribed formal pattern of cultural behavior, usually symbolic and often religious or ceremonial in character (see Keesing 1981).

In ethology, by an intended analogy, ritual refers to a

pattern of animal behavior, such as reproductive display, which has a distinctively stylized quality: and ritualization is the evolutionary or developmental process which brings a ritual into existence (see Immelmann 1980). Hypothetically, evolutionary ritualization originates with a non-ritual movement such as feeding, and proceeds by a gradual modification of the movement in which it also acquires the function of a social signal. The modified form of the movement may be exaggerated, formalized and repetitive, and may include the display of conspicuous colors or structures: these changes are considered to enhance the clarity of the communication involved (see also STEREOTYPY; TYPICAL INTENSITY).

Discussions between ethologists, anthropologists and others (e.g. Hinde 1972) have raised many issues of interest, but have also demonstrated that the different disciplines use "ritual" and "ritualization" in very different senses. See also RITUAL. RDA

Bibliography

Hinde, R.A. 1972 ed.: *Non-verbal communication*. Cambridge, New York, Melbourne: Cambridge University Press.

Immelmann, K. 1980 *Introduction to ethology*. New York, London: Plenum Press.

Keesing, R.M. 1981 *Cultural anthropology: a contemporary perspective*. 2nd ed. New York and London; Holt, Rinehart & Winston.

RNA, DNA The two major nucleic acids in virtually all living organisms. DNA (deoxyribonucleic acid) is found primarily in the nucleus of all cells and contains the genetic blueprint for the entire organism. It is present as a double-stranded helix whose backbone is comprised of an alternative arrangement of sugar and phosphate molecules. The stairs of the helix are formed by pairing four bases: cytosine, guanine, thymine and adenine. Base pairings are always complementary, with adenine binding to thymine and cytosine to guanine. A linear arrangement of these four bases forms the genetic code, which is read as a series of triplets, each coding for one amino acid. During transcription the two strands of DNA separate, breaking the base pairings, and a single stranded molecule of RNA (ribonucleic acid) is transcribed in complementary fashion

B_1 B_2

1′CH OH CH OH

O O 2′CH O O CH O O

HO—P—O—CH_2—CH—CH—O—P—O—CH_2—CH—CH—O—P—O----CH_2—CH

5′ 4′ 3′

O^- O^- O^-

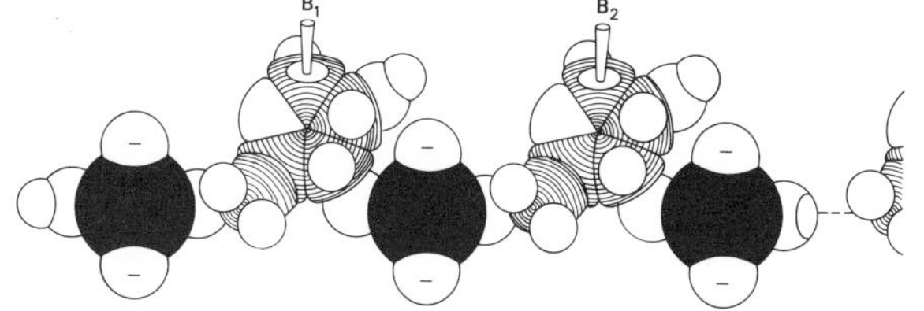

from the DNA template. In RNA, uracil replaces thymine. The messenger RNA thus formed migrates to the cytoplasm and associates with ribosomes to initiate protein synthesis, a process called translation. A separate species, transfer RNA, brings molecules of amino acids over to the ribosomes in an order specified by the sequence of bases in the messenger. These amino acids are joined sequentially by peptide bonding to form a polypeptide. When translation is complete, the polypeptide breaks away from the ribosome and assumes the configuration of a protein. GPH

role: animal A pattern of behavior that is characteristic of individuals holding a particular position within a social structure. The role concept is useful only if the behavior in question benefits other group members (Bernstein, 1966). An example is the exploratory behavior of a peripheral animal. In introducing the role concept to primate ethology Bernstein emphasized that the functions of animal social positions are not entirely defined by DOMINANCE. An animal may begin or cease a role behavior within days of a change of group structure. The assumption of a role may result from the evolved behavioral tendencies of the member and may be influenced by social interactions. Whereas human role behavior is partly enforced by group expectations, animals more often seem to suppress than to enforce role behavior in a group member. HK

Bibliography

Bernstein, I.S. 1966: Analysis of a key role in a capuchin (Cebus albifrons) group. *Tulane studies in zoology* 13, 49–54.

role ambiguity, conflict and overload Role ambiguity exists when an individual has inadequate information about his or her work role, where there is a lack of clarity about the work objectives associated with the role, about colleagues' expectations of the work role, and about the scope and responsibilities of the job. Role conflict exists when an individual in a particular work role is torn by conflicting job demands or troubled by having to undertake tasks which he or she does not want to do or does not think are part of the job specification.

French and Caplan (1973) have differentiated between quantitative and qualitative overload. Quantitative refers to having "too much to do", while qualitative overload involves work that is "too difficult". (See also WORK STRESS.) CLC

Bibliography

French, J.R.P. and Caplan, R.D. 1973: Organisational stress and individual strain. In *The failure of success* ed. A.J. Marrow. Amacon.

role-rule theory An approach to the analysis and explanation of the more formal kinds of social interaction. It is an integral part of the ETHOGENIC method in social psychology. In many of their social interactions people can be seen as performing in roles. The basic notion of role is taken from the stage but it has been developed in various different ways, so that the term is now to some extent ambiguous. A role may be simply a way of referring to some regular pattern in the way people of a certain category behave. We might, for instance, speak of "woman's role". There are no specific rules which need to be followed to create the role, and roles of this sort are usually associated with expectations. A more tightly defined notion of role has been used in the analysis of the way in which people behave in institutional settings. In this context role behavior is related to structural features of institutions, which locate roles in terms of the relations between functional units of the institution. For instance, in a hospital there may be distinctive roles for doctors, nurses, patients etc. In so far as these roles are officially defined they are associated with systems of rules which specify the behavior appropriate to this or that role.

The use of role-rule theory to analyse and explain other kinds of social interaction draws on the psychological features of institutional role behavior. In particular it assumes that the number of routine forms of interaction is greater than one might expect. Further, by extending the notion of role, role-rule theory proposes a hypothetical mechanism which could produce conforming, coordinated interaction between people, and so provides a necessary basis for explaining that behavior. "Role" is used in the analysis of social interactions and "rule" in the explanation of the regularities and patterns found by means of that analysis.

In studying institutional interactions microsociologists (particularly Goffman 1969, pp.37ff) have used the notion of role to identify a number of psychologically interesting phenomena. When a person is so located in an institution that more than one set of rules (and reciprocally of expectations) seems to be in play, they may experience "role-conflict", uncertainties as to the relative priorities to be given to each rule-system. In certain institutions the solemnity of role-fulfilling actions is sometimes a bar to the very best performance, and the leader of a team may sometimes reveal a "human side" by taking "role-distance", that is by acting in a way inconsistent with full immersion in his or her role.

Doubts have sometimes been expressed (Lindsey 1977) about the justification for using the rule metaphor to explain the regularity of the actions people produce in fulfilling the demands of their roles, whether it be in the looser or the stricter sense of "role". A somewhat similar doubt has also been expressed about using the notion of "grammatical rule" in the explanation of the ability of native speakers to produce grammatically correct sentences. Clearly there are many occasions on which people act in a coordinated and regulated way without reference to explicitly formulated rules. However, the use of the rule metaphor has been justified by the argument that any cognitive process by which patterned action is produced must draw on some body of knowledge or belief, whether this is done consciously or not. The fact that this body of knowledge often has normative force, and that when it is explicitly formulated it is often expressed in the form of rules, justifies the use of the rule-metaphor to describe it. RHa

Bibliography

Biddle, B.J. and Thomas, E.J. 1966: *Role theory: concepts and research*. New York: Wiley.

Collett, P., ed. 1977: *Social rules and social behavior*. Oxford: Blackwell; Totowa, N.J.: Rowman & Littlefield.

Goffman, E. 1969: *Where the action is*. London: Allen Lane.

Harré, R. 1979: *Social being: a theory for social psychology*. Oxford: Basil Blackwell; Totowa, N.J.: Littlefield Adams.

Lindsey, R. 1977: Rules as a bridge between speech and action. In Collett, *op. cit.*

roles: social psychology The term role is usually defined as the behavior which is associated with a particular position in a social system. A social role implies that the person who holds this particular position enacts the associated behavior, but it also carries expectations held by others about the behavior that is appropriate for the occupant of the position.

Since a person can hold more than one role at a time and the expectations for different roles may be incompatible, conflicts between roles can easily develop. Even a single role can have incompatible demands. Such role conflicts in everyday life have been illustrated in interesting and sometimes insightful ways by Goffman (1971). The concept of role recently gained some theoretical importance in the so-called dramaturgical model of man advocated by Harré (1979) and empirical significance in the psychological study of social situations by Argyle et al. (1981). In general the concept of role appears to be more important in sociological than in social psychological analyses. JMFJ

Bibliography

Argyle, M., Furnham, A. and Graham, J.A. 1981: *Social situations*, Cambridge University Press.

Collett, P., ed. 1977: *Social rules and social behavior*. Oxford: Basil Blackwell; Totowa, N.J.: Rowman and Littlefield.

Goffman, E. 1971: *Relations in public*. New York: Basic Books.

Harré, R. 1979: *Social being*. Oxford: Basil Blackwell; Totowa, N.J.: Littlefield Adams.

Rolfing (structural integration) *See* body-centered therapy

rosicrucians Dubious "secret society", almost certainly a kind of hoax. In 1614 there appeared in Kassel a pamphlet called *Famosa Fraternitas of the Worthy Order of the Rosy Cross*. It was anonymous, and stated that a man called Christian Rosenkreutz, who had lived to be 106, had, after a life in search of "occult wisdom", founded a brotherhood called the Rosy Cross. He had been buried for 120 years in a hidden tomb, his body surrounded by inextinguishable candles. Now a Brother had found the tomb, and the Brotherhood was openly announcing its existence and inviting learned men to become members . . .

The pamphlet caused widespread excitement, not least because it seemed to be a trumpet call announcing a new wisdom, no longer restricted by Aristotle and Galen. Since the pamphlet gave no address it was impossible for the many candidates to make their eagerness known, although many went to the trouble of publishing replies indicating their willingness to join. A second pamphlet, the *Confessio Fraternitatis,* a year later, kept the enthusiasm alive. Then, a year later, the third document appeared, a strange allegory called *The chemical wedding,* full of alchemical symbols. Scholars have been able to trace the authorship of this work to a minister named Johann Valentin Andreae. It seems probable that the Rosicrucians were a group of intellectual idealists who lived in Tübingen, and who, with the fervor of young men, hoped to start an intellectual revolution which never came about. But the legend has persisted down the centuries. The modern American organization, known as AMORC, has no kind of connection with the earlier group. However a belief has persisted that the "rosicrucians" had an esoteric psychological doctrine.

In *The Holy Blood and the Holy Grail,* Henry Lincoln alleges that Andreae actually created a network of secret societies; but his evidence, while interesting, is far from conclusive. CW

Bibliography

McIntosh, Christopher 1980: *The Rosy Cross unveiled.* London: Aquarian Press.

Lincoln, Henry, Baigent, Michael and Leigh, Richard 1982: *The Holy Blood and the Holy Grail.* London: Cape.

Yates, Frances 1972: *The Rosicrucian enlightenment.* London: Routledge & Kegan Paul.

A Christian Rosenkreutz Anthology. 1968. New York: Rudolph Steiner Publications.

rules The notion of rule is widely used in linguistics, philosophy and more recently psychology to explain the organization of behavior and its interpretation. In linguistics it has earned its greatest currency through the work of Chomsky, and in philosophy through the ideas of Wittgenstein. Rules may either be constitutive (in the sense of defining equivalent classes), generative (in the sense of defining constituent relations) or regulative (in the sense of defining actions which are permitted, prescribed or proscribed). Furthermore a rule may be inferred either through direct observation, articulation, recognition of infraction, or the application of sanction following infringement. (See ETHOGENICS.) PC

Bibliography

Chomsky, N. 1965: *Aspects of the theory of syntax.* Cambridge, Mass.: MIT Press.

Collett, P., ed. 1976: *Social rules and social behavior.* Oxford: Basil Blackwell; Totowa, N.J.: Rowman & Littlefield.

Shimanoff, S. 1980: *Communication rules.* New York: Sage.

Wittgenstein, L. 1953: *Philosophical investigations.* Oxford: Basil Blackwell; New York: Macmillan.

Russell, Bertrand (1872–1970) Russell was a logician, and his ideas in philosophy developed out of his ideas in logic (see ATOMISM). His early philosophical writings included several contributions to the philosophy of mind: an account of self-knowledge (1912 and 1914), an analysis of perceptual data (1912 and 1914b) and a critique of William James's BEHAVIORISM (1914a). He was strongly influenced by HUME and his theory of language was adapted very closely to Hume's theory of the mind. His main contribution to the philosophy of mind is a brilliant but hastily written book (1921), in which he tries to combine Hume's picture of the mind, derived from introspection, with behaviorism and depth psychology. He was arguably the greatest philosopher of this century and he also made important contributions to politics, economics and the discussion of the main social questions of his period. DP

Bibliography

Russell, Bertrand, 1912: *The problems of philosophy,* Oxford.

——— 1914a: *On the nature of acquaintance.* Reprinted in *Logic and knowledge.* ed. R.C. Marsh. London: Allen & Unwin.

——— 1914b: *Our knowledge of the external world.* London: Allen & Unwin.

——— 1921: *The analysis of mind.* London: Allen & Unwin.

*Ayer, A.J. 1972: *Russell.* London: Fontana.

Ryle, Gilbert (1900–1976) Wayneflete Professor of metaphysical philosophy in the university of Oxford, Ryle was one of the most influential philosophers of his generation. In the 1920s he became interested in philosophical methodology, and this led him to the study of philosophical logic, particularly the question of what distinguishes sense from nonsense, and of such philosophers as RUSSELL, HUSSERL and Frege, and later WITTGENSTEIN and the members of the Vienna Circle. Before the end of the second world war Ryle had come to some settled conclusions about the nature of philosophy (1932, 1938). Philosophy was essentially an inquiry into CONCEPTS and meaning with two intimately connected aims, one destructive and the other constructive. The former was to diagnose and remove fundamental conceptual confusions engendered by our tendency to be misled by certain superficial features of our language (1932). The latter (1938) was to enlighten us as to the nature of our concepts and their interrelations by a systematic investigation of what can and cannot be said without absurdity, and of which inferences are valid and which are not (See CONCEPT and CATEGORY). After the war his main concern was to illustrate these views by a sustained application of them to "some notorious and large-sized Gordian Knot". This he did in *The concept of mind* (1949), which was followed up by *Dilemmas* (1954), a work devoted to "the consolidation and diversification of what had been the meta-theme of *The concept of mind*". Latterly he wrote more on the philosophy of mind, especially in a series of papers concerned with "thinking", (1971, 1979). Because of his debunking of the "inner grotto" of the mind, he is often considered a philosophical behaviorist, although he himself denied the title. JMS

Bibliography

Ryle, G. 1932: Systematically misleading expressions. *Proceedings of the Aristotelian Society* 32.

——— 1938: Categories. *Proceedings of the Aristotelian Society* 38 189–206.

——— 1949: *The concept of mind.* London: Hutchinson; Totowa, N.J.: Barnes & Noble (1975).

——— 1954: *Dilemmas,* Cambridge: Cambridge University Press.

——— 1971: *Collected papers*. Vol. 2. London: Hutchinson.

——— 1979: *On thinking*. Oxford: Basil Blackwell; Totowa, N.J.: Rowman & Littlefield.

S

S–R, S–R–S, S–S models *See* behaviorism

sado-masochism Abnormal sexual practices (paraphilias) involving the infliction or suffering of pain. The term derives from the Marquis de Sade (1740–1814) in whose novel *Justine* sexual gratification was associated with pain, and L. von S. Masoch (1836–1895), an Austrian novelist who first described pain as a sexual stimulant. Sadism and masochism are found in both homo and heterosexual relationships, and in both sexes. Since these practices are complementary, clinical literature reports many couples, one of whom is a sadist and the other a masochist in a stable relationship; though masochism is apparently more common (Davison and Neale 1982).

Both psychoanalytic and conditioning theories have been proposed to explain the origins of the condition. The psychoanalytic theory connects sadism to castration fear (and so is inapplicable to women), while the conditioning theory depends on the rather implausible thesis that the arousal involved in inflicting and experiencing pain is similar to sexual excitement. Neither theory is well supported empirically. RHa

Bibliography

Davison, G.C. and Neale, J.M. 1982: *Abnormal psychology*, 3rd edn. New York: Wiley.

samsara The process of reincarnation, and endless change within a static world order. This transmigration of the individual through different lives was accepted as an obvious fact of worldly existence by most schools of Indian religion and philosophy. The exact circumstances of an individuals's rebirth depends upon his KARMA, which functions as a kind of spiritual capital. When he has accumulated a store of good karma, he is reborn in one of the many heavens, or in one of the higher castes of Hindu society. But when his merit has been exhausted through prolonged enjoyment of a higher state of life, or if he performs some bad actions, he is reborn in a lower caste or one of the many hells, where he suffers for some time until his debt is paid off.

Samsara is also used in a specialized sense to mean the transmigration in a single life from one set of circumstances to another. This is also governed by karma.

Samsara is thus a cycle of births and deaths, enjoyment and suffering, which carries on eternally unless the individual achieves LIBERATION. DA

Sartre, Jean-Paul (1905–80) Philosopher, novelist, playwright and political theorist, contributed to the philosophy of mind at the beginning of his career. He introduced the phenomenology of HUSSERL to France, concentrating on the imagination as the center of human freedom. In *L'Imaginaire* (1940) he analysed the relation between imagination, perception, art and action. In *L'Etre et le néant* (1945) he insisted on man's responsibility for his actions and his character, arising from his imaginative power to envisage possibilities as well as to perceive actualities. This belief in total freedom came to be regarded as typically Existentialist. To escape the oppressive burden of responsibility, people were said often to deceive themselves into believing that they were bound, by their character or their prior obligations. This deception was called *Mauvaise foi*. Sartre denied the existence of the unconscious mind, holding this itself to be an invention of bad faith. MW

Bibliography

Sartre, J.-P. 1948: *The psychology of imagination*. New York: Citadel Press.

——— 1956: *Being and nothingness*. New York: Philosophical Library.

Solomon, Robert C., ed. 1972: *Phenomenology and existentialism*. New York: Harper & Row.

satiation effects *See* emotion, satiation and starvation effects on

Saussure, Ferdinand de (1857–1913). Best known for his *Cours de linguistique générale* (1916 (*1960*)) which is based on his lectures at the University of Geneva and published by his students after his death. Among Saussure's most influential contributions to linguistics and psycholinguistics are:

(1) the distinction between "langue" and "parole" which is similar to that between COMPETENCE and PERFORMANCE

(2) the distinction between diachronic and synchronic language studies

(3) his distinction between paradigmatic and syntagmatic relations

(4) his concept of language as a system of interdependent terms in which the value of each term results only from the simultaneous presence of other terms

(5) his definition of the linguistic sign as consisting of a concept (signifié) and an acoustic image (signifiant) and his insistence that linguistic signs are arbitrary and linear. PM

Bibliography

Culler, Jonathan 1976: *Saussure*. Glasgow: Fontana.

Saussure, Ferdinand de, (*1960*): *Course in general linguistics*. London: Peter Owen.

schema Body of knowledge that provides a framework within which to locate new items of knowledge (plural *schemata* or *schemas*). Bartlett (1932) suggested that the schema is the active, organized setting within which new experiences are influenced by those previous reactions and experiences that are connected by some common aspect. In recent years interest in the schema has again become prominent in cognitive psychology and its role has been explored in, for example, the comprehension of text. This research has been influenced by work in ARTIFICIAL

INTELLIGENCE which emphasizes the importance of large schema-like data structures that have been termed *frames* or *scripts*. The development of different types of schema in children has been described by PIAGET. GVJ

Bibliography

Anderson, John R. 1980: *Cognitive psychology and its implications*, San Francisco: W.H. Freeman.

Bartlett, Frederic C. 1932: *Remembering: A study in experimental and social psychology*, London and New York: Cambridge University Press.

schizoglossia The term was introduced by Haugen (1963) to refer to the problems of speakers who are exposed to more than one variety of their own language. It reflects the fact that speaking is only partially a conscious process and that there can be a considerable gap between what speakers (want to) believe they are saying and their actual linguistic behavior (see DIGLOSSIA). PM

Bibliography

Haugen, Einar 1963: Schizoglossia and the linguistic norm. In *Monograph series on languages and linguistics* 15. Washington DC: Georgetown University Press.

schizophrenia A mental illness (or group of illnesses), in which there is a fundamental disturbance of the personality characterized by disturbances of thinking, motivation and mood together with DELUSIONS and HALLUCINATIONS, but in which cognition is normal. The peak incidence is in early adult life and approximately one per cent of adults suffer from it at some time in their lives. Amidst the wide range of symptoms and variability in their course, there are three basic groupings (1) acute syndrome, often precipitated by stress, with little chronic impairment (2) chronic schizophrenia with no acute episodes, and (3) acute episodes together with longterm abnormalities.

Schizophrenia may affect all aspects of the personality. The acute syndromes are characterized by positive psychological symptoms, such as DELUSIONS, HALLUCINATIONS and THOUGHT DISORDER as well as disturbance in mood and behavior. More chronic schizophrenia is dominated by negative symptoms which include social withdrawal, apathy, lack of volition and decreased emotional expression ("blunting of affect"). The symptoms are greatly worsened by lack of environmental stimulation, as in INSTITUTIONALIZATION. Four main clinical patterns have been described, although most recent evidence suggests that the subtypes cannot be clearly distinguished genetically or clinically:

1. *Hebephrenia* The prominent symptoms are changes of affect, shallowness of mood and thought disorder. Delusions and hallucinations are not obvious. It is said to begin in late adolescence or early adult life.

2. *Catatonia* Psychomotor symptoms of over or underactivity. Abnormal postures may be maintained for long periods or there may be stupor, excitement or abnormal movements. Said to have been common in the large asylums it is now rare.

3. *Paranoid* Most often seen with later onset, paranoid delusions are the most prominent symptom and personality is relatively well preserved. There is no clear distinction from "paraphrenia" of middle age or "late paraphrenia" of the elderly (see PARANOID STATES).

4. *Simple* Progressive decline in personality and social achievement without obvious psychiatric symptoms. The most doubtful category and one which it is difficult to diagnose.

The problem of definition
The greatest problem in describing schizophrenia is the difficulty in diagnosis, although most psychiatrists agree about patients with typical symptoms. The condition was first clearly identified by the German psychiatrist Emil Kraepelin (1919) who distinguished two major groups of psychiatric illness, dementia praecox and manic-depressive psychosis. In describing the former (later called schizophrenia), he emphasized the effects on personality, emotion and volition. Kraepelin based his account on descriptions of symptoms and observations of longterm outcome and his conclusions have remained the basis for all more recent concepts. Eugen Bleuler enlarged clinical understanding and also attempted to identify underlying basic symptoms. He introduced the term schizophrenia to emphasize "splitting" of psychic functions, and identified *fundamental* symptoms: disturbance of associations, thought disorder, changes in emotional reactions, autism. Inevitably the dependence of diagnosis upon psychopathological mechanisms rather than overt symptoms meant much less precision than in Kraepelin's approach. More recent attempts to define the concepts of schizophrenia have derived from these two different approaches. Schneider (1959) emphasized the importance of precise diagnosis and suggested the value of a number of symptoms of special diagnostic importance, "first rank symptoms". His criteria have been widely used in Europe and continue to have a major influence on later systems. This relatively narrow and precise definition is in contrast to the broader and vaguer definitions derived from Bleuler's account of psychological mechanisms which have been especially popular in the United States. In recent years increasing awareness of the problems caused by wide international variations in diagnostic criteria (WHO 1978) have led to considerable efforts to develop clear operational criteria. A number of overlapping definitions are available, the best known being that of the current American classification, DSM3 (American Psychiatric Association 1980). All these definitions require the presence of certain key symptoms and some also emphasize chronicity of course in terms of abnormal pre-illness personality or of prolonged duration of symptoms.

Related Syndromes Modern narrow definitions emphasize difficulties in classifying atypical illnesses. After careful examination some can be classified as AFFECTIVE DISORDER or PERSONALITY DISORDER while others can be placed in tentative categories such as PARANOID STATE. It is still uncertain whether there is an intermediate or subsyndrome of acute, good prognosis psychosis, precipitated by stress and characterized by persistent mood disturbance and perplexity. Among the overlapping terms are "good prognosis schizophrenia", schizophreniform state, cycloid psychosis, bouffée delirante and schizoaffective state. The last of these terms has been particularly widely used, both in this sense and also for conditions which satisfy diagnostic criteria for both schizophrenia and affective disorder.

Etiology Much the strongest evidence of predisposing factors comes from genetic studies. These show the occurrence of the condition in around 10 per cent of first degree relatives. Study of identical and non-identical twins and of children of a schizophrenic pair adopted at birth strongly suggest an inherited predisposition, although the mechanism and inheritance is uncertain (Shields 1978). However, it is clear that inheritance is not a complete explanation and this has encouraged much research on environmental factors, including social class, social deprivation and migration. Since FREUD's discussion (Freud 1958) of the autobiography of a paranoid judge, Schreber, there have been numerous psychodynamic theories but the most popular current interest is in the role of patterns of communications within the family (Wynne 1981). The central difficulty in evaluating hypotheses is that it is not possible to determine whether abnormal communication follows the onset of schizophrenia in a family member or precedes it. The limitations of retrospective evidence have led to "high risk research", that is prospective study of populations thought to have a greatly increased risk of schizophrenia. In addition to these *predisposing* factors there is evidence that physical factors and social stresses may precipitate the initial onset and relapse of illness. Study of mediating mechanisms is concentrated in two broad areas: first, psychological abnormalities in arousal, attention and thinking and secondly upon biochemical processes. Research in the latter area has been partly encouraged by advances in psychopharmacology. However, even though there is much evidence of the mode of action of antipsychotic drugs it cannot be concluded that similar mechanisms are the biochemical basis of schizophrenia. Most current interest centers on abnormalities in the neurotransmitter dopamine.

Prognosis The incorporation of evidence of chronicity in some diagnostic concepts makes it difficult to review and compare follow-up evidence. It would appear that about a fifth of patients suffering a first illness have a complete remission of symptoms and about a fifth have a poor prognosis with chronic or relapsing illness (M. Bleuler 1974). Others have further episodes of acute illness or social difficulties but manage with medical care and social support to live largely independent lives. Predictors of a good outcome are: sudden onset, good pre-morbid personality, good previous adjustment, and precipitation of the illness by an obvious stress. Prognosis is substantially affected by social influences. Understimulation encourages the signs of "institutionalization" whereas overstimulation (such as may be caused by stressful "life events" or stresses within families) may precipitate florid acute symptoms. There are some indications that the prognosis for social recovery is better in under-developed countries and this may be due to the better social support.

Treatment Treatment of the acute florid symptoms largely depends upon psychotropic medication, particularly the phenothiazine group, although sympathetic care is also essential. This is usually best provided in hospital. Patients with chronic handicaps or who have had recurrent illnesses require long-term treatment. This has two aims, the prevention of further acute episodes and rehabilitation to minimize chronic handicaps (Wing 1978). The former depends upon the reduction of social and family stresses and usually also upon long-term medication. Rehabilitation is primarily social although many patients also require maintenance medication for control of symptoms. The nature and complexity of their treatment plan will depend upon continuing clinical assessment. Those with the poorest outlook and the greatest handicaps may require considerable medical and social care over many years. A small minority will require sheltered employment and accommodation. The reform of the mental hospitals has rarely been accompanied by the development of adequate community services. This means that it is often difficult to provide the best long-term care for severely handicapped chronic patients. RAM

Bibliography

American Psychiatric Association 1980: *Diagnostic and statistical manual III.*

Bleuler, E. 1950: *Dementia praecox: the group of schizophrenias.* New York: International University Press.

Bleuler, M. 1974: The long term course of the schizophrenic psychoses. *Psychological medicine* 4, 244–54.

Freud, S. 1958: Psychoanalytic notes on a autobiographical account of a case of paranoia. *Standard edition of the psychological works of Sigmund Freud,* vol. XII. London: Hogarth; New York: Norton.

*Kaplan, H.I., Freedman and Sadock, B.J. 1980: *Comprehensive textbook of psychiatry.* 3rd ed. Baltimore: Williams and Wilkins.

Kraepelin, E. 1919: *Dementia praecox and paraphrenia.* Edinburgh: Livingstone.

Schneider, K. 1959: *Clinical psychopathology.* New York: Grune & Stratten.

Shields, J. 1978: Genetics. In *op. cit.* Ed. J.K. Wing.

*Wing, J.K., ed. 1978: *Schizophrenia: a new synthesis.* London: Academic Press.

World Health Organisation 1978: *Mental disorders: glossary and guide to their classification in accordance with the ninth revision of the international classification of diseases.* Geneva: WHO.

Wynne, L.C. 1981: Current concepts about schizophrenics and family relationships. *Journal of nervous and mental diseases* 169, 82–9.

school as a social organization This is a general concept which embraces a range of theoretical and methodological perspectives on the school as a complex social system which has a *structure* (a formal and informal organization, a system of management and administration, an allocation of roles with rights and duties etc.) and a *culture* (one or more systems of values, norms and sanctions among its members). From a psychological point of view these perspectives consider the impact of the school on the attitudes and achievements of individual teachers and pupils and on the interactions between individuals or groups of individuals.

The classic account of the school as a social system is that by Waller (1932), who pioneered many of the themes developed in later theory and research on the school – the distinctive culture of the school, the characteristics and social relations of the teachers, the transactions and conflicts between teachers and pupils, pupil subcultures, and the relations between the school and its local community. Waller skillfully combined functionalist, conflict and symbolic interactionist perspectives, showing that each was essential to an adequate account of the school as a social system.

Subsequent work lacks the coherence and range of Waller's book mainly because it treats in greater depth areas which Waller covered at a relatively superficial level. Later work, especially in the United States, initially specialized in the application of organization theory to the study of the school as a social system, drawing upon a large literature on other complex institutions such as hospitals and factories and on a burgeoning literature on bureaucracies in modern societies. This tradition continues, especially in North America, with a strong emphasis on functionalist theory and on quantification. Certainly this field is now highly fragmented, but it continues to yield applications for the management and administration of schools (see Davies 1982).

In Britain, by contrast, the dominant, but far from exclusive, preference has been for more ethnographic approaches (see Hammersley 1980) in which, under the influence of anthropology and symbolic interactionism, social psychological and microsociological concerns coalesce. Typically in ethnographic studies a single school, or one or more segments within a school, are closely examined, commonly with some attention to social class factors, in the spirit of Hollingshead's pioneering American investigation (1949). Of the smaller segments within the school as a social system, relations between the school principal and the teachers, and between the teachers and their colleagues, have until recent times been relatively neglected by ethnographers, whose primary focus has been TEACHER-PUPIL INTERACTIONS, pupil-pupil interactions and PEER GROUP influences. Usually ethnographic studies of the school rely heavily on naturalistic observation and qualitative evidence. Hargreaves (1967) examined the impact of streaming or tracking on teacher-pupil and pupil-pupil relations, with special reference to delinquency prone youth and DISRUPTIVE PUPILS, and making use of subcultural theory, group dynamics research and sociometric techniques. This approach to pupil differentiation has been consolidated by Ball (1981) in his study of a comprehensive school which introduced the organization of "mixed-ability" teaching. He offers a careful assessment of its impact on subject choice and pupil identity. In the United States, Jackson (1968) used ethnographic methods to elucidate the powerful impact of schools as social institutions on pupils, their feelings towards school and their consequent involvement or withdrawal. Because Jackson carefully related his analysis to more conventional psychological studies of pupils, his work exercised a profound influence on EDUCATIONAL PSYCHOLOGY, in part through the novel methodology and in part because it set psychological studies of pupils within a more adequate social psychological framework. Smith and Geoffrey (1968) used ethnographic methods for the more intensive study of classroom processes, paying special attention to teacher strategies and TEACHING TECHNIQUES. By 1979 in Britain Woods was able to offer a sophisticated account of pupil adaptations to school which greatly advanced the earlier and more simple division of pupils into "conformists" and "deviants", and to counterbalance this by an investigation of the ways in which a variety of teachers' adaptations to their situations are constrained by the social organization of the school.

In recent work, such as that by Sharp and Green (1975), the responses of teachers and pupils are set within a neo-marxist theoretical perspective, strengthening the links with macro-sociology but weakening the value for educational psychology. Complementing this, however, there has been a massive growth of classroom research which is essentially social psychological in character.

It is evident that the concept of the school as a social organization is now a vague, umbrella term under which an extremely wide range of theories, methodologies and substantive studies can be subsumed. In principle the school as a social organization could be a useful bridging concept between the sociological and psychological studies of schooling. Although there are notable continuities of theme pursued by these diverse studies, there has been little consistent theoretical development, and the absence of a cumulative set of empirical findings is striking: the different paths of both theory and empirical research seem to be diverging rather than converging. Since sociological work does not always overtly acknowledge the social psychological nature of its subject, educational psychologists have sometimes remained uninfluenced by research which carries a sociological label. These disciplinary boundaries are currently weakening and educational psychology is taking greater account of the vast literature on the school as a social organization. Rutter et al. (1979) in their study of school effectiveness, SCHOOL DIFFERENCES and EDUCATIONAL ATTAINMENT provide a good example of an influential psychological investigation which is likely to stimulate the interest of educational psychologists in the school as a social organization. DHH

Bibliography

Ball, S.J. 1981: *Beachside comprehensive*. Cambridge: Cambridge University Press.

*Davies, B. 1982: Organisational theory and schools. In *The social sciences in educational studies*, ed. A. Hartnett. London and Boston: Heinemann.

*Hammersley, M. 1980: Classroom ethnography. *Educational analysis* 2(2), 47–74.

Hargreaves, D.H. 1967: *Social relations in a secondary school*. London and Boston: Routledge & Kegan Paul.

Hollingshead, A.B. 1949: *Elmstown's youth*. London and New York: Wiley & Sons.

Jackson, P.W. 1968: *Life in classrooms*. London and New York: Holt, Rinehart & Winston.

Rutter, M. et al. 1979: *Fifteen thousand hours*. London: Open Books; Cambridge, Mass.: Harvard University Press.

Sharp, R. and Green, A. 1975: *Education and social control*. London and Boston: Routledge & Kegan Paul.

Smith, L. and Geoffrey, W. 1968: *The complexities of an urban classroom*. London and New York: Holt, Rinehart & Winston.

Waller, W. 1932: *The sociology of teaching*. New York: Wiley & Sons.

Woods, P. 1979: *The divided school*. London and Boston: Routledge & Kegan Paul.

school differences Many parents go to considerable lengths to place their children in particular schools thus demonstrating that they believe in the existence of school differences. Social researchers however have not always shared this belief, but rather have argued that apparent differences may result from variation in the social background and ability of pupils.

Large-scale American studies (e.g. Jencks 1973) failed to identify any school-related variables to account for differences in life chances. In comparison to individual characteristics and family background, they argued, school influence was trivial. (According to Jencks, school influence was less important than "luck".)

By their nature, however, these large scale studies focused only on relatively conspicuous school variables such as style of buildings, levels of resourcing and pupil-teacher ratios. They did not attempt to collect information on attitudes, values and styles of the teachers. Furthermore because they lacked information on pupil characteristics prior to secondary school entrance, they were unable to measure any increment in achievement which could be attributed to differences in effectiveness. Finally their findings are limited because of the use of verbal reasoning scores rather than measures of learning in subjects actually taught by schools.

More recent research in America and in the United Kingdom has re-opened the debate by demonstrating school differences in examination results (Brimer et al. 1978), delinquency (Power et al. 1972 and Gath et al. 1977) and attendance. The complex statistical study by Summers and Wolfe (1977) actually posed the question "Do schools make a difference?". After a series of analyses that utilized pupil-specific data gathered over several years of schooling they concluded that, even after allowing for a whole series of other influences, schools could make a difference.

The contribution to the debate by Rutter et al. (1979) is important for it attempted to control for intake variation to the schools. Having allowed for this, the researchers still found differences in outcome measures of attendance, behavior, delinquency and attainment between pupils from twelve inner-city schools. The need for such control is clear because Rutter et al. demonstrated substantial differences between the pupil intake to the schools studied. However, other researchers (Heath et al. 1980) have criticized the methodology and have argued that more careful control might have reduced the variation in the outcome measures. Replications of similar studies are needed to resolve the matter.

School differences in process – atmosphere, organization and style of teaching – have also been investigated both in the United States (Brookover et al. 1976) and in Britain (Rutter et al. 1979). The researchers have all argued that those differences are of crucial importance and are likely to have a direct effect on pupils' achievements. Further studies are needed to clarify these issues and to document the ways in which schools that are shown to be effective have created and sustained their pupils' achievements. PJM

Bibliography

Brimer, M.A. et al. 1978: *Sources of difference in school achievement.* Slough, Bucks: National Foundation for Educational Research.

Brookover, W.B. et al. 1976: *Elementary school climate and school achievement.* East Lansing: Michigan State University, College of Urban Development.

Gath, D. et al. 1977: *Child guidance and delinquency in a London borough.* Maudsley Monographs no. 24. Oxford: Oxford University Press.

Heath, A. et al. 1980: The seventy thousand hours that Rutter left out. *Oxford review of education* 6, 3–19.

Jencks, C. et al. 1973: *Inequality.* London and New York: Allen Lane.

Power, M.J. et al. 1972: Neighbourhood, school and juveniles before the courts. *British journal of criminology* 12, 111–32.

Rutter, M. et al. 1979: *Fifteen thousand hours.* London: Open Books; Cambridge, Mass.: Harvard University Press.

Summers, A.A. and Wolfe, B.L. 1977: Do schools make a difference? *American economic review.*

school failure Cannot be identified without some reference to the aims and objectives of education. However these are diverse, and their specification will vary considerably between individuals, social groups, cultures and countries. Furthermore many essential facets of education are not open to precise definition, measurement or evaluation. Much research on school failure has therefore had to use limited indices of education, such as competence in reading and computation or performance in public examinations. These indices have a measure of objectivity and are pertinent to education but cannot be equated with it. Other aspects of education, concerned with social behavior, knowledge of the world, self-sufficiency, independence of outlook and maintenance of mental health are arguably no less important but they are more difficult to define, objectify and assess.

In practice it is the broad spectrum of cognitive skills and knowledge that receives most attention in education. Children whose performance in such activities falls below the norm for their age group are considered as "failing", with those markedly below such a standard being identified as requiring special attention. Fully reliable methods of identifying school failure, even in these terms, do not exist, nor are there general prescriptions guaranteed to rectify it (see EDUCATIONAL ATTAINMENT; REMEDIAL READING, REMEDIAL MATHEMATICS). It is also difficult to specify the size of the problem. In the United Kingdom it has been estimated that some 20 per cent of the school population need some form of additional specialist attention during their school career but this estimate does not include children who meet the expected standard for their age but are capable of achieving very much more.

The possible reasons for less than optimal performance in school are numerous and varied and complex in their interactions, with the incidence, however defined, much more prevalent in boys than girls. In developing countries, where education is not freely or easily available, "school failure" as such is likely to be far less prevalent and more closely linked to physical health and nutrition.

In western developed countries it is estimated that about 2 per cent of the school population have moderate or severe learning difficulties attributable to their genetic endowment. However, it is being increasingly realized that such children can learn more and to greater effect if the teaching and learning experiences offered are appropriately structured in relation to existing skills and feasible objectives. The importance of early identification and appropriate action, to include increased involvement with parents, now receives much wider recognition. Regrettably, many educational systems still make insufficient provision for the continuing education of such children beyond their school years.

Other children are identified as failing in school because they lack the necessary component skills essential, for example, to be competent in reading (see REMEDIAL READING; READING: COGNITIVE SKILLS). Specific sensory and neurological deficits may contribute to such problems and in extreme cases perhaps cause them (see BLIND, THE: PSYCHOLOGY AND EDUCATION; HEARING IMPAIRED AND DEAF, THE PSYCHOLOGY AND EDUCATION; DYSLEXIC CHILDREN; LEARNING DIFFICULTIES). Some children who have had a learning disability nevertheless appear able to develop their own alternative strategies which enable them to achieve success.

Emotional stress and conflict, whether arising from organic factors, from family tensions or from poor relations with peers or teachers, may also contribute to school failure. Many normal children can experience difficulties with school work of course, but these often prove transient and remit spontaneously over time. The resilience of some children exposed to stress, or their ability to cope with it without any apparent disadvantage, require more investigation.

Many more children exist who appear normal in every respect except for their poor school performance. A disproportionate number of them come from low socio-economic group families living in the poorer city areas. This fact in itself provides no explanation, of course, and many exceptions are found that counter this general trend. Nonetheless the poor educational responses of such children has long caused concern to educationists and in recent years to central governments (see COMPENSATORY EDUCATION; EDUCATIONAL ATTAINMENT AND SOCIAL CLASS). Parental interest and involvement, particularly at the preschool stage, has been emphasized as important to later progress. Personality and temperamental characteristics are also relevant. Introverted children generally perform better than extroverts, at least at the secondary stage of their schooling. However, this could be partly a function of teaching style and the demands of an academic curriculum at this stage. The expectations of teachers as well as pupils have also been implicated (see EDUCATIONAL ATTAINMENT AND EXPECTATIONS). Other research has emphasized the importance of the child's orientation to learning (see EDUCATIONAL ATTAINMENT AND LOCUS OF CONTROL; LEARNED HELPLESSNESS). Children who play truant from school or who are delinquent usually fail in school but they also tend to come from the most disadvantaged sectors of the community (see ABSENCE FROM SCHOOL AND TRUANCY; DELINQUENCY). The effects of allergies, artificial additives in food and lead pollution from traffic fumes have recently been identified as other possible contributors to poor school performance and behavior. Simple explanations of school failure are therefore precluded by the number and complexity of interacting factors.

Learning has generally been found to be more efficient and better retained when it is based on intrinsic motivation – when the learning task elicits the natural curiosity and interests of the child. Extrinsic motivation is dependent on the use of external rewards or punishments and tends to be less effective. However, extrinsic motivation may provide the only basis or strategy that will induce learning some tasks, particularly in the early stages of development or at later stages when the task set may appear quite unrelated to any previous experience of the child (see COGNITIVE DEVELOPMENT: NON-PIAGETIAN THEORIES; PIAGET).

Schools and educational services may fail as well as pupils. The relevance of the school curriculum and the manner of its presentation obviously have crucial importance. Some countries and some schools seem more successful than others in providing valued alternatives to the prevalent academic emphasis. School organization and the management of pupils by their teachers is also being increasingly recognized as needing much closer examination (see SCHOOL DIFFERENCES; SCHOOL AS A SOCIAL ORGANIZATION).

Research on teaching, which may be considered the obverse of learning, remains inconclusive in offering solutions to the problem of school failure, because of the complexity of the interactions between teacher and pupil and the broader social context to learning (Entwistle, 1981). However, focussing on teaching rather than learning, by way of conclusion, may serve to highlight some of the more difficult issues that confront all parents, teachers and educational administrators concerned with reducing school failure and maximizing educational attainment. These may be summarized as follows:

(1) Children vary enormously in the rate and the manner in which they learn. Any educational provision to reduce school failure must take this into account.

(2) The requirement to teach groups in the classroom and to foster the development of individual children places extremely high demands on educational resources, particularly in relation to the personal qualities and skills of the teaching profession.

(3) Identifying children who are failing or who are likely to fail in school is a necessary first stage requirement but in itself resolves no problems.

(4) A more rigorous monitoring of the curriculum and its effectiveness in demonstrating relevance to the child and at least meeting basic employment demands in terms of literacy and numeracy, seem highly desirable.

(5) The acquisition of cognitive skills needed to reduce and prevent school failure cannot be divorced from their social context. However, it is often not possible to change this radically or quickly even when it appears patently desirable to do so. In such circumstances the only feasible alternative is to attempt to devise experimentally and pragmatically, learning programs tailored to the individual child that have some effect. Such an approach, which has already had some success in helping severely retarded children, requires not only competence in terms of the subject matter to be acquired but also specialized knowledge of the basic

psychological processes, involved, such as perception, learning, memory and reasoning. RM/AKW

Bibliography

Entwistle, Noel J. 1981: *Styles of learning and teaching*. Chichester and New York: John Wiley.

Holt, J. 1981: *Teach your own*. Brightlingsea, Essex: Lighthouse Books; New York: Delacorte Press, Seymour Lawrence.

Rutter, M. et al. 1979: *Fifteen thousand hours: secondary schools and their effects on children*. London: Open Books; Cambridge, Mass.: Harvard University Press.

school learning, evaluation The evaluation of effectiveness of school learning involves the attempt to judge the success and value of pupils' learning against specified criteria. In order to evaluate effectiveness, aims and objectives are needed against which pupils' performance is judged. This usually takes the form of specifying formal curricula and assessing pupils' knowledge or understanding of it, although there is also a "hidden" or informal curriculum which it is more difficult to evaluate. Techniques ranging from objective, quantitative measurement to more informal or qualitative description have been used for this purpose.

Until the 1970s, educational success in England was measured largely by national examinations, in particular the now defunct 11+ examination and the national GCE (General Certificate of Education) and CSE (Certificate of Secondary Education) examinations at 16+. In 1974 the Bullock committee made as the first of its principal recommendations the need for a system of monitoring, and the Assessment of Performance Unit (APU) was set up in 1975 as a unit within the Department of Education and Science (DES) to promote "the development of methods of assessing and monitoring the achievement of children at school". The APU is different from public examinations because its aim is to monitor national standards rather than assess individual learning. Using "light sampling" (i.e. testing about 2 per cent of all children) and an "item bank" of questions, the APU monitors national attainments in mathematics, language, science, aesthetics, and physical, personal and social development.

Whereas the centralized educational system of Britain is amenable to monitoring and public tests, the decentralized, highly local system in the US makes national monitoring difficult. The National Assessment of Educational Progress (NAEP) was set up by the federal government in 1967 to evaluate educational outcomes nationally for use in determining policy. Although national monitoring is an important part of educational evaluation, most evaluation of school learning aims at assessing individuals rather than large groups.

Tests

National Tests: The most widely-used and well-known technique of evaluating pupils' learning is still examinations, culminating in Britain at the end of the school career in the national public examinations (GCE and CSE) which attempt to measure the outcome of the educational process through a series of objective tests (NORMATIVE- AND CRITERION-REFERENCED TESTS). This is a national assessment, administered through different local examination boards, which caters for pupils considered to be sufficiently able to attempt courses leading to the national examination, normally about 60 per cent of the age cohort. Public examinations provide a summative or terminal assessment of the learned material, and claim high objectivity and validity (see TESTS, INTELLIGENCE). The criterion of validity they use is known as content validity, and involves describing a given body of knowledge and measuring the pupils' mastery of it, i.e. what they have learned. In the USA, there are no public tests administered to the majority of pupils but a variety of norm-referenced tests of academic skills are administered by local school boards and used for comparative purposes.

Local Tests: Many schools use their own internal examinations to assess pupils' learning; these tests may take place once a year or more frequently as part of continuous assessment and are set and marked by teachers. Objective tests (whether administered nationally through the examination boards or the DES in Britain, or locally through the school boards in the USA) for monitoring progress and evaluating the effectiveness of learning aim at high validity, objectivity, and reliability. Tests however tend to evaluate the "product" of learning rather than the "process", thereby missing out on an important aspect of education.

Examination results are only a small part of what are generally considered to be desirable outcomes. Bloom's taxonomy of educational objectives includes the cognitive, affective and psychomotor domains, but very few formal tests attempt to assess more than the cognitive "product". Research has shown (Raven 1977) that the vast majority of teachers, pupils and parents "want schools to foster such qualities as ... independence, the ability to make their own observations and learn without instruction, the ability to apply facts and techniques to new problems, to develop their characters and personality". Yet the fact that the product of learning is so much easier to define and evaluate than the process has led to a concentration on the cognitive areas of assessment.

Behavioral Observations: Partly for this reason, observational methods are sometimes used to evaluate learning, particularly with children under the age of eleven. Some "process" objectives refer to *specific activities* on the part of pupils rather than an increase in knowledge. For example the teacher may wish pupils to work collaboratively with one another. One direct way to assess whether such an objective is achieved is to observe and record children's classroom behavior. Galton and Croll (1980) used this method to study the effect of different kinds of teaching strategies in the primary school. Individual "target pupils" were observed for short periods to see whether they were working alone, with others, attending to or interacting with the teacher, or socializing among themselves. They found that pupils in a large sample of classrooms spent no more than 5 per cent of lesson time in group-work, despite exhortations of the Plowden Committee (1967) about the effectiveness of this form of learning.

Sylva, Roy and Painter (1980) used direct behavioral observation to assess the effectiveness of different kinds of preschool curriculum. They observed target children in a variety of preschools and found that those attending "structured" programs engaged in more imaginative pretend and problem solving play. In most observational studies classroom process is assessed and not the performance of individuals.

Informal school-based assessments: Teachers often devise less formal methods of measuring progress, although still striving for objectivity, when they assess course work and make pupil profiles. The teacher specifies the nature and amount of coursework to be assessed (and sometimes graded) and completes a profile on each pupil as part of a formative (as opposed to summative) assessment. "Formative assessment ... is an aid to teaching and learning, it takes account of work at present by looking back over the past in order to look forward to future development ... summative assessment tends to freeze time, to isolate performance and competence from their developmental context and, because it can be imagined to deal in absolute, objective values, lends itself to being thought of as a means of conclusively classifying people" (in Burgess and Adams 1980). Informal methods have the advantage of providing continuous feedback as part of the evaluation, and of including all the pupils and not just those who are college-bound. As well as assessing pupils' learning in this way, teachers are increasingly using self evaluation systems (Simons 1980) to evaluate the effectiveness of the whole curriculum and different teaching methods.

Pupil Self-assessment: In Britain Burgess and Adams (1980) describe an ambitious scheme whereby pupils are involved both in the planning (objectives) of the content of the curriculum and in the recording of outcomes (evaluation) of their education; "at the heart of our proposals is a statement which every sixteen-year-old will have on leaving school, showing his experience, competence, interests and purposes, which he can show to parents and employers alike". They propose that this system of evaluation should be nationally validated and accredited so that it carries the same validity and objectivity (and therefore status, particularly to those outside the education system) as the present public examinations. Developments along these lines provide evaluation of the effectiveness of the learning process as well as the product.

School Inspections and Investigations: Inspections are a means of evaluating the effectiveness of individual schools and often include examination of the results of the four methods listed above. In Britain a team of Her Majesty's Inspectors (HMI) or local advisers, visits a school for a few days to inspect different records, observe teaching and learning, interview staff and sometimes pupils, look at test results, and then publish a full report for the school and the Local Education Authority. In the US similar investigations into one or more schools may be undertaken by the School Board to evaluate effectiveness.

The means of evaluation will vary according to its purpose, which in turn depends on the role of those carrying it out. While evaluation of learning takes place throughout the school career, it is at 16–18 years that the issue becomes crucial. National evaluation, carried out in Britain by the Assessment of Performance Unit or by the examination boards and in the US by the National Assessment of Educational Progress, allows national monitoring of standards or objective assessment of individuals for purposes of selection. The cost of objectivity, validity and quantifiable outcome is the neglect of areas of unquestionable educational validity, such as Bloom's affective area, the exclusion of the less able school-leaver in Britain, and the neglect of a qualitative description of the process of education. Intrinsic evaluation, carried out by the school or by teachers in conjunction with pupils provides continuous feedback which may be used for diagnosis and guidance about the learning process, but may be vulnerable to the biases of subjectivity.

While evaluation implies judgment, though this may be self-judgment, accountability refers to the obligation to describe one's activities to anyone who has a legitimate interest in them and to meet certain obligations in the fulfillment of duty. In schools three levels of accountability can be distinguished – (i) moral accountability (to the clients); (ii) professional accountability (to oneself and colleagues); and (iii) contractual accountability (to the employers). This raises important questions as to what teachers are to be held accountable for. Is it possible to show that a teacher has succeeded or failed in stated objectives? Although the clarity of the objectives determines the efficiency of the evaluation, the educational process is sufficiently complex to make it difficult to assign responsibility when objectives are not achieved. For example, there has been at least one case in the United States of America in which a school-leaver has sued the State Department of Education for failure to instil basic competencies in him (the criterion of minimum competencies for school leavers is fairly widespread in USA). Although accountability depends on the evaluation of educational outcome, clearly accountability procedures must be concerned with factors which are under the control of teachers and are stated as objectives by the schools themselves.

Psychology has made its greatest contribution to education in constructing methods of evaluation. While psychology can contribute greatly to measuring the success of pupils' learning, it cannot determine the value; this is a moral and political decision.

See also SCHOOL FAILURE. KS/IL

Bibliography

Bloom, B. ed. 1956: *The taxonomy of educational objectives.* London: Longman.

*Burgess, T. and Adams, E. 1980: *Outcomes of education..* London: Macmillan.

Galton, M. and Croll, P. 1980: 'Pupil progress in basic skills'. In *Progress and performance in the primary classroom*, ed. M. Galton and B. Simon. London: Routledge & Kegan Paul.

Holt, M. 1982: *Evaluating the evaluators.* London: Hodder and Stoughton.

Raven, J. 1977: *Education, values and society.* London: Lewis; New York: Psychological Corp.

Simons, H. 1980: Process evaluation in schools. In *Accountability and education*, ed. C. Lacey and D. Lawton. London and New York: Methuen.

Sylva, K., Roy, C., Painter, M. 1980: *Childwatching in playgroup and nursery school.* London: Grant McIntyre.

school phobia (Sometimes known as school refusal.) The principal manifestation of a neurotic disorder, characterized by severe reluctance to attend school. Reports of prevalence among children attending child guidance clinics in the United Kingdom range from 1 per cent to 8 per cent; there is no authoritative account of the overall prevalence within the country. Disturbed family relationships are reported in many cases. Hersov (1977) cites possible causes of school refusal, and emphasizes that it should be seen as occurring against a background of a variety of psychiatric disorders. The problem can occur at any age, though acute onset is seen most often in younger children. Common precipitating factors are a change of school or class, death or disturbance in the family, and illness. Clinicians have differed on the frequency of separation anxiety. The prognosis is good, irrespective of type of treatment, provided that the child is pre-adolescent, and is referred soon after onset, and that the school refusal is not associated with serious social problems. (See also ABSENCE FROM SCHOOL.) DMG

Bibliography

Hersov, L. 1977: School refusal. In *Child psychiatry: modern approaches*, ed. M. Rutter and L. Hersov. Oxford: Blackwell Scientific; Philadelphia: Lippincott.

school psychological services: general The scope, nature and organization of school psychological services vary so greatly throughout the world that no pattern or list of services is typical. Factors influencing services include the industrial level of the country, the proportion of school-age children attending schools, the extent to which individual human services are encouraged by a country's values and whether schools are located in urban or rural areas. In many countries it is difficult to determine what services should be called psychological because of overlap among the services offered by psychologists, social workers, counselors and special educators.

Among countries offering comprehensive services, including screening, assessment, counseling and consultation on pupil learning and adjustment, some tend to offer services through child guidance or specialized clinics; for example, Finland, Iceland, Israel, New Zealand and the United Kingdom. In Denmark, Norway and Sweden psychologists work directly in schools. In the United States and Canada services vary from nonexistent to sophisticated. Urban areas tend to have centralized district-wide arrangements. Moderately sized school districts mostly assign psychologists directly to a limited number of schools. Rural areas have cooperative service centers for a number of districts.

In countries offering services limited mainly to general guidance and assessment for special education, the clinic model is most often used by Australia, Belgium, Japan, Panama and Turkey (but only in the two largest cities). No clear patterns exist in Austria, France, West Germany, South Africa or Switzerland. Services of an even more limited kind appear to be offered in Poland and Mexico.

In some industrialized countries, school psychological services are of a very limited nature or nonexistent; for example, Greece (except in private schools), Italy, Spain and Taiwan. There are no known direct services in the USSR or the People's Republic of China.

Except as already noted, little is known to exist in most of the developing countries and regions, such as North and Central Africa, the Middle East, India, Southeast Asia, the Philippines and Latin and Central America. Some countries in these regions have shown interest in organizing services. Egypt, for instance, has opened guidance centers in some universities. Brazil, Peru and Venezuela appear to be encouraging school services. JIB

Bibliography

Catteral, C. D. 1982: International school psychology: Problems and promise. In *The handbook of school psychology*, ed. C. R. Reynolds and T. B. Gutkin. New York and Chichester: John Wiley.

school psychological services: in North America School psychological services have expanded greatly in North America during the last decade. This has come about because of public pressure and subsequent legislative mandate for in-school psychological services for children with special educational problems and needs. Virtually all larger school districts and most school districts in North America now employ school psychologists who possess at least a master's degree. School districts vary from providing extensive school psychological services to providing services at minimal levels and referring most cases to general agencies. The responsibilities of these professionals include administering a variety of diagnostic tests, supervising the conduct of large scale standardized tests, the counseling of teachers and parents on the values and limitations of psychological assessments and interventions, the counseling of students about available psychological services, delivering psychological interventions for minor psychological disturbances (e.g. acting out) and advising school administrations about how psychological principles can be used in schools. School psychologists often play a prominent role in special education units, such as classes for teaching disabled students. Training in school psychology usually includes work in psychological assessment, clinical psychology, developmental psychology, education and special education. Field work is almost always a part of the training. The number of training programs in school psychology, (especially doctoral programs) is increasing in the United States and Canada, although the absolute number of such programs is small relative to the number of clinical and experimental programs. MP

school psychological services: in the United Kingdom Schools' Psychological Services are formed by educational psychologists employed in the United Kingdom by local education authorities. These psychologists usually have a background of experience in teaching as well as professional qualifications in psychology. Their central functions have traditionally been the identification, assessment and treatment of individual children with special educational needs and emotional or behavioral problems. They offer a service of advice and consultation to schools and other agencies on these matters. They are also frequently involved in counseling parents, in-service training of teachers, the development of provision for children with special needs, advice on children to social services departments and systems intervention (see SYSTEMS THEORY) in institutions providing for children.

The first such psychologist employed by a local authority in the United Kingdom was Cyril Burt who was appointed by the London County Council as Schools Psychologist in 1913. Although other authorities appointed psychologists to similar posts between the wars, there was more rapid development in the parallel provision of multi-disciplinary child guidance clinics in which educational psychologists played a part. The 1944 Education Act defined the handicaps for which special educational provision could be made in a more comprehensive way than had existed previously. The need for objective and manifestly expert advice on the selection of children for this provision was a major factor in the expansion in Schools' Psychological Services that followed. In 1955 there were 140 educational psychologists (full-time equivalent) employed in England and Wales; by 1965 the figure was 326 (i.e. one for every 24,000 school children); by 1979 it was over 900. Services in Scotland were always more generously staffed. In the early 1960s there were shortages of trained educational psychologists, so that a government committee was commissioned to report on their qualifications and the facilities for training (Department of Education and Science 1968). More training courses were established. Once the supply of educational psychologists was assured, local authorities were advised that this profession should be consulted in all cases when children's special educational needs were assessed (Department of Education and Science, 1975). With a new Act of Parliament covering children's special educational needs a requirement to take psychological advice on the subject will become mandatory (Department of Education and Science 1980).

Schools' Psychological Services therefore have an assured support role in educational administration. But many Educational Psychologists are dissatisfied with this limited role and consider that psychology has a great deal more to offer in the field of education. Some services have developed a wider range of functions in relation to schools and the community (Loxley 1978; Acklaw 1979). The Schools' Psychological Service of the future is likely to be still more diverse in its activities while retaining certain core responsibilities for work with individual children. TIC

Bibliography

Acklaw, J. 1979: Educational psychology: am I deluded? *Bulletin of the British Psychological Society* 32, 283–4.

Department of Education and Science. 1968: *Psychologists in education services.* (The Summerfield Report). London: Her Majesty's Stationery Office.

Department of Education and Science. 1975: *The discovery of children requiring special education and the assessment of their needs.* Circular 2/75. London: Her Majesty's Stationery Office.

Department of Education and Science. 1980: *Special needs in education.* London: Her Majesty's Stationery Office.

Loxley, D. 1978: Community psychology. In *Reconstructing educational psychology*, ed. B Gillham. London: Croom Helm.

Williams, P. 1974: The Growth and Scope of the Schools' Psychological Service. In *The practice of educational psychology*, ed. M. Chazam et al. London: Longman.

school *See above, and also* absence from school and truancy

Schopenhauer, Arthur (1788–1860) A German post-Kantian philosopher whose main work, *Die Welt als Wille und Vorstellung* (1818, enlarged edition 1844, English trans. 1958), included a theory of human nature that was to have profound repercussions within the field of psychology. Not only did Schopenhauer's doctrine of the identity of body and will constitute a powerful challenge to the tenets of traditional psycho-physical dualism; he also provided an account of motivation which in important respects foreshadowed psychoanalytical conceptions of the mind and its workings. He maintained that subjective introspection was an unreliable guide to the true character of our desires and intentions, the latter often taking shape beneath the level of consciousness and independently of rational deliberation or control. Schopenhauer can be said to have anticipated Freud – as Freud himself admitted – both in his stress upon the role of the unconscious in human life and in the unique status he accorded to sexuality as a fundamental, if largely unacknowledged, source of behavior. PLG

Bibliography

*Fox, Michael, ed. 1980: *Schopenhauer: his philosophical achievement.* Brighton: Harvester Press; Totowa, N.J.; Barnes & Noble.

*Gardiner, Patrick 1963: *Schopenhauer.* London: Penguin.

*Hamlyn, D.W. 1980: *Schopenhauer.* London and Boston: Routledge & Kegan Paul.

Schopenhauer, A. 1958: *The world as will and representation*, translated by E.F.J. Payne. Colorado: Falcon's Wing Press.

scientific management The term used by Frederick Taylor and his followers (e.g. the Gilbreths) to describe a new approach to MANAGEMENT developed at the turn of the century. This school argued that decisions should be made scientifically (based on experimentation and quantitative analysis) rather than by tradition or rule of thumb. In addition it was claimed that there was a fundamental identity of interest between workers and management in that both would benefit from high productivity, low costs and higher wages. The techniques of scientific management included: time and motion study, standardization of tools and equipment, the use of tasks or assigned goals, large bonuses for task accomplishment, work simplification and extreme specialization, individualized work, management responsibility for training, scientific selection, shorter hours of work and rest pauses. Scientific management was enormously influential in later management thought and in personnel management (Wren 1979). Many criticisms have been made of Taylor and his followers but the majority of these are not entirely justified (see Locke 1982). EAL

Bibliography

Kelly, J.E. 1982: *Scientific management, job redesign and work performance.* London: Academic Press.

Locke, E.A. 1982: The ideas of Fredrick W. Taylor: an evaluation. *Academy of management review* 7, 14–24.

Taylor, F.W. 1911 (*1967*): *The principles of scientific management.* New York: Norton.

Wren, D.A. 1979: *The evolution of management thought.* 2nd edn. New York: Wiley.

search image A term with a variety of meanings. It is sometimes used in the context of a predator becoming more likely to eat a particular kind of prey as the result of experience: it might be said, for instance, that a bird which had learnt that a certain type of insect was good to eat had "adopted a search image" for that insect. The term is also used in a more restricted sense, reserving it for cases where there is evidence of a predator actually improving its ability to see camouflaged prey against its background. "Adopting a search image" here would be equivalent to learning to "break the camouflage" of the prey and implies a definite perceptual change on the part of the predator. (See also PREDATION.) MSD

Bibliography

M. Dawkins 1974: Perceptual changes in chicks: another look at the the Search Image concept. *Animal behaviour, 19,* 575–82.

second language acquisition A study closely associated with applied psycholinguistics (Slama-Cazacu 1976, Rieber 1979) and, in the case of untargeted second language acquisition, the development of pidgin and creole languages (see CREOLIZATION). For most of its history the study of second language acquisition has been dependent on prevailing psychological and linguistic theories, as well as on the requirements of foreign language teachers.

During the second half of the nineteenth century the development of second language skills was seen, under the impact of faculty psychology, to be a form of mind training which could promote concentration, reasoning and remembering. Both classicial and modern languages were taught according to the grammar-translation method, involving the memorization of grammatical rules, inflectional paradigms and vocabulary lists. Errors were regarded as signs of insufficient training. Grammatical correctness was the principal aim and language learning was not seen as involving the acquisition of wider communicative skills.

Around the turn of the century there was a growing body of opinion that second language acquisition was basically the same as first language acqusition and should therefore be taught accordingly. An application of this view is the direct method of second language teaching. Teaching is carried out entirely in the foreign language with no memorization of rules or learning of vocabulary via translation. Critics have pointed out that this method encourages inaccurate fluency in a second language.

Whereas both the faculty view and the view that first and second language acquisition are basically identical were founded on extremely limited experimental evidence, behaviorist psycholinguists began systematically to investigate second language acquisition during the 1950s. The central assumption of the behaviorists was that language is a system of verbal habits learnt by a process of building associations between concepts and sound structures. Learning was viewed as a mechanical process of making the right connections between a stimulus and the desired response.

As the second language learner already possessed well established native speech habits, transfer from L_1 (the mother tongue) to L_2 (the target or second language) could be expected in the form of either facilitation or interference. By carefully avoiding areas of contrastive difficulties (see CONTRASTIVE ANALYSIS OF LINGUISTIC SYSTEMS) it was hoped that errors in second language acquisition could be reduced to a minimum.

The behaviorist view of second language acquisition has been very influential, particularly in the derived audiolingual method of second language teaching, which has four main characteristics.

(1) Speaking rather than writing is taken as the primary manifestation of language. In the ideal classroom teaching proceeds along the natural hierarchy of listening, speaking, reading and writing.
(2) Second language acquisition differs from first language acquisition. Constructions may not be required in the same order.
(3) New linguistic habits are acquired by mimicry-memorization and pattern drilling, preferably in a language laboratory.
(4) Languages are invariant systems of habits such as described in a structuralist grammar, context-determined variation being regarded as non-significant and hence not part of the acquisition process.

The behaviorist view of language acquisition came under attack during the 1960s in the wake of Chomsky's contributions to psycholinguistics (see Chomsky 1959). Chomsky argued that behaviorist explanations could not account for the most basic aspect of human language, its creativity. The transformational cognitive criticisms of behaviorist accounts of language acquisition include:

(1) Language is stimulus free and innovative; an S-R model cannot capture the processes underlying acquisition.
(2) Speakers internalize highly abstract grammars without having been given explicit rules.
(3) Individual languages are not unique and randomly different but manifestations of more abstract universal principles of language; second language learners have (at least partial) access to such universal knowledge.
(4) Competence underlies performance. Therefore students must know the rules of a language before they can perform in it.

No full cognitive account of second language acquisition

has been developed, and the overall impact of transformational-generative grammar on second language teaching was accordingly minor.

By the late 1970s it had become clear that second language skills consisted of more than abstract competence, instead communicative competence was made a central concept, with some important consequences for second language research:

(1) Interest developed in the systematic aspects of learner's errors (cf. error analysis, interlanguage)
(2) The relationship between linguistic variability and language external factors was investigated (cf. LANGUAGE: VARIATION THEORIES)
(3) Large-scale longitudinal studies were undetaken.

In spite of some progress, a considerable amount of pre-theoretical work remains to be carried out. At present, research is somewhat compartimentalized. The questions which have received most attention include:

(1) The differences between first and second language acquisition.
(2) The question of a "universal syllabus"
(3) The role of motivation and related factors.

The differences between first and second language acquisition are related to differences in the critical learning age as well as the linguistic functions of the target language. Madden et al. (1974) have found significant differences between child first and second language acquisition, but no great distinction between adult and child second-language acquisition. Thus, it appears that the variable of learning age cannot explain differences in acquisition (see also GENIE).

A possible alternative explanation which is, however, in need of further substantiation is that differences between L_1 and L_2 acquisition are related to the *functions of language*.. Halliday (1974) has suggested that the functional development in first language acquisition proceeds as follows:

instrumental (function)
directive
phatic
expressive
heuristic
metalinguistic
poetic
referential (cognitive)

(Note that the names used to denote these functions differ from Halliday's original ones). Mühlhäusler (1980:47) suggests a very different hierarchy for natural second language acquisition, and the development of untargeted pidgin languages:

referential (cognitive) function
directive
heuristic
expressive
phatic
metalinguistic
poetic

Should structural development turn out to be dependent on functional development this could explain many of the differences between first and second language acquisition.

The close similarity between child and adult second language learning suggests that there may be an inbuilt "syllabus" which is activated in this situation and much recent research into pidginization and *inter-language* phenomena is designed to determine its nature. Research to date (see Corder and Roulet 1977) suggests that:

(1) the order in which new L_2 constructions are acquired is independent of the structures of L_1 and L_2
(2) L_2 learners make errors even where contrastive analysis would suggest facilitation.
(3) the nature of L_1 and L_2 can account for differences in the speed of learning.

Whereas such findings support the view that L_2 acquisition is a creative and universally determined process, there are some important restrictions:

(1) a distinction needs to be made between second language acquisition as a natural subconscious process and second language learning, i.e. the result of overt instruction. The extent to which the mastery of a second language involves "acquisition" and "learning" depends on such factors as motivation, age of the learner, relatedness between L_1 and L_2 and various others.
(2) in the absence of a formal learning context, L_2 learners will end up with a fossilized pidgin rather than a fully elaborated version of the target language.

The very complexity of the innate syllabus means that only descriptions of small parts are available at present. As the interrelationship between the various developing parts of *grammar* becomes better known valuable suggestions can be given to applied linguistics.

Second language acquisition does not take place in a social vacuum, though some classrooms may approach this situation. Much recent research has concentrated on the relationship between the learner as a social being and the learning or acquisition process. It appears that the two principal factors involved are individual differences between learners and differences in the learning context.

Individual differences said to influence second language acquisition include general learning ability, phonetic coding ability, grammatical sensitivity, inductive learning ability and associative memory (see Ingram 1975). It is not clear whether such factors affect the implicational order postulated as underlying the universal syllabus or merely the speed with which learning proceeds. This also applies to motivation, a factor which has received considerable attention, in particular Lambert's distinction (1967) between instrumental and integrative motivation. Instrumental motivation refers to the learner's desire to better him or herself materially by means of acquiring a new additional language, whereas integrative motivation refers to the desire to get to know and to become friendly with the speakers of another language. According to Lambert, an integrative motivation is more likely to lead to successful second language acquisition, though McNamara (1973) adduces a number of counter-examples, e.g. the fact that language shift such as that from Irish to English (see BILINGUALISM; LANGUAGE DEATH) has often been accompanied by unfavorable attitudes towards the conquering peoples and their language.

Factors external to the learner include hours spent in the classroom, size of class, teaching method, personality of instructor and others (cf. Fatham 1976).

It is impossible at this point to present a view of second language acquisition which integrates the various findings outlined here. However, with the shift in emphasis towards the description of actual speech rather than idealized abstract constructs in psycholinguistics and renewed interest in the speaker's performance, it may not be long before such an integrated view emerges.

See also FIRST LANGUAGE ACQUISITION. PM

Bibliography

*Chastain, Kenneth 1971: *The development of modern language skills.* Chicago: Rand McNally.

Chomsky, Noam 1959: Review of B.F. Skinner's *"Verbal behaviour". Language* 35, 26–58.

*Corder, S. Pit and Roulet, E., eds 1977: *The notions of simplification, interlanguages, and pidgins and their relation to second language pedagogy.* Geneva: Librairie Droz.

Fathman, Ann K. 1976: Variables affecting the successful learning of English as a second language. *Tesol Quarterly* 10, 433–49.

Halliday, Michael A.K. 1974: *Explorations in the functions of language.* London: Edward Arnold.

Ingram, Elisabeth 1975: Psychology and language learning. In *The Edinburgh course in applied linguistics* vol. 2, ed J.P.B. Allen and S.P. Corder. Oxford University Press.

Lambert, Wallace E. 1967: A Social Psychology of Bilingualism. *Journal of Social Issues* 23, 91–109.

Madden, C., Bailey, N. and Krashen, S. 1974: Acquisition of function words by adult learners of English as a second language. In *Papers from the Fifth Annual Meeting of the North Eastern Linguistic Society*, Harvard University Press: 234–24.

McNamara, John 1973: Attitudes and learning a second language. In *Language attitudes*, ed. R.W. Fasold and R.W. Shuy. Georgetown University Press, Washington D.C.

*Mowrer O. Hobart 1979: *Psychology of language and learning.* New York: Plenum.

Mühlhäusler, Peter 1980: "Structural expansion and the notion of creolization". In *Theoretical orientations in Creole studies*, ed. Albert Valdman and Arnold Highfield. New York and London: Academic Press 19–56.

Rieber, R.W., ed. 1979: *Applied psycholinguistics and mental health.* New York: Plenum.

*Rivers, Wilga M. 1964: *The psychologist and the foreign language teacher.* Chicago: University of Chicago Press.

Slama-Cazacu, Tatiana 1976: Applied psycholinguistics: its objects and goal. In *Proceedings of the Fourth International Congress of Applied Linguistics*, 27–64, ed. G. Nickel. Stuttgart: Hochschulverlag.

second messenger systems. *See* adenyl cyclase, cAMP and second messenger systems

selection *See* personnel selection; evolution

self: philosophical usage The dominant theory of self in western philosophy is plain enough: each of us is an incorporeal self or MIND; all of our psychological states are states of this self; and each of us has absolutely certain, though private, knowledge of it and its states whenever they occur.

This view, given embryonic form by St Augustine (*De quantitate animae*, chs. XIII–XIV; 400–22, bk. X; 413–26, bk. XI), owes its popularity to DESCARTES, who defended it with fascinating though perhaps specious arguments. A famous rationale emerges from Descartes's search in several works, for something he could know without any risk of error. It will be a convenience to adopt his terminology, and classify all our multifarious mental processes and states as forms of thinking (*cogitationes*). Accordingly, if someone feels chilled, experiences disappointment, indulges in phantasies, doubts something, seems to perceive objects – when objects are on display or when he is hallucinating or dreaming – then we say he is thinking. Now Descartes's reasoning proceeds approximately as follows: I could be mistaken if I assumed the existence of any material thing, including the body I call "mine". For instance, I might be dreaming when I believe, apparently on the basis of conclusive evidence, that my hand is here under my gaze. But even if I am constantly deluded, I cannot be wrong when I suppose that I am thinking – however erroneous or muddled my thinking is. More important, I cannot be wrong in supposing that I exist. Descartes goes on to draw four exciting but debatable conclusions: (i) I *know* that this "I" or self exists and thinks; (ii) specifically, I have some kind of direct experience or *introspective* knowledge of it and its operations; (iii) because I may be deluded about everything else, I do *not* know whether this "I" or self has any characteristics besides thinking; so the safe course is to say that it *only* thinks; (iv) inasmuch as I could be mistaken regarding my body, I do not know whether it exists; yet since I know my self exists, self and body must be distinct, and self non-bodily.

This concept of self was taken over, with appropriate additions by many subsequent theorists of PERSONAL IDENTITY. Their main further contentions were: (v) I manage to remain one and the same individual because my self endures uninterruptedly and unaltered throughout my career; (vi) I know that it does this because I periodically introspect my self. Bishop Butler evokes this enriched theory when he declares that "our ... bodies are no more ourselves, or part of ourselves, than any other matter around us". As for the *bona fide* self, he says: "upon comparing the consciousness of one's self ... in any two moments, there ... immediately arises to the mind the idea of personal identity ... reflecting upon ... my self now, and ... my self ... years ago, I discern they are ... the same self" (1736, ch. 1, dissertation 1).

HUME undermined most of this doctrine by examining claims (ii) and (vi) – asking, in effect, what Butler's "consciousness of one's self" might be like. What is one conscious *of*? In Hume's jargon: we seem to have no "idea of *self* ... For, from what impression could this idea be derived?" (1739, bk. I, part IV, sec. VI). But it might be argued that episodes of thought must belong to something? These and other "perceptions" are, however, "separable from each other ... and have no need of anything to support their existence"; we have no idea "after what manner ... they belong to self", how they are "connected with it". So Descartes suggested that we know with the greatest possible certainty that our self exists. But Hume's request for details about it and our supposed knowledge of it casts doubt on the whole theory, and should make us wonder whether the Cartesian term "self" is even intelligible. Of course Hume admits that his own proposal, that "the mind" or self is "nothing but a bundle ... of different perceptions", is barely cogent.

Some of Hume's successors adamantly reasserted the Descartes–Butler analysis. Thomas Reid insisted that the "self or I, to which [my thoughts] belong, is permanent, and has the same relation to all the ... thoughts ... which I call mine" (1785, Essay III, ch. IV). KANT agreed with Hume that there is no introspective or other knowledge of a self, but he argued that we necessarily regard our thoughts as belonging to a self – which we consider but do not know to be distinct from our bodies (1787, B157, B404–8). Finally, some twentieth century philosophers – RUSSELL, the early WITTGENSTEIN, and Moritz Schlick – tried to develop a variant of Hume's "bundle": the "no-ownership" theory of self (for references and criticism see Strawson 1958).

One cannot help inquiring, incidentally, why nearly all these debaters serenely ignored the way in which people carry on everyday discourse with the pronoun "I" and the noun "self". This might have shaken some theorists' confidence, for example, that the "I" or self must be a ghostly mind exclusively given over to thought and other supposedly ethereal pursuits. When people bathe themselves, dress themselves, look at themselves in a mirror, paint portraits of themselves, feed or starve themselves, could the self in question be a mind? The self they wash, etc., surely is a flesh and blood human being. Even when people pity themselves, condemn themselves, or betray themselves, more than a Cartesian phantom is involved. The noun "self" may turn up when no mental phenomena are in question. Some flowers are self-pollenating, some engines self-lubricating and some watches self-winding. Overall, then, the traditional account ignores many of the ordinary uses of the word "self". Against this the objection can of course be raised that people regard some aspects of their selves as more fundamental than others, and the parts of themselves they wash or offer to their fathers to be spanked are not necessarily as central as some of the inner states they cherish as their essential "selves". Naturally the slippery uses of words such as "self" in everyday speech can be a dangerous guide for philosophers. Cathy and Heathcliff in *Wuthering Heights* seemed to consider, somewhat romantically, that they had a sort of common self, while some people are said to experience affronts to their friends or property as literal affronts to themselves.

Nevertheless, many recent philosophers have assumed that everyday uses of language are at once a torch and something to be elucidated. Drawing on their novel insights into the logic of common speech they have replaced the immaterial thoughtful self with an embodied person who takes vigorous physical action and reasons out loud, at length and in public. But a new enigma has developed about how to analyse such a person's self-referential cognition, talk and purposive behavior. Suppose I am N.N., until yesterday chieftain of the local Mafia organization. Chagrined that I did not win re-election, I consider shooting myself. I announce my morbid thoughts, and then act on them. What does "myself" mean in this story? One cannot substitute my name, "N.N.", or a description that only fits me, "the recently deposed local Mafia chieftain". I might not recall that I am N.N. or the outgoing capo, although I can hardly have any difficulty in identifying the self which is myself. It is also, and obviously, not necessarily the case that *if* one were planning to do away with N.N. or the last Mafia leader, one would be planning to do away with himself. In a novelette one could hire a killer to murder someone described in a particular way without realizing that the description fitted oneself, or would do so by the time the killer got to work. It is certainly possible that one might misidentify an individual who is the object of one's hostile thoughts, exactly by misdescribing him. But while one might also misdescribe oneself one cannot so readily misidentify oneself and prescribe the wrong self. This is the sort of problem considered to be important by many modern philosophers who write about the self (see Perry 1979 and essays 1–5 of Diamond and Teichman 1979).

The relevance of such discussions to psychological theories of the self is that they frequently treat a person's self in terms of his self-concept. This is the sum of descriptions one would take to be true of oneself. According to many psychologists such descriptions necessarily situate one in a social world, as a person among persons. They do this because they are learnt from others and are not logically only applicable to oneself. What can truly be said of oneself can also, in principle, be truly said of someone else. But these modern philosophical discussions suggest that though one may describe and misdescribe oneself and others using similar terms and with similar liability to error, one's ability to identify oneself is necessarily not reliant on these descriptions in the way that one's ability to identify others may be. Hence, for all its vulgar embodiment, a person's relation to and cognition of himself does seem to have certain unique features, and these features do seem to be connected with incorrigibility and certainty. This of course was the point, although not the issue, at which Descartes began.

IGT

Bibliography

Augustine, St.: *De quantitate animae (On the greatness of the soul)*. Trans. J.M. Colleran. Ancient Christian Writers vol. 9. New York: Paulist-Newman Press 1950.

———: *De trinitate (On the trinity)*. Trans. J.J. O'Meara, Fathers of the Church vol. 45. Washington: Catholic University Press 1963.

———: *De civitate dei (The city of God)*. Trans. J.J. Wand. Oxford: Oxford University Press 1963.

Butler, J. 1736 (*1897*): The analogy of religion. In *Works of Bishop Butler*, ed. W.E. Gladstone. Oxford: Oxford University Press.

Diamond, C. and Teichman, J., eds. 1979: *Intention and intentionality*. Brighton: Harvester Press; Ithaca, New York: Cornell University Press.

Hume, D. 1739 (*1888*): *A treatise of human nature*, ed. L.A. Selby-Bigge. Oxford: Oxford University Press.

Kant, I. 1787 (*1929*): *Critique of pure reason*. Trans. Norman Kemp Smith. London: Macmillan.

Perry, J. 1979: The problem of the essential indexical. *Nous* 13, 3–21.

Reid, T. 1785 (*1941*): *Essay on the intellectual powers of man*, ed. A.D. Woozley. London: Macmillan.

Strawson, P. 1958: Persons. In *Minnesota studies in the philosophy of science*, ed. H. Feigl et al., vol. 2. Minneapolis: University of Minnesota Press.

self: psychological usage A person's framework of self-referential meaning – cognitive and affective perceptions of self-as-object, arising from innate dispositions and social interactions across a lifetime, characterized by thought, feeling and action relative to a social structure of roles, rules, norms and values.

From the moment of birth onward the child is committed to a world of socially interpreted and evaluated action. The child exhibits an inborn propensity for development from the biological to the social and the symbolic. Through a stream of behavior it is engaged in a complex blend of innately pre-adapted actions directed at the development of physical, social and psychological extension beyond mere survival. The human infant attends selectively to its own kind, to human features and human speech. It is not only sensitive to but also actively participates in interaction characterized by temporal sequencing. This sequencing – including turn-taking – is the logical and practical basis of communicating meaning, which minimally requires the acknowledgment, assignment and acceptance of mutally dependent roles of addressor and addressee. Reciprocal exchanges of verbal and non-verbal gestures, and patterns of gesture, founded upon a mutual recognition of identity and role enable successive approximation directed at the demonstration and derivation of meaning.

There appears to be a social imperative to seek out and embark upon dialogue. The child acts in the role of agent or initiator, an implicit "I" with an inbuilt propensity for social outcomes which will cast it in the role of recipient, the incipient "me". Interaction with dialogue makes possible the progression from recognition of reciprocal role to self-consciousness to consciousness of one's self. From simple sensation arises primitive perception in the form of SELF-AWARENESS of "me" – an identity based upon realization and interpretation of physical separation and differentiation.

Primitive perception yields to complex conceptions communicated, albeit approximately, through the expressive symbols of GESTURE and PLAY. The path from babbling through the idiosyncratic proto-language of the toddler, inevitably abandoned for adult language with its greater capacity to be comprehended, constitutes an extended experiment in the symbolic expression of experience with respect to social roles and rules. Play extends this process. The child enacts, through partial performances, the roles of observed others – particularly of parents and other family members. These performances in play, as in non-play contexts, reflect rules of relationship, of interdependent roles, attitudinally supported by norms and values.

From these processes of symbolization and performance a concept of self arises – a system of self-referential meaning, a synthesis of imagined notions of "me", culturally emergent and defined in social interaction. Interaction, therefore, engenders a global sense of identity, comprising "*I*", the experiencing aspect of self as knower, and "*me*", the empirical aspect of personal experience, the knowledge of self as object or self as known (see SELF-CONCEPT).

Attempts at systematic or economic description of the self concept are destined to be condemned as artificial, impoverished, impersonal and unreal. Self-theorists agree, however, that the self-concept evolves across a lifetime and does not change with the transition from adolescence into adulthood. It can be viewed as a continuing attempt to synthesize many *selves* or multiple facets of a single *self*. James (1890) spoke of three constituents of the empirical self: the *material self* deriving from bodily awareness, clothing, family, home and property; the *social self*, in effect a conglomeration of social selves which reflect two aspects of the individual's imaginations – on the one hand, perceptions or images of the individual that he assumes are held by other individuals, or groups of individuals, who are significant because their views of the individual are important to the individual, and, on the other hand, social values and norms couched in shared views of such issues as shame and honor; finally the *spiritual self*, the awareness of one's own frailties, disposition and one's own existence, that aspect "me" as self knowledge which is closest to the current experience, the subjective judging thought of "I".

Research into the self-concept of individuals at various ages supports the early descriptive efforts of James. The young child actively constructs the social world of others and self relative to others in terms of sex, appearance, age, kinship, social role, possessions and actions. From puberty onwards construing becomes more psychological, where persons are perceived and conceived in terms of personality.

Self-evaluation and the evaluation of others emerge as crucial aspects of the evolving self-concept. They contribute to *self-esteem*, when success and failure enter awareness as a notion of worth, reflecting the degree of congruence between pretensions and achievement, the similarity between self evaluation and the regard or value placed upon oneself by others. It has been suggested that the need to be viewed positively is a universal need, which becomes even more compelling than SELF-ACTUALIZATION, the need to assert or realize fully one's identity. Significant others are important in the generation and maintenance of a sense of continuity and coherence reflecting positive self evaluation. Although these contributors to the individual's self esteem change from parents to peers within the period of primary socialization and in the secondary socialization of adulthood include many diverse sources, common requirements foster a sense of high self-esteem. Irrespective of age or socio-economic status, self-esteem emerges as a function of a secure, accepting environment, in which initiative is encouraged within clearly defined bounds of behavior.

Closely related to descriptive abstractions of self based upon self-evaluation, self-esteem, positive regard and self-actualization is the *ideal self* – suggested to be that concept of self which the individual would most like to realize, being the one upon which the highest value is placed.

Perceptions of incongruity between what one is or is becoming and what one wishes to be, create anxiety which can assume pathological proportions. Incongruence between self as knower and self as known, disparity between the "real", "true", or "inner" self and the "unreal", "false" or "outer" enacted self, can lead to distortion, dissociation or disorganisation of the stream of experience and the self-concept. Such responses serve to emphasize that by the application of the self-concept, events within the social structure, involving persons and personal actions relative to the individual, have the potential to be rendered meaningful. The social world of self and others is comprehensible in terms of anticipated replication and outcome, identification and identity, acceptability and acceptance, evaluation and value.

Several self theorists indicate that the self concept operates as a guide to behavior and a criterion for conduct. This assertion needs to be approached with caution. The study of the self concept can render the student self-conscious and blind to the fact that as a system of self-referential meaning generated in a myriad of interactions across the life span, at any given time its contents of internalized roles, status, norms and values are bound to be mutually exclusive and contradictory. The very vagueness of the individual's multifaceted self concept can be seen as an effective mechanism for coping with co-existent illogicality. The extent to which the self-concept exerts an influence on personal conduct at any given time is necessarily a function of the content and degree of self-awareness – the amount and axis of attention focussed upon self and performance.

For the major part of daily life the individual's concept is accessed, edited and implemented preconsciously. Many, if not most, of its constituent constructs of individuality and sociality exist and operate at the pre-verbal level of emotion, "felt" disposition and action itself. Attempts to intellectualize these by raising them to consciousness and expression, to the level of logic, language and thought are necessarily fraught, revealing the mutually exclusive and contradictory. All attempts to gain access to the self-concept, to "measure" it by self-report techniques, are by definition destined to be equivocal. This is because the researcher seeks to render manifest that which for the most part is enacted preconsciously and which, by excluding the incongruous, the contrary and the ambiguous, ensures stability. Recognising this allows methodological problems of reliability, validity, social desirability and the acquiescence commonly found in self-concept research, to be placed into a sensible, self-conscious phenomenological perspective.

EWS

Bibliography

Burns, R.B. 1979: *The self concept: theory, measurement, development and behavior*. London: Longman.

Gergen, K.J. 1971: *The concept of self*. New York: Holt, Rinehart & Winston.

James, W. 1890 (1950). *The principles of psychology*. New York: Dover.

self: social psychology of Social psychology recognizes the interpersonally determined, and consequently malleable nature of the SELF while largely ignoring or rejecting the stabilizing and unifying qualities attributed to it in psychoanalytic and humanistic formulatons. This view owes much to the symbolic interactionist school of social psychology, in particular to Cooley's (1902) conception of the "looking glass self" which refers to the self as a construction built up of other people's attitudes toward us. For G.H. Mead (1934) this process of "reflection" develops into one of "self-reflexivity": what constitutes human selfhood is the capacity to take ourselves as objects of our own consciousness to which we make indications and respond. In Mead's theory, a major precondition to the development of self which marks it as an incipiently social phenomenon is the ability to take the role of the other, so that his attitudes toward us might be appraised and internalized.

If the self is constructed within the social context, rather than being an autonomous substance or an internal propulsion, it is subject to change with changes in social stimulation. Research has shown that people attend to cues from their own and others' behavior in order to infer such important components of their own self-systems as motives, emotions, beliefs, values, desires etc. (see Gergen 1977, for a review). Moreover, the functions for which a homuncular self was originally postulated are in the social psychological tradition seen to be largely illusory: the apprehension of personal identity over time is rather construed to be a reconstruction over time in terms of the end arrived at, and trans-situational consistency is accounted for by concomitants understood as specific self-interests. However, conceiving of the self as a wholly inter- rather than intra-psychic phenomenon can lead to an extreme situationism and thus to the reification of particular system boundaries, and if only to avoid this result an "ego psychology" is a justifiable and necessary enterprise.

BRS

Bibliography

Cooley, C.H. 1902: *Human nature and the social order*. New York: Scribner.

Gergen, K. 1977: The social construction of self knowledge. In T. Mischel, op. cit.

Mead, G.H. 1934: *Mind, self and society*. Chicago: University of Chicago Press.

*Mischel, T. ed. 1977: *The self: psychological and philosophical issues*. Oxford: Basil Blackwell; Totowa, N.J.: Rowman & Littlefield.

*Wegner, D.M. and Vallacher, R.R. eds. 1980: *The self in social psychology*. New York and Oxford: Oxford University Press.

self-actualization The inherent tendency towards self-fulfilment, self-expression and the attainment of autonomy from external forces. It is a process rather than an end state. A self-actualizing individual is deemed to be realistic, spontaneous and demonstrative, able both to engage and to transcend problems, being particularly resistant to social pressures.

According to Goldstein and Rogers self-actualization is the sole motive, with drives such as sex, hunger and achievement as aspects, or modes of this fundamental force. Although universal and innate, its expression varies in individuals, who differ in genetic endowment, environment and cultural background. Maslow considers self-actualization to be the highest level of need. The prospect of fulfilling the highest needs (meta-needs) such as beauty, goodness and wholeness, cannot arise until lower needs such as physiological deficiencies are satisfied. These also include a need for safety, love and esteem. Maslow believes that very few individuals achieve a degree of self-actualization. This is akin to Jung's view that self-actualization cannot come about until a person has fulfilled all of his or her capacities, and is individuated and whole. EWS

Bibliography

Chaplin, J.P. and Krawiec, T.S. 1968: *Systems and theories of psychology*. New York: Holt, Rinehart & Winston.

self-awareness The capacity to think in terms of one's SELF-CONCEPT, focussing attention, processing information and acting with regard to this concept. The content of self-awareness can be classified according to accessibility – those conscious aspects of self-information incorporating the open (public) self, known also to others, and the hidden self, known only to the individual. These contrast with the blind self, known only to others and the unknown self, known to no one, though its existence can possibly be inferred. Consciousness of self, open or hidden, as level of self-awareness, varies. It is low in situations seen to be routine or ritual and heightened when circumstances are viewed as enhancing, eroding, or demanding a revision of, the self-concept. Meditation, hypnosis, drugs (particularly alcohol), and provision of simultaneous or recorded feedback, particularly visual, can markedly affect self-awareness, self-concept and social performance. Indeed, it is believed that some degree of self-awareness is basic to all interpersonal behavior and the emergence and application of values and norms. Recent research indicates that self-awareness is not a uniquely human attribute. EWS

Bibliography

Gallup, G.G. 1979: Self-awareness in primates. *American scientist* 67, 417–21.

Kleinke, C.L. 1978: *Self-perception: the psychology of personal awareness*. San Francisco: W.H. Freeman.

self-awareness, objective The directing of attention inward so that consciousness is focused on the SELF, its reflex being "subjective self-awareness" wherein consciousness is focused on events external to the self. Duval and Wicklund (1972) assert that the former attentive condition generates self-evaluation by setting up an automatic comparison between the individual's current state or level of performance and an ideal state. The larger the perceived discrepancy between the two states the higher the degree of negative self-evaluation, an intrinsically uncomfortable affect which the individual seeks to avoid or dispel either by changing his or her present state towards the ideal or by reverting to the subjectively self-aware condition. Objective self-awareness may be induced by any cues which serve to remind one of oneself (e.g. mirror, tape recording of one's voice, comparison with others). A recent extension of the theory was the discovery of stable individual differences in chronic objective/subjective self-awareness, or what has been termed "private and public self-consciousness" (Fenigstein et al. 1975). BRS

Bibliography

Duval, S. and Wicklund, R.A. 1972: *A theory of objective self awareness*. New York and London: Academic Press.

Fenigstein, A., Scheier, M.F. and Buss, A.H. 1975: Public and private self consciousness: Assessment and theory. *Journal of consulting and clinical psychology* 43, 522–7.

*Wicklund, R.A. and Frey, D. 1980: Self-awareness theory: When the self makes a difference. In *The Self in social psychology*, ed. D.M. Wegner and R.R. Vallacher. New York and Oxford: Oxford University Press.

self-concept One of many terms (self-identity, self-image, self-ideal, perceived self, phenomenal self) relating to self-perception. To illustrate this, Allport (1965) wrote:

> Suppose that you are facing a difficult and critical exam. No doubt you are aware of your high pulse rate, and of the butterflies in your stomach (*bodily self*): also of the significance of the exam in terms of your past and future (*self-identity*); of your prideful involvement (*self-esteem*); of what success or failure may mean to your family (*self-extension*); or your hopes and aspirations (*self-image*); of your role as solver of problems on the examination (*rational agent*) and of the relevance of the whole situation to your long range goals (*self striving*).

Mead (1934) wrote of the social construction of the self-concept which is altogether a reflection of the opinions and attitudes communicated by significant others. In this sense, it is argued that society provides a looking glass in which people discover their image or self-concept.

The related concepts of ego and self form the core of many controversial areas of modern thinking in psychology. The two major approaches concern the self as the person perceives it (self as object), and the self as the agent of activity (self as subject). The self is seen as central for the integration and direction of the individual towards various forms of interaction with persons and objects.

Some of the more interesting questions on this topic are discussed by Epstein (1973) and Gergen (1961). AF

Bibliography

Allport, G. 1965: *Pattern and growth in personality*. New York: Holt, Rinehart & Winston.

Epstein, S. 1973: The self-concept revisited: or a theory of a theory. *American psychologist*.

Gergen, K. 1961: *The concept of self*. New York: Holt, Rinehart & Winston.

Mead, G.H. 1934: *Mind, self and society*. Chicago: University of Chicago Press.

self-consistency The stability of the self-concept across situations and time. Stability of the self-concept provides a point of reference within a changing environment and a point of projection of the self into the future. A variety of reasons are given for this cognitive tendency including the provision of a sense of personal control or the ability to regulate change, the economy in the organization of perceptions, the reduction of conflict among concepts, and avoidance of cognitions with conflicting implications for action. The pressure for change of the self-concept usually emerges from information from others which is inconsistent with the relevant facets of the self as perceived by the person. In response to the inconsistent information, the person may avoid or change his or her evaluation of those who provide the information, change the conception of the self as in therapy, and change or misperceive his or her own actions. Given the mutual influence of the self-concept and the environment, and the constant changes, in that environment, self-consistency can only be relative and the process of self-change must be considered along with self-consistency. RCZ

Bibliography

Jones, S.G. 1973: Self and interpersonal evaluations: esteem theories versus consistency theories. *Psychological bulletin* 79, 185–99.

self-control The ability to defer immediate instinctual pleasure and gratification to attain a future, usually socially valued, goal. The person who exercises self-control shows that innate needs have been socialized, that the culture's values are more significant than his or her desires and urges (see also SUBLIMATION). The term implies another way of stating the problem of the relationship between the idiosyncratic personality confronting the collective's need for conformity and the social rewards that can accrue from delaying instinctual satisfaction.

Self-control can be accounted for at two opposing levels: (i) consciously the person is aware of future goals and rewards and can plan and structure behavior for future goals. A person's commitment must also be a part of self-control. (ii) for behaviorism self-control is explained by the Law of Relative Effect in that the delay of behavior is accomplished by the relative size of the reward in the future. Organisms will distribute their behavior (responses) according to the relative gains connected with each action. The organism is for the most part unaware of this process.

The social learning theorist, Bandura, regards self-control as both external and internal. The person can reward himself and actively shape the external environment so as to be more rewarding. This is done through gaining control over reinforcements, and doing this is seen as a sign of maturity. JWA

self-deception The idea of self-deception presents difficulties to those philosophers who hold that the content of consciousness is infallibly revealed to consciousness itself. How can we be deceived, if we are directly aware of "inner experience?"

In Existentialist thought, on the other hand, especially that of J.-P. Sartre, self-deception, or Bad Faith has a central place. Only self-conscious beings can deceive themselves. This is possible because they are detached from their experiences, and can describe them truly or falsely, and this includes their experience of themselves. They are driven to self-deception by fear of their own freedom. They prefer to pretend to themselves that they are bound by necessity or moral considerations, rather than face the fact of their own total freedom and responsibility. (CF. AKRASIA.) MW

self-esteem A term given to the evaluation an individual makes of, and applies to, himself. It can express positive or negative feelings and indicates the extent to which the individual believes himself or herself to be significant, capable and worthy. (Although self esteem is a concept which may be applied to specific areas of experience, it is almost always applied to general feelings of worthiness). Studies show that the self esteem of an individual often remains constant for several years after middle childhood and is very difficult to change in an upward or downward direction. Even when faced with "objective" evidence, people prefer to accept their own "subjective" view of their worthiness. This may be because of the individual's need for psychological consistency when dealing with the world. RMCH

self-monitoring The storage of information about an individual's actions, thoughts, feelings, etc. The totality of information a person has about his or her actions is wider than the record of that to which he or she consciously attends. The phenomenon of self-monitoring is the basis of self reflective aspects of accounting. (See ETHOGENICS). It also forms the basis for a theory about individual differences in social behaviour (Snyder 1979). See SELF-MONITORING. RHa

Bibliography

Snyder, M. 1979: Self-monitoring processes. In *Advances in experimental social psychology*, vol. 12, ed. L. Berkowitz. New York: Academic Press.

self-perception theory A theory, proposed by Bem (1972) which suggests that people have no direct knowledge of their own internal states but infer their existence from observations of their own behavior. In Bem's view there is no essential difference between actor and observer in gaining access to one's internal state of mind. Bem's theory, which is a more precise revival of the James-Lange theory of emotion, attracted a good deal of attention by reinterpreting Festinger and Carlsmith's famous experiment in COGNITIVE DISSONANCE. According to Bem, a larger attitude change for a smaller bribe is what one would infer from the behavior of the subjects in the experiment. Bem's reinterpretation has been criticized on various grounds and the evidence appears to be equivocal. Nevertheless Bem's theory has served in many ways to renew interest in a classical problem of psychology. Research in ATTRIBUTION THEORY has shown that significant differences exist between actors and observers in making inferences about internal states. JMFJ

Bibliography

Bem, D. J. 1972: Self-perception theory. In *Advances in experimental social psychology* Vol. 6, ed. L. Berkowitz. New York: Academic Press.

self-presentation A concept often used synonymously with impression-management to refer to the numerous strategies that people employ to control and manage their outward images and the impressions of themselves which they present to other people. William James, C.H. Cooley, and G.H. Mead all stressed the idea that in social discourse and interaction people present different selves to different people usually in order to show their best profile or make a good impression.

Self-presentation is at the center of the work by Goffman (1959, 1963, 1967), who uses the theatrical analogy for social interaction. For Goffman each person (actor) attempts to maintain an image appropriate to the social situation and hence to be positively evaluated. Furthermore the rules of social life ensure that each participant will attempt to keep all members of the interaction "in face" or playing an acceptable role through appropriate self-presentation. Everyone therefore has a range of self-presentational images and tactics which he or she uses to sustain social interaction and a positive self image.

The idea of self-presentation has greatly influenced the work of Harré (1979) and Snyder (1979). The latter has extended this idea to the concept of self-monitoring, which refers to the extent to which people can and do exercise control over their verbal and non-verbal self-presentation. High self-monitors (those skilled in self-presentation) regulate and control their non-verbal and verbal behavior to make it situationally appropriate and hence demonstrate high cross-situational variability and a low correlation between attitudes and social behavior. Conversely low self-monitors (those not skilled in self-presentation) do not present themselves very well; are more cross situationally consistent and tend to express attitudes that do predict their behavior. AF

Bibliography

Goffman, E. 1959: *The presentation of self in everyday life.* Harmondsworth: Penguin.

——— 1963: *Stigma: notes on the management of spoiled identity.* Englewood Cliff, N.J.: Prentice-Hall.

——— 1967: *Interaction ritual: essays on face-to-face behavior.* Garden City: Doubleday.

Harré, R. 1979: *Social being.* Oxford: Basil Blackwell; Totowa, N.J.: Littlefield Adams.

Snyder, M. 1979: Self-monitoring processes. In *Advances in experimental social psychology* vol. 12, ed. L. Berkowitz. New York: Academic Press.

self-stimulation Electrical stimulation of certain brain regions, for example in the HYPOTHALAMUS and LIMBIC SYSTEM, is positively reinforcing in that animals will work to obtain the brain-stimulation. It has been speculated that the brain-stimulation involves activation of neural structures and pathways that subserve more conventional reinforcement (e.g. food and water). Neuroanatomical and neuropharmacological evidence suggests that the effects of the stimulation are mediated via catecholaminergic pathways. These originate in the midbrain and lower brainstem and connect to the hypothalamus, striatum and other forebrain areas employing the catecholamine NEUROTRANSMITTERS (see BRAIN AND CENTRAL NERVOUS SYSTEM: ILLUSTRATIONS, figs. 5 and 6).

Self-stimulation has been observed in man but regions that sustain it are not easily found. Most often sensations produced by such stimulation are rarely intensely pleasurable. One medical application of self-administered electrical brain stimulation has been in the relief of intense and otherwise intractable pain. RCS/BER

self *See above, and also* emotion and self

selfishness In human psychology the word is used with its normal meaning, but evolutionary biologists sometimes use it in a technical sense: selfish behavior increases the welfare of the individual at the expense of the welfare of others. "Altruistic" behavior is the opposite. A third technical term is sometimes defined in a similar way: a "spiteful" act is one that harms the perpetrator, but harms some other individual(s) even more. Mathematical models suggest that SPITE is unlikely to evolve in nature. Whether ALTRUISM is likely to evolve depends upon how welfare is defined. If it is taken to mean survival, ordinary parental care qualifies as an altruistic act. But if welfare is taken to mean Darwinian FITNESS or REPRODUCTIVE SUCCESS, parental care is not necessarily altruistic since a parent only achieves reproductive success through the survival of its offspring. Much the same can be said of apparent altruism towards other close genetic relatives. The history of the Darwinian study of altruism has been, in a sense, a process of explaining away apparent altruism at the level of the individual by showing that it follows from a more fundamental genetic selfishness. This has no connection with another kind of "explaining away" in the field of human motives: we may dismiss an apparently altruistic man as secretly selfish, doing good for his own ends. Darwinian explanations of selfishness at the genetic level make no reference to subjective motives. They are concerned solely with the effects of actions. RD

Bibliography

Dawkins, R. 1976: *The selfish gene.* Oxford: Oxford University Press.

semantic differential A measurement instrument, consisting of a number of carefully selected pairs of adjectives for eliciting the affective meaning of words and concepts. Developed by Osgood et al. (1957), it has been widely used in psychological research. Factor analysis has shown that semantic differentiations in this sense can be reduced to some extent (20 to 80 per cent of the total variance depending upon the domain from which words and concepts are chosen) to three independent dimensions of affective judgment: evaluation (good–bad), potency (strong–weak) and activity (fast–slow). Osgood has shown in a large number of cross-cultural studies that these dimensions are nearly universal. Semantic atlases which give the affective meaning of scores for a large number of concepts have been based on these and other studies. JMFJ

Bibliography

Osgood, C. E., Suci, G. J. and Tannenbaum P. H. 1957: *The measurement of meaning*, Urbana: University of Illinois Press.

semantic memory The term is used to describe general knowledge as opposed to episodic, personal memories. General knowledge is decontextualized as a consequence of repeated exposure: its origins are forgotten and no longer matter. Hence, it does not require for its reinstatement specific contextual cues, which are necessary for the retrieval of episodic traces. It is, therefore, more widely useful. However, the distinction between episodic and semantic memory is mainly one of convenience and does not imply the existence of separate, distinct systems. In general, the difference is one of degree, and episodic and semantic traces often function as units. WKi

sensation In its technical meaning, sensation is the capacity to have experiences through stimulation of the sense organs, or an exercise of that capacity. A sensation is the object of any such sense-experience; so used, the term "sensation" is a close synonym of SENSE DATUM. Sensation is often distinguished from perception as not involving conceptualization of the content; in sensation we experience colored patches which in perception are conceptualized as physical realities. This philosophical usage is much wider than that of modern non-technical usage, in which the term "sensation" is restricted to certain forms of bodily feeling. In this usage, we have no sensation from healthy vision, though the use of a diseased eye may involve such an occurrence. JOU

sense datum Commonly defined as being the immediate object of sense-experience. Such a definition is purely relational and leaves open the ontological status of sense-data, which might even be physical objects. But it is commonly assumed that they are more fundamental than physical objects and the problem then arises how they are related to physical objects (see PERCEPTION: PHILOSOPHICAL). "Idea of sense" or "impression" are approximate synonyms of "sense-datum", save that a sense-datum need not be mental. "Sensum" is an exact synonym of "sense-datum". JOU

senses: chemical and the nervous system The neural structures which participate in the detection of chemicals in the air or mouth and lead to the sensations and perceptions of taste and smell.

SENSORY TRANSDUCTION in the gustatory system occurs in the tastebuds of the tongue and palate. Tastebuds are associated with specialized papillae on the tongue (fungiform papillae on the front of the tongue, foliate papillae on the sides, and circumvallate papillae on the back of the tongue). Although individual taste afferent fibers are not selectively responsive to the four qualities of taste (sweet, salty, sour and bitter), sensitivity to sweet is greatest at the tip of the tongue; sensitivity to bitter, at the back; and to sour and salty, along the sides. Nonetheless, the encoding of gustatory information appears to involve the pattern of firing of the population of taste afferents since each fiber responds to some degree to a wide variety of stimuli. Tastebuds are innervated by the facial, glossopharyngeal and vagus nerves whose cell bodies lie in the geniculate, superior petrosal and nodose ganglia respectively. Taste afferents terminate in the solitary nucleus of the medulla. The gustatory relay nuclei lie in the ventromedial portion of the ventral posterior THALAMUS (see BRAIN AND CENTRAL NERVOUS SYSTEM ILLUSTRATIONS, fig. 19). Two gustatory cortical regions have been identified. One occupies a portion of parietal cortex next to the somatosensory cortex representing the oral cavity (figs. 2, 3 and 4). The other lies in the anterior opercular–insular cortex overlying the claustrum adjacent to the oral representation in the second somatosensory cortical field.

Olfactory receptors, located in the olfactory mucosa of the posterior nasal cavity, detect the presence of odorants. The receptors themselves bear axons which terminate in the glomeruli of the olfactory bulb (fig. 16). Like taste fibers, olfactory fibers are responsive to a variety of stimuli, and the spatial and temporal characteristics of the responses of the whole population of olfactory afferents may encode the perceived features of odor stimuli. The olfactory bulb projects to the anterior olfactory nucleus, the olfactory tubercule, the prepyriform cortex, the amygdaloid complex and the transitional entorhinal cortex. These structures variously project to the HYPOTHALAMUS (figs. 15 and 20) and the same regions of ventromedial, ventroposterior thalamus (figs. 15 and 19) that receive gustatory inputs. The projection from thalamus is to the same region of the parietal lobe of CEREBRAL CORTEX that receives gustatory projections. The olfactory system thus has two regions of primary cortex, one in palaeocortex (prepyriform cortex), which evolved early in the vertebrate line, and later connections through the thalamus to a second region in neocortex (parietal cortex). Like the auditory system, the olfactory system has a significant system of descending fibers. Centrifugal fibers from higher centers innervate the glomeruli of the olfactory bulb where they modulate the sensory input at the level of the second order of olfactory neurons. SCC

Bibliography

Beidler, L.M., ed. 1971: *Handbook of sensory physiology*, Vol. IV, *Chemical senses*, Part 2, *Taste*. Berlin and New York: Springer-Verlag.

——— 971: *Handbook of sensory physiology*, Vol. IV, *Chemical senses*, Part 1, *Olfaction*. Berlin and New York: Springer-Verlag.

——— 1980: The chemical senses: gustation and olfaction. In *Medical Physiology*, 14th edn., ed. V.B. Mountcastle. St. Louis and London: C.V. Mosby.

Shepard, G.M. 1979: *The synaptic organization of the brain*. 2nd edn. Oxford and New York: Oxford University Press.

Shepard, G.M., Getchell, T.V. and Kauer, J.S. 1975: Analysis of structure and function in the olfactory pathway. In *The nervous system*, Vol. 1, *The basic neurosciences*, ed. R.O. Brady. New York: Raven Press.

senses: electromagnetic The ability to detect electric or magnetic fields. Many fish are capable of electroreception. For example, dogfish and sharks have electroreceptive sense organs, called *ampullae Lorenzini*, which are distributed over the body surface and usually concentrated in the region of the head. Some dogfish even when buried under sand, can detect prey by the local distortion of the geophysical electric field.

Some fish, especially the gymnotid eels, generate their

own weak electric fields and are sensitive to distortions of their own field caused by objects in the environment. They usually live in conditions of poor visibility. The fish are sensitive to the electric discharges of other members of the species, and may communicate with each other through this medium.

Fish such as the electric ray and the electric eel produce strong electric discharges capable of stunning prey and some predators. However, they do not seem to be capable of electroreception.

Many different animals are sensitive to magnetic fields. Orientation to magnetic north has been found in bacteria, flatworms and snails. Magnetic sensitivity is also used in navigation in pigeons and in bees. Pigeons and other birds effectively have a magnetic compass which they deploy when the sun is obscured by clouds, or when navigating at night. There is some evidence for a similar ability in man (Baker 1981). DJM

Bibliography

Baker, Reginald R. 1981: *Human navigation and the sixth sense*. London: Hodder & Stoughton; New York: Simon & Schuster 1982.

senses: mechanical The detection of mechanical disturbances in the environment and within the animal's body. Mechanoreceptors are involved in many senses, including hearing, balance, pressure detection and touch.

Information from mechanoreceptors in the limb joints and muscles is particularly important in coordination and locomotion. Postural reflexes are triggered by receptors in the limbs and in the maculae, the organs of balance in the vertebrate ear. Invertebrates often have analogous mechanisms. Thus the statocysts of the octopus are analogous to the maculae of vertebrates and enable the animal to maintain its orientation with respect to gravity.

The array of mechanical senses with which an animal is equipped is partly determined by its way of life. Pigeons have a small vesicle in the ear which gives them a high sensitivity to barometric pressure. This organ is especially well developed in diving birds and is also found in sharks. Other fish detect hydrostatic pressure by means of mechanoreceptors attached to the swim bladder, an organ which does not occur in sharks. DJM

sensibile This term, introduced by Bertrand Russell, was defined by him as follows: "I shall give the name *sensibilia* to those objects which have the same metaphysical and physical status as sense-data, without necessarily being data of any mind" (Russell 1914). A sensibile is to a SENSE DATUM as a man is to a husband; it is something which becomes a sense-datum by becoming the object of a mind. Russell admitted that there might be no sensibilia that were not sense-data, but did not regard sense-data as essentially mental. What Russell called sensibilia have sometimes been called possible sense-data. JOU

Bibliography

Russell, B.A.W. 1914: The relation of sense-data to physics. *Scientia* 4.

sensitization An increase in response to a repeated stimulus not due to pairing with another stimulus. It often requires intense or noxious stimuli to be observed.

sensori-motor stage In Piagetian theory, the first stage of development from birth to approximately eighteen months. It is so called because the connection between infant and environment consists in particular motor responses to classes of sensory stimuli. Development begins with reflexive responses to a strictly limited range of sensory events and proceeds through the coordination and elaboration of motor responses to more complex combinations of eliciting stimuli. Throughout the sensori-motor period actions are controlled by direct sensory stimulation. The end of this stage is marked by the development of representation (the ability to retrieve information from memory) and the regulation of action by stored knowledge. During the sensori-motor stage, the infant develops concepts of space, time causes and objects, expressed in the control of motor activities. GEB

Bibliography

Piaget, Jean 1936 (*1953*): *The origin of intelligence in the child*. London: Routledge and Kegan Paul; New York: International Universities Press (1966), *The origins of intelligence in children*.

sensory deprivation and enrichment Rearing in either enriched or deprived multi-sensory environments may produce significant effects upon the adult nervous system, including biochemical, anatomical and behavioral changes (see also CRITICAL PERIODS AND THE NERVOUS SYSTEM). For example cells in the cortex show greater dendritic branching, more dendritic spines, and larger synaptic regions in animals reared in complex environments relative to littermates reared in impoverished environments. There is also a consistent increase in the overall cortical thickness of rats reared in enriched environments, which is accompanied by a greater cortical weight. The increased weight is at least partially due to greater protein and RNA content in brain tissue, and there is a greater ratio of RNA to DNA, suggesting increased metabolic activity.

At the behavioral level, selective rearing in an enriched environment produces more efficient maze learning, but the results on tasks such as visual discrimination learning are less consistent. In general, the evidence supports the conclusion that differential rearing produces behaviorally different animals, but it may be misleading to use terms like "intelligence" to refer to such differences. Selective rearing is known to produce longlasting effects upon emotionality and exploration: multi-sensory deprivation decreases exploratory tendencies and increases diffused, undirected fear reactions, whereas enrichment conditions produce more purposeful patterns of exploratory and avoidance behavior. It is these changes which may account for the deprived animal's inferior performance on learning tasks. BER/RCS

sensory enrichment *See* sensory deprivation and enrichment

sensory neglect A set of abnormalities exhibited by patients with cerebral lesions usually characterized by the failure to respond to sensory stimuli presented to the side contralateral to the lesion, even though there is no peripheral sensory or motor defect. The neglect syndrome accompanies lesions, most often caused by cerebral infarction or rapidly-growing malignant tumors, to the inferior parietal lobule, dorsolateral frontal lobe, cingulate gyrus, neostriatum, or thalamus.

Clinically patients often fail to turn towards stimuli contralateral to the lesion (hemiakinesia). They may fail to use extremities on the contralateral side. Some patients refer contralateral sensory stimuli to the ipsilateral side (allesthesia), for example reporting that they were touched on the same side as the lesion when the tactile stimulus is applied to the side opposite the lesion. When asked to draw, patients may produce only half of an object and may quarter rather than bisect a line (hemispatial neglect). Patients may fail to dress the abnormal side, may deny that affected extremities belong to their bodies (anosognosia) or may read only part of a word ("grandmother" may be read as "mother") (paralexia). Finally, patients showing sensory neglect are often also hypokinetic, showing little interest in their environment, and appearing unconcerned about their illness and apathetic about events in general. Patients with initial hemisensory neglect who ignore contralateral stimuli or refer them to the unaffected side often improve later and are able to lateralize stimuli successfully to the affected side. These patients still often fail to report stimulation of the affected side when both sides are simultaneously stimulated (sensory extinction).

The mechanisms of sensory neglect have proved difficult to determine. The combinations of symptoms shown by patients are variable and depend greatly on what is measured clinically and how. Numerous theories have been advanced to explain the symptoms and sets of symptoms of sensory neglect. Of these the hypothesis that neglect results from defects in the attention-arousal mechanisms is consistent with much of the extant data (Heilman and Valenstein 1972). SCC

Bibliography

*Heilman, K.M. 1979: Neglect and related disorders. In K.M. Heilman and E. Valenstein, eds, *Clinical neuropsychology*. Oxford and New York: Oxford University Press.

Heilman, K.M. and Valenstein, E. 1972: Frontal lobe neglect in man. *Neurology* 22. 660-64.

sensory systems, neural bases of The mechanisms by which the nervous system responds to physical energy in the environment to produce sensory experience. A number of different sensory systems can be distinguished on the basis of the kinds of environmental stimulation to which they respond. These systems fall into three broad categories. The first, called exteroceptive, is concerned with stimuli arising outside the body and provides information about events in the external world. There are five exteroceptive sensory systems: the olfactory system is concerned with the sense of smell, the gustatory system with taste, the visual system with sight, the auditory system with hearing, and the somatic system with feeling stimuli that contact the body surface. The second broad category of sensory systems, called proprioceptive, is stimulated by the action of the body itself and provides information about the activity and position of the body and limbs. Within this category the vestibular system is concerned with the static position of the head (relative to gravity) and with linear or rotational movement of the head. The kinesthetic system is concerned with sensations originating from the muscles, tendons, and joints and provides information about the position of the limbs and body. The third category of sensory systems is called interoceptive, and is stimulated by the internal organs and viscera. This system is concerned with sensations of pain, pressure, and temperature of the internal organs.

The first step in neural processing for each of these sensory systems is conversion of environmental stimuli into the electrochemical activity of NEURONS. This conversion, called SENSORY TRANSDUCTION, is accomplished by specialized sensory receptors. In many sensory systems, the environmental stimulus directly contacts the receptors. For example the soluble molecules that produce tastes come into direct contact with the gustatory receptors on the tongue and other regions of the mouth and throat. However some sensory systems have accessory structures that focus, amplify, or otherwise modify the environmental stimulus before it impinges upon the receptor. For example external and middle ear structures collect sound waves (vibrations) in the air, amplify the pressure of the vibrations, and convert them into moving waves in a fluid in the inner ear. These moving waves cause a membrane in the inner ear to vibrate in the fluid. The auditory receptors contact this membrane, and are stimulated by its vibration. Thus, sensory receptors may be stimulated only indirectly by complex accessory structures.

In general the receptors are specialized cells that are uniquely sensitive to particular kinds of environmental stimuli. For example olfactory receptors are cells with membranes that are particularly sensitive to airborn gaseous molecules. Visual receptor cells contain pigments that absorb light of particular wavelengths. Auditory receptors have specialized hairs (or cilia) that are sensitive to the vibrations of the inner ear membrane that they contact. In each case stimulation of the receptor cell produces a small voltage change (a few thousandths of a volt) across the receptor cell membrane. This results in release of a chemical transmitter substance from the receptor cell, which makes contact (see SYNAPSE AND SYNAPTIC TRANSMISSION) with one or more neurons. The neurons in turn generate electrochemical impulses (see ACTION POTENTIAL) that are propagated along their axons into the sensory pathways of the brain.

In some sensory systems (somatic, kinesthetic, and interoceptive), the sensory receptors are specialized nerve endings of neurons rather than separate receptor cells. In these cases, environmental stimulation produces a small voltage change directly in the nerve ending, and this results in action potential generation.

Thus, in every sensory system, environmental stimulation leads directly or indirectly to action potentials in neurons. It is this activity of the neurons, transmitted along axons into the sensory pathways of the brain, that forms the neural basis of sensory experience. Which sensory modality we experience (taste, sound, touch, etc.) depends upon which of these pathways is activated.

Within each sensory system specific properties of sensory stimulation (type of stimulus, its location, intensity, etc.) as well as complex perceptual phenomena are coded by the action potentials generated in neurons. Because all action potentials of all neurons have basically the same form specific sensory information can be coded in only two ways: by which neurons are active, and by the frequency or pattern of action potentials generated by the neurons. Both these methods of stimulus coding appear to be utilized by all sensory systems.

In many sensory systems the location of a stimulus in the environment is coded according to which neurons are active. This happens because the spatial layout of the receptor surface is projected into the brain in a topographic manner by the sensory neurons. Thus, throughout the somatic sensory pathways there is a topographic representation of the body surface, and stimulation of a particular location on the body activates the neurons that receive inputs from that location. Likewise the visual receptor cells lie in a sheet at the back of the eye (the retina), and this receptor sheet is represented topographically in the visual pathways of the brain. Consequently stimulation of a particular retinal location by a light source activates only particular neurons in the visual system.

Stimulus quality may also be coded according to which neurons are active. For example, light touch, pressure, or temperature changes on the skin lead to activation of different neurons in the somatic sensory system. This is due largely to the presence of specific sensory receptors in the skin, each of which activates different sensory neurons. Specific tastes, odors, sound frequencies (pitch), and other sensory qualities may also be coded in a similar fashion.

In general the frequency of action potentials generated by sensory neurons is related to stimulus intensity. More intense stimuli (brighter lights, louder sounds, etc.) cause larger voltage changes in the receptors and this leads to more action potentials (higher discharge frequency) in the sensory neurons. However discharge frequency can also code stimulus quality, and in some cases both discharge frequency and the discharging neurons can be involved in stimulus coding. Color information is coded this way in the visual system. Certain colors produce activity in certain neurons but not in others. In addition, different colors may activate the same neurons with different patterns of activity. Thus for some neurons blue light increases discharge frequency and yellow light decreases it. For other neurons red light increases activity while green light decreases it. In a similar manner some vestibular system neurons increase their activity when the head turns in one direction and decrease their activity for movement in the opposite direction.

Relatively little is known about the neural bases of more complex sensory experience and perception. Some neurons have been found to discharge only to certain perceptual or abstract aspects of sensory stimuli. For example some neurons in the visual system discharge only when contours of certain orientations move in certain directions with specific velocities through the visual field. It is possible that other neurons (yet to be found) respond selectively to more complex aspects of the environment, such as specific visual objects or spoken words. However, the most widely held view is that such complex sensory stimuli are coded by the discharges of many thousands (perhaps millions) of neurons, each of which responds to specific components of the overall stimulus. For example when we look at an object different neurons discharge in different patterns to the various contours, colors, and light intensities that occur in different locations in the object. It is this ensemble of neuronal activity that is thought to form the neural basis of complex sensory experience. See also AUDITORY NERVOUS SYSTEM; SENSES, CHEMICAL, AND THE NERVOUS SYSTEM; PAIN AND THE NERVOUS SYSTEM; SOMATOSENSORY NERVOUS SYSTEM; VISUAL NERVOUS SYSTEM. PDS

Bibliography

Geldard, Frank A. 1972: *The human senses* 2nd edn. New York and London: John Wiley & Sons.

Thompson, Richard F. 1967: *Foundations of physiological psychology*. New York: Harper & Row.

Uttal, William R. 1973 *The psychobiology of sensory coding*, New York and London: Harper & Row.

sensory transduction The conversion of physical stimuli into electrical activity within a cell, the sensory receptor. Sensory transduction is an early stage in the function of all sensory systems. In the visual system it occurs in the rods and cones of the retina; in the auditory system, in the hair cells of the cochlea; in the somatosensory system, in the Meissner corpuscles, Merkel discs, Pacinian corpuscles, etc., of the skin; in the olfactory system, in the olfactory receptors of the sensory epithelium in the nose; in the gustatory system, in the receptors of the tastebuds; in the proprioceptive system, in the muscle spindles and joint receptors; in the vestibular system, in the hair cells of the utricle, saccule and semicircular canals. Since the sensitivity and fidelity of the transduction process ultimately determines what an organism can hear, see, taste, etc., the receptor cells in which sensory transduction occurs are all specialized for exquisite sensitivity to the particular physical stimuli to which they respond.

Although the details vary from receptor to receptor, and in most systems much remains to be worked out, sensory transduction of all sorts appears to involve the encoding of the physical stimulus at the molecular level. At some point in a complex chain of events triggered by a physical stimulus, a channel or pore in the receptor cell membrane is opened or closed, modulating a flow of ions and producing a change in the receptor cell membrane potential and/or membrane resistance. Information about this change is relayed to secondary neurons and ultimately leads to sensation and perception. SCC

Bibliography

Cold Spring Harbor Symposium on Quantitative Biology, Vol XXX. Sensory receptors. 1965: Cold Spring Harbor, NY: Cold Spring Harbor Laboratory of Quantitative Biology.

Loewenstein, W.R. 1971: *Handbook of sensory physiology*, Vol. I. *Principles of receptor physiology*. Berlin and New York: Springer-Verlag.

Miller, W.H. 1981: *Current topics in membranes and transport*, vol. 15. *Molecular mechanisms of photoreceptor transduction*. London and New York: Academic Press.

Uttal, W.R. 1972: *Sensory coding. selected readings*. Boston: Little, Brown.

sentiment A configuration of emotional dispositions orientated about one cognition (of object, person, group, or symbol) and existing as a structured, relatively abiding element in individual character and social tradition. Established when instinctual dispositions are activated in relation to one particular object (e.g. sex – with *this* partner; parental feelings – for *this* child) they are an inward shaping of the "self" (a core of character-formation) focusing the individual's experience upon one specific range of objects (home, family, region, nation) and tending to exclude others. In this, they are also the experienced, regulatory side of the individual's accommodation to the constraining social structure; constituting an inwardly established set of preferences, prejudices, attachments, values, ideals, which are the ground for a relatively enduring pattern of directed motivation, and a *self*-regulation of behavior within the external regulations of the institutional order. In individual and society, sentiments are thought so important that closely correlated *sanctions* arise to uphold, enforce, and prevent the breaking of them. (See INSTINCT for related theories and bibliography). RF

separation A term derived from psychoanalytic theory to describe the anxiety held to be generated by the absence of a person believed necessary for survival (prototypically the mother) and to denote a major developmental process – separation-individuation (Mahler, Pine and Bergman 1975). Mahler and her co-workers described sub-phases of differentiation, practicing and rapproachment to account for development from a symbiotic phase in the middle of the first year when the infant and mother are still primarily a unit, to the autonomy or separation of the three-year-old from its mother. More widely known are the three phases – protest, despair and detachment – described by Bowlby as the young child's response to separation from its primary caregiver and his hypothesis relating maternal loss or deprivation and psychiatric illness. Research in the past thirty years has supported and clarified this proposed relationship but also shown the need to distinguish between bonding failure and bond disruption, between qualitative differences in care and their effects on intellectual, social and emotional factors, between long and short term effects and the influence of individual differences on outcomes (Rutter 1981). (See also ATTACHMENT; DEPRIVATION.) BBL

Bibliography

Mahler, M.S., Pine, F. and Bergman, A. 1975: *The psychological birth of the human infant*. London: Hutchinson; New York: Basic Books.

Rutter, M. 1981: *Maternal deprivation reassessed*, 2nd edn. Harmondsworth and New York: Penguin.

sequential analysis A family of research methods which detect and summarize the regularities with which one event or behavior follows another. The commonest techniques begin by calculating transitional probabilities, the conditional probabilities with which each type of event occurs given the types of immediately preceding events. In the simplest case a Markov chain is formed – a sequence of events having as its defining regularity a fixed pattern of probabilities of occurrence for each event, conditional only upon the one event immediately before.

Such methods require three assumptions to be met, which may frequently be a problem with real behavioral data: stationarity (meaning that the transitional probabilities are fixed parameters of the pattern); homogeneity (meaning that the probabilities have not been produced by the unwitting mixture of several different behavior patterns); and order (meaning that probabilities have been used which are conditional on the appropriate number of preceding events).

Other approaches to sequential analysis include methods based on the rule systems of generative grammar and the methods of time series analysis which is used with continuous variables. DDC

serial learning In serial learning items (e.g. nonsense syllables) are always presented in the same serial order, and the subject learns to anticipate the next item of the list in response to each item, with a special stimulus signaling the beginning of the sequence. The early work on serial learning concentrated on finding the functional stimulus in the serial learning task, since each item serves both as a stimulus and a response term. Modern research, instead, looks at serial learning as a problem in memory encoding and retrieval, where the same kind of processes play a role as in other memory tests, viz. subjective organization and chunking processes. A striking empirical regularity observed in most serial learning task is the serial position effect: when performance in a serial learning task is plotted with the percentage of the total errors on the ordinate and serial position on the abscissa, an inverted U-shaped curve is obtained, with a slight asymmetry since more errors occur in the second half. This function can be shown to be the result of the learning strategies used in serial tasks. WKi

serial vs. parallel processing The sense organs receive information in parallel: many receptors are stimulated simultaneously in normal life. Central information processing however appears often to deal with only one message at a time. For example, we can visually fixate either a picture on our left or on our right. Conscious decision making and thought can deal with only one message at a time even if the receptors do not point to a source, such as trying to attend to two conversations at once. Central processing is therefore serial. The main exception is in the case of highly practised skills. When behavior becomes automatic it can often be performed in parallel with other behavior. NM

serotonin A monoamine neurotransmitter in both the peripheral and central nervous systems. Serotonin is synthesized from the amino acid, tryptophan, the primary source of which is dietary. Centrally, serotonergic cell bodies are located in the pineal gland, and in discrete nuclei of the BRAIN STEM, especially in the nuclei of the raphe system. Descending serotonergic neurons form synapses in the SPINAL CORD. Ascending serotonergic fibers include projections from the raphe nuclei to a number of other neural structures, including the RETICULAR ACTIVATING SYSTEM (some serotonergic cell bodies are also found here), HYPOTHALAMUS, HIPPOCAMPUS, CEREBRAL CORTEX, CEREBELLUM, and portion of the BASAL GANGLIA. The majority of serotonergic synapses seem to be inhibitory. Serotonergic pathways appear to be involved in a number of physiological functions, including thermoregulation, sleep and the perception of pain, as well as mediating the action of certain hallucinogens. GPH

sex: social psychology Until recently, "sex" was simply treated as an independent variable in many social psychological studies, because variations in social behavior depend to some extent upon the sex or gender of subjects. Research has emphasized differences between men and women in aggression, conformity, achievement-orientated behaviors and the perception of non-verbal cues. Although many sex differences in these forms of social behavior have been reported, no simple differential pattern has emerged from this research.

The social psychological study of sexual behavior has only just begun to attract the attention of researchers, presumably because the investigation of intimate behavior is still regarded as taboo. Nevertheless interesting findings about the social aspects of sexual behavior are beginning to emerge with respect to changes in sexual attitudes and practices (e.g. contraception), differences and similarities between male and female sexual behavior and reactions to erotica and pornography. JMFJ

Bibliography

Baron, R.A. and Byrne, D. 1981: *Social psychology*. Boston, Mass.: Allyn and Bacon.

sex differences in development A field of study concerned with the measurement and explanation of differences in the behavior of males and females as they appear throughout the lifespan. These differences embrace aspects of intellectual functioning, temperament and interests relating to work and leisure. The psychological study of differences is not directly concerned with primary sexual characteristics such as those involving hormones and reproduction or such secondary characteristics as size and bone structure. Psychological differences are often uncovered incidentally when experimenters compare the performance of males and females before combining scores for the two groups. The lack of systematic study is reflected in the variety of reported differences. Not surprisingly controversy surrounds the conclusions which have been drawn from the empirical evidence and conflicting theoretical accounts are offered to explain alleged differences.

Maccoby and Jacklin's landmark survey (1974) of over 1,600 studies reported reliable differences in only four areas and challenged many stereotypic beliefs. They concluded that the evidence supported the belief that females have greater verbal skills although it was unclear whether these are present in early childhood or emerge shortly before puberty. Males were found to have higher visual-spatial and mathematical abilities; these appear reliably in adolescence. In addition boys displayed more aggression both physical and verbal; differences could be observed in the play of toddlers. On the other hand Maccoby and Jacklin concluded that the evidence failed to support beliefs that girls are more sociable or suggestible, that girls are better at simple tasks and rote memory while boys are better able to deal with complex intellectual tasks or those requiring analytical thinking, that girls lack achievement motivation and self-esteem, that boys are visually orientated while girls are auditorially orientated, or that boys are more responsive to environmental factors while girls' development is more influenced by heredity. They noted that the evidence was inconclusive concerning sex differences in tactile sensitivity, anxiety and fear, activity level, competitiveness, dominance, compliance and nurturance.

Although Maccoby and Jacklin have provided a starting point for much further study their survey has been attacked both for the limited nature of its conclusions and for its lack of stringency (Block 1976; Fairweather 1976). Block argues that the fortuitous reporting of differences in studies which were not designed to reveal them and the reliance on subjects from a restricted age range (over three-quarters of the studies reviewed by Maccoby and Jacklin were of children below the age of thirteen years) challenges the conclusions which are drawn. In addition she questions Maccoby and Jacklin's decision procedures, for example giving equal weight to statistically weak and powerful studies, omitting some significant reports and failing to achieve conceptual clarity in their own analysis. Block believes that the evidence can just as well support many of the differences which Maccoby and Jacklin reported as unproven and is often clearer than they indicated. In contrast Fairweather, examining studies of intellectual ability, challenged the evidence for differences in verbal and mathematical skills although he supported the view that males and females differ in their visual–spatial abilities.

This lack of consensus has not deterred psychologists from seeking and providing explanations for the differences they believe they have found. These explanations are generally not derived directly from psychological theory but are as wide-ranging and controversial as the evidence they attempt to explain.

Common-sense accounts of sex differences link psychological traits to biological differences of form and reproductive function. Psychological explanations often reveal their origins in naïve accounts. So pervasive has the common-sense view been that Victorian scholars sought women's alleged intellectual inferiority in their smaller absolute brain size. This belief has been discredited; when comparisons of intelligence are made across species the ratio of the mass of the brain to the total mass of the individual is employed. Even this alleged relationship is doubtful.

The contemporary and competing naïve explanation of differences in terms of social conditioning has gained impetus from the women's movement. It emphasizes that the differences which we are trying to trace reflect the roles which men and women in our society are expected to fulfill – the preparation of girls for motherhood and undemanding low status work and of boys for achievement and competition for society's most prestigious positions. These expectations and aspirations are believed to be differentially inculcated by conditioning, a term which owes little to Pavlov but is used in everyday speech to explain the learning of social rules and values.

Psychologists acknowledge the influence of both biological and environmental factors in development but many emphasize the former at the expense of the latter. Typically, volumes reviewing theories and evidence of sex differences in intellectual ability devote one section to social factors but one each to the effects of genes, hormones and the brain (Wittig and Petersen 1979).

In discussing genes, spatial ability has been linked to a recessive gene on the X chromosome. The evidence for such an inheritance pattern is not strong nor is that for the variability hypothesis which suggests that male heterozygosity (X and Y chromosomes) results in greater extremes in the male on a variety of traits. Hormones which have been shown to affect reproductive behavior in rats are often implicated in explaining temperamental differences as well as intellectual ability. Varying effects of greater lateralization of the right or the left hemisphere of the brain have been used to account for differences in verbal and spatial abilities. None of these explanations has gone unchallenged.

The superior performance of males in educational and occupational domains involving mathematical and visual–spatial abilities has enlivened the debate. There is fairly wide consensus concerning the contribution of biological factors to differences in spatial ability (McGee 1979) and the relation of these to mathematical achievement (Sherman 1978). However, psychologists such as Sherman argue for including the impact of sex-role factors in any account of differential performance in mathematics. She has measured children's beliefs about their chances of being successful in mathematics, about the usefulness of it in their lives and about their parents' evaluations of their achievement and shown that they influence performance as much as visual–spatial ability. Sherman's explanation is interactive in that mathematical achievement is shown to reflect biological and social processes. Although interactional explanations of many varieties are widely considered they are still challenged. A recent study of almost 10,000 adolescents of superior mathematical ability in the United States demonstrated a male superiority and its authors ascribed this difference to inherent factors which distinguished males and females (Benbow and Stanley 1980).

The vehemence of the controversy focuses attention on the nature of the differences being explained. Primary sex characteristics such as genital structure yield categorical differentiations: males and females show no overlap; while psychological traits are distributed along a continuum, most average differences are small and there is much overlap. The magnitude of difference in visual–spatial abilities is medium to large yet 25 per cent of females perform better than the male average.

Categorical differentiation based upon genitals may be important in subtle ways. Maccoby and Jacklin reported few differences in the socialization of boys and girls but by the time children begin to speak they correctly label themselves. Both social learning and cognitive–developmental theory offer explanations: the former in terms of rewards and punishment as well as imitation and learning through observation and the latter according to the child's developing understanding of the social world and its place in the sex role system (Mischel 1970, Kohlberg 1966).

Undoubtedly the processes described by social learning theorists contribute to the acquisition of differences in behavior. A particular advantage of the cognitive–developmental approach is its emphasis on the child's active participation in constructing its own identity. A new approach to sex differences, which derives from ethnomethodology, begins by attacking the term "sex" and by noting that the processes through which individuals are categorized as male or female are social and problematic in their precise operation (Kessler and McKenna 1978). To mark the social construction of the categories "man" and "woman" the term "gender" is being used increasingly to designate psychological differences and sex is reserved for reference to biological distinctions. The introduction of the term "gender" provides no explanation in itself but accentuates the need for caution before accepting exclusively biological accounts of psychological differences. In addition it stresses that the very situations in which differences are recorded, be they surveys or experiments are social situations differently interpreted by men and women. The explanation of psychological differences observed in them will require understanding of these situations as well as of biological and intrapsychic phenomena (Deux 1976).

BBL

Bibliography

*Archer, J. and Lloyd, B. 1982: *Sex and gender in society*. Harmondsworth: Penguin.

Benbow, C.P. and Stanley, J.C. 1980: Sex differences in mathematical ability: fact or artifact? *Science* 210, 1262–4.

Block, J.H. 1976: Issues, problems and pitfalls in assessing sex differences: a critical review of 'The psychology of sex differences'. *Merrill-Palmer quarterly* 22, 283–308.

Deux, K. 1976: *The behavior of men and women*. Belmont, California: Wadsworth Publishing Company.

Fairweather, H. 1976: Sex differences in cognition. *Cognition* 4, 231–280.

Kessler, S.J. and McKenna, W. 1978: *Gender: an ethnomethodological approach*. New York: Wiley.

Kohlberg, L. 1966: A cognitive-developmental analysis of children's sex role concepts and attitudes. In E.E. Maccoby, ed., *The development of sex differences*. Stanford, California: Stanford University Press; London: Tavistock Publications (1967).

Maccoby, E.E. and Jacklin, C.N. 1974: *The psychology of sex differences*. Stanford, California: Stanford University Press; Oxford: Oxford University Press (1975).

McGee, M.G. 1979: Human spatial abilities: Psychometric studies and environmental, genetic, hormonal and neurological influences. *Psychological Bulletin* 86, 889–918.

Mischel, W. 1970: Sex-typing and socialization. In P.H. Mussen, ed., *Carmichael's manual of child psychology* Vol. III, 3rd edn. New York: Wiley.

*Sherman, J.A. 1978: *Sex related cognitive differences: an essay on theory and evidence*. Springfield, Illinois: Charles C. Thomas.

Shields, S.A. 1975: Functionalism, Darwinism, and the psychology of women: a study in social myth. *American psychologist* 30, 739–54.

Wittig, M.A. and Petersen, A.C. 1979: *Sex-related differences in cognitive functioning: developmental issues*. New York and London: Academic Press.

sex-related speech differences Cultural definitions of femaleness and maleness can vary greatly, and accordingly, in a society emphasizing set specifity, differential linguistic behavior can develop as a result of the close interrelationship between language and culture.

Our perception and consequently our analysis of sex-linked aspects of language is shaped by the prevalent representations of sex roles in our own culture. The division of a given society in terms of sex roles is not always clear-cut, however, and cross-culturally a large number of intermediate patterns exist, resulting in a continuum at one end of which lies the reversal of sex roles as we know them.

While it is generally agreed that western (and probably all) cultures have assigned certain linguistic markers to female and male roles, it must be pointed out that such sex-related differences are unlikely to reflect significant differences at the level of linguistic competence, but are associated with differential performance or differential culture-derived communicative COMPETENCE. It is not the linguistic structures themselves but their use in communication which display sex-associated patterns.

The two most commonly given explanations of the relationship between a speaker's sex and speech variations are the dominant economic relations in society and biological factors. Consequently, no study of sex-related speech varieties is possible without taking an interdisciplinary standpoint involving linguistic, psychology, biology, anthropology, ethology, economics and politics. As stated by Smith (1979, p.136) "sex alone is probably not the best determinant of any isolated feature, either marker or stereotype".

Interest in sex-linked speech varieties was awakened in the last century following the reports of travelers, missionaries and ethnographers in "exotic" parts of the world. These reports consisted principally of anecdotal descriptions of lexical and morphological asymmetries, and hardly any attempt was made to connect observed speech differences to semantic, psychological and economic factors. An over-estimation of sex-related speech differences resulted, since the linguists who used such information (e.g. Max Mueller 1975) were mostly male western academics who analysed language from their own perspective, assuming that standard language was that spoken by males and that female speech was accordingly deviant. These early observers thus ignored the fact that sex-specific speech patterns may have different significance in different cultures. It was only because male and female patterns were seen with reference to the western model that an opposition between the sexes became expected.

Attempts to study sex-related speech differences in a systematic way began in the early 1970s, drawing partly on the anthropological investigations of Mead (1935, 1949). One of the most important distinctions introduced at this point was that between sex-exclusive and sex-preferential speech markers.

Every society or culture selects and standardizes certain human traits and assigns to them the status of social markers according to its needs. Thus:

(1) criteria other than sex (e.g. age, profession or ethnic origin) can be emphasized;
(2) the selection of biological features such as sex and age is favored, because they are both immediately perceptible and "irreversible";
(3) human traits can be suppressed or encouraged to meet the needs or wishes of society. This leads to a promotion of positively evaluated markers of sex.

It must be stressed that the features selected tend to be of a cultural rather than a biological nature, and that they are only subsequently assigned sexual value. A sexual explanation of non-sexual events tends to be given in such a manner that cause and effect can become interchanged. Where culture determines sexual role behavior, every member of a culture will have a culturally determined sexual personality. As speech reflects cultural processes, sex-specific behavior is also manifested at the linguistic level.

Recent research in bio- and neurolinguistics has pointed to the fact that biological and physiological differences between the sexes must also be considered in connection with sex-specific speech differences (see NEUROLINGUISTICS). In addition to possible (but not necessary) phonetic variations of pitch relating to the length and thickness of the vocal folds and supralaryngeal vocal tract size, there is sex-specific specialization tied to brain LATERALIZATION. The specialization of the left half of the brain (language setting) and the right half (spatial perception) is laid out differently in each sex. Similarly, the perception of emotions varies with a person's sex. There may thus be a genuine connection between lexico-semantic choice of emotional utterances and referential reality. (See WHORF.)

The principal task facing the analyst is to relate observed speech markers such as voice quality, tempo or prosodies to the culturally and biologically determined sex differences, specifying in each case the extent to which speech expresses the psychological reality of individual speakers and/or the collective experience shared with other members of a social group. In this connection it must be pointed out that speakers belong to many different groups at once, e.g.

groups defined by age, profession or ethnic origin, in addition to sex.

Next to socially and biologically conditioned speech markers the study of sex-related language differences is concerned with the ways in which sexual differences are expressed in the lexicon of language (see LEXICAL ANALYSIS). First, there is the unequivocal case of lexical items denoting some specific aspect in the sexual life of individuals. Verbs expressing the idea of "to lactate" or to "menstruate" are associated with female subjects cross-linguistically, whereas verbs expressing the meanings of "pulling back one's foreskin" or "to be impotent" are predicated of males only.

In other cases of lexical analysis there is considerable confusion, the most common examples being (1) the unsystematic listing of synchronic asymmetries (e.g. pairs such as master–mistress; spinster–bachelor where the female has negative connotations) without considering their socio-historical background, and (2) the inability to distinguish between the speech of a subject (e.g. the use of the interjection *eek*! by women) and speech about a subject (e.g. the use of the adjective *buxom* and the noun *wench*). It has been argued that the lexical inventory must be made to conform to biological reality and it is widely assumed that the absence of lexical information about the referent's sex in the title and names of professions (e.g. the use of *doctor* rather than "*he-doctor*" or "*she-doctor*") is a form of discrimination. One could argue, however, that an overmarked distinction such as actor vs. actress reinforces rather than diminishes the division between the sexes.

Frequently adduced examples of sexism in language are the fields of morphology and pronominal usage. The most common misunderstanding concerns the relationship between gender (grammatical genus) and sexus (natural sex).

The primary function of gender is that of a classificatory device and instead of maleness and femaleness, shape, size, edibility or animateness can be its basis. The incorporation of this feature in languages such as French or German and its manifestation in articles, derivational morphology, adjective agreement or pronominalization serves little synchronic function, as it does not carry any information relevant to social interrelationships. One reason for the discrepency between grammatical gender assignation and social reality may be sought in the transition from a pre-industrial to an industrial society, and it may be the case that gender could serve a social function in a very different society.

The question of the basic, or more natural (see LINGUISTIC NATURALNESS) value of masculine forms remains unresolved. It can be shown that alleged universals of grammar, such as "masculine comes before feminine in conjuncts" or that "the male gender is more comprehensive than the female gender" (as in: mind that child, *he* may be deaf), are highly culture-specific as well as being fairly recent developments. If one agrees with claims made by biologists that the female sex is the more basic because it is irreversible, the male sexual personality appears as unstable. One could then argue that the constant need for definition may have led to the linguistic consequence of elaborating forms of expression where maleness is lasting and stable! This may also account for the fact that speakers generally feel the need to associate gender with sex in languages where sex-linked gender is overtly expressed. We are dealing here with some of the roots of tension between linguistic, social and biological explanations.

The existence of sex-related varieties of language at the syntactic level is not generally accepted, the reason for this being that we are leaving the domain of performance and reaching that of competence in the sense of the ability of speaker–hearers to generate well-formed surface structures. Lakoff (1975) has pointed out that the more frequent use of tag questions and conditional mood, among other things, points to a less secure position of women. Her claims have recently been challenged (Smith 1979 : 135) by findings that syntactic differences appear to be related more closely to a sex-neutral powerless speech style which is distributed differently within and between societies.

Recent findings (Richter 1979) indicate that even non-verbal or pragmatic elements (see NON-VERBAL COMMUNICATION) are largely culture-determined, and associated with different sexual values in different societies.

From the above discussion it would seem to follow that it is insufficient to describe sex-related speech differences in terms of innate biological factors. It seems equally one-sided to relate them simply to their economic dependence or other forms of discrimination against women. The two factors are interrelated in a complex way. The status of any single member of a society is multidimensional and dynamically changing. There are many more forms of behavioral and speech patterns than those reflecting maleness or femaleness. Furthermore, speech attitudes and behavior need to be considered beside the sex role expectations in a given society at a given time.

A potential new approach to the question of sex-related language differences would attenuate the differences where they are less relevant (i.e. in the domains of social competence), and assign observed linguistic differences to a linguistic continuum rather than measuring them against a preselected (culturally determined) standard. By changing the speakers' attitudes to this topic one could eliminate some forms of discriminatory behavior and promote a better fit between language and society. MV

Bibliography

Farb, P. 1973: *Word play: what happens when people talk.* New York: A.A. Knopf.

Key, M.R. 1972: Linguistic behavior of male and female. *Linguistics* 88, 15–31.

*——— 1975: *Male/female language.* Metuchen, N.J.: Scarecrow Press.

Lakoff, R. 1975: *Language and women's place.* New York: Harper & Row.

Mead, M. 1935: *Sex and temperament.* New York: William Morrow.

——— 1949: *Male and female.* New York: William Morrow.

Meditch, A. 1975: The development of sex-specific speech patterns in young children. *Anthropological linguistics.* 17/9, 421–33.

Miller, C. and Swift, K. 1976: *Words and women, language and the sexes.* New York: Anchor Press/Doubleday; London: Pelican Books (1979).

Mueller, M. 1975: *Science of language.* London: Longman.

Richter, M. 1980: *Aspekte der Frauensprache.* M.A. thesis, Berlin: Technische Universität.

Sachs, J., Lieberman, P. and Erickson, D. 1973: Anatomical and cultural determinants of male and female speech. In *Language attitudes: current trends and prospects.* ed. R.W. Shuy and R. W. Fasold. Washington, D.C.: Georgetown University Press, 74–84.

Smith, M. 1979: Sex markers in speech. In *Social markers in speech,* ed. K.R. Scherer and H. Giles, Cambridge and New York: Cambridge University Press.

*Thorne, B. and Henley N., eds 1975: *Language and sex: difference and dominance.* Rowley, Mass.: Newbury House.

Trudgill, P. 1974: Language and sex. Ch 4 of *Sociolinguistics: an introduction.* London: Penguin.

sex roles A repertoire of attitudes, behaviors, perceptions and affective reactions which are more commonly associated with one sex than the other. Over the last fifteen years, social scientists have documented the content of sex roles and considered their implications for the treatment of men and women by various social institutions such as education, mental health, criminal justice and the labor force.

Ancillary but separate from the study of sex roles is the investigation of sex differences (or gender differences) in human performance. Empirical studies suggest that the most reliable sex differences are to be found in IQ tests (with males performing on average higher on spatial–mathematical subscales, females higher on verbal subscales) and aggressive behavior (males on average displaying spontaneously higher levels). The interaction of sex differences and sex roles has been variously explained by different disciplines. Some anthropologists (e.g. Tiger 1970) have argued that originally small morphological and neuroanatomical differences between the sexes were augmented by early bifurcation of social responsibilities; men's hunting behavior leading to increases in aggression and spatial discriminations, and women's child-rearing resulting in increased verbal ability and decreased aggression. Neuroendocrine bases of sex differences have been documented by Gray and Buffery (1971) and related to evolutionary processes. Other anthropologists and sociologists have stressed the mutability of sex roles, noting cultures in which men perform "women's" work (Mead 1935), and the way in which economic and social changes have altered the prevailing notions of appropriately "feminine" activities (Rowbotham 1973).

Developmental psychologists have pursued three major approaches to sex role acquisition in children. The psychoanalytic school directs attention to the Oedipus complex and its successful resolution as crucial for appropriate identification, while at the same time positing the passive and active nature of women and men respectively as relatively fixed (Strachey and Richards 1973). Social learning theorists believe that behavior appropriate to sex role results from differential positive reinforcement (Mischel 1970). Cognitive developmentalists suggest that only after the acquisition of the concept of permanence can the child understand the immutability of gender which is a prerequisite for sex role learning (Kohlberg 1966).

Studies of sexually anomalous babies by Money and Erhardt (1972) have shed more light on the plasticity of sex role learning. One of two male identical twins had his penis amputated as a result of a surgical accident. The child received plastic surgery and endocrine treatment resulting in an appearance of femininity although remaining genetically male. While exhibiting heightened levels of rough-and-tumble play more characteristic of a male, the child's behavior by the age of four-and-a-half years was significantly different from the brother's, and virtually indistinguishable from other females. This indicates the critical importance of socialization in sex role development.

AC

Bibliography

Gray, J.A. and Buffery, A.W.H. 1971: Sex differences in emotional and cognitive behaviour in mammals including man; adaptive and neural bases. *Acta psychologia* 35, 89–111.

Kohlberg, L. 1966: A cognitive developmental analysis of children's sex role concepts and attitudes. In *The development of sex differences,* ed. E.E. Maccoby. Stanford, Calif.: Stanford University Press.

Maccoby, E. and Jacklin, C.N. 1974: *The psychology of sex differences.* Stanford, Calif.: Stanford University Press.

Mead, M. 1935: *Sex and temperament in three primitive societies.* New York: Morrow.

Mischel, W. 1970: Sex typing and socialization. In *Carmichael's manual of child psychology,* ed. P.H. Mussen, vol. 1. New York: Wiley.

Money, J. and Erhardt, A.A. 1972: *Man and woman, boy and girl.* Baltimore, Maryland: Johns Hopkins University Press.

Strachey, J. and Richards, A., eds. 1973: *New introductory lectures on psychoanalysis.* Harmondsworth: Penguin. (Lectures by Freud 1925 and 1931.)

Tiger, L. 1970: *Men in groups.* New York: Random House.

Weitz, S. 1977: *Sex roles.* New York: Oxford University Press.

sexual behavior and the nervous system The nervous system plays a complex role in controlling sexual behavior through the interaction of neuronal and hormonal activity. The HYPOTHALAMUS initiates and regulates sexual behavior by controlling the pituitary gland's production of gonadotrophic hormones which stimulate the sex organs (gonads). The amount of sex hormones produced by the gonads at the sequential stages of sexual behavior is monitored by the hypothalamus via feedback through the blood. Although these hormones play an important role in the activation of such behavior, the nervous system controls its form and direction.

The hypothalamus does not act alone within the nervous system in controlling sexual behavior. The LIMBIC SYSTEM, and particularly the AMYGDALA, is important for the discrimination of environmental and social factors which dictate the appearance of sex behavior and its appropriate expression. The amygdala achieves this control by inhibiting the hypothalamic influence on the pituitary gland. In cases where the amygdala has been removed in man and animals, inappropriate sexual behavior is elicited.

RCS/BER

sexual behavior in animals Behavior associated with reproduction. In many animals there are three phases of the reproductive cycle: (1) preparation, which may include building a nest, establishing a territory, etc. (2) sexual behavior, including courtship and fertilization of eggs. (3)

parental behavior, including incubation, nursing, feeding and guarding the young.

In most species reproductive behavior is organized on a cyclical basis, determined directly by changes in hormone balance, and indirectly by seasonal or climatic factors. The reproductive cycle is usually organized so that the young are born at the most favorable time of year, when food is plentiful. For example, great tits (*Parus major*) in southern England lay their eggs in April, the exact date being strongly influenced by the average daily temperatures during March. Hatching occurs in May and June.

In vertebrates the combined influence of changes in day-length and temperature stimulates the pituitary gland to secrete gonadotrophic hormones, which stimulate the sexual organs to produce the sex hormones responsible for maintaining sexual behavior and physiology. In some species the endogenous circannual clock has a strong influence on the timing of reproductive behavior, and may override climatic factors (Pengelley 1974).

In addition to the seasonal reproductive cycle, many mammals have a shorter cycle of sexual activity, or heat, called the estrous cycle. There may be a series of such cycles throughout the breeding season, as in rodents, cats and rabbits, or there may be a few, as in dogs. Within each cycle there is a short period of heat, when the female is receptive and when males are attracted to females as a result of special chemical attractants, called pheromones, which are released at this time. In a few mammals, such as the cat and rabbit, ovulation occurs only after copulation, but in the majority ovulation occurs irrespective of sexual intercourse. In some primates, including man, the female is receptive most of the time, there is no estrous cycle, and ovulation occurs at a particular point in a cycle of a different type, called the menstrual cycle.

Sexual intercourse, or copulation, is normally preceded by some type of courtship. In some invertebrates, fish, amphibians and reptiles the courtship is perfunctory, but some communication must take place for the female to be able to discriminate between sexual and aggressive advances on the part of the male. A male house fly (*Musca*) jumps on the female's back without any apparent preliminary, but the chemical senses of the female have to be properly stimulated for mating to be successful. The male fruit fly (*Drosophila*) performs an elaborate dance before attempting to mount the female. Here the stimulation provided by the male is primarily visual and auditory.

Elaborate courtship usually takes place in the context of coyness on the part of the female. In many species it is important that the female should appear to be reluctant to mate initially. Coyness encourages competition among males and gives the female a chance to choose between different suitors. Mate selection is especially important in those species in which the female provides the greater parental investment, because the male has greater time and opportunity for promiscuous mating and is less likely to take particular care in choosing among females. In those species in which the female is primarily responsible for care of the offspring it is the female that exercises choice during courtship. In the rare cases of male parental care, such as the three-spined stickleback, it is the male that is primarily active in choice of mate.

Courtship involves some kind of display during which visual, auditory, chemical or tactile communication occurs between the participants. The display may serve a number of functions, including advertisement, warning to rivals, and identification and greeting between established breeding partners. The courtship may involve a single male–female pair, or it may be communal as in the case of the sage grouse (*Centrocercus mophasianus*). Male sage grouse are conspicuous birds which aggregate at communal breeding arenas, called leks, where they compete for females. The dull coloured females visit various leks and appear to be choosing a suitable mate. Communal displays occur in a number of bird species and in some antelopes.

In many species the courtship of the male brings the female to a state of sexual readiness. In the smooth newt (*Triturus vulgaris*) the probability of successful fertilization increases with the duration of the male display. In doves and pigeons the calls of the male induce changes in female hormones which bring her to a state of sexual receptivity.

Mating techniques vary enormously among animals. In general, fertilization of eggs by sperm is external to the body in fish and amphibians. Internal fertilization takes place in birds, but is highly developed in mammals which have intromission in which the female vagina is penetrated by the male penis. Single or multiple intromissions may be required before there is ejaculation of sperm into the vagina. In some animals, such as dogs, there is a genital lock which prevents disengagement during intromission. Ejaculation is followed by a refractory period during which no further ejaculation can occur. In rats it is known that the refractory period facilitates sperm transport inside the female, and that this is disrupted if copulation from another male occurs during this period. It is possible that the refractory period is a device enabling the male to ward off rival males and thus prevent sperm competition within the female.

After fertilization the initial phase of parental care is the sole responsibility of the female in those species in which fertilization is internal. Where fertilization is external it may be the male which assumes the parental role. In the three-spined stickleback, for example, the male chases the female away from the nest as soon as he has fertilized the eggs which she deposited there. The male then guards the nest against rival males which may attempt to steal or eat his eggs.

The pattern of parental care that is characteristic of a species is an important part of its social organization, and is a major factor in the evolution of the mating system. Male birds are just as well equipped to care for the eggs and young as are female birds and in 90 per cent of bird species there is a monogamous mating system with the sexes taking roughly equal parental roles. Female mammals, on the other hand, are specially equipped to feed the young and the male cannot play an equivalent part in parental care. The majority of mammals show polygamy, in which one male mates with a number of females. DJM

Bibliography

*Beach, Frank A., ed. 1965: *Sex and behavior*. New York and London: Wiley.

*Hutchinson, John B. 1978: *Biological determinants of sexual behaviour*. Chichester and New York: Wiley.

Pengelley, Eric T., ed. 1974: *Circannual clocks*. New York and London: Academic Press.

sexual differentiation and the nervous system Adult sexual behavior may be influenced by circulating levels of hormones, but its expression is controlled by the neural circuitry of the brain and spinal cord (see SEXUAL BEHAVIOR AND THE NERVOUS SYSTEM). This neural organization is determined early in development, when the presence of sex hormones may act to organize brain circuitry differentially in males and females. For example, exposure to androgens, male sex hormones, around the time of birth is known to influence sexual behaviour in adult rodents long after the circulating effectiveness of the hormones has ceased. Anatomical differences between the sexes in the pre-optic area of the HYPOTHALAMUS can be abolished by giving androgen to newborn females or by castrating newborn males. Likewise, the presence of ESTROGENS, female sex hormones, may influence both brain development and consequent adult sexual behavior.

While such studies help to elucidate the role of hormones in neural development, they continue to elicit controversy regarding their relevance to the psychological study of sex differences in humans (see SEX DIFFERENCES IN DEVELOPMENT). BER/RCS

shame *See* guilt and shame

shift working The need to work shifts arises when work must be done outside the normal working day. This need can arise for three main reasons; firstly a service may be required outside normal working hours, e.g. hospitals; secondly a process may need to run continuously to avoid the cost of starting up and shutting down e.g. steel making; thirdly the capital cost of equipment may need to be amortised quickly by intensive use, e.g. air transport. It will be noted that as technology advances, all these reasons become more cogent. From a human viewpoint shift work is inherently undesirable but for the above reasons it is often essential. There has been extensive research on shift work starting with the Industrial Fatigue Research Board in Britain during the first world war and now supported extensively by the European Coal and Steel Community.

The evidence in terms of opinions, performance or health does not indicate that shift-work is seriously detrimental. This may be partly due to self selection: some individuals apparently have a much greater tolerance than others and may choose or continue to work shifts. Shift working can be made more acceptable through incentives, sensitive consideration of social variables and judicious selection of the most appropriate shift system. The systems vary from the double day shift (one team on a long morning, one on a long afternoon, with a nightly shut down except for maintenance) to a continuous twenty-four hour system requiring successive teams working for eight hours on a rotating schedule. WTS

Bibliography

Colquhoun, W.P. and Rutenfranz, J., eds. 1975: *Studies of shift work*. London: Taylor & Francis.

short term memory The memory system that holds information in temporary storage for a minute or so is usually referred to as short term memory (STM) or immediate memory. The capacity of STM is limited to approximately seven items of information, a finding which stands in contrast to the very large capacity of LONGTERM MEMORY (LTM). Memories stored in STM can either be forgotten or, through the processes of CONSOLIDATION OF MEMORY, be transferred to LTM. Retrieval of information from STM has been extensively studied using reaction-time procedures. These studies suggest that retrieval from STM is based on serial rather than parallel search processes.

See also MEMORY; SHORT TERM AND LONG TERM. RAJ

sibling rivalry (sib-competition) Competitive interactions between the offspring of the same parent(s). Resources available to litter-mates may be in short supply. In sexually-reproducing species siblings will not be identical genetically, and so a gene that causes its bearer to behave selfishly will not always harm the same gene in others. The extent and nature of sib-competition will be moderated by kin selection (see ALTRUISM); full sibs will, all things equal, be less aggressively competitive than half sibs because of their greater relatedness. An early form of sib-competition can be competition over resources provided by the parent (i.e. competition over PARENTAL INVESTMENT). It will generally be in the parent's interests to reduce such competition where possible. Sib-competition can, under extreme circumstances, lead to fratricide. There is good evidence for this in birds (O'Connor, 1979). GAP

Bibliography

O'Connor, R.J. 1979: Brood reduction in birds: selection for fratricide, infanticide and suicide? *Animal behavior* 26, 79–96.

sign stimulus In instinctive behavior, that aspect of a normally complex stimulus which evokes the strongest response. It has been demonstrated that the red breast feathers of a male European robin alone evoke more attack from a rival than the combination of all other features. This is a typical example. The response can occur in the absence of the sign stimulus (robins lacking the red feathers are still attacked) but far less strongly. There is sometimes evidence from animals reared in social isolation that responsiveness to sign stimuli develops normally in the absence of exposure to them. Sign stimuli are usually specially evolved signal structures, crests, bright patches, calls or scent glands, which trigger appropriate responses in con-specifics. Lorenz called such structures releasers and they are much employed in intraspecific communication. Not all sign stimuli are releasers in this sense. The speckling pattern of some birds eggs is an important sign stimulus for incubation, but it is likely to have evolved as camouflage. (See also SUPERNORMAL STIMULUS). AWGM

simulators Are designed to replicate the essential characteristics of a task or group of tasks that are necessary for learning and the transfer of training. Simulators come in many forms from those stressing "physical fidelity" or the maximization of operational equipment realism such as airplane flight simulators to those focusing on "psychological fidelity" or the close approximation of cognitive and behavioral processes necessary for successful job performance such as role-playing. There are many reasons for the development and use of simulators, most notable among them being safety considerations, controlled reproducibility, and cost. With regard to safety, the airplane simulator is an example where the final task, successfully piloting a plane under various flight conditions, requires much training; without a simulator the lives of pilots, instructors and others would be severely endangered. Controlled reproducibility refers to the fact that many conditions can be not only simulated, but repeated again and again, and events can be reproduced to a different time frame; for instance a business simulation encompassing many years of activity might unfold during a two-day workshop. Finally, while building a simulation exercise may be costly, this expense is often far less than the expense which might be incurred via on-the-job trial and error efforts. RRJ

skills Capabilities to perform particular tasks or to achieve particular goals. Many skills can be acquired, sometimes after a long period of training and practice. However, the essence of a skill is its effectiveness, so does not necessarily have to be learnt, but can develop largely as a result of the normal maturation process and be hardly at all dependent on a specific training program.

The difference between the everyday use of the term and its use by psychologists is particularly obvious in the industrial context, in which the concept of a "skilled worker" is conventionally used. The skilled worker is frequently so defined in terms of his or her completion of an extended period of training, but from a psychological point of view the more important distinction has to be made in terms of the special skills that may be demanded by industrial tasks. A task which depends only on skills that people learn in the informal school of experience may be performed just as skilfully as another task which makes unusual performance demands that can only be met after a special course of training. This distinction accentuates the quality of performance rather than the procedures that have led up to achieving it.

"Skill" covers a wide range of acts and behavior. Some skills, such as playing tennis, are easily observed. Others, such as mental skills, are so structured that the underlying skill has to be inferred. It is useful to define three major categories of skill: (1) perceptual skills which depend mainly on the mechanisms which underlie perception, particularly of complex patterns; (2) perceptual-motor skills which emphasize the coordinated contribution of both perceptual (input) and motor (output) processes and mechanisms; and (3) mental skills such as reasoning. Thinking and reasoning, though logically inseparable from other kinds of skill, have been studied separately. It is not clear whether the ultimate analysis of different categories of skill will reveal a common set of underlying processes, or whether different contents will demand different underlying mechanisms.

To date the bulk of psychological research on skill has been concentrated on the nature and acquisition of perceptual-motor skills with considerable emphasis being placed on those with easily observable dynamic variations in input and output. While ball-games offer an interesting source of information it has been found convenient to invent new tasks in controlled (laboratory) situations with which to investigate the processes which underlie skilled performance. Tasks have been devised which make differential demands on hypothetical underlying processes including, for example, speed of decision, spatial and temporal accuracy of response and the capacity to share attention among a number of more or less simultaneous demands (Legge and Barber 1976).

The defining attributes of skill are effectiveness and flexibility. Effectiveness means that the act in question can be achieved quickly and accurately, and with economy which confers stamina. At a lower level of performance, in contrast, even if the right thing is done, it may have taken a long time to determine, it may be done clumsily and it may be done with less than the desired (or required) degree of accuracy. Furthermore, the actor/operator will probably appear harassed by the situation instead of seeming to have time in hand.

The flexibility which epitomizes skill is, however, the more important and less obvious characteristic. In real life, the same problem hardly ever occurs twice. When receiving service at tennis, badminton or squash, it is very unlikely that the same problem will be presented in terms of speed, position and trajectory of the flight of the ball. Yet a successful return demands that the receiver's racquet be in a particular place at a particular time, moving in a particular trajectory at a particular speed. Countless millions of service return shots would have to be learnt if the return was to be matched to the service. Skilled players can accomodate vast ranges of services, including those they have never seen before, and still produce effective return shots. They have a flexible skill which can deal with widely varying circumstances. A very simple (and untrained) example of this is the way in which relatively small boys can throw stones which vary quite widely in weight without the accuracy of the throw being significantly affected. An automatic allowance is made for the mass of the stone and the signals sent to the throwing muscles are adjusted accordingly.

Underlying mechanisms

The flexibility which characterizes skill also points to the sorts of processes and mechanisms which must underlie it. It places skill in stark contrast with, for example, habit. When stimulus-response (S-R) conceptualizations held sway it was postulated that all behavior could be analysed into a series of S-R connections, each S being a sufficient condition for the occurrence of its associated R. This Behaviorist Scheme was initiated by Watson and continues in the work of Skinner and his students. Unfortunately the S-R framework does not offer a rich enough theoretical structure to accommodate the flexibility which characterizes skill. A different level of analysis is needed which incorporates a more complex building block than the S-R link. This was provided by the growing interest of engineers in control theory and the self-stabilizing feature of the negative feedback circuit in which the output of the system is fed back and matched against a demand signal which defines the state that should be achieved.

A negative-feedback controlled system such as a thermostatically controlled refrigerator is stable in the sense that it always strives to produce the demand state even though there are factors in the system's environment that tend to disturb its output. The thermostat will produce an appropriate response regardless of whether it has "experienced" the specific environmental condition before. It operates according to a principle rather than producing a specific associative response.

Open-loop and closed-loop operation

Although feedback systems offer attractive models of the processes underlying human skills there is considerable debate about the extent to which skills actually operate as feedback systems. In an open-loop system the response is not connected back to the stimulus, while a closed-loop system is one in which, by feedback, the system can respond to its own output. If a performance is closed-looped, cutting the loop should cause a marked deterioration in performance. For example, when a car windscreen shatters at speed the driver has only his residual memory of the road and his position on it, and he will crash unless he manages to stop first. However, it can be shown that there are many skilful movements, such as aiming, playing a keyboard instrument etc that are unaffected by blocking the feedback and thereby cutting the loop. These quick responses are completed too fast for any feedback from them to influence their execution. These responses are called ballistic (Legge and Barber 1976).

Analysis of skilled performance indicates that the key to high levels of skill is to be found in open-loop operation. For while a number of skills such as car-driving clearly have a closed-loop aspect, it is equally clear that the individual movements that make up the sequence of control adjustments are themselves selected and executed in an open-loop mode. For example it is the antithesis of skilful driving to make a random series of alterations to the setting of the front-wheels of the car. The essential question is about how the skilled driver finds the right steering-wheel movement and then programs his motor system to produce that movement with virtually no further supervision.

A stimulus-response theory would argue that responses that fit a particular situation are learned and as skill increases a larger and larger repertoire of responses is compiled. As this bank of responses grows the chances of meeting a situation for which no at least approximately suitable response is available decrease. This theory offers a credible account but it also provokes a number of problems. First it would seem to require that all skills be learned since it is almost inconceivable that a person could inherit the specific patterns necessary to respond to particular stimuli, except in the gross sense of, say, turning to look at a source of noise. Secondly, it implies that the selection of an appropriate response would have to be a remarkable process carried out extremely rapidly. Otherwise the larger the repertoire the slower would be the selection of each response. Experimental studies of the time it takes people to choose one from among varying numbers of alternatives indicates that choice or selection time increases quite steeply as the number of alternatives increases. Although this relationship is logarithmic rather than linear (that is the gradient of the increase becomes less and less steep as the number of alternatives expands) it is clear that a process that depended upon sorting through and choosing from a very large repertoire would still be very time consuming (Welford 1976). It would be inconceivable that such a time-consuming process could produce the very rapid precise responses demanded by fast ball games such as tennis.

It is necessary, therefore, in all but the simplest choice problems (where the repertoire of responses is really very small, probably less than about fifteen) for a different principle to operate. Instead of selecting from among pre-programmed, learned responses it would be necessary for the responding mechanism to have a way of building an appropriate response from basic units using a set of design principles that have been acquired from training and practice. In this scheme what has been learned is not specific responses associated with specific stimuli but a set of algorithms or operational rules for building a program that will, when executed, produce a response. The skill of the performer will then be determined by the efficiency of those algorithms.

Of course, there will be many circumstances when a habitual movement will be adequate and when it would be inefficient to go through the time-consuming business of building a response from scratch. However, such responses may be relatively rare. Even in situations such as hitting a golf ball it is likely that the actual stroke will be produced by modulating the basic swing. The swing will have been incorporated as a unit within the algorithm. These variations will be needed to compensate for the lie of the ball and in order for example to introduce bias in flight to counteract a cross-wind.

Since the majority of skilled actions take place in a dynamic context an important component of skill is anticipation. Some mechanism or process must operate to predict the state of affairs in the future, at the time when the movement which is being planned will actually take place.

Tennis players need to aim at where the ball will be when the racquet gets there, not where the ball is when they are preparing their shot. An essential feature of increasing skill is the increasing precision of the prediction processes which make major contributions to the spatio-temporal coordination of movements allowing the right movements to be made at the right times.

Skill Acquisition
There is an important distinction between practice and training: in training a deliberate scheme to assist learning is defined and followed by the trainee. In many cases this scheme involves a trainer who both guides the trainee towards making more satisfactory movements and attending to more appropriate feedback and gives the trainee encouragement and an evaluation of progress. Practice may simply involve using the skills that have been acquired, sometimes imperfectly. There will be a fuzzy area between training and practice in which the benefits are greater than those which arise from simple repetition, but the guidance and feedback is considerably less precise than would be provided in a properly managed training program.

Psychologists have been much exercised by the nature of learning, probably because many have taken the view that the adult is very largely a product of the countless learning experiences that characterize development. However, a relatively small proportion of the effort that has been devoted to studying learning in general has been dedicated to the question of how skills are acquired.

Clear recommendations about how to promote skill acquisition have been very well covered by Holding (1965).
(1) Guidance (verbal or physical) which helps the learner to produce approximately the right sort of responses. For example, special contraptions have been made to ensure that a golf-club is swung only in the near-ideal arc, giving the beginning golfer a chance to feel what the swing should be like.
(2) Feedback informs the learner how close he or she is to producing the desired performance. Some kinds of feedback are knowledge of results. Feedback may involve a trainer or special equipment but often the situation produces a considerable amount without further enhancement, for example, failing to connect with an on-coming tennis-ball or the dart failing to hit its target.

An important landmark in the development of skill is when sufficient progress has been made for further improvement to follow simply from further practice. This could not be provided by a simple stimulus-response model of learning, but one that entails the learning of algorithms could accommodate it.

Perhaps one of the most remarkable ways of improving a skill is by "immobile" practice. The trainee goes through the activity mentally but makes no movements at all. Although probably much less effective than actual practice, this kind of mental rehearsal can help maintain a skill when circumstances prevent full scale practice. DL

Bibliography

Annett, J. 1969: *Feedback and behavior*. London: Penguin.

Fitts, P.M. and Posner, M.I. 1967: *Human performance*. Belmont, Cal: Brookes-Cole.

Holding, D.H. 1965: *Principles of training*. Oxford and New York: Pergamon.

——— *Experimental psychology in industry*. London: Penguin.

——— ed. 1981: *Human skills*. New York and Chichester: Wiley.

Legge, D., ed. 1970: *Skills*. London: Penguin.

——— and Barber, P.J. 1976: *Information and skill*. London and New York: Methuen.

Schmidt, R.A. (1975) *Motor skills*. New York: Harper & Row.

Stammers, R. and Patrick J. 1975: *The psychology of training*. London: Methuen.

Stelmach, G.E., ed. 1976: *Motor control: issues and trends*. New York and London: Academic Press.

Welford, A.T., 1968: *Fundamentals of skill*. London: Methuen.

——— 1976: *Skilled performance: perceptual and motor skills*. Glenview, Ill.: Scott Foresman.

skin *See* galvanic skin responses

Skinner, Burrhus Frederic (born 1904.) Experimental psychologist responsible for the development of operant techniques. Skinner was born in Pennsylvania and from 1922 to 1926 attended Hamilton College, N.Y., where he majored in English. He then entered Harvard College to study psychology, and remained there for five years after taking his doctorate. He joined the faculty at the university of Minnesota in 1936, and moved to the university of Indiana in 1945. In 1948 he returned to Harvard where he remained for the rest of his career.

Skinner showed that animal and human behavior could be modified by reinforcement and that animals could in this way be trained to carry out particular tasks to obtain reward, or avoid punishment. His belief that any reinforcer could be used to modify any aspect of behavior was subsequently shown to be incorrect (see REINFORCEMENT). Nevertheless, his OPERANT CONDITIONING techniques came to be widely used in training and studying animals, and in the modification of human behavior in teaching and clinical situations.

Skinner developed a thorough-going philosophy of BEHAVIORISM which he promulgated in his many books. The most important of these were *The behavior of organisms*, *Verbal behaviour* and *About behaviorism*. He also published three autobiographical works: *Cumulative record*, *Particulars of my life* and *The shaping of a behaviorist*. DJM

Bibliography

Skinner, B.F. 1938: *The behavior of organisms*. New York and London: Appleton-Century.

——— 1957: *Verbal behavior*. New York: Appleton-Century-Crofts; London: Methuen 1959.

——— 1959: *Cumulative record*. New York: Appleton-Century-Crofts; London: Methuen 1961.

——— 1974: *About behaviorism*. New York: Knopf; London: Cape.

——— 1976: *Particulars of my life*. New York: Knopf; London: Cape.

——— 1979: *The shaping of a behaviorist*. New York: Knopf; Oxford: Holdan Books.

sleep: human paradoxical The stage of sleep during which most dreaming is assumed to occur. If an individual is awakened during a period of paradoxical sleep, he or she is more likely to claim to have been dreaming than in any other stage of sleep. The term REM sleep comes from the observation that rapid eye movements occur during this phase of sleep. In addition to eye movements, characteristic features of REM sleep include loss of muscle tone, an increase in neural activity, and an electroencephalogram (EEG) record that is paradoxically very similar to that of a person awake. Paradoxical sleep occurs four or five times during the night at approximately ninety-minute intervals with the first episode following a period of slow-wave sleep (SWS), about ninety minutes after sleep onset. (See also SLEEP AND AROUSAL; PHYSIOLOGICAL BASES.)

sleep: in animals Sleep is a state characterized by prolonged periods of immobility during which a species-typical posture may be adopted. By international agreement sleep is defined either in terms of raised thresholds of arousal, or in terms of electroencephalograph (EEG) patterns.

A sleeping animal is less easily aroused by a sound or touch stimulus than is an animal which is awake. Some fish can be lifted out of the water while asleep. Depth of sleep is gauged by the magnitude of the stimulus required to arouse the animal. To some extent, the response to stimulation is selective. Familiar sounds for example are less arousing than unfamiliar ones. Some animals, such as cattle, deer and horses, are very light sleepers, being aroused from sleep by the slightest sign of danger.

Sleep can be diagnosed, among birds and mammals, on the basis of electrical potentials measured in the brain, or on the scalp, by means of an electroencephalograph. So called quiet sleep is characterized by the presence of high amplitude slow wave changes in potential, whereas during active sleep the EEG pattern resembles the waking state with rapid low voltage changes in potential. The situation is somewhat paradoxical because arousal tests show that depth of sleep is usually greater during active sleep than during quiet sleep. Active sleep is often accompanied by sporadic episodes of rapid eye movement. If woken up during such episodes, humans often report that they were dreaming. Many other animals show signs of dreaming, such as limb movements or vocalizations. The alternation of quiet and active sleep is widespread among birds and mammals, but other species do not appear to have these two kinds of sleep. Among reptiles, for example, the electrical activity of the brain is intermediate between that characteristic of quiet sleep and active sleep.

Most animals sleep during particular periods of the day, though there is great variation between species. Some sleep at night, some during the day, while others are active only at sunrise and sunset. Sleep is no different from many other aspects of behavior in fitting into a daily routine that is characteristic of the species in its natural environment. The timing of sleep is partly influenced by the animal's endogenous clock and partly by other aspects of the state of motivation. Animals do not usually sleep until they have found a suitable site, free from disturbance by predators or rivals.

The duration of sleep also varies widely from one species to another. Some mammals, such as the two-toed sloth, armadillo and opossum, sleep up to twenty hours per day. At the other extreme, Dall's porpoise and the swift appear not to sleep at all, being constantly on the move. Herbivores generally sleep less than carnivorous animals, and this is probably due to their need to spend a large proportion of the day feeding. Herbivores are often vulnerable to predators when asleep and their need for vigilance is therefore higher than that of an animal which can sleep in a safe place.

Differences between species are sometimes difficult to interpret, because of lack of knowledge arising from the difficulty of diagnosing sleep under natural conditions. While sleep can be readily identified in the laboratory, by EEG or arousal tests, it cannot be claimed that sleep follows a natural pattern under laboratory conditions. On the other hand there have been very few studies of sleep in the natural environment which have used proper diagnostic tests. In one study arousal tests were administered to herring gulls in the wild and it was discovered that a certain rate of eye-blink was characteristic of sleep with a raised threshold of arousal. Sometimes the animals adopted a sleep posture, but did not have raised thresholds of arousal or show the typical eye-blink rate (Amlaner and McFarland 1981). By using the eye-blink criterion to distinguish between true- and pseudo-sleep, it was discovered that the sleep patterns of herring gulls are different in different phases of the breeding cycle. The birds sleep less during the courtship phase, when territorial defense is at a premium, than they do during the incubation phase. It is also thought that migrating birds sleep less than usual, both in the wild and if they are confined to the laboratory during the migratory period. It appears that sleep patterns adapt to the animal's way of life, even when this changes markedly with the seasons of the year.

In animals other than birds and mammals EEG diagnosis is not possible, and assessment of sleep must be based upon behavioral considerations. Some reptiles show obvious symptoms of sleep, but others, including alligators, crocodiles, and snakes, may remain immobile for days without giving much clue to their motivational state. The chameleon (*Camaeleo melleri*) retires to a branch at sunset and adopts a typical sleep posture with its eyes closed. Some reptiles and amphibians have a lowered respiration rate during sleep and are less easily disturbed during such periods. Fish spend long periods immobile, some at night and others during the day. Color changes occur in some fish, probably to enhance camouflage during sleep. By similar behavioral criteria, some insects would appear to sleep. Moths and butterflies rest at specific sites which offer good camouflage. They often adopt a typical rest posture and may sometimes be touched without being disturbed.

Arousal in animals may range from deep sleep, through various waking stages, to great excitement. The term is also used to denote the degree of responsiveness to particular types of stimulation. The responsiveness of a male rat to a female is often described in terms of sexual arousal. The concept of general arousal presents considerable difficulties of measurement and interpretation. Behavioral indices are inevitably specific to the type of behavior employed and physiological indices, such as the rate of the heart beat, are difficult to interpret. Although aroused animals generally have an elevated heart rate, this also occurs in other situations, such as exertion. Hebb (1955) suggested that arousal level, as measured by brain activity (electroencephalograph), is the physiological equivalent of the behavioral concept of general drive (see MOTIVATION, ANIMALS), and that there is an optimal arousal level for performance of particular behavior patterns. The numerous attempts to substantiate this theory have not been particularly successful, and the arousal concept is no longer widely used.

Prolonged periods of torpid immobility are found in many animals, especially during periods of unfavorable climate, such as the desert summer or the arctic winter. In the torpid state the animal is able to conserve energy, as in hibernating mammals, or conserve water, as in aestivating desert rodents. It has been suggested that sleep also enables animals to conserve energy at times when activity is not likely to be profitable, as when food is unattainable or predators prevalent. Many small birds reduce their body temperatures at night and this enables them to reduce energy expenditure on THERMOREGULATION. Some small mammals sleep in a warm insulated nest which serves a similar purpose. Sleep can therefore be seen as a means by which animals conserve energy and avoid danger.

The whole question of the function of sleep is, however, controversial. Traditionally, sleep has been seen as a restorative process, necessary for the maintenance of some as yet unknown brain process. Animals and people deprived of sleep become irritable and aggressive. When allowed to sleep after deprivation they to some extent catch up on the sleep they have missed. In these respects sleep seems to be like hunger and thirst, part of the physiological HOMEOSTASIS.

All sleep researchers recognize that there is a mechanism which induces an increasing tendency to sleep, which is satisfied by periods of sleeping. However, this does not necessarily mean that sleep is an essential recuperative process. It shows only that animals can have a strong MOTIVATION to sleep. Some scientists doubt the recuperative theory because of the great variation in sleep duration that is found when different species are compared. Careful studies have shown that there is no correlation between sleep pattern and intelligence or degree of evolutionary development, as might be expected if sleep were important in the regulation of brain activity. Sleep is thought to be of great evolutionary age and sleep patterns appear to be carefully tailored to the life-style of the animal. Animals in danger of predation either sleep less than other animals or take trouble to sleep in an especially safe place. As mentioned above, sleep patterns generally complement the periods when foraging opportunities are good, and they appear to vary as the demands on the animal's time vary with the seasons.

The ecological view of the function of sleep, that it has evolved to keep animals out of trouble at certain times of day, does little to explain the complex alternation of quiet and active sleep that is found in birds and mammals. It has been suggested that sleep may have evolved as an aid to time-budgeting, but that it may have acquired secondary functions among the more advanced animals. So it is possible that both sides of the argument may be justified. DJM

Bibliography

Amlaner, C.J.Jr. and McFarland, D.J. 1981: Sleep in the herring gull (*Larus argentatus*). *Animal behavior* 29, 551–56.

Hartmann, Ernest L. 1973: *The functions of sleep*. New Haven and London: Yale University Press.

Hebb, D.O. 1955: Drives and the central nervous system. *Psychology review* 62, 243–54.

sleep: psychological features A state of temporary loss of consciousness and of unresponsiveness to external stimuli. Its nature and functions are not clearly understood. Using an electroencephalograph to monitor the electrical activity of a sleeping brain reveals five discernible stages of sleep which occur in cycles of about ninety minutes. Stages 1 ("light sleep") to 4 ("deep sleep") are characterized by an absence of, or only slow, eye movements, and are conventionally referred to as non-rapid eye movement or non-REM sleep. (stages 3 and 4 are often combined and called "delta sleep".) The fifth stage is associated with rapid eye movements and known as REM or "dreaming" sleep. Delta sleep occurs mainly in the first third of the night, REM sleep in the latter third. The sleep cycle shows wide individual variations whose significance is unknown.

During the onset of sleep individuals are easily awakened and often report dreamlike fantasies. Waking thresholds are higher during stage 2, with mental content more thoughtlike and fragmentary, and recall is sparse and less reliable. Waking thresholds in delta sleep are generally high, with poor dream recall. There is mixed evidence on waking thresholds from REM sleep in humans, though they are low compared to delta sleep. Dream recall after REM awakenings is characteristically abundant and detailed.

Both the total time spent asleep and the distribution of particular sleep stages are closely related to age. In general, total sleep time is greatest in infancy. During the first year of life a reduction in the amount of sleep is accompanied by a change in its pattern towards a combination of one long sleep at night and daytime naps. Through the early years sleep totals continue to decline towards the pattern of young adulthood, with its average of between seven-and-a-half and eight hours concentrated into a single period at night. Old age sees a recurrence of napping and more frequent awakening during the night. The proportion of REM sleep is highest in infancy and childhood, amounting to half or more of total sleep time in the newly born. Both males and females show a marked decrease in the proportion of REM sleep from infancy to puberty, followed by a more gradual drop until the late twenties, when it levels off at between a fifth and a quarter of total sleep time until late adulthood. In men the proportion of REM sleep drops again in old age. Women, however, show no further decline after their twenties.

Variations in the amount of time preceding sleep ("prior wakefulness") affect both the length of time taken to go to sleep ("sleep latency") and the length of time spent asleep. Generally speaking, the longer an individual has been awake the stronger the urge to sleep and the shorter sleep latency, though there is only a weak relationship between prior wakefulness and sleep length. Sleep latency is strongly influenced by when in the day an attempt to sleep occurs.

This is the case even when the length of prior wakefulness is held constant, and helps to explain why jet travellers and workers on irregular shifts often experience difficulties in falling and staying asleep. Sleep during the day, or what an individual's "biological clock" tells him is daytime, differs in a number of ways from regular night sleep. The timing of sleep stages is radically altered, and day sleep is more likely to be broken or curtailed. Performance of a variety of tasks during the period when an individual would usually be asleep deteriorates sharply. However, if this new timetable is maintained for any length of time, sleep patterns revert to their original form and performance improves. Again there are variations among individuals. Changes in the time of going to sleep are likely to affect sleep only if they are erratic or significantly different from usual. Although any departure from routine impairs performance, occasional or limited variations are unlikely to have much effect on basic rhythms. Prior wakefulness is also directly related to the amount of different types of sleep which follow. A few hours only of wakefulness result in very little stage 4 or "deep" sleep, and sleep will be broken or finished early. Up to twenty hours of wakefulness, the amount of stage 4 sleep steadily increases and awakenings become fewer. Beyond twenty hours, the subsequent sleep is likely to be at its deepest and most uninterrupted.

Subjects experimentally deprived of sleep find it difficult to concentrate on undemanding tasks, and report feelings of confusion, disorientation and irritability. Prolonged sleep loss of up to between 150 and 200 hours may on occasion be associated with hallucinations and fantasies of persecution; but even here there are no apparent long term psychological effects. The main consequence of sleep deprivation seems to be overwhelming fatigue and desire for sleep. The effects of extended wakefulness on subsequent sleep patterns have also been studied. There is an increase in stage 4 during the first night of recovery, and in REM on the second night, compared to baseline sleep. Subjects deprived of a particular sleep stage experience an excessive amount of that stage when allowed to sleep uninterrupted again. This is the phenomenon of "rebound".

There are wide differences between individuals in the length, depth and quality of their sleep. We simply do not know why people should differ in their need for sleep. There is disagreement, for example, about variations in the waking personalities of naturally short and long sleepers. These individual differences should not be confused with "sleep disorders" such as insomnia and narcolepsy. Dissatisfaction with the brevity and poor quality of sleep, or insomnia, is most common in women and the elderly. Difficulty in getting to sleep is related to waking anxiety; difficulty in staying asleep or waking too early to depression. The use of hypnotic drugs to induce sleep rarely provides a "normal" night of sleep: REM is usually reduced, with consequent withdrawal from the drug often leading to REM rebound, nightmares and further insomnia. In contrast, narcolepsy is excessive or irresistible sleepiness, often involving periods of involuntary sleep during the day which may prove acutely socially embarrassing.

See also DREAM, HALLUCINATION. RPE

Bibliography

Cartwright, R.D. 1978: *A primer on sleep and dreaming*. Reading, Mass. and London: Addison-Wesley.

Cohen, D.B. 1979: *Sleep and dreaming: origins, nature and functions*. Oxford and New York: Pergamon.

Oswald, I. 1980: *Sleep*. 4th edn. Harmondsworth and New York: Penguin.

Webb, W.B. 1975: *Sleep, the gentle tyrant*. Englewood Cliffs, N.J.: Prentice-Hall.

sleep and arousal: physiological bases States characterized by changes in consciousness leading in the former, to a decreased responsiveness to the external

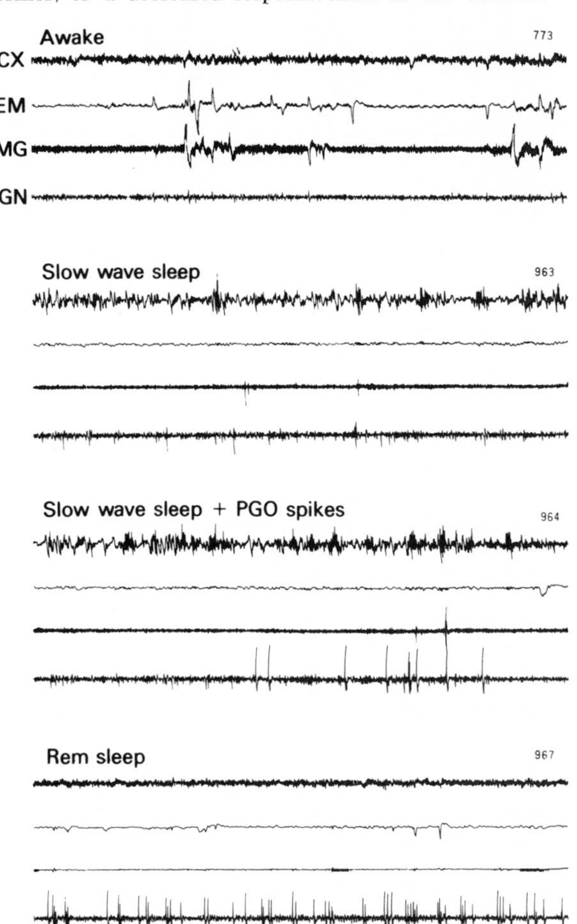

Electrophysiological signs of sleep and wakefulness in the cat. Cortex (CX) movements (EM) electromyogram (EMG) geniculate nucleus (LGN)

environment, and in the latter to an efficient interaction with it. Although these two extremes of activity can easily be distinguished by visual observation, a more reliable definition has to describe sleep and wakefulness as a biological rhythm only accurately identified by electrophysiological recording techniques. Using such techniques, it is well accepted that birds, mammals and primates, including man, present at least two basic patterns of sleep. The first, called slow wave sleep (SWS) or non-REM sleep, is characterized electroencephalographically (EEG) by the appearance of 14 to 18 Hz cortical spindles, which as sleep deepens are replaced by 2–4 Hz slow waves. At the same time high voltage (500-800μV) sharp waves are recorded from the hippocampus (see BRAIN AND CENTRAL NERVOUS SYSTEM: ILLUSTRATIONS, fig. 17), while the electromyogram (EMG) or muscle tone decreases slightly. Usually after 30 to 40 min. the rapid-eye-movement (REM) sleep phase appears (see PARADOXICAL SLEEP), characterized by the appearance of low voltage fast activity in the cortical EEG, a regular hippocampal theta rhythm (5–6 Hz), an isoelectric EMG (total loss of muscle tone) and bursts of rapid eye movements. Approximately half a minute before the onset of the REM sleep phase (and continuous throughout it), high-voltage EEG spikes appear in the pontine reticular formation (fig. 6), the lateral geniculate nucleus (LGN) and the occipital cortex (fig. 23). These spikes are called PGO and have a fairly constant daily rate of about 14,000 in the cat.

Human EEG sleep stages are more differentiated and consist of four non-REM sleep stages: Stage I, loss of alpha; Stage II, spindles and isolated short waves called K complexes, on a low voltage background activity; Stage III, high amplitude delta activity (slow waves 1–3 Hz); Stage IV, with over 50 per cent of delta activity, and one REM stage characterized by low-voltage theta activity, with no spindles or K complexes, and accompanied of course by eye movements and loss of muscle tone (figs. 33 and 34). It is in this stage that dreaming occurs. During this stage there is also generally speaking an increase in mean value and variability of the heart rate, respiratory rate and blood pressure (see NEUROMETRICS).

The events occurring during REM sleep have been classed as phasic and tonic. The phasic events are represented by activities such as eye movement bursts, middle ear muscle activity (MEMA), cardiovascular irregularities, respiratory changes, muscular twitches, changes in pupil diameter, fluctuations in penile erection, and PGO spikes. The tonic events are represented by low-voltage fast EEG activity, EMG suppression, temperature elevation and increased blood flow.

Since the discovery of REM sleep in the 1950s physiologists have attempted to locate the brain structures responsible for the two phases of sleep through experiments whereby specific areas of the brain are lesioned and subsequent effects on sleep analyzed. Although it is now thought highly doubtful that specific centers exist, there is relative agreement that the sleep-wake rhythm is a brain stem regulated phenomenon with the added involvement of the basal forebrain in regulating SWS. It should be pointed out, however, that in animals which have very definite sleep and waking rhythms, i.e., rodents, the suprachiasmatic nucleus (SCN) seems to play an important role (see fig. 20). For example rodents sleep mostly during the day and are active at night. If the SCN is lesioned this rhythm is disrupted, but interestingly the total amount of sleep and waking remains unchanged. It therefore seems that sleep is controlled by several interrelated mechanisms originating from widespread areas of the brain. One group of structures around the hypothalamus would seem to regulate its basic rhythms, while other structures mainly located along the brain stem would be responsible for triggering its onset and/or maintaining its duration.

Coincident with the search for brain regulating structures in sleep there has been a great deal of interest in identifying the chemical substances utilized by these structures in producing sleep. Here again it is more than likely that several substances participate, although theories favoring one over another have been put forward. The most commonly known is the monoamine theory which suggests that slow wave sleep is initiated by the release of serotonin (5–HT) from neurons of the dorsal raphe nuclei

Electrophysiological and Behavioral Correlates of Sleep and Wakefulness in the Cat

	Arousal		Sleep	
	attentive	relaxed	slow wave sleep	REM sleep
Cortical activity	low-voltage fast waves	spindles mixed with mostly low-voltage fast waves	spindles and high voltage slow waves	low voltage fast waves
Hippocampal activity	regular rhythmic theta waves	rhythmic theta waves	irregular high-voltage slow waves	very regular rhythmic theta waves
EMG	high amplitude	medium amplitude	low amplitude	isoelectric with twitches
Eye movements	biphasic continuous	practically none	none	biphasic bursts
PGO	none	none	present only before transition to REM	present (14,000 per day)
Behavior	exploratory attentive	sitting up or lying, head up, eyes open	lying on the side, eyes closed, respiration and heart beat slow	lying curled up, twitching of extremities, neck muscles and vibrissae, irregular respiration
Time spent 24 hr/day	35% alternating between the two		50%	15%

in the brain stem, while REM sleep is triggered by the release of 5–HT from neurons of the caudal raphe nuclei. Once initiated, the 'executive' mechanisms of REM sleep are governed by catecholamines: the catecholamine (NE) containing neurons of the caudal third of the locus coeruleus are responsible for the muscle atonia associated with REM sleep, and those of the medial third of the locus coeruleus function as a pacemaker for PGO activity. On the other hand wakefulness and cortical arousal are dependent on NE-containing neurons of the anterior locus coeruleus, dopamine-containing neurons of the midbrain reticular formation and cholinergic neurons in the cortex. In other theories the monoamines do not play such a central role, and the main triggering mechanisms of sleep revolve around peptides. Although some such peptides have been isolated, and have been referred to as sleep factors there is as yet no conclusive evidence that they are in fact sleep inducing substances. Other hypotheses revolve around the idea that protein synthesis or a particular group of proteins are most likely to be involved in the production of REM sleep through a kind of "gating" mechanism which modulates the excitability levels of the various neuronal groups involved in producing the electrophysiological signs of REM sleep episodes. Whatever the eventual answer to the neurochemistry of sleep will be, it is more than likely that all these systems and probably more are involved through a rather complicated interaction.

Besides the attempts to understand the mechanisms by which the brain produces the sleep-wake cycle, one of the most nagging questions is the function of sleep. Several theories have been advanced, most of which have some points in common, and which boil down to the following five: (1) the restorative theory which holds that sleep is a period of restoration of physiological and/or psychological states, with SWS restoring the body and REM sleep restoring the brain; (2) the protective theory which suggests that sleep gives the organism a period whereby it can protect itself from excessive wear and tear; (3) the energy conservation theory which holds that sleep serves the function of conserving energy by limiting metabolic requirements; (4) the ethological theory which holds that sleep and wakefulness are control systems which enhance survival and thus protect the species; and (5) the instinctive theory which holds that sleep is an instinct and therefore to be seen as innate behavior rather than as a need. Probably none of these theories alone can explain the function of sleep, but a combination of all might answer the question why we sleep.

Finally, it is important to note that although sleep abnormalities have dramatic influences on waking performances and moods, it is only recently that a reasonable understanding of sleep pathologies has been reached. Sleep disorders can essentially be divided into primary and secondary.

Primary sleep disorders are those in which the abnormalities related to sleep are the cardinal signs or symptoms from which the patient suffers. In these cases a malfunction of the basic neurophysiological and/or neurochemical mechanisms involved in regulating the sleep-wake cycle is presupposed. There are four principal primary sleep disorders. One is narcolepsy, in which the patient goes directly from waking to REM sleep. It is characterized by four symptoms (the so called narcolepsy tetrad): (a) short, but almost irresistible, daytime sleep attacks (b) cataplexy (ranging from transient weakness to total paralysis of all voluntary muscles) (c) sleep paralysis, a disorder characterized by a sudden inability to execute voluntary movements either at the onset of sleep or upon awakening during the night or in the morning, and (d) hypnagogic hallucinations, so called because they occur as the patient is falling asleep. Another primary sleep disorder is apnea: in this disease the patients literally stop breathing whenever they fall asleep. Three types of apneas are typically observed: central apneas, defined by an absence of any respiratory effort; upper airway apneas which involve a collapse of the upper airway; mixed apneas in which there is a combination of both. There are three clinical subtypes of the sleep apnea syndrome: (a) hypersomnia-hypoventilation syndrome, in which upper airway apneas predominate and which occurs mostly but not necessarily in overweight (Pickwickian) patients (here patients complain of excessive daytime sleepiness on account of the frequent awakenings at night due to the apneas); (b) insomnia-sleep apnea syndrome, in which central sleep apneas predominate and although patients awaken often during the night they do not sleep during the day; (c) sleep apnea in children, which is thought to cause the sudden infant death syndrome (SIDS), although SIDS is itself a much more complicated syndrome. In the remaining two primary sleep disorders, primary insomnia and hypersomnia, the patients do not present significant medical, psychiatric and/or behavioral pathologies, and the disorder is therefore probably associated with a basic dysfunction of the physiology and chemistry of sleep.

The secondary sleep disorders are those in which the basic pathology is medical, i.e., neurological or psychiatric, and sleep disturbances are one of many symptoms. As such we have epilepsies, thyroid dysfunctions, drug and alcohol abuse, depression, schizophrenia and so on.

Finally, there are a series of activities which are normal in waking but erupt in sleep and create various problems. These are the parasomnias, among which are: somnambulism, enuresis (bedwetting), nightmares and night terrors, bruxism (teeth grinding), to name only a few.

The fields of pharmacology of sleep, dreams and development are being very actively pursued in various laboratories and it is only through the interactions of all these fields of sleep research that a solid understanding of the sleep-wakefulness cycle will be forthcoming. RD-C

Bibliography

Dement, William C. 1972: *Some must watch while some must sleep*, Stanford, Calif.: Stanford Alumnic Assoc.; reptd 1978: New York and London: Norton.

Drucker-Colín, René R., Shkurovich, M. and Sterman, M.B. eds. 1979: *The functions of sleep*, New York and London: Academic Press.

Jouvet, M. 1972: The role of monoamines and acetycholine in the regulation of the sleep-waking cycle. *Ergebnisse der Physiologie* 64, 166–307.

McConnell, P.S., Boer, G.J., Romijn, N.J., van der Poll, N.E. and Corner, M.A. 1980: *Adaptive capabilities of the nervous system*. Amsterdam, Elsevier. Section III, pp.253–356.

Moruzzi, G. 1972: The sleep-waking cycle, *Ergebnisse der Physiologie* 66, 1–165.

Orem, John and Barnes, Charles D. eds 1980: *Physiology in sleep*. New York and London: Academic Press.

Roffwarg, H.P., Chairman. 1979: Association of Sleep Disorders Centers. *Diagnostic classification of sleep and arousal disorders*, First Edition, prepared by the Sleep Disorders Classification Committee, *Sleep* 2: 1–137.

sleep *See above and also* emotion and sleep

small group intervention Group dynamics, as a branch of social psychology, is perhaps one of the most applied areas of social psychological research. T (training) groups were first developed in the National Training Laboratories at Bethel in Maine, in 1947. Many forms of group training have since been developed aiming at personal and organizational change but their positive and negative effects are still disputed. Research has begun to move beyond the stage of simply showing whether or not such small group interventions do have a positive effect and concentrates more on the social and psychological processes which might bring such change about. JMFJ

Bibliography

Hartman, J.J. 1979: Small group methods of personal change. *Annual review of psychology* 30, 453–476.

smell *See* taste and smell (in animals)

smiling: developmental Can be minimally defined as a facial expression which involves the corners of the mouth turning up, but there are many variations on this even in infancy. The conditions which elicit smiling at this time are equally varied.

Smiling may occur in neonates without external stimulation, but during the first month after birth is likely to be elicited by sounds, including voices, and in the second month by visual stimulation which is usually human faces.

The appearance of the smile is not dependent on visual experience, for it emerges at the same age since conception rather than at the same chronological age since birth, and at similar ages in blind and sighted children.

Nevertheless the frequency of smiling has been shown to be different for children reared in institutions and at home, and can be increased almost immediately by the experience of contingent responses of smiling, talking and touching from a social partner. Furthermore, smiling tends to become restricted to familiar people after about six months of age. AW

Bibliography

Sroufe, L.A. and Waters, E. 1976: The ontogenesis of smiling and laughter: A perspective on the organisation of development in infancy. *Psychological review* 83, 173–89.

social behavior A term used synonymously with interpersonal behavior and social interaction to denote the subject matter of social psychology. The study of social behavior may include the study of such things as attitudes, values and beliefs, which are taken to influence overt behavior, as well as the study of such things as face-to-face interaction.

See also EMOTION AND SOCIAL BEHAVIOR. AF

social categorization Has been suggested as an important and fundamental process in intergroup behavior (see PREJUDICE). Tajfel (1982) has argued that social categorization leads to an accumulation of perceived between-group differences and assimilation of within-group differences. Research has confirmed the first of these two hypotheses but there is as yet no clear evidence with respect to assimilation. Tajfel has also argued that social categorization is a sufficient condition for discrimination; but so-called minimal group studies show that people use discrimination of outgroup members only as a means of achieving a positive self-evaluation where discrimination is the only way in which a positive identity can be achieved. JMFJ

Bibliography

Tajfel, H. 1982: Social psychology of intergroup relations. *Annual review of psychology* 33, 1–39.

social class. *See* educational attainment and social class

social comparison Festinger (1954) has suggested that we use other people as sources for comparison in order to evaluate our own attitudes and abilities when comparison with objective standards is not possible. The theory predicts a preference for associating with others who hold similar attitudes or have slightly superior abilities because such interactions provide the most informative social comparisons.

Social comparison processes also play an important role in the development of a positive social identity, as suggested in Tajfel's (1982) theory of intergroup differentiation.

A similar notion can be found in the primus-inter-pares (p.i.p.) principle, which suggests that social interaction is in part governed by the desire to be similar to others and at the same time different from others, which results in the paradoxical finding that on average we feel ourselves to be superior to the average other. JMFJ

Bibliography

Festinger, L. 1954: A theory of social comparison processes. *Human relations* 7, 117–40.

Tajfel, H. ed. 1982: *Social identity and intergroup relations*. Cambridge and New York: Cambridge University Press.

social Darwinism. *See* Darwinism, social

social disadvantage The concepts of social disadvantage and cultural deprivation were invoked to explain the disproportionately high rate of SCHOOL FAILURE found among children from lower-class families. The concepts were derived from studies of animal behavior which found that deprivation of sensory input in early life resulted in organisms with impaired intellectual and affective functioning (Hebb and Thompson 1954). Similar detrimental effects were found in human infants reared in the atypical and under-stimulating environment of orphanages and institutions (Hunt 1961). Based on results such as these, the idea of SENSORY DEPRIVATION was extended to apply to the home environments of the poor – hence the terms social disadvantage and cultural deprivation (Deutsch 1967). The school failure of children from these groups was then seen as the inevitable consequence of this hypothesized deprivation, and educational efforts were made to overcome the children's deficiencies (see COMPENSATORY EDUCATION). In recent years the concepts of social or cultural deprivation have been challenged. The claim has been made that while child-rearing practices of various subgroups are different from those of the dominant group, they are not deficient (Labov 1970). The controversy has caused these terms to fall increasingly into disuse. However, the social and educational problems of the children have not abated. (See also EDUCATIONAL ATTAINMENT AND SOCIAL CLASS.) MB/JM

Bibliography

Hebb, D.O. and Thompson, W.R. 1954: The social significance of animal studies. In *Handbook of social psychology*, ed. G. Lindzey. Reading, Mass.: Addison-Wesley.

Hunt, J.M. 1961: *Intelligence and experience*. New York: Ronald Press.

Deutsch, M. et al. 1967: *The disadvantaged child: studies of the social environment and the learning process*. New York and London: Basic Books.

Labov, W. 1970: The logic of nonstandard English. In *Language and poverty*, ed. F. Williams. Chicage: Markham.

social exchange Entails reciprocal giving and receiving between individuals, between individuals and groups, or between individuals representing groups. At its most basic, social exchange expresses the reciprocal rule: that an individual gives and another returns, in some measure, what is given. An imbalance between what is given and received may reflect differences in status or resources between donors and recipients, thus placing one or other in debt and so assuring the continuity of the reciprocal relationship. Social exchange theory is a body of explanations having as their core principle that much of social interaction involves exchanges of material things, of behavior or of ideas.

Exchange can be studied at the individual level of strategies and consequences, or at the level of interdependency of two or more individuals, but it would be mistaken to conceptualize social exchange only as a matter of individual motivations. It may involve some calculation and rational planning of relative rewards and costs by each party, but the form and content of the exchange itself (how much, of what, and how frequently) are influenced or even determined by social conventions and norms prevailing within given societies and groups. Studies of social exchange have often brought a close focus to bear on individual motivations but much of the vast literature on this topic also recognises that the questions of why and *with whom* exchanges take place and the manner in which they do take place, are socially determined issues.

Social exchange attracts research and discussion from an interdisciplinary range that spans social anthropology, sociology, social psychology and evolutionary biology. This gives some warning also that it is no easy matter to attempt to compress the currently existing theory of social exchange explanations into a few representative statements. There is a variety of possible interpretations depending on whether social exchange is discussed by anthropologists, sociologists, psychologists or biologists. These differing interpretations can be summarized as follows: social anthropologists tend to emphasize the classification of the exchanges, their non-material implications and the symbolic meanings of the exchanges that permeate a given society; sociologists tend to interpret social exchange within the context of groups and power relations; social psychologists focus on the interpersonal significance of reciprocal behavior and place some emphasis on motivation; sociobiologists seem influenced also by this latter interpretation, conceptualizing some forms of animal social behavior especially in primates and carnivores in reinforcement terminology.

Together with this variety of interpretations there are large differences in methodology: anthropologists using descriptively based analyses, sociologists using survey methods and taking up the critical discussion of theory, social psychologists following experimental research models and sociobiologists referring to ethological field studies. The result of this variety of approaches is a formidable empirical and theoretical literature on social exchange, much of the latter consisting of critical appraisals contributing to further developments in the theory (Chadwick-Jones 1976). Social exchange explanations have been remarkably well criticized and have survived the criticisms remarkably.

Explanations of social behavior in terms of social exchange first emerged substantially from the work of anthropologists – Mauss, Malinowski, Lévi-Strauss (see Turner 1978) whose work has been influential in sociology but much less so in social psychology. Here the major starting point was provided by George Homans (1961) who applied reinforcement hypotheses, borrowed from experimental studies of learning, to a broad range of empirical evidence and research illustrations. In addition to reinforcement concepts, Homans used analogies from economics and notions of profit and loss, gain and cost. From these analogies what tended to emerge was a model of human motivation in terms of cost/benefit, rational behavior. Homans, however, introduced a superb qualification to this type of conclusion – the Aristotelian principle of distributive justice. Clearly, it had to be admitted that there is no social exchange that does not involve some consideration of justice and there can be no justice if not to resolve some issue of social exchange. (This area of theory in social psychology is sometimes labeled "exchange-equity" theory.) Further questions arise over what *kind* of justice should operate – equity or equality, distributive justice or social justice?

These issues were discussed in a richly illustrative text by

Blau (1964), whose discussion of exchange and power, while sharing the emphasis on reinforcement motives and economic analogies, at the same time broadened the area of the explanations to comprise competing social groups, innovations in society and the forms of social exchange that can be observed in loving relationships and in families. In the latter context, critics of social exchange theory have often raised questions implying its basic weakness, such as: how can the giving of love and care to children be explained in terms of calculating returns? On the contrary, family studies provide useful instances of the highly moral aspects of social exchange involving rights and obligations.

The operation of social exchange in the interdependency between two persons was explored very extensively by Thibaut and Kelley (1959). They interpreted exchange as a pattern of behavior rather than merely as an exchange of material values. These two authors contributed a fascinating range of conjectures, using matrices adapted to social psychology from earlier game-theory formats. Thibaut and Kelley, while not themselves claiming a major interest in social exchange, do much to explore the nature of interdependency between individuals. Their work has influenced a very large number of experimental studies on negotiation, trust, bargaining and on the effects of threats and other inducements in producing agreement over the sharing of outcomes between individuals.

Tendencies towards a reductionist view of social behavior are apparent in some introductory textbooks (a rather similar tendency to the simplification and smoothing-over of theories in economics textbooks) in which the label "exchange theory" appears to refer only to "the individual's" opportunist orientations to gains or losses and completely ignores any broader reciprocal scope of social exchanges: for example, their expression of important symbolic meanings, sustaining social structures and, in Sahlins's words (1972) "provisioning society". It might, of course, be observed that behavior, in many situations, is influenced by its consequences but this assumption seems no more than commonplace and what is much more problematical is why some consequences are considered important and others disregarded; and how, in different social groups, do certain consequences come to be valued more than others?

Sahlins's analysis of pre-market, primitive societies provides a historical perspective on social exchange (see also Ekeh 1974). So much so that social exchange, as the expression of reciprocal relations in society, seems to have universal relevance. Lévi-Strauss (1969), in particular, argued along these lines. Nevertheless, within a given society there may be many forms of social interaction including exploitation and coercion that do not bear out either the rational or the reciprocal rule. The boundaries or limits of a social exchange explanation and the circumstances under which behavior becomes more calculating and less trusting seem to provide an especially interesting topic for research.

One of the features of this body of theory is the expression of its influence through a great variety of research designs. Gergen, Greenberg and Willis (1980) provide excellent examples of the creative diversity of both theoretical and research approaches; a chapter by Befu, "Structural and Motivational Approaches to Social Exchange" gives a discussion of the moral compulsions in social exchange. Burgess and Huston's useful collection of essays (1979) includes a view from sociobiology, as expounded in Alexander's "Natural Selection and Social Exchange". Important contrasts between economic and social exchange are brought out by Foa and Foa (1974) and, lastly, the work of John and Jeanne Gullahorn on computer modeling of social exchange sequences (see Chadwick-Jones 1976) is a further example of the many possibilities involving a very broad scope of experiments, observational studies and theoretical enquiry. JKC-J

Bibliography

Blau, P.M. 1964: *Exchange and power in social life*. New York: Wiley.

*Burgess, R.L. and Huston, T.L., eds. 1979: *Social exchange in developing relationships*. New York and London: Academic Press.

*Chadwick-Jones, J.K. 1976: *Social exchange theory: its structure and influence in social psychology*. London and New York: Academic Press.

Ekeh, P.P. 1974: *Social exchange theory: the two traditions*. Cambridge, Mass.: Harvard University Press.

Foa, U.G. and E.B. 1974: *Societal structures of the mind*. Springfield, Ill.: Charles C. Thomas.

*Gergen, K.J., Greenberg, M.S. and Willis, R.H. 1980: *Social exchange: advances in theory and research*. New York and London: Plenum Press.

Homans, G.C. 1961: *Social behavior: its elementary forms*. New York: Harcourt Brace Jovanovich; London: Routledge & Kegan Paul.

Lévi-Strauss, C. 1969: *The elementary structures of kinship*, 2nd edn. Boston: Beacon.

Sahlins, M.D. 1972: *Stone age economics*. Chicago: Aldine.

Thibaut, J.W. and Kelley, H.H. 1959: *The social psychology of groups*. New York: Wiley.

Turner, J.H. 1978: *The structure of sociological theory*. Homewood, Ill.: Dorsey Press.

social facilitation The first experimentally-discovered effect in social psychology indicating that the presence of another person has a motivational effect upon the performance of a subject by enhancing dominant responses. Initial research led to seemingly contradictory findings because performance is sometimes improved, and sometimes affected negatively, by the presence of others. Zajonc (1965) argued, however, that these contradictory findings could be reconciled by assuming that the presence of another person increases the drive of the subject, as formulated in the Hull-Spencer behavior theory. This would lead to improved performance when correct responses are dominant and worse performance when errors are dominant (as in the early stages of a learning process).

Recent reviews of the literature suggest that the evidence for Zajonc's explanation is far from conclusive. JMFJ

Bibliography

Triplett, N. 1897: The dynamogenic factors in pacemaking and competition. *American journal of psychology* 9, 507–533.

Zajonc, R.B. 1965: Social facilitation. *Science*. 149, 269–274.

social influence Any change which a person's relations with other people (individual, group, institution or society) produce on his intellectual activities, emotions or actions. We usually think that others are free, that they weigh up alternatives and carry out their choices rationally. Everyone seems to be his own master. In reality this is only a western belief. It utterly denies that fundamental phenomenon of social life which we call influence. This is one of the most important concepts in social psychology. Usually we are not even conscious of such influence and we do not know why or how it takes place.

In the late nineteenth century, when hypnosis was a popular object of public curiosity and scientific development, influence was considered a consequence of hypnotic suggestion under which one was transformed into something like a robot: one's conduct under the control of someone else who can restrict one's awareness and destroy one's critical faculties and independence. Tarde believed that individuals were in a state of hypnotic suggestion whenever they are together. This produced imitation, the mechanism by which everything individual became social, thereby creating the uniformity common to all societies. Lebon believed that openness to mutual influence, accompanied by a loss of sense of responsibility and of normal intellectual capacities, causes a spread of ideas through emotion and thereby produced mental unity in a group. This conception of social life as a regression to more primitive states of mind is no longer popular in France. It was badly received in the United States where social psychology was developing on a more optimistic and matter-of-fact basis.

In 1936, Sherif experimentally investigated how groups construct shared rules and norms. He made such rules the criterion of the passage from individual functioning to social functioning. He chose an ambiguous situation in which individuals did not have established rules at their disposal. Using a visual illusion, the autokinetic effect (the impression that a fixed point of light is moving when it is seen in total darkness) he showed how members of groups come to agree in their estimation of the displacement of the light until their shared opinion remains stable even if they are subsequently asked to do the experiment on their own.

Even though he was a fugitive from Nazism, Asch wanted to show that influence has not necessarily the power of suggestion, that the individual can resist, at least if he knows that the influence is misleading. He did not believe that people imitate blindly; whether alone or in a group the individual adopts the opinions of others deliberately and rationally, and can remain independent if circumstances permit. Nevertheless Asch's experiments did not confirm this criticism. On the contrary, they demonstrated the power of pressures to conform, and the tendency of the group to follow blindly even to the extent of denying objective reality. To conform to a majority made up of confederates of the experimenter who give false responses, the subject declares against all the evidence that unequal lines are the same length. From this experiment onwards, social influence *in* a group was confused with individuals' conformity *to* the group, seen in its extreme form in the blind obedience displayed in Milgram's famous experiments where more than 60 per cent of subjects did not hesitate to give someone apparent electric shocks on the orders of the experimenter.

Festinger showed that the individual is defenseless in the face of shared beliefs. To attain an objective vision of things he needs to rely on others. In a situation of uncertainty or ambiguity it is necessary to arrive at a collective definition, to create a social reality. Error can only be individual while truth is social and spontaneously imposes itself on the majority. Everyone's adherence to the same belief produces a majority effect creating an influence which never needs to manifest itself as such. There is no sign of constraint or overt pressure. Everyone accepts the collective belief and all share collectively in the same social reality. If this pressure to uniformity proves ineffective the group can get rid of deviants.

If, in this model of majority influence, groups effectively eliminate deviants and obtain support for the majority view-point, it is not clear how social change could occur, even if only to maintain contact with reality. It seems a fundamental contradiction that a group's uniformity is detrimental to the group's success and adaptation. So groups must be capable of reacting against the rigid forces of conformity. To understand innovation we must assume minority influence. Innovation then becomes, in the face of conformity, a fundamental form of impact which individuals have on each other and on their group. The problem of influence is to understand how the norms of a society are maintained or overturned. Within this framework, majorities and minorities can both exercise an influence in different areas.

Every society functions on the basis of agreements about fundamental principles, i.e. consensus. The power of the minority lies in its ability to refuse the consensus. Certainly the group will bring pressure to bear to re-establish its homogeneity. But the more it knows that exclusion is unusual or even impossible, the more the minority can resist. The group must then resign itself to negotiating with this uncooperative minority and that is where the process of influence begins. Besides, deviance is not necessarily the bogy suggested by the psychology of conformity. Eccentric or unusual behavior has an undoubted attraction.

For a minority to have an influence it must prove its determination by its behavioral style. It is the combination of behavior and its context that produces its instrumental and symbolic significance. It is consistency in the minority's behavioral style which initially determines its power of persuasion. A consistent style is assertive. It demonstrates the individual's involvement and independence to the extent that, even in a hostile environment, it displays his assurance and his determination not to modify his own point of view. Even if perceived as aggressive this style of behavior exercises an incontestable and complex influence.

First it was necessary to prove that minority influence really exists. This was demonstrated by Moscovici, Lage and Naffrechoux (1969). They projected blue transparencies to groups of two confederates and four naive subjects. The confederates systematically judged the transparencies to be green. The subjects' threshold of discrimination between blue and green changed: among the intermediate tones between pure blue and pure green they perceived green earlier. In this case, consistency lay in repeating the same response. This demonstrated a refusal to change and an indifference to others' responses. In experiments more specifically concerning attitudes (Mugny 1982; Paicheler 1976) consistency is shown in a firm, coherent statement of an unchanging viewpoint and a refusal to be influenced by others. These experiments again demonstrate the effectiveness of minority influence in conjunction with the persuasiveness of a consistent behavioral style.

The effectiveness of a minority influence comes from the handling of the conflict caused by the disagreement between the source and the target of the influence. This conflict acts as a "thaw". It causes individuals or groups who are open to the influence to question their own positions. The resolution of conflict with a majority comes through passive acceptance or "compliance" expressed in a change of public response but an unchanged private belief. The resolution of conflict with a minority involves reexamining the object itself. While not expressing itself in a modified public response this may operate more indirectly or latently, whether through a halo effect or a profounder modification of the structure of response.

A minority or deviant group and its influence may often be explicitly rejected. Equally, this influence may be avoided by tracing unusual behavior to mental disturbance (Mugny 1982). Nevertheless a consciously rejected influence can develop underground and have unexpected results. Mugny (1982) demonstrates how minority influence acts not on its explicit concerns but on connected issues. Subjects do not have an impression of giving way to a minority influence. Yet, while they "forget" or deceive themselves about the influence's source, because the source is a minority it is more effective. This is found after a lapse of time, in the minority "sleeper-effect". It is also found in the modification of perception apparent in judgements of after-images in a replication of the blue–green experiment. An after-image is the complementary color seen when one looks at a white screen after staring at a color for several seconds. Moscovici and Personnaz (1980) demonstrated that there is no modification of the after-image under majority influence, but under minority influence the subject's after-image is displaced towards the complement of green.

Majorities and minorities have distinct influences. Majority influence helps maintain social uniformity. Minority influence introduces processes of social change, processes of differing complexity which are difficult to discern. The fundamental progress in studying minority influence lies in passing beyond appearances, to throw light on the underlying levels of this process. SMo and GP

Bibliography

Moscovici, S., Lage, E. and Naffrechoux M. 1969: Influence of a consistent minority on the responses of a majority in a color perception task. *Sociometry*. 32, 265–79.

Moscovici, S. and Personnaz, B. 1980: Studies in social influence, v: minority influence and conversion behavior in a perceptual task. *Journal of experimental social psychology*. 16, 270–82.

Mugny, G. 1982: *The power of minorities*. London: Academic Press.

Paicheler, G. 1976: Norms and attitude change I: polarization and styles of behavior. *European journal of social psychology*. 6, 405–27.

social interaction The social behavior between two or more people at the level of verbal utterances and non-verbal signals. Utterances alternate, apart from interruptions, while non-verbal signals are sent continuously and simultaneously. The two kinds of messages however are closely linked. It is useful to distinguish between encounters, like interviewing and teaching, where one person is in charge, two-sided encounters, like discussion and negotiation, where each side is pursuing certain goals, and casual encounters, where each person responds mainly to what happened last. Social interaction occurs with or without other activities, such as work, games, eating and drinking. There may be a task, or the meeting can be primarily social.

Events in social interaction can be categorized as, for example, "suggestions" or "questions", as is done in interaction recording. The twelve categories devised by Bales have been used in a variety of settings, but it has been found that special categories are needed for the kinds of interaction which occur in particular settings, such as psychotherapy or management–union bargaining. In addition special activities take place for example in doctor–patient interviews and when playing games. On the other hand the repertoire of non-verbal communication is much the same in all settings.

Verbal utterances of the kind just described play an important part in most social interaction, but **non-verbal communication** (NVC) is also important. Non-verbal communication consists of social signals conveyed by FACIAL EXPRESSION, GESTURES and bodily movements, GAZE, spatial position, TOUCH, appearance and tone of voice. Some are fairly slow or static, like proximity, others are fast-moving, such as gestures, and may be closely coordinated with speech. The sender encodes an emotional or other state into a NV signal, which is decoded by the receiver. Often encoding is unconscious and decoding conscious, but both may be below the threshold of awareness, as with pupil dilation which is a signal for sexual attraction, or with signals governing the synchronizing of speech. The meaning of a NV signal can be found by seeing how states of the sender are encoded, and how signals are decoded, or how they affect others' behavior.

NVC conveys several different kinds of message. It is the main way of indicating interpersonal attitudes, such as like-dislike; the author and others have found that NVC is much more powerful than words for this purpose. NVC is the main channel for expressing emotions; these are often concealed, though there may be "leakage" to less controlled areas, such as the voice or feet. It plays an important part in conversation — completing and elaborating on utterances, for example by gesture and tone of voice, providing feedback from listeners, for example showing surprise or annoyance in the face, and controlling the synchronizing of utterances by means of glances and head nods. NVC is the main method of self-presentation, via appearance and by manner of speaking, and it plays an important part in greetings and other rituals.

One way of analysing sequences of interaction is to find the probability that one kind of social act leads to another. This produces "adjacency pairs" of which the commonest is question–answer; others are joke–laugh, accuse–deny, request–comply. There are also pairs linking two acts by the same person, such as accept–thank. Another important short sequence is response–matching, for example of head nods, smiles or jokes. Reinforcement by agreement, smile, head nod etc. increases the frequency of the behavior reinforced, while negative reinforcement reduces it, usually without much awareness on either side. There are rules governing two-step sequences: for example an utterance should be relevant to what has just been said, and also add something new to it. Longer sequences than two can be discovered by further statistical analysis. This has been quite successful in the study of stereotyped non-verbal sequences like greetings and partings, but less successful for conversation. One case in which two-step links do build up to longer sequences is in the formation of repeated cycles. For example part of a class in school may consist of a repeated cycle of interaction, for example, teacher explains — teacher asks question — pupils reply. This illustrates a limitation of interaction recording, since the repeated cycles would consist of a continuous build-up of complexity, and not a repetition of the same questions and answers. Part of the difficulty of this approach to conversation is that there is often embedding, so that question and answer may be separated, for example by another question and answer. In addition, interactors may be looking ahead to the intended goal of the interaction. Encounters divide into a number of partly independent phases, with different sequences of interaction in each, though the phases themselves come in a certain order, as in the different parts of a selection interview, a doctor–patient encounter, or a dinner party.

A model which has helped with the interpretation of longer sequences is the motor-skill model, which uses the similarity between social behavior and the performance of motor skills. In each case the performer is trying to attain some goal, and makes corrections to his behavior as the result of feedback. This suggests a basic four-step sequence, for example interviewer asks question — respondent gives unsatisfactory answer — interviewer repeats, clarifies or sharpens question — respondent gives useful answer. As in motor skills, there is a hierarchical structure, in which larger plans consist of smaller ones. The motor-skill model fits one-sided encounters, like interviews, though in other cases both interactors can be found to be pursuing plans and taking corrective action at the same time. This model makes use of two-step sequences, such as the effects of reinforcement. However there are several differences between social and motor skills, so that the model needs some elaboration. It is essentially a one-way model, and does not fully describe the interaction of two independent interactors; it does not incorporate the rules of sequence or the properties of different social situations; interactors have elaborate cognitive structures which enable them to consider another's point of view, knowledge of rules of sequence, and of moral or other principles.

A model of interaction which takes more account of the independent but coordinated activity of different interactors is the game model. Games, including competitive and aggressive ones. are not possible unless both sides keep to the same rules, and the same is true of social interaction. Every kind of encounter is like a kind of game, with particular goals, repertoire and rules. As with games, although there may be competition and conflict of interests, there must also be co-operation to keep the rules. Interactors must work out a pattern of interaction which is agreeable to both, including a degree of intimacy, dominance relations, activity, topic of conversation, timing of speech, etc. The relationship between two people greatly affects the game and the nature of the social interaction, depending on whether they are in love, enemies, of different status, and so on.

Socially skilled behavior depends on the mastery of patterns of social interaction. Failures of social competence show aspects of interaction which most people can perform unthinkingly. These include lack of rewardingness, failure to initiate interaction, inaccurate perception of the other, inability to see the other's point of view, failure to master conversation sequences, failure to deal with the rules or other properties of situations. These basic skills are needed for all kinds of social encounter; to make friends and influence people, to be a teacher or doctor, further interaction skills are needed. Social skills training is given to mental patients with social difficulties, to members of the public in the form of assertiveness and heterosexual training, to managers, teachers and others, and for those going to work overseas. A number of methods are in use, and follow-up studies show that role-playing, with video-tape playback, modelling, coaching, and "homework" is the most effective.

See also COMMUNICATION, NON-VERBAL. JMA

Bibliography

Argyle, M. 1969: *Social interaction*. London: Methuen.

——— 1975: *Bodily communication*. London: Methuen.

——— 1978: *The psychology of interpersonal behaviour*. 3rd edn. Harmondsworth: Penguin Books.

Argyle, M., Furnham, A. and Graham, J.A. 1981: *Social situations*. Cambridge and New York: Cambridge University Press.

Bellack, A.S. and Hersen, M. 1979: *Research and practice in social skills training*. New York and London: Plenum.

Clarke, D.D. in press: *Conversation: strategy and structure*. Oxford and New York: Pergamon.

Fraser, C. and Scherer, K., eds. in press: *Social psychology of language*. Cambridge and New York: Cambridge University Press.

Knapp, M.L. 1978: *Nonverbal communication in human interaction*. 2nd edn. New York: Holt, Rinehart & Winston.

Morris, D. 1977: *Manwatching*. London: Cape.

Singleton, W.T., Spurgeon, P. and Stammers, R.B., eds. 1979 *The analysis of social skill*. New York & London: Plenum.

Wrightsman, L.S. and Deaux, K. 1980: *Social psychology in the eighties*. 3rd edn. Monterey, Calif.: Brooks/Cole.

social learning theory A loosely organized collection of hypotheses which state that social behavior develops mainly as a result of observing others and of reinforcement. In a series of famous experiments, Bandura (see Bandura

1977) showed that imitation of an aggressive adult model could explain aggressive behavior in children. But the effect of reward and punishment on learning to behave aggressively has also been demonstrated.

More recently Bandura has shown that children, especially in the case of moral development, learn not by imitating the exact behavior they witness, but by extracting the common attributes exemplified in different modelled responses and formulating rules for generating behavior with similar structural characteristics. JMFJ

Bibliography

Bandura, A. 1977: *Social-learning theory*. Englewood Cliffs, N.J.: Prentice-Hall.

social motivation A term used for the *description* as well as for the *explanation* of human social behavior. In the case of description, social motivation either refers to a differential property of the person (e.g. some persons are seen as more aggressive than others) to a differential property of the situation (e.g. some situations are seen as more powerful to instigate aggression than others), or to a differential property of persons and situations at the same time. In the case of explanation, social motivation is merely social behavior in general.

The term has become more and more accepted in psychology, as illustrated for example by the growing number of chapters about social motivation in standard works of psychology (e.g. Cofer and Appley, 1964, Walters and Parke 1964, Berkowitz, 1969; DeCharms and Muir 1978, Brody 1980). In earlier publications (roughly before the 1960s), it was more common to use terms such as ego-forces (typical of clinical- and personality-psychologists and also of general psychologists concerned with the problem of the integration of fragmentary biological needs), group dynamics (typical of the Lewinian school), or simply values and attitudes. Today social motivation is also more or less synonymous with cognitive or human motivation.

The descriptive use of social motivation

The description of persons is an inherent part of personality- and differential- psychology. Many of the personality concepts which are used for that purpose actually refer to social motivational tendencies of the individual. For example, the trait concept anxiety, which was long the dominant concept in personality research, certainly refers to the way in which an individual relates to himself and to others. For other concepts such as social dependence, achievement motivation and power motivation, which have been the object of research in the last couple of decades, the relation to social motivation is explicitly present in the concept itself. A recent development in the differential study of social motivation has been the use of abstract geometrical frames for both the definition and measurement of an individual's typical motivation (e.g. McClintock 1972, MacCrimmon and Messick 1976). For example, if, in a Cartesian framework, X represents the outcome for the Self and Y the outcome for the Other, competition can be defined as the tendency to maximize X in comparison with Y, aggression as the tendency to minimize Y, etc. Starting from such a definition, measuring people's social motivation is a matter of deriving their tendency to minimize or maximize X or Y or the relation between X and Y from their actual choices of points in that framework. Several studies of that kind have been performed and their outcomes successfully correlated with more "real life" indices of social motivation.

The *description of situations* in terms of the extent to which they elicit certain forms of social behavior is more typical of experimental social psychology. Many experiments in social psychology are not as one might expect, a test of a theory, but a more analytic description of how most people of a given culture behave under certain contrived social conditions. For example it has been found that most westerners have a strong tendency to obey the instructions of an experimenter whom they have previously accepted in that role, even though the instructions may lead to severe harm either to themselves or to others. It has also been found that most people conform to a certain extent with the clearly incorrect responses of a majority, provided that this majority is unanimous. And it has been found that most people are less prone to help a victim when many people are present. The description of the motivating power of a situation is essentially an empirical generalization of such findings. Of course, these findings may also serve either as a starting point or as a check point for a more abstract theory of social behavior in general.

An idea which has gained more and more ground in personality- research as well as experimental social psychology is that social behavior is often a function of a characteristic *combination of person and situation.* For example it has been found that some people cheat in situation A and behave honestly in situation B, whereas other people do just the reverse. It has also been found that some people try to achieve in one situation and not in another, whereas others do the reverse. The idea that persons and situations interact has led some researchers to the construction of specific educational or instructional programs for specific groups of children, but it must be said that this interactionist approach to education has had less success than was originally hoped.

The diagnostic efforts of psychologists are not only directed at individual persons, but often at larger *categories of persons*, such as for example men and women. An important modern area of research is directed to finding out how men and women differ with respect to achievement motivation. The results of that research suggest that women tend to fear success in many domains where men typically try to obtain success.

Other research efforts, typically within so called cross-cultural psychology, are directed at the description of the typical motivation of certain cultures.

Some authors use the word "cultural" in a very broad sense, as an indication of what is typical of human behavior and motivation in contrast with nonhuman or animal behavior and motivation. It is certainly true, that human motivation is culturally transformed. It is by contact with educated members of his species that an individual learns to think and speak in a conceptual way, which enables him to develop an ego-concept and to relate his needs to that concept. For example, hunger is experienced by a human individual as "I am hungry" or "my hunger". Also the objects which a human individual uses to reduce his needs are typically manmade or cultural. A hungry individual tries to purchase some bread or looks for a restaurant. It is on a basis of this cultural transformation of needs that one could say that all human motivation is by definition social motivation.

The explanatory use of social motivation
There are many small- or middle range theories in psychology about the dynamics of human social behavior. Broad theories, however, which try to reduce a large variety of seemingly unrelated and even seemingly contradictory aspects of human social behavior to a limited set of principles or concepts are quite rare.

One such is the attempt to explain human social behavior as much as possible in terms of non-social or general principles of learning.

Whether certain forms of human social behavior are learned (secondary) or unlearned (primary) in nature has been a matter of vehement discussion.

Another theory which also deals with human social behavior in terms of learning is so called social learning theory. In contrast with the reduction to non-social principles of learning, this approach stresses precisely the fundamental social mediation of human learning and perception. Symbolic processes and modelling are considered of pivotal importance in the development of human personality and motivation.

Two theoretical models which have exerted a strong influence on thinking and research in the domain of human motivation are the so called FIELD THEORY and ROLE THEORY. Field theory, created by Lewin, conceives motivation as the system of forces which guides a person through the regions of his psychological field, whereas role theory conceives motivation in terms of the conscious demands which operate on a person because of his position in a social structure.

Finally, during the last decade or so social motivation has been more and more conceived as a dynamic property of a man's SOCIAL REPRESENTATION, that is his concept of himself and others. For example it has been demonstrated that a large number of typically human forms of motivation, such as non-instrumental rivalry, neurotic anxiety, the reciprocation of friendship and hate, the need for equity and other forms of social justice, etc. can be logically derived from three fundamental cognitive processes in the Self-Other conception, viz social attribution, social comparison and social validation. JBR

Bibliography

Berkowitz, L. 1969: Social motivation. In *Handbook of social psychology*, ed. G. Lindzey and E. Aronson. Reading Mass., Addison-Wesley Publishing Company.

Brody, N. 1980: Social motivation. *Annual review of psychology*. 31, 143–68.

Cofer, C.N. and Appley, M.H. 1964: *Motivation: theory and research*. New York: Wiley.

DeCharms, R. and Muir, M.S. 1978: Motivation: social approaches. *Annual review of psychology* 29, 91–113.

MacCrimmon, K.R. and Messick, D.M. 1976: A framework for social motives. *Behavioral science* 21, 86–100.

McClintock, C.G. 1972: Social motivation: a set of propositions. *Behavioral science* 17, 438–54.

Walters, R.H. and Parke, R.D. 1964: Social motivation, dependency, and susceptibility to social influence. In *Advances in experimental social psychology*, ed. L. Berkowitz. New York, Academic Press.

social perception The term social perception is used in at least two different ways in social psychology. On the one hand it refers to the social determinants of perception, on the other to perception of the social environment. The main emphasis of research during the past decades has been on perception of the social environment, especially the judgment of other people's characteristics.

The term perception is used here in a broad and extended sense. It includes processes of inference which are often classified as cognition rather than perception.

The traditional areas of research have been the judgment of emotions from facial and other forms of expression; the judgment of personality characteristics from various external signs and the formation of impressions of the personality of other people. In the first two areas of research initial results were interesting, statistically significant and exasperatingly inconsistent. The highly contradictory results in earlier studies of the accuracy of the recognition of emotional expressions have by and large been resolved by the obvious discovery that errors of recognition of emotion are a function of the psychological distance between emotions and the context in which the emotions are expressed (see EMOTIONS, RECOGNITION OF). More recent work by Ekman (Ekman and Oster 1979) has shown the universal nature of a small number of emotions.

The study of the accuracy of person perception gave way to an interest in studying the process of impression formation, after it had been shown that many of the early findings were artefacts of the procedures used.

Impression formation was originally thought to be a Gestalt-like process in which information about another person was integrated in a complex way, taking into account its specific configuration (sequential and otherwise). It is clear now that information integration processes in social judgment are predominantly additive. Integration is in most cases achieved by adding or averaging processes. Recent research has shown that social judgment is largely based on simple cognitive heuristics (rules of thumb), such as the representativeness and availability of information, which might explain the many shortcomings of human judgment. (Kahneman, Slovic and Tversky 1982; Nisbett and Ross 1980). Related to this approach is the suggestion by Rosch (Mervis and Rosch 1981) that prototypes play an important role in impression formation.

One of the aspects of information integration which has attracted a good deal of interest during the last two decades is the effect of inconsistency of the available information (COGNITIVE CONSISTENCY). In general it appears that inconsistency does affect social judgment processes but the effect is much less strong and less general than was originally suggested. Its effects depend to a large extent upon the cognitive representation underlying the representation of the stimuli to be judged (see Eiser 1980).

Impressions of other people are often based on observed behavior. But Heider has argued convincingly that final judgments are arrived at by inferring more or less invariant underlying or latent dispositions of the person and/or situation from observed or assumed variations in behavior. ATTRIBUTION theories have been concerned with the cognitive processes in making such inferences and in general with the explanation of our own and other peoples' behavior.

In addition to the study of attribution and integration processes, research in person perception has also studied the cognitive representations which result from these processes. The study of IMPLICIT PERSONALITY THEORIES analyses the associations which the observer assumes to exist between inferred personality traits. The same idea has been extended to the study of emotional states, social episodes and social behavior.

A neglected area of research has been the relationship between social cognition and social behavior. Although social perception has been studied in the context of non-verbal communication and social interaction, the results of these studies have so far not been integrated with the more cognitively oriented information processing approach in social perception. JMFJ

Bibliography

*Eiser, J.R. 1980: *Cognitive social psychology*. London and New York: Methuen.

Ekman, P and Oster, H. 1979: Facial expressions of emotion. *Annual review of psychology* 30.

Kahneman, D.G., Slovic, P. and Tversky, A. 1982: *Judgment under uncertainty*. Cambridge and New York: Cambridge University Press.

Mervis, G.B. and Rosch, E. 1981: Categorization of natural objects. *Annual review of psychology* 32, 89–115.

Nisbett, R.E. and Ross, L. 1980: *Human inference: strategies and shortcomings of social judgment*. Englewood Cliffs, N.J.: Prentice-Hall.

social power Although social power has been characterized as a fundamental concept in the social sciences, it has not been exhaustively studied in social psychology. Perhaps this is due to the lack of clarity in defining social power and in separating it from related concepts such as leadership, dominance, influence and control.

FIELD THEORY defines power as the maximum resultant force that a person A can bring to bear on another person B with respect to a particular region of B's life space. According to French and Raven (1959), the power of A over B can be based on the mediation of rewards by A for B, coercion, legitimacy, identification and expertness. Other authors, who are mainly concerned with decision making, have equated power and influence, suggesting that power is manifested by changes in the probability of eliciting a response from another person B. In the context of game theory (see GAMES) power has been defined as the ability to affect the quality of the partner's outcome.

The Dutch psychologist Mulder (see Ng 1980) has developed and tested an exhaustive theory which maintains in essence that social power is a basic form of motivation which by itself leads to satisfaction. It is addictive and leads less powerful persons to attempt to reduce the power distance from the more powerful, but the more they succeed the stronger this tendency tends to become. JMFJ

Bibliography

French, J.R.P.Jr. and Raven, B.H. 1959: The bases of social power. In *Studies in social power*, ed. D. Cartwright. Ann Arbor: University of Michigan Press.

Ng, S.K. 1980: *The social psychology of power*. London and New York: Academic Press.

social psychiatry. *See* social therapy; epidemiological methods in psychiatry

social psychology Can be defined as the study of behavioral dependence and interdependence. However, this view of social psychology which regards the study of social behavior essentially as a sub-discipline of psychology, can be interpreted in different ways. Behavioral (inter)dependence implies that behavior is studied as both the cause and effect of the behavior of others, but the definition leaves open the possibility that others may be actually present, imagined or merely implied by the situation. In the former case we are concerned with such phenomena as SOCIAL FACILITATION, IMITATION, CONFORMITY, SOCIAL INTERACTION etc., whereas the latter includes the effect of social structure and culture on human behavior.

Because the boundaries of the study of SOCIAL BEHAVIOR are vague, social psychology has concerned itself with a wide variety of problems. A recent survey of topics in one of the most important journals shows the following topics as the most active areas of contemporary research: attribution processes, group processes, helping, attraction and affiliation, aggression, crime, attitude and attitude change, social cognition, social and personality development and cross-cultural research.

Historically, social psychology emerged at the beginning of this century as a reaction to the asocial nature of general psychology. The year of its birth is usually given as 1908 when the first two textbooks in social psychology appeared, but recent historical research has shown that interest in the study of social behavior developed during the second part of the nineteenth century, perhaps beginning with Auguste Comte's notion of La Morale Positive, but also influenced by Folk psychology as developed by Lazarus, Steinthal and Wundt in Germany. It appeared as if social psychology had been given the task of socializing psychology and personalizing the study of society. Under the influence of the experimental methodology which social psychology began to adopt between the two world wars, this integrative task was largely reduced to the study of the effect of a manipulable social environment upon individual behavior under laboratory conditions. The price which social psychology had to pay for its experimental rigor was a loss of relevance of its findings. The disenchantment with the experimental approach led to a crisis in the 1960s and

1970s, in which a variety of alternative approaches were suggested. Virtually all of these have remained programmatic in nature and have as yet not produced any substantive contributions to the study of social behavior. The crisis did, however, have the effect of liberalizing social psychology and freeing it from the artificiality of the laboratory experiment. In recent years much more attention has been paid to the study of social behavior in its natural surroundings and its social and cultural context, making use of careful observation and advanced correlational methods.

Social psychology is traditionally divided into three or four areas of research. The study of individual social behavior, the study of dyadic social interaction and communication processes, the study of small groups and the psychological study of social issues.

In the study of individual social behavior both cognitive and motivational factors are important. Cognitive processes have been studied in two different ways in social psychology: there has been research on the effect of social factors on perception, but most attention has been given to the perception of other people. In perceiving and judging other people we tend to attribute the observed behavior to more or less invariant latent characteristics of the person and/or the situation which we interpret as the causes of that behavior. We infer emotional states of other persons to a large extent from subtle nonverbal cues which manifest themselves in facial expressions. In order to interpret and explain our own behavior and that of others we rely to a very large extent upon the pattern of behavior which we observe or presuppose. ATTRIBUTION THEORIES have suggested and demonstrated various ways in which such patterns lead to specific inferences about the person and/or the situation. An additional problem in social perception is the question of how all available information is integrated in an overall impression or judgment. In general it appears that we integrate information about other people in a relatively simple fashion, making use of cognitive heuristics and perhaps also of prototypes. When a comparison with objective judgment is possible it appears that social judgment is often suboptimal due to the shortcomings which arise from simplifying rules of thumb.

Closely related to the study of social perception is the study of ATTITUDES. In general attitudes are regarded as acquired behavioral dispositions of an evaluative nature. To what extent attitudes do in fact influence behavior is still a moot question, but recent research has convincingly shown that under certain conditions attitudes, as measured by traditional attitude scales, have some predictive value in this respect. Research on attitude change has for a long time been the most prolific area of research in social psychology. Most theories of attitude change are based upon the notion that change is brought about by the perceived discrepancy between one's initial attitude and the one advocated by the source of new information. This source can either be the stimulus or attitude object itself (see MERE EXPOSURE EFFECT), an external communicator (persuasive COMMUNICATION) or the behavior of the receiver (forced compliance). Recent French research and work in computer simulation suggest that attitudes might be fruitfully regarded and studied as part of social representations and belief systems.

Applied attitude research has been concerned in a very important way with questions of prejudice and discrimination. Early theories emphasized the importance of personality factors (see AUTHORITARIAN PERSONALITY) but more recent work has shown that evaluative differentiation is related to social categorization and the general tendency of group members to achieve a social identity.

Motivational aspects of individual social behavior have been studied most often in relation to dyadic interaction processes. Analysis of everyday interaction reveals two basic dimensions of social behavior: a dimension of domination, status or power versus submissive behavior and a dimension of positive social behavior (attraction, affiliation, love, helping) versus negative social behavior (aggression).

Factors which have been shown to affect initial attraction to another person are propinquity, repeated exposure, one's emotional state, need for affiliation, physical attractiveness in the other person and (attitude) similarity. Recent research has moved away from studying such superficial contacts and is concentrating more on long term relationships in friendship and marriage. Altruism and helping as another form of (pro) social behavior is currently one of the most active areas of research. It appears that helping is less likely to occur when a person does not accept responsibility in the situation (diffusion of responsibility, bystander effect) and when the benefits are low and the costs are high. Sociobiological theories of altruism have taken in particular the latter view, emphasizing in addition the evolutionary significance of altruistic behavior and its relation to kinship.

Aggression is again an area of research where both biological and social psychological theories have made important contributions. Early biological approaches as suggested by Freud and Lorenz, stressing such phenomena as catharsis, have given way to social learning explanations and approaches which have developed the original frustration–aggression hypothesis of Dollard and Millar. Present views consider aggression very much as any other form of social behavior which is determined by motivational and habit factors.

Various attempts have been made to formulate general theories of social interaction. Most of these theories consider social interaction as a form of social exchange in which the participants attempt to maximize their own benefits and minimize their costs. This may be true in an absolute sense as in bargaining and negotiation, in a relative sense as in competition and cooperation or with respect to a standard of fairness as equity theory suggests.

Considering the effect of groups on individual behavior and studying small groups as social entities of a super-individual nature have been of special interest to social psychology in the period of and around the second world war. Apart from basic work concerned with communication and interaction in small groups, research revealed the social influence of unanimous majority opinion in such groups, which yields strong uniformity.

Recently it has been shown that even minorities can have an important effect. Strong obedience to authority is another effect which has attracted a good deal of attention. In recent years interest in small group research has waned particularly because many of the groups studied were collections of strangers in laboratory conditions. Generalization from such groups to real life groups is hazardous, as e.g. group polarization effects show. It has been observed in laboratory conditions that groups are willing to make more extreme decisions than individuals but this effect has been very difficult to replicate in natural groups.

The application of social psychology to social issues has been a longstanding tradition of social psychologists. The application to prejudice and discrimination has already been mentioned. Application to clinical, organizational and educational problems has also attracted a good deal of attention from social psychologists. Currently the impact of our man-made environment and social psychological processes in legal proceedings are studied intensively. In addition interest is increasing in problems of a cross-cultural nature.
JMFJ

Bibliography

Argyle, M. 1978: *The psychology of interpersonal behavior*. Harmondsworth and Baltimore: Penguin.

Baron, R.A. and Byrne, D. 1981: *Social psychology: understanding human interaction*. Boston: Allyn and Bacon.

Tajfel, H. and Fraser, C. 1978: *Introducing social psychology*. Harmondsworth: Penguin.

social representation The concept of social representation as developed during the last twenty years, mainly by French researchers, has its theoretical origins in the notion of "collective representation" introduced by Durkheim (1898) to refer to the characteristics of social thinking compared to individual thinking.

Further study of this genuinely social psychological phenomenon was delayed by the dominating influence of two main scientific currents: behaviorism in psychology and the positivistic tradition in the philosophy of science.

The social representations approach, stressing symbolic functions and their role in the construction of reality, was introduced by Moscovici, who defines them as "systems of values, ideas and practices with a two-fold function; first, to establish an order which will enable individuals to orient themselves in and master their material social world, and second, to facilitate communication among members of a community by providing them with a code for naming and classifying the various aspects of their world and their individual and group history" (Moscovici 1961).

The concept differs from related concepts such as opinion, attitude or image which constitute a response to an external stimulus and thus a preparation for action. A social representation defines both the stimulus as well as the response it evokes. More than a simple guide to behavior, the social representation remodels and reconstitutes the elements of the environment in which the behavior will take place; this gives the behavior meaning and integrates it into a larger behavioral and relational system.

The notion of social representation implies simultaneously a process and a content. The latter can be analysed according to different dimensions: the attitude, the information and the field of representation concerning a given social object.

Comparative studies of the content and coherence of these dimensions may consider the division between groups in terms of their social representations. It is possible to determine the boundaries of a group through its vision of the world.

The way in which a social representation is produced and functions depends on two main processes: objectification and anchoring.

The process of objectification gives material reality to an abstract entity. First, objectification implies the strengthening of the iconic representation of a possibly ill-defined idea; that is, the "doubling" of a concept with an image. From the mass of information in circulation regarding the object of representation certain aspects are selected. Drawn from their original context the selected elements are arranged in a specific structure. This figurative model–"iconic cast"–reproduces in a nearly visual manner a certain abstract organization. It constitutes the central part of the representation. Second, the process of objectification "naturalizes" the abstract concept: the figurative model is reified. For the group it has become a category in language; and as such it is identified as objective reality.

Objectification thus involves two converging processes: the first leads from the concept to its image, the second from the image to the social elaboration of reality.

Through the process of anchorage the social object is classified within the society's network of categories. Fitting it into the existing hierarchy of social norms, values and productions, society transforms the object of representation into a serviceable instrument.

This implies that a social representation is a mode of knowledge peculiar to a particular society and irreducible to any other mode.

In sum, the role of the representation is to make the strange familiar. The mode of reasoning underlying this process is characterized by the conclusion controlling the premises. This is true of social thinking in general and it is the opposite of the mode of reasoning that science observes or tries to observe. But social thinking and scientific thinking are not only opposed. The way in which they are complementary, the way in which they nourish each others' productions appears in the orientation of scientific advance as well as in the diffusion of science in society.

Numerous experimental studies have illustrated the close relationship between social representations and behavior. It appears that different representations of the same object (task, partner, situation, group, etc.) determine different types of behavior.

More complex and dynamic functions of social representations have also been addressed by experimental studies. In the field of intergroup relations Doise (1978) investigated the functioning of anticipatory and justificatory representations: they are determined by group interaction which they in turn influence.

The empirical studies of social representations concern mostly very broad or complex objects (psychoanalysis, culture, illness, childhood, body, education among others). Observing the processes of generation and evolution of social representations, the correspondence between their production and their function, or their role in communication and social behavior, these studies suggest the generality and the relevance of the phenomenon. EF/SM

Bibliography

Abric, J.C. 1971: Experimental study of group creativity: task representation, group structure, and performance. *European journal of social psychology* 1–3.

Chombart de Lauwe, M.J. 1971: *Un monde autre: l'enfance. De ses représentations à son mythe.* Paris: Payot.

Codol, J.P. 1974: On the system of representations in a group situation. *European journal of social psychology.* 4–3.

Doise, W. 1978: *Groups and individuals: explanations in social psychology.* Cambridge and New York: Cambridge University Press.

Durkheim, E. 1898 (*1967*): Représentations individuelles et représentations collectives. In *Sociologie et philosophie.* Paris: Presses Universitaires de France.

Farr, R.M., ed. 1982: *Social representations.* Cambridge and New York: Cambridge University Press.

Gorin, M. 1980: *A l'école du groupe. Heurs et malheurs d'une innovation éducative.* Paris: Dunod. 1980.

Herzlich, C. 1972: La représentation sociale. In *Introduction à la psychologie sociale*, ed. S. Moscovici. Paris: Larousse.

——— 1973: *Health and illness: a social psychological analysis.* London: Academic Press.

Jodelet, D. 1976: *La représentation sociale du corps.* Paris: Ecole des hautes etudes en sciences sociales.

Kaes, R. 1968: *Images de la culture chez les ouvriers francais.* Paris: éditions Cujas.

Moscovici, S. 1961: *La psychanalyse, son image et son public.* Paris: Presses Universitaires de France.

——— 1973: Preface to: *Health and illness: a social psychological analysis.* London: Academic Press.

social skills A concept widely but loosely used to describe the skills employed when interacting at an interpersonal level with other people. Attempts have been made to define social skills in both behaviorist and intentionalist terms. For instance, social skills have been defined as "the ability to emit both positively reinforcing behavior toward others and to avoid emitting behavior that involved punishment by others" (Libert and Lewisohn 1973) "the extent to which a person can communicate with others in a manner that fulfills one's rights, requirements, satisfactions or obligations to a reasonable degree without damaging the other person's similar rights ..." (Phillips 1978). The concept has been used synonymously with "social competence", "social adequacy", and even "assertiveness" though each is associated with a particular theory of social interest. Talking of "skills" rather than "skill" emphasizes the complexity and variety of the kinds of actions that can be performed completely or partially. Van Hasselt's definition of social skills (1979) highlights three main elements which are seen to be crucial: social skills are situation-specific; they are acquired capacities to display appropriate responses, both verbal and nonverbal, and they should enable people to behave in a way which does not hurt or harm others. Continuing ambiguity as to the definition and empirical realizations of social skills means that social skills training subsumes a huge variety of techniques which range from behavior therapy to non-directive counseling, and have been aimed at widely different kinds of behavior. AF

Bibliography

Libert, J. and Lewisohn, P. 1973: Concept of social skills with special reference to the behavior of depressed persons. *Journal of consulting and clinical psychology* 40, 304–12.

Phillips, E. 1978: *The social skills bases of psychopathology.* London: Grune and Stratton.

Van Hasselt, V., Hersen, M., Whitehill, M. & Bellack, A. 1979: Social skills assessment and training for children: an evaluative review. *Behavioral research and therapy* 17, 417–37.

social skills training A practical procedure by means of which new forms of social behavior can be learned, or existing behavior modified. The aim of SST is to help clients to organize or improve their social skills, namely behavioral sequences which conform to social norms and which enable people to achieve desired social goals more efficiently and acceptably. SST has been developed and scientifically tested by many university, hospital and business based research teams, and has acquired variable support (modest to good) for its effectiveness. The training consists of instruction (description of applicable skills); modelling or demonstration by competent others; imitation and rehearsal by the client; teaching and feedback from others or from video-recordings; reinforcement for achieving set standards; homework practice in which the client applies the new skill in a real-life situation. SST is used for training psychiatric patients, as well as managers and other industrial and business personnel, teachers, social workers, doctors and other professionals. It is also used for improving intercultural communication. PET

Bibliography

Trower, P., Bryant, B.M. & Argyle, M. 1978: *Social skills and mental health.* London: Methuen.

social therapy This is a form of psychiatric treatment in which the patients' social setting is specifically designed and operated so as to be in itself a major therapeutic factor.

The late eighteenth century, the "Age of Reason", saw a gradual awareness of the cruel manner in which the mentally ill were often treated: in prisons, in private "madhouses", and in institutions such as Bethlem in London and the Bicêtre and the Salpêtrière in Paris. Pinel, as physician-in-chief of the Bicêtre, in 1793 released the patients from chains and forbade many of the traditional treatments such as bleeding, purging and drugs. (Pinel 1801, 1809). In England the Quaker Tuke in 1796 opened "The Retreat" at York which was run on humanitarian lines (Tuke 1813). The "non-restraint" movement flourished under the leadership of men such as Conolly (1856) at the many institutions built in England after the passing of the Asylums Act 1845. These reforms, however, were not merely humanitarian: Pinel, Tuke and Conolly all subscribed to the theory of treatment called "moral management". (In the mid nineteenth century the word moral was still a synonym for psychological). Moral treatment consisted of providing a peaceful and pleasant environment together with purposeful activities. The normality of the patients was emphasized rather than their sickness.

In the second half of the nineteenth century, however, many asylums grew unmanageably large and the staff in them grew increasingly pessimistic as to the curability of the mentally ill. These institutions tended to develop restrictive and repressive regimes encouraging the development of institutionalism (see REHABILITATION). When active treatment was provided it was usually according to the MEDICAL MODEL in which the patient is a passive recipient, and little emphasis is placed upon the treatment environment.

Before the second world war psychodynamic theories (see PSYCHOANALYSIS) had had little influence upon the treatment of the institutionalized mentally ill, but during the war a number of analysts became responsible for hospital wards catering for psychoneurotic ex-soldiers. Experiments were conducted into forms of patient self-government and the use of the newly developing forms of GROUP THERAPY. Following his experiences at Northfield Hospital, Birmingham, Main coined the term "therapeutic community" which he described as "an attempt to use a hospital not as an organisation run by doctors in the interests of their own greater technical efficiency, but as a community with the immediate aim of full participation of all its members in its daily life and the eventual aim of resocialisation of the neurotic individual for life in ordinary society" (Main 1946).

Maxwell Jones continued work in social therapy after the war at the Industrial Neurosis Unit at Belmont Hospital (later renamed Henderson Hospital) where most of the characteristic features of the therapeutic community were developed. The most important perhaps is the emphasis upon the therapeutic potential of all activities and interactions, summarized by Jones's phrase the "living–learning situation". Every therapeutic community has a community meeting, usually daily, in which the day's events can be analysed. These meetings, which are attended by all residents and all staff working in the unit, vary in detail, but all concentrate upon "here and now" problems and tasks. In most communities the rest of the day is divided between formal psychotherapeutic activities, often group therapy, and the carrying out of daily living tasks such as cleaning and cooking.

A team of sociologists led by Rapoport studied the Henderson Hospital (1960) and concluded that the therapeutic regimen could be summarized by four themes: democratization, communalism, permissiveness and reality confrontation. The therapeutic community approach, like "moral management", tends to emphasize its clients' normality rather than their illnesses, but in addition every community member is also seen as having therapeutic potential. The therapeutic community would appear to be the treatment of choice for certain PERSONALITY DISORDERS (Whiteley 1972).

The post war years also saw the start of the "open door movement" within mental hospitals, followed in the 1950s by the introduction of effective major tranquillizers such as chlorpromazine. Clark (1981) described the application of social therapy in a large psychiatric hospital in terms of "activity, freedom and responsibility". The provision of sheltered workshops and industrial therapy units has become very widespread, but it would appear that the opportunity to experience freedom and responsibility are equally important. Wing and Brown (1970) in a comparative study of three mental hospitals clearly demonstrated the effectiveness of social therapy in institutionalism and SCHIZOPHRENIA. Social therapeutic programs have also been used in a variety of other settings, for example prisons and hostels, (see Jansen 1980).

Social therapy is an empirical treatment developed in response to clinical problems and is, therefore, not directly based upon any one particular theory. Historically it has tended to be associated with liberal and radical values, with a rejection of the MEDICAL MODEL of man. Attempts have, however, been made to describe social therapy using psychodynamic concepts. Cumming and Cumming (1962) in a theoretical analysis suggested that the therapeutic community, "encourages ego growth through successful crisis resolution". Therapeutic communities have also been studied by sociologists (e.g. Rapoport 1960), social psychologists and anthropologists.

In general, it seems to be agreed that social therapy, by providing a model social group ("communal" and "democratic") permits the learning by experience ("permissiveness") of more appropriate forms of behavior. The most important treatment factor is probably a communication system (usually including the community meeting) which ensures prompt and accurate feedback to the individual and to the group ("reality confrontation").

GPP

Bibliography

*Clark, D.H. 1981: *Social therapy in psychiatry.* 2nd edn. Edinburgh: Churchill Livingstone.

Conolly, J. 1856: *The treatment of the insane without mechanical restraints.* London: Smith, Elder.

Cumming, J. and Cumming, E. 1962: *Ego and milieu.* New York: Atherton Press; London: Prentice Hall International.

*Hinshelwood, R.D. and Manning, N.P., eds. 1979: *Therapeutic communities: reflections and progress.* London and Boston: Routledge and Kegan Paul.

*Jansen, E., ed. 1980: *The therapeutic community outside the hospital.* London: Croom Helm.

Jones, M. 1968: *Social psychiatry in practice.* London: Penguin.

Main, T.F. 1946: The hospital as a therapeutic community. *Bulletin of the Menninger Clinic* 10, 66–70.

Pinel, P. 1801 *(1962)*: *A treatise on insanity,* 2nd English edn. New York: Hathner Publishing Co.

Rapoport, R.N. 1960: *Community as doctor.* London: Tavistock; Springfield Illinois: Charles C. Thomas.

Tuke, S. 1813: *Description of the retreat.* York: W. Alexander.

Whiteley, S. 1972: Henderson. In *Dealing with deviants,* ed. S. Whiteley, D. Briggs and M. Turner. London: Hogarth Press; Toronto: Clarke, Irwin & Co.

Wing, J.K. and Brown, G.W. 1970: *Institutionalism and schizophrenia*. Cambridge: Cambridge University Press.

socialization A technical term which gained currency in anthropology, psychology and sociology during the late 1930s to describe the processes through which an individual becomes a competent member of society. Interest in the experiences which influence the young and their participation in the community is as old as the Bible and readily found in the writings of philosophers and diarists as well as the founding fathers of modern social science such as Durkheim and Freud. Emphases differ within disciplines; anthropologists stress cultural transmission or enculturation, personality psychologists focus on impulse control, while sociologists concentrate on role learning. In each field the term has a unique history and meaning but its popularity coincided with the rise of positivism in the social sciences, with efforts to deal with social policy issues such as education in a scientific, value-free manner, and with a model of the child as a passive recipient of social experiences which transforms a biological organism into a human being.

According to Whiting (1968) the term "socialization" was first used formally in anthropology in 1935 but it was Freud's *Totem and Taboo*, published in 1913, which launched the study of childhood, not as a cataloguing of rituals and their cultural diffusion, but as the period in which culture had its most profound impact on the individual. Within anthropology the study of socialization is associated with the particularly American speciality known as Personality and Culture. Among its hallmarks is reliance on psychoanalytic theory. Prototypical of this approach is the collaborative work of Kardiner, a psycho analyst, and Linton and Dubois, anthropologists. The merging of their disciplinary interests is seen in concepts such as "basic personality structure" (Kardiner 1945). The term reflects both the concern of depth psychologists with that which is enduring, central or genotypic rather than merely surface or phenotypic and of anthropologists with that which is common or modal across individuals in a society. "Basic personality structures" were assumed to differ as a function of culturally specific socialization experiences. Learning theory, particularly Hullian theory with its emphasis on drive reduction as the central mechanism of reinforcement and compatible with psychoanalytic instinct theory, was later added to Culture and Personality formulations. Disenchantment with grand theories, global concepts and deductive systems in the 1960s produced a new anthropology of childhood characterized by interest in cognitive development and concerned with precise observations of behavior typical of ethological research. (British social anthropologists have not espoused the Culture and Personality approach and have generally eschewed psychological explanations.)

A variety of conceptual and methodological perspectives are included in reviews of psychological studies of socialization (Danziger 1971, Zigler and Child 1973). This diversity reflects the different theoretical orientations and research strategies employed by psychologists to explain the influences of the social world on individual development. Initially psychoanalysis provided impetus for psychological studies of socialization and its influences are found even in Piaget's early work. The term "socialization" is, however, most often linked in psychology as in anthropology with general behavior theory – the positivist amalgam of psychoanalysis and Hullian learning theory developed at Yale University by an interdisciplinary group of psychologists, anthropologists and sociologists. Complex processes such as imitation and identification were explained within this behaviorist learning framework (Miller and Dollard 1941). It had a major influence in the 1940s, 1950s and early 1960s both on psychological studies of socialization and in Personality and Culture (Whiting and Child 1953). In socialization studies the dominant strategy was to measure, in adults or older children, molar traits held to be enduring, such as aggression, dependence or conscience, and to relate these measures to early childhood experiences. The complex character descriptions of psychoanalysis became the quantified traits or consequent variables which were linked to a host of child rearing or antecedent variables by a variety of learning mechanisms such as generalization and avoidance learning.

Patterns of Child Rearing (Sears, Maccoby and Levin, 1957) is typical of the general behavior theory approach to socialization. It is the report of almost 400 interviews with mothers of five-year-olds and contains quantified data on antecedent dimensions such as feeding and the training of aggression and obedience. As a scientific study it was considered an authoritative source of information about American socialization practices for many years. Methodologically it was flawed by reliance on mothers' reports both for information on child rearing and for assessment of consequent variables such as strength of a child's conscience. Criticisms of the approach have come from many quarters. Learning theorists questioned Hullian assumptions about reinforcement and in developmental psychology, the observational learning theory of Bandura provided a more fruitful model with which to explain the influence of parents, peers and others.

Dissatisfaction with the dominant socialization approach extended well beyond learning theorists. In the attacks upon behaviorism in the 1960s Bandura's neo-behaviorist model was a target as well as the passive view of the infant as a lump of clay needing to be shaped by social forces. The unidirectional influence of adults or experienced members of society upon the young and inexperienced was questioned and a need to recognize individual differences among infants stressed. The unique and fundamental importance of early experience was queried. So pervasive were the negative attitudes attached to the term "socialization" that Richards offered a detailed explanation for rejecting the word as part of the main title of a volume on early development even though he and other contributors were writing about processes which in a general sense would be described as socialization (Richards 1974). Crucial to their position and that of many contemporary investigators is a view of the human infant as an active participant in the socialization process and of the interaction as based upon reciprocity.

Attention to biological factors was re-introduced in studying socialization, and the infant's biological potential became a focus alongside any effects of culture. The rediscovery of biology has engendered new controversies. The extent of the innate social propensities of the infant is contentious. Some psychologists describe the new born as presocial, a highly developed biological organism ready to learn to live in society (Schaffer 1979) yet other theorists maintain that at birth the human infant has rudimentary social skills (Trevarthen 1980). Nonetheless, most psychologists now take care not to underestimate the contribution of the infant to its socialization.

The sociological study of socialization has undergone a similar reassessment of theoretical and research priorities. The Parsonian position, influential during the 1950s, viewed socialization as the psychological process through which the role-differentiated nuclear family ensured that children developed human personalities, e.g., systems of socially appropriate action (Parsons and Bales 1955). These personality systems were held to reflect the social structures which the individual had experienced. Parsons was criticized for presenting an over-socialized view which left little scope for individual differences or innovation in society (Wrong 1961). In a spirit akin to that of psychologists, sociologists rejected the passive and malleable child model which had suited the positivist, determinist orientation of the social sciences in the mid-twentieth century. In search of a model which recognized the child's view of his social world, sociologists returned to the writings of G. H. Mead (White 1977). Crucial elements in Mead's work are its emphases on a reflexive self and on symbols. In order to construct and to understand the language or primary symbol system of society the child needs to interact with others. Mastery of language equips the child to understand itself and others.

Depth and detail were sacrificed in order to consider socialization from anthropological and sociological as well as psychological perspectives. This strategy has led to recognition of wider epistemological issues such as the nature of the explanatory theory employed and the model of the child which was its object, but it has resulted in a neglect of many other dimensions and changes. There has also been a marked shift in emphasis from the study of personality and motivation to concern with intellectual abilities and social understanding. Childhood is no longer the sole focus of interest and processes of socialization are investigated in adolescence, adulthood and old age. Socialization is generally viewed as an interactive process and no longer the passive receipt of expertise by a novice. Along with a diversity in content psychological research also presents a variety of theoretical positions. Social psychological studies drawing inspiration from the symbolic interactionist theory of Mead take their place alongside Piagetian explorations of the social world and Vygotskian analyses of the internalization of socially constructed tools of thought. BBL

Bibliography

Danziger, K. 1971: *Socialization.* Harmondsworth, Penguin.

Kardiner, A. 1945: The concept of basic personality structure as an operational tool in the social sciences. In *The science of man in the world crisis* ed. R. Linton. New York: Columbia University Press.

Miller, N.E. and Dollard, J. 1941: *Social learning and imitation.* New Haven: Yale University Press; London: Greenwood Press (1979).

Parsons, T. and Bales, R.F. 1955: *Family, socialization and interaction process.* Glencoe, Ill.: Free Press; London: Routledge & Kegan Paul (1956).

Richards, M.P.M. ed. 1974: *The integration of a child into a social world.* Cambridge and New York: Cambridge University Press.

Schaffer, H.R. 1979: Acquiring the concept of dialogue. In *Psychological development from infancy: image to intention,* ed. M. Bornstein and W. Kesson. Hillsdale, N.J.: Erlbaum; London: Halstead (1979).

Sears, R.R., Maccoby, E.E. and Levin, H. 1957: *Patterns of child rearing.* Evanston, Ill.: Row, Peterson.

Trevarthen, C. 1980: Neurological developmental and the growth of psychological functions. In *Developmental psychology and society,* ed. J. Sants. London: Macmillan; New York: St. Martin.

White, G. 1977: *Socialization.* London and New York: Longman.

Whiting, J.W.M. 1968: Socialization: Anthropological aspects. In *International Encyclopedia of the social sciences* vol 14, ed. D.L. Sills. New York: Macmillan and Free Press.

Whiting, J.W.M. and Child, I. 1953: *Child training and personality.* New Haven: Yale University Press.

Wrong, D. 1961: The over-socialized conception of man in modern society. *American sociological review* 26, 184–193.

Zigler, E.F. & Child, I.L., eds. 1973: *Socialization and personality development.* Reading, Mass.: Addison-Wesley.

socialization: in developmental psychology A term used to describe the process of growing up, in which children learn the norms of their society and acquire their own distinctive values, beliefs and personality characteristics. In a broad sense it refers to any form of social development; in a specific sense it is particularly concerned with MORAL DEVELOPMENT. Early studies were to some extent influenced by PSYCHOANALYSIS. Traditionally, questions relating to sex differences, the ordinal position of the child in the family, maturation, critical periods, the effects of deprivation and child-rearing practices received a great deal of attention. Under the influence of the work of Piaget and Kohlberg, recent research has concerned itself more with moral development.

Anthropology and cross-cultural psychology have contributed in many ways to the comparative study of socialization processes. Sociology and political science have focused in particular on adult (re)socialization. JMFJ

Bibliography

Triandis, H.C. and Heron, A. 1981: *Handbook of cross-cultural psychology,* Vols 1–6. Boston: Allyn and Bacon.

socialization, occupational The influence process by which an individual is taught and learns the norms, VALUES, ATTITUDES and behaviors appropriate for success in an occupational role. Socialization generally proceeds through a series of stages: anticipatory (before entering the occupational role), encounter (or initial entry) and adaptation. Occupational socialization is a continuous process, but it may be highly intensified at certain points, eg on initial entry, on promotion to a higher level. Some writers (Katz 1977) draw a distinction between the socialization of newcomers and the resocialization of veterans making some kind of an occupational change, such as a transfer to a different job.

An organization has various means, such as induction programs, at its disposal to bring about the socialization of employees. Early socialization experiences, and the part in them played by the individual's immediate supervisor, are important for later CAREER success. Not all socialization is the result of formal, organizationally directed activities. The informal social influence of the work group has a particularly powerful effect. To the extent that most occupational roles exist within an organizational setting of some kind, the term organizational socialization is sometimes preferred. RSW

Bibliography

Katz, R. 1977: Job enrichment: some career considerations. In *Organizational careers: some new perspectives*, ed. J. Van Maanen. London, New York, Sydney, Toronto: Wiley.

Louis, M.R. 1980: Surprise and sense making: what newcomers experience in entering unfamiliar organizational settings. *Administrative science quarterly* 25, 226–51.

sociobiology The study of the biological basis of social behavior. Although the word was being used in the early 1960s (Altmann 1962), the birth of sociobiology as a discipline is clearly identified with the publication of Wilson's major review (1975).

The field is derived from two separate biological traditions, evolutionary biology and ethology. Sociobiology is properly concerned with the causation and development of social behavior, as well as with functional and evolutionary questions which ask how specific traits serve as adaptations. Research on the causation and ontogeny of social behavior is reviewed by Hinde (1970). However the impetus for Wilson's 'new synthesis' came from theoretical considerations of apparent evolutionary anomalies.

Natural selection acts on individuals and results in changes of population gene frequencies. Genes which cause the fitness of their bearers to be enhanced are selectively favored. A tradition in ethology, evident in the writings of Lorenz, has been the belief that animals behave for the benefit of the group or the species rather than in their own individual interests. Selection among groups was seen as a potent evolutionary force. Wynne-Edwards (1962) was explicit about the importance of group selection as a force moulding social behavior. He argued that animals restrict their population density and rate of reproduction so that the maximum sustainable yield is maintained from the available food supplies. He postulated the existence of epideictic displays (see CONVENTIONAL AND EPIDEICTIC BEHAVIOUR) which allow members of a population to assess the density of the population. Although group selection *is* an evolutionary force, it is a weak one compared with individual selection: biologically unacceptable models of population structure have to be envisaged for group selection to outweigh the importance of individual selection (Maynard Smith 1976).

If animals are generally selected to behave in their own selfish interests, why is altruism such a common component of many animal societies? Although both Fisher and Haldane anticipated his result, Hamilton (1964) described a mechanism whereby genes coding for altruistic behavior would be selectively favored: an individual helping a close relative may be favoring the spread of its own genes because kin are particularly likely to share copies of the altruist's genes through identity by descent. Indeed, parental investment might be seen as one manifestation of such kin selection theory. Another may be that the peculiar kind of inheritance found among some social insects (the hymenoptera – ants, bees and wasps) whereby sisters share more genetic material than do mothers and daughters, predisposes these animals to develop societies founded on altruistic behavior. Not all cases of altruism result from kin selection. Trivers (1971) suggested that under certain conditions reciprocal altruism may evolve in which one animal helps another to its own disadvantage in the expectation that the altruism may be reciprocated later. This process is distinct from mutualism (see SYMBIOSIS) where there is no delay between giving and receiving help.

The currency of sociobiology is units of fitness. Since the advantages of social behavior will result from the summation of individual interactions it is important to understand that the best strategy for an animal to adopt in a social context will depend upon the behavior of others. This realization has led to the identification of the EVOLUTIONARILY STABLE STRATEGY.

Sociobiologists cannot assume that patterns of behavior are inherited (see BEHAVIOR GENETICS). Many will be learned or culturally transmitted. Since it is often impractical to determine the heritability of variation in social behavior among animals sociobiologists normally recognize adaptation by a difference between two phenotypic traits which leads to a difference in fitness between the individuals possessing them. The animal with the higher fitness is said to be more adapted than the other. This reasoning does not imply that adaptations necessarily have genetic causes since adaptation is defined by its effects rather than its causes.

The scientific methodology used by sociobiology has been criticized by Lewontin (1979). In addition to cautioning against genetic assumptions he argues that hypotheses are too often accepted without test, and points out that a functional approach to the interpretation of social behavior and the difficulty of testing hypotheses can often lead to the 'imaginative reconstruction' of evolutionary scenarios which are later accepted as facts. Furthermore he claims that if the results of tests, when made, do not closely fit predictions the hypotheses are not discarded but merely modified since animals are thought to optimize their behavior. Lewontin calls this technique "Progressive ad hoc optimization".

Functional explanations for patterns of variation in social behavior almost always claim some degree of generality and are, therefore, testable. When similar selective forces act on independently evolving lineages we might expect convergent evolution to produce traits that are correlated in similar ways within different taxonomic groups. This is the nub of the comparative method that was extensively used by Darwin to test functional evolutionary hypotheses. Constellations of functionally related characters are expected to recur in similar ecological circumstances among different taxonomic groups. For instance, in different mammalian families group structures correlate with the distribution of resources. In turn males respond to and influence grouping patterns in their attempts to gain mating access to females. The breeding systems that result correlate with differences in morphology between the sexes (Clutton-Brock and Harvey 1978).

However, there is a tendency among sociobiologists to treat all behavioral differences as adaptive. This is an unfounded assertion, and Lewontin (1979) lists several causes for non-adaptive evolution. One of the major methodological problems facing sociobiologists (and evolutionists in general) is that, although it is often possible to demonstrate the adaptive nature of a character difference, it is not possible to be sure that a particular difference is non-adaptive.

Wilson (1975) saw sociobiology as a potential unifying discipline embracing both social psychology and sociology. It is conceivable that cross-cultural analyses will demonstrate correlates of social life and ecology among humans, while comparison with other mammalian groups might suggest the importance of universals in human societies. It must be understood that human social behavior is extremely malleable, and that behavioral differences among individuals from various cultures probably result from cultural rather than genetic transmission. PHH

Bibliography

Altmann, S.A. 1962: A field study of the sociobiology of rhesus monkeys, *Macaca mulatta*. *Annals of the New York Academy of Sciences* 102, 338–435.

*Clutton-Brock, T.H. and Harvey, P.H. 1978: Mammals, resources and reproductive strategies. *Nature* 273, 191–95.

Hamilton, W.D. 1964: The genetical evolution of social behavior. *Journal of theoretical biology* 7, 1–52.

Hinde, R.A. 1970: *Animal behaviour: a synthesis of ethology and comparative psychology*. New York, McGraw-Hill.

*Lewontin, R.C. 1979: Sociobiology as an adaptationist program. *Behavioral science* 24, 5–14.

Maynard Smith, J. 1976: Group selection. *Quarterly reviews of biology* 51, 277–83.

Trivers, R.L. 1971: The evolution of reciprocal altruism. *Quarterly Reviews of Biology*. 46, 35–57.

*Wilson, Edward O. 1975: *Sociobiology, the new synthesis*. Cambridge, Mass.: Harvard University Press.

Wynne-Edwards, V.C. 1962: *Animal dispersion in relation to social behaviour*. Edinburgh: Oliver & Boyd; New York: Hafner.

sociobiology: human The scope and definition of work of human ethologists, especially those who considered themselves to be working in the wider, framework of evolutionary biology and the adaptiveness of human behavior, shifted markedly in the 1970s with the growing influence of sociobiology. The adaptive value of behavior was seen no longer in terms of species survival, but in terms of individual and inclusive fitness. Observational and traditional ethological methods became only one of many ways of studying this. The sociobiological assumption of genetic influences on behavior, applied to the human case, has led to vigorous attacks and controversy. It has been stressed by those objecting to this assumption that many of the fundamental processes of human interaction are based on the expectations of individuals about each other which in turn are based on rights and duties embodied in human institutions. These are held to be man-made, and not subject to genetic influence. Such objections are directed against what may be called naive (genetic) sociobiology. For a balanced review see Ruse (1979).

General expositions of human sociobiology include Wilson (1978) and Alexander (1980). Among numerous areas of human behavior approached from a sociobiological perspective are the following: marriage systems: the rareness of polyandry, and the relation of monogamy/polygyny to resource ecology and parental care, sexuality and sexual dimorphism, different reproductive strategies of males and females; kinship terminologies and unilineal and bilineal descent: their relationship to sexual strategies and to paternity and certainty; choice of marriage or mating partners: for example the effects of early co-socialization on later incest avoidance; altruism, reciprocity and exchange: their relationship to kinship; territoriality and aggression: for example circumstances predicting human tribal warfare; parental care and investment: for example the occurrence of preferential female infanticide in highly stratified societies, and adoption of kin and non-kin.

Human sociobiology, even more than human ethology, has the potential to bring together a variety of disciplines other than psychology – notably anthropology, sociology, politics, economics and history (Chagnon and Irons 1979), as well as population genetics and demography. However, in so doing it is likely to be transformed into a wider theory of gene-culture evolution and the interaction of both genetic and cultural factors in human behavior. Recent attempts to consider such interaction are typified by Lumsden and Wilson (1981). In general such approaches lead to the conclusion that human behavior will not always be adaptive in the way that naive human sociobiology would predict, not only because the human environment has changed so much from that of our hominid ancestors, but also because culture itself can be considered an evolutionary process, embodying selection, variation and retention, which may co-evolve with but can also conflict with the pressures of biological evolution. PKS

Bibliography

Alexander, R.D. 1980: *Darwinism and human affairs*. London: Pitman; Seattle: University of Washington Press.

Blurton Jones, N.G., ed. 1972: *Ethological studies of child behaviour*. Cambridge and New York: Cambridge University Press.

Bowlby, John 1969: *Attachment and loss, vol. 1: Attachment*. London: Hogarth Press; New York: Basic Books.

Chagnon, N.A., and Irons, W. 1979: *Evolutionary biology and human social behavior: an anthropological perspective*. Massachusetts: Duxbury Press.

Eibl-Eibesfeldt, I. 1979: Human ethology: concepts and implications for the sciences of man. *Behavioural and brain sciences* 2, 1–57.

Ekman, P., and Friesen, W.V. 1976: Measuring facial movement. *Environmental psychology and nonverbal behaviour* 1, 56–75.

Lumsden, Charles J. and Wilson, Edward O. 1981: *Genes, minds and culture.* Cambridge, Mass: Harvard University Press.

McGrew, W.C. 1972: *An ethological study of children's behaviour.* London and New York: Academic Press.

Ruse, M. 1979: *Sociobiology: sense or nonsense?* Dordrecht, Holland: D. Reidel.

Smith, P.K. 1983: Human sociobiology. In *Psychology Survey IV*, ed. B.M. Foss and J. Nicholson.

Smith, P.K., and Connolly, K.J. 1980: *The ecology of preschool behaviour.* British Psychological Society. Cambridge and New York: Cambridge University Press.

Wilson, Edmund O. 1978: *On human nature.* Cambridge, Mass.: Harvard University Press.

sociolect Any combination of observable variable features of a language which can be associated with a certain social group. A distinction must be made between folk-classifications (such as the U versus non-U versions of British English) and forms of speech found within well-defined social isoglosses, i.e. boundaries of usages (see LABOV; VARIATION THEORIES).

As with regional *dialects*, linguists have experienced considerable difficulties in correlating extralinguistic and linguistic variables.

Of particular interest to psycholinguistics is the question of subjective reactions to the speech of socially stigmatized groups and to what extent efficient communication is possible between users of distinct social dialects. PM

Bibliography

Wolfram, W. and Fasold, R.W. 1974: *Social dialects in American English.* London and Englewood Cliffs, N.J.: Prentice Hall.

sociolinguistics The study of the relationship between linguistic and social phenomena. It began to establish itself as a sub-discipline of linguistics in the 1960s as a result of the realization that many linguistic patterns cannot be studied without also studying the users of such patterns (i.e. there is an indexical aspect to linguistic signs) and that social interaction is carried out, to a significant extent, through the medium of language.

The various subdivisions that are found within sociolinguistics relate to developments within linguistics and sociology and to differential emphasis on social and linguistic phenomena.

The principal directions within sociolinguistics, in their order of development, are: the language and society approach, embracing the study of linguistic CODES, the relationship between language and culture (see WHORF), etc; VARIATION THEORIES of language; and the communicative COMPETENCE approach. PM

Bibliography

Grimshaw, Allen D. 1978: Language in society: four texts. Review article, *Language* 54, 156–69.

Neustupny, J.V. 1974: Sociolinguistics and the language teacher. *Linguistic communications* 12, 1–24.

sociopathic personality Refers to a typical cluster of character traits in an individual who is repeatedly at variance with society. He is unable to make deep and stable relationships, is lacking in concern for others and incapable of guilt and remorse; he is self-centered, irritable and impatient, being liable to emotional and aggressive outbursts in the face of frustrations and delays in the gratification of his wishes. The term is virtually synonymous with PSYCHOPATHIC PERSONALITY, with the exclusion of the inadequate (that is, neurotic) and the creative psychopathic subgroups.

The sociopath is said to score high on tests of extroversion and low on neuroticism, and to be relatively resistant to attempts to modify his behavior through psychotherapy or behavioral treatments, although slow improvement usually occurs through delayed maturational processes. However, sociopathic personality should probably not be seen as a clear-cut diagnostic entity, but rather as part of the wide and varied spectrum of PERSONALITY DISORDERS. DLJ

Bibliography

Craft, Michael 1966: *Psychopathic disorders and their assessment.* London: Pergamon.

sociotechnical system The conceptualization of organizations as the integration of a social component (the organization of people and work) and a technical component (equipment and the production process layout). The concept originated with the Tavistock Institute's study of production problems arising from technological changes in British coal mining (Trist and Bamforth 1951). They concluded that different work tasks and technical requirements have different psychological and social consequences. Even with similar work technologies, alternative social structures may exist, each with a unique impact on people. With its concern for the social component of organizations, the sociotechnical approach has provided an impetus for the HUMAN RELATIONS SCHOOL and many ORGANIZATION DEVELOPMENT projects. SGH/NMT

Bibliography

Trist, E.L. and Bamforth, K.W. 1951: Some social and psychological consequences of the long-wall method of coal-getting. *Human relations.* 4, 3–38.

somatosensory nervous system Those neural structures which participate in the conversion of the stimulation of body tissues into the sensations and perceptions of touch, position, temperature, and pain. As a physically large system with several submodalities, the somatosensory system has several identifiable subsystems. Spatially, all parts of the body except the face are innervated by somatic afferents from segments of the spinal cord. The face is innervated by afferents of the trigeminal nerve. Functionally and structurally the spinal segmental system is subdivided into the dorsal column–medial lemniscal system and the anterolateral system. The same dichotomy is present in the trigeminal system.

The dorsal column–medial lemniscal system subserves touch, pressure and position sense. (See BRAIN AND CENTRAL NERVOUS SYSTEM: ILLUSTRATIONS, fig. 28). Its primary afferents are all myelinated fibers from peripheral mechanoreceptors (e.g. Pacinian corpuscles, Meissner corpuscles, Merkel disks, etc.) where SENSORY TRANSDUCTION occurs. The cell bodies for these fibers are in the dorsal root ganglia of the spinal cord. Afferent axons ascend ipsilaterally in the dorsal columns of the spinal cord to the dorsal column nuclei. These project contralaterally via the medial lemniscus to the posterior nuclear group and the ventral posterior lateral (VPL) nucleus of the thalamus (fig. 19). VPL projects to two somatosensory cortical regions, the primary cortex (SI) of the post central gyrus of the parietal lobe and the secondary cortex (SII) on the upper bank of the Sylvian fissure (figs. 2 and 3). The posterior nuclear group projects primarily to SII and the somatosensory association cortex just behind SI. All these structures are somatotopically organized with continuous mapping of body site onto neural structure (fig. 4).

The anterolateral system subserves pain, temperature sense and crude touch (fig. 29). Primary afferents whose cell bodies lie in the dorsal root ganglia, synapse on neurons in the dorsal horn of the spinal cord. These cells project contralaterally in the lateral spinal columns to the reticular formation of the brainstem (figs. 6 and 9) and to the same regions of the thalamus innervated by the dorsal column nuclei. Projections from thalamus to the CEREBRAL CORTEX (SI, SII, and somatosensory association cortex) follow the patterns of the dorsal column–medial lemniscal system.

Like other neocortex, somatosensory cortex is organized into vertical columns. Each column contains vertical sets of neurons sensitive to the same submodality and innervated from the same small region of peripheral sensory organ (see VISUAL NERVOUS SYSTEM for another example of the columnar organization of neocortex).

Descending connections directly from the cortex and those through subcortical relays influence the afferent input at many levels down to the dorsal horn of the spinal cord. These centrifugal neurons appear to contribute to the shaping of sensory input, perhaps selectively increasing spatial resolution in a particular region. They also play a role in facilitating portions of afferent pathways about to be stimulated by body movement. SCC

Bibliography

Iggo, A., ed. 1973: *Handbook of sensory physiology*. vol. II, *Somatosensory system*. Berlin and New York: Springer-Verlag.

Kandel, E.R. and Schwartz, J.H., eds. 1981: *Principles of neural science*. New York and Oxford: Elsevier/North-Holland.

Mountcastle, V.B. 1980: Neural mechanisms in somesthesia. In *Medical physiology*, 14th edn. vol. I, ed. V.B. Mountcastle, St. Louis and London: C.V. Mosby.

sound symbolism (phonetic symbolism) Means that the relationship between the signifier (form) and the signified (meaning) part of a linguistic sign is not arbitrary but that sound expresses meaning directly and intrinsically. For example, the vowel [i] with its high pitch and small oral opening is associated with the meaning "smallness" in many languages whereas the vowel [a] with a prominent low pitch and a large oral opening is frequently found in lexical items denoting "largeness". when confronted with the nonsense words "sug" (phonetically [sag]) and sig (phonetically [sig]) as names for animals, speakers of English would assign "sug" to the large animal.

The extent to which the association between words and their meanings is non-arbitrary in natural languages has been debated for a long time. The origin of the argument is found in Plato's dialogue "Cratylus", where the view presented by Hermogenes that language is purely a matter of convention and that one can give whatever name one desires to any object is contrasted with that of Cratylus, who claims that a name is naturally suited to its object and that one only needs to know the name in order to know the natural properties of the associated thing.

Most modern linguists and psycholinguists accept Saussure's view that no motivation for the phonetic constitution of a sign is to be found in the thing for which it is a sign, and that cases of onomatapoeia (see below) are not sufficiently numerous or important in language to invalidate the basic principle of arbitrariness. However there has recently been renewed interest and substantial research in the area of sound symbolism in connection with the question of linguistic universals and linguistic naturalness. A good summary of the psycholinguistic research is provided by Taylor (1976, 307–31) and the linguistic implications are discussed by Harris (1980, 102–12).

The phonetic symbolism hypothesis exists both in the form of a universal and a language specific phonetic symbolism claim. Two arguments are commonly adduced against the stronger universal version.

The first is that different languages can have quite different names for the same or similar concepts: English *big* corresponds to German *gross* and Enga (a non-melanesian language of the New Guinea Highlands) *andake* (for inanimates) and *putuko* (for animates). The second is that different languages often have the same, or similarly pronounced, words for very different concepts. Haas (1957: 338–41) for instance adduces numerous examples of lexical items from other languages which bear close phonetic similarity to English four-letter words and therefore produce a special form of interference in second language learning.

Proponents of the universal phonetic symbolism hypothesis would reply that phonetic symbolism is found in restricted parts of the lexicon only, notably with regard to the semantic areas of size, shape, weight and colour. They refer to the results of experiments such as the antonym pair test in which native speakers of one language listen to antonym pairs in another (preferably unrelated) language and then have to guess which foreign word translates the equivalent in their own language (Brown 1970: 258–73).

A second area for which universal phonetic symbolism is commonly claimed is that of onomatopoeia, i.e. cases where the sound structure of a word imitates the sound of an animal or object. For example, the sound commonly attributed to roosters in various languages is:

Afrikaans	koekelekoe [kukeleku]
Danish	kykeliky [kikeliki]
English	cock-a-doodle-doo
Greek	kokkux [kokuks]
Japanese	kokekokyo [kokekio]

However at present there is insufficient comparative evidence and virtually no evidence from first and second language acquisition for the universality of onomatopoeia.

Until recently it had been widely assumed that the results of such tests support the universal phonetic symbolism claim. However Taylor (1976, 315–25) points to many instances of experimental bias invalidating the evidence. More comparative language data and better controlled psycholinguistic experiments are needed in this area.

New promising fields for the investigation of universal phonetic motivation are the study of relative motivation in syntagmemes and suprasegmental phonology. Syntagmemes include complex and compound lexical items as well as syntactic constructions. Recent work on constructional iconism (Mayerthaler 1978) has shown a number of language-independent principles of morphonological motivation. Languages of the inflectional type, for instance, will have either no affix or a shorter one with unmarked grammatical categories and a longer affix with marked categories. Thus singular, positive and present tense forms are shorter than the corresponding plural, comparative and minus present tense forms (see LINGUISTIC NATURALNESS).

Evidence from newly emerging linguistic systems such as pidgins and creoles (see SECOND LANGUAGE ACQUISITION; CREOLIZATION) suggests that there is a universal motivation for certain basic types of intonation.

While the question of a universal phonetic motivation remains unsolved, firmer support is available for language-specific phonetic symbolism, though, again, a number of principled objections must be mentioned:

Languages can have randomly associated homophones, such as English *sound* (meaning: healthy, what is heard, narrow passage) and *bank* (meaning: margin of river or establishment for custody of money).

Languages have randomly associated synonyms such as English *small* and *little* with very different phonetic properties.

Both the form and meaning of linguistic signs can change in the course of history.

Thus phonetic symbolism is restricted to a larger or smaller range of phenomena in a given language. Languages which are historically related are more likely to exhibit similarities than are unrelated ones. According to Taylor (1976, 326) an important factor accounting for cross-linguistic differences is that of differing language habits: "Initial [t] is associated with smallness, probably because in English some frequently used 'small' words start with [t]: tiny, teeny, tip, trifle, tinge". Taylor's observations are supported by the fact that language-specific phonetic symbolism becomes more consistent with increased age.

A promising new area of research into language-specific phonetic symbolism is the investigation of syntactic freezes, i.e. fixed word order in conjuncts in the right hand column are significantly less grammatical (see GRAMMATICALNESS) than those in the left (Cooper and Ross 1975, 63–111).

perfectly grammatical	*less gramatical or ungrammatical*
sooner or later	later or sooner
friend or foe	foe or friend
once or twice	twice or once

The regularities governing the grammaticalness of such freezes appear to be language-specific and include both semantic and phonological factors. Examples are:

semantic conditions	*examples of underlying freezes*	*phonological conditions*
here before there	(at home and abroad)	place two element contains more syllables (wild and woolly)
adult before child	(father and son)	place two element has more initial consonants (helter skelter)
positive before negative	(pluses and minuses)	place two element has fewer final consonant (sink or swim)
solid before liquid	(field and stream)	place two element has a longer vowel nucleus (trick or treat)

Cooper and Ross (1975, 92) suggest that "frozen conjunct order reflects a perceptual processing principle whereby conjuncts, which are easier to process tend to occupy place one in a freeze, enabling the listener to handle the preliminary processing of this conjunct while new information is still to be presented to him by the speaker."

The restrictions underlying freezes are not only language-specific but vary in their restrictiveness. The interrelationship between phonetic and semantic restrictions in such syntagmemes and their relationship to discourse structure rules remain poorly understood.

In conclusion, it would seem that the importance of the question of phonetic symbolism lies in the fact that it brings together a number of areas of research in linguistics and psycholinguistics. A meaningful discussion of the phenomenon appears to be possible only within the wider framework of the study of: linguistic universals; LINGUISTIC NATURALNESS; comparative linguistics; developmental psycholinguistics; and NEUROLINGUISTICS.

The results in the area of freezes suggest that the restriction of the investigation to individual lexical items is unnecessarily narrow and that in order to obtain useful answers to the question of phonetic symbolism, syntagmemes and discourse structure should also be examined. PM

Bibliography

Brown, Roger 1970: Phonetic symbolism in natural languages. In *Psycholinguistics*, ed. R. Brown *et al.*. New York: Macmillan. 258–73.

Cooper, William A. and Ross, John R. 1975: World order. In *papers from the Parc session on functionalism*. Illinois: Chicago Linguistic Society. 63–111.

Haas, Mary 1957: Interlingual word taboos. *American anthoropologist* 53, 338–41.

Harris, Roy 1980: *The language makers*. London: Duckworth.

Mayerthaler, Willi 1978: *Morphologische Natürlichkeit*. Habilitations-thesis, Technical University, Berlin (West) English trans. to be published by Karoma Publ, Ann Arbor.

Taylor, Insup 1976: *Introduction to psycholinguistics*. New York: Holt Rinehart & Winston.

space: psychological aspects Three fields of interest have dominated psychological studies of space; mechanisms of spatial perception, the modes of representation of spatial knowledge, and the social interpretations of space.

The psychology of spatial perception has been dominated by two main kinds of theory: that the perception of spatial relations is based on visual and perhaps other sensations, and in contrast that it is a cognitive process involving visual information (Gibson 1968) and/or is of the nature of hypotheses (Gregory 1970). For a judicious review of the candidate theories for visual perception see Cartarette and Friedman (1974). For detailed accounts of the psychology of spatial perception see PERCEPTION. Visual ways of perceiving space dominate the literature, but considerable effort has been devoted to the study of spatial perception by the blind, which is based on tactile, auditory and kinesthetic experience (Hunter 1964).

Mental mapping

Most research has been carried out on route-finding in large urban environments. Early research focused on the "legibility" of cities (Lynch 1960). High legibility is reported to be related to emotional security. The following elements are commonly found in descriptions of cities; paths or routes, districts, nodes (strategic junctions or breaks) and landmarks. It is reported that people structure cities either by paths or by districts. Appleyard (1970) examined the way people represent cities and found two discrete mapdrawing styles, a sequential style which creates a network representation of a city and a spatial style which creates a mosaic patterned representation. Recent research has used distance and angle estimation to explore mental maps (Byrne 1981). This research supports a model in which urban spatial areas are represented as network maps, consisting of strings of locations forming a network of paths known to be traversable, but vector distance is not preserved.

Another line of research examines geographical knowledge, exploring the effects of conceptual categorization on judgments of relative geographical relations. Systematic errors in judgment support a model in which spatial information is stored hierarchically (Stevens and Coupe 1978).

The texturing of space with meaning often determined by the nature of the social episode proceeding in that space involves two basic structures: the division of the space into regions relative to rights of access (Harré 1979) and the "loading" of the regions so defined for psychologically derived and relevant attributes (Lewin 1935; Goffman 1971). The ecological concept of *Umwelt* has been borrowed to express the differential texturing of space for persons of different status and position, or occupying different roles in society, which uses a certain total spatial region. RHa/ME

Bibliography

Appleyard, D. 1970: Styles and methods of structuring a city. *Environment and behavior* 2, 100–17.

Byrne, R.W. 1981: Geographical knowledge and orientation. In *Normality and pathology of cognitive function*, ed. A. Ellis. London: Academic Press.

Cartarette, E.C. and Friedman, M.E. 1974: *Handbook of perception volume 1*. New York and London: Academic Press.

Gibson, J.J. 1968: *The senses considered as perceptual systems*. Boston: Houghton; London: George, Allen & Unwin.

Goffman, E. 1971: *Relations in public*. London: Allen Lane; New York: Basic Books.

Gregory, R.L. 1970: *The intelligent eye*. London: Weidenfeld.

Harré, R. 1979: *Social being*. Oxford: Basil Blackwell; Totowa, N.J.: Rowman, Littlefield & Adams (1980), 192–204.

Hunter, W.F. 1964: An analysis of space perception in congenitally blind and in sighted individuals. *Journal of general psychology* 70, 325–9.

Lewin, K. 1935: *Principles of topological psychology*. Trans. F. and G.M. Heider. New York: McGraw-Hill.

*Lynch, Kevin 1960, 1964: *The image of a city*. Cambridge, Mass.: Technical Press.

*Stevens, A. and Coupe, P. 1978: Distortions in judged spatial distances. *Cognitive psychology* 10, 422–437.

spacing The term used in ethology to refer to the distance an animal puts between itself and a fellow member of its own group. When there is no spacing, as for instance in the mother-infant relationship in mammals, we can speak of a BOND between the two individuals. In most species, spacing distributes the members of a group in such a way that they are in sensory contact with each other but do not infringe each other's personal space. This is the case, for instance, in birds that form flocks and shoaling fish. The actual mechanisms by which spacing is maintained in these species are still not fully understood, but in some fish it is clear that fry do not show the precisely aligned spacing characteristic of adults, and it is probable that learning is at least partly involved in the ontogeny of spacing.

In territorial species, spacing may be very pronounced. Birds of prey lay claim to a large hunting ground and defend it against all other birds of prey, not merely their own species. For predators, spacing is a permanent state, whereas for other species, such as grouse, it may be a complex phenomenon, related mainly to distribution during the breeding season.

Studies of primates and human children have shown that when spacing is insufficient, (a condition that can be called "crowding"), the frequency of aggressiveness increases. Among adults, there are different spacing norms in different human cultures. The close spacing characteristic of Arab countries, for example, can puzzle Europeans, and the significance of close spacing, particularly touching, differs both within and between cultures: closeness in general goes with intimacy, while wide spacing may express either lack of warmth or differences in social status. (See also TERRITORIALITY; CONVENTIONAL AND EPIDEICTIC BEHAVIOR.) VR

species and speciation In modern evolutionary biology, species usually refers to the biological species concept, whereby a species is a set of actually or potentially interbreeding natural populations that is reproductively isolated from other such sets (see Mayr 1963). In practice, the existence of reproductive isolation cannot always be determined directly, and other features such as differences in form may be used to distinguish between species: but generally these criteria are intended as reflections of reproductive isolation, not as good criteria in themselves.

Speciation refers to the evolutionary processes whereby species originate – usually, the splitting of one species into two or more distinct ones. The mechanism usually thought responsible is geographic speciation – the development of reproductive isolation between populations during a period of geographic isolation. Other mechanisms, however, are sometimes proposed (White 1978). See also EVOLUTION, NATURAL SELECTION. RDA

Bibliography

Mayr, E. 1963: *Animal species and evolution*. Cambridge, Mass: Harvard University Press.

White, M.J.D. 1978: *Modes of speciation*. San Francisco: W.H. Freeman.

speech: telegraphic The term "telegraphic speech" was introduced by Brown (1970) to describe the short incomplete utterances produced by children after the two-word stage of *first language acquisition*. (See LANGUAGE ACQUISITION). The use of telegraphic speech reflects a constraint on the length of utterance children are able to produce. This limitation grows less restrictive with age.

Forms most likely to appear in telegraphic speech are nouns, verbs and adjectives, in that order. Forms likely to be omitted (when compared with adult speech) are inflections, the *copula*, auxiliary verbs, articles and conjunctions. As the telegraphic speech stage progresses such function words are gradually added.

The appearance of telegraphic speech rather than a three-word stage after the two-word stage is still in need of explanation. It may be a reflection of the fact that most syntactic and semantic relations are binary rather than ternary.

A possible objection to the term "telegraphic speech" is that it may misleadingly imply that a child's utterances are merely reductions of adult models and not novel creations.

PM

Bibliography

Brown, Roger 1970: *Psycholinguistics*, New York and London: MacMillan.

speech act A term introduced by Bühler (1934) and subsequently taken up by Austin (1962) who stresses that in saying things speakers are actually doing things. According to Austin, we perform three kinds of acts in speaking a language: Acts of saying something, i.e. locutionary acts, or, more precisely, phonetic acts of uttering noises, phatic acts of uttering certain words of a certain vocabulary and in a certain grammatical form, and rhetic acts of using those variables with a certain sense and reference. Acts *in* saying something, i.e. illocutionary acts such as "asking questions", "giving orders", "making promises". Acts *by* saying something, i.e perlocutionary acts of producing certain intended or unintended effects upon the feeling, thoughts or actions of other persons such as "persuading" or "convincing". How an utterance has to be interpreted and what we achieve with speech therefore depends on the illocutionary force of the utterance and its perlocutionary effects. Research has mainly focused on illocutionary acts which can be *direct* or *indirect*. The illocutionary force of direct speech acts corresponds to the literal meaning of the sentence/utterance. For indirect speech acts the force of a literal interpretation is inappropriate and the analyst has to rely on contextual information. It is therefore essential to establish the rules constituting specific speech acts, i.e. constitutive rules (Searle 1969, Kreckel 1981). MK

Bibliography

Austin, J.L. 1962: *How to do things with words*. Cambridge, Mass.: Harvard University Press.

Bühler, K. 1934: *Sprachtheorie: die Darstellungsfunktion der Sprache*. Jena: Gustav Fischer.

Kreckel, M. 1981: *Communicative acts and shared knowledge in natural discourse*. New York and London: Academic Press.

Searle, J.R. 1969: *Speech acts*. Cambridge and New York: Cambridge University Press.

speech differences *See* sex-related speech differences

speech disorders Pathological disturbances in an individual's behavior, the study of which is speech pathology. This is not the only possible definition. At one time the term "speech disorder" referred only to disabilities involving the motor function of the vocal organs, thereby ruling out the more "central" disorders such as aphasia. At the other extreme some therapists have taken the term to apply to all mental and physical disabilities which hinder verbal communication, including SCHIZOPHRENIA, DEAFNESS AND HEARING IMPAIRMENT, cleft palate, and reading and writing disorders such as DYSLEXIA. "Speech disorders" here refers only to those communicational disorders which specifically concern the production and reception of speech. This excludes abnormalities of speech which arise as repercussions from other non-language disturbances: for instance, the distinctively disordered speech of the schizophrenic or of many of the deaf.

Speech disorders can arise from a variety of causes. If a particular disorder can be traced to a lesion or malfunctioning in the brain or nervous system, the disorder will be referred to as "organic". If no such cause can be found, or assumed, the disorder will be deemed "functional". The most common types of organic speech disorders result from cerebro-vascular accidents or "strokes". Speech disorders may also be caused by brain tumors, birth injury, infectious diseases (such as meningitis), headwounds, etc.

Although speech disorders are mentioned in texts dating as far back as the ancient Egyptian era, they did not become the subject of scientific investigation until the nineteenth century. Medical scientists, such as Pierre Broca (1865) and Carl Wernicke (1908) first undertook the study of speech disorders with the aim of locating the area(s) in the brain specifically concerned with speech (see BRAIN AND CENTRAL NERVOUS SYSTEM: ILLUSTRATIONS). These investigations centered on the CEREBRAL CORTEX or surface gray matter covering the major part of the brain. The areas which these early investigators found to be the seat of language functions were located in the left of the cortex (for right-handed people: see LATERALIZATION) at or near the junction between the temporal, frontal, and parietal lobes. Two such areas were found to be essential to coherent speech. The first, Broca's area, is located at the inferior gyrus of the left frontal lobe. A second speech area, known as Wernicke's area, is found in the superior gyrus of the left temporal lobe. Lesions in Broca's area were said to lead to "motor" or "expressive" speech disorders: that is, disorders affecting the production of speech. Lesions in Wernicke's area were thought to be the cause of "sensory" or "receptive" disorders: i.e. disorders affecting the reception of speech.

Much of this early medical framework is still part of speech pathology today. Both the expressive/receptive dichotomy and the notion of speech centers in the brain continue to exert an influence on contemporary theories of NEUROLINGUISTICS and speech pathology. Recent work, however, has turned more to the specification of the behavioral aspects of speech disorders, framed in the vocabulary of modern linguistics. The linguistic character of a disorder had hitherto been analysed only in very general, pre-theoretical terms. The dominant notion was that of language modalities: speaking, hearing, reading, and writing. Today these commonsense descriptions have largely been replaced by a variety of competing descriptive frameworks, culled from contemporary linguistic theories. As yet, there is little conclusive evidence about the relative merits of these frameworks; consequently there is no standard classification of speech disorders. However, it is convenient (and not uncommon) to group them into three basic types: central disorders, output (or production) disorders, and input (or reception) disorders.

Most central disorders are grouped under the general heading of *aphasia*, which has received more scientific attention than any other speech disorder primarily because it is thought to reveal the nature of the speaker/hearer's knowledge of his language as well as of the ways in which that knowledge is cognitively processed.

Whether, in the contemporary theoretical context, aphasia is to be seen as a disorder of competence or performance is, however, controversial (see Whitaker 1970; Wiegl and Bierwisch 1970).

One influential analysis of aphasia was first suggested by Roman Jakobson (1964) on the basis of investigations by the Soviet psychologist A.R. Luria (1970, 1976). This linguistic classification has been modified and extended (see Sabouraud, Gagnepain, and Sabouraud 1963, and Gagnepain 1973 and forthcoming). Gagnepain and the Sabourauds model their analysis on two fundamental linguistic dichotomies. The first concerns the distinction between syntagmatic (combinatory) and paradigmatic (selectional) processes (see PARADIGMATIC AND SYNTAGMATIC RELATIONS IN GRAMMAR). Aphasics with a lesion in Broca's area are said to have difficulty combining linguistic items in coherent sequence. On the other hand, a Wernicke's aphasic is unable to make an effective selection of appropriate linguistic items. The second dichotomy is drawn between two types of linguistic unit: the phoneme and the word. This is sometimes referred to as "the dual articulation of language" and is a dichotomy between the primary significant units of language (words) and the primary non-significant units (phonemes) (see SPEECH UNITS). While phonology concerns the language-user's ability to select and combine phonemes in order to construct words; semiology, according to this theory, refers to the ability to select and combine words in the construction of utterances.

As a result of the intersection of these two dichotomies, the earlier distinction between "expressive" and "receptive" aphasia has been replaced by a more complex division into four fundamental types of aphasia. The Broca's aphasic with a semiological disorder is unable to combine words effectively into a syntactic structure. His vocalizations are often described as telegraphic (see TELEGRAPHIC SPEECH) or as exhibiting a-grammatism. When there is a-grammatism an absence of the grammatical markers (prepositions, conjunctions, inflectional endings) needed to combine words into sentences is observed. Should a phonological disorder affect the Broca's aphasic he will be unable to combine phonemes into coherent words. This may result in utterances consisting of many unconnected syllabic fragments spoken with an a-rhythmical and monotonous pitch pattern.

The Wernicke's aphasic with a semiological disorder will produce a fluent stream of words, with no lack of grammatical markers, but a word-finding difficulty (anomia) may be observed. This may in turn lead to frequent circumlocution in order to avoid selection difficulties and/or to the use of vague pronouns and "semantically empty" words such as *thing*, *whatsitsname*, and *the one*. In addition paraphasia (the production of inappropriate words) or jargon (the production of meaningless words) may occur. The speech of the Wernicke's aphasic with a phonological disorder will be characterized by frequent inappropriate selections from the stock of phonemes. Again, jargon and paraphasia may result, but at the syllabic level. Related to this will be the inability, often attributed to dysarthria (see below), to realize the basic paradigmatic oppositions which distinguish one phoneme from another. Thus the word *bit* may be pronounced as *pit* or *bid* or *bet*.

The most frequently studied output disorders are stuttering (or "stammering") and cluttering. A variety of features characterize stuttering. These include erratic rhythm and tempo patterns, abnormal prolongations of sound segments, and greater than usual amounts of pausing, repetition, self-correction, and incomplete grammatical structures. In addition there may be blocking – a unique characteristic of the stutterer resulting from the inability to release the tension built up prior to articulation. There has, as yet, been no accepted organic explanation of stuttering, but much progress has been made in its functional study, including the specification of psychological factors which may cause a child to acquire a stutter.

Cluttering is often confused with stuttering. The clutterer tends to speak too quickly, omitting linguistic units of various levels, telescoping units into one another, and even inverting the sequential order of units. There is also the characteristic "flat" intonation of the clutterer. Because general personality differences have been found between clutterers and stutterers – the former tend to be aggressive and extroverted while the latter are timid and introspective – there are some speech pathologists who take them not as disorders specific to speech, but as resulting from an influence of character traits on speech.

On the borderline between central and output disorders are dysarthria and apraxia (or dyspraxia) of speech. Both involve disability in the articulation of speech and may result either from malfunctioning in central linguistic processes or from more general malfunctions in the neuromuscular command of articulatory performance. Since there are other behaviorial apraxias – for instance, apraxia of tool use (which affects writing ability) and apraxia of dress – all of which involve a difficulty in performing voluntary and purposive movements, it has been argued (Gagnepain 1973 and forthcoming) that apraxia is not a disability specific to language, and so not, strictly speaking, a speech disorder.

Two disorders are primarily concerned with input. Auditory agnosia is diagnosed when the hearer is not able to recognize what should be familiar speech sounds. He is not able to recognize as instances of the same linguistic unit two occurrences of a particular phoneme or syllable. With "pure word deafness", on the other hand, the recognition of sounds is not impaired. But the patient is unable to take a group of sounds as forming a recognizable word. As with many of the types of speech disorders the distinction between agnosia and "pure word deafness" is largely theoretical, in practice it is difficult to distinguish between them. The inexplicitness of both the linguistic and the neurological criteria which define such categories is a problem which continues to plague the study and remedial treatment of speech disorders. (See also NEUROLINGUISTICS.)

TJT

Bibliography

Broca, P. 1865: Sur la siège de la faculté du language articulé. Reprinted in *La Naissance de la neuropsychologie du language*, ed. H. Hécaen and J. Dubois. Paris: Flammarion. 1969.

*Crystal, D. 1980: *Introduction to language pathology*, London: Edward Arnold.

Crystal, D., Fletcher, P., and Garman, M. 1976: *The grammatical analysis of language disability*. London: Edward Arnold.

*Dalton, P. and Hardcastle, W. J. 1977: *Disorders of fluency*. London: Edward Arnold.

Gagnepain, J. 1973: Discours et methode, *Actes du Colloque International d'Aphasiologie*. Brussels.

——— forthcoming: *Du vouloir dire*, Oxford and New York: Pergamon.

Jakobson, R. 1964: Towards a linguistic typology of aphasia impairments. In *Disorders of language* ed. A. De Reuck and M. O'Connor. London: Churchill.

*Lesser, R. 1978: *Linguistic investigations of aphasia*. London: Edward Arnold.

Luria, A. R. 1970: *Traumatic aphasia*. The Hague: Mouton.

——— 1976: *Basic problems of neurolinguistics*. The Hague: Mouton.

Sabouraud, O., Gagnepain, J., and Sabouraud, A. 1963: *Vers une approche linguistique des problèmes de l'aphasie*, Rennes. (Also in *Revue de Neuropsychiatrie de l'Ouest*, 1963.)

Weigl, E. and Bierwisch, M. 1970: Neuropsychology and linguistics: topics of common research. *Foundations of language* 6, 1–18.

Wernicke, C. 1908: The symptom-complex of aphasia, in *Disorders of the nervous system*. ed. A. Church. New York: Appleton.

Whitaker, H. 1970: Linguistic competence: evidence from aphasia, *Glossa* 4, 46–53.

speech units The unit of speech is the segment of the linguistic material about which statements are to be made. They can be either units of grammar, units of intonation, and psychological units.

Units of grammar or linguistic units: Language is a patterned activity. The category set up to account for the stretches that carry grammatical patterns is the "unit" – a component of a specific theory of grammar. In general, three questions must be asked about a linguistic unit: (1) What is it? (2) What does it do? (3) Where does it occur? The answers to these questions identify first the form as a member of a definite form class: second how this form functions within language/speech; and third the *distribution* of the unit. Up to this point theory of grammar has accounted for these three aspects in studying (1) units of varying forms going from "large" to "small", e.g. sentence, clause, phrase, word, morpheme; (2) grammatical relationships between units that make up the patterns, e.g. subordinate and superordinate clauses, subject, object, and so forth; (3) the respective occurrence of specific units in specific functions (Quirk and Greenbaum 1973; Halliday 1976).

Units of intonation or phonological units: In spoken English units of intonation are tone units. A tone unit does not correspond to any grammatical unit in spite of the fact that in conversational English it often coincides with a clause. According to Quirk and Greenbaum (1973) tone units are the principal ordering device the speaker has at his disposition to transmit the messages he wishes to convey. That is, tone units segment the continuous stretch of discourse into message blocks or units of information (Halliday 1976). This implies that the message of an utterance may change according to where the tone unit boundaries fall. For instance,

//she should have phoned her//mother was worried//.
//she should have phoned//her mother was worried//.

The physical features that define tone unit boundaries are patterns of voice, pitch, rhythm, and loudness. The end of the tone unit is signalled at the point of discontinuity where all these features change.

The problem of boundaries has been discussed by different authors under different headings. Trager and Smith (1951) coined the term "phonemic clause", a term which has been taken up by most linguists working in the American tradition. They distinguish between three types of 'terminal' junctures that modify the intonation contour. Other writers in contrast, speak of "rhythm units" and of "tentative" and "final pauses". The terms "intonation groups", "sense group", "syntagmas", and "idea unit" have also been used.

Within each tone unit one lexical item stands out from the rest of the utterance because of its prominence in pitch, rhythm and loudness. This item is called the nucleus (Quirk and Greenbaum 1973). This feature of intonation contributes largely to the kind of message conveyed (Kreckel 1981). It is discussed under different names: "tonic" (Halliday 1976), "intonation center" (Chomsky and Halle, 1968), (The terms "countour center", "primary contour", "accent", "center" and "primary stress" have also been used).

Research has shown (Kreckel 1981) that tone units have psychological reality. That is, linguistically naive, native speakers equate tone units with the smallest meaningful unit, i.e. with the unit used for encoding and decoding messages.

Psychological units: The aim of psychological and psycholinguistic research is to identify units of speech which correspond to the explicit and implicit linguistic knowledge of native speakers. Starting from the assumption that language has a structure with different degrees of cohesiveness researchers make use of the experimental paradigm in order to explore where the continuous flow of speech breaks under different severity of strain into differently sized elements. Experimental designs either focus on the breakpoints or on stretches of assumed cohesiveness.

The most common experimental procedures are "click-monitoring", "phoneme-monitoring", and "transient memory-load". These and other procedures have produced differently sized units of speech (for a review see Levelt and Flores d'Arcais 1978; for a critique Kreckel 1981). MK

Bibliography

Austin, J. L. 1962: *How to do things with words*. Cambridge, Mass.: Harvard University Press.

Bühler, K. 1934: *Sprachtheorie: die Darstellungsfunktion der Sprache*. Jena: Gustav Fischer.

Chomsky, N. and Halle, M. 1968: *The sound pattern of English*. New York: Harper & Row.

Crystal, D. 1969: *Prosodic systems and intonation in English*. Cambridge and New York: Cambridge University Press.

*Crystal, D. 1975: *The English tone of voice*. London; Edward Arnold; New York: St Martin's.

Grice, H. P. 1975: Logic and conversation. *In Syntax and semantics. vol 3. Speech acts*, ed. P. Cole and J. L. Morgan, New York and London: Academic Press.

Habermas, J. 1976: Some distinctions in universal pragmatics. *Theoretical sociology* 3, 155–167.

*Halliday, M. A. K. 1976: *System and function in language: selected papers*, ed. G. Kress. Oxford: Oxford University Press.

*Kreckel, M. 1981: *Communicative acts and shared knowledge in natural discourse*. New York and London: Academic Press.

Levelt, W. J. M. and Flores d'Arcais, G. B. 1978: *Studies in the perception of language*. New York: Wiley.

Lyons, J. 1977: *Semantics*. vols. 1 and 2. Cambridge and New York; Cambridge University Press.

Quirk, R. and Greenbaum, S. 1973: *A university grammar of English*. London: Longman; New York: Harcourt Brace.

Searle, J. R. 1969: *Speech acts*. Cambridge and New York: Cambridge University Press.

Silverstein, M. 1976: Shifters, linguistic categories, and cultural description. In *Meaning in anthropology*, ed. K. H. Basso and H. A. Selby. Albuquerque: University of New Mexico Press.

Trager, G. L. and Smith, H. L. 1951: *An outline of English structure*. Studies in linguistics, occasional papers, 3. Norman, Oklahoma: Battenberg Press.

speech *See above, and also* displaced speech

spelling This term refers to two different psychologically interesting areas: first the letter-by-letter structure of words, and second the letter-by-letter production of words. Spelling in the sense of letter-by-letter structure of words (orthography) only applies to alphabetic writing systems. The basic principle of these systems is that continuous speech sound can be represented by discrete letters. However, the relationship between units of speech sound (phonemes) and units of the visible word (graphemes) is fraught with problems (Gleitman and Rozin 1977).

In many languages spelling deviates from the sound of the spoken word. Deviations are the more marked the older the history of the orthography. Pronunciation changes over time, and successive spelling reforms have their effect. English orthography is especially complex as different languages with different orthographic systems have contributed to its form, the main ones being Germanic and Romance (Scragg 1974). The origin of many English words is still preserved in their spelling even if the sound has changed considerably (e.g. psychology, preserving the Greek *ps* and *ch*, which are sounded *s* and *k*).

Spelling can convey information about words on a number of important linguistic levels: not only the sound of a word, but often also a previous pronunciation (the *b* in lamb was once pronounced), a word's language origin, sometimes its syntactic form (*-ed* ending for past tense in English, capital letters for nouns in German), relationships between words that belong together (sign-signature), and distinctions between words that do not belong together even though they sound the same (to, two, too). These factors all contribute to spelling which means that spelling knowledge is not a trivial accomplishment (Haas 1970). This knowledge is not usually conscious but it can be demonstrated that people use it in rapid word recognition (see READING) and word production. Languages with very recent spelling reforms based solely on representing speech sound by spelling (Finnish, Serbocroat, or Turkish) have as a result much less orthographic complexity and script is considered phonetically accurate.

A description of letter-to-sound correspondences in English is provided by Venezky (1970) who classifies words according to the degree of predictability of spelling from the sound in context. If letter position is taken into account, as well as morphological units, regularity of spelling is much greater than is usually thought. Besides regularity or predictability, frequency of occurrence and length of a word influence how well its spelling is perceived and remembered. Morton (1979) provides a truly remarkable model that succeeds in taking into account the many processes involved in word recognition and yet simplifies their overwhelming complexity. The influence of linguistic factors on spelling is less clear than that of cognitive ones since a systematic linguistically based analysis of English orthography is not available.

Orthography not only determines letter-by-letter structure of words, but also whether small or capital letters are to be used and rules of punctuation. There are also conventions about abbreviation and hyphenation or separation of words. All these aspects of written language are subject to continual change. Spelling conventions are greatly influenced by social and political factors (Venezky 1980).

The *production* of words, either when writing, typing or orally naming the constituent letters is the other meaning of spelling. This process of production or reproduction can be contrasted with the process of recognition. Clearly, one is not the inverse of the other. Dissociations can occur, so that a person can be an excellent reader but an atrocious speller, or that a child may be able to spell a particular word but may not be able to recognize it, and vice versa (Bryant and Bradley 1980).

Spelling skill is acquired during the early school years and according to the orthographic complexity of the language, may take a long time to become automatic and may loom large in LEARNING DISABILITIES. Despite the artificial nature of spelling skill and its dependence on learning, young pre-readers with bare knowledge of the letters of the alphabet can be observed to invent their own spellings. Read (1971) has analysed linguistically these early productions and has been able to relate them to the child's own conceptions of phonology. Children at this stage write as they speak, or rather as they consciously analyse their own speech. They are usually not able to read back what they have written.

Much of the early stages of learning to spell is taken up by learning to segment words into those sound units that often arbitrarily correspond to letters, or letter strings (e.g. the sound ʃ is *sh* in English, *ch* in French, *sch* in German, *sci* in Italian, *s* in Portuguese).

One particular problem for conscious segmentation are such consonant clusters as in hi*n*t or pu*m*p (Marcel 1980). Many beginners tend to reduce these clusters, so that *n* or *m* are omitted. This exactly parallels what happens in normal early speech development and is therefore particularly fascinating. It occurs consistently in certain cases of severe spelling disability, as are found with DYSLEXIA. It is by no means clear whether phonological segmentation skills are a prerequisite or a consequence of being able to spell: both processes are normally acquired at the same time by young children. Illiterate adults in a peasant community have been shown to have poorer awareness of speech as a sequence of phonemes than those who had learned to read (Morais et al. 1979).

Later stages of learning to spell require two main strategies: one has to do with the application of general spelling rules, the other with the memorizing of specific word spellings. Both strategies are needed and INSTRUCTIONAL TECHNIQUES have been devised to promote these skills. The aim is a fully automatic production process: a skilled speller can write a word effortlessly and correctly. Automatic sequences are presumably governed by internal programs that precede specific motor programs. The speller is equally able to write, type, print or orally spell the word correctly. The nature of the internal representation is not accessible to introspective awareness. Many good spellers believe that they rely on visual images of spellings. However, these visual images are more likely to be a later and optional manifestation of the internal program. Seymour and Porpodas (1980) have found a directional quality to these programs from left to right in the letter string, in experiments where people had to produce either the preceding or following letter in a string. Also there are clear relationships between the position of a letter in sequence and error probability. Initial letters are almost always correctly produced, middle positions, and especially vowels, least well (Wing and Baddeley 1980).

Level of spelling skill is assessed by educational attainment tests. These tests usually consist of dictation of word lists. Mostly they are of little use in diagnosing particular spelling problems. The quality of a spelling mistake can potentially pinpoint the source of spelling difficulty. For instance, errors that involve the type of cluster reduction mentioned above can be diagnostically useful. They point to problems with phonological analysis and/or awareness. A tendency to such errors can best be revealed with nonsense words. The spelling of real familiar words can of course be learned by various means and thus this problem may be hidden. In general, serious nonphonetic errors are likely to betray difficulties with phonological analysis. Minor nonphonetic errors, that is, those that still preserve the syllable structure of the word, often mean that the child does not yet know the sound-to-letter rules very well. This error would be especially noticed in very regular or predictable words. Remedial teaching needs to distinguish this type of nonphonetic error from the more serious one mentioned above. Minor errors can also simply be slips of the pen.

Phonetically plausible errors account for a large proportion of misspellings in English. They are of course a very rational way of representing spoken words that have not been encountered before or that one cannot remember in letter-by-letter detail. They imply good phonological analysis and good knowledge of sound-to-letter rules. Nevertheless, neither of these important steps in spelling progress are sufficient. In many orthographies (especially English, French or German) the exact letter-by-letter structure needs to be known for many unpredictable or irregular words and those word pairs that sound alike but have otherwise little to do with each other. At the highest level of spelling skill, it is this aspect that discriminates most between individuals. This may well be a matter of learning specific words by rote. Interestingly, some people have lifelong difficulties specifically with this stage in spelling. One possible cause might be their disinclination to take in the full letter-by-letter detail of words, when reading (Frith 1980). Such a strategy works perfectly well in reading but for spelling the full detail is essential. This again serves to demonstrate that reading and spelling strategies are relatively independent and each deserves to be looked at in its own right. UF

Bibliography

*Frith, U. (ed.) 1980: *Cognitive processes in spelling.* London and New York: Academic Press. (Contains articles by Baker; Bryant and Bradley; Frith; Marcel; Morton; Seymour and Porpodar; Venezsky (1980); and Wing and Baddeley cited in text.)

Gleitman, L. and Rozin, P. 1977: The structure and acquisition of reading, I: Relations between orthographies and the structure of language. In *Toward a psychology of reading*, ed. A.S. Reber and D.L. Scarborough. Hillsdale, N.J.: Erlbaum.

Haas, W. 1970: *Phonographic translation.* Manchester: Manchester University Press.

*Kavanagh, J.F. and Venezky, R.L., eds. 1980: *Orthography, reading and dyslexia.* Baltimore: University Park Press, 1980.

Morais, J., Cary, L., Alegria, J. and Bertelson, P. 1977: Does awareness of speech as a sequence of phones arise spontaneously? *Cognition* 7, 323–31.

Morton, J. 1979: Word recognition. In *Structures and processes*, ed. J. Morton, and J. C. Marshall, Psycholinguistics series, 2. London: Paul Elek.

Read, C. 1971: Preschool children's knowledge of English phonology. *Harvard educational review* 41, 1–34.

Scragg, D.G. 1974: *A history of English spelling.* Manchester: Manchester University Press.

Venezky, R.L. 1970: *The structure of English orthography.* The Hague: Mouton.

spinal cord A portion of the central nervous system that begins at the base of the brain and extends caudally as a long tapering tube within the spinal column (see BRAIN AND CENTRAL NERVOUS SYSTEM: ILLUSTRATIONS fig. 10). The spinal cord of humans is composed of 24 segments which divide into cervical, thoracic, lumbar, and sacral regions. A cross-section of the spinal cord at any level reveals a central canal, containing cerebrospinal fluid, surrounded by a butterfly-shaped core of gray matter, made up mainly of three types of cell bodies: (1) sensory neurons (generally located in the dorsal aspect of the cord), which receive input conveyed by peripheral nerves from receptors; (2) motor neurons (concentrated in the ventral portions), which project motor signals to response or effector mechanisms; (3) interneurons, which connect spinal neurons in proximity to each other. The gray matter is surrounded by a mass of white matter, consisting of myelinated fiber columns that carry ascending and descending information between spinal segments and higher brain regions. An additional function of the spinal cord is the mediation of reflexes (i.e. simple, involuntary responses) under the control of specific stimuli (e.g. knee-jerk reflex). In its most elementary form this is accomplished when a stimulus excites a sensory fiber that synapses directly with the cell body of a motor neuron which, in turn, projects directly to a muscle, activating a response. This is an example of a monosynaptic reflex; other reflexes, also mediated within the spinal cord, have more complicated neural circuitry, involving one or more interneurons. GWi

Spinoza, Baruch (1632–77) Dutch philosopher, known chiefly for the austere metaphysical system presented in his *Ethics* (1677). His premise was that the universe is a single complex unity – as he put it, that there is only one "substance", for which the words "God" and "Nature" are alternative names. Apart from eliciting unjust accusations of atheism, this view led Spinoza to revise Descartes's dualism (see DESCARTES). While accepting much of Descartes's account of the mental and the physical, Spinoza argued that they were really two "attributes" of the single substance of the universe, rather than two different kinds of thing. Any event, according to Spinoza, could be conceived in terms either of the mental or of the physical attribute, and would accordingly be explicable by reference either to a series of mental causes or to a series of physical ones. However, given the substantial unity of the two attributes, Descartes's view that they might interact was incoherent. To every physical occurrence there corresponded an idea (though no one need be aware of it), and conversely. An individual mind was the idea of a particular body, and God's mind was the idea of the physical world as a whole.

The concept of "free will" had no part in this scheme: to be free was to escape the domination of one's emotions by understanding them in universal or rational terms, and hence becoming directly subject to the causality of the universe as a whole. (See also MIND-BODY PROBLEM). JR

Bibliography

Spinoza, Baruch 1924: *Spinoza Opera.* 4 vols. Ed. C. Gebhardt. Heidelberg.

——— 1883: *The chief works of Spinoza translated from the Latin.* 2 vols. Trans. R.H.M. Elwes. London: George Bell.

spite Behavior that lowers the genetic fitnesses of both the perpetrator and the target animal. Spite has to be understood in relation to kin selection. Since only behavior that increases an individual's fitness will spread, spiteful behavior would normally be selected against. If, however, spite is directed against an unrelated individual, related ones may benefit, and genes underlying the behavior will proliferate. In practice spite is difficult to demonstrate in nature, though efforts have been made (Hamilton 1970). Spite in animals clearly differs from the lay usage with its wider implication of any harmful action perpetrated by an individual who feels himself to have been harmed. VR

Bibliography

Hamilton, W.D. 1970: Selfish and spiteful behaviour in an evolutionary model. *Nature* 228, 1218–20.

split-brain preparation A surgical procedure in which the corpus collosum and other fibers connecting the two cerebral hemispheres are severed (see BRAIN AND CENTRAL NERVOUS SYSTEM: ILLS 1 and 6). This operation eliminates interhemispheric transfer of information and, when the optic chiasm (fig. 23) is also cut abolishing interocular transfer, the effect is to create virtually two functionally independent brains. Used initially in experiments with animals, this technique has proved useful in studying how the brain integrates and processes information. Surgical sectioning of the corpus collosum has also been performed on humans to prevent the spread of epileptic seizures in the brain. Observations based on such patients have confirmed the functional asymmetry of the human brain. Thus stimuli can be identified verbally by split-brain patients when projected to the left but not the right hemisphere. Conversely, nonverbal tasks can be performed better when the information is processed in the right hemisphere. These and related findings emphasize the respective dominance of the left and right hemispheres with respect to linguistic and nonverbal operations. GWi

Spoonerism The Warden of New College, Oxford, the Revd W.A. Spooner (1844–1930) is often credited as the originator of a verbal slip involving accidental or purposeful metathesis of sounds as in "rag and bug" for "bag and rug".

Spoonerisms, like other slips of the tongue, can provide important evidence about the psychological reality of abstract linguistic representations. Thus, the question whether the phonetic units [k] and [k^{h}] as in [ska^{i}] "sky" and [k^{h}i] "key" should be represented as a single abstract phoneteme or as two abstract segments, can be resolved by appealing to the spoonerism *with scare and kill* [skeə əŋ k^{h}ɪɫ] instead of *with care and skill* [k^{h}eə əŋ skɪɫ]. The mere transposition of the initial phonetic symbols would have resulted in the phonetically unacceptable unaspirated [kil] and the equally unacceptable [sk^{h}ɛə]. The fact that aspiration is automatically introduced when [k] is followed by a vowel suggests that [k] and [k^{h}] should be represented as a single abstract unit in the mental representation or deep structure. PM

Bibliography

Fromkin, V., ed 1973: *Speech errors as linguistic evidence*. The Hague: Mouton.

sport, psychology of The scientific study of human behavior in sport. Sport, as typically understood in this sense, includes recreational physical activities as well as highly organized, competitive athletics. Psychological interest in sport tends to be rather narrow, emphasizing the sub-areas of personality and social psychology.

In North America the psychology of sport emerged as a recognizable subdiscipline within physical education during the 1960s. Before 1960 sport psychology consisted of a few isolated studies, often a-theoretical personality studies of athletes. During the 1960s and 1970s experimental social psychology theories and methods dominated the psychology of sport. In the 1980s the psychology of sport has focussed increasingly on sport-specific, applied issues and incorporated clinical and counseling psychology approaches.

Psychology of sport research falls into the three general areas of personality, motivation and social influence. Personality is a long-standing research topic in sport psychology, but much of that research has been poorly conceived and conducted. An inappropriate emphasis on the trait approach and general personality measures yielded few findings of either theoretical or practical value. In general, personality traits do not differentiate athletes from non-athletes, or various athlete subgroups from each other. Morgan (1980) is one of the few sport psychologists to report consistent relationships between personality measures and success in sport. Morgan's mental health model proposes that success in athletics and positive mental health are directly proportional, and that psychopathology and success are inversely proportional. Morgan's research with wrestlers, runners and oarsmen indicates that successful athletes, in comparison to norms and less successful athletes, exhibit higher levels of vigor and lower levels of tension, depression, anger, fatigue and confusion.

The investigation of sport-specific individual differences, exemplified by Martens's competitive anxiety work (1977), is a more promising sport personality research approach. Martens developed the Sport Competition Anxiety Test (SCAT), which measures competitive trait anxiety, the predisposition to high levels of anxiety in competitive sport. He demonstrated the reliability and validity of SCAT through a systematic series of lab and field studies and reported that SCAT predicted anxiety in sport competition better than did general trait anxiety measures. Further investigations of competitive anxiety reveal a strong win–loss influence with winners decreasing and losers increasing in state anxiety, and an increase in state anxiety as the time of competition nears, especially for high competitive trait anxious persons.

Motivation has always been a prominent topic in sport psychology research and practice. Much sport psychology work focusses on arousal, the intensity dimension of behavior, and its relationship to performance. Sport folklore suggests that the best athletes increase arousal to peak levels just before performance, and many coaching tactics aim to increase arousal levels. The empirical evidence runs counter to popular practice and suggests that most athletes should calm down or decrease arousal before competing. There are exceptions; some top athletes, especially those in strength or endurance events such as weight lifting, may effectively use arousal-increasing techniques to improve performance.

Most sport psychologists accept the inverted-U hypothesis as a general maxim; performance is best at a moderate, optimal arousal level and progressively poorer as arousal increases or decreases from that optimal point. In typical sport settings many factors operate to increase arousal levels to or beyond the optimal level, and added arousal-increasing techniques are seldom needed. Furthermore, research pinpoints several detrimental effects of arousal on performance. Arousal tends to narrow attentional focus and highly aroused performers may lose sensitivity to relevant environmental cues. Studies using EMG measures show that highly anxious or aroused persons use more muscular energy and exhibit less efficient movement patterns than less anxious persons.

Successful performers are not simply less aroused or anxious than less successful performers. Instead, successful performers appear better able to control arousal and focus attention on the task. Differences in arousal patterns of better and poorer performers was illustrated in a series of studies with parachutists (Fenz 1975). Continuous monitoring of arousal indicated that novice parachutists increased in arousal from the night before the jump up to the time of the jump and were at their highest arousal levels immediately before jumping. Experienced jumpers, in contrast, reached their peak arousal levels early in the jump sequence and decreased or controled arousal immediately before the jump. The empirical evidence, then, suggests that calming strategies are more appropriate than arousal-increasing techniques, and this is especially true for less skilled and less experienced sport participants.

As well as considering the intensity dimension of behavior, sport psychologists are also concerned with directing behavior. Behavioral approaches and reinforcement techniques have been effective in modifying some sport behaviors, but the prevailing trend in sport psychology, as in general psychology, is toward cognitive approaches. Research demonstrating that extrinsic rewards can undermine intrinsic motivation has considerable application to sport. Extrinsic rewards, such as trophies, uniforms, scholarships and media attention, are common in sport. Psychologists and sport psychologists have demonstrated that rewards, including athletic scholarships and perhaps even competition itself, may be interpreted as controlling sport behavior, thus undermining intrinsic motivation and the desire to participate when rewards are no longer available.

The drawbacks of extrinsic rewards and behavioral approaches have led sport psychologists to turn to attributional and cognitive approaches. Much sport attribution research is descriptive examination of the causal attributions of winners and losers in sport competition. Many of the findings reflect the egocentric bias found in general attribution research with successful sport participants reporting more internal causal attributions than unsuccessful participants. Other research suggests that sport may prompt some unique attribution patterns, especially in team competition, and those patterns should be considered in cognitive approaches to sport. Sport psychologists are actively investigating achievement cognitions and attributions, but few conclusive findings have emerged. Initial work suggests that teaching strategies, such as participant modelling, which aim to increase self-efficacy (the belief that one can perform the required task) and reduce state anxiety yield positive achievement cognitions and enhanced performance.

Social influence in sport was a dominant topic during the 1960s and 1970s, and social influence continues as an important aspect of the psychology of sport. A number of studies examined the influence of the presence of others as spectators, coactors or competitors on motor performance. Generally research with motor tasks supports Zajonc's predictions (1965). The presence of others tends to increase arousal and impair performance during early learning stages, but to facilitate the performance of speed and endurance tasks and well-learned skills. However, evidence for the impairment of learning is much weaker than the evidence for facilitation of simple and well-learned tasks, and the findings have not been generalized to field settings in sport.

A number of sport psychologists have examined special behavior within sport, particularly aggressive behavior. Indeed, highly competitive sports are often advocated as healthy outlets for aggressive urges. Research, though, does not support the role of sport as a catharsis for releasing aggression. In fact, studies show that highly aggressive sports tend to increase hostility and aggression. Furthermore, most aggression research suggests that aggressive behavior is socially learned in sport through modelling and reinforcement of aggressive behavior.

Social interaction and relationships within sport groups are also of concern within the psychology of sport. Cohesiveness or attraction-to-group, has been an especially popular topic. Common wisdom suggests that cohesiveness facilitates team performance, but sport psychology research reveals that the cohesion–performance relationship is weak at best.

The current trend in North American sport psychology, and a long-standing practice in Europe, is for sport psychology knowledge to be put into practice by work directly with athletes and teams. The focus of most applied sport psychology programs is to help athletes develop psychological skills to improve performance and enhance the sport experience. One of the most common applied techniques is anxiety management. A variety of techniques have been used with athletes, including progressive relaxation, autogenic training, biofeedback, hypnosis and cognitive–behavioral approaches. Other components of typical applied programs are imagery, either as a relaxation technique or as mental practice, attentional control, goal-setting and interpersonal relationship training. Although research is limited, several sport psychologists report positive results in numerous cases, especially in helping athletes to control anxiety and consequently enhance performance. Psychology of sport research continues in the areas of personality, motivation and social influence. The current trend is toward identifying individual and situational variables relevant to sport performance and behavior and examining those variables with multivariate, interactive approaches. As the research continues to provide sport-specific psychological principles as a basis for applied programs, these programs will increase in popularity and credibility. DLG

Bibliography

Fenz, W. 1975: Coping mechanisms and performance under stress. In *Psychology of sport and motor behavior II*, ed. D.M. Landers. University Park, PA: Pennsylvania State University.

*Martens, R. 1975: *Social psychology and physical activity*. New York: Harper & Row.

——— 1977: *Sport competition anxiety test*. Champaign, Ill.: Human Kinetics.

Morgan, W.P. 1980: The trait psychology controversy. *Research quarterly for exercise and sport*, 51, 50–76.

*Straub, W.F., ed. 1978: *Sport psychology: An analysis of athlete behavior*. Ithaca, N.Y.: Mouvement Publications.

*Silva, J.M. and Weinberg, R. S., eds. 1983: *Psychological foundations of sport and exercise*. Champaign, Ill.: Human Kinetics.

Zajonc, R.B. 1965: Social facilitation. *Science* 149, 269–74.

squish The term was introduced by Ross (1972) to replace the notion that the grammatical categories "verb", "adjective" and "noun" are distinct and unrelated. Instead it is argued that these categories are points in a linear squish, or hierarchy, of the type: verb → present participle → passive participle → adjective → preposition → adjectival noun → noun.

Whether a given item is more nouny or more verby depends on the grammatical processes to which it is susceptible. While gradient descriptions of the type proposed by Ross have become widely accepted in linguistics, they are unlikely to be of great interest to psycholinguists since:

i) squishes are set up within strictly *synchronic* grammars and are therefore unsuited to the description of linguistic development

ii) the various points on a squish are traditional categories of grammar whose psychological reality and universality is not beyond doubt.

Recent research has shown that both these restrictions can be overcome. PM

Bibliography

Ross, John R. 1972: Endstation Hauptwort: the category squish. In *Papers from the Eighth Regional Meeting*. Chicago Linguistic Society.

starvation effects *See* emotion, satiation and starvation effects on

state dependence *See* memory, state dependence

state-dependent learning *See* learning, state-dependent

statistical methods Procedures for the planning of data collection in experiments and surveys together with techniques for describing and summarizing sample data so that inferences may be made about populations from which the samples were taken. They offer a rigorously based approach to the design and analysis aspects of investigations. Methods for analysis are usually pre-determined by the particular experimental or survey design employed and its implementation. Knowledge of (a) the design and its characteristics, (b) the methods of analysis which may be associated with the design, (c) the amount of precision required for estimation and (d) the variation in the population may be used to determine the sample sizes which will be necessary for a satisfactory investigation.

Following the collection of statistical data the first requirement is usually a description. In the light of the nature of the variables, whether they are nominal, ordinal, interval or ratio in character, appropriate graphical methods are used for presentation. For the first two types of variable a bar chart, pie chart or pictogram is normally used whereas for the last two a histogram or a frequency diagram suffices. Certain probability distributions may be confirmed by plotting sample frequencies on special graph paper. Multivariate data is treated by plotting scatter diagrams or frequency contours for two variables at a time. Graphical methods are used for exploratory data analysis and residual analysis which allow the validity of assumptions made by classical methods to be examined and appropriate action taken.

Following graphical descriptions, statistical measures are calculated from the observations to provide estimates of population characteristics. These may be quantities which describe the distribution of the values of a variable in the population in terms of its location (e.g. mean, median, mode, mid-range) or its dispersion (e.g. standard deviation, mean deviation, range, semi-interquartile range) or its shape (e.g. skewness, kurtosis). Where single values are calculated to represent these population characteristics, the estimates are called "point estimates". More useful are "interval estimates" which consist of two values between which the true value of the population parameter in question will be expected to lie with some stated probability. Such intervals are known as "confidence intervals".

Whereas it is possible to proceed to make inferences about hypotheses involving population parameters using confidence intervals, it is more common to compute "test statistics" for this purpose. These are quantities calculated from samples which are standardized so that their distributions over repeated samples can be derived theoretically and "critical values" obtained and tabulated for use in statistical tests.

Statistical tests are said to be "parametric" if they refer to the form of the underlying distribution of the observations and "nonparametric" or "distribution-free" if they do not. Parametric tests are concerned with hypotheses which mention the population values of parameters of this underlying distribution. The most common parametric tests are based on the sample mean and test a hypothesis regarding the population mean (e.g. normal z-test, Student's t-test) whereas non-parametric tests often use the ranked sample values for testing a hypothesis about the population median (e.g. Mann–Whitney U-test, Wilcoxon test, sign test). The advantage of the latter is that the specific test used will be more valid over a wide range of underlying distributions and the main disadvantage, where both may apply, will be a loss of power. Parametric tests often assume that the sample values follow a normal distribution, or at least that the sample mean is approximately normally distributed and this is true in practice unless the sample sizes are very small because of the Central Limit Theorem.

Non-parametric tests are used for testing the goodness-of-fit of an observed distribution to a theoretical one or may compare two observed distributions. The chi-square (χ^2) test and the Kolmogorov–Smirnov tests are both suitable for these purposes with the latter being more sensitive to the largest deviation between two distributions. Where individuals are classified into categories by two attributes the resulting contingency table may be analysed using a chi-square test for association between the attributes. Fisher's exact test is used in this situation for small frequencies. Where the samples are correlated, another non-parametric test, McNemar's, is used to test for a difference between the proportions in the categories.

Tests of means for a single population or for two populations are based on the standard normal z- or the t-distribution according as the variance in the population sampled is known or unknown. Tests for proportions use a test statistic which is taken to be approximately normal for large samples. Where there are more than two populations, an analysis of variance is applied using an F-statistic for difference between means or a chi-square statistic for a difference between proportions.

As well as providing for the testing of means of several samples, the analysis of variance, due to R.A. Fisher, is used to test for the effects of several factors which are varied in a systematic way in the same experiment. Such uses of the analysis of variance are examples of linear models which describe the measured response in terms of a sum of effects due to the factors and the interactions between them. For a single factor the simplest design is known as the "completely randomized" design in which the levels of the factor (or treatments) are applied randomly to the experimental units. Where these units are arranged in groups or "blocks" and complete sets of treatments are applied in each block the design is known as a "randomized block design". This very commonly used design allows for independent testing of treatment and block effects by means of an analysis of variance.

Whereas the randomized block design may be seen to exploit the heterogeneity of experimental units in one dimension, an extension of the design known as the "Latin Square" design caters for two dimensions. If the two dimensions are thought of as "rows" and "columns" then the rows constitute blocks within which all treatments appear and the columns likewise. This balanced but restricted design allows for independent tests of the "rows", "columns" and treatments factors. Extensions of the randomized block design provide for additional treatment factors and for incomplete blocks containing subsets of the available treatments. The latter include confounded designs in which main effects are estimated with full precision and only those interactions which are of interest are deliberately estimated in the analysis. In balanced incomplete designs, some of the interactions may be estimated with lower precision than main effects. This is also achieved by "split-plot" designs in which less important factors are applied at the level of plots within blocks and more important factors are applied to sub-plots which are formed by splitting main plots. Whereas factorial designs in which all levels of all factors appear in every possible combination are known as "crossed" designs, the split-plot design is an example of a "hierarchical' or "nested" design.

The analysis of variance F-tests are based upon underlying assumptions that the observations are normally distributed and have equal variance within groups. When these assumptions are untenable recourse is made either to transformation of the variable to restore the desired properties or to ranking and a non-parametric test. In the single factor experiment the Kruskal–Wallis test is used and for several factors, Friedman's test for matched samples is applied for each factor separately.

Where the factors may be expressed in the form of quantitative variables, the analysis of variance may be used to test the significance of the trend or response function. The levels of a factor may be equally spaced on an appropriate scale and it is then convenient to consider the response function by fitting orthogonal polynomials. For a factor with two levels, a linear component is tested, with three levels, a quadratic component, etc. If there are several factors of this type operating simultaneously, interactions between these components are investigated also.

As well as the response variable, a concomitant variable is sometimes measured. Adjustment for the effect of this concomitant variable is by an analysis of covariance. This procedure is able to deal with several concomitant variables.

Regression and correlation methods are applied to investigate the relationships between two or more variables. In the case of simple regression, one variable which is statistically varying is seen to depend upon another mathematical variable which is not subject to statistical variation. There are applications, however, where both variables involved are statistical but the "dependent" variable is subject to more variation than the "independent" one. The form of the relationship is most often linear but can also be a higher degree polynomial or exponential or any other mathematical continuous function. Correlation refers more generally to the relationship or interdependence between two variables and therefore applies to situations where regression may be inappropriate. Measures of correlation include the "product–moment correlation coefficient" which measures the degree of linear correlation between two continuous variables and, for ranked variables, Kendall's "tau" and Spearman's "rho".

Multiple linear regression is a method for fitting a relationship in which the "dependent" variable is a linear function of several "independent" variables. Multiple correlation refers to the degree of interdependency between variables in a group and is often calculated as a coefficient in the multiple regression context where it represents the measured correlation between observed values of the dependent variable and the values predicted by the multiple regression equation.

Factor analysis and associated techniques in multivariate analysis seek to explain the relations between the variables in a set, using the correlation matrix for the set. Principal component analysis establishes a set of uncorrelated combinations of the original variables which explain in decreasing order of magnitude the variation in the sample. Ideally, most of the variation is accounted for by the first few components and the remainder may be discarded. Where the set of original variables is structured with two subsets, one "regressor", the other "independent", canonical analysis is relevant. Discriminant analysis deals with the problem of a single set of variables which have different mean values but identical correlations in two or more populations. A discriminant function is estimated using individuals from known populations and then used to classify unknown individuals. Other techniques such as multi-dimensional scaling and cluster analysis are employed to explore the structural relationships between individuals for whom multiple observations are available.

Finally, it should be remarked that some research workers prefer to incorporate "prior" information with experimental evidence in a formal way when making inferences. Bayesian inference, which originates from a theorem of Thomas Bayes on inverse probability, provides for this by requiring a specification of the prior distribution of parameters. This can involve some complicated mathematics and non-Bayesians are concerned by the difficult and arbitrary choice of this prior distribution. The arguments for Bayesian analysis are that this generalizes the inferential procedure so that nothing of the conventional approach is lost, that it encourages the formulation of prior knowledge and that it provides a decision-theoretic approach which is relevant to many situations. Bayesians and non-Bayesians all use prior information and mostly arrive at the same conclusions despite the differences in approach. RWH

Bibliography

Fisher, R.A. 1935: *The design and analysis of experiments*. Edinburgh: Oliver & Boyd.

Guilford, J.P. and Fruchter, B. 1956: *Fundamental statistics in psychology and education*. New York: McGraw-Hill.

Marriott, F.H.C. 1974: *The interpretation of multiple observations*. London: Academic Press.

Siegel, S. 1956: *Non-parametric statistics for the behavioral sciences*. New York: McGraw-Hill.

Winer, B.J. 1962: *Statistical principles in experimental design*. New York: Holt, Rinehart & Winston.

status The extent to which a person or group is esteemed, admired or approved of by other people and groups. Status is essentially the rank or position of an individual in the prestige hierarchy of a group or community. Nearly all societies have status systems such as class or caste and these status systems significantly determine the social environment and power of the individual.

Psychologists have studied status differences in terms of conformity to group norms, openness to change (social mobility), leadership, organizational structure etc. Ideas of social status and related concepts appear in Tajfel's theory of intergroup relations. For instance when groups of unequal status interact, they may each show different degrees of intergroup discrimination as a function of their perceptions of the legitimacy and stability of the difference in status. Social and group status is often marked by status symbols which are visible marks which serve as cues that enable the members of a group or organization to perceive the status of other members accurately and hence as guides to appropriate behavior. In time, status symbols come to be admired and prized in their own right as symbols of success. AF

stereotypes May be considered to be oversimplified, rigid, and generalized beliefs about groups of people in which all individuals from the group are labelled with the perceived characteristics of the group. Thus stereotypes of members of a certain national, religious or racial group may affect the impressions people form of single individuals who are identifiable members of that particular group.

There are individual differences in stereotypes which form part of a person's "implicit personality theory", stereotypes however, tend to be widely shared by members of a given society. Whereas stereotypes of other groups (to which one does not belong) are simplistic and homogeneous the stereotypes of one's own group are usually complex and highly differentiated. Stereotypes may lead to overgeneralization, negative memory bias and polarized judgments, as well as to an overestimation of differences between groups; an underestimation of the variation within a group and distortions of reality or justification of hostility or oppression (Campbell 1967).

Although usually considered undesirable because they tend to sustain social prejudice, stereotypes function to help interaction. They often contain a "grain of truth" which helps to create social order and are based on sufficient truth to be useful in predicting other people's behavior. Occasionally they may be very accurate. Even people who are the targets of negative stereotypes may agree with the facts upon which they are based.

Extensive research has been done on stereotypes since the turn of the century, mainly restricted to the study of national characteristics. AF

Bibliography

Campbell, D. 1967: Stereotypes and the perception of group differences. *American psychologist* 22, 812–29.

stereotypy Stereotyped behavior patterns are those which show a high degree of fixity or constancy from one occasion to the next or even from one individual to another. The courtship patterns of ducks, which are typical of each species and are often performed with "clockwork" regularity, are a classic example. In fact, many animal signals have a fixed character, often being repeated with little variation (see TYPICAL INTENSITY).

Stereotypies may, however, emerge in a completely different context. Animals (particularly active ones like monkeys and wolves) may sometimes develop stereotyped actions such as bobbing up and down or pacing out a fixed path if they are confined in small cages. It has been argued that such stereotypies can be used as an indication that the animals are suffering from their confinement. MSD

Bibliography

Barlow, G.W. 1977: Modal action patterns. In *How animals communicate*, ed. T.A. Sebeok. Bloomington: Indiana University Press.

steroids – adrenal and gonadal Two important groups of hormones which are structurally related to cholesterol. In humans, the primary adrenal steroid is cortisol. The synthesis and release of cortisol is promoted by stressful stimulation (see ACTH). Increased cortisol levels stimulate glucose formation from protein, suppress inflammation and inhibit the further release of ACTH (inhibitory feedback control). Aldosterone, another adrenal steroid, is involved with the regulation of the concentration of sodium ions in body fluids. There are three major gonadal steroid hormones, each of which is important in SEXUAL DIFFERENCES IN DEVELOPMENT, (see also SEXUAL BEHAVIOR AND THE NERVOUS SYSTEM). In addition, testosterone, the primary male gonadal steroid, interacts with other hormones in the development, maturation and maintenance of sperm formation and secondary sexual characteristics. The primary female gonadal steroids, estrogens and progesterone, play an integral role in the monthly menstrual cycle of nonpregnant adult females. GPH

stimulants *See* drugs, stimulant

stimulus *See* sign stimulus; supernormal stimulus; behaviorism; conditioning

STM *See* memory: short term and long term

stochastic rules Probabilistic rules for predicting event-sequences. A subclass of stochastic rules which has been thought to be psychologically important contains rules governing Markov processes, in which the probability of event *E* is determined by all *E*'s predecessors in the series. Stochastic rules contain the focus of statistical learning theory and are compatible with behaviorist approaches in general. Chomsky (1957) argued that behaviorist theories of language in principle could not account for the learning, the grammar, or the creativity of language because language learning requires the assimilation of an infinite number of Markov rules and because Markov processes cannot generate structurally embedded sentences, for example (*The man who said that (John believes that (power corrupts) is false) is arriving today*). MAB

Bibliography

Chomsky, Noam 1957: *Syntactic structures*. The Hague: Mouton.

stream of consciousness *See* consciousness, stream of

stress The definition of the term "stress" has been the source of much debate: there are at least three different ways of defining it and thus of approaching its study (Cox 1978). The simplest definitions are those that have been termed the stimulus-based (used by engineers) and the response-based (favored by clinical practitioners and physiologists). The former concept treats and measures "stress" as a noxious or aversive characteristic of the person's environment, in terms of degrees of temperature, for example, as sound pressure level (excessive noise), as hours of restraint (animal studies), or as speed of machine-paced work. Conversely, and largely following from the work of Hans Selye (1976) the response-based approach defines and measures stress in terms of the non-specific elements of the (physiological) response to noxious or aversive stimuli. In practice, there has been a tendency to concentrate on sympathetic–adrenal medullary activity and on pituitary-adrenal cortical activity as representative of the non-specific stress response. For a variety of reasons these approaches have been seen as inadequate by most psychologists, who have advanced more interactive models. These have tended to focus on the person's dynamic relationship with their environment, and to emphasize the critical importance of perceptual-cognitive processes and of individual differences (e.g. Lazarus 1976). Several models of stress now treat it, not as "stimulus" or "response", but as a process. The process is that which describes the way in which people realize and identify their problems, how they react to them and attempt to cope with them, and the "cost" of doing so. Such models usually combine social psychological and psycho-physiological perspectives, and attempt to identify the structural characteristics of problems in terms of the demands made on the person, the support and resources made available for coping (or problem solving), and the constraints on coping. Situations involving high demand and high constraint, but involving poor problem-solving resources or low support are perceived and reported as aversive or problematic, and are often associated with the sort of changes in behavior and in physiological state which have been taken as diagnostic of stress. The term "stress" is thus to be treated as an economic descriptor of a particular problem-oriented process.

Given the confirmed existence of "stressful" problems, and the reactions they evoke, the individual shows increased risk of a number of psychological and physical disorders. Among those chronic physical disorders commonly associated with the existence of "stress" are coronary heart disease, gastric ulcers and, more recently, disorders of the immune system. Attempts at coping with stress may involve direct action (eg. avoidance or escape behavior, aggression or palliative behavior) or may be more cognitive (cognitive defense). TRC

Bibliography

Cox, Tom 1978: *Stress*, London: Macmillan.
Lazarus, Richard, S. 1976: *Patterns of adjustment*. New York: McGraw-Hill.
Selye, Hans 1976: *Stress in health and disease*. Reading, Mass.: Butterworth.

stress *See* "life events"; work stress

structural integration *See* body-centered therapy

structuralism A contemporary theory attempting to identify universal organizing principles underlying the surface of cultural, social, psychological, linguistic and literary expressions. Although structural analyses have existed since classical philosophy the contemporary approach developed since the second world war on the Continent, particularly in France, has had its greatest impact in the English speaking world over the past decade or so.

Two forms of structuralism have become prominent in the United States and Britain since 1945; they warrant distinction. One form of structural analysis conceives of the repetitive patterns of interaction among persons codified into the institutions of social life as a structuralism. The myriad visible social institutions which individuals, by means of their interactions create, and in which they live their lives, such as the family, polity, economy, etc., are the foci of these structural analyses. This structuralism is identified with anthropological and sociological structural-functionalism, and American empiricism and symbolic interactionist analyses.

The second type of structuralism is more Platonic, seeking form and not content, bypassing institutional, cultural, and linguistic variation in order to establish universal sources for content. It is the focus upon, and search for, these invariant structures and the lack of involvement with surface appearances which separates this school from the previous one and gives it the appellation structuralism.

This is the structuralism to which the term is now most commonly applied. The authors whose works are associated with this structuralism include for example, Althusser, Lévi-Strauss, Foucault, Freud, Lacan, Piaget, de Saussure and Derrida.

The apparent inconsistency in the suggestion that structuralism has had its greatest influence in Britain and the United States in the last ten years and the inclusion of Marx, Freud and Saussure among the structuralists is explained by the knowledge that the contemporary structuralists attribute their intellectual heritage to these earlier thinkers or continue to develop their structuralism through a dialogue with, and reinterpretation of, these nineteenth and early twentieth century theorists. Shared epistemological principles harking back to these earlier theorists unite their interests. Sigmund Freud's psychoanalysis can help to illustrate some of these unities.

Freud formulates two realms of psychic activity, one observable the other not. Regarding the observable realm it is possible to become witness to particular mental processes such as those in conscious thinking, dreams, slips of the tongue, symptoms, etc. The contents of these observable activities varies from person to person across a societal population and from society to society. However, there is another, more fundamental psychic reality, a shared structure which exists across populations, societies, and cultures. This reality is the unobservable realm of unconscious activity. This is the realm of the organization of psychic drives and defenses which makes up every individual's unconscious mental life. It is this structure which determines and unites the varieties of observable, and sometimes conscious, mental life of individuals and societal populations. Despite the variety of observable psychical and mental processes, and their content, they are unified by a shared and universal psychic structure present in every individual. The particularity of observable psychical activity is the result of the unique combination of the unobservable factors but in every individual the structural factors combined are the same. These structural universals for Freud are such as the Id, Ego and Superego, the Oedipus complex, etc.

A coherence among structuralist's approaches to knowledge can be extrapolated from this illustration of Freudian theorizing. There is a shared assumption among structuralists that the determining reality exists at an empirically unobservable level; scientific knowledge cannot be induced from observable manifestations, it can only be inferred from theoretical knowledge of this deeper reality. Thus, the structuralist theorists cut through the observed reality to formulate a more fundamental one. In this assumption also resides structuralism's criticism of naive empiricism.

While surface or conscious subjectivity of persons, such as in conversations, kinship descriptions, descriptions of symptoms, etc., are data for structuralists they are only signs of deeper invariant underlying structures. For example, Lévi-Strauss (1963) suggests that diametrically opposite incest systems are expressions of the same underlying organizing principle, i.e., the need for the reciprocal exchange of women for marriage among clans. Structuralists do not build their theories upon subjective report but by imaginative conceptual leap which goes beyond subjective expression, so structuralists' analyses bypass human subjectivity, subjective consciousness.

Cultural idiosyncracy is treated similarly. Cultural variation, so influential in relativistic cultural anthropology, is dealt with by structuralists as forms of manifest or surface appearances; culture is the temporal and spatial expression of the unique organization of underlying structural reality. Thus, cultural variation is relegated to secondary importance in structuralism.

Similar to structuralism's denigration of cultural influences, its conception of causation denies the importance of historical influences. Structuralism distinguishes synchronic from diachronic causation, emphasizing the former. Synchronic causation suggests that surface appearances are understood best in terms of the interaction of the factors which create them at the particular point in time. This type of causal analysis is achieved without regard to the historical evolution of the structural factors creating appearances. Diachronic analyses stress the historical development of causal factors; that is, the history of causal factors in shaping the appearance of the phenomena. Thus, within the framework of structuralist analyses, it can be said of the example from psychoanalysis, that while historical factors in personal biography are crucial in the development of an individual's character, however for an individual's public display of personal characteristics, such as, symptoms, cognitive abilities, etc. at a particular point in time, the structure and process of unconsious drives and defenses, at that moment, are determining. Although, the theoretical distinction between synchronic and diachronic causation has been drawn sharply by structuralists it has not always been possible for them to maintain it in their empirical analyses.

Structuralists also posit a complex relation between appearances and causation. This aspect of causation structuralists refer to as overdetermination. By overdetermination structuralism means that a phenomenon is determined by many factors; surface appearances are the product of several causes at once. Accordingly, in psychoanalytic theory the appearance of a personal attribute, e.g., symptom, may have its origins in the effects of an early fixation, an unconscious organizational residue of an early biographical relationship and simultaneously may be caused by the effects of a personal relation in the present. The symptom is the result of the psychic residue and the effects of the immediate relationship operating synchronically.

Althusser offers another example of overdeterminism from political action. He suggests that revolutions do not result from a simple conflict between opposing classes, that is, the struggle between workers and the capitalists, but, he writes (1969 p.99), "if this contradiction is to become '*active*' in the strongest sense, to become a ruptural principle, there must be an accumulation of 'circumstance' and 'currents' so that whatever their origins and sense (and many of them will *necessarily* be paradoxically foreign to the revolution in origin and sense, or even its 'direct opponents'), they 'fuse' into a *ruptural unity* . . ." (emphasis in the original). For Althusser this "ruptural unity" is overdetermined and it causes class revolutions.

Lévi-Strauss's writings stand out in contemporary structuralism for their priority and popularity. His work is significant too because it represents the confluence of a number of influences and in turn has been exceedingly influential in the structuralist movement.

Lévi-Strauss's theorizing developed at the intersection of the two contemporary forms of structuralism. He draws upon the writings of Émile Durkheim, an armchair anthropological fieldworker, whose theoretical, epistemological and substantive focus upon social order influenced structural-functionalism and structuralism alike. Simultaneously, Lévi-Strauss claims as his intellectual forefathers (with proper adjustment to his own thinking) Marx, Freud and Saussure. In addition, Lévi-Strauss is a critic of, and his theorizing developed in reaction to, post-second-world-war French subjectivist and humanist philosophy of the Sartrean and Bergsonian types.

Lévi-Strauss's structural analysis is based on two principles; the polarity of binary opposites and homology or analogy. By polarity Lévi-Strauss means that underlying any society are sets of opposing linguistic and psychological formulations acting as organizing principles. The polar opposites are such as, sacred-profane, pure-impure, male-female, superior-inferior, etc. Further, these opposites are divisible into homologous groupings. The result being that pure, sacred, male, superior, etc., constitute one set and the other homologous group is constituted by the opposites. It is the object of Lévi-Straussian analysis to describe these polar-homologous groupings and to explain the way they achieve their underlying coalescence which is expressed in the visible organization of the particular society. Lévi-Strauss supposes that the principles of this simple scheme underlie all surface appearances. Thus, he uses similar classificatory schemes to analyse poetry, Greek myths and preliterate societies' attitudes to food.

An additional impulse unites Lévi-Strauss, Althusser and other structuralists; this is their desire to develop, at last, a truly scientific theory of human phenomena–one that cuts through all human diversity and is everywhere applicable. But despite their unities in approach to knowledge and in their mission, there are disagreements among them too. For example, Althusser has accused Lévi-Strauss of undermining Marxist materialism with his idealism. And Piaget has been critical of his fellow structuralists (1970). However, structuralism has received special ire not from within but from humanists outside its gates. Humanists have suggested that structuralism's epistemology eliminates from theorizing exactly what is constitutive of humanity, its consciousness, its cultural and historical development, influences, uniqueness. Humanists suggest that there can be no science of humanity without theoretical provision for these characteristics of social life. The result is a continuing controversy between humanists and structuralists and no where is this controversy more intense than between the Marxist on both sides of these issues (Thompson 1978; Williams 1977). GMP

Bibliography

Althusser, Louis. 1969: *For Marx*, Trans. Ben Brewster. New York: Pantheon.

Barthes, Roland. 1979: *Images, music, text.* Essays selected and translated by Stephen Heath. New York: Hill and Wang.

Derrida, Jacques. 1976: *Of grammatology.* Trans. Gayatri Spivak. Baltimore: Johns Hopkins University Press.

——— 1978: *Writings and difference.* Trans. Alan Bass. Chicago: University of Chicago Press.

Foucault, Michel. 1972: *The archaeology of knowledge.* Trans. Sheridan Smith. New York: Pantheon.

Glucksmann, Miriam. 1974: *Structuralist analysis in contemporary social thought: A comparison of the theories of Claude Levi-Strauss and Louis Althusser.* London: Routledge and Kegan Paul.

Harrari, J.V. 1971: *Structuralists and structuralism: A selected bibliography of contemporary thought (1960–1970)* Ithaca, New York: Diacritics.

Lacan, Jacques. 1978: *The four fundamental concepts of psychoanalysis.* Trans. Alan Sheridan. New York: Norton.

Levi-Strauss, Claude. 1963: *Structural anthropology.* Trans. Claire Jacobson and Brooke Grundfest Schoef. New York: Basic Books.

Miller, Joan M. 1981: *French Structuralism: a multidisciplinary bibliography with checklist of sources for Louis Althusser, Roland Barthes, Jacques Derrida, Michel Foucault, Lucien Goldmann, Jacques Lacan and an update of the works on Claude Lévi Strauss.* New York: Garland.

Piaget, Jean. 1970: *Structuralism.* Trans. Chaninah Maschler. New York: Basic Books.

Saussure, Ferdinand de. 1959: *Course in general linguistics.* Translated by Wade Baskin, New York: McGraw-Hill.

Seung, T.K. 1982: *Structuralism and hermeneutics.* New York: Columbia University Press.

Thompson, E.P. 1978: *The poverty of theory and other essays.* New York: Monthly Review.

Williams, Raymond. 1977: *Marxism and literature.* Oxford, England: Oxford University Press.

stupor A condition of mutism and lack of movement and responsiveness in which there is evidence of relative preservation of consciousness. The term has been used in various senses but it is agreed that it must be clearly distinguished from coma, in which consciousness is impaired, and that it has organic and psychiatric causes. Among the former are lesions of the upper mid brain (e.g. tumors, strokes, meningitis and encephalitis), senile and pre-senile dementia, and raised intracranial pressure and severe alcohol or drug intoxication. The most common psychiatric causes are DEPRESSION and SCHIZOPHRENIA, but HYSTERIA and other neuroses are also rare causes. Diagnosis depends upon meticulous physical examination and a detailed psychiatric history from other informants. RAM

Bibliography

Lishman, W.A. 1978: *Organic psychiatry: the psychological consequences of cerebral disorder.* Oxford: Blackwell Scientific; St Louis, Missouri: C.V. Mosby.

subception The phenomenon of autonomic response to a stimulus which is not consciously recognized. McCleary and Lazarus (1949) introduced the term subception to suggest an apparently autonomic, perhaps subcortical form of perception. Subjects were shown nonsense syllables, half of which had previously been associated with shock, and the other half of which were neutral. With tachistoscopic exposures too short for conscious recognition, subjects still showed an elevated galvanic skin response to the syllables previously paired with shock. This important study led to a series of investigations concerning the possible effects of unconscious phenomena on bodily processes and overt actions. Although there is considerable controversy, it is possible to interpret the findings as consistent with views of defensiveness promulgated by personality theorists such as Freud and Rogers. SRM

Bibliography

McCleary, Robert A. and Lazarus, Richard S. 1949: Autonomic discrimination without awareness. *Journal of personality* 18, 171–9.

subculture A subdivision of the culture of the whole population or a major section of it at a particular period, consisting of persons who share special concepts and mores whilst adhering to the dominant characteristics of the wider culture. Significant subcultures are determined by social class, racial and religious affiliations. Their emergence is explicable in terms of mutual facilitation and support in groups facing common problems that cannot be solved by traditional methods (Cohen 1955). By sharing beliefs, objectives and ways of behaving, a sense of corporate identity is created, distinctive perspectives about values are provided and role strain, caused by conflict between ideology and role expectations, is reduced. The protective effect of subculture variation on early socialization is especially important. This is mediated initially through the family, then the PEER GROUP. Deviant sub-cultures have been related to the occurrence of DELINQUENCY in certain geographical areas, although it is more adequately understood in the context of intrafamilial and small group processes. WLLP-J

Bibliography

Cohen, A.K. 1955: *Delinquent boys: the culture of the gang*. Chicago: The Free Press of Glencoe, Ill.

sublimation The most mature form of defensiveness, according to Freud and his followers, in that only the object of the instinct is altered, permitting considerable instinctual gratification to take place without ensuing anxiety or guilt. In psychoanalytic theory sublimation is the major defensive operation of the genital (or most mature) stage of psychosexual development. For example the true object of an adult male's sexual instinct may be his mother (who was the first female he loved when his sexual instinct was maturing sufficiently to involve his sexual organs *per se*). But the knowledge of, and action upon this would provoke intolerable anxiety and guilt. Therefore, the male sublimates by substituting for the true object another female (not related to him, and available for marriage) who resembles his mother in some fashion he does not consciously recognize. In having sexual relations with this other woman, he gains satisfaction for his originally incestuous impulse in a socially acceptable manner. Achieving this sublimation involves the interplay of various defense mechanisms. SRM

subpersonal psychology The attempt to describe subsections of what we normally call persons with the predicates that we typically first learn to apply to persons as wholes (Dennett 1978). In everyday terms, persons are entities that have sensations, plans, beliefs, intentions, actions, capacities and a robust cognitive and appetitive existence. Companies, nations and varieties of animals (and, presumably, intelligent extra-terrestrials) are often spoken of as if they they had similar characteristics. Subpersonal psychology supposes that there is much to be gained from characterizing subsections of persons as having many of the features of persons; equally, it understands much of what looks to be successful in recent psychology (in the broadest sense) as exercises in subpersonal psychology. Just as persons may be said to have physical and mental character, so may the subsections of persons treated in modular psychology, faculty psychology, component psychology, localizationist and lateralizationist psychoneurology, and indeed in the most basic brain delineations (into the metaphorical reptile, mammalian, and sapient brains). Perhaps less warrantably, some would add the clinical phenomena of multiple and split personality and even its humble everyday miniature, mixed feelings.

An obvious feature of personality is competitive desire, a sense of self against others. In commissurotomy, the apparent difference in attitudes and desires between right and left hemispheres has particularly impressed those who would speak of the split brain splitting the person into two persons. The multiple personalities of the psychoanalytic literature belong with these cases in that what is suggested is an attitudinal and appetitive psychological splitting which must presumably have some neurological realization. A similar case could be made for the ego, superego, and id of classical Freudian psychology.

The personality features that are more central to subpersonal psychology are cognitive and representational. The commissurotomy cases suggest that one hemisphere may know something the other does not, and one hemisphere may be able to produce representations that the other is much less able to handle. The common suggestion is that linguistic representations are the left hemisphere's domain and visual representations the speciality of the right. Facial recognition in particular appears separable from general visual processing and also peculiarly detached from language. But these sorts of claims must rest on independent psychological distinctions between various forms of representation and various cognitive processes. Noam Chomsky's work, for example, purports to separate an autonomous (see 1957) syntactical–phonological component from other cognitive components on developmental and information-processing grounds; the direct neurological evidence could only supplement this in mapping the "speech-centers" in the brain. The subpersonal psychologist would claim to replace the black box of holistic psychology with a more explanatory *collection* of black boxes. This can succeed to the degree that these boxes can be distinguished in terms of different functions and levels of representation, inputs and outputs, and differential rates of development. In view of the widely held opinion that much of our cognitive life is unconscious, consciousness itself may come to be understood as distinguished by particular levels of representation and a particular role as an interface between inputs of visual, linguistic, etc., components and some executive processing component with outputs to motor control components (see EMOTION AND PERSONALITY). JFL

Bibliography

Chomsky, Noam 1957: *Syntactic structures.* The Hague: Mouton.

Dennett, Daniel 1978: *Brainstorms.* Cambridge, Mass.: Bradford Books.

substance Defined by Aristotle as an entity of which something may be predicated but which cannot itself be predicated of anything. In this sense Socrates, Marathon and the Athenian State are substances, but wisdom is not since it can be predicated of Socrates. The word has been defined, more narrowly, as what requires nothing else for its own existence. "Requires nothing else" is ambiguous, but this definition has typically been taken to exclude such items as battles and societies, which could not exist unless people existed. In this sense no composite object, and no LOGICAL CONSTRUCTION, could count as a substance. Perhaps nothing could; but minds and momentary sense-data are among items which have at one time or another been assigned that status. Two other notions of substance, closely related to this one and to each other are those of a center of change – something which remains one and the same while capable of admitting contrary qualities – and of that which underlies and supports the attributes of an object. In a familiar, but very different sense a substance is the material or stuff of which a number of individual things may be composed. The gold of which coins, rings, etc. are sometimes made would count as a substance, though the individual coins etc. would not. In metaphysics and science a substance has sometimes been more narrowly defined as a material that is permanent, subject to some law of conservation. JMS

sufism The term for a particular network of related orders of mystics. Historically they were shaped by Islam. The earliest orders came into being in the Middle East and were brought by travelling initiates to North Africa, Spain and India. Sufism is a living tradition with growing membership in Europe and America.

The two understandings that are a constant in the Sufi experience are first, that nothing exists except God, and second, that the most accurate and powerful understanding of the nature of God is that he is Love, Lover and Beloved. The goal of the Sufi is the annihilation of the false self in union with the Beloved, or God understood as Love.

Each order has a lineage of guides. The Sufi initiate works with a guide who facilitates the process of transformation. The method of teaching includes the assignment of mantras, the use of the many-levelled teaching story or parable, and the use of breathing and walking practices. These forms of instruction are now being studied in the West as ways of bringing about specific non-linear or indirect learning processes. It should be of interest to the psychologist that Sufi philosophy, like that of ZEN BUDDHISM and TAOISM, generally takes the form of poetry and story, in contrast to works of philosophy in the western tradition.

Common to all orders is emphasis on learning by experience rather than on the mastering of a body of dogma. Still, there is a voluminous heritage of written teachings, prominant among which are the works of Jelal al-Din Rumi and Ibn Arabi. The written works of the Sufis are slowly becoming available to English speakers in translation. VJ

Bibliography

Khan, Hazrat Inayat 1979: *The Sufi message of Hazrat Inayat Khan.* Geneva: International Headquarters Sufi Movement.

Shah, Idries 1964: *The Sufis.* Garden City: Doubleday.

suicide The deliberate act of taking one's life; the term attempted suicide is often more loosely used of acts which carry some risk but are not necessarily aimed at death – parasuicide is an alternative term. Durkheim (1951) described four types of motivation: egoistic, anomic (where the individual is poorly integrated into society), altruistic and fatalistic. In western cultures suicide tends to be slightly more common among men than women, and for both sexes the risks are higher in the elderly, those living alone, in poor health or suffering from psychotic depression (especially with delusions of guilt and worthlessness; see AFFECTIVE DISORDERS). The majority give some prior warning of their suicidal intentions. Alcoholism and drug abuse greatly increase the risk of suicide. DLJ

Bibliography

Durkheim, Emil 1951: *Suicide.* Glencoe, Ill.: Free Press.

*Stengel, E. 1973: *Suicide and attempted suicide.* Harmondsworth: Penguin; New York: Jason Aronson.

Sullivan, Harry Stack *See* neo-Freudian theory

superego In PSYCHOANALYTIC PERSONALITY THEORY that part of the mind from which emanate evaluative and moralistic prohibitions or recommendations about actions and mental life. These directives have been internalized from childhood experience of (or perhaps rather fantasy about) parental controls. It cannot be equated with "conscience" because its activity is often unconscious, and because these continuing pressures may actually be at odds with the person's conscious values. The severity of those pressures also reflects the strength of the person's own aggressive impulses, and therefore does not reflect the actual severity of parents. In Freudian theory the superego develops out of the EGO as a result of the OEDIPUS AND ELEKTRA complexes, and is especially apparent in obsessional neuroses. Although Freud places such development in the fourth–fifth years of life Kleinian theory (Segal 1979) puts it earlier.

Since the superego's pressures are essentially non-rational, and at least partly unconscious (hence totems and taboos), psychoanalytic treatment aims at bringing them more under ego-control. See also EGO IDEAL.

Bibliography

Freud, Sigmund 1923: *The ego and the id. Standard edition of the complete psychological works of Sigmund Freud.* Vol. 19. London: Hogarth Press; New York: Norton.

Segal, Hannah 1979: *Klein.* London: Fontana.

supernormal stimulus A stimulus, commonly artificial, evoking a stronger response than the stimulus to which the response normally occurs. Supernormal stimuli often exaggerate aspects of SIGN STIMULI. Thus an elongated yellow pencil shape with two red rings near the tip will evoke more food soliciting pecks from a herring gull chick than the parent's bill, which is broader and carries a single red spot. Some experiments have shown that an animal's responsiveness to certain stimuli can be open-ended: many birds prefer to incubate larger than normal eggs; even huge eggs larger than the bird's own body are preferred. Some male fish will always choose to court the larger of two females and hence females of a foreign species may prove abnormally attractive. The supernormal, bright orange gape of a young cuckoo is one of the means whereby its foster parents are induced to feed it, often to the exclusion of their own young. (See also RELEASER; PARASITISM.) AWGM

superstition An irrational belief or practice. Usually employed in a pejorative sense to refer to the apparently irrational beliefs and/or practices of others. Superstition was a word frequently used by nineteenth-century writers to refer to the religions of pre-literate people. This was normally the result of failure to appreciate the premises on which such religious ideas were based. With a deepening understanding of such practices and beliefs the use of superstition to describe them has fallen into disuse among social scientists. However, individuals will admit to being superstitious and will avoid certain things. Members of certain occupations, sailors for example, are often regarded as more superstitious than others. It is sometimes possible to explain superstitions of this sort in practical terms, but more often not. Most superstitious avoidances are likely to be only peripheral to a major belief system and thus difficult to explain in terms of it. PGR

survey feedback A type of data-based intervention within ORGANIZATION DEVELOPMENT whereby survey results are reported back to the members of a client system for a check on the validity of the findings, for interpretation, and for development of action plans for change and improvement.

Five stages are involved in the process (Nadler 1977). (1) Planning to use data: Specific plans are formulated for data collection and use, with an explicit understanding of the implications of this process for feedback and later use of the data. (2) Collecting data: Plans are made to gather information about the organization through the utilization of a survey instrument, usually a structured questionnaire completed by all members of the organization. (3) Analyzing data: The raw data (collected information from survey questionnaires) are interpreted and prepared for presentation. (4) Feeding back data: The interpreted material is fed back to the members of the organization to check on its validity and to initiate change activities to remedy problems which have been revealed. (5) Following up: Plans are executed to initiate and sustain change in order to improve organizational effectiveness.

In the top-down approach data are fed back to the organization, beginning with the top executive team and proceeding down the organization in an interlocking chain of meetings. Each supervisor participates as a group member in a feedback session with his or her manager and peers before the material is discussed with subordinates. As the process moves down through the hierarchy ideas and suggestions are filtered up through the chain of discussion groups and contribute to the development of action plans for change. In bottom-up or subordinate-oriented feedback, subordinates receive data and work with it with the assistance of the consultant before supervisors see it.

CCB/NMT

Bibliography

Nadler, D.A. 1977: *Feedback and organizational development.* Reading, Mass.: Addison Wesley.

symbiosis In evolutionary biology, a relationship of close ecological dependence between members of two different SPECIES. Generally the relationship is of a complex kind, and probably reflects adaptation in each species to the presence of the other. Three kinds of symbiosis are distinguished: commensalism, where one partner benefits and the other is not greatly affected; PARASITISM, where one partner benefits and the other is disadvantaged; and mutualism, where both partners benefit. Sometimes symbiosis is used in a narrower sense, equivalent only to mutualism as just defined. Symbioses are often seen at the level of ecological and behavioral interactions between individuals, but symbiotic relationships have also been described involving whole societies, and these cases are referred to as social symbioses. See Wilson (1975). RDA

Bibliography

Wilson, Edward O. 1975: *Sociobiology: the new synthesis.* Cambridge, Mass.: Harvard University Press.

symbolic interaction A theoretical perspective on social life which emphasizes the meaningfulness of human life and action. The perspective additionally emphasizes the pluralistic and conflictual nature of society, the relative openness of social life, the indeterminancy of social structure, the importance of subjective interpretations, the cultural and social relativity of moral and social rules, and the socially constructed nature of the self. The direct intellectual antecedents of the interactionist perspective are commonly traced to the turn of twentieth-century America, and its first empirical researches done at the University of Chicago between 1900–30. One way to appreciate the distinctive nature of symbolic interactionism is to understand its long-standing opposition to many of the central tenets of scientific positivism. This includes the rejection by symbolic interactionism of the organic analogy, scientific hypothesis formulation and testing, cause and effect relationships, universalistic laws of the social world, and the positivist version of scientific objectivity. By contrast, symbolic interactionism has stressed naturalism, analytical induction as a general methodology, indeterminent relationships, culturally and socially specific laws or rules, and an empathic understanding gained from participation or immersion in social life.

The direct philosophical antecendents of symbolic interactionism can be found in the works of the early pragmatists in America, especially those of Charles Sanders Peirce (1839–1914), William James (1842–1910), and John Dewey (1859–1952). Peirce developed an early pragmatic maxim concerning the meaningfulness of human action, namely, that one should not see meanings as being inherent in the objects or relationships themselves, but rather as being displayed in specific, concrete social situations. Furthermore, one must know the practical consequences of a given action in order to know its meaning for the human actor. For William James, who avowed clinical and therapeutic interests in addition to scholarly ones, meaning was even more individualistic and subjective than as conceived by Peirce. James's *Principles of psychology* (1890) articulates his version of pragmatism and its implications for psychology, and in it he asserts that a person has as many social selves as there are other people who carry around some conception or definition of that person. John Dewey further extended many of these ideas, and emphasized the inevitability of pluralism in society as a result of these continuing processes of human interpretation and meaning. Dewey stressed the processual nature of reflective experience, meaning that human existence is necessarily and inevitably open-ended and "incomplete", as individuals continually reflect on, reconstruct, and thereby modify all "past" actions and behavior, preparing the scene for future actions. Dewey was responsible for bringing George Herbert Mead to the University of Chicago, where they enjoyed a long friendship. For many, Mead's name is associated with the early origins of interactionism in sociology and social psychology.

Early symbolic interactionism flourished at the University of Chicago, where three scholars are of central importance, William I. Thomas (1863–1947), Charles Horton Cooley (1864–1929), and George Herbert Mead (1863–1931). The last is seminal in the development of early interactionism, and the one most responsible for taking the abstract philosophical ideas of the pragmatists and grounding them in empirical, social reality. Mead's student Herbert Blumer is the one responsible for creating the term symbolic interactionism.

Charles Horton Cooley tried to combine hereditary factors with environmental (social) factors, and emphasized the role of emotion in human meanings. He is known for his idea of the "looking glass self", which means that individuals try to imagine the impression they are making on others by their actions and, according to Cooley, try to imagine some judgment of their actions, and then experience an emotional reaction to this perceived evaluation by others. From this early idea it is possible to see the beginnings of a central tenet of interactionism, that the meanings of an act for the individual emerge in the context of interactions with other people, that individuals perceive and take into account others' perceptions and judgments of an act. William I. Thomas formulated another idea which is akin to this, concerning an actor's definition of the situation. The Thomas Theorem states "if men define situations as real, they are real in their consequences". This well known theorem is one of the central ideas of symbolic interactionism, and highlights the extent to which human actions and meanings are framed by the situation or context in which they occur.

The central figure in early interactionism is George Herbert Mead, who crystallized many ideas of the early pragmatists with those of his scientific colleagues. Mead regarded the individual as the basic unit of analysis for interactionism, and emphasized the role of language and symbols in the creation of human meaning. The human mind, for Mead, was not a fixed, organic entity, but rather a continuous process of interpretation, reflection, and judgment of experience. Individuals act towards other individuals and physical objects because of the symbolic meaning those have for the individual. These meanings are not fixed, however. They are not given by the nature of culture or society. They are open-ended, and may change in specific situations of human social interaction. When the meaning of a given gesture or communication is shared between a sender and receiver, then a significant symbol is involved, says Mead, and humans are distinguished from animals precisely because they can share, build on, change, and communicate such symbolic meanings through a shared language and interactional competence.

Recent decades have seen the emergence of three distinct branches of symbolic interactionism. These are the neo-Chicago school which has centered around Herbert Blumer, the Iowa school which is associated with the work of the late Manfred H. Kuhn, and the dramaturgy popularized by Erving Goffman and his students. These three branches of symbolic interactionism are distinct, but they share several basic assumptions about human social life. They agree that individuals do things because of the meanings their actions have, and that these meanings must be central to any scientific understanding of behavior. They agree that the central focus of attention is in social interaction, when two or more individuals come into each other's presence, either actually or potentially. Blumer's emphasis tends to be on the fluid, situational, contextual nature of meaning. He views meaning as something which arises when two or more persons come into interaction. Humans are essentially rational, says Blumer, and when they encounter a social situation they engage in an open and problematic process of interpretation, to discover the intentions of the other, and the meaning of the existent action. By contrast, Kuhn's work tends to emphasize the more stable, unchanging, unproblematic aspects of social life. His work expresses a close affinity with several key positivist assumptions about human life and the nature of science. Both Blumer (1969) and Kuhn (1970) are concerned about the nature of the self, what individuals think about their selves, how they arrive at such definitions, and what this means when thrust into an interactional context. Again, the work of Blumer and his followers tends to emphasize the openness of self-definitions and human experience more generally, whereas the work of Kuhn and his followers tends to emphasize the relative stability of social life and the unproblematic nature of human interactions.

The work of Erving Goffman is significantly responsible for the sustained vigor of interactionist thought in sociology and social psychology. His early work *The presentation of self in everyday life* (1959) utilized theatrical metaphors to capture certain essences of social life, namely, the devices, strategies, tactics, and procedures used by individuals, either separately or in unison, to present to others the *appearance* of order, normality, and rationality in social situations. He contrasted back-stage preparations with front-stage appearances in social life, and his unique perspective is called dramaturgy, as key theatrical and performative notions are brought to interpret everyday, mundane social scenes. For Goffman, there is an inherent conflict between individuals and the social forms of communication and interaction, and his work concentrates on the many ways individuals present their selves to others, and how they influence each other in face-to-face interaction. Goffman's book *Behavior in public places* (1963) extends these dramaturgical ideas, and together with the essays in *Asylums* (1961), form the crucial early statements of *labeling theory* in the sociology of deviant behavior. According to this view, no actions are inherently deviant or abnormal, but such definitions emerge in the context of face-to-face interaction. This insight has produced an entire genre of innovative research in the field of deviance.

In the late 1970s and early 1980s symbolic interactionism remains a vigorous and creative perspective and research program. To some extent this results from the emergence of creative research and theoretical work in other disciplines, those which share some or all of the theoretical concerns of symbolic interactionism. These include PHENOMENOLOGY, ETHOGENICS, ETHNOMETHODOLOGY, existential sociology, humanistic psychology, conversational analysis, ATTRIBUTION THEORY, socio-linguistics, and the sociology of emotions. Through many discussions and debates, symbolic interactionists have incorporated many key ideas from these other disciplines. The interactionism of today is a more complicated, empirically grounded, scientific perspective than that which began in Chicago during the 1890s. JMJ

Bibliography

Blumer, H. 1969: *Symbolic interactionism.* Englewood Cliffs, N.J.: Prentice-Hall.

Goffman, E. 1959: *The presentation of self in everyday life.* Garden City, N.Y.: Doubleday.

——— 1961: *Asylums.* Garden City, N.Y.: Doubleday.

——— 1963: *Behavior in public places.* New York: The Free Press.

James, W. 1890: *Principles of psychology.* New York: Holt.

Kuhn, M.H. 1970: Self-Attitudes by age, sex, and professional training. In *Social psychology through symbolic interaction,* ed. Gregory Stone and Harvey Farberman. Waltham, Mass.: Xerox Publishing Co.

*Manis, J.G. and B.N. Meltzer, eds. 1980: *Symbolic interaction.* Boston, Mass.: Allyn and Bacon.

*Rosenberg, M. and Turner, R.H., eds. 1981: *Social psychology: sociological perspectives.* New York: Basic Books.

symbol/symbolism In its most general sense the word is used as roughly synonymous with "whatever stands for something, or has representative function". Objects satisfying this description would be words, images, pictures, diagrams, maps or codes. Individual instances of any of these kinds of objects may be identified as "tokens". The letters "r" "e" "d" written in order, form a token of the English word "red" for example. However, in psychology, a token is regarded as "symbolic" when interest in its referential meaning is suspended, and focussed instead, on the *content* articulated (see CONSCIOUSNESS). The intention, as a psychological factor in this content, may be unconscious. The emotional state one is in when "seeing red", for instance, may be a determiner of the selection of this token on occasion for communicative purposes, without one being aware of it. FREUD suggested that many tokens were selected in such ways. We could call these "symbolic" uses of "red". Symbols, in the psychological sense, would be distinguished from "signs", as contents are distinguished from objects of reference – the latter being correlated with signs through the relation of reference, the former being correlated with symbols through the unconscious part of the content. This agrees with C. G. JUNG's distinction which assigns reference, and the use of referring tokens in directed thinking, to the work of conscious thought, and symbols to the work of conscious and unconscious thought, together.

There is a strong connection between the symbolic use of tokens and ALTERED STATES. Jung pointed out that the same themes, images, figures, dramatic situations, etc., are to be found in dreams, religious representations and mythology, hallucinations of demented persons, as well as appearing regularly in other type of fantasy-tinged products: fairy tales, legends, folk stories, ballads, novels and the like. Later, drug-induced states were also found to manifest these same recurrent patterns. Hypnosis had already demonstrated that memory content inaccessible in ordinary states could be obtained by state-altering techniques. Certain types of MEDITATION also use symbols, either to reach an altered state, or to contemplate while in one. This regular connection between altered states and symbolically articulated content is explicable in contemporary physiological theory in terms of arousal of different psychic systems, each responsible for contributing something to the complex of factors making up a given content. The "archetypal", or common-collective character of the basic themes would then require the hypothesis of a kind of self-experience that is retained, probably in an emotionally-charged form, which posits an organization of human experience below the level of consciousness. Altered states would be sought for their expressive content, in order to by-pass the "ego-" organization of ordinary waking experience. This is the classical depth-psychological understanding of symbols: the return, in more or less distorted form, of demi-urges, feelings, ideas, impulses, that are incompatible with the predominant conscious attitude, and are therefore split off from it. SBT

Bibliography

Jung, C. G. 1969: *Man and his symbols*. Garden City, N.Y.: Doubleday.

Erich Neumann: *The origins and history of consciousness*. Bollingen Series XLII. Princeton: Princeton University Press.

synapse and synaptic transmission The site and process of the communication of information from one neuron to another (see BRAIN AND CENTRAL NERVOUS SYSTEM: ILLUSTRATIONS, figs. 30 and 32). The term synapse describes the junction between two neurons or other excitable cells. The conduction of nervous impulses along a neuron is an electrical process, while the transmission of information from one neuron to the next is (with few exceptions) chemical and is termed synaptic transmission (see NEUROTRANSMITTER SYSTEMS). The presynaptic axon terminals of a neuron contain many synaptic vesicles, which in turn contain molecules of neurotransmitters. In general, any one neuron contains only one type of neurotransmitter. When an ACTION POTENTIAL reaches the axon terminal, it effects a quantal release of neurotransmitter into the synaptic cleft, a 200 ångström gap between the presynaptic and postsynaptic neural elements. The interaction of the neurotransmitter and its receptor on the postsynaptic neural membrane causes certain changes in the permeability of that membrane to specific ions. This permeability change makes it either more or less likely that the postsynaptic neuron will initiate an action potential. Since each neuron may receive input from 1,000 or more synapses, the "decision" to fire is based on the spatial and temporal summation of these various signals. Once released, the action of the neurotransmitter may be terminated by enzymatic degradation or by reuptake into the presynaptic neuron. GPH

synaptic structure *See* memory and learning, synaptic structure theories

synchronic linguistics *See* linguistics, synchronic

syntagmatic relations *See* paradigmatic and syntagmatic relations in grammar

systems theory An aggregate of theoretical conceptions within the frames of which both general peculiarities of structures and functions of objects which are systems and methods to cognize them, the different special classes and types of systems (e.g. mathematical, physical, chemical, biological, psychical, social, economic, linguistic) are being analysed. A multitude of diverse variants of systems theory advanced mainly in the second half of the twentieth century are known under different names: general systems theory, systems approach, systems analysis, mathematical, biological, linguistic, psychological, sociological, etc. systems theories. The concept of "system" is a key concept in all these. It means an aggregate of interrelated and interconnected elements which form a whole.

The concept of "system" has a very long history. The thesis that the whole is more than the sum of its parts was formulated in Antiquity. In the course of the philosophical development beginning with Plato, Aristotle, Euclid and others much attention has also been paid to an interpretation and elaboration of specific features of systems of knowledge. Stoics interpreted system as the universal order. In modern times the encyclopedic views of Leibniz have played an outstanding part in our understanding of the ontology of systems. The system character of cognition was especially stressed by Kant (1781): "This completeness of science cannot be accepted with confidence on the guarantee of its existence in an aggregate formed only by means of repeated experiments ... [but] only because of their connection in a system ... The sum of its knowledge constitutes a system determined by and compromised under an idea; and the completeness and articulation of this system can at the same time serve as a test of the correctness and genuineness of all the parts of knowledge that belong to it". This line was developed further in the works of Schelling and Hegel. The latter wrote, in particular (1817): "Unless it is a system, philosophy is not a scientific production. Unsystematic philosophising can only be expected to give expression to personal peculiarities of mind, and has no principle for the regulation of its contents". From the seventeenth to the nineteenth centuries in different special sciences some types of system (geometrical, mechanical, etc.) were subjected to investigation. Marxism, leaning upon a materialist and dialectical tradition in philosophy, formulated general philosophical and methodological foundations for the scientific understanding of integral developing systems. Dialectical-materialism presupposes: (1) integrity of objects of the external world and those of knowledge; (2) the interrelation of the parts of an object, and that object with others as the parts of yet other objects; (3) the dynamic nature of any object; (4) functioning of any object caused by interaction of this object and its environment, with primacy of inner laws of functioning and object's development over outer ones.

At the beginning of the twentieth century special analytic methods of various systems in Bogdanov's tectology, Gestalt psychology, different organismic, biological and psychological conceptions, etc. were developed, but it was during the late 1940s that the Austrian biologist L. von Bertalanffy advanced a program for general systems theory. The main objects of this were: (1) to formulate general principles and laws of systems independent of their special type, or the nature of their components and the relations between them; (2) to establish strict laws by analysis of biological, social and behavioral systems; (3) to build a basis for a synthesis of modern scientific knowledge by establishing the isomorphism of the laws of different spheres of reality (von Bertalanffy 1971). Cybernetics (Wiener 1948) and a family of scientific disciplines connected with it were of a great importance in understanding the mechanisms of control systems. In particular, the set of methods and methodologies to elaborate and make a decision in the design and control over complex and supercomplex sociotechnical systems has been developed in various conceptions which have become successively more complete. These were: systems engineering (1950s–60s), operation research (1960s–70s) and systems analysis, which has gradually become widely accepted within the last fifteen to twenty years. Simultaneously in recent years research in the theoretical and methodological foundations of the systems approach, systems modeling and general systems research have been in the process of development.

A system is characterized not only by the connections and relations between its components (its definite organization), but also by the mutual interactions of the system and its environment. It is in the latter relation that a system expresses its integrity. Usually any system can be regarded as an element of a higher level system, while for some problems its elements can be represented as systems of a lower level. Invariant aspects of a system are defined by its structure. The morphology, structure and behavior of a system and its functioning are of a hierarchic, multi-level character. Integral functioning comes about as a result of the interaction of all the levels of the hierarchy. Natural, technical and social systems are characterized by their processes of information and control. Some of the most complex systems are goal-orientated systems, and self-organizing systems capable of changing their organization and structure while functioning.

In the twentieth century there has been a development of systems research methods and a widespread use of these methods for solving applied problems of science and technology (for instance, in the analysis of various biological systems, in the construction of transport systems, and in the organization of systems of industrial control). This has demanded the elaboration of strict formal definitions of the concept of "system". Such definitions are being constructed with the help of set theory, mathematical logic, cybernetics, etc. Summing up the main approaches to the definition of the concept, a system may be understood as a class of sets $S = \{M_s^\alpha\}$ for each pair of which a many-too-one correspondence $Yd\beta$: $M_s^\alpha \rightarrow M_s^\beta$ is established. Specific interpretations are given to set class elements depending on the problems concerned (Shreider 1971; Sadovsky, 1974).

Psychology is one of the scientific disciplines in which methods and principles of systems theory are widely and effectively applied. Psychological functioning represents a typical example of a system, but of course psychology has only adopted this approach in the twentieth century. The first stages of psychology's development in the experimental psychology of Wundt, in associationism and classical behaviorism were marked by the dominance of an "atomistic" viewpoint. Some components of mental functioning were isolated for research from the general context of man's mental activity conditioned by biological and social factors. The aspect of behavior studies such as reflexes were regarded as the elements of mental functioning and thought to be irreducible into simpler components. At the same time this approach was regarded as the only one which was compatible with the rigorous demands of a scientific psychology. The rise of different forms of reductionism – physiological, sociological and later cybernetics – has been a consequence of this approach, and has led not only to the loss of any specifically "psychological" object of research, but also to a belief that this represents a deep crisis in the science of psychology.

Psychology has overcome this crisis as a result of the acceptance (for the most part unrecognised) of a systems view of both its subject matter and its research methods. Vygotsky said, as long ago as 1930, "The most essential achievement of psychology in recent years is that the analytical approach to psychological processes has been replaced by a holistic or structural approach . . . The essence of this new viewpoint consists in the fact that the concept of the 'whole' has moved into the foreground. The 'whole' possesses its own attributes and defines the attributes and functions of the objects which constitute it" (Vygotsky, 1962–1978). The first steps in this direction were connected with William James's doctrine of the stream of consciousness and more particularly with Gestalt psychology. Upholders of this view based their theories on the Gestalt-Qualitäten discovered in 1890 by Ch. von Ehrenfels. Gestalt-Qualitäten are perceptible structures of objects as wholes which cannot be explained only on the basis of a knowledge of the attributes of the elements which constitute these structures. Gestalt-psychologists systematically and holistically interpreted various mental functions (perceptions, thinking, etc.) in accordance with their basic methodological credo: "There are relations which lead to a state in which the causes and nature of the processes of the whole cannot be learned from the knowledge of its elements which exist allegedly in the form of separate pieces, later put together and interconnected. On the contrary any behavior of a part of the whole is governed by the inner structural laws of the whole" (Wertheimer 1945). Having decided that mental structures were systems of this kind, gestalt psychologists simply made this an a priori assumption. That is why their work was not a complete success.

Essential progress in the comprehension of the systems nature of genetic psychology was made by J. Piaget and by L.S. Vygotsky. Piaget claimed on the basis of an enormous amount of empirical data, collected over more than fifty years, that intellect is a system of reversible and coordinated operations. He stressed that the operations of inner thought derive from the child's actions on external objects. He singled out the successive stages in the formation of intellect and other mental functions, i.e. the stages in the formation of successively more complicated operational systems. The essence of his anti-elementarist approach to research is expressed in his assertion that "an isolated operation could not be an operation, because the essence of operations is to form systems" (Piaget 1947).

The ideas advanced by Vygotsky during the late 1920s and early '30s utilized systems principles in the description of human development. Within this framework Vygotsky and his disciples from the 1940s onwards succeeded in: (1) singling out and describing the main levels in the holistic development of mental structures; (2) showing how these structures grew from an interaction between biological peculiarities and culture; (3) showing how essential the use of signs is in higher functions; (4) working out a general scheme to describe how actions are "internalized" to form the basis of internal, intellectual functions.

In the course of the development of psychology over the last thirty to forty years the systems structure of the mind has been understood first of all as a result of the "activity" approach in psychology. The concept of "activity" was one of the key concepts in German classical philosophy (see Kant). It was interpreted from a dialectical-materialistic viewpoint in Marxist philosophy. Activity is a specific human form of behavior directed to the transformation of an object. "Activity" as a special system includes the elements of subject and object to which the actions of the subject are directed. These two components are not completely separated from each other (as they were in the psychology of the nineteenth century and earlier). There is a fixed systems structure belonging not only to each of them separately (as was supposed in most psychology of the first half of the twentieth century), but also to them both together as they form an organic unity. The conception of the coordination of movements worked out by Bernstein (1967) is an excellent example of a systems analysis of a psychophysiological object and it demonstrates the productivity of such an analysis. In modern psychology the systems approach appears in various forms: e.g. the theory of the psychological field (see FIELD THEORY); the psychological theory of activity (see MARXIST ACTIVITY PSYCHOLOGY); the conception of activity and psychological unity (Rubinstein 1957); theories of personality (e.g. Allport 1961); and psycholinguistics (see CHOMSKY). In the last fifteen to twenty years the systems approach has been widely used in applied psychology, in the psychology of learning, for example, and ergonomics, and also in science connected with psychology, e.g. psychiatry (Gray, Duhl and Rizzo, 1969).

In modern psychology a systems integrated interpretation of cognitive processes is embodied in the consideration of them as forms of information processing (Neisser 1967). Practically all cognitive processes, from finding stimulation to decision making are best treated as part of a complex and intricate interaction. VNS

Bibliography

Allport, G.W. 1961: *Pattern and growth in personality*. New York and London: Holt, Rinehart & Winston.

Bernstein, N. 1967: *The coordination and regulation of movements*. Oxford: Pergamon.

Bertalanffy, L. von 1968: *Organismic psychology and systems theory*. Worcester, Mass.: Clark University Press.

Blauberg, I.V., Sadovsky, V.N., and Yudin, E.G. 1977: *Systems theory: philosophical and methodological problems*. Moscow: Progress Publishers.

Gray, W., Duhl, F.J., and Rizzo, N.D., eds. 1969: *General systems theory and psychiatry*. Boston: Little Brown; London: Churhill.

Kornblum, S., ed. 1973: *Attention and performance IV*. New York: Academic Press.

Marx, M. and Hillix, W. 1973: *Systems and theories in psychology*. New York: McGraw-Hill.

Mead, G.H. 1934: *Mind, self and society*. Chicago: Chicago University Press.

Neisser, U. 1967: *Cognitive psychology*. New York: Appleton-Century-Crofts.

Piaget, J. 1946: *La psychologie de l'intelligence*. Paris.

Rubinstein, S.L. 1957: *Being and consciousness*. Moscow (in Russian).

Sadovsky, V.N. 1974: Problems of a general systems theory as a metatheory. *Ratio* Vol. XVI, No. 1, 33–50.

Shreider, Y.A. 1971: On the definition of system. *Nauchno-tekhicheskaya informatsiya*, Series 2, No. 7, 5–8 (in Russian).

Vygotsky, L.S. 1962: *Thought and language*. Cambridge, Mass.: MIT Press.

——— 1978: *Mind is society: the development of higher psychological processes*. Cambridge, Mass.: MIT Press.

Wertheimer, M. 1945: *Productive thinking*. New York and London: Harper.

Szasz, Thomas Born in Budapest in 1920, and studied medicine, psychiatry and psychoanalysis in the United States. In 1956 he was appointed Professor of Psychiatry at the State University of New York at Syracuse. His prolific writings have established him as one of the foremost critics of conventional psychiatry and its relationship with the State. His main thesis is that in using the concept of mental illness to categorize some unusual types of behavior we collude with those elements in society which seek to stigmatize, segregate and persecute certain of its members. He argues that just as in the Middle Ages deviant individuals were stigmatized as witches, now they are designated as mentally ill and compulsorily hospitalized.

Szasz's views have been strongly challenged, for example by Roth (1976). DLJ

Bibliography

Roth, M. 1976: Schizophrenia and the theories of Thomas Szasz, *British journal of psychiatry* 129, 317–26.

Szasz, T.S. 1961: *The myth of mental illness*. New York: Hoeber-Harper.

——— 1971: *The manufacture of madness*. London: Routlege & Kegan Paul.

T

T-group (training group) A method for improving individuals' sensitivity to themselves and others. The primary objectives are to increase individuals' awareness of their own feelings, the reactions of other people, and their impact on others, as well as their awareness of how people interrelate and of how groups operate. The T-group seeks to improve the individual's skills in listening to people, in understanding them empathically, in expressing feelings, and in providing feedback to other people.

The T-group is not structured at the outset but evolves its own organization. The evolving structure is continuously examined by members through looking at the social process of the group. The interactions that take place focus on the sharing of feelings about interpersonal behavior. Lectures, skill-building games, process observation experiences, simulations, and other structured experiences are sometimes used to support T-group activities.

The T-group is helped by a trainer whose role is to participate and provide some leadership in helping people get in touch with themselves and to share their thoughts openly with each other. There are two main types of trainer: those who emphasize the personal growth of the individual participant, and those who focus on the processes of group development and operation. T-groups are most commonly found in educational and business settings. Each group consists of approximately ten to fifteen people, including one or two trainers. The group is usually scheduled for one or two meetings each day over a period of one or two weeks. The meetings typically last for around two hours. ALP/NMT

taboo A word of Polynesian origin quickly adopted into the English language in the eighteenth century to refer to behavior (involving people or objects) which is socially disapproved of or forbidden, although not necessarily legally prohibited. In a more technical sense the word is used by anthropologists to refer to relationships to which danger adheres. Failure to observe the conditions of a taboo is regarded as resulting in automatic mystical or supernatural sanctions. For example the breach of the incest taboo is thought to result in some retribution falling on the culprits themselves or perhaps on the whole community.

A precise definition of taboo has never been agreed upon, and even within Oceanian languages its meaning shifts from one society to another. Accordingly its status as an analytic category is questionable, and in recent anthropological literature the term has often been replaced by the word pollution. PGR

tacit knowledge: perceptual, cognitive In perception, we construe objects or events as, e.g., "trees" or "accidents," respectively, by combining the sensory input with our knowledge. Similarly, in reading a newspaper article, various knowledge sources are needed for comprehension, ranging from the lexical and syntactic levels up through knowledge or episodic experiences relevant to the material being read to knowledge about newspaper style and pragmatics. While it can be shown that this knowledge is used and activated in perception and comprehension, it is not usually conscious and hence is referred to as tacit knowledge. Note that not only general knowledge proper plays such a role, but that personal, episodic experiences are also part of the tacit background that enters into processing. (See PERCEPTION) WKi

tacit knowledge: social psychological A term used to refer to the wide variety of things a person has to know or assume in order both to make sense of other peoples' utterances and activities, and to produce ones that are intelligible to others.

The view that orderly social interaction can only be produced when participants tacitly share a range of common background expectancies that normally remain unexplicated and taken for granted has been particularly important in the development of phenomenological sociology and ethnomethodology. A series of experiments by Harold Garfinkel (1967), for example, demonstrated how easily various mundane interactions (such as greetings sequences) could be dramatically disrupted if one party began to ask questions about things that are normally assumed or taken for granted. And one general conclusion that can be drawn from this and similar studies is that it is necessary to develop an approach to the analysis of social behavior that comes to terms with the "seen but un-noticed" ways in which tacit knowledge features in its production and interpretation.

See also ETHNOMETHODOLOGY; INDEXICAL EXPRESSIONS.

JMAt

Bibliography

Garfinkel, Harold 1967: *Studies in ethnomethodology*. Englewood Cliffs, N.J.: Prentice Hall.

Schutz, Alfred 1962: *Collected papers I: the problem of social reality*. The Hague: Martinus Nijhoff.

Tantric psychology A term used by interpreters of the Hindu and Buddhist Tantras. The word *Tantra* refers primarily to a special group of sacred scriptures, but is also used to denote the systems of magico-religious belief and practice expounded in these scriptures. The Tantras do not put forward psychological theories to explain human behavior, but contain instructions for various kinds of meditation and ritual worship, methods for gaining magical powers, and metaphysical theories asserting the fundamental identity of man as microcosm with God and the world as macrocosm. The aim of Tantric practice is two fold: to gain LIBERATION and/or enjoyment. The former usually means rebirth as controller of one of the heavenly worlds, plus the attainment of magical powers (which are often used for political purposes).

Tantric practice uses many different media for the realization of unity between the practitioner and the deity. The four most notable of these media are sexual intercourse, mantras, visual images and breathing techniques.

The *sexuality* in Tantric ritual is seen not as human sexuality, but as the divine intercourse between God and Goddess. The male and female practitioners imagine themselves as God and Goddess, and experience the bliss of consciousness which is said to be the source of the universe. As with all Tantric practices, the sexual rituals may only be performed by those who have been inititated by a Tantric guru, and the aspirant must have attained a certain level of spiritual development before he is allowed to take part in the sexual rituals, which also involve the use of meat and wine and other substances which produce intoxication. The tantras distinguish three subjective states in which a person might use intoxicants: divine, heroic and bestial. Indulging in sex, alcohol etc. in a bestial (lustful) state of mind is said to lead straight to hell. The heroic state is characteristic of the practitioner who has brought his passions under control and can maintain his meditative awareness even when his senses are stimulated to the maximum. The divine state is that in which the practitioner is completely identified with the deity and all craving has been transcended.

Although Tantric practice is characterized by strong

antinomian tendencies, Tantra was not a revolutionary movement aimed at changing orthodox social values and behavior. Caste and purity rules were ignored in the ritual context but most Tantrics maintained a strict orthodox puritanism outside the initiatory circle. Women were worshipped during Tantric rites, but still treated as social inferiors in the Tantrics' everyday life. In this sense Tantra is just as conservative and other-worldly as the orthodox Indian religions, and its reversal of normal moral and social values in the ritual context actually serves to strengthen these norms in the everyday world.

The second element of Tantric practice referred to above is the use of *mantras*. These are sacred sounds which, if received from a guru as part of an initiation ritual (and *only* if received in this way), have a *magic* power of their own. This power can be utilized by the practitioner who recites the mantra either in a whispered voice or mentally, in order to gain union with his chosen Deity. Mantras may be anything from one to hundreds of syllables long, and may include single mystic syllables which express the essence of certain deities, praises to deities, and/or syllables expressing metaphysical categories. For example, the syllable ra expresses the element of fire. It is not merely a *symbol* for fire, but the very essence of fire in sound form. By meditating on his mantra the practitioner achieves unity with it, and therefore unity with the essence of the deity or metaphysical element which it expresses. Thus he gains both liberation from and magical power over the world.

The *visual images* used in Tantric practice are of two kinds: (a) iconographic mental representations of the deity being worshipped, and (b) external diagrams called *mandalas* or *yantras*. The former are particularly important in Buddhist Tantra. Here the meditator produces vivid and detailed mental pictures of a deity, who may be gentle or fierce. Each iconographic element has a religious significance: for example a knife held by a fierce deity symbolizes the cutting away of pride and wrong-doing; a trident symbolizes the end of the three defilements (*kleshas*) of passion, hatred and delusion (*raga*, *dvesha* and *moha*) (see BUDDHIST PSYCHOLOGY).

The mandalas or yantras differ in the Buddhist and Hindu Tantric schools in that the Buddhist mandalas usually contain highly intricate iconographic representations of deities, whereas the Hindu ones are usually abstract diagrams often with mantras written in the different segments of the pattern. The mandala represents all or part of the structure of the universe, and is used in ritual worship as the abode of the deity, who is worshipped as present in the mandala. (There is no simple way of distinguishing between the terms mandala and yantra, and they are often used interchangeably.) JUNG used the terms 'mandala' to refer to any diagram which uses combinations of squares and circles, with flower-like or wheel-like circular layers radiating from a central point. He sees the mandala, whether drawn with intentional symbolic significance according to a religious tradition or produced spontaneously, for example by schizophrenic patients, as a means for reintegrating a fragmented psyche and developing a harmony in the self between the conscious and unconscious.

The last of the major elements of Tantric practice is the use of *breathing techniques*. These are part of the Tantric Yoga, which is known as *Kundalini Yoga*. The mystical physiology of Kundalini Yoga shows a great deal in common with that of *Hatha Yoga*. The practitioner contemplates the junction point between the in-going and out-going breaths which symbolize (or from the Tantric point of view *express*) objectivity and subjectivity. At the same time he contemplates the rise of the energy called Kundalini, which moves through the *chakras* located along the spinal cord rising from the rectum up to the top of the head. At the climax of this meditation the yogi experiences the full bliss of universal consciousness, in which all his individual limitations are transcended in his identity with the infinite. (See YOGA PSYCHOLOGY.)

A wide variety of Hindu Tantric schools became popular in India between 500 and 1,000 AD. The Buddhist Tantric schools had their origin in India at about the same time, but soon became exclusively confined to Tibet. The doctrines and practices of the different schools were so diverse that it is difficult to generalize about Tantric psychology. The deity worshipped may be fierce or benevolent, male or female, in the last case often one of the forms of the Mother Goddess. Tantric sects worshipping the Mother can, with some confidence, be interpreted as desiring to return to the primordial unity of the Mother's womb, but the Buddhist Tantras do not lend themselves to this interpretation so easily.

Some orthodox sects confined the ritual performance of impure acts such as eating meat to imagination. Other sects, in which the quest for magical power rather than liberation dominated, went to the extremes of eating raw human flesh during rituals conducted in cremation grounds at midnight.

One theme which is present in all Tantric sects, however, is the unification of opposites, whether these are the opposites of male and female, subject and object, limited and unlimited or pure and impure. DA

Bibliography

*Goudriaan, T. *et al* 1979: *Hindu Tantrism*. Lieden: E.J. Brill.

*Sierksma, F. 1966: *Tibet's terrifying deities*. The Hague and Paris: Mouton.

*Tucci, G. 1961: *The theory and practice of the Mandala*. London: Rider.

*Jung, C.G. 1959: *Concerning mandala symbolism: Collected Works* Vol. IX, part 1: London: Routledge & Kegan Paul; Princeton: Princeton University Press (1969).

taoism Chinese philosophy founded by Lao Tsu in the sixth century BC. The *Tao te Ching* expresses this simple philosophy of life, often dismissed for its paradoxical character. "Empty and be full; Wear out and be new; Have little and gain; Have much and be confused." Although Taoism is not a psychology, *per se*, its many recommendations about life and comportment are relevant in any discussion of psychological health. Taoist practices include: effortless, yet effective action that proceeds gently, without force; modesty and sincerity in social relationships; an awareness of one's own energetic processes (*tai chi*); and a transcendence of the dualizing limitations of percepts and concepts. The latter entails an epistemology that goes beyond the distinction between knowing subject and known object, towards an experienced unitary metaphysics (mysticism) that allows the participant to merge with and be guided by the Tao (the ultimate source and unifying principle of all that exists, or is in process). The fundamental intent is towards the experience of the unification of all opposites, falsely dichotomized by the seduction of reason, towards the gradual attainment of clarity and openness in a creative balance. "Therefore the sage avoids extremes, excesses, and complacency" (see BI-MODALITY). DAL

Bibliography

Lao Tsu 1972: *Tao te Ching*. Trans. Jane English and Gia-Fu Feng. New York: Vintage Books.

Wilhelm, Richard (trans.) 1978: *I Ching (Book of Changes)*. Bollingen Series XIX. Princeton University Press.

Chaung Tsu 1974: *Inner chapters*. Trans. Jane English and Gia-Fu Feng. New York: Vintage Books.

task analysis A series of activities designed to determine the relevant knowledge, skills, and abilities necessary for successful task performance. While specific procedures vary with respect to how task analysis is done, in general they all converge on the idea that what is needed is a list of steps for the performance of a given task. One illustrative procedure breaks task analysis down into two basic components, the task description and the task specification. The task description is a statement of the global activities performed on the job as well as the environmental conditions under which the job takes place. This description details the essential job activities as well as the physical, social and psychological milieu of the job. The task specification attempts to list the actual steps necessary to perform each task and to attach importance weights to each task. In moving from task description to task specification, the task analysis becomes more fine-tuned or detailed in its delineation of the activities required to perform the job. The results of a task analysis are often used for such organizational activities as defining appropriate training strategies for new employees and developing evaluation devices used to measure employees' performance. RRJ

teacher–pupil interactions It is generally agreed that the encounter between teachers and pupils is at the heart of the process of schooling, so teacher-pupil interactions have been a major research topic in EDUCATIONAL PSYCHOLOGY. All theories of learning and cognitive development have their implications for teacher strategies and TEACHING TECHNIQUES, especially with reference to the work of Piaget and Bruner, though it must be conceded that psychologists have paid far less attention to theories of instruction than to theories of learning. The pedagogical aspects of teacher-pupil interactions have been the subject of more sustained research when the pupils experience LEARNING DIFFICULTIES, require remedial help of various kinds, or are considered to be DISRUPTIVE PUPILS (see also BEHAVIOR CHANGE IN THE CLASSROOM). Various research methodologies have been used to investigate the nature and effects, especially on educational attainment, of teacher-pupil interactions. The oldest and most popular method is that of *systematic observation* in which, on the basis of time-sampling, each observed teacher and pupil behavior is assigned to one of a set of pre-determined categories which comprise the observation schedule. The earliest schedules concentrated almost entirely on the teacher's verbal behavior, but later schedules greatly expanded the categories of pupil talk and of non-verbal behavior. Systematic observation is considered to provide not only a technique for the quantification of teacher-pupil interactions, but also a means of evaluating classroom innovations and of training teachers. Very few generalizable research findings have been generated by the use of systematic observation schedules. More recently ethnographic methods of observation (see SCHOOL AS A SOCIAL ORGANIZATION) have become a second method for investigating teacher-pupil interactions. Naturalistic observation combined with the use of lesson transcripts and of interviews for the elicitation of participants' accounts (see ETHOGENICS) have proved to be powerful tools for uncovering important aspects of teacher-pupil interactions neglected by systematic observation, though the two approaches should be seen as complementary. Both have, for example, made a significant contribution to the study of the self-fulfilling prophecy in classrooms, a topic which brings together the substantial research on teachers' and pupils' perceptions of one another and their effects on interaction, and then the consequences of this interaction. A third approach to teacher-pupil interactions derives from socio-linguistics (and sometimes ethnomethodology and conversational analysis). These studies have yielded significant insights into the structure of classroom interactions and the ways in which teachers, through their talk, control meanings and maintain their authority over pupils. DHH

Bibliography

Brophy, J.E. and Good, T.L. 1974: *Teacher-student relationships: causes and consequences*. New York and London: Holt, Rinehart & Winston.

Edwards, A.D. and Furlong, V.J. 1978: *The language of teaching*. London: Heinemann.

McIntyre, D.I. 1980: Systematic observation of classroom activities, *Educational analysis* 2(2), 3–30.

Rogers, C. 1982: *A social psychology of schooling*. London and Boston: Routledge & Kegan Paul.

teaching techniques

Points of origin

Some teaching techniques follow from psychological theories. For instance, programmed instruction was developed from classical learning theory (Skinner 1961) and cognitive conflict techniques for presenting social studies materials are based on Piagetian-cognitive developmental models of cognitive growth (Johnson and Johnson 1979). At the other extreme many instructional techniques are based just "on what someone feels ought to work".

Focus of application

Some instructional/teaching techniques involve changing

what teachers do, and others involve modifying the activities of children. For instance, in direct instruction the focus is on changing what teachers do. Direct instruction approaches to classroom organization (as contrasted to open classroom techniques) involve "academically focused, teacher-directed classrooms" (Rosenshine 1979, p.38) with clear goals for students, many low-level questions from teachers, strict monitoring of student performance, and immediate, academically-focused feedback from the teacher to the student (Peterson 1979, Rosenshine 1979). In contrast, other instructional approaches rely on changing the ways children teach each other. A great deal of attention has been paid recently to having children serve as tutors in classrooms with particular interest in cross-age tutoring (e.g. Allen 1976). Also, the major instructional content of the cognitive conflict models of education referred to above are the differing views of different children about difficult social problems.

Degree of curriculum materials modification
Many instructional techniques involve changing the format of materials that are presented to learners. Instructional television, programmed instruction, pictorial presentation of materials, and the addition of questions to text are but a few of the format changes that have been researched in recent years (see LEARNING STRATEGIES). In contrast, other instructional variations require no change in materials, merely a change in the way in which materials are presented. For example in personalized systems of instruction (Johnson and Ruskin 1977) traditional texts are typically used, but the text is broken down into smaller units with the student required to pass quizzes on each of these units. Particularly striking format changes involve the application of recent developments in electronic technology into classroom settings (e.g. computer and hand-held calculators).

Effectiveness
The available data do not show whether any particular instructional technique is "the best". The research on many of the instructional techniques referenced in this article has been conducted in only a limited number of situations. For example most of the research on direct instruction versus open classrooms has been conducted in primary schools with most of the interpretable data emanating from studies of reading and mathematics achievement (Rosenshine 1979). Also, many instructional strategies are suited only to particular purposes and particular populations. Instructional techniques have been specifically devised for teaching such diverse subjects as mathematics, psychomotor skills, creativity, clinical medical skills and foreign languages. There are also population-specific instructional strategies for children of all ages and abilities.

A third constraint on establishing a best strategy is that it has long been believed that some children are going to benefit more than others from some instructional techniques. In recent years the study of such potential aptitude/treatment interactions (ATI henceforth) has been formalized with the development of sophisticated methodology for evaluating whether or not an ATI exists (Cronbach and Snow 1977). The various types of instruction that can be given to children in school can be thought of as treatments and any dimension of an individual "that predicts response to instruction" (Snow 1976) can be regarded as an aptitude. There are occasions when a treatment will affect one group of learners and have no effect on another group. When this occurs, the interaction is said to be ordinal. If the treatment causes harm to some people and has no effect on others it is obvious that it should be dropped. If the treatment is helpful to some and has no effect on others, administering the treatment on an across-the-board basis can be defended, unless it is expensive in terms of time or money. In that case, it is difficult to defend giving it to the people who do not need it. In addition to the ordinal interactions there are also cases in which a given treatment helps one population and harms another group relative to an alternative instruction. It would be difficult to make a case for all-or-none adoption when this type of disordinal interaction exists.

Although it is not possible to decide on a "best" instructional technique, there is a growing awareness that the "best" way to evaluate instructional treatments is through the use of true experiments. Experimental psychologists have made great strides in specifying how the experimental method can be applied in real-world settings (Riechen and Boruch 1974), and it has been possible for educational psychologists to devise tests of a number of large-scale instructional treatments. Because of this increasing methodological sophistication, researchers in the area have become aware of errors of the past. For example in many studies in the literature classroom 1 with teacher X was asked to use instructional treatment A, while classroom 2 with teacher Y used treatment B. The performance of pupils in classroom 1 was then compared with the performance of those in classroom 2, and an inference was made about the relative efficacy of treatments A and B. Researchers are now aware that such a design confounds a number of factors, most obviously teacher and treatment. There is a growing realization that when the unit of instructional treatment is the classroom, the unit of analysis should be the classroom, and not the individual learner within the classroom, as has been the case in the past (Riecken and Boruch 1974; Rosenshine 1979). A large number of instructional treatments have been proposed but much more research is needed to establish the conditions for effectiveness of each of these instructional/teaching techniques. MP

Bibliography

Allen, V.A., ed. 1976: *Children as teachers: theory and research on tutoring.* New York, San Francisco and London: Academic Press.

Cronbach, L.J., and Snow, R.E. 1977: *Aptitudes and instructional methods: A handbook for research on interactions.* New York: Irvington.

Johnson, D.W., and Johnson, R.T. 1979: Conflict in the classroom: Controversy and learning. *Review of educational research* 49, 51–70.

Johnson, K.R., and Ruskin, R.S. 1977: *Behavioral instruction: An evaluative review.* Washington, D.C.: American Psychological Association.

Peterson, P.L. 1979: Direct instruction reconsidered. In *Research on teaching: concepts, findings, and implications,* ed. P.L. Peterson and J. Walberg. Berkeley, Cal.: McCutchan.

Riechen, H.W., and Boruch, R.F. 1974: *Social experimentation: a method for planning and evaluating social intervention.* New York, San Francisco and London: Academic Press.

Rosenshine, B.V. 1979: Content, time, and direct instruction. In *Research on teaching: Concepts, findings and implications*, ed. P.L. Peterson and J. Walberg. Berkeley, Calif.: McCutchan.

Skinner, B.F. 1961: *The technology of teaching.* New York: Appleton-Century-Crofts.

Snow, R.E. 1976: Aptitude–treatment interactions and individualized alternatives in higher education. In *Individuality and learning*, ed. Samuel Messick et al. San Francisco, Washington and London: Jossey-Bass.

team development A process for helping groups within organizations to work more effectively. The overall goal is the creation of a team that engages in a continuous process of collaborative self-diagnosis in order to improve its effectiveness. The process is based on the belief that it is often necessary to change a culture, that is the shared norms and ideologies which regulate team behavior, to one which is supportive of open, direct problem solving and more effective interactive working relationships. Initially, a consultant works with the team in carrying out the process; however, the consultant and the team work to institutionalize and build in the capacity for the team to carry on the process without reliance on the consultant. (See also ORGANIZATION DEVELOPMENT.)

Discussions during team development aim to impart knowledge and behavioral skills so as more effectively to manage several areas: goal and priority setting; role allocations and leadership functions; structural issues (e.g., technical layout of work, links between roles); team processes (e.g., decision making, conflict management, problem solving, communication processes); team norms and values; interpersonal relationships, individual style; and team interface with its environment; that is, with the larger organization or with other groups. CCB/NMT

technology *See* educational technology

telegraphic speech *See* speech, telegraphic

teleology The study of purpose; also the claim that a phenomenon exists for a purpose (extrinsic teleology), or has a purpose of its own (immanent teleology). Explanations in terms of purpose have a peculiar logic; doubts about their scientific validity used to be common among psychologists. With the rise of cybernetics and artificial intelligence since the second world war, goal-directed animal behavior has come to be better understood.

The new paradigm recognizes that an intelligent problem-solver must be able to represent internally the desired state of affairs, and the actual state of affairs, and must construct a possible route from the actual to the desired. The old problems of teleology, such as "How can the future affect the present?", are replaced by problems about representation, such as "How does the system represent alternative possible futures, and how does it select between them?".

A further advance has been the clearer separation made between the concept of goal-directedness and the concept of functional adaptiveness. Natural functionality can be understood in purely biological terms with the help of Darwin's theory of natural selection, without the need for cognitive notions like "goal" or "internal representation". ARW

Bibliography

Miller, G.A., Galanter, E. and Pribram, K. 1960: *Plans and the structure of behavior.* New York: Holt, Rinehart & Winston.

Wiener, N. 1949: *Cybernetics, or control and communication in the animal and the machine.* New York: Wiley.

Woodfield, Andrew 1976: *Teleology.* Cambridge and New York: Cambridge University Press.

temperature regulation *See* thermoregulation in the nervous system.

territoriality The tendency of animals to defend a particular area, usually against members of the same species. The concept was first elaborated by Howard (1920) with particular reference to birds, and this group remains the most studied.

Territories vary enormously in size: among birds the least flycatcher (*Empidonax minimus*) has a feeding territory of just 0.07 ha while the golden eagle (*Aquila chrysaetos*) defends almost 10,000 ha. Territories are most easily seen where there is overt aggression between animals, but often this is not the case, and territory boundaries are maintained by conventional signals; under these circumstances the best indication of territoriality will be the distribution of animals on the ground, which will not be random.

Animals may occupy a territory singly, as for example male ruffs (*Philomachus pugnax*) on the breeding ground, as a pair (eagles), or in much larger groups, such as the herds of African buffalo (*Syncerus caffer*) that divide up the savannah plains. Animals often invest considerable resources in territory defense, which will be profitable only if in the long run the benefits to be had are even greater. These benefits will not be the same in all cases, and for convenience one may divide territories into those maintained primarily for feeding and those for breeding (predator avoidance may also be important).

Comparative studies of a wide range of species have shown that territory is often intimately linked to food supply. In the case of birds, for example, there is a strong relationship between body weight and territory size, which implies that the territory is being used to supply the animal's food requirements – bigger animals need more food (Schoener 1968). Territoriality also varies with food availability within a single species. The dunlin (*Calidris alpina*) is a small wading bird that breeds (among other places) in Alaska. Holmes (1970) discovered that in an arctic area, where they are few ponds and an unpredictable food supply, the territories were considerably larger than in a subarctic area where there were more ponds and where the food was more abundant.

Davies (1978a) has made a thorough study of the economics of feeding and territoriality. His own work on the winter feeding territories of the pied wagtail (*Motacilla alba yarrellii*) reveals the nice balance struck between the costs of defense and the benefits gained as a result. The pied wagtail eats insects washed up onto the banks of small streams, defending its riparian rights to a stretch of stream. The size of the territory is such that by the time the bird has searched methodically along both banks a fresh supply of insect food has been washed ashore. When food is less abundant the wagtail will abandon its territory and go off to feed in a flock elsewhere, though it returns from time to time to chase intruders and reassess the availability of insects. When food is particularly abundant it may permit another bird, often a juvenile, to share the territory, but if the supply should diminish it chases the satellite bird away.

The pied wagtail balances food and defense accurately, and the same probably applies to other species. Nectar feeding sunbirds defend territories that vary greatly in size but nevertheless contain a similar number of flowers, and the number of flowers is just sufficient to supply the bird's daily energy needs (Gill and Wolf 1975).

Breeding is a second reason for the defense of territories. It may be that the male is able to defend some resource that the female needs; by controlling that resource the male gains access to females. Female elephant seals (*Mirounga angustirostris*) haul out on beaches to give birth, and mate shortly after parturition. Males defend the beach against all comers and so gain the right to mate with the females.

In many birds the female needs a good nest-site, or ample food for the nestlings, or both. Males that can offer these resources within the territory will attract females. If the resource is very patchily distributed it may pay a female more to be the second female on a good territory than the only one on a poor territory, and hence territoriality can influence the development of specific mating systems, in this case polygyny.

Territory size may influence breeding success. In the stickleback (*Gasterosteus aculeatus*) males with bigger territories do better. This is because a primary source of danger for the eggs in the male's nest is other male sticklebacks, and a larger territory keeps intruders at bay. Females prefer to mate with a male with a larger territory (van den Assem 1967).

Some breeding territories are very small and contain no resources. These include the tiny nesting areas of gulls, spaced apart by the distance that two incubating adults can stretch. These territories are a compromise between the advantages of colonial nesting in terms of mass defense against predators and the disadvantages of such behavior as cannibalism. A small territory may contain only the male defending it. Such aggregations of males are called leks, and they are found in many species. The lekking ground is often maintained from season to season over many years, succeeding generations adhering to the tradition. Usually it is the males occupying central positions in the lek who attract the most females, but the peripheral males may gain some matings and will also, as they grow older, come to control central territories.

The female's role in lek behavior is not clear. She may prefer to visit certain territories, or to mate with certain males. In the Uganda kob (*Kobus kob*) there is no discernible difference in the display of central and peripheral males, and the females continue to visit the central territories even after the males that formerly occupied them have been removed. Probably in leks the females' preference for the central places sets up an artificial prize for which males compete. Once the males have sorted out their relative worth the females confer the ultimate prize – reproduction – on the winners.

Territoriality often seems to regulate population numbers. In red grouse (*Lagopus scoticus*) individuals who do not acquire a territory not only fail to breed, but also pay the ultimate cost and die. When territory holders are removed, their places are taken by non-territorial birds, who now survive, and so Watson (1967) suggested that territorial behavior set an upper limit on population size. Population regulation may be a consequence of territoriality, but cannot be its function, because this would require natural selection to act at the level of the group, and there are good theoretical reasons why this is seldom the case.

Territories are defended by means of a series of specialized behavior patterns. Many animals, particularly carnivores, mark the boundaries of the territory with urine, faeces, or the secretions of special scent glands. Neighbors respect these signs and intruders too will avoid fresh scent marks.

In general there are three tiers to territorial defense. A long-distance signal – scent or specific warning vocalizations – serves to keep intruders away. In one study (Krebs et al. 1978) great tits (*Parus major*) were removed from their territories and replaced by loudspeakers that broadcast great tit song. Intruders were kept away by song alone, whereas they quickly invaded territories with no song broadcast. If an intruder should ignore the signals of the occupant there will often be a display, and in the case of persistent intruders this will escalate into a fight. At almost all stages the resident has a clear advantage, by virtue of its knowledge of the territory. Sometimes, as in the case of the speckled wood butterfly (*Pararge aegeria*), this advantage is absolute; the resident always wins (Davies 1978b). In other cases there is an overwhelming "home field" advantage to the resident. The red-winged blackbird (*Agelaius phoeniceus*) will dominate a rival on its own territory but succumb on the rival's territory (Yasukawa 1979).

A concept related to territoriality is that of individual distance. Rather than a fixed geographic area, this is a space around the animal within which others are not permitted. Individual distance is exemplified by large flocks of starlings (*Sturnus vulgaris*) sitting at regular intervals along a telephone wire (see SPACING). Such behavior may prevent interference in escape or when feeding and hinder the spread of parasites.

JJCh

Bibliography

Assem, J. van den. 1967: Territory in the three-spined stickleback *Gasterosteus aculeatus* L., *Behaviour supplement* 16, 1–164.

Davies, N.B. 1978a: Ecological questions about territorial behavior. In *Behavioural ecology: an evolutionary approach*, ed. J.R. Krebs and N.B. Davies. Oxford: Blackwell Scientific; Sunderland, Mass.: Sinauer Assoc.

*Davies, N.B. 1978b: Territorial defence in the speckled wood butterfly (*Pararge aegeria*): the resident always wins. *Animal behaviour* 26, 138–47.

Gill, F.B. and Wolf, L.L. 1975: Economies of feeding territoriality in the golden-winged sunbird. *Ecology* 56, 333–45.

Hinde, Robert A. 1982: *Ethology*. London: Fontana; New York and Oxford: Oxford University Press (hard covers).

Holmes, R.T. 1970: Differences in population density, territoriality and food supply of dunlin on arctic and subarctic tundra. In *Animal populations in relation to their food resources*, ed. A. Watson. Oxford: Blackwell Scientific.

Howard, H. Eliot 1920: *Territory in bird life*. London: John Murray; reprinted 1978: New York: Arno Press.

Krebs, J.R., Ashcroft, R. and Webber, M. 1978: Song repertoires and territory defense in the great tit (*Parus major*). *Nature* 271, 539–42.

Schoener, T.W. 1968: Sizes of feeding territories among birds. *Ecology* 49, 123–41.

Watson, A. 1967: Population control by territorial behavior in red grouse. *Nature* 215, 1274–75.

Yasukawa, K. 1979: A fair advantage in animal confrontations. *New scientist* 84, 366–68.

tests: educational attainment (USA – achievement) Systematic procedures devised to sample and measure educationally relevant knowledge or skills. Reading, spelling and number (mathematics) attainment tests are the ones most commonly used by teachers and psychologists, but tests are available to cover many other areas of the school curriculum. The same principles of "measurement" are used as for intelligence tests (see also TESTS: NORM- AND CRITERION-REFERENCED). The main difference being that the content of attainment tests is more circumscribed, the individual being required to read a standard list of words, or several prose passages, or solve mathematical problems. The number of correct answers or solutions is converted to an index of educational attainment in the particular subject. This may take the form of a reading (or number) quotient (see INTELLIGENCE QUOTIENT) or an "age" score. A child with a "reading age" of ten years, in effect reads correctly the same number of words as did a reference group of children with a chronological age of ten years. MBe

tests: intelligence One or more sets of tasks or problems, the solution of which is assumed to be a function of "intelligence". "Intelligence" is a hypothetical construction, an assumed property or capacity of the individual introduced *post hoc* to account for individual differences in certain classes of performance, for example, academic accomplishment or an ability to solve complex problems. The selection of tasks for a test reflects the test constructor's theory of "intelligence". There is some consensus as to the sorts of tasks which expose the operation of "intelligence". However, as there is no generally accepted theory or definition of intelligence, the tasks which comprise a particular test will usually reflect the theoretical orientation of the test's author as well as the intended use of the test. For instance, tests designed for use with children will contain items which differ from those in tests for adults.

The more widely used tests usually require the definition of words, answering general knowledge and reasoning questions and the completion of jigsaw-like puzzles. Tests are available for different age ranges, for individual or group administration and for testing people with certain handicaps. When devised for administration to children below about two years of age, they are called developmental tests but they are less reliable. Performance on each task is scored and the total score is transformed to IQ.

IQ's, for a variety of possible reasons, have some predictive power in terms of both current and future performance in a range of activities. However, prediction is by no means perfect and large changes in IQ over time for some individuals are well documented. (See also PSYCHOLOGICAL ASSESSMENT.) MBe

tests: normative- and criterion-referenced Norm-referenced tests utilize the performance of some reference group as a standard against which the performance of an individual can be compared. An "above average IQ" is an abbreviated description for a score obtained by an individual which is above the average of the scores obtained by comparable individuals on the same test.

Criterion-referenced tests use as their basis for comparison or reference a specified set of performances or actions, the criteria. The purpose of the test is to quantify or describe in some standard systematic way, the extent to which the individual has achieved or possesses the criterion behavior. The immediate aim of the test is to describe an individual's behavior or competence rather than to draw a comparison with some reference group. Such a test might for instance be developed to index knowledge of basic arithmetic skills, or self-sufficiency among handicapped people. Self-sufficiency, for example, would be defined in terms of a number of components (able to cope with eating, or dressing unaided) which would then be broken down further into a hierarchy of unitary subskills, such as holding a fork or doing up buttons. Criterion-referenced testing would then involve ascertaining which of the component skills were present, and thereby the extent to which the individual had achieved the criterion of self-sufficiency.

It should be noted that "errors" of measurement can be identified fairly precisely in normative- but not in criterion-referenced tests, where the tester's own notional standards are used. MBe

tests: personality Personality is a term, used in different ways by different psychologists, and can include in its definition, intelligence, physique, skills, and, more commonly, emotional and social qualities, interests and attitudes. The study of personality is concerned with individual differences, specifically those which seem to particular theorists to be most essential for understanding and predicting idiosyncratic behavior. Some personality tests aim to identify and measure "traits" (sociability, anxiety, impulsiveness, honesty, etc.). Others are concerned with "types" (clusters of traits which tend to occur together).

A variety of procedures is used to index these characteristics, including interviews, self-ratings or the judgments of others, specially devised questionnaires, direct observation of behavior, and projection techniques. The last mentioned may involve the use of abstract pictures – such as "ink blots" – or semi-structured pictures which the individual is asked to describe. It is assumed that he will "project" his own personality into the descriptions, thereby making "it" accessible to the tester.

Personality tests are sometimes used to complement other information for clinical or guidance purposes, in trying to teach a fuller understanding of the patient. It is claimed, for instance, that better predictions about educational accomplishment can be achieved by using personality tests in addition to intelligence tests. There are many theories of personality and many tests available. The particular procedure chosen will be strongly influenced by the theoretical orientation of the user.

Tests have been devised to quantify a great variety of human characteristics such as creativity, anxiety, impulsivity, styles of thinking, motivation to achieve, interests, and there are batteries (a standard collection) of tests for vocational and career guidance. The standard compendium of psychological tests has been compiled by Buros (1978). MBe

Bibliography

Buros, O.K. 1978: *The eighth mental measurement yearbook.* New Jersey: Gryphon Press.

tests: reliability of The extent to which a measure is free from random error. An observed score on any measure (including, of course, psychological tests) consists of two parts, one of them random (chance events) and the other systematic. A reliability estimate shows the relative size of these two parts. Methods for estimating the reliability of scores involve studying their consistency on a single occasion or their stability over two of more occasions. Different methods might give different estimates, depending on which components of the score are regarded as random and which are regarded as systematic. The systematic portion of the score may be composed of a single component or of several independent effects which are added together in a composite. For example, if a mathematics examination is given to a group of people on two occasions, some portion of the score on the second occasion will consist of the examinee's memory of answers to the questions on the first occasion. The memory component would be a systematic effect, and from the researcher's viewpoint it may or may not be desirable. In any event, it is not random, so it increases the systematic or reliable portion of the score. MDH

Bibliography

Campbell, J.P. 1976: Psychometric theory. In *Handbook of industrial and organizational psychology*, ed. M.D. Dunnette. Chicago: Rand McNally.

tests: validity of The extent to which scores on tests or other measures are justified or supported by evidence. Validity refers to the relationship between a test and what it is purported to measure or predict. Researchers gather evidence for the validity of a measure from three different angles: content, criterion, and construct. Until recently it has been believed that validity evidence is specific to the research setting in which it was gathered. However, Schmidt and Hunter (1977) and many others have reported investigations showing that under some circumstances validity evidence may be generalized to new settings. MDH

Bibliography

*Cascio, Wayne F. 1982: *Applied psychology in personnel management.* 2nd edn. Reston, Virginia: Reston Publishing Company.

Schmidt, F.L., and Hunter, J.E. 1977: Development of a general solution to the problem of validity generalization. *Journal of applied psychology*, 62, 529–40.

tests *See also* projective tests; word associations test

thalamus (Greek, thalamos, bedchamber) A major structure in the diencephalon, located centrally in the brain between the third ventrical and posterior limbs of the internal capsule (see BRAIN AND CENTRAL NERVOUS SYSTEM: ILLUSTRATION). A Y-shaped band of myelinated fibers anatomically divides the thalamus into several nuclear groups containing nuclei which fall into three functional categories. (1) Sensory relay nuclei which receive input from ascending sensory pathways and project to specific cortical projection areas. This category includes lateral and medial geniculate bodies which, respectively, are parts of the visual and auditory systems, and the postero-ventral nucleus which represents somasthetic and kinesthetic senses. The postero-ventral nucleus is also the termination point for pain, temperature, and gustatory senses. The lateral ventral nucleus relays motor signals between subcortical areas (e.g., cerebellum, basal ganglia), and the frontal cortex. (2) Association nuclei which have reciprocal connections with association areas of the cortex and are concerned with memory and integrative functions. They include pulvinar, dorsolateral, and dorsomedial nuclei. (3) Mid-line nuclei which include periventricular and intralaminar nuclei which receive input from the brain stem reticular formation as well as other thalamic and subcortical nuclei. As part of the ascending activating system, these nuclei project diffusely throughout the cortex, serving a cortical arousal function. GWi

theosophy The word means divine wisdom or the wisdom of the gods. It was a term originally used in the third century AD by the Alexandrian philosopher Ammonius Saccas who was the originator of the Eclectic Theosophical system (also referred to as Neo-Platonism). This system attempted to reconcile all religions by demonstrating their underlying sameness through the interpretation of all their sacred mysteries, myths, legends and symbols by means of comparative analysis and the Hermetic principles of analogy and correspondences. Eclectic Theosophy had three principal beliefs: (1) belief in a supreme boundless and immutable principle that is both indivisible and yet the root of the many; (2) belief in humanity's immortality with each person being a radiation of the universal oversoul; (3) belief in theurgy which is an ancient mystical process similar to certain forms of *tantra* and YOGA through which practitioners purify themselves physically, emotionally and mentally in order to invoke the goods (symbolic of the higher or inner self) to impart the divine mysteries (illumination).

These beliefs flourished in a culture that was the legacy of Alexander the Great's conquests which had linked much of the ancient world politically and economically. The door to the East that the Macedonian opened with the sword provided the way for many sacred mystery teachings, cults and religions such as Mithraism, Manichaeism, Buddhism and Hinduism to mix with the Egyptian teachings of Osiris and Serapis, Gnosticism, Christianity and Judaism.

These ideas were revived in the later part of the nineteenth century by the Theosophical Society, when European conquests in the East seemed to have repeated the ancient pattern of events instigated by Alexander. Many ancient Sanskrit, Persian, Chinese and Egyptian texts were translated into European languages. The Theosophical Society founded by Helena Petrovna Blavatsky and Henry Olcott claimed to present the higher spiritual interpretation of this literature.

The Society played a significant role in the reawakening of the East to a more self-confident appreciation of its own literature and served as a catalyst for the popularization and the spreading of the eastern religions in the West and as an indirect prime mover in the later Holistic and Transpersonal movements. The Russian born Helena Blavatsky wrote more than 20 volumes on the subject of occultism including her magnum opus *The secret doctrine*. Claiming inspiration from Raja-yogins, the doctrine she presented was said to be ageless; a portion of the ancient mysteries that belonged to no single land or religion and formed the inner esoteric infrastructure upon which all outer exoteric religions are built.

The "Secret Doctrine" claims that not only is there one life which when manifesting itself through matter produces a third factor of *consciousness* which is the soul of all forms whether atom, man, planet, solar system etc., but that the purpose for which life takes form is the evolution of consciousness. It rejects both the theory of the creationists that depend on the miracle of an anthropomorphic god and the Darwinian theory of evolution that limits itself to the chance evolution of physical forms. According to her, as the unexplained fossil gaps prove, natural selection might account for minor variations of color, size, etc., but has never been able to explain the origin of species.

Teaching that all lives evolve through the developmental stages of the mineral, plant, animal, human and superhuman kingdoms by means of the cyclic process of *reincarnation*, the "Secret Doctrine" extends its theory of evolutionary unfolding into pre-physical and post-physical states by stating that occult evolution is based on the infinite divisibility of the atom and the existence of *planes* of nature other than the physical. Consequently, Blavatsky's theosophy extended the theories of Freud, Erikson, Levinson, etc. on life stage development by incorporating reincarnation into personality development. All psychological and physiological problems are seen to be the results of inhibited soul life, KARMA, and evolution.

According to Blavatsky, the soul manifests through the mechanisms of the mental body, astral or emotional body, etheric or vital body and the physical body. The energy of the soul and the mental and emotional forces are distributed through the physical body by the agents of the etheric vehicle, the nervous system, the endocrine system and the blood stream. The etheric energy body is said to underly the cerebrospinal and sympathetic nerve-systems forming seven major *chakras* or centers which correspond to the seven major glands (pineal, pituitary, thyroid, thymus, pancreas, gonads, adrenal) and other minor centers (basis of acupuncture). This extends the theories and findings of neuro and behavioral scientists because the hormonal imbalance or balance of the physical body is said to be responsive through the etheric to first the emotional or mental bodies and finally to the soul. Physical heredity and environmental object relations are perceived as secondary causes controlled by the karma and state of unfolding of the reincarnating soul.

Likewise, an understanding of *dreams*, according to theosophical writings, depends on the facts of the soul, reincarnation, the activity during sleep of the mental and emotional bodies, and the consequent protective interference with the memory of this by the chakras and their etheric protective webs. The psychological techniques which explore dreams and the basic determining conditions hidden in the events of childhood which initiate adult behavioral patterns are said to lead into possible confusion with past-life patterns of experience that are sometimes better left unexplored. In theosophical writings this method forms only the first part of a "path psychology" which is divided into three major approaches for people who are seeking psychological help or improvement. Dream work is the first, while the second, although sometimes combined with the previous method, attempts to fill the present with new engrossing interests and to kindle the creative drive. The third approach involves the conscious attempt to bring in the dynamic power of the soul. In this process creativity, love and selflessness are not perceived as merely sublimations of the sexual instinct but as the outcome of the development process. Dietary purification, right emotional control, study, *yoga*, meditation, and a life of service become the elements in this attempt to cleanse the lower nature and merge with the consciousness of the soul. Hence, these three methods are considered to be useful for the differential developmental stages of consciousness that are exhibited in modern civilization. CFH

Bibliography

Blavatsky, H.P. 1888 (*1977*): *The secret doctrine*. 2 Vols. Pasadena Calif: Theosophical University Press.

——— 1889 (*1975*): *The voice of the silence*. Pasadena Calif: Theosophical University Press.

Collins, Mabel 1885 (*1980*): *Light on the path*. Wheaton Illinois: Quest Books, Third Quest Printing of 1885 original.

thermoregulation The maintenance of an optimal temperature. Animals function most effectively at a particular temperature, below which their metabolism progressively slows down. Above the optimal temperature the metabolic rate rises rapidly and energy is utilized wastefully. For most species there is a lethal limit in the region of 47°C.

Animals are able to influence their own body temperature by appropriate behavior and by specialized physiological mechanisms. In both cases some degree of thermoreception is essential. Nerve endings sensitive to the temperature at the surface of the animal have been studied in insects, fish, amphibia, reptiles, birds and mammals. The temperature sense is especially well developed in pit vipers (*Crotalidae*) which have special sense organs sensitive to infra-red radiation. These endow the animal with a directional temperature sense and enable it to attack warm-blooded prey when visibility is poor. Some animals also have thermoreceptors in the internal organs, particularly the brain. In mammals there are distinct heat and cold receptors in the skin, and there are also thermoreceptors in the veins, spinal cord and brain. The thermoreceptors in the veins and spinal cord can initiate shivering even though the temperature of the brain and at the skin remains constant. This sometimes happens when people drink a large quantity of cold water.

The metabolic reactions of the body produce heat continuously and animals can easily become overheated, especially when they are active. Overheating can also occur in especially hot environments or when heat dissipation is impaired. Because the lethal body temperature is not much above the normal body temperature of many animals, cooling mechanisms have to be especially rapid and effective.

There are four principle ways of losing heat from the body. (1) Conduction of heat occurs through the tissues and between the body and external objects, such as the ground. The degree of conduction depends upon the temperature differences between these, and upon the degree of insulation. Insulation is provided by layers of fat within the body and by layers of air trapped in hair or feathers at the body surface. Animals can to some extent control the rate at which the body cools by altering these insulating properties, Long-term regulation can be effected by increasing deposition of fat and hair growth in winter and decreasing these in summer. Short-term changes can be achieved by raising or lowering hair and feathers, and by altering body posture in relation to the prevailing weather. Surface insulation is influenced by wind and wetness. Wet hair increases heat loss by conduction. When a mammal lies or sits on the ground the hair is compressed and holds less air. Heat is then conducted into the ground, particularly when the ground is wet. It is for this reason that cows frequently lie down before rain comes.

(2) Convection occurs as a result of the circulation of warm blood from the interior of the body to the cooler surface tissues. The control of blood flow provides an important means of temperature regulation. When the hand of a European is plunged into cold water there is an increase in the flow of blood to the hand, but his is only half the increase an Eskimo could obtain, to keep his hand warm and usable. The Lapps, a people of European origin, respond in the same way as other Europeans even though they inhabit conditions similar to those of Eskimos.

Convection is also important at the surface of the body. Free convection occurs as warm air ascends from a heated surface, and is of some importance in warm-blooded animals. Forced convection occurs when the surface is subject to an airstream so that heat lost from the body is quickly removed. The angle at which wind strikes the body and the direction of hair growth in relation to wind direction can to some extent be controlled by the animal. Much more heat is lost if the wind blows against the direction of hair or feather growth and most resting mammals and birds face into the wind to prevent this.

(3) Radiation heat loss is proportional to the area of the radiating surface and is roughly proportional to the temperature difference between the animal and its environment. An animal's color makes no significant difference to its heat loss by radiation, but it does affect heat gain. Thus black animals gain more heat by absorption of radiation than do white ones which have greater reflection. Animals can affect radiant heat losses by behavioral means. For example, certain fiddler crabs (*Uca*), ground squirrels (*Ammospermophilus leucurus*), and other burrowing animals, make sorties between their cool burrows and the warm external environment. In this way they can easily cool off by radiation if they become overheated. Camels (*Camelus dromedarius*) allow their body temperature to rise during the day time and dissipate the excess heat by radiation during the cold desert night.

(4) Evaporation from the body surface occurs in most animals, but its extent depends upon the type of body covering. Insects which have a hard surface covered with wax lose very little water by evaporation, but earthworms (*Lumbricus*) suffer rapid dessication of the surface of the body in a dry atmosphere. Most animals also lose water in respiration and this form of water loss is particularly important as a means of cooling in reptiles and birds.

Evaporative water loss through the skin is uncontrolled in amphibians, reptiles and birds, but in mammals it is regulated by the sweat glands. These are present in all higher mammals except rodents and lagomorphs (rabbits). In man, the sweat glands on the palms are emotionally controlled, while those on the rest of the body normally respond to thermal control. Sweating is controlled by thermoreceptors in the brain and not by those in the skin. Thus we usually sweat during exercise but not when sitting by a hot fire. Some animals enhance evaporative cooling by moistening the body surface with saliva, or wetting themselves with water as in the case of elephants.

Respiratory evaporation is to some extent controlled in most animals. Crocodiles, snakes and some lizards gape widely when hot. The desert iguana (*Dipsosaurus*) pants like a dog. Because so much water is lost in respiratory evaporation it tends to be used only in emergencies. Birds and mammals pant only when their body temperature approaches the lethal temperature. Flying birds generate a lot of heat and rely primarily upon respiratory evaporation to dissipate it. The camel does not pant at all, but relies on radiant cooling during the night. Camels do not store water to a greater extent than other species, and cannot afford to expend water in keeping cool.

Animals can increase their body temperature in two main ways: by increasing heat production or heat gain and by reducing heat losses. Many invertebrates are cold-blooded in the sense that their body temperature tends to conform to that of their environment. Because the rate of metabolic reactions is determined by the temperature at which they occur, it is difficult for such animals to increase metabolic rate in response to cold. They can raise their body temperature only by moving to a warmer environment. In warm-blooded animals heat production can be raised by muscular activity such as shivering, and by raising metabolic rate under the influence of hormones. Food intake also serves to increase heat production, because heat is released during digestion.

Heat losses can be reduced by increasing insulation at the body surface. Birds fluff their feathers, mammals raise their fur, and people put on extra clothes when cold. These rapid responses can be supplemented in the long term by increasing the amount of fur or subcutaneous fat. Heat losses can also be reduced by behavioral means. The most effective of these is to move to less cold surroundings. Heat loss by radiation can be reduced by curling up and so reducing the apparent area of the body surface. The warming effects of sunlight can be exploited by color change. Many lizards change color in accordance with their thermal requirements. In the early morning when temperatures are low they adopt a dark coloration which aids the absorption of radiant heat. As the temperature rises throughout the day, the lizards become pale, thus reflecting solar radiation to a greater extent. Heat can also be obtained by conduction from hot surfaces. The lizard *Aporosaura anchietae*, which inhabits the Namib desert, emerges from beneath the sand where it spends the night and presses its body against the sun-warmed surface of the sand so that it can quickly raise its body temperature and become active.

Some animals, called poikilotherms, have a body temperature that is the same as the environmental temperature. This is particularly true for small invertebrates and for fish. Aquatic animals cannot lose water from the body by evaporation and so can never achieve a body temperature that is lower than that of their surroundings. The heat generated by muscular exercise is rapidly removed from the body by conduction and this can be prevented only by efficient insulation as in marine animals such as whales. Heat lost from the body is rapidly removed by convection due to the flow of water over the surface.

Poikilotherms have a difficult time on land, because temperatures fluctuate much more widely on land than in water. The necessity to avoid temperature extremes severely restricts the range of behavior of such animals. These restrictions can to some extent be overcome by behavior which enables the animal to attain a body temperature higher than that of the environment. Sun bathing serves this purpose in many animals and reptiles. For example, the frog *Rana clamitans* can maintain a body temperature 17°C. above that of the environment by basking in full sun. Such animals are generally called ectotherms (heat source from without) in contrast to endotherms (heat source from within) which applies to mammals, birds and large reptiles which control body temperature on a basis of internally produced heat.

Most ectotherms are able to regulate their body temperature to a limited extent. Amphibia can keep cool by evaporation of water from the body surface. The frog *Rana pipiens* can maintain a body temperature of 36.8°C. at an environmental temperature of 50°C. Reptiles have a more limited ability to cool themselves and tend to avoid very hot conditions. The Namib desert lizard *Aporosaura achietae* burrows into the sand when the midday temperature climbs above 40°C.

True thermal HOMEOSTASIS is found in birds and mammals, which are able to maintain a constant body temperature despite fluctuations in environmental temperature. Their high metabolic rate provides an internal source of heat and their insulated body surface prevents uncontrolled dissipation of this heat. Birds and mammals maintain a body temperature that is generally higher than that of their surroundings. The brain receives information about the temperature of the body and is able to exercise control over the mechanisms of warming and cooling. When the brain temperature becomes too high the cooling mechanisms are activated, and if it becomes too cool heat losses are reduced and warming mechanisms are activated. This FEEDBACK principle is the same as that found in a thermostatically controlled electric heater.

Fine control of body temperature occurs in man who has an early warning system consisting of numerous thermoreceptors in the skin. On the basis of this type of information people are able to take anticipatory action and so forestall any undue fluctuations in body temperature. Controlled temperature changes do occur in birds and mammals, often on a diurnal basis. The phenomenon is particularly marked in birds which generally reduce their body temperature by several degrees at night, probably as a means of energy conservation. The average human body temperature is 36.7°C in the early morning and 37.5°C. in the late afternoon.

The degree of thermoregulation varies considerably among species within the animal kingdom. Although partly due to the requirements of different ways of life, this variation reflects evolutionary advances. Primitive animals tend to conform to the dictates of the environment. The ability to control body temperature in the face of environmental changes is characteristic of higher mammals and birds and enables them to exploit a wide range of habitats. DJM

Bibliography

*Hokanson, J. E. 1969: *The physiological bases of motivation*. New York: J. Wiley and Sons.

*Whitlow, G. C ed. 1970: *Comparative physiology of thermoregulation*. vols. I and II. New York: Academic Press.

thermoregulation in the nervous system To maintain an optimal body temperature the brain receives information about temperature in the environment via thermoreceptors in the skin, and exercises control over physiological and behavioral mechanisms for warming and cooling. Thermoregulatory behaviors and reflexes play a large part in maintaining thermal-homeostasis.

As with other primary needs (see HUNGER AND THE NERVOUS SYSTEM; THIRST AND THE NERVOUS SYSTEM and SEXUAL BEHAVIOR AND THE NERVOUS SYSTEM) thermoregulatory neural control resides in the HYPOTHALAMUS. The hypothalamus obtains information about core-body temperature, compares it with the desired optimal temperature and then triggers, if necessary, the appropriate thermoregulatory mechanisms. Experiments with animals have indicated that the hypothalamus achieves thermal-homeostasis via two populations of neurons, "heat sensitive" and "cold sensitive". If an increase in body core-temperature above optimal is anticipated, "heat-sensitive" cells are activated initiating heat loss mechanisms (e.g. sweating). If a decrease below optimal temperature is anticipated, the "cold sensitive" are activated initiating heat conservation mechanisms (e.g. shivering). RCS/BER

thinking, lateral Lateral thinking can be defined both in terms of the operations of an information processing system; and in terms of the result or outcome.

In our usual passive information systems the information is recorded as marks on paper or magnetic tape. From these marks we would hope faithfully to reproduce the input information – as in playing a tape on a hi-fi set. In an active information system there is an environment in which the incoming information organizes itself into patterns. There is no longer a faithful record but an "organization" of integrated experience which can now be triggered by only a small part of that experience. For a "passive" information system, think of a towel on to the surface of which spoonfuls of ink are placed and leave a mark recording where they were placed. For an "active" information system, think of a shallow dish of gelatine and heated ink. The hot ink melts the gelatine. If a second spoonful is placed anywhere near the first, the ink flows into the depression left by the first spoonful (after emptying the melted geltatine and cooled ink). A succession of spoonfuls produces channels on the gelatine surface. The analogy is between Newtonian space and Einsteinian space. In an active information system the information is "curved" or altered as it is recorded. In short the information both creates the contours and is altered by them. Active information systems are pattern-making systems. Lateral thinking is pattern-switching in an active information system.

In terms of its outcome, lateral thinking is concerned with perceptual and conceptual changes. This is the underlying process of insight, creativity and humor. Many so called creative people are quite rigid. They may have a different way of looking at the world but are rigidly locked into that way. Others are simply producers in an area where the next production is unlikely to be exactly the same as the last one. Unlike the vague term creativity, lateral thinking can be defined in operational terms (as above). Lateral thinking can be used as a deliberate process and a key operation is "provocation". There may not be a reason for saying something until after it has been said. That is the definition of provocation. The provocation allows us to escape from one pattern and switch into another. In lateral thinking we look for the "movement" value of an idea – not just the judgment or truth value. The word "po" acts as an indicator to show that a statement is being made outside the judgment system and for its provocative value. In considering the problem of river pollution we might have the statement: "Po the factory is placed downstream of itself". From this apparently illogical statement comes the idea that legislation could insist that the factory intake of water be placed downstream of its own outflow. In considering a central town parking problem we might say: "Po the cars organized their own parking". From this comes the idea that drivers might park anywhere they liked – provided the car headlights were left fully on (hence limiting the parking time). There are many other deliberate techniques in lateral thinking, for example the use of random stimulation. EdeB

Bibliography

de Bono, Edward 1969: *The mechanism of mind.* London: Jonathan Cape; New York: Simon and Schuster (1970).

——— 1972: *Lateral thinking.* London: Ward Lock Educational; New York: Harper & Row (1973).

——— 1975: *Po: beyond Yes and No.* Harmondsworth: Penguin; New York: Simon and Schuster.

thirst and the nervous system Thirst is a subjective sensation aroused by a lack of water, and which subsides shortly after water consumption. Cellular dehydration, a loss of water from inside the cells of the body, is a powerful stimulus for drinking, and is thought to be monitored by a specialized population of cells within the brain. These osmoreceptors reside in the pre-optic area of the HYPOTHALAMUS, and lesions in this region decrease drinking, even in response to stimuli producing cellular dehydration, while small injections of hypertonic saline in this region stimulate drinking.

Depletion of the extra-cellular fluid volume (in particular, the blood volume) is also a powerful stimulus for drinking, which may indirectly result in an increase of angiotensin in the blood, via the kidney. Intravenous or intracerebral injections of angiotensin are known to elicit drinking, and receptors for this vasoactive peptide may reside in structures around the ventricles of the brain. For example, cells in the subfornical organ respond to local application of angiotensin, while lesions of this structure abolish drinking in response to intravenous injections of angiotensin. RCS/BER

Bibliography

Rolls, B.J. and Rolls, E.T. 1982: *Thirst.* Cambridge and New York: Cambridge University Press.

thirst *See above, and also* hunger and thirst: physiological determinants

Thorndike's Law *See* learning, Thorndike's laws

thought disorder This term is employed in its broadest sense to describe four types of abnormality in thinking: the form of thought (the way in which thoughts are linked together by logical associations), possession of thought (the feeling that one's thoughts are not one's own), content of thought (delusions and other related morbid ideas), and stream of thought in which the speed and abundancy of thoughts is abnormal. The term is also sometimes used in a narrow sense restricted to formal thought disorder. This includes phenomena such as thought blocking (a feeling that thoughts have come to a sudden stop), flight of ideas and a general loosening of associations. The latter may be so severe that the result is totally incoherent speech. Thought disorder has been classified in a variety of ways, none entirely satisfactory. There have also been a range of explanatory theories. Thought disorder is characteristic of SCHIZOPHRENIA, MANIA and ORGANIC MENTAL STATE and precise description of its nature has diagnostic significance.

JC

Bibliography

Fish, F. 1967: *Clinical psychopathology*. Bristol: John Wright.

Kaplan, H.I., Freedman and Sadock, B.J. 1980: *Comprehensive textbook of psychiatry*. 3rd edn. Baltimore: Williams & Wilkins.

threat in animal ethology A ritualized gesture, (including vocalizations and scents) of AGGRESSION. It is usually evolved from signals associated with large size and strength, such as deep-pitched vocalizations, or erect posture that enlarges apparent size. It may, also, be derived from signals of confident attack, such as a direct stare or mock lunge. See also COMMUNICATION; RITUAL AND RITUALIZATION.

AJ

time: psychology of Two major research areas have developed in the psychological study of time; the acquisition of temporal concepts and the development of time symbolization, and the awareness or perception of time. The most detailed studies of the acquisition of temporal concepts are due to Piaget (1971), who showed that temporal concepts are derived from more fundamental concepts which reflect process phenomena, rather than temporal phenomena *per se*. Voyat (1977) has shown how children develop temporal concepts from their understanding of velocity/distance relations, and in the early stages of life a child has no conception of time *per se* but only "as embodied in changes and assimilated to the child's own actions". Various ways in which temporal concepts are represented can be found in Leach (1974).

The existence of biological "clocks" is well proven for both animals (see RHYTHMS) and man (Luce 1971). However, it seems unlikely that the perception of temporal intervals and the assessment of their relevant length makes any essential use of these rhythms (Doob 1971). Various temporal features of daily life, such as "time pressure" and "time utilization" have been related to personality characteristics (Calabrasi and Cohen 1968). Considering the interest of the field, many quite basic issues have not been deeply explored. For example, the relation of the "specious present" (the atomizing or chunking of events) to the experience of time as a continuous flow of events; nor has the puzzling phenomenon of the apparent acceleration of time perception in later life been satisfactorily explained.

RHa

Bibliography

Calabrasi, R. and Cohen, J. 1968: Personality and time attitudes. *Journal of abnormal psychology* 73, 431–439.

Doob, L. 1971: *Patterning of time*. New Haven: Yale University Press.

Gorman, B.S and Wessman, A.F. 1977: *Personal experience of time*. New York and London: Plenum Press.

Leach, E. 1974: In *The Presence of things future*, ed. T.J. Cottle and S.L. Klineberg, New York: Free Press.

Luce, G.G. 1971: *Body time*. New York: Pantheon.

Piaget, J. 1971: *The child's conception of time*. New York: Ballantyne Books.

Voyat, G. 1977: Perception and concept of time: a developmental perspective. In: Gorman and Wessman (1977).

time series Statistical method for analysing the change of phenomena over time. It consists of a number of time-ordered observations of a process. The observations are usually at the interval level of measurement and the time separating the observations is constant. The goal of the social scientist is to make inferences about the process underlying the time series. This is accomplished using either time-domain models or frequency-domain models. The use of the former is also referred to as regression analysis (see REGRESSION) and the latter as harmonic analysis (McCleary and Hay 1980). Using the time-domain model the goal is to predict the present from the past; mathematically, this is formulated as a regression equation. In the case of frequency-domain models the goal is to break down the time series into its basic frequency units and to analyse the variation in frequencies that any given frequency accounts for (Gottman 1981). Regression approaches to time series analysis have been the most common ones in social sciences.

MG

Bibliography

Gottman, J.M. 1981: *Time series analysis: a comprehensive introduction for social scientists*. Cambridge and New York: Cambridge University Press.

McCleary, R. and Hay, R.A., Jr. 1980: *Applied time series for the social sciences*. Beverly Hills: Sage.

Tinbergen, Nikolaas Born in The Hague in 1907 and studied and later taught at Leiden University, while making observations of insect and bird behavior. Interned from 1942 to 1945, he returned to Leiden but moved to the Zoology Department at Oxford University in 1949, becoming a Reader in 1960 and Professor in 1966. His 1951 book *The study of instinct*, following LORENZ's work, was the culmination of instinct theory in ETHOLOGY, envisaging a hierarchical system of instinctive behavior ending up in a consummatory act (see HIERARCHY). At Oxford Tinbergen was profoundly influential on the development of British ethology, through his graduate students and through his own work, notably on gulls. Tinbergen's "four whys" (see ETHOLOGY) have become distinctive of the modern discipline. With his wife, he later studied autistic children (*Early child autism*, 1972). He shared the Nobel Prize for Physiology or Medicine in 1973 with von Frisch and Lorenz. PKS

Bibliography

Tinbergen, N. 1972, 1973: *The animal in its world: explorations of an ethologist 1932–1972*. 2 vols. London: Allen and Unwin; Cambridge, Mass.: Harvard University Press.

tool using The use of tools is widespread in the animal kingdom, ranging from the solitary wasp *Ammophila umaria*, which uses a pebble as a hammer to pound soil into its nest burrow, to the chimpanzee which uses a twig to probe for ants or termites. Tool using is defined by biologists as the use of an external object as a functional extension of the body, to attain an immediate GOAL. This definition excludes cases where food items are dropped onto a hard surface to smash them open, which is common among birds, or where the animal scratches itself by rubbing against a tree, although it includes cases where the animal picks up a stick to scratch itself, as has been observed in elephants and horses (Lawick-Goodall 1970). A bird's nest could be considered as a tool for rearing the young, but this is not really a short-term goal.

Tool using involves problem solving, particularly where a tool is not readily available. Some animals display intelligence in fashioning suitable tools. Thus the Galapagos woodpecker finch (*Lactospiza pallida*) probes for insects in crevices by means of a twig or cactus spine held in the beak. The birds select a tool that is appropriate to the task and may even break a twig to a convenient length. DJM

Bibliography

Lawick-Goodall, von J. 1970: Tool-using in primates and other vertebrates. In *Advances in the study of behaviour*, ed. D.S. Lehman, R.A. Hinde and E. Shaw. New York and London: Academic Press.

topological psychology The psychological geometry formulated by Lewin (1936) to represent diagrammaticaly certain structural concepts of field theory. Its psychological applications were suggested by the complex mathematical discipline of topology, which deals with the properties of figures that remain unchanged under continuous transformation or stretching. In other words, one can say that mathematical topology deal with the qualitative relationships of connection and position. Mathematicians have not always been able to see the relationship between their geometric precepts and the topology developed by Lewin. However, despite less rigorous mathematical constraints, Lewin's topology investigates spatial relations in a psychological sense, particularly such relationships as "part–whole", "belongingness" and membership characteristics.

The most basic construct in Lewin's topological system is that of the LIFE SPACE, which is the psychological field or total situation. It encompasses the totality of facts which determine the behavior of an individual at a given moment. Any distinguishable part of the life space or person is defined as a region, and this refers to present or contemplated activities rather than to any objective area in which these activities might occur. A region may contain various degrees of differentiation, a term referring to the number of subparts within a region.

Locomotion refers to any change of position of the behaving self within the life space. Movement from one region to another involves locomotion through a path of neighbouring regions. Two regions are considered neighboring if they have a common boundary but are otherwise foreign to each other. The boundary of a region is formed by those cells in the region for which there is no surrounding boundary that lies entirely within the region. Finally, Lewin introduced hodological space in an attempt to develop a geometry whose basic spatial concepts could be integrated with dynamic concepts. In hodological space, the distinguished path between any two regions is the preferred or psychologically best path; it is the path the individual expects to take if he chooses to proceed from one region to another.

These are the major concepts of Lewin's topology, and they function within his theoretical framework to allow one to determine which events are possible in a given life space and which are not. In order to determine which of the possible events will occur in a given case, it is necessary to refer to Lewin's dynamic concepts. MDe

Bibliography

Lewin, K. 1936: *Principles of topological psychology*. New York: McGraw-Hill.

touch in social interaction Contact between adults usually implies intimacy and warmth, but there are different kinds of contact, some of which are aggressive. Among non-aggressive touches not all are affiliative, nor are all mutual. Some manual touches are controlling. A distinction must also be made among parts of the body touched and among parts used to do the touching. Jourard (1966) found that females reported being touched far more than males did, a result also found in 1976 by Rosenfeld. Henley too found that women were touched more than men. Henley argued that since superiors and those who might be trying to control others would touch inferiors and those being controlled, the accessibility of women to touch symbolized inferior social status. Argyle however has argued that the sex difference may not symbolize power differences. Men and women are more likely to tell women significant or intimate secrets. Hence women's role as recipients of touch and secrets may reflect society's expectation that women will be warm and supportive, and it may have little to do with control.

Touch is also perceived rather differently by men and women. Fisher and others (1976) found that students who had been touched by a librarian, sometimes without knowing it, liked the librarian (and even library) more than did the untouched. The effect was greater among women. Whitcher and Fisher (1979) found greater sex differences in a hospital. Touch from a nurse before an operation lessened women's anxiety, and their blood pressure, but the effects were the opposite for men. This perhaps supports the connection with control, though not necessarily status. Men may have been unhappy about the symbol of loss of control. Nguyen and others (1975, 1976) investigated the perception of receiving different kinds of touch (pat, squeeze, brush and stroke) on different body areas from someone of the opposite sex. Women distinguished touches signalling desire from those signalling love, whereas men did not. But married women and unmarried men found sexual touching "warmer" than married men and unmarried women. Among women touch may increase liking for a man when there are other reasons to like him, but decrease it when there are not (Touhey, 1974).

Contact may also be formalized, as in handshakes and other greetings, but contact greetings tend to imply more intimacy than non-contact ones, as Victorian distinctions between bowing and handshaking show. There are also cultural differences. "Contact cultures" such as Arabs and Southern Europeans, seem to have more touch than "non-contact cultures", such as Northern Europeans and Indians. Jourard reported that couples in cafes touched 180 times per hour in Puerto Rico, 110 times in France, twice in America, and not at all in England. It is unclear whether such differences are caused by differences in friendliness or merely in conventions. Italians appear to use gestures and touch to control conversations and conversational turn-taking where English and Americans use gaze and intonation. RL

Bibliography

*Knapp, M.L. 1978: *Nonverbal communication in human interaction.* New York: Holt, Rinehart & Winston.

*Montagu, A. 1978: *Touching.* 2nd edn. New York: Harper and Row.

Touhey, J.C. 1974: Effects of dominance and competence on heterosexual attraction. *British journal of social and clinical psychology* 13, 22–6.

Whitcher, S.J. and Fisher, J.D. 1979: Multidimensional reaction to therapeutic touch in a hospital setting. *Journal of personality and social psychology* 37, 87–96.

All other references will be found in Knapp.

trace storage A term used by Melton (1963) to refer to the retention of experienced events, in contradistinction to trace formation and trace utilization. (A memory trace is usually defined as the neurophysiological record of an attended-to event.) Trace storage is said to intervene between trace formation, or the initial acquisition of information, and trace utilization, or the retrieval of information that has been stored.

The Gestalt psychologists of the 1930s believed that the memory trace undergoes systematic changes in the course of storage; but the results of well controlled experiments have failed to support that hypothesis. There is no evidence, moreover, that memory traces decay autonomously in time while they are in storage. NCW

Bibliography

Melton, A.W. 1963: Implications of short-term memory for a general theory of memory. *Journal of verbal learning and verbal behavior* 1, 1-21.

training Training can be viewed as any activity designed systematically to improve job knowledge, skills, and/or abilities of individuals, or to modify their attitudes and social behavior in a particular direction. Traditionally, the word training has referred to something narrower than education since training tends to be far more specific and practical in scope. Such a distinction is unnecessary in this context and this discussion treats training as simply an educational process which utilizes the knowledge and procedures suggested by years of investigation of various learning theories and their application.

Training Needs

Any explanation of training is best approached by presenting a chronological analysis of the events of a training course. The primary event within this sequence is the determination of training needs. This first step requires the establishment of training objectives, a procedure which leads to a list of tasks, knowledge and attitudes to be learned by a specified group of individuals. This analysis can be broken down into three areas; training needs relevant to the organization as a whole, training needs of specific operations within the organization and individual employees' training needs. The establishment of organizational training needs is one involving the current performance levels of all units of an organization and its resources including personnel, facilities and finances. At this level of analysis the organization must attempt to identify the areas where training is needed and then set priorities and schedules for conducting training in each area. Few organizations can afford to offer training in all areas which require performance improvement. The results of an organization's training needs analysis allows it to formulate a long term plan which will enable it to train its members expediently.

Training needs analysis at the operations level specifies the tasks associated with a particular job or activity which would benefit from a training program. The determination of these needs is the result of a job analysis which specifies the behavior of organizational members and evaluates current levels of performance against a relevant performance metric. When performance levels for a group of employees are depressed, training programs are indicated. Often the content of these training programs is already delineated by the job analysis. Operation level analysis of training needs focusses on the jobs and tasks within jobs across a group of employees.

The final level of training needs analysis involves the individual organization member. It is important that each member of the organization be made aware of her or his strengths and weaknesses. When problems of performance occur the employer should be made aware of how performance can be improved, which can often be via a formal training program. The implication of the individual member analysis is that while many workers may find a given task or group of tasks quite difficult not all workers in the same job will be having performance problems. Inclusion of these workers in a training program would be an unnecessary expense. Conversely, jobs which are performed well by most workers may be problematic for a few. Analysis of training needs at the individual level can help to identify those individuals who might benefit from training.

With respect to the identification of training needs it seems clear that an integrated approach is necessary. We must consider the organization, the jobs or operations, and the individuals.

Efficient Training

Having shown how an organization needs to train its members, the next step in the process is the setting up of an efficient training program. While it is impossible to specify the best way to conduct training on account of the diversity of training materials and settings, it is possible to identify the issues which must be considered. Gagne and Rohwer (1969) claim that the direct application of principles of learning to training programs is problematic because (1) the conditions under which learning is investigated in the laboratory are different from those in an applied setting and (2) the tasks the learner must engage in in the laboratory are not like everyday tasks. Nevertheless, research on learning has highlighted many areas for training programs to consider. The following list is more fully explained by Campbell, et al. (1970).

(1) Massed versus distributed learning sessions, i.e. the degree to which training is spread out over time.

(2) Whole versus part learning, i.e. whether tasks and sub tasks are broken down for training or whether the activity to be learned is presented as a unified whole.

(3) Reinforcement, i.e. what rewards are associated with the successful performance of the task for which people are being trained. This is not a simple issue since what is reinforcing to one individual is not necessarily so to another. Another important point is how this "association" between performance and reward is formed.

(4) Feedback or knowledge of results: in training it is important that the learner be made aware of how she/he is doing. This information can be qualitative or quantitative and should not only convey direct evaluation of correct versus incorrect behavior, but should also tell the learner how to change the incorrect behavior.

(5) Transfer of training, i.e. that the improvement observed during training carries over to the job.

While it is difficult, if not impossible, to outline the "best way" to put together a training program due to the many issues delineated above, Gagne (1965, 1967) and Gagne and Rohwer (1969) have suggested a sequence of steps we should consider in preparing and conducting a training program.

The road to the successful development of a training program is filled with potholes. The complexities of learning interact with the variety of settings and materials encompassing the total training needs of any organization. Training programs are as diverse in content as the people who attend them. Examples include training for simple motor tasks in an assembly line to training for leadership skills in management development programs.

See also T-GROUPS; EVALUATION OF TRAINING; GROUP TRAINING.

RRJ

Bibliography

Campbell, J.P. et al. 1970: *Managerial behavior, performance and effectiveness.* New York: McGraw-Hill.

Gagne, R.M. 1965: *The conditions of learning.* New York: Holt, Rinehart & Winston.

——— 1967: *Learning and individual differences.* Columbus, Ohio: Merrill.

——— and Rohwer, W.D., Jr. 1969: Instructional psychology. *Annual review of psychology.*

traits A trait is a characteristic of a person or animal which varies from one individual to another. Traits may be physical (e.g. height, eye color) or psychological (e.g. intelligence and aggressiveness). The concept is one of particular relevance to personality psychology because the major effort in recent years has been directed at establishing the main dimensions of temperament on which people differ as a first step towards explaining these individual differences. Traits are conceived as reasonably stable and enduring attributes, distinguishing them from *states,* which are temporary behavioral predispositions. Because a person is anxious in the dentist's chair this does not mean he or she is necessarily anxious in general.

It has been estimated that there are about 4500 trait-descriptive adjectives in the English language, many of which are heavily overlapping (e.g. pompous, vain, arrogant, conceited, presumptuous, egotistical, snobbish, smug and haughty). The first task of the psychologist is therefore, to reduce the list to manageable proportions and identify those that are of central importance. A statistical method for doing this is called *factor analysis.* This is a technique of classification which starts with a matrix of correlations among test items and looks for the simplest patterns that might account for it. Not uncommonly, a hierarchial pattern emerges; a large number of trait clusters are found at what is called the *primary factor level* which, because they are themselves intercorrelated, may be reduced to a smaller number of more independent *high-order factors.* Some critics of factor analysis claim that the method yields contradictory results on different occasions, but this is usually not true; apparent contradictions arise because researchers favor solutions at different levels of generality. American psychologists, notably R.B. Cattell, have generally concentrated upon the primary factor level (the *Sixteen Personality Factor Questionnaire* being a well known measuring instrument) while European psychologists, such as H.J. Eysenck, have preferred to work with a more general but reliable higher order level.

Eysenck stresses the importance of three major dimensions which are largely independent of one another: extroversion versus introversion, neuroticism versus stability and psychoticism versus empathy. These are the three scales provided in the Eysenck Personality Questionnaire. If three dimensions seems a very small number within which to describe the many different personalities that we encounter it is worth remembering that all of the 25,000 or so colors we can distinguish may be identified by their positions in relation to just three variables: hue, saturation and brightness. Indeed, research has shown that the multi-trait profiles yielded by many personality tests such as the MMPI can be reduced to three scores with little loss of information.

Eysenck has devoted a great deal of research to the question of the biological basis of these three main dimensions. His theory of extroversion concerns the level of *arousal* typically prevailing in the cerebral cortex, which in turn depends upon the physiological functioning of the brain-stem reticular activating system. Introverts are believed to have a higher level of chronic arousal than extroverts, who are therefore less in control of their impulses and more sensation-hungry in their behavior. Neuroticism is thought to be related to the degree of lability of the emotional midbrain (which controls the autonomic nervous system and therefore factors such as fearfulness and irritability). Psychoticism is assumed to have some kind of biochemical basis that is as yet unknown but involves the balance of sex hormones or the chemistry of synapses. Jeffrey Gray has proposed a rival theory that anxiety and impulsiveness are basic temperamental variables, relating at the neurological level to pain avoidance and reward-seeking mechanisms respectively. Both theories have assembled considerable experimental support but there are many issues still to be settled.

Other personality variables that have been widely researched because of their theoretical and practical significance are authoritarianism, dogmatism, internal versus external control, aggressiveness, achievement motivation and field dependence. Within the clinical field there are other particularly relevant variables, such as depression, obsessionality, anxiety and thought disorder.

Measurement of traits is most commonly undertaken with questionnaires and adjective check-lists, although there are many other techniques that may be used for special purposes, such as behavioral observation and ratings, projective devices and performance in laboratory tasks. All such measures are samples of behavior that have direct or theoretical relevance to the trait in question. Color preferences, for example, may be used as a clue to extroversion since it is known that extroverts tend to choose bright, garish colors while introverts prefer subtle, reserved colors.

In recent years, some psychologists, such as W. Mischel, have questioned the usefulness of the trait concept, claiming that situational factors are much more important determinants of behavior. They illustrate this argument by referring, among others, to a 1928 study by Hartshorne and May which found that dishonesty in school children did not generalize greatly from one situation to another. Thus a child who cheated in exams would not necessarily steal from a shop or lie to his parents. Since only low correlations are found among such behaviors Mischel has argued that behavior is very largely situation-specific.

Trait theorists such as Eysenck reply that the low correlations occur because these different situations place variable degrees of stress on the child's honesty and that a whole battery of such items is needed before stable and valid trait measurement is achieved. They cite the parallel case of intelligence in which a child may pass one IQ test item and fail another because one is more difficult than the other. This does not mean that intelligence does not exist as a trait, merely that a large number of problems are needed to comprise a satisfactory IQ scale.

The specificity theory gained considerable popularity among American psychologists because it was consonant with the environmentalist *Zeitgeist* of the 1960s and 70s. Today, however, it is recognized that although situational factors need to be considered in a full account of human motivation and behavior, the measurement of temperamental traits is also a necessary exercise for many purposes. Developmental studies have confirmed that emotional tendencies, strongly predictive of similar characteristics in later childhood, can be identified in infants within a few weeks of birth.

Another criticism of the trait approach is the argument that every individual is totally unique and therefore it is not possible to classify people with respect to preselected factors. This is a misunderstanding of the nature of scientific thought, which depends heavily upon classification and generalization. It is true that nobody is perfectly duplicated, not even by their identical twin, but such a statement is utterly unhelpful. Every banana is unique, but it is sometimes useful to classify bananas as large or small, straight or bent, green, ripe or bad. The unique individual may be of interest to the novelist, dramatist or clinician, but it would be difficult even to describe him without resort to higher order (summary) concepts.

Trait measurement is of particular interest in the field of behavioral genetics, where concern is with the degree of heritability of factors such as height, intelligence, musical ability, and psychoticism. Modern techniques of genetic analysis based on comparisons of identical and fraternal twins can also reveal the approximate number of different genes that are involved in determining the individual's position on a trait and whether the family or other aspects of the environment are the more influential in modifying it. The old, naive heredity versus environment argument has given way to a comprehensive partitioning of variance of a trait into different kinds of genetic and environmental influence.

Among the complications of genetic analysis are assortative mating, dominance and epistasis. *Assortative mating* refers to the fact that humans tend to marry or pair on the basis of similarity on a great number of traits such as height, intelligence, attractiveness and political conservatism. This causes a certain degree of polarization within the population on the trait in question and an increase in the kinship correlations that has to be put into the equations of the behavioral geneticist.

Dominance refers to the fact that some genes predominate over others (called recessives) in terms of the degree to which they are manifested in body or behavior. The best known example is eye color, in which brown is dominant over blue. In the field of behavior it is found that most of the genes determining high IQ are dominant (some evidence for this being seen in the phenomena of *inbreeding depression* and *hybrid vigour*), but neither end of the extroversion–introversion dimension predominates over the other. It is likely that this reflects the fact that high extroversion and introversion are roughly equally adaptive to the individual in evolutionary terms.

Epistasis refers to the fact that the expression of a gene may be modified by the action of a non-coinciding gene, possibly even one that is located on a different chromosome. Since the effect of this is to lower all kinship correlations except those for identical twins, epistasis is often difficult to distinguish from dominance. It may, however, account for some part of the variance in IQ and other traits that has previously been attributed to the environment.

Trait psychology (and indeed the science of psychometrics) may be said to have originated in the last century when Sir Francis Galton took a variety of anatomical and behavioral measurements on a large sample of visitors to the great Crystal Palace Exhibition in Kensington and sought to intercorrelate them. We have come a long way since then in terms of measurement techniques, experimental procedures and genetic analysis, although there are problems yet to be solved. Criticisms of the trait concept have had little impact on this progress, and with the decline of psychoanalytic approaches to the explanation of behavior, the psychology of personality has increasingly come to be regarded as synonymous with the study of traits. GDW

Bibliography

Blass, T., ed. 1977: *Personality variables in social behavior*. Hillsdale, N.J.: Lawrence Erlbaum.

Lynn, R. 1981: *Dimensions of personality*. Oxford and New York: Pergamon.

Mischel, W. 1968: *Personality and assessment*. New York and London: Wiley.

transactional analysis (TA) A theory of personality and social behavior, used as a vehicle for psychotherapy and more general social change. It was born out of Eric Berne's early interest in intuition (1949) and his desire to produce a language of behavior which would be universally under stood (1972).

Central to TA is the concept and practice colloquially known as "stroking" – the process of stimulating and giving recognition to fellow human beings. Stroking patterns form a common theme in the main sub-sections of TA.

Personality structure is formed by the interrelationship of Parent, Adult and Child. These labels do not bear their common meaning but denote "egostates", coherent systems of external behavior and internal process. They are formed from the early beginnings of human development. The Parent egostate is based on limit-setting and nurturing as modelled by an individual's own parent figures. The Adult comprises reality testing and probability computing. The Child is an expression of feelings, creativity or adaptations which were originally experienced during actual childhood. TA prescribes methods for achieving a balance of energy among the egostates which is held to be essential for the well-being of the individual, the family or the organization.

Communication is defined as a series of stimuli and responses from the egostates between individuals. TA pays particular attention to the stimuli and responses which occur at a psychological level, usually non-verbally and outside the awareness of the participants. These are "ulterior" transactions and it is believed they decide the real outcome of an exchange. They are the powerful means which we adopt to influence each other.

Games, arguably the most original construct in TA (Berne 1964), are created by a regular use of ulterior transactions leading to a conclusion in which all participants lose. They are played from the psychological roles of Persecutor, Rescuer or Victim and constitute set routines to structure time, provide excitement and avoid intimacy. They can range from low-level teasing to criminal involvement and occupy a large part of everyday activity.

Feelings analysis is focused on the possible repertoire of anger, fear, sadness and joy or those feelings like guilt, hurt, boredom or jealousy which are compounds of two or more of the basic four. They can be experienced as reactions – appropriate contemporary responses; as "rubberbands" – old feelings reactivated by a trigger in the present; or as "rackets" – favorite permitted or displaced feelings generated as a background accompaniment to living.

Script analysis examines plans decided upon in early childhood under parental influence, which are intended to shape the most important aspects of life. They consist of myths arising out of messages received about self and the world and are perpetuated by games and rackets. They fall into the main categories of "winner", breeding success, "non-winner", which are tolerable but unsatisfying, and "loser", which presents problems of varying degree. Scripts may be changed through redecisions which will replace old internal frames of reference with a realistic and more accurate world view. CT

Bibliography

Berne, E. 1949: The nature of intuition, *Psychiatric quarterly* 23, 203–26. Reprinted in E. Berne, 1977, *Intuition and egostates*, San Francisco: TA Press.

——— 1972: *What do you say after you say hello?* New York and London: André Deutsch (1974).

——— 1964: *Games people play*. New York: Grove Press; London: André Deutsch (1966).

Woollams, S. and Brown, M. 1978: *Transactional analysis*. Michigan: Huron Valley Press.

transfer of learning The effect of a previous learning episode or episodes upon performance in a later task. Transfer may be positive, if later performance is facilitated by previous learning, or negative if it is impaired. Transfer may be specific, when the same knowledge is applied in detail in two situations; it may result from GENERALIZATION, where the second task is similar to the first in some way; or it may be abstract or conceptual, where performance on the second task is based on some general principle or rule which the two tasks share. LEARNING SETS provide a classic example of the latter; so does the "learned helplessness effect" where previous experience of response-independent reinforcement results in difficulty in learning a wide range of response-reinforcer relations. Finally, transfer may depend on inference, previously learned information being combined with new information to generate novel behavior. EAG

translation: indeterminacy of When we translate from one communication system, language, dialect or ideolect to another there will be a range of more or less plausible translations compatible with all we may know, or even can know, about the behavior, observable sensory inputs and physical and cultural surroundings of the would-be communicators. Quine speaks of the worst case of this as RADICAL TRANSLATION in which we imagine the human anthropologist investigating human "natives" who speak a totally unfamiliar language. He writes that "the firmer the direct links of a sentence with non-verbal stimulation, of course, the less that sentence can diverge from its correlate under any such mapping (translation scheme)" (1960, p.27).

Since Quine has in mind human non-verbal stimulation, he sees less indeterminacy respecting sentences that describe humanly-observed everyday-for-humans physical objects. This writes empiricism into indeterminacy of translation. However the bent of science has been to strive for theories in which this dependence is minimized. Indeed, those who have been interested in sending messages to possible extra-terrestrial intelligences have assumed that the theoretical foundations and truths of mathematics and physics will be the more invariant under translation. For this reason it may be argued that indeterminacy of translation is no more or less than the underdetermination of all empirical theories.

How much indeterminacy of translation there is among human languages is also a complex problem in anthropological and psychological research. We now seem quite far from the *linguistic relativity* that was an anthropological and linguistic commonplace of the time when Quine formulated his views. For example, it was then supposed that the visual spectrum was sectioned differently from language to language and that this sectioning not only ruled out one-to-one mappings of color terms but also determined how speakers conceptualized about colors. More recent work suggests that the color terms of any human language are an ordered selection from native universals (Berlin and Kay 1969) and that speakers of languages with few color terms will none the less section the spectrum in the same way as those speaking a language rich in color terms. JFL

Bibliography

Berlin, Brent and Kay, Paul 1969: *Basic color terms: their universality and evolution*. Berkeley: University of California Press.

Quine, W.V.O. 1960: *Word and object*. New York: Wiley.

translation: radical Translation between two languages when there is neither a bilingual interpreter nor the equivalent of a translation manual such as the Rosetta Stone. Some way must be sought to individuate linguistic items and structures in the foreign language and to relate these, systematically, to conditions and behavior in the surrounding non-linguistic environment before translation can succeed. Quine (1960) speaks of the native and the anthropologist, supposing a situation in which the anthropologist has individuated the native sentence "gavagai" and connects it with an environmental occurrence to which he would respond with "Lo, a rabbit". Quine stresses the INDETERMINACY OF TRANSLATION in that other translations such as "Lo, rabbit stages" or "Lo, a manifestation of rabbitness" might be "behaviorally equivalent", but this is clearly parochial. Obviously, there are degrees and dimensions of radicalness. Assuming a human, English-speaking "anthropologist", the native (perhaps an extra-terrestrial intelligence) might have different sense organs, might have different ways of conceptualizing the non-linguistic environment, or might have different ways of conceptualizing the linguistic environment, of individuating linguistic items and structures. The actual assumption made in the case of interstellar messages has been that the "natives" will share what conceptual base our knowledge of physics and mathematics requires. The linguistic nativist assumes that humans share a narrow and powerful way of individuating linguistic items and structures. To the degree to which this is so, the human native and anthropologist will not have as radical a problem as Quine supposes. Chomsky (1975) has suggested that *indeterminacy of translation* is just the familiar lack of determination of all empirical theories relative to the data upon which they are based. If we treat a tentative translation as a theory based on the available data, including the sentence to be translated, there is no special problem of translation as such. JFL

Bibliography

Chomsky, Noam 1975: *Reflections on language*. New York: Pantheon.

Quine, W.V.O. 1960: *Word and object*. New York: Wiley.

translation *See above, and* also machine translation

transmitter substances: neurotransmitters Chemical entities which are synthetized and stored in neurons (see NEURON) and released into the synaptic cleft during nerve activity. They interact with specific receptors on post synaptic membranes, thereby inducing a change in the activity of the post synaptic cells (see SYNAPSE AND SYNAPTIC TRANSMISSION).

Criteria have been formulated which need to be met before a substance can be considered to be a transmitter (Eccles 1964; Elliott and Darchas 1980). There is not yet definite proof of a transmitter role for many putative transmitters, both in the periphery and in the central nervous system. A further complication is that it seems likely that substances traditionally classified as transmitters may also be neuromodulators or have a neuromodulator function (see NEUROMODULATORS).

In 1921 the German physiologist Otto Loewi provided the first conclusive evidence for the concept of neurohumoral transmission. He made the classical demonstration that a chemical substance released by one frog heart *in vitro* could inhibit the activity of a second heart. The "Vagusstoff" of Loewi was later shown to be ACETYLCHOLINE, the transmitter of the postganglionic parasympathetic nerves. Similarly, a cardiac excitatory substance was called "Acceleransstoff" by Loewi, who believed it to be EPINEPHRINE. In 1946 Von Euler was finally able to end a long and sometimes heated dispute by proving that, in higher vertebrates including man, NOREPINEPHRINE rather than epinephrine is the transmitter of the postganglionic sympathetic nerves. Other chemical substances which might also be acting as transmitter substances in the periphery include DOPAMINE, SEROTONIN (=5-hydroxytryptamine) and adenosine nucleotides. Acetylcholine, norepinephrine, dopamine, adrenaline, serotonin and γ-amino acid (GABA) are well known and proven transmitter substances in the central nervous system. Evidence for a transmitter role has been presented for a number of amino acids, among which are glycine, glutamate, aspartate, histidine, proline and taurine. At least some of the many peptides which have been shown to occur in distinct neuronal systems in the central nervous system are very likely candidates for a transmitter role (see NEUROMODULATORS). DHGV

Bibliography

Eccles, John C. 1964: *The physiology of synapses*. Berlin: Springer-Verlag.

Elliott, G.R. and Darchas, J.D. 1980: Changing concepts about neuroregulation; neurotransmitters and neuromodulators. In D. De Wied and P.A. Van Keep, eds, *Hormones and the brain*, Lancaster: MTP Press.

transpersonal psychology Transpersonal psychology concerns itself with ultimate questions about human existence. As Walsh and Vaughan (1980) define it:

> Transpersonal psychology is concerned with expanding the field of pyschology to include the study of optimal psychological health and well-being. It recognizes the potential for experiencing a broad range of states of consciousness (see ALTERED STATES), in some of which identity may extend beyond the usual limits of the ego and personality.

The applied side of transpersonal psychology, transpersonal psychotherapy, is similarly defined by them:

> Transpersonal psychotherapy includes traditional areas and concerns, adding to these an interest in facilitating growth and awareness beyond traditionally recognized limits of health. The importance of modifying consciousness and the validity of transcendental experience and identity is affirmed.

Transpersonal experiences of people are the basis for this psychology rather than philosophical convictions. Where philosophical or ethical arguments, e.g. might argue that we should treat each other as if we were an interdependent organism, with our individual welfare related to the general welfare, transpersonal psychology would put its emphasis on the fact that sometimes people have profound experiences in altered states of consciousness where they *experience* being one with all other living beings. Regardless of how we later interpret this such experiences are not abstract considerations but feel "realer than real", and so can profoundly change the experiencers' orientation and behavior. Transpersonal psychology is thus distinguished from academic philosophy by its emphasis on studying the experiences people actually have. Although many of these experiences have been labeled "religious" or "spiritual" in the past, it is distinguished from religion or theology by its desire to base itself in empirical, scientific study, and by the incorporation of modern knowledge about psychopathology of cognition, rather than having a dogmatic *a priori* belief system that experience must be forced to fit.

Anthony Sutich (1907 – 1976), founder and editor of the *Journal of transpersonal psychology*, listed the topics of central empirical interest in transpersonal psychology as including: individual and species-wide meta-needs, ultimate values, unitive consciousness, peak experiences, being-values, ecstasy, mystical experience, awe, being, self-actualization, essence, bliss, wonder, ultimate meaning, transcendence of the self, spirit, oneness, cosmic awareness, individual and species-wide synergy, maximal interpersonal encounter, sacralization of everyday life, transcendental phenomena, cosmic self-humor and playfulness, maximal sensory awareness, responsiveness and expression.

To illustrate the differences in approach of major psychological schools consider an individual suffering from strong feelings of nonacceptance by his peers and a meaningless quality to his life. Psychoanalytic therapy would concentrate on finding the childhood causes of these feelings and treating them so that the patient would feel accepted and find as much fulfillment as is reasonable in life work with others: fulfillment would be implicitly seen as inherently limited because of the psychoanalytic conception of the ego as a reality factor doomed to making compromises between a primitive and irrational id and a rigid and socially necessary superego. The behavior therapist would look for the situational contingencies that elicited the feelings of unacceptance and meaninglessness and teach the patient alternate reaction and control techniques in these situations. Both psychoanalytic therapy and behavior therapy implicitly accept society as sound and stress adjustment to it. A humanistic therapist would use some traditional knowledge about psychopathology to help the patient, but the emphasis would be on developing the satisfaction that is believed to be inherent in open communication with others, and stressing the patient's needs to explore his or her own unique human potentials and developing ways to express and satisfy these potentials. Some prevailing cultural values are directly questioned in humanistic approaches insofar as they limit an individual's personal growth and happiness. A transpersonal therapist might use any of the techniques of the former three schools, but also guide the patient to a recognition that while a reasonable degree of satisfaction within socially defined realms is fine, the ego is an instrument for adapting to a particular culture, and the patient has a fuller and deeper self than can ever be provided by any amount of ego functioning. The patient might be taught meditation exercises, e.g. that teach him not to identify with any aspect of ego functioning but sense a more universal core of being within himself: voluntary disidentification (when not carried to extremes) provides a very effective means to avoid the effects of stress. Other techniques might involve learning to enter some altered states in which mystical experiences occur that provide an intense experiential foundation for a sense of meaning in life, etc. The transpersonal approach stresses effectiveness in ordinary life but not identification with it as the ultimate definer of human potentials.

Transpersonal psychology is in its infancy, and much of its knowledge base is more hint and intimation, mixed with generous amounts of mistakes, than highly factual data. Transpersonal therapy is far more art than science at this time. Since the deepest and most enduring human experiences and values are treated in this area of psychology, however, its extensive development is vital to a full understanding of human life. CTT

Bibliography

Green, E. and A. 1977: *Beyond biofeedback*. New York: Delacorte Press.

Maslow, A. 1964: *Toward a psychology of being*. Princeton, N.J.: Van Nostrand.

Pearce, J. 1974: *Exploring the crack in the cosmic egg: split minds and meta-realities*. New York: Julian Press.

Pelletier, K. and Garfield, C. 1976: *Consciousness East and West*. New York: Harper Colophon.

Tart, C. 1969: *Altered states of consciousness*. New York: Wiley.

——— 1975: *Transpersonal psychologies*. New York: Harper & Row.

Walsh, R. and Vaughan, F. 1980: *Beyond ego: transpersonal dimensions in psychology*. Los Angeles: J.P. Tarcher.

twilight state *See* consciousness, disorders.

twin studies The comparison of genetically identical with genetically similar humans, with a view to establishing the interaction between biological and environmental factors that give rise to behavior.

The usual method involves comparisons between monozygotic (identical) twins and dizygotic (fraternal) twins. Where both sets have been reared in similar environments, the lesser variability of behavior between identical twins is taken to reflect their greater genetic similarity for that trait. Various measures of heritability (some controversial) for different traits have been derived. Heritability is the proportion of variance in behavior due to genetic factors that appeared over generations, when environmental factors were held to be constant. The best known example concerns the intelligence quotient for which heritability estimates vary between .4 and .8.

Other methods compare identical twins reared together with those reared apart, to establish more precisely the role of the environment in behavioral development. It is generally found that adopted monozygotic twins reared apart are nevertheless more similar to each other (and to their biological parents) than to their adoptive siblings (or adoptive parents). Although this does not rule out a general contribution of a common human environment to development, it suggests that specific effects of the environment as in the development of particular interests or aspects of personality, may occur only in relation to genetic predispositions shared by parent and child.

Another method has been to compare identical twins who are dissimilar (discordant) for a particular trait. This has proved very useful in establishing that environmental factors are crucial to the etiology of schizophrenia. GEB

Bibliography

Mittler, P. 1971: *The study of twins*. Harmondsworth: Penguin.

two factor theory Developed by Herzberg (1966) who argued that certain elements of a job (e.g. interesting work, achievement, responsibility) led to high work motivation and job satisfaction when present but not to their opposite when absent, while other elements (e.g. pay, organizational policies, supervision) led to low motivation and to dissatisfaction when poor, but not to their opposite when good. Underlying these two sets of factors, according to Herzberg, were two sets of needs (growth needs and animal needs), which also operated only in one direction: the growth needs allegedly produced satisfaction when fulfilled but no dissatisfaction when frustrated, and the animal needs supposedly produced dissatisfaction when frustated but no satisfaction when fulfilled. There is little empirical support for this theory except when Herzberg's own methods of investigation and analysis are used. These methods have been widely criticized (see Locke 1976). The theory is also dubious on logical grounds, since needs and values all have two directions rather than one (see WORK MOTIVATION). The technique of job enrichment grew out of this theory, although job enrichment is an application of only a small part of the theory. Nor does the theory give any clear explanation of the mechanisms by which job enrichment produces higher work motivation. EAL

Bibliography

Herzberg, F. 1966: *Work and the nature of man*. Cleveland: World Publications.

Locke, E.A. 1976: The nature and causes of job satisfaction. In *Handbook of industrial and organizational psychology*. ed. M.D. Dunnette. Chicago: Rand McNally.

type-A personality Friedman and Rosenman (1974) observed a statistically significant relationship between certain behavior patterns and the prevalence of coronary heart disease (CHD). Individuals significantly at risk were referred to as exhibiting "the coronary-prone behavior pattern, Type A" as distinct from Type B (low risk of CHD). Type A people showed the overt behavioral syndrome or style of living characterized by "extremes of competetiveness, striving for achievement, restlessness, hyper-alertness, explosiveness of speech, tenseness of facial musculature and feelings of being under pressure of time and under the challenge of responsibility". Type Bs possess the opposite extremes of the attributes above.

In the early studies, persons were designated as either Type A or Type B on the basis of clinical judgments by doctors and psychologists or through peer ratings. These studies found higher incidence of CHD among Type A than Type B. Many inherent methodological weaknesses were overcome by the classic Western Collaborative Group Study (Rosenman, Friedman and Strauss, 1964, 1966). This was a prospective national study of over 3,400 men free of CHD. All these men were rated as Type A or B by psychiatrists after intensive interviews, without knowledge of any biological data about them and without the individuals being seen by a cardiologist. Diagnosis was made by an electrocardiographer and independent medical internist, who were not informed about the subjects' behavioral patterns. Results included the following: after two and a half years of the study, Type A men between the ages of forty and forty-nine and fifty and fifty-nine had 6.5 and 1.9 times respectively the incidence of CHD than Type B men. (See CORONARY-PRONE BEHAVIOR.) CLC

Bibliography

Friedman, M. and Rosenman, R.H. 1974: *Type A behavior and your heart.* Greenwich, Connecticut: Fawcett Publications, Inc.

Rosenman, R.H., Friedman, M., and Strauss, R. 1964: A predictive study of CHD. *Journal of the American Medical Association* 189, 15–22.

——— 1966: CHD in the Western Collaborative Group Study. *Journal of the American Medical Association* 195, 86–92.

types *See* authoritarian personality; extroversion and introversion; Jung, Carl.

typical intensity The high degree of stereotypy observed in many patterns of behavior that have a communicative function. Display movements or sounds are generally much more stereotyped in form than the behavior patterns from which they have evolved. For example, many male woodpeckers drum on dead branches to signal their possession of a territory to other males and to attract females. Display drumming is performed with a characteristic rhythm which shows much less variation than the sound made by a male excavating a nest hole, the behavior from which the drumming display is apparently derived. The adaptive significance of typical intensity is that it means that animal signals convey unambiguous information. Typical intensity is one of the properties that displays acquire during the process of ritualization and is a particularly important feature of displays that indicate an individual's species. (See also COMMUNICATION; TERRITORIALITY.) TRH

U

Umwelt (pl. *Umwelten*) The portion or aspect of the environment which is significant for a human or animal being (see ENVIRONMENTAL PSYCHOLOGY). First introduced into biology by Jacob von Uexküll, it was meant to signify the subjective environment corresponding to the structure and state or "inner world" of an organism. As sensory *(Merkwelt)* as well as motor environment *(Wirkwelt)* the *Umwelt* is species- and organism-specific. Generalized to the human level (by Uexküll himself) *Umwelt* has now become the technical term for the subjectively meaningful surroundings of an individual or group. That is why social scientists emphasize the social character of *Umwelten* as ensembles of meaning (Harré 1979). Conceptualized as the environment-as-experienced-and-acted-upon-by-individuals, the psychological usage of *Umwelt* is quasi synonymous with phenomenological and interactional conceptions of situation (Magnusson 1981; see also PHENOMENOLOGY IN PSYCHOLOGY). As ego-centered, the *Umwelt* moves with the individual (Goffman, 1971, p.255).

In every-day German *Umwelt* is equivalent to environment in differential psychology – the whole class of external factors capable of influencing behavior, as contrasted with hereditary influences. CFG

Bibliography

Goffman, E. 1971: *Relations in public: micro-studies of the public order.* New York: Harper & Row.

Harré, R. 1979: *Social being: a theory for social psychology.* Oxford: Basil Blackwell; Totowa, N.J.: Littlefield Adams.

Magnusson, D., ed., 1981: *Toward a psychology of situations: an interactional perspective.* Hillsdale, N.J.: Erlbaum.

von Uexküll, J. 1909: *Umwelt und Innenwelt der Tiere.* Berlin: Springer.

*——— 1957: A stroll through the worlds of animals and men. In *Instinctive behavior*, ed. C.H. Schiller. New York: International Universities Press.

unconscious drive A psychoanalytic concept used to describe a basic urge that is associated with a state of psychic energy and which leads to a specific form of behavior that discharges the energy. The word drive is used interchangeably with instinct, both being derived from the German word *Trieb*. There is no agreed classification of drives, and terms overlap. Examples are sex, life, death and aggressive drives. The expression of drives is affected by the DEFENSE MECHANISMS. RAM

unconscious mind The hypothetical location of those mental processes and properties which cannot be consciously recalled but which nevertheless influence actions and mental life, often (but not necessarily) by disrupting them in puzzling ways. Thought by the ancients, mystics and Jungians to be a means of access to external spiritual or transcendental powers. Many philosophers from Plato onwards have felt compelled to postulate its existence in order to explain certain aspects of memory, selective perception or intuition. Thus in the *Meno* Plato depicts Socrates eliciting "unconscious knowledge" of a geometric theorem from an illiterate boy; and at the beginning of *Republic* IX he in effect attributes to the mind an unconscious layer whose incestuous desires break out in dreams. Although the concept gradually became more familiar to European philosophy after Aquinas, so that it was even "topical" by 1800, it was not investigated empirically by clinicians or experimenters until the last decades of the nineteenth century. As Whyte shows (1960, chs. 6–8), there were several fairly specific statements of the ubiquity, importance and passionate nature of unconscious processes even before 1800 (e.g. Rousseau, Herder), and the current state of speculation by the mid-nineteenth century was reviewed massively, derivatively and somewhat uncritically by von Hartmann (1869) whose work made a strong impact in France and England as well as his native Germany. But earlier, in 1846, the German physician C.G. Carus (whose works were known to Freud) had written that "the key to the understanding of the conscious life lies in the region of the unconscious"

(Whyte 1960, p.149). This view was echoed and emphasized by British psychiatrist Henry Maudsley (1867); and his work was reviewed by Freud's philosophy teacher at Vienna University, Franz Brentano, in 1874, just as Freud was beginning his studies, and a few years before Francis Galton published some experimental studies of memory which required him to think in terms of unconscious mental processes.

Freud initially studied these processes clinically as the determinants of neurotic symptoms in hysteria; in which case they were identified as painful memories and anxiety-laden wishes which had been subjected to repression, to which he gained access through hypnosis, free-association and dream-interpretation. The last of these came to be called the "royal road" to the Unconscious (see dream theories). He soon began to illustrate the general hypothesis, that the pattern of much normal behavior and mental life is also determined unconsciously by memories, associations and wishes that have been repressed, in the investigation of dreams, mishaps and jokes drawn from everyday life (1900; 1901; 1905). Seen in this way the forgotten appointment is not just due to a faded memory-trace etc. but is positively, if indirectly, determined by an unconscious (repressed) wish to avoid it.

Since, however, that wish is unconscious it has been subject to the transformations of "primary process" ideation and to the motivation of the "pleasure-principle", and has achieved only indirect expression. The primary process is non-rational, and does not acknowledge logical contradiction: an idea and its opposite are the same. In this process, an idea may be "displaced", and hence represented in consciousness or action, by another which is contingently, concretely (or otherwise non-rationally) connected; or it may become "condensed" with others into a composite symbol. Both transformations are evident in dream imagery, and the former, in the form of irrelevant perceptual similarity, also in the acoustic *Klang* – associations which divert the course of psychotic thinking. When such transformations are deployed consciously, in the context of (and not instead of) a rational train of thought (reality-principle) then that is a source of humor – as when a *Klang* association is perceived as a pun (Freud 1915, ch. 5).

That association between conscious and unconscious processes Freud called "Preconscious", for he realized that much of what was unconscious in a descriptive sense had not actually been repressed from consciousness in a dynamic sense, but was "latent" and available to voluntary recall in certain conditions (e.g. one's knowledge of a foreign language). The other main component of the Unconscious is the "mental representations" of the instincts.

Freud was definite that his concept of the Unconscious was a system or structure in the "topography" of the mental apparatus; it is not just the logical class of unconscious processes, or the figure of speech that Janet seemed to want to make it (Freud 1917; ch. 17). This insistence upon the spatial metaphor makes for philosophical embarrassment, especially after the strictures of Ryle (1949), and may by symptomatic of his having the early neurological model of the *Project*... (Freud 1895) at the back of his mind. Problematical also is Freud's insistence that all psychological processes that occur consciously can also occur unconsciously, or *in* the Unconscious. This applies even to those, such as feeling and awareness, of which consciousness seems a necessary quality; and he explicitly defends the concept of "unconscious emotion", and even "unconscious consciousness of guilt", recognizing the apparent contradiction, in the essay on *The Unconscious* (1915; ch. 3).

Freud argued that his clinical data (especially) compelled him to such a postulate: it was both "necessary" and "legitimate" (ibid. ch. 1). But it may be objected (i) that such data were contaminated by his own methods and expectations, so that what has to be explained is something less elaborate which can be accommodated more parsimoniously by the conditioning theories of Pavlov or Skinner (see Wolpe and Rachmann 1960; Conway 1978); (ii) that references to unconscious processes are necessarily untestable and therefore scientifically worthless (but see Cheshire 1975, chs 5 and 6); (iii) that everything Freud needs to say, for the sake of his system, can be construed logically into propositions about learned dispositions, underlying neurological processes or (after Harré 1970) into conceptual models of the unknown mechanisms which generate certain actions and experiences (Cheshire *ibid.*); (iv) that Freud's hypotheses and concepts can be translated adequately into an "action-language" qualified with similes and adverbs (Schafer 1976; cf. MacIntyre 1958). The analogy of language and translation, with respect to the organisation of unconscious processes, was much elaborated by Lacan, and resisted by Wittgenstein.

For Jung's distinction between the "personal" and the "collective" Unconscious, see DREAM THEORIES NMC

Bibliography

Cheshire, Neil M. 1975: *The nature of psychodynamic interpretation*. London and New York: Wiley.

Conway, A.V. 1978: Little Hans: misrepresentation of the evidence? *Bulletin of the British Psychological Society* 31, 285–7.

Ellengerger, Henri F. 1970: *The discovery of the unconscious*. New York: Basic Books.

Freud, Sigmund 1895, 1900, 1901, 1905, 1915, 1916–17: Project for a scientific psychology (vol. 1); The interpretation of dreams (vols. 4–5); The psychopathology of everyday life (vol. 6); *Jokes and their relation to the unconscious (vol. 8); The unconscious (vol. 14); Introductory lectures on psychoanalysis (vol. 16); *Standard edition of the psychological works of Sigmund Freud*. Vols as indicated. London: Hogarth Press; New York: Norton.

Harré, Rom 1970: *The principles of scientific thinking* London: Macmillan.

MacIntyre, Alistair C. 1958: *The unconscious*. London: Routledge & Kegan Paul.

Miles, T.R. 1966: *Eliminating the unconscious*. Oxford: Pergamon.

Ryle, Gilbert 1949: *The concept of mind*. London: Hutchinson; Totowa, N.J.: Barnes & Noble (1975).

Schafer, Roy 1976: *A new language for psychoanalysis*.

Whyte, Lancelot L. 1960: *The unconscious before Freud*. New York: Basic Books; London: Tavistock (1962).

Wolpe, J. and Rachmann, S. 1960: Psychoanalytic evidence. *Journal of nervous and mental diseases* 131, 135–48.

unconscious, the *See* Jung, Carl

unemployment: psychological effects of Inability to find paid work is becoming increasingly common in many countries. Research has indicated that unemployed people tend to report more symptoms of depression and anxiety than do those in work. Not surprisingly their major problems are financial and an inability to fill the time. Unemployment is often socially isolating, with diminishing identity-supports and social rewards. It has been suggested that the transition into and through unemployment involves successive psychological phases. Initially there is said to be indignation and shock, followed by a relatively optimistic phase. The person is said next to become increasingly depressed and bored with continuing unsuccessful job seeking. After several months he or she is likely to have settled down to being unemployed; anxiety, struggle and hope all decline to some extent. The evidence for discontinuous phases is in practice extremely sparse, although a general progression and subsequent psychological adaptation seems very likely.

Most investigations have covered middle-aged married men, and evidence about the effects of unemployment on women and young people is limited. However, research interest in the topic has expanded recently, and it has been established that unemployment leads to decline in self-esteem, psychological well-being and general life satisfaction for young people of both sexes. It also seems likely that young people habituate to the effects of unemployment faster than older workers. GMB

Bibliography

Hayes, J. and Nutman, P. 1981: *Understanding the unemployed: the psychological effects of unemployment.* London: Tavistock; New York: Methuen.

universal The word has typically been used to describe whatever it is that explains the generality we recognize in things when we see them as alike. The concept is also invoked to explain our recognition of that generality and of our ability to use general terms. It is noted that a given word (beautiful, horse, between etc.) can be used to describe a variety of different individual things existing in different times and places, and it is asked what makes this possible. Answers count as theories of universals. Traditional answers are classified under the headings of Realism, Conceptualism, and Nominalism. According to Realism a universal is a non-mental entity, a property existing independently of (Plato) or in (Aristotle) the things having that property. Things partake in such universals and this is what makes them alike and explains our ability to classify them as we do. A conceptualist (e.g. Locke) holds that realism does not afford an adequate explanation – to recognize an object as being of a certain sort we need certain mental entities, namely abstract ideas (or concepts or images). Nominalism is the theory that generality is solely a property of words, and the use to which they are put, so that neither common characters nor abstract ideas are needed to explain how we can classify. On an extreme view of this sort certain objects are cats only because we call them "cats" – other versions allow similarity, but not common characters. JMS

universals (social) Structures, traits, and properties of persons, or groups of persons, and their behavior. Social universals are supposed to exist, or are empirically demonstrated to hold, independently of historical and cultural conditions. According to Lonner (1980, p.165), the study of psychology is "*de facto* the study of universals", whatever the definition of its scope as to geographic, temporal, or other domains may be. It aims at the exploration of simple universals such as human sexuality, aggression, communication; of functional universals such as, e.g., need achievement (McClelland 1961). Psychology furthermore analyses ethologically-oriented universals of behavior with a definite link to the phylogeny of *homo sapiens* such as inherited facial expression of anger or of fear (Ekman 1972). Ekman asserts that some facial expressions are universal, i.e. not bound to learning of whatever kind, whereas other authors maintain that nonlinguistic and paralinguistic modes of expression cannot be understood across cultures (Birdwhistell 1970).

With regard to universals in interpersonal structures, the results of cross-cultural psychology vary greatly. Some authors distinguish between just two universals, viz. association/dissociation and superordination/subordination (e.g. Brown 1965), whereas others list up to eight (Foa 1961). AM

Bibliography

Birdwhistell, R.L. 1970: *Kinesics and context.* Philadelphia: University of Pennsylvania Press.

Brown, R. 1965: *Social psychology.* New York: Free Press.

Ekman, P. 1972: Universality and cultural differences in facial expressions of emotion. In *Nebraska symposium on motivation,* ed. J.K. Cole. Lincoln: University of Nebraska Press.

Foa, U.G. 1961: Convergences in the analysis of the structure of interpersonal behavior. *Psychological review* 68, 341–53.

Lonner, W.J. 1980: The search for psychological universals. In *Handbook of cross-cultural psychology,* ed. H.C. Triandis and W.W. Lambert. Boston and London: Allyn & Bacon.

McLelland, D.C. 1961: *The achieving society.* Princeton, N.J.: Van Nostrand.

universals *See above, and also* linguistic universals

unofficial psychologies: concepts Unofficial psychology is marked, among other things, by using terms in the description of persons that originate in popular use as slang and metaphor. Drug-using subcultures, political movements, racial and social minorities, electronic technology in the arts and communication media, rock music, folk poets and general literature have all contributed special terms for psychological states ("high", "stoned", "blissful", "clear", etc.); conditions ("burned out", "uptight", "righteous", "sanpaku", etc.); reactions ("freaked out") and dispositions ("straight", "hung up", "twisted", "macho") that are used "unofficially".

In addition to popular terms that have arisen more or less spontaneously, there are also a number of regular unofficial systems: entire vocabularies, originating from sources outside the stream of standard academic psychology, but merging with the latter to provide new vehicles for common expression and reference. In the United States during the 1960s a period of relatively unfettered experimentation with new modes of awareness and self-description was followed by a wave of new psychological systems and their vocabularies, originating mainly from non-European sources: India, China, Japan, Tibet, Persia, Africa; as well as from variously distributed sects and cults of a more esoteric sort based on supposed traditions of ancient knowledge: ROSICRUCIANS, SPIRITUALISM, KABALISM, alchemists, witchcraft, THEOSOPHY and OCCULT societies, among others.

Terms of these systems often have technical uses in the context of their respective traditions (e.g. "enlightenment" in Zen; "Samadhi" and "Jhana" in Pali BUDDHISM; "Maya" in YOGA PSYCHOLOGY; "baraka" in SUFISM), defined by master practitioners, gurus, adepts, initiates, etc., and represented in "official" texts (I Ching, Tao te Ching, Urantia). In practice the random and individualistic usage these terms have borrowed makes it questionable whether the traditional vocabularies have any common definable meaning at all, in terms of contemporary usage, except possibly in strict initiatic contexts. They have acquired currency by being picked up and applied vaguely to the experiences of altered awareness resulting from all manner of practices (see ALTERED STATES). The issue is further complicated by the fact that the systems in which these vocabularies originate generally impose disciplined self intervention on their adherents.

A third unofficial group of terms for describing persons is derived from philosophical analysis and criticism. These are construed as categories imposed on psychological description by the nature of personal existence in general. In as much as they do not arise out of natural, in the sense of spontaneous, untutored uses, these descriptions, when applied to experience (as opposed to arising from it by reflection) are sanctioned only by the particular philosophical standpoint or school. The result of the dissemination of philosophical vocabularies in practice is a spread of the recognition of the conceptual differences on which they are based throughout the general stream of psychological discourse. From the standpoint of the individual language user, such well-known terms as "ressentiment", "bad faith", "authenticity", "alienation", "identity crisis" and the like, even when backed by systematic philosophical reflection, present themselves alongside "KARMA", "right mindfulness", "samsara", "prajna" and the like, as terms of self-description occurring outside vocabularies of official psychology, requiring justification in terms of applicability to experience.

A fourth major group of unofficial psychologies use descriptive terms taken from mythological or religious contexts. The analytical psychology of C.G. JUNG deserves special recognition in any list of these, since it is elaborated around the hypothesis that such terms of common use symbolize collective deep-structures appearing at all times and places under different cultural tokens and images. "Soul", "spirit", "inner man", "evil", "God", "Christ", "idols" are examples of terms from the Christian tradition recognized as symbolic in this sense. Others such as "heaven", "the lower world", "the cross", "ascent", "creation", "rebirth", are taken to symbolize features of the topography of the "psyche" and its dynamics. Thus, in addition to "scientific" terms used for psychological description (if by these are meant terms whose use is controlled by weaker or stronger observational criteria) these psychologies use terms that are straightforwardly mythic or symbolic in character ("anima", "animus", "pysche", "shadow" for instance), derived from an analysis of the inferred archetypal structures. It also employs terms taken from various other (non-psychological) analytic studies(e.g. "mana personality", "participation mystique", "the numinous", "in illo tempore", from anthropology and the history of religion) when their use fits the general framework.

These psychologies cannot be regarded as "unofficial" in the same sense as those deriving from straight philosophical analysis, since it is not merely the result of a conceptual analysis that they claim to import into the description of persons. Nevertheless, a distinction persists between terms that arise from descriptions used in "counter-cultural" contexts and those that are deliberately reapplied, in counter-cultural contexts, after analytical work, for purposes of understanding and explaining alleged psychological novelties. The claim that the reflectively refined use of mythological terms is only a reapplication to the psyche of the terminology it itself spontaneously posits for its own self-description is still a claim that is highly theoretical in character, although neither self-contradictory nor obviously false. Indeed, it provides a broader "natural" context of appeal for justification than that provided by the philosopher's appeal to mere conceptual analysis. It subjects the latter to a kind of criticism. Further, it may perhaps be assumed that the *inner appropriation* of the mythico/religious vocabulary may accompany a process of personal transformation at those points spoken of in its own transformation terminology, e.g. "reborn", "enlightened", "become two-in-one", "development", "self-realization", "conscious moment". Some religions (e.h. Voudoun) name specific mythological figures ("deities") after particular states, so that to refer to *that* deity without having been in *that* state might be impossible; therefore the name of that deity could not be used by everyone in the same way. The vocabulary of any non-mythological descriptions of such a process would have this peculiar semantic twist also. Keyed as they are to special experiences, they can only be regarded from the standpoint of general psychology as "unofficial".

This leads finally to the concept of a genuinely esoteric vocabulary, the meaning of whose terms is consciously preserved for those who have prepared themselves to understand them in the proper way. The chief contemporary example of such a system is that of G. GURDJIEFF. A true esoteric vocabulary would be one whose terms of self-description and other-description were based entirely on criteria arising from experiences outside the addressee's current level or capacity of experiential understanding. Such an external standpoint might be viewed as either lying wholly outside one's own kind of awareness (i.e. in the way a being from another solar system might understand human consciousness from the standpoint of its own); or else as having resulted from a development that retains continuity with prior phases through memory. In the second case, the vocabulary would be "esoteric" only to those whose own experiences did not provide sufficient ground for understanding the full meanings. This is the sense in which Gurdjieff's "legomonisms" and some Sufi poetry are esoteric.

Such language use is based not merely on descriptions of personal transformation as a possible process, but on the assumption of its successful accomplishment by the users of esoteric vocabularies, who left markers for those who would advance through the stages. A continuity of the sequence of experiences is provided for by the concept of the initiate's "work". This factor distinguishes esoteric psychologies proper from the "momentary deity" psychologies of the mythico/religious tradition. SBT/DAL

V

vacuum activity Behavior manifested in the absence of any appropriate stimulus, as a result of abnormally high motivation. In practice it is never possible to be certain that no stimulus is present, but this is unimportant for the term draws attention to the extreme lowering of thresholds of responsiveness which can result if an instinct is thwarted over a long period. In such cases, it has been argued, there is an accumulation of a specific DRIVE relating to the activity. The original example described by LORENZ related to captive starlings performing the full sequence of fly-catching activities in the absence of any fly and when fully fed in their cage. Paired Bengalese finches at the nest-building stage of their reproductive cycle but deprived of nesting material will attempt to carry items of food or even their own droppings to the chosen nest site. In a completely bare cage they can be observed to go through all the movements of carrying material, placing and weaving it into the nest, with nothing in their bills. AWGM

values What individuals consider good or beneficial to their well being. Unlike needs values are not innate but are acquired through experience (actively and conceptually in some cases; passively, by "osmosis" and conformity in others). Values are the link between needs and action; they serve to allocate attention and effort to various needs (see NEEDS), and are also the basis for emotions. Values exist on different levels with moral values being most fundamental; at a more concrete level values may involve tastes in food, clothing and music, etc. People are not necessarily aware of all of their values; some may be held subconsciously and may even conflict with conscious values. EAL

Bibliography

Rand, A. 1964: *The virtue of selfishness.* New York: Signet.

variation. *See* language variation theories

vedanta The most well-known school of Hindu philosophy, really a system of hermeneutics. Its most famous exponent was Shankara, who wrote commentaries on the Upanishads which form the end (*anta*), of the sacred texts called the Veda) in the eighth century AD.

Vedanta asserts that there is only one truly existing entity called Brahman, and its nature is existence, consciousness and bliss. The everyday world of SAMSARA is said to be simply illusion (*maya*) caused by ignorance (*avidya*). Shankara's favorite analogy is that of the rope and snake; in poor light one mistakes a distant rope for a snake, but upon close inspection one realizes it is really just a rope, and the illusory "snake" vanishes. Similarly, due to ignorance man thinks the world is real, but when ignorance is removed by the reachings of Vedanta he realizes that what he thought was the world is in fact simply Brahman; the illusory world of samsara disappears, and he thus gains LIBERATION. DA

verstehende Psychologie An approach to psychology applying the method of *Verstehen,* i.e. understanding mental processes in others through observation of physical processes and analogy to one's own (directly accessible) mental processes. Though the term was coined by JASPERS, W. Dilthey is considered the first to have advocated this "descriptive and analytic" approach which he opposes to a causally explanatory psychology. The latter follows natural sciences in searching for general (causal) laws, neglecting individuality, meaning, sense and value. *Verstehende Psychologie* is idiographic, employing description, empathy, interpretation and sympathetic understanding.

(See also HERMENEUTIC INTERPRETATIVE THEORY; GEISTESWISSENSCHAFTLICHE PSYCHOLOGIE; IDIOGRAPHIC METHODS.) HUKG

vigilance A state of readiness to detect specific unpredictable events in the environment. Vigilance is closely related to ATTENTION and the type of event that is most likely to be detected may vary according to motivation.

In humans the prototype was the wartime development of radar and sonar: an operator was required to pay attention to a "noisy" situation and very occasionally a signal appeared just above the noise level – a blip on the screen or an echo in the earphones. Vigilance became important in psychology after the classical experimental studies of N. H. Mackworth who discovered that in conditions requiring vigilance there was a marked deterioration in human performance in a relatively short time – less than half an hour. The problem proved to be susceptible to analysis by a specialized form of decision theory known as signal detection theory which emphasizes the distinction between two kinds of errors: those due to the missing of stimuli which did appear, and those due to responding to stimuli which in fact had not appeared. It also led to an interest in the concept of AROUSAL.

In relation to industrial psychology there is an obvious

parallel with inspection tasks. Here the original findings of Mackworth remain apposite: namely that the performance decrement is reduced by incentives, drugs, increasing the signal strength, providing variety in stimulation and optimizing the work environment in terms of noise, heating and lighting.

Vigilance has recently become the subject of study in animals. For example, resting herring gulls attend preferentially to alarm calls from other members of the species. Vigilance in foraging for food may take the form of a specific SEARCH IMAGE, as a result of which the animal pays attention to certain types of food items, while ignoring other equally palatable ones. Vigilance is particularly important in SOCIAL situations, where a few members of the herd or flock keep watch for predators while the others feed or sleep. DJM/WTS

Bibliography

Broadbent, Donald E. 1971: *Decision and stress*. London and New York: Academic Press.

visual discrimination selective attention of an object or event in the visual modality. Discrimination is usually inferred from an attentional preference, or some selective response such as a directional eye movement, which suggests that the perceiver has differentiated a target attribute from others in the field of view.

Visual discrimination techniques have been useful in the study of perceptual development. Robert Fantz (1965) pioneered a method in which the baby is presented with pairs of dissimilar stimuli for comparison. Attentional preferences for one of the stimuli show that discrimination of color, movement and some aspects of form are innate. Other types of visual discrimination, especially those requiring fine distinctions within a category of objects, continue to develop throughout the lifespan. GEB

Bibliography

Fantz, R.L. 1965: Visual perception from birth as shown by pattern selectivity. *Annals of the New York Academy of Sciences* 118, 793–814.

visual illusions Stimuli that surprise or disturb the observer because the resulting perception does not conform exactly to some of the physical characteristics of the stimulus. Indeed, such stimuli seem to violate the simple or implicit expectancies that the observer has about the degree of correspondence between the physical and the perceived worlds. As such, they often provide important insights into the processing mechanisms of visual perception (see VISUAL PERCEPTION).

Consider the first drawing in the figure opposite, the so-called Vertical–Horizontal Illusion. To most observers, line a (the vertical) appears longer than line b (the horizontal). They nevertheless are exactly the same length. If they were placed side by side they would appear equal. But placed perpendicular, a continues to look longer even after the observer has verified with measuring instruments that it is not. Illusions of this sort have been known and studied since antiquity. For example, Ictinus and Callicrates, when designing the Parthenon (447–432 BC), slightly bowed the entablature convexly and slanted the columns outwardly to prevent the building's eastern front from appearing to sag in the middle and to tilt inwards (an optical illusion caused by the building's long horizontal lines and tapering vertical ones).

Some idea of the wide range of stimuli eliciting striking visual illusions is given in the accompanying figure. Included here are: geometrical–optical illusions in which size, orientation or shape is misjudged (drawing 1–16); figural after-effects in which the perception of contours is temporarily altered (drawing 17); illusory or subjective contours in which lines or shapes appear that have no physical reality (drawing 18); spatio–temporal illusions in which subjective color phenomena are evoked by moving patterns differing only in total reflectance or lightness (drawing 19); and contrast illusions in which the lightness (or color) differences between parts of the figure are misjudged (drawing 20).

The exact causes of most of these illusions are not known, but implicated are such diverse factors as the dioptic limitations of the eye (resulting in stimulus degradation), the neural interactions of the retina and cortex (resulting in stimulus rearrangement), and, most importantly, the inappropriate application of cognitive–judgmental mechanisms (resulting in erroneous inferences and unconscious hypotheses about the constancy scaling of depth, linear perspective and size). LTS

Figure Captions

1. The Horizontal–Vertical illusion (lines a and b are actually the same length).
2. The Sander Parallelogram illusion (the dashed lines a and b are the same length).
3. The Müller–Lyer illusion (line segments a and b are the same length).
4. The Ponzo illusion (lines a and b are the same length).
5. The Zöllner illusion (the long vertical lines, a, b, c, and d are all parallel).
6. The Pogendorff illusion (the line segments a and b form a straight line).
7. The Delboeuf illusion (the inner circles a and b are the same size).
8. The Ebbinghaus illusion (the inner circles a and b are the same size).
9. The Ehrenstein illusion (structure a is a perfect rectangle).
10. The Fraser Spiral illusion (the curved lines all form perfect circles, not a continuous spiral).
11. The Jastrow illusion (crescents a and b are the same size).
12. The Orbison illusion (structures a and b are respectively a perfect square and circle).
13. The Hering illusion (the vertical lines a and b are parallel).
14. The Wundt illusion (the vertical lines a and b are parallel).
15. The Ehrenstein or Pin Cushion illusion (structure a is a perfect square).
16. The corridor illusion (cylinders a and b are the same size).
17. Two figural aftereffects (after staring for a minute at the differently tilted gratings on the top (a), by looking up and down along the black bar between them, the vertical gratings in the middle (b) appear to be tilted in opposite directions. Likewise, after staring for a minute at the pair of different spatial frequency gratings on the bottom (c) the identical spatial frequency gratings in the middle (b) appear to have different stripe widths).

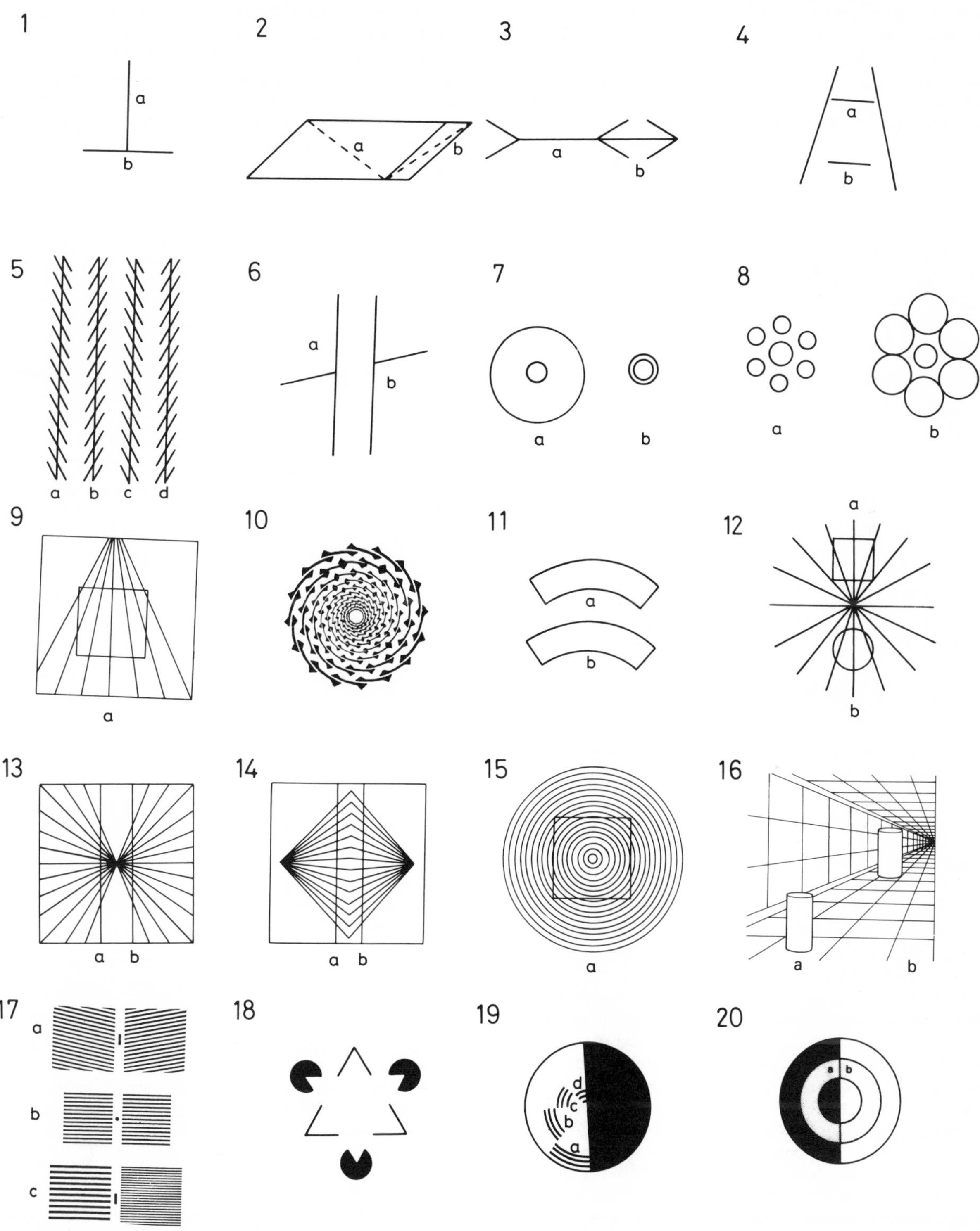
1
a
b
2
a
b
3
a
b
4
a
b
5
a b c d
6
a
b
7
a
b
8
a
b
9
a
10
11
a
b
12
a
b
13
a b
14
a b
15
a
16
a
b
17
a
b
c
18
19
a
b
c
d
20
a b

18. The Kanizsa illusory triangle.
19. The Benham top (a black and white disc which when rotated at about 5–10 Hz clockwise induces subjective color arcs at various radii: the lines labeled a appear bluish, b olive-greenish, c reddish, and d magenta).
20. A contrast pattern (the two halves, a and b, of the grey ring are identical in lightness and reflectance).

Bibliography

Coren, S. and Girgus, J.A. 1978: *Seeing is deceiving: the psychology of visual illusions*. Hillsdale, N.J.: Lawrence Erlbaum.

Gregory, R.L. and Gombrich, E.H., eds. 1973: *Illusion in nature and art*. London: Duckworth; New York: Scribner.

Jastrow, J. 1891: A study of Zöllner's figures and other related illusions. *American journal of psychology* 4, 381–98.

Robinson, J.D. 1972: *The psychology of visual illusion*. London: Hutchinson; Atlantic Highlands, N.J.: Humanities Press.

visual nervous system (See BRAIN AND CENTRAL NERVOUS SYSTEM: ILLUSTRATIONS, fig. 23) The neural structures which participate in the conversion of light into the sensations and perceptions of vision. Light rays are focused by the cornea and lens of the eye onto the retinal mosaic of rods and cones (figs. 24 and 25). Absorption of photons of light by these photoreceptors causes SENSORY TRANSDUCTION, initiating the chain of neural events that result in seeing. The retina, unlike the peripheral neural structures of other sensory systems, is an evagination of the brain and complex processing occurs before information is forwarded along the optic nerve. There is a trend toward ENCEPHALIZATION of visual processing in the retinae of vertebrates with lower animals performing more processing peripherally and higher animals doing more centrally. Central projections of the optic nerve innervate six areas of the brain in vertebrates: the HYPOTHALAMUS (suprachiasmatic nuclei: fig. 20) and accessory optic tract nuclei, the dorsal THALAMUS (dorsal lateral geniculate nucleus), the ventral thalamus (ventral lateral geniculate nucleus) (fig. 19), the pretectal region and the optic tectum (superior colliculus: figs 6 and 7). In most of these structures, the organization of the optic nerve fiber terminals preserves the arrangement of their source in the retina producing a retinotopic map.

These various retinal inputs serve identifiable, separate, visual systems which are interconnected in complex ways to produce visually guided behavior. The connections to the hypothalamus serve to synchronize biological rhythms to the light–dark cycle of the environment, and may not lead directly to visual perception. The connections to the pretectal areas mediate the pupillary response to light and likewise do not lead directly to visual perception. The functions of the accessory optic system and the ventral lateral geniculate nucleus are not yet clear. The two most studied visual subsystems are the retina–geniculate–striate cortex system which serves form vision, and the retinotectal system which moves the eyes.

Optic nerve fibers from corresponding parts of the retinae of both eyes innervate adjacent layers of the dorsal lateral geniculate nucleus (LGN), bringing into registration retinotopic maps from the two eyes. The LGN projects via the optic radiation to the striate cortex (area 17) on the banks of the calcarine fissure in the parietal lobe of CEREBRAL CORTEX (figs 2 and 3). The striate cortex projects to the peristriate cortex (areas 18 and 19) which finally projects to the infratemporal cortex in the temporal lobe. The connections in this subsystem appear to be hierarchical with simpler response properties in cells closer to the retina leading to more and more complex response properties in cells further up the neuronal chain. Striate cortex has highly structured arrangements of cortical columns to abstract stimulus pattern information from retinogeniculate inputs (see Hubel and Wiesel 1977).

Besides visual inputs, the superior colliculus also receives sensory inputs from other modalities and interconnects directly or indirectly with visual cortex, the pulvinar of the thalamus, the CEREBELLUM, (fig. 6), vestibular nuclei and the motor nuclei of the extraocular muscles which move the eyes. The retinotectal system is involved with voluntary and involuntary eye movements, with the direction of visual gaze toward the source of a sensory stimulus, with preservation of gaze during body movements, etc. The retinotectal and geniculostriate subsystems are strongly interconnected.

Descending connections from striate cortex to the LGN are well known in mammals. Neural feedback to the retina itself, however, has only recently become a relatively popular concept with the suggestion that centrifugal fibers in the optic nerve may regulate photoreceptor membrane turnover (see Teirstein et al. 1980; Itaya 1980). SCC

Bibliography

Cornsweet, T.N. 1970: *Visual perception*. New York and London: Academic Press.

Ebbeson, S.O.E. 1970: On the organization of central visual pathways in vertebrates. *Brain, behavior and evolution* 3, 178–94.

Gregory, R.L. 1966: *Eye and brain, the psychology of seeing*. New York: World University Library, McGraw-Hill.

Hubel, D.H. and Wiesel, T.N. 1977: Ferrier Lecture: Functional architecture of macaque monkey visual cortex. *Proceedings of the Royal Society of London, Series B, biological sciences* 198: 1–59.

Itaya, S.K. 1980: Retinal efferents from the pretectal area in the rat. *Brain research* 201, 436–41.

Jung, R., ed. 1973: *Handbook of sensory physiology*, Vol. VII/3, *Central visual information, A: integrative functions and comparative data*; and *B: Visual centers in the brain*. Berlin and New York: Springer-Verlag.

Kandel, E.R. and Schwartz, J.H., eds. 1981: *Principles of neural science*. New York and Oxford: Elsevier/North-Holland.

Rodieck, R.W. 1973: *The vertebrate retina*. San Francisco: W.H. Freeeman.

——— 1979: Visual pathways. *Annual review of neuroscience* 2, 193–225.

Teirstein, P.S., Goldman, A.I. and O'Brien, P.J. 1980: Evidence for both local and central regulation of rat rod outer segment disc shedding. *Investigative ophthalmology and visual science* 19, 1268–73.

Van Essen, D.C. 1979: Visual areas of the mammalian cerebral cortex. *Annual review of neuroscience* 2, 227–63.

visual perception The subjective experience arising from sensory stimulation of the visual system and brain. Its complete and proper study encompasses not only the visual domains of neurophysiology, psychophysics and psychology, but also encroaches upon the related fields of learning, memory and ARTIFICIAL INTELLIGENCE (pattern recognition).

The process of visual perception starts with the

absorption of photons in the four types of retinal photoreceptors, the rods and cones (see COLOR VISION). These sensory transducers receive a two-dimensional image of external objects, reduced and blurred by the lens and other ocular media interposed in front of the retina. They convert it into a code of electro-chemical impulses, which is subsequently analysed by a multitude of neurons into many different dimensions: contrast, orientation, spatial frequency, color, stereoscopic disparity, direction, velocity, and so forth. Such analysis unavoidably alters the input so that an object's representation becomes an abstraction with certain elements enhanced or elaborated and others degraded or lost.

The abstraction begins in the retina where ganglion cells with concentric receptive field organization (see VISUAL NERVOUS SYSTEM) code an object by its spatial changes in contrast: accentuating regions of change (contours or edges) and disregarding regions of uniformity. At higher levels in the cortex, other neurons advance the process of feature extraction. They respond selectively to specific elements such as edges of a particular orientation or moving in a particular direction. Of course the activity of individual neurons *per se* does not code orientation or direction. This is probably done by the relative distribution of activity among neurons with different but overlapping sensitivities. Such groups of neurons, hierarchically arranged within parallel processing networks, compose what are frequently referred to as neural channels. Much psychophysical and electrophysical evidence suggests that distinct channels exist for coding the various stimulus dimensions. However, there is still considerable debate about how separate and independent the channels are and to what degree they are localized in separate cortical areas (see SENSORY SYSTEMS NEURAL BASES). After all, it must not be forgotten that any given neuron may transmit information about a number of different stimulus dimensions (for example, contrast, orientation and spatial frequency) and may therefore contribute to a number of different analysing systems.

Regardless of the precise neurophysiological details, one way or another the visual system has the necessary machinery for analysing the visual image into values along particular stimulus dimensions. This, obviously, is an essential preliminary to recognizing or perceiving objects in the visual world, but it must not be mistaken for the process of perception itself. Perception requires not only detecting the presence or absence of features in the visual image, but also defining their relationship to one another and assigning them to separate objects. To achieve this end, perception cannot merely be a passive extracting process. It must also be an active integrating one, associating and organizing the sensory information (see PERCEPTION).

Consider first scene analysis, which is so fundamental to perception that we generally take it for granted. This is the process of dividing the visual image into discrete objects. It involves organizing the extracted elements of the retinal image so that information corresponding to the boundaries between surfaces and objects can be recognized. This is in itself a difficult task because boundaries may be marked by differences in reflectance (or luminance), orientation and texture or by discontinuities in stereoscopic depth and relative movement (see below). Even more difficult, however, is the task of identifying those regions of the retinal image that are not part of any particular object or figure, but compose the background. This organizing of extracted elements into figure and ground seems to be fundamental to vision in that it is present at first sight as far as can be determined from the early behavior of infants and from the behavior of the congenitally blind who are given sight at maturity.

Figure–ground analysis segregates an image into objects and results in them appearing qualitatively very different from the background. It does not provide detailed information about their size, shape, distance or their position in visual space. Further perceptual processes must be involved in making these precise visual judgments. For instance we have considerable perceptual information available to us about the distance of objects or their depth in the visual field; a three-dimensional awareness that cannot be simply obtained from feature analysing and reconstructing the two-dimensional retinal image. Some information about depth is provided by straightforward binocular cues that vary monotonically with distance: the accommodation of the lens, the convergence of the eyes, and the disparity of the two retinal images (i.e. they differ slightly in size, shape and location as the result of the geometry of the light rays). More information, however, is provided by monocular cues derived from further organizing and processing of the extracted elements of the retinal image: (i) *Interposition*, perceiving that nearer objects often partially occlude those further away; (ii) *Kinetic Parallax*, perceiving that moving objects have typical expansive and constrictive patterns associated with them; (iii) *Motion Parallax*, perceiving that head or body movements differentially displace objects at different distances in the visual field; (iv) *Attached Shadows*, perceiving that the attached shadows of objects change with distance and relative position in the visual field; (v) *Size Perspective*, perceiving that the retinal image of familiar objects whose true size is roughly known get progressively smaller with increasing distance; and (vi) *Linear Perspective*, perceiving that the convergence of parallel lines and texture gradients leading away from the observer provide frameworks of relative distance for locating objects.

The perceptual processes also extract from the retinal image considerable information about object direction and movement in space. And they do this despite two major problems. First, they must overcome the limitation that visual neurons have spatially discrete receptive fields and can only resolve the continuous motion of objects transversing the retina into a series of discrete excitations. Second, they must overcome the confounding effects of eye movements which shift the image of fixed objects around the retina. Thus, there must be active compensatory mechanisms restoring perceived motion and subtracting out the constantly changing position of the eyes. Information about eye position may come from monitoring the proprioceptive signals originating from the eye muscles and the central (efferent) signals originating from the cortical neurons commanding head, body and eye movements.

Besides permitting us to locate reliably the distance and direction of objects in visual space, perceptual processes allow us to judge accurately their size, shape and colour. And they allow us to do this, despite wide changes in the viewing conditions that significantly vary the retinal image. For example, a jet airliner viewed from afar is still perceived as being large even though its retinal image is very small, much smaller than tiny objects near at hand (i.e. perceived size cannot correspond exactly with visual angle subtended at the retina). Likewise, a round object viewed obliquely is still perceived as circular even though its retinal image is elliptical (i.e. perceived shape cannot correspond exactly with the object's retinal image); and white paper viewed under moonlight is still perceived as white even though it reflects less light than carbon paper viewed under direct sunlight (i.e. perceived lightness/color cannot correspond exactly with the incident retinal illumination). In short, objects are generally judged to be constant in size, shape and lightness/color over an enormous range of viewing conditions that change their phenomenological appearance. The perceptual system must derive this constancy from the various retinal images by taking into account other information obtained directly from the adjacent objects and surfaces and indirectly from the short term memory stores (see SHORT TERM MEMORY). (This problem of how we recognize objects as being constant is related to the more complex problem of pattern recognition in general, of how we recognize a very diverse set of objects as belonging to a single significant category).

The few examples that could be discussed above should suffice to demonstrate that perception is not determined merely by passive neural analysis of the retinal input, but also involves active organizing of the sensory information. This fact has several consequences. First, it means that perception is not immediate. Time is required to extract perceptual information either from the retinal image or from the accessible memory stores. Second, it means that perception is not a fixed, immutable process. It is affected not only by a general knowledge of what are likely properties of objects, but also by the specific knowledge of what sorts of objects are likely to be met in particular situations (i.e. the role of expectancy and selection in recognition). Third, it means that perception is fallible. Our perceptual hypotheses about objects may conform to the sensory information, but they are by no means inevitably proven by it. They may be false, nonsensical or nonveridical (see VISUAL ILLUSIONS). Fourth, it means that perception may be modified by experience and learning (see MEMORY AND LEARNING: PHYSIOLOGICAL BASES). Early visual exposure during maturation and specific environmental conditions even in adulthood can affect the development and functioning of perceptual mechanisms. LTS

Bibliography

Boring, E.D. 1942: *Sensation and perception in the history of experimental psychology*. New York: Appleton-Century Crofts.

Braddick, O.J. and Atkinson, J. 1982: Higher functions in vision. In *The senses*, ed. H.B. Barlow and J.D. Mollon. Cambridge and New York: Cambridge University Press.

*Frisby, J. 1979: *Seeing*. Oxford and New York: Oxford University Press.

Gibson, J.J. 1966: *The senses considered as perceptual systems*. Boston: Houghton Mifflin.

*Gregory, R.L. 1970: *The intelligent eye*. London: Weidenfeld & Nicolson; New York: McGraw Hill.

Jung, R. 1973: Visual perception and neurophysiology. In *Handbook of sensory physiology*, ed. R. Jung. vol VII/3, Central processing of visual information, Part A. Heidelberg: Springer-Verlag.

*Held, R., Leibowitz, H.W. and Teuber, H.-L., eds. 1978: *Handbook of sensory physiology*, vol VIII, Perception. Heidelberg: Springer-Verlag.

——— and Richards, W., eds. 1972: *Perception: mechanisms and models* (Readings from Scientific American). San Francisco: W.H. Freeman.

vocational choice Generally used by laymen to mean either: the choice of a type of occupation, or the choice of a career, or both. Although the two terms are often used as synonyms, even by psychologists and sociologists, they have more precise meanings the use of which is favored by many specialists. An *occupation* is a group of similar jobs in which people perform essentially the same tasks, drawing on the same body of knowledge and using the same basic skills; the occupation exists independently of the person pursuing it. A *career* is the sequence of positions, jobs or occupations which a person has filled during the course of his or her life; these may differ considerably or they may all be in the same field with or without vertical movement. The term *vocation*, in the literature of the behavioral sciences, is used both to denote an occupation, and to characterize an occupation which has some of the personal meaning of career: it borrows from religious usage, signifying being called by something or someone greater than oneself to perform a given kind of work, but denotes a personal conviction that the occupation in question is most appropriate for oneself.

Historical Perspective. Although studies of vocational choice and services designed to help young people and adults in the making of such choices are now taken for granted, interest in these matters did not become institutionalized until just before the first world war when large numbers of young people were entering the workforce, and in some countries large numbers of immigrants needed to be assimilated. This led to the establishment of employment bureaux and vocational counseling services, with the emphasis on occupational and job choice, on the present and the immediate future – careers, the long term, were not the issue.

Approaches and Theories. This approach to vocational *choice* led to the first scientific work on what has since come to be seen as just one phase of vocational or career development (Super 1957). The rapid development of psychological tests for occupational selection and vocational guidance that resulted from their use during the first world war put assessment instruments and data for their interpretation in the hands of vocational counselors, who during the 1920s and 1930s became increasingly familiar with vocational psychology and, in countries such as France and the United States, trained in at least the most directly relevant aspects of psychology, sociology and economics.

This first scientific approach has become known as *Trait-and-Factor Theory* and is exemplified by books on aptitude and interest testing (e.g. Super and Crites 1962). It is also known as matching theory, for it consists of matching the abilities and interests of the client with those known to be typical of men and women in the occupations which are, or might be, of interest. This development of information concerning occupations led, when combined with older methods, to improved job descriptions, making possible such important manuals as the American *Dictionary of occupational titles* and *Occupational outlook handbook*, both revised periodically by the US Department of Labor and emulated in a number of other countries. The methods and materials of matching people and jobs proved very useful in the manpower shifts caused by the second world war and later by the return of military personnel and war-industry employees to civilian life.

But, with developments in the psychology of personality and of adulthood, a new approach, a new type of theory, came into being. Differential psychology, useful though it had proved as a theoretical basis for vocational choice, was found not to be enough. Ginzberg (1951) and Super (1953, 1957) studied the work of a group of Austrian psychologists which for the first time collected and organized data on the unfolding of careers, the emergence and changing of vocational choices, throughout the life span. Ginzberg entitled his book *Occupational choice* and focussed on development only until entry into the labor force; he and his colleagues viewed choice as the outcome of a developmental process beginning in early childhood. Super and his associates went further, considering the entire life span and viewing choices as evolving constantly with personal and social changes. This work led to many studies of the processes and outcomes of vocational or career development and to the emergence of a new body of theory (Hall 1976; Levinson 1978; Lowenthal 1975; Watts, Super and Kidd 1981).

Developmental Theory recognizes that, although much of a child's thinking about occupations and career is fantasy, it is based on personal needs such as that to explore, to be powerful and to be loved, and furthermore it leads to and results from identification with key persons who serve as role models. This is the basis for adolescent interest in occupations with preferences changing with experiences of success and failure, of praise and ridicule, and of acceptance or rejection by adult role models.

The tools of developmental theory have, in the nature of things, been neither so accessible, nor so practical as those of differential theory. The understanding of a person's development and of the kinds of continuities that may be seen in it, is obtained by means of time-consuming interviews, projective techniques and autobiographical essays, the interpretation of which is much more subjective, and therefore unreliable, than is that of standardized tests and inventories. Understanding the nature of possible future development is even more difficult, for not only is the client developing, but so is the society in which he or she functions.

It is these complexities, and their focus on society rather than on the person, that have led many sociologists, particularly in Great Britain, to develop *structural theories* of vocational choice. Impressed by the limits imposed upon choice by the accident of birth into a particular social class, by the relationship between the socioeconomic status of a child's parents on the one hand, and the amount and type of education, the employment opportunities, and the friends available to the child on the other, these sociologists tend to view the child and youth as placed at an early age on a conveyor belt which takes him or her inevitably toward an occupation like that of the parents. Roberts states that vocational counseling should aim, not at helping the individual to implement a conception of himself or herself as a worker, nor at helping a person to find an occupation really suited to his or her abilities and interests, but at assisting the individual to fit into the socially assigned niche.

The views of "opportunity structuralists" have been examined, and in the eyes of many vocational counselors and psychologists, refuted by writers such as Daws (in Watts, Super and Kidd 1981). Others such as Cherry (in Watts, Super and Kidd 1981) have adduced new and better data which show that individual differences are important, and that a significant number of young people do, by the time they are young adults, escape from the Procrustean bed of the structuralists and find their way into more "self-actualizing" occupations. Career development, we now know, is a long process and one in which both psychological and socioeconomic variables play a part.

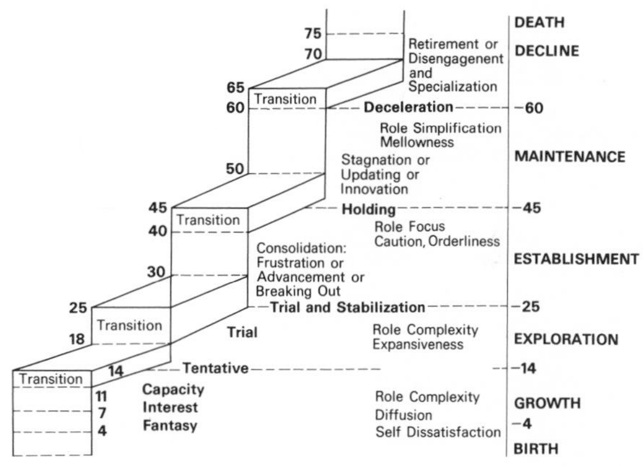

Life Stages and Sub-stages: A composite model

Life Span and Life Space. Central to the theory of career development are the concepts of life stages and developmental tasks, and those of life space and the roles that fill it. The diagram brings together notions of life stage theory as formulated by a number of the developmentalists cited, showing the major life stages of growth, exploration, establishment, maintenance and decline, together with their sub-stages and their role and personality characteristics, with the approximate ages of each stage and transition from one stage to the next. It is too often assumed that because the developmental tasks of exploration, establishment, etc. can be assigned approximate ages and because they follow in a sequence throughout the life cycle, the ages are biologically fixed and the stages must succeed each other in orderly and inevitable sequence. But most life stage theorists do not now take this point of view, for it has been shown that there are important individual differences in development, some maturing early and others late; and it has been shown that people recycle through the several stages of growth, exploration, establishment, maintenance and decline (there are minicycles within the maxicycle) as they make transitions from one stage or substage to another. Each new situation calls for exploration of its characteristics, which may lead to growth, which may in turn lead to a new establishment. Furthermore it is evident that the normal sequence of stages in the maxicycle is not inevitable, for some people virtually skip exploration as a result of what sometimes proves to be premature fixation or closure, and some keep on innovating, i.e. establishing, until well into what should chronologically be decline and skip that stage by dying at the peak or on the high plateau of their careers, well beyond the normal retirement age.

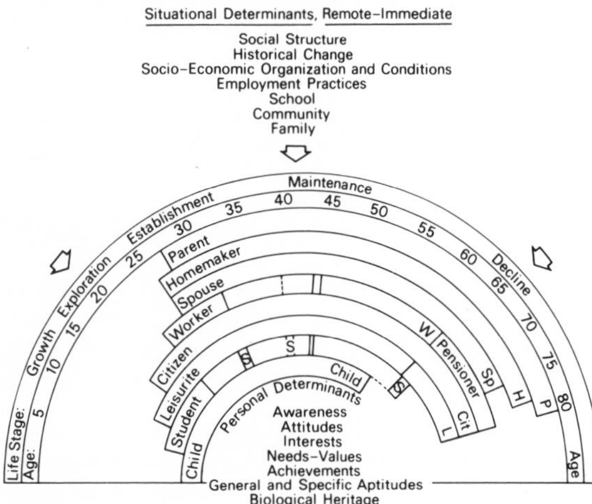

The Life-Career Rainbow: Nine life roles in schematic life space.

The concept of life space recognizes that the life course is made up of a number of roles, some played in sequence, others played simultaneously (Super 1980). A youth may be a child, a student, a pursuer of leisure activities and a citizen active in the community all at the same time, as in the case of the person whose career is depicted in the rainbow diagram. These roles were not all taken on at once, however, but appear in the life-career rainbow in sequence. (The roles of spouse and homemaker were taken on simultaneously in this career.) It is obvious that, when too many roles are engaged in, with time and emotional demands which may be excessive, role conflict results: each role has impact on the others. But the impact may also be positive, the role of part-time student enriching the worker role or the homemaking role, etc. One of the objectives of sound vocational guidance, or well-rounded career education, is to help people to view their roles as a changing constellation, some of which provide outlets for some abilities and values and meet some needs, while others are better suited to other abilities, interests, and needs.

Vocational Guidance and Counseling. Helping young people and adults to make vocational choices has long been a function of educational institutions, social service agencies and employment services. Although the location and nature of the services, and the training of the personnel performing them, varies somewhat from country to country it is to those institutions and ministries that the public should turn for information and counseling. Universities often offer courses taking one or two years, sometimes four, to complete: in Great Britain they are called counseling or careers advisory courses (for school counselors or careers officers); in the USA and Canada they are usually called either counseling or counseling psychology courses. Sources of information are the British Association for Counselling, the British Psychological Society, the American Personnel and Guidance Association, the American Psychological Association, the Canadian Association for Guidance and Counselling, the Canadian Psychological Society, and similar associations in other countries. See also LIFE-SPAN PSYCHOLOGY. DES

Bibliography

Ginzberg, E. *et al.* 1951: *Occupational choice.* New York: Columbia University Press.

Hall, D. T. 1976: *Careers in organizations.* Pacific Palisades, Calif.: Goodyear Publishing Co.

Levinson, D. J. 1978: *The seasons of a man's life.* New York: Ballantine.

Lowenthal, M. F. 1975: *Four stages of life.* San Francisco: Jossey-Bass.

Super, D. E. 1953: A theory of vocational development. *American psychologist* 8, 185–90.

——— 1957: *The psychology of careers.* New York: Harper.

——— 1980: A life-span, life-space, approach to career development. *Journal of vocational behavior* 13, 282–98.

——— and Crites, J. O. 1962: *Appraising vocational fitness.* New York: Harper.

Watts, A. G., Super, D. E. and Kidd, J. M. 1981: *Career development in Britain.* Cambridge: Hobson's Press.

volition A private mental act which, in traditional action theory, was thought to precede all voluntary acts, and to be that whose presence distinguished voluntary from involuntary acts. This tidy answer to the ancient question of that distinction has run, in more recent times, into a number of troubles. For one thing many voluntary acts do not seem to be preceded by such private volitions; if they are postulated in such cases nonetheless, then volitions, the quintessentially voluntary acts, may sometimes be acts we do not know we are doing. Another trouble is that many acts seem neither voluntary nor involuntary – steps taken in walking or running, for example, or abstractedly braking a car at a red light: how can these fit the volition analysis? Thirdly, are volitions themselves voluntary or involuntary acts? If voluntary, must they be preceded by further volitions, and so ad infinitum? Philosophy now regards the voluntary and involuntary as a highly complex conceptual terrain, not likely to be analysable with so simple a device as volitions. See also INTENTIONAL ACTION. JT

Bibliography

Ryle, Gilbert, 1949: *The concept of mind.* London: Hutchinson; Totowa, N.J: Barnes & Noble (1975).

Vesey, G.N.A. 1961: Volition. *Philosophy* 36, 352–65.

voluntarism (from the Latin *voluntas* = will) A theory of behavior in which a presumption of wilful action is being made. In philosophical discourse voluntarism is opposed to rationalism, which places human reason over the presumably less measured, more spontaneous actions of voluntarism. In psychology, voluntarism is usually opposed to mechanistic theories which explain behavior without positing willed actions in the human being. Voluntarism is therefore a teleological theory with the added suggestion carried over from philosophical precedents that ends (purposes, intentions) are framed spontaneously (i.e. emotively, intuitively) rather than calculatingly or rationally. There is often the suggestion in voluntaristic theory that a complete psychology of the person is impossible owing to the inscrutable and subjective nature of human experience. (See also MECHANISTIC THEORY, PURPOSIVISM.) JFR

voluntary behavior Behavior in which the subject is, to some extent, a free agent. Some behavioral scientists believe that voluntary behavior is the product of a free will, but others take a more deterministic attitude. Many psychologists equate voluntary behavior with operant behavior that is produced in order to attain some GOAL. Physiologists regard it as being the product of the somatic nervous system, in contrast to the autonomic activity which is reflex and involuntary. The somatic nervous system supplies the striated skeletal muscles responsible for the movement of limbs, etc.

Although the major part of overt behavior is controlled through the somatic nervous system, it is by no means all voluntary. Examples of involuntary somatic reflexes are the startle response and the orienting response. Other involuntary reflexes may be the result of conditioning. Voluntary behavior does not include automatic responses to a situation, but scientists disagree as to whether observed behavior, however apparently voluntary, is always an inevitable consequence of the stimulus situation and the animal's internal state (see MOTIVATION, ANIMAL; OPERANT CONDITIONING). DJM

von Frisch, Karl Born in Vienna in 1886 and educated in the Universities of Vienna and Munich. He has been Professor in Zoology at a number of universities, notably Munich. Initially working in fish biology, his interest in color changes in fish led him to research in color vision, especially in lower organisms. His researches on the sensory physiology of honey-bees were facilitated by his discovering how to train bees to forage at artificial feeding stations. It became clear that odor information could be passed to other bees by foragers returning to the hive. Later, von Frisch concluded that returning foragers use a "dance language" to communicate the distance and direction of the food source, by means of the speed and orientation of the dance (see COMMUNICATION: ANIMAL). This work in particular (von Frisch 1967) raised profound issues about the nature of symbolic communication, although criticisms and re-interpretations have not been lacking (e.g. Rosin 1980). It led to his sharing the Nobel Prize for Physiology or Medicine in 1973 with Lorenz and Tinbergen. PKS

Bibliography

von Frisch, K. 1967: *The dance language and orientation of bees.* Cambridge, Mass.: Harvard University Press.

Rosin, R. 1980: Paradoxes of the honey-bee "dance language" hypothesis. *Journal of theoretical biology*, 84, 775–800.

W

Watson, John Broadus (1878–1958). The founder of the psychological school known as BEHAVIORISM. This doctrine was first stated in Watson's classic paper "Psychology as the behaviorist views it" (1913) and developed during a relatively short academic career. Watson's own words from this paper best summarize his position and also illustrate the vigor with which he set out the new psychology.

> "Psychology as the behaviorist views it is a purely objective branch of natural science. Its theoretical goal is the prediction and control of behavior. Introspection forms no essential part of its methods, nor is the scientific value of its data dependent upon the readiness with which they lend themselves to interpretation in terms of consciousness. The behaviorist, in his efforts to get a unitary scheme of animal response recognises no dividing line between man and brute. The behavior of man, with all of its refinement and complexity, forms only a part of the behaviorist's total scheme of investigation."

This captures the essence of Watson's new departure: psychology as a natural science, of the continuity in nature and the form of study of animal and man, and antimentalism (opposition to the belief that understanding mental events is central to understanding behavior). One further element present in his scheme was reductionism, the doctrine that human behavior is ultimately explicable in terms of physiology. In this respect Watson's thinking was more subtle than that of some of his followers. He warned that though it may be taken for granted that the organism is a machine, "the machine should not be made too simple for the multitudinous demands" that the behaviorist's findings require.

Watson was born in Greenville, South Carolina and entered the town's Baptist University, Furman, at the age of fifteen. In 1900 he joined the psychology department of Chicago University to read for his doctorate. He graduated as the university's youngest ever PhD in 1903 and his thesis was published in the same year. Watson's early work bore some of the hallmarks of his later doctrine: close observation and an absence of anthropomorphism. During his stay at Chicago, where he was appointed instructor, he worked feverishly both on his research and to support himself. He was plagued by a shortage of money for much of his academic life. During this period he began to win public recognition and started to edit the *Psychological Bulletin*. In 1908, at the age of twenty-nine he was appointed Professor of Psychology at Johns Hopkins University. In 1910 he published an article in *Harpers* in which he argued for a "new science of animal behavior", using only observation and experiment and refraining from absurd speculations on animal consciousness.

The turning point in Watson's career and, indeed, in academic psychology came in 1913. In a series of lectures at Columbia University he delivered the lecture which was published as "Psychology as the behaviorist views it" and was in effect a manifesto for the new science.

Watson was reacting against not only the introspectionism of Tichener and Wundt but also the dominant school of animal psychology, functionalism. This Watson considered to be anthropomorphic and therefore unscientific. He wanted to end the distinction between animal and human psychology and place them both in the evolutionary tradition of Darwinian biology.

Watson regarded behavior as the product of the interplay of heredity and environment. The task of psychology is to determine what is instinctive and what is learned. (The extreme environmentalism for which he became notorious was expounded in his later popular articles).

Watson's book *Psychology from the standpoint of a behaviorist* (1919) further elaborated the behaviorist program. In it he reported his observations of children and attempted to show how behaviorism could deal with the most diverse and complex human actions.

In 1920 Watson divorced his wife in favor of a student many years his junior. The scandal caused by this forced him to resign his chair and he never returned to an academic post. He took up a second career with the advertising agency J. Walter Thompson where he made a considerable contribution to the developing business of advertising, rendering it much more psychological in character. During the 1920s Watson became a great popularizer of psychology and *The psychological care of infant and child* (1928) became a best seller. Two years later he produced a revised edition of "Behaviorism". Among the revisions was the adoption of a more strongly environmentalist position, judging conditioning to be more important than heredity.

After his wife's death in 1936 Watson gradually withdrew from active life and retired in 1947. He was treated with hostility, derision and indifference by many of his academic contemporaries for much of his career, but in 1957, the year before he died, the American Psychological Association honored its pasts Presidents, including Watson. Its tribute to him remains an apt summary

> To John B. Watson, whose work has been one of the vital determinants of the form and substance of modern psychology. He initiated a revolution in psychological thought and his writings have been the point of departure for continuing lines of fruitful research. APO

Bibliography

Cohen, D.: 1979: *J.B. Watson: the founder of behaviourism*. London and Boston: Routledge & Kegan Paul.

Larson, C.A., Harris, B. and Semelson, F. 1981: On the other hand. *Contemporary psychology* 26, 62–4.

Watson, J.B. 1913: Psychology as the behaviorist views it. *Psychological bulletin*.

——— 1919: *Psychology from the standpoint of a behaviorist*. 1st edn. Philadelphia: Lippincott.

——— 1930: *Behaviorism*. Rev. edn. New York: Harpers.

Wechsler scales Tests of general intelligence devised by David Wechsler for individual assessment. There are three scales: the Wechsler Adult Intelligence Scale – Revised (WAIS–R) for use with people aged 16 to 74 years; the Wechsler Intelligence Scale for Children – Revised (WISC–R), age range 6 to 16 years 11 months; and the Wechsler Preschool and Primary School Scale of Intelligence (WPPSI), age range 4 to 6 years 6 months.

The basic element of each scale is an item, a question or task, such as "Who invented the jet engine?", "What important part is missing in the picture?", "Put this jig-saw together as quickly as you can". Each item is scored as correct or incorrect. For some items, extra points are added according to the degree of generality of the answer and the speed with which a correct solution is provided.

Items sampling a particular area of intelligence, such as numerical skills, word knowledge, reasoning, are grouped into a sub-test (collection of homogenous items), and presented in ascending order of difficulty. Administration of the sub-test is discontinued after a pre-determined number of failures. Several sub-tests are grouped together to form a *sub-scale*. This is done partly for theoretical reasons and in part because of empirical evidence that, despite their specific characteristics and the special information or skill required for correct solution, they also appear to tap a higher level of organization of intellect. The Wechsler Scales have two sub-scales, the Verbal and the Performance. The former indexes the more general verbal ability of the testee (the ability to record, manipulate and reproduce language-related information), indexed by the Verbal Scale IQ. The Performance Scale IQ provides a measure of the ability to manipulate visual–spatial relationships. Although the sub-scales provide separate IQ's, the abilities which contribute to each overlap.

The WAIS–R has six sub-tests in the Verbal Scale, five of which are used to compute the IQ. The Performance Scale has five sub-tests. The WISC–R has six sub-tests in each sub-scale, five from each being used to compute the respective IQ's. The WPPSI has 10 sub-tests, five for each sub-scale, and two supplementary sub-tests.

All the Wechsler Scales enable the computation of the Full Scale IQ, a measure of general intelligence. Like all tests of intelligence, the choice of items, their organization within the scale and their scoring reflect the test originator's underlying model of the organization of human abilities (see TESTS, INTELLIGENCE; INTELLIGENCE QUOTIENT).

Specific items in the sub-tests reflect the age group for which the particular scale is intended, with some overlap of content to enable continuous coverage of the age-spectrum. Each scale has the same basic structure, and most of the sub-tests have common titles across the three scales. All three are standardized tests, with NORMS derived from the USA population. None of the current versions have UK norms but the test manuals have been modified to take account of cultural differences between the two countries.

Score levels on single sub-tests, or differences between scores on several sub-tests, or between the Verbal and Performance Scale IQ's are sometimes used for differential diagnosis of cognitive dysfunctions or psychological disturbance. This is a complex task for reasons to do with intricacies of the theory and practice of psychological measurement. Conclusions from such exercises in diagnostic testing are more often than not of dubious validity. See Kaufman (1979) and Sattler (1974) for more detailed discussion of the WPPSI and WISC–R and their use in assessment of intelligence, and Anastasi (1982) for a more detailed description of the three scales. MBe

Bibliography

Anastasi, A. 1982: *Psychological testing, 5th edn.* New York: Macmillan.

Kaufman, A.S. 1979: *Intelligence testing with the WISC–R.* New York: John Wiley

Sattler, J.M. 1974: *Assessment of children's intelligence.* Philadephia: W. B. Saunders.

Wernicke's syndrome (or Wernicke's encephalopathy) An acute neurological disorder described by Wernicke in 1881. Its main features are impaired consciousness, disorientation, ataxia (uncoordinated bodily movements) and ophthalmoplegia (paralysis of eye movements). As Wernicke demonstrated, post mortem examination of the brain reveals hemorrhagic lesions in the gray matter around the third and fourth ventricles and the aqueduct. The condition sometimes occurs after many years of alcohol abuse, and is often followed by KORSAKOV'S SYNDROME. DG

Whorf, Benjamin Lee (1897–1941). Studied chemistry at the Massachusetts Institute of Technology and worked in the chemical and insurance industries for most of his life. Whorf became a student of the famous anthropologist and linguist Edward Sapir, and lecturer in anthropology at Yale University in 1937.

Whorf is best known for his views on the relationship between language and thought. According to the Sapir-Whorf hypothesis of linguistic relativity, people are not led to the same picture of reality unless their language backgrounds are the same. This view was acceptable in the structuralist period of linguistics but is in direct conflict with universalist views, such as those held by Chomsky (see CHOMSKY; LANGUAGE ACQUISITION DEVICE).

Evidence which could either confirm or disconfirm Whorf's claims is still very limited. Tests carried out by Carrol and Casagrande (1958) indicate that grammar can influence behavior under certain conditions. Recent developments in Whorfian linguistics are discussed in Pinxten (ed. 1976). PM

Bibliography

Carrol, John B. and Casagrande, Joseph B. 1958: The function of language classification in behavior. In *Readings in social psychology* ed. E.E. Maccoby et al. New York: Holt, Rinehart & Winston.

Pinxten, Rik, ed. 1976: *Universalism versus relativism in language and thought.* The Hague and Paris: Mouton.

Whorf, Benjamin L. 1956: *Language, thought and reality.* Cambridge, Mass.: MIT Press.

will In traditional psychology, the faculty which produces voluntary actions. Anatomists regularly characterize the body's muscles as subject to the will, e.g. finger muscles, or as not subject to the will, e.g. the muscles of the heart. The distinction is straightforward enough, and answers our experience. But the difficulty begins when one tries to say what being subject to the will amounts to. A physiologist may approximate the distinction by thinking of it as that between muscles controlled by reflex arcs and those controlled by "higher centers" of the brain, though this dichotomy – clear enough as far as it goes – soon blurs. But a psychologist or philosopher who tries to analyse will as a concept belonging to the apparatus of psychology will have a harder time. He might suggest that for a muscular action to be produced by the will is for it to be performed knowingly; but this is an inadequate criterion, for many unwilled muscular actions occur with the subject's knowledge – e.g. the chattering of teeth. One might then suggest that the mark of the willed muscular action is that it is *preceded* by knowledge that it will happen. But this won't do either, for a sneeze is preceded by the knowledge that it will happen, but is not willed. Again, one might suggest that the willed muscular action effects a desire; and while that may be true it is not what *makes* the action willed, for a sneeze is not willed but it effects a desire. The failure of these and like attempts led psychologists to regard the will as a faculty irreducible to those of knowledge or appetite. But the concept of will is unsatisfactorily obscure. In some versions the will produced only VOLITIONS; in others it could directly produce any BASIC ACT. Will is prima facie a problem for MATERIALISM, and some of the most telling arguments against it have been elaborated in defense of that position. In the above we have spoken only of muscular actions; matters are much more complex if the scope is widened to include all INTENTIONAL ACTION. The question of the existence of will is often not distinguished from that of free will, though it should be; the matter of akrasia, weakness of will, shows a very different aspect of this concept. JT

Bibliography

Horsburgh, H.J.N. 1956: Freedom and real will theories. *Australian journal of philosophy* 34, 92–105.

James, William 1890 (*1950*): *Principles of psychology.* New York: Dover.

Mackay, D.M. 1957: Brain and will. *The Listener* 57, 745–6, 788–9.

Ryle, Gilbert. 1949: *The concept of mind.* London: Hutchinson; Totowa, N.J.: Barnes & Noble

Wittgenstein, Ludwig 1953: *Philosophical investigations.* Trans. G.E.M. Anscombe. Oxford; Basil Blackwell: New York: Macmillan.

Wittgenstein, Ludwig Josef Johann (1889–1951) Wittgenstein was preoccupied in most of his work by the character of certain central psychological concepts (such as sensation, intention, explanation, hope) and with the question whether certain concepts commonly assumed by philosophers to be psychological (meaning, understanding, belief, certainty, for example) are really so. His discussions of these issues are of great importance for our understanding of the nature and limits of psychology. Nevertheless Wittgenstein's contribution to this subject will not be properly grasped unless it is realized that his interest in it was not typically that of a psychologist, or even that of a philosopher of psychology.

The questions which mainly concerned Wittgenstein were about the nature of language, about the relation of logic to language, and about the application of both logic and language to "the world". His reflections on these questions first ran into difficulties engendered by the peculiarities of (apparently) psychological concepts in his early work *Tractatus Logico-Philosophicus*, where he had developed an account of language resting on a distinction between "elementary" and "non-elementary" propositions. The sense of elementary propositions consisted in their capability of being either true or false – truth and falsity being regarded here as involving a relation between the proposition and a "state of affairs". Non-elementary propositions, on the other hand, were constructed by way of simple logical operations applied to elementary propositions and their truth or falsity depended in determinate ("truth-functional") ways on the truth and falsity of the elementary propositions from which they were constructed.

However it was not clear how this account could apply to propositions such as "John believes that it is raining". This does not appear to be elementary, in that the proposition "it is raining" occurs in it as a constituent. But neither is it in any obvious way related to its constituents "truth-functionally" (in the sense sketched in the previous paragraph): the truth or falsity of "John believes that it is raining" seems logically independent of the truth or falsity of "it is raining".

For Wittgenstein an acceptable account of belief or judgment would have to "show that it is impossible for a judgment to be a piece of nonsense" (1922, § 5.5422); and he thought that this requirement was not met by any account of belief, etc as a relation between a conscious subject and certain other elements, concluding that "there is no such thing as the soul – the subject, etc – as it is conceived in the superficial psychology of the present day" (ibid. § 5.5421).

Though Wittgenstein's approach to these questions underwent radical change in his later writings the issues that continued to exercise him in the philosophy of psychology flowed from similar preoccupations with logical questions. This continuity is evident, for example, in the close connection between his discussion of belief in the *Tractatus* and his interest in the paradox expounded by G.E. Moore. (See 1953, part II, sect. x.) The paradox is that whereas the sentence "John believes that it is raining but it isn't" seems to be in perfect logical order, the sentence "I believe that it is raining but it isn't" does not. And yet if believing that it is raining is a (psychological) state of affairs quite distinct from the state of the weather, it is hard to see how this second sentence can be contradictory, as it seems to be.

Wittgenstein's treatment of "Moore's Paradox" in his later writings is typical of his approach to other questions in the philosophy of psychology. He questions whether it really is adequate to regard sentences of the form "I believe that ..." as expressing a perfectly definite psychological state of affairs. This was of course to reject the whole account of language, as articulated in the *Tractatus*, as composed of propositions clearly expressing absolutely determinate states of affairs. In line with this general re-alignment of his views about language, Wittgenstein vigorously questioned the highly tempting – and not the less so for being usually unspoken – assumption that the terms in which human beings characteristically express and discuss their mental life are names or descriptions of distinct psychological processes.

This trend in Wittgenstein's thinking has led to a widespread conviction that he was a "behaviorist". Nothing, however, could be further from the truth. On Wittgenstein's view, behaviorists – who believe that psychological concepts are descriptive of bodily processes of one sort or another – commit precisely the same mistake at a fundamental level as do those who interpret psychological concepts as descriptive of processes, or states in some non-physical medium. The following remarks are quite explicit about this.

> How does the philosophical problem about mental processes and states and about behaviorism arise? – The first step is the one that altogether escapes notice. We talk of processes and states and leave their nature undecided. Sometimes perhaps we shall know more about them – we think. But that is just what commits us to a particular way of looking at the matter. For we have a definite concept of what it means to learn to know a process better. (The decisive movement in the conjuring trick has been made, and it was the very one we thought quite innocent.) – And now the analogy which was to make us understand our thoughts falls to pieces. So we have to deny the yet uncomprehended process in the yet unexplained medium. And now it looks as if we had denied mental processes. And naturally we don't want to deny them. (1953, pt I, § 308).

This important passage shows how careful one needs to be in interpreting Wittgenstein's position. He certainly does not reject as improper any talk of mental "states" or "processes". He does, however, try to show that, if our aim is the philosophical one of clarifying what, say, belief, hope, expectation, pain are, we shall get into trouble if we assume that this must be a matter of explaining the nature of certain states or processes; because the concepts in question have other uses where they function quite differently from the way in which names of states or processes function, and these other uses, moreover, are presupposed by those uses in which the concepts are plausibly regarded as referring to states or processes. For example, to say of someone in the third person "He believes that so and so" may in some circumstances be acceptably characterized as ascribing psychological states to him. But, as "Moore's Paradox" brings out, there are severe logical objections to characterizing the first person use "I believe that so and so" in this way. Yet the sense of the third person use would be considerably impoverished did the first person use not exist alongside it. This is evident, for instance, in the very restricted use we have for speaking of the beliefs of animals – which do not have the capacity for expressing beliefs in the first person.

Points like this underlie the remark with which Wittgenstein concludes his posthumously published book *Philosophical investigations*, about the "confusion and barrenness of psychology", which he takes to spring from the "conceptual confusion" which underlies its experimental methods, as a result of which "problem and method pass one another by" (1953, pt II, § xiv). PGW

Bibliography

Wittgenstein, Ludwig 1922: *Tractatus Logico-Philosophicus*. (*1961*) London: Routledge & Kegan Paul; New York: Humanities Press.

——— 1953: *Philosophical investigations*. Oxford: Basil Blackwell; New York: Macmillan.

——— 1980: *Remarks on the philosophy of psychology*. 2 vols. Oxford: Basil Blackwell; Chicago: University of Chicago Press.

word association test A word association test (WAT) is elegantly simple: provide someone with a stimulus word, and ask for the first word that comes to mind. For example, say "table", and the response may well be "chair". Psychologists examine the nature and probabilities of response words, and sometimes how long it takes for a response. Word associations reveal people's verbal habits, the structure of their verbal memory, thought processes, and occasionally even emotional states and personality. They can be used both to understand individual people and to study the structure of language itself.

Response patterns. The father of WAT was the British scientist Galton, who in the nineteenth century tested one subject, himself. In a less personal WAT in 1901 the German linguist-psychologist team Thumb and Marbe used eight subjects and sixty stimulus words. They found the following response trends, which have also been found in many subsequent WATs.

Words of one type evoked a response of the same type: e.g., "brother" led to "sister"; a noun led to another noun.

More common responses occurred more rapidly than less common ones: e.g., to "table", the most frequent response "chair" might occur within 1.3 sec; the next most frequent "furniture", within 1.6 sec; the third "eat", within 2 sec, and so on.

A given stimulus word often elicited an identical response from different subjects.

In the first large scale WAT, Kent and Rosanoff (1910) tested 1,000 subjects' responses to 100 stimulus words, establishing a set of norms for future WATs. Between 1910 and 1954, there was an increase in primary (the most frequently given) responses. For example, to "table", the primary response "chair" was given by 26.7% in 1910; 33.8% in 1928; and 84.0% in 1954. Idiosyncratic responses (such as "mensa", which was given to "table" by 1 out of 1,008 subjects) became rarer. These trends may be due to the influence of mass media, to advertising, and to the standardization of school instruction. We are in the "group-think" age.

Response patterns of various groups of people differ. Among speakers of three kindred languages – American-English, German, and French, primary responses are similar, but the American group tend to react much more uniformly to a stimulus word than do the German and French groups.

Between men and women, response times tend to be faster for men (1.3 sec for educated, 1.8 for uneducated) than for women (1.7 sec for educated, 2.2 for uneducated) (Jung 1918). Males tend to respond with antonyms and females with synonyms (Goodenough 1946). At every age female subjects may be characterized as stereotyped: compared to males, females give fewer different responses to each stimulus, and are more likely to give one of the four most frequent responses.

Conformity-minded people or people who are exposed to uniform mass media are likely to show more common responses, or less richness. All groups may be moving toward giving more common responses over the years.

Adults vs. children. The character of WAT responses changes with age. The table compares how often four US age groups gave the primary response (for the age group) to nine Kent-Rosanoff words, chosen because they elicited large (65% or more) primary responses in adults.

Comparison of Primary Responses by Four Age Groups

Stimulus	*Response*	*Adult*	*Grade V*	*Grade I*	*Kindergarten*
bitter	sweet	65.2	24.2 (sour)	6.8 (butter)	5.0 (better)
black	white	75.1	36.2 (dark)	12.1	6.5 (crayon)
dark	light	82.9	40.4	30.4	13.5 (night)
hard	soft	67.4	34.2	19.6	8.0 (rock)
high	low	67.5	46.4	21.8	8.5
long	short	75.8	47.0	20.0	8.0 (grass)
man	woman	76.7	18.8	12.9	9.5
slow	fast	75.2	51.6	35.7	18.0
table	chair	84.0	39.2	36.1	32.0

(Children's responses that differ from those of adults are given in parentheses.) Data of adults from Russell and Jenkins, 1954; of Grade V from Palermo and Jenkins, 1964 of Grade I and Kindergarten from Entwisle 1966).

The table reveals the following trends:

(1) Primary responses are more probable for adults than for children.

(2) In adults, all adjective stimuli elicited adjective antonyms. According to Deese (1965), contrast is the basic association pattern for adjectives. He notes that dictionaries often define an adjective by giving its opposite.

(3) At age 10 some stimuli and responses are from the

same word class but are synonyms rather than antonyms ("bitter-sour" and "dark-black").

(4) At age 6 the stimulus and response are from different word classes, and are related in sound but not in meaning ("bitter-butter"). Children are responding to superficial, phonetic aspect of words.

(5) At kindergarten (age 5), in "bitter-better", the stimulus and the response are from the same word class (perhaps fortuitously), but are related in sound rather than in meaning. In "black-crayon", "dark-night", "hard-rock" and "long-grass", the stimulus and the response are from different word classes, but are likely word sequences in running speech.

Adults typically respond to a noun with another noun, to an adjective with another adjective; they give *paradigmatic* responses. Children, by contrast, respond to an adjective (black) with a noun (crayon) that follows the stimulus in a sentence; they give syntagmatic responses.

The shift from syntagmatic to paradigmatic occurs between ages five and nine. Between 1916 and 1961, paradigmatic responses among school children increased for both nouns and adjectives by 10 per cent or more. And paradigmatic responding was associated with increased use of contrasts. Both effects may be related to test-taking practice and linguistic sophistication through mass-media.

Diagnostic use of WAT.
WATs can reveal a person's emotional state. The noted Swiss psychoanalyst Jung (*1918*) pioneered the use of word association in clinical diagnosis. He used emotionally loaded words to probe into patients' repressed images, wishes, or emotions. Both the time it takes for a person to produce a response word and the type of response word are supposed to reflect the emotional state. For example, a thirty-seven year old female teacher, single, came to him with a severe case of insomnia. She responded with an unusual word "home-sick" to the stimulus "foreign", taking 14.8 sec (compared to normal people's 2 sec in responding to neutral words). In a subsequent interview, she revealed her love affair with a foreigner who left her without saying good-bye.

Generally, people who give a large number of unusual responses are considered to have some form of mental disturbance. Goodenough (1946) reports that single and divorced women, compared to married women, give many unusual responses.

In earlier times, schizophrenics were believed to have unusual and "unlogical" associations, remote associations and clang associations (or rhymes). Modern word association tests show that schizophrenics have intact associative structure, though they tend to have longer response times, fewer common responses, and more repetitions, than do normals (Mefford 1979).

Rapaport and his associates at the Menninger Clinic developed a diagnostic WAT, containing sixty stimulus words, of which twenty are such "traumatic" words as "love, breast, suicide, masturbate, bite", and the rest are such neutral words as "hat, chair, man, city". Here is one illustrative case. A thirty-two year old surgeon, married and childless, with severe anxiety, responded to "breast" with "mammary gland", taking an extraordinarily long time of 4 min 5 sec. The diagnostician's comment on this response was "neurotic intellectualizing" (Rapaport, Gill and Schafer 1946). Out of sixty stimulus words twelve elicited responses requiring specific comments.

Shiomi (1979) in Japan used the words of Rapaport, et al. to study personality of normal people. For male adults response times of extroverts to "traumatic" words were shorter than those of introverts. According to Shiomi, introverts defend themselves against responding to traumatic words whereas extroverts do not.

Goodenough (1946) used WATs to test leadership among a large number of women in the US Army. The proportion of active verbs (e.g., "fish", rather than "fishing" to "rod") among the responses given by officer candidates was many times greater than by the enlisted women.

In a WAT a person is free to respond, free to reveal, unconsciously, aspects of his or her inner life. IT

Bibliography

Deese, J. 1965: *The structure of associations in language and thought*. Baltimore: Johns Hopkins University Press.

Entwisle, D. 1966: *Word associations of young children*. Baltimore: Johns Hopkins University Press.

Goodenough, F.L. 1946: Semantic choice and personality structure. *Science* 104, 451–6.

Jung, C.G. *1918: Studies in word- association*. London: W. Heinemann.

Kent, H.G. and Rosanoff, A.J. 1910: A study of association in insanity. *American journal of insanity*. 67, 37–96.

Mefford, R.B.Jr. 1979: Word association: capacity of chronic schizophrenics to follow formal semantic, syntactic, and instructional rules. *Psychological reports* 45, 431–42.

Palermo, D.S. and Jenkins, J.J. 1964: *Word association norms. Grade school through college*. Minneapolis: University of Minesota Press.

Rapaport, D., Gill, M. and Schafer, R. 1946: *Diagnostic psychological testing*. Chicago: Yearbook Publications.

Russell, W.A. and Jenkins, J.J. 1954: *The complete Minnesota norms for responses to 100 words from the Kent- Rosanoff word association test*. Minneapolis: Technical Report No. 11, 1954.

Shiomi, K. 1979: Differences in RTs of extraverts and introverts to Rapaport's word association test. *Psychological reports*, 45, 75–80.

work attitudes The sub-set of attitudes which are directed to paid employment. Principal types of work attitudes are job satisfaction, alienation, organizational commitment, job and work involvement, and job motivation (Cook et al. 1981).

Job satisfaction was the first of these to be investigated (in the 1930s), and is now viewed in terms either of overall job satisfaction or of specific job satisfaction (e.g. Smith, Kendall and Hulin 1969; Locke 1976). In the former case an overall attitude to the job is measured in respect of both direction and intensity, in the latter attitudes towards specific job features are tapped. Most commonly studied are satisfaction with the boss, pay, colleagues, promotion prospects, the actual work undertaken, and the organization in general. Specific satisfactions are usually found to be significantly intercorrelated, contributing to overall satisfaction, but they are differentially responsive to job and organizational characteristics. Specific satisfactions are sometimes grouped together in respect of intrinsic and extrinsic job satisfaction (see TWO-FACTOR THEORY). "Intrinsic job satisfaction" refers to attitudes towards features of work content: amount of responsibility granted to the person, freedom to choose his or her own method of working, recognition for good work, opportunity to use abilities, etc. (see WORK REDESIGN). "Extrinsic job satisfaction" refers to attitudes towards features of the work context: physical work conditions, colleagues, pay, boss, hours of work.

Alienation is a second work attitude, often viewed in terms of an employee's sense of powerlessness and isolation, and a feeling that his or her job has no meaning or personal value. In many respects alienation is similar to very low job satisfaction. Research has usually failed to reveal widespread alienation from work, although specific attitudes to unattractive or demeaning jobs are of course typically negative.

A third important work attitude is organizational commitment. This is a general attitude towards the organization, rather than a reaction to a particular job. High organizational commitment is defined in terms of three factors: a strong belief in, and acceptance of, the organization's goals and values; a readiness to exert considerable effort on behalf of the organization; and a strong desire to remain a member of the organization (Mowday, Porter and Steers 1982). Longer-tenure employees usually exhibit greater organizational commitment, sometimes to the extent of being psychologically "locked in" to their place of employment.

Job involvement has also been widely studied as a person's attachment to his or her present job. That is to be distinguished from a more general "work involvement", the personal salience of having paid employment. Recognizing that "work" has several meanings in addition to that of a paid job (it is present in housework and voluntary work, for example), it has recently become more usual to refer to "employment commitment" rather than to work involvement. Such an attitude strongly mediates the negative impact of being unemployed; those unemployed people with high employment commitment have higher scores on measures of psychological distress than do those with low employment commitment (Warr 1983).

Job motivation, the willingness to expend effort in the attainment of job goals, has been viewed in terms of intrinsic and extrinsic components. Intrinsic motivation is defined in terms of the expenditure of effort to achieve intrinsic satisfaction, through enhanced self-esteem, satisfaction with work quantity and quality, etc. Extrinsic motivation is that driven by rewards in terms of money or other non-intrinsic gains (see WORK MOTIVATION.)

Work attitudes of these kinds are often measured through standardized questionnaires, of tested reliability and validity. Positive work attitudes are widely held to be desirable on two counts. First, paid employment is a major feature of most people's lives and it is important to strive for personally satisfying jobs which enhance self-esteem. Research has thus sought to reduce WORK STRESS and to improve the quality of working life as a goal in its own right. Work attitudes are often measured as part of ORGANIZATION DEVELOPMENT projects, in which attempts are made to alter behavior and the structure of organizations for the benefit of their members.

A second basis for interest in work attitudes is the notion that more positive attitudes will be reflected in improved work quantity or quality. This is to be expected in respect of motivation, but the link between other attitudes and work behavior is more tenuous. For example, level of overall job satisfaction is not in general significantly associated with level of personal work performance. Current thinking is that work attitudes and behavior are intercorrelated only in specific conditions (see e.g. Warr 1978). For example, there must be personal freedom of choice about behavior, ability levels must be high enough to permit raised performance levels, and social pressures from work colleagues should not be so strong that they have greater influence upon individual behavior than do more direct work attitudes. In general, then, the latter are on their own often poor predictors of work performance. This is also true in respect of ABSENTEEISM, where attendance at work is often found to be strongly influenced by family commitments, transport arrangements, and workgroup norms about what is a tolerable number of absences in the course of a year (Chadwick-Jones, Nicholson and Brown 1982). PBW

Bibliography

Chadwick-Jones, J.K., Nicholson, N. and Brown, C. 1982: *Social psychology of absenteeism*. New York: Praeger.

Cook, J.D. et al. 1981: *The experience of work: a compendium and review of 249 measures and their use*. London: Academic Press.

Locke, E.A. 1976: The nature and causes of job satisfaction. In *Handbook of industrial and organizational psychology*, ed. M.D. Dunnette. Chicago: Rand McNally.

Mowday, R.T., Porter, L.W. and Steers, R.M. 1982: *Employee-organization linkages: the psychology of commitment, absenteeism and turnover*. New York: Academic Press.

Smith, P.C., Kendall, L.M. and Hulin, C.L. 1969: *The measurement of satisfaction in work and retirement*. Chicago: Rand McNally.

Warr, P.B., ed. 1978: *Psychology at work* 2nd edn. Harmondsworth: Penguin.

——— 1983: Job loss, unemployment and psychological well-being. In *Role transitions*, ed. E. van de Vliert and V. Allen. New York: Plenum Press.

work ethic Originally known as the Protestant ethic, this is the view that hard work and career progress are moral virtues in themselves, independent of any practical results. In the early part of this century the German sociologist Max Weber put forward the idea that the rise of capitalism was helped on by the Protestant Reformation which fostered the notion that hard work was a moral duty and that a person's good works constituted proof that he had been chosen by God for salvation; people therefore worked hard to prove that they had been chosen. The work ethic is a secularization of the Protestant ethic. It is widely held to be declining in western society as a result of such influences as welfare state policies, increasing wealth, the declining influence of religion, and more relaxed child rearing practices. Research by Cherrington (1980) supports this claim, especially among younger workers. Cherrington estimates that one third of the current US workforce believes in the work ethic. Those people who do are slightly more likely to be high producers and to be satisfied with their work than those who do not. Cherrington found work ethic values to be related to child rearing practices which encouraged firm discipline, personal responsibility and high standards of personal conduct. EAL

Bibliography

Cherrington, D.J. 1980: *The work ethic*. New York: AMACOM.

Weber, Max 1904–05: *The Protestant ethic and the spirit of capitalism*. Trans. Talcott Parsons 1958. New York: Scribner.

work redesign The redesign of work in organizations has been primarily concerned with creating jobs which enhance employee motivation, satisfaction and productivity. Traditional approaches to job design were heavily influenced by scientific management and classical management theory. Frederick Taylor, the most influential spokesman for scientific management, argued that jobs should be studied scientifically and quantitatively in an effort to achieve maximum worker efficiency (Taylor 1911). Scientific management advocated the simplification of jobs into component tasks that could be performed most efficiently, matching employee physical and mental skills to task requirements, training employees to perform in the most efficient manner and providing incentives for high performance. Classical management theory stressed principles to enhance the rational design and efficiency of organizations, including simplification of tasks and a division of labor in which employees perform specialized task functions. The division of labor was thought to enhance efficiency through the development of specialized skills, increased concentration possible on simplified tasks, and fewer interruptions due to changes in work demands (Hackman and Oldham 1980).

Emphasis on the rational design of jobs to achieve maximum efficiency and effectiveness provided the foundation for industrial engineering approaches to job design. During the 1950s and 1960s, however, a number of writers began to question whether the types of jobs created by this approach were beneficial for employees or organizations (Kornhauser 1965; Walker and Guest 1952). Simplified jobs in which employees perform a repetitive series of specialized tasks were thought to result in higher levels of employee dissatisfaction and alienation, which in turn caused absenteeism, staff turnover, and lower productivity. Concern with the impact of jobs on employees resulted in a number of suggested approaches to the redesign of work. In contrast to industrial engineering, most of these approaches emphasize the motivating characteristics of tasks themselves. (See also WORK ATTITUDES.)

"Job enlargement" stressed the expansion of simplified tasks so that employees could perform tasks of a more varied nature. The primary emphasis of job enlargement was to increase the number of different tasks performed and thus increase work variety, although consideration was also given to increasing employee discretion over work pace and methods, responsibility for work quality and opportunities to complete a whole task.

"Job enrichment" is most clearly associated with the work of Herzberg and his colleagues (Herzberg, Mausner and Snyderman 1959; Herzberg 1966, 1976). Herzberg's early research on job attitudes suggested that satisfaction and dissatisfaction were caused by different sets of factors. Job satisfaction was primarily influenced by "motivators" associated with the content of the task itself, including opportunities for achievement, recognition, growth and challenge. Job dissatisfaction was primarily influenced by "hygiene" factors associated with the work context, including pay, fringe benefits, job security and company policies and administration. Job enrichment approaches to work redesign advocate increasing the number of motivators associated with a job. A series of job redesign efforts following Herzberg's approach were carried out with reported success, although the original job attitude research upon which job enrichment was based has been widely criticized (Campbell and Pritchard 1976).

Recent efforts at work redesign have been heavily influenced by Hackman and Oldham's work (1976, 1980) on job characteristics. Following earlier efforts this approach provided a more comprehensive theoretical framework by identifying the basic psychological processes through which job characteristics enhance intrinsic work motivation and job satisfaction. Three "critical psychological states" were identified. Experienced meaningfulness of the work was thought to be influenced by the core job characteristics of skill variety, task identity and task significance. Experienced responsibility for the outcomes of work is primarily influenced by employee autonomy in work procedures and scheduling. Knowledge of the actual results of work is influenced by feedback from the job itself. Job characteristics theory suggests that important relationships in the model are moderated by several factors, including the skills and knowledge of the employee and his or her growth-need strength, and satisfaction with contextual factors. A major element of the job characteristics approach has been to provide the analytical tools necessary for managers to determine when work redesign is necessary and what specific aspects of the job should be redesigned. Towards this end, the Job Diagnostic Survey was developed and tested in several organizations. Research on this model has been reviewed by Roberts and Glick (1981) and several work redesign efforts based on this approach are reviewed in Hackman and Oldham (1980).

Recent work redesign projects in organizations have also been heavily influenced by sociotechnical systems theory. Based on the pioneering work of Trist, Emery and their colleagues at the Tavistock Institute, this approach seeks the joint optimization of the technical and social systems in organizations. The sociotechnical approach to work redesign generally stresses the work group rather than individual employees as the fundamental unit of analysis. Job design principles that emerge from this approach include an optimum variety of tasks, meaningful pattern of tasks that relate to an overall task, optimum length of the work cycle, discretion in setting work standards, performance of "boundary" tasks and creation of tasks that require a degree of skill worthy of respect and that make a recognizable contribution to an overall product. The historical development of sociotechnical systems theory has been described by Trist (1981) and work redesign efforts based on the approach have been summarized in Trist (1981) and Davis and Cherns (1975). A somewhat critical perspective on work redesign has been provided by Kelly (1982). RTM

Bibliography

Campbell, J. and Pritchard, R. 1976: Motivation theory in industrial and organizational psychology. In *Handbook of industrial and organizational psychology*, ed. M. Dunnette. Chicago: Rand McNally.

*Davis, L. and Cherns, A. 1975: *The quality of working life*. 2 vols. New York: Free Press.

Hackman, J. and Oldham, G. 1976: Motivation through the design of work: test of a theory. *Organizational behavior and human performance* 16, 250–79.

*——— 1980: *Work redesign*. Reading, Mass.: Addison-Wesley.

Herzberg, F. 1966: *Work and the nature of man*. Cleveland: World.

——— 1976: *The managerial choice*. Homewood, Ill.: Dow Jones-Irwin.

———, Mausner, B. and Snyderman, B. 1959: *The motivation to work*. New York: John Wiley.

Kelly, J.E. 1982: *Scientific management, job redesign and work performance*. London: Academic Press.

Kornhauser, A. 1965: *Mental health of the industrial worker*. New York: Wiley.

Roberts, K. and Glick, W. 1981: The job characteristics approach to task design: a critical review. *Journal of applied psychology*, 66, 193–217.

Taylor, F. 1911: *The principles of scientific management*. New York: Harper.

*Trist, E. 1981: The evolution of sociotechnical systems as a conceptual framework and as an action research program. In *Perspectives on organizational design and behavior*, ed. A. Van De Ven and W. Joyce. New York: Wiley–Interscience.

Walker, C. and Guest, R. 1952: *The man on the assembly line*. Cambridge, Mass.: Harvard University Press.

work sample tests A form of PERSONNEL SELECTION in which an applicant is required to perform tasks which have been sampled as central components of the job in question. Testing job applicants in this way has recently become more prevalent, as legal and social pressures for demonstrable fairness in selection have increased. Work sample tests are thus used in conjunction with more conventional intelligence or aptitude tests (Robertson and Kandola 1982). PBW

Bibliography

Robertson, I.T. and Kandola, R.S. 1982: Work sample tests: validity, adverse impact and applicant reaction. *Journal of occupational psychology* 55, 171–83.

work stress Many of the current definitions of stress come from homeostatic, energy-exchange models of physical phenomena espoused by earlier scientists such as Boyle, Cannon, etc. (Hinkle 1973), suggesting that stress results from the interaction of stimuli and an organism. Lazarus (1971) summarizes the definition in human stress terms thus: "Stress refers to a very broad class of problems differentiated from other problem areas because it deals with *any demands which tax the system*, whether it is, a physiological system, a social system, or a psychological system, *and the response of that system*."

In any form of paid employment there are a large number of potential sources of stress: the characteristics of the job itself, the role of the person in the organization, interpersonal relationships at work, career development pressures, the climate and structure of the organization, and problems associated with the interface between the organization and the outside world.

Factors intrinsic to the job were a first and vital focus of study for early researchers in stress. Stress can be caused by too much or too little work, time pressures and deadlines, having to make too many decisions, fatigue from the physical strains of the work environment (e.g. an assembly line), excessive travel, long hours, having to cope with changes at work, and the expenses (monetary and career) of making mistakes.

Another major source of work stress is associated with a person's role in the organization. A great deal of research in this area has concentrated on ROLE AMBIGUITY AND CONFLICT.

A third major source of stress at work has to do with the nature of relationships with superiors, subordinates, and colleagues. A number of writers (e.g. Argyris 1964; Cooper and Marshall 1978) have suggested that good relationships between members of a work group are a central factor in individual and organizational health.

Buck (1972) focused on the attitude of workers and managers to their immediate bosses and their relationships with them, using Fleishman's (1969) leadership questionnaire on consideration and initiating structure. As described in Chapter 10, the consideration factor is associated with behavior indicative of friendship, mutual trust, respect and a certain warmth between boss and subordinate. Buck found that those workers who felt that their bosses were low on consideration reported feeling more job pressure. Workers who were under pressure reported that their bosses did not give them criticism in a helpful way, played favourites with subordinates, "pulled rank", and took advantage of them whenever they got a chance. Buck concludes that the "lack of considerate behaviour of supervisors appears to have contributed significantly to feelings of job pressure."

Officially one of the most critical functions of a manager is his supervision of other people's work. It has long been accepted that "inability to delegate" can be a problem, but now a new strain is being put on the manager's interpersonal skills: he must learn to work "participatively". In respect of relationships with colleagues more generally stress can be caused not only by interpersonal rivalry and competition but also by a lack of adequate social support in difficult situations (Lazarus 1966). At highly competitive managerial levels, for example, it is likely that problem sharing will be inhibited for fear of appearing weak, and much American literature identifies the isolated life of the top executive as an added source of strain.

Two major clusters of potential stressors have been identified in the area of career development: lack of job security and fear of redundancy, obsolescence or early retirement; and status incongruity (under- or over-promotion) or frustration at having reached a career ceiling.

For many workers, especially managers and professional staff, CAREER progression is of overriding importance: by promotion they earn not only money, but also enhanced status and the new job challenges for which they strive. Typically, in the early years at work this striving and the ability to come to terms quickly with a rapidly changing environment is fostered and suitably rewarded by the company. At middle age a person's career becomes more problematic, and most employees find their progress slowed if not actually stopped. Job opportunities become fewer, those jobs that are available take longer to master, past (mistaken?) decisions cannot be revoked, old knowledge and methods become obsolete, energies may be flagging or demanded for family activities, and there is the press of fresh young recruits to face in competition.

A fifth potential source of work stress is simply "being in the organization", and the threat to an individual's freedom, autonomy and identity that this poses. Criticisms such as little or no participation in the decision making process, no sense of belonging, lack of effective consultation and communication, restrictions on behavior (e.g. through tight budgets) and office politics are frequent.

The sixth and final source of work stress is more a "catch-all" for all those exchanges between life outside and life inside the organization that might put pressure on an individual: family problems (Pahl and Pahl 1971), life crises (Cooper and Marshall 1978), financial difficulties, conflict of personal beliefs with those of the company, and the conflict of company with family demands.

The individual worker has two stress-related problems with respect to his family and his work. The first is that of managing time and conflicting commitments. Not only does the busy work life leave few resources to cope with other people's needs, but in order to do a job well, the individual usually needs support from others to cope with the details of home management, to relieve stress when possible, and to maintain contact with the world outside work. The second problem, often a result of the first, is the spill-over of crises or stresses from one system to the other.

CLC

Bibliography

Argyris, C. 1964: *Integrating the individual and the organisation.* New York: Wiley.

Buck, V.E. 1972: *Working under pressure.* London; Staples Press; New York: Crane Rusak.

Cooper, C.L. and Marshall, J. 1978: *Understanding executive stress.* London: Macmillan.

Fleishman, E.A. 1969: *Manual for the leadership opinion questionnaire.* Science Research Associates.

Hinkle, L.W. 1973: The concept of "stress" in the biological and social sciences. *Science, medicine and man* 1, 31–48.

Lazarus, R.S. 1966: *Psychological stress and the coping process.* New York: McGraw-Hill.

Lazarus, R.S. 1971: The concepts of stress and disease. In L. Levi, ed., *Society, stress and disease.* Oxford: Oxford University Press.

Pahl, J.M. and R.E. 1971: *Managers and their wives.* London: Allen Lane.

writing systems A set of visual symbols used to represent the words and sentences of a language. Writing systems are always parasitic upon a pre-existing spoken language, but they vary greatly in their relation to the phonetic structure of the language they represent.

Phonetic writing systems, such as those used for all of the Indo-European and most of the rest of the written languages in the word, are "alphabetic". The letters of an alphabet, which may number from a couple of dozen to a couple of hundred, each typically stand for a unit consonant or vowel of the spoken language, though no alphabet is perfect. Not every sound of every word is represented. The same letter may stand for different sounds in different words, and spellings are often highly discrepant from actual pronunciations. But similarities in spelling do nearly invariably reflect actual or historical similarities in pronunciation.

Not so with non-phonetic writing systems, such as that used for *Chinese*, which is almost purely "logographic": the characters each typically stand for a different whole word of Chinese. In many cases, graphic similarities between characters reflect similarities in meaning between the words they stand for, occasionally in pictorially explicable ways, but these recurring graphic elements scarcely ever reflect similarities in sound. The non-phonetic nature of Chinese characters meshes well with the fact that they are used by people whose diverse spoken dialects defy representation in a common phonetic writing system.

The Japanese use the only major mixed phonetic/non-phonetic writing system of the present day. Phonetic symbols representing the syllables of *Japanese* coöccur with logographic characters borrowed from the Chinese. Each syllabic symbol stands for a complete consonant-plus-vowel or vowel-only syllable. No graphic similarity marks the fact that these syllables contain recurrent component vowels and consonants. One "syllabary", the *hiragana*, is used for affixes and other affix-like grammatical particles, while another, the *katakana*, is used for foreign words and sounds. The logographic characters, on the other hand, are used to represent the uninflected root nouns, verbs, and adjectives.

Recent research on aphasia and on developmental reading disorders suggests that phonetic writing systems require more skill of their users in the phonetic aspects of language than do non-phonetic systems. Therapists have successfully employed artificially constructed logographic writing systems to help hearing-impaired and other phonetically disabled patients acquire or maintain linguistics abilities.

HSS

Bibliography

Gelb, I.J. 1963: *A study of writing.* Chicago: University of Chicago Press.

Wundt, Wilhelm (1832–1920). Philosopher, physiologist, psychologist, at the universities of Heidelberg and (from 1875) Leipzig. In Heidelberg, after his medical training, Wundt moved into research in sensory and neural physiology and then into specifically psychological experimentation, thereby elaborating his ideas for a new, scientific psychology anchored in physiology which he expounded in *Grundzüge der physiologischen Psychologie* (1st edn. 1873/74). As professor of philosophy in Leipzig he became the celebrated organizer of psychology as an autonomous and scientific discipline: he founded the prototypical psychological institute around a laboratory, wrote influential treatises and textbooks, edited journals and attracted an international group of students (the Wundt-school). They disseminated the institutional structure. Wundt had given to the field (including some idiosyncrasies, among them a relative neglect of differential, animal, child and applied psychology). For many years this school was so predominant that most opposing views chose to define themselves in contrast to it.

Yet there is no brief way in which to summarize Wundt's psychology since it was constantly remodelled in the course of his research which spanned simple sensory impressions, reaction time, and highly complex mental processes. Though close to the associationist tradition Wundt criticized it for its disregard of volitional processes and proposed the principle of creative synthesis by which a combination of mental elements acquires new, emergent properties not contained in the elements themselves.

In psychological method Wundt perceived a basic dichotomy. Simpler mental processes are the object of experimental physiological psychology. This is unsuitable for the more complex which are explored through the study of their transindividual products (e.g. language, custom, myth, religion), and are the domain of *Völkerpsychologie* (social psychology, mis-termed "folk psychology"). Important for an understanding of Wundt's methodology is the philosophy of science as put forward in his *Logik*. Wundt embedded his psychology in an elaborate philosophy to which belong the conception of mind as an activity, not a substance; psychological (not metaphysical) voluntarism; the a priori unity of consciousness; and the dominant role assigned to apperception. HUKG

Bibliography

*Bringmann, W.G. and Scheerer, E., eds. 1980: Wundt centennial issue. *Psychological research* 42, 1–189.

*——— and Tweney, R., eds. 1980: *Wundt studies: a centennial collection.* Toronto: Hogrefe.

*Rieber, R.W., ed. 1980: *Wilhelm Wundt and the making of scientific psychology.* New York: Plenum.

Wundt, Wilhelm 1907: *Outlines of psychology,* 3rd edn. Trans. C.H. Judd. Leipzig: Engelmann.

——— 1908–1911: *Grundzüge der physiologischen Psychologie,* 6th edn. 3 vols. Leipzig: Engelmann.

——— 1917–1926: *Völkerpsychologie,* 1st to 4th edns. 10 vols. Leipzig: Kröner.

——— 1919: *System der Philosophie,* 4th edn. 2 vols. Leipzig: Kröner.

Y

yoga psychology A system for the cultivation of self-control, due to the second century Indian sage, Patanjali. The yoga conception of "mind" involves a personal essence (*atman*), a thinking-substance (*buddhi*) which produces knowledge (*bodha*). In ordinary life the mind is distracted, infatuated with real and ideal objects, and restlessly in flux. Yoga psychology is largely concerned with the practices by which change and infestation of the self by objects can be overcome.

By distancing himself from immediate experience the yogin achieves both passionlessness and mastery. Indeed they are one and the same. "Passionlessness is the consciousness of being master on the part of one who has rid himself of thirst for seen or revealed objects". Amongst revealed objects are some we would ordinarily take to be the very point of religious practices, such as the attainment of heaven.

To reach a state in which the "Intellect which unites not with objects is conscious of its own thinking-substance when the mind stuff takes the form of that [thinking-substance] by reflecting it" one must pass through a sequence of deletions of the contents of consciousness. From *vitarka,* deliberation on ordinary sense-experience delete direct experience (*abhoga*); from reflection, the state thus achieved, delete deliberation; from the resulting stage, joy, delete reflection; and from the last stage delete joy and one has *samvid,* pure "sense-of-personality" without content.

The essence of the technique is concentration. "When the yogin's mind-stuff has become concentrated he gains as his portion, the discrimination of insight, by which he perceives things as they really are". All this is facilitated by the repetition of a Mystic Syllable to attain singleness-of-intent.

A complicated structure of hindrances have to be overcome which are essentially a psychology of ordinary thought, involving *prakhya* (vividness), *pravrtti* (activity); and *sthiti* (inertia). It is by the use of mind-energy that the Self (*purusha*) is revealed as independent of even the purified *sattra,* mind-stuff's momentary properties, which are, paradoxically the means by which a grasp of the distinction between Self and the stream of particular experiences is acquired. The final condition is not only passionless, but stable. All fluctuations have been restricted. (The quotations in this article are all from Wood (1914)). RHa

Bibliography

Rawlinson, A. 1981: Yoga psychology. In *Indigenous psychologies,* eds P. Heelas and A. Lock. London and New York: Academic Press.

Woods, J. H. 1914: *The yoga-system of Patanjali.* Cambridge, Mass: Harvard University Press.

Young–Helmholtz theory *See* color vision.

Z

Zen Buddhism A tradition found in Japan, from the twelfth century AD, which blends certain elements from Chinese Buddhism and TAOISM. It has permeated Japanese life and values, from poetry and the visual arts to the military class of samurai warriors (see Suzuki 1959). The word *zen* is derived from the Chinese *ch'an,* in turn derived from Sanskrit *dhyāna,* "meditation". There is, accordingly, a very large amount of meditation in Zen religious practice, particularly in the sitting position of *za-zen*. Zen thought marries that form of BUDDHIST PSYCHOLOGY which emphasizes "emptiness" and the inadequacy of words to depict reality with the Taoist aesthetic of mystical quietism and "naturalness". The two major schools of Zen are *Soto*, which lays heavy stress on *za-zen*, and *Rinzai*, which stresses the need to arrive by any and every means at "sudden enlightenment" (*satori*). SC

Bibliography

Suzuki, D.T. 1959: *Zen and Japanese culture*. London: Routledge & Kegan Paul; Princeton N.J.: Princeton University Press.

Zipf's Law Zipf's Law implies that there is an inverse relation between the length of a word and its frequency (Zipf 1949). Devito (1970), in discussing the relevance of this principle to research into stuttering, points out that since the amount of information carried by a word increases with its length and as its frequency decreases, stuttering increases with decreasing redundancy. PM

Bibliography

Devito 1970: *The psychology of speech and language*. New York: Random House.

Zipf, G.K. 1949: *Human behavior and the principle of the least effort*. Cambridge, Mass.: Addison-Wesley.

zoological theories of dominance Dominance has two meanings. It is usually the ranking of one animal over another in a fairly stable hierarchy of threats. It may also mean the priority of one animal over another for access to scarce resources, particularly food or mates. Much of the work on dominance deals with the relationship between the two meanings, that is, the question does high status in the threat hierachy increase an animal's survival and reproduction?

Dominance originally seemed a unitary, and all-embracing idea. Schjelderupp-Ebbe (1931), working on peck-order in chickens and other birds, pictured dominance as a despotic ordering of the universe. Maslow (1936) realized that the apparently sexual mounting and presenting of macaque monkeys is often a ritualized gesture of threat or appeasement. Thus dominance relations apparently pervaded the monkeys' lives. Maslow studied monkeys competing for a piece of food. He found that the mounter or threatener obtained the food, except occasionally when a subordinate presented, and then was "allowed" to feed. A stable dominance hierarchy can, in fact, reduce tension, since only a few situations are contested (Hall and DeVore 1965). It soon became clear, however, that threat ranking and food and mating priorities are not always correlated. Their relation varies in different species and situations (Gartlan 1968).

In the most straightforward situations the threat hierarchy does correlate with access to food or mates. These threats may be a direct function of body size, as in bighorn sheep, which grow more massive and curly horns year by year. They can assess each other's appearance as a "threat", and do not challenge sheep better armed than themselves (Geist 1971). A similar signal is the roaring of red deer. The length and pitch of a stag's rutting roar is closely correlated to the size of his harem, presumably because the roar is an index of his size, stamina, and fighting ability (Clutton-Brock et al 1979).

However, there are more complicated situations, such as when status has a geographical factor, when threat and food priority differ between the two sexes, or when the most advantageous strategy depends on the strategy of competitors.

If status has a geographical component, it verges on TERRITORIALITY. Territorial animals successfully chase rivals from their core areas, but at the territorial boundaries the rivals simply chase each other back to their own sides. In this case, winning the fight implies control of the territory's resources, whether food, nesting sites or other crucial resources. A classic intermediate case is Stellar's jay, which is territorial in summer but has a dominance hierarchy in winter. In winter flocks, however, both threat and food priority are determined by distance from the summer territory – the bird feeding nearest its own nest site dominates the others (Brown 1963). Several mammals, such as rabbits, also have geographical dominance, in which members of one clan overlap others, but proximity to the warren influences the hierarchy.

In several primate species the sexes are ranked separately, and females have priority to food while males maintain a threat hierarchy among themselves with little reference to the females. This is true in ringtailed lemur, brown lemur, and white sifaka on Madagascar. These lemurs suggest that female food priority may be a strongly inherited trait – it appears in all four social lemurs that have been studied, including the monogamous indri. Among the true monkeys and apes all but a few species apparently have male priority over females for food. The South American squirrel monkey, and the African talapoin and patas monkeys, at least show that the monkey stock can evolve female priority in exceptional circumstances. It is not clear quite what those circumstances are. Squirrel monkey and talapoin are very similar: small greenish river-edge species which forage in multi-male troops of 40-100 animals or more. The patas, however, is a large harem-forming monkey of the savannah and desert edge. Jones (1980) suggested that female dominance evolves in species which are highly food-limited. It may be that food priority is just one of a number of strategies open to females, such as foraging alone, out of immediate competition, like chimpanzees and orangutans (Wrangham 1979) or limiting body size, like, perhaps, Sykes monkeys and savannah baboons (Coelho 1979).

In still more complicated situations, the threat hierarchy is only loosely correlated with priority for resources. Hausfater (1975) found that in one baboon troop the first ranking male selectively mated on the third day of estrus, when a female baboon is most likely to conceive. However, individual preference also played a part: not all females mated with a first-ranking male. Other adult males formed consort bonds, and mated on as many cycle days as possible. Again, particular females were likely to consort with particular males. Finally, subadult males copulated behind bushes, particularly on the most fertile cycle days, whenever an estrus female escaped the adult males' vigilance. Hausfater (1975) points out that differing strategies are appropriate to different phases of the life cycle. Dominance must be understood over time, not just at a given moment. A similar conclusion emerges from Glander's study (1980) of howler monkeys. Young adult howler females dominate older ones in the threat hierarchy. However, the younger ones, like many primipares, had much lower survival of infants than the second-rank females, and they in turn than third rank, and so on, with the oldest and lowest ranked females raising fewer infants than any but the dominant. In this case, it may be an advantage to a young female to enter the hierarchy at the top, though the advantage only appears when she is displaced to second rank.

The costs and benefits of high rank depend on the strategies of one's opponents. In some species, or social situations, one may find an EVOLUTIONARILY STABLE STRATEGY (ESS), in which some animals achieve partial reproductive priority by social dominance, while others may "choose" to remain subordinates or avoiders. The advantages of being subordinate depend on both the number and ferocity of the dominants, while the advantages of being dominant depend on the number and meekness of subordinates (Maynard-Smith 1972, 1979). This is true both for the young baboons sneaking copulations behind bushes, and for species where the alternate behavior may be genetically programmed, as in solitary bees. Thus, threat-submission strategies form part of the general theory of SOCIOBIOLOGY and reproductive advantage, as well as bearing on the question of when it is advantageous to escalate threat into fighting (see AGGRESSION).

Finally, high threat rank may be transmitted from an animal to its descendants. This may be done genetically, as in inbred strains of aggressive rats. It may be done environmentally, as the young of social animals in good condition, with ample food supply, tend to be larger and survive better than those raised with poor food supply, and therefore at an advantage when the threat hierarchy corresponds to physical size and stamina. It may be done socially, as when a young Japanese macaque learns from its mother whom it may or may not threaten, and in maturing acquires a rank just below its mother (if female), or loosely correlated with hers (if male) (Kawai 1958). Thus entire female lineages may dominate others in threat. During food shortage, this threat dominance does indeed translate, in the macaque, into differential food access, infant growth, and survival (Mori 1979).

In summary, dominance began in the 1930s as a simplifying and unifying concept. Now, the real interest is in analysing "dominance" into its not-so-simple components, and in seeing how these components increase evolutionary fitness.

AJ

Bibliography

Brown, J.L. 1963: Aggressiveness, dominance, and social organization in the Stellar Jay. *Condor* 65, 460–484.

Clutton-Brock, T.H., Albon, S.D., R.M. Gibson and F.E. Guinness 1979: The logical stag: adaptive aspects of fighting in red deer (*Cervus elaphus* L.). *Animal behavior* 27: 211–225.

Coelho, A.M. Jr. 1979: Socio-bioenergetics and sexual dimorphism in primates. *Primates* 15, 263–269.

*Gartlan, J.S. 1968: Structure and function in primate society. *Folia primatologia* 8, 89–121.

Geist, V. 1971: *Mountain sheep: a study in behavior and evolution.* Chicago: University of Chicago Press.

Glander, K.E. 1980: Reproduction and population growth in free ranging mantled howler monkeys. *American journal of physical anthropology* 53, 25–36.

Hall, K.R.L. and Devore, I. 1965: Baboon social behaviour. In *Primate behavior*, ed. I. Devore. New York: Holt, Rinehart and Winston.

Hausfater, G. 1975: Dominance and reproduction in baboons (*Papio cynocephalus*) *Contributions to primatology* 7.

Jolly, A. in prep. *The evolution of primate behavior.* 2nd edn. New York. Macmillan.

Jones, C.B. 1980. The functions of status in the mantled howler monkey. *Primates* 21, 389–405.

Marler, P. and Hamilton, W.J.III 1966: *Mechanisms of animal behavior.* New York, London and Sydney: John Wiley & Sons.

Maslow, A.H. 1936: The role of dominance in the social and sexual behavior of infrahuman primates III: A theory of the sexual behavior of infrahuman primates. *Journal of genetic psychology* 48, 310–38.

Maynard-Smith, J. 1972: *On evolution.* Edinburgh: Edinburgh University Press.

*—— 1979: Game theory and the evolution of behavior. *Proceedings of the Royal Society* (London). Series B 205, 475–88.

McKinnon, J. 1978: *The ape within us.* London: Collins.

Mori, A. 1979: Analysis of population changes by measurement of body weight in the Koshima troop of Japanese monkeys. *Primates* 20, 371–8.

Schjelderupp-Ebbe, T. 1931: Die Despotie im sozialen Leben der Vögel, *Forschungsbericht Völkerpsychologische Sozialogie* 10: 77–140.

Wrangham, R. 1979: Sex differences in chimpanzee dispersion. In *The great apes*, ed. D.A. Hamburg and E.R. McCown. Menlo Park, California: Benjamin/Cummings.

INDEX AND GLOSSARY

Page references in bold are to articles in which the index headword appears in the title. Rough and ready definitions are provided for some terms; other terms are supplied with one or two page-references to lead to a definition or to a typical use of the term. Further information can be found by following the cross-references in the text; and for authors by referring to the article bibliographies.